*Pallmann's*
# ALLITERATION GUIDE

*Abridged Edition*

By Lee Pallmann

ISBN-13: 978-0615993027
ISBN-10: 0615993028

*Pallmann's Alliteration Guide* (*Abridged Edition*) © 2014 by FBP Publishing and Lee Pallmann. Rev. 1.0. All rights reserved. No part of this book may be copied, reproduced or stored in an electronic retrieval system without the prior written permission of the author. All synonyms are solely the opinion of the author. All trademarks, registered trademarks, service marks, etc., mentioned in this work are the property of the respective owners thereof. An attempt has been made to identify such trademarks in this volume, however the user of this volume is ultimately responsible for not violating any law regarding this property.

DEDICATION

To my loving wife, Valerie, who has stood by me
and suffered through the writing of this book.
I love you with all my heart.

# INTRODUCTION

Alliteration helps your audience remember your points, adds polish to your outlines, and brings an air of professionalism to your work. *Pallmann's Alliteration Guide* was written to help you beautifully alliterate your outlines or to assist in the creation of acrostics, acronyms, and alliterated sentences. More than a thesaurus, *Pallmann's Alliteration Guide* gives you at least twenty-six synonyms (or near-synonyms) for each entry, covering the entire alphabet from A to Z, thus providing twenty-six possible matches for the points in your outline, or helping you to find "just the right word" for your acrostic or acronym.

## PHILOSOPHY OF THIS BOOK

This book is intended to help authors, preachers, teachers, poets, and speech writers to alliterate their outlines or messages. This book contains commonly used words in the English language (excluding connective words such as "the", "and" and "is"), along with at least twenty-six synonyms, listed alphabetically, for each entry.

When a preacher, speech writer, etc., has the points of his outline figured out, he can name them with the most natural, logical name that comes to mind. Of course, these points would not normally all begin with the same letter of the alphabet. He may then look up each of these words in the *Alliteration Guide,* and find twenty-six sets of corresponding words, for each of his points. From this selection, a suitable match can usually be found.

For example, if a speech writer had three points to his speech: "Mercy", "Freedom", and "Prosperity", he could then look up each of these words in the *Alliteration Guide*, and compare the words in their respective entries. Upon doing this, he might decide to alliterate the points of his speech with the letter "A" (altruism—autonomy—affluence). Or, he might prefer the letter "F" (forgiveness—freedom—fortune). Or, he might choose to use the letter "L" (leniency—liberty—luxury). Alternately, he may prefer one of the twenty-three other combinations. This makes it easier to alliterate one's points.

There are very few exact synonyms in the English language. This is because each word has its own connotations and shades of meaning. For this reason, a given word found in an entry may or may not be appropriate for a particular application. It is beyond the scope of this work to define and delineate the meaning or shade of meaning for each word contained in an entry. Therefore, the user of this guide must choose his sets of words wisely in order to convey the point he wishes to convey.

Political correctness has been conscientiously avoided in this volume, as the author believes that such conformity to liberal ideals has a castrating effect on the language as well as on the freedom of speech. Thus, words that might be considered offensive, though synonymous, have been included with the qualifier "[off.]" following the word, when the author felt it might be an offensive term to some people.

Obviously, there are many cases where an exact synonym could not be found. In these cases, the *closest* word that could be found is used, and is italicized. In many cases, for a given key word, more than one synonym exists. In these cases, all such words are included. When more than one word is listed for the same letter of the alphabet, the author has attempted to list them from "least to most" order as much as possible. For example, under the heading "tiny", one will find three words listed for the letter "m". They are placed in the following order: "microscopic;

minute; miniature;" Of these words, "microscopic" is the least, that is the *smallest* in meaning. The word "minute" would mean something tiny, yet generally larger than microscopic. While "miniature" (as a miniature car or pony) still means tiny, yet it would normally refer to something larger than "microscopic" or "minute."

This volume provides the author with the tools to help find that "perfect" word—or set of words—that will make his finished product beautifully alliterated. Many a dedicated author will not only alliterate his main points, but secondary and tertiary ones as well.

## HOW TO USE THIS VOLUME

The basic format of this work is as follows: each included English word (called a *key word*) is listed in alphabetical order followed by its part of speech and one or more synonym for each letter of the alphabet. This "paragraph" is called an *entry*.

Each entry begins with the key word in bold print. This is the word that you are looking up. Following the key word is the part of speech, parenthesized and in italics. The part of speech is abbreviated as follows:

| | | | |
|---|---|---|---|
| (*adj.*) | adjective | (*n.*) | noun |
| (*adv.*) | adverb | (*prep.*) | preposition |
| (*conj.*) | conjunction | (*pron.*) | pronoun |
| (*interj.*) | interjection | (*v.*) | verb |

In order to shorten the size of this volume, many adverbs have been intentionally left out. This was done when simply adding the suffix *-ly* to the adjective provides the adverbial form of the word. Thus, one wishing to find the word "intelligently", need only to look up the word "intelligent", and place the synonyms they find in that entry in adverbial form.

Following the part of speech, the synonyms (and near-synonyms) for the key word are listed. The goal of the author was to find at least twenty-six synonyms for each key word, one for each letter of the alphabet. The letters Q, X, Y, and Z, were particularly challenging, and synonyms beginning with these letters may at times seem strained or bordering on silly. The author begs grace from the reader in such cases.

When multiple synonyms exist for the same letter of the alphabet, all synonyms are listed in the entry. This is because multiple synonyms present more than one shade of meaning, allowing you to choose the word that best suits your present usage. In such cases, the general rule followed to determine the order of listing is from "less" to "more", regarding the intensity of the word. In cases where no exact synonym was found, the closest word (in the author's judgment) was used, but placed in italics. In some applications, you may find the italicized word works for you; in other situations, it will not.

At the end of the entry, there may be a related word that is recommended for you to consider. Such entries are indicated in brackets and the indicator *"see"*, as:

[*see* arctic; cold]

In the above example, one could look up the key word "arctic" and also the key word "cold" for further possibilities in determining the alliteration to be used. The user may determine whether he wants to look up the related key words based on whether (a) he has already found the word he wants to use, or (b) the related words are consistent with the theme and direction he wishes to go.

Finally, when an alliterated antonym (word with an opposite meaning) could be found, it will be indicated in brackets, with the indicator "*Ant.* ", as:

[*Ant.* odd]

The above example is the alliterated antonym for the word **ordinary**, since "odd" has the opposite meaning of "ordinary."

## EXAMPLE OF AN ENTRY

Following is an example of an entry:

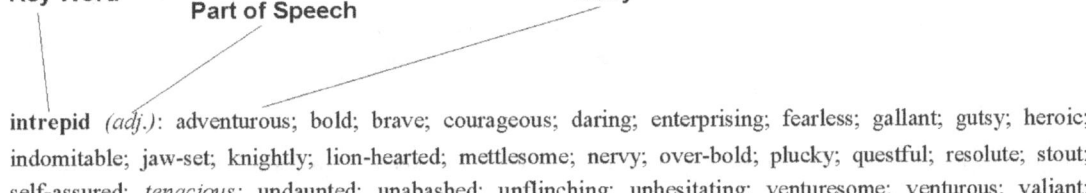

**intrepid** *(adj.)*: adventurous; bold; brave; courageous; daring; enterprising; fearless; gallant; gutsy; heroic; indomitable; jaw-set; knightly; lion-hearted; mettlesome; nervy; over-bold; plucky; questful; resolute; stout; self-assured; *tenacious;* undaunted; unabashed; unflinching; unhesitating; venturesome; venturous; valiant; well-hearted; *xtry.;* yieldless; zealous; [*Ant.* insecure]

In the above example, the entry is for the key word *intrepid,* which appears in bold print. It is followed by the part-of-speech in parenthesized italics "*(adj.)*", signifying that it is an adjective. Following this is a list of synonyms for the word *intrepid*. Notice that there are two *b* words ("bold" and "brave"). Often, the *Alliteration Guide* will give you more than one word for a given letter. When this occurs, it gives you more of a choice in selecting the word that is right for your application.

Note also, that in the above sample entry, the word "tenacious" is italicized. This indicates that the word "tenacious" is not an exact synonym for the word *intrepid*, but merely the closest word in meaning beginning with the letter "t".

Finally, the entry concludes with the bracketed phrase: "[*Ant.* insecure]" indicating that the word "insecure" is the antonym for *intrepid.* Antonyms are only suggested when they are alliterated with the key word. The alliterated antonym is given when possible as an aid, because in some cases the outline will employ the use of opposites.

Although not seen in the above example, an entry may also end with a bracketed phrase beginning with "[*see*...". The word contained herein is suggested for your consideration. When the suggested word matches the meaning of your point, it may be a good idea to look up this entry as well, which will yield you more choices of words to select from.

When looking up a key word, it is generally best to look up the more common word rather than the more obscure, as the latter may not have an entry for it (e.g. it is better to look up the word *dog* than the word *cur*). Commonly used words for which there are entries are listed in this book, even when considered synonymous. This is because each entry caters to the specific shade of meaning or connotation of the key word. This was also done to aid in the speed of lookup, rather than redirecting the reader to another entry, thus saving time and minimizing frustration.

## SEPARATE LISTINGS FOR HOMOGRAPHS

In some cases, there may be two English words that have the same spelling, yet completely different meanings (known as *homographs*). For example, the word *apology* can mean (a) an admission of wrongdoing; or (b) a defense of a doctrine or system of faith. In such cases, each word is listed separately, and following the part of speech (within the parentheses) is a brief definition of the word, to help the reader distinguish which definition the entry refers to. Thus:

**apology** *(n. admission of wrong)*: admission; begging forgiveness; concession; declaration of wrongdoing; eating humble pie; fessing up [improper]; guilt-admission; humble pie; imploration for absolution; just say sorry; keening; looking for forgiveness; mea culpa [L.]; mav; non-justification; owning up; peccavi; quittance; request for forgiveness; sincere ~; taking blame; utterance; voicing sorrow; well-worded ~; xfer; yearning; zeroing in;

**apology** *(n. defense)*: apologetic; advocation; backing; championing; defense; explanation; furtherance; grounded defense; holding forth; interpretation; justification; key arguments; logical argument; making a case for; noble defense; outline; promotion; questionless; ready defense; substantiation; thought-out argument; upholding; vindication; well-thought-out argument; xtry. defense; yeme; zealous defense;

While definitions are not included for every key word, they are given in this situation in order to alert the reader to the presence of another listing, and to allow the reader to distinguish between the different meanings. In a few cases, a definition is given when a homograph exists, even if that homograph is not listed in the *Alliteration Guide*.

## EXAMPLE OF ALLITERATING AN OUTLINE

In order to alliterate the points of your outline, you must first decide what your points are. As you create your outline, simply choose the most natural words that come to mind for each point (obviously, they need not begin with the same letter). Then, look up each key word corresponding to your points. If the key word you are looking up is not contained in the *Alliteration Guide,* try looking up a word with similar meaning. Bookmarks are suggested to save each page containing the key word you are looking up. By comparing each of the entries that correspond to your point names, you may then select the best matching set that "works" for your application.

For the sake of example, suppose the outline to alliterate was:  I. The Beginning; II. The Middle, III. The Conclusion. By looking up the key words "**beginning**", "**middle**", and "**conclusion**", several possibilities surface. Following are the actual entries for the above words:

**beginning** *(n.)*: arrival; advent; birth; coming; commencement; creation; dawn; debut; embarkment; entry; establishment; first; founding; genesis; hatching; introduction; inception; initiation; instigation; jump off; kickoff; launching; manifestation; *making;* naissance; onset; outset; origin(ation); *presentation;* production; *quickening;* rudiment; rise; start; take-off; *unveiling;* ushering in; *verge;* welcoming; *xenogenesis; youth; zygogenesis;*

**middle** *(n.)*: axis; belly; body; center(point); core; crux; dead center; epicenter; fesse point; golden mean; halfway point; hub; heart; interior; inside; *just exactly centered;* kernel; *lodged;* midpoint; midway; midst; midrange; midstream; nucleus; nave; ophalos; par; pith; *quotidian;* right in the middle; smack in the middle [slang]; thick; umbilic; *via media;* waist(line); *within; x-section;* yolk; *zenith;* [*Ant.* margin]

**conclusion** *(n.)*: apogee; bringing to an end; close; closure; consummation; culmination; destination; end; epilogue; finish; finale; fruition; *good bye;* hatching; illation; *judgment;* killing; *limit;* matter's end; *non-continuation;* outcome; peroration; product; quittance; result; resolution; summation; termination; upshot; *verge;* windup; *xy-coordinate;* year-end; zenith;

Some sets that could be used are:

| Key Word | Words beginning with "C" | Words beginning with "D" | Words beginning with "E" | Words beginning with "T" |
|---|---|---|---|---|
| **beginning** | commencement | dawn | embarkment | take-off |
| **middle** | center | dead-center | epicenter | thick |
| **conclusion** | close | destination | end | termination |

As you can see, other possibilities exist as well. In fact, at least twenty-six possibilities exist for any outline. While many of these may be inappropriate for your application, you can usually find at least one (if not several) possible matches that will work. Keep in mind that the key word itself may be the perfect word to use in your outline (e.g. in the above example, in the column for the letter "c", the word *conclusion* may be used instead of the word *close*).

It is generally best, when outlining, to select more than one possible word for each point to be alliterated (these may be similar or overlapping concepts). This gives you more "options" to look up, and a greater probability of finding just the right word. For example:

**1st Point:** The Problem/Situation/Breakdown → I. The Condition
**2nd Point:** The Request → II. The Cry
**3rd Point:** The Solution/Fix → III. The Cure

The fact that points one and three had more than one word to look up gave the writer greater options to choose from, and yielded a perhaps better outline than if he had only looked up one word for each point.

## USE OF ITALICS

In the actual entry paragraph (the "A-Z list of synonyms"), the use of italics is reserved for four purposes:

(a) **Inexact synonyms.** When a word appears in italics as a regular entry word, it indicates that the italicized word is *not* an exact synonym for the key word. It is, however, the word closest in meaning beginning with that letter of the alphabet. On occasion, an entry will include multiple synonyms for the same letter of the alphabet. These may include an italicized (nearly synonymous) word that the editor felt ought to be included for your consideration.

(b) **Different part of speech or tense.** When a suitable synonym could not be found for a given letter, but a word was found which had a similar meaning albeit a different part of speech (or a different tense), then that word was included, but italicized. For example, the word "went" appears among the entries for the key word *go*, but is italicized since it is the *past tense* form of the word "go."

(c) **Foreign and archaic words.** Words or phrases that are borrowed from another language are italicized, but followed by the abbreviated name of the language it comes from, enclosed in brackets (see Appendix A, for a list of abbreviations used in this book). An example of this would be:

*à la carte* [F.]

The above example shows that the term *à la carte* is a foreign phrase. The bracketed abbreviation following the phrase indicates that the phrase comes from the French language. The fact that the brackets and the "F." are *not* italicized indicates that the phrase is an exact synonym for the key word. If the foreign word is *not* an exact synonym, then the bracketed indicator following the phrase will also be italicized, as in the following example:

*à la carte [F.]*

Archaic words are also italicized, followed by the indicator "[arch.]." When this indicator is non-italicized, it indicates an exact synonym. When the indicator is also italicized, it indicates a near-meaning, but not an exact synonym.

(d) **Articles.** Occasionally, an entry will contain a phrase that has an article (*a, an,* or *the*) preceding it. These articles are not counted with regards to matching the intended alliteration letter. In such cases, the article of the word will be italicized, as in the example:

*the* right

The above phrase is included in the entry for the key word *conservatism*. It is one of the words suggested for the letter "r" *not* the letter "t". To help clarify this to the reader visually, the word *the* is italicized.

## LIST OF EXAMPLES

For some entries, a separate indented paragraph (in smaller, sans-serif type) will follow the main entry. This is called a *list of examples*. The *list of examples* gives you, not synonyms of the key word (as the main entry does), but actual examples or types of the thing represented by the key word.

For example, the key word *dog* would contain words in the main entry such as: "canine. cur, hound, mongrel, pooch, and whelp." The *list of examples* would contain a list of various *types* of dogs, as: "beagle, collie, dachshund, French poodle, and German Shepherd." The purpose of this list is to provide further possibilities for you to choose from which may or may not work for your particular application.

## SPECIAL SYMBOLS USED IN THIS BOOK

Some special symbols are employed in this book which indicate certain things. These are:

**1. Star ∗:** When a star appears in an entry following the part-of-speech, it indicates that the entry includes items that may be examples of types of the key word. When a star indicator is present, words that are types or examples will not be italicized in the entry.

**2. Tilde ~ :** A tilde ( ~ ) symbol in an entry indicates that it should be replaced with the key word. This system is used to reduce space in this volume and save pages in this book, thereby reducing its cost. An example of an entry containing tildes follows:

write *(v.)*: annotate; address; author; blazon; compose; chronicle; correspond; draft; denote; enter; expatiate; enface; engrave; emblazon; etch; fabulize; grave; hand~; indite; inscribe; indicate; imprint; jot; keep record; log; mark; *make;* notate; *over~;* pen; put down; print; quill; redact; record; register; scribble; scrawl; sign; scratch; take down; transcribe; *under~; vellum;* write down; *x; yak; zay;* [*Ant.* white out]

In the above example, the word *hand~* should be understood "handwrite", the word *over~* should be understood "overwrite", and the word *under~* should be understood "underwrite." What the tilde stands for is defined by whatever the key word is; in this example, it stands for the word *write*.

## USE OF PARENTHESES WITHIN THE LISTING

In some cases, an insertion of letters into an existing word or phrase provides another useful phrase. In such cases, the inserted letters appear in parentheses. For example, "big (ugly) foot" should be read as "big foot" or "big ugly foot." Another example might be the word "(con)cede" should be read as "concede" or "cede."

If a hyphenated part of a phrase is optional, it will be listed as in the following example:

(bleach-)blonde.

This should be read as "bleach-blonde" or "blonde."

Sometimes a part of a phrase may be replaced by another word. In such cases, the replacement phrase appears following the phrase it may replace, with a leading hyphen (-) surrounded in parentheses. Thus, a listing of "air force (-corps)" should be read as "air force" or "air corps." This may also occur when a common prefix is used more than once. For example, a listing of "hypersensitive (-active; -charged);" should be understood to mean "hypersensitive", "hyperactive" or "hypercharged."

## OTHER USES OF THE *ALLITERATION GUIDE*

Besides alliterating outlines, this guide may be used to accomplish other forms of alliterations, such as:

(a) **Alliterated Sentences.** This is a sentence where all or many of the words begin with the same letter. An example of an alliterated sentence would be:

Alice, an American actress accompanied Alex and Andrea always.

(b) **Acrostics.** This is a paragraph where the first letter of each line follows an alphabetical pattern (such as following the alphabet from A to Z, or in spelling out a word). Example:

America, so sweet a land,
Beautiful and very grand!
Come one, come all, on every hand,
Dare ye now the ocean span
Every woman, every man,
Freedom waits, Providence's plan!

(c) **Acronyms.** The *Alliteration Guide* can be useful in the creation of acronyms (a term where each letter of the term stands for another word). An example of an acronym is:

S.W.O.R.D. = S)pecial W)eapons O)rganization of the R)oyal D)efenders

The *Alliteration Guide* can be useful when looking for a word that stands for a particular letter you are looking for. By looking up the key word for the meaning you desire, at least one synonym for the desired letter will be presented.

## NOTES FOR POETS

The *Alliteration Guide* is a valuable tool when creating an acrostic or acronym. By looking up the desired words, you can create an acrostic by selecting the appropriate letter from the alphabet. For example, my wife is:

V) irtuous
A ) mazing!
L ) ovely
E ) ver-faithful
R ) ighteous
I ) ntelligent
E ) xceptional!

The *Alliteration Guide* may also be used to write acrostic poetry. For example, if one wanted to alliterate the sentence "Small dogs eat much food." with each word beginning with a consecutive letter of the alphabet, one could change it to: "<u>A</u>dolescent <u>b</u>eagles <u>c</u>onsume <u>d</u>isproportionate <u>e</u>dibles."

If the desire were to have each word of the sentence start with the same letter, we could use any of the following:

| Small | Dogs | Eat | Much | Food |
|---|---|---|---|---|
| callow | canines | chew | considerable | comestibles |
| developing | dogs | devour | disproportionate | dinners |
| half-pint | hounds | have | heaping | hash |
| minute | mutts | munch | many | meats |
| pint-sized | pooches | partake | plenteous | provisions |

Other possibilities exist also, as becomes evident when one compares the entries for each of these key words.

In addition, the *Alliteration Guide* is valuable to poets and song writers as a thesaurus. When a particular word that you wish to use does not fit the meter that you are working with (in your poem or lyrics), that word may be looked up as a key word in this book, providing the writer with several alternative words that could be used. Many times, a good substitute word will be found containing less or more syllables than the original word, fitting the desired meter.

## NOTES FOR PREACHERS

When working on a sermon, one must, of course, prayerfully select the passage that will be preached. After the text has been selected, read the passage over and over. You may find it helpful to photocopy the text; then you can mark the photocopy and make notes on the margin. Divide the text up into your points. Give the points names that come naturally and which truly reflect the meaning of the point to be made in the text. After this is done, look up the names that you gave to your points in the *Alliteration Guide*. Select from twenty-six sets of words (one for each letter of the alphabet), the matching set which best represent the points to be made. Often there will be several good choices, and you, the preacher, must select the one that is best for your sermon.

On rare occasion, there will be no matches that work. When this is the case, never twist or change your message to "fit" a nicely alliterated outline. It is better to not have your points alliterated, then to change the message that God, through His Word, is trying to convey. In such cases, it is often best to phrase all three points alike (such as: "I. Joseph served his father; II. Joseph served his brethren; III. Joseph served God".)

In most cases, however, finding a well-alliterated outline that truly reflects the points will be possible. Consider the example on the following page. A relatively short biblical text has been chosen, allowing the chart to fit on one page, but the length of the text is irrelevant.

| Step 1. | Step 2. | Step 3. | Step 4. |
|---|---|---|---|
| Select a text. | Outline the text. | Look up Your Key Words in the *Alliteration Guide*. | Select best match. Your outline is done. |

Mark 4:37-41

**37** And there arose a great storm of wind, and the waves beat into the ship, so that it was now full.

**38** And he was in the hinder part of the ship, asleep on a pillow: and they awake him, and say unto him, Master, carest thou not that we perish?

**39** And he arose, and rebuked the wind, and said unto the sea, Peace, be still. And the wind ceased, and there was a great calm.

**40** And he said unto them, Why are ye so fearful? how is it that ye have no faith?

**41** And they feared exceedingly, and said one to another, What manner of man is this, that even the wind and the sea obey him?

1. The Trial (vv. 37-38a)

2. The Appeal (v. 38b)

3. The Calm (v. 39)

4. The Lesson (vv. 40-41)

*(You can also alliterate your secondary and tertiary points!)*

**trial** *(n.)*: adversity; burden; complication; calamity; difficulty; distress; endangerment; encumbrance; fix; grief; hardship; incommodity; jam; kink; load; misfortune; nuisance; ordeal; (problem); quandary; rattle; strait; test; trouble; tribulation; upheaval; vexation; woe; worry; *xerotripsis; yuckiness; zinger;*

**appeal** *(n.)*: adjuration; behest; call; cry; *cri de coeur* [F.]; desire; entreaty; forewish; great desire; humble entreaty; importunity; impassioned plea; imploration; juration; *known need; looking for;* making request; *need;* obsecration; obtestation; petition; (plea;) quiritation; request; supplication; *try;* urging; voice; wish; XQ; yarning; *zikr;*

**calm** *(n.)*: ataraxy; becalming; composure; coolness; dignity; evenness; equanimity; friendliness; gentleness; harmony; idyll; jarlessness; keeping peace; *laid-back;* motionlessness; mildness; non-turbulence; order; (peace;) placidity; poise; quiescence; restfulness; relaxedness; stillness; serenity; sedateness; tranquility; tameness; undisturbed; *very calm;* well-relaxed state; *xenophilious; yielding;* zero trouble;

**lesson** *(n.)*: axiom; book ~; class; coaching; direction; education; formal ~; guidance; *homework;* instruction; *junior class;* knowledge; lecture; lection; maxim; moral; *message; noetic;* object lesson; period; (principle;) qualification; rudiment; schooling; session; seminar; teaching; training; tutorial; tenet; unit; vitalism; worksheet; *xenagogue; yielding; zoology ~;*

Mark 4:37-41

I. The Problem (vv. 37-38a)

II. The Plea (v 38b)

III. The Peace (v. 39)

IV. The Principle (vv. 40-41)

* Easy-to-use

* Designed for Sermon-preparation

* Every word has synonymps or nearest-matches for every letter of the alphabet.

# A

**abandon** *(v.)*: abdicate; abjure; bow out; back out; cast off; desert; discard; depart; ditch; disown; evacuate; forsake; forswear; fling; go; give up; hand over; *ignore;* jettison; jump ship; jilt; junk; kest; leave; maroon; neglect; opt out; pitch; quit; relinquish; renounce; resign; relent; strand; surrender; shed; stop; throw out (-away); toss; unload; vacate; walk out; waive; withdraw; *xfer;* yield; zip away; [*Ant.* abide]

**abandonment** *(n.)*: abdication; abjuration; apostasy; backing out; casting off; dereliction; departure; desertion; defection; disowning; evacuation; forfeiture; forswearing; forsaking; giving up; handing over; ignoring; jilting; junking; jumping ship; kesting; leaving; marooning; neglecting; opting out; pitching; quitting; relinquishment; resignation; rejection; renunciation; stranding; surrender; *shedding;* throwing out (-away); unloading; vacating; withdrawal; *xfer;* yielding; *zipping away;* [*Ant.* abiding]

**abase** *(v.)*: abnegate; belittle; chaff; cut down; degrade; demean; denigrate; *execrate;* fleer; gibe; humiliate; insult; jibe; knock; laugh at; malign; mock; *name-calling; offend;* put down; quib; ridicule; slur; tease; trivialize; *utter against;* vex; wipe; *xuld [arch.];* yock; zeroize; [*Ant.* advance]

**abasement** *(n.)*: abnegation; belittlement; condescension; degradation; effacement; facetiousness; gibing; humiliation; ignominy; indignity; jibing; knocking; lowering; mortification; *name-calling;* obloquy; pridelessness; *quivering;* reproach shame; *timidity;* upbraiding; verecundity; wite; xtry. ~; *yowling;* zeroization; [*Ant.* advancement]

**abate** *(v.)*: assuage; alleviate; break; bate; curb; *cut;* decrease; decline; diminish; dwindle; dissipate; ease; ebb; fade; fall; go down; hush; *impair; improve;* jade; knock down; languish; lessen; lower; mitigate; *narrow; outgo;* peter out; quell; recede; reduce; remit; subside; taper; *undo; vanish;* wane; waste; *xerosis;* yield; zap; [*Ant.* accrete]

**abatement** *(n.)*: assuagement; bating; contraction; decrease; diminishment; easing; ebbing; fading; falling; going down; hushing; *impairment; improvement;* jading; knocking down; lessening; lowering; mitigation; *narrowing; outgo;* petering out; quelling; receding; subsidence; tapering; *undoing; vanishing;* waning; *xerosis*; yielding; zapping; [*Ant.* accretion]

**abbey** *(n.)*: ascetic community; basilica; convent; cloister; commune; *dorm; edifice;* friary; glebe; hermitage; incloister; *jong [Tib.]; kibbutz;* lamasery [Tib.]; monastery; minster; nunnery; *oratorio;* priory; *Qumran;* religious community; sacrarium; temple; *upper room;* vicarage; wat [Bud.]; *xenodocheum; yogic house;* zawiyah [Mos.];

**abbot** *(n.)*: abbé; abbess [fem.]; beadsman; brother; cenobite; dean; ecclesiastic; friar; grand prior; hieromonach; *individual; jubilarian;* kirkman [Scot.]; lay ~; monk; *nun [fem.]; Observant;* prior; *Qumranite;* rector; stylite; *talapoin [Bud.]; underling;* votary; white friar; *Xaverian;* yogi *[Hind.];* zetetic;

**abbreviate** *(v.)*: abridge; boil down; cut; curtail; condense; contract; decrease; diminish; encapsulate; foreshorten; *go down;* halve; *initials; just shorten;* knock down; lower; lessen; minimize; nip; *omit;* pare; *quicken;* reduce; shorten; shrink; truncate; *undersize; vell;* welk; *x-sect; yank; zeroize;*

**abbreviation** *(n.)*: abridgement; acronym; abbreviature; breviature; contraction; condensation; *diminishment;* encapsulation; foreshortening; *gone down; halving;* initials; *just shorter; knocking down;* lessening; minimization; *non-complete;* optimization; precis; *quickening;* reduction; shortening; truncation; *undersize; velling;* welking; *x-secting; yanking;* zeroizing;

**abdicate** *(v.)*: abandon; bow out; back out; cede; desert; disclaim; evacuate; forfeit; forswear; give up; hand over; *interrupt;* jump off; kest; leave; make an end; *nullify;* opt out; *pitch;* quit; relinquish; resign; renounce; step down; surrender; throw away (-in the towel); terminate; unload; vacate; waive; *xfer;* yield; *zip away;* [*Ant.* abide]

**abdomen** *(n.)*: abomasum; belly; crop; duodenum; epigastrium; front; gut; *huge ~;* ingluvies [zoo.]; jejunum; kyte; lower belly; mesothorax; middle midriff; *notum [zoo.];* omasum [zoo.]; pannel [zoo.]; *qualmish;* rumen [zoo.]; stomach; tummy; underbelly; vitals; venter; wame; *waist; xenometra ~; yellow-bellied;* zonite;

**abdominal** *(adj.)*: abdominous; belly; celiac; digestive; enteric; *front;* gastric; *heart;* intestinal; jejunal; *kyte; load;* mesothoractic; nephrogastric; omasum-related; pertaining to the belly; *qualmish;* related to the stomach; stomachic; tummy-related; underbelly; ventral; *waist; x-section; tallow-bellied; zonal;*

**abduct** *(v.)*: apprehend; betake; capture; *detain; ensnare; fetch;* grab; hold hostage; hijack; *imprison; jail;* kidnap; lasso; lay hands on; make off with; nab; nobble; overpower; pick up; *quash;* remove; rustle; seize; shanghai; steal; snatch; take (by force); usurp; *vacate;* wrest; *xfer; yank; zip away;*

**abductee** *(n.)*: arrestee; *behind bars;* captive; detainee; *encaged; fettered;* guest [joc.]; hostage; internee; *jailbird;* kidnapped person; *locked up; man;* niffer; *overtaken;* prisoner; *questionee; rustled;* surety; taken; under lock and key; victim; *ward; x,;* yard bird [slang]; *zek [Rus.];*

**abduction** *(n.)*: apprehension; abducting; betaking; capture; depredation; *ensnaring; fetching;* grabbing; hostage-taking; hijacking; impressment; *jailing;* kidnapping; *lassoing; make off with;* nabbing; overpowering; pick-up; *quashing;* rustling; seizure; snatching; shanghai; taking; usurpation; *vacating;* wresting; *xfer; yanking; zipping away;*

**abductor** *(n.)*: assailant; *buster;* captor; *detainer; ensnarer; fetcher; grabber;* hostage-taker; hijacker; imprisoner; *jailor;* kidnapper; *lassoer;* man-stealer; nabber; overpowerer; *procurer; quasher;* rustler snatcher; taker; usurper; *violator;* wrester; *xenotransplanter; yanker; zipper;*

**aberration** *(n.)*: anomaly; abnormality; bizarreness; curiosity; deviation; eccentricity; foible; glitch; heterotypicality; irregularity; *jarring ~;* kookiness; lapse; malformation; non-usualness; oddity; peculiarity; quirk; ridiculousness; strangeness; twist; unusualness; variance; weirdness; *xenomorph;* yaw; zaniness; [*Ant.* averageness]

**abhor** *(v.)*: abominate; *balk at;* contemn; comminate; despise; detest; deplore; disdain; execrate; find repugnant; *gall;* hate; *inexpiably hate; jaded; keck;* loathe; mislike; not like; *odious; pshaw; quad;* reject; scorn; take an aversion to; utterly ~; vilipend; *wrathful; xenophobic; yucky; zero love;* [*Ant.* adore]

**abhorrence** *(n.)*: abomination; badness; contemptibleness; deplorableness; evil; foulness; grossness; horridness; ignobleness; *jadedness; kitsch;* loathsomeness; miserableness; malignance; nefariousness; offensiveness; putridity; *quad;* repugnance; reprehension; shamefulness; terribleness; uncouthness; vileness; wretchedness; *xenophobia;* yuckiness; zhlubbiness; [*Ant.* adoration]

**abide** *(v.)*: await; bear; bide; continue; dwell; encamp; endure; follow on; *go to;* harbor; hang one's hat; inhabit; *journey;* keep on; linger; lodge; live; *move in; nest;* occupy; pause; peregrinate; quarter; remain; reside; stay; sojourn; settle; tolerate; tarry; *use; voyage to;* wait; *winter;* xenize; *yerde* [arch.]; *zip to;* [*Ant.* abandon]

**ability** *(n.)*: authorization; ableness; adeptness; aptitude; bravura; capability; capacity; competence; deftness; dowry; enablement; expertise; faculty; flair; gift; habilitation; instinct; *jurisdiction;* knack; know-how; long suit; means; natural ability; *old-hand;* potential; power; proficiency; qualification; resources; sufficiency; skill; talent; usefulness; virtuosity; wherewithal; ways; *xenium; yaup* [arch.]; *zeal;*

**abject** *(adj.)*: awful; bleak; contemptible; dismal; despicable; execrable; forlorn; grim; humble; hopeless; ill-favored; *jarring;* keen; lowly; lamentable; mean; miserable; morose; nasty; *odious;* paltry; pitiful; pathetic; qualityless; rank; sorry; sorrowful; terrible; utter; vile; wretched; woeful; xtry. bad; yucky; *zestless;* [*Ant.* advantaged]

**abjection** *(n.)*: abjectness; bleakness; contemptibleness; despicableness; despondency; execrableness; forlornness; grimness; humbleness; hopelessness; ill-favoredness; *jarring;* keen ~; lowliness; meanness; misery; moroseness; nastiness; *odiousness;* paltriness; pitifulness; *quite poor;* rankness; sorriness; terribleness; utter ~; vileness; wretchedness; woe; *xtry. ~;* yuckiness; *zero;* [*Ant.* advantage]

**abjure** *(v.)*: abnegate; break with; cast off; disclaim; disavow; end; forsake; forswear; give up; hand over; impugn; *jump off;* kiss goodbye; leave; make relinquishment; not claim; *overturn;* pitch; quit; renounce; shun; surrender; turn away; *undo;* void; withdraw; x; *yield; zero claim;* [*Ant.* affirm]

**abjuration** *(n.)*: abnegation; breaking with; casting off; disclaiming; disavowal; ending; forsaking; giving up; handing over; impugnation; *jumping off;* kissing goodbye; leaving; making ~; negation; *overturning;* palinody; quitting; quitclaim; renunciation; surrender; turning away; *undoing;* voiding; withdrawal; x-ing; *yielding; zero claim;* [*Ant.* affirmation]

**ablaze** *(adj.)*: alight; afire; burning; blazing; conflagrant; deflagrating; enflamed; flaming; glowing; hot; ignited; *jeopardized;* kindled; lit (up); *miskindled; nightfire;* on fire; *pyric;* quick-matched; razing; red-hot; raging; smoldering; scorching; torching; ustion; *volcanic;* white-hot; *xylophyrographic; yellow-flamed; zapped;* [*see* burn]

**able** *(adj.)*: adept; authorized; bodily capable; competent; capable; certified; deft; empowered; effective; efficacious; fit; *flair;* good; gifted; having know-how; *instant; just right;* knowledgeable; keen; *learned;* mighty; *means;* naturally ~; overqualified; proficient; powerful; qualified; ready; sufficient; strong; skilled; talented; up to; versed; well-able; *xtry. qualified;* yarkened; *zealous;*

**able-bodied** *(adj.)*: able; brawny; capable; dynamic; energetic; fit; good; healthy; in shape; *jusqu'au bout [F.]; keen;* lusty; muscular; non-hindered; okay; proficient; qualified; robust; strong; *tough;* unflagging; vigorous; well; x-strong; yauld; zippy; [*Ant.* ailing]

**ablution** *(n.)*: abstersion; bathing; cleansing; decontamination; depuration; expurgation; februation; *germ-removal;* headbath; hallowing; *implunging; jalap; knee-bath;* lavation; lustration; mundification; *non-polluted;* outwashing; purification; *quintessentialize;* rinsing; ritualistic washing; sanctification; *tubbing; unpolluted; vacuation;* washing; *xylol; yellow soap; zinc oxide;* [*Ant.* adulteration]

**abnormal** *(adj.)*: atypical; anomalous; bizarre; curious; crazy; different; deviant; erratic; enigmatic; eccentric; extraordinary; funny; freakish; goofy; heterotypical; irregular; jarring; kooky; loony; malformed; mad; mysterious; nonstandard; odd; outlandish; peculiar; queer; remarkable; rare; strange; *twisted;* unusual; unconventional; unnatural; variant; weird; xenomorphic; *yawed*; zany; [*Ant.* average]

**abnormality** *(n.)*: anomaly; aberration; bizarreness; craziness; deviation; enigma; eccentricity; foible; goofiness; *heterotypical;* irregularity; idiosyncrasy; *jarring ~;* kookiness; looniness; malformation; non-usualness; oddness; peculiarity; queerness; ridiculousness; strangeness; twist; unusualness; variation; weirdness; *xenomorph;* yaw; zaniness; [*Ant.* averageness]

**abode** *(n.)*: address; base; cottage; dwelling place; den; edifice; family residence; *guest house;* house; home; habitation; inhabitance; joint [slang]; *ken;* lodging; manse; nest; occupancy; pad [slang]; place; quarters; residence; roost; seat; spot; stead; tenancy; *utility apartment; villa;* whereabouts; *x-house; yali; zwinger;*

**abolish** *(v.)*: abrogate; annul; ban; blot; cancel; do away with; destroy; end; eliminate; extinguish; eradicate; finish; get rid of; *halt;* illegalize; invalidate; *junk;* kibosh; kill; *let go;* make void; nullify; negate; outlaw; put an end to; purge; quash; rid; stop; terminate; undo; void; vitiate; *wipe out;* x-out; *yank;* zero out; [*Ant.* approve]

**abolition** *(n.)*: abrogation; abolishment; banning; closing down; disallowance; end; elimination; finishing; *giving up;* halting; illegalization; *junking;* killing; *leaving off;* making an end; negation; nullification; outlawing; obliteration; putting away; quashing; rescindment; stopping; termination; undoing; voidance; *withdrawal;* x-ing out; *yielding; zero out;* [*Ant.* advancement]

**abominable** *(adj.)*: abhorrent; bad; baneful; crude; coarse; detestable; despicable; evil; execrable; filthy; foul; gross; horrible; heinous; immoral; jaded; kitsch; loathsome; malevolent; nefarious; nauseating; offensive; odious; perverted; polluted; *quad;* repulsive; reprehensible; sinful; shameful; terrible; treacherous; unholy; vile; wicked; *x-rated;* yucky; zhlubby; [*Ant.* adorable]

**abomination** *(n.)*: abhorrence; anathema; baseness; bane; crime; curse; detestation; evil; filthiness; gross sin; horror; iniquity; *jadedness; knavery;* loathsomeness; malignance; nefariousness; offense; outrage; perversion; plague; *quad;* reprehension; shame; terribleness; uncouthness; vileness; wickedness; *x-rating;* yuckiness; zhlubbiness; [*Ant.* adoration]

**aboriginal** *(adj.)*: ancient; barbaric; crude; dated; early; endemic; first; *germinal;* heathen; indigenous; *Jurassic; kipper [Aus.];* low-technology; *makeshift;* native; original; primal; primitive; *quintessential;* rough; simple; savage; time-forgotten; uncivilized; unrefined; *vulgar;* way-old; XO; *ylem; zero-sophistication;*

**abort** *(v.)*: abandon; break off; butcher; cancel; dispose of; destroy; eliminate; end; exterminate; forbear; *give up;* halt; interrupt; jib; kill; *liquidate;* murder; *nullify; obliterate;* prevent; quit; quench; *resign;* relent; stop; terminate; *undo;* vitiate; waste; x-out; *yank;* zap;

**abortion** *(n.)*: abandoning; aborting; *butchery;* clinical ~; deletion; ending; feticide; filicide; *giving up;* halting; interruption; infanticide; *jab;* killing; *life-taking;* misbirth; miscarriage; nullification; *obliteration;* prevention; procedure; quitting; quenching; *ruination;* stopping; snuffing out; termination; undoing; void; willful termination; x-ing out; *yank; zap;*

**abound** *(v.)*: *abundant;* brim; bourgeon; crowd; do well; enlarge; flourish; greaten; gain; have much; increase; jam; *keen;* luxuriate; multiply; *much; nourish;* overflow; overabound; prosper; proliferate; *quantify;* rise; run over; succeed; super~; thrive; upsurge; *verdant;* wax greater; *xtry.; yain* [arch.]; *zoom ahead;*

**about-face** *(n.)*: about turn; back-turn; change of heart; come back; doubleback; *entwist;* face opposite direction; *go back;* hairpin turn; *inflection; jag; knuckle; loop around;* make 180° turn; *nonlinear;* overturning; pivot; *quit;* right-about; repent; reversal; spin on heel; turnabout; turnaround; turn 180°; U-turn; volte-face; *wind; xy-curve; yaw; zag;* [*Ant.* abide]

**aboveboard** *(adj.)*: angelic; blameless; correct; deceitless; ethical; fair; genuine; honest; ingenuous; just; kosher; legitimate; moral; noble; on-the-level; plain-dealing; qualmless; reputable; square; straightforward; trustworthy; upright; *up and up;* virtuous; without deception; *Xn.;* yet unquestioned; zero deceit;

**aboveground** *(adj.)*: above-ground; *based-on-ground;* clerestory; directly on the ground; epigeal; *floor;* ground-level; higher-than-ground; *increased; jacked-up; kaolin;* lying on the ground; *meadow;* non-buried; on-ground; *planar; quoit;* resting on the ground; surface; topside; up top; visible; *way up top; x=0; yonder; zenithal;* [*Ant.* all-underground]

**abrade** *(v.)*: abrase; bray; burr; chafe; dig; deburr; erase; erode; file (down); grind; graze; grate; hack; irk; injure; *jag;* knock off; lacerate; levigate; mash; mill down; nick; *open;* plane; *quash;* rub; rasp; reduce; roughen; scuff; sand; scrape; scratch; scour; take away; triturate; use ~; *violent;* wear away (-down); xyster; yedder; *zip;*

**abrasion** *(n.)*: attrition; buffing; cut; chafing; digging; deburring; erasure; erosion; filing; friction; grinding; grazing; grating; hack; injury; *jag;* knocking off; laceration; levigation; mashing; milling; nick; *open;* planing; *querry;* rubbing; rasping; scuffing; sanding; scrape; scratch; scouring; trituration; urtication; *violence;* wearing; wound; xystering; yedder; *zipping;*

**abreast** *(adj.)*: apace; apprised; *au courant* [F.]; briefed; current; *disclose;* enlightened; filled in; *goings-on;* highly informed; informed; in touch; in-the-know; *just in; kept informed; latest;* made aware; *news; oral report;* posted; quaint [arch.]; report; scoop; tell; up-to-date; updated; versed in; well-informed; *xfer; yield; zero in;*

**abridge** *(v.)*: abbreviate; boil down; curtail; condense; contract; cut; decrease; diminish; edit down; expurgate; foreshorten; geld; halve; *initials; jist; knock down;* lower; lessen; minimize; nip; omit; pare; *quicken;* reduce; shorten; truncate; trim down; *undersize; vell;* welk; *x-sect; yank; zeroize;*

**abridgement** *(n.)*: abbreviation; boiling down; condensation; *diminishment;* expurgation; foreshortening; gelding; *halving;* initials; *jist; knocking down;* lessening; minimization; nipping; *non-complete;* optimization; paring down; *quickening;* reduction; shortening; truncation; trimming; *undersize; velling;* welking; *x-secting; yanking; zeroizing;*

**abroad** *(adv.)*: away; at large; beyond; *cast out;* distant; elsewhere; far off; *foreign soil;* gone away; *homesick;* in foreign lands; journeying; *known world;* lands ~; *make trip;* not here; overseas; *peregrine; quest; roaming;* sojourning; traveling; transmarine; ultramarine; voyaging; vacationing; widely; xenizing; *yeard [Scot.]; zipping;*

**abrogate** *(v.)*: annul; break; cancel; do away with; end; finish; get rid of; *halt;* invalidate; *junk;* kill; *let go;* make an end of; nullify; *outlaw;* put an end to; quash; revoke; rescind; stop; terminate; undo; void; *wipe out;* x-out; *yank;* zero out; [*Ant.* annul]

**abrogation** *(n.)*: annulment; breaking; cancellation; doing away with; ending; finishing; getting rid of; *halt;* invalidation; *junking;* killing; *letting go;* making an end of; nullification; *outlawing;* putting an end to; quashing; revocation; rescindment; stopping; termination; undoing; voiding; *wiping out;* x-ing out; *yanking;* zeroing out; [*Ant.* annulment]

**abrupt** *(adj.)*: abridged; brief; brusque; concise; curt; direct; economical; fine; gruff; hasty; harsh; impolite; *just little; knee-high;* laconic; matter-of-fact; neat; *overly short;* pithy; quick; reduced; short; sudden; snappy; snippy; terse; ungracious; uncivil; very small; wee; XS; *yea big; zeroized;*

**abscond** *(v.)*: abandon; bolt; break away; cut out; *depart;* desert; defect; decamp; disappear; escape; flee; go; hightail; *intervert;* jump; *katabasis [Gr.];* leave; levant; make off; *neglect; on the run;* part; *quit;* run off (away); slip away; steal away; skip off (-town); take off; up and leave; vacate; walk off; *xfer;* yead; zip away; [*Ant.* abide]

**absconder** *(n.)*: absentee; bolter; *cut out;* deserter; escapee; fugitive; *get away; hastener;* infractor; jail-breaker; *knuck;* leaver; man on the run; *non-prisoner;* outlaw; parter; quitter; runaway; runner; skedaddler; truant; *unapprehended; vacate;* withdrawer; *xfer;* yegg; zip away; [*Ant.* abider]

**absence** *(n.)*: absenteeism; break; casting off; dearth; desertion; *excused ~;* forsaking; going off; hooky; *inexcusable ~;* jejuneness; keeping away; lack; miss; nonattendance; nonappearance; *out;* privation; playing hooky; *quitting; running away;* skiving [Br.]; *shirking;* truancy; unaccounted-for ~; vacancy; want; *xenization; yellow-bellied;* zero-attendance; [*Ant.* attendance]

**absent** *(adj.)*: away; AWOL; *breaking; clear;* displaced; deserting; disappeared; devoid; elsewhere; forsaking; gone; *hooky;* introuvable; jejune; keeping away; lacking; lost; missing; misplaced; not present; needful; out; played hooky; *privation; quitting;* removed; somewhere else; truant; unaccounted for; vacant; wanting; *xenization; yellow-bellied;* zero; [*Ant.* attending]

**absentee** *(n.)*: absconder; *break away; clear;* deserter; *empty seat;* forsaker; *goer;* hooky-player; *inexcused absence; jaunter;* keeper away; leaver; lost person; malingerer; no-show; *out;* person not attending; *quitter;* runaway; shirker; truant; trivant; *unaccounted for;* vacant; withdrawer; *xenizer; yieldless; zero;* [*Ant.* attender[

**absent-minded** *(adj.)*: *amnesia;* brainless; careless; distracted; distrait; *elsewhere;* forgetful; *goffish;* harebrained; inattentive; *Jehu;* knuckle-headed; *lackadaisical;* mindless; neglectful; oblivious; preoccupied; *quirky; reckless;* scatter-brained; thoughtless; unthinking; unfocused; vacant-minded; without regard; *x'ed;* yonderly; *zero thought;* [*Ant.* attentive]

**absent-mindedness** *(n.)*: *amnesia;* brainlessness; carelessness; disregard; *escapes one;* forgetfulness; gap in memory; heedlessness; irretention; *just forgot;* knuckleheadedness; lapse of memory; memorylessness; memory lapse (-loss); neglectfulness; obliviousness; poor memory; *quirkiness;* regardlessness; *scatterbrained;* thoughtlessness; unmindfulness; unthinkingness; vagueness; wandering mind; *x'ing;* yonderliness; *zero remembrance;* [*Ant.* attentiveness]

**absolute** *(adj.)*: assured; beyond doubt; certain; complete; categorical; definite; downright; entire; for sure; *glaring; high;* indisputable; just; keen; *literally;* most (certainly); notable; outright; positive; perfect; pure; quite; real; sure; true; utter; unequivocal; veritable; whole; 'xactly [slang]; ywis [arch.]; zenithal;* [*Ant.* approximate]
**absolutely** *(adj.)*: assuredly; beyond doubt; certainly; definitely; downright; entirely; for sure; *glaringly; highly;* indisputably; just; keenly; *literally;* most (certainly); notably; outright; positively; quite; really; surely; signally; truly; utterly; unequivocally; veritably; wholly; 'xactly [slang]; ywis [arch.]; 'zactly [dial.];* [*Ant.* approximately]
**absolution** *(n.)*: amnesty; acquittal; blotting out; clemency; clearing; disregard; excusing; exculpation; exoneration; forgiveness; grace; *help;* indemnity; justification; kindness; leniency; mercy; non-prosecution; overlooking; pardon; quittance; remittance; remission; reprieve; shrift; stay; taking away; *tolerance; tabula rasa* [L.]*; unshackling;* voiding; *washing; x-ing out; yanking;* zeroing out; [*Ant.* avengement]
**absolve** *(v.)*: acquit; blot out; clear; disregard; excuse; exculpate; exonerate; forgive; grant pardon; *humaneness;* indemnify; justify; *kindness;* let go; make slate clean; *mercy;* non-execution; not hold accountable; overlook; pardon; quit; remit; release; remember no more; spare; shrive; show mercy; take away; *tolerate;* unvengefulness; void; wipe clean; *wash; x out; yank;* zero out; [*Ant.* avenge]
**absorb** *(v.)*: assimilate; *bloat; carry;* drink in; engulf; *fill; get; hold;* incorporate; imbibe; *juice-fill; keep; lap up;* metabolize; *not leak;* osmose; occlude; pick up; *quaff;* retain; re(ab)sorb; soak up; sop up; sponge; take in; *understand; volume;* wipe up; *xfer; yolp [arch.]; zimocca;* [*Ant.* avert]
**absorbent** *(adj.)*: absorptive; absorbfacient; bibulous; chemisorbent; drinking-in; *engulfing; fill; grantia;* hygroscopic; imbibing; *juice-drinking; keeping; lap up;* metabolizing; *non-leaking;* occluding; permeable; porous; *quantity;* resorbent; retentive; spongy; siccative; sorbefacient; thirsty; uptaking; vauxia-like; wiping; *xenophyophoric; yolp [arch.]; zoophyte;*
**absorption** *(n.)*: assimilation; blotting; combination; drinking; endosmosis; fusion; getting; *holding;* incorporation; imbibing; *juice-filling; keeping; lapping up;* metabolization; *non-leakage;* osmosis; occlusion; picking up; *quantity;* retention; re(ab)sorbtion; soaking up; sopping up; sorption; taking in; uptake; *volume;* wiping up; *xfer; yolp [arch.]; zimocca;*
**abstain** *(v.)*: avoid; abjure; bow out; cease; desist; deny oneself; *don't;* eschew; forbear; forego; give up; hold back; inhibit; just say no; keep from; leave off; make an end to; not do; *omit;* pass up; quit; refrain; stop; spare; terminate; *undo; voluntarily ~;* withdraw; x; yield; *zero;* [*Ant.* accept]
**abstinence** *(n.)*: abstaining; bowing out; ceasing; desistance; eschewal; forbearance; giving up; holding back; inhibiting; *just say no;* keeping from; leaving off; making an end to; non-participation; *omitting;* passing up; quitting; refraining; restraint; self-denial; self-restraint; termination; *undoing;* voluntary refraining; withdrawal; x; yielding; *zero indulgence;* [*Ant.* association]
**abstract** *(adj.)*: academic; *bodiless;* conceptual; distinct; ethereal; fanciful; generalized; hypothetical; intangible; inconcrete; *jumbled;* kuriologic; *logical;* mental; notional; obscure; perceptual; quasi-philosophical; rational; speculative; theoretical; unsubstantial; vague; whimsical; *xenagogic;* yet hard to grasp; zetetical; [*Ant.* absolute]
**abstruse** *(adj.)*: arcane; bewildering; complicated; complex; difficult; deep; elaborate; esoteric; foggy; fuzzy; formidable; grueling; hard; highbrow; hairy; intricate; involved; inextricable; jarring; knotty; labyrinthine; mysterious; mind-boggling; non-easy; obscure; perplexing; puzzling; *question-filled;* recondite; shadowy; technical; tough; tricky; unsearchable; vexatious; wildering; *xenagogic;* yet undiscovered; zany;
**absurd** *(adj.)*: abnormal; bizarre; crazy; cockamamie; daft; *eccentric;* funny; farcical; far-fetched; gonzo; goofy; haywire; illogical; incongruous; incredible; *jokey;* kooky; ludicrous; mad; nonsensical; nutty; outrageous; preposterous; *quacky;* ridiculous; silly; strange; *twisted;* unreasonable; *variant;* weird; whacky; *xenomorphic; yo-yoish;* zany; [*Ant.* acceptable]

**absurdity** *(n.)*: absurdness; bizarreness; craziness; daftness; *eccentricity;* fatuity; goofiness; harebrainedness; inanity; joke; kookiness; ludicrousness; madness; nonsensicality; outlandishness; preposterousness; quackery; ridiculousness; senselessness; *twistedness;* unreasonableness; *vanity;* weirdness; *xiaoren; yokelishness;* zaniness;

**abundance** *(n.)*: amplitude; a lot; bounty; copiousness; disproportionateness; excess; fullness; *flood;* generous amount; glut; galore; heaps; immensity; jumbo amounts; *king-sized amount;* lots; loads; liberality; much; many; multiplicity; multitude; myriad; numerousness; oodles; overabundance; overmuch; plenty; plenitude; plethora; plenteousness; preponderance; profusion; prolificacy; quantities; repleteness; richness; surplus; superfluity; super~; tons; teemingness; uberty; volumes; vastness; wealth; x.; *yards; zillion;* [Ant. absence]

**abundant** *(adj.)*: ample; abounding; beaucoup; bountiful; copious; disproportionate; excess(ive); full; fruitful; great; generous; galore; heaps; immense; jumbo; *king-sized amounts;* lots; loads; liberal; lavish; many; much; numerous; overflowing; overabundant; plentiful; profuse; prolific; quantitative; *replete;* rich; surplus; superfluous; super~; tons; uberous; unreserved; voluminous; vast; wantless; x.; *yards; zillions;* [Ant. absent]

**abuse** *(n.)*: abusiveness; bother; cruelty; discommode; exploitation; *force; galsome;* harm; ill-treatment; *jadedness;* kindlessness; *lovelessness;* misuse; mistreatment; maltreatment; molestation; neglect; overexploit; perversion; *quad;* ravaging; raping; *self-abuse;* terrible treatment; unkindness; violence; verbal ~; wrong use; *xenophobia; yanking down; zero respect;* [Ant. aid]

**abuse** *(v.)*: abominate; bother; brutalize; contravene; despoil; exploit; *force; go against;* hurt; injure; ill-treat; *jaded;* knock about; *lapse;* milk; mishandle; misuse; mistreat; maltreat; molest; *neglect;* obloquy; persecute; *quad;* rough up; ravage; rape; *sin against;* transgress; use; violate; victimize; wrong; *x-out; yank down; zeroize;* [Ant. aid]

**abusive** *(adj.)*: atrocious; bad; cruel; disdainful; execrable; flagitious; grueling; harsh; invective; jackboot; kindless; loathsome; mean; nasty; odious; overbearing; pitiless; *quad;* rough; severe; terrible; unkind; violent; wicked; *xenophobic; yeffell* [arch.]; *zero-mercy;* [Ant. assistive]

**abysmal** *(adj.)*: abyssal; bottomless; chasmed; deep; endless; fathomless; gaping; huge; immense; immeasurable; *jumbo; katavothron [Gr.];* limitless; measureless; never-ending; *ongoing;* profound; *quenchless;* ravine-like; sempiternal; terrible; unfathomable; vast; wide-open; *xtry.;* yawning; *zero end;* [see terrible]

**abyss** *(n.)*: abysm; bottomless pit; chasm; depth; deep; endless space; Erebus; fissure; gulf; gap(e); hell; *infinite; immense;* jaw-hole; *katavothron* [Gr.]; *limitless; measureless;* never-ending pit; netherworld; outer darkness; pit; *quenchless fire;* ravine; *sea;* scissure; Tartarus; unbottomed pit; void; world beneath; xibalba; yawn; *zone;*

**academia** *(n.)*: academic world; academe; *bookworms; cognoscenti* [It.]; college circles; doctors; educational circles; *erudition; fellow;* great minds; higher education; intelligentsia; intellectuals; ivory tower; *judicial minds; the* knowledgeable; literati; *mentally astute; noetic; over-educated;* philomaths; *professors;* quantrophrenia; *readers;* scholars; savants; universities; *valedictorians;* world of academics; *xenagogues;* Yale; zetetics;

**academic** *(adj.)*: academical; bookish; collegiate; didactical; educational; erudite; *formal; gifted;* higher learning; heuristic; intellectual; judicious; knowledgeable; learned; mentally astute; noetic; owlish; pedantic; *quick-witted; rational;* scholastic; scholarly; *teaching; thinking;* university; *valedictorian;* well-read; xenagogic; yaup; *zippy;*

**academics** *(n.)*: *achievement;* book-learning; coming along; didactics; education; erudition; formal education; guidance; higher education; instruction; *judiciousness;* knowledge; learning; *memorization;* neogenesis; operant conditioning; preparation; *qualification;* research; scholarship; schooling; training; undergraduate studies; university training; *valedictorian; well-prepared;* xenagogy; *yapp; zealous studying;*

**academy** *(n.)*: academe; boy's school; college; day school; elementary school; finishing school; grade school; halls; institution; junior college; *K-12; leading edge school;* military ~; night school; one-room schoolhouse; private school; police ~; *quarter;* religious school; school; trade school; upper school; vocational school; Waldorf ~; *xenagogy;* year-round school; *zone;*

**accede** *(v.)*: assent; agree; back; consent; *do;* endorse; fall in; grant; homologate; indorse; join; keep; line up; *match;* nod; okay; permit; *questionless;* ratify; sanction; *togetherness;* unite; validate; warrant; *xel [arch.];* yield; *zealously ~;*

**accelerate** *(v.)*: advance; book [slang]; career; drive; expedite; fly; go faster; hasten; hurry; hustle; increase speed; june; *kite; leave in the dust;* move faster; nail it; *onward;* pick up speed; quicken; rush; speed up; step up; take off; *undergo; velocity;* wherret; whir; *x-speed; yede* [arch.]; zip; zoom; [*Ant.* abort]

**acceleration** *(n.)*: accelerating; briskness; celerity; dexterity; dispatch; expedition; fastness; *going;* hastening; hurrying; *intensity;* jildi [mil.]; keenness; liveliness; *movement;* nimbleness; *overhastiness;* picking up; quickening; rapidity; speed; taking off; *uninhibited;* velocity; whipping; *x-speed; yar;* zippiness; zooming; [*Ant.* aborting]

**accentuate** *(v.)*: accent; bring out; concentrate on; draw attention to; emphasize; evince; feature; give emphasis to; heighten; highlight; *inflate; jump out;* keep emphasis on; lay emphasis upon; mark; *notice; overemphasize;* point out (-up); play up; punctuate; *quite overstress; red letter;* stress; spotlight; *target;* underscore; *value; weight; xtry. emphasis; yed;* zero in;

**accept** *(v.)*: acknowledge; accept; allow; agree; approve; adopt; bear; believe; consent; condone; deal with; endorse; embrace; face; get; harmonize; have; imbibe; jive [slang]; know; line up; make do; nod; own; permit; pass; *qualified;* recognize; receive; ratify sanction; tolerate; take (in); understand; *validate;* welcome; *xfer;* yes; *Zufriedenheit* [G.]; [*Ant.* abandon]

**acceptability** *(n.)*: adequacy; bearableness; conventionalism; correctness; *decency; enough;* fitness; goodness; *honky-dory; indication;* jakeness [Br.]; *keenness;* legitimacy; measuring up; norm(alcy); orthodoxy; properness; qualification; quality; reasonableness; satisfactoriness; sufficiency; suitableness; tolerability; usualness; validness; *well; xel [arch.]; yenough* [arch.]; *Zufriedenheit* [G.]; [*Ant.* abomination]

**acceptable** *(adj.)*: adequate; appropriate; agreeable; bearable; believable; conventional; credible; condonable; decent; endurable; enough; fair; fitting; fine; good enough; honky-dory; honorable; innocuous; justifiable; kosher; livable; legitimate; minimal; meet; normal; okay; passable; permissible; proper; pleasing; *quantum sufficit* [L.]; reasonable; sufferable; satisfactory; sufficient; suitable; standard; tolerable; usual; valid; warrantable; *x-parent; yes; zero problem;* [*Ant.* abominable]

**acceptance** *(n.)*: acceptation; acquiescence; agreement; approval; adoption; belief; credence; concordance; *dealing with;* embracing; facing; getting; harmoniousness; imbibing; jiving [slang]; keeping; lining up; making do; nod; owning; passing; permitting; *qualifying;* receipt; reception; *sanction;* tolerance; toleration; taking; take-up; *unopposed; validating;* welcome; *xfer;* yes; *Zufriedenheit* [G.]; [*Ant.* abandonment]

**access** *(n.)*: admittance; admission; approach(ability); *blessing;* clearance; door; entry; entrance; *freedom;* getting in; *have;* in(gress); *joint-permission; the* key; license; means; *may; non-barred;* open door; permission; passage; *qualified;* right of entry; route; reception; readmission; readmittance; sufferance; tunnel; ticket; unbarred entry; *uninhibited; validation;* way in; *xfer;* Y. [mil.]; *zero hindrance;*

**access** *(v.)*: approach; board; come in; *descend;* enter; *find;* go in; gain entry; head into; irrupt; jump in; *knock;* let oneself in; make an entrance; *near;* open; pass; penetrate; *quest;* reach; sail into; travel into; *unlock; venture;* walk through; *xfer;* yede; zip in;

**accessible** *(adj.)*: available; acquirable; *buyable;* clear; directly ~; easily reached; findable; gettable; havable; *ingress;* just there for the taking; *keepable;* left unguarded; *may;* non-barred; open; obtainable; procurable; quite easily found; reachable; readily ~; spare; there; takable; usable; unrestricted; *valid; workable; xtr;* yours for the taking; *zero problem;*

**accessory** *(adj.)*: add-on; appurtenance; accouterment; bells & whistles; commodity; complement; do-dad; extra; equipment; frill; *gear;* habiliment; incidental; *item; joining; keen; luxury item; more;* non-essential; option; plus; *quality; remaining;* supplemental item; thing; utility; *vehicle ~; with; xtr; yard work ~; zippy ~;*

**accident** *(n.)*: *alarming;* blunder; bump; bang-up; coincidence; collision; crash; calamity; catastrophe; disaster; error; fault; fender-bender; goof-up; hitch; *hit;* impact; jolt; kink; *lapse;* mistake; mishap; misfortune; mess-up; *non-purposive;* ordeal; *pile up; pranging;* quirk; random happening; smash; snafu; serendipity; twist of fate; unexpected occurrence; upset; *violent;* wreck; *x; yipes!; zing;* [*Ant.* aim]

**accidental** *(adj.)*: auspicious; blundering; casual; coincidental; chance; disastrous; erroneous; fluky; fortuitous; *goof-up;* haphazard; *happenstance;* inadvertent; *just by chance; kink;* lucky; mistaken; misfortunate; non-purposeful; odd; occasional; providential; quirky; random; serendipitous; totally unintended; unintentional; unplanned; *via accident;* wrong; *xtry. circumstance;* yet unexpected; zero planning; [*Ant.* aimed]

**acclaim** *(n.)*: accolades; applause; blessing; commendation; devotion; exaltation; extolling; fame; glorification; honor; idolization; *jubilation;* kudos; laud; magnification; *notoriety; over-praise;* praise; *quality;* rejoicing; singing; tribute; uplifting; veneration; *worship; xtry.; yichus;* zealous ~; [*Ant.* abhorrence]

**acclamation** *(n.)*: acclaim; applause; approbation; bowing; compliments; commendation; delight; esteem; favor; glory; hailing; idolization; *joy;* kudos; laureateship; love; mitting [slang]; nowel; *outstanding;* plaudit; praise; *quality;* regard; salute; tribute; *unmitigated ~;* veneration; *worship; xtry.;* yelling; *ziraleet* [Arab.]; [*Ant.* abhorrence]

**acclimate** *(v.)*: adjust; adapt; accustom; assimilate; acclimatize; become accustomed to; conform; desensitize; dispose; ease into; enure; familiarize; get used to; habituate; inure; jibe [slang]; *kit; line up;* mesh; *naturalize;* orient(ate); prepare; qualify; readjust; reconcile; synchronize; *season;* tailor; unite; verse; *well-adjusted; xenize;* yarken; *zero foreignness;*

**acclimation** *(n.)*: adjustment; adaptation; assimilation; acclimitization; becoming accustomed; conformity; desensitization; disposing; easing into; enuring; familiarization; fitness; getting used to; habituation; harmonization; homogenization; inurement; jibing [slang]; *kit; lining up;* meshing; *naturalization;* orientation; preparation; qualification; readjustment; reconciliation; synchronization; tailoring; uniting; versing; *well-adjusted; xenization;* yarking; *zero discord;*

**accolade** *(n.)*: award; acclaim; blessing; credit; commendation; devotion; encomium; exaltation; extolling; fame; glorification; honor; idolization; *jubilation;* kudos; laud; lifting up; magnification; *notoriety; over-praise;* praise; *quality;* raving; singing; tribute; uplifting; veneration; worship; *xtry.; yichus;* zealous ~; [*Ant.* animadversion]

**accommodate** *(v.)*: assist; adapt; bestead; contain; *cooperate;* do a favor; ease; furnish; fit; facilitate; fashion; garnish; give; help; handle; hold; house; *inclose; just-in-time; kindness;* lend a hand; minister; *not hinder;* oblige; put up; *quick-to-help;* render; service; supply; take; temper; tailor; unburden; *valet;* work for; *xtry.;* yield help; *zero hindrance;*

**accommodation** *(n.)*: assistance; adaptation; besteading; containment; *dorm;* enclosure; facilitation; garnishing; handle; housing; *inclosure; just-in-time; kindness;* living ~s; ministration; *not hinder;* obligement; putting up; *quickness to help;* rendering; supply; servicing; taking in; *unburden; valet;* working for; *xtry.;* yielding help; *zero hindrance;*

**accompany** *(v.)*: attend; be present with; come with; complement; convoy; drive together; escort; follow; go with; *hitch;* inosculate; join; keep company with; *lead;* move together; *near; out with; present; quicken;* ride with; supplement; tag along; travel together; usher; visit with; walk together; *xfer.;* yoke; *zero loneliness;* [*Ant.* abandon]

**accomplice** *(n.)*: associate; assistant; abettor; buddy [slang]; confederate; collaborator; cohort; co-conspirator; *defender; engineer;* fellow; friend; *good-fellow;* helper; insider; joint-ally; *kith; loyal friend;* mate; *neighbor;* offsider; partaker; partner (in crime); *quondam friend;* ringer; right-hand man; supporter; succorer; teammate; *upholder;* varlet; workmate; *xel [arch.];* yokefellow; zealot;
**accomplish** *(v.)*: achieve; attain; bring about; complete; carry out; consummate; do; execute; effect(uate); finish; (ful)fill; get done; gain; hit; handle; implement; *jump to it;* keep; *lead to;* make; *not resist;* obey; *outcome; overachieve;* produce; perform; pull off; *quick-to-comply;* reach; realize; satisfy; succeed; tackle; undertake; *victory;* wreak; *win; xfer;* yield; zip to it;
**accomplishment** *(n. completion)*: achievement; bringing about; completion; doing; execution; fulfillment; finishing; getting done; *handling;* implementation; *job well done;* keeping; *living out;* making; *nothing left; outcome;* performance; *qualification;* realization; reaching; success; transaction; triumph; *undertaking; victory;* working; wrapping up; *xfer;* yield; *zealous ~;*
**accomplishment** *(n. exploit)*: act; achievement; *brought about; crowning achievement;* deed; exploit; feat; geste; heroic act; *intrepidity;* job; key move; level of achievement; move; *noble thing;* occurrence; *outcome;* performance; *quest;* renowned ~; success; thing; triumph; undertaking; victory; (wonder)work; *xtry.;* yield; *zealous act;*
**accord** *(n.)*: agreement; accordance; affinity; bond of harmony; concurrence; concert; *delight;* empathy; fellowship; *getting along;* harmony; identification; identity; *joy;* keeping; like-mindedness; meeting of the minds; meshing; non-discord; oneness; peace; quarrel-lessness; rapport; solidarity; togetherness; unity; *voluntary fellowship; willingness; xenia; yedinstvo* [Rus.]; *zero discord;* [Ant. argument]
**accord** *(v.)*: afford; bestow; confer; deliver; endow; furnish; give; grant; hand (over); impart; *judge worthy; kit; leave;* make to agree; *non-retention;* offer; present; *qualify;* render; settle; transfer; unhand; *vest; weigh; xfer;* yield; *zip;* [Ant. appropriate]
**accordant** *(adj.)*: agreeable; *balanced;* choral; concordant; canorous; *delightful;* euphonious; *fit; good;* harmonious; instrumental; *joyous;* keen-sounding; lyrical; melodic; *nice-sounding;* orchestral; pleasant-sounding; *quality; rewarding;* symphonious; sweet; tuneful; *uplifting; very nice;* well-sounding; *xylophonic; yed; zero discordance;* [Ant. argumentative]
**accost** *(v.)*: approach; buttonhole; come up to; confront; corner; draw near; *detain;* engage; face; grab; *halt;* intercept; *join; key in; lay into;* move in on; nobble; *oppose;* pull aside; quickly intercept; *remark;* stop; speak to; take one aside; talk to; utter; *voice;* waylay; *xfer;* yank aside; *zero in;* [Ant. avert]
**account** *(n.)*: archive; audit; annals; books; balance; computation; credit; cartulay; description; details; explanation; financial report; *general ~;* history; information; invoice; journal; kept record; log; ledger; muniment; notation; noctuary; official record; postea; *quantity;* rendition; record; register; report; registry; story; score; sheet; statement; tab(ulation); tally; user ~; version; written ~; *xenodocheionology;* yellow sheet [crim. law]; *zet [dial.];*
**accountability** *(n.)*: answerability; blamableness; chargeableness; duty; errand; *function; guilt;* holding responsible; incumbency; job; *key role;* liability; mission; necessity; obligation; place; post; *quest;* responsibility; subjectability to blame; task; undertaking; vituperability; work; *xci; yoke; zing;*
**accountable** *(adj.)*: amenable; answerable; accusable; blamable; chargeable; directly responsible; *errant; faulty; guilty;* held responsible; imputable; *judged; kept ~;* liable; *mistaken; non-innocent;* obliged; punishable; *questionable;* responsible; subject; to blame; trusted; to blame; *upbraided; vituperable; witting; xfer; yoke; zero passing-the-buck;*
**accountant** *(n.)*: auditor; analyst; bookkeeper; cash-keeper; check-writer; *depositor;* economist; financial advisor; fiscal advisor; geoeconomist; house ~; *intendant; job;* keeper of the books; *ledger;* moneybag-holder; number-cruncher; officer; purser; payer; questor; record keeper; reckoner; secretary; treasurer; *underling;* verifier; *worker; xaraf; yeme; zum [dial.];*

**accounting** *(n.)*: account-keeping; bookkeeping; computation; documentation; electronic ~; figuring; financial record-keeping; general ~; *house accountant;* inventorying; *journal;* keeping records; ledger-keeping; maintaining the books; number-crunching; office work; paper trail; quantification; reckoning; record-keeping; settlement; tabulation; *unpaid balance;* verification; *work; xaraf; yeme; zet [dial.];*

**accredit** *(v.)*: ascribe; approve; blame; credit; deem; *entitle;* fix; give credit; hold responsible; impute; *judge; know;* lay at the door; *make; notion;* owe to; officially recognize; put down to; *questionless;* recognize; suppose; think; *understand;* validate; warrant; *xfer;* yield as due; *zay [dial.];*

**accreditation** *(n.)*: approval; bearing out; certification; deeming; establishment; final certification; giving recognition; homologation; imputation; justification; *kithe [Scot.];* legitimization; *making; notarization;* official recognition; proving; qualification; recognition; stamp of approval; *testimonial;* upholding; validation; warrant; x-certification; *yes; zero doubt;*

**accrual** *(n.)*: accumulation; accretion; amassment; buildup; collection; deposit; enlargement; forgathering; growth; gathering; heap; hoard; ingathering; jam [slang]; kit [coll.]; lot; mass; multitude; number; overflow; pack; quantity; ruck; set; throng; unit; volume; waxing; *xuld [arch.];* yelm; *zoo;*

**accrue** *(v.)*: accumulate; amass; build up; collect; compile; *develop;* expand; form; grow; gather; garner; heap up; hoard; increase; jump; keep growing; *largen;* mount up; *nob; overstock;* pile up; *quadruplicate;* rack up; rise; store; stockpile; *take off;* upbuild; *varia;* wax greater; *XL;* yard; *zoologize;*

**accumulate** *(v.)*: assemble; accrue; amass; build; bank; collect; cumulate; draw together; enlarge; *fatten;* gather; grow; heap up; hoard; increase; *jump up;* keep growing; lay up; largen; multiply; mount; *number; overgrow;* pile up; *quadruplicate;* rise; reposit; save; store up; *strengthen;* take off; upbuild; *volume;* wax larger; *XL; yain [arch.]; zoom;* [*Ant.* abate]

**accumulation** *(n.)*: accrual; accretion; agglomeration; amassment; buildup; collection; deposit; enlargement; forgathering; group; gathering; growth; heap; hoard; ingathering; jam [slang]; kit [coll.]; lot; mass; multitude; number; overflow; pack; quantity; ruck; set; session; squad; swarm; turnout; throng; tribe; troop; unit; variety; vestry; wisp; wheen; *xuld [arch.]; yelm; zoo;* [*Ant.* abatement]

**accumulative** *(adj.)*: accretionary; aggregate; *broad;* collective; cumulative; *detailed;* entire; full; group; *high; intact;* joint; *kept intact;* lump; mass; non-abridged; overall; panoramic; *quantified; ready;* summative; total; united; *veritable;* whole; x-total; *yare; zet [dial.];*

**accuracy** *(n.)*: accurateness; *bona fide;* correctness; certainty; dependability; detail; exactness; faithfulness; genuineness; honesty; indubitability; *justness;* keenness; legitimacy; literalness; meticulousness; non-fictitiousness; *ontic;* precision; *quaecumque sunt vera* [L.]; reliability; sureness; technicality; trueness; *unerring;* verity; well-tried; x-parent; *yes; zero error;* [*Ant.* approximation]

**accurate** *(adj.)*: actual; bona fide; correct; definite; exact; faithful; genuine; honest; indubitable; justifiable; known; legitimate; *mean it;* never-failing; open; precise; questionless; right; reliable; sure; sound; true; unerring; valid; veritable; well-tried; warrantable; *x-parent; yes;* 'zactly [dial.]; [*Ant.* amiss]

**accursed** *(adj.)*: accurst; anathematized; blighted; cursed; doomed; execrable; fated; *grieved;* hexed; ill-fated; jinxed; *karakia [Maori]; lash out;* menaced; nettled; *ordeal;* plagued; *quashed;* riled; *spell;* troubled; under a curse; vexed; witched; *xuld [arch.]; yerked; zapped;* [*Ant.* advantaged]

**accusation** *(n.)*: assertion; allegation; arraignment; blame; claim; charge; denunciation; denouncement; exprobation; finding fault; finger-pointing; grievance; gravamen; holding one responsible; indictment; jactitation; knock; laying guilt before; making ~; *naming; oppugning;* pointing finger at; *questioning; reproach; statement; summons;* testimonial; upbraiding; *vituperation;* witness; *xfer; yammer; zero in;*

**accusatory** *(adj.)*: apprehensive; *blaming;* criminatory; distrustful; exprobrative; fault-finding; finger-pointing; *guarded;* highly ~; indictive; *jealous;* keenly ~; leery; mistrustful; non-believing; over-suspicious; paranoid; querulent; *reluctant;* suspicious; *tentative;* upbraiding; very suspicious; wary; *xenophobic;* yare-handed; *zärtlich* [G.]; [*Ant.* absolving]

**accuse** *(v.)*: assert; allege; arraign; blame; charge; delate; dispraise; denounce; exprobrate; fault; *guilt;* hold responsible; indict; implead; incriminate; impeach; *j'accuse; knock;* lay guilt before; make allegation; name; *oppugn;* point finger at; *question;* recriminate; saddle with; tax; *utter; vituperate; word; xfer; yak; zero in;* [*Ant.* argue for]

**accuser** *(n.)*: adversary; arraigner; blamer; challenger; complainant; delater; charger; exprobrater; faulter; guilt-finder; *hold responsible;* incriminator; indictor; jaunderer; kibitz; *knocker;* litigant; magpie; *newsmonger;* opponent; petitioner; prosecutor; quidnunc; rumormonger; slanderer; tattletale; *utterer; vituperator;* whistleblower; *xferer;* yammerer; *zero in;* [*Ant.* advocate]

**accustom** *(v.)*: adapt; adjust; acclimate; assimilate; become adjusted; conform; desensitize; dispose; ease into; familiarize; fit in; get used to; habilitate; *harden;* inure; jibe [slang]; *kitted; line out;* mesh; *naturalize;* orient(ate); prepare; *qualify;* readjust; ready; reconcile; suit; synchronize; train; tailor; *used;* verse; *well-adjusted; xenize;* yarken; *zealously ready;*

**ache** *(n.)*: ailing; affliction; boo-boo; crick; cramp; discomfort; distress; dolor; *excruciating;* flare; galling; hurt; irritation; inflammation; jabbing; *kibe; laceration;* misery; *nip; ouch!;* pang; pain; quab; ranking; soreness; smarting; stinging; twinge; tenderness; throbbing; *unpleasantness;* vexation; woefulness; writhing; *xiphodynia;* yearning; yaik; zing; [*see* suffering]

**ache** *(v.)*: ail; bleed; burn; cramp; cause woe; disserve; *excruciating;* feel pain; grieve; hurt; *injury;* jeel; *killing;* languish; mourn; *nocument; ouch!;* pine; pound; pain; *quash; rack; sore;* smart; sting; twinge; throb; trouble; *unpleasant;* vex; writhe; *x.;* yearn; *zap,* [*Ant.* aid]

**achieve** *(v.)*: accomplish; attain; bring about; carry out; complete; do; execute; effect(uate); finish; fulfill; get done; gain; hit; implement; *jump to it;* keep; *lead to;* make; *not resist;* obtain; over~; pull off; perform; *quick-to-comply;* realize; reach; succeed; take care of; up and do; *victory;* wreak; win; *xfer;* yield; zip to it;

**achievement** *(n.)*: accomplishment; bringing about; completion; doing; execution; finishing; fulfillment; gaining; hitting; implementation; *job well done;* keeping; *leading;* making; *notoriety;* obtainment; over~; performance; *quick-to-comply;* realization; reaching; success; triumph; undertaking; victory; wonderwork; *xtry.;* yield; *zipping to it;*

**achiever** *(n.)*: agent; big producer; completer; doer; executor; finisher; go-getter; high-flyer; implementer; *jump to it; keeper; leader;* mover and shaker; *not lazy;* operant; over~; performer; producer; *quickener;* reacher; success; *triumphant;* undertaker; *victory;* worker; *xtry.;* yielder; zealous worker;

**acknowledge** *(v.)*: admit; accept; affirm; broadcast; concede; confess; disclose; divulge; declare; express; fess up; grant; hold forth; indicate; *jaw;* know; let out; make known; notice; notify; own up; profess; proclaim; *quoth;* recognize; regard; state; salute; tell; utter; voice; word; *xenagogy; yield; zero in;*

**acknowledgement** *(n.)*: admission; acceptance; affirmation; broadcast; cognizance; concession; confession; disclosure; declaration; expression; formal recognition; granting; holding forth; indication; *judgment;* knowledge; *let out;* making known; notice; notification; owning up; profession; proclamation; *quoth;* recognizance; recognition; regard; statement; salutation; telling; utterance; *voice;* word; *xenagogy;* yielding; zeroing in;

**acme** *(n.)*: apex; best; climax; *destination;* extremity; *farthest point;* greatest height; high point; *increase;* kop; limit; lofty height; meridian; nib; *overmost;* peak; pinnacle; *quoif; ridge;* summit; top; utmost; vertex; *way up; xtry; yonder point;* zenith;

**acquaint** *(v.)*: accustom; brief; cause to know; *dispose;* explain; familiarize; get to know; habituate; introduce; inform; inure; jibe [slang]; know; *line out; meet;* notify; orient(ate); prime; *quaint* [arch.]; ready; *school;* tell; update; verse; *well- ~ed; xenize;* yarken; *zero foreignness;*

**acquaintance** *(n.)*: associate; business associate; contact; colleague; *dude; employee;* friend; fellow; guy [masc.]; gal [fem.]; *him; her;* individual; *joe;* knowledge; kith; *lad; lass;* man [masc.]; *name;* neighbor; one; person; *quadragenarian;* recent ~; somebody; townsman; *unity; villager;* worker; *xenizer;* yokefellow; *zhlub;* [*Ant.* alien]

**acquiesce** *(v.)*: accede; agree; accept; bow; consent; (con)cede; comply; do; endorse; fall in; go along with; harmonize; *indulge;* join; knuckle under; line up; mind; not resist; obey; permit; perform; *quick-to-accept;* relent; resign; succumb; submit; *toe the line;* undertake; *verify; weaken; xel [arch.];* yield; *zip to it;*

**acquiescence** *(n.)*: agreement; *buxom;* compliance; deference; endorsement; favorableness; gameness; heedfulness; *implement; jumping (to it);* knuckling (under); listening; morigerousness; nonresistance; obsequiousness; passiveness; quietism; reactivity; submissiveness; tractability; *unresisting; very submissive;* willingness; *xtry.;* yieldedness; *zero resistance;*

**acquiescent** *(adj.)*: agreeable; buxom; compliant; deferential; ever-obedient; fawning; game; heedful; *implemental; jumps (to it);* knuckling (under); listening; morigerous; non-resistant; obsequious; passive; quietistic; reactive; submissive; tractable; unresisting; *very submissive;* willing; *xtry.;* yielding; *zero-resistance;*

**acquire** *(v.)*: attain; buy; come by; develop; exact; fetch; get; gain; have; inherit; *jump at;* kep; land; make off with; nab; obtain; procure; purchase; *quoff;* receive; seize; take; usurp; *vest;* win; wrest; xfer; yank away; *zip away;* [*Ant.* award]

**acquisition** *(n.)*: attainment; buying; belonging; catching; *development;* emption; *finding;* getting; gaining; having; inheriting; *jet; kep;* landing; making off with; netting; obtainment; procurement; possession; purchase; *quantity;* receipt; retrieving; seizing; taking; *thing; usurping; vest;* win; *xfer;* yanking; zipping away;

**acquit** *(v.)*: *avenge; blameless;* clear; deraign; declare innocent; exonerate; find not guilty; get off; hold not-guilty; *illustrate;* justify; *kithe;* let off; liberate; *maintain; not guilty; open;* prove (innocence); propugn; quit; remove blame; restore; set free; totally ~; undo damage; vindicate; withdraw charges; *x-out; yele [arch.];* zero out charges; [*Ant.* accuse]

**acquittal** *(n.)*: acquittance; *blamelessness established;* clearance; disculpation; exculpation; exoneration; freedom; getting off; holding not guilty; *invalidation;* justification; *kithing;* letting off; liberation; *maintaining;* name-clearing; *opening;* pardon; quittance; restitution; restoration; setting free; total ~; upholding; vindication; withdrawal of charges; *xing-out; yele [arch.]; zero guilt;* [*Ant.* accusation]

**acre** *(n.)*: *acreage;* arpent; back ~; croft; *division; estate;* farm; glebe; grounds; hide; hectare; *item;* juger [Rom.]; khet [Ind.]; land; lot; *mile;* nook; oxgang; plot; patch; plat; parcel; quadrat; run; section; tract; unit; virgate; *wedge; x-mal [G.];* yard(land); *zone;*

**acrimony** *(n.)*: anger; acrimoniousness; bitterness; contempt; displeasure; disgust; exasperation; fury; gall; hatred; indignation; jadedness; *kindlessness; kindle;* loathing; malevolence; negativism; offense; pique; querulousness; rancor; resentment; spite; *tetchiness;* umbrage; virulence; venom; wrath; *xenophobia; yawping; zoilism;* [*Ant.* agreeableness]

**across** *(prep. + adv.)*: athwart; bridging; crosswise; crossways; directly through; edgewise; from end to end; *go over;* horizontal; intersecting; *juncture; kittycorner;* longways; *moving through; non-vertical;* over; passing through; *quicken;* right through; sideways; transversely; through; *underway; vertically ~;* westward; *x-wise;* yede; *zip ~;* [*Ant.* apeak]

**act** *(v. behave)*: affect; accomplish; behave; conduct oneself; carry; comport; do; demean; experience; engage (in); execute; function; give; hand(le); indulge; *job; keep;* live; *make; notion;* operate; over~; overre~; perform; proceed; produce; *quicken;* react; *schesis;* take; undertake; *venture;* walk; work; wreak; *xfer;* yede [arch.]; *zealously do;*

**act** *(v. role-play)*: appear; behave; be; con; dramatize; dissemble; enact; fake; feign; *guile;* ham it up; impersonate; *just make-believe; keep ~ing; live; like; lead;* make-believe; mum; mislead; melodramatize; *non-reality;* over~; play-act; pretend; perform; present; put on an ~; *quasi;* role-play; re-enact; stage; simulate; theatricize; *use; vaunt; work; xenophonia;* yield performance; *zealously pretend;*

**acting** *(n.)*: *act out; the* boards; *choreography; cinema; company;* drama(tization); enactment; faking; feigning; *the* footlights; *gallery;* histrionism; impersonation; job; *kinderspiel* [G.]; land of make-believe; *lines;* melodrama; *non-reality;* onstage; over~; play-acting; pretending; performing (arts); *quasi-acting;* rehearsal; re-enactment; stage; show business; theater; thespian art; *underacting;* virtu; Vaudeville; *work; Xanthopoulos;* yielding a performance; *zarzuela* [Sp.];

**action** *(n.)*: act(ivity); behavior; comings and goings; doings; deed; dealings; effort; exploit; function; feat; gest(ure); help; handling; initiative; job; *knee-action;* life; move(ment); motion; maneuver; measure; *notorious act;* operation; performance; praxis; *quick;* reaction; step; thing; transaction; undertaking; *venture;* work(ing); x-action; *yaw; zeal;*

**activate** *(v.)*: actuate; begin; commence; debut; establish; found; get going; *hatch;* initiate; impel; jump-start; kick off; launch; make a start; *new;* originate; push-start; quicken; rouse; re~; start; turn on; trigger; undertake; unleash; *vivify;* waken; *xon; yede;* zip;

**activation** *(n.)*: actuation; beginning; commencement; debut; establishment; founding; getting going; *hatching;* initiation; jump-start; kickoff; launching; making a start; *new;* origination; push-start; quickening; reactivation; start; turning on; triggering; undertaking; unleashing; vivification; waking; *xenogenesis; yede;* zipping;

**active** *(adj.)*: animated; brisk; *cheerful;* diligent; energetic; forceful; *gung-ho;* hurried; high-energy; intense; *jumpy;* keen; lively; mobilized; nippy; operational; overactive; peppy; pert; quick; rapid; springy; *thrilled; upbeat;* vigorous; vivacious; working; wimble; *x-energy;* yeasty; zippy; [*Ant.* asleep]

**actively** *(adv.)*: aggressively; briskly; *cheerfully;* diligently; energetically; forcefully; *gung-ho;* hurriedly; intensely; *jumping;* keenly; *lively; mobilized;* nimbly; over~; peppily; pertly; quickly; rapidly; *speedily; thrilled; upbeat;* vigorously; vivaciously; *wimble; x-energy; yauld;* zippily;

**activist** *(n.)*: advocate; believer; campaigner; crusader; devotee; extremist; fanatic; gainsayer; *heart-impassioned;* insurrectionist; Jacobin; *kicker;* loyal ~; militant; non-conformist; objector; poissarde [fem.]; quixote; radical; revolutionary; supporter; *troublemaker;* ultra-zealot; votary; *withstander; xenocentrist; yieldless;* zealot;

**activity** *(n. busyness)*: action; activeness; busyness; bustle; commotion; doings; enterprise; flurry; goings-on; hustle and bustle; impulse; jee; kinetic; locomotion; motion; movement; *non-stationary;* operation; *progression;* quickening; relocation; stir; turmoil; *underway;* vigor; working; *xfer;* yeastiness; zipping;

**activity** *(n. event)*: away day; break; *car ride;* day trip; event; fun day; getaway; *game; hike;* itineration; *jaunt; kip;* leisure trip; mini-vacation; night out; outing; pleasure trip; planned ~; quest; ride; scheduled event; shebang; *show; sport;* thing; trip; *unwind;* vacation; *workbench; xtry. time; yong* [arch.]; zugunruhe;

**actor** *(n.)*: actress [fem.]; barnstormer; character; *cast* [pl.]; *company* [pl.]; dramatist; entertainer; farceur; *gallery* ~; ham; hypocrite; impersonator; ingénue; *idol;* juvenile (~); kid-star; leading man [masc.] (-lady [fem.]); luvvie [Br.]; movie star; *non-reality;* onstage performer; play- ~; performer; *querencia [Sp.];* re-enactor; stage-player; star; thespian; *troupe* [pl.]; utility man; understudy; *vaudeville;* walk-on; *Xanthopoulos;* young ~; Ziegfeld girl [fem.];

**actual** *(adj.)*: authentic; accurate; bona fide; concrete; definite; existent; exact; factual; genuine; honest; indubitable; *justifiable;* known; legitimate; literal; matter-of-fact; non-fictitious; ontic; physical; precise; questionless; real; right(ful); substantial; tangible; true; unquestionable; valid; veritable; well-tried; *x-parent; yes;* 'zactly [dial.]; [*Ant.* artificial]

**actuality** *(n.)*: authenticity; accuracy; being; certainty; definiteness; existence; fact(uality); genuineness; hypostasis; indubitability; *justification; knowledge;* legitimacy; materiality; non-fiction; *ontic;* precision; *quaecumque sunt vera* [L.]; reality; substantiality; tangibility; truth; unquestionability; validity; veracity; *the* way it is; *x-parent; yes;* zero error; [*Ant.* artificiality]

**actually** *(adv.)*: accurately; beyond question; correctly; definitely; exactly; factually; genuinely; honestly; indubitably; just(ly); knowledgably; literally; most truly; *non-exaggeratedly; outright;* precisely; quite; really; straightforwardly; truly; truthfully; unquestionably; very; verily; well; 'xactly [slang]; *ywis* [arch.]; 'zactly [dial.];

**acumen** *(n.)*: acuity; astuteness; brightness; braininess; brainpower; brilliance; *common sense;* cleverness; discernment; expertise; farsightedness; genius; highbrowism; intelligence; judiciousness; keenness; logic; mental shrewdness; nimble-wittedness; *on the ball;* perspicuity; quickness; *reason;* sharpness; *thinking; ultra-quick; very sharp;* wit; wisdom; *xenagogy; yaup; zippiness;* [Ant. asininity]

**acutely** *(adv.)*: absolutely; *beyond compare;* completely; deeply; extremely; fully; glaringly; highly; intensely; *just;* keenly; *literally;* most (certainly); notably; *outright;* positively; quite; really; severely; sharply; terribly; utterly; very; wholly; 'xactly [slang]; ywis [arch.]; 'zactly [dial.];

**adage** *(n.)*: axiom; aphorism; byword; cliché; dictum; epigram; formulary; guideline; *hackneyed saying;* instruction; *judgment; koine;* law; maxim; neology; oracle; proverb; quote; rule; saying; truism; universal truth; verse; wisdom; *xenophonia; Yogism;* zeteticism;

**adamancy** *(n.)*: *absolute certainty;* bull-headedness; contrariness; determination; *ever-stubborn;* firmness; grimness; headstrongness; hardness; insistence; inflexibility; *jaw-set; keeping; lastingness;* mule-headedness; non-yieldedness; obduracy; pertinacity; *querulousness;* rigidity; renitency; stubbornness; tenacity; unyieldingness; *volition;* willfulness; *x-grained;* yieldlessness; *zero give;* [Ant. acquiescence]

**adamant** *(adj.)*: adamantine; bull-headed; contumacious; determined; ever-stubborn; firm; grim; headstrong; hard; insistent; inflexible; jaw-set; *keep; lasting;* mule-headed; non-bending; obdurate; pertinacious; quite strong; rigid; renitent; stubborn; tenacious; unyielding; very stubborn; willful; *x-grained;* yieldless; *zero give;* [Ant. acquiescent]

**adapt** *(v.)*: adjust; accustom; acclimate; become ~ed; change; customize; condition; conform; dispose; equip; fit; get ready; habilitate; inure; improve; jibe [slang]; key to; *labile;* make ready; naturalize; outfit; prepare; qualify; ready; retrofit; set; suit; transition; tailor; *ultra-prepared;* verse; whet; work out; *well-readied; xenize; yarken; zealously ~;*

**adaptable** *(adj.)*: adjustable; bendable; changeable; conformable; ductile; editable; fixable; flexible; giving; handy; impressionable; *jibe [slang]; knock into shape;* lithesome; modifiable; non-fixed; *outfit;* pliable; protean; *qualifiable;* revisable; settable; switchable; shapeable; tailorable; unfixed; versatile; workable; *xenomorphic;* yielding; *zero constancy;*

**adaptation** *(n.)*: adaption; alteration; betterment; change; conversion; difference; edition; enhancement; ecesis; fitting; gradual change; *horotely;* innovation; improvement; *jumping; key to;* *lowering; lengthening;* modification; *newness;* overhaul; permutation; *qualification;* revision; refitting; switch; substitution; transformation; tailoring; *upgrade;* variation; version; warping; *xenomorph; yaw; zigzag;*

**add** *(v.)*: append; annex; *bind;* combine; compendiate; do the sum; *expand; fasten; glue;* hitch; introduce; increase; join; knit; link; merge; *new; overgrow;* put together; *quasi-fuse;* reannex; *reunite;* superinduce; sum; supplement; super~; total; tally; tack on; unite; *vise; wed; xenograft;* yoke; *zip;*

**addict** *(n.)*: addicted person; acidhead; buff; cocain- ~; devotee; drug-user; dope-head; enthusiast; fan(atic); groupie; hophead; hype; habitué; ideologue; junkie; *keen;* LSD-user; marijuana smoker; methead; nut; narcie [slang]; narocomaniac; *obsessed;* practitioner; pothead; *pusher; quacked; radical;* slave; tripper; user; *votary; want it; xenocentrist;* yearner; zealot;

**addicted** *(adj.)*: *abusing;* bound; controlled; dependent; enslaved; fettered; *grip;* hooked; in the grip; *junky;* kept a slave; led captive; manacled; *not free;* obsessed; pinioned; *quashed;* reliant; shackled; taken captive; under the influence; *victimized; wasted; xtc;* yoked; *zoned out;*

**addiction** *(n.)*: addictedness; bad habit; bondage; compulsion; craving; dependency; entanglement; fixation; fetish; *got to have;* habit; infatuation; *idée fixe* [F.]; jones; *keenness;* longing; mania; need; narcomania; obsession; physical dependence; *problem;* preoccupation; passion; *quandary;* reliance; slavery; thing; urge; *vassalage; withdrawal; xenocentrism;* yearning; zeal;
**addictive** *(adj.)*: addiction-forming; *bondage;* compulsive; dependency-forming; entangling; enslaving; fixating; *got to have;* habit-forming; infatuating; *jones; killing; longing; mania; narcotic;* obsessive; *problematic;* preoccupying; *quandary;* reliant; shackling; *thing;* urge-producing; *vassalage; withdrawal; xenocentrism;* yearning; *zeal;*
**addition** *(n.)*: adding; accumulation; appendix; building; calculation; development; extension; figuring; gaining; heightening; increasing; insertion; joining; *knitting;* linking; math; mounting; *new;* obtainment; plus; *quantities;* raising; summation; supplementation; super~; totaling; tallying; uniting; *volume;* waxing; *xenograft;* yoking; *zipping together;*
**additional** *(adj.)*: added; bonus; back up; contributory; *different;* extra; further; farther; *gobs; heightened;* increased; joining; *king-sized amounts;* leftover; more; new; other; plus; *quantities;* residual; remaining; supplemental; *too;* ulterior; unused; *volumes; with;* x.; yet more; *zillions;*
**address** *(n.)*: allocution; bespeaking; communication; discourse; declamation; elocution; filibuster; formal speech; greeting; homily; instruction; indiction; *inaugural ~;* jeremiad; *kerygma;* lecture; message; monologue; *narration;* oration; oratory; public address; proclamation; pronouncement; *quotation;* recitation; rhetoric; speech; sermon; talk; utterance; vocalization; valediction; word(s); *xenophonia; yawner [off.]; zinger [slang];*
**address** *(v.)*: articulate; bespeak; converse; delineate; express; *foremention;* give speech; hold forth; instruct; *jaw; key in;* let out; mention; *notify;* opine; pipe up; quoth; relay; remark; relate; speak; state; tell; utter; voice; word; *xenophonia;* yak; *zero in;*
**adept** *(adj.)*: able; artful; brilliant; commanding; capable; deft; expert; familiar; good; gifted; handy; incredible; jolly good; knowledgeable; *laudable;* masterful; notable; nimble; outstanding; *old hand;* proficient; qualified; remarkable; seasoned; talented; unequalled; virtuosic; wonderful; xtry.; *you-beaut [Aus.]; zippy;*
**adeptness** *(n.)*: adroitness; bent; craftsmanship; cunning; deftness; expertise; flair; genius; handicraft; instinct; *jack-of-all-trades;* know-how; long suit; mastery; natural ability; occupation; proficiency; quickness; readiness; skill; talent; usefulness; virtuosity; way; *xenium;* years of experience; zest;
**adequacy** *(n.)*: adequateness; bearableness; *correctness; decency; enough;* fitness; goodness; *have; indication;* jakeness [Br.]; *keenness;* legitimacy; measuring up; norm(alcy); orthodoxy; properness; qualification; quality; reasonableness; satisfaction; satisfactoriness; sufficiency; tolerability; usualness; validness; *well; xel [arch.]; yenough* [arch.]; *Zufriedenheit* [G.];
**adequate** *(adj.)*: acceptable; bearable; conventional; *decent;* endurable; enough; fit; fine; good (enough); happy; honky-dory; *indicate;* jake [Br.]; kosher; legitimate; livable; minimal; normal; okay; passable; pleasing; *quantum sufficit* [L.]; reasonable; satisfactory; sufficient; tolerable; usual; valid; well (enough); *xel [arch.]; yenough* [arch.]; zero complaint; [Ant. abominable]
**adhere** *(v.)*: agglutinate; attach; affix; bond; cling; cohere; cement; dure; *embed;* fasten; glue; hold (together); *inviscate; imbed;* join; keep; latch; mount; *nail; oneness;* paste; *quick-dry;* remain; stick; secure; tack; unite; *viscous;* weld; *xenograft;* yoke; zip; [see believe]
**adherence** *(n.)*: agglutination; bond; cleaving; *daub; embedment;* fastening; gluing; holding (together); *inviscation;* joining; keeping; latching on; mounting; *nailing; oneness;* pasting; *quick-dry;* remaining; sticking; tacking; uniting; *viscosity;* weld; *xenograft;* yoke; *zipping;* [see belief]
**adherent** *(n.)*: advocate; believer; convert; devotee; enthusiast; follower; gillie; *holder;* imbiber; janissary; *kirsen [dial.];* liegeman; member; neophyte; *one;* proselyte; *questor;* recruit; receiver; supporter; truster; upholder; votary; *won over; Xnize; yielder;* zealot;

**adhesion** *(n.)*: adherence; bond; coherence; *daub; embedding;* fusing; fixing; grip; hold; invisication; joining; keeping; latching on; mounting; *nailing; oneness;* pasting; *quick-dry;* remaining; sticking; tenacity; union; viscousness; weld; *xenograft;* yoke; *zipping;*
**adhesive** *(adj.)*: adhering; bonding; clinging; dauby; emplastic; fastening; gummy; goopy; gooey; gluey; glutinous; holding; *inpissated;* joinable; *knit;* lentous; mucilaginous; *non-separable;* oozy; pitchy; *quince-mucilge;* ropy; sticky; tacky; tenacious; *-unite;* viscid; viscous; *weldable; xenograft;* yoke; *zip;*
**adjacency** *(n.)*: abutment; butting up; contiguity; contiguousness; connection; direct connection; *engrafted: flush against; go up to;* hardness by; *interconnection;* joining; knitting; linkage; meeting; nearness; *over one;* proximity; *quasi-fused; related;* sharing a wall; touching; union; verging; wedding; *xenograft;* yoking; *zero in on;*
**adjacent** *(adj.)*: against; attached; adjoining; abutting; by; beside; bordering; butting up against; close; contiguous; connected; directly joining; *engrafted:* flush against; *go up to;* hard by; *interconnect;* joined; joining; knitted; linked; meeting; nearby; nigh; next to; neighboring; *over one;* put together; *quasi-fused; related;* stuck-together; touching; united; verging; vicinal; wedded to; with; *xenograft;* yoked; *zero in on;*
**adjoin** *(v.)*: abut; attach; affix; border; butt up against; connect; dovetail; *engraft;* fasten; *glue;* hitch; interconnect; join; knit; link to; meet; neighbor; *over one;* put together; *quite close; reattach;* stick; touch; tie; unite; *vise;* wed; *xenograft;* yoke; *zip;*
**adjourn** *(v.)*: *abort;* break; close; conclude; delay; defer; end; finish; *go home;* hang; halt; interrupt; intermit; *just over; knock off;* leave; *motion to stop; non-continuance; over;* pause; postpone; quit; rest; recess; *readjourn;* suspend; stop; take a break; terminate; *unanimous motion to end;* vacate; wind up; *x; yield; zero convening;* [Ant. assemble]
**adjournment** *(n.)*: adjourning; break; continuance; closing; concluding; delay; deferment; end; finishing; *going home;* hanging; halting; interruption; intermission; jauking; *knocking off;* leaving; *motion;* non-continuance; *over;* pause; postponement; quitting; recess; suspension; stopping; termination; *unanimous motion to end;* vacating; winding up; *x-rest;* yielding; *zero convening;* [Ant. assembly]
**adjure** *(v.)*: appeal; beg; bid; beseech; call; cry; charge; command; desire; direct; dictate; demand; entreat; enjoin; *foreadmonish;* govern; *harass;* implore; *juration;* kneel to; *long for;* make request; mandate; necessitate; ordain; obsecrate; order; plead; press; *query;* request; require; supplicate; tell; urge; *vocalize;* wish; *XQ.;* yearn for; yark; *zakon [Rus.];*
**adjust** *(v.)*: align; attune; alter; bring into line; *bend;* correct; calibrate; change; dispose; doctor; enhance; fiddle with; fine-tune; fix; gear to; harmonize; improve; *jury-rig;* key to; *level off;* make aligned; modify; *non-fixed;* overhaul; *overcorrect;* proportion; put right; *quick-fix;* regulate; reset; right; rectify; revise; synchronize; switch; set; tweak; tune (up); *upbuild;* vary; work on; *xfer;* yark; zet [dial.];
**adjustment** *(n.)*: alignment; attunement; *bending;* calibration; correction; disposing; evening up; fine-tuning; gearing to; harmonization; improvement; jibing [slang]; keying to; *leveling off;* making aligned; *non-fixed;* overhaul; proportioning; *quick-fix;* re~; synchronization; tweaking; tuning; tune-up; *upbuilding;* vamping; *well-adjusted; xfer;* yarking; *zero discord;*
**administer** *(v. give)*: apportion; bestow; contribute; curate; dispense; endue; furnish; give; hand out; impart; *justly divide; kit;* let one have; mete out; *non-retention; offer;* portion (out); *quantify;* render; supply; *transfer; unitize;* vest; weigh; *xfer;* yield; zone; [Ant. appropriate]
**administer** *(v. oversee)*: administrate; boss; control; direct; *exhort;* force; govern; handle; head; influence; instruct; judge; keep; lead; manage; *nobble;* oversee; preside over; *quality control;* run; supervise; superintend; take over; *upkeep; vanquish;* watch over; *wield; XO;* yeme; *zero delta;*
**administration** *(n.)*: authority; *bishopric;* control; charge; direction; enforcement; *fatherhood;* governance; government; headship; *instruction;* jurisdiction; kingship; leadership; management; *necessitation;* oversight; power; *queenship;* running; rule; supervision; sovereignty; *taking the lead;* use of authority; *vizierate;* wardenship; *xenagogy;* yard; *zakon [Rus.];*

**administrative** *(adj.)*: administerial; bureaucratic; congressional; diet-related; executory; federal; governmental; heteronomous; institutional; judicatory; *kakistocratically;* legislative; ministerial; *mayoral;* nomothetic; national; official; political; parliamentary; quasi-legislative; ruling; senatorial; *throne; unicameral; viceroyal; ward; xenocratic; yard; zemstvo [Rus.];*
**administrator** *(n.)*: authority; bureaucrat; boss; chief; chairman; comptroller; director; executive; foreman; governor; head; intendant; jefe; keeper; leader; manager; *nazir [Mos.];* overseer; procurator; principal; *queen [fem.];* ruler; superintendent; supervisor; trustee; undershepherd; viceroy; warden; XO; yardboss; zayim;
**admirable** *(adj.)*: admired; beloved; commendable; distinguished; estimable; excellent; favorable; fine; great; honorable; highly sought-after; impressive; jake [Br.]; keen; laudable; meritorious; marvelous; nice; outstanding; praiseworthy; *qualified;* remarkable; splendid; terrific; ultra-good; very good; virtuous; worthy; wonderful; xtry.; yichus; *zealously loved;* [Ant. abominable]
**admiral** *(n.)*: ~ of the fleet; brass; captain; commodore; *director; executive officer;* flag officer; fleet ~; grand ~; high-ranking officer; head of fleet; *intendant; jarl; keeper;* lord; lieutenant ~; master; naval officer; *navarch* [Gr.]; officer; *pilot; quartermaster;* rear ~; skipper; shipmaster; *satrap* [Ind.]; *top brass; ultimate authority;* vice-admiral; *x-chaser; yachtsman; zayim;*
**admiration** *(n.)*: appreciation; approbation; adoration; *bowing;* cherishing; deference; delight; esteem; favor; glorification; honor; high regard; idolization; *justness;* kudos; love; marveling; *non-contempt;* obeisance; pleasure; *quality;* respect; regard; *salutation;* tribute; *unmitigated respect;* veneration; wonderment; worship; *xtry.; yielding;* zeal;
**admire** *(v.)*: appreciate; adore; applaud; *bow to;* commend; delight in; esteem; fancy; favor; go for; honor; hail; hold in high regard; idolize; *joy in; keen;* like; love; marvel at; notice; *outstanding;* praise; *quick to compliment;* respect; salute; think highly of; *uplift;* venerate; worship; *xtry.;* yearn; zeal; [Ant. abhor]
**admirer** *(n.)*: aficionado [masc.]; applauder; beau; cat; devotee; enthusiast; fan; groupie; hound; idolizer; junkie; *keen;* lover; maven; noticer; *obsessed;* praiser; *quack;* regarder; swain; *secret ~; thrilled;* ultraist; venerator; well-wisher; worshiper; *xenocentrist;* yearner; zealot; [Ant. abhorer]
**admission** *(n. confession)*: acknowledgement; blame-taking; confession; declaration; *enunciation;* fessing up [improper]; *granting; guilt; honesty;* indication; jurat; *keeping; lining up; message;* notification; owning up; profession; *question-and-answer; reassurance;* self-conviction; testimonial; *utterance;* verification; witness; *xenagogy; yielding; zero in;*
**admission** *(n. entry)*: admittance; access; *blessing;* clearance; *door;* entrance; entry; *freedom;* getting in; *have;* ingress; initiation; *joint-permission;* the key; license; *may; non-barred;* open door; permission; *qualified;* right of entry; reception; *re~;* sufferance; taking in; unbarred entry; *uninhibited; validation;* way in; *xfer;* Y. [mil.]; *zero hindrance;*
**admit** *(v. acknowledge)*: acknowledge; agree; allow; bear testimony; confess; come clean; concede; disclose; divulge; declare; express; fess up [improper]; give; grant; hold forth; indicate; inform; *jaw; key in;* let out; make known; notify; noise; own up; profess; *plea guilty;* proclaim; quoth; *quit denying; realize;* relate; state; tell; take the blame; utter; voice; word; *xenagogy;* yield; zero in; [Ant. argue]
**admit** *(v. allow entrance)*: allow; accept; *bless;* clear; *door;* embrace; *forbear;* give access; homologate; *have;* invite in; induct; *justify; key;* let in; motion on; *nod;* open door for; permit; pass; *qualify;* receive; *readmit;* suffer; take in; usher in; validate; welcome; wave on; *x on the dotted line;* yes; yield; *zero hindrance;*
**admittance** *(n.)*: access; admission; *blessing;* clearance; *door;* entrance; *freedom;* getting in; *have;* ingress; induction; *joint-permission;* the key; license; *motion on; non-barred;* open door; permission; *qualified;* right of entry; reception; *re~;* sufferance; ticket; unbarred entry; *uninhibited; validation;* way in; *xfer;* Y. [mil.]; *zero hindrance;*

**admixture** *(n.)*: amalgamation; blend; combination; concoction; *dash;* elixir; ester; farrago; formula; fusion; *grouping;* hodgepodge; intermixture; jumble(ment); kava; *lumping;* mishmash; minglement; mixture; merging; *non-homogenous ~;* olio; pasticcio; potion; *queer;* recipe; salad; *temperament;* union; ule; *variety; wedding; xanthate;* yanggoma; *zipping together;*

**admonish** *(v.)*: advise; berate; caution; counsel; direct; excoriate; fault; give advice; harangue; instruct; jaw; knock; lecture; lay into; *macerate; notify;* objurgate; *punish; question;* rebuke; reprove; scold; tell off; upbraid; vituperate; warn; *xuld [arch.];* yell at; *zap;* [*Ant.* applaud]

**admonition** *(n.)*: admonishment; berating; correction; denunciation; excoriation; faulting; faultfinding; going-over; haranguing; increpation; jawing; knocking; lecture; lambasting; monitory; nagging; objurgation; *punishment; questioning;* rebuke; reprimand; scolding; telling off; upbraiding; vituperation; warning; *xuld [arch.];* yelling at; *zapping;* [*Ant.* acclaim]

**ado** *(n.)*: activity; bustle; bother; commotion; doings; excitement; flurry; goings on; hubbub; intranquility; jumble; kerfuffle; labor; movement; non-orderliness; *ordeal;* pother; *quantity;* ruckus; stirring; to-do; trouble; upheaval; vexation; wasting time; *xtry. commotion; yelling;* zealous carrying on;

**adolescence** *(n.)*: adolescent years; boyhood [masc.]; childhood; development; early years; formative years; growing; girlhood [fem.]; greenness; *hatchling;* immaturity; juvenility; juvenescence; kidhood [joc.]; *little;* may; nonage; *over-young;* puberty; pubescence; *quite young; rawness;* springtime of life; tenderness; underdevelopment; verdancy; *weanling;* XS; youth; *zero-experience;* [*Ant.* agedness]

**adolescent** *(n.)*: anklebiter; bobby soxer [fem.]; *child;* damsel [fem.]; *eighteen-year old; fifteen-year old;* guy [masc.]; gal [fem.]; high-schooler; *individual;* juvenile; kid; lad [masc.]; lass [fem.]; minor; *nineteen-year old;* older kid; pubescent; quincearian; rose [fem. slang]; *seventeen-year old;* teenager; *underage; virgin; vandal;* whippersnapper; *xbred;* youth; *zit-faced kid;*

**adopt** *(v.)*: accept; affect; bring in; borrow; co-opt; copy; *desire; do;* embrace; filial; *get;* have; *interest; imitate; join;* keep; legally ~; make one's own; naturalize; obtain legal rights; *procure; qualify;* receive; raise; *re~;* support; take in; *undertake;* vouch for; welcome; *xfer;* yoke; zet [*dial.*]; [*Ant.* abandon]

**adoption** *(n.)*: acceptance; adfiliation; assumption; bringing in; co-optation; *doing;* embracing; filiation; *get; have; imitating; joining;* keeping; legal ~; making one's own; naturalization; obtaining; *procuring; qualification;* receiving; *supporting;* taking in; *undertaking; vouching for; welcoming; xfer;* yoking; zet [*dial.*]; [*Ant.* abandonment]

**adoration** *(n.)*: admiration; affection; adulation; *bowing; celebration;* devotion; esteem; *fondness;* glorification; honor; homage; idolization; *jubilation;* kneeling; love; laudation; magnification; never-failing love; *obeisance;* praise; *quixotic;* reverence; *song of praise;* tribute; undying love; veneration; worship; *xenophilia;* yearning; zeal; [*Ant.* abhorrence]

**adore** *(v.)*: admire; *beloved;* cherish; delight in; enjoy; endear; feel affection for; greatly love; have feelings; idolize; joy in; *kiss;* love; *melt; non-selfish;* overlove; praise; *quixotic;* relish; regard; show love; *tenderness; utmost esteem;* value; venerate; worship; *xenophilic;* yearn for; zeal; [*Ant.* abhor]

**adorn** *(v.)*: array; bedeck; beautify; bedizen; clothe; dress; decorate; dandify; deck (out); embellish; enhance; emblazon; enchase; fancify; florid; grace; garnish; habilitate; inwrought; jazz up; jewel; kit; *let be adorned;* make prettier; *nicer;* ornament; prettify; pretty up; prank; *quaintise [arch.];* render lovely; *readorn;* spruce; trim; *use ornaments;* vest; *wear; xtry.; yclad [arch.];* zizz; [*Ant.* abase]

**adult** *(adj.)*: *aged;* big; *complete;* developed; *elder;* full-grown; grown(-up); high-grown; *in one's prime; just ripe; king-size;* legal-aged; mature; not a kid; old; of legal age; *perfect;* quadragenarian; ripe; *senior;* thoroughly grown; unchildlike; voting-aged; well-grown; XL; *yain; zero immaturity;*

**adult** *(n.)*: *aged person;* big person; *citizen;* daddy [masc.]; elder; full-grown person; grown-up; high-grown man; *individual;* joe [slang, masc.]; jane [slang fem.]; *kins(wo)man; legal-aged;* mature person; man [masc.]; mommy [fem.]; non-minor; old(er) person; *parent;* quadragenarian; *registered voter; senior; twenty-year old; up in years;* voter; woman [fem.]; *xenic;* young ~; *zaftig [fem.];*

**adulterate** *(v.)*: alter; bend; corrupt; debase; entwist; foul up; garble; *harm;* injure; *jade;* knot; *louse up;* mutilate; *nullify; obloquoy; oppress;* pollute; prostitute; *quade* [arch.]; ruin; spoil; taint; *undo;* vary; warp; *xenomorph*; *yaw; zad;*
**adulterer** *(n.)*: adulterous man; belswagger; carouser; debauchee; evil man; fornicator; gigolo; home-wrecker; immoral-man; john [slang]; *keeper or a mistress;* libertine; lecher; libidnist; Lothario; mistress-keeper; *(married) man;* non-faithful; *outparamour;* paramour; philanderer; palliard; *quad;* rake; *Romeo;* satyr; two-timer; unfaithful man; vow-breaker; whoremonger; womanizer; wencher; *x-rated;* yoke-breaker; *zipless;* [*see* sinner]
**adulteress** *(n.)*: advoutress; bawd; courtesan; doxy; evil woman; fornicator; gamester; harlot; immoral woman; jade; kittock; lady of the evening; mistress; *non-faithful; obscene woman;* prostitute; put; paramour; quean; *rig;* seductress; strange woman; temptress; unfaithful woman; vixen; whore; *x-rated;* yaud; *zipless;* [*see* sinner]
**adulterous** *(adj.)*: abandoned; adulterative; bad; base; concupiscent; dissolute; extramarital; fornicative; fescennine; godless; *harlotry;* immoral; illicit; jadish; *kinky;* lascivious; lewd; libertine; licentious; meretricious; non-pure; obscene; profligate; perversel *quad;* reprobate; sinful; slattern; trampy; unchaste; unlawful; unfaithful; venereous; wicked; wanton; whorish; x-rated; *youthful list; zipless;*
**adultery** *(n.)*: affair; betrayal; cuckolddom; cheating; *concupiscence;* debauchery; disloyalty; *eroticism; evil;* fornication; gross infidelity; *harlotry;* immorality; infidelity; *jade; kinkiness;* lasciviousness; *looseness; mischief;* non-faithfulness; odure; promiscuity; *perversion;* playing the harlot; *queanery;* revelry; (sexual) sin; treachery; unfaithfulness; uncleanness; venery; whoredom; whoremongery; *x-rated behavior; youthful lust; zizziness;*
**adulthood** *(n.)*: adultness; *bigness;* coming of age; driving age; *enlargement;* full-bloom; fullness of years; grown (up); *heightening; increase; judiciousness; knowledge;* luxuriating; legal age; maturity; manhood [masc.]; *non-child; of age;* prime of life; parenthood; *quality;* ripeness; *sprouting; thriving; upshooting;* virility [masc.]; womanhood [fem.]; *XL;* years; *zoomed up;*
**advance** *(v.)*: *approach;* better; come; continue; draw on; edge; forge ahead; further; foster; go forward; help; *hurry; headway;* improve; journey on; jet; *kindle;* leap; move ahead; *non-stationary; ongoing;* progress; proceed; promote; press on; push; *quicken;* run; rise; set forward; sail on; travel; *underway;* venture ahead; walk; *xfer; yede;* zip; [*Ant.* abandon]
**advanced** *(adj.)*: *ahead of its time;* brand-new; complex; cutting-edge; *des nous jours* [F.]; *enhanced;* forward-looking; ground-breaking; high-tech; improved; *just out; keen; the* latest; leading-edge; (most) modern; new; *outstanding;* progressed; *quantum leap;* revolutionary; sophisticated; state-of-the-art; technologically ~; up-to-date; ultramodern; very ~; *world-shattering; xtry.;* years ahead of its time; *zoomed ahead;* [*Ant.* archaic]
**advancement** *(n.)*: approach; appointment; betterment; continuance; coming along; development; expansion; elevation; furtherance; growth; gain; helping; heightening; improvement; increase; jump; *knowledge;* leap; maturity; melioration; *non-stationary;* ontogeny; progress(ion); promotion; preferment; quantum increase; raising; sailing on; traveling; upswing; upturn; upgrading; venturing ahead; walking; *xfer; yede;* zipping; [*Ant.* abatement]
**advantage** *(n.)*: avail; asset; benefit; *capital gain; cumulation;* dominance; edge; favor; gain; help; head start; improvement; increase; *jump;* kinch; lead; *makings;* net gain; obtainment; pro(fit); *quick asset;* reward; superiority; *takings;* upper hand; usefulness; upside; vantage; whip hand; *worthwhile; x-div;* yield; *zillions;* [*Ant.* adverseness]
**advantageous** *(adj.)*: assistive; beneficial; constructive; conducive; desirable; expedient; fair; favorable; good; gainful; handy; helpful; instrumental; *judicious;* keen; *lucrative; mutualism;* nice; outstanding; profitable; propitious; *quality;* rewarding; salutary; serving; *terrific;* useful; valuable; worthwhile; xtry.; yieldful; *zillions;* [*Ant.* adverse

**advent** *(n.)*: arrival; birth(day); beginning; coming; dawn; entrance; founding; formation; genesis; giving birth; hatching; inception; *jump off; kickoff; launching;* manifestation; nativity; naissance; origination; presentation; *quickening;* rise; start; *take-off;* ushering in; *unveiling;* visitation; *welcoming* xenogenesis; *youth;* zygogeneis; [*Ant.* abandonment]

**adventure** *(n.)*: *action-packed;* bold undertaking; challenge; dare; escapade; excursion; experience; expedition; exploration; epic; emprise; foray; glory-seeking; *hunt; hazard;* intrepidity; journey; jeep safari; knight-errantry; lark; mis~; *night voyage;* odyssey; pilgrimage; quest; *risk;* sojourn; safari; trek; undertaking; venture; voyage; *wayfaring; xenize; yong* [arch.]; *zugunruhe* [G.];

**adventurer** *(n.)*: adventure-seeker; buccaneer; challenger; dare-devil; explorer; forayer; glory-seeker; (hitch-)hiker; intrepid individual; journeyer; knight; *lark; musketeer; night voyager; odyssey;* pioneer; questor; *renown;* sojourner; swashbuckler; traveler; trekker; *undertaking;* venturer; voyager; wayfarer; *xenizer; yong [arch.]; zugunruhe [G.];*

**adventurous** *(adj.)*: adventuresome; action-packed; bold; courageous; daring; enterprising; epic; fearless; gutsy; heroic; intrepid; *journey; knightly; lion-hearted;* manly; nervy; *outstanding;* plucky; *quick-witted;* rash; risk-taking; strong; spirited; stout; thrill-seeking; temerarious; undaunted; venturesome; *wherewithal; xtry.;* yare; *zealous;* [*Ant.* apprehensive]

**adversarial** *(adj.)*: antagonistic; adversative; belligerent; confrontational; competitive; disputing; enemy; *fierce; galsome;* hostile; inimical; *jeopardizing;* kindless; *low-down;* malicious; non-friendly; oppositional; pugnacious; quarrelsome; rivalrous; striving; *threatening;* unfriendly; violent; warlike; *xenophobic; yieldless;* zealotic; [*Ant.* amicable]

**adversary** *(n.)*: antagonist; attacker; bad guy; contender; competitor; disputant; enemy; foe; *garrison;* hostile; instigator; jangler; kemper; *legion; litigant;* match; nemesis; opponent; *player; quarreler;* rival; striver; *threat; unfriendly;* vier; warling; *xenic; yuon* [arch.]; *zeke [off];* [*Ant.* ally]

**adverse** *(adj.)*: antagonistic; bad; contrary; disagreeable; difficult; detrimental; execrable; foul; grievous; hard; harmful; inauspicious; ill-favored; inimical; jarring; kindless; lousy; miserable; negative; objectionable; poor; *quad; rotten;* severe; terrible; undesirable; unfavorable; very bad; wicked; *xtry. bad;* yucky; *zero pleasure;* [*Ant.* advantageous]

**adversity** *(n.)*: affliction; bind; calamity; difficulty; encumbrance; endangerment; fix; grief; hardship; infelicity; jam; kink; load; misfortune; nuisance; opposition; problems; quandary; rattle; strait; trouble; trial; unhappiness; upheaval; vexation; worries; woe; *xerotripsis; yuckiness; zhlubby;* [*Ant.* advantage]

**advertise** *(v.)*: announce; ballyhoo; bill; broadcast; circulate; disseminate; endorse; exhibit; further; flaunt; give notice; hard sell; inform; *joint-advertisement; known;* let be known; make known; market; notify; *overspread;* plug; promote; publish; pitch; push; *quarter-page ad;* reveal; spread the word; solicit; sell; soft sell; sponsor; tell; tout; *televise;* unmask; *voice;* woo; *xmit; yell; zine ad;*

**advertisement** *(n.)*: ad; announcement; brochure; bill; blurb; broadcast; *billboard;* color ad; circular; commercial; display ad; endorsement; flyer; four-page spread; *general public;* handbill; information; insert; *joint- ~; kid's TV show ad;* leaflet; magazine ~; notice; newspaper ~; *over the air;* promotion; poster; publicity; quadrifoliate ad; radio spot; spot; TV ad; unifoliate ~; *vignette;* want ad; *xmit;* yellow pages ad; zine ad;

**advice** *(n.)*: assistance; admonition; *befriending; bad ~;* counsel; direction; exhortation; free ~; guidance; good ~; help; instruction; judgment; *kibizing* [Yid.]; *leading; mentorship; notification;* opinion; piece of ~; *quick ~;* recommendation; rede; suggestion; tip; *urging;* voice; word of ~; *xenagogy; yammering; zeroing in;*

**advisable** *(adj.)*: advantageous; beneficial; constructive; desirable; expedient; favorable; good; helpful; *intelligent;* judicious; *keen; lucrative;* meet; *no-nonsense; operative;* prudent; *quartful* [arch.]; recommended; sensible; *tenable;* useful; valuable; wise; well-advised; *xtry.; yieldful; zero-problem;* [*Ant.* absurd]

**advise** *(v.)*: admonish; *be a friend to;* counsel; direct; exhort; foreadvise; guide; give counsel; help; inform; instruct; judge; kibitz; lead; *mention;* notify; offer one's opinion; postulate; *quicken;* recommend; suggest; tender one's opinion; *urge;* voice; warn; *xenagogy; yammer; zero in;*
**advisor** *(n.)*: adviser; *bearer of advice;* counselor; consultant; consigliere; cabinet member; Dutch uncle; expert; friend; guide; guru; helper; instructor; informer; *judge;* keen ~; *leader;* mentor; nestor; oracle; *postulator;* prophet; *quain [arch.];* recommender; seer; tip-giver; *urger;* very wise man; wise man; *xenagogue; yammerer; zero in;* [*Ant.* adversary]
**advisory** *(adj.)*: admonitory; *beware;* counseling; directing; exhortive; foreadvising; guiding; hortatory; instructive; informative; *judicious; knowledgeable;* leading; monitory; notifying; *opinionative;* postulational; *quickening;* recommending; suggestive; tendering one's opinion; *urging; voice;* warning; *well-advised; xenagogic; yet unsafe; zeroing in;*
**advisory** *(n.)*: alert; *beware;* caution; caveat; *distress;* emergency; forewarning; grim warning; *hue and cry;* injunction; *jeopardy;* klaxton; larum; monition; notification; *omen;* precaution; *quivering;* red alert; sign(al); siren; tip; *urging; vatic;* warning; *xenagogy;* yellow alert; *zealous alert;*
**advocacy** *(n.)*: advancement; advocating; backing; championing; defending; endorsement; encouragement; furtherance; getting behind; help; intercession; judicial pleading; *keen on;* lending support; making a case for; *non-enmity; overspread;* promotion; *quickening;* recommendation; support; taking up for; upholding; *vindication; wishing well; xtry. backing; yes; zeal;* [*Ant.* attack]
**advocate** *(n.)*: advocator; advancer; *attorney;* backer; champion; defender; exponent; friend; favorer; great supporter; helper; intercessor; *joiner;* keen supporter; *laureate; mate; non-enemy; overcomer;* proponent; promoter; patron(ess); protagonist; partisan; *questor;* representative; supporter; *teammate;* upholder; voice; votary; well-wisher; *xtry. backer; yokefellow;* zealot; [*Ant.* adversary]
**advocate** *(v.)*: advance; back; champion; defend; declaim; endorse; encourage; elevate; favor; foster; further; get behind; help; indorse; *join; keen on;* lend support; make a case for; *non-enmity; overspread;* plead; promote; push; *quicken;* recommend; sympathize; stand behind; support; take up for; uphold; *vindicate; wish well; xtry. back; yes; zeal;* [*Ant.* attack]
**aerial** *(adj.)*: aeronautical; airborne; atmospheric; birdlike; cloudbourne; *darting;* ethereal; flying; fledge; *gliding;* high-up; in-flight; *jetting; kiting;* lofty; mid-air; non-grounded; overhead; pneumatic; *quickened; rising;* superterrene; *taking flight;* upper-atmospheric; volplaning; windborne; *x-plane; yonder; zooming o'er;*
**affair** *(n. adulterous relationship)*: adultery; betrayal; bawdishness; cheating; dalliance; extracurricular activity [joc.]; fling; fornication; *gross infidelity;* hanky-panky; immorality; infidelity; jadery; *kinkiness;* liaison; *mischief;* non-faithfulness; odure; promiscuity; *perversion; queanery;* relationship; shamelessness; sin; two-timing; treachery; unfaithfulness; venery; whoredom; whoremongery; *x-rated behavior; yielding; zhlubbery;*
**affair** *(n. happening)*: activity; business; *befall;* chapter; concern; development; event; episode; experience; fact; function; *goings on;* gathering; happening; incident; issue; job; key event; *lot;* matter; notable event; occasion; occurrence; proceeding; *question;* reception; situation; social event; thing; undertaking; *venture; work out; xtr. event; yield;* zinger;
**affect** *(v.)*: act on; bring about; cause; drive; engender; foster; generate; *have result;* initiate; instigate; induce; infect; *jump-start;* kindle; lead off; make happen; move; *nudge;* occasion; produce; quicken; result; redound; set off; touch; trigger; *unlock; vivify;* work; *xuld [arch.];* yield; *zip into motion;*
**affection** *(n.)*: amorousness; adoration; *beloved;* care; closeness; devotion; desire; dearness; endearment; fondness; feelings; good will; heart; infatuation; *joy;* kindness; love; *motherly love;* niceness; *overlove;* passion; *quixotic;* romance; sentiment; tenderness; *unselfishness; vehemence;* warmth; *xenophilia;* yearning; *zealous love;*

**affectionate** *(adj.)*: amorous; becharmed; caring; cuddly; cozy; doting; devoted; endearing; friendly; gentle; gushy; huggy; infatuated; intimate; *jealous;* kissy; loving; mushy; nice; *open;* passionate; quixotic; romantic; sentimental; sweet; snuggly; tender; *unreserved; Valentine;* warm; xenial; *yearnful; zealous;* [*Ant.* aloof]

**affidavit** *(n.)*: attestation; affirmation; *binding document;* citation; confirmation; declaration; document; expression; *form;* given statement; *holding forth;* indication; jurat; *kept;* legal notification; manifestation; notification; notice; official declaration; profession; proclamation; protestation; quotation; report; statement; signed ~; testimonial; testimonium; *ukase* [Rus.]; validation; verification; venue; witness; written declaration; *x-form;* yeme; *zet [dial.];*

**affiliate** *(v.)*: associate; belong to; connect; correlate; consort; deal; *enlist;* fraternize; fellowship; get together; have to do with; hitch up; involve; implicate; join; *knit;* link; make a league; *nail; one;* partner; *quinquevirate;* relate; socialize; tie; unite; *vise;* work together; *xenograft;* yoke; *zip together;* [*Ant.* avoid]

**affinity** *(n.)*: agreement; accord; bond; camaraderie; delight; empathy; fellowship; good will; harmony; identification; joint-agreement; kinship; like-mindedness; meeting of the minds; nearness; oneness; partiality; quarrel-lessness; rapport; solidarity; trust; unity; *voluntariness; willingness; xenia; yedinstvo* [Rus.]; *zeal;* [*Ant.* adversity]

**affirm** *(v.)*: acknowledge; attest; assert; aver; bear out; confirm; declare; establish; fix; guarantee; hold forth; indicate; join; kith [Scot.]; line up; legitimize; make known; maintain; nail down; okay; profess; prove; quoth; reassure; say; substantiate; tell; uphold; verify; warrant; *xenagogy;* yes; *zero doubt;* [*Ant.* abjure]

**affirmation** *(n.)*: assertion; averment; *broadcast;* confession; confirmation; declaration; enunciation; *falling in;* green light; holding forth; indication; jactitation; *keeping; lining up; message;* nod; okay; pronouncement; predication; *quotation;* reaffirmation; statement; testimonial; utterance; verification; witness; *xenagogy;* yeme; *zero in;* [*Ant.* abjuration]

**affix** *(v.)*: attach; bind; connect; dovetail; engraft; fasten; fix; *glue;* hitch; interlink; infix; implant; ingraft; join; knit; link; mount; nail; *oxreim;* put together; *quasi-fuse;* relate; reunite; rivet; stick; set to; splice; secure; tie; tack; unite; *vise;* wed; weld; *xenograft;* yoke; *zip;*

**afflict** *(v.)*: abuse; ail; brutalize; cause suffering; disserve; damage; engrieve; endamage; fix [slang]; grieve; hurt; injure; impair; inflict damage; jeel; *kick; knock;* lift hand against; maim; *nocument;* oppress; pain; persecute; *quail* [arch.]; *ruin;* smite; scath; trouble; torture; torment; *unsafe;* vitiate; victimize; vex; wound; wreak havoc; *x.; ydrad [arch.]; zap;* [*Ant.* aid]

**affliction** *(n.)*: adversity; burden; calamity; difficulty; endangerment; evil; foul-treatment; grief; hardship; infelicity; jam; *killing; loss;* misfortune; malady; misery; nocument; opposition; ordeal; pain; plague; *quandary; rigor;* suffering; sorrow; trouble; trial; tribulation; torment; unhappiness; vexation; worries; woe; *xerotripsis; yuckiness; zhlubby;* [*Ant.* aid]

**affluence** *(n.)*: assets; abundance; bounty; capital; *dollars;* estate; fortune; gold; holdings; *income; jewels; krugerrands* luxury; money; means; *notes;* opulence; prosperity; *quantities;* riches; substance; success; treasure; trappings (of success); uberty; *valuables;* wealth; *xenocurrency; yellow boy [Br.];* zillions [slang]; [*Ant.* abjection]

**affluent** *(adj.)*: abounding; bountiful; comfortable; *dollars;* extravagant; filthy rich; *gold;* high-class; *haves;* independently wealthy; jet set; *king's ransom;* loaded; moneyed; *notes;* opulent; privileged; prosperous; *quartful* [arch.]; rich; successful; treasure-filled; upper class; vested; well off; wealthy; *xenocurrency; yellow boy [Br.]; zillionaire;* [*Ant.* abject]

**afford** *(v.)*: allow; allocate; bear; confer; dispense; expend; furnish; grant; have (funds for); indulge; invest; justify; *keep;* let; manage (to pay for); *net;* offer; pay for; *quantify;* ration; render; supply; *transfer;* use up; validate; well ~; *xfer;* yield; *zum [arch.];*

**affront** *(n.)*: aspersion; blast; criticism; crushing remark; dig; defamation; epithet; *fleer;* gibe; humiliating remark; insult; jibe; knock; libel; maligning; name; offense; outrage; put-down; quip; rude comment; slight; slur; smear; traducement; unkind name; violence; wipe; *xuld [arch.]; yock;* zinger; [*Ant.* applause]

**affront** *(v.)*: asperse; attack; belittle; criticize; denigrate; disparage; excoriate; *fleer;* gibe; humiliate; insult; jibe; knock; libel; malign; *name-calling;* outrage; put one down; quib; revile; run down; slight; slander; smear; traduce; upset; vilify; wipe; *xuld [arch.];* yock; *zing;* [*Ant.* applaud]

**afloat** *(adj.)*: adrift; buoyant; *coasting;* drifting; *evolation;* floating; *going;* hovering; inaquating; *jetting;* kiting; loose; *moving;* natant; on the water; planing; *quickened; resting;* seaborne; take to the seas; unmoored; unanchored; *voyage;* waterborne; *xuld [arch.]; yern;* zero mooring;

**afoot** *(adv.)*: arisen; befalling; coming to pass; developing; ensuing; falling; going on; happening; intervening; *jumping up; kep;* lighting; materializing; *nearing;* occurring; proceeding; *quickening; rising;* springing up; transpiring; up; venturing; *work; xpire;* yield; zip;

**aforementioned** *(adj.)*: abovementioned; aforesaid; aforenamed; before mentioned; cited previously; *declared earlier;* earlier cited; foresaid; foregoing; *gone before;* having been previously cited; *initially referred to;* just-mentioned; *known already; last reference;* mentioned earlier; named before; originally referred to; previously mentioned; *quoted earlier;* referenced earlier; stated previously; supra; *talked about previously; used before; viz.; whilom; xel [arch.]; y-aforsayde* [arch.]; *zet [dial.];*

**afraid** *(adj.)*: apprehensive; alarmed; *bothered;* careful; concerned; cowardly; distressed; distraught; edgy; fearful; frightened; fretful; faint-hearted; gutless; *hesitant;* horrified; insecure; jittery jumpy; kitten-hearted; lily-livered; milk-livered; nervous; overanxious; paranoid; pluckless; panicky; phobic; petrified; quivering; *reluctant;* scared; spooked; terrified; terror-stricken; *troubled;* uneasy; unnerved; vexed; worried; *xenophobic;* yellow(-bellied); *zapped;* [see aghast]

**Africa** *(n.)*: Abyssinia; Black Continent; Congo; Dark Continent; Ethiopia; East ~; *faraway ~;* Gambia; Ghana; Ham; Ivory Coast; jungle; Kenya; Land of Ham; Madagascar; Nigeria; negrodom; *Orange Free State;* Pretoria; Qwaqwa; *Rwanda;* South ~; *Tanzania;* Uganda; *Venda;* West ~; *Xhosa; Yamoussukro;* Zaire; Zambia;

**African** *(adj. + n.)*: Abyssinian; black; colored; dark-skinned; Ethiopian; *Fingo; Gambian;* Hamite; Hottentot; *Ibibio;* jetty [off.]; klonkie; *Kenyan; Liberian;* melanochroid; Negro; *Orange Free State;* Pygmy; Quashi [off.]; *Rhodesian; Sudanese; Tanzanian;* ulotrichous; umfaan [off.]; *Venda; Watuzi; Xhosa; Yoruba; Zulu; Zambian;*

**afterlife** *(n.)*: afterworld; by and by; coming eternity; destiny; eternity; ever-after; future life; *the great beyond;* hereafter; immortality; *jusqu'au bout [F.]; keeps going;* life after death; *measureless;* next life; over the river (of death); postexistence; *quadrillion;* rest of eternity; sweet by and by; time without end; *unending; vast;* world to come; *x-life;* yonder; *zillions;* [see eternity]

**aftermath** *(n.)*: after-effects; byproduct; consequence; development; effects; fruit; following events; *get;* harvest; impact; *just desserts; known outcome;* lattermath; *matter; necessarily;* outcome; product; quantum effect; results; sequent; termination; upshot; *validity;* work; wake; *xenagogy;* yield; *zeug [G.];*

**afternoon** *(n.)*: after noon; beyond noon; siesta; directly after lunch; evening; following the noontide; *going for 4:00;* heat of the day; *interval;* just past noon; *kilocycle;* later in day; mid~; *noontide;* one o'clock; *the* p.m.; post meridiem; pip-emma; *quarter past one; right after lunch;* second half of the day; teatime; under the sun; vesper; *Wednesday ~; xiawu* [Chin.]; *yesterday ~; Zeit [G.];*

**afterward** *(adv.)*: afterwards; after that; beyond that; coming next; directly following; eventually; following; going next; henceforth; in a while; just behind; *key position;* later; *much later;* next; on the heels of; past that; *quickly following;* right after; soon after; subsequently; successively; then(ceforth); thereafter; ultimately; *virtually;* whenceforth; *x-list;* yond; *Z-position;* [*Ant.* afore]

**against** *(v.)*: at odds with; anti-; bucking; contrary; disagree with; expostulatory; fighting ~; 'gainst [slang]; have a quarrel with; in disagreement with; *jangle;* kick at; lock horns with [slang]; *make fur fly;* not supportive of; opposed to; *pitted ~;* quarrel with; resist; stand ~; strongly oppose; take issue with; *undermine;* versus; withstand; *x.; yieldless; zero agreement;*

**agape** *(adj.)*: astonished; bowled over; confounded; dumbfounded; *enchanted;* flabbergasted; gaping; *held in awe;* impressed; *jaw dropped; keeled over; lo!;* marveling; nonplused; open-mouthed; poleaxed; quite amazed; *remarkable;* speechless; totally in awe; *un belief; vexed;* wide open; *xtry.;* yawning; *zing;*

**agapé** *(n.)*: affection; brotherly love; charity; devotion; endearment; fealty; goodwill; heart; *interest; joy;* kindness; love; mutuality; niceness; oneness; pure love; *quite selfless;* real love; selflessness; tender love; unselfishness; *vehemence;* warmth; *xtry. love;* yearning; zeal; [*Ant.* abhorrence]

**age** *(n.)*: adulthood; amount of time; bit; *century;* dotage; day; dispensation; elderliness; era; epoch; *fortnight;* generation; golden ~; hour; historical period; *heyday;* interval; *juncture; kilocycle;* lifetime; maturity; millennium; *new ~;* oldness; old ~; period; quarter; *run time;* senility; span; time (span); undetermined time period; *vintage;* wear and tear; *week;* x-time; *yog* [Ind.]; years; *zone;*

**age** *(v.)*: advance in years; become older; come into one's own; develop; deteriorate; *educe;* flower; grow (older); gray; *heighten;* increase; *jump up;* keep growing; *length of years;* mature; *not getting any younger; overripen;* progress (through life); *quantum increase;* ripen; shoot up; *thrive;* upshoot; *vegetate;* wax older; wane; *xfer;* yellow; *zip through life;*

**agency** *(n.)*: association; bureau; branch; company; *catchery* [Ind.]; department; division; establishment; federal ~; group; *house;* incorporation; jura; *kongsi* [Chin.]; location; ministry; nexus; organization; office; *partnership;* quango; regional office; society; town office; *unit;* village office; *workers' union; x-class; yuan* [Chin.]; zonal office;

**agenda** *(n.)*: arranged plan; blueprint; bill; calendar; docket; design; *engineering;* foredesign; ground-work; *hidden ~;* itinerary; *journal;* key objectives; layout; list; lineup; master plan; *notion;* outline; program; plan; *quo mode [L.]; reason;* schedule; strategem; scheme; timetable; things to be done; underlying plan; *visual; way; wile; x-chart; yantra [Hind.];* zenithal projection;

**aggravate** *(v. annoy)*: annoy; bug; bother; chafe; disturb; exasperate; frustrate; gall; grate on; harass; irritate; jangle; key up; *livid;* menace; madden; nettle; *offend;* pester; pique; provoke; *queach [arch.];* rankle; rile; *steam;* test; upset; vex; wig; weary; *x-ing;* yerk; *zing;* [*Ant.* appeal]

**aggravate** *(v. make worse)*: augment; build up; compound; drive; exacerbate; fire up; get worse; heighten; intensify; inflame; *just making it worse;* kindle; *louse up;* multiply; magnify; *not help; outgo;* put fuel on the fire; provoke; *quickly degenerate;* rile; ramify; stir up; trouble; *undo; verge downward;* worsen; *x; yield more trouble; zero help;* [*Ant.* assist]

**aggravation** *(n.)*: annoyance; bother; crossness; dissatisfaction; displeasure; enragement; frustration; gall; hassle; irritation; irksomeness; *jarring; kindling;* lividness; madness; nuisance; *outrage;* perturbation; provocation; quick-temperament; *ruffle; steaming;* temper; *upset;* vexation; weariness; *xerothermia;* yelling; zealousy [arch.]; [*Ant.* appeal]

**aggregate** *(adj.)*: accumulative; *broad;* cumulative; collective; *detailed;* entire; full; group; heaped; *intact;* joint; *kept intact;* lump; mass; non-abridged; overall; panoramic; *quantified; ready;* summative; total; united; *veritable;* whole; *xtry.; yare; zet [dial.];*

**aggression** *(n.)*: antagonism; assault; attack; belligerence; blitz(krieg); charge; drive; depredation; escalade; forage; foray; *going after;* hostility; invasion; *jump; kampf* [G.]; lashing out; militancy; *nastiness;* onset; onrush; offensive; onslaught; push; *quarreling;* raid; sortie; strike; *threat;* unfriendliness; violence; warring; *x-fire; yed;* zapping; [*Ant.* aid]

**aggressive** *(adj.)*: antagonistic; belligerent; confrontational; destructive; encroaching; fierce; *go-getter;* galsome; hostile; inimical; *jingoist; killing;* lion-like; militant; nasty; non-peaceful; offensive; odious; pugnacious; quarrelsome; rancorous; savage; truculent; threatening; unfriendly; unpeaceful; violent; warlike; *xenophobic; yieldless; zealotic;*

**aggressor** *(n.)*: antagonist; assaulter; assailant; belligerent; bully; contender; *doer;* enemy; fighter; *getter;* hitter; initiator; invader; *jumper;* kemper; lasher out; *militarist; nemesis;* opponent; provoker; *quarreler;* raider; striker; troubler; threat; *user; violence;* warling; *xenic; yuon [arch.];* zapper; [*Ant.* ally]

**aghast** *(adj.)*: astonished; affrighted; afraid; alarmed; appalled; *burdened; care;* distressed; deadstruck; *exasperated;* frightened; gastered; horrified; intimidated; jittery; jarred; kiaughed [Scot.]; *languished;* made nervous; nervous; overburdened; panicked; quivering; rattled; revolted; scared; spooked; shocked; taken back; terrified; unnerved; vexed; worried; *xenophobic;* yelling; *zealless;*

**agile** *(adj.)*: active; brisk; clever; dexterous; energetic; fast; frisky; graceful; hurried; intense; *jiffy;* keen-footed; lissome; limber; mercurial; nimble; on the ball; peart; quick; rapid; sharp; spry; swift; *twinkle toes;* ultrafast; volitant; vigorous; wimble; *x-speed;* yar; zippy; [*Ant.* awkward]

**agitate** *(v.)*: arouse; bestir; betoss; churn; disturb; excite; flutter; grieve; hassle; *ignite;* jar; kirn [Scot.]; kindle; *lurch;* move; *nudge; overagitate;* provoke; quicken; rouse; rock; stir up; trouble; upset; vellicate; whisk; *xuld [arch.];* yerk; *zing;*

**agnostic** *(adj.)*: *atheistic; beware;* cynical; doubtful; disbelieving; ever-cynical; faithless; guarded; hesitant; irresolute; jangler; knocker; leery; mistrustful; nonbelieving; nontheistic; oppugning; polemical; pessimistic; questioning; rejecting; skeptic; suspicious; trustless; unsure; unbelieving; vacillating; wary; *x-careful;* yet-unconvinced; zetetic;

**agnostic** *(n.)*: *atheist;* balker; cynic; doubter; disbeliever; *enquirer;* freethinker; *guarded; hesitator;* infidel; jangler; knocker; *leery;* materialist; nonbeliever; nontheist; oppugner; polemic; Pyrrhonist; questioner; rejecter; somatist; truth-challenger; unsure; unbeliever; vacillator; *wet blanket; x-careful; yawper;* zetetic;

**agnosticism** *(n.)*: apprehension; *atheism; being unconvinced;* cynicism; doubt; *ever-cynical;* faithlessness; *guardedness;* hesitation; incredulity; *jangling; knocking;* leeriness; mistrust; misbelief; non-belief; oppugning; pessimism; questioning; rejection; skepticism; somatism; truth-rejecting; unbelief; vacillation; wariness; *x-careful; yieldlessness;* zeteticism;

**agonize** *(n.)*: anguish; burn; chafe; distress; experience pain; feel pain; grieve; hurt; *inflame; jabbing; killing [slang];* lament; lancinating; *misery; noise; outcry;* pain; pierce; *quiver; rack;* strive; suffer; *tormented;* undergo suffering; *vex;* wrestle; writhe; *xiphodynia;* yowl; *zing;*

**agony** *(n.)*: affliction; anguish; biting; burning; chafing; dolor; distress; extreme pain; *excruciating;* feeling bad; grief; galling; hurt(ing); injury; inflammation; jabbing pain; *killing [slang];* lamenting; misery; *nip; ouch!;* pain; passion; *quivering;* rack; ranking; suffering; torment; *unpleasantness;* vexation; writhing; woe; *xiphodynia;* yowling; *zing;*

**agree** *(v.)*: accept; assent; accede; acquiesce; allow; approve; authorize; be in accord; back; correlate; chime; correspond; consent; concur; cohere; condone; *do; delight;* endorse; fall in; go along with; grant; homologate; harmonize; indorse; jive [slang]; join; keep; line up; *like-minded;* match; nod; okay; permit; *questionless;* ratify; see eye to eye; synchronize; settle (on); subscribe to; sanction; support; *togetherness;* unite with; *unwithstood; vow;* warrant; *xel [arch.];* yes; yield; zealously ~; [*Ant.* argue]

**agreeable** *(adj. acceptable)*: acceptable; bearable; *credible;* decent; endurable; fair; fitting; good; happy; innocuous; justifiable; *known;* legitimate; meet; non-objectionable; okay; passable; quite sensible; reasonable; sufferable; sensible; suitable; satisfactory; tolerable; unobjectionable; viable; valid; wise; workable; *xenial; yes; zealous;* [*Ant.* adverse]

**agreeable** *(adj. pleasant)*: accordant; appealing; biddable; congenial; compliant; concordant; congruous; delightful; endurable; enjoyable; fine; friendly; fun; good; genial; harmonious; happy; heartwarming; invigorating; joyful; keen; lovely; *minimally ~;* nice; okay; passable; pleasing; *quantum sufficit [L.];* rewarding; satisfying; superb; tolerable; terrific; uplifting; valid; well-pleasing; xenial; *yeah!; zestful;* [*Ant.* abominable]

**agreement** *(n. accord)*: assent; affirmation; accord(ance); approval; affinity; bargain; commonality; correlation; consonance; congruity; consent; *delight;* empathy; fellowship; good rapport; harmony; *identification; joy;* keeping; like-mindedness; meeting of the minds; nodding; one-mindedness; oneness; predication; quarrel-lessness; rapport; solidarity; sympathy; single-mindedness; togetherness; understanding; unanimity; unity; *voluntariness; willingness; widespread ~; xenia;* yielding; *yedinstvo* [Rus.]; zeal; [*Ant.* argument]

**agreement** *(n. pact)*: arrangement; alliance; bargain; bond; compromise; contract; commitment; concord(at); compact; covenant; deal; entente; federation; formal ~; gentleman's ~; guarantee; happy medium; hypothecation; indenture; joint understanding; *kept promise;* league; mutual ~; nonaggression pact; oath; promise; pledge; (peace) pact; *qualified promise;* resolve; settlement; treaty; understanding; vow; word; *x-one's heart;* yoke; *zealous agreement;* [*Ant.* animosity]

**agricultural** *(adj.)*: agrarian; agrestic; bucolic; country; *dairy farm; esne;* farm(land); geoponic; georgic; husbandry; inurbane; *joskin; kolkhoz* [Rus.]; landward; *manse;* non-urbanized; *olericultural;* predial; *quaint;* rustic; rural; *simple; tillage;* undeveloped; viticultural; wheatland; *xeriscape®; yokelish; zemledelie* [Rus.];

**aid** *(n.)*: assistance; backing; coming to help; deliverance; *deed;* easing; facilitation; giving of help; help; intercession; *just-in-time;* kindness; lightening the load; ministering; *non-hindrance; outpouring;* pitching in; *quick-to-help;* relief; succor; support; subvention; *taking of help;* upholding; *valet;* working for; *xtry.; yielding; zero hindrance;* [*see* assistant; *Ant.* attack]

**aid** *(v.)*: abet; assist; bail out; come to the rescue; do a favor; deliver; encourage; ease; extricate; facilitate; further; give assistance; help; intercede; *just-in-time; keep;* lend a hand; minister; *not hinder;* open doors; pitch in; *quick-to-help;* relieve; rescue; succor; support; *take under one's wing;* uphold; *valet;* work for; *xtry.; yield; zero hindrance;* [*Ant.* attack]

**ailment** *(n.)*: ailing; bug; condition; disease; *epidemic; fever; germ;* health problem; infirmity; *jaundice; kings evil;* lesion; malady; nausea; *ordeal;* pip; problem; queasiness; *remittent;* sickness; trouble; *upset;* virus; *weakness; x-virus; yellow fever; zero comfort;*

**aim** *(v. endeavor)*: attempt; assay; be after; choose to pursue; dare; do one's best; endeavor; follow after; go for; have a crack; hazard; intend; incline; *jeopardize;* kemp; labor; make an effort; *nitency; object;* push for; purpose; pursue; *question [arch.];* risk; seek; strive; try; undertake; venture; work at; *xuld [arch.];* yearn; *zealously attempt;*

**aim** *(v. target in)*: adjust; bear down on; close (in); direct; draw a bead; *endeavor;* focus; fix(ate); guide; get a bead; hone (in); incline; indicate; *jaeger;* kithe [Scot.]; level; mark; nock; *obtain a bead;* (pin)point; *quick-aim;* range; single out; sight; train; take ~; target (in); use sights; verge; *work out; x-y coordinate; ypointing [arch.];* zero in;

**aimless** *(adj.)*: absurd; blithering; *clueless;* directionless; empty; futile; goalless; *hopeless;* inane; ignoble; jerkwater; ketty; lacking direction; meaningless; mindless; non-purposive; otiose; purposeless; pointless; *questionable; ridiculous;* senseless; *sorry; trivial;* useless; undirected; unfocused; unaiming; vain; worthless; *xiaoren; yet futile;* zero-aim;

**aimlessness** *(n.)*: *absurdity; blithering; cluelessness; directionless;* emptiness; futility; futileness; foolishness; goallessness; *hopelessness;* imprudence; inanity; ignobleness; *jerkwater;* kettiness; lack of purpose; *mindlessness;* non-purpose; nugcity; otiosity; purposelessness; pointlessness; *questionable; ridiculousness; senselessness; triviality;* uselessness; vanity; worthlessness; *xiaoren; yet futile;* zero aim;

**air** *(n.)*: atmosphere; breathable ~; *the* blue; clear ~; *deep blue sky;* ether; environment; fug [slang]; *gas; gray skies;* heavens; inhalable ~; jove; *keen ~; liquid ~;* mososphere; *night ~;* oxygen; open skies; plenum; quality ~; *region;* space; sky; troposphere; upper atmosphere; vault of heaven; wind; *xerosere;* yonder; *zone;*

**airborne** *(adj.)*: aerial; *blue;* cloudbourne; *darting;* ethereal; fledge; flying; gliding; high-up; in-flight; jetting; *kiting; levitational;* mid-air; non-grounded; overhead; plane-related; *quickened; rising;* superterrene; *taking flight;* up; volant; windborne; *x-plane; yonder;* zooming o'er;

**airflow** *(n.)*: airstream; blast; current; draft; exhalation; flow; gust; headwind; harmattan; indraft; jet stream; katabatic wind; levanter; movement; *notus; overdraft;* puff; quarter-wind; *rush;* stream; tailwind; undercurrent; *velocity;* wind; x-wind; *yaw; zephyr;*

**air force** *(n.)*: air corps; battle planes; *bombers;* combat planes; defenses; *engines;* force; flying corps; *group; high command;* interceptors; *jets; kamikazes;* Luftwaffe [G.]; military airplanes; *number; over;* planes; *qualified pilots;* R.A.F. [Br.]; squadron; tactical ~; team; U.S.A.F. [U.S.]; *vehicles;* warplanes; *x-plane; yonder;* zeppelins;

**airplane** *(n.)*: aircraft; airliner; biplane; *bomber;* bird [slang]; combat plane; double-prop plane; *executive jet;* flying machine; *fighter; glider;* heavier-than-air craft; *interceptor;* jet(liner); *kamikaze [Jap.];* landplane; mailplane; multiplane; *naval fighter; observation plane;* puddle jumper; plane; quadruplane; ramjet; seaplane; transport; triplane; turbojet; *utility plane; vehicle;* warplane; wide-body; *x-plane; yoke;* Zero;
  **Types of aircraft**: Albatross D.1; B-12; Cessna; Douglas F3D; Euler D.1; F-14; F-16; Gloster Grebe; helicopter; IAR-80; Junker J-2; KAI FA-50; Lockheed YF-12; Messerschmitt Me 410; Northrop XFT; Ornithopter; Pfaltz D-3; Q-5 Fantan; Rex D; Sopwith Camel; Thulin K; Villers V; Westland Wizard; X-1; Yokosuka D4Y2-S; Zero; 707; 727; 747;

**airport** *(n.)*: airstrip (-field); *base; clearing;* Dullas; *environs;* flying field; *ground;* hub; heliport; *hangar;* international ~; *jungle clearing; key location;* landing strip (-field); municipal ~; national ~; *outlying field; place;* quick-service ~; runway; strip; *takeoff;* USAFB; vicinity ~; *way to land;* XIY; yard; *zone;*

**airship** *(n.)*: aerostat; blimp; craft; dirigible; *engine;* fire balloon; *Goodyear® Blimp; Graf Zeppelin;* hydrogen blimp; *investigator; jumbo balloon; kite balloon;* lighter-than-air craft; montgolfier; *Norge;* observation balloon; pilot balloon; *quicken;* rockoon; ship; sausage [slang]; *transport; unidentified object;* vessel; *weather balloon; x-port; yonder;* zeppelin;

**airworthy** *(adj.)*: air-worthy; able to fly; *bi-wing; check;* dependable; ever-faithful; flyable; flightworthy; good-condition; *having wings;* in working order; *justifiable; keen;* large-winged; most trustworthy; never-failing; *okay;* perfect working order; questionless; reliable; safe; sound; sky-worthy; trustworthy; unfailing; volant; working; xtry. condition; *yet flyable; zero doubt*

**aisle** *(n.)*: alley; *berth;* center ~; corridor; *division; entryway; exit; floorage;* gangway; *hall;* isle; journey-way; *kosher* ~; lane; middle ~; nave- ~; outer ~; passageway; quire-wing; right-hand ~; side ~; transept; *uninhibited;* vennel; (walk)way; walk; *xystus;* yle; *zone;*

**akin** *(adj.)*: allied; alike; blood-related; *brethren;* connected; *daughter; equivalent;* family; german; homologous; interrelated; *just the same;* kindred; linked; matching; *non-differing; one;* parallel; *quae est eadem* [L.]; related; similar; sister [fem.]; *tantamount;* uniform; very similar; *word-perfect;* xerographed; *yes;* zincograph;

**alarm** *(n.)*: anxiety; burden; bell; care; distress; *emergency;* fear; fire ~; gastness; horror; insecurity; jitteriness; kiaugh [Scot.]; *lily-livered;* monition; nervousness; over-anxiety; panic (button); quaking; red alert; stress; signal; trepidation; terror; uneasiness; vexation; worry; whistle; *xenophobia;* yellow-belliedness; yellow flag; *zeallessness;* [see alert]

**alarm** *(v.)*: affright; *burden; care;* daunt; distress; dismay; *exasperate;* frighten; gaster; horrify; *insecurity; jitters;* kiaugh [Scot.]; *languish;* make nervous (-afraid); nerve; overburden; panic; *quicken;* raise apprehensions; scare; terrify; unnerve; vex; worry; *xenophobia;* yelping; zealless; [see warn]

**alarmist** *(n.)*: alarmer; brooder; Cassandra; doomsayer; *exasperated;* fearmonger; gloom-monger; *horrifier;* insecure; jittery; kiaugher [Scot.]; *lily-livered;* mistruster; newsmonger; *over-anxious;* prophet of doom; *quitter;* rumor-monger; scaremonger; terrormonger; *uneasy;* vexer; worrier; *xenophobia;* yeller; zealless;

**alcohol** *(n.)*: ale; booze; *the* bottle; cocktail; drink; eyewater; firewater; grog; hard drink; intoxicant; joywater; *kirschwasser;* liquor; mixed drink; moonshine; neck oil; oil of joy [both slang]; potable; *quass; rum;* spirits; strong drink; tipple; *undiluted drink;* verjuice; wine; whisky; *xanthoxylin; yill;* zymotic concoction;
   **Kinds of alcoholic drink**: ale; beer; brandy; champagne; cognac; daiquiri; eggnog; flip; gin; hock; Irish whiskey; jake; kirsch; lager; martini; mead; negus; ouzo; pulque; quass; rum; rye; saki; schnapps; scotch; tequila; usquebaugh; vodka; whiskey; wine; xanthoxylin; yarke; zubrowka;
**alcoholic** *(adj.)*: alcohol-based; brewed; *containing alcohol; drunk;* eighty-proof; fermented; fuddling; *gin-laced;* hard; intoxicating; intoxicative; inebriating; jag; *kaylied;* laced; *moonshine-laced;* nippy; overproof; plastering; quafferous; *rum-laced;* strong; spiked; spiritous; *tipsy;* underproof; vinolent; winy; *xanthoxlic;* yeasted; zymotic; [*Ant.* alcohol-free]
**alcoholic** *(n.)*: alcohol-drinker; bibber; boozer; carouser; drinker; drunk(ard); elbow-bender; fuddler; guzzler; hooch hound; inebriate; Jimmy Woodser [slang]; *kaylied;* lush; muddler; nipper; oenphilist; pot companion; plonko; quaffer; rummy; sot; tippler; *underage drinker;* vinolent; winebibber; wino; wassailer; *xanthoxylic;* yiller; *zubrowka-drinker;*
**alcoholism** *(n.)*: addiction; boozing; crapulence; compotation; drinking; dipsomania; elbow-bending; fuddlement; guzzling; hard drinking; insobriety; intemperance; *joywater;* keif [Arab]; liquor-drinking; moonshining; nipping; obfuscation; potation; quasi-soberness; *rum; sot;* tippling; *user;* vinolency; winebibbing; *xanthoxylin; yveresce* [arch.]; zubrowka; [*Ant.* abstinence]
**alcove** *(n.)*: *area;* booth; bay; cranny; cubicle; cavity; den; enclosure; *fissure; grotto;* hole; hollow; indentation; *jaw-hole;* krater; *lacuna; mouth;* nook; opening; partition; *place; quarry-pit;* recess; secluded place; *tokonoma* [Jap.]; *unit;* vug; *well; xystus;* yawn; zanja;
**alert** *(adj.)*: attentive; *beware;* careful; discerning; ever-watchful; fabian; guarded; heedful; intentive; judicious; keeping in mind; leery; mindful; *noting;* observant; on guard; precautious; *qui vive* [F.]; quick-witted; regardful; *suspicious; tending;* ultra-careful; vigilant; watchful; wary; *x-careful;* yare-handed; *zärtlich* [G.]; [*Ant.* asleep]
**alert** *(n.)*: advisory; alarm; bell; caution; distress signal; *emergency;* forewarning; *fire alarm; gastness;* hue and cry; *insecurity; jitters;* klaxton; larum; monition; notice; *noise; overpanic;* prewarning; panic bell; *quivering;* red ~; *siren; trumpet; unease; verbum sapient* [L.]; warning; *x-alert;* yellow ~; *zinger;*
**alert** *(v.)*: advise; admonish; bode; caution; *dissuade; exhort;* forewarn; give warning; hue and cry; inform; *jeopardy; klaxon;* let one know; make known; notify; opine; precaution; presage; *quicken;* ready; signal; sound the alarm; tell; tip off; *urge; vocalize;* warn; *xenagogy; yellow alert; zero in;*
**alertness** *(n.)*: attentiveness; *beware;* consciousness; cautiousness; *discernment; ever-watchful; fabian;* gingerness; heedfulness; intentiveness; *judicious;* keeping watch; leeriness; mindfulness; nimbleness; observation; precaution; quickness; regard; *suspicion;* tending; ultra-carefulness; vigilance; watchfulness; *x-careful;* yare-handedness; *zeal;*
**alibi** *(n.)*: account; answer; *basis;* claim; defense; explanation; excuse; fish story; grounds; *hard proof; intellection;* justification; *key reason;* lame excuse; legitimization; *motivation; notion;* out; pretext; *questionable;* reason; story; *thinking; ulterior motive;* vindication; *witnesses; x-out; yeme; zeal;*
**alien** *(adj.)*: astral; *being;* cosmic; deep space; extraterrestrial; *from afar;* galactic; heavenly; interplanetary; *jovial; kosmos* [Gr.]; lunar, *Martian;* non-earth; off-earth; planetary; quasi-stellar; *rocket-man;* space; *traveler;* unearthly; *visiting; world; x-ray star; yonder;* zonic; [*see* foreign]
**alien** *(n.)*: *afar;* being; cosmic visitor; creature; deep space traveler; extraterrestrial; *from afar;* galactic traveler; green man; *humanoid;* intergalactic traveler; *invader;* Jovian; *kosmos;* life-form; Lunarian; little green man; Martian; nonhuman; outworlder; *Plutonian;* quasi-humanoid; rocket-man; space man; stranger; traveler; unearthly visitor; UFO man; visitor; Venusian; wayfarer; *xenology; yonder; Zorkon invader;* [*see* foreigner]

**alienate** *(v.)*: aliene; blackball; coldshoulder; distance; disaffect; estrange; forebear; give cold shoulder to; have nothing to do with; ignore; isolate; *jink;* keep out; *leave alone;* move away from; not accept; ostracize; push away; quit on; reject; separate; turn away; *unfriendly; vault;* withdraw from; x-out; *yard [arch.]; zero fellowship;* [Ant. attract]

**alienation** *(n.)*: anomy; abstraction; avoidance; blackballing; cold shoulder; distancing; estrangement; *fleeing;* giving the cold shoulder; *hostility;* isolation; *jinking;* keeping out; *loathing;* moving away from; non-acceptance; ostracism; ostracizing; pushing away; quite [Sp.]; rejection; separation; turning away; unfriendliness; *vaulting;* withdrawal; *xenelasy;* yarding [arch.]; *zero fellowship;* [Ant. attraction]

**align** *(v.)*: adjust; attune; bring into line; calibrate; correct; dispose; *enhance;* fine-tune; fix; gear to; harmonize; improve; *jury-rig;* key to; *level off;* make ~ed; *newly* ~; overhaul; overcorrect; proportion; *quick-fix;* re~; set; synchronize; tweak; tune (up); *upbuild;* vamp; *work on; xfer; yarken;* zet [dial.];

**alike** *(adj.)*: akin; *balanced;* comparable; duplicate; equivalent; *further; greatly* ~; homologous; invariable; indistinguishable; identical; just the same; kindred; like; matching; non-differing; *one;* parallel; *quae est eadem* [L.]; resembling; similar; same; tantamount; uniform; unvaried; verbatim; *word-perfect; xerographed; yes; zincograph;* [Ant. alien]

**alive** *(adj.)*: animate; breathing; biological; *cheerful; disquieted;* enlivened; fit; frisky; going; healthy; inextinct; invigorated; jaunty; kicking [slang]; living; lively; moving; non-dead; organic; perky; quick; *raring;* surviving; sensate; spright; thriving; unslain; vitalized; vibrant; well; warm; *xel [arch.];* yauld; zoetic; zippy;

**allay** *(v.)*: appease; alleviate; becalm; calm; diffuse; ease; fix; *gratify;* hush; *incline; jarless;* knock *down;* lay to rest; mitigate; *nullify; overcome;* pacify; quell; relieve; soften; soothe; settle; tranquilize; unruffle; *vanquish; work out;* x-out; *yield; zeroize;* [Ant. augment]

**allegation** *(n.)*: assertion; averment; accusation; blame; claim; charge; declaration; exprobation; formal charge; grievance; holding one responsible; indictment; jactitation; key ~; laying guilt before; making ~; *naming;* overment; profession; *questioning; reproach;* statement; *throwing the book at;* unproven assertion; *vituperation; word; xfer; yammer; zero in;*

**allege** *(v.)*: assert; aver; accuse; blame; claim; declare; exprobate; fault; *guilt;* hang on; incriminate; *j'accuse; knock;* lay at one's door; make allegation; *non-proven;* offer; point finger at; *question;* recite; state; saddle with; testify; uphold; *vituperate; word; xfer; yet unconvicted; zero in;*

**allegiance** *(n.)*: adherence; bond; commitment; constancy; dependability; dedication; devotion; devotedness; *ever-faithful;* faithfulness; fealty; fidelity; *goodwill;* heart- ~; integrity; immovability; *joining;* keenness; loyalty; mateship; *non-failing;* obligation; *partnership; quite loyal;* reliability; steadfastness; trueness; trustworthiness; unwaveringness; unfailingness; *verity; well-tried; xtry.; yeoman's service; zeal;*

**allegorical** *(adj.)*: allegoric; abstract; Bunyanesque; comparative; curiologic; descriptive; emblematic; figurative; figural; *general;* hieroglyphic; illustrative; *journalistic;* kuriologic; *likening;* metaphoric(al); non-literal; *only comparative;* pictorial; parabolic; poetical; *quarto;* representative; symbolic; typical; umbratical; vignette; word-picture; *xenodoceionological; yarn;* zeugmatic; [Ant. actual]

**allegory** *(n.)*: allusion; apologue; *book;* comparison; dissimile; emblem; figure; gest; hyperbole; imagery; *journey; kind;* likening; metaphor; *narrative; only a comparison;* picture; parable; *quarto;* representation; simile; similitude; symbolism; type; umbratic; vignette; word picture; *xenodocheionology; yarn;* zeugma; [Ant. actuality]

**allergy** *(n.)*: aversion; bad reaction; *break out;* condition; disorder; erubescence; food ~; genetics-related ~; hypersensitivity; *hay fever;* intolerance; *jackfruit* ~; keen sensitivity; late-phase response; malady; non-tolerance; oversensitivity; pollen fever; *queasy;* reaction; *rash;* sensitivity; tenderness; urticaria; *V14;* wheat ~; *xerodermia; yellow spots; zero tolerance;*

**alleviate** *(v.)*: abate; assuage; bate; break; contract; condense; curb; *cut;* decrease; diminish; dissipate; ease; ebb; fade; fall; go down; *hush; halt;* improve; *jump down;* knock down; lessen; lower; minish; moderate; mitigate; *narrow; outgo;* palliate; quell; quail; reduce; recede; subside; taper; temper; *undo; vanish;* wane; *xerosis;* yield; *zap;* [Ant. augment]

**alleviation** *(n.)*: abatement; assuagement; bating; breaking; curbing; decrease; diminishment; easing; fading; going down; *halting;* improvement; *jump down; knock down;* lessening; lightening; moderation; *narrowing; outgo;* palliation; quelling; receding; reduction; salving; subsiding; tapering; *undoing; vanishing;* waning; *xerosis*; yielding; *zapping;* [Ant. augmentation]

**alley** *(n.)*: aisle; alleyway; byway; corridor; causeway; dirt road; esplanade; footpath; *go-between;* horse path; isle; journey-way; *kotal;* lane(way); means; *narrow way;* outlet; path(way); passage(way); *quo mode* [L.]; road; route; street; track; *underpass;* vennel; way; xystum; *yong* [arch.]; zwinger;

**alliance** *(n.)*: agreement; association; bond; brotherhood; bloc; coalition; confederation; cartel; deal; entente; fellowship; federation; group; guarantee; *help;* indenture; joint-coalition; kinship; league; mis~; mutual agreement; mateship; merger; nonaggression pact; oneness; oath; pact; quinquevirate; rapport; settlement; society; treaty; understanding; union; *vow;* working ~; *x-treaty;* yoke; *zonal agreement;* [Ant. animosity]

**allocate** *(v.)*: apportion; admeasure; allot; assign; appoint; bestow; consign; distribute; deal; divide; dole; divvy; earmark; furnish; give; hand out; issue; *justly divide;* kit; let; mete; measure; *non-retention;* outfit; portion (out); part; parcel; quantify; ration; separate; *transfer;* unitize; vest; *weigh; xfer;* yield; *zone;* [Ant. appropriate]

**allocation** *(n.)*: apportionment; allotment; bestowal; consigning; distribution; dealing; doling; dose; earmarking; *furnishing;* giving out; handing out; issuance; *just division; kitting;* lot; measurement; *non-retention;* outfitting; portion; part; purparty; quantum; quota; ration(ing); share; *transferal;* unitization; vesting; *weighing; xfer;* yielding; *zoning;* [Ant. appropriation]

**allot** *(v.)*: allocate; bestow; consign; designate; equip; furnish; give; hand out; issue; *jettison;* kit; let; mete; *measure; non-retention;* outfit; provide; *quantum;* ration; supply; transfer; *unhand;* vest; *weigh;* xfer; yield; *zone;* [Ant. appropriate]

**allotment** *(n.)*: allocation; apportionment; allowance; bestowal; consigning; designation; earmarking; furnishing; giving out; handing out; issuance; *just division; kitting;* lot; measurement; *non-retention;* outfitting; portion; quantum; ration; share; *transferal;* unitization; vesting; *weighing; xfer;* yielding; *zoning;* [Ant. appropriation]

**allow** *(v.)*: authorize; bless; consent to; deem okay; decriminalize; enable; empower; facilitate; give permission; grant; humor; indulge; judge acceptable; *knowingly ~;* let; legalize; make possible; not oppose; *nod;* okay; permit; *qualify; rationalize;* suffer; sanction; tolerate; *unhindered;* validate; vouchsafe; warrant; *x on the dotted line;* yield; yes; *zealously approve;*

**allowable** *(adj.)*: acceptable; admissible; bearable; *correct;* decent; endurable; *forbear;* fine; good; *humor; indulge;* justified; *kosher;* livable; legal; minimal; not bad; okay; permissible; *quantum suffict* [L.]; reasonable; sufferable; tolerable; up to standard; *veritable;* warrantable; *x on the dotted line; yenough* [arch.]; *zero opposition;* [Ant. abhorrent]

**allowance** *(n. money allotted)*: amount; allotment; annuity; *base pay;* cash; disbursement; emolument; financing; grant; *hire;* income; *justification;* kickback; *lot;* money; *net pay; overcompensation;* payment; *quid pro quo [L.];* recompense; stipend; tret; *unindebtedness;* virement; *wage; xfer; yield; zapping;*

**allude** *(v.)*: advert; betoken; connote; drop hint; drive at; denote; *express; foreadvise;* give indication; hint at; imply; infer; insinuate; *judge; known;* lead; make out; mention; *nuance; overtone;* postulate; point; quiddit; refer; suggest; *tacit; undercurrent; undertone;* vaguely express; wink; *xfer; yammer; zone;*

**allure** *(v.)*: attract; bait; charm; captivate; draw; entice; ensnare; entrap; fascinate; get (attention of); *have come;* invite; interest; intrigue; infatuate; jade; *keen;* lure; lead; move; magnetize; *nudge; outwit;* persuade; *quibbling [arch.];* rivet; seduce; spellbind; transfix; tempt; tole; *urge; vie for;* woo; *xuld [arch.];* yerk; zygotaxis; [*Ant.* alienate]
**allurement** *(n.)*: allure; attraction; bait; beauty; charm; coaxing; drawing; deception; enticement; ensnarement; fascination; gudgeon; honeypot; hook, line and sinker; inducement; incitement; japing; *knavery;* lure; magnetism; *nudge; outwitting;* prodding; provocation; *quiblin* [arch.]; roping; seduction; test; temptation; tantalizing; trap; urging; *vie;* wooing; *xuld [arch.];* yearning; zygotaxis [biol.]; [*Ant.* alienation]
**ally** *(n.)*: associate; abettor; benchfellow; *buddy;* collaborator; consociate; confederate; cobelligerent; defender; *entente partner;* friend; fellow; good-fellow; helper; *involve; joint-forces;* kith [pl.]; *loyal friend;* mate; ministrant; neighbor; offsider; partner; *quondam friend;* right-hand man; *reciprocal;* supporter; teammate; *united;* voice; workfellow; workmate; *xenophile;* yokefellow; *zealous friend;* [*see* brother; *Ant.* adversary]
**ally** *(v.)*: align with; assist; band together; collaborate; confederate; defend; enter into a league; federate; give assistance; help; *involve;* join (forces); *knit;* league; make league; *non-aggression pact; one;* partner; *quick-to-help; reciprocal;* support; side with; team up with; unite; *vouch for;* work together; *xenophile;* yoke; *zealously support;* [*Ant.* attack]
**almighty** *(adj.)*: all-powerful; boundless; completely powerful; *divine;* entheastic; *force; greatest; highest power;* invincible; infinite; *Jehovah; King of kings;* limitless; mighty; *multipotent;* non-limited; omnipotent; plenipotent(iary); *powerful; qi;* ruling; supreme; totally powerful; unstoppable; *very strong;* without limitation; *xtry. power;* Yahweh; zero limitations;
**almost** *(adv.)*: about; approximately; approaching; basically; close (to); drawing nigh to; essentially; *functionally;* generally; give or take; *honorarily;* implicitly; just about; *known as;* like; more or less; nearly; *on the right track;* practically; proximally; proximately; quasi; roughly; slightly; *somewhat;* touching on; up near; upon; virtually; very nearly; well-nigh; *xtry. close; yede [arch.];* zeroing in on; [*see* resemblance; *Ant.* altogether]
**alms** *(n.)*: aid; benefaction; *beau geste* [F.]; charity; dole; donations; *endowment;* favors; gift; help; *investment; joyful giving;* kind deeds; liberality; largesse; money; noble gifts; offering; philanthropy; *quarter; rendering;* selfless gifts; thoughtful donation; *unselfishness; virtuousness;* warmth; xenium; yielding help; zeda-kah [Heb.];
**almsgiver** *(n.)*: almoner; altruist; benefactor; contributor; donor; endower; favorer; giver; humanitarian; imparter; *joyful giver;* kind person; liberal giver; Maecenas; *noble ~; open-handed;* patron; philanthropist; *quantity;* rich benefactor; sponsor; thoughtful person; unselfish one; *vester;* welldoer; *xferer;* yielder; zealous supporter;
**alone** *(adj.)*: abandoned; by oneself; cast off; deserted; desolate; *evacuated;* forlorn; forsaken; grief-stricken; *hopeless;* isolated; individual; just by oneself; *kept ~;* lonesome; *miserable;* non-accompanied; only; *piteous;* quite ~; *recluse;* solo; solitaire; sole; *single-handedly;* totally ~; unaccompanied; unchaperoned; unaided; very much ~; without company; *xfer; yearnful;* zero company; [*Ant.* accompanied]
**aloof** *(adj.)*: apart; away from; alienated; *breach;* cool; cold; detached; distant; estranged; formal; far; *gruff; hostile;* insocial; inaccessible; *jaded;* kindless; loveless; *mean;* non-friendly; offish; *pitiless;* quiet; remote; silent; standoffish; taciturn; unfriendly; unapproachable; very distant; withdrawn; *xenophobic;* yet estranged; zealless;
**aloud** *(adj.)*: audibly; *blaringly;* clearly; *distinctly spoken;* enunciactorily; *forte; greatly;* hearably; in the hearing of; *jamming; keenly;* loudly; multisonously; noisily; out loud; orally; pronounced; quietlessly; reading out loud; resonantly; *spoken;* sonorously; *told;* using one's voice; verbally; with one's voice; *x-loud;* yelling; zero quietude;

**altar** *(n. front of church)*: area; bench; bema; church ~; down front; elevated place; front; gradin; holy place; *introspection; justification;* kneeling bench; *libation;* mourner's bench; *nave;* offering place; predella; *place; quickening;* retable; soleas; table; *unburden; vestry;* weeping bench; *Xn. ~; yield; zone;*
**altar** *(n. place of sacrifice)*: atonal ~; bronze ~; chantry; *death;* eschara; elevated place; *fire; grove;* high place; heap of stones; *horns;* immolation place; *joss-house;* krioboly; libational ~; mound; non-tooled ~; offering place; place of sacrifice; quartz-stone ~; rock-pile; stone table; table; unhewn stone ~; *votive offering;* worship-place; *xenium; yajna [Hind.]; zone;*
**alter** *(v.)*: adjust; *bend;* change; deviate; edit; fiddle with; fix; *grow; heighten;* improve; *jib; key to; lower;* modify; novate; overhaul; *put right; qualify;* revise; switch; transform; tailor; upgrade; vary; *work; xenomorph; yaw; zigzag;*
**altercate** *(v.)*: argue; bicker; contend; dispute; *earful;* fight; gainsay; have words; impugn; *jarring;* kas-kas [Jam.]; lock horns [slang]; make fur fly; *negate;* oppose; pick fight; quarrel; resist; strive; tiff; *unharmonious;* vie; withstand; *x-purposes; yain* [arch.]; *zealously disagree;* [Ant. agree]
**alteration** *(n.)*: adjustment; amendment; *betterment;* change; difference; edition; enhancement; fixing; *growth; heightening;* innovation; improvement; *jumping; key to; lowering; lengthening;* modification; *newness;* overhaul; permutation; *qualification;* revision; switch; substitution; tailoring; transformation; *upgrade;* variation; *warping; xenomorph; yaw; zigzag;*
**alternate** *(v.)*: alter; *bounce;* crisscross; change; *dither;* exchange; fluctuate; *go up and down; hump;* interchange; jump; *kedge; laciniate;* meander; *non-fixed;* oscillate; pendulate; *quiver;* reel; reciprocate; shift; switch; swing; teeter; totter; twist; turn; undulate; vacillate; vary; waver; *x-ing;* yo-yo; zigzag;
**alternation** *(n.)*: altering; *bouncing;* changing; *dithering;* erraticism; fluctuation; flux; *going back and forth; hopping around;* instability; *jiggling; kedging; lacination;* mutability; non-stability; oscillation; pendulating; *quivering;* rocking; shifting; swinging; turning; unstableness; undulation; vacillation; wavering; waffling; *x-ing;* yo-yoing; zigzagging;
**alternative** *(adj.)*: alternate; *beyond the accepted norm;* contingency; different; elective; *funny; going instead;* heterogeneous; irregular; innovative; just-in-case; *keen;* logical ~; modified; new; nontraditional; other; peculiar; *queer; replacement;* substitute; totally different; unusual; unconventional; variant; weird; *xtr.;* yet another; *zwap;*
**alternative** *(n.)*: another option; *best ~;* choice; decision; determination; elective; final judgment; first ~; favorite; *gauging; heart; inclination;* judgment; *knowledge; like; liberty; mind; nomination;* option; possibility; pick; preference; pleasure; *quibble;* ruling; selection; take; top ~; *ultimatum;* vote; verdict; wish; will; *x; yes; zeal;*
**although** *(conj.)*: albeit; but though; contradictorily; despite; even though; *for;* granting; howsoever; in spite of the fact; *just because;* knowing this; *laying that aside;* minding; notwithstanding that; on the other hand; *putting that aside; qheche* [arch.]; regardless; seeing this; though; *understanding that; variance;* while; *x.;* yet; *zeroing in on;*
**altitude** *(n.)*: aerial climb; boost; celsitude; climb; degree of elevation; elevation; flight level; feet above sea level; *going up;* highth; height; increase; *jacking up;* kanjira; level; loftiness; measure of height; number of feet; *overgrowth; putting high up; quantum increase;* rise; surmounting; transcendence; upward elevation; vertical measurement; *way up; xfer; yain [arch.]; zenith;*
**always** *(adj.)*: at all times; alway; *boundless;* continuously; constantly; ceaselessly; *durably;* ever; endlessly; eternally; for life; forever(more); going on forever; *habitually;* invariably; interminably; infinitely; *jusqu'au bout [F.]; keep;* lastingly; *measureless;* never-endingly; *ongoing;* perpetually; *quadrillion;* round-the-clock; sempiternally; timelessly; 24-7; uniformly; unceasingly; unendingly; unchangeably; *vast;* without end; *xgressing;* year-after-year; *zero end;*
**amalgamate** *(v.)*: admix; blend; combine; *develop; entwine;* fuse; *group; hodge-podge;* intermix; join; knit; *lump together;* mix; merge; meld; *node;* overmix; *pass into; queach [arch.];* run together; synthesize; temper; unite; *voluble;* wed; *xenograft; yerk together; zip together;*

**amalgamation** *(n.)*: admixture; blend; combination; *development; entwining;* fusion; *grouping;* hodgepodge; intermixture; joining; knitting; *lumping together;* mixture; merging; melding; *non-homogenous ~;* olio; putting together; *queaching [arch.];* running together; synthesis; tempering; union; *variety; wedding; xanthate;* yanggoma; *zipping together;*
**amass** *(v.)*: accumulate; aggregate; build; collect; conglomerate; deposit; enlarge; *fatten;* gather; grow; hoard; increase; join together; *keep growing;* lay up; mount up; *number; overgrow;* pile up; *quadruplicate;* reposit; store up; stockpile; take off; upbuild; *volume;* wax larger; XL; yain [arch.]; zoom;
**amateur** *(n.)*: apprentice; beginner; cadet; disciple; empiric; first-timer; greenhorn; ham; inceptor; jackeroo; kook; learner; mentee; nonprofessional; novice; newcomer; *one inexperienced;* probationer; protégé; prentice; *quick learner;* rookie; starter; tenderfoot; undertaker; *venturer; wannabe; xon; yet inexperienced; zero experience;* [*Ant.* authority]
**amateurish** *(adj.)*: amateur; beginner; crude; dorky; empirical; feeble; goofy; hokey; inexpert; inexperienced; jackleg; kooky; *lacking; moronic;* non-professional; novice; *only a beginner;* pathetic; quasi-standard; rag-tag; substandard; skill-less; terrible; unprofessional; *verdant;* wanting; *xiaoren;* yokelish; zhlubby; [*Ant.* authoritative]
**amaze** *(v.)*: astonish; astound; awe; bedazzle; bowl over; confound; dazzle; dumbfound; *enchant; excite;* flabbergast; floor; gape; hold one's breath; impact; impress; jolt; keel over; look aghast; make marvel; *nonplus;* overwhelm; overawe; poleax; *quite amazed;* render speechless; surprise; stun; shock; take back; unable to believe; *very impressed; wonder;* wow; *xtry.; yerk; zing;*
**amazement** *(n.)*: astonishment; awe; bedazzlement; confounding; dumbfounding; *enchantment;* flabbergasting; gastness; holding one's breath; impression; jolt; keeling over; looking aghast; marveling; *nonplus;* overwhelming; poleaxing; *quite amazed;* rendering surprise; speechlessness; stun; shock; taking back; unbelief; *very impressed;* wonder(ment); *xtry.; yerk;* zonking;
**amazing** *(adj.)*: astonishing; astounding; awesome; breathtaking; *commendable;* divine; extraordinary; fantastic; great; heavenly; incredible; impressive; jolly good; keen; laudable; marvelous; notable; outstanding; prodigious; *quantum* [L.]; remarkable; stupendous; terrific; tremendous; uncanny; unequalled; very good; virtuous; wondrous; xtry.; you-beaut [Aus.]; *zestful;*
**ambassador** *(n.)*: agent; bearer of tidings; consul; commissary; dispatch; diplomat; dignitary; envoy; emissary; foreign minister; government minister; high commissioner; intendant; *janker;* kurveyor; legate; liaison; minister; missionary; nuncio; official; plenipotentiary; *questor* [It.]; representative; *servant;* tidings-bearer; *updater;* vice-consul; V.I.P.; *walking delegate; xeno-representative; yamen* [Chin.]; *zip;*
**ambassadorship** *(n.)*: ambassage; *bishoprick;* consulate; commission; diplomatic office; envoyship; foreign ministry; government appointment; high commission; intendance; *janker; kurveying;* legateship; ministry; *nuncio;* office; *proclaimer;* questorship [It.]; *representative;* service; *tidings-bearer; updater;* vice-consulate; *work; xeno-representation; yamen* [Chin.]; *zip;*
**ambiguity** *(n.)*: abstruseness; bewilderment; confusion; doubt; equivocalness; fogginess; grayness; haziness; inconclusiveness; *jumble;* kiaugh [Scot.]; *lightlessness;* murkiness; non-certainty; obscurity; polysemy; questionability; *reservation;* shakiness; turbidity; uncertainty; vagueness; wooliness; *xtry. doubt; yet uncertain;* zero clarity;
**ambiguous** *(adj.)*: abstruse; borderline; confusing; cryptic; doubtful; double-meaning; dubious; equivocal; fuzzy; gray; hazy; indefinite; inconclusive; *jumbled; known to few; lightless;* murky; nebulous; obscure; polysemous; questionable; *reservations;* sketchy; turbid; unclear; uncertain; vague; woolly; *xeroophthalmic; yet uncertain; zero clarity;* [*Ant.* absolute]
**ambition** *(n.)*: aspiring; ambitiousness; *bidding;* craving; desire; *enthusiasm;* fancy; *greed;* hope; hubris; itching; *intention; juration;* keen desire; longing; *mania;* nisus; notion; objective; pruriency; quest; *restlessness;* strong desire; thirst; urge; velleity; want; wish; will; *xel [arch.];* yearning; *zeal;* [*Ant.* apathy]

**ambitious** *(adj.)*: aspiring; *burning;* committed; determined; driven; enthusiastic; fervent; *go-getter;* high-reaching; *impassioned;* just raring; keen; *longing;* motivated; *need;* overzealous; passionate; *quick;* ready; success-oriented; spirited; *thrilled; unwavering;* vaulting; wholehearted; *wannabe; xtry.;* yare; zealous; [*Ant.* apathetic]

**amble** *(v.)*: ambulate; bear along; continue; drift; *enter; flânerie* [F.]; go; gad; gravitate; hoof; *interlope;* journey; *keep pace;* lumber; mosey; night-walk; outwalk; promenade; pootle; *quicken;* ramble; stroll; saunter; tramp; traipse; *underway;* venture; walk; wander; xfer; yaw; *zigzag;*

**ambush** *(n.)*: assault; attack; ambuscade; ambushment; bushwhacking; concealment; deception; ensnarement; foray; *get;* hit; incursion; jumping; *kampf* [G.]; lying in wait; mugging; *nabbing;* onrush; *pouncing; quick raid;* raid; strike; surprise attack; trap; *usurping;* veney; *violence;* waylaying; *x-fire; yerd [arch.]; zapping;*

**ambush** *(v.)*: await; attack; ambuscade; belay; beset; bushwhack; catch offguard; deceive; ensnare; foray; *get; hide;* insidiate; jump; jap [coll.]; *keep in hiding;* lie in wait; lurk; mug; *nab; overtake; overwhelm;* pounce upon; *quad;* raid; surprise attack; trap; *usurp; violence;* wait; waylay; *x; yerd [arch.];* zap;

**ambusher** *(v.)*: attacker; bushwhacker; *crook; despoiler;* ensnarer; forelayer; guerilla; hedge-creeper; *highwayman;* insidiator; jumper; *knuck;* lier in wait; lurker; mugger; *nab;* outlaw; prowler; *quad; robber;* spoiler; *thief; usurper; villain;* waylayer; *x; yob [arch.]; zob;*

**amend** *(v.)*: adjust; alter; better; change; correct; develop; edit; enhance; fix; *get right; help;* improve; *jib; key to;* lengthen; modify; mend; *novate;* overhaul; *put right;* qualify; reform; revise; redress; remedy; rectify; set right; *switch; transform;* update; *vary; work; xenomorph; yaw; zigzag;* [*Ant.* aggravate]

**amendment** *(n.)*: adjustment; alteration; betterment; change; correction; difference; deviation; edition; enhancement; *fluctuation; growth; heightening;* improvement; *joining; key addition; lengthening;* modification; *new part;* overhaul; permutation; qualification; revision; switch; shift; transformation; update; variation; *warping; xenomorph; yaw; zigzag;*

**amenity** *(n.)*: affability; *bonus;* civility; courtesy; comfort; delicacy; dainty; daintrel; elegancy; favor; fine point; goody; *high-style; indulgence; jimp;* kindness; luxury; *manners;* nicety; *obligingness;* pleasantry; *quality;* refinement; subtlety; small point; tactfulness; urbanity; *virtue;* well-treated; xenium; yeff [arch.]; zealous care;

**American** *(adj. and n.)*: *Arkansan; Bostonian;* Columbian; *Delaware; East St. Louis; Floridian;* gringo [off.]; *Hoosier; Idahoan; Jacksonian; Kentuckian; Louisianan; Missourian;* new-world; *Oklahoman;* patriot(ic); *Quakertown;* "red, white and blue"; Sammy [slang]; *Texan;* U.S. citizen; *Virginian; Washingtonian; Xenian;* Yankee; *Zonian;* [*Ant.* alien]

**amiable** *(adj.)*: amicable; affable; benevolent; congenial; delightful; easygoing; friendly; gentling; gregarious; good-natured; hospitable; harmonious; intimate; jovial; kindly; likable; mellow; nice; outgoing; pleasant; *quilting bee;* responsive; sociable; *thoughtful;* uplifting; very friendly; warm; xenial; *yokefellow; zealous;* [*Ant.* adversarial]

**amicable** *(adj.)*: amiable; brotherly; congenial; delightful; engaging; friendly; genial; harmonious; *intimate; jovial;* kind; *likable; mild;* neighborly; outgoing; personable; polite; *quilting bee;* responsive; sociable; *thoughtful;* uplifting; very nice; welcoming; xenial; *yokefellow; zestful;* [*Ant.* antagonistic]

**amnesia** *(n.)*: agnosia; blackout; *carelessness;* disrememberance [dial.]; *escapes one;* fugue; gap in memory; *heedlessness;* irretention; *just forgot; knock on the head;* loss of memory; memory loss; non-remembrance; obliviousness; *poor memory; quirkiness; regardlessness; scatterbrained; thoughtlessness;* unmindfulness; *void; wandering; x-out;* yonderliness; zero remembrance;

**amnesty** *(n.)*: acquittal; absolution; blotting out; clearing; cancelling; dismissal; excusing; exculpation; exoneration; forgiveness; general pardon; *humaneness;* indemnification; justification; keeping no account; letting go; *mercy;* non-execution; oblivion; pardon; quittance; remittance; release; sparing; taking away; *unvengefulness;* voidance; wiping clean; *washing; x-ing out; yielding;* zeroing out;

**amoral** *(adj.)*: anti-religious; *blasphemous;* carnal; dishonorable; earthly-minded; faithless; godless; *humanistic;* indevout; jackeen; knavish; latitudinarian; libertine; miscreant; nonmoral; overcredulous; profane; *questionable;* reprobate; secular; *transgressing;* unprincipled; unscrupulous; unmoral; *villainous;* worldly-minded; *x-gressing; yieldless;* zero-morals;
**amorphous** *(adj.)*: amoebic; *blurry;* changeable; dimensionless; erratic; formless; featureless; free; *gelatin-like;* hazy; inchoate; indistinct; ill-defined; jellyish; *kedging;* loose; labile; multiversant; mutable; nebulous; *obscure; omniform;* protean; quasi-morphous; *revamping;* shapeless; transmutable; unformed; undeveloped; unclear; unshaped; unstructured; vague; *wavering; x-bodied;* yeasty; zaggy; [*Ant.* absolute]
**amount** *(n.)*: aggregate; bottom line; count; degree; extent; figure; group; grand total; horde; *ingathering;* jag; *kit;* load; level; mass; measure; number; *offset;* part; (pro)portion; quantity; reckoning; ratio; size; sum; total; units; volume; weight; whole; *x; yard; z-score;*
**ample** *(adj.)*: adequate; abundant; bountiful; copious; *disproportionate;* enough; full; generous; *heaps; immense;* jumbo; *king-sized amounts;* liberal; more than enough; necessary; overabundant; plentiful; quantitative; rich; sufficient; tons; unreserved; voluminous; vast; wantless; x.; *yards; zillions;*
**amplification** *(n.)*: amplitude; boost; clamorousness; decibels; elevation; fullness; greatness; highness; intensity; jacking up; *kilawatts;* loudness; *level;* magnitude; noise; *outsound;* phon; quantity; raising; sound volume; *turned up;* upping; volume; widening; watts; *x-loud;* yelling; zero quietness;
**amplify** *(v.)*: augment; broaden; crank up; deepen; enlarge; exaggerate; fatten; greaten; grow; heighten; increase; intensify; jack up; *keep growing;* largen; make louder; magnify; *nourish;* overstress; progress; *quadruplicate;* rise; strengthen; turn up; up; *volume;* widen; wax greater; *XL; yain* [arch.]; *zoom;*
**amplitude** *(n.)*: abundance; bounty; copiousness; disproportion; excess; *flood;* generous amount; galore; heaps; immensity; jumbo amounts; *king-sized amount;* liberality; largeness; multiplicity; myriad; numerousness; overabundance; plenty; plethora; profusion; quantities; repleteness; surplus; superabundance; tons; uberty; volumes; wealth; x.; *yards; zillion;*
**amputate** *(v.)*: abscind; bob; cut off; dismember; excise; *forehew; gouge;* hack; incise; jigsaw; knife; lop; *mutilate; nip;* obtruncate; prune; *quarter;* remove; resect; sever; take off; truncate; transfix; *undo; vell;* whack off; *x-sect;* yerk; *zigsaw* [arch.]; [*Ant.* add]
**amputation** *(n.)*: abscission; *bobbing;* cutting off; dismemberment; excision; exsection; *forehewn;* getting rid of; hacking; *incision; jigsawing; knife;* lopping; medical removal; *nipping;* obtruncation; pruning; *quartering;* removal; rescection; severing; surgical removal; taking off; truncation; transfixion; *undoing; velling;* whacking off; *xfer;* yerking; zigsaw [arch]; [*Ant.* addition]
**amuse** *(v.)*: absorb; bedazzle; cheer; divert; delight; entertain; fascinate; gratify; humor; have fun; interest; jollify; keep entertained; *leisure;* make one smile; *non-serious;* occupy; please; *quality time;* regale; *spellbind;* tickle one's fancy; *unwind; view; watch; xenization;* yippee; zappy; [*Ant.* agitate]
**amusement** *(n.)*: avocation; buffoonery; clowning around; comedy; cheer; diversion; distraction; delight; entertainment; enjoyment; fun; glee; hobby; idle ~; jollity; kill-time; lighthearted play; leisure; mirth; *non-serious; overjoying;* pastime; play; pleasure; *quality time;* recreation; sport; tomfoolery; *unwind; vanity;* whit; *x-play;* yippee; zaniness; [*Ant.* agitation]
**analogy** *(n.)*: alikeness; *bearing resemblance;* comparison; correlation; *duplication;* exemplum; figure; *gemination;* homology; homogeneity; illustration; juxtaposition; *kind;* likeness; metaphor; nearness; *oneness;* parallelism; *quasi-similitude;* resemblance; similarity; *type;* uniformity; very image; *with comparison; xfer;* yoke; *zeugma;*
**analysis** *(n.)*: assay; assessment; breakdown; check (up); critique; diagnostic; examination; field study; *finding;* going over; *herborization;* investigation; *judgment;* knowledge-gathering; lab analysis; look-over; microanalysis; *neuroanalysis;* overhaul; probe; query; research; results; study; scrutiny; test; *urinalysis;* volumetric analysis; winnowing; *xenodiagnosis;* yield results; *zootomy;*

**analyze** *(v.)*: assess; break down; consider; check; dissect; examine; explore; find; go over; *hone in on;* investigate; *judge; knowledge;* look at (-over); make a study of; *notice;* observe; probe; question; review; re-examine; research; study; scrutinize; test; *understand;* verify; *watch;* xenodiagnose; yeme; *zero in;*
**anarchist** *(n.)*: *anti-establishment; activist;* beatnik; *criminal;* dissenter; dissident; *enemy;* free spirit; guerilla; *heterodox;* insurrectionist; *jaw-set; kabouter* [Du.]; lawless person; mutineer; nonconformist; oppositionist; poissarde [fem.]; *queer;* revolutionary; seditionary; troublemaker; *unconventional;* villain; wiggy; *x-grained; yieldless;* zealot;
**anarchy** *(n.)*: anarchism; bewilderment; bedlam; chaos; disorder; embroilment; farrago; gastness; havoc; intranquility; jumble; kerfuffle; lawlessness; mayhem; non-orderliness; *obscurity;* pandemonium; *quandary; quizzical; rebellion;* stupefaction; turmoil; upheaval; vexation; welter; xaos; *yo-yo;* zoo;
**ancestor** *(n.)*: ascendant; blood-relative; clan member; distant relation; *derived; eight generations removed;* forebearer; (fore)father; foremother; forerunner; *generations;* (great-)grandfather; (great-)grandmother; *heredity;* immediate ~; *inherited; Jewish ancestry;* kin; lineal ~; *man; non-paternal ~;* originator; parent; predecessor; progenitor; primogenitor; quatrayle; relative; *stock;* tribal head; *unilineal; vein; white race; x-linked; yellow race; zygogenetic;*
**ancestral** *(adj.)*: agnatic; atavistic; blood; clannish; derivational; ethnic; familial; genetic; hereditary; inherited; *joined;* kin-related; lineal; maternal [fem.]; nibiliary; national; old; original; past; paternal [masc.]; phyletic; *quarter;* racial; stock-related; tribal; *unilineal; vein; whakapapa* [Maori]; *x-linked; yoni [Skr.]; zygogenetic;*
**anchor** *(n.)*: anchorage; bower; cock-bill; claw ~; Danforth ~; *equipment;* fluke; grapnel; grappling; hawse; iron ~; *join;* kedge; killick; *landing;* Martin ~; *moorings;* northill ~; *object;* plough ~; quick-release ~; rochna ~; stabilizer; ship's ~; *tripping;* unit; vignette; wasi; *xtr. hold;* yacht ~; *zero drift;*
**anchor** *(v.)*: affix; brace; cast ~; *dock; engage;* fasten; grip tight; hook; interlock; join; kedge; latch on; moor; *nail; oxreim;* place at ~; *quit;* rest at ~; secure; *tie up;* unite; *very firm hold; well-anchored; xuld [arch.];* yoke; *zero drift;*
**ancient** *(adj.)*: antiquated; archaic; age-old; antediluvian; bygone; *chronicled;* dated; early; *former; gray;* historic; immemorial; *jaded; kept;* long-standing; *musty; nostalgic;* olden; prehistoric; preadamic; *quondam; ripe(ned); retired;* senescent; stricken in years; time-honored; time-worn; *up in years; used;* venerable; well-worn; XO; *yore; zillions of years old;*
**anesthesia** *(n.)*: anesthetization; analegia; benumbment; cloudedness; dullness; deadness; etherization; *frozenness;* general ~; *hibernation;* insensitivity; insensibility; *jadedness;* knockout drug; local ~; making numb; non-feeling; non-sensitivity; obtundency; putting under; *quiescence; resting;* senslessness; sleep; torpor; torpidity; unfeelingness; *very numb; without feeling; xylocaine; yet insensitive;* zero feeling;
**anesthetize** *(v.)*: attenuate; benumb; cloud; dull; deaden; etherize; *freeze;* go ~; hebetate; *insensitive; jade;* knock out; lay out; make ~; numb; obtund; put under; *quiescent; reduce feeling;* sedate; stultify; take the edge off; *unfeeling; void; without feeling; xylocaine; yet insensitive;* zonk; [*Ant.* awaken]
**angel** *(n.)*: arch~; *being;* cherub(im); celestial; dominions [pl.] ethereal being; *fairy;* guardian ~; *Gabriel;* heavenly being; host [pl.]; holy ~; hierarch; invisible helper; Jehovah's messenger; *King's servant; light-bearer;* messenger; ministering spirit; *Michael;* nonhuman messenger; *ocellated being;* putto; principalities [pl.]; powers [pl.]; quadrafrontal; righteous ~; seraph(im); spirit; son of God; *transmundane; Uriel;* virtues [pl.]; *wonderful being; Xgazd; yonder;* zonic being; [*see* demon]
**angelic** *(adj.)*: angel-like; angelical; beautiful; cherubic; celestial; divine; ethereal; *fabulous;* good; glorified; heavenly; innocent; *just; keen;* lovely; *moral; majestic;* non-earthly; otherworldly; pure; *quality;* righteous; seraphic; *transmundane;* unfallen; virtuous; *worshipful;* xtry.; *yonder;* zonic; [*see* good; demonic]

**anger** *(n.)*: aggravation; bitterness; *boiling;* crossness; choler; displeasure; enragement; fury; gall; hotness; indignation; ire; infuriation; incensement; *jealous rage; kindling;* lividness; madness; *nettling;* outrage; perturbation; quick-temperament; ruffle; rage; *steaming;* temper; *upset;* unmixed wrath; *virulence; venting;* wrath; *xerothermia; yelling; zealousy* [arch.];

**anger** *(v.)*: aggravate; boil; cross; disturb; displease; disgust; embitter; exasperate; enrage; frustrate; fluster; fume; gall; *hamper; heat;* irritate; infuriate; incense; *jar;* kindle; lose it (-one's temper); miff; madden; nettle; *offend;* outrage; *provoke;* pique; perturb; *quick-tempered;* rankle; rile; *slow burn;* steam; seethe; tick off; upset; vex; vent; work up; *xerothermic; yell; zealousy [arch.];* [*Ant.* appeal]

**angle** *(n.)*: acclivity; bevel; bias; cock; degree; declivity; *diagonal;* el(evation); fall; gradient; hade; hip; incline; jag; knick; lean; *movement; natural slope;* obliqueness; pitch; quoin; rise; ramp; slant; slope; tilt; trajectory; upslope; verge; vector; wind; *xy-gradient;* yaw; zag;

**angry** *(adj.)*: annoyed; aggravated; angered; boiling; beside oneself; cross; disgusted; exasperated; enraged; fuming; furious; galled; hot; irate; infuriated; incensed; jumping mad; *kindled;* livid; mad; nettled; outraged; peppery; perturbed; quick-tempered; riled; raging; sore; ticked off; upset; violent; wroth; *xerothermic; yond* [arch.]; *zealousy [arch.];*

**anguish** *(n.)*: agony; *bleakness;* chafing; distress; dolor; extreme pain; *excruciating;* feel bad; grief; hurt(ing); inconsolableness; joylessness; *killing;* lowness; misery; *negativism; overmuch sorrow;* pain; *quivering;* ruefulness; suffering; torment; *unhappiness;* vexation; wrenching; writhing; *xiphodynia; yearning; zing;*

**animal** *(n.)*: *amphibian;* beast; creature; domestic ~; *ectotherm;* fauna [pl.]; game; *herbivore; insectivore;* jument; *koala;* livestock; life form; *mammal; marsupial; non-vertebrate;* organism; pose [heraldry]; quadruped; *reptile;* stock; soliped; *thing;* ungulate; varmint; *vertibrate;* wildlife [pl.]; wilding; *xerocole; yearling;* zoic;
   **Kinds of animals**: ape; bird; cow; dog; elephant; fox; goat; horse; ibex; jaguar; kangaroo; lion; monkey; newt; otter; pig; quail; rabbit; sheep, tiger; uakari; vulture; walrus; xeme; yak; zebra;

**animate** *(v.)*: awaken; bestir; bring to life; *come back;* disquiet; enliven; energize; *fix;* give life; hearten; invigorate; *jar; kindle;* liven; move; make alive; *not inert; over-agitate;* perk up; quicken; revive; rouse; stir; *thrive;* uplift; vitalize; vivify; wake; *xenenthesis; yerk; zip;*

**animated** *(adj.)*: active; bouncy; *cheerful;* dynamic; energetic; enthusiastic; frisky; *gung-ho;* high-spirited; intense; *jumpy;* keen; lively; *motivated;* nippy; overactive; peppy; quick-moving; rapid; spirited; springy; *thrilled; upbeat;* vigorous; wimble; *x-energy;* yeasty; zestful;

**animation** *(n.)*: activity; breath; consciousness; disquieting; enlivening; *friskiness;* go; heartening; invigoration; *jarring;* kick; life; movement; *non-stationary; over-agitation;* perkiness; quickening; rousing; stirring; *thriving; uplift;* vitality; vigor; vivaciousness; verve; *wake;* xenenthesis; yeastiness; zip;

**animosity** *(n.)*: antagonism; bitterness; contrariness; dislike; enmity; fight; gainsaying; hostility; ill-will; *jangling; knocking;* loathing; malice; negativism; opposition; *polarity;* querulousness; resentment; spite; *tetchiness;* unfriendliness; venom; *withstanding; xenophobia; yawping;* zoilism; [*Ant.* accord]

**annihilate** *(v.)*: abolish; atomize; blot out; crush; destroy; demolish; disintegrate; expunge; exterminate; finish off; *grind; havoc; incinerate; junk;* kill; lay waste; liquidate; level; *massacre;* nullify; obliterate; pulverize; quash; raze; ruin; reduce to naught; smash; snuff out; *terminate;* unbuild; vaporize; wipe out; *x-ing; yank down;* zap;

**annihilation** *(n.)*: abolishment; atomization; blotting out; crushing; dissolution; death; expunction; extermination; finishing off; *grinding; havoc;* incineration; *jaws of death;* killing; liquidation; *massacre;* nullification; naught; obliteration; pulverization; quashing; *ruination;* snuffing out; *termination;* undoing; vaporization; wiping out; *x-ing out; yanking down; zapping;*

**anniversary** *(n.)*: annual celebration; birthday; bicentary; bicentennial; celebration; centenary; centennial; decentennial; *eightieth ~;* fanfare; *golden ~; hundredth ~; ivory ~;* jubilee; *keen remembrance; lace ~;* milestone; novennial; occasion; *platinum ~;* quadricentennial; remembrance; special day; *silver ~;* triennial; undecennial; vigintennial; wedding *~; xtry. celebration;* year-mind; yahrzeit; yearly *~; zeit [G.];*
**announce** *(v.)*: annunciate; broadcast; convey; declare; exclaim; *fame; give;* herald; inform; *jaw; key in;* let out; *mention;* make known; notify; noise; *orate;* proclaim; quoth; report; rehearse; relay; say; state; tell; utter; voice; word; *xenagogy;* yell; *zero in;*
**announcement** *(n.)*: address; annunciation; bulletin; broadcast; communication; communiqué; dispatch; declaration; enunciation; edict; full disclosure; general ~; holding forth; intimation; indiction; jactitation; *keynote address; letter;* message; manifesto; notification; notice; oration; pronouncement; press release; promulgation; proclamation; *quotation;* report; revelation; statement; testimonial; utterance; verbalization; word; written notice; *xenagogy;* yeme; *zealous message;*
**annoy** *(v.)*: aggravate; antagonize; acerbate; bother; bug; badger; chafe; disturb; exasperate; frustrate; fluster; grate (on); gravel; gall; hassle; harass; incommode; irritate; jangle; *kindle; livid;* menace; nettle; nag; *offend;* peeve; pester; perturb; *queach [arch.];* ruffle; rankle; *steam; stir up;* tease; test; tee off; unnerve; vex; *weary; x-ing;* yerk; *zing;* [*see* mock; nuisance; *Ant.* appeal]
**annoyance** *(n.)*: aggravation; antagonizing; botheration; chafing; disturbance; exasperation; frustration; grating; hassle; harassment; irritation; jangling; *kindling; lividness;* menace; nettling; nag; *offence;* pestering; perturbation; provocation; *queach [arch.];* rankling; scourge; testing; umbrage; vexation; *weariness; x-ing; yerk; zinging;* [*see* nuisance]
**annoying** *(adj.)*: aggravating; bothersome; cursed; disturbing; exasperating; frustrating; grating; grievous; galling; harassing; irritating; jarring; *knotty;* lousy; menacing; nettling; overburdensome; pesky; problematic; quisquose; rankling; sore; tiresome; trying; unnerving; vexatious; wearying; *xerotripsis; yucky; zinging;* [*Ant.* appealing]
**annul** *(v.)*: abrogate; break up; cancel; call off; disannul; dissolve; end; eliminate; finish; get rid of; *hang it up;* invalidate; *judicial separation;* kill; leave; make void; nullify; negate; *opt out;* put away; quit; rescind; split up; terminate; unmarry; undo; void; withdraw; *x-out; yank;* zero out;
**annulment** *(n.)*: abrogation; breakup; cancellation; divorcement; dissolution; elimination; *filing for ~; gulf; hanging it up;* invalidation; *judicial separation;* keeping separate; leaving; making an end of; nullification; *opting out;* putting away; Petrine dissolution [R.C.C.]; quittance; rescinding; splitting up; termination; unmarrying; voidance; withdrawal; *x; yawn; zipping apart;*
**anoint** *(v.)*: appoint; bestow; consecrate; daub; dedicate; embrocate; *furnish;* grease; hallow; invest; install; instate; *jubilate; king;* lay hands on; make; *massage;* nard; oint; *oil;* ordain; pour; place; pomade; *qualify;* rub; *recognize;* spread; smear; separate; set apart; sanctify; *throne; unction;* vest; wash; wipe; *xfer;* yark; *zet [dial.];*
**anointed** *(adj.)*: appointed; blessed; consecrated; daubed; dedicated; embrocated; *furnish;* greased; hallowed; invested; *jubilate; king; lay hands on;* massaged; *Messiah;* narded; ointed; ordained; pomaded; *qualified;* rubbed; spread; smeared; separated; set apart; sanctified; *throne; unction;* vested; washed; *xfer;* yarkened; *zet [dial.];*
**anointing** *(n.)*: anointment; blessing; chrismation; conferring; consecration; dedication; embrocation; *furnishing; giving;* hallowing; instating; *jubilate; king; laying hands on;* making; *Messiahship; nard;* ointing; outpouring; ordaining; pouring; *qualifying;* rubbing; sanctification; *throne;* unction; vesting; *washing; xfer;* yarkening; *zet [dial.];*
**anomaly** *(n.)*: abnormality; aberration; bizarreness; craziness; deviation; eccentricity; *foible;* glitch; hitch; irregularity; incongruity; *jarring ~;* kink; looniness; *malformation;* non-usualness; obliquity; peculiarity; quirk; ridiculous thing; strange thing; *twist;* unusual thing; variation; weird thing; *xenomorph; yaw;* zany item;

**anonymous** *(adj.)*: anon; *baffling;* concealed; *disguised; empty;* faceless; guess who; hidden; innominate; John Doe [masc.]; Jane Doe [fem.]; known to none; *little known;* mysterious; nameless; not-named; one; person; *quidam [L.]; revealed to none;* secret; *somebody; top secret;* unknown; unnamed; unspecified; unidentified; undisclosed; undesignated; unsigned; veiled; without name; X; you-know-who; Y.Z. [Br.]; zero identity;
**answer** *(n.)*: argument; *backtalk;* counter; comeback; declaration; defense; elucidation; explanation; finding; general reply; handling; input; judgment; *key input; letter;* message; *note;* outcome; *pronouncement;* quotient; riposte; response; respondence; reply; rejoinder; rebuttal; retort; resolution; sally; short ~; statement; solution; *treatment;* utterance; unriddling; verdict; word; *witty reply; words; xtry.; ~; yes-answer;* zealous reply;
**answer** *(v.)*: advise; *argue;* back ~; counter; come back with; deal with; declare; *echo;* express; explain; elucidate; figure out; give ~; handle; intimate; input; judge; *key in;* lay to rest; make reply; *note;* orate; *pipe up; quotient;* ripost(e); respond; reply; return; rejoin; rebut; retort; say; snap back; state; solve; tell; utter; voice; work through; *x;* yes; zero in; [*Ant.* ask]
**antagonism** *(n.)*: animosity; bitterness; contrariness; dislike; enmity; *fight;* gainsaying; hostility; ill-will; jangliness; *knocking;* loathing; malice; negativism; opposition; *polarity;* querulousness; resentment; spite; *tetchiness;* unfriendliness; variance; *withstanding; xenophobia; yawping;* zoilism; [*Ant.* accord]
**antagonist** *(n.)*: adversary; bad guy; challenger; disputant; enemy; foe; *garrison; hostile;* instigator; jangler; kemper; *legion; litigant;* match; nemesis; opponent; *player; quarreler;* rival; striver; *traitor; unfriendly;* vier; warling; xenic; yuon [arch.]; zoilist; [*Ant.* ally]
**antagonistic** *(adj.)*: adverse; belligerent; contentious; dangerous; enemy; *fierce; galsome;* hostile; inimical; *jeopardizing;* kindless; low-down; mean; malicious; nasty; odious; pugnacious; pernicious; quarrelsome; rough; *savage;* tough; threatening; unfriendly; violent; warlike; *xenophobic; yieldless; zealotic;* [*Ant.* assistive]
**antagonize** *(v.)*: annoy; acerbate; bother; chafe; disturb; exasperate; frustrate; gall; harass; irritate; jangle; *kid; livid;* miff; menace; nettle; *offend;* pester; *queach [arch.];* rankle; rile; *steam;* tease; taunt; tempt; unnerve; vex; *weary; x-ing;* yerk; *zing;* [*Ant.* assist]
**antelope** *(n.)*: addax; bushbuck; chamois; deer; doe [fem.]; eland; elk; fawn; gazelle; hart [masc.]; hind [fem.]; impala; *jumping deer;* kudu; lechwe; mohr; nyala; oryx; pronghorn; quanga; reebok; saiga; stag [masc.]; topi; *ungulate; venison;* whitetail; *x-breed;* yakin; *zoic;*
**anthem** *(n.)*: arietta; *arrangement;* ballad; carol; ditty; étude; folksong; gallimaufry; hymn; *inspired music;* jingle; kasida; laud; march; music; *national anthem;* ode; piece; quodlibet; refrain; song; tune; tract; undersong; *Volkslied* [G.]; war song; *xylophone song;* yed; zemirah;
**antic** *(n.)*: act; beguilement; caper; deception; escapade; farce; gag; hoax; imposture; joke; knavishness; lark; mischief; naughtiness; *outrageous;* prank; questionable activity; ruse; stunt; shenanigan; trick; *untruth; vandalism;* waggery; *xuld [arch.];* yock; zinger;
**antichrist** *(n.)*: anti-Christ; *the* Beast; charismatic one-world leader; *the* Devil's man; *enemy of God;* false messiah; god-impersonator; hell's man; *individual; jab jab [Carib.];* king; little horn; man of sin; nemesis; one-world leader; *prince; quad;* ruler; Satan's man; *666;* Tribulational leader; unifier of earth; *vile one;* wicked one; Xargi; yet future one-world leader; zar; [*Ant.* Alpha and Omega]
**anti-Christian** *(adj.)*: antichristian; antievangelical; antimoralist; Bible-hating; Christ-rejecting; devilish; evil; fiendish; Gospel-hating; humanistic; irreligious; Jesus-hating; *Kirchenkampf* [G.]; *loathing;* malevolent; non-godly; opposed to Christianity; pernicious; *quad; rejecting Christ;* sinful; satanic; *treacherous;* un-Christian; villainous; worldly; wicked; *xgressing; yeffell [arch.]; zero godliness;*
**anticipate** *(v.)*: await; believe; bide; count on; calculate; desire; envision; expect; forethink; foresee; *guess;* hope for; *imminence; just wait;* keenly await; look forward to; make preparations for; *non-idle; overcompensate;* plan for; predict; *quait [arch.];* ready oneself for; see coming; think likely; *use patience;* visualize; wait for; *xel [arch.];* yarken; zealously await; [*see* prepare]

**anticipation** *(n.)*: alacrity; *bated breath;* calculation; desire; expectation; eagerness; foresight; *guess;* hope; *imminence; just waiting;* keenness; looking forward to; making preparation; *non-idleness;* officiousness; preoccupation; prevision; prediction; quicksightedness; readiness; seeing ahead; thinking likely; *using patience;* visualization; waiting; *xel [arch.];* yearning; zealous ~; [*see* readiness]

**antidote** *(n.)*: alexiteric; antipoison; antitoxin; bezoar; cure; counterpoison; *drug;* elixir; *febrifuge; glycerol;* help; injection; *julep; kola; lohock;* medicine; mithridate; neutralizer; orvietan; *pill; quinine;* remedy; serum; treacle; theriac; unpoison; vaccine; wonder drug; xenoantiserum; *yanggona; zopissa [arch.];*

**antique** *(adj.)*: antiquated; bygone; classic; dated; early-style; *former days; good old;* historic; *immemorial; jaded; kept;* long-standing; mossgrown; nostalgic; olden; old-fashioned; *past;* quaint; *relic;* senescent; time-honored (-worn); *unfashionable;* very old; well-aged; Xanthian; *yesteryear; zillions of years old;*

**antique** *(n.)*: artifact; bygone; curio; classic; collectible; conversation piece; dated; *early-style; furniture; garage sale item;* heirloom; *item; junk;* knick-knack; long-retired item; monument; nostalgic item; old thing; piece; *quaintry;* relic; showpiece; treasure from the past; uncommon thing; vintage item; well-aged object; *xtry. piece; ye olde; zillions of years old;*

**anti-Semetic** *(adj.)*: anti-Jewish; bigoted; *chauvinistic;* discriminatory; *ethnic cleansing; fiendish; godless;* Hebrew-hating; Hitleresque; *intolerant;* judeophobic; Jew-hating; *klannish;* loathing; *malevolent;* Nazi; opposing the Jews; pro-Nazi; *quick to judge;* racist; Semite-opposing; *terrorizing; unkind; villainous;* wicked; *xenophobic;* Yiddish-hating; Zionist-rejecting; [*Ant.* Abrahamic]

**antisocial** *(adj.)*: anti-social; bashful; cold; dissocial; eremitical; *fearful; gentle;* hermitical; introverted; isolationist; jackalent; keeping to oneself; *lonely; mortified;* non-social; *overmodest; petrified;* quiet; reserved; reclusive; secluded; timid; unfriendly; unsocial; *verecund;* withdrawn; xenophobic; yarrow; *zealless;*

**antitype** *(n.)*: archetype; basis; correspondent figure; fulfillment; *distillation;* epitome; exemplar; fugler; fulfillment; guide; holotype; ideal; jewel; *kit-cat; lead;* model; neotype; original; prototype; pattern; quintessence; referent; standard; template; ule; *virtual; way; xenagogue;* yardstick; *zincograph;*

**anxiety** *(n.)*: apprehension; burden; concern; care; consternation; distress; *exasperation;* fear; gloom; *horror;* insecurity; jitteriness; kiaugh [Scot.]; lather; misgivings; nervousness; over-anxiety; paranoia; panic; quaking; *reluctance;* solicitude; stress; trepidation; uneasiness; vexation; worry; *xenophobia;* yellow-belliedness; *zeallessness;*

**anxious** *(adj.)*: apprehensive; bothered; *bated breath;* concerned; dread; distraught; edgy; fretful; fearful; faint-hearted; gutless; hesitant; insecure; jittery; jumpy; keyed up; lily-livered; misgiving; nervous; overanxious; paranoid; phobic; quivering; reluctant; squirmish; scared; troubled; unsure; uneasy; vexed; worried; *xenophobic;* yellow(-bellied); *zapped;*

**apart** *(adv.)*: asunder; broken; *bifurcated;* cleft; divided; disunited; disjoined; disassembled; *excluded;* forked; *gone; halved;* in parts; *jigsawed; knived;* laniated; made separate; not connected; opened; parted; quinquefid; riven; separate; split; *torn* ~; uncombined; unglued; unassembled; verging away; *wedge; x'ed; yandied; zoned;*

**apartment** *(n.)*: abode; bed-sitter; building; condominium; dorm; dwelling; duplex; efficiency ~; frontroom; flat (house); garage ~; home; high-rise; inhabitance; *jacal; ken;* lodging; living quadplex; quarters; maisonette; manor ~; *nest;* outbuilding; place; pad [slang]; penthouse; quarters; room; residence; rent house; studio ~; suite; summerhouse; tenement; *utility apartment;* villa; walk-up; x-house; *yali; zwinger;*

**apathetic** *(adj.)*: aloof; blithe; cool; disinterested; *easygoing;* fainéant; groggy; half-hearted; indifferent; jaded; knark; listless; mopish; non-interested; oscitant; phlegmatic; quiescent; *relaxed;* spiritless; torpid; uninterested; uncommitted; vapid; workshy; *xenarthrous;* yareless; zealless; [*Ant.* ambitious]

**apathy** *(n.)*: abulia; blitheness; *boredom;* coolness; casualness; disinterest; ennui; *faint-heartedness; grogginess;* half-heartedness; indifference; *jem'enfichism* [F.]; *knark;* lassitude; lack of concern; mopishness; nonchalance; oscitance; passiveness; quiescence; regardlessness; spiritlessness; torpidity; unconcern; vapidity; *weariness; xenarthrous;* yarelessness; zeallessness; [*see* insignificance; *Ant.* ambition]

**apex** *(n.)*: acme; apogee; brow; climax; crest; *distance;* extremity; *fastigium* [L.]; *greatest height;* head; high point; height; *increase; important; jut;* kop; limit; mountaintop; nib; *overmost point;* peak; pinnacle; *quoif; ridge;* summit; top; upper extremity; vertex; *way up; xtry; yonder point;* zenith;

**apocryphal** *(adj.)*: apocrypha-related; *bogus;* counterfeit; dubious; extracanonical; fictitious; *guileful; hoax;* invented; *japed; kiddy;* look-alike; mythical; non-canonical; non-authentic; *omitted from the canon;* pseudepigraphical; *phony;* questionable; *rejected;* spurious; *totally false;* uncanonical; unauthentic; *vain; wily; xeno-; yichus;* zero validity;

   **Apocryphal books:** Baruch; Ecclesiasticus; *the* Idol Bel and the Dragon; Judith; I & II Macabees; Prayer of Manasses; Rest of Esther; Story of Suzanna; Tobit; Wisdom;

**apologize** *(v.)*: admit; beg forgiveness; confess; desire pardon; eat crow (-humble pie); fess up [improper]; *go to; humble oneself;* implore for absolution; *just say sorry; keen;* look for forgiveness; make amends (-up); *non-justification;* own up; plead for pardon; pray for forgiveness; *quit denying;* request forgiveness; *recompense;* say sorry; seek absolution; supplicate; take the blame; utter apology; *voice sorrow over;* want forgiveness; *xfer; yearn;* zero in; [*Ant.* accuse]

**apology** *(n. admission of wrong)*: admission; begging forgiveness; concession; declaration of wrongdoing; eating humble pie; fessing up [improper]; guilt-admission; humble pie; imploration for absolution; *just say sorry; keening; looking for forgiveness; mea culpa* [L.]; mav; *non-justification;* owning up; peccavi; *quittance;* request for forgiveness; sincere ~; taking blame; *utterance;* voicing sorrow; *well-worded ~; xfer; yearning;* zeroing in; [*Ant.* accusation]

**apology** *(n. defense)*: apologetic; advocation; *backing;* championing; defense; explanation; *furtherance;* grounded defense; holding forth; *interpretation;* justification; *key arguments;* logical argument; logomachy; making a case for; *noble defense; outline;* promotion; *questionless;* ready defense; substantiation; thought-out argument; upholding; vindication; well-thought-out argument; *xtry. defense; yeme;* zealous defense;

**apostasy** *(n.)*: abandonment; breaking away; casting off; departure; desertion; error; forsaking; going off; *heresy;* infidelity; *jumping ship; knavery;* leaving the truth; mass- ~; *neodoxy;* obliquation; parting; *quitting;* renunciation of the faith; *surrender;* tergiversation; unfaithfulness; *vacating;* walking away; *xfer; yielding;* zero faithfulness;

**apostate** *(n.)*: arch- ~; betrayer; *collaborator;* defector; *evildoer;* false teacher; *guiler;* heretic; insurgent; Judas; *knave;* leaver; mutineer; *non-loyal; opposer;* perverter; *quisling;* renegade; *sedition;* traitor; turncoat; *unfaithful; vacater;* wicked; *xfer; yegg;* zero loyalty;

**apostatize** *(v.)*: abandon; betray one's beliefs; cast off; depart; *evacuate;* forsake; go off; *head the wrong way; insurgent; jump ship;* know the truth, yet leave it; lapse; leave the truth; make about-face; *non-faithfulness;* overturn; pitch; quit; relinquish; renounce faith; sell out; turn back on; tergiversate; *unfaithful;* volte-face; walk away; *xfer; yield;* zero faithfulness;

**apostle** *(n.)*: advocate; *believer; Christian;* disciple; *evangelist; eye-witness;* follower; gospeler; holder-forth; *instructed;* Jesus disciple; *kerygma;* liegeman; *loyal follower;* men; messenger; myrmidon *neophyte; orator;* preacher; *quoter; redeemed;* sent one; servant; *the* Twelve [pl.]; *utterer;* voice; witness; *Xn; yielder;* Zebedist;

**apparatus** *(n.)*: appliance; *brainchild;* contrivance; contraption; device; engine; equipment; *function;* gear; gadget; *hardware;* instrument; instrumentation; invention; *jigger;* kit; labor-saving device; mechanism; machine; "nuts and bolts"; *object; operation;* piece of equipment; quaint device; *robot;* system; tackle; unit; *vade mecum* [L.]; *workings; X-Y recorder; you-know-what; Zeug* [G.];

**apparent** *(adj.)*: *appearing;* blatant; clear; discernable; evident; *flagrant;* glaring; *heedless; intentional; just plain to see;* kenspeckle; lucid; manifest; noticeable; obvious; plain; palpable; quite obvious; recognizable; seeming; seeable; self-evident; transparent; unmistakable; visible; watchable; *x-parent; yare; zero-disguised;*
**appeal** *(n. attraction)*: attraction; beauty; charm; draw; desirableness; enjoyableness; fascination; geasa; heavenliness; interest; joyousness; keenness; lure; magnetism; magic; niceness; *over joyousness;* pleasantness; queme; *reward;* satisfaction; thrill; *uplifting; vivaciousness;* wonderfulness; *xenia; yeah! zygotaxis [biol.];* [*Ant.* abomination]
**appeal** *(n. request)*: adjuration; bid; call; cry; *cri de coeur* [F.]; desire; entreaty; *forewish; great desire; humble entreaty;* importunity; impassioned plea; imploration; juration; *known need; looking for;* making request; *need;* obsecration; obtestation; petition; plea; quest; request; supplication; try; urging; *voice;* wish; *XQ;* yarning; *zikr* [Mos.];
**appeal** *(v.)*: ask; adjure; beg; beseech; call for; crave; conjure; desire; entreat; *file for; go begging; humbly ask;* implore; impetrate; *juration; kneel;* lift up one's voice for; lobby; make request; *need;* obsecrate; prevail upon; petition; plead; *quiritation;* request; solicit; supplicate; trouble one for; *try to get;* urge; vocalize; wish; *XQ.;* yearn for; *zealously plead;*
**appealing** *(adj.)*: attractive; blithe; charming; desirable; endearing; enthralling; fascinating; *good;* happy; heartwarming; inviting; interesting; intriguing; *joyous;* keen; lovely; *merry;* nice; *overjoyed;* pleasing; *queme;* rewarding; stimulating; thrilling; uplifting; *vivacious;* welcome; *xenial; yeah!; zestful;* [*Ant.* appalling]
**appear** *(v.)*: arise; *arrive;* become visible; come; *develop draw near;* emerge; *form; grow;* happen; irrupt; *jump in;* kithe [Scot.]; look; materialize; manifest; *near; non-concealed;* occur; pop up; *quicken;* reappear; rise; show up; turn up; uprise; visit; *visible; walk up; xfer;* yede; *zip out;*
**appearance** *(n. look)*: aesthetic; bearing; countenance; display; deportment; exterior; face; form; guise; *how it looks;* imagery; *just for looks; ken;* look; manner of ~; manifestation; *notice;* outside; outward ~; ostentation; *perception;* quale; resemblance; semblance; *take;* unveiling; visage; way it looks; *xtry. ~;* yeme; *zero in;*
**appearance** *(n. manifestation)*: appearing; arrival; advent; becoming visible; coming; dawn; emergence; founding; formation; genesis; hatching; incarnation; *jump off; kick off; launching;* materialization; manifestation; naissance; origination; presence; *quickening;* realization; reappearance; rising; start; *take-off;* ushering in; *visitation; welcoming; xenogenesis; yielding; zygogenesis;*
**appease** *(v.)*: assuage; allay; becalm; calm; conciliate; diffuse; dulcify; ease; fulfill; gratify; humor; hush; indulge; *justify; knock down;* lull; mollify; make peace; mend fences; *nullify; overcome;* pacify; placate; propitiate; quell; reconcile; render favorable; resolve; soothe; satisfy; tranquilize; unruffle; *vanish;* win favor; *x-out; yield; zeroize;* [*Ant.* anger]
**appeasement** *(n.)*: assuagement; becalming; conciliation; diffusing; dulcification; easing; fulfillment; gratification; humoring; indulging; *justification; knocking down;* lulling; mollification; *nullification; overcoming;* pacification; placation; propitiation; quelling; reconciliation; satisfaction; tranquilization; unruffling; *vanishing;* winning favor; x-ing out; *yielding; zeroizing;* [*Ant.* anger]
**append** *(v.)*: add; attach; amend; annex; *bind;* combine; dovetail; engraft; fasten; fix; *glue;* hitch; inosculate; join; knit; link; marry; merge; *nail; oxreim;* put together; *quasi-fuse;* relate; stick; secure; splice; tag on; tack on; tie on; unite; *vise;* wed; weld; *xenograft;* yoke; *zip;*
**appetite** *(n.)*: appetency; belly-pinching; craving; desire; *edge of starvation;* famish(ment); famine; greed; gluttony; hunger; inclination; itch; *jejune; keenness of ~;* longing; lust; *malnourishment;* need; *over-hungry;* pangs; *quenchless;* ravenousness; starvation; taste; thirst; urge; vacuity; voracity; want; xenorexia; yen; *zapped;*

**appetizing** *(adj.)*: agreeable; *bon!* [F.]; *captivating;* delicious; enjoyable; flavorful; good; gustable; heavenly; irresistible; *juicy;* keen; luscious; mouth-watering; nice; *outstanding;* pleasing; palatable; *quite good;* relishable; savory; toothsome; tantalizing; *tempting; unbelievably good;* very good; wonderful; XF; yummy; zesty; [*Ant.* appalling]

**applaud** *(v.)*: acclaim; approve; bless; clap; congratulate; *delight;* express approval; *favor;* give applause; hail; *impact; joy;* kudize; laud; magnify; *nod; ovation;* praise; put hands together [slang]; *quicken;* rave about; support; *thrill; uplift; venerate; well-pleased; xtry.;* yell; zest;

**applause** *(n.)*: acclaim; approval; blessing; clapping; *delight;* eclat; *favor;* glorification; handclapping; *impact; joy;* klap [var.]; laud; magnification; *noise;* ovation; putting hands together [slang]; praise; *quickening;* round of ~; support; standing ovation; *thrill; uplift; veneration; well-pleased; xtry.* response; yelling; zest;

**application** *(n. relevance)*: appliance; bearing; connotation; directive; employment; essence; effect; function; gist; guideline; heart; inference; implication; idea; importance; impact; jist; *knowledge;* lesson; meaning; message; moral; maxim; *nexus;* operation; purpose; point; pertinence; principle; quintessence; relevance; rule; significance; truth; tenet; use; value; worth; weight; *warning;* xenenthesis; *yoke; zeug [G.];*

**appoint** *(v.)*: assign; bestow; choose; *crown;* designate; earmark; entrust; establish; fix; give; handsel; install; institute; invest; instate; inaugurate; *join; keep; let;* make; name; ordain; pick; place; *qualify; re~;* select; set; *take; title; use;* vest; *work; xfer;* yark; *zet [arch.];*

**applicant** *(n.)*: aspirer; *business* ~; candidate; desirer; entreater; filer; *go-getter;* hopeful; interviewee; job-seeker; *kither; looking for employment; man;* nominee; ordinand [rel.]; prospect; petitioner; postulant [rel.]; qualified ~; requester; runner; seeker; *try for; uninterviewed* ~; vier; wannabe [slang]; x-search; yearner; zealous;

**apply** *(v. spread over)*: anoint; bedaub; brush; cover; daub; dab; embrocate; *fan out; grease;* hand-spread; inflict; infucate; *jigger;* knead; lay on; *make use of; nard;* overspread; put it on; paint; *quab;* rub; *reapply;* spread; smear; transfer; use; *varnish;* wipe; xfer; yark; *zip;*

**apply** *(v. use)*: avail; benefit from; *come to use;* direct; *do;* employ; execute; find application; *function;* get benefit from; harness; implement; *jump to it; keep; learn from;* make application; *not ignore;* operate; pertain; put into practice; *quickly implement;* relate; set to use; take to heart; use; utilize; *vocation;* work; *xfer; yoke; zealously* ~;

**appraisal** *(n.)*: assessment; belief; conclusion; deeming; estimation; evaluation; feeling; finding; gauging; *hypothesis; idea; input;* judgment; *knowledge;* leaning; measurement; notion; opinion; perspective; pricing; quotation; review; surmising; take; thoughts; *unbiased* ~; valuation; *wisdom; xenodiagnosis; yankering;* zeal;

**appraise** *(v.)*: assess; adjudge; *believe;* consider; deem; estimate; evaluate; figure; gauge; *hold;* inspect; judge; *know; list;* measure; *notion; opinion;* price; *quote;* review; rate; surmise; set at; size up; think on; use brain; valuate; value; weigh; *xenodiagnose; yeme; zazen;*

**appraiser** *(n.)*: assessor; *beholder;* connoisseur; checker; deemer; estimator; evaluator; figurer; gauger; *held;* inspector; judge; *know-it-all;* lister; measurer; *notate; opinion;* pricer; qualified ~; rater; surmiser; trained ~; *use skill;* valuator; weigher; *xenodiagnoser; yeme; zazen;*

**appreciate** *(v.)*: acknowledge; *bless;* consciously thank; *debt of gratitude;* express gratitude; enjoy; *forever thankful;* give thanks; *heartfelt thanks; indebted;* joy in; know; *laud; mindful;* not forget; *owe;* perceive; praise; *quick-to-thank;* realize; recognize; salute; show gratitude; thank; understand; value; welcome; *xenium; yet thankful; zealously* ~;

**appreciation** *(n.)*: appreciating; *blessing;* credit; delivering of thanks; expression of thanks; *forever thankful;* gratefulness; honor; indebtedness; *joy;* kind-thoughtedness; *love;* mindfulness; non-forgetfulness; *owing;* praise; *quick-to-thank;* recognition; spirit of thankfulness; *salute;* thankfulness; understanding; value; *wholehearted thanks; xtry. gratitude;* yielding thanks; *zeal;*

**apprehend** *(v.)*: arrest; betrap; bust; capture; detain; entrap; fasten upon; get; grab; *hold; hook; imprison; jail; keep;* lay hold; lasso; *make off with;* nab; overtake; obtain; pick up; *quarantine;* run in; seize; take; usurp; *vanquish;* whisk away; wrest; x.; *yard; zip away;*

**apprehension** *(n.)*: anxiety; burden; care; concern; distress; *exasperation;* fear; gloom; horror; insecurity; jitteriness; kiaugh [Scot.]; leeriness; *mistrust;* nervousness; over-anxiety; paranoia; qualmishness; reservation; *reluctance;* solicitude; stress; trepidation; uneasiness; vexation; worry; *xenophobia;* yellow-belliedness; *zeallessness;* [*Ant.* audacity]

**apprehensive** *(adj.)*: anxious; afraid; burdened; concerned; distressed; edgy; fearful; fretful; faint-hearted; gutless; hesitant; insecure; jittery; keyed up; lily-livered; much-concerned; nervous; overanxious; phobic; paranoid; qualmish; reluctant; squirmish; scared; terrified; *troubled;* unsure; uneasy; vexed; worried; *xenophobic;* yellow(-bellied); *zapped;* [*Ant.* audacious]

**apprentice** *(n.)*: assistant; beginner; cadet; disciple; employee; first-year ~; gofer [slang]; helper; intern; jackaroo; *knowledge;* learner; menial; neophyte; offsider; pupil; *quick learner;* student; trainee; underling; *venturer;* worker-in-training; wannabe [slang]; *xenagogy;* yeoman; *zaikai [Jap.];* [*Ant.* authority]

**apprenticeship** *(n.)*: assistance; beginner-training; cadetship; discipleship; education; *first timer;* guidance; helping; internship; *jackaroo; knowledge;* learning; *menial; new; offsider;* prenticeship; *quick learner;* schooling; training; *underling; venture; working; xenagogy;* yeoman; *zaikai [Jap.];*

**approach** *(v.)*: advance; appulse; bear down on; come near; close in; draw nigh; ease up to; enter upon; face; go toward; hone in; impend; *join; keep by;* lead up to; line; loom; move near; near; *oncoming;* proximate; pass near; *quite close;* reach; step up to; touch on; *threshold; upon; upcoming;* verge on; wax close; *xfer; yede [arch.];* zero in on; [*see* ask; *Ant.* abandon]

**approachable** *(adj.)*: affable; accessible; benign; congenial; *delighted;* easygoing; friendly; genial; gregarious; hospitable; interested; *jovial;* kindly; *loving; merciful; non-fearful;* open(-minded); pleasant; *quick to embrace;* receptive; sociable; *take to;* uncritical; very gregarious; warm; welcoming; *xenial; yes; zealous to help;*

**appropriate** *(adj.)*: approved; apt; apposite; apropos; becoming; befitting; corresponding; correct; *comme il faut* [F.]; decorous; due; expedient; fit(ting); good; *honorable;* ideal; just; *kosher;* legitimate; meet; *not out-of-place;* okay; proper; qualified; right; suitable; seemly; *tolerable; unselfish;* valid; well(-suited); worthy; *xtry.; yielded; zealous;*

**appropriate** *(v.)*: assume; betake; confiscate; commandeer; dispossess; divest; exact; fetch; get; grab; have; haul away; intercept; impound; *jerk away;* keep; lay hold on; make off with; nab; obtain; procure; *quirk;* remove; seize; sequester; take; usurp; *vellicate;* wrest; xfer; yank; zip away; [*Ant.* abhorrent]

**appropriateness** *(n.)*: aptness; appositeness; *biensénce* [F.]; correctness; comeliness; decorum; demureness; dignity; expedience; fitness; good taste; gentility; *honor; idoneous; justness; judiciousness; keenness;* legitimacy; meetness; modesty; mannerliness; *not out-of-place; okay;* politeness; potitesse; propriety; qualification; restraint; rightness; sedateness; suitableness; seemliness; tact; *unselfishness;* validity; worthiness; *xtry.; yieldedness; zero fault;* [*Ant.* abhorrence]

**appropriation** *(n.)*: assumption; betaking; confiscation; commandeering; dispossession; divesture; exaction; fetching; getting; grabbing; having; hauling away; interception; impounding; *just take;* keeping; laying hold on; making off with; nabbing; obtainment; procurement; possession; *quick seizing;* removal; seizure; sequestering; taking (over); usurpation; *vellication;* wresting; xfer; yanking; zipping away;

**approval** *(n.)*: approbation; authorization; blessing; consent; commendation; *delight;* endorsement; favor; go-ahead; green light; hear to [reg.]; imprimatur; joint-permission; *knowingly allowed;* license; leave; liking; *liberty; may;* nod; okay; permission; *qualified yes;* ratificaion; support; sign-off; thumbs up [slang]; unreluctance; *unopposed;* vouchsafement; willingness; *x on the dotted line;* yes; *zealous ~;* [*Ant.* animadversion]

**approve** *(v.)*: allow; accept; authenticate; authorize; back; bless; consent; certify; commend; *decriminalize;* endorse; favor; grant; homologate; indulge; justify; knowingly allow; let; make *nod;* okay; pass; qualify; ratify; suffer; sign off; sanction; support; *tolerate; unopposed;* validate; warrant; *x on the dotted line;* yes; yield approbation; *zealously ~;* [*Ant.* animadvert]
**approximate** *(adj.)*: about; ballpark; crude; close; drawing near to; estimated; *forthcoming; guess;* hard by; imprecise; inexact; just about; *kept close;* loose; more or less; near; on or about; proximate; projected; quite close; rough; similar; touching on; *upon;* vague; very close; well-nigh; *x-differential; yede [arch.];* zeroing in; [*Ant.* absolute]
**approximate** *(v.)*: approach; be near; come close to; draw nigh; estimate; fix closely; guess; hone in; impend; *just about;* keep close; loom; move close to; near; *overdo;* proximate; project; *quite close;* reckon; round; simulate; touch on; *upon;* verge on; wax close; *xfer; yede [arch.];* zero in on;
**approximation** *(n.)*: approximateness; ballpark; calculation; *drawing nigh;* estimation; *figure;* general idea; *hunch;* inexactness; immediacy; idea; *just about;* keep close; *like;* more or less; nearness; *official estimate;* proximation; *quote;* reckoning; speculation; *theory; unofficial;* vicinity; *wild guess; x; yeme;* zeroing in;
**apron** *(n.)*: *attire;* baker's ~; carpenter's ~; *dress;* ephod; *finery; garb; habiliments;* item; jumper; kitchen ~; leather ~; mother's ~; nail ~; *outerwear;* pinny; *quaintry [arch.];* raiment; smock; slipper; slop; *togs; uniform;* vesture; workman's ~; *XL; yelek [Turk.]; zari;*
**aquatic** *(adj.)*: abyssopelagic; bathymetrical; *channel;* deep-sea; *estuary; freshwater; grallatorial* [zoo.]; hydrographic; *inlet; jheel [Ind.]; keld;* limnetic; lacustrine; marine; natatory; neptunian; oceanic; pelagic; *quai;* river(-dwelling); subaquatic; sea; thalassic; undersea; *voe;* water-dwelling; *xyrisic; yeo; Zee [G.];*
**Arab** *(n.)*: Arabian; Bedouin; *Cubbabeesh;* desert-dweller; Edomite; *fakir; Ghassanids; Himyarite;* Ishmaelite; *Jordinian; Kababish;* Libyan; Mideasterner; nomad; Omani; oil-rich ~; Palestinian; Qatari; *Rashidun;* Saudi Arabian; *sheik;* tent-dweller; *Umayyed; Vallahades;* wanderer; *xeque;* Yemeni; *Zaidi;*
**arbitrary** *(adj.)*: arbitrable; *aimless;* based on whim; chance; draw of the hat; *empty;* fortuitous; groundless; habnab; *happen;* indiscriminate; *jumbled; keg-meg;* left to chance; motiveless; nonsystematic; *only by chance;* purposeless; purely ~; *quirky;* random; subjective; *totally ~;* unsystematic; very random; wanton; *whim; x; yet indiscriminate;* zero reason;
**arbitrate** *(v.)*: assess; *bench;* consider; decide; determine; evaluate; *figure out;* gauge; hear; intercede; interplead; interpose; judge; *knowledge; list [arch.];* moderate; mediate; negotiate; oversee; pass judgment; *qua [L.];* referee; resolve; settle; sit in judgment; try; umpire; valuate; weigh; XQ; *Your Honor; zamorin;*
**arbitration** *(n.)*: arbitrating; benching; considering; determination; evaluation; *figuring out;* gauging; hearing; intercession; intermediation; interposition; judgment; *knowing; listening;* mediation; negotiation; oversight; presiding; *qua [L.];* refereeing; settling; trying; umpirage; valuation; weighing; XQ; *Your Honor; zamorin;*
**arbitrator** *(n.)*: arbiter; bencher; connoisseur; chief justice; circuit ~; decider; determiner; district-judge; domesman; evaluator; *forejudge;* go-between; Honor; *hakeem* [Mos.]; intermediary; inspector; judge; kadi; *lud [Br.];* mediator; moderator; magistrate; negotiator; official; officer; presider; pretor; *qadi* [Mos.]; referee; *sentencer; settler;* trier; umpire; *vindicator;* weigher; *XQ.; Your Honor; zamorin;*
**arch** *(n.)*: arc; bow; bend; curve; dome; *el(bow); foil;* groined vault; hemisphere; intrados; *jag;* kavadi; lancet ~; *meandering; nonlinear;* ogee; over~; parabola; quadrantal; roof; *rounded;* semicircle; turn; U; vault; *wagon vault; xy-curve; ypsiliform;* zygomatic ~;
**arch** *(v.)*: arc; bend; curve; dome; *el(bow);* fold; *groined vault;* hunch; incline; *jag;* knuckle; *lean; move; nonlinear;* overbend; *ply; quoil [arch.];* round; *swerve;* turn; U; vault; *wind; x-curve; ypsiliform; zag;*

**archaic** *(adj.)*: antiquated; bygone; classical; dated; early; *former; feeble; gray;* historic; *in times past; jaded; kept;* long-standing; Middle English; *medieval;* no-longer-used; old-fashioned; outdated; obsolete; primitive; *quondam;* retired; senescent; time-worn; *unused;* very old; worn; *xanthian; yore;* zillions of years old;

**archer** *(n.)*: arbalister; bowman; bowyer; crossbowman; deadeye ~; expert shooter; *fighter; game hunter;* hunter; *individual; jaeger; keen shot;* longbowman; marksman; *non-combat archery; one;* precision bowman; *quill;* Robin Hood; shooter; toxophilite [joc.]; *user; veteran ~; warrior;* x-bowman; *yager; zero in;*

**archery** *(n.)*: arrow-shooting; bowmanship; bow and arrow; crossbow-shooting; dart-shooting; expert shooting; *fletching; game hunting; hunting;* infrared bow-hunting; *jaeger; keen shooting;* longbow shooting; marksmanship; non-combat ~; *operation;* precision shooting; *quill; recurve crossbow ~;* shooting; toxophily; use of bow and arrow; *violence; warfare;* x-bow-shooting; *yager; zeroing in;*

**architect** *(n.)*: architectural engineer; builder; creator; chief ~; designer; draftsman; draughtsman; drafter; engineer; founder; fashioner; framer; father; *graduate ~;* house-wright; inventor; *job; key ~;* landscape ~; maker; mother; mastermind; master builder; *naval ~;* originator; planner; project manager; *qualified ~; redesigner; state ~;* technical designer; urban designer; *vamper; wager;* x-builder; *yard engineer; zone ~;*

**arduous** *(adj.)*: agonizing; backbreaking; challenging; demanding; exhausting; fatiguing; grueling; hard; intense; *jading;* killing; laborious; moiling; not easy; onerous; *painful; quite hard;* rigorous; strenuous; toilsome; tiresome; unrelenting; very hard; *vigorous;* wearisome; *x-heavy; yare;* zapping;

**area** *(n.)*: acreage; berth; corner; coverage; capacity; division; district; extent; expanse; floorage; field; ground; *hugeness;* immediate ~; jurisdiction; *kray* [Rus.]; locale; municipality; niche; neighborhood; *oblast [Rus.];* place; part; province; quadrant; quarter; region; range; spot; section; sector; sphere; territory; ubiety; vicinity; ward; *x-section; yard;* zone; [*see* topic]

**arena** *(n.)*: amphitheatre; building; coliseum; drama; edifice; field house; grandstand; grounds; hippodrome; indoor ~; *ice rink; judgment hall; kabuki* [Jap.]; lyceum; multiplex; *naumachy* [Rom.]; odeum; park; *pit; querencia* [Sp.]; rink; stadium; theatre; *upper circle;* venue; *wing; xenodocheum;* yard; *zone;*

**argue** *(v.)*: altercate; bicker; contend; clash; disagree; differ; debate; expostulate; fuss; feud; gainsay; hold; have words with; impugn; jangle; kemp; lock horns [slang]; maintain; make fur fly; niff; oppose; parley; quarrel; reason; resist; retort; ratiocinate; remonstrate; squabble; spar; tiff; *unharmonious;* vie; wrangle; *x-purposes;* yell; *zap;* [*Ant.* agree]

**argument** *(n. dispute)*: altercation; bickering; brawl; controversy; contention; disagreement; debate; dispute; dissent; exchange; fuss; fight; feud; gainsaying; hairsplitting; heated exchange; incongruity; jangling; kagg; *locking horns;* misunderstanding; negativism; odds; opposition; polemic; quibble; quarrel; run-in; row; resistance; retort; remonstrance; strife; squabble; spat; tussle; unharmoniousness; *unpleasantness;* variance; wrangling; *x-fire;* yed; *za-zum [Rus.];* [*Ant.* agreement]

**argument** *(n. defense)*: answer; basis; contention; case; confutation; defense; explanation; fundamental ~; grounds; hypobole; *hold;* interpretation; justification; key ~; logical ~; *making intelligible;* notion; objective; *outreason;* point of view; philosophical ~; *quickening;* reasoning; refutation; sorites; sophism; syllogism; thinking; unfailing logic; validation; view; way of thinking; well thought-out ~; *xenodiagnosis; yeme; zealous ~;* [*Ant.* attack]

**argumentation** *(n.)*: arguing; apagogy; apologetics; basic ~; contending; disputation; discursiveness; debate; explanation; formal logic; *grounds;* holding forth; *interpretation;* justification; key ~; logic; many-valued logic; *non-flawed logic;* oratory; philosophical ~; pure logic; *quickening;* reasoning; syllogism; sophistry; *thinking;* unfailing logic; verificationism; *way of thinking; xenodiagnosis; yeme; zealous ~;* [*Ant.* attack]

**argumentative** *(adj.)*: aggressive; agonistic; belligerent; contentious; contrary; disagreeable; disputatious; emulous; factious; gainsaying; hot-tempered; irritable; jangly; knaggy; liverish; mean; nasty; ornery; pugnacious; quarrelsome; resistant; ratiocinative; striving; temperamental; umbrageous; vinegary; wranglesome; *xenophobic;* yieldless; *za-zum* [Rus.]; [*Ant.* agreeable]
**arid** *(adj.)*: anhydrous; barren; bone-dry; chapped; dry; evaporated; fountainless; *gone dry;* hot; insolated; jejune; kibe; *languishing; mummified;* non-watered; overhot; parched; quenchless; rainless; scorched; thirsty; torrid; unwatered; vaporated; waterless; xerothermic; *yarrish; zapped;* [*Ant.* arctic]
**aristocracy** *(n.)*: aristocrats; bluebloods; crachach; *dukes;* elite; *earls;* family; gentry; high-born; *important;* jarldom; *knights;* lords and ladies; *marquis;* nobility; optimacy; patricians; *queen's men; royalty; sirs;* titled; trueborn; upper class; V.I.P.'s; well-bred; *xtry.; younkers; zayim;*
**aristocrat** *(n.)*: archduke; blueblood; *baron; count; duke; earl;* feudal superior; gentleman; hidalgo [Sp.]; *important;* junker; knight; laird; lord; *marquis;* nobleman; optimate; patrician; *queen; ruler; sir;* titled person; toff; upper cruster; *viscount; waldgrave; XO;* younker; *zayim;* [*Ant.* agrarian]
**ark** *(n.)*: *afloat;* box; barge; crate; chest; cupboard; coffer; craft; depository; enclosure; *floating; gopher wood ~;* holder; *inclosure; jack-boat;* kist; locker; moving carton; Noah's ~; *ocean-going ship;* pod; *quaddy;* repository; strongbox; ship; trunk; *ungula;* vessel; wooden chest; *xebec; yadzutsu [Jap.]; zabra;* [see boat; vessel;]
**arm** *(v.)*: accouter; *bestow upon; confer;* deck; equip; fore~; furnish; gear; heel up; issue; *jibe [slang];* kit; load; make ready; *near-ready;* outfit; prepare; provide; *qualify;* ready; supply; *transfer;* train; *unhand;* vest; *well-armed; xfer;* yarken; *zap;*
**Armageddon** *(n.)*: *armed conflict;* battle; bloodbath; *conflict;* doomsday; day of the Lord; end of the world; final battle; *Gog and Magog; har megiddo* [Heb.]; *invasion;* Jezreel valley; Judgment Day; *Kishon; luctation;* Megiddo; *no-return; onslaught;* planetary conflict; *Qiyamah* [Arab.]; *Rev. 16;* Second Coming; tribulation; undoing of the anti-Christ; valley of ~; war to end all wars; *x-fire; yed; zero-hour;*
**armed** *(adj.)*: ~ to the teeth; battle-ready; combat-ready; dangerous; *defensible;* equipped; fortified; gun-brandishing; heavily ~; *inimical; javelin-bearing;* keenly equipt; light- ~; munitions-carrying; *non-peaceful;* outfitted; prepared for war; *quill-carrying;* rifle-bearing; sword-toting; toting a weapon; *unfriendly; violent;* weapon-toting; *xiphos-wielding;* yataghan-carrying; *zone;*
**armor** *(n.)*: armour; armature; brigandine; body ~; bard; coat (of mail); chain mail; *defense;* esquire; *fortification; gauntlet; greaves;* habergeon; hauberk; iron suit; jambeaux; jupon; *keiko* [Jap.]; lame; mail; *nanban-gusoku* [Jap.]; outer shell; *o-yoroi* [Jap.]; panoply; plate ~; quirré; reinforced ~; suit; shell; tace; *uchidashi* [Jap.]; vambrace; *warrior; xia; yoroi* [Jap.]; *zertsalo* [Chin.];
   **Kinds of armor**: armet; breastplate; cowter; doublet; elbow cop; fauld; gauntlet; greaves; helmet, jack of plate; kneelet; lower bevor; mail; nasal helm; pauldron; poleyn; queue; rondel; sabatan; shield; skirt; solleret; tasset; upper bevor; vambrace; visor; wakibiki [Jap.];
**armory** *(n.)*: arsenal; battery; *bomb-chest;* cache; depot; entrepot; firearms; gunroom; headquarters; *iron rations [slang]; javelin room; keep; load;* munitions store; magazine; *naval munitions store;* ordnance; promptuary; *quantity;* repository; storehouse; *treasure; utility room; volume;* weapons store; *xiphos;* yard; *zone;*
**arms** *(n.)*: ammunition; armaments; bombs; batteries; battlements; combat equipment; *defense; deterrent;* equipment; fire~; guns; *handguns;* instruments of war; *javelins; kit; load;* munitions; missiles; *nuclear ~;* ordnance; projectiles; *quantities; rifles;* swords; stores; tools of war; *Uzis; violence;* weapons; weaponry; warheads; *xiphos; y-gun; zweihander;*
**army** *(n.)*: armed force; band; battalion; cavalry; defense; encampment; force; ground forces; host; infantry; junior service [Br.]; *kerns;* land-force; legion; military; nonconscripted army; occupation force; peace-keeping force; *quingenary* [Rom.]; regiment; reinforcements; ranks; soldiers; standing ~; troops; unit; vanguard; warriors; war machine; x-force; *yeald; Zahal* [Isr.];

64

**aroma** *(n.)*: aura; balm; *cense;* delightful scent; essence; fragrance; good ~; *heavenly smell;* incense; joyous aroma; keen smell; *lovely smell; musk;* nidor; *nose; odor;* pleasant smell; quality; redolence; smell; scent; (sweet) savor; terrific fragrance; unforgettable ~; very pleasant ~; whiff; *xtry. scent;* yummy scent; *zedoary;*
**aromatic** *(adj.)*: ambrosial; balmy; censed; *diffusing; delightful;* essenced; fragrant; good-smelling; *heliotrope;* incensed; *jasmine; keen; lovely; musky; nidorous;* odorous; perfumed; *queme;* redolent; scented; sweet-smelling; thuriferous; *unoffensive; very nice;* well-scented; *xanthoxylene; yummy; zedoary;*
**arouse** *(v.)*: awaken; bestir; *call;* disquiet; excite; *fuel;* grab; hearten; incite; jar; kindle; *lead;* move; motivate; nudge; *overagitate;* provoke; pique; quicken; rouse; stir; trouble; *upset; vex;* wake(n); *xuld [arch.];* yerk; *zing;*
**arrange** *(v.)*: assemble; array; *be;* configure; collate; display; distribute; *exhibit;* fix; group; *have;* index; *judge; kit;* lay out; make plans; *nicely order;* order; organize; place; put in order; prepare; *qualify;* rank; rearrange; set (out); sort; systematize; *tabulate;* unitize; *valuate; work; xfer; yield; zonate;*
**arrangement** *(n.)*: array; *behold;* configuration; display; exhibit(ion); format(ion); grouping; *how it's arranged;* indication; infrastructure; *justification; kithe [Scot.];* layout; method; *manner;* non-concealment; outline; order; organization; plan; position; permutation; panoply; *quo mode [L.];* rearrangement; re-formation; reorganization; scheme; structure; setup; spread; *tabulation;* ultrastructure; view; way; *xfer; yielding; zooming in;* [see agreement]
**array** *(n.)*: arrangement; assortment; *breadth;* collection; demonstration; exhibit(ion); full ~; gamut; *hodgepodge; indication; jumble; kithe [Scot.];* layout; multiplicity; matrix; non-concealment; organized layout; presentation; panoply; *quality;* range; selection; spread; spectrum; *ton; unveiling;* variety; *window; xtry.; yielding; zillions;*
**array** *(v.)*: adorn; accouter; bedeck; clothe; decorate; deck (out); dress; embellish; fancify; garnish; *habit;* inwrought; jewel; kit; lay on; make prettier; *nicer;* ornament; prettify; prank; pretty up; *quaintise [arch.];* render lovely; spruce; trim; *use; vest; wear; xy-coordinates; yclad [arch.]; zizz;*
**arrest** *(v.)*: apprehend; bust; capture; *charge;* detain; entrap; fasten upon; *fetter;* get; grab; hold; *haul;* imprison; incarcerate; jail; keep; lay hold; lasso; *make off with;* nab; overtake; pick up; *quarantine;* run in; seize; take (into custody); *usurp;* vanquish; whisk; wrest; x.; *yard; zip away;*
**arrival** *(n.)*: attainment; appearance; advent; breaking in; coming; *descending;* entrance; flow; getting in; *happening;* influx; introduction; *journey; kickoff; letting in;* making entrance; *nearing;* occurrence; passing onto the scene; *quickening;* reaching; showing up; transpiring; *upspringing;* visitation; *walking in; xfer; yede; zipping;*
**arrive** *(v.)*: attain; *become;* come to; drive up; *descend upon;* enter; fetch; find; gain; get to; hit; *in; just in; kick off;* land; make; *near; obtain;* pull up to; *quicken to;* reach; show up; touch down; *upspring; visit;* walk in; *xfer; yain [arch.]; zoom to;*
**arrogance** *(n.)*: audacity; bigheadedness; conceit; condescension; cockiness; disdain; egotism; flatulence; gloating; haughteur; impudence; inflatedness; jackanapes; *know-it-all;* loftiness; magisterialness; narcissism; overconfidence; pride; pompousness; *quilicom [arch.]; ridicule;* smugness; self-importance; turgidity; uppityness; vanity; vainness; wind; *xenophobia; yieldless; zero humility;* [Ant. abasement]
**arrogant** *(adj.)*: audacious; big-headed; boastful; conceited; cocky; condescending; disdainful; egotistical; fastuous; full of oneself; glass-glazing; haughty; imperious; *jackanapes; know-it-all;* lofty; *magnificent;* narcissistic; overweening; proud; quick-to-boast; *reassured;* self-important; superior; smug; supercilious; turgid; uppity; vain; wrapped up in oneself; *x-proud; yelping; zero humility;* [Ant. abased]
**arrow** *(n.)*: aerial; bolt; chested ~; *caret;* dart; *elf-shot;* fescue; fléchette [F.]; fire- ~; flaming ~; gypsy ~; head; indicator; *judo-point; koshi [Jap.]; launch;* missile; nock; *offensive weapon;* pointer; pheon; projectile; poison ~; quarrel; reed; shot; shaft; spright; tackle; *unfriendly fire;* vire; *volley;* war ~; *weapon; xyston;* yad; zinger;

**arrowhead** *(n.)*: arrow-head; barb; broadhead; coronel; dart; *end;* forkhead; *gypsy arrow;* head; hastate; Indian ~; judo point; *koshi [Jap.];* lancet; missile-head; *nock; offensive weapon;* point; pile; quarrel-head; *reed;* spearhead; *sagittate;* tip; *unfriendly fire; verge; weapon;* xyston; *yano-ne* [Jap.]; *zinger;*
**arsenal** *(n.)*: armory; battery; *bomb-chest;* cache; depot; entrepot; firearms; gunroom; hold; *iron rations [slang]; javelin room; keep; load;* munitions store; *naval munitions store;* ordnance; promptuary; *powder room; quantity;* repository; stockpile; *treasure; utility room; volume;* weapons store; *xiphos;* yard; *zone;*
**arson** *(n.)*: *ablaze;* burning; combusting; *crime;* defraudment; enkindling; fire-rising; *fraud; gutting; heat;* incendiarism; *jeopardization;* kindling; lighting up; miskindling; *neal; overburn;* pyromania; quickfire; razing; setting afire; torching [slang]; *ustion; vesicate; waste; xylophyrography; yegg; zinger;*
**arsonist** *(n.)*: *ablaze;* blaze-starter; burner; charer; deflagrater; enkindler; fire-starter; firbug; *gut; hot;* incendiarist; incendiary; *jeopardizer;* kindler; *lighter up;* miskindler; *no-good; overburn;* pyromaniac; *quick-match;* razer; scorcher; torcher; *ustion; villain; wrongdoer; xgressor; yegg; zapper;*
**art** *(n. graphic art)*: artwork; artistry; brush; canvas; coloring; depiction; drawing; *etching;* fine ~; folk ~; graphic design; handiwork; illustration; ink-drawing; *juvenilia; kapnography;* landscape painting; pop ~; masterpiece; masterwork; *neo-impressionism;* opus; oeuvre; oil painting; picture; portraiture; quattrocento; rendering; sketch; *sculpture;* talent; *usefulness;* verism; vignette; work (of ~); watercolor; wash drawing; *xylography;* Yamato; zoomorphism;
    **Types of art**: calligraphy, charcoals, ceramics; oils; finger paint; paint; pastel; pencils; photography; sculpture; watercolor;
**art** *(n. skill)*: ability; *bent;* craft; capability; deftness; expertise; finesse; genius; habilitation; *instinct; jack-of-all-trades;* knack; long suit; mastery; natural ability; occupation; proficiency; *qualification; readiness;* skill; talent; usefulness; virtuosity; wherewithal; *xenium;* yaup; zest; [*Ant.* awkwardness]
**article** *(n.)*: *analysis;* blurb; column; composition; commentary; dissertation; editorial; *facts; gossip column;* handiwork; item; journalism; *kapnography;* letter; leader; literature; magazine ~; newspaper ~; *opinion column;* paragraph; piece; paper; *the quill; revision;* study; treatise; *uncials;* vignette; writing; *xiaozhuan; yellow journalism;* zine; [*see* thing]
**articulate** *(adj.)*: adroit; *beautiful;* coherent; communicative; clear; *debonair;* expressive; eloquent; fluent; graceful; honey-mouthed; influential; inspiring; *jim-dandy; keen;* lucid; moving; *noteworthy;* outstanding; polished; *quantum* [L.]; refined; suave; smooth; talkative; *uttering;* voluble; well-expressed; *xtry.; yare; zealous;*
**articulate** *(v.)*: address; assert; bespeak; convey; delineate; enunciate; express; *foremention; give; gab;* hold forth; impart; *jaw; key in;* let out; mention; note; observe; opine; pronounce; quoth; remark; speak; state; tell; utter; verbalize; voice; word; *xenophonia;* yak; *zero in;*
**artificer** *(n.)*: artisan; builder; craftsman; designer; expert; fashioner; guildsman; hand-crafter; handicraftsman; *industrial worker;* journeyman; *key man;* laborer; master; maker; *notoriety; operator;* professional; qualified worker; ready worker; specialist; skilled worker; talented ~; *useful; versed;* workman; worker; *xylographer;* yeoman; *zaikai [Jap.];* [*Ant.* apprentice]
**artificial** *(adj.)*: artificially-made; bionic; bogus; contranatural; *duplicitous;* ersatz; false; factitious; *glib;* heterogenial; irreal; insincere; *Janus-faced; kidding;* lab-produced; man-made; non-real; *outward;* phony; plastic; prosthetic; *quasi-;* reproduction; synthetic; *two-faced;* unnatural; unreal; *vain; wrought; x; yentzing;* zelig; [*Ant.* actual]
**artist** *(n.)*: artiste; brush ~; caricaturist; colorist; cartoonist; drawer; easel man; futurist; graphics ~; handcrafter; illustrator; idyllist; *juvenilia; kapnographer;* limner; *mannerist; mosaicist;* Nabis; *niellist;* oil painter; painter; portrayer; portraitist; *qualified;* Rembrandt [slang]; sketcher; still-life painter; technical ~; urban ~; verist; watercolorist; *xfer;* Yamato ~ [Jap.]; zoographer;

**ascend** *(v.)*: arise; amount; become higher; climb; *develop;* elevate; *fly up;* go up; heighten; increase; jump up; *keep rising; largen;* mount; move upward; *nudge higher;* overclimb; *outclimb; overcome;* progress; *quantum increase;* rise; scale; surmount; transcend; upclimb; verge upward; wax higher; *xfer; yain* [arch.]; *zoom up;*

**ascension** *(n.)*: ascent; ascending; becoming higher; climb; *developing;* elevation; *flying up;* going up; heightening; *homegoing; increase;* jumping up; *keep rising; largen;* mounting; movment upward; *nudging higher;* overclimbing; progress; *quantum increase;* rising; scaling; surmounting; transcendence; upgoing; uprising; verging upward; waxing higher; *xfer; yain [arch.]; zooming up;*

**ascent** *(n.)*: ascendance; *bias;* climb; *dune; elevation; foothill;* going up; hill; *hike;* inclination; *jag; knoll;* lift; mounting; *natural slope;* obliqueness; pitch; *quantity of increase;* rise; slope; scaling; taking off; upward slope; verge; way up; *zy-gradient;* yaw; zag; [*Ant.* abseiling]

**ascertain** *(v.)*: adjudge; *bear out;* confirm; determine; discern; discover; establish; find out; get; *have;* identify; judge; know; learn; make certain; *notice;* observe; perceive; *qualify;* resolve; settle; tell; uncover; verify; *wist; xenagogy; yeme; zero in;*

**ascetic** *(n.)*: abstainer; *brother;* cenobite; *druid [pagan];* ecclesiastic; friar; grand prior; hesychast; hermit; *imam [Mos.]; jubilarian;* kirkman [Scot.]; lay abbot; monk; *nun [fem.]; Observant;* prior; *Qumranite;* religious (man); stylite; *talapoin [Bud.]; underling;* votary; white friar; *Xaverian;* yogi *[Hind.];* zetetic;

**ascribe** *(v.)*: attribute; accredit; *belong; believe;* blame; credit; chalk up to; deem; *entitle;* fix; give credit; hold responsible; impute; *judge; know;* lay at the door; *make;* notion; owe to; put down to; *questionless;* recognize; suppose; think; *understand; view; written; xfer;* yield as due; *zay [dial.];*

**ash** *(n.)*: *ashes;* black grime; cinder; dust; ember; fly ~; grime; *hard coal; incinerated; jet black;* kollow; lampblack; *matter;* nast; oven ~; powder; *quadrel;* rapil; soot; slag; *turbidity;* urry; volcanic ~; wood-soot; xylanthrax; *yucky; zable;*

**ashamed** *(adj.)*: abashed; brought low; blushing; crushed; discomfited; discountenanced; disgraced; embarrassed; flustered; grieved; humiliated; *indignity; jackalent;* knocked down; *low;* mortified; *not proud; overtaken;* perplexed; *quiet;* reproached; shamed; taken down a peg; *uneasy;* very ~; *wite; xtry.* humiliated; yowling; *zero honor;* [*see* remorseful]

**ask** *(v.)*: appeal; adjure; bid; beg; beseech; cross-examine; *call;* desire; enquire; entreat; *find out;* grill; *get;* hit up; inquire; invite; implead; importune; implore; interrogate; *just want to know; know;* look for answers; make query; *nose;* obsecrate; oppugn; pose; pray; plead; prevail upon; petition; probe; question; quiz; query; raise; request; seek; supplicate; solicit; take counsel; test; urge; vocalize; want; XQ.; *yearn; zetetic;* [*Ant.* answer]

**asleep** *(adj.)*: aestivating; *abed* [arch.]; *bedded down;* crashed [slang]; dormant; dozing; estivating; *fallen asleep; gone to bed;* hibernating; *idle; just sleeping;* knocked out; land of Nod; *Morpheus;* napping; out; *passed out;* quiescent; retired; resting; sleeping; slumbering; snoozing; *taking a nap;* under; unawakened; unconscious; *vegetating;* wakeless; x-sleep; yawning; zonked out; [*Ant.* awake]

**aspect** *(v.)*: attribute; appearance; angle; bearing; characteristic; detail; dimension; element; feature; facet; *given detail;* hand; issue; *judgment; key ~;* look; *mannerism; notion;* outlook; part; property; position; quality; regard; side; trait; thing; *understanding;* view(point); ways of looking at it; *x-factor; yield; zero in;*

**aspersion** *(n.)*: attack; belittlement; calumny; defamation; denigration; evil-speaking; false words; gossip; *hearsay;* insult; injurious remark; jaunder; knock; libel; malediction; name-calling; obtrectation; put-down; *quidnunc;* running down; slander; slur; smear; traducement; unkind remark; vilification; *wickedness; x-ing;* yellowing; *zeroization;* [*Ant.* assistance]

**asphyxiate** *(v.): afflict; bind;* choke; deprive of oxygen; extinguish; *flood;* gag; hang; *inhibit;* jugulate; kill; *lynch; murder; nullify;* overwhelm; *put out;* quench; *repress;* suffocate; smother; throttle; *undo; void;* whirken [arch.]; *xuld [arch.]; yote; zeroize;*

**asphyxiation** *(n.)*: asphyxia; *binding;* choking; deprivation of oxygen; extinguishment; *flooding;* gagging; garroting; hanging; *incapacitation;* jugulation; killing; *lynching; murdering; nullification;* overlaying; *putting out;* quenching; *repression;* suffocation; smothering; throttling; *undoing; voiding;* wringing; *x-ing; yote;* zeroizing;

**aspiration** *(n.)*: ambition; *bidding;* craving; desire; dream; endeavor; fancy; *greed;* heart's desire; hope; itching; inclination; *intention; juration;* keen desire; longing; *mania; need;* notion; objective; pruriency; quest; *restlessness;* strong desire; thirst; urge; velleity; wish; *xel [arch.];* yearning; *zeal;*

**aspire** *(v.)*: aim; *bid;* crave; desire; dream; endeavor; fancy; *got to have;* hope; itch; *just got to have; keen desire;* long for; *mania; notion; objective;* pant after; pursue; *quest for; reach for;* seek; thirst for; *urge; velleity;* want; wish; *xel [arch.];* yearn for; *zeal;*

**assailant** *(n.)*: assailer; attacker; beater; clasher; *doer;* enemy; fighter; foe; *get;* hitter; invader; *jumper;* kemper; lasher out; mugger; *nemesis;* opponent; pillager; *quarreler;* raider; striker; troubler; *violence;* warling; *xenic; yuon [arch.];* zapper; [*Ant.* ally]

**assassin** *(n.)*: annihilator; bravo; contract killer; dispatcher; eliminator; *finisher;* gunman; hired gun; immolator; *job;* killer; liquidator; murderer; *ninja;* obliterator; paid killer; quencher; *ruthless;* slayer; terminator; *undoer;* victimizer; waster [slang]; *x-out;* yegg; *zapper;*

**assassinate** *(v.)*: annihilate; bump off [slang]; *cancel;* destroy; dispose of; eliminate; finish off; gun down; *homicide;* immolate; *jab;* kill; *liquidate;* murder; *nip;* obliterate; put to death; quench; run through; slay; terminate; *unseat;* vitiate; waste [slang]; x-out; *yataghan;* zap;

**assault** *(n.)*: attack; assail; beating; battery; charge; *dispute;* escalade; foray; *get;* hit; incursion; invasion; *jarring; kampf* [G.]; lashing out; *march on; non-peaceful;* onslaught; offensive; pounce; *quarrel;* raid; strike; take the offensive; *unrest;* violence; war(fare); *x-fire;* yed; *zonk;* [*Ant.* assistance]

**assault** *(v.)*: attack; blast; beating; charge; depredation; escalade; foray; *get;* hit; invade; jump; *knock out;* lashing out; launch attack; *march on; naval warfare;* onrush; pillage; *quick raid;* raid; strike; *take; unrest;* veney; *war(fare); x-fire; yed;* zap; [*Ant.* assist]

**assemble** *(v.)*: accumulate; amass; bring together; convene; congregate; converge; come together; draw together; *encounter;* flock; gather; group; huddle; have a meeting; horde; intersect; join; *knit;* link up; meet; muster; *negotiate; overcrowd; party; quorum;* rally; reconvene; *summon;* turn out; unite; *visit; work together; x.;* yoke together; *zone;* [*Ant.* adjourn]

**assembly** *(n.)*: assemblage; body; congregation; convocation; discussion; *ekklesia* [Gr.]; forgathering; forum; gathering; horde; ingathering; jam [coll.]; kit [coll.]; lot; meeting; *number; opportunity;* people; party; plenum; *quorum;* regathering; reunion; session; turnout; throng; unit; vestry; *worshipers;* witan; *x.;* yain [arch.]; *zayat [Burm.];*

**assent** *(n.)*: acceptance; acquiescence; agreement; blessing; consent; *delight;* endorsement; favor; *freedom;* go-ahead; here to [reg.]; indorsement; *joining;* keeping; leave; *liberty;* meeting of the minds; nod; okay; permission; predication; *qualified agreement; ratification;* sufferance; sanction; thumbs up [slang]; unreluctance; *voluntariness;* willingness; *xenia;* yielding; *zeal;* [*Ant.* argument]

**assent** *(v.)*: agree; accede; acquiesce; accept; allow; be in accord; back; consent; *do;* endorse; fall in; grant; go along with; homologate; indorse; join; keep; *like-minded;* line up; *match;* nod; okay; (be) one; obsignate; permit; *quoth;* ratify; support; *together;* unite; *verify;* warrant; *xel [arch.];* yield; *zealless;* [*Ant.* argue]

**assert** *(v.)*: aver; bespeak; claim; declare; express; *fame; give;* hold forth; indicate; *jaw; key in;* let out; mention; noise; opine; proclaim; quoth; report; relay; state; tell; utter; voice; word; *xenophonia;* yak; *zero in;*

**assertive** *(adj.)*: assured; bold; certain; convinced; doughty; dogmatic; ever-confident; firm; gallant; heroic; intrepid; *jarless; knightly;* lion-hearted; manly; never-fearing; obstinate; poised; positive; questful; resolute; self-confident; sure; trusting; unafraid; very sure; *wherewithal; xtry.;* yare; zealous; [*Ant.* apprehensive]

**assess** *(v.)*: appraise; *believe;* consider; check; deem; evaluate; figure; gauge; *hold;* inspect; judge; *know;* list; measure; *notion; opinion;* peg; price; *quote;* rate; reckon; surmise; size up; think on; use brain; valuate; vet; weigh; *xenodiagnose; yeme; zazen;*

**assessment** *(n.)*: appraisal; belief; critique; conclusion; decision; evaluation; estimation; feeling; gauging; *hypothesis;* inspection; investigation; judgment; *knowledge;* leaning; listing; mind; notion; opinion; perspective; point of view; *quot homines tot sententiae* [L.]; reckoning; surmising; thoughts; take; *unbiased opinion;* valuation; word; *xenodiagnosis; year-end audit;* zetetic;

**assets** *(n.)*: affluence; belongings; capital; *dollars;* equity; estate; fortune; gains; holdings; investments; *jewels; krugerrands;* lucre; money; net worth; opulence; possessions; property; *quantities;* resources; substance; treasure; uberty; valuables; *venture capital;* worth; *xenocurrency; yellow boy [Br.]; zillions [slang];*

**assign** *(v.)*: allocate; allot; bestow; consign; designate; delegate; earmark; equip; furnish; give; hand over; issue; *job;* kit; let; make; *non-retention; outfit;* portion (out); *qualify;* release; saddle with; transfer; *unhand;* vest; *work;* xfer; yield; *zone;*

**assignment** *(n.)*: accountability; business; burden; charge; commission; duty; errand; *function; goal; handling;* incumbency; job; *key role;* liability; mission; necessity; obligation; project; quest; responsibility; *station;* task; undertaking; vocation; work; xci.; *yoke; zealous task;*

**assimilate** *(v.)*: acclimate; adapt; absorb; acculturate; blend in; conform; *dispose;* embrace; enculturate; *fit in;* gradually absorb; habituate; integrate; jibe [slang]; *kit; line up;* make a part of; *naturalize;* orient; prepare; qualify; regularize; *suit; train; unite; verse; well-adjusted; xenize;* yarken; *zero foreignness;*

**assimilation** *(n.)*: acclimation; adaptation; absorption; acculturation; blending in; conforming; *disposing;* enculturation; *fitting in;* gradual absorption; habituation; integration; *jibing [slang]; kit; lining up;* making a part of; *naturalization;* orientation; preparation; qualification; regularization; *suiting; training; uniting; versing; well-adjusted; xenization;* yarken; *zero foreignness;*

**assist** *(v.)*: aid; abet; bolster; back; cooperate; do a favor; ease; facilitate; further; give assistance; help (out); intercede; *just-in-time; kindness;* lend aid; minister; *not hinder;* open doors; pitch in; *quick-to-help;* reach out; relieve; succor; serve; support; *take under one's wing;* uphold; *valet;* work for; *xtry.;* yield; *zero hindrance;* [*Ant.* afflict]

**assistance** *(n.)*: aid; bolstering; backing; cooperation; deliverance; *expertese;* facilitation; financing; giving of help; hand; help; intercession; *joint cooperation;* kindness; lending a hand; ministration; *non-hindrance; overprotection;* pitching in; *quick-to-help;* respite; relief; rescue; succor; service; support; subvention; *technical ~;* usefulness; *valet;* working for; *xtry.;* yielding; *zero hindrance;* [*Ant.* affliction]

**assistant** *(n.)*: apprentice; aide; acolyte; adjunct; attendant; associate; butler; collaborator; cleric; coadjutant; demiurge; deputy; employee; famulus; gofer [slang]; helper; intern; jackman; knipper; legman; liason; menia; minion; minister; nipper; offsider; page; porter; *personnel;* partner; *qaimaquam [Turk.];* retainer [arch.]; servant; succorer; *trusty servant;* underling; undersecretary; valet; viceroy; worker; x-man; yeoman; *zaikai;* [*Ant.* adversary]

**associate** *(n.)*: affiliate; bedfellow; cohort; consort; companion; *devoted friend; equal;* fellow; friend; good-fellow; helper; intimate; joint owner; kith [pl.]; *loyal friend;* mate; *neighbor;* one associated; partner; *quinquevirate;* right-hand man; sidekick; teammate; *unfailing friend; votary;* workmate; *x-class;* yokefellow; *zealous friend;*

**associate** *(v.)*: affiliate; band; connect; correlate; consort; deal; *establish;* fraternize; fellowship; *go with; group together;* have to do with; hitch up; involve; implicate; join; *knit;* link; *merge;* nail; *one;* partner; *quinquevirate;* relate; socialize; tie; unite; *vise;* work together; *xenograft;* yoke; *zip together;* [*Ant.* avoid]

**association** *(n. connection)*: affiliation; band; *bedfellows;* connection; correlation; conjunction; cooperation; cahoots; consort; dealings; *establishment;* fraternization; fellowship; *grouping together;* having to do with; involvement; implication; joining; *knitting;* link; *merge;* nexus; *one;* partner; quinquevirate; relation; socialization; tie; union; *vise;* working together; *xenograft;* yoke; *zone;*

**association** *(n. organization)*: affiliation; alliance; brotherhood; consortium; club; coalition; confederation; *department;* establishment; fellowship; fraternity; federation; group; guild; *horizontal union;* incorporation; joint coalition; *kongsi* [Chin.]; league; *mutual;* nexus; organization; partnership; quinquevirate; *registered guild;* society; syndicate; troop; union; *vertical union; workers' union; x-class;* yeald; zollverein;

**assortment** *(n.)*: array; bunch; big selection; collection; choice; diversity; extensive ~; full array; *grouping;* hodgepodge; heterogeneity; *interesting ~;* jumble; keen ~; *load;* large quantity; miscellany; mixture; mixed bag; multiplicity; number; olio; options; pastiche; quantity; range; selection; *ton; uberous;* variety; wide selection; wealth; xtry. selection; *yelm; zillions;*

**assuage** *(v.)*: abate; attenuate; alleviate; bate; break; curb; contract; condense; decrease; decline; diminish; ease; ebb; fade; go down; *hush; halt;* improve; *jump down;* knock down; languish; lower; lessen; moderate; mitigate; *minimize; narrow; outgo;* peter out; quell; quail; recede; reduce; subside; taper; temper; *undo; vanish;* wane; *xerosis;* yield; zap; [*Ant.* augment]

**assume** *(v.)*: *adopt;* believe; conjecture; deduce; expect; figure; guess; hypothesize; imagine; just thought; *know; led to believe;* make assumption; *notion; occur;* postulate; presume; *question;* reckon; suppose; take for granted; think; *use brain; venture;* wis; *xenodiagnose; yeme; zazen;*

**assumption** *(n.)*: assuming; belief; conjecture; deduction; educated guess; expectation; fancy; guess(work); hunch; hypothesis; idea; judgment; *knowledge;* lemma; mind; notion; opinion; postulation; presumption; qualified opinion; reckoning; supposition; self-evident fact; theory; *urge;* view; *wild guess; xenodiagnosis; yankering; zeal;*

**assurance** *(n.)*: assuredness; belief; confidence; certainty; declaration; *entrusting;* faith; guarantee; hope; insurance; *just believe; knowledge;* lock; *mainstay;* non-doubt; oath; promise; questionlessness; reliance; resting assured; rock-solid faith; sureness; surety; security; trust; *unwaveringness;* vow; warrant; *xel [arch.]; y'faith* [arch.]; *zeal;* [*see* pledge]

**assure** *(v.)*: affirm; avow; behight; comfort; confirm; declare; encourage; establish; *fix;* give assurance; guarantee; *help;* hold forth; insure; *justify; know; let out;* make certain; notify; *overconfident;* promise; pledge; *quoth;* reassure; reaffirm; swear; testify; uphold; verify; vouch; warrant; *xenagogy; yield; zero in;* [*Ant.* abjure]

**astonish** *(v.)*: amaze; astound; bowl one over; confound; dazzle; *enchant;* flabbergast; gape; hold one's breath; impact; jolt; knock for six; look aghast; make marvel; *nonplus;* overwhelm; *puzzle; quite amazed;* render speechless; surprise; stun; take back; unable to believe; *very impressed;* wonder; *xtry.; yerk; zing;*

**astonishing** *(adj.)*: amazing; awesome; brilliant; breathtaking; confounding; divine; extraordinary; fantastic; great; heavenly; incredible; just amazing; keen; laudable; marvelous; notable; outstanding; prodigious; *quantum* [L.]; remarkable; stupendous; tremendous; unbelievable; very good (-high); wondrous; xtry.; you-beaut [Aus.]; *zizzy;* [*Ant.* aweless]

**astonishment** *(n.)*: amazement; bewilderment; confounding; dumbfounding; *extraordinariness;* flabbergasting; gastness; holding one's breath; impression; jolt; keeling over; looking aghast; marveling; *nonplus;* overwhelming; poleaxing; *quite amazed;* rendering speechlessness; surprise; shock; stun; taking back; *unbelievable; very impressed;* wonder(ment); *xtry.; you-beaut* [Aus.]; zonking; [*Ant.* awelessness]

**astound** *(v.)*: amaze; astonish; bedazzle; confound; dumbfound; *excite;* floor; gape; hold one's breath; impress; jolt; keel over; look aghast; make marvel; *nonplus;* overwhelm; poleax; *quite amazed;* render speechless; stupefy; shock; throw; unable to believe; *virtually ~;* wonder; *xtry.; yerk; zing;*

**astrologer** *(n.)*: astrologist; augerer; *bewitcher;* clairvoyant; diviner; ephemerist; fortune-teller; *geomancer; horoscopic; incantation; jadoo-wallah; karakia* [Maori]; *lithomancer;* mystic; medium; necromancer; oracle; occultist; predicter; *quad; rhabdomancer;* stargazer; soothsayer; theurgist; *unveiler; voodooist;* witch; *xylomancer; yogist;* zodiacist;

**astrology** *(n.)*: astromancy; black magic; clairvoyance; divination; enchantment; fortune-telling; genethliac; horoscopy; incantation; juju; *Keltic religion; legerdemain*; magic; new age; occult; prediction; *quad; rune;* star-gazing; sorcery; *theurgy; under a sign;* voodoo; witchcraft; *xylomancy; yogism;* zodiac;
**astronomical** *(adj.)*: astral; astronomic; *body;* cosmic; cosmological; celestial; deep space; extraterrestrial; *four quarters of the universe;* galactic; heavenly; interplanetary; interstellar; intergalactic; *jovial; kosmos [Gr.];* lunar; metagalactic; *nebular;* outer space; planetary; polygalactal; quasi-stellar; *relating to planets;* space; solar; stellar; *terrestrial;* universal; *vacuum;* worldwide; *x-ray star;* yonder; zonic;
**astronomy** *(n.)*: astrophysics; astrography; *beholding;* cosmography; *discipline; examination; field;* galactic observation; *the heavens; investigation; Jupiter; Kepler's laws;* looking at the stars; *magnetar; nebula; observation;* planetary science; quantum ~; radar ~; rocket science; research; science; stargazing; selenography; *stars; telescope;* uranography; ultraviolet ~; *volumetric analysis;* watching the stars; x-ray ~; *yellow star;* zetetic ~;
**astute** *(adj.)*: artful; bright; clever; discerning; eagle-eyed; *farsighted;* gifted; highly intelligent; incisive; judicious; keen; *longsighted;* Maciavellian; nimble-witted; on the ball; perceptive; quick; razor-sharp; shrewd; sharp; tricky; ultra-smart; vulpine; wise; *xtry.;* yepe; *zippy;* [Ant. air-headed]
**asylum** *(n.)*: *area;* booby hatch; bug house; crazy house; dementia ward; *eccentric;* funny farm; *goofy;* home; haven; hospital; insane ~; *jail;* kook house; loony bin; lunatic ~; madhouse; mental ward; nuthouse; *off one's rocker;* psychiatric ward; padded cell; *quacked; raving;* sick house; shelter; *straitjacket; taken leave of senses; unbalanced; volatile;* ward; *xtr. loony; yo-yo;* zany house;
**atheism** *(n.)*: *agnosticism;* Bible-rejecting; cynicism; disbelief; denial; epistemology; faithlessness; freethinking; godlessness; humanism; incredulity; irreligion; Jehovah-rejecting; *knocking;* logical positivism; miscreancy; non-belief; naturalism; objectivism; over-credulousness; polemicism; *questioning;* rationalism; skepticism; total rejection; unbelief; *vanity; worldly-mindedness; Xt-rejecting; yieldlessness;* zero belief;
**atheist** *(n.)*: *agnostic;* anti-Christian; Bible-rejecter; critic; doubter; epistemological ~; freethinker; God-rejecter; humanist; infidel; *Jehovah-rejecter; knocker;* logical positivist; minimifidianist; miscreant; nontheist; nonbeliever; oppugner; polemic; questioner; rationalist; rejecter; skeptic; somatist; *secularist;* total rejecter; unbeliever; *vanity;* worldling; *Xt-rejecting; yet unconvinced;* zetetic;
**atheistic** *(adj.)*: agnostic; anti-Christian; atheistical; Bible-rejecting; cynical; *Christ-rejecting;* disbelieving; epistemologically ~; faithless; freethinking; God-rejecting; godless; humanistic; incredulous; irreligious; *Jehovah-rejecting; knocking;* logically positivistic; *misological;* non-believing; naturalistic; overcredulous; *practical atheism; questioning;* rationalistic; skeptical; truth-rejecting; unbelieving; *vain;* worldly; *Xt.-rejecting; yieldless;* zetetic;
**athlete** *(n.)*: athletic man; ballplayer; contestant; competitor; decathlete; *entrant;* finalist; gymnast; gamester; half-blue; ironman; jock [slang]; kemp; *libero;* miler; multiventer; *nimble;* Olympian; player; participant; pent~; qualifier; quarterback; runner; sprinter; sportsman; trainee; teammate; *unflagging; vigorous;* well-trained ~; *Xenakis; yauld; zippy;*
**athletic** *(adj.)*: able-bodied; agile; brawny; *capable;* durable; energetic; fit; goodly; healthy; iron; *jusqu'au bout [F.]; keen;* lusty; muscular; nimble; olympean; pancratic; physical; *quality;* rugged; robust; sturdy; strapping; *sports;* tough; *unflagging;* vigorous; well-set; x-strong; yauld; *zippy;*
**atmosphere** *(n. firmament)*: air; *the blue;* clouds; deep blue sky; environment; ether; empyrean; fug [slang]; firmament; first heaven; *gray skies;* heavens; ionosphere; *jumbo cloud; KH instability; layer;* mid-heaven; mesosphere; *night sky;* open-skies; pressure; *quality; region;* sky; stratosphere; thermosphere; upper ~; vault of heaven; welkin; *xerosere;* yonder; *zenith;*
**atmosphere** *(n. mood)*: ambiance; aura; air; backdrop; climate; character; disposition; environment; feel; *genius loci* [L.]; general feeling; *humor;* impression; *just a feeling; knowledge;*

*location;* mood; milieu; *nature;* overall feel; *place;* quality; *reaction;* sense; spirit; surroundings; setting; tone; tenor; *upper ~;* venue; *way; xfer; yaw;* zeitgeist;
**atom** *(n.)*: anion; bit; *crumb; dram;* electron; fermion; gluon; grain; hadron; ion; jot; kaon; lepton; monad; meson; molecule; mite; neutron; ounce; proton; pion; particle; quark; *remnant;* subatomic particle; *tidbit; trace; unit;* valence electron; whit; *w-particle; xi particle; yngot [arch.];* z-particle;
**atone** *(v.)*: appease; bring together; conciliate; do penance; expiate; *fulfill; gratify;* harmonize; immolate; *justify; kill sacrifice; libation;* make reparation (-peace; -up for); *nullify;* offset; pacify; propitiate; *qualification;* reconcile; satisfy; set right; *sacrifice; together again;* unruffle; *void;* win favor; x-out; *yield; zeroize;*
**atonement** *(n.)*: amends; appeasement; bringing together; conciliation; doing penance; expiation; full ~; *gratification;* harmonization; *immolation; justification; killing sacrifice; lulling;* making reparations; *non-indebtedness;* offering; *oneness;* peace-offering; propitiation; quittance; reparation; reconciliation; redemption; satisfaction; sacrifice; salvation; *togetherness;* unruffling; *voidance;* winning favor; x-ing out; *yield; Zufriedenheit* [G.];
**atoning** *(adj.)*: atonal; appeasing; becalming; conciliatory; *drawing together;* expiatory; *forgiving; gratifying;* harmonizing; *immolating; justifying; killing sacrifice; lulling;* mollifying; *nullifying; overcoming;* piacular; quelling; reconciliatory; sacrificing; *together;* unifying; *voiding; working out; x-ing; yielding; zeroizing;*
**atrocity** *(n.)*: abomination; breach; cruelty; crime; depravity; evil; flagitiousness; gross sin; heinousness; iniquity; *jadedness;* knavishness; *liability;* misdeed; nefariousness; offense; perverseness; *quad;* rebellion; sin; treachery; unrighteousness; villainy; violence; wickedness; *xgression; yetzer hara* [Heb.]; *zhlubbiness;*
**attach** *(v.)*: affix; adhere; anchor; bind; connect; dovetail; engraft; fasten; *glue;* hitch; interconnect; infix; implant; inosculate; join; knot; knit; link; mount; meld; *nail; oxreim;* put together; *quasi-fuse;* relate; reunite; reattach; stick; secure; splice; subjoin; tack; tie; unite; *vise;* wed; weld; *xenograft;* yoke; *zip;* [Ant. abstract]
**attachment** *(n.)*: affixation; adherence; anchoring; bond; connection; dovetail; *elbow joint;* fitment; *graft;* hookup; interconnection; joining; joint; knitting; link; meld; nexus; *oxreim;* putting together; *quasi-fuse;* relation; *re~;* splice; tie; union; *vise;* weld; *xenograft;* yoke; *zipping together;* [Ant. abstraction]
**attack** *(n.)*: assault; aggression; blast; beating; bout; *Blitzkrieg* [G.]; camisado; charge; drive; depredation; escalade; forage; foray; *get;* hit; incursion; invasion; *jump; kampf* [G.]; lashing out; *march; naval warfare;* onset; onrush; offensive; onslaught; pillaging; *quick raid;* raid; sortie; strike; surprise ~; *take; unrest;* veney; *violence; war(fare); x-fire; yed;* zap; [Ant. assistance]
**attack** *(v.)*: assail; aggress; assault; blast; beat; clash with; *drive;* engage; fight; foray; get; hit; harry; invade; jump; knock; lash out; levy war against; light into; march on; *naval warfare;* oppugn; *onslaught;* pillage; pounce; quab; raid; strike; storm; smite; *take; unrest;* victimize; war; *x-fire; yed;* zap; [Ant. aid]
**attacker** *(n.)*: assailant; aggressor; beater; clasher; *doer;* enemy; fighter; foe; *get;* hitter; invader; *jumper;* kemper; lasher out; mugger; *nemesis;* opponent; pillager; *quarreler;* raider; rapist; striker; troubler; *unprovoked;* victimizer; warling; *xenic; yuon [arch.];* zapper; [Ant. abettor]
**attain** *(v.)*: arrive; achieve; accomplish; become; come to; *do;* effect; fulfill; get; gain; hit; *inherit; jet;* kep; *land;* make; nab; *obtain;* procure; pull off; *quicken to;* reach; *secure; succeed;* touch; take; usurp; *victory;* win; *xfer; yain* [arch.]; *zoom to;*
**attainable** *(adj.)*: achievable; accomplishable; *become; come to; doable;* effectible; findable; gettable; havable; *inheritable; jet; keepable;* landable; makeable; nabbable; obtainable; procurable; quite ~; reachable; *secureable;* takable; *utilizable; victory;* winnable; *xfer;* yours for the taking; *zero problem;*

72

**attainment** *(n.)*: achievement; accomplishment; becoming; completion; doing; execution; fulfillment; gaining; hitting; implementation; job; keeping; *landing;* making; nabbing; *obtainment;* performance; *quickening to;* reaching; realization; success; taking; usurpation; victory; wonderwork; *xtry.; yield; zooming;*
**attempt** *(n.)*: *aspiration;* bid; crack; dare; effort; endeavor; full-blown effort; go; *hazarding; intent; jeopardizing;* kemp; *like to; move;* nisus; *the* old college try; proffer; push; quest; *reattempt;* shot; stab; try; undertaking; venture; *work; xuld [arch.]; yearning; zeal;* [*Ant.* abandonment]
**attempt** *(v.)*: assay; *battle; compete;* dare; endeavor; essay; follow after; go for; hazard; *intend; imperil; jeopardize;* kemp; *like to;* make an effort; *nitency; offer;* push for; proffer; *question [arch.];* risk; seek; strive; try; tackle; undertake; venture; wing it; work at; *xuld [arch.];* yearn; *zealously endeavor;* [*Ant.* abandon]
**attend** *(v. be present)*: appear; accompany; be present; be there; come (out); *draw; darken the doorstep;* enter in; forsake not; go to; hit; *honor; in;* join; keep; *link up;* make; not miss; observe; present oneself at; participate; *quorum;* regard; remain; show up; turn out; *unite with;* visit; wait; *xfer;* yede; *zip to;*
**attend** *(v. serve)*: assist; bestow service; care for; do (one's bidding); *exert;* function; give care; help; *industry; job;* keep; lackey; labor for; minister; *nurse;* obey; perform; *quick-to-obey;* regard; serve; tend; take care of; *use; valet;* wait on; *xfer;* yeme; *zealously ~;*
**attendance** *(n.)*: appearance; audience; being there; count; *draw; ever-present; figure;* group; headcount; ingathering; joining; *keeping; linking up;* mass; number; *observation;* presence; quantity; *quorum;* regular ~; showing; turnout; *united with;* volume; *with; xfer; yede; zealous ~;* [*Ant.* absence]
**attendant** *(n.)*: assistant; butler; chamberlain; demiurge; eye-servant; footman; *gofer* [slang]; gallopin; handmaid(en) [fem.]; henchman; indentured servant; jackman; knave; lackey; minister; man(servant) [masc.]; maid(servant) [fem.]; neif; offsider; porter; page; *personnel;* quarter-maid; retinue [pl.]; servant; *trusty servant;* underservant; valet; wench [fem.]; x-man; yeoman; zaikai; [*Ant.* assailant]
**attention** *(n.)*: awareness; attentiveness; brainwork; concentration; consideration; care; deliberation; diligence; ear; emphasis; engrossment; focus; gaze; heed; interest; *judgment;* kindness; looking into; mind; notice; observation; observance; *on one's mind;* pondering; precision; quality time; regard; single-mindedness; spotlight; thought; ultra-mindfulness; *valuating;* watching; *xtr. consideration;* yeme [arch.]; zeroing in;
**attentive** *(adj.)*: aware; alert; *bethink;* conscious; conscientious; dutiful; diligent; ever-mindful; focused; gazeful; heedful; intentive; judicious; keeping in mind; listening; mindful; *non-distracted;* observant; open-eared (-eyed); paying attention; quick-witted; regardful; *sagacious;* thoughtful; ultra-mindful; vigilant; watchful; x-careful; yare-handed; *zärtlich* [G.]; [*Ant.* apathetic]
**attentiveness** *(n.)*: awareness; alertness; *behold;* consciousness; conscientiousness; dutifulness; empressment; focus; gazefulness; heedfulness; *intentness;* judiciousness; keeping in mind; listening; mindfulness; *non-distraction;* observance; paying of attention; quick-wittedness; regardfulness; *sagaciousness;* thoughtfulness; ultra-mindfulness; vigilance; watchfulness; *x-careful;* yare-handedness; *zärtlich [G.];* [*Ant.* apathy]
**attest** *(v.)*: affirm; bear out; confirm; document; establish; fix; guarantee; homologate; *indicate;* justify; kithe [Scot.]; legitimize; *maintain;* nail down; *okay;* profess; prove; *questionless;* reassure; substantiate; testify; uphold; verify; warrant; witness; x-certify; *yes; zero doubt;*
**attestation** *(n.)*: affirmation; bearing out; confirmation; documentation; establishing; fixing; guarantee; homologation; *indication;* justification; kithing [Scot.]; legitimization; *maintaining;* notification; open ~; profession; *questionless;* reassurance; substantiation; testimony; upholding; verification; witness; *x-certification;* yeme; *zero doubt;*
**attic** *(n.)*: *area; barn loft;* cockoft; dormer; *extension; floor;* garret; *hayloft; inclosed area; jube; keep;* loft; *mezzanine; niche;* overhead loft; place; *quadrant;* room above; storage area; sky parlor; top-loft; upper floor; *volume; wall; xtr. storage; yu [Chin.]; zone;*

**attire** *(n.)*: apparel; array; bedizenment; clothes; dress; ensemble; finery; fashion; garb; getup; habiliments; investiture; *jumper; knitwear;* livery; mufti; *menswear; national dress;* outfit; outerwear; *palliament [arch.]; quaintry* [arch.]; raiment; *regalia;* suit; threads [slang]; *uniform;* vestment; wardrobe; XL; *yelek [Turk.]; zari;*
**attire** *(v.)*: accouter; apparel; bedeck; bedrape; clothe; dress; enrobe; *fancify;* garb; habit; invest; jacket; kit; *loungewear; make prettier; nice;* outfit; put on; prink; *quaintise [arch.];* reapparel; slip into; trim; uniform; vest; wrap; wear; *xuld [arch.]; yclad* [arch.]; zip on;
**attitude** *(n.)*: angle; air; bearing; belief; bent; bias; countenance; conception; cast; disposition; demeanor; estimation; feeling; frame of mind; ground; heart; impression; idea; inclination; judgment; *known inclination;* leaning; mind(set); mood; mentality; notion; outlook; perception; posture; position; perspective; point of view; *quot homines tot sententiae* [L.]; reaction; reckoning; sentiment; slant; standpoint; spirit; tendency; thinking; temperament; tone; take; *urge;* visage; vein; view(point); way of thinking; *xenodiagnosis;* yaw; zeal;
**attorney** *(n.)*: advocate; barrister; criminal ~; counselor; defender; essoiner; *fiduciary;* general ~; indicter; jurist; King's Counsel; lawyer; man of law; non-prosecuting ~; *outer bar;* prosecutor; pettifogger; practitioner; Pennsylvania ~; *paralegal;* Queen's Counsel; *quibbler; questmonger;* representative; solicitor; *scrivener;* shyster [derog.]; templar; *unethical ~; vakil* [Asia]; *wakil* [Asia]; XQ; Yankee lawyer; *zonal practitioner;*
**attract** *(v.)*: allure; bewitch; charm; captivate; draw; entice; engage; enthrall; fascinate; get (attention of); *have come;* interest; intrigue; infatuate; *jill-flirt; keen;* lure; lead; magnetize; *nudge; outwit;* persuade; *quibbling [arch.];* rope in; seduce; tout; tempt; *urge; vie for;* woo; *xuld [arch.];* yerk; *zygotaxis [biol.];* [*see* engross]
**attractive** *(adj.)*: appealing; bonny; beautiful; charming; desirable; delectable; eye-catching; fair; good-looking; handsome; *irresistible; jolie laide [F.];* killing [slang]; lovely; magnificent; nice-looking; *outstanding;* pretty; quite beautiful; ravishing; striking; tantalizing; *unsurpassed;* voluptuous; well-favored (-looking); *xtry.;* you-beaut [Aus.]; zizzy; [*Ant.* appalling]
**attribute** *(n.)*: aspect; *badge;* characteristic; detail; element; facet; feature; *good quality;* highlight; ingredient; *jist;* key feature; lineament; mark; *nature; object;* peculiarity; particularity; part; point; property; quality; reality; *side;* trait; undeniable quality; virtue; way; *x-factor; yetzer* [Heb.]; *zero in;*
**attribute** *(v.)*: ascribe; accredit; account; *belong; believe;* blame; count; credit; charge; deem; *entitle;* fix; give credit; hold responsible; impute; *judge; know;* lay at the door; *make; notion;* owe to; put down to; pin on; *questionless;* recognize; suppose; think; *understand;* view; *work of; xfer;* yield as due; *zay [dial.];*
**atrophy** *(v.)*: ail; break down; consume; deteriorate; degenerate; erode; fade; flaccid; fugacious; *go down;* hone; impair; *jade; knock off;* languish; marasmus; *narrow; outgo;* pine; perish; quail; *reduce;* shrivel; *taper; undo; vanish;* weaken; waste away; wither; xeroma; yellow ~; *zap;*
**atypical** *(adj.)*: anomalous; abnormal; aberrant; *bizarre; curious; crazy;* different; deviant; enigmatic; erratic; funny; gonzo; *goofy;* heterotypical; irregular; *jarring;* kooky; loony; mysterious; malformed; mad; nonstandard; odd; peculiar; queer; *remarkable; rare;* strange; *twisted;* unusual; uncharacteristic; variant; weird; xenomorphic; *yo-yoish;* zany; [*Ant.* average]
**authoritarian** *(adj.)*: austere; bossy; commanding; controlling; demanding; domineering; dictatorial; *evil-hearted;* forceful; fascistic; grave; harsh; high-handed; Hitleresque; influential; imposing; imperious; iron-fisted; *jaded;* kindless; loveless; magisterial; *nasty;* overbearing; *powerful; quede [arch.];* repressive; strict; strong; tyrannical; totalitarian; unreasonable; undemocratic; unassailable; *virulent; way too strict; xenophobic;* yieldless; *za-zum* [Rus.];
**awful** *(adj.)*: abhorrent; atrocious; bad; crummy; crude; contemptible; despicable; deplorable; detestable; evil; foul; gross; horrible; heinous; indecent; jaded; kitsch; loathsome; malevolent; nasty; nefarious; offensive; odious; pathetic; perfidious; *quad;* revolting; reprehensible; sinful; terrible; unenviable; vile; wretched; wicked; *x-rated;* yucky; zhlubby; [*Ant.* appealing]

**auction** *(n.)*: auctioning; bidding; Chinese ~; Dutch ~; *event; for sale; going for;* highest bidder; *hawking;* intercourse; jam [slang]; *kommers* [G.]; *let go;* mart; *no-nonsense ~; outcry;* public ~ (-sale); *quarter-priced; retail;* sale; sell-off; subhastation; silent ~; *trade; unload;* vendue; *white sale; x-change; yard sale; 0% down sale;*

**audacious** *(adj.)*: arrogant; bold; brazen; brash; courageous; daring; enterprising; foolhardy; gutsy; hardy; intrepid; *jaunty; know-it-all; lofty;* malapert; nervy; overconfident; presumptuous; *quick-witted;* risky; rude; spirited; temerarious; unafraid; vainglorious; *wherewithal; xtry.; yare; zealous;* [Ant. apprehensive]

**audacity** *(n.)*: arrogance; boldness; brazenness; brashness; cheekiness; contempt; daringness; disrespect; effrontery; flagrancy; gall; haughtiness; impudence; insolence; impertinence; *jackanapes; know-it-all; lip;* malapertness; nerve; overconfidence; presumption; pertness; *quilicom* [arch.]; rudeness; surliness; sassiness; sauciness; *turgidity;* uppityness; *unruliness;* vanity; *wherewithal; xenophobia; yahoo; zero humility;* [Ant. apprehension]

**audible** *(adj.)*: articulate; *aloud; being clear;* clear; coherent; detectable; discernable; enunciatory; fine; *gettable;* hearable; identifiable; *judicable; knowable;* loud enough; *listenable;* measurable; noticeable; *observable;* perceptible; quantifiable; recognizable; sonant; traceable; understandable; vocal; *volume;* within earshot; *x-parent;* yet perceivable; *zeroing in;*

**audience** *(n.)*: assembly; bystanders; beholders; crowd; congregation; *descriers;* eyewitnesses; forgathering; gathering; group; gazers; hearers; *interview; janata* [Asia]; *kith;* lookers; listenership [radio]; mass; multitude; *nonplayers;* onlookers; observers; passers-by; people; press; *quelet* [arch.]; ruck; *regarders; rubberneckers;* spectators; throng; *unbiased observers;* viewers; watchers; witnesses; *x.; yain* [arch.]; *zoa;*

**audit** *(n.)*: assessment; *background check;* check; *diagnostic;* examination; field examination; going over; hearing; inspection; *jerquing; knowledge test;* look-over; mandatory ~; *non-mandatory ~;* official check; *perquisition;* questioning; review; scrutiny; trial; *undertaking;* verification; *weighing; XQ;* year-end ~; *zeroing in;*

**audit** *(v.)*: assess; *behold;* check; do ~; examine; *find;* go over; *have examination;* inspect; *jerque; keek;* look over; make inspection; *note;* overlook; pick over; *question;* review; scrutinize; try; *undertake;* verify; weigh; *xenodiagnose; yeme; zero in;*

**audition** *(n.)*: audience; bench test; *conference;* dry run; examination; field test; going over; hearing; interview; job interview; key ~; *look;* mock run; night ~; *oral examination;* prelim; *qualification;* rehearsal; recital; run-through; screen test; trial; test run; tryout; *unoffical run;* viva; walkout; walk-through; *xenagogy; yarking; zet [dial.];*

**auditorium** *(n.)*: amphitheater; arena; building; common hall; coliseum; *domed ~;* edifice; field house; grounds; hall; *indoor seating; judgment hall;* kabuki [Jap.]; lecture hall; meeting hall (-place); *naumachy* [Rom.]; odeum; *place;* public seating; *querencia* [Sp.]; *rostrum; seating;* sanctuary; theater; *upper circle;* venue; wing; *xenodocheum; yard; zone;*

**augment** *(v.)*: amplify; boost; climb; compound; *develop;* enhance; escalate; fortify; grow; heighten; increase; intensify; jack up; *keep increasing;* largify; magnify; *new growth;* overload; *progress; quantum increase;* raise; step up; strengthen; turn up; up; *volume;* wax; *XL; yain* [arch.]; *zoom;* [Ant. assuage]

**aura** *(n.)*: afterglow; brilliance; candescence; *dazzle;* emanation; fulgency; glow; haze; halo; irradiance; *jet; kindle;* light; lucence; *moonlight;* nimbus; *overlight;* phosphorescence; radiance; refulgence; shine; shining; splendor; *thermoluminescence; ultraviolet light;* vividness; white light; *xenon light;* yellow light; *zodiacal light;*

**austere** *(adj.)*: ascetic; authoritarian; *bitter;* cruel; dour; exacting; firm; flinty; gruff; grave; glowering; grim; harsh; hard(-nosed); humorless; incompassionate; inconsiderate; *jaded;* kindless; *lousy;* mean; merciless; negative; overbearing; pitiless; *quarrelsome;* rough; rigorous; rigid; serious; stern; strict; torvous; totalitarian; unmild; unmerciful; unkind; uncompassionate; unpitying; unreasonable; very hard; *wrathful; xtry. harsh; yucky;* zero tolerance;

**austerity** *(n.)*: asceticism; bareness; *cruelty;* difficulty; economy; frugality; graveness; harshness; impoverishment; *jarring; keen ~; lowliness;* meanness; *nastiness;* onerousness; plainness; *quantity;* rigor; simplicity; self-denial; strictness; severity; torvity; *unpitying;* very simple; *wrath; xtry. conditions;* yuckiness; zero mercy; [Ant. abundance]

**authentic** *(adj.)*: actual; bona fide; correct; definite; exact; faithful; genuine; honest-to-goodness; indubitable; justifiable; known; legitimate; *mean it;* non-reproduced; *open;* proper; qualified; real; *sincere;* true; truthful; unerring; valid; well-proven; x-parent; *yes;* 'zactly [dial.]; [Ant. artifical]

**authenticate** *(v.)*: affirm; attest; bear out; check; certify; confirm; corroborate; demonstrate; document; establish; ensure; fix; give proof; homologate; illustrate; jerque; justify; kithe [Scot.]; legitimize; *maintain;* nail down; notarize; *okay;* prove; *questionless;* reconfirm; show; sustain; substantiate; stamp; try; testify; uphold; verify; validate; warrant; x-certify; *yes; zero doubt;*

**authentication** *(n.)*: attestation; bearing out; certification; confirmation; demonstration; documentation; establishment; final ~; giving of proof; homologation; illustration; insurance; justification; *kithe [Scot.];* legitimization; *maintenance;* notarization; okay; proof; *questionlessness;* reconfirmation; substantiation; seal; stamp of approval; testimony; upholding; verification; validation; warrant; witness; x-certification; *yes; zero doubt;*

**authenticity** *(n.)*: actuality; *bona fide;* certainty; dependability; exactness; factuality; genuineness; honesty; indubitability; *justification; knowledge;* legitimacy; *measuring up;* non-fictitiousness; *okay;* properness; quality; reliability; sureness; truth; trustworthiness; *unaltered;* validity; *well-proven; x-parent; yes; zero error;*

**author** *(n.)*: annotator; authoress [fem.]; blazoner; columnist; commentator; co- ~; dialogue-writer; essayist; epistolizer; fabulizer; ghostwriter; hedge-writer; inscriber; journalist; *keeper of journal;* leafleteer; man of letters; makar [Scot.]; novelist; observator; penman; playwright; quill-driver; remarker; scribe; tragedian; *underwriter;* volumist; writer; *Xenophon; yellow journalist; Zola;*

**author** *(v.)*: annotate; *book;* compose; draft; enter; fabulize; *grave;* handwrite; indite; jot down; keep record; log; make; notate; originate; pen; quill; redact; scrawl; take down; underwrite; *vellum;* write; *x; yak; zay;*

**authoritative** *(adj.)*: assertive; bold; bossy; commanding; dogmatic; dominating; ever-confident; firm; *gallant;* hard; imposing; *jarless; knowing;* lion-hearted; manly; masterly; magisterial; non-fearful; *obstinate;* peremptory; *questful;* resolute; respected; self-assured; take-charge; unafraid; very convincing; well-confident; *xtry.; yet undaunted; zealous;*

**authority** *(n.)*: auspices; *badge;* clout; control; command; *crown;* dominion; domination; empowering; faculty; government; headship; horn [Bible]; helm; hegemony; influence; imperium; jurisdiction; kingship; lordship; *legal right; leverage;* mastery; name; oversight; power; *quo warranto* [L.]; right; rule; rod [Bible]; rod of iron; regency; sway; say-so; sanction; sovereignty; *scepter; throne;* umpirage; virtue; warrant; weight; *x-pass;* yard; zorch;

**authorization** *(n.)*: approval; backing; consent; *delight;* empowerment; *freedom;* green light; hear to [reg.]; imprimatur; joint-permission; *knowingly allowed;* license; licensure; *may;* nod; okay; permission; papers; *qualified yes; right;* support; sanction; thumbs up [slang]; unreluctance; *unopposed;* visa; *warrant; x-pass;* yes; *zealous ~;*

**authorize** *(v.)*: allow; approve; *bless;* consent; confer; *decriminalize;* empower; establish; facilitate; give permission; homologate; indulge; *justify;* knowingly allow; let; make possible; *nod;* okay; permit; *qualify;* ratify; set; sanction; *tolerate; unopposed;* validate; warrant; *x on the dotted line; yes; zealously approve;*

**automatic** *(adj.)*: automated; button-operated; conditioned; computerized; *des nous jours* [F.]; electronic; fast; *guaranteed;* habitual; immediate; involuntary; instinctive; industrialized; *just lay back;* knee-jerk; *leading-edge;* mindless; mechanized; natural; non-voluntary; *new-fangled;* operated-by-computer; Pavlovian; preset; pre-conditioned; plug-in; *quick;* reflexive; self-operating; *technologically advanced;* unconscious; very advanced; world-class; *xtry.; yet unsurpassed; zippity;*

**automobile** *(n.)*: auto; bucket (of bolts); clunker; car; dragster; *Edsel®;* flivver; gas-guzzler; hatchback; hardtop; horseless carriage; *Infiniti®;* jalopy; kit-car; lemon; *low rider;* motor car (-vehicle); notchback; off-road vehicle; passenger car; quad; roadster [slang]; subcompact; sedan; sports car; transportation; *truck; undercarriage;* vehicle; wheels [slang]; wagon; *X-C90; Yugo®; Zis* [Rus.];
  **Kinds of vehicles**: buggy; convertible; hearse; hot rod; jeep; limo(usine); minivan; racecar; sports car; station wagon; truck; van;
**autonomous** *(adj.)*: able to govern self; bondless; *control; direct control;* empowered; free; governing oneself; *headship;* independent; *justified; kept free;* liberated; managing own affairs; non-subjugated; open; particularistic; quite independent; ruling self; self-governing; sovereign; totally independent; unsubjected; *very independent; warranted; xel [arch.];* yokeless; *zero hierarchy;*
**autonomy** *(n.)*: ability to rule self; bondlessness; control; *dominion; empowered;* freedom; governing oneself; home rule; independence; *justification; kept free;* liberty; management of own affairs; non-subjugation; open; particularism; *quite free;* rule by self; self-government; self-rule; sovereignty; total liberty; *unsubjected; very independent;* warrant; *xel [arch.];* yokelessness; *zero hierarchy;*
**auxiliary** *(adj.)*: assisting; back up; contributory; *different;* extra; *emergency;* further; *gaining;* helping; increased; joining; *king-sized amounts; leftover;* more; new; other; plus; *quantities; remaining;* spare; supporting; subsidiary; supplemental; *too; unused; volumes; wealth;* x.; yet more; *zillions;*
**avail** *(n.)*: advantage; benefit; *cause; conduciveness; dividend;* expediency; favor; good; gain; help; increase; *justification; keep; logical advantage;* makings; net profit; obtainment; purpose; *quittal;* reward; service; takings; use; vantage; winnings; x-div; yield; *zillions;*
**avail** *(v.)*: apply; benefit from; *control;* deploy; *do;* employ; exercise; further; *get benefit from;* harness; *implement;* jockey; *keep; let;* make use of; *nobble;* overuse; put to use; *qualify;* run; *set to use;* take advantage of; use; *vocation;* work; *xuld [arch.]; yain* [arch.]; zeal;
**availability** *(n.)*: accessibility; acquirability; *buyable;* convenience; disposal; eligibility; findability; gettability; handiness; *idoneous; just there; keepability; leftover; marriageability;* nearness; obtainability; possibility; *quite easily found;* readiness; supply; *takable;* usability; vacancy; *workability; xtra; yet unclaimed; zero problem;*
**available** *(adj.)*: accessible; acquirable; at one's disposal; buyable; claimable; *a* dime a dozen; eligible; easily reached; free; findable; gettable; havable; *idoneous;* just there for the taking; *keepable;* leftover; *marriageable;* non-claimed; numerous; open; obtainable; possible; procurable; quite easily found; reachable; readily ~; spare; *sequesterable;* there; takable; untaken; unoccupied; unsold; unclaimed; unmarried; up for grabs; usable; vacant; *workable; xtra;* yours for the asking; *zero problem;*
**avalanche** *(n.)*: *avalange* [arch.]; barrage; *collapse; cover;* downslide; earthflow; falling rock; *glide; heaping;* icefall; inundation; *jet; klip;* landslide; landslip; lahar; mudslide; *mudflow;* noise-induced ~; *outflow;* plummeting; *quake;* rockslide; rockfall; slide; snow-slip; torrent; uncontrolled landslide; *volcanic eruption;* washaway; *xfer; yuki [Jap.]; zip down;*
**avenge** *(v.)*: *afflict;* bring to justice; come back; *despiteful;* even the score; fix; get (back); have vengeance; *inflict; justice* [arch.]; kindless; *lex talionis [L.];* make one pay; *nemesis;* offset; pay back; punish; *quittal;* revenge; requite; settle; take vengeance; *unkindness;* vindicate; *whip; x-out; yet unavenged;* zealously ~; [Ant. absolve]
**avenger** *(n.)*: *amercer;* bitter person; chastiser; corrector; despiteful individual; evener; executioner; *foe; gall;* harrier; inflicter; justicer; *killer; lex talionis [L.];* merciless man; nemesis; *obdurate;* punisher; *quittal;* retaliator; revenger; settler; taker of vengeance; *unforgiveness;* vindicator; venger; vigilante; *whip; x-out; yet unavenged;* zealous ~; [Ant. absolver]
**avenue** *(n.)*: alley; artery; boulevard; course; drive; esplanade; freeway; *going;* highway; interstate; journey-way; king's highway; lane; motorway; non-toll road; outstreet; outlet; pike; parkway; queen's highway; road; street; thoroughfare; *underpass;* vennel; way; xyst; *yong [arch.]; zwinger;*

**average** *(adj.)*: archetypic; basic; common; center; *dull;* everyday; familiar; generic; general; halfway; ho-hum; intermediate; inelaborate; *juste-milieu* [F.]; *known;* lackluster; mean; middle; medium; median; medial; mediocre; middle-of-the-road; normal; ordinary; plain; quotidian; regular; run-of-the-mill; simple; standard; so-so; typical; usual; *via media* [L.]; *worldly;* xymedian; yawnsome; zestless; [*Ant.* atypical]

**averse** *(adj.)*: against; begrudging; *chary;* disinclined; ever-opposed; flat against; grudging; hesitant; indisposed; just not in favor; keenly opposed; loath; much-opposed; non-desirous; opposed; plumb against; *questioning;* reluctant; soured; totally against; unfavorable; unwilling; unforthcoming; very opposed; *wary; x-out;* yet unwilling; zealless; [*Ant.* assistive]

**aversion** *(n.)*: abhorrence; *bête noire* [F.]; contempt; dislike; detestation; enmity; *fiendfulness;* gall; hatred; intense dislike; *jadedness;* kindlessness; loathing; malice; nolition; odium; *poison;* querulousness; revulsion; spite; *tetchiness;* uncharitableness; unwillingness; vitriol; *withstanding;* xenophobia; yuckiness; zero interest; [*Ant.* affection]

**avert** *(v.)*: avoid; block; circumvent; deter; divert; escape; forestall; *go away;* halt; inhibit; jink; keep (from); look away; *move away from; nullify;* obviate; prevent; *quite* [Sp.] redirect; stop; turn away; *undo;* veer; ward off; x; *yank;* zilch; [*Ant.* accelerate]

**avoid** *(v.)*: avert; bypass; circumvent; dodge; detour; elude; evade; eschew; forestall; flee; get around; *hedge; ignore;* jink; keep away from; let alone; leave be; miss; *negotiate around;* obviate; prevent; parry; *quite* [Sp.]; run away from; sidestep; skirt; shun; turn away from; utterly ~; *veer away;* withdraw; *x-out;* yerk; zero contact;

**await** *(v.)*: anticipate; abide; bide; *continue; dwell;* expect; *forsee; go to;* hope; idle; *just wait;* keep on; look for; *motionless; nide;* occupy; pause; *quait* [arch.]; remain; stay; tarry; *use patience; veg out* [slang]; wait for; *xenize; yerde* [arch.]; *zip to;*

**awake** *(adj.)*: alert; aware; bestirred; conscious; disquieted; excited; fired up; *gotten up; hyped-up;* incited; *jarred;* keyed up; liminal; *moving;* newly-waked; out of bed; open-eyed; *provoked;* quickened; roused; stirred; *troubled;* up; *vivified;* wakened; wakeful; wide- ~; wide-eyed; *xuld* [arch.]; *yet ~; zesty;* [*Ant.* asleep]

**awaken** *(v.)*: arouse; awake; bestir; *call;* come alive; disturb; disquiet; excite; *fuel; goad;* hearten; incite; jar; kindle; *lead; move; nudge; overagitate;* provoke; quicken; rouse; roust; recrudesce; stir; trouble; *upset; vex;* wake (up); waken; *xuld* [arch.]; yerk; *zip;*

**award** *(n.)*: accolade; approbation; blue ribbon; credit; citation; compensation; cup; crown; decoration; *embellishment; fee;* guerdon; gift; gold cup; glory; honor; high honors; indemnity; incentive; jackpot; *king's ransom;* laurel wreath; loving cup; medal(lion); *Nobel Prize; ornament;* prize; plaque; payment; quittance; reward; ribbon; requital; remuneration; recompense; satisfaction; trophy; *utu* [N.Z.]; *victory crown; wage;* xenium; *yeff* [arch.]; yellow jersey [sports]; *Zion's crowns;*

**award** *(v.)*: assign; bestow; confer; decorate; endow; *furnish;* give; grant; hand (over); honor with; issue; *judge; kit;* laurel; make gift; *notable; outfit;* present; *quicken;* recognize; render; reward; *supply;* transfer; *unhand;* vest; *weigh;* xfer; *yield; zip;*

**award-winner** *(n.)*: achiever; *bronze-medalist;* champ(ion); defeater; dominator; expunger; frontrunner; *gold-medalist;* hero; *individual; jubilant;* kemp; laureate; medalist; *Nobel prizewinner;* overcomer; prizewinner; *qualified;* recipient; *silver medalist;* triumphant; undefeated champ; victor; winner; *xtry.; yell; zealous;*

**aware** *(adj.)*: awake; alert; *bethink;* cognizant; discerning; ever-mindful; focused; *grasp; heedful;* informed; *judicious;* knowing; knowledgeable; leery; mindful; *non-ignorant;* observant; perceptive; quick-witted; responsive; *sense;* thoughtful; understanding; vigilant; wary; well- ~; x-careful; yare-handed; *zärtlich* [G.];

**awareness** *(n.)*: alertness; attentiveness; *bethink;* consciousness; cognizance; discernment; *ever-mindful;* focus; grasp; *heedful; insight; judiciousness;* knowledge; leeriness; mindfulness; notice;

*observant;* perception; quick-wittedness; responsiveness; recognition; sense; thoughtfulness; understanding; vigilance; wakefulness; *x-careful;* yare-handed; *zärtlich [G.];*
**awe** *(n.)*: amazement; bedazzlement; confounding; dread; dazzling; *enchantment;* flooring; gaping; holding one's breath; impressing; jolting; keeling over; looking aghast; marveling; *nonplus;* overwhelming; *perplexing; quite amazed;* rendering speechlessness; stunning; terror; *unable to believe; very impressed;* wonder; *xtry.; yerk; zing;*
**awe** *(v.)*: amaze; astonish; bedazzle; confound; dazzle; dumbfound; *enchant;* floor; gape; hold one's breath; impress; jolt; keel over; look aghast; make marvel; *nonplus;* overwhelm; poleax; *quite amazed;* render speechless; stun; take one's breath away; unable to believe; *very impressed;* wonder; *xtry.; yerk; zing;*
**awesome** *(adj.)*: amazing; astonishing; awe-inspiring; breathtaking; *capital;* dazzling; extraordinary; fantastic; grand; great; heavenly; incredible; *jolting;* keen; lofty; magnificent; noteworthy; overwhelming; prodigious; *quantum* [L.]; remarkable; spectacular; tremendous; unequalled; unbelievable; *virtuous;* wondrous; xtry.; *yippee!; zestful;*
**awestruck** *(v.)*: awed; bowled over; confounded; dumbfounded; *enchanted;* flabbergasted; gaping; *holding one's breath;* impressed; jolted; keeled over; looked aghast; marveling; *nonplused;* overwhelmed; perplexed; *quite amazed;* rendered speechless; speechless; thunderstruck; unable to speak; *very impressed;* wonderstruck; *xtry.; yerk; zing;*
**awkward** *(adj.)*: artless; bulky; bumbling; clumsy; cumbersome; difficult; dowdy; *étourderie* [F.]; embarrassing; fumbly; gangly; gawky; graceless; gimpy; hard; heavy-handed (-footed); hulky; inelegant; inept; jumbly; klutzy; kayu; lumbering; maladroit; non-graceful; oafish; plumbeous; *quirky;* restive; socially inept; slovenly; troublesome; ungainly; ungraceful; unwieldy; uncoordinated; unhandy; untoward; uncomfortable; uneasy; *vexatious;* wooden; xtry. ~; yokelish; zhlubby; [*see* shy; Ant. artful]
**awry** *(adj.)*: amiss; askew; bad; crooked; chim-cham; defective; erroneous; flim-flam; flooey [slang]; false; *goofy; haywire;* incorrect; ill; jim-jam; kim-kam; lopsided; muddled; not right; off-kilter; *problem; quirky; rotten;* skewed; twisted; *unacceptable; unplanned;* very wrong; wrong; *x'ed; yo-yo;* zonky; [*Ant.* accurate]
**awkwardness** *(n.)*: artlessness; bulkiness; clumsiness; cumbersomeness; difficulty; dowdiness; *étourderie* [F.]; fumbliness; gawkiness; gracelessness; heavy-handedness (-footedness); hulkiness; inelegance; indexterity; jumbliness; klutziness; lumbering; maladroitness; non-gracefulness; oafishness; *plumbeous; quirkiness; rube;* slovenliness; troublesomeness; ungainliness; uneasiness; *vexation;* woodenness; xtry. ~; yokelishness; zhlubbiness; [*Ant.* artfulness]
**awning** *(n.)*: arch canopy; baldachin; cover; canvas ~; canopy; dorse; electric retractable ~; fabric ~; *gore;* half-circle canopy; *item; job;* kitchen-window ~; laced ~; metal ~; non-retractable ~; orange-peel canopy; panoply; porte-cochère; quarter-round ~; retractable ~; sunshade; terrace canopy; tentory; *tarp; umbrella; veil;* window ~; *xillinous;* yellow ~; *zeta;*
**axe** *(n.)*: ax; blade; battle-~; broadax; cleaver; celt; chopper; double-bi ~; edge; fire- ~; francisca; glair; gisarme; hatchet; hand ~; halberd; holing-ax; ice ~; *jelman [Turk.];* kukri; lochaber ~; meat-cleaver; *navaja;* ovate hand~; pickax; poleax; partisan; *quarrel; razor;* sparth; tomahawk; twilbill; utility; Valencia knife; whin-ax; *xyster;* yaxe [dial.]; zax;
**axel** *(n.)*: axis; arbor; bore; car ~; disselboom; *equipment;* fust; gudgeon; hinge; half shaft; interconnecting ~; jimmer; keyway; live ~; mechanical shaft; notched ~; open shaft; pin; quill; rod; shaft; spindle; trans~; *underworkings;* verge; wheel ~; *xfer; yedder;* zinc-coated ~;
**axiom** *(n.)*: adage; aphorism; byword; cliché; dictum; expression; epigram; formulary; generality; guideline; *hackneyed saying;* instruction; *judgment; koine;* law; maxim; neology; oracle; proverb; quote; rule; saying; truism; universal truth; veracity; wisdom; *xenophonia, Yogism;* zeteticism;

# B

**babble** *(n.)*: argot; baby-talk; blather; chatter; claptrap; drivel; double-talk; empty words; fudge; gibberish; guff; hot air; inarticulate sounds; jabber; jargon; kelter; *lard;* mumbo-jumbo; nonsense; *outlandishness;* prattle; queer speech; rambling; slaver; twaddle; tarradiddle; utterance; vain talk; wishwash; xenoglossy; yabber; *zeug [G.];*
**babble** *(v.)*: argot; blather; chatter; double-talk; *empty words;* fudge; gibber; gab(ble); haver; idly chatter; jabber; *kelter; lard;* mutter; natter; *outlandish;* prattle; prate; patter; *quatsch;* ramble; rattle; rant; slaver; twaddle; talk; utter; vocalize; witter; *xenoglossy;* yabber; yabble; *zeug [G.];* [see gurgle]
**baby** *(n.)*: arrival; bantling; child; doll; *daughter [fem.]; enfant [F.];* firstling; girl [fem.]; hatchling; infant; *just-born;* kid; little one; manling [masc.]; newborn; neonate; nursling; offspring; poupetan; *quintuplet;* recent arrival; suckling; toddler; tot; *ungrown; very young one;* wee one; weanling; *XS;* young(ling); yeanling; yearling; *zon [dial. masc.];*
**baby carriage** *(n.)*: apparatus; buggy; carriage; *doll carriage; equipment;* foldup ~; gig; hooded carriage; infant stroller; jogging stroller; kid cart; *light pushchair; means;* newborn; *outdoor;* perambulator; pram; pushchair; quad stroller; roller; stroller; twin ~; umbrella stroller; *vehicle;* wheeler; *x-fold ~;* young child's stroller; *zip;*
**babyhood** *(n.)*: *arrival;* boyhood [masc.]; childhood; development; early years; formative years; growing; girlhood [fem.]; *hatchling;* infancy; juniority; kidhood [joc.]; *littleness;* maturing; newborn stage; neonatal period; *offspring;* period right after birth; *quite young; raising;* suckling stage; springtime of life; tenderness; toddlerhood; underdevelopment; verdancy; weanling years; *XS;* youth; *zero-maturity;*
**babyish** *(adj.)*: *adolescent;* baby(-like); childish; dollish; early; fledgling; *growing;* hastive; infantile; immature; juvenescent; kiddish; little; maidenly [fem.]; namby-pamby; nektonic; *over-young;* puerile; *quite young;* raw; small; silly; tiny; undeveloped; vernal; wee; *XS;* young; *zero-experience;*
**babysit** *(v.)*: attend; be there for; care for; deal with; *enforce; feed;* give attention to; handle; *infant; job;* keep watch; look after; mind; *nanny; operate; perform; quality time;* run things; sit; take care of; tend; *undertake; visit;* watch; *xfer; yeme; zealously watch;*
**bacchanalian** *(adj.)*: abandoned; bad; carousing; drunken; debauched; dionysian; effete; epicurean; frolicsome; godless; hedonistic; intemperate; jadish; *knavish;* libertine; mischievous; nontemperate; overindulgent; orgiastic; partying; *quad;* reveling; riotous; sinful; shameless; tainted; unrestrained; *venery;* wanton; *x-rated; yahoo;* zizzy; [*Ant.* blameless]
**bachelor** *(n.)*: available man; boy; celibate; *dude;* eligible young man; *free;* gentleman; handsome young man; *individual;* joe [slang]; *kid;* lad; master; man; *Mr. Right;* non-married man; *open; person;* qualified young man; quirkyalone; *rascal;* single man; *terrific young man;* unmarried man; *virile;* wifeless; *x-linked;* young man; *zon [dial.];* [*Ant.* bridegroom]
**bachelorette** *(n.)*: available young lady; beauty; *colleen [Ire];* damsel; eligible young lady; femme-sole; girl; *gold-digger; her; individual;* jane [slang]; *kid;* lass; miss; maiden; nymph [poet.]; old maid; *peri;* quirkyalone; rose; spinster; *terrific young lady;* unmarried woman; virgin; *woman; x-chromosome;* young lady; *zitella [It.];* [*Ant.* bride]
**back** *(n.)*: abaft; aft; arrear; backside; behind; butt; croup [zoo.]; *dorsal;* end; flipside; fro; gammon [zoo.]; hinder; hindmost; ischiadic; jacksy; *keister;* latter part; most rearward place; nether (part); notum; *oddments;* posterior; quarterdeck [naut.]; rear; stern; tail; underside; *verge;* waning; xyz end; yondmost; Z-position; [*Ant.* beginning]

**back** *(v.)*: agree; approve; abet; advocate; be in accord; bankroll; condone; champion; defend; declaim; endorse; finance; fund; give support to; help; indorse; join; keep; line up; maintain; *nod;* obsignate; patronize; pay for; promote; *qualify;* ratify; sympathize; stand behind; subsidize; support; *togetherness;* uphold; underwrite; *validate;* warrant; *xel [arch.];* yes; *zealously support;* [Ant. battle]

**backbite** *(v.)*: attack; belittle; badmouth; blast; calumniate; criticize; defame; denigrate; *execrate;* falsely accuse; gossip about; harangue; insult; jab; knock; libel; mudsling; malign; name-call; obloquy; put down; *quib;* run down; slander; traduce; *use;* vilify; wipe; *x-ing;* yellow; *zap;*

**backbiter** *(n.)*: asperser; belittler; calumniator; defamer; evil-speaker; false accuser; gossip; hatchet man; insulter; jaunderer; knocker; libeler; maligner; mudslinger; name-caller; *over-critical;* put down; *quib;* railer; slanderer; traducer; tarnisher; *unfair;* vilifier; *wicked; x-ing;* yellower; *zeroizer;*

**backbiting** *(n.)*: aspersion; belittlement; calumny; character assassination; defamation; denigration; evil-speaking; false words; gossip; *hearsay;* insult; injury; jaunder; *klatsch;* libel; mudslinging; malediction; name-calling; obtrectation; putting down; *quidnunc;* running down; slander; traducement; tarnishing; unfair criticism; vilification; *wickedness; x-ing;* yellowing; *zeroization;*

**backbreaking** *(adj.)*: arduous; burdensome; challenging; demanding; exhausting; fatiguing; grueling; grinding; hard; heavy; intense; jading; killing; laborious; moiling; not easy; operose; *painful; quite hard;* rigorous; strenuous; taxing; unrelenting; *vigorous;* wearisome; *x-heavy; yare; zapping;*

**backflow** *(n.)*: *afflux;* backwash; crosscurrent; deflow; ebb; flow back; *gush; hurl;* issue; influx; jet(stream); *kickback; liquid;* movement back; naid; *outflow; profluence; quell;* reflux; reflow; rift; stream; tide; undercurrent; undertow; *vomiting;* wash; *x-current; yern; zwoosh;*

**background** *(n.)*: area view; backdrop (-cloth); conditions; circumstances; drop; education; environment; fond; field; *ground;* history; habitat; immediate area; *juncture; knowledge;* landscape; locale; *mise en scène* [F.]; milieu; nature; overlook; personal training; panorama; *qualifications;* region; scene(ry); set(ting); surroundings; training; terrain; upbringing; venue; vista; waterscape; *xerosere;* yonder; *zone;*

**backlog** *(n.)*: accumulation; buildup; collection; *deposit;* excess; *forgathering;* glut; heap; *in-box;* jam [slang]; *kit [coll.];* lot; load; mass; number; overplus; pile; quantity; *ruck;* surplus; *to-do list;* unfinished work; volume; workload; *x-tra; yet unfinished work;* zillions;

**backpack** *(n.)*: *alligator bag;* bag; carry-all; daypack; *equipment-pack;* fanny pack; gear bag; haversack; *implement;* journey-sack; knapsack; *luggage;* matilda [Aus.]; molle [mil.]; musette; nunny bag [Can.]; *overnight case;* pack(sack); *quiver;* rucksack; shoulder bag; sack; tote bag; utility pack; valise; walking sack; x-bag; yannigan bag [slang]; zipper-bag;

**backslidden** *(adj.)*: away from God; backset; changed back; disfellowshipped; *escheated;* fallen back; gotten away from God; harked back; *impeded;* jumped back; *knocked back;* lapsed back; moved back; not right with God; out of fellowship with God; plunge; *quit;* relapsed; regressed; slid back; turned back; *undone;* veered away from God; way far away; *xfer;* yielded to the flesh; *zapped;*

**backslide** *(v.)*: apostatize; backset; change back; downslide; *escheat;* fall back; go back; hark back; *impede;* jump back; *knock back;* lapse; lose fellowship with God; move back; *non-advancement; over again;* plunge; *quit;* relapse; revert; regress; return; sideline; slide back; turn back; *undo;* veer away from God; wander; *xfer;* yield again; *zoom downward;*

**backslider** *(n.)*: apostate; backsetter; *changer back;* defaulter; *evildoer;* fallen one; goer back; harker back; *iniquity;* jumper back; *knave;* lapser; misdoer; *not right;* offender; *plunger;* quitter; recidivist; reverter; sinner; transgressor; *ungodly;* veerer; wanderer; *xfer;* yielder; *zero righteousness;*

**backsliding** *(n.)*: atavism; backslide; backset; change back; downslide; *escheat;* falling back; going back; heading back; *impediment;* jump back; *knock back;* lapse; move backward; *non-advancement; over again;* plunge; *quitting;* relapse; reversion; regression; retroversion; return; setback; slide; turnabout; *undoing; vacating;* wandering; *xfer;* yielding again to; *zoom downward;*

**backstab** *(v.)*: attack; betray; commit treachery; double-cross; *err;* frame; guile; hand over; *insurrect;* jilt; *kick at;* let down; *mutiny; not loyal;* overthrow; plunge the knife; quisle; rise up; stab in the back; turn on; *underhanded;* violate trust; *withstand; x-gress; yieldless; zero loyalty;*
**backstabber** *(n.)*: absconder; arch-traitor; betrayer; collaborationist; double-crosser; *evildoer;* false friend; fiend; guiler; highbinder; insurgent; Judas; *knave; liar;* mutineer; *non-loyal;* opportunist; plotter; Quisling; rat; subversive; turncoat; *unloyal; villain; wicked; xfer; yegg; zero loyalty;*
**backtalk** *(v.)*: argue; bicker; cavil; dispute; *erupt;* fuss; gainsay; hassle; *inharmonious;* jangle; kick up dust; *lock horns [slang];* make a problem; niff; object; parley; quibble; retort; sass; talk back; *unharmonious;* vie; wrangle; *x-purposes;* yell; *zap;* [*Ant.* bow]
**backup** *(n.)*: archive; auxiliary; backed up copy; copy; disk; daily ~; *extra copy;* facsimile; *flash drive; gigabyte; hard copy;* information; *just in case; keep; log;* monthly ~; nightly ~; off-site ~; protected copy; *quadruplicate;* record; spare (copy); tape; *unit;* verified ~; weekly ~; *x-file;* yesterday's ~; zip file;
**backward** *(adv.)*: aback; astern; arsy-versy; back(wards); counter; downside-up; everted; fakie; going the wrong way; hindward; inside out; inverted; just the opposite; *knocked back; loused up;* misoriented; non-forward-facing; opposite-facing; postic; *quirky;* rearward; reversed; retrograde; retroverse; sternward; towards the back; turned around; upside down; vice-versa; wrong-facing; widdershins; *x-grained; yet reversed; zero orientation;*
**bacteria** *(n.)*: amoeba; bacilli; bug; cell; *coccus; disease;* E. coli; fomite; foreign body; germs; *heterameba;* infection; *jelly-like; kernel; listeria;* microorganism; microbes; *nanobacterium;* organisms; pathogens; *Q fever;* rotifers; spores; superbug; supergerm; *taint;* ultravirus; *virus; wee organism; xanthomonad;* yersinia; *zygote;*
**bad** *(adj.)*: adverse; awful; abominable; baneful; crummy; corrupt; contemptible; cruel; dreadful; debauched; errant; execrable; evil; foul; fiendish; godless; horrible; heinous; invalid; ill; injurious; iniquitous; jaded; knavish; lousy; licentious; mischievous; malevolent; negative; naughty; nasty; nefarious; ornery; odious; pernicious; *questionable;* rotten; rapacious; ruthless; sinful; sinister; terrible; treacherous; undesirable; unacceptable; unhealthy; unscrupulous; unrighteous; vile; villainous; wrong(ful); wicked; *xgressing;* yucky; *zhlubby;* [*Ant.* beneficial]
**badge** *(n.)*: award; *authority;* button; credentials; designation; emblem; *figure;* gold ~; hallmark; *heraldry;* I.D.; insignia; insigne; icon; *jack; key; logo;* mark; medal; name ~; *object;* pin; *qualifications;* representation; symbol; shield; star; token; *umbo; vexillum; wafer;* X; *yeoman's insignia; zeug;*
**badger** *(v.)*: antagonize; bug; chafe; disturb; exasperate; frustrate; gall; harass; irritate; jangle; *kid; livid;* menace; nag; *offend;* pester; *queach [arch.];* rankle; *steam;* tempt; try one's patience; unnerve; vex; weary; *x-ing;* yerk; *zing;*
**badmouth** *(v.)*: abase; attack; belittle; criticize; disparage; excoriate; fault; give bad name; harangue; impugn; jangle; knock; lambaste; mock; niggle; *object;* pan; *quarrel;* run down; slam; traduce; *unkind words;* vilify; whine about; *xuld [arch.];* yammer; *zing;* [*Ant.* bless]
**badness** *(n.)*: awfulness; baseness; cruelty; despicableness; evil; fellness; foulness; godlessness; heinousness; ill-will; *jadedness;* kindlessness; loathsomeness; meanness; nastiness; nefariousness; odiousness; perniciousness; querulousness; ruthlessness; sinfulness; terribleness; treachery; unhealthiness; ungodliness; vileness; virulence; wickedness; *xenophobia;* yuckiness; *zoilism;* [*Ant.* beneficialness]
**baffle** *(v.)*: addle; boggle; confuse; confound; discomfit; escape one; elude; flummox; gravel; hamper; *incoherent;* jumble; kittle; lose; mix up; nonplus; obscure; puzzle; quiz; rattle; stump; tangle; *unclear;* vex; wilder; *x; yo-yo; zero understanding;*
**bag** *(n.)*: * alligator-skin ~; brown paper ~; cod; canvas ~; drawstring ~; *earth~;* flaxen ~; gunnysack; hand~; *in;* jute sack; kit~; leather ~; mail~; money~; *nunny ~;* overnight ~; paper ~; plastic ~; pouch; poke; *quiver;* receptacle; shopping ~; sack; scrip; tote; utility ~; *velvet pouch;* work~; x-bag; yannigan ~; zipper- ~;

**baggy** *(adj.)*: *abundant;* billowing; *comfortable;* droopy; ever-so-loose; floppy; generous; hanging; ill-fitting; *jumbo-sized; king-size;* loose-fitting; much-too-loose; not tight; oversized; pendulous; *quantitative;* roomy; slack; sagging; too big; unshapely; voluminous; way too big; *XL; yet too big; zero tightness;*

**bagpipes** *(n.)*: aerophones; biniou; chanter; cornemuse; doodlesack; English ~; *flabiol;* gaida; hornpipe; Irish organ; *instrument; jirba;* Keltic pipes; loure; miskin; musette; Northumbrian smallpipe; *organ;* pipes; qrajna; reed-pipes; sordellina; Scottish ~; *tulum;* uilleann pipes; veuze; Welsh pipes; xeremia; *ykaida* [Gr.]; zampogna;

**bail** *(n.)*: assessment; bond; collateral; *debt;* earnest money; frankpledge; fidejussor; guarantee; hypothecation; insurance; jail-bond; *kickback; legal tender;* mainpernor; *note; outlay;* payment; pledge; parole; *quittance;* release-money; security; surety; *transfer; U.S. currency; vigorish;* warrenty; *xfer; yardage; zum* [dial.];

**bailiff** *(n.)*: attendant; bobby; court official; deputy; enforcer; *functionary;* guardian; *helper; intendant;* jurat; keeper of the peace; law enforcement officer; marshal; *notary;* officer; official; police officer; *questura* [It.]; representative; steward; sheriff; tipstaff; uniformed deputy; *viscount;* warden; *xeriff;* yeoman; *zayim;*

**bailout** *(n.)*: assistance; burden-shouldering; *covering;* deliverance; *extrication;* financial rescue; government ~; help; *investment; just-in-time; kindness;* lending aid; money; *non-taxable; overpayment;* pay; *quick help;* rescue; salvage; *transfer;* unburdening; *vest;* working capital; *xtr. money; yielding; zero hindrance;*

**bait** *(n.)*: attraction; allurement; berley; chum; draw; *decoy;* enticement; fly; gaff; hackle, inducement; *jape; knavery;* lure; morsel; *night crawler;* outwitting; provocation; *quiblin* [arch.]; *roping in;* seduction; temptation; trap; urging; *vie;* worm; *xuld* [arch.]; yearning; zygotaxis;

**bake** *(v.)*: anneal; brown; broil; cook; dry out; *evenly ~; furnace- ~; griddle;* heat; harden; *improvise; jumbal;* kiln- ~; *lightly ~;* make; *neal* [arch.]; oven- ~; overheat; prepare; pan-broil; quick- ~; roast; swelter; sun- ~; toast; undercook; *very hot;* whip up; *xeo;* yark; *zwieback;*

**bakery** *(n.)*: *area ~;* bake shop; bakehouse; cake shop; dainty shop; *establishment;* French ~; German ~; *honey bun;* Italian ~; *jumbal; kolach;* local ~; market; *napoleon;* outlet; patisserie; pastry shoppe; *quick mart;* retail outlet; shoppe; torte shop; *unit; variety;* workshop; *xeo;* yeast cake; *zwieback;*

**balance** *(n. equilibrium)*: antithesis; balancing; counterpoise; counterweight; dynamic symmetry; equilibrium; equi~; fairness; geometric symmetry; homogeny; *identicalness;* justice; *knotted score;* levelness; micro~; manageability; non-difference; *offset;* poise; parity; *quits; remainder;* steadiness; symmetry; stability; tension; uniformity; vertigo; *weight; xy-balanced; yet alike; zero imbalance;*

**balance** *(n. scale)*: *apparatus;* bathroom scale; *contrivance;* digital scale; electronic scale; fish scale; *gadget; hydraulic ~; instrument;* just weights; kitchen ~; laboratory ~; *level;* medical scale; milligram ~; *net weight; object;* postal scale; *quantity;* retail ~; scale; two-pan ~; *tip;* union scale; vernier; weight; weighing scale; *xci,; yeme; zeug* [G.];

**balance** *(v.)*: adjust; attune; bring to equilibrium; compensate; counter~; *deal with;* even up; equilibrate; equalize; fix; get even; harmonize; *identicalness;* juggle; keep ~d; librate; level; match; manage; neutralize; offset; poise; *quicken;* readjust; regulate; stabilize; symmetrize; *tip the scales;* use ~; *vertigo;* weigh; *x-balance; yeme; zero drop;*

**balanced** *(adj.)*: alike; axisymmetic; balancing; commensurable; *duplicate;* even; equiponderant; equilibrated; fair; geometrically ~; harmonious; holohedral; isonomic; justified; kept in balance; *kilter;* level; matching; mirror-image; non-discriminatory; objective; omniparous; proportioned; quite ~; right-looking; symmetrical; *true;* uniform; unbiased; *very ~;* well- ~; *xy- ~; yet alike;* zygomorphic;

**balcony** *(n.)*: *area;* box; circle; choir loft; deck; *extension;* floor; fly gallery; gallery; hayloft; Italian ~; jube; king's loft; lanai; loft; loggia; mirador; mezzanine; *nook;* overhang; platform; quarter-gallery [naut.]; roodloft; skybox; terrace; top-loft; upper level; veranda; *walkway; xyst; yu [Chin.];* zayat;

**bald** *(adj.)*: acomous; balding; bare-headed; bald-headed; baldpate(d); clipped; depilous; defollicled; exfoliatory; forehead-bald; follicle-less [joc.]; glabrescent; glabrous; hairless; implumed; *jejune;* kerfed; lacking hair; *missing hair;* naked-headed; *off;* pieled; quite ~; receding; skinhead; shaved; shorn; smooth-headed; tonsured; thin (on top); unadorned; *void of hair;* without hair; *waxed; xyrao [Gr.]; yakiba [Jap.]; zero hair;* [Ant. bushy]

**baldness** *(n.)*: alopecia; baldheadedness; *combover;* depilousness; exfoliation; follicle-lessness [joc.]; glabrousness; hairlessness; implumation; *jejuneness;* kerfed look; loss of hair; *missing hair;* naked-headedness; *off;* pattern ~; *quite hairless;* receding hairline; smooth-headedness; thinness (of hair); unadornment; *void of hair;* want of hair; *xyrao [Gr.]; yakiba [Jap.];* zero hair; [Ant. bushiness]

**balk** *(v.)*: aback; avoid; blench; cringe; draw back; *edgy;* flinch; go back; hesitate; *involuntary;* jib; jump; kick; *lose courage;* move back in fear; *nervous;* ouch; *palter;* quail; recoil; shrink; tremble; *uneasy; vexed;* wince; withdraw; *xuld [arch.];* yerk; zip aback;

**ball** *(n.)*: annulus; *bezant;* circle; *disk; ellipse; felly;* globe; hand~; hard~; incirclet; *juggling ~; kinch; lacrosse ~;* micro-ball; marble; *non-square;* orb; *object; plaything; quasi-circular;* round thing; rubber ~; sphere; soft~; *tennis ~;* unicircular; vesica; wheel; *x-radius; y-radius; zone;* [see dance]
  Kinds of balls: basket~; base~; beach ~; cannon ~; eight ~; foot~; golf ~; hand- ~; juggling ~; king- ~; medicine ~; ogress; ping-pong ~; round shot; soft~; snow~; soccer ~; tennis ~; volley~; whiffle- ~; xare- ~;

**ballerina** *(n.)*: artist; ballet dancer; coryphée; dancer; *entertainer;* figurante; girl dancer; *her; individual; jane;* kicker girl; lead dancer; *morisk; nymph; orchel;* prima ~; performer; *quadrille; refined;* sujet; tutu girl; *uptown; valse;* woman dancer; *xaxado; yang-ko [Chin.]; zapateado;*

**ballpark** *(n.)*: arena; ball field; coliseum; dome; edifice; field house; grandstand; grounds; hippodrome; indoor ~; *judgment hall; kabuki* [Jap.]; lyceum; *multiplex; naumachy* [Rom.]; odeum; playing field; park; *querencia* [Sp.]; *range;* stadium; *theatre; upper circle;* venue; *wing; xenodocheum;* yard; *zone;*

**balm** *(n.)*: abirritant; balsam; cream; demulcent; embrocation; emollient; fomentation; gel; harquebusade; *item; jojoba; kamachili;* lotion; medication; *nard;* ointment; palliative; *quinine;* rub; salve; treatment; unguent; vulnerary; wash; xylobalsamum; *yellow ~;* zinc ointment;

**bam** *(n.)*: assault; bang; boom; clunk; crack; din; *explosion;* fragor; *get; hit; impact;* jolt; klop; knock; lam; mash; *nail;* oompf; pow; *quash;* rap; slam; thud; thwack; *undo; violence;* wham; *xuld [arch.];* yedder; zing;

**bamboozle** *(v.)*: *allure;* beguile; con; dupe; deceive; ensnare; fool; guile; hoodwink; insnare; jape; *kid;* lie to; mislead; nobble; outfox; pull the wool over one's eyes; *quiblin [arch.];* rook; sucker; trick; use; verneuk; wangle; *xuld [arch.];* yank one's chain; *zing;*

**ban** *(v.)*: *avert;* bar; curb; disallow; debar; estop; exclude; forbid; *gum up;* halt; inhibit; interdict; *jam;* keep out; *limit;* make illegal; nullify; outlaw; prohibit; proscribe; quash; restrain; stop; turn away; *upset;* veto; withhold; *x; yank;* zero;

**band** *(n. group)*: amassment; bunch; crowd; drove; *en masse;* faction; group; gang; horde; ingathering; jam [slang]; kit [coll.]; lot; mob; number; *ones;* party; pack; quantity; roundup; rabble; squad; turnout; unit; variety; wisp; *xtry. crowd; yardful; zillions;*

**band** *(v. music players)*: * *artists;* brass ~; concert ensemble; *duet;* ensemble; folk-music ~; group; *harmonizers;* instrumentalists; jug- ~; jazz- ~; *kapelle* [G.]; ligature; marching ~; musicians; *notes;* one-man ~; oom-pah ~; orchestra; performers; parquet; philharmonic; *quadrille;* rock ~; symphony; *trio;* unit; *violins;* wind ensemble; *xylophone;* yé-yé ~; *zouk;* [see choir]

**band** *(n. stripe)*: *aspect;* bar; belt; cingulum; *diagonal ~; edge;* fess; fascia; *gray-banded;* hairline; *impression; jet black ~; key marking;* line; marking; *narrow-banded;* one-inch ~; pinstripe; pale; *quillstroke;* row; ribbon; *ring;* stripe; streak; striation; *thin-striped; underline;* vitta; weal; wale; *wing bar* [zoo.]; *x'ed; yellow ~;* zona;

**bandage** *(n.)*: ∗ Ace® ~; binding; compress; dressing; *eye-patch;* finger ~; fascia; *first aid;* gauze; hand ~; *injury; junk;* knee- ~; leg ~; ligature; medicated compress; nose- ~; *over;* pledget; pad; patch; poultice; plaster; *quoil [arch.];* roller; swath; sear-cloth; tourniquet; *upbind; volar wrist splint;* wrapping; *xillinous; yedder; zinc hydroxide;*

**bandit** *(n.)*: armed man; brigand; *bandito* [Sp.]; crook; *delinquent; evildoer;* filcher; ganef; hood; intruder; *jailbird;* klepht; larcenist; mugger; nimmer; outlaw; pirate; *quad;* robber; stealer; thief; *unscrupulous;* villain; waddy; *xiaoren;* yegg; *zhlub;* [Ant. bobby]

**bandy** *(v.)*: air; bring up; cite; discuss; exchange; *foremention; give; have say; indicate; jaw; key in;* let out; mention; name; *overhear; point out;* quoth; remark; say; toss around; talk about; utter; voice; word; *xfer;* yak; *zero in;*

**bane** *(n.)*: annoyance; aggravation; bother; blight; curse; difficulty; displeasure; execration; *evil;* frustration; foulness; gadfly; grief; hardship; hex; irritation; jinx; *karakia* [Maori]; *loathsome;* menace; nuisance; *ordeal;* pest; *qualm* [arch.]; *ruination;* scourge; trouble; unrest; umbrage; vexation; woe; *x-ing;* yellow blight; *zauber* [G.]; [Ant. blessing]

**bang** *(n.)*: airburst; boom; burst; blow; blast; clatter; crash; crunch; din; detonation; eruption; explosion; fulmination; going off; hit; impact; jolt; knock; ka-pow; kaboom; *lam; mine; noise;* outburst; plunk; pop; pow; *quake;* rumble; reverberate; racket; roar; sound; shot; slam; smash; sonic boom; thump; thwack; thud; thunder; unleashing; vroom; whack; wallop; wham; *xuld* [arch.]; *yield;* zonk;

**banish** *(v.)*: alienate; boot; cast out; drive out; deport; expel; exile; expatriate; force out; get rid of; heave out; *impulse; jettison;* kick out; lock out; make leave; *non-residency;* oust; proscribe; *quant;* relegate; send away; throw out; *unhouse;* vomit out; *wale; xenelasy; ybanysshed* [arch.]; *zing;* [Ant. beckon]

**banishment** *(n.)*: alienation; booting; banishing; casting out; driving out; deportation; expulsion; exile; expatriation; forcing out; *getting rid of;* heaving out; *impulsion; jettison;* kicking out; locking out; making to leave; *non-retention;* ousting; proscription; quitture; relegation; sending away; throwing out; *unseating;* vomiting out; *walking papers;* xenelasy; *yanking; zero admittance;* [Ant. beckoning]

**bank** *(n.)*: ∗ accepting house; banking institution; credit union; central ~; commercial ~; depository; *economic institution; financial institution; government ~; home mortgage lender; international ~; institution; junior mortgage;* keep; land ~; lender; merchant ~; national ~; out-of-state ~; *private ~; piggy ~; questuary;* repository; savings ~; state ~; Swiss ~; trust company; U.S. ~; *vault;* World ~; *xaraf; yeme;* Zurich ~;

**banker** *(n.)*: *auditor;* bank employee; creditor; cambist; debtee; *economist;* funder; financier; *greenbacks;* home mortgage official; investor; junior loan officer; *keeper;* lender; loan officer; moneychanger; money-lender; mortgager; mortgage-holder; *number-cruncher;* officer; *payer;* questuary; representative; state bank employee; trust officer; usurer; *vice president; worker;* xaraf; *yeme;* Zurich ~;

**bankroll** *(v.)*: abet; back; capitalize; *disburse funds to; expend;* fund; finance; grubstake; help; habilitate; invest; *just-in-time;* keep; lend aid; maintain; *numbers; overpay;* pay for; patronize; *quick;* refinance; subsidize; support; *take on;* underwrite; *vest; well-supported; xfer; yield; zealously support;*

**bankrupt** *(adj.)*: absolutely penniless; broke; belly up; *closed;* destitute; defunct; economically failed; foreclosed; gone bust; *hard-luck;* insolvent; *jarring;* kaput; liquidated; moneyless; non-solvent; out-of-business; penniless; quisby; ruined; successless; *tragedy;* undone; *void;* washed-out; *x-ed out; yedder; zip;* [Ant. bountiful]

**bankruptcy** *(n.)*: *abatement;* bust; collapse; downfall; destitution; economic failure; foreclosure; folding; going broke; hang up one's hat; insolvency; *jarring defeat; knock-out;* liquidation; *moneyless;* non-solvency; *out-of-business;* pennilessness; poverty; *quit;* ruination; successlessness; *tragedy;* undoing; *void;* washout; *x-ing; yedder; zip;* [Ant. bountifulness]

**banner** *(n.)*: *arms;* banderole; colors; *designation;* ensign; flag; gonfalon; hanging; insignia; jack; King's colors; *labarum; mark;* national colors; *oriflamme [F.];* pennant; pennon; Queen's colors; *red, white, and blue [U.S.];* standard; streamer; *tricolor;* union jack; vexil; whip; *xeno-flag; yacht ensign; zeug;*

**banquet** *(n.)*: ambigu; *barbeque;* celebration; dinner; entertainment; *event;* feast; gala; grand ~; high tea [Br.]; ingesta; junket; kale-time; luncheon; meal; nourishment; *occasion;* provisions; *quelque-chose [F.];* reception; regale; supper; spread; table; *unassimilated food;* victuals; wassail; *xarque; yams; ziti;*

**banshee** *(n.)*: apparition; bodiless entity; cacodemon; disembodied spirit; entity; fetch; ghost; haunt; incorporiety; jumby; *kelpie;* lemures; materialization; nonmaterial being; oracle; phantom; *quickened spirit;* revenant; spirit; *taunter;* undead; visitant; wraith; *xenenthesis; yaksha* [Ind.]; zumby;

**banter** *(v.)*: *anecdote;* badinage; chaff; chitchat; *discussion;* exchange; *fun;* good fun; humoring; *insult;* jesting; joking; kidding; light teasing remarks; levity; making fun; *nifty; outjest;* playful talk; quipping; repartee; raillery; sport; teasing; *utter; vex;* wordplay; *xuld [arch.];* yocking; *zing;*

**baptism** *(n.)*: *adult ~;* baptismal; believer's ~; Christian ~; dipping; dunking; demersion; *engulfing;* full immersion; going under; *hidden;* immersion; *John's ~; keelhaul;* lowering; *mersion* [arch.]; 'neath; *ordinance;* plunge; *queven [arch.];* re~; submersion; total immersion; underwater dipping; *verging;* wetting; water ~; *xuld [arch.]; ybaptized [arch.]; zet [dial.];*

**Baptist** *(n.)*: Ana- ~; Albigensian; Bible-believer; Biblicist; ~ Brider; *Christian;* Donatist; Dunkard [G.]; *evangelized;* Fundamental ~; GARB ~; Hutterite; Independent ~; Immersionist; *Jehovist;* Knipperdolling; Landmark ~; Missionary ~; Northern ~; Old Paths ~; Paulician; Petrobrussian; *quickened;* Regular ~; Southern ~; separatist; *tunkers;* ultra-independant ~; *vehement Bible-lover;* Waldensian; Xn.; *Yahwist;* Zwickau prophet [G.];

**baptistry** *(n.)*: *aquatic tank;* baptismal tank; baptistery; *cistern;* dunk-tank; enclosed ~; fiberglas ~; glass-front ~; heated ~; indoor pool; *jacuzzi; kier;* lake; *mersion [arch.];* nap; open ~; press; pot; *quarter-tank;* receptacle; steeper; tank; *underwater; vat;* water tank; *xfer; yield; zun;*

**baptize** *(v.)*: *absorb;* bury; cover; dip; dunk; engulf; fully immerse; go under; *hide;* immerse; *jawp; keelhaul;* lower; merge; 'neath; overwhelm; plunge; put under; plant; *queven* [arch.]; re~; submerge; *totally under;* under (the water); verge; whelm; *wet;* water- ~; *xuld [arch.]: ybaptized [arch.]; zet [dial.];*

**bar** *(n. rod)*: aluminum ~; block; barrier; caber; dowel; el- ~; *furule;* gooseneck ~; *gold ~;* hunk; handspike; ingot; iron ~; jackstay; kilhig; length; metal ~; *narrow band; object;* piece; pole; *quarter-post;* rod; shaft; stick; stave; *tack claw;* upright; virgulate; wedge; x- ~; *yedder; zygon;*

**bar** *(n. tavern)*: ale-house; beer joint; barroom; cabaret; cantina; drinking-house; establishment; fern ~; groghouse; hostelry; inn; joint; kiddleywink; lounge; mughouse; night-house; *open ~;* pub; *queme house;* roadhouse; rathskeller; speakeasy; saloon; taphouse; tavern; *utility ~; vinery;* wine ~; *xenodocheum;* youth club; *zubrowka;*

**bar** *(v.)*: *avert;* ban; curb; debar; exclude; forbid; *gum up;* hinder; impede; inhibit; interdict; *jam;* keep out; lock out; *moderate;* nullify; obstruct; preclude; prohibit; quash; restrict; stop; turn away; *undo;* veto; withhold; *x; yank; zap;*

**barb** *(n.)*: acicula; brier; burr; cusp; denticle; *edge;* fleam; fluke; *graver;* hairpin; *incisor;* jag; *keen edge; lancet;* mucro; needle; *object;* prick(er); prickle; point; quadrille; quill; razor; sticker; spike; thistle; tip; thorn; tooth; tine; *unthreaded ~; venus' comb; wimble;* xyston; yucca; *zinger;*

**barbaric** *(adj.)*: atrocious; barbarous; bellicose; brutal; crude; cruel; devilish; *evil;* feral; fierce; ferocious; godless; heathen; ill-mannered; jungli; *kaf* [arch.]; *lewd;* mean; nasty; odious; pagan; *querulous;* rude; rapacious; savage; terrible; uncivilized; uncouth; vulgar; vicious; warlike; wild; *xenophobic; yefell [arch.]; zero-mercy;*

**barbarity** *(n.)*: atrociousness; barbarism; brutality; cruelty; despicableness; evil; foulness; godlessness; harshness; incivility; ignominy; *jangliness;* kindlessness; licentiousness; meanness; nastiness; odiousness; pitilessness; querulousness; rudeness; ruthlessness; savageness; savagism; terribleness; unkindness; viciousness; wickedness; *xenophobia;* yuckiness; *zhlubbiness;*
**barbecue** *(n.)*: *athanor;* barbeque; charbroiler; *device;* electric grill; freestanding grill; (gas) grill; *hotdog cooker; item; jet;* kerosene stove; *light; mesquite; neal [arch.];* outdoor grill; *pit;* propane grill; *qualm [arch.]; range;* stove; tripod grill; uniform-heat stove; *vulcan; weenie; xeo; yellow-hot; zap;*
**barbecue** *(v.)*: *anneal;* barbeque; broil; charbroil; decrepitate; *evenly cook;* flame(-broil); griddle; grill; heat; *incinerate; jet; kiln-bake; light;* make; *neal [arch.];* overcook; put on the grill; *prepare; qualm* [arch.]; roast; sear; toast; *undercook; very hot;* whip up; *xeo;* yark; *zoutch;*
**barber** *(n.)*: *artiste;* beautician; coiffeur; dresser; *expert;* friseur; gentleman's hairdresser; haircutter; *individual; job; kudumi;* licensed ~; men's hair stylist; nonprofessional ~; *owner/operator;* poller; professional ~; *quaifer* [arch.]; razor cutter; stylist; trimmer; unlicensed ~; *varlet; worker; xerasia; yield; zakai [Jap.];*
**bare** *(adj. empty)*: airy; blank; clear; desolate; devoid; empty; evacuated; fistular; futile; forlorn; gant; hollow; inane; jejune; *kaput;* load-less; meaningless; nothing; non-filled; out; *plucked;* quaffed; *reduced;* stark; tapped out; unoccupied; void; wiped out; "x"; *yielded;* zero; [*Ant.* bountiful]
**bare** *(v.)*: appear; bring out; *carry;* display; expose; exhibit; flash; flaunt; give; hold out; illustrate; *jut;* kithe [Scot.]; lay out; manifest; make visible; *non-concealment;* open up; present; *qualify;* reveal; show; take out; unveil; uncover; wear; vaunt; *wave; x-ray;* yomp; zip out;
**barefoot** *(adj.)*: *arches;* barefooted; *bootless; clog-less;* discalced; excalceated; foot-bare; going without shoes; hillbilly-style; in bare feet; *just feet; keep one's shoes off; loaferless;* minus the shoes; naked-footed; *open-toed; ped;* quite unshod; redshank [contempt]; shoeless; sockless; toe-bare; unshod; unsandaled; void of footwear; without socks and shoes; *x-out;* yet unshod; *zero shoes;*
**barely** *(adv.)*: almost not; *but; cannot; close;* dearly exception; few; gauntly; hardly; infrequently; just; jumply; jejunely; *keenly scarce;* leanly; meagerly; narrowly; obscurely; paltrily; *quasi;* rarely; scarcely; sparsely; seldom; tenuously; uncommonly; very seldom; *wheenly* [arch.]; *xtry.;* yet uncommonly; *zero;*
**bareness** *(n.)*: *the* altogether; *the* buff; barrenness; clotheslessness; disrobement; dishabille; exposure; flaunting; garblessness; *heedlessness;* immodesty; indecency; *jadedness; kinkiness;* lewdness; *manifestation;* nakedness; *obscenity;* peeling; *quad; the* raw; shame(lessness); *tout ensemble* [F.]; undress; unadornment; *vileness;* without clothes; x-rated; yuckiness; zero clothes;
**bargain** *(n.)*: absolute steal [slang]; big deal; cost-saving venture; deal; discount; extraordinary savings; fantastic price; good deal (-buy); huge savings; *half-off;* incredible savings; *jumbo sale; keen deal;* low price; money's worth; *no-brainer; on sale;* pennyworth; *quarter-priced; reduced;* steal [slang]; *sale; savings;* terrific buy; unbelievable deal; very good price; wonderful ~; *xtry. buy;* yard sale ~; *0% interest;*
**bargain** *(v.)*: argue; bicker; cavil; contend; deal; dispute; *equivocate;* fuss; gainsay; haggle; *inharmonious;* jangle; kick up dust; lock horns; make a problem; negotiate; *object;* palter; quibble; *resist;* squabble; trifle; *unharmonious;* vie; wrangle; *x-purposes;* yell; *zap;*
**barge** *(n.)*: ark; boat; bulk carrier; craft; cargo boat; Dutch ~; *export;* freight boat; galleyfoist; hulk; hopper ~; *import;* junk ~; *keelboat;* lighter; lake freighter; *mover; naval boat;* open ~; pontoon; *q-ship;* river freighter; self-propelled ~; transport; *ultralarge crude carrier;* vessel; watercraft; *xfer;* yacht; *zabra;*
**barge** *(v.)*: *attack;* butt; cut in; drive; elbow; force; *go;* heave; interrupt; jolt; knock; *lash out;* muscle in; nudge; ooch; push; quant; rush; shove; thrust; *upthrust; violence;* walk (in); *xowyn* [arch.]; yerk; zonk;
**barn** *(n.)*: *area;* byre; cowshed; cow~; dairy ~; *edifice;* fruitloft; *farm;* granary; henhouse; hayloft; *inhabitance;* jacal; kipsie [Aus.]; loft; milking ~; *nitch;* outbuilding; place; *quinta;* red ~; *receptacle;* stable; *silo;* storage ~; *two-story ~;* utility building; vaccary; woodshed; x-house; *yakutat hut; zayat;*

**barnyard** *(n.)*: *area;* barn yard; croft; *dairy farm;* enclosure; farmyard; *greens-stall;* haw; inclosure; *jail;* kraal [S. Afr.]; *list;* mew; *narrow; outside;* pen; paddock; quad; *run; stockyard;* tigh [dial.]; *utility pen; vollery;* wynd [dial.]; *xystus;* yard; *zariba;*

**baron** *(n.)*: aristocrat; baronet; boyar; count; duke; earl; feudal superior; grand duke; graf [G.]; hidalgo [Sp.]; *industrialist;* Junker; knight; landowner; landgrave; lord; marquis; *mogul;* noble(man); optimate; patrician; *queen; ruler; sir;* thane; *tycoon; upper crust;* viscount; waldgrave; *xtry. person;* younker; *zayim;*

**baroness** *(n.)*: aristocrat; baron's wife; countess; duchess; dame; *earl [masc.]; feudal lady;* grand duchess; *heiress; important lady; jarl [masc.]; khanum* [Ind.]; lady; marquise; noblewoman; optimate; patrician; *queen; ruling class; silk-stocking;* titled woman; *upper crust;* viscountess; woman of breeding; *xtry; woman; younker; zayim;*

**barracks** *(n.)*: abode; billet; cantonment; casern; dwelling (place); edifice; field quarters; garrison; hut; inhabitance; *jacal; ken;* living quarters; military housing; Nissen hut; outbuilding; place; quarters; Quonset hut; residence; structure; shack; tent; *utility apartment;* villa; *wicker hut;* x-house; *yakutat hut; zwinger;*

**barrage** *(v.)*: assault; bombardment; connonade; discharge; enfilade; expulsion; foray; *get;* hit; *invasion; jolt; kesting;* lobbing; mortaring; nonstop ~; onslaught; pommel; *quash;* raid; shower; salvo; torrent; *unleashing;* volley; wale; *x-fire; yed; zero hour;*

**barrel** *(n.)*: *aluminum keg;* butt; cask; cylinder; drum; *earthenware pot;* firkin; *gas can;* hogshead; *insulated container;* jar; keg; *locker; milk can; noggin;* oil drum; puncheon; quinderkyn; runlet; *shipping container;* tun; tierce; ungula; vessel; wine-cask; x-barrel; *yabba; zun;*

**barren** *(adj.)*: addle; bleak; childless; desolate; destitute; devoid; empty; effete; forlorn; fallow; fruitless; *grassless;* heirless; infertile; infecund; jejune; *kept from bearing;* lacking; meager; non-bearing; *nullipara;* olated; paltry; *quenchless;* resourceless; *reedless;* sterile; teemless; treeless; unfruitful; uninhabited; uninhabitable; unproductive; unverdant; verdureless; void of children; wanting; *woodless;* xerarchic; yeld; yieldless; *zero fruit;* [*see* dry, *Ant.* bountiful]

**barrenness** *(n.)*: addling; bareness; childlessness; desolation; emptiness; fallowness; fruitlessness; *grasslessness;* heirlessness; infertility; infertileness; infecundity; jejuneness; *kept from bearing;* lack of bearing; meagerness; non-fruitfulness; olation; paltriness; *quenchlessness;* resourcelessness; sterility; teemlessness; unfruitfulness; void; want of children; *xerarchic;* yieldlessness; zero fruit; [*Ant.* bounty]

**barricade** *(n.)*: abatis; barrier; battlement; cordon; countervallation; defense; earthwork; embankment; fortification; gabion; hedge; immure; *junkpile;* kraal; *line;* mudwall; *non-admittance;* obstruction; perpend; *quickset hedge;* roadblock; rampart; revetment; separator; *traverse; utility wall;* vallation; wall; weir; *x-fence; yard wall; zero admittance;*

**barrier** *(n.)*: *area fence;* blockade; brick wall; countervallation; divider; difficulty; encumbrance; fence; gully; hindrance; hurdle; impediment; impasse; *jailhouse wall;* kraal; line; limit; *moat; no entry;* obstruction; pale; palisade; *quickset hedge;* rampart; roadblock; stone-wall; *trench; utility fence;* vallation; wall; *x-fence; yard fence; zigzag fence;* [*see* blockage]

**bartender** *(n.)*: alehouse-keeper; alewife [fem.]; barkeep(er); barman; barmaid [fem.]; counterman; drink mixer; *employee;* flairbrasil; ganneker; hosteller; *innkeeper; jigger man;* kaniker; liquor-man; mixer; *neif;* owner; publican: *quinta;* rummy; skinker; sommelier; tapster; *underservant;* vintner; wine steward; *xeres; yarke server; zymologist;*

**barter** *(v.)*: *alternate;* bargain; change; countertrade; deal; exchange; *for;* give in exchange; haggle; interchange; *jockey; key trade;* let one have for; make trade; *negotiate; overtrade;* permute; *quick-change;* replace; swap; trade; upgrade; *vamp; wissel* [arch.]; xfer; *yaw; zwap* [dial.];

**base** *(adj.)*: appalling; abominable; brutish; boorish; beastly; crude; coarse; crass; detestable; despicable; degenerate; disgusting; evil; filthy; foul; gauche; graceless; horrible; horrid; indecent; ill-mannered; jadish; knavish; lewd; low; licentious; loutish; mean; nasty; nauseating; obnoxious; offensive; perverted; pathetic; *questionable;* raw; rude; rough; sinful; shameful; terrible; tasteless; tactless; uncouth; unclean; unrefined; vile; vulgar; wretched; wicked; *x-rated;* yucky; zhlubby;
**base** *(n. fortress)*: army ~; bastion; center; citadel; donjon; *enclosure;* fortress; garrison; hub; headquarters; installation; *joint command headquarters;* keep; *laager;* muniment; military ~; naval ~; outpost; propugnacle; *quarters;* redoubt; stronghold; tower; unit headquarters; vault; watchtower; *x-house; yamen* [Chin.]; zwinger;
**base** *(n. foundation)*: aft; bottom; butt; basis; cornerstone; dado; end; foundation; floor; foot(ing); ground; hinder part; *infrastructure; jacksy;* keystone; low(est) point; *minimum;* nether side; origin; plinth; platform; premise; quadra; quoin; rock-bottom; root; sub~; socle; sole; surface; source; *terra firma* [L.]; underside; underlying foundation; *valley; way down;* xenolith; *yoni* [Skr.]; zaccho;
**baseless** *(adj.)*: absurd; beyond reason; causeless; dumb; erroneous; fallacious; groundless; *hollow;* idiopathic; just for no reason; *kim-kam;* lacking basis; misconceived; not justified; off base; poor; questionable; reasonless; random; silly; *tenuous;* uncaused; unfounded; unwarranted; unjustified; *vague;* without cause; *x-out; yawed; zero-justification;*
**basement** *(n.)*: ale cellar; bunker; cellar; downstairs; *equipment storage;* finished ~; *garage;* half-dugout; hypogeum; *ice house; jaw-hole;* keller; look-out ~; mattamore; non-finished ~; *over-filled ~;* partially-finished ~; *quarters; recreation room;* subcellar; storm shelter; *TV room;* undercroft; unfinished ~; vault; wine-cellar; walk-up ~; *xystum; you* [Chin.]; zone;
**baseness** *(n.)*: abjection; brutishness; crudeness; degradation; depravity; evil; filthiness; grossness; horridness; ignobleness; indecency; *jadishness;* knavery; lowness; meanness; nastiness; offensiveness; perversion; perfidiousness; *questionability;* rudeness; rawness; sinfulness; terribleness; uncouthness; vileness; wretchedness; *x-rating;* yuckiness; zhlubbiness;
**bash** *(v.)*: assault; beat; bang; c(l)onk; crush; dash; dent; *elbow;* flail; grind; hit; impact; jab; jam; knock; kick; levigate; mash; *nullify; overcome;* punch; quash; rap; smite; smash; thump; uppercut; veney; whack; wallop; *x;* yerk; zonk;
**bashful** *(adj.)*: apprehensive; blushful; coy; diffident; embarrassed; fearful; gentle; hesitant; introverted; insecure; jackalent; keenly shy; lily-livered; modest; mortified; nervous; over-modest; petrified; qualmish; quiet; reserved; shy; sheepish; shamefaced; timid; unpretentious; verecund; withdrawn; *xenophobic;* yarrow; *zealless;* [*Ant.* bold]
**bashfulness** *(n.)*: apprehension; blushing; coyness; diffidence; embarrassment; fearfulness; gentleness; hesitancy; introversion; insecurity; *jitteriness;* kitten-heartedness; lily-liveredness; modesty; mortification; nervousness; over-modesty; petrification; quietness; reservedness; shyness; shamefacedness; timidity; unsureness; verecundity; withdrawal; *xenophobia;* yarowness; *zeallessness;* [*Ant.* boldness]
**basic** *(adj.)*: average; basal; bare-bones; critical; *deep-seated; daily;* entry-level; essential; familiar; generic; ho-hum; indispensable; *just regular;* key; *lackluster;* main; necessary; normal; ordinary; plain; principle; quotidian; regular; run-of-the-mill; rudimentary; simple; straightforward; typical; unsophisticated; uncomplicated; vanilla; vital; *wonted; x-type; yawnish; zestless;*
**bask** *(v.)*: apricate; *benefit from;* cherish; delight in; enjoy; fancy; glory; have delight; indulge; joy; *keen on;* lounge; laze; *make one happy; nice; own;* please one; *queme;* relax; relish; revel; soak up; savor; take pleasure in; *uplift; value;* wallow; *xtry.; yearn for; zestful;*
**basket** *(n.)*: alms- ~; bushel; corb; creel; *container;* dosser; egg ~; fruit ~; frail; flasket; gabion; hand~; holder; hask; *inclosure;* junket; kipe; kit; laundry ~; maund; nacelle; osier ~; pannier; *quiver; receptacle;* rush- ~; scuttle; *tumbril; ungula;* voider; wisket; x-weave ~; *yadzutsu* [Jap.]; zipper ~;

**bastard** *(n.)*: adultery's child; bantling; child of whoredom; daughter of whoredom [fem.]; *excluded son;* foul-gotten child; *guy;* horeson; illegitimate child; *junior; kid;* love child; misbegotten child; not rightful heir; *odure;* putain; queanling; *rig's son;* son of whoredom [masc.]; trollop's son; unclean child; *venal child;* whoreson; *x-rated;* yaud; *zero inheritance;*
**bastion** *(n.)*: acropolis; bulwark; bastille; citadel; defense; *enclosure;* fort(ification); fortress; garrison; hold; *imperial palace; jong* [Tib.]; keep; *lasting;* mainstay; nest; outpost; propugnacle; *quarters;* refuge; rock; stronghold; tower; *unbeatable;* vault; watchtower; *x-house;* yamen [Chin.]; zwinger;
**bat** *(n. club)*: alpenstock; bludgeon; billy club; club; cudgel; dagger-staff; espantoon; fungo ~; godendag; hurl- ~; *instrument;* jitte; knobkerrie; lathi; mace; nightstick; *officer's staff;* partisan; quarterstaff; rod; stick; truncheon; ununke [Afr.]; *verge;* war club; waddy; *xylon;* yam stick; zagaye;
**batch** *(n.)*: assemblage; bunch; collection; drove; *extra;* forgathering; group; heap; ingathering; jam [slang]; kit [coll.]; lot; mass; number; *overflow;* pack; pile; quantity; *ruck;* set; tally; *ton;* unit; variety; wisp; *xuld [arch.];* yelm [straw]; *zillion;*
**bath** *(n.)*: ablution; bubble ~; bathing; cleaning; cleansing; dip; expugation; flush; *get clean;* head- ~; immersion; Japanese ~; knee-bath; lavation; *milk ~;* natation; *over-clean; purification;* plunge ~; quick ~; rinsing; sponge ~; shower; spa; tub- ~; unsullying; *vat;* wash(tub); *xylol; yellow soap; zierlich* [G.];
**bathe** *(v.)*: *ablution;* bath; clean(se); dip; expurgate; foment; get clean; hose (off; down); imbathe; *jawp; kill germs;* lave; make oneself clean; *non-sullied; over-clean;* purify; *quite clean;* rinse; soak; shower; *scrub;* take a bath; tub; unsully; *verge;* wash; *xuld [arch.]; ybaptized [arch.];* zet *[dial.];* [Ant. bemire]
**bathroom** *(n.)*: amenities; *baño* [Sp.]; boy's room [masc.]; commode; duck [slang]; earth closet; facilities; garderobe; girl's room [fem.]; head [naut.]; *indoor plumbing;* john; karzy; lavatory; ladies' room [fem.]; loo [Br.]; men's room [masc.]; *night-chair;* outhouse; potty; powder room; *quarters;* restroom; services; toilet; urinal [masc.]; *vanity;* washroom; water closet; woman's room [fem.]; xysma; yu [Chin.]; zone;
**baton** *(n.)*: alpenstock; billy club; battoon; caduceus; *dagger-staff; emblem;* ferule; *godendag;* handstaff; *instrument;* jambee; kecky; langet; *mantle;* night stick; *officer's staff;* pointer; *quarterstaff;* rod; (swagger) stick; truncheon; ununke [Afr.]; verge; wand; *xylon;* yard [arch.]; zagaye; [*see* responsibility]
**battalion** *(n.)*: army; band; brigade; company; detachment; division; *encampment;* force; group; host; infantry; junior service [Br.]; *kerns;* legion; militia; *nonconscripted army;* outfit; platoon; quantity; regiment; squad; troops; unit; vanguard; warriors; x-force; *yeald;* zouave;
**batter** *(v.)*: assault; beat; bruise; clobber; drub; *efface;* flail; *get;* hit; *impact;* jab; knock; lam; maul; nubble; *overhit;* pelt; pound; punch; quab; rap; smite; strike; thrash; uppercut; veney; whack; welt; work over; *x-sect;* yedder; zonk;
**battle** *(n.)*: attack; armed conflict; bout; brawl; *Blitzkrieg* [G.]; confrontation; conflict; clash; combat; campaign; crusade; dispute; encounter; embroilment; fight; fray; *gunnery;* hostilities; hand-to-hand combat; irregular warfare; *imbroglio;* jihad [Mos.]; *kampf* [G.]; *luctation* [arch.]; mêlée; naval warfare; occursion; onslaught; pitched ~; quarrel; run-in; squabble; scuffle; skirmish; struggle; tussle; unrest; vying; war(fare); *x-fire;* yed; *zapping;*
**battle** *(v.)*: altercate; attack; brawl; contend; clash; dispute; duke it out [slang]; engage; fight; feud; grapple; *have fight with; invade;* jangle; kemp; *levy war;* make war with; *naysay;* oppose; oppugn; pick fight; quarrel; resist; struggle; scuffle; strike; strive; tangle; *unharmonious;* vie; wrangle; (wage) war; *x-purposes;* yain [arch.]; *zap;*
**battlefield** *(n.)*: arena; battleground; battlefront; combat zone; disputed area; *enemy lines; fox hole;* firing line; front (lines); field of honor; ground; *hill; hellhole; invaded territory; jousting arena;* knoll; *line;* mine field; *non-safe zone; operation;* place of battle; *quadrant;* region; salient; trenches; theater; *upland; vicinity;* war zone; *xy-coordinate;* yard; zone of conflict;

**battlement** *(n.)*: *area wall;* barricade; bulwark; countervallation; defense; embankment; earthwork; fortification; glacis; hedge; immure; *jardang; knoll;* line; muniment; *non-endangered;* obstruction; perpend; parapet; *quai;* rampart; revetment; stone wall; terraplein; *utility wall;* vallation; wall; *x-fence; yard wall; zariba;*
**bawd** *(n.)*: agent; bordel; brothel-house madam; conciliatrix; *doxy;* escort service; fleshmonger; gigolo [masc.]; *hireling; innkeeper; jade;* keeper of brothel; lady-pander; madam; negotiator; procuress; purveyor; pimp [masc.]; *quean-procurer;* runner; strumpet-provider; truller; *unprincipled; venal;* wench-provider; *x-rated;* yaud-girl; *zipless;*
**bawl** *(v.)*: *appeal;* blubber; cry; despair; erupt into tears; *fret;* grieve; howl; *inveigh; judder;* keen; lachrymate; lament; mewl; moan; *noise;* outcry; outweep; pout; *quistle [arch.];* roar; sob; snivel; shed tears; squall; tear; *ululate; vociferate;* whimper; whine; weep; wail; *xenophthalmia;* yawp; yowl; *zowie;* [Ant. beam]
**bay** *(n.)*: arm(let); bosporus; bight; cove; *deep;* embayment; fjord; gulf; harbor; inlet; *jheel [Ind.];* kyle [Scot.]; lagoon; mouth; narrows; opening; *port;* quai; recess; sound; *tarn; underground pool;* voe; *water; xyrisic; yeo; Zee [G.];* [see; lake; river]
**bazaar** *(n.)*: auction; boutique; *convenience store;* depot; exchange; emporium; fish (-flea) market; galleria; *haggle; industry; jumble-shop; key store; location;* market(place); *newsstand;* open air market; plaza; *quick mart; resellers;* street market; shambles; souk; trading post; *unit;* variety store; warehouse; *xfer; yard sale; zoco* [Arab.];
**beach** *(adj.)*: *aquatic;* beachfront; coastal; coastline; *dockside; estuary; frontal; gulf front;* hinterland; *inlet; jetty side; key side;* lakeshore; mudflat; near-shore; nip; oceanfront; oceanside; public ~; plage; *quost [L.];* riviera; shore; seaside; seacoast; *tidal; unhindered view; voe;* waterfront; *xyrisic; yeo; Zee [G.];*
**beach** *(n.)*: *area;* bank; beachfront; coastline; *dockside;* edge; *front;* gulf front; hinterland; inception; *jetty; keys;* lido; lakeshore; leeshore; mudflat; nearshore ~; oceanside; *periphery; quost* [arch.]; riviera; sands; shore(line); seaside; seashore; seacoast; seaboard; threshold; ulterior; verge; waterline; waterfront; *x-border; yonder; zone;*
**beachhead** *(n.)*: advance; bridgehead; captured shoreline; *development;* established hold; foothold; *grip;* hold; headway; initial success; jump-off point; *kept position;* lodgement; *movement; non-vulnerable;* outguard; position; *quantum leap; railhead;* spearhead; toehold; *unit;* vantage point; *work; xy-coordinate; yain [arch.];* zone of occupation;
**bead** *(n.)*: * abacus ~; bone ~; bodom; cloisonné ~; dichronic ~; ethnic ~; faux natural ~; glass ~; hair pipe ~; ivory ~; Job's tears; *jewelry;* kaolin ~; love ~; millefiori ~; necklace ~; ornament; plastic ~; prayer ~; quahog ~; rosary ~; stone ~; trinket; ultraviolet-sensitive ~; vintage ~; wampum; xtal ~; yellow ~; zircon ~;
**beak** *(n.)*: * aerial fishing ~; bill; culmen; dip-netting ~; *entrance;* fruit-eating ~; grain-eating ~; *hole;* insect-catching ~; *jaws;* knobbed bill; lancing ~; mouth; nib; *orifice;* pecker; *quadrate;* rostrum; scything ~; trap; *unopened ~; voice;* woodpecker ~; *xerochilia;* yap; *zosterops;*
**beam** *(n. light ray)*: *aura;* beacon; candescence; *dazzle;* emission; flow; flood; gleam; *headlight;* issuance; *jet; kilowatt;* leam [Br.]; light ~; *moon~; nimbus;* output; *patch;* quiver; ray; signal; stream; sun~; twinkle; *ultraviolet ray; violet ray;* wave; *x-ray; yellow ray; zap;*
**beam** *(n. rafter)*: *axle;* board; brace; cross~; deal; *elm;* four by four; girder; hardboard; *ironwood ~;* joist; knee-timber; lumber; lath; *maple ~; nemoral;* one-by-four; plank; quarter-cleft; rafter; stud; strut; support ~; timber; two-by-four; underlayment; veneer; wood; *xylon; yew; zingara;*
**beam** *(v.)*: *aura;* brighten; coruscate; dazzle; effluge; emit; flash; gleam; glisten; glow; give off; *halo;* irradiate; *jet;* kindle; light; luster; make light; *nitency;* outshine; *polish;* quiver; radiate; shed; shine; twinkle; throw off; transmit; *ultraviolet light; vividness; waver;* xmit; yield light; *zap;*

**bean** *(n.)*: * azuki ~; brown ~; *chickpea; detarium senegalense; edible;* French ~; green ~; *haricot* [F.]; *inga edulis* [L.]; jumping ~; jack ~; kidney ~; legume; lima ~; lentil; Mexican jumping ~; navy ~; *orphanodenron bernalii* [L.]; pulse; *quesadilla;* runner ~; string ~; tepary ~; *urad; vetch;* wax ~; xylia; yam ~; *zakuski [Rus.];*

**bear** *(n. forest animal)*: * *animal;* black ~; cub; *den-dweller;* European brown ~; Floridian ~; grizzly ~; Himalayan brown ~; *ichtyophagous;* jungle- ~; Kodiak; *koala (~); lesser panda; mammal;* Manchurian ~; Newfoundland ~; *omnivore; panda (~);* polar ~; *quadruped; red panda;* sun ~; she- ~; *teddy ~;* ursus; *varmint; wildlife;* white ~; *x-breed;* yakutat ~; *zoic;*

**bear** *(v. carry)*: abide; accept; bring; bide; carry; cadge; convey; countenance; deliver; endure; forbear; get; have; haul; *indulge;* janker; keep; lug; live with; move; *nest; overcarry;* put up with; *quarter-cart;* relay; suffer; stand; stomach; shoulder; take; tolerate; transport; uphold; undergo; van; wear; xfer; yomp; *zip;*

**bear** *(v. give birth)*: animate; birth; cast; calve [zoo.]; deliver; drop [slang]; ean [arch.]; found; foal [zoo.]; give birth; generate; have; hatch [zoo.]; *initiate; jump-start;* kid; kindle [both zoo.]; *labor;* mother; *nativity; out;* produce; propagate; *quicken; raise up; spring;* throw [zoo.]; usher into the world; vivify; whelp [zoo.]; *xenogenesis;* yean; yield; *zygogenesis;* [see beget]

**bearable** *(adj.)*: acceptable; *bear; co-existing;* decent; endurable; *forbear;* fine; good; *humor; indulge;* jake [Br.]; *kosher;* livable; minimal; manageable; not bad; okay; passable; *quantum sufficit* [L.]; reasonable; sufferable; so-so; tolerable; up to standard; veritable; welcome; warrantable; well; *xenial; yenough* [arch.]; *zero opposition;*

**beard** *(n.)*: * *awn;* bushy ~; balbo; chin-hairs; donegal; extended goatee; facial hair; fuzz; fluff; five o'clock shadow; goatee; hair; *item;* junco; kesh; *long ~;* mane; neard; *orange-bearded;* parted ~; *quiff;* royale; stubble; tuft; unshaven; unrazored; vandyke; whiskers; *xerasia; yellow ~;* ziff;

**bearded** *(adj.)*: awned; bewhiskered; barbate; chin-haired; downy-chinned; *extended goatee;* furry-chinned; goateed; hairy-chinned; *in need of a shave;* jubate; kesh-sporting; lanate; maned; *non-shaven; orange-bearded;* pappose; *quiff;* red- ~; shaggy- ~; stubbly; tufted; unshaven; villous; whiskered; whiskery; *white ~; xerasia; yellow- ~; ziff;* [Ant. beardless]

**beardless** *(adj.)*: awnless; bare-faced; clean-shaven; *docked; exscinded; furrless;* glabrous; having no beard; *incised; jejune; kiddish;* lacking a beard; *mown;* non-bearded; *open-chinned; puerile;* quite ~; razored; shaven; shorn; smooth-faced; *trimmed;* unbearded; *void;* well-shaven; whiskerless; *xyrao [Gr.]; young-looking;* ziff-less; [Ant. bearded]

**beast** *(n.)*: animal; brute; creature; cattle [pl.]; domestic animal; *elk;* fauna [pl.]; game; hellcat; *insectivore;* jument; *koala;* livestock; *mammal;* man-eater; monster; *non-vertebrate;* organism; *pony;* quadruped; *reptile;* stock; *tiger;* ungulate; varmint; wild ~; work animal; *xolotl; yearling;* zoic;

**beastly** *(adj.)*: animalistic; brutish; bestial; beastlike; crude; dreadful; *evil;* freal; ferocious; gluttonous; gruff; hoggish; ill-mannered; junglish; *kaf [arch.]; lionlike;* mean; mammalian; nasty; obnoxious; piggish; *quad;* rude; rapacious; savage; terrible; uncouth; uncivilized; vicious; voracious; wild; *xolotl;* yahoo; zoonic;

**beat** *(v. strike)*: attack; bash; bang; batter; buffet; clobber; clock; conk; cudgel; drub; deck; *efface;* flail; flog; *get;* hit; *impact;* jab; knock; larrup; maul; mash; nubble; nail; *overhit;* pound; punch; pelt; quab; rap; sock; strike; smite; swinge; thump; thwack; thrash; uppercut; veney; whack; wallop; *x-sect;* yedder; zonk;

**beat** *(v. triumph over)*: annihilate; best; conquer; defeat; expugn; foil; *gut;* halt; *impede; junk* [slang]; knock out; kill; lick; master; *neutralize;* overcome; prevail; quash; rout; subjugate; trounce; unseat; vanquish; worst; whip; win; *x-ing; yank down;* zap;

**beatitude** *(n.)*: attitude of blessing; blessedness; bliss; consecration; declaration of blessedness; *ethereal blessings;* felicity; *gift;* happiness; *impeccability;* joy to the full; *kindness; liberality;* munificence of God; *narrow way; outstanding character;* path to blessing; *quality; righteous way;* sublimity; true blessings; *uprightness;* virtues that produce blessing; way of blessing; *xtry.;* yield; *Zion's favor;*

**beautiful** *(adj.)*: attractive; aesthetic; beauteous; comely; charming; dainty; desirable; elegant; eye-catching; fair; good-looking; gorgeous; handsome; *irresistible; jolie* [F.]; killing [slang]; lovely; magnificent; nice-looking; *ornate; outstanding;* picturesque; pleasing; pretty; pulchritudinous; quite ~; ravishing; striking; sublime; terrific-looking; *unsurpassed;* voluptuous; well-favored (-looking); *xtry.;* you-beaut [Aus.]; zizzy; [Ant. bad-looking]

**beautify** *(v.)*: adorn; aestheticize; bedeck; brighten; clothe; decorate; deck (out); dress up; dazzle up; embellish; fancify; glamorize; habilitate; improve; jazz up; jewel; kit; *let be adorned;* make prettier; *nicer;* ornament; prank; prettify; pretty up; *quaintise* [arch.]; render lovely; spruce up; trim; *use ornaments;* vest; *wear; xtry.;* yclad [arch.]; zizz; [Ant. bemangle]

**beauty** *(n. attractiveness)*: attractiveness; allure; beauteousness; comeliness; charm; desirableness; elegance; fairness; goodliness; good looks; glamour; gorgeousness; grandeur; grace; handsomeness; *irresistibility; jolie [F.];* keenness; loveliness; magnificence; niceness; *outstanding;* prettiness; pulchritude; *quaintrelle* [arch.]; radiance; shapliness; splendor; *terrific; unsurpassed;* voluptuousness; winsomeness; *xtry.;* yugen [Jap.]; zizz; [Ant. badness]

**beauty** *(n. good-looking woman)*: angel; belle; babe; beaut(y); cutie; doll; *eye-catcher;* fair maiden; good-looker; handsome woman; irresistibly charming lady; jewel; juno; knockout; lovely lady; looker [slang]; maid; model; *morsel;* nymph; *outstanding;* princess; pretty little thing; queen; ravishing ~; sweetheart; *toots;* unrivaled ~; voluptuous woman; woman of great ~; *xtry.* ~; yummy morsel; zizzy;

**because** *(conj.)*: as; being; 'cause; due to the fact; *effectual;* for; given; having known that; inasmuch; insomuch; *just ~;* knowing that; *learn;* motivated by; *notion;* observing that; *purpose;* quia [L.]; reason being; since; seeing as; taking into consideration; understanding that; *valuation;* whereas; *xfer; yeme;* zeroing in;

**beckon** *(v.)*: ask one to come; bid; call; cry; desire; entreat; flare; gesture; holler; invite; *jingle;* knell; *loudly call;* motion; nempne; outcry; petition; page; *quo minus [L.];* request; signal; send for; summon; tell; *utter; urge;* vociferate; *will; xmit;* yell; *zealously bid;* [Ant. banish]

**become** *(v.)*: affect; ascend to; assume; be; come to be; develop into; emerge as; fall; get; grow; *happen; increase; jump into; keep growing; let oneself be;* move toward; *make;* mature; *novate; own;* pass into; progress; *quicken;* realize; start to be; turn into; transform; undergo; *vary;* wax; *xfer;* yield; zero in;

**becoming** *(adj.)*: appropriate; befitting; correct; due; ever-appropriate; fit; good; *honorable;* idoneous; just; *kosher;* legitimate; meet; nice; okay; proper; qualified; right; suitable; *tolerable; unselfish;* valid; well-suited; *xtry.;* yielded; zealous;

**bed** *(n.)*: air~; bunk; cot; couch; crib; cradle; divan; day~; down- ~; double- ~; *estivate;* feather ~; foldaway ~; futon; *gurney;* hammock; infant ~; *inflatable ~; journey's end;* king-size ~; kip [Br.]; *laying down;* mat(tress); Murphy ~; nest; *oversleep;* pallet; press- ~; *pad;* platform ~; queen-size ~; rollaway; single- ~; sofa~; twin ~; trundle- ~; toddler ~; *unconscious; vegetation;* waterbed; *x-sleep;* yawning; zotheca [Rom.];

**bedazzle** *(v.)*: astound; awe; bowl over; confound; dazzle; enchant; floor; gape; hold one's breath; impress; jolt; keel over; look aghast; make marvel; *nonplus;* overawe; *perplex; quite amazed;* render speechless; surprise; stun; strike; take back; unable to believe; *very impressed;* wow; wonder; *xtry.;* yerk; zing; [Ant. bore]

**bedeck** *(v.)*: adorn; beautify; bedizen; clothe; decorate; deck (out); dress; embellish; enhance; emblazon; enchase; fancify; grace; garnish; habilitate; inwrought; jewel; kit; *let be adorned;* make prettier; *nicer;* ornament; prank; prettify; pretty up; *quaintise* [arch.]; render lovely; spruce; trim; *use ornaments;* vest; *wear; xtry.;* yclad [arch.]; zizz;

**bedfellow** *(n.)*: amigo; buddy; companion; *defender; equal partner;* fellow; good-fellow; helper; intimate; *Jonathan;* kith [pl.]; lodger; mate; *neighbor; other;* pal; partner; *quondam friend;* roommate; sidekick; *teammate; unfailing friend;* visitor; workfellow; *xenophile;* yokefellow; *zealous friend;*

**bedlam** *(n.)*: anarchy; *bustle;* chaos; disorder; entanglement; farrago; gastness; helter-skelter; intranquility; jumble; kerfuffle; lunacy; mayhem; non-orderliness; *obscurity;* pandemonium; *quandary; restlessness;* stupefaction; turmoil; upheaval; vexation; welter; xaos; *yo-yo;* zoo;
**Bedouin** *(n.)*: Arab; Bedouin; booley [Ire.]; camel-rider; desert people [pl.]; drifter; *emigrant;* floater; gadabout; gypsy; *hadji* [Arab.]; itinerant; journeyer; *Kenite;* landlouper; migrant; nomad; *oberration;* pilgrim; *quick-mover;* rover; roamer; sojourner; transient; tent-dweller; *unfixed;* vagrant; wanderer; *xerophile;* Yahgan; *zingaro* [It.]
**bedraggled** *(adj.)*: *awful;* bad; chaotic; disheveled; entangled; frowzy; grubby; haggard; incomposed; jumbled; keg-meg; *ludicrous;* messy; mangy; non-organized *orderless;* poky; quaggy; rumpled; scruffy; straggly; tousled; unkempt; vile; windswept; *wild; x'ed;* yucky; *zany;*
**bedroom** *(n.)*: apartment; area; bedchamber; bower; boudoir; chamber; den; end room; flat; guest chamber; houseroom; inhabitance; *joint ~; keeping room;* lodging; loft; *middle room;* night-chamber; outer ~; parlor; place; quarters; room; space; suite; *terrace ~;* upper room; *vestry;* wardroom; *xystum; yu* [Chin.]; *zeta;*
**bedtime** *(n.)*: afterhours; bed time; close of the day; curfew; day's end; evening; fall of the sun; going down of the sun; *hibernation; idleness; jammies; kip;* lights out; *moonlight;* nighttime; naptime; *overnight; pernoctation; quarter-past nine;* rest time; slumbertime; time for bed; *unconsciousness;* vespers; *wakelessness; x-ing;* yawning; *zero light;*
**bee** *(n.)*: ∗ apis; bumble~; carpenter ~; drone; European honey~; *fig wasp;* gold ~; honey bee; *insect; jarfly; kallobombus;* leafcutter ~; mining ~; nitter; orchid ~; *pestilence; paper wasp;* queen ~; Russian honey~; sweat ~; swarm [pl.]; tawny mining ~; *ufo abei* [L.]; vespid; worker; *wasp; xylocopa;* yellow jacket; *zoic;*
**beef** *(n.)*: ∗ angus; black angus; brisket; beeves; corned ~; *darkcutter; European ~;* flesh; grass-fed ~; Hereford ~; *hamburger;* Irish molted; jerky; Kobe ~; *London Broil;* meat; neck- ~; organic ~; pot roast; *quality ~;* red meat; roast; steak; sirloin; tenderloin; USDA choice ~; veal; *wisent; xarque; yukhoe;* zingara;
**beehive** *(n.)*: apiary; alveolus; bee's nest; comb; *domicile; elm tree;* fixed-frame hive; *gold bee;* hive; honeycomb; *infestation; jarfly;* Kenya-hive; Langstrith hive; mud hive; nest; *orchid bee; place; quarters; repository;* skep; top-bar hive; *unit;* vespiary; wasp nest; *xylocopa;* yellow jacket hive; *zuph* [Heb.];
**beep** *(n.)*: alarm; blow; bleep; choo-choo; *ding; echo;* fweet!; *gong;* honk; *intonation; jow; knoll;* loud ~; *music;* noise; ooga-ooga; peep; *quake;* ring; sound; toot; *utterance;* vweet!; whistle; *xtr. loud; yammer; zap;*
**beer** *(n.)*: alcohol; brew; cocktail; dark ~; *eyewater;* fito; German ~; *head;* ice ~; *joywater;* keg ~; kvas; lager; microbrew; mum; *mug;* nip; *oil of joy;* pilsener; quaich; *runlet;* snifter; spruce ~; tipple; table ~; tap; umqombothi [S. Afr.]; *vessel;* wort; *xtal.;* yeast; *yaourt;* zyzomys;
**before** *(prep.)*: afore(time); ahead of; antecedently; afront; beforehand; beforetime; *ci-devant; day ~;* ere; earlier; erst; fore; *gone by;* heretofore; in front of; just ~; *kept;* leading; *morning;* née; of old; *originally;* prior; previous; past; proceeding; protatic; quondam; retrospectively; *starting ~; timely;* up till now; very early; whilom; *xtry, early; yore; zero in;*
**befriend** *(n.)*: aid; buddy up; cooperate with; do a favor for; encourage; favor; give help to; help; *interceded; joy-giving; kindness;* latch onto; make friends with; *nice; overprotect;* pal up; *quick-to-help;* relieve; show kindness to; take to; *unselfish; virtue;* win as a friend; *xenia; yield; zealous;*
**beg** *(v.)*: ask; appeal; adjure; beseech; cadge; crave; desire; entreat; freeload; *grovel;* hit up; implore; *juration; knock;* look for; make request; *need;* obsecrate; panhandle; petition; plead; pray; *quête* [F.]; request; solicit; seek; supplicate; tap; urge; *vocalize;* wish; *XQ.;* yearn for; *zetetic;*
**beget** *(v.)*: *actuate;* bring forth; begin; cause; *develop;* engender; father; generate; gender; have (offspring); initiate; *jump-start;* kittle; lead to; make; *new;* originate; occasion; *offspring;* produce; procreate; propagate; *quicken; result in;* sire; spawn; *trigger; unleash; vivify;* work; *xenogenesis;* yield; *zip;* [*see* bare]

**beggar** *(n.)*: almsman; bum; beggar-woman [fem.]; cadger; derelict; *estivator;* floater; *growtnol;* hobo; *idler;* javel; kern; loafer; mendicant; maunder; *night-wanderer; oberration;* panhandler; *quisby;* rolling stone; scavenger; tramp; *urchin;* vagabond; vagrant; wanderer; *xenarthra*; yahoo; *zhlub;* [*see* sluggard; *Ant.* benefactor]

**beggarly** *(adj.)*: *abbreviated;* bitty; *compact;* derisory; exiguous; feeble; *gnat-sized; hardly;* inadequate; insubstantial; *just little;* ketty; little; meager; measly; negligible; *overly small;* paltry; *quantité négligeable* [F.]; runty; reduced; scanty; small; teeny; ungenerous; very small; wretched; wee; XS; *yea big; zero;*

**begin** *(v.)*: activate; arise; bring into being; beget; commence; debut; embark; establish; form; found; get started; generate; *hatch;* initiate; instigate; instate; institute; ignite; jump-start; kick off; *kindle;* lead off; launch; make a start; mastermind; *new;* originate; proceed; push-start; *quicken;* reactivate; set out; sally; start; turn on; trigger; *take up (-root);* undertake; unleash; *venture; vivify; work out; xon; xenogenesis;* yede; zip;

**beginner** *(n.)*: amateur; abecedarian; apprentice; *beginning;* cadet; debutant; disciple; embarker; first-timer; *green; hatchling;* inceptor; jackeroo; *kid;* learner; mentee; novice; neophyte; nonprofessional; only a novice; pupil; prentice; *quick learner; recruit;* starter; trainee; tyro; undertaker; *venturer; wannabe; xon; yard worker; zero experience;*

**beginning** *(n.)*: arrival; advent; birth; coming; commencement; creation; dawn; debut; embarkment; entry; establishment; first; founding; genesis; hatching; introduction; inception; initiation; instigation; jump off; kickoff; launching; manifestation; *making;* naissance; onset; outset; origin(ation); *presentation;* production; *quickening;* rudiment; rise; start; take-off; *unveiling;* ushering in; *verge;* welcoming; *xenogenesis;* youth; *zygogenesis;*

**begrudge** *(v.)*: abhor; bear ill-will; covet; deeply resent; envy; *fester over;* grudge; hold against; *indignant; jealous; kindless;* loathe; mind; *not like; offended;* pinch; *querulous;* resent; stint; take offense at; utterly loathe; vilipend; *wrathful; xenophobic; yucky; zero joy;*

**beguile** *(v.)*: *allure;* belie; buffalo; con; cheat; dupe; deceive; delude; ensnare; fool; guile; hoodwink; insnare; jape; kid; lie to; misguide; nobble; outfox; put one over; *quiblin* [arch.]; rook; shyster; swindle; snow; trick; *utter falsehood;* verneuk; wangle; *xuld [arch.]; yentz; zing;*

**behave** *(v.)*: act; *be good;* conduct oneself; carry; comport; do; demean; deport; execute; experience; engage (in); function; give; hand(le); indulge; *job; keep;* live; *make; notion;* operate; *overreact;* perform; *quicken;* react; *schesis;* take; undertake; *venture;* walk; *xfer; yede* [arch.]; *zealously ~;*

**behavior** *(n.)*: actions; bearing; conduct; carriage; comportment; deeds; deport(ment); demeanor; expression; etiquette; form; front; guise; habitude; *inclination; job; keeping;* life; movements; manner; mien; *nature;* observance; performance; practice; pattern of ~; *quickening;* response; role; schesis; testimony; *undertaking; venturing;* ways; *x-action; yede; zeal;*

**behead** *(v.)*: axe; butcher; chop head off; decapitate; execute; *finish off;* guillotine; head; *incide; jugular;* kill; lop head off; *make die;* neck; *off with one's head;* perform execution; *quench;* remove head; *separate; sever;* take off one's head; *undo;* victimize; violence; whack off one's head; *x-out; yerk; zip off;*

**behold** *(v.)*: acknowledge; *alas!;* become aware; consider; descry; espy; face; feast eyes on; gaze; *hone in on; hear ye!* inspect; *judge;* ken; look; *lo!;* mind; notice; observe; *perceive; qua* [L.]; regard; see; survey; spy; take in; *understand;* view; watch; witness; *x-ray vision;* yeme; *zero in;*

**belabor** *(v.)*: *add to;* beat a dead horse; camp on; dwell on; *extend; further;* go on; harp; *iterate; jangle;* keep going on; labor on; make too repetitive; *nag;* overdo; overstress; pound; *queach [arch.];* repeat; rehash; spend time on; thrash; *utter again; vex;* work; wear out; *xuld [arch.]; yet again; zillionth time;*

**belief** *(n.)*: adherence; assent; believing; confidence; certainty; conviction; creed; dependence; entrusting; faith; *grasping;* hope; *heart- ~;* identification; ideology; judgment; *knowledge; looking to;* mindset; *mainstay;* non-doubt; opinion; *overconfidence;* position; persuasion; questionlessness; reliance; resting assured; rock-solid faith; stand; stance; surety; trust; ule; understanding; view; *wholehearted ~; xel [arch.]; y'faith* [arch.]; *zeal;* [*see* conviction]

**believable** *(adj.)*: acceptable; authentic; bearable; conceivable; convincing; credible; conclusory; down-to-earth; defensible; *endurable;* fair; good-sounding; heart-convincing; impressive; justifiable; *knowledgeable;* likely; logical; matter-of-fact; not doubtful; ostensible; plausible; probable; persuasive; *questionless;* reasonable; realistic; satisfactory; supportable; swaying; tenable; true-to-life; unquestioned; valid; well-taken; workable; *xenodiagnosis; yieldful; zealous;*
**believe** *(v.)*: account; accept; adhere; bank on; buy into; confess; commit; depend on; embrace; follow; faith- ~; *give heart to;* have faith; hold; imbibe; judge faithful; *know;* look to; maintain; *non-doubt;* own; *overtrust;* profess; *persuaded; questionless;* rest in; repose; rely; swallow; stand on; trust; uphold; very much ~; wholeheartedly ~; *xenodiagnose; y'faith [arch.];* zealously embrace; [*see* faith]
**believer** *(n.)*: adherent; advocate; born again ~; brother [masc.]; convert; Christian; churchgoer; devotee; *evangelical;* follower; *God's people;* heaven-bound; *imbiber;* janissary; *kirsen* [dial.]; lover of God; member; neophyte; *orthodox;* proselyte; possessor; *quickened;* relier; redeemed; saint; saved person; sister [fem.]; truster; upholder; votary; washed; Xn.; yielder; Zionite;
**belittle** *(v.)*: abase; badmouth; chaff; cut down; degrade; demean; denigrate; *execrate;* fleer; gibe; humiliate; insult; jibe; knock; laugh at; malign; mock; *name-calling; offend;* put down; quib; ridicule; slur; tease; trivialize; underrate; vex; wipe; *xuld [arch.];* yock; zap;
**bell** *(n.)*: * alarm; buzzer; chime; church~; cow~; dinner ~; door~; *emergency ~;* firehouse ~; gong; hand~; *intonation;* jingle ~; jangler; knell; lunch ~; market- ~; noon ~; *object;* passing- ~; peal [pl.]; *quickener;* ringer; signal; sleigh- ~; school ~; tocsin; tower- ~; tam-tam; university ~; vesper; wing- ~; whistle; *xfer; yanglour* [arch.]; z-z-z-t;
**belligerent** *(adj.)*: antagonistic; bellicose; contentious; confrontational; disruptive; enemy; fierce; *grievous;* hostile; inimical; jeopardous; *kindless;* lion-like; militant; nasty; odious; pugnacious; quarrelsome; *rough;* savage; threatening; unfriendly; violent; warlike; *xenophobic; yieldless; zealous;* [*Ant.* benevolent]
**belly** *(n.)*: abdomen; breadbasket; crop; *digestive; eat;* front; gut; gizzard; *huge ~;* ingluvies [zoo.]; *jelly- ~ [slang];* kel [slang]; *load;* midsection; maw; midriff; *notum [zoo.];* omasum [zoo.]; *organ;* pot [slang]; paunch; *qualmish;* rumen [zoo.]; stomach; tummy; underbelly; underside; venter; wame; *waist; xiphosternum; yellow-bellied; ziphosternum;* [*see* womb]
**belong** *(v.)*: appertain; be part of; befit; concern; connect to; *dear; encompass;* fit in; go with; have to do with; inhere; *justified; known link;* link with; match; *non-outcast; owned by;* pertain; *quality;* relate; *suit; take; used with;* vest in; *with; xel [arch.]; yours; zero foreignness;*
**belongings** *(n.)*: articles; baggage; chattels; commodities; *duffel bag;* effects; feedstock; goods; gear; habiliments; holdings; items; *junk;* kit; luggage; *matter;* needments; objects; possessions; property; paraphernalia; personal effects; *quantity; raw material;* stuff; things; trappings; *useful;* valuables; *wares; wanigan; xenenthesis; yannigan; zeug* [G.];
**beloved** *(adj.)*: admired; adored; best-loved; cherished; dear; darling; estimable; endeared; favored; greatly loved; heart-dear; important; jake [Br.]; keen; kissable; loved; much-loved; *noteworthy; outstanding;* popular; prized; *qualified; remarkable;* significant; treasured; ultra-popular; very dear; valued; well-loved; xtry.; yearned-for; *zealously loved;*
**below** *(n.)*: adown; beneath; *covered;* down from; *entombed;* fewer; *gone down; hidden by;* inferior; inside; *just underneath; keeled under;* lower; less than; *masked;* 'neath; nether; on earth; *poorer;* put under; quite buried; roofed by; ranked lower than; subordinate; thereunder; under(neath); *veiled;* within; worse; *x-out; yielding to; zero equality;*
**belt** *(n.)*: aorter; amma; band; baldrick; cincture; *cingulum* [Rom.]; deerskin ~; elk hide ~; fur ~; girdle; girth; *harness; inclosure;* jadam ~; karate ~; leather ~; money ~; Naugahyde® ~; *obi* [Jap.]; pigskin ~; *quirboilly ~;* restraint; sash; *suspenders;* strap; shoulder- ~; surcingle; sword- ~; tie- ~; utility ~; vinyl ~; wanty; *waistband; xanthation; yoke;* zona;

**bench** *(n.)*: aluminum ~; banquette; bank; courting ~; church ~; deck ~; exedra; *furniture;* garden ~; *hassock;* iron ~; *joggling board;* kissing ~; lawn ~; *mahogany ~; nine-seater; ottoman;* park ~; piano ~; pew; *place; quiver leg;* row; rusbank; settee; seat; stall; settle; *tête-à-tête [F.];* upholstered ~; *vinyl-covered sofa;* wooden ~; x- ~; yew ~; *zeug [G.];*

**bend** *(n.)*: angle; arc; buckle; bow; curve; curvature; crook; corner; dip; el(bow); fold; *geometric curve;* hook; hunch; incline; incurve; *jag;* kink; knee; knuckle; L; left turn; *loop;* meander; *nonlinear;* offset; ogee; oxbend; parabola; quat; quarter ~; right turn; refold; round; stoop; turn; twist; *uncinate;* verge; wind; warp; xy-curve; yaw; zig; zag;

**bend** *(v.)*: angle; arc(h); buckle; bow; crouch; curve; crook; dip; double; enfold; flex; fold; *geniculate;* hunch; hunker; hinge; incline; jog; jackknife; kink; knuckle; kneel; knee-bend; keel over; lap; meander; *non-rigid;* overlap; ply; quat; refold; sag; stoop; squat; sway; twist; turn; *uncinate;* vary; *wind; xy-curve;* yield; zigzag; [*see* compromise]

**bendable** *(adj.)*: adaptable; bendy; compliant; ductile; elastic; flexible; foldable; *give;* hand- ~; infirm; *jiggly; knuckle;* limber; lithe; manipulable; non-rigid; *open;* pliant; pliable; *queachy [arch.];* resilient; responsive; rubbery; supple; tensile; unfirm; versatile; workable; willowy; *xapuri;* yielding; *zingy;*

**benediction** *(n.)*: adieu; approval; blessing; closing; conclusion; *done;* ending prayer; farewell; good-bye; *host;* inspirational closing; *juration;* kind wishes; last words; *motivational closing; night-parting; officiate;* prayer; parting words; *quittance; resolution;* sanction; termination; *utterance;* vale(diction); *wrapping up; xfer; yielding; zay [dial.];*

**benefaction** *(n.)*: almsgiving; aid; benignity; backing; charitableness; charity; donation; *endowment;* favor; funding; financing; generosity; giving; help; *investment; joyful giving;* kindness; liberality; largesse; magnanimity; munificence; nobleness; open-handedness; patronage; philanthropy; *quantity-giving; righteousness;* support; *thoughtfulness;* unselfishness; *virtuousness;* warmth; *xenophilia; yieldedness; zealous support;*

**benefactor** *(n.)*: almsgiver; bestower; benefactress [fem.]; backer; contributor; do-gooder; donor; donator; endower; favorer; furtherer; giver; grantor; helper; *investor; joyful giver;* kind-hearted person; liberal giver; *magnanimous; noble ~; open-handed;* patron; promoter; perficient; *quantity; rich ~;* sponsor; supporter; *thoughtful person;* unselfish person; *vester;* wealthy ~; *xferer; yielder; zealous supporter;*

**beneficial** *(adj.)*: advantageous; benefitting; constructive; conducive; *decent;* encouraging; expedient; fair; favorable; good; gainful; helpful; handy; instrumental; jim dandy; keen; *lucrative; mutually ~;* nice; outstanding; profitable; propitious; *quality;* rewarding; salutary; serving; *terrific;* useful; valuable; worthwhile; *xtry.;* yieldful; zillions; [*Ant.* bad]

**beneficiary** *(n.)*: award-winner; benefitter; contribution-receiver; donee; endowment-recipient; favor recipient; getter; grantee; haver; *heir;* inheritor; *joint heir;* keeper; largess-recipient; *make off; nabber;* offering-receiver; payee; *qualified ~;* recipient; sponsored (-supported) person; taker; transferee; *user; vest;* winner; *xfer; yank; zealous;*

**benefit** *(n.)*: advantage; betterment; *cumulation;* dividend; edge; favor; good; gain; help; increase; *jump;* kind deed; *livelihood; makings; net profit;* obtainment; perk; profit; *quittal;* return; reward; subsidy; *takings;* use; *usury;* vantage; welfare; *x-div;* yield; *zillions;*

**benevolence** *(n.)*: altruism; beneficence; charity; *deference; endearing;* favor; generosity; good will; helpfulness; *interest; joyful giving;* kindness; liberality; *love;* munificence; nobleness; open-handedness; philanthropy; *quality; righteousness;* selflessness; *thoughtfulness;* unselfishness; virtue; *warmth; xenophilia; yieldedness to God; zeal for God;* [*Ant.* belligerence]

**benevolent** *(adj.)*: altruistic; beneficent; benign; charitable; caring; *deferential;* ever-kind; friendly; good; gracious; generous; humane; hospitable; *indulgent; jovial;* kind(-hearted); liberal; munificent; nice; openhanded; Pickwickian; *quick to help; regardful;* sympathetic; softhearted; thoughtful; tender(hearted); unselfish; very kind; warmhearted; xenial; xenophilous; *yielding;* zealous of good works [Tit. 2:4]; [*Ant.* belligerent]

**benign** *(adj.)*: amiable; benevolent; congenial; *dear; endearing;* friendly; genial; gentle; good; harmless; innocuous; *jovial;* kind; loving; merciful; nice; non-threatening; *obliging;* pleasing; *quick to help; regardful;* sympathetic; tenderhearted; unselfish; very kind; well-natured; xenial; *yielding; zero threat;* [*Ant.* bad]

**bent** *(adj.)*: angled; aduncous; arcuate; arched; buckled; bowed; curved; crooked; declivous; escarped; embowed; flexuous; geniculate; hooked; hunched; inclined; jim-jam; kim-kam; *leaning; markedly ~;* non-linear; oblique; pitched; quinque-angular; repandous; retroflexive; recurvate; stooped; tilted; uneven; unstraightened; U-shaped; verging; varus [med.]; winding; *xuld [arch.];* yawing; ypsiliform; zad; [*Ant.* bendless]

**bequeath** *(v.)*: award; bestow; confer; commit; designate; devise; devolve; endow; *furnish;* gift; give; hand down; impart; *join to; kit;* leave; make to inherit; *non-retention; offer;* provide; *quoth;* render; *supply;* transfer upon death; *unhand;* vest; will; xfer; yafe; *zip;*

**bequest** *(v.)*: acquisition; bequeathal; birthright; co-parcenary; devisal; dower; endowment; estate; fellow-heirdom; gift; heritage; inheritance; jointure; *kindness;* legacy; movable; *no corporeal hereditament; ownership;* parcenary; *quoff;* reversion; succession; settlement; trust; ultimogeniture; *valuables;* wealth; *xmission; yain [arch.]; zillions;*

**berate** *(v.)*: admonish; baste; bash; bawl out; chide; castigate; denounce; excoriate; flay; give talking to; harangue; inveigh; jaw; knock; lecture; *macerate;* nag; objurgate; *punish; question;* reprimand; scold; tell off; upbraid; vituperate; *warn; xuld [arch.];* yell at; *zap;* [*Ant.* bless]

**bereavement** *(n.)*: attrition; bemoaning; bewailing; crying; deprivation; despair; emotion; feeling sorrow; grief; howling; inconsolableness; joylessness; keening; loss; lamentation; mourning; noise; outcry; plaint; quiritation; remorse; sorrow; tears; unhappiness; *vapors;* weeping; wailing; woe; *xuld [arch.];* yowling; *zing;* [*Ant.* birth]

**beseech** *(v.)*: ask; adjure; beg; crave; conjure; desire; entreat; *foreadmonish; go begging;* humbly ask; implore; implead; impetrate; *juration; kneel to; look for;* make request; *need;* obsecrate; petition; pray; *quiritation;* request; supplicate; throw oneself at the feet of; urge; *vocalize;* wish; *XQ;* yearn for; *zealously plead;*

**besiege** *(v.)*: assail; beset; beleaguer; blockade; circle; cordon; contain; draw around; encircle; environ; frame; gird; hem in; inclose; *joint forces;* kirtle; lay siege; leaguer; *move around; non-broken circle; overwhelm;* put around; *quoil [dial.]; rein in;* siege; surround; starve out; trap; *unrest; volt;* whelm; *x-fire;* yard; zone;

**best** *(adj.)*: A-1; ablest; *blue ribbon;* choicest; dandiest; elite; finest; first-rate (-class); favorite; greatest; highest; *impressive; jim-dandy;* keenest; loftiest; most desirable; maximal; No. 1; nonesuch; optimal; optimum; premium; prime; *the* pick; *quintessence;* rosiest; superior; select; top(most); top-notch; top-rated; ultimate; unrivaled; unsurpassed; unequalled; unmatched; very ~; world-class; winning(est); xtry.; yondmost; zenithal;

**bestow** *(v.)*: award; bequeath; confer; designate; endow; furnish; give; hand (over); impart; *jettison;* kit; lay upon; make gift; *non-retention; offer;* present; *quicken;* render; supply; show; transfer; *unhand;* vest; *weigh;* xfer; yield; *zip;*

**bet** *(n.)*: ante; *beat the odds;* chance; dice-roll; exacta; *faites vos jeux* [F.]; gamble; game; high stake; *indulging;* jeopardy; *kitty;* loo; lay wager; longshot; monet; noddy; *off-track betting;* parlay; pledge; perfecta; punt; quinella; risk; *roll of the dice;* stake; set; superfecta; taking a chance; *up the ante;* venture; wager; *xiaoren;* Yarborough; zet [dial.];

**bet** *(v.)*: anticipate; ante; *beat the odds;* chance; depone; endanger; *faites vos jeux* [F.]; gamble; go; hazard; *indulge; iffy;* jeff; *kitty;* lay bets; make bet; *not abstain; odds;* parlay; pledge; punt; *quick-money;* risk; *roll the dice;* squander; stake; take chance; *think; up the ante;* venture; wager(r); *xfer;* Yarborough; *zealously ~;*

**better** *(adj.)*: ascendant; *beat;* choicer; dandier; enhanced; enriched; finer; greater; higher; improved; *jim-dandy;* keener; lovelier; loftier; more fine; much ~; nicer; nobler; *over;* prepotent; preponderant; *quality;* rosier; superior; transcendent; *upper;* very much improved; worthier; XF; *yummier; zizzier;*

**betray** *(v.)*: *assail;* bewray; backstab; commit mutiny (-treachery); deceive; desert; double-cross; defect; *err;* frame; guile; hand over; *insurrect;* jilt; *knife-in-the-back;* let down; *mutiny; not loyal;* overthrow; play Judas; quisle; rise up; stab one in the back; turn on; *unloyal; violate; withstand; x-gress; yieldless; zero loyalty;*

**betrayal** *(n.)*: artfulness; backstabbing; crookedness; disloyalty; desertion; duplicity; defection; *evil;* faithlessness; guile; honorlessness; infidelity; jadery; knife-in-the-back; *lying;* mutiny; *malevolence;* non-loyalty; *opportunism;* perfidy; quislingism; roguery; sedition; sellout; stab-in-the-back; treachery; traitorousness; unfaithfulness; violation of trust; wickedness; *x-ing; yegginess; zero honor;*

**beverage** *(n.)*: aliment; *blend;* cold drink; *cup;* drink; *elixir;* fluid; *glass;* hot drink; infusion; juice; *kava;* liquid (refreshment); long drink; *mixed ~;* nectar; *orange juice;* potation; potion; potable; pick-me-up; *quench;* refreshment; refection; refresco; substance; soft drink; tonic; tall drink; thirst-quencher; *undiluted; volume;* wet drink; *xeres;* yaffle; *zubrowka;*

**beware** *(v.)*: attend (to); be vigilant; careful; *dire;* exercise caution; *forewarned;* give heed; heed; *imminent danger; jeopardy awaits;* keep watch; look out; mind; notice; *observe;* proceed with caution; *questionable;* realize the danger; steer clear; take heed; use caution; *vigilance;* watch out; *x; yield; zing;*

**bewilder** *(v.)*: addle; baffle; confuse; disconcert; *entangle;* fuddle; gravel; hamper; *incoherent;* jumble; kittle; lose; moider; mystify; nonplus; obscure; perplex; quiz; *ravel;* stump; tangle; *unorganized;* vex; wilder; *x; yo-yo; zero understanding;*

**bewilderment** *(n.)*: amazement; bafflement; confusion; disorientation; embroilment; farrago; gastness; *havoc;* incomprehension; jumble; kerfuffle; *lunacy;* mystification; non-comprehension; *obscurity;* puzzlement; perplexity; *quizzical; raveled;* stupefaction; turmoil; uncertainty; vexation; wilderment; *xtry. confusion; yo-yo;* zoo;

**bewitch** *(v.)*: attract; becharm; charm; cast spell on; draw; enchant; fascinate; get (attention of); *have under a spell;* intrigue; *jade; keen;* lure; mesmerize; *notion;* overcome; put under s spell; *quibbling [arch.];* rivet; spellbind; transfix; use magic; *vie for;* woo; *xuld [arch.];* yerk; *zygotaxis;*

**bias** *(n.)*: *attitude;* bent; bigotry; cast; chauvinism; disposition; discrimination; *election;* favoritism; *gauging;* headset; inclination; *jaundiced; keen;* leaning; *mind;* narrow-mindedness; one-sidedness; partiality; prejudice; *quibble; ruling;* slant; tendency; tilt; unfairness; verging; warp; *x; yaw; zeal;*

**biased** *(adj.)*: *attitude;* bent; bigoted; chauvinistic; discriminatory; *elect;* fond of; *gauging; headset;* inclined; jaundiced; *know already;* leaning; *minded;* nonobjective; narrow-minded; one-sided; partial; prejudiced; predisposed; *quibble;* racist; slanted; subjective; tilted; unfair; *verged;* warped; xenophobic; *yawed; zealotic;*

**Bible** *(n.)*: Authorized Version; *the* Book; canon; divine revelation; double-edged sword; *English ~; family ~;* God's Word; Good Book; Holy ~ (-Scriptures; -Writ); inspired Word; *Jehovah's Word;* King James Version; *the* Law; manual; *New Testament;* oracles of God; Old Black Book; *Old Testament;* Pentateuch; pocket Testament; *quick and powerful;* revelation; Scripture(s); sword of the Spirit; statutes; two-edged sword; Testament; *unadulterated Word of God;* version; *the* Word (of God); *Xn. ~; yesod mora* [Heb.]; *Zechariah;*

    **Biblical Books:** Acts; Amos; Colossians; Deuteronomy; Exodus; Ephesians; First Corinthians; Genesis; Galatians; Habakkuk; Hebrews; Isaiah; Jeremiah; John; Leviticus; Luke; Micah; Matthew; Nehemiah; Obadiah; Psalms; Philippians; Ruth; Romans; Song of Solomon; Titus; Zechariah;

**biblical** *(adj.)*: authoritative; biblically accurate; Bible-based; canonical; divine; defensible; *exact;* firm; *grounds; honest;* in the Book; *inerrant;* justifiable; known; legitimate; *maintainable;* non-heretical; nouthetic; orthodox; proper; questionless; right; *reliable;* scriptural; sound; true; theological; unerring; valid; *well-grounded; x-parent; yes; zero-error;*

**bid** *(n.)*: attempt; business offer; crack; *dare;* endeavor; full-blown effort; go; hit; invitation; job proposal; kemp; last-ditch effort; *move; nisus* [L.]; offer; proposal; proffer; quest; *reattempt;* submission; try; undertaking; venture; *work; xuld [arch.]; yearning; zeal;*

**big** *(adj.)*: ample; abundant; astronomical; bonny; broad; beefy; bulky; chubby; corpulent; capacious; colossal; deep; disproportionate; expansive; extensive; elephantine; enormous; flabby; full-size; fat; generous; great; grand; giant; heavy(-set); huge; hulking; immense; jumbo-sized; king-size; large; massive; *noteworthy;* overweight; oversized; portly; ponderous; plump; prodigious; quantitative; roomy; rotund; stout; sizable; substantial; tubby; tremendous; titanic; *unmanageable; unwieldy;* voluminous; vast; wide; weighty; whopping; XL; *yet unsurpassed; zaftig;* [*Ant.* bitty]

**bigness** *(n.)*: amplitude; bulk; chubbiness; chunkiness; capaciousness; disproportion; extent; enormity; fullness; greatness; hulkiness; hugeness; immensity; jumboness; *king-sized;* largeness; magnitude; *noteworthiness;* obesity; overlargeness; prodigiousness; quantity; rotundity; size; tremendousness; *unbelievable;* volume; vastness; wideness; weightiness; XL; *yet unsurpassed; zaftig;*

**bigotry** *(n.)*: anti-Semitism; apartheid [S. Af.]; bias; chauvinism; discrimination; ethnocentrism; favoritism; *gall; hatred;* intolerance; jaundice; klanism; leaning; *minority-hating;* narrow-mindedness; onesidedness; prejudice; *quick to judge;* racism; supremism; segregationism; *terror;* unfairness; *vexation;* Waspishness; xenophobia; *yahooism; zealotry;*

**bill** *(n.)*: account; balance due; charge; check; damage; debit; expected payment; financial responsibility; *gross amount; history;* invoice; *journal;* knock [slang]; list of charges; money due; noctuary; *overcharge; payable; quantity;* record; statement; sight draft; ticket; tab; *undercharge; value;* written ~; *xaraf;* yellow copy; *zum [dial.];*

**bill-collector** *(n.)*: accounts payable; banker; collector; collection agency; credit card company; debt-collector; exiseman; financial institution; gabeler; *heartless creditor; institution; junior officer;* khalsah [Ind.]; lender; mortgager; nobber; *officer;* publican; questman; receiver of debts; shylock; skip tracer; tax collector; *usurer;* vulture [slang]; *worker; xaraf;* yeoman; zamindar [Ind.];

**bin** *(n.)*: *area;* box; basket; carton; container; dump~; *enclosure; five-by-seven ~; garbage ~* holder; in-box; junk drawer; kist; *lunchbox;* mailbox; moving carton; *newspaper ~;* out-box; open container; plastic ~; *quantity;* receptacle; storage container; tin; *ungula;* vessel; wooden crate; *xfer ~; yellow ~;* zone;

**bind** *(v.)*: attach; *around;* band; bale; bundle; begird; connect; chain; draw around; enwrap; enfetter; fasten; fetter; gird; handcuff; inwrap; join; knit; knot; link; manacle; moor; *non-liberated; overwind;* put around; pinion; *quoil [arch.];* ravel; restrain; secure; swaddle; shackle; strap; tie; truss; upbind; unite; *volt;* wrap; wind; *xenograft;* yoke; *zone;*

**binge** *(n.)*: *affair;* bout; carouse; *drinking bout;* extravaganza; fit; fling; *gorge;* hellbender; indulgence; jag; *keg; lost control; moment;* non-restrained spree; orgy; *outburst; overdo;* period; *quickening;* rampage; splurge; spree; tear; *uncontrolled time; vent;* wallow; *x-time; yielding to; zealous indulgence;*

**bird** *(n.)*: *auk;* birdie; cock [masc.]; *dove; eagle;* fowl; fledgling; game ~; hen [fem.]; *ibis; jay; kiwi; lark;* martlet; *needletail; oscine; ornithology;* passerine; poultry; quab; reclaim; *robin; raptor;* song~; sea~; squab; *thrush; umbrella bird;* volery [pl.]; wildfowl; waterfowl; *xenops; yellowfinch; zugvogel [G.];*

> **Birds**: albatross; bluebird; buzzard; chicken; canary; cardinal; condor; duck; egret; eagle; flamingo; finch; falcon; grouse; hummingbird; heron; hawk; ibis; jay; kiwi; kite; lark; mockingbird; nightingale; oriole; ostrich; owl; parrot; pelican; petrel; quail; quetzal; rooster; robin; raven; sparrow; thrush; toucan; upright pershing; vulture; warbler; wren; xema; yellowfinch; zebra finch;

**birth** *(n.)*: advent; arrival; birthday; beginning; bearing; bringing forth; childbirth; coming; debut; delivery; entrance; founding; formation; generation; genesis; hatching; having a baby; inception; introduction; *jump off; kickoff;* labor; *making; mothering;* nativity; nascence; origin(ation); parturition; *quickening;* rise; start; spawning; travail; ushering in; *unveiling; visitation; welcoming;* xenogenesis; yielding; zygogenesis; [*Ant.* bereavement]

**birthmark** *(n.)*: angel kiss; blemish; café au lait spot; discoloration; *envermeiled; figure; growth;* head blemish; imperfection; identifying mark; *jot; kink;* leg ~; mark; mole; nevus; *oddity;* port wine stain; *quirk;* red spot; stain; strawberry mark; stork bite; splotch; telangiectatic nevus; *undesirable; voglie* [It.]; *wiham* [Arab.]; *x; yod; zone;*

**biscuit** *(n.)*: *angu* bun; *bread;* cross bun; cracknel; dinner roll; *edible;* finger roll; *gingerbread;* hardtack; *Italian bread; jannock;* kaiser roll; *light cake;* muffin; morning roll; *naan bread;* oat ~; popover; *quick bread;* roll; scone; *toast; unleavened bread;* wheat ~; *x-bun; yuan hsiao* [Chin.]; zwieback;

**bishop** *(n.)*: arch~; biretta; *brother;* cleric; cardinal; diocesan; ecclesiastic; *episcopate;* friar; grand prior; hieromonach; *imam [Mos.]; Jesuit;* kirkman [Scot.]; leader; minister; metropolitan; *nun [fem.];* overseer; priest; prelate; *Qumranite [Jew.];* reverend; suffragan; *top brass; undershepherd;* vicar; *white friar; Xaverian; yogi [Hind.]; zealoter;*

**bit** *(n.)*: *amount;* bunch; crumb; chip; chunk; daud; drop; *ens;* fleck; flake; fraction; fragment; *gob;* hunk; iota; jib; junt; jigger; kernel; lump; lamia; little piece; mite; morsel; modicum; mammock; mass; nugget; ounce; ort; piece; part; portion; *quantity;* remnant; speck; spot; smidgen; smattering; scrap; small piece; tad; tid~; *unit; vestige;* whit; wee ~; wedge; *xylon; yngot [arch.]; zum [dial.];*

**bite** *(v.)*: attack; *ate;* begnaw; chomp; clamp down on; *dine;* eat; *feed;* gnaw; have by the teeth; *intake; junket;* knab; *lacerate;* mump; munch; nip; nibble; *overeat;* pinch; *quill [arch.]; rip;* snap; sink teeth into; tear; take chunk out of [slang]; *use teeth; vicious;* wound; *xenophagy;* yaffle; *zing;*

**bitter** *(adj. bad tasting)*: acerb(ic); acrid; astringent; awful; bad; bitter-tasting; *crummy;* disagreeable; evil-tasting; foul-flavored; galled; hard; ill-tasting; *jarring; keen;* lousy; *miserable;* nasty; *offensive;* peccant; quite awful; *repulsive; stomach-turning;* terrible; unpleasant; unpalatable; *vile;* wersh; *xtry. bad;* yucky; *zestless;*

**bitter** *(adj. hateful)*: acrimonious; angry; *bad;* critical; despiteful; embittered; foul; galled; hateful; indignant; jaundiced; jaded; kindless; loathsome; mordacious; malicious; malignant; nasty; offended; peppery; querulous; resentful; spiteful; sour; *terrible;* ugly; vicious; *wicked; xenophobic; yucky;* zoilean;

**bitterness** *(n.)*: acerbity; animosity; anger; acrimoniousness; bile; choler; contempt; disgust; enmity; *embittered; foulness;* grudge; gall; hate; indignation; jadedness; *kindlessness;* loathing; malice; non-forgiveness; *nastiness;* offense; perturbation; poison; *querulousness;* resentment; sourness; spite; *trouble;* umbrage; unpleasantness; venom; virulence; wormwood; *xenophobia; yuckiness;* zoilism;

**bizarre** *(adj.)*: absurd; berserk; crazy; daft; egg-headed; funny; freakish; goofy; haywire; irrational; insane; jokey; kooky; loony; mad; nonsensical; nutty; odd; outrageous; outlandish; outré; peculiar; quacked; ridiculous; rum; surreal; twisted; unbelievable; *variant;* weird; wacky; warped; *xtry.; yuk yuk;* zany;

**blabber** *(n.)*: *absurdity;* blather; blab; chatter; drivel; empty words; fudge; gossip; hot air; idle talk; jabber; kelter; leak; mumbo-jumbo; nonsense; *outlandishness;* prattle; queer speech; rambling; ranting; slaver; twaddle; talk; utterance; vain talk; wishwash; xenoglossy; yap; yammer; *zeug* [G.];

**blabber** *(v.)*: *assert;* blather; blab; chatter; disclose; drivel; *expose; fudge;* gabble; gossip; *hot air;* inform; jabber; jaunder; kelter; leak; mention; notify; *open;* prattle; *quidnunc;* ramble; rat; snitch; talk; tell; tattle; utter; *vocalize; whistleblower; xenoglossy;* yap; yammer; *zeug* [G.];

**blabbermouth** *(n.)*: aspersion-caster; bigmouth; cummer; defamater; echoer; *fink;* gossiper; *hearsay;* idle chatterer; informer; informant; jaunderer; kibitz; *loose-tongued;* magpie; newsmonger; *obtrectation;* prater; quidnunc; rumormonger; rat; slanderer; snitch; tattletale; tattler; *utterer; vicious voice;* whistle-blower; *xiaoren;* yakker; *zeroizer;*

**black** *(adj.)*: anthracite; blue- ~; coal- ~; dark; dwale [heraldry]; ebon(y); Frankfurt ~; gray-black; heben; hell- ~; inky; jetty; jet- ~; kettle- ~; lamp~; midnight; nigrine; onyx ~; pitch- ~; *Quaker-gray;* raven; sable; swarthy; tar- ~; ungreenable ~; violet- ~; wadd; *xylanthrax;* yenite; zable; [*see* evil; African]

**blacken** *(v.)*: *alter;* bedim; black; cloud; darken; denigrate; encloud; eclipse; ebonize; *fuliginous;* gloom; hide; incloud; infuscate; japan; *kettle-black;* lower light; make dim; melanize; nigrify; obscure; obfuscate; *pitchy;* quench; *rayless;* shade; smutch; tan; umbrate; *veil; well-darkened; xerophthalmic; yenite; zero light;* [*Ant.* bleach]

**blackness** *(n.)*: absolute darkness; black; *cloud;* darkness; *encloud;* fadedness; *gloom; haze;* infuscation; inkiness; jettiness; *kettle-black;* lightlessness; *midnight;* night; nigritude; obscurity; pitch ~; *quirkiness;* raylessness; shadow; total darkness; *umbrage; very dark; wadd; xeropthalmic;* yeming; zero light;

**blacksmith** *(n.)*: artisan; *anvilsmith; bronzesmith; coppersmith; die-maker; expert;* forger; *goldsmith;* hammer-man; *handicraftsman;* ironsmith; *jacksmith;* kettler; *locksmith;* metal-worker; *nail-maker; ore-worker; picksmith;* quartarian; *refiner;* smith; *tinsmith; unwrought metal; vulcanian;* wright; *xanthoconite;* yetter; *zinc smith;*

**blade** *(n.)*: army knife; barber knife; cutter; *dagger;* edge; fine edge; galvanized ~; *hand knife; instrument; jack knife;* knife-edge; lancet; *metzenbaum; navaja;* Ottoman knife; parer; quarrel; razor; sharp edge; twin-blade ~; utility knife; *vell;* whetted edge; *xyrao* [Gr.]; *yakiba* [Jap.]; *zip;*

**blame** *(n.)*: accountability; accusation; blameworthiness; culpability; charge; condemn; dispraise; denunciation; *error; encumbrance;* fault; guilt; *harangue;* indictment; *judgment; knock;* liability; *mistake; non-innocence;* onus; peccancy; *question;* responsibility; recrimination; reproach; shame; taking to task; *upbraiding; vice;* wrong; xci.; *yoke; zing;*

**blame** *(v.)*: accuse; bring to court; charge; censure; denounce; exprobate; fault; formally charge; give credit to; *guilt;* hold responsible; indict; incriminate; judge guilty; *j'accuse* [F.]; knock; lay guilt before; make allegation against; *non-innocent; oppugn;* point finger at; *question;* reproach; scapegoat; saddle with; tax; *upbraid;* vituperate; *word; xci; yell at; zero in;*

**blameless** *(adj.)*: aboveboard; blemishless; clean; *decent;* exemplary; faultless; good; guiltless; godly; honorable; holy; innocent; impeccable; just; *keen;* law-abiding; moral; *noble;* outstanding; pure; questionless; righteous; spotless; taintless; unblamable; virtuous; without blame; *xtry.;* yet unblamed; *zero guilt;*

**blameworthy** *(adj.)*: at fault; blamable; culpable; deserving blame; errant; flagitious; faulty; guilty; *halt;* indictable; *judged; knocked;* liable; mistaken; notorious; odious; peccant; punishable; *quirky;* responsible; reprehensible; subject to blame; shameful; to be blamed; upbraided; vituperable; wrong; *x-out; yoke; zing;*

**bland** *(adj.)*: average; boring; banal; *colorless;* dull; drab; empty; flat; flavorless; gentle; ho-hum; insipid; intastable; jejune; *known;* lackluster; mild; mediocre; nondescript; ordinary; plain; prosaic; *quotidian; regular;* savorless; stale; tasteless; *tame;* uninteresting; unexciting; unimpressive; unremarkable; vapid; weak; *x-out;* yawnsome; zestless;

**blank** *(adj.)*: airy; bare; clean; devoid; empty; fistular; futile; forlorn; gant; hollow; inane; jejune; *kaput;* load-less; meaningless; nothing; out; plain; quaffed; *reduced;* stark; tapped out; unoccupied; vacant; white; wiped out; "x"; *yielded;* zero;

**blank check** *(n.)*: absolute authority; *boundless; carte blanche* [F.]; dominion; empowering; free hand; *governance; headship; influence;* justification; *king;* license; liberty; mastery; no restrictions; open access; permission; *quite free;* rule; *right;* sanction; total freedom; unrestricted use; *visa;* whatever one wishes; *xenium;* yet unrestricted; zero limitations;

**blanket** *(n.)*: afghan; bedspread; bedcover; comforter; cover; duvet; eiderdown; electric ~; fuzzy ~; goathair ~; hyke; horse ~; Italian quilt; jersey ~; *kaross* [S. Afr.]; layer; lap ~; mohair ~; *night time;* over~; patchwork quilt; quarter ~; quilt; receiving ~; sugan; throw; tester; thermal ~; under~; Victorian quilt; wagga; *x-pattern; yellow ~; zigzag quilt;*

**blaspheme** *(v.)*: abominate; berate God; curse; commit sacrilege; disrespect; defile; desecrate; execrate; foment; *goad; hate;* inquinate; *jade;* knowingly disrespect; *kindle; loathe;* malign; not respect God; offend; profane; pollute; *quad;* revile; swear; *taint;* utter blasphemies; unhallow; violate; *wickedness; x-ing; yieldless; zing;* [*Ant.* bless]

**blasphemer** *(n.)*: abominator; berater; curser; defiler; desecrator; execrator; foul mouth; God-hater; heretic; *irreverent; jade; knowingly disrespect; loather of God;* maligner; non-respecter; offender; profaner; polluter; *quad;* reviler; swearer; *tarnisher;* unhallower; violator; wretch; *x'er; yieldless; zinger;* [*Ant.* blesser]

**blasphemous** *(adj.)*: abominable; berating; calumnious; disrespectful; defiling; desecrating; execrable; foul; God-dishonoring; *heretical; horrifying;* impious; irreverent; *jadey;* knowingly disrespectful; *loathing;* maledictive; non-respectful; offensive; profane; polluting; *quad;* reproachful; sacrilegious; terrible; unholy; unpious; violating; wicked; *x-ing; yieldless;* zero respect;

**blasphemy** *(n.)*: abomination; blaspheming; cursing; disrespect; desecration; execration; flagrance; gross disrespect; heresy; irreverence; insolence; juration; knowing disrespect; *loathing;* malediction; non-respect; offense; outrage; presumption; profanity; profanation; *quad;* reviling; sacrilege; *tainting;* unhallowing; vulgarity; *violation;* wickedness; *x-rated speech; yieldlessness;* zero respect; [*see* impudence]

**blatant** *(adj.)*: apparent; bold; conspicuous; deliberate; explicit; flagrant; glaring; *heedless;* intentional; *just plain to see;* kenspeckle; *lucid;* manifest; noticeable; overt; open; patent; *quite obvious;* recognizable; shameless; transparent; unmistakable; visible; witnessable; *x-parent; yare; zenithal;*

**bleach** *(n.)*: *agent;* blancher; calsimine; colorsafe ~; decolorant; etiolation agent; fading agent; *gallon;* hue-remover; industrial ~; javel water; kalsomine; lightener; madder ~; *non-colored; object;* perborate; *quite white;* remover; *substance;* treatment; uncolorer; *vanish;* whitener; *xeesal; yellow-remover; zero color;*

**bleach** *(v.)*: achromize; blanch; blench; *candescent;* dealbate; decolorize; etiolate; fade; grow pale; *hue-remover; industrial bleach; javel water; kalsomine;* lighten; make white; *non-colored;* obliterate; pale; *quite white;* remove color; *stain-remover;* take color out; uncolor; *vanish;* whiten; *whited;* xanthochroic; *yellow-remover; zero color;*

**bleary** *(adj.)*: *ambiguous;* blurry; cloudy; dim; enclouded; fuzzy; groggy; hazy; indistinct; *just blurred; knotty;* lowery; misty; nebulous; out-of-focus; obscure; puffy; *qually* [arch.]; *rheum;* shadowy; tired; unclear; vague; watery; *xtry. ~; yawnful; zero-zero;*

**bleat** *(v.)* appeal; baa; cry; *complain; discharge;* exclaim; fuss; *groan; holler;* inveigh; *jubilate; keen;* lament; moan; noise; outcry; *protest; quiritation; resonate;* sound; *talk;* utter; *vociferate;* wail; *xenophonia;* yammer; *zow;*

**bleed** *(v.)*: abate; *bloody;* come out; drip; drain; emit; exudate; flow; gleet; hemorrhage; issue; *jet; kest;* lose blood; *make bloody;* nose~; ooze blood; phlebotomize; *quail;* run; seep; shed; spill; siphon; trickle; *use up;* venesect; *vein;* went [p.t.]; *xude;* yield blood; *zap;*

**blemish** *(n.)*: abnormality; blotch; *carbuncle;* discoloration; defect; *eruption;* flaw; growth; *hive;* imperfection; jarble; knub; lentigo; mark; nevus; *oddity;* pimple; patch; quirk; rash; spot; smudge; stain; tarnish; taint; *ulcer; verruca;* wart; xanthoma; yedder; *zit;*

**blend** *(n.)*: admixture; amalgamation; bemingling; combination; *diverse; entanglement;* fusion; *gallimaufrey;* hybrid; interminglement; intermixture; integration; inosculation; joining; *kirning; lumping together;* mix(ture); mergence; meld; *node; overmixing;* putting together; *queaching* [arch.]; *raveling;* synthesis; throwing together; union; *volubility;* wedding; *xenograft; yerking together; zipping together;*

**blend** *(v.)*: admix; amalgamate; bemingle; combine; *diverse;* emulsify; fuse; *get together; hodge-podge;* intermingle; intermix; integrate; inosculate; join; *kirn; lump together;* mingle; mix; marry; merge; meld; *node;* orchestrate; pass into; *queach* [arch.]; *ravel;* shake together; stir; synthesize; throw together; toss; unite; *voluble;* wed; *xenograft; yerk together; zip together;*

**bless** *(v.)*: aid; assist; advance; benefit; bestow ~ing; confer ~ing; cheer; do good unto; exalt; favor; give; gladden; help; honor; invoke ~ing upon; *joy; kindness;* lift up; make happy; magnify; *nice;* overjoy; offer praise; prosper; praise; *quicken;* relieve; show favor; *tender mercies;* uplift; *vivify;* work for; *xtry. blessing;* yield; *zealously help;* [see praise]
**blessed** *(adj.)*: advantaged; blest; *contented;* delighted; exultant; favored; glad; God-favored; happy; heaven ~; *in high spirits;* joyous; kindly treated; *loved;* made to prosper; much- ~; never-so-much ~; overjoyed; privileged; prospered; *quite ~; regarded;* satisfied; treated well; unusually favored; very ~; well- ~; *xenium; yet favored;* zeal;
**blessing** *(n.)*: approval; advantage; benefit; benevolence; bounty; consent; divine favor; *endearing;* favor; goodwill; gift; godsend; happiness; help of God; *immoderacy; joy;* kindness; liberality; munificence; nicety; open-handedness; permission; present; provision; prosperity; *quarter; regard;* sweet ~; tender mercies; underserved favor; *virtue;* wealth; *xenium; yield;* Zion's favor;
**blind** *(adj.)*: amaurotic; blinded; benighted; cannot see; dim-sighted; darkened; eclipsed; eyeless; *faulty sight;* groping; hemeralopic; impaired; *just can't see;* kept from seeing; legally ~; mole-eyed; night- ~; non-seeing; nyctalopic; ophthalmic; pur~; quite ~; rayless; sightless; stone- ~; totally ~; unseeing; unsighted; visually impaired; visionless; weak-sighted; without vision; *xerophthalmia;* yet unable to see; *zero visibility;*
**blindness** *(n.)*: amaurosis; ablepsy; benightedness; cecity; day ~; darkness; eyelessness; flash ~; *glaucoma;* hemeralopia; impairment; invision; *just can't see; keeping in-the-dark; legally blind;* metamorphopsia; non-sightedness; nyctalopia; obscurity; obfuscation; ophthalmy; pur~; quadrantanopia; *raylessness;* sightlessness; total ~; unseeingness; visionlessness; weak-sightedness; want of sight; xerophthalmia; *yet unable to see;* zero visibility;
**bliss** *(n.)*: animation; blitheness; cheer; delight; elation; exhilaration; felicity; gladness; glee; happiness; intoxication; joy; keenness; lightheartedness; merriment; *niceness;* overjoy; pleasure; *queme;* rejoicing; satisfaction; thrill; *uplifted; vivacity;* winsomeness; *xanadu; yeah!;* zestfulness; [*Ant.* badness]
**blissful** *(adj.)*: agreeable; beautific; blithe; *beaming;* cheerful; delighted; elated; exhilarated; felicitous; glad(some); gleeful; happy; invigorated; joyful; keen; lighthearted; merry; *nice;* overjoyed; pleased; *queme;* rejoicing; satisfied; thrilled; uplifted; *vivacious;* well-pleased; *xanadu; yeah!* zestful; [*Ant.* bad]
**blister** *(n.)*: abscess; bleb; boil; carbuncle; *defect;* eruption; furuncle; growth; hydatid; *imperfection;* jog; kibe; lump; *mark;* node; *oddity;* pustule; quirk; *raised area;* swelling; tumor; umbo; vesicle; wen; *xyloma;* yedder; *zit;*
**blob** *(n.)*: accumulation; bunch; clump; drip; drop; *element;* fleck; glob(ule); gob; glop; gout; hunk; *inkstain;* junt; *knot;* lump; mass; nubble; *ounce;* piece; quantity; *roll;* splotch; tad; *unit; viscid;* water-drop; wad; *x-mal [G.];* yelm; *zum [dial.];*
**block** *(n.)*: adobe; brick; *cinder ~; chopping ~;* chunk; disruption; extruded brick; firebrick; *glass ~; hard material; item;* junt; klompie; lump; mud brick; mass; module; nugget; *object;* obstruction; piece; part; quarle; red brick; slab; *stone ~;* tablet; unit; *veneer stone;* wood ~; wedge; xblock; *yard ~; zone;*
**block** *(v.)*: avert; bar; blockade; check; close off; deter; *defeat;* embar; forestall; foil; gum up; hinder; impede; jam; *keep from; limit;* mess up; *manacle; no access;* obstruct; oppilate; obstipate; occlude; parry; prevent; portcullis; *quash; restrain;* stop (up); shut (out); thwart; *undo; void;* ward off; *x.; yank; zeroize;*
**blockade** *(n.)*: abatis; barrier; barricade; beseigment; cordon; defense; embankment; fortification; gabion; hedge; impasse; *jam; kirtle; line; mudwall;* naval ~; obstruction; perpend; *quickset hedge;* rampart; revetment; siege; stranglehold; *traverse; utility wall;* vallation; wall; *x-fence; yard wall; zero admittance;*
**blockage** *(n.)*: arrest; barrier; cumbrance; clog; difficulty; encumbrance; *frustration;* glitch; Gordian knot; hindrance; holdup; hurdle; interference; impediment; impasse; jam; kink; *lodgment; mess;* nuisance; obstacle; obstruction; problem; quandary; roadblock; stoppage; trouble; *upset;* vigia; wall; x; *yowler; zinger;*

**blonde** *(adj.)*: aureate; ash ~; (bleach-)blond; *canary;* dirty- ~; *ecru;* fair-haired; flaxen; golden (-haired); hair of gold; *Indian yellow; jonquil; king's yellow;* light-colored; leucous; marigold; natural ~; *ocherous;* pale; platinum ~; *quince; royal yellow;* strawberry- ~; sandy; tow-headed; *uranite;* vitelline; washed-out; xanthotrichous; yellow(-haired); *zante;*

**blood** *(n.)*: *afflux;* bloodiness; bleeding; ~stream; claret; corpuscles; *drops; erythrocytes;* fluid; gluten; gore; hemoglobin; ichor [myth.]; juice [slang]; *ketone;* life~; *mass; nasty; ooze;* plasma; *quart;* red ~ cells; sanguine; *thin/thick ~; trickling; type A+ ~; unshed;* vital fluid; white ~ cells; *xantorubin; yellow ~; zymome;* [see bloodline]

**bloodless** *(adj.)*: amicable; blood-less; concordant; *diplomatic;* exsanguinous; ever-peaceful; *friendly;* gentle; *harmonious;* irenic; *jarless; keeping peace; loving;* mild; nonviolent; *orderly;* peaceful; *quiet;* resolved without blood; sanguineless; tame; unhostile; unbloody; unbloodied; violence-avoiding; without blood; *xenophilious; yielding;* zealous of peace; [*Ant.* bloody]

**bloodline** *(n.)*: ancestry; blood; clan; descent; derivation; ethnicity; extraction; family; genetics; genotype; heredity; *inheritance; jus soli [L.];* kindred; lineage; *mores;* nationality; origin; people; *quarter;* race; stock; tribe; *ubiety; Vaterland [G.]; white race; x-link; yoni* [Skr.]; *zoe;*

**bloodshed** *(n.)*: atrocity; butchery; carnage; destruction; evil; ferocity; gruesomeness; harm; inclemency; injuries; *jeopardy;* killing; loss of life; murder; massacre; *nefariousness;* odiousness; perniciousness; *quashing;* riotousness; slaughter; treachery; *upheaval;* violence; waste of life; wartime; *x-ing out; yanking down; zealotry;*

**blood-stained** *(adj.)*: *afflux;* bloody; blood-spotted (-splattered; -drenched); crimson; dampened by blood; ensanguined; *flow;* gory; *hemorrhage;* imbrued; *jeopardized; killing; lethal;* messy; nasty; over-bloody; plethoric; *quad;* red-stained; sanguinary; *tinged; unclean;* vermillion; wounded; *xantorubin;* yucky; *zymome;*

**bloodthirsty** *(adj.)*: aggressive; barbaric; bloody; beastly; brutal; cruel; cutthroat; destructive; deadly; evil-intentioned; fierce; ferocious; gory; hostile; injurious; jeopardizing; killing; lethal; murderous; nefarious; odious; pernicious; *quad;* ruthless; rapacious; savage; sanguinary; treacherous; *unpeaceful;* violent; warlike; *xenophobic; yeffell* [arch.]*; zero-mercy;*

**bloody** *(adj.)*: *aggressive;* bleeding; blood-stained; cruel; crimson; disgusting; ensanguined; foul; gory; hurt; hemorrhaging; horrible; injured; imbrued; *jeopardized; killing; lethal;* messy; murderous; nasty; over-bloody; plethoric; *quad;* red-stained; sanguinary; slaughterous; treacherous; *unpleasant;* violent; wounded; *xantorubin;* yucky; *zymome;* [*Ant.* bloodless]

**bloom** *(v.)*: abloom; blossom; come into maturity; develop; effloresce; flourish; flower; grow; *heighten;* increase; *jump up; keep growing;* leaf; mature; *nourish;* open; produce; prosper; *quadruplicate;* ripen; shoot; thrive; unfold; vegetate; wax larger; *XL;* yield; *zoom;*

**blossom** *(v.)*: *advance;* bloom; come into flower; do well; enhance; flower; grow; *heighten;* irrupt; jump up; *keep growing;* luxuriate; mushroom; *nourish;* open up; prosper; *quantum growth;* rise; sprout; thrive; *upgrow* [arch.]; vegetate; *wax larger; XL;* yield flowers; *zoom;*

**blot** *(n.)*: abnormality; blotch; blemish; *chit;* defect; *engrained;* flaw; *grease spot; hue; imperfection;* jaup; kink; *line;* mark; macula; naeve; *object;* patch; quirk; *ring;* spot; stain; splotch; tarnish; unsightly spot; vice; wart; wem; *X; yedder; zit;*

**blow** *(n.)*: assault; bash; cuff; clobber; clip; clout; clock; crack; dash; deck; *efface;* flogging; *get;* hit; impact; jolt; knock; *kick;* lick; mauling; nob; open-handed ~; punch; *quab;* rap; smack; sock; swipe; shot; strike; slam; thwack; thump; uppercut; veney; wap; whack; wallop; *x-sect;* yedder; zonk;

**blow** *(v.)*: aerate; *afflation;* breathe; bluster; blast; *cool;* drive air; emit; exhale; fan; gust; huff; insufflate; inflate; impel; jet; *kest;* let out; make air blow; *non-stagnant;* outblow; output; overinflate; overproportion; puff; *quake;* rupture; *snort;* stream; shoot air; squall; throw air; *unleash;* vent; whiff; wind; wuther; waft; wheeze; *xuld [arch.];* yirr; zephyr; [*see* explode]

**blue** *(adj.)*: azure; baby ~; bice; cobalt; cyan; dark ~; electric ~; French ~; gentian ~; hyacinth; indigo; jay; jazel; kyanite; light ~; marine; midnight ~; navy; old ~; peacock ~; Prussian ~; queen's ~; robin's egg; sky ~; sea- ~; turquoise; sapphire; ultramarine; vivid ~; watchet; *xerces ~; yellow- ~;* zaffer;

**bluff** *(v.)*: *allure;* beguile; con; dupe; ensnare; fake; guile; hornswoggle; insnare; jape; kid; lead astray; lie; mislead; nobble; outknave; pretend; *quiblin* [arch.]; rook; sucker; trick; *utter falsehood;* verneuk; weasel; *xuld [arch.]; yentz; zing;*

**blunt** *(adj. frank)*: *abrupt;* brusque; brutally honest; candid; direct; ever-truthful; frank; forthright; *gruff;* honest; inconsiderate; janty; keenly ~; *lay it out;* maladroit; no-nonsense; non-tactful; outspoken; outright; obtuse; plain-spoken; *qualified;* raw; straight; truthful; tactless; upfront; undiplomatic; untactful; *veritable;* without subtlety; *x-parent; yieldless; zero tact;*

**blunt** *(adj. not sharp)*: *abraded;* blunted; coarse; dull(ed); edgeless; *flat;* gone dull; hebetate; in need of sharpening; just not sharp; *knocked;* lacking sharpness; much-dulled; non-sharp; obtuse; obtundent; pointless; *quelled;* rounded; retuse; *soft;* too dull; unpointed; unsharpened; very ~; well-rounded; *x-out; yet unsharpened; zero sharpness;* [Ant. barbed]

**blunt** *(v. to dull)*: attenuate; become dull; come to be dull; dull; disedge; deaden; *errode;* fail; go dull; hebetate; impair; *jade; knock; lacking sharpness;* make dull; *non-sharp;* obtund; *pointless; quell;* rebate; retund; round; soften; *too dull;* unsharpen; *very dull;* wear smooth; *x-out; yet unsharpened; zeroize;*

**blur** *(n.)*: abstraction; blear; blurriness; cloudiness; distortion; enclouding; fuzziness; *ghost;* haze; indistinctness; jumble; *keif [Arab.];* low visibility; muddle; non-distinctness; obscurity; poor picture; quasi-visibility; *reverie;* shadow; *tangle;* uncertainness; vagueness; whir; *xerophthalmia; yet unfocused;* zero resolution;

**blur** *(v.)*: addle; becloud; cloud; confuse; dim; eclipse; encloud; *fuzzy;* go (-get) blurry; haze; infuscate; *jag;* keep unclear; lose definition; muddle; not be clear; obscure; put out of focus; *quat* [arch.]; *repress;* shadow; soften; see double; take out of focus; umbrate; *unclear; vague;* wimple; *xerophthalmic;* yeme; zeroize;

**blurry** *(adj.)*: ambiguous; blurred; bleary; clouded; dim; enclouded; fuzzy; *gray;* hazy; indistinct; *jellylike; known to few; lightless;* murky; nebulous; obscure; *poor;* quaggy; rough; shadowy; turbid; unclear; unfocused; vague; woolly; *xeroophthalmic;* yet unclear; *zero clarity;*

**blush** *(v.)*: *ashamed;* be embarrased; crimson; *disgraced; embarrass;* flush; get embarrassed; heat; *indignity; jackalent; knock off one's horse;* look red; mantle; *nither [arch.];* out~; pinken; *quiet;* redden; rose; suffuse; turn red; *uneasy;* very embarrassed; wax red; *xtry.; yet modest; zero composure;*

**blustery** *(adj.)*: airy; breezy; blowy; blusterous; *crosswind;* drafty; eolian; flawy; gusty; howling; inclement; *jet stream;* katabatic; *line squall;* moderately windy; *not calm;* over-windy; puffy; *quarter-wind;* rough; squally; stormy; turbulent; *uncontrolled;* violent; windy; *x-wind; yaw;* zephyrous;

**board** *(n. council)*: assembly; advisory; body; board of advisors (-trustees; etc.); committee; cabinet; council; diet; eldership; *forum;* governing body; *heads;* illuminati; junto; *kit;* legislative body; *meeting; nominative committee; organization;* panel; presbytery; quinquevirate; ruling body; session; synod; *tribunal; union;* vestry; *ward; xenocracy; yain [arch.]; zemstvo [Rus.];*

**board** *(n. wooden plank)*: acacia; beam; crossbeam; deal; *elm;* floor~; gangplank; hard~; *item;* joist; knee-timber; lumber; lath; *maple; nemoral;* one-by-four; plank; piece of wood; press~; quarter-cleft; rafter; slat; stud; scantling; timber; two-by-four; underlayment; *veneer;* wood; *xylon; yew; zingara;*

**board** *(v.)*: abate [law]; *aboard;* barge in; come in; descend upon; embark; *forge ahead;* get on; head into; irrupt; jump in; *kite; let on;* make an entrance; *navigate into; open;* pass onto; *quest;* re-enter; set oneself aboard; transcend into; *use;* venture into; walk onto; *xfer;* yede; zip into;

**boast** *(n.)*: avowal; assertion; brag; bravado; claim; *delighting;* exaggeration; flatulence; gasconade; heroics; *immodesty;* jactitation; *kompology; loftiness; maintain; narcissism; ostentation;* pretension; *quacking;* rodomontade; swaggering; triumphing; ululation; vaunt; vainglorying; wallowing; *x-proud; yelp; zestfulness;*

**boast** *(v.)*: advertise; brag; crow; *disdain;* exult; flaunt; glory; gasconade; huff; *inflated;* jubilate; kvell; loudly proclaim; magnificate; *narcissist;* overween; pride oneself on; preen; presume; *puff up;* quack; roister; show off; swank; talk big; ululate; vapor; whoop; *x-proud;* yap; *zero humility;*
**boaster** *(n.)*: *arrogant;* braggart; bragger; braggadocio; crower; *delighter;* egotist; fanfaron; gloater; huff; *immodest;* Jack-the-lad; know-it-all; loudmouth; magnificator; narcissist; ostentator; popinjay; quidnunc; rodomont; rooster; swaggerer; *trumpeter;* talker; *ululator;* vaunter; *wallower; x-proud;* yelper; *zestful;*
**boastful** *(adj.)*: arrogant; bragging; conceited; disdainful; egotistical; fastuous; gloating; haughty; high-sounding; inflated; *kompology;* lofty; magnificating; narcissistic; overconfident; overweening; proud; pompous; quick-to-boast; rodomont; superior; snobbish; stuck-up; self-glorifying; thrasonical; unhumbled; vainglorious; wrapped up in oneself; *x-proud;* yelping; *zero humility;*
**boat** *(n.)*: ark; barge; bark [poet.]; craft; *dinghy; eight-oar;* fly~; ferry; galley; house~; *ice*~; jack- ~; *ketch;* lugger; laker; long~; motor~; navy ~; *outrigger;* paddle~; pinnace; quadruple scull; rig; row~; river~; scull; sail~; steam~; ship; *tug*~; *udema;* vessel; watercraft; *xebec;* yawl; *zabra;*
**bodily** *(adj.)*: animate; body-related; corporeal; *disquieted; earthly;* fleshly; *genuine;* hylic; innate; jejune; *known;* living; materiate; mortal; non-spiritual; outward; physical; *quotidian;* reified; somatical; temporal; unspiritual; *vapid; worldly; xfer; yourself;* zoetical;
**body** *(n.)*: anatomy; biology; clay vessel; *developed;* earthly ~; flesh; frame; figure; *growing;* human ~; *individual; joined together; katabolism;* living ~; mortal ~; non-spiritual part; organism; physique; physical ~; *quarron* [arch.]; *real flesh and blood;* self; soma; tabernacle; unit; vessel; whole ~; *xbreed; yourself;* zootomy; zoarium; [*see* corpse]
   **Body parts**: appendix; bladder; colon; digits; eye; finger; gall bladder; hand; intestines; jaw; kidney; liver; muscle; neck; *organ;* pancreas; rib; spleen; toe; uriary tract; vein; xiphosternum;
**bog** *(n.)*: *aikraw;* bottomland; bayou; carr; *damp;* everglade; fen; glade; haugh; inland marsh; *jheel* [Ind.]; kavir; *lagoon;* marsh; moor; *nanoplankton; overgrown;* peat~; quagmire; *reeds;* swamp; tarn; *usnea;* vlie [S. Afr.]; wetlands; xyrisic; yarpha; *zoocarpous area;*
**boggle** *(v.)*: amaze; bewilder; confuse; discomfit; *entangle;* fluster; gravel; hamper; *incoherent;* jumble; kittle; lose; muddle; *mind-boggling;* nonplus; obscure; pother; quiz; *ravel;* stump; scramble; tangle; *unorganized;* vex; wilder; *x;* yo-yo; *zero understanding;*
**boggy** *(adj.)*: alluvial; bog-like; carr-like; damp; *everglade;* fenny; gouty; *heavy; icky; jheel* [Ind.]; kavir-like; lutose; *loamy;* marshy; miry; *never-dry; oozy;* paludal; peaty; quaggy; *reedy;* swampy; *turbid;* uliginose; *vlie [S. Afr.];* water-logged; xyrisic; yucky; *zoocarpous;*
**bogus** *(adj.)*: artificial; *bad;* counterfeit; deceitful; ersatz; false; fake; fraudulent; falsified; gag; guileful; hoax; imaginary; imitation; japed; kiddy; *lying;* make-believe; mendacious; non-real; *outfoxed;* phony; quacky; quasi; rip off; replicated; spurious; sham; trick; unreal; vain; wily; *xeno-;* yeggy; *zero authenticity;* [*Ant.* bona fide]
**boil** *(n.)*: abscess; blister; carbuncle; decoction; eruption; fistula; growth; hive; hemorrhoid; *inflammation;* jog; kyle; lump; *mar;* node; *oddity; pustule; quirk; raised area;* sore; tumor; ulcer; vesicle; wen; *xanthoma;* yedder; *zit;*
**boil** *(v.)*: agitate; braise; bubble; cook; decoct; estuate; effervesce; *ebullient;* foam; gently ~; heat; hard- ~; *irritate;* jump; kier; *liquid; move;* neal [arch.]; overheat; poach; par~; *quicken;* rage; *rebullition;* simmer; slow ~; stew; seethe; *sodden;* sterilize; trouble; *upset; violent;* vaporize; wallop; *xeo; yerk;* zoutch;
**boisterous** *(adj.)*: agitated; angry; blustery; cyclonic; *destructive;* enraged; furious; gusty; hostile; inclement; *Jupiter Pluvius; knot floater;* loud; monsoonal; *non-peaceful;* over- ~; pandemoniac; quakeful; raging; roaring; stormy; turbulent; tempestuous; unstable; violent; windy; wild; *xude; yond [arch.];* zinging; [*Ant.* becalmed]

**bold** *(adj.)*: audacious; brave; bodacious; brash; brazen; confident; courageous; doughty; daring; enterprising; ever-bold; forward; fearless; gutsy; gallant; heroic; intrepid; *jarless;* knightly; lion-hearted; manly; nervy; never-fearing; outspoken; presumptuous; plucky; *quick-witted;* rash; self-assured; *saucy;* stout; temerarious; unafraid; unflinching; undaunted; valiant; well-spirited; *xtry.;* yare; zealous; [Ant. bashful]

**boldness** *(n.)*: audacity; bravery; brazenness; courage; doughtiness; daring; enterprise; emprise; fortitude; fearlessness; guts; gumption; hardiness; heroism; intrepidity; *jarless;* knightliness; lion-heartedness; manliness; nerve; *obstinacy;* pluck; *quakeless;* rashness; resolve; spirit; stoutness; strength; temerity; undauntedness; valiance; wherewithal; *xtry.;* yung [Chin.]; zealousness; [Ant. bashfulness]

**bomb** *(n.)*: atomic ~; bombshell; canister; dynamite; device; daisy cutter; dirty ~; explosives; fire~; fougade; fireball; grenade; hand grenade; high explosives; H- ~; *ignite; jet;* keg; landmine; letter ~; mail ~; mine; *missile;* nail ~; nuclear ~; oyster mine; powder (keg); petard; pipe ~; *quake;* robot ~; shell; sonic mine; TNT; time ~; thermonuclear weapons; UXB; *V-1;* warhead; *xyloiden; yield; zap;*

**bombard** *(v.)*: attack; bomb; barrage; blitz(krieg); *camisado;* drop bombs; dive bomb; *engage; fight; get;* hurl bomb at; *hit; invade; jolt; kemp;* let bombs fall; mortar; *nuke; onslaught;* pound; *pelt; quash;* ravage; release bombs; shell; *strike; torpedo; unleash;* volley; whomp; *x-fire; yed;* zeppelin;

**bombardment** *(n.)*: air raid; attack; bombing; barrage; blitz(krieg); cannonade; dropping bombs; *engaging; foray; get;* hit; *invasion; jolt; kemp;* letting bombs fall; mortaring; nonstop ~; onslaught; pelting; pounding; *quash;* raid; shelling; *strike; torpedo; unleashing;* volley; whomping; *x-fire; yed;* zero hour;

**bombastic** *(adj.)*: arrogant; big-sounding; blustering; *condescending;* dignified; extravagant; florid; flowery; grandiloquent; highfalutin; high-sounding; impressive; inflated; Johnsonian; *know-it-all;* lofty; long-winded; magniloquent; noble-sounding; orotund; overblown; pompous; pretentious; puffy; *quantitative;* rhetorical; swelling; turgid; tumid; uppity; verbose; well-sounding; xtry.; *yammering; zesty;*

**bond** *(n.)*: attachment; affixation; binding; connection; cement; *dovetail; embedding;* fitment; fuse; glue; *hookup;* interconnection; joining; joint; knitting; link; *league;* linkup; marriage; meld; nexus; oneness; permanent ~; *quasi-fuse;* relation; sticking; splice; tie; union; *vise;* wedding; weld; *xenograft;* yoke; *zipping together;*

**bond** *(v.)*: adhere; affix; bestick; cohere; cement; dure; *embed;* fasten; fuse; glue; grip; hold (together); *imbed;* join; keep; latch; meld; *nail; oneness;* paste; *quick-dry;* remain; stick; stay; set; secure; tack; unite; *viscous;* weld; *xenograft;* yoke; zip; [Ant. break]

**bondage** *(n.)*: assiento; burden; bondservice; captivity; drudgery; enslavement; forced labor; fetters; grip; hardship; hard ~; helotism; inthrallment; *job; keeping down;* labor; mancipation; niefdom; oppression; *overlabor;* peonage; *quelling;* repression; slavery; toil; thralldom; *under;* vassalage; work; *xibalo;* yoke; Zeug [G.]; [Ant. bondlessness]

**bone** *(n.)*: * ankle ~; back~; carpal; dolos; *exoskeleton;* femur; *good luck ~;* humerus; involucrum; jaw~; knee-bone; long ~; lamina; lamella; mandible; marrowbone; neck- ~; os; phalanges; *quadratojugal;* ramus; rib; *skeleton;* scapula; tibia; ulna; vertebra; whale~; wish~; xiphoid; Y- ~; zygoma;

**boneless** *(adj.)*: abstracted; bone-out; *cut-out;* deboned; exossated; exosseous; filleted; *get rid of;* having no bones; *infirm; jiggly; knife-cut;* limp; *malleable;* non-boned; *over-soft; pliable;* quite ~; rubbery; strengthless; *tender;* unboned; *vacated;* without bones; *x-out; yanked;* zero bones; [Ant. bone-in]

**bonus** *(n.)*: award; advantage; benefit; bells & whistles [pl.]; boon; *contribution;* dividend; extra; freebie; frill; gain; gratuity; godsend; hand out; honor; incentive; *jumbo ~; kickback;* leftover; lagniappe; monthly ~; nicety; overplus; plus; perk; perquisite; *quantity above;* reward; sweetener; *treat; unused; value;* windfall; x.; year-end ~; *zillions;*

**bony** *(adj.)*: attenuated; *bones;* constricted; delicate; emaciated; frail; gaunt; horny; *half-starved;* insubstantial; jimp; knobby; lanky; meager; malnourished; narrow; osseous; overthin; pencil-thin; *quantité négligeable [F.];* ribby; skinny; skeletal; thin; underweight; virgate [bot.]; wiry; *xiphisternal; yieldless;* zero body fat;

**book** *(n.)*: album; booklet; *bestseller;* codex; copy; digest; *encyclopedia; edition; exposé;* folio; flip~; *gazetteer;* hardcover; *imprinting; journal; kappa book;* literature; manual; novel; octavo; paperback; primer; prose; publication; quarto; reader; scroll; story~; soft cover; softback; text(~); tome; *unpublished work;* volume; writing; work; xylographica; yellowback; *zipper- ~;*

**book** *(v.)*: arrange; bespeak; charter; *decide on;* engage; *find help;* get; hire; hold; ink; *join the team;* keep; line up; make reservation; *name:* order; organize; prearrange; pencil in; *qualified;* reserve; schedule; take on; use; *vocation; work; xtr. hours;* yes; *zet [dial.];*

**bookkeeper** *(n.)*: accountant; bean counter [slang]; creditor; chamberlain; check-writer; *depositor;* economist; financial advisor; geoeconomist; *holder; intendant; job;* keeper of the books; ledger-keeper: moneybag-holder; number-cruncher; officer; purser; questor; record keeper; reckoner; secretary; treasurer; *underling;* verifier; *worker; xaraf; yeme; zakai [Jap.];*

**boom** *(n.)*: airburst; bang; blast; burst; blow; clatter; crunch; crash; din; detonation; explosion; eruption; fulmination; going off; hit; *impact; jolt;* knock; ka-pow; kaboom; *let rip; mine; noise;* outburst; plunk; pop; pow; *quake;* reverberate; racket; rumble; roar; shot; smash; slam; sound; sonic ~; thud; thump; thwack; thunder; unleashing; vroom; whack; wham; wallop; *xuld [arch.]; yedder;* zonk;

**boor** *(n.)*: *agrarian;* bawdy; churl; cretin; dolt; egghead; funk; gink; hobbledehoy; insensitive person; jackanapes; jerk; kern; knark; lout; mompara; non-sensitive person; oaf; put; peasant; *quack;* rube; swain; turkey; *unsophisticated;* vulgarian; whig [Br.]; *xiaoren;* yazzihamper; yokel; zob; zhlub;

**boost** *(v.)*: advance; augment; bring up; *climb; develop;* elevate; further; go up; hoist; heighten; increase; jack up; *keep going up;* lift; move up; *new growth; overgrow;* push up; promote; quicken; raise; strengthen; take a turn up; uplift; verge upward; wax higher; *XL; yain [arch.]; zoom up;*

**booth** *(n.)*: *area;* box; bay; carrel; cubicle; dispensary; enclosure; *food ~;* gunyah; hut; *isolation ~;* jacal; kiosk; *lean-to;* makeshift hut; nook; outbuilding; pagoda; place; partition; *quarters;* rotunda; room; stall; stand; shack; tent; *ticket ~; telephone ~; utility hut; voting ~;* wickup; *x-house;* yakutat hut; zotheca [Rom.];

**border** *(n.)*: abuttal; boundary; brim; borderline; coast; crossing; dawn; edge; frame; fringe; frontier; *gilded edge;* hem; inception; *imbordered; jurisdiction; kept limit;* line; limit; margin; march; *narrow;* orle; outskirts; perimeter; quadra; rim; side; skirt; threshold; tressure; *ulterior;* verge; *without; x-ing;* yonder; *zone;*

**bore** *(v. disinterest)*: *awearied;* bore stiff; care nothing for; dull; disinterest; exhaust; fatigue; *grieve; hate;* irk; jade; *known;* lose interest; make disinterested; numb; *over-bored;* put to sleep; *quail;* run out of patience; stultify; tire; turn off; *uninteresting; very ~d;* weary; *xerosis;* yield; zero interest; [*Ant.* bedazzle]

**bore** *(v. drill)*: auger; *broach; cut;* drill; empierce; fix [arch.]; gore; hole; impale; jab; knife; lance; make hole; *nail; needle;* open; pierce; penetrate; *quill;* ream; stab; spear; thirl; *undercut; ventilate;* wimble; *xylotomy;* yerk; *zing;*

**bored** *(adj.)*: awearied; bored stiff; *commonplace;* disinterested; exhausted; fatigued; *grieved; ho-hum;* indifferent; jaded; *known;* listless; made disinterested; non-enthused; over-bored; *pathetic; quailed;* run out of patience; sick (and tired); tired; turned off; uninterested; unenthused; very ~; weary; xtry. ~; yet unamazed; zealless; [*Ant.* bemused]

**boredom** *(n.)*: *averageness;* boredness; commonplaceness; dullness; dullsville; ennui; flatness; *generic;* humdrum; heigh-ho; insipidity; jejuneness; *keen ~;* losing interest; monotony; non-excitement; over-boredom; prosaicism; *quotidian;* repetitiveness; savorlessness; tedium; tediousness; *uninteresting;* vapidity; weariness; *xtry. ~;* yawning; zestlessness; [*Ant.* bemusement]

**boring** *(adj.)*: average; bland; banal; commonplace; drab; dull; eventless; flat; frumpy; generic; humdrum; ho-hum; insipid; jejune; *known;* lackluster; livelong; laborious; longsome; mundane; monotonous; non-exciting; nondescript; operose; old-hat; ponderous; pedestrian; platitudinous; prosy; prosaic; quotidian; repetitious; repetitive; *rut;* soporific; savorless; tedious; tiresome; uninteresting; unimaginative; uneventful; unoriginal; vapid; wearisome; *xtry. ~;* yawnful; zestless; [*Ant.* bedazzling]

**born again** *(adj.)*: alive in Christ; blood-bought (-washed); Christian; delivered; elect; forgiven; glory-bound; gloriously saved; heaven-bound; in Christ; justified; kingdom-bound; *life eternal; mercifully saved; no condemnation; on one's way to heaven; purchased;* quickened; redeemed; regenerated; reborn; saved; *son; transformed;* united in Christ; *unshackled; vivified;* washed; Xn.; *yonder-bound;* Zion-bound; [*Ant.* bound for hell]

**borrow** *(v.)*: adopt; ask; beg; bum; cadge; commandeer; *desire;* employ; *for;* get on loan; have on loan; *implement; just ask;* keep for a while; *lease;* mooch; *need temporarily; overuse;* put to use; *qualmless;* run into debt; scrounge; sponge; (temporarily) take; twock; advantage of; use; *volition; want; xfer;* yain [arch.]; zeal;

**bosom** *(n.)*: arms; breast; chest; décolleté [fem.]; embrace; embonpoint; *feelings; gird;* heart; inner man; *imbosomed; jog;* kirtle; *love;* midsection; *nestle; oxtercog; passion; quiddity; recline;* soul; *sternum;* torso; upper body; *value; warmth; xiphoid; yield; ziphosternum;*

**boss** *(n.)*: authority; big cheese (-wig) [both slang]; chief; CEO; director; employer; executive; foreman; governor; head; intendant; jefe; keeper; leader; lord; manager; master; magnate; *nobleman; night manager; nibs* [Br.]; overseer; principal; prefect; president; patriarch; queen [fem.]; ringleader; ruler; superior; supervisor; superintendent; top-dog; *top brass; ultimate authority;* vizer; warden; XO; *yokemaster;* zayim; [*Ant.* bondservant[

**bossy** *(adj.)*: authoritarian; *brutal;* controlling; domineering; *evil-hearted;* fascistic; grouchy; harsh; high-handed; imposing; imperious; *jaded;* kindless; loveless; micro-managing; *nasty;* overbearing; powerful-hungry; *quede [arch.];* repressive; strict; tyrannical; unreasonable; *virulent;* way too strict; *xenophobic;* yieldless; *za-zum [Rus.];* [*Ant.* biddable]

**botch** *(v.)*: *abort;* bungle; bollix; crash; disappoint; *disqualify;* err; foul up; fumble; go bad; hash; *impropriety; jolt; kaput;* louse up; muff; mess up; not succeed; *omit; pratfall; poor;* quit; ruin; slip; stumble; spoil; trip; underachieve; *violate;* wash out; *"x"; yedder;* zorch;

**bother** *(v.)*: annoy; bug; badger; chafe; disturb; dog; exasperate; frustrate; grate (on); harass; irritate; jangle; *kid; livid;* menace; miff; nag; nettle; *offend;* pester; *queach [arch.];* rile; *steam;* taunt; test; unnerve; vex; weary; *x-ing;* yerk; zing; [*Ant.* bless]

**bothersome** *(adj.)*: annoying; burdensome; *cursed;* difficult; exasperating; frustrating; grating; galling; hard; irksome; inconvenient; jarring; knotty; *lousy; messy; nuisance;* overburdensome; problematic; quisquose; rattling; *steamed;* troublesome; tiresome; unpleasant; vexatious; wearisome; *xerotripsis;* yucky; *zhlubby;*

**bottle** *(n.)*: acetabulum; beaker; borachio; cruet; carafe; cruse; container; decanter; ewer; flacon; flask; flagon; galipot; gallon; half gallon; *inurn;* jug; jeroboam; kit; lachrymatory; *liter;* mickey; magnum; *neck;* olla; phial; quart container; receptacle; soldier [slang]; salmanazar; thermos; urn; vial; wineskin; winchester; *xeres jug;* yabba; zun;

**bottom** *(adj.)*: *aft;* basal; bottommost; *cirque; down;* endmost; foundational; ground; hindermost; *intervale; jacksy; keel-side;* low(est) point; lowermost; minimum; nethermost; *on the ~;* pit; quoit; rock- ~; *sole; tail;* undermost; underneath; valley; *way down; xtr. low;* yunga; *zero altitude;*

**bottom** *(n.)*: *aft;* butt; bottom side; base; *cirque;* downside; end; earth; foot; floor; foundation; ground; hinder part; *intervale; jacksy; keel-side;* low(est) point; *minimum;* nether side; nadir; *on the ~; pit; quoit;* rock- ~; *root;* sole; *terra firma* [L.]; *tail;* underneath; underside; underbody; undersurface; underpart; undercarriage; valley; *way down; xtr. low;* yunga; *zero altitude;*

**boulder** *(n.)*: *aplite;* bedrock; crag; *dolomite;* enormous rock; formation; great stone; *Gibraltar;* huge rock; immense stone; jumbo-sized rock; *kunzite;* large rock; mass; monolith; megalith; *notable rock; obsidian;* prodigious stone; *quartz;* rock; stone; tremendous rock; *uranite;* volcanic rock; weighty rock; *xenoblast; yenite; zircon;*
**bounce** *(n.)*: *axel;* bound; capriole; curvet [horses]; *dart;* elevation; flying ~; gambol; hop; hurdle; *issue;* jump; jounce; *kite;* leap; *movement; nimble;* overleap; pounce; pannade [horses]; *quersprung;* rise; skip; spring; tour jete; upspring; vault; *whiz; xfer; yerk;* zoom;
**bounce** *(v.)*: *arise;* bob; bound; cavort; carom; *dart; elevate;* fly; gambol; glance; hop; *issue;* jump; jounce; kick back; leap; make jounce; jump; *nimble; overleap;* pogo; pounce; *quersprung;* resile; ricochet; saltate; spring; skip; take leap; *underleap;* vault; *whiz; xfer;* yerk; zoom;
**bouncy** *(adj.)*: animated; brisk; cheerful; dynamic; energetic; effervescent; frisky; *gung-ho;* high-spirited; intense; jumpy; kedge; lively; *motivated;* nippy; overactive; peppy; quick; rapid; springy; *thrilled; upbeat;* vivacious; wimble; *x-energy;* yary; zippy;
**boundary** *(n.)*: ambit; abuttal; brink; bounds; border; coast; confines; dawn; dividing line; edge; frontier; *gate;* hem; interface; *jurisdiction; kept limit;* limit; line; margin; *narrow;* outskirts; periphery; purlieu; quadra; rim; *state line;* threshold; *ulterior;* verge; *without; x-border; yonder;* zone;
**bountiful** *(adj.)*: abundant; beaucoup; bursting; copious; disproportionate; excessive; *fruitful;* great; generous; galore; heaps; immense; jumbo; *king-sized;* liberal; multitudinous; numerous; overflowing; overabundant; plentiful; profuse; quantitative; rich; superabundant; terrific; uberous; voluminous; vast; wantless; x.; *yards; zillions;* [*Ant.* bare]
**bouquet** *(n.)*: arrangement; bunch; *corsage;* dozen roses; *edelweiss;* flowers; *geraniums; hyacinths; irises; jasmines; knotweed; lilies;* mixed ~; nosegay; *orchids;* panicle; posy; *quantity;* roses; spray; *tulips;* uncut ~; *verticillaster;* wildflower ~; *xeranthemums; yarrows; zinnias;*
**bout** *(n.)*: attack; binge; bender; carouse; drinking ~; extravaganza; fit; *gorge;* hellbender; interlude; jag; *kick; lost control; moment;* non-restrained spree; orgy; potation; *quickening;* run; spell; spree; surfeit; turn; *uncontrolled moment; vent;* wallow; *x-time; yielding to; zealous indulgence;*
**bow** *(n. archer's weapon)*: * arbalest; balister; composite ~; cross~; *drawn ~;* English long~; flat~; game ~; *hoal* [Kor.]; *instrument; jolt;* kaman; long~; Mongol ~; *Nottingham; object;* Penobscot ~; quarrel; recurve cross- ~; short~; self- ~; *teppo yumi* [Jap.]; *unbent ~; violin ~;* windlass; *weapon; x-bow;* yew ~; *yumi* [Jap.]; zyhgyr ~ [Pers.];
**bow** *(n. stoop)*: arch; bend; crouch; curtsy; dip; droop; enfolding; flex; fold; geniculation; hunching over; inclination; *jump down;* kneel; kowtow; lapping over; *movement;* namaste; *obeisance;* pilé; quat; refolding; salaam; squat; turn; *uncinate; verge; wind; x-curve;* yield; zemnoy ~;
**bow** *(n. trimming on a gift)*: adornment; bedecking; curling ribbon; decorative ~; embellishment; fontage; garnish; gift- ~; *highlight; item; jazzing up; kit; loops;* metallic ~; *nicety;* ornament; *prettify;* quaintise [arch.]; ribbon; sash; trimming; *upscale;* velvet ~; *well-trimmed; xtry.;* yclad [arch.]; zizz;
**bow** *(v.)*: arch; *acquiesce;* bend; crouch; curtsy; duck; droop; dip; enfold; fall; flag; fold; geniflect; hunch; hang; incline; *jag;* knuckle; kowtow; *kneel;* loll; lower; lean over; *move (down);* nod; overbend; ply; quat; refold; stoop; sag; squat; twist; *uncinate; venerate;* weaken; *x-curve; yield; zing;*
**bowels** *(n.)*: *appendix;* blind gut; cecum; *duodenum;* entrails; fry; gut(s); humbles; haslet; innards; insides; intestines; jejunum; *kishke* [Yid.]; *large intestines;* mid-gut; numbles; offal; organs; puddings [dial.]; quarry; ropes [birds]; stuffings; *small intestines;* tripes; umbles; viscera; workings; *xysma; yucky; ziphoid;*
**bowl** *(n.)*: *article;* basin; crock; dish; *earthenware ~;* fictile ~; glass ~; hazel-earth ~; *item;* jasperware ~; *kuel* [Chin.]; *large ~;* mixing ~; mazer; monkey dish; *noggin;* olla; porringer; punch ~; quart-vessel; ramekin; soup ~; salad ~; tureen; tazza; urn; vessel; work ~; *xeo;* yan; zegedine;

**box** *(n.)*: ark; bin; bunker; carton; crate; chest; container; depository; *egg carton; fire~; gift ~;* holder; *hat~;* hope chest; *inro* [Jap.]; *jewelry ~;* kist; lockbox; moving carton; *naulage; open ~;* pyx; *pill~;* package; *quinderkyn;* receptacle; repository; shoe ~; strong ~; shipping container; *tinder~;* trunk; *unopened ~;* vasculum; vessel; wooden ~; *xtr. storage;* yakhdan; *zipper-bag;*
**boy** *(n.)*: adolescent; begotten; bo [slang]; bairn; child; dude; *enfant* [F.]; fellow; guy; hobbledehoy; *increase;* juvenile; knave; kid; lad; man-child; nipper; *offspring; preschooler; progeny;* quinquennarian; *relative;* stripling; son(ny); school~; shaver; sprout; swain; tyke; teenager; urchin; *vandal;* waif; *xbred;* youth; zon [dial.]; [*Ant.* babe]
**boyfriend** *(n.)*: admirer; beau; caller; *date;* esquire; fellow; fiancé; guy; gallant; heartthrob; inamorato; joe [slang]; knight in shining armor; lad; *loverboy;* man; noble suitor; *one;* paramour; questor; Romeo; suitor; sweetheart; swain; true love; torch; *unmarried;* valentine; wooer; *x-linked;* young man; *zon [dial.]:* [*Ant.* beloved]
**boyhood** *(n.)*: adolescence; being a boy; childhood; development; early years; formative years; growing-up years; *hatchling;* immaturity; juniority; kidhood [joc.]; *knee-high to a grasshopper; littleness;* maturing; *non-adult; over-young;* pre-adulthood; *quite young;* raising; state of being a boy; tenderness; underdevelopment; verdancy; weanling years; *XS;* youth; *zero-maturity;*
**boyish** *(adj.)*: adolescent; boylike; childish; *developing;* early; fledgling; green; hastive; immature; juvenile; kiddish; laddish; *mannish; new; over-young;* puerile; *quite immature;* raw; small; tender; trifling; underage; vernal; wee; *XS;* young; youthful; *zero-experience;*
**bracelet** *(n.)*: armlet; adornment; bangle; chain- ~; charm ~; diamond ~; *embellishment;* fandangle; gold ~; hand jewelry; identification ~; *jewelry; karats; ligure;* manil; name ~; ornament for wrist; pearl ~; *quaintry;* ring ~; silver ~; tennis ~; *uvarovite;* vervel; wristlet; xtal. ~; YAG ~; zonule;
**brag** *(v.)*: assert; boast; crow; *disdain;* exult; flourish; glory; *gloat;* huff; *inflated; jactitation;* kvell; loudly proclaim; magnificate; noise; overween; plume; *pride;* quack; rant; rodomontade; rave; roister; show off; swagger; triumph; ululate; vaunt; *wallow; xtr. proud;* yelp; *zestful;*
**braggart** *(n.)*: arrogant; bragger; boaster; braggadocio; crower; *disdainer;* egotist; fanfaron; gloater; huff; *inflated;* Jack-the-lad; know-it-all; loudmouth; magnificator; narcissist; ostentator; popinjay; *proud;* quidnunc; roisterer; rodomont; swaggerer; *trumpeter;* ululator; vaunter; vain person; *wallower; xtr. proud; zero humility;*
**bragging** *(n.)*: arrogance; boasting; crowing; *disdain;* egotism; egoism; fanfaronade; glorying; gloriation; haughtiness; inflatedness; jactitation; kompology; *loud-mouthed;* magnificating; narcissism; ostentation; pride; quacking; roistering; showing off; talking big; ululating; vaunting speech; *wallowing; xtr. proud;* yelping; *zero humility;* [*Ant.* brokenness]
**braid** *(n.)*: aiguillette; bullion; corn ~; Dutch ~; double- ~; *entwined;* French ~; girl's ~; gold ~; hair-plating; inverted French ~; *jill;* knit; lace; *merging; net; ornamentation;* plaiting; pigtail; queue; rickrack; soutache; *style;* thong; *topknot; under; vemp;* weave; wattle; *x-ing; youthful ~;* zigzag ~;
**braid** *(v.)*: arrange; bind; cue; Dutch- ~; *do;* double- ~; entwine; French- ~; *fix; girl; hair;* interweave; interlace; *jill;* knit; lace; make ~ed; *net; ornament;* plait; queue; *rickrack; style;* twine; *topknot;* use ~s; *vamp;* weave; wattle; *x-ing;* yede [arch.]; zigzag ~;
**brain** *(n.)*: anatomy; brains; cerebrum; *devise;* encephalon; fore~; gray matter; head; hypothalamus; *intellect; jole* [zoo.]; *kopf* [G.]; left lobe; mind; neocortex; noodle [slang]; occiput; pink matter; quadrigeminal; right lobe; skull; thinker; thalamus; *understanding;* vertex; wonder; *xtry. thought;* yead [arch.]; *zenith;* [*see* leader]
**brainwash** *(v.)*: *affect;* brain-wash; condition; convince; *deceive; deprogram; educate;* foster; give misinformation; *hype;* indoctrinate; inculcate; *justify; knowledge;* lead astray; misinstruct; nobble; *overpersuade;* program; propagandize; persuade; *qualify;* re-educate; reprogram; reindoctrinate; steep; talk into; *undermine; verbiage;* win over; xula [arch.]; *yellow journalism;* zhdanovism;

**branch** *(n.)*: arm; branchlet; bough; chat; *dogwood ~; extremity;* faggot; *grafted ~; hickory ~; ironwood;* jackstraw; kipper; limb; *maple ~;* nicky; offshoot; osier; plash; *quaker;* rame; runner; rod; shoot; sprig; switch; stave; stick; tendril; twig; *upas ~; vimineous;* withe; wattle; *xylem; xenograft; yard* [arch.]; *zamia;* [*see* tree; root, division]

**brand** *(n.)*: *analysis;* breed; class(ification); category; designation; denomination; estate; fashion; genre; group; heading; ilk; *jack;* kind; label; make; *nature;* order; persuasion; *quarter;* rank; species; style; stripe; sort; type; *unit;* variety; *way; x-class;* year-class; zoological classification;

**brand** *(v.)*: *annotate;* burn; *char;* designate; engrave; fix mark; grave; *heat;* imprint; *jot; kenmark;* label; mark; name; *overwrite;* put mark on; *quality; red hot;* sear; *token;* use branging iron; *vest;* write on; *xylograph; yard mark; zay;*

**brash** *(adj.)*: audacious; bold-faced; cocky; discourteous; disrespectful; *effrontery;* foolhardy; glib; haughty; impetuous; jaunty; *know-it-all;* lippy; malapert; nervy; overbold; pert; *quick-to-speak;* rash; saucy; temerarious; unabashed; vain; *wicked; x-proud; yieldless; zero respect;* [*Ant.* bashful]

**brass** *(adj.)*: *admiralty ~;* brazen; bronze; bronzy; *common- ~; deaurated;* electroplated; fine- ~; gold-colored; *high ~; inaurate; jewel-encrusted; karat; leafed;* manganese; *naval ~;* orichalcum; *parcel-gilt; quince;* royal ~; *shiny;* tombac; uranite; vermeil; white ~; *xanthous;* yellow; *zante;*

**brass** *(n.)*: admiralty ~; *alloy;* bronze; copper-zinc alloy; common ~; DZR ~; *electrum;* fine ~; gilding metal; high ~; *inaurate; jewel-encrusted ~; karats;* leaded ~; manganese; (Muntz) metal; naval ~; orichalcum; ormolu; prince's metal; *quality;* rivet ~; *substance;* tonval ~; *uranite;* vermeil; white ~; *xanthous;* yellow ~; zinc-copper alloy;

**brat** *(n.)*: annoyer; botherer; bugger; chafer; displeaser; demon; exasperator; frustrater; griever; galler; harasser; imp; jangler; kidder; kicker; little ~; menace; nettler; nuisance; naughty boy; nagger; needler; oppressor; provoker; pest; *queach [arch.];* riler; spoiled ~; taunter; urchin; vexer; *weary; x-er;* yerk; *zhub;* [*Ant.* blessing]

**brave** *(adj.)*: audacious; adventurous; bold; courageous; daring; dauntless; enterprising; fearless; gallant; heroic; intrepid; *jarless;* knightly; lion-hearted; manly; nervy; noble; never-fearing; obstinate; plucky; questful; *resolute;* strong; spirited; stout; *tenacious;* unafraid; undaunted; unflinching; unfrightened; valiant; valorous; *wherewithal; xtry.; yare;* zealous;

**bravery** *(n.)*: audacity; boldness; courage; daring; enterprise; fortitude; fearlessness; guts; gumption; grit; gallantry; heroism; intestinal fortitude; intrepidity; *jarless;* knightliness; lion-heartedness; manliness; mettle; nerve; nobleness; *obstinacy;* pluck; prowess; *quakeless;* resolve; stoutness; strength; spirit; *tenacity;* undauntedness; valor; wherewithal; *xtry. ~; yung* [Chin.]; *zealousness;*

**brawn** *(n.)*: ability; brawniness; capability; dint; energy; force; gusto; heartiness; horsepower; *intensity; jet-power; kilowatt;* lustiness; might; muscle; *natural ability; omnipotence;* power; *qualifications;* ruggedness; robustness; strength; thewiness; *usefulness;* vim; vigor; wherewithal; *xenium; yare;* zip; zing; [*Ant.* brittleness]

**brawny** *(adj.)*: able-bodied; burly; bullish; *capable;* durable; energetic; fit; good; husky; iron; *jusqu'au bout [F.]; keen;* lusty; muscular; manly; *nervy;* obstinate; powerful; *quality;* rugged; robust; strapping; stalwart; tough; unflagging; vigorous; well-set; *x-strong;* yeomanly; *zippy;* [*Ant.* brittle]

**brazen** *(adj.)*: audacious; bold; brash; courageous; daring; enterprising; foolhardy; gutsy; hardy; intrepid; *jaunty; know-it-all; lofty;* malapert; nervy; overconfident; presumptuous; *quick-witted;* risky; rude; spirited; temerarious; unafraid; vainglorious; *wherewithal; xtry.; yare;* zealous; [*see* brass; *Ant.* bashful]

**brazenness** *(n.)*: audacity; boldness; brashness; contempt; cheekiness; disrespect; effrontery; flagrancy; gall; haughtiness; hauteur; impudence; insolence; *jackanapes; know-it-all;* loftiness; malapertness; nerve; overconfidence; presumption; pertness; *quilicom* [arch.]; rudeness; surliness; sassiness; sauciness; *turgidity;* uppityness; *unruliness;* vanity; *wind; xenophobia;* yahoo; zero humility; [*Ant.* bashfulness]

**breach** *(n.)*: aperture; break; crack; dilaceration; *excavation;* fissure; gap; hole; incavation; jaw-hole; krater; lacuna; *missing part; niche;* opening; parting; *quarry-pit;* rent; *split;* tear; *umbilicus; violation; widening; x-ing;* yawn; zanja;

**bread** *(n.)*: * angu ~; brioche; corn~; date~; *edible;* French ~; flat~; ginger~; haver~; heel; Italian ~; jannock; kettle- ~; loaf; light ~; muffin; *manna;* naan ~; oat ~; pumpernickel; pita; panini; pan loaf; plain loaf; quick ~; rye ~; spoon ~; tea ~; toast; unleavened ~; veda ~; white ~; wastel; wave-loaf; *xtr. dark ~; yuan Hsiao [Chin.];* zwieback;

**breadth** *(n.)*: amplitude; broadness; capacity; *distance;* extent; *finger~;* fullness; girth; *hair~; hand~;* hugeness; immensity; jumboness; *king-sized;* length; measurement; *non-abridged; overlargeness;* prodigiousness; *quantity;* reach; span; thickness; *upper limit;* volume; width; *x-coordinate;* yardstick measurement; *zone;*

**break** *(n. rest)*: adjournment; abeyance; breather; *coffee ~; discontinuance;* ease; forbearance; *gala day;* hold; holiday; hiatus; idleness; intermission; *journey's end; kip;* letup; lunch ~; *motionlessness;* non-activity; *off;* pause; quietude; rest; repose; respite; recess; suspension; time-out; *unwinding;* vacation; wait; *x-rest; yawning; zizz;* [*Ant.* busy oneself]

**break** *(n. severance)*: aperture; breach; crack; cleft; division; divide; *efforce;* fracture; fissure; fork; gulf; gap; hiatus; interstice; *junction;* knapple; laceration; *mincing; mashing;* non-continuum; opening; parting; partage; *quadrisection;* rift; rupture; rend; split; severance; schism; tear; uncoupling; *veering; waste; x-ing out;* yawn; zap; [*see* pause; *Ant.* bond]

**break** *(v. bust)*: *axe;* bust; burst; crack; crush; cut; damage; destroy; disunite; *efface;* explode; fracture; ground; harm; injure; *jab;* knock apart; lacerate; mar; *nullify;* olate; prang; pull down; quash; rout; ruin; ravage; rupture; rend; snap; shatter; sever; split; smash; tear; uproot; vitiate; wreck; *x-ing;* yank down; zap; [*Ant.* bind]

**break** *(v. stop working)*: *abort;* break down; burn out; conk (out); discontinue working; *end;* fail; fall apart; go (kaplooie); halt; *interrupt;* jam; konk (out); *kaput;* leave off functioning; *motionless; ot work; off-kilter;* park it; quit; rest; stop working; terminate; undo; veto; walk off; *x;* yield; zero;

**breastplate** *(n.)*: armor; breast-plate; corselet; cuirass; chestplate; *defensive armor;* ephod; *fortification;* gorget ~; habergeon; iron plate; *jupon;* knight armor; leather ~; lorica; *mail;* Norse ~; *outer shell;* plastron; poitrel; *quirré;* Roman ~; steel ~; *segmentata* [Rom.]; torso armor; upper body armor; vest; *wear; xia; yoke; zeug [G.];*

**breath** *(n.)*: air; aspiration; breathing; *cough; drawing;* exhalation; flow; gasp; gust; huff; inhalation; *judder; katabatic; lung; mains; nose;* outblow; pant; puff; *quill [arch.];* respiration; *respiratory; rale;* single respiration; souffle; *thing; upper respiratory;* ventilation; whiff; wind; *xuld [arch.];* yawn; zephyr;

**breathable** *(adj.)*: acceptable; befitting; *clear; decent;* environmentally safe; fit to breathe; good; *high-quality;* innocuous; just fine; *keen; legitimate;* meet; *nice;* okay; pure; quality; respirable; suitable; taintless; *untainted; valid;* well-suited; *xtry.;* yes; zero toxins; [*Ant.* bad]

**breathe** *(v.)*: aspirate; *air; blow; circulate air;* draw air; exhale; fill lungs; gasp; huff; hyperventilate; inhale; inbreathe; inspire; *judder;* keep on; let air out; *lung;* move; *nose;* outblow; puff; *plosion;* quill *[arch.];* respire; suspire; take in air; *use oxygen;* ventilate; wheeze; *xuld [arch.];* yolp; *zephyr;*

**breathtaking** *(adj.)*: amazing; awesome; astonishing; brilliant; confounding; divine; extraordinary; fantastic; great; grand; heavenly; incredible; impressive; *jarring;* keen; lofty; magnificent; mind-boggling; notable; overwhelming; prodigious; *quantum* [L.]; remarkable; spectacular; tremendous; unequalled; unbelievable; very good; wondrous; xtry.; you-beaut [Aus.]; *zestful;* [*Ant.* boring]

**breed** *(n.)*: ancestry; brand; class(ification); descent; derivation; ethnicity; extraction; family; genre; group; genus; heredity; ilk; *jus soli [L.];* kind; lineage; mores; nationality; origin; people; pedigree; parentage; *quarter;* rod; stock; sort; species; strain; stripe; type; tribe; *ubeity;* variety; vein; *way; x-class;* year-class; zoological classification;

**breed** *(v.)*: assemble; bring up; create; cause; develop; engender; form; generate; give birth to; hatch; institute; initiate; *job;* keep; *labor;* make; multiply; *newly formed;* originate; produce; procreate; *quicken;* raise; reproduce; spawn; shape; turn out; *upbuild; vary;* work; *xenogenesis;* yield; *zygogenesis;*
**brevity** *(n.)*: abbreviation; briefness; conciseness; cursoriness; curtness; *diurnal;* economy; ephemerality; fugaciousness; *germinal;* hurriedness; *instance; just little; knocked down;* laconicism; momentariness; non-lengthiness; *overly small;* pithiness; quickness; rapidity; shortness; succinctness; to the point; terseness; use of few words; *very short; wee; XS; yea big;* zippiness;
**brew** *(v.)*: alcoholize; bring to readiness; concoct; distill; decoct; *effervesce;* ferment; get ready; *habilitate;* infuse; *jibe; keg; light beer;* make; *near-ready; outfit;* prepare; *quality;* re-ferment; *set;* turn into alcohol; use yeast; vintage; well-readied; *xfer;* yarken; *yeast; zymotic;*
**bribe** *(n.)*: allurement; blood money; carrot; douceur; enticement; fee; gift; grease; hire; hush money; inducement; *jewel;* kickback; kola [Afr.]; lure money; money; nobbling; *outlay;* payment; payoff; payola; present; price; palm-grease; quiet-money; reward; sop; subornation; tea money; *usury;* vigorish; venal; *wile; xenium; yield; zero ethics;*
**bribe** *(v.)*: allure with money; buy (off); *compensate; disburse;* entice; *finance;* grease one's palm; hire; induce; *jewel; kickback; lure;* make ~; nobble; *outlay;* pay off; *quiet-money;* reward; suborn; *temp; usury; vig;* weigh out; *xenium; yield; zero ethics;*
**bribery** *(n.)*: allurement; buying off; *compensation; disbursement;* enticement; embracery; *financing;* grease; gift-giving; hiring; inducement; *jewels;* kickbacks; *lure; malversation;* nobbling; *outlay;* paying off; *quiet-money;* rewarding; shelling out; *temp; usury; venal;* weighing out; *xenium; yield; zero ethics;*
**brick** *(n.)*: adobe; block; cement block; cinder block; cobblestone; dry-pressed ~; extruded ~; firebrick; *glass block;* hewn stone; industrial block; *jib;* klompie; kiln-dried ~; *lateritous;* masonry; mud ~; nog; *opus vittatum;* pavement ~; quarle; quadrel; red ~; stone block; sett; *tile; undressed stone; veneer stone;* Wienerberger ~; xblock; yard block; *zeug;*
**bricklayer** *(n.)*: artificer; brickworker; craftsman; *doer; employee;* freemason; granite worker; hodman; industrial worker; *jobber; kiln-dried;* laborer; mason; nogger; *operator;* paver; quarler; rubbleworker; stonemason; tiler; *underling;* veneer stone-worker; worker; xblock layer; yard block layer; *zaikai [Jap.];*
**bridal** *(adj.)*: alliance; bond; conjugal; *deuterogamy; espousal; frankmarriage;* getting together; hymeneal; *intermarriage;* joining; knot; league; marriage; matrimonial; nuptial; opetide; *partnership; quixotic; relationship;* spousal; *tying the knot;* union; vow-taking; wedding; *x; yoke; zonam solvere* [L.];
**bride** *(n.)*: amorist; beauty; *coquette;* daughter; *enjoined; female;* girl; handmaiden; honeymooner; *inamorata; jeune fille* [F.]; *kitten;* lass; lady love; lovebird; maiden; newlywed; *other;* prize; *quedam [arch.];* rose [slang]; sweetheart; *true love; unmarried woman;* virgin; woman; wife; war ~; *x-chromosome;* young ~; *zitella* [It.]; [Ant. bridegroom]
**bridegroom** *(n.)*: *adult;* benedict; *chap; dude; eligible bachelor;* fellow; groom; honeymooner; husband; inamorato; *joe [slang]; key man;* lucky fellow; man; Mr. Right; newlywed; *one; prince charming;* querry; *right one;* sir; *tuxedo;* usher; virile; working man; *x-linked;* young man; zoon; [Ant. bride]
**bridesmaid** *(n.)*: attendant; best friends; *companion;* damsel; *endeared;* friend; *flower girl;* girl; handmaiden; *individual; jeune fille [F.]; kith;* lass; maiden; maid (matron) of honor; newlywed; *one;* person; *quedam [arch.];* rose [slang]; *sidekick;* trainbearer; usherette; virgin; woman; wedding party [pl.]; *x-chromosome;* young lady; *zitella* [It.]; [Ant. brideman]
**bridge** *(n.)*: arch ~; box girder ~; crossing; covered bridge; draw~; extradosed ~; foot~; floating ~; girder ~; humpback ~; ice ~; *jhula* [Himalayas]; K-7 ~; log ~; moon ~; *natural ~;* overpass; over~ [Br.]; pontoon ~; pontifice; passage; Q- ~; rope ~; railroad ~; suspension ~; trestle ~; toll ~; underpass; under~ [Br.]; viaduct; walkway; x-ing; Y-bridge; zig-zag ~;

**bridge** *(v.)*: arch; build ~s; connect; cross; *decussate;* extend across; fix together; go across; hook up; interconnect; join; *knit;* link; move across; *nitch [Scot.]; over;* put together; pass over; *quicken; relate;* reunite; span; tie together; traverse; unite; *venture; wed; xenograft;* yoke; zet [dial.];

**brief** *(adj.)*: abbreviated; abridged; brusque; concise; cursory; curt; diurnal; economical; ephemeral; fugacious; *germinal;* hurried; *instant; just little; knocked down;* little; laconic; momentary; not lengthy; *overly short;* pithy; passing; quick; rapid; shortness; succinct; to the point; terse; temporal; transient; using few words; very short; wee; *XS; yea big;* zippy; [*Ant.* big]

**bright** *(adj.)*: argent; brilliant; beaming; cheery; colorful; dazzling; effulgent; enlightened; fulgent; florid; gleaming; high-colored; intense; illuminated; *joyous;* keen; luminous; light; lit; lustrous; lambent; magnificent; nitid; orthochromatic; *powerful;* quite ~; radiant; shining; sparkling; splendid; transplendent; utterly ~; vibrant; vivid; *wondrous; xtry.; yellow;* zippy; [*Ant.* bedimmed]

**brighten** *(v.)*: adorn; brighten up; cheer up; cast light; dazzle; enlighten; engild; fully light; gild; glow; highlight; irradiate; illuminate; intensify; jazz up; *kindle;* lighten; make brighter; *non-dimmed;* outshine; *polish; quiver;* radiate; shine; throw light; *undimmed;* vivify; wax brighter; *xtry;* yield light; *zap;* [*Ant.* bedim]

**brightness** *(n. illumination)*: aura; brilliance; candescence; dazzle; effulgence; fulgency; glow; glory; haze; *halo;* illumination; *jacklight; keenness;* light; luminosity; luster; *moonlight;* nitency; oriency; prefulgency; *quality;* radiance; refulgence; shine; sheen; transplendency; utter shine; vividness; whiteness; *xenon light;* yellow light; *zodiacal light;*

**brilliance** *(n. illumination)*: aura; brightness; candescence; dazzle; emanation; fulgency; glow; glory; heavenliness; irradiance; intensity; *jacklight; kindle;* luster; lucence; magnificence; nitency; *overlight; phosphorescence; quality;* radiance; resplendence; splendor; *translucency; ultraviolet light;* vividness; white light; *xenon light;* yellow light; *zodiacal light;*

**brilliant** *(adj.)*: *aglow;* bright; beaming; cheery; dazzling; effulgent; enlightened; fulgent; florid; gleaming; glowing; glorious; high-colored; intense; illuminated; *joyous;* keen; luminous; light; lit; lustrous; lambent; magnificent; naif; orthochromatic; *powerful; quality;* radiant; resplendent; shining; sparkling; splendid; transplendent; utterly ~; vibrant; vivid; *wondrous; xtry.; yellow;* zippy; [*see* smart]

**brim** *(n.)*: abuttal; border; *circumference; derby;* edge; fore-edge; *gilded edge;* hem; *imbordered;* jut; *kepi-brim;* lip; margin; *narrow;* outskirts; perimeter; *quadra;* ridge; rim; *side;* top; upper edge; verge; *welt;* x-border; yonder; zone;

**bring** *(v.)*: accompany; *attract;* bear; carry; conduct; convey; deliver; *export;* fetch; get; haul; *import;* janker; kurvey; lug; lead; move; *non-retention; overcarry;* pass; quarter-cart; relay; retrieve; ship; transport; take; uptake; *van; walk;* xfer; yomp; zip;

**brink** *(n.)*: abuttal; border; boundary; bank; coast; circumference; dawn; edge; environs; fringe; gate; hem; inception; *jurisdiction; kept limit;* limit; margin; *narrow;* outskirts; perimeter; quadra; rim; *sevlage;* threshold; *ulterior;* verge; *without;* x-border; yonder; zone;

**brisk** *(adj.)*: accelerated; *bouncy; celerity;* dexterous; expeditious; frisky; *geared up;* hurried; intense; *jiffy; keen;* lively; *moving;* nimble; *on the double;* pronto; quick; rapid; snappy; spirited; timely; *ultrasonic speed;* vigorous; wimble; x-speed; yauld; zippy;

**bristle** *(n.)*: awn; acicula; brush hair; coarse hair; *dark hair; ever-rigid;* frenulum; fiber; *gris;* hair; *item; juba [L.];* kemp; *long ~; mane;* nylon ~; *object;* prickle; quill; rigid hair; stubble; seta; thick hair; *unbending;* vibrissa; whisker; *xerasia; yieldless; zapata;*

**bristly** *(adj.)*: acanaceous; bushy; bristled; brambly; coarse; *dark hair;* ever-prickly; flocculent; glochidiate; hispid; hirsute; *itchy; jubate;* kempy; lanuginous; maned; *non-bald;* overgrown; prickly; *quiff;* rough; setaceous; setiferous; setose; spiny; thorny; unshorn; velutinous; whiskery; *xerasia; yellow-haired; zapata;*

**Britain** *(n.)*: Albion [poet.]; Britannia; *Caledonia* [L.]; *Devonshire;* England; *Finchley;* Great ~; *Hampshire; island kingdom;* John Bull [pfn.]; *the* Kingdom; Land (of the Rose); Mercia; *Nottingham;* Old Dart [slang]; *Prydain Fawr* [Welsh]; *the* Queen's Land; Queuetopia [joc.]; *the* Realm; Sovereign of the Seas; Tight Little Island [slang]; United Kingdom; *Victorian England; Wessex; Xylophone; Yorkshire; Zennor;*

**British** *(adj.)*: Anglo-Saxon; Britannic; Commonwealth; *Devonshire;* English; *from Britain; Great Britain;* His (Her) Majesty's; Iceni; Irish ~; John Bullish; *King's;* Limey [off.]; Mercian; *Northern Irish;* Old ~; pongo [Aus. slang]; *Queen's; Red Coat [U.S.];* Scotch ~; *tommy [slang];* U.K.; Victorian; Welsh ~; *xanthochroic; Yinglish*; *Zennor;*

**brittle** *(adj.)*: arenaceous; breakable; crackable; delicate; easily broken; embrittled; frangible; fragile; frail; glasslike; hard; *inflexible; jimp; krisp;* likely to shatter; *mar;* non-flexible; *overly ~; prang;* quite ~; rigid; shatterable; *too ~;* ultrahard; very fragile; weak; *x-hard;* yieldless; zero give;

**broach** *(v.)*: approach; bring up; comment; discuss; express; *foremention;* get on the subject; *holf forth;* introduce; *jaw; key in;* launch into; mention; *note;* open; *present; quoth;* raise; speak of; talk about; utter; verbalize; word; *xenophonia; yak;* zero in;

**broad** *(adj.)*: askant; big; capacious; *disproportionate;* extended; expansive; far-reaching; *great;* horizontal; *immense;* jacent; *king-sized;* lengthways; lengthwise; lateral; large; *massive; non-vertical;* obtuse; prodigious; quantitative; *roomy;* sideways; sidelong; thick; uncondensed; vast; wide; x-axis; *yawning;* zoomed out; [*see* comprehensive]

**broad** *(n. a woman)* [all offensive terms]: *amoret;* babe; bimbo; chick; dame; doll; *escort;* fem; goil; hen; *individual;* Jane; kitten; Lolita; moll; nancy; ol' gal; petticoat; quean; rig; skirt; tramp; *unkind;* venal; *woman; xanthippe;* yaud; *zaftig;* [*see* woman]

**broadcast** *(v.)*: air; bestrew; circulate; disseminate; diffuse; effuse; fan out; give out; *hurl;* inseminate; intersperse; *jawp; known;* litter; make dispersed; *non-localized;* overspread; propagate; publicize; *publish; quantity;* radiate; re~; *redisperse;* scatter; spread; *send;* thinly spread; transmit; televise; *universalize; very widespread;* widespread; xmit; yield; *zealously propagate;*

**broaden** *(v.)*: augment; become broader; *cross-widened;* dilate; enlarge; extend; flare; fan out; greaten; grow; *heighten;* increase; jumboize; *keep growing;* largify; make broader; *newly-widened;* outspread; *post-expansion; quantum increase; revamp;* stretch; spread out; thicken; upbuild; *very broad;* widen; wax bigger; *XL; yawn; zoom;*

**brochure** *(v.)*: advertisement; booklet; *circular;* double-fold; *essay;* flier; flysheet; *gospel tract;* handbill; handout; informational leaflet; *journalism; key thoughts;* leaflet; literature; *message; notations; opus;* pamphlet; paper; prospectus; quadrifoliate; reading matter; *sources;* tract; unifoliate ~; *vignette;* writing; *xenagogy; yeme; zeug;*

**broken** *(adj.)*: *agitato* [mus.]; broke; busted; cracked; conked out; defective; defunct; *exploded;* faulty; *grinded to a halt;* hurt; inoperative; imperfect; inadequate; *junk;* kaput; lost; malfunctioning; non-operative; out-of-order; peccant; quashed; ruined; smashed; severed; split; *shot;* torn; *trouble;* undone; useless; *void;* wrecked; x'ed; *yanked; zapped;*

**brood** *(v.)*: agonize; *bother;* contemplate; dwell on; despond; *evaluate;* fret; glower; huff; *incubate; jangle;* kick; languish; mope; muse; *not happy;* over-ponder; pout; pine; *question;* ruminate; sigh; sulk; think about; *upset;* vex; worry; *xenodiagnose; yeme; zero in;*

**brook** *(n.)*: arroyo; bourn; branch; bogan [Can.]; creek; *deep;* effluent; freshet; gully; *headwaters;* inlet; *jheel [Ind.];* kill [Du.]; lough; millstream; nant; outlet; prong; quebrada; river; rivulet; runnel; stream; tributary; *underground stream; voe;* waterway; *xyrisic;* yeo; *Zee [G.];*

**broom** *(n.)*: angle ~; besom; corn ~; *dust-brush; enamel brush;* flag~; garage ~; house ~; *instrument;* janitor's ~; kitchen ~; long-handled ~; *malkin;* nylon-bristle ~; outdoor ~; push~; *quillbrush;* rigger; sweeper; shop ~; straw ~; *trim brush;* utensil; *varnish brush;* whisk; xtr. wide ~; yard ~; *zeug [G.];*

**brothel** *(n.)*: *adultery;* bordello; bagnio; bawdy-house; cathouse; den of harlots; *embrothel;* fleshpot; gamester-house; hothouse; *immorality;* juke; kip; *lady of the evening;* meretrix-house; notch-house; *ordure;* prostitute-house; queanery; rookery; stew; trullhouse; *ungodliness; venery;* whorehouse; x-rated; yaup-house; *zoo;*

**brother** *(n.)*: agnate; big ~; blood ~; brethren [pl.]; *cadet* [arch.]; *dear ~;* elder ~; *flesh and blood; german;* half- ~; identical twin; *junior;* kid- ~; kin(sman); little ~; *ménage;* near kinsman; older ~; *pal; quintuplet;* relative; relation; sibling; *twin ~; uterine ~; virile;* ward; *x-linked;* younger ~; *zon [dial.];*

**brotherhood** *(n.)*: affinity; bond; camaraderie; comradeship; devotion; endearment; friendship; fraternity; fellowship; goodwill; *helping;* intimacy; joining; kinship; loyalty; mateship; nearness; oneness; partnership; *quondam friendship;* relationship; solidarity; trust; unity; *value;* warmth; *xenia;* yoke; *zeal;*

**brown** *(adj.)*: auburn; beige; brick; brunette; chocolate; coffee; chestnut; dark ~; *embrowned; earthen;* filemot; fuscous; gray- ~; hazel; *imbrowned;* java; khaki; light ~; melanic; mahogany; nutmeg; ocher; puce; queen's brown; russet; reddish-brown; sandy; sepia; tawny; tan; taupe; umber; Vandyke ~; wheatish; *xanthomelanoid;* yellowish- ~; *zerda- ~;*

**bruise** *(n.)*: affliction; black and blue mark; black eye; contusion; discoloration; ecchymosis; flesh wound; gall; hurt; injury; *jolt;* knock; *lesion; lump;* mark; *nubbling; offense;* prang; query; *riven;* shiner; *thrash; uppercut; violence;* welt; *xtry. pain;* yedder; *zonked;*

**bruise** *(v.)*: afflict; batter; bash; bang; contuse; clobber; dinge [Br.]; *efface;* flog; frush [arch.]; give one a black eye; hurt; injure; *jolt;* knock; lam; maul; mash; nubble; *overhit;* pound; punch; pelt; quab; rap; smite; thrash; uppercut; veney; whack; *x-sect;* yedder; zonk;

**brush** *(n.)*: angle ~; broom; baster; *catt ~;* duster; dust ~; enamel ~; fire~; feather duster; grooming ~; hair~; *instrument;* jack-handle ~; kid- ~; long-handled ~; lint ~; malkin; nylon ~; nail~; *oval-sash ~;* paint~; quill~; rigger; spreader; sweeper; trim ~; tooth~; *utensil;* varnish ~; wire ~; wall ~; xtr. fine ~; yard broom; *zeug [G.];*

**brush** *(v.)*: apply; broom; baste; *color; cover;* daub; *dust;* embrocate; fucate; groom; hand-paint; infucate; *jostle;* kemb; limn; *make;* neaten; overspread; paint; *quab; reapply;* spread; slubber; sweep; stroke; *tidy (-touch) up; transfer;* upsweep; *vamp;* whisk; wipe; *xfer; yark; zip;*

**brutal** *(adj.)*: atrocious; brutish; barbaric; crude; dreadful; evil; ferocious; gruff; harsh; inhuman; ill-mannered; junglish; *kaf [arch.]; loutish;* mean; nasty; overbearing; *painful; quad;* rough; savage; severe; terrible; truculent; unkind; violent; wicked; *xtry. ~; yahoo; zooid;* [*Ant.* benign]

**brutish** *(adj.)*: awful; atrocious; base; boorish; beastly; bestial; crude; coarse; crass; despicable; degraded; evil; filthy; foul; graceless; gross; horrendous; indecent; ill-mannered; jaded; kitsch; loutish; loutish; mean; nefarious; nasty; obnoxious; offensive; oafish; pathetic; *quad;* repugnant; raw; rude; rough; sordid; sinful; shameless; terrible; treacherous; uncouth; uncivilized; unrefined; vile; vulgar; wretched; wicked; *x-rated;* yucky; zhlubby; [*Ant.* benign]

**bubble** *(v.)*: agitate; burble; bleb; blister; cavitate; decoct; effervesce; fizz(le); foam; ferment; gurgle; hard-boil; imboil; *jet; jump;* kier; lather; murmur; *neal [arch.]; over-boil;* popple; *quietly burble;* regurgitate; seethe; simmer; sud; *trouble; uprush;* vescicate; well; wallop; *xuld [arch.]; yote;* zoutch;

**bubbly** *(adj.)*: airy; animated; bouncy; cheerful; delightful; effervescent; fun; gay; happy; *inspiring;* joyful; *keen;* lively; merry; *nice; overjoyed;* poppling; *quite cheerful; rejoicing;* sparkly; spunky; *thrilled;* uplifting; vivacious; *winsome; xtr. happy; yeah!;* zesty;

**bucket** *(n.)*: *aluminum pail; bin;* can; container; debe; *excavator ~;* fire ~; grain ~; hod; ice ~; *jug;* kibble; lard ~; *load;* milk pail; mop ~; *nook;* oyster pail; pail; *quinderkyn;* receptacle; scuttle; sand pail; tin ~; *utility ~;* vessel; water ~; wooden ~; *xtr. large ~; yellow ~;* zinc-coated ~;

**buckle** *(v. bend)*: *acquiesce;* bend; bow; crumple; collapse; dip; enfold; flex; fold; *geniculate;* hunker; incline; *judder;* knuckle; lap; *move; non-rigid; overbend;* ply; quat; refold; stoop; twist; *uncinate;* vary; *warp; x-out;* yield; zigzag; [*see* compromise]

**buckle** *(v. fasten)*: attach; bind; connect; clasp; *do; engage;* fasten; *grip;* hitch; interlock; join; *knot;* link; latch; *mount; non-opened; over-tighten;* put together; *quite secure;* reunite; secure; *tack;* unite; *Velcro®; wed; xfer; yoke; zip;*

**bud** *(v.)*: *appear;* blossom; *climb;* develop; *emerge; flourish;* germinate; *heighten;* inoculate; *jump up;* knop; luxuriate; mature; *nourish; outgrow;* pullulate; *quantum growth; rise;* sprout; shoot; take root; thrive; upshoot; vegetate; wax greater; *xin yi [Chin.]; yain* [arch.]; *zoom up;*

**budge** *(v.)*: advance; bestir; creep; dislodge; edge; *force;* go; haul; inch; jar; *kite;* leave; move; nudge; ooch; push; quicken; *relocate; remove;* shove; *traverse; underway;* verge; *walk;* xfer; yede; *zip;* [*Ant.* bide]

**budget** *(n.)*: annual ~; *allotment;* blueprint; corporate ~; *design;* economic spending plan; formula; general ~; *high;* itemized ~; *joint ~; key spending plan; layout;* master plan; *missions ~; national ~;* outline; plan; *quo mode [L.]; ratified ~;* spending plan; total spending plan; *underlying plan; voted-for;* working plan; *x-chart;* yearly ~; *zenithal projection;*

**budget** *(v.)*: *austerity;* be careful; cut back; curb; decrease; economize; *frugal;* get by; hold back; *illiberal; judicious;* keep from overspending; limit; make cuts; *niggardly; omit;* plan; *quail;* retrench; scrimp; spend less; tighten one's belt; use sparingly; *very cheap;* watch it; *x; yeme; zero-expenditure;*

**buffet** *(v.)*: attack; batter; clobber; *drub; efface;* flail; *get;* hit; *impact;* jab; knock; lam; maul; nubble; *overhit;* pound; quab; rap; smite; strike; thrash; uppercut; veney; wallop; *x-sect;* yedder; zonk;

**bug** *(n.)*: *ant;* beetle; critter; creepy-crawly; *drainfly; earwig; fly; flea;* gnat; *housefly; hornet;* insect; *June bug; king weevil;* leaf insect; *menace; mosquito; nun moth; orchid mantis;* pest; plague; *quadripennate; roach;* spider; *tick; union jack butterfly;* vermin; wasp; weevil; *xyleborus; yucca borer; zyzzogeton;* [*see* plague; swarm]

**bug** *(v.)*: annoy; antagonize; aggravate; bother; badger; chafe; disturb; exasperate; frustrate; fluster; grate (on); gall; harass; hassle; irritate; irk; jangle; kid; *livid;* menace; nettle; nag; *offend;* pester; *queach [arch.];* rankle; rile; *steam;* tease; taunt; trouble; unnerve; vex; *weary; wherret; x-ing;* yerk; zing; [*see* mock; nuisance; *Ant.* bless]

**buggy** *(n.)*: *apparatus;* barrow; carriage; coach; dray; equipage; fiacre; gig; hackney; Italian coach; jaunting car; karrozzin; landau; mail-coach; noddy; *oxcart;* pleasure-carriage; *quadricycle;* rig; surrey; tandem; *undercarriage;* vehicle; wagon; *x-port;* yanker [Br.]; *Zis [Rus.];*

**build** *(v.)*: assemble; bring into being; create; construct; design; develop; erect; edify; engineer; fashion; fabricate; form(ulate); found; forge; generate; *hew;* institute; invent; *job;* knock together; *labor;* make; manufacture; mass produce; *new-built;* originate; output; produce; put together; put up; pump out; quick-build; raise; rebuild; reassemble; shape; strengthen; turn out; upbuild; *vamp;* wage; *xenomorph;* yield; zip together; [*Ant.* break]

**builder** *(n.)*: assembler; architect; bricklayer; creator constructer; contractor; carpenter; designer; developer; erecter; edifier; engineer; fashioner; fabricator; formulator; founder; forger; generator; house-raiser; institutor; inventor; *job; knock together;* labor; maker; manufacturer; mass producer; *new-built;* originator; producer; *quick-build;* rebuilder; shaper; subcontractor; *trained carpenter;* upbuilder; *vamper;* wright; wager; *xenomorph;* yielder; *zip together;* [*Ant.* breaker]

**building** *(n.)*: architecture; *apartment ~; business;* complex; domed ~; edifice; facilities; frame; *garage;* house; high rise; *institution; junior college;* kamienica; low rise; mid-rise; nine-story ~; office ~; pile; palazzo; quadriplex; residential ~; (super)structure; skyskraper; tower; two-story ~; utility ~; vertical structure; wing; xenodocheion; yardhouse; *zone;*

**Kinds of buildings**: apartment; barn; church house; domicile; eatery; factory; farmhouse; garage; house; high-rise; industrial ~; joss house; low-rise; mall; nursing home; office; police station; Quonset hut; restaurant; store; store; townhouse; utility building; villa; warehouse; xenodoceion; yardhouse; ziggurat;

**bulge** *(v.)*: *augment;* bloat; balloon; *climax;* distend; expand; fatten; grow; *huff;* inflate; jumboize; *keep growing;* largen; *maximize; nob;* oversaturate; puff up; protrude; *quantum increase;* rise; swell; tumulate; *thicken; upbuild; voluminous;* wax greater; *XL: yaw; zoom;*
**bulk** *(n.)*: amplitude; body; bigness; corpulence; *disproportion;* extensiveness; fullness; greatness; hugeness; immensity; jumboness; *king-sized;* largeness; mass; *noteworthiness;* obesity; prodigiousness; quantum; *ruck;* size; *tremendousness; unladen weight;* volume; weight; *XL; Ymir; zaftig;*
**bull** *(n.)*: apis; *animal;* bovine; cattle [pl.]; draft-ox; *el Toro* [Sp.]; fatling; gelding; Holstein; *Irish moiled;* jument; Jersey; kyloe; leppy; *mammal;* neat; ox; *polled shorthorn; quadruped; red heifer;* steer; Taurus; *Toro* [Sp.]; Texas longhorn; ure; vituline; Welsh; *x-breed;* yearling; *zebu;* [*see* beast]
**bulletin** *(n.)*: announcement; broadcast; brochure; communication; church ~; dispatch; *enunciation;* flyer; general announcement; headlines; information brochure; journal; *key thoughts;* leaflet; magazine; *message;* notice; newsletter; official ~; program; publication; periodical; quadrifoliate; report; release; *source;* tract; trifold ~; unifoliate ~; *vignette;* word; *xenagogy;* yeme; *zine;*
**bullock** *(n.)*: aurochs; bovid; *cow; creature;* draft- ~; *ennstal;* fatling; gaur; heifer; *Irish moiled; jument;* kouprey; *livestock;* musk ox; neat; ox; *polled shorthorn; quadruped;* red heifer; sarlac; Tartary ox; urus; vu quang ~; water buffalo; *x-breed;* yak; zebu; [*see* beast]
**bully** *(n.)*: aggressor; brow-beater; coercer; *daunter; evildoer;* fanfaron; *good-for-nothing;* hector; hackster; intimidator; *jackanapes;* kill-cow; *lowlife;* menace; *no-good;* oppressor; *pick on;* quarreler; ruffian; scrapper; tough-guy; terrorizer; *unruly;* varlet; warrior; *xiaoren;* yobo; *zabernism;*
**bully** *(v.)*: aggress; browbeat; buffalo; coerce; daunt; *endanger;* frighten; *go after;* harass; hector; intimidate; *jeopardize;* keep down; lean on; menace; *nerves;* oppress; pressure; pick on; *quash;* ramp; strong-arm; threaten; terrorize; tyrannize; unnerve; victimize; walk on; *xenophobia; yieldless; zabernism;*
**bulrush** *(n.)*: *arundinaceous;* bog-rush; cattail; *durra; eelgrass;* flag; grass; haugh-grass Indian ~; *jheel* [Ind.]; kamish [Rus.]; lagoon-grass; mace-reed; *nanoplankton; overgrowth;* papyrus; quill; reed; rush; sedge; typha; *tall reeds; usnea;* vetiver-grass; water-flag; *xyris;* yedda; *zea;*
**bulwark** *(n.)*: *abatis;* battlement; bastion; bank; contravallation; defense; embankment; earthwork; fortification; guard; glacis; hornwork; intrenchment; *jardang;* knoll; line (of defense); mound; muniment; *non-endangered;* outwork; parapet; *quai;* rampart; sconce; talis; *upholding;* vallation; wall; *x-ed; yeming* [arch.]; *zone;*
**bum** *(n.)*: almsman; beggar; bindlestiff; cadger; deadbeat; derelict; *estivator;* floater; gallivant; hobo; *idler;* javel; kern; loafer; mendicant; ne'er-do-well; *oberration;* panhandler; *quisby;* rolling stone; scavenger; skell; tramp; *urchin;* vagrant; wastrel; wretch; *xenarthra;* yahoo; *zhlub;* [*see* sluggard; *Ant.* billionaire]
**bumbling** *(adj.)*: awkward; bungling; clumsy; dowdy; *étourderie* [F.]; fumbly; gangly; heavy-handed; inelegant; jumbly; klutzy; lumbering; maladroit; non-graceful; oafish; plumbeous; *quirky; rube;* socially inept; troublesome; ungainly; ungraceful; *vexatious;* wooden; *xtr. clumsy;* yokelish; zhlubby;
**bump** *(n.)*: amassment; bulge; *clod; contusion;* daud; *eruption; furuncle;* goiter; hump; inflation; jog; knob; knot; mound; nodule; nub; *oddity;* protuberance; quat; raised area; swelling; *tumor;* umbo; varix; wart; welt; xyloma; *yedder; zit;*
**bump** *(v.)*: *assault;* bang; clobber; dash; *elbow; flog; grind;* hit; impact; jolt; knock; lam; mash; nail; *overhit;* pound; quab; rap; strike; thump; uppercut; *veney;* whack; *x-sect;* yerk; zonk;
**bumpkin** *(n.)*: agrarian; boor; backwoodsman; country ~; chuff; dolt; *egghead;* farmer; funk; goff; hick; hillbilly; ignoramus; joskin; kern; knuff; lout; larrikin; mountaineer; numbskull; oaf; provincial; peasant; plebeian; plowboy; quack; rube; rustic; redneck; swain; tike; *unsophisticated; vassal;* whig [Br.]; *xiaoren;* yokel; zhlub;
**bumpy** *(adj.)*: *amassed;* bulgy; clumpy; *coarse;* daudy; *eruptive;* full of lunps; gibbos; humpy; *irregular;* jagged; knobby; lumpy; *mounds;* nubby; overly ~; papular; *quat;* rough; salebrous; *tumor;* umbonate; uneven; *varix;* whelky; *xyloma; yedder;* zitty;

**bun** *(n.)*: *angu bread;* biscuit; cross ~; croissant; dinner roll; *edible;* finger roll; *gingerbread;* hot cross ~; honey ~; *Italian bread; jannock;* kaiser roll; *light cake;* muffin; *naan bread;* oat ~; pan dulce; *quick bread;* roll; sweet roll; simnel; *toast; unleavened bread;* wheat ~; x- ~; *yuan hsiao* [Chin.]; zwieback;

**bunch** *(n.)*: assemblage; amassment; band; batch; bundle; collection; cluster; drove; *eight;* forgathering; group; hoard; heap; ingathering; *jam [slang];* kit [coll.]; lot; mass; multitude; number; overflow; pack; quantity; ruck; raft; set; turnout; unit; variety; wisp; *xtr.; yelm; zillions;*

**bundle** *(n.)*: array; assemblage; batch; bale; cluster; draught; *embale;* fascicle; fagot; group; heap; herd; hulk; hank; *ingathering; juba* [L.]; knitch; lot; mass; *nugget; overabundance;* pack(et); package; quantity; quire; roll; sheaf; set; shock; truss; tuft; *unit;* volley; wisp; wad; *xtr.;* yelm; *zonic;*

**buoyancy** *(n.)*: airiness; buoyance; *carrying;* driftability; *etherealness;* floatability; flotability; *going;* hoverability; inaquation; *jetting; kiting;* levitability; *lightness; moving on water;* natability; ocean-worthiness; *planing; quickening; resting;* seaworthiness; suspendibility; suspensibility; *transcendence; upbearing; volplaning;* waftability; *xuld [arch.]; yet unsinkable; zooming;*

**buoyant** *(adj.)*: *afloat;* being able to float; *carry;* driftable; *easily floats;* floatable; flotable; floaty; *going;* hoverable; inaquation; *jetting; kiting;* levitatable; lighter-than-air; *moving on water;* natant; ocean-worthy; *planing; quickened; resting;* seaworthy; suspendible; suspensible; *transcent; upbear; volplaning;* waftable; *xuld [arch.];* yet unsinkable; *zooming;*

**burden** *(n.)*: albatross; burthen; burdensomeness; brunt; burning desire; care; charge; carrying; craving; duty; dead weight; encumbrance; *fretting; goal; heaviness;* imposition; job; *key role;* load; liability; longing; millstone; mission; necessity; need; obligation; onus; over~; pack; *quest;* responsibility; strain; task; tote; undertaking; unction; vocation; weight; xci.; yoke; yearning; *zeugma [Gr.];* [*see* job; *Ant.* blessing]

**burden** *(v.)*: aggrieve; bother; bear down; concern; cumber; disturb; encumber; *fret;* grieve; *give;* heap on; impose; *jam-pack; kibble;* load; lade; lay on full; make ~ous; *nerve;* over~; overload; overweigh; put on one's shoulders; press; *quash; ram;* saddle; strain; trouble; *upset;* vex; worry; weigh down; *xuld [arch.];* yoke; zap; [*Ant.* bless]

**burdensome** *(adj.)*: arduous; bothersome; *complicated;* difficult; distressing; exasperating; fatiguing; grievous; heavy; hard; *irksome;* jarring; knotty; *lousy; messy;* noisome; onerous; oppressive; problematic; quisquose; repressive; straitened; trying; troublesome; tiresome; unpleasant; vexatious; wearisome; weighty; *xerotripsis; yucky; zhlubby;*

**bureau** *(n. agency)*: agency; branch; cabinet; committee; department; division; establishment; federal ~; government ~; group; headquarters; incorporation; jura; *kongsi* [Chin.]; location; ministry; nexus; organization; office; *power;* quango; records ~; subdivision; service; town office; *unit; village office; workers' union; x-class; yuan* [Chin.]; zonal office;

**burglar** *(n.)*: armed man; bandit; crook; cat ~; cracksman; *delinquent; evildoer;* filcher; gangster; housebreaker; intruder; *jailbird;* knuck; kleptomaniac; larcenist; mugger; nimmer; outlaw; prowler; *quad;* robber; stealer; thief; *unscrupulous;* villain; waddy; *xiaoren;* yegg; *zhlub;* [*Ant.* bobby]

**burglary** *(n.)*: abstraction; breaking and entering; brigandage; *crime;* deprivation; excoriation; extortion; filching; grand larceny; hoist; heist; holdup; housebreaking; *impalming; identity theft; japery;* kleptomania; larceny; mugging; michery; nimming; *obtaining;* pilfering; purloining; petty larceny; *quad;* robbery; stealing; shoplifting; theft; thievery; unpursings; *underhandedness;* violence; villainy; wresting; *xfer; yanking; zipping away;*

**burial** *(n.)*: act of burying; burying; cemetery service; committal; dirge; entombment; funeral (service); graveside; *hearselike;* internment; joint ~; knell; *lyke-wake;* memorial service; *mausolean; necropolis;* obsequies; planting; quieting; requiem; sepulture; *service;* tombing; undertaking; viaticum; wake; *xat; yizkor* [Heb.]; *zoothapsis;* [*see* cemetery]

**burn** *(n.)*: ambustion; *affliction;* burn-mark; blister; char-mark; *damage;* evil; first degree ~; gall; hurt; injury; *jarring;* kindle; leg- ~; mat- ~; *mark;* neck wound; over~; patch; *quirk; redness;* second degree ~; scorch mark; sear; third degree ~; *ustion;* vesication; wound; *xtr. hot;* yedder; *zapping;*

**burn** *(v.)*: alight; *ablaze;* blaze; combust; char; cremate; *consume;* deflagrate; *devour;* enflame; enkindle; *engulf;* flame; flare; glow; go up in smoke; gut; *heat;* ignite; incinerate; inflame; *jeopardize;* kindle; light (up); *miskindle;* neal; overburn; *pyric;* quick-match; raze; roast; *rage;* scorch; smolder; sear; singe; scald; torch; ustion; vesicate; *waste;* wreck; *xylophyrography; yearn; zap;* [*see* flame]

**burnish** *(v.)*: apply ~; buff; *coat; develop shine; enamel;* furbish; *finish;* gloss; glaze; *high-gloss; inceration;* jigger; *keen;* lacquer; luster; make shiny; *nigrosine;* overglaze; *overpolish;* overgild; polish; *quartz sand;* rub; shine; sleek; shellac; topcoat; *urethane;* varnish; wax; *xesturgy; yare; zinc flourosilicate;*

**burnt** *(adj.)*: adust [arch.]; *ashes;* burned; ~ to a crisp; charred; deflagrated; encindered; fire- ~; gone up in smoke; gutted; *hot;* incinerated; *jejune;* kindled; *lit up; match-lit;* nealed; overbaked; *pyric; quick-match;* razed; scorched; singed; torched; *ustion;* vesicated; well-cooked; *xylophyrography; yellow-hot;* zapped;

**burrow** *(n.)*: aperture; breach; cranny; dugout; den; excavation; fissure; gap; hole; home; incavation; jaw-hole; krater; lodge; maze; nook; opening; pit; *quarry-pit;* rabbit hole; sett; tunnel; underground passageway; vug; warren; *xystus pit;* yawn; *zanja;*

**burrow** *(v.)*: advance; break through; channel; dig; excavate; *fodient;* grub; hollow; hole; *intrench; jenkin;* kip; *lower;* mole; *notch; open; prospect;* quarry; *remove dirt;* shovel; tunnel; undermine; *venture;* worm; *xfer; yede; zanja;*

**burst** *(n.)*: accelerate; breaking (forth); coursing; dehiscence; eruption; flow; gush; hurling; issue; jet; *ka-pow;* letting go; *movement; naid;* out~; outpouring; pouring; *quickening;* rush; surge; torrent; uprush; vomiting; wave; *xfer; yead;* zipping;

**burst** *(v.)*: *accelerate;* bust; break open; *crack;* course; come unglued; dehisce; erupt; explode; flow; gush; hurl; issue; jet; *ka-pow;* let go; *move; non-containment; out~;* pour out; *quicken;* rip; rupture; stream; shoot; spurt; surge; *tear apart;* unleash; vent; *wham; xfer;* yead; *zap;*

**bury** *(v.)*: *arrange;* burrow; begrave; cover; conceal; commit; consign to grave; deposit; embed; entomb; fix; funeralize; ground; hide; implant; inter; inhume; *jacket;* kist; lodge; lay to rest; *make; mantle; nuzzle;* overlay; obscure; plant; put in (the ground); pit; *quat [arch.];* reset; *rebury;* sink; subdeposit; sepulchre; set; tuck; *underground; verge;* whelm; *xenotransplant;* yird; zet [dial.]; [*Ant.* bring out]

**bush** *(n.)*: acer; arboret; brush; *caper-bush; dendroid; elemi;* frutex; *gorse;* hedge; heath; *item; juba* ~; *kalmia; lantana; may-bloom; narra;* oleander; *piperidge; plant; queach; rosa;* shrub(bery); thicket; thorn ~; topiary; *ulex;* vegetation; *whin; xylopia; yawshrub; zereba;*

**bushy** *(adj.)*: abundant; bristly; *copious;* dense; *entangled;* fluffy; flocculent; *gris;* hairy; *intertwined; jubate;* kempy; luxuriant; *maned; non-bald;* overgrown; plush; *quiff;* really hairy; shaggy; thick; unkempt; villous; wooly; *xerasia; yellow-haired; zapata;* [*Ant.* bare]

**business** *(n.)*: activity; buying and selling; commerce; dealings; enterprise; *exportation; furnish; goods;* handling; intercourse; *importation; job; kommers* [G.]; *labor;* merchandising; marketing; *oversell;* private enterprise; *qualified sale;* retailing; selling; shipping; trade; trading; traffic; *undersell;* vending; wholesale; *xfer; X12;* yardage; *zaikai* [Jap.];

**busy** *(adj.)*: abuzz; bustling; *cluttered; crazy;* doing (something); eventful; full; going nonstop; helter-skelter; hopping; industrious; jumping; *kicking;* laboring; moving; *non-quiet;* overburdened; occupied; *problem;* quite ~; *routine;* swamped; *T-commerce;* unavailable; very ~; working; *x-full;* yet cluttered; *zero free time;* [*Ant.* bored]

**busybody** *(n.)*: *arbitrator;* busy-body; buttinsky; crasher; disturber; encroacher; *force oneself in;* gossip; *horning in;* interferer; *jump right in;* kibitz; *louser up;* meddler; nose; *officious;* pest; pry; quidnunc; rumormonger; snoop; tamperer; troublemaker; *utterer;* violator; *whisperer;* x; yenta; *zealously intermeddle;*
**busyness** *(n.)*: activity; bustle; business; commotion; doings; energy; flurry; goings-on; hubbub; hurrying; hullabaloo; intercourse; *jumping; keeping busy;* labor; movement; *non-stationariness; ongoing;* productivity; quickening; running to and fro; stirring; *traffic; teeming; underway;* vigor; work; *xfer; yede; zipping;* [see work]
**butler** *(n.)*: attendant; *bondman;* chamberlain; cup-bearer; demiurge; employee; footman; *gofer* [slang]; gallopin; house steward; *indentured servant; Jeeves;* keeper; lackey; minister; man(servant); major-domo; naperer; offsider; pantler; *quartermaid* [fem.]; *retainer* [arch.]; servant; suffragi [Arab.]; *trusty servant;* under ~; valet; waiter; x-man; yeoman; zaikai; [*Ant.* boss]
**buttress** *(n,)*: abutment; butment; brace; crutch; clasping ~; diagonal ~; *edifice;* fulcram; flying ~; fortification; *girder;* hold; *item;* joist; *keep;* leg; main support; non-clasping ~; *object;* prop; pillar; *quarter-arch;* reinforcement; support; setback ~; *truss;* undergirding; underpin; underprop; vang; *wall; well-supported; xfer; yieldless; zaccho;*
**buy** *(v.)*: acquire; bring money for; *come by;* deal; *engage in sale; fetch;* get; *have;* invest; *jump at; kep; lay down money for;* make purchase; *nab;* obtain; *over~;* pick up; procure; pay for; purchase; quoff; re~; shop; secure; sink money into; take home; *use money; vest;* wholesale; *xfer; yafe* [arch.]; *zealously acquire;*
**buyer** *(n.)*: *acquirer;* bargain-hunter; customer; client; dealer; end-user; *financier;* guest; *haggler;* interested party; investor; *junk-dealer;* keener; lunchbreak shopper; *man(ciple);* non-risk ~; *oligopsony; outpatient;* purchaser; qualified ~; *reseller;* shopper; trader; user; vendee; walk-in; *xfer; youth; zealous ~;*
**buzzword** *(n.)*: adage; byword; catchword; catch phrase; dictum; epigram; formula; guideline; household word; *instruction; judgment; koine;* law; maxim; neology; oracle; proverb; platitude; quote; rule; saying; shibboleth; truism; tenet; universal phrase; verse; wisdom; *xenophonia; Yogism;* zeteticism;
**bylaw** *(n.)*: *act;* behest; code; directive; enactment; *fatwa* [Mos.]; governance; *halacha* [Heb.]; injunction; *jus gentium* [L.]; *keleusmatically;* law; measure; *natural (-national) law;* ordinance; precept; *quo minus* [L.]; rule; statute; *technicality;* ukase; *voice; word;* XO mandate; yardstick; *zakon* [Rus.];
**bypass** *(v.)*: avoid; *beat around;* circumvent; detour; evade; find way around; get around; *hedge; ignore;* jink; keep away from; *let alone;* move around; navigate around; obviate; parry; *quite* [Sp.]; *redirect; roundabout;* sidestep; skirt; turn away from; utterly avoid; *vacate;* walk away from; x-out; yerk; *zero contact;*
**bystander** *(n.)*: audience; attestant; beholder; considerer; *crowd;* deponent; eyewitness; *forgathering;* gazer; *gathering; group;* hearer; innocent ~; *janata* [Asia]; keeker; looker-on; man; *mass;* noticer; onlooker; person; *press;* passer-by; *quelet* [arch.]; regarder; *rubbernecker;* spectator; *throng; unbiased observer;* viewer; watcher; witness; x.; *yain* [arch.]; *zoa;*
**byway** *(n.)*: avenue; boulevard; corridor; dirt road; esplanade; footpath; *going;* horsepath; *ice road;* journey-way; *kotal;* lane; mews; means; non-toll road; outstreet; path(way); *quo mode* [L.]; road; side road; trail; *underpass; vennel;* way; *xystus; yong* [arch.]; *zwinger;*
**byword** *(n.)*: axiom; buzzword; catchword; dictum; epigram; epitome; formulary; guideline; household word; *instruction; judgment; koine;* law; maxim; neology; oracle; proverb; principle; quote; rule; slogan; truism; tenet; universal saying; verse; well-known example; *xenophonia; Yogism;* zeteticism;

# C

**cab** *(n.)*: *Austin FX3;* black cab [Br.]; *bus;* car; *driver;* electric ~; for-hire ~; hack [slang]; *item; jitney; kit-car;* limo; mini~; *notchback; operator;* paid ride; private-hire ~; *quad;* ride; *rickshaw;* service; taxi(~); *unit; vehicle; water taxi; xfer;* yellow ~; *zem* [Benin];

**cab driver** *(n.)*: auriga; buggy driver; cabby; cabbie; carman; charioteer; driver; *employee; fella; gharry-wallah [Ind.];* hackneyman; *individual;* jarvey; *kurumaya* [Chin.]; limo driver; *motorist; navigator;* operator; paid driver; qualified driver; rig-driver; *servant;* taxi driver; *uhlan;* valet; wheelman; *x-port;* yanker operator; *zain-driver;* [*see* chauffeur]

**cabin** *(n.)*: abode; building; bungalow; cottage; chateau; cuddy; deckhouse [both naut.]; domicile; dwelling (place); edifice; *flat house; guest house;* house; hovel; inhabitance; *izba* [Rus.]; jacal; *ken;* log ~; lodge; *manor house; nest;* outbuilding; place; quinta; residence; structure; shack; *townhouse; utility apartment;* villa; wanigan; *x-house; yakutat hut; zwinger;*

**cabinet** *(n. council)*: advisory; board; body of advisors; council; diet; eldership; forum; *government; heads; illuminati;* junto; *kit;* legal advisors; *meeting; nominative committee; organization;* panel; quinquevirate; *ruling body;* session; *tribunal; union;* vestry; *ward; xenocracy; yain* [arch.]; *zemstvo [Rus.];*

**cabinet** *(n. cupboard)*: armoire; buffet; closet; china ~; display case; *equipment; furniture;* glass case; hutch; *item; junk drawer;* kitchen ~; locker; mahogany ~; *nook;* oak ~; *place;* quadrilocular; *room; sideboard;* tallboy; unit; vitrine; vargueno; wardrobe; *xtr. storage; youth dresser; zeta;*

**cable** *(n.)*: *abb;* braid; cord; cablet; chain; down-haul; earing; *fiber;* gantline; hawser; *intertwined;* jack-line; keel-rope; line; lead; mooring ~; nautical rope; *osier rope;* port-rope; painter; prolonge; qiviut; rope; restraint; steel ~; twine; towline; *uncoil;* vang; wire; x-braid; yard-rope; zein;

**cackle** *(v.)*: *arride* [arch.]; boff [slang]; crow; *deride; erupt; frolic;* guffaw; hoot; irrision; *jolly;* keckle; laugh; *mirth;* nicker; *outburst; peep;* quack; roar; squawk; titter; utter laughter; *vibrate with laughter;* whicker; *xuld [arch.];* yuk; *zeal;*

**cactus** *(n.)*: *ariocarpus;* barrel ~; cereus; desert ~; *eulychnia;* foshhook ~; *glochid;* hoodia; Indian ~; *jasminocereus;* keg ~; lava ~; melon-thistle; nopal; opuntia; pimpillo; peyote; *quiabentia; rebutia; saguaro;* torch-thistle; *uebelmannia; vegetation; weberocereus;* xerophyte; yucca ~; zygo~;

**cadet** *(n.)*: apprentice; beginner; *comer;* disciple; enlistee; *freshman;* greenhorn; *ham;* inductee; *junior ~;* kook; learner; mentee; newcomer; *one;* pupil; *quick learner;* recruit; student; trainee; undergraduate; *venturer;* wannabe; *xon;* young trainee; *zealous student;* [*Ant.* coach]

**cadaver** *(n.)*: *ashes;* body; corpse; dead body; *exhumation; facecloth;* goner; *human body;* inanimate body; *just died;* ket; lifeless body; mummified body; *non-living body; one; pall; quarry;* remains; stiff; *tomb; unlaid; vestiges; wrapped ~; x-man; yielded up the ghost; zombie;*

**cadaverous** *(adj.)*: *alarming;* baleful; corselike; deathly; eerie; funereal; ghastly; hideous; icky; jarring; *knee-knocking;* lurid; morbid; necrophilious; ominous; pale; *queer;* repulsive; sepulchral; *terrifying;* unnerving; *vexatious;* wan; xanthous; yucky; *zonky;*

**cadet** *(n.)*: apprentice; beginner; *comer;* disciple; enlistee; *freshman;* greenhorn; *ham;* inductee; *junior ~;* kook; learner; mentee; newcomer; *one;* pupil; *quick learner;* recruit; student; trainee; undergraduate; *venturer;* wannabe; *xon;* young trainee; *zealous student;* [*Ant.* coach]

**Caesar** *(n.)*: autocrat; *Augustus; boss;* chief; *czar [Rus.];* dynast; emperor (of Rome); first consul; *governor;* Highness; imperial ruler; *Julius;* king; lord; monarch; magistrate; *Nero;* overlord; potentate; *queen [fem.];* ruler; Roman emperor; sovereign; *tyrant; ultimate authority; vice-regent; warlord; xabandar;* Yao [Chin.]; *zar* [Rus.]; [*Ant.* citizen]

**café** *(n.)*: automat; bistro; cafeteria; diner; eatery; fonda; grill; hash house; inn; *joint;* kitchen; luncheonette; mess hall; *nightclub; oriental restaurant;* porterhouse; quick-lunch counter; restaurant; steakhouse; snack bar; tearoom; *urban café; vent* [arch.]; *Western steakhouse;* xenodocheum; *Yokohama steakhouse; zonal chain restaurant;*

**cafeteria** *(n.)*: automat; buffet; café; dining room; establishment; food court; grill; hash house; *Italian restaurant; joint;* kitchen; lunchroom; mess hall; *nightclub; oriental restaurant;* porterhouse; quick-lunch counter; refectory; restaurant; snack bar; tearoom; *urban café; vent* [arch.]; *Western steakhouse;* xenodocheum; *Yokohama steakhouse; zonal chain restaurant;*

**cage** *(n.)*: aviary; bull pen; bird~; corral; coop; cote; cow-pen; close; *dove-house;* enclosure; fence; *garth;* hutch; hencoop; hogpen; inclosure; jail; kennel; lock-up; mew; *narrow;* oxstall; pen; pinfold; pound; quad; run; sty; sheepcote; tigh [dial.]; terrarium; utility pen; vollery; wynd [dial.]; *xystus;* yard; zariba;

**cage** *(v.)*: *arrest;* box in; coop up; detain; enclose; fence in; get in ~; hold; inclose; *jail;* keep; lock up; mew up; *nab; on ice;* pen up; *quad;* rail in; shut in; trap in; *use ~; victimize;* wall in; *xystus;* yard; *zet;*

**calamitous** *(n.)*: adverse; bad; catastrophic; disastrous; devastating; earth-shattering; *fateful;* grievous; hapless; ill-fated; Jonabesque; *killing; loss;* misfortunate; nightmarish; *ordeal;* pitiable; queer-lucked; ruinous; shattering; tragic; unfortunate; violent; woeful; *xerotripsis; yucky; zapping;* [*Ant.* constructive]

**calamity** *(n.)*: adversity; accident; blow; catastrophe; disaster; devastation; evil; fiasco; grief; hardship; heartbreak; incommodity; jam; kettle of fish [slang]; loss; misfortune; nightmare; ordeal; predicament; quandary; ruination; strait; tragedy; upheaval; violence; woe; *xerotripsis;* yedder; zinger;

**calculate** *(v.)*: analyze; *brainstorm;* compute; conceive; determine; estimate; figure; forethink; gauge; *hypothesize; ideate;* judge; *know; lucubrate;* meditate; *notion; observe;* ponder; quantulate; reckon; *study;* think; *use brain; valuate;* work out; *xenodiagnose; yeme; zazen;*

**calendar** *(n.)*: agenda; appointment book; *book;* calendar book; datebook; engagment ~; eighteen-month ~; four-month ~; *Gregorian ~;* hanging ~; *itinerary;* Julian ~; *kalendar* [arch.]; *lunisolar ~; monthly ~; notebook;* ordo [R.C.C.]; picture ~; *qua mode [L.];* rota; schedule; twelve-month ~; timetable; *unscheduled; view;* wall ~; *xia ~* [Chin.]; yearly ~; *zeug [G.];*

**calf** *(n.)*: angus; baby cow; boss; bulchin; cow; dogie; *ennstal;* freemartin; gelding; heifer; infant; Jersey; kyloe; leppy; maverick; neat; *ox;* polled shorthorn; *quadruped; red meat;* stirk; Texas longhorn; *ungulate;* veal; Welsh; *x-breed;* yearling; *zho;*

**call** *(n.)*: appeal; bellow; beckoning; cry; contact; *discharge;* exclamation; *fretting;* growl; holler; *inveighing; jubilation;* keen; loud shout; *lamentation;* moan; noise; outcry; outcalling; phone ~; quiritation; resonation; shout; thunder; ululation; *uproar;* vociferation; wail; whoop; *xmission;* yell; *zindabad;*

**call** *(v. cry out, beckon)*: appeal; bellow; beckon; cry; convoke; dial; exclaim; *erupt; fret;* growl; holler; invite; *jubilate;* keen; loudly say; *lament;* moan; noise; outcry; outcall; phone; *quiritation;* resonate; shout; summon; *thunder;* ululate; vociferate; wail; whoop; *xmit;* yell; *zindabad;*

**call** *(v. give name to)*: appellation; brand; christen; designate; dub; denominate; entitle; forename; give title to; hail as; identify; *jurisdiction; known as;* label; *misname;* name; *ordain;* phrase; *quiring;* refer to; surname; style; term; tag; *use; vocable;* word; *xenonym;* yclept; zoon;

**calligraphy** *(n.)*: artwork; beautiful handwriting; characters; cursive; decorative writing; engraving; fine hand; graphics; handwriting; inscription; *jot; kapnography;* lettering; *markings; notation;* Old English; penmanship; *the quill;* Roman; script; text; uncials; *vignette;* writing; xiaozhuan; ye olde; *zeug;*

**callous** *(adj.)*: austere; *barbaric;* cold-hearted; disdainful; *excessive;* flint-hearted; *galsome;* heartless; hardhearted; incompassionate; jaded; knark; *loveless;* merciless; non-sparing; obdurate; pitiless; *querulous;* ruthless; severe; thick-skinned; uncompassionate; unfeeling; *violent; wicked;* xenophobic; yieldless; *zoilean;* [*Ant.* compassionate]

**calm** *(adj.)*: accordant; becalmed; composed; cool(-headed); degage; easeful; equable; even-tempered; friendly; gentle; hushed; harmonious; halycon; idyllic; imperturbable; *jarless; keeping peace;* laid-back; motionless; mild; nonviolent; *orderly;* peaceful; pacific; placid; poised; quiescent; quiet; restful; relaxed; still; serene; sedate; subdued; tranquil; tame; undisturbed; untroubled; unflappable; unalarmed; unruffled; *violence-hating;* well-relaxed; worriless; wrathless; *xenophilious; yielding; zealous of peace;* [Ant. crazy]
**calm** *(n.)*: ataraxy; becalming; composure; coolness; dignity; evenness; equanimity; friendliness; gentleness; harmony; idyll; jarlessness; keeping peace; *laid-back;* motionlessness; mildness; non-turbulence; order; peace; placidity; poise; quiescence; restfulness; relaxedness; stillness; serenity; sedateness; tranquility; tameness; undisturbed; *very calm;* well-relaxed state; *xenophilious; yielding;* zero trouble;
**calm** *(v.)*: allay; alleviate; appease; anesthetize; be~; cool; diffuse; ease; *friendly; gratify;* hush; *intercept; jarless; knock down;* lull; mitigate; milden; mollify; *nullify; overcome;* pacify; quiet; quell; relieve; redress; still; soothe; settle; sedate; tranquilize; unruffle; *vanquish;* wind down; *x-out; yield; zeroize;*
**Calvary** *(n.)*: altar of sacrifice; *Blood; bore our sins; the* Cross; *the* Crucifixion; *death; expiation;* finished work; Golgotha; *the* Hill; *immolation; Jesus' death; killed; libation;* Mt. ~; *nails; the* Old Rugged Cross; place of Crucifixion; (-a skull); *quietus;* a Roman Cross; *the* Skull; *total sacrifice; unspeakable gift; violent death;* without Jerusalem; X; *yielded up the ghost; zeal for sinners;*
**Calvinism** *(n.)*: appointment of God; *before-ordained;* Covenant Theology; determinism; election; foreordination; Genevanism; hardshellism; involuntary salvation; *John Knox;* Knoxian theology; *limited atonement;* Moderate ~; necessitarianism; *non-Arminian; ordained beforehand;* predestination; *quondam selection;* Reformed Theology; supralapsarianism; *sovereignty;* TULIP theology; *unchangeable plan of God; verdict; will of God; x-cending; yonder; zero choice;*
**Calvinist** *(n.)*: advocate of Calvinism; *before-ordained;* Covenant Theologian; determinist; electionist; five-point ~; Genevanist; hardshell; *involuntary; John Knox;* Knoxian; *limited atonement;* Moderate ~; necessitarianist; *non-Arminian;* one-point ~; predestinarian; *quondam selection;* Reformed; supralapsarian; three-point ~; *unchangeable plan of God; verdict; will of God; x-cending; yonder; zero choice;*
**camaraderie** *(n.)*: affinity; bond; brotherhood; comradeship; commonality; devotion; empathy; friendship; *goodwill;* harmony; identification; *joining;* kinship; like-mindedness; love; meeting of the minds; nearness; oneness; partnership; *quarrel-lessness;* rapport; solidarity; togetherness; unity; *voluntariness; warmth; xenia;* yoke; zeal; [Ant. contrariness]
**camel** *(n.)*: animal; Arabian ~; Bactrian ~; beast (of burden); camelid; *creature;* dromedary; *even-toed;* feral ~; guanaco; humpster [slang]; *Injaz; jumxeroticent;* kameel [S. Afr.]; lowland Indian ~; *mammal; non-humped cama;* oont; one-humper; *packo; quadruped; ruminantia;* ship of the desert [slang]; two-humper; *ungulate;* vicuna; wild ~; xeroid; yak; zoic;
**camp** *(n.)*: assemblage; base; bivouac; ~ground; castrametation; Christian ~; *dwelling;* day ~; encampment; *force;* garrison; hutment; *inhabitance;* joint ~; *kibitka;* lodgment; laager [S. Afr.]; military headquarters; motor ~; night ~; outpost; post; quarters; *refugee* ~; *regiment; station;* tentage; *unit; velarium;* war ~; *xenizing;* yayla; zariba;
**camp** *(v.)*: abide; bivouac; bide; continue; dwell; encamp; follow on; go camping; *hang out;* inhabit; *journey;* keep; lodge; make camp; *nest;* occupy; pitch; quarter; remain; stay; tent; tarry; *use; voyage to;* wait; xenize; yerde [arch.]; *zip to;*
**campaign** *(n.)*: assault; boom; crusade; *charge;* drive; electioneer; fight; fundraiser; *general election;* hustings; invasion; joint ~; *krieg [G.];* line of attack; march; *nationwide* ~; operation; offensive; push; political ~; *politicking; quick raid;* run; race; struggle; *speechmaking;* team effort; united push; vying; war(fare); *x-fire; yed; zap;*

**camp meeting** *(n.)*: assembly; *bestirring;* church service; *declaration;* evangelistic meeting; forgathering; gathering; *hellfire and brimstone preaching;* ingathering; *jubilee;* kindling hearts; *local church meeting;* meeting; *new life;* open air meeting; outdoor revival; praise meeting; *quickening;* revival; service; tent meeting (-revival); *upheaval; vivification;* worship; *x.; yielding; zealous preaching;*

**campus** *(n.)*: area; *buildings;* compound; college ~; dorm; estate; facilities; grounds; *high school ~; institution; jurisdiction; key location;* location; mall; *nook; organizational ~;* property; quad; *range;* site; school grounds; square; *territory;* university ~; *vicinity;* ward; *x- ~;* yard; *zone;*

**can** *(n.)*: aluminum ~; *butt;* canister; container; cylinder; drum; *earthenware pot;* firkin; *gas ~;* hogshead; *item;* jar; *keg; label;* milk ~; *noggin;* oil ~; *puncheon; quinderkyn;* receptacle; *shipping container;* tin ~; *urn;* vessel; *water butt; x-barrel; yabba; zun;*

**Canaan** *(n.)*: Abraham's possession; Beulah land; Canaanland; *Dan;* Eschol; *Faithful City;* glorious land; Holy Land; Israel; Jordan valley; Judah; *Kadesh;* land of promise; (-milk and honey); *Middle East; Negev; other side;* promised land; Palestine; *Queen City; Reuben; Simeon; Trans-jordan; Urusalim [Egy.];* victorious Christian life; west of the Jordan; x-ing the Jordan; Yisreael; Zion;

**Canada** *(n.)*: *Alberta; British Columbia;* Canadian homeland; Dominion of ~; *Edmonton;* French ~; Great White North; *Halifax; Iberville;* Johnny Canuck; Keewatin; *Lower ~; Montreal; Nova Scotia;* Ottawa; *Prince Edward Island;* Quebec; *Roblin; Silver Bay; Tadoussac; Ungava; Upper Canada; Vancouver;* Western ~; *Xena;* Yukon; *Zionz;*

   **Canadian provinces:** Alberta; British Columbia; Manitoba; Newfoundland; Ontario; Prince Edward Island; Quebec; Saskatchewan; Yukon;

**Canadian** *(n.)*: *Albertan; British Columbian;* Canadien [masc.]; Canadienne [fem.]; Canuck [slang]; citizen of Canada; *Deep River;* English- ~; French- ~; *Great White North; Halfax;* individual from Canada; Jean Baptiste [slang]; *Keewatin;* lower ~; *Manitoban; Nova Scotian; Ontarian; peasouper;* Québecois [F.]; *royal ~; Saskatchewanian; Torontonian; Ungavan; Vancouverian;* Western ~; *xanthocroic;* Yukoner; *Zionz;*

**canal** *(n.)*: arm(let); acequia; bosporus; channel; *deep;* estuary; firth; fairway; *gulf; harbor;* inlet; irrigation ~; *jheel [Ind.];* kyle [Scot.]; *loch; mouth;* narrows; opening; passage(way); quanat; route; seaway; *tarn; underwater passageway;* voe; water passageway; *xyrisic; yeo;* Zee [G.];

**cancel** *(v.)*: annul; abandon; blot out; cross out; delete; end; forbear; *give up;* halt; interrupt; jib; kill; leave off; make of none effect; nullify; negate; obliterate; prevent; quit; revoke; stop; scrub; terminate; undo; veto; withdraw; *x; yield; zero;* [Ant. continue]

**cancerous** *(adj.)*: adverse; *bad;* cankerous; carcinomatous; deadly; diseased; exulcerate; fatal; galsome; harmful; hostile; injurious; *jeopardous;* killing; life-threatening; leukemic; malignant; malefic; noxious; *ominous;* parenclymic; *quad; rancid;* sarcomatous; *tumoral;* ulcerous; viperous; wasting; xanthopsic; *yellow fever; zonal;*

**candid** *(adj.)*: *abrupt;* blunt; *curt;* direct; explicit; frank; forthright; *gruff;* honest; ingenuous; janty; keenly ~; *lay it out;* maladroit; non-tactful; obtuse; outspoken; open(hearted); outright; plain-spoken; *qualified;* raw; straight; tactless; truthful; untactful; upfront; undiplomatic; *veritable;* without subtlety; *x-parent; yieldless; zero tact;* [Ant. circuitous]

**candidate** *(n.)*: aspirant; applicant; baby-kisser; campaigner; contender; contestant; competitor; challenger; dark horse; entrant; *favorite son;* gerrymanderer; hopeful; handshaker; incumbent; jerrymanderer; *key ~; legislator;* man; nominee; office-seeker; politician; politicaster; *quango;* runner; statesman; *Tammany man; upper house;* vote-getter; wannabe; whistle-stopper; *xenocrat; yearner; zenocrat;*

**candle** *(n.)*: aromatic ~; alnight; bayberry ~; cierge; dip; *enlighten;* flame; fuse; farthing dip; *glow;* halo; *illuminant;* joss stick; *kandel* [arch.]; light; luminaria; *maple-scented ~;* night- ~; *object;* percher; quarion; rushlight; scented ~; shammash; taper; tallow; *unlit ~;* vanilla ~; wax ~; watch-light; *wick; xtr. wide ~;* yellow wax ~; *zayat ~;*

**candlestick** *(n.)*: *aura; bulb;* candleholder; candelabrum; *Davy lamp; emission;* flambeau; girandole; *holder; incandescent lamp;* jesse; *kerosene lamp;* lamp(stand); menorah; nightlight; oil lamp; pricket; *quartz lamp; radiance;* sconce; stand; torchère; *uplight; vase; worklight; xenon lamp; yellow light; zircon light;*

**cane** *(n.)*: alpenstock; baton; crook; dagger-staff; espantoon; ferule; grain~; handstaff; *instrument;* jambee; kebbie; langet; malacca; nibby; officer's staff; packstff; quarterstaff; ratan; staff; tipstaff; *ununke* [Afr.]; *virgulate;* walking stick; *xylon;* yam stick; *zagaye;*

**canine** *(adj.)*: animalistic; bestial; *cur;* doggish; doglike; *evil-mannered;* foxlike; *greyhound-like;* hound-like; ill-mannered; jackalesque; *K-9 [slang];* lupine; mongrel; *nonhuman; ossivorous;* puppyish; quadrupedal; rach-like; savage; terrier-like; uncouth; vulpine; vixenish; wolflike; wolfish; *xolotl;* Yorkshire terrier-like; *zerda;*

**canine** *(n.)*: animal; birddog; cur; dog; *elkhound;* feist; *greyhound;* hound; *Irish setter;* jackal; *K-9 [slang];* lapdog; mongrel; mutt; night-dog; *ovtcharka;* pooch; *quadruped;* retriever; *sheepdog;* terrier; *ululator;* vizsla; whelp; *xolotl; yellow dog; zerda;* [*see* dog]

**cannibal** *(n.)*: anthropagi(te); barbarian; cannibalistic person; devil [derog.]; eater of humans; ferine; *gnawer;* headhunter; *individual;* jungli; *killer; lover of human flesh;* man-eater; *native; odious; pagan; querulous; rude;* savage; tribesman; uncivilized person; vandal; wild man; *Xhosa;* yahoo; *Zulu;*

**cannibalism** *(n.)*: anthrophagism; anthrophagy; barbarism; cannibalizing; devilry; eating people; endo~; exo~; flesh-eating; gnawing flesh; human flesh-eating; *incivility; jangliness; kaf [arch.]; licentiousness; meanness;* necro- ~; *odiousness;* people-eating; *querulousness;* rapaciousness; savagery; *terribleness; unkindness;* viciousness; *wickedness; xenophobia;* Yagaism; *zhlubbiness;*

**cannibalistic** *(adj.)*: anthropophagous; anthropophagist; barbarous; *cruel;* devilish; *eating humans;* ferocious; *gruesome;* human-eating; *ill-mannered;* jungli; *kaf [arch.]; licentious;* man-eating; *nasty; odious;* people-eating; *querulous;* rapacious; savage; *tribal;* uncivilized; *vicious; wild; xenophobic;* yahoo; *Zulu;*

**cannibalize** *(v.)*: *ate; banquet;* cannibalise [Br.]; consume; devour; eat; feast on; gnaw; gobble; have for dinner; ingest; *junket;* kill and eat; *lunch; munch; nosh; overeat;* prey upon; partake; *quill [arch.];* raven; scarf down; tear into; *undereat; victimize;* wolf down; *xerophagy;* yaffle; *zip down;*

**cannon** *(n.)*: artillery; antiaircraft; battery; big gun; culverin; chaser; demi-culverin; dog [slang]; engine of war; field gun; falcon; gun; heavy artillery; howitzer; iron culverin; *jolt;* katyusha; Long Tom; mortar; naval ~; ordnance; Parrott rifle; quadrant; rabinet; saker; stern-chase; trench ~; *unleash; volley;* weapon; *x-fire; yed;* zumbooruk;

**canonical** *(adj.)*: authoritative; biblical; credible; defensible; efficacious; factual; God-authored; Holy Spirit-inspired; inspired; justified; *known;* legitimate; *merited;* non-counterfeit; *official;* proper; qualified; recognized; sound; true; unapocryphal; valid; *well-tried; x-parent; yes;* zero-error; [*Ant.* counterfeit]

**canonize** *(v.)*: *ascend;* besaint; consecrate; dub a saint; enroll among the saints; *favor;* give sainthood; honor with sainthood; invest with sainthood; *jalap; keen;* lustrate; make a saint; number with the saints; ordain a saint; *purify; qualified; reconsecrate;* saint; *take; unction;* vest with sainthood; *wrought; xtry.; yield; zet [dial.];*

**canopy** *(n.)*: awning; arch ~; baldachin; cover; dorse; electric retractable ~; fabric ~; *gore;* half-circle ~; *item; job;* kitchen-window awning; laced ~; metal ~; Naugahyde® ~; orange-peel ~; panoply; porte-cochère; quarter-round ~; retractable ~; sunshade; tester; tilt; terrace ~; *umbrella; veil;* waterfall ~; *xillinous; yellow* ~; *zeta;*

**canteen** *(n.)*: army ~; bottle; container; *decanter; ewer;* flask; *gallon; half gallon; inurn;* jerrican; *jug;* kit; lota; munga; *neck; olla; phial; quart container;* receptacle; *skin;* tin; thermos; *urn;* vessel; water bottle; *xtr. water;* yabba; *zun;*

**canter** *(v.)*: *advance; breeze; charge;* dash; *elan;* flow; gallop; hasten; *interlope;* jog; *keep pace;* lope; move; *night-walk;* outstride; *proceed;* quicken; run; stride; sprint; trot; *underway;* venture; whiz; xfer; yern; *zip;*

**canyon** *(n.)*: arroyo; break; box ~; coulee; clough; defile; deep valley; *excavation;* flood meadow; gorge; gulch; hollow; intervale; *Jackson Hole;* krantz; lowlands; *meadow;* nadir; opening; *pit; quarry;* ravine; slade; *Tremola;* underlands; valley; water gap; *xyrisic;* yunga; *zanja;*

**cap** *(n.)*: alpine hat; boater; chapeau; coif; derby; *Easter bonnet;* felt ~; *glengarry;* hat; *item; jingasa* [Jap.]; kepi; *leghorn;* mitre; night ~; *overseas ~;* peci; quoif; riding hat; shaki; toque; *ushanka; visor;* wimple; XS; yarmulke; zarcole;

**capability** *(n.)*: ability; *background; brawn;* capacity; deftness; expertise; efficacy; faculty; gift; genius; habilitation; *instinct; jurisdiction;* know-how; legerdemain; means; natural ability; *over-qualification; old-hand;* power; potential; qualification; resources; sufficiency; skill; talent; usefulness; virtuosity; wherewithal; *xenium; yare; zeal;*

**capable** *(adj.)*: able; adept; bodily able; competent; deft; effective; fit; *flair;* good; gifted; having know-how; *instant; just right;* knowledgeable; *knack;* learned; mighty; *means;* naturally able; overqualified; proficient; qualified; readied; strong; skilled; talented; up to; versed; well-able; *xtry. qualified;* yarkened; *zealous;*

**capacious** *(adj.)*: abundant; ample; airy; big; commodious; disproportionate; expansive; full-size; giant; generous; huge; immense; jumbo-sized; king-size; large; massive; non-cramped; open; oversize; prodigious; quantitative; roomy; spacious; sizeable; tremendous; uncramped; voluminous; wide; XL; *Ymir; zaftig;* [*Ant.* compact]

**capaciousness** *(n.)*: amplitude; bigness; commodiousness; disproportion; extensiveness; fullness; greatness; hugeness; immensity; jumboness; *king-sized;* largeness; magnitude; *non-cramped;* overlargeness; prodigiousness; quantity; roominess; spaciousness; tremendousness; *uncramped;* vastness; wideness; XL; *Ymir; zaftig;* [*Ant.* compactness]

**capacity** *(n.)*: ability; *boundary;* capability; *deftness; dimensions;* efficacy; facility; *gift;* habilitation; *instinct; jurisdiction;* know-how; *level;* means; *natural ability; office;* power; quality; resources; *room;* sufficiency; *talent;* usefulness; virtuosity; volume; wherewithal; *xenium; yare; zeal;*

**cape** *(n. cloak)*: *apparel;* black ~; cloak; cope; domino; *enrobing;* fanon; *garment;* huke; *item of clothing; jelab* [Morocco]; *kit;* loose outer garment; mantle; mantelet; mozzetta; muleta; *night ~;* orale; poncho; pall; pelerine; pluvial; pashmina; phulkari; prayer shawl; *quaintry [arch.];* roquelaur; shawl; stole; tippet; *uniform;* veil; wrap; whisk; XL; *yelek;* zendalet;

**cape** *(n. headland)*: *arm;* bluff; chersonese; delta; *extension;* foreland; *ground;* headland; hook; isthmus; jut(ting); *knob; landstreight* [arch.]; morro; neck; noup; naze; ness; outcrop; peninsula; promontory; point; *quirk; ridge;* spit; tongue; upper ~; *volcanic island; weal; xtr. piece; yelld [arch.]; zenith;*

**caper** *(n.)*: antic; beguilement; cantrip; deception; escapade; farce; gag; hoax; imposture; joke; knavishness; lark; mischief; naughtiness; *outfoxing;* prank; questionable activity; ruse; stunt; shenanigan; trick; *untruth; vandalism;* waggery; *xuld [arch.];* yock; zinger;

**capital** *(n.)*: *autonomy; big city;* chief city; dominant city; eminent city; foremost city; governmental seat; headquarters; imperial seat; *jurisdiction;* key city; leading city; main city; national capital; official ~; prime city; queen city; ranking city; seat; state ~; top city; *unofficial ~;* Vienna; Washington D.C.; XO; *yard*: zone;

  **National capitals**: Amsterdam; Berlin; Copenhagen; Dublin; Edinburgh; Freetown; Guatemala City; Helsinki; Islamabad; Jerusalem; Kabul; Lisbon; London; Madrid; Moscow; New Delhi; Oslo; Ottawa; Paris; Peking; Quito; Rome; Stockholm; Tokyo; Ulan Bator; Vienna; Washington D.C.; Yaren; Zagreb;

**capitalism** *(n.)*: achievement-based system; *American dream;* business; commercialism; *dare-taking;* entrepreneurism; free enterprise (-market system); *go-getter; hard work;* industrialism; *John-a-dreams; keen-dreamer;* laissez-faire; mercantilism; *non-socialist; ownership;* private

enterprise; *quick profit;* reward-system; self-regulating market; *system; trade;* U.S. system; *venture;* world of ~; *xtr. profit; yettie; zeal for business;* [*Ant.* Communism]
**capitalist** *(n.)*: achiever; bourgeois; businessman; commercialist; *dare-taker;* entrepreneur; factory owner; go-getter; *hard worker;* industrialist; *John-a-dreams; keen-dreamer;* legal owner; money-maker; non-socialist; owner; proprietor; questor; risk-taker; self-starter; *thinker;* upstart; venture ~; *working for self; XO;* yettie; *zealous businessman;* [*Ant.* Communist]
**capricious** *(adj.)*: arbitrary; bouncy; changeable; *dangerous;* erratic; fickle; giddy; heady; inconstant; impetuous; jumpy; *kaleidoscopic;* labile; moody; non-stable; out-of-control; precarious; quirky; random; stormy; tumultuous; unstable; unpredictable; volatile; whimsical; *x-ing;* yo-yo; zany; [*Ant.* constant]
**capsize** *(v.)*: agitate; *bottom up; culbuter;* disturb; dump over; *excite;* fall; flip over; go over; *headlong;* invert; *jolt;* keel (over); *lean over; make nose-five; non-righted;* overturn; overset; pitchpole; quickly ~; roll over; somersault; turn (-tip) over; tump; upset; *violence; whop; xuld [arch.];* yerk; zonk;
**capsulize** *(v.)*: abridge; boil down; condense; densify; epitomize; encapsulate; *foreshorten;* go over; *heart; idea; jist; knock down; lessen;* minimize; *newsbrief;* outline; perorate; quickly review; recap; review; sum up; *thumbnail; use summary; vitals; work; xenenthesis; yetzer [Heb.]; zoe [Gr.];*
**captain** *(n.)*: authority; admiral; bargemaster; boss; brigadier-general; chief; commander; commodore; director; executive; flag officer; governor; head; intendant; *jarl; king(fish);* leader; lord; master; *naval officer;* overseer; officer; pilot; *quartermaster;* ruler; rear-admiral; sea ~; superior; shipmaster; skipper; taskmaster; *ultimate authority;* vice-admiral; warden; XO; *yokemaster; zayim;*
**caption** *(n.)*: annotation; blurb; cutline; comment; description; epigraph; footer; *graphic;* heading; inscription; *journalism; key;* legend; message; notation; *observations;* preamble; *quotation;* remark; subtitle; title; *uncials; verbiage;* writing; *xiaozhuan; yellow journalism; zeug;*
**captivate** *(v.)*: attract; bewitch; charm; draw; enthrall; ensnare; fascinate; get (attention of); *have interested;* interest; intrigue; infatuate; *jade; keen;* lure; make prisoner; mesmerize; *nudge;* overpower; persuade; *quibbling [arch.];* rivet; seduce; tempt; *urge; vie for;* woo; *x-fix; yerk; zygotaxis [biol.];*
**captive** *(n.)*: arrestee; *behind bars;* convict; *captured;* detainee; *encaged; fellow-prisoner;* gaol-bird [Br.]; hostage; internee; jailbird; *kriegie* [G.]; lagger; maximum security inmate; *niner; oubliette;* prisoner; quod inmate; *rattle;* stir bird [slang]; trusty; *under lock and key;* villain; ward-bird [slang]; *x,;* yard bird [slang]; *zek* [Rus.]; [*Ant.* captor]
**captivity** *(n.)*: *apprehension;* bondage; captivation; domination; enslavement; forced labor; grip; holding; imprisonment; inthrallment; *jail;* keeping as slave; *labor;* mancipation; *non-freedom;* oppression; peonage; *quelling;* repression; subjugation; thralldom; *under one's mastery;* vassalage; *work;* xibalo; yoke; *zone;*
**capture** *(n.)*: arrest; busting; confinement; captivity; detention; encagement; *force;* guarding; holding; imprisonment; jail; keeping; *locked up;* making captive; *non-freedom;* oppression; pinioning; *quarantine;* restraint; subduing; taking into custody; *under lock and key; vanquishment;* withholding; *x.;* yarding; *zone;*
**capture** *(v.)*: apprehend; betrap; bust; catch; detain; entrap; fasten upon; get; grab; *hold; hook; imprison; jail; keep;* lay hold; lasso; *make off with;* nab; net; overtake; obtain; pick up; *quarantine;* recapture; *restrain;* seize; subdue; take; usurp; *vanquish; whisk; wrest; x.; yard; zip away;*
**car** *(n.)*: auto(mobile); bucket (of bolts); clunker; coupe; convertible; dragster; *Edsel®; flivver;* gas-guzzler; hatchback; hardtop; horseless carriage; *Infiniti®; jalopy; kit-car;* lemon; *low rider;* motor car (vehicle); notchback; off-road vehicle; passenger ~; quad; roadster [slang]; sedan; sports ~; transportation; *truck; undercarriage;* vehicle; wheels [slang]; wagon; *X-C90; Yugo®; Zis* [Rus.];
**caravan** *(n.)*: array; band; convoy; cavalcade; *drove; envoy; flock;* group; *horde; individuals; journeyers;* kafila; *line; laager;* motorcade; merchant train; *naval convoy; operation;* procession; *questors; ruck;* succession; train; *traders; unit; visitors;* wagon train; *xfer; yellow bus; Zug* [G.];

**carcass** *(n.)*: *ashes;* body; corpse; cadaver; decedent; dead body; *exhumation; facecloth;* goner; *hearse;* inanimate body; *just died;* ket; lifeless body; morkin; *non-living body; one; pall; quarry;* remains; stiff; *tomb; unlaid;* victim; *wrapped ~; x-man; yielded up the ghost; zombie;*

**cardinal** *(n.)*: archbishop; bishop; cleric; diocesan; ecclesiastic; *friar;* grand vicar; hieromonach; *important; Jesuit;* kirkman [Scot.]; *legate; monk; non-laity; official; priest; Qumranite;* religious man; *superintendent; top brass; ultramontane;* vicar; *white friar; Xaverian; yogi [Hind.]; zealoter;* [see bird]

**care** *(n. attention)*: attention; affection; assistance; attendance; benevolence; compassion; concern; devotion; empathy; feelings; goodwill; gentleness; heart; help; *infatuation; joy;* kindness; love; minding; ministration; nurture; *overlove; pity;* love; *quixotic;* regard; sympathy; solicitude; tenderness; tending; treatment; *understanding; virtue;* warmth; *xenophilia;* yearning; yeme; *zeal;* [*Ant.* callousness]

**care** *(n. anxiety)*: anxiety; burden; bother; caution; concern; distress; *exasperation;* fretting; gingerliness; guardedness; headache; insecurities; *jitteriness;* kiaugh [Scot.]; lather; *mindfulness;* nervousness; over-anxiety; problem; *quaking;* recking; stress; trouble; unrest; vexation; worry; *xenophobia;* yearning; *zealessness;* [*Ant.* confidence]

**care** *(v.)*: attend to; appreciate; bear in mind; consider; care for (-about); cherish; devote oneself to; empathize; esteem; favor; feel affection; *guard;* have interest in; *interested;* joy in; *kindness;* look after; like; love; mind; *nurture;* oversee; prize; *quixotic;* reck; regard; relish; see to; show love; tend; take an interest in; *unselfishness;* value highly; watch over; want; *xenophilic;* yearn for; *zeal;*

**careen** *(v.)*: accelerate; barrel; cruise; dart; *elan;* fly; go fast; hurtle; *incline;* jet; kite; light; move fast; nutate; *outrun;* pitch; *quicken;* rocket; race; speed; tear; *uprush;* volutate; whiz; *xuld [arch.];* yern; zip;

**career** *(n.)*: activity; business; craft; calling; commission; duty; day job; employment; field; grind [slang]; handicraft; industry; job; key position; livelihood; line of business; métier; mission; *night employment;* occupation; profession; *quest;* responsibility; service; trade; *undertaking;* vocation; work; walk of life; xci. *yoke; zealous duty;*

**carefree** *(adj.)*: airy; buoyant; casual; degage; easygoing; fun-loving; *gay;* happy-go-lucky; imperturbable; insouciant; jaunty; keg-meg; lighthearted; mellow; nonchalant; optimistic; playful; *quick;* relaxed; stress-free; *thoughtless;* unconcerned; vivacious; worry-free; wareless; *xenarthrous;* yeasty; zippy; [*Ant.* careworn]

**careful** *(adj.)*: aware; alert; attentive; assiduous; *beware;* cautious; circumspect; conscious; delicate; discerning; deliberate; ever-careful; fabian; guarded; heedful; hesitant; *intentional;* judicious; *kid gloves;* keeping in mind; leery; mindful; *nervous;* observant; overcautious; prudent; quick-witted; *reluctant;* suspicious; sensible; thoughtful; tender; ultra-careful; vigilant; wary; well-discerning; witty; x-careful; yare-handed; *zärtlich [G.];* [see beware; *Ant.* careless]

**carefulness** *(n.)*: awareness; alertness; assiduousness; *bewaring;* caution; cautiousness; circumspection; discretion; *ever-careful;* fastidiousness; guardedness; heedfulness; *intent;* judiciousness; kid gloves; leeriness; mindfulness; nervousness; *observation;* prudence; paranoia; quick-wittedness; *reluctance;* suspicion; tenderness; thoughtfulness; umbrateous; vigilance; wariness; watchfulness; *x-careful;* yare-handedness; *zeal;* [*Ant.* carelessness]

**careless** *(adj.)*: apathetic; blasé; casual; cavalier; dispassionate; easygoing; forgetful; foolhardy; *gay;* happy-go-lucky; haphazard; hasty; heedless; inattentive; jaunty; keg-meg; lackadaisical; mindless; madcap; negligent; nonchalant; over-hasty; playful; *questionable;* reckless; sloppy; slipshod; slapdash; thoughtless; uncircumspect; unconcerned; unmindful; *vapid;* wareless; wild; *xenarthrous;* yareless; zealless; [*Ant.* careful]

**carelessness** *(n.)*: apathy; *blasé;* casualness; dispassion; *easygoing;* forgetfulness; *gaiety;* hastiness; heedlessness; inattention; jauntiness; *keg-meg;* lackadaisicalness; mindlessness; negligence; over-hastiness; playfulness; *questionableness;* recklessness; sloppiness; thoughtlessness; unmindfulness; *vapid;* warelessness; wildness; *xenarthrous;* yarelessness; zealessness; [*Ant.* carefulness]

**caress** *(v.)*: *affection;* brush; cosset; dally; embrace; feel; fondle; graze; hug; *inwrap; just barely touch;* kiss; lightly touch; massage; nuzzle; osculate; pet; pat; *quab;* rub; stroke; touch; *upstroke; voluptuary; whisk; X; yank; zip;*

**caretaker** *(n.)*: attendant; administrator; *boss;* custodian; concierge; conservator; curator; director; *executive; foreman;* guardian; *helper; individual; janitor;* keeper; legal protector; manager; *night watchman;* overseer; officer; porter; protector; *quarter master; representative;* steward; trustee; upholder; verger; warder; watchman; warden; XO; yeoman; *zeloter;*

**careworn** *(adj.)*: anguished; burdened; concerned; drawn; exhausted; fraught; gaunt; haggard; heavy-laden; hollow-eyed; *impaired;* jaded; keenly worn; laden; languid; much-wearied; *non-enthused;* overwrought; old; pinched; *quaking;* raddled; rueful; strained; tired; *unrest; vexation;* worn; weary; *xtry, weary;* yearnful; *zealessness;* [*see* carefree]

**cargo** *(n.)*: articles; batch; burden; *boxes;* consignment; delivery; *equipment;* freight; goods; haulage; handling; horseload; items; *jetsam;* kit; load; lading; moveables; merchandise; naulage; *objects;* payload; piece goods; quantity; *railroad car;* shipment; stowage; shipload; stuff; trainload; truckload; things; *undelivered goods;* valuables; vanload; wagonload; *xfer goods;* yard goods; *zeug [G.];*

**caring** *(adj.)*: attentive; affectionate; benevolent; compassionate; concerned; devoted; empathetic; feeling; gentle; humane; impassioned; *joy-imparting;* kind(hearted); loving; merciful; nice; *openhanded;* passionate; quick-to-help; regardful; romantic; sympathetic; sensitive; sympathetic; thoughtful; tender(hearted); unselfish; very kind; warm(hearted); xenial; *yielding; zealous of good works* [Tit. 2:4]; [*Ant.* callous]

**carnage** *(n.)*: atrocity; bloodshed; bloodbath; bodies; casualties; destruction; dead bodies; *evil; ferocity;* gruesomeness; havoc; human bodies; *injuries; jab-wound;* killing; loss of life; massacre; *nefariousness; odiousness; people; quashing;* ruination; slaughter; treachery; *upheaval;* violence; waste of life; *xuld [arch.]; yielded souls; zealotry;*

**carnal** *(adj.)*: animal; bodily; corporeal; depraved; earthly; *erotic;* fleshly; fallen; *godless;* human; impure; *jadish; knavish;* lascivious; lustful; *malevolent;* natural; *obscene;* physical; *quad;* reprobate; sensual; tangible; unspiritual; voluptuous; worldly; *x-rated;* yielded to the flesh; zoetical; [*see* sinful; worldly; *Ant.* chaste]

**carnality** *(n.)*: abominatino; badness; corruption; depravity; debasement; debauchery; earthly-mindedness; fleshliness; godlessness; human nature; immorality; *jadishness; knavishness; lewdness;* mundaneness; naturalness; obduracy; physical; *quad;* reprobation; sensuality; temporality; ungodliness; vice; vileness; worldliness; wickedness; *x-rated; yetzer hara* [Heb.]; *zoetical;* [*see* sin; worldliness; *Ant.* chasteness]

**carnival** *(n.)*: amusement park; bazaar; country fair; celebration; circus; *display;* extravaganza; expo(sition); eisteddfod [Welsh]; fair; festival; gala; *horse fair; international festival;* jamboree; kermis; *London Expo;* mas; midway; *undination;* Oktoberfest; panegyris; *quilting;* renaissance fair; raree show; state fair; traveling ~; theme park; *unveiling;* vernissage; World's Fair; *x-po [slang]; youst [arch.]; zoo;*

**carnivore** *(n.)*: animal; beast; creature; dermaphage; equivore; flesh-eater; game; harpy; insectivore; jument; killer; *lives off prey;* meat-eater; necrophage; omophage; predator; *quadruped; rapacious;* sarcophage; *tiger; uraeus;* varmint; wilding; *xolotl; yanking off flesh;* zoophage;

**carnivorous** *(adj.)*: animal-eating; beast-eating; *carnivore;* dermaphagous; equivorous; flesh-eating; game-eating; *hunting;* insectivorous; ichthyophagous; *jungly; killing;* living off prey; meat-eating; necrophagous; omophagous; predaceous; *quite hungry;* rapacious; sarcophagous; *tearing flesh off; uraeus; vicious;* wildlife-eating; *xarque; yanking off flesh;* zoophagous;

**carol** *(n.)*: anthem; ballad; chorus; ditty; étude; folksong; gallimaufry; hymn; inspirational; jingle; kasida; *lied* [G.]; laud; music; melody; noel; ode; piece; quodlibet; refrain; song; tune; undersong; vocalization; *warbling; xylophone song;* yed; *zemirah;*

**carpenter** *(n.)*: *artisan;* builder; constructionist; contractor; *cabinetmaker; developer;* erector; fabricator; *generator;* house-raiser; industrial ~; joiner; *knock together;* laborer; maker; *new-built; originator; producer; quick-build;* rebuilder; ships- ~; turner; upbuilder; *vamper;* woodworker; woodcrafter; *xylographer;* Xerez; *yew-worker; zealous worker;*

**carpentry** *(n.)*: *art;* building; barn raising; construction; *cabinetmaking; development;* erecting; fabrication; *generation;* house raising; industrial ~; joinery; *knocking together; laborering;* making; *new-built; origination; producing; quick-build;* rebuilding; ships- ~; timber-work; upbuilding; *vamping;* woodworking; woodcraft; *xylography; yew-working; zealous work;*

**carpet** *(n.)*: area rug; broadloom ~; carpeting; cabistan; drugget; *eight-foot runner;* floor covering; flokati; fragment; gul; hearthrug; industrial ~; juruk; kirman; living room ~; mat; needlepunch; numdah; outdoor ~; Persian ~; plush ~; qum rug; rug; shag ~; thick ~; *unshampooed ~; villous;* wall-to-wall; *xillinous;* yuruk; *zeta rug;*

**carriage** *(n.)*: *apparatus;* buggy; coach; dray; equipage; fiacre; gig; hackney; horse-drawn ~; Italian coach; jaunting car; karrozzin; landau; mail-coach; noddy; *omnibus;* pleasure-carriage; *quadricycle;* rig; surrey; stagecoach; tandem; *undercarriage;* vehicle; wagon; *x-port;* yanker [Br.]; Zis [Rus.];

**carry** *(v.)*: *accept;* bear; bring; convey; cadge; cart; deliver; *endure;* freight; ferry; *get;* hold; haul; *include;* janker; keep; lug; move; *nest; overcarry;* pass; pack; port; *quarter-cart;* relay; ship; support; tote; transport; take; uptake; *van; wield; with;* xfer; yomp; yanker [Br.]; *zip;*

**cart** *(n.)*: *apparatus; apple ~;* barrow; carriage; corf; dray; *equipment;* farm wagon; gig; handcart; *iron chariot;* janker; *karrozzin;* light ~; motorized ~; *neap;* ox- ~; pushcart; quadricycle; rig; red wagon; shopping ~; truck; trundle; tea ~; tumbrel; trailer; trolley; *undercarriage;* vehicle; wagon; *x-port;* yanker [Br.]; Zis [Rus.];

**cartoon** *(n.)*: animation; black & white ~; caricature; comic strip; drawing; *entertainment;* funnies; graphic character; *humorous; item;* japanimation; *kooky;* laughable; manga [Jap.]; newspaper funnies; *object;* picture; political ~; *quality animation; ridiculous;* sketch; strip; toon [slang]; *uncolored ~; volume;* weekend funnies; xylograph; yo-yo; zany;

**carve** *(v.)*: *art;* bisect; cut; dig; exect; engrave; fashion; gouge; hew; insculpt; *jag; knife; lop;* mold; *notch; overcut;* pare; *quarter;* reshape; rough-hew; sculpt; shape; slice; tool; trim; *unveil; vell;* whittle; write; *x-sect;* yerk; *zip off;*

**case** *(n.)*: *ark;* box; chest; container; carton; cassone; caddy; drum; etui; *firkin;* grip; holder; *inro* [Jap.]; jumbuck; jacket; kist; lockbox; moving carton; *nécessaire* [F.]; *object;* packing ~; pod; *quinderkyn;* receptacle; sleeve; shell; sheath; suit~; trunk; utility ~; vanity; wrapper; *xfer container; yadzutsu [Jap.];* zipper ~;

**cashier** *(n.)*: assistant; bank clerk; bursar; clerk; checker; collector; check-out lady; desk lady [fem]; *drawer; employee;* financial secretary; *girl;* helper; *individual; junior loan officer; keeper; lady;* money-taker; *note-holder;* officer; paymaster; questuary; receiver; secretary; teller; *usurer; vault;* worker; *window;* xaraf; *yeme; zaikai [Jap.];*

**cask** *(n.)*: *aluminum keg;* butt; barrel; canister; container; drum; *earthenware pot;* firkin; *gas can;* hogshead; *incask; jug;* keg; *locker;* milk can; noggin; *oil drum;* puncheon; pipe; quinderkyn; rundlet; scuttle-butt; tun; tierce; ungula; vessel; water butt; wine-cask; x-barrel; *yabba;* zun;

**casket** *(n.)*: *aluminum ~;* bier; (bone)box; chest; coffin; depository; *entomb;* feretory; grave-box; hearse; *inclosure; joint-marker;* kist; *lockbox;* mummy case; *nail; necropolis;* ossuary; pall; *quietus;* reliquary; sarcophagus; trunk; *unopened ~;* vault; wooden box; xat; yew box; ziarat [Mos.];

**cast** *(v.)*: *abandon;* betoss; chuck; discard; discharge; eject; fling; give the heave-ho; hurl; impel; jettison; kest; lob; launch; *move; non-retention; outthrow;* pitch; *quoit;* relinquish; sling; shoot; throw; toss; upcast; vault; wale; *xuld* [arch.]; york; *zing;*

**castaway** *(n.)*: abandoned person; banished man; castoff; derelict; exile; foundling; *goner;* hellbound sinner; irredeemable person; *judged; knave;* lost person; marooned person; *non-redeemable* maroon; outcast; pariah; *questrel;* reject; survivor; *transgressor;* unredeemable man; *villain;* waif; *xci.; ybanysshed [arch.];* zero redemption;
**castigate** *(v.)*: admonish; berate; censure; denounce; excoriate; fulminate; give talking to; harangue; impugn; jump down one's throat; knock; lambaste; *macerate;* nag; objurgate; *punish;* question; rebuke; reprove; scold; tell off; upbraid; vituperate; wig [Br.]; *xuld [arch.];* yell at; *zap;* [*Ant.* commend]
**castigation** *(n.)*: admonishment; berating; correction; discipline; emendation; fulmination; *giving talking to;* haranguing; impugnation; jumping down one's throat; knocking; lambasting; *maceration;* nag; objurgate; *punish;* question; rebuke; reprove; scold; tell off; upbraid; vituperate; wig [Br.]; *xuld [arch.];* yell at; *zap;* [*Ant.* commendation]
**castle** *(n.)*: alcazar; bastion; berg; citadel; chateau; donjon; *defense;* estate; fortress; garrison; hold; imperial palace; *jong* [Tib.]; keep; l-plan ~; martello; motte and bailey; nest; outpost; palace; quadrangular ~; redoubt; rath; refuge; stronghold; tower; *unbeatable;* vault; watchtower; walls; ward; *x-house; yamen* [Chin.]; z-plan ~;
**castrate** *(v.)*: alter; bowdlerize; cut; caponize; demasculinize; desex; emasculate; fix; geld; *hack;* hysterectomy; "it"; *jemmy;* kern; lib; make sexless; neuter; *operate;* poulardize [fem.]; queenie; *remove;* spay [fem.]; sterilize; *truncate;* unsex; vasectomy; weaken; x-sect; yedder; zip;
**casual** *(adj.)*: airy; blithe; careless; carefree; chance; degage; easygoing; familiar; glib; happy-go-lucky; insouciant; informal; jaunty; keg-meg; laid-back; lackadaisical; mellow; nonchalant; offhand; *playful; quick;* relaxed; stress-free; *slipshod; thoughtless;* unhurried; unceremonious; *vapid;* wareless; *xenarthrous;* yareless; zealless;
**cat** *(n.)*: alley ~; bangal; calico; *critter; Dutch rex; exotic shorthair;* feline; grimalkin; gib; house ~; *Indian ~; Javanese ~;* kitten; kitty; longhair; mouser; malkin; *nepelung; ocicat;* puss(y); pussy~; quoll; rex; shorthair; tom~; tabby (~); *ultra; victoria rex; wampas; xenosmilus;* York chocolate; zibeline ~;
**cataclysm** *(n.)*: act of God; breaking up; catastrophe; calamity; disaster; devastation; evil; fiasco; grief; hardship; infelicity; judgment; *knock-out; leveling;* misfortune; natural disaster; *ordeal; predicament;* quake; ruin; *setback;* tragedy; upheaval; violence; wreck; woefulness; *xerotripsis;* yedder; zinger;
**catacomb** *(n.)*: alcove; *below ground;* cave(rn); chambers; den; enclosure; fissure; grotto; hollow; incavation; jaw-hole; *krater;* labyrinth; maze; niche; *network;* opening; passage; *quarry-pit;* recess; *room; refuge;* souterrain; *shelter;* tunnels; underground tunnels; vault; warren; *xenolith;* yawn; *zanja;*
**catalog** *(n.)*: advertisement; booklet; catalogue; directory; equipment list; flier; general ~; handlist; information; *journal; key products;* listing; log; magalog; *national ~;* official ~; pricelist; prospectus; product ~; *quadrifoliate; reading matter;* sourcebook; *trifold; unifoliate;* vending ~; wares; *xenagogy; yeme; zine;*
**catalog** *(v.)*: arrange; assort; assign; *bestow;* class(ify); catalogue; divide; evaluate; file; group; hold; index; *judge; kit;* list; methodize; *make; notch;* organize; order; pigeonhole; peg; place; *qualify;* rank; rate; sort; systemize; tabulate; unitize; valuate; *work; xfer; yield; zonate;*
**catapult** *(n.)*: arbalest; ballista; cestrosphendone; carroballista; *device;* engine; *fire; gadget;* hurler; *instrument of war; jaculate; kest;* launcher; mangonel; *nignay;* onager; projector; *quoit; rocket-launcher;* spingard; trebuchet; *unit; vault;* woomera; war engine; *weapon; xuld [arch.];* york; zeug [arch.];
**catapult** *(v.)*: attack; barrage; cast; discharge; eject; fling; *go flying;* hurl; impel; jaculate; kest; launch; lob; *move; navigate; over;* propel; quant; rocket; send; sling; thrust; upcast; vault; wale; *xuld* [arch.]; york; *zing;*
**catastrophe** *(n.)*: adversity; accident; blow; calamity; disaster; debacle; evil; fiasco; grief; hardship; incommodity; *judgment;* knock-out blow; loss; misfortune; nightmare; ordeal; predicament; quake; ruin; *strait; setback;* tragedy; upheaval; violence; wreck; woefulness; *xerotripsis;* yedder; zinger;

**catastrophic** *(adj.)*: adverse; bad; calamitous; disastrous; devastating; earth-shattering; *fateful;* grievous; hapless; ill-fated; Jonahesque; *killing; loss;* misfortunate; nightmarish; *ordeal;* pitiable; queer-lucked; ruinous; shattering; tragic; unfortunate; violent; woeful; wreckful; *xerotripsis; yucky; zapping;*
**catch** *(v.)*: apprehend; betrap; capture; detain; ensnare; entrap; fasten upon; get; grab; hook; *imprison; jail; keep;* lay hold; lasso; mesh; nab; net; overtake; obtain; pick up; *quarantine;* recapture; seize; snatch; take; trap; tackle; trammel; usurp; *vanquish; whisk; wrest; x.; yard; zip away;*
**catchword** *(n.)*: adage; buzzword; byword; catch phrase; dictum; epigram; formula; guideline; household word; *instruction; judgment; koine;* law; maxim; neology; oracle; proverb; platitude; quote; rule; saying; shibboleth; truism; tenet; universal phrase; verse; wisdom; *xenophonia; Yogism;* zeteticism;
**catechism** *(n.)*: adjuration; basic manual; catechization; catechesis; discipleship; education; fostering; guidance; hortation; indoctrination; instruction; *justification;* knowledge; lessons; mentoring; nurture; *oversight;* preparation; qualification; religious instruction; schooling; training; *upbringing; verbiage; work; xenagogy;* yarking; *zakon [Rus.];*
**categorical** *(adj.)*: absolute; beyond doubt; clear-cut; definite; express; firm; *glaring; high;* indisputable; just plain; keen; *literal;* most certain; notable; outright; perfect; *quite;* resounding; sound; total; unconditional; uncontested; unquestionable; *verily;* whole; *'xactly [slang]; ywis [arch.]; zenithal;*
**categorize** *(v.)*: arrange; assort; assign; *bestow;* catalog; divide; evaluate; file; group; grade; *hold;* index; *judge; kit;* label; methodize; *make; notch;* organize; order; pigeonhole; peg; place; *qualify;* rank; rate; sort; systemize; subdivide; tag; unitize; valuate; *work; xfer; yield; zonate;*
**category** *(n.)*: area; brand; breed; branch; class(ification); cast(e); designation; division; estate; family; form; fashion; feather; genre; group; genus; heading; ilk; *jack;* kind; *kingdom;* lot; label; make; manner; model; mold; nature; order; phylum; persuasion; *quarter;* rubric; rating; sort; set; species; strain; style; stripe; type; *unit;* variety; *way; x-class;* year-class; zoological classification;
**cater** *(v.)*: accommodate; baby; coddle; *do;* epicurize; furnish; give; gratify; help; indulge; *justify;* kit; let have; make provision; *non-retention;* outfit; provide; pamper; *quarter;* render; supply; satisfy; serve; tailor; unhand; vest; *weigh; xfer;* yield to; *zip;*
**cathedral** *(n.)*: *auditorium;* basilica; chapel; church building; *duomo* [It.]; edifice; *fane* [arch.]; gathering place; house; *ingathering; joss house;* kirk [Scot.]; *location;* minor bascilica; nave; *naos* [Gr.]; oratorium; place of worship; *Quadragesimarian; rectory;* sacrarium; temple; *upper room; vestry;* worship center; xystum; *yele* [arch.]; *zayat* [Burm.];
**Catholic** *(adj.)*: Augustinian; bishop; Church of Rome; *denominational; ecclesiastical; Franciscan; Guelph; High Church;* iconolatrous *[derog.]; Jesuit; Knights of Columbus; liturgical;* Mariolatrous [derog.]; *Nicene; Orthodox;* papal; popish; papist [both derog.]; *Quadragesimarian;* Roman Catholic; Romanist; Romish; Romist [both off.]; sacramentalist; Sacerdotalist; transubstantiationist; universal; ultramontane; Vatican; *worshipping; Xaverian; Yagoua; Zentrumspartei [G.];*
**Catholicism** *(n.)*: *Augustinianism; bishops;* Catholicity; Church of Rome; dulia; *episcopacy; Franciscan; Guelph; High Church;* iconolatry; *Jesuit; Knights of Columbus;* Latin Church; Mother Rome; Mariolatry [derog.]; *Nicene Creed; nunnery; Orthodox;* Papal system; popery [derog.]; priestcraft; *Quadragene;* Roman Catholicism; Romanism; sacramentalism; Sacerdotalism; *sect;* Scarlet Woman [off.]; *transubstantiation;* ultramontanism; universal church; Vatican; Western Church; *Xaviarianism; Yagoua; Zentrumspartei [G.];*
**cattle** *(n.)*: animals; beasts; beef ~; cows; dairy ~; dhan; *ennstal;* farm animals; *Guernseys;* heifers; *Irish moiled; juments;* kine; livestock; milch cows; neats; *oxen;* Polled Shorthorn; *quadrupeds;* rother-beasts; steers; stock; Texas longhorns; *ungulates;* veal; Welsh; *x-breed;* yearlings; *zebus;*
**Caucasian** *(adj.)*: Anglo-Saxon; Alpine; Aryan; buckra; Caucasoid; *Danish;* European; fair-skinned; *Germanic;* Hesperian; Indo-European; Japhetic; *kabloona* [Innuit]; light-skinned; lani [S. Afr.]; *Monacan; Nordic;* Occidental; paleface [Am. Ind.]; *Québecois; Russian; Scandinavian; Teutonic; Ukrainian; Viennese;* white-skinned; Western; WASP; xanthochroic; *Yugoslav; Zeelander;*

**cauldron** *(n.)*: alchemist's crucible; boiling pot; caldron; *dishpan; electric frying pan;* fleshpot; *griddle;* hot pot; *iron pot; jackshea;* kettle; large pot; metal ~; nog; ovenware; pot; quart-pot; roaster; seething pot; *teapot; urn;* vessel; *wok; xeo; yetling; zone;*
**cause** *(n.)*: agent; basis; beginning; causation; driving force; determinant; explanation; foundation; grounds; *happening;* impetus; inducement; justification; key reason; *lead to;* motive; *need;* origin; occasion; provocation; *qualification;* reason; root; rationale; source; thrust; underlying cause; venter; wherefore; *xenenthesis; yoni* [Skr.]; *zeal;*
**cause** *(v.)*: affect; begin; bring about; beget; conduce; change; drive; engender; effect; foster; foment; generate; gender; goad; hasten; *happen;* initiate; instigate; induce; *jump-start;* kindle; lead to; make happen; move; *nudge;* occasion; produce; provoke; prompt; precipitate; quicken; rouse; result; *reactivate;* set off; start; trigger; use influence upon; *vivify;* wreak; work; *xuld* [arch.]; yield; *zip into motion;*
**caustic** *(adj.)*: acerbic; belittling; cynical; derisive; embittered; fleering; gibing; *hateful;* ironic; jaded; kindless; ludificatory; mordant; narky; opprobrious; pyrotic; *quede [arch.];* ridiculing; sarcastic; taunting; unkind; virulent; wry; *xuld [arch.]; yah;* zinging;
**caution** *(v.)*: advise; *bode;* counsel; *dissuade;* exhort; forewarn; give warning; *help;* inform; *jeopardy; knowledge;* let one know; make known; notify; opine; precaution; prewarn; *quicken; remind; speak;* tell; tip off; urge; *vocalize;* warn; *xenagogy; yellow alert; zero in;*
**cautious** *(adj.)*: alert; *beware;* careful; circumspect; discerning; ever-careful; fabian; guarded; heedful; *intentional;* judicious; *kid gloves;* leery; mindful; *nervous;* observant; over~; precautious; prudent; quick-witted; restrained; sensible; suspicious; thoughtful; ultra-careful; vigilant; wary; x-careful; yare-handed; *zärtlich* [G.]; [*Ant.* careless]
**cavalry** *(n.)*: army; band; company; dragoons; encampment; force; garrison; horsemen; Ironsides; *junior service [Br.];* kerns; light-horse; mounted unit; *nonconscripted army;* outpost; *peace-keeping force;* quadrille; riders; soldiers; troopers; unit; vedettes; warriors; x-force; yeomanry; zouave;
**cave** *(n.)*: alcove; *breach;* cavern; den; enclosure; fissure; grotto; hollow; incavation; ice cave; jaw-hole; *krater;* lava ~; *lair; main entrance;* niche; opening; pit; *quarry-pit;* recess; *room; refuge;* sea ~; subterranean room; *shelter;* talus ~; *underground;* vault; *weem* [arch.]; *Xerri's grotto;* yawn; *zanja;*
**cavity** *(n.)*: aperture; abscess; breach; crevice; crater; druse; excavation; fissure; gap(e); hole; hollow; incavation; jaw-hole; *khor* [Arab.]; lacuna; maw; niche; opening; pit; *quarry-pit;* recess; *sump;* trench; *umbilicus;* vug; well; *xystus pit;* yawn; zanja;
**cavort** *(v.)*: *advance;* bound; caper; dance; *enter;* frolic; gambol; horse around; *interlope;* jaunce; *keep pace;* leap; march; *night-walk; outwalk;* prance; *quicken;* romp; swagger; tramp; *underway;* venture; walk; *xfer; yaw; zigzag;*
**cease** *(v.)*: abort; abandon; belay; block; cut out; desist; end; forbear; fold; give up; halt; interrupt; jib; kill; leave; *moderate; nullify;* obstruct; prevent; quit; resign; relent; stop; terminate; undo; veto; walk off; *x; yield; zero;* [*Ant.* continue]
**ceasefire** *(n.)*: armistice; break; breather; cessation of hostilities; declaration of peace; end of hostilities; *fains* [arch.]; *guarantee;* hold one's fire; interval; joint-agreement; *keep peace;* lull; moratorium; negotiation; *ordinance;* peace; quittance; respite; reprieve; settlement; truce; understanding; *vow; word; x-rest; yafery* [arch.]; *zero-fighting;*
**ceaseless** *(adj.)*: abiding; *boundless;* continuous; continual; day and night; endless; *forever;* going on; gapless; *hourly;* infinite; incessant; *jusqu'au bout* [F.]; keeping-on; lasting; limitless; *maintaining;* never-ending; ongoing; perpetual; *quadrillion;* remaining; relentless; repeated; repeating; steady; 24/7; unceasing; unbroken; uninterrupted; unending; *vast;* without end; *xferring;* year-round; *zillion;* [*Ant.* ceased]
**cede** *(v.)*: abandon; bow out; back out; concede; capitulate; disclaim; *evacuate;* forego; forswear; give up; hand over; *ignore;* jump off; *kest;* lose; make an end; *nullify;* outgo; *pitch;* quit; relinquish; renounce; surrender; throw away (-in the towel); unload; vacate; waive; *xfer;* yield; *zip away;* [*Ant.* capture]

**celibacy** *(n.)*: abstinence; bachelorhood; continence; *decency;* *eunuch;* freshness; friarhood; *goodness;* honor; innocence; *justness;* keeping pure; *lily-white;* misogamy; morality; monkery; non-marriage; *only;* purity; *questionless;* refraining; singleness; taintlessness; undefilement; virginity; withdrawal; x-out; *yieldlessness;* zeal for purity;
**celibate** *(adj.)*: abstaining; blameless; continent; *decent;* *eunuch;* fresh; *good;* honorable; innocent; *just;* kept pure; *lily-white;* misogamic; moral; non-married; *only;* pure; *qualmless;* refraining; single; taintless; unmarried; virgin; vestal; *wholesome; x-out; yet undefiled; zealous for purity;*
**celebrate** *(v.)*: attend; beam; bless; cheer; delight; *dance;* exult; elate; fete; glory; glee; honor; *imparadised;* jubilate; keep; live it up; make merry; maffick; memorialize; *nowell;* observe; praise; party; *quiver;* rejoice; remember; solemnize; *shout;* triumph; *thrill; uplift;* venerate; vociferate; wonder; wallow; xmassing [off.]; *yeme;* yell; zealous; [*Ant.* cry]
**celebration** *(n.)*: array; ball; banquet; bash; celebrating; carousal; *display;* extravaganza; fanfare; festivity; fete; fiesta [Sp.]; feast; gala; hoopla; holiday; *international ~;* jamboree; joyance; jubilance; kermis; *laughing;* merriment; merrymaking; *nundination;* occasion; party; parade; pomp and circumstance; pageantry; pachanga; *quindene;* revel; shindig; show; ticker-tape parade; *unveiling;* vernissage; winging; *x-po [slang]*; yahoo!; zeal; [*Ant.* crying]
**celebrator** *(n.)*: adorer; banqueter; celebrant; dancer; exulter; frolicker; glorier; honorer; *individual;* jubilarian; keeper of the feast; *laugher;* merrymaker; *nowell;* observer; partier; *queme;* rejoicer; reveler; rolicker; singer; *shouter;* triumphant; *uplifter; venerator;* whoopie; xmasser [off.]; yeller; zealous celebrant; [*Ant.* crier]
**celebrity** *(n.)*: *actor;* big name; celebrated person; distinguished individual; eminent person; famous person; great person; high-profile individual; idol; icon; jeune premier; kid actor; legend; luminary; movie star; notable person; outstanding individual; personality; personage; pop star; *quality;* renowned person; super(star); *talked-about; universally known;* venerated person; well-known individual; *xtry.; yichus; zealously loved;*
**cellar** *(n.)*: ale ~; basement; *crawl space;* downstairs; *equipment storage;* finished basement; *garage;* hypogeum; half-dugout; *ice house; jaw-hole;* keller; look-out basement; mattamore; non-finished basement; *over-filled ~;* partially-finished basement; *quarters; recreation room;* storm shelter; subcellar; *TV room;* undercroft; vault; wine- ~; *xystum;* you [Chin.]; zone;
**cement** *(n.)*: asphalt ~; *béton brut* [F.]; concrete; ducrete; eternit®; fibre ~; geopolymer ~; *glue; hardened ~;* industrial ~; *Jennite;* kieselkalk; *lift slab construction;* magnesia concrete; non-hydaulic ~; *opus mixtum* [L.]; Portland ~; quick-setting ~; ready-mix concrete; sorel ~; tabby; *unsolidified ~;* Vicar morter; white Portland ~ xenolith; *yet unhardened ~;* zinc oxide concrete;
**cemetery** *(n.)*: ancient burial grounds; burying place; boneyard; boot hill; churchyard; *the* dead; *epitaphs; footstones;* graveyard; graves; headstones; *interred; iron gates; joubt-markers* kirk-garth [Scot.]; *lych-gate;* memorial park; mausoleum; necropolis; ossuaries; park; *quartz headstones;* repository; sepulchers; tombs; *urn;* vaults; *whited sepulchers; xats;* yard; ziarats; [*see* gravestone]
**censor** *(v.)*: *abridge;* blue-pencil; bowdlerize; bleep; control; *doctor;* edit; emasculate; fix; gag; *hold back; inhibit; jam;* koro; leave out; muzzle; *nullify;* oppress; precheck; pre~; *quash;* repress; suppress; stifle; take out; *unprintable; vitiate;* watch; *x;* yank; *zero out;*
**censorship** *(n.)*: alteration; bowdlerization; control; doctoring; editing; expurgation; "fixing"; government control; *hegemony; inhibition; jurisdiction;* keeping out; limiting; modification; non-freedom; *oversight;* pre~; quashing; restriction; revision; suppression; *tailoring; unfit; vitiation;* withholding; x-out; yanking; *zeroization;*
**censure** *(n.)*: admonition; berating; criticism; condemnation; denunciation; disapprobation; excoriation; flaying; going-over; haranguing; increpation; *judgment;* knocking; lambasting; monitory; nagging; objurgation; *punishment; questioning;* rebuke; scolding; telling off; upbraiding; vituperation; *warning; xuld [arch.];* yelling at; *zapping;*

**censure** *(v.)*: admonish; berate; criticize; denounce; excoriate; fault; fulminate; give talking to; harangue; inveigh; jaw; knock; lambaste; *macerate;* nag; objurgate; pan; *question;* reprove; revile; scold; tell off; upbraid; vituperate; wig [Br.]; *warn; xuld [arch.];* yell at; *zap;* [Ant. commend]

**census** *(n.)*: analysis; *breakdown;* citywide survey; decentennial ~; evaluation; field study; *form;* Gallup poll; household ~; inquiry; *judge; key survey;* listing; *mandated ~;* nationwide ~; opinion poll; poll; questionnaire; research; *results;* survey; town-wide survey; *undertaking;* vox populi [L.]; vote; *wishes; xenodiagnosis;* yearly ~; *zonal census;*

**center** *(n.)*: axis; belly; centre; centerpoint; core; crux; dead ~; epi~; fesse-point; *geological ~;* heart; hub; halfway point; interior; inside; *just exactly centered;* kernel; *lodged;* middle; midpoint; midst; midway; mid; nucleus; nave; *origin;* pith; prokaryon; *quotidian;* right in the middle; smack in the middle [slang]; thick; umbilic; *via media; within; x-section;* yolk; *zenith;*

**central** *(adj.)*: axial; *basic;* center; centric; core; chief; dominant; equidistant; epi~; eminent; first; foremost; focal; great; halfway; hub; interior; intermediate; *just exactly centered; kernel;* located centrally; middle; midway; midmost; main; nucleal; overriding; prominent; prime; preeminent; *uotidian; right in the middle;* supreme; topmost; umbilic; *via media; within; x-section; yolk; zenithal;*

**centrality** *(n.)*: all-importance; *bigness;* centricity; distinction; equidistance; fundamental importance; gravity; greatness; hub; importance; *just exactly centered; key;* leading role; magnitude; notability; obtrusiveness; prominence; preeminence; *quantum; right in the middle;* significance; toploftiness; umbilic; visibility; weight; *x-section; yolk; zenithal;*

**ceramic** *(adj.)*: argil; bisque; clay; china; crockery; celadon; delft; earthen(ware); fictile; graniteware; hazel-earth; ironstone; imari; jasperware; kaolinic; loam; murrhine; majolica; Meissen; *Nyon;* oven-baked clay; porcelain; pottery; porcelaneous; queensware; *red clay;* Sèvres; slipware; terracotta; *urry;* Victorian majolica; wally; *xtry. piece;* yellowware; *Zurich ware;*

**ceremonial** *(adj.)*: august; *big to-do;* ceremonious; *duteous;* established; formal(istic); *grandiose;* holy; initiatory; institutional; inveterate; judicatory; *kept tradition;* liturgical; mannered; *native;* official; proper; punctilious; procedural; pedantic; *qualified;* ritualistic; rigid; solemn; sacramental; traditional; *unquestioned;* very traditional; wonted; *xtry.;* yearly; *zoetic;* [Ant. casual]

**ceremony** *(n.)*: amenities; *big to-do;* ceremonial; commencement; *duty;* exercise; event; formality; function; *gathering;* holy rite; initiatory; institution; *jubilee; kept tradition;* liturgy; *mass; nuptial ~;* obsequies; observance; procedure; practice; pomp; *quadrisacramentalism;* ritual; rite; service; solemnization; solemnity; service; sacrament; traditional ~; *unquestioned tradition;* venerated institution; wont; *xtry. ~;* yearly ~; *zoetic;*

   **Types of ceremonies**: academic graduation; baccalaureate; baptism; bar mitzvah; communion; dedication; encaenia; funeral; graduation; inauguration; marriage; memorial service; nuptials; ordination; religious ~; ribbon-cutting ~; sacrament; wedding;

**certain** *(adj.)*: assured; beyond doubt; confident; convinced; definite; dependable; doubtless; evident; firm; guaranteed; highly confident; indisputable; incontestable; inarguable; incontrovertible; just sure; keenly sure; *legitimate;* mistake-proof; non-questionable; 100% sure; positive; quite sure; questionless; reliable; sure; self-evident; true; unfailing; unquestionable; undeniable; unmistaken; unarguable; unshakable; verified; well-tried; without doubt; xtry. sure; *yes;* zero doubt;

**certainly** *(adj.)*: absolutely; assuredly; beyond doubt; clearly; completely; definitely; decidedly; doubtlessly; entirely; for sure; fully; *glaringly;* highly; indeed; inevitable; indisputably; incontestably; inarguably; *just; keenly; literally;* most (certainly); notably; no doubt; *outright;* positively; peremptorily; quite; really; surely; truly; undoubtedly; unquestionably; verily; wholly; without a doubt; 'xactly; yessiree [both slang]; 'zactly [dial.];

**certainty** *(n.)*: actuality; assurance; assuredness; *bona fide;* certainness; confidence; correctness; dependability; dogmatism; exactness; factuality; genuineness; honesty; inevitability;

indubitability; *justification; knowledge;* legitimacy; *made sure;* non-fictitiousness; *okay;* precision; proof; questionlessness; reality; reliability; sureness; truth; trustworthiness; unmistakability; veracity; validity; *whole truth; x-parent; yes; zero error;* [*Ant.* confusion]

**certification** *(n.)*: authentication; attestation; bearing out; confirmation; demonstration; documentation; establishment; final ~; giving of proof; homologation; illustration; insurance; justification; *kithe [Scot.];* legitimization; *maintenance;* notarization; okay; proof; *questionlessness;* reconfirmation; substantiation; seal; stamp of approval; testimony; upholding; verification; validation; warrant; witness; x-certification; *yes; zero doubt;*

**certify** *(v.)*: attest; authenticate; bear out; confirm; *demonstrate;* establish; ensure; fix; give proof; guarantee; homologate; *illustrate;* justify; kithe [Scot.]; legitimize; make certain; *nail down;* okay; prove; *questionless;* reassure; rubber-stamp; substantiate; try; uphold; verify; warrant; x-certify; *yes; zero doubt;*

**cessation** *(n.)*: aborting; belaying; ceasing; discontinuation; end; forbearance; giving up; halting; interruption; jettisoning; killing; leaving off; *motionlessness; nix;* opting out; prevention; quitting; rest; suspension; termination; *undoing; vacating;* withdrawal; *x-ing; yielding; zero;* [*Ant.* continuance]

**cesspool** *(n.)*: *aperture;* basin; cesspit; drain; drywell; excrement tank; feces container; *gutter; holding tank;* in-ground ~; jaw-hole; *jube; keytonuria; laystall; management; night soil;* open drain; *pit; quagmire; ring;* septic tank; sump; sewer; tank; *underdrain; vessel;* waste tank; *xysma; yucky; zone;*

**chaff** *(n.)*: argal; *buildup;* canaille; dross; emptyings; flysch; grouts; husks; impurities; junk; kaff [dial.]; lees; matter; *non-wanted matter;* offscouring; *paleous;* quittor; refuse; sordes; throwaway part; *threshings;* unwanted; vinasse; waste; *xysma; yuckiness; zero;*

**chaff** *(v.)*: abuse; banter; chide; dig; *enmity;* fleer; gibe; harass; insult; josh; kid; laugh; make fun; *names;* outrage; poke fun; quip; rib; sneer; tease; utter against; verbally abuse; wipe; *xuld [arch.];* yock; zing;

**chain** *(n.)*: * aluminum ~; ball ~; catenation; double-loop ~; *enchained;* fob; galvanized ~; *held;* iron ~; incatenation; jack-chain; kedge- ~; linkage; metal ~; navy ~; O-ring ~; proof-coil ~; *quasi-fused;* roller ~; safety ~; top- ~; *unite; vulcanized steel ~;* weldless ~; *xtr.-reinforced ~; yoke;* zinc-coated ~;

**chain** *(v.)*: attach; anchor; bind; connect; catenate; *darbies;* enchain; fasten; fetter; *glue;* hitch; interlink; join; knit; link; lock up; mount; *nitch [Scot.]; oxreim;* put together; *quasi-fuse;* relate; restrain; secure; shackle; tie; unite; *vise;* weld; *xenograft;* yoke; *zip;*

**chair** *(n.)*: arm~; barrel ~; *bench;* chaise; deck ~; easy ~; *fauteuil; furniture;* gig; *hassock;* ice cream ~; jump seat; kack [slang]; lawn ~; lounger; *mercy seat; nursing ~;* ottoman; *palanquin;* quiver leg; recliner; *rocker;* seat; side ~; *throne;* upholstery; *vice chair;* wing ~; x- ~; yacht ~; *zeug [G.];*

**chairman** *(n.)*: administrator; boss; chief; director; executive; *foreman;* governor; head; intendant; jefe; keeper; leader; manager; master; notable; overseer; presiding officer; president; *queen [fem.];* ruler; speaker; trustee; *ultimate authority;* vizer; warden; XO; *yokemaster;* zayim;

**challenge** *(v.)*: arrogate; brave; call out; contest; defy; dare; extend ~; face up to; give ~; hold out ~; invite; *jangle;* kick against; lay claim to; make ~; nempne; offer duel; object; provoke; question; raise ~; stand up against; summon; throw down the glove; take on; urge to fight; voice ~; want a fight; *xenophobia; yafe [arch.];* zealously ~;

**challenger** *(n.)*: adversary; bad guy; contender; combatant; defier; disputer; dueler; enemy; foe; *garrison; hostile;* instigator; jangler; kemper; *legion; litigant;* match; nemesis; opponent; *player;* quarreler; rival; striver; *taker; unfriendly;* vier; *warrior; xenic; yuon* [arch.]; *zeke [off];*

**chamber** *(n.)*: ante~; bedroom; compartment; den; end room; front room; guest ~; houseroom; hall; inhabitance; *joint room;* keeping room; lodging; lounge; *middle common room;* nook; out-room parlor; place; quarters; room; space; *TV room;* utility room; *vestry;* ward; *x-ray room; yu* [Chin.]; zeta;

**champion** *(n.)*: advocate; brave warrior; champ; deliverer; exponent; folk hero; frontrunner; guardian; hero; *invader; jubilant;* kemp; knight; legend; lifesaver; liberator; laureate; messiah; non-loser; overcomer; paladin; *queller;* rescuer; supporter; title-holder; triumphant; upholder; victor; vanquisher; warrior; winner; white knight; *xtry.; yell; zealous;* [*Ant.* coward]

**championship** *(n.)*: *achievement; brilliant ~;* conquering; domination; debellation; exultation; feat; glory; gain; *historic ~; invincibleness;* jubilee; knockout; *lordship;* mastery; *nike* [G.]; overcoming; prevailing; prize; *quashing; reward;* success; triumph; title; uncontested win; victory; win; *xtry. win; yell;* zenith;
**chance** *(n.)*: ability; accident; break; capability; *definite ~;* expectation; *fighting ~; fat ~;* feasibility; fluke; *good ~;* gamble; hope; indetermination; *just a ~; known risk;* likelihood; *luck;* maybe; *non-guaranteed;* opportunity; occasion; possibility; probability; prospect; potential; *qualified ~;* risk; *special ~;* try; uncertainness; venture; window; *xtry. chance; yet possible; zone;*
**change** *(n.)*: alteration; betterment; conversion; correction; difference; deviation; development; edition; evolution; effect; enhancement; fluctuation; *growth; heightening;* interchange; innovation; improvement; jump; *key ~; lowering;* modification; *newness;* overhaul; obliquation; permutation; qualification; revision; reformation; redesign; replacement; shift; substitution; switch; shake-up; transformation; transition; *upgrade;* variation; vagary; *warping;* xenomorph; *yaw;* zigzag; [*Ant.* continuance]
**change** *(v.)*: alter; adjust; affect; amend; become; *better;* convert; *correct;* deviate; develop; dissimilate; doctor; edit; evolve; exchange; enhance; fiddle with; fix; *grow; heighten;* innovate; improve; interchange; *jib; jump; key to; lower;* modify; metamorphose; modulate; make over; novate; overhaul; permute; *qualify;* redesign; reform; remake; revise; replace; revamp; renovate; rearrange; revolutionize; restructure; switch; swap; substitute; shift; turn; transform; transition; tailor; trade; tack; upgrade; vary; work; warp; xenomorph; *yaw;* zigzag; [*see* pervert; *Ant.* continue]
**changeable** *(adj.)*: alterable; adaptable; adjustable; bendable; betterable; convertible; developable; editable; exchangeable; erratic; flexible; fickle; *growable; handy; helpable;* inconstant; irresolute; interchangeable; *jumpy;* kaleidoscopic; labile; light-minded; modifiable; mutable; moveable; manipulable; non-fixed; *overhaul;* protean; precarious; plastic; positionable; qualifiable; revisable; substitutable; switchable; translatable; transferable; transposable; transmutable; unsteady; uncertain; unpredictable; unsettled; variable; volatile; wavering; whiffling; *xenomorphic;* yeasty; *zero constancy;* [*Ant.* changeless]
**changeless** *(adj.)*: absolute; bound; constant; definite; ever the same; enduring; eternal; fixed; guaranteed; hard; immovable; immutable; inalienable; *just the same;* kept the same; lasting; motionless; non-moveable; obdurate; permanent; quite frim; rigid; stationary; *transcending;* unchanging; vested; without change; *x-cending;* ypight [arch.]; *zet;* [*Ant.* changeable]
**channel** *(n. frequency)*: AM signal; band; communication frequency; direct signal; electromagnetic signal; frequency; FM signal; *grid-dip oscillator;* high-frequency signal; intermediate frequency; *jansky;* kilocycles; long wave; medium frequency; network; *omnidirectional range;* pickup; *quasi-clear signal;* radio frequency; station; setting; (shortwave) signal; television frequency; ultra high frequency (UHF); very high frequency (VHF); wavelength; x-wave; *yagi; zinc radio;*
**channel** *(n. waterway)*: arm(let); aqueduct; arroyo; breach; bosporus; canal; conduit; duct; estuary; firth; flume; gap; gully; gat; groove; headrace; inlet; irrigation canal; *jheel [Ind.];* kyle [Scot.]; lough; leat; mouth; moat; narrows; neck; nullah; nappe; outlet; passage; quanat; runnel; reigle; route; strait; spillway; sluice; swash; trench; tide-way; tailrace; u-groove; voe; vasa; waterway; *xyrisic;* yawn; zanja;
**channel** *(v.)*: *advance;* burrow; chafer; dig; excavate; furrow; grub; hollow; *intrench; jenkin;* kip; *lower;* mole; *notch; open; prospect;* quarry; *remove dirt;* shovel; tunnel; *trench;* undermine; *vacate;* worm; *xfer; yede; zanja;*
**chant** *(n.)*: antiphon; ballad; bellow; cantillation; croon; dirge; elegy; *funeral song; gallimaufry;* hymn; intone; incantation; *jingle;* keen; lay; litany; mantra; nenia; oratorio; plainsong; paean; quadrille; refrain; song; trill; utterance; vocalization; warble; *xylophone song;* yed; ziraleet;
**chant** *(v.)*: articulate; bellow; cant(illate); drone; echo; *funeral song; gallimaufry;* holler; intone; jodel; key in; let out; make a chant; *nonet; outbreak;* perform; quaver; recite; sing; troll; utter; vocalize; *well-sung; xoeoemei;* yell; *zemirah;*

**chaos** *(n.)*: anarchy; bedlam; confusion; disorder; entanglement; farrago; gastness; havoc; intranquility; jumble; kerfuffle; lawlessness; mayhem; non-orderliness; *obscurity;* pandemonium; *quandary; restlessness;* stupefaction; turmoil; upheaval; vexation; welter; xaos; *yo-yo;* zoo; [*Ant.* control]

**chaotic** *(adj.)*: anarchic; bewildering; confused; disorderly; disorganized; entangled; frenzied; *grungy;* hectic; incomposed; jumbled; keg-meg; littered; muddled; neglected; orderless; pell-mell; quaggy; *ruffled;* sloppy; slovenly; slattern [fem.]; slipshod; topsy-turvy; unorganized; *vexing;* wild; *x'ed; yucky;* zoo-like; [*Ant.* controlled]

**chaperone** *(n.)*: attendant; bodyguard; chaperon; companion; duenna; escort; fellow traveler; guardian; helper; *interested party; journeyer;* keeper; lookout; monitor; noble protector; overseer; protector; *questor; reporter;* safeguard; trustee; upholder; vigil; watcher; *xenagogue; yeoman; zealot;*

**chaplain** *(n.)*: army ~; Bible-teacher; cleric; *declarer;* expositor; field preacher; gospeler; homilist; *itinerant preacher; josser* [Aus. slang]; *kerygma;* lecturer; minister; navy ~; orator; pastor; *quoter;* revivalist; speaker; *teacher; utterer;* voicer; *warner;* xenagogue; *yeller [derog.]; zealous preacher;*

**chapped** *(adj.)*: aching; blistered; cracked; dry; *excruciating; fret; grievous;* hasky; *inflammation; jabbing;* kibed; *lip-chapping; miserable;* nipped; overly ~; painful; *quenchless;* rimose; raw; sore; split; tender; uncomfortable; very cracked; waterless; windburned; *xerocheilia; yanked; zapped;*

**chapter** *(n.)*: affiliate; branch; book-division; component; division; episode; fascicle; *group;* heading; installment; *joint-authorship; key part;* lesson; macrodivision; *notation; opening ~;* part; *quarter;* rubric; section; subdivision; text heading; unit; *volume; weekly episode; x-mal [G.]; yet further divided;* zone;

**character** *(n. mark)*: *ABC's;* brand; capital; designation; engraving; *etching;* figure; glyph; hierogram; imprint; initial; jot; ken-mark; letter; mark; majuscule; notation; numeral; *object;* phonetic ~; printed ~; *question mark;* representation; symbol; *type;* uncial; *variable;* waymark; *x; yod; zeug;*

**character** *(n. nature)*: attributes; *badge;* characteristic; constitution; disposition; ethos; essence; fiber; *gist;* heart; humor; inclination; intrinsicality; *jist; kind;* lineament; makeup; nature; overall makeup; property; personality; quality; reality; suchness; spirit; temperament; tendency; underlying ~; virtue; *xenenthesis; yetzer* [Heb.]; *zoe;*

**character** *(n. principles)*: *above reproach;* blameless ~; Christian ~; decency; ethics; *faultlessness;* godliness; honor; integrity; *justness; kalokagathia* [Gr.]; lineaments; morals; moral fiber; name; *over-scrupulousness;* principles; qualms; reputation; righteousness; scruples; *truthfulness;* uprightness; virtue; *wholesomeness; xtry; yieldedness to God; zero-blame;* [*see* holiness]

**characteristic** *(adj.)*: archetypical; *badge;* common(place); customary; distinguishing; everyday; familiar; general; habitual; individual; indicative; *jist; kuriologic;* long-established; *mark;* normal; ordinary; particular; quotidian; representative; standard; symptomatic; typical; usual; very typical; wonted; *xenenthesis; yetzer* [Heb.]; *zoe;*

**characteristic** *(n.)*: attribute; *badge; character;* detail; element; feature; *good quality;* highlight; ingredient; *jist;* key feature; lineament; mark; *nature; object;* property; point; peculiarity; particularity; part; quality; reality; *side;* trait; undeniable quality; virtue; way; *x-factor; yetzer* [Heb.]; *zero in;*

**characterize** *(v.)*: *articulate;* brand; clarify; constitute; describe; explain; formulate; give description; gloss; *hit* [arch.]; illustrate; identify; *judge; keynote;* limn; line out; mark; *notify;* outline; portray; paint; *quaint [arch.];* represent; signalize; spell out; tell; *utter; version;* word; *xenagogy; yak; zero in;*

**charade** *(n.)*: act; bogus imitation; caricature; dramatization; deception; emulation; farce; *game; hoke;* impersonation; *just alike; keep;* look-alike; mock-up; mimcry; *non-genuine; overacting;* pretense; parody; *questionable;* representation; sham; travesty; trick; *unreal; virtual;* work; *xtry. act; yet another; zinger;*

**charge** *(n. task)*: assignment; bidding; behest; business; commission; command; custody; care; directive; duty; errand; *function; goal; halidom;* instruction; incumbency; job; *key role; law; liability; load;* mission; necessity; obligation; post; *purpose; quest;* responsibility; *station;* task; undertaking; vocation; work; xci.; *yoke; zealous task;* [see job]

**charge** *(n. fee)*: assessment; *burden; custom;* dues; debit; excise; fee; fine; gabelle; handling charge; impost; interest; jettage; keelage; levy; mulct; nuisance tax; octroi; penalty; quarterage; *revenue;* surcharge; tax; *usury;* vigorish; withholding; x-int; yardage; *zakat* [Mos.];

**charge** *(v. command)*: adjure; *ask;* bid; command; direct; demand; dictate; enjoin; *exhort; foist;* govern; *have;* instruct; *juration; kaleusmatic;* lay on; mandate; necessitate; order; ordain; *pronounce; quo minus [L.];* require; *stipulate;* tell; *utter; voice; word; xenagogy;* yark; *zakon [Rus.];*

**charge** *(v. formally blame)*: accuse; arraign; aver; blame; contend; delate; *exprobate;* fault; *guilt;* hold responsible; indict; incriminate; *j'accuse; knock;* lay guilt before; make allegation; *non-innocent; oppugn;* point finger at; *question; reproach; saddle with;* tax; *utter; vituperate; word; xfer; yak; zero in;*

**charge** *(v. rush)*: attack; assault; accelerate; bolt; chase; dash; elan; flash; gallop; hurry; invade; jet; *kite;* lope; move; *nimble; overrun; progress;* quicken; rush; stampede; storm; tear; tilt; tear; *uprush; velocity;* whiz; *xuld [arch.];* yern; zip;

**chariot** *(n.)*: *apparatus;* buggy; berlin; curricle; dray; *encoach;* fiacre; gig; hackney; Italian coach; jaunting car; karrozzin; landau; mail-coach; *neap; oxcart;* pontoon-carriage; quadriga; rig; rath; surrey; trap; *undercarriage;* vehicle; war-~; wagon; *x-port;* yanker [Br.]; *Zis [Rus.];*

**charismatic** *(adj. charming)*: alluring; *bewitching;* charming; debonair; enamoring; enthralling; fascinating; *gripping;* highly influential; intriguing; *jolie laide [F.];* keen; likeable; magnetic; *nice;* outstanding; pleasant; *quaint;* riveting; suave; taking; urbane; very appealing; well-favored; witching; *xtry;* you-beaut [Aus.]; *zizzy;*

**charismatic** *(adj. tongues-speaking)*: Asuza Street; *barking-like-dogs;* Corinthian; demon-casting; exorcising; *feminist;* gift-crazed; *hand-raising; interdenominational; juddering; kerygma; laughing; movement;* neo-Pentecostal; *organizational;* Pentecostal(ist); *quaking;* rolling-in-the-aisles; sign-craving; tongues-speaking; *unconventional;* Vintage; *way-out;* xenoglossic; *yelping-like-dogs; zealous;*

**charitable** *(adj.)*: altruistic; benevolent; caring; condolent; *dear;* eleemosynary; freehanded; generous; giving; high-minded; ingenuous; *joyful;* kind; liberal; munificent; noble-minded; open-handed; philanthropic; quick-to-give; *regardful;* selfless; tenderhearted; unselfish; ungrudging; very kind; warmhearted; *xenophilous; yielded; zealous of good works;*

**charity** *(n.)*: alms; altruism; aid; bigheartedness; benevolence; charitableness; contributions; dole; donations; *endowment;* favor; freehandedness; goodwill; generosity; giving; help; humanity; handout; *investment; joyful giving;* kindness; love; liberality; largesse; magnanimity; munificence; mercy; nobleness; open-handedness; philanthropy; quarter; *righteousness;* sympathy; selflessness; *thoughtfulness;* unselfishness; *virtuousness;* warmth; *xenophilia; yieldedness; zeda-kah* [Heb.]; [see love]

**charlatan** *(n.)*: *actor;* bluffer; con artist; deceiver; empiric; fake; fraud; grifter; hoaxer; huckster; haberdasher; imposter; jape; knave; *liar;* mountebank; nostrum; *oily;* phony; pretender; panhandler; quack; racketeer; snake-oil salesman; sham artist; swindler; trickster; *untruther;* verneuker; wheeler-dealer; *xiaoren; yantzer; zinger;*

**charm** *(n. appeal)*: appeal; allure; attraction; beauty; charisma; desirableness; enchantment; fascination; geasa; hold; inducement; junu; kinch; lure; likeableness; loveliness; magnetism; magic; *niceness; overcoming;* pull; quaintness; riveting; spell; temptation; *unequalled; voluptuousness;* winsomeness; *xtry.; yearning;* zap; zygotaxis [biol.]; [see spell]

**charm** *(n. lucky item)*: amulet; bloodstone; *curio; doodad; entity;* fetish; good-luck charm; grigri; hoodoo; *horseshoe;* image; item; juju; *kappe;* lucky charm; magic charm; mojo; night-spell; oracle; obeah; *object;* periapt; query stone; rabbit foot; scarab; talisman; token; totem; toadstone; *unit;* voodoo; *whatchy;* xoanon; *yantra;* zogo;

**charm** *(v.)*: attract; allure; becharm; bewitch; captivate; draw; enamor; ensorcell; enchant; fascinate; get (attention of); *have come;* interest; intrigue; infatuate; *jade; keen;* lure; magnetize; *nudge;* overcome; persuade; *quibbling [arch.];* rivet; seduce; transfix; use magic; *vie for;* woo; *xuld [arch.]; yerk; zygotaxis;*

**charming** *(adj.)*: appealing; beautiful; captivating; charismatic; delightful; enamoring; enchanting; elegant; fascinating; goodly; handsome; inviting; intriguing; *jolie laide [F.]; keen;* lovely; magnificent; *nice; outstanding;* pretty; pleasant; picturesque; quaint; riveting; suave; taking; *unsurpassed;* very attractive; well-favored; *xtry;* you-beaut [Aus.]; *zizzy;*

**chart** *(n.)*: atlas; blueprint; charting; diagram; *engineering;* foredesign; floor plan; graph; house plan; illustration; journal; *key location map;* layout; map; navigational ~; outline; plan; pictograph; *quo mode [L.];* road map; schedule; schematic; table; *undersea ~;* visual; wall~; x-chart; *yantra* [Hind.]; zenithal projection;

**chart** *(v.)*: artwork; *blaze;* copy down; draw; depict; draft; delineate; diagram; etch; form picture; graph; handwrite; illustrate; jot down; *key;* limn; layout; map (out); notate; navigate; outline; plan; plot out; *quo mode [L.];* render; sketch; trace out; use instruments; *vector;* work; write; x-chart; *yield; zet [dial.];*

**chase** *(v.)*: *after;* be after; come after; drive; dog; *entrap;* follow (after); go after; hound; hunt for; *interlope;* jack; *keenly seek; look for;* make one's prey; *non-leader;* overcome; pursue; quest; run after; stalk; seek; trail; *undertake;* venture; *wild goose chase; xfer; yearn after; zealously follow;* [Ant. catch]

**chasm** *(n.)*: abyss; breach; cleft; crater; deep abyss; *excavation;* fissure; gap; gorge; gulch; hole; incavation; jaw-hole; krater; lacuna; maw; *niche;* opening; parting; *quarry-pit;* ravine; rift; split; *trench; umbilicus;* void; widening; *x-ing;* yawn; zanja;

**chaste** *(adj.)*: aboveboard; blameless; clean; decent; exemplary; fair; good; guiltless; honorable; holy; innocent; *just; keen;* lily-white; moral; *nice; old-fashioned;* pure; qualmless; righteous; respectable; stainless; taintless; untarnished; unspotted; undefiled; virtuous; wholesome; *xtry.;* yet undefiled; *zero blame;* [Ant. corrupt]

**chasten** *(v.)*: afflict; beat; chastise; correct; discipline; *enlighten;* flog; *guide;* hit; *inflict; jolt;* knock; lick; make one sorry; *nubble; open one's eyes;* paddle; punish; quab; reprimand; spank; smite; thrash; tan one's hide; use the rod; *vituperate;* whip; *x-sect;* yerk; *zap;* [Ant. commend]

**chastise** *(v.)*: *assault;* beat; censure; discipline; *enlighten;* flog; *guide;* hit; inflict; *jolt;* knock; keep in line; lick; mulct; *nubble; open one's eyes;* punish; quab; reprimand; spank; thrash; *use the rod; vituperate;* whip; *x-sect; yerk; zap;* [Ant. crown]

**chastity** *(n.)*: abstinence; *blamelessness;* chasteness; *decency; ever-faithful;* faithfulness; goodness; honor; innocence; immaculateness; *justness; keenness; limpidness;* modesty; morality; *newness;* old-fashioned morals; purity; pudicity; *quality;* righteousness; sinlessness; taintlessness; uprightness; virtue; virginity; wholesomeness; *xtry; yieldedness to God; zeal for God;* [Ant. corruption]

**chat** *(n.)*: argument; bearing heart; chit-chat; causerie; colloquy; conversation; discussion; dialogue; exchange words; *fraternization;* gabbing; huddle; interchange; *jangle; key discussion;* little talk; meeting; natter; oral treaty; persiflage; quadrilogue; reasoning; speech; talk; *uttering; vocalization;* words; *xenophonia;* yarn; *zero in;*

**chat** *(v.)*: allege; bear hearts; chit-chat; converse; discuss; exchange words; *fraternize;* gab; have discussion; interact; jaw; kibitz; *little ~;* make small talk; natter; *outtalk;* parley; *quarrel;* reason; shoot the breeze; speak; twitter; talk (over); *utter; vocalize;* words; *xenophonia;* yak; *zero in;*

**chatter** *(n.)*: *absurdity;* blather; clack; drivel; empty words; fudge; gabble; hot air; idle talk; jabber; kelter; *lard;* mumbo-jumbo; nonsense; *outlandishness;* prattle; queer speech; rambling; ranting; slaver; twaddle; talk; utterance; vain talk; wishwash; xenoglossy; yabber; *zeug [G.];*

**chauffeur** *(n.)*: auriga; buggy driver; coachman; driver; employee; fellow; *gharry-wallah;* hackneyman; *individual;* jarvey; kurveyor; limo driver; *man; nagsman;* operator; pilot; paid driver; *quadrille;* rig-driver; servant; tandem operator; *uhlan;* valet; wheelman; *x-port;* yanker operator; *zain-driver;*

**cheap** *(adj. inexpensive)*: affordable; *bon marché* [F.]; bargain-priced; cost-effective; dirt- ~; discounted; economical; frugal; good price; *half-priced;* inexpensive; *justified; knock-out prices;* low-cost; moderately-priced; not expensive; *on sale;* pennyworth; quite ~; reasonable; reduced; sixpenny; thrifty; uncostly; value-priced; *worth it; xtry.; yellow tag sale;* zero-profit; [*Ant.* costly]

**cheap** *(adj. miserly)*: avaricious; begrudging; chintzy; *derisory;* economical; frugal; grudging; hard-fisted; illiberal; *judicious; kitsch;* laggard; miserly; meager; niggardly; overcautious; parsimonious; penny-pinching; *quick-to-refuse;* reluctant; stingy; sparing; thrifty; ungenerous; *vacillating;* wary; *xtry.* ~; yieldless; zero-generosity; [*Ant.* charitable]

**cheap** *(adj. shoddy)*: awful; base; cheesy; chintzy; cheapo; catchpenny; dumpy; downmarket; *embarrassing;* faulty; gimcrack; *horrible;* inferior; junky; jimcrack; jerrybuilt; keg-meg; lousy; low-grade; low-quality; *meager;* non-quality; *otious;* poor; pathetic; quisquillous; rubblishy; shoddy; slapdash; substandard; trashy; tinpot; two-bit; third-rate; unprime; *vile;* wretched; *weak; x-bad; yucky;* zero-quality;

**cheapen** *(v.)*: abase; belittle; cut prices; disvalue; denigrate; demean; depreciate; degrade; devaluate; *execrate;* fall; *go down; horrible;* insult; *jibe;* knock (down); lessen value; lower; make cheaper; mark down; *negate; otious;* put down; *quib;* reduce; slash prices; slump; trivialize; undervalue; underrate; undercut; *vilify;* wipe; *x-out;* yield; *zeroize;*

**cheapness** *(n.)*: awfulness; baseness; chintziness; despicability; dumpiness; economicalness; faultiness; gimcrackery; horribleness; inferiority; jimcrackery; *keg-meg;* lousiness; low quality; meanness; non-quality; *otious;* poorness; *quality;* reasonableness; shoddiness; trashiness; unworthiness; vileness; wretchedness; *x-badness; yuckiness;* zero-quality;

**cheat** *(v.)*: *allure;* beguile; bilk; burn; chouse; chicane; cozen; con; diddle; defraud; ensnare; fleece; gyp; hornswoggle; insnare; jape; kid; *lie;* misrepresent; nobble; outfox; put one over; *quiblin* [arch.]; rook; rip off; swindle; trick; take advantage; *utter falsehood;* verneuk; weasel; wangle; *xuld [arch.]; yentz; zing;*

**cheater** *(n.)*: *allurer;* beguiler; cheat; con artist; cozener; deceiver; defrauder; ensnarer; fraud; finagler; guiler; gypper; hoaxer; Indian giver; jackal; knave; liar; misrepresentor; no-good; open liar; phony; quacksalver; rook; swindler; shyster; trickster; untruther; verneuker; wangler; *xgressor;* yarn-spinner; *zinger;*

**check** *(v.)*: assess; analyze; behold; consider; compare; diagnose; examine; find; feel; go over; *hone in on;* inspect; investigate; *jerque;* keek; look at (-over); make inspection; note; observe; overlook; pick over; pore; question; quiz; research; review; re-examine; study; scrutinize; scan; test; *understand;* verify; view; vet; watch; weigh; *xeque; yeme; zero in;*

**cheer** *(n.)*: animation; bliss; cheerfulness; contentedness; delight; exuberance; felicity; glee; gladness; happiness; hilarity; intoxication; joy(fulness); jubilation; *keenness;* lightheartedness; merriment; *niceness;* overjoy; pleasure; *queme;* rejoicing; sunniness; satisfaction; thrill; *uplifted;* vivacity; winsomeness; *xanadu; yeah!;* zestfulness; [*Ant.* cheerless]

**cheer** *(v.)*: applaud; *bellow;* celebrate; clap; delight; *dance;* exult; *fanfare;* glory; glee; hail; holler; *idolize;* jubilate; *keen;* laud; make merry; noise; *ovation;* praise; *quiritation;* root on; rejoice; roar; shout; thunder; *triumph;* urge on; vociferate; whoop; *xenophonia;* yell; zindabad [Arab.]; [*see* praise; *Ant.* criticize]

**cheerful** *(adj.)*: animated; bubbly; blissful; bright; cheery; chipper; delighted; exuberant; effervescent; ebullient; felicitous; gleeful; happy; intoxicated; joyful; jubilant; jovial; *keen;* lively; lighthearted; merry; mirthful; *nice;* overjoyed; pleased; *queme;* riant; rejoicing; sunny; satisfied; thrilled; uplifted; *vivacious;* winsome; *xanadu;* yeasty; zestful; [*Ant.* cheerless]

**cheerfulness** *(n.)*: alacrity; blissfulness; brightness; cheer(iness); delightfulness; enjoyableness; felicity; gladness; happiness; invigoration; jocundity; *keenness;* lightheartedness; *merriness;* niceness; *over joyousness;* pleasantness; queme; rosiness; sunniness; satisfaction; thrill; *uplifting;* vivaciousness; winsomeness; *xenia; yeah!* zestfulness; [*Ant.* cheerlessness]

**cheese** *(n.)*: * American ~; bleu ~; *caerphilly;* dairy ~; *Edam;* feta; gouda; gratin; haloumi; *item;* jack ~; kebbuck; Limburger; mozarella; Muenster ~; Monterey Jack; Neufchâtel; *object;* Parmesian; paneer; quince- ~; ricotta ~; Swiss ~; *taleggio;* unsliced ~; vacherin; white ~; *whey; xynomizithra;* yellow ~; *zeiger* ~;
   **Kinds of cheese**: American; bleu ~; brie; cheddar; dimsi; esrom; feta; gouda; haloumi; ircano; jack; katiki; Limburger; Muenster; mozzarella; Neufchatel; ossau-iraty; parmesan; quark; roquefort; Swiss; tomme des savorie; ubriaco; vacherin; Wensleydale; xynomizithra; Yorkshire blue; zeiger;
**chef** *(n.)*: artist; baker; barbequer; cook; culinary expert; dinner ~; expert ~; fry cook; griller; gourmet ~; head ~; hash slinger [slang]; *Italian* ~; *Japanese* ~; kitchener; lunch ~; *man [masc.];* nourisher; Oriental ~; pastry-cook; padrone; *qualified* ~; restaurant ~; sous- ~; trained ~; uber~; victual-preparer; well-trained ~; *woman [fem.]; xeo user;* yarker; *zesty;*
**cherish** *(v.)*: adore; *beloved;* care for; cleave to; devote oneself to; esteem; feel affection for; greatly love; hold dear; idolize; joy in; *kiss;* love; *melt;* nurture; overlove; prize; *quixotic;* relish; show love; treasure; *unselfishness;* value; worship; *xenophilic;* yearn for; *zeal;* [Ant. contemn]
**chest** *(n. bosom)*: *area;* bosom; breast; bust; cleavage [fem.]; décolleté [fem.]; embonpoint [fem.]; front; *gird;* heart; *imbosomed; jog;* kirtle; *love;* midsection; *nestle;* oxtercog; pectoral; *quiddity;* ribs; sternum; torso; trunk; upper body; *venter; warmth;* xiphoid; *yield;* ziphisternum;
**chest** *(n. box)*: ark; box; cassone; container; coffer; *drum;* enclosure; *firkin; gift box* hope ~; hutch; *iron* ~; *jarahwood* ~; kist; lockbox; locker; *moving carton;* night safe; oak ~; pod; *quinderkyn;* receptacle; strongbox; sea ~; trunk; treasure ~; *ungula;* vanity; vessel; wooden ~; *xtr. space; yadzutsu [Jap.];* zebrawood ~;
**chew** *(v.)*: *ate;* begnaw; chomp; dine; eat; feed; gnaw; graze; have; intake; junket; knabble; lunch; masticate; munch; nosh; *overeat;* partake; *quill* [arch.]; ruminate; sup; *taste; undereat; victual;* wolf; *xerophagy;* yaffle; *zip down;*
**chicken** *(n.)*: asil; *animal;* bird; biddy; broiler; chick; domestic fowl; egger; *fowl;* fryer; gump; hen; *ixworth; java; kadaknath;* leghorn; minorca; nankin; *orloff;* poultry; pullet; quachilto; rooster [masc.]; *silkie; tomaru; uncooked* ~; vorwerk ~; *wyandotte;* white meat; x-breed; yurlov crower; zoic;
**chide** *(v.)*: admonish; blame; criticize; denounce; excoriate; fault; give talking to; harangue; impugn; jaffock; knock; lambaste; *macerate;* nag; objurgate; pan; *question;* reprimand; rebuke; reprove; scold; take to task; upbraid; vituperate; wig [Br.]; warn; *xuld [arch.];* yell at; *zap;* [Ant. commend]
**chief** *(adj.)*: absolute; big; central; dominant; eminent; foremost; greatest; highest; important; *judicious;* key; leading; main; notable; overriding; prime; quintessential; ranking; supreme; top; ultimate; vital; weighty; *xenenthesis;* yet unsurpassed; zenithal;
**chief** *(n.)*: autocrat; authority; boss; chieftain; director; dynast; dictator; executive; *foreman;* governor; Grand Sachem; head; intendant; Indian ~; jemander [Ind.]; king; leader; master; monarch; nobleman; overseer; overlord; potentate; president; prime minister; principal; prefect; patriarch; queen [fem.]; ruler; sachem; sagamore; supervisor; tyrant; *ultimate authority;* vizer; village ~; warden; warlord; XO; *yardboss;* zayim;
**child** *(n.)*: adolescent; born one; begotten; bairn; boy [masc.]; chip off the old block; descendant; dependent; daughter [fem.]; *enfant [F.];* fruit (of the womb); flesh and blood; firstling; girl [fem.]; gamin; hobbledehoy [masc.]; increase; issue; junior; kid; little one; lad [masc.]; lass [fem.]; minor; neophyte; nipper [Br.]; offspring; progeny; preschooler; peewee; quinquennarian; rug rat [joc.]; *relative;* scion; son [masc.]; sprout; tot; urchin; *vandal;* whippersnapper; waif; whelp; *xbred;* youngster; youth; young'un [dial.]; zon [dial. masc.]; [see fruit]
**childbirth** *(n.)*: accouchement; bearing; coming; conception; delivery; entrance; engendering; *founding;* formation; generation; geniture; giving birth; hatching; having a baby; *incubation; jump off; kickoff;* labor; mothering; nativity; origin; parturition; *quickening;* reproduction; spawning; travail; ushering in; *visitation; welcoming; waiting; xenogenesis;* yielding; zygogeneis;

**childish** *(adj.)*: adolescent; babyish; boyish; callow; childlike; doited; early; fledgling; green; hastive; immature; juvenile; kiddish; little; maidenly [fem.]; nascent; *over-young;* puerile; *quite young; ridiculous;* silly; trifling; unadult; vernal; wee; *XS;* young; youthful; *zero-experience;*
**childishness** *(n.)*: adolescence; babyishness; boyishness [masc.]; callowness; *development; earliness; fledgling;* greenness; girlishness [fem.]; hastiveness; immaturity; juvenility; kiddishness; lack of maturity; neoteny; non-maturity; *over-young;* puerility; *quite young;* rawness; silliness; trifling; undevelopment; *vernal;* witlessness; *XS;* youth; *zero-experience;*
**childless** *(adj.)*: aching; barren; bereaved; child-deprived; desolate; empty; effete; forlorn; *grieving;* heirless; infertile; jejune; *kept from bearing;* lacking; *made ~;* non-bearing; olated; orbate; *poor; quenched;* resourceless; sterile; *sine prole* [L.]; teemless; unfruitful; void of children; without issue; x'ed; yeld; *zero fruit;*
**children** *(n.)*: adolescents; brood; begotten; born ones; *covey* [zoo.]; descendants; daughters [fem.]; *enfant [F.];* fruit (of the womb); generations; *heirs; hatch* [zoo.]; issue; increase; juvenile; juniors; kids; little ones; munchkins [joc.]; mouths to feed; *next generation;* offspring; progeny; posterity; *quinquennarian;* rug rats [joc.]; sons; tikes; *urchins; vandals;* wee ones; whelps; xbred; young; zons [dial.]; [see fruit]
**chilly** *(adj.)*: airish; brisk; cold; cool; chilling; *dead; east wind;* frigid; gelid; *glacial;* heatless; icy; *Jack Frost;* keen; low temperature; *moderately cold;* nippy; overcold; parky; *quite cool;* refrigerated; snappy; *thawless;* unheated; *very cold;* wintry; xeric-less; ycie [arch.]; *zero degrees;*
**chimney** *(n.)*: apparatus; brick ~; chimney stack; *duct;* escape; flue; funnel; granite ~; high ~; *item; j-bend pipe;* kitchen- ~; lum; main ~; outlet; pipe; *quarter-high ~; release;* smokestack; stovepipe; shaft; turret; uptake; vent; *way out; xfer,* Y-branch; zone;
**China** *(n.)* Asia; *Beijing;* Communist ~; *Cathay* [arch.]; *dynasty;* East Asia; *Far East; Gobi;* Hong Kong; inland ~; *Japan;* Keeman; land of ~; Mainland ~; Nationalist ~; Orient; People's Republic of ~; *Peking;* Qinghai; Red ~; *Shenzhou* [Chin.]; *Tsingtao; Urumqi; Van Leng;* western ~; *Xi'an;* Yunnan; zimu;
**Chinese** *(adj.)*: Asian; *Beijing;* Cantonese; *dynastic;* Eastern; *Far Eastern; Gobi;* Hunan; *Indo- ~; Japanese;* Keemun; *Liaoning;* Mandarin; Manchurian; Nationalist ~; Oriental; Putonghua; *Pekingese;* Qin; *Red ~;* Sinaean; *Tsingtao; Ueumqi; Van Leng;* western ~; xanthoderm; Yunnanese; zimu;
**chip** *(n.)*: amount; bit; chip; chunk; crumb; clod; clump; daud; drop; *ens;* fragment; flake; fleck; fraction; *gob;* hunk; *iota;* jib; junt; jigger; kernel; lump; lamia; little piece; morsel; mammock; mass; mite; nugget; ounce; ort; piece; part; portion; *quantity;* remnant; small piece; speck; sliver; shard; spall; smidgen; shaving; tidbit; *unit; vestige;* wedge; wee bit; *wood shaving;* xylon; yngot [arch.]; zum [dial.];
**chip** *(v.)*: axe; break; crack; damage; *efface;* fracture; flake; *grind; harm;* injure; *jab;* knock apart; *little pieces;* make ~; *nugget;* olate; pull down; *quash;* rupture; spall; splinter; tear; uproot; vitiate; wreck; *x-ing;* yank down; zap;
**chisel** *(n.)*: adze; bolster; *bezel;* caulking iron; *device;* edge; flat-blade ~; gouge; *hand tool; instrument;* J-groove ~; knapper; *likeness; means;* notcher; *object;* paring tool; *quality; retrencher;* socket-chisel; tool; *utensil;* V-groove ~; weeding-chisel; xyster; yerk; zeug;
**chisel** *(v.)*: ax; *bob;* cut; carve; *design;* engrave; fashion; gouge; grave; hew; hammer; incise; inscribe; *jot;* knap; *lop;* mold; make; notch; *object;* pare; quadrisect; *retrench;* shape; sculpt; tool; *unseam; undercut;* vell; whittle; *xylograph;* yerk; zigsaw [arch.];
**chivalrous** *(adj.)*: altruistic; brave; courteous; decorous; *enterprising;* fair-spoken; gallant; gentlemanly; heroic; intrepid; *judicious;* knightly; lion-hearted; mannerly; manful; noble; obliging; polite; *quick-to-help;* respectable; stouthearted; thoughtful; unselfish; valiant; well-mannered; *xtry.; yare; zealous;* [Ant. crude]
**choice** *(n.)*: alternative; *best ~;* choosing; decision; determination; election; final judgment; first ~; favorite; *gauging; heart; inclination;* judgment; *knowledge; like; liberty; mind; nomination;* option; pick; preference; pleasure; *quibble;* ruling; selection; take; top ~; *ultimatum;* verdict; vote; will; wish; *x; yes;* zeal;

**choir** *(n.)*: assemblage; body of singers; chorus; duet; ensemble; foregathering; group; glee club; hymn singers; *intoners;* jingle ~; *key singer; lot;* musicians; *number;* octet; performers; quartet; quintet; resonators; singers; *trio; utterers;* vocalists; voices; warblers; worshipers; *xoeoemei;* yodelers; zealous ~;

**choke** *(v.)*: asphyxiate; *bind; cover; constrict;* deprive of oxygen; extinguish; *finish off;* gag; garrote; *hush; incapacitate;* jugulate; kill; *lynch; murder; nullify;* overlay; *put out;* quackle; quench; *repress;* strangle; suffocate; smother; stifle; throttle; *undo; void;* wring (one's neck); whirken [arch.]; *xuld [arch.]; yote; zeroize;*

**choose** *(v.)*: ascertain; *best choice;* cull; decide; determine; elect; favor; go with; hand-pick; indicate; judge between; *know; list* [arch.]; *like;* make a choice; *nominate;* opt; pick; prefer; please; *quibble;* resolve; select; settle on; specify; single out; take; *use;* vote; want; *well-chosen; x; yes; zealous for;*

**choosy** *(adj.)*: austere; *bull-headed; careful;* demanding; difficult; discriminating; exacting; fussy; finicky; fastidious; *griping;* hard to please; implacable; *insistent; just so; kvetch [Yid.]; like; malcontented; meticulous;* nitpicky; overparticular; picky; particular; quiddle; *repining;* selective; tough; unappeasable; very ~; *whining; xuld [arch.]; yieldless; zero give;* [Ant. carefree]

**chop** *(v.)*: ax; abscind; bisect; bob; cut; crop; cleave; dissever; dice; exscind; fragment; *gouge; grate;* hack; hew; hash; incise; *jag;* knife; lop; mince; *notch;* obtruncate; pole-axe; prune; poll; quarter; retrench; slice; slash; sever; trim; take off; *undercut;* vell; whack; x-sect; yerk; *zip;* [Ant. connect]

**choppy** *(adj.)*: *angry;* broken; crackly; difficult; disconnected; erratic; fitful; *grating;* herky-jerky; irregular; intermittent; jerky; *keeling; lousy;* much-broken; non-smooth; *overly ~; problematic; quirky;* rough; shifting; temperamental; uneven; volatile; wavering; wavy; *xuld [arch.];* yeasty; *zealous;* [Ant. continuous]

**chore** *(n.)*: assignment; business; charge; duty; errand; field; grind [slang]; hard job; industry; job; *key position; livelihood;* mission; *necessity;* odd job; *profession; quest;* responsibility; service; task; undertaking; vocation; work; xci. *yoke; zealous duty;*

**chorus** *(n. group of singers)*: assemblage; barbershop quartet; choir; chorale; duet; ensemble; folk singers; group; hymn singers; *intoners;* jingle-chanters; *key singer; love song;* musicians; *nonet;* octet; performers; quartet; quintet; resonators; singers; trio; *unit;* voices; worshipers; *xoeoemei; yodelers;* zealous singers;

**chorus** *(n. refrain of song)*: anthem; burden; chorale; descant; *étude; folksong; gallimaufry;* hymn; *inspirational;* jingle; *kasida;* laud; melody; *notes;* ode; *piece;* quodlibet; refrain; strain; theme; undersong; *vocalization; warbling;* xylophone song; *yed; zemirah;*

**chosen** *(adj.)*: appointed; before-ordained; *choice;* determined; destined; elect(ed); favored; foreordained; *God-appointed;* hand-picked; heaven-ordained; indicated; instituted; *judged; known; listed; liked;* made afore; *nominated;* opted-for; ordained; picked; preferred; pre-determined; predestinated; preordained; *qualified;* resolved; selected; singled out; taken; *used;* voted-for; wanted; well-chosen; *x; yes; zealous for;*

**Christ** *(n.)*: Advocate; Almighty; Ancient of Days; Author and Finisher of the Faith; alpha; Branch; Blessed Son; Bread of Life; ~ Child; Chief Shepherd (-Cornerstone); Counselor; Consolation of Israel; Deliverer; Door; Dayspring; Day Star; Desire of Nations; Emmanuel; Everlasting Father; Faithful and True; firstborn of the dead; God the Son; God Incarnate; Good Shepherd; Great Shepherd (-Physician; -High Priest); Head; Holy Child (-One of Israel); High Priest; Heir of All Things; Immanuel; I AM; Jesus (Christ); Judge; King (of kings); Lamb (of God); Lord (of lords); Light (of the world); Life; Lily of the Valley; Lion of the Tribe of Judah; Living Water; Locus; Master; Messiah; Mighty God; Man of Sorrows; Morning Star; Nazarene; Only begotten Son; omega; Prince of Peace; *Quickener;* Redeemer; Rock; Righteous; Rabbi; Rose of Sharon; Savior; Son of God (-man); Shepherd; Seed of the woman; Second Adam; Truth; Teacher; Unspeakable Gift; Vine; Victor; Word (of life; of God); Wonderful; Way; Xt.; Yeshua; *Yahweh;* Zion's Hope; [see God]

**christen** *(v.)*: asperse; besprinkle; call; dedicate; designate; dub; decant; entitle; effuse; *font;* godparent; *holy water;* infuse; *jawp; kirk;* label; *moisten;* name; *outpour;* purify; *queven [arch.];* resperse; sprinkle; tinkle; title; *undried; vapor;* wet; *xpn.; ybaptized [arch.]; zet [dial.];*
**Christian** *(adj.)*: alive in Christ; believing; born-again; Blood-washed; Christ-centered (-honoring); Christlike; delivered; elect; evangelical; forgiven; God-fearing; godly; heaven-bound; in Christ; justified; kirsen [dial.]; living in Christ; *moral;* Nazarene; orthodox; professing Christ; quickened; redeemed; saintly; saved; *Trinitarian;* united in Christ; *victorious; washed;* Xn. *Yahwist;* Zionite;
**Christian** *(n.)*: *alive in Christ;* believer; brother [masc.]; brethren [pl.]; child of God; *churchgoer;* disciple; *do-gooder;* elect; follower of Christ; God's child; holy roller [derog.]; *in Christ;* Jehovist; kirsen [dial.]; lover of God; *moralist;* Nazarene; orthodox; professor of Christianity; *quickened;* redeemed man; *the* righteous [pl.]; saint; saved person; *Trinitarian; unshackled; victor; washed;* Xn. *Yahwist;* Zionite;
**Christianity** *(n.)*: *alive in Christ;* Bible- ~; Christianism; *Christendom;* discipleship of Christ; evangelical ~; *the* Faith; Gospel; *Hamoousianism; in Christ;* Jesus; Kingdom of God; life in Christ; *morality;* NT ~; *the* old paths; old-time religion; personal relationship with Christ; *quickening of God; relationship with God; righteousness of Christ;* Spirit-filled life; *truth; unshackled; victorious Christian living; the* Way; Xnty. *Yahwism; Zionite;*
**Christlike** *(adj.)*: altruistic; benevolent; blameless; Christianlike; decent; ever-faithful; faithful; godly; high-minded; impeccable; irreproachable; just; *keen; loving;* moral; *noble; outstanding;* pure; principled; *quality;* righteous; saintly; *truthful;* upright; virtuous; wholesome; *Xn.; yielded; zaddik* [Heb.];
**chronic** *(adj.)*: abiding; binding; continual; *durative;* enduring; *fixed;* going on and on; *habitual;* inveterate; *jusqu'au bout* [F.]; *keeps going;* long-lasting; maintaining; nonstop; ongoing; prolonged; perpetual; *quadrillion;* remaining; steady; *termination-free;* unceasing; *vast;* without end; *x-cending;* year-round; *zero break;*
**chronicle** *(n.)*: account; archive; annals; book; chronography; diary; experiences; factual account; *goings on;* history; *incident;* journal; *knowledge;* life story; lore; memoirs; narrative; *oral history;* past history; *quarto;* record; story; tale; *unabridged story; version;* written history; *xenodocheionology; yesteryear; zine;*
**chronicle** *(v.)*: annotate; *book;* compose; draft; enter; *facts;* grave; handwrite; indite; indicate; journalize; keep record; log; mark down; narrate; *overwrite;* put down; preserve; quill; record; recount; set down; take down; undertake to write; *vellum;* write (down); *x; yak; zay;*
**chronological** *(adj.)*: as it occurred; blow-by-blow; chronologic; date-order; ensuing; following each other; going in order; historical-order; in order; junctural; keyed-by-date; linear; *methodical; non-random;* ordered; progressive; *queue; real-time;* sequential; successive; time-order; *uninterrupted; verging;* with historical ordering; *x-pire;* year-order; *Zeit [G.];*
**chuckle** *(v.)*: *arride* [arch.]; burst out; chortle; die laughing [slang]; exult; *frolic;* giggle; ha ha; irrision; *jolly;* keckle; laugh; *mirth;* nicker; *outburst; peal; quib;* roar; snicker; snigger; tee-hee; twitter; utter laughter; *vibrate with laughter;* whicker; *xtr. funny;* yuk; *zeal;* [Ant. cry]
**chunk** *(n.)*: amount; bit; bunch; chip; clump; clod; daud; *ens;* fragment; *gob;* hunk; *iota;* junt; kernel; lump; morsel; mass; mammock; nugget; ort; ounce; piece; part; portion; *quantity;* remnant; small piece; tidbit; *unit; vestige;* wedge; *xylon; yngot [arch.]; zum [dial.];*
**church** *(n.)*: assembly; body (of Christ); bride of Christ; congregation; *deployment; ekklesia* [Gr.]; flock; *gathering; group;* house of God; ingathering; *jam* [coll.]; *kirk* [Scot.]; local church; ministry; members; *mission; number;* NT ~; *overflow; people;* pillar and ground; *quorum;* regathering; *sheep; session;* temple of the Holy Ghost; *turnout; unit; vestry;* work; *worshipers;* Xn.; *Yahweh's church; zayat* [Burm.]; [*see* church house]

**churchgoer** *(n.)*: attender; believer; brother [masc.]; church member; congregant; disciple; *elect;* follower; faithful attender; goer; *holy roller [derog.];* ingatherer; *Jehovist;* kirsen [dial.]; layman; member; *non-clergy;* oblate; proselyte; parishioner; *quickened;* regular; saint; saved person; tither; *unshackled;* votary; worshiper; Xn.; *Yahwist; Zionite;*

**church house** *(n.)*: *auditorium;* building; church building; chapel; cathedral; *domicile;* edifice; Ebenezer [Br.]; facility; fane [poet.]; gathering place; God's house; house (of God); *ingathering; Jesus' house;* kirk [Scot.]; *the* Lord's house; meeting place; meetinghouse; mission; minster; nave; oratorio; oratory; oratorium; place of worship; *parvis;* Quaker church; *rectory;* sanctuary; tabernacle; temple; *upper room;* vestry; worship-house; Xn. church; *yele* [arch.]; *zayat* [Burm.];

**churlish** *(adj.)*: argumentative; bad-mannered; base; brutish; crude; coarse; crass; discourteous; evil-mannered; fractious; gruff; homebred; ill-mannered; jaded; *kitsch;* loutish; mean; nasty; obnoxious; *pathetic;* quarrelsome; rude; surly; truculent; uncivil; vulgar; wretched; *x-rated;* yokelish; zhlubby; [*Ant.* congenial]

**churn** *(v.)*: agitate; blend; convulse; *crank;* disturb; *excite; fold; gyrate; harrow; intermix;* jabble; kirn [Scot.]; *lash;* mix; moil; *nutate; overagitate;* paddle; queach; roil; stir; turn; *use beater;* vigorously stir; whip; *xuld [arch.]; yerk; zwoosh;*

**circle** *(n.)*: annulus; ball; bezant (heraldry); circlet; cycle; circuit; disk; enclosure; ellipsoid; *felly;* gyre; globe; hoop; incirclet; Jordan curve; kinch; loop; micro- ~; *non-square;* orb; *oval;* perimeter; *quasi-circular;* ring; round; radius; rigol; sphere; turn; *unicircular;* vesica; wheel; *x-radius; y-radius; zone;*

**circle** *(v.)*: *around;* begird; besiege; circuit; cordon; draw around; encircle; enclose; environ; encompass; frame; gird; hem in; hedge; inclose; *Jordan curve;* kirtle; loop around; make ~ around; *non-broken circle;* orbit; outline; put around; *quoil [dial.];* ravel; revolve; round; surround; *twine; upwind; volt;* wrap; wreathe; *xy-curve;* yard; zone;

**circuit** *(n.)*: annulus; beat; bout; circle; *doughnut;* eyre; *felly;* gradation; *hoop;* incirclet; *Jordan curve; kinch;* loop; micro-circle; *nexus;* orbit; *path; queue;* ring; round (circle); route; sphere; tour; usual route; *voyage;* wheel; *XOR circuit; y-radius; zone;*

**circular** *(adj.)*: annular; annulary; ball-shaped; curved; circulative; cycloid; cylindrical; discoid; disk-like; encyclical; *elliptical;* falcade; globous; globular; gyre; hooplike; incirclet; *j-curve; kinch;* looping; *moving circularly;* nodular; orbicular; perispheric; *quasi-circular;* round(ed); rotund; ringlike; spherical; spheroidal; turning; unangular; verticil; wheel-shaped; *x-radius; y-radius;* zonical;

**circulate** *(v.)*: advertise; broadcast; circularize; distribute; diffuse; expose; fame; give out; go around; hand out; issue; intermix; *join; known;* let others know; move (in circle); *notify;* openly report; pass around; publicize; *querl;* raise awareness; run; spread; tell others; *uphold; well-known; xmit; yell; zip;*

**circumcise** *(v.)*: abscind; *bris;* cut away; dissever; exscind; *foreskin; gouge;* hew; incide; *jag; knife; lop; mul* [Heb.]; *nick;* obtruncate; *pare; qualify;* recise; remove foreskin; surgically remove prepuce; take off foreskin; *unattach; vell; work; x-sect; Yiddish practice; zip;*

**circumcision** *(n.)*: abscission; bris; cutting away; dissevering; eighth-day ~; foreskin-removal; *gouging;* hewing; incision; *jag; knife; lop;* mohel [Heb.]; *nick;* obtruncation; paring; qualification; recise; removal of the foreskin; *rite;* sign of the covenant; *surgery;* taking off; *unattaching; velling; work; x-sect; Yiddish practice; zip;*

**circumspect** *(adj.)*: alert; *beware;* careful; cautious; discerning; ever-careful; fabian; guarded; heedful; *intentional;* judicious; *kid gloves;* leery; mindful; *nervous;* observant; prudent; quick-witted; restrained; sensible; thoughtful; ultra-careful; vigilant; watchful; wary; x-careful; yare-handed; *zärtlich* [G.]; [*Ant.* careless]

**circumstance** *(n.)*: attribute; *ailment; being;* bind; condition; case; *details;* estate; fashion; fix; fare; fact; guise; happening; incident; immediate ~; juncture; kilter; lot; manner; mode; *new development;* occurrence; order; particulars; posture; place; predicament; plight; position; quality; *result;* situation; state; status; shape; tenor; tone; *unusual ~;* venue; vein; way; *xenenthesis; yield; zet [dial.];*

**circumstantial** *(adj.)*: attending; belief-based; conjectural; deductive; *estimated; feeling;* guessed; hypothetical; incidental; inferred; *just supposed; keenly suspected; lemma; minded;* non-proven; opinionative; putative; Q.E.D.; reckoned; situational; suppositional; seeming; *theoretical;* unproven; virtual; *way it seems; xenenthesis;* yet unproven; *zealous;*

**circumvent** *(v.)*: avoid; bypass; circumnavigate; detour; evade; flank; go around; *hedge; indirect;* jink; *keep away from; let alone;* move; miss; navigate around; obviate; pass by; *quite [Sp.];* roundabout; skirt; sidestep; tiptoe around; *use other route; vault; walk around; xuld [arch.];* yerk; *zip around;*

**circus** *(n.)*: act; *amusement park;* big top; carnival; *display;* entertainers; event; fun park; festival; gilly; hippodrome; international ~; *juggler;* kermis; *lion-tamer;* midway; *noveau cirque; occasion;* performance; playland; *quality production;* ridotto; show; traveling ~; three-ring ~; *unicyclist show;* vernissage; water park; *xtry.; yahoo!;* zoo;

**cistern** *(n.)*: artesian well; basin; container; draw-~; *exploration ~;* font; *fountain; gush;* headspring; issue; *jubb [Heb.];* keld; *lake;* mickery; namma hole; *oil ~;* pump ~; Persian ~; quell; qanat; reservoir; spring; source; step~; sluice; tank; underground ~; vat; well(spring); *XO; YP; zemzem;*

**citizen** *(n.)*: *abider;* burgess; civilian; countryman; dweller; denizen; *ethnic;* fellow ~; *gentleman;* habitant; inhabitant; *jake; kipper [Aus.];* local; legal ~; member; national; oppidan; occupant; person; *quiritian [L.];* resident; subject; taxpayer; townsman; townie [slang]; *townsfolk; ubeity;* villager; voter; working man; *xenophile; yokel; zonal;*

**citizenship** *(n.)*: *abiding;* birthright; *citizenry;* dwelling; *ethnic;* fellowship; *group;* habitance; inhabitance; *jus soli [L.]; jus sanguinis [L.]; kipper [Aus.];* legal ~; membership; naturalization; occupancy; part; *quiritian [L.];* residency; *subject; taxpayer; ubeity;* villager; voting-rights; *working class; xenophile; yokel; zonal;*

**city** *(n.)*: *autonomy;* borough; burg; center; *capital ~; district;* emporium; exurb; faubourg; free ~; greater ~; hamlet; inner ~; imperial ~; *jurisdiction;* kirk-town [Scot.]; *location; limits;* metropolis; *native ~;* outport; *oppidum [Rom.];* port (~); place; *quarter; rancho;* seaport; town; treasure- ~; urban center; ville; whistle stop [slang]; ward; *Xining; yokel town; zone;* [*see* town; *Ant.* country]
    **U.S. cities**: Atlanta; Boston; Chicago; Denver; Eugene; Fresno; Greenville; Houston; Indianaoplis; Jacksonville; Kansas City; Los Angeles; Memphis; New York; Orlando; Philadelphia; Quakertown; Richmond; Seattle; Topeka; Urbana; Ventura; Washington D.C.; Xenia; Youngstown; Zanesville;
    **Foreign cities**: Amsterdam; Berlin; Cairo; Dublin, Edinburgh, Frankfurt, Glascow, Hong Kong, Istanbul, Jerusalem, Kalingrad, London; Madrid; Moscow; Naples; Ottowa; Paris; Quebec, Rome, Stockholm, Tokyo, Ulm, Vienna, Venice, Warsaw, Xining, Yokahama, Zurich;

**civil** *(adj.)*: amiable; becoming; courteous; decorous; elegant; fitting; gentlemanly; high-style; *interpersonal;* judicious; kind; *likable;* mannerly; *nice;* obsequious; polite; *queme;* respectful; sociable; tactful; urbane; very polite; well-mannered; *xenial; yielding; zero offense;* [*Ant.* crude]

**civilian** *(n.)*: *anyone;* bystander; citizen; dude; everyday person; fellow; gentleman; human (being); individual; joe [slang masc.]; jill [slang fem.]; *kid;* living soul; man; nonmilitary individual; noncombatant; outsider; person; *quadragenarian;* regular person; soul; townsfolk [pl.]; urbanite; villager; woman [fem.]; *xenic;* yokel; *zoon;*

**civility** *(n.)*: appropriateness; amenity; breeding; *behavior;* courtesy; courtliness; decorum; elegance; fitness; good manners; gentility; high-style; *impressive; jimp; kindness; loveliness;* manners; *niceness;* obligingness; propriety; politeness; *quaintness;* refinement; social correctness; table manners; urbanity; *Victorian; well-mannered; xtry.; younker; zero offense;* [*Ant.* crudeness]

**civilization** *(n.)*: advancement; body; building up; culture; Christianization; development; establishment; enculturation; *federation;* group; *habituation;* institution; joint coalition; *key ~;* league; mutual interest group; modernization; nation; organization; open ~; public; progress; *quinquevirate;* refinement; society; technologically advanced ~; urbanization; *values;* way of life; westernization; white man's burden; *x-class; yeald;* zonta;

**civilize** *(v.)*: acculturate; Americanize; bring up-to-date; Christianize; develop; enlighten; Europeanize; *further; guide;* help become ~d; improve; *jump; key values; lead;* modernize; *non-savage; open one's eyes;* progress; *quantum leap;* refine; sophisticate; teach; tame; urbanize; *verse;* Westenize; *xenophilia;* yankeefy; *zoom ahead;* [*Ant.* corrupt]

**clad** *(p.p.)*: appareled; attired; bedecked; clothed; dressed; decked; decent; enrobed; fully clothed; garbed; habited; invested; jacketed; kit; *loungewear;* modest; *nice;* outfitted; prinked; *quaintised [arch.];* reappareled; shrouded; trimmed; *uniformed;* vested; well-appareled; wearing clothes; wrapped; *xuld [arch.];* yclad [arch.]; zipped on; [*Ant.* clothesless]

**claim** *(n.)*: assertion; allegation; affirmation; arrogation; averment; boast; contention; declaration; droit; demand; entitlement; *finding; gotten;* holding forth; insistence; jactitation; *keynote address;* legal ~; *maintaining;* notification; opining; profession; postulation; *quotation;* right; reclamation; statement; testimonial; utterance; vocalization; word; *xenagogy;* yeme; *zealous affirmation;*

**claim** *(v.)*: assert; allege; affirm; avow; arrogate; boast; contend; declare; express; *foremention; give;* hold; insist; jointly ~; *keep saying;* lay ~ to; maintain; *name;* opine; purport; profess; postulate; proclaim; *questionless;* report; reclaim; *reassert;* say; state; swear; testify; unequivocally ~; vouch; *word; xfer; yak; zealously affirm;* [*Ant.* cast off]

**clap** *(n.)*: applaud; applause [pl.]; bang; *clobber; din;* eclat; *fan; get;* hit; hand~; impact; *jolt;* klap [var.]; knock; licking; *mitting [slang]; nob;* ovation [pl.]; pat; put hands together [slang]; *praise; quab;* rap; slap; smack; *standing ovation;* tap; uppercut; *veney;* whack; *x-sect;* yedder; *zonk;*

**clap** *(v.)*: applaud; bang; click; clock; *din;* eclat; *fan; give applause;* hit; hand~; impact; *jolt;* klap [var.]; knock; lick; *mit [slang]; nob;* ovation [pl.]; put hands together [slang]; *quab;* rap; slap; smack; tap; uppercut; *veney;* whack; *x-sect;* yedder; *zonk;*

**clarify** *(v.)*: *address;* break down; comment; clear up; delineate; define; demystify; disambiguate; explain; expound; enlighten; expand; elaborate; elucidate; formulate; gloss; help one understand; illuminate; justify; *key in;* lay open; make clear; note; open up; put clearly; *qualify;* reword; resolve; show; shed light on; spell out; throw light on; uncloud; *verse;* write out; *xenagogy;* yak; zero in on;

**clarity** *(n.)*: apparentness; *brightness;* clearness; contrast; crispness; definition; distinctness; decoloration; explicitness; *fineness; glass; hydrophanous;* identifiableness; *just plain; kenspeckle;* lucidity; lucidness; limpidness; markedness; non-vagueness; obviousness; precision; perspicuity; pellucidity; plainness; *quickly identified;* relucency; sharpness; transparency; uncloudiness; understandableness; visibility; *well-defined;* x-parency; yeme [*arch.*]; zero confusion;

**class** *(n.)*: assembly; body; convocation; *college* ~; discussion group; *education;* English ~; forgathering; group; graduating ~; hour; *history* ~; ingathering; junior ~; kit [*coll.*]; lot; *language* ~; meeting; *math* ~; *number; object lesson* pupils; period; *quorum;* regathering; reunion; students; session; seminar; training ~; unit; *violin* ~; *worshipers; workshop; xenagogy;* Yiddish ~; zoology ~;

**classic** *(adj.)*: ageless; acclaimed; beloved; celebrated; dateless; enduring; esteemed; famous; great; honored; immortal; *Julian; known and loved by all; loved by millions;* memorable; noteworthy; olden; outstanding; popular; *quality;* respected; revered; standard; time-honored; timeless; traditional; unforgettable; universally acclaimed; venerated; *world-class;* xtry.; *year-after-year; zet [dial.];*

**classical** *(adj.)*: ageless; beloved; classic; dateless; enduring; famous; great; honored; immortal; *Julian; known and loved by all; loved by millions;* memorable; neo~; outstanding; *popularized; quality;* revered; *standard;* traditional; timeless; universally acclaimed; venerated; well-beloved; xtry.; *year-after-year; zet [dial.];* [*Ant.* contemporary]

**classification** *(n. category)*: arrangement; brand; breed; branch; class; category; categorization; cast(e); *class;* designation; denomination; distribution; estate; family; fashion; filing; genre; group; genus; heading; ilk; indexing; *jack;* kind; *kingdom;* lot; label; manner; model; mold; methodization; nature; nomenclature; order; organization; phylum; persuasion; placement; *quarter;* rank; rating;

ranging; sort; species; systemization; strain; style; superclass (-order); subclass (-group; -order); stripe; type; taxonomy; unitization; *unit;* variety; *way; x-class;* year-class; zootaxy;
**classify** *(v.)*: arrange; assort; assign; *bestow;* class; categorize; catalog; cull; classis; divide; distribute; evaluate; file; group; grade; *hold;* index; *judge; kit;* list; methodize; *make; notch;* organize; order; pigeonhole; peg; place; *qualify;* rank; rate; sort; systemize; subdivide; tabulate; unitize; valuate; *work; xfer; yield; zonate;*
**claw** *(n.)*: appendage; barb; *clutches; dorsum; extremity;* foot; frush; falcula; grabber; hook; hand; horn-foot; *interceptor; jag;* knuckles; left ~; meat hook [slang]; nail; nipper; *open ~;* pincer; pounce; *paw; quick;* retractile; spur; talon; toenail; unguis; ungula; *volar; wolf's ~; xema ~; yads;* zygodactyl;
**clay** *(n.)*: argil; bole; china ~; *dirt;* earth; fire~; gault; hazel-earth; iron- ~; *jet-clay;* kaolin; loam; marl; mud; *nast;* ocher; potter's earth; putty; pug; *quagmire;* red ~; *shist;* terra cotta; under~; urry; *virgin soil;* white clay; *xysma;* yellow-earth; zonal ~;
**clean** *(adj.)*: aseptic; bathed; cleansed; cleanly; disinfected; expurgated; fresh; germless; germ-free; hygienic; immaculate; jimp [Br.]; *kempt;* laundered; mopped; machine-washed; neat; orderly; pure; pristine; *quaint;* rinsed; spotless; sanitary; sparkling; sterile; shipshape; spic-and-span; tidy; trim; unsullied; undefiled; uncontaminated; unsoiled; vacuumed; washed; well-scrubbed; *xylol; yellow soap; zierlich* [G.]; [*see* empty; *Ant.* collied]
**clean** *(v.)*: absterge; bathe; clear out; cleanse; deterge; declutter; disinfect, degrease; dust; elute; flush; get clean; hose (off; down); house~; *immerse; jalap;* kill germs; launder; mop; machine-wash; neaten; outwash; pick up; purify; preen; *quintessentialize;* remove dirt; rinse; rid; sanitize; scrub; scour; sterilize; sweep; tidy; tub; unsully; vacuum; wash; wipe; *xylol; yellow soap; zierlich* [G.]; [*Ant.* colly]
**cleanliness** *(n.)*: asepsis; bathing; cleanness; disinfection, elution; freshness; *getting clean;* hygiene; immaculateness; *jalap;* killing germs; *laundering; mopping;* neatness; orderliness; purity; *quintessentialize; rinsed;* sanitation; spotlessness; tidiness; unsulliedness; *vacuumed; washed; xylol; yellow soap; zierlich* [G.]; [*Ant.* collying]
**cleanse** *(v.)*: absterge; bathe; clean out; depurate; decontaminate, detoxify; expurgate; flush; get clean; hygienize; *implunge; jalap;* kill germs; lustrate; mundify; *non-polluted;* outwash; purify; purge; *quintessentialize;* rinse; refine; sanctify; *tub;* unsully; *vacuate;* wash; *xylol; yellow soap; zierlich* [G.]; [*Ant.* contaminate]
**cleansing** *(n.)*: ablution; bathing; cleaning; depuration; decontamination; depuration; detoxification; expurgation; februation; *germ-removal;* headbath; *hallowing; implunging; jalap;* knee-bath; lavation; lustration; mundification; *non-polluted;* outwashing; purification; *quintessentialize;* rinsing; refinement; sanctification; *tubbing; unpolluted; vacuation;* washing; *xylol; yellow soap; zierlich* [G.]; [*Ant.* contamination]
**clear** *(adj.)*: apparent; blatant; clean; cloudless; colorless; crisp; crystal; distinct; diaphanous; evident; explicit; fine; *glass;* hydrophanous; identifiable; *just plain;* kenspeckle; lucid; luculent; limpid; marked; non-vague; obvious; overt; open; pure; pellucid; perspicuous; plain; perspicuous; quickly seen; relucent; see-through; sheer; sharp; transparent; translucent; univocal; unsubtle; uncolored; unclouded; understandable; visible; well-defined; *xparent; yeme [arch.];* zero confusion; [*see* understandable; *Ant.* clouded]
**clear** *(v.)*: absolve; acquit; blot out; clean; clarify; dissipate; dispel; disculpate; evaporate; exculpate; exonerate; free; find innocent; go away; grant pardon; *have free;* indemnify; justify; *kindness;* let go; make clean; not hold accountable; overlook; prove innocent; quit; rid of obstructions; remit; release; set free; take away; unblock; void; vindicate; wipe clean; *x out; yank;* zero out;
**clearing** *(n.)*: area; *bush; bare ground;* cleared area; dell; *earsh;* field; glade; haugh [Scot.]; ile [Welsh]; *jebel; knoll;* lea; meadow; milpa; *natural ~;* open space; opening; plot; *quadrat; range; sod;* turf; upland; *vega;* woodless area; *xyris;* yard; *zea;*

**cleave** *(v. cling)*: abide by; bind; cling; clutch; draw around; embrace; firmly hold; grasp; hold on; inwrap; *join;* keep hold; link; *make firm; nestle;* oxtercog; put arms around; *questionless;* remain faithful; stick to; take hold of; *unite; volt; with; x; yoke; zone;* [Ant. cut off]

**cleave** *(v. sever)*: ax; bisect; cut; chop; divide; exect; fissure; *gap;* hack; halve; incise; *jigsaw; knife;* lop; *miter; nick;* obtruncate; prescind; *quadrisect;* rive; split; sever; *trim;* truncate; *undo;* vell; whack; x-sect; yerk; *zip;* [Ant. connect]

**cleft** *(adj.)*: *apportioned;* bisected; bifid; cloven; divided; exscinded; forked; fissured; gapped; halved; incided; *jagged; knifed; lopped; mitered;* notched; opened; parted; *quadrisect;* rent; rifted; split; severed; *torn; unyoked; velled; ways; x-sect;* yandied; *zoned;*

**cleft** *(n.)*: aperture; break; breach; crack; division; *efforce;* fracture; fork; fissure; gap; hiatus; interstice; indentation; *junction;* knapple; *laceration; mincing; mashing;* non-continuum; opening; parting; *quadrifid;* rift; rend; split; torn; *uncoupling; veering; ways; x-cut;* yawn; *zip;*

**clergy** *(n.)*: *abbots;* bishops; clerics; *devoted men;* elders; friars; gospelers; homilists; *itinerant preachers;* jossers [Aus. slang]; *kerygma; lecturers;* ministers; non-laity; ordained individuals; preachers; *priesthood; quoter;* revivalists; servants of God; teachers of the Bible; *utterers; voicers; warners; xenagogues; yogists; Zadokites;*

**clergyman** *(n.)*: abbé; archpresbyter; bishop; churchman; chaplain; cardinal; diocesan; ecclesiastic; father; grand prior; high ~; presbyter; prior; hierarch; *intermediary; Jesuit ~;* kirkman [Scot.]; *legate;* minister; monsignor; *non-laity;* overseer; priest; pastor; parson; *qumranite;* rector; reverend; sacramentalist; theologian; *ultramontane;* vicar; *worship-leader; Xaverian; yogi [Hind.];* zadokite;

**clever** *(adj.)*: astute; bright; cunning; deft; expertly; furtive; gifted; *hollow;* ingenious; judicious; Jesuitical; knowing; *longsighted;* Maciavellian; nifty; *overwise;* pawky; quick; roguish; shrewd; tricky; underhanded; vulpine; wise; witty; *xtry.;* yepe; *zinger;* [Ant. clownish]

**cleverness** *(n.)*: astuteness; brightness; cunning; deviousness; evasiveness; foxiness; gift; *hoax;* ingenuity; judiciousness; know-how; *longsightedness;* Machiavelism; niftiness; outfoxing; policy; quick-wittedness; roguishness; shrewdness; trickiness; underhandedness; *vulpine;* wittiness; *xtry, ~; yepe;* zinging;

**cliché** *(n.)*: adage; aphorism; byword; common saying; dictum; expression; formulary; generality; *hackneyed saying;* instruction; *judgment; koine;* line; maxim; neology; overused expression; platitude; quote; rule; saying; truism; universal truth; verse; wisdom; *xenophonia; Yogism;* zeteticism;

**click** *(v.)*: *abrupt hit;* bang; beat; clock; clack; drum; *echo;* flick; graze; hit; *impact; jab;* klick; *knock;* lightly hit; martel; *nail; overhit; pound;* quab; rap; strike; snap; tap; tick; *unlock;* veney; whack; *x-sect; yerk;* zonk;

**client** *(n.)*: *acquirer;* buyer; customer; *dependant;* end-user; *fan;* guest; *haggler;* individual; *junk-dealer; keener;* loyal customer; *man(ciple); non-repeat customer; oligopsony; outpatient;* patron; purchaser; prospect; paying ~; *patient;* qualified buyer; repeat customer; *reseller;* shopper; *subject;* trader; user; vendee; walk-in; xfer customer; *yoke; zet [dial.];*

**clientele** *(n.)*: audience; base of customers; customer base; clientage; dependants; end-users; following; group of customers; *have;* investors; *junk-dealers;* kind of customers; loyal customers; market; *names; outpatients;* patrons; qualified buyers; regulars; shoppers; type of customers; *users;* vendees; walk-ins; *xfer customers; yoke; zum [dial.];*

**cliff** *(n.)*: aslope; brim; brink; bluff; crag; drop (off); descent; edge; escarpment; fall; face; *glacial ridge;* hogh; head wall; hogback; *ice ridge;* jardang; *khud* [Ind.]; ledge; mountainside; nip; overhang; outcrop; precipice; pali; *quoif;* ridge; rim; spur; scarp; saddle; *top; upland ridge;* verge; *waterfall; Xiao;* yardang; *zenith;*

**climax** *(n.)*: apex; apogee; best part; culmination; denouement; *extremity;* end; *fastigium* [L.]; *finale;* greatest height; height; highlight; *important part; jut;* key moment; *lofty height;* mountaintop; *nib; overmost point;* peak; pinnacle; *quoif; ridge;* summit; top; *uppermost;* vertex; *way up; xtry; yonder point;* zenith;

153

**climb** *(n.)*: ascent; *bias;* climb; *dune;* elevation; *fly up;* going up; hike; incline; jump; *knoll;* leap; mounting; *natural slope;* obliqueness; pitch; *quantity of increase;* rise; slope; *tilt;* upward slope; verge; way up; *xfwe; yaw; zoom up;*

**climb** *(v.)*: ascend; become higher; clamber; *clear; develop;* elevate; escalade; *fly up;* go up; heighten; increase; jump up; *keep rising; largen;* mount; move upward; *nudge higher;* overclimb; *outclimb; overcome;* progress; proceed; *quantum increase;* rise; raise; *reascend;* scale; surmount; scramble; shinny; transcend; *tower; upward;* verge upward; wax higher; *xfer; yain* [arch.]; *zoom up;* [Ant. come down]

**cling** *(v.)*: adhere; attach; *bound;* clutch; clench; cinch; cleave; cohere; dure; embrace; engrasp; fasten on; grip; grasp; hang on; hold; infold; *join;* keep to; latch onto; make secure; nobble; *oxtercog;* persevere; *quelch;* retain; stick; take hold; usurp; *vice;* wrap hand around; *xfer; yank; zone;*

**clip** *(v. cut)*: *abridge;* bob; cut; crop; dock; exect; *fissure;* graze; hack; incise; *jag; knife;* lop; *mow;* nip; obtruncate; pare; poll; *quarter; remove;* shear; snip; take off; *undercut;* vell; whittle; *x-sect;* yerk; *zip off;*

**clique** *(n.)*: alliance; band; cabal; coterie; circle; club; *drove;* elite group; friends; faction; group; *horde;* in-group; *just the group; kit;* loyal friends; mates; *number; organization;* party; *quantity;* ruck; sympathizers; society; troop; unit; *vertical union;* "we four, no more"; *x-class;* yokefellows; *zip together;*

**cloak** *(n.)*: apparel; burnoose; cape; coat; capote; capuchin; domino; disguise; *enrobing;* fanon; garment; *hyke; inwrap; jacket; kit; loose outer garment;* mantle; night ~; outer garment; poncho; pall; pelerine; *quaintry [arch.];* roquelaur; riding hood; shroud; serape; tippet; upper ~; vesture; wrap; *XL; yelek;* zendalet;

**cloak** *(v.)*: *artfulness;* bemask; cover; conceal; disguise; envelop; *fool;* garb; hide; *incognito; jape;* keep hidden; lay low; mask; *non-recognizable;* obscure; put out of view; *quat* [arch.]; *recluse;* shroud; tuck away; *under cover;* veil; wrap; *xenomorph; yashmak; zero recognition;*

**clock** *(n.)*: alarm ; analog~; bracket ~; chronometer; digital ~ electric ~; *flyback chronograph;* grandfather ~; horologe; *hourglass;* hour-hand; *instrument;* jeweled ~; knock; longcase ~; mechanical watch; nock; *observatory chronometer;* pocket watch; quartz ~; radio ~; stopwatch; *sundial;* timepiece; *Uhr* [G.]; *voice ~;* wall clock; watch; xtal.; year ~; *Zytglogge ~;*

**clod** *(n.)*: amassment; bunch; clump; daud; drift; *enlargement;* fascicle; group; gob; heap; hunk; *ingathering; juba* [L.]; knot; lump; mass; mound; nugget; *overabundance;* pack; passel; quantity; rick; stack; tuft; *unit; volley;* wad; *x-mal [G.];* yelm; *zum [dial.];*

**clog** *(n.)*: arrest; blockage; cumbrance; difficulty; encumbrance; *frustration;* glitch; holdup; impediment; jam; *kink;* lodgment; *mess; nuisance;* obstruction; problem; plug; *quandary;* roadblock; stopping-up; *trouble; upset; vigia; wall;* x; *yowler; zinger;*

**clone** *(v.)*: ape; *borrow;* copy; duplicate; emulate; *follow;* geminate; *holotype;* imitate; *just like; keep;* look alike; make a replica of; *near; overdub;* parrot; *quadruplicate;* replicate; *simulate; transcribe; virtual; watch closely;* xerox copy; *yield; zincograph;*

**close** *(adj.)*: approaching; adjacent; *by; beside;* bordering; close by; drawn up to; dear; *edging; forthcoming; gone up to;* hard by; hot; intimate; impending; *juxtaposed; kept by;* local; more or less; near; nearby; nigh; *oncoming;* proximate; *point-blank;* quite ~; *roughly; soon;* touching on; upon; upcoming; vicinal; well-nigh; *xferred; yede [arch.];* zeroing in on;

**close** *(v.)*: act; bolt ~d; catch; close up; deadbolt; *engage;* fasten; *guard;* have locked; interlock; *jail;* keep ~d; latch; lock; make fast; *narrow;* occlude; push closed; *quickly ~;* reclose; shut; secure; seal; slam; tighten; *unopened; vault; well-secured; x-tight; yank;* zip ~d;

**closeknit** *(adj.)*: affectionate; bonded; close; dear; endeared; familiar; *genial;* habituated; interdependent; joined; *kind;* loving; loyal; mutually supportive; near-and-dear; *over-protective; protective; quilting bee; relationship;* supportive; tightknit; unreserved; very close; warm; *xenial;* yoked; zealous;

**closet** *(n.)*: ambry; *area;* bedroom ~; cabinet; den ~; *étagère;* footlocker; *gallery;* hall ~; *incavation;* janitor ~; keep; linen ~; locker; *mantelshelf;* nacelle; *open;* press; pantry; quadrilocular; *room;* storage compartment; supply ~; *tack;* utility ~; *vitrine;* walk-in; wardrobe; *xtr. storage; youth dresser;* zeta;

**cloth** *(n.)*: *androsia;* broad~; *bolt;* cotton; cloot; *dush ~; entrelac;* fabric; *geotextile;* hair~; *Irish linen; jaconet;* knit; linen; loose-weave; material; *madras;* nylon; *oil~;* pattern- ~; Queen's ~; rag; *roll; silk;* textile; threads; tight-weave; *ulos;* viscose; weave; warp and woof; *xanthation;* yardage; *zibeline;*

   **Types of fabric**: acetate; brocade; canvas; cotton; denim; eyelet; flannel; gabardine; haircloth; iridescent; jaconet; kersey; linen; muslin; nylon; organdy; polyester; poplin; quentin; rayon; satin; silk; terry; twill; union cloth; voile; wincey; zibeline;

**clothe** *(v.)*: attire; accouter; bedeck; clad; dress; enrobe; *fancify;* garb; habit; invest; jacket; kit; *loungewear; make prettier; nice;* outfit; put on; prink; *quaintise [arch.];* reapparel; slip into; trim; uniform; vest; wear; *xuld [arch.]; yclad* [arch.]; zip on; [*Ant.* cast off]

**clothed** *(p.p.)*: appareled; bedecked; clad; dressed; decent; enrobed; fully ~; garbed; habited; invested; jacketed; kit; *loungewear;* modest; *nice;* outfitted; prinked; *quaintised [arch.];* reappareled; shrouded; trimmed; *uniformed;* vested; wearing clothes; *xuld [arch.]; yclad* [arch.]; zipped on; [*Ant.* clothesless]

**clothing** *(n.)*: apparel; attire; bedizenment; clothes; covering; dress; daywear; duds; ensemble; finery; fashion; garb; garments; getup; habiliments; investiture; *jumper;* knitwear; livery; mufti; *menswear; national dress;* outfit; outerwear; prêt-à-porter; playwear; *quaintry* [arch.]; raiment; suit; togs; toggery; threads [slang]; *uniform; undergarments;* vesture; vestment; wardrobe; *womenswear; XL; yelek [Turk.]; zari;*

   **Kinds of clothing**: apron; blouse; cap; dress; ephod; frock; gown; hat; ivy league sweater; jumper; kilt; long johns; muffs; nightgown; overalls; pants; robe; shirt; skirt; socks; t-shirt; uniform; vest; waistcoat; yelek; zari;

**cloud** *(n.)*: atomization; alto-cumulus; aura; breath; brume; billow; cloudlet; cirrus; cumulus; contrail; dust ~; exhalation; exhaust; fog; fume; gas; gauze; gloom; haze; high fog; ice ~; *jumbo ~; KH instability;* lightning ~; mist; miasma; nimbus; obscurity; overcast; puff; pall; pollution; pother; *quasi-vaporous;* rain ~; rack; scud; steam; smoke; spray; swirl; stratus; storm ~; smog; thunder~ (-head); uncinus; vapor; wisp; woolpack; *xenon ~; yellowy ~; zodiacal dust ~;*

**cloud** *(v.)*: adumbrate; becloud; blur; confuse; darken; dim; eclipse; encloud; fog; *get in the way;* hide; infuscate; *jape;* keep unclear; *lightless;* mask; muddle; nubilate; obnubilate; overshadow; obscure; put out of view; *quat* [arch.]; repress; shroud; suppress; tuck away; umbrate; veil; *wimple; xerophthalmic;* yeme; *zeroize;*

**cloudless** *(adj.)*: azure; blue; clear; distinct; *empty;* fine; *great; high visibility; identifiable; just plain;* keen; lucid; *mostly clear;* non-clouded; open (skies); plain; quite clear; *relucent;* sky blue; *totally ~;* unclouded; *visible;* without clouds; *xparent;* yet unclouded; *zero cloudiness;* [*Ant.* cloudy]

**cloudy** *(adj.)*: addled; beclouded; clouded; dusty; dull; dark; dank; dim; enclouded; foggy; fumy; gloomy; gray; gaseous; hazy; inclouded; *jumbo cloud; KH instability;* lowery; lour; misty; murky; murksome; nebulous; nebulose; overcast; obscure; overclouded; puffy; qually; *rainy;* reeky [dial.]; sunless; steamy; smoky; turbid; thick; umbered; vaporous; wispy; wet; *xenon cloud; yellowy cloud;* zero-zero; [*Ant.* clear; cloudless]

**clout** *(n.)*: authority; *badge;* command; dominion; effectuality; faculty; *government;* headship; influence; jurisdiction; *kingship;* leverage; mastery; name; *oversight;* power; *quo warranto* [L.]; rule; sway; *throne;* umpirage; virtue; weight; *xtry.* influence; yard; *zonal control;*

**cloven** *(adj.)*: apart; breach; cleft; divided; *excinded;* forked; *gapped;* halved; indented; *jag;* knappled; *lacerated; mitered;* notched; opened; parted; *quadrifid;* rent; rifted; split; two-sectioned; uncoupled; velled; *with a cleft; x-sect;* yandied; *zoned;*

**clown** *(n.)*: antic; buffoon; comic; dummy; entertainer; fool; goof(ball); harlequin; humorist; half-wit; idiot; jester; joker; knuff; knucklehead; lout; merry-andrew; moron; nitwit; oaf; performer; punch; quack; rattlebrain; simpleton; slapstick comedian; turkey; *unwise; vacant;* wacko; *xtry.;* yo-yo; zany;

**club** *(n. bat)*: alpenstock; bat; bludgeon; billy ~; bastinado; cudgel; dagger-staff; espantoon; fakir's crutch; godendag; hurl-bat; *instrument;* jitte; knobstick; lathi; mace; nightstick; nulla-nulla; *officer's staff;* partisan; quarterstaff; rod; stick; shillelagh; truncheon; *ununke* [Afr.]; *verge;* war club; waddy; *xylon;* yam stick; zagaye;

**club** *(n. society)*: association; brotherhood; confraternity; coalition; *department;* establishment; federation; fraternity; guild; group; *horizontal union;* institution; joint-coalition; *kongsi* [Chin.]; league; lodge; *mutual;* nexus; organization; partnership; quinquevirate; *registered guild;* society; syndicate; troop; union; *vertical union; workers' union; x-class;* yeald; youyh ~; zonta;

**clue** *(n.)*: allusion; bit of information; *corpus delicti* [L.]; dead giveaway; evidence; *fact;* giveaway; hint; indication; inkling; *junt;* key; lead; link; *mention; nuance; overtone;* pointer; proof; queen's evidence; *remnant;* sign; suspicion; trace; umbrage; vestige; witness; wind; *xtry. ~; yet undiscovered; zum* [dial.];

**clumsy** *(adj.)*: awkward; bumbling; cumbersome; dowdy; *étourderie* [F.]; fumbly; gangly; gawky; graceless; gimpy; heavy-handed (-footed); inelegant; jumbly; klutzy; lumbering; maladroit; non-graceful; oafish; plumbeous; *quirky; rube;* socially inept; troublesome; ungainly; ungraceful; unwieldy; uncoordinated; *vexatious;* wooden; *xtry. ~;* yokelish; zhlubby; [*Ant.* clever]

**clutter** *(n.)*: accumulation; bunch; confusion; disorder; entanglement; farrago; guddle; heap; hodgepodge; intertanglement; jumble; kerfuffle; litter; mess; mass; muddle; *number; obscurity;* pile; *quantity; ravel;* stuff; tangle; things; untidiness; *vexation; wreck;* xtry. mess; yelm; *zoo;* [*Ant.* cleanliness]

**clutter** *(v.)*: *abstruse; break up;* cover; confuse; disarrange; disorganize; dishevel; disorder; encumber; fill; get messy; *heap;* intertangle; jumble; *knot;* litter; mess up; *non-tidied; overcomplicate;* put out of order; *quirk; rumple;* strew; trash; upset; *vandalize;* wreck; *x-out; yet disorganized; zorch;* [*Ant.* clean]

**coach** *(n. buggy)*: *apparatus;* buggy; carriage; dray; equipage; fiacre; gig; hackney; Italian coach; jaunting car; karrozzin; landau; mail-coach; noddy; *omnibus;* pleasure-carriage; *quadricycle;* rig; surrey; stage~; tandem; *undercarriage;* vehicle; wagon; *x-port;* yanker [Br.]; *Zis* [Rus.];

**coach** *(n. sports instructor)*: abecedarian; ball ~; conditioner; driller; edifier; faculty [pl.]; guide; head ~; instructor; *jobation;* kickball ~; *leader;* master; *nurture;* overseer; pedagogue; *qualifier;* riding instructor; schooler; trainer; *under-teacher; varsity ~; worker;* xystarch; *yeller;* zealot;

**coachman** *(n.)*: auriga; buggy driver; cabman; drayman; driver; employee; *fast rider;* gharry-wallah [Ind.]; hackneyman; hacky; *individual;* jarvey; kurveyor; liveryman; mail-coach driver; nagsman; operator; postilion; quadrille; rig-driver; stagecoach driver; tandem operator; *uhlan; voiturier* [F.]; wagoner; whip; *x-port;* yamstchik; *zain-driver;*

**coagulate** *(v.)*: *alter;* become hard; congulate; densen; *enharden;* firm up; gelatinate; harden; inspissate; jellify; knot; lump; make hard; *non-fluid; overharden;* pectize; quarle; *reform;* solidify; thicken; *unite; vary;* work to thicken; *xerogel;* yearn; zet [dial.];

**coal** *(n.)*: anthracite; bovey- ~; char~; *culm;* day~; empyrical; fuel; fusain; glance- ~; gleed; hard ~; *ignitable;* jet; judd; kolm; kiln- ~; lignite; metage; nut ~; oven ~; pit- ~; quarry- ~; *rock;* soft ~ tunnel-kiln; urry; vitrain; wood- ~; xylanthrax; yard-coal; *zinkenite;*

**coalition** *(n.)*: alliance; bond; bloc; confederation; *defense;* establishment; federation; guild; group; *horizontal union; incorporation;* joint ~; *kongsi* [Chin.]; league; mergence; mutual bond; nexus; organization; partnership; quinquevirate; *rapport;* society; *trade union; troop;* union; *vertical union;* workers' union; *x-treaty;* yoke; zollverein;

**coarse** *(adj.)*: abominable; boorish; crude; degraded; defiling; defiled; disgusting; earthy; foul-mouthed; gauche; gross; horrid; ill-mannered; jadish; kitsch; loutish; mean; nasty; offensive; obscene; piggish; *quad;* rude; rough; shocking; tasteless; uncouth; vulgar; wretched; *x-rated;* yucky; zhlubby;

**coast** *(n.)*: *abuttal;* border; brink; coastline; *dockside;* edge; fringe; *gate;* hinterland; inception; *jurisdiction; kept limit;* lido; lakeshore; limit; margin; nearshore; nip; outskirts; oceanside; periphery; *quost* [arch.]; rim; shore(line); seaside; seashore; seacoast; seaboard; threshold; ulterior; verge; waterline; *x-border; yonder; zone;*

**coastal** *(adj.)*: *aquatic;* beachfront; coastline; dockside; *estuary;* frontal; *gulf front;* harbor side; *inlet; jetty side; key side;* lakeside (-front); mere side; near-shore; oceanfront (-side); *pier side;* quayside; riparial; seafront; seaside; sublittoral; *tidal; unhindered view; voe;* waterfront; *xyrisic; yeo; Zee [G.];* [Ant. central]

**coat** *(n.)*: anorak; *buff ~;* cloak; duster; Eskimo ~; fur ~; gilet; huke; inverness; jacket; jerkin; kirtle; long~; mink ~; mantle; *Norfolk jacket;* over~; parka; quentin ~; redingote; rain~; spencer; trench ~; top~; ulster; vented jacket; windbreaker; *xillinous;* yakskin ~; zamarra;

**coax** *(v.)*: allure; bear on; cajole; draw; entice; encourage; *flatter;* goad; *hoodwink;* inveigle; *jape; knavery;* lead; *make; nudge; outwit;* persuade; *quiblin [arch.]; rope;* sweet-talk; tempt; urge; *vie;* wheedle; *xuld [arch.];* yerk; zealously convince;

**cobbler** *(n.)*: artisan; bootmaker; cordwainer; designer; *expert ~;* farrier; guildsman; heeler; *industrial workwe; journeyman;* kibbler; *laborer; leprechaun;* mender; mustelid; *needle-man; outfitter;* professional ~; qualified ~; repairman; shoemaker; *tanner; underling; versed;* worker; *x-sandal;* yeoman; *zapatero* [Sp.];

**cocky** *(adj.)*: arrogant; brash; biggity; conceited; disdainful; egotistical; flatulent; gally; haughty; impudent; *jackanapes;* know-it-all; lifted up; most brazen; nervy; overconfident; puffed up; quick-to-boast; roisterous; sassy; think highly of oneself; unabashed; vaunting; wrapped up in oneself; *x-proud;* yelping; zero humility; [Ant. childlike]

**cocoon** *(n.)*: aurelia; *bundle;* chrysalis; case; cocalon; dupion; encasement; *fold; gird;* hull; inclosure; *jacket; kid;* larva-case; moth-case; nympha; nest; outer case; pupa; pod; quod; *receptacle;* sack; shell; theca; *urtucating hair ~; vessel;* wrap; *x-ing;* yoke sack; *zonule;*

**coddle** *(v.)*: *attend to;* baby; cosset; do everything for; dote over; excessively ~; fuss over; gratify; humor; indulge; *jump to it; keep;* lavish; molly~; mother; *nurse;* overprotect; overindulge; pamper; pander; *quadle* [arch.]; *rave;* spoil; take care of; tend; *undertake; vigorously ~; worry too much; x-care;* yield to; *zip right to it;*

**code** *(n.)*: argot; *binary ~;* cipher; cypher; *designation;* encryption; *form of expression;* glossa; *hidden meaning;* idioglossia; jargon; *key;* language; markings; morse ~; *message;* notation; *object ~;* pictogram; *questionable; reckoning;* secret ~; symbols; top-secret ~; *text;* unintelligible; *vocabulary;* wordage; *x-code; yet undeciphered ~; zeug;*

**coerce** *(v.)*: admonish; bully; compel; constrain; drive; exhort; force; *get;* hurry; intimidate; *jump on; knock;* lean on; make; *must; nudge;* oblige; press; *quicken;* require; strong-arm; sandbag; twist one's arm; urge; *vie;* weigh upon; *xuld [arch.];* yank; zealously urge;

**coercion** *(n.)*: *admonishment;* bullying; compelling; constraining; driving; duress; exhorting; force; *getting;* hurrying; intimidation; *jumping on; knocking;* leaning on; making; *nudging;* obliging; pressure; *quickening;* requiring; strong-arming; twisting one's arm; urging; *vying;* weighing upon; *xuld [arch.]; yanking; zealously urging;*

**coexist** *(v.)*: accept; bear with one another; cohabit; coincide; *dure;* exist together; forbear; get along with; harmonize; *indulge; jive;* keep harmony with; live with; maintain coexistence; *non-discord; one;* put up with; *quality; reconcile;* suffer with; tolerate; understand; *very tolerant;* wink at; *xenobiosis;* yield to; *zero discord;* [Ant. clash]

**coffer** *(n.)*: *assets;* box; chest; deposit box; *ebony chest;* firebox; *gold;* holder; *iron chest; jewel chest;* keep-chest; lockbox; money bin; *notes; opulence; prosperity; quinderkyn;* receptacle; strongbox; trunk; treasure chest; *ungula;* vault; wooden chest; *xenocurrency; yadzutsu [Jap.]; zechin;*

**coffin** *(n.)*: *aluminum ~;* bier; bonebox; casket; cist; *depository; encapsulation;* feretory; grave-box; hearse; *inclosure; joint-marker;* kist; *lockbox;* mahogany casket; *necropolis;* ossuary; pine box; *quietus;* reliquary; sarcophagus; trunk; *unopened ~;* vault; wooden box; *xat;* yew box; *ziarat* [Mos.]; [*Ant.* cradle]
**cog** *(n.)*: *article; bolts;* component; cam; cogwheel; drive wheel; *equipment;* flywheel; feature; gear; hopper; inner workings; *joint; keyway; lantern pinion;* mechanism; mill~; notched wheel; *nuts; object;* part; pinion; *quill-pin;* ratch; *spring;* sprocket; toothed wheel; *unit; valve;* wheel; *x-part; yod; zeug;*
**cohabit** *(v.)*: abide together; be together; co-exist; cohabitate; dwell with; exist together; *forbear;* get along with; harmonize; inhabit together; jointly inhabit; keep home together; live together; move in with; *non-separate;* occupy the same quarters; put up with; *quarters;* roommate; share a home; shack up; take up with; *understand; use; venery; winter; xenobiosis; yfere* [arch.]; *zero discord;*
**cohere** *(v.)*: adhere; agglutinate; bond; cement; cleave; dure; *embed;* fasten; glue; grip; hold (together); *imbed;* join; keep; latch; meld; *nail; oneness;* paste; *quick-dry;* remain; stick; stay; tack; unite; *viscous;* weld; *xenograft;* yoke; *zip;* [*Ant.* come apart]
**coherence** *(n.)*: adherence; bond; cohesion; cementing; cleaving; *dovetailing; embedment;* fastening; gluing; holding (together); *inviscation;* joining; keeping; latching on; mounting; *nailing; oneness;* pasting; *quick-dry;* remaining; sticking; tacking; uniting; *viscosity;* weld; *xenograft;* yoking; zipping; [*Ant.* coming apart]
**cohort** *(n.)*: accomplice; abettor; buddy; confederate; collaborator; co-conspirator; crony; *defender; engineer;* follower; *good-fellow;* helper; *instigator;* joint-ally; *kith; loyal friend;* mate; *neighbor;* offsider; partner (in crime); partaker; *quondam friend;* right-hand man; succorer; supporter; teammate; *upholder;* varlet; workmate; *xiaoren;* yokefellow; *zealot;*
**coil** *(n.)*: *alternation;* braid; curl; convolution; *downward spiral;* entwisting; frounce; gyre; helix; *intwisting; jag;* kink; *looping; meandering; nonlinear; overwound;* pin curl; *peristaltic;* querl; ringlet; spiral; spring; twist; turbinate; tendril; upwinding; volute; winding; *x-ing; yaw;* zigzag;
**coil** *(v.)*: *alternate;* becurl; curl; convolve; *downward spiral;* entwist; furl; glomerate; hankle; intort; involute; *jag;* keckle; loop; meander; *nonlinear; overwind; prewind;* quoil [dial.]; ravel; roll; spiral; twist; upwind; volt; wind; *x-ing; yaw;* zigzag;
**coin** *(n.)*: * aluminum ~; brass ~; coinage [pl.]; currency; change [pl.]; disc; dime; *ex-change;* farthing; fido; gold dollar; guilder; gold ~; half dollar; *Indian head nickel;* jacobus; kopeck [Rus.]; lira [It.]; loose change [pl]; money; *mite; numismatic;* nickel; *obol;* penny; pence [pl.]; piece; quarter; red cent; *ruble; rupee; rial;* shekel; sixpence; shilling; silver ~; *specie;* threepence; token; *unit;* vering; *wooden nickel;* xu; yokindale; zac; zechin;
  **Coins**: anna; batzen; cent; dime; drachma; doubloon; eagle; euro; florin; guilder; half-dollar; krugerrand; lek; mark; nickel; pence; penny; quarter; repee; shekel; shilling; talent; xerafeen; yen; zechin;
**coincide** *(v.)*: align; be together; concur; *direct; exact; fine-tune;* go together; happen together; *indicate accordance;* jive [slang]; keep pace; line up; match; *non-disparity;* occur together; overlap; *pace; qualify; readjust;* synchronize; simultaneously occur; *together; timing;* unite; *verse;* work together; *x-harmonize; yark; zero difference;*
**coincidence** *(n.)*: accident; *bad luck;* chance; destiny; Dame Fortune; *ensue;* fortune; fate; fluke; freak; fortuity; *good luck;* happenstance; *intervene;* just by chance; kismet; karma [eastern rel.]; luck; *mozzle;* Norns; *occurrence;* providence; quirk; quinky-dink [joc.]; *roll of the dice;* simultaneous occurrence; twist of fate; *unplanned; vicissitude;* wheel of fortune; *xtry. ~; yield; zero planning;* [*see* providence]
**coitus** *(n.)*: aphrodisia; breeding; copulation; *desire; experience; familiarity;* going into; gendering; *heterogamy;* intercourse; intimate relations; joining; knowledge; lovemaking; lying together; mating; marriage bed; nuptial privileges; *outbreeding;* physical relations; *quiff* [arch.]; relations; reproduction; sex; *two becoming one;* union; venery; whoopee [vulg.]; *xbreed;* yum-yum [nav. slang]; zatch [vulg. slang]; [*see* fornication]

**cold** *(adj.)*: algid; arctic; bitter; brisk; biting; cool; chilly; crisp; deadening ~; *extreme;* frigid; freezing; frosty; frozen; gelid; heatless; icy; ice-cold; *Jack Frost;* keen; low-temperature; *miserable;* nippy; numbing; over~; polar; *quivering;* raw; refrigerated; snappy; stone ~; subzero; severe; thawless; unheated; *very ~;* wintry; *xeric-less;* ycie [arch.]; zero degrees; [*see* aloof, shiver]
**cold** *(n.)*: arctic; bitter ~; briskness; coolness; chill; deadness; *distemperature; extreme temperatures;* frigidity; frigidness; frost; frozenness; gelidity; *heatless;* iciness; *Jack Frost;* keenness; low temperatures; *much-chilled;* nip; nippiness; *numbness;* over~; polar regions; *quivering;* refrigeration; subzero temperatures; *unheated;* very low temperature; wintriness; xtr. ~; *ycie [arch.];* zero degrees; [*see* snowstorm]
**collaborate** *(v.)*: abet; both work together; complicit; cooperate; do together; enter into alliance; federate; get together; help; involve oneself; *in cahoots;* join forces; *knit;* liaise; league with; mutually support; make league; *not hinder;* operate with; partner; *quick-to-help;* render assistance; succor; support; team up; unite; *vie together;* work together; *xenophile;* yoke up; *zealously support;* [*Ant.* contend]
**collaboration** *(n.)*: abetting; bearing together; cooperation; doing together; entering into alliance; federation; getting together; help; involvement; *in cahoots;* joining forces; *knitting;* league; mutual effort; *non-hindrance;* operating together; partnership; participation; *quick-to-help;* rendering assistance; succor; support; teamwork; uniting; *vying together;* working together; *xenophilia;* yoking up; *zealous support;* [*Ant.* contention]
**collapse** *(n.)*: *annihilation;* breakdown; bankruptcy; crumbling; crash; disintegration; end; fall; failure; giving way; *havoc;* implosion; *jumping down;* keeling over; *loss; melting away;* nervous breakdown; *nose-dive; overthrow;* plummet; *quick demise;* ruin; sinking; toppling; *undoing; volting;* wreck; *x-cend;* yielding; *zapping;* [*Ant.* continuance]
**collapse** *(v.)*: *annihilated;* break down; cave in; crumble; disintegrate; deflate; end; fall (down; apart); fail; give way; *havoc;* infold; implode; *jump down;* keel over; *loss; melt away;* nose-dive; overthrow; plummet; *quick-fall;* ruin; subside; topple; *undo; volt;* wreck; *x-cend;* yield; *zap;* [*Ant.* continue]
**collapsible** *(adj.)*: able to be collapsed; *break down;* compactable; contractible; deflatable; easy-to-collapse; extendible; foldaway; foldup; folding; *goes away;* handy; infolding; *jump-down;* keen; *little;* movable; nesting; *one-step;* portable; quick-folding; retractable; retractile; sheathable; telescoping; *travel; unfixed;* variable-length; wrap-up; *xfer;* yanker; *zip-close;*
**collar** *(n.)*: ∗ ascot ~; button-down ~; crewneck; double-round ~; eton ~; *fichu* ~; gorget; hame; imperial ~; jabot; *keyhole;* lapel; mandarin collar; mock ~; neckline; neckband; *object;* partlet; pickardil; quellio; ruff; rabato; rollneck; scoopneck; turtleneck; upright ~; v-neck; wing ~; *xtr.-low neckline;* Y- ~; *zhido;*
**colleague** *(n.)*: acquaintance; business associate; confrère; counterpart; *dear friend;* equal; fellow professional; good-fellow; *good friend; human; individual; juror; kith;* loyal friend; mate [Aus.]; *neighbor; one;* peer; *qualified peer;* right-hand man; sidekick; teammate; *unfailing friend; varsity teammate;* workmate; *x-class;* yealing; yokefellow; *zealous friend;*
**collect** *(v.)*: accrue; accumulate; amass; build up; compile; draw up; *expand;* form; grow; gather; garner; hoard; heap up; increase; jump; keep growing; *largen;* mount up; *nob; overstock;* pile up; *quadruplicate;* rack up; rise; store; stockpile; take up; upbuild; *varia;* wax greater; *XL;* yard; *zip together;*
**collection** *(n.)*: accumulation; assemblage; build-up; compilation; cluster; drove; *extensive ~; full array;* group; gathering; heap; hoard; ingathering; *juba* [L.]; kit; load; mass; number; overabundance; pile; panoply; quantity; ruck; stockpile; stack; store; treasure; *unit;* varia; *wagonload; x-section; yelm;* zet [dial.];
**collective** *(adj.)*: aggregate; amassed; accumulative; *broad; big;* combined; cumulative; comprehensive; corporate; *detailed;* entire; full; group; *high; intact;* joint; *kept intact;* lump; mutual; mass; non-abridged; overall; panoramic; *quantified; ready;* shared; summative; total; united; *veritable;* whole; *xtry.;* yare; zet [dial.];

**collector** *(n.)*: accumulator; amasser; builder up; *coin ~;* compiler; *developer;* enthusiast; *expander; former;* gleaner; gatherer; hobbyist; hoarder; *increase; jump; keep growing; largen;* mounter; *nob; overstock;* piler; packrat; *quantifier; rack up; stamp ~;* stockpiler; *take up;* upbuilder; *volume; warehouse; xfer;* yarder; *zealous ~;*
**college** *(n.)*: academy; *alma matter;* business school; boys ~; Bible ~; business school; campus; day school; educational facility; finishing school; four-year ~; graduate school; girls' ~; halls; institution; institute; ivory tower; junior ~; *knowledge; lower school;* multiversity; night school; normal school; *Oxford;* place of higher learning; *quarter; religious school;* school; *seminary;* trade school; technical ~; university; varsity [Br.]; vocational school; village ~; *women's ~; xenagogue;* yard; *yeshiva* [Heb.]; *zone;*
**collide** *(v.)*: assault; bash; bang into; broadside; crash; clobber; dash against; *efface; flatten;* grind; hit; impact; jolt; jam; knock; lam; mash; nail; *occursion;* plow into; quash; ram; run into; strike; smack; smash; slam; thump; thwack; *undo; veney;* whack; *x;* yedder; zonk; [*Ant.* clear]
**colloquial** *(adj.)*: *average; basic;* common; casual; *daily;* everyday; familiar; *general;* habitual; idiomatic; informal; *jargon; known; long-established; modern;* natural; ordinary; popular; *quotidian;* regular; slang; *typical;* usual; vernacular; vulgar; widespread; *xtr. common; yet nonstandard; zum [dial.];*
**cologne** *(n.)*: aftershave; balsam; *calamus; diapasm;* essence; *eau de ~* [F.]; fragrance; *good-smelling; heavenly scent;* incense; jasmine; keora oil; *lotion;* musk; nidor; odor; perfume; *quality perfume;* redolence; scent; toiletry; *unguent;* volatile oil; *whiff;* xanthoxylene; ylang-ylang; zedoary;
**colonial** *(adj.)*: *area; buffer state;* colony-related; *dominion;* expansionist; *force; governing; highness;* imperialist; jurisdictional; *king's; land; mandated; nome;* outpost-related; provincial; *queendom; regional;* settlement-related; territorial; *under;* viceroyal; *waywodeship [Turk.];* xenizing; *yard; zonal;*
**colonialism** *(n.)*: annexation; building empires; colonization; domain-expanding; expansionism; empire-building; founding colonies; *gaining territories;* homesteading; imperialism; *jurisdictional expansion;* kingdom-building; land-acquisition; *manifest destiny;* neo~; *occupation;* province-acquisition; *queendom;* realm-expansion; *sovereignty;* territory-collecting; *upbuilding;* viceroyship; *world power;* xenization; *yede; zone;*
**colonize** *(v.)*: annex; abide; begin a colony; claim; displace; establish colony; expand; ensconce; empeople; found a colony; *get;* homestead; immigrate; *jurisdiction; key territory;* lay claim to; migrate to; *nestle;* occupy; *own;* plant colony; *quarter;* relocate; settle; take over; *under the crown; voyage; warrant;* xenize; *yede; zone;*
**colony** *(n.)*: area; burgage; country; crown ~; dependency; dominion; eparchy; *feudal territory;* governance; *habitation;* imperial ~ (-domain); *jurisdiction; kingship;* land; legal possession; mandate; *nome;* outpost; overseas territory; protectorate; possession; plant; *queendom;* region; settlement; satellite; territory; *under;* viceroyalty; *waywodeship [Turk.];* xenization; *yard; zone;*
**color** *(n.)*: accent; blush; cool ~; coloration; coloring; complexion; chroma; dye; distemper; engrain; fucus; flush; *glow;* hue; halftone; hint; ingrain; *japan;* key; lake; medium; *nigrosine; orange;* pigment(ation); paint; *quercitron; red;* shade; stain; tint; tinge; tone; tincture; tempera; tinct; undertone (-tint); vehicle; wash; warm ~; *xanthone;* yarn-dye; *zaffa;*
  **Colors**: amber; aqua; beige; black; blue; brown; cyan; dark blue; emerald; flesh; gray; green; hot pink; indigo; jet black; kettle black; light blue; maroon; navy; orange; pink; peach; purple; Quaker gray; red; rose; scarlet; turquoise; ultramarine; violet; white; xanthic; yellow; zaffer;
**color** *(v.)*: adorn; bedye; blush; colorize; dye; engrain; enliven; flush; glaze; *hue;* imbue; ingrain; infuse; *japan; key to;* lacquer; make; *nigrosine;* overdye; paint; pigment; *quercitron;* ruddle; shade; stain; tint; tinge; tincture; tone; *umber;* vat-dye; woad; wash; *xanthene;* yarn-dye; *zaffer;*

**colorful** *(adj.)*: *attention-getting;* bright; chromatic; daedal; diverse-colored; *entertissued;* full-color; gay; heterochromatic; irised; inshaded; iridescent; jazzy; keenly colored; lively; multicolored; *nitid; orthochromatic;* parti-colored; prismatic; polychromatic; *quatri-couleur* [F.]; rich; rainbow; splashy; tri-colored; *utterly vivid;* variegated; vivid; vibrant; varicolored; *wondrous; x-ray spectrum; xtry.; yellow-red-green;* zippy; [*see* descriptive; *Ant.* colorless]

**colorless** *(adj.)*: achromatic; albino; bleached; clear; diaphanous; decolorated; etiolated; filmy; glassy; hydrophanous; invisible; *just plain;* keenly visible; limpid; mealy; muted; non-colored; *obvious;* pellucid; pale; *quit [arch.];* relucent; see-through; transparent; uncolored; visible; water-colored; white; *xparent;* yet uncolored; zero-color; [*see* dull; pale; *Ant.* colorful]

**colossal** *(adj.)*: astronomical; big; considerable; disproportionate; enormous; fantastic; gigantic; Goliath; gargantuan; huge; humongous; immense; jumbo-sized; king-size; large; massive; mammoth; monstrous; *noteworthy;* oversize; prodigious; queen-size; rotund; sizable; tremendous; *unbelievable;* voluminous; whopping; XXL; *Ymir; zaftig;* [*Ant.* compact]

**colt** *(adj.)*: animal; beast; *charger;* dobbin; equine; foal; gelding; horse; *Indian pony;* jennet; *kelpy; livery; mustang;* neddy; *organism;* pony; quad; *racehorse; steed;* thoroughbred; *ungulate; unicorn; varmint;* workhorse; *x-breed;* yeanling; yearling; *zebra;*

**column** *(n.)*: ante; archpillar; buttress; *colonade; doorpost; epistyle;* fulcrum; *gatepost;* herm; intercolumniation; jackstay; *kabber; load-bearing;* main support; newel-post; *octostyle;* pillar; queen post; rest; support; shaft; tige; upright; vertical; *weight-bearing post; xystus; yard; zaccho;* [*see* article]

**columnist** *(n.)*: author; *blazoner;* contributor; diaskeuast; essayist; featured ~; *ghostwriter;* hedge-writer; interviewer; journalist; *key journalist;* linkman; magazine ~; newspaper ~; observator; pressman; quill-driver; remarker; syndicated ~; transcriber; *underwriter;* volumist; writer; *XYZ;* yellow journalist; *zine ~;*

**coma** *(n.)*: abstraction; blackout; comatose state; daze; entrancement; fuddling; *gibbered; haze;* incoherence; infratentoral ~; jag; knocked out; locked-in syndrome; *mesmerism;* nar~; out; period of unconsciousness; *quaffing;* reverie; stupor; sleep; supertentoral ~; trance; *tentorium cerebelli* [L.]; unconsciousness; vegetative state; *whacked (out); xanthoxylin; yarked;* zonking;

**comb** *(n.)*: *arrange;* brush; card; *device; enhance;* fine-toothed ~; grooming device; hairbrush; hatchel; hot ~; *instrument; jumbo- ~;* kemb; *line up; metal ~;* nit ~; *over-neaten;* pick; pecten; quin; rake; styling brush; *tool;* unbreakable ~; *vamp;* wool-comb; xtr. fine-toothed ~; yarn-comb; *zip;*

**comb** *(v.)*: align; brush; *correct;* disentangle; *enhance;* fix; groom; hatchel; *instrument; jerque;* kemb; *line up;* make aligned; neaten; *over-neaten;* pick; pheese; preen [zoo.]; quannet; rake; run through; style; straighten; take a comb to; untangle; *vamp;* wool- ~; *xtr. fine-toothed ~; yarn-comb; zip;*

**combat** *(n.)*: altercation; battle; clash; dispute; embroilment; fight; *gunnery;* hostilities; hand-to-hand ~; *imbroglio; jihad* [Mos.]; *kampf* [G.]; *luctation* [arch.]; mêlée; occursion; physical ~; quarrel; run-in; struggle; skirmish; striving; scuffle; scrap; tussle; unrest; vying; war(fare); *x-fire; yed; zone;* [*Ant.* calm]

**combination** *(n.)*: admixture; amalgamation; aggregation; blend; compound; concoction; consolidation; decoction; elixir; ester; formula; fusion; farrago; farraginous; *grouping;* hodgepodge; intermixture; incorporation; joining; knotting; lumping together; mixture; merging; minglement; marriage; medley; mélange; mishmash; *non-homogenous ~;* olio; potion; pasticcio; *queer;* recipe; salad; *temperament;* ule; union; unification; *variety; wedding; xanthate;* yanggoma; *zipped together;*

**combine** *(v.)*: aggregate; amalgamate; adjoin; add; blend; conjoin; coalesce; commingle; compound; conflate; draw together; entwine; fuse; group together; hitch; integrate; intermix; join; knit; link; lump together; mix; merge; mingle; marry; meld; *network; overmix;* put together; *quasi-fuse;* reunite; stick together; syndicate; tie; toss; unite; *voluble;* wed; xenograft; yoke; zip together;

**combust** *(v.)*: alight; ablaze; burn; catch fire; char; cremate; *consume;* deflagrate; enflame; enkindle; flame; flare; glow; gut; *heat;* ignite; incinerate; inflame; *jeopardize;* kindle; light (up); *miskindle;* neal; overburn; pyrolyze; *quick-match;* raze; roast; *rage;* scorch; smolder; sear; singe; scald; torch; ustion; vesicate; *waste; wreck; xylophyrography; yearn; zap;* [*see* flame]

**combustion** *(n.)*: *aflame;* burning; conflagration; deflagration; enflaming; fire; *glow; hot;* ignition; *jungle-fire;* kindling; light; *miskindle; night-fire;* overburning; pyrolysis; *quick-match; raging ~;* spark; *torch;* ustulation; *vulcanization; wildfire; xylophyrography; yearning; zap;*
**come** *(v.)*: attain; approach; arrive; appear; advance; befall; betide; call; draw (near); enter; eventuate; emerge; fall; follow; *find;* get to; happen; *hike;* irrupt; *incur;* journey; *kite; lumber;* move; navigate; near; occur; proceed; pass; progress; *quicken;* reach; *sail;* show up; travel; traverse; transpire; upspring; visit; voyage; *walk;* xfer; yede; zip;
**comedian** *(n.)*: *anecdotic;* buffoon; cutup; comic; droll; entertainer; farceur; funny-man; gagster; humorist; ham; *insulter;* joker; jokester; kidder; larrikin; merry-andrew; *nut; one-liner;* punster; quipster; riddler; sporter; stooge; tummler; *unserious; vexer;* wit; wag; *xtry.; yo-yo,* zany;
**comedy** *(n.)*: amusement; buffoonery; burleque; comicalness; comicality; drollery; *entertainment;* funniness; gag; humor; hilarity; *indulgence; insanity;* jocoseness; kookiness; levity; laughs; light ~; *madness;* nuttiness; outrageousness; puns; quackiness; ridiculousness; raw ~; sport; slapstick; tongue-in-cheek ~; *unserious; vainness;* wit; waggishness; *xtry. funny; yuk-yuk;* zaniness;
**comet** *(n.)*: acontias; bolide; *coma; dust tail;* evening star; fireball; falling star; *green fireball;* Halley's comet; *icarus; jetting; Kreutz sungrazer; Leonid;* meteor(ite); meteoroid; near-earth object; *object;* Oort cloud; parhelion; quadrantids; *rock;* shooting star; streak; *tail; uranite; velocity; whoosh!;* xiphias; yellow-tailed ~; *zoom;*
**comfort** *(n.)*: alleviation; bed of roses; coziness; complacency; consolation; disburdening; ease; fleshpots; great ~; homeyness; indulgence; *joy; kip;* luxury; making one feel better; *non-essential; optimism;* placating; quietude; rest; relaxation; relief; solace; *total ~;* unburdening; voluptuousness; well-being; *x-soft; yielding; zest;*
**comfort** *(v.)*: assuage; allay; alleviate; becalm; comfort; console; calm; cheer; condole with; disburden; ease; free from grief; give ~; help; *indulge; joy; kindness; luxury;* make one feel better; *nice; optimize;* placate; put arm around; quell; reassure; relieve; recomfort; soothe; solace; take ~; unburden; *very sweet; wellbeing; x-soft;* yield help; *zest;*
**comfortable** *(adj.)*: air-filled; *bouncy;* cozy; comfy; contented; complacent; cushy; disburdening; easy; easeful; fine; good; happy; homey; *indulged; joy;* keen; luxurious; *mild;* nice; over-soft; pleased; placid; padded; *quilted;* relaxed; soft; snug; satisfying; *temder;* unstrained; voluptuous; warm; *x-soft;* yielding; *zizzy;* [*Ant.* comfortless]
**comforter** *(n.)*: assuager; becalmer; consoler; condoler; cheerer; disburdener; easer; friend; giver of comfort; helper; *indulger; joy; kindness; luxury; mitigator; nice; optimize;* pacifier; paraclete; queller; reassurer; reliever; soother; solacer; *take ~; unburden; very present help; wellbeing; x-soft;* yielder of help; *zero hardship;* [*see* Holy Spirit; quilt]
**comical** *(n.)*: amusing; berserk; bizarre; clown-like; droll; entertaining; funny; farcical; goofy; giddy; hilarious; humorous; hysterical; insane; jokey; kooky; laughable; loony; mad; nutty; outrageous; pun-filled; quacked; ridiculous; slapstick; side-splitting; silly; tittering; unserious; *vain;* wacky; *xtry. funny; yokelish;* zany;
**coming** *(n.)*: advent; arrival; appearing; birth(day); beginning; commencing; dawn; entrance; ETA; emergence; founding; formation; forth~; genesis; giving birth; hatching; incoming; *jump off; kickoff;* landing; manifestation; naissance; origination; presentation; *quickening;* rise; start; touchdown; ushering in; up~; visitation; *welcoming* xenogenesis; *youth;* zygogeneis;
**command** *(n.)*: adjuration; behest; bidding; charge; commandment; decree; directive; demand; diktat; exhortation; edict; fiat; governance; halidom; instruction; injunction; imperative; juration; jussive [gram.]; *keleusmatically;* law; mandate; mittimus; *necessitate;* order; obtestation; precept; pronouncement; *quo minus [L.];* requirement; statute; *tyranny;* utterance; ultimatum; unction; *voice;* word; *xenagogy;* yelling; *zakon [Rus.];* [*see* rule; *Ant.* compliance]

162

**command** *(v.)*: adjure; *ask;* bid; charge; demand; decree; direct; dictate; enjoin; *exhort;* force; *foist;* govern; give an order; *have;* instruct; insist; *juration; kaleusmatic;* lay down; *lead;* mandate; make a demand; necessitate; order; ordain; *pronounce; quo minus [L.];* require; rule; stipulate; *say;* tell; utter; *voice; word; xenagogy;* yark; yell; *zakon [Rus.];* [*Ant.* comply; countermand]

**commandeer** *(v.)*: appropriate; betake; confiscate; dispossess; divest; expropriate; force into service; grab; hijack; impound; *just take;* keep; lay hold on; make off with; nab; obtain; procure; *quirk;* requisition; sequester; seize; take; *use; vest;* wrest; xfer; yank; zip away;

**commander** *(n.)*: authority; boss; captain; director; dictator; executive; *foreman;* governor; head; intendant; jarl; *king;* leader; master; *nobleman;* overseer; potentate; president; principal; queen [fem.]; ruler; superior; taskmaster; *ultimate authority;* vizer; warden; warlord; XO; *yokemaster;* zayim;

**commandment** *(n.)*: act; bill; behest; command; decree; edict; *fatwa* [Mos.]; governance; *halacha* [Heb.]; injunction; *jus gentium* [L.]; *keleusmatically;* law; mandate; *natural (-national) law;* ordinance; precept; *quo minus* [L.]; rule; statute; *tenet;* ukase; *voice; word;* XO mandate; yardstick; *zakon* [Rus.];

**commemorate** *(v.)*: appreciate; bear in mind; celebrate; call to mind; dedicate; esteem; fête; give regard to; honor; insoul; *jog one's memory;* keep in mind; *laud;* memorialize; *not forgotten;* observe; pay tribute to; *quicken mind;* remember; ritualize; summon up; think of; *unforgotten;* venerate; *well-remembered; xtry. honors; yet remembered;* zealously observe; [*Ant.* condemn]

**commemoration** *(n.)*: appreciation; bearing in mind; celebration; dedication; esteeming; enshrining; fête; giving regard to; honoring; *insoul; jog one's memory;* keeping in mind; *lauding;* memorial; *not forgotten;* observation; paying tribute to; *quickening the mind;* remembrance; solemn remembrance; shrine; tribute; *unforgotten;* veneration; *well-remembered; xtry. honors; yet remembered;* zealous observation; [*Ant.* condemnation]

**commemorative** *(adj.)*: appreciative; bearing in mind; commemorating; celebratory; consecrative; dedicatory; enshrining; *fête;* giving regard to; honoring; insouling; in memory; *journaling;* keeping in mind; *laudative;* memorializing; monumental; *not forgotten;* observing; paying tribute; *quickening;* remembering; solemnizing; tributary; *unforgotten;* venerating; *well-remembered; xtry. honors; yet remembered;* zealously observing;

**commence** *(v.)*: activate; begin; create; debut; embark; establish; form; found; get started; generate; *hatch;* initiate; instate; institute; jump-start; kick off; launch; make a start; *newfound;* originate; proceed; push-start; *quicken;* reactivate; start; set out; turn to; trigger; undertake; *venture; work out; xenogenesis; yield; zip;* [*Ant.* cancel]

**commencement** *(n.)*: advent; beginning; commencing; dawn; debut; embarkment; establishment; exercises; founding; genesis; graduation ceremony; hatching; initiation; jump off; kickoff; launching; making; naissance; onset; proem; *quickening;* rise; start; solemnity; take-off; triggering; undertaking; *unveiling;* ushering in; *verge;* welcoming; xenogenesis; *youth; zygogenesis;* [*Ant.* cancellation]

**commend** *(v.)*: acclaim; applaud; bless; credit; do honor; extol; fame; glorify; honor; *idolize; jubilate; kudos;* laud; magnify; *note; obeisance;* pangyrize; praise; *quiritation;* recognize; sing praises; thank; tout; uplift; venerate; *worship; xenophilia; yichus;* zealously ~; [*see* commit; *Ant.* criticize]

**commendable** *(adj.)*: admirable; beloved; creditable; distinguished; estimable; excellent; favorable; fine; great; honorable; impressive; jake [Br.]; keen; laudable; meritorious; marvelous; nice; outstanding; praiseworthy; *qualified;* remarkable; splendid; terrific; ultra-good; virtuous; very good; worthy; wonderful; xtry.; yichus; *zealously loved;* [*Ant.* contemptible]

**commendation** *(n.)*: appreciation; award; blessing; credit; citation; decoration; exaltation; encomium; *fame;* glorification; honor; high praise; idolization; *jubilation;* kudos; laud; medal; *notoriety; over-praise;* praise; promotion; *quality;* recognition; special recognition; thanks; tribute; *uplifting;* veneration; *worship; xtry.; yichus;* zealous praise;

**comment** *(n.)*: annotation; *bon mot* [F.]; commentary; descant; epigraph; footnote; general ~; handwritten ~; inscription; journal entry; *key ~; letter; message;* note; notation; observation; opinion; postil; *quick note;* remark; statement; text; utterance; *verbiage;* words; *xfer;* yakking; *zero out;*
**comment** *(v.)*: annotate; bespeak; communicate; declare; express; footnote; give comment; *have say;* indicate; *jaw; key in;* let out; mention; make a comment; notate; observe; postil; pipe up; quoth; remark; say; state; tell; talk about; utter; voice; write; *xenophonia;* yak; *zero in;*
**commentary** *(n.)*: annotation; book; catena; clarification; *document;* exposition; explanation; *form;* guide; gloss; handiwork; interpretation; *journal; kerygma;* literature; *masterpiece;* notes; observations; postil; *the quill;* reference work; remarks; scholium; text; *utterance; vignette;* work; writing; *x-reference; yield; zeug;*
**commerce** *(n.)*: activity; business; buying and selling; chaffery; dealings; enterprise; *exporting; furnish; goods;* handling; interchange; intercourse; *importing; job; kommers* [G.]; legal trade; merchandising; mercantilism; marketing; *oversell;* purveying; *qualified sale;* retailing; selling; shipping; trade; trading; traffic; *undersell;* vending; wholesale; *xfer; X12;* yardage; *zyalde [arch.];*
**commercial** *(adj.)*: activity; business; corporate; *dealing;* economic; for-profit; *goods-handling;* handling; industrial; *job-creating; kommers* [G.]; *legal trade;* mercantile; merchant; *oversell;* purveying; profit-making; *qualified sale;* retail; selling; trade; trading; *undersell;* vending; wholesale; *xfer; X12;* yardage; *zyalde [arch.];*
**commercial** *(n.)*: advertisement; business ad; corporate advertising; display; enterprise; endorsement; *flyer; goods; handling;* industrial advertising; *job; kommers* [G.]; *layout;* marketing; mercantile; *network;* one-minute ~; promotion; *qualified sale;* radio spot; spot; spread; TV spot; *undersell;* vendor ad; *weekly ad; xfer; X12;* yardage; *zyalde [arch.];*
**commission** *(n.)*: assignment; anointing; business; charge; calling; duty; errand; enterprise; end; function; goal; *handling;* injunction; industry; job; key responsibility; labor; mandate; mission; necessity; obligation; objective; office; purpose; post; quest; responsibility; *station;* task; undertaking; unction; vocation; work; xci.; *yoke; zealous task;*
**commission** *(v.)*: appoint; anoint; bid; charge; consecrate; decree; employ; *foist;* give assignment; *have;* instruct; *job; key charge;* lay down; mandate; necessitate; obligate; ordain; *pronounce; quo minus [L.];* require; sanction; tell; utter; *voice; word; xenagogy;* yark; *zealously command;*
**commissioner** *(n.)*: administrator; *boss;* commissary; chief; director; executive; foreman; governor; head; intendant; jefe; keeper; leader; manager; *night manager;* overseer; officer; principal; *quartermaster;* representative; superintendent; trustee; undershepherd; viceroy; warden; XO; yardboss; zayim;
**commit** *(v. dedicate)*: assign; bestow; commend; charge; delegate; dedicate; devote; entrust; furnish; give; guarantee; hand over; *intrust* [arch.]; *jet over; kit; let; mete;* necessitate; offer; obligate; promise; *qualify; recommit;* surrender; set aside; transfer; undertake; vest; vow; *word;* xfer; yafe; *zeal;*
**commitment** *(n.)*: allegiance; bestowment; committal; dedication; devotion; entrusting; faithfulness; guarantee; *heart;* immovability; *joining;* keeping; loyalty; *mateship; necessitation;* obligation; promise; pledge; *qualification;* reliability; *recommitment;* spirit; trueness; *unwavering;* vigor; wholeheartedness; *xtry,; yeomanliness;* zeal;
**committed** *(adj.)*: allegiant; *by;* confirmed; devoted; dedicated; ever-faithful; faithful; *good; heart;* immovable; *joined;* keen; loyal; *mateship;* never-failing; *one; partnership;* quite ~; reliable; steadfast; staunch; sold-out; true; unwavering; unswerving; vigorous; wholehearted; *xtry.; yeomanly;* zealous; [Ant. careless]
**committee** *(n.)*: advisory; assembly; board; body; council; cabinet; diet; eldership; forum; group; *heads; illuminati;* junta; *kit;* legislative body; *meeting; nominative committee; organization;* panel; presidium; quinquevirate; ruling body; sub~; session; synod; trustees; *union;* vestry; *ward; xenocracy; yain* [arch.]; *zemstvo [Rus.];*

**common** *(adj.)*: average; basic; commonplace; customary; conventional; communal; daily; everyday; familiar; frequent; generic; general; habitual; inveterate; joint; known; *long-established;* mundane; mutual; normal; ordinary; plain; par (for the course); plebeian; quotidian; regular; simple; typical; usual; universal; very ~; widespread; well-known; *x-type;* yare; *yawnsome;* zestless; [*see* profane]

**commonality** *(n.)*: agreement; affinity; bond of harmony; correlation; camaraderie; *delight; empathy;* fellowship; *generality;* harmony; identification; *joy;* kinship; like-mindedness; meeting of the minds; *nodding;* oneness; *parallelism;* quarrel-lessness; rapport; solidarity; synchronization; single-mindedness; togetherness; unanimity; unity; *voluntariness;* willingness; widespread agreement; *xenia; yedinstvo* [Rus.]; zeal;

**common sense** *(n.)*: average sense; brain; *common knowledge;* discretion; everyday sense; *foresight;* good sense; horse sense; intelligence; judgment; kop; level-headedness; logic; mother wit; native wit; normal intelligence; ordinary sense; practicality; *quickness of mind;* realism; roadwalking sense; sense; *the* sense one was born with; *thinking;* usual intelligence; *valuation;* wit; walking sense; *xtr. thought; yepe [arch.];* zero stupidity; [*Ant.* craziness]

**commotion** *(n.)*: activity; ado; agitation; bustle; brouhaha; commess; disturbance; excitement; flurry; goings on; hubbub; intranquility; jumble; kerfuffle; *lunacy;* melee; non-orderliness; *obscurity;* pother; *quandary;* ruckus; restlessness; shindy; tizzy; tumult; unrest; vexation; wilderment; *xtry. mess; yo-yo;* zoo; [*Ant.* calm]

**commune** *(n.)*: abbey; basilica; convent; community; *dorm; edifice;* friary; *facility;* group; hermitage; house; incloister; *jong [Tib.];* kibbutz; lamasery [Tib.]; mir; nunnery; *oratorio;* priory; *Qumran;* religious community; sacrarium; *together; upper room; village;* wat [Bud.]; *xenodochium;* yogic house; *zawiyah* [Mos.];

**commune** *(v.)*: associate; affiliate; *bandy words;* communicate; converse; consort; deal; engage in conversation; fellowship; get with; have fellowship; interact; interface; intercommunicate; join with; *keep in touch;* link; maintain good relations; *nearness; oneness; partner; pray;* quietly ~; relate; socialize; share; speak; talk together; *unity;* visit; warmly speak; *xenia;* yoke; *zeal;*

**communicate** *(v.)*: articulate; bespeak; converse; declare; express; *foremention;* get across; have conversation with; indicate; *jaw; key in;* let out; mention; noise; *note;* observe; *proclaim;* quoth; relate; relay; say; speak; state; tell; talk; utter; verbalize; voice; word; *xenophonia;* yak; *zero in;*

**communication** *(n.)*: address; bespeaking; contact; communiqué; discourse; elocution; expression; *filibuster; glossa;* homily; *inaugural address;* indiction; *jabbering; kerygma;* lecture; message; *narration;* oration; proclamation; pontification; *quotation;* recitation; speech; sermon; statement; talk; transmittance; utterance; vocalization; word(s); *xenophonia; yawner [off.]; zinger [slang];*

**communion** *(n.)*: accord; brotherhood; communing; closeness; *devotion;* empathy; fellowship; *goodwill;* harmony; intimacy; *joining; koinonia* [Gr.]; kinship; *league;* mateship; nearness; oneness; participation; quiet ~; (right) relationship; sweet ~; togetherness; unity; *virtue;* warmth; *xenia; yoke; zeal;* [*Ant.* contention]

**Communion** *(n.)*: assembly; *the* Bread; *the* Cup; *divine ~; the* Elements; *the* feast; grape juice; holy ~; housel; intinction; *juice; keeping the feast; the* Lord's Table (-Supper); *memorial;* NT *ordinance;* ordinance; *Passover;* quarterly; rite; *the* Supper; *the* Table; *unleavened bread; unfermented grape juice; viaticum;* wafer; *x-substantiation;* yeastless bread; zonic ~;

**Communism** *(n.)*: anti-capitalism; Bolshevikism; Communist principles; despotism; *empire; Fabian;* government-control; *the* Hammer & Sickle; *ideology;* Jacobinism; Kremlinism; Leninism; Marxism; Maoism; New Left; Naxalism; neo- ~; one-party system; *People's Republic;* quango; red plague; Socialism; Stalinism; *totalitarianism; undemocratic; violence;* welfarism; *Xinhua [Chin.];* Y.C.L.; *za-zum [Rus.];* [*see* totalitarianism; *Ant.* capitalism]

**Communist** *(n.)*: anti-capitalist; Bolshevik; Commie; *deviant; Eastern; Fabian; guerrilla; Hammer & Sickle; iron curtain; Jacobin;* Komsomol; Kremlinist; leftist; Leninist; Marxist; Maoist; New Leftist; Naxalite; neo-Communist; *oppressor;* pinko; *quede [arch.]; red;* Soviet; socialist; Stalinist; *subversive;* totalitarian; *undemocratic;* Viet Cong; *welfarist;* Xinhua [Chin.]; *Y.C.L.;* Zengakuren [Jap.]; [*Ant.* capitalist]

**Communistic** *(adj.)*: anti-capitalist; Bolshevik; Communist; *dictatorial; Eastern block; Fabian;* government-controlled; Hammer & Sickle; Iron Curtain; *Jacobin;* Komsomol; Kremlinist; leftist; Leninist; left-wing; Marxist; Maoist; New Leftist; Naxalite; neo-Communism; *oppressive;* pink(o); *quede [arch.];* Red; Soviet; socialist; Stalinist; *subversive;* totalitarian; undemocratic; *Viet Cong;* Warsaw Pact; *Xinhua [Chin.]; Y.C.L.; Zengakuren* [Jap.]; [*see* oppressive; *Ant.* capitalistic]

**commute** *(v.)*: *aggravation;* betake oneself; come and go; *carpool;* drive; *everyday; find one's way;* go back and forth; head to and fro; hurry; *itinerate;* journey; *kite;* locomote; *move; navigate; outrun;* pass; *quicken;* rail; ride; shuttle; travel; *underway; voyage; wayfare; xenize; yede* [arch.]; *zip;*

**compact** *(adj.)*: abridged; brief; concise; compacted; condensed; compressed; dense; *efficient;* fugacious; foldup; *germinal; half-pint;* itsy-bitsy; *jitney; knee-high;* little; mini(ature); neat; *overly small;* packed; pocket-sized; *quaint;* reduced; small; squeezed; serried; tiny; trim; undersized; very small; wee; *XS; yea big; zero;* [*Ant.* capacious]

**companion** *(n.)*: ally; associate; buddy; bedfellow; comrade; compatriot; devoted friend; escort; friend; good-fellow; girlfriend [fem.]; helper; intimate; Jonathan; kith [pl.]; loyal friend; mate; neighbor; other self; playmate; partner; *quondam friend;* roommate; schoolmate; sidekick; *teammate;* unfailing friend; *votary; watcher; xenophile;* yokemate; *zealous friend;* [*see* spouse; *Ant.* competitor]

**companionship** *(n.)*: affinity; brotherhood; company; camaraderie; devotion; endearment; friendship; fellowship; goodwill; *helping;* intimacy; joining; kinship; love; *loyalty;* mateship; marriage; nearness; oneness; partnership; *quondam friendship;* rapport; solidarity; time spent together; *unfailing ~; value;* warmth; *xenia; yoke; zeal;*

**company** *(n.)*: *AB;* business; corporation; chain; conglomerate; *dba; dummy corporation;* establishment; enterprise; firm; factory; franchise; group; *holding ~;* industry; job; joint-venture; *kongsi [Chin.]; limited ~;* manufacturer; mill; mutual company; national (-non-profit) corporation; organization; outfit; operation; partnership; plant; quasi-public corporation; *refinery;* small business; shop; *team; unlimited ~;* venture; workplace; workshop; *x-div.; YK; zaibatsu* [Jap.];

**comparable** *(adj.)*: alike; analogous; *balance;* corresponding; duplicate; equivalent; *further; geminated;* homologous; identical; just the same; kindred; like; matching; non-differing; *one;* parallel; *quae est eadem* [L.]; resembling; similar; tantamount; unimproved; unmodified; very similar; *word-perfect;* xerographed; *yet the same; zero difference;* [*Ant.* contradistinctive]

**comparative** *(adj.)*: analogous; balancing; comparing; *deeming;* evaluative; *fair;* gauging; *holding comparison;* involving comparisons; juxtapositional; *knowing similarities;* likening; *measuring;* noting similarities; *observing;* proportional; quantifying; relative; reasonable; setting together; thinking on similarities; using comparison; valuative; weighing; *xenodiagnostic;* yeming; *zeroing in;* [*Ant.* contradistinctive]

**compare** *(v.)*: *appraise;* balance; compare; contrast; check; *deem;* evaluate; *find;* gage; hold comparison; *inspect;* juxtapose; *know similarities;* liken; measure; match; note similarities; *observe;* put side-by-side; quantify; relate; set together; think on similarities; use comparison; valuate; weigh; *xenodiagnose;* yeme; *zero in;* [*Ant.* contrast]

**comparison** *(n.)*: analogy; assessment; *bearing resemblance;* contrast; correlation; *duplication;* equivalence; *finding; gauging;* homogeneity; illustration; juxtaposition; *kind;* likeness; metaphor; nearness; *oneness;* parallelism; *quasi-similitude;* resemblance; similarity; *throwing side-by-side;* uniformity; very image; weighing; *xfer; yoke; zeroing in;* [*Ant.* contrast; contradistinction]

**compartment** *(n.)*: area; box; bin; bay; cubby-hole; cargo space; division; enclosure; file cabinet; *glove box;* hole; holding ~; incavation; *jar; kiosk;* locker; luggage ~; moving carton; nook; overhead ~; place; pigeonhole; partition; *quarter-holder;* recess; storage ~; secret ~; space; trunk; underground ~; *vessel;* wall ~; *xtr. storage; you* [Chin.]; zone; zarf;

**compassion** *(n.)*: affection; benevolence; care; *dearness;* empathy; feelings; grace; heart; *interest; joy-giving;* kindness; love; mercy; niceness; oneness; pity; *quick-to-help;* respects; sympathy; soft(hearted)ness; tender(hearted)ness; understanding; *virtue;* warmth; *xenophilia;* yearning; zeal to forgive; [*Ant.* callousness]

**compassionate** *(adj.)*: affectionate; benevolent; clement; caring; *dear;* empathetic; feeling; gentle; humane; *intimate; joy-imparting;* kindhearted; loving; merciful; nice; *openhanded;* piteous; *quick to help; regardful;* sympathetic; sensitive; softhearted; thoughtful; tender(hearted); unselfish; very kind; warm(hearted); xenial; yearnful; *zealous of good works* [Tit. 2:4]; [*Ant.* callous]

**compatibility** *(n.)*: agreement; *befitting;* compatibleness; consistency; downward ~; *expedience;* fit; going together; harmony; *hand and glove; idoneous; just right;* keen match; like-mindedness; match; *non-erroneous;* oneness; parity; qualification; right fit; suitability; *tuning;* uniformity; upward ~; *version;* well-suitedness; xtry. ~; *yieldedness;* zero incompatibility;

**compatible** *(adj.)*: agreeable; *befitting;* corresponding; consistent; downward ~; equivalent; fitting; going together; harmonious; *hand and glove;* idoneous; just right; keenly matched; like-minded; matched; *non-erroneous; okay;* perfect; qualified; right; suitable; *tuned;* upward ~; *uniform;* very well suited; well-matched; xtry. ~; *yielded;* zero incompatibility;

**compel** *(v.)*: *admonish;* bear on; constrain; coerce; drive; exhort; force; *get;* hurry; impel; *jump on; knock;* lean on; make; *must;* necessitate; oblige; pressure; *quicken;* require; strong-arm; tell; urge; *vie;* warn; *xuld* [arch.]; *yank; zealously urge;* [*see* command]

**compensate** *(v.)*: *attend to;* balance (out); counteract; counterbalance; *disburse;* equlize; fix; gratify; give back (-for); *help;* indemnify; *justly ~; kick in;* level out; make up for; make payment; *non-retention;* offset; pay (back); *quid pro quo* [L.]; recompense; redress; remunerate; reward; requite; repay; set right; square (up); take care of; *undo; vest;* weigh out; *xfer;* yield; *zero-out one's debt;*

**compensation** *(n.)*: amount; base pay; cash; commission; disbursement; damages; earnings; finances; guerdon; hire; income; just desserts; *kickback; livelihood; minimum wage; net pay; overcompensation;* pay(ment); quittance; *quid pro quo* [L.]; recompense; return; reimbursement; redress; salary; solatium; take-home pay; *unindebted;* virement; wage(s); xfer; yield; *zero-out one's debt;*

**compete** *(v.)*: antagonize; battle; contend; dispute; enter; endeavor; fight; grapple; have contest with; *involve; jarring;* kemp; lock horns [slang]; make fur fly; *non-partial;* oppose; outvie; participate; play; *quarrel;* run; rival; strive; try to win; *unfriendly;* vie; wrestle; war; *x-purposes; yed; zealously ~;*

**competence** *(n.)*: ability; adeptness; basic ~; capability; competency; deftness; experience; expertise; fitness; *gift;* habilitation; *influence; justification;* knack; know-how; legerdemain; means; nous; *old-hand;* proficiency; qualification; readiness; skill; sufficiency; talent; *usefulness;* virtuosity; wherewithal; *xtry. qualifications;* yarkening; *zeal;*

**competent** *(adj.)*: adept; able; adequate; bodily capable; capable; deft; expert; fit; good; *healthy;* intelligent; *just right;* knowledgeable; legally ~; mighty; *natural ability; overqualified;* proficient; qualified; ready; skilled; sufficient; *sui juris* [L.]; talented; up to; versed; well-able; *xtry. qualified;* yarkened; *zealous;*

**competition** *(n.)*: antagonism; battle; bout; contention; clash; contest; dispute; emulation; enmity; fight; *grappling;* hostility; *imbroglio;* jockeying *kampf* [G.]; *luctation* [arch.]; mêlée; match; *non-agreement;* opposition; *position warfare;* quarrel; rivalry; struggle; striving; tussle; tournament; unfriendliness; vying; war; *x-fire;* yed; *zonal ~;*

**competitive** *(adj.)*: adversarial; antagonistic; belligerent; competing; confrontational; disputanting; *enemy; fierce; galsome;* hostile; inimical; *jeopardizing;* kindless; *low-down;* malicious; non-friendly; oppositional; pugnacious; quarrelsome; rivalrous; striving; *threatening;* unfriendly; vying; warlike; *xenophobic; yieldless; zealotic;*

**competitor** *(n.)*: adversary; agonist; bad guy; contender; disputant; entrant; enemy; foe; gladiator; *hostile;* instigator; jangler; kemper; *legion; litigant;* match; nemesis; opponent; *player;* quarreler; rival; striver; squabbler; tussler; *unfriendly;* vier; *warrior;* xenic; *yuon [arch.]; zeke [off.];* [*Ant.* compatriot]

**compilation** *(n.)*: accumulation; assemblage; build-up; collection; *drove; embale; file;* gathering; heap; hoard; ingathering; *juba* [L.]; kit; load; mass; number; organization; pile; quantity; ruck; stockpile; stack; *treasure; unit;* varia; *written collection; x-section; yelm; zone;*

**compile** *(v.)*: accumulate; assemble; amass; build up; collect; draw together; *expand; form;* gather; hoard; increase; *jump; keep gathering; largen;* make up; *nob;* organize; put together; *quadruplicate;* record; store; stockpile; take up; upbuild; *varia;* write; XL; *yard; zone;*

**complacency** *(n.)*: apathy; bliss; complacence; contentment; comfort; *droopiness; ennui;* fatuousness; gratification; happiness; indulgence; *joy; keen;* lack of concern; *merry;* non-concern; overconfidence; pleasure; *queme; rejoicing;* (self-)satisfaction; smugness; *thrilled;* unconcern; *vivacious; well-pleased; xanadu; you-beaut [Aus.];* zero concern; [*Ant.* concern]

**complacent** *(adj.)*: apathetic; blissful; content; comfortable; *droopy;* easy-going; fatuous; gratified; happy; indifferent; *just satisfied;* kef; Laodicean; *mawmish;* non-motivated; overconfident; placid; pleased; *quiescent; remiss;* (self-)satisfied; smug; *torpid;* unconcerned; very content; well-pleased; *xenarthrous;* yareless; zealless; [*Ant.* concerned]

**complain** *(v.)*: *accuse;* bewail; bellyache; beef; balk; criticize; carp; disparage; decry; *explode;* fault; fuss; grumble; gripe; gainsay; harangue; hone; inveigh; jangle; knock; lambaste; mutter; moan; murmur; niggle; nitpick; object; pick; protest; quetch; repine; squawk; traduce; *ululate;* vituperate; whine; *xuld [arch.];* yammer; zing; [*Ant.* commend]

**complainer** *(n.)*: *accuser;* bellyacher; carper; disparager; *explode;* fusser; griper; haranguer; impugner; jangler; kvetch; libelant; murmurer; nitpicker; objector; protester; quibbler; remonstrator; slammer; *tear into;* unhappy camper; vituperator; whiner; *xuld [arch.];* yawper; Zoilus; [*Ant.* commender]

**complaint** *(n.)*: argument; beef; criticism; decrial; denunciation; dispute; exception; fuss; grievance; gripe; *hairsplitting;* impugnation; increpation; jeremiad; kvetch; knocking; *locking horns;* maundering; murmuring; niggle; objection; protest; peeve; plaint; problem; quarrel; quarimony; querele; resistance; repining; stricture; *strife; tussle;* unharmoniousness; variance; vice; withstanding; *x-fire;* yawping; *za-zum [Rus.];* [*Ant.* commendation]

**complement** *(n.)*: accompaniment; balance; counterpart; completion; *deal;* exact match; fit; fullness; fulfillment; *go with;* harmonization; *increase; join; kilter;* looking good; match; *number;* one of two; perfecting part; quota; *the* rest; remainder; supplement; totality; *unit;* very good match; *work together; xy-balanced; yet agreeing;* zero imbalance;

**complement** *(v.)*: accompany; balance out; blend; correlate; complete; do nicely with; enhance; fit well with; finish; (ful)fill; go with; harmonize; integrate; *just perfect; keep;* look great with; make up for; *non-clashing; orchestrate;* perfect; *quite nice;* round out; set off; suit; supplement; *total; unify; very good;* wrap up; *xfer; yain [arch.]; zet [reg.];*

**complete** *(adj. comprehensive)*: aggregate; all-encompassing; broad; comprehensive; *diligent;* entire; exhaustive; full; general; gross; *high;* inclusive; integral; jimbang; *kit and caboodle; long; lump;* macroscopic; non-abridged; overall; plenary; perfect; *quantitative;* round-circle; sheer; sweeping; total; thorough; unabridged; undivided; uncut; utter; universal; veritable; whole; *xtry.;* yare; *zealous;*

**complete** *(adj. finished)*: accomplished; brought to an end; completed; concluded; consummate; done; ended; finished; fulfilled; finalized; full-circle; *grown; here;* intact; *just finished; kept; long-awaited;* made; *non-abridged;* over; perfect; *qualified;* ready; resolved; secure; through; undertaken; *veritable;* whole; *xtry.; yare;* zeroed;

**complete** *(adj. whole)*: absolute; big; completed; done; entire; exhaustive; ended; finished; full (-length); fulfilled; full-circle; general; grown; high; intact; *just finished; kit and caboodle; long-awaited;* mature; non-abridged; *overall;* perfect; pure; plenary; *qualified;* ready; *sum total;* total; unabridged; undivided; uncut; unbroken; unedited; veritable; whole; *xtry.;* yare; *zero incompletion;*

**complete** *(v.)*: accomplish; bring to fruition; conclude; consummate; complement; carry out; do; execute; end; finish; (ful)fill; get done; handle; implement; *jump to it;* keep; leave nothing undone; make an end; *not fail;* obey; perform; pass; *quick-to-comply;* reach; realize; satisfy; succeed; tackle; transact; undertake; *victory;* wrap up; *xfer; yain* [arch.]; zip to it;

**completely** *(adv.)*: absolutely; aggregately; altogether; broadly; comprehensively; *done;* entirely; fully; flatly; *generally;* heart and soul; inclusively; *jimbang; keenly; long;* macroscopically; *non-partially; overall;* plenarily; *quite;* roundly; sweepingly; totally; thoroughly; *tout à fait* [F.]; utterly; unconditionally; universally; veritably; wholly; *xtry.;* yarely; *zero incompletion;*

**completeness** *(n.)*: amplitude; breadth; completion; consummation; doneness; entireness; fullness; *grown; high;* integrity; *just finished; kept intact; long and short;* maturity; *non-abridged; overall;* perfection; plenitude; plenariness; *quantity;* readiness; roundness; *success;* thoroughness; totality; unity; *veritable;* wholeness; *xtry.; yare; zone;*

**completion** *(n.)*: accomplishment; achievement; bringing about; conclusion; close; doing; execution; entirety; end; fulfillment; finishing; fruition; getting done; *handling;* implementation; inclusiveness; *job well done;* keeping; *living out;* making an end; *no more remaining; outcome;* performance; perfection; quitting; realization; reaching; success; totality; triumph; transaction; *utterly; victory;* wholeness; wrapping up; windup; *xfer; yield; zero remaining;* [*see* end]

**complex** *(adj.)*: abstruse; byzantine; complicated; difficult; elaborate; formidable; grueling; hairy; hard; involute; intricate; jarring; knotty; labyrinthine; mind-boggling; non-easy; overwhelming; perplexing; *question-filled;* recondite; reticular; spaghetti-like; tough; thorny; unsearchable; vexatious; wildering; *xenagogic; yucky; zany;*

**complexity** *(n.)*: abstruseness; *byzantine;* complexness; difficulty; elaborateness; formidableness; grueling; hardness; involution; intricacy; *jarring;* knottiness; *labyrinth; mind-boggling;* non-easiness; *overly involved;* perplexity; *question-filled;* reconditeness; *spaghetti-like;* toughness; unsearchableness; vexing; wilderment; *xenagogic; yuckiness; zaniness;*

**compliance** *(n.)*: acquiescence; agreement; bowing; conformity; deference; execution; fulfillment; giving in; heeding; implementation; *jumping on it;* keeping; listening; mindfulness; non-resistance; obligingness; obedience; performance; *questionlessness;* regard; submission; *toeing the line;* upholding; vigorous ~; *work; xlation;* yieldedness; *zeal;* [Ant. contravention]

**compliant** *(adj.)*: acquiescent; biddable; conforming; deferential; ever-obedient; following; *good;* heedful; implementing; *jump right to it;* keeping; *kowtow;* listening; law-abiding; mindful; non-resistant; obedient; perfect; performing; questionless; regardful; right on it; submissive; *true;* unresisting; *vigilant;* willing; *xtr. ~;* yielded; zealous; [Ant. contumacious]

**complicate** *(v.)*: *abstruse;* bewilder; confuse; compound; *disarrange;* entangle; *fuddle; gnarl; hamper;* intertwine; *involve;* jumble; knot; *labyrinth;* make more complex; *nonplus;* over~; obfuscate; obscure; perplex; *quirk;* ravel; *scramble;* tangle; *unstraightened;* vex; weave; *x-ing; yarn;* zigzag;

**complicated** *(adj.)*: abstruse; bewildering; complex; convoluted; difficult; elaborate; formidable; grueling; hard; involved; inextricable; jarring; knotty; labyrinthine; multifaceted; non-easy; over~; puzzling; problematic; *question-filled;* rough; spaghetti-like; technical; tough; tangled; unsearchable; vexatious; wildering; *xenagogic; yucky; zany;*

**complication** *(n.)*: adversity; bind; complexity; difficulty; encumbrance; fix; glitch; headache; hitch; inconvenience; jam; kink; knottiness; load; mess; *matter;* nuisance; obstacle; problem; quandary; rattle; snag; trouble; upheaval; vexation; worry; *xerotripsis; yuckiness;* zinger;
**compliment** *(n.)*: accolade; bouquet [slang]; commendation; *delight;* encouragement; flattery; felicitation; glorification; honor; *idolization; jubilation;* kind remark; kudo; laudatory comment; *magnification;* nice remark; *obeisance;* pat-on-the-back; praise; *quiritation;* rave remark; salute; tribute; uplifting remark; veneration; warm fuzzy; *xtr. nice; yichus;* zealous praise;
**compliment** *(v.)*: applaud; bow to; commend; congratulate; *delight;* encourage; flatter; glorify; honor; *idolize; jubilate; kudos;* laud; magnify; note; *obeisance;* praise; *quiritation; regard; rave;* salute; thank; uplift; venerate; *warmness; xtr. nice; yichus;* zealously praise; [*Ant.* criticize]
**complimentary** *(adj.)*: admiring; acclamatory; adulatory; blarneying; congratulatory; *delightsome;* encouraging; flattering; fulsome; glowing; honoring; *idolizing; jubilate;* kind; laudatory; magnifying; *nice;* oily-tongued; praiseful; *quiritation;* raving; sycophantic; thankful; uplifting; venerational; *warm; xtr. nice; yichus;* zealously; [*see* free; *Ant.* critical]
**comply** *(v.)*: attend; bow; conform; do; execute; fulfill; give in; heed; harken; indulge; jump (to it); keep; listen to; mind; not resist; obey; perform; *questionless; regard;* submit; toe the line; undertake; vigorously obey; *work; wholly; xlate;* yield; zip to it; [*Ant.* contravene]
**component** *(n.)*: appurtenance; *bit;* constituent; cog; division; element; feature; *gear;* hunk; ingredient; item; *jib; kernel;* little piece; member; *nugget;* ought; part; piece; quantity; *remnant;* section; *thing;* unit; *vestige;* widget; *x-mal [G.]; yngot* [arch.]; *zum [dial.];*
**compose** *(v.)*: author; build; constitute; compile; create; draft; embody; enter; fabricate; form; generate; handwrite; indite; invent; jot down; keep record; log; mark; make; melodize; notate; originate; pen; put together; quill; redact; scribble; shape; take down; *undertake; vellum;* write; *xfer;* yield; *zet [dial.];*
**composer** *(n.)*: author; ballader; creator; doggerelist; elegist; framer; *glossator;* harmonist; hymnist; hymnwriter; inspirational songwriter; jongleur; kasida-writer; librettist; lyricist; melodist; musician; *noel;* odist; psalmist; *quadrille; rhymester;* songwriter; sonneteer; symphonist; tunesmith; *undersong;* versifier; writer; *Xenakis;* yedder; zemirah-writer;
  **Composers**: Amram; Bach; Beethoven; Brahms; Chopin; Dvorak; Elgar; Franck; Gluck; Handel; Haydn; Ibert; Janacek; Khachaturian; Liszt; Mendelssohn; Mozart; Nielsen; Offenbach; Prokofiev; Quantz; Rachmaninoff; Schubert; Schumann; Strauss; Tchaikovsky; Ullmann; Vivaldi; Wagner; Xenakis; Yost; Zwilich;
**composition** *(n.)*: article; *booklet;* commentary; dissertation; essay; feature; *graving;* handiwork; *item; journal; kapnography;* literature; letter; monograph; *note;* opus; *opinion;* paper; *the quill; revision;* study; treatise; thesis; term paper; *uncials;* vignette; writing; work; *xiaozhuan; yellow journalism; zeug;*
**composure** *(n.)*: aplomb; becalmed state; calmness; cool [slang]; *dignity;* equanimity; *friendliness;* gentleness; harmony; idyll; *jarless; keeping peace; laid-back;* motionlessness; mildness; non-turbulence; *orderliness;* poise; phlegm; quiescence; repose; self-possession; sang-froid; tranquility; unflappability; *very calm; well-relaxed; xenophilious; yieldlessness; zero stress;*
**compound** *(v.)*: add; admix; blend; couple; coalesce; combine; complicate; *develop;* enlarge; fuse; *get together;* heap together; increase; intermix; intermingle; intensify; join; knit; link; lump together; mix; mingle; meld; multiply; *network; overmix;* put together; proliferate; *quasi-fuse;* reunite; ramify; synthesize; toss together; unite; *voluble;* wed; *xenograft;* yoke; zip together;
**comprehend** *(v.)*: apprehend; become aware of; conceptualize; digest; discern; experience; fathom; grasp; get; have in one's heart (-brain); identify; *judge;* know; *learn;* make acquaintance; naw [dial.]; observe; own; perceive; *plumb; questionless;* realize; recognize; see; take in; understand; *value;* wis(t); wot; wit; *xenodiagnose; yeme;* zero in;

**comprehensible** *(adj.)*: apprehensible; *basic;* clear; comprehendible; discernable; easy-to-understand; fathomable; graspable; *handleable;* intelligible; *just plain;* knowable; logical; manifest; non-confusing; obvious; perceivable; plain; questionless; recognizable; straightforward; transparent; understandable; very easy; well-structured; *xparent; yet ~; zero confusion;* [*Ant.* confusing]

**comprehension** *(n.)*: apprehension; *brains;* command; conception; discernment; erudition; fix; grasp; grip; heart-understanding; *hindsight;* ideation; insight; illumination; judgment; knowledge; learning; *light;* mental apprehension; mastery; notion; ownership; perception; perceptiveness; percipience; *quick-sighted;* realization; recognition; sense; *take; thought;* understanding; *visualization;* wit; *xtry. ~; yeme [arch.]; zero problem;* [*Ant.* confusion]

**comprehensive** *(adj.)*: all-inclusive; across-the-board; broad; complete; *done;* exhaustive; full; far-reaching; general; *high;* inclusive; *joint; known; long-range;* macroscopic; non-abridged; overall; panoramic; *quantified; ranging;* summative; total; thorough; unabridged; universal; veritable; whole; wide-ranging; *xtry. coverage;* yare; *zonal;* [*Ant.* cursory]

**compress** *(v.)*: astringe; bear down; clamp; compact; crush; depress; express; flatten; force; grind; hug; *impair;* jam; keep down; levigate; mash; minimize; narrow; *overcome;* press; quash; reduce; squeeze; smash; tamp; tighten; *undo; void;* wring; x; *yank down;* zap;

**compression** *(n.)*: astriction; binding; clamping; compressing; depression; *exerting force;* flattening; force; grinding; hugging; *impairment;* jamming; keeping down; levigation; mashing; minimizing; narrowing; *overcoming;* pressing; quashing; restriction; squeezing; tightening; *undoing; voiding;* wringing; x-ing; *yanking down;* zapping;

**compromise** *(n.)*: arrangement; agreement; accommodation; bending; buckling; bargain; concession; cooperation; deal; *ensuring;* folding; giving in; happy medium; indulging; *juste milieu* [F.]; knuckling (under); *league;* middle-course; *modus vivendi* [L.]; negotiation; *oath; pact; qualified promise;* relenting; settlement; taking the mean; *understanding; vow;* wimping out; *xfer;* yielding; *zero conviction;*

**compromise** *(v.)*: arrange; agree; accommodate; bend; buckle; bow; bargain; concede; dip one's colors; *ensure;* fold; give in; *halfway;* indulge; just give in; knuckle (under); *league;* make concession; meet halfway; negotiate; *oath; promise; qualified ~;* relent; settle for; soften; slacken; take the mean; *use; violate;* wimp out; *xfer;* yield; *zero conviction;*

**compulsion** *(n.)*: admonishment; bearing upon; constraint; coercion; duress; driving; exhortation; force; *get;* hurrying; impulsion; *jumping on; knocking;* leaning on; making; mandatoriness *must;* necessitation; obligation; pressure; *quickening;* requirement; strong-arming; *telling;* urging; *vying;* warning; *xuld [arch.]; yanking; zealous urging;* [*Ant.* choice]

**compulsory** *(adj.)*: absolutely required; binding; constraining; demanded; enforced; forced; *got to; have to;* irremissible; indispensable; *jump to it; key;* law; mandatory; *must;* necessary; no-option; obligatory; pressing; *quantum;* required; *serious;* top-priority; unavoidable; vital; without choice; *yieldless;* zero-option;

**compunction** *(n.)*: apprehension; *bone;* conscience; doubt; demurral; ethics; foreboding; guilt; hesitation; issues; *jarred;* keen sense of guilt; *light of conscience;* misgiving; niggle; objections; pricking; problem; pang of conscience; qualm; reservations; scruple; shame; trepidation; uneasiness; vacillation; worry; *x-ing; yieldedness; zeroing in;*

**computation** *(n.)*: analysis; brainwork; calculation; determination; estimation; figure; gauging; *hypothesis; idea;* judgment; *knowledge; lucubration;* meditation; *notion; observation;* pondering; *quite;* reckoning; *study;* thinking; totaling; *use of brain;* valuation; working out; *xenodiagnosis; yeme; zazen;*

**compute** *(v.)*: analyze; *brainstorm;* calculate; conceive; determine; estimate; figure; gauge; *hypothesize; ideate;* judge; *know; lucubrate;* meditate; *notion; observe;* ponder; *question;* reckon; *study;* think; total; *use brain; valuate;* work out; *xenodiagnose; yeme; zazen;*

171

**comrade** *(n.)*: ally; buddy; companion; compatriot; *devoted friend; endeared;* friend; fellow; good friend; helper; intimate; Jonathan; kith [pl.]; *loyal friend;* mate; *neighbor; ouboet [S. Afr.];* partner; *quondam friend; repository;* sympathizer; *tovarich [Rus.];* unfailing friend; *votary; watcher; xenophile;* yokemate; *zealous friend;* [*Ant.* contender]

**con** *(v.)*: *allure;* bilk; beguile; buffalo; cheat; defraud; ensnare; fool; fleece; guile; hornswoggle; insnare; *jape;* kid; lie; misrepresent; nobble; outfox; put one over; *quiblin* [arch.]; rook; shyster; sucker; swindle; snow; trick; take advantage; *utter falsehood;* verneuk; weasel; wangle; *xuld [arch.]; yentz; zing;*

**con artist** *(n.)*: *allurer;* beguiler; charlatan; cheat; crook; con man; defrauder; ensnarer; fraud; fake; guiler; hornswoggler; *jape;* knave; liar; misrepresenter; nobbler; outfoxer; ploy-maker; quacksalver; rook; swindler; shyster; trickster; *untruther;* verneuker; weasel; *xgressor; yentzer* [Heb.]; *zinger;*

**conceal** *(v.)*: *artfulness;* bury; bemask; cloak; cover; disguise; entomb; foil; *garb;* hide; *incognito;* imbosk; *jape;* keep hidden; lay low; mask; mantle; not let on; obscure; obfuscate; put out of view; *quat* [arch.]; *recluse;* shroud; stash; shelter; tuck away; *under cover;* veil; withhold; *xenomorph;* yird; *zeroize;*

**concede** *(v.)*: acknowledge; admit (defeat); agree; bow; bend; confess; cede; *declare;* eat humble pie; forfeit; give in; grant; hold forth; *indicate; jump off;* knuckle (under); lay down arms; make known; *notify;* own up; put away claim; *quit;* relinquish; surrender; throw in the towel; *unvictorious;* voice concession; withdraw; *x;* yield; *zero success;* [*Ant.* conquer]

**conceit** *(n.)*: arrogance; bigheadedness; condescension; dandyism; egotism; flatulence; fullness of self; gloating; haughtiness; immodesty; inflatedness; *jackanapes; know-it-all;* loftiness; magisterialness; narcissism; overproudness; pride; pomposity; *quilicom* [arch.]; *ruff* [arch.]; self-admiration; self-importance; stuck-upness; turgidity; *unhumbled;* vanity; vainness; vauntery; wind; *xenophobia; yieldless; zero humility;*

**conceited** *(adj.)*: arrogant; big-headed; condescending; dandified; egotistical; flatulent; full of oneself; glass-glazing; haughty; inflated; *jackanapes; know-it-all;* lifted up; much- ~; narcissistic; overproud; proud; puffed up; pompous; peacockish; quick-to-boast; *reassured;* smug; stuck-up; self-admiring; self-glorious; thrasonic; unhumbled; vain; vaunting; wrapped up in oneself; *x-proud; yelping; zero humility;*

**conceivable** *(adj.)*: appreciable; believable; credible; devisable; expectable; fanciable; feasible; *get idea;* humanly possible; imaginable; inventable; *judge; knowable;* likely; *mind; notion; originate;* possible; *quixotic;* reckonable; supposable; thinkable; *utilizable;* viable; workable; *xenodiagnose; yeme; zazen;*

**conceive** *(v.)*: *apprehend;* believe; *brainstorm;* create; conceptualize; devise; dream of; dissemble; envision; fancy; formulize; fantasize; get idea; hatch; imagine; invent; *judge; know; lucubrate;* make believe; *notion; originate;* picture; pretend; *quixotic;* reckon; see; suppose; think; use imagination; visualize; ween; *xenodiagnose; yeme; zazen;*

**concentrate** *(v.)*: analyze; bear in mind; consider; dwell; digest; evaluate; focus; give thought; hone in; *ideate;* judge; *know; lucubrate;* meditate; *notion;* observe; ponder; pore; *question;* reflect; study; think; use brain; valuate; weigh; *xenodiagnose; yeme;* zero in;

**concentration** *(n.)*: attention; brainwork; consideration; contemplation; deliberation; evaluation; focus; going over; headwork; hunch; intellection; judgment; *knowledge;* lucubration; meditation; *notion;* observation; *on one's mind;* pondering; *questioning;* rumination; study; thought; using one's brain; valuation; weighing; *xtr. consideration; yeme* [arch.]; zeroing in;

**concept** *(n.)*: abstraction; apprehension; belief; basic idea; conception; *deliberation;* evaluation; fancy; gist; head-knowledge; idea; imagination; image; *judgment;* knowledge; lucubration; *musing;* notion; objectification; perception; point; *quot homines tot sententiae* [L.]; reckoning; sense; thought; understanding; view; weighing; *x-factor; yeme* [arch.]; *zazen* [Bud.];

**conception** *(n. origination)*: apperception; breeding; conceiving; *development;* engendering; formation; fathering; generation; having children; inception; *jump off;* kicking off; launching; *making; naissance;* origination; procreation; *quickening;* reproduction; start; spawning; *travail;* ushering in; *visitation; waiting;* xenogenesis; yielding; zygogenesis;

**conception** *(n. understanding)*: apprehension; angle; belief; concept(ualization); comprehension; cogitation; *disposition;* envisioning; fancy; grasp; *heart;* idea; image; judgment; *knowledge;* learning; *mentality; mind;* notion; outlook; opinion; picturing; perception; *quot homines tot sententiae* [L.]; realization; *standpoint;* take; thinking; understanding; visualization; *wisdom; xenodiagnosis;* yaw; *zeal;*

**concern** *(n.)*: apprehension; burden; bother; care; disquiet; *exasperation;* fear; *gloom;* headache; interest; incertitude; insecurities; joint-interest; kiaugh [Scot.]; lather; matter; nervousness; over-anxiety; problem; *quaking;* recking; stress; special interest; trepidation; trouble; uneasiness; vexation; worriment; *xenophobia;* yearning; zeal;

**concern** *(v.)*: appertain; apply; burden; bother; *care;* distress; *eye askance; fret;* get anxious; have anxiety; interest; involve; *jumpy;* kiaugh [Scot.]; *load;* matter; *nervous; over-anxious;* pertain; *quiver;* regard; relate; set on edge; touch; *uneasy; vulnerable;* worry; weigh down; *xfer; yield anxiety; zero in;*

**concerning** *(prep.)*: about; anent [Scot.]; bearing on; *connected with;* directly relating to; *encompassing;* for; *gist;* having to do with; involving; *joining; known;* linking; *meant; namely;* over; pertaining; *quo ad* [L.]; respecting; regarding; relating to; specifically about; touching; *unto;* vis-à-vis; with reference to; *xref; yoked to; zeroing in;*

**concert** *(n.)*: *act;* band ~; benefit; cantata; caberet; choral presentation; dinner & show; event; floorshow; gig; hootenanny [slang]; indoor ~; jam session; *kapellmeister [G.];* live performance; music ~; night performance; outdoor ~; performance; *querencia [Sp.];* recital; session; show; theatre show; *upper circle;* vocal ~; *work; xylophone act;* yard show; *zarzuela;*

**concert hall** *(n.)*: arena; amphitheatre; building; coliseum; complex; drama; edifice; field house; grandstand; grounds; hall; *ice rink; judgment hall; kabuki* [Jap.]; lyceum; multiplex; *naumachy* [Rom.]; odeum; playhouse; *pit; querencia* [Sp.]; *ring;* stage; theatre; *upper circle;* venue; *wing; xenodocheum;* yard; *zone;*

**concession** *(n.)*: acknowledgement; acquiescence; admission (of defeat); bowing; bending; buckling; ceding; compromise; confession; dispensation; dedition; eating humble pie; forfeiture; granting; giving in; granting; handover; indulgence; *jumping;* knuckling (under); listening to; making relinquishment; non-resistance; owning up; putting away claim; quadregene; relinquishment; succumbing; sop; surrender; throwing in the towel; *unvictorious;* verbal admission; withdrawal; *xfer;* yieldance; *zero success;*

**conciliate** *(v.)*: appease; becalm; calm; diffuse; ease; *fulfill;* gratify; hush; indulge; *justify; knock down;* lull; make peace; mend fences; mollify; *nullify; overcome;* pacify; quell; reconcile; soothe; tranquilize; unruffle; *vanish;* win favor; *x-out; yield; zeroize;*

**concise** *(adj.)*: abridged; brief; compact; decurtate; economical; fine; *germinal; half-pint; itsy-bitsy; just little; knee-high;* little; laconic; miniature; neat; *of few words;* pithy; pocket-sized; *quick;* reduced; short; succinct; to the point; terse; unloquacious; very small; wee; *XS; yea big; zero;*

**conciseness** *(n.)*: abbreviation; brevity; compactness; diminutiveness; economy; fineness; *germinal; half-pint; itsy-bitsy; just little; knee-high;* laconicalness; minuteness; neatness; over-smallness; pithiness; *quantity;* runtiness; succinctness; terseness; unloquaciousness; *very small;* weeness; *XS; yea big; zero;*

**conclude** *(v.)*: accomplish; assume; bring to an end; close; construe; consummate; *done;* deduce; end; educe; finish; get it done; halt; hypothesize; infer; *judge; kill;* leave off; make an end of; *notion; over;* put an end to; presume; perorate; quit; resolve; reckon; shut; stop; suppose; terminate; *undertake to finish; venture to close;* wrap up; *x-out; yeme; zero question;*

**conclusion** *(n.)*: apogee; bringing to an end; close; closure; consummation; culmination; destination; end; epilogue; finish; finale; fruition; *good bye; hatching;* illation; *judgment;* killing; *limit;* matter's end; *non-continuation;* outcome; peroration; product; quittance; result; resolution; summation; termination; upshot; *verge;* windup; *xy-coordinate;* year-end; *zenith;*

**conclusive** *(adj.)*: absolute; authoritative; beyond doubt; convincing; certain; decisive; definite; desitive; determinate; definitive; ending; final; guaranteed; highly ~; indisputable; *just sure;* keenly sure; last; *mistake-proof;* non-questioned; 100% proven; positive; questionless; reliable; sure; *true;* unquestionable; *verified;* without question; *xtry. sure; yet irrefutable;* zero question;
**conclusiveness** *(n.)*: absoluteness; *beyond doubt;* certainty; decisiveness; definiteness; *ending;* finality; *guaranteed;* high degree of certainty; indisputability; *just sure;* keenness; *last; mistake-proof; non-questioned; 100% proven;* positivity; questionlessness; reliability; sureness; *truth;* unquestionability; verification; wrap-up; xtry. sureness; *yet irrefutable; zero question;*
**concoct** *(v.)*: *analyze;* birth; brew; contrive; cook up; dream up; devise; engineer; fabricate; *get idea;* hatch; invent; *judge;* kiddy; *lucubrate;* make up; *notion;* originate; prepare; plot; *quick; ruminate;* scheme; think (up); *use brain;* vamp up; work up; *xenodiagnose; yeme;* zero in;
**concoction** *(n.)*: admixture; blend; brew; combination; compound; *dash;* elixir; formula; gallimaufry; hodgepodge; intermixture; jumblement; kava; *lumping;* mixture; minglement; *non-homogenous ~;* olio; potion; *quart;* recipe; solution; *temperament;* ule; variety; work; *xanthate;* yanggoma; *zany ~;*
**concourse** *(n.)*: atrium; assembly place; byway; boardwalk; courtyard; domus; esplanade; forecourt; gathering place; hall; *isovist;* junction; *key passageway;* large open space; mall; *node;* open-air court; promenade; quad; rambla; rotunda; square; town square; university ~; *vomitory;* (walk)way; *xyst; yong* [arch.]; zocalo [Mex.];
**concrete** *(n.)*: asphalt ~; *béton brut* [F.]; cement; ducrete; eternit®; fibre cement; geopolymer ~; *glue; hardened ~;* industrial ~; *Jennite; kieselkalk; lift slab construction;* magnesia ~; non-hydaulic cement; *opus mixtum [L.];* pavement; Portland cement; precast ~; quick-setting ~; ready-mix ~; sorel cement; tabby; *unsolidified ~; Vicar morter;* white Portland cement; *xenolith; yieldless;* zinc oxide ~;
**concubine** *(n.)*: *attendant;* bond wife; consort; doxy; enslaved woman; *er nai* [Chin.]; feme-covert; goodwife; handmaid; inferior wife; *jill; kadin* [Mos.]; lover; mistress; non-exclusive wife; odalisque; paramour; *quaedam [arch.]; retained woman;* slave wife; thrall-wife; ux.; *vrouw* [S. Afr.]; wife; *xenobiosis;* yokemate; *zayat;*
**concur** *(v.)*: agree; accede; acquiesce; affirm; accept; authorize; approve; allow; assent; be in accord; back; consent; concur; correlate; condone; cohere; *do;* endorse; *empower;* fall in; *fadge* [arch.]; grant; go along with; homologate; harmonize; *indulge; indicate;* jive [slang]; join; keep; *like-minded;* line up; *match;* nod; okay; permit; quite agree; rapport; ratify; sanction; see eye to eye; synchronize; *togetherness;* unite; understand; *verify;* warrant; *xtry. agreement;* yes; yield; *zealously ~;*
**concurrence** *(n.)*: agreement; bond of harmony; conjunction; consent; *delight;* empathy; fellowship; *getting along with;* harmony; *identification;* joining of forces; keeping; like-mindedness; meeting of the minds; nodding; oneness; predication; *quick to agree;* rapport; solidarity; togetherness; unity; unanimity; *voluntariness;* willingness; xenia; yielding; *zeal;*
**condemn** *(v.)*: accuse; blame; *banish;* convict; damn; doom; destroy; denounce; denunciate; deprecate; exprobate; foredoom; *guilty;* hold responsible; *hang;* interdict; judge; *knock; kill;* lambaste; make one pay; *non-innocence;* ordain punishment; proscribe; punish; *quash;* reprobate; ruin; sentence; traduce; upbraid; vitiate; wreck; *xci.; yell at; zero out;*
**condemnation** *(n.)*: attainder; annihilation; blame; censure; conviction; denunciation; damnation; doom; death penalty; excoriation; fall; guilt; *gallows; hell;* indicting; judgment; just recompense; *killing; liability; mortality;* nemesis; opprobrium; proscription; perdition; punishment; *qua [L.];* reprobation; ruination; retribution; reprobation; sentence; *torment; undoing;* verdict; vitiation; wreck; x-out; *yelling; zapping;* [*see* hell; tribulation; judgment]
**condemnatory** *(adj.)*: accusatory; belittling; censorious; condemning; critical; disapproving; disparaging; damnatory; damnable; *explosive;* fault-finding; griping; hypercritical; impugning; judgmental; knocking; lambasting; *mean;* negative; overcritical; pejorative; *querulous;* rebukeful; scornful; traducent; unfavorable; vindictive; whingy; *xenophobic;* yauping; zoilean;

**condense** *(v.)*: attenuate; abridge; become smaller; contract; constrict; densen; downsize; extenuate; encapsulate; filter; get littler; *halve; improve; jump down;* knock down; lose weight; make thinner; narrow; *omit;* pack down; quail; reduce; slenderize; shorten; squeeze; thin; *undersized; vanish;* wane; waste; *XS; yield;* zeroize;

**condescend** *(v.)*: abase; bend down; come down; deign; descend; *evacuate; forfeit;* go down; humble oneself; imbrute; *jackalent; knock down;* lower oneself; make lower; *non-retention;* oblige; patronize; *quail;* recede; *reduce;* stoop; take down; unbend; vouchsafe; *wane; x-cend;* yield; *zero arrogance;*

**condescending** *(adj.)*: arrogant; big-headed; contemptuous; disdainful; egotistical; fastuous; gloating; haughty; imperious; jibing; knocking; lofty; mocking; narcissistic; overweening; patronizing; quick-to-boast; ridiculing; scornful; superior; turgid; uppity; vain; wrapped up in oneself; *x-proud; yelping; zero humility;*

**condescension** *(n. disdain)*: arrogance; bigheadedness; contempt; disdain; egotism; flatulence; gloating; hauteur; imperiousness; jibing; knocking; loftiness; magisterialness; narcissism; overconfidence; pomposity; *quilicom* [arch.]; *ruff* [arch.]; smugness; self-importance; snobbery; turgidity; unkindness; vanity; wind; *xenophobia; yieldless; zero humility;*

**condescension** *(n. stooping)*: abasement; bending down; coming down; deigning; *evacuation; forfeiting;* going down; humbling; ignominy; *jackalent; knocking down;* lowering; making lower; *non-retention; obsequious;* patronizing; *quail;* receding; resignation; stooping; taking down; *underneath one's place; vouchsafe;* willing submission; *x-cend;* yielding; *zero arrogance;*

**condition** *(n. state)*: attribute; ailment; being; circumstance; *details; development;* estate; fashion; fitness; guise; happening; incident; juncture; *jam;* kilter; lot; manner; mode; *nightmare;* order; particulars; posture; place; predicament; plight; position; quality; repair; situation; state (of being); status; standing; shape; tenor; tone; *usefulness;* vein; way; *xenenthesis; yowler; zinger;*

**condition** *(n. stipulation)*: *adjuration;* basic qualification; criterion; caveat; determining factor; demand; expectation; find point; ground rules; habilitation; indispensable criterion; *juration;* key factor; limitation; must; mandate; necessity; *obligation;* prerequisite; proviso; provision; qualification; requirement; rider; restriction; stipulation; specification; terms; ultimatum; vital qualification; want; *XO requirement; yarking; zero option;*

**conditional** *(adj.)*: according to terms; bound by; contingent; circumstantial; dependent; depending; *expectation; first prerequisite;* gauging; hypothetical; *if; just if; key factor;* limited by; *must;* non-automatic; *only if;* provisory; provisional; predicated on; qualified; reliant; restricted; stipulatory; subject; static; situational; *terms;* upon conditions met; *vital qualification;* with a condition; *XO requirement; yet ~; zeroing in;*

**condone** *(v.)*: agree with; accede; acquiesce; affirm; accept; authorize; approve; allow; assent; be in accord; back up; consent; concur; correlate; condone; cohere; *do;* endorse; *empower;* fall in; *fadge* [arch.]; grant; go along with; homologate; harmonize; *indulge; indicate;* jive [slang]; join; keep; *like-minded;* line up; *match;* nod; overlook; permit; quite agree; rapport; ratify; sanction; see eye to eye; synchronize; tolerate; think it okay; unite; understand; *verify;* warrant; *x on the dotted line;* yes; yea-say; *zealously ~;* [*Ant.* challenge]

**conducive** *(adj.)*: aidful; advantageous; beneficial; contributing; conducible; *does;* expedient; encouraging; favorable; fostering; good; helpful; inservient; instrumental; *judicious; keen;* leading to; *meet; non-harmful;* operative; promoting; *quartful* [arch.]; resulting in; serving; tending to; useful; viable; workable; *xtr. helpful;* yieldful; *zero harm;* [*Ant.* cumbering]

**conductor** *(n.)*: artiste; bandmaster; choir director; choirmaster; director; ensemble director; *first;* guide; head; *individual;* jam-leader; kapellmeister; leader; maestro; music-master; *manuductor; nipilersortuni ussersortuusoq* [Greenlandic]; *orchestrator;* precentor; quirister; régisseur; songleader; *top banana* [joc.]; *utingo* [Swahili]; *veteran ~;* wind ensemble director; *Xenakis; yard foreman; zouk;*

**conduit** *(n.)*: aqueduct; black pipe; channel; duct; electrical ~; flume; gutter; groove; hosepipe; irrigation canal; *j-bend pipe; kyle;* line; main; nullah; outlet; pipe; *quill* [arch.]; route; steel pipe; spillway; tube; trench; *underground pipeline;* ventiduct; water pipe; way; *x-ray tube; Y-branch; zanja;*
**confederacy** *(n.)*: alliance; brotherhood; confederation; coalition; defense alliance; establishment; federation; guild; group; *help;* incorporation; joint coalition; *kongsi* [Chin.]; league; mutual agreement; nexus; organization; partnership; quinquevirate; *regiment;* society; troop; treaty; union; *vow;* working alliance; *x-class;* yoke; yeald; zollverein;
**confederate** *(adj.)*: allied; affiliated; bound; confederative; *deal; entente;* federated; *group; help;* in league; joined; *kith [pl.]; league; linked;* mutually bound; *nexus;* oath-bound; partnered; *quinquevirate; regiment;* supporter; teammate; united; voice; working together; *xenophile;* yokefellow; *zealous friend;*
**confederation** *(n.)*: association; alliance; brotherhood; bloc; cartel; coalition; confederacy; *deal;* entente; federation; group; *helping;* indenture; joint coalition; kinship; league; mutual agreement; *misalliance;* nexus; organization; partnership; pact; quinquevirate; *rapport;* society; treaty; understanding; union; *vow;* working agreement; *x-treaty;* yoke; *zonal agreement;*
**confer** *(v. discuss)*: advise; bear hearts; collogue; consult; discuss; exchange words; *fraternize;* gab; huddle; interact; *jangle; key discussion; little chat;* meet about; negotiate; *outtalk;* parley; *quarrel;* reason; speak; talk over; *utter; vocalize; words; xenophonia;* yak; *zero in;*
**confer** *(v. give)*: award; bestow; commit; deliver; endow; furnish; give; grant; hand (over); impart; *join to;* kit; lavish; mete; *non-retention;* offer; present; *quicken;* render; supply; transfer; unhand; vest; *will;* xfer; yield; *zip;* [*Ant.* confiscate]
**conference** *(n.)*: assembly; business meeting; convention; consultation; discussion; encounter; forgathering; forum; gathering; group discussion; huddle; interchange; *jangle;* kit [coll.]; *little chat;* meeting; negotiations; oral treaty; public meeting; parley; powwow; quadrilogue; round table; session; summit; symposium; talks; *union meeting; vestry; videoconference;* words; *x.;* yarn; *zero in;*
**confess** *(v.)*: admit; acknowledge; broadcast; come clean; concede; declare; disclose; express; fess up; give; grant; hold forth; indicate; inform; *jaw; key in;* let it be known; make known; noise; notify; own up; proclaim; profess; quoth; relate; *realize;* shrive; state; tell; take the blame; utter; voice; word; *xenagogy;* yield; *zero in;* [*Ant.* contradict]
**confession** *(n.)*: admission; acknowledgement; affirmation; *belief;* concession; disclosure; declaration; exposure; fessing up [improper]; *granting;* guilt; held; honesty; indication; jurat; *keeping; lining up;* making known; notification; owning up; profession; *question-and-answer;* report; reassurance; shrift; statement; self-conviction; testimonial; utterance; ule; verification; witness; *xenagogy; yielding; zero in;* [*Ant.* contradiction]
**confide** *(v.)*: admit; believe in; confess; count on; depend on; disclose; entrust; *faith; give;* have faith in; intimate; *judge faithful; keep a secret;* let one know; *mention; never doubt; overconfidence;* privately tell; *questionless;* rely on; share a confidence; trust; tell secret; unload; *voice;* whisper; xfer; *y'faith [arch.]; zero doubt;*
**confidence** *(n.)*: assurance; belief; boldness; conviction; certainty; credulity; dependence; entrusting; faith; *guarantee;* hope; *inspiration; just believe;* knowledge; *looking to; mainstay;* non-doubt; *over~;* persuasion; questionlessness; reliance; resting assured; rock-solid faith; sureness; trust; undauntedness; unwavering faith; utter ~; *vow;* warrant; *xel [arch.]; y'faith [arch.]; zeal;* [*Ant.* consternation]
**confident** *(adj.)*: aplomb; assured; assertive; bold; certain; convinced; composed; calm; cool; collected; doughty; dogmatic; ever- ~; fearless; firm; fully assured; grave; gallant; heroic; intrepid; *jarless; knightly;* lion-hearted; manly; never-fearing; obstinate; positive; poised; questful; resolute; reliant; sure; self-assured; sanguine; staid; trusting; temerarious; unafraid; unworried; very sure; wholly certain; *xtry.;* yare; zealous;

**confidential** *(adj.)*: arcane; *behind-the-scenes;* classified; concealed; dark; exclusive; furtive; guarded; hush-hush; intside; *just between us;* known only to a few; *locked;* mysterious; non-public; off-the-record; private; privileged; *quiet;* restricted; secret; sensitive; top-secret; undisclosed; veiled; *wary; xeno-; yieldless; zero sharing;*

**configure** *(v.)*: arrange; build up; constitute; design; distribute; *engineer;* fix; form; group; *have; index; jury-rig; key to;* lay out; make; *nicely order;* order; organize; place; put in order; *qualify;* rearrange; set up; *tabulate;* unitize; *valuate;* work; *xfer; yield;* zet [dial.];

**confine** *(v.)*: arrest; bind; capture; curb; detain; encage; fence; fetter; guard; hold; imprison; incarcerate; jail; keep; lock up; localize; limit; *manacle;* nab; *on ice;* pen; quarantine; restrict; restrain; shut one up; sequester; seclude; take into custody; *under lock and key; vile durance; ward; x.;* yard; *zone;*

**confinement** *(n.)*: arrest; binding; capture; captivity; detention; encaging; fettering; guarding; holding; imprisonment; incarceration; jail; keeping; locking up; *manacling; non-freedom; on ice;* prison; quarantine; restriction; restraint; sequestering; seclusion; taking into custody; *under lock and key;* vile durance; withholding; *x.;* yarding; *zone;*

**confirm** *(v.)*: affirm; acknowledge; attest; bear out; corroborate; declare; establish; ensure; fix; guarantee; hold forth; indicate; justify; *key in;* let out; make known; notify; own up; proclaim; *quoth;* reassure; substantiate; tell; uphold; verify; validate; warrant; *xenagogy; yield; zero in;* [Ant. contradict]

**confirmation** *(n.)*: affirmation; attestation; assurance; authentication; bearing out; corroboration; confession; declaration; evidence; final verification; guarantee; homologation; indication; jurat; *keeping;* legitimization; *message;* notification; okay; proof; *questionless;* reconfirmation; reassurance; substantiation; testimonial; upholding; verification; witness; x-certification; yeme; *zero doubt;* [Ant. contradiction]

**confiscate** *(v.)*: appropriate; betake; commandeer; dispossess; divest; expropriate; *force;* grab; haul away; impound; *just take;* keep; lay hold on; make off with; nab; obtain; procure; *quirk;* requisition; seize; sequester; take; *use; vest;* wrest; xfer; yank; zip away; [Ant. confer]

**confiscation** *(n.)*: appropriation; attainder; betaking; commandeering; dispossession; divesting; expropriation; *force;* grabbing; hauling away; impounding; *just taking;* keeping; laying hold on; making off with; nabbing; obtaining; procurement; *quirk;* requisitioning; seizure; sequestering; taking; *using; vesting;* wresting; xfer; yanking; zipping away; [Ant. conferral]

**conflict** *(n.)*: argument; altercation; battle; bout; confrontation; contention; clash; dispute; disagreement; encounter; fight; *gunnery;* hostilities; *imbroglio; jihad* [Mos.]; *kampf* [G.]; *luctation* [arch.]; mêlée; *non-agreement;* occursion; *position warfare;* quarrel; run-in; struggle; strife; tussle; unrest; vying; war(fare); *x-fire; yed; zero concord;* [Ant. concord]

**conform** *(v.)*: acquiesce; agree; bend; comply; do; execute; fit; follow; give in to; heed; *indulge;* jump (to it); kowtow; knuckle (under); listen to; match; mold; not resist; obey; observe; perform; *questionless;* relent; succumb; shape; toe the line; undertake; *vigorously obey; work; wholly ~; xlate;* yield; zip to it;

**conformist** *(n.)*: acquiescent one; Babbit; conformer; *do like everyone else;* emulator; follower; *go wuth the flow;* heeder; *indulger; just alike;* kowtower; *listener;* mold-fitter; mimick; non-resister; one of the group; parrot; *questionless; relenter;* sheep; traditionalist; *undertaker; very obedient; willing conformer; xerograph;* yes-man; yielder; *zero variance;*

**conformity** *(n.)*: acquiescence; agreement; bending; compliance; doing; execution; fitting; following; giving in; heeding; *implementation; jumping on it;* kowtowing; listening; matching; molding; non-resistance; obedience; performance; *questionlessness;* relenting; succumbing; toeing the line; undertaking; *vigorous compliance; work; xlation;* yieldedness; *zeal;*

**confound** *(v.)*: addle; baffle; confuse; disconcert; *entangle;* flummox; fluster; gravel; hamper; *incoherent;* jumble; kittle; lose; mystify; *mind-boggling;* nonplus; obscure; pother; perplex; quiz; *ravel;* stump; scramble; tangle; unsettle; vex; wilder; *x; yo-yo; zero understanding;*

**confront** *(v.)*: accost; battle; buttonhole; challenge; contend with; deal with; encounter; face; grapple; handle; *intercept; join; kill;* look toward; lie opposite; meet; nobble; oppose; *put up fight;* query; rencounter; reckon with; stand face-to-face; tackle; undertake; verge on; war against; *x-purposes; yain* [arch.]; *zero in;* [*Ant.* circumvent]

**confrontation** *(n.)*: argument; bout; conflict; dispute; encounter; face-off; fight; grappling; hostility; *imbroglio; jarring; kampf* [G.]; *luctation* [arch.]; mêlée; nobbling; opposition; *punches;* quarrel; run-in; strife; showdown; tussle; unrest; vying; war; *x-fire;* yed; *zero agreement;* [*Ant.* circumvention]

**confrontational** *(adj.)*: argumentative; belligerent; contentious; disagreeable; emulous; fractious; gainsaying; hot-tempered; irascible; jangly; knaggy; *loud-mouthed; litigious;* mean; nasty; objectionable; pugnacious; quarrelsome; resistant; striving; temperamental; umbrageous; vying; wranglesome; *xenophobic;* yieldless; *za-zum* [Rus.]; [*Ant.* concordant]

**confuse** *(v.)*: addle; bewilder; boggle; confound; disorient; discomfit; embroil; entangle; fuddle; foil; gravel; hamper; intermix; jumble; kittle; lose; mystify; mix up; muddle; nonplus; obscure; puzzle; perplex; quiz; *ravel;* stump; scramble; tangle; *unorganized;* vex; wilder; *x; yo-yo; zero understanding;*

**confused** *(adj.)*: addled; addlepated; bewildered; baffled; boggled; bemused; befuddled; confounded; disorderly; discomfited; dazed; discombobulated; *exasperated; entangled;* fascinated; foggy; graveled; habnab; hazy; incoherent; jumbled; *kapakari* [Haw.]; *lost;* mystified; messed up; muzzy; nonplussed; overly ~; puzzled; perplexed; pixilated; pothered; quizzical; *quandary;* raveled; stumped; troubled; tangled; turbid; unorderly; unorganized; unarranged; vexed; wildered; *x'ed; yo-yo; zany;*

**confusion** *(n.)*: anarchy; bewilderment; bedlam; chaos; disorder; discombobulation; entanglement; farrago; gastness; havoc; incomprehension; jumble; kerfuffle; lunacy; mystification; mayhem; mix-up; non-orderliness; obscurity; puzzlement; pandemonium; questionability; restlessness; stupefaction; snafu; turmoil; tumult; tizzy; uncertainty; upheaval; vexation; wilderment; xtry. mess; *yo-yo;* zoo; [*Ant.* comprehension]

**confutation** *(n.)*: annulment; *breaking;* controverting; disproof; exclusion; falsification; gainsaying; having disproved; invalidation; *junking; knocking out; licking; mastery;* negation; overthrow; proving false; quashing; refutation; repudiation; subversion; *trouncing;* undoing; vitiation; voidance; *whipping;* x-ing out; *yanking down;* zeroization; [*Ant.* confirmation]

**confute** *(v.)*: annul; *break;* controvert; disprove; exclude; falsify; gainsay; have disproved; invalidate; *junk; knock out; lick; mastery;* negate; overthrow; overturn; prove false; quash; refute; repudiate; subvert; *trounce;* undo; vitiate; void; *whip;* x; *yank down;* zeroize; [*Ant.* confirm]

**congeal** *(v.)*: alter; become hard; congeal; densify; *engross* [arch.]; firm up; gel(atinize); harden; incrassate; jell(y); knot; lump; make hard; *non-fluid;* obdure; pectize; quarle; regelate; set; thicken; *unyielding; variate;* waulk; *xerogel;* yearn; zet [dial.];

**congenial** *(adj.)*: amiable; affable; benevolent; cordial; delightful; extroverted; friendly; genial; gregarious; hospitable; intimate; jovial; kindly; likable; mellow; neighborly; nice; outgoing; pleasant; polite; *quilting bee;* responsive; sociable; *thoughtful;* uplifting; very friendly; warm; xenial; *yokefellow;* zealous; [*Ant.* contentious]

**congest** *(v.)*: accumulate; build; crowd; densen; enlarge; *fatten;* gather; grow; heap up; hoard; increase; jam(-pack); *keep growing;* lay up; largen; multiply; mount; *number;* overcrowd; pile up; *quadruplicate;* rise; reposit; save; store up; *strengthen;* take off; upbuild; *volume;* wax larger; XL; *yain* [arch.]; *zoom;*

**congestion** *(n.)*: accumulation; amassment; buildup; collection; deposit; enlargement; forgathering; gathering; hoarding; ingathering; jam; kit [coll.]; lot; mass; number; overflow; pack; quantity; ruck; swarm; throng; traffic; *unit; variety;* wheen; XL; *yelm; zoo;*

**conglomerate** *(v.)*: amass; build; collect; draw together; enlarge; *fatten;* gather; grow; hoard; increase; *jump up;* knot; lay up; mass together; *number;* overgrow; pile up; *quadruplicate;* reposit; store up; stockpile; take off; upbuild; *volume;* wax larger; XL; *yain* [arch.]; *zone;*

**conglomeration** *(n.)*: accumulation; buildup; collection; deposit; enlargement; forgathering; group; growth; gathering; hoard; heap; ingathering; jam [slang]; kit [coll.]; lot; mass; multitude; number; overflow; pack; quantity; ruck; set; session; squad; swarm; throng; turnout; troop; tribe; unit; variety; vestry; wisp; wheen; *XL; yelm; zoo;*
**congratulate** *(v.)*: applaud; bless; *best wishes;* compliment; commend; do honor; encourage; felicitate; give honor; honor; *idolize; jubilate; kudos;* laud; magnify; *note;* overpraise; praise; *quite pleased;* recognize; salute; tout; uplift; venerate; *way to go; xtry.; yichus;* zealously commend; [*Ant.* censure]
**congratulatory** *(adj.)*: appreciative; admiring; acclamatory; *best wishes;* complimentary; celebratory; *devoted; eclat;* fulsome; flattering; glowing; honoring; *idolizing; jubilation; kudos;* laudatory; magnifying; *nice; overly flattering;* praiseful; *quite pleased;* raving; sycophantic; *special;* triumphant; uplifting; venerating; *well-received; xtry.; yichus; zealous;*
**congregant** *(n.)*: attender; believer; brother [masc.]; church member; disciple; *elect;* faithful attender; goer; *holy roller [derog.];* ingatherer; *Jehovist;* kirsen [dial.]; layman; member; *non-clergy;* oblate; parishioner; *quickened;* regular; saint; tither; *unshackled;* votary; worshiper; *Xn.; Yahwist; Zionite;*
**congregate** *(v.)*: assemble; amass; bring together; convene; converge; come together; draw together; embody; flock; gather; have a meeting; *include;* join; *knit;* link up; meet; *negotiate;* organize; overcrowd; put together; *quorum;* rally; reconvene; *summon; socialize;* turn out; unite; *visit; work together; x.; yoke; zone;*
**congregation** *(n.)*: assembly; body; convention; church; diet; embodiment; *ekklesia* [G.]; forgathering; flock; gathering; group; horde; ingathering; jam [coll.]; kit [coll.]; lot; meeting; *number;* organization; people; party; plenum; quorum; rally; roundup; regathering; session; throng; turnout; unit; vestry; *worshipers; work; x.; yain* [arch.]; *zayat* [Burm.];
**congress** *(n.)*: assemblage; body of legislators; convocation; diet; *envoys;* forgathering; government; house; *ingathering; judiciary; king;* legislature; lower house; members of congress; national assembly; *Oireachtas* [Ire.]; parliament; *quorum;* representatives; senate; session; *turnout;* upper house; *vote; witan; xenarchy; yield; zet* [dial.];
**congressional** *(adj.)*: *administrative;* bicameral; congress-related; deliberative; enacting; *federal;* governmental; heteronomous; *institutional;* judicatory; *kakistocratically;* legislative; *mayoral;* nomothetic; ordaining; parliamentary; *quasi-legislative;* representative; rule-making; senatorial; *town council;* unicameral; voter-elected; *ward; xenocratic; yard; zemstvo* [Rus.];
**congressman** *(n.)*: assemblyman; *bureaucrat;* counselor; diet member; elder; elected representative; floor leader; governmental leader; *house leader; individual; jurisdiction;* Kentucky ~; legislator; lawmaker; member of congress; *nomothetic; official;* parliament member; *politician; qualified;* representative; senator; statesman; solon; *Tennessee* ~; upper house member; *voter; Wyoming* ~; *xenarch; yes-man; zealous* ~;
**congruence** *(n.)*: agreement; balance; congruity; congruency; consistency; *duplication;* equivalence; *fitness; goodness;* harmony; identicalness; *just alike;* keeping; likeness; match; non-difference; oneness; parity; quits; resemblance; sameness; similarity; *togetherness;* uniformity; *very similar; with; xenia; yielding; zero difference;*
**congruent** *(adj.)*: agreeing; balanced; congruous; duplicate; equivalent; *fit; good;* harmonious; identical; *just alike;* kindred; like; matching; non-differing; *one;* parallel; *quae est eadem* [L.]; resembling; similar; tantamount; uniform; very similar; *with; xerographed;* yes; *zero difference;* [*Ant.* contradistinct]
**congruous** *(adj.)*: agreeable; befitting; congruent; corresponding; due; euphonic; fitting; good; harmonious; idoneous; justifiable; *kosher;* like-minded; matching; nice; obliging; proper; qualified; right; suitable; synchronous; *tolerable;* unisonous; valid; well-suited; *xtry.;* yummy; *zero incongruity;* [*Ant.* contradistinctive]

**conical** *(adj.)*: A-frame; bristlecone; conic; cone-shaped; coniform; deltoid; *equilaterally triangular;* funnel-shaped; geographically ~; hastate; *isosceles;* jib-shaped; *knee pine;* leg-of-mutton; *monterey pine;* narrowing; outspreading; pineal; pyramidal; pointed; quartzoidal; *reducing;* sagittate; tapered; triangular; *umbrella pine; V-shaped;* wedge-shaped; *X-mas tree shaped [off.]; yellow pine; zanthoxylum;*
**conjure** *(v.)*: adjure; bring up; bid; call up; desire; evoke; entreat; *force; go to; have come;* invoke; *jurate; kneel to;* lift up one's voice to; muster up; *need;* obsecrate; petition; pray; *quiritation;* raise; summon; trouble; urge; *voodoo;* wish; *xylomance;* yearn for; *zealously plead;*
**connect** *(v.)*: attach; affix; adhere; anchor; bind; bond; bolt; conjoin; combine; clasp; couple; clinch; chain; catenate; dovetail; engraft; fasten; fix; fuse; glue; hitch; hinge; interlock; interlink; interconnect; infix; ingraft; implant; inosculate; join; jack into; knit; knot; link; latch; lace; marry; merge; mount; nitch [Scot.]; *nail; oxreim;* put together; plug in; *quasi-fuse;* relate; reunite; stick; secure; splice; set to; tie; tack; unite; *vise;* wed; weld; *xenograft;* yoke; zip; [*Ant.* cleave]
**connection** *(n.)*: attachment; affixation; appending; annexation; association; bond; concominance; dovetail; *elbow joint;* fuse; fitment; *graft;* hookup; installation; joining; joint; jack; juncture; knitting; link; *league;* linkup; marriage; nexus; outlet; plug-in; *quasi-fuse;* relation; *reattachment;* securing; splice; tie; union; *vise;* wedding; weld; *xenograft;* yoke; *zipping together;* [*Ant.* cleaving]
**connective** *(adj.)*: attaching; binding; connecting; conjunctive; copular; *dovetailing; engrafting;* fastening; *grafting;* hinge; interconnecting; joining; *knitting;* linking; mounting; *nitch [Scot.];* oxreim; pairing; *quasi-fuse;* relative; securing; tying; uniting; *vise;* wedding; *xenograft;* yoking; *zip together;*
**connive** *(v.)*: *analyze;* birth; concoct; contrive; cook up; devise; engineer; formulate; *get;* hatch; invent; *judge;* kiddy; *lucubrate;* manipulate; machinate; *notion;* originate; plot; plan; quick-plot; *ruminate;* scheme; think (up); *use brain; visualize;* work up; *xenodiagnose; yeme;* zero in;
**conniver** *(n.)*: allurer; beguiler; concoctor; deviser; ensnarer; formulator; guiler; hatcher; inventor; jesuit; knave; *liar;* manipulator; misleader; machinator; *no-good;* originator; plotter; planner; quacksalver; rook; schemer; thinker; trickster; *untruther;* verneuker; wheeler-dealer; *xgressor; yentzer* [Heb.]; *zinger;*
**connoisseur** *(n.)*: authority; buff; *chief;* doyen; epicure; expert; *food ~;* gourmet; *hotshot; in the know;* judge; knowledgeable person; leader; master; maven; notable expert; one expert in; professional; *qualified;* recognized authority; specialist; taster; uncontested master; veteran; wonk; whiz; *xtry. judge; yeoman; zealous ~;*
**connotation** *(n.)*: association; betokening; connoting; denotation; essence; *foreshadow;* gist; intension; hint; implication; *jab; know; leading into;* meaning; nuance; overtone; postulation; quiddit; reference; sense; suggestion; touch; undertone; undercurrent; vague inference; *winking; xfer; yammering; zay;*
**conquer** *(v.)*: annihilate; *annex;* beat; crush; capture; defeat; expugn; foil; fell; flatten; *gut;* hammer; *invincible; junk [slang];* kill; knock out; lick; master; *massacre; neutralize;* overcome (-power; -take; -run); obliterate; prevail; quench; quash; rout; raze; subjugate; subdue; smite; subject; surmount; triumph (over); trounce; take (over); unseat; vanquish; win; worst; whip; *x-out; yank down;* zap; [*Ant.* capitulate]
**conqueror** *(n.)*: award-winner; beater; champion; defeater; expugner; frontrunner; *great;* hero; *invader; jubilant;* kemp; laureate; master; non-loser; overcomer; prevailer; *quasher; ruler;* subduer; subjugator; triumpher; undefeated champ; vanquisher; victor; winner; *xtry.; yell; zealous;* [*Ant.* conquered]
**conquest** *(n.)*: acquisition; annexation; *buyout;* capture; domination; expugnation; *feat;* grab; gain; *historic victory;* invasion; *jump on;* knockout; *lordship;* military ~; *marching in;* national takeover; overthrow; occupation; overtaking; prevailing; *quest;* routing; re- ~; seizure; subjugation; takeover; *upheaval;* victory; win; *xfer; yong [arch.];* zapping; [*Ant.* capitulation]
**conscience** *(n.)*: ability to judge right and wrong; better judgment; consciousness; *deem;* ethics; feeling; God-given ~; heart; inner light; judgment; knowledge of right from wrong; light; moral sense; natural sense of right; *open eyes;* principles; qualm; *realization;* sense of right; scruples; spirit; superego; *twinge;* understanding of right and wrong; voice of ~; *within; xenenthesis; yearning; zoe [Gr.];*

**conscientious** *(adj.)*: assiduous; busy; careful; diligent; exacting; fastidious; *great detail;* hard-working; industrious; just so; keen; laborious; meticulous; nit-picking; onerous; over~; painstaking; *quiddle;* rigorous; scrupulous; solicitous; thorough; tedious; upstanding; vigilant; *wholehearted;* xtry.; *yare; zealous;* [*Ant.* careless]

**conscious** *(adj.)*: awake; aware; bestirred; cognizant; disquieted; *excited;* focused; *gotten up; heedful; incited; jarred;* knowing; liminal; mindful; *non-ignorant;* out of bed; open-eyed; perceptive; quickened; responsive; sentient; supraliminal; *thoughtful;* up; understanding; vivified; wakened; wakeful; wide-awake; *xuld [arch.];* yet ~; zoetic; [*Ant.* comatose]

**consciousness** *(n.)*: awareness; *bethink;* cognizance; discernment; *ever-mindful;* faculties; grasp; *heedful;* insomnolence; *judiciousness;* knowledge; leeriness; mindfulness; notice; observance; perception; quick-wittedness; responsiveness; realization; recognition; sense; thoughtfulness; understanding; vigilance; wakefulness; *x-careful;* yare-handed; *zärtlich [G.];*

**consecrate** *(v.)*: anoint; bless; cleanse; commit; devote; dedicate; depurate; expurgate; *favor; give over;* hallow; *invest; jalap; keep separate;* lustrate; make holy; *nard;* ordain; purify; *quicken; re~;* set apart; solemnize; sanctify; *taintless;* unsully; vest; wash clean; *xfer; yield; zierlich [G.];* [*Ant.* corrupt]

**consecration** *(n.)*: anointing; blessing; cleansing; commitment; dedication; depuration; expurgation; *favor; giving over;* hallowing; *investment; jalap; keeping;* lustration; making holy; *nard;* ordination; purification; *quickening; re~;* setting apart; solemnization; sanctification; *taintless;* unction; vesting; washing clean; *xfer; yielding; zierlich [G.];* [*Ant.* corruption]

**consecutive** *(adj.)*: adjacent; back-to-back; contiguous; directly following; *each following the last:* following each other; *going one before the other;* hard by; in order; joining; kept-together; linked; *mounting;* neighboring; ordered; placed together; *qualtified; repeated;* successive; sequential; succeeding; touching; together; unbroken; *uninterrupted;* verging; without interruption; *xenograft;* yoked; *zero break;*

**consent** *(n.)*: approval; assent; allowance; blessing; consensus; *delight;* endorsement; favor; go-ahead; hear to [reg.]; imprimatur; joint-permission; *knowingly allowed;* license; leave; *liberty; may;* nod; okay; permission; *qualified yes; right;* sufferance; sanction; thumbs up [slang]; unreluctance; vouchsafement; willingness; *x on the dotted line;* yes; *zealous approval;* [*Ant.* condemnation]

**consent** *(v.)*: allow; agree; accede; acquiesce; accept; authorize; approve; allow; assent; bless; concur; correlate; condone; cohere; *do;* endorse; *empower;* fall in; grant; go along with; give permission; have; homologate; indulge; jive [slang]; join; keep; let; make possible; nod; okay; permit; *qualify;* rapport; ratify; suffer; sanction; *tolerate; unhindered; understand;* vouchsafe; warrant; *x on the dotted line;* yield; *zero opposition;* [*Ant.* condemn]

**consequence** *(n.)*: aftermath; aftereffects; backwash; *bring;* consummation; corollary; derivative; development; destiny; effect; end result; eventuality; fruit; *get;* harvest; impact; issue; just desserts; *known outcome;* lattermath; *matter; necessarily;* outcome; outgrowth; product; quantum effect; ramification; result; repercussion; significance; sequent; side effect; termination; upshot; *validity;* work; wake; *xenagogy;* yield; *zeug [G.];* [*see* conclusion]

**conservatism** *(n.)*: anti-liberalness; *Bible-believing;* conventionalism; diehard ~; *ever-conservative;* family-values; *GOP;* hardhat ~; *illiberality;* John Birch; *keeping;* liberal-opposing ~; misoneism; narrow-mindedness; neo~; New Right; old-time values; political ~; preservationism; *quaint;* right-wing; *the* right; standpatism; staunch ~; traditionalism; Toryism; ultra~; *vieux jeu [F.]; way it was;* Xty.; *Young Conservativism; zero liberalness;*

**conservative** *(adj.)*: anti-liberal; *Bible-believing;* conventional; conformist; diehard; ever- ~; fundamentalism; *GOP; God-fearing;* holdout; hardhat; hidebound; imperialist; *John Birch;* keep-it-the-same; long-established; liberal-opposing; misoneist(ic); Middle America; moderate; narrow-minded; neo~; old-fashioned (-school; -line); orthodox; old paths; old guard; politically ~; preservationist; purist; *quaint;* right(-wing); rightist; standpatter; slow-to-change; traditional(ist); traditionist; ultra~; *vieux jeu* [F.]; Victorian; wary; *Xn.; Young Conservative; zero liberalness;* [*see* frugal]

**conserve** *(v.)*: *assure;* be careful; *continue; defend; ever-kept;* fend; guard; hold; insure; *jaga;* keep; look after; maintain; *not jeopardize; ongoing;* protect; preserve; *quia timet [L.];* retain; save; take care of; use sparingly; vallate; withhold; *x-guard; yeme* [arch.]; *zero danger;*
**consider** *(v.)*: analyze; bear in mind; contemplate; deliberate; dwell; evaluate; examine; entertain; figure; gauge; *hypothesize;* imagine; judge; *know; lucubrate;* meditate; mull; *notion; occur;* ponder; question; reflect; reconsider; study; think; use brain; valuate; weigh; *xenodiagnose; yeme; zazen;*
**considerable** *(adj.)*: astronomical; big; colossal; disproportionate; extensive; fat; generous; huge; immense; jumbo-sized; king-size; large; massive; noteworthy; oversized; prodigious; quantitative; real big; sizable; substantial; tremendous; *unbelievable;* voluminous; weighty; XL; *yet uncounted;* zillion;
**considerate** *(adj.)*: attentive; *benevolent;* caring; conscientious; deferential; *endeared; friendly;* gracious; giving; heedful; intentive; *judicious;* kind(-hearted); loving; mindful; nice; observant; polite; qui vive; regardful; sensitive; solicitous; selfless; thoughtful; understanding; very kind; warm; xenial; *yielding; zealous of good works* [Tit. 2:4]; [*Ant.* careless]
**consideration** *(n.)*: attention; brainwork; contemplation; deliberation; evaluation; focus; figuring; graveness; headwork; intellection; judgment; *knowledge;* lucubration; meditation; *notion; on one's mind;* pondering; *questioning;* reflection; rumination; solicitude; study; thought; using one's brain; valuation; weighing; *xenodiagnosis; yeme* [arch.]; *zazen;*
**consign** *(v.)*: assign; bestow; commit; deliver; entrust; forward; give; hand over; issue; *jet over; kit; let; mete; necessitate; obligate;* put in custody; *qualify;* relegate; remit; send; transfer; *unhand;* vest; *with;* xfer; yafe; *zone;* [*Ant.* confiscate]
**consist** *(v.)*: *also;* break down into; comprise; contain; *defined by;* entail; feature; *group;* have; inhere; include; incorporate; *joint; kept; lie;* made of; *necessitate;* own; possess; *quantity; require;* subsist; take in; *under; volume;* within; x.; *yard; zone;*
**consistency** *(n.)*: alikeness; balance; consistence; constancy; coherency; dependability; evenness; faithfulness; fixity; glabriety; homogeny; harmony; invariableness; intransience; *just the same;* kindredness; likeness; *matching;* normalcy; order; predictability; *quae est eadem [L.];* reliability; regularity; steadiness; stability; steadfastness; trustworthiness; uniformity; *verbatim; well-trusted; xerographed; yes;* zero variableness; [*Ant.* capriciousness]
**consistent** *(adj.)*: alike; abiding; balanced; constant; coherent; dependable; even(-keeled); faithful; fixed; *going steady;* homogenous; harmonious; invariable; just the same; kindred; like; lasting; matching; never-failing; ordered; predictable; *quae est eadem* [L.]; reliable; regular; steady; stable; set; steadfast; trustworthy; uniform; unfailing; unfaltering; unswerving; unchanging; unvarying; *verbatim; well-trusted; xerographed; yes; zero variableness;* [*Ant.* capricious]
**consistently** *(adj.)*: always; *balanced;* constantly; conscientiously; continually; dependably; dutifully; devotedly; evenly; every time; faithfully; *going steady;* homogenously; invariably; *just the same; kindred;* loyally; *matching;* never-failingly; *ordered;* predictably; perpetually; perseveringly; *quae est eadem [L.];* reliably; regularly; religiously; strictly; steadily; steadfastly; trustworthily; uniformly; unfailingly; *verbatim;* without fail; *xerographed; yes; zero variance;* [*Ant.* capriciously]
**consolation** *(n.)*: alleviation; bed of roses; comfort; disburdening; ease; fleshpots; great ~; help; indulgence; *joy; kip;* luxury; making one feel better; *non-essential; optimism;* placating; quietude; rest; relief; solace; *taking comfort;* unburdening; voluptuousness; well-being; *x-soft.;* yielding help; *zizziness;*
**console** *(v.)*: assure; becalm; comfort; cheer; condole; disburden; encourage; feel with; give comfort; hearten; inspirit; *jump-start; kindness;* lift; make one feel better; *non-depressed;* offer solace; palliate; *quell;* reassure; relieve; soothe; *take comfort;* unburden; vivify; weep with; *xtr. comfort;* yield help; *zest;*
**consolidate** *(v.)*: amalgamate; bring together; combine; draw together; *entwine;* form into one; fuse; gather; *harden;* integrate; join; knit; link; merge; *network;* organize; put together; *quasi-fuse; relate;* syndicate; tie in; unite; *verge;* weave; *xenograft;* yoke; *zip together;*

**consort** *(n.)*: amoret; beloved; companion; darling; escort; feme-covert; goodwife; honey; helpmeet; intimate; *jealous spouse; kadin* [Mos.]; lover; mate; mistress [fem.]; *nuptial;* other half; partner; *queen- ~; ravish;* sweetheart; spouse; *trusted spouse;* ux [fem.].; *vrouw* [S. Afr.]; wife [both fem.]; *xtry.;* yokemate; *zaftig [fem.];*

**consort** *(v.)*: associate; band; correlate; *dealings; escort;* fraternize; go around; hang out; hobnob; interact; join; *knit;* link; mix; *non-separate; overly fond;* place oneself by; *quite comfortable;* rub elbows; socialize; *tie;* unite; *vise;* work together; *xenograft;* yoke; *zip together;*

**conspicuous** *(adj.)*: apparent; blatant; clear; discernable; evident; eye-catching; flagrant; glaring; *heedless;* in full view; *just plain to see; kenspeckle;* lucid; manifest; marked; noticeable; open; overt; obtrusive; plain; palpable; pointed; quite obvious; recognizable; seeable; salient; shameless; tangible; unmistakable; visible; watchable; well-defined; *x-parent; yare; zero-disguised;* [*Ant.* covert]

**conspiracy** *(n.)*: artifice; *blueprint;* collusion; design; enginery; foredesign; gambit; huggermugger; intrigue; jape; King's gambit; *layout;* machination; *non-loyalty; overthrow;* plot; perfidiousness; *quo mode* [L.]; ruse; scheme; sedition; treachery; *usurpation;* villainy; wile; *x-chart; yantra [Hind.];* zenithal projection;

**conspirator** *(n.)*: accomplice; archtraitor; backstabber; conspirer; caballer; conniver; colluder; deviser; engineer; formulator; guiler; highbinder; inventor; Judas; knave; *lucubrator;* machinator; *no-good;* originator; plotter; Quisling; *rebel;* schemer; subversive; traitor; treasonist; underminer; verneuker; *working against; xenodiagnosis; yentzer [Heb.]; zero in;*

**conspire** *(v.)*: arrange; brew; cabal; connive; collude; devise; engineer; formulate; grift; hatch; invent; jockey; kiddy; lay a plot; machinate; *notion;* originate; plot; *questionable; rig;* scheme; think (up); *unite; visualize;* work against; *xenodiagnose; yeme;* zero in;

**constant** *(adj.)*: abiding; around-the-clock; *breakless;* continual; chronic; daily; endless; even; fixed; going on and on; *hourly;* invariable; *jusqu'au bout* [F.]; *keeps going;* lasting; maintaining; nonstop; never-ending; ongoing; perpetual; *quadrillion;* regular; 'round the clock; steady; twenty-four-hour; unchanging; uninterrupted; unvarying; unrelenting; *vast;* without end; *x-cending;* year-round; *zillion;* [*Ant.* capricious]

**consternation** *(n.)*: anxiety; alarm; bewilderment; concern; dismay; *exasperation;* fear; gloom; horror; insecurity; jitteriness; kiaugh [Scot.]; lather; muddlement; nervousness; over-anxiety; panic; paranoia; quaking; *reluctance;* stress; solicitude; trepidation; terror; uneasiness; vexation; worry; *xenophobia;* yellow-belliedness; *zeallessness;* [*Ant.* calm]

**constitute** *(v.)*: aggregate; become; compose; consist of; comprise; develop; embody; form; *generate; have;* incorporate; *justify; keep; let;* make up; *newly formed; originate;* put together; *quantify; reform;* shape; take shape; *upbuild; vamp; whole; xfer;* yield; *zip together;*

**constitution** *(n. make-up)*: arrangement; articles; being; composition; disposition; essence; framework; formation; general make-up; hypostasis; inherence; *justification; keleusmatic;* law; makeup; nature; organization; *precepts; quintessence;* structure; temperament; *unchangeable law; volume;* wherewithal; *xenenthesis; yu [Chin.]; zoe [Gr.];*

**constitution** *(n. law or code)*: amendment; bylaws; charter; civil code; *directive;* enactment; framework; governing law; *high court; international law; jus gentium* [L.]; *keleusmatic;* law; mandate; national law; *organizational law;* precepts; *penal code; quo minus* [L.]; rules; statute; *tolerated;* U.S. ~; *validity;* word of the law; *XO mandate;* yardstick; *zakon* [Rus.];

**constitutional** *(adj.)*: allowed (by law); *blameless;* correct; *de jure* [F.]; endorsed; formal; good; heteronomous; innocent; judicial; *keen;* legal; *moral; not illegal;* ordained; permitted; *questionless;* rightful; *strict; tolerated;* unprohibited; vested; warranted; *Xn;* yet to be outlawed; *zero problem;*

**constrain** *(v.)*: *admonish;* bear on; bind; compel; drive; exhort; force; *get;* hurry; impel; *justify; knock;* lean on; make; necessitate; oblige; pressure; *quicken;* require; strong-arm; tell; urge; *vie;* weigh upon; *xuld [arch.];* yank; *zealously urge;* [*see* restrict]

**constrict** *(v.)*: apply pressure; bind; contract; compress; draw together; extrude; *force;* grow smaller; *halve;* inhibit; *jam; kibble;* limit; make tighter; narrow; overply; press; quash; restrict; straiten; squeeze; tighten; *uncomfortable; vice;* wring; *xuld* [arch.]; *yote; zeroize;*

**construct** *(v.)*: assemble; build; create; confect; develop; erect; fabricate; form; generate; *hew; institute; job;* knock together; *labor;* make; *new-built;* originate; output; produce; put together; quick-build; raise; shape; turn out; upbuild; *vamp;* wage; *x-build;* yield; zip together;

**construction** *(n.)*: assembling; building; constructing; development; erection; edification; fabrication; forming; generation; house-building; *industry; job;* knocking together; *labor;* making; *new-built;* origination; putting together; *quick-built;* raising; shaping; turning out; upbuilding; *vamp;* work; *x-building;* yielding; zipping together; [*Ant.* collapse]

**constructive** *(adj.)*: advantageous; beneficial; conducive; definitional; edifying; furthersome; favorable; gainful; good; helpful; instrumental; *jim dandy;* keen; *lucrative; mutually beneficial;* nice; *outstanding;* profitable; productive; *quality; rewarding;* salutary; tending to; useful; valuable; worthwhile; xtry.; yieldful; *zero problem;*

**construe** *(v.)*: assume; believe; conclude; deduce; evaluate; figure (out); gather; get; *hypothesize;* interpret; infer; judge; *know; led to believe;* make out; *notion; occur;* perceive; presume; *qualified judgment;* read; see; take; understand; *view;* work out; *xlate; yeme; zero in;*

**consult** *(v.)*: ask; bid advice; check with; confer; discuss; enquire of; find out; *get opinion; have ~ation;* inquire; *just ask; know;* look to; make inquiry; *negotiate; obsecrate;* prevail upon; query; request opinion; refer to; seek advice; take counsel; *use; venture to ask;* want opinion; *x; yearn for counsel; zet* [dial.];

**consultation** *(n.)*: advice; advisement; *beseeching;* counsel; conference; direction; deliberation; expert opinion; free advice; guidance; hortation; instruction; judgment; *kibizing* [Yid.]; leading; meeting; *notification;* opinion; piece of advice; *quick advice;* recommendation; session; talk; *urging;* voice; word of advice; *xenagogy; yammering; zeroing in;*

**consume** *(v.)*: annihilate; burn up; crush; destroy; devour; expend; eat (up); finish off; go through; have; incinerate; *junk;* kill; lay waste; *mangle;* neutralize; obliterate; put away; quash; ruin; ravage; spend; spoil; take away; use up; vitiate; waste; *x-ing;* yank down; zap; [*Ant.* conserve]

**consummate** *(adj.)*: accomplished; brought to fruition; complete(d); culminate; concluded; done; ended; finished; fulfilled; get done; *have; implement; just finished; kept; long-awaited;* mature; made complete; *non-deficient;* over; perfect; *qualified;* resolved; *settled;* thorough; total; unsurpassed; utter; virtuosic; whole; *xtry.; yare;* zenithal;

**consummate** *(v.)*: accomplish; bring to fruition; complete; conclude; do; effectuate; finalize; get done; *have;* implement; *justify; keep; let;* make an end of; nail it; *over;* perform; *qualify;* reach; realize; resolve; see it through; tie down; *undertake; victory;* wrap up; *xfer; yare; zero deficiency;* [*Ant.* cancel]

**contact** *(n.)*: association; brushing against; contingence; connection; communication; depression; embosoming; feeling; getting in touch; handling; intersection; *juncture;* kissing; light ~; meeting; *nexus; overhandle;* physical ~; *quab;* reaching; stroking; touching; union; verbal communication; writing; *xmission; yoke; zero gap;*

**contact** *(v.)*: affect; brush against; connect; communicate; depress; embosom; feel; get in touch; handle; intersect; *juncture;* kiss; lightly touch; meet; *nab; overhandle;* pat; quab; reach; rub; stroke; touch (base); *use;* verbally communicate; write; *xmit; yank; zonk;*

**contagious** *(adj.)*: able to be passed; *breeding;* contaminating; catching; communicable; contractible; *disease;* easily-transmitted; *foul;* givable; gettable; *horrible;* infective; infectuous; *jading; known to be ~;* life-threatening; multiplying; non-contained; overspreading; pestiferous; *quick-spreading; rabid;* spreadable; transmittable; uncontained; very ~; *wreak; xfer; yet ~; zoonosis;*

**contain** *(v.)*: accommodate; box in; comprise; *draw around;* enclose; encompass; fix; *gird;* house; hold; have; hem in; include; inclose; *jail;* keep within; lock up; mure; *nest; own;* pen; pavilion; *pent-up;* quarantine; repress; restrain; surround; suppress; shelter; *take in; under; vessel;* wrap; x.; yard; *zone;*

**container** *(n.)*: ampoule; ark; box; bin; bushel; bunker; case; crate; carton; chest; depository; ewer; firkin; flask; *gift box* holder; *iron chest*; jug; jar; kettle; lockbox; magazine; *nest; osier basket;* package; pod; pyx; *quinderkyn;* receptacle; repository; storage ~; tub; trunk; tin; utility ~; vessel; wooden box; *xtr. space; yadzutsu [Jap.];* zipper bag;
**containment** *(n.)*: accommodation; boxing in; comprising; corraling; *drawing around;* enclosure; encompassing; fixing; girding; housing; holding; having; hemming in; inclusion; inclosing; inhibition; jailing; keeping; locking up; limiting; muring; nonproliferation; *overseeing;* penning; *pent-up;* quarantine; repression; restraint; suppression; *taking in; under control; vessel;* wrapping; *x.;* yarding; *zoning;*
**contaminate** *(v.)*: adulterate; attaint; bastardize; corrupt; defile; empoison; foul; *go bad; hoar;* infect; jade; *ketty; lace;* mortify; *necrosis; oxidize;* pollute; poison; queer; ruin; spoil; sully; taint; *undo;* vitiate; welk; *x- ~;* yellow; *zorch;* [*Ant.* cleanse]
**contemplate** *(v.)*: analyze; brainstorm; consider; cogitate; devise; deliberate; dwell; evaluate; figure; gauge; *hypothesize;* ideate; judge; *know; lucubrate;* mull over; muse; meditate; *notion;* observe; ponder; pore; question; ruminate; reflect; study; think; use brain; valuate; weigh; *xenodiagnose; yeme; zazen;*
**contemplation** *(n.)*: analysis; brainwork; brooding; consideration; concentration; cogitation; deliberation; evaluation; focus; fancy; fabrication; *genius;* headwork; intellection; judgment; *knowledge;* lucubration; musing; meditation; *notion; on one's mind;* pondering; *questioning;* rumination; reasoning; speculation; thinking; thought; using one's brain; valuating; weighing; *xenodiagnosis; yeme* [arch.]; *zazen* [Bud.];
**contemplative** *(adj.)*: absorbed; brooding; cogitative; concentrative; considering; deliberating; deep in thought; engrossed; evaluative; figuring; gauging; heart-searching; introspective; judging; *knowing;* lost in thought; meditative; musing; museful; *notional;* occupied; pondering; pensive; *quiet;* reflective; studious; thoughtful; thinking; ultra- ~; valuating; wistful; *xenocratic; yearnful; zetetic;* [*Ant.* careless]
**contemporary** *(adj.)*: avant-garde; brand-new; current; *designer; developed;* existing; fashionable; green; hot; hip; in-vogue; just-out; *kickoff;* latest; modern; new; original; of our time; present-day; *questionable;* recent; stylish; twenty-first century; up-to-date; ultramodern; unconventional; *vogue; world-wise; xenogenetic; young; zygogenetic;* [*Ant.* classic]
**contempt** *(n.)*: abhorrence; brazenfacedness; condescension; disdain; enmity; fight; gall; hatred; ill-will; indignation; jangliness; knocking; loathing; malice; odium; *polarity;* querulousness; revulsion; scorn; *tetchiness;* utter dislike; venom; *withstanding; xenophobia; yawping; zoilism;* [*Ant.* cherishing]
**contend** *(v.)*: argue; altercate; bicker; battle; compete; dispute; engage; fight; gainsay; grapple; have words with; *impugn;* jangle; kemp; lock horns [slang]; *levy war;* make war with; *naysay;* oppose; pick fight; quarrel; run against; resist; strive; tangle; *unharmonious;* vie; (wage) war; wrangle; *x-purposes; yain* [arch.]; *zap;* [*Ant.* condone]
**contender** *(n.)*: adversary; battler; challenger; competitor; disputant; enemy; foe; gainsayer; *hostile;* impugner; jangler; kemper; *litigant;* match; nemesis; opponent; *player;* quarreler; rival; striver; *troubler;* underminer; *villain;* vier; wrangler; *warrior; xenic; yuon* [arch.]; *zapper;* [*Ant.* condoner]
**content** *(adj.)*: appeased; blissful; contented; delighted; elated; (ful)filled; gratified; happy; indulged; joyful; *keen; like; merry; no complaint;* overjoyed; pleased; placable; plaintless; pacified; *queme;* reconciled; resigned; satisfied; thrilled; unrepining; *vivacious;* well-pleased; *xanadu; you-beaut [Aus.];* zestful; [*Ant.* critical]
**content** *(n.)*: appurtenance; body; contents; *data;* effects; focus; facts; goods; gist; guts; *have;* items; insides; information; jist; *kit; load;* material; matter; *nub; objects;* presented facts; quintessence; *raw material;* substance; subject matter; stuff(ing); things; topic; theme; *unit ~s; volume;* what's inside; *xenenthesis; yield; zeug* [G.];
**content** *(v.)*: appease; befit; comfort; delight; execute; fulfill; fill; gratify; hush; ingratiate; *joy;* keep happy; *like;* make happy; meet; mollify; not displease; overjoy; please; pacify; quell; *reward; reach;* satisfy; soothe; suit; *thrill; uplift; victory; wrap up; xtry.; yain* [arch.]; *zero problem;* [*Ant.* critical]

**contention** *(n.)*: argument; bickering; conflict; controversy; disagreement; discord; embroilment; fight; fussing; gainsaying; headshaking; incongruity; jangling; kagg; *locking horns; making fur fly;* negativism; odds; opposition; polemic; quarrel; resistance; strife; tussle; unharmoniousness; variance; wrangling; *x-fire;* yed; *zapping;* [*Ant.* concord]

**contentious** *(adj.)*: argumentative; belligerent; cantankerous; contrary; disagreeable; emulous; factious; grouchy; gainsaying; hot-tempered; hard to get along with; irritable; jangly; knaggy; liverish; mean; nasty; ornery; pugnacious; quarrelsome; resistant; ratiocinative; snappy; temperamental; umbrageous; vinegary; wranglesome; *xenophobic;* yieldless; *za-zum* [Rus.]; [*Ant.* concordant]

**contentment** *(n.)*: appeasement; bliss; contentedness; complacency; delight; ease; felicity; gratification; happiness; indulgence; joy(fulness); kicks; lightheartedness; merriment; *niceness;* overjoy; pleasure; quiet pleasure; resting; satisfaction; transport; *uplifted; vivacity;* winsomeness; *xanadu; yeah!;* zestfulness; [*Ant.* criticalness]

**contest** *(v.)*: argue; bicker; challenge; dispute; *engage;* fight; gainsay; have words with; impugn; jangle; kemp; lock horns [slang]; make fur fly; naysay; oppose; pick fight; question; resist; strive; tiff; *unharmonious;* vie; withstand; *x-purposes; yell; zap;* [*Ant.* condone]

**continual** *(adj.)*: abiding; *boundless;* continuous; constant; daily; enduring; *forever;* gapless; *hourly;* incessant; *jusqu'au bout* [F.]; *keeps going;* lasting; maintaining; nonstop; ongoing; perpetual; *quadrillion;* remaining; relentless; repeated; round-the-clock; seamless; steady; twenty-four-hour; unceasing; unbroken; uninterrupted; *vast;* without end; *xferring;* year-round; *zillion;* [*Ant.* choppy]

**continuation** *(n.)*: addendum; addition; *again;* beginning again; continuance; continuing; *doing over;* extension; furtherance; going on; *have again; immortalize; journeying on;* keeping on; lengthening; maintaining; *non-stop; ongoing;* proceeding; pressing on; perpetuation; prolongation; *quickening;* resumption; starting again; sustaining; taking up; upholding; *voyaging on; wax; xenization; yede; zooming ahead;* [*Ant.* cancellation]

**continue** *(v.)*: abide; bear; brave; carry on; conduct; do; endure; extend; flow; follow after (- on); go on; hold on; harbor; *immortalize; journey on;* keep (up; on); last; maintain; *non-stop;* outlast; proceed; persist; prolong; perpetuate; pursue; plug away; press on; perdure; propagate; *quicken;* remain; resume; run; sustain; stay; spread; tarry; uphold; *voyage on;* wax; wage; *xenize;* yede; *zoom ahead;* [*Ant.* cease]

**continuous** *(adj.)*: abiding; *boundless;* constant; continual; chronic; durative; enduring; endless; *forever; fixed;* gapless; *hourly;* incessant; infinite; *jusqu'au bout* [F.]; *keeps going;* lasting; maintaining; nonstop; ongoing; perpetual; perennial; *quadrillion;* remaining; repeated; recurring; surviving; steady; twenty-four-hour; uninterrupted; unceasing; unbroken; *vast;* without end; *xferring;* year-round; *zillion;* [*Ant.* ceased]

**contort** *(v.)*: alter; bend; change; distort; entwist; foul up; garble; *hurl;* injure; *jade;* knot; *louse up;* mutilate; *nullify; obloquoy; oppress;* pervert; *quade* [arch.]; ruin; spoil; skew; twist; upbend; variate; warp; writhe; *xenomorph; yaw;* zigzag.

**contortion** *(n.)*: alteration; bending; changing; distortion; entwisting; fouling up; garbling; *hurling;* injuring; *jading;* knotting; *lousing up;* mutilation; *nullification; obloquoy;* perversion; *quade [arch.];* ruination; skewing; twisting; *undo;* variation; winding; warping; writhing; *xenomorph; yaw;* zigzag.

**contour** *(n.)*: ambit; bend; curve; curvature; delineation; exact shape; form; geometric curve; *half circle;* incurvature; *J-curve; kind;* lineation; *meandering;* nonlinear; outline; profile; quat; relief; shape; turns; tournure; *upbend;* verge; winding; xy-curve; *yaw; zag;*

**contract** *(n.)*: agreement; binding agreement; covenant; deal; *enforceable ~;* federation; gentleman's agreement; *happy medium;* indenture; joint agreement; key agreement; legal ~; manufacturing ~; *non-negotiable ~;* oath; pledge; *papers;* qualified agreement; *rental agreement;* signed ~; terms; understanding; vow; written agreement; *X on the dotted line;* yoke; yellow-dog ~; *zet [dial.];*

**contract** *(v.)*: abate; become smaller; compress; constrict; diminish; decrease; extenuate; fall off; get (thinner); *halve; impair; jump down; knock down;* lessen; minimize; narrow; *outgo;* pare down; quail; reduce; slenderize; straiten; taper; thin; *undersize; vanish;* wane; welk; *XS; yield; zeroize;*

**contraction** *(n.)*: abridging; abbreviation; astringency; becoming smaller; compression; constriction; diminishment; drawing together; *elasticity;* falling off; getting smaller; *halving; impairing; jumping down; knocking down;* lessening; minimizing; narrowing; *outgo;* paring down; quailing; reducing; shrinking; shortening; tapering; *undersize; vanishing;* welking; *XS;* yielding; zeroizing;

**contradict** *(v.)*: argue; belie; controvert; challenge; counter; contravene; disagree with; deny; dispute; disaffirm; expostulate; fight; gainsay; *have words with;* impugn; jangle; kick at; lock horns [slang]; make fur fly; negate; oppose; pick fight; quarrel; refute; strive; show to be wrong; take issue; undo; undermine; vie; withstand; *x-purposes; yell; zap;* [Ant. confirm]

**contradiction** *(n.)*: antilogy; antimony; bickering; challenge; conflict; clash; discrepancy; disagreement; disparity; dissimilarity; expostulation; fight; gap; *hostility;* impugnation; inconsistency; incompatibility; incongruity; jangling; kicking at; *lapse;* making fur fly; negation; opposition; occursion; oxymoron; picking fight; quarrel; refutation; striving; taking issue; unlikeness; variation; withstanding; *x-purposes; yelling; zapping;* [Ant. confirmation]

**contradictory** *(adj.)*: abjuratory; *bad; broken;* conflicting; dissonant; differing; discrepant; erratic; *false; glitchy;* having inconsistencies; incongruent; incompatible; inharmonious; inconsistent; *just doesn't match; known discrepancies;* lacking conformity; mismatched; non-uniform; noncoherent; *opposite;* paradoxical; problematic; *questionable;* renunciatory; self-contradicting; *trouble;* uncoherent; varying; with discrepancies; *x-out;* yet inconsistent; *zero consistency;* [Ant. consistent]

**contraption** *(n.)*: apparatus; *brainchild;* contrivance; device; engine; *function;* gizmo; gadget; *hardware;* instrument; invention; jiggumbob; *jalopy;* kickumbob; labor-saving device; machine; "nuts and bolts"; *object;* piece of equipment; *quantum leap;* rig; system; technological marvel; unit; *vade mecum [L.];* widget; *X-Y recorder; you-know-what; zeug [G.];*

**contrary** *(adj. conflicting)*: at variance; *bucking;* conflicting; differing; divergent; expostulatory; factious; greatly divergent; highly incompatible; incompatible; jangly; *kicking; liverish;* mismatched; non-compatible; opposing; pugnacious; quite contradictory; refutative; self-contradicting; totally incompatible; utterly ~; varying; wrongheaded; *x-ing; yieldless; zero agreement;* [Ant. corresponding]

**contrary** *(adj. disagreeable)*: antithestical; argumentative; bucking; conflicting; contradictory; differing; divergent; disagreeable; expostulatory; factious; gainsaying; hindersome; inhibitive; jangly; knaggy; liverish; murmuring; negative; opposing; petulant; querulous; resistant; self-willed; touchy; unkind; vying; waspish; *x-purposes; yell; zero agreement;* [Ant. cooperative]

**contrast** *(n.)*: antithesis; antipathy; *bearing dissimilarity;* contradistinction; difference; differentiation; dissimilarity; dissimilitude; evaluation; *foil; gap;* heterogeneity; inharmoniousness; juxtaposition; *kind; likeness;* marked difference; non-resemblance; otherness; opposition; putting side-by-side; *quite different;* relation; setting together; *throwing side-by-side;* unlikeness; varying; weighing; *xfer; yeme; zeroing in;* [Ant. comparison]

**contrast** *(v.)*: analogize differences; *balance;* compare; contradistinguish; distinguish; differentiate; evaluate differences; foil; gage; hold comparison; *inspect;* juxtapose; *know differences;* list distinctions; measure; note differences; *observe;* put side-by-side; *quantify;* relate; set together; think on dissimilarities; use ~; valuate; weigh; *xenodiagnose;* yeme; *zero in;* [Ant. compare]

**contribute** *(v.)*: add; back; confer; donate; endow; fund; grant; help; impart; *join in;* kit; lend; make contribution; *non-retention; offload;* pay; plow in; participate; *quick-to-give;* relinquish; subsidize; transfer; underwrite; *vest;* work toward; xfer; yield; *zip;*

**contribution** *(n.)*: alms; bestowal; check; donation; endowment; *favor;* gift; generosity; handsel; investment; *joy-giving;* kindness; liberality; largess; munificence; *nicety;* offering; present; *quantity; reward;* support; tithe; *unselfishness;* vouchsafement; *work;* xenium; *yeff* [arch.]; *zealous support;*

**contrite** *(adj.)*: ashamed; broken; conscience-stricken; crushed; despairing; expiatory; feeling sorry; grieving; heart-repentant; humble; *inveighing; juddering;* keenly ~; lamenting; mourning; *non-stubborn;* outcrying; penitent(ial); *quaking;* rueful; repentant; sorry; turning; *U-turn; volte-face* [F.]; woeful; *x-out; yearning;* zealous to repent; [*Ant.* conceited]

**contrition** *(n.)*: attrition; about-face; brokenness; contriteness; change of heart; despair; expiatoriness; feeling sorry; grief; high-repentance; *inveighing; juddering; keening; lamentation;* mourning; mortification; *non-stubbornness; outcry;* penitence; *quaking;* repentance; sorrow; turning; *U-turn; volte-face* [F.]; woefulness; *x-ing out; yamim nora'im* [Heb.]; zeal to get right; [*Ant.* conceit]

**contrive** *(v.)*: arrange; birth; brew; concoct; conceive; devise; design; engineer; fabricate; formulate; *get;* hatch; invent; *judge;* kiddy; *lay out;* machinate; *notion;* originate; plot; plan; *quick-thinking; rustle up;* scheme; think (up); *use brain;* vamp up; work up; *xenodiagnose; yeme;* zero in;

**control** *(n.)*: authority; *badge;* clutches; custody; command; charge; dominance; dominion; direction; empowering; faculty; grip; government; guidance; hands; headship; hegemony; *the helm;* influence; jurisdiction; keeping; kingship; lordship; mastery; manipulation; name; oversight; power; *quo warranto* [L.]; right; restrict; rule; say-so; sway; *throne;* umpirage; virtue; warrant; weight; *xtry.* ~; yard; *zonal* ~; [*Ant.* compliance]

**control** *(v.)*: abuse; boss; command; dominate; direct; dictate; exploit; force; govern; guide; head; handle; influence; jockey; keep under ~; lead; lord over; manipulate; manage; *nobble;* oversee; oppress; prevail; predominate; *quell;* regulate; run; rule; subdue; take over; *use; under ~; vanquish; weight; xtr.* ~; yeme; zeal; [*Ant.* comply]

**controversial** *(adj.)*: arguable; bickered about; contestable; controvertible; divisive; disputatious; disputable; disputative; disputed; debatable; debated; ever-debated; fussed over; *gainsay;* hot; *interchange; jangle;* keenly debated; liable to be questioned; much-debated; non-settled; oft-debated; polemic(al); questionable; ratiocinative; strived over; *tiff;* unsettled; up for debate; very ~; wrangled over; *x-fire; yell; zero agreement;* [*Ant.* concordant]

**controversy** *(n.)*: argument; bickering; contention; disagreement; dispute; embroilment; fight; gainsaying; hairsplitting; incongruity; issue; jangling; kagg; *locking horns; making fur fly;* negativism; opposition; polemic; quarrel; resistance; strife; tussle; unharmoniousness; variance; wrangling; *x-purposes;* yed; *zapping;* [*Ant.* consonance]

**convenience** *(n.)*: accommodation; benefit; commodiousness; *desirableness;* ease; expedience; facility; *good;* handiness; inservience; *just so easy; keen;* leisure; luxury; meetness; non-difficulty; opportunity; *problem-free; queme;* relief; seasonableness; self-service; timeliness; usefulness; utility; *very convenient;* wieldableness; *xtry. opportunity;* yarage; *zipity;*

**convenient** *(adj.)*: accommodating; *adapted;* befitting; commodious; *desirable;* easy; expedient; fitting; good; handy; inservient; just so easy; keen; *local;* meet; nice; opportune; problem-free; queme; *result-oriented;* stress-free; seasonable; self-serving; timely; useful; very ~; well-timed (-placed); *xtry. easy;* yielding; *zero problem;* [*Ant.* challenging]

**convention** *(n.)*: assembly; body; convocation; discussion; *ekklesia* [G.]; forgathering; gathering; horde; ingathering; jam [coll.]; kit [coll.]; lot; meeting; *number; opportunity;* powwow; *quorum;* regathering; reunion; session; throng; turnout; *union;* vestry; *working; witan, x.; yain* [arch.]; *zayat* [Burm.];

**conventional** *(adj.)*: accepted; behavioral; customary; cultural; common; dominant; established; familiar; general; habitual; inveterate; jake [Br.]; known; long-established; main; normal; ordinary; orthodox; predominant; *qualified;* regular; routine; standard; typical; traditional; usual; *venerated;* well-established; *x-cultural; ye olde; zealous tradition;*

**converge** *(v.)*: approach; amass; bear down on; come together; congregate; draw together; *encounter;* forgather; gather; have a meeting; intersect; join; *knit;* link with; meet; merge; near; *overlap;* pass together; *quorum;* run into; rally; reconvene; rendezvous; stream together; touch; unite; verge together; *work together; x.;* yoke; *zone;*

**conversation** *(n.)*: argument; bearing heart; chat; colloquy; conference; discussion; dialogue; discourse; exchange words; *fraternization;* gabbing; heart-to-heart; huddle; interchange; jangle; *key ~; little chat;* meeting; negotiation(s); oral treaty; parlance; quadrilogue; reasoning; speech; (table-) talk; *tête-à-tête* [F.]; *uttering; vocalization;* words; *xenophonia;* yarn; yakking; ya-ta-ta; *zero in;*
**converse** *(v.)*: articulate; bespeak; communicate; commune; chat; declare; discuss; dialogize; discourse; express; *fraternize;* gab; have words; interact; jaw; *key in;* let out; mention; *notify; outtalk;* parley; *quarrel;* relate; reason; ramble; relay; speak; talk (over); utter; verbalize; word; *xenophonia;* yak; *zero in;*
**conversion** *(n.)*: alteration; becoming a believer; change(over); commutation; *development;* evangelization; flip-flop; going over; *have; improvement; justification; key ~; let;* move; modification; *new;* overhaul; proselytization; proselytism; *qualification;* renovation; switch; transformation; turning; transmutation; *upgrade;* vamping; *winning over; xfer; yielding; zwap [dial.];*
**convert** *(n.)*: adherent; advocate; believer; catechumen; churchgoer; disciple; devotee; enlistee; follower; factionary; *gung-ho;* holder; imbiber; janissary; *kirsen [dial.];* liegeman; member; myrmidon; neophyte; *overcomer;* proselyte; *qualify;* recruit; receiver; supporter; truster; *trainee; united;* votary; *wannabe; Xnize; yielder;* zealot;
**convert** *(v.)*: alter; adapt; become; believe; change (over); convince; *develop;* evangelize; exchange; fix; go over; gain; *heighten;* improve; interchange; *jump; key to; lead to Christ;* modify; move; make over; *novate;* overhaul; proselytize; persuade; *qualify;* retrofit; revise; recruit; revamp; renovate; switch; sway; transform; translate; turn into; upgrade; vamp; win (over); *work; Xnize; yaw; zigzag;*
**convey** *(v.)*: *airlift;* bring; bear; carry; conduct; deliver; eloin; *export;* freight; forward; ferry; give; get; haul; impart; janker; *jet;* kurvey; locomote; move; *navigate; overcarry;* pass; quarter-cart; relay; ship; send; transport; take; uptake; *van;* waft; wheel; xfer; yanker [Br.]; zip; [*see* communicate]
**convict** *(n.)*: arrestee; bad guy; criminal; deviant; ex- ~; felon; gangster; hardened criminal; inmate; jailbird; knuck; lawbreaker; malefactor; no-good; offender; prisoner; quod inmate; rogue; *robber;* stir bird [slang]; transgressor; underboss; villain; ward-bird [slang]; *xgressor;* yardbird; *zek* [Rus.]; [*Ant.* cop]
**convict** *(v.)*: affect; aggrieve; burden; convince; condemn; determine guilt; *encumber;* find guilty; get; grieve; have under ~; impress; inveigle; judge guilty; know guilt; lay guilt; made to feel guilty; not leave alone; *overburden;* persuade; prick (in heart); *questionless;* ring one's bell; sway; tug (at heart); unsettle; *very convicted;* weigh down; *xfer guilt; yield ~ion; zap;* [*Ant.* clear]
**conviction** *(n.)*: assurance; belief; burden; confidence; certitude; doctrine; determination; *encumbering;* faith; *genuine ~;* heavy burden; Holy Spirit ~; ideology; *judgment; knowledge; looking to;* mindset; non-doubt; opinion; persuasion; questionlessness; religious ~; resolve; sureness; standard; sense of ~; trust; unwaveringness; view; value; wholehearted ~; *xel [arch.]; y'faith* [arch.]; *zero innocence;* [*see* guilt; *Ant.* clearing]
**convicting** *(adj.)*: affecting; burdening; cutting; convincing; *dealing; encumbering; forceful;* guilt-bringing; heavy; impressing; *judging;* keen; laying guilt; majorly ~; *non-easy; overburdened;* piercing; quite ~; reproving; self-reproving; tugging; unsettling; very ~; weighing down; *xtry. ~;* yielding conviction; *zero innocence;* [*Ant.* confidence-building]
**convince** *(v.)*: argue; bring around; cajole; disabuse; encourage; *force;* gain; hook in; influence; induce; inveigle; incite; *justify; know;* lead into; motivate; make see; nobble; outtalk; persuade; *questionless;* re-educate; sway; sell; talk into; *urge; vie for;* win over; *xuld [arch.]; yerk;* zorch;
**convoluted** *(adj.)*: abstruse; bewildering; complicated; difficult; entangled; frustrating; gnarled; hard; intertwined; jumbled; knotty; labyrinthine; mazy; nodated; overcomplicated; perplexing; *question; recondite;* scrambled; tangled; twisted; unsolvable; vexatious; wildering; *xtry.; yucky;* zany; [*Ant.* clear]
**convulsion** *(n.)*: agitation; bestirring; *contraction;* diddering; *excitement;* fluttering; gyration; hustling; *instability;* juddering; knocking; lurching; *movement; nodding;* oscillation; pitching; quivering; rattling; shaking; twitching; *unstable;* vibration; wobbling; *xuld [arch.];* yerking; *zigzagging;*

**cook** *(n.)*: *army ~;* baker; barbequer; chef; dinner chef; expert chef; *fry ~;* griller; hash slinger [slang]; *Italian chef; Japanese chef;* kitchener; lunch *~; man [masc.];* nourisher; *oriental chef;* pastry- *~; qualified ~;* restaurant chef; sous-chef; trained *~;* uberchef; victual-preparer; well-trained *~; woman [fem.];* xeo user; yarker; zesty;

**cook** *(v.)*: *anneal;* braise; bake; broil; brown; concoct; decrepitate; evenly *~;* fry; grill; griddle; heat; harden; *improvise; jumbal; kitchen; let ~;* make; microwave; *neal [arch.];* over~ (-heat); oven-roast; prepare; pan-fry; pan-broil; quick-bake; roast; steam; seethe; toast; *undercook; very hot;* whip up; warm up; *xeo;* yark; *zap;* [*Ant.* cool]

**cool** *(adj.)*: algid; air conditioned; brisk; chilly; *damp; electronically cooled;* frosty; gelid; heatless; icy; *Jack Frost; keel;* low temperature; moderate; nippy; *overcold; pleasant; quite cool;* refrigerated; snappy; temperate; unheated; *ventilated;* wintry; *xtr. chilled; ycie* [arch.]; *zealless;* [*see* shiver]

**cooperate** *(v.)*: agree; bow; comply; collaborate; do; execute; follow; go along with; heed; harmonize; implement; jump (to it); knuckle under; liaise; mind; not resist; oblige; perform; *questionless; regard;* submit; truckle; *undertake;* voluntarily submit; work together; *x-help;* yield; *zip to it;* [*Ant.* challenge]

**cooperation** *(n.)*: assistance; backing; co~partnering; *devotion; enterprise;* friendship; full *~;* giving of help; help; *interest;* joint *~; kinship;* league; lending a hand; mutual aid; non-resistance; *over-helpful;* partnership; quinquevirate; *relationship;* support; teamwork; *undertaking;* voluntary submission; working together; *x-class;* yoke; *zero hindrance;* [*Ant.* contrariness]

**cooperative** *(adj.)*: accommodating; *beneficial;* compliant; complaisant; deferential; ever-helpful; favorable; *good;* helpful; *implementing; joint; kowtowing;* listening; mutual; non-resistant; obliging; passive; questionless; ready to help; submissive; supportive; tractable; unresisting; *vigilant;* willing; *xtry;* yielded; *zealous;* [*Ant.* contrary]

**coordinate** *(v.)*: align; bring together; co-ordinate; *direct; exact;* fine-tune; go together; harmonize; *in sync;* jive; keep together line up; match; mesh; *non-discord;* organize; orchestrate; put together; quadrate; reconcile; readjust; synchronize; *timing;* unite; verse; well- *~d; x-harmonize;* yark; zero difference;

**coordination** *(n.)*: alignment; bringing together; co-ordination; *direction;* exact alignment; fine-tuning; going together; harmonization; *in sync;* jiving [slang]; *keying in;* liaison; meshing; *non-discrepancy;* organization; preparation; *qualification;* readjustment; reconciliation; synchronization; timing; *uniting; versing;* well-coordinated; *x-harmonize;* yarking; zero difference; [*Ant.* chaos]

**cope** *(v.)*: accept; bear; counter; deal; endure; *equal;* fare; get by; handle; hack; hold up; *interact;* jockey; keep under control; live with; manage; make do; muddle through; *notion;* overcome; put up with; *quicken;* respond; stand; *survive;* tolerate; *uphold; victory;* work through; *xfer; yomp; zet [dial.];*

**copious** *(adj.)*: abundant; bountiful; countless; disproportionate; excessive; fruitful; great; generous; galore; heaping; immense; jumbo; king-sized; liberal; multitudinous; numerous; overflowing; overabundant; plentiful; profuse; quantitative; *replete;* rich; superabundant; terrific; uberous; voluminous; vast; wantless; *x.; yards;* zillions;

**copy** *(n.)*: apograph; apery; borrowing; clone; counterfeit; duplicate; ditto; emulation; estreat; ectype; *forged ~;* gemination; *holotype;* imitation; impersonation; *just like;* knockoff; look-alike; mimicry; mirror image; mock-up; model; mimeograph; *near; offprint; overdub;* parroting; personation; photocopy; *quadruplicate;* reproduction; replication; simulation; semblance; transcript(ion); tenor; *unretouched; virtual ~; wide-margin ~;* xerox; *yielding;* zincograph;

**copy** *(v.)*: ape; borrow; clone; counterfeit; duplicate; ditto; dub; emulate; echo; exscribe; estreat; follow; forge; feign; geminate; gesticulate; *holotype;* imitate; impersonate; *just like;* keep; *look alike;* mimic; mirror; mock; model; mimeograph; *near; offprint; overdub;* parrot; personate; photocopy; plagiarize; *quadruplicate;* reproduce; replicate; repeat; simulate; semble; transcribe; take; *use copier; virtual; watch closely;* xerox; *yield;* zincograph; zoomimic;

**cord** *(n.)*: app; braid; clevy; *drawstring; entangle;* filament; *goldthread;* halter; *intertwine;* jute; knittle; line; ligature; lash; monofilament; natural fiber; organzine; ply; packthread; *qiviut;* rope; string; twine; thread; *uncoil;* vang; watap; *xylem;* yarn; zein;

**core** *(n.)*: axis; belly; center(point); crux; deepest recess; epicenter; fesse-point; *geological ~;* heart; hub; interior; *just exactly centered;* kernel; *lodged;* middle; nucleus; *origin;* pith; prokaryon; *quotidian;* recesses; smack in the middle [slang]; thick; umbilic; *via media; within; x-section;* yolk; *zone;*

**corn** *(n.)*: aliment; *boiled ~;* cob; ceres; dent ~; ear; field ~; flint ~; grain; hominy; ile; Indian ~; *jumbo ~;* kernels; *load;* maize; mealie; *nubbin;* organiz ~; pop ~; *querned ~;* rash; sweet- ~; spike; table ~; uncooked ~; *viands;* white ~; *xanthophyll;* yankee ~; zein;

**corner** *(n.)*: angle; ancone; bend; curve; dip; el; fold; *geomeric curve;* hook; incurve; *jag;* knee; left turn; *move;* nook; offset; oxbend; *parabola;* quoin; right angle; sharp ~; turn; *uncinate;* verge; wind; *xy-curve;* yaw; zag; [*see* monopolize]

**cornerstone** *(n.)*: acrogonieis [Gr.]; basis; basic building block; corner-stone; *dado; establishment;* foundation (stone); ground; headstone; *important;* joining-stone; keystone; *litho; masonry; naissance;* original stone; *petros;* quoin; *rock;* stone of the corner; tri-cornered rock; *unit;* vital part; *wedge; xenolith; yoni [Skr.]; zaccho;*

**coronate** *(v.)*: anoint; bestow; crown; *deliver;* enthrone; *furnish; give; hand over;* install; invest; instate; inthrone; *jubilate; king; lautu* [Inca]; make; *nobility;* ordain; place; *queen; re-enthrone;* set up; throne; *unction;* vest; *worship; xfer;* yark; Zar;

**corporate** *(adj.)*: AB; business; company; commercial; *dealer; economic; executive;* factory; *group; holdings;* industrial; job-related; *kongsi* [Chin.]; Ltd.; mercantile; *non-profit organization;* office; organizational; *production; quasi-public; rat-race;* small-business; shop; *trading;* united; *venture;* workplace; x-corporation; YK; *zaibatsu* [Jap.];

**corporation** *(n.)*: AB; body; business; company; conglomerate; chain; *dummy ~;* enterprise; empire; firm; group; *holding company;* industry; *incorporated;* job; joint-venture; *kongsi* [Chin.]; *limited company;* multinational ~; mega~; national (-non-profit) corporation; organization; public ~; quasi-public ~; *refinery;* small business; shop; trade ~; *unlimited company;* venture; workplace; x- ~; YK; *zaibatsu* [Jap.];

**corpse** *(n.)*: *ashes;* body; cadaver; carcass; dead body; *exhumation; facecloth;* goner; *hearse;* inanimate body; *just died;* ket; lifeless body; morkin; mummified body; *non-living body;* one; pall; *quarry;* remains; stiff; *tomb; unlaid;* victim; vestiges; *wrapped ~; x-man; yielded up the ghost;* zombie;

**corral** *(n.)*: area; bull pen; cage; cattlefold; cow-pen; croft; *divider; dove-house;* enclosure; fold; fence; *greens-stall;* hogpen; hok; inclosure; *jail;* kraal [S. Afr.]; list; mew; *narrow;* oxstall; pen; quad; run; sheepcote; sty; stockyard; tigh [dial.]; *utility pen; vollery;* wynd [dial.]; *xystus;* yard; zariba;

**corral** *(v.)*: accommodate; *bound;* cage; close in; contain; coop up; digladiate; enclose; encage; enmew; fence in; *get;* hold in; inclose; incage; include; immure; *jail;* kennel; lock up; mew; *nab;* oxstall; pen; *quad; round up;* shut up; stable; trap; *utility pen; vollery;* wall in; *x;* yard; zariba;

**correct** *(adj. accurate)*: accurate; bona fide; *checked;* definite; exact; factual; genuine; honest; indubitable; inerrant; justifiable; known; legitimate; *mean it;* never-failing; orthodox; precise; proper; questionless; right; sound; true; unerring; unmistaken; veritable; well-tried; *x-parent;* yes; 'zactly [dial.];

**correct** *(adj. fitting)*: appropriate; befitting; *comme il faut* [F.] due; expedient; fitting; good; *honorable;* idoneous; just; *kosher;* legitimate; meet; *not out-of-place;* okay; proper; qualified; right; suitable; seemly; *tolerable; unselfish;* valid; well(-suited); *xtry.; yielded; zero fault;*

**correct** *(v.)*: adjust; amend; better; change; cure; *develop; darn;* edit; enhance; emend(ate); fix; *get right; heal;* improve; *jib; key to; legitimize;* mend; novate; overhaul; put right; patch up; *qualify;* rectify; right; repair; switch; transform; tweak; update; vamp; *work; xenomorph; yaw; zigzag;*

**correction** *(n.)*: amendment; adjustment; betterment; change; development; edition; enhancement; emendation; fix; *growth; heightening;* improvement; *jibbing; keying to; legitimization;* modification; *new;* overhaul; permutation; qualification; revision; redesign; switch; substitution; tweak; update; variation; *work out; xenomorph; yaw; zigzag;*
**correlate** *(v.)*: associate; be in accord; correspond; draw a parallel; *endorse;* fall together; go along with; harmonize; *indicate agreement;* jive [slang]; join; keep; line up; link; match up; *nexus;* order; parallel; *quinquevirate;* relate; synchronize; *together; unite; verify;* warrant; *xenia* yoke; *zero disagreement;*
**corrode** *(v.)*: atrophy; attaint; break down; corrupt; canker; disintegrate; deteriorate; decay; decompose; eat away; erode; encanker; ferruginate; go bad; gnaw; hoar; hydrolyze; *infect; junk; ketty; labelfaction;* make worse; mortify; nibble away; oxidize; pervert; putrefy; queer; ruin; rust; rot; spoil; taint; *undo;* vitiate; welk; *xylaria;* yellow; *zorch;*
**corrosion** *(n.)*: atrophy; breakdown; corruption; disintegration; deterioration; decomposition; eating away; erosion; ferrugination; *goethite;* hydrolysis; *iron oxide; junking; killing;* labelfaction; mordication; *nullification;* oxidation; pejoration; queering; rust; rotting; spoiling; turning into dust; undoing; viciation; wearing (away); waning; worsening; weakening; *x-ing; yellowing; zinc pest;*
**corrosive** *(adj.)*: acidic; breaking down; caustic; disintegrative; deteriorative; eroding; ferruginating; *going bad;* hydrolyzing; *infectious; junky; ketty; labelfactious;* mortifying; *necrosis;* oxidizing; putrefactive; queering; rusting; rotting; spoiling; tainting; *undo;* vitiable; welking; *xylaria;* yellowing; *zorching;* [Ant. calorized]
**corrupt** *(adj.)*: adulterated; bad; corrupted; crooked; distorted; damaged; dishonest; evil; foul; godless; *horrible;* impure; *jaded; ketty; lousy; misguided;* morbid; nasty; oxidized; pretorian; peccant; *queer;* rotten; shiftless; tainted; unclean; underhanded; venal; wicked; *x-rated; yucky; zorch;* [*see* evil; dishonest; *Ant.* chaste]
**corrupt** *(v.)*: adulterate; attaint; break down; corrode; canker; carnalize; distort; deprave; decay; erode; encanker; fail; ferruginate; go bad; hoar; hydrolyze; infect; jade; *ketty; labelfaction;* make worse; mortify; *necrosis;* oxidize; pervert; poison; putrefy; queer; ruin; rust; rot; subvert; spoil; taint; *undo;* vitiate; welk; *xylaria;* yellow; *zorch;* [Ant. cleanse]
**corruptible** *(adj.)*: *adulterant; bad;* corrodible; *decay;* erodible; fugacious; *going bad;* hydrolyzable; impermanent; *jading; ketty;* liable to spoil; *mortifying;* nondurable; oxidizable; perishable; pervertible; *queering; rotting;* spoilable; *tainting;* unpreserved; vitiatable; *welking; xylaria; yellowing; zeroize;*
**corruption** *(n.)*: abuse; adulteration; breakdown; corruptness; crookedness; contamination; corrosion; canker; dishonesty; depravity; distortion; deterioration; decay; evil; exploitation; fraudulence; foulness; guile; honorlessness; improbity; impurity; jobbery; knavery; lying; misconduct; mordication; non-truthfulness; ordure; perfidy; perversion; putrescence; pollution; queering; roguery; skullduggery; taint; unfairness; venality; wickedness; warpage; *x-ing;* yegginess; *zxnrbl;* [Ant. chasteness]
**cosign** *(v.)*: assure; be security; certify; *declare;* ensure; *for another;* guarantee; *hazard oneself;* indemnify; jurate; *keep guaranteed; lend one's name;* make sure; *non-conditional promise;* obligate oneself; pledge; promise; *qualify; resolve;* swear; take responsibility for; undersign; vouch; *warrant;* x on the dotted line; *yafery* [arch.]*; zealously confirm;*
**cosigner** *(n.)*: assurer; backer; cosignatory; *declarer;* ensurer; *for another;* guarantor; *hazarder;* indemnifier; jurator; *keep guaranteed; lend one's name; make sure; non-conditional promise;* one obligated; pledger; *qualified ~; resolver;* swearer; taker on of the responsibility; undersigned; voucher; *warrantor;* x on the dotted line; *yafery* [arch.]*; zealous confirmer;*
**cosmetics** *(n.)*: *articles;* beauty aids; cosmetic aids; darkener; eye shadow; foundation; gels; *hues; items; jellies;* kohl; lipstick; make-up; maquillage; *mascara;* nail polish; *objects;* powder; paint; *quaintries;* rouge; shadow; toiletries; *undercoat;* visagiste aids; war paint [slang]; *xfer paint;* yolk-based ~; *zeug;*

**cosmic** *(adj.)*: astral; astronomical; *body;* cosmological; celestial; deep space; extraterrestrial; *four quarters of the universe;* galactic; heavenly; interplanetary; interstellar; intergalactic; *jovial; kosmos [Gr.];* lunar; metagalactic; *nebular;* outer space; planetary; quasi-stellar; *relating to planets;* stellar; space; *terrestrial;* universal; *vacuum;* worlds; *x-ray star;* yonder; zonic;

**cost** *(n.)*: amount; bulk price; charge; dollar figure; damage [slang]; expense; expenditure; fee; fare; going price; *handling fee;* impost; jettage; keelage; list price; loss; mise; metage; *number;* outlay; outgo; price(-tag); *quote;* retail price; rate; sum; sacrifice; sale price; *tag;* unit ~; value; worth; wholesale price; *x-tax;* yardage; *zakat;*

**costly** *(adj.)*: *at great cost; bleed dry;* cutthroat; dear(-bought); expensive; exorbitant; *fine;* greatly-priced; high-cost (-dollar; -priced); invaluable; inordinate; immoderate; *judged worthy; king's ransom;* lavish; money-grubbing; not cheap; of great price; outrageous; overpriced; precious; pricey; quality; *rich;* sumptuous; steep; top-dollar; upscale; upmarket; unreasonable; usurious; valuable; worth it's weight in gold; *xtry.; yieldful; zestful;* [*Ant.* cheap]

**costume** *(n.)*: attire; ball-room ~; cover; camouflage; cloak; disguise; dress; *enrobed;* facemask; fancy dress; façade; front; get-up; guise; garb; hood; help-mask; *incognito;* jest; *kept disguised;* loup; mask; make-up; mumm; maskery; *non-recognizable;* outfit; persona; play-clothes; *quat [arch.];* robe; shroud; *transformed; uniform;* veil; vizard; *wardrobe;* xenomorph; yashmak; *zero recognition;*

**cottage** *(n.)*: abode; bungalow; bower; bothy; chalet; chateau; cabin; domicile; dwelling (place); dacha [Rus.]; edifice; *flat house; guest house;* home; house; inhabitance; jacal; *ken;* lodging; manor house; *nest;* outbuilding; place; quinta; residence; structure; summerhouse; *townhouse; utility apartment;* villa; *wanigan;* x-house; *yali; zwinger;*

**couch** *(n.)*: armchair; *accubita* [Rom.]; bench; bergère; chaise lounge; divan; davenport; daybed; *exedra;* futon; *furniture;* fold-out sofa; genuine leather ~; hassock; *item;* Jacobean bench; kippan sofa; loveseat; lounge; *muslin-covered ~;* Naugahyde® ~; *ottoman;* pull-out ~; (padded) pew; *quaint;* recamier; sofa (bed); settee [Br.]; tête-à-tête; takht; upholstery; *vinyl-covered ~;* Winnipeg ~; *x-chair; yew bench; zafu;*

**cough** *(n.)*: *asthma;* bronchitis; bark; croup; dry ~; discharge; expectorate; *forceful ~; germ;* hack; haust; *illness; judder;* koff [var.]; *lung; malady; noise; obstruction-expulsion;* phlegm; quinsy; *release;* smoker's ~; tussis; tickle (in throat); *unhealthiness;* violent ~; whoop; *x-disease; yex; zap;*

**council** *(n.)*: advisory; assembly; board; body; cabinet; committee; consistory; curia; diet; eldership; *forum; government; heads; illuminati;* junto; judicature; *kit;* legislative body; *meeting; nominative committee; organization;* panel; presbytery; quinquevirate; ruling body; session; synod; tribunal; union; vestry; *ward; xenocracy; yain* [arch.]; *zemstvo [Rus.];*

**counsel** *(n.)*: advice; *befriending;* charge; consultation; direction; exhortation; free advice; guidance; hortation; instruction; judgment; kibizing [Yid.]; *leading; mentorship; notification;* opinion; piece of advice; *quick advice;* recommendation; suggestion; tip; *urging;* voice; word of advice; *xenagogy; yammering; zeroing in;*

**counsel** *(v.)*: advise; *be a friend to;* coach; consult; direct; exhort; foreadvise; guide; give counsel; help; instruct; inform; judge; kibitz; lead; *mention;* notify; offer one's opinion; postulate; *quicken;* recommend; suggest; steer; tender one's opinion; *urge;* voice; warn; *xenagogy; yammer; zero in;*

**counselor** *(n.)*: advisor; *bearer of advice;* consultant; cabinet member; Dutch uncle; expert; friend; guide; guru; helper; instructor; informer; *judge;* keen ~; *leader;* mentor; nestor; opinion-offerer; prophet; *postulator; quain [arch.];* recommender; seer; tip-giver; teacher; *urger;* very wise man; wise man; *xenagogue; yammerer; zet [dial.];*

**consult** *(v.)*: ask; *be a friend to;* check with; confer; discuss; exhort; foreadvise; guide; give counsel; help; instruct; inform; judge; kibitz; lead; *mention;* notify; offer one's opinion; postulate; *quicken;* recommend; see; steer; talk with; *urge;* voice; warn; *xenagogy; yammer; zero in;*

**consultant** *(n.)*: advisor; *bearer of advice;* counselor; consigliere; doctor; expert; *friend;* guide; helper; instructor; *judge;* keen ~; *leader; medical ~; notifier; opinion; officer;* paid ~; professional ~; *quain [arch.];* recommender; *seer; teller; urger;* very wise man; wise man; *xenagogue; yammerer; zet [dial.];*
**count** *(n. aristocrat)*: aristocrat; baron; countess [fem.]; duke; earl; feudal superior; grandee; graf [G.]; hidalgo [Sp.]; *important;* jarl; *knight;* lord; marquis; nobleman; optimate; palatine; palsgrave; *queen; ruler; sir;* titled person; *upper crust;* viscount; waldgrave; *XO;* younker; *zayim;*
**count** *(n. sum)*: amount; bulk; computation; degree; extent; figure; *group; horde;* inventory; jag; *kit;* level; load; measure; mass; number; *offset;* portion; part; quantity; reckoning; range; sum; strength; score; total; tally; units; volume; whole; weight; *x; yard; z-score;*
**count** *(v.)*: add up; aggregate; *bulk; bottom line;* calculate; do the sum; enumerate; figure; foot; gage; *have totaled;* increment; inventory; *join;* keep score; *learn the amount;* mete; measure; number; numerate; *over~ (-measure);* paginate; put tick mark down; quantitate; quantify; reckon; recense; re~; sum up; tally; total; *unite; valuate; work out; x-count; yeme;* zum [dial.];
**countenance** *(n.)*: appearance; attitude; air; bearing; cast; composure; carriage; disposition; demeanor; deportment; expression; face; frame of mind; ground; heart; impression; judgment; *known inclination;* look; manner; mien; mood; *notion;* outward appearance; outlook; phiz [derog.]; port; presence; quale; reaction; sentiment; spirit; temperament; *urge;* visage; *whim; xenodiagnosis;* yaw; *zeal;*
**counterattack** *(n.)*: answer; backlash; counteroffensive (-force); defense; *equibalance;* forced response; *get back;* hit back; *interchange; judgment; knock-out; lash back;* military response; *non-belligerent response;* onset; push; *quashing;* response; retaliation; strategic response; *treatment; undoing;* vengeance; war against; *xtry. defense;* ~; *yes-answer;* zealous reply; [*Ant.* conquest]
**counterfeit** *(adj.)*: artificial; bogus; counterfeited; dissembling; deceitful; ersatz; forged; fake; falsified; guileful; hoax; imitation; japed; kiddy; look-alike; make-believe; mendacious; non-real; *outfoxed;* phony; postiche; quacky; quasi; rip off; replicated; spurious; sham; trick; unreal; vain; wily; *xeno-; yeggy; zero validity;*
**counterfeit** *(n.)*: apery; *bogus copy;* copy; duplication; emulation; forgery; fake; gesticulation; hand-forged copy; imitation; *japery; keep;* look-alike; likeness; mock-up; near-duplicate; offprint; phony; *quadruplicate;* replica; simulation; similitude; transcription; *unreal; virtual; work; xerograph; yield; zoomimic;*
**counterfeit** *(v.)*: ape; *borrow;* copy; duplicate; emulate; forge; *gesticulate; holotype;* imitate; *just like; keep; look alike;* mimic; *near; offprint; overdub;* personate; *quadruplicate;* replicate; simulate; transcribe; *unreal; virtual; watch closely; xerox; yield; zincograph;*
**countless** *(adj.)*: *a lot;* boundless; *crawling with; disproportionate;* endless; fathomless; *great; huge;* inestimable; innumerable; jillion; kazillion; limitless; myriad; multitudinous; numberless; *ongoing;* plethoric; *quadrillion; remarkable;* sumless; tremendous; untold; unnumbered; uncounted; uncountable; unreckonable; vast; without number; x; yet unnumbered; zillion.
**country** *(adj.)*: agricultural; agrarian; bucolic; countrified; countryside; *dairy farm; esne;* farm(land); geoponic; georgic; husbandry; inurbane; *joskin; kolkhoz [Rus.];* landward; *manse;* non-urbanized; *olericultural;* predial; *quaint;* rural; rustic; *simple; tillage; undeveloped;* viticultural; wheatland; *xeriscape®;* yokeldom [joc.]; zemledelie [Rus.]; [*Ant.* city]
**country** *(n.)*: area; *archduchy; buffer state;* commonwealth; colony; domain; democracy; demesne; dominion; empire; free state; fatherland; government; homeland; irredenta; *jurisdiction;* kingdom; land; mother ~; motherland; monarchy; nation; *old ~;* power; polity; queendom; realm; republic; state; soil; territory; toparchy; *united kingdom; Vaterland* [G.]; world power; *xerifdom; yard; zemstvo [Rus.];* [see government; farmland]
    **Countries**: Albania; Brazil; Canada; Denmark; England; France; Germany; Hungary; Italy; Japan; Korea; Luxembourg; Mexico; Netherlands; Oman; Poland; Qatar; Russia; Sweden; Turkey; United States; Venezuela; Wales; Yemen; Zambia;

**countryside** *(n.)*: *agricultural;* backwoods; bush [Aus.]; country; cropland; *dairy farms; estates;* farmland; fields; georgic; heartland; hinterland; hayfield; implanted land; *jillaroo; kolkhoz [Rus.];* layland; landscape; middle of nowhere; moorland; *non-urban;* outback; outdoors; plowland; quaint countryside; rural; rustic; sown land; tillage; undeveloped; *vineyards;* wheatland; wold; *xeriscape®;* yokeldom [joc.]; *zemledelie [Rus.];*

**county** *(n.)*: area; borough; canton; district; *element; field; ground;* hundred; *isolated location; jagir* [Asia]; *kray* [Rus.]; locality; municipality; nomarchy; *oblast [Rus.];* province; quadrant; region; section; shire; territory; township; ubiety; viceroyalty; *vicinity;* ward; *x-sector; yard;* zone;

**coup d'état** *(n.)*: annexation; bouleversement; bloodless revolution; coup; defiance; *ever-defiant; fight; general disregard;* high treason; insurgence; *jolting;* knock over; *lèse majesté* [F.]; mutiny; noncompliance; overthrow; purge; quake; revolution; subversion; takeover; upheaval; violence; *war; xgression; yellow flu; zapping;*

**couple** *(n.)*: acoupling; both; brace; couplet; duo; deuce; dyad; doublet; *even match; few;* gemel; husband and wife; *inseparable pair;* joining; kipple [Scot.]; *linked;* match; mates; *marriage; newlyweds; ordered pair;* pair; qualified ~; *reunite;* set; two(some); team; twain; unit; *value-pack; wed; x-pair;* yoke; *zygo-;*

**couple** *(v.)*: attach; bind; connect; double-team; *entwine;* fasten; group; harness; hitch; hook up; *inosculate;* join; *knit;* link; match up; *network; order together;* pair; put together; *quasi-fuse;* relate; *reunite;* stick together; team; twin; unite; *vise;* wed; wive; *xenograft;* yoke; *zygo-;* [Ant. cleave]

**courage** *(n.)*: audacity; backbone; bravery; boldness; bravado; chivalry; daring; *determination;* enterprise; fearlessness; fortitude; gallantry; guts; gumption; grit; hardiness; heroism; intrepidity; intestinal fortitude; *jarless;* knightliness; lion-heartedness; manliness; mettle; nobleness; nerve; *obstinacy;* pluck; prowess; *quakeless; resolve;* stoutness; strength; *spirit; tenacity;* undauntedness; valor; wherewithal; *xia* [Chin.]; *yung* [Chin.]; *zealousness;* [see strength; Ant. cowardice]

**courageous** *(adj.)*: adventurous; audacious; brave; bold; chivalrous; daring; dauntless; enterprising; fearless; gutsy; gritty; gallant; heroic; hardy; intrepid; *jarless;* knightly; lion-hearted; manly; mettlesome; nervy; never-fearing; *obstinate;* plucky; *quick-witted; resolute;* strong; spirited; stouthearted; *tenacious;* unafraid; undaunted; unflinching; unfrightened; valiant; valorous; *wherewithal; xtry.; yare; zealous;* [Ant. cowardly]

**courier** *(n.)*: announcer; bearer of tidings; correspondent; dispatch; emissary; estafet; *foreign minister; gofer;* herald; informer; *just in; kurveyor;* liaison; letter-carrier; messenger; nuncio; *official;* proclaimer; post; *questor* [It.]; runner; rider; representative; *servant;* tidings-bearer; updater; *voicer;* walking delegate; x-man; *yamen* [Chin.]; *zip;*

**course** *(n.)*: avenue; bearing; channel; direction; *esplanade;* footpath; flight path; fashion; gateway; highway; *itinerary;* journey-way; king's highway; lane; means; non-toll road; orientation; option; path(way); *quo mode* [L.]; road; route; *street;* track; tack [naut.]; trail; trajectory; tide; *underpass;* vector; way; *xystus; yong* [arch.]; *zwinger;*

**court** *(n.)*: arbitration; appellate; bench; board of inquiry; courthouse; curia; district ~; ecclesiastical ~; eyre; forum; federal (-family) court; gemot; hearing; high ~; inquisition; intermediate ~; judgment hall (-seat); judicature; kings ~; kangaroo ~; law ~; leet; manorial ~; night ~; oyer; open ~; *piepoudre;* quarter session; rota; superior ~; Supreme Court; session; seat of justice; tribunal; trial; United States Supreme ~; venue; wardmote; *xabandar;* youth ~ [Can.]; *zamorin [Hind.];*

**court** *(v.)*: *addresses;* bill and coo; cozy up to; date; *encourage;* flatter; go with; *have out;* ingratiate; *join;* keep company; *love;* match-make; *nubility; out together;* pursue; *quest;* romance; see; suit; serenade; take out; *undying love;* visit; woo; wine and dine; *xenia; young love; zero in;*

**courteous** *(adj.)*: amiable; benign; civil(ized); deferential; *encouraging;* friendly; gracious; gentlemanly; *harmonious; interpersonal;* judicious; kind; *likable;* mannerly; nice; obsequious; polite; *queme;* respectful; sociable; tactful; urbane; very polite; well-mannered; *xenial; yielding; zero offense;* [Ant. crass]

**courtesy** *(n.)*: *appropriateness;* breeding; civility; decorum; etiquette; fineness; good manners; gentility; good manners; high-style; *impressive; jimp;* kindness; *loveliness;* manners; niceness; obligingness; politeness; *quaintness;* refinement; social correctness; table manners; urbanity; *Victorian; well-mannered; xtry.; younker; zero offense;* [*Ant.* crassness]

**courtyard** *(n.)*: arcade; *boardwalk;* court; colonade; district; esplanade; forecourt; garden; garth; haw; *Italian garden; Japanese garden;* keep-yard; lapa; mall; *niche;* open-air court; patio; quad; rose garden; square; terrace; *ubeity; vomitory;* walkway; xystus; yard; zocalo [Mex.];

**cousin** *(n.)*: agnate; brother; blood kin; coz [slang]; cross ~; *dear ~;* elder ~; first ~; german; *half-brother; interrelation; junior;* kin(sman [masc.], -swoman [fem.]); kissing ~; *little ~; ménage;* near-kinsman; next of kin; older ~; people; parallel ~; quater- ~; relative; relation; second ~; third ~; uncle's son; *vein; ward; x-linked;* younger ~; *zon [dial.];* [see family]

**covenant** *(n.)*: agreement; *bond;* contract; commitment; deal; *engagement;* forswearing; guarantee; hypothecation; indenture; joint agreement; jurament; *kept promise;* league; *making of vows;* non-conditional promise; oath; pledge; promise; *qualified promise;* resolution; sworn statement; solemn oath; testament; undertaking; unconditional promise; vow; word (of honor); *x-one's heart; yafery* [arch.]; zealous ~;

**covenant** *(v.)*: adjure; assure; assert; *bind;* commit; deign; *ensure;* forswear; guarantee; give word; hypothecate; interpledge; jurate; *keep word;* legitimize; make promise; *nobly vow;* obligate; pledge; promise; *qualify;* resolve; swear; testify; *unconditionally promise;* vow; warrant; *x-ones heart; yafery [arch.]; zealously vow;*

**cover** *(n.)*: *article;* blanket; case; casing; covering; cap; canopy; ceil; *disguise;* envelope; flap; front; *go over;* hood; *inveil;* jacket; *kist;* lid; mantle; mask; *non-revealed;* overlay; patch; pall; *quat [arch.];* roof; slip~; sleeve; shroud; sheath; shell; top; *unopened ~;* veil; wrapper; *x-out;* yapp; zigzag quilt;

**cover** *(v.)*: arrange; bespread; blanket; bury; cloak; conceal; canopy; coat; ceil; deck; enclose; entomb; *fix;* get ~ed; hood; hide; inhume; jacket; kist; lay over; mantle; mask; *non-revealed;* overspread (-lay; -canopy); put over; pall; *quat [arch.];* relay; roof; spread over; shelter; superpose; *top; umbrate;* veil; whelm; wrap around; *x-out;* yird; *zet [dial.];*

**covering** *(n.)*: *atop;* blanket; cover(ture); casing; coating; cloak; canopy; ceil; *drape;* enwrapment; enclosure; flap; *gusset;* hood; inveil; jacket; *kick plate;* lid; loose ~; mantle; *non-revealed;* outer ~; overlay (-blanket); opercula [zoo.]; pavis; potlid; pall; panoply; packaging; *quat [arch.];* roof; slick cover; slip-cover; shell; tarp; top; *umbration;* veil; wrapper; wimple; *x-out;* yashmak; zip- ~; [see atonement]

**covet** *(v.)*: ache for; begrudge; crave; desire; envy; *fancy; fret;* grudge; hunger for; itch; *just got to have; keenly desire;* lust after; long for; *mine; need; over-greedy;* pant; *quest for;* repine; *seek;* thirst for; *urge; velleity;* want; *xel [arch.];* yearn for; *zoilism;*

**covetous** *(adj.)*: avaricious; acquisitive; begrudging; craving; desirous; discontent; envious; evil-eyed; *fretting;* greedy; hard-fisted; insatiable; jealous; kitish; longing; materialistic; *non-generous;* over-greedy; prurient; quenchless; rapacious; sateless; thirsty; unsatisfied; venal; wanting; *xtry. greed;* yearnful; zoilean; [*Ant.* charitable]

**covetousness** *(n.)*: avarice; acquisitiveness; begrudging; craving; cupidity; desire; envy; *fretting;* greed(iness); hunger; insatiability; *jealousy; keen desire;* lust; materialism; *non-generosity;* over-greediness; pruriency; quenchlessness; repining; satelessness; *thirst; unsatisfied;* voraciousness; want; *xtry. ~;* yearning; zoilism; [*Ant.* charitableness]

**cow** *(n.)*: angus; *animal;* bovine; beast; bull; *beef;* calf; cattle [pl.]; dairy ~; dogie; *ennstal;* fatted calf; fatling; gelding; Guernsey; heifer; Holstein; *Irish moiled;* Jersey; kyloe; kine [pl.]; longhorn; leppy; *livestock;* milch ~; milker; neat; *ox;* Polled Shorthorn; quey; red heifer; steer; shorthorn; Texas longhorn; *ungulate; veal;* vituline; Welsh; *x-breed;* yearling; *zho;* [see beast]

**coward** *(n.)*: alarmist; baby; brooder; caitiff; chicken; dastard; deserter; *ever-fearful;* fraidy cat; feardie [Scot.]; funk; gutless; hesitator; invertebrate; jellyfish; *kitten-hearted;* lily liver; milquetoast; niding; *overanxious;* poltroon; pogue; quitter; recreant; runaway; sop; sissy; scaredy-cat; trembler; *unmanly; vexed;* weakling; wimp; *xenophobe;* yellow-belly; zob; [Ant. champion]
**cowardice** *(n.)*: affright; *burden;* cowardliness; dread; edginess; faintheartedness; fear; funk; gutlessness; horror; insecurity; jitters; kiaugh [Scot.]; *lily-livered;* mousiness; nervousness; over-anxiety; pusillanimity; poor-spiritedness; quaking; recreance; *scared; stress;* timidity; timorousness; terror; unmanliness; vexation; weakness; wimpiness; *xenophobia;* yellowness; zealessness; [Ant. courage]
**cowardly** *(adj.)*: afraid; *bothered;* cravenly; chicken; dreading; edgy; ever-fearful; fearful; faint-hearted; gutless; hesitant; insecure; jittery kitten-hearted; lily-livered; milk-livered; nerveless; overanxious; pusillanimous; quivering; recreantly; reluctant; spineless; scared; timid; timorously; terrified; unmanly; vexed; weak-kneed; worried; *xenophobic;* yellow(-bellied); zealless; [Ant. courageous]
**cower** *(v.)*: *affright;* balk; buckle; cringe; dip; *enfold;* flinch; *grimace;* hunker down; have fear; *intimidated;* jump back; *knuckle;* lose courage; *move away; nervous; overwhelmed; panic;* quiver; recoil; shrink back; tremble; *uneasy; vulnerable;* wince; *xenophobic; yield; zealless;*
**cozy** *(adj.)*: appealing; buddy-buddy; comfortable; comfy [slang]; cushy; *delightful;* embosomed; *fine;* good; homey; happy; intimate; *indulged; joy; kept close;* loving; made comfortable; nice; over-soft; pleasant; *quaint;* relaxing; snug; tight; *under the covers;* very ~; warm; *x-soft;* yielding; zero discomfort;
**crack** *(n.)*: aperture; break; breach; chink; crevice; crevasse; chap; chink; divide; division; *exscind;* fissure; gape; hole; interstice; jaw-hole; kin; krack; kibe; laceration; microgroove; mar; niche; nook; opening; parting; *quadrisection;* rip; snap; stridor; split; *tear; uncoupling;* vug; *wreckage;* x; yawn; *zap;*
**crack** *(v.)*: *apart;* bust; break; chink; chap; cut open; damage; divide; *efface;* fracture; go to pieces; gap; harm; injure; *jab;* krack; *lacerate;* mar; *nullify;* open; part; *quash;* ruin; rupture; shatter; split; tear; *undone;* violence; wreck; *x-ing;* yank apart; *zap;* [see decode; hit]
**cracker** *(n.)*: animal ~; biscuit; crispbread; *digestive biscuit; edible; food;* Graham ~; hotel ~; *item;* jewel ~; *krack;* luncheonette ~; matzo; nacho cheese ~; oyster ~; prawn ~; Quaker cookie; rye ~; saltine; thin; unleavened bread; vanilla wafer; wafer; water biscuit; *x-crunchy ~; yellow ~;* zwieback;
**cradle** *(n.)*: *airbed;* bassinet; baby bed; crib; *down-bed; estivate; feather bed;* gurney; hatchery; hotbed; incubator; infant bed; *journey's end;* kip [Br.]; *laying down;* mattress; *manger;* nest; *oversleep;* playpen; *quietude;* rocker bed; straw mattress; soft bed; toddler ~; *unoccupied ~; vessel;* waterbed; *x-sleep; yawning;* zotheca [Rom.];
**cradle** *(v.)*: *around;* bind up; cuddle; draw around; embrace; fold; gird; hold; infold; *join;* keep close; lull; *make safe;* nestle; oxtercog; put arms around; *quietly hold;* receive; rock; support; take; *tenderly;* upbind; *value;* wrap arms around; X; yoke; zone;
**craft** *(n.)*: ability; art; *bent;* capability; craftwork; discipline; expertise; forte; gift; handicraft; handcraft; instinct; *job;* know-how; long suit; manual skill; natural ability; occupation; panurgy; qualification; readiness; skill; talent; *usefulness;* virtuosity; *wherewithal; xenium;* yaup; zest;
**craft** *(v.)*: *assemble;* build; create; construct; design; develop; engineer; fashion; generate; *hew;* invent; *job;* knock together; *labor;* make; *new-built;* originate; put together; produce; *quality-built;* raise; shape; sculpt; turn out; upbuild; *vamp;* whittle; wage; *xlate;* yield; *zeal;*
**craftiness** *(n.)*: artfulness; beguiling; cunning; cleverness; deviousness; deceitfulness; deception; evasiveness; foxiness; guile; *hoax;* ingenuity; insidiousness; Jesuitry; jiggery-pockery; knavishness; *lying;* mendacity; non-trustworthiness; outfoxing; perspicacity; *quaintise* [arch.]; roguishness; subtlety; shrewdness; slyness; trickiness; underhandedness; *vulpine;* wiliness; *xtry, cleverness;* yepship [arch.]; zinging; [Ant. credulity]
**craftsman** *(n.)*: artificer; artisan; artist; builder; craftworker; designer; expert; fashioner; guildsman; hand-crafter; handicraftsman; handyman; handworker; *industrial worker;* journeyman; *key man;* laborer; master; maker; *notoriety; operator;* professional; qualified worker; ready

worker; specialist; skilled worker; tradesman; *useful; versed;* workman; worker; wright; *xylographer;* yeoman; *zaikai [Jap.];*
**craftsmanship** *(n.)*: ability; adeptness; adroitness; art(work); bent; command; capability; cunning; deftness; expertise; familiarity; finesse; genius; handiwork (-craft); instinct; *job;* knack; know-how; long suit; mastery; masterfulness; masterpiece; natural ability; occupation; proficiency; quality; readiness; skill(fulness); talent; usefulness; virtuosity; work(manship); *xenium; years of experience;* zest;
**crafty** *(adj.)*: artful; beguiling; Bismarckian; cunning; clever; devious; deceptive; evasive; foxy; guileful; *hollow;* illusive; insidious; jady; knavish; *longsighted;* misleading; Maciavellian; non-trustworthy; *overwise;* pawky; *quaintise [arch.];* roguish; subtle; sly; sneaky; shrewd; slick; silver-tongued; tricky; underhanded; untrustworthy; unscrupulous; vulpine; wily; wise; *xtry.;* yepe; zinger; [*see* wise; evil; devilish; *Ant.* credulous]
**cram** *(v.)*: arrange; *bear down on;* crunch; crowd; depress; *enfold;* fill; force; get in; gorge; *hammer; infarce* [arch.]; jam(-pack); knock in; load; mush; *niche;* overstuff (-fill); pack; press; quash; ram; stuff; squeeze; tamp; *up thrust; volume;* wedge; *xuld [arch.];* yerk; zip;
**cramp** *(n.)*: ache; *biting;* crick; discomfort; excruciating pain; flare; grief; hurt; intense pain; jab; kink; lancinating pain; misery; *nagging ~; osteocope;* pain; quab; *rack;* spasm; stitch; shooting pain; twinge; *unpleasantness; vexation;* wrenching; *xiphodynia;* yaik; zing;
**crane** *(n. boon)*: *apparatus;* arm; boon; capstan; derrick; davit; elevator; *forklift;* gantry ~; hoist; *instrument;* jenny; *kickumbob;* lift; machine; non-telescoping ~; *outstretch;* pully; *parbuckle; quantitative;* rigger; sheers; sheerlegs; tower ~; tripaston; *unit;* vertical lift; windlass; *xfer;* yarder; *zeug;*
**crash** *(n.)*: accident; bang; boom; crunch; crack; *disaster; explosion;* fragor; *grind;* hit; impact; jolt; kaboom; knock; *lam;* mash; *noise; occurrence;* pow; *quash;* rap; smash; thwack; *undo; vroom;* wham; whack; wreck; *xuld [arch.];* yedder; zing;
**crash** *(v.)*: assault; bash; bang into; collide; clobber; collapse; dash; *explode;* fall into; grind; hit; impact; jam; knock; lam; mash; nail; *overhit;* pound; quash; run into; smash; thump; *undo; void;* whack; wreck; *x;* yedder; zonk;
**crate** *(n.)*: ark; box; bunker; container; case; chest; carton; coffer; *drum;* encasement; *firkin; gift box* holder; *iron chest; jute sack;* kist; lockbox; moving carton; *nook; oil drum;* pod; *quinderkyn;* receptacle; shipping container; trunk; *ungula;* vessel; wooden crate; *XL box; yadzutsu [Jap.]; zet [dial.];*
**crater** *(n.)*: aperture; basin; cavity; caldera; depression; excavation; fissure; gulch; gap; hole; hollow; incavation; jaw-hole; krater; lacuna; maar; *niche;* opening; pit; *quarry-pit;* ravine; sump; trench; *umbilicus;* valley; vug; well; *xystus pit;* yawn; zanja;
**crave** *(v.)*: ask; ache; beseech; beg; bespeak; covet; desire; entreat; fancy; *got to have;* hanker; itch; *just got to have; keen on;* long for; need; obsecrate; pant for; *quiritation;* request; supplicate; trouble one for; urge; *velleity;* want; *xuld [arch.];* yearn for; *zealously desire;* [*Ant.* contemn]
**crawl** *(v.)*: amble; *budge;* creep; drag; edge; footslog; gimp; hitch; inch; jiffle; keep advancing; lumber; limp; move slowly; nudge; ooch; plod; quaddle; *real slow;* scoot along; toddle; totter; *under; very slow;* wriggle; wamble; *xfer;* yaw; *zigzag;*
**crazy** *(adj.)*: absurd; berserk; bonkers; bananas; batty; cracked; cuckoo; deranged; demented; daft; disturbed; eccentric; funny; goofy; haywire; insane; *jokey;* kooky; lunatic; loony; mad; mental (case); nutty; neurotic; outlandish; off ones rocker; psycho(tic); psychopathic; quacked; raving; *ridiculous;* screwy; sick (in the head); twisted; taken leave of senses; unstable; unbalanced; *volatile;* wacky; warped; weird; wild; *xtry. mad; yo-yo;* zany; [*see* silly; *Ant.* commonsense]
**creak** *(n.)*: *acute tone;* bemoaning; crick; drone; *echo;* forced; groan; harsh noise; *irk;* jangle; keen; *lament;* moan; noise; *open;* pule; querk; rasp; squeak; *tone; unflexing; vibration;* whine; *xtr.;* yerr; zip;
**cream** *(n.)*: afterings; *best part;* crème; *dairy;* emulsion; foremilk; *goat's milk;* heavy ~; ice ~; junket; kreme [arch.]; *lactose;* milk; *nutrition; over-rich; pale; quart;* rich ~; single ~; topping; udder; Vitamin D milk; whipped ~; *xanthine oxidase;* yarrum; 0% milk;

**creamy** *(adj.)*: adularescent; *buttery;* cream-like; *dairy;* emulsive; fatty; *goat's milk; heavy; inclouded; junket; kremie [arch.];* luscious; milky; *non-watery;* over-rich; *pale; qually [arch.];* rich; smooth; semiflulidic; thick; *utterly ~;* velvety; wheyey; *xanthene oxidase;* yellowish; *zet [dial.];*

**create** *(v.)*: *assemble;* build; bring into being; construct; craft; design; erect; fashion; fabricate; form; found; generate; *hew;* institute; initiate; invent; *job;* knock together; *labor;* make; *newly form;* originate; produce; *quicken;* raise; shape; speak into existence; turn out; upbuild; *vamp;* wage; *xenomorph;* yield; *zip together;*

**creation** *(n.)*: advent; beginning; commencement; dawn; establishment; formation; genesis; *hatching;* inception; jump off; kickoff; launching; making; nascency; origination; production; *quickening;* rising; start; take-off; *unveiling; verge; welcoming; xenogenesis; youth; zygogenesis;*

**creative** *(adj.)*: artistic; bold; clever; *demiurgic;* enterprising; fanciful; full of ideas; fecund; gifted; heaven-gifted; imaginative; illustrative; innovative; inventive; ingenious; *judicious;* keen-minded; *laboring; make;* novel-notioned; original; *prolific;* quick-witted; right-brained; resourceful; sharp; talented; *unique;* vivid; witty; *xtry.;* yepe; yeasty; *zesty;*

**creator** *(n.)*: assembler; artisan; builder; constructor; craftsman; designer; erector; engineer; fashioner; fabricator; founder; generator; handicraftsman; inventor; *journeyman; key man; laborer;* master builder; maker; *notion;* originator; producer; *qualified builder; rebuilder;* shaper; *tooler;* upbuilder; *vamper;* wright; *xylographer;* yeoman; *zaikai [Jap.];* [Ant. creature]

**creature** *(n.)*: animal; being; critter; creation; domestic animal; entity; fauna [pl.]; game; *herbivore;* individual; jument; *koala;* life form; man; mammal; monster; *non-vertebrate;* organism; person; *pony;* quadruped; *reptile; scavenger; tiger;* ungulate; varmint; wilding; wildlife [pl.]; *xiphopagus;* yearling; zoic; [Ant. creator]

**credible** *(adj.)*: accurate; believable; convincing; dependable; ever-faithful; faithful; genuine; honest; infallible; justifiable; known; likely; most faithful; never-failing; *open-and-shut case;* plausible; questionless; reliable; sound; trustworthy; unfailing; veritable; well-trusted; *xtry;* yeomanly; *zealous;*]

**credit** *(n.)*: acknowledgement; appreciation; believability; credence; distinguishing; estimation; *fess up;* glory; honor; indebtedness; justification; *kudos; laurels;* mindfulness; note; owning up; praise; *quick-to-recognize;* recognition; *salute;* tribute; thanks; *understanding; value;* weight; *xtry. gratitude;* yielding thanks; *zeroing in;*

**credit** *(v.)*: ascribe; attribute; ac~; *believe;* blame; charge; count; chalk up to; deem; *entitle;* fix; give ~; hold responsible; impute; *judge; know;* lay at the door; *make;* notate; owe to; put down to; *questionless;* recognize; suppose; think; *understand; view; well-donw; xfer;* yield as due; *zay [dial.];*

**creed** *(n.)*: article of faith; belief; credo; doctrine; *entrusting;* faith; general beliefs; heart-belief; ideology; *jist;* key beliefs; *loyalty; mainstay; notion;* oracles; persuasion; *quote;* religion; statement of faith; theology; ule; *view;* way of believing; *xel [arch.]; y'faith* [arch.]; *zet [dial.];*

**creek** *(n.)*: arroyo; brook; crick [reg.]; *deep;* effluent; freshet; gully; *headwaters; inlet; jheel [Ind.]; kill [Du.];* lough; millstream; *narrows;* outlet; *passage;* quebrada; rill; stream; tributary; *underground stream; voe;* waterway; *xyrisic;* yeo; Zee *[G.];*

**creep** *(v.)*: *amble;* budge; crawl; drag; edge; *falter;* gimp; hitch; inch; jiffle; *keep advancing;* lumber; move (slowly); *non-speedy; obambulate [arch.];* plod; quaddle; *relocate;* scuttle; scoot; totter; *underway; very slow;* wriggle; *xfer;* yaw; *zigzag;*

**cremate** *(v.)*: alight; burn; combust; deflagrate; enflame; flame; *gut; heat;* incinerate; *jeopardize;* kindle; light (up); *miskindle; nightfire;* overburn; *pyre; quick-match;* raze; scorch; torch; ustion; vesticate; *waste; xermothermic; yellow-hot; zap;*

**crest** *(n.)*: apex; brow; crown; *destination;* extremity; *farthest point; greatest height;* high point; *hillcrest; increase; jut;* kop; limit; mountaintop; nib; *overmost point;* peak; pinnacle; *quoif;* ridge; summit; top; upper extremity; vertex; *way up; xtry;* yardang; zenith;

**crew** *(n.)*: assembly; A-team; bunch; company; detachment; employees; faction; group; hired help; ingathering; jam [slang]; kit [coll.]; lot; mass; number; *outworkers;* party; quantity; *rally;* squad; staff; team; troop; unit; *variety;* wisp; x-unit; *yeomen;* zonal ~;
**crib** *(n.)*: airbed; bassinet; (baby) bed; cradle; *down-bed;* enclosure; *feather bed; gurney; hammock;* infant bed; Jenny Lind ~: kip [Br.]; *laying down;* mini ~; mattress; *manger; nest; oversleep;* playpen; *quietude;* rocking bed; straw mattress; stock; toddler ~; travel ~; *unconscious; vegetation;* waterbed; x-sleep; *young; zotheca [Rom.];*
**crier** *(n.)*: announcer; bellman; courier; dispatch; envoy; forewarner; *giver of tidings;* herald; informer; *just in;* keener; liaison; lamenter; messenger; notifier; *official;* proclaimer; *quidnunc [L.];* representative; reporter; *speaker;* town ~; updater; *utterer;* voice; walking delegate; wailer; x-man; yeller; *zip;*
**crime** *(n.)*: atrocity; breach; criminal offense; debauchery; evil; felony; fault; guilt; heinousness; infraction; injustice; *judgment; killing;* law-breaking; malefaction; misdemeanor; malfeasance; misdeed; *naughtiness;* offense; outrage; outlawry; peccadillo; perpetration; *quad;* rebellion; sin; transgression; tort; unlawful act; violation; villainy; wrong(doing); war ~; *xgression; yetzer hara [Heb.]; zero innocence;*
**criminal** *(n.)*: archfiend; bad guy; crook; convict; culprit; delinquent; *deviant;* evildoer; extortionist; felon; gangster; gunsel [slang]; highwayman; highbinder; infractor; jailbird; knuck; lawbreaker; malefactor; misdemeanant; *murderer;* no-good; outlaw; offender; perpetrator; *quad;* rogue; recidivist; *robber;* scoundrel; transgressor; tortfeasor; thug; *thief;* underboss; villain; wrongdoer *xgressor;* yardbird; yegg; *zhlub;* [*Ant.* constable]
**cringe** *(v.)*: aback; balk; blench; cower; draw back; *edgy;* flinch; grimace; girn; *hesitate; involuntary;* jump; *kick;* lose courage; move back in fear; *nervous; ouch; palter;* queck; quiver; quail; recoil; *react;* shrink; tremble; *uneasy; vexed;* wince; *xuld [arch.];* yerk; zip aback;
**cripple** *(v.)*: *afflict; be~;* crush; disable; enfeeble; *feeble; game;* hamstring; hough [Scot.]; injure; immobilize; *jake-legged;* knock out; lame; maim; *nullify;* obstruct; paralyze; *query;* render inoperative; *stop; thwart; undo; victimize; wound;* wing; wreck; x-out; yedder; zap;
**crisis** *(n.)*: adversity; bind; *breakdown;* critical moment; dilemma; emergency; fix; *gathering clouds;* height; impasse; jam; kadooment [Carib.]; life ~; mess; nightmare; ordeal; predicament; quandary; *rattle; ruin;* situation; trauma point; trial; upheaval; vexation; woe; *xtry. circumstance;* yedder; zero hour; [*see* calamity]
**criterion** *(n.)*: accepted standard; benchmark; condition; deciding factor; established standard; factor; gauge; habilitation; indispensable ~; judgment standard; key ~; *limitation;* measure; norm; *obligation;* prerequisite; qualification; requirement; rule; stipulation; specifications; standard; terms; *ultimate deciding factor;* vital condition; want; *XO requirement;* yardstick; *zero option;*
**critic** *(n.)*: attacker; balker; criticizer; doubter; *enemy;* faultfinder; grumbler; haranguer; impugner; jangler; knocker; lambaster; momus; nonbeliever; oppugner; polemic; questioner; rejecter; skeptic; traducer; *unfavorable;* vituperator; whinger; *xiaoren; yeller;* Zoilus; [*Ant.* commender]
**critical** *(adj. disparaging)*: animadversive; belittling; captious; condemnatory; censorious; disapproving; disparaging; deprecatory; *explosive;* frowning; fault-finding; griping; hypercritical; harsh; impugning; judgmental; knocking; lambasting; *mean;* negative; over- ~; pejorative; peppery; *querulous;* rebukeful; rough; sharp-tongued; traducent; unfavorable; vindictive; whingy; *xenophobic;* yauping; zoilean; [*Ant.* complimentary]
**critical** *(adj. essential)*: acute; *bad;* crucial; dangerous; essential; *fundamental;* grave; heavy; imperative; important; *jeopardized;* key; life-threatening; major; matter of life or death; necessary; *oligatory;* perilous; *quintessential;* required; serious; threatening; urgent; vital; weighty; *xtry.; yearnful; zero hour;*
**criticism** *(n.)*: assessment; admonishment; bashing; blame; beef; censure; critique; decrial; denunciation; excoriation; evaluation; flack; faultfinding; gripe; haranguing; hypercriticism; increpation; judgment; knocking; lambasting; monitory; niggle; objection; protest; quarrel; reproach; review; swipe; stricture; slam; telling off; upbraiding; vitriol; whingeing [Br.]; *x-fire;* yawping; zoilism; [*Ant.* compliment]

**criticize** *(v.)*: asperse; attack; blast; castigate; condemn; decry; denounce; disparage; excoriate; fault; gripe; harangue; impugn; jangle; knock; lambaste; make criticism; *murmur;* nitpick; object; pan; question; remonstrate; slam; traduce; *ululate;* vituperate; whine; *xuld [arch.];* yell at; *zing;* [*Ant.* compliment]

**critique** *(n.)*: assessment; appraisal; breakdown; criticism; deeming; evaluation; feeling; finding; gauging; *herborization;* idea; judgment; *knowledge-gathering;* leaning; mind; *notion;* opinion; perspective; *quot homines tot sententiae* [L.]; review; surmising; take; thought; *unbiased opinion;* valuation; write-up; *xenodiagnosis;* yield results; *zinger;*

**crooked** *(adj.)*: awry; angular; bent; curved; cockeyed; declivous; escarped; flexuous; *gradient;* hunched; inclined; jim-jam; kim-kam; lopsided; *markedly ~;* non-linear; oblique; pitched; quinque-angular; repandous; sloped; slanted; stooped; tilted; uneven; unstraightened; verging; varus [med.]; winding; *xuld [arch.];* yawing; zad; [*see* dishonest, *Ant.* curveless]

**crop** *(n.)*: agricultural yield; byproduct; bumper ~; cash ~; *corn;* dividend; earing; fruit(age); farm ~; *grain; gathering;* harvest; ingathering; *juglans;* kirning [Scot.]; land yield; *maize;* nurse ~; outgrowth; produce; quantities; reaping; rowen; return; seedlings; takings; *underutilized ~; vegetation;* wheat; *xanthocarpous;* yield; *zafra;*

**crop** *(v.)*: *abridge;* bob; clip; dock; exscind; *fix;* graze; hack; incise; *jigsaw;* knife; lop; *miter;* nip; obtruncate; pare; poll; *quarter;* retrench; shear; shorten; trim; *undercut; vell;* whittle; x-sect; *yerk; zip off;*

**crops** *(n.)*: acquisition; bumper crop; crop; *deposit;* ears; *fields;* firstfruits; fruit; gatherings; garner; harvest; increase; ingathering; *jam [slang];* kirning [Scot.]; *load;* mass; *net;* output; plants; produce; quantity; reaping; *store;* takings; unharvested ~; vintage; winter- ~; x-crop; yield; zafra;

**cross** *(adj.)*: angry; boiling; chagrined; displeased; exasperated; furious; galled; hot; irate; *jumping mad; kindled;* livid; mad; nettled; outraged; perturbed; quick-tempered; raging; sore; ticked off; upset; violent; wroth; *xerothermic; yond [arch.]; zealousy [arch.];*

**cross** *(n.)*: *across;* bisection; crossroad; connection; conjunction; cleche; crossing; crosslet; decussation; *emblem; fylfot;* gibbet; heraldic ~; intersection; junction; juncture; jointure; *khachkar; lauburu;* mark; *nexus;* overlapping; pommette; potence; quadrivial; rood; saltire; T-junction; union; *Victoria ~; western ~;* X; x-ing; *yew ~; zeug;*

   **Kinds of crosses**: Armenian ~; Byzantine ~; Christian ~; Eastern ~; florian ~; Greek ~; high ~; iron ~; Jerusalem ~; knight's ~; Latin ~; Maltese ~; neolithic ~; Occitan ~; Pisan ~; Red ~; Swiss ~; two-barred ~; Victoria ~; X;

**Cross** *(n.)*: alter of sacrifice; *atonement; bodily suffering;* Calvary; Crucifixion; death of Christ; *execution; flogging;* gibbet; Golgotha; Holy Cross; *infliction;* Jesus' sacrifice; *kinosis; lashing; murder; nails;* old rugged ~; passion; *quietus;* Roman cross; shedding of Blood; *stauros* [Gr.]; *suffering;* tree; *ultimate sacrifice; veil rent; way of suffering;* X; *xylos* [Gr.]; *yielding up the ghost; zapping;* [*see* Calvary]

**cross** *(v.)*: *across; advance;* bridge; ~ over; ~-sect; criss~; decussate; *encounter;* fly over; go over; *hurry;* intersect; juncture; *kindle; locomote;* move over; *nudge;* overlap; pass over; *quicken; run; recross;* span; traverse; transverse; *underway; voyage; venture;* walk; x; x-intercept; *xfer; yede;* zip over;

**crossroad** *(n.)*: *alternative;* bisection; crossroads; connection; crossway; *decision;* exit; fork; *gateway;* highway intersection; intersection; interchange; junction; *key decision;* lane crossing; meeting point; node; *nexus;* option; *point of decision;* quadrivial; road crossing; six-way intersection; T in the road; union; *vennel;* waypoint; x-ing; Y in the road; *zone;* [*see* decision]

**crouch** *(v.)*: *acquiesce;* bend; bow; curve; dip; duck; enfold; flex; fold; *geniculate;* hunker; incline; *jag;* knuckle; kneel; lie low; *move down; namaste;* overbend; ply; quat; *refold;* squat; stoop; scrooch; *turn; uncinate; vary;* wind; *xfer;* yield; *zip;*

**crowd** *(n.)*: assemblage; amassment; audience; bunch; company; cluster; clique; drove; *everyone;* forgathering; faction; flock; group; gang; gathering; horde; host; ingathering; jam [slang]; kit [coll.]; lot; mass; multitude; mob; number; *overflow;* pack; press; quantity; ruck; rabble; shoal; swarm; throng; turnout; troop; unit; variety; wisp; *xtr. people; yardful;* zoo;

**crowd** *(v.)*: amass; *burden;* cram; clutter; condense; compress; congest; cumber; densify; densen; encumber; fill; gorge; horde; inundate; incumber; jam-pack; *kibble;* load; mass; maximize; *no room;* over~ (-populate -stuff; -fill; -load; -people); press; pack; *populous;* quash full; rally; replenish; swarm; stuff; saturate; squeeze; *serried;* throng; use up; *volume;* wedge in; *x-people; yield; zero space leftover;*

**crown** *(n.)*: archducal ~; bycoket; corona; diadem; *emblem;* floral ~; grass ~; headpiece; hat; hedjet; imperial ~; jeweled ~; kingly hat; laurel ~; monarchial ~; naval ~; ornament: pschent [Egy.]; queenly hat; rigol; stephanos; state ~; tiara; tonsure; uraeus; victor's ~; wreath; *xtal. tiara; yark; Zar's ~; [see* reward]

**crown** *(v.)*: anoint; bestow; coronate; *deliver;* enthrone; *furnish; give; hand over;* install; invest; instate; inthrone; *jubilate; king; lautu* [Inca]; laurel; make; *nobility;* ordain; place; queen; re-enthrone; set up; throne; *unction;* vest; *worship; xfer;* yark; *Zar;*

**crucial** *(adj.)*: all-important; *big;* critical; compelling; dire; exigent; essential; *fundamentally important;* grave; heavy; imperative; important; *jump to it;* key; life-or-death; major; matter of life or death; needful; *oligatory;* pressing; paramount; priority; *quintessential;* required; serious; terribly important; urgent; vital; weighty; *xtry.; yearnful; zero hour;*

**crucify** *(v.)*: afflict; *agony; blood sacrifice;* cause to die; deliver to be crucified; execute; excruciate; *finish off;* give death penalty; hang on a cross; inflict pain; immolate; *jab;* kill; lancinate; make to suffer; *murder;* nail to a cross; offer; put to death; punish; *pierce; quash;* rack; slay; shed blood; sacrifice; torment; take life; *unjustly kill;* victimize; *wound; x-out; yield; zero mercy;*

**crude** *(adj.)*: abominable; base; coarse; degraded; defiling; defiled; disgusting; earthy; filthy; gauche; gross; horrid; ill-mannered; jadish; kitsch; lewd; mean; nasty; offensive; obscene; piggish; *quad;* raw; rude; shocking; tasteless; unrefined; uncouth; vulgar; wretched; *x-rated;* yucky; zhlubby; [*Ant.* civil]

**cruel** *(adj.)*: atrocious; brutal; callous; disdainful; execrable; flagitious; *gruff;* heartless; harsh; inhuman; jackboot; kindless; loathsome; merciless; mean; nasty; odious; overbearing; pitiless; *quad;* ruthless; sadistic; severe; terrible; unmerciful; unkind; vicious; wicked; *xenophobic; yeffell* [arch.]; *zero-mercy;* [*Ant.* charitable]

**cruelty** *(n.)*: atrociousness; brutality; cruelness; devilishness; evil; ferociousness; *galsomeness;* harshness; inhumanness; *jadedness;* kindlessness; *lovelessness;* meanness; nastiness; odiousness; pitilessness; *querulousness;* ruthlessness; sadism; savagery; severity; terribleness; unmercifulness; viciousness; wickedness; *xenophobia; yelling; zero-mercy;* [*Ant.* charitableness]

**crumb** *(n.)*: *atom;* bit; chunk; chip; clod; daud; *ens;* fragment; flake; *gob;* hunk; *iota;* junt; kernel; lump; little piece; morsel; mite; nugget; ort; ounce; piece; *quantity;* remnant; speck; tidbit; *unit; vestige;* wedge; wee bit; *xylon; yngot* [arch.]; *zum* [dial.];

**crumble** *(v.)*: *annihilate;* break apart; comminute; collapse; disintegrate; explode; fall apart; fragment; grind; *hunks; impair; junk; kill;* lay waste; levigate; mash; *nullify; obliterate;* pulverize; powder; quash; reduce to powder; smash; squash; turn into dust; *topple; unbuild; violence;* waste away; *x-ing;* yank apart; *zap;* [*Ant.* construct]

**crusade** *(n.)*: attack; battle; campaign; drive; expedition; fight; *gunnery;* holy war; *invasion; jihad* [Mos.]; *kampf* [G.]; *luctation* [arch.]; movement; *naval warfare;* onslaught; *position warfare;* quarrel; religious war; struggle; *total war; unrest;* venture; war; *x-fire;* yed; *zealous war;*

**crush** *(v.)*: *annihilate;* bash; compact; destroy; *expunge;* flatten; grind; *humiliate; immobilize;* jam; *kill;* levigate; mash; nullify; *obliterate;* press; pulp; pulverize; quash; ruin; squash; smash; throttle; tamp; *undo;* void; wreck; *x;* yank down; zap;

**crust** *(n.)*: *atop; buildup;* covering; coating; dry ~; encrustation; formation; *granular;* hard layer; incrustation; *jarring;* kirtling; layer; mellit [zoo.]; *natural encrustation;* overgrowth; outer part; *pie ~; quat;* rigid ~; shell; skin; scab; *top;* upper layer; verge; *wax hard; x-hard;* yucky; *zet* [dial.];

**cry** *(n.)*: *appeal;* bellow; call; discharge; declamation; ebullition; exclamation; fit of ~ing; growl; holler; hoot; howl; *inveighing; jubilation;* keen; loud shout; lamentation; moan; noise; outcry; *proclamation;* quiritation; resonation; reverberation; roar; shout; scream; shriek; sob; tearful ~; ululation; vociferation; wail; whoop; whine; *xenophonia;* yell; yowl; *zindabad;*
**cry** *(v. bawl)*: *attrition;* bawl; boo-hoo; *contrition;* despair; erupt into tears; *feel sorrow;* grieve; gush; howl; *inveigh; judder;* keen; lachrymate; moan; *noise;* outcry; outweep; *pout;* quistle *[arch.];* roar; sob; snivel; shed tears; squall; tear; *ululate; vociferate;* weep; wail; whimper; *xenophthalmia;* yowl; yawp; *zowie;* [*Ant.* chuckle]
**cry** *(v. shout)*: appeal; bellow; beckon; call; declaim; exclaim; *erupt; fret;* growl; holler; *inveigh; jubilate;* keen; loudly say; moan; noise; outcry; *proclaim; quiritation;* roar; shout; scream; *thunder;* ululate; vociferate; whoop; *xenophonia;* yell; *zindabad;*
**cryptic** *(adj.)*: arcane; *abstruse;* baffling; coded; cabalistic; curious; dark; enigmatic; esoteric; furtive; gnomic; hidden; inexplicable; jumbled; *knotted; labyrinthine;* mysterious; non-legible; obscure; puzzling; queer; recondite; secret; top-secret; unsolved; unrevealed; veiled; weird; *xeno-; yieldless;* zany;
**crystal** *(n.)*: *aventurine;* blown glass; clear glass; double-glass; etched ~; flint glass; glass; heavy glass; Iceland ~; *jume ~; kaleidoscope;* lead ~; *mineral; non-glare glass;* opaline; pure ~; quartz; rock ~; sparkling glass; *transparent; uniform;* vitreous (silica); *wavellite;* xtal; *yard; zizzy;*
**cuddle** *(v.)*: *affection;* burrow; cozy up; croodle; dandle; draw close; embrace; embosom; *fondle;* grip; hug; infold; *jam; keep close; love;* make comfortable; nestle; nuzzle; *overply;* press; *quash; rub;* snuggle; *tenderly hug;* upbind; *very cozy;* wrap; X; yoke up with; zone;
**culmination** *(n.)*: apex; apogee; *best part;* climax; consummation; *destination;* end; finale; *greatest height;* height; *important; jut;* key part; *lofty height;* mountaintop; meridian; *ne pas ultra* [F.]; *overmost point;* peak; pinnacle; *quoif;* ridge; summit; top; *uttermost;* vertex; windup; *xtry; yonder point;* zenith;
**culprit** *(n.)*: *accused;* bad guy; crook; criminal; doer of evil; evildoer; felon; guilty party; *highbinder;* infractor; jackanapes; knave; lawbreaker; malefactor; no-good; offender; perpetrator; *questrel;* rogue; scoundrel; sinner; transgressor; *ungodly;* villain; wrongdoer *xgressor; yob; zhlub;*
**cult** *(n.)*: affiliation; belief-system; church group; denomination; *eastern religion;* false religion; group; *hierarchy;* integrated system; *junta;* Krishnaism; *liegdom;* man-centered sect; *neo-orthodox;* organization; philosophy; *quasi-Christian;* religious group; sect; *theology;* ule; *viewpoint;* wing; *Xenu;* yogi; zoism; [*Ant.* Christianity]
**cultivate** *(v.)*: *advance;* breed; cultivate; dress; develop; encourage; farm; foster; grow; garden; help bring about; husband; inspire; *jump ahead; keep;* labor to produce; make grow; nurture; *outweed;* produce; quicken; raise; rotovate; sow; till; undertake to produce; *vivify;* work; weed; *xfer;* yield; *zealously promote;*
**cultural** *(n.)*: accepted; behavioral; customary; dominant; expected; familiar; general; habitual; inveterate; jake [Br.]; known; long-established; main; normal; ordinary; prevalent; *qualified;* routine; societal; traditional; usual; *unwritten;* venerated; well-established; *x-cultural; ye olde; zealous tradition;*
**culture** *(n.)*: accepted way; behavior; customs; daily routine; established practice; folk ways; general behavioral pattern; habitude; institution; *jake [Br.]; kultur* [G.]; long-established tradition; manner; mores; meme; norm; old ways; practice; *quo mode* [L.]; *routine;* society; social behavior; tradition; usage; values; way (of life); *x-cultural; ye olde; zealous tradition;*
**cumbersome** *(adj.)*: awkward; bulky; clumsy; difficult; encumbering; fumbly; graceless; hard; hulky; impeditive; inelegant; jumbly; klutzy; lumbering; maladroit; non-graceful; oafish; ponderous; *quirky; rube; socially inept;* troublesome; ungraceful; unwieldy; unmanageable; vexatious; wearisome; *xtr. difficult; yokelish; zhlubby;*
**cumulative** *(adj.)*: all-encompassing; broad; collective; combined; *done;* entire; full; group; *high;* inclusive; joint; *known;* lump; macroscopic; non-abridged; overall; plenary; quantitative; *ranging;* summative; total; unabridged; *vast;* whole; *xtry.; yare; zonal;*

**cunning** *(adj.)*: artful; beguiling; crafty; clever; deceitful; devious; evasive; foxy; fraudful; guileful; *hollow;* illusive; insidious; jady; jesuitical; knavish; *longsighted;* mischievous; non-trustworthy; *overwise;* pawky; *quaintise [arch.];* roguish; subtle; shrewd; tricky; underhanded; vulpine; wily; *xtry.;* yepe; zinger; [*Ant.* credulous]
**cup** *(n.)*: ama; beaker; chalice; calix; demitasse; decanter; *egg~;* flute; glass; goblet; highball glass; *imbiber;* jigger; krug; *liquid container;* mug; mazer; noggin; *olla;* pannikin; quaich; receptacle; stein; tumbler; tea~; tassie; *urn;* vessel; water glass; wineglass; xtal.; yard; zegedine;
**cupbearer** *(n.)*: attendant; butler; cup-bearer; chamberlain; demiurge; eunuch; *food-taster;* gallopin; house steward; indentured servant; jackman; king's attendant; lackey; manservant; naperer; official ~; pantler; queen's attendant; royal ~; servant; *trusted servant;* underbutler; valet; worker; x-man; yeoman; *zaikai;*
**cupboard** *(n.)*: armoire; buffet; closet; cabinet; *dairy; étagère;* footlocker; *gallery;* hutch; *item; jar shelf;* kitchen cabinet; keep; locker; mahogany ~; nook; overhead ~; *opening;* pantry; quadrilocular; *room;* sideboard; *tansu; utensil chest;* vitrine; wraparound cabinet; *xtr. storage; yam box;* zeta;
**curable** *(adj.)*: ameliorable; *betterable;* correctable; doctorable; emendable; fixable; *get fixed;* helpable; improvable; *jury-rig; kilter; level out;* mendable; medicable; *neogenesis; overhauling;* patchable; *quick-fix;* rectifiable; remediable; sanable; treatable; *upbuild; vamp;* workable; *x-fix; yanggona; zip back together;* [*Ant.* cureless]
**curative** *(adj.)*: advantageous; antidotal; beneficial; convalescent; corrective; doctor-endorsed; effective; favorable; gainful; good; healing; healthful; iatric; *julep;* kinic; life-extending; medicable; medicinal; *nourishing; outstanding;* profitable; quinic; remedial; recuperative; restorative; salutary; therapeutic; useful; vulnerary; wholesome; *xenobiotic; yieldful; zopissa [arch.];* [*Ant.* corrupting]
**curb** *(v.)*: avert; block; curtail; check; decrease; encumber; *frustrate; gum up;* hold back; impede; *jam;* keep (from); limit; *let* [arch.]; moderate; *nullify;* obstruct; parameterize; qualify; restrict; restrain; shorten; thwart; *undo;* veto; withhold; *x; yank; zap;* [*Ant.* continue]
**cure** *(n.)*: antidote; balm; *cure-all;* drug; elixir; *first aid; glycerol;* healing agent; *injection; julep;* key; lohock; medicine; natural ~; *oxacillin;* pharmaceutical; *quinine;* remedy; serum; treatment; ule; vaccine; wonder drug; xenobiotic; yanggona; *zopissa* [arch.];
**cure** *(v.)*: aright; better; correct; doctor; *enhance;* fix; get better; heal; improve; *jury-rig; kilter; level out;* medicate; mend; make well; *neogenesis;* overhaul; patch up; *quick-fix;* remedy; restore; right; set aright; tune up; *upbuild;* vamp; work a ~; *x-fix; yanggona; zip back together;*
**curiosity** *(n. inquisitiveness)*: agog; burning desire; curiousness; desire to know; eagerness; *fancy; got to know;* hungering; inquisitiveness; interest; *just need to know;* knowledge-seeking; *longing;* meddlesomeness; nosiness; over~; probing; prying; questioning; *really want to know;* snooping; *trying to find out; unsatisfied; very strange;* wonder; *xtry.;* yearning; zeal to know; [*Ant.* coolness]
**curiosity** *(n. novelty)*: article; bauble; curio; *decoration; effects;* fallal; gewgaw; habiliment; item; *junk;* knickknack; *lovely item; merchandise;* novelty; object; piece; *quelque-chose* [F.]; rare object; showpiece; trinket; thing; unusual item; *valuable;* whigmaleerie; *xylograph; yannigan; zeug [G.];*
**curious** *(adj.)*: agog; *burning desire;* concerned; desirous (-dying) to know; eager; *fancy; got to know;* hungering; inquisitive; inquiring; interested; *just need to know;* keen; knowledge-seeking; looking for answers; meddlesome; nosy; over~; probing; prying; quizzical; questioning; questful; rogatory; searching; snooping; *trying to find out;* unsatisfied; voyeuristic; wondering; *xtry. ~;* yuky [Scot.]; zealous to find out; [*Ant.* cool]
**curl** *(n.)*: alternation; *becurled;* coil; circlet; convolution; *downward ~;* entwisting; frizz(le); frounce; gyre; helix; hank; *intwisting; jag;* kink; *looping; meandering; nonlinear; overwound;* pin curl; *peristaltic;* querl; ringlet; spiral; swirl; twist; twirl; *tress;* upwinding; volution; whirl; whorl; *x-ing; yaw; zigzag;*

**curl** *(v.)*: *alternate;* becurl; bend; coil; corkscrew; *do wrap;* entwist; frizz; gnarl; hankle; intwist; *jag;* kink; loop; meander; *nonlinear; overwind; prewind;* querl; ravel; ringlet; spiral; twist; tong; upwind; *underwind;* volt; wind; *x-ing; yaw;* zigzag;

**curly** *(adj.)*: *alternating;* becurled; curled; *do wrap;* entwisted; frizzy; *gnarled;* hankled; intwisted; *jag;* kinky; looped; meandering; *nonlinear; overwound; prewound;* querly; raveled; spiraled; twisted; *tight curls;* ulotrichous; volute; wound; *x-ing; yaw;* zigzagged; [*Ant.* curveless]

**current** *(adj.)*: at hand; *by and by;* contemporary; *direct;* existing; existent; *forthwith;* going on now; *here;* immediate; incumbent; *just now; known; lately;* modern; *now;* of today; present; prevailing; *quickly;* recent; sitting; serving; this moment; *today's;* up-to-date; very newest; *without ado; x-speed; yet; zealously;*

**current** *(n.)*: *airflow;* blast; backset; course; circulation; direction; drift; discharge; ebb; flow; gushing; *hurl;* issue; jet(stream); Kuroshio; line; movement; millrace; naid; outflow; profluence; pouring; quell; rush; rip ~; stream; tide; torrent; under~; undertow; *vomiting;* wafting; *water flow; xfer;* yern; *zwoosh;*

**curriculum** *(n.)*: academic materials; books; course; classroom lessons; *didactic;* educational material; formal lessons; *guide;* home school ~; instruction; *journal; knowledge;* lessons; material; minicourse; *noetic; outlines;* primers; *quantity;* readers; schoolbooks; textbooks; university textbooks; trivium; verse-books; workbooks; xenagogue; *yarking; zine;*

**curse** *(n.)*: anathema; bewitchment; commination; demonifuge; execration; *foulness; grief;* hex; incantation; jinx; *karakia [Maori]; loathsome ~;* malediction; night-spell; *ordeal;* pox; qualm [arch.]; *ruination;* spell; *trouble; undoing;* voodoo; woe; weird [Scot.]; *xala; yellow blight; zauber* [G.]; zapping;

**curse** *(v.)*: anathematize; afflict; *accursed;* bewitch; cast spell; comminate; denounce evil against; enchant; execrate; foment; get; grieve; hex; harass; imprecate; jinx; *karakia [Maori]; lash out;* menace; nettle; *ordeal;* plague; put ~ (-spell) on; *quash;* rile; scourge; torment; trouble; upset; unnerve; vex; witch; *xuld [arch.];* yerk; *zap;*

**cursory** *(adj.)*: ankle-deep; brief; casual; desultory; external; fast; glib; hurried; inconsiderable; *jaunty; keg-meg;* light; mere ~; meager; non-thorough; *on the surface;* perfunctory; passing; quick; rapid; superficial; *trivial;* unmeticulous; *visual;* without close attention; *x-fast;* yar; *zippy;* [*Ant.* comprehensive]

**curt** *(adj.)*: abrupt; brusque; curtal; direct; *economical;* forthright; gruff; harsh; inconsiderate; *jaded;* kindless; laconic; *mean;* non-tactful; offhanded; pointed; quick; rough; rude; short; snippy; terse; unkind; unceremonious; *violent; withdrawn; xuld [arch.]; yeesy [arch.]; zhlubbily;* [*Ant.* civil]

**curtail** *(v.)*: abridge; bring down; cut short; curb; decrease; *edit;* foreshorten; *go down;* hold back; impede; *jam;* knock down; limit; make shorter; minimize; narrow down; obtruncate; pare down; *quail;* reduce duration; shorten; trim; truncate; *undo; vell;* whittle; *x-sect; yeme* [arch.]; *zeroize;*

**curtain** *(n.)*: *apparatus;* bed-hangings; *blinds;* cottage ~; drapes; drapery; end ~; front ~; *furnishing;* Gobelin; hangings; *item;* Japanese ~; *kitchen curtains;* lace ~; mantling; net ~; noren [Jap.]; nightshade; *object;* portière; purdah [Ind.]; *q-bond ~;* roll-down ~; skirt; shower ~; swag; sheer ~: tableau ~; *tapestry;* uprising ~; veil; *valance;* wimple; window curtain; *x-weave ~; yellow ~;* zibeline;

**curve** *(n.)*: angle; arc; bend; bow; curvature; crook; dip; el(bow); fold; geomeric ~; hook; hunch; incline; *jag;* knee; knuckle; kink; left turn; meniscus; *nonlinear;* ogee; oxbend; parabola; quat; right turn; rondure; stoop; sheer; turn; twist; *uncinate;* verge; vault; wind; warp; xy-curve; yaw; zig; zag;

**curve** *(v.)*: arc(h); bend; bow; change direction; crook; curl; down~; *enfold;* fold; *go;* hook; incline; jag; *kink;* lean; *move; non-linear;* out~; *ply; quoil [arch.];* round; swerve; turn; U-turn; up~; verge; *wind;* x-curve; yaw; zag;

**cushion** *(n.)*: air pillow; bolster; cow pillow; dampener; eiderdown pillow; feather pillow; goosefeather pillow; headrest; inflatable ~; *Japanese pillow;* kahili pillow [Haw.]; lace pillow; *mat;* neck pillow; overstuffed ~; pillow; *quilt;* rest; sofa ~; seat; throw pillow; upholstery; velvet ~; Winnipeg ~; *xillinous; yellow ~;* zabuton;

**cussword** *(n.)*: abuse; *anathematizing;* blasphemy; curse; coarse language; dirty word; expletive; foul language; *gross disrespect; hex;* irreverence; invective; juration; *kitsch; lewd word;* malediction; *nasty language;* oath; profanity; *quadriliteral;* ribaldry; swearword; sacrilege; tasteless speech; ungodly language; vulgarism; *vernacular; wickedness; XXXX; yawp; zinger;*

**custodian** *(n.)*: attendant; broom-pusher; caretaker; curator; concierge; *day laborer;* employee; *fix-it man;* gatekeeper; *hand(yman);* hireling; industrial worker; janitor; keeper; *lackey;* maintenance man; night janitor; *offside; personnel; quarter-maid; roustabout;* sextant; sanitation engineer; turnkey; *underling;* verger; warden; x-man; *yeoman; zakai [Jap.];*

**custody** *(n.)*: accountability; *burden;* care; charge; *duty; ensuring; fending;* guardianship; holding; handling; intendancy; jurisdiction; keeping; *lordship;* management; *necessity;* oversight; protection; *quia timet [L.];* responsibility; stewardship; safekeeping; trusteeship; *upholding; vocation;* ward; watchcare; xci.; *yeming [arch.]; zamindari [Ind.];*

**custom** *(n.)*: assuetude; accepted way; behavior; culture; consuetude; daily routine; established practice; fashion; folk ways; general behavioral pattern; habit; institution; *jake [Br.]; kultur [G.];* long-established tradition; manner; mores; norm; old ways; pattern; *quo mode [L.];* rubric; routine; society; social behavior; tradition; usage; *venerated; vogue;* way; wont; *x-cultural; ye olde; zealous tradition;*

**customary** *(adj.)*: accepted; automatic; behavioral; customable; cultural; common; conventional; dominant; expected; established; familiar; general; habitual; habitudinal; inveterate; jake [Br.]; known; long-established; main; normal; *natural;* ordinary; prevalent; prevailing; popular; predominant; qualified; regular; routine; standard; societal; social; traditional; typical; tribal; time-honored; usual; *unwritten;* venerated; well-established; widespread; *x-cultural; ye olde; zealous tradition;*

**customer** *(n.)*: *acquirer;* buyer; consumer; client; *dependant;* end-user; fellow; guest; guy; *haggler;* investor; individual; *junk-dealer;* keener; *lad; man(ciple); non-cash ~;* one; *outpatient;* patron; purchaser; prospect; paying ~; *patient;* qualified buyer; regular ~; shopper; *subject;* trader; user; vendee; walk-in; *xfer ~; yokel; zhlub;*

**cut** *(n.)*: affliction; break; boo-boo; chop; crop; damage; *excision;* flesh wound; gash; graze; hack mark; incision; injury; *jab mark;* kerf; lesion; laceration; maim; *mischief;* nick; notch; opening; puncture; query; *riven;* sore; slash; scratch; tear; *unseaming;* violence; wound; x-section; yedder; *zip;*

**cut** *(v.)*: ax; abscind; amputate; bisect; bob; cleave; chop; crop; carve; clip; dissever; divide; dock; exscind; foreshorten; fissure; gouge; graze; grate; hack; hew; halve; incise; *jigsaw;* knife; lop; mince; mow; nip; nick; obtruncate; pare; prune; poll; part; quadrisect; retrench; remove; slice; slit; slash; shear; split; sever; snip; separate; trim; truncate; *unseam; under~;* vell; whack; whittle; x-sect; yerk; zip;

**cute** *(adj.)*: adorable; beautiful; charming; cuddly; delightful; endearing; fair; good-looking; handsome; irresistible; *jolie [F.];* kissable; lovely; *magnificent;* nice-looking; *outstanding;* pretty; quite ~; *regard; really ~;* sweet; taking; *unsurpassed;* voluptuous; well-looking; *xtry.;* yummy; *zizzy;* [*Ant.* contemptible]

**cycle** *(n.)*: annulus; bout; circle; circuit; consecution; course; *development;* epi~; *full-circle;* gradation; gamut; *hoop;* indiction; *Jordan curve; kilocycle;* loop; lap; micro-circle; nexus; orbit; phase; period; *queue;* ring; round; rotation; series; sequence; train; *unbroken ~; vesica;* wheel; *x-radius; y-radius;* zeitgeber;

**cynical** *(adj.)*: acerbic; bitter; caustic; disparaging; distrustful; embittered; fleering; gibing; hypercritival; ironic; jaded; kindless; ludificatory; mordacious; mistrustful; negative; negativistic; opprobrious; pungent; *quede [arch.];* ridiculing; suspicious; skeptical; satiric; sardonic; trenchant; ugly; virulent; wry; *xuld [arch.]; yah;* zinging;

**cynicism** *(n.)*: acerbity; bitterness; causticity; derision; embitterment; facetiousness; gibing; hypercriticism; irony; jadedness; kindlessness; ludification; mordacity; narkiness; opprobrium; pyroticism; *quede [arch.];* ridicule; sarcasm; sardonicism; satire; trenchancy; unkindness; virulence; wryness; *xuld [arch.]; yah;* zinging;

# D

**dab** *(n.)*: *application;* blotch; conglobulation; daub; *engrained;* flaw; glob; *hunk;* imperfection; jaup; kink; *lump;* mark; naeve; *ounce;* patch; *quantity; round spot;* splash; smudge; smear; touch; *unsightly spot;* verruca; wem; *X; yelm; zum [dial.];*

**dab** *(v.)*: apply; blotch; brush; cover; daub; dollop; embrocate; *fan out; get on;* hand-spread; infucate; *jigger; kirtle;* lay on; *make; non-smooth;* overspread; paint; *quab; reapply;* spot; smear; smudge; slap; touch; *use; varnish;* wipe; *xfer; yark; zip;*

**dabble** *(v.)*: amuse oneself; busy oneself; coquet; do as a hobby; experiment; fool around; fiddle; *gratify;* have fun; *interest;* jerk around; kill time; like to mess; mess around; *non-serious;* occupy oneself; play at; *quicken; realize;* spend time doing; tinker; *use; vigor;* work; *xel; yerde [arch.];* zeal;

**dagger** *(n.)*: army knife; bhuj; *blade;* creese; dirk; elephant ~; fleam; golok [Malay]; hamidashi [Jap.]; *instrument;* jambiya; kris; knife; landsknecht [G.]; machete; *navaja;* obelus; poniard; quarrel; roundel; stiletto; tanto; *utility knife; Valencia knife;* woodknife; xiphoid; yataghan; *zafar;*

**daily** *(adj.)*: abiding; by the day; continual; circadian; diurnal; day-by-day; every day; *forever;* going on; habitually; in a day's time; *jusqu'au bout [F.];* keeps going; *lasting;* maintaining; nonstop; ongoing; *per diem* [L.]; *perpetual;* quotidian; repeated; steady; *termination-free;* unbroken; *vast; without end; xferring; year-round; zillion;*

**dainty** *(adj.)*: appealing; breakable; brittle; *charming;* delicate; delicious; exquisite; frail; fine; frangible; graceful; *handle with care;* insubstantial; jimp; *keen;* lovely; luxurious; migniard; nice; neat; *ornate;* petite; pretty; pleasing; quaint; refined; soft; slight; sensitive; tender; tasty; ultrafine; very fragile; weak; XF; *yare-handed; zierlich [G.];*

**dale** *(n.)*: *aperture;* basin; combe; dell; *excavation;* flood meadow; glen; hollow; intervale; *Jackson Hole;* kar; lowlands; *meadow;* notch; *opening; pit; quarry;* recess; slade; trough; underlands; vale; water gap; *xyrisic;* yunga; *zanja;*

**dam** *(n.)*: aboiteau; barrier; back~; containment wall; check ~; dike; embankment; floodgate; garth; headgate; *inclosure;* jetty; keldwall; levee; milldam; mole; *nautical wall; obstruction;* powdike; presa; quai; restraining wall; sea wall; tide-gate; *utility wall; vallum;* weir; wall; *Xalala Dam; yard wall;* zariba;

**damage** *(n.)*: affliction; blast; breakage; *cost;* detriment; evil; foulness; *grief;* harm; injury; impairment; jeel; *knock;* loss; maiming; marring; nocument; *offense;* prang; *query; ruin;* scath; toll; *unsafe;* violence; wound; wrecking; *x-ing;* yedder; *zap;*

**damage** *(v.)*: afflict; break; cripple; disserve; en~; fix [slang]; *grieve;* hurt; injure; impair; inflict ~; jeel; *knock; lacerate;* maim; mar; nocument; olate; prang; persecute; *quash;* ruin; rend; scath; trouble; *uproot;* victimize; wound; wreck; *x-ing;* yank apart; zap; [*Ant.* develop]

**damnable** *(adj.)*: *avenging;* blamable; condemnable; damning; exprobating; foredooming; *guilty;* heinous; *interdictory; judging;* killing; *loathsome;* mortal; *non-innocence;* opprobrious; proscriptive; *quashing;* ruinous; soul-damning (-destroying); traducible; upbraiding; vitiating; wrecking; *xci.;* yell at; zero out;

**damnation** *(n.)*: anathematizing; *abyss;* blame; condemnation; doom; death; eternal punishment; fall; guilt; *guilty verdict;* holocaust; hell; *indicting;* judgment; *killing; liability; mortality;* nemesis; opprobrium; proscription; perdition; *quenchless fire;* reprobation; ruination; retribution; sentence; *torment; undoing; verdict;* vitiation; wreck; x-out; *yelling; zapping;* [*see* hell; *Ant.* deliverance]

**damp** *(adj.)*: awash; bedashed; clammy; *cold;* dampened; dewy; embrocated; fenny; *gooey;* humid; imbrued; *juicy; kept wet;* liquidy; moist; non-dry; *oozy; plashed;* quaggy; roric; soggy; *tear-stained;* undried; vapored; wet(tish); *xtr. moist;* yoted; ziment; [*Ant.* dry]

**dance** (n.): *allemande;* ball; barn ~; ballet; cotillion; cha-cha; divertisement; evening ~; folk ~; fandango; gyration; hustle; hoe-down; hop; hula; *Irish jig;* jig; *jitterbug;* kissing ~; *kolo [Slav.];* line ~; *minuet; moves;* masked ball; nautch; *orchel;* polka; prom; *pas de deux* [F.]; performance; quick-step; quadrille; romping; square ~; two-step; trot; twirl; tap ~; *tango; unglued;* valse; valeta; waltz; *xiphism; yang-ko* [Chin.]; zapateado;
    **Dances**: arial; barn ~; ballet; belly; Charleston; Cha cha cha; disco; eisa; foxtrot; gavot; hokey-pokey; Irish folk; Jitterbug; Kolo; Latin ~; Mambo; minuet; nutbush; Oberek; polka; quadrille; rain ~; square ~; tango; upa; valeta; waltz; xibelani; yowla ~; zouk;

**dance** (v.): *art;* boogie; bop; ballet; caper; do a ~; exult; foxtrot; frisk; float; gyrate; gambol; grind; hustle; hop; hoof [joc.]; *Irish jig; jeté [F.]; kolo;* leap; move; mosh; *ngoma* [E. Afr.]; *orchel;* polka; prance; *quadrille;* romp; rumba; square ~; skip; trot; twirl; tango; tap ~; *unglued;* valse; waltz; *xaxado; yang-ko* [Chin.]; *zapateado;*

**dancer** (n.): artist; ballerina; belly- ~; chorus girl; danseur [masc.]; danseuse [fem.]; *entertainer;* figurant; go-go ~; hustler; *individual;* jazz ~; kickshoe; leadman; morisk; *nautch; orchel;* performer; *quadrille;* rope- ~; swinger; tangoist; *unglued;* vaudevillist; waltzer; *xaxado; yang-ko* [Chin.]; *zapateado;*

**danger** (n.): adversity; *bad;* chance; dangerousness; endangerment; *exposure; foreboding; fear; gnarly;* harm; hazard; hurt; imperilment; jeopardy; jaws of death; known risk; *life-threatening;* menace; maleficence; non-safety; *ominous;* peril; *questionable;* risk; self-risk; threat; unsafety; virulence; venturesomeness; warning; woe; "x"; *yeopartie* [arch.]; *zero safety;*

**dangerous** (adj.): adverse; bad; chancy; dicey; endangering; foreboding; gnarly; hazardous; harmful; injurious; jeopardous; *known risk;* life-threatening; menacing; malefic; nocuous; *ominous;* perilous; parlous; questionable; risky; speculative; self-hazarding; suicidal; threatening; unsafe; venturesome; woeful; *x.; ydrad* [arch.]; *zero safety;*

**dangle** (v.): *around;* bounce; balance; coggle; droop; draggle; *equipoise;* fix; float; *gibbet;* hang; hover; *impend;* jiggle; *kite;* loom; lop; librate; make dependant; nutate; overhang; *pendulous; quat;* rest; suspend; sway; swing; totter; *unsteady;* vacillate; wave; *x-ing; yede; zoom;*

**dare** (n.): *action;* bet; challenge; defiance; endangerment; *facing up to;* gamble; *high stakes;* invitation; *jeopardy;* known risk; laying one's life on the line; *meeting the challenge; nempne; out~;* provocation; quest; risk; *something;* test; ultimatum; venture; wager; *xel* [arch.]; yerking [dial.]; *zeal;*

**dare** (v.): adventure; attempt; bet; challenge; *claim;* defy; durst [p.t.]; endanger; *face up to;* gamble; goad; have the nerve; hazard; invite; jeopardize oneself; *know the risk;* lay one's life on the line; make challenge; nempne; *out~;* provoke; *question;* risk; *strive;* test; urge; undertake; venture; wager; *xtry. act;* yerk [dial.]; *zealously attempt;*

**daring** (adj.): audacious; adventurous; brave; bold; courageous; dauntless; enterprising; fearless; gallant; gutsy; heroic; intrepid; *jarless; knightly;* lion-hearted; manly; nervy; *obstinate;* plucky; questful; *resolute;* stout; temerarious; undaunted; valiant; *wherewithal; xtry.; yare; zealous;* [Ant. distraught]

**dark** (adj.): adiaphanous; bedimmed; black; clouded; caliginous; darkened; dim; dismal; dingy; dusky; enclouded; fuliginous; gloomy; hidden; infuscated; jet black; kettle-black; lightless; memphian; murky; mysterious; *moonlit;* non-bright; obscure; opaque; pitchy; pitch-dark; *quirky;* rayless; swarthy; shady; shadowy; sunless; Stygian; tenebrous; umbrageous; unlit; very dim; *wadd; xerophthalmic; yenite;* zero light; [Ant. dazzling]

**darken** (v.): *alter;* bedim; blacken; cloud; dim; darkle; embrown; encloud; eclipse; fade; gloom; hide; incloud; infuscate; *jetty; kettle-black;* lower light; make dim; nigresce; obscure; obfuscate; *pitchy; quell; recess;* shade; *smutch;* tan; turn dark; umbrate; *veil; well-darkened; xerophthalmic;* yeme; *zero light;*

**darkness** (n.): absence of light; blackness; cloudiness; dusk; enclouding; fogginess; gloom; half-visibility; infuscation; jettiness; *kettle-black;* lightlessness; murk; murkiness; murksomeness; milkiness; night; obscurity; opaqueness; pitchiness; *quirkiness;* raylessness; shadow; shade; swarthiness; total ~; tenebrosity; umbrage; vagueness; *wadd; xerophthalmic;* yeming; zero light; [Ant. daylight]

**darling** *(adj.)*: admired; beloved; cherished; dear; endeared; favored; good; heart-dear; important; jake [Br.]; kissable; loved; machree; *noteworthy; outstanding;* prized; *quixotic; remarkable;* significant; treasured; unequaled; valued; well-beloved; *xenial; yearn; zealously loved;* [Ant. detested]

**dart** *(v.)*: accelerate; bolt; charge; dash; elan; flash; glide; hurry; *interlope;* jet; *kite;* lope; move; *nimble; outrun; overrun; proceed;* quicken; rush; race; streak; tear; *uprush; velocity;* whip; *xuld [arch.];* yern; zoom; [Ant. delay]

**dash** *(v.)*: accelerate; breeze; charge; dart; elan; fly; gallop; hurtle; *interlope;* jog; *kite;* lope; move; *nimble; outrun; proceed;* quicken; run; race; sprint; tear; *uprush; velocity;* whiz; *xuld [arch.];* yern; zip;

**date** *(v.)*: associate; bill and coo; court; call on; *dalliance;* escort; flatter; go out with; *have out;* ingratiate; *join;* keep company; *love;* match-make; *nubility; out together;* pursue; *quest;* romance; see; suit; serenade; take out; *undying love;* visit; woo; wine and dine; *xenia; young love; zero in;*

**dating** *(n.)*: addresses; billing and cooing; courtship; dalliance; escorting; *following;* gallantry; going with; *honeyed words; interaction; joining;* keeping company; love-suit; lovemaking [arch.]; match-making; *nubility; offer of marriage;* pursuit; *proposal;* quest; *relationship; rendezvous;* seeing; suiting; serenading; *taking out;* unchaperoned ~; visiting; wooing; *xenia;* young love; *zeroing in;*

**daughter** *(n.)*: adolescent; born one; child; descendant; damsel; eldest ~; female child; filial; girl; heiress; increase; junior; kid; little one; lass; minor; neophyte; offspring; progeny; *quinquennarian; relative;* step~; scion; teenage ~; *urchin; virgin; woman; x-chromosome;* youngest ~; young lady; *zitella [It.];*

**daunt** *(v.)*: alarm; bother; cause to faint; dismay; discourage; dispirit; engrieve; faze; *faint;* gaster; *horrify* intimidate; *jitters;* kiaugh [Scot.]; lower one's spirits; make nervous; nerve; overwhelm; panic; quench; rattle; scare; trouble; unnerve; vex; worry; *xuld [arch.]; yelping; zealless;*

**dawdle** *(v.)*: abide; bide; *continue;* (dilly-)dally; *ease; extend;* futz; fool around; goof off; hang around; idle; jauk; kick back; lollygag; loiter; loaf; mess around; *non-responsive; obstruct;* putter; piddle; procrastinate; quiddle; *remain;* stand around; stall; take one's time; twiddle thumbs; *unresponsive;* veg out; waste time; while (away); *xenize; yerde [arch.]; zealless;* [Ant. do]

**dawn** *(n. beginning)*: advent; arrival; birth; commencement; coming; dawning; dayspring; embarkment; founding; genesis; hatching; inception; jumping off; kickoff; launching; manifestation; naissance; onset; *production;* quickening; rising; start; take-off; *unveiling;* ushering in; *verge;* welcoming; *xenogenesis;* youth; *zygogenesis;* [Ant. demise]

**dawn** *(n. daybreak)*: aurora; A.M.; break of day; crack of dawn; daybreak; dayspring; daylight; *early morn;* first light; going up of the sun; half-light; *initial; jump off; kick off;* light of day; morning; *night's end; opening;* prime; *quite early;* rising of the sun; sunrise; sunup; *time; tomorrow; up-going of the sun;* very early; *wake up call; x-time; yeender; zone;* [Ant. dusk]

**day** *(n.)*: autumn ~; broad ~; cycle; *century;* daytime; *era;* fortnight; gilded morning [poet.]; *hour;* hey~; interval; *jiffy; kilocycle; light;* man-day; moon [Am. Ind.]; noctidal; nychthemeron; *one revolution;* period; *quarter;* revolution; sun(up); *summer ~;* 24 hours; *unclouded ~; vintage;* work~; week~; *x-time;* yom [Heb.]; *year; zone;* [Ant. dark]

**daybreak** *(n.)*: A.M.; break of day; cockcrow; dawn; *early morn;* first light; going up of the sun; half-light; *initial; jump off; kick off;* light (of day); morning; new day; *opening; period; quite early;* rooster; sunup; *time; tomorrow; up-going of the sun;* very early; *wake up call; x-time;* yestermorn; *zone;* [Ant. day's end]

**daydream** *(n.)*: abstraction; bemusement; contemplation; dream; engrossment; fantasm; fancy; *glassy-eyed; head in the clouds;* imagine; *inattention; jag;* kinching; lethe; musing; *non-attention;* obliviousness; preoccupation; pipe-dream; *quixotic;* reverie; stargazing; trance; *unconscious thought; vegging out;* wish; woolgathering; *x-fix;* yearnfulness; *zoning out;*

**daydream** *(v.)*: *abstraction;* build castles in the air; contemplate; dream; envision; fancy; fantasize; get idea in one's head; hatch; hallucinate; imagine; *judge; know; lucubrate;* make up; *notion; originate;* picture; *quixotic;* romanticize; stargaze; think; use imagination; visualize; woolgather; *xenodiagnose;* yearn for; *zazen;*

**daze** *(n.)*: abstraction; astonishment; befuddlement; bemusement; confusion; dream; delirium; enchantment; entrancement; fuddlement; gibbered; haze; incoherence; *inebriated;* jag; *knocked out;* lethe; *laid out;* muddlement; mesmerization; narcosis; out (of touch); preoccupation; *quaffing;* reverie; stupor; spell; shock; tizzy; trance; *under;* vexation; whirl; *xanthoxylin; yarked;* zonked;

**dazzle** *(v.)*: amaze; astonish; bedazzle; confound; daze; dumbfound; enchant; flabbergast; gape; hold one's breath; impress; jolt; keel over; look aghast; make marvel; *nonplus;* overwhelm; poleax; *quite amazed;* render speechless; stun; take one's breath away; unable to believe; *very impressed;* wonder; *xtry.; yerk; zing;* [Ant. disinterest]

**deacon** *(n.)*: assistant; arch~; *buttress;* church officer; *diakoneo* [Gr.]; elder; *full of the Spirit;* good man; head ~; *individual; Jesus' servant;* kirk-maister [Scot.]; lifetime ~; *layman; man;* non-ordained ~; officer; *pillar;* qualified man; right-hand man; servant; sub~; trustee; *usher;* verger; working ~; *Xn.;* yes-man [derog.]; *zealous Christian;*

**dead** *(adj.)*: annihilated; amort; asleep; breathless; buried; ceased; deceased; departed; done for; defunct; expired; ended; exterminated; extinct; faded away; failed; fallen; finished; gone; *had it;* inanimate; *just-killed;* kaput; lifeless; late; lost; motionless; non-living; no more; out of commission; perished; passed away; quenched; *resting;* sleeping; stone-dead; terminated; unliving; vanished; vanquished; went home (to be with the Lord); wiped out; *x-ed out; yielded up the ghost;* zombie-like;

**dead end** *(n.)*: abrupt end; brick wall; *cul e sac* [F.]; *difficulty;* end of the road; *fence; gate;* hindrance; impasse; *jam; keeping;* limit; *mark;* no outlet; obstruction; police blockade; *quandary;* roadblock; street blockade; *trouble; unopen;* vigia; wall; x; *yieldless; zero outlet;*

**deadliness** *(n.)*: *adversity;* banefulness; *contamination;* destructiveness; evil; fatality; fatiferousness; *grievousness;* harmfulness; *injuriousness;* jeopardy; killing-ability; lethality; mortality; noxiousness; *obliteration;* perilousness; poisonousness; *quench;* ruinousness; self-destruction; toxicity; *unsafe;* virulence; *widow-making; x-ing; ydrad* [arch.]; *zero safety;*

**deadlock** *(n.)* abeyance; break; cessation; cul-de-sac; draw; dead end; end of the road; *forced end;* gridlock; holdup; impasse; jam; knotted score; logjam; Mexican standoff; *non-operation;* obstruction; pause; *quietus;* rest; stymie; standstill; stalemate; standoff; *time out; unwinding; void;* wait; *x-rest; yawning; zero productivity;*

**deadly** *(adj.)*: *à la mort* [F.]; baneful; *contaminated;* destructive; doomful; death-dealing; eliminating; fatal; fell; *grievous;* harmful; injurious; internecine; jeopardous; killing; lethal; mortal; noxious; *obliterating;* perilous; poisonous; pernicious; perilous; *quenching;* ruinous; self-destructive; toxic; unsafe; virulent; *widow-maker; x-ing; ydrad* [arch.]; *zero safety;* [Ant. dangerless]

**deaf** *(adj.)*: ailment; bad hearing; completely ~; dull of hearing; deafened; ear-deafened; feeble-eared; *grievous;* hearing-impaired; hard of hearing; *impaired; jackleg; killed; loss of hearing; much-deafened;* non-hearing; *obstruction;* partially ~; quite ~; *reduced-hearing;* stone- ~; tone ~; thick of hearing; unhearing; unresponsive; very hard of hearing; weak-eared; word- ~; *x-out; yieldless; zero hearing;*

**deal** *(n.)*: agreement; arrangement; bargain; binding agreement; compromise; contract; covenant; *declaration;* exchange; federation; gentleman's agreement; happy medium; indenture; joint understanding; *key agreement;* letter of agreement; league; *misalliance; nonaggression pact;* offer; oath; *papers;* pledge; pact; qualified agreement; *resolution;* suggestion; settlement; terms; trade; transaction; understanding; vow; *way; x on the dotted line;* yellow-dog contract; yoke; *zet* [dial.];

**deal** *(v. distribute)*: allocate; *bestow;* consign; distribute; dole; *earmark;* furnish; give; hand out; issue; *justly divide; kit;* lay out; mete; *non-retention; offload;* portion (out); part; parcel; quantify; ration; share out; *transfer;* unitize; vest; *weigh; xfer;* yield; *zone;*

**dear** *(adj.)*: adored; beloved; cherished; darling; endeared; favored; greatly loved; highly prized; important; jake [Br.]; kissable; loved; machree; *noteworthy; outstanding;* prized; *quixotic; remarkable;* significant; treasured; unequaled; valuable; well-loved (-prized); *xenial;* yichus; *zealously loved;* [Ant. detested]

**dearth** *(n.)*: absence; bareness; *coming up short;* deficiency; destitution; emptiness; falling short; famine; grievous ~; *great need; hardly enough;* insufficiency; inadequacy; *just not enough; keen deprivation;* lack; meagerness; need; not enough; *out;* paucity; *quandary;* rareness; shortage; short supply; scantiness; scarcity; *too little;* unavailability; void; want; *xtry. deficiency; yearning; zero sufficiency:* [*Ant.* disproportionateness]

**death** *(n.)*: annihilation; abolition; abolishment; *bereavement;* cessation; casualty; decease; dying; demise; downfall; departure; dissolution; expiration; extermination; elimination; extinction; extinguishment; end; fatality; fall; *the* grave; Grim Reaper; home-going; *internment; jaws of* ~; Jordan-crossing; killing; king of terrors; lifelessness; loss; liquidation; mortality; murder; *necropolis;* Old Floorer [slang]; perishing; parting; *passing away;* quietus; rest; release; *the* Reaper; sudden ~; termination; undoing; vanishing; *Waterloo;* Xanatos; yielding (up the ghost); *zonking out [slang];* [*see* nonexistence; *Ant.* dawn]

**deathlike** *(adj.)*: ashen; breathless; charnel; cadaverous; *cold;* deathly; *dolesome;* eerie; funereal; gloomy; hushed; idle; jarless; *kaput;* lifeless; motionless; morose; non-moving; ominous; peaceful; pale; quiet; *resting;* silent; spooky; tenebrous; uncheerful; *vampirical;* wan; weird; *x'ed; yielded;* zombie-like;

**debar** *(v.)*: *avert;* bar; ban; cumber; disallow; exclude; forbid *gum up;* hinder; inhibit; *jam;* keep (from); limit; *moderate;* nullify; obstruct; prohibit; quash; restrain; stop; turn away; *upset;* veto; withhold; *x; yank; zero; zap;*

**debase** *(v.)*: abase; adulterate; belittle; bring low; cut down; crush; degrade; demean; dishonor; demote; efface; *fall; grime;* humiliate; humble; impair; imbrute; *jackalent;* knock down; lower; mortify; *nither* [arch.]; *offend;* put down; *quieten;* reduce; shame; sully; sink; taint; tarnish; upbraid; vitiate vulgarize; wipe; *x-out;* yellow; *zeroize;* [*Ant.* deify]

**debatable** *(adj.)*: arguable; *back and forth;* controversial; controvertible; confutable; doubtful; disputable; disputed; *engage; fussed over; go at it;* highly ~; iffy; indeterminate; *jangle; kemp; lock horns [slang];* maybe; much-debated; not settled; open for debate; perhaps; problematic; parleyed; questionable; ratiocinative; speculative; *topic of debate;* uncertain; unsettled; undetermined; up for debate; vied over; wrangled over; *x-purposes;* yet unsettled; *zero consensus;* [*Ant.* definite]

**debate** *(n.)*: argument; bearing heart; contest; controversy; discussion; dispute; deliberation; disagreement; exchange; friendly ~; give-and-take; hot ~; interchange; jangle; key ~; logomachy; meeting; negotiation(s); oral ~; *opponency;* parley; parlance; palaver [joc.]; panel discussion; pep talk; powwow; quadrilogue; reasoning; round; speculation; speech; talks; *uttering; vocalization;* words; XQ; yarn; *zero in;*

**debate** *(v.)*: argue; bicker; contend; dispute; deliberate; defend; engage in ~; fuss; feud; go at it; have words with; interchange; jangle; *kemp;* lock horns [slang]; *maintain; make fur fly;* niff; *oppose;* parley; quarrel; *question;* ratiocinate; reason; strive; *tiff; unharmonious;* vie; wrangle; *x-purposes;* yell; *yieldless;* zero in;

**debater** *(n.)*: arguer; apologist; bickerer; contravertist; contender; disputant; disputer; deliberator; defender; eristic; fusser; feuder; *guardian;* haranguer; *interchange;* jangler; jawsmith; *kemper;* logomachist; maintainer; *niff;* opposer; parleyer; panelist; quarreler; ratiocinator; striver; tub thumper; upholder; vier; wrangler; *x-purposes;* yeller; *zero in;*

**debauchery** *(n.)*: abomination; badness; corruption; depravity; evil; foul-behavior; godlessness; heinousness; immorality; jadishness; knavery; lasciviousness; mischief; naughtiness; obduracy; perversion; *quad;* revelry; sin; transgression; unrighteousness; virulence; wickedness; *xgression; yetzer hara* [Heb.]; *zymosis;* [*Ant.* decency]

**debris** *(n.)*: *atoms;* bits; clamjamfry; detritus; *elements;* fragments; granules; garbage; hunks; *ions;* junk; *kernels;* little pieces; mess; *nuggets;* offal; pieces; *quadrillion pieces;* remains; rubble; shards; smithereens; trash; *unsightly garbage;* vestiges; wreckage; waste; *x-mal* [G.]; *yngot* [arch.]; *zillions of pieces;*

**debt** *(n.)*: arrears; amount due; balance (due); commitment; deficit; encumberment; financial obligation; *gap;* hocking; *hardship;* indebtedness; *jejuneness;* known ~; liability; long-term debt; money owed; *nonpayment; need;* obligation; *owe;* paucity; pledge; *quisby;* responsibility; red ink; score (to settle); tab; unpaid balance; *vow; want; x-differential;* yearning; *zet amount [dial.];*

**debtor** *(n.)*: acquirer; borrower; *constrained; cosigner;* debtee; defaulter; *exacted; financially obligated;* grubstake receiver; holder of mortgage; *insolvent;* indebted person; *jumbo mortgage holder; key mortgagee;* lendee; mortgagee; *nonpayer;* ower; pledger; *qualified mortgagee;* responsible party; *subject; transgressor; uncollected debt;* vower; *welcher; x on the dotted line; yoked;* z-bond holder; [*Ant.* dun]

**debut** *(n.)*: arrival; beginning; commencement; coming; dawn; entry; first appearance; genesis; *hatching;* introduction; jump off; kickoff; launching; maiden performance; manifestation; naissance; onset; opening; premiere; *quickening;* rising; start; take-off; unveiling; *verge; welcoming; xenogenesis; youth; zygogenesis;* [*Ant.* disappearance]

**debt-collector** *(n.)*: accounts payable; bill-collector; creditor; collector; collection agency; credit card company; dun; exiseman; financial institution; gabeler; *heartless creditor; institution; junior officer; khalsah* [Ind.]; lender; mortgager; nobber; *officer;* publican; questman; receiver of debts; shylock; skip tracer; tax collector; *usurer;* vulture [slang]; *worker; xaraf; yob; zamindar [Ind.];* [*Ant.* debtor]

**debt-free** *(adj.)*: absolutely ~; *burn the mortgage;* commitment-free; debtless; even; free from debt; *good; honky-dory;* in the black; *justified; keen;* liability-free; mortgage-free; not in debt; non-indebted; out-of-debt; paid-up; *qualified; released;* solvent; totally ~; unencumbered; *vow is paid;* without debt; *x-out;* yet in the black; zero debt;

**debtor** *(n.)*: acquirer; borrower; *constrained; cosigner;* debtee; defaulter; *exacted; financially obligated;* grubstake receiver; holder of mortgage; *insolvent;* indebted person; *jumbo mortgage holder; key mortgagee;* lendee; mortgagee; *nonpayer;* ower; pledger; *qualified mortgagee;* responsible party; *subject; transgressor; uncollected debt;* vower; *welcher; x on the dotted line; yoked;* z-bond holder; [*Ant.* dun]

**debut** *(n.)*: arrival; beginning; commencement; coming; dawn; entry; first appearance; genesis; *hatching;* introduction; jump off; kickoff; launching; maiden performance; manifestation; naissance; onset; opening; premiere; *quickening;* rising; start; take-off; unveiling; *verge; welcoming; xenogenesis; youth; zygogenesis;* [*Ant.* disappearance]

**decadence** *(n.)*: adultery; badness; corruption; degeneracy; decadency; effeteness; fallenness; fornication; godlessness; harlotry; immorality; incontinence; jadery; *knavery;* lasciviousness; *mischief;* non-faithfulness; odure; profligacy; *queanery;* revelry; sinfulness; turpitude; unfaithfulness; uncleanness; vice; wantonness; *x-rated behavior; yielding to sin;* zero morality; [*Ant.* decency]

**decadent** *(adj.)*: adulterated; abominable; bad; corrupt; degenerate; depraved; effete; evil; fallen; godless; heinous; ignoble; immoral; jadish; *knavish;* lascivious; malevolent; *nasty;* obdurate; profligate; *quad;* rebellious; rotten; sordid; sinful; tainted; ungodly; *vitiated;* wicked; *xgressing; yieldless;* zero good; [*Ant.* decent]

**decapitate** *(v.)*: axe; behead; chop head off; decollate; execute; *finish off;* guillotine; head; *hack; incide; jugular; kill;* lop head off; *make die;* neck; *off with one's head;* perform execution; *quench;* remove head; *separate; sever;* take off one's head; *undo; victimize; violence;* whack one's head off; *x-out; yerk; zip off;*

**decay** *(n.)*: autolysis; breakdown; corruption; decomposition; delapidation; disintegration; deterioration; erosion; festering; foulness; gangrene; hoaring; impairment; *jade;* kettiness; labelfaction; mortification; necrosis; *off; oxidation;* putrefaction; queering; rot(ting); ruination; rancidness; spoilage; tainting; undoing; *vile;* welking; water-rot; xylaria; yellowing; *zorch;*

**decay** *(v.)*: *attrit;* break down; corrupt; decompose; delapidate; disintegrate; deteriorate; decline; erode; fester; fade; fail; go bad; hoar; impair; *jade; ketty; labelfaction;* mortify; mar; *necrosis; off; oxidize;* putrefy; queer; rot; spoil; taint; *undo; vile;* welk; *xylaria;* yellow; *zorch;*

**deceit** *(n.)*: artifice; beguilement; chicanery; deception; deviousness; defrauding; double-dealing; dishonesty; duplicity; ensnarement; fraud; guile; hoodwinking; illusiveness; improbity; japery; knavery; lying; misleading; monkey business; nobbling; outfoxing; perfidy; *questionableness;* roguery; skullduggery; shadiness; trickery; treachery; underhandedness; villainy; vice; wiliness; *xuld [arch.];* yegginess; *zero honesty;*
**deceitful** *(adj.)*: arch; bad; beguiling; crafty; cunning; clever; deceptive; dishonest; double-tongued; devious; evasive; ensnaring; fraudulent; fallacious; guileful; honorless; ingenious; jesuitical; jady; knavish; lying; misleading; non-trustworthy; opportunistic; perfidious; quasi-ethical; roguish; seedy; sly; shady; treacherous; tricky; two-tongued; unscrupulous; underhanded; vulpine; wily; weaselly; *x-ing;* yeggy; *zero integrity;*
**deceitfulness** *(n.)*: artfulness; beguiling; craftiness; cleverness; deviousness; evasiveness; foxiness; guile; *hoax;* ingenuity; jiggery-pockery; knavishness; *lying;* mendacity; non-trustworthiness; outfoxing; policy; *quaintise* [arch.]; roguishness; subtlety; slyness; trickiness; underhandedness; *vulpine;* wiliness; *xtry, cleverness;* yepship [arch.]; *zinging;*
**deceive** *(v.)*: allure; beguile; con; delude; defraud; dupe; ensnare; fool; guile; hoodwink; illude; jape; kid; lie; mislead; nobble; outfox; pull wool over one's eyes; *quiblin* [arch.]; *rook;* shyster; trick; take in; utter falsehood; verneuk; wangle; *xuld [arch.];* yentz; *zing;*
**deceiver** *(n.)*: allurer; beguiler; con artist; deluder; defrauder; debaucher; ensnarer; fraud; guiler; hoaxer; *imposter;* jape; knave; liar; misrepresenter; *no-good;* open liar; pretender; quacksalver; rook; swindler; tricker; trickster; untruther; verneuker; wangler; weasel; *xgressor;* yentzer [Heb.]; *zinger;*
**decency** *(n.)*: appropriateness; bienseance; chasteness; comeliness; decentness; demureness; decorousness; estimableness; fitness; goodness; honorableness; irreproachability; impeccability; *justness; kindness; lily-white;* modesty; morality; nobleness; outstanding moral character; propriety; probity; *quality;* respectability; suitability; tastefulness; uprightness; virtuousness; wholesomeness; *xtry.; yarrow; zero wrongdoing;* [Ant. debauchery]
**decent** *(adj.)*: appropriate; ample; becoming; chaste; comely; covered; demure; decorous; dressed; endurable; ethical; fine; fit; good; honorable; impeccable; just; kind; *lily-white;* modest; moral; noble; nice; *outstanding;* passable; presentable; proper; principled; pure; *quality;* respectable; suitable; sufficient; tasteful; true-dealing; uncorrupted; upright; virtuous; wholesome; *xtry.;* yarrow; *zero wrongdoing;* [Ant. dirty]
**deception** *(n.)*: artifice; allurement; beguilement; con; deceit(fulness); delusion; defrauding; ensnarement; farce; guise; hoodwinking; imposture; illusiveness; illusion; japery; knavishness; lie; misleading; nobbling; outfoxing; pretext; *quiblin [arch.];* ruse; sham; scam; subterfuge; trick(ery); untruth; verneuking; wiliness; *xuld [arch.];* yentzing; *zinger;*
**deceptive** *(adj.)*: artful; beguiling; cheating; deceitful; delusive; elusory; fraudulent; guileful; *hollow;* illusive; indirect; jady; jesuitic; knavish; lying; misleading; non-trustworthy; oversubtle; pawky; *quaintise [arch.];* roguish; shrewd; scheming; tricky; underhanded; vulpine; wily; *xtry.;* yepe; *zinger;* [Ant. direct]
**dechristianize** *(v.)*: apostatize; backslide; *corrupt;* demoralize; *err;* fall away; go back into sin; heathenize; *impair; jump down; keep getting worse;* lose ground; move away from God; *non-Christian;* oppress; paganize; *post-Christian;* quit on God; reject Christianity; sink; spiral downward; turn from Christianity; uproot; unchristianize; veer away from God; *worsen; x-out; yield to Satan; zeroize;*
**decide** *(v.)*: adjudge; ascertain; *best choice;* choose; determine; elect; favor; give choice; *hand pick;* indicate; judge between; *know; list* [arch.]; *like;* make a choice; *name;* opt; pick; please; prefer; *quibble;* resolve; select; settle on; take; try; *use;* vote; want; *well-chosen; x; yes; zealous for;*
**decipher** *(v.)*: ascertain; break; crack; decode; decrypt; *explain;* figure out; *get;* give the meaning; hash out; interpret; judge the meaning; know; *look at;* make out; *naw [dial.];* open up; perceive; *questionless;* read; solve; tell; uncode; understand; *verify;* work out; x-code; yield; *zero in;*

**decision** *(n.)*: arret; alternative; arbitration; *best choice;* choice; determination; election; final ~ (-judgment); gauging; *heart;* inclination; judgment; *knowledge; like; liberty; mind; nomination;* option; preference; pick; pleasure; *quibble;* resolve; ruling; selection; take; top ~; *ultimatum;* verdict; vote; will; wish; *x; yes; zeal;*

**decisive** *(adj.)*: absolute; beyond doubt; conclusive; certain; definite; definitive; ending; final; guaranteed; highly ~; indisputable; *just sure;* key; last; *made sure;* non-questioned; 100% sure; positive; questionless; resolved; sound; *true;* unquestionable; *verified;* without question; *xtry. sure; yet irrefutable;* zero question;

**deck** *(n.)*: after ~; boat ~; covered ~; decking; estrade; fore~; floor; gun ~; half ~; *intermediate story;* jube; kitchen ~; landing; level; lower ~; main ~; *nightingale floor;* orlop ~; platform; poop ~; quarterdeck; rear ~; shelter ~; sun ~; story; top ~; terrace; tier; upper ~; veranda; weather ~; xyst; *yew-wood ~; zaguan;*

**deck** *(v.)*: adorn; array; bedeck; cover; decorate; embellish; fancify; garnish; hang; inwreath; jazz up; kit; *let be adorned;* make prettier; *nicer;* ornament; prettify; *quaintise* [arch.]; render lovely; spruce; trim; *use ornaments;* vest; wreathe; *xtry.; yclad* [arch.]; *zizz;*

**declaim** *(v.)*: articulate; bespeak; blazon; cite; deliver; echo; elocute; *foremention;* give; hold forth; iterate; *jaw; keep coming;* lecture; *mouth; mention;* narrate; orate; pronounce; quote; recite; rehearse; say; state; tell; trumpet; *unfold;* utter; voice; word; *xenophonia; yak; zero in;*

**declaration** *(n.)*: announcement; affirmation; avowal; broadcast; bulletin; communication; confession; dispatch; enunciation; exclamation; *forewarning; give message;* holding forth; indiction; intimation; jactitation; *judgment;* keynote address; *letter; language;* message; manifesto; notification; oration; proclamation; pronouncement; *quotation;* report; revelation; statement; testimonial; utterance; vocalization; verbalization; word; *xenagogy;* yeme; *zealous message;*

**declare** *(v.)*: announce; affirm; avow; broadcast; bode; claim; confess; cry; convey; disclose; express; exclaim; *fame;* give out; hold forth; indicate; intimate; inform; *jaw; key in;* let out; make known; noise; notify; *outcry;* proclaim; profess; promulgate; quoth; relate; relay; state; say; tell; testify; utter; voice; word; warrant; *xenagogy;* yell; *zero in;* [*Ant.* disclaim]

**decline** *(n.)*: abatement; breaking (down); bating; contraction; decrease; drop; diminishment; downturn; ebbing; fall; fading; failing; going down; *halting;* impairment; jump down; *knock down;* lessening; move down; *narrowing; nosedive; outgo;* petering out; plunge; quailing; receding; reduction; subsiding; shrinking; slump; slippage; tapering; *undoing;* vanishing; waning; wasting; *xerosis;* yielding; *zapping;*

**decline** *(v.)*: abate; assuage; alleviate; break; bate; curb; contract; condense; cut; decrease; diminish; dissipate; dwindle; ease; ebb; fade; fall; go down; hit a slump; *impair; jump down;* knock down; languish; lessen; lower; minish; moderate; mitigate; *narrow; outgo;* peter out; pall; plummet; quell; quail; recede; reduce; sink; slide; subside; taper; *undo;* verge downward; *vanish;* wane; waste; *xerosis;* yield; zap; [*Ant.* develop]

**decode** *(v.)*: ascertain; break; crack; decrypt; decipher; descramble; *expose; explain;* figure out; *get;* give interpretation; have decoded; interpret; *judge;* know; *learn;* make out; *non-coded;* open up; perceive; *questionless;* read; render; solve; tell; uncode; *verify;* work out; x-code; yield; *zero in;*

**decompose** *(v.)*: *attrit;* break down; corrupt; decay; erode; fester; fade; go bad; hoar; impair; *jade;* ketty; labelfaction; moulder; mortify; necrose; *off; oxidize;* putrefy; queer; rot; ruin; spoil; taint; *undo; vile;* waste away; wem; *xylaria;* yellow; *zorch;* [*Ant.* develop]

**decomposition** *(n.)*: autolysis; bacterial decay; corruption; decay; erosion; festering; gangrene; hoaring; impairment; *jade;* kettiness; labelfaction; mortification; necrosis; *opprobrium; oxidation;* putrefaction; queering; rotting; returning to dust; spoilage; tainting; undoing; *vanishing;* welking; xylaria; yellowing; *zapping;* [*Ant.* development]

**decompress** *(v.)*: augment; blow up; cause decompression; *develop;* expand; fill with air; grow; heighten; inflate; *jack up; keep growing;* largen; make larger; *non-compressed;* open; pump up; *quadruple;* rise; swell; *take off;* upshoot; unzip; *volume;* wax greater; *XL; yain* [arch.]; *zoom;* [*Ant.* depress]

**decontaminate** *(v.)*: antisepticize; boil; cleanse; depurate; disinfect, detoxify; expurgate; flush; get clean; hygienize; *implunge; jalap;* kill germs; lustrate; mundify; neutralize; outwash; purify; *quarantine;* reclaim; sanitize; sterilize; *tub; unpolluted; vacuate;* wash; *xylol; yellow soap; zero contamination;* [*Ant.* defile]

**decontamination** *(n.)*: ablution; bathing; cleansing; depollution; depuration; detoxification; expurgation; fumigation; *germ-removal;* headbath; *implunging; jalap;* killing germs; lavation; lustration; mundification; *non-polluted;* outwashing; purification; purgation; *quarantine;* reclamation; sterilization; *tubbing; unpolluted; vacuation;* washing; *xylol; yellow soap; zero contamination;* [*Ant.* defilement]

**decorate** *(v.)*: adorn; bedeck; beautify; clothe; deck (out); embellish; fancify; garnish; habilitate; inwrought; jazz up; jewel; kit; *let be adorned;* make prettier; *nicer;* ornament; prettify; *quaintise* [arch.]; renovate; re~; spruce up; trim; tart up; *use ornaments;* vest; wallpaper; *xtry.; yclad [arch.]; zizz;*

**decorated** *(adj.)*: adorned; beautiful; bedeckt; charming; decorative; dressy; embellished; fancy; garnished; high-wrought; highly ~; intricate; *jewel-encrusted; keenly ornate;* lavish; much-decorated; *niggled;* ornate; ornamented; pretty; *pearled; quaint;* ritzy; swanky; snazzy; trimmed; upscale; very ornate; well-ornamented; *xtry.; yet unsurpassed; zierlich* [G.];

**decoration** *(n.)*: adornment; beautification; cosmetic; décor; embellishment; exornation; frill; falbala; fanciness; garnish(ment); *hall-decking;* improvement; jabot; *keen décor; luxurience;* marqutry; nicety; ornament(ation); pretty thing; quaintry; remodeling; sprucing up; trimming; titivation; *tinsel;* trappings; use of ornaments; *vignette; well-ornamented; xtry.; yclad [arch.]; zizziness;*

**decorative** *(adj.)*: adorning; aesthetic; beautifying; cosmetic; decorating; embellishing; fancy; garnishing; highlighting; improving; *jeweled; keenly ornamented;* luxurient; *much-decorated; nice;* ornamental; pretty; *quaint; ritzy;* superficial; trimming; *upscale; very fancy; well-ornamented; xtry.; yet unsurpassed; zizzy;*

**decoy** *(n.)*: allurement; bait; *con;* deception; ~ -duck; ensnarement; facsimile; gin; hunting ~; *imitation;* jig; *knavery;* lure; mock-up; *non-real; outfox; phony;* q-ship; red herring; snare; trap; *unreal; verneuking;* wooden ~; *xylograph;* yager ~; *zinger;*

**decrease** *(n.)*: abatement; breaking (down); curbing; contraction; condensation; cut; decline; diminishment; dissipation; dwindling; dropping; decrement; degression; easing; ebbing; falling; going down; *hush; halting; impairment;* jump down; *knock down;* lessening; lowering; lightening; moderation; minimization; narrowing; *outgo;* petering out; plunge; quailing; receding; reduction; subsidence; shrinkage; slump; tapering; *undoing; vanishing;* waning; wasting; *xerosis;* yielding; *zapping;*

**decrease** *(v.)*: abate; alleviate; break; bate; curb; contract; condense; cut; diminish; decline; dissipate; dwindle; drop; ease; ebb; fade; fall; go down; *hush;* impair; jump down; knock down; languish; lessen; lower; minish; moderate; mitigate; *narrow; outgo;* peter out; pare down; quell; quail; reduce; recede; roll back; subside; taper; tail off; *undo; vanish;* wane; *xerosis;* yield; zap; [*Ant.* develop]

**decree** *(n.)*: adjuration; *announcement;* behest; command; declaration; edict; fiat; *fatwa* [Mos.]; governance; *halacha* [Heb.]; injunction; judgment; *keleusmatic;* law; mandate; *national law;* order; proclamation; *quo minus* [L.]; rule; statute; sanction; *tyranny;* ukase; verdict; word; XO mandate; yardstick; *zakon* [Rus.];

**decree** *(v.)*: adjure; bid; charge; dictate; direct; enact; enjoin; *foist;* give an order; *have;* instruct; *juration; kaleusmatic;* lay down; mandate; necessitate; order; *pronounce; quo minus [L.];* require; stipulate; *say;* tell; *utter; voice; word; xenagogy;* yell; *zakon [Rus.];*

**decrepit** *(adj.)*: aged; ailing; broken-down; crumbling; dilapidated; *eroded;* falling apart; gerontic; *hurting;* infirm; *jaded; kept; last legs;* mummylike; neglected; old; poor; pathetic; *quite run-down;* run-down; rickety; stricken in years; time-worn; up in years; unfirm; very old; worn-out; wretched; XO; *yucky; zillions of years old;*

**dedicate** *(v.)*: assign; bless; commit; consecrate; devote; *establish; for; furnish;* give over; hallow; *invest; jalap;* keep; *lustrate;* make holy; *nard;* offer; promise; purify; *qualify;* recommit; set apart; sanctify; *transfer; unhand;* vest; *word; xfer;* yafe; *zeal;*

**dedication** *(n. ceremony)*: amenities; *blessing;* ceremony; christening; *duty;* encaenia; event; exercises; formality; *gathering;* holy rite; initiatory; *joyous occasion; kept tradition;* liturgy; *mass;* niceties; observance; ordination; *practice; quadrisacramentalism;* rite; service; solemnities; *tradition;* unveiling; vesting; *words; xfer;* yafing; *zeal;*

**dedication** *(n. commitment)*: allegiance; blessing; commitment; consecration; devotion; engagement; fixedness; giving allegiance; hallowing; *investing; jalap; key event;* loyalty; making holy; *nard;* offering; promise; purification; *qualification;* recommitment; setting apart; sanctification; *transfer;* undying loyalty; vow; *wholeheartedness; xfer;* yafing; zeal;

**deduce** *(v.)*: assume; bet; conjecture; calculate; conclude; deem; draw; estimate; expect; elecit; figure out; guess; hypothesize; infer; judge; *know; lucubrate;* muse; *notion; occur;* presume; *question;* read into; reckon; speculate; suppose; think; take; *use brain; venture;* work out; *xenodiagnose; yeme; zazen;*

**deduct** *(v.)*: abstract; *but; cross out;* delete; detract; defalcate; derogate; elide; except; fall off; ged rid of; *have removed;* impair; *jump down;* knock off; less(en); minus; *negative;* obliterate; purge; *quit;* remove; reduce; subtract; take away; unload; *void out;* withdraw; *x-out;* yank; *zeroize;*

**deed** *(n. action)*: act(ion); behavior; comings and goings; doings; exploit; feat; goings; hand; *indication;* job; *knee-action;* life; move(ment); *notorious act;* operation; performance; *quick response;* reaction; step; thing; transaction; *undertaking; venture;* work(ing); x-action; *yaw; zeal;*

**deed** *(n. title)*: article; book; charter; document; entitlement; *file;* government-issued ~; house ~; *item;* justification; *key document;* legal ~; land ~; *mine claim;* notarized ~; ownership papers; property title (~); *qualification;* recorded ~; *scroll;* title (~); *uncontested;* validated ~; *writing; xfer papers; yellow copy; zeug;*

**deem** *(v.)*: assess; adjudge; believe; consider; decide; evaluate; figure; gauge; *hold; ideate;* judge; *know; list;* measure; meditate; *notion;* opinion; price; *quote;* reckon; regard; surmise; think; use brain; valuate; value; weigh; *xenodiagnose; yeme; zazen;*

**de-emphasis** *(n.)*: abasement; belittlement; curbing; downplaying; *diminishment;* easing up; fading; *going easy;* hush; impairment; *jump down;* knocking off; lessening; lightening; minimization; non-emphasis; *out-of-the-spotlight;* playing down; quelling; *reduction;* subsiding; toning down; underplaying; *vanishing; waning; x-out; yet underplayed;* zeroization;

**de-emphasize** *(v.)*: *abase;* belittle; curb; downplay; *diminish;* ease up; fade; go easy; *hold back; impair; jump down;* knock off; lighten up; minimize; make light of; *not emphasize; out-of-the-spotlight;* play down; quell; *reduce;* scale down; tone down; underplay; underrate; understate; underemphasize; *very light;* withhold; *x-out; yet underplayed;* zeroize;

**deep** *(adj.)*: abysmal; bottomless; bridle- ~; chest- ~; depressed; *extensive;* four-foot ~; *great;* hidden; intense; *jump down;* knee- ~; low; *large;* massive; neck- ~; *overwhelming;* profound; *quantitative; really ~;* skin- ~; thick; *under;* very ~; vast; waist- ~; way-down; *x-deep;* yawning; *zoom;*

**deepen** *(v.)*: augment; become deeper; cut deeper; dig deeper; enlarge; excavate; *further;* grow deeper; *hide;* increase; *jump;* keep growing; lower; make deeper; *new depths;* overdig; *progress; quite deeper;* recede; sink; *trench;* undercut; verge downward; wax deeper; XL; *yain [arch.]; zoom;*

**deer** *(n.)*: antelope; buck [masc.]; caribou; doe [fem.]; elk; fawn; *fallow ~;* gazelle; hart; hind; impala; *jumping ~;* knobber; *lechwe;* musk ~; mule ~; nilgai [Asia]; *oryx;* pronghorn; *quadruped;* roe(buck); rein~; stag; *tragulidaei [L.]; ungulate;* Virginia ~; venison; whitetail; *x-breed; yearling; zoic;*

**deface** *(v.)*: abuse; butcher; cut off; disfigure; *exscind; fissure;* garble; hurt; injure; *jab; knife;* lacerate; mar; *notch;* olate; pull apart; *quade* [arch.]; ruin; spoil; tear asunder; twist; uglify; vandalize; wreck; *x-sect;* yank apart; *zap;*

**defamation** *(n.)*: aspersion; belittlement; calumny; denigration; disparagement; evil-speaking; false words; gossip; *hearsay;* insult; jaunder; *klatsch;* libel; mudslinging; malediction; name-calling; obtrectation; putting down; *quidnunc;* running down; slander; slighting; tarnishing; unfair criticism; vilification; *wickedness; xenophobia;* yellowing; *zeroization;*

**defamatory** *(adj.)*: attacking; backbiting; calumnious; disparaging; evil-speaking; foul; gossipy; harmful; insulting; injurious; jabbing; keenly ~; libelous; maledictive; non-truthful; *obnoxious;* pernicious; *quad;* reputation-slandering; slanderous; scurrilous; tarnishing; *untrue;* vilifying; *wicked; x-ing;* yellowing; *zeroizing;*

**defame** *(v.)*: asperse; belittle; badmouth; calumniate; denigrate; disparage; *execrate;* falsely accuse; gossip about; harm reputation; insult; jab; knock; libel; malign; name-call; obloquy; put down; *quib;* run down; slander; slur; traduce; *use;* vilify; wipe; *xuld [arch.];* yellow; *zap;*

**defeat** *(n.)*: *abatement;* breakdown; bust; conquest; downfall; debacle; expugnation; fall; *giving in; hitch;* improsperity; *jolt;* knock-out blow; letdown; loss; *malfunction;* nonsuccess; overthrow; pasting; quashing; rout; successlessness; tragedy; unsuccessfulness; utter ~; vanquishment; *washout;* wipeout; walloping; x-ing; yedder; zap; [Ant. domination]

**defeat** *(v.)*: ace; *annihilate;* beat; conquer; crush; discomfit; dominate; destroy; drub; expugn; eliminate; foil; flatten; gain victory; *gut; hammer; invade; junk [slang];* kill; knock out; lick; master; *massacre; neutralize;* overcome; overwhelm; overthrow; one-up; prevail; quash; rout; subjugate; smite; triumph (over); trounce; thrash; unseat; vanquish; worst; whip; whoop; wallop; *x-ing; yank down;* zap; [Ant. dominate]

**defeatism** *(n.)*: apprehension; bleakness; concern; despair; esistentialism; fatalism; finalism; gloom; hopelessness; insecurity; *jitters; kiagh [Scot.];* losing heart; malism; nihilism; negativism; over-anxiety; pessimism; *quaking;* resignation; *scared;* trepidation; uneasiness; vexation; Weltscmertz; *xenophobia;* yielding to despair; *zeallessness;*

**defeatist** *(n.)*: apprehensive individual; bleak one; cynic; despairer; esistentialist; fatalist; finalist; gloom & doomer; hopeless person; insecure individual; *jittery one; kiagh [Scot.]; lilly-livered;* malist; nihilist; negativist; over-anxious person; pessimist; *quaker;* resigned individual; *scared person; trepidation;* uneasy one; vexed one; worrier; *xenophobe; yellow-belly; zeallessness person;*

**defect** *(n.)*: accident; blunder; boo-boo; crack in one's armor; deficiency; error; flaw; fault; goof-up; hitch; imperfection; *jumble;* kink; lapse; lack; mistake; *nevus;* oversight; problem; quirk; *rough spot;* shortcoming; *typo; undoing; violation;* weakness; *xgression; yaw; zinger;*

**defect** *(v.)*: abandon; bow out; change sides desert; evacuate; forsake; go over; hand over; *ignore;* jump ship; kest; leave; move to the other side; *neglect;* opt out; pitch; quit; renounce; switch sides; turn traitor; *unload;* vacate; walk out; withdraw; *xfer;* yield; zip away;

**defective** *(adj.)*: amiss; bad; crummy; *damaged;* erroneous; faulty; flawed; groundless; *hopeless;* imperfect; inadequate; *jim-jam;* kaput; lacking; *lousy;* malfunctioning; non-working; out-of-order; peccant; quirky; *ruined;* substandard; *troublesome;* unreliable; vituperable; wanting; *x'ed; yawed;* zany;

**defector** *(n.)*: absconder; archtraitor; betrayer; collaborator; deserter; double-crosser; *evildoer; fiend;* guiler; *honorless;* insurgent; Judas; *knave; liar;* mutineer; *non-loyal;* opportunist; *perfidious;* Quisling; renegade; *sedition;* turncoat; traitor; *unloyal; villain; wicked; xfer; yegg;* zero loyalty;

**defend** *(v.)*: arm; argue (for); battle; cloak; contend for; drive back; ensconce; fend; fortify; guard; hold (the fort); insure; jaga; keep safe; look after; make safe; *nestle;* overshadow; protect; *quia timet [L.];* refuge; shield; take care of; uphold; vallate; watch (over); ward off; *x-guard; yeme [arch.];* zero danger;

**defendant** *(v.)*: appellee; accused; *blamed;* charged; disputant; *exprobrate;* faulted one; *guilty party; held responsible;* indicted man; *j'accuse; knock;* litigant; *libelee;* man accused; *non-innocent;* offender; party in question; *question;* resister; suspect; tried individual; undertrial; *vituperate;* wrangle; *xiaoren; yeming [arch.]; zero innocence;*

**defender** *(n.)*: armed guard; bodyguard; chaperone; defense personnel; escort; footguard; guardian; hyperaspist; home defense; imperial guard; jaga; keeper; *lookout;* mainstay; night-watch(man); outguard; protector; quarterman; rear-guard; sentry; safekeeper; *trooper;* upholder; vindicator; watchman; warden; *xiphos-bearer;* yeoman of the guard; zeloter;
**defense** *(n.)*: armature; bulwark; coverture; countervallation; defending; earthwork; fortress; fortifications; guardship; guardianship; hold; intrenchment; justification; keep; lunette; muniment; *nuclear ~;* outwork; protection; panoply; *quia timet [L.];* rampart; security; self- ~; tenaille; upholding; vallation; wall; wardship; *x-guard; yeming* [arch.]; zero vulnerability; [*Ant.* depredation]
**defenseless** *(adj.)*: at risk; brittle; barehanded; crippled; defenceless [Br.]; exposed; feeble; guardless; helpless; indefensible; justiciable; *knocked out;* liable; lame; much-weakened; non-helpable; naked; open; powerless; *queachy* [dial.]; *risky;* susceptible; *tired;* unprotected; unarmed; vincible; vulnerable; weak; weaponless; wide-open; *xtry. vulnerable; yawnish; zapped;* [*Ant.* defensible]
**defensible** *(adj.)*: attack-proof; battle-safe; *covered;* defendable; ever-safe; firm; great; hit-proof; impregnable; *jusqu'au bout [F.]; kept safe;* lasting; mighty; non-vulnerable; *over-protected;* powerful; *quartful* [arch.]; robust; secure; tenable; unconquerable; unassailable; very safe; well-protected; x-strong; yieldless; zap-proof; [*Ant.* defenseless]
**defensive** *(adj.)*: armed; attack-ready; battle-ready; cautious; distrustful; ensconced; fortifying; guarded; highly guarded; impenetrable; justifying; *keeping safe;* leery; mistrustful; non-vulnerable; overprotective; protective; *quick to justify;* ready-for-attack; self-justifying; shielding; *tough;* upholding; *vallate;* wary; *x-guard; yeme* [arch.]; zero danger;
**defer** *(v. concede)*: accede; bow; concede; do; *execute;* follow; give way; heed; *indulge; jump off;* knuckle (under); listen to; *mind;* not resist; obey; perform; *quit;* relent; relinquish; submit; *truckle; undertake; venerate; withdraw; x;* yield; zero resistance;
**deference** *(n.)*: acquiescence; biddableness; compliance; deferring; esteem; followership; giving in; heeding; *implementation; jumping to it; keeling in;* listening; mindfulness; non-resistance; obsequiousness; *politeness; questionlessness;* respect; submissiveness; *toeing the line;* upholding; veneration; *willingness to defer; xlation;* yieldedness; *zero resistance;* [*Ant.* disrespect]
**deferential** *(adj.)*: acquiescent; biddable; compliant; deferent; ever- ~; flexible; game; heedful; *inclined; jump right to it;* kowtowing; listening; meek; non-resistant; obsequious; passive; pliant; quick-to-defer; regardful; submissive; tractable; thoughtful; unresisting; very compliant; well-disposed; *xtry;* yielding; *zero resistance;* [*Ant.* disrespectful]
**deferment** *(n. putting off)*: adjournment; break; *concession;* deferral; *ease up; forbearance;* gap; holdup; interval; jauking; *keeping;* lapse; moratorium; *night rest;* obstruction; postponement; quietude; recess; rescheduling; rain check; suspension; time out; *unwinding;* vacation; wait; *x-rest; yearlong delay; zizz;*
**defiance** *(n.)*: affront; bucking; contravention; challenge; contumacy; disobedience; *ever-defiant;* flouting; *general disregard;* heading on; insubordination; *jadedness;* kicking; lawlessness; misbehavior; mutiny; noncompliance; obstinacy; *paying no regard; questioning;* rebellion; resistance; standing against; taking on; unyieldingness; violation; withstanding; *xgression;* yieldlessness; *zapping;* [*Ant.* deference]
**defiant** *(adj.)*: anti-authority; bad; bold; contravening; challenging; contumacious; disobedient; ever- ~; flouting; *glaringly disobedient;* headstrong; insubordinate; incompliant; incorrigible; insurgent; *jaded; knocking;* lawless; mutinous; noncompliant; obdurate; *pigheaded; querulous;* refractory; rebellious; self-willed; truculent; unyielding; unruly; unsubmissive; ungovernable; violating; willful; *x-grained;* yieldless; *zero give;* [*Ant.* deferential]
**deficiency** *(n.)*: absence; badness; coming up short; dearth; destitution; *empty;* falling short; flaw; gap; *hardly enough;* inadequacy; insufficiency; *just not enough; known deficiency;* lack; meagerness; need; outage; paucity; *quisby;* running short; shortage; shortfall; scarcity; shortcoming; *too little;* unavailability; vulnerability; want(age); weakness; *xtry. ~; yowling;* zero sufficiency; [*Ant.* disproportionateness]

**deficient** *(adj.)*: *abject;* bad; below standard; *crummy;* defective; *empty;* failing; falling short; greatly in need; *hard-pressed;* insufficient; *just not enough;* keenly ~; lacking; low; missing something; non-sufficient; needful; *out;* poor; partial; *questionable; ran out;* short; shy; slack; too little; unsufficing; unsatisfactory; *under;* very ~; wanting; *xtry. deficient;* yet ~; zero sufficiency: [Ant. disproportionate]

**deficit** *(n.)*: arrears; absence; *back rent; condition;* debt; dearth; deficiency; *emptiness;* financial ~; gap; *hardship;* insufficiency; inadequacy; *jejuneness; known ~;* lack; liability; *meagerness;* nonpayment; need; omission; *owe;* paucity; *quisby; responsibility;* shortfall; shortage; scarcity; scarceness; *too little;* ullage; *void;* want(age); *x-differential; yearning;* zero sufficiency; [Ant. disproportion]

**defile** *(v.)*: adulterate; besmirch; corrupt; contaminate; denigrate; debase; desecrate; dirty; *exploit;* foul; grime; *humble; harm;* injure; javel; kollow; *louse up;* make unclean; mire; *nullify; oppress; outrage;* pollute; *quade [arch.];* ruin; sully; spoil; tarnish; taint; *undermine;* violate; wrong; *x; yucky: zap;*

**defilement** *(n.)*: adulteration; besmirching; corruption; contamination; denigration; debasement; desecration; dirtying; defiling; *exploitation;* fouling; griming; *humbling; harm;* injury; javeling; kollowing; *lousing up;* miring; *non-respect; outrage;* pollution; *quade [arch.];* ruination; sullying; spoiling; tarnishing; *undermining;* violation; *warping; x; yucky: zapping;*

**define** *(v.)*: address; bespeak; clarify; characterize; describe; delineate; demarcate; explain; formulate; give meaning; hold forth; illuminate; *justify; key in;* line out; make clear; mark out; notate; outline; *precise; qualify; represent;* show; spell out; tell; *uncloud; verse;* write out; *xenagogy; yak;* zero in on;

**definite** *(adj.)*: accurate; beyond doubt; certain; dependable; exact; firm; guaranteed; honest-to-goodness; infallible; indisputable; incontestable; inarguable; justifiable; known; legitimate; mistake-proof; non-questionable; 100% sure; positive; proven; questionless; reliable; sure; trustworthy; undeniable; unarguable; verified; without doubt; *xtry. sure; yes;* zero doubt;

**definition** *(n.)*: acutance; book ~; clarification; description; dictionary ~; distinctness; explanation; formulation; giving the meaning; *helping one understand;* illumination; *justification; knowledge;* lexicon ~; limpidity; meaning; notation; outline; precise meaning; pellucidity; *qualification;* reddition; spelling out; telling; unambiguity; visibility; Webster's ~; *xenagogy; yak;* zeroing in;

**definitive** *(adj.)*: absolute; beyond doubt; conclusive; decisive; ending; final; guaranteed; highly conclusive; indisputable; incontrovertible; *just sure;* keenly sure; *last;* most authoritative; non-questioned; 100% certain; positive; questionless; reliable; sound; terminative; unquestionable; *verified;* without question; *xtry. sure; yet irrefutable;* zero question;

**deflate** *(v.)*: abate; *bate;* collapse; decrease; *ebb;* flatten; fold up; go down; *hide;* implode; *jump down; knock down;* lower; let air out; *minish; non-inflated; outgo;* poke hole in; *quell;* reduce; shrink; take air out of; un-inflate; *verge downward;* weazen; *x-out; yield;* zeroize; [Ant. distend]

**deflect** *(v.)*: avert; bounce; change direction; divert; diffract; *el; fend off;* glance; head another direction; *inhibit;* jump back; *keep at bay; light;* move away; *non-penetration; off;* ping; *quell;* rebound; richocet; refract; spring back; turn away; *U-turn;* veer; ward off; *xfer; yaw; zag;*

**deform** *(v.)*: adulterate; alter; bend; contort; distort; entwist; foul up; garble; gnarl; *harm; hideous;* injure; *jade;* knot; *louse up;* mutate; mutilate; malform; misshape; miscreate; *nullify; obloquy; oppress;* pervert; *quade* [arch.]; ruin; spoil; skew; twist; unform; vary; warp; *xenomorph; yaw; zad;*

**deformity** *(n.)*: abnormality; *blemish;* contortion; distortion; disfigurement; defect; evil-favoredness; fault; *gruesomeness;* hagardliness; hideousness; *imperfection; jadedness;* kyphosis; lordosis; malformation; monstrosity; non-normality; *obloquy;* perversion; queerness; repugnancy; *skewed;* truncation; ugliness; *variation;* warp(age); *xenomorph; yaw; zad;*

**defraud** *(v.)*: allure; beguile; bilk; cheat; dupe; ensnare; fleece; gyp; hornswoggle; insnare; jape; *kid;* lie to; misrepresent; nobble; outfox; put one over; *quiblin* [arch.]; rook; rip off; swindle; take advantage; *utter falsehood;* verneuk; weasel; wangle; *xuld [arch.]; yentz; zing;*

**defray** *(v.)*: *afford;* bear the cost of; cover; discharge; expend; forfeit; give; help with; *invest; justify;* kick in; lay out; meet; *non-retention;* outlay; pay for; *quid pro quo [L.];* recompense; subsidize; take care of; underwrite; *vest; weigh out;* xfer; yield; *zero-out one's debt;*

**deftness** *(n.)*: adroitness; *bent;* cleverness; dexterity; expertise; finesse; genius; habilitation; instinct; *jack-of-all-trades;* knack; long suit; mastery; natural ability; *occupation;* proficiency; quickness; readiness; skill; talent; usefulness; virtuosity; wherewithal; *xenium;* yaup; zest;

**defy** *(v.)*: affront; brave; buck; challenge; disobey; dare; *err;* flout; *go astray; head on;* infract; *jaded;* kick at; *lawless;* mutiny; not heed; outface; openly resist; *pay no regard to; quad;* rebel; resist; stand against; take on; *unheeded;* violate; withstand; *x-gress; yieldless; zero obedience;*

**degenerate** *(adj.)*: adulterous; bad; corrupt; debauched; dissolute; depraved; decadent; evil; fornicative; godless; *horrible;* immoral; jaded; *kitsch;* lascivious; morally bankrupt; non-moral; obscene; profligate; *quad;* reprobate; scrofulous; *trampy;* unchaste; vile; wicked; x-rated; *yucky; zero-morals;* [*Ant.* decent]

**degenerate** *(v.)*: alter; break down; crumble; dissolve; deteriorate; disintegrate; dwindle; decline; erode; fall apart; go down; hydrolyze; *impair; junk; kaput; lay waste;* mortify; *nullify; obliterate;* pall; quash; reprobate; regress; spoil; sink; turn into dust; unbuild; *vanish;* worsen; weaken; *x-ing; yield;* zap;

**degeneration** *(n.)*: attrition; abating; breakdown; corruption; corrosion; crumbling; deterioration; disintegration; decay; erosion; falling apart; going down; *hoaring;* impairment; *jade; kaput;* labelfaction; mortification; necrosis; oxidation; pejoration; queering; regression; rotting; spoiling; tainting; undoing; *vanishing;* worsening; waning; weakening; *xylaria; yielding; zapping;*

**degrade** *(v.)*: abase; belittle; cut down; demean; debase; disgrace; efface; *fall; go down;* humiliate; ill-treat; *jackalent;* knock down; lower; mortify; *nither* [arch.]; *offend;* put down; *quieten;* reduce; shame; sully; sink; taint; tarnish; upbraid; vitiate wipe; *x-out;* yellow; *zeroize;*

**degree** *(n.)*: amount; band; boundary; bigness; capacity; class; caliber; designation; extent; echelon; fullness; grade; height; increment; intensity; immensity; jurisdiction; knotch; limit; level; latitude; largeness; *lower limit;* magnitude; measure; notch; order of magnitude; plane; point; position; qua(ntity); reach; rank; rating; rung; step; severity; tier; tick; upper limit; vastness; wideness; *x-section; yield; zone;*

**dehumanize** *(v.)*: abase; brutalize; brutify; bestialize; coarsen; desensitize; *evil; fleer; gibe;* harden; imbrute; jade; *knock;* lower; make inhuman; *numb; offend;* put down; *quib; ruthless; slur;* treat terribly; *uncaring;* vulgarize; *wicked; xuld [arch.];* yock; zero zeroize; [*Ant.* dignify]

**dehydrate** *(v.)*: air-dry; bake; chap; dry up (-out); desiccate; demoisturize; evaporate; exsiccate; fire-dry; go dry; heat-dry; insolate; *jejune;* kipper; kiln-dry; lose moisture; make dry; *non-hydrated;* oven-dry; overdry; parch; *quail;* roast; sun-dry; shrivel; torrefy; towel-dry; *use up;* ventilate; *vacuum dry;* wizen; wither; *xeransis; yarrish;* zap;

**deify** *(v.)*: apotheosize; become a god; *consecrate;* divinize; exalt to rank of god; *fulgent;* god; highly exalt; idolize; *joss;* kneel before; laud as a god; make a god; *non-human; obeisance;* praise as a god; *quantum leap;* regard as a god; sanctify as a god; *transcend; uplift;* venerate as a god; worship; *xfer; yichus; zet [dial.];* [*Ant.* dehumanize]

**deity** *(n.)*: apotropean; *Baal;* carved image; divinity; demigod; *earth god;* false god; god; household god; idol; joss; *ka [Egy.];* lar; man-made image; naiad; orisha; pagan god; queen of heaven; river-god; statue; totem; *underworld ~;* vanir; wakanda; xoanon; yaksha; zeme; [*Ant.* Devil]

**dejected** *(adj.)*: *affected;* bleak; cheerless; depressed; despondent; *ejulation;* forlorn; gloomy; heavy-hearted; in the dumps; joyless; *keening;* lachrymose; miserable; mopish; melancholic; negative; overcast; pessimistic; pitiful; *quivering;* rueful; sad; sorrowful; tristful; unhappy; very sad; woeful; *xtry despondent;* yucky; zealless; [*Ant.* delighted]

**delay** *(n.)*: adjournment; breather; break; cumbrance; deferment; dawdling; dilly-dallying; dalliance; *ease up;* forbearance; gap; holdup; interval; jauking; keeping; killing time; lingering; lull; lag; lapse; lollygagging; moratorium; night rest; obstruction; pause; prolongment; putting off; postponement; procrastination; quietude; rest; setback; suspension; stall; time out (-lag); tarrying; *unwinding; vacation;* wait; *x-rest; yawning; zizz;*

**delay** *(v.)*: adjourn; break; cumber; detain; deter; dawdle; defer; (dilly-)dally; dither; drag; encumber; exclude; frustrate; forestall; *go slow;* hinder; hamper; hold up; hesitate; hem and haw; impede; inhibit; jauk; keep; kill time; linger; lag; loiter; linger; lolligag; moderate; *non-cooperation;* obstruct; postpone; put off; procrastinate; prolong; *quit;* rest; restrain; retard; slow; stall; shelve; tarry; temporize; *um and ah;* veto; wait; withhold; waste time; *x; yank; zap;*

**delegate** *(v.)*: assign; authorize; bestow; consign; commit; depute; entrust; farm out; give out; hand over; intrust; *job; kit; let; make; non-retention;* offload; put in ones hands; *qualify;* reassign; set on; turn over; *unhand;* vest; *work;* xfer; *yield;* zet [dial.];

**delegation** *(n.)*: ambassadors; body; commission; deputation; delegates; emissaries; forgathering; group; host; ingathering; *jurisdiction; kit;* lobby group; mission; number; officers; party; *quantity;* representatives; subcommittee; troop; unit; *volume;* walking ~; xfer; *yain [arch.];* zone;

**delete** *(v.)*: annihilate; blot out; cut; dele; erase; *free;* get rid of; *halve;* invalidate; *jump down;* kill; lift off; minus; negate; obliterate; *put back; quash;* rub out; remove; scratch; strike out; scrape off; scrub; take off; undo; *void;* white out; *x-out; yank;* zero out;

**deletion** *(n.)*: annihilation; blotting out; cutting; deleting; erasure; expunction; excision; *free;* getting rid of; *halving; invalidation; jumping down; killing;* lifting off; minusing; negation; obliteration; *putting back; quantity reduced;* rubbing out; removal; striking out; scrubbing; taking off; undoing; voidance; whiting out; *x-ing out; yanking;* zeroing out;

**deliberate** *(adj.)*: aware; by design; conscious; considered; calculated; done on purpose; ever-conscious; *forethought;* glaring; hasteless; intentional; *just plain to see;* knowing; *liking;* meaningful; non-accidental; on purpose; purposeful; (pre-)planned; premeditated; quite intentional; resolute; studied; thought-out; unhasty; volitional; willful; witting; *xtry. planned; yearnful; zealous;* [*Ant.* desultory]

**deliberate** *(v.)*: analyze; brood; chaw; consider; debate; evaluate; examine; figure; gauge; hem and haw; introspect; judge; *know;* lucubrate; mull over; muse; *notion;* overanalyze; ponder; question; reflect; study; think about; use brain; valuate; weigh out; *xenodiagnose; yeme; zazen;*

**delicate** *(adj.)*: *appealing;* breakable; brittle; crushable; dainty; easily broken; elegant; fragile; frail; fine; frangible; graceful; *handle with care;* insubstantial; jimp; *keen;* lovely; migniard; nice; *ornate;* pretty; quaint; refined; slight; sensitive; tender; ultrafine; very fragile; weak; XF; *yare-handed; zierlich [G.];* [*Ant.* durable]

**delicious** *(adj.)*: appetizing; appealing; *bon!* [F.]; comestible; delectable; delightful; enjoyable; exquisite; fine; flavorful; good; great-tasting; heavenly; irresistible; *juicy;* keen; luscious; mouth-watering; nice; *outstanding;* pleasing; palatable; *quite good;* relishable; savory; scrumptious; tasty; tantalizing; toothsome; titillating; unbelievably good; very good; wonderful; *XF;* yummy; zesty; [*Ant.* disgusting]

**delight** *(n.)*: appeal; afterglow; bliss; cheer; contentedness; delectation; elation; euphoria; felicity; gladness; glee; happiness; intoxication; joy; *keenness;* lightheartedness; merriment; *niceness;* over-joyfulness; pleasure; *queme;* rejoicing; relishing; rapture; satisfaction; thrill; *uplifted; vivacity;* winsomeness; *xanadu; yeah!;* zestfulness; [*Ant.* displeasure]

**delight** *(v.)*: appeal to; bring joy to; buoy up; cheer (up); *do backflips;* enthuse; enrapture; excite; felicitate; gladden; give pleasure to; glory in; hearten; inspire; joy; *keen;* lift up; make happy; *nice;* overjoy; *oblectation;* please; quicken; rejoice; *raptured;* satisfy; stir; thrill; uplift; vitalize; *well-pleased; xtry.; yeah!; zest;* [*Ant.* displease; disenchant]

**delightful** *(adj.)*: agreeable; appealing; blithe; blissful; cheerful; delightsome; delectable; enjoyable; fine; fun; fantastic; good; glad; heavenly; happy; invigorating; joyful; keen; lovely; mellifluent; nice; *overjoyed;* pleasant; quite nice; rewarding; satisfying; superb; terrific; thrilling; uplifting; very good; wonderful; well-pleasing; *xenial;* yummy; *zestful;* [*Ant.* disgusting]
**delineate** *(v.)*: articulate; bespeak; communicate; draw; define; describe; declare; demarcate; explain; *foremention;* give description; *hold forth;* indicate; *jaw; key in;* let out; limn; mark out; notate; outline; proclaim; picture; quoth; relate; relay; state; sketch; set; tell; trace out; utter; verbalize; word; write; *xenophonia;* yak; zet [dial.];
**delinquency** *(n.)*: abdication; bad debt; carelessness; dereliction; error; failure; *going unattended;* heedlessness; irresponsibility; *jumping ship; kesting;* laches; misdeed; negligence; omission; offense; passing over; *quick to forget;* remissness; recklessness; shirking; slight; *thoughtlessness;* unfaithfulness; *vagueness;* wrong; welshing; *xtry. irregard; yemeles* [arch.]; zero responsibility; [*Ant.* dependability]
**delinquent** *(adj.)*: aberrant; bad; careless; criminal; derelict; erroneous; failing; felonious; *guilty;* heedless; irresponsible; *jaded; kesting;* law-offending; misbehaving; negligent; offending; perfidous; *quick to forget;* remissive; reckless; shirking; *thoughtless;* unfaithful; *very careless;* welshing; *xtry. disregard; yemeles* [arch.]; *zero responsibility;* [*Ant.* dependable]
**delirious** *(adj.)*: astonished; bemused; confused; delirious; drugged; entranced; frenzied; floaty; flighty; feverous; glassy-eyed; hallucinating; incoherent; irrational; jagged; keif [Arab.]; lethe; mad; non-stable; nonrational; overexcited; pyretic; psychedelic; *quaffed;* restless; stupefied; *transfixed;* unstable; vegged out; whacked out [slang]; *xanthoxylin; yerking;* zoned out [slang];
**deliver** *(v.)*: affranchise; bring; convey; consign; distribute; emancipate; freight; forward; ferry; free; give; get; give; haul; hand ~; *import;* janker; kurvey; locomote; move; mail; manumit; *navigate; offload;* pass; purvey; put in one's hand; quarter-cart; relay; redeliver; ship; send; transport; transfer; take; uptake; unload; *van; waft; wheel;* xfer; yanker [Br.]; yield; zip; [*see* free; produce; surrender; save; *Ant.* dispossess]
**deliverance** *(n.)*: affranchisement; bringing through; clearing; delivery; emancipation; escape; emancipation; freedom; *getting out; help; imperishableness;* jailbreak; *keeping safe;* liberation; manumission; new chance; overcoming; prisonbreak; quittance; rescue; recovery; release; riddance; redemption; regeneration; salvation; setting free; *transport; unshackled;* vouchsafement; *win;* xfer; yielding; *zipping;* [*Ant.* dispossession]
**deliverer** *(n.)*: *advocate;* beater; champion; deliveryman; eleutherian; emancipator; freer; folk hero; *great;* hero; *invader; jubilant;* knight; liberator; messiah; *non-loser;* overcomer; paladin; *queller;* rescuer; redeemer; savior; triumphant; upholder; victor; white knight; *xtry.; yielder; zealous;* [*Ant.* dispossessor]
**delivery** *(n.)*: *airmail;* bringing; box; carriage; conveyance; consignment; distribution; delivering; express ~; envelope; freight; giving; haulage; importation; international ~; *junk mail;* kurveying; *logistics;* moving; next-day ~; overnight ~; post; package; parcel; quick- ~; relocation; sending; shipping; supply; shipment; transportation; transfer; *underway; unshackled; voyage;* wagoning; *wafting;* xfer.; yielding; *zipping;* [*Ant.* dispossession]
**delude** *(v.)*: allure; beguile; con; deceive; ensnare; fool; flam; finagle; guile; gull; gag; hoodwink; insnare; jape; kid; lead astray; mislead; nobble; outwit; pull wool over one's eyes; *quiblin* [arch.]; *rook;* string along; shyster; trick; utter lies; verneuk; weasel; wangle; wile; *xuld [arch.];* yenta; *zing;*
**deluge** *(n.)*: alluvion; burst; cataclysm; debacle; *eddy;* flood; gushing; high water; inundation; *judgment; killing;* lake; *movement of waters;* Niagra; overflow; partial ~; *quandary;* rush; stream; surge; swell; torrent; tide; uprush; upwelling; *violent ~;* water-flood; washout; whelm; xtry. surge; yeo; *Zee;*
**delusion** *(n.)*: aberration; beguilement; con; deception; ensnarement; fraud; guile; hoax; illusion; illusiveness; japery; knavery; lie; misconception; misbelief; non-reality; outwitting; pretext; *quiblin [arch.];* ruse; sham; trick; *unreal;* vision; wile; *xuld [arch.];* yaup; *zinger;*

222

**delusive** *(adj.)*: artful; beguiling; chimerical; delusory; deceptive; ensnaring; fraudulent; guileful; *hollow;* illusory; jady; knavish; lying; misleading; non-trustworthy; *overwise;* pawky; *quaintise [arch.];* roguish; specious; tricky; underhanded; vain; wily; *xtry.;* yepe; *zinger;*

**demand** *(n.)*: adjuration; behest; bidding; command; decree; exigency; enjoining; fiat; *governance;* halidom; injunction; juration; *keleusmatically;* laying on; *law;* mandate; necessity; order; *petition; precept; quo minus [L.];* requirement; stipulation; tasking; ultimatum; *voice; word;* XO mandate; yoke; *zakon [Rus.];*

**demand** *(v.)*: adjure; bid; call for; command; dictate; enjoin; *foist;* give an order; *have to;* insist; *juration; kaleusmatic;* lay down; mandate; necessitate; order; postulate; press; *quo minus [L.];* require; stipulate; say (so); tell; *utter; voice;* want; *xenagogy;* yark; *zakon [Rus.];*

**demeanor** *(n.)*: air; attitude; bearing; behavior; countenance; deportment; expression; feeling; frame of mind; guise; heart; impression; idea; judgment; *known inclination;* leaning; mindset; mood; mentality; notion; outlook; posture; quality; reaction; sentiment; spirit; temperament; undertone; visage; way; *xenodiagnosis;* yaw; *zeal;*

**democracy** *(n.)*: *autonomy;* bipartisan system; *constitutional republic; consensus;* democratic system; elected government; free country; government by the people; *have say;* independent ~; *justice; keen; liberty;* majority rule; *non-tyranny; overall consensus;* pure ~; *quite balanced;* representative ~; self-governing body; *two-party system; United States;* voting; Western republic; *xenocracy;* Yankee-style ~; *zero totalitarian;* [*Ant.* despotism]

**democratic** *(adj.)*: autonomous; *bipartisan; constitutional;* democracy-based; elected; egalitarian; free; governed-by-the-people; *honor;* independent; *just; keen; legislative;* majoritarian; *non-tyrannical; one nation under God;* people-governed; *quite balanced;* representative; self-governing; self-ruling; *two-party;* ultra-democratic; voter-run; *We the People; xenocatic;* Yankee; *zero totalitarian;* [*Ant.* despotic]

**demolish** *(v.)*: annihilate; break; bulldoze; bring to naught; blow up; crush; destroy; destruct; expunge; extirpate; flatten; grind to dust; havoc; *incinerate; junk;* knock down; level; *mangle;* neutralize; obliterate; olate; pulverize; quash; ruin; raze; smash; throw down; trash; topple; unroot; vitiate; waste; wreck; *x-ing;* yank down; zap; [*Ant.* develop]

**demolition** *(n.)*: annihilation; breakup; consumption; destruction; dismantlement; eradication; flattening; grinding up; havoc; *iconoclast; jarring;* knocking down; leveling; mashing; *non-existent;* obliteration; pulverization; quashing; ruining; razing; smashing; tearing down; undoing; violence; wrecking; *x-ing;* yanking down; zapping; [*Ant.* development]

**demon** *(n.)*: atua; *angel;* bad spirit; *being;* caco~; devil; evil spirit; fallen angel; foul (-familiar) spirit; fiend; ghoul; hellion; host of hell [pl.]; impure spirit; incubus; imp; jinnee; *kanaima* [Guyana]; *loa; minion;* numen; oni [Jap.]; orisha [Carib.]; puck; powers of darkness [pl.]; *quasi-demon; red cap;* succubus; spirit-being; *tempter;* unclean spirit; vile spirit; wendigo; *Xai;* yaksha [Ind.]; zar;

**demoniac** *(n.)*: asylum case; *berserk;* crazy man; demonomist; demon-possessed man; *evil spirit; freaky; ghost;* hellion; insane person; *judderer; kook;* lunatic; man with a devil; maniac; *neurotic;* one possessed with a devil; possessed person; *quasi-demon;* raving lunatic; spirit-infested man; tomb-dweller; *unclean spirit; volatile person;* wild man; *Xai;* yaksha [Ind.]; zany;

**demonic** *(adj.)*: atrocious; bedeviled; bad; cruel; devilish; demoniac; evil; foul; ghoulish; heinous; hell-bred; ignominious; *jaded; kindless;* luciferian; malevolent; nefarious; *odious;* pernicious; quad; ruthless; satanic; sinister; terrible; unholy; villainous; vile; wicked; *xgressing; yeffell* [arch.]; *zar-like;* [*Ant.* divine]

**demonstrate** *(v.)*: act out; affirm; bear out; characterize; display; exhibit; explain; epitomize; fix in ones mind; guide; hold out; illustrate; jerque; kithe [Scot.]; lay out; make plain; *nail down;* open up; portray; prove; *qualify;* reveal; show; typify; unveil; verify; *wave; x-certify; yield; zet [dial.];* [*Ant.* disprove]

**demoralize** *(v.)*: affect; agonize; bother; cause discouragement; dispirit; dishearten; discourage; engrieve; fall; grieve; hurt; *intimidate; jitters;* knock down; lower one's spirits; make sad; nerve; oppress; pall; quench one's spirit; rend one's heart; sorrow; trouble; undermine; vex; weaken spirits; *xuld [arch.];* yearn; zestless;

**demote** *(v.)*: *alleviate;* bring down; cut down; disrate; disbar; defrock; exauthorate; *fall;* give demotion; *have redress; impair; judge;* knock down; lower rank; move down; *non-promotion; off;* penalize; *quit;* relegate; strip; take away position; unfrock; unseat; *verge downward; wrench; x-out; yank;* zugzwang;

**den** *(n.)*: alcove; burrow; cave; delve; enclosure; fissure; grotto; hollow; hole; hideaway; home; inhabitance; ice cave; jaw-hole; *krater;* lair; *main entrance;* nest; opening; pit; *quarry-pit;* recess; *room;* refuge; shelter; talus ~; undercovert; vault; warren; *xtr. storage;* yawn; *zanja;*

**denial** *(n.)*: abnegation; abstinence; bickering; contraversion; contradiction; denegation; disavowal; disaffirmation; *expostulation;* fussing with; gainsaying; having disagreement with; impugnation; *jangling; knocking; lock horns [slang];* making ~; naysaying; negation; oppugnation; opposition; parleying; quarreling; repudiation; rejection; stint; traversal; *unequivocal ~; vehement ~; wrangling; x-purposes;* yelling; zero agreement;

**denomination** *(n.)*: affiliation; brand; creed; classification; church; designation; estate; ecclesiastical body; faith; faction; feather; group; *hierarchy;* ilk; ism; *jack;* kind; label; manner; *national ~;* order; organization; persuasion; *quarter;* religion; sort; stripe; sect; type; ule; variety; wing; *x-class; yoking; zollverein;*

    Religious Denominations: Anglican; Brethren; Catholic; Disciples of Christ; Episcopalian; Greek Orthodox; Jehovah's Witness; Lutheran; Methodist; Neo-charismatic; Orthodox; Presbyterian; Quaker; Reformed; Seventh Day Adventist; Theosophy; Unitarianism; Wesleyan;

**denominational** *(adj.)*: associational; *brand;* clerical; congregational; denomination-related; ecclesiastical; factional; *group;* hierarchical; *institutional; jurisdictional; kerygmatic; liturgical; monastic; nodal; order;* prelatical; *quoad sacra* [L.]; religious; sectarian; *trimestrial; ultramontane;* votary-related; *wing; Xavarian; yoke; zonal;*

**denounce** *(v.)*: accuse; attack; blame; condemn; criticize; deprecate; excoriate; fault; give talking to; harangue; impugn; jaw; knock; lambaste; *macerate; nag;* objurgate; pillory; *question;* reproach; scold; tell off; upbraid; vituperate; wig [Br.]; *xuld [arch.];* yell at; *zap;* [Ant. delight in]

**dense** *(adj.)*: amassed; *bunched;* compact; crowded; close; compressed; densified; *ever-close;* full; gorged; hard; *incumbered;* jam-packed; *kibbled;* loaded; micro-packed; maximized; nonporous; overstuffed; packed; *quashed;* rocklike; solid; semi-compact; serried; thick(set); tightly-packed; *up close;* very close; *wedged in; xtry. packed; yelm;* zero room;

**density** *(n.)*: amassment; *bunched;* compactness; closeness; denseness; *ever-close;* fullness; gorging; *heaping; incumbered;* jam-packing; *kibbling;* loading; micro-packing; *no space;* overstuffing; packing; *quashed;* rocklikeness; solidity; thickness; *up close;* very close; *wedged in; xtr. packed; yelm;* zero room;

**dent** *(n.)*: *affliction;* bend; buckle; (con)cavity; dig; dint; ding; dimple; depression; engrailing; fold; furrow; gash; hit; indentation; jag; *knock; loss;* mash; nick; *offense;* pock mark; pit; *quash;* ruin; smash; *toll; undoing;* violence; wound; *x-ing;* yedder; *zap;*

**dent** *(v.)*: afflict; bend; buckle; *crunch;* dint; engrail; fold; *grieve;* hit; indent; *jeel; knock into; lacerate;* mar; mash; nick; *olate;* pock; *quash;* run into; smash; trouble; *uproot;* victimize; wound; wreck; *x-ing; yank apart; zap;*

**deny** *(v.)*: argue with; bicker; contradict; contend with; disbelieve; disavow; disaffirm; denegate; disacknowledge; *expostulate;* fuss with; gainsay; have disagreement with; impugn; *jangle; kemp; lock horns [slang];* make denial; naysay; negate; oppose; parley; quarrel; repudiate; reject; squabble; spar; tiff; unbelieve; *vehemently ~;* wrangle; *x-purposes;* yell; *zap;*

**depart** *(v.)*: abscond; abandon; buzz off; be off; clear out; check out; disappear; deviate; desert; exit; flee; go; hightail; *immigrate; jilt; katabasis* [Gr.]; leave; mosey (along); migrate; *neglect; out;* part; quit; run off; remove; shove off; take leave; *uproot;* up and go; vacate; withdraw; xfer; yead; zip away;

**department** *(n.)*: area; branch; bureau; contingent; division; establishment; fraction; group; *house;* incorporation; jura; *kongsi [Chin.];* location; ministry; nexus; organization; office; part; quango; *records ~;* subdivision; territory; unit; *vicinity;* ward; *x-class; yuan [Chin.];* zone;

**departure** *(n.)*: abandonment; *begone;* coming out; departing; exit; egression; escape; evacuation; exodus; farewell; fleeing; going out; good-bye; *hightailing;* issuing out; *jumping out; kesting;* leaving; migration; *non-retention;* outgo; out-gate; off-ramp; parting; *quitting; riddance;* shoving off; separation; taking leave; *uprooting;* vacating; vanishing; withdrawal; x; *yead;* zipping away;

**depend** *(v.)*: accept; bank on; believe in; count on; deem trustworthy; entrust; embrace; *follow;* fully rely; *faith;* grab onto; have faith; hang on; hinge; inwardly trust; judge faithful; keep trusting; look to; lean on; *mainstay; non-doubt; overtrust;* put faith in; pivot; profess; *persuaded; questionless;* rest with; rely; stand on; swear by; trust; *unfailing;* very much ~; wholeheartedly ~; *y'faith [arch.];* zealously embrace;

**dependable** *(adj.)*: accurate; believable; committed; consistent; duteous; ever-faithful; faithful; firm; good; honest; incorruptible; indefatigable; *just; keen;* loyal; most faithful; never-failing; *obedient;* punctilious; principled; *questionless;* riskless; reliable; responsible; steadfast; sure(fire); true; trustworthy; trusty; unfailing; unfaltering; unerring; valid; well-tried; *xtry;* yeomanly; *zealous;* [Ant. disappointing]

**dependence** *(n.)*: assurance; belief; confidence; dependency; equidependency; faith; *guarantee;* hanging; hope; interrelation; inter~; *just believe; knowledge;* leaning; *mainstay;* non-doubt; need; *overconfidence;* pensility; *questionlessness;* reliance; resting on; sureness; tie; trust; unwavering faith; utter ~; *vow;* warrant; *xel [arch.]; y'faith* [arch.]; zeal;

**depict** *(v.)*: *appear;* bare; characterize; describe; draw; exhibit; fashion; give a picture of; hold out; illustrate; *justify;* kithe [Scot.]; lay out; limn; manifest; notate; open up; picture; picture; portray; paint; *qualify;* reveal; show; tell; trace out; typify; *uncover; visualize;* write; *xfer; yield; zet [dial.];*

**deplete** *(v.)*: *abate;* bleed; consume; drain; diminish; empty out; exhaust; expend; finish; fatigue; gobble up; hone; impoverish; jade; *kaput;* lessen; milk; *nullify;* overtax; overspend; *put out;* quail; reduce; rob; spend; sap; tax; tire; tap; use (up); vacate; weaken; weary; *xerosis; yield;* zap;

**deploy** *(v.)*: array; bring out; call up; distribute; employ; embattle; fan out; group; *have; in position; jump into action; kit;* lay out; move; *non-resting;* organize; outspread; position; *quantify;* ready; set (out); station; situate; transfer; use; *vest; well-readied;* xfer; *yarken;* zeal;

**deport** *(v.)*: alienate; banish; cast out; drive out; exile; expel; expatriate; force out; get rid of; heave out; *impulse; jettison;* kick out; *launch;* make leave; *non-residency;* oust; out-migrate; proscribe; *quant;* remigrate; repatriate; relegate; send away; throw out; *unhouse;* vomit out; *wale;* xfer; *ybanysshed* [arch.]; *zing;* [Ant. denize]

**depose** *(v.)*: *abase;* boot; can; divest; defrock; dethrone; disseat; expel; exauthorate; fleece; get rid of; heave-ho; impeach; *jettison;* kick out; lay aside; make to resign; *nab;* overthrow; oust; put off; *quit;* remove; rob; rid; strip; throw out; unseat; unfrock; unthrone; *vomit;* wrench; *x-out;* yank; *zip away;*

**deposit** *(n.)*: addition; accumulation; bed; buildup; collection; depositum; enlargement; furnishing; growth; gathering; heap; ingathering; *jam; kit;* load; lode; mass; *number;* overflow; pack; quantity; ruck; stowing; transfer; unloading; *volume; wedge;* xfer; *yield;* zet [dial.]; [Ant. deduction]

**deposit** *(v.)*: add; bestow; bank; consign; commit; credit; deliver; drop; dump; *endow;* furnish; give; hide away; insert; imbed; impart; *jettison;* kit; leave; lay down; lodge; *mete; non-retention;* offload; put; place; *quicken;* reposit; rest; stick; stow; transfer; unload; vest; *weigh;* xfer; *yield; zip;* [Ant. deduct]

**depravity** *(n.)*: abominableness; baseness; carnality; corruption; degeneracy; depravation; decadence; evilness; fallenness; godlessness; heinousness; iniquity; *jadedness;* knavishness; *leaven;* malignity; nefariousness; obduracy; perverseness; *quad;* reprobation; sinfulness; turpitude; unrighteousness; vileness; wretchedness; wickedness; *xgression; yetzer hara* [Heb.]; *zymosis;* [*Ant.* divinity]
**depress** *(v.)*: affect; agonize; bother; bring to tears; cast down; dishearten; discourage; demoralize; dispirit; enervate; faze; grieve; *hyp* [arch.]; *inconsolable; joyless;* knock down; lower one's spirits; make sad; *negative;* oppress; press down; quench one's spirit; rend one's heart; sadden; trouble; upset; vex; weigh heavily; *xuld [arch.]; yearn; zestless;*
**depression** *(n.)*: *affectedness;* blueness; cheerlessness; downheartedness; despondency; dejection; dysphoria; evil spirit; forlornness; gloom; hopelessness; heartsickness; *inconsolableness;* joylessness; *keening;* low spirits; misery; negative spirit; overcast mood; pessimism; quailing; ruefulness; sadness; tristesse; unhappiness; vapors; woefulness; xtry. ~; *yearnfulness; zealessness;* [*Ant.* delight]
**deprive** *(v.)*: *abuse;* betake; bereave; confiscate; dispossess; divest; deny; expropriate; *force;* grab; hold back; haul away; impoverish; *jerk away; keep away;* lose; *lacking;* make off with; not allow; *omit;* prevent; *quad;* rob; remove; reave; seize; sequester; take away; usurp; *vellicate;* wrest; wrench; *xfer;* yank away; *zip away;* [*Ant.* deliver]
**depth** *(n.)*: abyss; bottom; *chasm;* deepness; extensiveness; fathom; gap; *hidden;* introversion; intensity; jump down; knee- ~; lowness; level; measure; *number of feet; overwhelming;* profundity; *quantitativeness;* remoteness; severity; sounding; thickness; *unfathomable;* very ~; vastness; *way-down; x-deep; yawning; zoom;*
**derail** *(v.)*: avert; *backslide; come off;* divert; deter; distract; deflect; deviate; digress; excurse; foil; go off; *hinder; inhibit; jink;* keep from; lose one's focus; leave; maunder; move away; *not on course; off;* preoccupy; put on the back burner; *quell;* redirect; reroute; sidetrack; throw off course; turn away; upset; veer; wander; *wreck; x-ing;* yaw; *zip off;*
**deranged** *(adj.)*: aberrational; berserk; bonkers; crazy; disturbed; demented; *eccentric;* freaky; *goofy;* haywire; insane; *jolted;* kooky; loony; lunatic; mental (case); mad; neurotic; nuts; out of one's mind; outlandish; psycho(tic); psychedelic; quacked; *ridiculous;* sick (in the head); twisted; unstable; unbalanced; volatile; wacko; warped; *xanthoxylin; yo-yo;* zany;
**deride** *(v.)*: abase; belittle; chaff; denounce; *execrate;* fleer; gibe; humiliate; hiss; insult; jeer; jibe; knock; laugh at; mock; *name-calling; offend;* pillory; quib; ridicule; rail; scorn; scoff; sneer; taunt; tease; utter against; verbally abuse; vex; wipe; *xuld [arch.];* yock; zap; [*Ant.* delight in]
**derision** *(n.)*: abuse; belittlement; contempt; disdain; *eruption;* fleering; gibing; harshness; insult; jeers; kidding; laughter; mockery; name-calling; opprobrium; pillory; quibbing; ridicule; railery; ribbing; scorn; scoffing; taunting; unflattering terms; *unkindness;* vexation; wipes; *x-ing;* yah; *zinging;* [*Ant.* delight]
**derivation** *(n.)*: ancestry; background; birthplace; *came from;* clan; descent; extraction; eduction; family tree; genealogy; generation; heredity; *inherited; jet;* kin; lineage; line; link; maternal side; *nibiliary;* origin; paternal side; *provenance; quarter;* roots; source; tracing; *unilineal;* vein; whakapapa [Maori]; *x-linked; yoni* [Skr.]; *zygogenetic;*
**derive** *(v.)*: *attain;* bring out; come from; descend; draw out; extract; educe; force out; get; *have;* intercept; inherit; *jet;* keep; lixiviate; make of; *nibiliary;* obtain; proceed from; produce; *quarter;* receive; retrieve; *siphon;* take; *unilineal; vein;* worm out of; *xfer;* yield; *zygogenetic;*
**derogatory** *(adj.)*: abasing; belittling; critical; defamatory; detractory; disparaging; evil-intentioned; fleering; gibing; humiliating; insulting; jibing; knocking; *laughing;* mocking; *name-calling;* offensive; pejorative; *quib;* ridiculing; slanderous; traducible; unkind; vilifying; wiping; *xtry. bad;* yocking; *zinging;*
**descend** *(v.)*: abseil; belly-whop; climb down; come (down) from; drop; dive; decline; *ebb;* fall; go down; *high-dive;* immerge; jump down; keel over; lower; move downward; nose-dive; *over the cliff;* plummet; *quick-fall;* reduce; rappel; sink; slump; tumble; turn downward; *undo;* volt; whop; *x-cend; yank down;* zoom downward;

**descendant** *(n.)*: *adolescent;* begotten; child; daughter [fem.]; *enfant* [F.]; flesh and blood; firstling; grandchild; heir; inheritor; *junior; kindred;* little one; *minor; neophyte;* offspring; progeny; *quinquennarian;* relation; son [masc.]; *teenager; urchin; vein; whelp; xbred;* young; zon [dial. masc.];

**descent** *(n.)*: *angle;* belly-whop; climb down; drop; dive; decline; declivity; downturn; *ebb;* fall; going down; *headlong fall;* immergence; jump down; keeling over; leap down; movement downward; nose-dive; *over the cliff;* plunge; plummet; quick-fall; reduction; sinking; slump; slope; tumble; tailspin; *undoing;* volt; whop; *x-cend; yanking down;* zoom downward;

**describe** *(v.)*: *articulate;* bill; characterize; clarify; delineate; define; depict; depaint; explain; express; familiarize; formulate; give description; gloss; *hit* [arch.]; illustrate; *jot down; keynote;* limn; line out; make one understand; narrate; outline; *overpaint;* portray; paint; *quaint [arch.];* represent; *state;* spell out; tell; *utter; version;* word; *xenagogy; yeme; zero in;*

**description** *(n.)*: account; brief; blueprint; characterization; clarification; delineation; definition; depiction; explanation; formulation; gloss; *hit* [arch.]; illustration; *jotting down; keynote;* limning; *make clear;* narrative; outline; portrayal; pantography; *quaint [arch.];* recountal; representation; rendition; statement; telling; *utterance;* version; words; word-picture; *xenagogy; yarn; zero in;*

**descriptive** *(adj.)*: affective; *beautiful;* colorful; demonstrative; declarative; delineative; explanatory; expressive; enunciative; exegetical; exegetic; *frank;* graphic; highly poetic; illustrative; *jarring;* keenly ~; limning; moving; narrative; overly-graphic; poetic; picturesque; quantified; representative; raw; specific; telling; unequivocal; vivid; well-described; *xenagogic; yieldful;* zolaistic;

**desecrate** *(v.)*: abominate; blaspheme; commit sacrilege; defile; disrespect; execrate; *foment; grime; harm;* insult; javel; kollow; lay waste to; mire; *not respect; offend;* profane; *quade [arch.];* ruinate; sully; spoil; tarnish; *unhallow;* vandalize; violate; wreak havoc; *x-ing; yieldless:* zero respect;

**desensitize** *(v.)*: accustom; acclimatize; anesthetize; become accustomed to; callous; deaden; dull sensitivities; enure; familiarize; get used to; harden; inure; jibe [slang]; *kit; line up;* make less sensitive; numb; *ossify;* prepare; *qualify; ready;* stupefy; toughen; *unite; verse;* well-adjusted; *xenize;* yarken; *zet [dial.];*

**desert** *(n.)*: arid region; barrens; basin ~; badlands; *country;* desolate place; erg; *flatlands;* grassless place; hamada ~; *isolation; jejune;* kavir [Pers.]; lowveld [S. Afr.]; mesa; non-inhabited place; outback; plains; Qattara; reg; sands; savanna; *Sahara; torrid; trackless ~; uninhabited land; vast ~;* wilderness; wasteland; xerarchy; *yellow sands;* Zahara;
   **Deserts**: Arabian; Blue; Chihuahuan; Dasht-e Kavir; Egyptian; Gobi; Great Basin; Indus Valley; Judean; Kalahari; Libyan; Mojave; Nubian; Owami; Patagonian; Rub'al Khali; Sahara; Sinai; Tanami; White; Zaara;

**desert** *(v.)*: abandon; abdicate; bow out; back out; cut out; cede; depart; disown; drop; evacuate; forsake; go; give over; hand over; *ignore;* jump ship; jilt; kest; kiss goodbye; leave; maroon; neglect; opt out; pitch; quit; run away; relinquish; strand; shed; throw away; unload; vacate; walk out; withdraw; *xfer;* yield; zip away; [*Ant.* the deep]

**desertion** *(n.)*: abandonment; breaking away; casting off; dereliction; departure; evacuation; forsaking; giving up; handing over; ignoring; *jumping ship;* jilting; kesting; leaving; marooning; neglecting; opting out; pitching; quitting; relinquishment; revolt; running away; stranding; *shedding;* throwing out (-away); unloading; vacating; withdrawal; *xfer;* yielding; *zipping away;* [*Ant.* dependability]

**deserve** *(v.)*: *achieve;* be worthy of; call for; demand; earn; entitle; *fetch;* get to have; have coming; *incur;* justify; *kep; land;* merit; *need;* ought to have; *profit; quoff;* require; *right;* should have; *take in; unanimous agreement; valuate;* worth; warrant; work for; *well-earned; x-div; yield; zet [dial.];*

**design** *(n.)*: adornment; aim; *beautification;* cosmetic ornament; decorum; decoration; device; embellishment; emblem; figure; fashion; filigree; gadroon; goal; *highlight;* intent; jewel; *kory;* lovely embellishment; motif; mark; *nicety;* ornamentation; object; pattern; plan; purpose; quillons; repeating pattern; scrollwork; *structure;* theme; trimming; target; *upscale;* vignette; *well-trimmed; xenia motif; yclad [arch.];* zoophorus;

**design** *(v.)*: arrange; aim; *birth;* create; contrive; draw up; devise; engineer; fabricate; formulate; *get idea; hatch;* invent; intend; *judge; kiddy;* lay out; machinate; map out; mean; *notion;* originate; outline; (pre)plan; *quick-thinking;* ruminate; scheme; sketch; strategize; think (up); *use brain; visualize;* work out; *xenodiagnose; yeme;* zero in;

**designate** *(v. appoint)*: appoint; assign; *anoint;* betoken; choose; delegate; destinate; establish; earmark; *forechoose;* give (appointment); handsel; indicate; *jurisdiction;* key to; label; mark; name; ordain; pick; point out; *qualify;* refer to; specify; tag; *use;* vest; *well-chosen; x-ing;* yark; zero in;

**designate** *(v. give name to)*: assign; brand; call; dub; denominate; entitle; forename; give title to; hail as; identify; indicate; *jurisdiction; known as;* label; *mention; misname;* name; ordain; *phrase; quiring;* refer to; style; term; tag; *use; vocable; word; xenonym;* yclept; *zoon;*

**desirable** *(adj.)*: agreeable; attractive; appealing; bonny; choice; charming; coveted; desired; enviable; first-rate; good; handsome; irresistible; *just want; killing [slang];* looked-for; longed-for; much sought-after; *needed; outstanding;* pleasing; quite ~; *ravishing;* sought-after; tantalizing; *unsurpassed;* very appealing; wanted; *xtry.;* yearned-for; *zizzy;* [Ant. detestable]

**desire** *(n.)*: aspiration; appeal; aim; avarice; bidding; craving; choice; delight; desirousness; entreaty; fancy; fondness; goal; great ~; hope; heart's ~; hunger; itch; inclination; impulse; *just want to;* keen ~; longing; lust; *mind; need;* obsession; pleasure; plea; prayer; *quiritation;* request; self-will; strong ~; thirst; urge; velleity; whim(sey); will; wish; want; *xenenthesis;* yen; yearning; *zeal;* [Ant. detestation]

**desire** *(v.)*: aspire; ache; bid; covet; crave; desiderate; *eagerly ~;* fancy; got to have; hanker; hope for; hone; itch; implead; jump at; *keen desire;* lust after; long for; *mine; need; order;* pant; *please; quest for; reach for;* seek; thirst for; *urge; velleity;* want; wish; would like; *xel [arch.];* yearn for; *zeal;* [Ant. detest]

**desirous** *(adj.)*: ambitious; appetent; *badly desiring;* craving; desiring; desireful; eager; fain; game; hopeful; inclined; *jealous;* keen; longing for; lusting; minded; *not disinclined;* of a mind to; optative; pleased; *prepared;* quick; ready; set; too happy; unreluctant; very ~; willing; wishing; *xtry. happy;* yearnful; yare; zestful; [Ant. deplorable]

**desk** *(n.)*: acacia ~; bedside ~; counter; davenport; escritoire; fold-up ~; gateleg table; head table; imbenching; *jarahwood ~;* kitchen table; lap desk; lapboard; *mensal;* night table; nightstand; *overhang;* parsons table; quercine table; roll-top ~; scrutoir; table; utility table; vanity ~; workbench; workdesk; writing-desk (-table); work surface; x-table; *yew ~; zingana ~;*

**desolate** *(adj.)*: airy; annihilated; barren; bare; clean; clear; deserted; devoid; empty; forlorn; gant; hollow; inane; jejune; kithless; leveled; meaningless; nothing; obliterated; plain; quashed; ruined; stripped; tapped out; unoccupied; vacant; wiped out; wasted; x'ed; *yanked down;* zeroized;

**desolation** *(n.)*: annihilation; barrenness; consumption; destruction; devastation; expunction; fall; flattening; *gant;* havoc; incineration; iconoclast; *judgment;* kithlessness; leveling; mangling; mutilation; *non-existent;* obliteration; pulverization; quashing; ruin; spoiling; smashing; *terror;* undoing; violence; waste; wreckage; x-ing; *yanking down;* zapping; [Ant. development]

**despair** *(n.)*: anxiety; bleakness; *care;* despondency; exasperation; fretting; gloom; hopelessness; insecurity; *joylessness;* kiaugh [Scot.]; *lily-livered; mistrust;* nervousness; over-anxiety; panic; quaking; *reluctance; scared; stress;* trepidation; unrest; vexation; weariness of life; *xenophobia; yellow-belliedness; zeallessness;* [Ant. delight]

**despair** *(v.)*: anguish; abandon hope; brood; *contemplate;* despond; *end hopes;* fret; give up hope; have no hope; *inconsolability; joyless;* kiaugh [Scot.]; lose hope; *mope; nervous breakdown;* overponder; pall; question; ruminate; sink in hopelessness; throw in the towel; *upset;* vex; worry; *xenodiagnose;* yield to ~; zero in; [Ant. delight in]

**desperate** *(adj.)*: at wit's end; beside oneself; *critical;* distressed; distraught; despairing; dire; *extreme;* frantic; frenzied; *grave;* harried; intense; jittery; *keyed up;* last-hope; *mad;* nervous; needy; overanxious; panicked; *quivering;* reckless; scared; stressed; terrified; upset; *urgent;* vexed; worried; woeful; xtry. ~; *yemelich [arch.];* zero hope;

**desperation** *(n.)*: anxiety; burden; care; distress; despair; *exasperation;* fear; *gloom;* hopelessness; insecurity; jimjams; kiaugh [Scot.]; *lather; mistrust;* need; over-anxiety; panic; paranoia; quaking; *reluctance;* stress; solicitude; trepidation; unrest; vexation; worry; *xenophobia;* yearning; *zeallessness;*
**despise** *(v.)*: abhor; *balk at;* contemn; detest; deplore; execrate; *feel contempt for;* grudge; hate; *inexpiably hate; jaded;* kick at; loathe; mislike; not like; *odious; pshaw; querulous;* reprobate; spurn; treat with contempt; utterly loathe; vilipend; *wrathful; xenophobic; yucky; zero love;* [*Ant.* delight in]
**despiteful** *(adj.)*: abhorrent; bitter; cynical; cruel; disdainful; embittered; foul; galsome; hateful; inimical; jaded; kindless; loathsome; malicious; mean; nasty; odious; pernicious; *quede* [arch.]; rancorous; spiteful; terrible; unkind; virulent; wicked; xenophobic; *yucky; zealotic;*
**despot** *(n.)*: autocrat; boss; commander; dictator; executive; *Führer [G.];* gauleiter; Hitler; high-mockery-muck [derog.]; intendant; jemander [Ind.]; king; leader; lord; monocrat; *Nazi;* overlord; oligarch; potentate; prefect; queen [fem.]; ruler; *Shogun* [Jap.]; tyrant; *ultimate authority;* vizer; warlord; *xenarch; yokemaster;* zayim;
**despotic** *(adj.)*: authoritarian; autocratic; brutal; bossy; cruel; domineering; dictatorial; *evil-hearted;* exploitive; fascistic; gruff; harsh; Hitlerian; iron-fisted; *jaded;* kindless; loveless; monocratic; *nefarious;* non-democratic; overbearing; oppressive; *powerful; quede [arch.];* repressive; strict; tyrannical; unreasonable; unassailable; undemocratic; *virulent;* warmongering; *xenarchic;* yieldless; *za-zum* [Rus.]; [*Ant.* democratic]
**despotism** *(n.)*: authoritarianism; absolute power; *brutality; bossiness;* cruelty; *Communism;* dictatorship; *exploitation;* fascism; *gauleiter;* harshness; Hiterism; iron-fistedness; *jadedness;* kindlessness; lording over; monocracy; *Nazism;* oppression; *oligarchy;* police state; *quenching;* rule by force; supreme command; tyranny; *unchecked power;* violence; *warlord; xenarchy;* yieldlessness; *za-zum [Rus.];* [*Ant.* democracy]
**destination** *(n.)*: arrival; bourne; country of ~; destiny; end; final ~; goal; *hope; intention;* journey's end; *key place;* last stop; mark; *need;* objective; port; *place;* quintain; *rail stop;* stop; terminus; termination point; ultimate end; *view;* windup; x; yonder; zero in;
**destine** *(v.)*: appoint; *before selected;* choose; determine; decree; destinate; *doom;* elect; establish; foreordain; fate; *God-appointed; heaven-ordained;* intend; *judge; kismet;* lot; mark; *meant; necessitate;* ordain; predestine; predestinate; *quondam selection;* reserve; resolved by God; select; set for; *tag; unchangeable;* verdict; wheel of fortune; willed by God; x.; yonder; *zet [dial.];*
**destiny** *(n.)*: appointment; *bound to happen;* certain ~; destination; divine appointment; end; fate; fortune; future; God's will; happy chance; inevitability; journey's end; kismet; lot; *meant; necessary end;* outcome; *ordained end;* providence; portion; predetermined end; *qismet* [Arab.]; *result;* sovereign ~; terminus; ultimate end; *volition of God;* wheel of fortune; will of God; *x; yonder; zet [dial.];*
**destitute** *(adj.)*: abject; beggarly; *comfortless;* deprived; dirt-poor; down-and-out; empty-handed; forlorn; gant; humble; hard-luck; impoverished; indigent; jejune; *keenly poor;* lacking; moneyless; needy; overcome with poverty; poor; penniless; *quisby; rags;* suffering; *terribly poor;* unfortunate; void; wanting; without; *xtry ~; yowling;* zero;
**destroy** *(v.)*: annihilate; break; blot out; bring to naught; consume; crush; demolish; devastate; devour; destruct; expunge; eradicate; extirpate; efface; finish off; grind to dust; havoc; incinerate; *junk;* kill; lay waste; level; *lose; mangle; mar;* neutralize; obliterate; olate; prang; pull down; quash; rout; ruin; ravage; rack; raze; spoil; slay; swallow up; shipwreck; throw down; take apart; unroot; vitiate; waste; wreck; wrack; *x-ing;* yank down; zap; [*Ant.* develop]
**destruction** *(n.)*: annihilation; breakup; consumption; devastation; demolition; desolation; dissolution; eradication; expunction; fall; grinding; havoc; incineration; iconoclast; *judgment;* killing; loss; mangling; mutilation; *non-existent;* obliteration; perdition; pulverization; quashing; ruin(ation); spoiling; smashing; *terror;* undoing; violence; vastation; vandalism; vitiation; waste; wreck(age); x-ing; *yanking down;* zapping; [*Ant.* development]

**destructive** *(adj.)*: *adverse;* baneful; calamitous; cataclysmic; consumptive; devastating; disastrous; deadly; deleterious; desolatory; direful; eliminating; fatal; fell; *grievous;* harmful; hurtful; injurious; internecine; jeopardous; killing; lethal; mortal; malevolent; nocent; noxious; *obliterating;* perilous; poisonous; pernicious; ruinous; self-destructive; toxic; unsafe; virulent; vitiable; wounding; wasteful; *x-ing; ydrad [arch.]; zapping;* [Ant. developmental]

**detach** *(v.)*: abstract; break off; cut off; come apart; disconnect; disengage; extract; extricate; free; get out; *halve;* isolate; jerk apart; *kill; laniate;* make separate; *non-continuous;* open; part; *quarter;* remove; separate; take off; unfasten; uncouple; unyoke; *unattached; vell;* wrench; *x-sect;* yandy; *zip off;*

**detail** *(n.)*: attribute; *badge;* characteristic; distinguishing characteristic; element; feature; fact(or); fine point; *good quality;* highlight; ingredient; *judgment;* key feature; lineament; mark; niceties; *object;* point; peculiarity; particular(ity); part; quality; reality; specific; trait; undeniable characteristic; virtue; way; *x-factor; yetzer* [Heb.]; *zero in;*

**detain** *(v.)*: arrest; bust; capture; confine; delay; encumber; forestall; fix; guard; hold; impede; imprison; jail; keep; lay hold; *make one wait; nab;* obstruct; pinion; *quarantine;* restrain; secure; take into custody; *under lock and key; vanquish;* withhold; *x.;* yard; *zone;*

**detainment** *(n.)*: arrest; busting; confinement; captivity; detention; durance; encumbering; forestalling; guarding; holding; house arrest; imprisonment; jailing; keeping; laying hold; *making one wait; non-freedom;* obstruction; pinioning; *quarantine;* restraint; security prison; taking into custody; *under lock and key; vanquish;* wait; *x.;* yarding; *zone;*

**detect** *(v.)*: ascertain; become aware of; come across; discover; discern; espy; encounter; expose; find (out); get back; hit on; identify; *jaeger;* kithe [Scot.]; locate; make a discovery; notice; observe; perceive; *quick-to-learn; reveal;* sense; stumble on; spot; *see;* track down; uncover; view; *work out; x-search; yead;* zero in;

**detective** *(n.)*: agent; beagle [slang]; cop; *counterintelligence;* dick [slang]; examinant; flatfoot; federal agent; gumshoe; G-man; hawkshaw; investigator; inspector; jack [Br.]; *keen eye; lead-man;* man-hunter; nose [slang]; officer; operative; private eye (-investigator); P.I.; plainclothes man; questman; *researcher;* sleuth; snoop; shadow; tail; tec [slang]; tracker; undercover agent; *viewer;* watcher; *XQ; Yard man; zetetic;*

**detention** *(n.)*: arrest; busting; confinement; detainment; encumbering; forestalling; guarding; holding; imprisonment; jail; keeping; locking up; making a prisoner; *non-freedom;* obstruction; pinioning; *quarantine;* restraint; security prison; taking into custody; *under lock and key; vanquish;* withholding; *x.;* yarding; *zone;*

**deter** *(v.)*: avert; block; cumber; discourage; encumber; forestall; forefend; frustrate; foil; *gum up;* hinder; impede; inhibit; *jam;* keep (from); limit; *moderate;* negate; obstruct; prevent; quash; restrain; resist; stop; thwart; *upset;* veto; withhold; *x; yank;* zilch;

**deteriorate** *(v.)*: attrit; abate; break down; crumble; corrupt; decline; degenerate; diminish; depreciate; ebb; enfeeble; exhaust; fade; go down; *halt;* impair; *jump down; knock off;* languish; moderate; *negate; outgo;* pall; quail; reduce; regress; revert; subside; sink; taper; take a turn for the worse; *undo; vanish;* worsen; wane; weaken; worsen; *xerosis; yield; zap;*

**deterioration** *(n.)*: attrition; abating; breakdown; corruption; corrosion; crumbling; decline; degeneration; disintegration; decay; erosion; falling apart; going down; *hoaring;* impairment; *jade; kaput;* labelfaction; mortification; necrosis; oxidation; pejoration; queering; regression; rotting; spoiling; tainting; undoing; *vanishing;* worsening; waning; weakening; xylaria; *yielding; zapping;*

**determination** *(n. choice)*: appointment; *best choice;* choice; decision; election; finding; gauging; *heart;* inclination; judgment; knowledge; like; liberty; mind; nomination; opinion; pick; *quibble;* ruling; selection; take; *ultimatum;* verdict; will; *xel [arch.];* yes; zeal;

**determination** *(n. perseverance)*: assiduity; bulldog-tenacity; continuance; doggedness; endurance; foursquare; gumption; grit; headstrongness; indefatigableness; *insistence; jaw-set;* keeping at it; *leave no stone unturned; mettle;* not giving up; obstinacy; perseverance; persistence; *quit-free;* relentlessness; resolve; resolution; sticktoitiveness; steadiness; spirit; speddum; tenacity; unyieldingness; *volition;* willpower; *xel [arch.];* yieldlessness; *zealous continuance;* [*Ant.* despair]

**determine** *(v.)*: ascertain; adjudge; *best choice;* choose; decide; elect; favor; give choice; *hand pick;* indicate; judge between; *know; like;* make a choice; *nominate;* opt; pick; prefer; please; *quibble;* resolve; settle on; select; take; *use;* vote; want; *well-chosen; xel [arch.];* yes; *zealous for;*

**determined** *(adj.)*: adamant; bound (and ~); contumacious; dogged; dour; ever-stubborn; firm; foursquare; grim; headstrong; insistent; jaw-set; *keep; lasting;* mule-headed; mulish; non-bending; obstinate; persistent; *querulous;* resolute; steadfast; set; tenacious; unyielding; untiring; *volitional;* willful; *xel [arch.];* yieldless; *zero give;* [*Ant.* despondent]

**detour** *(n.)*: alternate route; bypass; change in route; deviation; emergency ~; *fork;* going a different way; heading around; interstate; *jink; keeping away;* lane; *means;* navigation around; *other way;* passage; *quite [Sp.];* redirection; rerouting; *sidestep;* turning away; *updated route;* veer; variation; *withdrawal; x-route; yaw; zag;*

**detour** *(v.)*: avoid; bypass; circumvent (-navigate); divert; evade; find a way around; go around; *head around; interstate; jink; keep away from; lane;* make alternate route; *negotiate around;* obviate; *prevent; quite [Sp.];* redirect; reroute; sidestep; turn away from; *utterly ~; veer away;* withdraw; *x-route; yaw; zag;*

**detract** *(v.)*: abase; belittle; cheapen; diminish; derogate; erode; *fleer; go down;* hurt; impair; *jeel; knock;* lessen; *minimize; non-edifying;* omit; *pull down;* quell; reduce; subtract; take away from; undermine; *vanish;* weaken; *xerosis; yank down; zeroize;*

**detriment** *(n.)*: affliction; blast; *cost;* damage; disadvantage; evil; foulness; *grief;* harm; injury; impairment; *jeel; knock;* loss; *mischief;* nocument; *offense;* prang; *query; ruin;* scath; troubling; *unsafe;* violence; wounding; *x-ing;* yedder; *zap;*

**devastate** *(v.)*: annihilate; bring to naught; crush; destroy; desolate; *expunge;* finish off; grind to dust; havoc; *incinerate; junk;* kill; lay waste; level; *mangle; mar; non-existent;* obliterate; pulverize; quash; ruin; spoil; smash; throw down; unroot; vitiate; waste; wreck; *x-out;* yank down; zap; [*Ant.* develop]

**devastation** *(n.)*: annihilation; bloodshed; carnage; consumption; destruction; desolation; *eradication; expunction;* fall; grief; havoc; incineration; iconoclast; *judgment;* killing; loss; mangling; *non-existent;* obliteration; pulverization; quashing; ruin(ation); ravage; spoiling; smashing; *terror;* undoing; violence; wreck(age); x-ing; *yanking down;* zapping; [*Ant.* development]

**develop** *(v.)*: advance; blossom; become; change; crystallize; deepen; educe; enlarge; flourish; grow; heighten; increase; jump up; *keep growing;* luxuriate; mature; *nourish;* outgrow; progress; *quantum increase;* ripen; sprout; shoot up; thrive; upshoot; upgrade; vegetate; wax bigger; *XL; yain [arch.]; zoom;* [*Ant.* devolve]

**development** *(n.)*: advancing; blossoming; becoming; change; developing; deepening; eduction; enlargement; flowering; growth; heightening; increase; instruction; jumping up; *keen growth;* luxuriating; learning; maturity; mental ~; neogenesis; operant conditioning; progress; *quantum increase;* ripening; raising; sprouting; thriving; upbringing; *vegetation;* waxing bigger; *xtry.* achievement; *youth; zooming up;* [*Ant.* devolution]

**deviate** *(v.)*: alter; bend; branch off; change; derogate; diverge; depart; excurse; fiddle with; go off; hook; invurve; jump off; *knocked off;* lean; maunder; move; modify; novate; *oscillate;* part from; *queer;* revise; stray; turn; *update;* verge; veer; vary; wander; *xenomorph;* yaw; zigzag;

**deviation** *(n.)*: aberration; alteration; bias; change; declination; divergence; derogation; *editing; fluctuation;* gyre; *heading away; innovation;* improvement; jumping off; *knocking off; leading away;* movement; nonconformism; overhaul; perversion; *queerness;* revision; straying; turning; unconformism; verging; variation; wandering; *xenomorph;* yaw; zigzag;

**device** *(n.)*: apparatus; *brainchild;* contraption; contrivance; *doodad;* engine; *function;* gadget; *hardware;* instrument; invention; invention; *jigger; kickumbob;* labor-saving ~; mechanism; machine; means; "nuts and bolts"; *object;* piece of equipment; *quick-fix;* robot; scheme; tool; unit; *vade mecum [L.];* widget; *X-Y recorder; yield; Zeug [G.];*

**Devil** *(n. Satan)*: Adversary; accuser; *Apollyon* [Gr.]; *Abaddon* [Heb.]; *the* archfiend; Beelzebub; Belial; *the* corrupter; Dragon; Deceiver; Diablo; *the* Evil One; *the* Enemy; Fiend; father of lies; god of this world; *Hell;* Instigator; *jab jab* [Carib.]; *Kali;* liar; lord of the flies; Lucifer; Mephisto(pheles); murderer; *Nick;* old serpent; Old Nick (-Scratch); Prince of Darkness (-devils; -the power of the air; -this world); *quad;* ruler of darkness; red dragon; Satan; serpent; *slanderer;* Tempter; *the* Unholy One; *the* Vile One; *the* Wicked One; *Xargi; yeffell [arch.]; zar;* [*Ant.* Deity]

**devil** *(n. demon): afreet;* bad spirit; cacodemon; demon; evil spirit; fallen angel; foul (-familiar) spirit; ghoul; hellion; impure spirit; jinnee; *kanaima* [Guyana]; *loa; minion;* numen; orisha [Carib.]; puck, *quasi-demon; red cap; spirit-being; tempter;* unclean spirit; vile spirit; wendigo; *xoanan; yaksha* [Ind.]; zar; [*Ant.* divine messenger]

**devilish** *(adj.)*: abominable; bedeviled; bad; conniving; cruel; diabolical; evil; fiendish; guileful; heinous; hell-bred; iniquitous; jaded; knavish; luciferian; malevolent; nefarious; *odious;* pernicious; *quad;* ruthless; satanic; sinister; treacherous; unholy; ungodly; vicious; vile; wicked; *xgressing;* yucky; *zero godliness;* [*Ant.* divine]

**devious** *(adj.)*: artful; byzantine; bad; crafty; cunning; deceitful; evil; foxy; fraudful; guileful; honnorless; insidious; jady; knavish; lying; mischievous; manipulative; non-trustworthy; *ornery;* pawky; *quaintise [arch.];* ruthless; roguish; sneaky; scheming; sinuous; tricky; tortuous; underhanded; vulpine; wily; *xtry.;* yepe; *zinger;* [*Ant.* dependable]

**devise** *(v.): analyze;* birth; conceive; concoct; dream up; *evaluate;* fabricate; formulate; *get;* hatch; invent; imagine; *judge;* kiddy; *lucubrate;* machinate; *notion;* originate; plan; *quick invent; ruminate;* scheme; think (up); use brain; *visualize;* work up; *xenodiagnose; yeme; zazen;*

**devoid** *(adj.)*: absent; bereft; clear; destitute; empty; free from; gant; hollow; *inane;* jejune; *kaput;* lacking; missing; not having; omitting; *plain;* quaffed; *resourceless;* stripped; totally ~; *unsupplied;* void; without; *x;* yeld; *zero;*

**devote** *(v.)*: assign; bless; commit; dedicate; *entrust;* follow; give; hallow; *invest; jalap;* keep *separate; lustrate;* make dedicated; *nard;* offer; promise; *qualify; recommit;* set apart; *transfer;* unhand; vest; *word; xfer;* yafe; *zeal;*

**devotion** *(n.)*: allegiance; bond; commitment; consecration; dedication; endearment; fidelity; *goodwill;* heart; *infatuation; immovability; joining;* keenness; loyalty; love; mateship; *motherly love;* niceness; *overlove;* passion; piety; *quixotic;* religiosity; separation; *selflessness;* trueness; *unselfishness; veneration;* warmth; *xenophilia;* yearning; zeal;

**devotions** *(n.)*: alone-time with God; Bible-reading; *consecration;* devotional time; daily ~; early-morning ~; family ~; God and I time; hour with God; *introspective;* just-God-and-me time; *keenness; love;* morning ~; *nightly prayers;* one-on-one time; prayer time; prayers; personal ~; quiet time; reading one's Bible; secret time; spending time with God; time with God; *unloading; voicing;* worship; *Xn.; yizkor [Heb.]; zet [dial.];* [*Ant.* devil-worship]

**devour** *(v.): ate; bite;* consume; descend upon; depredate; engorge; eat; feast; gobble; *have;* intake; junket; *kill* [joc.]; lunch; *munch; nibble; overeat;* prey upon; *quill* [arch.]; raven; scarf; swallow; tear into; *use up; voracious;* wolf; *xerophagy;* yolp; *zip down;*

**devout** *(adj.)*: adorant; believing; committed; deferential; earnest; fearing; grave; God-fearing; holy; humble; *introspective; jubilating; kneeling;* laudatory; magnifying; *non-presumptuous; obeisance;* prayerful; pious; *quaking;* religious; reverent(ial); spiritual; *thoughtful; uplifting;* venerative; worshipful; *Xn.; yielding; yearnful;* zealous; [*Ant.* disloyal]

**dexterity** *(n.)*: agility; briskness; celerity; deftness; dextrousness; expertness; fastness; *greased lightning;* hurriedness; ingenuity; *jildi* [mil.]; knack; legerdemain; *mastery;* nimbleness; *overhastiness; pronto;* quickness; rapidity; swiftness; skill; sleight; *trickiness; uninhibited; velocity;* wimbleness; *x-speed; yar;* zip; [*Ant.* dragginess]

**diabolic** *(adj.)*: abominable; bedeviled; bad; cruel; devilish; diabolical; evil; foul; ghoulish; heinous; hell-bred; ignominious; *jaded;* knavish; luciferian; malevolent; nefarious; ogreish; pernicious; quad; reprehensible; sinister; treacherous; ungodly; villainous; wicked; *x-rated; yucky; zar-like;* [*Ant.* divine]

**diagnosis** *(n.)*: analysis; *breakdown;* critique; diagnostic testing; examination; field study; *finding;* going over; *herborization;* investigation; *judgment;* knowledge-gathering; lab analysis; look-over; microanalysis; *neuroanalysis; overhaul;* probe; query; research; results; study; scrutiny; test; *urinalysis;* volumetric analysis; winnowing; *xeno~;* yield results; *zootomy;*

**diagnostic** *(adj.)*: analytical; *breaking down;* checking; *directional;* exploratory; finding out; going over; *honing in on;* investigative; *judging; knowledge-getting;* learning; making a study of; *nanoanalytic;* observational; prognostic; question-answering; researching; studying; testing; *urinanalytical;* verifying; *watching;* xeno~; *yielding; zeroing in;*

**diagonal** *(n.)*: aslant; angled; aslope; biased; catty-cornered; crossways; descending; *elevation;* falling; gradient; heel; inclined; *jagged; kinked;* leaning; moving at an angle; *natural slope;* oblique; port; *queer;* sloping; slanted; slantwise; traverse; upsloping; verging; *winding upward; xy-gradient;* yawing; *zigzag;*

**diagram** *(n.)*: analytic ~; blueprint; chart; drawing; *engineering;* floor plan; graph(ic); *hatched;* illustration; *journal; key location map;* layout; map; *navigational ~;* outline; plan; pictograph; *quo mode [L.];* road map; schedule; schema(tic); *topographical map; undersea ~;* visual; wallchart; x-chart; *yantra* [Hind.]; zenithal projection;

**dial** *(n.)*: *adjustable;* bulb; control; *digital readout;* equipment; face; gage; hand- ~; indicator; instrument; *joystick;* knob; *lever; mechanism; needle; oscillate;* pointer; *quick-switch;* rotary switch; switch; *turn;* up/down switch; *volume control;* wall switch; *x-y switch; yield; zeug;*

**dialogue** *(n.)*: argument; bearing heart; conference; conversation; discussion; exchange words; *fraternization;* gabbing; heart-to-heart; interchange; jangle; *key ~; little chat;* meeting; negotiation(s); oral treaty; parlance; quadrilogue; reasoning; speech; talks; *uttering; vocalization;* words; *xenophonia;* yarn; *zero in;*

**dictate** *(v.)*: adjure; bid; command; decree; enjoin; *foist;* govern; *have;* instruct; *juration; kaleusmatic; lead;* mandate; necessitate; order; pronounce; *quo minus [L.];* require; stipulate; *say;* tell; utter; *voice; word; xenagogy;* yell; *zakon* [Rus.];

**dictator** *(n.)*: autocrat; authority; boss; commander; caudillo; despot; demagogue; executive; *Fuehrer [G.];* governor; head; intendant; *jemander* [Ind.]; king; leader; lord; master; *Negus [Afr.];* overlord; oligarch; potentate; prefect; queen [fem.]; ruler; superior; superintendent; supervisor; tyrant; *ultimate authority;* vizer; *warlord;* XO; *yokemaster;* zayim;

**dictatorial** *(adj.)*: authoritarian; bossy; commanding; controlling; despotic; domineering; *evil-hearted;* fascistic; grave; high-handed; imposing; imperious; *jaded;* kindless; loveless; magisterial; *nasty;* overbearing; peremptory; *quede [arch.];* repressive; strict; strong; tyrannical; totalitarian; unreasonable; undemocratic; unassailable; *virulent; way too strict; xenophobic;* yieldless; *za-zum* [Rus.];

**die** *(v.)*: abate; *asphyxiate;* bite the dust; cease; croak; conk out; disappear; depart; decease; drop dead; expire; end; fade away; fail; fall; go (home); give up the ghost; *hazard; heir; inevitable; jaws of death;* kick the bucket [slang]; *lifeless;* meet one's Maker; *non-living; over;* perish; pass away; quell; quail; rest; succumb; terminate; *undo;* vanish; wane; wither; "x"; yield one's spirit; *zapped;* [*Ant.* dure]

**diet** *(adj.)*: *alterative;* burn-it-off; calorie-free; dietary; dietetic; *eating less;* fat-free; *guaranteed weight-loss;* half-calorie; *improvement; just one calorie; keen;* low-fat (-cal(orie); -carb); *meager;* non-fat(tening); one-calorie; *pencil-thin; quick-loss;* reduced fat; special ~; *trim; under;* very low-carb; weight-watching; *xerophageous;* yogurt; zero calorie (-transfat, etc.);

**differ** *(v.)*: argue; belie; beg to ~; contradict; disagree; diverge; expostulate; flite; *gainsay;* have difference; incombine; jar with; keenly ~; lock horns [slang]; *must disagree;* not agree; *object;* pick *fight;* quarrel; run counter; strive; take issue; *unharmonious;* vary; wrangle; *x-purposes; yell; zap;*

**difference** *(n.)*: assortment; alteration; asymmetry; *bizarreness;* contrariety; conflict; change; dissimilarity; diversity; dissimilitude; distinctness; deviation; disparity; *enigma;* funniness; gap; heterogeneity; inequality; incongruity; incompatibility; individuality; inequality; *jumble;* keen ~; *looniness;* modification; *mix;* nonequivalence; novelty; non-match; opposition; originality; oddness; peculiarity; queerness; reverse; separateness; strangeness; transformation; unlikeness; unevenness; unconformity; uncommonness; uniqueness; variation; *wide range;* weirdness; *x-differential; yaw; zaniness;*

**different** *(adj.)*: another; atypical; assorted; altered; bizarre; contrary; conflicting; changed; differing; dissimilar; diverse; distinct; deviant; disparate; erose; funny; *gapping;* heterogeneous; individual; incongruous; incompatible; irregular; *jumbled; kooky; loony;* modified; miscellaneous; mixed; nonsimilar; novel; non-matching; new; other; opposing; original; odd; peculiar; queer; reverse; rare; separate; sundry; strange; transformed; unalike; unlike; unequal; unusual; uncommon; unique; variance; varied; various; weird; wide-ranging; world apart; *xenomorphic; yawed; zany;* [see distinct]

**difficult** *(adj.)*: awkward; abstruse; adverse; bewildering; bad; complicated; deep; elaborate; formidable; grueling; hard; hairy; intricate; jarring; kittle; knotty; labyrinthine; mind-boggling; non-easy; overcomplicated; onerous; perplexing; puzzling; *quisquose* [arch.]; rough; strenuous; straitened; tough; thorny; tricky; ticklish; unsearchable; vexatious; wildering; *xenagogic; yucky; zapping;*

**difficulty** *(n.)*: awkwardness; adversity; bind; burden; complication; dilemma; encumbrance; fix; glitch; grief; hitch; hardship; impasse; jam; kink; load; mess; nuisance; obstacle; problems; quandary; rattle; struggle; snag; trouble; trial; upheaval; vexation; worries; *xerotripsis; yuckiness; zapping;*

**diffuse** *(v.)*: *advance;* broadcast; circulate; disperse; disseminate; effuse; fan out; go away; *hurl;* intersperse; *jawp; known; litter;* make widespread; *non-localized;* overspread; permeate; *quantity;* radiate; redisperse; refract; scatter; strew; spread; *send;* thinly spread; *universalize;* vanish; *widespread; xmit; yonder; zap;*

**dig** *(v.)*: *abstract;* burrow; coal-mine; delve; dredge; dig up (-out); disinter; explore; excavate; *find;* get out; hollow (out); investigate; *jenkin;* kip; *lower;* mine; *notch;* open; prospect; quarry; remove dirt; sap; search; scoop; shovel; trench; take out; tunnel; unearth; *venture;* work with spade; *xfer; yede; zanja;*

**digest** *(v.)*: assimilate; absorb; break down; *chew on;* decoct; eat; *feed; gustate;* handle; ingest; *junket;* kill [joc.]; *lunch;* metabolize; *nosh; overeat;* process; peptonize; *quill* [arch.]; *ruminate;* swallow; take in; *use; victual; wolf; xfer;* yaffle; *zip down;* [*Ant.* discharge]

**digestion** *(n.)*: assimilation; absorption; breaking down; catabolism; digesting; decoction; eupepsy; food-processing; *gastric juices;* handling; ingestion; *juices;* katabolism; *lunch;* metabolism; *noshing; overeat;* processing; peptonization; *quill [arch.];* rumination; stomachal metabolization; taking in; *use;* ventral processes; *wolf; xfer;* yaffling; *zipping down;*

**digestive** *(adj.)*: alvine; *breaking down;* coeliac; catabolic; digesting; eupeptic; *food-breakdown;* gastric; *humbles;* intestinal; jejunal; katabolic; lower abdominal; metabolic; nephrogastric; omasum-related; processing; *qualmish; ruminal;* stomachal; *transforming;* utilitarian; ventral; *working; xfer; yummy; zonal;*

**dignified** *(adj.)*: august; blue-blooded; commanding; decorous; distinguished; elegant; fabulous; grand; high-born; honored; illustrious; impressive; *judicious;* kingly; lofty; lordly; magisterial; majestic; masterly; noble; *ostentatious;* portly; queenly [fem.]; regal; stately; seemly; *tsarish;* uncommon; venerated; well-born; xtry.; yorkist; *zarish* [arch.]; [*Ant.* debased]

**dignity** *(n.)*: augustness; bigheadedness; command; decorum; distinction; esteem; *formality;* greatness; grandeur; honor; highness; impressiveness; *judiciousness;* kingliness; loftiness; majesty; magnificence; majesty; nobleness; *ostentation;* portliness; prestige; pride; *queenliness [fem.];* respect; stateliness; self-respect; *tugidity; unhumbled; virtue;* worthiness; *xtry.;* yichus; *zarishness* [arch.]; [*see* pride; *Ant.* debasement]

**digress** *(v.)*: alter; *break away;* change; divagate; depart; excurse; *fill out;* get off track; head off on a goose trail; *involved;* jump off topic; *kick off; lots;* maunder; not stay on course; *off the topic;* part from; *quite off the topic;* roam; stray; turn away from; *unload;* verge; wander; *xfer;* yaw; *zag;* [*Ant.* develop]

**digression** *(n.)*: ambages; *breaking away;* circuity; divagation; departing; excursion; excursis; *filling out;* goose-trail; *heading away; involved;* jumping off topic; *kick off; lots;* maundering; not staying on course; *off the topic;* parting from; *quite off the topic;* rabbit-trail; straying; tangent; *unloading;* verging; wandering; *xfer;* yaw; *zag;* [*Ant.* development]

**dilemma** *(n.)*: adversity; bind; crisis; difficulty; *endangerment;* fix; glitch; grief; headache; impasse; imbroglio; jam; kink; *load;* mess; nightmare; obstacle; predicament; plight; quandary; rattle; strait; stalemate; trouble; trial; upheaval; vexation; worry; *xerotripsis; yuckiness; zinger;* [*see* calamity]

**diligence** *(n.)*: assiduity; business; *commitment;* drive; determination; energy; fervency; good work ethic; hard work; industry; intensity; jauntiness; keen determination; laboriousness; mindfulness; motivation; non-laziness; oomph; persistence; pep; *quick-to-work;* responsibility; sedulousness; tirelessness; unslothful; vigor; work; *xtry. ~; yare;* zeal; [*Ant.* dragginess]

**diligent** *(adj.)*: assiduous; busy; *committed;* determined; enduring; *fervent;* gung-ho; hard-working; industrious; jaunty; keen; laborious; mindful; motivated; not lazy; overdiligent; persistent; *quick-to-work;* responsible; relentless; sedulous; tireless; unflagging; unslothful; vigorous; weariless; *xtry.; worker;* yare; zealous; [*Ant.* draggy]

**dilute** *(v.)*: attenuate; blend; *combine;* diminish potency; enervate; fade; *go down;* hydrate; immix; jade; kill; lessen potency; mitigate; mix; *not full strength;* offset; put water in; *quail;* rarefy; *sodden;* thin; *tenuous;* undercut; *very ~d;* weaken; water down; *xtr. weak; yet diluted;* zeroize; [*Ant.* distillate]

**dim** *(adj.)*: *ashen;* bedimmed; badly lit; clouded; caliginous; darkened; dull; dingy; dusky; enclouded; faint; faded; gloomy; hazy; indistinct; *jumbled; kaleidoscopic;* lightless; murky; nebulated; not bright; obscure; pale; prescripted; *quirky;* rayless; soft; shadowy; tenebrious; unlit; unclear; vague; weak; *xerophthalmic; yenite; zero visibility;* [*Ant.* distinct]

**diminish** *(v.)*: abate; assuage; alleviate; break; bate; curb; contract; condense; cut; decrease; decline; dissipate; dwindle; ease; ebb; fade; fall; go down; *hush;* impair; *jump down;* knock down; languish; lessen; lower; moderate; mitigate; minimize; *narrow; outgo;* peter out; quell; quail; recede; reduce; subside; slacken; taper; *undo; vanish;* wane; waste; *xerosis;* yield; zap; [*Ant.* develop]

**dine** *(v.)*: *ate;* banquet; consume; digest; eat; feast; fare; gobble; have; indulge; interdine; junket; kill [joc.]; knabble; lunch; munch; nibble; *overeat;* partake; *quill* [arch.]; raven; sup; *tuck away; taste; undereat; victual;* wine and ~; *xerophagy;* yaffle; *zip down;* [*Ant.* discharge]

**dinner** *(n.)*: aliment; bread; banquet; cuisine; diet; eating; fare; grub; haute cuisine; ingesta; junket; kitchen-meat; luncheon; meal; nourishment; *organic food;* provisions; *quelque-chose [F.];* repast; supper; *table; unprocessed food;* victuals; *whole food; xarque; yams; ziti dinner;*

**dip** *(v.)*: *angle;* bend; bow; bathe; bob; crouch; curve; dab; drop; dunk; duck; descend; engulf; fall; go down; hunker; incline; immerse; *jag; kink;* lower; lessen; *lade;* move down; *namaste; overwhelm;* put in; quat; rinse; sink; stoop; squat; slope; scoop; stick in; submerse; submerge; turn downward; *under;* verge; wet; *x-curve:* yaw; *zet [dial.];*

**diplomacy** *(n.)*: amiableness; *benignancy;* carefulness; consideration; delicacy; discretion; elegance; fragility; gentility; heedfulness; inoffensiveness; judgment; kid gloves; *lovingkindness;* Machiavellism; non-offensiveness; over-politeness; politesse; *queme;* regard; sensitivity; skill; statesmanship; tact; *unoffensive; virtue;* wisdom; *xenagogically; yepe;* zero offense;

**diplomat** *(n.)*: ambassador; attaché; bearer of tidings; consul; commissary; dignitary; diplomatist; envoy; emissary; foreign minister; government minister; high commissioner; intendant; *janker;* kurveyor; legate; liaison; minister; nuncio; official; plenipotentiary; *questor* [It.]; representative; statesman; tidings-bearer; *updater;* vice-consul; V.I.P.; *walking delegate; xeno-representative; yamen* [Chin.]; *zip;*

**diplomatic** *(adj.)*: ambassadorial; *benignancy;* consular; careful; delegatory; delicate; discrete; elegant; fragile; gentile; heedful; inoffensive; judicious; kind; *lovingkindness; mannerly;* non-offensive; over-careful; political; polite; *queme;* regardful; sensitive; skillful; tactful; *unoffensive;* very careful; wise; wily; *xenagogic; yepe; zero offense;*

**direct** *(adv.)*: as the crow flies; *breakless;* continuous; directly; express; *fast; go fast; hastily;* immediate; *just like that; keenly;* linear; *momentarily;* nonstop; on the spot; promptly; quickly; right; straight; speedily; *termination-free; tour de suite* [F.]; undelayed; very quick; without delay; *x-speed; yare; zero-wait;*

**direct** *(v.)*: administer; boss; control; dictate; exploit; focus; guide; head; influence; *jockey;* keep under control; lead; manage; *nobble;* oversee; point; *qualify;* run; show the way; tell; *use; vanquish; weight; xenagogy;* yeme; *zip;*

**direction** *(n.)*: *altering; bearing;* cardinal point; directional bearing; *east;* focus; *forth;* geographical ~; guidance; hinge; *instructions; journey; key;* latitude; movement; *north; over;* point; *quo mode* [L.]; route; *south;* tack; *underway;* vector; way; *xy-coordinate; yonder; zenith;*
  **Directions**: backward; down; east, forward; left; nadir; north, over; right; south, true north, under; up; west; zenith;

**director** *(n.)*: administrator; boss; controller; chief; *dean;* executive; foreman; governor; head; intendant; jefe; keeper; leader; lord; manager; *night manager;* overseer; procurator; *quartermaster;* reeve; supervisor; trustee; undershepherd; vice president; warden; XO; yardboss; *zayim;*

**dirt** *(n.)*: *acid soil; bemire;* colly; clay; crud; dust; earth; filth; ground; grime; grunge; *hazel-earth; iron-clay; jet;* kollow; loam; mud; marl; nast; ordure; pedalfer; quadrel; red soil; smut; soil; sod; topsoil; undersoil; virgin soil; waste; *xysma;* yellow soil; zonal soil; [*see* filth]

**dirty** *(adj. soiled)*: *awful;* bemired; black; collied; contaminated; dirtied; dingy; *disgusting;* earth-smudged; filthy; feculent; foul; grimy; grungy; grubby; germy; hoggish; insanitary; jarbled; kollowed; loamy; muddy; murky; messy; mucky; mired; nasty; oozy; polluted; piggish; puddly; quaggy; red-soiled; soiled; stained; slimy; squalid; sullied; turbid; uliginous; unbathed; unwashed; unsanitary; unhygienic; unclean; vile; well-stained; well-dirtied; *xysmic;* yucky; *zero cleanliness;* [*Ant.* disinfected]

**dirty** *(adj. x-rated)*: adulterous; bad; base; carnal; crude; degrading; explicit; filthy; fleshy; gauche; horrid; indecent; immoral; jadish; kinky; lewd; meretricious; *nasty;* obscene; perverse; *quad;* raunchy; sleazy; smutty; tasteless; trashy; unchaste; vulgar; whorish; x-rated; *yucky; zipless;* [*Ant.* decent]

**dirty** *(v.)*: adulterate; besmirch; bemire; befoul; bedaub; begrime; colly; contaminate; *cloud;* defile; daggle; distain; draggle; drabble; *earthy;* foul; grime; *hoggish; infect;* javel; jarble; kollow; *loamy;* muddy; mire; make ~; *non-sterile; oozy;* pollute; queer; rub dirt on; soil; sully; smudge; smirch; stain; tarnish; *uliginous; vitiate;* welk; *xysmic; yellow; zorch;* [*Ant.* disinfect]

**disable** *(v.)*: *afflict;* becripple; cripple; disenable; deactivate; disarm; *enfeeble; feeble; game;* hamstring; handicap; hough [Scot.]; inactivate; incapacitate; *jake-legged;* knock out; lame; maim; neutralize; *obstruct;* paralyze; *quash;* render inoperative; shut down; turn off; *unplug;* victimize; wing; *wound; x-out; yedder; zeroize;*

**disadvantage** *(n.)*: adverseness; bad quality; con; drawback; downside; *encumbrance;* foible; *glitch;* handicap; hindrance; impairment; incapacitation; *jeopardy; kink;* liability; *mistake;* negative; *obstruction;* pitfall; *quirk; restriction;* snag; shortcoming; *trammel;* undesirable quality; vulnerability; *vantageless;* weakness; *x; yet vulnerable; zero benefit;*

**disadvantageous** *(adj.)*: adverse; bad; *crummy;* damaging; erroneous; foul; *grievous;* hurtful; injurious; *jeopardous; kooky;* lousy; *mistaken;* non-beneficial; *obstructive;* prejudical; *quirky;* rotten; *shortcoming;* terrible; undesirable; unfavorable; unhelpful; very bad; wrong; *x; yucky; zero benefit;*

**disagree** *(v.)*: argue; bicker; cavil; contend; contradict; differ; dissent; dispute; expostulate; fight; gainsay; hold opposite view; *impugn;* jangle; kemp; lock horns [slang]; make fur fly; naysay; object; pick fight; quarrel; row; squabble; strive; struggle; take issue; tiff; *unharmonious;* vie; vary; withstand; *x-purposes;* yell; *zap;*

**disagreement** *(n.)*: argument; bickering; contention; controversy; dispute; discord(ance); disunity; dissent; disharmony; disaccord; embroilment; expostulation; fight; feud; fuss; gainsaying; hairsplitting; headshaking; incongruity; inaccordance; issue; jangling; kagg; *locking horns;* misunderstanding; negativism; odds; opposition; polemic; paradox; quarrel; quibble; resistance; rift; strife; squabble; tussle; unharmoniousness; unlikeness; variance; wrangling; *x-purposes;* yed; *zapping;*

**disappear** *(v.)*: *abate;* become invisible; cease to be seen; dematerialize; depart; dissipate; evanesce; evaporate; fade (away); go away; hide; immaterialize; *just ~;* keep out of view; *killed;* leave no trace; melt away; not be found; *out of sight;* pass off the scene; *quick-vanish;* recede; sink away; turn invisible; *unseen;* vanish; withdraw; wither; *xeromatous; yield;* zip away; [*see* perish]

**disappearance** *(n.)*: *abatement;* becoming invisible; ceasing to be seen; dematerialization; departure; dissipation; evanescence; evaporation; fading; going away; hiding; immaterialization; *jarring ~;* keeping out of view; leaving no trace; melting away; *non-visualization; out of sight;* passing off the scene; *poof!; quick-vanish;* receding; sinking away; turning invisible; *unseen;* vanishing; withdrawal; *xeromatous; yielding;* zipping away; [*Ant.* debut]

**disappoint** *(v.)*: aggrieve; burst one's bubble; bring reproach; crash; disenchant; dissatisfy; dishearten; disillusion; *embarrass;* fail; frustrate; grieve; hurt; *impropriety; jolt;* knock down; let one down; make ashamed; not succeed; *overwhelm;* pierce through; *quench;* rend one's heart; sadden; shame; thwart; *underachieve;* vex; wound; *"x"; yedder; zorch;* [*Ant.* delight]

**disappointment** *(n.)*: anticlimax; blow; crushing; disenchantment; disillusionment; *embarrassment;* failure; frustration; grief; hurt; *impropriety;* jolt; *knock down;* letdown; making ashamed; non-success; *overwhelming;* pain in one's heart; *quench;* rending one's heart; setback; thwarting; unsuccessfulness; vexation; wound; *"x"; yedder;* zero; [*Ant.* delight]

**disapproval** *(n.)*: abhorrence; berating; censure; criticism; condemnation; disapprobation; displeasure; dislike; disfavor; excoriation; flaying; flak; going-over; haranguing; increpation; *judgment;* knocking; lambasting; monitory; negativity; objurgation; putting down; *questioning;* rebuke; scolding; telling off; unhappiness; vituperation; withstanding; *xuld [arch.];* yelling at; *zapping;*

**disapprove** *(v.)*: abhor; berate; condemn; censure; dislike; disfavor; discountenance; execrate; frown on; gripe about; have a problem with; increpate; jib; knock; loathe; mislike; not approve; object; oppose; protest; quibble; resist; raise objection; reject; squawk; take issue; *urge against;* veto; withstand; whine; *x-fire;* yawp; *zing;*

**disarm** *(v.)*: *arms removal;* betake; confiscate arms; defuse; deactivate; expropriate; *fix;* give up weapons; haul away arms; *impound;* jerk away; *keep away; lose; lacking;* make weaponless; neutralize; *open to attack;* prevent from having arms; *quad;* remove arms; strip; take arms away; unarm; *void;* wrest arms away; *x-out;* yank away; *zeroize;*

**disarmament** *(n.)*: arms removal; *betaking;* confiscation of arms; defusing; double-zero option; expropriation; *fixing;* giving up weapons; hauling away arms; *impounding; jerking away; keeping away; lacking;* making weaponless; neutralization; *opening to attack;* preventing from having arms; *quad;* removal of arms; stripping; scrapping arms; taking arms away; unarming; *voiding;* wresting arms away; *x-ing out;* yanking away; zero-zero option;

**disarray** *(n.)*: anarchy; bewilderment; confusion; chaos; disorder(liness); entanglement; farrago; gastness; havoc; incoherence; jumble; kerfuffle; *lunacy;* mess; non-orderliness; *obscurity;* pell-mell; *quandary;* randomness; stupefaction; topsy-turvy; unorderliness; untidiness; vexation; welter; *xtry. mess; yo-yo;* zoo;

**disassemble** *(v.)*: *apart;* break up (-down; -apart); collapse; dismantle; dismember; disaggregate; *end;* fracture; get apart; *hew down; in parts; jerk apart;* knock apart; limb; make separate; *nullify; opened;* pull apart; *quick takedown;* remove pieces; *repack;* separate; take apart; tear down; undo; unscrew; *unassembled; very many parts;* wreck; *x-ing;* yank apart; zip apart;

**disaster** *(n.)*: adversity; blow; breakup (-down); calamity; catastrophe; debacle; devastation; evil; fiasco; failure; grief; heartbreak; hammer blow; infelicity; *judgment;* killer; loss; misfortune; nightmare; ordeal; predicament; quandary; ruin; *snafu; setback;* tragedy; upheaval; violence; woe; *xtry. blow;* yedder; zinger

**disastrous** *(adj.)*: adverse; awful; bad; calamitous; devastating; earth-shattering; *fateful;* grievous; hapless; ill-fated; Jonahesque; *killing; loss;* misfortunate; nightmarish; *ordeal;* pitiable; queer-lucked; ruinous; shattering; tragic; unpheaving; violent; woeful; wreckful; *xerotripsis; yucky; zapping;*

**disband** *(v.)*: *alienate;* break up; come apart; come apart; dissolve; end; fractionate; go separate ways; have a falling out; *isolate;* just fly away; *keep apart;* lose unity; move in different directions; *not together; outspread;* part ways; *quit; redisperse;* separate; split up; scatter; *tear apart;* unyoke; *vanish; wither; x-sect;* yank apart; *zeroize;*

**disbelief** *(n.)*: apprehension; *baffling;* cynicism; doubt; distrust; *equivocalness;* fear; guardedness; hesitation; incertitude; incredulity; *jitteriness;* kiaugh [Scot.]; leeriness; mistrust; non-trust; overcriticalness; pessimism; qualm; reservations; suspicion; scepticism; trepidation; unbelief; *vacillation;* worry; wariness; *xtry. doubt; yieldlessness;* zero confidence; [*Ant.* denial]

**disbelieve** *(v.)*: *asperse;* beware; challenge; dispute; discount; distrust; discredit; doubt; *ever-doubtful;* fear; get nervous; hesitate; *iffiness; jittery;* keep doubting; *leery;* mistrust; not believe; naysay; oppugn; *pessimistic;* question; ridicule; scoff; suspect; *skeptical;* take issue with; unbelieve; *vacillate;* worry; *x-out; yet doubt;* zero confidence; [*Ant.* deny]

**disburse** *(v.)*: afford; buy; compensate; distribute; expend; fork over; give; hand over; *indemnify; justify;* kick in; lay out; make payment; *non-retention;* outlay; pay; quit; remit; shell out; settle; tender; unhand; *vest;* write check; xfer; yield; *zero-out one's debt;*

**disbursement** *(n.)*: amount; *base pay;* cost; damages; expense; expenditure; finances; giving out; handing over; *imbursement; justification; kickback; liquidation; money; net pay;* outlay; outgo; payment; quittance; remittance; spending; transfer; *unindebted;* virement; wage(s); xfer; yielding; *zapping;*

**discard** *(v.)*: abandon; betoss; cast off; drop; dump; dispose of; dispense with; ditch; eliminate; forsake; fling; get rid of; heave-ho; ignore; jettison; junk; kest; leave; *move into garbage;* neglect; oust; pitch; *quit;* rid oneself of; relinquish; reject; shed; scrap; throw out (-away); trash; toss; unload; *vacate;* waste; *x-out;* yield; zero out;

**discern** *(v.)*: apprehend; become aware of; comprehend; distinguish; experience; fathom; grasp; *have; hear;* identify; judge; know; learn; make out; notice; observe; perceive; *qualify;* recognize; separate; see; tell; understand; view; wist; *xenodiagnose; yeme;* zero in;

**discernable** *(adj.)*: appreciable; apparent; *becomes clear;* clear; detectable; distinct; evident; fathomable; gaugeable; *hearable;* identifiable; *judicable;* knowable; *learnable;* measurable; marked; noticeable; observable; perceptible; quantifiable; recognizable; seeable; traceable; understandable; visible; watchable; *x-parent; yare; zeroing in;*

**discernment** *(n.)*: acumen; *better judgment;* common sense; discretion; eye-mindedness; foresight; feeling; good sense; horse sense; insight; judgment; keenness of judgment; level-headedness; *maxim;* non-foolishness; *overwiseness;* perception; quick-sightedness; rationality; sagaciousness; taste; understanding; *value;* wisdom; *xenagogy; yepe [arch.];* zeroing in;

**discharge** *(n.)*: afflux; *blast;* confluence; deflow; emission; excretion; efflux; flow; going out; *hurl;* issue; *jet; kesting;* leakage; movement; *naid;* outflow; pouring out; *quantity;* release; seepage; secretion; transudation; unleashing; *vomiting;* wash; *xfer;* yield; *zwoosh;*

**discharge** *(v. release)*: allow to leave; boot; cut loose; dismiss; expel; free; fire; give leave; *heads roll [joc.];* inactivate; jettison; kick out; let go; make unemployed; no longer employ; oust; put out; *quash;* release; secrete; send out; terminate; unemploy; *vote out;* withdraw employment; *x-out; yank; zeroize;*

**discharge** *(v. shoot)*: *abandon;* betoss; bolt; cast; chuck; catapult; discard; eject; fling; give out; hurl; impel; issue; jaculate; kest; launch; *move; nudge out;* outthrow; propel; *quoit;* relinquish; shoot; thrust; upcast; vault; wale; whip; *xuld* [arch.]; york; zing;

**disciple** *(n.)*: adherent; apprentice; apostle; believer; convert; devotee; epigone; follower; good follower; homager; *instructed;* janissary; *keeper;* learner; member; neophyte; *one;* proselyte; pupil; quester; recruit; student; trainee; undergraduate; votary; *witness;* Xn.; *yielder;* Zebedist; zealot; [arch.]; [*Ant.* detractor]

**disciple** *(v.)*: admonish; *bring up;* condition; catechize; direct; educate; foster; ground; home school; instruct; *jobation; knock into;* lecture; mentor; nurture; open one's eyes; pedagogue; qualify; ready; school; train; *unlock;* verse; work with; xenagogue; *yak; zealously instruct;*

**discipleship** *(n.)*: apprenticeship; bringing along; coaching; catechization; direction; educating; fostering; guidance; hortation; instruction; *jobation; knowledge; lessons;* mentoring; nurture; *oversight;* pedagogy; qualification; readying; schooling; training; *upbringing;* versing; *working with;* xenagogy; yarking; Zebedist [arch.];

**discipline** *(v.)*: amerce; afflict; bring to justice; chastise; correct; chasten; disciple; drill; educate; *enforce;* fleague; *give stripes;* have redress; instruct; *judge;* keep in line; lay into; mulct; *nail; open one's eyes;* prepare; penalize; *qualify;* reprimand; regulate; school; spank; *scourge;* train; teach (a lesson); *upbraid; vitiate; whip; x-out;* yard [arch.]; zap;

**discomfort** *(n.)*: anxiety; affliction; *burning; biting;* cramp; crick; chafing; distress; *excruciating; embarrassment;* feel bad; grief; hurt(ing); irritation; irking; jabbing; kink; lamentability; misery; *malaise; nip; ouch!;* pain; pang; quab; rawness; soreness; smarting; sting; sensitiveness; tenderness; twinge; throbbing; unpleasantness; uneasiness; vexation; woe; *xiphodynia;* yaik; zing;

**disconnect** *(v.)*: abstract; break off; cut off; detach; disjoin; disassociate; disunite; extract; extricate; free; get out; *halve;* isolate; *jerk apart; knock apart; laniate;* make separate; *non-continuous;* open; part; *quarter;* remove; separate; take off; unhook; uncouple; unyoke; *vell;* wreck; *x-sect;* yank apart; *zip off;*

**discontent** *(adj.)*: angry; bellyaching; critical; dissatisfied; discontented; ever-grumbling; frustrated; grumbling; hypercritical; *implacable;* joyless; *knocking; low opinion;* malcontent; nitpicking; not pleased; objecting; petulant; querimonious; repining; scowling; *troubled;* unsatisfied; very unhappy; whining; *xtry. critical;* yelling; zero joy; [*Ant.* delight]

**discontentment** *(n.)*: anguish; bellyaching; criticalness; dissatisfaction; discontent; *ever-grumbling;* frustration; grumbling; hypercriticalness; inquietude; implacability; joylessness; knocking; *low opinion;* malcontentedness; non-satisfaction; objection; petulance; querimoniousness; restlessness; repining; scowling; *troubled;* unhappiness; vapors; woe; *x-out;* yeastiness; *zero joy;* [*Ant.* delight]

**discontinue** *(v.)*: abort; break off; cease; desist; end; forbear; fold; give up; halt; interrupt; jib; kill; leave; *moderate; nullify;* obstruct; prevent; quit; resign; stop; terminate; undo; veto; withdraw; *x; yield; zero;*

**discord** *(n.)*: argument; bickering; contention; disaccord; disagreement; disharmony; disunion; embroilment; friction; gainsaying; hairsplitting; headshaking; incongruity; inaccordance; jangling; kagg; *lack of harmony; making fur fly;* negativism; odds; opposition; polarization; quarrel; resistance; strife; *tussle;* unharmoniousness; variance; wrangling; *x-fire;* yed; *zapping;*

**discount** *(n.)*: abatement; break; cut(back); decrease; *easing; falling;* going down; *half-priced; incentive;* jump down in price; *knocking down;* lowering; minimization; *non-profit; off;* price reduction; percentage off; quantity ~; reduced rate; reduction; rebate; *sale;* taking something off; *unit price; value; white sale; x-out*; yellow-tag sake; *zeroize;*

**discount** *(v. disregard)*: *abandon;* brush aside; close one's eyes; disregard; dismiss; elide; flout; go over; *heedless;* ignore; *jump over; kest;* look the other way; misattend; neglect; overlook; pass over; pay no heed; *quick-to-forget;* reject; sweep aside; toss aside; *unfaithful; violate;* write off; *x-ing; yemeles [arch.];* zero responsibility;

**discount** *(v. reduce)*: *alleviate; break;* cut; decrease; drop; *ease; fall;* go down; *halve; improve; jump down;* knock down; lower; make lower; *non-profit; offer lower price;* put on sale; *percentage off; price reduction; quantity- ~;* reduce; shrink; *sale;* take something off; *undo; volume ~;* weaken; x-out; yellow-tag sale; zap;

**discourage** *(v.)*: *affect;* bother; cast down; dismay; dishearten; depress; demoralize; dispirit; daunt; deject; dissuade; deter; engrieve; faze; *faint;* grieve; *give up; heart-discouraged; hopeless;* inhibit; *joyless;* knock down; keep from; lower one's spirits; lose hope; make demoralized; *negative;* oppose; press down; quench; *rend one's heart;* sadden; shake; trouble; *undermine;* vex; weigh upon; *xuld [arch.];* yearn; zap; [Ant. delight]

**discouragement** *(n.)*: *affectedness;* blueness; cheerlessness; depression; dejection; demoralization; *damper; ejulation;* forlornness; gloom; hopelessness; *inconsolableness;* joylessness; *keening;* low spirits; mournfulness; negative spirit; overcast mood; pessimism; quailing; ruefulness; sadness; tristesse; unhappiness; vapors; weight; xtry. ~; *yearnfulness; zealessness;* [Ant. delight]

**discourse** *(n.)*: address; bespeaking; communication; declaration; elocution; expression; filibuster; formal speech; *glossa;* homily; indiction; jeremiad; *jabbering; kerygma;* lecture; message; monologue; narrative; oration; proclamation; *quotation;* recitation; speech; sermon; talk; utterance; vocalization; word(s); *xenophonia;* yakking; zinger *[slang];*

**discover** *(v.)*: ascertain; bring to light; come across; detect; determine; dig up; dredge up; encounter; excavate; espy; find (out); get back; hit on; identify; *jaeger;* kithe [Scot.]; learn; locate; light on; make a discovery; notice; observe; pinpoint; *quick-to-learn;* realize; re~; stumble on; spot; see; track down; unearth; uncover; unveil; venture upon; *witness; x-search; yead;* zero-concealment; [Ant. disguise]

**discovery** *(n.)*: ascertaining; bringing to light; breakthrough; coming to light; disclosure; detection; encounter; espial; find(ing); godsend; *hitting on;* invention; *just discovered;* knowledge; location; mystery unveiled; new ~; opening up; pinpointing; *quantum leap;* revelation; scientific ~; serendipity; trove; trouvaille; unearthing; uncovering; vermissage; wit-craft; *widget; x-view; yead;* zero-concealment;

**discredit** *(v.)*: attack; *answer;* belittle; belie; cast doubt; confute; disparage; doubt; disbelieve; disprove; expose; falsify; *gravel;* harm reputation of; invalidate; *jar;* knock the bottom out of; *lambaste;* make to appear untrustworthy; negate; *overturn;* prove false; question; run down; refute; slur; shoot down; show to be false; try to demean; *undo; vilify; whip; x-out;* yank down; zeroize;

**discreet** *(adj.)*: astute; *beware;* careful; cautious; diplomatic; discerning; ever-careful; fabian; gracious; *harmless;* inoffensive; judicious; kind; *loving; mannerly;* nondirect; over-careful; prudent; *queme;* restrained; subtle; tactful; unobtrusive; very careful; wise; wary; *xenagogic;* yepe; *zärtlich [G.];*

**discriminate** *(v.)*: abuse; *bias;* contradistinguish; differentiate; distinguish; discern; *expect;* forejudge; *generalize;* harass; individualize; ill-treat; judge; know which is which; *leaning;* make a distinction; *notice;* oppress; particularize; pick on; *prejudge; quick to judge;* recognize; *racism;* separate; segregate; single out; tell apart; treat differently; *unfair; valuate; wist; xenophobia; yeme;* zero in;

**discrimination** *(n.)*: anti-Semitism; apartheid [S. Afr.]; bias; bigotry; chauvinism; discriminatory behavior; ethnocentrism; favoritism; *gall; hatred;* inequitableness; intolerance; judging; klanism; leaning; *minority-hating;* non-equitableness; one-sidedness; partiality; prejudice; *quick to judge;* respect of persons; supremism; segregationalism; *tilted;* unfairness; *vexation;* Waspishness; xenophobia; yahooism; zealotry;

**discriminatory** *(adj.)*: anti-Semetic; anti-black, *etc.*; biased; bigoted; chauvinistic; discriminating; ethnocentric; favoring; *galsome hateful;* inequitable; intolerant; jaundiced; klannish; lopsided; minority-hating; nonequitable; one-sided; partial; prejudiced; *quick to judge;* racist; supremist; tilted; unfair; *venal;* wrongful; xenophobic; *yahooist; zero justice;*

**discuss** *(v.)*: argue; allege; bear hearts; chat; converse; confer; consult; debate; deliberate; exchange words; *fraternize;* gab; have discussion; huddle; interchange; interact; *jangle; key discussion; little chat;* meet about; negotiate; *outtalk;* parley; *quarrel;* reason; speak; talk (over); utter; vocalize; write about; *xenophonia;* yak; *zero in;*

**discussion** *(n.)*: argument; bearing hearts; conversation; conference; consultation; colloquy; chat; debate; dialogue; discourse; deliberations; exchange; *fraternization;* gabbing; heart-to-heart; huddle; interchange; interlocution; jangle; *key ~; little chat;* meeting; negotiation(s); oral treaty; parley; parlance; palaver [joc.]; panel ~; pep talk; powwow; quadrilogue; reasoning; rap session; speech; talk(s); *uttering; vocalization;* words; *xenophonia;* yarn; yakking; *zero in;*

**disdain** *(n.)*: abhorrence; bitterness; contempt; detestation; embitterment; foulness; gall; hate; inimicality; jadedness; kindlessness; loathing; malice; *nastiness;* odium; perniciousness; *querulousness;* resentfulness; scorn; spite; *tetchiness;* unkindness; virulence; *withstanding; xenophobia; yuckiness; zealotry;* [*Ant.* delight]

**disdain** *(v.)*: abhor; *bewail;* condemn; detest; eschew; execrate; frown upon; *grieve about;* hate; *indignation; jangling; keck;* loathe; mislike; not like; *odious; pshaw; querulous;* reprobate; revile; scorn; treat with contempt; utterly loathe; vilipend; *wrathful; xenophobic; yucky; zero love;* [*Ant.* delight]

**disdainful** *(adj.)*: abhorrent; bitter; cynical; cruel; despiteful; embittered; foul; *galsome;* hateful; inimical; jaded; kindless; loathsome; mean; nasty; odious; pernicious; *quede* [arch.]; resentful; scornful; terrible; unkind; virulent; wicked; xenophobic; *yucky; zealotic;* [*Ant.* delighted]

**disease** *(n.)*: ailment; affliction; blight; bug; *bacteria;* condition; contagious ~; consumption; distemper; disorder; endemic; *epidemic;* fever; *grievance;* humoral; illness; infirmity; indisposition; illness; infectious ~; *jitteriness; killer;* lesion; malady; non-contagious ~; organic ~; *ordeal;* plague; pertilence; polio; pox; *quirk;* qualm [arch.]; rockiness [slang]; sickness; scourge; taint; *thorn in the flesh;* upset; unhealthiness; *virus;* venereal ~; woe; *x-disease; yellow fever;* zoonosis;

> **Diseases**: anemia; bubonic plague; consumption; cancer; diphtheria; dropsy; dysentery; encephalitis; fascioliasis; gout; hepatitis; influenza; jaundice; king's evil; ketosis; leprosy; malaria; measles; mumps; nephrosclerosis; osteoporosis; palsy; pleurisy; pneumonia; quinsy; q-fever; rickets; rubella; scarlet fever; scurvy; small pox; tonsillitis; typhoid; uremia; vives; West Nile virus; xerdermia; yellow fever; zygomycosis;

**disembark** *(v.)*: *abandon;* be off; come out of; debark; discharge; deplane; debus; exit; *flee;* get off; *hightail; immigrate;* jump off; *kest;* land; move out; *navigate; outpace;* put on shore; *quit;* remove; set off (-out); transfer; unload; unship; vacate; withdraw; xfer; yead; *zip away;*

**disembowel** *(v.)*: *abstract;* bowel; clean out; disbowel; draw; eviscerate; exenterate; embowel; fillet; gut; *haul; intestinal removal; jerk out;* open the bowels; paunch; *quarry;* remove bowels; scoop guts out; take out bowels; unbowel; viscerate; *wrench; xfer;* yank out intestines; *zero out;*

**disenchant** *(v.)*: *affect;* break the spell; clear the curse; decharm; eliminate curse; free from enchantment; get rid of curse; *have spell removed; invalidate; jar; kill;* lift curse; make curse null and void; normalize; negate spell; *obliterate;* put at liberty; *quell;* remove spell; set free; take spell away; uncurse; undo curse; *void;* wake up; *x-out; yokeless; zeroize;* [*Ant.* delight]

**disentangle** *(v.)*: *arrange;* brush; correct; comb; disencumber; disembroil; disengage; extricate; enucleate; free; fix; get out; *hatchel; improve; justify; kinkless;* loose; make right; neaten; outwind; open; put right; quannet; release; separate; straighten out; take a comb to; *tangle-free;* un(en)tangle; unravel; unscramble; unbraid; unwind; unloose; unsnarl; *vamp;* work out; *xfer; yarn-comb; zero entanglements;* [*Ant.* disarrange]

**disfavor** *(n.)*: aversion; *bêtes noires* [F.]; censure; contempt; disapproval; displeasure; dislike; disesteem; excoriation; *fallen; gall;* hatred; ill-will; *judgment;* knocking; loathing; low esteem; *malice;* non-approval; odium; *punishment; questioning;* rejection; repugnance; *scorn; turn;* unpopularity; vitriol; *withstanding; xenophobia; yawping; zealessness;* [*Ant.* delight]
**disfigure** *(v.)*: *abuse;* butcher; cut off; deface; disfeature; endamage; *fissure;* garble; hackle; injure; jeel; *knife;* lacerate; mangle; maim; *notch;* olate; pull apart; *quade* [arch.]; ruin; spoil; tear asunder; twist; uglify; victimize; wound; warp; *x-sect;* yank apart; *zap;*
**disgrace** *(n.)*: ashamedness; abasement; bashfulness; contempt; dishonor; debasement; degradation; disrepute; dispraise; disreputation; embarrassment; *fall; grief;* humiliation; indignity; ignominy; *infamy;* ill repute; *joylessness; kettiness;* lowering; letdown; loss of face; mortification; *notorious incident;* opprobrium; public disgrace; putting to shame; *quad;* reproach; shame; tarnishing; under a cloud; verecundity; wite; *xtry. shame; yuckiness; zero honor;* [*Ant.* distinction]
**disgrace** *(v.)*: abash; bring reproach; chagrin; debase; dishonor; embarrass; foreshame; *grieve;* humiliate; *indignity; jackalent; knock down;* let down; mortify; *nither [arch.]; out of countenance;* put to shame; *quieten;* reproach; shame; tarnish; *upbraid; vitiate;* wrong; *xtry. humiliated; yield; zero honor;* [*Ant.* delight]
**disgraceful** *(adj.)*: awful; appalling; bad; blameworthy; contemptuous; debasing; dishonorable; execrable; embarrassing; flagitious; *guilty;* humiliative; ignominious; inglorious; *jaded; ketty;* loathsome; miserable; nasty; opprobrious; pathetic; *quad;* reproachful; reprehensible; shameful; scurrilous; terrible; unacceptable; vile; wretched; *xtry. shameful;* yucky; *zero honor* [*Ant.* delightful]
**disgruntle** *(v.)*: anger; bother; chafe; displease; disaffect; dissatisfy; discontent; estrange; foment; grieve; *harass;* irritate; jangle; kick; *lose it;* miff; nettle; offend; peeve; pique; *queach [arch.];* rile; steam; turn off; upset; vex; weary; *xuld [arch.];* yearn [arch.]; *zero pleasure;* [*Ant.* delight]
**disguise** *(n.)*: attire; ball-room costume; costume; cover; camouflage; cloak; dress; *enrobed;* facemask; fancy dress; façade; front; get-up; guise; garb; hood; help-mask; *incognito;* jest; *kept disguised;* loup; mask; make-up; mumm; maskery; *non-recognizable;* outfit; persona; play-clothes; *quat [arch.]; robe;* shroud; *transformed;* uniform; veil; vizard; *wardrobe; xenomorph; yashmak; zero recognition;*
**disguise** *(v.)*: attire; bemask; costume; cover; camouflage; cloak; conceal; dissemble; *enrobe;* feign; garb; hide; hood; immask; jest; keep concealed; *loup;* mask; masquerade; *non-recognizable;* outfit; play the part of; pretend to be; *quat [arch.];* redo; shroud; transform; *unrecognizable;* veil; wear ~; *xenomorph; yashmak; zero recognition;* [*Ant.* discover]
**disgust** *(n.)*: abhorrence; *baseness;* contempt; detestation; execrableness; fetidness; gall; hatred; indignation; jarring; kettiness; loathsomeness; malice; nausea; odium; perturbation; queerness; revulsion; repugnance; sickness; scorn; turning one's stomach; unpleasantness; vileness; *wretchedness; xenophobia;* yuckiness; *zorillo;* [*see* annoyance; *Ant.* delight]
**disgust** *(v.)*: appall; *bring displeasure; contempt;* displease; detest; enrage; frustrate; gross one out; horrify; *indignation;* jar; *keck; loathe;* misaffect; nauseate; offend; perturb; *quad;* repel; repulse; revolt; sicken; turn one's stomach; upset; *vile;* ward off; *xuld* [arch.]; *yucky; zealously hate;* [*Ant.* delight]
**disgusting** *(adj.)*: awful; abhorrent; appalling; *ad nauseam* [L.]; bad; contemptible; disagreeable; detestable; execrable; foul; fetid; gross; ghastly; horrible; hideous; icky; jarring; ketty; loathsome; mawkish; nasty; nauseating; objectionable; offensive; putrid; *queasy;* repulsive; revolting; repelling; repugnant; sickening; stomach-turning; terrible; unpleasant; undesirable; unappetizing; upsetting; vile; verminous; wretched; *xysmic;* yucky; *zorillo;* [*Ant.* delightful]
**dish** *(n.)*: *article;* bowl; basin; china; crock; casserole ~; *container;* dinnerware; dinner plate; entremet; fictile ~; glass plate; hazel-earth ~; *item;* jasperware ~; *kuel* [Chin.]; *large plate;* mazer; monkey ~; nut ~; *olla;* plate; platter; quart-vessel; ramekin; saucer; serving ~; salver; side plate; teacup; tea-saucer; trencher; urceole; vessel; work bowl; *xtl* ~; yabba; yandy; *zegedine;* [*see* cup]

**dishearten** *(v.)*: affect; agonize; bother; bring to tears; cast down; cause sorrow; dismay; depress; demoralize; discourage; deject; dispirit; eat at; fall; grieve; *hyp* [arch.]; *hopeless; inconsolable; joyless;* knock down; lower one's spirits; make sad; *negative; overcast;* plunge into sorrow; quench one's spirit; rend one's heart; sadden; sorrow; trouble; upset; vex; weigh upon; *xuld* [arch.]; *yearn; zestless;*

**dishonest** *(adj.)*: artful; bad; crooked; corrupt; deceitful; dishonorable; devious; disreputable; evasive; *evil;* fraudulent; guileful; *greedy;* honorless; ignoble; jady; knavish; lying; louche; misconducted; non-credible; opportunistic; perfidious; quasi-ethical; ruthless; roguish; seedy; shady; treacherous; tricky; thieving; unscrupulous; underhanded; venal; wily; *x-ing;* yeggy; *zero honesty;* [*Ant.* dependable]

**dishonesty** *(n.)*: artfulness; *betrayal;* crookedness; cheating; corruption; deceit; duplicity; dishonorableness; deviousness; evasiveness; evil; fraudulence; guile; honorlessness; improbity; jadery; knavery; lying; misconduct; non-truthfulness; *opportunism;* perfidy; questionableness; roguery; skullduggery; shadiness; treachery; trickery; untrustworthiness; untruthfulness; unfairness; villainy; wickedness; *x-ing;* yegginess; *zero honesty;* [*Ant.* dependability]

**dishonor** *(n.)*: ashamedness; belittling; contempt; disgrace; disrepute; embarrassment; fraudulence; *grief;* humiliation; indignity; *joylessness; kettiness;* loss of face; mortification; *notorious incident;* opprobrium; public disgrace; *quad;* reproach; shame; tarnishing; upbraiding; verecundity; wite; *x-ing;* yuckiness; *zero honor;* [*Ant.* distinction]

**dishonorable** *(adj.)*: abominable; base; characterless; disreputable; disgraceful; disloyal; *evil;* fraudulent; guileful; honorless; ignominious; jady; knavish; low-down; misconducted; non-trustworthy; opportunistic; perfidious; quasi-ethical; reprehensible; shameful; treacherous; untrustworthy; unprincipled; unethical; vile; wily; *x-ing;* yeggy; *zero honesty;* [*Ant.* distinguished]

**disinfect** *(v.)*: antisepticize; bleach; boil; cleanse; decontaminate; elute; fumigate; get rid of germs; hygienize; *immaculate; jalap;* kill germs; *launder;* make germ-free; neutralize; outwash; purify; *quench;* rid of germs; sterilize; sanitize; *tub;* unsully; *vacuum;* wipe; *xylol; yellow soap; zierlich [G.];* [*Ant.* dirty]

**disinherit** *(v.)*: abandon; banish; cut off; disown; *deprive;* exheredate; exclude; forsake; give up; *hate; ignore; jilt; kick out;* leave out; make an outcast; not claim; *ostracize;* put out; *quit on;* remove from will; *spurn;* take away inheritance; utterly reject; *veto;* write out of one's will; x-out; yank; zero out;

**disintegrate** *(v.)*: atomize; annihilate; break down; crush; crumble; collapse; corrode; demolish; dissolve; decompose; degenerate; deteriorate; destroy; disappear; expunge; erode; fall apart; grind to dust; hydrolyze; *incinerate; junk; kill; lay waste;* mash; mortify; *nullify;* obliterate; pulverize; quash; *rot; ruin;* smash; spoil; turn into dust; unbuild; vaporize; wipe out; wear (away); *x-ing; yank apart;* zap;

**disintegration** *(n.)*: atomization; annihilation; breakdown; crumbling; collapse; corrosion; corruption; demolishing; dissolution; destruction; disappearance; decomposition; degeneration; deterioration; erosion; falling apart; grinding to dust; hydrolysis; *incineration; junking; killing;* labelfaction; mortification; *nullification;* obliteration; pejoration; putrefaction; queering; rotting; ruination; spoiling; turning into dust; undoing; vitiation; wearing (away); waning; worsening; weakening; *x-ing; yanking apart;* zapping;

**disinterest** *(n.)*: apathy; blitheness; boredom; coolness; casualness; dispassion; *easygoing; frigidness; grogginess;* half-heartedness; indifference; *jem'enfichism* [F.]; *knark;* lassitude; lack of concern; mopishness; nonchalance; oscitance; *phlegmatic;* quiescence; *repression;* spiritlessness; torpidity; unconcern; vapidity; withdrawnness; *xenarthrous;* yarelessness; zealessness; [*see* boredom; *Ant.* dazzle]

**disinterested** *(adj.)*: apathetic; blasé; businesslike; cold; dispassionate; detached; emotionless; frigid; *glaring;* hard(-hearted); insensitive; indifferent; jaded; knark; loveless; matter-of-fact; non-sympathetic; objective; pitiless; *quiet;* repressed; steel-like; tough; unsympathetic; unmoved; unbiased; *viewless;* withdrawn; *xerothalmic;* yareless; zombie-like; [*Ant.* dazzled]

**dislike** *(n.)*: aversion; *balking at;* contempt; disliking; disapprobation; disapproval; distaste; disinclination; enmity; *frown upon;* gall; hatred; *indignation;* jadedness; *knocking;* loathing; misliking; negativism; odium; *polarity;* quarrel; revulsion; shuddering; *tetchiness;* unpopularity; vice; *withstanding; xenophobia; yawping; zeallessness;* [*Ant.* delight]

**dislike** *(v.)*: abhor; abominate; bear malice; contemn; disfavor; disesteem; disdain; disapprove; disrelish; execrate; *fie; frown; gall;* hate; *inexpiable ~; jaded; kick at;* loathe; lote; mislike; misaffect; not care for; *outscorn; odious; pshaw; querulous;* reject; reprobate; shudder; shrink from; take an aversion; utterly loathe; vilipend; *war with; xenophobic; yucky; zero liking;* [*Ant.* delight in]

**dislodge** *(v.)*: abstract; break free; cut loose; dislocate; detach; extricate; extract; free; get out; *help;* isolate; jerk away; *kip;* luxate; loose; *move; non-retention;* open; pull loose; pluck; *quarry;* remove; separate; take out; unfix; unseat; unhinge; unjoint; uproot; *verge;* winkle out; *xuld [arch.];* yank out; *zip;*

**disloyal** *(adj.)*: artful; betraying; backstabbing; crooked; deceitful; dastardly; evil; faithless; guileful; honorless; inconstant; *infidel;* jadish; knavish; lying; mutinous; non-loyal; *opportunistic;* perfidious; quisling; recreant; seditious; treacherous; unloyal; unfaithful; untrue; violent; wicked; *x-ing; yeggy; zero honesty;* [*Ant.* dependable]

**dismal** *(adj.)*: abject; bleak; cheerless; depressing; drear(y); doleful; darksome; ever-gloomy; forlorn; gloomy; glum; grim; hopeless; *inconsolable;* joyless; keenful; lugubrious; morose; melancholic; non-hopeful; overcast; pessimistic; *quivering;* rueful; sad; sorrowful; sullen; tenebrous; tristful; unhappy; vexing; woeful; wretched; *xtry. ~;* yucky; *zestless;* [*Ant.* delightful]

**dismay** *(n.)*: anxiety; burden; consternation; discomposure; distress; dread; *exasperation;* fear; gloom; *horror;* insecurity; jitteriness; kiaugh [Scot.]; lather; *mistrust;* nervousness; over-anxiety; panic; paranoia; quaking; *reluctance;* stress; solicitude; trepidation; uneasiness; vexation; worry; *xenophobia;* yellow-belliedness; *zeallessness;*

**dismay** *(v.)*: alarm; bring to tears; cast down; disconcert; discourage; engrieve; fall; grieve; *hopeless; inconsolable;* jar; knock down; lower one's spirits; mourn; *negative; overcast;* pain; quench one's spirit; rend one's heart; sadden; trouble; upset; vex; wring heart; *xuld [arch.]; yearn; zestless;*

**dismiss** *(v.)*: allow to leave; brush aside; close one's eyes; discount; disregard; discharge; elide; flout; go over; give notice; *heedless;* ignore; jump over; kick out; look the other way; let go; make light of; neglect; overlook; pooh-pooh; *quick-to-forget;* reject; release; shrug off; send away; treat lightly; unseat; *violate;* write off; *x-ing; yemeles [arch.]; zero responsibility;*

**dismissal** *(n.)*: authorization to go; brush-off; congé; discharge; departure; end; farewell; good-bye; halting; *issue; jumping off;* kicking out; leave; manumission; non-detention; ousting; putting out; quitting; release; sending away; time to leave; unseating; *voidance;* walking papers; *xfer; yokeless; zoneless;*

**disobedience** *(n.): abuse;* bad behavior; *breaking;* contravention; challenge; contumacy; defiance; disregard; *evildoing;* failure to comply; flouting; *general disregard; headstrongness;* insubordination; infringement; *jadedness;* kicking; lack of compliance; misbehavior; noncompliance; naughtiness; obstinacy; paying no attention; *questioning;* rebellion; refusal; stubbornness; sin; transgression; trespass; unruliness; unyieldingness; violation; willfulness; *xgression;* yieldlessness; *zapping;* [*Ant.* doing]

**disobedient** *(adj.): abusive;* bad; contravening; contumacious; defiant; ever-stubborn; flouting; *glaringly ~;* headstrong; insubordinate; *jaw-set; knocking;* lawless; misbehaving; noncompliant; obdurate; pay no attention; *querulous;* rebellious; self-willed; truculent; unsubmissive; unruly; violating; willful; wayward; *x-grained;* yieldless; *zero give;* [*Ant.* duteous]

**disobey** *(v.)*: abuse; break; buck; contravene; challenge; disregard; defy; err; flout; go astray; *harden one's heart;* infringe; infract; ignore; *jaded;* kick; leave the straight and narrow; mutiny; misbehave; not heed; offend; pay no regard to; *quad;* rebel; refuse; resist; revolt; sin; transgress; trespass; *unheeded;* violate; withstand; *x-gress; yieldless; zero obedience;* [*Ant.* do]

**disorder** *(n.)*: anarchy; bedlam; chaos; disarray; distemper; disorganization; entanglement; farrago; gastness; haphazardness; incoherence; jumble; kerfuffle; *lawlessness;* mess; non-orderliness; *obscurity;* pandemonium; *quandary;* rumbustiousness; stupefaction; turmoil; unruliness; vexation; wildness; *xtry. mess; yo-yo;* zoo;

**disorganized** *(adj.)*: anarchic; bedraggled; cluttered; disheveled; entangled; *filthy;* grotty; higgledy-piggledy; incomposed; jumbled; keg-meg; littered; muddled; messy; neglected; orderless; pell-mell; *quaggy;* rumpled; sloppy; tangled; untidy; unorganized; *vexing;* wild; *x'ed;* yucky; zoo-like;

**disorient** *(v.)*: addle; bewilder; confuse; disorientate; ensnarl; enbroil; fuddle; foil; gravel; hamper; *incoherent;* jumble; kittle; lose; mystify; mix up; nonplus; obscure; puzzle; quiz; *ravel;* stupefy; throw; *unorganized;* vex; wilder; *x; yo-yo; zero understanding;* [*Ant.* direct]

**disown** *(v.)*: alienate; abandon; break with; cut off; cast out; disclaim; dispossess; exheredate; forsake; give up; have nothing to do with; impugn; *jilt;* kiss goodbye; kick out; let go; make an outcast; not claim; ostracize; put out; quit on; renounce; reject; repudiate; spurn; throw out; *unload; vomit own;* withdraw; wash one's hands of; *x-out; yank; zero fellowship;*

**dispatch** *(v.)*: assign; *bus;* convey; consign; despatch; deliver; *export;* forward; give; *hurl;* issue; *jet;* kurvey; launch; mail; *noise; overnight;* post; *quarter-cart;* relay; send; transfer; *unload; van; waft; xfer; yield;* zip;

**dispensable** *(adj.)*: *absurd;* beyond-basics; *can do without;* disposable; expendable; frivolous; *garbage; hoity-toity;* insignificant; *jerkwater;* ketty; *little;* minor; nonessential; *overmuch; petty;* quisquillos; redundant; replaceable; superfluous; trivial; *throwaway;* unnecessary; unessential; unimportant; vain; worthless; xtr.; yet unneeded; *zero;*

**dispensation** *(n.)*: age; bestowment; *century;* dealing of God; era; epoch; *frame; generation; hour; interval; juncture; key time;* law; *life;* ministration; *new ~;* ordering; phase; *quarter; rule;* system; stewardship; time; *undetermined time period; vintage;* week; *x-time;* years; *zone;*

   **Biblical dispensations**: Innocence; Adamic; Noahic; Abrahamic; Mosaic; Law; Grace; Church Age; Tribulation; New Earth;

**disperse** *(v.)*: *away;* break up; broadcast; circulate; diffuse; disband; disseminate; dissipate; effuse; *further; fizzle out;* go all over; *hurl;* intersperse; *jumble; known; litter;* make interspersed; *non-localized;* overspread; *part; propagate; quantity;* radiate; *re~;* scatter; strew; spread; *send;* thinly spread; *universalize; very widespread;* widespread; *xmit; yank;* zeroize; [*see* propagate]

**display** *(n.)*: array; arrangement; baring; *case;* demonstration; exhibit(ion); éclat; floorshow; *gathering; glass case; holding out;* indication; *justification; kithe [Scot.];* layout; manifestation; non-concealment; ostentation; presentation; panoply; *quality;* revelation; show; spread; spectacle; *trade show;* unveiling; viewing; *window; xtry.; yielding; zooming in;*

**display** *(v.)*: array; bare; *carry;* disclose; exhibit; expose; flaunt; flash; *give;* hold out; illustrate; *justify;* kithe [Scot.]; lay out; manifest; make visible; *non-concealment;* open up; present; *qualify;* reveal; show; *typify;* unveil; uncover; vaunt; *wave; x-ray; yield;* zoom in on; [*Ant.* disguise]

**displease** *(v.)*: anger; annoy; aggravate; bother; chafe; dissatisfy; disgust; exasperate; foment; grieve; *harass;* irritate; jangle; kick; *lose it;* miff; nettle; offend; provoke; peeve; pain; *queach [arch.];* rile; steam; tick off; upset; vex; weary; *xuld [arch.];* yearn [arch.]; *zero pleasure;* [*Ant.* delight]

**displeasure** *(n.)*: anger; bitterness; *boiling;* choler; disgust; enragement; fury; gall; hotness; indignation; *jealousy; kindling;* lividness; madness; *nettling;* outrage; perturbation; quick-temperament; *resentment;* sore ~; temper; umbrage; virulence; wrath; *xerothermia; yelling; zealousy* [arch.]; [*Ant.* delight]

**disposable** *(adj.)*: *absurd;* beyond-basics; *can do without;* dispensable; expendable; frivolous; *garbage; hoity-toity;* insignificant; *jerkwater;* ketty; *leftover;* minor; nonessential; non-reusable; *overmuch;* petty; quisquillos; replaceable; superfluous; throwaway; unneeded; vain; worthless; xtr.; yet unneeded; *zero;*

**disposal** *(n.)*: abstraction; booting [slang]; clearance; discarding; dumping; elimination; *forsaking;* getting rid of; hauling away; *incineration;* junking; *knocking off;* leaving; *moving out;* nullification; offloading; purging; pitching; *quitting;* removal; scrapping; throwing away; unloading; *vacating;* wasting; *xfer;* yielding; *zero out;*
**dispose of** *(v.)*: abandon; betoss; cast away; discard; dump; expel; eliminate; forsake; get rid of; hurl; *incinerate;* junk; jettison; kill; leave behind; move out; nullify; oust; offload; purge; pitch; *quash;* rid; scrap; trash; throw out; unload; *vacate;* waste; *x-out; yank;* zero out;
**disposition** *(n.)*: attitude; bent; cast; demeanor; estimation; frame of mind; ground; humors; *heart;* inclination; judgment; *known* inclination; lineament; leaning; mindset; nature; outlook; personality; propensity; proclivity; *quintessence;* readiness; suchness; spirit; temperament; tendency; tenor; *urge;* vein; way; xenenthesis; *yetzer* [Heb.]; *zoe;*
**disprove** *(v.)*: annul; belie; confute; controvert; debunk; disconfirm; exclude; expose; falsify; *gravel;* have disproved; invalidate; *junk; knock out; lick; mastery;* negate; overthrow; overturn; prove false; quash; refute; repudiate; subvert; *trounce;* undo; vitiate; void; *whip;* x; *yank down;* zeroize; [*Ant.* demonstrate]
**dispute** *(n.)*: argument; altercation; bickering; contention; disagreement; dissent; embroilment; fight; feud; gainsaying; hairsplitting; incongruity; jangling; kagg; logomachy; *making fur fly;* negativism; odds; opposition; *polemic;* quarrel; row; strife; tussle; unharmoniousness; variance; wrangling; *x-fire;* yed; *zapping;*
**dispute** *(v.)*: argue; altercate; bicker; contend; challenge; controvert; disagree; *engage;* fight; gainsay; have words with; *impugn;* jangle; kemp; lock horns [slang]; make fur fly; naysay; oppose; pick fight; quarrel; resist; squabble; tiff; *unharmonious;* vie; withstand; *x-purposes;* yell; *zap;* [*Ant.* demonstrate]
**disqualify** *(v.)*: *abrogate;* ban; bar; boot out; cast aside; disallow; debar; delegitimize; eliminate; forbid; get rid of; *halt;* invalidate; incapacitate; indispose; *jettison;* kick out; *lock out;* make unfit; negate; outlaw; oust; put out; prohibit; *quit;* rule out; reject; superannuate; *suspend;* take out; throw out; *unqualified;* void; vitiate; *withhold;* x-out; *yank;* zero out;
**disregard** *(n.)*: audacity; brashness; contempt; disrespect; disdain; effrontery; flagrancy; gall; *haughtiness; hatred;* indifference; irreverence; jangliness; *knocking;* laches; malapertness; neglect; nonconformance; *odium;* profanation; presumption; *quilicom [arch.];* rudeness; spite; temerity; unruliness; *venom; wickedness; xenophobia; yieldlessness;* zero respect; [*Ant.* deference]
**disregard** *(v.)*: abdicate; belittle; *culpa;* disesteem; disrespect; disdain; elide; forget; go over; *heedless;* ignore; irregard; jump over; *knock;* let go; miss; neglect; overlook; pass over; pretermit; *quick-to-forget; remiss;* slight; spurn; turn a blind eye; *unfaithful; void;* wink at; *x-ing; yemeles [arch.];* zero responsibility; [*Ant.* defer]
**disrespect** *(n.)*: audacity; brashness; contempt; disregard; disesteem; effrontery; flagrancy; gall; *hatred;* insolence; impertinence; irreverence; jangliness; *knocking; lesse majesty* [F.]; *lip;* malapertness; *nerve; odium;* profanation; pertness; presumption; *quilicom [arch.];* rudeness; sassiness; sauciness; temerity; unruliness; *venom; wickedness; xenophobia; yieldlessness;* zero respect; [*Ant.* dignify]
**disrespect** *(v.)*: affront; belittle; criticize; censure; cag; denigrate; disparage; *execrate; fleer;* gibe; humiliate; insult; jibe; knock; kagg; libel; malign; *not respect;* offend; put one down; quib; revile; slight; traduce; upset; vilify; wipe; *xuld [arch.];* yock; *zing;* [*Ant.* dignify]
**disrespectful** *(adj.)*: audacious; brash; contemptuous; disregardful; *effrontery;* flagrant; galsome; haughty; insolent; impertinent; irreverent; jady; *kindless; lesse majesty* [F.]; *lousy;* malapert; non-respectful; *overconfident;* profane; pert; presumptuous; *quilicom [arch.];* rude; sassy; saucy; *temerarious;* unruly; uncivil; *vulgar; wicked; xenophobic; yieldless;* zero respect; [*Ant.* deferential]
**disruptive** *(adj.)*: *awful;* boisterous; crazy; disorderly; distracting; *evil; foul; grievous;* hog-wild; irregular; jungli; *kaf* [arch.]; loutish; mad; noisy; outrageous; problematic; querulous; reckless; rip-roaring; *savage;* troublesome; upsetting; violent; wild; *xtr. ~;* yahoo; zany;

**dissatisfaction** *(n.)*: annoyance; bothering; chafing; displeasure; disaffection; disgruntling; discontent; displeasure; estrangement; frustration; grief; *harassment;* irritation; jangling; kicking; *lack of satisfaction;* misery; nettling; offence; peeving; *queach [arch.];* riling; *steamed;* turning off; unhappiness; vexing; weariness; *xuld [arch.]; yearn* [arch.]; *zero pleasure;* [*Ant.* delight]

**dissatisfy** *(v.)*: annoy; bother; chafe; displease; disaffect; disgruntle; estrange; foment; grieve; *harass;* irritate; jangle; kick; *lose it;* miff; nettle; offend; peeve; *queach [arch.];* rile; steam; turn off; upset; vex; weary; *xuld [arch.]; yearn* [arch.]; *zero pleasure;* [*Ant.* delight]

**dissent** *(n.)*: antipathy; bucking; contrariety; disagreement; disputation; dissidence; exception; fighting; gainsaying; hostility; incongruity; jangling; kicking; loathing; malice; non-agreement; opposition; protestation; querulousness; resistance; strife; *troublemaking;* unharmoniousness; variance; withstanding; *x-fire;* yawping; *zeallessness;*

**dissent** *(v.)*: argue; balk; contradict; disagree; dispute; expostulate; fight; gainsay; have disagreement with; *impugn;* jangle; kick against; lock horns [slang]; make waves; naysay; oppose; pick fight; quarrel; rebel; stand opposed; take issue; *unlikeness;* vary; withstand; *x-purposes; yell*; zealously oppose;

**dissipate** *(v.)*: abate; assuage; break up; bate; come to naught; decrease; decline; diminish; disperse; dissolve; ease; ebb; fade; fritter away; go away; *hush; impair; jade;* knock down; lessen; lower; mitigate; melt; *narrow; outgo;* peter out; philander; quell; recede; reduce; subside; scatter; taper; take flight; *undo;* vanish; wane; waste; *xfer;* yield; zap;

**dissolve** *(v.)*: atomize; break down; colliquate; deliquesce; disintegrate; dissipate; disband; evaporate; fall apart; fluidify; go separate ways; hydrolyze; *integrate; join; kill;* liquefy; melt; *nullify;* obliterate; pulverize; *quail;* resolve; redissolve; solubilize; turn into dust; *thaw;* turn into dust; unfix; vanish; wear (away); *x-ing;* yeet; zap;

**dissuade** *(v.)*: argue against; avert; bring around; convince not to; discourage; daunt; divert; encourage not to; expostulate; frighten; *guide; help;* intimidate; *jink;* keep from; lead away from; make one not want to; *non-agreement; oppose;* persuade against; quench; remonstrate; sway; talk out of; urge against; *vie;* win over; *xuld [arch.]; yerk away;* zorch; [*Ant.* drive]

**dissuasion** *(n.)*: advice against; bringing around; convincing against; discouragement; daunting; exhortation against; expostulation; frightening; *guidance; help;* intimidation; *jinking;* keeping from; leading away; making one not wasn't to; *non-agreement; opposition;* persuading against; quenching; remonstration; swaying; sureness; talking out of; urging against; *violent opposition;* winning over; *xel [arch.]; yerking away;* zorch;

**distance** *(n.)*: *away; afar;* breadth; continuous miles; *duration;* expanse; *equi~;* farness; girth; how far away; interval; *jumboness;* kilometers; length; longinquity; miles; milage; *nautical miles;* overall length; *prodigiousness;* quartile; remoteness; reach; run; space; travel ~; *umbratile; vastness;* width; *xy-coordinates;* yards; *zone;*

**distant** *(adj.)*: afield; *afar; beyond; cool;* detached; divided; *equidistant;* far(-away); far-off; *girth;* hundreds of miles away; isolated; *jump; kilometers; long way;* many miles away; not close; outlying; *parted;* quartile; remote; secluded; secludinous; thousands of miles away; umbratile; very far; worlds apart; *xfer; yards; zillions of miles;* [*see* aloof]

**distill** *(v.)*: alcoholize; boil; brew; bootleg; condense; concoct; concentrate; cohobate; decoct; depurate; distil; extract; extill; essentialize; filer; glean; *hard liquor;* infuse; *joy water; kirsch;* make alcohol; make moonshine; *negus;* obtain; operate a still; purify; *quaffed;* refine; run moonshine; sublimate; trickle; *turn out;* use a still; volatilize; *whisky-making; xenenthesis;* yeast; zygotic; [*Ant.* detoxify]

**distinct** *(adj.)*: apparent; blatant; clear(-cut); distinctive; definite; different; defined; express; evident; ferly; fine; glaring; *hearable;* identifiable; individual; *just plain;* kenspeckle; *keen;* lucid; marked; noticeable; obvious; one-of-a-kind; plain; peculiar; *quite;* queer; recognizable; specific; separate; trenchant; transparent; unmistakable; unique; unusual; visible; well-defined; *XF; yeme [arch.]; zero confusion;* [*Ant.* dim]

**distinction** *(n.)*: antithesis; *bearing dissimilarity;* contrast; contra~; difference; end of resemblance; fine point; *gap;* heterogeneity; individuality; *juxtaposition;* key ~; logical ~; marked difference; non-resemblance; otherness; peculiarity; quiddity; real difference; singularity; separateness; *thing;* unlikeness; uniqueness; variation; *wide range; xtry; difference yeme; zeroing in;*
**distinctive** *(adj.)*: all one's own; *brand;* characteristic; distinguishing; especial; *famous;* giveaway; *heterotypical;* idiosyncratic; individual; identifying; inimitable; *just one; known by;* legendary; *marked;* notable; one-of-a-kind; peculiar; particular; proper; quite ~; recognizable; special; signature; *sui generis* [L.]; typic; trademark; unique; very ~; *well-known; xtry.;* yet unreproduced; *zany;*
**distinguish** *(v.)*: *aware;* behold; catch; comprehend; discern; discriminate; differentiate; *eye;* fathom; get; *have; hear;* identify; judge; know; learn; make a distinction; notice; observe; perceive; *qualify;* recognize; separate; *see;* tell apart; understand; view; wist; *xenodiagnose; yeme;* zero in;
**distort** *(v.)*: adulterate; alter; bend; contort; disfigure; deform; entwist; foul up; garble; *harm;* injure; *jade;* knot; *louse up;* mutilate; *nullify; obloquoy; oppress;* pervert; *quade* [arch.]; ruin; spoil; skew; twist; *undo;* vary; warp; *xenomorph; yaw; zad;*
**distortion** *(n.)*: alteration; bending; corruption; deformation; *evil;* frowardness; godlessness; horridness; iniquity; impurity; jadedness; *knavery;* lewdness; misrepresentation; nefariousness; obfuscation; perversion; queeringness; reprobation; slanting; twisting; unrighteousness; violence; warping; *x-rated; yuckiness;* zigzag;
**distract** *(v.)*: avert; befuddle; catch one's attention; disrupt; divert; derail; draw away; enthrall; forestall; get off track; *hinder;* interrupt; *jam;* keep from; lose one's focus; make one ~ed; *non-attention; off-track;* preoccupy; *quell;* redirect; sidetrack; throw off course; turn away; *unseat;* veer; wander; *xuld [arch.];* yank off course; zag;
**distraction** *(n.)*: addling; befuddling; *commotion;* disruption; diversion; enthrallment; forestallment; getting off track; *hindrance;* interruption; interpellation; *jamming; keeping from;* losing one's focus; making one distracted; non-attention; *off-track;* preoccupation; *quelling;* redirection; sidetracking; trouble; *unseating;* veering; wandering; *xuld [arch.];* yonderliness; *zagging;*
**distress** *(n.)*: anxiety; burden; care; dread; despair; emotionalism; fear; gloom; heartache; insecurity; jitteriness; kiaugh [Scot.]; lather; mortification; nervousness; over-anxiety; panic; quaking; restlessness; stress; trepidation; uneasiness; vexation; worry; *xenophobia; yellow-belliedness; zeallessness;*
**distress** *(v.)*: alarm; burden; concern; disturb; *exasperate;* frighten; gaster; horrify; *insecurity; jitters;* kiaugh [Scot.]; *languish;* make nervous; nerve; overburden; panic; quicken; *red alert;* scare; trouble; upset; vex; worry; *xenophobia; yelping; zealless;* [*Ant.* delight]
**distribute** *(v.)*: administer; assign; allocate; bestow; confer; commit; dispense; deal; dole; endue; furnish; give out; hand out; issue; *jettison;* kit; lavish; mete; *non-retention;* outfit; offload; part with; pass on; present; provide; *quicken;* relay; render; relinquish; supply; surrender; transfer; unhand; vest; *weigh;* xfer; yield; *zip;*
**distribution** *(n.)*: allocation; bestowal; consigning; dispersal; dispensation; enduing; furnishing; giving out; handing out; issuing; *justly dividing;* kitting; *letting;* meting; *non-retention;* outfitting; offloading; portioning; quantifying; rationing; supply; sharing; transferring; unloading; vesting; *weighing; xfer;* yielding; zipping;
**district** *(n.)*: area; borough; county; division; exurb; *field; ground; hundred; imperial territory;* jurisdiction; *kray* [Rus.]; location; locale; municipality; nome; nomarchy; *oblast [Rus.];* parish; precinct; purlieu; part; province; quadrant; region; section; sector; territory; ubiety; vicinity; viceroyalty; ward; *x-sector; yard;* zone; zillah [Ind.];
**disturb** *(v.)*: agitate; arouse; bestir; bother; *concern;* distract; disquiet; distemper; excite; faze; goad; harrow; interrupt; incite; jostle; kittle; *lead;* move; nudge; *overagitate;* perturb; provoke; quicken; rouse; stir; shake; trouble; upset; vex; whip up; *xuld [arch.];* yerk; *zing;* [*Ant.* delight]

**disturbance** *(n.)*: agitation; bedlam; commotion; disquieting; excitement; fracas; fuss; goading; havoc; hullabaloo; insurrection; *jumble;* kick-up; loud ~; mayhem; noise; *outcry;* pandemonium; *quandary;* ruckus; rumpus; riot; shouting; stushie; tumult; upheaval; violence; wildness; xtry. uprising; *yerking; zoo;* [*see* annoyance]

**ditch** *(n.)*: *aperture;* boyau; channel; dugout; dike; excavation; escarp; furrow; fosse; gully; hollow; incavation; jaw-hole; kerf; *long furrow;* moat; *niche; opening;* pit; quadrisulcate; *ravine; sump;* trench; *umbilicus;* vallum; ward; *xystus pit;* yawn; zanja;

**dive** *(n.)*: *angle;* belly-whop; crash ~; drop; descent; downturn; *endeavor;* fall; gainer; go below; header; high- ~; header; immergence; jump down; jackknife; keeling over; leap down; *movement downward;* nose- ~; *over the cliff;* plunge; quick-fall; running- ~; swoop; swan~; tumble; tailspin; *under;* volt; whop; *x-cend; yanking down;* zoom downward;

**dive** *(v.)*: *angle;* belly-whop; crash ~; drop; descend; delve; deep-sea ~; *endeavor;* fall; freefall; go down; *headlong;* immerge; jump down; jackknife; keel over; leap; make nose~; *over the cliff;* plunge; plummet; quick-fall; running- ~; *reduce;* sink; sky- ~; skin- ~; sound [zoo.]; submerge; tumble; turn downward; *under;* volt; whop; *x-cend; yank down;* zoom down;

**diverge** *(v.)*: *apart;* branch; cleave; deviate; depart; divide; excurse; fork; go off; *halve; isolate; jump apart; keep apart;* leave; move away; *non-parallel; open;* part; *quarter;* rend; recede; run off; separate; split; stray; turn away; *unyoke;* vary; withdraw; *xfer;* yawn; zigzag;

**diverse** *(adj.)*: assorted; another; atypical; *bountiful;* conflicting; different; differing; diversified; dedallian; dissimilar; distinct; diversiform; eclectic; fully- ~; *general;* heterogeneous; individual; incompatible; *jumbled; kaleidoscopic; loony;* miscellaneous; motley; mixed; multifarious; manifold; multifaceted; multiform; non-matching; other; opposing; peculiar; queer; ranging separate; sundry; *tons;* unalike; varied; various; varisized; variegated; variform; wide-ranging; xeno-; *yawed; zany;*

**diversify** *(v.)*: alter; branch out; broaden; change; deviate; expand; fiddle with; *grow; heighten;* innovate; *jib; key to; lower;* modify; novate; overhaul; *put right; qualify;* revise; spread out; sub~; take on new things; *upgrade;* vary; widen; xenomorph; yaw; zigzag;

**diversion** *(n.)*: amusement; befuddling; *commotion;* distraction; digression; entertainment; forestallment; getting off track; hobby; interruption; *jamming; keeping from;* losing one's focus; making one distracted; non-attention; *off-track;* preoccupation; pastime; *quelling;* redirection; sidetracking; trouble; *unseating;* veering off-track; wandering; *xuld [arch.];* yaw; zagging;

**diversity** *(n.)*: assortment; bunch; big selection; collection; commixture; disconformity; dissimilitude; *eclectic mix;* full array; *general;* hodgepodge; inharmoniousness; jumble; *kaleidoscopic; lots;* multiplicity; mixture; multiformity; nonconformity; olio; otherness; pastiche; *quantity;* range; selection; *ton;* unsimilarity; variety; wide range; *xtry. mix; yelm; zillions;*

**divert** *(v.)*: avert; branch off; change course; derail; deter; distract; deflect; deviate; detour; excurse; entangle; forestall; go off; head off; inflect; *jink;* keep from; lose one's focus; move away; *non-attention; off-track;* preoccupy; put on the back burner; *quell;* redirect; reroute; refract; sidetrack; turn; *unseat;* veer; ward off; *wander;* x; *yaw;* zag;

**divest** *(v.)*: *appropriate;* betake; carry off; deprive; dispossess; expel; exauthorate; fleece; get rid of; *heave out;* impoverish; impeach; *jettison; kest;* lose; make one give up; *nab; offload;* overthrow; put off; part from; *quit;* remove; rob; rid; strip; take (away); unfrock; unseat; *vote out;* wrench; *x-out;* yank; *zip away;*

**divide** *(v.)*: abscind; bisect; break; bifurcate; cut; cleave; dissever; disunite; dichotomize; exscind; fork; fissure; *gouge;* halve; incide; intersect; *jigsaw;* keep apart; lop; *miter; notch;* obtruncate; part(ition); parcel; *quadrisect;* rend; rive; sever; separate; split; sunder; sub~; transect; unyoke; *vell;* wall off; whack apart; x-sect; yandy; zone;

**dividend** *(n.)*: annuity; bonus; commission; divvy; earnings; fruit; gain; guerdon; *hire;* income; interest; *justification; kickback;* lagniappe; money; meed; net receipts; *overcompensation;* perk; payment; proceeds; quarterage; recompense; royalty; surplus; sum; transfer; unearned income; virement; wage(s); x-div.; yield; *zapping;*

**divination** *(n.)*: augury; black magic; conjuring; divining; enchantment; fortune-telling; geomancy; hocus pocus; horoscopy; incantation; juju; *Keltic religion; legerdemain;* magic; necromancy; occult; *palmistry; quad;* rune; soothsaying; theurgy; *ungodliness;* voodoo; witchcraft; xenomancy; *yogism; zodiac;*

  **Types of divination**: austromancy; botanomancy; chiromancy; divining; eromancy; favomancy; gastromancy; heiromancy; horoscopy; isopsephy; jiaobei; keraunonabcy; lithomancy; meteormancy; necromancy; onomancy; pyromancy; qiu qian; rhabdomancy; spodomancy; tarot reading; uromancy; videomancy; water witching; xylomancy; ydromancy; zoomancy;

**divine** *(adj.)*: angelic; blissful; celestial; deific; ethereal; empyreal; fabulous; godly; Godlike; heavenly; *incarnated;* joyous; *keen;* lofty; magnificent; numinous; other-worldly; paradisian; *queme; radiant;* supernatural; supernal; supermundane; superlunary; *theological;* unworldly; virtuous; wonderful; *xtry.; yet unparalleled;* zonic; [*Ant.* devilish]

**divine** *(v.)*: augur; bode; cry; declare; envisage; foretell; give prophecy; hariolate; inform; *jobation; kurvey; legerdemain;* make predicition; notify; orate; predict; prognosticate; presage; *quain* [arch.]; read palms (-tea leaves, etc.); scry; tell the future; utter; vaticinate; warn; *xenomancy; yell; zay [arch.];*

**diviner** *(n.)*: astrologer; bewitcher; clairvoyant; dowser; enchanter; fortune-teller; geomancer; haruspice; *incantation;* jadoo-wallah; keraunonabcist; lithomancer; mystic; medium; necromancer; oracle; psychic; palm-reader; *quacksalver;* rhabdomancer; soothsayer; seer; theurgist; *unveiler;* voodooist; wizard; xylomancer; *yogist;* zodiacist; [*see* witch];

**divinity** *(n.)*: angelicalness; *bliss;* celestiality; divineness; deity; ethereality; fabulousness; godhood; godness; godhead; godship; heavenliness; *incarnation;* Jesus; *keenness;* loftiness; magnificence; numen; other-worldliness; *paradisaical; queme; radiance;* supernaturalism; *theology;* unworldliness; virtue; wonder; *xtry.; yet unparalleled;* zonic;

**division** *(n.)*: abstraction; break; breach; cleavage; cleft; disjunction; disconnection; disunion; divorce; disharmony; exscinding; fork; fissure; gap; gulf; hiatus; isolation; judicial separation; keeping separate; leaving; marked ~; non-unity; otherness; partition; parting; quinquefid; *quartering;* rift; separation; sub~; severance; split; schism; taking apart; uncoupling; unyoking; vacating; withdrawal; weeding out; *xiphopagotomy;* yawn; zoning;

**divisive** *(adj.)*: argumentative; bickering; contrary; controversial; disputatious; emulous; factious; grumbling; hot-tempered; ill-tempered; jangly; knaggy; liverish; murmuring; negative; opposing; petulant; querulous; repining; striving; touchy; *unsatisfied;* vinegary; wranglesome; *xenophobic; yawping;* zoilean;

**divorce** *(n.)*: annulment; breakup; broken marriage; calling it quits; divorcement; dissolution; *end; filing for ~;* going separate ways; hanging it up; *isolation;* judicial separation; keeping separate; leaving; making an end of; nullification; *opting out;* putting away; parting; quittance; *rending;* split-up; separation; severance; talaq [Mos.]; *termination;* unmarrying; voidance; *vacating;* walking papers [slang]; x; *yawn; zoning;*

**divorce** *(v.)*: annul; break up; call it quits; dissociate; dissolve; end; file for ~; go separate ways; hang it up; *isolate; judicial separation;* keep separate; leave; make an end of; nullify; *opt out;* put away; part; quit; *rend;* split up; separate; terminate; unmarry; unyoke; *vacating;* walk out; *x; yawn;* zip apart;

**dizzy** *(adj.)*: awhirl; befuddled; confused; disoriented; emptyheaded; faint; giddy; hinky; incoherent; jumbled; *kapakari [Haw.];* lightheaded; mixed-up; non-stable; over- ~; *pixilated;* quirky; rattlebrained; shaky; swimming; *turbid;* unstable; unbalanced; vertiginous; woozy; whirly; *x'ed; yo-yo; zany;*

**do** *(v.)*: accomplish; act; achieve; bring about; complete; carry out; discharge; execute; effect; engage; fulfill; get done; handle; implement; jump to it; keep; lend oneself to; make; *not resist;* obey; perform; practice; pull off; *questionless;* realize; see it through; transact; undertake; *vigor;* work; *xuld [arch.];* yield; zip to it; [*Ant.* dawdle]

**doctor** *(n.)*: archiater; animal ~; attending physician; brain surgeon; country ~; consultant; doc [slang]; externe; family ~; general practitioner; house ~ (-physician); head surgeon; intern; *joe;* knife-man [slang]; laser surgeon; M.D.; neurosurgeon; *obstetrician;* physician; Ph.D.; practitioner; paraclesian; *quack;* restorer; sawbones [slang]; specialist; surgeon; *Th.D.;* urologist; veterinarian; worker; *xenoparaste specialist; yeoman; zambuk [Aus.];*
    **Types of doctors**: allergist; brain surgeon; cardiologist; dermtologist; endocrinologist; family practitioner; general practitioner; gynocologist; heart doctor; immunologist; lithotomist; microbiologist; neurologist; obstetrician; podiatrist; rhematologist; spine surgeon; thoracic surgeon; urologist; veterinarian;

**doctrine** *(n.)*: article; belief; creed; credo; concept; cardinal ~; dogma; *education;* fact; great truth; *hierology;* idea; instruction; indoctrination; ideology; "ism"; *judgment;* knowledge; learning; *lessons;* maxim; notion; oracles; opinion; precept; principle; position; philosophy; *qualification;* rhetoric; stance; stand; tenet; teaching; theology; truth; *understanding;* view; *wisdom; xenagogy; yarking;* zeteticism;

**document** *(n.)*: article; *booklet;* chirograph; composition; deed; dossier; essay; file; *government papers;* handiwork; item; journalism; *kapnography;* literature; letter; legal paper; manuscript; *notation;* oeuvre; official ~; paper; piece; *the quill;* record; *scroll;* treatise; thesis; text; *uncials;* vignette; writ(ing); work; *xiaozhuan; yellow journalism; zeug;*

**documentation** *(n.)*: authentication; bearing out; certification; credentials; documents; establishment; final certification; giving of proof; homologation; identification; justification; *kithe [Scot.];* legitimization; muniments; necessary paperwork; okay; paperwork; paper trail; proof; *questionlessness;* records; substantiation; testimonial; upholding; verification; validation; warrant; x-certification; *yes; zero doubt;*

**dog** *(n.)*: *animal;* birddog; bitch [fem.]; *beast;* canine; cur; doggy [slang]; *elkhound;* feist; griffon; hound; *Irish setter; jackal;* K-9 [slang]; lapdog; mongrel; mutt; night-dog; *ovtcharka;* pooch; pup(py); *quadruped;* rach; sheep~; terrier; *ululator; vizsla;* whelp; woofer [joc.]; watch~; *xolo;* yard ~; *zerda;*
    **Kinds of dogs**: Alsatian; beagle; collie; dachshund; elkhound; foxhound; French poodle; German shepherd; greyhound; husky; Irish setter; Jack Russell; kelpie; Labrador; mastiff; Newfoundland; otterhound; pitbull; pug; Queensland heeler; retriever; rottweiler; sheepdog; schnauzer; St. Bernard; spaniel; terrier; utonagan; vizsla; whippet; wolfhound; xolo; Yorkshire terrier; zerda;

**dogmatic** *(adj.)*: adamant; absolute; bendless; confident; certain; dogmatical; emphatic; firm; grim; headstrong; intolerant; inflexible; jaw-set; *keep; lasting;* mulish; narrow; opinionated; peremptory; positive; pronunciative; *querulous;* rigid; strict; *tenacious; tough;* unbending; very rigid; *willful; x-grained;* yieldless; zero-give;

**doll** *(n.)*: antique ~; baby ~; corn- ~; dollie [slang]; dress-up figure; earthen ~; figurine; golliwog; hazel-earth ~; *item;* jumeau; kewpie; lifelike ~; mopsey; *novelty; object;* paper ~; porcelain ~; *quelkshaw;* rag~; rag-baby; Steiner ~; talking ~; toy; *undressed ~;* vinyl ~; wax ~; xoanon; *youngling; zizz;*

**dollar** *(n.)*: almighty ~; buck banknote; cash; currency; *coin;* dough; Eisenhower ~; folding money; funds; greenback; gold (certificate); gold ~; hard cash; *item; jiggy; Krugerrand; loot;* money; moolah; note; one- ~ bill; paper money; peso; *quetzal [Guatemala]; riches;* silver (certificate); security; silver ~; simoleon; smacker; *thaler* [arch.]; U.S. ~; *valuables;* wampum; *xenocurrency;* yellowback; *zechin;*

**domain** *(n.)*: area; border; country; department; demesne; dominion; extent of influence; estate; empire; field; governance; hemisphere; influence; jurisdiction; kingdom; land; limits; monarchy; nation; orb; purview; principality; possession; queendom [fem.]; realm; sphere of influence; state; territory; *unit; viscounty;* world; *xerifdom; yard;* zone of influence;

**domestic** *(adj.)*: at-home; *born-here;* connubial; conjugal; domesticated; *everyday-life;* family; *gentilitious;* household; homebred; internal; *jake;* kin-related; local; marital; matrimonial; non-foreign; national; *of that place; paisano;* quasi-marital; residential; *statewide;* tribal; *ubeity;* village-dwelling; wedded; *xenophile; yield; zadruga* [Slav.];
**dominant** *(adj.)*: ascendant; biggest; chief; controlling; domineering; eminent; foremost; focal; greatest; highest; in control; influential; *judge;* key; leading; main; notable; overriding; prime; principle; pre~; prevailing; *quintessential;* ruling; ranking; supreme; top; *ultimate; vital;* weighty; *xenenthesis; yet unsurpassed;* zenithal;
**dominate** *(v.)*: abuse; boss; control; direct; dictate; domineer; enslave; force; govern; head; handle; influence; jockey; keep under control; lead; lord over; manipulate; manage; *nobble;* oversee; oppress; prevail; predominate; *quell;* run; rule; subdue; take over; *use;* vassalize; wear the pants; *x-out;* yeme; zero in;
**domination** *(n.)*: authority; bossing; control; dominion; dominance; empowering; faculty; government; headship; influence; jurisdiction; kingship; lordship; mastery; name; oversight; ownership; power; *quo warranto* [L.]; rule; supremacy; thrall; umpirage; virtue; *warrant; weight; x-out;* yard; *zonal control;*
**domineer** *(v.)*: afflict; browbeat; control; dominate; enslave; force; govern; *hold;* intimidate; *jurisdiction;* keep down; lord over; master; *not reasonable;* oppress; persecute; predominate; quell; repress; rule; subjugate; suppress; tyrannize; use; vanquish; weigh; *xuld [arch.];* yoke; *zap;*
**domineering** *(adj.)*: authoritarian; bossy; commanding; controlling; demanding; dictatorial; exacting; forceful; fascistic; grave; harsh; high-handed; heavy-handed; imposing; imperious; *jaded;* kindless; loveless; magisterial; *nasty;* overbearing; pushy; peremptory; *quede [arch.];* repressive; strict; strong; tyrannical; totalitarian; unreasonable; undemocratic; unassailable; *virulent;* weighty; *xenophobic;* yieldless; *za-zum* [Rus.]; [*Ant.* deferential]
**dominion** *(n.)*: authority; *badge;* command; *crown;* domination; empery; faculty; government; headship; influence; imperium; jurisdiction; kingship; lordship; mastery; name; ownership; oversight; possession; power; *quo warranto* [L.]; rule; realm; say-so; supremacy; territory; *throne;* umpirage; virtue; *warrant; weight; x-pass;* yard; *zonal control;* [see kingdom]
**donate** *(v.)*: award; bestow; contribute; distribute; endow; furnish; give; gift; hand (over); impart; *jettison;* kick in; lavish; mete; *non-retention;* offer; provide; *quality;* render; supply; transfer; unhand; vest; *weigh;* xfer; yield; *zip;*
**donation** *(n.)*: award; alms; bestowal; blessing; bequest; contribution; donative; endowment; favor; gift; handsel; impartation; *joy-giving;* kindness; liberality; largess; lagniappe; munificence; nicety; offering; present; *quantity;* reward; *surprise;* tribute; *unselfishness;* vouchsafement; *wherewithal;* xenium; *yeff* [arch.]; *zealous support;* [see grace]
**done** *(adj.)*: accomplished; brought to fruition; complete(d); concluded; consummate; developed; ended; executed; finished; fulfilled; *grown; high;* intact; *just finished; kept; long-awaited;* mature; made; *non-abridged;* over; performed; perfect; *qualified;* resolved; ready; *sweeping;* through; terminated; *utterly finished; veritable;* whole; x'ed; yare; *zipped up;*
**donkey** *(n.)*: ass; burro; *beast;* cuddy [Scot.]; colt; domestic ass; equid; *equus* [L.]; fussock; foal; genet; he-ass [masc.]; *Indian pony;* jackass [masc.]; jenny; jennet [both fem.]; kiang; longear; moke; *mule;* neddy; onager; *pack mule;* quagga; *racehorse;* she-ass [fem.]; sumpter; tame ass; *ungulate; varmint;* wild ass; *xilingol; yard ass;* zonkey;
**donor** *(n.)*: awarder; bestower; benefactor; contributor; donator; endower; furnisher; giver; granter; hander (over); imparter; issuer; imputer; *jettison;* kitter; lavisher; meter; *non-retention;* outfitter; offerer; provider; patron; *quickener;* renderer; supplier; transferer; tither; unhander; vester; *weigher;* xfer; yielder; *zip;* [*Ant.* donee]

**doom** *(n.)*: annihilation; *burning;* calamity; condemnation; destruction; death; damnation; evil; fall; *the grave; hell; internment;* judgment; *killing;* laying waste; *mortality;* nemesis; olation; perdition; punishment; *quashing;* ruin(ation); reprobation; *sentence; torment;* undoing; *vitiation;* woe; wrecking; *x-out; yanking down; zapping;*

**door** *(n.)*: archway; access; adit; antipope; back~; *cellar ~;* doorway; entrance; entryway; exit; front ~; French ~; flap; folding ~; gate(way); gorge; hatch; ingress; jib-door; *kick plate; knocker;* liftgate; main entrance; *notch;* opening; outlet; passage; portcullis; private entrance; quadrivalve; rear ~; sliding ~; threshold; trap- ~; utility ~; vomitory; wicket; x-door; yett; zeta ~;

**doorpost** *(n.)*: *area;* beam; crossbeam; doorframe; doorjamb; *edifice;* frame; gatepost; heelpost; *item;* jamb; korupe; lintel; *molding; nebule; ovolo;* post; platband; quarter-post; *reglet;* sidepiece; sidepost; transom; upright; upper ~; *vertcal; wood; xsome; yett; zeug;*

**dormant** *(adj.)*: asleep; buried; concealed; dozing; estivating; fallow; gone to sleep; hibernating; inactive; idle; *jarless;* kip; latent; motionless; non-active; out; passive; quiescent; resting; sleeping; torpid; unawakened; vegetating; wakeless; *x-sleep;* yet to awaken; *zero activity;*

**dose** *(n.)*: allocation; amount; bestowal; consignment; dosage; *extent; furnishing;* given amount; *heaping teaspoon;* issuance; *just right amount; kit;* lot; measure; *number; ounce;* portion; pre-measured amount; *pill;* quantity; *ration;* spoonful; *transferal;* unit; *vesting;* weighed out; *xfer; yielding; zoning;*

**dot** *(n.)*: *abnormality;* blot(ch); black ~; chit; dapple; defect; *engrained;* fleck; freckle; *grease spot; hue; imperfection;* jaup; *jot;* kink; *line;* mark; map~; naeve; *orb;* polka- ~; pip; quirk; round ~; spot; speck; *tarnish; unsightly spot;* verruca; wem; X; *yedder;* zit;

**double-minded** *(adj.)*: astable; bouncy; changeable; dithering; erratic; fluctuating; going back and forth; hinky; instable; irresolute; *jumpy; kaleidoscopic;* labile; moody; non-stable; oscillating; pendular; *questionable;* roving; shaky; tottering; undetermined; unsettled; unstable; vacillatory; wavering; *x-ing;* yeasty; *ziggety;*

**doubt** *(n.)*: apprehension; bringing into question; *confusion;* cynicism; contravertibility; doubtfulness; disbelief; distrust; dubiousness; dubiety; *equivocalness;* faithlessness; fear; *guardedness;* hesitation; incredulity; infidelity; iffiness; *jitteriness; knocking;* leeriness; misbelief; mistrust; misgiving; non-belief; negativism; *over-anxiety;* pessimism; question; qualm; questionability; reservations; skepticism; suspicion; trepidation; unbelief; uncertainty; *vacillation;* worry; wariness; *xtry. doubt; yieldlessness;* zero confidence;

**doubt** *(v.)*: *apprehension;* bring into question; challenge; disbelieve; dispute; discount; distrust; discredit; *ever-doubtful;* falter; fear; get nervous; hesitate; *iffiness; jittery;* keep doubting; *leery;* mistrust; not believe; naysay; oppugn; *pessimistic;* question; raise a question; ridicule; scoff; suspect; *skeptical;* take with a grain of salt; unbelieve; *vacillate;* worry; waver; *xtry. ~;* yet doubt; zero confidence;

**doubter** *(n.)*: agnostic; *atheist;* balker; cynic; disbeliever; *enquirer;* freethinker; *guarded;* hesitator; irresolute; infidel; jangler; knocker; *leery;* misanthropist; nonbeliever; oppugner; polemic; pessimist; questioner; rejecter; skeptic; somatist; truth-challenger; unbeliever; vacillator; *wet blanket; x-careful; yawper;* zetetic;

**doubtful** *(adj.)*: ambiguous; amphibological; borderline; confusing; disbelieving; distrustful; diffident; dubious; equivocal; fishy; *guarded;* hesitant; incredulous; improbable; *jittery;* kiaugh [Scot.]; lacking certainty; *misgivings;* not likely; negative; *of doubtful meaning;* pessimistic; puzzling; questionable; reticent; suspensive; trustless; uncertain; unconvinced; unsure; unlikely; very unlikely; wavering; *xtry, ~;* yet unconvinced; *zero probability;*

**doubtless** *(adj.)*: almost certainly; assuredly; beyond question; certainly; definite; evident; firm; guaranteed; highly confident; indisputable; incontestable; incontrovertible; just sure; keenly sure; *legitimate;* mistake-proof; non-questionable; 100% sure; positive; probably; questionless; reliable; sure; true; unquestionable; verified; without a doubt; xtry. sure; *yes;* zero doubt;

**dove** *(n.)*: *animal;* bird; cock [masc.]; *creature;* domestic pigeon; *emerald ~;* finnikin; *fowl; ground ~;* house pigeon; *imperial pigeon; jacobine; kereru; luzon bleeding-heart;* mourning *~; nun ~;* oenas; pigeon; queest; ring~; squab [young]; turtle~; *unspeckled ~; victoria crowned pigeon;* white-winged ~; *xenops [L.]; yellow-footed ~; zenaida ~;*

**down** *(prep.)*: at the bottom; bottomward; collapsing; downward(s); declining; earthward; falling; groundward; hellward; inclined ~; *jump; kill;* low; *meridional;* netherward; on the ground; *pointed ~; quite ~ward;* right ~; straight ~; south; toward the earth; *under(neath);* verging ~; way ~; x=0; *yielded; Z- [Cartesian];*

**downfall** *(n.)*: *annihilation;* breakup; bringing down; collapse; *coup de grâce* [F.]; demise; defeat; death(blow); end; fall; folding; final blow; going down; *humiliation; internment; insolvency; just desserts;* knocking out; labefaction; loss; *malfunction; nonsuccess;* overthrow; perishing; *quashing;* ruin; subversion; toppling; undoing; *vanishment;* wreck; Waterloo; Xenophon; *yielding; zeroing out;*

**downward** *(adj.)*: adown; bottomward; coming down; down(wards); declining; earthward; falling; groundward; hellward; inclined ~; *jumping down; keeling over;* low; *moribund;* netherward; on the descent; plummeting; *quickly falling;* reduced altitude; sliding; southward; toward the earth; *under(neath);* verging down; way down; *x-cend; yet ~; Z- [Cartesian];*

**dowry** *(n.)*: amount; bride price; compensation; dowery; dot; *extent; fee;* gift; *handsel;* indemnification; *jewels; kiddushin* [Heb.]; *labola* [Afr.]; money; *number;* offering; price; *quantity;* recompense; specified amount; tocher; *unload;* value; *worth; xenium;* yield; *zitella;*

**drab** *(adj.)*: average; boring; cheerless; dull; dingy; *empty;* flat; gray; ho-hum; insipid; jejune; *ketty;* lackluster; monotonous; non-exciting; ordinary; plain; quotidian; repetitive; somber; subfusc; tedious; tiresome; uninteresting; vapid; wearisome; *xtry. ~;* yawnful; zestless;

**draft** *(n. levied troops)*: admission; bidding; conscription; compulsory enlistment; draught; enlistment; forced enlistment; general enlistment; *hiring;* inlistment; impress; *joining; kerns;* levy; Landstrum; mandated enlistment; *nempne;* order; press; *qualification;* recruitment; summoning; taking; *using;* volume; wartime levy; *xfer; yoke; zet [dial.];*

**draft** *(n. rough plan)*: *artwork;* blueprint; catagraph; drawing; etching; first ~; general idea; house plan; imprecise plan; ichnography; *kiaugh [Scot.];* layout; *map; not set in stone;* outline; plan; *questionable;* rough ~ (-outline); sketch; tentative plan; *uncertain;* vague idea; working drawing; *x-chart; yet uncertain; zenithal projection;*

**draft** *(v. levy troops)*: admit; bid; conscript; call; draught; enlist; enroll; *force;* get; *hire;* impress; join; *kerns;* levy; muster; *nempne;* order; press; *qualify;* recruit; *raise;* sign up; summon; *shanghai;* take; *use;* volume; *wartime; xfer; yoke; zet [dial.];*

**draft** *(v. write)*: author; blazon; compose; draw up; enface; fill out; grave; handwrite; inscribe; jot; keep record; limn; mark; make up; notate; outline; pen; quill; redact; scribble; *take down;* underwrite; *vellum;* write out; *x; yak; zay;*

**drag** *(v.)*: *action;* bring; *carry;* draw; evulse; force along; *get;* haul; heave; hale; *involve;* jerk along; kedge; lug; move; muscle; *nudge; out~;* pull; *quarter-cart;* rake; *ship;* take; tow; tug; trice; troll; *uptake; vellico* [L.]; *wimple; xfer;* yank; *zip;*

**dragon** *(n.)*: *animal; amphithere;* basilisk; black ~; chimera; cockatrice; *Chinese ~;* draco; eight-headed ~; firedrake; green ~; hydra; iron ~; *Japanese ~;* knucker; lindworm; *monster;* nidhogg; Orochi; platinum ~; quadra-headed ~; *reptile;* red ~; (sea) serpent; three-headed ~; *unleashed ~; varmint;* wivern; *xana* [Bulgarian]; yellow ~; *zahhak* [Pers.]; [see Devil]

**drain** *(v.)*: *abate;* bleed; clean out; consume; deplete; empty; exhaust; expend; empty; flow out; fatigue; finish; go down; hone; *impoverish;* jade; *kill;* let out; leach; *minimize; nullify;* ooze; *overspend;* pour out; pump out; quail; reduce; run out; sap; siphon off; spend; trickle out; tax; tire; tap; use (up); unplug; vacate; weaken; weary; *xerosis; yield;* zap;

**drama** *(n.)*: acting; antimasque; *the* boards; *cinema; comedy;* dramatization; enactment; feigning; *the* footlights; *gallery;* histrionism; impersonation; job; *kinderspiel* [G.]; land of make-believe; masque; melo~; *non-reality;* onstage; overacting; performing (arts); play-acting; *quasi-acting;* re-enactment; stage; show business; theater; theatrics; thespian art; underacting; virtu; *work;* Xanthopoulos; *yielding; zarzuela* [Sp.];
**dramatic** *(adj.)*: astonishing; breathtaking; *cinematic;* dramatized; dramatical; exciting; extraordinary; fabulous; gripping; *great;* histrionical; impressive; jarring; keen; *laudable;* melo~; magnificent; *noteworthy;* overwhelming; prodigious; *quantum [L.];* remarkable; spectacular; staged; thrilling; theatrical; unparalleled; vivid; wonderful; xtry.; *yippee!;* zizzy;
**dramatize** *(v.)*: act (out); behave; be; con; dissemble; enact; feign; *guile;* ham it up; impersonate; *just make-believe; keep ~ing; live; like;* mum; melo~; *non-reality;* overplay; over~; perform; play-act; play up; *quasi;* role-play; re-enact; stage; simulate; theatricalize; *use; vaunt; work;* xenophonia; yield performance; *zealously pretend;*
**drastic** *(adj.)*: acute; big; comprehensive; critical; dire; desperate; dramatic; extreme; far-reaching; grave; huge; intense; jarring; *keenly severe; large;* marked; major; *needful;* onerous; *painful;* quantum; radical; severe; strong; *titanic;* urgent; vast; very marked; *weighty;* xtry.; yet unconventional; *zealous;*
**draw** *(v.)*: *artwork;* block in; copy; doodle; draft; depict; diagram; etch; form picture; grave; handwrite; illustrate; jot; *kapnograph;* limn; make drawing; mark out; notate; outline; portray; pencil; plot; *quill;* represent; render; redraw; redraft; scrawl; sketch; *stylize;* trace; turn out; use pen; *vignette;* write; *xylography; yield; zet [dial.];*
**drawing** *(n.)*: artwork; blueprint; caricature; cartoon; depiction; doodle; draft; etching; figuration; graving; handiwork; illustration; *jot;* kapnography; limning; likeness; *masterpiece; notations;* outline; picture; portrayal; *quill;* representation; rough sketch; sketch; technical ~; *unfinished ~;* vignette; woodcutting; xylograph; *yield; zet [dial.];*
**dread** *(n.)*: alarm; apprehension; burden; care; cowardice; cold sweat; distress; *exasperation;* fear; fright; gloom; gastness; horror; insecurity; jitteriness; kiaugh [Scot.]; *lily-livered; mistrust;* nervousness; over-anxiety; panic; quaking; *reluctance;* stress; scariness; terror; uneasiness; vexation; worry; *xenophobia;* yellow-belliedness; *zeallessness;*
**dread** *(v.)*: affright; be scared; *careful;* despair; eye askance; fear; get nervous; have qualms; *intimidated; jump; knees knocking;* lose courage; misgive; moither; *nervous wreck;* overwhelm; panic; quake; *recoil;* scare; *shake;* tremble; terror; take fright; *uneasy; unnerved; vulnerable;* worry; wig out; *xenophobic; ydrad; zoophobic;*
**dream** *(n.)*: abstraction; *appearance;* bemusement; bad ~; *consumed;* delusion; *entrancement;* fantasy; fancy; *gibbered;* hallucination; hypnologic image; illusion; imagery; *incubus; jag; knocked out;* lethe; *mesmerism;* nightmare; oracle; phantasm; pipe ~; *quaffed;* reverie; sweven; trance; *unconsciousness;* vision; wraith; *x-fix; yumemi [Jap.]; zoned out;*
**dream** *(v.)*: *appearance;* bemuse; conjure up; conceive of; day~; envisage; evoke; fancy; fantasize; *gibber;* have ~; hallucinate; imagine; *jag;* knock out; *lethe; mesmerized; nightmare; oracle;* picture; *quaffed; reverie;* see (in one's ~s); stargaze; think of; *unconscious;* visualize; *woolgathering; x-fix; yumemi [Jap.]; zone out;*
**dreamer** *(n.)*: abstract-thinker; *builder;* creative person; day~; enthusiast; futurist; fancier; great visionary; hallucinator; imaginer; idealizer; John-a-dreams; keen-dreamer; *look ahead;* musard; *notional;* oracle; prophet; quixote; romanticist; stargazer; thinker; utopian; visionary; *woolgatherer; xtry.; yumeni [Jap.]; zetetic;*
**dreary** *(adj.)*: awful; bleak; cheerless; drab; dismal; drear(isome); enclouded; funereal; foreboding; gray; grim; gloomy; hazy; ill-omened; joyless; *keening;* lugubrious; murky; miserable; melancholic; *negative;* overcast; plaintive; *quad;* rayless; sombrous; tristful; unexciting; very glum; weariful; *xtry. gloomy;* yucky; *zestless;*

**drench** *(v.)*: *aqua;* bedrench; *clean;* douse; dunk; drouk; embrocate; flood; get soaked; humectate; indrench; jawp; *keelhaul;* lave; madefy; *non-dry; overwhelm;* plunge; *queven [arch.];* ret; soak; souse; teem; *under; vapor;* water-soak; *xtr.* wet; yote; zwish; [*Ant.* dry]

**dress** *(n. clothing)*: apparel; attire; bedizenment; clothing; clothes; duds; enrobing; finery; fashion; garb; garments; habiliments; investiture; *jumper;* knitwear; *loungewear;* mufti; *menswear; national dress;* outfits; *palliament [arch.]; quaintry* [arch.]; raiment; suit; trappings; togs; *uniform;* vesture; wardrobe; *XL; yelek [Turk.]; zari;*

**dress** *(n. woman's garment)*: apparel; attire; ball gown; clothing; caftan; chemise; durndel; deshabille; evening gown; frock; fillibeg; gown; home ~; *item of clothing;* jumper; kirtle; kimono; lounge ~; mini~; *muu muu* [Haw.]; night- ~; negligee; outfit; pinafore; polonaise; *quaintry [arch.];* rig; shirt~; sweater~; *skirt;* sacque; sari; sun~; tent ~; un~ [arch.]; vesture; whittle; wedding gown; *XS ~;* yelek [Turk.]; yukata; zari; [*see* garment]

**dress** *(v.)*: attire; apparel; adorn; array; bedeck; bedizen; clothe; clad; don; deck; enrobe; *fancify;* gird; get dressed; garb; habilitate; habit; invest; jacket; kit; *loungewear; make prettier; nice;* outfit; *overdress;* put on; palliate; prink; put on; *quaintise [arch.];* reapparel; rig; slip into; suit up; trim; uniform; vest; wear; *xuld [arch.];* yclad [arch.]; zip on; [*Ant.* disrobe]

**dresser** *(n.)*: armoire; bureau; chiffonier; chest (of drawers); *drawers; equipment; furniture;* garderobe; highboy; *item; jeans-drawer; keep;* lowboy; mahogany ~; *nook;* oak ~; *place; quadrilocular; room; sideboard;* tallboy; tansu; utility chest; vanity; wardrobe; *xtr. storage;* yew-wood ~; *zeta;*

**dribble** *(v.)*: *abate;* bleed; come out; drip(ple); emit; filter; *flow;* gleet; *hemorrhage;* issue; *jet;* kest; leak; *move; non-retention;* ooze; *pour; quicken;* rain; *run;* salivate; spill; secrete; trickle; *uprush;* vomit; weep; *xfer;* yote; *zip;* [*see* bounce]

**drift** *(v.)*: *afloat; adrift;* buoy; coast; deflow; *evolation;* float; flow; glide; hover; hang; *issue; jet;* kite; levitate; move on; *natant; oceanborne;* plane; *quicken;* rest; swim; sail; travel; upbear; volplane; waft; *xuld [arch.];* yede; *zip;*

**drill** *(n.)*: auger; borer; brace; carpenter's brace; drillpress; eggbeater ~; fraise; gimlet; hand ~; *item;* jadder; keyway ~; lancer; *machine; needle; object;* press; push ~; pneumatic ~; *quill;* reamer; screw starter; screwgun; tap; transfixer; *utility; ventilator;* wimble; *xylotomy;* Yankee push ~; *zeug;*

**drill** *(v.)*: auger; bore; *cut; drive;* empierce; fix [arch.]; gore; hole; impale; jab; knife; lance; make hole; *nail; needle;* open; pierce; puncture; *quill;* run through; ream; stab; thirl; transfix; *undercut; ventilate;* wimble; *xylotomy;* yerk; *zing;*

**drink** *(n. alcohol)*: alcoholic ~; bevvy; brew; chaser; deochandorius; *elixir;* fermented substance; *glass;* hard ~; intoxicating beverage; *jug; kava;* liquor; mixed ~; nerver; one for the road; potation; quaff; refection; substance; stirrup cup; *tequila; unmixed; vodka; wine; xeres;* yaffle; *zun;*

**drink** *(n. beverage)*: aliment; beverage; cold ~; concoction; *cup;* decoction; elixir; fluid; *glass;* hot ~; infusion; juice; *kava;* liquid (refreshment); long ~; *mug;* nectar; *one;* potion; potable; pick-me-up; quaff; refreshment; refection; refresco; substance; soft drink; tea; tonic; tisane; tall drink; thirst-quencher; *undiluted; volume;* wet drink; *xeres;* yaffle; *zero-calerie ~;*

**drink** *(v. consume alcoholic beverages)*: *absorb;* bib; booze; bevvy; carouse; down; *excess;* fuddle; guzzle; have one; imbibe; *jigger;* knock back; *liquor; mug;* nip; overdrink; outdrink; *partake;* quaff; *resorb;* swig; tipple; tope; *use; volume;* wash down; *xeres;* yaffle; *zip down;*

**drink** *(v. swallow)*: absorb; assimilate; bib; consume; chug; down [both slang]; extract; fuddle; gulp; guzzle; have; hydrate; imbibe; infuse; *juice;* knock back; lap (up) [zoo.]; lush; *milk;* nip; *overdrink; outdrink;* partake; quaff; *quench;* resorb; rehydrate; sip; swallow; swill; suck; slurp; swig; take in; tipple; *use; voracity;* wash down; *xeres;* yaffle; yolp; *zip down;* [*Ant.* discharge]

**drip** *(n.)*: accumulation; bead; conglobulation; drop(let); dribblet; eyedrop; *fleck;* globule; *hunk; iota;* jigger; *knot; liquid;* mass; *nugget;* ooze; *particle; quantity; raindrop;* splash; tear; trickle; *unit; vestige;* water-drop; *XL ~;* yelm; *zum [dial.];*

**drip** *(v.)*: *afflux;* bleed; come down; drizzle; emit; filter; fall; go down; *hurl;* issue; *jet;* kest; leak; lixiviate; *move; non-retention;* ooze; plummet; *quick-fall;* rain; secrete; *seep;* spill; tear; trickle; *unsealed; vent;* weep through; *xfer;* yote; *zip;*

**drive** *(v. force)*: actuate; boost; cast; direct; eject; force; goad; hammer; hurl; impel; jam; knock; *lunge;* move; nudge; over~; push; propel; pound; quant; ram; shove; thrust; upcast; vault; wale; *xuld* [arch.]; york; *zing;*

**drive** *(v. operate vehicle)*: actuate; accelerate; bring; bus; convey; *deliver; export;* fly [slang]; go; head; *impel;* jeep; journey; kepp going; locomote; move; navigate; operate; *onward;* proceed; *quick;* ride; run; stream; truck; travel; tootle; use car; van; wheel; xfer; yanker [Br.]; zip;

**driven** *(adj.)*: ambitious; ardent; bound and determined; burning; committed; determined; enthusiastic; eager; fervent; *go-getter;* high-reaching; impassioned; indefatigable; *jarred;* keen; lively; motivated; *non-lazy;* overzealous; pushing; passionate; *quickened;* resolved; self-motivated; self-starting; totally committed; untiring; vigorous; wholehearted; *xtry.;* yare; zealous;

**driver** *(n.)*: auriga; bus ~; buggy ~; coachman; cab ~; commuter; deliverer; *employee;* fellow who drives; *guy;* hackneyman; *individual;* jarvey; Jehu; kurveyor; limo ~; licensed ~; muleteer; motorist; *navigator;* operator; paid ~; pilot; *qualified ~;* reinsman; rig- ~; rider; stage coach ~; *servant;* truck ~; traveler; *user;* valet; vehicle operator; wagonman; wheelman; *x-port;* yanker operator; *zip;*

**droop** *(v.)*: arch; bow; curve; dangle; *enfold;* flop; go down; hang (down); *incline; jiggle; kneel;* lop; loll; move down; *nose-dive;* overhang; *pendulous; quat;* rest; sag; sink; slump; tire; turn down; *uncinate; verge;* wilt; *x-curve;* yield; *zero rigidness;*

**drop** *(n. decline)*: angle; belly-whop; crash dive; dive; descent; decline; *ever-downward;* fall; freefall; gainer; going down; headlong fall; *immergence;* jump down; keeling over; leap down; lowering; movement downward; nose-dive; *over the cliff;* plunge; plummet; quick-fall; reduction; sinking; slump; tumble; *undoing;* volt; whop; *x-cend; yanking down;* zoom downward;

**drop** *(n. drip)*: accumulation; bead; blob; conglobulation; dribble; drip; droplet; dew~; eye~; fleck; glob; *hunk; iota;* jigger; *knot;* leaking; mass; *nugget; ounce;* particle; quantity; rain~; smidgen; splash; trickle; tear(~); *unit; vestige;* water- ~; *x-cend;* yelm; *zum [dial.];*

**drop** *(v.)*: angle down; belly-whop; crash dive; dive; descend; *ever-downward;* (free)fall; go down; hurl down; immerge; jump down; keel over; let fall; lower; make nose-dive; nose-dive; *over the cliff;* plunge; plummet; plop; plump; quick-fall; release; reduce; sink; slump; tumble; unclench; vail; whop; *x-cend; yank down;* zoom down;

**dross** *(n.)*: argal; buildup; chaff; castoffs; dregs; emptyings; flysch; grouts; *heap;* impurities; junk; kaff [dial.]; lees; leavings; *matter; non-wanted matter;* orgal; offscourings; *pulp;* quittor; recrement; slag; scum; slag; scoria; tartar; *unclean;* vinasse; waste; *xysma; yuckiness; zero;*

**drought** *(n.)*: aridness; barrenness; crisis; drouth; dearth; extreme thirst; *famine;* grievous ~; *haskiness;* insufficiency; jejuneness; *keen thirst;* lack; *meagerness;* need; *over-thirsty;* parchedness; polydipsia; *quenchlessness;* rainlessness; shortage; scarcity; thirst; *under-hydrated;* vacuity; waterlessness; xerotes; xerosis; *yearning; zero water;*

**drown** *(v.)*: asphyxiate; bury; cover; deluge; demerse; deep six [slang]; douse; die; engulf; flood; go under; *hold;* inundate; *jawp;* keelhaul; *lower; merse; non-living;* overwhelm; overflow; plunge; perish; *queven [arch.];* ruin; sink; submerge; suffocate; *take one's life; under (the water); victimized;* whelm; *xuld* [arch.]: *ybaptized* [arch.]; *zet [dial.];*

**drudgery** *(n.)*: *action;* burden; chore; drudgework; effort; factory work; *fatigue;* grunt work; hard work; industry; job; *kitchen work;* labor; menial labor; moil; *night-work; occupation;* production; *quantity;* rigor; slog; toil; undesirable work; vocation; work; *wrought; xtry. ~; yardwork; zealous labor;*

**drug** *(n.)*: ∗ agent; antibiotic; amphetamine; angel dust; *barbiturate;* castor oil; crack; cocaine; controlled substance; dope; downer; electuary; fix; flucoxacillin; generic ~; galenical; grass; herb; hemp; heroin; illegal ~; jalap; joint; *kola;* laudanum; *LSD;* medication; marijuana; methane; mind-altering ~;

narcotic; opium; over-the-counter ~; pharmaceutical; penicillin; pills; quinine; *remedy;* substance; steroid; treatment; upper; vice; vancomycin; weed; xenobiotic; xtc; yarb [dial.]; yage; *zopissa [arch.]*

**drug** *(v.)*: analgize; benumb; *confer;* dope; desensitize; embrocate; fix; give medicine to; hit; *inject; jack;* knock out; lace; medicate; narcotize; numb; opiate; poison; physic; *quade [arch.];* relax; sedate; treat; tranquilize; *under- ~;* vaccinate; well- *~ed; xfer;* yield; zip;

**drum** *(n.)*: * ashiko; bass ~; bongo; canister; davul; *equipment;* frame ~; gangan; hand ~; *instrument;* Japanese ~; kettle~; *loud ~;* membranophone; *ngoma* [Afr.]; omele; percussion; pan; qilaut; raban; snare ~; tenor ~; tom-tom; tabor; tof; timbrel; *udukai* [Ind.]; *V-drum®;* water ~; *xam; yak bera* [Sri Lanka]; zabumba;

**drumbeat** *(n.)*: *action;* (back) beat; cadence; chamade [mil.]; drumming; *echo;* flam; gallop beat; hit; *heavy ~;* isorhythm; jam; knock; lam; *meter; noise;* ostinato beat; polt; quab; rhythm; rat-at-at; rock- ~; rataphan; sound of ~; tapping; tuck; *usul; vibration;* whack; "x"; yerk; *zafer [Turk.];*

**drunk** *(adj.)*: addled; besotted; blitzed; crocked; drunken; ebrious; fuddled; giddy; high; heady; intoxicated; inebriated; jag; kaylied; lit up; maudlin; nappy; overcome; plastered; pixilated; quaffed; reeling; soused; sottish; smashed; sloshed; tipsy; unsober; under the influence; *vineous;* well-oiled; woozy; *xanthoxylin;* yarked; zonked; [*Ant.* dry]

**drunkard** *(n.)*: alcoholic; bibber; boozer; carouser; drunk; drinker; elbow-bender; fuddler; guzzler; hooch hound; inebriate; *Jimmy Woodser [slang];* kirsch-drinker; lovepot; muddler; nipper; oenphilist; pot companion; quaffer; rummy; sot; toper; *underage drinker;* vinolent; winebibber; wino; wassailer; *xanthoxylic;* yiller; *zubrowka-drinker;*

**drunkenness** *(n.)*: alcoholism; befuddlement; crapulence; dipsomania; *ebrious;* fuddlement; guzzling; hard drinking; *hangover;* inebriation; intoxication; jag; katzenjammer; liquor-drinking; moonshining; nipping; obfuscation; potation; quasi-soberness; *rum; sot;* tipsiness; *unsober;* vinolency; winebibbing; *xanthoxylin; yveresce* [arch.]; zubrowka; [*Ant.* dryness]

**dry** *(adj.)*: arid; anhydrous; barren; bone- ~; brittle; chapped; dried; dehydrated; droughty; dryshod; evaporated; exsiccated; fountainless; *gone ~;* hot; hasky; insolated; jejune; kibe; *leakless; mummified;* non-watered; overhot; parched; quenchless; rainless; *roasting;* sun-dried; scorched; sere; torrid; thirsty; unwatered; vaporated; waterless; withered; wizened; warm; xeric; *yarrish; zapped;* [*Ant.* drenched]

**dry** *(v.)*: aerate; air out; air-dry; bake; chap; ~ up (-out); desiccate; demoisturize; dehydrate; evaporate; exsiccate; fire-dry; go ~; heat-dry; insolate; *jejune;* kiln-dry; lose moisture; make dry; *non-hydrated;* oven-dry; overdry; parch; *quail;* rub down; *roast;* sun-dry; torrefy; towel-dry; *use up;* ventilate; *vacuum dry;* weather; wither; *xeransis; yarrish; zap;* [*Ant.* drench]

**dryness** *(n.)*: aridity; aridness; barrenness; chapping; dehydration; drought; exsiccation; *emaciation; fire-dried;* grimness; heat; insolation; jejuneness; *kiln-dried;* lack of moisture; moisture-deprivation; non-moistness; over~; parchedness; quenchlessness; rainlessness; siccity; torridity; unmoisturization; vaporation; waterlessness; want of rain; *withering;* xerotes; xerosis; xeracity; *yarrish; zero moisture;* [*Ant.* dampness]

**dub** *(v.)*: anoint; brand; call; designate; ennoble; entitle; forename; give title to; hail as; identify; *jurisdiction;* knight; label; make known as; make noble; name; nobilitate; nickname; ordain; *phrase;* qualify; refer to; surname; style; term; tag; *use; vocable; word; xenonym;* yclept; *zoon;*

**duct** *(n.)*: aqueduct; black pipe; conduit; ductwork; electrical ~; flume; gutter; groove; hosepipe; irrigation canal; *j-bend pipe; kyle;* line; main; nullah; outlet; pipe; *quill* [arch.]; route; steel pipe; spillway; tube; trench; *underground pipeline;* ventiduct; water pipe; *x-ray tube;* Y-branch; zanja;

**duel** *(n.)*: affray; battle (of honor); challenge; contest; combat; confrontation; dispute; *dare;* encounter; face-off; fight to the death; gunfight; hand-to-hand combat; *incongruity;* jangle; knock-down-drag-out fight; *loggerheads;* monomachy; needle match [Br.]; occursion; *pick fight;* quarrel; run-in; showdown; sole combat; tussle; *unrest;* vying; warfare; *x-fire;* yed; *zapping;*

**dull** *(adj. boring)*: arid; average; boring; commonplace; drab; *empty;* flat; generic; humdrum; ho-hum; insipid; jejune; *known;* lackluster; mundane; monotonous; non-exciting; nondescript; operose; ponderous; quotidian; repetitive; soporific; savorless; tedious; tiresome; unexciting; uninteresting; uneventful; unoriginal; vapid; wearisome; *xtry. ~;* yawnful; zestless; [*Ant.* dynamic]
**dull** *(adj. not sharp)*: abraded; blunt; *curved;* dulled; edgeless; flat; gone ~; hebetate; in need of sharpening; *just not sharp; kibbled;* lacking sharpness; much-dulled; non-sharp; obtuse; obtundent; pointless; *quelled;* rounded; retuse; *smooth;* too ~; unpointed; unsharpened; very blunt; well-rounded; *x-out; yet unsharpened; zero sharpness;*
**dull** *(v.)*: assuage; blunt; cloud; disedge; deaden; *errode;* fail; get blunt; hebetate; impair; *jade; knock; lacking sharpness;* make ~; muffle; *non-sharp;* numb; obtund; *pointless; quell;* reduce; round; soften; *too dull;* unsharpen; *very dull;* wear smooth; *x-out; yet unsharpened; zeroize;*
**dumb** *(adj.)*: air-headed; brainless; clownish; dense; egg-headed; foolish; goofy; harebrained; half-witted; ignorant; imbecilic; jackass; knuckleheaded; lame-brained; mindless; moronic; nit-witted; obtuse; pea-brained; quacky; ridiculous; stupid; slow; senseless; thick(-witted); unintelligent; vacuous; *wacky; xtry. stupid; yokelish;* zany; [*see* mute]
**dumbfound** *(v.)*: astonish; amaze; bowl one over; confound; dazzle; *enchant;* flabbergast; gape; hold one's breath; impress; jolt; keel over; look aghast; make marvel; *nonplus;* overwhelm; perplex; *quite amazed;* render speechless; shock; stun; take back; unable to believe; *very impressed;* wonder; *xtry.;* yerk; zing;
**dumbstruck** *(adj.)*: astonished; awestruck; bowled over; confounded; dumbfounded; *enchanted;* flabbergasted; gobsmacked [Br.]; hushed; incredulous; *jolted;* knocked for six; *looking aghast;* much-awed; *nonplused;* overwhelmed; *perplexed;* quiet; rapt; speechless; thunderstruck; unable to believe; very stunned; *wonder; xtry.; yareless;* zitti [It.];
**dump** *(n.)*: *amassment; bags;* city ~; compost pile; dumping ground; *elimination; foul;* garbage ~; heap; *incineration;* junkyard; junk pile; kitchen midden; landfill; mound; midden; nuisance grounds [Can.]; *outskirts;* parkout; *pile;* quisquilliary; refuse pile; rubbish dump; scrapyard; scrapheap; trash heap; tip [Br.]; *useless items; vile;* wastelot; *xysma pit;* yard; zone;
**dung** *(n.)*: argol; buffalo chips; compost; cow chips; droppings; doo-doo; excrement; feces; fertilizer; guano; horsedung; intestinal discharge; jakes; *keytonuria; laystall;* manure; night soil; ordure; poop; *quisquillous;* refuse; stool; soil; sordes; scat; top-dressing; turd [vulg.]; *urine; vileness;* waste; xysma; *yuckiness;* zigg;
**dungeon** *(n.)*: *arrest;* bastille; cell; confinement; detention; encagement; *fetters;* gaol [Br.]; guardhouse; hold; incarceration; jail; keep; lockup; maximum security; *manacles;* oubliette; prison; quod; roundhouse; slammer; tollbooth; under lock and key; vile durance; ward; x; yard; zipper [coll.];
**duplicate** *(n.)*: apery; borrowing; (carbon) copy; clone; duplication; double; ditto; emulation; facsimile; *gesticulation;* holotype; *image; just alike; keep;* likeness; mimeograph; mirror-image; near-duplicate; offprint; photocopy; quadruplicate; reproduction; same; stat; triplicate; *unofficial copy;* very image; word-perfect; xerograph; *yellow copy;* zincograph;
**duplicate** *(v.)*: ape; borrow; copy; dub; emulate; follow; *geminate; holotype;* imitate; *just like; keep; look alike;* make copy; mimic; model; mimeograph; *near; offprint; overdub;* parrot; photocopy; quadruplicate; reprint; reproduce; replicate; re~; simulate; transcribe; use copier; *virtual; watch closely;* xerox; *yield; zincograph;*
**durable** *(adj.)*: abiding; *bearing through;* continuing; diuturnal; enduring; firm; good; hearty; heavy-duty; indissoluble; immortal; *just keeps going;* keen; lasting; long-lived; long-lasting; maintaining; never-tiring; obstinate; per~; perpetual; *quickening;* resilient; robust; rock-solid; sturdy; strong; stable; tough; time-tested; unbreakable; vibrant; well-built; *x-heavy;* yieldless; *zero perishing;* [*see* tough; *Ant.* delicate]

**duration** *(n.)*: amount; biding; continuation; diuturnity; extent; fixedness; gap; *happening;* interval; interspace; *journey; keeps going;* length; lapse; longevity; *magnitude; nonstop;* outriding; period; perpetuity; *quartile* [L.]; *ride out;* span; space; timespan; undisclosed amount of time; *voyage;* while; *xfer; yieldless; zet [dial.];*

**duress** *(n.)*: admonishment; bullying; coercion; compulsion; driving; exhorting; force; *getting;* high pressure; intimidation; *jumping on; knocking;* leaning on; making; necessitation; obliging; pressure; *quickening;* requiring; strong-arming; threat; urging; *violence;* weighing upon; *xuld [arch.];* yanking; zealously urging;

**dusk** *(n.)*: *after hours;* bedtime; close of the day; darkness; day's end; (early) evening; *fall of the sun;* gloam; *hour;* infuscation; *jettiness; kettle-black;* last light; moderate darkness; nightfall; night(time); *obscurity;* pitchiness; *q.n.; rest;* sunset; twilight; umbrage; vespers; *wink; x-ing; yester-evening; zone;* [*Ant.* dawn]

**dust** *(n.)*: ashes; bits; cinders; comminution; dirt; empasm; fragments; granules; grindings; household dirt; *ions; jot;* konis [Gr.]; lint; microparticles; *nast; obliterated;* pilm; particles; powder; *quashed;* rapil; smeddum; soil; sand; smithereens; talc; triturate; *undusted;* volcanic ash; white ash; *xeraphium; yttria;* zodiacal ~;

**dutiful** *(adj.)*: allegiant; bound by duty; committed; duteous; devoted; ever-faithful; faithful; *good;* heedful; inerrable; *jump to it;* keenly loyal; loyal; meticulous; never-failing; obedient; principled; questionless; responsible; submissive; true; unquestioning; vigilant; well-committed; *xtry.;* yielded; zealous; [*Ant.* delinquent]

**duty** *(n.)*: assignment; burden; business; charge; commission; demand; errand; *encumbrance;* function; grave responsibility; heavy demand; incumbency; job; key role; liability; mission; necessity; orders; obligation; place; post; position; *purpose; quest;* role; responsibility; service; *station;* sworn ~; task; undertaking; unction; vocation; work; *xci.; yoke;* zealous task;

**duty-bound** *(adj.)*: allegiant; bound by honor; constrained; compelled; duteous; ethically bound; forced; *good;* honor-bound; impelled; *just have to;* keenly compelled; liable; *loyal;* morally required; *necessity;* obliged; pledged; *questionless;* responsible; *submissive;* trusted; *unquestioning;* vigilant; well-committed; *xtry.; yielded;* zealous; [*Ant.* delinquent]

**dwell** *(v.)*: abide; bide; continue; domicile; exist; follow on; *go to;* hang one's hat; harbor; inhabit; *journey;* keep on; live; linger; lodge; make one's home; nest; occupy; pause; peregrinate; quarter; remain; reside; stay; sojourn; tarry; tabernacle; *use; voyage to;* wait; xenize; yerde [arch.]; *zip to;*

**dwindle** *(v.)*: abate; assuage; alleviate; break; bate; curb; contract; condense; *cut;* decrease; decline; diminish; dissipate; ease; ebb; fade; fall; go down; *hush; halt;* impair; *jump down;* knock down; languish; lessen; lower; minish; moderate; mitigate; *minimize; narrow; outgo;* peter out; quell; quail; reduce; recede; shrink; subside; taper; *undo; vanish;* wane; waste; *xerosis;* yield; zap;

**dying** *(adj.)*: almost dead; breathing one's last breaths; chemical- ~; departing; *deathbed;* expiring; fading away; going; half-dead; *ingraining; jaws of death;* kicking the bucket [slang]; leaving this life; moribund; near-dead; *over;* perishing; quelling; receding; rare; succumbing; taking leave; *undo;* vanishing; waning; *x-ing;* yield; *zapping;*

**dynamic** *(adj.)*: active; animated; brisk; bouncy; compelling; driving; energetic; forceful; fiery; go-getter; high-energy; intense; impassioned; *jumpy;* keen; lively; motivated; nippy; *overactive;* peppy; powerful; quick-moving; rapid-moving; rip-roaring; spirited; *take-charge; upbeat;* vibrant; vigorous; wimble; white-hot; *x-energy;* yeasty; zestful; [*Ant.* dull]

**dynasty** *(n.)*: ancestors; bloodline; clan; descent; empire; *era;* family; gens; house; imperial family; *jus soli* [L.]; kin; line; ménage; *Ming; near kinsman; offspring; people; period; quarter;* relations; ruling family; regime; sept [Ire.]; sovereignty; tribe; *umunna* [Afr.]; *vein; whanau* [N.Z.]; Xia; Yuan; zadruga [Slav.];

# E

**eager** *(adj.)*: anxious; ardent; avid; ambitious; bursting; committed; devoted; enthusiastic; excited; fervent; gung-ho; hungry; impatient; *jumping;* keen; keyed up; *lively;* motivated; *non-bored;* overzealous; passionate; quick; ready; raring; solicitous; spirited; thrilled; unreserved; vehement; wholehearted; *xtry. ~;* yare; zealous;

**eagerness** *(n.)*: anxiousness; avidness; alacrity; ardor; *burning desire;* commitment; devotion; enthusiasm; fervency; *gusto;* heart; impatience; *joy;* keenness; *liveliness; militancy; nationalism;* overzealousness; passion; quickness; readiness; spirit; *thrill;* unreservedness; vehemence; wholeheartedness; *x-fervor;* yareness; zeal;

**eagle-eyed** *(adj.)*: alert; acute-visioned; *behold;* conscientious; discerning; ever-watchful; *fine; good;* hawk-eyed; intentive; *judicious;* keen-eyed; longsighted; mindful; *noticing;* observant; perceptive; quick-eyed; *razor sharp;* sharp-sighted; *trained eye;* ultra-careful; vigilant; watchful; *xiphoidal;* yare; zero in;

**earlier** *(adj. + adv.)*: aforetime; antecedently; ahead; before(hand); beforetime; *commencing; day ~;* erst; former(ly); *gone on ~;* heretofore; in front of; in time past; just before; *kickoff;* leading; *morning; née;* onetime; *originally;* prior; previous(ly); past; preceding; protatic; quondam; retrospectively; *starting ~;* timely; unseasonable; very early; whilom; *xtry, early; yore; zero in;*

**early** *(adj.)*: antecedent; archaic; bygone; before (sunup, etc.); betimes; *commencing;* directly; embryonic; ere long; first; *genesis;* hatchling; initial; *jiffy; kick off;* leading; *morning;* number one; original; premature; preceding; quick; red-eye; rath; starting; soon; too soon; timeful; untimely; unseasonable; very ~; wee hours; *xenogenesis;* young; *zero tardiness;*

**earn** *(v.)*: achieve; attain; bring in; clear; collect; deserve; *exact;* fetch; gain; get (paid); gross; have coming; *increase;* justify; knock down; *land;* make; merit; net; ought to have; obtain; pull in; *profit; quoff;* receive; reap; secure; take in; *usury; valuate;* warrant; work for; *x-div; yield; zillions;* [*Ant.* expend]

**earnest** *(adj.)*: authentic; bona fide; confiding; definite; ever-faithful; frank; genuine; grave; honest; heartfelt; ingenuous; *just; known; legitimate; meant;* non-nonsense; open; pure; questionless; real; sincere; solemn; truthful; unperjured; veritable; *well-tried;* x-parent; *yare;* zealous;

**earring** *(n.)*: adornment; bauble; clip-on ~; diamong ~; elench; 14K ~; gold ~; hoop ~; *intaglio;* jewelry; *kickshaw;* ladies' ~; magnetic ~; *navette ~;* ornament; pendant; pearl ~; *quaintry; ruby ~;* stud; *trinket;* uvarovite; *valuables; water sapphire; xtal.;* yag; zircon ~;

**earth** *(n.)*: all the ~; blue marble [poet.]; *ball; cosmos; dirt;* domain of man (-Satan); *earthrise; everything; field;* ground; globe; geosphere; God's footstool; home; *humanity; inhabitants; joint nations of the ~; known world; large-scale;* macrocosm; natural world; orb; our world; *the* planet; *quaquaversal; real world;* sphere; Terra; universe; vale (of tears); world; *xtry. planet;* yeard [Scot.]; *zoa;*

**earthling** *(n.)*: anyone; *being;* citizen of earth; dweller of earth; earthman; earth-dweller; earther [derog.]; figure; guy [masc.]; human (being); homo sapiens; inhabitant of earth; joe [slang]; *kid; living soul;* man; mortal; *name; one; organism;* person; *quadragenarian;* resident; soul; tellurian; terrestrial; *underling; villager;* wight; worldling; woman [fem.]; *xenic;* yokel; zoon; [*Ant.* extraterrestrial]

**earthly** *(adj.)*: alluvial; bodily; corporeal; carnal-minded; *down here;* earthy; earthborn; earthen; fluvioterrestrial; fleshly; global; geotic; human; irreligious; just secular; *known; life down here;* material; mortal; mundane; natural; non-spiritual; of this earth; physical; profane; *quite normal; routine;* sublunary; subastral; subcelestial; secular; terrestrial; temporal; tellurian; terrene; under the sun; unspiritual; vile; worldly; *xenenthesis;* yeard [Scot.]; zoetical; [*Ant.* etheral]

**earthquake** *(n.)*: agitation; aftershock; bestirring; cataclysm; crack; diastrophism; disquieting; *earthdin* [arch.]; *fault (line);* geological disturbance; *heaving;* isoseismic; judder; *knocking;* lurching; *movement; natural disaster; opening;* primary wave; quake; rumble; seism; shaking; seaquake; temblor; tremor; upheaval; *vibration; wabble; xuld [arch.];* yaw(n); *zigzag;*

**eathquake-proof** *(adj.)*: aseismic; *base-isolated; covered;* danger-proof; earthquake-safe; *fortified; good; high quality;* insulated; indestructable; *just fine;* kept safe; *low-risk;* made ~; non-vulnerable; *okay;* protected; quakeproof; risk-free; rated earthquake-safe; shockproof; tremor-proof; unthreatened; very secure; well-protected; *xtry;* yet unendangered; *zero danger;*

**earthshaking** *(adj.)*: all-important; big; critical; devastating; earth-shattering; fantastic; great; grave; history-making; important; incredible; *jump to it;* key; life-threatening; momentous; newsworthy; *obligatory;* pressing; quantum; required; remarkable; significant; stunning; tremendous; urgent; vital; weighty; xtry.; *yearnful;* zero hour;

**earthwork** *(n.)*: *abatis;* bulwark; battlement; contravallation; defense; embankment; fortification; glacis; half-moon; intrenchment; *jardang;* knoll; line (of defense); mound; muniment; *non-endangered;* outwork; parapet; *quai;* rampart; sconce; talis; *upholding;* vallation; wall; *x-ed; yeming* [arch.]; *zone;*

**ease** *(n.)*: alleviation; break; comfort; *doing;* easiness; effortlessness; forbearance; gentleness; handiness; idleness; *journey's end;* kip; leisure; luxury; moderation; non-difficulty; *off;* pause; quiet(ude); rest; relaxation; slacking off; simplicity; time out; unwinding; vacation; *waning; x-rest; yawning;* zizz; [Ant. encumberance]

**ease** *(v.)*: abate; alleviate; break; bate; cut; decrease; diminish; dissipate; ebb; fade; go down; *hush;* improve; *jump down;* knock down; lessen; lighten; moderate; mitigate; minish; *non-difficult; outgo;* palliate; peter out; quail; quell; relieve; reduce; redress; subside; taper; take pressure off; unwind; vacation; wane; *xerosis;* yield; zap; [Ant. encumber]

**easel** *(n.)*: adjustable stand; *bear;* cat; canterbury; display ~; *equipment;* frame; *gadget;* holder; *instrument; jib;* kapellmeister stand; *leg;* music stand; neap; *object;* portable ~; quadripod; rest; stand; tripod; tetrapod; unipod; *vice;* wooden ~; x-stand; *yew-wood stand; zeug [G.];*

**easy** *(adj.)*: artless; basic; comfortable; cushy; *a* cinch; done easily; effortless; ergonomic; facile; *good;* handy; incomplex; *just simple;* kindergarten-level; low-brow; low-impact; laborless; mere; not difficult; non-strenuous; non-complex; oversimplified; piece of cake; quick-and- ~; relaxing; simple; *a* snap; too ~; uncomplicated; undemanding; very ~; way too ~; *x-type;* yare; *zero complexity;* [Ant. elaborate]

**easygoing** *(adj.)*: airy; affable; blithe; carefree; degage; even-tempered; fancy-free; good-natured; happy-go-lucky; indulgent; jaunty; keg-meg; laid-back; lighthearted; mellow; nonchalant; over-casual; pleasant-hearted; *quick-to-comply;* relaxed; sweet-tempered; tolerant; unambitious; unconcerned; *vapid;* work-shy; winsome; *xenarthrous;* yielding; *zealless;* [Ant. edgy]

**eat** *(v.)*: absorb; *ate;* break bread; banquet; consume; chew; chow down; digest; down; dine; devour; engorge; feed; fare; feast; graze; gustate; gobble; gorge; have; intake; ingest; indulge; junket; kill [joc.]; lunch (on); munch; nibble; nosh; over~; partake; *quill* [arch.]; raven; sup; swallow; *taste;* take in; tuck away; *under~; victual;* wolf (down); *xerophagy;* yaffle; *zip down;*

**eavesdrop** *(v.)*: *attend;* bug; *comprehend;* discern; espy; *follow;* give ear; hear; identify; *judge;* keep listening; listen in; mark; nose around; overhear; perceive; *pry; quietly listen; regard;* snoop; spy; try to listen; tap; *understand; volume;* wiretap; *xenodiagnose;* yield; *zero in;*

**ebb** *(v.)*: abate; assuage; alleviate; break; bate; curb; contract; condense; decrease; dwindle; decline; diminish; dissipate; ease; evanesce; fade; fall; go down; *hush;* halt; *impair; improve; jump down;* knock down; languish; lessen; lower; moderate; mitigate; *narrow; outgo;* peter out; quail; quell; recede; reduce; subside; taper; *undo; vanish;* wane; waste; *xerosis;* yield; zap; [Ant. efflux]

**eccentric** *(adj.)*: anomalous; balmy; bizarre; curious; deviant; eccentrical; funny; gonzo; heterotypical; irregular; jarring; kooky; loony; mad; nonstandard; nutty; odd; peculiar; queer; quacked; ridiculous; strange; scatty; screwball; totally weird; *senses;* unusual; unconventional; *variant;* weird; *xenomorphic; yokelish*; zany;

**eccentric** *(n.)*: abnormal individual; bizarre person; character; coot; deranged man; enigma; fruitcake; goof-ball; *hairbrain;* insane man; *just a little off;* kook; loony-bird; mental case; nut(case); oddball; peculiar man; quack; rare bird; strange bird; *type;* unusual person; very strange one; weirdo; *xtry. character;* yo-yo; zany;

**echo** *(n.)*: answer; boom; concurrent ~; duplication; echoing; feedback; *go again; hear again;* iteration; iterant ~; *just like; keep going; likeness;* mimicry; noise; *over again;* parroting; *quadruplicate;* resonance; reverberation; sound reflection; *tautological; utterance; verbigeration;* whisper; *xerograph; yielding; zoomimicry;*

**echo** *(v.)*: answer; bounce back; boom; copy; duplicate; emulate; feed back; give reverberation; *hear again;* iterate; imitate; *just like;* keep sounding; *likeness;* mimic; *noise; over again;* parrot; quote; repeat; reverberate; rebound; re-echo; resound; redouble; rumbling; sound back; thunder; *undergo; verbatim; words; xerograph; yield; zoomimic;*

**eclectic** *(adj.)*: assorted; broad-ranging; composite; diversified; derived; empirical; fully-diverse; *general;* heterogeneous; inclusive; jumbled; *kinds;* liberal; miscellaneous; mixed; *non-matching; other;* peculiar; pied; queer; rationalistic; sundry; selected; thrown-together; universal; varied; wide-ranging; *xeno-; yawed;* zany;

**eclipse** *(v.)*: *alter;* block; beat; cloud; cover; darken; encloud; exceed; fully ~; *garb;* hide; immerge; *jade;* keep hidden; lay over; mask; *not seen;* overshadow; obscure; partially ~; *quat [arch.]; run in front of;* shroud; *saronic;* surmount; thwart; transcend; umbrate; veil; *withdrawn; x; yank;* zero light;

**ecology** *(n.)*: animal ~; bioscience; conservationism; deep ~; environmentalism; field ~; *green;* habitat conservationalism; *ideology; jove; kind of thinking;* love of nature; marine ~; nature; *outdoors;* preservationism; quantitative ~; *recycling;* sere; syn~; tree-hugging [derog.]; *upper atmosphere; values;* world conservationism; xerosere; *yonder;* zoo- ~;

**economic** *(adj.)*: asset-control; budgetary; capitol-related; dollars-and-cents; economical; financial; fiscal; geo~; *hard cash;* inter-economic; *jiggy; kale;* lucrative; *tender;* monetary; macro~; *numbers; obol;* pecuniary; *quid [Br.];* riches; socio- ~; trade; *U.S. economy;* venture *capitol;* world ~; *xenocurrency; yen; zechin;*

**economical** *(adj.)*: affordable; *bon marché* [F.]; bargain-priced; cost-effective; discounted; dollar-stretching; dirt-cheap; economizing; frugal; good price; *half-priced;* inexpensive; *justified; knock-out prices;* low-cost; moderately-priced; nominal; *on sale;* pennywise; quite good; reasonable; reduced; scrimping; sixpenny; thrifty; uncostly; unexpensive; value-priced; within means; *xtry.; yellow tag sale; zero-profit;* [*Ant.* expensive]

**economize** *(v.)*: *austerity;* budget; cut back; curb; *decrease;* eke out; *frugal;* get by; hold back; *illiberal; judicious;* keep within means; limit; make cuts; *niggardly;* omit; pinch; *quail;* retrench; reduce; scrimp; skimp; spend less; tighten one's belt; use sparingly; *very cheap;* watch it; *x; yield; zero-expenditure;* [*Ant.* expend]

**economy** *(n.)*: affairs; brevity; conciseness; circulation; commerce; closed ~; diversified ~; economic situation; financial shape; geo~; GNP; *home ~;* international trade; *J effect; krugerrands;* local ~; market; managed ~; national ~; open ~; planned ~; *quantity; recession;* succinctness; spending; stock market; trade; *U.S. ~;* venture capital; world ~; *xenocurrency; yen; zechin;*

**ecosystem** *(n.)*: animal habitat; biosphere; biocenosis; closed system; cycle; *deep ecology;* environment; *food chain;* gestalt; habitat; inhabitance; *jungle; kept alive;* life system; microhabitat; nature; *outskirts;* purlieus; *qualified ~; rain forest;* system; sere; terrarium; unit; vicinage; world; xenosere; *yonder;* zoological-botanical ~;

**ecstasy** *(n.)*: afterglow; bliss; cheerfulness; delirium; elation; euphoria; felicity; fulfillment; glee; gratification; happiness; hilarity; intoxication; joy; *keenness;* levity; merriment; *nice feeling;* overjoy; pleasure; *queme;* rapture; seventh heaven; satisfaction; thrill; transport; *uplifted; vivacity;* winsomeness; *xanadu;* yeastiness; zestfulness; [*Ant.* enragement]

**ecstatic** *(adj.)*: animated; blissful; cheerful; delighted; elated; euphoric; felicitous; gleeful; gratified; happy; intoxicated; joyous; *keen;* lighthearted; merry; *nice;* overjoyed; pleased; *queme;* rhapsodic; satisfied; thrilled; transported; uplifted; *vivacious;* well-pleased; *xanadu;* yeasty; zestful; [*Ant.* enraged]

**ecumenical** *(adj.)*: all-faith; broad-minded; co-operative; cross-denominational; catholic; *denominational;* ecumenic; ecumenistic; faith-community; global; *heterogeneous;* irenic; interdenominational; interfaith; joint-faith; Judeo-Christian-Islamic; *keeping an open mind;* liberalistic; multi-faith; noninsular; one-world church; polychurch; pluralistic; *quasi-Christian;* reunionist; *sympathetic;* transdenominational; universal; *Vatican II;* wide-minded; *x-denominational; yielding; zero-separation;*

**ecumenicism** *(n.)*: all-faiths; broad-mindedness; co-operation; denominational co-operation; ecumenism; ecumenicism; faith community; global ~; *heterogeneous;* irenicism; interdenominationalism; joint operation; *keeping an open mind;* large-mindedness; *liberalism;* multi-faith co-operation; noninsularity; N.C.C.; one-world church; polychurchism; pluralism; *quasi-Christian;* reunionism; spirit of unity; transdenominationalism; *unity; Vatican II;* wide-mindedness; W.C.C.; *x-denominationalism; yielding; zero-separation;*

**eddy** *(n.)*: around; backset; counterflow; downward spiral; *effect;* funnel; gurge; gyre; hurling; hurricane; ill wind; *jee; keel; loop;* maelstrom; nutation; *orb;* purling; querl; rotary; swirl; twirl; turbillion; *undercurrent;* vortex; whirligig; whirlpool; *x-ing; yede; zwoosh around;*

**edge** *(n.)*: abuttal; border; boundary; bounds; brim; brink; coast; circumference; dawn; environs; fringe; frontier; fore-edge; *gilded edge;* hem; inception; interface; *imbordered; jurisdiction; kept limit;* line; limit; margin; *narrow;* outskirts; perimeter; quadra; rim; side; skirt; selvage [fabric]; threshold; ulterior; verge; *without; x-border; yonder;* zenith; [*see* advantage]

**edgewise** *(adj.)*: across; breadthways; crosswise; crabwise; dead level; edgeways; flat; *ground;* horizonal; incumbent; jacent; *knocked over;* longways; longwise; *mean;* non-vertical; on-edge; procumbent; *quasi-horizontal;* recumbent; sideways; sidelong; turned; unsloping; *vegetating;* wide; x-axis; *yede; zero verticalness;*

**edgy** *(adj.)*: anxious; apprehensive; bothered; concerned; disturbed; distressed; easily upset; fretful; gutless; hesitant; insecure; ill at ease; jittery; jumpy; keyed up; lily-livered; much-bothered; nervous; overanxious; perturbed; peaceless; quaky; restless; stressed; tense; uneasy; vexed; worried; *xenophobic;* yeasty; *zapped;* [*Ant.* easygoing]

**edible** *(adj.)*: alimental; *bearable; chewable;* consumable; comestible; cibarious; digestible; decoctable; eatable; esculent; fit-to-eat; *food; gnawable;* good for food; healthy-to-eat; ingestible; *just fine; keen; legitimate;* meant-to-eat; manducable; nourishing; okay to eat; palatable; queme; risk-free; suitable; *tasty;* usable; *victual;* wholesome; *xarque;* you can eat it; yummy; *zero problem;*

**edict** *(n.)*: act; behest; bill; commandment; decree; diktat; enactment; fiat; government order; hest; injunction; interdict; *jus gentium* [L.]; *keleusmatic;* law; mandate; *necessity;* order; pronouncement; proclamation; *quo minus* [L.]; rule; statute; *tenet;* ukase; ultimatum; *verdict; word;* XO mandate; *yardstick; zakon* [Rus.].

**edification** *(n.)*: amelioration; advancement; building (up); construction; development; education; enhancement; expansion; furtherance; growth; help; instruction; improvement; *jumping ahead; keep growing;* lifting up; melioration; *new-vamp;* optimization; progression; perfecting; *quantum increase;* refinement; strengthening; teaching; upbuilding; *vamping;* working good; *xtry.;* yielding better things; *zest up;* [*Ant.* erosion]

**edify** *(v.)*: ameliorate; advance; build (up); construct; develop; educate; enhance; further; grow; help; instruct; improve; *jump ahead; keep growing;* lift up; make better; *new-vamp;* optimize; progress; perfect; *quantum increase;* refine; strengthen; teach; upbuild; *vamp;* work good; *xtry.;* yield better things; *zest up;* [*Ant.* erode]

**edit** *(v.)*: alter; blue-pencil; change; doctor; emend; enhance; fix; go over; *help;* improve; jib; *key to; legitimize;* modify; novate; overhaul; put right; *qualify;* revise; redact; switch; tweak; touch up; tailor; update; vamp; work on; *xenomorph; yaw; zigzag;*

**editor** *(n.)*: annotator; book publisher; *boss;* checker; censurer; copyreader; copy ~; diakeuast; editor-in-chief; feature ~; general ~; gazetteer; *helper;* improver; journalist; *key to;* lead writer; managing ~; newspaper ~; overhauler; paragrapher; pressman; *qualify;* reader; reviser; redactor; sub~; sports ~; textual ~; updater; vamper; war correspondent; *xenomorph; yokemaster; zaikei;*

**educate** *(v.)*: acquaint; bring up-to-date; condition; catechize; disciple; enlighten; foster; guide; ground; home school; instruct; impart; *jobation; knock into;* lecture; *misteach;* mentor; nurture; *open one's eyes;* prime; pedagogue; qualify; ready; rear; re- ~; school; teach; unlock; verse; work with; xenagogue; *yak; zealously instruct;*

**education** *(n.)*: apprenticeship; academics; book-learning; coaching; *the* classroom; catechization; discipleship; erudition; fostering; formal ~; guidance; grounding; higher ~; instruction; impartation; indoctrination; *junior college; knowledge;* lessons; lecturing; learning; mentoring; nurturing; *oversight;* pedagogy; preparation; qualification; readying; *re~;* studies; schooling; scholarship; teaching; training; upbringing; versing; vocational training; *working with;* xenagogy; yarking; *zealous studying;*

**educational** *(adj.)*: academic; bookish; catechetical; didactic; educating; *formal;* guiding; heuristic; instructive; judicious; knowledge-gaining; learning; mentoring; noetic; *over-educated;* pedagogical; preceptive; *qualifying; readying;* rabbinical; scholastic; teaching; tutorial; university; *verse; working;* xenagogic; yarking; *zealous to learn;*

**eerie** *(adj.)*: abnormal; bizarre; creepy; daunting; evil; foreboding; frightful; ghastly; ghostly; ghoulish; haunted; intimidating; jarring; knee-knocking; lurid; macabre; nerve-racking; ominous; peculiar; queer; rattling; spooky; terrifying; unnerving; unnatural; *vampirical;* weird; *xenophobic; ydrad* [arch.]; zonky;

**effect** *(n.)*: aftermath; byproduct; consequence; derivative; end result; éclat; fruit; *get;* harvest; impression; impact; influence; *just desserts; known outcome;* lattermath; *matter; necessarily;* outcome; product; perlocution; quantum ~; ramification; result; side ~; significance; sequent; termination; upshot; *validity;* work; wake; *xenagogy;* yield; *zeug [G.];*

**effect** *(v.)*: achieve; accomplish; bring about; carry out; create; do; engineer; fashion; generate; have; implement; *job; knock together; labor;* make; *necessary;* originate; produce; *quick-build;* realize; shape; turn out; upbuild; *vamp;* work; *x-effect;* yield; *zet [dial.];*

**effective** *(adj.)*: active; adept; able; *beneficial;* capable; deft; effectual; efficacious; functioning; good; helpful; impacting; influential; *just what's needed;* keen; *lattermath;* mighty; nonfailing; operative; proficient; powerful; potent; *qualified;* resulting; serviceable; sufficient; successful; tenable; useful; valuable; well-able; working; workable; *xtry. qualified;* yarkened; *zealous;*

**effectiveness** *(n.)*: ability; *beneficialness;* capability; deftness; efficacy; force; good; helpfulness; impact; *just what's needed;* keenness; *lattermath;* mightiness; *natural ability;* operativeness; power; *qualification;* results; success; *tenability;* use; value; weight; workability; *x-effect;* yarkening; *zeal;*

**effeminate** *(adj.)*: androgynous; *beautiful;* bisexual; camp; delicate; epicene; enervated; feminized; girlish; gynandromorphous; hermaphroditical; inter-sexual; jemmy; *khanith* [Arab.]; lace-on-your-underwear; moffie; mampala [Carib.]; muliebrous; namby-pamby; overly ~; pantywaist; queenie; *real ~;* sissified; soft(ling); tender; transvestite; unmanly; unmanlike; unmasculine; *voluptuous;* womanly; womanish; womanlike; *weak;* xanith [Arab.]; *yellow;* zero manliness; [*Ant.* ever-manly]

**effervescent** *(adj.)*: active; animated; aerated; bubbly; *cheerful;* dynamic; energetic; enthusiastic; frisky; fizzy; foaming; frothing; *glowing; gaseous;* high-spirited; impassioned; *jumpy;* kedge; lathering; lively; light-hearted; mirthful; nippy; *overactive;* pert; pétillant; quickened; robust; sibilant; spirited; sprightly; sparkling; *thrilled;* upbeat; vivacious; wimble; *x-energy;* yeasty; zippy; zesty;
**efficiency** *(n.)*: adeptness; *best way;* cost-effectiveness; *dynamic;* economy; *fuel- ~; good;* high ~; *impact; just what's needed; keenness;* labor- ~; minimal effort; non-wastefulness; organization; proficiency; quantum ~; resource conservation; sensibility; streamlining; top ~; ; unwastefulness; *virtuously;* waste- ~; *xtry. management;* yieldfullness; *zero waste;*
**efficient** *(adj.)*: adept; best; cost-effective; dynamic; economical; *fuel- ~;* good; highly ~; *impressive; just what's needed; keen;* labor-saving; minimal-effort; managed well; maximum-efficiency; non-wasteful; organized; proficient; *quick;* resource- ~; sensible; streamlined; thrifty; top-efficiency; unwasteful; virtually waste-free; well-managed (-handled); *xtry.;* yieldfully; zero-waste;
**effigy** *(n.)*: alikeness; *bearing resemblance;* carving; dummy; exact likeness; figure; *guy; head;* image; *just like; kind of like;* likeness; mock-up; manequin; near-likeness; *object;* portrayal; *quirk;* representation; similitude; *scarecrow; thing; use;* visual representation; *with comparison;* xoanon; *yet alike; zeug [G.];*
**effort** *(n.)*: attempt; bid; crack; determination; endeavor; energy; exertion; full-blown attempt; go; hard work; intensity; *jeopardizing;* kemp; labor; *move;* nisus; *offer;* push; physical exertion; quest; *reattempt;* shot; stab; striving; try; toil; undertaking; venture; work; *xuld [arch.];* yearning; zeal; [*Ant.* ease]
**egalitarian** *(adj.)*: anti-discriminatory; believing in equality; classless; democratic; equal(itarian); fair-minded; free; *good;* honest; impartial; just; keeping justice; *legitimate; moral;* non-discriminatory; objective; plain-dealing; *quality;* righteous; square; true; unbiased; virtuous; *worthy; Xn.; yet unblamable;* zero-bias;
**egotism** *(n.)*: arrogance; bigheadedness; conceit; disdain; egocentricity; fullness of self; gloating; haughtiness; inflatedness; *jackanapes; know-it-all;* loftiness; megalomania; narcissism; overconfidence; pride; *quilicom* [arch.]; *ruff* [arch.]; self-adoration; self-importance; snobbery; turgidity; *unhumbled;* vanity; wind; *xenophobia; yieldless; zero humility;* [*Ant.* effacement]
**egotist** *(n.)*: *arrogant;* braggart; boaster; crower; *delighter;* egoist; fanfaron; gloater; huff; *inflated;* Jack-the-lad; know-it-all; loudmouth; monopolist; narcissist; ostentator; popinjay; quidnunc; roisterer; swaggerer; *trumpeter;* ululator; vain person; *wallower; x-proud;* yelper; *zero humility;*
**egotistical** *(adj.)*: arrogant; big-headed; conceited; disdainful; egocentric; flatulent; glass-glazing; haughty; inflated; *jackanapes; know-it-all;* lofty; much-inflated; narcissistic; overproud; proud; puffed up; quick-to-boast; *reassured;* stuck-up; turgid; unhumbled; vain; wrapped up in oneself; *x-proud; yelping; zero humility;* [*Ant.* effaced]
**Egypt** *(n.)*: Arab Rep. of Egypt; *Aegypt* [L.]; *Alexandria; Bahnamuh;* Cairo; desert; Egyptian Empire; *Faris; Goshen;* Ham; *Idku; Jabal;* Kingdom of ~; Kimi [Coptic]; Land of Ham; Mizraim; Nile Region; North Africa; *Ofira;* pharaonic ~; Qattara; *Ramsis; Sadaqa; Tag El-lzz;* Upper Nile; *valley of the Nile; the world; xerarch; Yasdenia;* Zaqaziq;
**Egyptian** *(adj.)*: ancient ~; *Alexandrian; Bedouin;* Coptic; *Cairene; Demotic;* Egypt; *Faris; Goshen;* Hamitic; *Heiroglyphic; Idku; Jabal; Kafr Abaza; Lahun;* Mizraim; *Middle Kingdom;* Nile; North African; of Egypt; Old Kingdom; *pharonic; Qattara; Ramsis; Sadaqa; Tag El-lzz;* Upper Nile; valley of the Nile; *Wafd; xanthomelanoi; Yasdenian;* Zaghlulist;
**eject** *(v.)*: *abandon;* betoss; cast; catapult; discharge; expel; fling; force; fire off; go out; hurl; impel; jettison; kest; launch; make to expel; *non-retention;* outthrow; oust; project; propel; *quoit; recast;* sling; shoot; throw; thrust; upcast; vomit; vault; wale; *xuld* [arch.]; york; *zing;* [*Ant.* eat]
**elaborate** *(adj.)*: abstruse; bewildering; complicated; complex; detailed; embellished; fancy; gordian; high-wrought; intricate; involved; *jarring;* knotty; labyrinthine; mind-boggling; non-easy; overly involved; overwhelming; perplexing; *question-filled;* recondite; sophisticated; tricky; unsearchable; vexatious; well-wrought; wildering; *xenagogic; yucky; zero easiness;* [*Ant.* easy]

**elaborate** *(v.)*: add to; build on; comment; develop; explain; expound; enlarge; extend; further discuss; go into detail; heighten; *illuminate; jump up; keep growing;* largen; make bigger; *nourish; outgrow;* particularlize; *quadruplicate; rise;* spell out; *throw light on; uncloud; verse;* write; work up; *xtn; yain* [arch.]; zoom-in;

**elapse** *(v.)*: advance; *betide;* come and go; *drift by;* expire; flow; go by; *happen;* intervene; *journey; kep;* lapse; move by; *number;* occur; pass; *quicken;* roll by; spend; slip away; take place; transpire; use up; vanish; waste; *wait; went; xfer;* yede; zip by;

**elastic** *(adj.)*: adjustable; adaptable; bouncy; contractile; ductile; expandable; flexible; flexile; *give;* highly contractile; infirm; *jiggly; keen;* lithe; latex; limber; *moveable;* non-rigid; *overstretch;* pliant; *quivering;* rubbery; resilient; supple; springy; stretchy; stretchable; tensile; *unfixed;* variable; visco~; whippy; *xapuri;* yielding; *zingy;*

**elasticity** *(n.)*: adjustability; adaptability; bounciness; contractility; changeableness; ductility; expandability; flexibility; *give;* high contractility; infirmness; *jiggliness; keenness;* litheness; limberness; mutability; non-rigidity; *overstretch;* pliability; pliancy; *quivering;* rubberiness; resiliency; stretch; stretchability; tensility; *unfixed;* visco~; willowiness; *xapuri;* yielding; *zinginess;*

**elate** *(v.)*: applaud; beam; bless; cheer; delight; exult; *frisk;* glory; *hurray; imparadised;* joy; kill the fatted calf; lilt; laugh; make merry; *nowell;* overjoy; praise; party; *quiver;* rejoice; *shout;* thrill; uplift; vivify; *wonder; xanadu;* yell; *zestful;* [*see* praise]

**elation** *(n.)*: animation; bliss; cheerfulness; delirium; exultation; exuberance; euphoria; felicity; glee; gaity; hilarity; intoxication; jubilation; *keenness;* lightheartedness; merriment; *niceness;* overjoy; pleasure; *queme;* rejoicing; rapture; seventh heaven; thrill; transport; *uplifted; vivacity;* winsomeness; *xanadu;* yeastiness; zestfulness;

**elder** *(adj.)*: adult; bigger; *chronicled;* dated earlier; earlier; first-born; former; grown (up); historic; inveterate; *jaded; kept;* longer-lived; more mature; *nostalgic;* older; past; quondam; *ripened;* senior; time-honored; *upper;* vintage; well-matured; *XO; yellowed; zet* [dial.];

**elder** *(n.)*: ancient men; *boss;* church officer; doyen; deacon; elderly man; *first;* gray-headed man; hoary head; inveterate man; *judicious;* kirk-maister [Scot.]; *layman;* mature man; *non-ordained deacon;* old man; officer; *pillar;* qualified man; right-hand man; senior; trustee; *usher;* venerable old man; wise man; *xenagogue; years; zet* [dial.];

**elderly** *(adj.)*: aged; anile; bygone; *chronicled;* dated; decrepit; early; full-grown; *feeble;* geriatric; gray-headed (-haired); *hoary; infirm; jaded; kept;* long-standing; mature; *nostalgic;* over-the-hill; old; *prehistoric; quondam;* ripe(ned); *retired;* senior; senescent; stricken in years; time-honored; time-worn; tottering; *up in years;* veteran; well-along in years; well-worn; *Xanthian; yore; zillions of years old;*

**eldest** *(adj.)*: *aged;* beginning; commencing; debuting; earliest; first(born); *genesis; hatched first;* initial; *judicious; knowledgeable; leading;* most-aged; number one; oldest; primigenial; *quickened; rising;* starting; *top; unprecedented; vaunt* [arch.]; *wisest;* xenogenesis; *years;* zygogenesis;

**elect** *(adj.)*: appointed; before-ordained; chosen; determined; destined; elected; elite; foreordain; foreappointed; forechosen; foreknown; God-appointed; hand-picked; heaven-ordained; institute; *judge; known; let be known;* made afore; *necessitated;* ordained; predestinated; predetermined; preordained; preselected; *qualified;* resolved; selected; sovereignly chosen; taken; *used; verdict;* well-chosen; *x-scending; yonder;* zero choice;

**elect** *(v.)*: accept; appoint; *ballot;* choose; decide; *election;* favor; foreordain; give choice; hand-pick; indicate; judge; *keen on; like;* make choice; mandate; *nominate;* opt for; ordain; pick; predestinate; predetermine; *qualify;* resolve; select; sovereignly choose; take; *use;* vote for; want; x; *yes; zealous for;*

**election** *(n.)*: alternativity; ballot; choice; decision; determinism; electing; favoring; foreordaining; gall; *hand-picked;* indication; judgment; *key choice;* local ~; majority vote; national ~; opinion; poll; pick; preference; plebiscite; predestination; predeterminism; *qualification;* referendum; resolve; suffrage; selection; show of hands; *taking; usage;* vote; write-in ballot; X; *yes; zeal for;*

**electrocute** *(v.)*: annihilate; burn; cook; do in; electrify; fry; give the electric chair; *high voltage; incinerate;* jolt; kill; liquidate; *melt; newton;* obliterate; put to death; *quell;* rub out; slay; shock; take one's life; *unseat; volts;* waste; *x-out; yowtch;* zap;

**elegance** *(n.)*: appeal; beauty; charm; class; daintiness; delicacy; elegancy; exquisiteness; fanciness; fashionableness; fineness; grace(fulness); high-style; impressiveness; jimp; *keenness;* loveliness; manners; magnificence; niceness; *over~;* poise; polish; quaintness; refinement; swank; stylishness; tastefulness; *uncommonness; Victorian; well-refined; xlty.; younker; zierlich [G.];*

**elegant** *(adj.)*: appealing; beautiful; charming; dainty; delicate; exquisite; fancy; graceful; genteel; high-society; impressive; impeccable; jimp; *keen;* lovely; mannered; neat; nice; ornate; *overelegant;* prim; poised; polished; posh; quaint; refined; swank; stylish; suave; tasteful; uptown; *uncommon;* Victorian; well-refined (-dressed); XF; *younker; zierlich* [G.]; [*Ant.* earthy]

**element** *(n.)*: aspect; atomic ~; bit; building block; component; constituent; division; degree; essential part; faction; factor; feature; *group; hint; habitation;* ingredient; item; *jib; kernel; landform ~;* member; molecule; *nugget; ought;* part; quantity; *remnant;* segment; section; substance; thing; trait; *touch; unit; vestige; wee thing; x-mal [G.]; yngot* [arch.]; zum [dial.]; [*Ant.* entirety]
    **Elements**: Argon; Barium; Carbon; Dysprosium; Einsteinium; Fermium; Gallium; Hydrogen; Iridium; Krypton; Lithium; Magnesium; Nitrogen; Oxygen; Plutonium; Radium; Sodium; Titanium; Uranium; Vanadium; Xenon; Yttrium; Zinc;

**elemental** *(adj.)*: absolute minimal; basic; constituent; deep-seated; essential; fundamental; *greatest; highest;* intrinsic; *just the basics;* kernel; key; *leading; main;* necessary; *original;* primary; quintessential; rudimentary; *supporting; top;* underlying; vital; *warp and woof; xenenthesis; yod;* zoetic; [*Ant.* entire]

**elevate** *(v.)*: advance; arise; boost; bring higher; climb; *develop;* escalade; ennoble; *fly;* go up; heighten; honor; increase; jack up; *keep going up;* lift (up); make higher; *new heights; overgrow;* put high up; promote; *quantum increase;* raise; surmount; *stand upright;* transcend; uphoist; uplift; verge upward; wax higher; *xfer; yain* [arch.]; *zoom up;*

**elevation** *(n.)*: altitude; boost; climb; degree of ~; *distance;* elevating; feet above sea level; going up; height; increase; jacking up; kanjira; lifting (up); level; loftiness; making higher; number of feet; *overgrowth;* putting high up; promotion; *quantum increase;* rise; surmounting; transcendence; upward ~; verticalness; waxing higher; *xfer; yain* [arch.]; *zenith;*

**eligibility** *(n.)*: availability; adequateness; *befitting;* capability; *deserving;* eligibleness; fitness; goods; *highly recommended; idoneous;* justification; *kosher;* legitimacy; makings; marriageableness; *not barred; over-qualification;* properness; qualification; rightness; recommendation; suitableness; *trueness; untaken;* validity; worthiness; *xtry.; yichus; zero problem;*

**eligible** *(adj.)*: available; adequate; befitting; capable; deserving; eminently qualified; fit(ting); good; highly deserving; idoneous; justified; *keenly ~;* legitimate; marriageable; meritorious; *notable; outstanding;* proper; qualified; right; suitable; single; *true;* untaken; unmarried; up for; valid; worthy; well-suited; *xtry.;* yichus; *zealous;*

**eliminate** *(v.)*: abolish; *ban;* cut off; cancel; destroy; do away with; dispense with; eradicate; exterminate; finish; get rid of; *halt; illegalize;* jettison; kill; *let go;* liquidate; make an end of; nullify; outlaw; put an end to; quash; rid; remove; stop; throw out; terminate; undo; void; vitiate; wipe out; x-out; *yank;* zero out; [*Ant.* erect]

**elimination** *(n.)*: abolishment; annihilation; *banning;* cutting off; cancellation; destruction; eradication; extermination; finishing (off); getting rid of; *halting; illegalization;* jettisoning; killing (off); liquidation; making an end of; nullify; outlawing; obliteration; putting an end to; quashing; ridding; removal; stopping; termination; undoing; voiding; wiping out; x-out; *yanking;* zeroing out; [*Ant.* erection]

**elixir** *(n.)*: admixture; brew; blend; concoction; compound; drink; decoction; emulsion; formula; go-go juice; *hypnotic potion;* intermixture; *juice; karakia [Maori]; love potion; liquid;* mixture; medicine; *nectar; old recipé;* potion; quintessence; remedy; recipé; serum; suspension; tonic; *ule; volatile substance;* witches' brew; *xenophobic;* yanggona; *zauber [G.];*
**eloquence** *(n.)*: articulateness; beauty; charm; charisma; dynamism; expression; eloquentness; fluency; facundity; grandiosity; grace; *honey-mouthed;* influence; inspiration; *jim-dandy;* keenness; lucidity; magnificence; noteworthiness; oratory; polish; persuasiveness; power; *quantum [L.];* refinement; skill; suavity; speechcraft; *touching; unbelievable skill;* volubility; wordcraft; *xtry. skill;* yareness; zeal;
**eloquent** *(adj.)*: articulate; beautiful; charismatic; dynamic; elocutionary; fluent; facund; grandiloquent; graceful; honey-mouthed; heart-stirring; influential; inspiring; *jim-dandy;* keen; lucid; moving; magnificent; noteworthy; oratorical; polished; persuasive; powerful; *quantum* [L.]; refined; resplendent; suave; silver-tongued; skillful; touching; *unbelievable;* voluble; well-spoken (-articulated; -penned); xtry.; yare; zealous;
**elude** *(v.)*: avoid; beguile; circumvent; dodge; evade; escape; forestall; flee; get away; *hide; insnare;* jink; keep away from; leave; miss; *negotiate around;* obviate; outfox; outflank; parry; *quite [Sp.];* run away from; skirt; turn away from; utterly ~; *veer away;* withdraw; *x-out;* yerk; zip away;
**elusive** *(adj.)*: abstract; baffling; cunning; deceptive; elusory; evasive; fleeting; foxy; guileful; hard to find; illusive; *judicious;* knavish; *lying;* mysterious; non-trustworthy; obscure; pawky; *quiet; roguish;* subtle; slippery; stealthy; tricky; *underhanded;* vague; wily; *xtry.;* yepe; *zinger;*
**emanate** *(v.)*: *aura;* beam; come; discharge; emit; exude; flow; give off; go forth; gush; *hurl;* impart; issue; jet; *knock out; leak; mete out; naid;* ooze; output; produce; proceed from; *quick flow;* radiate; shed; stream; throw; unleash; *vection; waft; x-radiate;* yield; zap;
**emasculate** *(v.)*: alter; bowdlerize; castrate; demasculinize; effeminate; eunuchate; fix; geld; hamstring; *inert; jemmy;* kern; lib; make sexless; neuter; *operate;* poulardize [fem.]; queenie; remove; sissify; sterilize; *truncate;* unsex; *vasectomy;* weaken; *x-sect; yield one's masculinity;* zeroize;
**embalm** *(v.)*: *aromatize;* bind up; coil up; dry-cure; enwrap; eternalize; *formaldehyde;* gird; *hold;* imbalm; *jaga;* keep; lie in state; mummify; *necropolis;* overwrap; pickle; prepare (for burial); preserve; *quoil [arch.];* ravel; stuff; treat; taxidermy; upbind; *volt;* wrap up; *xerodermic;* yeme; *zone;*
**embargo** *(n.)*: absconding; ban; constraint; debarment; exclusion; forbiddance; government interdict; hindering; injunction; interdiction; jurisdictional bar; *keeping out;* lockout; *mandate;* nonadmission; order; prohibition; proscription; *quell;* restriction; stoppage; *thwarting; unpermitted; veto;* withhold; *xeno-prohibition; ybarred [arch.];* zoning laws;
**embark** *(v.)*: activate; board; begin; commence; debut; enter in; *found;* get started; get on; go (ahead); head; initiate; jump-start; kick off; launch; make a start; *new;* originate; proceed; push-off; *quicken; reactivate;* start; set out; sail off; take ship; tackle; undertake; venture; weigh anchor; *xon;* yede; *zip away;* [Ant. exit]
**embarrass** *(v.)*: abash; *ashamed;* bring down; bother; *blush;* chagrin; crush; discomfit; discountenance; disgrace; devastate; efface; fluster; *grieve;* humiliate; *indignity; jackalent;* knock down; *lower;* make uncomfortable; mortify; nonplus; *overtake;* put to shame; perplex; *quiet;* rattle; reproach; sheepishness; shame; take down a peg; upset; *vitiate;* weigh down; *xtry. humiliated;* yowl; zero honor;
**embarrassing** *(adj.)*: awkward; bothersome; *blushing;* crushing; discomfiting; effacing; flustering; *grieving;* humiliating; *indignity; jackalent;* kayu; *low;* mortifying; nonplusing; oafish; perplexing; *quieting;* rattling; shameful; *troubling;* uneasy; vexing; worrying; *xtry. low;* yucky; zero honor;
**embarrassment** *(n.)*: awkwardness; ashamedness; abashment; blushing; coyness; discomfiture; disgrace; effacement; fuddlement; *grief;* humiliation; indignity; ignominy; *joylessness; kettiness;* loss of face; mortification; *notorious incident;* opprobrium; public disgrace; *quad;* reproach; shame; timorousness; *upbraiding;* verecundity; wite; *xtry. ~;* yuckiness; zero honor;

**embassy** *(n.)*: ambassage; *building;* consulate; diplomatic office; embassade; foreign consulate; government office; home office; intendant's office; *jurisdiction; key location; location;* ministry; *nuncio;* office; proconsulate; *quarters;* regional office; *suite; tower;* United Nations; *unit;* vice-consulate; *work place; xeno-representative; yamen* [Chin.]; zonal office;

**embed** *(v.)*: *affix;* bury; conceal; cement; deposit; entrench; fix; ground; graft; hide; imbed; implant; join; keep within; lodge; *make; non-moveable; obscure;* plant; put in; *quat [arch.];* root; reset; sink; set in; sandwich; *tuck; underground; verge;* wedge; xenograft; yird; zet [dial.]; [*Ant.* extract]

**embezzle** *(v.)*: appropriate; *bilk;* cabbage; defalcate; defraud; exploit; filch; grift; *help oneself; impalm;* jape; *klick [Scot.];* loot; misappropriate; misuse; *nick;* outdo; peculate; purloin; *quad;* rob; steal; siphon; skim; take; thieve; *use illegally; villainy;* walk off with; weasel; *xfer;* yentz; *zap;*

**embezzlement** *(n.)*: appropriation; *bilking;* cabbaging; crime; defrauding; exploitation; fraud; grifting; *helping oneself; impalming;* japery; *klick [Scot.];* larceny; misappropriation; *non-integrity;* outdoing; peculation; *quad; redirection;* stealing; skimming; siphoning; thievery; *use illegally;* violation; white-collar crime; *xfer;* yentzing; *zapping;*

**embezzler** *(n.)*: appropriator; beguiler; cheater; defalcator; exploiter; fraud; guiler; hoaxer; *impalmer;* japer; knave; *liar;* misappropriator; *no-good;* outdoer; peculator; *quad;* rook; swindler; thief; *untruther;* verneuker; weasel; *xgressor;* yentzer [Heb.]; *zinger;*

**embitter** *(v.)*: acerbate; become bitter; cross; disaffect; disgust; estrange; fluster; gall; *heat;* incense; jaundice; kindle; *lose it;* madden; make bitter; nettle; offend; poison; *quick*-turn sour; rankle; sour; tick off; upset; vex; worsen; *xerothermic; yell; zealousy [arch.];*

**emblem** *(n.)*: arms; brand; blazon; badge; character; crest; coat of arms; designation; device; ensign; figure; glyph; hierogram; heraldry; icon; insignia; *jack;* key; logo; mark; *notation; object;* picture; pictogram; *quarter;* representation; symbol; sign(et); seal; *type; uncial;* vexillum; watermark; *X; yacht ensign; zeug;*

**embodiment** *(n.)*: *attributes;* bodiliness; being; constitution; corporality; distillation; essence; epitome; fundamentality; *gist;* heart; incarnation; jet; kernel; lifeblood; makeup; nature; *ontology;* personification; quintessence; reification; substance; soul; *thing; underneath;* vitality; warp and woof; *xenenthesis; yetzer* [Heb.]; *zoe [Gr.];*

**embrace** *(n.)*: acceptance; begirding; clinch; drawing around; embracement; fastening on; grip; grasp; hug; infolding; *joining;* kinch; *looping around; mushy;* nobble; *nestle;* oxtercog; putting around; *quashing;* reception; squeeze; throwing arms around; upbinding; *volting;* welcoming; *x;* yoke; *zone;*

**embrace** *(v.)*: accept; adopt; begird; believe; cleave to; draw around; enwrap; embosom; enclasp; fold; gird; hug; inwrap; *join;* kirtle; *loop around; mushy; nestle;* oxtercog; put around; *quash;* receive; squeeze; take; throw arms around; use; upbind; *volt;* wrap around; welcome; *x; yoke; zone;* [*Ant.* exclude]

**emerge** *(v.)*: arise; appear; burst forth; come out; debouch; develop; distill; emanate; flow out; get out; hatch; happen; issue; *journey; known; look;* materialize; *non-hidden;* occur; proceed out of; *quicken;* rise out of; reappear; sally; surface; show up; survive; turn up; transpire; upspring; venture out; *walk out; xfer;* yede; zip out;

**emergence** *(n.)*: appearing; budding; coming; development; emersion; forthcoming; growing; hatching; issuing; *just coming; key development;* late development; manifestation; *new; opening;* procession; *quickening;* rising up; surfacing; turning up; *upcoming;* venturing out; *will be; xfer; yeding;* zipping out;

**emergency** *(n.)*: adversity; breakdown; crisis; direness; exigency; *fix;* grave situation; *height; impasse;* jam; knotty situation; life crisis; *medical ~; nightmare;* ordeal; problem; predicament; *quandary;* red alert; situation; trauma point; urgent situation; vexation; woe; *xtry. circumstance;* yedder; zero hour;

**eminence** *(n.)*: acclaim; bigness; celebrity; distinction; eminency; fame; glory; honor; illustriousness; *jubilation; known;* legend; magnificence; notoriety; outstandingness; prominence; *quality;* renown; status; super~; *talked-about; universally known;* veneration; world-renown; *xtry.;* yichus; *zealous love;*

**eminent** *(adj.)*: acclaimed; beloved; big; celebrated; distinguished; everywhere-known; famous; great; highly regarded; illustrious; *jubilated over;* known; legendary; lustrious; magnifical; noted; notable; outstanding; prominent; *quality;* renowned; super~; *star;* talked-about; universally known; venerated; well-known; world-famous; *xtry.;* yichus; *zealously loved;*

**emissary** *(n.)*: agent; bearer of tidings; courier; consul; diplomat; delegate; envoy; foreign minister; government minister; high commissioner; intendant; *janker;* kurveyor; liaison; legate; minister; nuncio; official; *proxy; questor* [It.]; representative; *servant;* tidings-bearer; *updater;* vice-consul; *walking delegate; xeno-representative; yamen* [Chin.]; zip;

**emission** *(n.)*: atomization; broadcast; casting off; discharge; emitting; emanation; flow; giving off; hurling; issue; jetting; *kesting;* letting off; *moving; non-retention;* output; pouring out; *quantity;* release; stream; trajection; unleashing; venting; went out [p.t.]; *xfer;* yield; *zip;*

**emit** *(v.)*: *atomize;* beam; cast; come forth; discharge; dart; diffuse; emanate; fling; fall; fire; flash; flow; give (off); generate; hurl; issue; irradiate; *jet;* kest; let out; *make; non-retention;* ooze; output; produce; pour; *quoit;* release; radiate; secrete; seep; send forth; shoot; shine; transude; throw; transmit; unleash; vault; *wale; x-radiate;* yield; *zap;*

**emotion** *(n.)*: affect; attitude; bearing one's heart; concern; disposition; expressiveness; feeling(s); gut; hormone; humor; heart; inclination; *jarring; kindle; love; leaning;* mood; *notion; opinion;* passion; pang; pathos; *quivering; romance;* sentiment; temper(ament); *urge;* vein; way of thinking; *xenenthesis; yearning; zeal;*

   **Emotions**: alarm; amusement; anger, annoyance; boredom; contempt; delight; despair; disappointment; disgust; dread; elation; embarrassment; envy; excitement; fear; frustration; gladness; grief; guilt; happiness; hate; irritation; joy; love, melancholy; outrage; pleasure; remorse; revulsion; rage; sadness; sorrow; shame; surprise; tension; unhappiness; warmth; worry; zeal;

**emotional** *(adj.)*: affective; *bowels;* choked up; *crying;* disturbing; dramatic; expressive; effusive; emotive; feeling; glandular; gut-wrenching; hormonal; hysterical; histrionic; *inspired;* jarring; keenly ~; lachrymose; moving; moody; mind-stricken; mushy; misty-eyed; novelettish; overwhelming; overdramatic; overwrought; passionate; poignant; quixotic; rhapsodic; stirring; sensitive; sentimental; soulful; touching; tender(-hearted); tearful; teary; unrestrained; visceral; weepy; *xtry. ~; yet unquenched;* zealous; [*Ant.* emotionless]

**emotions** *(n.)*: affect; bowels; *countenance;* disposition; emotionalism; expression; feelings; gut (feeling); heartstrings; hormones; *impressions; jarring; kindle; love;* mood; nerves; *outpouring;* pathos; passion; *quivering; romance;* sentiment; sensibilities; sensitivities; temperament; *urge;* vein; whim; *xtry.;* yearning; *zeal;*

**empathy** *(n.)*: affinity; *bond;* compassion; *desire;* emotional bond; feeling; *graciousness;* heart; identification; *jarred;* kinship; like-mindedness; mercy; *niceness;* oneness; pathos; *quarter;* ruth; sympathy; togetherness; understanding; vibrations; warmth; *xenia;* yearning; zeal; [*Ant.* ennui]

**emperor** *(n.)*: autocrat; authority; boss; Caesar; crowned head; dynast; executive; *Fuehrer* [G.]; *governor;* head; highness; imperial majesty; jemander [Ind.]; king; kaiser; lord; monarch; nobleman; *Negus* [Afr.]; oligarch; potentate; *queen* [fem.]; ruler; regent; sovereign; *tyrant; ultimate authority; vice-regent; warden;* XO; *younker;* zayim;

**emphasis** *(n.)*: accent; attention; *big;* center; *dominance;* eminence; focus; feature; fore(front); fixation; *greatest;* highlight; high spot; importance; ictus; *judged most important;* key point; limelight; main thing; *notable;* overriding consideration; prominence; priority; paralipsis; *quintessence;* red lettering; spotlight; stress; thrust; underscoring; *vital; value;* weight; *xtry. point; yellow highlight; zest;*

**emphasize** *(v.)*: accentuate; bring into focus; call attention to; draw attention to; emphatically state; focus; give emphasis to; highlight; italicize; *jump out;* keep emphasis on; lay stress upon; major; make emphasis; narrow down; over~; point out; play up; *quite overstress;* red-underline; stress; *target;* underscore; *value; weight; xtry. emphasis; yed;* zero in; [*Ant.* ease up]

**emphatic** *(adj.)*: ardent; burning; compelling; categorical; definite; emphatical; forceful; glaring; hearty; hardline; insistent; jaw-set; *keen;* loud; motivating; non-deterred; overzealous; positive; passionate; quite ~; resounding; strong; torrid; unequivocal; vehement; wholehearted; *xtry.;* yieldless; zealous;

**empire** *(n.)*: archduchy; body politic; country; colonies; domain; empery; fatherland; grand duchy; *homeland;* imperium; imperial power; jurisdiction; kingdom; land; monarchy; nation; *oligarchy;* power; queendom [fem.]; region; realm; reich [G.]; state; territory; *united kingdom; viscounty;* world power; xerifdom; *yard;* zenocracy;

**employ** *(v.)*: add to staff; avail; apply; bring in; busy; charter; contract; *drive;* enlist; engage; exercise; exploit; *function;* give job to; hire; harness; *implement; join the team;* keep; *labor;* make an employee; *name:* operate; pay; put to work; *qualify;* recruit; retain; sign-on; take on; use; utilize; *vocation;* work; *xtr. hours; yain [arch.]; zet [dial.];*

**employee** *(n.)*: associate; blue-collar worker; co-worker; crewmember; day laborer; drone [derog.]; executor; fellow laborer; floozy [derog.]; gofer [slang]; grunt [derog.]; hireling; hand; industrial worker; jobholder; jack; *kitchen worker;* laborer; moiler; menial; navvy [Br.]; operator; producer; *qualified laborer;* roustabout; staff member; subordinate; toiler; underling; *vassal;* worker; workman; wage earner; *xylographer;* yeoman; zaikai [Jap.]; [Ant. employer]

**employer** *(n.)*: authority; boss; chief; director; executive; *foreman;* goodman; head; intendant; *jarl; kingpin;* leader; manager; nibs [Br.]; owner; proprietor; *qualified ~;* ruler; supervisor; *taskmaster;* ultimate authority; vice president; warden; XO; yardboss; *zayim;* [Ant. employee]

**employment** *(n.)*: activity; assignment; business; *burden;* career; craft; calling; drudgery; duty; enterprise; field; *grind;* handwork; industry; job; *key position;* living; livelihood; métier; mission; *necessity;* occupation; profession; *quest;* retaining; responsibility; service; trade; undertaking; vocation; work; xci. *yoke; zealous duty;*

**emptiness** *(n.)*: airiness; barrenness; bareness; blankness; cleanness; desolation; evacuation; futility; gantness; hollowness; inaneness; jejuneness; *kaput;* loneliness; meaninglessness; nothingness; *out; poured out; quaffed; reduction;* sterility; total ~; ullage; vanity; void; vacancy; vacuity; vacuum; worthlessness; *"x";* yieldlessess; zero;

**empty** *(adj.)*: airy; bare; blank; barren; clean; clear; desolate; deserted; devoid; evacuated; fistular; futile; forlorn; gant; hollow; inane; jejune; *kaput;* load-less; meaningless; nothing; naked; out; poured out; quaffed; *reduced;* stark; tapped out; tumed [Scot.]; unoccupied; vain; void; vacant; wiped out; waste; "x"; yieldless; zero;

**empty** *(v.)*: abate; baseless; clear; clean out; drain; discharge; divest; deplete; exhaust; evacuate; finish; gush out; hone; *impoverish; jejune; kaput;* let out; *minimize; nullify;* olate; pour out; quaff; run out; spend; tap out; tume [Scot.]; use up; vacate; weaken; weary; wane; waste; wipe out; *xfer; yield;* zap;

**emulate** *(v.)*: ape; be like; copy; duplicate; ditto; echo; follow; fashion; forge; *geminate; holotype;* imitate; impersonate; *just like; keep; look alike;* model; mimic; *near; offprint; overdub;* parrot; plagerize; pattern; *quadruplicate;* repeat; reproduce; replicate; shadow; simulate; transcribe; *use copier; virtual; watch closely;* xerograph; *yield;* zincograph;

**emulation** *(n. imitation)*: apery; borrowing; copying; duplication; echoing; following; *going after; holotype;* imitation; impersonation; *just like; keep;* likeness; mimicry; *nearing; offprint;* parrotry; plagerization; personification; *quadruplicate;* reproduction; replication; repeating; simulation; take-off; use; *virtual; watching closely;* xenograph; *yield;* zoomimic;

**emulation** *(n. competition)*: antagonism; bad blood; competition; dispute; enmity; fighting; gamesmanship; hostility; inimicalness; jealousy; *knavery;* lifemanship; mêlée; noncooperation; outdoing; *pugnaciousness;* quarrel; rivalry; strife; tug-of-war; unfriendliness; vying; war; *x-fire;* yed; *zeal;*

**enable** *(v.)*: allow; authorize; bless; consent to; capacitate; *do;* empower; facilitate; give power; help; *indulge; justify;* kit; let; make possible; *means; nod;* okay; permit; qualify; ready; suffer; sanction; *tolerate; unhindered;* validate; warrant; *x on the dotted line; yes; zealously approve;*

**enamor** *(v.)*: attract; allure; bewitch; charm; captivate; draw; enchant; fascinate; get (attention of); *have come;* infatuate; inspire; incite to love; *jade; keen;* lure; magnetize; *nudge; outwit;* persuade; *quibbling [arch.];* rivet; seduce; tempt; *urge;* vamp; woo; *xuld [arch.]; yerk; zygotaxis [biol.];*

**encase** *(v.): around;* beset; cover; coat; case; draw around; envelop; enclose; encapsulate; frame; gird; hem in; inclose; incase; jacket; kirtle; *lay over;* mummify; *non-broken;* overlay; put around; *quoil [dial.];* ravel; sheathe; sandwich; *twine; upwind; volt;* wrap; *x-border;* yard; zone;

**enchant** *(v.):* allure; bewitch; charm; conjure; delight; enthrall; fascinate; get (attention of); hold captive; infatuate; *jolt;* kinch; *lure;* mesmerize; *narcosis;* overwhelm; put under a spell; *quaffed;* rivet; spellbind; transfix; use magic; *veg out;* woo; wow; *x-fix; yield; zone out;*

**enchantment** *(n.):* attraction; bewitchment; charm; conjuring; draw; enticement; entrancement; fascination; glamour; hypnosis; incantation; junu; *karakia* [Maori]; lithomancy; magic; night-spell; *overwhelming;* power; *qualm* [arch.]; rhabdomancy; spell; transfixation; *under; voodoo;* weird [Scot.]; xylomancy; *yoga trance;* zauber [G.];

**enclose** *(v.): all around;* begird; circle; contain; draw around; encircle; encompass; fence in; frame; gird; hem in; immure; inclose; *jacket;* kirtle; *loop around; lay siege to;* mure; *non-broken circle;* outline; put around; palisade; pavilion; *quoil [dial.];* ravel; surround; seal in; sandwich; swallow; twine; *upwind; volt;* wall-in; wrap; *x-border;* yard; zone;

**encode** *(v.): alter;* bring into; code; convert; *denote;* encrypt; encipher; *formulate;* get into code; have coded; *issue;* jumble; *key to; language;* make encoded; *newly ~d; over;* put into code; *qualify;* render in code; scramble; translate; transcribe; use code; *vamp;* write in code; xlate; yield in code; *zay [dial.];*

**encompass** *(v. surround): around;* begird; circle; draw around; encircle; frame; gird; hem in; inclose; include; *Jordan curve;* kirtle; *loop around;* move around; *noose;* outline; put around; *quoil [dial.];* ravel; surround; siege; twine; *upwind; volt;* wrap; *x-border;* yard; zone; [*Ant.* exclude]

**encounter** *(v.):* alight upon; bump into; come across; chance upon; draw near; *enter;* fall upon; *greet;* happen upon; *intersect;* just meet; *key meeting;* light upon; meet; *near; occur;* pass by; *quicken;* run into; re~; stumble upon; *transpire;* unexpectedly meet; *visit;* walk by; *x.; yede; zip;*

**encourage** *(v.):* assure; back; bolster; cheer; console; dynamize; egg on; fillip; foster; give confidence; hearten; incite; inspire; inspirit; *jump-start;* kindle; lift; make confident; motivate; *nudge; openhearted;* pat on the back; prod; provoke; promote; quicken; raise spirits; root for; reassure; support; stimulate; *take heart;* uplift; urge; vitalize; warm; *xuld [arch.]; yerk [dial.];* zealously back; [*Ant.* engrieve]

**encouragement** *(n.):* assurance; backing (up); bolstering; cheering; consolation; dynamizing; encouraging; exhorting; fillip; fostering; goading; gladdening; heartening; inciting; inspiration; *jump-start;* kindling; lift; motivation; nudge; *openhearted;* prodding; pep talk; provocation; promotion; *quickening;* raising spirits; support; stimulation; *taking heart;* urging; uplifting; vivifying; well-wishing; *xtry.; yeah!;* zest;

**encourager** *(n.):* assurer; Barnabas; consoler; disburdener; edifier; *fillip;* gladdener; helper; inspirer; *jump-starter;* keen ~; lifter up; motivator; *nudge;* one who encourages; provoker unto good works; *quickener;* reassurer; son of consolation; true friend; uplifter; vivifier; well-wisher; *xtry. ~; yipee!;* zealous supporter;

**encouraging** *(adj.):* assuring; bolstering; consoling; comforting; driving; exhilarating; *fillip;* good; gladdening; horatory; heartening; inspirational; inspiring; *jump-start; kindly;* lifting; motivational; motivating; *nudging; opening;* parentical; promising; quickening; reassuring; supportive; *taking heart;* uplifting; vivifying; *well; xuld [arch.]; yerk [dial.]; zealous;*

**encroach** *(v.):* advance upon; breach; creep in; *disregard;* entrench; flout; force; go into; horn in; impinge; infringe; intrude; interlope; *jurisdiction; keep on; lapse;* make inroads into; *neglect;* overstep; obtrude; presume upon; *quad; raid;* squat; trespass; usurp; violate; worm in; *xfer; yieldless;* zero consideration;

**encumber** *(v.)*: *avert;* burden; cumber; *delay;* ensnarl; frustrate; *get in the way; gum up;* hinder; hamper; impede; *jam;* keep (from); limit; moderate; mess up; *nullify;* obstruct; *prevent; quash;* restrain; stop; thwart; *upset;* veto; weigh down; x; *yank; zap;* [*Ant.* ease]

**encumbrance** *(n.)*: albatross; burden; cumbrance; difficulty; encumbering; *frustration;* gumming up; hindrance; hang-up; impediment; jamming; keeping back; logjam; *mess;* nuisance; obstruction; problem; quandary; roadblock; stumbling block; trouble; *upset;* vigia; wall; x; *yowler; zinger;* [*Ant.* ease]

**end** *(n.)*: aft; apogee; bottom; base; butt; bounds; conclusion; consummation; destination; extremity; edge; farmost; farthermost; finish; *gotten through;* hindermost part; *implementation; just desserts;* killing; limit; margin; nadir; outer limit; outcome; omega; product; posterior; quittance; result; rock-bottom; rear; summation; termination; tail(- ~); upper limit; uttermost; *verge;* windup; *x-ing out;* year-end; Z; [*Ant.* embarkment]

**end** *(v.)*: abort; abolish; abrogate; break off; cease; close; conclude; cancel; cut short; discontinue; desist; extinguish; eliminate; finish; get rid of; halt; invalidate; *junk;* kill; leave off; make an end of; nullify; *oust;* put an end to; quash; resign; relent; stop; terminate; undo; *void;* wrap up; x-out; *yield;* zero out; [*Ant.* establish]

**endanger** *(v.)*: attempt; bare; compromise; *dare;* expose; *foreboding;* gamble with; hazard; imperil; jeopardize; *knowingly ~;* lay open; make vulnerable; *non-protected;* open to danger; put at risk; peril; *questionable;* risk; *subject to danger;* take risk; *unprotected;* venture; wager; "x"; *yeopartie [arch.];* zero guarantee; [*Ant.* ensure]

**endeavor** *(n.)*: attempt; bid; crack; dare; effort; full-blown effort; go; header; *intent;* jab; kemp; labor; *move;* nisus; old college try; push; proffer; quest; *reattempt;* shot; stab; try; undertaking; venture; whack; *xuld [arch.];* yearning; zeal;

**endeavor** *(v.)*: attempt; assay; bid for; *compete;* dare; do one's best; essay; follow after; go for; have a crack; hazard; *intend;* jab; kemp; labor; make an effort; *nitency; offer;* push for; proffer; *question [arch.];* risk; seek; strive; try; undertake; venture; work at; *xuld [arch.];* yearn; zealously attempt;

**endless** *(adj.)*: *always;* boundless; continual; ceaseless; day-after-day; deathless; eternal; fadeless; *forever;* gapless; *huge;* incessant; interminable; inexhaustible; *jointless;* keeps going; lasting; limitless; month-after-month; never-ending; ongoing; perpetual; *quadrillion;* round-the-clock; sempiternal; time without end; termless; unending; *vast;* without end; *xtry.;* year-after-year; zillion; [*Ant.* ended, exhaustible]

**endow** *(v.)*: award; bestow; bequeath; confer; donate; endue; furnish; grant; hand (over); impart; *jettison;* kit; lavish; *measure; non-retention; outgive;* provide; *quicken;* render; supply; transfer; *unhand;* vest; *weigh;* xfer; yield; *zip;* [*Ant.* expropriate]

**endowment** *(n.)*: award; benefaction; bequest; contribution; dower; endowment; favor; gift; grant; handsel; inheritance; income; *joy-giving;* kindness; liberality; largess; lagniappe; munificence; nest egg; offering; present; provision; *quality gift;* revenue; subsidy; trust; *unselfishness;* vouchsafement; *white elephant gift;* xenium; *yeff* [arch.]; *zealous support;* [*see* grace]

**endurance** *(n.)*: abiding; bearing; continuance; duration; determination; *endlessness; energy;* forbearance; fortitude; grit; holding out; imperishability; *jaw-set;* keeping on; longevity; lastingness; *mettle;* not giving up; obstinacy; perseverance; patience; *quit-free;* resoluteness; sustaining; sufferance; toleration; unyieldingness; *vivacity; willpower; x-scend;* yieldlessness; *zealous continuance;* [*Ant.* expiration]

**endure** *(v.)*: abide; bear; bide; brave; continue; carry on; dure; do; extend; follow on; go on; have; hold on; *intense; journey on;* keep (going); last; live through; maintain; *non-stop;* outlast; outride; persist; persevere; put up with; perdure; *quiet;* remain; suffer; survive; stand; sustain; thole; tolerate; take; tough it out; undergo; *voyage on;* weather; withstand; *xtry.; yieldless;* zet [dial.]; [*Ant.* expire]

**enemy** *(n.)*: adversary; antagonist; bad guy; belligerent; contender; disputant; defier; emulator; foe; *garrison;* hater; instigator; jangler; kemper; *legion;* match; nemesis; opponent; public ~; *quarreler;* rival; striver; *traitor; troops;* troubler; *unfriendly;* villain; warling; *xenic; yuon* [arch.]; *zeke [off];*

**energetic** *(adj.)*: active; animated; brisk; bouncy; *cheerful;* diligent; dynamic; enthusiastic; forceful; frisky; feisty; *gung-ho;* high-spirited; high-energy; high-powered; intense; *jumpy;* kedge; keen; lively; lusty; *motivated;* nippy; overactive; peppy; pert; quick; rapid; robustious; spirited; springy; spry; *thrilled; upbeat;* vigorous; vivacious; wimble; *x-energy;* yare; yeasty; zippy; [*Ant.* exhausted]

**energize** *(v.)*: activate; animate; boost; *cheer;* disquiet; empower; *fix;* give power; hearten; invigorate; jar; kindle; liven; motivate; make alive; *nippy; overactive;* pep up; quicken; revive; revitalize; switch on; strengthen; turn on; *uplift;* vitalize; wake; *xuld [arch.];* yerk; zip; [*Ant.* enervate]

**energy** *(n.)*: ability; brawn; capability; dint; drive; dynamism; élan; electricity; force; generant; get-up-and-go; horsepower; intensity; juice; kick; kilowatts; lustiness; might; muscle; nuclear ~; operativeness; pep; power; *qualifications;* resources; strength; smeddum; solar ~; thewiness; *usefulness;* vim; vigor; vitality; voltage; wherewithal; wattage; *xenium; yare;* zip;

**enforce** *(v.)*: adhere to; bind; carry out; compel; constrain; discharge; execute; force; guarantee; hold to; implement; impel; *jurisdiction;* keep; *law ~ment;* make; necessitate; oblige; police; press; *quicken;* regulate; require; support; set in motion; throw the book at; uphold; *violence;* wam; *xuld [arch.];* yoke; zealously keep;

**engage** *(v.)*: associate; *active;* become a part; busy oneself; connect; contract; *do;* employ; engross; *full-support;* get ~d; hire; have a part; involve; join; *knit;* link arms with; mix up in; *non-detached;* occupy; partake in; *quicken;* relate; retain; secure; take part; use; *volition;* wrap up; work; *xfer;* yoke; *zealously participate;* [*see* espouse]

**engaged** *(adj.)*: altar-bound; affianced; betrothed; committed; desponsated; espoused; fianced; *guaranteed;* handfasted; intended; joined in engagement; *knot; love;* marriage-bound; *nuptials;* obligated; promised; pledged; *qualified; retained;* spoken for; to be wed; trothed; *unconditionally promised; vow;* wed; *x;* yoked; *zet [dial.];* [*see* espouse]

**engagement** *(n.)*: affiancing; betrothal; commitment; desponsation; espousal; *fiance;* giving to marry; handfasting; *intended marriage; jurament;* kowl; *love knot;* marriage-promise; nuptial covenant; *oath;* promise; *qualified commitment; ring;* speaking for; trothing; *unconditional promise; vow;* written engagement; *x; yafery [arch.]; zitella [It.];* [*see* espousal; marriage]

**engine** *(n.)*: apparatus; boiler [slang]; contraption; diesel ~; electric motor; flat-four; gasoline ~; heat ~; internal-combustion ~; *j-series;* kicker ~; *labor-saving device; locomotive;* motor; machine; "nuts and bolts"; *outdrive;* piece of equipment; powerhouse; q-type; rotary ~; steam ~; turbine ~; *train;* unit; V- ~; V6; V8; Wankel ~; water- ~; x-type; Y-block ~; *Zeug [G.];*

    **Car Engine Parts**: air filter; battery; crankshaft; distributor; engine block; fan belt; fuel pump; gas tank; heater; intake valve; manifold; nuts; oil pan; pistons; radiator; sump; thermostat; universal joint; wiring; valve spring; water pump;

**engineer** *(n.)*: architect; builder; creator; chief architect; designer; draftsman; erector; founder; fashioner; framer; *gripman;* house-wright; inventor; *job;* key ~; *leader;* maker; mastermind; *naval ~;* originator; planner; *qualified ~; redesigner;* shaper; technical designer; urban designer; *vamper; work;* x-builder; yard ~; zonal ~;

**engineer** *(v.)*: *achieve;* assemble; build; bring about; contrive; construct; craft; design; develop; erect; fashion; fabricate; frame; generate; *hew;* institute; invent; *job;* knock together; *labor;* manipulate; make; *newly form;* originate; plan; produce; *quicken;* raise; shape; turn out; upbuild; *vamp;* wangle; work up; *xenomorph;* yield; *zip together;*

**engraft** *(v.)*: attach; affix; bind; connect; *dovetail;* embed; fasten; fix; graft; hitch; heterograft; ingraft; infix; join; knit; knot; link; mount; merge; *nail;* oxreim; plant; *quasi-fuse; relate;* splice; tie; unite; *vise;* wed; xenograft; yoke; *zoograft;* [*Ant.* extract]

**engrave** *(v.)*: annotate; burn; carve; cut; chase; damasken; etch; emblazon; enchase; fabricate; grave; gouge; *hew;* inscribe; *jot; kaplography;* letter; mark; notch; overprint; print; put down; quill; redact; record; scribe; score; tool; *underwrite; vignette;* write (down); *x-scribe; year mark; zay;* [*Ant.* expunge]

**engross** *(v.)*: absorb; arrest; bemuse; captivate; draw; enthrall; fixate; grip; hold; involve; immerse; *jag;* kinch; *like;* monopolize; *narcosis;* occupy; preoccupy; *quaffed;* rivet; *rapt;* spellbind; transfix; *under a spell; veg out;* welter; *x-fix; yield; zone out;*

**engulf** *(v.)*: *absorb;* begird; circle; *contain;* draw around; encircle; envelop; enclose; encase; *frame;* gird; hem in; inclose; incase; *Jordan curve;* kirtle; *loop around;* mure; *non-broken circle;* overwhelm; put around; *quoil [dial.];* ravel; surround; swallow; twine; *upwind; volt;* wrap; *x-cend;* yard; zone;

**enhance** *(v.)*: advance; augment; better; boost; change; convalesce; develop; enrich; embellish; fine-tune; further; get better; help; hone; heighten; improve; jump ahead; *keen;* lift; meliorate; make better; new-vamp; optimize; overhaul; progress; perfect; polish; *quantum leap;* raise; refine; succor; tweak; titivate; upgrade; upbuild; uprate [Br.]; vamp; work on; *xtry.; yarken; zizz;*

**enhancement** *(n.)*: augmentation; betterment; boost; change; development; deepening; enrichment; embellishment; fine-tuning; furtherance; growth; heightening; *headway;* improvement; increase; *jumping ahead; keen;* lifting; made better; *new-vamping;* optimization; overhaul; progression; quantum increase; raising; supplementation; transcendence; upgrade; vamping; waxing; *xtry; yarkening; zizz;*

**enjoy** *(v.)*: appreciate; bask in; benefit from; cherish; delight in; *enthused;* fancy; glory in; have; *invigorate;* joy in; *keen on;* like; love; luxuriate; *make one happy;* nice; own; please one; *queme;* relish; revel in; savor; take pleasure in; *uplift; value;* wallow in; *want; xtry.;* yearn for; *zestful;* [*Ant.* execrate]

**enjoyable** *(adj.)*: agreeable; blithe; cheerful; delightful; exquisite; fine; fun; fantastic; good; gratifying; heavenly; happy; invigorating; joyous; keen; lovely; *merry;* nice; *overjoyed;* pleasant; *queme;* rewarding; satisfying; terrific; uplifting; *vivacious;* wonderful; *xtry.; yeah!; zestful;* [*Ant.* execrable]

**enjoyment** *(n.)*: amusement; bliss; cheer(fulness); contentedness; delight; elation; fun; gratification; happiness; intoxication; joy; *keenness;* lightheartedness; *laughter;* merriment; *niceness;* overjoy; pleasure; *queme;* relishing; satisfaction; thrill; *uplifted; vivacity; well-pleased; xtry. joy; yeah!;* zestfulness; [*Ant.* execration]

**enlarge** *(v.)*: aggrandize; add to; augment; broaden; climb; distend; dilate; expand; extend; fatten; greaten; grow; heighten; increase; inflate; jump up; *keep growing;* largen; multiply; make bigger; numerically increase; outgrow; progress; *quadruplicate;* rise; spread; swell; thicken; take off; *upgrow* [arch.]; *vegetate;* widen; wax greater; *xtn; yain* [arch.]; zoom up (-in); [*Ant.* ebb]

**enlargement** *(n.)*: aggrandizement; augmentation; adding on; broadening; climb; distension; dilation; expansion; extension; fattening; growth; heightening; increase; inflation; jumping up; *keep growing;* largening; multiplication; making bigger; numeric growth; outgrowth; progress; *quadruplicate;* rise; rising; spreading; swelling; thickening; takeoff; upgrowth; *vegetation;* widening; waxing greater; xtn; *yain [arch.];* zooming up (-in); [*Ant.* ebbing]

**enlighten** *(v.)*: apprise; bring up-to-date; brighten; clear up; disclose; elucidate; educate; explain; *fulfil;* give instruction; *help;* illuminate; *just tell; keep informed;* light(en); let one know; make known; notify; open one's eyes; *point out; qualify;* report; show; shed light on; tell; update; verse; witness; warn; *xenagogue; yield up; zealously instruct;*

**enlightenment** *(n.)*: awareness; bringing up-to-date; brightening; clarification; disclosure; elucidation; education; explanation; éclaircissement; *fulfillment;* giving of instruct; *help;* illumination; *just tell;* knowledge; light(ening); making known; notification; opening one's eyes; *pointing out; qualify;* report; show; shed light on; tell; understanding; versing; wisdom; *xenagogue; yielding up; zealously instruct;*

**enlist** *(v.)*: admit; bid; conscript; call; draft; draught; enroll; *force;* get; hire; impress; induct; join; *key men;* levy; muster; *nempne;* order; press; *qualify;* recruit; register; *raise;* re- ~; sign up; summon; *shanghai;* take; *use;* volunteer; work; xfer; yield; zet [dial.]; [*Ant.* expel]

**enmity** *(n.)*: antipathy; animosity; bitterness; contrariness; dislike; *evil;* fight; gall; hostility; inimicality; ill-will; jangliness; *knocking;* loathing; malice; *negativism;* opposition; odium; *polarity;* querulousness; resentment; rancor; spite; *tetchiness;* unfriendliness; virulence; wrangling; *xenophobia; yawping; zoilism;* [*Ant.* endearment]

**enough** *(n.)*: adequate; ample; bare minimum; *capable; deft;* efficacious; fine; good; handsome; *influence;* jake [Br.]; just right; keen; *legitimate; liberal; much;* nuff [slang]; not lacking; okay; plenty; *quantum sufficit* [L.]; reasonable amount; sufficient; satisfactory; *tolerable; usual;* very ample; well; *xenium; yenough* [arch.]; *zero need;*

**enrage** *(v.)*: anger; boil; cross; disturb; disgust; exasperate; fluster; gall; *heat;* infuriate; incense; *jar;* kindle; lose one's temper; madden; nettle; outrage; *provoke;* perturb; *quick-tempered;* rile; steam; tick off; upset; vex; work up; *xerothermic; yell; zealousy [arch.];* [*Ant.* ease]

**enrapture** *(v.)*: *affect;* bring joy to; cheer (up); delight; elate; exhilarate; felicitate; gladden; hearten; inthrall; joy; *kindle;* lift up; make happy; *nice;* overjoy; please; quicken; rejoice; stir; thrill; unsadden; uplift; vitalize; wow; *xtry.; yippee!; zeal;* [*Ant.* eat at]

**enrich** *(v.)*: augment; better; boost; *correct;* develop; deepen; enhance; further; grow; help; heighten; improve; *jump ahead; keen;* lift; make better; *new-vamp; overhaul;* progress; *quantum leap;* raise; refine; richen; supplement; transcend; upgrade; vamp; wax; *xtry.; yarken; zizz;* [*Ant.* exhaust]

**enrichment** *(n.)*: augmentation; betterment; boost; *correction;* development; deepening; enhancement; furtherance; growth; heightening; improvement; increase; *jumping ahead; keen;* lifting; made better; *new-vamping; overhaul;* progression; quantum increase; raising; refinement; supplementation; transcendence; upgrade; *vamping;* waxing; *xtry; yarkening; zizz;* [*Ant.* exhaustion]

**enroll** *(v.)*: add one's name; admit; begin; come in; *draft;* enter; enrol; enlist; *find;* go in; head into; insert name; join; *kite; let into;* matriculate; note down; *open;* put name on the roll; *qualify;* record; register; sign up; take; *use; venture;* write down; xfer; yede; zip into; [*Ant.* exit]

**enslave** *(v.)*: *addict;* bind; bethrall; captivate; dominate; enthrall; force to work; govern; hold in bondage; impress; inthrall; *jail;* keep as slave; lead captive; mancipate; master; *not free;* oppress; *persecute;* quell; repress; subjugate; suppress; take captive; thrall; *under one's mastery;* vassal; work; xeno-dominate; yoke; *zone;* [*Ant.* emancipate]

**ensnare** *(v.)*: abuscade; betrap; catch; capture; decoy; entangle; entrap; fool; get; gin; hook; inveigle; *jump; keep;* lure; lay hold; mesh; nab; net; overtake; pick up; *quick-catch;* reel in; snare; seize; trap; usurp; *vanquish;* waylay; *x.; yard; zip away;* [*Ant.* emancipate]

**ensure** *(v.)*: assure; *bind to oath;* certify; determine; *establish;* fix; guarantee; homologate; insure; jurate; *keep; legitimize;* make sure; *nail down; okay;* prove; *questionless;* reassure; see to it; safeguard; try; uphold; vow; warrant; x-certify; *yes; zero doubt;* [*Ant.* endanger]

**entanglement** *(n.)*: abstruseness; bind; contortion; complication; chaos; disarrangement; entwinement; fix; farrago; gnarl; hodgepodge; intertanglement; jumble; kink; knot; labyrinth; mess; node; *ordeal;* problem; quandary; ravel; snarl; tangle; unorderliness; *voluble;* weave; xyloma; *yucky; zigzag;* [*Ant.* extrication]

**enter** *(v.)*: abate [law]; appear; *aboard; admission;* barge; board; cross over into; come in; descend; enroll; embark; *find;* go in; head into; irrupt; jump in; *knock;* let oneself in; matriculate; make an entrance; *near; open;* pass; penetrate; *quest;* reach; re- ~; sail into; travel into; *unlock;* venture; walk through; wedge; *xfer;* yede; zip in; [*Ant.* exit]

**enterprising** *(adj.)*: adventurous; bold; confident; daring; entrepreneurial; fearless; gutsy; hardy; intrepid; jarless; *keen; lion-hearted;* mercantile; not afraid; *overconfident;* plucky; *quick-to-act;* resourceful; self-assured; *taking the bull by the horns;* unafraid; venturesome; *well-hearted; xtry.;* yare; zealous;

**entertain** *(v. amuse)*: amuse; bedazzle; cheer; divert; delight; *enjoyment; feed;* gratify; humor; interest; jollify; *kill time; leisure;* make merry; *non-serious; overjoy;* please; *quality time;* regale; satisfy; tickle one's fancy; *unwind; view;* wow; *xenization; yippee; zizz;*

**entertain** *(v. show hospitality)*: accommodate; board; bestead; cater to; dine with; embower; feed; give food; host; have over; invite over; *join;* keep; lodge; *minister to; nourish; oblige;* provide with a meal; *quarter;* receive into home; serve dinner; treat with hospitality; *unburden;* victual; *well-please; xenial; yield victuals; zone;*

**entertaining** *(adj.)*: amusing; absorbing; blast [slang]; cheering; diverting; delightful; enjoyable; exciting; engrossing; fun(ny); gleeful; gay; humorous; interesting; indulgent; joyous; *kill-time;* larky; merry; moving; *non-serious; overjoyed;* pleasurable; *quality time;* recreative; sportive; thrilling; upbeat; very ~; well-pleasing; whimsical; xtry.; *yippee;* zany;

**entertainment** *(n.)*: activity; avocation; amusement; bedazzlement; cheer; diversion; distraction; enjoyment; fun; glee; hobby; indulgence; jollity; kill-time; leisure; light ~; mirth; *nightlife; overjoyed;* pastime; pleasure; performance; *quality time;* regaling; sport; treat; *uplifting;* viewing; vaudeville; *watching;* xtry.; *yippee; zest;*

**enthuse** *(v.)*: arouse; bestir; cheer; delight; excite; fire up; *goad;* gladden; hype-up; hearten; incite; joy; kindle; lift up; motivate; move; *nudge;* overjoy; provoke; quicken; rouse; *rejoice;* stir; thrill; unglue; vivify; whet; *xuld [arch.]; yerk; zing;*

**enthusiasm** *(n.)*: ardor; bestirring; commitment; devotion; eagerness; élan; fervency; gusto; heart; intensity; *joie de vivre [F.];* keenness; liveliness; motivation; *non-boredom; obsession;* passion; *quickening;* robustness; spirit; *thrill; ultra-zealous;* vehemence; wholeheartedness; *x-fervor;* yareness; zeal; [*Ant.* emotionlessness]

**enthusiast** *(n.)*: admirer; activist; buff; *crazed;* devotee; extremist; follower; fan(atic); groupie; *hobbyist;* ideologue; jock; *keen; liegeman;* maven; maniac; nut; *nympholept; obsessed; passionate;* quack; radical; supporter; *thrilled;* ultraist; votary; well-wisher; *xtry.;* Young Turk; zealot;

**enthusiastic** *(adj.)*: ambitious; ardent; burning; committed; devoted; excited; enthused; fervent; gung-ho; hearty; impassioned; *jingoist;* keen; *loyal;* motivated; mad; *non-apathetic;* overzealous; *on fire;* passionate; perfervid; quick; ready; raring; spirited; thrilled; unreserved; vehement; wholehearted; *xenocentric;* yare; zealous;

**entice** *(v.)*: allure; bait; coax; draw; ensnare; fool; goad; hoodwink; induce; jape; *knavery;* lead on (-astray); lure; mislead; *nudge; outwit;* prod; provoke; *quiblin [arch.]; rope;* seduce; tempt; urge; *vie;* woo; *xuld [arch.];* yerk; *zygotaxis;*

**enticement** *(n.)*: allurement; bait; come-on; coaxing; drawing; deception; ensnarement; *fooling;* gudgeon; hook, line and sinker; honeypot; inducement; incitement; japing; knavery; lure; misleading; *nudge; outfoxing;* prodding; provocation; *quiblin* [arch.]; roping in; seduction; temptation; urging; *vie;* wooing; *xuld [arch.];* yearning; zygotaxis [biol.];

**entire** *(adj.)*: absolute; all-encompassing; broad; complete; cumulative; comprehensive; *done;* exhaustive; full; general; high; intact; inclusive; *jim-bang;* known; *large-scale;* macroscopic; non-abridged; outright; overall; perfect; pure; plenary; quantitative; *ranging; round;* sheer; summative; thorough; total; undiminished; unabridged; uncut; undivided; utter; *vast;* whole; *x-cending;* yare; *zonal;*

**entrance** *(n.)*: access; archway; back door; corridor; door(way); entryway; front door; gateway; hatch; ingress(ion); inlet; *jib-door; knock;* liftgate; lobby; main ~; *narthex;* opening; private ~; passage(way); portcullis; portal; quadrivalve; rear ~; sliding door; threshold; tunnel; utility door; vestibule; vomitory; way in; x-door; yett; *zeta door;* [*Ant.* exit]

**entreat** *(v.)*: ask; appeal; adjure; beg; beseech; call for; conjure; desire; *endeavor; foreadmonish; go begging; humbly ask;* intercede; implead; implore; *juration; kneel to;* lift up one's voice for; make request; *need;* obsecrate; petition; plead; prevail upon; *quiritation;* request; seek; supplicate; try to get; urge; *vocalize;* wish; *XQ.;* yearn for; *zealously plead;*

**entrepreneur** *(n.)*: *achiever;* businessman; capitalist; dare-taker; enterprising young man; factory owner; go-getter; *hard worker;* industrialist; intrapreneur; *John-a-dreams; keen-dreamer;* legal owner; mover and shaker; *nabob;* owner; propieter; proprietress [fem.]; questor; risk-taker; self-starter; *thinker;* undertaker; upstart; venture capitalist; *worker; XO;* yettie; *zealous businessman;*

**entrepreneurial** *(adj.)*: ambitious; business; capitalistic; darin; enterprising; free-market; go-getter; *hard-working;* industrialist; intrapreneurial; *John-a-dreams; keen-dreamer; lawful; mover & shaker; nabob;* owner-; proprietary; proprietorial; *quest-taking;* risk-taking; success-oriented; *trade; upstart;* venturing; *working; XO;* yettie; *zealous;*

**entrust** *(v.)*: assign; bestow; consign; commit; delegate; *enlist; furnish;* give; hand over; *intrust* [arch.]; *judge faithful;* keep in one's trust; *let;* make responsible; *necessitate;* obligate; put in charge; *qualify; recommit;* set on one's shoulders; transfer; trust; *unhand;* vest; *wholeheartedly trust;* xfer; yafe; zeal;

**envelop** *(v.)*: *around;* begird; cover; draw around; engulf; encase; frame; gird; hem in; incase; ingulf; jacket; keep around; *loop around;* mummify; *net;* overlay; overwhelm; put over; *quoil [dial.];* ravel; sheathe; surround; twine; *upwind; volt;* wrap; *x;* yard; zone;

**envelope** *(n.)*: airmail ~; business ~; bangtail; cover(ing); dust jacket; enclosure; flat; *gem case;* holder; inclosure; integument; jacket; kirtle; letter-size ~; legal-size ~; mailer; No. 10 ~; office ~; packet; package; padded mailer; quick-seal ~; routing ~; security ~; *thing;* utility ~; vellum ~; window ~; wrapper; *xfer;* yellow ~; *zip-lock® bag;*

**enviable** *(adj.)*: agreeable; appealing; attractive; bonny; charming; choice; coveted; desirable; envied; first-rate; good; handsome; irresistible; *jim dandy;* keen; looked-for; much sought-after; *needed; outstanding;* pleasing; quite ~; *real good;* sought-after; tantalizing; *unsurpassed;* very appealing; wanted; *xtry.;* yearned-for; *zizzy;* [Ant. execrable]

**envious** *(adj.)*: askant; begrudging; covetous; desirous; envying; evil-eyed; fully ~; grudging; green; *hateful;* invidious; jealous; keenly ~; lusting; malignant; non-trusting; overly ~; protective; piqued; *quirky;* resentful; squint-eyed; suspicious; *troubled;* untrusting; vain; watchful; *xtry. ~;* yearnful; *zealous* [arch.];

**environment** *(n.)*: air; atmosphere; ambiance; backdrop; climate; clime; climature; conditions; *development;* environs; firmament; feel; geocorona; habitat; immediate surroundings; *jove; kind;* locale; milieu; mood; nature; oxygen; ozone layer; purlieu; *quintessence; region;* surroundings; setting; terrain; tone; *upper atmosphere;* venue; welkin; *xerosere; yonder; zone;*

**environmental** *(adj.)*: aireal; atmospheric; *background;* climatic(al); circumstantial; *developmental;* ecospheric; firmamental; geocoronal; habitat-related; immediate-surrounding; *jove;* key; *locational; man's environment;* natural; ozone-related; *place; quintessential;* regional; surrounding; tonal; upper atmospheric; *venue;* welkin; *xerosere; yonder;* zonal;

**envision** *(v.)*: anticipate; behold; conceive; conceptualize; dream of; devise; envisage; fancy; foresee; get idea; hatch; imagine; just see; *know;* look upon; make up; *notion;* objectify; picture; *quick-sighted;* realize; reify; see; think; use imagination; visualize; ween; *xenodiagnose; yeme;* zero in;

**envy** *(n.)*: avarice; begrudging; covetousness; desire; enviousness; fancying; greed; green-eyed monster; hunger; invidiousness; jealousy; *keenly covetous;* lust; malignity; *non-graciousness;* odium; pique; protectiveness; *quad;* repine; resentment; spite; *troubling; unhappiness;* vexation; want; *xry. avarice;* yearning; *zealousy* [arch.]; [*see* desire]

**envy** *(v.)*: ache for; begrudge; covet; desire; eat one's heart out; fret over; fancy; grudge; hunger for; itch; *jealous; keenly desire;* long for; lust after; *mind; non-gracious; over-greedy;* pant; *quest for;* repine; resent; stint; thirst for; *urge; velleity;* want; *xel* [arch.]; yearn for; *zoilism;*

**ephod** *(n.)*: apron; breastplate; *clothing; dress;* embroidered apron; *flamenical;* gem-studded ~; *garment;* high priestly ~; *Israelite; Jewish ~;* knee-apron; linen ~; *me'il* [Heb.]; *notable;* outfit; pectoral; priestly breastplate; *queyu* [Guyana]; *raiment;* sacerdotal habit; *tunic;* uniform; urim; vestment; *wardrobe; xtr. ~; Yiddish;* Zadok;

**epic** *(adj.)*: amazing; bigger-than-life; colossal; *disproportionate;* enormous; fantastic; great; heroic; huge; immense; *jumbo-sized; king-size;* larger-than-life; massive; noteworthy; oversize; prodigious; *quantitative;* really large; substantial; tremendous; *unbelievable;* very large; vast; whopping; xtry.; yet unsurpassed; zillions;

**epic** *(n.)*: adventure; blockbuster; cinematic triumph; *daring adventure;* extravaganza; *fantastic;* grand production; heroic production; incredible event; *journey; knightly errand;* large-scale production; much-celebrated production; *notable;* odyssey; pilgrimage; quest; *risk;* sojourn; trek; undertaking; venture; *wayfaring; xtry. production; yet unsurpassed;* zugunruhe [G.];

**episode** *(n.)*: affair; *bout;* chapter; *development;* event; experience; flare-up; *goings-on;* happening; incident; *jaunt; key event; lesson;* matter; notable event; occurrence; period; *quindene; report; record; retelling;* showing; time; unit; viewing; written story; x-po; yarn; zet [dial.];

**epistle** *(n.)*: autograph; *book;* communication; correspondence; dispatch; *essay;* fan mail; *glyph;* handwriting; inscription; *instruction; journal; kapnography;* letter; message; mail; missive; note; *open letter;* post; *the quill; roll;* scribbling; thoughts; text; *uncials;* vignette; writing; *xiaozhuan; yellow envelope; zeug;*

**epitaph** *(n.)*: annotation; *burying words;* caption; commentary; dedication; epigraph; final words; graving; *handwriting;* inscription; *journalism; kapnography;* legend; message; notation; *observations;* paragraph; *quotation;* remarks; superscription; text; *uncials; verbiage;* writing; *xiaozhuan;* year stamp; zet [dial.]; [see eulogy]

**epithet** *(n.)*: adjective; brand; characterization; description; expressive term; *first name;* given designation; handle; identifying term; *jurisdiction; known as;* label; moniker; nickname; *over title;* pet name; *quiring;* representation; surname; tag; *unofficial name;* vocable; word; xenonym; yu [Chin.]; zoon;

**epitome** *(n.)*: archetype; *beau ideal* [F.]; characterization; distillation; essence; embodiment; fugler; guide; height; ideal; jewel; *kept specimen; leader;* model; neotype; *original;* personification; quintessence; representation; standard; spirit; shining example; touchstone; ule; very essence; *way to be; xenagogue;* yardstick; zeroing in; [Ant. exception]

**equal** *(adj.)*: alike; balanced; commensurate; co~; duplicate; equivalent; equipollent; fair; *generally the same;* homologous; identical; just the same; kindred; like; level; matching; non-differing; one and the same; *parallel; quae est eadem* [L.]; resembling; same; tantamount; unchanged; verbatim; *word-perfect; xerographed; yes;* zero variation;

**equality** *(n.)*: alikeness; balance; commensurability; co~; draw; evenness; equivalence; equipollence; equity; egalitarianism; fairness; *gemination;* homogeny; identicalness; *just alike; knotted score;* likeness; levelness; match; non-difference; owelty; parity; quits; resemblance; sameness; *tie;* uniformity; *verbatim; word-for-word; xerograph; yes;* zero discrimination;

**equip** *(v.)*: accouter; bestow; confer; deliver; endow; furnish; give; hand (over); issue; impart; jibe [slang]; kit; *line out;* make ready; *needed item;* outfit; provide; prepare; *quicken;* rig; ready; supply; train; *uniform;* vest; *well-equipped;* xfer; yarken; *zip;*

**equipment** *(n.)*: appurtenance; accouterments; *belongings;* commodities; *devices;* effects; field ~; gear; hardware; items; *junk* [joc.]; kit; *load;* machines; needed items; *objects;* paraphernalia; *quantity; resources;* stuff; things; tools; tackle; utensils; *valuables; whirligig; xyster;* yarken; zeug [G.];

**equity** *(n.)*: anti-discrimination; blamelessness; *consistency;* disinterest; equitableness; equality; fairness; goodness; honesty; impartiality; justness; *keenness; legitimacy;* morality; non-discrimination; objectivity; propriety; *quality;* rectitude; sameness; truth; uprightness; virtue; what is right; *x-cending justice; yet the same;* zero bias;

**equivalence** *(n.)*: alikeness; basic likeness; commensurateness; *draw;* evenness; equality; *fairness; generally the same;* harmoniousness; indistinguishability; identicalness; *just alike; keeping;* likeness; match; non-difference; oneness; proportionateness; parity; quits; resemblance; sameness; similarity; *tantamount;* uniformity; *verbatim; word-for-word; xtry. similarity; yes;* zero imbalance;

**equivalent** *(adj.)*: akin; balanced; comparable; duplicate; equal; *fairly equal; generally the same;* homologous; indistinguishable; identical; just like; kindred; like; matching; non-differing; *one;* parallel; *quae est eadem* [L.]; resembling; similar; tantamount; uniform; very similar; *word-perfect; xtry. similar; yes; zero variation;*

**equivocate** *(v.)*: avoid; beat around the bush; circumvent; dodge; dither; dissemble; evade; elude; fudge; get around; hedge; *indirect;* jink; *keep from telling;* let alone; mislead; negotiate; outwit; prevaricate; quibble; *resist;* sidestep; skirt; trifle; tiptoe around; tergiversate; *unclear;* vacillate; waffle; *x-purposes; yell; zap;*

**era** *(n.)*: age; bit; *century;* day; dispensation; epoch; *fortnight;* generation; golden age; hour; historical period; *heyday;* interval; *juncture; kilocycle; lifetime;* minute; moment; month; millennium; *new ~; old times;* period; quarter; *run time;* span; time(span); undetermined time period; *vintage;* week; x-time; *yog* [Ind.]; years; *zone;*

**eradicate** *(v.)*: annihilate; bring to naught; blot out; crush; consume; destroy; eliminate; extirpate; exterminate; finish off; grind to dust; havoc; *incinerate; junk;* kill; *lose;* lay waste; level; *mash;* neutralize; obliterate; pull down; quash; ruin; stamp out; throw down; take apart; unroot; vitiate; wipe out; x-out; yank down; zap; [*Ant.* establish]

**erase** *(v.)*: annihilate; blot out; *correct;* delete; efface; exise; eliminate; eradicate; expunge; *free;* get rid of; *hide; invalidate; junk; kill;* lift off; *make correction;* negate; obliterate; *put back; quash;* remove; rub out; strike out; scrape off; scrub; take off; undo; *void;* white out; *x-out; yank;* zero out;

**erect** *(adj.)*: aligned; apeak; bendless; columnar; direct; ever-straight; fully-standing; *guided; high-reaching;* in a vertical line; *jagless; kink-less; linear; made straight;* non-curved; on end; perpendicular; plumb; quite ~; rectilinear; straight; standing; tall; unbent; upright; vertical; *waveless; x-straight; y-axis; zero horizontality;*

**erect** *(v.)*: assemble; build; construct; *develop;* engineer; fabricate; generate; hoist; institute; *jerk up;* knock together; lift up; make; *new-built;* originate; put up; quick-build; raise; set up; turn out; upbuild; *vertical;* wage; *x-type;* yield; zero give; [*Ant.* efface]

**erode** *(v.)*: attrit; break down; corrode; deteriorate; eat away; fade; grind away; *havoc;* impair; *jump down; knock down;* lessen; *minimize;* nibble away; outwear; *pall; quail;* remove; subside; take away; undermine; *vanish;* wash; wear away; *waterworn; waveworn; x-out;* yank down; zeroize; [*Ant.* edify]

**erosion** *(n.)*: attrition; bating; corrosion; corrosion; deflation; detrition; eroding; fading; going down; *havoc;* impairing; jading; knocking down; lessening; minishing; *narrowing;* outwearing; *palling; quailing;* receding; removal; shrinking; subsiding; tapering off; undermining; *vanishing;* wearing away; washout; *xerosis;* yielding; zeroizing; [*Ant.* edification]

**err** *(v.)*: abort; botch; bungle; blunder; crash; disappoint; *error;* foul up; fumble; goof up; go wrong; hash; *impropriety; jolt; kaput;* louse up; muff; mess up; make a mistake; not succeed; offend; *pratfall; poor; quit;* ruin; slip; stumble; trip; underachieve; *violate;* wash out; "x"; *yedder;* zorch;

**errand** *(n.)*: assignment; business; chore; charge; duty; *encumbrance; function; goal; handling;* incumbency; job; *key role;* liability; mission; necessity; obligation; *purpose;* quest; responsibility; *station;* task; undertaking; vocation; work; xci.; *yoke; zealous task;*

**erratic** *(adj.)*: arbitrary; bouncy; capricious; deviating; enigmatic; fluctuating; fitful; *goofy;* herky-jerky; haywire; irregular; jumpy; jerky; kaleidoscopic; labile; meandering; moody; *mad;* non-stable; out-of-control; precarious; queer; roving; random; shaky; tempolabile; unstable; unpredictable; volatile; wild; *x-ing; yo-yoish;* zany; [*Ant.* even]

**erroneous** *(adj.)*: amiss; bogus; bad; baseless; confused; *contradictory;* deficient; defective; erring; faulty; flawed; fallacious; false; groundless; *hollow;* heretical; inaccurate; incorrect; jim-jam; kim-kam; *lying;* mistaken; misguided; misconceived; misunderstood; non-orthodox; not true; off base; peccant; *quite wrong; repudiated;* spurious; specious; solecistical; *trick;* untrue; unsound; *void of truth;* wrong; *x-gressing; yawed; zero-truth;* [*Ant.* exact]

**error** *(n.)*: accident; boo-boo; blunder; breach; corrigendum; defect; evil; *faux pas* [F.]; fallacy; fault; failure; false doctrine; goof-up; hitch; howler [Br.]; inaccuracy; *jumble;* kink; lapse; miscalculation; mistake; *non-purposive;* oversight; problem; quirk; *responsibility;* slip(-up); solecism; typo; transgression; undoing; *violation;* weakness; wrong(doing); *xgression; yaw;* zinger;

**erupt** *(v.)*: *accelerate;* break out; burst forth; *cast off;* discharge; displode; explode; flare up; go off; hurl; issue; jet; *kest;* let off; *move; nova;* outburst; pop; *quake;* release; spew; spout; throw; unleash; vent; vomit; *whoosh; xuld* [arch.]; yield; *zap;*

**eruption** *(n.)*: *acceleration;* breaking (forth); burst; coming forth; discharge; explosion; flare-up; going off; hurling; issue; jet; *ka-pow;* letting go; *movement; naid;* outburst; outbreak; outpouring; pouring out; *quickening;* release; spouting; *torrent;* upsurge; venting; vomiting; *whoosh; xfer; yead; zap;*

**escalate** *(v.)*: augment; boost; climb; compound; *develop;* expand; enlarge; enhance; further; grow; greaten; heighten; increase; intensify; jack up; jump up; *keep increasing;* largify; make worse; magnify; *new growth;* overload; *progress; quantum increase;* raise; step up; strengthen; turn up; up; *volume;* wax greater; XL; *yain* [arch.]; zoom; [Ant. ease]

**escape** *(n.)*: absconding; break(out); charge; decampment; escaping; flight; getaway; hegira; *interloping;* jailbreak; *kiting away;* lam; making off; *non-captive;* outrunning; prison break; *quickening;* running away; *the* slip [slang]; sally; *tear out; up and away;* vanishing; withdrawal; *xfer;* yard-break; zipping away; [Ant. entrapment]

**escape** *(v.)*: avoid; abscond; break away; charge; decamp; evade; flee; get away; *hurtle; interlope;* jump away; *kite away;* lam; make off; *non-captive;* outrun; *prison break; quicken;* run; slip away; scape [poet.]; sally; take off; *up and away;* vamoose; vanish; withdraw; *xfer; yern;* zip away; [Ant. entrap]

**escort** *(n.)*: attendant; bodyguard; chaperone; companion; date; ensurer; friend; fellow traveler; guide; guard; helper; intimate; *journeyer;* keeper; lead; mate; *night watch;* other self; partner; *quickener;* rider; sidekick; scout; safe-conduct; *teammate;* usher; *votary;* watcher; *xenophile;* yeoman; *zealous friend;* [see enemy]

**escort** *(v.)*: accompany; be present with; bring along; come with; complement; convey; conduct; drive together; ensure; fend; go along with; help; inosculate; join; keep company with; lead; move with; *nearby; out with; present; quicken;* ride with; see; safeguard; travel with; usher; visit with; walk together; *xfer.;* yoke; *zero loneliness;*

**espousal** *(n.)*: arrangement; affiancing; betrothal; betrothment; commitment; cowle; desponsation; engagement; *fiancé; giving to marry;* handfasting; *intended marriage; jurament;* kowl; *love knot;* marriage-promise; nuptial covenant; *oath;* promise; pledge; *qualified commitment; resolution;* speaking for; trothing; taking; *unconditional promise; vow;* written engagement; *x; yafery* [arch.]; *zitella* [It.]; [Ant. estrangement]

**espouse** *(v.)*: arrange; affiance; betroth; commit; covenant; desponsate; engage; fiancé; give one's hand; handfast; *involved; jurate;* kowl; *love knot;* make ~d; *nuptials; oath;* promise; pledge; plight one's troth; *qualified;* resolve; *spoken for;* troth; *taken; unconditionally promise;* vow; write engagement; *x; yafery* [arch.]; *zitella* [It.];

**essay** *(n.)*: article; *booklet;* composition; dissertation; disquisition; editorial; *form; graving;* handiwork; *inscription;* journal; *kapnography;* letter; leader; literature; monograph; *note;* opus; *opinion;* paper; *the quill;* revision; study; treatise; thesis; *uncials;* vignette; writing; work; *xiaozhuan; yellow journalism; zeug;*

**essence** *(n.)*: *attributes;* being; composition; constitution; crux; disposition; distillate; distillation; entity; embodiment; flower; fundamentality; gist; heart; hypostasis; inbeing; inscape; *intrinsic;* jet; jist; kernel; keest; long-and-short; lifeblood; makeup; nub; nature; ontology; pith; *personification;* quiddity; quint~; root; stuff; substance; soul; thing; *underneath;* vitals; warp and woof; xenenthesis; *yetzer* [Heb.]; *zeug* [G.]; [see person]

**essential** *(adj. basic)*: absolute minimal; bare; basic; constituent; core; deep-seated; elemental; fundamental; foundational; *general;* *highest;* inherent; intrinsic; indispensable; *just the basics;* key; kernel; *leading;* minimal; main; necessary; nitty-gritty; original; primitive; primary; quiddative; quint~; rudimentary; supporting; substantive; *top;* underlying; vital; *whole; xenenthesis; yet indispensable;* zoetic; [Ant. extra]

**essential** *(adj. imperative)*: all-important; *big;* critical; dire; *expedient;* eminent; foundational; fundamental; great; high; important; imperative; integral; indispensable; *jump to it;* key; leading; life-and-death; main; mission critical; needed; needful; necessary; *obligatory;* paramount; *quantum;* required; significant; *terribly ~;* urgent; ultimate; vital; weighty; *xtry.; yearnful;* zero hour; [Ant. expendable]

**establish** *(v.)*: actuate; begin; build; create; charter; *debut; develop;* erect; form; found; fix; generate; *hatch;* institute; initiate; jump-start; kick off; launch; make; *newly form;* originate; produce; *quicken;* raise; start; set (in motion); settle; turn on; unleash; unveil; *venture;* work out; *xenogenesis; yield;* zet [dial.]; [Ant. end]

**establishment** *(n.)*: advent; beginning; creation; dawn; embarkment; foundation; formation; genesis; *hatching;* inception; jump off; kickoff; launching; making; naissance; origination; onset; *presentation; quickening;* rising; start; setting up; take-off; *unveiling; verge; welcoming; xenogenesis; youth;* zet *[dial.];* [Ant. end]

**estate** *(n. assets)*: assets; belongings; capital; demain; *dollars; domain;* earnings; fortune; gains; holdings; investments; *jewels; krugerrands* lands; life- ~; money; net worth; opulence; possessions; property; quinta; resources; substance; treasure; uberty; valuables; wealth; *xtry. wealth; yellow boy [Br.];* zillions;

**estate** *(n. manor)*: abode; barton; *castle;* demesne; *edifice;* farm; great house; homestead; inhabitance; joclet; konak; living quarters; manor; mansion; *nest; opulent;* property; plantation; quinta; residence; ranch; structure; townhouse; *upper class;* villa; wealthy home; x-house; yoklet; *zwinger;*

**esteem** *(n.)*: admiration; *bowing;* consideration; deference; devoirs; estimation; fear; favor; *giving honor;* honor; high regard; *impressiveness; justness; kneeling;* love; *merit;* non-contempt; obeisance; politeness; *quality;* respect; regard; repute; reverence; *salutation;* tribute; *unmitigated respect;* veneration; wonder; *xtry.;* yielding; *zero contempt;*

**esteem** *(v.)*: admire; bow to; consider; count; defer to; *estimate;* fear; give honor; honor; *idolize;* judge; kneel to; look up to; make obeisance to; notice; *obeisance;* prefer; praise; *quality;* respect; regard; revere; salute; think of; *unmitigated ~;* venerate; worship; *xtry.;* yield; *zero contempt;*

**estimable** *(adj.)*: assessable; appraisable; admirable; *believed;* calculable; deserving; enumerable; figurable; gaugeable; good; highly esteemed; *incrementable; judged; knowable;* laudable; measurable; numerable; *opinion;* possible to estimate; *quote;* reckonable; surmisable; *thought to be worth; unitizable; valuate;* venerable; *workable;* x-count; yeme; zum *[dial.];*

**estimate** *(v.)*: assess; appraise; *believe;* consider; deem; evaluate; figure; gauge; *hold; ideate;* judge; *know; list;* measure; *notion; opinion;* price; *quote;* reckon; surmise; think on; use brain; valuate; value; weigh; *xenodiagnose;* yeme; zum *[dial.];*

**estimation** *(n.)*: assessment; appraisal; belief; conjecture; deduction; estimate; evaluation; feeling; guess; hunch; hypothesis; idea; judgment; *knowledge; lemma;* mind; notion; opinion; presumption; quote; reckoning; speculation; surmising; thought; theory; *urge;* view; weighing; *x; yankering; zeal;*

**estranged** *(adj.)*: aloof; at odds; alienated; *breach;* cool; cold; detached; distant; *enmity;* formal; far; *giving cold shoulder;* hostile; insocial; inaccessible; *jaded;* kindless; loveless; *mean;* non-friendly; offish; *pitiless;* quiet; remote; standoffish; silent; taciturn; unfriendly; unapproachable; very distant; withdrawn; *xenophobic;* yet estranged; zealless;

**estrangement** *(n.)*: alienation; breach; cold shoulder; distancing; estranging; falling-out; giving cold shoulder; hostility; isolation; *jinking;* keeping out; *loathing;* moving away from; non-fellowship; ostracism; pushing away; *quite* [Sp.]; rift; separation; turning away; unfriendliness; *vaulting;* withdrawal; *xenelasy; yarding* [arch.]; *zero fellowship;* [Ant. endearment]

**eternal** *(adj.)*: atemporal; ageless; *boundless;* ceaseless; deathless; endless; everlasting; fadeless; *forever;* going on forever; *heavenly;* interminable; *jusqu'au bout [F.]; keeps going;* lasting; limitless; *measureless;* never-ceasing; olamic; perpetual; *quadrillion; remaining;* sempiternal; timeless; unending; *vast;* without end; *x-cending;* year-after-year; *zillion;* [*Ant.* evanescent]

**eternity** *(n.)*: all time; *afterlife;* by and by; *ceaseless; duration;* endlessness; ever(more); forever(more); *going on; the* hereafter; infinity; *jusqu'au bout [F.];* kingdom come; limitlessness; measurelessness; never-endingness; *the* next life; *ongoing;* perpetuity; permanence; *quadrillion; remaining;* sempiternity; time without end; unceasingness; *vastness of ~;* world without end; *x-cending;* yonder; *zillions of years;* [*Ant.* evanescence]

**ethical** *(adj.)*: appropriate; blameless; correct; Christian; decent; equitable; fair; good; honest; *impartial;* just; kosher; legitimate; moral; noble; orthodox; proper; principled; *questionless;* right; respectable; square; scrupulous; true-dealing; upright; virtuous; *worthy;* Xn.; *yet to be blamed; zero-blame;* [*Ant.* evil-minded]

**ethnic** *(adj.)*: ancestral; blood; clannish; cultural; derivational; ethnical; family; genetic; hereditary; *inherited; Japhetic; Jewish;* kin-related; lineal; *mankind;* national; original; phyletic; *quarter;* racial; stock-related; social; tribal; *unilineal; vein; white race; x-linked; yellow race; zygogenetic;*

**ethnicity** *(n.)*: ancestry; bloodline; country; descent; extraction; family; *group;* gens; genetics; heredity; *inheritance; jus soli [L.];* kindred; lineage; *mores;* nationality; origin; people; *quarter;* race; stock; tribe; *ubiety; vein; white race; x-link; yoni* [Skr.]; *zoe;*

**etiquette** *(n.)*: amenities; behavior; breeding; custom; correctness; courtesy; civility; code of conduct; decorum; elegance; fitness; good manners; gentility; gallantry; high-style; *impressive; jimp; kindness; loveliness;* manners; niceness; nobleness; obligingness; propriety; protocol; proper manners; procedure; politeness; properness; p's and q's; punctilio; *quaintness;* right; refinement; social correctness; table manners; urbanity; *Victorian ~;* wonting; *xtry.; younker; zero unrefinement;*

**eucharist** *(n.)*: *aifreann* [Gael.]; *alter bread;* bread and wine; breaking of bread; Blessed Sacrament; consubstantiation; Communion; divine ~; elements; *the* Feast; *grape juice;* host; Holy Communion; intinction; *juice; keeping the feast; the* Lord's body; Liturgy; Mass; *non-symbolic;* oblation; Postcommunion; *quarterly;* real presence; *rite; the* synaxis; Sacrament (of the Table); *the* Table; *union; viaticum;* wafer; *x-substantiation;* yeastless bread; *zonic rite;*

**eulogize** *(v.)*: acclaim; belaud; bless; commend; *devote;* extol; flatter; glorify; honor; *idolize; jubilate over; known;* laud; magnify; *note; orate;* pay tribute; praise; panegyrize; *quiritation; reward;* set off; sing praises; talk about; uplift; venerate; wax lyrical; *xenophilia; yichus;* zealously commend;

**eulogy** *(n.)*: address; accolade; *bespeaking;* citation; commendation; discourse; epitaph; encomium; eulogium; flattering words; glorification; homage; *identification; jabbering; knowledge;* laudative; message; *narration;* oration; panegyric; plaudit; *quotation;* remarks; speech; tribute; utterance; *vocalization;* words; *xenophobia; yuchus;* zealous oration;

**eunuch** *(n.)*: attendant; bondman; castrated man; chamberlain; demasculinized servant; emasculated manservant; fixed servant; gelding; guard; halfer; indentured servant; jaga; kerned guard; *lackey;* manservant; neutered servant; outguard; porter; quarterman; retainer; slave; servant; *trusted servant;* unsexed servant; vigil; ward; *x-guard;* yeoman; *zeloter;*

**euphemism** *(n.)*: anathematization; *byword;* code word; *darn;* euphemistic expression; figure of speech; *gesture; hex;* idiom; *juration;* ketch-word; *line;* metonym; near swearword; *oath; phrase; quote;* replacement word; softening; term of equivalence; *used instead; vernacularism; word; xenonym; yell-word; zinger;*

**euphoria** *(n.)*: animation; bliss; cheerfulness; delight; elation; ecstasy; felicity; glee; hilarity; intoxication; jubilation; *keenness;* levity; merriment; *niceness;* overjoy; pleasure; *queme;* rapture; seventh heaven; transport; *uplifted; vivacity;* winsomeness; *xanadu; yeah!;* zestfulness;

**euphoric** *(adj.)*: animated; blissful; cheerful; delighted; elated; ecstatic; enrapt; felicitous; gleeful; happy; intoxicated; jubilant; *keen;* lighthearted; merry; *nice;* overjoyed; pleased; *queme;* rejoicing; sunny; satisfied; thrilled; transported; uplifted; *vivacious;* well-pleased; *xanadu; yeah!* zestful; [*Ant.* exasperated]

**euthanize** *(v.)*: annihilate; blot out; *cut off;* dispose of; end (one's life); finish; *get rid of; homicide; inject; jab;* kill; *liquidate;* mercy-kill; *nip;* obliterate; put to sleep; put out of one's misery; quell; rub out; slay; terminate; *unseat;* vitiate; wipe out; x-out; *yataghan; zap;*

**evacuate** *(v.)*: abandon; be off; clear out; depart; desert; exit; empty; flee; go; hightail; *immigrate; jet; kest;* leave; medevac; make tracks; *not remain;* olate; part; pull out; quit; remove; skedaddle; take off; uproot; vacate; withdraw; *xfer;* yern; zip away;

**evade** *(v.)*: avoid; bilk; bypass; circumvent; dodge; elude; *fudge;* go around; hedge; *indirect;* jink; *keep away from; leave;* move away from; niddle; obviate; parry; prevaricate; *quite* [Sp.]; run away; skirt; sidestep; tiptoe around; tergiversate; *unclear; vacillate; waffle; xfer;* yern; zip away;

**evaluate** *(v.)*: assess; appraise; *believe;* consider; deem; estimate; figure; gauge; *hold; ideate;* judge; *know; list;* measure; meditate; *notion; opinion;* price; *quote;* reckon; study; surmise; think on; use brain; valuate; value; vet; weigh; *xenodiagnose; yeme; zazen;*

**evaluation** *(n.)*: assessment; appraisal; belief; conclusion; deeming; decision; estimation; estimate; feeling; finding; gauging; *hypothesis; idea; input;* judgment; *knowledge;* leaning; mind; notion; opinion; perspective; point of view; pricing; quotation; *quot homines tot sententiae* [L.]; reckoning; rating; slant; surmising; take; thoughts; *unbiased ~;* verdict; valuation; *wisdom; xenodiagnosis; yankering; zeal;*

**evangelical** *(adj.)*: *ardent;* Bible-believing; Christian; disciple-making; evangelizing; fervent; gospel-spreading; heavenly-minded; *interested in souls; justified; kirsen* [dial.]; Lutheran; missions-minded; new ~; neo- ~; orthodox; Protestant; *quickened; reformed;* soul-winning (-conscious); *Trinitarian; undertaking; vehement; washed;* Xn. *Yahwist;* zealous for souls;

**evangelism** *(n.)*: *ardor;* biblical witnessing; conversion; door-knocking; evangelization; fervency for souls; Great Commission; house visitation; *inviting people; Jesus;* knocking doors; leading souls to Christ; missionary work; *ministry;* neighborhood outreach; outreach; personal ~; *quest for souls;* reaching the lost; soul-winning; trying to win souls; *undertaking;* visitation; witnessing; *xenagogy; yede;* zeal for souls;

**evangelist** *(n.)*: *apostle;* Bible-teacher; circuit rider; *declarer;* evangel; field preacher; gospeler; herald; hot-gospeler; itinerant preacher; josser [Aus. slang]; *kindler;* lecturer; messenger; man of God; *noiser;* orator; open-air preacher; preacher; *quoter;* revivalist; speaker; sermonizer; servant of God; trumpeter; *utterer;* voicer; *warner;* xenagogue; *yeller* [derog.]; *zealous preacher;*

**evangelize** *(v.)*: *affect;* birth; convert; Christianize; *deliver;* exhort; *further; get saved; herald; indoctrinate; Jesus; kerygma;* lead to Christ; make converts; *minister; noise abroad;* obey Great Commission; proselytize; persuade; *quote the Bible;* recruit; sway; see one saved; turn to Christ; urge; victory; work; win (souls); *Xnize;* yank from hell; *zelous for Christ;*

**evaporate** *(v.)*: aerate; become dry; change into vapor; dry (up, out); dissipate; etherize; exsiccate; fade; gasify; *heat; incloud; jumbo cloud;* kier; *lour;* mist; nebulize; *overspread;* pass off into vapor; *quicken; ret;* sublimate; turn into vapor; *upset;* vaporize; wither; *xerosis; yield;* zoutch; [*Ant.* enharden]

**evaporation** *(n.)*: aeration; becoming dry; changing into vapor; drying; dissipate; exsiccation; evaporating; evanescence; etherization; fading; gasification; *heat;* inclouding; *jumbo cloud;* kiering; *lour;* misting; nebulization; *overspread;* passing off into vapor; *quickening; ret;* sublimation; turning into vapor; *upset;* vaporization; withering; xerosis; *yield;* zoutching; [*Ant.* enhardening]

**evasion** *(n.)*: avoidance; bilking; circumvention; dodging; equivocation; escape; *fudging;* getting around; hedging; inveracity; jinking; *keeping from telling; lying;* misleading; niddling; obviation; parrying; prevarication; qubbling; *resisting;* skirting; sidestepping; tiptoeing around; tergiversating; *untruth; vacillation;* whiffling; *xfer;* yerning; *zinger;*

**evasive** *(adj.)*: ambiguous; *beating around trhe bush;* cagey; coy; deceptive; elusory; furtive; guarded; *hidden;* indirect; *jinking;* knavish; *lying;* misleading; noncommittal; oblique; pawky; *quaintise [arch.];* roundabout; slippery; tricky; *underhanded;* vague; wily; *xtry.;* yepe; *zinger;*

**even** *(adj.)*: abiding; balanced; constant; consistent; dead ~; evened; e'en; flush; flat; firm; fixed; geometrically balanced; homaloidal; invariable; *jusqu'au bout* [F.]; *keeps the same;* level; measured; non-bumpy; ongoing; plane; *quiet;* regular; steady; stable; tabulate; uniform; unbroken; unvarying; unswerving; unfaltering; *very ~;* without variation; *x-cending;* yet; *zero variation;* [*Ant.* erratic]

**evening** *(n.)*: after-hours; bedtime; close of the day; dark (hours); eve(n); eventide; fall of the sun; gloaming; *half past six;* in the night; *jammies; kip;* lights-out; late-night; *midnight;* moonlight; night(fall; -time); *overnight; pernoctation;* quarter-moon; *rest;* sunset; *soir* [F.]; twilight; *under the cover;* vesper(s); wee hours; *weeknight; x-ing; yesternight; zero light;*

**event** *(n.)*: affair; *ball;* chapter; *dance;* experience; episode; function; *formal ~;* gathering; happening; incident; instance; *jaunt; key ~; lawn party;* meeting; notable event; occasion; occurrence; outing; period; *quindene; reunion;* shebang; *special ~;* thing; time; *upshot;* vernissage; wingding; *x-po; year-end party; zeit [G.];*

**eventual** *(adj.)*: anticipated; at length; by and by; bound-to-come; consequent; down-the-road; ensuing; final; *going;* hindmost; inevitable; *just a bit later; key;* latter; last; *much later; next;* overall; prospective; *quite some time later;* resulting; resultant; subsequent; terminal; ultimate; *very end; waiting; xtr.;* yondmost; *zet;*

**everlasting** *(adj.)*: always; *boundless;* continuous; continual; ceaseless; durative; eternal; fadeless; *forever;* going on forever; *huge;* interminable; immortal; incorruptible; infinite; *jusqu'au bout* [F.]; keeps going; lasting; limitless; month-after-month; never-ending; olamic; *ongoing;* perpetual; *quadrillion; remaining;* sempiternal; time without end; unending; unceasing; *vast;* without end; *x-cending;* year-after-year; *zillion;* [*Ant.* ended]

**every** *(adj. + adv.)*: all; apiece; *bar none; collective; direct;* each; *fully; group; high;* ilka [Scot.]; individually; *just all; known; the lot of them; many;* none excluded; omitting none; per; *plenary; quantity-unlimited;* respectively; singly; *totality; unabridged;* vast lot; *the* whole; *xtry.;* yet all; *zet [dial.];*

**evict** *(v.)*: abstract; boot; clear; cast out; dispossess; debar; expel; expulse; force out; get out; heave out; isolate; *judicially dispossess;* kick out; *leave out;* make leave; *negate;* oust; put out; *quit on;* remove; send away; throw out; unhouse; *vomit out; walking papers; xenelasy;* yank; *zip away;*

**eviction** *(n.)*: abstraction; booting; clearing; casting out; dispossession; debarring; expulsion; forcing out; getting out; heaving out; isolation; *judicial dispossession;* kicking out; *leaving out;* making to leave; *non-remaining;* ousting; putting out; quitture; removal; sending out; throwing out; unhousing; *vomiting out; walking papers; xenelasy;* yanking; *zero retention;*

**evidence** *(n.)*: attestation; authentication; backup; confirmation; *corpus delicti* [L.]; demonstration; documentation; exhibit; facts; *grounds;* hearsay ~; hard facts; indication; justification; *key ~;* legitimization; manifestation; notarization; obsignation; proven fact; qualification; reason (to believe); remonstrance; substantiation; testimony; undeniable proof; verification; witness; *xtry. ~; yes; zero doubt;*

**evident** *(adj.)*: apparent; blatant; clear; discernable; eye-catching; *flagrant;* glaring; *heedless; intentional; just plain to see; kenspeckle;* lucid; manifest; noticeable; obvious; plain; quite obvious; recognizable; self- ~; transparent; unmistakable; visible; watchable; *x-parent; yare; zero-disguised;*

**evil** *(adj.)*: abominable; bad; corrupt; devious; dastardly; debauched; diabolical; devilish; errant; execrable; evil-minded; foul; flagitious; fiendish; guileful; godless; heinous; iniquitous; immoral; jaded; knavish; licentious; mischievous; malicious; malevolent; maledictory; naughty; nefarious; ornery; obdurate; perverse; pernicious; *quad;* rotten; rapacious; ruthless; sinful; sinister; satanic; transgressing; treacherous; unrighteous; unscrupulous; villainous; vicious; wicked; *xgressing; yeffell* [arch.]; *zymotic;* [*Ant.* exemplary]

**evil** *(n.)*: abomination; badness; corruption; dark; debauchery; devilishness; devilry; evilness; fiendishness; godlessness; heinousness; iniquity; *jadedness; knavishness; lawlessness; licentiousness;* malevolence; nefariousness; obduracy; perniciousness; quad; rebellion; rottenness; sin; transgression; turpitude; ungodliness; villainy; wickedness; *x-gression; yeffell* [arch.]; *zhlubbiness;* [Ant. exemplariness]

**evoke** *(v.)*: ask one to come; bid; beckon; call forth; convoke; draw forth; entail; foregather; gather; *holler; invite; jar;* knell; look back; muster; nempne; order; pull up; *quicken;* rouse; summon; tell; use; vociferate; *will; xfer; yell for; zealously bid;*

**evolution** *(n.)*: amelioration; advancement; betterment; change; development; evolving; furtherance; gradual change; horotely; improvement; *jumping up; keen development; leading to;* macro~; micro~; *nonmenialism; operant conditioning;* progression; *quantum leap;* revision; slow change; transformation; upgrading; variation; waxing better; *xenim orphism; yawing; zapping;*

**evolutionary** *(adj.)*: accidental; by process of time; chance; casual; developmental; evolving; fortuitous; gradual; horotelic; improving-over-time; just-by-chance; *keen development;* little-by-little; mutational; *non-designed; over the years;* progressive; *quantities of years;* resulting from evolution; slow; tachytelic; upgrading; *vast eons; without design; xtry. chance; years; zillons of years;*

**Evolutionism** *(n.)*: adaptation; Big-Bang Theory; cladogenesis; *cosmic ~;* Darwinism; Evolution; foredating; gradualism; geogony; hypothesis; *infinite monkey theorem; Jurassic; koinophilia;* Lamarckism; macroevlution; neo-Darwinism; natural selection; orthogenesis; pseudoscience; progressivism; paleontology; quantum evolution; rapid evolution; speciation; theory; theistic ~; uniformitarianism; variation; *wave; xengeneic;* ylem ideology; zoopaleontology; [see atheism]

    **Supposed ages of Evolution**: Archean; Boreal; Cambrian; Devonian; Eocene; Furongian; Guadalupian; Hadean; Ioanian; Jurassic; Kimmeridgian; Lower Paleolithic; Mesolithic; Neogene; Oligocene; Precambrian; Quaternary; Rhyacian; Silurian; Triassic; Upper Paleolithic; Valangian; Wuchiapingian; Ypresian; Zanclean;

**Evolutionist** *(n.)*: advocate of Evolution; *atheist;* Big-Bang Theory advocate; *cosmic ~;* Darwinist; Evolution advocate; *follower of Darwin;* gradualist; hypothesis-believer; *individual; justifier of Evolutionism; koinophilia;* Lamarckist; macroevlutionist; *monkey's uncle;* neo-Darwinist; orthogenesis advocate; pseudo-scientist; progressivist; paleontologist; quasi-scientist; rapid evolution advocate; scientist; Theistic ~; uniformitarianist; *variationist; wave; xenomorphist;* ylem ideologist; zoopaleontologist;

**evolve** *(v.)*: ameliorate; advance; better; *become;* change; co~; devolve [neg.]; develop; evolute [joc.]; enhance; *fix;* gradually change; heighten; improve; *jump up; keep changing; lead to;* modify; metamorph [slang]; *new; overhaul;* progress; *quantum leap;* revise; *shift;* transform; upgrade; vary; *warp; xenomorph; yaw; zap;*

**exact** *(adj.)*: accurate; absolute; bona fide; correct; designated; definite; dead-on; explicit; express; faithful; *genuine;* hypercorrect; indubitable; inerrant; just (so); known; literal; lifelike; *mean it;* nonfigurative; on the mark; proper; precise; peremptory; questionless; right; sure; specific; technical; true; unerring; unequivocal; veritable; very; *well-tried;* x-act [slang]; *yes;* 'zact [dial.]; [Ant. estimated]

**exacting** *(adj.)*: assiduous; *busy;* careful; conscientious; diligent; detailed; exact; fastidious; finicky; fussy; *great detail;* hypercorrective; heedful; hard(line); industrious; inflexible; just-so; keen; logical; laborious; meticulous; nit-picking; orderly; operose; picky; particular; persnickety; punctilious; painstaking; precise; quiddle; rigorous; scrupulous; systematic; thorough; tedious; technical; *unhasty;* vigilant; *wholehearted;* x-act [slang]; yare; zealous; [Ant. easygoing]

**exaggerate** *(v.)*: amplify; aggrandize; blow out of proportion; *change; draw attention to;* embellish; *fish story;* greaten; hyperbolize; inflate; jazz; *keep growing;* lay it on thick; magnify; make too much of; *non-literal;* overstate; overplay; overrate; *overblown;* play up; pile it on (thick); *quite overstated;* romanticize; stretch; strain; tell fish story; *underscore; verneuk; wangle; xtry.;* yed; *zinger;*

**exaggeration** *(n.)*: amplification; aggrandization; blowing out of proportion; *change; drawing attention to;* embellishment; fish story; greatening; hyperbole; inflation; jazz; *keep growing;* largening; lie; magnification; nonrealism; overstatement; overemphasis; playing up; piling it on (thick); *quite an overstatement; raising;* stretch; telling a fish story; *underscoring;* vast ~; white lie; *xtry. ~;* yedding; *zinger;* [Ant. exactness]

**exalt** *(v.)*: acclaim; bless; commend; *devote;* exuberate; extol; elevate; fame; glorify; honor; idolize; *jubilate;* kneel before; lift up; laud; magnify; *note; obeisance;* praise; *quiritation;* rejoice; sing praises; thank; tout; uplift; venerate; worship; *xenophilia; yichus;* zealously ~;

**exaltation** *(n.)*: acclaim; blessing; celebration; devotion; elevation; extolling; falling down; glorification; glorifying; honor; *idolatry;* jubilation; *kneeling;* lifting up; laud(ation); magnification; *never-failing love;* obeisance; praise; *quiritation;* reverence; *song of praise;* tribute; uplifting; veneration; worship; *xenophilia;* yielding; zeal;

**examination** *(n.)*: assessment; audit; analysis; *background check;* check; cross- ~; consideration; diagnostic; disquisition; exam; enquiry; evaluation; field test; final (exam); graded exam; hearing; inspection; inquiry; interrogation; investigation; jerquing; *knowledge test;* look-over; midterm; make-up ~; meta-analysis; *non-mandatory ~;* oral exam; open book ~; pop quiz; perquisition; palpation; quiz; questioning; re-examination; research; scrutiny; search; test; trial; *ultimate test;* viva; verification; written ~; *XQ;* year-end exam; zetetic; [*see* scrutiny]

**examine** *(v.)*: assess; analyze; audit; behold; consider; check out; diagnose; eye; find; feel; go over; *hone in on;* inspect; investigate; *jerque;* keek; look at (-over); make an examination; notice; note; observe; overlook; pick over; pore; palpate; probe; question; quiz; research; review; re-examine; study; scrutinize; scan; test; *understand;* verify; view; vet; watch; weigh; *xenodiagnose; XQ;* yeme; zero in;

**example** *(n.)*: apotheosis; archetype; *beau ideal* [F.]; case (in point); *distillation;* ensample; exemplum; *fashion; footsteps;* fugler; guide; holotype; illustration; instance; jewel; *keen specimen;* lead; model; neotype; one to follow; precedent; prototype; paradigm; praxis; paragon; *quintessence;* representative; role model; sample; shining ~; touchstone; ule; *virtual;* working model; *xenagogue;* yardstick; *zealous;* [*see* instance; Ant. exception]

**exasperate** *(v.)*: annoy; anger; boil; cross; disturb; disgust; enrage; frustrate; fluster; grate; *heat;* irritate; infuriate; incense; jangle; kindle; lose it; madden; miff; nettle; outrage; *offend;* peeve; pique; perturb; provoke; *quick-tempered;* rankle; rile; steam; tick off; upset; vex; worsen; *xerothermic;* yell; zealousy [arch.];

**excavate** *(v.)*: abstract; burrow; coal-mine; dig (out; up); ditch; delve; disinter; dislodge; disentomb; extract; exhume; ferret out; get out; hollow; *intrench; jenkin;* kip; *lower;* mine; *notch; open;* prospect; quarry; remove (dirt); sap; shovel; scoop out; trench; take out; unearth; untomb; *venture;* work with spade; *xfer; yede;* zealously dig; [Ant. entomb]

**excavation** *(n.)*: abstraction; archeological site; burrowing; colliery; coal mine; dig(ging); deterration; excavating; effossion; *fodient;* getting out; hole; howk [Scot.]; *industry; jenkin;* kirving; land-removing; mine; *ninety-foot dig; opening;* pit; quarry; removal; suffossion; *site; trench;* unearthing; *venture;* wheal; *xfer; yede;* zanja; [Ant. entombment]

**exceed** *(v.)*: advance past; bypass; better; beat; cap; do more; excel; *further;* go beyond; *higher;* improve upon; *just pass; kill;* lick; master; *no contest;* outdo; outnumber; outperform; overstep; overrun; pass (by); *quash;* rise above; reach higher level; surpass; transcend; top; unseat; venture further; win; *x-cend; yare;* zip past;

**excel** *(v.)*: advance past; beat; bypass; cap; do more; exceed; *further;* go beyond; *higher;* improve upon; *just pass; kill;* lick; master; *no contest;* outstrip; outdo; outperform; pass (by); *quash;* rise above; surpass; shine; transcend; top; unseat; *vanquish;* whip past; win; *x-cend; yeah!;* zip past;

**excellence** *(n.)*: admirableness; *brilliance;* class; distinction; exquisiteness; fineness; greatness; *highest quality;* heavenliness; impressiveness; *jim-dandy;* keenness; loftiness; merit; mastery; notoriety; outstandingness; prominence; pre-eminence; perfection; quality; remarkableness; superiority; transcendence; *unsurpassed;* virtue; worthiness; *xtry; you-beaut [Aus.]; zero-defect;*

**excellent** *(adj.)*: admirable; *bon!* [F.]; bonny; boffo; brilliant; capital; crackerjack; divine; exceptional; fantastic; first-rate; great; high(-quality); impressive; incredible; jolly good [Br.]; keen; lofty; laudable; magnificent; masterful; noteworthy; nonpareil; outstanding; phenomenal; praiseworthy; prime; *quality;* remarkable; sublime; splendid; superb; superlative; stupendous; top-notch; unequalled; virtuous; wonderful; xtry.; *you-beaut* [Aus.]; *zero-defect;*

**except** *(prep.)*: aside from; but; bar; besides; 'cept [slang]; dispense; excepting; excluding; *forget;* go over; however not; ignore; just not; *kest;* leave out; *miss;* not; omit; only not; putting aside; *quite free;* releasing; save; *toss out;* unless that; *void;* without; x; yet without; *zero effect;*

**exception** *(n.)*: *aside from;* barring; charter; debarment; exclusion; freeing; *government waiver; hold out;* immunity; *just not;* keeping out; leaving out; *missing;* noninclusion; omission; putting aside; *quittance;* release; special case; *tax ~; unaffected;* variance; waiver; *xfer; yet without; zero effect;*

**exceptional** *(adj.)*: astonishing; breathtaking; brilliant; *capital;* divine; extraordinary; fabulous; great; high; heavenly; incredible; jim-dandy; keen; lofty; laudable; magnificent; notable; outstanding; prominent; phenomenal; praiseworthy; *quantum* [L.]; remarkable; spectacular; tremendous; unequalled; unbelievable; unrivaled; very good; virtuous; wonderful; xtry.; *you-beaut* [Aus.]; zizzy; [*Ant.* everyday]

**excess** *(n.)*: abundance; amplitude; bounty; copiousness; disproportionateness; extra; fullness; generous amount; galore; heaps; immensity; jumbo amounts; *king-sized amount;* lots; loads; multiplicity; nimiety; overabundance; overmuch; overkill; plenty; plethora; preponderance; profusion; quantities; repleteness; superabundance; surplus; tons; uberty; volumes; wealth; x.; *yards; zillion;*

**excessive** *(adj.)*: above and beyond; beyond reason; crapulent; *crazy;* disproportionate; *de trop* [F.]; extreme; far above; gouging; high; inordinate; immoderate; *jumbo;* king-sized; *large; more than enough;* not needed; overmuch; overboard; overgenerous; *plenty; quantitative;* ridiculous; substantial; too much; undue; unwarranted; unnecessary; unreasonable; very high; wanton; xtry.; yet unwarranted; *zillions;*

**exchange** *(n.)*: alternation; barter; buying and selling; change; conversion; deal; even ~; flip; giving in ~; hand-over; interchange; *jockeying;* key trade; *link;* market; network; overhaul; put right; *quid pro quo* [L.]; reversal; replacement; reciprocation; switch; swap; substitution; trade; transposal; upgrade; *vary; work;* xfer; *yaw;* zwap [dial].

**exchange** *(v.)*: alternate; barter; change; convert; commute; cash in; deal; *even- ~;* flip; give in ~; horse-trade; interchange; invert; *jockey; key trade;* let one have for; make a trade; *network; overhaul; put right; quadrate;* reverse; replace; re-exchange; reciprocate; reconvert; switch; swap; substitute; trade; transpose; upgrade; *vary; work;* xfer; *yaw;* zwap [dial].

**exhaustion** *(n.)*: *aweary [poet.];* bleariness; comatose; drowsiness; extreme weariness; fatigue; *grogginess;* hypersomnia; inanition; *jetlag;* kef; languor; mopishness; nappiness; overtiredness; peplessness; plumb tuckered [reg.]; *quiet; run down;* sleepiness; tiredness; *unenthusiasm; vapidity;* weariness; *xenarthrous;* yawning; *zonked out;* [*Ant.* energizing]

**excitable** *(adj.)*: agitable; *bouncy;* concerned; delicate-nerved; edgy; fearful; galvanic; high-strung; hyper; insecure; jittery; jumpy; keyed up; lily-livered; *moody;* nervous; overstrung; paranoid; quivering; restless; skittish; tense; touchy; tight-wound; unstrung; volatile; wired; *xenophobic; yellow;* zippy; [*Ant.* easygoing]

**excite** *(v.)*: agitate; arouse; bestir; *cause;* drive; disturb; enthuse; fire up; gladden; *goad;* hearten; hype-up; inspire; ignite; joy; jar; kindle; *keyed up;* lift up; *lead;* motivate; *nudge;* overjoy; provoke; pique; quicken; rouse; stir; stimulate; titillate; thrill; trouble; unglue; vivify; whet; work up; *xuld [arch.];* yerk; *zing;* [*Ant.* ease]

**excitement** *(n.)*: amazement; anticipation; bedazzlement; conturbation; disturbance; enthusiasm; exhilaration; furor; frisson; goose bumps; hype; inspiration; joy; kick; lift; motivation; *non-boring;* overjoy; piquing; quickening; rousing; rage; stirring; stimulation; thrill; titillation; *unglued;* vivification; wonderment; *xtry. mood;* yerk; zeal; [*see* jubilation]

**exciting** *(n.)*: arousing; breathless; climactic; daring; exhilarating; *fired up;* great; heady; intense; jarring; *kindling;* lifting; moving; *non-boring;* overly stimulating; provocative; piquing; quickening; rousing; rip-roaring; stirring; stimulating; thrilling; uptempo; vivifying; wondrous; *xtry.; yerking;* zingy; [*Ant.* eventless]

**exclaim** *(v.)*: appeal; bellow; beckon; boom; brag; burst out; cry out; call; declaim; express; *fret;* growl; holler; howl; *inveigh; jubilate;* keen; loudly say; *lament;* mewl; noise; outcry; proclaim; *quiritation;* reclaim; resonate; reverberate; roar; rave; shout; trumpet; ululate; vociferate; wail; *xenophonia;* yell; yowl; *zindabad;*

**exclude** *(v.)*: alienate; bar; banish; blackball; cold-shoulder; disallow; debar; except; excommunicate; forbid; give the cold shoulder; hinder; illegalize; *jam;* keep out; limit; leave out; *make feel bad;* not accept; nix; outlaw; prohibit; proscribe; pill; quit on; restrict; reject; stop; shun; shut out; turn away; *unkind; veto;* withhold; x; *yard* [arch.]; *zero admittance;* [*Ant.* embrace]

**exclusion** *(n.)*: alienation; banishment; barring; cold shoulder; debarment; excluding; forbidding; *give cols shoulder;* hindering; illegalization; *jam;* keeping out; leaving out; *making feel bad;* non-acceptance; outlawing; prohibition; proscription; quitting on; restriction; rejection; shunning; shutting out; turning away; *unkindness; veto;* withholding; x; *yarding* [arch.]; zero admittance; [*Ant.* embrace]

**excommunicate** *(v.)*: anathematize; alienate; banish; boot; cut off; church; court-martial; disfellowship; discipline; debar; discharge; expel; eject; fire; get rid of; heave out; imban; interdict; interscind; *jettison;* kick out; *let go;* make leave; *negate;* oust; put out; proscribe; purge; quit of; remove; spew out; throw out; unchurch; unseat; vomit (out); *walking papers; xenelasy; yard* [arch.]; *zero out;* [*Ant.* embrace]

**excommunication** *(n.)*: alienation; banishment; cold shoulder; *cherem* [Heb.]; disfellowship; debarring; exclusion; expulsion; *fleeing;* giving cold shoulder; having nothing to do with; isolation; *jinking;* keeping out; *loathing;* moving away from; non-acceptance; ostracizing; proscription; *quite* [Sp.]; rejection; shuning; turning away; unchurching; vomiting out; walking papers; *xenelasy; yarding* [arch.]; *zero fellowship;* [*Ant.* embrace]

**excusable** *(adj.)*: admissible; allowable; bearable; condonable; defensible; explainable; forgivable; *good; helpable;* indemnifiable; justifiable; *kosher;* legitimate; maintainable; necessary; okay; pardonable; quite ~; reasonable; suitable; tenable; understandable; valid; vindicable; warrantable; *xferable;* yet ~; *zero problem;*

**excuse** *(n.)*: alibi; basis; cause; cop-out; defense; explanation; essoin; *escape;* exemption; foundation; *final cause;* grounds; *hold;* intellection; justification; key reason; logic; lame ~; legitimization; *motivation; notion;* out; pretext; put-off; poor ~; *quittance;* reason; rationalization; rationale; reasoning; story; salvo; self-justification; *thinking;* underlying reason; validation; *the wherefore; xenodiagnosis; yeme;* zeal;

**excuse** *(v.)*: absolve; apologize; *argue;* beg pardon; *clear up;* defend; explain; exempt; *forgive;* give reason; *have reason; illuminate;* justify; *key reason;* legitimize; let off; make ~ for; *not blame; overlook;* palliate; put off; pardon; *qualify;* rationalize; release; *reason;* self-justify; substantiate; tolerate; use excuses; vindicate; validate; worm out of; whitewash; warrant; *xenodiagnosis; yeme;* zeal; [*see* pardon]

**execute** *(v. do)*: accomplish; bring about; carry out; do; effect; fulfill; get done; handle; implement; jump to it; keep; lend oneself to; make; *not fail;* obey; perform; *questionless;* realize; see it through; transact; undertake; *vigor;* work; *xfer;* yield; zip to it;

**execute** *(v. kill)*: annihilate; behead; *cancel;* destroy; eliminate; exterminate; *electrocute;* finish off; gun down; hang; *inject; judge;* kill; *lethal injection; lapidate;* make to pay; *nip;* obliterate; put to death; quench; run through; slay; *stone;* terminate; *unseat;* vitiate; wipe out; x-out; *yank down;* zap; [*Ant.* establish]

**execution** *(n.)*: auto-da-fé; burning at the stake; condemnation; crucifixion; death; electric chair; firing squad; government-sanctioned ~; hanging; *injection;* judgment; *just desserts;* killing; lethal injection; making to pay; necktie party; obliteration; public hanging; *quenching;* running through; slaying; *stoning;* termination; *undoing;* vitiation; wiping out; *x-ing out; yanking down;* zapping; [*Ant.* establishment]

**executioner** *(n.)*: axe-man; assassin; butcher; *crony;* dispatcher; extirpator; *finisher;* gunman; hangman; headsman; hatchet man; hooded figure; *individual; job;* ketch; killer; liquidator; *mangler; ninja;* official; punisher; *quencher;* rope-man; slaughterer; terminator; *undoer;* vitiator; *widow-maker;* x-man; yardmaster; *zapper;*

**exemplary** *(adj.)*: awesome; brilliant; capital; dandy; excellent; fine; good; honorable; ideal; jim-dandy; keen; laudable; magnificent; notable; outstanding; perfect; praiseworthy; quality; remarkable; superb; splendid; tremendous; unblamable; very good; wonderful; xtry.; *you-beaut* [Aus.]; *zesty;*

**exemplify** *(v.)*: *archetype;* be; characterize; demonstrate; exhibit; epitomize; *fugle;* give as example; hold out; illustrate; *justify;* kithe [Scot.]; lay out; manifest; model; *noticeable;* open up; personify; *quality;* represent; show (forth); typify; *use;* validate; *wonderful example; xenagogue; yardstick;* zero in;

**exempt** *(adj.)*: absolutely impervious; *bondless;* clear; discharged; excepted; excluded; free; *given variance; hold;* immune; impervious; insusceptible; *just fine;* klendusic [bot.]; let off; made free; non-affected; off the hook; protected; privileged; quite free; released; resistant; safe; *tax- ~;* unsusceptible; unaffected; unliable; very safe; waved; x; yet impervious; *zap-proof;*

**exempt** *(v.)*: *aside; besides;* clear; discharge; except; free; give variance; *hold;* immunize; *just not; kest;* let off; miss; make free; *not liable;* overlook; omit; *protect; quite free;* release; *special case; tax ~;* unaffected; variance; wave; x; *yet unaffected; zero effect;*

**exemption** *(n.)*: absolute imperviousness; *bondlessness;* clearance; dispensation; diplomatic immunity; exception; freedom; free pass; *gratis; hold;* immunity; imperviousness; insusceptibility; impunity; *justification;* klendusity [bot.]; letting off; mandated ~; non-susceptibility; omission; protection; pass; quittance; resistance; safety; special status; *ticket:* tax ~; unaffectedness; variance; waiver; x; *yeming* [arch.]; *zap-proofness;*

**exercise** *(n.)*: activity; athletics; bodily ~; bodybuilding; calisthenics; *chin-ups;* daily ~; exercising; fartlek; floor ~; *fitness;* group ~; gymnastics; honing; interval training; isometrics; *jumping jacks;* keeping fit; leg ~; muscle-building; morning ~; natural ~; outdoor ~; plyometrics; physical ~; *pushups;* quantity; *running; shintaido* [Jap.]; training; toning up; *tai chi* [Chin.]; *underarm weightlifting; very intense ~;* warm-up; workout; weight-lifting; x-ercise [slang]; *yanking;* zealous ~;

**exhaust** *(n.)*: atomization; black smoke; cloud; discharge; emission; eduction; fumes; gas; *haze; incloud;* jet propulsion fumes; *KH instability;* leakage; miasma; noxious fumes; output; pollution; *quasi-vaporous;* release; smoke; toxic fumes; *unbreathable;* vapor; waste gases; *xenon gas; yellowy gas; zero health;*

**exhaust** *(v.)*: *abate;* bleed; bankrupt; consume; deplete; expend; finish; fatigue; *gone;* hone; impoverish; *jade; kaput;* lessen; lose; *minimize; nullify;* overextend; overspend; overexert; poop out; quail; run out; sap; spend; tire (out); tap out; tire; use (up); vacate; wipe out; wear out; *xerosis; yield;* zap; [*Ant.* energize]

**exhausted** *(adj.)*: aweary [lit.]; bone-weary; cachectic; drained; ever-so-weary; fatigued; forespent; groggy; half dead; *indolent; jaded;* knocked-out; lethargic; most tired; noddy; overspent; overexerted; pooped; *quiescent;* run down (-ragged); spent; tired; unrested; very tired; wiped out; *x'ed;* yawnish; zapped; [*Ant.* energized]

**exhaustible** *(adj.)*: able to be depleted; bleedable; consumable; drainable; depletable; expendable; finite; *given amount;* having limits; impoverishable; *just so much;* known amount; limited; *minimize;* non-renewable; *only so much; preset;* quite limited; *run out;* sappable; *tire out; using up;* very limited; with limitations; *x'ed;* yea so much; zappable; [*Ant.* endless]

**exhaustive** *(adj.)*: all-encompassing; broad; comprehensive; complete; *done;* entire; full; general; high; inclusive; *jim-bang; known; long-awaited;* macroscopic; non-abridged; overall; perfect; pure; plenary; quantitative; *ranging;* sheer; sweeping; total; thorough; unabridged; uncut; *veritable;* whole; *xtry.;* yare; *zonal;*

**exhort** *(v.)*: appeal; admonish; advise; bid; charge; declare; encourage; forcefully urge; goad; *herald;* implore; *jurate; key in;* lecture; make ~ation; *notify; order;* preach; press; prod; *quote scripture; rant;* remonstrate; reprove; spur; tell; urge; vocalize; warn; *xenagogy;* yell; *zealously urge;*

**exhortation** *(n.)*: admonition; bidding; beckoning; charge; call; counsel; caution; direction; encouragement; forewarning; guidance; hortation; imploration; incitement; injunction; juration; *kibitz;* lecture; monition; *nudge;* obtestation; preaching; preachment; pressing; *quo minus* [L.]; remonstration; reproof; sermon; telling; urging; *voice;* word; warning; warning; *xenagogy;* yelling; *zakon* [Rus.];

**exhibit** *(v.)*: array; bare; *carry;* display; demonstrate; expose; flaunt; *give;* hold out; illustrate; *just show;* kithe [Scot.]; lay out; manifest; *non-concealment; open up;* present; *qualify;* reveal; show (off); set out; *typify;* unveil; vaunt; *wave; xuld* [arch.]; yield; *zero concealment;*

**exhibition** *(n.)*: array; *behold;* carnival; display; expo(sition); floorshow; gathering; *horse show;* items on display; *jamboree;* kermis; local ~; manifestation; nundination; *occasion;* private showing; presentation; quality production; ridotto; show(ing); song and dance; spectacle; trade show; theatre performance; *unveiling;* vernissage; wingding; *xtry.;* yield; *zero concealment;*

**exhilarate** *(v.)*: animate; bestir; cheer; delight; excite; enthuse; elate; enliven; *ecstatic; frisk;* gloat; *happy;* hearten; invigarate; joy; *kill the fatted calf;* lift; *motivate; nowell;* overjoy; pep up; *quicken; rouse;* stimulate; stir; thrill; uplift; vivify; wow; *xanadu; yell;* zip up;

**exhilaration** *(n.)*: animation; bliss; cheerfulness; delight; elation; exuberance; felicity; glee; hilarity; happiness; intoxication; jubilation; *keenness;* lightheartedness; merriment; *niceness;* overjoy; pleasure; *queme;* rejoicing; seventh heaven; satisfaction; thrill; transport; *uplifted; vivacity;* winsomeness; *xanadu; yeah!;* zestfulness;

**exile** *(n. deportation)*: alienation; banishment; casting out; displacement; expatriation; expulsion; forcing out; *getting rid;* heaving out; *impel to leave; journeyer;* kicking out; legal ~; migration; *not allowed in;* ostracism; proscription; *quit;* relegation; separation; throwing out; uprooting; vacating; *without;* xenizing; *yet ousted; zero permission;*

**exile** *(n. deported person)*: alienated person; banished person; castaway; deportee; displaced person; diaspora; evacuee; expatriate; *forced out; gone;* heaved out; *impulse; jettison;* kicked out; *living abroad;* man without a country; migrant; *non-resident;* outcast; pariah; *quant;* reject; refugee; stateless person; *thrown out; uproot;* vomited out; *wale; xenelasy; ybanysshed* [arch.]; *zing;*

**exile** *(v.)*: alienate; banish; cast out; deport; drive out; expel; expatriate; force out; get rid of; heave out; *impulse; jettison;* kick out; *launch;* make leave; *non-residency;* oust; proscribe; *quant;* relegate; send away; throw out; *uproot;* vomit out; *wale; xenelasy; ybanysshed* [arch.]; *zing;* [*Ant.* embrace]

**exist** *(v.)*: abide; *am; alive;* be; consist; continue; dure; endure; fare; go on; habit; hold on; is; inhabit; *just ~;* keep alive; live; make it; not die; occur; outlast; persevere; *quick;* remain (alive); *real;* survive; subsist; stand; *tarry;* uphold; *vitality;* walk on the earth; *xenenthesis; yieldless; zero harm;* [*Ant.* expire]

**existence** *(n.)*: authenticity; being; consciousness; consistence; corporeality; continuation; duration; essence; entelechy; fact(uality); going on; happening; hypostasis; inherence; *just alive;* keeping alive; life; making it; non-death; ontology; occurrence; presence; presentness; quickening; reality; subsistence; substantial; truth; upholding; vitality; whereness; xenenthesis; *yu* [Chin.]; *zoe* [Gr.]; [*Ant.* expiration]

**exit** *(n.)*: abandonment; *begone;* coming out; departure; egress; escape; evacuation; exodus; farewell; fleeing; going out; good-bye; *hightailing;* issuing out; *jumping out; kesting;* leaving; migration; *non-retention;* outgo; out-gate; outcoming; off-ramp; parting; *quitting; ramp;* shoving off; taking leave; turnoff; *uprooting;* vacating; withdrawal; x; *yead;* zipping away; [*Ant.* entrance]

**exit** *(v.)*: abandon; be off; clear out; depart; egress; evacuate; emigrate; flee; go; hightail; immigrate; jump off; *kest;* leave; mosey (along); migrate; move out; *navigate; outcoming;* part; *quit;* remove; shove off; take leave; *uproot;* vacate; withdraw; xfer; yead; zip away; [*Ant.* enter]

**exodus** *(n.)*: abandonment; *begone;* coming out; departure; exit; egress; escape; evacuation; exode; farewell; fleeing; going out; good-bye; *hightailing;* issuing out; *jumping out; kesting;* leaving; migration; *non-retention;* outcoming; outgoing; out-gate; off-ramp; parting; *quitting; riddance;* shoving off; separation; taking leave; *uprooting;* vacating; withdrawal; x; *yead;* zipping away;

**exonerate** *(v.)*: acquit; *blameless;* clear; deraign; declare not guilty; exculpate; free; *guiltless;* hold not-guilty; *illustrate;* justify; *kithe;* liberate; maintain; *non-guilty; open;* prove (innocence); propugn; quit; remove blame; restore; set free; totally acquit; undo damage; vindicate; withdraw charges; *x-out; yele [arch.];* zero out charges; [*Ant.* excoriate]

**exoneration** *(n.)*: acquittal; *blamelessness established;* clearing; disculpation; exculpation; freedom; *guiltlessness established;* holding not guilty; *invalidation;* justification; *kithing; liberation; maintaining;* name-clearing; *opening;* proof; quittance; restoration; setting free; total acquittal; upholding; vindication; withdrawal of charges; *xing-out; yele [arch.];* zero guilt; [*Ant.* excoriation]

**exorcise** *(v.)*: adjure; banish; cast out; drive out; expel; force out; free; get rid of; *heave out; isolate; jettison;* kest; *launch; leave;* make leave; *non-residency;* oust; put out; *quant;* rid; send away; throw out; unseat; vanquish; *wale; xfer; yank; zap;*

**exorcism** *(n.)*: adjuration; banishment; casting out; driving out; expelling; exsufflation; forcing out; freeing; getting rid of; *heaving out; isolation; jettison;* kesting; *leaving;* making to leave; *non-residency;* ousting; putting out; *quant;* ridding; sending away; thrusting out; *unseating;* vanquishing; *wale; xfer; yanking; zap;*

**expand** *(v.)*: aggrandize; broaden; climb; develop; dilate; distend; enlarge; extend; fatten; grow; greaten; heighten; increase; inflate; jump up; *keep growing;* largen; lengthen; mount; maximize; *non-stable;* open out; progress; *quadruplicate;* rise; spread; swell; *thrive; upgrow* [arch.]; *vegetate;* wax larger; widen; xtn; *yain [arch.];* zoom; [*Ant.* ebb]

**expandable** *(adj.)*: adjustable; broadening; changeable; *collapsible;* dilatant; distensible; expansile; extendable; fold-out; growable; *heighten;* inflatable; *jump up; kaleidoscopic;* lengthenable; metamorphic; *non-confined;* opening; pullout; *quadruplicate;* retractable; stretchable; spreadable; telescoping; *upgrow [arch.];* variable; *wax larger;* xtn; yet ~; *zoom out;*

**expanse** *(n.)*: area; breadth; coverage; *depth;* extent; field; gulf; huge area; immense area; *jaw-hole; kilometers;* lapse; length; many-mile ~; *nadir;* open space; plane; *quadrant;* region; range; space; span; stretch; tract; unmeasurable gap; vastness; width; *xibalba; yawn;* zone;

**expansion** *(n.)*: advance; broadening; climbing; development; dilation; enlargement; furtherance; growth; heightening; increase; jumping up; *keen ~;* luxuriance; multiplication; new growth; outgrowth; *overgrowth;* progression; quantum increase; rising; spreading; swelling; thriving; upsurge; *vegetation;* waxing greater; xtn.; *yain [arch.];* zoom; [*Ant.* ebbing]

**expansive** *(adj.)*: abundant; big; capacious; distensive; extensive; fantastic; great; huge; immense; *jumbo-sized; king-size;* large; massive; *noteworthy;* open; prodigious; quantitative; roomy; spacious; sizable; *tremendous;* uncrowded; vast; wide; *xtry.; yawn;* zillions; [*Ant.* eensie-weensie]

**expect** *(v.)*: anticipate; believe; count on; *demand;* envision; forethink; *guess;* hope; *imagine;* insist; *just ~;* keep looking; look for; *mindful;* need; overtrust; plan for; presume; *questionless;* ready oneself for; *require;* suppose; think; trust; *urge; volition;* wait for; *xel [arch.];* yearn (for); zeal;

**expectation** *(n.)*: anticipation; belief; confidence; *desire;* expectancy; eagerness; faith; great hope; hope; *imminence; just expectation; keenness;* looking forward to; *mindful;* non-despair; optimism; prospect; *questionless; reliance;* sanguinity; trust; *unastonishment; vehemence;* wish; *xel [arch.];* yearning; *zeal;*

**expedience** *(n.)*: advisability; benefit; convenience; desirability; expediency; feasibility; gainfulness; helpfulness; *immediate;* judiciousness; *keenness; legitimacy;* meetness; no-nonsense; operability; practicality; prudence; *quartful [arch.];* reasonableness; sensibility; *tenability;* usefulness; value; wisdom; *xtry. appropriateness; yieldful;* zero problem; [*Ant.* erroneousness]

**expedient** *(adj.)*: advisable; advantageous; beneficial; convenient; conducive; *dernier ressort;* effective; favorable; good; helpful; *intelligent;* judicious; *keen;* logical; meet; no-nonsense; operative; practical; pragmatic; prudent; *quartful* [arch.]; trealistic; self-serving; *tenable;* useful; viable; workable; well-advised; *xtry. appropriate;* yieldful; zero problem; [*Ant.* erroneous]

**expedite** *(v.)*: accelerate; *burst;* cruise; dart; *erupt;* fly; go fast; hurry; *intense;* jet; *kite; lightning-fast;* move quickly; *non-delayed; outrun;* push through quickly; quicken; rush; speed; tear; *uprush; velocity;* whip; *xuld [arch.];* yern; zip; [*Ant.* ease up]

**expedition** *(n.)*: adventure; boat voyage; course; drive; excursion; exploration; experience; foray; going; *hadj* [Mos.]; itineration; journey; knight-errantry; lark; mission; *night voyage;* odyssey; outing; pilgrimage; quest; *ride;* sally; safari; trek; undertaking; voyage; venture; wayfaring; *xenize; yong* [arch.]; *zugunruhe* [G.];

**expel** *(v.)*: alienate; banish; cast out; disseize; eject; force out; get rid of; heave out; *impulse; jettison;* kick out; *launch;* make leave; *non-residency;* oust; put out; *quant;* reject; send away; throw out; thrust out; unseat; vomit (out); withdraw; *xenelasy; ybanysshed* [arch.]; *zing;* [*Ant.* embrace]

**expend** *(v.)*: apply; burn (up); consume; disburse; deplete; exhaust; *fatigue;* give (out); hand out; incur cost; *jiggy [Br.]; kill;* lay out; let go; lose; *lavish;* make payment; *non-retention;* outlay; pay out; *quaff; reduce;* spend; tap; use (up); *vest;* wear down; *xfer; yield;* zap; [*Ant.* earn]

**expendable** *(adj.)*: adjunct; beyond-basics; consumable; dispensable; disposable; extraneous; frivolous; *get rid of; hoity-toity;* insignificant; *jerkwater;* ketty; *leftover;* minor; nonessential; *overmuch;* petty; quisquillos; replaceable; superfluous; throwaway; unneeded; unessential; unimportant; vain; worthless; xtr.; yet unneeded; zero; [*Ant.* essential]

**expenditure** *(n.)*: amount; *base pay;* cash out; disbursement; expense; *finances;* giving out; handing over; *imbursement; justification; kickback; liquidation; money out; non-indebted;* outlay; outgo; outflow; payment; *quittance;* remittance; settlement; transfer; *unindebted;* virement; wage(s); xfer; yielding; zapping; [*Ant.* earnings]

**expensive** *(adj.)*: astronomical; big-ticket; costly; dear; exorbitant; fine; greatly-priced; high-priced; immoderate; inflated; *judged worthy; king's ransom;* lavish; money-grubbing; not cheap; out-of-range; overpriced; outrageous; precious; pricey; quality; *rich;* steep; top-dollar; uneconomical; unreasonable; very high; *worth it's weight in gold; xtry.; yieldful; zestful;* [*Ant.* economical]

**experience** *(n. happening)*: affair; adventure; *befall;* chapter; circumstance; drama; episode; encounter; event; fortuity; going on; happening; incident; *juncture;* key event; life ~; matter; melodrama; notable event; occurrence; ordeal; phenomenon; *quandary;* reality; situation; time; thing; *unfolding;* venture; work; *xtr. event; yield; zinger;*

**experience** *(n. skill)*: acquaintance; adeptness; basic training; competence; deftness; exposure; expertise; familiarity; going over; hours; habilitation; *instruction;* job training; know-how; knowledge; labor ~; mastery; *night hours;* on-the-job training; practice; qualification; readiness; skill; training; understanding; virtuosity; working with; *xenagogy;* years of ~; *zest;*

**experience** *(v.)*: *affect;* be subjected to; bear; come across; do; endure; feel; face; go through; have the ~; *happen to;* intimately know; *just happen;* know; live through; make acquaintance with; not avoid; *occurrence;* put through; *quab; ready;* suffer through; take; touch; undergo; *vibes;* work; *xfer; yeme; zet;*

**experiment** *(n.)*: analysis; *basic ~;* check; *development;* evaluation; field *~; findings; great ~; hopeful;* information-gathering *~; invention; justification;* knowledge-gaining ~; lab ~; making of tests; *new work;* operation; process; procedure; qualified research; research; scientific ~; test; trial; *unofficial ~; valuation;* work; x.; yield; zeroing in;

**experiment** *(v.)*: analyze; *behold;* conduct test; dabble; explore; find out; fool around with; get knowledge; *have tests;* investigate; *judge; know;* learn; make tests; *new work;* observe; play with; *quest for knowledge;* research; study; test; try out; *understand;* vet; work on; x.; yield; zero in;

**experimental** *(adj.)*: analytical; brand new; beta-test; *check;* developmental; exploratory; empirical; first-stage; *going through tests; hopeful;* investigational; *just out;* knowledge-gaining; laboratory; mostly-working; new; *operation;* pre-release; procedural; probational; pioneer; *questionable;* recently-developed; still-new; sample; tentative; trial; test; untested; untried; unproven; verificatory; *working on it;* x. young; zero debugging; [*Ant.* established]

**expert** *(adj.)*: adept; accomplished; brilliant; cunning; capable; deft; experienced; familiar; gifted; good; heaven-gifted; incredible; jolly good; knowledgeable; *leading;* masterful; notable; nimble; outstanding; proficient; qualified; remarkable; seasoned; skilled; talented; unequalled; virtuosic; wonderful; xtry.; *years of experience; zippy;*

**expert** *(n.)*: authority; boffin; connoisseur; doyen; dabster [arch.]; doyenne [fem.]; experienced master; *fine;* guru; hotshot; *individual; journeyman;* knowledgeable person; leader; master; maven; non-amateur; old hand; professional; pundit; *qualified ~;* real genius; specialist; technician; unrivaled master; veteran; wonk; well-informed; whiz; *xtry.; years of experience; zealous teacher;*

**expertise** *(n.)*: ability; adeptness; aptitude; bent; craftsmanship; command; cunning; deftness; experience; familiarity; genius; habilitation; *instinct; jack-of-all-trades;* know-how; long suit; mastery; *natural ability; occupation;* proficiency; qualification; quality; readiness; skill; talent; usefulness; virtuosity; wherewithal; *xenium;* years of experience; *zest;*

**expiration** *(n.)*: *abolition; bad;* cessation; discontinuation; end(ing); finishing; *going bad; halting; invalidation; jaws of death; killing;* liquidation; *mortification; nulling;* omega; perishing; parting; quietus; running out; stopping; termination; undoing; *vanishing;* withering; x-ing out; yielding; zapping; [*Ant.* existence]

**expire** *(v.)*: *abate;* be over; cease; decease; end; elapse; fail; go bad; give up the ghost; have its end; invalidate; *jaws of death;* kick the bucket [slang]; *lifeless;* meet one's Maker; *non-valid; over;* perish; pass expiration date; quail; run out; *succumb; spoil;* terminate; *unusable; vanish;* wane; "x"; yield one's spirit; *zapped;* [*Ant.* exist]

**explain** *(v.)*: answer; *address; bespeak;* clarify; comment; clear up; clue in; delineate; define; explicate; expound; enlighten; elaborate; elucidate; exposit; *footnote;* get across; gloss; help one understand; illuminate; justify; *key in;* lay open the meaning; make clear; note; *open up; precise; qualify; reword;* show; shed light on; spell out; throw light on; uncloud; *verse;* write out; *xenagogy; yak;* zero in on;

**explainable** *(adj.)*: answerable; *breakable;* clarifiable; delineable; definable; explicable; *findable; gettable;* helpable; intelligible; illustratable; justifiable; knowable; *logical; making clear; non-clouded;* openable; *perceivable;* qualifiable; resolvable; solvable; translatable; *tellable;* uncoverable; understandable; very ~; *workable; xlate;* yet ~; zero in on; [*see* forgivable]

**explanation** *(n.)*: account; briefing; clarification; description; definition; defense; dilatation; details; elucidation; explication; exposition; excuse; *foundation;* grounds; *hypothesis; intention;* interpretation; intendment; illustration; justification; key (reason); logical ~; light; laying open; making intelligible; narrative; *objective;* pretext; *quickening;* reason; rede; statement; specifics; thought; *understanding;* validation; words; written ~; *xenodiagnosis; yeme;* zero in;

**explanatory** *(adj.)*: advisory; *beautiful;* clarifying; descriptive; delineative; explicatory; expressive; enunciative; exegetic(al); expository; enlightening; elucidative; *foundational;* graphic; helpful; illustrative; illuminative; instructive; justifying; keenly educational; *learning; masterfully;* narrative; overly-graphic; pedagogic; qualifying; rationalistic; specific; telling; unequivocal; vivid; well-described; *xenagogic; yieldful;* zolaistic;

**explicit** *(adj.)*: apparent; blatant; clear; categorical; distinct; express; exact; *flagrant;* glaring; graphic; *heedless;* identifiable; *just plain;* keenly understandable; lucid; marked; non-vague; obvious; overt; open; plain; perspicuous; *quite obvious;* recognizable; specific; transparent; unequivocal; uninhibited; vivid; well-defined; *xparent; yeme [arch.];* zero confusion; [see x-rated; *Ant.* equivocal]

**explode** *(v.)*: apart; blow up; blast; burst; crash; detonate; erupt; fulminate; go off (-up in smoke); *hit;* ignite; *jet; ka-boom;* let go; mine; nova; outburst; pop; *pow!; quake;* release; rupture; set off; *smithereens;* tear apart; unleash; *up in smoke;* vent; *wham!;* x-bomb; yead; *zap;*

**exploit** *(n.)*: act(ion); behavior; coup; deed; effort; feat; going; heroic act; *intrepidity;* job; *knightliness; life;* move; *notorious act;* operation; performance; *quick act; reaction;* step; tour de force; thing; undertaking; venture; work(ing); x-action; *yaw; zeal;*

**exploit** *(v.)*: abuse; benefit from; capitalize on; despoil; *extract;* finagle; *get;* harm; ill-use; jockey; knock about; lig; manipulate; misuse; mishandle; milk; *nobble;* oppress; over~; profit from; push; *quad;* ravage; rape; sponge; suck dry; take advantage of; utilize; use; violate; victimize; walk all over; *x-out;* yeme; *zap;* [*Ant.* edify]

**exploitation** *(n.)*: abuse; bad use; capitalization; despoiling; *extraction;* finagling; *force; getting;* harm; ill-use; *jiggery-pokery;* knocking about; *ligging;* misuse; mistreatment; manipulation; maltreatment; molestation; neglect; overexploitation; profiting; *quad;* ravaging; raping; sucking dry; taking advantage; utilization; using; violation; wrong use; *x-ing out; yanking down; zapping;* [*Ant.* edification]

**exploration** *(n.)*: ascertaining; *braving;* combing; discovering; examination; foraging; going out into; hunt; investigation; jerquing; *kith;* looking over; mission; nosing around; overlooking; patrol; quest; reconnoiter; search; survey; trailblazing; uncovering; venture; watch; *x-search; yearn for; zealous ~;*

**explore** *(v.)*: ascertain; *bring to light;* comb; discover; examine; forage; go into; hunt; investigate; jerque; kithe; leave no stone unturned; make a search; *nose;* open up; probe; quest for; rake; rummage; reconnoiter; search (out); survey; trailblaze; uncover; *venture;* wade thru; x-search; *yearn for; zealously ~;*

**explosion** *(n.)*: aerial ~; blast; bang; boom; burst; *crack;* detonation; eruption; fulmination; flash; going up in smoke; hypernova; igniting; *jangle;* ka-boom; lashing out; mushroom cloud; nova; outburst; *pow; proruption;* quasar; rupture; supernova; *thunder; up in smoke;* venting; *violence;* wham-bang; *x-ray burster;* yield [nuclear science]; *zap;*

**explosive** *(adj.)*: agitable; bad-tempered; capricious; dangerous; erratic; feiry; grumpy; hot-tempered; irascible; jangly; *jeopardous; kaleidoscopic; labile;* mean-tempered; non-stable; out-of-control; precarious; quick-tempered; *risky;* stormy; tumultuous; unstable; volatile; violent; vesuvial; wild; *x-ing;* yeasty; *zoilean;* [*Ant.* easygoing]

**export** *(v.)*: *airlift; bring;* convey; deliver; *exit;* freight; furnish; give; handle; *issue;* janker; kurvey; locomote; move; *node; offload; overseas;* pass; produce; *quarter-cart;* relay; re~; ship; send out; supply; sell (abroad); trade; transport; uptake; *van; waft;* xfer; yanker [Br.]; *zip;*

**exportation** *(n.)*: *airlift; bringing;* conveyance; delivery; exporting; freighting; *going;* haulage; international shipping; *janker;* kurveying; *logistics;* movement; *node;* out-shipping; *pass;* quick-ship; relaying; shipping; trade; *underway; voyage;* waftage; xfer; *yield; zip;*

**expose** *(v.)*: advertise; bare; crack; display; disclose; exhibit; flaunt; give away; hold out; incur danger; *jut;* kithe [Scot.]; lay open; manifest; make visible; make known; manifest; muckrake; *non-concealment;* open up; *overexpose;* present; put on view; *qualify;* reveal; show; tout; take out; uncover; unveil; unmask; *visible; vulnerable; wave;* x-pose; *yield;* zero concealment; [*Ant.* entomb]

**exposit** *(v.)*: *address; bespeak;* clarify; comment; clarify; clear up; delineate; declare; define; expound; explain; exegete; *footnote;* give sense; help one understand; interpret; illuminate; *justify; kerygma;* lay open; make clear; *notate;* open up; preach; *qualify;* read and explain; shed light on; show; throw light on; uncloud; *verse;* write about; *xenagogy;* yell; zero in on;

**expositor** *(n.)*: annotator; Bible-teacher; commentator; clarifier; *declarer;* exegesist; exegete; expository preacher; *field preacher; gospeler;* hermeneut; homilist; interpreter; josser [Aus. slang]; *kerygma;* lecturer; messenger; minister; *noiser;* orator; preacher; pulpiteer; pastor; *quoter; revivalist;* speaker; sermonizer; teacher; *utterer;* voicer; writer; xenagogue; *yeller [derog.];* zealous preacher;

**expound** *(v.)*: acquaint; *bring up;* construe; describe; develop; delineate; explain; enlarge upon; *fugle;* guide; hold forth; interpret; *jobation; knowledge;* lay open; make clear; *notate;* orate; *outline;* preach; qualify; *ready;* school; sermonize; teach; unlock; *verse;* work with; *xenagogue; yak; zealously instruct;*

**express** *(adj.)*: accelerated; breakneck; *celerity;* direct; expeditious; fast; *greased lightening;* hurried; *immediate; jiffy; keen;* lickety-split; most direct; nonstop; overnight; pronto; prompt; quick; rapid; speedy; *timely; ultrasonic speed;* vigorous; without delay; x-speed; yar; zippy;

**express** *(v.)*: articulate; bespeak; communicate; convey; declare; enunciate; formularize; get across; *have say;* indicate; *jaw; key in;* let out; mention; noise; note; observe; proclaim; quoth; relate; remark; relay; say; state; tell; utter; verbalize; voice; word; write; *xenophonia;* yak; zero in;

**expression** *(n.)*: adage; byword; catchword; colloquialism; dictum; epigram; figure of speech; graphicness; hackneyed saying; idiom; *judgment;* ketch-word; line; localism; metonym; neologism; oracle; proverb; phrase; quote; rule; saying; term; universal truth; vernacularism; verbalism; word; *xenophonia; Yogism;* zeteticism;

**expressionless** *(adj.)*: *apathetic;* blank-expressioned; cold; deadpan; empty-expressioned; flat-expressioned; glassy; having no expression; impassive; irresponsive; inexpressive; *jaded; knocked out;* lacking expression; mechanical; non-expressive; obdurate; poker-faced; *quiet; repressed;* straight-faced; solemn; serious; stone-faced; *totally ~;* unexpressive; unsmiling; unresponsive; void of expression; wooden; *xylocaine;* yet ~; zero-expression;

**expulsion** *(n.)*: *alienation; action;* banishment; casting out; discharge; driving out; eviction; extrusion; forcing out; *getting rid of;* heaving out; issue; jettison; kicking out; launching; moving out; *non-remaining;* ouster; ousting; proscription; quitture; removal; riddance; separation; transportation; thrusting out; unchurching; vomiting out; *withdrawal;* xenelasy; *yanking; zero retention;* [Ant. embracement]

**exquisite** *(adj.)*: attractive; beautiful; charming; delicate; exceptional; fine; fabulous; gorgeous; heavenly; incomparable; *jeweled;* keen; lovely; magnificent; nice; outstanding; pleasant; *queme;* rewarding; superb; tasteful; unequalled; *valuable;* wonderful; xtry.; yummy; zizzy; [Ant. evil-favored]

**extend** *(v.)*: add on; broaden; continue; draw out; exsert; expand; further; fold out; go beyond; hang over; increase; jut; keep going; lengthen; make longer; *non-collapsed;* outlie; outspread; outstretch; overhang; over- ~; project; protrude; *quantity;* reach forth; stretch; stick out; thrust out; uncurl; *vary;* widen; wax longer; XL; *yield; zoom;*

**extension** *(n.)*: add-on; broadening; continuation; drawing out; expansion; enlargement; furthering; growth; heightening; increase; inflation; jutting; *keep going;* lengthening; making longer; *node; outgrowth;* prolongation; quantum increase; rising; spreading; *taller;* upgrade; *variation;* widening; waxing greater; xtn; *yearlong ~;* zooming up (-in);

**extensive** *(adj.)*: astronomical; abundant; big; considerable; disproportionate; enormous; expansive; far-reaching; great; huge; humongous; immense; jumbo-sized; king-size; large; massive; *noteworthy;* overmuch; prodigious; quantitative; *ranging; ridiculous;* substantial; sweeping; tremendous; *unbelievable;* vast; widespread; XL; *Ymir;* zealous;

**extent** *(n.)*: ambit; area; amount; bounds; bigness; coverage; capacity; degree; depths; extensiveness; fullness; farness; *gamut;* highness; hugeness; intensity; intenseness; immensity; jurisdiction; *kaza [Turk.];* limit; level; latitude; length; largeness; *lower limit;* magnitude; *neighborhood;* overall length; order of magnitude; point; qua; reach; scope; scale; span; severity; tier; upper limit; verge; vastness; wideness; *x-section;* yardage; *zone;*

**extenuating** *(adj.)*: acute; blame-mitigating; *clear;* desperate; extenuative; extreme; *free from blame;* grave; highly unusual; *intense;* justifying; *keenly severe; large;* mitigating; *needy;* onerous; palliative; qualifying; real grave; severe; *tremendous;* unusual; understandable; very unusual; weighty; xtry.; *yondmost; zeroizing;*

**exterior** *(adj.)*: apparent; beyond; circumambient; displayed; external; extrinsic; facial; *general appearance; hull;* integumental; *just outside; known; looks;* manifest; non-internal; outer; outward; outdoors; physical; perceptible; *quasi-aesthetic;* recognizable; surface; superficial; topical; temporal; unhidden; visible; without; x.; *yare; zenithal;*

**exterminate** *(v.)*: annihilate; *butcher;* cut off; destroy; eliminate; expunge; finish off; gun down; *homicide; incinerate; jab;* kill; *liquidate;* murder; massacre; *nip;* obliterate; purge; quench; *ruin;* slaughter; terminate; *undo;* vitiate; wipe out; x-out; *yank down;* zap;

**extermination** *(n.)*: annihilation; *butchering;* cessation; death; eradication; elimination; extinction; finishing off; *gunning down; homicide; incineration; jabbing;* killing; liquidation; mortality; *nullification;* obliteration; perishing; quashing; *ruination;* slaughter; termination; undoing; vitiation; wiping out; x-ing out; *yanking down; zapping;*

**external** *(adj.)*: aesthetic; apparent; beyond; circumambient; dermal; epidermal; exterior; extrinsic; facial; *general appearance; hull;* integumental; *just outside; known; looks;* manifest; non-internal; outside; outer; outward; outlying; physical; peripheral; *quasi-aesthetic;* recognizable; surface; surficial; superficial; topical; unhidden; visible; without; x.; *yare; zenithal;*

**extinct** *(adj.)*: archaic; bygone; ceased; died out; dead; extinguished; fallen; fossilized; gone; *has-been;* inexistent; *jurassic;* kaput; lost; *mortality;* nonexistent; no more; outmoded; perished; quenched; *relic;* snuffed out; terminated; unliving; vanished; wiped out; x-ed out; *yielded;* zeroized; [Ant. extant]

**extinction** *(n.)*: annihilation; *bygone;* cessation; destruction; death; extermination; fatality; *the grave; has-been*; inexistence; *jurassic;* killing; loss; mortality; mass ~; nonexistence; obliteration; perishing; quenching; *ruination;* snuffing out; termination; undoing; vanishing; wiping out; x-ing out; *yanking down; zapping;* [Ant. existence]

**extinguish** *(v.)*: asphyxiate; becalm; cover; douse; end; finish off; get it over; hush; immerse; *jam;* kill; *lay to rest;* make go out; nullify; overwhelm; put out; quench; *rid;* smother; snuff out; stifle; *terminate; undo;* void; wet; x-out; yote; zeroize; [*see* kill; Ant. establish]

**extort** *(v.)*: appropriate; betake; capture; divest; extract; exploit; force; grab; haul away; *intercept; jump at;* keep; lay hold of; make off with; nab; obtain; procure; *quirk;* remove; seize; take; usurp; *vest;* wrest; xfer; yank; zip away;

**extortion** *(n.)*: *aggression;* blackmail; coercion; duress; exaction; exploitation; forcing; *go after;* harassing; intimidation; *jeopardizing;* keeping down; larceny; menacing; *non-honesty;* overassessment; pressure; *quash;* robbery; stealing; shakedown; threatening; unnerving; violence; wresting; *xfer; yegg; zob;*

**extortionist** *(n.)*: appropriator; bloodsucker; crook; coercer; *depriver;* extortioner; felon; *greedy;* harpy; impropriator; *jailbird; knuck; lawbreaker;* malefactor; *no-good;* outlaw; profiteer; *quad;* robber; stealer; thief; *usurper;* villain; *waddy; xiaoren; yegg; zob;*

**extra** *(adj.)*: additional; auxiliary; bonus; contributory; *de trop* [F.]; extraneous; excess; further; *gobs* [slang]; *hoards;* increased; *joining; king-sized amounts;* leftover; more; *numerous;* other; plus; *quantities;* remaining; supplemental; surplus; spare; too; unused; *very; with;* xtr.; yet more; *zillions;* [Ant. essential]

**extract** *(v.)*: abstract; break out; *cant;* decoct; disconnect; divorce; disjoin; dislodge; evulse; extricate; free; get out; haul out; isolate; jerk out; kep; loose; lixiviate; make separate; *nab;* obtain; pull out; pluck out; quill; remove; separate; take out; unearth; *vell;* wrest; *x-sect;* yank out; *zip out;* [*Ant.* embed]
**extraction** *(n.)*: abstraction; boiling; breaking out; colature; decoction; dislodgement; drawing out; extrication; filtration; forcing out; getting out; heaving out; isolation; jerking out; *kep;* loosing; lixiviation; microfiltration; mining; *nabbing;* obtainment; pulling out; quilling; removing; separation; taking out; unearthing; *vellication;* wrenching; winkling out; *xuld [arch.];* yanking; zipping; [*Ant.* embedding]
**extradite** *(v.)*: *assign;* bring back; convey; deliver; export; fork over; give over; hand over; *issue; jettison;* kurvey; let have; *move; non-retention; offload;* pass; *quicken;* relinquish; surrender; send back; turn over; transfer; *unhand; volley; waft;* xfer; yield; *zero retention;*
**extraneous** *(adj.)*: additional; beside-the-point; contributory; disrelated; extrinsic; excess; extra; foreign; *gobs [slang]; hoards;* irrelevant; just not needed; *king-sized amounts;* leftover; *minor;* non-pertinent; outside; off-the-point; peripheral; *questionable;* redundant; superfluous; *too much;* unneeded; unrelated; *very much; with;* xtr.; *yards; zillions;* [*Ant.* essential]
**extraordinary** *(adj.)*: amazing; brilliant; breathtaking; capital; divine; excellent; exceptional; fantastic; fabulous; great; grand(iose); heavenly; incredible; *jim-dandy;* keen; lofty; laudable; marvelous; magnificent; noteworthy; notable; outstanding; prominent; phenomenal; *quantum* [L.]; remarkable; stupendous; superb; splendid; special; terrific; tremendous; uncommon; very good; wonderful; xtry.; *yippee!;* zizzy; [*Ant.* everyday]
**extraterrestrial** *(adj.)*: alien; beyond-earth; cosmic; deep space; *elsewhere;* from afar; galactic; heavenly; interplanetary; *jovial; kosmos [Gr.];* lunar; *Martian;* non-earth; off-earth; planetary; quasi-stellar; *rocket-man;* space; *traveling;* unearthly; *visiting; world; x-ray star; yonder;* zonic; [*Ant.* earthly]
**extraterrestrial** *(n.)*: alien; being; cosmic visitor; creature; *deep space;* extraterrestrial creature; *from afar;* galactic traveler; green man; *humanoid;* intergalactic traveler; *invader; Jovian; kosmos;* life-form; Lunarian; little green man; Martian; nonhuman; outworlder; *Plutonian;* quasi-humanoid; rocket-man; space man; traveler; unearthly visitor; UFO man; visitor; Venusian; wayfarer; *xenology; yonder; Zorkon invader;* [*Ant.* earthling]
**extravagant** *(adj.)*: abundant; affluent; bountiful; costly; classy; *decorated;* expensive; excessive; elaborate; fulsome; fabulous; grand; high;-class immoderate; indulgent; jet-set; *kingly;* luxurious; lavish; magnificent; non-frugal; opulent; overdone; plush; posh; *quartful* [arch.]; rich; sumptuous; spectacular; splendid; thriftless; upscale; voluptuous; wealthy; wasteful; xtry.; *yet unsurpassed; zierlich* [G.]; [*Ant.* economical]
**extreme** *(adj.)*: absolute; acute; best; complete; drastic; exorbitant; exceptional; full; fulminant; great; highest; intense; *just too much;* keen(est); large; most; maximum; *notable;* overly; peracute; perfect; quantitative; rank; radical; severe; stark; total; tremendous; utmost; utter; ultra; very; vehement; whole; xtry.; *yondmost; zenithal;*
**exuberant** *(adj.)*: animated; blissful; cheerful; delighted; elated; exhilarated; felicitous; glad; gleeful; happy; intoxicated; joyful; *keen;* lighthearted; merry; *nice;* overjoyed; pleased; *queme;* rejoicing; sunny; satisfied; thrilled; uplifted; *vivacious;* well-pleased; *xanadu;* yeasty; zestful;
**exult** *(v.)*: *applaud;* beam; bless; crow; cheer; celebrate; delight; dance; exuberate; elate; frisk; gloat; glory; *hurray; imparadised;* jubilate; *kill the fatted calf;* lilt; make merry; *nowell; ovation;* praise; *quiver;* rejoice; shout; triumph; *uplift; vivify;* wonder; *xanadu;* yell; zealous; [*see* praise]
**eye** *(n.)*: *adnate;* blue ~; brown ~; cornea; *descry;* eyeball; *field of view;* greenish ~; hazel ~; iris; *jerque; keek;* lid; *lash;* multiocular; *nye* [arch.]; orb; peeper; pupil; *quick glance;* retina; seeing; two ~s; uvea; vision; watcheye; walleye; x organ [zoo.]; *yeux [F.];* zero in;
**eyewitness** *(n.)*: attestant; bystander; beholder; *crowd;* descrier; eyer; *fellow;* gazer; hearer; innocent bystander; *janata [Asia];* keeker; looker-on; *multitude; man;* noticer; onlooker; person; passer-by; *quelet [arch.]; regarder;* spectator; testifier; *unbiased observer;* viewer; witness; *x.; yain* [arch.]; *zero in;*

# F

**fable** *(n.)*: apologue; allegory; bestiary; crock; *drama;* epic; folktale (-lore); *ghost story; hogwash;* imposture; invention; *journal; kappa book;* legend; myth; narrative; old (oft-retold) story; parable; *quarto;* retelling; story; (tall) tale; *untruth; version;* work of fiction; *xenodocheionology;* yarn; *zipper book;* [*Ant.* fact]

**fabricate** *(v. lie)*: allure; belie; concoct; contrive; dream up; equivocate; fake; gonk; hoodwink; invent; jazz; knowingly lie; lie; make up; manufacture; nobble; *outlie;* prevaricate; *quiblin* [arch.]; *rook;* stretch the truth; tell falsehood; trump up; *untruth;* verneuk; wangle; *xuld [arch.];* yentz; *zing;*

**fabricate** *(v. make)*: assemble; build; construct; devise; engineer; fashion; generate; hatch; invent; *job;* knock together; *labor;* make; manufacture; *new-vamp;* output; produce; quick-build; reproduce; shape; turn out; *upbuild;* vamp up; work out; *xenomorph;* yield; *z-bar;* [*see* lie]

**fabrication** *(n.)*: *alteration of truth;* big lie; contrivance; deception; equivocation; falsehood; false witness; gonk; half-truth; invention; jactitation; *kid;* lie; mendacity; non-truth; oath-breaking; perjury; *quiblin [arch.]; rook;* stretch; trick; untruth; *verneuking;* white lie; *xuld [arch.];* yarn; zinger; [*Ant.* fact]

**fabulous** *(adj.)*: astonishing; breathtaking; commendable; divine; extraordinary; fantastic; great; grandiose; heavenly; incredible; *jim-dandy;* keen; laudable; marvelous; noteworthy; outstanding; prodigious; phenomenal; *quantum* [L.]; remarkable; stupendous; terrific; tremendous; unbelievable; very good; wonderful; xtry.; yummy; zizzy;

**façade** *(n.)*: appearance; bemasking; covering; deception; exterior; face; (false) front; facade; guise; hood; integument; japery; *kept disguised;* loup; mask; *not real;* outer covering; pretense; Potemkin village; *quat [arch.]; repressing;* shroud; semblance; *transform; unreal;* veneer; window-dressing; *xylotechnigraphy;* yare; *zero reality;*

**face** *(n.)*: appearance; air; bearing; countenance; demeanor; expression; exterior; façade; front; gaze; *head; heart;* image; *judgment; knowledge;* look; mug; *notion;* obverse; outer surface; puss; phiz; quale; *reaction;* semblance; surface; top; *urge;* visage; veneer; way of looking; *xenenthesis; yaw; zeal;*

**face** *(v.)*: aim; accept; behold; confront; directly ~; deal with; encounter; fix eyes upon; gaze at; *handle; indicate; jerque;* keep looking; look (toward); lie opposite; meet; not avoid; oppose; point; *quick look;* recognize; stand opposite; turn toward; *understand;* view; *watch; xfer; yeme;* zero in; [*Ant.* flee]

**face-to-face** *(adv.)*: alone; before one; chin-to-chin; direct; eye-to-eye; facing it; *going head-on;* head-to-head; in front of; *just in front; keeping near; looking; meeting;* nose-to-nose; one-on-one; opposite; person-to-person; quite close; right before; *shoulder-to-shoulder;* toe-to-toe; upon; very close; with; xtry.; *yieldless; zeroing in;*

**facet** *(n.)*: aspect; angle; *bearing;* cutlet; characteristic; dimension; element; face; feature; *gradient;* hand; incline; issue; jag; kink; level; *makings; notion;* outlook; plane; perspective; pavilion; quality; *ruby;* side; surface; slant; *take; turn; understanding;* view; ways of looking at it; x-factor; *yaw; zag;*

**facilitate** *(v.)*: aid; accommodate; be of service; bolster; back; cooperate; do a favor; ease; enable; further; give assistance; help; *improve; just-in-time; kindness;* lend a hand; make easier; *not hinder;* oblige; promote; *quick-to-help;* relieve; serve; succor; support; take; unburden; *valet;* work for; xtry.; *yield; zero hindrance;* [*Ant.* frustrate]

**fact** *(n.)*: actuality; authenticity; being; *the* case; datum; existence; factuality; given ~; hypostasis; information; *judgment;* known truth; lemma; material ~; naked truth; *order of things;* presence; proven ~; qualified ~; reality; *statistic;* truth; unarguable ~; verity; well-known ~; witness; *x-fact;* yes; *zero doubt;* [*Ant.* fiction]

**faction** *(n.)*: assembly; bloc; circle; division; element; forgathering; group; horde; ingathering; jam [slang]; kit [coll.]; lot; mass; number; offshoot; part(y); portion; quantity; rally; rabble; *some;* splinter group; section; troop; *unit; variety;* wheen; x-cut; *yet some; zum [dial.];*

**factious** *(adj.)*: argumentative; belligerent; contentious; discordant; emulous; fractious; gainsaying; huffy; irritable; jangly; knaggy; liverish; mean; negative; objectionable; pugnacious; quarrelsome; resistant; striving; temperamental; unpeaceable; vying; wranglesome; *xenophobic;* yieldless; *za-zum* [Rus.];

**factor** *(n.)*: aspect; agent; angle; *bearing;* cause; consideration; detail; determinant; element; fact; facet; given fact; *hidden ~;* issue; *judgment;* known fact; level; matter; *naked truth;* object; part; plane; question; reason; side; thing (to consider); *unit;* variable; *way;* x-factor; *yet another; zeug;*

**factory** *(n.)*: assembly line; business; *cannery;* company; *developer;* establishment; facility; group; *holding company;* industrial plant; *joint-venture; kongsi [Chin.];* location; manu~; mill; national corporation; outfit; operation; (processing) plant; quasi-public corporation; *refinery;* small business; shop; *tooling up; union shop;* venture; works(hop); x-div.; yard; *zaibatsu* [Jap.];

**factual** *(adj.)*: actual; bona fide; correct; definite; exact; faithful; genuine; honest; indubitable; justifiable; known; legitimate; literal; *mean it;* never-failing; *open;* precise; questionless; right; sure; true; unerring; veritable; veracious; well-tried; *x-parent;* yes; 'zactly [dial.]; [*Ant.* fictional]

**faculty** *(n.)*: ability; *background; brawn;* capability; capacity; deftness; doctors; expertise; efficacy; facility; gift; genius; habilitation; instinct; intelligence; *jurisdiction;* know-how; learning; means; *natural ability; over-qualification;* power; professorate; quality; resources; sense; sufficiency; talent; teachers; *usefulness;* virtuosity; wherewithal; wits; *xenium; yare; zeal;*

**fad** *(n.)*: ardor; buzz; craze; design; desire; *enthusiasm;* fashion; fever; general inclination; high fashion; hysteria; in thing; inclination; *jaunty;* keenness; look; love; mania; notion; obsession; passion; quirk; rave; rage; style; trend; thing; urge; vogue; whim; *xtry.;* yankering; zeal;

**faddish** *(adj.)*: ardor; big; current; dandy; *enthusiasm;* fashionable; grody; hip; in; jaunty; keen; *the* latest; modish; nardy; *outstanding;* popular; quite ~; real neat; stylish; trendy; up-to-date; voguish; with-it; xtry.; you-beaut [Aus.]; zooty;

**fade** *(n.)*: abate; bate; condense; decrease; diminish; dissipate; disappear; ebb; fail; go down; *hush; invisible;* jade; knock down; languish; lessen; minish; minimize; narrow; *outgo;* peter out; quail; recede; reduce; shrink; subside; taper; *undo;* vanish; wane; waste; *xerosis;* yield; zap; [*Ant.* flourish]

**fail** *(v.)*: *abort;* botch; bust; bungle; break (down); bankrupt; conk out; collapse; crash; disappoint; *disqualify;* err; falter; flunk; fumble; foul up; flop; fall; fold; get goose egg; go bad; halt; *impropriety; jolt; kaput;* lay an egg; louse up; lapse; lack; lose; muff; muck; malfunction; *miss;* not succeed; omit; *pratfall; poor;* quit; run short; stumble; sink; tank [slang]; underachieve; *violate;* wash out; "x"; yield; zorch; [*Ant.* fulfill]

**failure** *(n.)*: abatement; botch-up; botching; breach; bust; breakdown; bankruptcy; crash; collapse; dud; disappointment; delinquency; downfall; defeat; debacle; error; flunk; flub; failing; flop; fall; fold; fiasco; goof-up; hitch; improsperity; insolvency; *jolt;* kink; lack; lemon; letdown; *lead balloon;* malfunction; nonsuccess; omission; pratfall; quitter; *ruin;* stumble; setback; tragedy; unsuccessfulness; *violation;* wipeout; washout; *winless;* "x"; yedder; zero; [*Ant.* fulfillment]

**faint** *(adj.)*: aweary [lit.]; bushed; beat; catatonic; *dizzy;* dog-tired; drained; enervate; exhausted; fatigued; *groggy;* haggard; half dead; *indolent;* jaded; knocked-out; lethargic; light-headed; *moiled;* noddy; oscitant; pooped; *quiescent;* run down; sluggish; sleepy; tired; unlively; vertiginous; weary; weak; *xenarthrous;* yawnish; zapped; [*Ant.* full-strength]

**faint** *(v.)*: *asphyxy;* black out; collapse; drop; enervate; fall (unconscious); grow weary; gray out; hit the floor; *inertness; jar;* keel over; *knocked out;* lose consciousness; make drop; *numbed; out;* pass out; *quothe* [arch.]; *rest;* swoon; syncope; tumble; *unconsciousness; vertiginous;* weaken; *x-cend;* yield; zonk out;

**faintness** *(n.)*: *anemia;* bleariness; catatonia; drowsiness; enervation; exhaustion; fatigue; grogginess; heaviness; inertia; jetlag; kef; languor; lipothymy; mopishness; nappiness; oscitancy; peplessness; *quiet; run down;* sluggishness; sleepiness; tiredness; unliveliness; vertiginousness; weariness; *xenarthrous;* yawning; zonking out; [*Ant.* full-strength]

**fair** *(adj.)*: anti-discriminatory; balanced; commensurable; *disinterested;* even-handed; equitable; faithful; good; godly; honest; honorable; impartial; just; *keen;* level; moral; non-discriminatory; objective; plain-dealing; *quite balanced;* reasonable; righteous; square; true; unbiased; unprejudiced; upright; virtuous; well-balanced; *Xn.; yieldless;* zero-bias; [*Ant.* false]

**fair** *(n.)*: agricultural show; amusement park; bazaar; ball; carnival; country ~; celebration; *display;* exhibition; extravaganza; expo(sition); *eisteddfod* [Welsh]; festival; fete; festivity; gala; *horse ~; international festival;* jamboree; kermis; local ~; midway; mas; *nundination; occasion; Oktoberfest;* panegyris; *quilting;* renaissance ~; state ~; traveling carnival; theme park; *unveiling;* vernissage; World's ~; *x-po [slang]; youst [arch.];* zoo;

**fairness** *(n.)*: auspiciousness, blamelessness; cleanness; *disinterest;* equity; fair-mindedness; goodness; godliness; honesty; honor; impartiality; justness; justice; *keenness;* legitimacy; morality; non-discrimination; objectivity; plain-dealing; probity; *quality;* rectitude; righteousness; squareness; truth; uprightness; virtue; *worthiness; Xty.; yieldlessness;* zero-bias; [*Ant.* favoritism]

**fairy** *(n.)*: aos si; brownie; boggart; Corrigan; dryad; *elf;* fay; ~ godmother; good folk; genie; hamadryad; *imp;* jinni; korrigan; lele; *minotaur;* nymph; ouphe; peri; pixie; *Queen Mab;* redcap; sylph; sprite; *Titania;* undine; *vetter;* white lady; xana; *yokai* [Jap.]; zane;

**fairytale** *(n.)*: account; adventure; beastary; chronicle; *drama;* epic; fable; fairy tale; folktale; Grimm tale; *hogwash;* imposture; *journal;* knight story; legend; *lore* [pl.]; myth; narrative; *oral narrative; portrayal; quarto;* retelling; story; tale; *unabridged story;* version; *writing;* xenodocheionology; yarn; *zipper book;* [*Ant.* fact]

**faith** *(n.)*: assurance; assuredness; blind ~; belief; confidence; certainty; credulity; credence; conviction; dependence; entrusting; following; firmness; fear of God; *great ~;* hope; ideology; *just believe;* knowledge; *looking to; mainstay;* non-doubt; *overconfidence;* old-time religion; persuasion; questionlessness; reliance; resting assured; rock-solid ~; sureness; surety; saving ~; trust; unwaveringness; volitional ~; wholehearted ~; *xel [arch.]; y'faith* [arch.]; *zeal;* [see conviction; *Ant.* faithlessness]

**faithful** *(adj.)*: accurate; *believable;* committed; consistent; dependable; ever-faithful; faithworthy; good; honest; inerrable; *just; keen;* loyal; most ~; never-failing; *open-and-shut case;* precise; perfect; *questionless;* reliable; steadfast; sure; *semper fidelis* [L.]; trusty; trusted; true; trustworthy; unfailing; unfaltering; valid; well-trusted; *xtry;* yeomanly; *zealous;* [see. performance; duty; *Ant.* faithless]

**faithfulness** *(n.)*: accuracy; adherence; *believableness;* consistency; dedication; dependability; evenness; fealty; fidelity; *goodness;* honor; *integrity; justness; keenness;* loyalty; *most faithful;* non-variableness; *outstanding;* precision; piety; *questionlessness;* reliability; steadfastness; trustiness; trueness; trustworthiness; unfailingness; verity; *well-trusted; xtry;* yeomanliness; zeal; [*Ant.* faithlessness]

**faithless** *(adj.)*: anti-religious; anti-Christian; amoral; *bad;* capricious; Christ-rejecting; disbelieving; disloyal; earthly-minded; freethinking; godless; *humanistic;* irreligious; jackeen; *knavish;* latitudinarian; libertine; lost; misbelieving; miscreant; nonbelieving; nonreligious; non-Christian; overcredulous; *profane;* questioning; remiss; reprobate; slack; secular; sinful; *transgressing;* unfaithful; unreligious; unbelieving; unsaved; *vile;* worldly-minded; worshipless; *x-gressing; yieldless;* zero-faith; [*Ant.* faithful]

**faithlessness** *(n.)*: adultery; betrayal; capriciousness; disloyalty; *evil;* falseness; godlessness; heedlessness; infidelity; *jadishness; knavishness;* laxness; miscreancy; neglectfulness; odure; perfidy; *quirkiness;* remissness; slackness; treachery; unreliability; unfaithfulness; *violation of trust; variableness;* whoredom; *x-gression; yielding;* zero-reliability; [*Ant.* faithfulness]

**fake** *(adj.)*: artificial; bogus; counterfeit; dissembling; deceitful; ersatz; false; fictitious; feigned; falsified; forged; fraudulent; gag; guileful; hoax; inauthentic; imaginary; imitation; japed; kiddy; *lying;* make-believe; mock; mendacious; non-real; *outfoxed;* pretend; phony; quacky; quasi-; replicated; rip off; simulated; synthetic; sham; spurious; trick; unreal; vain; *wily; xeno-; yeggy; zero validity;* [*see* hypocrite; *Ant.* factual]

**fake** *(v.)*: act out; beguile; counterfeit; dupe; dissemble; *ensnare;* feign; falsify; forge; guile; hoax; impersonate; *just make-believe; kid; lie;* make-believe; nobble; *overact;* pretend; *quiblin* [arch.]; role-play; replicate; simulate; take on the part; use deceit; verneuk; wangle; *xfer;* yentz; *zealously play at;*

**fall** *(n.)*: *angle;* belly-whop; collapse; crash dive; decline; drop; descent; dive; *ejection;* free~; gainer; header; high-dive; header; immergence; jump down; keeling over; leap down; movement downward; nose-dive; overthrow; plunge; plummet; pratfall; quick-fall; running-dive; *roll;* slump; sinking; spill; swoop; tumble; tailspin; toppling; undoing; volt; whop; *x-cend; yanking down;* zoom downward;

**fall** *(v.)*: *aaah!;* belly-whop; collapse; crash dive; droop; drop; descend; dive; *eject;* free~; go down; have a ~; immerge; jump down; keel over; *leap down;* make nose-dive; nose-dive; *over the cliff;* precipitate; plunge; plummet; plump; pratfall; quick-fall; reduce; sink; slump; tumble; topple; *undo;* volt; whop; *x-cend; yank down;* zoom down; [*Ant.* fly]

**fallen** *(adj.)*: adulterated; base; corrupt; degenerate; depraved; effete; foul; godless; heinous; ignoble; jaded; knavish; low; mean; morally corrupt; *nasty;* obdurate; profligate; *quad;* rebellious; sinful; tainted; ungodly; vile; wretched; *xgressive; yieldless; zero good;* [*see* defeat; *Ant.* faithful]

**fallibility** *(n.)*: *amiss;* baseness; capability of failure; defectiveness; errancy; faultiness; *guilt;* humanness; imperfection; *just fallen; kink;* lack; mortality; non-perfection; *omission;* problem; quirk; *reprehension;* shortcoming; trouble; unsoundness; *vice;* weakness; *xgression; yaw; zaniness;* [*Ant.* faultlessness]

**fallible** *(adj.)*: *amiss;* bad; capable of fault; defective; errable; faulty; *groundless;* human; imperfect; *judgment-impaired; kim-kam;* limited; liable to error; mortal; not perfect; open to error; peccant; questionable; *rickety;* sinful; tending to err; unsound; unreliable; *vulnerable;* weak; *xgress; yawed; zany;* [*Ant.* faultless]

**false** *(adj.)*: artificial; bogus; bad; baseless; confused; counterfeit; defective; deficient; erroneous; erring; fake; faulty; fallacious; groundless; *hollow;* hoax; heretical; inaccurate; incorrect; jim-jam; kim-kam; lying; mistaken; misunderstood; made-up; misleading; not true; non-orthodox; off base; phony; put-on; *questionable; repudiated;* spurious; specious; *trick;* untrue; unsound; unfounded; *variant; void of truth;* wrong; *x-out; yawed; zero-truth;* [*Ant.* factual]

**falsify** *(v.)*: *allure;* belie; con; deceive; equivocate; fake; forge; gonk; hoodwink; hide the truth; invent; illude; jape; knowingly lie; lie; misrepresent; nobble; *outlie;* perjure; *quiblin* [arch.]; rig; shyster; trick; utter falsehood; verneuk; wangle; *xuld [arch.];* yentz; *zing;*

**fame** *(n.)*: acclaim; *beloved;* celebrity; distinction; eminence; famousness; glory; hearsay; hailing; honor; infamy; illustriousness; *jubilation; kudos;* legend; magnificence; note; name; notoriety; *outstanding;* popularity; prestige; *quality;* rumor; recognition; respect; réclame; renown; status; stardom; *talked-about;* universal knowledge of; veneration; world-renown; *xtry.;* yichus; *zealous love;* [*Ant.* famelessness]

**fame** *(v.)*: acclaim; broadcast; circulate; declare; disseminate; endorse; *famous;* get the word out; *hail;* immortalize; *jubilate in;* keep advertising; let be known; make famous; nowel; overspread; publicize; popularize; *quantity;* raise awareness; spread; tell others; *televise;* universalize; *venerate; widespread; xtry.;* yell from the rooftops; *zizzy;*

**familiar** *(adj.)*: acquainted; accustomed; buddy-buddy; chummy; conversant; close; comfortable; cozy; dear; easy; familiarized; friendly; gregarious; habituated; household; identifiable; intimate; *just regular;* known; long-recognized; memorable; near; old hat; over~; personal; quotidian; recognizable; standard; typical; usual; used to; *valued;* well-acquainted; wont; *x-linked;* yarkened; *zestless;* [*Ant.* foreign]

**familiarity** *(n.)*: acquaintance; *buddy-buddy;* casualness; closeness; *dearness; easiness;* familiarness; friendliness; gregariousness; habitude; intimacy; *jibing [slang];* knowledge; *long-recognized; memorable;* nearness; overfriendliness; *personal; quotidian;* relaxedness; social ~; tenderness; usualness; *very familiar;* wontedness; x-linked; yarkened; zestless; [Ant. foreignness]
**familiarize** *(v.)*: acquaint; accustom; acclimate; become accustomed to; conform; dispose; desensitize; ease into; fit; get used to; habituate; inure; jibe [slang]; *kit;* look over; mesh; *naturalize;* orient(ate); prepare; qualify; ready; *suit; season;* train; unite; *verse;* wont; *xenize;* yarken; zero foreignness;
**family** *(n.)*: adoptive ~; belongings [reg.]; blood relations; brethren; brood; connections; clan; dynasty; *domestic;* estate; extended ~; flesh and blood; ~ unit; gens; house(hold); *in-laws; jus soli [L.];* kinsmen; kin(folk); loved ones; ménage; near kinsman; nuclear ~; *offspring;* people; *quarter;* relations; relatives; sub~; *sept* [Ire.]; tribe; *umunna* [Afr.]; vein; whanau [N.Z.]; x-linked; yoni *[Skr.];* zadruga [Slav.];
**famine** *(n.)*: *aridity;* barrenness; crisis; dearth; destitution; extreme hunger; food shortage; famishment; *great need;* grievous ~; hunger; insufficiency; jejuneness; *keen deprivation;* lack; meagerness; need; *over-hungry;* paucity; *quandary;* ravenousness; scarcity; shortage; *thirst; undernourished;* vacuity; want; xerophagy; yearning; zero food; [Ant. feast]
**famous** *(adj.)*: acclaimed; big-name; beloved; celebrated; distinguished; eminent; famed; folkloric; gestic; great; high-profile; infamous; iconic; illustrious; *jubilated over;* known; legendary; magnifical; notable; *notorious;* outstanding; popular; prestigious; *quality;* recognized; renowned; *star;* talked-about; universally known; venerated; well-known (-liked; -loved); world-famous; *xtry.;* yearned-for; yichus; *zealously loved;* [Ant. fameless]
**fan** *(n. blower)*: aerator; agitator; box ~; blower; cooler; ceiling ~; *device;* electric ~; flabellum; *gust;* handheld ~; *instrument;* Japanese ~; kickumbob; *light breeze; machine; notus;* oscillating ~; punka; *quarter-wind;* rotary blade; stream; thermantidote [Asia]; *uchiwa* [Jap.]; *unit;* ventilator; window ~; x-wind; yandy; zephyr;
**fan** *(n. devotee)*: admirer; buff; *crazed;* devotee; enthusiast; follower; fanatic; groupie; hound; ideologue; idolizer; Jacobin; *keen;* lover; maven; *noticer; obsessed; passionate;* quack; regarder; supporter; *thrilled;* ultraist; votary; well-wisher; *xenocentrist;* Young Turk; zealot;
**fan** *(v.)*: air; aerate; blow air; cool; drive air; emit air; *fling air;* get cool; *huff;* insufflate; *jet; kest;* let air blow; make air blow; *non-stagnant;* output; puff; *quick;* recirculate; shoot air; throw air; *unleash;* ventilate; winnow; *xuld [arch.];* yandy; zephyr;
**fanatic** *(n.)*: activist; buff; *crazed;* devotee; enthusiast; extremist; fan; follower; groupie; *hobbyist;* ideologue; Jacobin; kook; *lover;* maniac; militant; nut; *obsessed;* proselyte; quack; radical; supporter; *thrilled;* ultraist; votary; *weirdo; xenocentrist;* Young Turk; zealot;
**fanatical** *(adj.)*: ardent; besotted; crazed; devoted; enthusiastic; extreme; fanatic; fervent; gung-ho; hearty; impassioned; *jingoist;* keen; keyed up; *loyal;* mad; nuts; overenthusiastic; obsessed; passionate; quacky; radical; spirited; *thrilled;* ultraistic; vehement; wild-eyed; *xenocentric;* yare; zealotic; [see crazy]
**fanaticism** *(n.)*: activism; ardor; *burning desire;* commitment; civism; devotion; extremism; fervor; *glorying;* heartiness; immoderation; *joy;* keenness; liveliness; militancy; mania; nationalism; obsession; passion; *quickness;* radicalism; spirit; *thrill;* ultraism; vigor; wholeheartedness; *xenocentrism;* yareness; zeal(otry);
**fancy** *(adj.)*: adorned; beautiful; charming; dressy; decorative; elegant; elaborate; fanciful; garnished; high-wrought; highly decorated; intricate; *jewel-encrusted;* keenly-looking; *ornate;* lavish; much-decorated; *niggled;* ornate; ornamented; *pretty; quaint;* ritzy; snazzy; swanky; sumptuous; trimmed; upscale; Victorian; well-ornamented; *xtry.; yet unsurpassed; zierlich* [G.];

**fancy** *(n.)*: aspiration; *bidding;* choice; desire; dream; *enthusiasm;* fantasy; general desire; hope; illusion; *just want to; keenness;* longing; megrim; notion; *obsession;* pleasure; *quiritation;* reverie; *self-will; true desire;* urge; vagary; velleity; whim; wish; *xenenthesis;* yen; yearning; *zeal;* [Ant. fear]

**fanfare** *(n.)*: ado; bustle; celebration; display; elaborateness; festivity; gaiety; hoopla; impressive display; *joyance;* kerfuffle; loud celebration; merry-making; *nundination;* observance; pomp (and circumstance); *quindene;* rejoicing; show; trumpeting; to-do; *upheaval; veneration; wingding; xtry.;* yelling; yippee; zest;

**fantasize** *(v.)*: *abstraction;* build castles in the air; contemplate; (day)dream; envision; fancy; get idea in one's head; hatch; hallucinate; imagine; just imagine; *know; lucubrate;* make up; *notion; originate;* picture; *quixotic;* romanticize; suppose; think; use imagination; visualize; woolgather; *xenodiagnose; yeme; zazen;*

**fantastic** *(adj.)*: amazing; breathtaking; commendable; divine; excellent; exceptional; fabulous; great; heavenly; incredible; jolly good; keen; large; *laudable;* marvelous; magnificent; notable; outstanding; phenomenal; *quantum* [L.]; remarkable; super; sublime; splendid; spectacular; terrific; tremendous; unequalled; very good; virtuous; wonderful; xtry.; *yippee!;* zizzy; [Ant. foul]

**fantasy** *(n.)*: air castle; bubble; chimera; (day)dream; envisionment; fancy; *ghost;* hallucination; invention; illusion; *jape; knavery;* lie; mirage; *nonexistent;* outform; pink elephant; phantasy; quantum effect; reverie; *simulation;* trip; utopia; vision; whimsy; *Xanadu; yaksha [Ind.];* zoopsia; [Ant. fear]

**far** *(adj.)*: afield; aloof; away from; alienated; afar off; by far; *cool;* distant; *estranged;* faraway; far-off; *girth;* hundreds of miles away; isolated; inaccessible; *just as ~ as possible; kilometers; long way;* light years; many miles away; not close; outlying; *parted; quite a ways;* remote; secluded; secludinous; thousands of miles away; very ~; worlds apart; *xfer; yet estranged; zillions of miles away;* [see aloof]

**fare** *(n. ticket cost)*: amount; *bill;* charge; *due;* expense; fee; going price; handling charge; *itinerary;* jettage; keelage; levy; money; naulum; *outlay;* price; *quid [Br.];* rate; *surcharge;* ticket-price; undiscounted fee; voyage fare; *wharfage; xfer fee; yardage; zip;*

**fare** *(v. eat)*: *ate;* break bread; consume; dine; eat; feast; *gobble; gorge;* have; ingest; indulge; *junket; kill* [joc.]; lunch; munch; *nibble;* overeat; partake; *quill* [arch.]; *raven;* sup; tuck away; *undereat; victual;* wolf; *xerophagy;* yaffle; *zip down;*

**far-fetched** *(adj.)*: amazing; bizarre; crazy; *disagreeable;* exaggerated; extraordinary; fanciful; fantastic; greatly exaggerated; hard to believe; implausible; *joke;* kooky; ludicrous; mind-blowing; non-believable; outlandish; preposterous; *questionable;* ridiculous; *stupefying; terrible;* unbelievable; *vain;* wild; xtry.; y.; *za-zum* [Rus.]; [Ant. feasible]

**farm** *(n.)*: acreage; barnyard; croft; dairy (~); estate; farmstead; grange; homestead; hacienda [Sp.]; *intercrop; joclet; kolkoz* [Rus.]; land; lactary; *latifundium* [Rom.]; manse; *non-urban;* orchard; patch; pig- ~; plantation; *quinta;* rustic; ranch; subsistence ~; smallholding; tract; toun [Scot.]; *usable ~land;* villa; working ~; werf; *xeriscape®; yeomanship; zemledelie [Rus.];*

**farm** *(v.)*: *agriculture;* breed; crop; cultivate; dibble; dress; *eke out; establish; fertilize;* garden; *grow;* harvest; husband; homestead; intercrop; *job;* kippin; labor; *make; manure; non-urban;* operate a ~; plow; plant; *quat [arch.];* raise; sow; seed; sharecrop; till; *toil; use; veld;* work; *xeriscape®; yield; zafra;*

**farmable** *(adj.)*: arable; *befitting;* cultiv(at)able; *doable; expedient;* fertilizable; good; harvestable; *idoneous; justifiable;* keen; *legitimate;* meet; *nutrient;* okay; plowable; plantable; qualified; *reapable;* suitable; tillable; usable; valid; workable; *xeriscape®; yerabyll [arch.];* zafra;

**farmer** *(n.)*: agriculturalist; bean grower; cultivator; cornhusker; dirt ~; dairy ~; *esne;* farmwoman [fem.]; granger; grower; husbandman; harvester; harvestman; *intercrop;* jillaroo [fem.]; *kulak* [Rus.]; land-worker; *man; manse-owner;* milker; *non-urbanite;* orchardist; plowman; planter; pig ~; *quadrat;* ruralist; reaper; sower; subsistence ~; sharecropper; swineherd; tiller; tenant ~; *under~* [arch.]; villein; workman; *xeriscaper;* yokel; yeoman; *zhlub;* [see peasant]

**farmhand** *(n.)*: assistant; barnyard hand; *cowhand;* drudge; employee; farm hand; granger; (hired) hand; harvestman; *intern;* jillaroo [fem.]; *knave;* laborer; man; nipper; offsider; plowman; *quarterer;* reaper; sower; spalpeen; tiller; underling; vassal; worker; *xeriscaper;* yeoman; *zaikai [Jap.];*
**farming** *(n.)*: agriculture; barnyard work; cultivation; crofting; dairy; dressing; dry ~; *estate;* farming; geoponics; gardening; husbandry; harvesting; horticulture; *implanting; joclet; kolkhoz [Rus.];* land-working; manse-work; *nursery;* orcharding; plowing; planting; *quinta;* ranch work; ruralizing; soil; sharecropping; sowing; seeding; tillage; *undeveloped;* viniculture; working; *xeriscaping;* yeomanship; *zemledelie* [Rus.];
**farmland** *(n.)*: acreage; bush [Aus.]; country(side); cropland; dairyland; *estates;* farms; fields; georgic; heartland; hinterland; hayfield; implanted land; *jillaroo; kolkhoz [Rus.];* layland; landscape; meadows; *non-urban; outland;* plowland; pastures; *quaint countryside;* rural; rustic; sown land; tillage; undeveloped land; *vineyards;* wheatland; wold; *xeriscape®;* yokeldom; *zemledelie [Rus.];*
**far-reaching** *(adj.)*: all-pervading; broad; common; diffuse; extensive; *epidemic;* far-flung; general; huge; *indiscriminate; international; joint; known world;* large-scale; major; non-localized; overall; pervasive; pandemic; quaquaversal; rife; *serious; trans-world;* universal; very ~; widespread; wide-reaching; *x-world; yonder; zonic;*
**farther** *(prep.)*: after; beyond; clear of; *distant;* extralimitary; further; gone over (past); hereafter; in another place; just past; kept ~; longer; more distant; next; over; outside; past; quite ~; remoter; surpassing; thither; ulterior; *very far;* without; x.; yonder; *zooming past;*
**farthest** *(adj.)*: aftermost; backmost; caudal; distant; endmost; extreme; furthest; farthermost; final; greatest distance; headmost; *in another place; just past; kept ~;* last; most distant; *nethermost;* out(er)most; *past;* quite ~; remotest; *surpassed;* terminating; ut(ter)most; very ~; without; *xy-coordinate;* yondmost; *zillions;*
**fascinate** *(v.)*: amaze; bedazzle; captivate; draw; enthrall; flabbergast; grip; hold; intrigue; *jag;* kinch; *like;* mesmerize; *non-boring;* overwhelm; preoccupy; *quicken;* rivet; spellbind; transfix; *under a spell; very impressed;* welter; wow; *x-fix; yield; zeal;*
**fascination** *(n.)*: amazement; astonishment; awe; bedazzlement; captivation; disbelief; dazzlement; enthrallment; flabbergastation; grip; hold; incredulity; *joy; keenness;* liking; marvel; *nonplus; overwhelmed;* preoccupation; *quickening;* riveting; spellbinding; transfixation; unbelief; *very impressed;* wonder(ment); *x-fix; yerk; zeal;*
**fashion** *(n.)*: approach; *bravura;* cast; design; décor; *estate;* form; *genus;* high style; in thing; *jaunty;* kind; look; latest; manner; model; make; *newest; obsession;* pattern; *quality;* rave; rage; sort; style; trend; taste; thing; usage; vogue; way; *x-class;* yankering; *zeal;*
**fashion** *(v.)*: assemble; build; craft; create; design; efform; engineer; erect; form; generate; *hew;* invent; *job;* knock together; *labor;* make; *new-built;* originate; produce; quick-build; raise; shape; turn out; upbuild; *vamp;* wage; *xfer;* yield; *zip together;*
**fashionable** *(adj.)*: *au courant* [F.]; *best;* chic; current; dandy; elegant; faddish; genteel; hip; in; jaunty; keen; *the* latest; modish; nardy; *outstanding;* popular; quite ~; real neat; stylish; trendy; up-to-date; voguish; with-it; xtry.; you-beaut [Aus.]; zooty;
**fast** *(adj.)*: apace; accelerated; agile; brisk; breakneck; charging; double-speed; dexterous; expeditious; express; fleet; *geared up;* hurried; hasty; high-speed; intemperate; jet-speed; *keeping pace;* lissome; lickety-split; mercurial; *moving;* nimble; *on the double;* prompt; pronto; posthaste; quick; rushed; rapid; swift; speedy; *timely;* turbo; ultrasonic; volitant; wimble; whizzing; x-speed; yar; zippy; [see secure]
**fast** *(n.)*: abstinence; Barmecide feast; *cleansing; denial;* eat nothing; *fasting;* go hungry; hunger strike; *intercession; jejunery;* keeping ~; lenten diet; *macerate;* not eating; *opting out; punishment;* quadragesimal; refrain from eating; strict ~; time of ~ing; *uneating;* vigil; *waste away;* xerophagy; *yo-yo dieting; zero food;* [Ant. feast]

**fast** *(v.)*: abstain; be fasting; *cleanse;* diet; deny flesh; eat nothing; forego; famish; go without; hunger; *intercede; jour maigre* [F.]; keep ~; lay aside eating; *macerate;* not eat; observe a ~; put off eating; quit eating; refrain from eating; spare to eat; starve; *time of fasting; uneating; vigil;* withdraw from food; *xerophagy; yield one's spirit; zero food;* [*Ant.* feast]

**fasten** *(v.)*: attach; affix; anchor; button; buckle; bind; bolt; bond; clasp; couple; clinch; chain; close; connect; *dovetail;* engraft; engraft; frap; fix; glue; hook; hitch; interconnect; infix; interlock; inosculate; join; knit; knot; latch; lace; link; lock; mount; nail; *oxreim;* pin; put together; *quasi-fuse;* relate; reunite; rivet; snap; secure; tack; tie; unite; *Velcro®;* weld; *xenograft;* yoke; zip; [*Ant.* free]

**fastener** *(n.)*: *attach;* button; buckle; bolt; clip; coupling; clasp; closure; connector; *dowel;* eyebolt; eyescrew; *floor nail;* grappler; hook; hasp; inkle; joiner; *kevel;* latch(et); locknut; machine screw; nail; nut; *oval brad;* pin; quick-snap; rivet; staple; snap; screw; screw-eye; tack; toggle; U-bolt; *Velcro®;* woodscrew; wing nut; *xenograft;* yoke; zipper;

**fasting** *(n.)*: abstinence; Barmecide feast; *cleansing;* dieting; denial; *endure hunger;* famishment; going hungry; hunger (strike); *intercession;* jejunery; *knowing God;* Lenten diet; *macerate;* not eating; *opting out; punishment;* quadragesimal; refraining; starvation; time of ~; *uneating;* vigil; withdrawal from food; xerophagia; *yielding one's spirit; zero food;* [*Ant.* feasting]

**fat** *(adj.)*: abundant; beefy; big; chubby; corpulent; disproportionate; enormous; elephantine; flabby; full-size (-figured); great; heavy(-set); hefty; huge; immense; jumbo-sized; king-size; large; massive; *noteworthy;* overweight; obese; ponderous; plump; pudgy; portly; quantitative; queen-size; rotund; sizable; tubby; *unwieldy;* ventricose; voluminous; wide; weighty; XL; *Ymir;* zaftig; [*Ant.* frail]

**fat** *(n.)*: adipose; animal- ~; body fat; blubber; cholesterol; corpulence; drippings; excess ~; flab; flick; grease; heaviness; insulation; jelly [slang]; keech; lard; marbling; *non-skinniness;* obesity; padding; pounds; *quantitativeness;* rotundity; suet; trans- ~; tallow; unsaturated ~; volume; wideness; x- ~; *Ymir;* zero leanness;

**fatal** *(adj.)*: *adverse;* baneful; calamitous; deadly; eliminating; fatiferous; fell; *grievous;* harmful; ill-fated; injurious; internecine; jeopardous; killing; lethal; mortal; noxious; *obliterating;* poisonous; pernicious; perilous; ruinous; self-destructive; terminal; toxic; unsafe; virulent; wreckful; x-ing; *ydrad* [arch.]; *zero safety;* [*Ant.* fine]

**fatalism** *(n.)*: apprehension; bleakness; concern; defeatism; despair; existentialism; finalism; gloom; hopelessness; insecurity; *jitters; kiugh* [Scot.]; lowness of spirit; *mistrust;* negativism; nihilism; over-anxiety; pessimism; *quaking;* resignation; sinking into despair; trepidation; uneasiness; vexation; weariness of life; Weltscmertz; *xenophobia; yielding; zeallessness;*

**fate** *(n.)*: appointment; *the* breaks; chance; dole; destiny; end; future; fortune; God's will; handwriting on the wall; inevitability; journey's end; kismet; karma; lot; Moirai; *meant;* necessity; *outcome;* ordained end; portion; *qismet* [Arab.]; *result; sovereign destiny;* terminus; ultimate end; *volition of God;* wheel of fortune; will of God; *x; yonder;* zodiac;

**fateful** *(adj.)*: auspicious; big; crucial; decisive; earthshaking; foredoomed; great; historic; ill-fated; important; *jinxed;* key; lucky; leading; momentous; noteworthy; ominous; portentous; *quantum; relevant;* significant; top-rated; unstoppable; vital; weighty; xtry.; *yearnful; zero hour;*

**father** *(n.)*: abba [Gr.]; ancestor; begetter; biological ~; *commander;* dad(dy); *elder;* forebearer; genitor; head; *institutor; judge;* king of his castle; *leader;* male parent; *near of kin;* old man [derog.]; originator; pop; pa(ppy); papa; pater; parent; progenitor; patriarch; procreator; *quickener; relative;* step ~; sire; *trainer; undershepherd; Vater* [G.]; *warden;* XO; *young ~; zealous dad;* [*see* parent]

**father** *(v.)*: *actuate;* beget; cause; *develop;* engender; found; generate; gender; have (offspring); initiate; *jump-start;* kittle; lead to; make; *new;* originate; *offspring;* produce; propagate; procreate; *quicken; result in;* sire; *trigger; unleash; vivify;* work; *xenogenesis;* yield; *zip;*

**fatherhood** *(n.)*: authority; being a dad; command; dominance; empowering; *eldership;* fatherliness; government; headship; influence; jurisdiction; *king of his castle;* lordship; *lineage;* mentoring; *near of kin;* oversight; parenthood; paternity; *quo warranto [L.];* rule; rod [Bible]; *responsibility; say-so; trust; undershepherd; virtue;* warrant; x-link; yauld; zeal;
**fatherless** *(adj.)*: *alone;* bereaved; *child without a father;* deprived; *expropriated; forsaken; grieved;* having no father; *in need of a dad;* just-orphaned; *kid without a father;* lacking a father; missing a father; *no father;* orphaned; orbate; parentless; *quite ~;* robbed of a father; *so alone; taken away; uncared for;* void of a father; without father; *x-out; yanked away; zero father;*
**fatherliness** *(n.)*: authoritativeness; *bravery;* care; dominance; *ever-confident;* fatherhood; *gallant;* hardiness; intrepidity; *judiciousness; knowledgeableness;* leadership; manliness; nobleness; *ordering;* paternalness; *questful;* ruggedness; respect; strength; trustworthiness; undauntedness; virility; *wherewithal;* x-link; *yauld*; zeal;
**fatherly** *(adj.)*: authoritative; *brave;* caring; dominating; ever-confident; fatherlike; *gallant;* hard-working; imposing; *judicious; knowledgeable;* loving; manly; noble; *ordering;* protective; parental; paternal; *questful;* rugged; respected; strong; supportive; trustworthy; unafraid; virile; *well-confident; xtry.;* yauld; *zealous;*
**fathom** *(v.)*: apprehend; become aware of; comprehend; discern; experience; figure out; gauge; grasp; have in one's heart (-brain); identify; *judge;* know; ken; *learn;* measure; naw [dial.]; *own; observe;* probe; perceive; *questionless;* recognize; realize; sound; see; *think;* understand; *value;* work out; xenodiagnose; *yeme;* zero in;
**fathomless** *(adj.)*: arcane; *amazing;* beyond comprehension; *confusion;* deep; ever-mysterious; forever mysterious; great; hard-to-comprehend; *high;* inconceivable; incomprehensible; *just too high;* kithless; *limitless;* mind-blowing; non-fathomable; over one's head; profound; quantum; remarkable; staggering; too deep (-great); unimaginable; unknowable; unfathomable; vast; wondrous; xtry.; y.; *zero understanding;*
**fatigue** *(n.)*: *awearied;* bleariness; *comatose;* drowsiness; exhaustion; faintness; grogginess; heaviness; indolence; jetlag; kef; lethargy; mopishness; nappiness; overtiredness; peplessness; *quiet; run down;* sleepiness; tiredness; *unenthusiasm; vapidity;* weariness; *xenarthrous; yawning;* zero energy; [Ant. friskiness]
**fatigue** *(v.)*: *awearied;* bleed; consume; drain; defaticate; do in; exhaust; frazzle; get tired; hone; *impoverish; jade; kaput;* lessen; make tired; *nullify; overspend;* peter out; quail; run out of energy; sap; tire (out); use up all one's energy; *void;* weary; wear out; *xerosis; yield;* zap;
**fatness** *(n.)*: *abundance;* bigness; chubbiness; disproportion; enormity; flabbiness; giganticness; heftiness; immensity; jumboness; *king-size;* largeness; massiveness; *noteworthiness;* obesity; plumpness; portliness; quantitativeness; rotundity; stoutness; tubbiness; unwieldiness; voluminousness; weightiness; *XL; Ymir; zaftig;* [Ant. frailness]
**fatten** *(v.)*: aggrandize; broaden; build up; beef up; cram; distend; enlarge; expand; feed; gorge; grow; get fat; *heavy;* increase; *jump up; keep growing;* lard; make fat; nourish; overfeed; pinguefy; plump up; put on weight; *quantify;* rise; swell; spread; thicken; tallow; *upgrow* [arch.]; *vegetate;* widen; *XL; yain* [arch.]; *zoom up;* [Ant. fade]
**fattening** *(n.)*: aggrandizing; buttery; calor(if)ic; diet-defeating; *enlarging;* fatty; *grow;* high-calorie; *increase; jaggery; keep growing;* lardy; meaty; non-dietetic; *oversweet;* pound-adding; quite ~; rich; *sweet;* too ~; un-dietetic; very ~; waist-expanding; *xylose; yain [arch.]; zuccary [arch.];* [Ant. fat-free]
**faucet** *(n.)*: *apparatus;* bibcock; basin ~; compression ~; cock; drain cock; *equipment;* fireplug; *gate valve;* hydrant; *instrument;* jet; kitchen sink ~; *lever;* monitor; *mouth;* nozzle; output; petcock; *quantity control;* regulator; spigot; spout; tap; *unit;* valve; water gate; *x-switch; yield; zeug [G.];*

**fault** *(n.)*: accountability; blame(worthiness); culpability; defect; error; flaw; foible; failing; fallacy; guilt(iness); hole; human error; hamartia; imperfection; jeofail; *kink;* liability; mistake; non-innocence; oversight; omission; onus; problem; *quirk;* responsibility; shortcoming; transgression; *unrighteousness;* vice; wrong; want; weakness; *xgression; yaw; zinger;*
**fault** *(v.)*: attribute; blame; criticize; denounce; excoriate; find ~ with; give criticism; hold responsible; incriminate; *j'accuse;* knock; lay guilt before; make allegation; *non-innocent; oppugn;* pick at; point finger at; question; reproach; *saddle with;* traduce; upbraid; vituperate; *whine; xci.; yell at; zero in;*
**faultless** *(adj.)*: accurate; blameless; certain; correct; definite; error-free; flawless; good; *honest;* inculpable; infallible; inerrant; impeccable; immaculate; *justifiable; keenly accurate; legitimate;* mistake-proof; non-fallible; *open-to-scrutiny; orthodox;* perfect; question-less; reliable; sure; true; unerring; unmistaken; unimpeachable; veritable; verifiable; without error; *x-parent; yes;* zero-defect; [*Ant.* fallible]
**faulty** *(adj.)*: amiss; bad; confused; defective; erroneous; errant; flawed; groundless; halt; incorrect; inaccurate; jim-jam; kim-kam; lousy; mistaken; misconceived; non-working; not true; off base; peccant; quirky; *repudiated;* specious; spurious; sophistical; troublesome; unsound; vituperable; wanting; wrong; *xtry.* errant; yawed; zany; [*Ant.* faultless]
**fauna** *(n.)*: animals; beasts; creatures; *denizen; elk;* forest animals; game; *herbivores; insectivores;* jungle animals; *koala;* livestock; *mammals; non-vertebrates;* organisms; *ponies;* quadrupeds; *reptiles;* stock; *tigers;* ungulates; varmints; wildlife; *xeme; yearling;* zoics;
**faux pas** *(n.)*: accident; blunder; clanger [Br.]; *defect;* error; fault; gaffe; howler [Br.]; indiscretion; *jumble; kink; lapse;* mistake; *non-purposive;* oversight; pratfall; *quirk; real blooper;* slip; solecism; social blunder; *transgression;* unintentional slip-up; *violation;* wrong; *xgression; yaw;* zinger;
**favor** *(n. goodwill)*: aid; assistance; approval; benevolence; bias; compassion; delight; *endearing;* friendliness; fancy; grace; goodwill; help; indulgence; *joviality;* kindness; love; mercy; niceness; obligingness; partiality; preference; *quarter;* regard; sympathy; thoughtfulness; unselfishness; *virtuousness;* warmth; xenia; yonste [arch.]; *zealousness;*
**favor** *(n. kind act)*: act of kindness; blessing; benefaction; courtesy; deed of kindness; errand; facilitation; good turn (-deed); grace; helping hand; indulgence; *joy;* kind act; *love;* mercy; *niceness;* obligement [Scot.]; pleasure; *quell; relishing;* service; thoughtful deed; unselfish act; volutation; wallowing; *xuld [arch.];* yielding; *zero opposition;*
**favor** *(v.)*: aspire; *best choice;* choose; desire; elect; fancy; give choice; have a preference; indicate; judge; *keen desire;* like better; make a choice; *nominate;* opt; prefer; *questionless;* rather; select; take; *use;* vote for; want; *xel [arch.];* yearn for; zealous for;
**favorable** *(adj.)*: auspicious; advantageous; beneficial; benign; cooperative; delightful; encouraging; fine; favonian; good; helpful; hopeful; *invigorating; jack-a-dandy;* kind; *likely;* marvelous; nice; obliging; promising; preferable; profitable; propitious; *quality;* really good; sympathetic; terrific; uncritical; useful; very good; well (-favored); *xenophilious; xenial; yes; zealous;* [*Ant.* foul]
**favorite** *(adj.)*: all-time best; best-loved; choice(st); desired; darling; *elite;* first; foremost; greatest; hobbyhorse; *incredible; jim-dandy;* keenest; leading; most favored (-admired; -praised); minikin; minion; number one; optimal; pet; preferred; *quality;* remarkable; select; top(most); unsurpassed ~; valued; V.I.P. well-favored; *xtry.; yondmost; zenithal;*
**favoritism** *(n.)*: altruism; bias; *choosiness;* discrimination; *elitism;* favoring; giving favor; having favorites; injustice; inequality; jaundiced eye; *keenest;* liking one better; *minikin;* nepotism; one-sidedness; partiality; preference; prelation; prosopolepsy; *quality;* remarkable; special privileges; *teachers pet;* unfairness; valuing; *well-favored; xenophobia; yondmost; zenithal;* [*Ant.* fairness]
**faze** *(v.)*: affect; bother; bestir; concern; daunt; excite; fluster; goad; harrow; intimidate; jostle; kittle; *lead;* move; nudge; overwhelm; provoke; quicken; rouse; stir; trouble; throw; unnerve; vex; whelm; *xuld* [arch.]; yerk; *zing;*

**fear** *(n.)*: apprehension; anxiety; alarm; affright; *bother; burden;* cowardice; care; distress; dread; despair; *exasperation;* fright; gastness; horror; insecurity; jitters; kiaugh [Scot.]; lily-liveredness; *mistrust;* nervousness; over-anxiety; phobia; paranoia; panic; quivering; quaking; *reluctance;* reverence; scaredness; shuddering; stress; trepidation; terror; uneasiness; *unrest;* vexation; worry; *xenophobia;* yellow-belliedness; *zeallessness;* [*Ant.* fearlessness]
  **Fears**: acrophobia [heights]; bibliophobia [books]; claustrophobia [closed in spaces]; demophobia [crowds]; elurophobia [cats]; frigophobia [cold]; gamophobia [marriage]; hydrophobia [water]; ichthyophobia [fish]; Japanophobia [the Japanese]; kainotophobia [change]; lachanophobia [vegetables]; melophobia [music]; necrophobia [dead]; ochophobia [vehicles]; pyrophobia [fire]; quadraphobia [the number four]; ranidaphobia [frogs]; selachophobia [sharks]; technophobia [technology]; urophobia [urinating]; verminophobia [germs]; wiccaphobia [witches]; xenophobia [foreigners]; ylophobia [forests]; zoophobia [animals];
**fear** *(v.)*: affright; be scared; *careful;* distress; dread; eye askance; fret; get nervous; have qualms; *intimidated; jump; knees knocking;* lose courage; misgive; moither; *nervous wreck; overwhelm;* panic; quake; *recoil;* scare; tremble; take fright; *uneasy; vulnerable;* worry; *xenophobic; ydrad* [arch.]; *zoophobic;* [*Ant.* fancy]
**fearful** *(adj.)*: anxious; afraid; *bothered;* careful; concerned; cowardly; distressed; edgy; faint-hearted; fretful; frightened; gutless; *hesitant;* horrified; insecure; jittery jumpy; kitten-hearted; lily-livered; milk-livered; nervous; overanxious; pluckless; panicky; petrified; quivering; *reluctant; restless;* scared; sore afraid; troubled; terrified; terror-stricken; uneasy; unnerved; vexed; worried; *xenophobic;* yellow(-bellied); *zapped;* [see aghast; cowardly; *Ant.* fearless]
**fearless** *(adj.)*: audacious; brave; bold; courageous; daring; enterprising; *fortitude;* gallant; hardy; heroic; intrepid; *jarless;* knightly; lion-hearted; manly; nervy; never-fearing; non-intimidated; *obstinate;* plucky; *quick-witted; resolute;* spirited; stout; strong; *temerarious;* unafraid; unflinching; unfrightened; undaunted; valiant; *wherewithal; xtry.;* yare; zealous; [*Ant.* fearful]
**fearsome** *(adj.)*: alarming; awesome; bad; chilling; distressing; dreadful; endangering; fearful; fretful; formidable; frightful; galling; hysterogenic; horrific; intimidating; jittery; knee-knocking; *lily-livered; mistrustful;* nightmarish; nervous; obsessive; phobic; quivering; *rueful;* stressful; terrifying; unsettling; unnerving; vexing; worrisome; woeful; *xenophobic; ydrad* [arch.]; *zealless;* [*Ant.* feared]
**feasible** *(adj.)*: achievable; *believable; bearable;* credible; doable; effective; expedient; functional; good; helpful; intelligent; judicious; *knowledgeable;* logical; likely; meet; no-nonsense; *okay;* possible; plausible; practicable; practical; quite sensible; reasonable; realistic; sensible; tenable; useful; viable; workable; *x in the box; yieldful; zero problem;* [*Ant.* far-fetched]
**feast** *(n.)*: ambigu; banquet; celebration; dinner; eating; food; gala; high tea [Br.]; ingesta; junket; kale-time; luncheon; meal; nourishment; *occasion;* provisions; potluck; *quelque-chose [F.];* repast; regale; supper; spread; table; *unassimilated food;* victuals; wassail; *xarque; yams; ziti;* [*Ant.* fast]
**feast** *(v.)*: assimilate; break bread; consume; dine; eat; fare well; *gorge;* have; indulge; junket; *kill fatted calf;* lunch; munch; nosh; overeat (-indulge); partake; pig out; party; *quill* [arch.]; raven; sup; tuck away; tear into; *undereat; victual;* wine and dine; *xerophagy;* yaffle; *zip down;* [*Ant.* fast]
**feat** *(n.)*: act; achievement; behavior; coup; deed; exploit; fine act; going; heroic act; *intrepidity;* job; *knightliness; life;* move; notable act; operation; performance; *quick act; reaction;* step; thing; tour de force; undertaking; venture; work(ing); x-action; *yaw; zeal.*
**feather** *(n.)*: aia- ~; beard; covert; crissum; *chicken- ~;* crest; down [pl.]; eiderdown; filoplume; goose-quill; hackle; *ibis- ~; jay- ~;* kahili [Haw.]; *lark- ~;* mail [pl.]; *nuptial plumage; neossoptile; oriole- ~;* penna; pinion; plume; plumage [pl.]; panache; quill; ruff; remiges; remex; scalpular; tail ~; tuft; *upright perching ~;* vibrissa; vane; *wren- ~ xema- ~; yellow finch- ~;* zoofulvin;
**featherless** *(adj.)*: acomous; bald; bare; callow; de-feathered; exposed; fledgeless; glabrous; having no feathers; implumous; *jerked out;* kepped; laid bare; *made bare;* naked; *open;* plumeless; plucked; quill-less; *revealed;* squab; stark naked; tuftless; unvaned; unfeathered; unfledged; unplumed; *visible; without feathers; x-out;* young; *zero feathers;* [*Ant.* feathery]

**feathery** *(adj.)*: abundant-feathered; *birdlike;* chicken-feathered; downy; downed; enfeathered; feathered; featherlike; goose-feathered; hirsute; *ibis-feathered; jay-feathered; kahili [Haw.];* lanate; lanuginous; mailed with feathers; *nappy; oriole-feathered;* penniform; pinnate; plumy; plumed; plumous; plumigerous; plumate; quilled; quill-like; remigial; scalpular; tomentous; tuftlike; unplucked; vibrissa-filled; well-plumed; *xema-feathered; yellow-feathered;* zoofulvious; [*Ant.* featherless]

**feature** *(n.)*: aspect; attribute; *bit; benefit;* component; characteristic; detail; element; facet; good quality; highlight; ingredient; *judgment;* key ~; lineament; mark; notable ~; *nature; object; outline;* part; property; quality; *reality; side; selling point;* thing; trait; *unit;* virtue; *way; x-mal [G.]; yetzer [arch.];* zero in;

**federation** *(n.)*: affiliation; association; alliance; brotherhood; confederation; confederacy; *department;* establishment; fraternity; group; guild; *horizontal union; industrial union;* joint coalition; *kongsi [Chin.];* league; *mutual bond;* nexus; organization; partnership; quinquevirate; *regiment;* society; *trade union; troop;* union; *vertical union; workers' union; x-class;* yeald; zollverein;

**fee** *(n.)*: assessment; *bill;* charge; dues; excise; fine; gabelle; handling charge; impost; interest; jettage; keelage; levy; mulct; nuisance tax; octroi; penalty; quarterage; rate charge; surcharge; toll; tariff; tax; usury; vigorish; *wharfage;* x-int; yardage; *zakat* [Mos.];

**feeble** *(adj.)*: anile; brittle; cachectic; doddery; defenseless; etiolated; enfeebled; frail; gimp; helpless; impotent; *jejune; knocked out;* lame; meager; nugatory; overweak; powerless; *queachy* [dial.]; *run down;* shaky; thin; tenuous; unable; unconvincing; vulnerable; weak; *x-out; yawnish; zapped;* [*Ant.* fit]

**feebleness** *(n.)*: anility; brittleness; cachexia; dodderiness; defenselessness; enfeeblement; frailty; *gimp;* helplessness; impotency; *jejuneness; knocking out;* limpness; lameness; meagerness; non-ability; over-weakness; powerlessness; *queachiness* [dial.]; *reduced ability;* shakiness; thinness; *unprotected;* vulnerability; weakness; *x-out; yielding; zapped;* [*Ant.* fitness]

**feed** *(n.)*: animal food; barley; chicken ~; durra; ensilage; fodder; grain; haver; ile; *Japanese millet;* kemple; lovegrass; meal; *nubbins;* oats; provision; provender; quill; redtop; silage; tow; *unprocessed grain;* victual; wild oats; xyris; yedda; zacate;

**feed** *(v.)*: allot food; bestow aliments; cater; distribute food; *entertain;* fortify; fill; give food; gorge; hand- ~; *help;* inviscerate; *jam-pack;* kit; *lavish;* make to eat; nourish; over~; provide; provision; provender; *quarter;* regale; repast; stall-feed; serve; sustain; *take care of;* under~; victual; winter~; *xenial;* yield victuals; zacate; [*Ant.* famish]

**feel** *(n.)*: atmosphere; body; consistency; character; distillation; embodiment; feeling; grain; handle [Br.]; impression; *jist;* keest; *like;* makeup; nature; overall ~; perception; quality; runniness; roughness; sensation; touch; texture; *understanding;* vibes [slang]; weftage; way of feeling; *xenenthesis; yetzer [Heb.]; zeug [G.];*

**feel** *(v.)*: affect; brush; believe; contact; caress; *deem;* examine; experience; finger; fondle; gently touch; grope; handle; have a feeling; inspect; *judder; know; like;* manipulate; *notion;* overhandle; pat; palpate; perceive; quab; rub; stroke; suffer; seem; sense; touch; think; undergo; *vibes [slang]; work; wis; xfer; yeme; zip;*

**feeling** *(n.)*: affection; aesthesia; attitude; bearing; belief; compassion; cast; disposition; emotion; estimation; frame of mind; gut ~; hunch; heart; inclination; impression; intuition; judgment; *known inclination;* leaning; love; mood; notion; opinion; perspective; passion; *quintessence;* reaction; sense; sensation; sentiment; touch; temperament; *urge;* vibes [slang]; *whim; xenodiagnosis; yearning; zeal;*

**feet** *(n.)* arches; bare ~; clodhoppers; dogs [slang]; *extremities;* footsies [slang]; *goers;* hooves; heels; *insoles; jut;* kickers; legs; *metatarsi; nectopods;* outsoles; paws; peds; *quadrisulcate; right foot;* soles; stocking ~; sandles; shoes; *toes;* tootsies [slang]; ungulas; volars; *webbed ~; xfer;* yads; zygodactyl;

**feign** *(v.)*: act; affect; *behave;* be; bluff; claim; con; dream; dissemble; envision; fake; fantasize; *guile;* hoax; imagine; invent; *just make-believe; keep dreaming; live; like;* make-believe; *non-reality; overact;* pretend; *quasi;* role-play; romanticize; simulate; sham; *take on the part;* use imagination; visualize; whimsy; *xfer;* yede; *zealously play at;*

**feisty** *(adj.)*: aggressive; belligerent; contentious; disagreeable; energetic; fractious; grumpy; huffy; irascible; jangly; knappy; lively; mean; nasty; ornery; petulant; querulous; resistant; spunky; spirited; temperamental; umbrageous; vinegary; wranglesome; *x-ways;* yieldless; zoilistic; [*Ant.* feeble]

**fellow** *(n.)*: associate; bloke; chap; companion; dude; *earthling;* feller; fella [both slang]; guy; gentleman; human; individual; joe [slang]; *kid;* living soul; man; mate; *name;* one; person; partner; *quadragenarian; rube [off.];* soul; teammate; *underling; virile;* worldling; *x-linked;* yokel; young man; zhlub; [*Ant.* female]

**fellowship** *(n.)*: agreement; accord; brotherhood; communion; *devotion;* empathy; friendship; getting along; harmony; interaction; *joining;* kinship; *koinonia* [Gr.]; like-mindedness; mutuality; nearness; oneness; *partnership;* quarrelessness; rapport; right relationship; solidarity; togetherness; *table;* unity; *voluntariness; warmth; xenia;* yoke; *zealous love;* [*Ant.* friction]

**fellowship** *(v.)*: associate; affiliate; be with; commune; consort; deal; engage in conversation; fraternize; get along with; hobnob; have harmony; interact; interface; intercommunicate; identify; join together; *keep in touch;* link; maintain good relations; *nearness; oneness; partner; pray;* quietly commune; run with; relate; speak; socialize; share; talk together; *unity;* visit; warmly speak; *xenia; yoke; zeal;* [*Ant.* fight]

**felon** *(n.)*: assailant; bad guy; criminal; deviant; extortionist; *fugitive;* gangster; highwayman; infractor; *jailbird;* knuck; larcenist; malefactor; no-good; outlaw; perpetrator; *quad;* rogue; scoundrel; transgressor; *underboss;* violator; wrongdoer; *xgressor;* yegg; *zhlub;*

**female** *(n.)*: amoret; beauty; belle; chick [off.]; citess; daughter; distaff; *effeminate;* femme; girl; *her; individual;* jane [slang]; *kinswoman; khanum* [Pers.]; lady; maiden; madam; matron; nymph [poet.]; *one; person; quaedam* [arch.]; *red-head;* squaw [Am. Ind.]; señora [Sp.]; sister; *termagant; temptress; unmanly; virgin; vrouw* [Du.]; woman; *x-chromosome; young lady;* zaftig; [*Ant.* fellow]

**feminine** *(adj.)*: attractive; beautiful; charming; dainty; delicate; ever-womanly; female; girlish; gynic; gentle(womanly); *her; inobtrusive; jeune fille* [F.]; *kinswomanly;* ladylike; maidenly; muliebrile; nymphish; non-masculine; *over-womanly;* petticoat [dated]; *quiet; quedam* [arch.]; *ravishing;* sweet; soft; sylphic; shewomanly; tender; unmanly; *virtuous; voluptuous;* womanish; womanlike; womanly; x-linked; *yokemate; zaftig;*

**femininity** *(n.)*: attractiveness; beauty; charm; decorum; delicateness; *effeminacy;* femaleness; girlishness; gentle(womanli)ness; *hers; inobtrusiveness; jeune fille* [F.]; *kinswomanliness;* ladylikeness; meekness; maidenliness; muliebrity; nymphishness; *over-womanliness; prissiness;* quietness; *ravishing; sissiness;* sweetness; softness; tenderness; unmanliness; *voluptuousness;* womanliness; x-chromosome; *yokemate; zaftig;*

**feminism** *(n.)*: "affirmative action"; blurring gender lines; *cause; cross-dressing; defiance;* ERA; female suffrage; feminist movement; girl power; *her rights;* insubordination; jadedness; *kicking the pricks;* libbers; misandrism; militant ~; *NOW;* obstinacy; pro- ~; *post*~; quasi- ~; rights of women; suffragism; *transgression;* ultra- ~; *violation of God-given roles;* woman's rights (-lib); *x-chomosome;* yieldlessness; zealotry; [*Ant.* femininity]

**feminist** *(adj.)*: *anti-traditional;* Bible-hating; crusading; defiant; ERA; feministic; feminazi [off.]; girl-power; *her rights;* insubordinate; *Jezebel [off.];* kicker; libber; man-hating; misandrist; militant ~; non-traditionalist; *offended;* pro- ~; *post*~; quasi- ~; radical; suffragist; traditional role-hating; ultra- ~; *violating God-given roles;* women's lib; womanist; *x-chromosome; yieldless; zealotic;*

**feminist** *(n.)*: advocate of women's rights; Bible-hater; crusader; *defier;* ERA advocate; feminazi [off.]; *girl power; her rights;* insubordinate; *Jezebel [off.];* kicker; libber; man-hater; misandrist; militant ~; non-traditionalist; *offended;* pro- ~; *post*~; quasi- ~; radical ~; riot girl; suffragist; traditional role-hater; ultra- ~; *violator of God-given roles;* women's libber; womanist; *x-chromosome; yieldless;* zealot;

**feminize** *(v.)*: *alter;* beautify; castrate; demasculinize; effeminize; feminise [Br.]; *glamorize; hers; innovate; jemmy; kern; lib;* make feminine; *non-masculine; overhaul;* prettify; *quality;* render feminine; sissify [off.]; *transform;* unsex; *vary;* weaken; *xfer;* yield to the feminine; *zero masculinity;*

**fen** *(n.)*: *aikraw;* bog; carr; *damp place;* everglade; fenland; glade; holm [Br.]; inland marsh; *jheel* [Ind.]; kavir; *lagoon;* marsh; *nanoplankton; overgrown;* peatbog; quagmire; rosland; swamp; tarn; *usnea;* vlie [S. Afr.]; wash; xyrisic; yarpha; *zoocarpous area;*

**fence** *(n.)*: area ~; boundary; barrier; barbed wire ~; chicken wire; chain-link ~; divider; enclosure; fence-line; guide-rail; *garth;* hawhaw; inclosure; *jail;* kraal; line; log ~; mere-fence; *narrow ~; obstruction;* picket ~; paling; palisade; quickset hedge; railing; ring ~; stockade; sunk ~; trellis; *thorn hedge;* utility ~; Virginia ~; worm ~; weir; wall; x-fence; yard ~; zigzag ~;

**fence-sitting** *(n.)*: ambitendency; anythingarianism; *back and forth;* capriciousness; dithering; erraticism; fence-straddling; fickleness; going back and forth; hedging; indecision; indecisiveness; *jumping; kedging; lack of decisiveness;* middle-of-the-road; non-decisiveness; *on the fence;* pendulating; quasi-resoluteness; reluctance; shifting; teeter-tottering; uncertainty; vacillation; wishy-washiness; *x-ing;* yo-yoing; zigzagging; [Ant. firmness]

**ferment** *(v.)*: acidify; alcoholize; bubble; brew; concoct; distill; effervesce; fizz; *get ready;* heat; infuse; *jibe; keg;* leaven; make; moil; *near-ready;* overflow; *prepare; quality;* ripen; re- ~; seethe; sour; turn into alcohol; *use yeast; vintage;* work; *xfer;* yarken; *yeast; zymotic;*

**fermentation** *(n.)*: alcoholization; breakdown; corruption; dark ~; ethanol ~; fermenting; glyoxylate ~; *hard drink;* industrial ~; *joy water; kirsch;* lactic acid ~; mixed-acid ~; *negus;* oenology; photo~; *quafferous;* re-ferment; sourness; spumescence; turning; *under-proof; vinolent; winemaking; xanthoxylin;* yeasting; zymosis;

**ferocious** *(adj.)*: aggressive; beastly; cruel; destructive; *evil;* fierce; *growling; grievous;* harsh; intense; jungli; *kaf* [arch.]; lionlike; mean; non-domesticated; nasty; outrageous; pugnacious; *querulous;* rabid; raging; rapacious; savage; terrible; truculent; unrestrained; unbridled; vicious; wild; *xtr. mean;* yahoo; *zany;* [Ant. friendly]

**ferociousness** *(n.)*: aggressiveness; beastliness; cruelty; destructiveness; evil; ferocity; *gruffness;* harshness; intensity; *jangliness; kindlessness;* lion-likeness; meanness; nastiness; odiousness; pugnaciousness; *querulousness;* rapaciousness; savageness; terribleness; truculence; uncivility; viciousness; wildness; *xenophobia; yelling; zaniness;*

**fertile** *(adj.)*: abundant; bearing; copious; child-bearing; *deliver; endowed;* fecund; fruitful; generative; *good; highly productive;* inter~; *juvenescent;* keenly abundant; life-giving; *many; mother;* non-sterile; overabundant; *omniferous; pomiferous;* productive; prolific; *quantitative;* rank; rich; *superabundant; tons;* uberous; viviparous; well-fruited; *x.;* yielding; yieldful *zero-sterility;* [Ant. fruitless]

**fertility** *(n.)*: abundance; bountifulness; bearing; child-bearing; *delivering; endowed;* fecundity; fruitfulness; generativeness; gravidity; *high productivity;* inter~; *juvenescence;* keen abundance; luxuriance; *many; mother;* non-sterility; overabundance; productiveness; prolificacy; *quantity;* richness; *superabundance; tons;* uberousness; viviparousness; *well-fruited; x.;* yielding; *zero-sterility;* [Ant. fruitlessness]

**fertilize** *(v.)*: *ash;* batten; compost; dung; enrich; fructify; *good [arch.];* horsedung; improve; *jee; keytonuria;* lime; manure; marl; mulch; nitrogenize; *overspread; prepare;* quicklime; rejuvenate; spread manure; sidedress; stercorate; top-dress; *treat; urinate; vitalize; waste; xenogamy; yote; zet;*

**fertilizer** *(n.)*: argol; ash; bone meal; composture; dung; enrucher; feces; gypsum; horsedung; *item; jakes; keytonuria;* lime; manure; nitrogenizer; ordure; plaster-stone; *quality ~; refuse;* side-dressing; top-dressing; *urine; vitalization;* waste; xysma; *yote;* zigg;

**fervency** *(n.)*: ardency; burning; commitment; devotion; enthusiasm; fervor; gusto; heart; impassionedness; *joie de vivre [F.];* keenness; liveliness; *motivation; nationalism; officiousness;* passion; *quickness;* readiness; spirit; *thrill; ultra-zealous;* vehemence; wholeheartedness; *x-fervor;* yareness; zealousness; [Ant. feebleness]

**fervent** *(adj.)*: ardent; burning; committed; devoted; enthusiastic; fanatical; gung-ho; hearty; impassioned; *jingoist;* keen; *loyal;* motivated; mad; *nationalistic;* overzealous; passionate; quick; ready; spirited; tireless; unreserved; vehement; wholehearted; *xenocentric;* yare; zealous; [*Ant.* feeble]
**fervor** *(n.)*: ardor; burning; commitment; devotedness; enthusiasm; fervency; gusto; heart; intensity; *joy;* keenness; liveliness; *militancy; nationalism;* obsession; passion; *quickness;* robustness; spirit; tirelessness; *ultra-zealous;* vigor; wholeheartedness; *x-fervor;* yareness; zeal; [*Ant.* feebleness]
**fester** *(v.)*: aggravate; break out; canker; deteriorate; eat at; fret; gnaw; gall; *hoar;* infester; *jade; ketty; labelfaction;* mold; *non-healthy; oxidize;* pus; putrefy; queer; rankle; rot; smolder; spoil; *taint;* ulcerate; *virulent;* worsen; *waste; xylaria; youster* [arch.]; *zorch;*
**festive** *(adj.)*: *animated;* bright; cheerful; celebratory; delighted; *dazzling;* exuberant; festal; gleeful; gay; happy; high-spirited; intense; joyful; *keen;* lighthearted; merry; mirthful; *nice;* overjoyed; *pleasant; queme;* rejoicing; radiant; splendid; triumphant; upbeat; vibrant; vivacious; wonderful; *xtry.;* yeasty; zestful; [*Ant.* funereal]
**fetish** *(n.)*: amulet; bloodstone; charm; *doodad; entity;* fetich; grigri; hoodoo; image; *juju; kappe;* lucky charm; magic charm; mojo; *night-spell;* obeah; *object;* periapt; query stone; rabbit foot; scarab; talisman; *unit;* voodoo; *whatchy;* xoanon; *yantra;* zogo;
**fetter** *(n.)*: ankle-band; band; bond; cuffs; *chain;* darbies; *enfettered;* fettering; gyve; hamper; handcuff; hand-fetter; irons; jail-bands; *keeping;* ligature; manacle; nipper; *oppression;* pinion; *quell;* restraint; shackle; stocks; trammel; *unliberated; vervel;* wristband; Xica; yoke; zoster; [*Ant.* freedom]
**fetus** *(n.)*: *atom;* blastula; baby; *child;* developing baby; embryo; fruit (of the womb); *girl [fem.];* hatchling; infant; *juvenile; kid;* little one; morula; *non-full term;* ovule; *person; quite small;* rudiment; *son [masc.]; tiny baby;* unborn child; vitellus; womb-infant; *xenogenesis;* yolk; zoon;
**feud** *(n.)*: argument; bad blood; blood ~; contention; dispute; embroilment; fight; grudge; hostilities; *incongruity; jangling;* kagg; *locking horns; making fur fly;* negativism; opposition; odds; *polemic;* quarrel; row; strife; tussle; unharmoniousness; variance; war(fare); *x-fire;* yed; *zapping;* [*Ant.* friendship]
**feud** *(v.)*: argue; battle; contend; dispute; *engage;* fight; *grapple;* have words with; *impugn;* jangle; kick up dust; lock horns [slang]; make fur fly; *naysay;* oppose; pick fight; quarrel; row; strive; tiff; *unharmonious;* vie; war; *x-purposes;* yain [arch.]; *zap;* [*Ant.* friendship]
**feudal** *(adj.)*: Arthurian; barbaric; Byzantine; Crusade-period; dark age; *era;* feudalistic; gestic; historical; *iconic; jousting; knights; legendary;* medieval; manorial; non-enlightened; olden; predial; quasi- ~; Robin Hood-era; superannuated; *times gone by;* unenlightened; vassal; *warlords; xtr. old;* yore; *ziamet [Turk.];*
**feudalism** *(n.)*: *Arthurian;* baronage; collectivism; castles and nights; dark ages; *era;* fiefdom; *gestic;* homage-system; *iconic; jousting; knights and castles;* lords and ladies; manorialism; *non-enlightenment;* olden days; predial times; *quasi-feudal; Robin Hood era;* serfdom; serfhood; seignorialism; *times gone by; unenlightened;* vassalage; *warlords; xtr. old; yore; ziamet* [Turk.];
**fever** *(n.)*: * ague; burning; brucellosis; calenture; dengue; eruptive ~; febricity; gallsickness; hyperthermia; hyperpyrexia; high ~; intermittent ~; jungle ~; *kindled;* Lassa ~; low-grade ~; Malta ~; *99 degrees;* o'nyong-nyong ~; pyrexia; quartan; Q-fever; recurring ~; remittent ~; scarlet ~; temperature; typhus; undulant ~; verruga ~; warmness; *xerothermic;* yellow ~; *zich [arch.];*
**feverish** *(adj.)*: aguish; burning up; calid; *diseased;* enfevered; febric; *galled;* hot; hectic; *ill; jaundiced;* kindled; lightly ~; *malaise;* not well; *99 degrees;* overhot; *103 degrees;* pyretic; *quicksilver;* real warm; roasting; sick; sweltering; scarlatinous; *temperature;* unwell; violently ill; warm; xerothermic; *yellow fever; zich [arch.];* [*Ant.* fit]
**few** *(adj.)*: *abject;* below the needed amount; coming up short; deficient; exiguous; falling short; greatly insufficient; hardly enough (-any); infrequent; insufficient; *just not enough;* keenly deficient; less; lacking; meager; not many; occasional; paltry; quantity insufficient; rare; scant; trifling; thin; unfrequent; *under;* unsatisfactory; very ~; wanting; *xtry. deficient;* yet ~; *zero sufficiency:*

**fewer** *(adj.)*: *amount;* below; *concise;* dinkier; *excepting;* fewer; *greatly reduced; half;* inferior; *just ~; known to be ~;* lesser; lower amount; more modest; much less; not as much; *outclassed;* puisne; quite a bit less; reduced; smaller amount; tinier; under; unsubstantial; *very small;* weaker; *xtry. small; younger; zeroize;*

**fiancé** *(n.)*: affianced; betrothed; *committed;* darling; espoused; fiance; groom-to-be; husband-to-be; inamorto; intended; *joe; knight in shining armor; lover;* man; Mr. Right; *nuptial;* one-and-only; promised; *questor; Romeo;* sweetheart; true love; *unmarried; valentine; wedding; xtr. special one; yokemate; zon [dial.];* [*Ant.* fiancée]

**fiancée** *(n.)*: affianced; betrothed; bride-to-be; *committed;* darling; espoused; fiancee; *girlfriend;* honey; inamorta; intended; *jeune fille [F.]; kadin;* ladylove; maiden; *nuptial;* one-and-only; promised bride; *quedom [arch.]; rose [fem.];* sweetheart; true love; *unmarried; valentine;* wife-to-be; *xtr. special one; yokemate; zitella [It.];* [*Ant.* fiancé]

**fib** *(n.)*: *alteration of truth;* bluff; con; deceit; equivocation; flam; falsehood; gonk; half-truth; invention; jactitation; *kid;* lie; misrepresentation; non-truth; *outknavery;* putting one over; *quiblin [arch.]; rooking;* stretch; tall tale; untruth; *verneuking;* white lie; *xuld [arch.];* yarn; *zinger;* [*Ant.* fact]

**fib** *(v.)*: *allure;* belie; con; deceive; equivocate; fudge; feign; gonk; hoodwink; invent; *jackal;* knowingly lie; lie; misrepresent; nobble; *outfox;* perjure; *quiblin* [arch.]; *rook;* stretch the truth; tell falsehood; utter falsehood; verneuk; weasel; *xuld [arch.]; yentz; zing;*

**fiber** *(n.)*: app; *braid;* cord; *drawstring; entangle;* fibre; filament; *goldthread;* halter; *intertwine;* jute; knittle; line; ligature; *micro~; natural ~;* organzine; ply; *qiviut; rope-yarn;* strand; thread; *uncoil;* vang; warp; woof; xylem; yarn; zein;

**fickle** *(adj.)*: arbitrary; alternating; bouncy; changeable; capricious; double-faced; erratic; fluctuating; faithless; frivolous; giddy; *heady;* inconsistent; jumpy; *kaleidoscopic;* light-minded; mercurial; non-stable; out-of-control; precarious; quicksilver; *random;* shaky; temperamental; unsteady; unpredictable; volatile; whimsical; *x-ing;* yo-yo; zigzag; [*Ant.* firm]

**fickleness** *(n.)*: alternation; bouncing around; capriciousness; *disturbed;* erraticism; fluctuation; faithlessness; giddiness; *heady;* indecisiveness; jumpiness; *kaleidoscopic;* likeliness to change; mutability; non-stability; *out-of-control;* precariousness; *questionable;* randomness; shakiness; tergiversation; uncertainty; variableness; volatility; wavering; *x-ing; yo-yo;* zigzag; [*Ant.* firmness]

**fictitious** *(adj.)*: air-built; bogus; cooked-up; chimerical; dreamt-up *epic;* fictional; fictive; gag; hoax; invented; imaginary; japed; kiddy; *legendary;* made-up; mythical; nonexistent; *opinionative;* phony; quacky; *rendered;* sham; spurious; trick; trumped-up; unreal; *vain;* well-imagined; *xeno-;* yichus; *zero validity;* [*Ant.* factual]

**fidgety** *(adj.)*: antsy; bouncy; *churning;* discontent; edgy; fiddling; goosey; *hoppity;* impatient; jiggety; *kick; leaning;* moving around; *nervous;* overstrung; playing; *queachy;* restless; squirmy; twitchy; uneasy; unsettled; *vacillating;* wiggly; *xuld [arch.];* yanky; *zaggy;*

**field** *(n. area of land)*: acre; *bush;* clearing; *corn~; dale; earsh;* farmland; ground; haugh [Scot.]; ile [Welsh]; *jebel; knoll;* lea; meadow; milpa; *nature; outdoors;* pasture; playing ~; plot; quadrat; range; sod; steppe; turf; tract; upland; vega; vineyard; *water meadow; xyris;* yard; zea;

**field** *(n. line of work)*: area; business; career; craft; discipline; enterprise; emphasis; focus; *general ~; handcraft;* industry; job; *key position;* livelihood; line of work; métier; *notion;* occupation; profession; *quest; responsibility;* service; sphere; trade; undertaking; vocation; work; xci.; yoke; zone;

**fiendish** *(adj.)*: abominable; bad; corrupt; diabolical; evil; foul; fiendlike; guileful; heinous; iniquitous; jaded; knavish; licentious; malevolent; nasty; ornery; pernicious; *quad;* ruthless; sinister; treacherous; unethical; villainous; wicked; *xgressing;* yucky; zymotic; [*Ant.* friendly]

**fierce** *(adj.)*: ardent; aggressive; brutal; crazed; disorderly; *extreme;* fell; ferocious; *grievous;* harsh; intense; jungli; *kaf* [arch.]; lionlike; mad; nasty; outraged; passionate; *querulous;* raving; rampant; severe; terrible; truculent; turbulent; tempestuous; untamed; violent; wild; *xtr. mean;* yahoo, zany; [*Ant.* feeble]

**fiery** *(adj.)*: ablaze; blazing; burning; combusting; deflagrating; enflamed; flaming; glowing; hot; high-flaming; igneous; inflamed; *jejune;* kindled; lighted; *match-lit;* nealing; overhot; pyrogenic; quenchless; red-hot; smoldering; scarlet; sizzling; scorching; torrid; ustorious; unquenched; volcanic; *white-hot;* xerothermic; yellow-hot; *zealous;* [*Ant.* frozen]

**fight** *(n.)*: altercation; argument; attack; affray; brawl; battle; conflict; clash; dispute; dust-up; encounter; fist~; fray; gunfight; hostilities; hand-to-hand combat; irregular warfare; *jihad* [Mos.]; *kampf* [G.]; knock-down-drag-out ~; *loggerheads;* mêlée; *naval warfare;* occursion; onslaught; pugilism; quarrel; run-in; rumble; ruction; squabble; scrap; skirmish; scuffle; struggle; tussle; taking up arms; unrest; vying; war(fare); *x-fire;* yed; *zapping;*

**fight** *(v.)*: altercate; attack; bicker; brawl; battle; contend; clash; dispute; duke it out [slang]; engage; embroil; fist~; feud; grapple; *have words with; impugn;* jangle; kemp; levy war; make war with; *naysay;* oppose; pick fight; quarrel; resist; scrap; squabble; scuffle; struggle; strive; tangle; take up arms; *unharmonious;* vie; wrangle; (wage) war; *x-purposes; yain* [arch.]; *zap;*

**fighter** *(n.)*: aggressor; brawler; battler; combatant; crusader; duelist; defender; *enlisted man;* feuder; fighting man; gladiator; hoplite [Gr.]; infantryman; janissary [Turk.]; knight; lansquenet; legionnaire; mercenary; military man; *naysayer; officer;* pikeman; quarreler; rifleman; scrapper; squabbler; struggler; swordsman; soldier; tussler; tangler; *uniformed men;* velite [Rom.]; wrangler; warrior; *xiphos-bearer; yardbird; zoauve;*

**figment** *(n.)*: abstraction; *bogus;* creation; delusion; dream; *excogitation;* fabrication; fantasy; genesis; hallucination; invention; idea; *just imaginary; keen imagination; lethe;* musing; notion; origination; product (of one's imagination); *quickening; ruse; scheme;* thought; *unreality;* vapor; whim; *x-fix; yeme* [arch.]; *zazen;* [*Ant.* fact]

**figurative** *(adj.)*: allegorical; *Bunyanesque;* curiologic; comparative; descriptive; emblematic; figural; *general;* hieroglyphic; illustrative; *juxtaposed;* kuriologic; *likening;* metaphoric(al); *non-literal; operative;* pictorial; poetical; parabolic; prefigurate; *quarto;* representative; symbolic; typical; umbratical; vignette; word-picture; *xenodoceionological; yarn;* zeugmatic; [*Ant.* factual]

**figure** *(v.)*: assess; *brainstorm;* calculate; determine; evaluate; formulate; gauge; hatch; hypothesize; *ideate;* judge; *know; lucubrate;* muse; *notion; observe;* ponder; quantify; reckon; study; think; use brain; valuate; weigh; *xenodiagnose; yeme; zazen;*

**file** *(n. place of records)*: account; archive; book; cartulary; data(base); *evidence;* folder; *get down;* history; information; journal; *kept ~;* log; muniment; *notebook;* official record; postea; *quill;* record; *statement;* tally sheet; *underwritten;* vertical ~; written record; *xenagogy;* yellow sheet [crim. law]; *zet;*

**file** *(n. rasp)*: *abrasion;* barrette ~; checkering ~; dreadnought ~; equaling ~; flat ~; frower; grater; hand ~; *instrument;* joint-round edge ~; knife ~; *linishing;* millenicut ~; nail ~; needle ~; *ovate handaxe;* pippin; quannet; rasp; riffler; rattail; scraper; scourer; *tool;* triangular ~; *unifacial tool;* varnish scraper; wood rasp; xyster; *yataghan; zester;*

**file** *(v.)*: abrade; bray; burr; chafe; deburr; even out; file down; grind; grate; hone; *impair; jar;* knock off; level; levigate; manicure; make smooth; *nullify; overbear;* plane; *quash;* rub; rasp; smooth; scrape; take away; use ~; *very smooth;* wear away; xyster; *yerk; zeroize;*

**fill** *(v.)*: accomplish; burden; cover; cram; crowd; *diffuse; enough;* fulfill; flood; get in; gorge; *have;* imbue; jam-pack; *kibble;* load; make full; *niche;* occupy; overfill; overload; overstuff; pack; permeate; pervade; quash full; replenish; stock; stuff; suffuse; surfeit; saturate; sate; take up; top off; *tamp;* use; *volume;* wedge in; *xfer; yield; zero space leftover;*

**film** *(n. unwanted buildup)*: accumulation; buildup; coating; crust; creosol; deposit; *emptyings;* flysch; grouts; *hazmat;* impurities; junk; kaff [dial.]; lac; membrane; matter; *non-wanted matter;* offscouring; outer layer; pellicle; plaque; quinoldine; residue; residuum; resin; skin; scum; silt; tartar; *unwanted;* varve; waste; *xylene; yacca gum; zero;*

**filter** *(n.)*: *aerator;* bolter; cribble; *device; ethmoid;* filtre; *grate;* hand-held ~; *instrument;* jiggety sieve; kitchen strainer; lixiviator; mesh strainer; *net; operation;* percolator; purifier; *quaff;* riddle; strainer; screen; tammy; ultra~; *ventilate;* wilch; *xfer;* yandy; zaru;

**filter** *(v.)*: *aerate;* bolt; cribble; drain; elutriate; filtrate; go through; *highly ~ed; interstices; jiggety; kitchen strainer;* lixiviate; make separate; *non-combined; ooze;* pass through; perk; percolate; seep; quaff; riddle; screen; sift; strain; separate; transcolate; *use ~; ventilate;* winnow; *xude;* yote; zaru;

**filth** *(n.)*: *acid soil; bemired;* crud; debris; dirt; earth; foul matter; filthiness; grunge; grime; *hazel-earth;* impurities; *jet;* kirn; loam; mess; mud; muck; mire; nast; ordure; *pig manure;* quagmire; refuse; soil; scum; scuzz; squalidness; sewage; turbidness; uncleanness; vileness; waste; xysma; *yellow soil; zonal soil;* [*see* wickedness]

**filthy** *(adj.)*: *awful;* bemired; cruddy; collied; contaminated; dirty; dungy; *extremely dirty;* foul; feculent; grubby; germy; grungy; grimy; hoggish; insanitary; jarbled; kollowed; muddy; nasty; *oozy;* polluted; quaggy; *ruined;* soiled; squalid; scuzzy; turbid; uliginous; unbathed; vile; well-dirtied; *xysmic;* yucky; *zero cleanliness;*

**filtration** *(n.)*: aeration; bolting; colature; diffusion; drip ~; elutriation; filtering; *grinds; highly filtered; interstices; java; kitchen;* leakage; lixiviation; micro- ~; *non-combined; outflow;* percolation; quaffing; running (down); seepage; straining; sifting; sieving; trickling down; ultra~; *ventilation;* weeping; *xude;* yoting; zaru;

**final** *(adj.)*: absolute; *bottom;* concluding; closing; decisive; dying; endmost; eventual; ending; farmost; finishing; *grand finale;* hindermost; irreversible; irrevocable; *just the last; killing;* latest; last(-ditch); latter; *margin;* nth; outermost; posterior; *quitting;* remaining; surviving; terminal; ultimate; very last; *winning; xyz;* yondmost; year-end; *zenithal;* [*see* examination; *Ant.* first]

**finale** *(n.)*: apex; big ending; climax; culmination; denouement; ending; finis(h); grand ~; height; *incredible ending;* jubilee; *key movement;* last hoorah; *movement;* mountaintop; *nadir;* outcome; peak; *quittance;* resolution; summation; swan song; termination; upshot; *vertex;* windup act; xtry. finish; *yondmost;* zenith;

**finalize** *(v.)*: affirm; bring to an end; confirm; clinch; close; decide; establish; finish; guarantee; *halt; implement; judge; knowledge;* let it stand; make final; *non-changeable; over;* put an end to; *questionless;* resolve; settle; seal; *terminate; uphold;* verify; wrap up; x-out; yes; zet *[dial.];* [*Ant.* form]

**finally** *(adv.)*: at last; by and by; conclusively; decisively; eventually; forever; *grand finale;* hereafter; in the end; in conclusion; *just the last; killing;* lastly; *margin; nth;* once and for all; permanently; *quitting; remaining;* so then; terminally; ultimately; *verified; winning; xyz;* yet; yondmost; *zenithal;* [*Ant.* firstly]

**financial** *(n.)*: asset-control; budgetary; capitol-related; dollars-and-cents; economic; fiscal; geoeconomic; *hard cash;* inter-economic; *jiggy; kale; lucrative; tender;* monetary; macroeconomic; *numbers; obol;* pecuniary; *quid [Br.];* riches; *silver;* trade; *usurious;* venture *capitol;* world ~; *xenocurrency;* yen; zechin;

**financier** *(n.)*: abettor; backer; bankroller; capitalist; defrayer; entrepreneur; funder; financer; grubstaker; helper; investor; junior partner; *keep;* loaner; lender; mainstay; money lender; *numbers;* operator; partner; payer; *quick cash;* rich person; silent partner; subsidizer; supporter; tycoon; underwriter; *vest;* Wall Street ~; xaraf; *yield;* zillions;

**find** *(v.)*: ascertain; *attain to;* bring to light; come across; dig up; dredge up; discover; detect; determine; espy; encounter; find out; get; happen upon; identify; isolate; *jaeger;* kithe [Scot.]; light on; *learn;* locate; meet; *new-found;* obtain; pinpoint; *pick up; quick-to-discover;* regain; recover; stumble on; solve; *see;* turn up; track down; uncover; unearth; venture upon; work out; *x-search;* yead; zealously track; [*Ant.* forget]

**fine** *(adj.)*: attenuated; bitty; constricted; delicate; elongated; frail; gracile; hairbreadth; insubstantial; jimp; knife blade-thin; little; minute; narrow; overthin; paper-thin; pencil-thin; *quantité négligeable [F.];* real ~; slender; slim; super~; tenuous; threadlike; thin; ultra~; virgate [bot.]; wafer-thin; XF; *yieldless; zero thickness;* [*Ant.* fat]

**fine** *(n. charge)*: assessment; *bill;* charge; dues; duty; excise; fee; gabelle; handling charge; impost; interest; jettage; keelage; levy; mulct; nuisance tax; octroi; penalty; quarterage; *revenue;* surcharge; tax; usury; vigorish; *wharfage;* x-int; yardage; *zakat* [Mos.];

**finesse** *(n.)*: adeptness; beauty; cunning; deftness; elegance; flair; grace; hability; instinct; jimp; know-how; luster; mastery; natural ability; *overelegance;* proficiency; poise; quickness; refinement; skill; savvy; talent; *uncommon;* virtuosity; way; *xenium;* yaup; zest;

**finest** *(adj.)*: A-1; ablest; best; choicest; cream; dandiest; elite; first-rate; greatest; highest; *impressive; jim-dandy;* keenest; loftiest; most desirable; nicest; No. 1; optimal; prime; pick; premium; *quality;* rosiest; select; superior; top; unrivaled; very best; world-class; xtry.; yondmost; zenithal; [*Ant.* foulest]

**finger** *(n.)*: appendage; big ~; center ~; digit; dactyl; extremity; ~tip; fore~; *green thumb;* hook [slang]; *hand;* index ~; *jewel-encrusted ~; knuckle;* little ~; medius; middle ~; *nail; outstretched ~;* pointer; pinky; pollex; quadridigitate; ring ~; *stroke;* thumb; trigger ~; tentacle; *unmanicured ~; very narrow extension; well-manicured; xylaria;* yad; *zircon-jeweled ~;*

**finicky** *(adj.)*: austere; bull-headed; choosy; difficult; demanding; exacting; fussy; finical; *griping;* hard to please; impossible to please; *just so; kvetch [Yid.]; lousy; meticulous;* nitpicky; over- ~; picky; particular; persnickety; quiddle; *repining;* selective; tough to please; unappeasable; very ~; *whining; xuld [arch.]; yieldless; zero give;*

**finish** *(n.)*: alkyd; *brilliance;* coating; cloisonné; *Danish oil;* enamel; French polish; gloss; glaze; high-gloss ~; *inceration;* japan; *keen;* lacquer; marine spar; nigrosine; overglaze; polish; *quartz sand;* resin coat; shellac; topcoat; urethane; varnish; wax; wood ~; xesturgy; *yare; zinc flourosilicate;*

**finish** *(v.)*: accomplish; bring to an end (-fruition); close; complete; conclude; do (away with); dispatch; end; fulfill; get done; *halt; implement; junk;* kill; leave off; make an end of; *nullify; over;* put an end to; play out; polish off; quash; resolve; stop; see it through; terminate; *undertake; victory;* wrap up; wind up; *x-out;* yield; *zero-out;* [*Ant.* form]

**finite** *(adj.)*: *abuttals;* bounded; confined; determinate; established; fixed; greatly limited; having limits; insular; jurisdictional; known; limited; moderated; not unlimited; *nippet;* only so much; preset; parameterized; quite limited; restricted; set(tled); terminable; *unvested;* very limited; with limitations; *x'ed;* yea so much; *zoned;*

**fink** *(n.)*: *abomination;* blabbermouth; cummer; delator; echoer; *fickle;* gossiper; *hearsay;* informer; informant; jaunderer; kibitz; loose-tongue; magpie; newsmonger; *obtrectation;* prater; quidnunc; rat(~); snitch; tattletale; tattler; *utterer; vicious voice;* whistle-blower; *xiaoren;* yakker; *zeroizer;*

**fire** *(n.)*: *aflame;* blaze; burning; brush~; bon~; combustion; camp~; conflagration; deflagration; electrical ~; flame; flare; forest ~; ~storm; glow; hearth; *heat; hell~;* ignition; incineration; ingle; inferno; *jungle- ~; kindled;* light; *match;* night- ~; oxidation; pyre; *quick-match;* raging ~; sparks; *torch;* ustulation; *volcano;* wild~; watch ~; *xylophyrography; yearning; zap;* [*see* hell; spark; passion]

**fire** *(v. end employment)*: ax; boot [both joc.]; can; court-martial; dismiss; discharge; disemploy; eliminate; expel; *fix;* give leave; *heads roll [joc.];* impeach; *job loss;* kick out; let go; make unemployed; no longer employ; offload; pink slip; *quash;* remove; sack; terminate; unload; unemploy; *vote out;* withdraw employment; *x-out;* yank; *zeroize;*

**fire** *(v. shoot a gun)*: assault; blaze; *crack!;* discharge; *enfilade; function;* gun down; *hurl;* impel; *jaculate;* kill; let off; *machine-gun;* nuke; open fire; pull the trigger; *quick-fire;* release; *riddle;* shoot; take pot shot; unleash; volley; *work; x-out; yield;* zap;

318

**fireplace** *(n.)*: *andiron;* brick ~; chimenea; *dog-iron; electric ~;* fireside; fireboard; granite ~; grate; hearth(side); inglenook; *jamb;* kitchen-hearth; killogie; *log;* mantel(-piece); *night-fire;* open hearth; prefabricated ~; *potbelly stove; Quebec heater;* Rumford ~; stone ~; taboon; *ustulation; Vesta;* wood-fired oven; *xylophyrography;* Yule log; *zap;*

**fireproof** *(adj.)*: *asbestos;* asbestine; apyrous; burn-resistant; combustion-resistant; *defended; ensured;* flameproof; flame-retardant; *guarded;* heat-resistant; incombustible; incremable; *just won't burn; kept safe; lightless; made ~;* non-combustible (-flammable); *overprotected;* protected; *quasi-protected;* refractory; *resistant;* salamandrine; totally ~; unburnable; unflammable; *vallated; well-protected;* xylotile; *yeme [arch.]; zero danger;*

**firm** *(adj.)*: adamant; bendless; concrete; determined; definite; ever-rigid; fixed; glued; hard; inflexible; *jarless; keep;* lithified; *lasting;* mulish; nonflexible; obstinate; petrous; *querulous;* rigid; resolved; stiff; stubborn; sound; solid; tough; tenacious; unbending; unpliable; unyielding; *valid;* willful; *x-grained;* yieldless; *zero give;* [*Ant.* feeble, flaccid, flexible]

**firmament** *(n.)*: atmosphere; *the* blue; clouds; deep blue sky; empyrean; first heaven; gaseous covering; *gray skies;* heavens; ionosphere; *jumbo cloud; KH instability; layer;* mid-heaven; *night sky;* open skies; *patchy sky; quality air; region;* sky; *thermosphere;* upper atmosphere; vault of heaven; welkin; *xtr. thin air;* yonder; zenith; *zone;*

**firmness** *(n.)*: adamancy; bendlessness; concreteness; determination; *ever-rigid;* fixedness; *grimness;* hardness; inflexibility; *jaw-set; keeping;* lastingness; mulishness; non-flexibility; obstinacy; pertinacity; *querulousness;* rigidity; stiffness stubbornness; solidness; toughness; unyieldingness; *very rigid;* willfulness; *x-grained;* yieldlessness; *zero give;* [*Ant.* feebleness]

**first** *(adj.)*: archetypal; alpha; beginning; commencing; debuting; erst; earliest; firstfruits; former; foremost; *greatest; head;* initial; imprimis; *jump off; kick off;* leading; launching; maiden; number original; oldest; opening; *new;* primal; prototype; pioneer; primary; *quickened;* ruling; starting; top; unprecedented; very ~; virgin; *welcoming;* xenogenesis; *young;* zygogenesis; [*Ant.* final]

**firstborn** *(adj.)*: archical; born-first; commencing; debuting; eldest; eigne; first-begotten; *genesis; hatched first;* initial; *jump off; kick off;* leading; *made first;* number one; oldest; primigenial; *quickening;* rising; starting; senior; *top;* unprecedented; vaunt *[arch.];* welcomed; xenogenesis; *young;* zygogeneis; [*Ant.* final]

**firstfruits** *(n.)*: *arriving;* beginning; *commencement; debut; entry;* first part; firstlings; *genesis; hatching;* initial blessings; jump-off; kickoff; *launching; manifestation; new harvest;* onset; *primitial; quantity;* rudiments; start; tithe; *unveiling;* very first; *work; xfer;* year's first; *zygogenesis;*

**fish** *(n.)*: alepidote; *bass;* creature; *dace; eulachon;* freshwater ~; flat~; fillet; gold~; *herring;* ichthyoid; *jack~; krill; lady~;* mullet; *marine animal;* nekton; *needlefish;* ocean ~; parr; pan ~; quillback; river ~; sea ~; saltwater ~; *trout; umbra; vieja;* whitefish; *xenomi;* yabby; zope;

   **Types of fish**: anchovy; blue~; carp; dog~; eel; flounder; guppy; haddock; ide; jack crevalle; krill; ladyfish; mackerel; needle~; oarfish; perch; quill~; rudd; salmon; tuna; umbra; vieja; whiting; xurel; yabby; zander;

**fish** *(v.)*: angle; *bring out;* cast net; *catch ~;* dap; *explore;* find; go after; hunt for; ice ~; jig; kithe; look for; make a search; nose around; *obtain;* probe; prawn; quest for; *rummage; reel;* search; seek; spear~; trawl; troll; *uncover;* venture after; *work for; x-search; yearn for;* zetetic;

**fisher** *(n.)*: angler; bayman; catcher of fish; dragman; *enthusiast;* fisher(man); flyfisherman; halver; ice ~; jacker; *kipperer;* lake- ~; macarel; night angler; netsman; offshore angler; oysterman; packrodder; piscator; rodder; sportsman; seaman; trawler; troller; upcountry angler; *venturer;* winkler; whaler; *xurel-catcher; yabby-fisher; zander-catcher;*

**fishing** *(n.)*: angling; blue-fishing; catching fish; deep sea ~; *eel ~;* fish-catching; fly- ~; guddling; ice- ~; jigging; jug- ~; kiping; line ~; *mackerel ~;* night angling; net ~; offshore ~; ocean ~; piscation; *quillfish ~;* river ~; rod and reel; spear ~; sportsmanship; trawling; trolling; underwater spear ~; *vieja ~;* winkling; whaling; *xurel catching;* yair; *zope ~;*

**fit** *(adj. appropriate)*: appropriate; apropos; becoming; correct; due; ever-appropriate; fitting; good; *honorable;* idoneous; just; *kosher;* legitimate; meet; not out-of-place; okay; proper; qualified; right; suitable; seemly; *tolerable; unselfish;* valid; well(-suited); *xtry.; yielded; zero problem;*

**fit** *(adj. healthy)*: athletic; bodily well; *capital;* dandy; entire; fine; good; healthy; *incredible;* just fine; keen; lusty; mighty fine; nurtured; okay; peak; *quartful* [arch.]; robust; sound; strong; trim; tip-top; unimpaired; vigorous; well; *xtry.;* yaul; zippy; [*Ant.* fat]

**fit** *(n. temper tantrum)*: anger; blowup; conniption; dudgeon; enragement; furor; gall; hissy ~; infuriation; jumping ~; *kindling;* lividness; madness; *nettling;* outburst; pique; paroxysm; *quick-temper;* rage; *storm;* (temper) tantrum; *upset; unglued;* venting; wrath; xerothermia; yelling ~; *zealousy* [arch.];

**fitness** *(n.)*: appropriateness; becomingness; correctness; deservingness; expedience; fitness; felicity; grig; health; invalescence; justness; keenness; lustiness; might; *non*-rosiness; ruddiness; *okay;* patness; propriety; qualification; robustness; rightness; suitability; strength; trimness; *tip-top; unimpaired;* validity; vigor; wellness; well-being; worthiness; *xtry. health;* yaul; *zippiness;*

**fitting** *(adj.)*: appropriate; apt; befitting; correct; condign; due; deserved; expedient; fit; good; *honorable;* idoneous; just; *kosher;* legitimate; meet; *normal;* okay; proper; qualified; right; suitable; *tolerable; unselfish;* valid; well(-suited); *xtry.; yielded; zealous;*

**fix** *(v.)*: adjust; amend; *better;* correct; cure; darn; debug; doctor; expiate; establish; enhance; fiddle with; get working; harmonize; heal; improve; jury-rig; *kilter; level out;* mend; make good; *neogenesis;* overhaul; *overcorrect;* patch up; quick-fix; right; redress; rectify; repair; remedy; restore; service; stitch; set (aright); touch up; tinker; tune up; *upbuild;* vamp; work on; *x-fix; yieldless; zip back together;* [see affix; cure]

**fixable** *(adj.)*: adjustable; amendable; betterable; correctable; curable; doctorable; emendable; *fix; get fixed;* helpable; improvable; *jury-rig; kilter; level out;* mendable; medicable; *neogenesis; overhauling;* patchable; *quick-fix;* rectifiable; reversible; reparable; repairable; restorable; serviceable; sanable; treatable; tunable; *upbuild; vamp;* workable; *x-fix;* yet ~; *zip back together;* [*Ant.* fruitless]

**fixed** *(adj.)*: absolute; bound; changeless; definite; ever the same; firm; fast; guaranteed; hard; immovable; irremovable; irreversible; inalienable; inclavated; immutable; *just the same;* kept the same; lasting; locked-in; made whole; non-moveable; *one;* permanent; quite firm; reverseless; stationary; *transcending;* unshakable; unmodifiable; unmovable; unchangeable; unalterable; unalienable; vested; without change; *x-cending;* ypight [arch.]; *zero movement;* [*Ant.* fluctuating]

**flabby** *(adj.)*: atonic; baggy; chubby; droopy; *extra body fat;* full-figured; flaccid; *gimp; hanging;* infirm; *jiggly; king-size;* limp; *massive;* non-fit; overweight; pudgy; *quantitative;* roly-poly; sagging; tubby; unfit; ventricose; weak; XL; *yielding; zero tone;* [*Ant.* fit]

**flag** *(n.)*: American ~; banner; colors; *designation;* ensign; fanion; gonfalon; *heraldry;* insignia; jack; King's colors; *labarum; mark;* national colors; *Old Glory [U.S.];* oriflamme *[F.];* pennant; Queen's colors; *red, white, and blue [U.S.];* standard; streamer; *Stars & Stripes [U.S.];* tricolor; union jack; vexil; whip; *xeno-flag; yacht ensign; yellow jack; zeug;* [see bulrush]

**flagrancy** *(n.)*: audacity; brazenness; cheekiness; contempt; disrespect; egregiousness; forwardness; *fearlessness;* gall; haughtiness; insolence; impertinence; jadedness; *know-it-all; lipping;* malapertness; nerve; overconfidence; pertness; presumption; *quilicom [arch.];* rudeness; sassiness; sauciness; surliness; temerity; unruliness; vanity; *wind; xtry. audacity; yieldlessness; zero respect;* [*Ant.* furtiveness]

**flagrant** *(adj.)*: apparent; blatant; conspicuous; deliberate; egregious; flaring; glaring; *heedless; intentional; just plain to see;* kenspeckle; *lucid;* manifest; noticeable; open; patent; *quite obvious;* recognizable; shameless; transparent; undisguised; visible; *witting; x-parent; yare; zero shame;* [*Ant.* furtive]

**flair** *(n.)*: aptitude; bent; bravura; chic; dash; enthusiasm; finesse; gift; genius; hability; instinct; jimp; knack; lustiness; métier; natural ability; oomph; panache; *quality;* real ability; skill; style; talent; *usefulness;* verve; wherewithal; *xenium;* yaup; zest;

**flak** *(n.)*: aggravation; bellyaching; complaining; criticism; disapproval; excoriation; fuss; flack; fire; grumbling; griping; hassle; increpation; jangling; knocking; lambasting; murmuring; *niggling;* opposition; protesting; querulousness; repining; squawking; trouble; upbraiding; vitriol; whining; *x-ing;* yawping; Zoilism; [*Ant.* favor]

**flake** *(n.)*: *amount;* bit; chip; chunk; daud; *encrustation;* fragment; *gob;* hunk; *iota;* junt; kernel; little piece; lump; morsel; nugget; ort; ounce; piece; *quantity;* remnant; small piece; sliver; shard; scale; tidbit; *unit; vestige;* wee bit; wedge; *xylon; yngot [arch.]; zum [dial.];*

**flamboyance** *(n.)*: audacity; brightness; bedazzlement; colorfulness; dazzle; elaborateness; flashiness; gaudiness; garishness; *haughtiness;* intensity; jazziness; kick; loudness; *malapertness; nerviness;* oomph; ostentation; pickedness; pretentiousness; *quivery;* resplendence; showiness; tastelessness; tawdiness; uppitiness; vividness; *wowing; xanthene; yahoo;* zizz;

**flame** *(n.)*: *aflame;* blaze; conflagration; deflagration; *enflamed;* fire; glim; *heat;* incineration; *jungle-fire;* kindling; light; *miskindle;* night-fire; overburning; pyre; *quick-match;* raging fire; sparks; *torch;* ustulation; *volcano;* watch fire; wildfire; *xylophyrography; yearning; zap;*

**flammable** *(adj.)*: accendible; burnable; combustible; deflagrable; easily enkindled; *fire; glow;* hypergolic; ignitable; inflammable; *jeopardous; kindling;* lightable; *match;* non-fireproof; *overburning;* phlogistic; *quick-light; raging fire;* susceptible to flame; touchy; *unprotected; vulnerable;* wildfire; *xeric; yellow flame; zappable;* [*Ant.* flameproof]

**flap** *(n.)*: atop; bit; cover; door; *enclosure;* fold; *gusset;* hood; inveil; jacket; *kit;* lappet; lid; lappet; luff [naut.]; mantle; *non-revealed;* overlap; piece; *quantity; remnant;* slip; tab; trap; *umbration;* veil; wimple; *x-out; yank; zipper-pocket;*

**flare** *(n.)*: attention-getter; beacon; conflagration; distress signal; emergency signal; firebare; fusee; gleam; *heat;* incineration; *jungle-fire;* kindling; light; *match;* non-perchlorate ~; *overburning;* pyre; *quick-match;* rocket; signal; SOS; torch; *ustulate;* Very ~; warning signal; *xylophyrograph;* yellow ~; *zap;*

**flash** *(n.)*: *aura;* burst; coruscate; daze; emission; flicker; flare; glimmer; glint; gleam; *halo;* irradiance; *jet; kindle;* light; luster; *movement; nitency; overlight;* phosphorescence; quiver; reflection; ray; sparkle; shine; scintillate; twinkle; *ultraviolet light;* vividness; white light; *xenon light; yellow light;* zap;

**flask** *(n.)*: alembic; beaker; bottle; container; cuvette; carafe; decanter; ewer; flagon; galipot; hip ~; *inurn;* jug; kit; lachrymatory; mickey; noggin; olla; phial; *quart container;* receptacle; stoup; *thermos;* urn; vial; vessel; *winchester; xeres jug;* yabba; zun;

**flat** *(adj.)*: accumbent; bulldozed; compressed; deflated; even; flattened; flush; *ground;* horizontal; *ironed; jammed down;* kibbled; level; made ~; non-bumpy; oblated; planar; plano-horizontal; quashed; rolled over; smooth; tabulate; unrough; unrumpled; very smooth; waveless; *x-axis; yerked own; zero bumpiness;*

**flatly** *(adj.)*: absolutely; beyond doubt; categorically; downright; emphatically; flat-out; *glaringly; highly;* indisputably; just; keenly; *literally;* most (certainly); *notably;* outright; point-blank; quite; really; surely; totally; utterly; *very;* wholly; *'xactly [slang]; ywis [arch.]; 'zactly [dial.];*

**flatness** *(n.)*: accumbency; *bulldozed;* creaselessness; deflation; evenness; flushness; *ground;* horizontalness; *ironed; jammed down;* kibbling; levelness; *mashing;* non-bumpiness; oblateness; planarity; *quashing; rolled over;* smoothness; thinness; uniformity; *very smooth;* wavelessness; *x-axis; yerked own; zero bumpiness;*

**flatten** *(v.)*: apply pressure; bulldoze; compress; crush; depress; deflate; exert pressure; even out; fasciate; grind; *hurt; iron;* jam; kibble; knock down; level; make flat; mash; *nullify;* oblate; press down; quash; roll over; smooth(en); squash; tamp down; uncurl; uncrumple; *very flat;* wreck; *xuld [arch.]; yerk; zeroize;* [*see* crush]

**flatter** *(v.)*: adulate; butter up; blandish; bootlick; charm; curry favor; cajole; daub; entice; fawn; gloze; *honor;* ingratiate; inveigle; *jape;* kowtow; lead on; lickspittle; make points with; *nice; outfawn;* praise; paw; *quick to compliment; run after;* smooth talk; seduce; spaniel; toady; *unctuous; venerate;* wheedle; *xuld [arch.];* yabber; *zing;*
**flatterer** *(n.)*: adulator; blandisher; bootlicker; complimenter; charmer; coaxer; cajoler; dauber; enticer; fawner; glaverer; glozer; *honorer;* ingratiator; jabberer; *kind;* lickspittle; mamaguiler; *nice;* outfawner; pleaseman; *quick-to-compliment; rat;* smooth talker; sycophant; seducer; toady; *user; unctuosity; vain person;* wheedler; *xuld [arch.];* yes-man; *zinger;*
**flattering** *(adj.)*: adulatory; buttery; cajoling; daubing; enticing; fawning; gratifying; honey-mouthed; ingratiatory; *japing;* kowtowing; lickspittle; mamaguiling; *non-sincere;* obsequious; praise-filled; *quick-to-compliment; run after;* smarmy; toadyish; unctuous; *venerating;* wheedling; *xtry.;* yabbering; *zinging;*
**flattery** *(n.)*: adulation; buttering up; blandishment; bootlicking; coaxing; cajolery; daubing; enticing; flattering; flummery; fawning; fulsomeness; gloze; glaver; *high compliment;* ingratiation; jabbering; kind words; leading on; mamaguile; *niceness;* obsequiousness; palaver; *praise; quick to compliment; round;* sweet talk; smooth talk; smarm; sycophancy; seduction; toadyism; unctuosity; vanity; wheedling; *xuld [arch.];* jabbering; *zinging;*
**flaunt** *(v.)*: advertise; brandish; *carry;* display; exhibit; flash; gasconade; hold out; *in one's face; jactitation;* kithe [Scot.]; lay out; manifest; *non-concealment;* open up; parade; *qualify;* reveal; show off; tote; uncover; vaunt; wave; *xuld [arch.]; yieldless; zip out;*
**flavor** *(n.)*: aroma; *bite;* character; *delicious;* essence; flavoriness; *good taste; hint;* intrinsicality; *juicy; keen taste; liking; mouth-watering; nature; overall taste;* pungency; quality; relish; saltiness; sapor; savor(iness); taste; *unusual taste;* vim; way of tasting; *xenenthesis;* yumminess; zest;
    **Flavors**: apple; almond; banana; chocolate; cherry; cola; coconut; dark chocolate; elderberry; French vanilla; fig; grape; hazelnut; ircano cheese; jalapeño; kiwi; lemon; mango; nut; orange; peach; quince; raspberry; strawberry; tangerine; tootie-fruity; ugli® fruit; vanilla; watermelon; xigua; yuzu; ziziphus;
**flavorless** *(adj.)*: *average;* bland; *colorless;* dull; empty; flat; *gant;* humdrum; insipid; intastable; jejune; *kaput;* lifeless; lackluster; mundane; non-flavored; *ordinary;* plain; *questionable; regular;* savorless; tasteless; unflavored; vapid; watery; wersh; *x-out;* yucky; zestless; [*Ant.* flavorful]
**flaw** *(n.)*: *accident;* blemish; crack; defect; error; failing; fault; goof-up; gaffe; hitch; imperfection; *jumble;* kink; lapse; mistake; *non-purposive;* oversight; problem; quirk; *rift;* shortcoming; slip (-up); *typo;* unintentional mistake; *violation;* weakness; *xgression; yaw;* zinger; [*Ant.* flawlessness]
**flawless** *(adj.)*: accurate; blameless; blemishless; correct; *done perfectly;* error-free; faultless; guiltless; harmless; holy; infallible; inerrant; impeccable; *justified; known-innocent;* lamblike; mistake-proof; non-flawed; offenseless; perfect; qualmless; questionless; righteous; spotless; sinless; taintless; unreprovable; unimpeachable; unerring; virtuous; witeless; white; *xtry.;* yet unblamed; zero-defect; [*Ant.* flawed]
**flay** *(v.)*: abrade; *beat;* bark; cut; decorticate; debone; excarnate; flench; *get skin off;* husk; *incise;* julienne; *knife; lash; mince; negate;* open; peel; pare; pick clean; *quick-husk; remove skin;* strip; skin; take skin off; uncase; *vell;* whittle; *xyster; yerk; zip;*
**fleck** *(n.)*: *amount;* bit; chip; dot; daud; flake; *gob;* hunk; *iota;* jib; jigger; junt; kernel; little piece; morsel; nugget; ounce; piece; *quantity;* remnant; speck; tidbit; *unit; vestige;* wee bit; *xylon; yngot [arch.]; zit;*
**flee** *(v.)*: abscond; abandon; be off; bolt; clear out; depart; escape; fly; fugitate; go; hightail; *immigrate; jet;* kest; leave; make tracks; *neglect; outrun;* part; *quit;* run; shove off; scramble; turn tail; take off; *uproot;* vacate; *vanish;* withdraw; xfer; yead; zip away; [*Ant.* face]
**fleet** *(n.)*: assemblage; armada; boats; convoy; division; *escort;* flotilla; force; group; horde; *ironclads; junks; keelboats; longboats;* marine force; navy; *operation; PT boats; quinqueremes; R.N.;* ships; squadron; task force; *U.S.N.;* vessels; warships; *xebecs; yeomanry; zebecs;*

**flesh** *(n.)*: *animal ~;* body; cutis; carnality; dermis; depravity; epidermis; earthly body; fell; fallen nature; *godlessness;* hide; humanity; integument; *jacket; knavishness;* lamina; layer; manhood; natural body; outer surface; pelt; physical body; *quad;* rind; *reprobation;* skin; tegument; *unspiritual;* vellum; weak ~; *xerodermia;* yet unredeemed ~; *zest;* [*see* weakness]

**fleshly** *(adj.)*: Adamic; bodily; carnal; depraved; earthly; fallen; *godless;* human; *impure; jadish; knavish;* lustful; lascivious; *material;* natural; *only human;* physical; *quad;* reprobate; sensual; sinful; this-worldly; unspiritual; voluptuous; worldly; *xerodermatous;* yieldful; zoetical; [*see* sinful]

**flexibility** *(n.)*: adaptability; bendability; compliance; ductility; elasticity; flimsiness; formability; give; hand-bendability; impressionability; *jelutong; kinkiness;* limberness; manipulability; malleability; malleableness; nimbleness; non-rigidity; *openness;* pliancy; pliantness; plasticity; pliability; *quick-flex;* rubberiness; resilience; suppleness; stretchiness; tractability; *unset;* versatility; workableness; *xapuri;* yieldedness; *zingy;* [*Ant.* firmness]

**flexible** *(adj.)*: adaptable; bendable; conformable; changeable; ductile; elastic; flexile; formable; *give;* hand-bendable; infirm; *jiggly; kinked;* limber; lithe; lissome; manipulable; nimble; non-rigid; open; pliant; pliable; *queachy [arch.];* rubbery; resilient; responsive; supple; stretchy; tensile; tractable; unfirm; versatile; willowy; withy; workable; *xapuri;* yielding; *zingy;* [*Ant.* firm]

**flick** *(v.)*: *abandon;* betoss; cast; discharge; eject; fling; *give;* hurl; impel; jettison; kest; launch; *move; non-retention;* outthrow; pitch; *quoit;* rocket; shoot; throw; upcast; vault; wale; *xuld* [arch.]; york; zing;

**flicker** *(v.)*: *agitate;* bounce; coruscate; dance; *excite;* fluctuate; flitter; flutter; glimmer; gleam; hop; *irregular;* jump; *knock; lambency;* move; *nitency;* oscillate; prance; quiver; *reel;* shimmer; tremble; twinkle; *unsteady;* vacillate; waver; *x;* yerk; zip;

**flight** *(n.)*: aviation; blasting off; cruising; darting; evolation; flying; gliding; *hovering; instrument flying;* jetting; kiting; lighting; lifting off; *moving; night ~;* over~; passage; plane ~; *quickening;* rocketing; soaring; taking ~; upbearing; volitation; wing; whiz; *x-plane; yonder;* zoom; [*see* escape]

**flimsy** *(adj.)*: *adaptable;* bendable; cheap; droopy; enfeebled; feeble; floppy; flaccid; gimp; *hanging;* infirm; inferior; *junky; kinked;* limp; meager; non-rigid; *overweak;* pliant; pathetic; quisquillous; *relaxed;* sagging; soft; shoddy; *thin;* unfirm; *vulnerable;* weak; washy; *xapuri;* yielding; *zingy;* [*Ant.* firm]

**flinch** *(v.)*: *aback;* balk; blench; cringe; cower; draw back; *edgy;* flummox; go back; *hesitate; involuntary;* jump; *kick; lose courage;* move back in fear; nonplus; *ouch; palter;* queck; recoil; react; shrink; shy away; tremble; *uneasy; vexed;* wince; withdraw; *xuld [arch.];* yerk; zip aback; [*see* fear]

**fling** *(v.)*: *abandon;* betoss; cast; discard; eject; flick; give a flick; hurl; impel; jettison; kest; launch; make fly; *non-retention;* outthrow; pitch; *quoit;* recast; sling; toss; upcast; vault; whip; *xuld* [arch.]; york; zing;

**flip** *(v.)*: *abandon;* betoss; chuck; discharge; eject; flop; fling; *give;* hurl; impel; *jump;* kest; launch; make fly; *non-stationary;* outthrow; pitch; *quoit;* recast; sling; spin; toss; upcast; vault; whip; *xuld* [arch.]; yerk; *zing;*

**flippancy** *(n.)*: audacity; brazenness; cheekiness; *chutzpah* [Yid.]; disrespect; effrontery; frivolity; flagrancy; gall; *hutzpah* [Yid.]; impertinence; jadedness; *know-it-all;* levity; lip; mouthiness; nerve; overconfidence; pertness; *quilicom [arch.];* rudeness; sauciness; surliness; temerity; unruliness; vanity; waggishness; *x-pride; yieldlessness; zero respect;* [*Ant.* fear]

**flippant** *(adj.)*: audacious; brazen; cavalier; contemptuous; disrespectful; *effrontery;* facetious; frivolous; glib; hoity-toity; impertinent; insolent; irreverent; joking; jaunty; *know-it-all;* light; malapert; nervy; offhand; pert; presumptuous; *quilicom [arch.];* rude; surly; temerarious; unreverend; unhallowed; vain; waggish; *x-proud; yieldless; zero respect;* [*Ant.* fearful]

**flirt** *(n.)*: allurer; *bewitcher;* charmer; coquette; dallier; enticer; flatterer; gill- ~; heartbreaker; *inveigler;* jill- ~; *jilt; kidder;* leader on; man-catcher; *nictitate;* ogler; philanderer; *quixotic; rouser;* seductress; siren; tease; über- ~; vixen; wanton; *xuld [arch.];* yanker; *zip away;*

**flirt** *(v.)*: allure; bat eyelids; coquet; dally; entice; flatter; *glance; have eyes for; inveigle; jill- ~; keen on;* leer; lead on; make eyes at; *nictitate;* ogle; play; philander; *quick-look; rouse;* seduce; toy; tease; titillate; *unabashed;* vamp; wink; *xuld [arch.];* yank; *zip away;*

**flirtation** *(n.)*: alluring; batting eyelids; coquetry; dallying; eyelid-batting; enticing; flirting; goo-goo eyes; *hot-to-trot; inveigling; jill-flirt; kidding;* leading on; making eyes; *nictitation;* ogling; philandering; *quixotic;* rousing; seduction; toying; teasing; *unabashedness;* vamping; winking; *xuld [arch.];* yerking; zipping away;

**flirtatious** *(adj.)*: alluring; *bewitching;* coquettish; dallying; eyelid-batting; flirting; flirty; *gill-flirt;* hot-to-trot; *inveigling; jill-flirt; keen;* leading one on; *making eyes at; nictitating;* ogling; playful; philandering; *quixotic; rousing;* seductive; teasing; unabashed; vixen-like; winking; *xtry. brash;* yerking; *zippity;*

**float** *(v.)*: *afloat; adrift; ascend;* bob; buoy; coast; drift; *evolation;* fly; glide; hang; hover; inaquate; *jet;* kite; *lift;* levitate; move over; *natant; oceanborne;* poise; plane; *quicken;* rest; ride on; send; swim; sail; soar; *transcend;* upbear; volplane; waft; *xuld [arch.]; yern;* zoom; [*see* fly, glide]

**floatation** *(n.)*: airiness; buoyancy; *carrying;* drifting; evolation; flotation; *gliding;* hovering; inaquation; *jetting;* kiting; levitation; *mounting;* natation; *oceanborne;* planing; *quickening;* resting; seaworthiness; suspension; *transcending;* upbearing; volplaning; wafting; *xuld [arch.]; yern;* zoom;

**flock** *(n.)*: assemblage; bunch; bevy; collection; cluster; drove; *en masse;* fold; group; gregal; herd; ingathering; jam [slang]; kit [coll.]; lot; mass; number; *overflow;* pack; passel; quantity; regathering; roundup; set; swarm; throng; trip; unit; variety; wisp; *xillinous; yardful;* Zaanan; [*see* group]

**flock** *(v.)*: amass; bring together; congregate; draw together; *en masse;* forgather; gather; huddle; ingather; join; *knit;* link up; meet; *nest; overcrowd; pack; quorum;* rally; swarm; turn out; throng; unite; *visit; work together;* x.; yoke; *zone;*

**flog** *(v.)*: afflict; beat; chastise; *draw;* excoriate; flagellate; gird; give a whipping; hit; inflict; *jeel;* knout; lash; lam; lay stripes on; mark; *nail; oxgoad;* plow; quirt; razor-strap; *rend;* scourge; thrash; *unleash; victimize;* whip; *xuld [arch.];* yerk; *zing;*

**flood** *(n.)*: alluvion; *breaking;* cataclysm; deluge; debacle; *eddy;* freshet; flush; flash~; gushing; *the Great Flood;* high water; inundation; *judgment; killing; lake; mass; natural disaster;* neap tide; *Noah's ~;* overflow; partial ~; *quandary;* rush; surge; spate; swell; tide; torrent; uprush; upwelling; *violent ~;* washout; whelm; water- ~; *xtry. amounts of water;* yeo; *zwoosh;*

**flood** *(v.)*: abound; break; cascade; deluge; drown; engulf; fill; flush; gush; *heap;* increase; inundate; *jawp; keep rising; large;* mass; *niagara;* outswell; overfloat (-fill; -flow; -run; -swell; -whelm); onrush; pour; *quicken;* rush; *rise;* swamp; surge; swell; swamp; submerge; torrent; *uprush; verge upward;* wash out; whelm; *xuld [arch.];* yeo; zwoosh;

**floodgate** *(n.)*: aquatic barrier; barrier; control; containment wall; dam; embankment; floodwall; flowvalve; gate; headgate; hatch; *inclosure; jetty; keldwall;* levee; *mure; nautical wall;* obstruction; partition; quai; restraining wall; sluice(gate); *traverse; utility wall;* valve; warping-sluice; Xiaolongdi Dam; yard wall; zariba;

**floor** *(n.)*: *absolute bottom;* bottom; base; carpet; contabulation; dirt ~; deck; *entresol;* foundation; flooring; floorboards; ground; hardwood ~; *intervale; judaicum;* kitchen ~; level; laminate ~; *mezzanine; nightingale floor;* oak ~; plancher; planching; *quarterdeck;* rock-bottom; *rug;* surface; story; sub~; tier; tile ~; undersurface; *vinyl flooring;* wood ~; *xyst;* yew ~; *zone;*

**flop** *(v.)*: arch; bow; collapse; droop; *enfold;* flip; flex; flag; go down; hang (down); *incline; jiggle;* knuckle; lie; laze; loll; lop; *move down; non-rigid;* overhang; plop down; *quat;* relax; sag; sprawl; slump; turn down; *uncinate; verge;* wallop; wilt; *x-curve;* yield; zigzag;

**flounder** *(v.)*: *agitate;* beat; *crippled;* dither; *effort;* flap; flounce; get into trouble; helplessly thrash; *indefensible;* jiggle; jump around; kick; lash about; move uncontrollably; *nubble;* over-struggle; *powerless;* quab; *roll;* struggle; thrash; *upset;* volutate; wave arms; wallow; *xuld [arch.];* yerk; *zonk;*

**flour** *(n.)*: * all-purpose ~; bread- ~; cornmeal; *dough;* elubo; enriched ~; farina; ground wheat; hand-ground meal; *ingredient; jasmati ~;* koniak; ladu ~; meal; maizena; *nocake;* oat ~; plain ~; pollinar; padar; *powder;* quinoa ~; rye ~; smeddum; tapioca ~; unbleached ~; *volume;* wheatmeal; white ~; *xtr. fine ~;* yam ~; *zea mays;*

**flourish** *(v.)*: advance; blo(ss)om; burgeon; climb; develop; do well; enlarge; flower; grow; heighten; increase; jump up; *keep growing;* luxuriate; mature; *nourish;* overgrow; outgrow; prosper; *quadruplicate;* rise; sprout; succeed; thrive; upspring; upsprout; vegetate; wax; *XL;* yain [arch.]; *zoom;*

**flow** *(n.)*: afflux; blast; circulation; current; course; confluence; direction; discharge; drift; deflow; deluge; efflux; flush; flux; fluency; flood; gush; *hie;* issue; influx; jet(stream); *katabatic; leak;* movement; naid; niagara; out~; over~; onslaught; pouring; profluence; quell; rush; river; stream; surge; tide; torrent; undercurrent; upsurge; *vomiting;* wash; water ~; well; *xfer;* yern; *zwoosh;*

**flow** *(v.)*: afflux; *billow;* circulate; course; cascade; drift; emit; empty; flush; flood; gush; hurl; issue; *influx;* jet; *kite;* leave; move; naid; outpour; *over~;* purl; pour; quicken; run; rush; spray; squirt; spurt; spring; spout; stream; spew; travel; uprush; vomit; verge; wash; xfer; yern; zip;

**flower** *(n.)*: annual; *arrangement;* blo(ss)om; *bouquet;* cluster; *corsage;* disk floret; efflorescence; floret; *garland;* head; inflorescence; *jasmine; knotweed;* lily; may~; *nosegay;* orchid; posy; perennial; *quatrefoil; rose;* spray; *triennial; unfoldment;* umbel; vine ~; wildflower; *xerophyte; yarrow; zinnia;*
  **Kinds of flowers**: aster; azalea; buttercup; chrysanthemum; daffodil; daisy; edelweiss; forget-me-not; geranium; heather; hyacinth; iris; jasmine; knotweed; lilac; lily; magnolia; narcissus; orchid; pansy; poinsettia; queen-cup; rose; sunflower; tulip; umbrella plant; violet; wisteria; xeranthemum annum; yarrow; zinnia;

**flowery** *(adj.)*: *anthesis;* blossoming; crysanthemum-lined; daisied; edelweiss-filled; floral; floriferous; florescent; *gay;* hortulan; heathery; inflorescent; jasmine-filled; *keenly flowered;* lily-lined; multiflorous; *nosegay; ornate;* pollinary; primrose; *quatrefoil;* rosaceous; rosy; sunflowery; tulip-lined; *uniflorous;* violaceous; wildflower-filled; *xeranthemum;* yarrow-trimmed; zinnia-filled; [*see* pompous]

**fluctuate** *(v.)*: alter(nate); bounce; change; dither; *exchange;* flounder; go up and down; hump; *interweave;* jag; jump; *kedge;* librate; meander; nutate; oscillate; pendulate; *quiver;* reciprocate; reel; shift; swing; sway; turn; twist; teeter; totter; undulate; vacillate; vary; waver; *x-ing;* yaw; *yo-yo;* zigzag;

**fluency** *(n.)*: articulation; ability; *bilingual;* confidence; command; deftness; ease; effluence; eloquence; flow; fluidity; glossiness; gracefulness; *honey-mouthed;* inspiration; *jimp;* knowledgeableness; lucidity; mastery; non-hesitancy; *operativeness;* proficiency; profluency; *quickness;* refinement; smoothness; *talent;* unbrokenness; volubility; wherewithal; xtry. command; *yare; zippiness;*

**fluent** *(adj.)*: articulate; *bilingual; beautiful;* clear; comprehensible; conversant; deft; eloquent; flowing; graceful; honey-mouthed; *inspiring; jimp;* knowledgeable; lucid; masterful; *nimble; operative; overelegant;* proficient; polished; profluent; *quick;* refined; smooth; *talented;* unbroken; voluble; well-versed; xtry.; *yare; zippy;*

**fluid** *(n.)*: aqua; broth; colliquament; *drink;* eliquation; *flow;* goo; hot liquid; *infirm;* juice; *kiloliter;* liquid; moisture; *non-frozen; outpouring; pool;* quantum liquid; *runny;* succus; solution; substance; thawed substance; unfrozen substance; vapor; wetness; watery substance; *xanthoxylin; yeet;* zep;

**flurry** *(v.)*: *affuse;* besprinkle; come down; drop; *effuse;* fall; float; flake; *go; humectate;* intersperse; *jawp; keep coming; lap; move; névé; overspread;* plummet; *queven [arch.];* resperse; sprinkle; snow; tinkle; *unleash; volley;* winter ~; xpn.; *yote; zip down;*

**flush** *(v.)*: *activate;* burst; clean; drain; empty; flood; gush; hurl; issue; jet; *kite; let out;* move out; naid; outpour; pour; *quicken;* rinse; rush; sluice; stream; *travel;* uprush; vomit; wash; *xuld [arch.];* yead; zwish;

**fluster** *(v.)*: aggravate; bother; confuse; cross; disquiet; disturb; exasperate; frustrate; gall; *heat;* incense; *jar;* kindle; lose one's temper; miff; nettle; *outrage;* perturb; *quick-tempered;* rile; steam; tick off; upset; vex; *wrath; xerothermic; yell; zap;*

**flute** *(n.)*: alto ~; bass ~; cornamute; dactylic ~; eunuch ~; fife; gaita; halil; *instrument; jubal;* kaval; love ~; *musical instrument;* nay; ocarina; pipe; piccolo; quena; recorder; shinobue; tanso; *union pipe;* venu [Ind.]; whiffle; *wind instrument;* xirula; xiao; yokobue; zufolo;

**flutter** *(v.)*: agitate; bate; beat wings; *convulse;* didder; *excite;* flit(ter); flap; glide; hover; *instability;* jitter; kite; light; make flap; nutate; oscillate; palpitate; pitch; quiver; quaver; quake; rattle; rale; shake; shiver; shudder; twitter; *unstable;* vibrate; wabble; *xuld [arch.];* yerk; *zoom;*

**fly** *(v.)*: aviate; arise; *airborne;* breeze; blast; cruise; dart; elapse; float; flutter; flit; glide; hover; *issue;* jet; kite; light; lift; mount up; make off; *nimble;* overfly; *outfly;* plane; *quicken;* rise; rip; roar; rocket; swoop; sail; soar; shoot; streak; take flight; tear; upbear; volplane; wing; whiz; *xuld [arch.];* yern; zoom; [*see* swoop; float]

**foam** *(n.)*: aeration; bubbles; cream; despumation; effervescence; froth; *gurgling;* head; *imboil; jet; kier;* lather; *murmur;* nap; *over-boil;* poople; *quick lather; regurgitate;* (soap) suds; spume; sea ~; top froth; *uprush; vault;* white foam; *wash; xuld [arch.];* yeast; *zoutch;*

**foam** *(v.)*: aerate; burble; bubble; cavitate; decoct; effervesce; fizz(le); froth; gurgle; hiss; imboil; *jet; jump;* kier; lather; murmur; *neal [arch.]; over-boil;* poople; *quietly burble; regurgitate;* seethe; *trouble; uprush; vault;* wallop; *xuld [arch.];* yeast; zoutch;

**foamy** *(n.)*: aerated; bubbly; barmy; creamy; despumating; effervescent; frothy; *gurgling;* heady; *imboil; jet; kier;* lathery; *murmur;* nappy; *over-boil;* puffy; *quick lather; regurgitating;* sudsy; soapy; spumy; spumous; thick-foamed; *uprush; vault;* whipped; *xuld [arch.];* yeasty; *zoutch;*

**focus** *(n.)*: attention; bull's eye; center; *dominance;* emphasis; fore(front); focal point; fixation; *greatest;* highlight; importance; *judged most important;* key point; limelight; main thing; *notable;* overriding consideration; prominence; *quintessence; red letter;* spotlight; target; *ultimate; vital;* weight; *xtry. point; yellow highlight; zero in;*

**focus** *(v.)*: accentuate; bring to the fore; concentrate on; draw attention to; emphasize; feature; focalize; fixate; give emphasis to; highlight; *important; jump out;* keep emphasis on; lay emphasis upon; make the focal point; *noticeable;* overemphasize; point up; *quite overstress; red letter;* stress; spotlight; set sights on; target; underscore; *value; weight; xtry. emphasis; yed;* zero in;

**foe** *(n.)*: adversary; bad guy; contender; disputant; enemy; *fiend;* fighter; *garrison;* hostile person; instigator; jangler; kemper; *legion;* litigant; match; nemesis; opponent; *player; quarreler;* rival; striver; *traitor; troops; unfriendly;* vier; villain; warling; *xenic; yuon* [arch.]; *zeke [off.];* [Ant. friend]

**fog** *(n.)*: atomization; aura; brume; cloud; dust-cloud; effuvium; fume; gas; gauze; gloom; haze; high ~; *incloud; jumbo cloud; KH instability;* London ~; mist; murk; miasma; nebula; obscurity; pea soup; *quasi-vaporous;* reek; smoke; steam; smog; turbidity; unclarity; vapor; wisp; *xenon cloud; yellowy cloud;* zero-zero;

**foggy** *(adj.)*: *adularescent;* brumous; billowy; cloudy; dusty; dim; dull; enclouded; fumy; gray; gloomy; hazy; inclouded; jumbled; *KH instability;* lowery; misty; nebulous; overcast; puffy; *qually* [arch.]; *rain clouds;* teamy; smoky; smoggy; sturbid; soupy; thick; unclear; umbered; vaporous; wispy; wet; *xenon cloud; yellowy cloud;* zero-zero; [Ant. fine]

**foible** *(n.)*: affectation; bad habit; characteristic; deeds; eccentricity; funny habit; fault; gesticulation; habit; idiosyncrasy; *jerking;* kink; *living;* mannerism; *notion;* oddity; peculiarity; quirk; *reaction;* shortcoming; trait; unconventional behavior; vice; weakness; x-action; *yede;* zanism;

**foil** *(v.)*: avert; block; bring to naught; check; discomfit; defeat; encumber; frustrate; *gum up;* hinder; impede; jam up; kibosh; limit; mess up; nullify; obstruct; outsmart; prevent; quash; ruin; stop; spoil; thwart; upset; vanquish; void; ward off; "x"; *yank;* zeroize; [Ant. facilitate]

**fold** *(n.)*: angularity; bend; crease; doubling; enfolding; flounce; fan~; ~over; gathering; *hem;* infolding; *j-bend;* kirtle; lappet; make ~; *non-rigid;* overlap; over~; patagium; pleat; ply; plica(ture); plication; quadriplanar; ripple; rumple; ridge; scrunch; tuck; undercrease; *volt;* wrinkle; whelk; *x-ing; yard; zone;*

**fold** *(v.)*: angle; bend; crinkle; crease; double; enfold; flex; flip over; fan~; gather; *hem;* infold; *j-bend;* kirtle; lap over; make ~; *non-rigid;* overlap; pleat; quill; rumple; scrunch; tuck; turn; undercrease; volt; wrap; wrinkle; *x-ing; yard; zone;* [*Ant.* flatten]

**folder** *(n.)*: *area;* business ~; *cover;* dust jacket; envelope; file; green hanging file; holder; inclosure; jacket; *kirtle;* legal-size ~; manila ~; *note-file;* organizer; portfolio; *place; quantity;* receptacle; security ~; *thing;* utility ~; *vertical file;* wallet; *xfer;* yellow envelope; *zip file;*

**folklore** *(n.)*: annals; body of knowledge; custom; *drama;* epic; fables; folk tales; *Grimm; history;* immemorial stories; *journal;* knowledge of yore; legends; lore; myth; narrative; oral tradition; popular legend; *quillcraft;* retelling; superstition; stories; tradition; *urban myths; version;* word; *xenodocheionology;* yarns; *zay;*

**follow** *(v.)*: adhere; bedog; chase; come after; dog; ensue; *find;* go after; happen next; hunt; hound; *interlope; jack;* keep after; lag behind; monitor; nose out; observe; obey; pursue; quest after; run after; succeed; shadow; stalk; tag along; tail(gate); trail; trace; track; understand; venture after; watch; walk behind; *xfer; yield; zealously chase;* [*Ant.* flee]

**follower** *(n.)*: admirer; adherent; buff; backer; believer; convert; devotee; disciple; enthusiast; fan; factionary; *gung-ho;* homager; habitué; ideologue; janissary; *kirsen [dial.];* liegeman; lackey; minion; member; *neophyte;* observer; protégé; proselyte; quester; recruit; supporter; sidekick; tagalong; toady; *united;* votary; worshiper; *Xnize; yielder;* zealot;

**folly** *(n.)*: absurdity; buffoonery; craziness; dumbness; egg-headedness; foolishness; giddiness; gullibility; harebrainedness; imprudence; idiocy; juvenility; kookiness; ludicrousness; madness; nonsensicality; naivety; outrageousness; preposterousness; quackery; ridiculousness; senselessness; stupidity; thoughtlessness; *unwise; vanity;* wackiness; *xtry. ~; yokelishness;* zaniness;

**fond** *(adj.)*: affectionate; *bow to;* caring for; doting; esteeming; fancying; favoring; going for; highly regarding; inclined to love; joying in; keen; loving; much liking; *nice;* overtrustful; partial; *quick to choose;* regardful; satisfied; tender; *uplift;* venerating; warm; *xtry.;* yearning for; *zealous;*

**fondness** *(n.)*: affection; bent; bias; caring; delight; dearness; endearment; favor; goodwill; heart; inclination; *joy;* keenness; liking; *much prefer;* natural liking; over infatuation; partiality; penchant; *quick-to-choose;* regard; sweetness; tenderness; unmitigated love; *value;* warmth; *xenophilia;* yen; zeal;

**food** *(n.)*: aliment; bread; cuisine; chow; comestibles; diet; delicacy; daily bread; dinner; edibles; fast ~; foodstuff; fare; grub; groceries; hash; haute cuisine; ingesta; intake; junk ~; keep; lunch; morsel; mess; munga [slang]; meat; meal; nutrition; nourishment; organic ~; provisions; *quelque-chose [F.];* rations; repast; supplies; sustenance; supper; *travel rations;* table [poet]; *unprocessed ~;* victuals; vittles; viands; *wheat; xarque; yams; zakuski [Rus.];*

> **Kinds of food**: apple; bread; casserole; deviled egg; eggplant; fish; gyro; hamburger; ice cream; jalapeño; kale; lasagna; macaroni; nuts; orange; pie; quince; radish; salad; steak;tangelo; ugli® fruit; venison; watermelon; xarque; yams; ziti

**fool** *(n.)*: airhead; blockhead; clown; dummy; egghead; featherbrain; goof(ball); harebrain; ignoramus; idiot; jackass; knot-head; knucklehead; lame-brain; moron; nitwit; ninny; numbskull; oaf; pea-brain; quack; rattlebrain; simpleton; turkey; tom~; unwise; *vacant-headed;* woodenhead; *xiaoren;* yo-yo; zob;

**fool** *(v.)*: *allure;* beguile; con; deceive; delude; ensnare; fob; finagle; guile; hoodwink; insnare; jape; kid; lie to; mislead; nobble; outfox; put one over; *quiblin* [arch.]; rook; shyster; trick; *utter falsehood;* verneuk; weasel; wangle; *yentz; zing;*

**foolish** *(adj.)*: absurd; bumbling; clownish; dumb; egg-headed; feeble-minded; fatuous; goofy; giddy; goffish; gullible; half-witted; ignorant; indiscreet; ill-advised; imprudent; idiotic; insensible; injudicious; imbecilic; jackass; knuckleheaded; lame-brained; loggerheaded; misadvised; mawmish; moronic; nit-witted; naive; obtuse; oafish; pound- ~; quacky; ridiculous; simple; silly; stupid; thoughtless; tom~; thick; unwise; unadvised; vacant; verdant; witless; *xtry. ~; yokelish;* zany;

**foolishness** *(n.)*: absurdity; buffoonery; childishness; clownery; dumbness; *eccentricity;* foolery; folly; giddiness; gullibility; hebetude; imprudence; idiocy; *innocence;* juvenility; kookiness; lame-brainedness; madness; naivety; outlandishness; preposterousness; quackery; ridiculousness; simplicity; stupidity; tomfoolery; *unwise;* vertigo; witlessness; *xtry. ~; yokelishness;* zaniness;

**fool-proof** *(adj.)*: airtight; bound to work; certain; definite; efficacious; flawless; failsafe; guaranteed; *highly reliable;* infallible; *just sure;* keenly certain; *low-risk;* most certain; non-fallible; 100% sure; perfect; quite flawless; riskless; sure-fire; thought-out; unfailing; very safe; well thought-out; *warranteed; xtry.* sure; *yes;* zero doubt;

**foot** *(n.)* arch; base; bottom; clodhopper; dog [slang]; *extremity;* fore~; *goer;* hoof; heel; *insole; jut; kicker;* left ~; *metatarsus; nectopod;* outsole; paw; pes; ped; *quadrisulcate;* right ~; sole; *toes;* tootsie; trotter; ungula; volar; *webbed ~; xfer; yads; zygodactyl;*

**foothold** *(n.)*: advantage; base; control; *dug in;* encampment; footing; grip; hug; hold; *infold; join; kinch;* lodgment; military ~; niche; *operations;* place; *quartered regiment; retain;* secure position; toehold; *unit; vallation;* war machine; *xfer;* yayla; *zone;*

**footprint** *(n.)*: *animal tracks;* boot print; *camel tracks;* depression; dactylogram; *evidence;* footmark; foot print; footstep; *gazelle tracks;* hoofprint [zoo.]; ichnite [sci.]; imprint; impression; *jackal prints; kangaroo tracks; llama tracks;* mark; *nail print; ostrich tracks;* paw print; pug [both zoo.]; piste; prints [pl.]; *quadrisculate; racoon tracks;* slot; spoor [both zoo.]; shoe print; tracks; tread mark; *ungual;* volar imprints; *wolf tracks; xfer; yak tracks; zebra tracks;*

**footstool** *(n.)*: apparatus; bench; cricket; *divan; equipment;* footpeg; footrest; gig; hassock; *item; jack;* kneeler; leg rest; *mat; nub;* ottoman; pouffe; quilted ~; rest; support; stool; tuffet; *upholstery;* vice chair; wing chair; x-stool; *yacht chair; zeug [G.];*

**forage** *(v.)*: ascertain; bring; comb for; collect; *discover;* explore; fish; ferret; find; get; gather; hunt; *inquest;* jerque; kithe; look for; locate; make a search; maraud; nose out; *obtain;* probe; quest for; rummage; search; scavenge; scrounge; try to get; uncover; *venture;* wade through; wander; x-search; *yearn for; zealously search;*

**forager** *(n.)*: agent; *ascertainer; bringer;* comber; collector; *discoverer;* explorer; ferret; finder; gatherer; hunter(-gatherer); *inquest;* jerque; kennel-raker [arch.]; locator; marauder; noser; *obtainer;* prober; pillager; quester; rustler; ravager; searcher; scavenger; scrounger; *taker; uncoverer;* victualer; wader; *worker; x-search; yearn for; zealous searcher;*

**forbear** *(v.)*: abstain; bear with; cease; desist; deny; *don't;* eschew; forego; give up; hold back; inhibit; just say no; keep from; leave off; make an end to; not do; *omit;* put up with; quit; refrain; restrain oneself; spare; tolerate; *undo; voluntarily ~;* withhold; *x; yieldless; zero;*

**forbearance** *(n.)*: allowing; bearing; composure; desistance; endurance; forbearing; graciousness; holding back; indulgence; *just tolerating;* keeping ~; longsuffering; longsufferance; moderation; *non-anxiety;* over- ~; patience; *quietness;* restraint; self-control; sufferance; tolerance; unaggravation; *vasbyt;* waiting; *xtry. ~; yielding;* zero irritation;

**forbid** *(v.)*: *avert;* bar; ban; constrain; disallow; enjoin; exclude; forefend; fetter; *give injunction;* hobble; hinder; inhibit; interdict; *jam;* keep from; kibosh; limit; make illegal; nix; outlaw; prevent; prohibit; proscribe; *quash;* restrain; restrict; stop; thwart; *unpermitted;* veto; withhold; x; *ybarred* [arch.]; zero; [Ant. force]

**forbidden** *(adj.)*: *averted;* barred; banned; contraband; disallowed; denied; excluded; enjoined; felonious; government-banned; held back; impermissible; illegal; illicit; *jurisdictionally barred;* kept from; legally banned; *misguided;* nixed; not allowed; *nudum pacum* [L.]; off-limits; outlawed; prohibited; proscribed; *questionable;* restricted; shut out; *sinful;* taboo; unallowed; unauthorized; unlicensed; unlawful; *verboten* [G.]; vetoed; withheld; x-ed; *ybarred* [arch.]; *zonally outlawed;* [Ant. forced]

**force** *(n.)*: ability; brawn; brute ~; capability; compulsion; cogency; dint; duress; drive; energy; faculty; forcefulness; generant; gusto; horsepower; intensity; impact; juggernaut; knocking; lustiness; manpower; might; muscle; momentum; *nuclear power; omnipotence;* punch; pressure; power; *qualifications;* resources; strength; thewiness; thrust; *torque; usefulness;* vigor; wherewithal; *xenium; yare;* zip; [*Ant.* feebleness]

**force** *(v.)*: aggress; bear on; coerce; drive; dragoon; enforce; *fervor; get;* hurry; impel; jam; *knock;* lean on; make; *necessitate;* oblige; push; press(ure); *quicken;* require; strong-arm; tell; thrust; urge; vie; wam; *xuld* [arch.]; *yank; zealously urge;* [*Ant.* forbid]

**forceful** *(adj.)*: assertive; bearing down; bullying; cogent; convincing; compelling; dynamic; emphatic; energetic; forcible; fierce; *great;* hard; high-powered; heavy-handed; insistent; impelling; intense; *jetting;* keen; *lusty;* mighty; non-wimpy; overbearing; overwhelming; pushy; persuasive; powerful; quashing; robust; rigorous; strong; trenchant; unrelenting; vigorous; with great force; *x-energy;* yauld; zealous; [*Ant.* feeble]

**forcible** *(adj.)*: aggressive; bullying; compulsive; driving; effective; forceful; *great;* heavy (-handed); insistent; *jetting;* keen; *lusty;* mighty; non-wimpy; overpowering; ponderous; powerful; quashing; rigorous; strong; *tremendous;* unrelenting; violent; weighty; *x-energy;* yauld; zealous;

**forebode** *(v.)*: augur; bode; cry; declare; envisage; foreshadow; give notice; hint of; indicate; *jobation; kurvey;* look to; make a prediction; notify; omenate; point to; portend; premonish; prewarn; *quain* [arch.]; read the handwriting on the wall; signal; tell; threaten; utter warning; vaticinate; warn; *xenagogy; yell; zay* [arch.];

**forecast** *(v.)*: anticipate; bespeak; bode; calculate; conjecture; *declare;* estimate; foretell; foresee; guess; *herald; indicate;* judge; *know beforehand;* look ahead; make a prediction; notify; *orate;* predict; project; portend; *quain* [arch.]; read the future; speculate; see coming; tell the future; *utter;* vaticinate; warn; *xenagogy; yell; zay* [arch.];

**forefather** *(n.)*: ancestor; blood-relative; clan member; *derived; elder;* forebearer; father; (great-) grandfather; *heredity; inherited; judge;* kin; lineal ~; *man;* national head; originator; predecessor; progenitor; patriarch; *quarter;* relative; *stock;* tribal head; *unilineal; voortrekker* [Du.]; wise ~; *x-linked; yellow-race; zygogenetic;* [*Ant.* flesh and blood]

**forego** *(v.)*: abandon; bow out; cede; do without; discard; *eliminate;* forfeit; give up; *hand over;* ignore; junk; *kest;* leave; *miss;* neglect; overlook; pass (by); quit; relinquish; skip; sacrifice; throw away; unload; *vacate;* withdraw; *xfer;* yield; *zip away;*

**forehead** *(n.)*: above the eyebrows; brow; *caput; dew; eyebrows;* front(al bone); frons; furrowed brow; *gray matter;* head; *item; jole* [zoo.]; *kopf* [G.]; *lambda; metopic; noggin* [slang]; over the eyebrows; *pate; quadrigeminal; rim of one's hat;* sinciput; temples; upper head; *vertex;* wrinkled brow; *xerosis; yead* [arch.]; *zenith;*

**foreign** *(adj.)*: alien; *beyond;* curious; *distant land;* external; exotic; from overseas; *Greek; Hungarian;* imported; *Japanese; Korean; Libyan; Mexican;* non-native; outside; outborn; outland; overseas; peregrine; *queer; remote;* strange; tramontane; transmarine; unfamiliar; unknown; *visiting; Welsh;* xenic; *yonder; Zambian;* [*Ant.* familiar]

**foreigner** *(n.)*: alien; *Belgian; Czech; distant;* émigré; foreign devil [off.]; guest; habitué; immigrant; journeyer; *kwai-lo* [Chin. off.]; *lodger; Mexican;* non-resident; non-citizen; non-Israelite; outsider; outlander; peregrintor; *quidam; refugee; Russian;* stranger; tramontane; *uitlander* [S. Afr.]; visitor; *Welshman;* xenic; *yonder; Zambian;*

**foreignness** *(n.)*: alienage; alienness; bizarreness; curiousness; difference; exoticness; *foreign; Greek; heterotypical;* irregularity; *journey; Korean; land far away;* mysteriousness; non-usualness; oddness; peculiarity; queerness; *racial;* strangeness; total ~; unusualness; *variation; weirdness;* xeno-; *yet unknown; zero unfamiliarity;* [*Ant.* familiarity]

**foreknow** *(v.)*: anticipate; become aware of; comprehend ahead; discern; expect; foresee; grasp ahead; have insight; identify; *judge;* know; *made known; naw [dial.]; observe;* perceive; *questionless;* recognize; realize; sense; see; *tell beforehand;* understand; visualize; wot; *xenodiagnose; yeme;* zealously await;

**foreknowledge** *(n.)*: awareness; bodement; clairvoyance; divination; *envisioning;* ESP; foresight; foreseeing; foreknowing; forewarning; *grasp;* heads up; insight; *judiciousness;* knowledge; *learn; making aware; notion;* omniscience; prenotion; premonition; precognition; prescience; *quain [arch.];* revelation; (sixth) sense; total knowledge; *understanding;* vision; *wisdom; xylomancy; yeme;* zero ignorance;

**foreman** *(n.)*: administrator; boss; chief; director; *executive;* floorwalker; governor; headman; intendant; jefe; keeper; leader; manager; night manager; overseer; *proprietor;* quartermaster; ruler; supervisor; taskmaster; undershepherd; vizer; *warden;* XO; yardboss; zayim;

**foreordain** *(v.)*: appoint; bid; choose; determine; decree; destine; earmark; elect; forechoose (-appoint; -doom); give command; have it; *heaven-ordained;* intend; institute; *judge; kismet;* lay down; *lot;* make; *necessitate;* ordain beforehand; predetermine; predestine; predestinate; preordain; *quondam selection;* resolved by God; select; sovereignly choose; *take; unchangeable; verdict; willed by God; xel [arch.]; yonder; zero choice;* [see foreknow]

**forerunner** *(n.)*: announcer; bearer of news; crier; dispatch; emissary; forebearer; *fourrier* [F.]; *giver of news;* herald; harbinger; internuncio; *John the Baptist;* king-herald; liaison; messenger; nuncio; outrider; precursor; proclaimer; pursuivant; *questor [It.];* representative; *servant;* tidings-bearer; usher; voice; waymaker; *x-man; yamen* [Chin.]; *zealous announcer;* [Ant. follower]

**foreshadow** *(n.)*: adumbration; betokening; characterization; comparison; designation; *example;* foretoken; ~ing; figure; *glyph;* harbinger; illustration; image; *just like;* key ~; likeness; model; *notice; oracle;* picture; presage; pretype; prefiguration; *quain [arch.];* representation; shadow; sign; token; type; *umbrage;* very image; *word; xenenthesis; yichus;* Zeug [G.];

**foreshadow** *(v.)*: adumbrate; betoken; bespeak; bode; characterize; demonstrate; declare; epitomize; envisage; foretoken; foretell; give picture; *herald;* illustrate; indicate; *jobation; kithe;* likened to; model; *notify; omenate;* picture; presage; prefigure; *quain* [arch.]; represent; speak of; show forth; typify; tell of; *utter;* vaticinate; warn; *xenagogy; yet to come; zay [arch.];*

**foreskin** *(n.)*: article; bit; cutis prolongation; *doubling; enclosure;* flap; glans covering; *hide; item;* jacket; knife-cutting; lappet; *mul [Gr.]; natural covering;* outer flap; orlah [Heb.]; prepuce; *qualifier; recise;* skin; *tab;* uncircumcised prepuce; *vell;* whang [vulg.]; *xerodermia; yield; zum [dial.];*

**forest** *(n.)*: arbor; backwoods; bosket; bush; coppice; covert; dense woods; escarpment ~; forestland; greenwood; holt [poet.]; hurst [Br.]; *ironwood trees;* jungle; *kumquats; luxuriance; maple trees;* nemoral; overgrowth; pinewood; queach; *rain forest;* silva; trees; timberland; underwood; virgin ~; woods; wood(land); *the* wild(wood); wilderness; wildlands; *ximenia; yews; zamia;*

**foretell** *(v.)*: augur; bode; cry; declare; divine; envisage; foreshow; give prophecy; harbinger; herald; inform; *judge; know;* lament; make a prediction; notify; orate; predict; presage; portend; *quain* [arch.]; read the future; soothsay; tell beforehand; *utter;* vaticinate; warn; *xenagogy; yell; zay [arch.].*

**forever** *(adj.)*: always; *boundlessly;* continually; durably; eternally; for all time; going on ~; *habitually;* interminably; *jusqu'au bout [F.]; keep;* lastingly; measurelessly; never-endingly; on and on; perpetually; *quadrillion; remaining;* sempiternally; timelessly; tell the end of time; unceasingly; until the end of time; *vast;* without end; *xtry.;* year-after-year; *zillion;* [Ant. fleetingly]

**forever** *(adv.)*: all time; by and by; ceaselessly; duratively; endlessly; evermore; eternally; forevermore; gaplessly; hereafter; indefinitely; incessantly; *jusqu'au bout [F.]; keeps going;* limitlessly; measurelessly; never-endingly; *ongoing;* perpetually; *quadrillion; remaining;* sempiternally; *time without end;* unendingly; *vast;* without end; *x-cending; yonder;* zillions; [Ant. fleetingly]

**forfeit** *(v.)*: abandon; bow out; back out; cede; disclaim; escheat; forego; forswear; give up; hand over; *ignore;* jump off; kiss goodbye; lose; make an end; *non-retention; outgo;* part with; quit; relinquish; renounce; surrender; throw away (-in the towel); unload; vacate; waive; *xfer;* yield; *zero retention;*

**forgery** *(n.)*: *apery;* bogus replica; copy; counterfeit; duplication; emulation; fake; *gesticulation;* hand-forged copy; imitation; *just alike; keep;* likeness; look-alike; mock-up; near-duplicate; offprint; phony; *quadruplicate;* reproduction; replica; simulation; similitude; transcription; *unauthentic; virtual; work; xerograph; yet realistic; zincograph;*

**forget** *(v.)*: abandon; be forgetful; consign to oblivion; disremember; draw a blank; disregard; dismiss; desert; escape one's mind; fail to remember; *go out of one's head;* have no memory of; ignore; just ~; *knuckleheaded;* lose; *long-forgotten;* miss; misplace; neglect; not remember; overlook; pay no attention; pass over; *quick-to- ~;* remember no more; slip one's mind; slight; take no thought; unlearn; *void;* wipe memory clean; *x out; yemeles [arch.];* zero remembrance; [*Ant.* focus]

**forgetful** *(adj.)*: absent-minded; brainless; careless; disregardful; *elsewhere;* forgetting; *gap in memory;* harebrained; heedless; irretentive; irresponsible; *just forgot; knuckleheaded;* lethean; mindless; museless; neglectful; negligent; oblivious; poor-memoried; *quirky; remiss;* scatterbrained; thoughtless; unmindful; vague; wandering; *x out;* yonderly; *zero remembrance;* [*Ant.* focused]

**forgetfulness** *(n.)*: amnesia; absent-mindedness; brainlessness; carelessness; disremembrance [dial.]; disregard; *escaped;* forgetting; gap in memory; heedlessness; irretention; inconsideration; *just forgot; Korsakoff's psychosis;* lapse of memory; lethe; memory lapse (-loss); memorylessness; neglectfulness; obliviousness; poor memory; *quick to forget;* remissness; *scatterbrained;* thoughtlessness; unmindfulness; unthinkingness; vagueness; *wandering; x-ing out;* yonderliness; *zero remembrance;*

**forgivable** *(adj.)*: allowable; absolvable; *blot out;* can be forgiven; defensible; excusable; expiable; *forgiveness; grantable; helpable;* indemnifiable; justifiable; *kindness;* leniency-allowed; minor; non-irremissible; okay; pardonable; quite ~; remissible; slight; tolerable; understandable; venial; warrantable; *xferable;* yet ~; *zero out;*

**forgive** *(v.)*: acquit; absolve; blot out; cancel; clear; disregard; dismiss; excuse; exculpate; exonerate; forbear; grant pardon; *humaneness;* indemnify; justify; keep no account; let go; make slate clean; *mercy;* non-execution; not hold accountable; overlook; pass over; put away; pardon; quit; release; remit; remember no more; spare; show mercy; take away; *tolerate;* unvengefulness; void; wipe clean; *wash; x out; yield;* zero out; [*Ant.* fault]

**forgiveness** *(n.)*: amnesty; acquittal; absolution; blotting out; clemency; clearing; disregard; excusing; exculpation; exoneration; forbearance; grace; *help;* indemnity; justification; kindness; leniency; mercy; non-prosecution; overlooking; pardon; quittance; reprieve; remittance; remission; stay; taking away; *tolerance; tabula rasa* [L.]; *unshackling;* voiding; *washing; x-ing out; yielding;* zeroing out; [*see* grace; *Ant.* faulting]

**forgiving** *(adj.)*: altruistic; big-hearted; clement; *dear;* ever-gracious; forbearing; great-hearted; gracious; humane; *interested; joy-giving;* kind(hearted); lenient; merciful; non-harsh; *overlooking;* pitying; propitious; quick-to-forgive; ready to forgive; sparing; tolerant; tender-hearted; understanding; unrevengeful; very kind; warm; *xenial; yearnful; yielding;* zealous to forgive; [*Ant.* faulting]

**forgotten** *(adj.)*: abandoned; become ~; consigned to oblivion; disremembered; *empty;* failed to remember; gone from memory; having no memory of; ignored; just ~; *known no more;* lost; long- ~; misplaced; missed; non-remembered; neglected; overlooked; purged from memory; passed over; *quickly ~;* remembered no more; slipped one's mind; taken no thought; unrecollected; unremembered; unsung; *void;* wiped clean; *x'ed out; yemeles [arch.];* zero remembrance;

**fork** *(v.)*: *apart;* branch; bifurcate; cleave; divide; diverge; divaricate; *embranchment;* furcate; fissure; go off; *halve; interstice; juncture; keep apart;* leave; move apart; *non-parallel; open;* part; *quadrisect;* run off; ramify; rend; stray; separate; split; sprangle; turn away; *unseam;* vary; *ways; x-sect; yawn; zip apart;*

**forlorn** *(adj.)*: abandoned; bleak; cast off; dejected; deserted; *evacuated;* forsaken; grief-stricken; heartsick; inconsolable; jilted; *keening;* low; lonely; lorn; miserable; neglected; *overlooked;* piteous; *quit on;* rueful; shunned; sorrowful; tearful; unhappy; very sad; woeful; *xfer;* yearnful; *zestless;*

**form** *(n.)*: appearance; bearing; construction; design; exterior ~; figure; fashion; geometric shape; *hologram;* image; *just like;* kind; likeness; mold; moulage; model; manner; mode; *near;* outline; outward appearance; phylum; quale; resemblance; shape; similitude; silhouette; style; type; *unit;* visage; variety; *visible;* way; xenenthesis; yede; zootype;

**form** *(v.)*: assemble; arise; build; constitute; comprise; create; cast; construct; craft; design; develop; efform; erect; fashion; found; generate; *hew;* institute; *job;* knock together; *labor;* mold; make; *newly formed;* originate; produce; quick-build; raise; remake; reform; shape; style; sculpt; turn out; take shape; upbuild; *vamp;* whittle; *xenodiagnose;* yield; yote; *zip together;*

**formal** *(adj.)*: *authorized;* black-tie; correct; ceremonial; cold; *de jure* [F.]; established; formalistic; *great;* high-society; holy; initiatory; institutional; inveterate; judicial; *kept tradition;* legal; liturgical; modal; non-casual; official; ordained; proper; procedural; punctilious; pedantic; *quite proper;* ritualistic; rigid; solemn; sacramental; traditional; unemotional; *vested;* wonted; xtr. ~; yet traditional; *zero casualness;*

**formality** *(n.)*: affair; bienseance; custom; ceremony; duty; exercise; formal ceremony; *gathering;* habit; holiday; institution; *jubilation;* keeping; *liturgy;* ministration; norm; ordinance; ordinal; observance; practice; procedure; performance; *quadrisacramentalism;* ritual; rite; service; sacrament; tradition; use; venerated tradition; wont; *xtr.; yet traditional; zero casualness;*

**format** *(n.)*: arrangement; blueprint; configuration; design; *electronic* ~; form; *grouping;* how it's arranged; infrastructure; *justification; kithe [Scot.];* layout; manner; *notion;* organization; plan; *quo mode [L.];* rearrangement; setup; structure; scheme; *tabulation;* ultrastructure; *view;* way; *xfer; yielding; zet;*

**formative** *(adj.)*: admonishable; *biddable;* constructive; determining; effectual; formational; *growing up; heedful;* impressionable; influential; *junior;* knowledge-forming; *learning;* mentorable; *non-stubborn;* open; persuadable; *quicken;* receptive; seminal; shaping; teachable; unresisting; vulnerable; *willing to learn; xenagogic;* young; *zealous to learn;*

**former** *(adj.)*: anterior; beforetime; citavant; *days gone by;* earlier; first; *gone before;* historical; *initial; just before; known;* last; *most recent; née;* onetime; past; previous; prior; quondam; retrospective; said; *times gone by; unseasonable;* very early; whilom; x; *yesteryear; zero currentness;* [Ant. following]

**formidable** *(adj.)*: awesome; bad; chilling; daunting; *evil;* fearsome; galling; horrific; intimidating; jittery; knee-knocking; larger-than-life; menacing; nerve-racking; outstanding; phobic; *quad;* redoubtable; stressful; terrifying; unsettling; vexing; worrisome; *xtry; yieldless; zealess;* [Ant. frivolous]

**formula** *(n.)*: admixture; blend; blueprint; concoction; description; elixir; equation; formulation; guideline; *hatched;* intermixture; instructions; *jumble;* kava; linear equation; mixture; mathematical ~; *non-homogenous* mixture; *olio;* potion; proposition; principle; *quick recipe;* recipé; rubric; specifications; secret ~; theorem; ule; *variety;* written ~; *xanthate;* yanggoma; *zeroing in;*

**formulate** *(v.)*: *assemble;* birth; *brainstorm;* concoct; devise; engineer; fabricate; figure out; formularize; give as a formula; hatch; invent; *judge;* kiddy; *lucubrate;* machinate; *notion;* originate; prepare; *quick-build;* ruminate; scheme; think (up); use brain; vamp up; work out; *xenodiagnose; yeme; zero in;*

**fornicate** *(v.)*: adulterate; be immoral; commit immorality; debauch; *evil; faithlessness;* go into; have immoral relationship; *immorality; jade;* know immorally; lay with; *mischief; non-faithful; odure;* play the harlot; prostitute oneself; philander; *queanery;* rake; sleep; take immorally; use one's body lewdly; *venery;* womanize; wanton; whore; *x-rated; youthful lust; zhlubbery;*

**fornication** *(n.)*: adultery; baseness; cohabitation; debauchery; *evil;* faithlessness; godlessness; harlotry; impurity; incontinence; immorality; jadery; *kinkiness;* lasciviousness; looseness; moral laxness; non-faithfulness; odure; promiscuity; profligacy; *queanery;* revelry; shamelessness; (sexual) sin; treachery; turpitude; uncleanness; unchastidy; venery; whoredom; whoremongery; *x-rated behavior; yielder; youthful lust; zhlubbery;* [Ant. faithfulness]

**forsake** *(v.)*: abandon; abdicate; abjure; back out; bow out; cut out; cast off; discard; disown; desert; evacuate; forego; forswear; flat leave; give up (-over); hand over; ignore; jump ship; jilt; kest; leave; maroon; neglect; *omit;* pitch; quit; relinquish; resign; reject; renounce; shed; surrender; strand; turn back on; unload; vacate; waive; waste; walk out; withdraw; *xfer;* yield; zip away;

**forsaken** *(adj.)*: abandoned; *bereft;* cast off; derelict; deserted; evacuated; forlorn; given up; God- ~; *handed over;* ignored; jilted; kest; left; (lass)lorn; loveless; *miserable;* neglected; overlooked; *put away;* quitted; relinquished; stranded; spurned; thrown away; untended; unoccupied; unloved; vacant; walked away; *xfer; yielded; zipped away;*

**fort** *(n.)*: army base; blockhouse; base; bastille; castle; citadel; donjon; defense; *enclosure;* fortress; garrison; hold; *imperial palace; jong* [Tib.]; keep; log ~; martello; military post; nest; outpost; propugnacle; post; *quarters;* redoubt; rath; sconce; tower; *unbeatable;* vault; ward; walls; x-house; yamen [Chin.]; zwinger;

**forte** *(n.)*: ability; bent; bailiwick; capability; *deftness;* expertise; familiarity; gift; habilitation; *instinct; jimp;* know-how; long suit; métier; natural ability; *occupation;* proficiency; qualification; readiness; strength; talent; *usefulness;* virtuosity; *wherewithal; xenium; yaup;* zest;

**forthright** *(adj.)*: aboveboard; blunt; brutally honest; candid; direct; ever-truthful; frank; *give it to one straight;* honest; inconsiderate; janty; keenly ~; loud and clear; maladroit; no-nonsense; open(hearted); outright; outspoken; plain-spoken; *qualified;* raw; straight(forward); truthful; upfront; *veritable;* without subtlety; x-parent; *yieldless; zero guile;*

**fortify** *(v.)*: augment; build up; buttress; circumstantiate; develop; double; embattle; enhance; firm up; foster; grow; heighten; increase; *jump up; keep growing;* largen; make stronger; nourish; *overgrow;* prop; *quadruplicate;* rampart; reinforce; strengthen; toughen; undergird; vest; wax stronger; *XL; yain* [arch.]; *zoom up;*

**fortitude** *(n.)*: assiduity; bulldog-tenacity; courage; determination; endurance; fearlessness; grit; heartiness; intrepidity; *jaw-set;* keeping at it; lion-heartedness; mettle; nerve; nerviness; obstinacy; perseverance; *quit-free;* resolve; strength; stalwartness; tenacity; unyieldingness; vigor; willpower; xtry ~; yieldlessness; *zealous continuance;* [Ant. feebleness]

**fortress** *(n.)*: acropolis; berg; bastion; castle; citadel; defense; *enclosure;* fort(ification); garrison; hold; *imperial palace; jong* [Tib.]; keep; *laager;* motte and bailey; nest; octagon; palace; *qassbah* [Mos.]; refuge; redoubt; stronghold; tower; *unbeatable;* vault; watchtower; x-house; yamen [Chin.]; zariba;

**fortunate** *(adj.)*: auspicious; befortuned; blessed; charmed; *destined;* endowed with luck; felicitous; fortuitous; golden; gifted; happy; in luck; jammy; kissed by Dame Fortune; lucky; *meet; non-jinxed;* opportune; prosperous; providential; *quirky; ripe;* super-lucky; touched by an angel; ultra-lucky; *vissitudinous;* well; xtry. ~; *yellow boy [Br.];* zodiac; [Ant. fortuneless]

**fortune** *(n.)*: affluence; bounty; capital; *dollars;* estate; funds; gold; hoard; *income; jewels;* king's ransom; lucre; money; millions; *notes;* opulence; prosperity; *quantities;* riches; substance; treasure; uberty; valuables; wealth; *xenocurrency; yellow boy [Br.];* zillions [slang];

**fortune-teller** *(n.)*: astrologer; augur; bewitcher; clairvoyant; diviner; enchanter; foreteller; geomancer; haruspice; *incantation;* jadoo-wallah; *karakia [Maori];* lithomancer; medium; necromancer; oracle; palm-reader; *quad;* rhabdomancer; sibyl; soothsayer; theurgist; *ungodly;* vates; witch; xenomancer; *yogist;* zodiacist;

**forum** *(n.)*: assembly; board; convocation; discussion group; *event;* forgathering; group; *huddle;* ingathering; judiciary; *kit [coll.];* lot; meeting; *number;* opportunity; panel; query board; round table; session; symposium; talkboard; *unit;* vestry; witan; x.; *yain* [arch.]; *zayat [Burm.];*

**forward** *(adv.)*: ahead; along; before; *continuing;* directly ~; ever- ~; frontward; forth; going straight; headward; in front; *just straight; keenly ~;* looking ahead; *moving ahead; not to the right nor to the left;* on(ward); progressing; *quite straight;* right ahead; straight (ahead); to the fore; *unwavering;* vanward; *wax closer;* x-straight; *yawless; zip ahead;*

**foster** *(v.)*: advance; breed; cultivate; cause; develop; encourage; further; give rise to; help; improve; inspire; *jump ahead; keep;* let grow; make grow; nurture; nourish; *occasion;* promote; quicken; raise up; subserve; support; spawn; spread; teach; *upbuild; vivify; work on; xenagogy;* yield; *zealously promote;*

**foul** *(adj.)*: abominable; bad; corrupt; debauched; evil; fiendish; godless; hateful; iniquitous; jaded; knavish; licentious; malevolent; mephitic; nasty; ornery; polluted; perverse; *quad;* ruthless; sinful; treacherous; unclean; vicious; wicked; *x-bad;* yucky; *zhlubby;* [*Ant.* fair]

**foul-mouthed** *(adj.)*: abominable; base; blasphemous; crude; dirty; earthy; filthy; gauche; *horrid;* ill-mannered; jadish; kitsch; lewd; mean; nasty; offensive; obscene; *piggish; quad;* rude; scurrilous; tasteless; uncouth; unrefined; vulgar; wretched; *x-rated; yucky; zhlubby;*

**found** *(v.)*: assemble; begin; build; create; develop; erect; forge; fashion; generate; *hew;* incept; institute; *job;* knock together; lay foundations of; make; *new;* originate; produce; quick-build; raise; start; turn out; upbuild; *vamp;* wage; work; *xenogenesis;* yield; *zygogenesis;* [*Ant.* finish]

**foundation** *(n.)*: *aft;* base; basis; beginning; cornerstone; creation; dado; establishment; floor; footing; founding; ground(work); *hinder part;* inception; institution; *jacksy;* keystone; low(est) point; laying of the ~; *minimum; nether side;* origin(ation); premise; platform; plinth; quoin; root; rock-bottom; surface; start; *terra firma* [L.]; underpinning; *valley; way down; xenolith; yoni* [Skr.]; *zaccho;* [*Ant.* finishing]

**fountain** *(n.)*: ajutage; beginning; brine-spring; cascade; cistern; *derivation; estuary;* fount; font; geyser; headspring; issue; jet; keld; *lake;* mineral spring; *namma hole;* origin; *proceeding; qanat;* reservoir; spray; spout; spring; source; *traduction; upsurge;* venter; wellspring; *xenenthesis; yoni* [Skr.]; *zemzem;*

**fowl** *(n.)*: albatross; bird; chicken; *dove; eagle;* fledgling; game bird; hen [fem.]; *ibis; jay; kiwi; lark; migrant; needletail; oscine;* poultry; passerine; *quail; robin;* songbird; seafowl; *thrush; umbrella bird;* volery [pl.]; wildfowl; waterfowl; *xenops; yellowfinch; zugvogel* [G.];

**fowler** *(n.)*: aucupator; bird-catcher; catcher; decoy-man; ensnarer; fowl-catcher; *gunman;* hunter; *individual; jaeger* [G.]; *jacker; killer;* larker; *man; nimrod; outdoorsman;* poulterer; *quarry;* rifleman; snarer; trapper; *user of traps; venturer;* wild~; *xema;* yager; *zugvogel* [G.];

**fox** *(n.)*: * arctic ~; bushy-tail; corsack; *canine;* desert ~; *evasive;* fennec; gray ~; *hyena;* isatis; *jackal;* kit- ~; *lobo; maned wolf; night wolf; old ~;* pampas ~; *quadruped;* reynard; red ~; she- ~ [fem.]; tod [masc.]; *urocyon cinereoargenteus* [L.]; vixen [fem.]; *vulpine;* white ~; *wolf; xolotl; yabbi;* zerda;

**foyer** *(n.)*: antechamber; *balcony;* chamber; *den;* entryway; forecourt; gateway; hall; ingress; *jube; keyway;* lobby; *mudroom;* narthex; outer room; portal; *quarters;* room; stoa; *terrace;* utility room; vestibule; waiting room; xystum; *you* [Chin.]; zeta;

**fraction** *(n.)*: amount; bit; component; division; element; faction; *group;* hair [slang]; *half;* ingredient; *jib;* kernel; little bit; member; mite; *nugget; ought;* part; portion; percentage; quantity; *remnant;* small part; some; segment; section; tiny bit; tidbit; *unit; vestige; wedge; x-mal* [G.]; yngot [arch.]; zum [dial.]; [*Ant.* fullness]

**fractious** *(adj.)*: argumentative; bad-tempered; contrary; disagreeable; emulous; factious; grouchy; hard to get along with; huffy; irascible; jangly; kindless; liverish; mean; nasty; ornery; petulant; querulous; resistant; snappish; temperamental; umbrageous; vinegary; waspish; *xenophobic;* yieldless; zoilean;

**fragile** *(adj.)*: arenaceous; brittle; breakable; crackable; delicate; easily broken; frail; frangible; glasslike; highly ~; *inflexible; jimp; krisp;* likely to break; *mar;* non-flexible; overly brittle; perishable; quite ~; *rigid;* shatterable; temporal; undurable; ultra- ~; very ~; weak; *XF; yieldless;* zero give;

**fragment** *(n.)*: amount; bit; chip; chunk; daud; element; fraction; granule; hunk; *iota; item;* junt; kernel; lump; morsel; mass; nugget; ounce; ort; piece; quantity; remnant; scrap; segment; section; smithereen; tidbit; tad; unit; *vestige;* wad; wedge; *x-mal* [G.]; *yngot* [arch.]; zum [arch.];

**fragment** *(v.)*: atomize; break (up); burst; crack; crash; divide; disintegrate; *explode;* factionalize; fritter; grind; *halve; incomplete; jerk apart;* knock apart; levigate; make into pieces; *nullify; olate;* pulverize; quash; rupture; rend; splinter; smash; shatter; tear apart; *undo;* vitiate; *wreck; x-ing;* yank apart; *zap;*

**fragrance** *(n.)*: aura; aroma; balsam; cologne; *diapasm;* essence; fragrancy; *frankincense;* good-smelling; *heavenly scent;* incense; jasmine; keora oil; *lavender;* musk; *myrrh;* nidor; odor; perfume; *quality perfume;* redolence; scent; sweet smell; *toilet water; unforgettable aroma;* volatile oil; whiff; *waft; xanthoxylene;* yummy scent; *zedoary;* [*Ant.* fetor]

**fragrant** *(adj.)*: aromatic; balsamic; censed; delightful; essenced; fine-smelling; good-smelling; *heliotrope;* incensed; jasmine-scented; keen-odored; lovely-smelling; musky; nidorous; odorous; perfumed; *queme;* redolent; scented; sweet-smelling; thuriferous; thymy; *unoffensive;* very aromatic; well-scented; *xanthoxylene;* yummy-smelling; *zedoary;* [*Ant.* fetid]

**frail** *(adj.)*: anile; brittle; crumbly; delicate; enfeebled; fragile; gimp; helpless; insubstantial; infirm; *jejune; knocked out;* lame; light; meager; non-potent; overweak; old-womanish; *only human;* puny; *queachy* [dial.]; rickety; scrawny; slight; spindly; thin; tenuous; unhardy; vulnerable; weak; washy; *x-weak; yawnish; zapped;* [*Ant.* fat]

**frailty** *(n.)*: anility; brittleness; caducity; crumbliness; delicateness; enfeeblement; feebleness; fragility; gimpness; helplessness; informity; impotency; *jejuneness; knocking out;* lameness; *much-weakened;* non-ability; openness; powerlessness; *quirk; reduced ability;* softness; torpor; *unprotected;* vulnerability; weakness; *xtry. ~; yielding; zapped;*

**frame** *(n.)*: architecture; border; chassis; casing; construction; *door ~;* edge; enclosure; framework; guilloche; hem(line); *imbordered;* jack; *k-molding;* liner; lamella; margin; *notamy;* ossature; outline; orle; *picture ~; perimeter; purflew;* quadra; rim; skeleton; scaffold; sub~; substructure; shadow box; sash; tenter; under~; verge; window ~; x-frame; *yew-frame;* zone;

**frame** *(v. entrap)*: allure; beguile; con; defraud; ensnare; falsify; gaff; hornswoggle; insnare; jape; kep; lie to; *mesh;* nobble; outcraft; plant evidence; *quad;* rook; set up; trap; *utter falsehood;* verneuk; weasel; *xuld [arch.]; yentz; zing;*

**France** *(n.)*: *Aquitania;* Brittany; Burgundy; country; *Champagne; Dreux; Etampes;* French Republic (-Empire); Gaul; *heart of ~; Issoire;* Jean Crapaud; Kingdom of ~; *L'Hexagone* [coll.]; Metropolitan ~; *nation;* Normandy; *oriflamb;* Picardy; Paris; Quai d'Orsay; Republic of ~; *Southern ~; transalpine Gaul; Ussel;* Vichy ~; *Versailles; Western Europe; xalpine Gaul* [L.]; *Xures; Yvtot;* zone;

   **French regions**: Aquitaine; Burgundy; Champagne; Franche-Comte; Haute-Normandie; Ile-de-France; Languedoc; Midi-Pyrenees; Normandy; Picardy; Rhone;

**frank** *(adj.)*: aboveboard; blunt; candid; direct; ever-truthful; forthright; *give it to one straight;* honest; inconsiderate; janty; keenly ~; *lay it out;* maladroit; non-tactful; obtuse; outspoken; plain-spoken; *qualified;* raw; straight; tactless; unrestrained; untactful; undiplomatic; *veritable;* without subtlety; *x-parent; yieldless; zero tact;*

**frantic** *(adj.)*: anxious; agitated; brisk; busy; crazy; *diligent;* energetic; frazzled; feverish; frenzied; *gung-ho;* hopping; hurried; hectic; hysterical; intense; jumping; kedge; lymphated; mad; nippy; overbusy; panicked; quick-moving; raving; springy; *taxing;* uptight; vexing; worried; *xuld [arch.];* yeasty; zany;

**fraternity** *(n.)*: association; brotherhood; club; confrérie; *Delta Chi Omega;* establishment; fraternal order; guild; *house; inductee;* joint coalition; kinship; league; mateship; network; organization; partnership; *quinquevirate; relationship;* society; sorority [fem.]; trust; union; *value; working alliance; xenia; yeald;* Zeta Phi Sigma;

**fraud** *(n. deceit)*: allurement; beguilement; con; deception; defraudment; ensnarement; fraudulence; guise; guile; grift; hoodwinking; imposture; japery; knavishness; lie; misleading; misrepresentation; nobbling; outfoxing; pretext; *quiblin [arch.];* racket; swindling; sham; trickery; untruth; verneuking; wiliness; *xuld [arch.]; yentzing; zinger;* [*Ant.* fairness]

**fraud** *(n. hoaxer)*: allurer; beguiler; charlatan; cheat; defrauder; ensnarer; fake; guiler; grifter; hoaxer; huckster; imposter; jape; knave; liar; misleader; *no-good;* open liar; phony; quack(salver); rook; swindler; trickster; untruther; verneuker; wangler; weasel; *xgressor;* yentzer [Heb.]; *zinger;*

**fraudulence** *(n.)*: artfulness; beguilement; crookedness; dishonesty; deceit; ensnarement; fraud; guile; grifting; honorlessness; improbity; jadery; knavery; lying; misleading; non-truthfulness; *opportunism;* perfidy; questionableness; roguery; shadiness; skullduggery; trickery; treachery; untruthfulness; unscrupulousness; villainy; wiliness; *x-ing;* yegginess; *zero honesty;* [*Ant.* fairness]

**fraudulent** *(adj.)*: artful; bad; crooked; corrupt; dishonest; evasive; falsified; guileful; honorless; ignoble; jady; knavish; lying; misconducted; non-credible; opportunistic; perfidious; quasi-ethical; roguish; seedy; shady; tricky; treacherous; unprincipled; untrustworthy; underhanded; unscrupulous; venal; wily; *x-ing;* yeggy; *zero honesty;* [*Ant.* fair]

**freak** *(n.)*: aberration; beatnik; curiosity; deviation; eccentricity; ~ of nature; gazing-stock; *heterozygous;* irregularity; *joke; kink; laughingstock;* misfit; mutant; monstrosity; *non-usual;* oddity; peculiarity; queerity; *rarity;* singularity; side show; *twisted; unusual; variation;* weirdo; *xiphopagus; yawed;* zany;

**free** *(adj.)*: able; allowed; at liberty; bondless; complimentary; delivered; democratic; emancipated; expenseless; freed; footloose; fetterless; gratis; gratuitous; *honest;* independent; *justified; kept ~;* liberated; loose; manumitted; masterless; no-cost; non-captive; open; off; *pro bona* [L.]; permitted; quite ~; released; rid; scot- ~; set at liberty; totally- ~; *toll- ~;* unrestricted; unhindered; unrestrained; unencumbered; unshackled; unbound; unfettered; unentangled; unimpeded; unsuppressed; unbound; ungirt; unbridled; unconfined; unobstructed; uninhibited; voluntary; willing; welcome; without cost; *xenium;* yokeless; zero-cost; [*Ant.* fettered]

**free** *(v.)*: allow to go ~; bail (out); clear; deliver; disencumber; emancipate; *forgive;* give freedom to; *hand over; issue; justify; key;* liberate; loose; let go; manumit; not detain; *open;* put out; quit; release; set free; take out; unshackle; *volley; walk; xfer; yokeless; zoneless;* [*Ant.* fetter]

**freedom** *(n.)*: autonomy; bondlessness; clearance; deliverance; emancipation; free rein; gratuitousness; home rule; independence; *justification; key;* liberation; liberty; license; latitude; manumission; non-captivity; openness; privilege; *quite free;* release; self-determination; total ~; unrestraint; voluntariness; willingness; *xenium;* yokelessness; zero fetters; [*Ant.* fetters]

**free hand** *(n.)*: absolute authority; blank check; *carte blanche* [F.]; dominion; empowering; free rein; *governance; headship; influence;* justification; *king;* long rope; liberty; mastery; no restrictions; open access; *privilege; quite free;* rule; *right; sovereignty;* total freedom; *unrestrained; very free;* whatever one wishes; *xenium;* yet unrestricted; zero limitations;

**freeload** *(v.)*: abuse; *beg;* cadge; despoil; exploit; finagle; *get; hand-outs;* impose on; *jockey; knavery;* leech; live off others; mooch; *not work;* overexplot; parasitize; panhandle; *quad;* rely on others; sponge; take advantage; use others; victimize; walk all over; *x-out; yeme; zap;*

**freeloader** *(n.)*: *alms-taker;* barnacle; bloodsucker; bum; cadger; derelict; *easy living;* free-loader; gate-crasher; habitue; idler; javel; kern; leech; medicant; no-good; *oberration;* parasite; panhandler; *quisby; rolling stone;* sponge(r); scrounger; table-friend; user; vampire; welfare-taker; *xiaoren; yahoo; zhlub;* [*see* bum; sluggard]

**freely** *(adv.)*: as one pleases; bondlessly; complimentarily; deliberately; expenselessly; for free; gratuitously; *highly;* independently; *justifiedly; kept free;* loosely; lavishly; *masterless; no-cost;* openly; plainly; quitely; readily; spontaneously; totally- ~; unimpededly; voluntarily; willingly; without charge; *xenium;* yokelessly; *zero-cost;*

**freewill** *(adj.)*: as desired; by choice; chosen; discretionary; elective; free; gratuitous; *heart;* intentional; *just want to; kindness; like to; minded;* non-compulsory; optional; purposeful; quite optional; refusable; self-determined; totally optional; unforced; voluntary; willing; *xel [arch.]; yare; zealous;* [*Ant.* forced]

**free will** *(n.)*: autonomy; *by choice;* choice; desire; election; freedom to choose; general desire; heart desire; independent choice; *judgment; keenness;* liberty; mind; notion; objective; pleasure; *quiritation;* right to choose; *reckoning;* self-determination; *true desire;* urge; volition; voluntariness; will; *xenenthesis;* yearning; *zeal;* [*Ant.* foreordaining]

**freeze** *(v.)*: *arctic;* become hard; cool; chill; drop below 32 degrees; deep- ~; *enharden;* freeze over; glaciate; harden; infrigidate; ice (over); *Jack Frost;* keep frozen; lower temperature; make frozen; *non-thawed;* over- ~; put in ~er; quiver; quick- ~; rime; re~; shiver; solidify; turn to ice; *unthawed; very cold;* winterkill; *xtr. hard; ycie [arch.];* zero degrees; [*Ant.* fry]

**freight** *(n.)*: articles; batch; burden; carload; cargo; consignment; delivery; *equipment;* furnishings; goods; haulage; items; *jetsam;* kit; load; lading; moveables; naulage; objects; payload; quantity; railway ~; stuff; shipload; shipment; stowage; things; truckload; *unload;* valuables; wagonload; *x-load;* yard goods; *zeug [G.];*

**frenzy** *(n.)*: agitation; attack; bewilderment; brouhaha; bout; chaos; commotion; disturbance; excitement; embroilment; furor; flurry; free-for-all; *going;* hubbub; hysteria; insanity; jumble; kerfuffle; lather; mad rush; madness; *non-controlled;* overenthusiasm; pandemonium; *quickening;* rush; rage; ruckus; stirring; tizzy; tumult; upset; uproar; *vexation;* wildness; *xtry. fuss; yarked;* zeal;

**frequent** *(adj.)*: abundant; besetting; common; continual; daily; everyday; frequentative; habitual; inveterate; just as often as one can; *keep going;* lots; many; numerous; oftentime; oft-repeated; prevalent; perpetual; *quantitative;* repeated; regular; steady; thick-coming; usual; unceasing; very often; *well-traveled; x.; yet often; zillions;*

**fresh** *(adj.)*: anew; brand-new; crisp; dew- ~; ever- ~; fine; fructescent; farm ~; good; green; harvested; invigorated; juicy; just-harvested; keen; *latest;* mellow; nice; new; *other;* perfect; *quick-picked;* recent; ripe(ned); spanking-new; *to spare;* unspoiled; verdant; well-ripened; *xtry.;* young; zippy; [*Ant.* fusty]

**fret** *(v.)*: agonize; brood; chafe; dread; despair; eye askance; fray; fear; grow pale; have anxiety; *intimidated; jitter; knees knocking;* lose courage; languish; mither; *nervous wreck; overwhelm;* pother; quiver; recoil; *shake;* terror; *unnerved; vexed;* worry; wig out; *xenophobic; ydrad; zoophobic;*

**friction** *(n.)*: abrasion; *bickering;* chafing; confrication; disagreement; erosion; frication; grating; *hacking;* irritation; jar; kaceration; *mark; nick; opposition;* pounding; *quarreling;* rubbing; resistance; rasping; scraping; scouring; trituration; urtication; *violence;* wearing; xerotripsis; yedder; *zipping;*

**friend** *(n.)*: *amigo [Sp.];* ally; buddy; bosom (-best) ~; chum; companion; comrade; confidant; compatriot; defender; escort; fellow; good-fellow; helper; intimate; Jonathan; kindred spirit; kith [pl.]; *loyal ~;* mate; neighbor; other self; playmate; pal; partner; *quondam ~;* roommate; sidekick; sympathizer; teammate; *unfailing ~; voice; watcher; xenophile;* yokefellow; *zealous ~;* [*see* brother; *Ant.* foe]

**friendless** *(adj.)*: (all) alone; by oneself; companionless; disliked; estranged; friendless; forlorn; godforsaken; helpless; isolated; just oneself; kithless; lonely; lonesome; marooned; not befriended; ostracized; *piteous; quit on;* reclusive; solitary; shunned; *tearful;* unpopular; unbefriended; very alone; without a friend; *x'ed; yet unaccompanied; zero companionship;*

**friendliness** *(n.)*: amicability; amiableness; amity; affinity; benevolence; brotherliness; congeniality; companionableness; chumminess; *delightfulness;* esprit; familiarity; geniality; gregariousness; hospitality; harmony; intimacy; jocundity; kindness; likeableness; mutuality; neighborliness; oneness; pleasantness; queme; relationship; rapprochement; rapport; sociability; sisterliness [fem.]; thoughtfulness; unity; *virtue;* warmth; warm-heartedness; xenia; xenophilia; *yokefellow; zeal;* [*Ant.* fiendishly]

**friendly** *(adj.)*: amiable; amicable; affable; benevolent; brotherly; congenial; companionable; chummy; *delightful; extroverted;* familiar; genial; gregarious; hospitable; harmonious; intimate; just-folks; kindly; *likable;* matey; nice; neighborly; outgoing; personable; platonic; pally; *quite ~;* receptive; sociable; thick; uplifting; very friendly; welcoming; well-intentioned; warm; xenial; *yokefellow; zealous;* [*Ant.* fiendish]

**friendship** *(n.)*: amity; alliance; bond; brotherhood; commonality; companionship; closeness; camaraderie; comradeship; devotion; endearment; familiarity; friendliness; fellowship; fraternity; goodwill; harmony; intimacy; joining; kinship; knot; love; *loyalty;* mateship; nearness; neighborliness; oneness; partnership; *quondam ~;* rapport; relationship; sociability; sisterhood [fem.]; trust; unity; *unfailing ~; value;* warmth; xenia; yoke; *zeal;* [*Ant.* feud]

**fright** *(n.)*: affright; *burden; cowardice;* exasperation; fretting; gastness; heebie-jeebies; horror; insecurity; jitters; jitteriness; kiaugh [Scot.]; *lily-livered; mistrust;* nervousness; over-anxiety; panic; quaking; *reluctance;* startle; scare; terror; uneasiness; vexation; *the* willies; worry; *xenophobia;* yellow-belliedness; *zeallessness;* [*Ant.* fearlessness]

**frighten** *(v.)*: affright; alarm; *burden; care;* daunt; distress; *exasperate; fear;* gaster; horrify; intimidate; jolt; kiaugh [Scot.]; *languish;* make nervous; nerve; overburden; panic; quicken; rattle; scare; terrify; unnerve; vex; worry; *xenophobia;* yelping; zealless;

**frightful** *(adj.)*: alarming; blood-curdling; creepy; chilling; daunting; dreadful; eerie; foreboding; fearful; frightening; gruesome; ghastly; hair-raising; intimidating; jarring; knee-knocking; lurid; macabre; nightmarish; ominous; petrifying; queer; revolting; spooky; scary; terrifying; unnerving; vexatious; worrisome; *xenophobic; ydrad* [arch.]; zonky; [*Ant.* friendly]

**frill** *(n.)*: adornment; border; chitterling; decoration; edging; fringe; furbelow; gorget; *hem; imbordered;* jabot; knee-fringe; *lace; margin; narrow;* orfrays; purl; quadra; ruche; ruffle; *strip;* trimming; tassel; *ulterior;* valance; welt; *x-border; yonder;* zizith;

**fringe** *(n.)*: adornment; border; chitterling; decoration; edge; edging; frill; gorget; *hem; imbordered;* jabot; knee-fringe; *lace;* margin; *narrow;* orfrays; pleats; quadra; ruffle; strands; tassel; thrum; *ulterior;* valance; welt; *x-border; yonder; zone;* [*see* perimeter]

**frivolous** *(adj.)*: *absurd;* brainless; completely unimportant; dumb; empty; futile; giddy; hoity-toity; insignificant; inconsequential; irrelevant; jerkwater; ketty; little; light; minor; nugatory; negligible; otiose; petty; peripheral; picayune; quisquillous; ridiculous; silly; trifling; trivial; unimportant; vain; worthless; *XS;* yeasty; *zilch;*

**frizzy** *(adj.)*: *alternating;* becurled; curled; coiled; *distorted;* entwisted; frizzed; frizzled; *gnarled;* hankled; intwisted; *jag;* kinky; looped; meandering; *nonlinear; overwound; puffy;* querly; raveled; spiraled; twisted; tightly curled; upwound; volute; wound; *x-ing; yaw;* zigzagged; [*Ant.* flat]

**frog** *(n.)*: amphibian; bull~; croaker; *Dumeril's striped ~; edible ~;* froggy [slang]; *glass ~;* hyla; hopper; *Indian bull~; jiminez; kassina;* leap~; marsh ~; nototrema; ox~; paddock [Br.]; peeper; *quadruped; rain ~; spadefoot;* tree~; *toad; ugly toad; veined tree ~;* water ~; xenopus; *yellowbelly toad; Zetek's ~;*

**front** *(n.)*: anterior; beginning; commencement; *direct ~;* externals; face; façade; foreground; forepart; fore(~); *guise;* head; integument; *jib [naut.];* kisser; lead-in; *mug;* nose; obverse; proscenium [theater]; prow [naut.]; *quickening;* rostrum; start; tip; top; upfront; vaward; welcoming; xenogenesis; *yede;* zone;

**frown** *(n.)*: *affected;* black countenance; cringe; contortion; displeased expression; distortion; expression; fallen countenance; grimace; girn; glower; heavy countenance; *ill-humored;* joyless expression; *kick the dirt;* long face; lour; lower; miserable expression; nasty look; *overcast;* pout; *quite displeased;* rictus; simagre; scowl; *tearful; unhappy; very upset;* wince; wrinkle brow; *xtr. sad; yucky; zero joy;*

**frozen** *(adj.)*: arctic; bitter; cold; congealed; deep ~; *extreme;* frigid; freezing; fristy; frostbitten; gelid; hoary; hard(ened); icy; iced over; *Jack Frost;* keen; low-temperature; motionless; non-moving; over-frozen; polar; quite ~; rimy; raw; subzero; solidified; thawless; unthawed; *very cold;* wintry; *xtry. cold; ycie* [arch.]; zero degrees; [*Ant.* feiry]

**frugal** *(adj.)*: austere; begrudging; careful; conservative; dollar-pinching; economical; frugally-minded; grudging; hesitant; illiberal; judicious; *keenly ~;* low-budget; meager; niggardly; overcautious; parsimonious; pennywise; provident; *quick-to-refuse;* restrained; sparing; thrifty; unwasteful; *vacillating;* wary; *xtry. ~; yieldless;* zero-wastefulness; [*Ant.* free-handed]

**frugality** *(n.)*: austerity; begrudging; caution; cheapness; dollar-pinching; economicalness; frugalness; good husbandry; hoarding; illiberality; *Jack Benny;* knippering; laggardness; miserliness; niggardliness; over-frugality; parsimony; *quick-to-save;* restraint; scrimping; stinginess; thrift(iness); unwastefulness; *very miserly;* wariness; *xtry. ~; yieldlessness;* zero-wastefulness; [*Ant.* free-handedness]

**fruit** *(n. edible produce)*: achene; *berry;* byproduct; citrus; crop; drupe; end result; fruitage; *grapes;* harvest; issue; *jackfruit; kiwi; lime; melon; nectarine;* outgrowth; produce; *quince; reaping;* rape; sapote; tree-fruit; upshot; vintage; wall ~; wilding; xanthocarp; yield; zapote;
   **Types of fruit**: apple; banana; cherry; date; elderberry; fig; grape; huckleberry; Indian fig; jujube; kiwi; lemon; lime; mango; nectarine; orange; peach; pear; pineapple; quince; raspberry; strawberry; tangerine; ugli® ~; vista cherry; watermelon; xigua; yuzu; ziziphus;

**fruit** *(n. result)*: aftereffects; by-product; consequence; *derivative; development;* effect; end result; following effects; *get;* harvest; impact; issue; just desserts; *known outcome;* lattermath; manufacturing; natural outgrowth; outcome; outgrowth; product; quantum effect; ramification; result; reaping; repercussion; significance; sequent; termination; upshot; vintage; work; wake; *xenagogy;* yield; *zeug [G.];* [*Ant.* foundation]

**fruitful** *(adj.)*: abundant; bearing; copious; child-bearing; *diffuse;* effective; fertile; fecund; fructuous; fructiferous; generative; *good;* highly productive; interfertile; *just abounding; keenly abundant;* luxuriant; *many;* non-sterile; overabundant; productive; prolific; pomiferous; *quantitative;* rank; rich; seminal; superabundant; *thriving;* uberous; viviparous; worthwhile; well-fruited; *x.;* yielding; yieldful *zero-sterility;* [*Ant.* fruitless]

**fruitless** *(adj.)*: acarpous; abortive; barren; childless; desolate; devoid of fruit; empty; futile; gainless; *horrible;* ineffectual; improsperous; jejune; *kept from bearing;* lacking; manque; non-worthwhile; otiose; penurious; paltry; purposeless; *quenched;* rewardless; sterile; successless; *terrible;* unfruitful; unproductive; unsuccessful; vain; valueless; worthless; *xerarch;* yeld; yieldless; *zero fruit;* [*Ant.* fruitful]

**frustrate** *(v. annoy)*: annoy; aggravate; boil; chafe; cross; disturb; exasperate; fluster; grate; *hamper;* irritate; incense; *jar;* kindle; lose one's temper; madden; nettle; outrage; provoke; pique; perturb; *quick-tempered;* rile; rankle; steam; tick off; upset; vex; worsen; *xerothermic; yell; zealousy [arch.];*

**frustrate** *(v. thwart)*: avert; athwart; block; cumber; deter; encumber; foil; *gum up;* hinder; hamper; impede; *jam;* kibosh; limit; make void; nullify; obstruct; prevent; quash; restrain; stymie; thwart; undo; void; withhold; *x;* yank; zero; zap; [*Ant.* further]

**frustration** *(n.)*: aggravation; bafflement; bitterness; confounding; displeasure; dissatisfaction; discomfiture; enragement; foiling; flustering; gall; hotness; irritation; *jarring; kindling;* letdown; mental shock; nuisance; nullification; outmaneuvering; perturbation; quick-temperament; reversal; setback; temper; thwarting; upset; vexation; weariness; *xerothermia; yelling; zealousy* [arch.]; [*Ant.* furtherance]

**fry** *(v.)*: *anneal;* bake; brown; cook; deep- ~; *evenly ~;* frizzle; fricasee; *grill;* heat; *intense heat; jumbal;* kitchen; *let cook;* make; *neal [arch.];* ovenbake; pan- ~; quick-fry; *roast;* sizzle; stir- ~; sauté; *toast;* undercook; *very hot;* whip up; *xeo;* yark; zap; [*Ant.* freeze]

**fuel** *(n.)*: *auto ~; butanol;* combustible; *diesel;* energy; fossil ~; gasoline; hexamine; high-test; *item; jet ~; kerosine;* leaded ~; *motor oil;* nuclear ~; *oil;* petrol(eum); paraffin; propellant; *quart; rocket ~; red diesel;* synthetic ~; *tank;* unleaded ~; *virgin naphtha;* water gas; xylene; yealdon; zip [slang];

**fugitive** *(n.)*: absconder; *at large;* bolter; criminal; deserter; escapee; fleer; *goer; hastener; infractor;* jail-breaker; *knuck; leaver;* man without a country; nomad; outlaw; *on the run; price on one's head; quitter;* runaway; runner; refugee; skedaddler; truant; *unapprehended;* vagabond; withdrawer; wanted man; *xfer; yegg; zip away;*

**fulfill** *(v.)*: achieve; accomplish; bring about; carry out; complete; consummate; do; execute; effect(uate) fill; finish; get done; heed; implement; just do; keep; listen to; make; *not resist;* observe; perform; *qualified;* realize; satisfy; see through; transact; *undertake;* vigorously keep; work; *xfer;* yield; zip to it; [*see* satisfy; *Ant.* fail]

**fulfillment** *(n. completion)*: accomplishment; bringing about; completion; doing; execution; finishing; fruition; getting one; heeding; implementation; *jumping to it;* keeping; listening; *making;* non-resistance; observance; performance; *questionlessness;* realization; satisfaction; transaction; upholding; vigorous completion; *work; xlation; yain [arch.]; zet [dial.];* [*Ant.* failure]

**fulfillment** *(n. contentment)*: accomplishment; bliss; contentment; delight; enjoyment; felicity; gratification; happiness; *indulgence;* joy; kicks; liking; making good; nice feeling; overjoy; pleasure; quittance; rapture; satisfaction; titillation; *uplifted; vivacity;* winsomeness; *xanadu; yummy;* zeal; [*Ant.* failure]

**full** *(adj.)*: absolute; accomplished; all-encompassing; broad; brimming; chock- ~; crammed; complete; comprehensive; consummate; done; engorged; entire; exhaustive; fraught; full-circle (-length); (ful)filled; gorged; *high;* intact; inclusive; jammed; *kept; laden;* mature; macroscopic; non-abridged; outright; overall; packed; perfect; plenary; quite ~; replete; stuffed; sated; sweeping; thorough; total; unbroken; unedited; unqualified; uncut; utter; universal; veritable; whole; *xtry.;* yare; *zillions;*
    **Kinds of *full*:** armful; bagful; bellyful; bucketful; carful; cartful; cupful; earful; eyeful; forkful; handful; hatful; headful; houseful; jarful; jugful; kettleful; ladle-ful; lapful; mouthful; needleful; nestful; netful; pocketful; quartful; quiverful; roomful; sackful; spoonful; teacupful; wagonful; wheelbarrowful; worldful; yardful; yaffle; yearful; yepsen; zooful;

**fully** *(adv.)*: absolutely; altogether; beyond doubt; completely; definitely; entirely; for sure; globally; hundred percent; indisputably; intensely; just; keenly; *largely;* most (certainly); *notably;* 100%; positively; quite; really; surely; totally; utterly; *very;* wholly; 'xactly [slang]; *ywis* [arch.]; 'zactly [dial.]; [*Ant.* fractionally]

**fume** *(n.)*: afterdamp; atomization; breath; *bank;* cloud; *dust;* effuvium; exhaust; fog; gauze; gas; haze; *incloud; jumbo cloud;* KH instability; London fog; mist; miasma; noxious cloud; *overcast;* pall; pother; pollution; *quasi-vaporous;* reek; smoke; smog; trace; *umbered;* vapor; wisp; whiff; *xenon cloud; yellowy cloud; zirconium cloud;*

**fume** *(v. emit gas)*: atomize; breathe out; cast; discharge; emit; fumigate; give off; hydrogenate; issue; *jet; knock out;* let out; make ~s; *non-retention;* output; pollute; *quickly emit;* release; smoke; send out; transmit; *unload;* vapor; *wisp;* xfer; yield; *zap;*

**fume** *(v. seethe)*: anger; burn; cross; disgust; enrage; fluster; gall; huff; incense; infuriate; *jangle;* kindle; lose one's temper; miff; madden; nettle; *outrage;* pique; perturb; *quick-tempered;* rage; seethe; tick off; upset; vent; *wrath; xerothermic;* yell; *zealousy [arch.];*

**fun** *(adj.)*: amusing; blast [slang]; cheery; delightful; entertaining; enjoyable; exciting; frolicsome; fantastic; gleeful; gay; hilarious; indulgent; joyous; keen; light-hearted; merry; nice; *overjoyed;* pleasurable; *quality time;* recreative; sportive; satisfying; thrilling; uplifting; *vivacious;* wonderful; *xenial;* yet diversionary; *zany;*

**fun** *(n.)*: amusement; avocation; buffoonery; cheer; clowning around; diversion; delight; entertainment; enjoyment; excitement; frivolity; gas [slang]; gleefulness; gaiety; horseplay; hobby; idle amusement; jollity; kill-time; lighthearted play; leisure activity; merriment; merrymaking; mirth; *non-serious; overjoying;* pastime; play; pleasure; quality time; recreation; riot [slang]; sport; tomfoolery; *unwind; vaudeville; whimsical; x-play; yarn; zizz;*

**function** *(n.)*: action; activity; business; chore; design; duty; end; *for;* faculty; goal; high aim; intent; job; key reason; labor; meaning; mission; nisus; object(ive); purpose; qualifier; reason; service; task; use; *view;* work; x; *yielding; zeal;*

**function** *(v.)*: act; behave; carry on; do; drive; execute; *fulfill;* go; have effect; *industry; job;* keep (going); labor; make; minister; *nobble;* operate; perform; *quicken;* run; serve; tick; *undertake; useful; vigor;* work; *xuld [arch.];* yeme; *zip;*

**fundamental** *(adj.)*: absolute minimal; basic; constituent; deep-seated; elemental; essential; foundational; grassroots; heart; inherent; intrinsic; indispensable; *just the basics;* kernel; key; *least;* main; necessary; original; primitive; primary; quintessential; quiddative; rudimentary; supporting; *top;* underlying; vital; *warp and woof; xenenthesis; yod;* zoetic;

**Fundamentalism** *(n.)*: anti-modernism; Bible-belief; Baptists; conservative; die-hard conservatism; *evangelicalism;* Fundamental belief; *God-fearing;* historic Baptist position; *independent Baptist; Jesus-loving;* KJV; literalism; modernist-rejecting; *movement;* non-liberalism;

old paths; preservationism; *quasi- ~;* (religious) right; staunch conservatism; *theology; unswerving ~; verity;* Word-based belief; *Xty.; yet-to-compromise; zero liberalness;*

**Fundamentalist** *(adj.)*: anti-modernistic; Bible-believing; Baptist; conservative; die-hard; evangelical; Fundamental; God-fearing; hell-fire-and-brimstone; *independent Baptist; Jesus-loving; KJV-only;* literalist; modernist-opposing; non-progressive; old-paths; preservationist; *quasi- ~;* (religious) right; Scripture-based; theologically conservative; *"Thus saith the Lord"; unswerving ~; verity;* Word-based; *xenenthesis; yet-to-compromise; zealous;*

**Fundamentalist** *(n.)*: anti-modernist; Bible-believer; Bible-thumper; Baptist; conservative; die-hard ~; *evangelical;* Fundamental Christian; God-fearing ~; hell-fire-and-brimstone ~; *independent Baptist; Jesus-loving; KJV-defender;* literalist; modernism-rejector; narrow-minded ~; old-pather; preservationist; *quasi- ~;* (religious) right; separatist; true Baptist; unswerving ~; *verity;* Wesleyan; *Xn.; yet to compromise; zealot;*

**fundamentality** *(n.)*: *attributes;* being; constitution; *disposition;* essence; flower; gist; heart; inbeing; jet; kernel; lifeblood; makeup; nub; ontology; pith; quintessence; rudiments; soul; *thing; underneath;* vitals; warp and woof; *xenenthesis; yetzer* [Heb.]; *zoe [Gr.];*

**funds** *(n.)*: assets; bounty; capital; dollars; earnings; finances; gold; *holdings; income; jiggy; kitty;* lucre; money; net assets; opulence; prosperity; *quantities;* resources; substance; *treasury;* uberty; venture capital; wherewithal; *xenocurrency; yellow boy [Br.]; zillions [slang];*

**funeral** *(n.)*: *act;* burial; burying; ceremony; cortege; cemetery service; committal; dirge; exequies; entombment; feral; ~ service; gathering; graveside; *hearselike;* internment; joint ~; knell; kist; last rites; last post; memorial service; *necropolis;* obsequies; obit; procession; planting; quieting; requiem; service; train; *taps;* undertaking; viaticum; *visitation;* wake; *xat; yizkor* [Heb.]; *Zug* [G.]; [*see* cemetery]

**funny** *(adj.)*: amusing; blast [slang]; comical; daft; droll; entertaining; foolish; goofy; humorous; hilarious; hysterical; *insane;* jokey; jesting; knee-slapping; kooky; laughable; mirthful; nimble-witted; nutty; outrageous; preposterous; quick-witted; quacked; ridiculous; silly; side-splitting; tongue-and-cheek; uproarious; *vivifying;* witty; whimsical; *xtry.;* yare-handed; zany; [*see* strange, *Ant.* fearsome]

**fur** *(n.)*: animal ~; bristles; coat; down; *ermine;* fuzz; *genet;* hair; *imitation ~;* jaguar; kalgan; *lambskin;* mane; *mink; nebris;* oose; pile; pelage; pelt; qiviut; *rabbit;* shag; *timmer;* undercoat; vair; *wool; wolf; xerus; yak ~; zibeline;*

    **Kinds of furs**: Australian seal; bearskin; beaver; chincilla; dogskin; ermine; fox; genet; horsehair; imitation fur; jaguar; koala skin; leopard; mink; mohair; nutria; otter; possum fur; qiviut; rabbit; raccoon; sable; tigerskin; wolf; yak fir; zibeline.

**furious** *(adj.)*: angry; apoplectic; boiling; beside oneself; cross; disgusted; enraged; fuming; galled; hot; infuriated; jumping mad; *kindled;* livid; mad; nettled; outraged; perturbed; quick-tempered; raging; steaming; ticked off; upset; violent; wroth; *xerothermic; yond* [arch.]; *zealousy [arch.];*

**furlough** *(n.)*: absence; break; *coming home;* day off; excursion; flight; getaway; holiday; itineration; journey; *keeping in touch;* leave; liberty [nav.]; *misadventure; night voyage; off; personal day; periplus;* quest; retreat; shore leave [nav.]; sabbatical; sojourn; time off (-away); tour; trip; *travel; undertaking;* vacation; week off; *xenization; yong* [arch.]; zugunruhe;

**furnace** *(n.)*: athanor; burner; brick-kiln; calcar; *device;* electric oven; forge; grate; glass~; heater; hypocaust [Rom.]; incinerator; *jet;* kettle- ~; kiln; limekiln; muffle; *nut coal;* oil burner; oast; oven; potbelly stove; *quartz heater;* range; stove; tunnel-kiln; uniform-heat ~; *vulcan;* wind- ~; *xylophyrography; yellow-hot; zap;*

**furnish** *(v.)*: assign; award; accommodate; bestow; confer; deliver; equip; endow; fit; give; hand (over); impart; *jettison;* kit; *lend;* lavish upon; make available; *non-retention;* outfit; provide; provision; *quicken;* render; supply; transfer; *unhand;* vest; *weigh;* xfer; yield; *zip;*

**furrow** *(n.)*: arroyo; burrow; channel; dado; depression; excavation; flute; groove; hollow; impression; *jheel [Ind.]*; kerf; kloof; leat; microgroove; notch; opening; pleat; quirk; rut; slot; trench; U-groove; vallation; ward; wrinkle; *x-groove;* yawn; *zanja;*
**furry** *(adj.)*: *abounding in fur;* bushy; *cuddly;* downy; *ermine-lined;* fur-covered; fuzzy; fleecy; fluffy; *gris;* hairy; hirsute; *imitation fur-covered; jubate;* kempy; lanate; maned; nappy; over-fuzzy; pilous *quiff;* really fuzzy; soft; shaggy; tufty; unshorn; villous; wooly; *xerasia; yellow-haired; zapata;*
**fury** *(n.)*: anger; boiling; choler; displeasure; enragement; fuming; gall; hotness; infuriation; *jealous rage; kindling;* lividness; madness; *nettling;* outrage; perturbation; quick-temperament; rage; storminess; *steaming;* temper; uproar; *venting;* wrath; *xerothermia; yelling;* zealousness;
**fuse** *(v.)*: amalgamate; bond; connect; combine; deliquesce; *entangle;* form one; glue; *hold;* integrate; intermix; join; knit; liquesce; merge; meld; *node; overmix;* put together; *queach [arch.];* run together; solder; smelt; synthesize; temper; unite; *voluble;* wed; weld; *xenograft; yerk together; zip together;*
**fusion** *(n.)*: admixture; blend; combination; deliquescence; elixir; fusing; gluing; hookup; intermixture; joining; knitting; *linking;* merging; meld; *node;* oneness; putting together; *queaching [arch.];* reaction; synthesis; tempering; union; *volubility;* wedding; welding; *xanthate;* yanggoma; *zipping together;*
**fuss** *(n.)*: argument; big deal; bickering; complaint; controversy; dispute; exception; fight; gripe; hassle; impugnation; jangling; kicking; lodge a complaint; *murmuring;* nitpicking; objection; protest; quarrel; ruckus; spat; strife; to-do; *upset;* variance; wrangling; *x-fire;* yawp; *za-zum [Rus.];*
**fuss** *(v.)*: argue; bicker; contend; dispute; *entangle;* fight; gainsay; hassle; impugn; jangle; kick up dust; lock horns [slang]; make fur fly; nitpick; object; protest; quibble; roil; strive; tiff; *upset;* vie; wrangle; *xuld [arch.];* yell; zing;
**fussy** *(adj.)*: assiduous; busy; choosy; detailed; difficult; exacting; finicky; fastidious; *grumpy;* hard to please; inflexible; implacable; *just so;* keen; *laborious;* meticulous; nit-picking; over-finicky; picky; particular; quiddle; restless; selective; tough to please; *unreasonable; vigilant; wearying; xuld [arch.];* yare; *zero tolerance;* [Ant. fancy-free]
**futile** *(adj.)*: airy; barren; counterproductive; devoid of fruit; empty; fruitless; good for nothing; hopeless; ineffective; just no good; kooky; lousy; meaningless; non-effective; otiose; pointless; quisquillous; *ridiculous;* sorry; Sisyphean; trifling; to no avail; useless; unproductive; unavailing; vain; worthless; *x'ed;* yieldless; *zero effectiveness;* [Ant. functional]
**futility** *(n.)*: absurdity; barrenness; counterproductivity; dead letter; emptiness; fruitlessness; *goose egg;* hopelessness; ineffectiveness; *just no good;* kookiness; lousiness; meaninglessness; non-effectiveness; otiosity; pointlessness; *quisquillous; ridiculousness;* sorriness; trifle; uselessness; unproductiveness; vanity; worthlessness; *x'ed;* yieldlessness; *zero;* [Ant. functionality]
**future** *(adj.)*: approaching; beyond-the-present; coming; destined; ever-hastening; eventual; forthcoming; far-off; going-to-happen; hastening; impending; impending; just around the corner; *kingdom come;* later; long-range; *moving toward;* nearing; one-day; planned; prospective; pending; *quickening; reaching ahead; someday;* subsequent; scheduled; soon-to-come; to be; upcoming; ulterior; ultimate; very near ~; waiting; *xpire;* yet to come; *zooming ahead;*
**future** *(n.)*: awaiting day; beyond the present; coming; destiny; ever-hastening moment; finality; *going on;* hastening day; impending time; *just around the corner; kingdom come;* later; lot; morrow; near ~; offing; pending day; predestination; *quantum leap; remaining years;* someday; tomorrow; time to come; upcoming time; very near ~; waiting; *xpire;* years to come; *zillions of years from now;*
**fuzz** *(n.)*: animal fur; bushiness; coat; down; eiderdown; fluff; fur; *gris;* hair; *imitation fur; jaguar;* kalgan; *lint; mane;* nap; oose; peach ~; pile; qiviut; *rabbit;* shag; *timmer;* undercoat; vair; *wool; xerus;* yak fur; zibeline;
**fuzzy** *(adj.)*: *abounding in fur;* bushy; *coat; cute;* downy; *eiderdown;* furry; fluffy; *gris;* hairy; *indefinite; jubate;* kempy; lanate; *maned;* nappy; over-furry; pilous; plush; *quiff;* really furry; soft; tufty; *unshorn;* velvety; wooly; *xerasia; yellow-haired; zapata;* [*see* indistinct]

# G

**gadget** *(n.)*: apparatus; *bauble;* contrivance; contraption; device; *equipment;* flumadiddle; gizmo; hoosywhatsy; instrument; implement; jiggumbob; kickumbob; labor-saving device; mechanism; nignay; object; piece of equipment; *quaint object; the rage;* so-and-so; thingamajig; tool; utensil; *vade mecum* [L.]; widget; whirligig; x-device; you-know-what; *Zeug [G.];*

**gag** *(n.)*: antic; big joke; *canard* [F.]; *daftness; eccentricity;* funny; goofy prank; humor; hoax; *insult;* joke; kidding; levity; *madness;* nifty; *one-liner;* prank; practical joke; *quip;* ruse; sport; trick; *utterance; vexation;* witticism; *xuld [arch.];* yock; zinger;

**gag** *(v.)*: asphyxiate; block; choke; deprive of oxygen; extinguish; *finish off;* garrote; *hush;* inhibit; jugulate; kill; *lynch;* muffle; *nullify;* obstruct; plug up; quackle; repress; retch; smother; suffocate; throttle; *undo; void;* whirken [arch.]; *xuld [arch.];* yote; zeroize;

**gaiety** *(n.)*: afterglow; bliss; cheerfulness; delight; exhilaration; felicity; gladness; happiness; intoxication; joyfulness; *keenness;* lightheartedness; merriment; *niceness;* overjoy; pleasantness; *queme;* rejoicing; sunniness; thrill; *uplifted; vivacity;* winsomeness; *xanadu; yeah!;* zestfulness; [*Ant.* grouchiness]

**gain** *(n.)*: advantage; benefit; capital ~; cumulation; dividend; earnings; favor; gross profit; growth; help; increase; jump; killing; *lucre;* makings; net; obtainment; profit; *quittal;* return; reward; strengthening; takings; use; upsurge; *usury;* vantage; winnings; x-div; yield; *zillions;*

**gain** *(v.)*: acquire; attain; bag [slang]; buy; benefit; catch; develop; expand; find; get; have; increase; jump; kep; land; make off with; nab; net; obtain; procure; profit; *quoff;* receive; seize; take; usurp; *vest;* win; xfer; yank; zip away; [*Ant.* give]

**gainful** *(adj.)*: advantageous; beneficial; conducive; constructive; *decent;* excellent; favorable; good; helpful; instrumental; *jim dandy;* keen; lucrative; money-making; nice; *outstanding;* profitable; *quality;* remunerative; rewarding; salutary; *terrific;* useful; valuable; worthwhile; xtry.; yieldful; *zillions;* [*Ant.* gainless]

**gainsay** *(v.)*: argue; battle; contradict; dispute; *engage;* fight; grapple with; hassle; impugn; jangle; kick up dust; lock horns [slang]; make fur fly; naysay; object; pick fight; quarrel; resist; squabble; tiff; *unharmonious;* vie; wrangle; *x-purposes;* yell; *zap;*

**gall** *(n.)*: audacity; acrimony; anger; brazenness; bitterness; contempt; disgust; effrontery; foulness; grudge; hatred; hostility; indignation; insolence; jangliness; kindlessness; loathing; malapertness; nerve; nastiness; odium; perturbation; *querulousness;* resentment; sullenness; *tetchiness;* umbrage; venom; wrath; *xenophobia; yuckiness;* zoilism;

**gallant** *(adj.)*: adventurous; brave; courageous; daring; dauntless; enterprising; fearless; gutsy; great-hearted; heroic; intrepid; jaunty; knightly; lion-hearted; manly; noble; obstinate; plucky; questful; *resolute;* spirited; stout; strong; tigerish; unflinching; unafraid; valorous; *wherewithal; xtry.;* yare; zealous; [*Ant.* gutless]

**gallantry** *(n.)*: adventurousness; bravery; courage; daring; enterprise; fearlessness; gumption; grit; guts; heroism; intrepidity; jauntiness; knightliness; lion-heartedness; manliness; nobleness; *obstinacy;* pluck; *quakeless; resolve;* stoutness; tigerishness; undauntedness; valor; *wherewithal;* xtry. courage; *yung* [Chin.]; *zealousness;* [*Ant.* gutlessness]

**gallery** *(n.)*: arcade; art ~; bank; colonnade; collection; deck; exhibition hall; finery; galleria; hall; *institution;* jube; *keep;* loggia; museum; *non-enclosed* repertory; outroom; passageway; *porch; quarterdeck;* room; stoa; terrace; *upper deck;* veranda; walkway; xyst; *zeta;*

**gallop** *(v.)*: *accelerate;* barrel; canter; charge; dash; *elan;* fly; go; hurtle; *interlope;* jog; *keep pace;* lope; move; *nimble; outrun;* pace; quicken; run; sprint; tear; *underway; velocity;* whiz; xfer; yern; zip;

**gallows** *(n.)*: *ansa;* bargus; capital punishment; dule tree; execution; framework; gibbet; hangman; hanging tree; instrument of punishment; *jubbet* [arch.]; *justice;* killing-device; *loop; maple tree; makeshift ~;* noose; necktie party; *oak tree;* potence; *qiviut;* rope; scaffold; Tyburn ~; tree; *upright; victim; walnut tree; yew tree; zein;*

**gamble** *(n.)*: action; bet; chance; definite chance; endangerment; fling; fluke; game; good chance; hope; imperilment; just a chance; known risk; long shot; *maybe; non-guaranteed;* outside chance; possibility; qualified risk; risk; shot (in the dark); toss of the dice; uncertainty; venture; wager; *xtry. chance; yet possible; zone;*

**gamble** *(v.)*: attempt; bet; chance; depone; *dice;* endanger; *faites vos jeux* [F.]; go out on a limb; game; hazard; imperil; jeff; *kitty;* lay bets; make bet; *not abstain; opportune;* play (the odds); punt; place bet; *quick-money;* risk; roll the dice; stake; take chance; up the ante; venture; wager; *xfer; Yarborough; zealously ~;*

**gambler** *(n.)*: ante-placer; bettor; blackleg; carrow; chance-taker; cardshark; dice-roller; endangerer; *faites vos jeux [F.];* gamer; gamester; hazarder; high roller; *indulger;* jeopardizer; *kitty;* layer of bets; maker of bets; noddy; odds-player; player; petty ~; punter; *quick-money;* risk-taker; slotter; tinhorn; *up the ante;* venturer; wagerer; *xiaoren; Yarborough;* zealous card player;

**gambling** *(n.)*: *ante;* betting; chance-taking; casino-hopping; dicing; endangering; *faites vos jeux [F.];* gaming; hazardry; illegal ~; jeopardizing; *kitty;* lottery; making bets; noddying; odds-playing; playing; petty ~; quinella; roulette-playing; sporting; staking; sortilege; *sweepstakes;* taking bets; *up the ante;* vice; wagering; *x-factor;* Yarborough; *zeal for ~;*

    **Gambling Games**: Asian stud; bingo; blackjack; craps; dead pool; faro; gilet; high-low; jack; keno; loo; lotto; mambo stud; noddy; old maid; poker; quinze; roulette; slot machine; two-up; ultimate Texas hold'em; *vingt-et-un;* wapee; xoc dia;

**game** *(n.)*: amusement; board ~; competition; contest; diversion; entertainment; face-off; go [Br.]; horseplay; *interplay; jacks;* kemp; knockabout [Br.]; *luctation* [arch.]; match; matchup; meet; *novelty; Olympics;* pastime; pull; playoff; *quoits;* round; recreation; set; sport; simulation; struggle; tournament; *upmanship; video ~;* word ~; war(fare); *X and O's; yoking* [Scot.]; *zero work;*

    **Games**: arm-wrestling; backgammon; checkers; chess; dodgeball; English draughts; four square; grounders; hopscotch; I spy; jacks; kickball; leapfrog; marbles; nine men's morris; obsession; paddle ball; queenie, queenie, who's got the ball; ringtoss; stickball; tag; tic-tac-toe; under over; video game; wall ball; X and Os; Yahtzee®; zonk;

**gang** *(n.)*: amassment; army; band; clique; drove; detachment; *everybody;* faction; group; horde; ingathering; jam [slang]; junta; kit [coll.]; lot; mob; number; outfit; pack; peer group; posse; quantity; ring; squad; troop; unit; variety; wisp; *xiaoren; yobs; zhlubs;*

**gangly** *(adj.)*: awkward; bumbling; clumsy; dowdy; *étourderie* [F.]; fumbly; gawky; heavy-handed; inelegant; jumbly; klutzy; lumbering; maladroit; non-graceful; oafish; plumbeous; *quirky;* rangy; spindly; thin; ungraceful; ungainly; *vexatious;* wooden; *xtry.;* yokelish; zhlubby; [Ant. graceful]

**gap** *(n.)*: aperture; breach; crack; chink; cleft; cleuch; defile; *excavation;* fissure; gape; hole; interruption; interlude; incavation; jaw-hole; krater; lacuna; maw; moat; notch; nullah; opening; parting; pause; *quarry-pit;* recess; rift; ravine; split; trench; *umbilicus;* void; valley; wantage; wadi; *x-ing;* yawn; zanja;

**gape** *(v.)*: *amazed;* be agape; crack; eye; face (down); gaze; gaup; gawk; hang open; *jaw;* ken; look; make eyes; notice; open mouth; pore; *quick look;* rent; stare; take in; *unbelief; view;* watch; *x-ray vision;* yawn; zero in;

**garage** *(n.)*: attached ~; building; bay; bus shed; *barn;* carport; deteached ~; enclosure; four-car ~; garden shed; housing; hangar; *institution;* joined ~; *keep; lift;* mechanic; *nook;* one-car ~; port; quadriplex; repair station; structure; shop; shed; two-car ~; utility shed; van shed; *wing; xfer;* yardhouse; *zone;*

**garbage** *(n.)*: abatis; *brush; bag;* chaff; debris; *eliminate;* filth; *getting rid of; heap; items;* industrial waste; junk; ket; litter; mullock; *nihil [L.]; nuclear waste;* offscouring; offal; *pile;* quisquillous; recyclables; rubbish; refuse; sweepings; scrap; trash; unwanted items; vuilnis; waste; wastrel; *x-barrel; yucky; zero value;*

**garbage can** *(v.)*: *aluminun trashcan;* basket; bin; can; circular file [joc.]; container; dustbin; *eliminate; foul;* garbage bin; *holder; indoor trash bin; industrial bin;* junk bin; *kitchen garbage;* litter bin; *metal dumpster; nihil [L.];* office garbage; *pushcart; quisquillous;* receptacle; recycling bin; rubbish bin; skip; trashcan; trash bin; *unwanted items; vessel;* waste(paper) basket; wheelie bin; *x-barrel;* yard bin; *zero out;*

**garden** *(n.)*: alameda; *area;* bean patch; bowling green; botanical ~; cabbage-patch; Dutch ~; English ~; flower ~; grove; herb ~; hanging ~; Italian ~; Japanese ~; kitchen ~; lettuce patch; market ~; native ~; orchard; Oriental ~; (pea) patch; parterre; pleasance; *paradise;* queach; rose ~; seed plot; *spinach patch;* terrarium; tea ~; *udo patch;* vegetable ~; walled ~; winter ~; *xeriscape®;* yam patch; zen ~;

**gardener** *(n.)*: arboriculturalist; *botanist;* cultivator; *dendrologist;* electro-horticulturalist; floriculturalist; groundskeeper; green thumb; hoer; horticulturalist; *individual; jardinière* [F. fem.]; keeper; landscaper; market ~; nurseryman; orchardist; olericulturalist; planter; pruner; plantsman; *qualified laborer;* rose ~; *servant;* toiler; *underling;* viniculturalist; weeder; *xeriscape®;* yardman; *zucchini;*

**garment** *(n.)*: apparel; bedizenment; clothes; drapes; dress; enrobing; finery; garb; habiliments; item of clothing; *jacket;* knitwear; livery; leisurewear; *menswear; national dress;* outfit; *palliament [arch.]; quaintry* [arch.]; raiment; suit; threads [slang]; togs [pl.]; *uniform;* vestment; wear; *XL; yelek [Turk.]; zari;*

**garnish** *(v.)*: adorn; bedeck; *clothe;* deck; decorate; embellish; fancify; grace; habilitate; improve; jazz up; kit; *let be adorned;* make prettier; *nicer;* ornament; prettify; *quaintise* [arch.]; render lovely; spruce up; trim; *use ornaments;* vest; *wear; xtry.; yclad [arch.]; zizz;*

**gas** *(n.)*: aeriform substance; bottled ~; compressed ~; *defusing substance;* ether; exhaust; fumes; flatulence; gaseous fumes; hot air; *hydrogen;* inert ~; ideal ~; *jumbo cloud;* knall- ~; *laughing ~; mustard ~;* natural ~; *out~;* plasma; *quarter tank;* real ~; *substance; tank; trace ~; unliquefied;* vapor; *water vapor; xenon;* yperite; *zip;* [*see* fuel]

    **Kinds of gases**: argon; butane; chlorine; diborane; ethane; fluorine; germanium; helium; hydrogen; isobutane; krypton; laughing ~; methane; mustard ~; nerve ~; nitrogen; oxygen; poison ~; propane; radon; silane; trimethylborane; ununoctium; VX; xenon; yperite;

**gaseous** *(adj.)*: aeriform; beclouded; cloudy; defusive; ethereal; fumy; gassy; hazy; inclouded; *jumbo cloud; KH instability; lowery;* misty; miasmal; nebulous; *obscure;* puffy; *qually [arch.];* reeky; smoky; turbid; uncompressed; vaporous; wispy; *xenon; yellowy cloud; zero solidity;*

**gasp** *(n.)*: aspiration; blubber; breath; choke; *draw;* expiration; *flag;* gulp; huff; inhalation; *jolt; keen;* laboring breath; *mutter;* noisy inhalation; *outblow;* pant; puff; *quill* [arch.]; respiration; swallow; snort; thunder; *use oxygen;* ventilation; wheeze; *xuld [arch.];* yolp; *zinger;*

**gasp** *(v.)*: aspirate; *breath;* catch breath; draw breath; emit breath; *flag;* gulp; huff; inhale; *jolt; keep breath;* labor to breathe; *mouth;* noisily inhale; *outblow;* pant; poof; puff; *quill* [arch.]; respirate; swallow; struggle for air; snort; take in air; *use oxygen;* ventilate; wheeze; *xuld [arch.];* yolp; *zinger;*

**gate** *(n.)*: access; backdoor; cellarway; door; entrance; entryway; front ~; gateway; hinged ~; ingate; jib-door; kissing-gate; liftgate; main ~; *notch;* outgate; postern; portal; quadrivalve; rear ~; swinging gate; turnstile; tail~; toll- ~; utility ~; vomitory; wicket; x-door; yate [Scot.]; *zariba gate;*

**gatekeeper** *(n.)*: armed guard; beefeater; cordon; doorkeeper; eunuch; footguard; guard; hyperaspist; jaga; keeper; lookout; musketeer; night watch(man); ostiary; porter; quarterman; rear-guard; sentry; sentinel; *trooper;* uniformed guard; vigil; watchman; *xiphos-bearer;* yeoman; *zoauve;*

**gather** *(v.)*: assemble; aggregate; accumulate; bring together; collect; convene; come together; converge; congregate; draw together; encounter; forgather; flock; group; huddle; in~; join; *knit;* link up; meet; *near;* overcrowd; pile up; *quorum;* regroup; rally; sheave; throng; unite; *visit;* work together; *x.;* yoke; *zone;*

**gathering** *(n.)*: assembly; bunch; body; conference; congregation; convention; drove; encounter; event; forgathering; group; get-together; horde; ingathering; jamboree; kit [coll.]; lot; meet(ing); number; overcrowding; people; party; quorum; regathering; reunion; rally; session; seminar; symposium; summit; turnout; throng; unit; *vestry;* weekly ~; *x.;* yoking; *zayat [Burm.];*

**gauge** *(v.)*: assess; benchmark; calculate; determine; evaluate; figure; gage; hypothesize; identify; judge; *know; log;* make an estimate; measure; *notion; oversee;* plumb; quantify; reckon; rate; size up; scope; test; *uncover;* valuate; weigh; *xenodiagnose; yeme; zazen;*

**gay** *(adj.)*: animated; blissful; cheery; delighted; exhilarated; felicitous; glad(some); happy; intoxicated; joyful; *keen;* lighthearted; merry; *nice;* overjoyed; pleased; *queme;* rejoicing; sunny; thrilled; uplifted; vivacious; winsome; *xtry. happy; yeah!* zestful; [*Ant.* glum]

**gaze** *(v.)*: *admire;* behold; contemplate; descry; examine; face; fix eyes on; glare; have a look; inspect; *just have a look;* keep in sight; look; muse; notice; observe; peer; pore; *quick look;* regard; stare; take in; *understand;* view; watch; *x-ray vision;* yawn; zero in;

**gazing-stock** *(n.)*: aberration; butt; clown; *dummy;* embarrassment; fool; gazingstock; *heterozygous;* idiot; jestingstock; *kink;* laughingstock; mocking-stock; *non-usual;* object of ridicule; peculiarity; queerity; *ridiculous;* sight; target; *unusual;* victim; weirdo; *xtry. oddity; yawed;* zany;

**gear** *(n.)*: articles; belongings; chattels; commodities; duffel; equipment; furnishings; goods; habiliments; items; *junk [slang];* kit; *load;* matter; needments; objects; paraphernalia; *quantity;* rigging; stuff; tackle; trappings; utensils; valuables; works; *xenenthesis; yannigan; zeug* [G.];

**gel** *(n.)*: *article;* batter; congelation; *distillation;* emulsion; *flummery;* gelation; hydrogel; incrassation; jelly; *konfyt [S. Afr.];* lump; material; maringue; *nonliquid; object;* pudding; pectization; *quiddany; reset;* substance; semifluid; thick semisolid; *unyielding; viscid; waulk;* xerogel; *Yokan [Jap.];* zet [dial.];

**gel** *(v.)*: *alter;* become hard; congeal; coagulate; densify; *enharden;* firm up; gelatinize; harden; incrassate; jell(y); jellify; knot; lump; make hard; *non-fluid;* obdure; pectize; quarle; *reset;* set; solidify; thicken; *unyielding; vary; waulk; xerogel;* yearn; zet [dial.];

**gem** *(n.)*: *amethyst;* baguette; cabochon; crown jewel; *diamond; emerald; fire opal;* gemstone; *heliotrope;* intaglio; jewel; *karats; ligure;* mesomeles; navette; *onyx;* precious stone; *quartz;* rock; stone; *treasure;* uvarovite; *valuable; wealth;* xtal.; yag; *zircon;*
    **Kinds of gems**: amethyst; beryl; carbuncle, diamond, emerald, fire opal; garnet; heliotrope; iolite; jacinth; jasper; kyanite; ligure; marquis; onyx, opal; pearl; peridot, *quartz;* ruby, sapphire, topaz, turquoise; uvarovite; vesuvianite; water sapphire; yag; zirconium;

**gene** *(n.)*: allele; biological information; *blueprint;* chromosome; dominant ~; DNA; *endowment;* genome; hereditary characteristic; idiogram; information; *jus soli [L.];* karyomere; *lineal;* makeup; nucleotide; operon; poly~; *quarter;* recessive ~; RNA; structural ~; trans~; *unit;* unifactorial; *vein; whakapapa [Maori];* x-chromosome; y-chromosome; zygote;

**genealogy** *(n.)*: ancestry; background; bloodline; *clan;* derivation; descent; extraction; family tree; generation; heredity; history; *item; jus soli [L.];* kindred; list(ing); lineage; line; *mores;* nibiliary; origin; pedigree; *qualifications;* roots; record; source; traduction; *unabridged listing; vein; written ~; x-linked; yoni [Skr.]; zet [dial.];*

**general** *(adj.)*: all-purpose; broad; common; comprehensive; diversified; expansive; far-reaching; *for all;* generic; generalized; highly generalized; inclusive; *joint; known;* largely; main; nonspecific; open; ordinary; public; quaquaversal; regular; shared; typical; usual; unrestricted; universal; *very ~;* wide(spread); *x-type;* yare; *zero specifics;*

**general** *(n.)*: adjutant ~; brigadier ~; *brass;* commander; *director;* executive officer; five-star ~; field marshal; generalissimo; high ranking officer; head; *intendant; jarl; knight;* leader; lieutenant ~; military commander; *nobleman;* officer; one-star ~; *principal; quondam ~;* risaldar; *rank;* strategist; senior officer; three-star ~; *top brass; unmatched; V.I.P.;* warlord; *xanbika* [Chin.]; *yokemaster; zayim;*

**generality** *(n.)*: axiom; broad statement; cliché; dictum; *expression;* formula; generalization; *highly generalized;* inference; *judgment; koine;* law; maxim; neology; oversimplification; principle; *quotation;* rule; simplification; stereotype; truth; truism; universal truth; *verse; the* whole; *xenophonia; Yogism; zeteticism;*

**generalize** *(v.)*: axiomatic; broaden; *condense;* declutter; ease; *formula;* generalise [Br.]; *help;* improve; *just made easier;* keep simple; logicize; make easier; *non-specific;* over~; oversimplify; pare down; *quotation;* reduce to simple terms; simplify; stereotype; take a broad view; universalize; view simplistically; widen; xel [arch.]; yet ~d; zero confusion;

**generate** *(v.)*: assemble; breed; build; create; cause; develop; engender; form; give; hatch; *have;* institute; initiate; *job;* knock together; *labor;* make; manufacture; *newly formed;* originate; output; produce; *quicken;* raise; reproduce; spawn; shape; turn out; *upbuild; volts;* work up; *xenogenesis;* yield; *zygogenesis;*

**generation** *(n. beginning)*: advent; birth; begetting; beginning; creation; delivery; debut; entrance; formation; genesis; geniture; hatching; initiation; *jump off; kickoff; launching;* making; naissance; origination; production; quickening; rise; spawning; start; triggering; ushering in; *visitation; welcoming;* xenogenesis; yielding; zygogeneis;

**generation** *(n. wave of descendants)*: age group; *babies;* children; continuation; contemporaries; disemination; *enfant [F.]; future ~;* group; *heirs; inheritors; junior; kin;* lifetime; *little ones;* multiplication; next ~; older ~; progeny; propagation; peer group; *quinquennarian; relatives;* successive ~; spreading; times; *third ~; upcoming ~; vein;* wave; xfer of reigns; younger ~; *zon [dial.];*

**generic** *(adj.)*: all-purpose; basic; common; *dull;* everyday; featureless; general; ho-hum; inelaborate; *just regular; known;* lackluster; mundane; nonspecific; ordinary; plain; quotidian; regular; simple; standard; *typical;* unadorned; universal; *vague; wide;* x-brand; *yawnish; zestless;*

**generosity** *(n.)*: altruism; bigheartedness; benefaction; charitableness; do-goodism; extravagance; freehandedness; *favor;* giving; generousness; high-mindedness; *investment; joyful giving;* kindness; liberality; largesse; magnanimity; munificence; nobleness; open-handedness; patronage; philanthropy; *quantities;* richness; selflessness; *thoughtfulness;* unselfishness; *virtuousness;* warmheartedness; *xenophilia; yieldedness;* zealous support;

**generous** *(adj.)*: ample; altruistic; bountiful; big-hearted; benevolent; charitable; diffuse; extravagant; free-handed; giving; great-hearted; handsome; high-minded; *ingenuous; joyful;* kind; liberal; large-handed; lavish; magnanimous; munificent; noble-minded; open-handed; philanthropic; quick-to-give; rich; selfless; self-sacrificing; *thoughtful;* unselfish; ungrudging; *virtuous;* warmhearted; *xenial; yielded; zealous;* [Ant. grudging]

**genesis** *(n.)*: advent; beginning; creation; dawn; establishment; formation; generation; homo~; inception; jump off; kickoff; launching; making; naissance; origin(ation); production; *quickening;* rise; start; take-off; *unveiling; verge; welcoming; xeno~; yielding; zygo~;*

**genetic** *(adj.)*: ancestral; biological; chromosomal; DNA; elemental; foundational; gentilitious; hereditary; inherited; *joining;* kin-related; lineal; *makeup; natural;* operonic; parental; phyletic; *quarter;* racial; stock-related; *tribal; unilineal; vein; white race;* x-linked; y-linked; zoetic;

**genius** *(n. brilliance)*: acumen; ability; brilliance; cleverness; dexterity; efficacy; endowment; farsightedness; giftedness; highbrowism; intellect; judiciousness; knack; *logic;* mental capacity; nimble-wittedness; *on the ball;* perceptiveness; quickness; *reasoning;* sharpness; smarts; talent; ultra-braininess; virtuosity; wisdom; *xenagogy; yaup; zippiness;*

**genius** *(n. smart person)*: academic; brain [slang]; cogitator; deviser; Einstein; figurer; guru; highbrow; intellectual; inventor; *judger; knower;* luminary; mastermind; nonpareil; *oracular;* prodigy; quick-thinker; rocket scientist [slang]; scholar; thinker; *ultra-smart;* virtuoso; whiz (kid); wizard; *xenagogue; yauper; zippy;*

**genocide** *(n.)*: annihilation; butchering; blotting out; carnage; *death camp;* extermination; eradication; expunction; "final solution" [Nazi]; great slaughter; holocaust; *injustice; jaws of death;* killing (off); liquidation; mass killing; massacre; *nullification;* obliteration; purging; pogrom; quenching; *ruination;* slaying; snuff out; slaughter; termination; *undoing; vaporization;* wiping out; xenocide; *yanking down; zapping;*

**Gentile** *(n.)*: *alien;* barbarian; *Canaanite;* dog [derog.]; *European; foreigner;* Greek; *goyim* [Heb.]; *habitué; immigrant;* Japhethite; *Kelt; lost man; Moabite;* non-Jew; outsider; pig [derog.]; *peregrine;* Philistine; *quidam; remote;* stranger; swine; shegetz [both derog.]; *tramontane;* uncircumcised; *visitor; WASP;* xenic; *yonder; Zidonian;*

**gentle** *(adj.)*: affable; benign; calm; cautious; delicate; easy-going; forbearing; gracious; good-natured; humane; inobtrusive; judicious; kind; lamblike; light-handed; mild(-mannered); non-harsh; nice; *obliging;* placid; quiet; ruthful; soft; sweet; tame; tender; unagitating; very careful; well-natured; *xtr. mild;* yielding; *zärtlich* [G.];

**gentleman** *(n.)*: aristocrat; *bloke;* chap; cavalier; dude; *earl;* fellow; guy; good fellow; human being; individual; joe [slang]; *kid; lord;* man; *nobleman;* one; person; perfect ~; *quadragenarian;* real ~; sir; seignor; *true blue;* upper-class man; *viscount;* well-manered man; *x-linked; yokel; zhlub;*

**gentleness** *(n.)*: affability; benignity; calmness; delicateness; easiness; forbearance; good-naturedness; humaneness; inobtrusiveness; judiciousness; kindness; kid gloves; lamblikeness; mildness; mansuetude; non-harshness; *obligingness;* placidity; quietness; ruth; softness; sweetness; tenderness; tameness; *unagitated; velvetiness;* well-naturedness; *xenium; yieldedness; zärtlich* [G.];

**genuine** *(adj.)*: authentic; bona fide; correct; dinkum; definite; earnest; exact; factual; good; heartfelt; honest; indubitable; justifiable; known; legitimate; *mean it;* never-failing; open; pukka; qualified; real; sincere; true; unerring; veritable; *well-tried; x-parent; yes;* 'zactly [dial.]; [Ant. guileful, gag]

**germ** *(n.)*: *ameoba;* bug; bacteria; cell; *coccus; disease;* E. coli; fomite; foreign body; germen; hybrid pathogen; infection; *jot;* kernel; *listeria;* microorganism; microbe; *nanobacterium;* organism; pathogen; *Q fever;* rotifer; spore; superbug; super~; trypanosome; ultravirus; virus; *wee;* x-virus; yersinia; *zygote;*

**German** *(adj.)*: Alpine; *Bavarian;* Central European; *Deutsch* [G.]; *European;* East ~; *Fritz* [slang]; Germanic; Gothic; Hessian; Hanseatic; Indo-German; *Jerry* [slang]; *Kraut* [off.]; Low ~; Middle High ~; Nazi; *Ostrogoth;* Prussian; *Quadi;* Rhenish; Saxon; Teutonic; *Ulm;* Visigoth; West ~; *xanthochroid; Yach; Zwickau;*

**Germany** *(n.)*: Ashkenaz; *Berlin;* Bavaria; *country; Central Europe;* Deutschland [G.]; Empire; East ~; Fatherland; Federal Republic; Germania; Gomer; *Hesse;* Imperial ~; *Jerries* [slang]; *Jena;* Kaiserdom; *Leipzig; Mainz;* Nazi ~ [hist.]; Oldenburg; Prussia; *Quadi;* the Reich; *Saxony; Teutonic; Ulm; Visigoth; West ~* [hist.]; Weimar Republic [hist.]; Xanten; Yach; Zwickau;

   **German-speaking states**: Austria; Bavaria; E. Prussia; Hesse; Lower Saxony; Mecklenburg-Vorpommern; North Rhine-Westphalia; Prussia; Rhineland; Saxony; Silesia; Thuringia; Wurtemburg;

**germy** *(adj.)*: adulterated; bad; besmirched; contaminated; dirty; *earthy;* filthy; full of germs; germ-ridden; *harmful;* insanitary; infected; jarbled; kollowed; *loamy;* muddy; morbific; non-sterile; *oozy;* polluted; pathogenic; *queer; repugnant;* soiled; septic; tainted; unsanitary; unhygienic; vile; *welky; xysmic; yellow; zorch;*

**gestate** *(v.)*: *affect;* bring to fruition; conceive; carry; develop; educe; fabricate; grow; hatch; incubate; *juke; keep warm; largen;* make hatch; mature; nurture; *originate;* prepare; *quicken;* raise; sprout; *think of;* use incubator; *vegetate; warm; xeric; yarken; zazen;*

**gestation** *(n.)*: *anticipation; bigness;* conception; development; expectancy; formation; growth; gravidation; heaviness; incubation; *jumboize; klutziness; laden;* maturation; nine months; *outbreeding;* pregnancy; *quickening;* reproduction; ripening; sprouting; term; utero-gestation; *vivification;* waiting period; *xenogamy; young on the way; zygogenesis;*

**gesture** *(n.)*: action; beck; clue; cue; dactylology; *expressing;* finger-movement; gesticulation; hand motion; indication; *jab;* kinesics; *look;* movement; motion; nod; observable motion; prompt; *queue;* request; sign(al); token; use of sign-language; voiceless clue; wave; *xmission; yell; zealous bid;*

**gesture** *(v.)*: ask one to come; bid; beckon; cue; call; do motion; *express;* flag; give cue; gesticulate; hand-motion; indicate; *jab; knell;* let one know; motion; nod; observably motion; point; *queue;* request; sign(al); summon; tell; use sign-language; *urge;* voicelessly clue; wave; *xmit; yell; zealously bid;*

**get** *(v.)*: acquire; attain; buy; bag [slang]; catch; contract; develop; exact; fetch; find; gain; have; intercept; inherit; *include; jet;* keep; kep; land; make off with; nab; net; obtain; procure; *quoff;* retrieve; receive; reap; seize; take; usurp; *vest;* win; xfer; yank; zip away; [Ant. give]

**ghastly** *(adj.)*: alarming; blood-curdling; chilling; dreadful; eerie; frightful; grisly; gruesome; hair-raising; horrifying; intimidating; jarring; knee-knocking; lurid; morbid; nightmarish; ominous; petrifying; queer; repulsive; scary; terrifying; unnerving; *vexatious;* weird; *xenophobic;* yucky; zonky; [Ant. gorgeous]

**ghetto** *(n.)*: *alley;* barrio; bad neighborhood; city center; dive; dump; ethnic enclave; favela; *graffiti;* Hooverville; inner city; *Judengasse* [G.]; *Karjan* [Morocco]; *Lusnynai* [Lithuania]; minority neighborhood; midtown; *neighborhood; Orangi Town* [Pakistan]; poor neighborhood; *quartier* [F.]; run-down neighborhood; skid row; shantytown; slum; *trailer park;* urban dump; *villas miseria* [Argentina]; wrong side of the tracks; *x-sector; yard; zone;*

**ghost** *(n.)*: apparition; banshee; cacodemon; duppy; disembodied spirit; doppelganger; entity; eidolon; fetch; ghoul; haunt; haint; incorporiety; jumby; *kelpie;* lemures; manes; nonmaterial being; orc; phantom; phantasm; poltergeist; quickened spirit; revenant; spook; spirit; specter; *taunter;* unclean spirit; undead; visitant; wraith; *xenenthesis; yaksha* [Ind.]; zumby; [see spirit; demon; trace]

**ghostly** *(adj.)*: abnormal; asomatous; bizarre; creepy; dreadful; ethereal; eerie; eldritch; frightful; fey; ghastly; ghostlike; haunted; incorporeal; jarring; knee-knocking; lurid; morbid; macabre; nightmarish; ominous; paranormal; queer; *repulsive;* spooky; spectral; supernatural; terrifying; unnatural; unearthly; vaporous; wraithlike; *xenophobic; ydrad* [arch.]; zonic;

**giant** *(n.)*: Anakim; big ~; cyclops; colossus; *demon;* ettin; Fomorian; giantess [fem.]; Goliath; hulk; immense ~; jotun [Scand.]; king-sized brute; large man; monster; Nephilim [pl.]; ogre; ogress [fem.]; powerhouse; polyphemus; *quantitative; rotund;* stone ~; titan; *ugly ~; villain; whopping ~;* xiphopagus; Ymir; Zuzim;

**giant** *(adj.)*: astronomical; big; colossal; disproportionate; enormous; fantastic; great; gigantic; gargantuan; huge; humongous; immense; jumbo-sized; king-size; large; massive; mammoth; monstrous; *noteworthy;* oversize; prodigious; quantitative; rotund; sizable; substantial; tremendous; titanic; *unbelievable;* voluminous; vast; whopping; weighty; XXL; *Ymir; zaftig;*

**gift** *(n.)*: award; alms; bestowal; blessing; bequest; contribution; donation; endowment; favor; gratuity; giveaway; grant; handsel; impartation; *joy-giving;* kindness; liberality; lagniappe; largess; munificence; nicety; offering; present; *quality ~;* reward; surprise; tip; tribute; *unselfishness;* vouchsafement; white elephant ~; xenium; *yeff* [arch.]; *zealous support;* [see grace]

**gimmick** *(n.)*: attention-getter; artifice; beguilement; con; device; deception; ensnarement; flam; guile; hoax; instrument; japery; knavery; little game; maneuver; nobbling; outfoxing; ploy; *quiblin* [arch.]; ruse; stunt; sleight; trick; untruth; verneuking; wile; *xuld* [arch.]; yentzing; zinger;

**girder** *(n.)*: *angle-iron;* beam; crossbeam; double-T beam; extrusion beam; futtock; *girt;* H-beam; I-beam; joist; knee-rafter; lierne; metal; *non-galvanized ~; one-by-four; plank; queen-post;* rafter; rib; steel ~; strut; stud; support beam; tubular ~; universal beam; V-beam; W-beam ~; x-beam; y-bar; z-bar;

**girl** *(n.)*: abigail; babe; belle; beauty; colleen [Ire.]; cutie; *child;* damsel; *effeminate;* female; gal; handmaid(en); *inamorata;* jane [slang]; *kid;* lass; miss; maid(en); nymph [poet.]; *one;* peri; princess [slang]; *quedam* [arch.]; rose [slang]; *sister;* school~; sylph; teenybopper; tomato [slang]; *unmanly;* virgin; *woman; x-chromosome;* young lady (-thing); *zitella* [It.]; [*Ant.* guy]

**girlfriend** *(n.)*: admirer; beloved; coquette; darling; *endeared;* fiancée; flame; girl; gal; honey; inamorata; *Juliette;* jane [slang]; kitten [slang]; lass; lady friend; maiden; mistress; *nubility; one;* paramour; *quedom [arch.];* romantic attachment; sweetheart; spark; true love; *unmarried;* valentine; woman; *x-chromosome;* young lady; *zitella* [It.]; [*Ant.* guy]

**girlish** *(adj.)*: adolescent; *beautiful;* childish; cute; charming; dollish; *ever-womanly;* feminine; girl-like; hastive; immature; juvenile; kiddish; little; maidenly; nubile; *over-young;* puerile; *quite young; ravishing;* sweet; tender; unmanly; vernal; womanly; *weak; x-chromosome;* youthful; *zero-experience;*

**gist** *(n.)*: *attributes;* basic idea; crux; drift; essence; fundamentality; general idea; gravamen; heart; idea; jet; kernel; lifeblood; meaning; nub; *ontology;* pith; quintessence; root; substance; summation; thumbnail; thing; thrust; tenor; *underneath;* vitals; *warp and woof; xenenthesis; yetzer* [Heb.]; *zoe [Gr.];*

**give** *(v.)*: assign; administer; afford; award; bestow; cede; contribute; commit; confer; dole; deal; distribute; deliver; donate; endue; endow; fork over [slang]; furnish; grant; hand (over); issue; impart; *jettison;* kit; lavish; mete; *not retain;* offload; offer; outfit; part with; provide; pay; pass on; present; *quicken;* relinquish; remit; render; relay; surrender; supply; transfer; unhand; vouchsafe; vest; *weigh;* xfer; yield; *zip;* [*Ant.* get]

**giver** *(n.)*: assigner; awarder; bestower; contributor; conferrer; donor; endower; furnisher; granter; hander (over); issuer; imputer; imparter; *jettison;* kitter; lavisher; meter; *non-retention;* offerer; outfitter; provider; presenter; *quickener;* relinquisher; renderer; relayer; supplier; transferer; tither; unhander; vester; *weigher;* xfer; yielder; *zip;* [*Ant.* getter]

**glad** *(adj.)*: appreciative; blissful; cheerful; delighted; exuberant; felicitous; gladsome; gay; gleeful; happy; intoxicated; joyful; keen; lighthearted; merry; *nice;* overjoyed; pleased; *queme;* rejoicing; sunny; satisfied; thrilled; uplifted; *vivacious;* well-pleased; *xtry. happy;* yeasty; zestful; [*Ant.* grievous]

**gladness** *(n.)*: appreciation; bliss; cheer; delight; exuberance; felicity; gaity; glee; happiness; intoxication; jollity; *keenness;* lightheartedness; merriment; *niceness;* overjoy; pleasure; *queme;* rejoicing; sunniness; satisfaction; thrill; *uplifted; vivacity;* winsomeness; *xtry. happiness; yeah!;* zestfulness; [*Ant.* grief]

**glamorize** *(v.)*: *adorn;* beautify; *classy;* dress up; embellish; fancify; glam up; *hold up;* idealize; jazz up; *keen; lift up;* make glamorous; *new-vamp;* ornament; play up; present titillatingly; *quaintize;* romanticize; sensationalize; titivate; upgrade; wow; *xtry.; yarken;* zizzify;

**glamorous** *(adj.)*: attractive; alluring; beautiful; captivating; dazzling; elegant; exciting; flamboyant; fascinating; glittering; glitzy; gorgeous; high style; impressive; jazzy; killing; larger-than-life; modish; nice-looking; operatic; pleasing; quite nice; radiant; ritzy; showy; stylish; sophisticated; sensational; stunning; tawdry; tantalizing; uptown; vogue; wooing; xtry.; you-beaut [Aus.]; zizzy;

**glamour** *(n.)*: allure; beauty; captivation; dazzle; elegance; flamboyance; glam; glitz; high style; impressiveness; jazziness; *kick;* luster; modishness; *niceness;* ooh-laa-laa; pizzazz; *quaintrelle* [arch.]; radiance; style; sensation; tawdriness; tantalization; *uptown;* vogue; *wooing; xtry.; you-beat [Aus.];* zizz;

**glance** *(n.)*: *action;* beholding; casting of eyes; *coup d'oeil* [F.]; descrying; eyebeam; fleeting look; glimpse; *honing in on;* inspection; *just a look;* keek; look; momentary look; *notice;* oeiliad; peep; peek; quick look; *regard;* side-~; taking a quick look; *understand;* view; *watch; x-ray vision; yeme; zeroing in;*

**glance** *(v.)*: *acknowledge;* behold; cast eyes; descry; espy; eye; *find;* glimpse; *hone in on;* inspect; just quickly look; keek; look; make out; notice; note; observe; ogle; peek; *quick look;* regard; see; spy; take in; *understand;* view; watch; *x-ray vision; yeme;* zero in; [*see* look]

**glare** *(n.)*: angry look; black countenance; *countenance;* dirty look; evil eye; *frown;* glower; heavy countenance; *ill-humored;* joyless expression; *kick the dirt;* lour; lower; *the* look; miserable expression; nasty look; offended look; penetrating look; *quite displeased;* rictus; simagre; scowl; *tearful; umbrage; very upset;* wrinkled brow; *xtr. sad; yucky; zero joy;*

**glare** *(v.)*: angrily ~; *behold;* catch sight of; descry; eye; face (down); fleer; glower; *hone in on;* inspect; *judgment;* ken; leer; look; make eyes; notice; outstare; ogle; peer; *quick look;* recognize; stare; scowl; *take in; unkind eye;* view; wrinkle brow; *x-ray vision; yeme;* zero in;

**glaring** *(adj.)*: apparent; blatant; conspicuous; distinct; evident; flagrant; gross; highly visible; *intentional;* just plain to see; kenspeckle; *lucid;* manifest; noticeable; obvious; open; overt; plain; quite obvious; recognizable; salient; *transparent;* unmistakable; visible; well-defined; *x-parent; yeme [arch.]; zenithal;*

**glassy** *(adj.)*: *aventurine;* blank; crystal; dull; enamelar; flat; glasslike; glossy; hyaline; hyaloid; inexpressive; jaspery; *keen;* lucent; milky; non-opaque; opalescent; polished; *pearly;* quasi-transparent; reflective; smooth; sleek; translucent; unrough; vitreous; wet-looking; *xtl; yeme [arch.]; zeuxite;*

**gleam** *(n.)*: aura; brilliance; coruscation; dazzle; emanation; flicker; glint; glimmer; *halo;* irradiance; *jet; kindle;* luster; *majesty;* nitency; *overlight; phosphorescence; quivering;* radiance; sparkle; shimmer; shine; twinkle; *ultraviolet light; vividness; white light; x-ray;* yellow light; *zap;*

**gleam** *(v.)*: aura; beam; coruscate; dazzle; effluge; flash; glisten; *halo;* illuminate; *jet;* kindle; luster; make light; *nitency;* outshine; *phosphoresce; quiver;* radiate; sparkle; shine; twinkle; *ultraviolet light; vividness; waver; x-ray;* yield light; *zap;*

**glean** *(v.)*: accumulate; bring in; collect; draw in; *exact;* fetch; find; forage; gather; get; garner; harvest; *increase; job; keep;* lay hold upon; learn; *mow; nab;* obtain; pick (up); *quantity;* receive; return with; secure; take; *use; volume; work; xfer; yank; zip;*

**glib** *(adj.)*: artificial; bogus; casual; duplicitous; easy; facile; fluent; gushy; honey-mouthed; insincere; Janus-faced; *keen; lying;* mendacious; non-genuine; oily; persuasive; quick-tongued; relaxed; smooth; slick; shallow; two-faced; unconcerned; voluble; wangling; *xtry. superficial;* yentzing; *zelig;*

**glide** *(v.)*: *afloat;* breeze; balloon; coast; drift; effortlessly move; float; fly; glissade; hover; hydroplane; ice-skate; jet; kite; light; move; navigate; *outsoar;* pass over; *quicken;* run; rush; roll; slip; slide; sail; stream; take flight; upbear; volplane; wing; whiz; *xuld [arch.];* yern; zoom; [*see* slide]

**glimmer** *(n.)*: aura; brilliance; coruscation; *dazzle;* emission; flash; flicker; gleam; *halo;* irradiation; *jet; kindle;* luster; *move;* nitency; *overlight; phosphorescence;* radiance; sparkle; shimmer; twinkle; *ultraviolet light; vividness; white light; xenon light; yellow light; zing;*

**glimmer** *(v.)*: *aura;* blink; beam; coruscate; dance; effluge; flicker; gleam; glitter; glisten; *halo;* indication; *jet; kick;* luster; *move; nitency;* outshine; *pretty;* quiver; reflect; sparkle; shimmer; twinkle; *ultraviolet light; vividness; waver; x-ray;* yield light; *zap;*

**gloat** *(v.)*: *assert;* bluster; bask; crow; delight; exult; flaunt; flourish; glory; huff; *inflated;* joy; kvell; *lofty;* mantle; magnificate; noise; overween; plume; quack; rub it in; revel; swagger; triumph; ululate; vaunt; wallow; *x-proud;* yelp; *zero humility;*

**glob** *(n.)*: accumulation; blob; clump; drip; drop; daub; *element;* fleck; globule; gob; glop; gout; hunk; *iota;* junt; *knot;* lump; mass; nubble; *ounce;* piece; quantity; *roll;* splotch; tad; *unit; vestige;* wad; water-drop; *x-mass;* yelm; *zum [dial.];*

**global** *(adj.)*: all-earth; broad-reaching; comprehensive; *diffuse;* earthwide; four-quarters-of-the-earth; far-reaching; geopolitical; human-wide; international; joint-earth; *known-world;* large-scale; mondial; *the nations;* overall; over all the earth; panhuman; planetary; planetwide; quaquaversal; round-the-globe; supranational; *sweeping;* terrestrial; trans-world; universal; *very widespread;* worldwide; whole-earth; *x-world; yonder; zonic;*

**gloom** *(n.)*: abjectness; bleakness; cloudiness; dismalness; enclouded; forlornness; gloominess; hopelessness; infuscation; joylessness; *kindlesness;* lugubriousness; misery; nebulation; obscurity; pessimism; *Q.B.I.;* raylessness; shadowines; sadness; tenebrousness; unhappiness; vexing; woefulness; *xtry. depression;* yucky; *zealless;* [*Ant.* gladness]

**gloomy** *(adj.)*: abject; bleak; cloudy; cheerless; dour; dismal; enclouded; forlorn; funereal; gray; gloomful; hopeless; infuscated; joyless; *kindless;* lugubrious; miserable; nebulated; obscure; pessimistic; *Q.B.I.;* rayless; shadowy; sad; somber; tenebrous; unlit; uncheerful; vexing; woeful; *xtry. depression;* yucky; *zealless;* [*Ant.* glad]

**glorification** *(n.)*: apotheosis; bepraisement; conversion; dignification; elevation; exaltation; fulgency; greatening; gloriousness; glorifying; honor; immortalization; *joy; kudos;* laudation; luminosity; magnification; *new body; overpraise;* praise; *quantum leap;* resplendency; sanctification; translation; uplifting; veneration; *wondrousness; xlation; yichus; zeal;*

**glorify** *(v.)*: applaud; acclaim; adore; apotheosize; bless; cheer; *devote;* extol; exalt; fame; greaten; hail; honor; idolize; jubilate over; *kudos;* laud; lift up; magnify; *notoriety; overpraise;* praise; *quiritation;* rejoice in; sing praises; tout; uplift; venerate; worship; *xlate; yichus; zealously praise;* [*Ant.* gibe]

**glorious** *(adj.)*: awesome; brilliant; celebrated; dazzling; effulgent; exalted; famed; fulgent; great; grand; high; illustrious; *joyous; keen;* lauded; lustrous; lofty; magnificent; noble; numinous; outstanding; praised; *quality;* radiant; refulgent; resplendent; splendid; transplendent; *ultimate;* venerated; wondrous; xtry.; *yichus; zeal;*

**glory** *(n.)*: afterglow; adoration; aura; brilliance; celebrity; dazzlement; effulgence; exaltation; fame; fulgency; greatness; grandeur; honor; illustriousness; *joy; keenness;* light; magnificence; majesty; nimbus; numinousness; *outstanding;* pomp; praise; *quality;* radiance; refulgency; renown; resplendence; shining; splendor; transplendency; utter magnificence; vivid brightness; wonder; *xplendency; yichus; zeal;*

**glory** *(v.)*: adulate; bless; beam; celebrate; cheer; delight; *dance;* exult; *frisk;* gloat; glee; honor; *imparadised;* joy; jubilate; *kill the fatted calf;* laugh; lilt; laud; make merry; *nowell; ovation;* praise; *quiver;* revel; rollick; rejoice; sing; shout for joy; triumph; *uplift; vivify;* worship; *xtry. joy;* yell; *zealous;* [*see* praise; *Ant.* grieve]

**gloss** *(n.)*: alkyd; brilliance; coat; dazzle; enamel; finish; glaze; high-gloss finish; inceration; japan; *keen;* lacquer; marine spar; nigrosine; oil ~; overglaze; polish; *quartz sand;* refulgence; *resin;* shellac; spirit ~; shiny coat; sheen; topcoat; tung oil; urethane; varnish; wax; xesturgy; *yare; zinc flourosilicate;*

**glossy** *(adj.)*: *aura;* buffed; brilliant; coated; dazzling; enameled; finished; glossed; high-gloss; *intense;* japanned; *keen;* lacquered; *magnificent; non-matte;* over-polished; polished; *quality;* radiant; shiny; twinkly; urethane-coated; varnished; well-polished; waxed; *xesturgy; yary; zizzy;* [*Ant.* glare-free]

**glow** *(n.)*: aura; after~; brightness; brilliance; candescence; dim light; emanation; effulgence; fulgency; glimmer; gleam; glory; *halo;* illumination; irradiance; *joie de vivre [F.]; kindle;* light; luminosity; *moonlight;* nimbus; overlight; phosphorescence; radiance; refulgence; resplendence; shine; shining; splendor; *translucency; ultraviolet light;* vivacity; white light; warmth; *xenon light;* yellow light; *zest;*

**glow** *(v.)*: *aura;* brighten; burn; blare; beam; color; diffuse; emanate; exude; fulgurate; flare; glimmer; gleam; give light; *halo;* illuminate; *jacklight;* kindle; light; mantle; make light; *nimbus;* overflow with; phosphoresce; radiate; shine; twinkle; *ultraviolet light; vividness;* warm; *xenon light; yellow light; zest;*

**glue** *(n.)*: adhesive; binder; bond(ing agent); cement; *daub;* epoxy; fixative; goo(p); glutinate; *hold;* ichthyocolla; *join; knit;* library paste; mucilage; meld; *nail; one;* paste; quince-mucilage; rubber cement; stickum; super~; *tack; unite;* viscous; wood ~; weld; *xenograft; yoke; zet [dial.];*

**glue** *(v.)*: agglutinate; adhere; affix; bond; cohere; cement; *daub; embed;* fasten; glutinate; grip; hold (together); *inviscate; imbed;* join; knit; latch; mount; meld; *nail; oneness;* paste; *quick-dry;* rubber cement; stick; secure; tack; unite; *viscous;* weld; *xenograft; yoke; zip;*

**glutton** *(n.)*: avid eater; bottomless pit; belly-slave; connoisseur; devourer; epicure; foodie; gobbler; gulch; gourmand(er); hog; indulgent; junk-food junkie; *keyed up;* lurcher; mouth; *non-temperate;* overindulger; pig; *quenchless; rapacious;* surfeiter; trencherman; uncontrolled eater; *voracious; wolf; xtry. eater;* yevery; *zealous eater;*

**gluttonous** *(adj.)*: all-devouring; *boundless;* crapulent; devouring; excessive; edacious; ferocious; greedy; gormandizing; *hungry;* hoggish; indulgent; insatiable; *junketer; keyed up; lurcher;* meat-eating; non-satiated; overindulgent; openmouthed; piggish; polyphageous; quenchless; ravenous; rapacious; sateless; *starving; terrible;* unquenchable; unsatiable; unrestrained; voracious; wanton; xtry, greedy; yeverous; *zealous;*

**gluttony** *(n.)*: *abandon;* big appetite; crapulence; devouring; excess; edacity; feeding frenzy; gobbling; gula; greed; gulosity; hyperphagia; immoderacy; *junketer; keyed up;* lust; munching; non-satisfaction; overindulgence; overeating; polyphagia; *quenchlessness;* rapacity; self-indulgence; satelessness; *thirst;* unsatiability; voracity; wolfishness; xtry, greed; yevery; *zeal to eat;*

**gnarl** *(v.)*: *alternate;* bend; contort; distort; entwist; *furl; growth;* hankle; intertangle; joggle; knot; lump; meander; node; *over-twist; pervert;* querl; ravel; snake; twist; *ugly;* volt; wind; *xyloma;* yaw; zigzag;

**gnash** *(v.)*: *agony;* bite; *bruxism;* chew; chomp; clench; *distress; excruciating; frustration;* grind; have teeth grinding; *ire; jarring;* knash; *lividness;* munch; masticulate; nip; *overbite;* pinch; *quash;* rasp; ruminate; *suffer; torment; unhappy; vexation; writhe; xtry. pain; yaffle; zing;*

**gnaw** *(v.)*: *ate;* bite; begnaw; chew; dine; eat; feed; graze; have; ingest; *junket;* knabble; lunch; munch; masticate; nosh; nibble; *overeat;* partake; *quill* [arch.]; ruminate; *sup;* snack; taste; *undereat; victual;* wear away; *xerophagy;* yaffle; *zip down;*

**go** *(v.)*: accelerate; budge; book; circulate; depart; exit; fare; forge ahead; flow; get; head (off); *impelled;* jee; keep on; leave; move; navigate; operate; plod; proceed; progress; pass; quit; remove; run; sail; travel; undergo; venture; voyage; visit; walk; wend; *went;* xfer; yede; zip;

**goad** *(n.)*: actuator; bestirrer; cattle-prod; driver; electric cattle-prod; foin; gad; *heave; implement;* jabber; *kindle; lance; make; Neith;* ox ~; prick; prod; prong; poker; *quickener;* rowel; sticker; thruster; *urger;* valet; *whacker; xulder;* yerk [dial.]; *zapper;*

**goad** *(v.)*: actuate; bestir; coerce; drive; egg on; foin; get; gad; herd; incite; jab; *kindle; lance; make;* nudge; *oblige;* prick; poke; prod; quicken; *rouse;* stab; thrust; urge; *veney; whack; xuld* [arch.]; yerk [dial.]; *zing;*

**goal** *(n.)*: aim; aspiration; by-purpose; calling; design; end; function; great desire; hope; high aim; intent(ion); journey's end; key reason; last stop; meaning; notion; objective; purpose; point; quintain; reason; sake; target; ultimate aim; wish; will; x; *yearning;* zero in;

**God** *(n.)*: Almighty; *Adonai* [Heb.]; *Abba* [Gr.]; Beginning and End; Creator; Deity; Defender; Divine One; Everlasting ~; *Elohim; El Shaddai* [both Heb.]; Father (-of lights); ~ Almighty; Heavenly Father; Holy One; I AM; Jehovah; Judge; Just One; King (Eternal); LORD (of hosts); *the* Living ~; Maker; Master; Most High; *Nature's ~;* Omnipotent ~; Only Wise ~; Protector; Provider; Potentate; *Quickener;* Ruler; Righteous One; Sovereign; Sustainer; Supreme Being; Thrice-Holy ~; Three in One; *Theos* [Gr.]; Trinity; Unchanging ~; *voice from heaven;* Wise ~; *Xuda* [Arab.]; *Yahweh* [Heb.]; Zion's Hope; [see Christ; Trinity]

**god** *(n.)*: apotropean; beaten image; carved image; demi~; deva; divinity; deity; *earth ~;* false ~; fates; figure; goddess; godling; household ~; herm; idol; image; joss; *ka* [Egy.]; lar; likeness; man-made image; naiad; orisha; penate; pagan ~; queen of heaven; river- ~; statue; teraph; totem; *underworld ~;* vanir; wakanda; xoanon; yaksha; zeme; zemi; zootype; zoomorphism;

   **False gods**: Aphrodite; Ashtoreth, Baal; Chemosh; Dagon, Diana; Eros; Frita; Gaia; Hermes; Isis; Jupiter; Krishna; Kronos; Loki; Mars; Molech; Mercury; Nebo; Neptune; Nisroch; Oden; Pluto; Poseidon; Quetzalcoatl; Ra; Rimmon; Saturn; Tamuz; Thor; Titan; Uranus; Utu; Venus; Vishnu; Woden; Xango; Ymir; Zeus;

**goddess** *(n.)*: *Ashter;* beaten image; carved image; deess; demigoddess; *earth ~;* female deity; god; household ~; idol; *Isis;* joss; *ka [Egy.];* lady- ~; man-made image; naiad; orisha; pagan ~; *queen of heaven;* river- ~; statue; teraph; *underworld ~;* vanir; wakanda; xoanon; yaksha; zemi;
    **Goddesses**: Apaphrodite; Bia; Cytherea; Diana; Euthenia; Frita; Gaia; Hecate; Ibis; Isis; Juno; Kamira; Lyssa; Maat; Nike; Oizys; Pheobe; Quiritis; Rhea; Selene; Thalia; Urania; Venus; Wyrd; Xulsigiae; Yami; Zaria;
**godless** *(adj.)*: abominable; bad; corrupt; debauched; devilish; evil; foul; fiendish; guileful; heinous; iniquitous; *jaded;* knavish; licentious; malevolent; nasty; obdurate; polluted; pernicious; *quad;* rebellious; sinful; transgressing; unrighteous; virulent; wicked; *xgressing;* yucky; *zymotic;* [*Ant.* godly]
**godlessness** *(n.)*: abomination; badness; corruption; depravity; evil; foul-behavior; guiltiness; heinousness; iniquity; *jadedness;* knavishness; leaven; mischief; naughtiness; obduracy; pollution; perverseness; *quad;* rebellion; sin; transgression; unrighteousness; vice; wickedness; *xgression; yetzer hara* [Heb.]; *zymosis;* [*Ant.* godliness]
**godliness** *(n.)*: *aboveboard;* blamelessness; character; Christlikeness; divineness; *ever-faithful;* faithfulness; goodness; heavenly-mindedness; impeccability; justness; *keenness; love;* morality; *nobleness;* other-worldliness; piety; purity; *quality;* righteousness; saintliness; spirituality; sanctification; *truthfulness;* uprightness; ultramundaneness; virtue; wholesomeness; *Xty.; yieldedness; zaddik* [Heb.]; [*Ant.* godlessness]
**godly** *(adj.)*: aboveboard; angelic; benevolent; blameless; chaste; Christ-like; decent; ever-faithful; faithful; good; God-fearing; high-minded; irreproachable; impeccable; just; *keen; loving;* moral; *noble;* other-worldly; principled; pious; pure; *quality;* righteous; saintly; spiritual; Spirit-filled; sanctified; *truthful;* upright; virtuous; wholesome; *Xn.; yielded; zaddik* [Heb.]; [*Ant.* godless]
**gold** *(n.)*: AU; bullion; choice ~; *doubloons; electroplated;* fine ~; *gilded;* ~ nugget; *hoard; inaurate; jewelry;* karats; krugerrand; *lots; metal;* nugget; ore; precious metal; pure ~; *quality;* refined ~; *shekel;* treasure; tambac; 24K ~; *unrefined ~; vein;* white ~; wedge of ~; XAU; yellow (gold); *zillions;*
**golden** *(adj.)*: aureate; blonde; *cupreous;* deaurated; engilded; flaxen; gilded; gold; honey- ~; inaurated; *jacketed in gold; karat;* leafed; *metalic; nugget;* overlaid; *parcel-gilt; quince;* royal yellow; straw-colored; tow-colored; *uranite;* vermeiled; wheat-colored; xanthous; yellow; *zante;* [*see* costly]
**gold-plate** *(v.)*: aureate; *bronze-plate;* cover with gold; coat; deaurate; engild; electroplate; foil; foliate; gild; *have ~d;* inaurate; *jacket; kist;* leaf; metal; *nickel-plate;* overlay; overgild; plate; *quicksilver; roll;* saffron; *tin; upbind;* vermeil; white ~; *xanthous;* yellow-gold encrust; *zincify;*
**gone** *(adj.)*: absent; away; *behind;* consumed; disappeared; depleted; departed; dead; exhausted; elsewhere; expired; flat ~; finished; gone by the wayside; headed (off); irrecoverable; *jee; kited off;* lacking; left; lost; missing; moved out; not here; nonexistent; out; over; omitted; past; *quit;* removed; spent; shot; *too late;* un-accounted for; used up; vanished; went; *xferred; yede; zero;*
**good** *(adj.)*: advantageous; angelic; beneficial; benevolent; blameless; constructive; chaste; dandy; decent; excellent; exemplary; favorable; fair; fine; great; godly; honorable; holy; impeccable; immaculate; jim dandy; just; keen; lovely; moral; nifty; nice; noble; outstanding; profitable; peachy; principled; pure; quality; reputable; righteous; swell; sinless; terrific; useful; upright; unadulterated; virtuous; well; wholesome; worthy; *xtry.;* yummy; *zizzy;* [*Ant.* guileful, grievous, godless]
**goodness** *(n.)*: *amiableness;* beneficence; benevolence; blamelessness; chastity; divinity; exquisiteness; ethicalness; favorableness; fairness; fineness; good; godliness; honor; holiness; integrity; impeccability; justness; kindness; *love;* morality; niceness; nobility; *otherworldliness;* profitableness; probity; purity; quality; rectitude; righteousness; sinlessness; truthfulness; uprightness; usefulness; virtue; wholesomeness; *xtry; yieldedness to God; zeal for God;* [*Ant.* godlessness]
**good works** *(n.)*: acts; almsdeeds; behavior; charitable activities; deeds; efforts; feat; goings; good deeds; helping others; *industriousness; justifying oneself;* kindnesses; labors; meritorious acts; *nice things;* openhandedness; performance; *qualifications;* righteous acts; self-righteousness; things done; unselfish deeds; virtuous acts; works; *xtry, life;* your own righteousness; *zealous works;*

**gore** *(v.)*: auger; bore; cut; drive; en~; fix [arch.]; gouge; hole; impale; jab; knife; lance; make hole; *mutilate;* nail; open; pierce; *quill;* run through; stab; transfix; *undercut; ventilate;* wimble; *xylotomy;* yerk; *zing;*

**gorge** *(v.)*: *ate;* bolt; consume; cram; devour; en~; fill; gobble; *have;* ingurgitate; jam; *kill* [joc.]; load; munch; *nosh;* overeat; overindulge; overstuff; over~; pack in; *quill* [arch.]; raven; stuff; tuck away; *uncontrolled;* voraciously eat; wolf; *xfer;* yolp; *zip down;*

**gorgeous** *(adj.)*: attractive; beautiful; cute; charming; desirable; eye-catching; enchanting; fair; good-looking; heart-alluring; *irresistible; just fine;* killing [slang]; lovely; magnificent; nice-looking; *outstanding;* pretty; quite beautiful; ravishing; striking; *terrific;* uncommonly beautiful; voluptuous; well-favored (-looking); *xtry.;* you-beaut [Aus.]; zizzy; [*Ant.* ghastly]

**gory** *(adj.)*: *aggressive;* bloody; crimson; disgusting; ensanguined; *foul;* grisly; gruesome; hurt; horrible; injured; imbrued; *jeopardized; killed; lethal;* messy; murderous; nasty; over-bloody; *pernicious; quad;* red-stained; slaughterous; sanguinary; treacherous; *unpleasant;* violent; wounded; *xantorubin;* yucky; *zymome;*

**gospel** *(n.)*: account; *the Blood; the Cross;* death, burial, and resurrection of Christ; *evangel* [arch.]; faith in Christ; *the* Gospel; good news; glad tidings; heaven's ~; *immortality;* John 3:16; *Jesus; the* King's message; life-changing ~; message; *news;* only Way to heaven; preaching of the Cross; *quathrigan* [arch.]; redemption through Christ; salvation; *tidings; unshackled; veracity;* Word; *Xnty; yichus;* Zion; [*see* salvation]

**gossip** *(n.)*: aspersions; blather; backbiting; calumny; defamation; evil-speaking; false words; gab; grapevine; hearsay; hot air; idle chatter; jaunder; juicy ~; *klatch* [G.]; labrish [Carib.]; malignity; newsmongering; on-dit; obtrectation; prattle; prating; quidnunc; rumors; scuttlebutt; slander; scandal; talebearing; tidbit; tittle-tattle; tattling; tongue-wagging; unkind words; viciousness; whispering; *xgression;* yatter; yarn; *zay;*

**gossip** *(v.)*: *announce;* blather; badmouth; chatter; chinwag; circulate ~; declaim; echo; fame; gab; haver; iterate; insinuate; jaunder; *keep coming; loose tongue;* mention; natter; noise; opine; prattle; palaver; purvey; *quote;* repeat; rumormonger; say; tell; talk; utter; voice; wag ones tongue; *xgress;* yarn; *zero in;*

**gossiper** *(n.)*: aspersion-caster; busybody; backbiter; chatterbox; defamater; echoer; flibbertgibbet; gossip; *hearsay;* idle chatterer; jaunderer; kibitz; *loose-tongued;* magpie; newsmonger; *obtrectation;* prattler; prater; quidnunc; rumormonger; slanderer; talebearer; tattler; *utterer;* vicious voice; whisperer; *xiaoren;* yenta; *zeroizer;*

**gouge** *(v.)*: *avulse;* burrow; carve; dig; excavate; forehew; grub; gash; groove; hew; hollow; incise; incavate; *jag;* kerf; lacerate; *mole;* notch; *open;* plow; quarry; rip; root; scratch; shovel; scoop; tear; trench; uproot; vell; wound; *x-sect;* yerk; *zip;*

**gourd** *(n.)*: * adansonia; bottle- ~; calabash; *deciduous plant;* Ethiopian sour ~; *flora; growth;* herbage; *item;* jungle- ~; *kerf; lagenaria* [L.]; matrass; *nothoalsomitra [L.]; organic plant;* plant; *pumpkin; quickset; root;* squash; top; *undergrowth;* vine- ~; *weed;* warted ~; *xerophyte;* yarb [dial.]; zucca;

**govern** *(v.)*: administer; boss; control; direct; *execute; force;* guide; gubernate; handle; head; influence; jockey; keep under ~; lead; manipulate; manage; *navigate;* oversee; predominate; *quell;* run; rule; superintend; take oversight of; *undertake; vanquish;* wield authority; *XO;* yeme; *zayim;*

**governable** *(adj.)*: administrable; biddable; compliant; controllable; docile; *doable;* employable; *following;* guidable; handleable; *influence; justifiable;* keepable; law-abiding; manageable; non-rebellious; obedient; persuasible; *quellable;* rulable; subduable; tractable; unresisting; vanquishable; willing to be ruled; *xtry. docile;* yielding; *zero resistance;*

**governance** *(n.)*: administration; authority; *bishopric;* control; direction; dominion; *eldership; fatherhood;* government; headship; *instruction; jurisdiction; kingship;* leadership; management; *necessitation;* oversight; power; *queenship;* running; rule; reign; supervision; sovereignty; *taking the lead;* use of authority; *vizierate;* wardenship; *xenagogy;* yard; *zakon [Rus.];*

**governess** *(n.)*: *au pair* [F.]; *bonne* [F.]; babysitter; caretaker (-giver); duenna; *educator;* *forewoman;* granny; guardian; home teacher; instructress; *jefe;* keeper; *leader;* mammy; mistress; nanny; *overseer;* principle caretaker; *quartermaid;* rectress; sitter; trainer; tutoress; *undershepherd; vicereine;* warden; *xenagogue;* yaya; zookeeper *[joc.]*

**government** *(n.)*: administration; authority; aristocracy; bureaucracy; control; commonwealth; congress; direction; diet; *empire;* federal ~; governance; gubernation; headship; house; *imperial ~;* junta; kakistocracy; kingcraft; leadership; local ~; legislature; *mastery; monarchy;* national ~; officialdom; political science; polity; politics; provincial ~; parliament; *the* powers that be; quango; rule; regime(n); state ~; senate; town ~; throne; upper house; village ~; ward; *xenocracy;* yard; *zemstvo* [Rus.];

   **Types of government**: aristocracy; bureaucracy; chirocracy; democracy; dictatorship; ecclesiarchy; federalism; gerontocracy; gynarchy; hierocracy; imperial; juntocracy; kakistocracy; kritarchy; landocracy; monarchy; monocracy; nomocracy; ochlocracy; oligarchy; pentarchy; polycracy; plutocracy; queendom; republic; socialist; theocracy; *unicameralist;* whigarchy; xenocracy; zenocracy;

**governmental** *(adj.)*: administrative; bureaucratic; congressional; diet-related; *empire-related;* federal; government; heteronomous; institutional; judicatory; *kakistocratically;* legislative; *mayoral;* nomothetic; *national;* official; political; parliamentary; quasi-legislative; ruling; senatorial; *throne; unicameral; viceroyal;* ward; *xenocratic; yard; zemstvo [Rus.];*

**governor** *(n.)*: administrator; alderman; burgomaster [G.]; burgrave; bey [Turk.]; comptroller; director; elder; eparch; *foreman; general;* head; intendant; jurat; *kami* [Jap.]; leader; *lt. ~;* lord; magistrate; mayor; *nabob* [Arab.]; overseer; prefect; *quaimoqam* [Turk.]; ruler; supervisor; satrap [Pers.]; tirshatha; *ultimate authority;* viceroy; *warden;* xenarch; *yokemaster;* zayim;

**governorship** *(n.)*: authority; *badge;* control; command; dominion; *empowering;* faculty; government; headship; influence; jurisdiction; *kingship;* lordship; mayorship; *name;* office; position; premiership; *quo warranto* [L.]; rule; say-so; *top dog; umpirage;* vice regency; weight; *xenagogy; yamen* [Chin.]; *zonal control;*

**grab** *(v.)*: apprehend; arrest; *begird;* clutch; *draw around;* embrace; fasten on; grip; glom; grasp; hold; infold; *join;* kinch; latch onto; make secure; nab; *oxtercog;* put hands on; pluck; *quelch;* remove; snatch; take; usurp; *vice;* wrap hand around; *xfer;* yank; *zone;*

**grace** *(n.)*: altruism; amazing ~; benevolence; clemency; *delicacy;* easygoingness; favor; goodwill; heart; *helpfulness; interest; joy-giving;* kindness; leniency; mercy; niceness; *overpiteousness;* pity; quarter; ruth; slack; sympathy; tender mercies; unmerited favor; virtue; well-disposedness; *xenophilia; yearning;* zeal to forgive; [*see* mercy; gift]

**graceful** *(adj.)*: agile; balletic; beautiful; comely; dignified; effortless; elegant; flowing; fluid; gracious; heavenly; *inspiring;* jimo; *keen;* lovely; masterful; natural; *overelegant;* poised; polished; *quick;* refined; smooth; tasteful; unforced; unlabored; volant; willowy; well-polished; *xtry.; yaup; zierlich* [G.]; [*Ant.* gangly]

**gracious** *(adj.)*: amiable; benignant; courteous; charitable; diplomatic; ever- ~; elegant; forbearing; forgiving; favorable; graceful; great-hearted; humane; indulging; *joy-giving;* kind; lenient; merciful; nice; obliging; polite; propitious; pitying; quick-to-forgive; ready to forgive; sympathetic; tactful; tender-hearted; understanding; virtuous; warm; *xenial; yielding;* zealous to forgive;

**graciousness** *(n.)*: amiableness; benignancy; civility; consideration; compassion; deference; *endearing;* friendliness; favor; goodness; goodwill; humaneness; hospitality; *indulgence; joviality;* kindness; love; mercy; niceness; obligingness; pity; *quick to give;* regard; *sympathy; sweetness;* thoughtfulness; unselfishness; *virtuousness;* warmth; xenia; *yearning;* zealousness;

**grade** *(n.)*: *altitude;* bad ~; best ~; class; caliber; degree; evaluation; elevation; floor; grade-level; *height;* increment; journey level; *kind;* level; mark; notch; order; plane; quality; rank; rating; score; standing; tier; *unit;* varve; valuation; *way; x-class;* year; *zone;*

**grade** *(v.)*: assign ~; arrange; *bestow;* classify; categorize; distribute; evaluate; file; give ~; *hold;* index; judge; *kit;* list; label; mark; *notch;* order; peg; place; *qualify;* rank; rate; sort; tabulate; unitize; valuate; *work; xfer; yield; zonate;*

**gradual** *(adv.)*: a little at a time; bit by bit; crawling; delayed; ever-so- ~; foot-dragging; gentle; *halting;* inch-by-inch; incremental; *jog trot; known by few;* little-by-little; measured; non-hurried; ongoing; progressive; quite ~; regular; slow; turtlelike; unhurried; *unnoticed;* very ~; *wily; xtr. slow; yet slowly; zet;*

**graduate** *(n.)*: alumnus; *bachelor of arts;* collegiate; college ~; doctor; *elder;* fellow; graduate student; holder of degree; *individual; junior professor; kid;* licensed professional; *master of arts; next level; outgrow;* post~; qualified professional; *raise;* scholar; transcend; upgate; *verge upward;* walk the platform; *xfer; yain [arch.]; zoom up;*

**graduate** *(v.)*: advance; ascend; brevet; climb; develop, *degree;* elevate; exalt; finish; get diploma; *heighten;* increase; jump; kick upstairs; lift up; make the grade; move up; *next level; outgrow;* pass (on); promote; qualify; raise; step up; transcend; upgate; *verge upward;* walk the platform; *xfer; yain [arch.]; zoom up;*

**graft** *(n.)*: attachment; bond; connection; *drawn;* en~ing; embedding; fix; ~ing; homo~; hetero~; implantation; joint; *kidney ~;* link; mount; *node;* onlay; planting; *quasi-fuse; relation;* skin ~; splice; tie-in; union; *vise;* whip- ~; xeno~; yoke; zoo~;

**graft** *(v.)*: attach; affix; bond; connect; *draw;* entrench; embed; en~; fix; *get on;* homo~; hetero~; infix; inset; implant; imbed; join; knit; link; mount; *node;* onlay; plant; *quasi-fuse; re~;* splice; tie in; tack; unite; *vise;* wed; xeno~; yoke; zoo~;

**grain** *(n.)*: *amount;* bit; corn; cereal; durra; *ens;* feed; granule; grist; hyrse; inguinal; *junt;* kernel; little piece; millet; meal; nugget; *ounce;* particle; provender; *quantity; rice;* samp; *tidbit;* urge-wonder; *vestige;* wheat; *XAG; yngot [arch.]; zea [L.];*

   **Grains**: alfalfa; barley; corn; durra; English rye; Italian rye; kaffir; long-grained rice; millet; oats; paddy; rice; rye; sorghum; wheat; *zea mays* [L.];

**grand** *(adj.)*: amazing; brilliant; capital; distinguished; excellent; fabulous; great; grandiose; heavenly; impressive; incredible; jim-dandy; keen; lofty; laudable; magnificent; noteworthy; outstanding; prominent; *quantum* [L.]; remarkable; splendid; stupendous; tremendous; unbelievable; unequalled; very good; wonderful; xtry.; yet incomparable; zizzy;

**grandfather** *(n.)*: ayle; *ancestor;* bearded man; *codger;* dotard [off.]; elderly man; father's father; forefather; grandpa (-dad, -sire); *hoary head; individual; jack; kin; long beard;* maternal ~; nonagenarian; old man; pops; paternal ~; patriarch; *quite old;* relative; retiree; senior citizen; *time-worn; up in years;* very old man; white-haired man; *xtr. mature; years; zet [arch.];*

**grandiose** *(adj.)*: awesome; breathtaking; colossal; distinguished; extraordinary; fabulous; great; grand; high-flying; incredible; impressive; jim-dandy; keen; luxurious; magnificent; noteworthy; ostentatious; overwhelming; overdone; prestigious; *quantum* [L.]; remarkable; stupendous; turgid; tremendous; unbelievable; unparalleled; very impressive; wondrous; xtry.; *yippee!; zestful;*

**grandmother** *(n.)*: aged woman; *ancestor;* beldam; *babushka* [Rus.]; *clan member;* dear old ~; elderly lady; father's mother; grandma; *hag; individual; Jane; kin; lady;* mother's mother; maternal ~; matriarch; nana; old woman; paternal ~; *quite old;* relative; *senior; time-worn; up in years;* very old woman; white-haired lady; *xtr. mature; years; zet [arch.];*

**grant** *(n.)*: award; bestowal; contribution; donation; endowment; favor; funds; gift; government ~; handsel; individual gift; *joy-giving;* kindness; liberality; munificence; money; nicety; offering; present; *quality gift; reward;* subvention; tip; *unselfishness;* vouchsafement; *white elephant gift;* xenium; *yeff* [arch.]; *zealous support;*

**grant** *(v.)*: accord; award; bestow; confer; donate; endow; furnish; give; hand (over); impart; *jettison;* kit; lavish; make gift; *non-retention;* offer; provide; *qualify;* render; supply; transfer; unhand; vouchsafe; *weigh;* xfer; yield; *zip;*

**grape** *(n.)*: * azal; black grape; bunch [pl.]; cluster [pl.]; concord ~; dureza ~; elbing; fruit (of the vine); fox ~; grenache; himrod ~; interlaken; jonesville; klevner; lagrein; merlot; niagara; onaka ~; pais; *quince;* red ~; seedless ~; table ~; uveous; vine fruit; white ~; xarel-lo; *yayin [Heb.];* zéta;
**grapejuice** *(n.)*: *azal juice;* blood of the grape; concord ~; drink; *essence;* fruit juice; grape juice; *hermitage; item;* juice; klevner juice; *liquid;* must; nonfermented wine; new wine; onaka ~; *port wine; quince wine;* red ~; sugar-free ~; *table wine;* unfermented ~; vine juice; wine; white ~; *xeres; yayin [Heb.];* zep;
**grapevine** *(n.)*: azal vine; branch; creeper; climber; dureza vine; elbing ~; fruit vine; grape vine; *hopvine;* interlaken ~; jonesville ~; klevner ~; lagrein ~; muscadine; niagara ~; onaka ~; *plant; quartervine;* red grape vine; sympodium; trailer; *tendril;* uveous vine; vine; white grape vine; *xylem; yage; zebrina;*
**graphic** *(adj.)*: accurate; *blatant;* clear; descriptive; expressive; explicit; figurative; *gory; hard facts;* illustrative; *just plain;* keenly ~; lifelike; *marked; narrative;* open; pictorial; plain; *quite ~;* realistic; specific; *tasteless;* uninhibited; visual; veristic; vivid; well-described; *x-rated; yeme [arch.];* zolaistic;
**grasp** *(v.)*: apprehend; bite; clutch; clench; cinch; *draw around;* embrace; en~; fasten on; grab; grip; hold; infold; *join;* kinch; latch onto; make secure; nobble; *on;* pinch; *quelch; retain;* seize; take hold; usurp; *vice;* wrap hand around; *xfer; yank; zone;* [*see* comprehend]
**grass** *(n.)*: abature; blade; bulrush; crab~; *durra;* eel~; forage; flags; *grounds;* herbage; *Indian ~; Japanese lawn ~; knotgrass;* lawn; lea; *moss;* marram; *meadow; natural ~; orchard ~;* pasture; prairie; quitch; reed; rush; sedge; sward; sod; turf; undergrowth; *vetiver; weeds;* wiregrass; *xyris;* yard ~; zea;
**grate** *(v.)*: abrade; break up; chafe; dice; exect; file; grind; hash; incise; jag; *knife;* levigate; mince; nettle; *overcut;* pulverize; *quarter;* rasp; shred; tear up; *undercut;* vex; whittle; *xyster;* yerk; *zip off;*
**grateful** *(adj.)*: appreciative; beholden; conscious; duly ~; evangelian; full of gratitude; glad; *heartened;* indebted; *joyful;* kind-thoughted; *lavishing praise;* mindful; much obliged; non-forgetful; obliged; pleased; quite ~; remembering; *spirit of thanksgiving;* thankful; under obligation; very thankful; welcoming; *xtry. thankful;* yielding thanks; *zealous to give thanks;*
**gratification** *(n.)*: amusement; bliss; contentment; delight; enjoyment; fulfillment; gladness; happiness; indulgence; joy; kicks; liking; merriment; niceness; overjoy; pleasure; queme; rapture; satisfaction; titillation; *uplifted; vivacity;* want; *xtr. delight; yummy;* zest;
**gratify** *(v.)*: appease; befit; content; delight; *enjoy;* fulfill; gladden; humor; indulge; *joy;* keep happy; *like;* make happy; not displease; oblige; please; queme; reward; satisfy; titilate; *uplift; vivacity;* want; *Xanadu;* yield pleasure; *zest;*
**gratitude** *(n.)*: appreciation; *beholden;* credit; delivering of thanks; expression of thanks; *forever thankful;* gratefulness; honor; indebtedness; *joy;* kind-thoughtedness; *love;* mindfulness; non-forgetfulness; obligation; praise; *quick-to-thank;* recognition; spirit of thankfulness; thanks; understanding one's debt; *very thankful;* wah [Asia]; *xtry. ~;* yielding thanks; zeal; [*see* praise]
**gratuity** *(n.)*: acknowledgement; bonus; complimentariness; douceur; extra; 15%; favor; gift; honorarium; *interest; joy-giving;* kindness; liberality; *money;* nicety; offering; pourboire; perk; *quantity;* riptowell; show of appreciation; tip; *unselfish ~; vouchsafement; wage;* xenium; *yeff* [arch.]; *zealous gift;*
**grave** *(adj.)*: acute; bleak; catonian; crucial; dour; dire; earnest; foreboding; grim; great; humorless; heavy; highly important; important; *judicial; keening;* life-and-death; momentous; needful; ominous; po-faced; ponderous; *quantum;* resolute; serious; somber; solemn; thoughtful; unsmiling; urgent; vital; weighty; *xttr.; yearnful;* zoetic;
**grave** *(n.)*: *area;* burying-place; barrow; crypt; dolmen; entombment; final resting place; gravesite; grotto; hole; humation; house of death; home; interment; *jaw-hole;* kurgan; last home; mound; mausoleum; narrow house; ossuarium; pit; plot; pyramid; *quietus;* repository; resting place; sepulcher; tomb; *underground;* undercroft; vault; *watery ~* [poet.]; *xat; yawn;* ziarat [Mos.];

**gravestone** *(n.)*: arch; burial plaque; cairn; cemetery marker; cross; cenotaph; dolmen; *epitaph;* footstone; grave; headstone; *indicator;* joint marker; *knoll-marker; land marker;* marker; monument; memorial; mausoleum; *necropolis;* obelisk; plaque; pillar; *quartz headstone;* remembrance; stone (marker); sepulcher; shrine; tombstone; *urn;* vault plaque; *whinstone; writing;* xat; *yard stone;* ziarat [Mos.];
**graveyard** *(n.)*: ancient burial grounds; burying place; burial plot; cemetery; churchyard; *the* dead; *epitaphs; footstones;* graves; headstones; *interred;* iron gates; *joubt-markers* kirk-garth [Scot.]; lych-gate; memorial park; mausoleum; necropolis; ossuaries; park; *quartz headstones;* repository; sepulchers; tombs; *urn;* vaults; *whited sepulchers; xats;* yard; *ziarats;*
**gravitate** *(v.)*: *attraction;* bias; bear toward; conduce; drift; *edge;* float; go toward; have a predisposition; incline; jee; *keen tendency;* lean; list; move; *nudge; ongoing;* propend; *quicken;* rather; sink; set toward; tend; *usually tend;* verge; waft toward; *xel [arch.]; yaw; zip;*
**gravity** *(n. downward pull)*: attraction; *bottom; compulsion;* downward pull; earthward pull; force; gravitational force; G-force; heaviness; influence; *jump down; keel over; low;* magnetism; netherward pull; *overweight;* pull; ponderance; *quality; reduction;* sinking; tug; tendency downward; *under;* verging downward; weight; *x-force; yield; zone;*
**gravity** *(n. importance)*: acuteness; bigness; criticalness; direness; exigency; *force;* graveness; gravitas; heaviness; import(ance); *justification; keening; life-and-death;* momentousness; need; necessity; ominousness; press(ure); precedence; *quintessence;* resoluteness; seriousness; solemnity; thoughtfulness; urgency; vitalness; weight; *xtry.;* yearning; *zero hour;*
**gray** *(n.)*: acier; ashen; battleship ~; charcoal; drab; dapple; emery ~; frosty; grey; grayish; grizzle; hoary; iron ~; Jews-stone; kilbrickenite ~; lead- ~; mouse- ~; neutral; Oxford ~; pearl- ~; quartz; ragstone; smoky; slate; silver(y); taupe; urry- ~; violet- ~; whitish; xanadu; yellow- ~; zinc ~;
**graze** *(v. slightly cut)*: abrade; bark; cut; damage; exscind; fissure; gouge; hurt; injure; *jag;* kerf; lacerate; mar; nick; *open; puncture;* quail [arch.]; rasp; raze; shave; scrape; sideswipe; tear; *undercut; victimize;* wound; *xyster;* yedder; *zing;*
**graze** *(v. eat)*: ate; begnaw; chew; crop; depasture; eat; feed; gnaw; *have;* ingest; *jam;* knabble; lunch; masticate; nibble; *overeat;* pasture; *quill* [arch.]; ruminate; sustain; *taste; undereat; victual;* wolf; *xerophagy;* yaffle; *zip down;*
**greasy** *(adj.)*: adipose; blubbery; buttery; chrismaltory; *dauby; even;* fatty; freshly-greased; gunky; highly greased; *infucation;* just-greased; *known risk;* lubricated; lubric(ous); mucky; *no traction; oily;* pinguid; quite ~; regreased; slippery; slick; tallowy; unctuous; verk slick; *viscous;* wet; *xtr. ~;* yolky; *zero traction;*
**great** *(adj. eminent)*: acclaimed; beloved; celebrated; distinguished; eminent; extraordinary; famed; gestic; highly regarded; important; illustrious; impressive; iconic; *jubilated over;* known; legendary; lustrous; magnificent; notable; outstanding; popular; prominent; prestigious; *quality;* renowned; significant; superb; terrific; ultra-good; venerated; wonderful; xtry.; yichus; *zealously loved;*
**great** *(adj. large)*: abundant; amazing; astronomical; big; broad; considerable; colossal; disproportionate; deep; exceptional; extensive; enormous; expansive; fantastic; grand(iose); gigantic; huge; immense; jumbo-sized; king-size; lofty; large; marvelous; massive; noteworthy; outstanding; oversize; prestigious; prodigious; ponderous; quantitative; rotund; remarkable; sizable; substantial; tremendous; unmatchable; voluminous; vast; weighty; wonderful; XL; *yet unparalleled; zenithal;*
**greatest** *(adj.)*: above-all; best; chief; choicest; dominant; extreme; elite; finest; foremost; grandest; highest; *important; judged #1;* keenest; largest; leading; loftiest; main; most high; mightiest; No. 1; noblest; optimum; prime; paramount; quintessential; ranking; supreme; top; utmost; ultimate; unsurpassed; very best; weightiest; *xtry.;* yet unsurpassed; zenithal;

**greatness** *(n.)*: awesomeness bigness; caliber; distinction; enormity; excellence; fineness; grandness; grandeur; hugeness; immensity; jumboness; keenness; largeness; loftiness; magnitude; noteworthiness; overlargeness; prodigiousness; quality; quantity; rotundity; size; tremendousness; *unbelievable;* vastness; weightiness; *xtry.; yichus; zenith;*
**greed** *(n.)*: avidity; avarice; *begrudging;* cupidity; craving; covetousness; desire; esuriency; *fancying;* greediness; hunger; insatiability; *jealousy; keen desire;* lust; materialism; mammonism; niggardliness; overgreediness; pruriency; quenchlessness; rapaciousness; satelessness; thirst; usuriousness; voraciousness; want; *xtry. ~;* yearning; zoilism;
**green** *(adj.)*: * aquamarine; beryl- ~; celadon; dark ~; emerald; forest ~; grass- ~; glaucous; hunter ~; Irish ~; jade; Kelly ~; lime; myrtle; Nile ~; olive; pea- ~; Quaker ~; reseda; sea- ~; terra-verte; turquoise; uranite- ~; vert; wernerite- ~; xyris; yew- ~; zinc ~;
**greet** *(v.)*: acknowledge; *bow;* clasp hands; *due respect;* express greeting; *friendly;* grasp hand; hail; *indicate; joint-greeting;* kiss; *laud;* meet; nod; *obeisance;* pay regards; *quite courteous;* recognize; shake hands; salute; tip hat; utter greeting; voice ~ing; welcome; wave; *xenophilia; yain* [arch.]; *zdrav'stvuitye! [Rus.];*
**greeting** *(n.)*: acknowledgement; *ahoy!;* bow; clasping of the hands; devoirs; expression of ~; friendly ~; grasping of hand; hello; how-do-you-do; handshake; *indication;* joint- ~; kiss; *laud; meeting;* nod; observation; paying regards; *quite courteous;* recognition; reception; salutation; salute; tipping one's hat; uttering ~; voicing ~; wave; welcome; *xenophilia;* yo; yoo-hoo; *zdrav'stvuitye!* [Rus.]; [*Ant.* good-bye]
**grid** *(n.)*: adjoint; array; *board;* crisscross; diamond ~; *exhibit;* framework; grillage; *hub;* infrastructure; *joint; key link;* layout; *lines;* matrix; network; organized layout; panoply; plexus; *quality; range;* spread; system; tessaraic; *underpinning; variety;* wed; x-axis; y-axis; z-axis;
**grief** *(n.)*: anguish; bleakness; crestfallenness; dole; downheartedness; ejulation; forlornness; gloom; heartache; inconsolableness; joylessness; katzenjammer; lowness; low spirits; misery; *negativism;* overmuch sorrow; pain; *quivering;* ruefulness; sorrow; trouble; unhappiness; vapors; woe; *x-ing;* yearning; zestlessness;
**grief-stricken** *(adj.)*: anguished; broken-hearted; crushed; despondent; *ejulation;* forlorn; grieved; heartbroken; inconsolable; joyless; *keening;* low; miserable; negative; overcast; pessimistic; *quivering;* rueful; sorrowful; troubled; unhappy; very sad; woeful; *xtry. bleak; yucky;* zestless;
**grievance** *(n.)*: accusation; beef; complaint; dissention; exception; fuss; gripe; gravamen; hardship; impugnation; jeremiad; kvetching; *load;* murmuring; niggle; objection; plaint; problem; querimony; repining; striving; trouble; unharmoniousness; variance; withstanding; *x-fire;* yammering; *za-zum [Rus.];*
**grieve** *(v.)*: aggrieve; anguish; bemoan; bewail; cry; despair; distress; *embitter;* feel sad; gnash teeth; howl; injure; *judder;* keen; lament; mourn; noise; outcry; pain; quail; *reget;* sorrow; suffer; sadden; torment; upset; *vociferate;* weep; wail; *x-ing;* yowl; *zing;* [*Ant.* gladden]
**grievous** *(adj.)*: adverse; bad; burdensome; catastrophic; distressing; exasperating; fell; galling; hard; irksome; jarring; knotty; lamentable; mournful; noisome; onerous; problematic; quisquose; rattling; sorrowful; troublesome; unpleasant; vexatious; worrisome; *xerotripsis; yowling; zero joy;* [*Ant.* gladdening]
**grim** *(adj.)*: awful; bleak; cheerless; distressing; dismal; execrable; forbidding; frightening; gloomy; gruesome; ghastly; hopeless; horrible; hideous; invidious; jarring; kindless; loathsome; miserable; macabre; nasty; nauseating; ominous; poor; quisquose; repulsive; sickening; shocking; terrible; undesirable; uninviting; unpleasant; vile; wicked; *xerotripsis;* yucky; *zero pleasure;*
**grind** *(v.)*: abrade; bash; break up; bray; crush; destroy; disintegrate; *edge;* flatten; grate; granulate; hammer; *irritate;* jam; kibble; levigate; mash; mill; nibble; *overbear;* pound; pulverize; quash; rasp; ruin; sand; smash; triturate; *unbuild; vaporize;* wear away; x; *yank down;* zap; [*see* sharpen]

**grip** *(v.)*: apprehend; bite; cling to; clasp; clutch; clench; clinch; *draw around;* embrace; engrasp; enclasp; engrapple; fasten on; fix; grab; grasp; grapple; hold; hug; infold; *join;* kinch; latch onto; make secure; nobble; *on;* possess; *quelch;* rivet; seize; take; usurp; *vice;* wrap hand around; *wield; xfer; yank; zone;*

**grit** *(n. fortitude)*: audacity; bravery; courage; determination; enterprise; fortitude; gumption; hardiness; intestinal fortitude; *jarless;* knightliness; lion-heartedness; mettle; nobleness; nerve; *obstinacy;* perseverance; *quakeless;* resolve; strength; tenacity; undauntedness; valor; wherewithal; *xtry. ~; yung* [Chin.]; zeal; [Ant. gutlessness]

**grit** *(n. sand)*: attritus; bits of sand; bran; chafe; chippings; dust; detritus; earth; foreign matter; grains; gravel; *hard gravel; item; jolt;* kernels; lumps; matter; nast; *ocher;* particles; pebbles; *quicksand;* raspings; rock particles; sand; *talc; undesirable;* volcanic dust; whinstone; *xysma;* yellow sand; *zineb;*

**gritty** *(adj.)*: arenarious; abrasive; branlike; breccial; coarse-grained; detrital; *emery-like;* fine-grained; farinaceous; grainy; granular; granulated; *hard; irregular; juiceless;* kernelled; lumpy; lapideous; mealy; non-smooth; *ossified;* pebbly; *quartz;* rough-textured; sabulous; sandy; textured; unrefined; volcanic-ash; white-sanded; *xanthic;* yellow-sanded; *zet;*

**groan** *(v.)*: anguish; bemoan; cry out; creak; dissent; *express sorrow;* fuss; fret; grumble; grunt; heave a sigh; *inconsolable;* jangle; keen; lament; moan; murmur; *noise;* outcry; object; protest; querk; register one's displeasure sigh; sough; suspire; *tearful; utter;* vocalization; whimper; *xuld [arch.];* yammer; yawp; *zing;* [Ant. giggle]

**groom** *(n.)*: adult; bride~; *chap; dude; eligible young man;* fellow; guy; honeymooner; husband; inamorato; *joe [slang]; key man;* lucky fellow; man; newlywed; *one;* prince charming [joc.]; querry; *right one; sir; tuxedo; urbane; virile; wedding; x-linked;* young man; *zoon;*

**groom** *(v.)*: adapt; brush; comb; curry; cut; dress; develop; equip; fix; fettle; get ready; habilitate; improve; *jibe [slang]; kemp;* line out; make ready; manicure; neaten up; outfit; primp; preen; prepare; qualify; ready; set; suit; spruce up; tease; train; trim; *untangle;* verse; whet; *well-readied; xenagogue;* yarken; *zealously ~;*

**groove** *(n.)*: arroyo; bezel; cart-rut; chamfret; chase; channel; dado; embankment; furrow; flute; gouge; glyph; hollow; impression; *jheel [Ind.];* kerf; leat; micro~; nock; notch; open channel; pleat; *quarry;* quadrisulcate; rut; rabbet; slot; scissure; trough; track; trench; U-groove; vallation; wrinkle; ward; *x-groove;* yawn; zanja;

**groove** *(v.)*: *ax-cut;* bezel; channel; canaliculate; *cut ~; dig ~;* engrave; excavate; urrow; gouge; hew out; indent; *jag;* kerf; *lower; make ~;* notch; *open ~; pare; quarry;* rout; retrench; slot; score; scoop; *sulcate;* trench; U-groove; *vell;* work; *x-sect; yerk; zip;*

**grope** *(v.)*: attempt to find; beat about; *comb for;* desperately search for; explore; feel; fumble; grabble; hunt; *investigate;* jerque; kithe; look for; make a search; *nitency; oscillate;* probe; quest for; rummage; scrabble; thrash about; *unable; vain;* work to find; *x-search; yearn for; zero ability;*

**gross** *(adj.)*: appalling; bad; coarse; disgusting; evil; foul; ghastly; horrid; icky; jarring; *knarled;* loathsome; monstrous; nauseating; *offensive;* putrid; *queasy;* repulsive; sickening; terrible; ugly; vile; wicked; *xerophthalmic;* yucky; *zorillo-like;* [Ant. great]

**grouchy** *(adj.)*: argumentative; bad-tempered; crabby; cranky; cantankerous; disagreeable; emulous; feisty; grumpy; huffy; irritable; jangly; knaggy; liverish; mean; nasty; ornery; peevish; quarrelsome; resistant; snappy; testy; touchy; unpeaceable; vinegary; waspish; *xenophobic;* yieldless; *za-zum* [Rus.]; [Ant. gay]

**ground** *(n.)*: *absolute bottom;* bottom; base; court; dirt; dry land; earth; foundation; floor; ground-level; hinder part; *intervale; jacksy; krantz;* low point; lawn; land; *marl;* nether side; nadir; *ocean floor;* pavement; *quoit;* rock-bottom; *root;* surface; soil; sod; sward; seedbed; turf; *terra firma* [L.]; underside; valley; water level; *x=0; yunga;* zero altitude;

**groundless** *(adj.)*: *artificial;* baseless; chimerical; defective; deficient; empty; faulty; fallacious; gratuitous; *hollow;* inadequate; jim-jam; kim-kam; *lying;* misconceived; notional; off base; problematic; questionable; reasonless; speculative; shaky; tenuous; unfounded; unwarranted; unjustified; *vague;* weak; *x-out; yawed; zero-grounds;* [*Ant.* grounded]

**group** *(n.)*: accumulation; assemblage; assembly; amassment; army; bunch; bundle; batch; band; body; cluster; collection; crew; congregation; company; drove; deployment; ensemble; elite ~; faction; flock; forgathering; fellowship; gang; gathering; get-together; horde; host; ingathering; inner circle; jam [slang]; kit [coll.]; lot; mass; mob; meeting; number; order; passel; pack; phalanx; press; party; quantity; ruck; roundup; rally; swarm; set; troop; unit; variety; wheen; *x-class;* yelm; zoo;

  **Groups of animals:** aerie [eagles]; ambush [tigers]; band [gorillas]; barren [mules]; bevy [quail]; cackle [hyenas]; clutch [chickens]; crash [rhinos]; dole [doves]; drove [hogs]; exaltation [larks]; flock [sheep]; gaggle [geese]; gang [weasels]; herd [cattle]; infestation [lice]; kettle [hawks]; knot [frogs]; leap [leopards]; leash [foxes]; mob [emu]; murder [crows]; nest [hornets]; obstinacy [buffalo]; pack [coyotes]; parade [elephants]; pride [lions]; rookery [penguins]; school [fish]; sleuth [bears]; sounder [boar]; swarm [bees]; trip [goats]; troop [kangaroos]; unkindness [ravens]; volery [birds]; warren [rabbits]; yoke [oxen];

**grove** *(n.)*: arbor; bosket; bowling-green; coppice; copse; *dell; espalier;* firth; garden; heath; high place; hurst; intervale; *Japanese garden; kitchen-garden; luxuriance;* motte; nemoral; orchard; plantation; queach; *recess;* spinney; toft; tope; umbrage; *verge;* wood(let); xystus; *yawshrub;* zen garden;

**grovel** *(v.)*: abase; acquiesce; beg; cringe; crawl; demean; *eager-to-please;* fawn; grubble; humble oneself; ingratiate; *judder;* kowtow; lower oneself; mortify; *no dignity; obsequious;* prostrate; quiver; reclinate; slink; self-efface; toady; truckle; *unctuous; venerate;* worship; xenium; yield; *zip to it;*

**grow** *(v.)*: advance; accumulate; blo(ss)om; broaden; *become;* climb; creep up; develop; dilate; enlarge; expand; escalate; fatten; flower; gain; greaten; germinate; heighten; inflate; increase; intensify; jump up; *keep;* largen; lengthen; luxuriate; mount; mature; multiply; mushroom; nurture; over~; progress; *quadruplicate;* raise; rise; ripen; swell; sprout; shoot up; spread; strengthen; take off; thrive; upspring; vegetate; wax; widen; *XL; yain* [arch.]; *zoom;* [*see* flourish]

**growth** *(n.)*: advance; accretion; amplification; buildup; blossoming; broadening; betterment; climbing; development; dilation; enlargement; expansion; escalation; furtherance; growing; germination; heightening; hyperplasia; increase; increment; irruption; inter~; intensification; jumping; *keen ~;* luxuriance; maturity; multiplication; maturation; morphogenesis; new ~; out~; ontogeny; *over~;* progression; phytogenesis [bot.]; quantum increase; rising; swelling; sprouting; shooting up; skyrocketing; taking-off; thriving; *under~;* upsurge; up~; vegetation; waxing; *XL; yain* [arch.]; *zoom;*

**growl** *(n.)*: angry ~; bark; cry; discharge; eruption; *fume;* gnarl; howl; *inveighing;* jar; keen; loud cry; mewl; murmur; noise; ogganition; outcry; peal; *quiritation;* roar; snarl; thunder; ululation; vociferation; waul; *xolo;* yowl; yarr; *zing;* [*Ant.* groan]

**growl** *(v.)*: *air;* bark; cry; discharge; erupt; fuss; gnarl; howl; *inveigh;* jar; keen; loudly cry; mewl; murmur; noise; outcry; peal; *quiritate;* roar; snarl; thunder; ululate; vociferate; waul; *xolo;* yowl; yarr; *zing;* [*Ant.* groan]

**grudge** *(n.)*: animosity; bitterness; complaint; chip on one's shoulder; dispute; enmity; feud; grievance; hard feelings; ill will; *jangling;* kagg; *loathing;* malignity; non-forgiveness; ought; pique; quarrel; resentment; rancor; spite; *trouble;* umbrage; vindictiveness; war; *x-fire;* yed; *zoilism;*

**grudging** *(adj.)*: against one's will; bitter; be~; complaining; disinclined; envying; foul-spirited; grudge-bearing; halfhearted; indisposed; jackalent; kicking; loath; miserly; non-willing; opposed; penurious; *questioning;* reluctant; slow; *tightfisted;* unwilling; *vacillating;* wary; *xenophobic;* yarrow; zealless; [*Ant.* game]

**grueling** *(adj.)*: arduous; backbreaking; challenging; difficult; exhausting; fatiguing; grinding; hard; intense; jading; killing; laborious; moiling; not easy; onerous; painful; quite hard; rigorous; rough; strenuous; toilsome; unrelenting; vexatious; wearisome; *x-heavy; yare;* zapping;

**gruesome** *(adj.)*: alarming; bloody; chilling; dreadful; eerie; frightening; grisly; ghastly; horrific; *intimidating;* jarring; knee-knocking; lurid; morbid; macabre; nightmarish; ominous; petrifying; *quivering;* repugnant; shocking; terrifying; unpleasant; violent; *worrisome; xiphopagous; ydrad* [arch.]; zonky; [*Ant.* good]

**gruff** *(adj.)*: abrupt; brusque; curt; dour; *explicit;* forthright; grouchy; grumpish; harsh; inconsiderate; *jaded;* kindless; laconic; mean; non-tactful; offhanded; pointed; quick; rough; rude; stern; terse; uncivil; *violent;* wrathful; *xuld [arch.]; yeesy [arch.]; zhlubby;* [*Ant.* genial]

**grumble** *(v.)*: argue; bellyache; carp; complain; decry; *explode;* fuss; groan; hone; inveigh; jangle; *kvetch* [Yid.]; land on; maunder; moan; nitpick; object; pule; quibble; repine; snarl; thunder; *ululate;* vituperate; whine; *xuld [arch.];* yawp; zing;

**guarantee** *(n.)*: assurance; bond; commitment; collateral; certification; declaration; earnest; ensuring; faithful promise; gage; guaranty; hypothecation; imprest; jurament; *kept promise;* lifetime ~; mainpernor; *negotiable security;* oath; promise; pledge; *qualified promise;* resolution; security; testament; unconditional ~; vow; vouchsafing; warranty; word (of honor); *x-one's heart; yafery* [arch.]; zealous ~;

**guarantee** *(v.)*: assure; *bond;* commit; certify; declare; ensure; faithfully promise; give one's word; hypothecate; *imprest; justify; keep promise; lifetime ~;* make assurance; *negotiable security; oath;* promise; *qualify;* resolve; seal; testify; unconditionally ~; vouch; warranty; *x-one's heart; yafery [arch.];* zealously ~;

**guaranteed** *(n.)*: assured; bonded; certified; doubly-sure; ensured; failsafe; *given one's word;* hypothecated; ironclad; just as sure as can be; *kept promise; lifetime guarantee;* made sure; nailed down; open-and-shut; promised; pledged; questionless; reliable; secure; sure(-fire); totally sure; unrisky; unconditionally ~; vouchsafed; warrantied; *x-one's heart; yafery* [arch.]; zealously ~;

**guarantor** *(n.)*: assurer; backer; cosigner; deigner; ensurer; endorser; *faithful;* guaranty; hypothecator; insurer; jurant; *keeper;* legal ~; maker of vow; notary; oath-maker; promiser; *quality assurance;* resolution-maker; sponsor; surety; testifier; underwriter; upholder; voucher; warrantor; *x on the dotted line; yafery [arch.];* zealous ~;

**guard** *(n.)*: armed ~; body~; border patrol; chaperone; defender; eunuch; escort; foot~; gatekeeper; grenadier; garrison [pl.]; horse~; hyperaspist; home ~ [pl.]; imperial ~; jailor; jaga; keeper; lookout; musketeer; night-watch(man); out~; protector; patrol; *quarter ~;* quarter- ~ [pl.]; quaternion [pl.]; rear- ~; sentry; sentinel; security; trained ~; uniformed ~; vigil; watch(man); watcher; ward; *xiphos-bearer;* yeoman of the ~; *zoauve;*

**guard** *(v.)*: attend; *bless;* cover; defend; ensconce; fortify; fend; garrison; hold; insulate; insure; jaga; keep; look after; make safe; *nestle;* overshadow; protect; *qui vive;* refuge; shelter; shield; sentinel; safe~; take care of; tend; uphold; vallate; watch (over); *x-guard; yeme* [arch.]; *zero danger;*

**guardian** *(n.)*: attendant; advocate; bodyguard; caretaker; custodian; curator; champion; defender; escort; ensurer; foster parent; guard; *helper; interested party; jaga;* keeper; *lookout;* musketeer; noble protector; numen; overseer; protector; paladin; *quarter guard; ranger;* shepherd; sentinel; trustee; tutelar; upholder; vigil(ante); watchdog; warden; *xiphos-bearer;* yeoman of the guard; *zeloter;*

**guardianship** *(n.)*: administration; advocacy; *backing;* care; custodianship; curatorship; defense; ensuring; fending; guardship; headship; interest; jurisdiction; keepership; *looking out;* management; *no harm;* overseeing; protection; *qui vive;* responsibility; stewardship; security; tutelage; upholding; vigilance; ward(ship); *xiphos; yeming* [arch.]; *zealotry;*

**guess** *(n.)*: assumption; bet; belief; conjecture; deduction; estimate; estimation; fancy; feeling; gauging; hunch; hypothesis; idea; judgment; *knowledge; lemma;* mind; notion; opinion; presumption; *quote;* reckoning; stab; supposition; speculation; theory; *urge;* view; wild ~; *xenodiagnosis; yankering; zeal;*

**guess** *(v.)*: assume; believe; bet; conjecture; deduce; estimate; figure; gauge; hypothesize; imagine; judge; *know; lucubrate;* muse; *notion;* opine; presume; *question;* reckon; speculate; suppose; surmise; think; *use brain;* view; valuate; wager; *xenodiagnose; yeme; zazen;*

**guest** *(n.)*: arrival; alien; boarder; company; caller; denizen; entrant; friend; foreigner; frequenter; gate crasher; house ~; *habitué* [F.]; invitee; incomer; intruder; journeyer; key ~; lodger; moocher; newcomer; outsider; person; quarterer; roamer; sightseer; stranger; tablemate; tourist; unexpected guest; visitor; wayfarer; *xenos* [Gr.]; *yokefellow; zingaro [It.]*

**guidance** *(n.)*: advice; backing; counsel; direction; exhortation; free advice; guiding; hortation; instruction; information; judgment; *kibizing* [Yid.]; leading; mentorship; *notification;* opinion; piece of advice; *quick ~;* recommendation; suggestion; tip; thoughts; *urging;* voice; word of advice; *xenagogy; yarking; zeroing in;*

**guide** *(n.)*: attendant; bellwether; cicerone; cynosure; conductor; counselor; director; escort; forerunner; fugleman; group leader; governor; helper; head; intendant; *judge; king's ~;* leader; master ~; navigator; outrider; pathfinder; pilot; *queen's ~;* route-planner; scout; shepherd; tour ~; usher; vanguard; warden; xenagogue; *yokemaster; zayim;*

**guide** *(v.)*: advise; administer; bring in; counsel; conduct; control; direct; exhort; escort; foreadvise; give counsel; govern; help; instruct; jockey; judge; keep on track; lead; manipulate; mentor; navigate; oversee; point; pilot; *quicken;* recommend; run; show; steer; shepherd; tender one's opinion; usher; voice; warn; *xenagogy; yeme* [L.]; *zero in;*

**guideline** *(n.)*: axiom; belief; code; dictum; ethic; fundament; guiding principle; *horse sense;* ideal; institute; judgment; kernel of wisdom; lodestar; law; moral; norm; opinion; *organon;* principle; qualm; rule; standard; truism; universal truth; veracity; wisdom; *xenagogy;* yardstick; zeteticism;

**guile** *(n.)*: astuteness; beguilement; cleverness; craft; deceit; ensnarement; fraud; *guise;* hoodwinking; imposture; japery; knavishness; lying; misleading; nobbling; outfoxing; pretext; *quiblin [arch.];* ruthlessness; slyness; treachery; underhandedness; *vulpine;* wiliness; *xuld [arch.];* yentzing; *zinger;* [*Ant.* genuineness]

**guild** *(n.)*: association; affiliation; alliance; brotherhood; craft union; coalition; confederation; *department;* establishment; fraternity; federation; group; horizontal union; industrial union; joint coalition; *kongsi* [Chin.]; labor (-local) union; league; *mutual;* nexus; organization; partnership; quinquevirate; registered ~; society; syndicate; trade union; union; *vertical union;* workers' union; *x-class;* yeald; zollverein;

**guilt** *(n.)*: accountability; blame(worthiness); blood~iness; culpability; disgrace; *deserve;* embarrassment; error; fault; guiltiness; hamartia; *injustice;* jeofail; *kink;* liability; mistake; non-innocence; omission; onus; *problem; qualm;* responsibility; remorse; shortcoming; sinfulness; *transgression; unrighteousness;* vice; wrong(doing); *xgression; yaw; zinger;* [*see* remorse; *Ant.* guiltlessness]

**guiltless** *(adj.)*: aboveboard; blameless; blemishless; crimeless; clear; clean; dovelike; error-free; faultless; *good;* guilt-free; harmless; holy; innocent; *justified;* known-innocent; lamblike; *moral;* not guilty; offenseless; pure; qualmless; questionless; righteous; spotless; sinless; taintless; unresponsible; unguilty; unimpeachable; unblamable; unreprovable; virtuous; witeless; white; *xtry.;* yet unblamed; *zero-guilt;* [*Ant.* guilty]

**guilty** *(adj.)*: accountable; blameworthy; culpable; delinquent; errant; faulty; guilt-ridden; have guilt; indictable; *jaded; knavish;* liable; *mistaken;* non-innocent; opprobrious; offending; peccant; *questionable;* red-handed; reproachful; reprehensible; *shameful;* sinful; *treacherous;* unclean; unforgiven; unpardoned; vituperable; wrong; *xgressing; yobbish; zing;* [*Ant.* guiltless]

**gulf** *(n.)*: abyss; break; chasm; depth; deep; expanse; *fosse;* gap(e); hollow; *immense;* jaw-hole; *katavothron* [Gr.]; *lap; moat;* nadir; nullah; opening; pit; *quarry;* recess; rift; ravine; span; *trench;* unbottomed pit; void; width; *xibalba;* yawn; *zone;* [*see* bay]

**gullible** *(adj.)*: artless; befoolable; childlike; credulous; dupable; ever-so-trusting; feeble-minded; foolish; fatuous; goffish; half-witted; innocent; jackass; knuckleheaded; lame-brained; moronic; naïve; obtuse; pea-brained; quacky; ridiculous; simple; trusting; unwise; verdant; victimizable; witless; *xtry. ~;* yet unsuspecting; zany;

**gulp** *(v.)*: *assimilate; bib;* chug; drink; engorge; fuddle; guzzle; *have;* inhale; infuse; ingurgitate; *juice;* knock back [slang]; lap (up) [zoo.]; *mouthful;* nip; overdrink; partake; quaff; resorb; sip; suck; swig; swallow; swill; take in; tipple; *use; voracity;* wash down [slang]; *xeres;* yaffle; yolp; *zip down;*
**gun** *(n.)*: arms; breechloader; carbine; cannon; derringer; Enfeld; flintlock; firestick; firearm; gat; hand~; howitzer; iron rations; *jingal; kalashnikov;* Luger; musket; muzzle-loader; *machine ~;* needle ~; oscar [slang]; pistol; piece; *Quaker ~;* rifle; revolver; six-shooter; shot~; submachine ~; *tommy ~; Uzi;* volley ~; wind- ~; *weapon; x- ~; yager; zap ~;*
**gunfire** *(n.)*: ack-ack; burst; blasting; barrage; crossfire; discharges; drumfire; enfilade; firing; gunshot; handgun-fire; *impact; jet; ka-blam;* lamming; machine gun fire; *noise of guns; onslaught;* pistol fire; *quant;* rifle fire; rat-at-at; shooting; thundering; *Uzi fire;* volley; weapon-fire; *x-fire; yield; zapa-zapa-zap;*
**gurgle** *(n.)*: agitation; burble; *commotion;* dribbling; effervescence; fizz(le); guggle; gargle; gush; hissing; *imboil;* jet; ker-plash; *liquid;* murmur; *noise; over-rushing;* purl; plash; *quiet burble;* ripple; rambling; regurgitation; slush; slosh; sputter; seething; tinkle; uprush; *vault;* washing; *xuld [arch.];* yote; zwish;
**gurgle** *(v.)*: agitate; bubble; burble; babble; boil; *commotion;* dribble; effervesce; fizz(le); gargle; gush; hiss; *imboil;* jet; *ker-plash; liquid;* murmur; *noise; over-rush;* purl; plash; *quietly burble;* ripple; ramble; regurgitate; slush; slosh; sputter; seethe; tinkle; uprush; *vault;* wash; *xuld [arch.];* yote; zwish;
**guru** *(n.)*: avatar; Brahman; clairvoyant; dalai lama; enlightened one; fakir [Ind.]; guide; high avatar; instructor; jnana; knowledgeable one; leader; lama; maharishi; *nome;* oracle; pandit; *qualified teacher;* religious leader; rishi; sage; swami; teacher; *utterer;* vatul; wise one; xenagogue; yogi; *zetetic;*
**gush** *(n.)*: afflux; blast; current; discharge; efflux; flow; gushing; *hurl;* issue; jet; *kiting;* loosing; movement; naid; niagara; outflow; pouring; *quickening;* rush; surge; torrent; upsurge; *vomiting;* wash; water ~; *xfer;* yern; *zwoosh;*
**gush** *(v.)*: accelerate; burst; course; drain; empty; flow; go; hurl; issue; jet; *kite; loose;* move; naid; outpour; pour; quicken; rush; spring; spout; spew; surge; stream; swoosh; *travel;* upsurge; vomit; wash; *xfer;* yead; zoom;
**gust** *(n.)*: airstream; blast; current; crosswind; draught; east wind; flaw; gale; headwind; indraft; jet stream; katabatic wind; levanter; moderate gale; notus; outburst; puff; quiff; *rotary winds;* squall; tailwind; updraft; violent wind; wind; williwaw; x-wind; *yaw;* zephyr;
**gut** *(v.)*: *abstract;* bowel; clean out; disembowel; eviscerate; exenterate; fillet; get guts out; hollow; *intestinal removal; jerk out;* open the bowels; paunch; *quarry;* remove bowels; scoop guts out; take out bowels; unbowel; viscerate; *wrench; xfer;* yank out intestines; *zero out;* [*see* destroy; burn;]
**gutter** *(n.)*: aqueduct; *breach;* conduit; channel; duct; eaves spout; flume; groove; headrace; irrigation canal; *jheel [Ind.];* kennel; leat; mouth; nullah; outlet; passageway; quanat; rone; rindle; rain ~; spillway; trough; underdrain; vasa; wasteweir; *xyrisic; yawn;* zanja;
**guy** *(n.)*: *anthropos* [Gr.]; boy; bloke; chap; dude; earthling; fellow; gentleman; human being; individual; joe [slang]; *kid;* living soul; man; *name;* one; person; *quadragenarian; rube [off.];* soul; Terran; *underling; virile;* worldling; *x-linked; yokel; zhlub;* [*Ant.* gal]
**gymnasium** *(n.)*: athletic court; basketball court; court; *dome;* exercise room; field house; fitness center; gym; health spa; indoor sport complex; *jock;* kickball court; *lower level;* match; *naumachy [Rom.];* outdoor gym; palaestra; *quadriplex;* recreation center; sports club; spa; *tennis court; upper level; venue;* weight room; xystus; xyst; YMCA; *zone;*
**gyp** *(v.)*: *allure;* bilk; cheat; defraud; ensnare; finagle; gaff; hoodwink; insnare; jape; *kid;* lie to; misguide; nobble; outfox; put one over; *quiblin* [arch.]; rip off; swindle; trick; *utter falsehood;* verneuk; wangle; *xuld [arch.]; yentz; zing;*
**gypsy** *(n.)*: ambler; bohemian; *conniver;* drifter; *emigrant;* floater; gipsy; *homeless;* itinerant; journeyer; Kanjar; *landlouper;* migrant; nomad; *oberration;* peregrinator; *quick-to-move;* roamer; sojourner; transient; *unfixed;* vagrant; wanderer; *xoraxai;* Yahgan; zingaro;

# H

**habit** *(n.)*: assuetude; addiction; behavior; custom; daily routine; established practice; fashion; general behavioral pattern; habitude; inclination; *jake [Br.]; kultur* [G.]; long-established practice; manner; normal routine; old ways; practice; pattern; *quo mode* [L.]; routine; ritual; social behavior; tradition; usage; *vein;* wont; *x-cultural; ye olde; zealous tradition;*

**habitual** *(adj.)*: automatic; behavioral; customary; disciplined; established; familiar; *general;* habitudinal; inveterate; ingrained; *jake [Br.]; known;* long-established; mechanical; normal; ordinary; practiced; perfunctory; *quotidian;* repeated; routine; standard; typical; traditional; usual; *venerated;* wonted; well-established; *x-cultural; ye olde; zealous tradition;* [Ant. heterotypical]

**hack** *(v.)*: ax; break up; chop; divide; dissever; exscind; forehew; gouge; hew; incide; *jag;* knife; lacerate; lop; mince; nick; obtruncate; prescind; quadrisect; *rip; remove;* slice; thwack; *undercut;* vell; whack; *x-sect;* yerk; *zip off;*

**Hades** *(n.)*: abyss; blazes; condemnation; damnation; eternal death; flames; *Gehenna;* hell; inferno; jahannam; *killing;* lower world; *misery;* netherworld; *opprobrium;* place of the dead; perdition; quenchless fire; *retribution;* suffering; torments; *Tartarus;* underworld; *vengeance;* wailing; xanthate; yelling; zone; [Ant. heaven]

**hag** *(n.)*: aged woman; bunter; battle-axe; beldam; crone; devil-woman; enchantress; frump; grandam; harpy; *individual;* Jezebel; korrigan; lamia; madam; medium; nag; old woman; poor old woman; *quarreler;* rude woman; sorceress; termagant; *up in years;* virago; wretch; witch; xanthippe; yenta; *zodiacist;*

**haggard** *(adj.)*: aweary [lit.]; bedraggled; careworn; drawn; disheveled; exhausted; frazzled; gaunt; half-dead; incomposed; *jaded;* keg-meg; *lethargic;* messy; non-organized; overspent; pooped; *quaggy;* run down; straggly; spent; tired; tousled; tattered; unkempt; unrested; *vile;* wiped out; wild; *x'ed;* yawnish; zapped;

**haggle** *(v.)*: argue; bicker; bargain; chaffer; dispute; dicker; *equivocate;* fuss; gainsay; *hondle* [arch.]; *inharmonious;* jangle; kick up dust; lock horns; make a problem; negotiate; naggle; offer less; palter; quibble; resist; squabble; trifle; talk down; *unharmonious;* vie; wrangle; *x-purposes;* yell; *zap;*

**hailstone** *(n.)*: *article;* ball; baseball-sized ~; chunk of ice; dime-sized ~; *enhardened ice; frozen;* golfball-sized ~; hail stone; ice pellet; *junt; kittly-benders; lob;* mass; *nugget; object;* pellet; quarter-sized ~; *rime; sleet;* stone; tennis-ball sized ~; *unthawed;* volley; wallop; xfer; yowndrift [arch.] zero degrees;

**hair** *(n.)*: auburn ~; bristle; bangs; curls; *down; eyelash;* follicles; fiber; fuzz; fluff; fur; gris; haircut; *head; item; juba* [L.]; kemp; lock; mop; mane; *nab; orange-headed;* pigtail; ponytail; quiff; ringlets; ruff; strand(s); swirl; shag; shock; tuft; tress; thatch; *unshaven;* vibrissa; wisp; whiskers; *wig;* wool; *xerasia; yellow-haired; zapata;*

**haircut** *(n.)*: *action;* buzz [slang]; barber cut; cut; *dock; electric razor cut;* fashion; *gris;* hairstyle; *induction cut; job; kudumi;* layered cut; manner of hair; *nipping; overhaul;* professional ~; *perm; quaife* [arch.]; razor cut; scissor cut; salon cut; trim; updo; *variety; well-trimmed; xerasia;* youth ~; *zip;*

**hairdresser** *(n.)*: *artiste;* barber; beautician; colorist; coiffeur [masc.]; coiffeuse [fem.]; dresser; *employee;* friseur; gentleman's ~; haircutter; hair stylist; *individual; job; kudumi;* licensed ~; men's hair stylist [masc.]; nonprofessional ~; *owner/operator;* plater; professional ~; *quaifer* [arch.]; razor cutter; stylist; trimmer; unlicensed ~; *versed;* worker; xerasia; yuppie; *zakai [Jap.];*

**hairiness** *(n.)*: *abundance;* bushiness; curliness; *downiness; excess;* furriness; fuzziness; fluffiness; *gris;* hirsuteness; *immensity; jubate;* kempiness; *lots of hair; maned;* non-baldness; over- ~; pilosity; pubescence; quantity of hair; *really hairy;* shagginess; tuftiness; *unshorn;* villosity; weediness; wooliness; *xerasia; yellow-haired; zapata;* [Ant. hairlessness]

**hairstyle** *(n.)*: Afro; buzz; bangs; cut; coif; do [slang]; *earlocks;* fashion; *gris;* haircut; hairdo; *induction cut; jarhead; kudumi; layered hair; mullet; nab; odango;* professional ~; perm; quiff; razor cut; style; *tonsure;* updo; *vogue; way; wear; waves; wig; xerasia; youth side lock; zip;*
   **Type of hairstyles**: Afro; beehive; bob; bowl cut; brush cut; buzz cut; combover; crew cut; ducktail; emo; flattop; hi-top; induction cut; jarhead; kudumi; layered; mullet; mohawk; pompadour; quiff; rattail; tonsure; shag; short; upsweep; wave; youth side lock;
**hairy** *(adj.)*: asperous; bristly; bushy; comose; capillaceous; *downy; excess;* fuzzy; fluffy; furry; fleecy; flocculent; glochidiate; hair-covered; hispid; hirsute; horrent; *inch-high shag; jubate;* kempy; lanate; lanuginous; maned; nappy; overgrown; pilous pilose; *quiff;* really ~; shaggy; tufty; unshorn; unpolled; villous; whiskery; wooly; *xerasia;* yet unshorn; *zapata;* [*Ant.* hairless]
**half-breed** *(n.)*: admixture; blend; crossbreed; *diverse; ethnically impure;* fusion; gallimaufry; hybrid; half-caste; intermixture; jumart; *kirning; lumping;* mix(ture); mutt; mongrel; mule; mulatto; mestee; *non-pure;* olio; *polyethnic;* quadroon; racial mixture; *sundry; two-races;* union; *varied; wedded;* x-breed; *yanggoma;* zebrass;
**half-hearted** *(adj.)*: apathetic; blasé; cold; draggy; *etiolated;* fainéant; fervorless; groggy; heavy; indolent; irresolute; *jog trot;* kef; lackadaisical; mopish; non-motivated; otiose; pepless; quiescent; remiss; spiritless; torpid; unenthusiastic; vapid; workshy; *xenarthrous;* yareless; zealless [*Ant.* hearty]
**halitosis** *(n.)*: awful breath; bad breath; chronic ~; dog-breath; effuvium; foul breath; garlic breath; horrible breath; icky breath; *jarring; ketty;* lousy breath; morning breath; *need a mint;* offensive breath; onion-breath; putrid breath; *quite strong breath;* reeking; smelly (-strong) breath; terrible breath; unpleasant breath; vile breath; wicked breath; *xtry. bad;* yucky breath; *zero mercy;*
**hallelujah** *(interj.)*: alleluia!; amen!; bless the Lord!; Christ be praised!; *devote;* exalt His name!; *fantastic;* glory (to God)!; halleluiah!; hosanna! *in excelsis deo!;* Jehovah be praised!; *Kneel before Him!;* Lord be praised!; may God be praised!; *notable;* O, praise His name!; praise God (-the Lord)!; *quiritation; rejoice;* Sing His praises!; thanks be to God!; *unglued; veneration;* Worship the Lord!; *xtry.;* Yahweh be praised!; Zion be praised!
**hallmark** *(n.)*: authentication; brand; characteristic; distinguishing mark; earmark; *feature; good quality; highlight;* identifiable mark; *jist;* ken-mark; logo; mark of quality; *notation;* official mark; particularity; quality mark; remarque; signature; seal of quality; trademark; unique mark; verification; way (of recognizing); *x-factor; yacht ensign; zeug [G.];*
**hallow** *(v.)*: anoint; bless; consecrate; devote; dedicate; exalt; *favor;* glorify; have consecrated; *invest;* jalap; keep; lustrate; memorialize; make holy; *nard;* ordain; purify; *quicken;* revere; set apart; solemnize; sanctify; *take for holy;* unction; venerate; wash clean; *xfer; yield; zierlich [G.];*
**hallway** *(n.)* aisle; alley; arcade; anteroom; archway; *boulevard;* corridor; *direction;* entryway; foyer; gangway; gallery; hall; *interjacent;* journey-way; *keyway;* loggia; lobby; mall; *node;* outlet; passage(way); *quo mode [L.];* rotunda; slype; transept; *under-passage;* vennel; vestibule; vomitory; (walk)way; xystus; *yele* [arch.]; *zone;*
**halo** *(n.)*: aureole; brightness; corona; disk; effulgence; fluency; glow; halation; illustriousness; *joyous; kindle;* light; mandorla; nimbus; O; parhelion; *quality;* radiance; ring; shining; transplendency; unearthly glow; vesica; *wreath; x-radius;* yellow ~; *zone;*
**ham** *(n.)*: * *animal protein;* Black Forest ~; cured ~; daisy ~; *edibles;* fresh ~; gammon; haggess; *ingesta;* jambon; kebab; lunchmeat; middling meat; *nourishment;* oven-baked ~; pork shoulder; *pig-meat; quarry;* roast pork; spiral ~; smoked ~; *turkey-bacon;* uncured ~; Virginia ~; Westphalia ~; *xarque;* yark; zakuski [Rus.];
**hamburger** *(n.)*: * all-beef burger; burger; cheeseburger; double burger; *eats; food;* grilled ~; *hot dog; item;* jumbo burger; *ketchup; lunch;* mushroom burger; *meat; nacket;* onion; patty; quarter-pounder; *roast beef sandwich;* slider; Salisbury steak; *sandwich; turkey burger;* ultimate ~; *veggie burger; the* works; *xtr.* well-done ~; *yummy;* zakuski [Rus.];

**hamlet** *(n.)*: *assemblage;* burg; clachan [Scot.]; dorp; exurb; free city; *ghost town;* hick town; hometown; *invillaged;* junction; kirk-town [Scot.]; *location;* market town; *native town;* outpost; one-horse town; place; *quarter;* rancho; settlement; shire; thorp; town; *urban center;* village; whistle stop [slang]; *Xenia;* yokel town; *zone;*

**hammer** *(n.)*: * *article;* ballpein ~; claw ~; drop ~; *equipment;* fuller; gavel; *hand tool;* iron ~; jack~; kevel; Lucerne ~; maul; mallet; nail ~; *object;* pein ~; plexor; *quern;* rawhide ~; sledge; tack ~; tilt ~; tendon ~; trip ~; *utensil; vulcanized ~;* war ~; *x-sect;* yedder; *zeug [G.];*

**hammer** *(v.)*: assault; beat; clobber; drub; *efface;* flail; *get;* hit; impact; jow; knock; lam; mash; nail; *overstrike;* pound; quab; rap; strike; thwack; *uppercut; veney;* whack; *x-sect;* yedder; *zonk;*

**hamper** *(n.)*: *area;* basket; clothes basket; dosser; *enclosure;* flasket; *gabion;* holder; *item; junket;* kit; laundry basket; maund; nacelle; osier ~; ped; *quiver;* receptacle; scuttle; *tumbril; ungula;* voider; wisket; x-weave ~; *yadzutsu [Jap.];* zipper ~;

**hamper** *(v.)*: avert; block; cumber; delay; deter; discomfit; encumber; frustrate; *gum up;* hinder; impede; jam up; keep (from); limit; *moderate;* nullify; obstruct; prevent; quash; restrain; stop; trammel; thwart; *undo;* veto; withhold; *x; yank;* zilch; [*Ant.* help]

**hamstring** *(v.)*: *afflict;* becripple; cripple; disable; enfeeble; *feeble; game;* hough [Scot.]; immobilize; *jake-legged;* knock out; lame; maim; nullify; *obstruct;* paralyze; *query;* render inoperative; sabotage; trammel; thwart; *undo; victimize;* wing; *wound; x-ing;* yedder; *zap;*

**hand** *(n.)*: appendage; *bind;* claw; clutches [pl.]; dukes [pl.]; *embrace;* forepaw; falcula; fingers; forehand; fist; grip; hand; *instrument; jabber;* knuckle; left ~; meat hook [slang]; mitt; metacarpus; manus; *nieve; organ;* open ~; paw; palm; *quadridigitate;* right ~; *seize;* talon; table; upper ~; volar; *work; xylaria;* yads; *zet [dial.];*

    **Kinds of *handed***: big-handed; double-handed; four-handed; large-handed; left-handed; lily-handed; one-handed; right-handed; single-handed; two-handed;

**handbag** *(n.)*: accessory bag; bag; clutch; caryall; day purse; European ~; *fanny pack;* grip; holdall [Aus.]; inro; *journey-sack;* kit bag; *luggage;* money- ~; *nécessaire* [F.]; organizer; purse; pocketbook; *quiver;* reticule; shoulder bag; satchel; tote; utility case; valise; *vanity case;* wallet; *x-bag; yannigan;* zipper-bag;

**handbook** *(n.)*: authoritative text; book; bible; compendium; *digest;* enchirdion; field-book; field guide; guide(book); how-to book; instructions; *journal; kappa book; literature;* manual; *notes;* operations ~; procedure book; publication; *quarto;* rule book; sourcebook; textbook; utility guide; vade-mecum; *work;* xenagogy; *yearbook; zipper-book;*

**handicap** *(n.)*: ailment; *becrippling; burden;* cumbrance; disability; disablement; encumbrance; feebleness; *gimp;* hindrance; impairment; *joggling; keeping from;* lameness; *maimedness;* non-ability; obstacle; problem; *quirk;* reduced ability; stymie; *tough situation; unable; vulnerability;* weakness; *x-out; yielding; zapped;*

**handicapped** *(adj.)*: *ailing;* becrippled; challenged; cumbered; debilitated; disabled; encumbered; *feeble;* gammy; hindered; impaired; incapacitated; *joggling; kept from;* lame; maimed; *not able;* obstructed; physically challenged; *quirk; reduced;* stymied; *tough situation; unable; vulnerable;* weak; wheelchair-bound; *x'ed out; yielded; zapped;*

**handkerchief** *(n.)*: *animetta;* babushka; cloth; disposable wipe; *embroidered ~;* facial tissue; *garb;* hankie; handcloth; *item; jaconet;* kerchief; linen ~; monogrammed ~; nose rag; *object;* pocket ~; *querche* [arch.]; romal; rag; silk ~; *tissue; unused ~;* veil; white ~; *xanthation;* yashmak; *zeug;*

**handle** *(n.)*: ansa; bail; brake; broom~; crank; crop; drawer pull; *equipment;* finger-grip; grip; handgrip; handlebar; hilt; haft; helve; iron ~; jug- ~; knob; kilp; kimbo ~; lever; *maniglions;* neap; *object;* pommel; pull-handle; *quillion;* rounce; strap; snath; stale; stock; twist ~; umbo; *vellicate;* winch; winder; *xfer; yank; zeuglodon;*

**handle** *(v.)*: affect; behave toward; cope; control; deal with; do; drive; execute; feel; fare; finger; fell; fondle; grip; get working; govern; have under control; interact; jockey; keep (under control); *lead;* manage; manipulate; maneuver; navigate; operate; over~; perform; pick up; play with; *quicken;* run; supervise; treat; touch; tiffler; take the oversight of; use; *vivify;* work; wield; *xuld [arch.];* yeme; *zip;* [*see* cope]

**handmaiden** *(n.)*: attendant; bondmaid (-woman); *bonne* [F.]; cookmaid; dairymaid; eye-servant; famulus; girl; handmaid; housemaid; *indentured servant; jobholder;* kitchen-maid; lady-servant; maid(servant); neif; offsider; parlormaid; quarter-maid; *retainer* [arch.]; slave(girl); servant; tweeny; underservant; *vassal;* wench; waiting-maid; *x-man;* yardwoman; *zaikai* [Jap.];

**handsome** *(adj.)*: attractive; buff; bonny; comely; charming; dashing; dreamy; enchanting; fine-looking; fetching; goodly; heart-alluring; ideal; *jaunt;* keen; lovely; marvelous-looking; nice-looking; *outstanding;* pleasant-looking; *quaint;* ruddy; striking; suave; *terrific; urbane;* virile; well-favored (-looking); *xtry.;* you-beaut [Aus.]; zippy; [*see* beautiful; *Ant.* homely]

**handwriting** *(n.)*: autography; *backhand;* chicken scratch; characters; cursive; chirography; calligraphy; *document; epistle;* form; graphic form; hand-writing; inscription; *journalism; kapnography;* longhand; manuscript; notation; niggle; *original ~;* print; pencraft; *the quill; remarks;* scribbling; scawl; scrivening; script; *text; uncials; verbiage;* writing; xiaozhuan; yielding; zeug;

**handy** *(adj.)*: accessible; advantageous; beneficial; close by; convenient; *deft;* expedient; fine; good; helpful; instrumental; *jim dandy;* keen; *lovely; masterful;* nearby; *opportune;* profitable; quick; ready-to-use; serving; tractable; useful; valuable; within reach; *xtry.; yieldful;* zippy; [*Ant.* hard]

**hang** *(v.)*: attach; append; bow; bend; cling; droop; dangle; drape; depend; *endure;* flop; fasten; fix; float; grab; hold; hover; impend; incline; *join; kite;* loom; lop; make dependant; nail; overhang; pin; *quat;* rest; sag; slouch; slump; sling; suspend; tack; tower; *unite; vice;* wave; *x-out;* yede; *zero gravity;*

**happen** *(v.)*: arise; befall; betide; chance; crop up; come to pass; develop; ensue; eventuate; fare; fall; follow; fortune; go on; hap; hazard; hit; intervene; *jump up; kep;* light; materialize; *near;* occur; proceed; *quicken;* rise; *result; run into;* spring up; stir; supervene; take place; transpire; unfold; venture; *work; xpire; yield; zip;*

**happening** *(n.)*: affair; *befall;* chapter; development; event; experience; episode; fact; going on; happenstance; incident; *juncture;* key event; *lot;* matter; manifestation; notable event; occurrence; occasion; phenomenon; *quicken;* reality; situation; time; thing; *unfolding; venture;* work out; *xtr. event; yield;* zinger;

**happiness** *(n.)*: animation; afterglow; bliss; cheer(fulness); delight; elation; exhilaration; exuberance; felicity; gladness; gaity; glee; hilarity; intoxication; joy(fulness); jubilation; *keenness;* lightheartedness; merriment; *niceness;* overjoy; pleasure; *queme;* rejoicing; sunniness; satisfaction; thrill; transport; *uplifted; vivacity*; winsomeness; *Xanadu;* yeastiness; zestfulness; [*Ant.* heartbrokenness]

**happy** *(adj.)*: animated; appreciative; blissful; beaming; cheerful; content; delighted; exuberant; exhilarated; elated; exultant; felicitous; glad(some); gay; gleeful; high-spirited; intoxicated; jolly; joyful; jubilant; *keen;* lighthearted; merry; *nice;* overjoyed; pleased; *queme;* rejoicing; sunny; satisfied; thrilled; uplifted; *vivacious;* well-pleased; *xtry.;* yeasty; zestful; [*Ant.* heartbroken]

**harass** *(v.)*: antagonize; bother; beleaguer; chivy; chafe; disturb; exasperate; frustrate; gall; hassle; harry; irritate; jangle; knock; leaguer; menace; nettle; oppress; pester; *queach [arch.];* roust; rile; scathe; trouble; unnerve; vex; weary; *x-ing;* yerk; *zing;*

**harbor** *(n.)*: anchorage; asylum; berth; bay; cove; dock; embayment; fjord; gulf; haven; inlet; jetty; kyle [Scot.]; lodgment; lagoon; marina; narrows; opening; port; quay; refuge; slip; shelter; *tarn; use;* voe; wharf; *xyrisic; yeming* [arch.]; *zone;*

**harbor** *(v.)*: abet; billet; conceal; defend; ensconce; fend; give refuge to; hide; insulate; jaga; keep; look after; make safe; nestle; overshadow; protect; pavilion; quarter; refuge; shelter; take care of; uphold; vallate; ward; *x-guard; yeme* [arch.]; *zero danger;*

**hard** *(adj. difficult)*: abstruse; bewildering; complicated; complex; difficult; deep; elaborate; formidable; grueling; highbrow; hairy; hard-to-understand; intricate; involved; *jarring;* knotty; labyrinthine; mysterious; mind-boggling; non-easy; overwhelming; perplexing; puzzling; *question-filled;* recondite; *shadowy;* technical; tough; unsearchable; vexatious; wildering; *xenagogic; yucky; zapping;* [*Ant.* handy]

**hard** *(adj. laborious)*: arduous; back-breaking; challenging; difficult; exhausting; fatiguing; grueling; heavy; intense; jading; killing; laborious; moiling; not easy; operose; problematical; *quite ~;* rigorous; strenuous; toilsome; tough; *uphill; very difficult;* wearisome; *x-heavy; yare; zapping;*

**hard** *(adj. solid)*: adamant; bendless; buckram; callous; durable; dense; ever-rigid; firm; granitelike; hardened; inflexible; indurated; ironlike; impenetrable; impermeable; *jarless;* kiln-hardened; lapideous; mighty; non-pliant; oaky; petrous; *quartz;* rigid; rock-solid; stiff; solid; strong; tough; unbending; unbendable; unyielding; unbreakable; very ~; well-built; xtr. ~; yieldless; zero give;

**harden** *(v.)*: anneal; become hard; cure; callous; case- ~; densify; en~; firm up; get harder; ~ (up); indurate; jell; kern; lapidify; make hard; *non-soft;* ossify; obdure; over~; petrify; quick-set; rigidify; stiffen; solidify; set; strengthen; temper; toughen; *undergird;* vulcanize; wax hard; *xerogel;* yearn; zet [dial.]; [*see* congeal]

**hardhearted** *(adj.)*: austere; *brutal;* callous; cold-hearted; disdainful; *excessive;* flint-hearted; *galsome;* hardened; heartless; incompassionate; ironhearted; jaded; knark; *loveless;* merciless; non-sparing; obdurate; pitiless; *querulous;* ruthless; severe; thick-skinned; unmerciful; unpitying; unfeeling; *violent; wicked; xenophobic;* yieldless; *zoilean;* [*Ant.* humane]

**hardness** *(n.)*: adamancy; brittleness; callousness; durability; *ever-rigid;* firmness; *granitelike;* hardiness; inflexibility; impenetrability; *jarless;* keeping; ligature [med.]; might; non-pliability; oakiness; *petrous; quartz;* rigidity; rigidness; stiffness; solidity; solidness; strength; toughness; unyieldingness; *vulcanization; willfulness; x-hard;* yieldlessness; *zero give;*

**hardship** *(n.)*: asperity; adversity; burden; complication; difficulty; encumbrance; fix; grief; hard times; incommodity; jam; kettle of fish [slang]; load; misfortune; need; *ordeal;* problem; quandary; rattle; suffering; trouble; unrest; vexation; worries; woe; *xerotripsis; yuckiness; zero;*

**harlot** *(n.)*: adulteress; bawd girl; call girl; courtesan; doxy; escort; fornicator; gamester; hooker; hireling; *immoral woman;* jade; kittock; lady of the evening; mistress; meretrix; nightwalker; *obscene woman;* prostitute; quean; rig; romp; strange woman; slut; slattern; strumpet; streetwalker; tramp; trollop; *unfaithful woman;* venal; whore; *x-rated woman; yaud; zipless;*

**harlotry** *(n.)*: adultery; badness; *concupiscence;* debauchery; *evil;* fornication; godlessness; hooking; hustling; immorality; incontinence; jadery; *kittock;* lasciviousness; looseness; *malfeasance; non-faithfulness;* odure; pimping; profligacy; playing the whore; queanery; revelry; solicitation; streetwalking; trollopy; unchastidy; uncleanness; venery; wenching; whoredom; white slavery; *x-rated behavior;* yielding; *zhlubbery;*

**harm** *(n.)*: affliction; blast; calamity; disservice; detriment; damage; evil; foulness; greivance; hurt; injury; impairment; jeel; *knock;* loss; mischief; marring; maiming; nocument; offense; prang; persecution; *query;* ruin; scath; trouble; unhealthiness; victimization; violence; wound; *x-ing;* yedder; zinging; [*Ant.* help]

**harm** *(v.)*: afflict; blast; *cripple;* disserve; damage; endamage; fix [slang]; get; hurt; injure; ill-treat; impair; jeel; *kick; knock;* louse up; mar; maim; nick; *offend;* pain; persecute; *quash;* ruin; scathe; trouble; *unsafe;* victimize; wound; *x.; ydrad [arch.];* zing; [*Ant.* help]

**harmful** *(adj.)*: adverse; bad; counterproductive; corrupting; crippling; detrimental; deleterious; damaging; destructive; endangering; foul; gnarly; hurtful; injurious; jeopardous; *known risk;* lethal; malefic; nocuous; opposing; perilous; pernicious; *quashing;* ruinous; self-destructive; threatening; unbeneficial; unsafe; violent; wounding; *x.; ydrad [arch.]; zero safety;* [*Ant.* harmless]

**harmless** *(adj.)*: alright; benign; *condonable;* disarmed; dangerless; ever-safe; fine; good; hurtless; innocent; inoffensive; innocuous; innoxious; *just fine;* kind; *lovely;* made ~; non-harmful; okay; poisonless; powerless; quite safe; risk-free; safe; trustworthy; unoffending; unhurtful; unharmful; very well; well; *xtry; you beaut [Aus.]; zero danger;* [Ant. harmful]

**harmonious** *(adj.)*: agreeable; accordant; balanced; brotherly; concordant; dulcet; eurythmic; euphonious; friendly; genial; harmonic; imbellic; jovial; keen; like-minded; melodious; nice; orchestral; pleasing; *quality;* reciprocal; symphonic; symphonious; tuneful; unhostile; very friendly; well-balanced; welcoming; xenial; *yieldful; zero discordance;* [Ant. harse-sounding]

**harmonize** *(v.)*: agree; attune; balance; blend; correspond; complement; draw together; equalize; fit; go along with; homogenize; heal; integrate; jive [slang]; keep harmony with; line up; mesh; *normalize;* orchestrate; proportion; quiet; reconcile; reconciliate; symphonize; tune; unify; *validate;* work out; *x-harmonize; yield; zero discord;*

**harmony** *(n.)*: agreement; accord(ance); balance; blending; consonance; concert; *delight;* equilibrium; fellowship; good communion; harmonization; integration; jiving [slang]; keeping; like-mindedness; meshing; non-discord; oneness; peace; *quality;* rapport; synchronization; togetherness; unity; *very congruent; widespread agreement; x-harmony; yung* [Chin.]; *zero-discord;*

**harp** *(n.)*: ∗ aeolian ~; bell ~; cither; dulcimer; Eolian lyre; French ~; gittith; hammer dulcimer; Irish ~; *instrument;* Jew's ~; kinnor; lyre; MacArthur ~; nebel; ongnyugum; psaltery; qanon; rote; symphonia; *stringed instrument;* trigon; upright ~; veena; Welsh ~; xalam; yangkin; zither;

**harsh** *(adj.)*: austere; abrasive; abusive; bitter; brutal; cruel; difficult; extreme; fierce; graceless; grueling; hard; intense; jarring; killing; *lousy;* mean; nasty; onerous; painful; *quantitative;* rough; sour; stark; severe; tremendous; unrelenting; violent; wicked; xtry.; yieldless; *zero mercy;* [Ant. humane]

**harshness** *(n.)*: asperity; acerbity; austerity; brutality; bitterness; cruelty; difficulty; extremeness; fierceness; gracelessness; hardness; ill-temper; intensity; jangliness; *keenness;* lack of grace; meanness; nastiness; onerousness; painfulness; *quantity;* roughness; severity; sourness; starkness; torvity; unkindness; verjuice; wickedness; *xtry.;* yieldlessness; *zero mercy;* [Ant. humaneness]

**harvest** *(n.)*: accumulation; by-product; crop; *draw; ears;* effect; fruitage; fruit-time; gatherings; garner; gain; harvesting; ingathering; *jam;* kirning [Scot.]; *load;* mass; *net;* outgrowth; output; produce; quantity; reaping; return; storing; season; talings; upshot; vintage; *wheat ~; x-crop;* yield; zafra;

**harvester** *(n.)*: agriculturalist; binder; cutter; cropper; *doer;* excerptor; farmhand; farmer; gleaner; hired hand; harvestman; *indentured servant; jobholder;* kirner [Scot.]; laborer; manservant; neif; operator; picker; *quarterer;* reaper; servant; sharecropper; toiler; *underling;* villein; workman; *x-man;* yeoman; *zaikai;*

**hassle** *(n.)*: annoyance; bother; carrying-on; difficulty; embroilment; frustration; grief; hardship; inconvenience; jangling; kink; *lousy;* menace; nuisance; onerousness; problem; quibble; rigamarole; setback; trouble; unpleasantness; vexation; worry; wrangling; *xtry. menace; yuckiness; zoilean;* [Ant. help]

**hassle** *(v.)*: annoy; bother; contend; disturb; exasperate; frustrate; gall; harass; irk; jangle; *knock; livid;* menace; nag; nettle; *obtrude;* pester; *queach [arch.];* rile; squabble; test; trouble; unnerve; vex; weary; wrangle; *x-ing;* yerk; *zing;* [Ant. help]

**haste** *(n.)*: acceleration; alacrity; bustle; celerity; darting; expedition; fastness; foolhardiness; going fast; hurriedness; impatience; impetuousness; jildi [mil.]; keenness; liveliness; madcap; nimbleness; overhastiness; prematureness; quickness; rapidity; rashness; speed; tall stepping [slang]; urgency; velocity; wildness; *x-speed; yar;* zippiness; [Ant. hesitance]

**hasten** *(v.)*: accelerate; bustle; charge; dart; expedite; fly; flash; get moving; hurry (up); hustle; hie; impel; jet; *kite;* lope; move; make haste; *nimble;* open the throttle; pop; quicken; rush; race; speed (up); tear; urge; unblock; vitalize; whiz; *xuld [arch.];* yern; zip (to it); [Ant. hinder]

**hasty** *(adj.)*: abrupt; brash; careless; devil-may-care; expeditious; fast; gadarene; hurried; impulsive; impetuous; *jumping to it; keeping pace;* lively; madcap; nerve-shattering; over~; precipitous; premature; perfunctory; quick; rushed; rash; reckless; speedy; too soon; unconsidered; veloce; whizzing; x-speed; yar; zippy; [*Ant.* hesitant]
**hat** *(n.)*: * *article;* bonnet; cap; chapeau; derby; *ensemble;* felt ~; *garb;* headpiece; helmet; hard~; *investient; jingasa* [Jap.]; kepi; *livery;* mitre; nivernois; *object;* panama ~; *quoif;* riding ~; sun~; titfer; top ~; *ushanka;* visor; wimple; *xtr. tall top~;* yarmulke; zarcole;
**hatch** *(v.)*: appear; *arise;* birth; break out; brood; come out of; develop; emerge; fabricate; go out; *have;* incubate; issue; *jab;* keep warm; *let out;* materialize; *nurture;* originate; produce; *quicken; rise;* sit on; show up; *turn up;* upspring; *view;* warm; went [p.t.]; *xuld [arch.];* yede; *zip out;* [*see* contrive]
**hate** *(n.)*: aversion; animosity; abhorrence; bitterness; contempt; disdain; disgust; detestation; enmity; evilwishing; fiendfulness; gall; hatefulness; hatred; indignation; ill-will; *jadedness;* kindlessness; loathing; malice; no love; odium; odiousness; *poison;* querulousness; rancor; revulsion; spite; scorn; *tetchiness;* uncharitableness; venom; virulence; vitriol; *withstanding;* xenophobia; *yuckiness; zealotry;*
**hate** *(v.)*: abhor; abominate; bear ill-will; contemn; disdain; despise; detest; deplore; execrate; *fie; frown; gall;* hold in disdain; *ill-will; jaded; kick;* loathe; mislike; not like; *odious; pshaw; querulous;* resist; resent; reprobate; scorn; take an aversion to; utterly loathe; vilipend; *wrathful; xenophobic; yucky; zero love;*
**hateful** *(adj.)*: abhorrent; bitter; contemptible; disdainful; despiteful; embittered; execrative; evil-wishing; foul; galsome; hostile; intolerant; inimical; jaded; kindless; low-down; loathsome; mean; malicious; malevolent; nasty; odious; pernicious; querulous; resentful; spiteful; terrible; unkind; ugly; virulent; wicked; xenophobic; *yucky;* zoilean; [*Ant.* heart-endearing]
**hatred** *(n.)*: aversion; animosity; abhorrence; bitterness; contempt; dislike; disdain; disgust; detestation; enmity; fight; gall; hatefulness; hostility; ill-will; *indignation;* jangliness; *knocking;* loathing; malice; odium; *polarity; poison;* querulousness; resentful; repulsion; revulsion; spite; scorn; *tetchiness;* unpopularity; vice; venom; virulence; vitriol; *withstanding;* xenophobia; *yawping; zoilism;*
**haul** *(v.)*: *action;* bring; carry; drag; deliver; *export;* freight; get; heave; *impel;* janker; kedge; lug; move; *non-stationary; outdrag;* pull; *quarter-cart;* relay; ship; tow; tug; tote; transport; *uptake;* vellicate; *wheel;* xfer; yomp; *zip;*
**have** *(v.)*: apprehend; bear; claim; control; *draw; embrace;* fill; grip; get; gain; hold; inherit; *just have;* keep; lay hold of; maintain; *nab;* obtain; occupy; own; possess; *quantify;* retain; secure; tote; take (possession of); use; *vaunt;* wield; win; *xfer; yain* [arch.]; zip out;
**haven** *(n.)*: anchorage; asylum; *bay;* cove; dock; *exurb;* franchise; *gangway;* harbor; *inlet;* jetty; key town; lodging; lodgment; megaport; marina; *near-shore;* outport; port; protection; quarter; refuge; seaport; shelter; safe ~; sanctuary; *town;* urban center; *voe;* winter-quarters; wharf; *Xanadu; yeming* [arch.]; *zone;*
**hay** *(n.)*: alfalfa; *barley;* chaff; dry feed; forage; ensilage; fodder; grass; haylage; ile; *Japanese millet;* kemple; lovegrass; meslin; *natural grass; orchard grass;* provender; pasturage; quill; redtop; straw; tow; *unprocessed grain; vittles;* winter feed; xyris; yard; *zacate;*
**hazard** *(n.)*: adversity; *bad;* chance; danger; endangerment; *foreboding;* gamble; harm; imperilment; jeopardy; known risk; *life-threatening;* menace; maleficence; non-safety; *ominous;* peril; *quicksand;* risk; self-risk; threat; uncertainty; unsafety; vulnerability; warning; woe; "x"; *yeopartie* [arch.]; *zero safety;*
**hazard** *(v.)*: attempt; bechance; brave; chance; dare; endanger; face up to; gamble with; hazard; imperil; jeopardize; *knowingly ~;* lay open; make vulnerable; *non-protected;* open to danger; put at risk; peril; *questionable;* risk; subject to danger; take risk; *undertake;* venture; wager; *"x"; yeopartie [arch.]; zero guarantee;*

**hazardous** *(adj.)*: adverse; bad; chancy; dangerous; endangering; foreboding; gnarly; high-risk; harmful; injurious; jeopardous; *known risk;* life-threatening; malefic; nocuous; *ominous;* parlous; perilous; questionable; risky; self-hazarding; threatening; treacherous; unsafe; venturesome; woeful; *x.; ydrad [arch.]; zero safety;* [*Ant.* harmless]

**haze** *(n. mist)*: atomization; brume; cloud; dust; dimness; exhaust; fume; fog; gas; gauze; haziness; indistinctness; *jumble; KH instability;* London fog; mist; miasma; nimbus; obscurity; puff; pall; *quasi-vaporous; reverie;* spray; steam; smoke; smog; *tizzy; umbered;* vapor; wisp; *xenon cloud; yellowy cloud; zirconium cloud;*

**haze** *(n. lethargy)*: abstraction; bemusement; confusion; daze; engrossment; floatiness; glassy-eyed look; heaviness; incoherence; jag; *keif [Arab.];* lethargy; muddle; nystagmus; obscurity; preoccupation; reverie; stupor; trance; *under;* vegging out [slang]; wacking out [slang]; *x-fix; yarelessness; zoned out;*

**hazy** *(adj.)*: addled; blurred; cloudy; dim; enclouded; fuzzy; foggy; gray; halituous; indistinct; jumbled; *KH instability;* lowery; misty; nebulous; obscure; pea-soupy; *qually* [arch.]; rimy; smoky; turbid; unclear; vague; vaporous; veiled; wispy; *xenon cloud; yellowy cloud; zero-zero;*

**head** *(n. noggin)*: *apex;* block; bonce [Br.]; brain; caput; cranium; crown; dome [poet.]; *egg~; face; gray ~;* high point; *item;* jobbernowl; *jole [zoo.]; kopf* [G.]; *lambda; memento mori [L.];* nut; noodle; noggin [all slang]; occiput; pate; quadrigeminal; *red ~;* scalp; skull; *temple;* top; *upper extremity;* vertex; *whiskers; xerosis; yead* [arch.]; *zenith;*

**head** *(n. ruler)*: authority; boss; chief; director; executive; *foreman;* governor; headman; intendant; jarl; king; leader; lord; master; *nobleman;* overseer; oligarch; president; prime minister; potentate; queen [fem.]; ruler; superintendent; sovereign; taskmaster; *ultimate authority;* vizer; *warden; warlord;* XO; *yokemaster;* zayim;

**heading** *(n.)*: article header; banner head; cap text; designation; epigraph; *face; general ~;* header; headline; inscription; *journalism; key;* label; message; notation; outline ~; preamble; *quotation;* rubric; running head; subheading; sign; section ~; title; *uncials; verbiage;* writing; *xiaozhuan; yield; zeug;*

**headless** *(adj.)*: acephalous; beheaded; crownless; dismembered; decapitated; *executed; finished off;* guillotined; having no head; *incide; jugular; killed;* lopped-off (head); *mindless;* necked; *off; performed execution; quenched;* removed head; *severed; taken-off;* undone; victimized; without a head; *x-out; yerk; zip off;*

**headline** *(n.)*: attention-getter; banner; cap text; drop line; epigraph; feature ~; *gist;* header; heading; inscription; jump head; *key;* leader; motto; notation; *over;* poster text; *quote;* rubric; screamer; title; *uncials; verbiage;* words; *xiaozhuan; yield; zeug;*

**headquarters** *(n.)*: army base; *axis;* bastion; center; central office; capital; *dominion;* epicenter; fortress; general ~; hub; HQ; inmost command post; imperial palace; *joint ~;* kernel; *kommandantur* [G.]; *lodge;* main office; nucleus; nerve center; operations center; pith; *Quirinal;* royal palace; supreme ~; *throne room; unit; vault;* war room; XO; *yamen [Chin.]; zenith;*

**headship** *(n.)*: authority; *badge;* control; command; directorship; dominion; empowering; faculty; government; hegemony; influence; jurisdiction; kingship; lordship; mastery; name; oversight; power; *quo warranto* [L.]; right; rule; say-so; *throne;* umpirage; *virtue;* warrant; weight; *xenagogy;* yard; *zonal control;*

**heal** *(v.)*: ameliorate; *better;* cure; convalesce; deliver; *enhance;* fix; get better; help; improve; *jump ahead;* knit; *let cure;* mend; make well; nurse to health; *nurse; optimize;* patch (up); *quick-fix;* recuperate; recover; rectify; restore; scab over; *succor;* take a turn for the better; *undo; vamp;* wax stronger; *xtry. recovery; yele* [arch.]; *zero affliction;* [*Ant.* hurt]

**healing** *(adj.)*: analeptic; *better;* convalescent; curative; delivering; *enhancing;* fixing; *gaining;* helping; iatric; *jumping ahead;* knitting; *let cure;* medicinal; nursing; *optimizing;* patching (up); *quick-fix;* remedial; recuperative; restorative; strengthening; therapeutic; *undoing;* vulnerary; wholesome; *xtry. recovery; yele* [arch.]; *zero affliction;* [*Ant.* hurtful]

**health** *(n.)*: able-bodiedness; bodily ~; condition; *dandiness;* eupepsia; fitness; good ~; healthiness; invalescence; *iechd da* [Welsh]; *just fine; keen ~;* lustiness; medical ~; normalcy; overall ~; propriety; *qualification;* robustness; shape; strength; soundness; trimness; *unimpaired;* verdure; well-being; wellness; *xtry. ~; yaul;* zippiness;

**healthy** *(adj. nutritious)*: advantageous; beneficial; *conducive; dandy;* enjoying good health; fine; good; healthful; invigorating; just fine; keen; *life-giving; mighty fine;* nutritious; nourishing; *organic; pure; quartful* [arch.]; right; sound; salubrious; salutary; *tremendous; uncompromised;* vitaminic; well; wholesome; *xtry.; yaul;* zero detriment; [*Ant.* harmful]

**healthy** *(adj. well)*: able-bodied; bodily well; *capital;* dandy; entire; fit; fine; good; hearty; hale; *in good health;* just fine; keen; lusty; mighty fine; nurtured; okay; peachy; peak; *quartful* [arch.]; robust; sound; strong; trim; thriving; tip-top; unimpaired; vigorous; well; whole; *xtry.; yaul;* zippy; [*Ant.* hurting]

**heap** *(n.)*: amassment; batch; bunch; bank; bulk; collection; cluster; drift; deposit; embankment; *flock;* gathering; group; hill; ingathering; *juba* [L.]; knoll; koppie; lump; load; lade; mess; mass; mound; mountain; *number;* overabundance; pile; quire; quantity; rick; ruck; stack; stockpile; tussock; *unit; volley;* wad; whisk; windrow; wagonload; wheen; *xtry.* pile; yelm; *zet* [dial.];

**heap** *(v.)*: accumulate; amass; bank; collect; cumulate; deposit; enlarge; embale; *fatten;* gather; hoard; increase; *jump up; keep growing;* lay up; mound; *number;* overgrow; pile; *quadruplicate;* reposit; store up; stockpile; treasure up; upbuild; *volume;* wax larger; *XL; yain* [arch.]; *zoom;*

**hear** *(v.)*: ascertain; attend; bend an ear; comprehend; discern; distinguish; entertain; fathom; give ear; hark; hear out; heed; hearken; identify; *judge;* keep; listen; list [poet.]; lend ear; mark; mind; *note;* over~; pay attention; perceive; *quietly listen;* rehear; *sense;* tend; understand; *volume;* wot; xenodiagnose; yield; zero in;

**hearing** *(n.)*: audibility; *bear;* comprehension; discernment; ears; fathoming; giving ear; heeding; identification; *judgment;* keeping; listening; minding; noise-perception; *over~;* perception; *quality of ~; rehear;* sound-perception; *tending;* understanding; voice-recognition; *wot;* xenodiagnose; yield; zero in;

**heart** *(n. affections)*: affections; bosom; core; devotion; essence; feelings; *gut;* heart of hearts; inner self (-man; -nature); *joyous;* kernel; lifeblood; middle; nucleus; ontology; passion; quintessence; quiddity; root; soul; spirit; ticker; underneath; vehemence; will; *xenenthesis;* yearning; zeal;

**heart** *(n. center)*: axis; belly; center(point); crux; core; dead center; epicenter; fesse-point; *gizzard;* hub; interior; inmost part *just exactly centered;* kernel; limaçon; midst; midway; midpoint; middle; nave; nucleus; omphalos; pith; *quotidian;* right in the middle; smack in the middle [slang]; thick; umbilic; vitals; *within;* x-section; yolk; *zone;*

**heartbeat** *(n.)*: *arrhythmia;* beating; beats per minute; cadence; drubbing; *echo;* fibrillation; *going;* heartthrob; im; *judder; knock;* lam; *murmur; noise; occurrence;* pounding; palpitation; pace; pulse; pulsation; *quivering;* rhythm; rate; *sound;* throb; thumping; *uptempt; vibration; within;* xfer; yield; *zone;*

**heartbroken** *(adj.)*: *affected;* blue; crestfallen; downhearted; despondent; dejected; *emotional;* forlorn; grief-stricken; heartsick; heavy (of heart); inconsolable; joyless; *keening;* low; miserable; *negative;* overcome; piteous; *quivering;* rueful; sorrowful; tearful; upset; very sad; woeful; *xtry. downhearted; yearnful; zestless;* [*Ant.* happy]

**heartfelt** *(adj.)*: authentic; bona fide; cordial; deep-felt; earnest; fervent; genuine; honest; ingenuous; justifiable; keen; loving; *mean it;* never-failing; open; passionate; *questionless;* real; sincere; true; unfeigned; veritable; wholehearted; *x-parent; yes;* zero hypocrisy; [*Ant.* hypocritical]

**heartless** *(adj.)*: austere; businesslike; callous; cruel; disinterested; emotionless; flint-hearted; granitelike; hard(-hearted); indifferent; indurate; jaded; knark; loveless; matter-of-fact; merciless; non-sympathetic; obdurate; pitiless; *querulous;* repressed; ruthless; steel-like; stone-hearted; soulless; tough; unsympathetic; vindictive; wicked; *xerothalmic;* yieldless; zealless; [*Ant.* humane]

**heat** *(n.)*: *aflame;* burning; calidity; *deflagration;* estuance; excadescence; fieriness; *glow;* hotness; incandescence; *isothermal;* intense ~; *jet heater;* kerosene ~; *latent heat; muffle;* nealing; *overheat; pyre;* Q [phys.]; radiant ~; *scorching ~;* temperature; toastiness; torridity; ustulation; *volcanic ~;* warmth; warmness; white ~; *xeric;* yellow-hot; zapping;
**heat** *(v.)*: anneal; broil; bask; bake; calefy; cook; decrepitate; expose to ~; evenly ~; fry; fire; glow; grill; *harden;* incandesce; *jet heater;* kindle; *let cook;* microwave; neal; oven- ~; over~; put a flame under; quick-bake; re~; roast; set a fire under; *steam;* swelter; super~; toast; tepefy; temper; torrefy; *undercook; vulcanize;* warm (up); *xeric;* yark; *zap;*
**heathen** *(adj.)*: *aboriginal;* barbaric; coarse; devilish; *evil;* foul; gentile; godless; heathenish; idolatrous; *jungli;* kaf [arch.]; lost; *misinformed;* neopagan; *orisha-worshipping;* pagan(istic); *quad;* rude; savage; *tribal;* uncircumcised; uncivilized; unevangelized; unchristian; unmoralized; ungodly; vulgar; *wicked; xenon-worshipping; yantra;* zoolatrous;
**heathen** *(n.)*: animal-worshiper; Baal-worshiper; chthonian; devil-worshiper; ecclesiolater; fetishist; *god-maker;* heliolater; idolater; joss-worshiper; kore; lover of idols; moon-worshiper; neo-pagan; orisha-worshiper; pagan; *quad; rhabdomancer;* sun-worshiper; *temple-prostitute; ungodly;* voodooist; worshiper; xoanon-worshiper; *Ymir-worshipper;* zoolater;
**heathenism** *(n.)*: adultery; Baal-worship; chthonianism; devil-worship; ethnicism; fetishism; *god-making;* heliolatry; idolatry; joss-worship; *kore;* love of idols; moon-worship; neo-paganism; orisha-worship; paganism; *quad; rhabdomancy; Sabianism; theogony;* unenlightenment; voodoo; whoredom; xoanon-worship; *yantra;* zoolatry;
**heave** *(v.)*: apply pressure; budge; chuck; drag; eject; fling; *go;* hurl; impel; jam; kibble; lurch; move forward; nudge; ooch; push; propel; quant; ram; shove; throw; thrust; upthrust; vomit; wale; *xowyn* [arch.]; yerk; *zonk;*
**heaven** *(n.)*: Abraham's bosom; afterworld; bliss; Beulah land; *the* Celestial City; *dreamland;* everlasting life; eternal home; empyrean; *forever;* glory; heavenly home; Holy City; habitation of God; *indescribable;* jasper-walled city; kingdom (come); Land of Promise; Millennial Kingdom; mansion; *the* New Jerusalem; *our eternal home;* paradise; Pearly Gates; *peace; quietude; rest; reward;* streets of gold; third ~; throne of God; upper world; utopia; *victory; the* world above; Xanadu; yonder; Zion; [*Ant.* hell]
**heavenly** *(adj.)*: angelic; blissful; breathtaking; celestial; divine; ethereal; fabulous; grand; happy; higher; holy; incredible; joyous; keen; lofty; magnificent; nice; noteworthy; noble; outstanding; pleasant; queme; remarkable; splendid; sublime; supernal; supernatural; terrific; uplifting; unparalleled; virtuous; wonderful; xtry.; *yippee!;* Zionite; [*Ant.* hellish]
**heavenward** *(adj.)*: *above;* bound for heaven; *celestial;* delivered; *escalating; forgiven;* glorybound; Godward; heavenbound; in Christ; *Jesus-ward;* kingdom-bound; *lofty heights; mercifully saved; no condemnation;* out of here; paradise-bound; *quickened; rapture;* skyward; toward heaven; upward(s); up; vertical; washed in the Blood; *xfer;* yonder-bound; zionward; [*Ant.* hellward]
**heavy** *(adj.)*: abundant; big; bulky; corpulent; dense; deep; enormous; fat; gigantic; hefty; huge; immense; jumbo-sized; king-size; large; massive; non-light; oversize; overweight; ponderous; prodigious; quantitative; rotund; stout; sizable; substantial; thick; tremendous; *unmanageable; unwieldy;* voluminous; weighty; XL; *yet unlightened;* zaftig;
**Hebrew** *(adj.)*: Abrahamic; *Ben Israel* [Heb.]; *circumcised;* Danite; Eberite; *Far'Am;* Gadite; Hebraic; Israelite; Jewish; *Kohathite;* Levite; Mosaic; Manassite; *Naphtali;* Orthodox Jewish; *Parod; Qatara;* rabbinical; Semitic; *Tel Aviv; Udim; Vardiya; Wadi 'Ara; xtry. nation;* Yiddish; *Zionist;*
**Hebrew** *(n.)*: Asherite; *Benjamite;* chosen people [pl.]; *Danite;* Eberite; Ephraimite; *Far'Am;* Galilean; Gadite; Hebrewess [fem.]; Israelite; Jew; *Korathite;* landsman; Levite; Manassite; native Israeli; *Naphtalite;* Orthodox Jew; Pharisee; *Qumram;* Reubenite; Semite; son of Abraham; *Tel Aviv; Udim; Vardiya; Wadi 'Ara; Xn. Jew;* Yahudi; Yahwist; *Zebulunite;*

**heckle** *(v.)*: annoy; abuse; belittle; bullyrag; chide; deride; execrate; fleer; gibe; hector; insult; jeer; knock; laugh at; mock; needle; *offend;* pester; pillory; quib; razz; ridicule; rail; scoff; scorn; taunt; utter against; vex; wipe; *xuld [arch.];* yock; *zap;*

**hectic** *(adj.)*: anarchic; amok; busy; boisterous; crazy; confused; chaotic; disorderly; excited; flustering; frenzied; gadarine; heated; incomposed; jumbled; keg-meg; lively; madhouse; nutsy; orderless; pell-mell; quaggy; restless; riotous; *speedy;* topsy-turvy; tumultuous; unsettled; *vexing;* wild; *x'ed; yucky;* zoo-like;

**hedge** *(n.)*: arbor; bushes; barrier; *caper-bush; dendroid;* espalier; enclosure; frutex; fence; greenery; hedgerow; inclosure; *juba bush; kalmia; lantana; may-bloom; narra; oleander; plants;* protection; quickset; row (of bushes); shrubbery; thorn bush; thicket; *ulex;* verge; windbreak; wall of protection; *xylopia; yawshrub;* zeriba; [*see* barrier; protection]

**hedonism** *(n.)*: abandon; bacchanalia; carousing; decadence; epicureanism; frolicsomeness; gratuitousness; heedlessness; indulgence; *japery; knavery;* licentiousness; lasciviousness; *mischievousness;* naughtiness; overindulgence; pleasure-seeking; *quad;* revelry; reckless abandon; sensualism; self-indulgence; *trespass;* unrestraint; voluptuousness; wantonness; *x-rated;* yieldedness to the flesh; *zero restraint;* [*Ant.* heavenly-mindedness]

**hedonist** *(n.)*: *adulterer;* bad man; carnalist; debauchee; epicure(an); fornicator; gadabout; hedonistic man; immoral man; *jaded; kinky;* luxurist; libertine; man of the flesh; *nocceur [F.];* obscene man; pleasure-seeker; pleasurist; *quad;* reprobate; rake; sensualist; sybarite; *tramp;* ungodly person; voluptuary; worldling; wanton; *x-rated; yielder; zero morals;*

**hedonistic** *(adj.)*: abandoned; bad; carefree; dissipated; decadent; epicurean; frolicsome; gratuitous; gadabout; hedonic; indulgent; jadish; *kinky;* licentious; lascivious; libertine; *mischievous;* non-moral; overindulgent; pleasure-seeking; *quad;* reckless; self-indulgent; sensualistic; sybaritic; *trampy;* unrestrained; uninhibited; unchaste; voluptuous; wanton; *x-rated;* yeasty; zizzy; [*Ant.* heavenly-minded]

**heed** *(n.)*: attention; bowing; compliance; doing; execution; fear; giving in; hearing; implementation; *jump on it;* keeping; listening; mindfulness; notice; observation; obedience; performance; *questionless;* regard; submission; *toeing the line;* upholding; *veneration;* weight; *xlation;* yielding; *zeal;*

**heed** *(v.)*: attend (to); bear in mind; comply; do; execute; follow; give in; hearken; *indulge; jump (to it);* keep; knuckle (under); listen to; mark; mind; note; not resist; observe; obey; perform; *questionless;* regard; submit; succumb; tend to; undertake; *vigorously obey;* watch; *xlate;* yield; zip to it;

**heedful** *(adj.)*: attentive; biddable; careful; compliant; deferential; ever-mindful; following; *giving in;* hearkening; intentive; judicious; keeping in mind; listening; mindful; non-resistant; obedient; *prudent;* quick-to-listen; regardful; submissive; thoughtful; unresisting; vigilant; watchful; xtr. careful; yielded; *zealous;* [*Ant.* heedless]

**heedless** *(adj.)*: abdicating; abandoning; blasé; careless; disregardful; eliding; forgetful; *go unattended;* haphazard; irresponsible; inattentive; *jim-jam; kim-kam;* lax; *missing;* negligent; neglectful; oblivious; phlegmatic; quirky; remiss; slack; thoughtless; unheeding; very neglectful; without regard; *xtry. ~;* yet irresponsible; *zero responsibility;* [*Ant.* heedful]

**height** *(n. pinnacle)*: apogee; apex; brow; climax; crown; crest; *destination;* extremity; *fastigium* [L.]; greatness; high point; *increase; jut;* kop; limit; lofty ~; mountaintop; meridian; *ne pas ultra* [F.]; *overmost point;* peak; pinnacle; *quoif;* rising; summit; top; upper extremity; vertex; *way up; xtry;* yonder; zenith;

**height** *(n. tallness)*: altitude; bigness; climb; distance; elevation; fall; feet tall; greatness; highness; inches; increment; jump; kanjira; length; loftiness; measurement; number of feet tall; *overlong;* procerity; *quantity;* rise; stature; tallness; upward elevation; verticalness; vertical measurement; *way up;* x-height; *yonder;* zenith;

**heinous** *(adj.)*: atrocious; bad; criminal; depraved; evil; flagitious; godless; horrible; iniquitous; *jaded;* knavish; licentious; malevolent; nefarious; obdurate; perverse; *quad;* ruthless; sinful; treacherous; unrighteous; villainous; wicked; *xgressing;* yucky; *zero good;* [*Ant.* holy]

**heir** *(n.)*: apparent ~; acquirer; atheling; beneficiary; co- ~; co-parcener; devisee; descendant; *estate;* fellow- ~; *grandchild;* heritor; heiress [fem.]; inheritor; joint- ~; *kids;* legatee; legal ~; *ménage;* next-of-kin; obtainer; parcener; *quoff;* recipient; rightful ~; successor; sole ~; transmitee; uncontested ~; *valuables; widow; xmit; yain [arch.]; zadruga ;*
**hell** *(n.)*: abyss; blazes; condemnation; destruction; damnation; everlasting condemnation (darkness); eternal death; furnace; fire and brimstone; Gehenna; Hades; hellfire; inferno; judgment; *killing;* Lake of Fire; *misery;* netherworld; never-ending fire; outer darkness; punishment; *the* pit; perdition; quenchless fire; retribution; ruination; suffering; second death; Tartarus; Tophet; torment; underworld; *vengeance; wailing;* xibalba; *yelling; zone of the dead;* [*see* fire; damnation, *Ant.* heaven]
**helmet** *(n.)*: * army ~; Adrian ~; armet; barbut; brode ~; casque; cappellina; combat ~; diving ~; equestrian ~; field ~; *galea [Rom.];* hard hat; headgear; helm [poet.]; imperial ~; jockey-cap; kettle-hat; *kabuto [Jap.];* lightweight ~; morion; Nazi ~; *o-boshi [Jap.];* pith ~; *pickelhaube [G.]; QGF03; Russian ~;* sallet; spiked ~; topee; umbriere; *ventail;* visor; war ~; *xtr. protection; yoroi [Jap.]; Zischaegge;*
**help** *(n.)*: assistance; aid; backing; burden-shouldering; cooperation; doctoring; *deed;* deliverance; encouraging; easing; extricating; facilitation; giving of help; hand; intercession; *just-in-time;* kindness; lending aid; ministering; *non-hindrance; overprotection;* pitching in; *quick-to-help;* relief; respite; subvention; support; succor; service; *taking under one's wing;* upholding; unburdening; usefulness; *valet;* working for; *xtry. ~; yielding; zero hindrance;* [*Ant.* hindrance, harm]
**help** *(v.)*: abet; assist; aid; alleviate; befriend; back; bolster; bail out; cooperate; comfort; come to the rescue; cure; do a favor; deliver; encourage; ease; extricate; facilitate; further; give assistance; help out; *heal;* intercede; *just-in-time; kindness;* lend aid; lighten one's load; minister; *not hinder;* open doors; pitch in; *quick-to-help;* reach out; relieve; rescue; support; serve; succor; take care of; uphold; unburden; *valet;* work for; *xtry.;* yield; *zero hindrance;* [*Ant.* hinder, harm]
**helper** *(n.)*: abettor; assistant; aide; backer; cooperator; coadjutant; deliverer; encourager; easer; friend; facilitator; gofer [slang]; hand; intern; intercessor; jackman; knipper; legman; mate; minister; nipper; offsider; partner; *quick-to-help;* relief-giver; servant; supporter; succorer; *tender;* upholder; volunteer; *valet;* workfellow; *xtry.;* yokefellow; *zaikai;* [*see* friend; *Ant.* hinderer]
**helpful** *(adj.)*: assistive; advantageous; beneficial; conducive; constructive; developmental; edifying; effective; favorable; facilitating; gainful; good; handy; instrumental; *jim dandy;* keen; *lucrative;* ministering; nice; obliging; productive; propitious; profitable; quick-to-help; remedial; serving; salutary; therapeutic; useful; valuable; worthwhile; xtry.; yieldful; *zealous to help;* [*Ant.* harmful]
**helpless** *(adj.)*: aidless; *baffled;* crippled; dependent; defenseless; enfeebled; friendless; feeble; guardless; *hopeless;* indefensible; justiciable; *knocked out;* liable; lame; much-weakened; non-helpable; open; powerless; *queachy* [dial.]; *reduced;* succorless; *tired;* unsupported; unaided; unprotected; vulnerable; weak; wide-open; *x'ed; yawnish; zapped;*
**hemorrhoid** *(n.)*: ailment; bulge; cyst; dermoid; emerod; furuncle; growth; hunch [arch.]; *inflammation;* jarble; knot; lipoma; malady; *osteoma;* piles; *quirk;* rising; swelling; tumor; *ulcer;* varicose-swelling; wen; *xanthogranuloma; yedder; zoocyst;*
**hen** *(n.)*: asil; *bird;* broiler; chicken; domestic fowl; egger; *fowl;* fryer; ga noi; houdan; heeler; *ixworth; java; kadaknath;* leghorn; layer; minorca; nankin; *orloff;* pullet; quachilto; rooster [masc.]; roaster; setting ~; *tomaru; umbrella bird;* vorwerk ~; *wyandotte; white meat; x-breed; yurlov crower; zoic;*
**herald** *(n.)*: announcer; blazoner; crier; dispatch; emissary; forerunner; guide; harbinger; internuncio; *jaw;* king-herald; liaison; messenger; nuncio; outrider; proclaimer; *questor [It.];* representative; scout; tidings-bearer; *utterer;* voice; waymaker; *x-man; yamen* [Chin.]; *zealous announcer;*
**heraldry** *(n.)*: armory; blazonry; coat-armor; designation; emblazonry; figuration; graphics; heraldic symbolism; *identification; jambeaux;* knowledge of coat-of-arms; *legend;* markings; *national symbolism;* official markings; *pictures; quain [arch.];* representation; symbolism; tokenism; *unique designation; valor;* war arms; *xtry.; yichus; zeug [G.];*

**herb** *(n.)*: annual; biennial; cutting; *drug; evergreen;* fine ~; green; herbelet; houseplant; herbage; *item;* jungle- ~; keck; *legume;* medicinal ~; natural ~; organic ~; plant; pot~; *qat; root;* shoot; triennial; undergrowth; vulnerary; wort; *xyrid;* yarb [dial.]; yareta; *zymophyte;*
   **Kinds of herbs**: aconite; basil; clove; dill; ezov; filé powder; ginseng; hyssop; Indonesian bay leaf; jalap; kaffir lime; lungwort; maldmony; nepeta; oregano; perilla; quaking-grass; rosemary; sorrel; thyme; usnea; vervain; watercress; xyrid; yarrow; zallouh;
**herd** *(n.)*: assemblage; bunch; bevy; cavvy; drove; *en masse;* fold; group; horde; ingathering; jam [slang]; kit; lot; mass; neat; *overstock;* pack; passel; quantity; roundup; regathering; string; troop; unit; *variety;* whole lot; *xferer; yield zet [dial.];*
   **Animal groupings**: army [caterpillars]; bale [turtles]; band [gorillas]; brood [chickens]; cete [badgers]; colony [beavers]; down [hares]; dray [squirrels]; drove [oxen]; dule [doves]; flock [sheep; birds]; gaggle [geese]; gam [whales]; gang [elk]; herd [cattle; elephants]; knot [toads]; leap [leopards]; mob [emus]; murder [crows]; nest [rabbits; snakes]; ostentation [peafowl]; pack [dogs; rats]; parliament [owls]; pride [lions]; quiver [cobras]; rag [colts]; rafter [turkeys]; school [fish]; shrewdness [apes]; skulk [foxes]; sleuth [bears]; sounder [swine]; troop [monkeys]; wedge [swans];
**herd** *(v.)*: assemble; bunch together; corral; chouse; control; direct; escort; *force;* guide; *help;* ingather; *jockey;* keep; lead; move; *navigate;* oversee; punch; *quicken;* run; shepherd; take oversight of; usher; *volume;* wrangle; *xfer; yede; zip along;* [*see* group]
**hereafter** *(n.)*: afterlife; by and by; *ceaseless;* duration; eternity; future life; future; *going on;* here after; infinity; *jusqu'au bout [F.]; keeps going;* life after death; *measureless; the* next life; *ongoing;* perpetuity; *quadrillion;* remainder of eternity; sweet by and by; time without end; *unending; vast;* world without end; *x-cending;* yonder; *zillions;*
**hereditary** *(adj.)*: ancestral; blood; clannish; derivational; ethnic; family; genetic; heritable; inherited; *joined;* kin-related; lineal; *mankind;* national; original; phyletic; *quarter;* racial; stock-related; tribal; *unilineal; vein;* willed; *x-linked;* yellow race; *zygogenetic;*
**heresy** *(n.)*: apostasy; abberation; abberance; abberancy; blasphemy; *corruption; confusion;* deviation; damnable ~; error; false doctrine; *groundless;* heterodoxy; infidelity; *Judaizing;* known ~; lie; misbelief; miscreance; miscreancy; neodoxy; obliquation; parting; profanation; quirk; *revisionism;* sacrilege; twisted doctrine; unorthodoxy; untruth; unfaithfulness; *variant;* wrong doctrine; *xtry. lie;* yaw; *zero truth;* [*see* lie]
**heretic** *(n.)*: apostate; arch~; antichrist; blind leader of the blind; *corruptor;* derider; *evildoer;* false teacher (prophet); *godless;* heresiarch; infidel; *Judaizer; kicker;* liar; miscreant; Nicolaitan; *off-base teacher;* pseudo-apostle; Quaternarian; renegade; scorner; theologaster; unbeliever; vexer; *wrong doctrine; xiaoren;* yuker; *zendik [Mos.];*
**heretical** *(adj.)*: apostate; aberrant; bad; confused; corrupt; cultic; deficient; defective; erroneous; false; godless; heterodox; *infidel; jumbled;* kooky; *lying;* misbelieved; non-biblical; non-orthodox; neodox; off-base; peccant; *quemadero [Sp.];* recreant; specious; sacrilegious; twisted; unsound; unorthodox; *variant;* wrong; *xiaoren;* yawed; *zero-truth;*
**heritage** *(v.)*: acquisition; bequest; birthright; culture; co-heirship; dower; ethos; estate; fellow-heirdom; gain; hereditament; heirdom; inheritance; jointure; *Kultur [G.];* kept traditions; legacy; *memorial;* non-shared hereditament; *ownership;* primogeniture; parcenary; *quoff;* reversion; succession; tradition; ultimogeniture; *values; ways; xmission;* yain [arch.]; *zet [dial.];*
**hermit** *(n.)*: anchorite; ascetic; beadsman; cenobite; dervis; eremite; friar; grand prior; hermitess [fem.]; isolationist; *jubilarian; kithless;* loner; lone-wolf; marabout [Mos.]; mountain man; non-socialite; outcast; private person; *quietude;* recluse; solitairian; trappist; *unsocial; votary;* withdrawn; *xenodochium;* yokeless; *Zetetic;*
**hero** *(n.)*: *advocate;* brave warrior; champion; deliverer; exemplar; folk ~; guardian; he-man; heroine [fem.]; *idol; jarl;* knight; lifesaver; liberator; legend; laureate; messiah; *non-loser;* overcomer; protagonist; paladin; *queller;* rescuer; star; super ~; title-holder; triumphant; *upholder;* victor; war ~; white knight; *xia; yell; zealous;*

**heroic** *(adj.)*: adventurous; bold; brave; courageous; daring; dauntless; enterprising; fearless; gallant; herolike; Herculean; intrepid; *jarless;* knightly; lion-hearted; manly; mettlesome; never-fearing; *obstinate;* plucky; *quick-witted; resolute;* strong; spirited; stout; tremendous; undaunted; valorous; valiant; *wherewithal; xtry.; yare; zealous;* [*Ant.* heinous]

**hesitant** *(adj.)*: ambivalent; apprehensive; bashful; cautious; costive; demurring; diffident; *edgy;* fearful; guarded; hesitating; iffy; insecure; jackalent; *keeping back;* loath; mousy; non-resolute; nervous; overcautious; pausing; questioning; reticent; reluctant; shy; timid; uncertain; unsure; unforthcoming; vacillating; wary; *x-ing;* yarrow; zealless; [*Ant.* hasty]

**hesitate** *(v.)*: alternate; boggle; *careful;* demur; delay; *edgy;* falter; flinch; fumble; grudge; hedge; hem and haw; halt; *indecisive; jackalent; knees knocking; loath;* mouse around; mammer; *non-resolute; overcaution;* pause; question; recoil; shrink; stop; think twice; *uncertain;* vacillate; waffle; waver; *x-ing;* yo-yo; *zealless;*

**hesitation** *(n.)*: ambivalence; boggling; caution; demurral; diffidence; delay; edginess; faltering; guardedness; hack; hang up; hesitancy; iffiness; jackalence; *knees knocking;* leeriness; mistrust; mousiness; non-resolution; overcaution; pause; qualm; reluctance; shyness; timidity; uncertainty; vacillation; wavering; *x-ing;* yo-yoing; zealessness; [*Ant.* haste]

**heyday** *(n.)*: apex; best years; climax; day; *expansion; fame;* golden age; height; high point; *increased; important;* jump; *kop; largeness;* mountaintop; *noteworthy; outstanding;* prime; peak; *quicken; remarkable;* summit; time; *upper extremity;* vertex; *wonderful days; xtry; yonder point;* zenith;

**hibernate** *(v.)*: aestivate; *asleep;* bed down; *crash;* doze; estivate; fall asleep; go to sleep; hole up; idle; *jaded;* keep cover; latibulize; lie dormant; *Morpheus;* nap; overwinter; pass out; *quiesce;* repose; retire; sleep; *take rest; unconscious;* vegetate; winter; *x-sleep; yawn;* zonk (out);

**hidden** *(adj.)*: abstruse; buried; covered; couched; camouflaged; concealed; disguised; eclipsed; furtive; guarded; hooded; hid(ing); incognito; indiscoverable; invisible; *jape;* kept ~; latent; masked; mysterious; not revealed; out-of-view; obscured; private; *quat [arch.];* repressed; recluse; shrouded; secret; tucked away; unseen; unrevealed; undiscovered; unsighted; unspied; undetected; veiled; withdrawn; X; *yieldless; zero knowledge;*

**hide** *(n.)*: * animal skin; back; coat; dermis; epidermis; fell; goatskin; hareskin; integument; jacket; kangaroo skin; *layer;* leather; membrane; natural covering; outer surface; pelt; parfleche; *quarry;* raccoon skin; skin; slough; tanned hide; *upper shoe leather;* vellum; whang; *xerodermia; yak hide; zebra skin;* [*see* skin]

**hide** *(v.)*: *away;* bury; bemask; cover; cloak; conceal; disguise; envelop; foil; *garb;* hood; immerge; *jape;* keep hidden; lay low; *lurk;* mask; mantle; *non-recognizable;* obscure; obfuscate; put out of view; *protect; quat* [arch.]; *recluse;* shroud; secrete; *skulk;* tuck away; *under cover;* veil; wimple; withdraw; *xenomorph;* yird; *zero recognition;*

**hideous** *(adj.)*: appalling; abominable; bestial; contorted; disgusting; eye-offending; frightful; grotesque; horrid; icky; jackal-faced; *knarled;* loathsome; monstrous; nauseating; offensive; putrid; *queer;* repulsive; shocking; terrible; ugly; vile; wicked; *xerophthalmic;* yucky; *zit-faced;* [*Ant.* handsome]

**hierarchy** *(n.)*: authority-structure; *boss;* chain of command; due order; echelons; *formation;* grouping; hierarchical order; *indexing; jurisdiction; key position;* line of authority; *manner; network;* order; pecking order; pyramid; *queue;* ranking system; social order; structure; succession of command; top-down chart; *tree;* totem pole; *under; upper; value; way; xyz;* yield; *zet [dial.];*

**high** *(adj.)*: above; aloft; astronomical; big; costly; *degree;* elevated; expensive; exalted; eminent; foremost; great; high-reaching (-ranking); increased; important; jacked-up; *kingly;* lofty; mountain- ~; non-economical; over(looking); pinnacled; *queenly;* raised; steep; soaring; sky- ~; tall; up there; towering; unreachable; very ~; way up; *xy-height; y-axis; zenithal;* [*Ant.* humble]

**highest** *(adj.)*: absolute; biggest; chief; dominant; eminent; extreme; farthest; foremost; greatest; headmost; important; *judicious;* key; largest; leading; loftiest; maximum; main; most high; *notable;* nth; overriding; overmost; peak; prime; *quintessential;* ranking; supreme; tallest; topmost; uppermost; ut(ter)most; *vertex; weightiest; xenenthesis; yondermost;* zenithal; [*Ant.* humblest]

**highway** *(n.)*: avenue; boulevard; course; clearway; causeway; divided ~; expressway; freeway; *going; high road;* interstate; journey-way; king's ~; lane; motorway; multilane ~; non-toll road; *outstreet;* parkway; pike; queen's ~; roadway; route; super~; turnpike; thruway; thoroughfare; U.S. ~; *vennel;* way; *xyst; yong* [arch.]; *zwinger;*

**hike** *(v.)*: advance; ascent; backpack; continue; demarch; edge; footstep; go; haul; *interlope;* journey; *keep pace; lumber;* move; night-walk; outwalk; proceed; *quicken; ramble;* step; trek; *underway;* venture; walk; *xfer; yomp; zigzag;*

**hill** *(n.)*: ant~; acclivity; bluff; bank; butte; climb; dune; esker; eminence; foot~; fell; glacis; heap; hillock; incline; inselberg; jebel; knoll; kop; loma; mound; mole~; nab; oser; prominence; *Quirinal;* rise; ramp; slope; tor; upslope; versant; *wad; Xiao;* yunga; *zenith;*

**hilly** *(adj.)*: acclivity; bumpy; craggy; dune-filled; *esker;* full of hills; *glacis;* hillocky; *inclined;* jebel-filled; knolly; lumpy; mound-filled; nab-covered; oser-filled; *prominence; quite ~;* rugged; sloping; tumulous; upland; versant; *wold; xalpine;* yunga-covered; *zenith;* [*Ant.* horizontal]

**hinder** *(v.)*: *avert;* block; cumber; delay; deter; encumber; frustrate; gum up; hamper; hold back; impede; impair; inhibit; jam-up; keep (from); *let* [arch.]; manacle; *negate;* obstruct; prevent; quash; restrain; slow down; stop; thwart; *undo;* veto; weigh down; withhold; x; *yank;* zilch; [*Ant.* help]

**hindrance** *(n.)*: arrest; barrier; cumbrance; difficulty; encumbrance; frustration; glitch; hurdle; holdup; impediment; impasse; jam; kink; logjam; monkey wrench; nuisance; obstruction; obstacle; problem; quandary; roadblock; snag; stumbling block; trouble; *upset;* vigia; wall; x; *yowler;* zinger; [*Ant.* help]

**hinge** *(n.)*: * axis; butt ~; continuous ~; door- ~; elbow; fulcrum; gate- ~; gudgeon; hook; invisible ~; joint; jemer; jimmers; knee; loose-pin ~; mortise; *non-rigid; oarlock;* pivot; piano ~; *quick access; rest;* swivel; strap ~; T- ~; utility ~; *vomitory;* wheel; x-door; yett ~; *zeugma;*

**hinge** *(v.)*: await; bend; *carry;* dip; depend; enfold; *flex; fold;* gimbal; hang; incline; *jolt;* knuckle; lap; move; *non-rigid;* open and shut; pivot; *quick;* rest; swing; turn; *universal joint; verge;* wag; *xuld* [arch.]; *yaw; zeugma;*

**hint** *(n.)*: allusion; bit; breath; clue; connotation; disclosure; dead giveaway; evidence; foreshadowing; giveaway; helpful ~; indication; inkling; *jog;* key word; lead; mention; nuance; overtone; pointer; quiddit; reference; smack; suggestion; trace; tip; undertone; vestige; warning; *xtr. subtle; yield; zum* [dial.];

**hint** *(v.)*: allude; betoken; connote; drop ~; denote; drive at; evidence; foreshadow; give indication; help; intimate; infer; insinuate; *jog;* key in; *lead;* make out; mention; *nudge; overtone;* postulate; quiddit; refer; suggest; tip off; use undertones; vaguely express; *wink; xfer; yammer; zum* [dial.];

**hire** *(n.)*: amount; base pay; compensation; defrayment; earnings; fee; guerdon; hiring; income; *justification; kickback;* living wage; money; net pay; *overcompensation;* pay(ment); quittance; recompense; remuneration; salary; take-home pay; *unindebted;* virement; wage(s); xfer; yield; *zapping;*

**hire** *(v.)*: add to staff; acquire; busy; bring in; call; charter; contract; decide on; enlist; employ; engage; find help; give job to; have work; ink; *join the team;* keep; lease; make an employee; *name;* obtain; pay; put to work; *qualified;* recruit; retain; re~; sign-on; staff; take on; use; underemploy; *vocation;* work; *xtr. hours;* yes; *zet* [dial.];

**hireling** *(n.)*: associate; *breadwinner;* co-worker; drone; employee; floozy [derog.]; fellow laborer; grunt [derog.]; gofer [slang]; hand; industrial worker; jobholder; *kitchen worker;* laborer; menial; moiler; navvy [Br.]; operator; producer; performer; *qualified laborer;* roustabout; servant; subordinate; toiler; underling; *vassal;* worker; *xylographer;* yeoman; *zaikai* [Jap.];

**historic** *(adj.)*: actual; biographical; big; celebrated; documented; earth-changing; factual; for-real; famous; great; historical; important; *joyous;* key; legendary; landmark; momentous; non-fictitious; noteworthy; *outstanding;* provable; portentous; *quantum;* real; recorded; red-letter; significant; traditional; unforgettable; verifiable; very important; weighty; *Xenophontean; yore;* zenithal;

**historicity** *(n.)*: authenticity; *being;* certainty; *dependability;* exactness; factuality; genuineness; historicalness; integrity of information; *journal-accuracy; knowledge;* literalness; *meticulousness;* non-fiction; *ontic;* precision of facts; quality of information; reality; sureness; trueness; *unmistaken;* verifiability; whole truth; *Xenophontean; yes; zero error;*

**history** *(n.)*: account; annals; antiquity; background; chronicles; days gone by; experience; former days; *geo~;* historiography; *incidents;* journal; *known ~;* life story; lore; legend; memoirs; modern ~; narrative; nonfiction; olden days; past; *questionless;* record; story; tale; times past; *unabridged ~; version;* written ~; *XYZ affair;* yesteryear; *zet [dial.];*

**hit** *(n.)*: assault; box; bop; bump; belt; bang; blow; bash; cuff; clobber; clout; crack; deck; dash; *efface;* flogging; *get;* impact; jab; jolt; knuckle sandwich; karate-chop; kidney-punch; *kick;* knock; lick; mauling; nob; nevel; open-handed blow; punch; *quab;* rap; swat; slap; smack; spanking; shot; sock; slug; swipe; slam; strike; smite; tap; thump; thwack; uppercut; veney; whap; whack; wallop; *x-sect;* yedder; zonk;

**hit** *(v.)*: assault; box; bop; bonk; bump; belt; bang; bash; beat; broadside; cuff; clobber; conk; clout; clock; collide; deck; dash; *expunge;* flog; flail; *get;* hammer; impact; jab; knock; lam; mash; maul; nail; *overhit;* pelt; punch; pound; quab; rap; swat; slap; smack; smite; strike; sock; thump; thrash; thwack; *undo;* veney; whack; wallop; *x-sect;* yedder; zonk;

**hitch** *(v.)*: attach; affix; bind; connect; couple; *drag; engraft;* fasten; *grip;* hook; harness; interlink; interlock; interconnect; join; knit; knot; link; latch; mount; *nip;* oxreim; put together; *quasi-fuse;* relate; reunite; set to; stick; secure; tie; tether; unite; *vise;* wed; *xenograft;* yoke; zip;

**hoard** *(n.)*: amassment; accumulation; buildup; collection; deposit; *enlargement;* forgathering; group; gathering; heap; ingathering; jam [slang]; kit [coll.]; lot; mass; number; overflow; pile; quantity; ruck; reservoir; supply; store; takings; trove; treasure; volume; wheen; *xuld [arch.]; yield;* zillions;

**hoard** *(v.)*: amass; accumulate; build up; collect; deposit; enlarge; *flock;* gather; heap up; increase; *join;* keep; lay up; mount; multiply; *number; overgrow;* pile up; *quadruplicate;* reposit; reservoir; store up; take up; treasure up; uild; *volume;* wax larger; *x.; yain* [arch.]; *zone;*

**hoax** *(n.)*: artifice; beguilement; canard; deception; *ensnarement;* fraud; guile; hornswaggling; deception; *imposture;* japery; knavishness; lie; misleading; *nobbling; outfoxing;* prank; practical joke; *quiblin [arch.];* ruse; spoof; stunt; scam; trick; untruth; verneuking; wile; *xuld [arch.]; yentzing; zinger;*

**hobble** *(v.)*: *amble;* bungle along; creep; crawl; daddle; edge; festinate; gimp; hitch; inch; jiffle; *keep advancing;* limp; move unstably; *non-stable;* oscillate; plod; quaddle; reel; stagger; stumble; tramp; totter; *uneven;* vacillate; waddle; wobble; waggle; *xfer;* yaw; zigzag;

**hobby** *(n.)*: avocation; bag; cup of tea; diversion; entertainment; endeavor; fascination; game; *hobbyist;* interest; *jollity;* kill-time; *kicks;* leisure activity; mind-stimulating ~; *numismatics;* occupation; pastime; pursuit; *philately; quixote;* relaxing ~; sideline; *time; thing;* undertaking; *value;* work; *xtry. ~; yo-yo;* zeal;

**hobbyist** *(n.)*: aficionado; addict; buff; collector; devotee; enthusiast; fanatic; gatherer; hound; *individual; junior ~;* keen; *lover of;* maven; nut; one obsessed; pursuer; quixote; *relaxing;* stamp collector; scrapbooker; tinkerer; ultraist; votary; worker; *xare; yare;* zealot;

**hoist** *(n.)*: *apparatus; arm;* boost; crane; davit; derrick; elevator; forklift; gantry crane; heavy lifting equipment; *instrument;* jenny; *kickumbob;* lift; machine; mechanism; *new level; nine feet; object;* parbuckle; *pully;* quoin; rigger; sheerlegs; tripaston; *unit; verge;* winch; windlass; *xfer;* yard donkey; *zeug [G.];*

**hoist** *(v.)*: *advance;* boost; bear upwards; crane; derrick; elevate; forklift; go up; heave; haul up; heft; increase; jack; jenny; *knock up;* lift; move up; *new level; nine feet; overgrow;* pull up; quoin; raise; sway [naut.]; take up; upheave; uplift; upraise; verge upward; winch; windlass; *xuld [arch.];* yank; *zoom up;*

**hold** *(v.)*: apprehend; bear; clutch; clench; cling to; clasp; cleave; detain; embrace; fasten on; fix; grab; grasp; grapple; grip; have; hug; infold; jail; kinch; latch onto; make secure; nobble; own; possess; *quelch;* retain; seize; take; *use; vice;* wield; *xfer; yain* [arch.]; *zone;*

**hole** *(n.)*: air- ~; aperture; bore~; breach; cavity; ditch; excavation; fissure; gap(e); hollow; interstice; incavation; jaw-hole; krater; lacuna; maw; niche; nail- ~; opening; orifice; pin~; peep ~; pigeon- ~; pot~; post~; perforation; puncture; pit; quarry-pit; recess; rupture; spiracle; slot; socket; sink~; sump; thirl; undercovert; vent(age); vug; well; *xystus pit;* yawn; zanja;

**holiday** *(n.)*: *array;* big day; celebration; day of celebration; extravaganza; feast; festival; fete; great feast; holy day; high day; *important day;* jamboree; jubilee; kirn; legal ~; major ~; national ~; observance; public ~; panegyris; quindene; religious ~; sabbatical; special day; Sabbath; *ticker-tape parade; unusual;* vacation; *week-long; x-po [slang]; yom tov* [Heb.]; *zeal;*

    **Secular Holidays**: Arbor Day; Bastille Day [F.]; Columbus Day; Election Day; Fourth of July; Father's Day; Flag Day; Groundhog Day; Halloween; Independence Day; Labor Day; May Day; Memorial Day; Mother's Day; New Year's Day; President's Day; St. Patrick's Day; Thanksgiving; Valentine's Day; Veteran's Day; Washington's birthday;

    **Religious Holidays**: Advent; Ash Wednesday; Christmas; Day of Atonement; Easter; Feast of Weeks; Good Friday; Hanukkah; Jewish New Year; Lent; Mardi Gras; Orthodox Christmas; Palm Sunday; Passover; Quadragesima; Rosh Hashanah; Ramadan; Sukkoth; Thanksgiving; Xylophory; Yom Kippor;

**holiness** *(n.)*: absolute ~; blamelessness; consecration; divineness; divinity; *ethicalness;* flawlessness; faultlessness; goodness; hallowedness; impeccability; justness; *kalokagathia* [Gr.]; *light; morality;* non-sinfulness; numinousness; *otherworldliness;* perfection; piety; *quality;* righteousness; rectitude; sanctity; sanctimony; separateness; saintliness; sanctification; sinlessness; sacredness; sacrosanctity; taintlessness; uprightness; utter ~; virtue; virtuousness; worthiness; *xtry; yet undefiled;* zero-defect; [Ant. heinousness]

**holler** *(n.)*: *appeal;* bellow; call; cry; discharge; exclamation; eruption; fuss; growl; hoot; howl; *imploration; jubilation;* keen; loud shout; *lamentation; moan;* noise; outcry; protest; quiritation; resonation; roar; shout; scream; *thundering;* ululation; *uproar;* vociferation; whoop; wail; *xenophonia;* yell; *zindabad;*

**holler** *(v.)*: *appeal;* beckon; bellow; call; cry; dissent; exclaim; erupt; fuss; growl; hoot; howl; *inveigh; implore; jubilate;* keen; loudly say; *lament;* moan; noise; outcry; protest; *quiritate;* resonate; roar; shout; scream; thunder; ululate; vociferate; whoop; wail; *xenophonia;* yell; *zindabad;*

**hollow** *(adj.)*: airy; burrowed; concave; channeled out; dug out; devoid; empty; fistular; gutted; hollowed; incavated; jejune; keach; *lacunose;* meaningless; not solid; open; *pocket; quarried;* routed; scooped out; trenched; tunneled; unfilled; void; *worthless; x-groove; yawning;* zero;

**hollow** *(n.)*: aperture; breach; crevice; cavity; crater; dug out; depression; excavation; fissure; gouge; hole; intaglio; incavation; jaw-hole; krater; lacuna; maw; *mouse hole;* niche; nook; opening; pit; *quarry;* recess; socket; trench; *umbilicus;* vug; well; *xystus pit;* yawn; zanja;

**hollow** *(v.)*: *advance;* burrow; channel (out); cave; delve; dig (out); excavate; furrow; grub; gouge; hole; incavate; *jenkin;* keach; *lower;* mole; *notch;* open; *prospect;* quarry; root; shovel; scoop; tunnel; *trench;* undermine; vell; worm; *xfer; yede; zanja;*

**hollowness** *(n.)*: airiness; barrenness; concaveness; concavity; desolation; emptiness; futility; gantness; hollow state; inaneness; jejuneness; *keaching; loneliness;* meaninglessness; nothingness; *out;* pit; *quaffed; reduction;* scooped out; total ~; ullage; vanity; void; worthlessness; "x"; *yawning;* zero;

**holy** *(adj.)*: *angelic;* blameless; blemishless; consecrated; divine; *excellent;* faultless; flawless; good; godly; Godlike; hallowed; inviolable; impeccable; just; *kramat [Arab.]; luminous;* moral; numinous; *otherworldly;* pious; perfect; *qualified;* righteous; set apart; separate; sanctified; sinless; saintly; sacred; sacrosanct; taintless; undefiled; virtuous; worthy; *Xn.;* yielded (to God); zero-defect; [*Ant.* hellish]

**Holy of Holies** *(n.)*: adytum; behind the veil; bethel; cella; *divine presence; environs; the Father; God's very presence;* holy place; inner sanctum; *Jehovah's presence;* Koresh Hakodashim [Heb.]; *Lord's presence;* Most Holy Place; *mercy seat; not common;* oracle; penetralia; *Qidduse Qiddusan; restricted area;* sacred place; sanctuary; *sancta sanctorium* [L.]; *temple; untouchable; veil; work of the priest; Xuda;* Yom Kippur; Zion's temple;

**Holy Spirit** *(n.)*: *the* Almighty; Beginning and End; Comforter; Dove; Eternal Spirit; Father; Guide; God; Holy Ghost; Intercessor; Just One; King of Glory; Lord God; Maker; *Nature's God;* Omnipotent God; Paraclete; Quickener; Righteous One; Sanctifier; Spirit (of God); Teacher; Third Person of the Godhead; Unction; *Voice;* Wise God; *Xuda;* Yahweh; Zion's Hope; [*see* God; Trinity]

**home** *(n.)*: abode; birthplace; base; *brethren;* cottage; clan; castle; dwelling; edifice; family; *gens;* household; inhabitance; *jacal; ken;* lodging; living quarters; manse; nest; *origin;* place; quarters; *querencia* [Sp.]; residence; relations; summerhouse; townhouse; unit; villa; *walk-up; xerosere; yali; zwinger;*

**homeless** *(adj.)*: abandoned; *bankrupt; companionless;* displaced; exiled; forlorn; gant; houseless; harborless; home-deprived; itinerate; jejune; kithless; landless; mendicant; *nationless;* on the street; poor; *quisby;* removed; reduced to begging; street-dwelling; transient; unaccommodated; unsheltered; unhoused; vagabond; without; *x-ient; yowling; zaanaim;* [*see* poor]

**homemade** *(adj.)*: *artificer;* built-at-home; crafted-by-hand; custom-built; domestic; *experienced;* fashioned-by-hand; *gifted;* homespun; homebred; homestyle; *individually made; just for you; know-how; laborer;* made at home; mom-and-pop; not mass-produced; *original;* personally made for you; *quaint; rustic;* skillfully crafted by hand; *talented;* unique; *versed;* wrought by hand; *xylographer;* yet ~; *zero factory production;*

**homesick** *(v.)*: aching; *burning;* craving; desirous; evocative; *forlorn; grieved;* heartsick; itching; *just got to have; keen desire;* lonely; longing; melancholy; nostalgic; *overly sad;* pining; *quashed; reach for;* sick for home; thirst for; *urge; velleity;* wistful; *xel [arch.];* yearning; *zealously desire;*

**homiletic** *(adj.)*: apologetic; Bible-preaching; commentary; declarative; expository; *form;* gospel-preaching; homiletical; *instructive; jeremiad;* kerystic; lecture; message-writing; *notes;* oratory; preaching; *quotation;* religious; rhetorical; sermonic; teaching; *uttering; vocalizing;* Word; xenagogic; *yielding; zet [dial.];*

**homily** *(n.)*: address; allocution; bespeaking; communication; discourse; elocution; *filibuster; glossa;* hortatory address; indiction; *jabbering;* kerygma; lecture; monologue; *narration;* oration; public speaking; pontification; *quotation;* recitation; sermon; talk; utterance; vocalization; word(s); xenophonia; yawner [off.]; *zinger [slang];*

**honest** *(adj.)*: aboveboard; blameless; credible; decent; deceitless; ethical; fair; good; guileless; genuine; honorable; ingenuous; just; jannock; *keen;* legitimate; moral; noble; open; overscrupulous; plain-dealing; qualmless; reputable; righteous; square; scrupulous; straight(forward); sincere; trustworthy; upright; up-and-up; virtuous; *well-trusted; Xn.;* yet *unadulterated; zero deceit;* [*see* truthful; frank; *Ant.* honorless]

**honesty** *(n.)*: authenticity; blamelessness; correctness; directness; ethicalness; exactitude; faithfulness; goodness; genuineness; honor; integrity; ingenuousness; justness; *kalokagathia* [Gr.]; literality; morality; nobility; openness; plain-dealing; probity; *quaecumque sunt vera* [L.]; reliability; straightforwardness; truth; trustworthiness; uprightness; veracity; *worthiness; xtry; yieldedness to God; zeal for God;* [*Ant.* honorlessness]

**honor** *(n.)*: acknowledgement; admiration; blessing; consideration; courtesy; deference; devoirs; dignity; esteem; fear; great respect; high regard; homage; illustriousness; *jubilation;* kudos; laudation; magnification; nobility; obeisance; politeness; *quality;* regard; respect; repute; reverence; salience; tribute; *unmitigated respect;* veneration; wonder; *xtry.;* yielding; *zero contempt;* [*see* praise; *Ant.* hatred]
**honor** *(v.)*: acknowledge; admire; bow to; consider; defer to; dignify; esteem; fear; give ~; honour [Br.]; homage; idolize; *jubilate;* kneel to; look up to; make obeisance to; notice; observe; prefer; praise; *quick to* recognize; regard; respect; revere(nce); salute; think of; uplift; venerate; worship; *xtry.;* yield; *zero contempt;* [*Ant.* hate]
**honorable** *(adj.)*: aboveboard; admirable; blameless; *character;* decent; ethical; esteemed; exemplary; fine; fair; good; great; godly; honest; high; holy; illustrious; impeccable; just; knightly; laudable; magnifical; moral; noble; *overscrupulous;* proper; principled; prestigious; *qualified;* respectable; reputable; righteous; sinless; trustworthy; upright; virtuous; venerable; worthy; well-thought-of; well-respected; xtry.; *yichus; zero guile;* [*Ant.* hateable]
**hood** *(n.)*: attire; awning; bonnet; covering; capuche; cowl; domino; *eboshi [Jap.]; flat cap;* guise; habit; *item of clothing;* jacket; *kepi; leghorn;* mask; nightcap; *opera hat; poke bonnet;* quoif; riding ~; shade; top; upper cover; vestment; *veil;* wimple; *xtr. protection; yellow ~; zarcole;*
**hoof** *(n.)*: arch; bottom; cloot; cloven ~; dog; extremity; foot; fore~; *goer;* heel; *insole; jag; kicker;* leg; *left ~; metacarpus;* nail; *object;* ped; quadruped; right-front ~; *sole;* toe; unguis; ungula; *volar; wild; xtr. hard;* yads; *zebra ~;*
**hook** *(n.)*: * angle; bend; *bat ~;* catch; curve; *eye~;* elbow; *fish~; flesh ~;* gaff; grapnel; hanger; hitch; incurve; jag; kilp; latch; lure; meak; nabber; offset; *pot- ~;* quat; right turn; round; *screw ~;* trammel; turn; *tenter~;* uncus; verge; *wind; xy-curve; yaw;* zag;
**hope** *(n.)*: aspiration; anticipation; belief; confidence; comfort; desire; expectation; expectancy; forewish; faith; *great ~;* hopefulness; intention; *just expectation;* keen desire; longing; *mindful;* non-despair; optimism; prospect; *questionless;* resort; reliance; sanguinity; trust; *unastonishment;* velleity; wish; *xel [arch.];* yearning; *zeal;* [*Ant.* hopelessness]
**hope** *(v.)*: aspire; anticipate; believe; count on; crave; desire; expect; forewish; greatly desire; have in mind; itch for; *just desire;* keep looking; looking forward to; make request; *need;* overtrust; pray; *questionless;* rely on; so desire; trust; *urge; volition;* wish; *xel [arch.];* yearn (for); *zeal;* [*see* trust]
**hopeful** *(adj.)*: aspiring; anxious; believing; confident; desirous; expectant; full of hope; *gung-ho;* hoping; itching; *just anticipating;* keen; *longing; mindful;* non-despairing; optimistic; possible; positive; *questionless;* ready; rosy; sanguine; trusting; upbeat; *very ~;* wishful; *xel [arch.];* yearnful; *zealous;* [*Ant.* hopeless]
**hopeless** *(adj.)*: abject; bleak; cheerless; comfortless; despondent; desperate; despairing; *evil;* forlorn; glum; gloomy; grim; *heart-despairing;* impossible; joyless; *katzenjammer;* lugubrious; lorn; morose; negative; *overmuch sorrow;* pessimistic; Q.B.I. [RAF slang]; *rueful;* sad; *troubled;* unhopeful; very bad; woeful; without hope; *x'ed; yearnful; zestless;* [*Ant.* hopeful]
**hopelessness** *(n.)*: angst; bleakness; cheerlessness; despondency; despair; *ejulation;* forlornness; gloom; *heartache;* inconsolableness; joylessness; *katzenjammer;* loss of hope; melancholy; moroseness; negativism; overmuch sorrow; pessimism; pall; *quivering; ruefulness;* sadness; trouble; unhappiness; vapors; woe; *x-ing;* yearning; *zestlessness;* [*Ant.* hope]
**horde** *(n.)*: amassment; army; bunch; crowd; deployment; *ekklesia [G.];* forgathering; group; gang; host; ingathering; jam [slang]; kit [coll.]; lot; legion; mass; multitude; number; *overflow;* passel; pack; quantity; ruck; rabble; swarm; throng; *unit;* volume; wheen; *xtry. mass; yield;* zillions;
**horizontal** *(adj.)*: across; abscissa; *baseline;* cumbent; dead level; even; edgewise; flat; ground; homaloid; incumbent; jacent; *knocked over;* level; laying down; lying; lengthways; lengthwise; longwise; longways; landscape; lateral; longitudinal; mean sea level; non-vertical; *on-level;* prone;

prostrate; procumbent; *quasi-horizontal;* resting; recumbent; sideways; transversal; unsloping; *vegetating;* wide; west-east; x-axis; *y=0;* zero verticalness;

**horn** *(n. prong)*: antler; buck~; barb; cornicle; *dragon ~;* extremity; fore prong~; gazelle ~; harts~; ibex ~; *jut;* knag; *long~; moose antler;* nape; ox ~; prong; point; projection; quadricorn; rhino ~; spike; tusk; tine; *unicorn ~; violence;* wapiti ~; *xtr. sharp;* yak ~; *zoology;*

**horn** *(n. trumpet)*: alt~; bugle; cornet; *dawn bugle; euphonium;* French ~; flugel~; German bugle; hazora; *instrument;* jubil; klaxon®; lituus; matin trumpet; noisemaker; *ophicleide;* post ~; quadrivalve; rams ~; shofar; *signal;* trump(et); tooter; *unvalved ~;* valve trumpet; whistle; wind instrument; *xylophone; yak- ~;* zinke;

**horrible** *(adj.)*: awful; bad; crummy; crude; despicable; detestable; deplorable; evil; foul; gross; horrid; indecent; jaded; kitsch; loathsome; malevolent; nasty; offensive; odious; pathetic; perfidious; *quad;* revolting; shocking; sinful; terrible; unenviable; vile; wicked; wretched; *x-rated;* yucky; zhlubby; [*Ant.* heavenly]

**horrid** *(adj.)*: abhorrent; bad; contemptible; detestable; despicable; evil; foul; gross; horrendous; ignoble; *jaded; kitsch;* loathsome; miserable; nasty; offensive; pathetic; *quad;* reprehensible; shocking; terrible; uncouth; vile; wretched; *x-rated;* yucky; zhlubby; [*Ant.* heavenly]

**horrify** *(v.)*: affright; alarm; *bother; concern;* distress; dread; daunt; *exasperate;* frighten; gaster; horripiliate; intimidate; *jitters;* kiaugh [Scot.]; *languish;* make scared; nerve; overwhelm with fear; panic; quicken; repel; scare; terrify; unnerve; vex; worry; *xenophobia; yelping; zealless;* [*Ant.* settle]

**horror** *(n.)*: alarm; *burden;* consternation; dread; exasperation; fear; gastness; heebie-jeebies; horripiliation; insecurity; jitteriness; kiaugh [Scot.]; lancination; *mistrust;* nervousness; over-anxiety; panic; quaking; revulsion; scare; shock; terror; uneasiness; vexation; worry; *xibalba;* yellow-belliedness; *zeallessness;* [*Ant.* happiness]

**horse** *(n.)*: animal; ambler; *Arabian;* beast; broomtail; bay; bronco; colt; charger; courser; dobbin; draft- ~; dam [fem.]; equine; foal; filly [fem.]; gelding; garron; hack(ney); *Indian pony;* jade; jennet; *koulan; kelpy; livery; Lippizaner;* mount; mare; mustang; nag; *organism;* pony; plug; pack~; palomino; pacer; palfrey; quarter ~; race~; steed; stallion; stud; sumpter; thoroughbred; *ungulate; varmint;* work~; war~; *xilingol ~;* yearling; zain;

**horseman** *(n.)*: auriga; *buckaroo;* coachman; cavalier; drayman; driver; dragoon; equestrian; fast rider; gharry-wallah [Ind.]; horseback rider; hussar; *itinerant;* Jehu [slang]; jockey; *knight;* liveryman; mounted ~; nightrider; nagsman; outrider; puncher; postilion; postboy; quadrille; reinsman; rider; skinner [slang]; trooper; uhlan; *voiturier* [F.]; vedette; wagoner; whip; x-rider; yager; *zouave;*

**hose** *(n.)*: adjutage; black ~; conduit; duct; *equipment;* flex-pipe; fire~; garden ~; hosepipe; irrigation ~; *j-bend pipe; kyle;* line; *main; nozzle;* outlet; pipe; quill [arch.]; rubber ~; shaft; siphon; tube; *underground ~line; ventiduct;* water ~; *x-ray tube; Y-branch ~; zanja;*

**hospitable** *(adj.)*: amiable; benevolent; brotherly; cordial; congenial; *delightful;* entertaining; friendly; gregarious; gracious; *helpful; inviting; jovial;* kind; largehearted; magnanimous; neighborly; openhanded; pleasant; *quilting bee;* receptive; sociable; *thoughtful;* urbane; very friendly; welcoming; warm; xenodochial; xenial; *yokefellow; zealous;*

**hospital** *(n.)*: asylum; base ~ [mil.]; clinic; day ~; *detox center;* emergency room; first aid station; field ~ [mil.]; general ~; *hospice;* infirmary; *institution; Jewish ~;* karitane ~; lazaretto; medical center; *nurse station;* osteopathic ~; orphanotrophy; pesthouse; *psychiatric ward;* qualified healthcare clinic; *quarantine;* Red Cross station; sickbay; sanatorium; treatment center; unendowed ~; urgent care center; valetudinarian; V.A. ~; ward; xenodochia; youth clinic; *zoological ~;*

**hospitality** *(n.)*: amiableness; benevolence; cordiality; *deference;* entertainment; friendliness; graciousness; hospitableness; *help;* inviting guests; *joy-spreading;* kindness; liberality; magnanimity; niceness; neighborliness; open door; propitiousness; *quarter;* reception; sociableness; taking in; urbanity; *visitor reception;* warmth; xenodochy; *yieldedness; zealousness;* [*Ant.* hostility]

**host** *(n.)*: army; band; company; deployment; encampment; force; garrison; group; horde; infantry; junior service [Br.]; *kerns;* legion; mass; military; nonconscripted army; *outpost;* platoon; quarter-guard; regiment; soldiers; troop; unit; vanguard; warriors; x-force; *yeald; zouaves;*
**hostage** *(n.)*: abductee; *behind bars;* captive; detainee; earnest; *fettered;* guaranty; *held;* internee; *jailbird;* kidnapped person; *locked up; manacled;* niffer; *overtaken;* prisoner; *quashed; rope-tied;* surety; *taken; under lock and key;* victim; *ward; x,;* yard bird [slang]; *zek [Rus.];*
**hostile** *(adj.)*: antagonistic; aggressive; belligerent; contentious; dangerous; enemy; fierce; galsome; hateful; intimidating; ill-affected; inimical; jingoistic; kindless; low-down; mean; malicious; nasty; odious; pugnacious; quarrelsome; rough; savage; tough; threatening; unfriendly; violent; warlike; *xenophobic; yieldless; zealotic;* [Ant. harmonious]
**hostility** *(n.)*: animosity; antagonism; aggression; belligerence; contrariness; dislike; enmity; fight; gall; hatred; ill-will; inimicality; jangliness; *knocking;* loathing; malice; negativism; opposition; *polarity;* querulousness; resentment; rancor; spite; *tetchiness;* unfriendliness; virulence; *withstanding;* xenophobia; *yawping;* zealotry; [Ant. harmony]
**hot** *(adj.)*: ardent; burning; blistering; candent; *degrees;* enkindled; fervid; fiery; glowing; heated; inflammatory; *jejune;* kindled; lighted; *muggy; non-cooled;* over~; piping ~; quenchless; red- ~; sultry; sweltering; sizzling; scalding; toasty; thermal; torrid; uncomfortable; volcanic; well-heated; white- ~; xerothermic; yellow-hot; *zeta-warmed;*
**hotbed** *(n.)*: activity center; breeding ground; center; *developing; environment;* epicenter; *flourish;* fount; gathering-place; hub; heart; incubator; *jumping;* key center; *lodge;* major hub; nursery; nucleus; *origin; place; quicken;* rookery; source; *thick; umbilic; venter;* warren; x-section; yolk; zone;
**hotel** *(n.)*: *accommodations;* bed and breakfast; *caravanserai* [Arab.]; dosshouse; *efficiency apartment;* flophouse; fleabag motel; guesthouse; hostel; inn; joint; juke; kip-house; lodge; motel; *nook;* outspan; parador; public house; quinta; *quarters;* roadhouse; rooming house; resort; suites; ski lodge; tavern; *ubiety;* victualing-house; *ward;* xenodocheum; youth hostel; *zeta;*
**house** *(n.)*: abode; bungalow; building; cabin; cottage; chateau; domicile; dwelling (place); edifice; frontroom; flat house; guest house; hovel; habitation; home; inhabitance; jacal; konak; log cabin; lodging; manse; manor house; nest; outbuilding; place; quinta; residence; shack; structure; summer~; tenement; town~; unity ~; villa; wimpey ~; *xanadu ~; yali; zwinger;*
**house** *(v.)*: accommodate; board; bestead; contain; domicile; embower; enclose; facilitate; give shelter to; garrison [mil.]; harbor; hold; host; *inclose;* include; *jacal;* keep; lodge; *minister;* nest; *oblige;* put up; quarter; *retain; relieve;* shelter; take in; table; *uphold; valet;* wall-in; *x-border;* yard; zone;
**household** *(adj.)*: accustomed; *brood;* common; clan-related; domestic; domiciliary; everyday; family; *gens;* hearthside; ingleside; *jus soli* [L.]; kin-related; *loved ones;* manorial; normative; ordinary; popular; *quarter;* regular; *sept [Ire.];* tribal; usual; *vein;* well-known; *x-linked; yoni [Skr.];* zadruga [Slav.];
**household** *(n.)*: *accustomed;* belongings [reg.]; blood relations; brood; brethren; connections; children; clan; *domestic;* dynasty; extended family; family; gens; house; homestead; *in-laws; jus soli [L.];* kin(folk); loved ones; ménage; nuclear family; offspring; people; *quarter;* relatives; sept [Ire.]; tribe; toft; *umunna* [Afr.]; *vein; whanau* [N.Z.]; *x-linked; yoni [Skr.];* zadruga [Slav.];
**housing** *(n.)*: accommodations; board; bower; *cottage;* domicile; embowering; flat houses; government ~; house; inhabitance; *jacal; keep;* lodging; lodgement; *makeshift ~; niche; obligement;* place (to live); quarters; quartering; room; roof over one's head; shelter; space; tenement; *ubiety;* villa; walk-up; *xanadu house; yali;* zoned ~;
**hover** *(v.)*: *afloat;* buoy; coast; drift; *evolation;* float; glide; hang; inaquate; jet; kite; levitate; move above; *natant;* overhang; poise; *quicken;* rest; suspend; take off; upbear; *volplane;* waft; *xuld [arch.]; yern; zoom;*

**howl** *(n.)*: acclamation; bay; bellow; cry; dissent; exclamation; fuss; growl; holler; hoot; *inveighing; jeremiad;* keen; loud shout; lament; moan; noise; outcry; puling; quiritation; resonation; reverberation; roar; shout; shriek; scream; thundering; ululation; uproar; vociferation; whoop; wail; wrawl; *xenophonia;* yell; yowl; *zindabad;*

**howl** *(v.)*: *appeal;* acclaim; bay; bellow; call; cry; dissent; exclaim; erupt; fuss; growl; hoot; holler; *inveigh; jubilate;* keen; loudly say; *lament;* moan; noise; outcry; pule; *quiritation;* resonate; reverberate; roar; shout; shriek; scream; thunder; ululate; vociferate; vent; whoop; wail; *xenophonia;* yowl; yell; *zindabad;*

**hub** *(n.)*: axis; belly; base; center(point); core; dead center; epicenter; fesse-point; *geological ~;* heart; interior; *just centered;* kernel; *lodged;* middle; nucleus; nave; omphalos; pith; *quotidian;* radius; spindle; *top;* umbilic; *via media;* within; x-section; yolk; zenith;

**hug** *(n.)*: *arms;* bear ~; clinch; drawing around; embrace; fastening on; grip; grasp; group ~; *hold;* infolding; *joining;* kinch; *looping around; mushy;* nobble; *nestle;* oxtercog; putting around; *quashing;* reception; squeeze; throwing arms around; upbinding; *volting;* welcoming; X; yoke; zone;

**hug** *(v.)*: *around;* bind; begird; cling; clutch; draw around; embrace; fold; gird; hold; inwrap; *join;* kirtle; *latch onto; love;* make embrace; *nestle;* oxtercog; put arms around; *quash;* roll; *receive;* squeeze; throw arms around; upbind; *volt;* wrap arms around; X; *yearnful ~;* zone;

**huge** *(adj.)*: ample; abundant; big; bulky; capacious; colossal; deep; disproportionate; extensive; enormous; expansive; fat; generous; great; giant; heavy; hulking; humongous; immense; jumbo-sized; king-size; large; massive; *noteworthy;* overgrown; obese; ponderous; prodigious; quantitative; rotund; roomy; sizable; substantial; tremendous; *unmanageable; unwieldy;* voluminous; vast; wide; whopping; weighty; XL; *Ymir; zaftig;*

**hull** *(n.)*: aril; bark; body; case; casing; carapace; *defense;* exterior; frame; fuselage; glume; husk; integument; jacket; keel; *layer;* main body; *non-edible* peel; pod; outside; protective covering; *querned; rind;* skin; shell; tegument; underside; vessel body; wrapping; x.; yare; zest;

**human** *(adj.)*: Adamic; anthropological; bipedal; *creaturely; depraved;* earthly; earthborn; flesh-and-blood; fallible; *global;* hominoid; humanoid; *individual; jack; kipper; living;* manly; mortal; natural-born; *only ~;* people-related; *quadragenarian; residential;* social; Terran; *under the sun; villager;* worldling; xenic; *yokel;* zoid; [*Ant.* heavenly]

**human** *(n.)*: Adamite; *anyone;* being; biped; *creature; citizen;* descendant of Adam; earthling; figure; fellow man; guy [masc.]; ~ being; *homo sapien* [L.]; individual; jack [slang]; *kipper [slang];* living soul; man; mortal; name; one; organism; person; *quadragenarian;* resident; soul; someone; terran; *underling; villager;* worldling; woman [fem.]; *xenic; yokel;* zoon;

**humane** *(adj.)*: amiable; benevolent; compassionate; decent; empathetic; friendly; gentle; humanitarian; *indulgent; jovial;* kindhearted; loving; merciful; nice; *obliging;* piteous; *quick to help;* ruthful; sympathetic; tender(hearted); *unselfish;* very kind; *warm;* xenial; *yielding; zärtlich* [G.]; [*Ant.* heartless]

**humble** *(adj.)*: abased; abject; base; broken; childlike; contrite; debased; demissive; effaced; *fearful;* groveling; humble-hearted; humbled; inglorious; ignoble; *jackalent; kind;* lowly; lamblike; lamblike; modest; meek; mild; non-esteemed; obsequious; poor (in spirit); *quiet;* renownless; respectful; self-effacing; self-abased; submissive; servile; teachable; unassuming; unboastful; unpretentious; vanquished; without airs; *xtry. humility;* yielding; *zero pride;* [*Ant.* haughty]

**humble** *(v.)*: abase; bring down; condescend; confound; debase; degrade; deflate; efface; embarrass; *flattened;* grovel; humiliate; imbrute; *jackalent; keep low;* lower; mortify; *nither* [*arch.*]; overwhelm; put down; prostrate; quiet; reduce; self-efface; take down; *undo;* vulgarize; wite; *xtry. ~d;* yield; *zero pride;*

**humid** *(adj.)*: airless; *boggy;* clammy; damp(ish); dank; *enkindled;* full-hot; *gross;* hot; hydrous; icky; jejune; *kindled; loathsome;* muggy; *non-dry;* oppressive; pluvious; *quenchless;* roasting; sticky; sultry; steamy; torrid; uncomfortable; vaporous; warm; wet; *xerothermic; yucky; zealless;*

**humiliate** *(v.)*: abash; belittle; bring low; crush; debase; degrade; disgrace; embarrass; flout; gibe at; humble; imbrute; jerr at; knock off one's high horse; lower; make fool of; mortify; *nither [arch.];* offend; put down; quell; reproach; ridicule; stultify; shame; take down; unfrock; vulgarize; wither; xtry. *humbled; yowl; zero pride;* [*Ant.* honor]

**humiliation** *(n.)*: abashment; belittlement; bringing low; crushing; degradation; disgrace; devastation; embarrassment; feeling of ~; *gibe;* humility; ignominy; indignity; *jibe; knocking off one's high horse;* letdown; lowering; mortification; *notoriousness;* obloquy; opprobrium; putting down; quelling; reproach; self-abasement; shame; take-down; upbraiding; verecundity; wite; xtry. ~; *yowling;* zero pride; [*Ant.* honor]

**humility** *(n.)*: abjection; abasement; brokenness; condescension; debasement; effacement; *fall; grace;* humbleness; ignobleness; ingloriousness; juniority; *knocking off one's high horse;* lowliness; meekness; modesty; meanness; non-pride; over-humbleness; poorness; pridelessness; *quality;* repentance; self-effacement; servility; timidity; unpretentiousness; *vileness; woefulness;* xtry. ~; *yieldedness;* zero pride; [*see* humiliation; *Ant.* haughtiness]

**humor** *(n.)*: amusement; burlesque; black ~; comedy; drollery; dry ~; entertainment; funniness; gag; humorousness; hilarity; *insanity;* irony; jocoseness; joking; kookiness; levity; low comedy; *madness;* nuttiness; outrageousness; puns; quackiness; ridiculousness; sport; tongue-in-cheek ~; *unserious; vainness;* wit(ticism); waggishness; wry ~; xtry. *sport; yuk-yuk;* zaniness; [*Ant.* heaviness]

**humor** *(v.)*: accommodate; allow; bear with; consent to; do a favor; entertain; facilitate; go along with; gratify; *have;* indulge; *just do; knowingly allow;* let; make concession; *nod;* oblige; pacify; *quell; rationalize;* suffer; tolerate; *unhindered; validate; willing;* xtry. *indulgent;* yield; *zero opposition;*

**humorous** *(adj.)*: amusing; bizarre; comical; daft; entertaining; funny; goofy; hilarious; *insane;* jokey; kooky; laughable; mirthful; mad; nimble-witted; outrageous; punny; quick-witted; ridiculous; *a* riot; silly; tongue-and-cheek; uproarious; very funny; whimsical; witty; xtry. *funny;* yare-handed; zany; [*Ant.* humorless]

**hunch** *(n.)*: assumption; bet; conjecture; deduction; estimation; feeling; *gauging;* hypothesis; idea; judgment; *knowledge;* leaning; mind; notion; opinion; presumption; *quot homines tot sententiae* [L.]; reckoning; supposition; speculation; theory; *urge;* view; *vibe;* wild guess; wind; *xenodiagnosis; yankering; zeal;*

**hunger** *(n.)*: appetite; belly-pinching; craving; desire; emptiness; esuriency; edacity; famishment; famine; greed; gluttony; hungering; hungriness; itch; *jejune; keenness of appetite;* lack; longing; *malnourishment;* need; *omnivorism;* pangs; *quenchless;* ravenousness; starvation; *thirst;* unprovisioned; vacuity; voracity; want; xenorexia; yapness; yearning; *zero food;*

**hunger** *(v.)*: ache; *bid;* crave; desire; en~; enfamish [both arch.]; famish; got to have; hanker; itch; *just got to have; keen desire;* lack; long for; mania; need; *order;* pant after; pine; *quest for;* relish; seek; thirst for; *urge;* voracity; want; xel [arch.]; yearn for; *zealously desire;*

**hungry** *(adj.)*: *appetite;* belly-pinched; craving; desirous; eager; enhungered; esurient; edacious; *faint;* famished; gluttonous; hungered; hungering; half-starved; itching; insatiable; jejune; *keen;* longing; malnourished; *needy;* openmouthed; panged; peckish; *quenchless;* ravenous; starving; *thirsty;* unfed; voracious; weak; xenorexic; yearning; yeverous; *zapped;* [*Ant.* happy]

**hunk** *(n.)*: agglomeration; bit; bunch; chip; clump; clod; chunk; daud; *ens;* fragment; flake; glob; heap; *iota;* junt; kernel; lump; morsel; mammock; mass; nugget; ounce; piece; portion; *quantity;* remnant; small piece; sliver; tidbit; *unit; vestige;* wedge; wad; *xylon; yngot [arch.];* zum [dial.];

**hunt** *(n.)*: *after; big* ~; combing; chase; course; dogging; expedition; fishing; fox~; foxchase; *goose chase;* hounding; *investigation;* jacking; *kill;* looking for; mission; man~; nosing around; *open season;* prowl; pursuit; quest; *retracing;* search; tracking; trailing; *undertaking;* venture; *wild goose chase;* x-search; yager; *zealously find;*

**hunt** *(v.)*: *after;* be after; bring in; course; chase; dog; *entrap;* fish; forage; follow; fox~; foxchase; go after; hound; *interlope;* jack; *kill;* look for; make one's prey; *nose around; open season;* prowl; pursue; prey on; queue; quest; run after; seek; search; stalk; trace; track; trail; *undertake;* venture; *wild goose chase; x-gun; yager; zealously find;*

**hunter** *(n.)*: * *angler;* big-game ~; chaser; courser; deer ~; elephant ~; forager; fowler; fox~; gunman; huntsman; huntress [fem.]; *investigator; jaeger* [G.]; jacker; killer; lion ~; *muzzle-loader* ~; nimrod; *outdoorsman;* predator; pursuer; quester; rifleman; sportsman; stalker; trapper; tracker; *uakari* ~; venturer; wildfowler; woodsman; wolfer; *xeme* ~; yager; *zebra* ~;

**hunting** *(n.)*: *after;* being after; coursing; chasing; dogging; exploration; fox~; gunning; hunstmanship; *interloping;* jacking; *killing;* looking; making one's prey; *nimrod; open season;* pursuing; preying; questing; *retracing;* searching; stalking; shooting; sporting; sportsmanship; trapping; tracking; *undertaking;* venery; wildfowling; *x-gun; yager; zealously finding;*

**hurdle** *(n.)*: *article;* barrier; challenge; cumbrance; difficulty; encumbrance; fence; galandesprung; hindrance; impediment; jam; kink; *lodgment;* mountain; nuisance; obstacle; problem; *quandary;* railing; roadblock; stumbling block; trouble; *upset; vigia;* wall; x; *yowler; zinger;*

**hurry** *(v.)*: accelerate; bustle; cruise; dash; dart; expedite; fly; go fast; hustle; haste(n); *issue;* june; jet; kite; light; move; not procrastinate; *outrun;* press on; quicken; rush; race; speed; tear; *uprush; velocity;* whip; *xuld [arch.];* yern; zip (to it); [*Ant.* hem and haw]

**hurt** *(adj.)*: afflicted; abused; blasted; chafing; damaged; endamaged; *flaring;* galling; gammy; harmed; injured; impaired; jeeled; *killing [slang]; lacerated;* marred; maimed; *nocument;* offend; pranged; *quab;* rack; suffering; tormented; *undone; uneasy;* victimized; wounded; *xiphodynia; yaik [arch.];* zinging; [*Ant.* healed]

**hurt** *(n.)*: affliction; abuse; blast; *cost;* disservice; detriment; damage; evil; foulness; *grief;* harm; injury; impairment; jeel; *knock;* loss; mischief; marring; maiming; nocument; offense; prang; persecution; *query; ruin;* scath; *suffering;* trouble; *unsafe;* victimization; violence; wound; *x-ing;* yedder; *zap;* [*Ant.* healing]

**hurt** *(v.)*: afflict; abuse; blast; *cripple;* disserve; damage; endamage; fix [slang]; give pain; harm; injure; inflict damage; impair; jeel; kick; kill; lift hand against; mar; maim; *nip; offend;* pain; persecute; *quash;* rack; scathe; trouble; *upset;* victimize; wound; x.; *ydrad [arch.]; zap;* [*see* ache; *Ant.* heal]

**hurtful** *(adj.)*: adverse; bad; cutting; detrimental; damaging; endangering; foul; gnarly; harmful; injurious; jeopardous; *known risk;* lethal; malefic; nocuous; *ominous;* pernicious; perilous; *questionable;* ruinous; self-destructive; threatening; unbeneficial; virulent; wounding; *x.; ydrad [arch.]; zero safety;* [*Ant.* helpful]

**husband** *(n.)*: *authority;* breadwinner; companion; defender; ever-faithful ~; family man; goodman; honey; hubby; head; inamorato; *joint ;* king (of the castle); *love;* lord; man; mate; nuptial partner; *one;* partner; provider; *quadragenarian; rom* [Gypsy]; spouse; *toiler; upholder; virile;* wedded spouse; *worker; x-linked;* yokefellow; *zoon;* [*Ant.* helpmeet]

**husk** *(n.)*: aril; bark; covering; casing; *dermis;* exocarp; exterior; firm outer layer; glume; hide; hard outer layer; integument; jacket; *kind; layer;* membrane; *non-edible* pod; outer layer; peel; *querned;* rind; skin; shuck; shell; tegument; *throw-away part; unusable part; vessel;* wrapping; *x.; yellow* ~; zest;

**husk** *(v.)*: abrade; bark; cut; *debone;* decorticate; excoriate; flay; *get ~ off;* hew; *incise;* julienne; *knife;* lash; mince; *negate;* open; peel; pare; *quick- ~;* remove ~; skin; strip; shuck; take ~ off; uncase; *vell;* whittle; *xyster; yerk; zip;*

**hut** *(n.)*: abode; bungalow; beach house; bush house; barracks; cottage; cabin; chateau; dump; dwelling (place); edifice; frontroom; grass ~; gunyah; hovel; hok; inhabitance; jacal; kya; lean-to; log ~; mud ~; nipa ~; outbuilding; place; quarters; rancho; shed; shack; shanty; thatched-roof ~; *utility apartment;* villa; wickup; *x-house;* yakutat hut; *zayat;* [*see* barracks]

**hygiene** *(n.)*: asepsis; bathing; cleanliness; disinfection; elution; freedom from filth; *germ-free;* hygienics; immaculateness; *jalap;* keeping germ-free; *lavation; mundification; no germs; oral ~;* personal ~; *quintessentialize; rinsing;* sterilization; sanitation; *totally germ-free; unsullied; vacuumed;* washing; *xylol; yellow soap; zero filth;*
**hymn** *(n.)*: anthem; ballad; carol; chorus; canticle; descant; doxology; étude; folksong; gallimaufry; harmony; inspirational; jingle; kasida; lovesong; melody; motet; notes; offertory; psalm; quadrille; refrain; recessional; song; strain; sequence; trisagion; *tune;* undersong; vocalization; *warbling; xylophone song;* yed; zemirah;
**hymnal** *(n.)*: antiphoner; anthology; book; chorus book; *decimo-sexto; edition; folio;* gradaul; hymnbook; inspirational ~; *jingle;* kasida-book; *lyrics;* missal; music-book; *notes;* offertory book; psalmbook; psalter(y); *quire book* [arch.]; *recessional;* songbook; *tome; undersong;* vesperal; *work;* xenagogy; yed-book; *zemirah-book;*
**hypnosis** *(n.)*: abstraction; bemusement; catalepsy; daze; entrancement; fascination; *glassy-eyed;* hypnotization; incoherence; *jag;* kinching; lethe; mesmerism; narcosis; obliviousness; preoccupation; *quaffed; reverie;* stupefaction; subconscious state; spellbinding; trance; under (a spell); *vacancy;* wacking out [slang]; *x-fix; yielded;* zoning out;
**hypocrisy** *(n.)*: act(ing); bluffing; counterfeiting; duplicity; disingenuousness; dissembling; dissimulation; emulation; feigning; fraud; grandiosity; hollowness; hypocriticalness; insincerity; japery; *kidding;* lying; misleading; mendacity; non-genuineness; *ostensible;* pretending; pretense; pretext; play-acting; phoniness; pharisaicalness; quacksalving; rooking; simulation; sanctimony; superficiality; two-facedness; unauthenticity; verneuking; willful dissimulation; *xtry. ~; yentzer; zelig;* [*Ant.* honesty]
**hypocrite** *(n.)*: actor; bluffer; counterfeit; charlatan; dissembler; emulator; fraud; guiler; huckster; insincere person; imposter; jerry-sneak [Br.]; *kidder;* liar; make-believer; nobbler; *outside;* pretender; play-actor; phony; Pharisee; quacksalver; religious ~; sham; tartuffe; *unauthentic;* ventzer; whited sepulcher; *xiaoren;* yentzer; *zelig;*
**hypocritical** *(adj.)*: artificial; bogus; contrived; counterfeit; duplicitous; disingenuous; dissembling; deceitful; emulative; false; facile; feigned; guileful; hollow; hypercritic; insincere; Janus-faced; *kidding; lying;* make-believe; mendacious; non-genuine; ostensible; pretended; phony; pharisaical; quacksalving; *rooking;* superficial; sanctimonious; tartuffian; two-faced; untruthful; verneuking; wangling; *xtry. phony;* yentzing; *zelig;* [*Ant.* heartfelt]
**hypothesis** *(n.)*: assumption; belief; conjecture; deduction; educated guess; estimation; expectation; feeling; guess; hunch; idea; judgment; *knowledge; lemma;* mind; notion; opinion; postulation; proposal; qualified opinion; reckoning; speculation; theory; theorem; *urge;* view; *wild guess; xenodiagnosis; yankering;* zeal;
**hypothesize** *(v.)*: assume; bet; conjecture; deduce; estimate; expect; figure; guess; *hatch;* imagine; judge; *know;* logicize; muse; *notion; occur;* presume; *question;* reckon; suppose; speculate; theorize; use reason; *venture; wis; xenodiagnose; yeme; zazen;*
**hypothetical** *(adj.)*: abstract; belief-based; conjectural; deductive; epagogic; *feeling;* guessed; hypothetic; inductive; *just supposed; knowledgeable;* logicized; not proven; opiniative; presumed; postulatory; Q.E.D.; reckoned; speculative; suppositional; theoretical; unproven; virtual; *what if...; xenagogic;* yet unproven; *zazen;*
**hysterical** *(adj.)*: amok; beside oneself; ballistic [slang]; crazy; distraught; exasperated; falling to pieces; *grief-stricken;* haywire; irrational; *jittery; kooky; lost it;* mad; not rational; overly upset; out-of-control; panicky; quacked; raving; stressed; *troubled;* upset; *violently upset;* wild; *xuld [arch.];* yelling; zany; [*Ant.* hushed]

# I

**ice** *(n.)*: * *arctic;* black ~; cube ~; crystallization; diamonds; *enhardened ~;* frozen water; frost; floe; glaciation; hoar(frost); hail; iciness; ice cube; iceberg; *Jack Frost;* kittly-benders; *low temperature; mantle of snow;* névé; *overcold;* pack ~; permafrost; *quern* [arch.]; rime; serac; shelf ~; slush; *thawing ~;* unthawed ~; verglas; white frost; *xtr. cold; yowndrift [arch.]* zero degrees; [Ant. inferno]

**iceberg** *(n.)*: *aufeis;* block; berg; chunk of ice; drift ice; *eyot;* floe; frazil; growler; hunk of ice; ice berg; iceisle; *junt; kittly-benders;* large ~; mass; *névé;* oceanborne ~; pinnacle ~; *quaternary; remnant;* small ~; tabular ~; *unnoticed ~; vestige;* wedge; *xfer;* York berg; *Zemu;*

**ichorous** *(adj.)*: awful; bad; contaminated; disgusting; evil-looking; festering; gross; hydropical; infected; *icky; juicy; ketty;* loathsome; morbid; nasty; oozy; pus-filled; *queasy;* rancorous; secreting; terrible; unenviable; vile; watery; xtry, gross; yucky; *zich [arch.];*

**icing** *(n.)*: almond ~; butter cream; cake frosting; cream; *delicious; edible topping;* frosting; fondant; glaze; *hardened ~;* iced topping; *jelly-filled; kreme [arch.];* lemon ~; mock cream; *nut-filled;* overglaze; pastillage; *quart;* royal ~; sweet ~; topping; unsweetened topping; vanilla ~; whipped topping; *xtr. sugary; yellow ~; zerbet;*

**icon** *(n.)*: *arms;* badge; crest; coat of arms; depiction; emblem; figure; glyph; hierogram; image; *jack;* key; likeness; mark; notation; object; picture; *quarter;* representation; symbol; token; *universal symbol; vexillum; wafer; x; yacht ensign; zeug;*

**icy** *(adj.)*: arctic; bitter; cold; chilled; *dead; extreme;* frozen; frosty; glacial; hoary; ice-cold; iced over; *Jack Frost; keen;* low-temperature; *miserable;* nippy; numbing; overcold; polar; quick-frozen; rimy; subzero; thawless; unthawed; *very cold;* wintry; *xeric-less; ycie* [arch.]; zero degrees; [Ant. inflamed]

**idea** *(n.)*: apprehension; brainchild; conception; design; evaluation; fancy; fabrication; gist; hunch; headwork; inspiration; jist; *knowledge;* lucubration; mindset; masterstroke; notion; opinion; plan; *quintessence;* reasoning; scheme; thought; *urge;* vague ~; way of thinking; *xtry. ~; yeme* [arch.]; *zazen;*

**ideal** *(adj.)*: archetypal; best-case scenario; capital; *dreamy;* exemplary; fanciful; good; *hypothetical;* idealistic; just right; *kalon [Gr.]; leading;* model; neotypical; outstanding; perfect; quixotic; romantic; standard; terrific; ultimate; *virtual; wanted; xtry. perfect; yardstick; zero-defect;*

**ideal** *(n. perfect example)*: archetype; *beau ideal* [F.]; classic example; *dream;* exemplar; epitome; eidolon; fugler; guide; height; illustration; jewel; *kalon* [Gr.]; lodestar; model; neotype; *original;* pattern; paradigm; paragon; quintessence; representation; rule; standard; touchstone; ule; ultimate; very example; *wanted; xanadu;* yardstick; *zero-defect;*

**ideal** *(n. principle)*: axiom; belief; code; dictum; ethic; fundament; guideline; high goal; institute; judgment; kernel of wisdom; lodestar; law; moral; notion; opinion; *organon;* principle; qualm; rule; standard; truism; universal truth; veracity; wisdom; *xenagogy;* yardstick; zeteticism;

**idealistic** *(adj.)*: aspiring; bright; chimerical; dream-world; expectant; full of hope; great; hopeful; idealist; *just hoping;* keen-envisioned; Laputian; much-hoped-for; notional; nonviable; optimistic; over-hopeful; positivistic; Polyanna; quixotic; romantic-notioned; rosy; sanguine; starry-eyed; trusting; upbeat; unrealistic; untenable; very ~; wishful; well-believing; *xanadu;* yea-saying; zealous;

**identical** *(adj.)*: alike; *balanced;* comparable; congruent; duplicate; equal; following; *good likeness;* homologous; indistinguishable; just the same; kindred; like; matching; non-differing; one-in-the-same; parallel; *quae est eadem* [L.]; resembling; (self)same; twin; tantamount; uniform; verbatim; word-perfect; *xerographed;* yet undifferentiated; *zero difference;* [Ant. incongruous]

**identity** *(n.)*: *alias;* birth-name; *certificate of birth;* designation; distinctiveness; egohood; first ~; given ~; handle [slang]; hypocorism; identification; *jurisdiction; known by;* last name; legal ~; *me;* name; official ~; personal information; *quiring;* representation; selfhood; title; uniqueness; *vocable;* who one is; *xenonym; yu [Chin.]; zoon;* [*see* accord]

**ideological** *(adj.)*: absorbed; brooding; conceptual; doctrinal; ethology; fanciful; gazeful; heady [slang]; idealistic; judicious; *Kantian;* logical; maieutic; notional; *opinionative;* philosophical; quodlibetarian; rational; staid; Socratic; theoretical; *understanding; valuating;* wise; *xenocratic; yearnful;* zetetic;

**ideology** *(n.)*: adherence; beliefs; body of ideas; credo; doctrine; dogma; ethos; faith; *gospel;* human understanding; ism; *judgment;* known beliefs; line; mindset; notions; opinion; principles; philosophy; quodlibetary; reasoning; religion; system of beliefs; tenets; ule; understanding; view; way of thinking; world view; *xel [arch.]; y'faith* [arch.]; *zet;*

**idiocy** *(n.)*: asininity; brainlessness; craziness; dumbness; egg-headedness; foolishness; gullibility; goofiness; hebetude; imbecility; jackassery; kookiness; ludicrousness; madness; naivety; outrageousness; preposterousness; quackery; ridiculousness; stupidity; thoughtlessness; *unthinking;* vertigo; witlessness; *xtry. ~; yokelishness;* zaniness; [*Ant.* intelligence]

**idiosyncrasy** *(n.)*: abnormality; aberration; behavior; characteristic; deviation; eccentricity; foible; glitch; habit; irregularity; *jerking;* kink; looniness; malformation; non-usualness; oddity; peculiarity; quirk; *response;* strangeness; twist; unique way; variation; way; *xtry.;* yaw; zaniness;

**idiot** *(n.)*: airhead; blockhead; boob; birdbrain; cretin; clown; clod; chowderhead; dummy; dope; dimwit; ding-a-ling; dolt; dunderhead; egghead; fool; fathead; goof(ball); harebrain; half-wit; ignoramus; imbecile; jerk; knucklehead; lout; moron; numbskull; oaf; pea-brain; quack; rattlebrain; simpleton; twit; turkey; *unwise; vacant;* woodenhead; *xiaoren;* yo-yo; zob;

**idiotic** *(adj.)*: air-headed; bumbling; block-headed; bird-brained; clownish; dumb; dopey; dim-witted; egg-headed; foolish; goofy; harebrained; half-witted; ignorant; imbecilic; jackass; knuckleheaded; lame-brained; moronic; nit-witted; outlandish; pea-brained; quacky; ridiculous; rattle-brained; silly; stupid; thick(-skulled); unthinking; *vacant;* witless; xtry. dumb; *yokelish;* zany; [*see* ridiculous; *Ant.* intelligent]

**idle** *(adj.)*: at rest; *asleep;* becalmed; calm; dormant; easeful; fallow; goldbricking; hibernating; inactive; immobile; indolent; jarless; *kill time;* latent; lazy; motionless; non-moving; out of action; peaceful; quiescent; quiet; resting; recumbent; still; sleeping; sluggish; slothful; torpid; undisturbed; unoccupied; vacant; workless; *x'ed;* yet inactive; *zero activity;* [*Ant.* industrious]

**idleness** *(n.)*: apathy; *break;* calm; dawdling; easiness; fooling around; goofing off; heaviness; inactivity; joblessness; kip; laziness; motionlessness; non-movement; otiosity; pausing; quietness; rest; relaxation; recumbency; slacking off; time out; taking it easy; unemployment; vegetating; waiting; *x-rest; yawning;* zizz; [*Ant.* industriousness]

**idol** *(n.)*: Ashtoreth; *Baal; Beelzebub; Buddha;* carved image; deity; earth god; false god; figure; fetish; god; graven image; heathen god; image; icon; joss; *kore;* likeness; molten image (-god); *Mammon; netherworld god;* orisha; pagan god; penate; pagan deity; *query stone;* representation; statue; totem; teraphim; *unit; voodoo god;* wood carving; xoanon; yaksha; zeme; [*see* god; grove]

**idolater** *(n.)*: allotheist; Baal-worshiper; chthonian; devil-worshiper; ecclesiolater; fetishist; *god-maker;* heathen; idol-worshiper; idolatress [fem.]; joss-worshiper; kore; lover of idols; moon-worshiper; neo-pagan; ophiolater; pagan; *quad; rhabdomancer;* sun-worshiper; theriolater; *ungodly;* voodooist; worshiper; xoanon-worshiper; *Ymir-follower;* zemeist;

**idolatrous** *(adj.)*: allotheistic; barbaric; coarse; devilish; *evil;* foul; godless; heathen; idol-worshipping; *jungli;* kaf [arch.]; lost; *misinformed;* neopagan; ophiolatry; pagan; polytheistic; *quad;* rude; savage; *tribal;* unchristian; vulgar; *wicked; xenon-worshipping; yantra;* zemeistic;

**idolatry** *(n.)*: allotheism; Baal-worship; covetousness; devil-worship; ethnicism; ecclesiolatry; fetishism; *god-making;* heathenism; heliolatry; idol-worship; joss-worship; *kore;* love of idols; moon-worship; neo-paganism; orisha-worship; paganism; polytheism; *quad; rhabdomancy; Sabianism;* sun-worship; *theogony; ungodliness;* voodoo; whoredom; xoanon-worship; *yantra;* zemeism;
**idol-maker** *(n.)*: artificer; *builder;* carver; chiseler; deity-maker; engraver; fashioner; godsmith; handcrafter; image-maker; joss-maker; *kore; laborer;* maker of idols; *neo-paganist; operator;* producer of idols; *quad; ready worker;* statuemaker; silversmith; teraphim-maker; *ungodly; voodoo;* wood-carver; xylographer; *yeoman;* zoolater;
**ignite** *(v.)*: alight; burn; combust; deflagrate; enkindle; flame; *gut; heat;* incinerate; inflame; *jeopardize;* kindle; light (up); miskindle; motivate; *nightfire;* overburn; *pyre; quick-match;* raze; rekindle; set on fire; scorch; torch; ustion; *vulcanize; waste; xylophyrograph; yerk;* zap;
**ignoble** *(adj.)*: abased; base; contemptible; despicable; evil; foul; graceless; humble; inglorious; *jejune; kneeling;* lowly; lewd; mean; modest; nasty; nauseating; obnoxious; odious; pathetic; *quad;* repugnant; rude; sorry; shameless; terrible; uncouth; unholy; vulgar; wretched; *x-rated;* yucky; zhlubby;
**ignorance** *(n.)*: *asininity;* bad information; childlikeness; deceptability; empty-headedness; feeble-mindedness; gullibility; *harebrained;* innocence; inexperience; *juvenility;* knowing nothing; lack of knowledge; moronism; naïvity; nescience; obtuseness; obliviousness; philistinism; *quackiness;* raw stupidity; simplicity; stupidity; *trusting;* unawareness; verdant; witlessness; *xtry. ~; youth; zhlubbiness;*
**ignorant** *(adj.)*: *amateurish;* blind; clueless; decievable; empty-headed; feeble-minded; gullible; *harebrained;* inexperienced; innocent; illiterate; *juvenile;* know-nothing; lacking knowledge; moronic; naïve; nescient; non-educated; oblivious; obtuse; *philistine; quacky; rude;* simple; stupid; *trusting;* uninformed; unlearned; uneducated; unaware; unwitting; unschooled; verdant; weetless; *xtry. unaware; young; zhlubby;* [*see* foolish; young]
**ignorantly** *(adv.)*: accidentally; blindly; cluelessly; *deceived; easily-deceived;* feeble-mindedly; gullibly; *having no knowledge;* inadvertently; innocently; *juvenile; knowledge-deprived;* lacking knowledge; mistakingly; naïvely; obtusely; obliviously; *peasantly; quackily; rudely;* simply; stupidly; *trustingly;* unknowingly; unwittingly; unbeknownst; verdantly; without knowledge; *xtry. ignorant; yet unawares; zero knowledge;*
**ignore** *(v.)*: avoid; brush aside; close one's eyes; disregard; discount; dismiss; elide; flout; go over; *heedless; indifferent;* irregard [improper]; jump over; *kest;* look the other way; misattend; neglect; overlook; pass over; pay no heed; *quick-to-forget;* reject; skip over; sweep aside; slight; snub; tune out; toss aside; *unfaithful;* view with trviality; wink at; *x-ing; yemeles [arch.];* zero responsibility;
**ill** *(adj.)*: ailing; affected; bad; bedridden; consumptive; diseased; evil-affected; feverish; galled; *hurt;* indisposed; infected; *jaundiced;* ketty; laid up; malaise; nauseous; not well; off-color; poor-health; queasy; *rabid;* sick; *tabid* [arch.]; unhealthy; *vulnerable;* weak; *x-disease; yellow; yucky; zich* [arch.];
**ill-bred** *(adj.)*: abominable; boorish; coarse; crude; discourteous; dowdy; evil-mannered; foul; gruff; hoiden; hoblike; inelegant; ill-mannered; immorigerous; *jadish; kitsch;* loathsome; misbehaved; non-civil; offensive; poor-mannered; queer; rough; rude; sorry; shocking; tactless; terrible; ungracious; unmannered; uncultivated; unbred; unrefined; uncivil; uncouth; vile; vulgar; wretched; *xenophobic;* yahoo; zhlubby;
**illegal** *(adj.)*: adulterine; against the law; banned; barred; bootleg; contraband; criminal; disallowed; enjoined; extralegal; forbidden; government-banned; held back; illicit; *jurisdictionally barred;* kept from; lawless; misappropriated; not allowed; nixed; *nudum pacum* [L.]; nonconstitutional; off-limits; outlawed; prohibited; *questionable;* restricted; shut out; sinful; transgressive; unlawful; under the counter; *verboten* [G.]; wicked; *x-ed; ybarred* [arch.]; *zapoviednik* [Rus.];
**illegality** *(n.)*: against the law; breach (of the law); criminality; disallowed action; extralegal act; forbidden act; guiltiness; horrendous act; illegal act; *jurisdictionally barred; knavishness;* lawlessness; misdemeanor; non-legal action; outlawed act; prohibited action; *questionable act;* restricted act; sin; trespass; unlawful act; violation; wrongdoing; *x-ed; ybarred [arch.]; zapoviednik [Rus.];*

**illegible** *(adj.)*: *awful;* badly written; cluttered; cacographic; disorderly; *entangled; fuzzy; gray;* highly ~; ill-written; indecipherable; jumbled; keg-meg; *lousy;* messy; non-readable; obscured; poorly written; *quirky; reprehensible;* sloppy; *terrible;* unreadable; undecipherable; very sloppy; written illegibly; *x'ed;* yet indecipherable; *zero legibility;* [*Ant.* intelligible]

**illegitimacy** *(n.)*: *adulterine;* bastardy; criminal birth; dishonor; *exclusion;* foulness; *gross immorality;* highly questionable birth; impropriety; illicit birth; *jurisdictionally barred; kept from;* lawlessness; *misbegotten;* non-legitimate birth; out-of-wedlock birth; *putain;* questionable origin; reproach; spurious birth; *treachery;* uncleanness; vile birth; *whoredom; x-gression; yaud; zero legitimacy;*

**illegitimate** *(adj.)*: adulterine; base(born); bastard; criminal; dishonorable; *excluded;* foul; *grievous;* highly questionable; illegal; ill-gotten; improper; impure; illicit; justiciable; *kept from;* lawless; misbegotten; not rightful; *nullus filius* [law]; out-of-wedlock; outlawed; putain; questionable; *reprehensible;* spurious; treacherous; unlawful; unorthodox; unclean; vile; wicked; *x-gressive; yaud; zero legitimacy;* [*Ant.* incontestable]

**illicit** *(adj.)*: against the law; backstreet; banned; criminal; dishonest; erroneous; forbidden; *godless;* highly illegal; illegal; justiciable; *knavish;* legally-prohibited; malapropos; not allowed; outlawed; prohibited; *questionable;* restricted; sinful; transgressing; unlawful; vile; wrong; *xgressing; yucky; zero propriety:*

**illiterate** *(adj.)*: aboriginal; Biblically ~; cannot read; *deprived;* education-deprived; *feeble; gullible; heathen;* ignorant; *just can't read;* know-nothing; letterless; *mean;* non-educated; oral [sociology]; poorly-educated; quite ~; *rude; simple; tutorless;* unlettered; uneducated; unlearned; unschooled; void of education; *weetless; xtry. deprived; yokelish; zhlubby;*

**illness** *(n.)*: ailment; bug; *bout;* condition; disease; disorder; *epidemic; fever; germ;* health problem; infection; infirmity; *jaundice; king's evil;* lesion; malady; nausea; *ordeal;* pox; plague; queasiness; *remittent;* sickness; *thorn in the flesh;* unhealthiness; *upset; virus;* weakness; *x-disease; yellow fever;* zoonosis; [*see* sickness]

**illogical** *(adj.)*: absurd; baseless; crazy; demented; erroneous; foolish; groundless; haywire; irrational; illogical; *joking;* kooky; ludicrous; mad; nonsensical; outlandish; paralogistic; preposterous; queer; rationless; ridiculous; specious; twisted; unscientific; unreasoned; void of reason; whacky; xtry. absurd; *yo-yo;* zany; [*Ant.* intelligent]

**illuminate** *(v.)*: *alight;* brighten; beam; burn; cast light; demystify; enkindle; enlighten; emit light; effulge; flash; fluoresce; gleam; glow; highlight; ignite; irradiate; illumine; incandesce; *jacklight;* kindle; light; luminesce; make light; *neal;* outshine; put fire on; *quiver;* radiate; shine; throw light; *undimmed; vivify; well-lit; xtry.;* yield light; *zap;* [*Ant.* incloud]

**illumination** *(n.)*: aura; brightness; candescence; demystification; effulgence; fulgency; glow; highlight; irradiation; *jacklight; kindle;* light; luminosity; *moonlight;* nitency; overhead lighting; *phosphorescence;* radiance; refulgence; shining; thermoluminescence; *understanding;* vividness; white light; *xenon light;* yellow light; *zodiacal light;* [*Ant.* inclouding]

**illusion** *(n.)*: appearance; bedevilment; chimera; deception; delusion; dream; enchantment; effect; figment; fantasy; *ghost;* hallucination; invention; image; jape; *kidding;* lie; mirage; maya [Hind.]; *nonexistent;* outform; optical ~; pink elephant; psychosis; phantasy; quantum effect; ruse; semblance; trick; unreality; vision; wile; *xfer; yaksha [Ind.]; zoopsia;*

**illustrate** *(v.)*: *artwork;* betoken; copy; draw; depict; draft; etch; form picture; grave; handwrite; impicture; jot; *kind;* limn; make picture; mark; make plain; *non-confusing;* ornament; pencil; picture; portray; *quill;* render; represent; sketch; turn out; use pen; visually depict; write; *xfer; yield; zay [dial.];*

**illustration** *(n. picture)*: artwork; blowup; cross-section; chart; caricature; color ~; depiction; drawing; detail; diagram; enlargement; etching; figure; graphic (image); headshot; image; in-drawing; *juvenillo; kit-cat;* likeness; map; notational; oil painting; picture; plate; portrayal; *quattrocento;* representation; rendering; sketch; *table;* umbratic; visual image; wallchart; *x-chart; yield chart;* zoom shot;

**illustration** *(n. word picture)*: analogy; *bearing resemblance;* comparison; case in point; demonstration; example; exemplum; figure; for instance; graphic ~; homogeneity; instance; imagery; juxtaposition; *kind;* likeness; model; metaphor; nearness; *object lesson;* portrayal; *quasi-similitude;* representative; story; sermon ~; typical example; *uniformity; very image;* word picture; *xfer; yoke; zeugma;*

**image** *(n.)*: artwork; bust; carving; depiction; engraving; figure(ine); graphic; graven ~; *god; handiwork;* icon; illustration; *job; kore;* likeness; monument; *niche;* object; picture; piece; *quartz work;* representation; statue; torso; *unveiled work;* virtu; wood-carving; xylograph; xoanon; *yield;* zoophorus;

**imaginable** *(adj.)*: assumable; believable; comprehendible; conceivable; devisable; expectable; fanciable; feasible; *get idea; hatch;* inventable; *judge;* knowable; likely; *make-believe; notion; originate;* possible; plausible; *quixotic;* reasonable; supposable; thinkable; *utilizable;* viable; *workable; xenodiagnose; yeme; zazen;* [*Ant.* inconceivable]

**imaginary** *(adj.)*: air-built; abstract; Barmecidal; chimerical; dream; dissembled; delusory; envisioned; fictitious; fictional; fanciful; fantastic; fantasy; false; feigned; fantasmal; *ghostly;* humoring; illusory; imagined; invented; invisible; impalpable; inexistent; *judged; known-only-to-you; lucubrated;* made-up; make-believe; notional; nonexistent; ostensible; pretend; phantasmal; quixotic; *reckoned;* supposed; simulated; thought-of; unobservable; unreal; visionary; whimsical; *xenodiagnosed; yeme; zazen;*

**imagination** *(n.)*: abstract; brainwork; cognition; conception; creativity; dissembling; dreams; envisioning; fancy; fantasy; fertile ~; *genius;* head; imagining; inventiveness; *just think; knowledge;* lucubration; make-believe; mind('s eye); *notion;* originality; pretending; ponderings; *quixotic;* resourcefulness; supposition; simulation; thoughts; *using one's brain;* vision; vista; whimsicalness; *xenodiagnosis; yeme* [arch.]; *zazen;*

**imaginative** *(adj.)*: artistic; bold; creative; dreaming; enterprising; fanciful; full of ideas; fecund; gifted; heaven-gifted; inventive; ingenious; *judicious;* keen-minded; *laboring; mentally active;* novel-notioned; original; *perceptive;* quick-witted; resourceful; sharp; talented; *unique;* vivid; visionary; witty; *xtry.;* yeasty; *zesty;*

**imagine** *(v.)*: assume; believe; conceptualize; conceive; dream of; dissemble; devise; envision; expect; fancy; fantasize; get idea; hallucinate; hatch; invent; *judge; know; lucubrate;* make believe; *notion;* originate; pretend; picture; *quixotic;* reckon; suppose; simulate; see; think; use imagination; visualize; ween; *xenodiagnose; yeme; zazen;*

**imitate** *(v.)*: affect; ape; borrow; copy; counterfeit; duplicate; echo; emulate; follow; forge; feign; go like; hoke; impersonate; *just like; keep;* look like; mimic; mirror; mock; model; *near; offprint;* parrot; pattern; personate; personify; plagiarize; quote; reproduce; replicate; repeat; simulate; semble; transcribe; try to be like; *use copier; virtual; watch closely;* xerograph; *yield;* zany;

**imitation** *(adj.)*: artificial; bogus; counterfeit; duplicated; ersatz; fake; gag; hokey; inauthentic; japed; knock-off; look-alike; mock; non-real; *offprint;* pretend; phony; quacky; replicated; reproduction; simulated; synthetic; trick; unauthentic; unreal; *vain; wily;* xerographed; *yeggy; zero validity;*

**imitation** *(n. act of copying)*: apery; borrowing; copying; duplication; emulation; following; *ghost; holotype;* impersonation; *just like; keep; look alike;* mimicry; mockery; mimesis; *nearness; offprint;* pappyshow; parrotry; personation; personification; plagiarism; *quote;* reproduction; replication; repeat; simulation; take-off; *unreal; virtual; watch closely;* xerograph; *yield;* zoomimic;

**imitation** *(n. fake)*: *artificial;* bogus copy; (carbon) copy; counterfeit; clone; duplication; ersatz; emulation; fake; facsimile; forgery; *gesticulation; hoodwink;* image; *just alike;* knockoff; look-alike; mock-up; model; *non-genuine; offprint;* phony; *quadruplicate;* replica; reproduction; simulation; similitude; *transcription;* unreal; *virtual;* xerograph; *yet another;* zincograph;

**immature** *(adj.)*: adolescent; baby(ish); boyish [masc.]; childish; depauperate; developing; early; fledgling; green; girlish [fem.]; hastive; inexperienced; juvenile; kiddish; little; maidenly [fem.]; nubile; overly-young; puerile; *quite young;* raw; small; silly; tender; undeveloped; unripe; vernal; wee; *XS;* young; *zero-experience;*

**immaturity** *(n.)*: adolescence; babyishness; boyishness [masc.]; childishness; depauperation; development; *earliness;* freshness; greenness; girlishness [fem.]; hastiveness; inexperience; juvenility; kiddishness; lack of maturity; neoteny; *over-young;* puerility; *quite young;* rawness; smallness; silliness; tenderness; undevelopment; unripeness; virginity; want of maturity; *XS;* youth; *zero-experience;*
**immeasurable** *(adj.)*: *astronomical;* beyond measure; continual; *decillion;* endless; *fantastic;* great; *huge;* inestimable; illimitable; immensurable; interminable; *jillion; kazillion;* limitless; measureless; never-ending; numberless; *ongoing;* octillion; perpetual; *quadrillion; repeated; relentless;* sumless; termless; timeless; unending; untold; vast; *vigintillion;* without number; xtry; yet unnumbered; *zillion;*
**immediate** *(adj.)*: abrupt; at hand; *bang!;* current; direct; expedited; express; fast; gapless; high-priority; instant(aneous); just like that; *keenly-timed;* lickety-split; momentary; near; on the spot; prompt; quick; rapid; speedy; *timely;* undelayed; very quick; without delay; *x-speed; yare;* zero-delay;
**immerse** *(v.)*: absorb; bathe; bury; baptize; cover; dip; dunk; demerse; drown; engulf; flood; go under; *hide;* immerge; implant; *jawp; keelhaul;* lower; move down into; nosedive; overwhelm; plunge; put under; plant; *queven* [arch.]; *rinse;* submerge; sink; steep; take under; *under (the water);* verge; whelm; *xuld [arch.]: ybaptized* [arch.]; *zet [dial.];*
**immersion** *(n.)*: *absorption;* burial; baptism; covering; dipping; dunking; engulfing; flooding; going under; *hiding;* immergence; jawping; keelhauling; lowering; moving down into; nose-diving; overwhelming; plunging; *queven [arch.];* rinsing; submersion; sinking; taking under; *under (the water);* verging; whelming; *xuld [arch.]: ybaptized* [arch.]; *zet [dial.];*
**immigrant** *(n.)*: alien; backsettler; comer; dweller; émigré; foreigner; *greenhorn;* homesteader; in-mover; illegal alien; *journeyer; keeping;* legal ~; migrator; newcomer; outlander; pioneer; *quarterer; refugee;* settler; sojourner; transmigrant; *upstart;* visitor; wetback; xmigrant; *yerde [arch.]; zip to;*
**immigrate** *(v.)*: arrive; budge; come in; displace; emigrate here; fly; get here; *hurry;* in-migrate; journey; *key move; live;* move; nomadize; *ongoing;* proceed; *quicken;* relocate; resettle; settle; sojourn; transmigrate; transplant; *underway;* voyage; *wander;* xenize; xfer; yede; zip;
**imminence** *(n.)*: approaching; bearing on; closeness; *days away;* ever-hastening coming; forthcoming; *going to happen soon;* hastening; impending; *just ahead;* keen ~; looming; momentariness; nearness; oncoming; proximity; *quickness; reaching;* short time; time just ahead; *upcoming;* vicinity; *waiting; xpire; yet coming; zippiness;*
**imminent** *(adj.)*: approaching; about to happen; bearing on; close; coming (soon); days away; ever-hastening; forthcoming; *going to happen soon;* hastening; hanging over; happening soon; impending; just around the corner; keenly ~; looming; momentary; near; oncoming; proximate; pending; *quick; reaching;* soon-to-come; threatening; upcoming; very soon; *waiting; xpire;* yet coming; *zero waiting;*
**immobile** *(adj.)*: at a standstill; becrippled; *broken;* crippled; disabled; debilitated; enfeebled; frozen; fixed; gimp; game; gammy; *hobbling;* hiphalt; hamstrung; handicapped; halt(ed); immotile; immobilized; incapacitated; inoperative; jake-legged; *keeled over; limping;* lame; motionless; non-mobile; non-moving; out-of-commission; palsied; paralyzed; permanent; quadriplegic; remaining; still; stagnant; stationary; *torpid;* unmoving; very still; *weak; x-out; yawing; zeroized;*
**immobilize** *(v.)*: arrest; becripple; cripple; disable; enfeeble; freeze; *gammy;* hamstring; halt; injure; *jake-legged;* knock out; lame; maim; nail down; *obstruct;* paralyze; *quit;* render inoperative; stop; transfix; *thwart; undo;* victimize; wing; wound; x-out; yedder; zap;
**immoderate** *(adj.)*: astronomical; acute; beyond reason; crapulent; disproportionate; excessive; extreme; far above; great; high; inordinate; *jumbo;* king-sized; *large;* monstrous; not needed; outrageous; overgenerous; prodigal; preposterous; quantitative; ridiculous; substantial; too much; unrestrained; unwarranted; very high; wanton; wild; xtry.; yet unwarranted; *zillions;*
**immodest** *(adj.)*: *appalling;* bare; crude; disgraceful; exposed; frontless; gauche; half-naked; indecent; jadish; kinky; low-cut; lewd; *meager;* naked; obscene; provocative; *quad;* revealing; shameful; shocking; tasteless; uncovered; unchaste; unblushing; vulgar; wanton; whorish; x-rated; *yucky; zero-modesty;*

**immodesty** *(n.)*: *abhorrence;* bareness; crudeness; disgrace; exposing; forwardness; gaucheness; *half-naked;* indecency; jadishness; kinkiness; lewdness; *meagerness;* nakedness; obscenity; provocativeness; *quad;* revealing; shamefulness; tastelessness; unchasteness; vulgarity; whorishness; *x-rated; yuckiness; zero-modesty;*

**immoral** *(adj.)*: adulterous; base; bad; corrupt; dissolute; debauched; decadent; evil; fornicative; godless; hedonistic; *horrible;* impure; illicit; incestuous; iniquitous; jaded; *kitsch;* lascivious; lewd; libertine; meretricious; mischievous; naughty; obscene; profligate; *quad;* reprobate; sinful; sleazy; slattern; trampy; ungodly; unlawful; unfaithful; unchaste; vile; wicked; wanton; whorish; x-rated; yieldful; *zipless;* [*Ant.* impeccable]

**immorality** *(n.)*: adultery; badness; corruption; cuckoldry; dishonor; debauchery; depravity; decadence; eroticism; evil; free love; fornication; guiltiness; harlotry; intemperance; illicit sex; impurity; infidelity; jadery; *kinkiness;* looseness; lasciviousness; lewdness; misconduct; naughtiness; ordure; promiscuity; profligacy; *perversion; queanery;* revelry; reprobation; (sexual) sin; shamelessness; trampery; turpitude; ungodliness; uncleanness; venery wickedness; whoredom; whoremongery; wantonness; *x-rated; yielding to sin; zero morality;* [*Ant.* impeccability]

**immortal** *(adj.)*: amaranthine; boundless; ceaseless; continuous; deathless; ever-living; ever-young; everlasting; fadeless; *forever;* going on forever; *heavenly;* incorruptible; imperishable; *jusqu'au bout [F.];* keeps going; lasting; *measureless;* never-dying; *ongoing;* perpetual; quenchless; *remaining;* sempiternal; timeless; undying; *vast;* without end; *xcending;* year-after-year; *zillion;*

**immortality** *(n.)*: agelessness; boundlessness; ceaselessness; deathlessness; everlasting life; *forever; going on; heaven;* incorruption; incorruptibility; imperishability; *jusqu'au bout [F.]; keeps going;* lasting life; *measureless;* non-corruptibleness; *ongoing;* perpetuity; quenchlessness; *remaining;* sempiternity; timelessness; undyingness; *vastness; without end; xcendance;* years without end; *zero termination;*

**immovable** *(adj.)*: absolute; bound; changeless; definite; ever the same; firm; fast; fixed; guaranteed; hard; immutable; irremovable; inalienable; *just the same;* kept the same; lasting; motionless; non-moveable; obdurate; permanent; quite frim; reverseless; stationary; there to stay; unmovable; vested; without change; *x-cending;* ypight [arch.]; *zero movement;* [*Ant.* impermanent]

**immune** *(adj.)*: absolutely impervious; *bondless;* clear; *defense;* exempt; free; *guarded; hardy;* insusceptible; impervious; *just fine;* klendusic [bot.]; *let off;* medically unaffected; non-affected; *okay;* protected; *quartful* [arch.]; resistant; safe; *totally safe;* unsusceptible; unaffected; vaccinated; without susceptibility; *xenobiotic; yet impervious; zap-proof;* [*Ant.* infected]

**immunity** *(n.)*: absolute imperviousness; *bondlessness;* clear sailing; *dispensation;* diplomatic ~; exemption; freedom; grant; harmlessness; imperviousness; insusceptibility; impunity; *just fine;* klendusity [bot.]; *lastingness; medically unaffected;* non-susceptibility; *okay;* protection; quittance; resistance; safety; *total safety;* unaffectedness; unsusceptibility; vaccination; *without susceptibility; xenobiotic; yeming* [arch.]; *zap-proofness;* [*Ant.* infection]

**immutability** *(n.)*: absoluteness; binding; constancy consistency; changelessness; *dependable; ever the same;* fixedness; going on and on; homogeneity; invariableness; immovability; *just the same;* keeping the same; *long-standing; maintaining;* non-mutability; *obstinacy; ongoing;* permanence; *quality of ~;* rigidness; steadiness; staying the same; transcendence; unchangeableness; *very constant;* without variation; *x-cendence; yet unchanged;* zero change; [*Ant.* inconstancy]

**immutable** *(adj.)*: absolute; bound; changeless; durable; ever the same; firm; fixed; *going on;* having no change; inalterable; invariable; immovable; just the same; keeps the same; long-standing; *maintaining;* never-changing; *obstinate;* permanent; *quae est eadem [L.];* rigid; resolute; stable; transcending; unchanging; unchangeable; unalterable; *very constant;* without change; *x-cending; yet unchanging; zero change;* [*Ant.* inconstant]

**impact** *(n.)*: appulse; blow; bash; bump; bang; brunt; crash; collision; driving force; frontal ~; effect; force; *get;* hit; impingment; jolt; knock; lam; might; *nevel;* open-handed blow; punch; power; quake; ram; slam; side- ~; thrust; upshot; vigor; whack; weight; *xuld [arch.]; yedder; zonk;*
**impair** *(v.)*: afflict; break; cripple; damage; enfeeble; fix [slang]; *gammy;* hurt; injure; jeel; knock out; lessen strength; make worse; *nocument; offend; pull down; quell; ruin;* scathe; trouble; *undo;* victimize; weaken; *x.; ydrad [arch.]; zap;* [*Ant.* improve]
**impale** *(v.)*: auger; bore; cut through; drive; empale; engore; fix [arch.]; gore; hole; *incise;* jab; knife; lance; make hole; nail; open; puncture; pierce; *quill;* run through; stab; spear; transfix; *undercut; ventilate;* wimble; *xylotomy;* yerk; *zing;*
**impart** *(v.)*: administer; award; bestow; confer; donate; endow; furnish; give; hand (over); issue; *jettison;* kit; leave; mete; make gift; *non-retention; offer;* pass along; provide; *quicken;* render; supply; transfer; unhand; vest; *weigh;* xfer; yield; *zip;*
**impartial** *(adj.)*: anti-discriminatory; balanced; correct; disinterested; equitable; even-handed; fair; good; honest; honorable; indifferent; imprejudicate; just; keeping justice; *legitimate;* moral; non-discriminatory; objective; plain-dealing; *quite ~;* righteous; reasonable; square; true; unbiased; upright; unprejudiced; virtuous; *wholly ~; xtry. fair; yet unbiased;* zero-bias;
**impartiality** *(n.)*: anti-discrimination; blamelessness; *consistency;* disinterest; equity; equality; fairness; goodness; honesty; indifference; indistinction; justness; *keenness; legitimacy;* morality; non-discrimination; objectivity; propriety; *quality;* rectitude; sameness; truth; uprightness; virtue; *wholly impartial; xtry. fairness; yet unbribed;* zero-bias;
**impassable** *(adj.)*: absolutely impervious; blocked; barred; closed; *detour;* embarred; *forbidden; guarded;* hedged; impenetrable; innavigable; jammed; *kaput;* KOed; locked out; much-obstructed; non-passable; occluse; obstructed; passless; quite ~; road-blocked; shut; stopped up; totally blocked-off; unnavigable; *verboten [G.];* well-guarded; walled; *x'ed;* yieldless; *zoned-off;*
**impasse** *(n.)*: adversity; bind; complication; deadlock; encumbrance; fix; gridlock; hitch; *incommodity;* jam; kink; logjam; mess; *nuisance;* obstacle; predicament; quandary; rattle; stalemate; trouble; *unrest;* vexation; woe; *xerotripsis; yuckiness; zhlubby;*
**impatience** *(n.)*: anxiety; alacrity; annoyance; *bothered;* chafing; disquietude; edginess; eagerness; fretfulness; gusto; hastiness; intolerance; irritation; itching; impetuousness; jitteriness; keenness; lather; *must;* non-patience; overhastiness; precipitancy; quickness; readiness; restlessness; suddenness; solicitude; touchiness; umbrage; vexation; weariness; *x-fervor;* yearning; zest;
**impatient** *(adj.)*: anxious; annoyed; bothered; chomping at the bit; chafing; disquiet; edgy; fretful; *gung-ho;* hasty; intolerant; irritated; jittery; keenly desirous; *lather; must;* non-patient; overhasty; precipitous; *quick;* restive; restless; short; touchy; unenduring; vexed; weary; *x-fervor;* yare; zealous;
**impeach** *(v.)*: accuse; arraign; blame; charge; delate; exprobate; fault; *guilt;* hold responsible; incriminate; indict; *j'accuse; knock;* lay guilt before; make allegation; *non-innocent; oppugn;* point finger at; *question;* reproach; *saddle with;* tax; *utter;* vote out; word; xfer; yell; zero in; [*Ant.* inaugurate]
**impede** *(v.)*: avert; block; cumber; deter; encumber; frustrate; *gum up;* hinder; inhibit; *jam;* keep; limit; moderate; nullify; obstruct; prevent; quash; restrain; stop; thwart; upset; veto; withhold; *x.; yank;* zilch;
**impediment** *(n.)*: adverseness; barrier; cumbrance; difficulty; encumbrance; foot-dragging; glitch; hindrance; hurdle; impairment; jam; kink; *lodgment;* mountain; *nuisance;* obstruction; problem; *quandary;* roadblock; stumbling block; trouble; *upset;* vigia; wall; x; *yowler; zinger;*
**impel** *(v.)*: advance; bear on; coerce; compel; drive; energize; force; goad; hurl; induce; *jump on; knock;* lean on; make; move; nudge; oblige; push; propel; quicken; require; sling; strong-arm; thrust; urge; *vie;* warn; *xuld [arch.]; yank; zealously urge;*
**impend** *(v.)*: approach; border on; come soon; close; draw near; endanger; fall; *glare;* hang over; imperil; *just around the corner; kiaugh;* loom; menace; near; overhang; *proceed; quicken;* reach; soon; threaten; *upspring;* verge on; *worry; xfer;* yede; *zip;*

**impenetrable** *(adj.)*: absolutely safe; bullet-proof; bomb-proof; *completely ~; defense;* ensconced; fortified; *guaranteed safe;* hard; impervious; *just fine;* kept safe; *locked;* made ~; non-penetrable; over-protected; penetration-proof; *quartful [arch.]; risk-free;* secure; totally safe; unpenetrable; very safe; well-protected; *xtry;* yieldless; *zero danger;*
**impenitence** *(n.)*: arrogance; *badness;* contumacy; defiance; evil; flouting; grieflessness; hard-heartedness; irrepentance; impenitentness; jadedness; *kicking;* lack of repentance; lawlessness; *misbehavior;* nonrepentance; obduracy; pride; *querulousness;* remorselessness; sorrowlessness; shamelessness; seared conscience; terribleness; unrepentance; unremorsefulness; vileness; waywardness; wickedness; *xgression;* yieldlessness; *zeallessness to repent;* [*see* sin]
**impenitent** *(adj.)*: arrogant; bad; contumacious; defiant; ever-defiant; frontless; griefless; hard-hearted; hardened; indurate; jaded; *kicking;* lawless; *misbehaving;* non-repentant; obdurate; proud; *querulous;* remorseless; sorrowless; shameless; terrible; unrepentant; unremorseful; vile; wayward; wicked; *xgression;* yieldless; *zero repentance;* [*see* stubborn]
**imperative** *(adj.)*: all-important; burning; crucial; dire; essential; fundamental; grave; heavy; important; jussive; key; life-or-death; matter of life or death; needful; *obligatory;* pressing; paramount; *quintessential;* required; serious; terribly important; urgent; vital; weighty; *xtry.; yearnful; zero hour;*
**imperceptible** *(adj.)*: à perte de vue [F.]; behind the scenes; concealed; disguised; ever-invisible; furtive; *ghostlike;* hidden; invisible; *jape;* kept out of view; *latent;* mysterious; non-detectable; obscure; perceived not; quite unperceived; real quiet; silent; secretive; transparent; unnoticeable; undetectable; unperceivable; veiled; without notice; *xtry. ~;* yet undiscovered; zero perception;
**imperfect** *(adj.)*: amiss; blemished; bad; *cracked;* deficient; defective; errant; erroneous; faulty; flawed; *guilty;* half-completed; incomplete; incorrect; inadequate; jim-jam; kim-kam; lacking; limited; malfunctioning; non-perfected; on the blink; partial; poor; problematic; quirky; *reprehensible;* short; shaky; troublesome; unperfected; unfinished; vituperable; wanting; *x-mal [G.]; yo-yoish;* zany;
**imperfection** *(n.)*: accident; blemish; corruption; defect; deficiency; error; flaw; fault; failing; *goof-up;* hitch; inaccuracy; inadequacy; *jumble;* kink; lack; mistake; non-perfection; omission; problem; quirk; *reprehensible;* shortcoming; trouble; *unperfected;* vice; weakness; *xgression;* yaw; zaniness;
**impertinence** *(n.)*: audacity; brashness; cockiness; disrespect; effrontery; forwardness; flagrancy; gall; hauteur; *hutzpah* [Yid.]; impudence; insolence; jadedness; *know-it-all; lip;* malapertness; nerve; overconfidence; pertness; *quilicom [arch.];* rudeness; surliness; temerity; unruliness; vainness; *wind; xtry.* brazenness; *yieldlessness;* zero respect;
**impertinent** *(adj.)*: audacious; brazen; cheeky; cavalier; disrespectful; *effrontery;* flippant; glib; hoity-toity; impudent; joking; *know-it-all;* light; malapert; nervy; offhand; presumptuous; quite rude; rude; surly; temerarious; unreverend; vain; *willful; x-proud;* yieldless; *zero respect;*
**impervious** *(adj.)*: absolutely safe; bullet-proof; completely impenetrable; *defensible;* ensconced; fortified; *guarded;* hard; impenetrable; *just fine;* kept safe; *locked;* made ~; not penetrable; opaque; penetration-proof; *quartful [arch.];* resistant; safe; totally safe; unthreatened; very safe; well-defended; *xtry;* yieldless; *zero danger;*
**impetuous** *(adj.)*: ambitious; brash; bold; capricious; desultory; erratic; foolhardy; furious; fierce; giddy; hasty; heady; impulsive; jumpy; *keen; lively;* madcap; nervy; offhand; precipitate; passionate; quick-to-change; rash; reckless; spontaneous; temperamental; ultroneous; unabashed; violent; vehement; wild; *x-ing;* yeasty; zestful;
**implacable** *(adj.)*: always-dissatisfied; bellyaching; critical; difficult-to-please; ever-grumbling; fussy; griping; hard-to-please; impossible-to-please; *jaded; knocking; limitless;* merciless; non-pacifiable; over-picky; picky; quibbling; repining; scowling; *troubled;* unappeasable; unpacifiable; very dissatisfied; whiny; *xtry. critical;* yieldless; zero pacification;

**implant** *(v.)*: attach; affix; bind; connect; dibble; drill in; embed; fasten; fix; graft; hitch; heterograft; infix; ingraft; join; knit; lodge; link; merge; *nail; outgrow;* plant; *quasi-fuse;* root; reset; seat; seminate; splice; tie; transplant; unite; *vise;* wed; xenograft; yoke; *zip;* [*Ant.* isolate]

**implication** *(n.)*: allusion; betokening; clue; connotation; denotation; essence; *foreadvisement;* gist; general idea; hint; inference; innuendo; intimation; illation; insinuation; *jab;* knock; laying of charges; meaning; nuance; overtone; postulation; quiddit; reference; suggestion; subaudition; touch; undercurrent; undertone; veiled reference; *winking; xfer; yammering; zay;*

**implore** *(v.)*: adjure; beseech; beg; call upon; desire; entreat; *foreadmonish;* give entreaty; *humbly ask;* impetrate; importune; *juration; kneel to;* lift up one's voice for; make request; *need;* obsecrate; petition; plead; pray; *quiritation;* request; solicit; supplicate; *try to get;* urge; *vocalize;* wish; *XQ.;* yearn for; *zetetic;*

**imply** *(v.)*: allude; betoken; connote; drive at; denote; drop hint; evidence; *foreadvise;* give indication; hint at; imply; infer; insinuate; intimate; *jibber; known; lead;* make out; mention; *nuance; overtone;* point to; postulate; purport; quiddit; refer; suggest; *subtlety;* signify; *take for granted; undercurrent;* vaguely express; *wink; xfer; yammer; zay;*

**impolite** *(adj.)*: abominable; bad-mannered; coarse; discourteous; evil; foul; graceless; homebred; indecorous; inelegant; ill-mannered; *jadish;* kindless; loutish; mannerless; non-polite; over-crude; poorly-mannered; *questionable;* rude; shocking; tasteless; uncultivated; unmannered; unrefined; uncivil; vulgar; wretched; *xenophobic;* yahoo; zhlubby;

**import** *(v.)*: *airlift;* bring in; convey; *draw; enter;* freight in; get; *haul;* introduce; *jet;* kurvey; locomote; move; *next-day;* obtain; procure; *quicken;* relay; ship in; take in; uptake; *van;* waft; xfer; yanker [Br.]; *zip;*

**importance** *(n.)*: all- ~; bigness; concernment; centrality; criticalness; degree; direness; enormity; emergency; exigency; *fundamental* ~; gravity; greatness; heaviness; indispensability; import; imperativeness; *justification; key;* loftiness; meaning; magnitude; need; necessity; outstandingness; precedence; press(ure); portentousness; *quintessence;* relevance; requirement; seriousness; top-rating; urgency; value; vitalness; weight; *xtry.;* yearning; *zero hour;* [*Ant.* insignificance]

**important** *(adj.)*: all- ~; big; burning; consequential; central; chief; crucial; critical; dominant; dire; eminent; essential; earthshaking; fundamental; focal; great; grave; heavy; high; indispensable; imperative; *jump to it;* key; leading; life-and-death; momentous; major; main; noteworthy; needed; outstanding; pertinent; priority; portentous; pressing; principal; prominent; preeminent; quantum; relevant; required; significant; top-priority; urgent; ultimate; valuable; very urgent; vital; worthy; worthwhile; weighty; *xtry.; yearnful;* zero hour; [*Ant.* insignificant]

**importune** *(adj.)*: adamant; beseeching; constant; dogging; entreating; firm; going on; high-pressure; insistent; importunate; *jusqu'au bout* [F.]; keeping on; lasting; *making request;* never-ceasing; ongoing; pressing; persistent; *quitting never;* relentless; steady; tenacious; unremitting; very persistent; wearisome; *x-cending;* yieldless; *zealous;*

**impose** *(v.)*: appoint; bid; burden; command; disturb; enforce; force; foist; give; hit with; inconvenience; intrude; insist; *juration; kaleusmatic;* lay on; levy; mandate; necessitate; obtrude; ordain; put one out; push; *quo minus* [L.]; require; set; thrust upon; *unwelcome; verdict;* weigh down with; *xenagogy;* yoke with; *zakon* [Rus.];

**impossibility** *(n.)*: absurdity; *barred;* contradiction; dooming to failure; *excluded; fruitlessless;* grimness; hopelessness; impracticability; improbability; *just impossible;* known ~; ludicrousness; *madness;* non-possibility; outlandishness; oxymoron; preposterousness; Q.B.I. [RAF slang]; ridiculousness; self-contradiction; total ~; unfeasibility; *virtual* ~; *weird; x; yet unsolvable;* zero chance;

**impossible** *(adj.)*: absurd; beyond the realm of possibility; contrary to reason; doomed to failure; excluded; fanciful; grim; hopeless; impractical; improbable; illogical; just ~; *known to be* ~; ludicrous; *mad;* not possible; out of the realm of possibility; preposterous; Q.B.I. [RAF slang]; ridiculous; ruled-out; self-contradictory; totally ~; untenable; unfeasible; unviable; unworkable; *virtually* ~; without a chance; *x;* yet unsolvable; zero chance;

**imposter** *(n.)*: actor; beguiler; charlatan; con artist; deceiver; empiric; fake; fraud; guiser; hoaxer; impersonator; jape; knave; *liar;* masquerader; nostrum; *outsider;* pretender; personator; poser; quack; rip-off artist; sham; swindler; trickster; *untruther;* verneuker; wolf in sheep's clothing; *xenomorph; yantzer; zinger;*

**impotence** *(n.)*: atony; brittleness; cachexy; defenselessness; enfeeblement; feebleness; frailty; *gimp;* helplessness; impotency; inability; *jejuneness; knocking out;* lameness; *meagerness;* non-ability; over-weakness; powerlessness; *quirk; reduced ability;* softness; *tiredness;* unauthoritativeness; vulnerability; weakness; *x-out; yielding; zapped;*

**impoverish** *(v.)*: *abate;* bleed; bankrupt; consume; drain; deplete; depauperate; expend; empty; finish; *gobble up;* hone; *in debt;* jade; *kaput;* leach; make poor; *nullify;* overtax; overspend; pauperize; quail; reduce; ruin; sap; suck dry; tax; tap one out; use (up); vacate; weaken; *xerosis; yield;* zap;

**impractical** *(adj.)*: airy; beyond realistic; contrary to reason; doomed to failure; *extraordinary;* fanciful; grim; hopeless; impracticable; inefficient; idealistic; just impossible; *kooky;* Laputan; ludicrous; *mad;* non-practical; out of question; pie-in-the-sky; questionable; quixotic; ridiculous; starry-eyed; totally ~; unfeasible; unworkable; unrealistic; untenable; unviable; uneconomical; *virtually ~;* without a chance; *x;* yet untenable; zero chance;

**imprecise** *(adj.)*: approximate; ballpark; close; *doubtful;* estimated; foggy; give-or-take; hazy; inexact; indefinite; *jim-jam; kim-kam;* loose; lax; *maybe;* non-precise; off; patchy; projected; *questionable;* rough; roundabout; slipshod; surmised; *touching on;* unexacting; unprecise; vague; weak; *x [algebra]; yawed;* zero-precision;

**impress** *(v.)*: affect; amaze; bedazzle; confound; dazzle; enthuse; faze; floor; grab; gape; hit; impact; jolt; knock over; *like;* make an ~ion; move; *nonplus;* overawe; pique; poleax; *quite amazed;* render speechless; stir; strike; surprise; touch; take back; thrill; underscore; *very ~ed;* wow; *wonder(struck); xtry.; yerk; zing;*

**impression** *(n.)*: attitude; bearing; conception; disposition; evaluation; feeling; gut feeling; hunch; idea; inclination; *judgment; knowledge;* leaning; mindset; notion; outlook; opinion; perception; *questioning;* reaction; sentiment; stamp; thoughts; take; understanding; valuation; *weight; xenodiagnosis; yeme* [arch.]; *zazen* [Bud.];

**impressive** *(adj.)*: arresting; amazing; awe-inspiring; big; breathtaking; commanding; distinguished; extraordinary; fantastic; great; grandiose; heavenly; incredible; imposing; jarring; keen; *lofty; laudable;* magnificent; masterful; notable; outstanding; praiseworthy; *quantum* [L.]; remarkable; striking; stunning; stupendous; tremendous; unbelievable; very good; wonderful; xtry.; *yippee!;* zizzy;

**imprison** *(v.)*: arrest; bust; confine; cage; detain; encage; *fetter;* fence in; gaol [Br.]; hold; incarcerate; intern; immure; jail; keep; lock up; *manacle;* nab; *oubliette;* put away; put in ward; *quarantine;* remand; shut up; sequester; take into custody; *under lock and key; vile durance;* ward; *x.;* yard up; *zip away;*

**imprisonment** *(n.)*: arrest; behind bars; confinement; durance; detention; encagement; *fetters;* guard; house arrest; incarceration; immurement; jailing; keep; *life ~;* maximum security; *nabbing;* oubliette; prison sentence; quod; remand; sentence; term of ~; under lock and key; vile durance; ward; *x;* yarding up; *zipper* [coll.];

**improbability** *(n.)*: abnormality; *bleak;* curiosity; doubtfulness; dubiousness; exception; fat chance; *grim;* hardly a chance; implausibility; *just unlikely;* known unlikelihood; long shot; *much-doubted;* non-probability; one-in-a-million chance; poor bet; questionability; rarity; slim chance; total unlikelihood; unlikelihood; virtual impossibility; *weak;* xtry. chance; *yet unlikely; zero chance;*

**improbable** *(adj.)*: absurd; *bleak;* cannot be expected; doubtful; ever-doubtful; fishy; far-fetched; *grim;* hardly likely; implausible; *just unlikely; known unlikelihood;* ludicrous; much-doubted; not promising; not likely; one-in-a-million chance; probably not; questionable; ridiculous; seemingly false; totally unlikely; unlikely; unapt; unconvincing; unpromising; very unlikely; way-out; weak; xtry. chance; yet unlikely; *zero chance;*

**impromptu** *(adj.)*: adlib; *bang!;* cueless; *direct;* extemporaneous; fresh; free; *going in cold;* haphazard; improvised; just as it comes up; *keen; like that;* momentary; non-rehearsed; offhand; off-the-cuff; on the fly; precipitate; *quick; roll with the punches;* spontaneous; *think-as-you-go;* unpremeditated; unrehearsed; unbidden; unplanned; unpracticed; unprompted; voluntary; winging it; *xtry.; yare; zip;*
**improper** *(adj.)*: awful; amiss; bad; clumsy; crude; dreadful; erroneous; foul; grossly ~; horrendous; incorrect; inappropriate; impropriate; illicit; just wrong; *kim-kam;* lousy; mismatched; malapropos; non-suited; out-of-place; poor; questionable; reprehensible; rude; shocking; tasteless; terrible; unfit(ting); unbefitting; unmeet; unsuitable; unbecoming; undue; unapproved; unsanctioned; unseemly; untoward; vile; vulgar; wrong; *xgressing;* yucky; *zero propriety;*
**improve** *(v.)*: advance; ameliorate; boost; better; cure; convalesce; develop; enrich; enhance; embellish; forge ahead; get better; heighten; hone; help; innovate; jump ahead; *keen; lead upward;* meliorate; make better; new-vamp; overhaul; optimize; *over~;* polish; progress; perfect; quintessentialize; rally; revamp; recuperate; raise; refine; shape up; succor; soup up; titivate; upbuild; uprate [Br.]; upgrade; vamp; work on; *xtry.; yarken;* zest up; [*Ant.* impair]
**improvement** *(n.)*: advancement; amelioration; boost; betterment; change; convalescence; development; enrichment; enhancement; embellishment; fix; gain; heightening; headway; innovation; jump ahead; *keen ~; leap upward;* melioration; new-vamping; optimization; overhaul; polishing; progress; quintessentialization; revamping; refinement; succor; titivation; upgrade; upturn; vamping; work; *xtry.; yarken;* zesting; [*Ant.* impairment]
**improvise** *(v.)*: adlib; *ad hoc;* brainstorm; contrive; do the best one can; devise; extemporize; fake it; go unpracticed; have at it; invent; improvisate; just do it; kludge; *like that;* make due; make do; *non-prepared; off-the-cuff;* play by ear; *quickly;* roll with the punches; spontaneously do; think-as-you-go; *unprepared;* vamp; wing it; *xtry.; yare; zealously try;*
**impudence** *(n.)*: audacity; boldness; brazenness; cheekiness; contempt; discourtesy; disrespect; effrontery; flagrancy; gall; haughtiness; impertinence; insolence; *jackanapes; know-it-all;* lack of respect; mouthiness; nerve; overconfidence; presumption; *quilicom* [arch.]; rudeness; sassiness; temerity; uppitiness; vanity; *wind; xenophobia; yahoo; zero humility;* [see sacrilege]
**impudent** *(adj.)*: audacious; bold-faced; brash; cocky; discourteous; disrespectful; *effrontery;* flagrant; fresh; glib; haughty; impertinent; jaunty; *know-it-all;* lippy; malapert; nervy; overbold; pert; *quick-to-speak;* rude; saucy; temerarious; unabashed; vain; *wicked; x-proud; yieldless; zero respect;*
**impulsive** *(adj.)*: *abrupt;* brash; capricious; determined; erratic; free; foolish; *giddy;* hasty; impetuous; jumpy; knee-jerk; *loose;* madcap; non-thoughtful; overhasty; precipitous; quick-to-act; quixotic; rash; spontaneous; temperamental; thoughtless; unexpected; unthinking; volatile; whimsical; wild; *x-ing;* yeasty; zestful;
**impure** *(adj.)*: adulterated; besotted; contaminated; corrupted; dirty; defiled; erroneous; foul; grimy; *harm;* immund; imperfect; *javelled; kollowed; loused up;* made ~; non-pure; *off;* polluted; *quade [arch.];* ruined; sullied; sinful; tainted; unclean; vile; wanton; *x; yucky; zero cleanness;* [*Ant.* immaculate]
**impurity** *(n.)*: adulterant; adulteration; badness; contaminant; contamination; dirt(iness); defilement; error; evil; filth; grime; *harmful contaminant;* impureness; *javelling; kollowing;* lack of purity; maculacy; non-pure elements; *offense;* pollutant; pollution; *quade [arch.];* ruination; sullying; sin; tainedness; toxin; uncleanness; vileness; waste product; *x-out; yuckiness; zero cleanness;* [*Ant.* immaculateness]
**imputation** *(n.)*: accounting; ascription; attribution; bringing over; crediting; *deeming;* entering; *facts;* giving; hanging on; impartation; *journal; kept record;* laying to; marking down; notation; *overwrite;* putting to one's account; *quill;* reckoning; setting down; transfer; *unhand; vest;* writing (down); xfer; yafing; *zay;*
**impute** *(v.)*: ascribe; attribute; apply; bring over; credit; *deem;* enter; *facts;* give; hang on; impart; *journalize; keep record;* lay to; mark down; notate; *overwrite;* put to; *quill;* reckon; set down; transfer; *unhand; vest;* write (down); *wite* [arch.]; xfer; yafe; *zay;*

**inaccessible** *(adj.)*: aloof; away; barred; closed; distant; disallowed; exclusive; far; forbidden; *guarded; hopeless; inconvenient;* impractical; impassable; isolated; *just can't get there; kept from;* locked; *mysterious;* non-accessible; obscure; out-of-the-way; prohibited; quite ~; remote; secluded; *tricky;* unapproachable; *verboten* [G.]; *wild;* X; yet ~; *zero access;*

**inaccuracy** *(n.)*: accident; boo-boo; blunder; coloring; contradiction; defect; error; flaw; fault; goof-up; hitch; imperfection; *jumble;* kink; lapse; lack; mistake; nonrealism; oversight; omission; problem; quirk; *responsibility;* slip(-up); typo; twisting; uncorrectness; *violation;* wrong; *x'ed; yaw;* zinger; [*Ant.* inerrancy]

**inaccurate** *(adj.)*: amiss; bad; colored; contradictory; defective; erroneous; false; fallacious; groundless; *hollow;* imprecise; incorrect; jim-jam; kim-kam; *lying;* mistaken; misleading; non-trustworthy; off base; problematic; *questionable; repudiated;* spurious; specious; twisted; untrue; *vague;* wrong; *x'ed; yawed; zero-truth;* [*Ant.* inerrant]

**inactive** *(adj.)*: abeyant; at ease; becalmed; calm; dormant; easeful; fallow; groggy; hibernating; idle; inert; jarless; *keeping still;* listless; latent; motionless; non-active; out of action; pausing; peaceful; quiescent; quiet; resting; recumbent; slothful; stationary; suspended; stopped; tranquil; unmoving; vacuous; workless; *x'ed;* yet to awaken; *zero activity;* [*Ant.* intense]

**inactivity** *(n.)*: abeyance; *becalmed;* calmness; dormancy; ease; fixedness; grogginess; holding; inactiveness; jarlessness; *keeping still;* lapse; lull; latency; motionlessness; non-activity; over-quietness; pause; peacefulness; quiescence; remission; recess; resting; suspension; stillness; tranquility unresponsiveness; void of activity; wait; *x'ing; yareless; zitti* [It.] [*Ant.* intensity]

**inadequate** *(adj.)*: absolutely ~; below the need; coming up short; deficient; defective; effete; erroneous; falling short; greatly in need; hardly enough; insufficient; *jejune;* keenly deficient; lacking; much-deficient; not (good) enough; of no force; poor; quite ~; *ran out;* scarce; short; scanty; too little; under; unsatisfactory; unqualified; void; wanting; *xtry. need; yearning; zero sufficiency;*

**inadvertent** *(adj.)*: accidental; blundering; careless; distracted; erroneous; feckless; *goof-up;* hasty; involuntary; just accidental; *keg-meg; lightly;* mistaking; non-purposeful; over-hasty; precipitous; *quirky;* reckless; slipshod; thoughtless; unintended; unintentional; *very careless;* witless; *xtr. careless;* yet unintended; *zero intention;* [*Ant.* intentional]

**inalienable** *(adj.)*: absolute; assured; bound; changeless; definite; ever the same; fixed; firm; guaranteed; hard; immutable; irremovable; *just the same;* kept the same; lasting; made sure; non-moveable; *one;* permanent; quite firm; reverseless; sure; *transcending;* unshakable; unchangeable; unalterable; unalienable; vested; without change; *x-cending; ypight* [arch.]; *zero movement;* [*Ant.* isolatable]

**inanimate** *(adj.)*: azoic; breathless; calm; dead; exanimate; fixed; *gone;* hushed; inert; inorganic; insensate; jarless; *kaput;* lifeless; motionless; nonliving; *on hold; perished;* quiet; restful; stationary; still; spiritless; tranquil; unresponsive; unliving; vacant; without life; *x'ed;* yet to move; *zero motion;*

**inappropriate** *(adj.)*: amiss; bad; *criminal;* deficient; erroneous; false; *godless;* highly ~; improper; incorrect; *jadish;* kim-kam; *lawfully wrong;* mismatched; misplaced; mistimed; mistaken; malapropos; non-suited; out-of-place; poor; questionable; reprehensible; shocking; tasteless; unbecoming; unseemly; unfit(ting); unbefitting; undue; *vile;* wrong; *xgressing; yucky; zero propriety;* [*Ant.* ideal]

**inarguable** *(adj.)*: assured; beyond doubt; certain; definite; evident; firm; guaranteed; highly confident; indisputable; just sure; keenly sure; *legitimate;* mistake-proof; non-questionable; 100% sure; positive; questionless; reliable; sure; true; undeniable; unarguable; verified; without doubt; xtry. sure; *yes;* zero doubt;

**incarnate** *(adj.)*: assuming humanity; become human; carnified; *divested;* embodied; enrobed in flesh; enfleshed; *flesh;* God ~; humanate; in the flesh; incarnated; *Jehovah ~; kenosis; living among us;* made flesh; *nativity;* organic; personified; *quintessence; reincarnified; stoop;* taken on flesh; tangible; *unglorified;* vulnerable; the Word was made flesh; xfer; *yielded; zoon;* [*Ant.* incorporeal]

**incarnation** *(n.)*: assuming flesh; becoming flesh; carnification; *divestment;* embodiment; enfleshment; *form; going to earth;* humanation; incarnating; *Jesus' ~;* kenosis; *likeness of human flesh;* manifestation; *nativity; obsequiousness;* personification; *quintessence; resigned to flesh; stoop;* taking on flesh; *undergo; vulnerable; the Word was made flesh; xfer; yielding; zoon;*
**incense** *(n.)*: aroma; bal(sa)m; cologne; *diapasm;* essence; fragrance; *good-smelling perfume; heavenly scent;* incensation; joss stick; *keora oil; lavender;* musk; myrrh; nidor; odor; perfume; *quality perfume;* redolence; scent; sweet smell; thurification; unctuousness; volatile oil; *waft; xanthoxylene; yield up; zedoary;*
**incense** *(v.)*: anger; burn; cross; disgust; enrage; fluster; gall; heat up; infuriate; *jangle;* kindle; lose one's temper; madden; nettle; outrage; perturb; *quick-tempered;* rile; steam; tick off; upset; vex; work up; *wrath; xerothermic; yell; zealousy [arch.];*
**incentive** *(n.)*: allurement; bonus; carrot; driving force; enticement; *factor;* frill; guerdon; *hook;* honeypot; inducement; justification; *known ~; lure;* motivation; *nudge; objective;* provocation; prize; *quickening;* reason; spur; stimulus; *trigger; ulterior motive; vitality;* wooing; *x; yearning; zeal;*
**incite** *(v.)*: arouse; bestir; cause; drive; disquiet; excite; fuel; goad; hearten; induce; ignite; jar; kindle; *lead;* move; motivate; nudge; overexcite; prompt; pique; provoke; quicken; rouse; suborn; stir; spur; spark; trigger; urge on; *vivify;* whet; whip up; *xuld [arch.];* yerk; *zing;*
**inclination** *(n.)*: attitude; bent; bias; cast; disposition; eagerness; fondness; gravitation; heart for; inclining; *judgment; keenness;* leaning; mind; notion; outlook; propensity; proclivity; penchant; predisposition; *quality;* readiness; slant; tendency; urge; velleity; wanting; *xenenthesis;* yaw; *zeal;*
**incline** *(v.)*: *attract;* bias; bend; cant; drift; dispose; *edge;* favor; gravitate; have a predisposition; impel; jee; *keenly favor;* lean; move; *nudge; ongoing;* predispose; prefer; *quicken;* rather; slant; tend; tilt; *usually tend;* verge; want; *xel [arch.]; yaw; zip;*
**inclined** *(adj.)*: apt; bent; conducive; disposed; eager; favoring; gravitating toward; have a predisposition; in the mood; impelled; *jee; keen;* likely; leaning; moving; *nudging;* oriented; propense; prone; predisposed; quick; receptive; slanting; tending; *usually tending;* verging; well-disposed; wanting; *xel [arch.]; yawed;* zealous;
**include** *(v.)*: add; box in; bundle; comprise; consist; contain; *draw around;* encompass; embrace; feature; group; have; hold; incorporate; inclose; join; keep within; lump together; merge; number with; *own;* place; pair; *quantify;* roll into one; surround; subsume; take in; unite; *vessel;* within; x.; yoke; zone;
**inclusion** *(n.)*: addition; bundling; comprising; containing; *drawing around;* encompassing; featuring; grouping; having; including; incorporation; integration; joining; keeping within; lumping together; merging; numbering with; *owning;* placement; *quantification;* rolling together; surrounding; subsumption; taking in; union; *volume; within;* x.; yarding; zoning;
**inclusive** *(adj.)*: across-the-board; all-encompassing; broad; comprehensive; *done;* entire; exhaustive; encompassing; full; general; global; *high;* including; joint; *kept; long-range; mature;* non-abridged; overall; overarching; *perfect; quantity;* rolled-together; subsumptive; total; thorough; unqualified; unabridged; umbrella; universal; whole; *x.;* yare; *zonal;*
**incoherence** *(n.)*: astonishment; bewilderment; confusion; disjointedness; entrancement; farrago; garbledness; hodgepodge; irrationality; immiscibility; jumble; kerfuffle; lunacy; mix-up; noncohesion; obscurity; puzzlement; *quizzical;* randomness; stupefaction; turbidity; uncohesiveness; unreason; vexation; wilderment; *x'ed; yo-yo; zoo;*
**incoherent** *(adj.)*: astonished; bewildered; confused; disjointed; entranced; foggy; fey; garbled; hazy; irrational; inapprehensible; jumbled; *kapakahi* [Haw.]; loopy; muddled; noncoherent; *non sequitur* [F.]; orderless; patchy; psychedelic; quaggy; random; stupefied; turbid; unintelligible; vexed; wild(ered); *x'ed; yerking; zany;*

**income** *(n.)*: amount; base pay; bread and butter; compensation; defrayment; earnings; financial remuneration; gross pay; hire; intake; *justification; kickback;* living wage; money; net pay; *overcompensation;* pay; quittance; revenue; remuneration; recompense; salary; take-home pay; *unindebted;* virement; wage(s); xfer; yield; *zapping;*

**incompetence** *(n.)*: artlessness; bungling; clumsiness; defectiveness; experience-deprivation; footlessness; greenness; hopelessness; ineptitude; inexpertness; *jackleg; kyu [Jap.];* lack of proficiency; maladroitness; non-proficiency; *overly green;* poorness; *questionableness;* rawness; skillessness; *terrible;* unskillfulness; verdancy; want; *xtr. klutzy;* youth; zero skill;

**incompetent** *(adj.)*: artless; bad; bungling; clumsy; defective; experience-deprived; footless; green; hopeless; inept; inexpert; improficient; inexperienced; inconversant; jackleg; *kyu* [Jap.]; lacking proficiency; maladroit; non-proficient; *over-green;* pathetic; *quasi-skilled;* raw; skilless; *terrible;* undertrained; unskilled; unable; verdant; wanting; *xtr. klutzy;* young and inexperienced; *zero skill;*

**incomplete** *(adj.)*: abridged; *almost;* basic; constituent; choppy; deficient; embryonic; failing; faulty; fragmentary; *growing;* halfway; half-completed; inadequate; insufficient; imperfect; inoperative; inconsummate; *just part; kept from completion;* lacking; missing something; non-complete; *omission;* partial; partway; *quelque* [F.]; rough; short; shy; scant; sketchy; to be completed; unfinished; very ~; wanting; without; *x-mal [G.];* yet ~; *zero completion;* [Ant. integral]

**incompleteness** *(n.)*: abridgement; *basic;* choppiness; deficiency; defectibility; *embryo;* faultiness; failure; *growing;* hiatus; inadequacy; insufficiency; imperfection; incompletion; *just partway; keeping from completion;* lack; meagerness; need; omission; partialness; paucity; *quelque [F.]; real close;* scantiness; shortage; *to be completed;* ullage; *very incomplete;* want(age); *x-mal [G.];* yearning; zero completion;

**inconceivable** *(adj.)*: amazing; beyond comprehension; *crazy;* disagreeable; *extraordinary;* fantastic; fanciful; far-fetched; *grossly unacceptable;* hard-to-believe; implausible; just unimaginable; *kooky;* ludicrous; mind-boggling; non-believable; outrageous; preposterous; *questionable;* ridiculous; shocking; *terrible;* unthinkable; unconscionable; vaporous; *wild; xtry.;* y.; *za-zum* [Rus.]; [*Ant.* imaginable]

**incongruity** *(n.)*: argument; absurdity; bizarreness; clash; difference; disagreement; disharmony; embroilment; *friction; grumbling;* heterogeneity; imbalance; inaccordance; incompatibility; incoherence; inappropriateness; *jangling; kagg;* lack of congruity; mismatching; non-conformity; odds; paradox; quarrel; *rift;* strife; *tussle;* unconformity; unharmoniousness; variance; variation; wrangling; *x-fire;* yed; zapping; [*Ant.* invariableness]

**inconsistency** *(n.)*: antilogy; *brokenness;* conflict; contradiction; dissonance; difference; discrepancy; error; flaw; *glitch; hitch;* incongruency; incompatibility; incoherency; irreconcilability; *jumpiness; knot;* lack of conformity; mismatch; non-uniformity; noncohesion; noncoherency; oppositeness; problem; *questionableness; real ~;* self-contradiction; *trouble;* unsteadiness; variance; wavering; *x-out; yet inconsistent;* zero consistency; [*Ant.* invariableness]

**inconsistent** *(adj.)*: at variance; *bad; broken;* conflicting; contradictory; dissonant; differing; discrepant; erratic; fickle; flawed; glitchy; having inconsistencies; incompatible; inharmonious; incoherent; incongruent; irreconcilable; *jumpy; knotty;* lacking conformity; mismatched; non-uniform; noncoherent; opposite; paradoxical; problematic; *questionable; ridiculous;* self-contradicting; *trouble;* unsteady; uncoherent; varying; wavering; whiffling; *x-out;* yet conflicting; *zero consistency;* [*Ant.* invariable]

**inconvenience** *(n.)*: annoyance; bother; complication; difficulty; disutility; encumbrance; frustration; grief; hassle; hardship; impediment; irritation; *jam;* kink; load; menace; nuisance; obstacle; problem; *quirk;* rattle; setback; snag; spot; trouble; unpleasantness; vexation; worry; *xtry. ~; yuckiness; zero convenience;*

**inconvenience** *(v.)*: annoy; bother; cause a problem; discommode; encumber; frustrate; grieve; hassle; incommode; *jam;* kink; load down; menace; *nuisance;* obtrude; put out; *quirk; rigamarole;* set back; trouble; unsuitableness; vex; worry; *xtry ~; yucky;* zero convenience;

**inconvenient** *(adj.)*: annoying; bothersome; cumbersome; discommodious; difficult; encumbering; frustrating; grievous; hard; hassle; inconvenient; incommodious; inopportune; infernal; irksome; *jarring;* knotty; *lousy;* mistimed; nuisance; obtrusive; problematic; quirky; *rough; sticky;* troublesome; unsuitable; unseemly; vexatious; wearisome; x-out; yucky; zero-convenience;

**incorporate** *(v.)*: add; admix; assimilate; blend; combine; *diverse;* embody; fuse; *group;* hold; include; integrate; join; kirn; lump together; mix; number among; *organize; pass into; queach* [arch.]; *ravel;* stick together; temper; unite; *voluble;* wed; *xenograft; yerk together; zip together;*

**incorrect** *(adj.)*: amiss; bad; *confused;* defective; erroneous; false; *groundless; hollow;* inaccurate; improper; *jim-jam; kim-kam;* lousy; lying; mistaken; misleading; non-suited; off base; poor; *problematic; questionable;* reprehensible; spurious; specious; *tricky;* untrue; unsuitable; *vile;* wrong; *xgressing; yawed; zero-truth;*

**incorruptible** *(adj.)*: amaranthine; *boundless;* continual; deathless; everlasting; fadeless; going on; *heavenly;* imperishable; *jusqu'au bout [F.];* keeps going; lasting; *measureless;* never-dying; *ongoing;* perpetual; *quadrillion;* remaining; sempiternal; timeless; undying; *vast;* without end; x-cending; year-after-year; *zillion;*

**increase** *(n.)*: amplification; augmentation; accretion; accrual; boost; buildup; broadening; climbing; development; expansion; enlargement; escalation; fattening; growth; heightening; intensification; jump; *keep growing;* lengthening; multiplication; mounting; new growth; overgrowth; progression; proliferation; *quadruplication;* rise; strengthening; swelling; taking off; upsurge; verging upward; waxing larger; widening; XL; yain [arch.]; *zooming;*

**increase** *(v.)*: augment; amplify; accrete; accrue; build; boost; broaden; climb; develop; expand; enlarge; escalate; fatten; grow; heighten; increment; intensify; jack up; jump up; *keep growing;* lengthen; largefy; mount; multiply; *new growth;* overgrow; progress; proliferate; *quadruplicate;* rise; rocket; strengthen; swell; soar; skyrocket; take off; upshoot; verge upward; wax larger; widen; XL; yain [arch.]; *zoom;*

**incredible** *(adj.)*: amazing; astonishing; breathtaking; commendable; divine; extraordinary; exceptional; fantastic; great; heavenly; impressive; jolly good; keen; *laudable;* marvelous; magnificent; masterful; noteworthy; outstanding; prodigious; *quantum* [L.]; remarkable; spectacular; terrific; tremendous; unbelievable; very good; virtuous; wonderful; xtry.; *yippee!;* zizzy;

**incriminate** *(v.)*: accuse; arraign; blame; criminalize; charge; delate; entangle; fault; *guilt;* hold responsible; implicate; indict; impeach; *j'accuse; knock;* lay blame on; make allegation; *non-innocent; oppugn;* point finger at; *question;* reproach; *recriminate; saddle with;* tax; *trump up;* utter; vituperate; word; xfer; yak; zero in;

**incurable** *(adj.)*: *abject;* beyond recovery; chronic; cureless; *deadly;* ever-present; fatal; grave; helpless; hopeless; inoperable; irremediable; irrecoverable; *joyless; killing;* lethal; mortal; medically ~; non-treatable; *ongoing;* past hope; *Q.B.I.;* remediless; *serious;* terminal; untreatable; uncorrectable; unremediable; very bad; without hope; x-ing; yet ~; zero chance of recovery;

**indebted** *(adj.)*: acknowledging one's debt; beholden; bound in gratitude; *constrained;* debted; encumbered; *forced;* grateful; have a debt; in one's debt; *jejuneness;* keenly ~; liable; much- ~; not without obligation; obliged; owe; pledged; *quantity;* responsible; required; *so thankful;* thankful; under obligation; very much ~; *want; xtry. thankful;* yoked; *zero way out;* [Ant. in the black]

**indecency** *(n.)*: abomination; baseness; crudeness; degradation; evil; filthiness; gaucheness; godlessness; horridness; impropriety; *jadishness;* kitsch; lewdness; meanness; nefariousness; nudity; offense; putridity; *quad;* reprehension; shamefulness; terribleness; uncouthness; vulgarity; wretchedness; x-rating; yuckiness; zhlubbiness;

**indecent** *(adj.)*: *abhorrent;* bawdy; crude; disgraceful; dirty; explicit; fleshy; filthy; gauche; half-naked; immodest; jadish; kinky; lewd; licentious; malodorous; naughty; obscene; promiscuous; prurient; pornographic; perverted; *quad;* revealing; racy; raw; smutty; shameful; salacious; smutty; shocking; tasteless; uncouth; unseemly; vulgar; whorish; x-rated; *yucky; zero-modesty;* [Ant. impeccable]

**indecision** *(n.)*: alternation; *bouncing;* changeableness; dithering; erraticism; fence-sitting; fickleness; going back and forth; hesitancy; hesitance; indecisiveness; irresolution; *jumping; kedging;* lack of decisiveness; mutability; *non-decisive;* oscillation; pendulousness; questioning; reluctance; shifting; teeter-tottering; uncertainty; vacillation; waffling; wavering; *x-ing;* yo-yoing; *zigzagging;* [*Ant.* indomitability]

**indecisive** *(adj.)*: ambivalent; back-and-forth; changing; dithering; erratic; fluctuating; fickle; *giddy;* halting; hesitant; irresolute; *jumping;* kaleidoscopic; *lacking decisiveness;* mutable; non-resolute; oscillating; pendulous; questioning; reluctant; shifting; suspensive; teeter-tottering; unsettled; undecided; vacillating; vertiginous; wishy-washy; weak-minded; waffly; wavering; *x-ing;* yo-yoish; *zigzagging;* [*Ant.* indomitable]

**indecisiveness** *(n.)*: ambivalence; *bouncing;* changeableness; diffidence; erraticism; fluctuation; going back and forth; hesitancy; indecision; irresolution; jumping; kiaugh [Scot.]; lack of determination; mutability; non-decisiveness; oscillation; pendulating; *questioning;* reticence; shifting; suspensiveness; teeter-tottering; uncertainty; vacillation; waffling; wavering; *x-ing;* yo-yoing; zigzagging; [*Ant.* indomitableness]

**indefinite** *(adj.)*: ambiguous; blurry; clouded; dim; enclouded; fuzzy; gray; hazy; indistinct; indeterminate; *jumpy; known to few; lacking clarity;* murky; nebulous; open-ended; obscure; *poorly defined;* questionable; rough; sketchy; turbid; unsure; undefined; undetermined; vague; woolly; *x-ing;* yet unclear; *zero clarity;* [*Ant.* indisputable]

**independence** *(n.)*: autonomy; bondlessness; clearance; deliverance; emancipation; freedom; gratuitousness; *honest;* independent rule; *justification; kept free;* latitude; license; liberty; manumission; non-captivity; openness; privilege; *quite free;* release; self-government; self-reliance; total ~; unrestraint; voluntariness; willingness; *xenium;* yokelessness; zero fetters;

**independent** *(adj.)*: autonomous; bondless; *clear;* disconnected; empowered; free; governing oneself; *headship;* individualistic; *justified; kept free;* liberated; managing own affairs; non-affiliated; non-subjugated; open; particularistic; quite ~; ruling self; substantive; self-governing; self-reliant; sovereign; totally ~; unsubjected; *very ~; warranted; x.;* yokeless; *zero hierarchy;*

**indescribable** *(adj.)*: awesome; beyond words; *cannot be uttered;* dumbfounding; extraordinary; fantastic; ghastly; great; horrendous; heavenly; incommunicable; inexpressible; intransmissible; ineffable; *jolting; keen;* lofty; magnificent; non-utterable; *overwhelmed;* phenomenal; quite ~; remarkable; shocking; tremendous; unrepeatable; unnameable; unspeakable; unutterable; *vulgar; words fail;* wondrous; xtry.; yet ~; *zero words;*

**indestructible** *(adj.)*: armored; bullet-proof; changeless; durable; everlasting; firm; *going on;* Herculean; illacerable; inviolable; imperishable; insuperable; *javelin-proof; keeps;* lasting; *mighty;* non-breakable; olamic; permanent; quenchless; rock-solid; shatterproof; *tough;* timeless; unbreakable; unassailable; unperishable; *vigorous;* well-built; *x-cending;* yet ~; *zero destruction;*

**indeterminate** *(adj.)*: amorphous; boundless; countless; difficult-to-determine; endless; free; gray; hard-to-determine; ill-defined; indefinite; indeterminable; *just don't know; kithless;* loose; limitless; measureless; mysterious; non-determined; open-ended; pendent; protean; quite unknown; *rough;* shadowy; termless; unforeseeable; undetermined; unknown; undefined; unspecified; vague; without limit; *x; y.; zero limitation;*

**indicate** *(v.)*: assert; betoken; bespeak; convey; communicate; denote; evince; express; foretoken; gesture; give indication; hint; intimate; *jaw; key in;* let out; mention; make clear; notify; outline; point out (-to); quoth; relate; show; signify; signal; tell; utter; voice; word; *xenophonia;* yak; *zero in;*

**indication** *(n.)*: assertion; betokening; clue; communication; denotation; expression; foretokening; gesture; grounds; hint; intimation; *justification; key evidence;* letting one know; mention; manifestation; nod; notification; omen; prompt; proof; *quoth;* relating; reflection; signal; signification; telling; token; utter; voicing; word; *xfer; yes;* zeroing in;

**indifference** *(n.)*: apathy; blitheness; boredom; casualness; carelessness; coolness; callousness; disinterest; ennui; flippancy; giddiness; half-heartedness; iciness; *jem'enfichism* [F.]; *knark;* lassitude; lack of concern; mopishness; nonchalance; oscitance; pococurantism; passivity; quiescence; respectlessness; superciliousness; torpidity; unconcern; vapidity; weariness; *xenarthrous;* yarelessness; zeallessness; [*Ant.* interest]
**indifferent** *(adj.)*: apathetic; blithe; casual; complacent; cool; cold(-hearted); callous; detached; disinterested; emotionless; flinty; giddy; hard(-hearted); indurate; impassive; icy; impersonal; jaded; knark; loveless; matter-of-fact; nonchalant; non-sympathetic; objective; pococurante; passive; quiescent; respectless; suave; steel-like; supercilious; tough; uninterested; uncaring; unsympathetic; unfeeling; uncommitted; viewless; withdrawn; *xerothalmic;* yareless; zealless; [*Ant.* interested]
**indigenous** *(adj.)*: aboriginal; born-there; connate; domestic; ethnic; *from there; general;* home-born; homebred; inborn; *jake; kipper [Aus.];* local; *mainlander;* native(-born); natural-born; national; original; *paisano; quiritian* [L.]; *resident; racial; subject;* tribal; *ubeity;* villager; *wonted; xenophile; yield; zonal;* [*Ant.* imported]
**indigestion** *(n.)*: agita; apepsy; acid stomach; belly ache; cardialgia; dyspepsia; *excruciating;* flatulence; gut-pain; heartburn; inflammation; *jabbing pain;* knots; lower abdominal pain; *misery; nausea; ouch;* pyrosis; *qualmish; rumen;* stomach ache; tummy ache; upset stomach; ulcer; ventral discomfort; water brash; *xiphodynia; yaik; zinger;*
**indignant** *(adj.)*: aggravated; bitter; cross; disgusted; exasperated; fuming; galled; hot; incensed; *jumping mad; kindled;* livid; mad; nettled; offended; piqued; quick-tempered; resentful; steamed; temperamental; up in arms; vexed; wrathful; *xerothermic; yond* [arch.]; *zealousy* [arch.];
**indignation** *(n.)*: anger; bitterness; crossness; displeasure; enragement; fury; gall; hotness; infuriation; *jadedness; kindlessness;* lividness; madness; *nettling;* outrage; perturbation; quick-temperament; resentment; *steaming;* temper; umbrage; venting; wrath; *xerothermia; yelling; zealousy* [arch.];
**indirect** *(adj.)*: ambiguous; backdoor; convoluted; circuitous; circumforaneous; duplicitous; evasive; fuzzy; guileful; hinted; implicit; *jumbled;* knavish; labyrinthine; mazy; non-direct; oblique; periphrastic; quasi-direct; roundabout; rough; sidelong; sneaky; turbid; unclear; veiled; vague; winding; x-ing; yawed; zigzag;
**indiscriminate** *(adj.)*: arbitrary; based on whim; careless; capricious; designless; erratic; fortuitous; groundless; haphazard; indiscriminative; jumbled; *keg-meg;* left to chance; loose; making no distinction; non-discerning; nonjudgmental; orderless; purposeless; *quirky;* random; subjective; totally random; undiscriminating; very random; without discrimination; wanton; *x; yet without bias; zero discrimination;*
**indisputable** *(adj.)*: assured; beyond doubt; certain; definite; evident; firm; guaranteed; highly confident; incontestable; incontrovertible; just sure; keenly sure; *legitimate;* mistake-proof; non-questionable; 100% sure; positive; quite sure; reliable; settled; sure; true; undisputed; undeniable; verified; without doubt; xtry. sure; *yes;* zero doubt;
**indistinct** *(adj.)*: amorphous; blurry; cloudy; dim; equivocal; fuzzy; gray; hazy; ill-defined; imprecise; indefinite; indiscernable; indistinguishable; indefinable; *jellyish; kedging;* lour; misty; muzzy; nebulous; obscure; *protean; qually* [arch.]; *really difficult;* smoky; turbid; unclear; vague; wispy; *xtry. difficult; yet indistinguishable; zero clarity;* [*Ant.* identifiable]
**indistinguishable** *(adj.)*: alike; blurry; comparable; duplicate; equal; exact; fuzzy; *gray;* half-visible; homologous; indiscernable; identical; just alike; kindred; like; matching; non-differing; one and the same; parallel; *quae est eadem* [L.]; resembling; same; twin; undifferentiated; *verbatim;* without distinction; *xerographed; yes; zincograph;* [*Ant.* identifiable]
**individual** *(n.)*: *anyone;* being; boy [masc.]; character; *dude;* earthling; figure; fellow [masc.]; gentleman [masc.]; guy [masc.]; girl [fem.]; human (being); *inhabitant;* joker [derog.]; *kid;* living soul; man; *name;* one; person; party; *quadragenarian; resident;* soul; someone; terran; unique ~; *villager;* worldling; woman [fem.]; *xenic; yokel;* zoon;

**indoctrinate** *(v.)*: admonish; beat into; brainwash; condition; disciple; educate; foster; ground; *hype;* instruct; impress; *jobation;* knock into; lecture; mentor; misteach; *narrate; opine;* program; propagandize; *qualify;* ready; reeducate; re~; reprogram; school; subvert; train; *unteach;* verse; work on; xenagogue; yark; *zealously instruct;*

**indulge** *(v.)*: accommodate; baby; coddle; cater to; do; delight in; epicurize; facilitate; gratify; humor; ingratiate; *justify;* keep happy; let; make concession; mollycoddle; *nod;* oblige; please; pander; pamper; *quell;* regale; relish; revel; suffer; splurge; satisfy; spoil; tolerate; take pleasure in; treat; *unhindered;* volutate; wallow; *xuld [arch.];* yield to; *zero opposition;*

**indulgence** *(n. papal allowance to sin)*: absolution; blank check; cockering; dispensation; extrabagance; forbearance; freedom; go-ahead; *humoring;* imprimatur; justification; *knowingly allowed;* license; *may; nod;* obliging; papal allowance; quadragene; *recklessness;* sufferance; tolerance; *unreluctance;* vouchsafement; warrant; x; yes; *zero moderation;*

**indulgence** *(n. permission)*: accommodation; babying; coddling; catering; disregard; extravagance; facilitation; gratification; humoring; indulging; inabstinence; immoderateness; insobriety; ingratiation; *justification; kindness;* letting; laxity; making concession; *nod; okay;* permission; pandering; pampering; pleasing; *quell;* relishing; spoiling; splurging; sufferance; toleration; unreluctance; unrestraint; volutation; wallowing; *xuld [arch.];* yielding; *zero opposition;*

**indulgent** *(adj.)*: anything-goes; babying; crapulent; dissipated; dissolute; decadent; excessive; extravagant; fulsome; gratifying; humoring; immoderate; intemperate; *justifying; knowingly allowed;* lenient; latitudiarian; merciful; non-strict; over- ~; outré; pleasure-seeking; quadragene; reckless; self- ~; tolerant; unbounded; unprohibitive; voluptuous; wild; wanton; *xtry. ~;* yielded to the flesh; *zero moderation;*

**industrious** *(adj.)*: assiduous; busy; constructive; diligent; enduring; fruitful; gung-ho; hard-working; intense; job-conscious; keen; laborious; motivated; not lazy; overdiligent; persistent; *quick-to-work;* responsible; relentless; sedulous; tireless; unslothful; vigorous; weariless; *xtry.; energetic;* yare; zippy; [*Ant.* idle]

**industry** *(n.)*: *AB;* (big) business; company; dealings; enterprise; factory; grind; holding company; incorporated business; job; joint-venture; *kongsi [Chin.]; limited;* manufacturer; national corporation; outfit; operation; plant; quasi-public corporation; *refinery;* small business; shop; toil; *unlimited;* venture; work(shop); *xtr. work; YK; zaibatsu [Jap.];* [*Ant.* idleness]

**inedible** *(adj.)*: awful; bad; crummy; corrupt; dreadful; execrable; foul; *gross;* horrible; highly ~; indigestible; *jaded; kinked;* lousy; *malevolent;* non-edible; *offensive;* pathetic; *questionable;* rotten; *sour;* terrible; unpalatable; uneatable; vile; wicked-tasting; *x-out;* you can't eat it; *zero edibility;* [*Ant.* ingestible]

**ineffective** *(adj.)*: *absurd;* barren; counterproductive; devoid of fruit; empty; feckless; failed; fruitless; futile; good for nothing; hopeless; ineffectual; inefficacious; just no good; *kitty;* lousy; maladroit; manqué; non-effective; otiose; pointless; quisquillous; *ridiculous;* sorry; *token;* unsuccessful; useless; unavailing; unproductive; useless; vain; worthless; *x-out;* yieldless; *zero effectiveness;*

**inefficient** *(adj.)*: awkward; bumbling; clumsy; disorganized; *extravagant; foolish; graceless;* hulky; inadept; ineffective; *jumbled;* klutzy; lacking efficienty; mismanaged; non-frugal; over-wasteful; poorly-managed; quasi-effective; *ridiculous;* shiftless; thriftless; time-wasting; unorganized; uneconomical; unproficient; unskillful; very ~; wasteful; *xtry. ~;* yet ineffective; *zero efficiency;*

**inelegant** *(adj.)*: artless; awkward; bumbling; clumsy; dowdy; étourderie [F.]; fumbly; graceless; hulky; inept; jumbly; klutzy; lumbering; maladroit; non-graceful; oafish; plumbeous; *quirky; rube;* socially inept; troublesome; ungraceful; *vexatious;* wooden; xiaoren; yokelish; zhlubby;

**ineloquent** *(adj.)*: awkward; artless; bungling; crude; clumsy; dreadful; étourderie [F.]; farouche; gauche; hesitant; inarticulate; inelegant; jerky; *klutzy;* lame; mumbling; non-fluent; oafish; pathetic; *quirky;* rough; rude; slow of speech; tongue-tied; ungraceful; unpersuasive; unrefined; vile; wooden; *xtry, ~;* yokelish; *zero eloquence;*

**inerrancy** *(n.)*: absolute perfection; accuracy; *blemishlessness;* correctness; dependability; exactness; faithfulness; *genuineness; honesty;* infallibility; *justness;* keenness; legitimacy; *mistake-proof;* non-errancy; *ontic;* perfection; perfection; *quaecumque sunt vera* [L.]; reliability; sureness; trustworthiness; unfaultiness; verity; *well-tried; x-parent; yes;* zero defect; [*Ant.* inaccuracy]

**inerrant** *(adj.)*: accurate; bearing true; correct; definite; error-free; flawless; good; *honest;* infallible; *justifiable; keenly accurate;* legitimate; mistake-proof; non-fallible; 100% accurate; perfect; questionless; reliable; sure; true; unerring; unmistaken; unimpeachable; verifiable; well-verified; *x-parent; yes;* zero-defect; [*Ant.* inaccurate]

**inexhaustible** *(adj.)*: all-sufficing; boundless; ceaseless; diffuse; endless; full; *gazillion; huge;* indefatigable; inconsumable; interminable; infinite; *jillion; kazillion;* limitless; measureless; non-exhaustible; over-abundant; plentitudinous; perpetual; *quantum libet* [L.]; relentless; sumless; superabundant; tireless; unlimited; vast; without end; *xtry.;* yet without end; *zillion;*

**inexpensive** *(adj.)*: affordable; *bon marché* [F.]; bargain-priced; cheap; cost-effective; dirt-cheap; discounted; economical; frugal; good price; half-priced; inexpensively priced; *justified; knock-out prices;* low-cost; moderately-priced; nominal; *on sale;* pennyworth; quite cheap; reasonable; sixpenny; thrifty; uncostly; unexpensive; value-priced; within means; *xtry.; yellow tag sale; zero-profit;*

**inexperienced** *(adj.)*: amateur; budding; clueless; callow; dewey; experience-deprived; footless; green; *hardly any experience;* ignorant; inexpert; *juvenile;* know-nothing; less proficient; *most inexpert;* new; *novice;* oblivious; *pathetic; quirky;* raw; simple; *trusting;* unexposed; untrained; unfledged; unskilled; verdant; wet behind the ears; *xtry. naive;* young; *zhlubby;*

**infallible** *(adj.)*: accurate; beyond question; correct; certain; dependable; error-free; faultless; flawless; good; *honest;* inerrant; *justifiable; keenly accurate; legitimate;* mistake-proof; non-fallible; 100% guaranteed; perfect; question-less; right; sure; trustworthy; unerring; unfailing; verifiable; watertight; *x-parent; yes;* zero-defect; [*Ant.* inaccurate]

**infamous** *(adj.)*: arrant; atrocious; bad; contemptuous; disreputable; everywhere-known; evil; famous; flagitious; gestic; hated; iconic; ignominious; *Jesse James;* known; legendary; much-hated; notorious; odious; prominent; *quantity;* recognized; sinister; talked-about; universally known; villainous; well-known; wanted; *xtry.;* yichus; *zealously hunted;* [*see* evil; famous; *Ant.* illustrious]

**infamy** *(n.)*: abomination; bad repute; contempt; disrepute; execration; foulness; great reproach; horror; ill-repute; infamousness; *jolting; keening;* loathsomeness; misery; notoriousness; obloquy; odium; perfidiousness; *quad;* reproach; *shame;* treachery; unrespectability; upbraiding; villainy; wretchedness; *xenophobia;* yichus; *zapping;* [*Ant.* illustriousness]

**infancy** *(n.)*: advent; babyhood; beginning; childhood; development; early years; formative years; growing; girlhood [fem.]; *hatching;* immaturity; juniority; kidhood [joc.]; *little;* minority; newborn stage; nascence; newness; outset; period right after birth; *quite young; rise;* start; suckling stage; tenderness; undevelopment; verdancy; weanling years; *XS;* youth; *zygogenesis;*

**infant** *(n.)*: arrival; baby; child; doll; *entrant;* firstling; girl [fem.]; hatchling; innocent child; junior; kid; little one; manling [masc.]; newborn; neonate; nursling; offspring; poupetan; *quite young; really young;* suckling; tot; *underage; vernal;* wee one; weanling; *XS;* young; yeanling; youngling; yearling; *zon [dial. masc.];*

**infect** *(v.)*: affect; afflict; blight; communicate; contaminate; defile; embue; foul; give to; have effect; impart; inquinate; *jinx; knock out; let one get;* make ~ed; *nocuous; offload;* pass on; pollute; *quicken;* relay; re~; spread; smittle; taint; transmit; *unload;* vitiate; wreak havoc on; xmit; *yucky;* zap; [*Ant.* immunize]

**infected** *(adj.)*: affected; *blighted;* contaminated; defiled; diseased; evil-affected; envenomed; foul; *gross; horrible;* impure; inquinated; *jolted; ketty;* lousy; mortified; nocuous; *off;* polluted; *qualm; reinfected; rabid;* seropositive; sick; tainted; unhealthy; vitiated; *welked;* xmit; *yucky;* zich [arch.]; [*Ant.* immunized]

**infection** *(n.)*: affected area; ailment; bug; contagion; contamination; disease; envenoming; flu; germ; health problem; infirmity; impurity; illness; *jaundice; king's evil; lesion;* malady; *nastiness;* oozing; pollution; paronychia; *queasiness; remittent;* sickness; tainting; *unwholesomeness;* virus; whitlow; *x-virus; yuckiness; zoonosis;* [*Ant.* immunity]

**infectious** *(adj.)*: affecting; *breeding;* communicable; contagious; diseased; evil-affecting; *feverish; grievous; horrible;* impartable; *jarring; ketty; lousy;* mortifying; *nocuous;* oozing; pestiferous; *qualm; rabid;* spreadable; smittle; transmittable; transferable; unwholesome; veruliferous; *wreak; xmitting; yucky; zoonosis;* [*Ant.* immune]

**infer** *(v.)*: allude; assume; betoken; conclude; connote; deduce; denote; extrapolate; feel; gather; hint at; imply; insinuate; judge; *known; lead;* make out; mention; *nuance;* opine; postulate; quiddit; reckon; suggest; suppose; surmise; take; *undercurrent; undertone;* vaguely express; *wink; xfer; yammer; zay;*

**inference** *(n.)*: allusion; assumption; betokening; conclusion; connotation; deduction; extrapolation; *foreadvisement;* gathering; hint; implication; insinuation; illation; judgment; *know; leading into;* mention; nuance; overtone; postulation; quiddit; reckoning; suggestion; supposition; touch; undertone; undercurrent; vague express; *winking; xfer; yammering; zay [dial.];*

**inferior** *(adj.)*: ancillary; below-standard; cheap; dinky; deficient; *eclipsed;* fourth-rate; fewer; gimcrack; grade B; half as good; inadequate; junkier; *knocked out;* lesser; lower; low-grade; much lower; nethermore; outranked; outclassed; petty; poor(er); *quite ~;* reduced-quality; second-rate; shoddier; substandard; subordinate; tin-pot; third-rate; under; unequal; valued at less; worse; waur; *x'ed;* yielding; *zero contest;*

**inferiority** *(n.)*: aberrance; baseness; cheapness; deficiency; *eclipsed;* fourth-rateness; *grade B; half as good;* inadequacy; juniority; *knocked out;* lower quality; lowness; mediocrity; nethermost; outranking; outclassing; poorness; *quality;* reduced quality; second-rateness; shoddiness; subordination; third-rateness; unequality; valuing at less; weakness; *x'ed;* yielding; *zero comparison;*

**inferno** *(n.)*: *aflame;* blaze; bonfire; conflagration; deflagration; *enflamed;* fire; furnace; Gehenna; hellfire; incineration; jahannam; *kindled;* light; *miskindle; night-fire;* oven; pyre; *quick-match;* raging ~; sparks; *torch;* ustulation; *volcano;* wildfire; *xylophyrography; yearning; zapping;* [*Ant.* ice]

**infertile** *(adj.)*: arid; barren; childless; desolate; empty; effete; forlorn; gelded; *heirless;* infecund; jejune; kept from bearing; lacking; *menopausal;* nonfertile; olated; *poor; quenched;* resourceless; sterile; *teemless;* unfertile; unfruitful; verdureless; wanting; *x;* yeld; *zero fruit;*

**infest** *(v.)*: abide; bide; crawl; dwell; encroach; fill; go into; habitate; inhabit; *jam;* keep on; live; move in; nest; overspread; plague; quarter; riddle; swarm; teem; *use; voyage to;* wait; *xenize; yerde [arch.];* zip to;

**infestation** *(n.)*: arrival; barrage; *coming;* deluge; entry; flood; *growth;* horde; influx; invasion; *jillions; keeping on; lice ~;* myiasis [maggots]; nesting; onslaught; plague; pediculosis [lice]; *quickening;* riddling; swarm; teeming; *unwelcome ~;* vermination [worms]; wave; *xfer; yeo; zillions;*

**infidelity** *(n.)*: adultery; betrayal; cuckolddom; disloyalty; debauchery; entanglement; faithlessness; fornication; gross ~; harlotry; impurity; immorality; jadery; *knavery;* liaison; lasciviousness; moral impurity; *mischief;* non-faithfulness; odure; promiscuity; playing the harlot; queanery; revelry; sin; treachery; unfaithfulness; venery; whoredom; *x-rated behavior; yearning; zhlubbery;*

**infiltrate** *(v.)*: advance; break into; creep into; *dwell;* enter; encroach; find a way in; get in; gain access; honeycomb; horn in; interlope; jump in; *keep in;* leak in; leaven; make inroads; *non-detected;* osmose; penetrate; quietly enter; *re-enter;* sneak into; slip in; trespass; *undercover; venture;* worm in; *xfer; yede; zip into;*

**infinite** *(adj.)*: ageless; boundless; continual; deathless; endless; *far-reaching; gazillion;* huge; immeasurable; illimitable; interminable; inexhaustible; *jillion; kazillion;* limitless; measureless; numberless; never-ending; ongoing; perpetual; *quadrillion; repeated;* repeated; relentless; sumless; termless; timeless; transfinite; undying; unending; vigintillion; *vast;* without number (-end); *x-finite; yet unnumbered; zillion;*

**infinity** *(n.)*: *all time;* by and by; continuousness; duration; endlessness; foreverness; going on and on; gazillion; *high;* infiniteness; jillion; kazillion; limitlessness; measurelessness; numberlessness; never-endingness; *ongoing;* perpetuity; quadrillion; *remaining;* sempiternity; trillion; *unending; vastness;* without number (-end); *x-cending;* yieldless; zillion;

**inflate** *(v.)*: augment; blow up; bloat; balloon; climb; distend; develop; expand; fill with air; grow; heighten; increase; jump up; *keep growing;* largen; mount; maximize; *non-deflated;* over~; pump up; *quadruple in size;* rise; swell; sufflate; *take off;* upshoot; *volume;* wax greater; *XL; yain* [arch.]; *zoom;*

**inflation** *(n.)*: augmentation; blowing up; bloating; climbing; development; expansion; enlargement; furtherance; growth; heightening; increase; jumping; *keen ~;* largening; making bigger; *new growth;* overdistension; progression; *quantum increase;* rising; swelling; sufflation; tumidity; upgrowth; *verging upward;* waxing; *XL; yain* [arch.]; *zooming;*

**inflexible** *(adj.)*: adamant; bendless; catonian; determined; ever-rigid; firm; fixed; granitelike; hard; intransigent; inexorable; *jaw-set; keep; lasting;* mulish; nonflexible; obstinate; pigheaded; petrous; quite ~; rigid; stubborn; stiff; strong; tough; unbending; unyielding; very rigid; willful; *x-grained;* yieldless; zero-give;

**inflict** *(v.)*: amerce; afflict; bring about; cause; do(le out); exact; foist; foment; give out; hurl; impose; *jab; knife;* lay on; mete out; *non-volitional;* occasion; perpetrate; pain; *quicken;* render; subject; *target; undo;* visit; wreak; *xuld* [arch.]; yoke with; *zero mercy;*

**influence** *(n.)*: auspices; authority; *badge;* control; clout; dominion; effect; faculty; guidance; hold; impact; impression; jurisdiction; kingship; leverage; leadership; mortmain; mastery; name; oversight; pull; power; *quo warranto [L.];* rule; sway; *throne; umpirage; virtue;* weight; *xuld [arch.];* yard; zorch;

**influence** *(v.)*: affect; bias; cause; control; drive; effectiveness; force; get; guide; hold; inspire; instigate; induce; impact; *jump-start;* kindle; lead; militate; move; nobble; *occasion;* pressure; prompt; persuade; *quicken;* rouse; sway; turn; *unlock; vivify;* weigh; work; *xuld* [arch.]; *yield; zorch;*

**influential** *(n.)*: authoritative; *badge;* controlling; dominative; effectual; forceful; great; hegemonic; impacting; *jurisdiction;* kingly; leading; masterly; *name;* overseeing; powerful; persuasive; *quo warranto [L.];* ruling; swaying; *throne; umpirage; virtue;* weighty; *xuld [arch.];* yard; *zonal control;* [*Ant.* ineffectual]

**influx** *(n.)*: afflux; blast; current; deluge; efflux; flux; flood; gush; *hurl;* innundation; jet(stream); *keep coming; leak;* movement; naid; onslaught; profluence; quell; rush; surge; stream; torrent; upsurge; *vomiting;* water flow; *xfer;* yern; *zwoosh;*

**inform** *(v.)*: acquaint; advise; apprise; brief; communicate; divulge; disclose; debrief; detail; enlighten; fame; give report; help; illuminate; *jaw;* kithe [Scot.]; keep posted; let be known; lighten; make report; notify; open one's eyes; proclaim; *quaint* [arch.]; relate; relay; report; state; tell; update; utter; verse; witness; warn; *xenagogic; yak; zero in;* [*see* tattle; spy]

**informal** *(adj.)*: airy; blithe; casual; candid; degage; easygoing; familiar; *gay;* happy-go-lucky; *in dishabille* [F.]; jaunty; keg-meg; laid-back; mellow; nonchalant; offhand; plain; *quick;* relaxed; stress-free; *tolerant;* unhurried; unceremonious; *vapid;* wareless; *xenarthrous; yareless; zero-formality;*

**informant** *(n.)*: agent; bigmouth; communicant; double agent; eyewitness; fink; grass; *hearer;* informer; jaunderer; *kibitz; listener;* mole; monitor; notifier; newsmonger; *observer;* peacher; plant; *quidnunc;* reporter; rat; stool pidgeon; snitch; spy; talker; tattler; tipster; undercover agent; vedette; witness; whistle-blower; *xmit;* yakker; *zarp;*

**information** *(n.)*: account; bulletin; communication; communiqué; details; data; enlightenment; facts; figures; *the* goods; *headline news;* info; intelligence; just the facts; knowledge; *the* lowdown; material; notice; news; output data; pointer; *qualified facts;* report; scoop; specifics; statistics; tip; tidings; training; update; *verity;* word; *x-fact; yield; zero doubt;* [*see* ignorance]

**informative** *(adj.)*: assistive; beneficial; betraying; communicative; divulging; educational; enlightening; *favorable;* guiding; *good;* helpful; indicative; informational; illuminating; instructive; *judicious;* knowledge-giving; *learn;* most ~; noetic; *over- ~;* profitable; *quick-help guide;* revealing; self-teaching; telltale; telling; useful; valuable; *worthwhile;* xenagogic; yielding info; *zero in;*

**infrequent** *(adj.)*: austere; bare; *cannot;* dear; exceptional; few(-and-far-between); gant; hard to find; intermittent; jejune; jimp; keenly ~; limited; little; measly; meager; negligible; occasional; paltry; precious (few); *queer;* rare; scarce; sporadic; *thin;* uncommon; unfrequent; valuable; *wheen* [arch.]; *xtry.; you-beaut [Aus.]; zero;* [*Ant.* inveterate]

**infringe** *(v.)*: advance upon; breach; creep in; contravene; disregard; encroach; flout; go into; horn in; intrude; impinge; invade; *jump in;* know no bounds; *lapse;* make inroads into; *neglect;* overstep; pay no regard; *quad;* rush in; storm in; trespass; usurp; violate; worm in; *xfer; yieldless; zero consideration;*

**infringement** *(n.)*: abuse; breach; contravention; disregard; encroachment; error; flouting; *grievance;* heedlessness; infraction; intrusion; invasion; *jadedness; knowingly violate;* lapse; misdemeanor; malfeasance; neglect; offense; peccability; *quad;* refractoriness; sin; trespass; unlawful act; violation; wrongdoing; *xgression;* yieldlessness; *zero regard;*

**infuse** *(v.)*: add; blend; breathe; concentrate; diffuse; embue; entincture; fill; fuse; give; *homogenize;* introduce; imbue; instill; jet; *key;* leach; leaven; mingle; *naid; oil;* perfuse; pervade; permeate; *quicken;* render; suffuse; saturate; steep; temper; *undermine; vitiate;* wash; *xfer; yeo; zet;*

**ingenious** *(adj.)*: astute; brilliant; clever; daedal; ever-resourceful; farsighted; gifted; genius; heaven-gifted; inventive; imaginative; inspired; judicious; keen; *learned;* most ~; nimble-witted; original; perceptive; quick-witted; resourceful; subtle; smart; sharp; thinking; ultra-smart; very ~; witty; xtry.; *yaup; zippy;* [*Ant.* idiotic]

**ingenuity** *(n.)*: astuteness; brilliance; cleverness; deftness; expertise; farsightedness; guile; *handiness;* inventiveness; ingeniousness; judiciousness; keenness; *learnedness;* mastery; nous; originality; policy; quick-wittedness; resourcefulness; sharpness; *trickiness;* ultra-creativity; virtuosity; wittiness; wizardry; *xtry, cleverness; yaup; zippiness;* [*Ant.* idiocy]

**ingrain** *(v.)*: *admonish;* brainwash; condition; *cram;* drill; deep-dye; entrench; establish; embed; fix; *firm;* ground; hammer; instill; imbed; *justify; knock into; lead;* make to believe; *nobble; over-persuade;* program; *questionless;* root; set in deeply; steep; teach; *undercoat; verse; win over; xenagogue; yoke;* zealously instill;

**ingredient** *(n.)*: additive; *bit;* component; constituent; *detail;* element; feature; *gob; hint;* item; *jigger;* key ~; lump; makings; *nugget; object;* piece; part; *quantity; remnant;* substance; thing; unit; vestige; wedge; *x-mal [G.]; yngot [arch.]; zum [dial.];*

**inhabit** *(v.)*: abide; bide; continue; dwell; exist in; empeople; follow on; *go to;* hang one's hat; homestead; indwell; *journey;* keep on; live; move in; *nest;* occupy; perch; populate; quarter; reside; stay; tarry; *use; voyage to;* wait; xenize; yerde [arch.]; *zip to;*

**inhabitant** *(n.)*: abider; *bide;* citizen; dweller; denizen; ethnic; fellow citizen; *gentleman;* habitant; indweller; *jake; kipper [Aus.];* local; *mainlander;* native; national; occupant; occupier; people [pl.]; *quiritian [L.];* resident; resider; subject; tenant; *ubeity;* villager; *woman; xenophile; yokel; zonal;*

**inhale** *(v.)*: aspirate; *air;* breathe in; *circulate air;* drag; draw air; *exhale;* fill lungs; gasp; *huff;* inbreathe; *judder; keep on;* let air in; *lung; move; nose;* olfact; puff; *quill [arch.];* respire; sniff; smell; suck in; snort; suspire; take in air; *use oxygen;* ventilate; whiff; *xuld [arch.];* yolp; *zephyr;*

**inherit** *(v.)*: acquire; accede; become heir; come into; *descent; entrusted; fetch;* get; gain; heir; *intrusted; join to;* kep; legally ~; make off with; nab; obtain; procure; *quoff;* receive; secure; step into; succeed to; take (over); *usurp; valuables;* win; *xfer; yank; zip away;*

**inheritance** *(n.)*: acquisition; bequest; birthright; co-heirship; co-parcenary; descent; dower; estate; fellow-heirdom; gain; heritage; incorporeal hereditament; jointure; *keep;* legacy; movable; non-corporeal hereditament; *ownership;* primogeniture; parcenary; *quoff;* reversion; succession; takings; treasures; ultimogeniture; *valuables;* wealth; *xmission; yain [arch.];* zillions;
**initiate** *(v.)*: activate; begin; commence; debut; establish; form; found; forge; generate; *head up;* instigate; implement; institute; *jump-start;* kick off; launch; lead off; make a start; *newly found;* originate; produce; *quicken;* raise up; start; turn out; upbuild; *vivify;* work out; *xfer;* yield; *zip into motion;*
**initiation** *(n.)*: acceptance; advent; beginning; commencement; debut; dawn; entrance; embarking; founding; genesis; *heading up;* inception; introduction; instigation; implementation; institution; jump-off; kickoff; launching; *making;* naissance; origination; outset; production; *quickening;* rise; start; triggering; take-off; ushering in; *verge;* welcoming; xenogenesis; youth; zygogenesis;
**inject** *(v.)*: add; administer; blast; *charge; discharge;* emit; foist; force; get into; *hurl;* introduce; insert; infuse; immit; jack up; jet; *kest; launch;* make ~ion; *naid; output;* pump; perfuse; *quasi-fuse; rush;* squirt; shoot; transfuse; *use;* vaccinate; *went; xfer; yield;* zap;
**injection** *(n.)*: addition; boring; clyster; *discharge;* enema; fix [slang]; *give shot; hurl;* inoculation; jab; *kest;* lancet; *make hole;* needle; open; perfusion; *quill; run through;* shot; transfixion; *under the skin;* vaccine; *wimble; xylotomy; yield; zapping;*
**injure** *(v.)*: afflict; blast; cut; crack; chafe; damage; endamage; fix [slang]; gash; hurt; harm; impair; inflict damage; jeel; knock; louse up; lacerate; mar; *nocument; offend;* persecute; *quash;* rend; ruin; scathe; trouble; *unsafe;* victimize; wound; *x.; ydrad [arch.]; zap;* [*Ant.* improve]
**injurious** *(adj.)*: adverse; bad; counterproductive; contrary; detrimental; damaging; endangering; foul; grave; hurtful; harmful; insalubrious; jeopardous; *known risk;* lethal; malefic; nocuous; *ominous;* perilous; *questionable;* risky; ruinous; self-destructive; scatheful; tortious; unbeneficial; violent; wounding; *x.; ydrad [arch.]; zero safety;*
**injustice** *(n.)*: atrocity; bias; breach; crookedness; crime; discrimination; disingenuousness; dishonesty; *evil;* falseness; foulness; great wrong; *gap; hardly just;* incommensurateness; inequitableness; inequality; invidiousness; *justiceless; knavery;* lacking equality; malfeasance; non-equality; one-sidedness; partiality; *quad; ruthlessness;* slantedness; trespass; unfairness; unjustness; unrighteousness; villainy; wrong; *xgression; yegginess; zero justice;* [*Ant.* impartiality]
**inn** *(n.)*: *accommodations;* bed and breakfast; *caravanserai* [Arab.]; dosshouse; *efficiency apartment;* flophouse; *fleabag motel;* flotel; guesthouse; hostel; hotel; *imaret* [Turk.]; *joint;* juke; kip-house; lodge; motel; *nook;* outspan; parador; quinta; roadhouse; rooming house; resort; suites; ski lodge; tavern; *ubiety;* victualing-house; *ward;* xenodocheum; youth hostel; *zeta;* [*see* restaurant; pub]
**innkeeper** *(n.)*: *administrator;* bed and bedfast owner; chamberlain; *director; executive;* flophouse owner; guesthouse owner; host; hosteller; hotelier; innholder; *jefe;* kip-house owner; landlord; manager; night manager; owner; publican; *quinta;* roadhouse owner; supervisor; taverner; *ubiety;* victualer; warden; *xenodocheum;* youth hosteller; *zeta;*
**innocence** *(n.)*: *aboveboard;* blamelessness; cleanness; dovelikeness; *exoneration;* faultlessness; guiltlessness; harmlessness; innocency; inculpability; irreproachability; impeccability; *justification;* known ~; lamblikeness; *morality;* non-guiltiness; offenselessness; purity; qualmlessness; righteousness; spotlessness; sinlessness; taintlessness; unguiltiness; unblamableness; unimpeachableness; viridity; witelessness; *xtry.; yet to be blamed;* zero-guilt;
**innocent** *(adj.)*: aboveboard; blameless; blemishless; clean; clear; dovelike; exemplary; *exonerated;* faultless; guiltless; harmless; holy; ingenuous; inculpable; irreproachable; impeccable; *justified;* known-innocent; lamblike; *moral;* not guilty; offenseless; pure; qualmless; questionless; righteous; spotless; sinless; taintless; unresponsible; unblamable; unguilty; unreprovable; unimpeachable; virtuous; witeless; white; *xtry.; yet unblamed; zero-guilt;* [*Ant.* indictable]

**innovate** *(v.)*: alter; advance; better; change; develop; enhance; further; go one better; *help;* improve; *jib; key to;* lift to greater heights; make better; modify; novate; overhaul; progress; *qualify;* redesign; revise; reinvent; *switch;* transform; upgrade; vamp; work on; *xenomorph; yaw; zet [dial.];*

**innuendo** *(n.)*: allusion; betokening; clue; denotation; *expression; foreadvisement;* gentile hint; hint; inference; implication; insinuation; intimation; *jab; know; look;* mention; nuance; overtone; postulation; quiddit; reference; suggestion; touch; undertone; undercurrent; vague express; whisper; *xfer; yammering; zet [dial.];*

**innumerable** *(adj.)*: *a lot;* boundless; countless; *disproportionate;* enormous; endless; fathomless; fantastic; *great; huge;* inestimable; incalculable; infinite; *jillion; kazillion;* limitless; myriad; multitudinous; numberless; *ongoing;* plethoric; *quadrillion; remarkable;* sumless; tremendous; untold; unnumbered; uncountable; unreckonable; vast; without number; x; yet unnumbered; *zillion;* [*see* huge]

**inquire** *(v.)*: ask; behest; *call for;* cross-examine; drill; demand; enquire; feel out; grill; *hunt for;* interrogate; investigate; *juration; know;* look into; make query; nose out; obsecrate; oppugn; pump [slang]; petition; pose; probe; pry; query; question; request; seek; test; *urge; vocalize;* wonder; XQ.; *yearn for; zetetic;*

**inquiry** *(n.)*: analysis; *behest;* cross-examine; delving; demand; enquiry; examination; feeler; grilling; hearing; inquest; investigation; interrogation; jury trial; *knowledge;* legislative ~; *mission; nosing around;* oppugning; probe; query; question; request; search; scrutiny; testing; trial; *urging; valuation;* work-over; XQ.; *yearning for;* zetetic; [*Ant.* input]

**inquisitive** *(adj.)*: asking; analytical; behesting; curious; drilling; demanding; enquiring; forward; grilling; highly curious; inquiring; interested; investigative; interrogative; *juration;* knowledge-seeking; *looking for answers;* mettling; meddlesome; nosy; overcurious; probing; prying; querying; questioning; quizzy; rogatory; searching; snooping; testing; *urging;* voyeuristic; wondering; *XQ.;* yuky [Scot.]; zetetical; [*Ant.* indifferent]

**inquisitor** *(n.)*: asker; *behest;* cross-examiner; driller; enquirer; examiner; *find out;* griller; grand ~; *hard questions;* inquirer; interrogator; *juration; know;* lawyer; master questioner; *nosy;* obsecrator; poser; prier; quizzer; quizmaster; questionmaster; querist; questioner; *requester;* seeker; tester; *urge; voice;* work-over; *XQ; yearn;* zetetic;

**insane** *(adj.)*: abnormal; absurd; batty; bananas; bonkers; berserk; cuckoo; cracked; crazy; daft; disturbed; deranged; demented; eccentric; freakish; goofy; haywire; irrational; *just plain crazy;* kooky; loony; loco; lunatic; mental (case); mad; nutty; neurotic; outlandish; psychedelic; psychopath; psycho(tic); quacked; raving; screwy; sick (in the head); stark raving mad; taken leave of senses; twisted; unbalanced; unstable; volatile; weird; wacky; warped; *xtry. bizarre;* yo-yo; zany;

**insanity** *(n.)*: absurdity; berzerkness; craziness; daftness; derangement; dementia; eccentricity; freakiness; goofiness; harebrainedness; irrationality; instability; *just plain crazy;* kookiness; looniness; lunacy; madness; mania; nuttiness; outlandishness; psychopathy; quackery; raving lunacy; screwiness; twistedness; unstable condition; *volatility;* wackiness; weirdness; *xtry. daftness;* yo-yo; zaniness; zoanthropy;

**inscription** *(n.)*: annotation; blurb; comment; caption; *dedication;* epigraph; epitaph; etching; engraving; entry; form; graving; handwriting; hieroglyphics; inscribing; inscript; *indication; journalism; kapnography;* letters; lettering; message; markings; notation; *observations;* posting; *quotation;* remark; subtitle; superscription; tooling; text; title; *uncials; verbiage;* writing; xiaozhuan; *yellow journalism;* zeug;

**insect** *(n.)*: ant; bug; critter; creepy-crawly; *drain fly; earwig; fly; gnat; housefly; hornet; infestation; June bug; king weevil;* leaf ~; *menace; mosquito; nuisance; orchid mantis;* pest; plague; *queen bee;* roach; spider; tick; *union jack butterfly;* vermin; wasp; weevil; *xyleborus; yucca borer; zyzzogeton;* [*see* plague; swarm]

**insecure** *(adj.)*: anxious; bashful; coy; diffident; demure; embarrassed; fearful; gentle; hesitant; infirm; jumpy; *knees knocking; lily-livered;* mousy; nervous; overmodest; petrified; quiet; reticent; self-conscious; timorous; unsure; verecund; withdrawn; *xenophobic;* yarrow; *zealless;* [*Ant.* intrepid]

**insecurity** *(n.)*: anxiety; bashfulness; coyness; demure; embarrassment; fearfulness; *gastness;* hesitancy; insecureness; jackalence; *knees knocking;* lack of confidence; mousiness; nervousness; overmodesty; precariousness; petrification; quietness; reticence; self-consciousness; self-doubt; timorousness; uncertainty; verecundity; *withdrawn; xenophobia; yarrow; zeallessness;*

**insensitive** *(adj.)*: austere; blasé; cold; callous; dead; *excessive;* flint-hearted; grossly ~; hardened; inattentive; indifferent; inconsiderate; insensate; jaded; knark; loutish; mannerless; nonsensitive; numb; obtuse; pachydermatous; pitiless; *quirky;* reckless; selfish; thick-skinned; unthoughtful; uncaring; uncompassionate; unmoved; unaffected; void of humanity; without regard; *x-out;* yieldless; *zoilean;*

**insensitivity** *(n.)*: austerity; benumbed state; callousness; deadness; *excessiveness;* flint-heartedness; gross ~; hardness; insensitiveness; insensience; jadedness; *knark;* lack of feeling; mannerlessness; numbness; obtuseness; pitilessness; *quirkiness;* recklessness; selfishness; thoughtlessness; unfeelingness; vulgarity; *without feeling; x-out;* yieldlessness; *zoileanism;*

**inseparability** *(n.)*: attachment; bond; closeness; devotedness; endearment; friendship; *glue;* hitching; indivisibility; joining; knitting; link; merging; *network;* oneness; putting together; *quasi-fuse;* reunion; solidarity; togetherness; unity; *vise; with; xenograft;* yoking; *zero separation;* [*Ant.* isolatability]

**inseparable** *(adj.)*: attached; bound; connected; combined; *devoted;* entwined; fused; glued; hitched; indivisible; indissoluble; joined; knitted; linked; merged; non-separable; one; put together; *quasi-fused;* reunited; secured; together; thick; united; undividable; *vise; with; xenograft;* yoked; *zero separation;* [*Ant.* isolatable]

**insert** *(v.)*: add; bestow; *confer;* deposit; engraft; fix; force; graft; *have;* infix; interline; implant; introduce; jam; *kit;* lodge; *make; nudge; output;* put; place; pop; push; *quick-push;* run in re~; reimplant; stick; slip; tuck; thrust; *use; vest;* work in; wedge; *xuld [arch.]; yield;* zet [dial.];

**insight** *(n.)*: awareness; *belief;* clairvoyance; comprehension; discernment; erudition; ESP; farsightedness; foresight; grasp; *hindsight;* intuition; judgment; knowledge; light; mental apprehension; notice; *notion; opinion;* perception; percipience; *quick-to-understand;* realization; (sixth) sense; trenchancy; understanding; vision; wisdom; xtry. ~; *yeme [arch.]; zero confusion;*

**insightful** *(adj.)*: astute; bright; clear-sighted; discerning; ever-wise; farsighted; *good; hawk-eyed;* intelligent; intuitive; judicious; keen; *longsighted;* mindful; *noticing;* observant; on the ball; perceptive; percipient; quick; razor-sharp; sharp; shrewd; trenchant; understanding; vigilant; wise; *xtry.;* yepe; *zero in;*

**insignia** *(n.)*: arms; badge; crest; designation; differentia; emblem; *figure; glyph;* hierogram; heraldry; icon; indicator; image; *jack;* key; logo; mark; *notation; object;* pictogram; *quarter;* representation; regalia; symbol; shield; sign(et); seal; timbre; *uncial; vexillum; wafer; x;* yacht ensign; *zeug;*

**insignificance** *(n.)*: absurdity; *blithering; crummy;* dinkiness; *emptiness;* frivolousness; futility; *gnat-sized; hoity-toity;* immateriality; inconsequentiality; irrelevance; *jerkwater;* kettiness; littleness; marginality; meaninglessness; nonimportance; obscurity; pettiness; paltriness; *quantité négligeable [F.]; ridiculousness;* smallness; triviality; unimportance; unsignificancy; vanity; worthlessness; *XS; yea big; zero importance;* [*Ant.* importance]

**insignificant** *(adj.)*: absurd; back-burner; *crummy;* dinky; *empty;* frivolous; futile; *gnat-sized;* hoity-toity; immaterial; inconsequential; irrelevant; jerkwater; ketty; little; marginal; minor; meaningless; nonimportant; nugatory; obscure; petty; paltry; *quantité négligeable* [F.]; rinky-dink; *ridiculous;* small; trivial; unimportant; unsignificant; vain; worthless; *XS; yea big; zero importance;* [*Ant.* important]

**insincere** *(adj.)*: artificial; bogus; contrived; counterfeited; disingenuous; dishonest; emulative; feigned; false(hearted); facile; guileful; hollow; hypocritical; illusive; Janus-faced; knavish; lying; make-believe; mendacious; non-genuine; ostensible; pretended; phony; pharisaical; quacksalving; *rooking;* superficial; two-faced; untruthful; verneuking; wangling; *xtry. superficial;* yentzing; *zelig;* [*Ant.* ingenuous]

**insincerity** *(n.)*: affectation; *bogus;* contriving; disingenuousness; dishonesty; emulative; false(heartedness); guile; hollow; hollowness; hypocrisy; illusiveness; jesuitry; knavery; lying; mendaciousness; non-genuineness; ostensibility; pretense; phoniness; pharisaism; quacksalving; religiosity; superficiality; two-facedness; untruthfulness; verneuking; wangling; *xtry. superficiality;* yentzing; *zelig;* [*Ant.* ingenuous]

**insinuate** *(v.)*: allude; betoken; connote; drive at; evince; *foreadvise;* give indication; hint at; imply; *judge; known;* lead on; make out; *nuance; overtone;* postulate; quiddit; refer; suggest; tell; *undertone;* vaguely express; *wink; xfer; yammer; zay;*

**insist** *(v.)*: adjure; bid; contend; command; demand; expect; enjoin; force upon; give an order; *have; hold;* impose; *juration; kaleusmatic;* lay down; make a demand; maintain; necessitate; order; prescribe; *quick to demand;* require; say so; stipulate; tell; urge; *vow; word; xenagogy;* yark; *zakon [Rus.];*

**insistent** *(adj.)*: adamant; bull-headed; clamorous; determined; emphatic; firm; forceful; gritty; headstrong; inexorable; jaw-set; *keeps up; lasting;* mulish; non-yielding; obstinate; persistent; *querulous;* resolute; relentless; single-minded; stubborn; shrill; tenacious; unrelenting; *vigorous;* willful; *x-grained;* yieldless; *zero give;*

**inspect** *(v.)*: assess; analyze; *behold;* check (out); diagnose; evaluate; examine; find out; go over; have a look; investigate; jerque; keek; look over; make ~ion; *notice;* observe; probe; pry; quality check; review; survey; scrutinize; test; *understand;* view; verify; vet; watch; *XQ;* yeme; *zero in;* [*Ant.* ignore]

**inspection** *(n.)*: assessment; boning; check; diagnostic; evaluation; examination; field test; going over; hard look; investigation; jerquing; *knowledge;* look-over; *meta-analysis; non-optional ~;* observation; overhaul; prospect; quality control; re-examination; survey; scrutiny; test; trial *unscheduled ~;* verification; written ~; *XQ;* yearly ~; *zetetic;* [*Ant.* ignoring]

**inspector** *(n.)*: assessor; auditor; bailiff; checker; deputy; evaluator; examiner; federal examiner; foreman; general ~; headman; investigator; jerquer; keeker; licensed ~; monitor; *note;* observer; overseer; officer; proctor; probator; quality control; reviewer; scrutinizer; scrutineer; tester; *unit ~;* verifier; watcher; *XQ;* yeme; *zero in;*

**inspiration** *(n.)*: afflatus; breath by God; communication of divine knowledge; divine communication; *ethereal;* full ~; God-breathed words; Holy Spirit ~; inspiring; *Jehovah's words; knowledge; loftiness;* movement by God; *not of man;* origination from God; *purely of God; quickening;* revelation; Spirit ~; *theopneustos* [Gr.]; utterance of God; *venerated;* words of God; *xmit; yonder; zonic;*

**inspired** *(n.)*: *afflatus;* breathed by God; communicated by God; divinely-given; *ethereal;* fully- ~; God-breathed (-given); Holy Spirit-given; heaven-inspired; inbreathed; *Jehovah's words; knowledge; lofty;* moved by God; *non man-made;* originating from God; *purely of God; quickened;* revealed; Spirit-given; transmitted by God; uttered by God; *venerated;* written by God; *xmit; yonder; zonic;*

**instability** *(n.)*: alternation; *bounciness; brokenness;* changeableness; capriciousness; disequilibrium; dithering; erraticism; fluctuation; fickleness; flux; *going back and forth;* hinkiness; irregularity; inconstancy; imbalance; insecurity; jumpiness; *kedging; lacination;* mutability; non-stability; oscillation; precariousness; quavering; rocking; shakiness; tottering; teetering; unsteadiness; unstableness; unpredictability; variability; volatility; wavering; *x-ing;* yo-yoing; zigzagging; [*Ant.* immovability]

**instance** *(n.)*: aspect; *befallen;* case; detail; example; fact; given ~; *highlight;* item; *juncture; knowledge; lot;* manifestation; *new development;* occurrence; occasion; particular; *quote;* representative case; sample; time; technicality; *unfolding;* visage; *when; x-factor; yield; zet [dial.];*

**instant** *(n.)*: anon; bit; *currently;* delay; *ephemeral;* flash; *glimpse;* half a second; *immediate;* jiffy; *kilocycle;* little while; millisecond; minute; moment; nanosecond; one minute; *point in time;* quick ~; *rapidly;* second; short time; trice; time; *uptime; verge;* wink; while; *x-time; yet;* zeptosecond;
**instantaneous** *(adj.)*: abrupt; breakneck; current; direct; ever-prompt; expeditious; fast; *going fast;* hasty; instant; *jiffy; keen;* lightning-fast; momentary; *now;* overhasty; precipitate; prompt; punctual; quick; rapid; sudden; swift; transient; undelayed; very quick; without warning; *xtry. fast;* yet sudden; zippy;
**instigate** *(v.)*: activate; bring about; begin; cause; drive; engender; foster; goad; generate; heat up; initiate; incite; jump-start; kick off; kindle; lead to; motivate; make; nettle; originate; prompt; precipitate; provoke; *quicken; rally;* start; stir up; set off; trigger; urge; *vivify;* wreak; *xenogenesis;* yield; *zeal;*
**instigation** *(n.)*: advent; beginning; commencement; dawn; embarkment; founding; goad; genesis; *hatching;* initiation; incitement; jump off; kickoff; launching; making; naissance; origination; provocation; *quickening;* rising; start; stirring-up; triggering; ushering in; *verge; welcoming; xenogenesis; youth; zygogenesis;*
**instill** *(v.)*: admonish; beat; cultivate; drill; drum in; establish; entrench; embed; foster; further; fix; ground; hammer; impart; inculcate; implant; imbue; infuse; indoctrinate; *justify; knock into;* leaven; make to believe; nurture; *over-persuade;* put in; program; *questionless;* root; school; teach; *undermine; verse;* win over; *xenagogue; yoke;* zealously ~;
**instillation** *(n.)*: admonishment; beating; cultivation; drumming in; entrenching; fostering; grounding; hammering; impartation; inculcation; implantation; imbuement; infusion; indoctrination; *justify; knock into;* leavening; making to believe; nurturing; *over-persuade;* programming; *questionless;* rooting; schooling; teaching; *undermining; versing; winning over; xenagogue; yoke;* zealous ~;
**instinct** *(n.)*: automatism; biological drive; conatus; drive; *essence;* force; gut response; *habit;* impulse; innate ability; *just natural;* knack; *leaning;* makeup; nature; overall makeup; (pre)programming; *quality;* reflex; subconscious urge; tendency; underlying makeup; *virtue;* way; *xenenthesis; yet unexplainable; zoetic;*
**instinctive** *(adj.)*: automatic; built-in; conditioned; *driven; essential;* forced; genetic; *habitual;* involuntary; inborn; intuitive; instinctual; *just natural;* knee-jerk; libidinal; mindless; natural; organic; (pre)programmed; *quick;* reflexive; spontaneous; *tendency;* unconscious; visceral; *way; xenenthesis; yet unexplainable; zoologic;*
**institute** *(v.)*: assemble; begin; build; create; develop; establish; form; found; generate; give; *hatch;* initiate; *jump-start;* kick-off; launch; make; *newly form;* originate; produce; *quicken;* raise up; start; turn out; unveil; *venture;* work up; *xenogenesis;* yield; *zip together;*
**institution** *(n.)*: association; body; convention; custom; *department;* establishment; foundation; *group; house;* institute; joint coalition; *kongsi [Chin.];* league; *mutual interest group;* nexus; organization; partnership; quinquevirate; *regular assembly;* society; school; trust; tradition; union; *venture; work; x-class; yeald; zollverein;*
**instruct** *(v.)*: admonish; adjure; bid; coach; catechize; command; disciple; direct; educate; enjoin; familiarize; foster; guide; give ~ion; ground; home school; inform; impart; inculcate; illumine; *juration; kibitz;* let know; lecture; *misteach;* mentor; mandate; notify; orientate; order; prepare; prime; pedagogue; qualify; rear; ready; require; rule; show how; school; tutor; teach; train; tell; utter; *unlock;* verse; work with; xenagogue; yark; *zealously ~;*
**instruction** *(n. command)*: adjuration; bidding; charge; direction; enjoining; fostering; *fiat;* guidance; hortation; injunction; juration; *keleusmatic;* lessons; monition; mandate; *necessitate;* order; precept; *quo minus [L.];* readying; requirement; statute; telling; utterance; *voice;* word; *xenagogy; yawping; zakon [Rus.];*

**instruction** *(n. teaching)*: apprenticeship; book-learning; breeding; coaching; classes; catechization; discipleship; didactics; education; fostering; guidance; hortation; indoctrination; *juration;* knowledge; lessons; lecturing; mentoring; nurture; object lesson; *oversight;* preparation; pedagogy; preachment; qualification; readying; schooling; tutelage; teaching; training; upbringing; vocational training; word; xenagogy; yarking; *zakon [Rus.];*

**instrument** *(n.)*: apparatus; *bauble;* contrivance; contraption; doohickey; device; equipment; *function;* gadget; gizmo; gimmal; hootenanny; habiliments; *hardware;* implement; *jigger;* kit; labor-saving device; mechanism; *nignay;* object; piece of equipment; quaint device; *resourcefulness; such-and-such;* tool; utensil; *valuable tool;* widget; *X-Y recorder; you-know-what;* zeug; zampogna;

   **Musical instruments:** accordion; bassoon; clarinet; dulcimer; English horn, flute; glockenspiel; harp; Irish flute; jubil; kettledrum; lute; marimba; nai; oboe; piano; qanon; ramshorn; saxophone; trumpet; ukulele; violin; whistle; xylophone; yangkin; zither;

**instrumental** *(adj.)*: assistive; beneficial; contributory; *do;* effective; favorable; good; helpful; influential; *jim dandy;* keen; *letting;* ministering; nurtural; of service; *obliging;* profitable; *quick-to-help; responsible;* salutary; serviceable; *terrific;* useful; valuable; working; *xtry.;* yieldful; *zealous to help;* [*see* musical]

**insubordinate** *(adj.)*: abusive; bad; contravening; disobedient; defiant; ever-stubborn; flouting; *grim;* headstrong; incompliant; *jaw-set; knocking;* lawless; misbehaving; mutinous; naughty; noncompliant; obdurate; perverse; *querulous;* rebellious; self-willed; truculent; unyielding; uncompliant; violating; wayward; *x-grained;* yieldless; *zero give;*

**insubordination** *(n.)*: *abuse;* bad behavior; contravention; challenge; contumacy; disobedience; defiance; *ever-defiant;* flouting; *general disregard; headstrongness;* intractability; *jadedness; kicking at;* lawlessness; misbehavior; mutiny; noncompliance; nonobedience; obstinacy; perverseness; *questioning;* rebellion; *stubbornness; sin;* transgression; unruliness; violation; waywardness; *xgression;* yieldlessness; *zapping;*

**insufficient** *(adj.)*: abject; below; coming up short; deficient; *empty;* falling short; greatly in need; hardly enough; *hard-pressed;* inadequate; *just not enough;* keenly deficient; lacking; low; missing something; non-sufficient; *out;* poor; partial; *questionable; ran out;* short; shy; too little; *under;* unsatisfactory; unsuitable; unsufficing; unacceptable; very ~; wanting; *xtry. deficient;* yet ~; *zero sufficiency:*

**insult** *(n.)*: affront; aspersion; barb; blast; badmouthing; belittlement; criticism; crushing remark; dig; defamation; epithet; flout; gibe; humiliating remark; insulting remark; jibe; knock; libel; maligning; names; offense; outrage; put-down; quip; rude comment; slight; smear; slur; traducement; unkind name; violence; wipe; *xuld [arch.]; yock;* zinger;

**insult** *(v.)*: affront; belittle; badmouth; blast; cag; criticize; censure; dig; defame; denigrate; disparage; disrespect; *execrate;* flout; *fleer;* gibe; humiliate; injure; jibe; knock; kagg; libel; malign; mud-sling; *name-calling;* obloquy; offend; put one down; quib; run down; revile; slight; smear; slander; traduce; upset; vilify; wipe; *xuld [arch.];* yock; *zing;*

**insulting** *(adj.)*: abusive; backbiting; calumnious; disparaging; defamatory; evil-speaking; foul; gossipy; harmful; injurious; jabbing; *keenly ~;* left-handed; libelous; maledictive; malicious; non-truthful; obtrusive; pernicious; *quad;* reputation-slandering; slanderous; tarnishing; *untrue;* vilifying; *wicked; x-ing;* yellowing; *zeroizing;*

**insure** *(v.)*: assure; bond; cover; defend; ensure; fend; guarantee; have insurance on; indemnify; *jaga;* keep safe; look after; make safe; *nestle; over~;* protect; *quia timet [L.];* re~; shield; safeguard; take care of; underwrite; vouchsafe; warrant; *x-guard; yeme [arch.]; zero danger;*

**insurrection** *(n.)*: armed uprising; *breach;* coup d'état; defiance; émeute; *fight;* general uprising; high treason; insurgence; jacquerie; *kicking at; lèse majesté* [F.]; mutiny; noncompliance; overthrow; peasant uprising; putsch; *questioning;* rebellion; revolt; subversion; treason; takeover; uprising; violence; *war; xgression; yieldlessness; zapping;*

**intact** *(adj.)*: all together; *bodily ~;* complete; *downright fine;* entire; full; *good; healthy;* in one piece; *just fine;* kept; lasting; *mainly okay;* non-damaged; okay; pure; perfect; *qualified;* remaining; safe; standing; together; unharmed; unbroken; *veritable;* whole; *xtry.;* yare; *zero harm;*
**intangible** *(adj.)*: airy; abstract; bodiless; baseless; cloudy; difficult to grasp; ethereal; firmless; flimsy; foundationless; groundless; hard to describe; insubstantial; immaterial; *jellylike; kerfuffled;* light; *make-believe;* non-tangible; nonmaterial; nebulous; non-real; obscure; *pitiful;* quaggy; *ridiculous;* sketchy; shadowy; tenuous; turbid; unsubstantial; unreal; vague; vaporous; weak; *xenomorphous;* yet unsubstantial; *zero clarity;* [*Ant.* ironclad]
**integrate** *(v.)*: assimilate; blend in; combine; coalesce; desegregate; emulsify; fit in; *group;* harmonize; intermix; incorporate join together; knit; link; lump together; mix; merge; mingle; *node; organize;* put together; *queach [arch.];* ravel; roll into one; shake together; temper; unite; *voluble;* wed; *xenograft;* yerk together; zip together;
**integration** *(n.)*: assimilation; blend; combination; coalescence; desegregation; emulsification; fusion; *gallimaufrey;* harmonization; intermixture; incorporation joining; knitting together; *lumping;* mixture; mergence; mingling; *node; organizing;* putting together; *queaching [arch.];* raveling; rolling together; shaking together; tempering; union; *vertical ~;* wedding; *xenograft;* yerking together; zipping together;
**integrity** *(n.)*: *aboveboard;* blamelessness; character; decency; ethics; fairness; goodness; honor; impeccability; justness; *kalokagathia* [Gr.]; *legitimacy;* morality; nobility; *openness;* probity; *quaecumque sunt vera* [L.]; rectitude; scrupulousness; trustworthiness; uprightness; virtue; worthiness; *xtry; yieldedness to God;* zero-blame;
**intellect** *(n.)*: astuteness; acumen; brains; common sense; *discrimination; expertise; forebrain;* good judgment; head; intelligence; I.Q.; judgment; *knowledge; lobe;* mind; nous; *occiput; prudence;* quadrigeminal; reason; sharpness; thinking; understanding; vermis; wits; *xenenthesis; yead* [arch.]; zenith;
**intellectual** *(adj.)*: astute; academic; bookish; bright; brainy; brilliant; clued-up [Br.]; cerebral; clever; deep; educated; erudite; enlightened; farsighted; gifted; highbrow; intelligent; judicious; knowledgeable; learned; mental; nimble-witted; on the ball; perceptive; quick; rational; smart; scholarly; thinking; ultra-smart; university-taught; very intelligent; well-educated; *xenagogic;* yaup; *zippy;* [*Ant.* ignorant]
**intellectual** *(n.)*: academic; brain [slang]; collegiate; deliberator; Einstein; figurer; genius; highbrow; intellect; *judger; knowledge; learned;* marvel; *noetic; oracular;* prodigy; ponderer; *philosopher; questioner;* rocket scientist [slang]; scholar; thinker; *ultra-smart; valuator;* whiz (kid); *xenagogue; yauper; zippy;* [*Ant.* ignoramus]
**intelligence** *(n.)*: acumen; astuteness; acuity; brightness; braininess; brilliance; *common sense;* cleverness; *discretion; education;* farsightedness; giftedness; genius; highbrowism; intellectualness; judiciousness; keenness; knowledgeableness; kop; logic; mental capacity; mother wit; nimble-witted; *on the ball;* precociousness; quickness; rationality; reasonableness; reason; smartness; sharpness; smarts; thought; *ultra-smart; valedictorian;* wit; *xenagogy; yaup; zippiness;* [*Ant.* irrationality]
**intelligent** *(adj.)*: astute; bright; clever; *discreet;* educated; farsighted; gifted; highbrow; intellectual; judicious; keen; learned; mental; nimble-witted; on the ball; perceptive; precocious; quick(-witted); rational; smart; thinking; ultra-smart; very smart; *valedictorian;* witty; well-read; x-smart; yaup; *zippy;* [*Ant.* irrational]
**intend** *(v.)*: anticipate; aim; *bid;* contemplate; desire; design; determine; expect; figure on; go for; hope; have in mind; *insist on; just want to; keen on;* look forward to; Lord willing; mean; *mind; nearly;* ordain; propose; purport; purpose; plan; *quicken;* resolve; seek; schedule; strive; *shall;* try; *undertake; volition;* want to; *xel [arch.];* yearn; *zealous;*
**intense** *(adj.)*: active; arduous; ardent; big; concentrative; challenging; difficult; demanding; energetic; extreme; forceful; grueling; heavy; hairy; intensive; jading; keen; lively; moiling; nerve-racking; overtaxing; powerful; quick-moving; rigorous; strong; severe; taxing; unrelenting; vigorous; wearisome; xtry.; yary; zippy; zealous;

**intensify** *(v.)*: augment; amplify; build up; boost; climb; develop; deepen; double; expand; enhance; escalate; further; fatten; fortify; grow; heighten; increase; jack up; jump up; key up; largify; mount; make greater; magnify; *new growth; overinflate;* progress; quicken; raise; rise; redouble; step up; strengthen; spiral; turn up; triple; up; *volume;* wax; widen; *worsen; XL; yain* [arch.]; *zoom;*

**intensive** *(adj.)*: arduous; backbreaking; concentrative; difficult; exhaustive; fatiguing; grueling; hard; intense; jading; killing; laborious; moiling; not easy; onerous; powerful; quick-moving; rigorous; strenuous; thorough; unrelenting; vigorous; wearisome; xtry.; yary; zealous;

**intention** *(n.)*: aim; basis; by-purpose; cause; design; end; foundation; function; goal; high aim; intent; justification; key reason; long-range plan; meaning; motive; *notion;* object(ive); purpose; quintain; reason; sake; stimulus; target; *ultima Thule* [L.]; ulterior motive; *view;* wish; will; x; *yearning; zeal;*

**intentional** *(adj.)*: advised; aforethought; by design; conscious; calculated; deliberate; ever-conscious; *forethought; glaring; highly visible;* intended; *just plain to see;* knowing; *liking;* meant; meditated; non-accidental; on purpose; purposeful; (pre-)planned; premeditative; quite ~; *resolute;* studied; thought-out; unforced; volitional; willful; witting; willful; *xtry. planned; yearnful; zealous;* [*Ant.* inadvertent]

**interact** *(v.)*: *act towards;* behave toward; converse; deal; *execute;* fraternize; get together; hobnob; interrelate; interface; intermingle; *join;* keep up with; link; mingle; *non-solitary; overreact; party; quality time;* relate; socialize; schmooze; treat; *utter; verbalize; work; xfer; yeme;* zero in; [*Ant.* isolate]

**interaction** *(n.)*: association; behavior; contact; conversation; dealings; engagement; fraternization; goings-on; hobnobbing; interface; intercourse; interplay; *joint; keeping company;* linking; mingling; *non-solitary; overreaction; party;* quality time; relating; socialization; treatment; *uttering; verbalization;* words; *xfer; ya-ta-ta;* zero in; [*see* communion; *Ant.* isolation]

**interbreed** *(v.)*: admix; breed together; blend; cross(breed); conjoin; diversify; *entangle;* fuse; *group;* hybridize; intermix; join; kirn; link; mingle; mix; mate; marry; miscegenate; *node; overmix;* produce; *queach [arch.];* roll together; synthesize; tie; unite; *voluble;* wed; x-breed; *xenogamy;* yank together; zip together; [*Ant.* inbreed]

**intercede** *(v.)*: ask; appeal; arbitrate; beseech; conjure; desire; entreat; *foreadmonish;* go between; *humbly ask;* intervene; judge; *kneel to;* lift up one's voice for; mediate; negotiate; obsecrate; plead; *quiritation;* request; supplicate; speak on one's behalf; throw oneself at one's feet; urge; *vocalize;* wish; XQ.; yearn for; *zealously beseech;*

**intercept** *(v.)*: apprehend; *bring;* catch; draw; extract; fetch; grab; head off; interrupt; jerk; kep; *lift;* make off with; nab; obviate; pluck; *quirk;* remove; seize; snatch; trammel; uproot; uptake; *vellicate;* whisk; *xuld [arch.];* yank; zip;

**intercession** *(n.)*: arbitration; benching; considering; determination; evaluation; *figuring out;* gauging; hearing; interposition; intermediation; judgment; *knowing; listening;* mediation; negotiation; oversight; presiding; *qua [L.];* refereeing; settling; trying; umpirage; valuation; weighing; *XQ; Your Honor; zamorin;*

**intercessor** *(n.)*: arbitrator; bencher; conciliator; daysman; *emissary; facilitator;* go-between; harmonizer; intermediary; judge; *Kissinger;* liaison; mediator; negotiator; *olive branch;* peacemaker; queller; reconciler; statesman; trucemaker; umpire; *violence-ender; work on behalf; xenophile; yamen* [Chin.]; *zero hostility;*

**intercessory** *(adj.)*: arbitrational; *bringing reconciliation;* conciliatory; diplomatic; *emissary; facilitating;* going-between; harmonizing; intermedial; intermediary; judging; *Kissinger; liaison;* mediatorial; negotiating; officiating; peacemaking; quelling; reconciliatory; *statesman;* trucemaking; umpirical; *violence-ending; working on behalf; xenophilic; yamen [Chin.]; zero hostility;*

**interest** *(n.)*: amusement; appeal; attraction; bemusement; concern; captivation; desire; enthrallment; fascination; grip; hold; intrigue; infatuation; *jarring;* keen ~; liking; mesmerization; magnetism; notice; occupation; preoccupation; *quickening;* regard; stimulation; tranfixation; undispassionateness; vested ~; whet; *xtry. ~; yeah!;* zygotaxis [biol.]; [*Ant.* indifference; *see* usury]

**interest** *(v.)*: amuse; appeal; attract; bemuse; captivate; draw; excite; entice; fascinate; grip; hold one's attention; intrigue; infatuate; *jar;* keenly ~; *like;* lure; mesmerize; not bore; *occupy;* pique one's ~; preoccupy; *quest;* rivet; stimulate; take; tantalize; transfix; *undispassionateness; vivify;* whet one's ~; *x-fix; yeah!;* zygotaxis [biol.];

**interesting** *(adj.)*: appealing; absorbing; bemusing; bewitching; captivating; drawing; engaging; exciting; enthralling; fascinating; gripping; hypnotic; irresistible; intriguing; juicy; keenly ~; luring; lively; merseric; non-boring; *occupying;* piquant; provocative; *quest;* riveting; stimulating; transfixing; *uplifting; vivacious;* whetting; *x-fixing; yeah!; zestful;* [Ant. insipid]

**interfere** *(v.)*: *antagonize;* butt in; cut in; disturb; encroach; force one's way in; get involved; horn in; intermeddle; impinge; intrude; intervene; jump in; kibitz; *louse up;* meddle; mess with; monkey with; nose in; overstep; pry; *questionable; restrain;* stick one's nose in; tamper; touch; *unwanted;* violate; work against; *x; yank; zilch;*

**interior** *(n.)*: *axis;* belly; center; depths; epicenter; fesse-point; gut; heart(land); inside; *just exactly centered;* kernel; *local;* medial; middle; midst; nave; *origin;* pith; *quotidian;* recesses; secluded; secret; thick; umbilic; *viscernal;* within; *x-section;* yolk; *zone;*

**intermediary** *(adj.)*: arbitrational; *benching;* conciliatory; diplomatic; *emissary;* facilitating; going-between; harmonizing; intercessory; intermedial; judging; *Kissinger;* liaison; mediatorial; negotiating; officiating; peacemaking; quelling; reconciliatory; *statesman;* third-party; trucemaking; umpiring; *violence-ending; working on behalf;* xenophilic; *yamen* [Chin.]; *zero hostility;*

**intermediary** *(n.)*: arbiter; bencher; conciliator; diplomat; emissary for peace; facilitator; go-between; harmonizer; intermediary; intercessor; judge; *Kissinger;* legate; mediator; negotiant; *official;* peacemaker; queller; reconciler; statesman; third party; trucemaker; umpire; *vehicle; work on behalf;* xenophile; *yamen* [Chin.]; *zero hostility;*

**intermittent** *(adj.)*: at times; *blue moon;* casual; capricious; desultory; erratic; fitful; *given;* here and there; irregular; just here and there; *kooky; lacking consistency; moderately;* now-and-then; nonuniform; occasional; periodic; *quarterly;* random; recurrent; sporadic; *times;* uncommon; variable; without regularity; *x; yo-yo; zero regularity;* [Ant. incessant]

**internal** *(adj.)*: *axis; bosom;* core; domestic; deep (inside); essential; endopsychic; from within; gut; heart; interior; intrinsic; inner; inward; immanent; in(ner)most; *just inside;* kernel; *located inside;* medial; nuclear; on the inside; private; *quotidian; recesses;* spirit; soul; *therein;* underneath; viscernal; within; *xenenthesis;* yolk; *zonal;*

**international** *(adj.)*: all-inclusive; broad-reaching; cosmopolitan; *diffuse;* earth-wide; foreign; far-reaching; geopolitical; global; *human-wide;* intercontinental; *joint; known world;* large-scale; mondial; multinational; *the* nations; *over all the earth; overall;* panhuman; planetary; quaquaversal; *relating to the whole world;* supranational; trans-world; universal; *very widespread;* worldwide; *x-world; yonder; zoneless;*

**interpret** *(v.)*: annotate; *bespeak;* construe; clarify; decipher; explain; elucidate; expound; figure out; give the meaning; help one understand; infer; illuminate; judge the meaning; *know;* lay open the meaning; make out (-clear); *notate; open up;* put in English; *qualify;* render; shed light on; show; translate; take; unlock; *verbalize;* work out; *xlate;* yield; *zero in;*

**interpretation** *(n.)*: anagoge; basic ~; construing; clarification; deciphering; explanation; elucidation; *form;* gist; gloss; hermeneutic(s); intendment; *jist;* key; literal translation; meaning; *notation; opening up; oneirocritic;* paraphrase; phrasing; putting into English; *quintessence;* rendering; signification; translation; understanding; version; *wording; xenenthesis;* yielding; *zeroing in;*

**interpreter** *(n.)*: annotator; *bespeaker;* clarifier; drogman; decipherer; explainer; *fluent;* guide; glossographer; hierophant; hermeneut; illuminator; *judge; know;* language- ~; linguist; master; *notater;* oneirocritic; paraphrast; *qualified* ~; renderer; speaker; scholar; translator; truchman; *understanding; voicer;* worker; *xlator;* yield; *zero in;*

**interrupt** *(v.)*: arrest; abort; butt iu; break in; chime in; cut in; cease; disturb; disrupt; *end;* force comment; get a word in edgewise; halt; interject; intervene; interpellate; interpolate; jam; keep in check; leave off; mess up; *non-continuum;* obstruct; prevent; *quit; relent;* stop; supervene; suspend; trouble; unsettle; upset; violate; wade in; *x; yak;* zero in;
**interruption** *(n.)*: abeyance; break; cutting in; cessation; disturbance; disruption; *end;* forced comment; getting a word in edgewise; holding; interjection; intervention; interpellation; interpolation; jamming; *kill;* leaving off; messing up; *non-continuum;* obstruction; pause; *quitting; relenting;* suspension; stop; trouble; unsettling; upset; violation; wading in; *x; yaking;* zeroing in;
**intersect** *(v.)*: *across;* bridge; (criss)cross; connect; decussate; encounter; *forgather;* go over; have a meeting; interconnect; join; juncture; *knit;* link up; meet; *nexus;* overlap; pass over; *quadrivial;* run across; span; touch; transcend; unite; *venture; walk;* x.; *yede;* zip over;
**interview** *(n.)*: audience; *briefing;* conversation; conference; discussion; dialogue; exchange of words; *fraternization; gabbing;* hearing; interchange; interrogation; *jangle; key conversation; lamppost ~;* meeting; *negotiations;* oral ~; parley; phone ~; press conference; questioning; review; statement; talk; *uttering;* viva; words; *xfer; yarn;* zero in;
**intimacy** *(n.)*: affinity; bond; closeness; dearness; endearment; familiarity; geniality; *harmony;* interconnection; intercourse; joining; knowledge; love; mateship; nearness; oneness; privity; propinquity; *quixotic;* relationship; sociability; tenderness; union; *very close;* warmth; *xenia;* yoke; zeal;
**intimate** *(adj.)*: affectionate; bonded; bosom; close-knit; cozy; dear; endeared; familiar; *genial;* habituated; intime; joined; known; loving; mated; near; over-familiar; one; private; personal; *quixotic; related;* snug; tight-knit; tender; unreserved; very friendly; warm; well-acquainted; xenial; yoked; *zealous;*
**intimate** *(v.)*: allude; betoken; connote; drive at; denote; drop hint; express; *foreadvise;* give indication; hint at; imply; insinuate; indicate; *jibber; known; lead;* make out; mention; *nuance; overtone;* postulate; quietly hint; reckon; suggest; tell; *undertone; undercurrent;* vaguely express; wink; *xfer; yammer; zay;*
**intimidate** *(v.)*: *alarm;* bully; browbeat; coerce; cow; daunt; endanger; force; grind down; hector; imperil; jeopardize; keep under; lord over; menace; mau-mau; *nerve;* oppress; pressure; *quicken;* ramp; scare; threaten; unpersuade; *victimize;* walk all over; *xenophobia; yieldless;* zap;
**intolerable** *(adj.)*: agonizing; beyond the pale; *calamitous; distressing;* excruciating; exceptionable; far too much; grueling; hard; insufferable; just too much; *killing; lousy;* more than one can bear; not bearable; over-the-top; past bearing; quite ~; rough; rigorous; severe; too much; unbearable; unendurable; unacceptable; very hard; *writhing;* xtry.; yet insufferable; *zero-tolerance;*
**intoxicate** *(v.)*: addle; besot; blast; crock; dizzy; *entrance;* fuddle; get drunk; *high;* inebriate; jag; *kaylied; lit up;* make drunk; *nappy;* overcome; plaster; quaff; *reeling;* souse; stupefy; *tipsy; unsober; vineous;* woozy; *xanthoxylin;* yark; zonk;
**intoxicated** *(adj.)*: addled; blitzed; crocked; drunk(en); *entranced;* fuddled; giddy; high; inebriated; jag; kaylied; lit up; maudlin; nappy; overcome; plastered; quaffed; reeling; soused; tipsy; under the influence; *vineous;* woozy; *xanthoxylin;* yarked; zonked;
**intoxication** *(n.)*: alcoholism; befuddlement; compotation; drunkenness; *eyewater;* fuddlement; guzzling; hard drinking; inebriation; jag; *keif* [Arab]; liquor-drinking; moonshining; non-soberness; obfuscation; potation; quasi-soberness; *rum-drinking; sot;* tipsiness; *user;* vinolency; winebibbing; *xanthoxylin; yveresce* [arch.]; *zonked;*
**intrepid** *(adj.)*: adventurous; bold; brave; courageous; daring; enterprising; fearless; gallant; gutsy; heroic; indomitable; jaw-set; knightly; lion-hearted; mettlesome; nervy; over-bold; plucky; questful; resolute; stout; self-assured; *tenacious;* undaunted; unabashed; unflinching; unhesitating; venturesome; venturous; valiant; well-hearted; *xtry.;* yieldless; zealous; [*Ant.* insecure]

**intricate** *(adj.)*: abstruse; bewildering; complicated; complex; daedal; elaborate; formidable; grueling; gordian; hard; hairy; involute; jumbled; knotty; labyrinthine; mind-boggling; non-easy; obscure; overwhelming; perplexing; *question-filled;* recondite; super-hard; tough; tricky; tortuous; unsearchable; vexatious; wildering; *xenagogic; yucky; zero easiness;* [*Ant.* incomplex]
**intrigue** *(v.)*: attract; bemuse; captivate; draw; enthrall; fascinate; grip; hold one's attention; interest; *jar;* keenly interest; *like;* mesmerize; *not bore; occupy;* pique; preoccupy; *quest;* rivet; stimulate; take; transfix; *uplift; vivify;* whet; *x-fixing; yeah!; zygotaxis [biol.];*
**introduction** *(n.)*: advent; beginning; commencement; debut; establishment; exordium; founding; genesis; *hatching;* initiation; jump off; kickoff; lead-in; launching; manifestation; naissance; origin; opening; presentation; *quickening;* rising; start; take-off; unveiling; *verge;* welcoming; *xenogenesis; yede; zygogenesis;*
**introductory** *(adj.)*: advance; beginning; commencing; debuting; exordial; first; groundwork; heading; isogogic(al); initial; *jump-start; kick off;* leading; makeready; *new;* opening; preliminary; prefatory; prelusive; proemal; *quickening;* rudimental; starting; *tuitionary; undertake; venture;* welcoming; *xon; yede; zip;*
**introspection** *(n.)*: absorption; brooding; contemplativeness; deepness in thought; examination; engrossment; fancifulness; gazefulness; heart-search; inward-look; judicialness; *knowledge;* look inward; meditation; naval-gazing; occupation; pondering; probing; *questioning;* reflection; self-examination; self-analysis; soul-search; thought; *understanding;* valuation; wistfulness; *xenocratic; yearning; zealous probe;*
**introspective** *(adj.)*: absorbed; brooding; contemplative; concentrative; deep in thought; engrossed; fanciful; gazeful; heart-searching; inward-looking; judicial; *knowledge;* lost in thought; meditative; musing; museful; notional; occupied; pondering; pensive; *questioning;* reflective; self-examining; soul-searching; thoughtful; thinking; understanding; *valuating;* wistful; *xenocratic; yearnful; zetetic;*
**introvert** *(n.)*: anchoret; *by oneself;* cautious person; dervis; eremite; *fearful; gone off;* homebody; isolationist; *judicious; kithless;* loner; meek person; non-socialite; outcast; private person; *quietude;* recluse; shy person; timid one; *unsociable; votary; withdrawn; xenodocheum; yokeless; zoned;*
**introverted** *(adj.)*: apprehensive; bashful; coy; diffident; embarrassed; fearful; gentle; hesitant; insecure; jackalent; *known introvert; lily-livered;* modest; mousy; nervous; overmodest; petrified; quiet; reserved; shy; timid; timorous; unaffable; verecund; withdrawn; *xenophobic;* yarrow; *zealless;*
**intrude** *(v.)*: advance upon; bud in; barge in; creep in; disturb; encroach; force oneself upon; go into; horn in; infringe; interrupt; intermeddle; invade; jump in; kibitz; *lay claim;* meddle; move in; muscle in; nose in; overstep; obtrude; presume upon; *quad; raid;* rush in; stick one's nose in; trespass; usurp; *uninvited;* violate; worm in; *xfer; yieldless; zero consideration;*
**intrusion** *(n.)*: advancing; breach; creeping in; disturbance; encroachment; forced entry; going in; horning in; humbug; imposition; infringement; invasion; *jumping in;* kick-up; *laying claim;* meddling; moving in; muscling in; nosing in; obtrusion; penetration; *questing; raid;* sticking one's nose in; trespass; usurpation; violation; worming in; *xfer; yieldless; zero consideration;*
**intrusive** *(adj.)*: advancing; budding in; creeping in; disturbing; disruptive; encroaching; forward; *getting in one's face;* horning in; invasive; *jump in; kick-up; lay claim;* meddling; nosy; nervy; obtrusive; prying; pushy; personal; *questionable; rude;* snooping; trespassing; uninvited; unwelcome; violative; worming in; *xfer; yieldless; zero consideration;* [*Ant.* inoffensive]
**intuition** *(n.)*: awareness; *belief;* clairvoyance; discernment; *estimation;* feeling; gut feeling; hunch; insight; intuitiveness; *judgment;* knowledge; *leaning; mindfulness; notion; opinion;* perception; perceptiveness; *quick to recognize;* recognition; (sixth) sense; *thought;* understanding; vague feeling; woman's ~ [fem.]; *xtry. hunch; yeme [arch.]; zero in;*

**intuitive** *(adj.)*: automatic; astute; bright; clear-sighted; discerning; ever-wise; foresightful; gifted; *heedful;* instinctive; insightful; *judicious;* keen; longsighted; *mindful; noticing;* on the ball; perceptive; quick to understand; razor-sharp; sensitive; *tendency;* understanding; very sharp; wise; *xtry.; yepe; zip;*

**invade** *(v.)*: attack; barge in; come in; conquer; descend; encroach; foray; go into; *gain;* horn in; *harry;* intrude; impinge; *jump in; knock out;* land; move in; *non-invited;* overrun; push in; *quash;* raid; rush in; seize; storm; take over; *uninvited;* violate; warray; *xfer; yed; zap;*

**invader** *(n.)*: attacker; assaulter; belligerent; commando; conqueror; defeater; *expugner;* freebooter; *green beret;* harrier; interloper; *jumper; kemp;* looter; marauder; *non-invited;* overcomer; pillager; plunderer; quester; raider; storm trooper; subjugator; troops; *undefeated champ;* vanquisher; *winner; xfer; yieldless; zealot;*

**invalid** *(adj.)*: annulled; bad; cancelled; disapproved; erroneous; *expired;* flawed; groundless; *horrible;* improper; incorrect; illegitimate; *just not acceptable;* killed; lousy; *mistaken;* null; non-valid; *old;* objectionable; pathetic; *quad;* rejected; spurious; turned-down; unapproved; unacceptable; void; wrong; *x-out;* yucky; *zero validity;*

**invaluable** *(adj.)*: *advantageous;* beyond price; costly; dear; expensive; *fine;* greatly treasured; helpful; highly-valued; inestimable; *judged worthy; king's ransom;* loved; more precious than gold; non-replaceable; of great price; precious; priceless; *quality;* rich; *steep;* too precious for words; treasured; useful; valuable; without price; *xtry.; yieldful; zestful;* [Ant. insignificant]

**invariable** *(adj.)*: alike; balanced; constant; dull; even; fixed; *good;* homologous; inflexible; just the same; kindred; like; matching; non-differing; *ordered;* parallel; *quae est eadem* [L.]; regular; same; *trustworthy;* uniform; unchanging; unvarying; unwavering; *verbatim; word-perfect; xerographed;* yet unchanged; zero-change; [Ant. inconstant]

**invasion** *(n.)*: attack; bid; *blitzkrieg* [G.]; campaign; drive; entrance; foray; *gunnery; hit;* incursion; intrusion; *jihad* [Mos.]; *kampf* [G.]; *lashing out; march on; nonstop;* onrush; onslaught; offensive; overrunning; push; quest; raid; strike; surprise attack; seizure; takeover; usurpation; veney; *war(fare); x-fire; yed; zapping;*

**invent** *(v.)*: *assemble;* brainstorm; build; come up with; concoct; contrive; conceive of; create; discover; dream up; devise; design; develop; engineer; figure out; fabricate; formulate; get idea; hatch; ideate; imagine; innovate; *judge; know;* lead off; make up; *notion;* originate; perceive; pioneer; produce; *quantum leap;* raise up; start; think up; use brain; visualize; work out; *xenodiagnose;* yield; *zero in;*

**invention** *(n.)*: *apparatus;* better mousetrap; brainchild; breakthrough; contrivance; contraption; creation; discovery; device; development; excogitation; engineering marvel; finding; gadget; gimmick; handiwork; *hoosywhatsy;* innovation; *jump;* keen ~; *labor-saving device; leap;* machine; novelism; *object;* patented ~; *quantum leap;* resourcefulness; scientific ~; technological breakthrough; unpatented ~; *vade mecum* [L.]; *widget;* wit-craft; whirligig; x-device; *you-know-what; zeug* [G.];

**inventor** *(n.)*: artificer; builder; brain; contriver; concoctor; creator; developer; devisor; engineer; experimenter; formulator; gadgeteer; genius; hatcher; innovator; imagineer; *judicious; knower; lucubrator;* maker; minter; mastermind; novator; originator; pioneer; *quantum leap;* realizer; schemer; scientist; thinker; *un-thought-of;* visionary; *work out; xenodiagnosis; yield; zero in;*

**inventory** *(n.)*: account; *books;* count; direct count; enumeration; *findings;* goods; house ~; itemization; *journal;* kept records; listing; materials; *numbers;* official record; *posting;* quantity assessment; record-keeping; recount; record; *report;* stock; supply; tabulation; unit count; *volume;* working ~; *x-count; yield; zet* [dial.];

**invest** *(v.)*: *acquire;* back; bankroll; buy stocks; *cash;* devote; equitize; fund; finance; give; *help;* involve oneself; jointly ~; *keep;* lay out; make an ~ment; *non-identified ~or;* outlay; put money into; plow back; *quoff;* re~; spend; sink money into; *take on;* underwrite; vest; *well-supported; xfer; yafe* [arch.]; *zaitech;*

**investigate** *(v.)*: analyze; audit; *behold;* check out; dig; discover; examine; explore; find out; go over; hunt for; inspect; *jerque;* keek; look into; make a search; nose around; observe; overlook; probe; question; quest for; research; study; seek; search; scrutinize; test; *understand; uncover;* venture out; *work on; XQ;* yeme; *zero in;*

**investigation** *(n.)*: audit; *bringing to light;* check; delving; examination; exploration; finding out; go-over; *hunt;* inspection; jerquing; knowledge-gathering expedition; look into; mission; nosing around; observation; probe; questioning; research; scrutinization; search; test; *understand; uncover; venture;* witch-hunt; *work; XQ; yeme;* zetetic;

**investment** *(n.)*: acquirement; backing; chance; *development;* equitization; funding; financing; giving; *help;* involvement; joint- ~; jeopardy ~; key ~; *lending; money; non-identified investor;* outlay; *opportunity;* project; *quoff;* re~; support; *taking on;* underwriting; venture; *well-supported; xfer; yafe [arch.];* zaitech;

**investor** *(n.)*: acquirer; backer; bankroller; cash ~; capitalist; devoter; equitizer; financer; financier; *giver; helper;* investment-maker; *joint-investment;* key ~; lender; *money; non-identified ~;* outlayer; partner; *quoff;* re- ~; supporter; silent partner; stockholder; *taker;* underwriter; venture capitalist; *well-supported; xfer; yafe [arch.]; zaitech;*

**invigorate** *(v.)*: animate; boost; brisken; chirk up; disquiet; enliven; energize; freshen; give life to; hearten; innerve; jar; keel; liven; make alive; *nudge;* overjoy; perk up; quicken; refresh; revive; revitalize; rejuvenate; stir; strengthen; thrill; uplift; vitalize; vivify; warm; *xuld [arch.]; yerk;* zing up;

**invincible** *(adj.)*: attack-proof; battle-safe; *covered;* dauntless; deathless; ever-safe; firm; *garreted;* herculean; indomitable; inconquerable; impervious; irrefrangible; *jusqu'au bout [F.];* kept safe; *lasting;* more than a match; never-failing; over-protected; protected; quenchless; *rigid;* supreme; *tough;* unbeatable; unstoppable; unconquerable; very safe; well-protected; x-safe; yet to be defeated; yieldless; zap-proof; [*Ant.* indefensible]

**invisible** *(adj.)*: à perte de vue [F.]; behind-the-scenes; clear; cloaked; diaphanous; *dim; evident; faded;* glasslike; hidden; intangible; inobservable; imperceptible; *jape;* kept-out-of-view; latent; microscopic; *mysterious;* non-appearing; out-of-sight; pellucid; *quite ~; relucent;* see-through; transparent; unseen; unobservable; unperceivable; veiled; well-hidden; *x-parent; yeme [arch.];* zero perceptibility; [*Ant.* identifiable]

**invitation** *(n.)*: appeal; beseechment; call; *draw;* encouragement; entreaty; *feeler;* general ~; *humble entreaty;* invite; imploration; joint- ~; *know one is invited; letter;* lure; making request; *named;* offer; official ~; petition; *question;* request; solicitation; *tendered;* urging; *voicing;* wish; *xenia;* yearning; *zet [arch.];*

**invite** *(v.)*: ask; bid; beckon; call; desire; extend invitation; furnish invitation; give invitation; hold out; implore; *just ask; knell; loudly call;* make invitation; nempne; offer; postulate; *question;* request; solicit; summon; tender invitation; urge; volunteer; want; will; *xenia; yafe [arch.];* zealously bid;

**involve** *(v.)*: associate; attach; become a part; connect; deal; engage; engross; entangle; enwrap; embroil; *full-support;* get ~d; have a part; include; implicate; join; *knit;* link arms with; mix up in; *non-detached;* occupy; participate; plait; *qualified participation;* relate; suck into; subsume; take part in; *use; volition;* wrap up; *xfer;* yoke; zealously participate;

**inward** *(adj.)*: *axis;* beneath-the-exterior; concealed; deep down; essential; from within; gut; hidden; home-felt; heartfelt; inner; internal; inmost; *just inside;* kernel; located deep within; *middle;* non-public; *origin;* private; quiet; *recesses;* secret; *therein;* unseen; underneath; *via media;* within; *xenenthesis; yolk; zitti [It.];*

**iron** *(n.)*: ✻ *adamantine;* bog ~; cast ~; cold ~; damask-steel; *enhardened;* ferrum; *galvo;* hardened ~; *ironstone; jacutinga;* kentlage; limonite; *latten;* metal; mitis; *no galvanized ~;* ore; pig- ~; quenched steel; raw ~; steel; torsten; *ultra basic; vivianite;* wrought ~; white ~; woots; *xanthosiderite; yieldless; zinnwaldite;*

**iron** *(v.)*: apply ~; *bulldoze;* calender; do ~ing; *even out;* flatten; get wrinkles out; hot-press; *ironing; jam; knock out; level;* make smooth; mangle; *non-wrinkled; overdo;* press; *quick- ~; roller;* steam; take wrinkles out; unwrinkle; *very smooth; wrinkle-free; xtr. smooth; yield; zet;*
**ironclad** *(adj. armored)*: armored; *battle-safe;* cased; durable; encased; firm; *galvanized;* hard; iron-plated; *just sure; keen;* loricate; mailed; non-vulnerable; obdurate; panoplied; *questionless;* rigid; steel-plated; tough; *unassailable; very tough;* well-protected; *xtry.; yieldless; zinc-coated;*
**ironclad** *(adj. irrefutable)*: assured; beyond doubt; certain; definite; established; firm; guaranteed; held by all; irrefutable; incontrovertible; indisputable; just sure; keenly sure; *legitimate;* mistake-proof; non-questionable; 100% sure; positive; questionless; reliable; solid; true; unanswerable; unassailable; verified; watertight; xtry. sure; *yes;* zero doubt; [*see* intangible]
**ironic** *(adj.)*: anomalous; bizarre; curious; crazy; dry; enigmatic; funny; grim; heterogeneous; incongruous; *jarring; kink; loony; mad;* nonsensical; odd; oxymoronic; paradoxical; queer; rabelaisian; strange, *twisted;* unusual; *very odd;* wry; weird; *xtry.; yo-yo; zany;*
**irony** *(n.)*: asteism; bizarreness; curiosity; craziness; *disturbing; enigma;* freakiness; glitch; hitch; incongruity; *jarring ~; kink; looniness; madness; non-sense;* oddness; paradoxical; queer; *ridiculous thing;* strange thing; twist; *trope;* unusual thing; *very odd;* weird thing; wryness; *xtry.; yo-yo; zaniness;*
**irrational** *(adj.)*: absurd; baseless; crazy; demented; erroneous; foolish; groundless; haywire; illogical; *joking;* kooky; loony; mad; nonsensical; outlandish; preposterous; queer; rationless; ridiculous; senseless; twisted; unreasonable; void of reason; whacky; *xtry. ~; yo-yo;* zany; [*Ant.* intelligent]
**irreconcilable** *(adj.)*: arcane; beyond solution; confounding; discomfiting; estranged; firm; grim; hopeless; irresoluble; immitigable; irresolvable; just hopeless; *known impossibility;* litigant; most irresolvable; non-resolvable; out of the realm of solving; perplexing; Q.B.I. [RAF slang]; *ridiculous;* stumping; too hard; uresolvable; unreconcilable; vexing; wildering; *x;* yet unsolvable; *zero solution;*
**irrefutable** *(adj.)*: assured; beyond doubt; certain; definite; established; firm; guaranteed; held by all; indisputable; incontestable; irrefrangible; ironclad; just sure; keenly sure; *legitimate;* mistake-proof; non-questionable; 100% sure; positive; questionless; reliable; sound; true; unquestionable; undeniable; verified; watertight; xtry. sure; *yes;* zero doubt; [*Ant.* improbable]
**irregular** *(adj.)*: abnormal; bizarre; capricious; different; deviant; erratic; enigmatic; funny; gonzo; *goofy;* heterotypical; inconsistent; incongruous; jerky; kooky; *loony;* mad; malformed; mutable; nutty; non-usual; nonstandard; odd; peculiar; queer; random; strange; screwy; shifting; spotty; tortuous; unusual; uncharacteristic; uneven; varying; weird; *xenomorphic;* yawed; zany;
**irregularity** *(n.)*: abnormality; anomaly; aberration; bizarreness; craziness; difference; deviation; eccentricity; foible; glitch; heterotypicality; inconsistency; incongruity; jerkiness; kookiness; looniness; malformation; non-usualness; oddness; oddity; obliquity; peculiarity; quirk; queerness; randomness; strangeness; twist; unusualness; variation; weirdness; *xenomorph;* yaw; zaniness;
**irrelevant** *(adj.)*: alien; beside the point; completely ~; disconnected; extraneous; foreign; gratuitous; *having no relevance;* inapplicable; immaterial; ill-adapted; impertinent; *just not relevant; keyless;* lacking relevance; moot; non-relevant; nonapplicable; off-the-subject; pointless; quite ~; *ridiculous; separate;* tangential; unrelated; unimportant; *vain;* without relevance; *x-out; yonder; zero relevance;* [*Ant.* important]
**irreparable** *(adj.)*: annihilated; beyond repair; cureless; defunct; *exploded; the end;* forever gone; gone; hopeless; irretrievable; irrecoverable; irremediable; incurable; *junked;* kaput; lasting; *malfunctioning;* non-fixable; *out-of-order;* permanently broken; quashed; ruined; smashed; severe; shot; *torn;* unfixable; unsalvageable; *void;* wrecked; x'ed; *yanked; zapped;* [*Ant.* improvable]
**irreplaceable** *(adj.)*: absolutely ~; beyond replacement; cannot be replaced; distinctive; especial; exclusive; *finest; greatly treasured; hopeless;* inimitable; *just one; keen; loved;* matchless; non-replaceable; one-of-a-kind; peculiar; quite ~; *rare;* sole; *sui generis* [L.]; *treasured;* unique; very unique; without equal; *xtry.;* yet inimitable; *zero replacement;* [*Ant.* interchangeable]

**irresistible** *(adj.)*: appealing; beckoning; bewitching; charming; compelling; desirable; enthralling; fascinating; forcible; *great;* heart-alluring; intriguing; *just ~;* keen; lovely; mesmeric; non-resistible; overpowering; overwhelming; powerful; *queme;* resistless; seducing; tempting; tantalizing; uncontrollable; unresistible; *vigorous;* witching; *xenial;* yearned-for; *zestful;*
**irresponsible** *(adj.)*: abdicating; bad; careless; carefree; disregardful; devil-may-care; eliding; faithless; giddy; heedless; inattentive; impulsive; *jim-jam; kim-kam;* lax; mercurial; negligent; *omitting; passing over; quirky;* remiss; reckless; slack; thoughtless; unreliable; very neglectful; without regard; *xtry. ~;* yet irresponsible; *zero responsibility;*
**irresponsive** *(adj.)*: apathetic; anesthetized; benumbed; cold; deadened; expressionless; flinty; *glaring;* hardened; insensitive; jaded; knocked out; listless; made insensitive; not responding; numb; obtundent; pokerfaced; quiet; responseless; sluggish; stone-faced; thick-skinned; unresponsive; very dull; without response; *xylocaine;* yet ~; zero response;
**irreverence** *(n.)*: abomination; blasphemy; contempt; disrespect; effrontery; flippancy; gross disrespect; haughtiness; impertinence; impiety; juration; *kindless;* levity; mocking; nastiness; offense; presumption; profanation; quad; rudeness; sacrilege; ungodliness; vulgarity; wickedness; yieldlessness; *zero reverence;*
**irreverent** *(adj.)*: arrogant; brazen; cavalier; disregardful; *evil;* flippant; frivolous; glib; haughty; insolent; impious; joking; jaunty; *know-it-all;* light; mocking; malapert; nervy; offhand; presumptuous; *quirky;* rude; superficial; temerarious; unreverend; vain; *wicked; x-proud;* yieldless; *zero respect;*
**irrevocable** *(adj.)*: absolute; binding; changeless; determinate; enduring; fixed; *guaranteed;* hard-and-fast; irreversible; *just the same; kept;* lasting; mandatory; nonreversible; obligatory; permanent; quite ~; reverseless; set (in stone); *too late;* unrecallable; unalterable; vested; written in stone; *x-cending;* yet ~; *zero revocation;* [Ant. impermanent]
**irritable** *(adj.)*: annoying; bad-tempered; crotchety; disagreeable; eruptive; fractious; grouchy; gruff; huffy; irascible; ill-tempered; impatient; jangly; knaggy; liverish; mean; nasty; ornery; petulant; querulous; rankling; snappy; testy; touchy; umbrageous; vinegary; wranglesome; *xenophobic;* yieldless; *za-zum* [Rus.];
**irritate** *(v.)*: annoy; bother; bug; chafe; disturb; exasperate; frustrate; get on one's nerves; grate (on); harass; irk; jangle; kindle; *livid;* menace; miff; nettle; offend; peeve; pester; *queach [arch.];* rankle; rasp; set on edge; test; unnerve; vex; weary; *x-ing;* yerk; *zing;*
**irritation** *(n.)*: annoyance; botheration; crossness; displeasure; exasperation; frustration; gall; hotness; incensement; jangling; kindling; *lividness;* maddening; nettling; offense; perturbation; quick-temperament; rankling; sore spot; temper; upset; virulence; wrath; *xerothermia; yelling; zealousy* [arch.];
**island** *(n.)*: atoll; ait; *Bermuda;* cay; continent; desert ~; eyot; floating ~; ground; holm; isle; islet; *insular;* jungle ~; key; land(mass); mass; nation- ~; *ostrov* [Rus.]; pladdy; *place; queendom;* river ~; sea-holm; skerry; tropical ~; towhead; uncharted ~; volcanic ~; *weal; Xaltocan; yelld* [arch.]; *Zante;*
   **Islands**: Admiralty Is.; Britain; Bermuda; Crete; Devil's Is.; Elba.; Flores; Greenland; Hawaii; Ireland; Java; Kawai; Long Is.; Madagascar; New Zealand; Obira; Prince Edward Is.; Patmos; Qeqertarsuaq; Riker's Is.; Sumatra; Tasmania; Unimak; Victoria Is.; Wrangel; Xiamen; Yap; Zanzibar;
**isolate** *(v.)*: alienate; *apart;* be alone; banish; contain; cut off; detach; exclude; exile; enisle; *forlorn;* get alone; hold; insulate; *just by oneself;* keep apart; *lone;* make contained; *non-connected; out; part;* quarantine; restrict; remove; *remote;* separate; segregate; sequester; seclude; take out; uncouple; unyoke; *veil;* withdraw; *xuld [arch.];* yellow flag; *zero contact;* [Ant. include]
**isolation** *(n.)*: aloneness; apartness; being alone; closed doors; detachment; exclusion; forlornness; getting by oneself; hermitism; insulation; inaccessibility; *jejuneness;* kithlessness; loneness; moving apart; non-inclusion; *outside;* privacy; quarantine; reclusion; remoteness; seclusion; separation; *tranquility; unsociability; veiling;* withdrawal; *xuld [arch.]; yokelessness;* zoning; [Ant. inclusion]

**isolationist** *(adj.)*: apanthropist; *by oneself;* closed; detached; exclusionist; free spirited; *gone off;* hermitic; isolation-loving; *jubilarian; keeping to oneself;* lone-wolf; marabout; non-social; non-open; *outcast;* private *quiet-loving;* reclusive; solitairian; seclusionist; *talapoin [Bud.];* unsocial; *votary;* withdrawn; *xenodochium; yokeless; Zetetic;*

**Israel** *(n.)*: *Assur;* Beulah land; Canaan; *Dan; Ephraim; Faithful City;* glorious land; Holy Land; house of Jacob; *Isaac;* Jacob; Judea; Judah; Jewry; *the* Jewish State; kingdom of ~; land of ~ (-Abraham; promise; Canaan); *Medinat Yisrea'el* [Heb.]; nation of ~; *Olive Tree;* Palestine; Promised Land; *Queen City; Reuben;* State of ~; *the Twelve Tribes; Urusalim [Egy.]; Vardiya; west bank; xtry. nation;* Yisrael; *Yafo;* Zion;

   **Tribes of Israel**: Asher; Benjamin; Dan; Ephraim; Gad; Issachar; Judah; Levi; Manasseh; Naphtali; Reuben; Simeon; Zebulun;

**Israelite** *(adj.)*: Abrahamic; *Ben Israel* [Heb.]; *circumcised; Danite;* Eberite; *Far'Am; Gadite;* Hebrew; Israelite; Isreali(tish); Jewish; *Kohathite; Levite; Mosaic; Manassite; Naphtali;* Orthodox ~; *Parod man; Qatara man; Reubenite; rabbinical;* Semitic; *Tel Aviv; Udimite; Vardiya; Wadi 'Ara; xtry. nation;* Yiddish; *Zionist;*

**Israelite** *(n.)*: *Asherite; Benjamite;* chosen people [pl.]; *Danite;* Eberite; *rabbinical; Galilean; Gadite;* Hebrew; Israeli; Jew; *Korathite; landsman; Levite; Manassite;* native Israeli; *Naphtalite; Orthodox Jew; Pharisee; Qumram; Reubenite;* Semite; son of Abraham; *Tel Aviv; Udimite; Vardiya man; Wadi 'Ara man; Xn. Jew;* Yahudi; Yahwist; Zionite;

**issue** *(n. flow)*: afflux; blast; circulation; confluence; current; course; direction; drift; deflow; discharge; deluge; efflux; flow; flux; flood; gush; *hurl;* issuance; jet(stream); *katabatic;* leakage; movement; naid; niagara; outflow; overflow; onslaught; pouring; profluence; quell; river; rush; stream; surge; tide; torrent; undercurrent; upsurge; venting; well; water flow; wash; *xfer;* yern; *zwoosh;*

**issue** *(n. subject)*: area; basic theme; concern; case; discussion topic; emphasis; field; *gist;* heading; hobby horse; idea; *justification;* key ~; leading question; matter; main point; *notion;* overriding ~; premise; question; quodlibet; root (-real) ~; subject; sphere; topic; theme; underlying subject; *vital;* weighty matter; x-factor; *yield; zone;*

**issue** *(v. assign)*: assign; bestow; confer; distribute; equip; furnish; give; hand out; impart; *jettison;* kit; let have; lend; mete; *non-retention;* outfit; provide; *quantify;* release; supply; transfer; transmit; *unhand;* vest; *weigh;* xfer; yield; *zip;*

**issue** *(v. release)*: atomize; broadcast; cast off; discharge; emit; emanate; flow; give off; gush; hurl; impart; jet; *kest;* let off; manufacture; *move;* not retain; ooze; output; provide; pour; *quicken;* release; stream; spew; spout; transmit; uprush; vomit; went [p.t.]; xfer; yield; *zip;*

**Italian** *(adj.)*: *Arezzo; Bologna;* Cisalpine; *Doragli; Etruscan;* Friulian; Florentine; guinea [off.]; *Hermada;* Italic; *Jesolo; Kaggi; Latin; Lombardic; Mediterranean;* Neapolitan; Neo-Latin; northern ~; *Oscan; Pisa; Quadri;* Roman; Sicilian; Tuscan; *Umbrian; Venetian;* wop [off.]; xanthomelanoid; *Yvorne; Zara;*

**Italy** *(n.)*: *Arezzo; Bologna; Cosale; Dorgali; Eboli; Florence; Genoa; Hermada;* Italian homeland; *Jesolo;* kingdom of ~; *Lombardy; Milan; Magna Graecia; Naples; Olbia; Pisa; Quadri;* Republic of ~; Rome; *Sicily; Tuscany; Umbria; Venice;* western ~; *Xitta; Yvorne; Zara;*

   **Italian regions**: Abruzzo; Basilicata; Campania; Emilia-Romagna; Lombardy; Molise; Piedmont; Rome; Sicily; Tuscany; Umbria; Veneto;

**item** *(n.)*: article; *belonging;* commodity; doodad; *equipment;* feature; *goods;* hoosywatsy; *it;* jib; kickumbob; *load; matter; noun;* object; particular; piece; *quaint object; raw material; stuff;* thing; tidbit; *utility; valuable; watchamacallit;* widget; xylon; you-know-what; *Zeug [G.];*

# J

**jab** *(n.)*: assault; box; clock; dash; *elbow;* flail; *get;* hit; impinge; jolt; knock; knuckle sandwich; karate-chop; kidney-punch; kick; lam; mash; nail; open-handed blow; punch; quab; rap; sock; thump; uppercut; veney; whack; *x-sect;* yerk; zonk;

**jab** *(v.)*: assault; box; clock; dash; elbow; empierce; flail; goad; hit; impinge; jolt; knock; knuckle sandwich; karate-chop; kick; lam; mash; nail; *overhit;* punch; pierce; quab; rap; sock; thump; uppercut; veney; whack; *x-sect;* yerk; zonk;

**jacket** *(n.)*: anorak; bolero; coat; duster; *envelope;* fleece; flak ~; gilet; huke; inverness; jerkin; kirtle; longcoat; monkey ~; *Norfolk ~;* overcoat; pelisse; quilted vest; *raincoat;* sports ~; spencer; sleeve; tail coat; *ulster;* vented ~; windbreaker; XL ~; yakskin ~; zamarra;

**jaded** *(adj.)*: acerbic; bitter; cynical; distrustful; embittered; fleering; gibing; hateful; ironical; jadish; kindless; ludificatory; mistrustful; negative; opprobrious; pessimistic; *quirky;* ridiculing; suspicious; skeptical; taunting; untrusting; virulent; wary; *xuld [arch.]; yieldless;* zinging;

**jagged** *(adj.)*: asperous; barbed; crooked; dentated; erratic; *frayed; gnarly;* haggled; indented; irregular; jaggy; *kinked;* laciniate; *meandering;* notched; *oscillating;* pointy; *quadridentate;* rough; ragged; serrated; saw-toothed; scabrous; toothed; uneven; *variable; wriggling; xyresic; yaw;* zigzag; [see sharp; Ant. jagless]

**jail** *(n.)*: *arrest;* behind bars; bastille; cell; cage; clink [slang]; confinement; county ~; detention; debtor's prison; dungeon; encagement; *fetters;* federal prison; guardhouse; hold; hoosegow; incarceration; jailhouse; keep; lockup; *manacles;* maximum security; *nabbed;* oubliette; pokey; prison; penitentiary; quod; roundhouse; rattle; slammer; tolbooth; tank [slang]; under lock and key; vile durance; ward; *x; yard;* zindan [Pers.];

**jail** *(v.)*: arrest; bust; confine; cage; commit; detain; encage; *fetter;* gaol [Br.]; guard; hold; imprison; incarcerate; jug [slang]; keep; lock up; *manacle; nab; oubliette;* put away (-behind bars); *quarantine;* remand; shut up; sequester; take into custody; *under lock and key; vile durance;* ward; *x.; yard; zip away;*

**jailer** *(n.)*: armed guard; *border patrol;* captor; corrections officer; detainer; eunuch; *foot guard;* guard; gaoler [Br.]; *hyperaspist; imperial guard;* jailor; keeper; *lookout; musketeer;* night-watch; outguard; prison keeper; quarterman; *rear-guard;* sentry; turnkey; *uniformed guard; vigil;* warden; warder; *xiphos-bearer;* yeoman of the guard; zoauve; [Ant. jailbird]

**jam** *(v.)*: *apply pressure;* bear down; cram; crush; depress; *exert pressure;* force; grind; heave; impel; jam-pack; kibble; load; mash; nail; overfill; overstuff; pack; press; push; quash; ram; squeeze; stuff; tamp; upthrust; *violence;* wedge; *xuld [arch.]; yerk;* zonk;

**Japan** *(n.)*: *Asia; Bansho; Cipangu* [arch.]; *Dachi;* Empire of ~; *Fukuoka; Gipangu* [arch.]; Honshu; Imperial ~; *islands;* Japanese Empire; Kyoto; Land of the Rising Sun; *Mt. Fuji;* Nippon; *Oyashima* [Jap.]; *Orient;* people of ~; *Qinghai; Saitama;* Tokyo; *Uruku; Van Leng; Wakayama; Xiangdong;* Yamato; Zeppen [dial.];

**Japanese** *(adj.)*: Asian; Ainu; *bungo; Chiba; Dachi; Ebara; Fukuoka; Gejo;* Heian; hiragana; issei; Japonic; Jap [off.]; Japanesque; Japannish; *Kanji; Limuta; Machisi; Nipponese* [Jap.]; Nip [off.]; Oriental; *Poro; Qinghai; Ritu; Sansei;* Tokyo; *Uruju; Van Leng; Wakayama; xanthoderm;* yellow peril [WW II]; Zeke [off.]

**jar** *(n.)*: *article;* bottle; cruse; container; decanter; earthenware ~; flagon; glass ~; hipflask; *inurn;* jelly ~; kit; lachrymatory; mayonnaise ~; *neck; object;* pickle ~; *quart;* receptacle; screw-top ~; *surahi* [Ind.]; *thermos;* urn; vessel; winchester; *xeres jug;* yabba; zun;

**jar** *(v.)*: agitate; bump; *confound;* disturb; excite; faze; grate; hit; incite; jostle; jolt; knock; *lam;* move; nudge; *overagitate;* perturb; quicken; rouse; shake; trouble; upset; vex; whack; *xuld [arch.];* yerk; *zing;*

**jargon** *(n.)*: argot; blather; claptrap; double-talk; empty words; fudge; gibberish; gobbleygook; hot air; inarticulate sounds; jabber; kelter; lingo; mumbo-jumbo; nonsense; *outlandishness;* prattle; queer speech; rambling; slaver; twaddle; talk; utterance; vain talk; wishwash; xenoglossy; yabber; *zeug* [G.];

**jaunt** *(n.)*: activity; away day; break; car ride; day trip; excursion; fun day; getaway; *holiday;* itineration; journey; *kip;* leisure trip; mini-vacation; *night out;* outing; pleasure trip; quest; ride; spin; spree; trip; *unwind;* vacation; *week off; xenization; yong* [arch.]; zugunruhe;

**jealous** *(adj.)*: askant; begrudging; covetous; desirous; envious; evil-eyed; emulous; fully ~; grudging; green; horn-mad; invidious; insane with jealousy; jaded; jaundiced; keenly ~; lusting; malignant; non-trusting; overly ~; protective; piqued; *quirky;* resentful; suspicious; squint-eyed; threatened; untrusting; vain; watchful; *xtry.* ~; yearnful; *zealous* [arch.];

**jealousy** *(n.)*: avarice; begrudging; covetousness; desire; envy; enviousness; evil-eye; emulation; fancying; grudge; greenness; green-eyed monster; horn-madness; invidiousness; jealousness; *keenly covetous;* lust; malignance; *need;* over-protectiveness; pique; protectiveness; *quad;* repine; resentment; suspiciousness; spite; *troubling;* unfulfillment; vanity; want; *xry. avarice;* yearning; zelotypia;

**Jehovah** *(n.)*: Almighty; Beginning and End; Creator; Deity; Divine One; Everlasting God; Elohim; El Shaddai; Father; God; Holy One; I AM; Judge; King; LORD (of hosts); Living God; Maker; Most High; *Nature's God;* Omnipotent One; Potentate; Provider; *Quickener;* Ruler; Righteous One; Sovereign; Sustainer; Supreme Being; Thrice-Holy God; *Theos* [Gr.]; Unchanging God; *voice from heaven;* Wise God; Xuda; Yahweh; Zion's Hope; [*see* God]

**jejune** *(adj.)*: arid; boring; barren; commonplace; dull; dreary; empty; flat; generic; grassless; humdrum; insipid; *just normal; known;* lackluster; mundane; non-exciting; operose; ponderous; quotidian; repetitive; stodgy; sterilely; tedious; unexciting; vapid; wearisome; *x-out;* yawnful; zestless;

**jeopardize** *(v.)*: at risk; bare; compromise; *dare;* endanger; *foreboding;* gamble with; hazard; imperil; jeopard; *knowingly* ~; lay open; make vulnerable; *non-protected;* open to danger; put at risk; peril; *questionable;* risk; *subject to danger;* take risk; *unprotected;* venture; wager; "x"; *yeopartie* [arch.]; zero guarantee;

**jeopardy** *(n.)*: adversity; *bad;* chance; danger; endangerment; *fear; gathering clouds;* hazard; imperilment; jeopardizing; known risk; liability; menace; maleficence; non-safety; *ominous;* peril; *questionable;* risk; self-risk; threat; unsafety; virulence; venturesomeness; warning; woe; "x"; *yeopartie* [arch.]; zero safety;

**jerk** *(v.)*: abstract; bob; cant; draw; drag; extract; flounce; force; grab; heave; intercept; jig; kedge; lug; *move;* nab; *outdrag;* pull; pluck; quirk; *remove;* snatch; tug; *uncoif;* vellicate; wrench; *xuld* [arch.]; yank; yerk; zip;

**jerky** *(adj.)*: arbitrary; bouncy; capricious; deviating; erratic; fitful; *goofy;* haywire; irregular; jumpy; jerking; *kooky;* lurching; *mad;* non-smooth; *odd; pendulating;* queer; rough; shaky; twitchy; unpredictable; unsmooth; volatile; winding; *x-ing;* yanking; zigzag;

**Jerusalem** *(n.)*: al-*Quds* [Arab.]; Beth David; *the* City of David; *the* City (of God); *district; exurb;* Faithful City; *governmental seat;* Holy City; *Ir David;* Israel's capital; Jebus; Jewish capital city; *key city; location;* Mt. Zion; *national capital; the* Old City; *place;* Queen City of the Earth; *Rusalimum* [Egy.]; Salem; *Solyma* [L.]; *town;* Urusalim [Egy.]; *village; ward;* Xn. quarter; *Yerushalayim* [Heb.]; Zion;

**jest** *(v.)*: anecdotic; banter; bejape; crack; *daffy; eccentric;* fun; gag; humor; *insult;* joke; jape; josh; kid; *levity;* make fun; nifty; *outjest;* pun; quip; rag; sport; tease; *utter; vex;* wisecrack; *xuld* [arch.]; yock; *zing;*

**jester** *(n.)*: antic; bourder; court ~; clown; droller; entertainer; fool; gagster; ham; *idiot;* joker; kidder; larrikin; merry-andrew; nitwit; *oaf;* programmatist; quipster; riddler; sporter; *turkey; unserious; vexer;* wag; *xtry.;* yo-yo; zany;

**Jesus Christ** *(n.)*: Advocate; Almighty; Ancient of Days; Author and Finisher of the Faith; Alpha; Branch; Blessed Son; Bread of Life; Christ (Child); Chief Shepherd (-Cornerstone); Counselor; Consolation of Israel; Deliverer; Door; Dayspring; Day Star; Desire of Nations; Emmanuel; Everlasting Father; Faithful and True; firstborn of the dead; God the Son; God Incarnate; Good Shepherd; Great Shepherd (-Physician; -High Priest); Head; Holy Child (-One of Israel); High Priest; Heir of All Things; Immanuel; I AM; Jesus; Judge; King (of kings); Lamb (of God); Lord (of lords); Light (of the world); Life; Lily of the Valley; Lion of the Tribe of Judah; Living Water; Master; Messiah; Mighty God; Man of Sorrows; Morning Star; Nazarene; Only begotten Son; Omega; Prince of Peace; *Quickener;* Redeemer; Rock; Righteous; Rabbi; Rose of Sharon; Savior; Son of God (-man); Shepherd; Seed of the woman; Second Adam; Truth; Teacher; Unspeakable Gift; Vine; Victor; virgin-born Son of God; Word (of life; of God); Wonderful; Way; Xt.; Yeshua; *Yahweh;* Zion's Hope; [*see* God]
**jet** *(v.)*: accelerate; burst; course; dart; *erupt;* flow; fly; glide; gush; hurl; issue; *impelled; jump;* kite; light; move; *naid; outfly;* pour; quicken; rush; run; rocket; surge; shoot; stream; speed; travel; uprush; *vault;* whiz; xfer; yead; zip; zoom;
**Jew** *(n.)*: Ashkenazi; *Asherite; Benjamite;* chosen people [pl.]; *the* Circumcision [pl.]; *Danite;* Eberite; *Ephraimite; Far'Am; Galilean; Gadite;* Hebrew; Hebrewess [fem.]; Israeli(te); *Issacharite;* Jewess [fem.]; Judean; Judaist; *Korathite; landsman;* Levite; *Manassite;* native Israeli; *Naphtalite;* Orthodox ~; *Pharisee; Qumram;* Reformed ~; *Reubenite;* Semite; son of Abraham; sabra; *Simeonite; Tel Aviv man; Udimite; Vardiya man; Wadi 'Ara man; Xn. Jew;* Yahudi; Yiddish; Yahwist; Zionite; *Zebulunite;*
**jewel** *(n.)*: *amethyst; beryl;* crystal; *diamond; emerald; fire opal;* gem; *heliotrope;* intaglio; *jacinth; kimzeylite; ligure;* mesomelas; navette; *onyx;* precious stone; *pearl; quartz;* rock; *ruby;* stone; *sapphire; treasure; topaz; turquoise; uvarovite; valuable; wealth;* xtal.; yag; *zircon;* [*see* gem]
**jewelry** *(n.)*: * adornment; beads; bracelet; bangle; bauble; costume ~; charm; chain; caracoly; decoration; earring; fandangle; finery; gaud; girandole; hand ~; *intaglio;* junk ~; kickshaw; lace; *marquis;* necklace; ornament; parure; pearls; pendant; quaintry; ring; sparkler; trinkets; *uvarovite; valuables; whigmaleerie;* xtal.; YAG ring; zircon ring;
**Jewish** *(adj.)*: Abrahamic; *Ben Israel* [Heb.]; *circumcised; Danite;* Eberite; *Far'Am; Gadite;* Hebrew; Israeli(te); Judaic; Judaistic; *Kohathite;* Levite; Mosaic; *Manassite; Naphtali;* Orthodox ~; *Palmahim; Qisrah;* rabbinical; Semitic; *Tel Aviv man; Udimite; Vardiya man; Wadi 'Ara man; xtry. nation;* Yiddish; Zionist;
**Jews** *(n.)*: Abraham's seed; *Ben Israel* [Heb.]; *the* Circumcision; concision; children of Israel; chosen people; diaspora; *Danites;* Eberites; *Far'Am;* God's chosen seed; Hebrews; Israeli(te)s; Jacob's seed; *Korathites; Levites; Manassites;* nation of Israel; Orthodox ~; *Pharisees; Qumram;* Reformed ~; sons of Abraham; *the* Twelve Tribes; *Udimite; Vardiya man; Wadi 'Ara man; xtry. nation;* Yiddish; Zionists;
**jezebel** *(n.)*: Amazon; beldam; crab; devil-woman; demoness; evil woman; fishwife; grimalkin; hellcat; hussy; *incessant;* jade; *knocker;* lamia; monster; nag; ogress; princess; queen; rude woman; shrew; termagant; *unkind;* virago; witch; xanthippe; yenta; zantippe;
**jilt** *(v.)*: abandon; break off; cast off; drop; ditch; eighty-six; forsake; flat leave; give up; *hightail;* illude; jettison; kest; leave one flat; *move on; non-committed; opt out;* pitch; quit on; reject; spurn; toss out; unload; *vacate;* walk out; *xfer; yield;* zip away;
**jingle** *(n.)*: *acoustic;* bell; clanging; clink; chink; ding-a-ling; *echo; fweet!;* gong; *harsh sound; intonation;* jing; (jingle-)jangle; klink; *loud noise;* metallic sound; *noise; output;* ping; *quake;* rattle; ringing; *sound; shrill;* tinkle; ting; *utterance;* vibration; *wheetle;* x-ing; *yammer; zing;* [*see* song]
**job** *(n.)*: activity; assignment; billet; berth; business; chore; career; craft; charge; commission; calling; day ~; duty; errand; employment; field; grind [slang]; *home business;* industry; journeywork; *key position;* livelihood; métier; mission; night employment; occupation; profession; *quest;* responsibility; service; task; trade; undertaking; vocation; work; xci. *yoke; zealous duty;*

**join** *(v.)*: attach; affix; adjoin; associate; adhere; anchor; band; bind; bond; connect; conjoin; couple; combine; draw together; *engraft;* frap; fasten; fix; fuse; graft; *glue;* hinge; hitch; interlock; interlink; interconnect; inosculate; joint; jabble; knit; knot; latch; link; mount; marry; merge; meld; *nail; oxreim;* put together; *quasi-fuse;* relate; reunite; rejoin; stick; secure; splice; set to; tie; tack; unite; *vise;* weld; wed; *xenograft;* yoke; zip;

**joint** *(n.)*: abutment; bone- ~; clasp; coupling; cotyle; commissure; connection; *dovetail;* elbow ~; ferrule; flexure; geniculation; hinge; implantation; inseam; jimmer; join; junction; juncture; karabiner; knot; kotyle; ligature; *lap ~; mount;* notched ~; node; *object;* push fit; *quadricapsular;* rabbet; seam; T-joint; universal ~; vinculum; *well-greased ~; xenograft;* yoke; zeugma;

**joke** *(n.)*: anecdote; antic; banter; boff; *canard [F.];* crack; caper; drollery; escapade; farce; gag; humor; hoax; *insult;* jest; jab; jape; kidding; levity; mischief; nifty; one-liner; pun; puzzle; practical ~; paragram; quip; riddle; sport; tease; trick; *utterance; vexation;* witticism; *xuld [arch.];* yarn; yock; zinger; zanyism;

**joke** *(v.)*: *anecdotic;* banter; bejape; chaff; *canard [F.];* deceive; *eccentric;* fun; gag; humor; hoax; horse around; *insult;* jest; jape; josh; kid; laugh; make fun (-merry); needle; outjest; pun; quip; rib; sport; tease; *utter; vex;* wisecrack; *xuld [arch.];* yock; *zing;*

**jolly** *(adj.)*: amusing; bright; cheery; delightful; exuberant; fun; genial; glowing; happy; intoxicated; jovial; *kindly;* lighthearted; merry; *nice;* optimistic; pleasant; *queme;* radiant; sunny; thrilled; uplifting; vivacious; winsome; *xenial; yeah!* zestful; [*Ant.* joyless]

**jolt** *(n.)*: astonish; bump; blow; collision; cant; dash; *effect;* floor; *get;* hit; impact; jerk; jog; knock; lam; *movement;* nudge; *oomph;* push; *quab;* rock; shove; shock; thrust; upset; *vault;* whack; *xuld [arch.];* yerk; zonk;

**jot** *(n.)*: apostrophe; bit; comma; dot; etch-mark; fermi; *germ;* hair; iota; jod; *kernel;* little mark; mark(ing); notation; *object;* period; quill-stroke; *record;* stroke; tittle; *umlaut; vell;* whit; *x;* yod; *zum [dial.];*

**jot** *(v.)*: annotate; *book;* compose; draft; enter; fabulize; get down; handwrite; indicate; imprint; journalize; keep record; log; mark down; notate; *overwrite;* put down; quill; record; scribble; scrawl; scratch; take down; underwrite; *vellum;* write; *x;* yak; zay;

**journal** *(n.)*: account; annals; book; cartulary; commentary; diary; description; details; explanation; financial report; *general account;* history; information; jottings; kept record; log; muniment; notes; noctuary; official record; postea; *quantity;* record; register; story; statement; telling; *underwritten;* version; written ~; *xenodocheionology;* yellow sheet [crim. law]; *zet [dial.];*

**journey** *(n.)*: adventure; *advancement;* boat voyage; course; commute; drive; excursion; expedition; flight; foray; going; *honeymoon; hadj* [Mos.]; itineration; jaunt; knight-errantry; *look-in;* movement; migration; mission; *night voyage;* outing; overnighter; peregrination; pilgrimage; quest; ride; social visit; stay; sojourn; trip; tour; trek; travels; *undertaking;* vacation; venture; visit; voyage; whirl; wayfaring; xenization; *yatra* [Hind.]; zugunruhe; [*see* adventure]

**journey** *(v.)*: advance; betake oneself; come to; commute; draw (near); emigrate; fare; fly; go; head; itinerate; immigrate; *jet; kite;* locomote; move; migrate; nightfare; navigate; *outrun;* proceed; pass; peregrinate; *quicken;* relocate; reach; sail; sally; travel; traverse; trek; *underway;* venture; voyage; wayfare; xenize; *yede [arch.]; zip;* [*see* wander]

**joy** *(n.)*: afterglow; bliss; cheer(fulness); delight; enjoyment; elation; euphoria; felicity; gladness; glee; happiness; intoxication; joyfulness; jubilation; *keenness;* lightheartedness; laughter; merriment; mirth; *nice feeling;* over~; pleasure; *queme;* rejoicing; rapture; sunniness; satisfaction; thrill; *uplifted; vivacity;* winsomeness; *xanadu;* yeastiness; zestfulness; [*Ant.* joylessness]

**joy** *(v.)*: *affect;* buoy up; bring ~ to; cheer (up); delight; excite; enthuse; enrapture; felicitate; gladden; hearten; inthrall; inspire; jubilate; *keen;* lift up; make happy; *nice;* over~; *oblectation;* please; quicken; rejoice; *raptured;* satisfy; stir; thrill; uplift; vitalize; *well-pleased; xtry.; yeah!;* zest;

**joyful** *(adj.)*: appreciative; animated; blissful; cheerful; delighted; exuberant; elated; exultant; felicitous; glad; happy; intoxicated; joyous; jubilant; *keen;* lighthearted; merry; *nice;* overjoyed; pleased; *queme;* rejoicing; sunny; satisfied; thrilled; uplifted; *vivacious;* well-pleased; *xanadu;* yeasty; zestful; [*Ant.* joyless]

**jubilant** *(adj.)*: animated; blissful; cheerful; delighted; exuberant; enrapt; euphoric; felicitous; gay; gleeful; happy; intoxicated; joyous; *keen;* lighthearted; merry; *nice;* overjoyed; pleased; *queme;* rejoicing; radiant; sunny; satisfied; thrilled; transported; uplifted; *vivacious;* well-pleased; *xanadu;* yeasty; zestful; [*Ant.* joyless]

**jubilate** *(v.)*: applaud; bluster; beam; bless; celebrate; cheer; delight; *dance;* exult; flourish; gloat; glory; glee; gleam; *hurray; imparadised;* joy; *kill the fatted calf;* lilt; *laugh;* make merry; *nowell; ovation;* overjoyed; praise; party; *quiver;* revel; rejoice; shout; triumph; *thrill; uplift;* vaunt; whoop; *xanadu;* yell; zealous; [*see* praise]

**jubilation** *(n.)*: animation; bliss; cheer(fulness); delight; exuberance; euphoria; felicity; glee; gaity; hilarity; intoxication; joyfulness; *keenness;* levity; merriment; *niceness;* overjoy; pleasure; *queme*; rejoicing; rapture; satisfaction; seventh heaven; transport; *uplifted;* vaunting; winsomeness; *xanadu;* yeastiness; zestfulness; [*see* praise]

**Judaism** *(n.)*: Abrahamic; *belief;* conservative ~; *Cabala;* doctrine; Eastern European ~; *faith; God's chosen people;* Hebraism; Israelitism; Jewish religion; Karaism *the* Law; *menorah;* non-Atheism; orthodox ~; Pharisaism; progressive ~; *Qumram;* rabbinism; reformed ~; *sect;* Sadducceeism; Talmudism; *ule; values;* worship of Jehovah; *xenophagy;* Yahwism; *Zionism;*

**judge** *(n.)*: arbiter; arbitrator; bencher; connoisseur; circuit ~; chief justice; decider; determiner; district-judge; domesman; evaluator; *forejudge;* gauger; god; Honor; intermediary; inspector; justice; *jurat* [F.]; kadi; *lud* [Br.]; moderator; magistrate; negotiator; official; officer; presider; pretor; *qadi* [Mos.]; referee; *settler;* sentencer; trier; umpire; *vindicator;* weigher; *XQ.;* Your Honor; *zamorin;*

**judge** *(v.)*: assess; appraise; adjudge; arbitrate; *bench;* choose; criticize; consider; deem; discern; decide; determine; evaluate; elect; figure out; gage; hear; intermediate; *judicious; knowledge;* list [*arch.*]; moderate; make judgment; *negotiate;* oversee; officiate; preside; pronounce; pass judgment; *qua* [L.]; referee; resolve; rule; select; settle; sit in judgment; try; umpire; valuate; weigh; *XQ;* Your Honor; *zamorin;* [*see* criticize]

**judgment** *(n.)*: assessment; adjudication; arbitration; belief; blame; conclusion; condemnation; decision; decree; damnation; evaluation; excoriation; feeling; finding; gauging; harsh ~; *idea;* jankers [mil. slang]; judication; *knowledge; leaning; laid bare;* mediation; mind; notion; opinion; pronouncement; punishment; *question;* reckoning; resolve; ruling; reprobation; selection; sentence; thoughts; *understanding; undoing;* valuation; verdict; visitation; word; weighing; *x-out;* yard [arch.]; *zapping;* [*see* pronouncement; condemnation; wisdom]

**judgmental** *(adj.)*: *attacking;* belittling; critical; condemnatory; disapproving; disparaging; *explosive;* frowning; fault-finding; griping; hypercritical; haranguing; harsh; impugning; judging; knocking; lambasting; *mean;* negative; over-critical; peppery; pejorative; *querulous;* rough; rebukeful; scornful; traducent; unfavorable; vindictive; whingy; *xenophobic;* yauping; zoilean;

**Judgment Day** *(n.)*: Accounting Day; *blame; Bema Seat;* crack of doom; doomsday; domesday; end of the world; Final Judgment; Great White Throne; *infuriation; the* Judgment; *the King of all the earth;* Last Judgment; *majesty; non-respecter;* ordained; *punishment; quick and powerful;* Reckoning; Day; *second resurrection;* Tribunal of Reckoning; *undoing;* verdict; White Throne Judgment; *x-out; yard* [arch.]; *zapping;*

**judicial** *(n.)*: appellate; *bench;* court; *de jure* [F.]; decretory; *endorsed;* formal; forensic; *gemot; heteronomous;* institutional; jurisprudent; jural; judicatory; *key officials;* legal; lawyerly; magisterial; magistral; noetical; official; pretorial; *quasi-judicatory;* recognized; sanctioned; tribunal; *unbiased; venue; warranted; x-jurisdictional;* yard [arch.]; zet [dial.];

**judicious** *(adj.)*: astute; *bright;* commonsense; discreet; ever-wise; far-sighted; *good; heaven-gifted;* intelligent; judgmatic; *knowledgeable;* levelheaded; *museful;* noetic; oracular; prudent; *quick-witted;* rational; sensible; smart; *thinking;* understanding; *valid;* wise; *xenagogic;* yepe; *zetetic;*

**jug** *(n.)*: ale bottle; bottle; container; decanter; ewer; flagon; gallon jug; *half gallon; inurn; jeroboam; kovsh* [Rus.]; lachrymatory; milk ~; *neck;* olla; phial; *quart container;* receptacle; *soldier [slang];* thermos; urn; vessel; wineskin; *xeres bottle;* yabba; zun;

**juggle** *(v.)*: adequately handle; balance; circulate; *deal with;* entertain; firebrand ~; *get a handle on;* handle; *interchange;* jockey; keep going; *librate;* manage; *nobble;* out~; perform; *quicken;* regulate; *supervise; throw; use; venture; well-balanced; xuld [arch.]; yeme;* zero out;

**juice** *(n.)*: apple ~; beverage; blood [poet.]; *cranberry ~;* concoction; *cup;* drink; extract; fruit ~; fluid; *grape ~; hot apple cider;* infusion; *juicy;* kiwi ~; liquid; *mango ~;* nectar; orange ~; potable; *prune ~; quaff;* refresco; sap; substance; tonic; tisane; *undiluted;* ver~; watery substance; *xeres;* yaffle; zep;

**juicy** *(adj.)*: aqua; *bedashed; containing juice;* drippy; embrocated; *fruity;* gooey; hydric; imbrued; juiceful; *kept wet;* liquid; luscious; moist; nectarous; oozy; pulpy; *quenching;* ripe; succulent; thirst-quenching; *titillating;* unwithered; *vapored;* wet; watery; *xanthocarpous;* yoted; *zapote;*

**jumble** *(n.)*: assortment; blend; bind; complication; chaos; disarrangement; entanglement; fix; gnarl; hodgepodge; intertanglement; jumblement; knot; labyrinth; mishmash; node; *ordeal;* problem; pi; *puzzle;* quandary; ravel; snarl; tangle; *umbilication; voluble;* weave; xyloma; yaw; zigzag;

**jump** *(n.)*: axel; bounce; caper; capriole; curvet [horses]; *dart;* elevation; flying leap; gambol; hop; hurdle; *issue;* jounce; jeté; *kite;* leap; *movement; nimble; overleap;* pounce; pannade [horses]; *quersprung;* rise; spring; skip; saltation; take-off; upspring; vault; *whiz; xfer;* yerk; *zoom;*

**jump** *(v.)*: arise; bound; bounce; clear; cavort; curvet [horses]; *dart;* elevate; fly; gambol; hop; hurdle; *issue;* jounce; *kite;* leap; make ~; *nimble;* overleap; outleap; pounce; pannade [horses]; pole vault; *quersprung;* ramp; rise; spring; skip; take flying leap; *underleap;* vault; *whiz; xfer;* yerk; *zip over;*

**jumpy** *(adj.)*: abrupt; bouncy; capricious; disturbed; erratic; fluctuating; giddy; *haywire;* inconstant; jerky; *kaleidoscopic;* labile; moody; non-stable; out-of-control; precarious; quavering; random; shaky; *tumultuous;* unstable; variable; wavering; *x-ing;* yeasty; *ziggety;*

**juncture** *(n.)*: attachment; annexation; bond; connection; crossing; convergence; dovetail; elbow; fitment; gathering; hookup; intersection; joint; junction; knee; link(up); meeting; nexus; outlet; plug-in; *quasi-fuse;* relation; reunion; splice; tie-in; terminal; union; *vise;* weld; *xenograft;* yoke; *zipping together;* [see occasion]

**jungle** *(n.)*: arbor; bosket; bush; covert; chaparral; *dense woods;* exuberance; forest; greenwood; *holt* [poet.]; *hurst* [Br.]; *ironwood trees;* jungles; *kumquats; luxuriance;* morass; nemoral; overgrowth; *pinewood;* queach; rain forest; scrub; trees; tropical forest; underwood; undergrowth; *vegetation; vines;* woods; wildlands; *ximenia; yews; zoo;*

**junk** *(n.)*: abatis; *brush; bag;* clutter; debris; *eliminate;* filth; garbage; *heap; items; industrial waste; jetsam;* ket; litter; mullock; miscellany; *nihil* [L.]; *nuclear waste;* offscouring; offal; *pile;* quisquillous; refuse; rubbish; recyclables; scrap; sweepings; trash; unwanted items; vuilnis; waste; wastrel; *x-barrel; yucky; zero value;*

**junky** *(adj.)*: awful; base; cheap; cheesy; chintzy; dumpy; *embarrassing;* faulty; gimcrack; *horrible;* inferior; jimcrack; jerrybuilt; keg-meg; lousy; low-grade; *miserable;* non-quality; *otious;* poor; pathetic; quisquillous; rubblishy; shoddy; slapdash; substandard; trashy; tin-pot; third-rate; unprime; *vile;* wretched; *weak; x-bad; yucky;* zero-quality;

**jurisdiction** *(n.)*: area; authority; *badge;* control; dominion; empery; field; government; headship; influence; *judgeship; kaza* [Turk.]; lordship; mastery; name; oversight; purview; power; *quo warranto* [L.]; range; rule; realm; sphere; turf; umpirage; *virtue;* world; *xerifdom;* yard; *zeminary* [Ind.];

**juror** *(n.)*: adjudicator; assizor; *bearer;* councilman; dicast; *eyewitnesses; foregathering;* grand ~; hearer; head ~; impaneled individual; juryman [masc.]; jurywoman [fem.]; *key person; listener;* member of the jury; *names; opinion;* peer; *quiet listener;* recognitor; *special jury;* talesman; *understand;* venireman; *wot; xenodiagnose; yield; zero in;*

**jury** *(n.)*: adjudicators; body; board; council; deliberators; *eyewitness;* forum; grand ~; *hung ~;* inquest; impaneling; jurors; *key body; legal ~;* members of the ~; *names; organized;* petit ~; party- ~; panel; peers; *quarrel; ruling;* special ~; tribunal; *undecided;* venire; *word; xenodiagnose; yain* [arch.]; zero in;

**just** *(adj.)*: anti-discriminatory; *blameless;* correct; conscionable; *disinterested;* equitable; fair; good; honest; honorable; impartial; just-minded; keeping justice; *legitimate;* moral; non-discriminatory; objective; plain-dealing; *quality;* reasonable; righteous; square; true; unbiased; upright; unprejudiced; virtuous; *worthy; Xn.; yet to be blamed;* zero-bias;

**just** *(adv.)*: actually; barely; correctly; definitely; exactly; exclusively; *faithfully; genuinely;* hardly; indubitably; just about; *keenly;* literally; mere(ly); no one but; nobbut [dial.]; only; precisely; quite exactly; *really;* solely; sant(ily); singly; to the penny (-minute, etc.); truly; *unerringly*; verily; wholly; 'xactly [slang]; yea; 'zactly [dial.];

**justice** *(n.)*: amends; *blamelessness;* constitutionality; due process; equity; fairness; goodness; honesty; impartiality; justness; just desserts; *the king's ~;* legitimacy; morality; non-discrimination; objectivity; plain-dealing; propriety; poetic ~; *quality;* rectitude; righteousness; squareness; truth; uprightness; virtue; way of righteousness; *Xn.; yet unblamable;* zero-bias;

**justifiable** *(adj.)*: admissible; allowable; *becoming;* condonable; defensible; explainable; excusable; forgivable; *good; helpable;* indemnifiable; justified; *kosher;* legitimate; maintainable; necessary; okay; proper; quite ~; reasonable; suitable; tenable; understandable; valid; vindicable; warrantable; *xferable;* yet ~; *zero problem;*

**justification** *(n.)*: absolution; acquittal; *blamelessness established;* clearing; discharge; exuse; exoneration; freedom; *guiltlessness;* holding as valid; *indemnification;* justifying; *kithing;* legitimization; *maintaining;* non-blame; *off;* pardon; *quittance;* rationalization; substantiation; *toleration;* upholding; vindication; warrant; *x-out; yes; zero condemnation;*

**justify** *(v.)*: acquit; absolve; *back;* clear; defend; deraign; disculpate; declare righteous; explain; excuse; exculpate; exonerate; free from blame; give reasons for; hold as valid; *indemnify; justified; keep from condemnation;* legitimize; let off; make excuse for; not blame; *off;* pardon; *quit;* rationalize; substantiate; *tolerate;* uphold; vindicate; warrant; *x-out; yes; zero condemnation;* [*Ant.* judge]

**justness** *(n.)*: appropriateness; *blamelessness;* correctness; disinterestedness; equitableness; even-handedness; fairness; godliness; honor; integrity; justice; *keeping equity;* legitimacy; morality; neutrality; open-mindedness; probity; *quality;* reasonableness; straightness; trueness; uprightness; validity; *worthiness; Xn.; yet unblamable;* zero-bias;

**juvenile** *(adj.)*: adolescent; babyish; boyish [masc.]; childish; developing; early; fledgling; green; girlish [fem.]; hastive; immature; juvenescent; kiddish; little; maidenly [fem.]; new; *over-young;* puerile; *quite young;* raw; small; tender; underage; unadult; vernal; wee; *XS;* young; *zero-experience;*

**juvenility** *(n.)*: adolescence; boyhood [masc.]; childhood; development; early years; formative years; girlhood [fem.]; greenness; *hatchling;* immaturity; juniority; juvenescence; kidhood [joc.]; littleness; may; nonage; *over-young;* puberty; pubescence; *quite young; rawness;* springtime of life; tenderness; underdevelopment; verdancy; weanling years; *XS;* youth; *zero-experience;*

**juxtapose** *(v.)*: *apposition;* balance; *beside;* check; compare; contrast; differentiate; distinguish; evaluate; *find;* gage; hold comparison; *inspect;* juxtaposit; *know similarities;* lay side by side; match; note similarities; *observe;* place alongside; *quantify;* relate; set together; think on similarities; use comparison; valuate; weigh; *xenodiagnose; yeme; zero in;*

# K

**karate** *(n.)*: aikido; *black belt;* combat; *defensive training; Eastern; fighting;* green belt; *hand-to-hand combat;* ippon; judo; jujitsu; kung fu; *Lee;* martial art; ninjitsu; *orange belt; physical combat; quick moves;* ryu; self-defense; tae kwon do; unarmed combat; *vying;* wushu; *Xande; yellow belt;* zen;

**keep** *(v.)*: abide; be; continue; carry on; do; execute; follow; file; grip; have; hold (on); harbor; implement; *justify; knuckle under;* listen to; maintain; not let go; observe; perform; persist; preserve; *questionless;* retain; remain; store; save; sustain; *taintless;* uphold; *vigorously obey;* withhold; warehouse; *xlate;* yield; *zip to it;*

**keeper** *(n.)*: administrator; boss; chamberlain; director; *executive;* foreman; governor; head; intendant; jefe; keymaster; leader; manager; *night manager;* overseer; procurator; *quartermaster;* reeve; steward; trustee; undershepherd; viceroy; warden; xo; yardmaster; *zayim;*

**keepsake** *(n.)*: article; bric-a-brac; collectible; chachka; *decoration;* ephemera [pl.]; favor; *gewgaw;* heirloom; *item; jewel;* knickknack; *lucky charm;* memento; memorabilia [pl.]; novelty; nicknack; *object;* piece; *quelque-chose* [F.]; reminder; remembrance; souvenir; token; *unique;* vestige; whigmaleerie; *xylograph; yannigan;* zeug [G.];

**keg** *(n.)*: *aluminum cask;* butt; barrel; cask; drum; *earthenware pot;* firkin; *gas can;* hogshead; *incask; jug;* knag; kilderkin; *locker; milk can; noggin; oil drum;* puncheon; pipe; quinderkyn; runlet; scuttle-butt; tierce; tun; ungula; vessel; water butt; wine-cask; x-barrel; *yabba; zun;*

**kenosis** *(n.)*: abasement; *becoming flesh;* condescension; divestiture; emptying; *form; giving up;* humbling oneself; incarnation; *Jesus; kenotic;* laying aside; *making human; non-glory; obsequiousness;* putting aside; *quail;* relinquishing; stooping; *taking on flesh; unglorified; vacating;* willful emptying; *xfer;* yielding; *zeroing out;*

**kettle** *(n.)*: *article;* boiler; cauldron; *dishpan; electric fryingpan;* fleshpot; fish~; *griddle;* hotplate; iron pot; *jackshea;* kaffir pot; *lool;* meat-pot; nog; ovenware; pot; quart-pot; roaster; seething pot; teapot; tea- ~; *urn;* vessel; *wok; xeo;* yetling; *zoutch;*

**kick** *(v.)*: assault; buck; boot; *clobber;* dash; *flail;* fly- ~; *get;* hit; impact; jolt; kent [dial.]; lam; *mash;* nail; *overstrike;* punt; *place~;* quick ~; rap; swipe; strike; shin; sidefoot; thwack; *uppercut;* veney; wince; *x-sect;* yerk; zonk;

**kid** *(v.)*: *anecdotic;* banter; bejape; chaff; *canard* [F.]; deceive; *eccentric;* fun; gag; humor; hoax; *insult;* joke; jest; josh; kid around; *levity;* make fun; needle; *outjest;* pun; quip; rag; rib; sport; tease; *utter; vex;* wisecrack; *xuld* [arch.]; yock; *zing;*

**kidnap** *(v.)*: abduct; betake; capture; *detain; ensnare; fetch;* grab; hold hostage; *imprison;* jail; kid-steal; *lasso;* make off with; nobble; nab; overpower; pick up; *quash;* rustle; snatch; take; usurp; *vacate;* wrest; *xfer; yank; zip away;*

**kill** *(v.)*: assassinate; annihilate; bump off [slang]; blow away; behead; butcher; cut off; crucify; do one in; dispatch; dispose of; destroy; end (one's life); eliminate; euthanize; execute; extirpate; exterminate; expunge; finish off; gun down; pith; *hang;* immolate; *jab;* knock off [slang]; *lapidate;* murder; massacre; *nip;* obliterate; put to death; purge; quash; run through; rub out; slay; smite; slaughter; terminate; take one's life; *unseat; vaticide;* waste; wipe out; x-out; *yataghan;* zap; [see conquer]
  **Types of killing**: amicide [friend]; bovicide [cow]; capital punishment; ceticide [whale]; episcicide [bishop]; filicide [own child]; fratricide [brother]; genocide [race]; homicide [person]; infanticide [baby]; legicide [law]; manslaughter; matricide [mother]; neonaticide [newborn]; omnicide [everything]; parricide [relative]; regicide [king]; self-defense; sororicide [sister]; suicide [self]; tyrannicide [tyrant]; uxoricide [wife]; vaticide [prophet]; weedicide [weeds]; xenocide [alien];

**killer** *(n.)*: axe-man; assassin; annihilator; butcher; *criminal;* destroyer; executioner; extirpator; eradicator; expunger; *finisher;* gunman; hackster; hit man; hired gun; *impenitent murderer; jabber;* knifer; knife-man; *lyncher;* manslayer; mankiller; murderer; massacrer; ninja; *obliterator;* predator; quencher; ripper; slayer; serial ~; slaughterer; terminator; *undoer;* victimizer; vitiator; waster; widow-maker; *x-er; yegg;* zapper;

**kiln** *(n.)*: athanor; brick- ~; calcar; *device; electric oven;* furnace; grate; heater; incinerator; *jet;* kettle-furnace; *limekiln;* muffle; *nut coal;* oven; oast; potbelly stove; Quebec heater; range; stove(top); tunnel-kiln; tandoor; uniform-heat ~; *vulcan;* wood stove; *xylophyrography; yellow-hot fire; zap;*

**kin** *(n.)*: *adopted family;* brethren; blood relations; clan; *domestic;* extended family; family; gens; household; *in-laws; jus soli [L.];* kinfolk; loved ones; ménage; near kinsman; *offspring;* people; *quarter;* relations; sept [Ire.]; tribe; *umunna* [Afr.]; *vein; whanau* [N.Z.]; *x-linked; yoni [Skr.]; zadruga* [Slav.];

**kind** *(adj.)*: affable; benign; benevolent; big-hearted; considerate; caring; compassionate; charitable; deferential; *endeared;* friendly; forgiving; gentle; gracious; generous; good; humane; hospitable; *indulgent; jovial;* kindly; kindhearted; loving; large-hearted; merciful; nice; neighborly; openhearted; pleasing; *quick to help; regardful;* sympathetic; sweet; softhearted; thoughtful; tender(hearted); unrevengeful; unselfish; very kind; warm; xenophilic; *yielding;* zealous of good works [Tit. 2:4]; [*Ant.* kindless]

**kind** *(n.)*: *analysis;* breed; brand; branch; category; cast(e); class(ification); designation; denomination; estate; feather; family; form; fashion; group; genre; genus; heading; ilk; *jack; kingdom;* lot; label; make; manner; mold; model; nature; order; phylum; persuasion; *quarter;* rank; rating; subgroup; subclass; suborder; sort; stripe; strain; style; species; superclass; superorder; type; tribe; unit; variety; variation; vein; *way; x-class;* year-class; zoological classification;

**kindle** *(v.)*: alight; awaken; burn; combust; deflagrate; encourage; excite; en~; enflame; fire up; get going; *heat;* incite; ignite; inflame; *jeopardize;* knock; light (up); make fire; *nightfire;* overburn; provoke; *pyre;* quicken; rouse; re~; raze; stir-up; spark; set on fire; tinder; torch; ustion; vivify; *waste; xylophyrography; yearn; zap;* [*see* flame; stir]

**kindling** *(n.)*: *acacia;* brush; branches; brushwood; billet; cordwood; dry sticks; *elm branches;* firebrand; firewood; firebavin; *gopherwood;* hickory branches; ironwood; jackstraw; kindle-wood; kippers; lighterd; lightwood; *material;* nicky; *osiers;* pollenger; *quassia; runners;* sticks; stovewood; twigs; tinder; timber; underbrush; very; wood; *xylon;* yule log; zamia brush;

**kindness** *(n.)*: amiableness; benevolence; civility; consideration; compassion; deference; *endeared;* favor; friendliness; graciousness; goodwill; humaneness; *indulgence; joviality;* kindheartedness; loving-kindness; leniency; mercifulness; niceness; obligingness; pity; propitiousness; *quick to give;* regard; sympathy; sweetness; thoughtfulness; unselfishness; *virtuousness;* warmth; xenophilia; yearning; *zealousness;*

**kindred** *(n.)*: ancestry; blood-relations; clan; descent; extraction; family; *group;* genetics; generation; household; heredity; *inheritance; jus soli [L.];* kin; line; *mores;* nationality; origin; people; parentage; *quarter;* relations; stock; tribe; *ubiety; very closely related; whanau* [N.Z.]; *x-link; yoni* [Skr.]; *zadruga* [Slav.];

**king** *(n.)*: autocrat; authority; *boss;* chief; Caesar [Rom.]; czar [Rus.]; dynast; emperor; *figurehead; governor;* highness; interrex; jemander [Ind.]; kaiser [G.]; lord; monarch; majesty; *noble;* oligarch; overlord; potentate; *prince;* queen [fem.]; ruler; regent; *Royal Highness;* sovereign; *sire;* toparch; *tsar; tyrant; ultimate authority;* vice-regent; warden; xabandar; xenarch; *Yang Dipertuan* [Malaysia]; zamorin [Hind.];

**kingdom** *(n.)*: autocracy; *buffer state;* country; *duchy;* domain; dominion; empire; *feudal territory; grand duchy;* governance; *homeland; imperial;* jurisdiction; *jarldom;* kingship; *kaiserdom;* land; monarchy; nation; *oligarchy;* power; principality; queendom [fem.]; realm; scepter; sovereignty; territory; throne; *united kingdom; viscounty; world power;* xerifdom; *yard; zenocracy;*

**kingly** *(adj.)*: aristocratic; *authoritative;* blueblooded; commanding; dignified; excellent; fine; grand; high-born; imperial; impressive; *judicious;* kinglike; lordly; lofty; majestic; monarchal; noble; *ostentatious;* princely; pompous; queenly [fem.]; royal; regal; stately; sovereign; *tsarish;* uncommon; valiant; well-born; xtry.; yorkist; zarish [arch.];

**kink** *(n.)*: angle; bend; crimp; difficulty; entanglement; frizz; flaw; gnarl; glitch; hitch; impediment; jag; knot; loop; mistake; *notch; nuisance;* obstacle; problem; quirk; ravel; snarl; snag; twist; tangle; *undoing; volt; vexation;* wind; *x-ing; yaw;* zigzag;

**kink** *(v.)*: angle; bend; crook; *ding; entwist;* fold; gnarl; hook; *intwist;* jag; knot; *loop; mess up; nonlinear;* offset; *problem;* quirk; ravel; snarl; twist; *underwind;* volt; whirl; *x-ing; yaw;* zigzag;

**kinship** *(n.)*: affinity; brotherhood; commonality; closeness; devotion; empathy; friendship; *goodwill; harmony;* intimacy; joining; knot; loyalty; like-mindedness; mateship; nearness; oneness; partnership; *quite close;* relationship; singleness of heart; trust; understanding; *value;* warmth; *xenia; yoke;* zeal;

**kiss** *(n.)*: *affection;* buss; canoodle; caress; deosculation; embrace; French ~; *gripping; hongi* [Maori]; holy ~; *interlock; juicy ~; kissing;* lovebite; *making out; nuzzling;* osculation; peck; pass; pax; *quaint ~;* romantic ~; smack; smooch; *touch lips; uninvited ~; voluptuous;* wrap; X; *yearning; zip;*

**kiss** *(v.)*: *affection;* bekiss; bill and coo; canoodle; contact; deosculate; embrace; French ~; *grip; hongi* [Maori]; *interlock; juicy ~; kissable;* lip; *love;* make out; neck; *nuzzle;* osculate; pucker; peck; *quaint kiss; rub lips;* smack; smooch; touch lips; *upstroke; voluptuous;* wrap; X; yearn; *zip;*

**kit** *(n.)*: accouterments; belongings; bag; commodities; chattels; *duffel bag;* equipment; *feedstock;* gear; habiliments; items; junk; *kickumbob; load;* material; matter; necessities; objects; outfit; paraphernalia; pack; *quantity;* rig; set; supplies; stuff; things; tackle; utensils; *valuables; wanigan; xenenthesis; yannigan; zeug* [G.];

**kitchen** *(n.)*: automat; beanery; buffet; cookery; cafeteria; dining hall; eat-in; eatery; food prep area; grill; galley [naut.]; hash house; inn; *joint;* kitchenette; lunchroom; mess hall; *nightclub; oriental restaurant; porterhouse;* quick-lunch counter; restaurant; steakhouse; snack bar; scullery; tearoom; *urban café; vent* [arch.]; *Western steakhouse;* xenodocheum; *Yokohama steakhouse; zonal chain restaurant;*

**knack** *(n.)*: ability; *bent;* capability; deftness; expertise; flair; gift; habilitation; *instinct; judgment;* know-how; legerdemain; means; mastery; natural ability; *old-hand;* proficiency; qualification; resources; readiness; skill; savvy; technique; talent; touch; usefulness; virtuosity; wherewithal; *xenium; yare;* zeal;

**knapsack** *(n.)*: *alligator bag;* bag; backpack; carry-all; daypack; *equipment;* fanny pack; gear bag; haversack; *item;* journey-sack; kitbag; *luggage;* matilda [Aus.]; molle [mil.]; musette; nunny bag [Can.]; *overnight case;* pack(sack); *quiver;* rucksack; sack; shoulder bag; tote bag; utility pack; valise; walking sack; x-bag; yannigan bag [slang]; zipper-bag;

**knead** *(v.)*: *action;* bear down on; *clutch; compress;* double over; enfold; fold; *grasp;* handle; impaste; *jam; kirtle;* lap over; massage; manipulate; malaxate; *non-rolled; overfold;* pug; push; press; play; *quill;* rework; squeeze; *tamp;* unkink; *volt;* work; *xuld* [arch.]; *yank; zonk;*

**kneel** *(v.)*: *acquiesce;* bend (the knee); crouch; dip; enfold; flex; fold; genuflect; hunker; incline; *jump down;* knee-bend; *laud; magnify;* nod; *overbend; obeisance; praise;* quat; *refold;* stoop; *turn down; uncinate; venerate;* worship; *x-bend; yield;* zip down; [see worship; kowtow]

**knell** *(n.)*: *announcement;* bell; chime; clang; ding; dong; *echo; fweet!;* gong; *hum;* intonation; jangle; knelling; loud ~; metallic sound; *noise; ominous sign;* peal; *quake;* ring(ing); sound; toll; *uproar;* vibrating; *wail; x-ing; yammer; zoing;*

**knife** *(n.)*: ∗ army ~; blade; bowie ~; carving ~; cutter; cutlery [pl.]; dirk; dagger; Exacto® ~; fleam; golok [Malay]; hunting ~; *instrument;* jackknife; kris; *landsknecht* [G.]; *machete; navaja; Ottoman ~;* pen~; pocket~; paring ~; qama; *razor ~;* stiletto; switchblade; shiv; steak~; shop~; scalpel; table ~; *utensil;* utility ~; *Valencia ~;* wood~; *xyster;* yataghan; *zafar;*

**knight** *(n.)*: *adventurer;* banneret; black ~; champion; crusader; cavalier; defender; *esquire;* fighter; gallant; hero; housecarl; *infantryman;* jouster; knight-errant; lancer; man-at-arms; nobleman; *officer;* paladin; *quirré;* renown; swordsman; *sir;* templar; *undaunted;* vavasor; warrior; white ~; *xia* [Chin.]; *youxia* [Chin.]; *zoauve;*
   **Medieval orders of knights:** Aubrac; Calatrava; Dobrzyn; Hospitallers; Livonian; Mountjoy; Spanish; Templars; Teutonic;
**knit** *(v.)*: attach; bind; connect; combine; *darn;* entwine; fasten; fix; *graft;* hitch; interlock; interweave; join; knot; link; lace; mend; merge; net; *oxreim;* purl; put together; *quill;* renter; stick; secure; splice; set to; tie; twill; unite; *vise;* weave; *xenograft;* yoke; yarn over; *zip;*
**knob** *(n. grip)*: ansa; boss; crop; control; drawer pull; door~; dial; *extuberance;* furniture ~; grip; handle; handgrip; iron ~; *jut;* kilp; *lever; maniglions;* neap; opener; pommel; quick-grip; rounce; stock; *tiller;* umbo; *verge;* winch; *x-piece; yank; zeuglodon;*
**knock** *(n.)*: assault; blow; cuff; clobber; clout; clock; crack; daud; dash; deck; *efface;* flailing; *get;* hit; impact; jolt; kick; lick; lam; *mauling;* nob; *open-handed blow;* punch; *quash;* rap; smack; sock; slam; shot; smite; strike; thump; thwack; uppercut; veney; whack; wallop; *x-sect;* yedder; zonk;
**knock** *(v.)*: assault; bump; beat; bash; clobber; conk; drub; deck; *elbow;* flail; *get;* hit; impact; jab; jar; jolt; jow; *kidney-punch;* klunk; lam; *lash;* maul; mash; nubble; nail; *overhit; overstrike;* pound; quab; rap; strike; slam; thump; uppercut; veney; whack; *x-sect;* yedder; zonk;
**knot** *(n.)*: * anchor ~; bow ~; burl; clinch; double hitch; entanglement; fisherman's ~; granny ~; half hitch; Indian ~; jumble; *kink;* loop ~; mesh ~; node; overhand ~; prusik; *quandary;* reef ~; rosette; square ~; slip ~; tie; *umbilication; voluble;* wall ~; Windsor ~; *xyloma;* yoke; *zigzag;*
**know** *(v.)*: apprehend; become aware of; comprehend; discern; experience; fathom; grasp; have in one's heart (-brain); identify; *judge;* ken; *learn;* make acquaintance; naw [dial.]; overheard; perceive; *questionless;* realize; recognize; see; *think;* understand; *value;* wis(t); wot; wit; *xenodiagnose; yeme;* zero in;
**know-how** *(n.)*: ability; bravura; capability; deftness; experience; expertise; familiarity; gift; habilitation; ingeniousness; *judgment;* knack; long suit; masterfulness; *natural ability; old-hand;* proficiency; qualification; readiness; skill; training; usefulness; virtuosity; wherewithal; *xenium;* years of experience; zest;
**knowingly** *(adv.)*: advisedly; *aware;* by design; consciously; deliberately; ever-consciously; foxily; *glaringly; highly visible;* intentionally; judiciously; *knowing; liking;* meditatedly; non-accidentally; on purpose; purposely; purposively; quite intentionally; rationally; scienter; thoughtfully; understandingly; volitionally; wittingly; *xtry. planned; yearnfully; zealously;*
**knowledge** *(n.)*: awareness; acquaintance; book-learning; consciousness; cognizance; cognition; comprehension; data; education; erudition; facts; findings; grasp; higher learning; information; insight; *just the facts;* knowing; ken; learning; lore; light; mental grasp; notice; *over-qualification;* perception; *qualification;* recognition; schooling; teaching; truth; understanding; *veracity;* word; wisdom; *xenagogy; years of experience; zero doubt;*
**knowledgeable** *(adj.)*: abreast; academic; bright; clued-up [Br.]; discerning; educated; erudite; familiar; grounded; highbrow; informed; in the know; judicious; knowing; learned; mindful; *nimble-witted; on the ball;* prescient; percipient; quick-witted; *re-educated;* smart; thinking; up to snuff; ultra-smart; versed; well-read; well-informed; *x-smart;* yaup; *zippy;*
**kosher** *(adj.)*: approved; blessed; clean; decent; endorsed; fitting; good; halal; in keeping; *Jewish;* kashrut; lawful; meet; non-objectionable; okay; permitted; *qualified;* rabbi-blessed; right; suitable; *true;* undefiled; valid; within the law; *xtr. careful;* yes; *zero problem;*
**kowtow** *(v.)*: acquiesce; bow; comply; do; *execute;* follow; give way; heed; *implement; jump (to it);* knuckle under; keel in; listen to; *mind;* not resist; obey; pander to; *questionless;* resign; succumb; truckle; toady; *undertake; very low;* weaken; *xlate;* yield; zip to it;

# L

**label** *(n.)*: adhesive ~; appellation; brand ~; characterization; classification; decal; designation; epithet; foil seal; gummed ~; handle; identifier; *jurisdiction; known by;* little sign; marker; name tag; *object;* peel-off; price tag; *quality seal;* resin-backed ~; sticker; tag; ticket; *unit marker; viscous; wafer; xfer picture; yellow tag; zet [dial.];* [see name]

**label** *(v.)*: address; brand; call; dub; entitle; forename; give title to; hail as; identify; *jurisdiction; known as;* let one be named; mark; name; nickname; ordain; place ~; *quiring;* refer to; surname; saddle with [slang]; style; term; tag; *use; vocable; word; xenonym;* yclept; *zoon;*

**labor** *(n. childbirth)*: accouchement; bearing; birthing; bringing forth; childbirth; delivery; *entrance; engendering; founding;* generation; giving birth; hatching; having a baby; *inception; incubation; jump off; kickoff;* live birth; mothering; nativity; *origination;* parturition; *quickening; rise; start;* travail; ushering in; *visitation; woe; xenogenesis;* yielding; *zygogenesis;*

**labor** *(n. work)*: action; burden; craft; drudgery; effort; field work; grunt work; hard work; handicraft; industry; job; *kitchen work;* lapwork; manual ~; moil; night-work; occupation; output; performance; production; *quality work;* rigor; service; serving; slopwork; toil; *undertaking;* vocation; work; *xtry. effort;* yardwork; *zealous ~;* [Ant. leisure]

**labor** *(v.)*: act; busy oneself; craft; carry on activity; do; drudge; effect; exert; function; grind; hustle; *industry; job;* keep at; labour; moil; *night-work;* operate; *overwork;* produce; plod; ply; put out; plug away; *quietly work; run; rigor;* slave; strive; serve; slog; *sweat;* toil; *use; volunteer;* work; *xfer; yardwork;* zealously ~;

**laboratory** *(n.)*: *area; building;* chemistry lab; developmental ~; experimental room; facility; *garage; house;* institution; *jurisdiction; kamienica;* lab; medical lab; *nook; office;* observatory; private lab; *quadriplex;* research lab; shop; test lab; underground ~; *vial;* workshop; x-ray lab; *yardhouse; zeta;*

**laborer** *(n.)*: associate; artificer; breadwinner; craftsman; co-worker; doer; drone [derog.]; day ~; employee; fellow ~; gofer [slang]; grunt [derog.]; hireling; hand; industrial worker; jobholder; jack; *kitchen worker;* laboring man; manual worker; moiler; navvy [Br.]; operator; performer; producer; *qualified ~;* roustabout; servant; staff member; toiler; underling; vassal; worker; workman; *xylographer;* yeoman; *zaikai [Jap.];* [Ant. loafer]

**laborious** *(adj.)*: arduous; backbreaking; challenging; difficult; demanding; exhausting; fatiguing; grueling; hard; intense; jading; killing; labor-intensive; moiling; not easy; onerous; operose; painstaking; *quite hard;* rigorous; strenuous; toilsome; unrelenting; *vigorous;* wearisome; *x-heavy; yare;* zealous;

**labyrinth** *(n.)*: anarchy; brainteaser; conundrum; convolution; *corn maze; difficulty;* entanglement; *fix; chaos;* Gordian knot; hodgepodge; intricacy; jumble; knot; *labyrinthine;* maze; network; *obstacle;* puzzle; *quonundrum [arch.]; ravel;* skein; tangle; unsolved puzzle; *vexation;* warren; *winding path; xyloma; yaw; zigzag;*

**labyrinthine** *(adj.)*: abstruse; bewildering; byzantine; convoluted; difficult; entangled; elaborate; *frustrating;* gnarled; hard; intricate; intertwined; insoluble; jumbled; knotty; labyrinthian; mazelike; mazy; nodated; overcomplicated; puzzling; perplexing; *questionable;* rivose; roundabout; snarled; scrambled; tangled; unsolvable; vexatious; wildering; *xenagogic; yucky;* zigzagged;

**lace** *(n.)*: * adornment; bobbin ~; Cluny ~; *decoration;* eyelet; frill; guipure; galloon; gold~; Honiton ~; interlacement; jabot; knit- ~; lacework; mechlin; needlepoint ~; ornamental ~; point ~; quilling; ruffle; sewing ~; tatting; trim; *underlacing;* Valenciennes; weave; *x-lace;* yarn- ~; *zizz;*

**lace** *(v.)*: adulterate; bastardize; contaminate; drug; doctor; dope; empoison; foul (up); *grim;* hocus [slang]; impregnate; *jade; kill;* louse up; mingle; make tainted; *non-pure; over-pollute;* pollute; *quade [arch.];* riddle; spike; tinge; taint; *undermine; vitiate; warp;* x-lace; *yucky; zap;* [see tie]

**lacerate** *(v.)*: *afflict;* break; cut; dilacerate; *damage; exscind; fissure;* gash; hack; incise; jag; kerf; laniate; lance; main; *nick; open;* puncture; *quail [arch.];* rend; rip; serrate; slash; tear; *uptear; vell;* wound; *x-sect;* yerk; zip;

**lack** *(n.)*: absence; bareness; coming up short; deficiency; dearth; destitution; emptiness; falling short; famine; grievous ~; great need; *hardly enough;* insufficiency; inadequacy; jejuneness; *just not enough; keen deprivation;* low supply; meagerness; need; not enough; *out;* paucity; privation; *quandary;* reduction; rareness; shortage; scarcity; short supply; scantiness; *too little;* unavailability; ullage; void; want; *xtry. deficiency; yearning; zero sufficiency;*

**ladder** *(n.)*: * assault ~; *aluminum ~;* bridge ~; cat ~; dissipative ~; extension ~; étrier; fixed ~; folding ~; fire escape; *gyn;* hook ~; iron ~; jack ~; *kit; lightweight ~;* metal ~; notch- ~; orchard ~; platform steps; quick-access ~; rope ~; *rungs;* rung ~; steps; step~; telescopic ~; utility ~; vertical rising ~; wooden ~; x- ~; yard ~; *zeug [G.];*

**laden** *(adj.)*: *amassed;* burdened; borne; crammed; *delivery;* encumbered; fraught; filled; full; *gotten;* heavy- ~; *imbued;* jam-packed; *kibbled;* loaded (down); maxed out; *non-empty;* overloaded; overburdened; packed; piled high; quashed full; *rammed;* stuffed; taxed; *tonnage;* under a burden; *vexed;* well-packed; weighed down; *xuld [arch.]; yieldless; zero room;*

**lady** *(n.)*: *adult; amoret;* belle; beauty; chick [off.]; citess; daughter; dame [off.]; *empress;* female; gal; girl; gentlewoman; *her; individual;* jane [slang]; khanum [Pers.]; lass; miss(us); madam; nymph [poet.]; noblewoman; old ~; petticoat; *quaedam* [arch.]; *queen; rib;* señora [Sp.]; *termagant; temptress; unmanly; vrouw* [Du.]; woman; *x-chromosome; young lady;* zaftig;

**ladylike** *(adj.)*: appropriate; becoming; courteous; cultured; decorous; ever-womanly; feminine; gracious; genteel; gentlewomanly; highbred; *inobtrusive; jeune fille [F.];* kind; lovely; modest; mannerly; noble; *orderly;* prim; proper; *quiet;* refined; *suitable; sweet; tender;* urbane; *virtuous;* womanlike; well-mannered (-bred); *x-chromosome; yokemate; zierlich [G.];* [*Ant.* lewd]

**lair** *(n.)*: alcove; burrow; berm; cave; den; *enclosure;* fox hole; grotto; hole; hollow; home; inhabitance; jaw-hole; *krater;* lodge; maw; nest; niche; *opening; place; quarters;* retreat; shelter; treasure; *under;* vault; warren; *xystus;* yawn; *zanja;*

**laity** *(n.)*: assembly; brethren; churchgoers; *the* devout; ecclesiastical body; flock; general public; *humanity; ingatherer; just regular;* kirsten [dial.]; laymen; members; non-clergy; oblates; people; parish; *quorum; regulars; saved;* temporalty; unordained; voraries; *worshipers; Xn.; Yahwist;* Zionist;

**lake** *(n.)*: *arm;* body (of water); carr; deep; *drink;* estuary; fishpond; gullet; hole; horse pond; inland sea; *jheel* [Ind.]; kettle-hole; lough; loch [Scot.]; mere; nyanza; ostiary; pool; pond; *quai;* reservoir; sea; tarn; *underground pool;* volcanic ~; water (hole); *xyrisic; yeo; Zee [G.];* [*see* sea; river, bay; swamp]

**lamb** *(n.)*: *animal;* black ~; cosset; dall sheep; ewe; fauna; gigot; house~; Indian ~; jumbuck; karakul; lambkin; mufflon; New Zealand ~; *ovine;* persian ~; *paschal ~; quadruped;* ram [masc.]; sheep; teg; urial; *varmint;* woolly ~; *x-breed;* yeanling; *zoic;*

**lame** *(adj.)*: *ailing;* becrippled; *broken;* crippled; disabled; debilitated; enfeebled; feeble; gimp; game; halt; handicapped; immobilized; incapacitated; jake-legged; *kaput;* limping; *maimed;* non-mobile; *overweak;* paralyzed; palsied; *quadriplegic; reeling;* spavined; trammeled; useless; *vulnerable;* weak; *x-out; yawing; zeroized;*

**lameness** *(n.)*: *ailing;* becrippling; crippling; disability; enfeeblement; feebleness; *gimp;* handicap; *hobbling;* immobility; jake-leggedness; *kaput;* limping; maiming; non-mobility; *over-weakness;* paralysis; palsy; quadriplegia; *reeling;* spavin; *tottering; unable; vulnerability;* weakness; *x-ing out; yielding; zeroizing;*

**lament** *(v.)*: anguish; bemoan; bewail; cry; despair; elegize; *fret;* feel sad; grieve; gnash teeth; howl; *inconsolable; judder;* keen; lift up one's voice; mourn; noise; outcry; pine; quail; regret; repine; sigh; sorrow; *tearful;* ululate; *vociferate;* weep; wail; *xtr. sad;* yowl; *zing;* [*Ant.* laugh]

**lamentation** *(n.)*: attrition; bitter cry; bemoaning; cry; distress; despair; exclamation; feeling sorrow; grief; gnashing of teeth; howling; inconsolableness; jeremiad; keening; lachrimation; lament; mourning; noise; outcry; plaint; quiritation; remorse; sorrow; tears; unhappiness; *vapors;* wailing; *x-ing;* yowling; *zing;* [*Ant.* laughing]

**lamp** *(n.)*: *aura;* bulb; candle(stick); droplight; Davy ~; electric ~; fixture; flashlight; floodlight; *glow;* headlight; head~; halogen light; incandescent ~; jacklight; klieg light; key light; light; lantern; maglight®; night- ~; oil ~; penlight; quartz ~; *radiance;* sun~; shoplight; table ~; thermo ~; torchier; uplight; *visual;* worklight; xenon ~; *yellow light;* zircon light;

**land** *(n.)*: area; acreage; *back~;* country; dry ~; district; domain; earth; field; ground(s); holdings; *imperial district;* jurisdiction; kench; lot; mass; manor; nome; on~; property; province; place; plot; quadrant; region; realty; real estate; soil; terrain; tract; terra firma; ubiety; *viceroyalty; ward; x-sector;* yard; zone; [see country]

**land** *(v.)*: alight; arrive; belly- ~; come down; crash- ~; disembark; *end up;* fly in to; go ashore; harbor; *incoming; journey; kite;* light; make a ~ing; *nestle; over to;* perch; *quat;* rest; settle; set down; touch down; *undershoot;* verge on; *wing; xfer; yead; zero in;* [*Ant.* launch]

**landlord** *(n.)*: apartment owner; *administrator;* building superintendent; collector; *debt collector;* estate owner; freeholder; *gentleman;* house owner; hotelier; *innkeeper;* jamindar [Ind.]; *keeper;* lessor; landlady [fem.]; landholder; manager; *neighbor;* owner; property-owner; *questman;* renter; rentier; rent-collector; slumlord; sublessor; titleholder; *usurer; vested;* woman; *xaraf; yardboss;* zamindar [Ind.];

**landmark** *(n.)*: abuttal; *ancient ~;* boundary mark; cairn; designation; earthwork; field boundary; guidepost; hoarstone; indicator; *jurisdiction; kept limit;* (ley) line; marker; *national ~;* obelisk; *outskirts;* property line marker; *quadra;* rock wall; stone marker; threshold marker; *urban; verge;* wall; waypost; *x-border; yonder; zone;*

**language** *(n.)*: argot; *accent; byword; creole;* dialect; expression; form of expression; glossa; home ~; inter~; idioglossia; idiolect; jargon; *known tongue;* lingo; langue; mother tongue; nomenclature; native tongue; national ~; oenomel; parlance; *Queen's English; rendition;* speech; talking; tongue; utterance; *unknown tongue;* vernacular; verbiage; vocabulary; vulgate; words; wordage; writing; *xenography;* yawp; *Zulu;*
   **Languages**: Arabic; Aramaic; Burmese; Chinese; Danish; Dutch; English; French; German; Greek; Hebrew; Italian; Japanese; Korean; Latin; Mandarin; Nepalese; Old English; Polish; Portuguese; Quechuan; Russian; Spanish; Syrian; Turkish; Urdu; Visayan; Welsh; Xhosa; Yiddish; Zulu;

**languid** *(adj.)*: anemic; blah; blasé; crawling; dull; effete; flagging; groggy; heavy; indolent; *jog-trot;* kef; lethargic; mopish; non-motivated; oscitant; pepless; quiescent; retarded; sluggish; torpid; unenergetic; vapid; weary; *xenarthrous;* yareless; zealless; [*Ant.* lusty]

**languish** *(v.)*: abate; assuage; bate; contract; condense; decrease; decline; diminish; dissipate; dwindle; ease; ebb; fade; fail; go down; hit the skids; impair; jade; knock down; lessen; lower; minish; *narrow; outgo;* pine (away); quail; recede; reduce; shrink; shrivel; subside; taper; *undo; vanish;* wane; waste; wither; *xerosis;* yield; zap;

**languor** *(n.)*: anemia; blahness; catatonia; dullness; *exhaustion;* faintness; grogginess; heaviness; indolence; jadedness; kef; lethargy; languidness; *motionlessness;* numbness; oscitancy; peplessness; *quiescence; rest;* slothfulness; torpor; unenthusiasm; vapidity; weariness; *xenarthrous;* yarelessness; zealessness; [*Ant.* lustiness]

**lanky** *(adj.)*: awkward; bony; clumsy; delicate; elongated; frail; gangly; gawky; hairbreadth; inelegant; jimp; *kooky-looking;* long-limbed; meager; narrow; overthin; *peakish; quantité négligeable* [F.]; rangy; scrawny; skinny; thin; twiggy; ungraceful; virgate [bot.]; weedy; XF; *yieldless; zero body fat;* [*Ant.* large]

**lantern** *(n.)*: ∗ *aura; bulb;* candlestick; Davy lamp; electric lamp; flashlight; *glow;* halogen light; incandescent lamp; jacklight; klieg light; lamp; maglight®; night-lamp; oil lamp; penlight; quartz lamp; *radiance;* shoplight; torch; uplight; *visual;* worklight; xenon lamp; *yellow light;* zircon light;

**lapse** *(n.)*: abeyance; aberration; breach; cessation; delay; elapse; failure; gap; hold; interval; *just a minute; kip;* lag; moratorium; night rest; omission; pause; period; *quietude;* rest; space; time lag; *unwinding; vacation;* wait; *x-rest; yawning; zizz;*

**large** *(adj.)*: abundant; astronomical; big; considerable; capacious; copious; colossal; deep; disproportionate; extensive; expansive; enormous; fat; full-size; generous; goodly; great; gigantic; huge; immense; jumbo-sized; king-size; large-scale; massive; *numerous; overmuch;* oversize; overweight; ponderous; prodigious; quantitative; queen-size; rotund; roomy; sizable; spacious; substantial; thick; tremendous; *unwieldy; unmanageable;* voluminous; vast; wide; weighty; whopping; XL; *Ymir; ziphoid;* [*Ant.* little]

**last** *(adj.)*: aftermost; bottom; concluding; closing; decisive; dying; ending; endmost; final; finishing; *grand finale;* hindermost; irrevocable; *just; killing;* latter; latest; most recent; nth; outermost; posterior; *quitting;* remaining; rearmost; surviving; terminal; ultimate; very ~; *winning; x-end;* year-end; *zenithal;* [*Ant.* leading]

**lasting** *(adj.)*: abiding; *bearing through;* continuing; durable; enduring; fixed; good; hearty; heavy-duty; immortal; *just keeps going;* keen; long-lived; long-lasting; maintaining; non-perishing; out~; perpetual; *quickening;* remaining; reverseless; sturdy; strong; stable; tough; unbreakable; uninterrupted; vibrant; without perishing; *x-heavy;* yieldless; *zero perishing;* [*Ant.* limited]

**late** *(adj.)*: after the time; behind schedule; belated; *cumbered;* dilatory; delayed; deferred; eleventh-hour; fashionably ~; *gradual;* held up; *impeded;* jauking; keeping one waiting; lagging; moratory; non-timely; overdue; procrastinatory; past-time; past-due; postponed; quite ~; retarded; *recently;* slow; tardy; unpunctual; unseasonable; untimely; *vapid; workshy; xenarthrous; yareless; zealless;*

**latency** *(n.)*: abstruseness; *buried;* concealment; dormancy; expectancy; *facility; gone into remission;* hiding; inactivity; *jurisdiction; kip;* latentness; *makings; nap;* obdormition; potential; quiescence; *resting;* sleep; *talent;* underdevelopment; vegetation; waiting; *x-sleep; yet undetected;* zizz;

**lateness** *(n.)*: abeyance; belatedness; *cumbering;* delay; deferment; ever-lateness; following; *going slowly;* holdup; inexpedience; jauking; *keeping one waiting;* lagging; *moratorium;* non-timeliness; negligence; over-lateness; postponement; *quite late;* retardation; remissness; slowness; slackness; tardiness; tarrying; unpunctuality; *vapidity;* wait; *xenarthra; yarelessness; zeallessness;*

**latent** *(adj.)*: abstruse; buried; concealed; deedless; dormant; delitescent; embryonic; furtive; *gone into remission;* hid(den); inactive; idle; *jarless;* kip; lying uncovered; *lurking;* masked; neglected; obscured; passive; potential; quiescent; repressed; sleeping; tacit; underlying; undetected; unseen; veiled; *withdrawn; x-sleep;* yet undetected; *zero activity;*

**later** *(adv.)*: after; behind; coming after; directly following; ensuing; following; going next; henceforth; in pursuit of; just behind; *kept behind;* later on; *much ~;* next; *over;* past; *quickly following; right after;* since; subsequent; thereafter; ultimate; *very late;* whenceforth; *x-list;* yonder; *Z-position;* [*Ant.* leading]

**latitude** *(n.)*: allowance; breathing-space; choice; *deviation;* elbow-room; freedom; flexibility; give; *headroom; independence; judgment space; keep*; liberty; leeway; margin; *non-rigidity; opportunity;* play; *qua;* room; slack; space; tolerance; *unfixed;* variation allowance; wiggle room; *xy-margin;* yaw; *zigzag room;*

**latter** *(adj.)*: aftermost; back-end; concluding; closing; determinate; end(ing); eventual; following; final; *grand finale;* hindmost; *irrevocable; just; killing;* late(r); modern; *nth;* outermost; posterior; *quitting;* rearmost; second; terminal; ultimate; very last; waning; *x-end;* yondmost; *zenithal;* [*Ant.* leading]

**laud** *(n.)*: acclaim; adoration; blessing; credit; commendation; devotion; encomium; extolling; exaltation; fame; glorification; honor; idolization; *jubilation;* kudos; lifting up; magnification; *notoriety; over-praise;* praise; *quality;* rejoicing; singing; tribute; uplifting; veneration; worship; *xtry.; yichus;* zealous ~; [*Ant.* lambasting]

**laud** *(v.)*: applaud; acclaim; adore; bless; credit; commend; doxologize; extol; exalt; fame; glorify; honor; hail; idolize; *jubilate;* kneel before; lionize; lift up; magnify; *note;* offer praise; praise; *quiritation;* resound; rejoice; sing praises; thank; tout; uplift; venerate; worship; *xenophilia; yichus;* zealously ~; [*see* rejoice; sing; worship; *Ant.* lambaste]

**laudable** *(adj.)*: admirable; beloved; commendable; distinguished; estimable; excellent; favorable; fine; great; honorable; impressive; jake [Br.]; keen; likeable; meritorious; marvelous; nice; outstanding; praiseworthy; *qualified;* remarkable; splendid; terrific; ultra-good; virtuous; very good; worthy; wonderful; xtry.; yichus; *zealously loved;*

**laugh** *(n.)*: arrision [arch.]; boff; chuckle; cackle; chortle; cachinnation; *daffiness;* exult; *frolic;* giggle; guffaw; ha ha; hoot; irrision; *jolly ~;* keckle; laff [modern]; *mirth;* nicker; *outburst; peal; quib;* roar; snigger; snicker; tee-hee; titter; twitter; *utterance; vibration;* whicker; *xiphosternum;* yock [slang]; *zeal;* [*Ant.* lamentation]

**laugh** *(v.)*: arride [arch.]; burst out; chuckle; cackle; chortle; cachinnate; die ~ing [slang]; *erupt; frolic;* giggle; guffaw; ha ha; hoot; *irrision; jolly;* keckle; laff [modern]; *mirth;* nicker; *outburst; peal; quib;* roar; snicker; sniggle; snigger; tee-hee; titter; twitter; utter ~er; *vibrate with laughter;* whicker; *xiphosternum;* yock [slang]; yuk; yaw-haw; *zeal;* [*see* mock; *Ant.* lament]

**laughingstock** *(n.)*: aberration; butt; clown; dummy; dunce; *eccentricity;* fool; gazing-stock; *heterozygous;* idiot; joke; jestingstock; knucklehead; laughing-stock; moron; nitwit; nockingstock; object of ridicule; peculiarity; queerity; *ridiculous;* sight; target; *unusual;* victim; weirdo; *xtry. oddity;* yo-yo; zob;

**laughter** *(n.)*: amusement; belly laugh; chuckling; cackling; chortling; *derision; eruption; frolic;* giggling; *gayety;* hilarity; hooting; horselaugh; irrision; *jolliness;* keckling; laughing; mirth; nickering; *noise; outburst;* peal of ~; *quibbing;* roaring; snickering; twittering; *uttering; vibration;* whickering; *xiphosternum;* yocking [slang]; *zeal;* [*see* mockery; *Ant.* lamentation]

**lavish** *(adj.)*: abundant; bountiful; costly; decorated; extravagant; fulsome; gorgeous; grand; high;-class immoderate; indulgent; *jet-set; kingly;* lush; luxurious; magnificent; never-wanting; overabundant; opulent; plush; posh; *quartful* [arch.]; rich; ritzy; sumptuous; swanky; thriftless; undue; upscale; uptown; voluptuous; wealthy; xtry.; *yet unsurpassed; zierlich* [G.];

**lavish** *(v.)*: abundantly give; bestow; confer; dole; expend; freely give; heap; impart; *jam-pack; kit;* load up; mound; *non-retention;* over~; pour; pile; *quicken;* regale; smother; squander; *transfer;* use ~ly; *vest;* waste; *xfer; yield; zip;*

**law** *(n.)*: act; bill; bylaw; code; constitution; commandment; directive; decree; enactment; edict; fiat; governance; *halacha* [Heb.]; injunction; indiction; *jus gentium* [L.]; *keleusmatic;* legislation; mandate; necessity; ordinance; penal code; pandect; precept; proclamation; *quo minus* [L.]; regulation; rule; statute; sanction; *technicality;* ukase; *voice; word;* XO mandate; yardstick; *zakon* [Rus.];

**lawful** *(adj.)*: allowed; acceptable; bona fide; correct; due; *de jure* [F.]; endorsed; formal; good; heteronomous; innocent; judicial; kosher; legitimate; licit; legal; merited; mandated; *moral;* not illegal; okay; official; permitted; *questionless;* rightful; sanctionable; tolerated; unobjectionable; valid; warranted; Xn; yes; zero problem;

**lawless** *(adj.)*: anarchic; bad; criminal; disorderly; disobedient; evil; foul; godless; *honorless;* insubordinate; *jaded;* knavish; law-breaking; misbehaving; noncompliant; obdurate; profligate; *quad;* rebellious; sinful; truculent; unruly; uncontrolled; villainous; wayward; *x-grained;* yieldless; *zero obedience;* [*Ant.* law-abiding]

**lawsuit** *(n.)*: action; bill; complaint; claim; charge; class suit; court case; dispute; *engage a lawyer;* filed suit; grievance; *hearing;* indictment; impugnation; jeremiad; *key ~;* legal action; litigation; *million dollar ~;* negotiation; *objection;* proceedings; prosecution; *quarrel;* replevin; suit; trial; use of the law; *vengeance; work; XQ;* yawp; *zet* [dial.];

**lawyer** *(n.)*: attorney; advocate; barrister; criminal ~; counselor; defender; essoiner; *fiduciary;* guide; indicter; jurist; King's Counsel; legal advisor (-representative); man of law; negotiant; *outer bar;* prosecutor; pettifogger; practitioner; Pennsylvania ~; Queen's Counsel; *questmonger;* representative; solicitor; shyster [derog.]; templar; *unethical ~; vakil;* wakil [both Asia]; *XQ;* Yankee ~; zealous ~;
**lax** *(adj.)*: accepting; broadminded; careless; disregardful; easy-going; forbearing; gracious; hit-or-miss; indulgent; *justifying; kindly;* laid-back; loose; lenient; mellow; not strict; non-harsh; nonjudgmental; overly lenient; permissive; *questionable;* relaxed; soft; slack; tolerant; uncritical; unrestrictive; very loose; without regard; *xtry. slack;* yielding; *zero strictness;*
**laxness** *(n.)*: acceptance; broadmindedness; carelessness; disregard; easygoingness; freedom; grace; hands-off approach; indulgence; *justification; kindliness;* looseness; leniency; mellowness; non-harshness; over-leniency; permissiveness; *questionable;* relaxation; softness; slackness; tolerance; unrestrictiveness; *very lose;* willingness to please; *xenia;* yielding; *zero strictness;*
**lay** *(v.)*: arrange; bed down; cast oneself; deposit; ease; fall; grope; humicubate; *idle; jacent; keep;* leave; lean; mat down; *nap;* overlie; overlay; put; place; *quarter;* recline; repose; rest; set; take ease; use bed; under~; *vegetate;* wait; *x-rest; yield; zizz;* [*see* sleep]
**layer** *(n.)*: aspect; blanket; band; bed; coat; covering; course; degree; escrampment; echelon; film; gradation; husk; integument; *jacket; kind;* level; *mark; notch;* overlay; pellicle; plane; *quantity;* rung; sheet; story; (sub)stratum; stratification; table; tier; *unit;* varve; wrapping; *x-class;* y-level; zone;
**layman** *(n.)*: attender; believer; church member; constituent; *disciple; elect;* faithful attender; goer; *handler; individual; just regular guy;* kirsen [dial.]; laic; lay person; member; non-clergy; noncleric; oblate; person; parishioner; *quiritian [L.];* regular; secular; *tither;* untrained man; votary; worshiper; *Xn.; yokefellow; zealous church member;*
**laziness** *(n.)*: apathy; blahness; casualness; droopiness; dilatoriness; *dolce fariente* [It.]; *ennui;* faintness; grogginess; heaviness; idleness; *jadedness; kef;* listlessness; lackadaisicalness; laxness; *motionlessness;* negligence; otiosity; passivity; peplessness; *quiescence;* remissness; relaxation; slackness; sloth(fulness); torpor; unenthusiasm; *vapidity;* weariness; *xenarthrous;* yarelessness; zeallessness; [*Ant.* liveliness]
**lazy** *(adj.)*: apathetic; bone- ~; casual; disinclined; do-nothing; easygoing; fainéant; groggy; half-hearted; idle; indolent; *jog trot;* kef; lethargic; laggard; mopish; non-motivated; otiose; pepless; quiescent; remiss; slothful; torpid; unmotivated; unaspiring; vapid; workshy; *xenarthrous;* yareless; zealless; [*Ant.* lively]
**lead** *(v.)*: administer; bid; conduct; control; command; direct; dominate; domineer; escort; fix; guide; govern; head; instruct; *jurisdiction;* keep; lord over; manage; marshal; master; *necessitate;* order; oversee; preside; predominate; *queen;* regulate; run; rule; reign; shepherd; spearhead; superintend; take the ~; usher; *voice; word; xenagogue; yeme* [arch.]; *zakon* [Rus.];
**leader** *(n.)*: administrator; bellwether; boss; chief; captain; director; demagogue; executive; forerunner; foreman; guide; group- ~; governor; head; intendant; *jarl;* king; lord; liege; manager; master; notable; overseer; pacesetter; principal; prefect; prime minister; president; *queen [fem.];* ring~; ruler; supervisor; superintendent; sovereign; taskmaster; tyrant; *undershepherd;* vizer; warden; warlord; XO; *yokemaster;* zayim;
**leadership** *(n.)*: administration; authority; *bishopric;* burden of ~; control; command; direction; dominion; executive power; eminence; formanship; guidance; governance; government; headship; hegemony; *the* helm; influence; *jurisdiction;* kingship; lordship; management; *necessitation;* oversight; power; *queenship;* rule; reign; supervision; superintendence; sovereignty; top position; use of authority; *vizierate;* wardenship; *xenagogy;* yard; *zenith;*
**leaf** *(n.)*: acerous; blade; cotyledon; decursive ~; evergreen needle; foliage; frond; green ~; glume; *herb;* involucre; *jugum; kerf;* leaflet; lamina; *maple ~;* needle; nipa; ola; oak ~; petal; quadrifoliate; red ~; spear; sepal; tree ~; unijugate; unicostate; vegetation; *wreath; xanthophyllic ~;* yellow ~; *zymophyte;*

**leaflet** *(v.)*: advertisement; brochure; circular; double-fold; *essay;* flier; *gospel tract;* handbill; handout; informational ~; *journalism; key thoughts;* literature; *message; notations; opus;* paper; prospectus; pamphlet; quadrifoliate; reading matter; sheet; tract; trifold; unifoliate ~; *vignette; writing; xenagogy; yeme; zeug;*

**league** *(n.)*: association; alliance; band; brotherhood; club; coalition; confederation; *defense alliance;* establishment; federation; guild; group; *helping; industrial union;* joint coalition; *kongsi* [Chin.]; labor union; mutual-defense pact; nexus; organization; partnership; quinquevirate; ring; society; trade union; union; *vertical union;* workers' union; *x-class;* yeald; zollverein;

**leak** *(n.)*: aperture; bleeding; crack; drip; efflux; flow; gash; gush; hole; issue; influx; *jet; kaput;* leakage; *movement;* non-retention; outflow; puncture; *quickening;* rupture; rush; seepage; spillage; trickle; *unsealed; valve* ~; water-seepage; *xfer; yern; zwoosh;*

**leak** *(v.)*: *afflux;* bleed; come through; drain; escape; flow; give off; *hurl;* issue; *jet; kest;* let out; *move; non-retention;* ooze; *pour; quicken;* release; shed; spill; seep; trickle; *unstop; vent;* weep; *xude;* yield; *zip;*

**lean** *(adj.)*: attenuated; bony; constricted; delicate; emaciated; fine; fit; gracile; hairbreadth; insubstantial; jimp; *knife blade-thin;* lanky; meager; narrow; overthin; peakish; *quantité négligeable* [F.]; ribby; slim; slender; trim; undersize; virgate [bot.]; wiry; XF; *yieldless;* zero body fat; [*Ant.* large]

**lean** *(v.)*: angle; bend; cant; depend on; dispose; *enfold;* fall; favor; gravitate; give preference to; heel; incline; jee; *knuckle;* lie against; list; like better; move diagonally; *non-vertical; oblique;* prop; propend; prefer; *quat;* recline; rest; slouch; slant; tilt; tend; uphold; verge; *want; xfer;* yaw; *zag;*

**leanness** *(n.)*: attenuation; boniness; constriction; delicacy; emaciation; fineness; gauntness; *hairbreadth;* insubstantiality; jimpness; *knifeblade-thin;* lankness; meagerness; narrowness; overthinness; paucity; *quantité négligeable [F.];* ribbiness; slimness; skinniness; scrawniness; scantiness; slightness; thinness; *underweight; virgate [bot.];* wiriness; XF; *yieldless;* zero thickness; [*Ant.* largeness]

**leap** *(n.)*: advance; bounce; caper; capriole; curvet [horses]; *dart;* elevation; flying ~; gambol; hop; hurdle; *issue;* jump; *kite;* lollup; *movement; nimble; overleap;* pounce; pannade [horses]; *quersprung;* rise; ramp; spring; skip; take-off; upspring; vault; *whiz; xfer; yerk; zoom;*

**leap** *(v.)*: *arise;* bound; capriole; curvet [horses]; *dart;* elevate; fly; gambol; hop; hurdle; *issue;* jump; jeté; *kite;* lep [Ire.]; lollup; make jump; *nimble;* over~; out~; pounce; pannade [horses]; pole vault; *quersprung;* ramp; rise; spring; take flying ~; upspring; vault; *whiz; xfer;* yerk; *zip over;*

**learn** *(v.)*: absorb; ascertain; be taught; catch on; comprehend; discover; digest; *experience;* find out; get; glean; gather; get; hear; imbibe; *judicious;* know; ~ by heart; memorize; naw [dial.]; *observe;* own; pick up; *quality education;* realize; receive; remember; retain; study; take in; understand; *valuate;* wis; *xenodiagnose; yeme;* zero in;

**leash** *(n.)*: *app; bridle;* cord; clip-on ~; dog ~; *equipment; fasten; gear;* halter; inspan; jess; kneehalter; line; lead; leam; martingal; nylon webbing ~; *object;* pet- ~; *quinsell;* rope; restraint; strap; tie-up; tether; *unite; vang;* walking- ~; *xfer* ~; yard-rope; *zein;*

**least** *(adj.)*: *amount;* bottom amount; *concise;* dinkiest; eensy-weensiest; fewest; *gnat-sized;* hindermost; irreducible; infinitesimal; *jot; known* ~; littlest; lowest; minimal; minimum; minutest; nethermost; nadir; *one percent;* puniest; *quota; quorum;* reduced to minimum; smallest; slightest; shortest; teeniest; tiniest; undermost; very ~; *wee;* weakest; *xtry. small; youngest;* zero; [*Ant.* largest]

**leather** *(n.)*: animal hide; buckskin; buff; calfskin; *cuir* [F.]; cordovan; cowhide; deerskin; elk hide; fleece; goatskin; hide; *impermeable* ~; jucten; kip; lambskin; morocco; napa; oxhide; pelt; pigskin; quirboilly; rawhide; skin; shoe ~; suede; tanned hide; upper shoe ~; *vamp;* whit~; *xeroderma;* yuft; zug;

**leave** *(v.)*: ayo; abandon; abscond; back out; *begone;* be off; check out; clear out; cast off; depart; decamp; desert; exit; emigrate; embark; evacuate; flee; forsake; go; hightail; *immigrate; jilt; katabasis* [Gr.]; kiss goodbye; kennel [animals]; loose [naut.]; mosey (along); migrate; *neglect; omit;* part; quit; run off; remove; retreat; scat; scram; skedaddle; shove off; separate; take ~; *uproot;* vacate; walk off; withdraw; xfer; yead; zip away; [*Ant.* linger]

**leaven** *(n.)*: active dry yeast; *agent;* barm; baker's yeast; *chametz* [Heb.]; dough-yeast; enzyme; ferment; granulated yeast; hartshorn; *ingredient;* instant yeast; *jast* [Swed.]; *killer yeast;* leavening; *monocalcium phosphate;* newing; *over~;* pre-cultured yeast; *quickener;* rising agent; saccharomyces; top yeast; unprocessed yeast; *vegemite; wort; xiao;* yeast; zyme; [*see* sin]

**lecture** *(n.)*: address; bespeaking; communication; discourse; dissertation; elocution; *filibuster; glossa;* homily; instruction; *jabbering; kerygma;* lesson; line out; monologue; message; *narration;* oration; objuration; presentation; public speaking; pontification; *quotation;* recitation; spiel; speech; talk; tongue-lashing; utterance; vocalization; word(s); *xenophonia; yawner [off.]; zinger [slang];*

**lecture** *(v.)*: address; admonish; berate; bawl out; chide; chew out; denounce; excoriate; flay; give talking to; harangue; instruct; inveigh; jaw; knock; lambaste; *macerate;* nag; orate; objurgate; *punish; question;* reprimand; rake; scold; sermonize; teach; tell off; upbraid; vituperate; *warn; xuld [arch.];* yell at; *zap;*

**ledge** *(n.)*: *aslope;* brim; brink; berm; cliff; drop off; edge; fall; glacial ridge; hogh; *ice ridge;* jardang; kaim; loma; mountainside; nip; outcrop; osar; pleat; *quoif;* ridge; rim; saddle; serac; *top ~; upper ~;* verge; *wrinkle; Xiao;* yardang; *zenith;*

**ledger** *(n.)*: account (book); books; blotter; check ~; cash-book; daybook; entry book; factory ~; general ~; *history; information;* journal; kept record; lieger; logbook; monetary records; nominal ~; office ~; purchase ~; *quick books;* record (book); register; shopbook; sales ~; tally sheet; *underwritten;* verification; written account; *xfer; yellow sheet; zet [dial.];*

**leeriness** *(n.)*: apprehension; *bothering;* captiousness; doubt; distrust; dubiousness; *ever-leery;* fear; guardedness; hesitation; iffiness; *jealousy; kiaugh [Scot.];* leariness; lacking faith; mistrust; non-trust; over-suspicion; paranoia; questioning; *reluctance;* suspicion; skepticism; trepidation; unbelief; *vacillation;* wariness; *xenophobia;* yare-handedness; zero trust;

**leery** *(adj.)*: apprehensive; *bothered;* captious; doubtful; distrustful; dubious; ever- ~; *fishy;* guarded; hesitant; highly skeptical; iffy; *jealous;* keenly suspicious; leary; mistrustful; non-trusting; over- ~; paranoid; questioning; *reluctant;* skeptical; suspicious; *tentative;* untrusting; very ~; wary; *xenophobic;* yare-handed; *zärtlich* [G.];

**leeway** *(n.)*: allowance; breathing-space; choice; *deviation;* elbow-room; freedom; flexibility; give; *headroom;* independence; *judgment space; keep;* latitude; margin; *non-rigidity; opportunity;* play; *qua;* room; slack; space; tolerance; *unfixed;* variation allowance; wiggle room; *xy-margin;* yaw; *zigzag room;*

**leg** *(n.)*: appendage; *ankle;* bough; calf; crus; *demarch; extremity;* fore~; fibula; femoral; gam; gigot [meat]; hind ~; hough; *instep;* jigget [meat]; *knee;* limb; left ~; mid~; *member;* naked ~; *object;* pastern [contemptuously]; pro~ [zoo.]; pant~; quadriceps; right ~; shank; trunk; thigh; tibia; uncovered ~; *vericose;* wooden ~; *xfer; yomp; zet [dial.];*

**legal** *(adj.)*: authorized; allowed by law; binding; correct; constitutional; *de jure* [F.]; defensible; endorsed; formal; good; heteronomous; innocent; judicial; *keen;* lawful; legitimate; *moral; not illegal;* ordained; permitted; *questionless;* rightful; *strict; tolerable;* unprohibited; vested; warranted; *Xn;* yet to be outlawed; *zero problem;* [*see* judicial; *Ant.* lawless]

**legalism** *(n.)*: actions; bondage of ~; Catharism; dead works; effort-based salvation; following the law; *good works; hypocrisy; industry;* Judaizing; keeping the law; law-keeping; merit-based salvation; *non-grace; own effort;* Phariseeism; *qualifying through works;* rule-keeping; religiosity; salvation by works; trying to keep the law; *unscriptural; venturing;* works-salvation; *xtr. effort; yoke of the law; zero grace;* [*see* hypocrisy]

**legalist** *(n.)*: actions; bondslave; Catharist; *dead works; effort-based;* follower of the law; *good works; hypocrite; industry;* Judaizer; keeper of the law; law-keeper; *merit-based; non-grace; own effort;* Pharisee; *qualifying through works;* rule-keeper; religionist; salvation-by-works; *trier; unscriptural; venturer;* works-salvationist; *xtr. effort; yoke of the law; zero grace;* [*see* hypocrite]

**legality** *(n.)*: authorization; *blamelessness;* correctness; constitutionality; defendability; endorsement; *formality; good;* heteronomousness; innocence; justice; *keeping the law;* legitimacy; licitness; lawfulness; *morality; not illegal; ordaining;* permission; *questionlessness;* rightfulness; strict ~; toleration; *unprohibited;* validity; warrant; Xn; *yoke of the law; zero problem;*

**legalize** *(v.)*: allow; authorize; bless; consent to; decriminalize; enable; establish; formally approve; give permission; homologate; *indulge; justify; knowingly allow;* let; legitimize; make legal; *nod;* okay; permit; *qualify;* repeal; ratify; sanction; tolerate; *unopposed;* vote into law; validate; warrant; *x on the dotted line; yes; zero opposition;*

**legend** *(n.)*: account; belief; custom; *drama;* epic; fiction; fable; folktale; folklore; *great ~;* hearsay; *imposture; journal;* key; lore; myth; narrative; old story; *portrayal; quarto;* retelling; superstition; saga; story; tale; tradition; *unconfirmed story; version; written account;* xenodocheionology; yarn; *zipper book;*

**legendary** *(adj.)*: acclaimed; beloved; celebrated; distinguished; eminent; folkloric; famed; gestic; historical; high-profile; illustrious; iconic; *jubilated over;* known; lustrious; magnifical; notable; outstanding; popular; *quality;* renowned; *significant;* talked-about; universally known; venerated; well-known; world-famous; *xtry.;* yichus; *zealously loved;*

**legible** *(adj.)*: able to read; *be clear;* clear; comprehensible; decipherable; discernable; easy-to-read; fair; fine; good enough; *hone in on;* intelligible; *just plain;* knowable; *lucid; make out;* neat; *obvious;* perceptible; *quality;* readable; *straightforward; transparent;* understandable; *very easy; watchable; x-parent; yare; zero confusion;*

**legion** *(n.)*: army; brigade; company; division; encampment; force; garrison; host; infantry; junior service [Br.]; *kerns;* land-force; military; maniple; nonconscripted army; outfit; platoon; *quingenary* [Rom.]; regiment; soldiers; troop; unit; volunteer army; warriors; x-force; *yeald;* zouave unit;

**legislate** *(v.)*: approve laws; *bid;* create law; decree; enact; establish; form; give an order; *have;* implement; impose; *juration; kaleusmatic;* levy; make laws; *nomothetic;* ordain; pass; *quo minus* [L.]; ratify; require; set in stone; *tell; unanimously approve;* vote into law; *word; xenagogy;* yell; *zakon* [Rus.];

**legislation** *(n.)*: act; bill; charter; decree; edict; enactment; *fatwa* [Mos.]; governance; *halacha* [Heb.]; injunction; *jus gentium* [L.]; *keleusmatic;* law(making); measure; mandate; *national law;* ordinance; precept; prescription; proclamation; *quo minus* [L.]; rule; regulation; ratification; statute; *technicality;* ukase; validation; writ; XO mandate; *yardstick; zakon* [Rus.];

**legitimacy** *(n.)*: authenticity; bona fideness; correctness; definiteness; explicability; faculty; genuineness; heteronomy; incontestableness; justifiableness; *knowledge;* legality; lawfulness; *morality;* non-contestableness; orthodoxy; properness; qualification; rightfulness; sufficiency; truth; unquestionableness; validity; warrantability; *x'ed; yes; Zufriedenheit* [G.];

**legitimate** *(adj.)*: acceptable; actual; authentic; authorized; bona fide; correct; deserving; endorsed; fitting; factual; genuine; good; heteronomous; honorable; incontestable; justifiable; known; kosher; legal; lawful; meet; non-contestable; official; orthodox; proper; qualified; real; rightful; sufficient; true; unquestionable; valid; warranted; *x-parent; yes; zero question;*

**legitimize** *(v.)*: authenticate; bless; *consent to;* defend; excuse; *fend;* give reasons; hold as valid; insist it's okay; justify; *keep doing;* legalize; *maintain;* make acceptable; notarize; naturalize; okay; pass; permit; *qualify;* rationalize; substantiate; *tolerate;* uphold; validate; vindicate; warrant; *x;* yes; *zealously defend;*

**leisure** *(n.)*: amusement; break time; convenience; day off; diversion; ease; entertainment; enjoyment; fun; free time; *gaiety;* hobby; holiday; idle time; *joy; kick back;* liberty; *merriment;* non-working hours; off time; pastime; pleasure; quiet; recreation; relaxation; R & R; repose; spare time; time off; *unwind;* vacation; *week off; x-play;* yong [arch.]; *zugunruhe* [G.]; [*Ant.* labor]

**leisurely** *(adv.)*: ambling; blithely; casually; dilatorily; easy; foot-dragging; gently; happy-go-lucky; idly; jauntily; *kill time;* leisurably; *moderately;* non-hurriedly; over-casually; pokily; *quiescently;* relaxed; slowly; tardigrade; unhurried; very ~; *warelessly; xenarthrous;* yarelessly; zeallessly; [*Ant.* laborious]

**lend** *(v.)*: advance; *bank loan;* credit; *debt;* extend; fore~; grant temporarily; *hand over;* invest; *just temporarily; kit;* let use; loan; make a loan; *nonconforming loan;* oblige; provide loan; *qualified loan; remit;* supply; temporarily let use; *use; vest; wadsett; xfer; yafe* [arch.]; *z-bond;*

**length** *(n.)*: amplitude; bigness; *breadth;* clearance; coverage; distance; duration; extent; footage; farness; *girth;* hugeness; *inseam; jumboness; king-sized;* linear measurement; longness; measurement; mileage; *non-vertical;* oblongness; prodigiousness; quartile; reach; remoteness; stretch; span; total ~; *underlying ~; volume;* width; *x-coordinate;* yardage; *zoomed out;*

**lengthen** *(v.)*: augment; build onto; *broaden; change;* distend; draw (-drag) out; elongate; extend; further; grow; *heighten;* increase; *jack up; keep growing;* largen; make longer; *non-shortened;* outstretch; protract; prolong; *quadruplicate; raise;* stretch; tauten; *upgrade; vary;* wax longer; *XL; yain* [arch.]*; zoom;* [Ant. lessen]

**leniency** *(n.)*: altruism; benevolence; compassion; clemency; *delicate love;* easygoingness; forgiveness; grace; heart; *indulgence; joy-giving;* kindness; lenience; mercy; niceness; *overly compassionate;* pity; quarter; ruth; readiness to forgive; sympathy; *tender mercies;* understanding; *virtue;* warmth; *xenia;* yearning; *zeal to forgive;*

**lenient** *(adj.)*: assuasive; benignant; compassionate; clement; *delicate;* easy(going); forgiving; forbearing; gracious; humane; indulgent; *joy-giving;* kind(hearted); light; lax; lenitive; merciful; non-harsh; obliging; permissive; pitying; *quarter;* relaxed; soft; sparing; tolerant; *understanding; virtuous;* weak; warm; *xenial;* yielding; zealous to forgive;

**leper** *(n.)*: *affected man;* belepered man; castaway; diseased man; expelee; *flesh; galled; horrible;* infected man; *jaundiced; ketty;* leprous man; lazar; man with leprosy; *non-healthy;* outcast; pariah; *qualm; rabid;* scabious man; *tabid [arch.];* untouchable; vitiligo-infected; *white as snow; xanthodermal; yellow; zich [arch.];*

**leprosy** *(n.)*: alphus; black ~; *condition;* disease; exanthem; *flesh; gall;* Hansen's disease; infirmity; jungle rot; *king's evil;* leprous condition; malady; *not healthy; ordeal;* plague; *qualm; remittent;* scall; *taint; unhealthiness;* vitiligo; *whiteness; xanthosis; yellowness; zoonosis;*

**leprous** *(adj.)*: *affected;* belepered; *consumptive;* diseased; evil-affected; flesh-diseased; *galled; horrible;* infected; *jaundiced; ketty;* lazarly; morbillous; *not healthy; off;* polluted; *qualm; rabid;* scabious; snow-white; *tabid [arch.];* untouchable; vitiligo-infected; white with leprosy; *xanthodermal; yellow; zich [arch.];*

**less** *(adj.)*: abated; below; beneath; *concise;* dinkier; diminished; excepting; fewer; *greatly reduced; half;* inferior; *just ~; known to be ~;* lesser; lower; more modest; minus; not as much; *outclassed; outdone; outranked;* puisne; quite a bit ~; reduced; shortened; smaller amount; tinier; under; *very small;* weaker; without; *xtry. small; younger; zeroize;*

**lessen** *(v.)*: alleviate; abate; assuage; break down; bate; curtail; contract; curb; condense; cut; decrease; decline; diminish; drop; dwindle; deteriorate; ease; ebb; exhaust; fade; fall; foreshorten; go down; *hush; halt;* impair; *jump down;* knock down; lower; lighten; languish; minimize; minish; mitigate; moderate; *narrow;* obtund; palliate; pare down; peter out; quail; recede; reduce; subside; shrink; shorten; taper; use up; undercut; *vanish;* weaken; wane; waste; *xerosis;* yield; zap; [Ant. lengthen]

**lesson** *(n.)*: axiom; book ~; class; coaching; direction; education; formal ~; guidance; *homework;* instruction; *junior class;* knowledge; lecture; lection; maxim; moral; message; *noetic;* object lesson; period; principle; *qualification;* rudiment; session; seminar; schooling; tutorial; tenet; teaching; training; unit; vitalism; worksheet; *xenagogue; yielding; zoology ~;*

**let** *(v.)*: allow; bless; consent to; *decriminalize;* enable; empower; facilitate; give permission; humor; indulge; *justify;* knowingly allow; license one to; *legalize;* make possible; *nod;* okay; permit; *qualify; rationalize;* suffer; sanction; tolerate; *unhindered;* validate; warrant; *x on the dotted line;* yield; *yes; zealously approve;*

**letter** *(n. epistle)*: airmail; business ~; correspondence; communication; draft; dispatch; epistle; e-mail; fan mail; fax; *going;* hate mail; interoffice memo; *junk mail; kurvey;* love ~; message; missive; memo; mail; note; night-delivery; *open ~;* post; *quick note;* registered mail; scroll; special delivery; telegram; *unopened ~; undelivered ~; verbiage;* writing; *xfer; yellow envelope; zip code;*
**letter** *(n. character in alphabet)*: alphabetic character; *B;* character; designation; *etching;* figure; glyph; hierogram; imprint; initial; *jot;* katakana; ken-mark; lowercase ~; mark; majuscule; monogram; notation; *object;* phonetic symbol; *Q;* representation; rune; symbol; swash ~; *type;* uncial; uppercase ~; *vowel; W; X; Y; Z;*
**level** *(adj.)*: abiding; balanced; constant; dead even; even; flat; flush; geometrically ~; horizontal; invariable; *jusqu'au bout* [F.]; *keeps the same;* levelled; *measured;* non-bumpy; ongoing; plane; *quite ~;* regular; smooth; totally ~; unvarying; *very ~;* without variation; *x-cending;* yet; *zero variation;* [*Ant.* lopsided]
**level** *(n.)*: altitude; *aspect;* bed; belt; caliber; class; *category;* deck; degree; echelon; elevation; floor; grade; height; *increase;* journey ~; *kind;* layer; mark; *mezzanine;* notch; order; point; position; plane; plateau; quality; quantity; rung; rank; story; step; stage; scale; stratum; *strata;* tier; unit; varve; *way; x-class;* y-level; zone;
**level** *(v.)*: *apply pressure;* bulldoze; balance out; crush; compress; correct; depress; even out; flatten; grind; *hurt; iron; jam;* knock down; lay flat; make flat; *non-slanted;* oblate; press plateau; flat; quash; roll over; smooth(en); stabilize; *tamp down; unruffle; very flat;* wreck; *xuld [arch.];* y-level; zeroize;
**lewd** *(adj.)*: abhorrent; base; bawdy; crude; degraded; dissolute; evil; filthy; gross; godless; horrid; indecent; jadish; kitsch; licentious; mean; naughty; offensive; obscene; perverted; *quad;* raw; racy; risqué; salacious; tactless; tasteless; uncouth; unholy; vulgar; wanton; x-rated; yucky; zhlubby;
**liable** *(adj.)*: accountable; at fault; blamable; culpable; chargeable; deemed guilty; errant; faulty; guilty; held responsible; indictable; judged guilty; *known;* legally responsible; *mistaken; non-transferable;* obliged; prone; *peccant; question;* responsible; subject to blame; suable; to blame; *upbraided;* vituperable; worthy of reproof; *xtry. at risk; yoke; zing;*
**liar** *(n.)*: *actor;* beguiler; bluffer; charlatan; con artist; cheat(er); deceiver; deluder; defrauder; equivocator; fake(r); fibber; falsifier; finagler; flimflammer; fraud; false witness; guiler; hypocrite; hoaxer; imposter; Indian giver; jackal; knave; *losenger* [arch.]; misrepresenter; mythomaniac; *no-good;* open liar; pretender; phony; perjurer; quack(salver); rook; story-teller; swindler; tricker; trickster; untruther; verneuker; welcher; wangler; *xgressor;* yarn-spinner; *yentzer* [Heb.]; *zinger;*
**liberal** *(adj.)*: activist; broadminded; bleeding-heart ~; culture-accommodating; compromising; *Democrat; extreme ~;* forward-thinking; *generous;* humanistic; indulgent; Jacobin; *kind;* lax; ~ -minded; left-wing; modernist; non-conventionalist; non-conservative; neo-evangelical [rel.]; open-minded; over~; progressive; permissive; paleo~; politically ~; *quasi- ~;* rank ~; Sadducee; tolerant; theologically ~ [rel.]; unrestrained; ultra- ~; very ~; welfarist; *xenial;* Young Turk; *zero-conservatism;* [*see* generous]
**liberalism** *(n.)*: activism; broadmindedness; culture-accommodation; compromising; *Democrat; extreme ~;* forward-thinking; *generosity; humanism;* indulgence; Jacobinical; *kind;* liberality; *the* left; modernism; non-conventionalism; non-conservatism; neo-evangelicalism [rel.]; open-mindedness; progressivism; *quasi- ~;* rank ~; Sadduceeism; tolerance; theological ~ [rel.]; unrestraint; ultra- ~; *very liberal;* welfarism; *xenial; Young Turk; zero-conservatism;*
**liberality** *(n.)*: altruism; bigheartedness; beneficence; charitableness; *donations;* extravagance; freehandedness; generosity; high-mindedness; impartation; *joyful giving;* kindness; largesse; liberalness; magnanimity; munificence; nobleness; open-handedness; philanthropy; *quantities;* readiness; selflessness; *thoughtfulness;* unselfishness; *virtuousness;* warmth; *xenophilia; yieldedness;* zealous giving;

**liberate** *(v.)*: allow to go free; bail out; clear; disintrall; discharge; deliver; emancipate; free; *get out;* give freedom to; *hand over; issue; justify; kest;* loose; let go; manumit; not detain; *open;* put out; quit; release; set free; take out; unhand; unleash; unpen; unyoke; unchain; unshackle; *volley;* walk; xfer; yokeless; zoneless;
**liberation** *(n.)*: autonomy; bondlessness; clearance; deliverance; emancipation; enfranchisement; freedom; going free; *heroics;* independence; Juneteenth; *kept free;* loosing; manumission; non-captivity; opening; putting at liberty; quittance; quietus; release; setting at liberty; total freedom; unshackling; *victory; winning; xfer;* yoke-breaking; *zero fetters;*
**liberator** *(n.)*: advocate; brave warrior; champion; deliverer; emancipator; freer; *guardian;* hero; *individual;* judge [Bible]; knight (in shining armor); looser; messiah; *notable;* overcomer; paladin; *queller;* releaser; rescuer; savior; triumphant; unshackler; victor; white knight; *xia;* yoke-breaker; *zealous;*
**liberty** *(n.)*: autonomy; bondlessness; clearance; deliverance; emancipation; freedom; going free; *honest;* independence; *kept free;* latitude; manumission; non-captivity; openness; privilege; prerogative; *quite free;* release; self-determination; total ~; unrestraint; voluntariness; willingness; *xenium;* yokelessness; zero fetters;
**license** *(n.)*: approval; authorization; blessing; consent; clearance; *do;* endorsement; favor; freedom; go-ahead; green light; hear to [reg.]; imprimatur; joint-permission; *knowingly allowed;* leave; liberty; licensure; *may;* nod; okay; permission; permit; qualification; right; support; sufferance; sanction; thumbs up [slang]; *unreluctance;* vouchsafement; willingness; warrant; *x;* yes; *zealous ~;*
**lid** *(n.)*: *article;* bung; cap; cover; dome; *envelope;* flap; *gusset;* hood; *item; jacket; kist;* luff [naut.]; mantle; *non-revealed;* overlay; patch; *quat [arch.];* roof; screw-on ~; top; *unopened ~;* veil; wimple; *x-out;* yapp; zigzag quilt;
**lie** *(n.)*: *alteration of truth;* big ~; con; canard; deceit; deception; equivocation; fib; falsehood; fabrication; false witness; gonk; *good one;* half-truth; invention; imposture; inveracity; jactitation; *kid;* line; misrepresentation; mendacity; non-truth; oath-breaking; promise-breaking; perjury; *quiblin [arch.]; rooking;* stretch; trick; tall tale; untruth; *verneuking;* white ~; whole cloth; whopper; *xuld [arch.];* yarn; *zinger;*
**lie** *(v. deceive)*: allure; belie; bear false witness; con; deceive; deal falsely; equivocate; fudge; fib; fabricate; falsify; forswear; gonk; hoodwink; invent; illude; jazz; knowingly ~; *lure;* misrepresent; nobble; out-and-out ~; prevaricate; perjure; *quiblin* [arch.]; *rook;* stretch the truth; speak untruth; trick; tell falsehood; utter falsehood; verneuk; wangle; *whid* [arch.]; *xuld [arch.];* yentz; *zing;*
**lie** *(v. lay)*: *at rest;* be; bed down; *couchant; down; encradle;* fall; grope; humicubate; *idle; jacent;* keep; lounge; lay (down); *motionless; nap; non-erect;* over~; overlay; prostrate; *quiet down;* recline; rest; repose; sprawl; *sit;* sidle; stretch out; take ease; use bed; under~; *vegetate;* wait; *x-rest;* yield; *zizz;* [see sleep]
**life** *(n.)*: animation; activity; breath; being; consciousness; duration; days; existence; essence; *friskiness;* go; heart(blood); *inbeing; joie de vivre* [F.]; kick; living; life force; lifetime; *movement;* natural ~; *neck;* orgone; presence; personality; pulse; quickness; *real live;* subsistence; soul; time; *uplift;* vivaciousness; verve; vigor; vitality; *wake;* xenenthesis; youthfulness; years; zest; zoe; [*Ant.* lifelessness]
**lifelike** *(adj.)*: authentic; believable; convincing; depictive; *exact;* faithful; genuine; highly realistic; incredibly ~; *just like; keen;* life-like; *masterful;* natural; *outstanding;* precisely accurate; quite ~; realistic; so ~; true-to-life; *unerring;* vivid; well-copied; *xtry.; yet realistic;* zero phoniness;
**lifestyle** *(n.)*: actions; behavior; conversation; conduct; custom; daily life; existence; *fashion; guise;* habitude; *inclination; job; keeping;* living; life; manner of living; *notion; observance;* pattern of living; *quickening;* routine; schesis; testimony; *undertaking; venturing;* way of life; *x-action; yede; zeal;*
**lift** *(v.)*: arise; boost; bring up; carry; *drag (up);* elevate; fly; go up; hoist; increase; jack up; *keep going up;* lift up; move up; *new growth;* overgrow; put up; *quicken;* raise; *soar;* take up; up~; verge upward; wax higher; winch; windlass; *XL; yain* [arch.]; *zoom up;* [*Ant.* lower]

**light** *(adj. enlightened)*: aura; bright; cheery; dazzling; effulgent; enlightened; fair; faded; gleaming; glorious; high-colored; intense; illuminated; *joyous;* keen; light-colored; luminous; muted; magnificent; nitid; orthochromatic; pale; pastel; quite bright; radiant; sunny; shining; splendorous; transplendent; utterly bright; vibrant; well-lit; whitish; *xtry.; yellow; zippy;* [*Ant.* lightless]

**light** *(adj. not heavy)*: airy; arioso [mus.]; buoyant; *carriable;* driftable; easy-to-lift; feathery; flotable; gossamery; hoverable; insubstantial; *just ounces; kernel;* lightweight; meager; not heavy; *ounces;* portable; quite ~; *resting;* suspendible; *transcending;* ultra~; underweight; very ~; weightless; x-light; *yod; zero-gravity;*

**light** *(n. illumination)*: aura; beam; brightness; brilliance; candescence; day~; energy; effulgence; flash; fulgency; glow; gleam; glory; *halo;* illumination; *jack~; key ~;* lucence; luminosity; *moon~;* nitency; *over~;* phosphorescence; *particles; quartz ~;* radiance; rays; refulgence; shine(-ing); splendor; thermoluminescence; torch~; *ultraviolet ~;* vividness; white ~; *xenon ~;* yellow ~; *zodiacal ~;* [*Ant.* lightlessness]
  **Kinds of light**: artificial ~; black ~; candle~; day~; electric ~; fire~; gas~; head~; incandescent ~; jack~; lamp~; moon~; natural ~; pen~; refracted ~; star~; sun~; spot~; torch~; twi~; ultraviolet ~; white ~; xenon ~; yellow ~; zodiacal ~;

**light** *(v.)*: *alight;* beam; burn; brighten; cast ~; *dazzle;* effulge; emit ~; enkindle; enlighten; flash; fluoresce; gleam; glow; *high~;* ignite; incandesce; irradiate; illuminate; *jack~;* kindle; luminesce; light up; make ~; *neal;* outshine; put fire on; *quiver;* relume; radiate; shine; throw ~; *undimmed; vividness; well-lit; xtry.;* yield ~; *zap;*

**lighten** *(v.)*: alleviate; brighten; cut; diminish; ease; en~; fade; go down; *hue;* illume; *jump down; knock down;* lessen; lift; make lighter; *not so bright; output;* pale; *quail;* relieve; reduce; subside; tone down; unlade; *vanish;* weaken; whiten; *xerosis;* yield; zeroize;

**lighthouse** *(n.)*: alert; beacon; cresset; *day beacon;* edifice; *fog-signal; great light;* harbor-light; *illumination;* joule; *keen light;* lantern; light station; lodestar; marker; night-beacon; *operation;* pharos; *quay light;* range lights; signal; *tower;* torch [poet.]; *utility building; village ~;* watch-tower; *xenon gas light; yellow beacon; zircon light;*

**lightning** *(n.)*: *act of God;* ball ~; bolt; chain ~; dry ~; electrical storm; flash(ing); fork ~; fulguration; fulminating; *glint;* heat ~; *ionization;* Jove's ~; *keraunic level;* light; ~ bolt; *monsoon;* nitency; *onslaught;* positive ~; *quake;* ribbon ~; sheet ~; thunderbolt; *upper atmospheric ~;* voltage; wildfire; *Xango; yellow flash;* zap; [*see* thunder]

**likable** *(adj.)*: agreeable; blithe; congenial; delightful; enjoyable; friendly; genial; happy; heartwarming; invigorating; jovial; keen; lovely; *merry;* nice; *outgoing;* pleasant; personable; *queme; rewarding;* sociable; *thoughtful; terrific;* uplifting; *very friendly;* warm; xenial; *yokefellow; zestful;* [*Ant.* loathsome]

**like** *(prep.)*: approximating; akin to; *balance;* close to; comparable; deemed similar; equivalent to; favor; *give comparison; hold comparison; image of;* just ~; kindred to; likened to; *mirror-image;* not unlike; on a par; parallel to; quasi-; resembling; similar to; such as; typical of; uniform with; *the* very image; worthy of comparison; *xfer; yield similarities; zero in;*

**like** *(v.)*: approve of; admire; bask in; consider admirable; care for; delight in; esteem; enjoy; fancy; favor; go for; honor; hold in high regard; idolize; joy in; *keen on;* love; marvel at; notice; *outstanding;* prefer; *please; quick to compliment;* respect; salute; think highly of; *uplift;* value; venerate; wish for; worship [slang]; *xtry.;* yearn; *zeal;* [*Ant.* loathe]

**likelihood** *(n.)*: aptness; best hope; chance; degree of probability; expectation; fighting chance; *good chance;* hope; happening; *intention; just maybe;* known chance; liability; likeliness; *maybe; not unlikely;* odds; prospect; potential; probability; *questionable;* reasonableness; sporting chance; tendency; *unsurprising;* verisimilitude; vraisemblance; *waiting; xel* [arch.]; *yet possible; zero chance;* [*Ant.* long shot]

**likely** *(adj.)*: apt; anticipated; believed; calculated; disposed; expected; foreseen; given to; hoped-for; imaginable; inclined; *just waiting; keenly awaiting;* liable; more than ~; not unlikely; ostensible; promising; probable; quite probable; ready; seeming; thought ~; *unsurprising;* verisimilar; waiting for; *xel* [arch.]; yet probable; zealously awaiting;

**like-minded** *(adj.)*: agreeing; accordant; *brother;* concurring; *dear;* endorsing; falling in; *get along;* harmonious; in agreement; jiving [slang]; kindred-spirited; likeminded; matching; non-differing; one-minded; parallel-thinking; *questionless; rapport;* single-minded; similarly-minded; *sister;* together; united; virtually identical; *well-suited; xenial;* yet alike; *zero disagreement;*

**likeness** *(n.)*: alikeness; bearing resemblance; commonality; duplication; dead-ringer; equivalence; exactness; fashion; form; *gemination;* homogeneity; image; *just alike;* kind(red); life~; look-alike; match; model; mirror-image; nearness; *oneness;* pattern; parallelism; *quae est eadem* [L.]; resemblance; similarity; similitude; sameness; spitting image; twin; uniformity; very image; *with comparison; xoanon;* yet alike; *zincograph;*

**limb** *(n.)*: arm; appendage; branch; bough; chat; *dogwood branch;* extremity; *fork;* gamb; *hickory branch; ironwood;* jackstraw; kipper; *leg;* member; nicky; offshoot; plash; *quaker;* rod; shoot; trunk; upas ~; *vimineous;* wing; *xenograft;* yard [arch.]; *zamia;*

**limelight** *(n.)*: attention; *big;* center; dominance; emphasis; fore(front); focus; focal point; *greatest;* high spot; highlight; importance; ictus; *judged most important;* key point; lime-light; main thing; *notoriety;* overriding consideration; prominence; public eye; *quicktime;* renown; spotlight; *target;* ultimate; view; weight; *xtry. point; yellow light; zircon light;*

**limit** *(n.)*: ambit; abuttal; border; bounds; boundary; cap; cutoff; coast; demarcation; extent; frontier; *gate;* hem; interface; *jurisdiction; kept ~;* lower ~; line; limits; limitation; margin; *narrow;* outer ~; parameter; quadra; restriction; statutory ~; threshold; upper ~; verge; *without; x-border; yonder; zone;*

**limit** *(v.)*: *adjust;* block; control; curb; delimit; *encumber;* fetter; govern; hold back; inhibit; *jam;* keep within bounds; *let* [arch.]; moderate; narrow down; obstruct; parameterize; qualify; regulate; restrict; suppress; temper; *undo;* veto; withhold; *x; yeme* [arch.]; *zero freedom;*

**limitation** *(n.)*: abuttals; bounds; barrier; confinement; circumscription; drawback; *encumbrance;* forbearance; gyve; holding back; impedance; jurisdictional ~; keeping; line; limit; moderation; no-cross line; obstruction; prison; *quell;* restriction; suppression; trammel; *unliberated; vervel;* withholding; x; *yama* [Hind.]; *zoster;*

**limp** *(v.)*: amble; *bad leg;* crawl; claudicate; drag; edge; falter; gimp; hitch; hobble; halt; inch; jiffle; *keep advancing;* lumber; mince; *non-stable; oscillate;* plod; quaddle; *reel;* shuffle; stagger; stumble; totter; *uneven;* vacillate; wobble; *xfer;* yaw; zigzag;

**line** *(n.)*: ambit; bar; column; cathetus; drawn ~; diagonal ~; etched ~; file; graving; *graphic;* horizontal ~; *incline;* jack- ~; *keel-rope;* linear mark; mark; *non-curving; object;* perpendicular ~; queue; row; radius; score; secant; straight ~; trajectory; under~; vector; *white ~;* x-line; *y-coordinate; zeile* [G.];

**lineage** *(n.)*: ancestry; bloodline; clan; *country;* descent; ethnicity; extraction; family; generation; genealogy; heredity; *inheritance; jus soli* [L.]; kindred; line; male line; nationality; origin; people; parentage; pedigree; *quarter;* race; roots; stock; seed; strain; tribe; *ubiety;* vein; *white race; x-link; yoni* [Skr.]; *zoe;*

**linger** *(v.)*: abide; bide; continue; dwell; delay; *encamp; endure;* fool around; follow on; goof off; hang around; hesitate; idle; *just wait around;* kill time; loiter; lag; mosey; *nest;* overstay; pause; procrastinate; *quiet;* remain; stay; tarry; *use; vacillate;* wait; *xenize;* yerde [arch.]; *zero rush;* [*Ant.* leave]

**link** *(n.)*: attachment; association; bond; connection; coupling; concatenation; copula; down~; *entwining;* fastening; fix; go-between; *hooked into;* interconnection; joint; *key;* loop; ligature; linkage; marriage; nexus; *offshoot;* piece; *quasi-fuse;* ring; relationship; splice; string; tie; up~; union; *v-link;* weld; *x-link;* yoke; *z-link;*

**link** *(v.)*: attach; associate; bind; connect; couple; conjoin; concatenate; down~; *entwine;* fasten; *go-between;* hook into; inter~; inosculate; join; knit; knot; latch; marry; merge; *network; offshoot;* put together; partner; *quasi-fuse;* relate; secure; set to; tie; tack; unite; up~; *v-link;* wed; weld; *xenograft;* yoke; *zip;*

**lion** *(n.)*: animal; big cat; beast; cat; cougar; carnivore; *creature;* devourer; eater; *feline; growler;* hunter; *Iberian lynx;* jungle cat; *jaguar;* kitty [joc.]; king of beasts; lioness [fem.]; leopard; meat-eater; mountain ~; *native cat;* ocelot; puss(y) [joc.]; predator; panther; puma; *quadruped;* ravening ~; she-lion [fem.]; *tiger; uncia uncia [L.]; vicious beast;* wildcat; *x-breed;* young ~; *zibet;*

**liquid** *(n.)*: aqua; broth; beverage; colliquament; drink; eliquation; fluid; goo; hot ~; *infirm;* juice; *kiloliter;* liquor [arch.]; moisture; *non-frozen;* outpouring; pool; quantum ~; *runny; substance;* succus; solution; thawed substance; unfrozen substance; vapor; wetness; water(ish); *xanthoxylin; yeet; zep;*

**list** *(n.)*: alphabetized ~; bill; check ~; catalog; directory; enumeration; file; *given;* hand~; itemized ~; inventory; job ~; key ~ing; listing; *mailing ~;* notation; ordered ~; précis; posting; *qualifications;* register; rundown; record; roll; summary; tabulation; typewritten ~; *unabridged ~;* vita; written ~; x- ~; *yield; zet [dial.];*

**list** *(v.)*: alphabetize ~; bill; catalog; detail; enumerate; file; *give ~; history;* itemize; inventory; jot down; *key in;* list out; make a ~; number; notate; *order;* put down; post; *qualifications;* record; register; summarize; tabulate; *use; vita;* write out a ~; x- ~; *yield; zet [dial.];*

**listen** *(v.)*: attend; *bear;* comprehend; discern; distinguish; eavesdrop; *earshot;* follow; give ear; hark; hear (out); heed; hearken; identify; *judge;* keep; list [poet.]; lend ear; mark; mind; note; overhear; obey; perceive; pay attention; *quietly ~;* regard; submit; tune in; tend; tap; understand; *volume;* wiretap; *xenodiagnose; yield; zero in;*

**literal** *(adj.)*: accurate; bare; correct; direct; exact; factual; *genuine;* honest; indubitable; *just; keenly;* literalistic; most exact; non-figurative; *outright;* plain; precise; quite ~; real; strict; true; unembellished; verbatim; word-for-word; *'xactly [slang]; ywis [arch.]; 'zactly [dial.];*

**literate** *(adj.)*: able to read; *book;* cultivated; *deft; educated;* fluent; *grounded; habilitated; instructed; jobation;* knowledgeable; literate; lettered; *man of letters; non-ignorant; on the ball;* proficient (at reading); *qualified;* reading; schooled; taught; up to things; versed; well-read; *xenagogue; yellowback; zero ignorance;*

**literature** *(n.)*: art; belles-lettres; books; collective writings; *document; epistle;* fiction; great works; humanities; information; *journalism;* key works; literary works; manuscripts; materials; novels; oeuvre; prose; poetry; *the* quill; reading matter; sub~; stories; texts; *uncials;* version; writings; works; *xiaozhuan; yellow journalism; zeug;*

**litter** *(n.)*: abatis; *bottles;* clutter; debris; *eliminate;* fragments; garbage; hash; *items;* junk; ket; *left around;* mullock; *nihil [L.];* offal; *pile; papers;* quisquillous; rubbish; scattered trash; trash; unwanted items; vuilnis; waste; *x-barrel; yucky; zero value;*

**litter** *(v.)*: *abominate;* blemish; clutter; dirty; encumber; filthify; *garbage; heap; items;* jumble; *ket;* leave trash around; mess up; not pick up after oneself; *offend;* pile; *quisquillous;* ruin; scatter; spoil; strew; trash; *untidy; vuilnis;* wreck; *x-barrel; yucky; zero value;*

**little** *(adj.)*: abbreviated; baby; brief; compact; concise; dinky; dwarfed; diminutive; eensie-weensie; exiguous; fine; few; gnat-sized; half-pint; itsy-bitsy; insignificant; *jot;* knee-high; little-bitty; Lilliputian; microscopic; minute; minuscule; miniature; negligible; ounce-sized; puny; petite; pygmy; pint-sized; *quantité négligeable [F.];* runty; rinky-dink; scant(y); shrimpy; small (-scale); short; tiny; teeny; undersized; very small; wee; XS; *yea big; zero;* [*Ant.* large]

**littleness** *(n.)*: abbreviation; brevity; compactness; conciseness; dinkiness; exiguousness; fineness; fewness; gnat-likeness; *half-pint;* insignificance; *jot; knee-high;* little; minuteness; negligibility; over-smallness; puniness; pettiness; paucity; *quantity;* runtiness; scantiness; smallness; slightness; tininess; teeniness; unimportance; *vileness;* weeness; XS; *yea big; zero;* [*Ant.* largeness]

**liturgical** *(adj.)*: archiepiscopal; *baptismal;* ceremonial; church; *devotional;* ecclesiastical; formal; *governing;* high church; *holy; inveterate; jacobite; kerygmatic;* liturgic; ministerial; *non-secular;* ordinal; priestly; pontifical; *quoad sacra* [L.]; ritualistic; religious; rubrical; ritualistic; sectarian; sacramental; *traditional;* ultramontane; virtuous; worship-related; *Xavarian; yielded; zealous;*
**liturgy** *(n.)*: antiphonary; breviary; church book; canon; decretal; euchologion; formulary; farse; gradual; *high church;* invitatory; julotta; kyriale; litany; lectionary; missal; mass-book; *nunc dimittis;* ordinal; processional; penitential; prayer-book; pontifical; *quarto;* responsary; rubric; sastra; sacramentary; tonary; unified ~; vade-mecum; *words;* xenagogy; ypakoe; zend;
**live** *(v. be alive)*: alive; breathe; be alive; consist; dure; draw breath; exist; *function;* go on; have life; hold on; inhere; *journey through;* keep living; last; make it; *move;* not die; outlast; persevere; *quick;* respire; remain (alive); survive; subsist; *tarry;* uphold; *vitality;* walk on the earth; *xenize; yieldless; zero harm;*
**live** *(v. reside)*: abide; bide; continue; dwell; exist; follow on; get along; hang one's hat; homestead; inhabit; *journey;* keep on; lodge; make one's home; *nest;* occupy; *pause;* quarter; reside; survive; stay; subside; settle; tarry; *use; voyage to;* wait; xenize; yerde [arch.]; *zip to;*
**livelihood** *(n.)*: activity; assignment; business; career; craft; calling; duty; employment; field; *grind [slang]; handcraft;* industry; job; *key position;* living; métier; *necessity;* occupation; profession; *quest;* responsibility; service; task; trade; undertaking; vocation; work; xci. *yoke; zealous duty;*
**lively** *(adj.)*: active; animated; brisk; bouncy; chipper; dynamic; energetic; frisky; feisty; gung-ho; hardy; high-spirited; impassioned; jaunty; keen-spirited; light-hearted; moving; nippy; overactive; perky; peppy; pert; quickened; robust; spirited; sprightly; sparky; trenchant; upbeat; vigorous; vibrant; vivacious; wimble; *x-energy;* yare; zesty; zippy; [*Ant.* lackadaisical]
**load** *(n.)*: arm~; *amount;* burden; boat~; cargo; consignment; case~; delivery; encumbrance; freight; goods; haulage; items; *job;* kit; lading; movables; *merchandise;* naulage; *objects;* pile; pay~; plane~; quantity; *railroad car;* shipment; stockpile; tote; train~; truck~; *unit;* volume; van~; weight; wagon~; *xfer goods;* yard goods; *zeug [G.];*
    Kinds of *load*: arm~; boat~; bucket~; car~; cart~; case~; horse~; pay~; plane~; ship~; trailer~; train~; truck~; van~; wagon~; work~;
**load** *(v.)*: arrange; amass; burden; crowd; cram; deposit; encumber; fill; get in; heap; imbue; jam-pack; *kibble;* lade; lavish; make full; mound; *niche;* overstuff; overfill; over~; pre~; place; pile on; pack(age); quash full; ram in; set; stow; store; stack; stuff; stockpile; tamp; *upthrust; volume;* weigh down; *xuld [arch.]; yerk;* zet [dial.];
**loan** *(n.)*: advance; bank ~; business ~; credit; construction ~; debt; day ~; *extending;* financing; grubstake; home ~; imprest; *investment;* jumbo mortgage; *key ~;* long-term ~; lent amount; mortgage; *nonconforming ~;* overadvance; prest; *quick ~; refinancing;* student ~; short-term ~; take-out ~; underadvance; variable-rate ~; wadsett; *xfer; yeme;* z-bond;
**loan** *(v.)*: advance; afford; *bank ~;* credit; *debt;* extend; float; fund; give ~; *hand over;* invest; *just temporarily; kit;* lend; make a ~; *negotiate a ~;* offer; provide ~; *qualified ~; remit;* supply; temporarily let use; *use;* vest; wadsett; *xfer; yafe* [arch.]*; z-bond;*
**lobby** *(v.)*: appeal; apply pressure; beseech; bully; call for; demand; entreat; formally request; go to bat; *help a cause;* importune; insist; jawbone; keep asking; look for; make demand; *need;* obsecrate; petition; pressure; *quiritation;* request; supplicate; *try to get;* urge; vocalize; want; *xtry. pressure;* yearn; *zealously plead;*
**local** *(adj.)*: area; *branch;* confined; close; community; district; *environs;* friendly neighborhood; general-area; home(grown); insular; in-area; indigenous; jurisdictional; *kept ~;* limited; municipal; native; nearby; neighboring; *own;* proximate; parochial; provisional; *quadrant;* restricted; residential; regional; site; town; ubiety; village; vicinal; *whereabouts; xy-coordinate; yard;* zonic;

**locate** *(v.)*: ascertain; bring to light; come across; discover; detect; determine; emplace; find; fixate; go; get; hit on; identify; isolate; *jaeger;* kithe [Scot.]; *learn;* move; make certain; *note;* obtain; put; pinpoint; position; *quick-to-discover;* re~; recover; search for; situate; turn up; travel; uncover; venture; visit; verify; work out; *xenotransplant;* yead; zero in; [*Ant.* lose]

**location** *(n.)*: address; area; branch; *county;* district; emplacement; *environs;* footing; fixation; field; ground(-plot); habitat; immediate area; jurisdiction; *kray [Rus.];* locale; locality; *municipality;* niche; office; place; point; position; quadrant; region; scene; setting; site; spot; *territory;* ubiety; venue; vicinity; whereabouts; xy-coordinate; *yard;* zone;

**lock** *(n.)*: *apparatus;* bar; bolt; catch; combination lock; deadbolt; electronic ~; fastener; guard; hook and eye; iron bar; jail ~; keyed ~; latch; master ~; night latch; outdoor ~; pad~; *quality* ~; rim ~; security device; *toggle; under ~ and key;* vault ~; wafer tumbler ~; *xtr. security;* Yale® lock; zipper lock;

**lock** *(v.)*: *arm;* bar; bolt; catch; deadbolt; engage; fasten; *guard;* have ~ed; inter~; *jail;* keep under ~ and key; latch; make secure; *non-vulnerable;* outbar; pad~; *quash;* restrain; secure; tightly ~; under ~ and key; vault; well-protected; x-tight; *yeme [arch.];* zipper-lock; [*Ant.* loose]

**locust** *(n.)*: * *acrididae* [L.]; *bug;* cricket; cicada; *dark bush-cricket; European mole cricket; flying insect;* grasshopper; *house cricket; harvest fly; insect; jumper;* katydid; *locusta migratoria* [L.]; migratory ~; nymph [baby]; *oedipoda coerulescens [L.];* pestilence; *quedius [L.]; red cicada;* seventeen-year ~; *tropical leap katydid;* urrin; *vermin;* weta; xyleus; *yucca borer;* zoic; [*see* swarm]

**lodge** *(n.)*: accommodations; bed and breakfast; cabin; dosshouse; *efficiency apartment;* flophouse; guesthouse; hotel; inn; juke; kip-house; lodging; luxury resort; motel; *nook;* outspan; *place;* quarters; resort; suites; ski ~; tavern; *ubiety;* victualing-house; *ward;* xenodocheum; youth hostel; *zeta;*

**lodge** *(v.)*: abide; accommodate; bide; bower; continue; dwell; *endure;* follow on; *go to;* hang one's hat; inhabit; *journey;* keep on; live; *move in;* nest; occupy; put up; quarter; remain; reside; stay; sojourn; tarry; *use; voyage to;* wait; *winter;* xenize; *yerde* [arch.]; *zip to;*

**loft** *(n.)*: attic; barn- ~; cock- ~; choir ~; deck; extension; fly gallery; gallery; hay~; Italian balcony; jube; king's ~; loggia; mezzanine; *nook;* overhang; platform; quarter-gallery [naut.]; rood~; *sail- ~;* top- ~; upper level; *veranda;* walkway; xyst; *yu [Chin.];* zayat;

**log** *(n. record)*: account; archive; book; chronicle; cartulary; documentation; data; *evidence;* file; *got down;* history; information; journal; kept record; listing; muniment; notation; official ~; proof; postea; *quill;* record; register; *statement;* tally sheet; *underwritten; verification;* written account; *xenagogy;* yellow sheet [crim. law]; zipper-book;

**log** *(n. section of wood)*: acacia ~; billet; backstick; clog; *driftwood ~; elm ~;* fire~; *graft;* hunk of wood; *ironwood;* juniper ~; *kindling;* limb; *mahogany ~;* nicky; oak section; piece of wood; *quassia; rame;* saw~; stovewood; tree section; *upas ~; vert;* wood; *xylem;* yule ~; *zum [arch.];*

**log** *(v.)*: annotate; *book;* chronicle; denote; enter; file; get down; handwrite; indicate; journalize; jot down; keep record; list; mark down; notate; *overwrite;* put down; quill; record; set down; take down; underwrite; *vellum;* write (down); *x;* yak; *zay;*

**logic** *(n.)*: apagogy; argumentation; analytical thinking; *based on facts;* cogency; coherence; discussiveness; discursiveness; defensibility; epistemology; formal ~; good ~; *headiness;* intelligence; judgment; *knowledge;* keen ~; level-headedness; many-valued ~; method; non-randomness; *outreason;* pure ~; *quite logical;* reason; rational thinking; syllogism; sensibleness; sound reasoning; tenability; understanding; verificationism; *well thought-out argument; xenagogic;* yepe; *zero doubt;*

**logical** *(adj.)*: argumental; analytical; based on facts; cogent; coherent; discussive; discursive; defensible; explicable; epistemological; fair; good; *heady;* intelligent; judicious; justifiable; *knowledgeable;* level-headed; legitimate; matter-of-fact; methodical; non-random; no-nonsense; *outreason;* practical; quite ~; reasonable; rational; sequacious; sensible; sound; tenable; understandable; valid; well thought-out; *xenagogic;* yepe; *zero doubt;*

**loiter** *(v.)*: abide; bide; coquet; dally; delay; ease around; futz; goof off; hang out (-around); idle; jauk; kick back; linger; laze; lag; mess around; *non-responsive;* obstruct; piddle; quiddle; remain; saunter; tarry; *unresponsive;* veg out; waste time; *xenize; yerde [arch.]; zealless;*
**loneliness** *(n.)*: aloneness; being alone; closed doors; desolation; emptiness; exclusion; forlorness; getting by oneself; hermitism; isolation; *jejuneness;* kithlessness; lonesomeness; *misery;* non-inclusion; *out-of-the-way;* privacy; quiet; quarantine; reclusion; retirement; singleness; solitariness; solitude; seclusion; *tranquility; unbefriended; very alone;* withdrawal; *x-out; yokelessness; zero companionship;*
**lonely** *(adj.)*: (all) alone; by oneself; *cast off;* desolate; *empty;* forlorn; *grieved; hopeless;* isolated; just oneself; kithless; lonesome; lorn; *miserable; non-accompanied;* overlooked; outcast; *piteous;* quit on; reclusive; *remote;* solitary; secluded; *tearful;* unbefriended; very alone; without company; *x'ed out;* yet unbefriended; *zero companionship;*
**long** *(adj.)*: *abiding; bearing through;* continuing; drawn out; extensive; extended; elongate; expansive; far(-reaching); going on; great; *holding;* increased; *jutting out; keeps going;* lengthy; *maintaining; not brief;* over~; ongoing; prolix; prolonged; quite ~; *reaching;* stretched; sustained; tall; timely; *unending;* vast; wide; XL; *yonder; zero brevity;* [*Ant.* little]
**longevity** *(n.)*: abidingness; being alive; continuance; durability; endurance; fortitude; going on; holding out; imperishability; *just keeps going;* keeping on; long life; length of days; lastingness; *maintenance;* not giving up; old age; prolongation; *quit-free; ripe old age;* survivance; sustaining; stamina; transcendence; unyieldingness; vigor; *willpower; x-scend;* years; *zealous continuance;*
**long-lived** *(n.)*: abiding; ancient; *bearing through;* continuing; chronic; durable; enduring; *for years;* good; hearty; immortal; *just keeps going; keen;* lasting; long-lasting; longevous; maintaining; *non-perishing;* old; prolonged; *quickening;* resilient; remaining; sturdy; strong; stable; time-honored; unbreakable; very old; venerable; *without perishing; x-heavy;* years; *zero perishing;*
**longsuffering** *(adj.)*: accepting; bearing; composed; disciplined; enduring; forbearing; gracious; holding out; indulgent; *just waiting; keeping patient;* long-suffering; merciful; not easily provoked; over-patient; patient; *quiet;* restrained; stoic; self-controlled; tolerant; unwearying; vasbyt; willing to wait; *xtry. patient; yieldful; zero irritation;*
**longsuffering** *(n.)*: acceptance; bearing; composure; discipline; endurance; forbearance; graciousness; holding back; indulgence; *just waiting; keeping patience;* longsufferance; moderation; non-anxiety; over-patience; patience; *quietness;* restraint; self-control; tolerance; temperance; unhurriedness; *vasbyt;* waiting; *xtry, patience; yielding; zero irritation;*
**look** *(n.)*: *acknowledgement;* beholding; casting of eyes; *coup d'oeil* [F.]; check over; descrying; eyeful; fleeting ~; glance; gaze; gander; *honing in on;* inspection; *just a ~;* keek; long ~; momentary ~; *notice;* oeiliad; peek; peep; quick ~; *regard;* steal a ~; taking a quick ~; *understand;* view; *watch; x-ray vision; yeme; zeroing in;*
**look** *(v.)*: *acknowledge;* behold; consider; descry; espy; eye; examine; face; fleer; focus on; fix eyes on; feast eyes on; glance; gaze; *hone in on;* inspect; *jerque;* keek; ken; leer; lour; make out; notice; observe; peek; peer; *quick ~;* recognize; regard; see; stare; scan; study; survey; scrutinize; take in; *understand;* view; watch; *x-ray vision; yeme;* zero in;
**loop** *(n.)*: annulus; bight; *bezant* [heraldry]; circle; *disk;* ellipse; *felly;* gyre; hoop; incirclet; *Jordan curve;* kinch; looping; micro-circle; *noose;* oval; *parbuckle; quasi-circular;* ring; *sphere; turn; unicircular;* vesica; *wheel; x-radius; y-radius; zone;*
**loop** *(v.)*: arch; becurl; curl; circle; *downward;* eddy; furl; go around; hurtle; incurvate; *jee; keel;* lasso; move around; nutate; orb; purl; querl; revolve; roll; swirl; spin; twirl; turn; upsweep; volt; whirl; *x-ing;* yede; zwoosh;

**loose** *(adj.)*: ayo; at large; baggy; *careless; desultory;* ever-so-loose; flowing; free; generous; hanging; ill-defined; inexact; *jumbo-sized; king-sized;* lax; lank; loose-fitting; much-too-loose; not tight; oversized; *open;* pendulous; quantitative; roomy; slack; sloppy; too big; undone; unrestrained; unbridled; voluminous; wobbly; *XL; yet too big; zero tightness;*

**loose** *(v.)*: allow to go free; bail out; clear; discharge; emancipate; free; give freedom to; hand over; *issue; justify; kest;* loosen; let go (-down); liberate; manumit; *non-tight;* open; outspan [Aus.]; put out; *quit;* relax; release; slacken; set free (-at liberty); take out; unhand; untie; unfasten; unbuckle; uncouple; unstrap; unharness; unbind; unshackle; *volley; walk; xfer; yokeless; zoneless;* [*Ant.* lock up]

**looseness** *(n.)*: *abundance;* bagginess; bigness; carelessness; desultoriness; extra room; flaccidness; generousness; haphazardness; inattention; inadvertency; insouciance; *jumbo-size; king-size;* laziness; languor; listlessness; laxity; laxness; *much-too-big;* non-attention; negligence; openness; play; *quantitativeness;* roominess; remissness; sloppiness; sluggishness; slothfulness; slackness; *too big;* unwariness; *volume;* wobbliness; *xenarthrous; yemeles* [arch.]; *zero tightness;*

**loot** *(v.)*: *appropriate;* boot; carry off treasures; despoil; excoriate; freeboot; gut; harrow; *incursion; junk;* knock off [slang]; lay waste; maraud; nobble; *overexploit;* pillage; plunder; *quash;* ransack; spoil; sack; swag; take; *unlade;* violate; wrest; *xfer; yank; zap;*

**lord** *(n.)*: administrator; authority; autocrat; boss; chief; director; dictator; executive; employer; emperor; feudal ~; governor; head; intendant; jarl; king; leader; liege; master; nobleman; overseer; over~; president; prime minister; potentate; *queen [fem.];* ruler; regent; superior; seignior; sovereign; thane; taskmaster; tyrant; ultimate authority; vizer; warlord; XO; *yokemaster;* zayim;

**Lord** *(n.)*: Almighty; Ancient of Days; Beginning and End; Creator; Chief Shepherd; Deliverer; Everlasting Father; Emmanuel; Father; Faithful; God; Holy One; I AM; Jehovah; Jesus; King (of kings); Lord of lords; Living God; Master; Nazarene; Only Wise God; Prince of Peace; *Quickener;* Redeemer; Savior; Shepherd; Truth; Thrice-Holy God; Three in One; Unchanging God; Victor; Word; *Xt.;* Yahweh; Yeshua; Zion's Hope; [*see* God; Christ; Trinity; *Ant.* Lucifer]

**lordship** *(n.)*: authority; bishopric; baronage; control; command; dominion; empowering; faculty; government; headship; influence; jurisdiction; kingship; legal rule; mastery; name; oversight; power; *quo warranto* [L.]; rule; say-so; *throne; umpirage;* vizierate; warrant; weight; *xarifdom;* yard; *zonal control;*

**lose** *(v.)*: admit defeat; become deprived of; capitulate; drop; escheat; forget; forfeit; give up; hand over; incur loss; *just gone;* kiss goodbye; leave; misplace; mislay; *non-retention; outgo;* put in the wrong place; *quit;* relinquish; surrender; throw (-*taken*) away; unload; *vanish;* walk off without; *x out; yet unlocated; zero retention;* [*Ant.* locate]

**loss** *(n.)*: annihilation; blow; bereavement; beating; cost; capitulation; deficit; damage; defeat; *expugnation;* forfeiture; fall; *great ~;* harm; hammering; injury; *jolt;* knock-out; letdown; *maiming;* nonsuccess; overthrow; pasting; quashing; routing; shortfall; slaughter; surrender; trouncing; tragedy; unsuccessfulness; utter ~; *violation; washout;* walloping; wipeout; *x-ing;* yedder; zap;

**lost** *(adj.)*: astray; absent; become ~; completely ~; capitulated; disoriented; elsewhere; forlorn; gone; hopelessly ~; *inability to find; just gone; kissed goodbye;* left; misplaced; missing; nowhere to be found; off-course; put in the wrong place; quite ~; relinquished; stray; surrendered; taken away; unaccounted-for; vanished; *whereabouts unknown; x out; yet undiscovered; zero retention;* [*see* perish; unsaved; *Ant.* located]

**loud** *(adj.)*: aloud; audible; boisterous; booming; blaring; clamorous; deafening; earsplitting; full-mouthed; *great;* high-volume; intense; *jangling;* keen; loud-sounding; multisonous; noisy; obstreperous; piercing; penetrating; plangent; quietless; raucous; reverberating; sonorous; sharp; stentorian; strident; thunderous; unquiet; uproarious; vociferous; voluminous; *wailing; x-loud; yelling; zero quietude;* [*Ant.* low]

**love** *(n.)*: affection; adoration; benevolence; charity; compassion; care; devotion; dearness; endearment; fondness; feelings; goodwill; *gentleness;* heart; infatuation; *joy;* kindness; lovingkindness; motherly ~; mutual ~; niceness; oneness; passion; *quixotic;* romance; selflessness; tenderness; true ~; *unselfishness;* undying ~; value; veneration; warmth; XOXO; young ~; yearning; zeal; [*see* lust; mercy; *Ant.* loathing]

**love** *(v.)*: admire; adore; bask in; burn with ~; cherish; care (for); delight in; desire; devote; enjoy; endear; feel affection for; go for; have feelings for; idolize; joy in; *kiss; like;* long for; *melt; non-selfish;* over~; prefer; *quixotic;* relish; show ~; treasure; *unselfishness;* value; venerate; worship; *xenophilic;* yearn for; *zeal;* [*see* like; *Ant.* loath]

**lovely** *(adj.)*: appealing; beautiful; charming; delightful; enthralling; fine; gorgeous; great; heavenly; invigorating; irresistible; *jim dandy;* keen; lovesome; *merry;* nice; outstanding; pleasant; *queme;* ravishing; rewarding; superb; satisfying; terrific; thrilling; uplifting; voluptuous; well-pleasing; *xtry.; you-beaut [Aus.];* zizzy; [*Ant.* loathsome]

**lover** *(n.)*: amoret; amorist; amorado; adorer; beloved; *cutie;* darling; esquire [masc.]; flame; gallant [masc.]; girlfriend [fem.]; honey; heartthrob; inamorato; Juliet [fem.]; kitten [fem.]; love(bird); ladylove [fem.]; mavourneen [Ire.]; mistress [fem.]; *nice;* other; pet; *querida* [Sp. fem.]; *querido* [Sp. masc.]; Romeo [masc.]; sweetheart; true love; torch; *undying love;* valentine; wooer; *XOXO;* yearner; *zitella [It. fem.];* [*Ant.* loather]

**lovesick** *(adj.)*: adoring; besotted; cupid-shot; distracted; enamored; fallen in love; *gotten;* head-over-heels; infatuated; in love; jitterpated; *kiss;* love-pined; madly in love; numb with love; obsessed; pining; *quixotic; romantic;* smitten; taken with; *unhappy; vehemence;* well-taken; *XOXO;* yearnful; *zealous;*

**love-struck** *(n.)*: *affected;* besotted; cupid-shot; distracted; enamored; fallen in love; gaga; heart-enamored; infatuated; in love; jitterpated; kooky; lovesick; moonstruck; numb with love; obsessed; pining; *quixotic; romantic;* starry-eyed; smitten; twitterpated; *unhappy; vehemence;* well-taken; *XOXO;* yearnful; *zealous;*

**loving** *(adj.)*: affectionate; amorous; *becharmed;* caring; devoted; empathic; fond; gentle; *heart-smitten;* intimate; *jealous;* kissy; *lovesome; merciful;* nice; *open;* passionate; quixotic; romantic; sweet; snuggly; tender; *unreserved; Valentine;* warm; xenial; *yearnful; zealous;* [*Ant.* loveless]

**low** *(adj.)*: abased; base; cast down; diminutive; down; debased; depleted; *effaced;* fallen; gentle; *groveling;* humble; ignoble; inglorious; *jackalent; kind;* lowly; little; muted; minimal; mean; modest; not high; nadir; *obsequious;* poor; *prostrate;* quiet; quite ~; renownless; *respectful;* servile; soft; short; *trounced;* undersized; unpretentious; *vile;* without airs; *xtry. humility;* yielding; *zero height;* [*see* sad; *Ant.* lofty]

**lowest** *(adj.)*: *amount;* bear minimum; bottom(most); *concise;* dinkiest; deepest; desinent; downmost; extreme; eensie-weensiest; fewest; farthest; *greatest depth;* hindermost; irreducible; infinitesimal; *jot;* known ~; least; littlest; lowermost; lowliest; minimum; minimal; minutest; most low; nadiral; nethermost; *one percent;* puniest; *quota; quorum;* rock-bottom; smallest; tiniest; undermost; very ~; worst; weakest; *xtry. small; youngest; zero;* [*Ant.* loftiest]

**lowliness** *(n.)*: abasement; *bringing low;* condescension; debasement; effacement; *fall; grace;* humility; ignobleness; ingloriousness; *jejuneness; knocking off one's high horse;* lowness; lowlihood; meekness; modesty; meanness; non-pride; over-humbleness; poorness; pridelessness; *quality;* reduction; self-effacement; servility; *timidity;* unimportance; unpretentiousness; *vileness; woefulness;* xtry. ~; *yieldedness;* zero pride; [*see* humiliation; *Ant.* loftiness]

**lowly** *(adj.)*: abased; base; contrite; deprived; effaced; *fearful; groveling;* humble; ignoble; inglorious; *jackalent; kind;* low; lamblike; mean; modest; non-esteemed; ordinary; poor (in spirit); *quiet;* renownless; *respectful;* servile; simple; third rank; unimportant; unassuming; unboastful; unpretentious; vulgar; without airs; *xtry. humility;* yielding; *zero pride;* [*Ant.* lofty]

**loyal** *(adj.)*: allegiant; behind; committed; dependable; dedicated; devoted; ever-faithful; faithful; *good;* hearty; immovable; *joined;* keen; *love;* leal [Scot.]; *mateship;* never-failing; *obedient; partnership;* quite ~; reliable; steadfast; true(-blue); trustworthy; unswerving; unwavering; unfaltering; unfailing; very ~; well-tried; *xtry.; yeomanly; zealous;*

**loyalty** *(n.)*: allegiance; bond; constancy; commitment; devotion; dedication; dependability; devotedness; *ever-faithful;* fidelity; faithfulness; fealty; *goodwill;* heart- ~; integrity; immovability; *joining;* keenness; line of duty; *love;* mateship; *non-failing;* oneness; *partnership; quick-to-help;* reliability; steadfastness; trueness; trustworthiness; unwaveringness; unfailingness; *verity;* well-tried; *xtry.; yeoman's service;* zeal;

**luck** *(n.)*: accident; allotment; break; *bad ~;* chance; cess; dumb ~; dole; destiny; *ensue;* fortuitousness; fortune; fate; *the* Fates; *good ~;* happenstance; happenchance; *intervene; jinx;* kismet; karma [Bud.]; ~ of the draw; ~iness; lady ~; lot; lucky stars; mozzle; *Norns;* omen; opportunity; purple patch [Br.]; quirk; roll of the dice; stars; stroke of ~; taking a chance; *Urd; vicissitude;* wheel of fortune; xtry. ~; *yet favored; zodiac;* [*see* providence]
    **Luck symbols**: amulet; acorn; barnstar; chimney sweep; dreamcatcher; four-leaf clover; horseshoe; jade; leprechaun; number 7; rabbit's foot; rainbow; shooting star; talisman; wishbone;

**lucky** *(adj.)*: auspicious; befortuned; blessed; charmed; *destined;* endowed with luck; felicitous; fortuitous; fortunate; good-fortuned; golden; happy; in luck; jammy; kissed by Dame Fortune; luck-endowed; *made to be blessed; non-jinxed;* opportune; prosperous; providential; *quirky; real ~;* super-lucky; touched by an angel; ultra-lucky; *vissitudinous;* well-fortuned; *xtry. ~; yet favored; zodiac;* [*Ant.* luckless]

**lucrative** *(adj.)*: advantageous; abounding; beneficial; bountiful; constructive; conducive; *decent; excellent;* fruitful; gainful; high-income; *instrumental; jim dandy;* keen; lucre-making; money-making; *nice; outstanding;* profitable; questuary; rewarding; sweet; *terrific; useful;* valuable; worthwhile; xtry.; yieldful; *zillions;*

**lukewarm** *(adj.)*: apathetic; barely warm; *blasé;* complacent; droopy; *easygoing;* fainéant; fervorless; *groggy;* half-hearted; indifferent; just warm; kef; laodicean; moderately warm; non-zealous; otiose; placid; quiescent; *remiss;* self-satisfied; torpid; unenthusiastic; vapid; warm; *wanting; xenarthrous;* yareless; zealless;

**lump** *(n.)*: amassment; bump; bulge; clump; clod; contusion; daud; enlargement; *furuncle;* goiter; gibbosity; heap; hunk; hump; inflation; jog; knot; knob; lentigo; mass; mound; nub; nodule; *oddity;* protuberance; quat; raised area; swelling; *tumor;* umbo; varix; wart; welt; wad; xyloma; *yedder;* zit;

**lumpy** *(adj.)*: *amassed;* bumpy; bulgy; clumpy; chunky; *coarse;* daudy; *eruptive;* full of lumps; gibbos; humpy; irregular; *jagged;* knotty; knobby; lumped; massy; nubby; nurly; overly ~; papular; *quat;* roughhewn; *salebrous;* thickened; uneven; umbonate; *varix;* whelky; *xyloma; yedder;* zitty; [*Ant.* level]

**lunatic** *(n.)*: asylum case; basket case; crackpot; demoniac; deranged man; eccentric; fruitcake; goof; harebrain; insane person; *jolt-brain;* kook; loony-bird; madman; maniac; mental case; nut(case); odd-ball; psycho(path); psychedelic; quack; raving ~; screwball; twisted individual; unstable person; volatile person; wacko; weirdo; *xtry. mad;* yo-yo; zany;

**lunge** *(v.)*: attack; *blast;* camisado; *drive; engage; fight;* go for; hit; *invade;* jump out at; jab; *knock;* lash out; lurch; make assault; *nudge; onslaught;* pounce on; *quab;* rush; strike; strike; *stab;* thrust; *unprepared;* violently thrust; *war;* xuld [arch.]; yerk; *zap;*

**lure** *(n.)*: allurement; bait; carrot; decoy; draw; enticement; ensnarement; fishhook; gimmick; hook; inducement; jig; *knavery;* lariat; magnet; *nudge; outwitting;* pull; *quiblin* [arch.]; roping; seducement; temptation; trap; urging; *vie;* wooing; *xuld* [arch.]; yearning; *zygotaxis* [biol.];

**lure** *(v.)*: allure; attract; bait; captivate; draw; entice; fascinate; get one hooked; hook in; induce; jape; *knavery;* lead; mislead; *nudge;* offer bait to; pull in; *quiblin* [arch.]; rope in; suck in; seduce; trepan; tole; troll; tempt; urge; *vie;* woo; *xuld* [arch.]; yerk; *zygotaxis;*

**lurk** *(v.)*: abide; *ambush;* bide; crouch; creep; dwell; *encamp; follow on;* gumshoe; hang around; hide; *inhabit; just be around;* keep close; linger; loom; lie in wait; *menace; near; occupy;* prowl; *quarter;* remain; skulk; stalk; tarry; underlie; *veiled;* wait; *xenize; yerde* [arch.]; *zero departure;*

**lurker** *(n.)*: ambusher; bushwhacker; creeper; *despoiler;* ensnarer; forelayer; gumshoe; hedge-creeper; insidiator; jumper; *knuck;* lier in wait; lingerer; lier in wait; mugger; *nab; overtaker;* prowler; *quad; robber;* skulker; *thief; usurper; villain;* waylayer; *x; yob* [arch.]; *zob;*

**lush** *(adj.)*: abundant; blooming; cespitose; dense; enfoliated; fertile; flourishing; grassy; green; herbaged; infoliated; jungly; *keen;* luxuriant; meadowy; *natural;* overgrown; plush; *quitch-grass covered;* rich; swardy; turfy; unspoiled; verdant; wooded; *xerophilious; yewey;* zea-filled; [*see* luxurious; *Ant.* lifeless]

**lust** *(n.)*: appetite; burning; covetousness; carnality; concupiscence; desire; eroticism; envy; fleshly ~; goatishness; hunger; immorality; impurity; itch; *jadishness; kinkiness;* lustfulness; lasciviousness; lech; *mischievousness;* nymphomania; obsession; pruriency; *quad;* randiness; reprobation; sensualness; salacity; thirst; unrestraint; unlawful desire; voluptuousness; want(onness); *x-rated thoughts;* yearning; zeal; [*Ant.* loathing]

**lust** *(v.)*: ache; *bid;* covet; crave; desire; *eroticize;* fancy; *got to have;* hunger; itch; *just got to have; keen desire;* long for; *mine; need; obsessed;* pine; pant; *quest for; reach for;* seek; thirst for; *urge; velleity;* want; *xel [arch.];* yearn for; *zealously desire;* [*see* loath]

**luster** *(n.)*: aura; brilliance; candescence; dazzle; effulgence; fulgency; gleam; halo; irradiation; illustriousness; *jet; keenness;* lustre; luminosity; magnificence; nitency; opalescence; patina; radiance; reflet; shine; sheen; *translucency; ultraviolet light;* vividness; white light; *xenon light;* yellow light; *zing;*

**lustful** *(adj.)*: aphrodisiacal; base; concupiscent; desirous; dissolute; dirty; epithumetic; fornicating; fescennine; goatish; hot-blooded; impure; immoral; impure; jadish; *kinky;* lewd; licentious; loose; libidinous; lecherous; *mischievous;* non-pure; nymphomaniacal; obscene; profligate; perverse; *quad;* ruttish; randy; reprobate; salacious; tempted; unchaste; unrestrained; venereous; whorish; wicked; wanton; x-rated; yearning; zizzy;

**lusty** *(adj.)*: able-bodied; athletic; brawny; *capable;* durable; energetic; fit; husky; iron; *jusqu'au bout [F.];* keen; large; muscular; nervy; *overzealous;* powerful; *quality;* rugged; robust; sturdy; strapping; stout; tough; unflagging; vigorous; well-set; x-strong; yauld; zealous; [*Ant.* languid]

**luxurious** *(adj.)*: affluent; bountiful; cushy; costly; deluxe; extravagant; fabulous; gorgeous; grand; high;-class immoderate; impressive; indulgent; *jet-set; kingly;* lavish; lush; luxuriant; magnificent; never-wanting; opulent; prestigious; plush; posh; *quartful* [arch.]; rich; ritzy; swanky; sumptuous; taking; upscale; voluptuous; wealthy; xtry.; *yet unsurpassed; zierlich* [G.];

**luxury** *(n.)*: amenity; bed of roses; comfort; delightfulness; ease; extravagance; Easy Street; fleshpots; fat of the land; grandeur; good things of life; high on the hog; indulgence; *joie de vivre* [F.]; *keen;* (lap of) ~; luxuriousness; lavishness; life of Riley; milk and honey; needlessness; opulence; plushness; purple and fine linen; quietude; rest; relaxation; richness; ritziness; self-indulgence; sumptuousness; treat; unnecessariness; voluptuousness; wealth; *xtry.; yet unsurpassed; zizziness;*

**lying** *(adj. laying down)*: abscissa; *baseline;* couchant; decumbent; edgewise; flat; groveling; horizontal; incumbent; jacent; *kowtow;* laying down; laid out; *mean sea level;* non-erect; on the ground; prone; procumbent; prostrate; *quasi-horizontal;* reclining; recumbent; resting; sideways; supine; transversal; un-erect; *vegetate; wide;* x-axis; *yielded; zonked out;*

**lying** *(adj. untruthful)*: artful; bad; crooked; dishonest; equivocating; false; guileful; honorless; ignoble; jady; knavish; louche; mendacious; misleading; non-credible; *opportunistic;* perjurious; *quasi-ethical;* ruthless; seedy; shady; treacherous; untrustworthy; untruthful; unscrupulous; venal; wily; *x-ing;* yeggy; *zero honesty;*

# M

**machination** *(n.)*: artifice; *blueprint;* conspiracy; design; enginery; foredesign; gambit; huggermugger; intrigue; japery; King's gambit; *layout;* maneuvering; *non-loyalty; overthrow;* planning; plotting; *quo mode* [L.]; ruse; scheming; treachery; underplot; villainy; wile; *x-chart; yantra [Hind.]; zenithal projection;*

**machine** *(n.)*: apparatus; appliance; *binary* ~; contraption; contrivance; computer; device; electronics; engine; *function;* gizmo; gadget(ry); *hardware;* instrument(ation); invention; *jigger; kickumbob;* labor-saving device; mechanism; motor; machinery; "nuts and bolts"; *object;* piece of equipment; *quality handiwork;* robot; system; technology; technological marvel; unit; *vehicle;* widget; *X-Y recorder; yield; Zeug [G.];*

**mad** *(adj.)*: angry; boiling; beside oneself; cross; disgusted; enraged; furious; galled; hot; irate; incensed; infuriated; jumping ~; kindled; livid; miffed; nettled; outraged; perturbed; quick-tempered; raging; sore; ticked off; upset; vexed; wroth; *xerothermic;* yelling ~; *zealousy [arch.];* [*see* insane; *Ant.* merry]

**madam** *(n.)*: *adult; belle;* citess; dame [off.]; *effeminate;* female; goodwife; gentlewoman; housewife; heiress; *individual;* jane [slang]; *khanum* [Pers.]; lady; mistress; madame; matron; nullipara; *one; person; quaedam* [arch.]; *relict;* señora [Sp.]; *termagant; unmanly; vrouw* [Du.]; woman; *xanthippe; young lady;* zaftig;

**madden** *(v.)*: anger; boil; burn; cross; disgust; enrage; exasperate; frustrate; fluster; fume; gall; heat up; incense; infuriate; *jangle;* kindle; lose one's temper; miff; nettle; outrage; provoke; perturb; *quick-tempered;* rile; steam; tick off; upset; vex; work up; *xerothermic;* yell; *zealousy* [arch.]; [*Ant.* mollify]

**madhouse** *(n.)*: asylum; bedlam; booby hatch; crazy house; dementia ward; *eccentric;* funny farm; goofy house; home; hospital; insane asylum; *jail;* kook house; loony bin; lunatic asylum; mental ward; nuthouse; *off the streets;* padded cell; psychiatric ward; *quacked; raving;* sick house; *taken leave of senses; unbalanced; volatile;* ward; *xtr. loony; yo-yo;* zany house;

**madly** *(adv.)*: ardently; badly; crazily; deeply; extremely; furiously; frantically; *gung-ho;* hurriedly; hotly; head over heals; intensely; jarringly; keenly; ludicrously; like mad; much; nonsensically; nuttily; overly; overmuch; powerfully; passionately; quickly; really; recklessly; strongly; totally; utterly; uncontrollably; very; vehemently; wildly; *xtry.;* yarily; zealously; [*see* angry; *Ant.* mildly]

**madman** *(n.)*: *absurd;* basket case; crackpot; crazy man; deranged man; *eccentric;* fruitcake; fruit-case; *gone mad; haywire;* insane man; *jack-o;* kook; loony-bird; lunatic; mental case; maniac; nut(case); *off-his-rocker;* psycho; quack; raving lunatic; strange bird; screwball; *taken leave of his senses;* unstable person; *volatile;* wacko; *xtr. weird;* yo-yo; zany;

**madness** *(n.)*: absurdity; berzerkness; craziness; daftness; derangement; dementia; eccentricity; freakiness; goofiness; harebrainedness; insanity; *jungle fever;* kookiness; looniness; lunacy; mania; nuttiness; outlandishness; psychopathy; quackery; raving lunacy; screwiness; twistedness; unstable condition; *volatility;* wackiness; weirdness; *xtry. lunacy; yo-yo;* zaniness; zoanthropy; [*see* insanity; *Ant.* merriment]

**magazine** *(n. periodical)*: *article;* annual; bulletin; back issue; booklet; biweekly; bimonthly; circular; digest; edition; fanzine [slang]; feuilleton; gazette; house organ; intelligencer; issue; journal; *key publication; leaflet;* monthly; *media;* newsletter; news~; *newspaper;* organ; periodical; publication; quarterly; rag; review; slick; semiweekly; tabloid; trade ~; *unifoliate; volume;* weekly; *x-tra;* yellow press; zine [slang];

**magazine** *(n. munitions store)*: armory; battery; cartridge; cache; depot; entrepot; firearms; gunroom; hold; *iron rations [slang]; javelin room; keep;* locker; munitions store; *naval arms depot;* ordnance; promptuary; *quantity;* repository; storehouse; *treasure;* utility room; vault; weapons store; *xiphos;* yard; *zone;*
**magi** *(n.)*: astronomers; *Brahman* [Ind.]; contemplator; *disciple; eastern; far-off travelers;* great men; *heavens-studiers;* inquirer; *journeyers; kings;* learned men; magnus; night-sky watchers; *oracle;* philosophers; questors; *rider;* sage; seekers; stargazers; *three kings; travelers; understanding;* venturer; wise men; xenagogue; *yeme;* zetetics;
**magic** *(n.)*: art; alchemy; *abracadabra;* black ~ (-art); conjuring; diablerie; deep ~; enchantment; fortune-telling; fetishism; gramary; hocus pocus; incantation; juju; *Keltic religion; legerdemain;* mojo; necromancy; occult; prestidigitation; *presto chango!; quad;* rune; slight of hand; sortilege; sorcery; theurgy; thaumaturgy; *uncanny;* voodoo; white ~; witchcraft; wizardry; xenomancy; *yogism; zodiac;*
**magical** *(adj.)*: amazing; bewitching; charmed; diabolic; enchanted; fey; ghostly; *hexed;* incredible; *jolting; keen;* lustrous; magic; mystical; miraculous; notable; not explainable; oracular; powerful; *queer;* runic; supernatural; spellbinding; sorcerous; talismanic; telesmatical; thaumaturgic; uncanny; voodooistic; wondrous; wizardly; *xtry.; yielded to sorcery; zapped;* [see wonderful; *Ant.* mundane]
**magician** *(n.)*: alchemist; arch~; bewitcher; conjurer; diviner; enchanter; fancymonger; geomancer; haruspice; illusionist; jadoo-wallah; *karakia [Maori];* lithomancer; magus; mage; Merlin; necromancer; occultist; psychic; *quack;* rhabdomancer; sorcerer; thaumaturge; thaumaturgist; *uncanny;* voodooist; wizard; xylomancer; *yogist;* zendik [Mos.];
**magistrate** *(n.)*: arbitrator; bencher; court judge; decider; evaluator; *forejudge;* gager; headman; Honor; intermediary; jurat; judge; kadi; law officer; moderator; *negotiator;* official; presider; pretor; quaestor; referee; sentencer; trier; *umpire;* vice-secretary; weigher; *XQ.; Your Honor; zamorin;*
**magnanimity** *(n.)*: altruism; benevolence; bigheartedness; charitableness; *donations;* errantry; favor; freehandedness; generosity; high-mindedness; indulgence; *joyful giving;* kindness; largesse; liberality; munificence; nobleness; open-handedness; philanthropy; *quantity-giving; righteousness;* selflessness; *thoughtfulness;* unselfishness; *virtuousness; warmth; xenophilia; yieldedness; zealous support;* [*Ant.* miserliness]
**magnanimous** *(adj.)*: altruistic; benevolent; bighearted; charitable; distinguished; eminent; free-handed; generous; high-minded; indulgent; *joy-giving;* kind; liberal; munificent; noble-minded; open-handed; philanthropic; quick-to-give; *rich;* selfless; *thoughtful;* ungrudging; *virtuous; worthy; xenial; yielded; zealous;* [*Ant.* miserly]
**magnate** *(n.)*: *authority;* boss; baron; chief; director; entrepreneur; *foreman;* governor; head; intendant; jefe; kalhuna; kingpin; lord; mogul; nibs [Br. joc.]; noble; overseer; plutocrat; queen [fem.]; ringleader; ruler; supervisor; tycoon; top-dog; *ultimate authority;* vizer; warden; XO; *yokemaster;* zayim;
**magnetic** *(adj.)*: attractive; beckoning; clinging; charismatic; drawing; enthralling; electro~; fetching; ferro~; geo~; gravitational; hydro~; inviting; iso~; *jolting;* kapp; luring; magnetiferous; *non-repelling; oersted;* polarized; quadrupolar; remanent; sideritic; seductive; *sticking;* tugging; *U-shaped magnet; variometric; weber; xtr. powerful; yanking;* zoo~;
**magnetism** *(n.)*: attraction; alliciency; beguilement; cling; draw; electromagnetic pull; ferro~; geo~; hydro~; iso~; *jolt;* kapp; lure; magnetization; *nuclear-magnetic resonance; oersted;* polarity; pull; quality of attraction; residual ~; stick; strong attraction; tug; *U-shaped ~; variometric;* wooing; *xtr. powerful; yank;* zoo~;
**magnification** *(v.)*: augmentation; boost; close-up; distension; enlargement; fortification; growth; heightening; increase; intensification; jump; *keep growing;* largening; lens ~; multiple; *normal ~;* overemphasis; puffing up; quantum increase; *raising;* strengthening; *times ten; upping the ~; volume;* widening; *XL; yain* [arch.]; zooming in; [*Ant.* miniaturization]

**magnificent** *(adj.)*: amazing; brilliant; breathtaking; commendable; capital; divine; extraordinary; fantastic; great; glorious; heavenly; impressive; incredible; jim-dandy; keen; laudable; lofty; marvelous; noteworthy; outstanding; overwhelming; prestigious; praiseworthy; *quantum* [L.]; remarkable; splendid; stupendous; tremendous; unbelievable; unparalleled; very great; virtuous; wonderful; xtry.; *you beaut [Aus.];* zizzy;

**magnify** *(v.)*: amplify; augment; blow up; crescendo; *close up;* distend; enlarge; expand; *fatten; fortify;* grow; get close-up; heighten; increase; intensify; jumboize; *keep growing;* largen; make bigger; multiply; maximize; *narrow in;* overproportion; puff up; *quantum increase;* raise; strengthen; *times by ten;* up the magnification; *view x100;* wax greater; widen; XL; *yain* [arch.]; zoom in; [*see* worship; *Ant.* miniaturize]

**magnitude** *(n.)*: amount; bigness; consequence; degree; extent; enormity; fullness; greatness; hugeness; importance; jumboness; *king-sized;* level; massiveness; *noteworthiness;* overlargeness; prodigiousness; quantity; *reach;* size; strength; significance; tier; tremendousness; *unbelievable;* vastitude; weightiness; XL; *yield; zaftig;* [*Ant.* marginality]

**maid** *(n.)*: attendant; bond~; chamber- ~; dairy~; eye-servant; famulus; *gallopin;* housekeeper; hand~(en); house~ (-keeper); *indentured servant; jong;* kitchen- ~; lady-servant; maidservant; *neif; offsider;* parlor~; quarter- ~; *retainer* [arch.]; servant; serving-maid; soubrette; *trusty servant;* underling; *vassal;* wench; waiting- ~; *x-man;* yeoman; *zaikai [Jap.];* [*see* woman, virgin]

**maiden** *(n.)*: angel; beauty; belle; colleen; damsel; *eye-catcher;* female; girl; handmaiden; *individual;* jill [slang]; *jeune fille* [F.]; *kitchenmaid;* lass; miss; maid; nymph [poet.]; *one; person; quedam* [arch.]; rose [slang]; schoolgirl; tomato [slang]; *unmanly;* virgin; woman; *x-chromosome;* young lady; *zitella* [It.]; [*Ant.* man]

**maidenly** *(adj.)*: attractive; *beautiful;* charming; delicate; ever-womanly; feminine; girlish; *her;* innocent; *jane; kinswomanly;* ladylike; maidenlike; *meek;* nymphish; *over-womanly;* pure; petticoat [dated]; *quiet; ravishing;* sweet; tender; unmanly; virtuous; womanly; *x-chromosome;* young and beautiful; *zitella [It.];* [*Ant.* manly]

**mail** *(n.)*: air~; bulk ~; correspondence; carriage; certified ~; delivery; *envelope;* express; form letter; first class ~; general delivery; *hate ~;* inter-office ~; *junk ~; kurveying;* letter; *media rate; night delivery; next-day delivery;* overnight delivery; post; parcels; parcel post; *quick delivery;* rural delivery; registered ~; snail ~ [slang]; telegram; *undelivered ~; voyage;* wire; *x-man; xfer; yellow-padded envelope; zip code;*

**mail** *(v.)*: airmail; *bear;* convey; deliver; *e-mail; express;* freight; forward; get; haul; *international post;* janker; kurvey; *letter; move; next day air;* overnight; post; *par avion [F.];* quarter-cart; relay; send; ship; transport; *uptake; van; waft;* xfer; yanker [Br.]; zip;

**maim** *(v.)*: *abuse;* bemangle; chop up; damage; deface; dismember; *exscind; flay;* garble; harm; injure; *jab; knife;* lacerate; mutilate; mar; *notch;* olate; pull apart; *quade* [arch.]; ruin; spoil; tear asunder; uglify; victimize; wreck; *x-sect;* yank apart; *zap;*

**main** *(adj.)*: absolute; basic; big; core; central; chief; dominant; essential; eminent; focal; foremost; great(est); highest; important; *judicious;* key; leading; major; notable; overriding; predominant; principal; prime; primary; quintessential; ranking; supreme; top; utmost; *ultimate;* vital; weighty; *xenenthesis; yet unsurpassed; zenithal;* [*Ant.* marginal]

**mainland** *(n.)*: *area;* bank; country; continent; *dock; edge; fringe;* greater landmass; *hinterland;* inland; *jurisdiction; key landmass;* land(mass); main mass; non-island; *offshore;* principal landmass; *quay; region;* shore; subcontinent; *threshold; ultimate destination; vast;* whole; *x-border; yeo; zone;*

**mainline** *(adj.)*: accepted; big; chief; dominant; established; foremost; great; historical; highly influential; important; *judicious;* key; known; leading; main(stream); major; notable; overriding; principal; quite large; recognized; significant; top; utmost; *vast majority;* well-known; xtry.; *yet unsurpassed;* zenith

**mainstay** *(n.)*: anchor; backbone; core; dominant part; *essential;* foundation; greatest part; hold; *important; justification;* keystone; lifeblood; main thing; *notable;* overriding support; pillar; quoin; right-hand man; staple; top support; upholder; vital thing; *weightiest; xenolith; yoni [Skr.]; zet [dial.];*
**maintain** *(v.)*: advance; bear up; continue; care for; do; endure; fix; go on; hold on; *immortalize; justify;* keep; look after; make repairs; not waste; outlast; preserve; prolong; perpetuate; *quick-fix;* repair; retain; remain; sustain; take care of; upkeep; uphold; *voyage on;* wax; wage; *xenize;* yede; *zero change;*
**maintenance** *(n.)*: *abiding;* basic upkeep; care; doing repairs; *enduring;* fixing; going on; holding on; *immortalizing; journeying on;* keeping; looking after; maintaining; nurture; *outlasting;* preservation; *quick-fix;* repair; sustaining; TLC [slang]: upkeep; *voyaging on;* work; *xenization;* yeding; *zero change;*
**majestic** *(adj.)*: august; awesome; breathtaking; commanding; dignified; excellent; fabulous; grand; high-born; impressive; *judicious;* kingly; lofty; magnificent; noble; *outstanding;* princely; queenly [fem.]; royal; regal; stately; towering; uncommon; valiant; well-born; xtry.; yorkist; *zarish* [arch.];
**major** *(adj.)*: ascendant; big; chief; dominant; essential; eminent; foremost; great; highly important; important; *judicious;* key; large; leading; main; noteworthy; overriding; principal; quite important; ranking; significant; top; utmost; vital; weighty; *xtry.; yet unsurpassed; zenithal;* [*Ant.* minor]
**major** *(v.)*: accent; bring into focus; concentrate; cathect; draw attention to; emphasize; focus; give emphasis to; highlight; *importance; jump out;* keep emphasis on; lay stress upon; make emphasis; narrow down; overemphasize; put stress on; quite overstress; re-emphasize; specialize; stress; target; *underscore; value; weight; xtry. emphasis; yed;* zero in; [*Ant.* minor]
**majority** *(n.)*: almost all; bulk; chief part; dominant percentage; essence; fifty-one percent; greater part; highest percentage; *immoderate; judgment; keen ~;* largest percentage; lion's share; most; nearly all; overmost; preponderance; popular vote; *quorum; quantity;* ranking percentage; significant percentage; top-voted amount; *utmost; virtually all;* vast ~; weightier amount; *xtry. percentage; yondmost; zero contest;* [*Ant.* minority]
**make** *(v.)*: assemble; build; constitute; comprise; construct; craft; create; design; develop; effect; engineer; erect; form(ulate); found; forge; fabricate; fashion; generate; hand ~; institute; invent; initiate; *job;* knock together; *labor;* manufacture; mold; mill; mass produce; *nominate;* originate; output; produce; put together; put up; pump out; quick-build; realize; raise; reap; shape; turn out; upbuild; *vamp;* wage; *xenomorph;* yield; *z-bar;*
**makeover** *(n.)*: alteration; betterment; change; do-over; enhancement; facelift; *growth; help;* improvement; job; *keen new look; look;* metamorphosis; *new look;* overhaul; permutation; qualification; revamping; renovation; redesign; remake; switch; transformation; upgrade; variation; *work-over; xenomorph; youthfulness; Zoya;*
**maker** *(n.)*: assembler; artisan; builder; constructor; craftsman; creator; designer; erector; fashioner; fabricator; founder; generator; guildsman; handicraftsman; inventor; journeyman; *key man; laborer;* master builder; manufacturer; *notoriety;* originator; producer; qualified builder; realizer; raiser; *rebuilder;* shaper; tooler; technician; upbuilder; *vamper;* worker; workman; *xylographer; yeoman; zaikai [Jap.];*
**makeshift** *(adj.)*: ad hoc [L.]; basic; crude; done quickly; ersatz; for a time; *gimmick; hard;* improvised; jackleg; jury-rigged; *katchha* [Ind.]; lasting a short while; make-do; non-permanent; only temporary; provisional; quick; rough; stopgap; short-term; substitute; thrown-together; temporary; uncontrived; *under par; vile; while waiting; x-itory; yucky; zwischnzug* [G.];
**makeup** *(n. constitution)*: arrangement; attributes; balance; character; constitution; composition; disposition; essence; fiber; formation; grain; heart; intrinsicality; *jist; kind;* layout; lineament; makings; mettle; nature; overall ~; property; personality; quality; reality; suchness; spirit; structure; temperament; underlying character; virtue; warp and woof; *xenenthesis; yetzer* [Heb.]; *zoe;*
**makeup** *(n. cosmetics)*: ∗ *articles;* beauty aids; cosmetics; darkener; eye shadow; face paint; greasepaint; hues; *items;* jellies; kohl; lipstick; maquillage; nail polish; *objects;* powder; paint; *quaintries;* rouge; shadow; tones; intrinsicality; undercoat; visagiste aids; war paint [slang]; *xfer paint;* yolk-based ~; *zeug;*

**maladapted** *(adj.)*: astable; badly adapted; confused; dazed; *exasperated; foggy; grievous;* hinky; ill-equipped; ill-adapted; instable; just not working out; *knark; lousy;* maladjusted; non-acclimated; out of tune; poorly-adapted; questionable; *raveled;* shaky; troublesome; unsuited; unstable; unadapted; vexed; wildered; *x'ed;* yet unadjusted; *ziggety;*

**malady** *(n.)*: ailment; bug; condition; disease; evil; *fever; germ;* health problem; infirmity; *jaundice; king's evil;* lesion; misfortune; *nausea; ordeal;* problem; queasiness; *remittent;* sickness; trouble; *upset; virus;* woe; *x-virus; yellow fever; zymogenic;*

**malaise** *(n.)*: anxiety; blahs; cheerlessness; discontent; ennui; frustration; grogginess; heaviness; inquietude; implacability; illness; joylessness; kef; lethargy; malcontentedness; non-satisfaction; overtiredness; peplessness; quasi-lethargic; restlessness; sickness; torpidity; unease; vapors; woe; *x-out;* yucky feeling; zeallessness;

**malevolence** *(n.)*: antagonism; bitterness; contempt; devilishness; evil; foulness; fiendishness; gall; hostility; ill-will; *jadedness;* knavishness; loathing; malice; nastiness; nefariousness; orneriness; perniciousness; querulousness; rancor; spite; treachery; unscrupulousness; venom; wickedness; *xenophobia; yawping; zealotry;*

**malevolent** *(adj.)*: abominable; bad; corrupt; devilish; diabolical; evil; foul; fiendish; guileful; harmful; hateful; iniquitous; *jaded;* knavish; loathsome; malicious; nasty; nefarious; ornery; perverse; pernicious; querulous; rotten; spiteful; treacherous; unrighteous; unkind; vicious; wicked; *xenophobic;* yucky; *zoilean;*

**malice** *(n.)*: animosity; bitterness; contempt; dislike; detestation; enmity; fight; gall; hatred; hostility; inimicality; ill-will; jangliness; knavishness; loathing; malevolence; negativism; odium; perniciousness; querulousness; resentment; rancor; spite; treachery; unfriendliness; venom; wickedness; *xenophobia; yawping; zealotry;*

**malicious** *(adj.)*: atrocious; baneful; bitter; contemptible; despiteful; evil-minded; foul; guileful; hateful; inimical; jangly; knavish; loathing; malevolent; nasty; odious; pernicious; poisonous; querulous; resentful; spiteful; treacherous; unfriendly; vicious; wicked; *xenophobic;* yawping; *zoilean;*

**malignant** *(adj.)*: abhorrent; bitter; cruel; despiteful; disdainful; evil; foul; galsome; hateful; inimical; jaded; kindless; low-down; loathsome; mean; malicious; malevolent; nasty; odious; pernicious; querulous; rancorous; spiteful; terrible; unkind; ugly; virulent; wicked; xenophobic; *yucky;* zoilean;

**malignity** *(n.)*: abominableness; badness; criminality; depravity; evil; flagitiousness; gall; heinousness; iniquity; *jadedness;* kindlessness; leaven; malice; nefariousness; obduracy; perverseness; querulousness; rancor; spite; sinfulness; treachery; unrighteousness; virulence; wickedness; *xgression; yetzer hara* [Heb.]; *zymosis;*

**malinger** *(v.)*: avoid; bludge; call in sick; dodge; evade; feign illness; get out of; goldbrick; *hedge; ignore;* jink; keep from; let go; miss work; not pull one's weight; obviate; pretend to be sick; *quit;* run from; shirk; turn away from; *uninterested; veer away;* withdraw; *x-out; yerk; zero interest;*

**malnourished** *(adj.)*: attenuated; bony; constricted; delicate; emaciated; frail; gaunt; half-starved; insubstantial; jejune; knife blade-thin; lean; macerated; narrow; overthin; peakish; *quantité négligeable* [F.]; ribby; skinny; starved; thin; underfed; undernourished; *voracious;* wasting away; XF; *yawpish; zero body fat;*

**man** *(n.)*: adult; anthropos [Gr.]; *boy;* bloke; biped; chap; character; dude; earthling; fellow; feller; fella [both slang]; figure; guy; grownup; gentleman; human(-being, -kind [pl.]); *homo sapiens* [L.]; individual; joe [slang]; *kid;* living soul; male; mortal; mankind; *name; neighbor;* one; old ~; pedestrian; person; people [pl.]; *quadragenarian; rube [off.];* son (of Adam); sir; soul; terran; *underling; virile;* worldling; *x-linked;* young ~; *yokel;* zoon; [*Ant.* maid]

    **Male-given names**: Allen; Bart; Charles; David; Earl; Frank; Greg; Harvey; Irving; Jacob; Kevin; Lee; Michael; Nicholas; Oscar; Peter; Quentin; Ray; Steven; Thomas; Ulysses; Vance; William; Xaviar; Yannis; Zeb;

**man** *(v.)*: attend; be at; cover; control; do; engage; fill; go and do; handle; implement; *jockey; keep busy; lend oneself to;* manipulate; *navigate;* occupy; operate; oversee; *perform; quicken;* run; staff; tend; use; *vigor;* work; *xuld [arch.];* yeme; *zip to it;*

**manage** *(v.)*: administer; administrate; boss; control; direct; engineer; force; govern; head; handle; instruct; influence; judge; keep; lead; maintain; manipulate; micro- ~; *navigate;* oversee; operate; preside over; *quality control;* run; superintend; supervise; take over; undertake; *vanquish;* watch over; wield; *XO;* yeme; *zero delta;* [*Ant.* mismanage]

**manageable** *(adj,)*: administrable; bearable; controllable; doable; endurable; feasible; governable; handlable; instructable; *judicious;* keepable; livable; maintainable; manipulable; not bad; okay; practical; passable; quite ~; *reasonable; superintendence;* tractable; tolerable; under control; viable; wieldy; workable; *xenagogic; yard;* zero problem; [*Ant.* mind-boggling]

**management** *(n.)*: administration; *bishopric;* control; direction; engineering; front office; government; governance; headship; *instruction; jurisdiction;* keepership; leadership; lordship; middle ~; managership; *navigation;* oversight; procuration; power; *queenship;* responsibility; rule; running; stewardship; supervision; superintendence; *taking the lead;* use of authority; *vizierate;* wardenship; *xenagogy;* yard; *zakon [Rus.];*

**manager** *(n.)*: administrator; business ~; boss; controller; chamberlain; chief (steward); director; executive; foreman; governor; head; intendant; jefe; keeper; line ~; major-domo; master; night ~; overseer; procurator; padrone; *quartermaster;* reeve; *ruler;* steward; slavedriver; superintendent; supervisor; trustee; undershepherd; viceroy; warden; XO; yardboss; *zayim;*

**mandate** *(n.)*: act; behest; command(ment); diktat; decree; edict; fiat; governance; *halacha* [Heb.]; injunction; *jus gentium* [L.]; *keleusmatic;* law; mission; *national law;* order; proclamation; *quo minus* [L.]; rule; statute; task; ukase; *voice;* writ; XO ~; *yardstick;* zakon [Rus.];

**mandate** *(v.)*: adjure; bid; command; decree; enjoin; force; give an order; *have;* instruct; impose; *juration; kaleusmatic;* license; make a demand; necessitate; order; ordain; pronounce; *quo minus [L.];* require; say; tell; *utter; voice;* warrant; *XO order; yark; zakon [Rus.];*

**mandatory** *(adj.)*: absolutely required; binding; compulsory; demanded; enforced; essential; forced; *got to; have to;* irremissible; indispensable; *jump to it; key;* law-enforced; mandated; necessary; obligatory; pressing; *questionless;* required; statutory; top-priority; unavoidable; vital; *weighty; xtry.; yieldless;* zero-option;

**maneuver** *(n.)*: action; behavior; contrivance; doings; exercise; feat; going; handling; *intrepidity;* jig; jockeying; *knee-action; light-footed;* move; manoeuvre; *naval ~;* operation; performance; *quick act; reaction;* step; shunt; scheme; thing; trick; tactic; *undertaking; venture;* working; x-action; *yaw; zeal;* [*see* ploy]

**maneuver** *(v.)*: angle; beguile; control; direct; exercise; force; govern; handle; influence; jockey; keep under control; lead; manipulate; move; manoeuvre; navigate; oversee; pilot; quick move; *run;* steer; shunt; scheme; take control of; turn; use; *venture;* wangle; work; *xfer;* yeme; *zip;* [*see* plot]

**manger** *(n.)*: *area;* bin; box; crib; container; *device; embankment;* feeding trough; feeder; gully; gutter; holder; hack; hopper; *item;* jube; kneading trough; *leat;* meal-trough; nullah; *outlet; pit;* qanat; rig; trough; utility trough; vale; *vessel;* watering-trough; *x-groove; yew box; zanja;*

**mangle** *(v.)*: *abuse;* butcher; contort; cut up; deface; disfigure; endamage; flay; *garble;* hackle; injure; jeel; *knife;* lacerate; mutilate; *notch;* olate; prang; *quade* [arch.]; ruin; smash; shred; twist; tear apart; *uglify;* victimize; wreck; *x-sect;* yank apart; *zap;* [*Ant.* make (over)]

**manhood** *(n.)*: adulthood; becoming a man; coming of age; development; *ever-manly;* full age; grit; humanity; *iron; jack- [zoo.]; knightliness;* legal age; maturity; masculinity; manliness; non-femininity; *over-virility;* post-adolescence; prime of life; "quit you like men"; ripeness; ruggedness; strength; toughness; *unwomanly;* virility; *well-set; x-strong;* years of maturity; *zooming up;*

**manifest** *(adj.)*: apparent; blatant; clear; conspicuous; discernible; evident; flagrant; glaring; highly visible; in view; just plain to see; kenspeckle; laid bare; marked; noticeable; naked; observable; open; plain; *quite obvious;* recognizable; salient; transparent; unhidden; unmistakable; visible; witnessable; *x-parent; yeme [arch.]; zenithal;* [*Ant.* masked]

**manifest** *(v.)*: appear; array; bare; come out; display; demonstrate; expose; exhibit; flash; flaunt; give evidence; hold out; identify; indicate; *justify;* kithe [Scot.]; lay out; make visible; *non-concealed;* open up; present; *quite obvious;* reveal; show; tout; uncover; vaunt; *wave; x-parent; yield; zero concealment;* [*see* mask]

**manipulate** *(v.)*: *abuse;* boss; control; diddle; direct; dominate; exploit; force; govern; handle; head; influence; jockey; keep under control; lead; make; maneuver; negotiate; operate; orchestrate; pull the strings; *quell;* run; steer; take control of; use; *vanquish;* work; *xfer;* yeme; *zero in;*

**manipulation** *(n.)*: *abuse;* behind-the scenes control; control; direction; exploitation; force; governance; handling; influence; jockeying; keeping under control; leading; management; maneuvering; manipulating; negotiation; operation; pulling strings; *quelling;* running; steering; treatment; using influence; utilization; *voice;* working; *xfer; yeme; zonal ~;*

**manliness** *(n.)*: adventurousness; backbone; bravery; courage; daring; enterprise; fearlessness; gumption; hardiness; intrepidity; *Jack;* knightliness; lustiness; maleness; mettle; manfulness; nerve; *over-virility;* prowess; *quakeless;* ruggedness; strength; toughness; undauntedness; virility; *wherewithal; x-link; yareness; zippiness;*

**manly** *(adj.)*: able-bodied; brave; courageous; dauntless; ever-manly; firm; gallant; hulky; iron; *jusqu'au bout [F.];* knightly; lusty; masculine; manful; nervy; *over-virile;* plucky; powerful; quakeless; rugged; red-blooded; strong; tough; unflagging; virile; well-set; *x-strong;* yauld; *zealous;* [*Ant.* maidenly]

**man-made** *(adj.)*: artificial; bogus; contranatural; *duplicitous;* ersatz; engineered; fake; false; factory-produced; *glib;* heterogenial; inorganic; imitation; *just contrived; kidding; lying;* manufactured; non-natural; *outward;* phony; plastic; *quasi-real;* reproduced; simulated; synthetic; *talented;* unnatural; *versed;* wrought; *xylographer; yentzing; zelig;*

**manner** *(n.)*: approach; behavior; custom; doings; *execution;* fashion; form; going about; habitude; *idiosyncrasy; jobation;* kind; *life;* method; mode; mien; means; *nature;* order; process; *quo mode* [L.]; routine; system; style; sort; technique; *usage;* vein; way; *xenenthesis; yong* [arch.]; *zealous tradition;*

**mannerism** *(n.)*: affectation; behavior; characteristic; deeds; eccentricity; foible; gesticulation; habit; idiosyncrasy; *jerking; known habit; life;* manner; *notion; oddity;* peculiarity; quirk; *reaction;* schesis; trait; unconventional behavior; *variation;* way of behaving; *x-action; yede;* zanism;

**manners** *(n.)*: amenities; appropriateness; behavior; breeding; civility; correctness; courtesy; code of conduct; decorum; etiquette; fitness; good ~; gentility; gallantry; high-style; *impressive; jimp; kindness; loveliness;* mannerliness; mores; niceness; nobleness; obligingness; politeness; p's and q's; properness; propriety; protocol; procedure; punctilio; *quaintness;* right; refinement; social correctness; table ~; urbanity; *Victorian;* well-mannered; *xtry.; younker; zero offense;*

**mansion** *(n.)*: abode; building; castle; demesne; estate; fancy home; great house; house; haveli; hall; inhabitance; joclet; konak; living quarters; manor (house); *nest;* opulent house; palace; quinta; residence; structure; townhouse; *unity house;* villa; wealthy home; *x-house; yashiki* [Jap.]; *zwinger;*

**manual** *(n.)*: *authoritative text;* book; bible; compendium; directions; enchirdion; field guide; field-book; guide(book); handbook; instructions; *journal; kappa book; literature;* manufacturer's directions; *notes;* operations ~; procedure book; primer; *publication; quarto;* rulebook; sourcebook; textbook; utility guide; vade-mecum; *work;* xenagogy; *yearbook; zipper-book;*

**manufacture** *(v.)*: assemble; build; construct; crank out; develop; *erect;* fabricate; factory-build; generate; handcraft; *initiate; JIT/JIC;* knock out; *labor;* make; mass produce; *new-built;* output; produce; *quick-build;* refine; rebuild; spit out; turn out; upbuild; *vamp;* work up; *xfer;* yield; *zip out;*

**manufacturing** *(n.)*: *assembling;* building; construction; developing; *engineering;* fabrication; generation; handcrafting; *initiation; JIT/JIC;* knocking out; *laboring;* making; milling; mass production; *new-built;* output; production; *quick-build;* refining; rebuilding; *shaping;* turning out; upbuilding; *vamping;* work(manship); *xferring;* yield; *zipping out;*

**manuscript** *(n.)*: autograph; book; codex; copy; document; epistle; final draft; graphic; hierogram; holograph; handscroll; inscription; *journal; kept record;* letter; leaf; *the Law;* mezuzah; *makimono* [Jap.]; notation; original; paper roll; papyrus; parchment; *Qumran;* roll; record; scroll; script; tarp; text; uncial; vellum; writing; *xuan paper;* yellowed ~; *zeug;*

**many** *(adj. + pron.)*: abundant; a lot of; bounteous; beaucoup; copious; divers; disproportionate; excess(ive); fruitful; great; galore; heaps; immense; innumerable; jumbo; *king-sized amounts;* lots; loads; legion; manifold; much; numerous; overmuch; plentiful; plural(ity); quantitative; rife; several; sundry; tons; umpteen; uberous; various; voluminous; wantless; *x.;* yards; zillions;

**map** *(n.)*: atlas; blueprint; chart; drawing; diagram; *Ebstorf ~;* floor plan; geography; *globe;* hemisphere; homolosine projection; illustration; ichnography; *Jordan Transverse Mercator;* key location ~; layout; Mercator Projection; navigational (-nautical) chart; outline; plan(isphere); protraction; photo~; quadrangle ~; road ~ (-atlas); raster chart; schematic; sea chart; topographical ~; treasure ~; *undersea chart;* visual; vector chart; wallchart; world ~; x-chart; *yantra* [Hind.]; zenithal projection;

**mar** *(v.)*: abuse; butcher; cut off; damage; deface; disfigure; endamage; *fissure;* garble; hurt; injure; impair; jeel; *knife;* lacerate; maim; *notch;* olate; prang; *quade* [arch.]; ruin; spoil; taint; uglify; vandalize; wreck; *x-sect;* yank apart; *zap;* [*Ant.* mend]

**maraud** *(v.)*: assault; boot; *carry off;* despoil; depredate; excoriate; fleece; freeboot; gut; harrow; invade; *junk; knock off [slang];* loot; lay waste; molest; *nobble; overrun;* pillage; plunder; *quash;* raid; ravage; ransack; spoil; sack; take; *unlade;* violate; *whomp; xfer; yank; zap;*

**marauder** *(n.)*: assaulter; bandit; conqueror; despoiler; exploiter; freebooter; *grabber;* harrier; invader; *jackal; killer;* looter; molester; *nobbler;* outlaw; oppressor; pillager; plunderer; questor; raider; ransacker; ravager; spoiler; taker; thief; *uninvited;* violator; *wrecker; xfer; yanker; zapper;*

**march** *(n.)*: advance; *bearing;* continuation; demarch; euphatory; force- ~; gait; goosestep; hike; half step; *invasion;* jaunce; *keeping pace;* lockstep; movement; night- ~; *outmarch;* parade; quickstep; *roving;* step; slow time; tramping; transfer; *upbeat; venture;* walk; *xfer;* yomp; *zipping;*

**march** *(v.)*: advance; backpack; continue; demarch; defile; *enter;* footstep; file; go; goosestep; hike; *issue; invade;* jaunce; *keep pace;* lope; move; night-march; out~; prance; parade; quick march; *reposition;* step; stride; strut; trudge; tramp; tread; troop; *underway;* venture; walk; xfer; yomp; *zip;*

**margin** *(n.)*: abuttal; bottom ~; border; coast; dawn; edge; fringe; frontier; *gilded edge;* hem; *imbordered; jurisdiction; kept limit;* left ~; line; limit; march; *narrow;* outskirts; perimeter; quadra; rim; right ~; side; skirt; top ~; threshold; tressure; *upper limit;* verge; without; *x-border; yonder; zone;* [*Ant.* middle]

**marine** *(adj.)*: aquatic; amphibious; bathymetrical; coastal; deep-sea; *estuary; freshwater; grallatorial* [zoo.]; hydrographic; *inlet; jheel* [Ind.]; *keld;* limnetic; maritime; natatory; nautical; neptunian; oceanic; pelagic; *quai;* river(-dwelling); sea(going); seafaring; submarine; thalassic; undersea (-water); *voe;* water-dwelling; waterborne; *xyrisic; yeo; Zee* [G.];

**mark** *(n. symbol)*: *arms;* badge; blazon; brand; character; crest; coat of arms; downstroke; designation; *dele;* emblem; figure; glyph; hierogram; heraldry; impression; indication; imprint; image; inscription; insignia; jot; ken- ~; letter; logo; marking; minim; notation; object; pen- ~; pictogram; quillstroke; representation; remarque; stroke; score; sigil; superscription; sign(ification); symbol; seal; tittle; token; upstroke; *vexillum;* water~; way~; X; *yacht ensign; zeug;* [*see* symbol]

**mark** *(n. trait)*: attribute; *badge;* characteristic; detail; element; feature; *good quality;* highlight; ingredient; *jist;* key feature; lineament; major trait; *nature; object;* property; particularity; peculiarity; quality; reality; singularity; trait; undeniable quality; virtue; way (of recognizing); *x-factor; yetzer* [Heb.]; *zero in;*

**mark** *(v.)*: annotate; blazon; betoken; *compose;* denote; designate; *dele;* enter; etch; form ~; grave; handwrite; incise; indicate; imprint; impress; inscribe; jot down; keep record; log; make ~; notate; *overwrite;* put down; print; quill; redact; record; register; scribble; set down; scratch; take down; tiver; underwrite; *vellum;* write; x(ing); *yak; zay;*

**market** *(n.)*: agora; boutique; bazaar; convenience store; chain store; depot; department store; emporium; farmers ~; fish ~; five-and-dime; flea ~; grocery store; *high-priced ~;* industry; *jumble-shop; key store; location;* mart; ~place; *newsstand;* open ~; outlet; plaza; produce stand; PX [mil.]; quick mart; ~place; rialto; retail outlet; shambles; showroom; shopping center; shop; store; super~; strip mall; trading post; *unit;* variety store; warehouse (-room); *xyst;* yard sale; *zoco* [Arab.]

**marriage** *(adj.)*: alliance; bridal; conjugal; *deuterogamy;* endogamy; *frank~;* getting together; hymeneal; *inter~;* joining; knotting; love match; matrimonial; nuptial; opetide; *partnership; quixotic; relational;* spousal; *tying;* vow-taking; wedding; x; yoke; *zonam solvere [L.];*

**marriage** *(n.)*: adjoining; bond; conjoining; *deuterogamy;* elopement; *frank~;* getting together; hymeneals; intermarriage; joining; knot; love match; matrimony; nuptials; *oneness;* opetide; partnership; *queen-gold; relationship;* spousals; tying the knot; union; vows; wedlock; *x;* yoke; *zonam solvere [L.];* [*see* wedding; espousal]

**marriage-related** *(adj.)*: adjoining; bridal; conjugal; connubial; *deuterogamous;* espoused; *frankmarriage; gathering;* hymeneal; intermarriage-related; joint; *knot-tying;* love-related; matrimonial; nuptial; opetidal; partnership; *queen-gold; relational;* spousal; *tying the knot;* union; *vows;* wedding-related; x; yoking; *zonam solvere [L.];*

**marry** *(v. officiate a wedding)*: administer; be in charge; conduct; do wedding; *execute; fix;* govern; head up; hitch; *institute;* join; *knot;* lead; manage; *nuptial;* officiate; perform; preside over; *qualified;* run; superintend; tie the knot; *unite; vows;* wed; *xfer;* yoke; *zet [dial.];*

**marry** *(v. wed)*: adjoin; bind; conjoin; *desponsate;* exchange vows; elope; fix; get hitched; give oneself; have; hitch; *inter~;* join; knit together; link; lead to the altar; merge; mate; make vows; *nuptials; oneness;* pair (off); *queen-gold; relate;* settle down; spend rest of life with; take; tie the knot; unite; *vows;* wed; *x.;* yoke with; *zonam solvere [L.];*

**marsh** *(n.)*: *aikraw;* bog; carr; drain; everglade; fen; glade; haugh; inland ~; *jheel* [Ind.]; kavir; lowland; moor; marish; marshland; *nanoplankton; overgrown;* peatbog; quag(mire); reeds; swamp(land); tarn; *usnea;* vlie [S. Afr.]; wetland; xyrisic; yarpha; *zoocarpous area;*

**marshal** *(v.)*: assemble; activate; bring together; collect; draw together; employ; forgather; flock; gather; *hurry;* initiate; join; *kindle;* line up; muster; *negotiate;* organize; position; *quicken;* rally; regroup; summon; throng; unite; *venture; work;* xfer; *yede; zone;*

**marshy** *(adj.)*: alluvial; boggy; carr-like; damp; *everglade;* fenny; gouty; *heavy; icky; jheel [Ind.];* kavir-like; lutose; *loamy;* mucky; moorish; *never-dry;* oozy; peaty; paludal; quaggy; *reedy;* swampy; *turbid;* uliginose; *vlie [S. Afr.];* watery; washy; xyrisic; *yucky; zoocarpous;*

**martyr** *(n.)*: agonizer; *beheaded one;* Christian ~; dead one; *endurer;* faithful ~; *gazingstock; harmed party; individual; judderer;* killed saint; *lion-hearted;* ~ for Christ; *nockingstock;* one who died; *proto~; prey; quietus;* resting saint; sufferer; soul under the throne; *target; undergoer;* victim; witness; *Xn. ~; yare; zealous Christian;*

**martyrdom** *(n.)*: *abuse;* burning; beheading; *casualty;* decease; dying; elimination; fall; *faithful witness;* giving one's life; home-going; *internment; Jordan-crossing;* killing; loss of life; murder; martyrization; *non-living;* offering; perishing; quietus; *release; rest;* sacrifice; termination; *unto death; vanishing;* witness; *xfer to heaven;* yielding (up the ghost); *zeal;*

**masculine** *(adj.)*: andric; butch; boyish; *courageous; dauntless;* ever-manly; *fellow;* guy; gentlemanly; he-man; *iron; jack- [zoo.]; keen; lusty;* male; manlike; mannish; manful; manly; non-feminine; *over-virile;* potency; "quit you like men"; rugged; strong; spear; sire; tom; tough; two-fisted; unfeminine; virile; *well-set; x-strong;* y-linked; *zealous;* [*Ant.* maidenly]

**masculinity** *(n.)*: androgenic; boyishness; *courage; dauntlessness; ever-masculine; full-grown; grown;* he-man; iron; jack- *[zoo.];* keenness; lustiness; maleness; manfulness; mannishness; non-femininity; *over-virility;* potency; "quit you like men"; ruggedness; strength; toughness; two-fistedness; *unfeminine;* virility; *well-set; x-linked; y-chromosome; zeal;* [*Ant.* maidenliness]

**mash** *(v.)*: *apply pressure;* bash; compress; crush; depress; *destroy; expunge;* flatten; grind; hash; *impel;* jam; kibble; kill; levigate; mush; *nail; overcome;* press; pulverize; quash; ram; squeeze; squash; smash; tamp; *undo; void;* wring; *xowyn* [arch.]; *yank down; zap;*

**mask** *(n.)*: ante~; *attire;* ball-room ~; costume; disguise; *enrobed;* face~; façade; get-up; guise; hood; help- ~; *incognito; jest; kept disguised;* loup; maskery; *non-recognizable;* outfit; put-on; *quat* [arch.]; rig; shield; *transformed; uniform;* vizard; war~; *xenomorph;* yashmak; *zero recognition;* Zulu war ~;

**mask** *(v.)*: *artfulness;* bemask; conceal; disguise; enwrap; face; *garb;* hide; imbosk; *jape;* keep hidden; lay low; mantle; *non-recognizable;* obscure; put out of view; *protect; quat* [arch.]; *recluse;* shroud; shield; tuck away; *underneath;* veil; vizand; wrap; *xenomorph; yashmak; zero recognition;*

**mason** *(n.)*: *artificer;* bricklayer (-worker); craftsman; *doer; employee;* free~; granite worker; hodman; industrial worker; *jobber; kiln-dried;* laborer; mortar-and-brick man; nogger; *operator;* paver; quarler; rubbleworker; stonemason; tiler; *union-worker;* veneer stone-worker; worker; xblock layer; yard block layer; *zaikai [Jap.];*

**masonry** *(n.)*: adobe; brickwork (-laying); craft; *doing; employment;* free~; granite-work; herringbone bond; *industry; job; kiln-dried; lateritous;* mason work; nogging; *operation;* paving; quarle work; rubblework; stonework; tracery; *using bricks;* veneer ~; work; xblock laying; yard block layer; *zeal;*

**mass** *(n.)*: amassment; bunch; body; bulk; collection; densification; *enlargement;* flocking; gathering; heap; hoard; ingathering; jam; kit; load; mess; mound; mountain; *number;* overabundance; passel; pile; quantity; ruck; reservoir; slew; slather; ton; uniting; versant; wagonload; *xtry amount;* yardful; *zillions;*

**massacre** *(n.)*: atrocity; bloodbath (-shed); butchery; carnage; destruction; extermination; *final solution;* genocide; holocaust; *incident; jeopardizing;* killing; laying waste; *liquidation;* mass-murder; *nefariousness;* obliteration; purging; *quenching;* ruination; slaughter; *termination; upheaval;* violence; wiping out; x-ing out; *yanking down; zapping;*

**massacre** *(v.)*: annihilate; butcher; cut off; destroy; eliminate; exterminate; expunge; finish off; gun down; *homicide; incinerate; jab;* kill; *liquidate;* murder; *neutralize;* obliterate; purge; quench; rub out; slaughter; terminate; *unseat; vaporize;* wipe out; x-out; *yank down;* zap;

**master** *(n.)*: administer; authority; boss; chief; commander; captain; director; dictator; employer; executive; enslaver; emperor; *foreman;* governor; head; intendant; jarl; king; lord; leader; manager; monarch; nobleman; overseer; president; potentate; *queen [fem.];* ruler; regent; superintendent; superior; slaveholder; subjugator; sovereign; taskmaster; tyrant; *ultimate authority;* vizer; warden; warlord; XO; *yokemaster;* zayim; [*Ant.* manservant, maidservant]

**masterful** *(adj.)*: adept; brilliant; breathtaking; commanding; deft; expert; exceptional; fantastic; fabulous; great; gifted; heaven-gifted; incredible; jolly good; keen; knowledgeable; *laudable;* magnificent; notable; outstanding; proficient; qualified; remarkable; seasoned; skillful; talented; unequalled; virtuosic; wonderful; xtry.; *you-beaut [Aus.];* zizzy;

**mastermind** *(n.)*: architect; brain; chief architect; designer; engineer; fabricator; great mind; head; intelligence; *jesuit; know-it-all;* leader; main thinker; *non-amateur;* organizer; planner; *quick-thinker;* ringleader; supervisor; thinker; *ultimate leader; verneuker;* whiz; *xtry.; yet unsurpassed;* zenith;

**masterpiece** *(n.)*: achievement of a lifetime; best effort; *chef d' oeuvre* [F.]; *display piece; expertly-crafted piece;* finest work; greatest work; gem; highest achievement; *impressive;* jewel; *keenest piece;* life's work; masterwork; *magnum opus* [L. lit.]; *notable;* outstanding work; pride and joy; *quality; real piece of work;* showpiece; *tour de force* [F.]; unequalled achievement; very best work; work (of art); xtry. piece; *yet unsurpassed;* zenithal creation;

**mastery** *(n.)*: adeptness; authority; bravura; command; deftness; dominion; expertise; faculty; genius; headship; influence; jurisdiction; know-how; kingship; lordship; masterfulness; *ne plus ultra* [L.]; oversight; power; *quo warranto* [L.]; rule; skill; *talent; usefulness;* virtue; weight; *xenium;* yaup; zenith;

**match** *(n. counterpart)*: another (of the same kind); archrival; bedfellow; compeer; counterpart; duplicate; equal; fellow; good-fellow; *husband;* identical copy; *just alike; keep;* like kind; look-alike; mate; near-duplicate; *ouboet [S. Afr.];* peer; partner; perfect ~; qualified counterpart; *the* right one; rival; spitting image; teammate; *union; virtually the same;* workmate; *xtry. ~;* yoke(fellow); *zincograph;*

**match** *(v.)*: align; agree; bring together; blend; complement; coordinate; double; equal; fit with; go together; harmonize; imitate; jive [slang]; keep harmony with; line up; meet; mesh; *nearly imitate;* orchestrate; put together; quadrate; readjust; reconcile; suit; synchronize; tone with; team up; unite; *verse; well- ~d; xtry. harmony;* yoke; *zero difference;*

**matchmaker** *(n.)*: arranger; blind date arranger; cupid; *dating agency;* eHarmony.com; *friend;* go-between; *husband-finder;* intermediary; joiner; knot-tyer; *linker;* matcher; *nakhoda* [Jap.]; *old man under the moon* [Chin.]; pairer; qualified ~; *redirector; shadchan* [Heb.]; *svakha* [Rus.]; *twinner;* union-maker; *visionary; wife-finder; xenagogue;* yoker; *zero in;*

**mate** *(n.)*: associate; ally; buddy; bedfellow; companion; comrade; compatriot; devoted friend; *equal;* fellow(helper); friend; good-fellow; helper; help~; honey; husband [masc.]; intimate; joint-partner; kith [pl.]; loyal friend; match; neighbor; other half; partner; *quondam friend;* room~; school~; sidekick; spouse; team~; unfailing friend; *votary;* wife [fem.]; *xenophile;* yokefellow; yoke~; *zealous friend;* [*see* husband, wife, friend]

**mate** *(v.)*: associate; breed; correlate; cross; double; *draw together;* engender; fecundate; get together with; have babies; in(ter)breed; join; *knit;* link up with; marry; *nuptials;* outbreed; pullulate; *qualify;* reproduce; *sire;* twin; unite; *vein;* wed; x.; yoke; *zootrophy;*

**material** *(adj.)*: animate; bodily; corporeal; *down here;* elemental; earthly; fleshly; *genuine;* hylic; innate; jejune; *known;* living; materiate; mortal; natural; ordinary; physical; quotidian; real-life; sensual; temporal; tangible; unspiritual; *vapid;* worldly; *xbred; yourself;* zoetical;

**materialism** *(n.)*: avarice; buying things; covetousness; desire for things; earthly-mindedness; *fancying;* greed; hunger for possessions; insatiability; *jealousy; keen desire;* lust for things; mammonism; non-contentment; *over-greedy;* Philistinism; pruriency; quenchlessness; *rapaciousness;* self-indulgence; things; *thirst for possessions; unsatisfied; venal;* want of things; *xtry. ~;* yearning; zeal for new things;

**materialistic** *(adj.)*: acquisitive; *begrudging;* covetous; desirous; discontent; earthly-minded; *fleshly;* greedy; hard-fisted; insatiable; jealous; kitish; longing; money-hungry; non-contented; over-greedy; prurient; quenchless; rapacious; self-indulgent; thirsty; unsatisfied; *venal;* wanting; *xtry. greed;* yearnful; *zero contentment;*

**materialize** *(v.)*: appear; become manifest; crop up; develop; emerge; follow; go on; happen; intervene; *jump up; kep;* light; manifest; *near;* occur; pop up; *quicken;* rise; result; surface; take place; transpire; unfold; *venture; work; xpire; yield; zip out;*

**matriarch** *(n.)*: ancestor; begetter; clan leader; *dowager; elder;* foremother; genitor; (great-)grandmother; head; *inherited; jewel; kinswoman;* lineal mother; matriarchal leader; *near of kin;* originator; old woman; predecessor; *queen;* respected leader; *supreme;* tribal leader; *unilineal;* venerated mother; *woman; xanthippe; y-linked;* zaftig;

**matter** *(n. substance)*: appurtenance; bits and pieces; building blocks; constituents; *dust;* elements; *filling; fluff; goods;* hyle; items; *junk; kit; load;* material; *needments;* objects; physical ~; *quantity;* raw material; stuff; substance; things; *useable ~; valuables;* warf and woof; *xenenthesis; yannigan; zeug* [G.];

**matter** *(n. topic)*: affair; business; consideration; concern; discussion topic; development; emphasis; field; *gist;* heading; issue; *juncture;* key issue; *lot;* main point; *notion;* overriding issue; point (in question); problem; question; *root issue;* subject; topic; thing; underlying subject; *vital;* weighty ~; *xtr. topic; yield; zone;*

**mattress** *(n.)*: air ~; bed; child- ~; *cushion;* double ~; *estivate;* foam ~; *gurney; hard ~;* inflatable ~; *journey's end;* king-size ~; *lumpy ~;* mat; *nest;* overstuffed ~; pallet; paillasse; pad; queen-size ~; rollaway ~; straw ~; toddler ~; *unconscious; vegetation;* waterbed ~; *x-sleep; yawning; zotheca* [Rom.];
**mature** *(adj.)*: advanced; blossomed; big; complete; developed; *equipped;* full-grown; grown(-up); harvestable; increased; *juicy; keen;* large; mellow; matured; newly ripe; omy; progressed; pickable; perfect; *quite ready;* raised; ready; ripe; sprouted; supple; *tasty; unspoiled; very good;* well-ripened; XL; *yain [arch.]; zet [dial.];*
**mature** *(v.)*: age; blossom; come into one's own; develop; *expand;* flower; grow (up); *heighten;* increase; *jump up;* keep growing; luxuriate; mellow; maturate; *nourish;* overripen; progress; *quantum increase;* ready; ripen; shoot up; strengthen; *thrive;* upshoot; *vegetate;* wax greater; XL; *yain* [arch.]; *zoom up;*
**maturity** *(n.)*: advancing; adultness; adulthood; blossoming; becoming; change; coming of age; development; education; enlargement; flowering; growth; *heightening;* increase; instruction; *judiciousness; knowledge;* learning; luxuriating; mellowing; maturing; neogenesis; operant conditioning; progress; *quantum increase;* readying; ripening; sprouting; thriving; upshooting; *vegetation;* waxing greater; XL; *yain [arch.]; zooming up;*
**maximize** *(v.)*: aggrandize; broaden; capitalize on; develop; expand; exploit; fatten; grow; heighten; increase; jump up; *keep growing;* largen; mount; make the most of; *nth degree;* open out; progress; *quadruplicate;* raise; spread; swell; take full advantage of; *up;* use to the full; *very best use;* wax larger; widen; *xtn; yain* [arch.]; *zoom;* [*Ant.* ebb]
**maximum** *(adj.)*: allowed; biggest; climactic; *determined;* extreme; full; farthest; greatest; highest; *immoderate; jump; kop;* largest; most; maximal; *nth* degree; overmost; potential; *quota; reach;* supreme; top; utmost; ultimate; *vertex;* widest; *xtry.;* yondmost; zenithal; [*Ant.* minimal]
**maximum** *(n.)*: allowed amount; *apex;* biggest amount; ceiling; *determined;* extent; full (capacity); greatest level; highest level; *immoderate; jump; kop;* largest amount; lid; limit; most; nth degree; overmost; potential; quota; record; supreme; top; utmost; upper limit; vertex; *widest; xtry.;* yondmost height; zenith; [*Ant.* minimum]
**maze** *(n.)*: anarchy; brainteaser; conglomeration; conundrum; *difficulty;* entanglement; fuddlement; *gnarl;* hodgepodge; intricacy; jumble; *knot;* labyrinth; miz~; network; *obstacle;* puzzle; *quonundrum* [arch.]; ravel; skein; tangle; unsolved puzzle; *vexation;* warren; web; winding path; *x-ing; yaw; zigzag;*
**meadow** *(n.)*: area; bush; clearing; *dale; earsh;* field; grassland; hill country; haugh [Scot.]; ile [Welsh]; *jebel; knoll;* lea; mead; *nature; outdoors;* pasture; quadrat; range; sod; sward; steppe; turf; upland; vega; *water meadow; xyris;* yard; *zea;*
**meager** *(adj.)*: austere; bitty; chintzy; derisory; exiguous; feeble; gaunt; *hardly;* inadequate; insignificant; jejune; ketty; lacking; limited; little; measly; negligible; *overly small;* poor; paltry; perurious; *quantité négligeable* [F.]; runty; small; scanty; teeny; ungenerous; very small; wee; XS; *yea big; zero;*
**meagerness** *(n.)*: austerity; bittiness; chintziness; dinkiness; exiguity; feebleness; gauntness; *hardly;* inadequacy; insignificance; jejuneness; kettiness; lack; littleness; measliness; negligibility; *overly small;* paltriness; peruriousness; *quantité négligeable* [F.]; runtiness; scantiness; teeniness; undersize; *very small;* want; XS; *yea big; zero;*
**meal** *(n.)*: aliment; *breakfast; brunch;* bread; board [pl.]; buffet; banquet; chow [slang]; cuisine; dinner; eating; food; feeding; feast; groceries; *hash;* high tea [Br.]; ingesta; junket; kale-time; *lunch;* mess; meat; mealtime; nourishment; *organic food;* provisions; potluck; *quelque-chose [F.];* repast; refection; sustenance; supper; table; *unassimilated food;* vittles; victuals; *wheat; xarque; yams; ziti;*
**mean** *(adj.)*: antagonistic; belligerent; catty; contemptuous; despiteful; evil; fiendful; galsome; hateful; inimical; jaded; kindless; loathsome; malicious; malevolent; mean-spirited; nasty; odious; pernicious; quarrelsome; rancorous; spiteful; tawdry; unkind; ugly; virulent; wicked; *xenophobic; yucky;* zoilean; [*Ant.* merciful]

**mean** *(v.)*: add up to; aim; betoken; bespeak; connote; denote; *entail;* foreshadow; give token or sign; have in mind; indicate; intend; *jobation; known;* lead to; make known; *necessitate;* omenate; portend; picture; plan; *qualify;* represent; *reveal;* stand for; symbolize; *thinking;* typify; *utter;* very aptly denote; want; *x-type;* yield; zero in;

**meander** *(v.)*: amble; alternate; bend; curve; drift; expatiate; extravagate; flexuous; gallivant; hover; *inflect;* jag; jump; *kedge;* loop about; move back and forth; *non-linear;* oscillate; pendulate; *quiver;* ramble; sinuate; snake; twist and turn; *undulate;* vacillate; wander; wind; *x-ing;* yaw; zigzag;

**meaningful** *(adj.)*: all-important; big; consequential; deep; evocative; fraught with meaning; great; highly important; important; *jubilated;* key; *large;* major; momentous; noteworthy; *outstanding;* profound; *quantum;* remarkable; significant; telling; *ultimate;* valuable; very ~; weighty; xtry.; *yearnful; zero hour;* [*Ant.* meaningless]

**meaningless** *(adj.)*: absurd; blithering; *crazy;* designless; empty; foolish; futile; good-for-nothing; hollow; high-sounding; insignificant; jerkwater; ketty; little; minor; marginal; nonsensical; nugatory; *obscure;* paltry; pointless; quisquillous; ridiculous; senseless; trifling; useless; unfruitful; unmeaning; vain; worthless; *x-out;* yet pointless; *zero meaning;* [*Ant.* meaningful]

**meanness** *(n.)*: atrocity; awfulness; belligerence; cruelty; despicableness; evil; fellness; foulness; godlessness; heartlessness; ignominy; *jadedness;* kindlessness; loathsomeness; malice; nastiness; odiousness; pitilessness; quarrelsomeness; rancorousness; spitefulness; terribleness; unkindness; vindictiveness; wickedness; *xenophobia;* yuckiness; zoileanism; [*Ant.* mercy]

**means** *(n.)*: avenue; ability; background; brawn; bucks; capital; capacity; deftness; dowry; expertise; efficacy; funds; facility; *gift; genius;* habilitation; instrument; income; *jurisdiction;* know-how; *license;* medium; mechanism; method; might; money; natural ability; *opportunity;* power; *qualification;* road; resources; stepping-stone; system; sufficiency; technique; tactic; *talent; usefulness;* vehicle; wherewithal; way; wealth; *xenium; yare; zeal;*

**measure** *(v.)*: allot; allocate; apportion; assess; bestow; *check;* deal out; divide; dispense; dole out; determine; exact; *fixed amount;* give; gauge; hand out; issue; *justly allocate; know;* lay a ruler against; mete; mensurate; *number; outside ~ment;* portion (out); parcel; quantitate; quantify; ration; *salient; transfer;* unitize; *volume;* weigh; *xfer; yardstick; zone;*

**measurement** *(n.)*: amount; breadth; capacity; dimension; depth; extent; footage; gauge; height; inside ~; *just allocation; kilometers;* length; meting; metric capacity; measure; measuring; mensuration; numbering; outside ~; portioning; quantity; ration; size; total ~; tonnage; unit size; volume; width; *XAG;* yardage; *zak;*

**meat** *(n.)*: animal protein; *beef;* cutlet; confit; coldcuts; collop; *duck;* escalope; flesh; game; hock; ingesta; jerky; kebab; lunchmeat; mincemeat; nourishment; *offal; pot roast;* quarry; red meat; steak; turkey; uncooked meat; viand; white meat; *xarque; yak-meat; zebra-meat;* [*see* food]

   **Kinds of meat**: agneau de pre-sale; beef; chicken; duck; escaopes; frog legs; goat ~; ham; iguana ~; jerky; kangaroo ~; lamb; mutton; pork; quail; red ~; steak; turkey; veal; venison; white ~; xarque; yak ~; zebra ~;

**mechanical** *(n.)*: automatic; button-operated; computer-operated; *device;* engine-operated; *function; gadget;* hardware; instrumentation; *jigger;* knee-jerk; labor-saving; motorized; machinal; mechanistic; mechanized; non-human; *operational;* powered; quasi- ~; robotic; systematic; *spring-loaded;* technological; *unit; vamped;* well-automated; *xerothalmic; yarken; zeug [G.];* [*Ant.* man-powered]

**medal** *(n.)*: award; blue ribbon; *citation;* cross; decoration; emblem; fourragère; gold ~; honor; Iron Cross [G.]; *jewel; kudos; knight;* laurel; medallion; Navy Cross [U.S.]; ornament; prize; Pour le Merit [G.]; purple heart [U.S.]; *qualify;* ribbon; *recognition;* silver cross; *trophy; unit citation;* Victoria Cross [Br.]; war ~; *xenium; yellow bar; Zion's crowns;*

**meddle** *(v.)*: abuse rights; butt in; cut in; disturb; encroach; force one's way in; get involved; horn in; interfere; inter~; jump in; kibitz; *louse up;* mess with; nose in; obtrude; pry; *questionable; recommend;* snoop; stick one's nose in; touch; tamper; *unwanted;* violate; worm in; *x; yank; zilch;*

**meddlesome** *(adj.)*: arbitrating; butting in; cutting in; disturbing; encroaching; forcing one's way in; getting involved; horning in; interfering; intrusive; invasive; jumping in; kibitzing; *lousing up;* meddling; nosy; officious; prying; pushy; *questionable; right in the middle;* snooping; tampering; *unwanted;* violating; *whispering* ; *x; yenta; zealous;*

**mediate** *(v.)*: arbitrate; bench; consider; determine; decide; evaluate; facilitate; *fix;* gage; hear; intercede; intervene; judge; *knowledge; list [arch.];* moderate; negotiate; oversee; pass judgment; *qua* [L.]; referee; resolve; sit in judgment; settle; try; umpire; valuate; weigh; *XQ; Your Honor; zetetic;*

**mediation** *(n.)*: arbitration; benching; considering; determination; evaluation; facilitation; *fixing;* gauging; hearing; intercession; inter~; interposition; judgment; *knowing; listening;* modertion; negotiation; oversight; presiding; *qua [L.];* refereeing; settling; trying; umpirage; valuation; weighing; *XQ; Your Honor; zamorin;*

**mediator** *(n.)*: arbitrator; broker; conciliator; diplomat; daysman; *emissary;* facilitator; go-between; harmonizer; intermediary; judge; *Kissinger;* legate; moderator; middleman; negotiator; ombudsman; peacemaker; queller; referee; statesman; third party; umpire; *vehicle; words; xenophile; yamen* [Chin.]; *zero hostility;*

**medical** *(adj.)*: allopathic; bacteriological; clinical; curative; doctor-related; epulotic; esculapian; *forensic;* gynecological [fem.]; health; healing; iatric; *julep;* kinic; *lending aid;* medicinal; nursing; *neurological;* officinal; physician-related; professional; *quinic;* remedial; restorative; sanative; surgical; theriacal; *unit;* vulnerary; *wellbeing; xenobiotic; yarb [dial.]; zopissa [arch.];*

**medication** *(n.)*: ∗ antibiotic; amphetamine; balm; castor oil; controlled substance; drug; electuary; *first aid;* generic drug; herb; illegal drug; jalap; *kola;* laudanum; medicine; narcotic; over-the-counter ~; pharmaceutical; pills; quinine; *remedy;* substance; treatment; *upper; vancomycin; well-tested ~;* xenobiotic; yarb [dial.]; zopissa [arch.];

**medicinal** *(adj.)*: advantageous; antidotal; beneficial; curative; doctor-endorsed; effective; favorable; good; gainful; healing; healthful; iatric; *julep;* kinic; *lending aid;* medicative; *nostrum;* officinal; pharmaceutical; quinic; remedial; restorative; salutary; therapeutic; useful; vulnerary; *worthwhile; xenobiotic; yieldful; zopissa [arch.];*

**medicine** *(n.)*: antibiotic; antidote; balm; cure; *castor oil;* drug; elixir; electuary; febrifuge; generic ~; herb(al remedy); injection; *julep; kola;* lohock; medication; nonprescription drug; *oxacillin;* pill; *penicillin;* prescription; pharmaceutical; *quinine;* remedy; serum; tonic; tablet; treatment; ule; vaccine; vulnerary; virucide; wonder drug; *xenobiotic;* yanggona; *zopissa* [arch.];

**mediocre** *(adj.)*: average; basic; boring; common; dull; everyday; familiar; generic; ho-hum; inelaborate; *juste-milieu* [F.]; *known;* lackluster; mean; medium; normal; ordinary; plain; quotidian; regular; run-of-the-mill; simple; standard; typical; usual; undistinguished; *via media* [L.]; weak; *xy-median; yawnsome; zestless;* [Ant. magnificent]

**mediocrity** *(n.)*: averageness; boringness; commonness; dullness; *everyday;* familiarity; generality; *ho-hum;* inelaborateness; *juste-milieu* [F.]; *known;* lack of excellence; meanness; non-excellence; ordinariness; plainness; *quotidian;* regularity; simpleness; typicality; usualness; *via media [L.];* weakness; *xy-median; yawnsome; zestless;* [Ant. magnificence]

**meditate** *(v.)*: analyze; brainstorm; contemplate; cogitate; dwell; deliberate; evaluate; focus; *gauge;* have in mind; ingest; introspect; judge; *know;* look upon; logicalize; muse; mull over; *notion; occur;* ponder; pore; question; reflect; study; think; use brain; valuate; weigh; *xenodiagnose; yeme; zazen;*

**meditation** *(n.)*: analysis; brainwork; contemplation; deliberation; evaluation; focus; *gauge;* headwork; intellection; introspection; judgment; *knowledge;* lucubration; mentation; musing; *notion; on one's mind;* pondering; questioning; reflection; study; thought; using one's brain; *valuating;* weighing; *xenagogy; yeme* [arch.]; *zazen* [Bud.];

**meditative** *(adj.)*: absorbed; brooding; contemplative; deep-in-thought; engrossed; fanciful; gazeful; heart-searching; introspective; judicial; *knowledge;* lost in thought; museful; notional; occupied; pensive; *quiet;* reflective; studious; thoughtful; understanding; *valuating;* wistful; *xenocratic; yearnful; zetetic;*

**medium** *(adj.)*: average; basic; center; central; dead-center; equitorial; fair; general; halfway; in-the-middle; intermediate; *juste-milieu* [F.]; *known;* lackluster; mean; mid-way; median; medial; middling; moderate; middle(-of-the-road); normal; neutral; ordinary; plain; quotidian; regular; standard; so-so; smack-in-the-middle; typical; usual; unexcessive; *via media* [L.]; *well-centered; xy-median; yawnsome; zestless;*

**medium** *(n. soothsayer)*: astrologer; bewitcher; clairvoyant; diviner; enchanter; fortune-teller; geomancer; haruspice; *incantation;* jadoo-wallah; *karakia [Maori];* lithomancer; mystic; necromancer; oracle; psychic; *quad;* rhabdomancer; spiritualist; seer; theurgist; *ungodly;* voodooist; wizard; xylomancer; *yogist;* zodiacist; [*see* witch; means]

**meek** *(adj.)*: abstemious; benign; cool; calm; collective; controlled; deferential; even-keeled; forbearing; gentle; harmless; humble; inobtrusive; *judicial;* kind; lowly; mild; nice; over-quiet; peaceable; poor in spirit; quiet; restrained; self-controlled; softhearted; temperate; unassuming; unobtrusive; unostentatious; *velvet glove;* wrathless; *xenial;* yielding; *zero overbearingness;*

**meekness** *(n.)*: abstemiousness; benignity; control; calm; deference; equanimity; forbearance; gentleness; humbleness; inobtrusiveness; *judicial;* kindness; lowliness; mildness; non-aggressiveness; *obedience;* peaceableness; quietness; restraint; self-control; temperance; unobtrusiveness; *velvet glove;* wrathlessness; *xenia;* yieldedness; *zero overbearingness;*

**meet** *(v.)*: assemble; bring together; bump into; come together; converge; convene; congregate; draw together; encounter; forgather; flock; greet; get together; gather; happen upon; huddle; have a meeting; intersect; join; *knit;* link up; make acquaintance; muster; *nonavoidance;* oppose; put together; *qualify;* run into; reach; reconvene; rendezvous; rally; stumble upon; see; stretch to; touch; turn out; unite; visit; *work together; x.;* yoke; *zone;*

**meeting** *(n.)*: assembly; body; consultation; caucus; conference; congregation; convention; convocation; discussion; encounter; *ekklesia* [G.]; forgathering; forum; get-together; gathering; huddle; horde; ingathering; jam [coll.]; kit [coll.]; lot; mass; number; *opportunity; people;* pow-wow; parley; party; *quorum;* ruck; regathering; reunion; rally; session; summit; symposium; talks; throng; *turnout;* unit; vestry; *videoconference;* work; witan; *x.;* yoking ; *zayat [Burm.];*

**melancholy** *(adj.)*: atrabilious; bleak; blue; cheerless; downcast; dark; doleful; depressed; dismal; dejected; dissipirited; despondent; *ejulation;* fallen; forlorn; glum; gloomy; hopeless; *inconsolable;* joyless; *katzenjammer;* low; lugubrious; lachrymose; melancholic; morose; negative; *overly sad;* pitiful; pathetic; *quivering; rotten;* sullen; sad; sorrowful; saturnine; troubled; unhappy; *vapors;* wretched; woeful; *xtry. sad; yearnful;* zealless;

**melancholy** *(n.)*: atrabiliousness; blueness; blue funk; cheerlessness; downheartedness; ennui; forlornness; glumness; hopelessness; *inconsolableness;* joylessness; katzenjammer; low; moroseness; negativism; overmuch sorrow; pessimism; *quivering; ruefulness;* sadness; tristesse; unhappiness; vapors; woefulness; *xtry. sadness; yearning;* zestlessness;

**melody** *(n.)*: air; anthem; ballad; carol; chorus; ditty; euphony; folksong; *gallimaufry;* hymn; *inspirational;* jingle; kasida; lovesong; music; *notes;* ode; piece; quodlibet; refrain; song; tune; undersong; *Volkslied* [G.]; work-song; *xylophone song;* yed; *zemirah;*

**melt** *(v.)*: ablate; become liquid; colliquate; dissolve; deliquate; deliquesce; evanesce; fluidify; fade; fuse; get soft; go; heat up; infuse; *juicy; kindle;* liquefy; liquesce; merge; *molten; non-solid; over-soften;* pass away; *quail;* resolve; run; soften; solute; smelt; turn into liquid; thaw; unfreeze; vanish; warm up; waste away; *xfer;* yeet; *zeroize;* [*see* dissipate]

**member** *(n.)*: associate; affiliate; belonger; brother; constituent; card-holder; card-carrying ~; charter ~; dues-paying ~; enrollee; fellow; factionary; guildsman; group- ~; *honorary ~;* insider; joiner; janissary; *key ~;* lifetime ~; *man; neophyte;* organization ~; patron; part; qualified ~; recruit; supporter; sister [fem.]; team ~; *united;* votary; *workmate; xenizer;* yokefellow; *zealot;*
**membership** *(n.)*: affiliation; admission; association; *belonging;* body; brotherhood; constituency; charter ~; *dues;* enrollment; fellowship; group; *honorary ~; involvement;* inclusion; joint- ~; *key ~;* lifetime ~; members; *nexus;* organization; part; qualified ~; recruitment; *relationship;* sisterhood [fem.]; society; team ~; *uniting;* votaries; *workmates; xenizers;* yoke; *zealots;*
**memorable** *(adj.)*: amazing; big; catchy; celebrated; distinguished; extraordinary; fantastic; great; highly ~; impressive; *just amazing; keen;* life-changing; magnificent; notable; outstanding; prominent; *quantum [L.];* recallable; rememberable; remarkable; red-letter; significant; tremendous; unforgettable; very important; worth remembering; *well-remembered;* xtry.; *yet unforgotten; zestful;*
**memorial** *(adj.)*: appreciative; bearing in mind; commemorative; celebratory; dedicatory; enshrining; *fête;* giving regard to; honoring; insouling; in memory; *journal;* keepsake; laudative; memorializing; monumental; necrological; *not forgotten;* observing; paying tribute; *quickening;* remembering; solemnizing; testimonial; tributary; *unforgotten;* venerating; *well-remembered;* xtry. honors; *yet remembered; zealously observing;*
**memorial** *(n.)*: arch; burial plaque; cenotaph; cairn; dolmen; epitaph; footstone; gravestone; headstone; heap; indicator; inscription; *joint marker;* keepsake; land marker; legend; mound; memorative; monument; *necrology;* obelisk; pillar; pantheon; *quartz headstone;* reminder; remembrance; stone (marker); shrine; tombstone; tribute; testimonial; *urn; vault plaque; whinstone; writing;* xat; *yard stone;* ziarat [Mos.];
**memorize** *(v.)*: absorb; bear in mind; commit to memory; cram; *dig up memory; evoke;* fix in one's mind; get into one's head; have in one's heart; imbibe; insoul; *jog one's memory;* keep in memory; know; learn (by heart); master; *not forget;* own; put in one's heart; *quicken mind;* remember; retain; store in memory; *think;* understand; *versed; well-remembered; xenagogy; yeme; zero in;*
**memory** *(n.)*: awareness; bearing in mind; commemoration; cognizance; dwelling; evoking; flashback; going back; hypermnesia; impression; iconic ~; *jogging;* kept ~; long-term ~; memorial; nostalgia; observation; permanent ~; *quick-to-remember;* remembrance; recollection; reflection; retention; reminiscence; rote; short-term ~; thought; unaided recall; *veneration; well-remembered;* xtr. ~; *yesteryear; zero in;*
**menace** *(n.)*: annoyance; bane; chafer; danger; exasperator; frustration; grief; harasser; hazard; irritant; jangler; kidder; louse; miffer; nuisance; oppressor; pain; pest; peril; *queach [arch.];* riler; savage; troublemaker; threat; upsetter; vexer; wrongdoer; *x-er;* yerk; *zhub;*
**mend** *(v.)*: ameliorate; amend; better; cure; convalesce; darn; emend; fix; get well; help; heal; improve; *jump ahead;* knit; *lend aid;* make better; nurse to health; *on the ~;* patch; put right; *quick-fix;* repair; rectify; recuperate; restore; sew up; set right; *tack;* transform; upgrade; vamp; whole; *x-fix; yele* [arch.]; *zip back together;* [Ant. mar]
**menial** *(adj.)*: attending; blue-collar; common; drudge; ever-tedious; factory; *gofer;* helping; ignoble; jobholder; *kyu* [Jap.]; lowly; low-level; manual; non-skilled; operose; ponderous; *quotidian;* repetitive; servile; tedious; unskilled; unimportant; *vapid;* wearisome; xtry. *obsequious; yucky; zestless;* [Ant. main]
**mental** *(adj.)*: academic; *abstract;* brain-related; cognitive; cerebral; deep; erudite; *farsighted;* gifted; highbrow; intellectual; *judicious;* knowledge-gaining; learning; mind-related; meditative; noetic; *occiput;* psychic; perceptual; pensive; pontine; phrenic; *quick-witted;* rational; ruminative; subconscious; subliminal; subjective; *scholarly;* thinking; telepathic; *understanding; vermis;* wistful; *xenagogic; yaup; zippy;* [*see* crazy; Ant. manual]

**mentality** *(n.)*: attitude; belief; cast; disposition; esprit; feeling; *gray matter;* heart; idea; judgment; *knowledge;* leaning; mindset; notion; outlook; perception; *quot homines tot sententiae [L.];* reckoning; rationality; sentiment; temperament; *ule;* viewpoint; way of thinking; *xenodiagnosis;* yaw; *zeal;*

**mention** *(v.)*: articulate; adduce; bandy; bring up; comment; disclose; declare; express; *foremention; give;* hint at; intimate; *jaw; key in;* let out; make known; note; observe; point out; pipe up; quoth; relate; remark; say; touch on; tell; utter; voice; word; *xenophonia;* yak; *zero in;*

**mentor** *(n.)*: advisor; big brother; counselor; *Dutch uncle;* example; friend; guide; goombah; guide; *helper;* instructor; *job; keen;* leader; model; nestor; *overseer;* pedagogue; preceptor; *quain [arch.];* role model; succorer; teacher; trainer; *uncle; value;* wise friend; xenagogue; *yokefellow; zealous friend;*

**mentor** *(v.)*: advise; *be there;* counsel; direct; exhort; foreadvise; guide; help; influence; *job;* keep on track; lead; model; *nice; oversee;* prepare; *quain [arch.];* role model; show; steer; spend time with; teach; tutor; *undershepherd; value;* work with; *xenagogy; yarken; zero in;*

**merchandise** *(n.)*: articles; *batch;* commodities; *delivery;* equipment; furnishings; goods; housewares; habiliments; items; job lot; *kitsch;* line; movables; *necessities;* objects; open stock; pedlery; products; *quantity;* resellable items; stuff; supplies; stock; things; *useful goods;* vendables; wares; *x-stock;* yield; yard goods; *zeug [G.];*

**merchant** *(n.)*: agent; business owner; cadger; dealer; exporter; furnisher; grocer; handler; importer; jobber; kiddier; *local ~;* marketer; monger; *négociant [F.];* operator; peddler; purveyor; *qualified retailer;* retailer; reseller; seller; storekeeper; supplier; sutler; trader; tradesman; trafficker; *utterer;* vendor; wholesaler; xylopolist; yarn man; *zyalde [arch.];*

**merciful** *(adj.)*: altruistic; benevolent; compassionate; clement; *dear;* easygoing; empathic; forbearing; forgiving; gracious; humane; *interested; joy-giving;* kind(hearted); lenient; *merciable [arch.];* non-harsh; *overly gracious;* pitying; propitious; quick-to-forgive; ready to forgive; sympathetic; sparing; tolerant; tender-hearted; understanding; very kind; warm; *xenial; yearnful; yielding;* zealous to forgive; [*Ant.* merciless]

**merciless** *(adj.)*: austere; barbaric; callous; cold-hearted; cruel(-hearted); cutthroat; disdainful; evil-minded; flint-hearted; *grievous;* heartless; hardhearted; hardened; incompassionate; implacable; ironhearted; inhuman; *jaded;* knark; kill-crazy; loveless; mean; malevolent; non-sparing; obdurate; pitiless; *querulous;* relentless; ruthless; severe; tearless; terrible; unpitying; uncompassionate; unfeeling; unmerciful; unsparing; vicious; without mercy; xenophobic; yieldless; *zestful;* [*Ant.* merciful]

**mercy** *(n.)*: act of kindness; benevolence; compassion; clemency; *delicate love;* empathy; forgiveness; favor; grace; goodwill; heart; *interest; joy-giving;* kindness; leniency; loving-kindness; mercifulness; niceness; *overly compassionate;* piteousness; pity; pathos; quarter; readiness to forgive; ruth; sympathy; tenderness; tender mercies; understanding; *virtue; warmth; xenia; yearning;* zeal to forgive; [*see* love; forgiveness; *Ant.* mercilessness]

**merge** *(n.)*: aggregation; amalgamation; blend; combination; consolidation; *dash;* emulsion; fusion; *grouping;* horizontal merger; intermixture; joining; knitting; lumping together; mixture; merging; merger; *network; one;* putting together; *queaching [arch.];* raveling; synthesis; *together;* union; vertical ~; wedding together; *xanthate; yanggoma; zet [dial.];*

**merge** *(v.)*: amalgamate; become one; blend; conflate; combine; coalesce; draw together; emulsify; flow together; fuse; get together; have union; integrate; interflow; intermix; inosculate; join; knit; lump together; mix; meld; *network; overmix;* pool; *queach [arch.];* ravel; synthesize; temper; unite; *voluble;* wed; *xenograft;* yoke; *zip together;*

**merit** *(n.)*: assessment; ability; advantage; benefit; condignity; credit; deserving; evaluation; excellence; fineness; good; gain; help; intrinsic worth; just desserts; justification; *known value;* laudable act; meritoriousness; *notion; outstanding;* profit; praiseworthiness; quality; redeeming value; self-worthiness; *terrific;* usefulness; value; virtue; worth(iness); *xtry.; yichus;* zeal;

**merit** *(v.)*: attain; achieve; bring in; clear; collect; deserve; earn; fetch; get; gain; have coming; *incur;* justify; *kep; land;* make; *net;* ought to have; obtain; *profit; quoff;* receive; secure; take in; *undertake; valuate;* work for; warrant; *well-deserved; x-div; yield; zealously work for;*

**meritorious** *(adj.)*: admirable; beloved; commendable; distinguished; estimable; excellent; fine; favorable; great; honorable; impressive; jake [Br.]; keen; laudable; marvelous; nice; outstanding; praiseworthy; quite good; remarkable; splendid; terrific; ultra-good; virtuous; very good; worthy; wonderful; xtry.; yichus; *zealously loved;* [*Ant.* meritless]

**mess** *(n.)*: anarchy; atrocity; bedlam; clutter; confusion; chaos; dishevelment; dive; disorder; disarray; entanglement; eyesore; farrago; grubbiness; guddle; heap; imbroglio; jumble; junk heap; kerfuffle; litter; mayhem; monstrosity; non-orderliness; *neglect;* olio; pigpen (-sty); quagmire; ravel; shambles; *sight;* tizzy; tangle; turmoil; untidiness; *vexation;* wreck; xtry. mess; yuckiness; zoo;

**message** *(n.)*: announcement; address; broadcast; bulletin; communication; dispatch; declaration; enunciation; epistle; *forewarning; give;* holding forth; intimation; jactitation; *keynote address;* letter; memo(random); missive; note; oration; pronouncement; proclamation; *quotation;* report; revelation; statement; testimonial; utterance; vocalization; verbalization; word; *xenagogy;* yeme; *zealous ~;*

**messenger** *(n.)*: announcer; ambassador; angel; bearer of tidings; bellman; courier; correspondent; crier; consul; dispatch; delegate; diplomat; emissary; envoy; foreign minister; *gofer;* herald; intelligencer; internuncio; *just in; kurveyor;* letter-carrier; legate; liaison; message-carrier; *minister;* negotiant; nuncio; *official; officer;* post; proclaimer; *questor* [It.]; runner; rider; representative; *servant;* tidings-bearer; town crier; updater; *utterer;* voicer; walking delegate; x-man; *yamen* [Chin.]; *zip;*

**Messiah** *(n.)*: Anointed; *Babe;* Blessed Son; Christ; Deliverer; Emmanuel; firstborn of the dead; God Incarnate; Holy One of Israel; Immanuel; Jesus; King; Lamb (of God); Mighty God; Nazarene; Only begotten Son; Promised One; *Quickener;* Redeemer; Savior; Truth; Unspeakable Gift; Victor; Way; Xt.; Yeshua; Zion's Hope;

**messy** *(adj.)*: *awful;* anarchic; bedraggled; cluttered; chaotic; dumpy; disorderly; disorganized; disheveled; entangled; frowzy; filthy; grungy; higgledy-piggledy; incomposed; jumbled; keg-meg; littered; messed-up; neglected; orderless; pell-mell; quaggy; rag-tag; ratty; sloppy; slovenly; topsy-turvy; untidy; unorganized; vile; wild; *x'ed;* yucky; zoo-like;

**metal** *(n.)*: alloy; base ~; *copper;* diamond plate; *eglin steel; ferric;* galvanized ~; high-quality ~; *iron; jewelry; kentlage;* limonite; mineral; *nugget;* ochimy; ore; pot ~; precious ~; Queen's ~; raw ~; refined ~; sheet ~; slich; *steel; titanium;* unrefined ~; virgin steel; woots; *xanthoconite; yttrium; zinc;*
   **Kinds of metal**: aluminum; brass; copper; dubnium; erbium; francium; gold; hassium; iron; lead; magnesium; nickel; ochimy; platinum; Queen's ~; rhenium; silver; steel; tin; titanium; uranium; vermeil; yttrium; zinc;

**metamorphosis** *(n.)*: alteration; becoming; change; development; evolution; forming; *growth; heightening; improvement; jump;* key change; *large change;* makeover; *newness;* overhaul; permutation; quantum leap; remake; switch; transformation; *upgrade;* variation; *wonder; xenomorph; yaw; zapping;*

**metaphor** *(n.)*: allusion; allegory; *book;* comparison; dissimile; *equivalent;* figure; gemination; hyperbole; illustration; imagery; *juxtaposition; kind;* likening; metonym; *narrative; oracle;* picture; parallelism; parable; *quarto;* representation; similitude; symbol; simile; trope; type; umbratic; vignette; word picture; *xenodocheionology; yarn;* zeugma;

**metaphoric** *(adj.)*: allegorical; Bunyanesque; comparative; curiologic; descriptive; emblematic; figurative; geminating; hieroglyphic; illustrative; *juxtapositional;* kuriologic; *likening;* metaphorical; *non-literal; obscured;* pictorial; poetical; parallel; parabolic; prefigurate; *quarto;* representative; symbolic; typical; umbratical; vignette; word-picture; *xenodoceionological; yarn;* zeugmatic;

**meteor** *(n.)*: asteroid; bolide; *body;* chunk; chondrite; comet; dragon [slang]; earth-grazing fireball; falling star; fireball; green fireball; helion; icarus; *jetting; krypton;* luminous globe; meteorite; near-earth object; *orionid;* prester; planetoid; *quadrantids;* rock; space rock; siderolite; *travel; uranite;* velocity; *whack;* x-type asteroid; *yenite; zooming;*

**method** *(n.)*: approach; behavior; course of action; devices; *execution;* fashion; *going;* habitude; *ingenius ~; job;* key; line of attack; manner; mode; methodology; means; *modus operandi* [L.]; *notion;* order; operation; policy; practice; process; procedure; *quo mode* [L.]; routine; system; strategy; scheme; technique; tactic; tack; *usage; vein;* way; *xenagogy; yet unconventional ~; zet [dial.];*
**methodical** *(adj.)*: analytical; businesslike; careful; disciplined; exacting; formulaic; *grid pattern;* habitual; industrious; *just so; keen;* logical; methodic; *non-random;* orderly; precise; painstaking; *quasi-logical;* regular; rigid; regimented; systematic; tedious; uniform; *vigilant;* well-regulated; *xtry; yare; zealous;* [*Ant.* messy]
**meticulous** *(adj.)*: assiduous; busy; careful; conscientious; diligent; detailed; exacting; finicky; fussy; fastidious; *great detail;* heedful; hard(line); hypercorrective; industrious; inflexible; just so; keen; logical; laborious; methodical; nit-picking; orderly; operose; picky; particular; precise; punctilious; painstaking; *quiddle;* rigorous; scrupulous; systematic; solicitous; thorough; tedious; technical; *unhasty;* vigilant; *wholehearted; xtry;* yare; *zealous;*
**microscopic** *(adj.)*: atomic; bitty; corpuscular; diminutive; eensie-weensie; fine; germinal; hardly visible; infinitesimal; imperceptible; *just little; keenly small;* little(-bitty); minute; minuscule; molecular; non-seeable; *overly small;* puny; *quantité négligeable* [F.]; *reduced;* small; submicroscopic; tiny; unseen; unseeable; ultramicroscopic; very small; wee; XS; *yea big; zero;*
**middle** *(adj.)*: average; *belly;* center; central; dead-center; equidistant; *fesse-point;* golden mean; halfway; intermediate; inmost; *juste-milieu* [F.]; kernel; *lodged;* mean; mid; medium; median; midway; medial; middle-of-the-road; navel; omphalic; *par;* quotidian; *regular; standard; typical;* umbilic; *via media; well-centered; xy-median; yolk; zenith;* [*Ant.* marginal]
**middle** *(n.)*: axis; belly; body; center(point); core; crux; dead center; epicenter; fesse-point; golden mean; halfway point; hub; heart; interior; inside; *just exactly centered;* kernel; *lodged;* midpoint; midway; midst; midrange; midstream; nucleus; nave; ophalos; par; pith; *quotidian;* right in the middle; smack in the middle [slang]; thick; umbilic; *via media;* waist(line); *within;* x-section; yolk; *zenith;* [*Ant.* margin]
**midget** *(adj.)*: abbreviated; baby; compact; dwarf; eensie-weensie; elfin; fairly small; gnat-sized; half-pint; homuncular; itsy-bitsy; *just so big;* knee-high; little; Lilliputian; miniature; not very big; nanoid; *one-inch tall;* puny; pygmy; pint-sized; *quarter-length;* runty; short; stumpy; tiny; undersized; vertically challenged [joc.]; wee; XS; *yea big;* Zwerg-like; [*Ant.* massive]
**midget** *(n.)*: atomy; *bedwarfed;* compact; dapperling; dwarf; *elfin; four-feet tall;* grub [derog.]; homunculus; half-pint; imp; jack sprat; knarl; *kabouter* [Du.]; Lilliputian; minim; midge; munchkin; Nibelung; ouphe; peewee; pygmy; *quite tiny;* runt; shorty; squirt; shrimp [both derog.]; *Tom Thumb; undersized; vertically challenged [joc.];* wee one; XS; *yea big;* Zwerg; [*Ant.* monster]
**midwife** *(n.)*: accoucheur [masc.]; birth nurse; coach; doula; dhai; expert *~; female; gynocologist;* howdy [coll.]; *iatrine* [arch.]; *jane; kimmer [Br.];* licensed *~;* lay *~;* maia; medica; nurse; obstetrician; obstetrix; professional *~;* qualified *~;* registered *~;* skilled coach; trained *~;* unlicensed *~; very experienced ~;* woman; *xenagogue;* yaya; *zaftig;*
**might** *(n.)*: ability; brawn; capability; dint; energy; force; gusto; horsepower; intensity; influence; *jet-power;* keest; lustiness; manpower; muscle; mightiness; *natural ability; oomph;* power; qi; robustness; strength; thewiness; *usefulness;* vigor; wherewithal; weight; *xenium; yare;* zip; [*Ant.* mildness]
**mighty** *(adj.)*: able-bodied; brawny; commanding; durable; energetic; enduring; forceful; great; herculean; impregnable; influential; iron; *jusqu'au bout [F.]; keen;* lusty; muscular; *nervy; oaky;* powerful; *quality;* robust; strong; tough; unflagging; vigorous; well-built; well-set; x-strong; yauld; *zippy;* [*Ant.* mild]
**migrate** *(v.)*: advance; *budge;* change places; drift; displace; emigrate; flit; fly; go; *hurry;* immigrate; journey; *key move;* leave; move; nomadize; out- *~;* proceed; *quicken;* roam; relocate; settle; sojourn; trek; trans~; transplant; *underway;* voyage; wander; xenize; *xfer; yede; zip away;*

**mild** *(adj.)*: affable; benign; calm; delicate; easygoing; forbearant; gentle; humane; inobtrusive; jarless; kind; light-handed; lamblike; meek; mellow; moderate; non-harsh; nice; obliging; placid; quiet; room-temperature; soft; sweet; tender; temperate; tender; unagitating; *velvety;* well-natured; *xenial;* yielding; *zärtlich* [G.]; [*Ant.* militant]

**military** *(n.)*: army; battalion; cavalry; defense force; encampment; fighting machine; force; garrison; host; homeguard; infantry; junior service [Br.]; *kerns;* legion; militia; nonconscripted army; *outpost;* peace-keeping force; quarter-guard; regiment; service; soldiers; troops; unit; vanguard; war machine; x-force; *yeald;* zouaves;

**milk** *(n.)*: *afterings;* biestings; breast ~; *butter~;* cream; cow's ~; dairy; *emulsion;* fore~; *fluid;* goat's ~; *gallon;* hind ~; heavy cream; ice ~; *jibbings;* kirn- ~; lactose; lowfat ~; milch; *nutrition;* 1% ~; *powdered ~; quart;* raw ~; skim- ~; 2% ~; *utter;* Vitamin D ~; whole ~; *xanthine oxidase;* yarrum; yak's ~; 0% ~;

**mill** *(v.)*: abrade; bray; chop; *do; edge;* fragment; grate; granulate; grind; *hammer;* incise; jam; knurl; levigate; mince; mash; nibble; *overbear;* pound; pulverize; quash; rasp; refine; smash; triturate; *unbuild; vaporize;* wear away; x; *yank down;* zap;

**Millennium** *(n.)*: age of Christ's reign; *better day;* Christ's reign; dispensation of Christ's reign; earthly reign of Christ; *fantastic;* Golden Age; *hour; interval;* Jesus' reign; *the* kingdom (age); *literal reign of Christ;* millennial reign; new era; one-thousand year reign; *physical reign of Christ; quo warranto [L.];* reign of Christ; Second Coming; *span;* thousand years; universal reign of Christ; *victorious kingdom;* world kingdom; *x-time;* year of jubilee; *Zion's hope;*

**millionaire** *(n.)*: affluent man; billionaire; *CEO;* Dives; *eccentric ~;* filthy rich person; gazillionaire; *heiress;* independently wealthy person; *jet-set; kazillionaire [joc.];* loaded man; megabucks [joc.]; millionairess [fem.]; multi- ~; nabob; opulent fellow; plutocrat; *quintillionaire;* rich man; successful businessman; *treasures;* uppercrust individual; vested man; wealthy person; *xenocurrency; yellow boy [Br.];* zillionaire; [*Ant.* mendicant]

**mimic** *(v.)*: ape; be like; copy; duplicate; emulate; follow; *geminate; holotype;* imitate; *just like; keep;* look like; lampoon; mock; *near; outright copy;* parallel; parrot; personate; *quadruplicate;* repeat; simulate; shadow; try to be like; *use copier; virtual;* watch closely; *xerograph; yield;* zoo~;

**mind** *(n.)*: *aptitude;* brain; cerebrum; disposition; determination; encephalon; *focus;* gray matter; head; intellect; judgment; *knowledge;* lobe; marbles; mentality; nous; occiput; pink matter; quadrigeminal; reason; skull; thoughts; understanding; upstairs [joc.]; vermis; wit; *xenenthesis; yead* [arch.]; *zenith;*

**mindful** *(adj.)*: aware; attentive; *bethink;* conscious; conscientious; dutiful; ever- ~; focused; gazeful; heedful; intentive; judicious; keeping in mind; listening; *minded; nagging;* observant; paying attention; quick-witted; regardful; *sagacious;* thoughtful; ultra-heedful; vigilant; watchful; x-careful; yare-handed; *zärtlich* [G.];

**mindset** *(n.)*: attitude; belief; conception; disposition; evaluation; frame of mind; ground; heart; idea; inclination; judgment; *known estimation;* leaning; mentality; notion; outlook; perspective; point of view; *quot homines tot sententiae [L.];* reckoning; sentiment; thinking; *ule;* viewpoint; way of thinking; *xenodiagnosis;* yaw; *zeal;*

**mine** *(n.)*: ∗ *adit;* black coal ~; colliery; coal ~; dig; delf; diamond ~; excavation; flint ~; gold ~: hole; incavation; *jaw-hole;* kill; limestone ~; mineshaft; mineral quarry; *nugget;* open-pit ~; *operation;* pit; quarry; rock quarry; *shaft;* stannery; tunnel; tin- ~; *underground;* vein; wind-hatch; *xenolith; yawn; zanja;*

**mine** *(v.)*: abstract; burrow; coal- ~; dig out (-up); dredge; excavate; *find;* get out; hollow; *hunt; intrench; jenkin;* kip; look for; make search; *notch; open;* prospect; quarry; remove (dirt); shovel; search; trench; take out; unearth; under~; *venture;* work with spade; *xfer; yede; zanja;*

**miniature** *(adj.)*: abbreviated; baby-sized; compact; diminutive; eensie-weensie; fine; gnat-sized; half-pint; itsy-bitsy; *jitney;* knee-high; little; minute; mini; *not very big; overly small;* puny; pygmy; pocket-sized; *quantité négligeable* [F.]; runty; reduced; small-scale; tiny; undersized; very small; wee; XS; *yea big; zero;* [*Ant.* massive]

**minimal** *(adj.)*: *amount;* borderline; *concise;* dinkiest; eensiest; fewest; good enough; hindermost; irreducible; *jot; known ~;* least; lowest; minimum; negligible; *one percent;* puniest; *quorum;* reduced to minimum; smallest; tiniest; undermost; very ~; *wee; xtry. small; youngest; zero;* [Ant. maximal]

**minimize** *(v.)*: abbreviate; abridge; belittle; cut; curtail; decrease; diminish; epitomize; foreshorten; go down; halve; impair; *just the minimum;* knock; lessen; minify; make little of; *nip off; optimize;* pare; quail; reduce; shrink; shorten; trim; underrate; *very little;* welk; *x-sect; yank; zeroize;* [Ant. maximize]

**minimum** *(adj.)*: adequate; bottom; bare ~; *concise;* dinkiest; eensie-weensiest; fewest; *good enough;* hindermost; infinitesimal; just enough; *known ~;* least; lowest; minimal; nominal; *one percent;* puniest; *quota;* required; smallest; tiniest; undermost; very ~; whit; *xtry. small; youngest; zero;* [Ant. maximum]

**minister** *(n. clergyman)*: *admonisher;* Bible-teacher; clergyman; Doctor of Divinity; expositor; field preacher; gospeler; homilist; itinerant preacher; josser [Aus. slang]; *kerygma;* lecturer; ministrant; messenger; man of God; *noiser;* orator; preacher; parson; pastor; *quoter;* rector; reverend; revivalist; speaker; sermonizer; servant of God; teacher; *utterer;* voicer; vicar; *warner;* xenagogue; *yeller [derog.]; zealous preacher;*

    **Religious titles**: abbot; abbess; archbishop; beadsman; bishop; cleric; cardinal; deacon; divine; ecclesiastic; elder; friar; father; guru; grand friar; hieromonk; holy man; high priest; imam; jesuit; kohen; lay abbot; lector; Levite; mother superior; monk; metropolitan; nun; ostiarius; oracle; parson; presbyter; prior; priest; patriarch; prophet; pope; qadi; rabbi; reverend (mother); rector; shaman; scribe; tonsured cleric; vicar; worship; yogi;

**minister** *(n. servant)*: attendant; *butler;* chamberlain; demiurge; errand-boy; footman; footboy; *gofer* [slang]; helper; *indentured servant;* jackman; knave; legman; man(servant); minion; neif; offsider; porter; *quarter maid* [fem.]; reeve; servant; *trusty servant;* underservant; valet; worker; x-man; yeoman; zaikai;

**minister** *(v.)*: attend; bestow service; care for; do; exert; function; *good works;* help; *industry; job;* keep; look after; mind; nurse; operate; obey; perform; *quick-to-obey; run; rigor;* serve; tend; take care of; *use; valet;* wait (on); work for; *xfer; yeme; zealously ~;*

**ministerial** *(adj.)*: abbot-related; biblical; clerical; church(ly); clergical; divine; *devotional;* ecclesiastical; faith-related; gospel; homiletical; *inculcating; Jesuitic; kirk;* liturgical; ministral; non-laical; ordinal; pastoral; priestly; *questor;* religious; rectoral; sacerdotal; theological; *ultramondane;* votarist; worship-related; *Xn.;* youth ministry-related; *Zadokite;*

**ministry** *(n.)*: anointing; apostleship; appointment; bishoprick; calling; church (work); cloth; *devotion;* ecclesiastical; full-time ~; Gospel ~; help; holy orders; *industry;* job; *kirk [Scot.];* lay ~; ministerial office; *non-laity;* office; outreach; pastorate; pulpit; prelateship; prelatical; *quoad sacra* [L.]; religious work; service; teaching & preaching ~; *unselfishness; vow;* work; *Xn. ~;* youth ~; *zeal;*

**miracle** *(n.)*: act of God; blessing; curiosity; divine act; extraordinary act; fascinating act; gift; healing; incredible happening; *joy-giving ~; known ~;* life-changing ~; marvel; mighty act; *nonplus; overwhelmed;* portent; *quite a thing;* remarkable act; sign; thaumaturgy; token; unusual occurrence; *very impressive ~;* wonder; xtry. act; *yet unexplained happening; zowie;*

**miracle-worker** *(n.)*: apostle; blessing-giver; *celestial visitor;* doer of miracles; *extraordinary power; fantastic;* God's man; healer; *iatromantis;* Jesus; *kind; life-changing;* miracle-doer; man of God; notable ~; one who does miracles; prophet of God; *quite amazing; remarkable;* sign-doer; thaumaturge; *uncanny;* verified ~; wonderworker; *xtry.; yonder; zendik [Mos.];*

**miraculous** *(adj.)*: amazing; astounding; bewildering; *celestial;* divine; extraordinary; fantastic; great; *heavenly;* incredible; inexplicable; *joyous; keen;* like nothing ever seen; marvelous; numinous; *outstanding;* phenomenal; preternatural; *quantum* [L.]; remarkable; supernatural; tremendous; theurgical; thaumturgical; uncanny; unbelievable; very wondrous; wonderful; wondrous; *xtry.; yonder; zoic;*

**mirror** *(n.)*: *angled ~;* bathroom ~; catoptron; cheval glass; catopter; dielectric ~; *enameled; finished;* glass; hand ~; *instrument; japanned; keen;* looking-glass; mirrored surface; non-reversing ~; one-way ~; pocket ~; pier glass; polished surface; quicksilvered glass; reflective surface; rearview ~; seeing glass; speculum; two-way ~; ultra-high reflectivity ~; vanity; wall ~; *xesturgy; Yata no Kagami; zero in;*

**misapply** *(v.)*: abuse; badly use; contort; do violence to; distort; erroneously apply; exploit; *force;* get wrong; ill-treat; *jaded; knowingly ~; louse up;* misuse; misapprehend; mishandle; misemploy; *not correct; overexploit;* poorly apply; pervert; *quad;* ravage; strain the sense; twist; use wrongly; victimize; violate; wrench out of context; *x-out;* yank out of context; *zeroize;*
**misbehave** *(v.)*: act up; behave badly; commit transgression; do wrong; disobey; err; foully behave; *fall;* go wrong; horribly behave; infringe; *jaded; knavish;* leave the straight and narrow; misconduct; not behave; *overstep; pay no regard to; quad;* rebel; sin; transgress; *unfaithful;* violate; wrongly behave; *x-gress;* yetzer hara [Heb.]; *zero righteousness;*
**miscalculate** *(v.)*: analyze incorrectly; botch; compute wrongly; determine incorrectly; err; figure wrongly; goof; *hypothesize incorrectly; incorrect;* judge wrongly; *kaput;* louse up; misestimate; miscompute; misjudge; not calculate right; overestimate; *problem; quirk;* reckon inaccurately; slip up; terribly ~; underestimate; *valuate wrongly;* wrongly judge; *x-out; yet incorrect; zero reliability;*
**mischief** *(n.)*: antics; badness; crime; devilment; evildoing; foul-behavior; godlessness; heinousness; iniquity; joke; knavishness; licentiousness; misdeed; misconduct; naughtiness; orneriness; perniciousness; questionable behavior; rebellion; sin(fulness); trouble; unrighteousness; villainy; wrongdoing; *xgression;* youthful playing; *zymosis;*
**mischievous** *(adj.)*: atrocious; bad; criminal; debauched; elfish; evil; foul; godless; heinous; impish; ill-behaved; incorrigible; jokey; knavish; licentious; misbehaving; naughty; ornery; playful; pernicious; *quad;* rascally; sinful; troublesome; unruly; vexatious; waggish; wanton; *xgressing;* yucky; *zymotic;*
**misconduct** *(n.)*: atrocity; breach; badness; crime; delinquency; error; fault; guiltiness; heinousness; infraction; injustice; irrectitude; iniquity; insidiousness; *jadedness;* knavishness; leaven; misbehavior; malfeasance; nonfeasance; naughtiness; offense; peccability; *quad;* rebellion; sin; tresspass; unrighteousness; violation; wrongdoing; *xgression;* yetzer hara [Heb.]; *zymosis;*
**miser** *(n.)*: accumulator; begrudger; cheapskate; dollar-saver; *economist;* Ebenezer Scrooge; *frugal;* gnoff; hoarder; *illiberal; Jack Benny;* knipper; laggard; muckerer; moneygrubber; niggard; *overcautious;* penny-pincher; pinchpenny; piker; *quick-to-save; reluctant;* skinflint; scrooge; tightwad; *ungenerous; vacillator; wary; xtry. ~; yieldless; zero-generosity.*
**miserable** *(adj.)*: abject; blue; baleful; crummy; crestfallen; calamitous; despondent; disconsolate; elegiac; forlorn; groanful; heartbroken; inconsolable; joyless; keening; low; mournful; negative; out of sorts; piteous; *quivering;* rueful; sad; tristful; unhappy; very sad; woeful; wretched; *x'ed; yearnful; zestless;* [Ant. merry]
**miserliness** *(n.)*: *accumulation;* begrudging; cheapness; dollar-saving; economicalness; frugality; good husbandry; hoarding; illiberality; *Jack Benny;* knippering; laggardness; minginess; niggardliness; over-frugality; penny-pinching; *quick-to-save; reluctance;* stinginess; tight-fistedness; ungenerosity; *very miserly; wary; xtry. ~; yieldlessness; zero-generosity;* [Ant. munificence]
**miserly** *(adj.)*: avaricious; begrudging; cheap; chintzy; close-fisted; dollar-conscious; economical; frugal; grudging; greedy; hard-fisted; illiberal; *judicious; kitish;* laggard; meager; mingy; niggardly; overcautious; penny-pinching; parsimonious; penurious; *quick-to-refuse;* reluctant; scrimping; sparing; stingy; thrifty; tight(fisted); ungenerous; *vacillating;* wary; *xtry. parsimoniousness;* yieldless; *zero-generosity;* [Ant. munificent]
**misery** *(n.)*: agony; blueness; crestfallenness; calamitousness; dole; dolor; despondency; evil-affected; forlornness; grief; heartache; inconsolableness; joylessness; katzenjammer; low spirits; melancholy; negativism; overmuch sorrow; pain; *quivering;* ruefulness; suffering; sorrow; trouble; unhappiness; vapors; woe; *xiphodynia;* yearning; *zestlessness;*
**misfit** *(n.)*: abnormal person; bizarre person; character; deranged man; eccentric; freak; gonzo; horse marine; irregular person; *jackass;* kook; loner; maladjusted individual; nonconformist; oddball; peculiar person; queer; *ridiculous;* singularity; square peg; twisted individual; unconventional person; *variant;* weirdo; *xenomorphic;* yo-yo; zany;

**misfortune** *(n.)*: accident; adversity; bad luck; catastrophe; disaster; evil; financial reverse; grief; hardship; ill fortune; *judgment; knock-out blow;* loss; mischance; misadventure; mishap; nightmare; ordeal; problem; quandary; reverse; setback; trouble; unlucky happening; *violence;* woe; *x-ing out; yedder; zinger;*

**misgiving** *(n.)*: apprehension; boding; compunction; conscience; doubt; ethics; fear; guilt; hesitation; issues; *jarred;* keen sense of guilt; leeriness; mistrust; niggle; objections; problem; qualm; reservations; scruple; trepidation; uneasiness; vacillation; worries; wariness; *x-ing; yieldedness; zeroing in;*

**misguided** *(adj.)*: amiss; *botched;* confused; deluded; deceived; erroneous; fooled; groundless; heedless; ill-advised; *jim-jam; kim-kam; lying;* misadvised; mistaken; misled; non-trustworthy; off base; *problematic; questionable; reckless;* self-deceived; tricked; unwise; *void of truth;* wrong trained; *x-gressed; yawed; zero-truth;*

**mislead** *(v.)*: allure; beguile; con; deceive; delude; ensnare; fool; guile; gull; hoodwink; insnare; jape; kid; lie to; misguide; nobble; obfuscate; put one over; *quiblin* [arch.]; rook; shyster; trick; *utter falsehood;* verneuk; weasel; *xuld [arch.];* yank one's chain; *zing;*

**misrepresent** *(v.)*: allure; beguile; color; con; deceive; equivocate; falsify; guile; hoodwink; illude; *jape;* knowingly lie; lie; mislead; nobble; overstate; perjure; *quiblin* [arch.]; *rook;* stretch; slant; trick; understate; verneuk; wangle; *xuld [arch.]; yentz; zing;*

**misrepresentation** *(n.)*: alteration of the truth; big lie; coloring; con; distortion; equivocation; falsehood; gonk; half-truth; inveracity; jactitation; *kid;* lie; line; misstatement; mendacity; non-truth; oath-breaking; perversion; *quiblin [arch.]; rooking;* stretch; slanting; twisting; untruth; *verneuking;* white lie; *xuld [arch.];* yarn; yellow journalism; *zinger;*

**miss** *(v. not hit what was aimed at)*: aim badly; botch; come short; clear; didn't hit; err; fail; goof; go off; hit the wrong mark; *incorrect; just ~; kaput;* louse up; muff; not succeed; overshoot; pass over; *quirk; run short;* shoot past; tank [slang]; undershoot; *veer off;* wide off; *xuld [arch.]; yedder; zero;*

**miss** *(v. overlook)*: avoid; *but;* clear; disregard; elide; exclude; fail to see; go over; *hide;* ignore; jump over; *kest;* lack; leave out; muff; neglect; omit; overlook; pass over; *quick-to-forget; remiss;* skip (over); turn the other way; *unfaithful; void;* want; *x-ing; yemeles [arch.]; zero responsibility;*

**miss** *(v. pine for)*: ache for; brood over; crave; desire; *ebb;* fret over; *get lonely;* hunger; itch for; *just want one back;* keenly desire; lack; long for; much ache for; need; *overly ~;* pine for; *quail; really ~; seek;* truly *~; upset; very much ~;* wish for; want; *x-out;* yearn for; *zero happiness;*

**mission** *(n.)*: assignment; *apostolate;* business; charge; commission; duty; errand; enterprise; expedition; *function; goal; handling;* incumbency; job; *key role;* liability; mandate; necessity; operation; obligation; pursuit; purpose; quest; responsibility; sortie; task; undertaking; venture; work; xci.; *yoke; zealous task;*

**missionary** *(n.)*: ambassador; apostle; Bible-preacher; church-planter; disciple-maker; emissary; evangelist; foreign ~; gospeler; home ~; itinerant preacher; josser [Aus. slang]; *kindler;* lay- ~; messenger; man of God; missioner; *noiser;* open-air preacher; preacher; propagator; proselytizer; *questor; revivalist;* soul-winner; teacher; *utterer;* venturer; witness; xenophile; *yeller [derog.]; zealous preacher;*

**missions** *(n.)*: *ambassadorship;* biblical ~; church-planting; disciple-making; evangelism; foreign ~; faith promise; global evangelism; home ~; international evangelism; *Jesus; knocking doors;* leading souls to Christ; *ministry;* missionary work; nationwide church-planting; outreach; planting churches; *quest for souls;* reaching the lost; soul-winning; trying to win souls; *undertaking; venturing;* world missions (-evangelism); xenocentrism; yede; zeal for souls;

**mist** *(n.)*: atomization; brume; cloud; dust; exhaust; fog; fume; gas; gauze; haze; high fog; ice cloud; *jumble; kerfuffle;* London fog; mistiness; murk; miasma; nimbus; obscurity; puff; pall; *quasi-vaporous; rain cloud;* steam; smoke; spray; smog; *tizzy; umbered;* vagueness; vapor; wisp; *xenon cloud; yellowy cloud; zero visibility;*

**mistake** (*n.*): accident; boo-boo; blooper; blunder; corrigendum; defect; error; fluke; faux pas; flaw; fault; failing; failure; goof-up; gaffe; howler [Br.]; inaccuracy; imperfection; *jumble;* kink; lapse; lack; misprint; mix-up; miscalculation; *non-purposive;* oversight; problem; pratfall; quirk; *responsibility;* slip(-up); solecism; typo; undoing; *violation;* wrong; weakness; *xgression;* yaw; zinger;

**mistaken** (*adj.*): amiss; baseless; bogus; bad; confused; deficient; defective; erring; erroneous; faulty; flawed; fallacious; false; groundless; hollow; heretical; inadequate; incorrect; inaccurate; jim-jam; kim-kam; *lying;* misbelieved; misunderstood; misconceived; misguided; not true; non-orthodox; off base; peccant; *queer; repudiated;* specious; spurious; sophistical; *trick;* untrue; unsound; unfounded; *variant; void of truth;* wrong; *x-ing; yawed; zero-truth;*

**mistreat** (*v.*): abuse; batter; bullyrag; brutalize; *cruelty;* despoil; exploit; *force; go against;* harm; ill-treat; *jaded;* knock about; *lapse;* misuse; maltreat; mishandle; *neglect;* obloquy; persecute; *quad;* rough up; *sin against;* treat badly; use; vandalize; wrong; *x-out; yank down; zeroize;* [*Ant.* mollycoddle]

**mistress** (*n. lady in charge*): authority; boss lady; chatelaine; dame; employer; forewoman; governess; homemaker; head; instructress; *jade;* keeper; lady; madam; noblewoman; overseer; proprietress; *queen;* ruler; superintendent; *tyrant; under-keeper; vrouw* [Du.]; woman-of-the-house; *XO;* yoke-mistress; *zaftig;*

**mistress** (*n. paramour*): amoret; beauty; courtesan; doxy; escort; femme; girl(friend); *harlot;* immoral woman; jezebel; kept woman; lady; meretrix; *naughty girl; odalisque;* paramour; quean; querida; *rig;* strange woman; temptress; *unfaithful woman;* vixen; woman; *wench; x-rated;* yaud; *zitella* [It.];

**mistrust** (*n.*): apprehension; *beware;* caution; caginess; distrust; doubt; *ever-suspicious;* fear; guardedness; hesitation; incredulity; *jitteriness; kiaugh* [Scot.]; leeriness; misgiving; non-belief; *over-suspicious;* paranoia; questioning; qualms; reservations; suspicion; skepticism; trepidation; unbelief; uncertainty; *vacillation;* wariness; *xtry. doubt; yet unconvinced;* zero confidence;

**mistrust** (*v.*): *apprehensive;* beware; call in question; distrust; *ever-doubtful;* fear; get nervous; hesitate; *iffiness; jittery;* keep doubting; *leery;* misbelieve; not believe; oppugn; *pessimistic;* question; raise a question; suspect; *skeptic;* take with a grain of salt; unbelieve; *vacillate; wary; xtry. ~; yet doubt; zero confidence;*

**misunderstand** (*v.*): *amiss;* believe erroneously; confuse; discern erroneously; erroneously believe; falsely understand; get the wrong idea; have ~ing; interpret erroneously; *judge wrongly; kerfuffle; louse-up;* misread; miscomprehend; misconstrue; misinterpret; misconceive; misapprehend; mistake; misjudge; not comprehend; *off base;* perceive flasely; *questionable;* read wrongly; see erroneously; take wrongly; understand wrongly; *vexation;* wrongly perceive; *x-out; yaw; zero understanding;*

**misunderstanding** (*adj.*): *amiss;* bad conceptualization; confusion; defective understanding; error; fallacy; false idea; garbling; heretical idea; incorrect understanding; jumble; *kerfuffle; louse-up;* misconception; mistaken idea; misapprehension; mix-up; non-correct idea; off base idea; poor understanding; *quarrel; real goof-up;* specious idea; *terrible ~;* unsound concept; *vexation;* wrong idea; *x-gression; yawed; zero understanding;*

**mite** (*n.*): *atom;* bit; bagatelle; crumb; drop; *ens;* flea; fragment; *frivolous;* groat; *hunk;* iota; impertinence; jack; joke; kernel; little bit; modicum; nothing; ounce; pittance; *quiddle;* remnant; smidgen; trifle; *unimportant; vestige;* whit; whiffle; *XAG; yngot* [arch.]; *zippo;*

**mitigate** (*v.*): assuage; bate; curb; diminish; ease; fade; go down; *hush;* improve; *jump down;* knock down; lessen; lighten; moderate; narrow; *outgo;* palliate; quell; relieve; soften; temper; *undo; volume;* wane; *xerosis;* yield; *zap;*

**mix** (*v.*): admix; amalgamate; bemingle; blend; combine; conflate; coalesce; disarrange; *entangle;* fuse; *group; hodge-podge;* intersperse; intermix; intermingle; integrate; incorporate inosculate; join; jabble; kirn; lump together; mingle; muddle; marry; merge; meld; *node; overmix;* put in random order; *queach* [arch.]; roll together; shake together; stir; toss; temper; unite; *voluble;* wed; *xenograft; yerk together; zip together;* [*see* stir]

**mixture** *(n.)*: admixture; amalgamation; blend; combination; concoction; compound; *diversity;* elixir; ester; formula; farrago; fusion; gallimaufry; hodgepodge; intermixture; inosculation; jumble(ment); kava; *lumping;* mishmash; mélange; mingling; mix; medley; marriage; meld; mergence; *non-homogenous ~;* olio; pouring together; pasticcio; potion; *queer;* recipe; salad; synthesis; tempering; ule; union; *variety; wedding; xanthate;* yanggoma; *zipping together;*

**moan** *(n.)*: agonizing; bawk; cry; despairing; elegizing; fretting; groan; grumble; grunt; howl; *inconsolable;* jeremiad; keen; lamentation; moaning; *noise;* outcry; puling; querk; roar; sigh; sough; suspiration; *tearful;* ululation; *vociferation;* whine; whimper; wail; *xuld [arch.];* yammer; yowl; *zing;*

**moan** *(v.)*: anguish; bemoan; cry out; despair; elegize; fret; groan; grumble; grunt; heave a sigh; *inconsolable; judder;* keen; lament; murmur; *noise;* outcry; *object;* pule; querk; repine; sigh; sough; suspire; *tearful;* ululate; *vociferate;* whine; whimper; wail; *xuld [arch.];* yammer; yowl; *zing;*

**moat** *(n.)*: abysm; breach; channel; ditch; entrenchment; fosse; gully; ha-ha; *irrigation canal; jheel [Ind.]; kyle;* leat; mole; nullah; *outlet;* passage; quanat; rampart; sunk fence; trench; *u-groove; vasa;* waterway; *xyrisic; yawn;* zanja;

**mob** *(n.)*: amassment; bunch; crowd; clanjamfry [Scot.]; drove; deluge; *everybody;* flock; group; gathering; horde; ingathering; jam [slang]; kit [coll.]; lot; mass; multitude; number; *outfit;* pack; party; quantity; quorum; rabble; swarm; throng; troop; *unit; variety;* wisp; *xtry. number; yobs;* zoo;

**mobile** *(adj.)*: ambulatory; *budgable;* conveyable; dynamic; drifting; drivable; ever-changing; flyable; going; *hurry;* itinerant; in motion; *jet-propelled;* kinematic; locomotive; moveable; moving; migratory; migrant; motile; non-stationary; nomadic; *ongoing;* peripatetic; portable; quick-moving; relocatable; roving; roaming; self-moving; transporting; traveling; unfixed; vagile; wandering; *xfer; yare;* zaanaim; [*Ant.* motionless]

**mobility** *(n.)*: ability to move; *budging;* conveyability; dynamic movement; downward ~; *emigration;* fluidity; going; *hurrying;* impermanence; *jet-propelled; kinematic;* locomotion; movement; nonstationariness; *ongoing;* portability; *quick-moving;* rising; speed; transportation; transfer; upward ~; vertical ~; walking; *xfer; yield; zip;* [*Ant.* motionlessness]

**mobilize** *(v.)*: actuate; bring together; call to arms; drum up; employ; *flock;* group; *hurry;* initiate; join; *kindle;* line up; move; muster; marshal; *nudge;* organize; position; quicken; rally; summon; throng; *underway; venture;* whip up; xfer; *yede;* zone;

**mock** *(v.)*: abuse; belittle; chide; deride; *execrate;* fleer; gibe; hiss; heckle; humiliate; insult; jeer; jibe; knock; laugh at; make fun (-sport); *name-calling; offend;* pillory; quib; ridicule; rail; scoff; sneer; scorn; tease; taunt; utter against; verbally abuse; wipe; *xuld [arch.];* yock; *zap;* [*Ant.* magnify]

**mocker** *(n.)*: abuser; belittler; chider; derider; execrator; flouter; faulter; giber; humiliator; insulter; jeerer; kidder; laugher; mocker; niggler; offender; *pillory;* quipper; ridiculer; railer; ribber; scoffer; scorner; teaser; taunter; *utterer;* vexer; *wiper; xuld [arch.];* yuker; *zapper;* [*Ant.* magnifier]

**mockery** *(n.)*: abuse; belittlement; chiding; derision; *eruption;* fleering; gibing; humiliation; insult; jeering; knocking; laughter; ludification; making fun; name-calling; opprobrium; pillory; quibbing; ridicule; railery; ribbing; sport; scoffing; scorn; taunting; *unkindness;* vexation; wipes; *x-ing;* yah; *zinging;* [*Ant.* magnification]

**mode** *(n.)*: approach; behavior; course of action; *do; execution;* form; genre; habitude; *indication; job;* kind; line of attack; manner; means; method; *notch;* operation; process; *quo mode* [L.]; routine; sort; setting; technique; tactic; tack; *usage;* variation; way; *xenagogy; yield; zet [dial.];*

**model** *(n.)*: archetype; antitype; basis; copy; criterion; duplication; example; epitome; exemplar; fugler; guide; holotype; ideal; jewel; key example; lead; mock-up; miniature; maquette; neotype; original; pattern; prototype; precedent; paragon; *quintessence;* replica; reproduction; representative; rule; specimen; standard; shining example; type; template; ule; very image; working prototype; *xenagogue;* yardstick; *zincograph;*

**moderate** *(adj.)*: average; abstemious; balanced; controlled; disciplined; easy; even; ever- ~; fair; governed; holding back; intermediary; judicious; keeping within limits; limited; moderated; medium; middle-of-the-road; non-excessive; *ordinary;* proportionate; *quite reasonable;* reasonable; sensible; sparing; temperate; unassuming; *voluntary discipline;* well-tempered; *xtry. ~;* yepe; *zero excess;*
**moderate** *(v.)*: alleviate; bate; curb; diminish; ease; fade; go down; hold in check; improve; judge; knock down; lessen; lighten; limit; mitigate; negotiate; obtund; palliate; quell; reduce; soften; temper; *undo; volume;* wane; *xerosis;* yield; *zap;*
**moderation** *(n.)*: abstemiousness; balance; control; denial; equanimity; forbearance; governance; gentleness; holding back; inhibition; judiciousness; keeping in check; limiting; longsuffering; moderateness; meekness; non-extremeness; *non troppo* [It.]; *orderliness;* parameterizing; patience; *quietness;* restraint; regulation; self-control; temperance; *under control;* volume-control; withholding; *xy mean; yama* [Hind.]; *zero excess;*
**modern** *(adj.)*: all-new; brand-new; contemporary; *des nous jours* [F.]; existing; fashionable; *green;* hot-off-the-press; highly developed; in-vogue; just out; *kickoff;* latest; modernistic; new; original; present-day; *quite new;* recent; stylish; *sleek;* twenty-first century; up-to-date; ultramodern; *virgin;* world-class; *xenogenetic; young; zygogenetic;*
**modernize** *(v.)*: advance; bring up-to-date; contemporize; develop; *electrify; forge ahead;* get better; *headway;* improve; *jump ahead; keep up; leading edge;* make modern; *new;* overhaul; *progress; quantum leap;* renovate; streamline; *technology;* update; vamp; *work on; xtry.; yain [arch.]; zoom ahead;*
**modest** *(adj.)*: appropriate; bashful; covered; demure; diffident; discreet; decent; ever- ~; fully dressed; good; *gentlewomanly;* humble; inconspicuous; jackalent; *kitted;* lowly; meek; nice; over- ~; plain; proper; quiet; reserved; shamefaced; self-effacing; timorous; unassuming; unpretentious; verecund; wholesome; *xtry. ~;* yarrow; *zero indecency;*
**modesty** *(n.)*: appropriateness; bashfulness; *covering;* demure; diffidence; discreetness; decency; *embarrassment; fully dressed; goodness;* humbleness; inconspicuousness; jackalence; *kitted;* lowliness; meekness; niceness; over- ~; pudency; plainness; propriety; quietness; reserve; shamefacedness; self-effacement; timorousness; unpretentiousness; unassumingness; verecundity; wholesomeness; *xtry. ~;* yarrowness; *zero indecency;*
**modification** *(n.)*: alteration; *betterment;* change; deviation; edition; fix; *growth; heightening;* innovation; improvement; *jumping; key to; lowering;* modulation; makeover; *newness;* overhaul; permutation; qualification; revision; switch; shift; transformation; tailor; *update; upgrade;* variation; *warping; xenomorph; yaw; zigzag;*
**modify** *(v.)*: alter; *bend; better;* change; deviate; doctor; develop; edit; fiddle with; fix; *grow; heighten;* innovate; improve; jib; *key to; lower;* make over (-worse; -better); novate; overhaul; personalize; qualify; revise; switch; tweak; transform; update; upgrade; vary; *work; xenomorph; yaw; zigzag;*
**moist** *(adj.)*: awash; bedashed; clammy; dewy; damp; embrocated; *flooded;* gooey; humid; humective; imbrued; juicy; *kept ~;* liquidy; mesic; non-dry; *oozy;* plashed; *quaggy;* rorid; soggy; teary; undried; vapored; wet; *xpn.;* yoted; *zero dryness;*
**moisten** *(v.)*: asperge; bedew; *clean;* dampen; embrocate; *fill;* get wet; humectate; humidify; imbrue; jawp; *keep wet;* launder; madefy; *non-dry; overwhelm;* plash; *quaggy;* ret; sprinkle; spatter; soak; *tear; undried;* vapor; wet; xpn.; yote; *zero dryness;*
**moldable** *(adj.)*: adaptable; bendable; conformable; compliant; ductile; easy-to-form; formable; governable; hand-bendable; infirm; impressionable; *jiggly; knuckle;* lithe; mouldable; malleable; *non-rigid; obedient;* pliable; plastic; *queachy [arch.];* responsive; soft; shapeable; teachable; tractable; *unfirm;* variable; workable; *xapuri;* yielding; *zero-rigidity;*
**moldy** *(n.)*: aging; *awful;* bad; blasted; crusty; corrupt; decaying; *encankered;* fusty; green; hoared; impairing; *jading;* ketty; *labefaction;* musty; mildewy; *nasty;* off; old; peccant; queering; rotting; stale; tainted; *unpleasant;* vinnewed; welking; *xylaria;* yellowed; *zapped;*

**moment** *(n.)*: *anon;* bit; *currently; delay; ephemeral;* flash; *glimpse;* heartbeat; half a minute; instant; jiffy; juncture in time; *kilocycle;* little while; minute; nanosecond; one minute; *point in time;* quick ~; *rapidly;* short time; second; time; trice; *uptime; verge;* while; wink; x-time; *yet;* zeptosecond;
**momentary** *(adj.)*: abbreviated; brief; cursory; *done quickly;* ephemeral; evanescent; fleeting; *germinal;* hurried; impermanent; *just a moment; katchha* [Ind.]; little; moment-long; momentaneous; non-permanent; only ~; passing; quick; rapid; short-lived; temporary; unstable; *very short;* wee; *x-itory;* yet fleeting; *zippy;*
**momentous** *(adj.)*: *all-important;* big; critical; decisive; earthshaking; fateful; great; historic; important; *jumbo;* key; leading; life-and-death; magnitudinous; noteworthy; *ominous;* portentous; quantum; red-letter; significant; top-rated; ultimate; vital; weighty; xtry.; *yearnful;* zero hour; [*Ant.* minor]
**momentum** *(n.)*: *activity; bearing;* compulsion; drive; energy; force; gait; *hustle;* impulse; impetus; *jet;* kinetic energy; *locomotion;* movement; *non-stationary; ongoing;* push; propulsion; *quickening;* rate; speed; thrust; *uninhibited;* velocity; *wherewithal; xuld [arch.]; yede;* zip;
**monarch** *(n.)*: autocrat; authority; *blueblood;* chief; crowned head; czar; caesar; dynast; emperor; *Führer [G.];* governor; highness; imperial majesty; *jemander [Ind.];* king; kaiser; lord; magistrate; majesty; noble; oligarch; potentate; queen [fem.]; ruler; regent; sovereign; tsar; *tyrant; ultimate authority;* vice-regent; warlord; xabandar; *younker;* zar; [*Ant.* minion]
**monarchy** *(n.)*: autocracy; *body politic;* crown; country; domain; dominion; *duchy;* empire; *earldom; feudal territory; grand duchy;* governance; home rule; *imperial;* jurisdiction; *jarldom;* kingdom; kingship; limited ~; land; monocracy; nation; *oligarchy;* power; principality; queendom [fem.]; realm; sovereignty; territory; throne; *united kingdom; viscounty; world power;* xerifdom; yard; zenocracy;
**monastery** *(n.)*: abbey; basilica; convent; commune; *dorm; edifice;* friary; glebe; hermitage; incloister; *jong [Tib.]; kibbutz;* lamasery [Tib.]; motherhouse; mir; minster; nunnery; *oratorio;* priory; *phalanstery;* Qumran; religious community; sacrarium; *talapoin [Bud.]; upper room;* vicarage; ward; wat [Bud.]; *xatra [Ind.]; yogic house;* zawiyah [Mos.];
**monastic** *(adj.)*: ascetic; abbatical; abbatial; *brotherhood;* communal; conventual; cenobitical; cloistral; claustral; *devout;* eremitical; friarly; God-seeking; hermitic; *institutional; jong [Tib.]; kirk; lamasery;* monkish; monachial; monastical; monasterial; non-worldly; *order; pious;* quasi-monastic; reclusive; religious; *simple; spiritual; theistic; uncomplicated; vow;* withdrawn; *xatra [Ind.]; yogic;* zetetic;
**money** *(n.)*: assets; bill; banknote; *coins;* currency; cash; capital; dough; dinero; dollars; economics; filthy lucre; finances; funds; green; *gold;* hard cash; *investment capital;* jiggy [slang]; kale [slang]; lucre; loot; legal tender; moolah [slang]; notes; *opulence;* pelf; pocket ~; paper ~; *q-ratio;* quid [Br.]; riches; siller; *silver;* till; treasure; *untaxed income;* venture capital; wampum; working capital; wealth; xenocurrency; *yens;* zechin;
   **Kinds of money**: austral; balboa; cruzado; dollar; drachma; euro; franc; fluid ounce; guilder; hwan; inti; Jamaican pound; krone; lira; mark; naira; ouguiya; pound; peso; quetzel; rank; ruble; schilling; shekel; tala; unit; vatu; won; xu; yen; zloty;
**moneychanger** *(n.)*: *agent;* banker; clerk; cambist; debtee; exchanger; financier; *greenbacks; helper;* investor; *junior officer; keeper;* lender; money-handler; *note broker;* officer; *payer;* questuary; *reckoner; secretary;* teller; *usurer; vault; worker;* xaraf; yeme; zaikai [Jap.];
**monk** *(n.)*: abbot; ascetic; bonze [Bud.]; *brother;* cenobite; dervis; ecclesiastic; friar; gymnosophist; hesychast; hermit; *isolationist; jubilarian;* kirkman [Scot.]; lay abbot; minorite; mendicant; *nun [fem.];* Observant; prior; primate; Qumranite; recollet; stylite; *talapoin* [Bud.]; *underling;* votary; white friar; Xaverian; *yogi [Hind.];* zetetic;
**monopolize** *(v.)*: absorb; bogart; corner; control; dominate; engross; *force;* grab; gobble up; have controlling interest; hog; *influence; jockey;* keep; *lay hold of;* make monopoly; *nab;* obtain monopoly; own; procure 51%; *quash;* rule; seize control; take over; use up; *vanquish;* wrest; *xfer; yank; zip away;*

**monopoly** *(n.)*: *all;* bogart; corner; control(ling interest); domination; expropriation; exclusive control; fifty-one percent; *governance;* holding; industry-control; *jurisdiction;* kingship; lordship; monopolization; natural ~; oligopoly; power; *quo warranto* [L.]; rule; supremacy; total control; *unfair advantage; vast majority; weight; xtry.;* yoke; zonal control;
**monotonous** *(adj.)*: *arduous;* boring; continuous; dull; *everlasting;* flat; generic; humdrum; insipid; incessant; jejune; *known-boring;* livelong; longsome; laborious; mundane; non-exciting; neverending; operose; ponderous; quotidian; repetitive; samely; tiresome; tedious; uninteresting; unexciting; vapid; wearisome; *xtry. boring;* yawnful; zestless; [*Ant.* modulated]
**monster** *(n.)*: ahaitzotl; beast; behemoth; creature; colossus; demon; *evil creature;* fiend; gowl; gorgon; horror; *imp; jinx; kraken;* leviathon; monstrosity; *nasty creature;* ogre; *Python; quinotaur; roc;* sea serpent (-monster); thing; troll; terror; *unicorn;* villain; *wivern; xiphopagus; yeti;* zombie;
   **Monsters**: abominable snowman; bigfoot; Count Dracula; cyclops; dragon; Ettin; Frankenstein; green slime; ghost; Godzilla; Gorgon; Hydra; Incubus; Jaud; kraken; leviathan; Loch Ness ~; medusa; mummy; nidhogg; ogre; puck; quinataur; roc; swamp creature; troll; undead; vampire; werewolf; xiphopagus; yetti; zombie;
**monstrous** *(adj.)*: awful; bad; creepy; distorted; dreadful; evil; frightful; grotesque; gruesome; hideous; horrifying; icky; jarring; *knarled;* loathsome; monster; nightmarish; odious; pernicious; *quad;* revolting; *rapacious;* shocking; terrible; ugly; voracious; warped; *wicked;* xiphopagous; yeverous; zombielike; [*see* huge; *Ant.* mediocre]
**monument** *(n.)*: acknowledgement; arch; burial plaque; bust; commemorative plaque; column; cenotaph; cairn; depiction; dolmen; *epitaph;* emblem; footstone; figure; grave-marker; heap; herm; headstone; indicator; icon; image; *joint-marker; korum;* likeness; landmark; marker; monolith; memorial; national ~; obelisk; plaque; pylon; pillar; *qubba* [Mos.]; representation; remembrance; stone (marker); symbol; shrine; statue; tomb; tribute; testimonial; tower; *U.S.* ~; vault; witness; xat; yard stone; ziarat [Mos.];
   **U,S, National Monuments**: Gateway Arch; Jefferson Memorial; Liberty Bell; Lincoln Memorial; Mt. Rushmore; Statue of Liberty; St. Louis Arch; Tomb of the Unknown Soldier; Washington Monument;
**monumental** *(adj.)*: amazing; big; breakthrough; celebrated; dominating; epic; earthshaking; famous; great; ground-breaking; historic; important; jumbo; key; landmark; legendary; milestone; major; momentous; notable; outstanding; ponderous; portentous; quantum; red-letter; revolutionary; significant; tremendous; unequalled; vital; weighty; xtry.; *yet unsurpassed;* zenithal; [*Ant.* minor]
**mood** *(n.)*: air; affect; attitude; ambiance; atmosphere; bearing; countenance; cast; disposition; demeanor; emotion; frame of mind; feeling; *good ~;* humor; inclination; impression; *judgment; known inclination;* leaning; mindset; notion; outlook; posture; quality of mind; reaction; sentiment; temper(ament); tone; tenor; *urge;* vein; visage; whim; *xenodiagnosis; yaw; zeal;* [*see* anger]
**moody** *(adj.)*: affected; bad-tempered; capricious; deviable; emotional; explosive; fickle; glum; grumpy; huffy; irritable; jangly; knaggy; labile; mutable; non-stable; overdramatic; pendulous; *querulous;* restless; sulky; temperamental; unpredictable; volatile; weepy; *xtry. ~;* yo-yo; ziggety; [*Ant.* merry-hearted]
**moon** *(n.)*: arch; blue ~; crescent; Cynthia; demu-lune; earth's ~; full ~; gibbous ~; half ~; Iapetus; *jag; kavadi;* lune; *lunar;* luminary; medallion [poet.]; new ~; orb of night; Pheobe; quarter ~; round ~; satellite; three-quarter ~; *undimmed;* vault; waxing ~; Xquic; Yohaulticetl; Zislbog;
**moonlight** *(n.)*: aura; beam; candescence; dimness; evening light; *fulgency;* glow; *halo;* illumination; *jacklight; kindle;* light; moonglow; moonshine; noctiluscence; *overlight; phosphorescence;* radiance; starlight; *twilight; ultraviolet light;* vividness; white light; xenon light; *yellow light;* zodiacal light;
**mope** *(v.)*: agonize; brood; chafe; despond; eat one's heart out; fret; glower; have pity-party; *incubate; joyless; kick;* languish; moan; *not happy;* over-ponder; pout; pine; *question;* ruminate; sulk; think about; *upset;* vex; worry; *xenodiagnose;* yearn; *zero in;*

**moral** *(adj.)*: aboveboard; blameless; chaste; decent; ethical; fair; good; godly; honorable; immaculate; just; *kalokagathia [Gr.];* law-abiding; morally pure; noble; observant; pure; principled; *questionless;* right(eous); respectable; sinless; taintless; upright; virtuous; wholesome; xtry.; yielded to God; *zaddik* [Heb.]; [Ant. meretricious]

**moral** *(n.)*: axiom; application; belief; code; dictum; ethic; fundament; guideline; *horse sense;* ideal; judiciousness; kernel of wisdom; lesson; message; *noble;* oracle; point; principle; quote; rule; significance; truism; universal truth; veracity; wisdom; *xenagogy;* yardstick; zeteticism;

**morale** *(n.)*: assurance; belief; confidence; dependence; esprit; faith; *good ~;* heart; hopes; *high ~;* inspiration; *just believe; keenness;* level of confidence; motivation; non-doubt; object lesson; outlook; pulling together; *quality;* resolve; spirits; self-confidence; trust; unwavering faith; vigor; way; *xel [arch.]; y'faith [arch.];* zeal;

**morality** *(n.)*: angelicalness; blamelessness; chastity; decency; ethics; faithfulness; goodness; godliness; holiness; honor; integrity; immaculateness; justness; *kalokagathia* [Gr.]; *legitimacy;* mores; morals; *nobility; over-scrupulousness;* principles; probity; *quality;* righteousness; rectitude; saintliness; scrupulousness; *taintlessness;* uprightness; virtuousness; wholesomeness; *xtry; yieldedness to God; zero-blame;* [Ant. meretriciousness]

**moralize** *(v.)*: attack; blast; criticize; decry; excoriate; fault; *gripe;* harangue; impugn; judge; knock; lecture; make judgments; nag; over- ~; preach; *question;* remonstrate; sermonize; traduce; *ululate;* vituperate; whine; *xuld [arch.];* yell at; *zing;*

**moralizing** *(adj.)*: admonitory; belittling; critical; disapproving; exhortative; fault-finding; *griping;* holier-than-thou; impugning; judgmental; knocking; lecturing; moralistic; negative; over-critical; preachy; *querulous;* rebukeful; sententious; traducent; *unappreciated;* vituperative; whingy; *xenophobic;* yauping; *zero mercy;*

**morbid** *(adj.)*: abhorrent; baleful; chilling; dark; eerie; funereal; grisly; gruesome; ghastly; hideous; icky; jarring; *knee-knocking;* lurid; macabre; necrophilious; ominous; *petrifying; queer;* repulsive; sepulchral; *terrifying;* unnerving; unpleasant; *vexatious; weird; xenophobic;* yucky; *zonky;* [Ant. merry]

**mores** *(n.)*: accepted way; behavior; customs; daily routine; ethics; folk ways; general behavioral pattern; habits; institution; *jake [Br.]; kultur [G.];* long-established tradition; manner; meme; morals; norm; old ways; practice; *quo mode* [L.]; rules; standards; traditions; usage; values; way (of life); *x-cultural; ye olde; zealous tradition;*

**morning** *(n.)*: the A.M.; break of day; cockcrow; dawn; daybreak (-spring; -time); *diurnal;* early part of the day; forenoon; going up of the sun; *half-light; inception; joy; kickoff; light;* morn; mid~; morrow; new day; next day; *opening of the day;* prime; *quite early;* rising (of the sun); *rooster crow;* sunrise; tomorrow; *up-going of the sun;* very early; wake up call; *xfer; yestermorn; zone;* [Ant. moonlight]

**morose** *(adj.)*: abject; bleak; cheerless; despondent; evil-affected; forlorn; gloomy; hopeless; impossible; joyless; keening; lorn; melancholic; negative; *overcast;* pessimistic; Q.B.I. [RAF slang]; rueful; sad; tristful; unhopeful; very sad; woeful; *x'ed; yearnful; zestless;* [Ant. merry]

**morsel** *(n.)*: *atom;* bit(e); crumb; dainty; edible; fragment; granule; hunk; iota; jib; kernel; lump; mite; modicum; nugget; ounce; particle; piece; quid; remnant; scrap; tad; *unit; viand;* whit; *x-particle; yummy bit; zum [dial.];*

**mortal** *(adj.)*: Adamic; baneful; corporeal; deadly; deathly; destructive; doomful; eliminating; fatal; *grievous;* harmful; injurious; internecine; jeopardous; killing; lethal; mortiferous; noxious; only-human; perilous; poisonous; pernicious; perilous; ruinous; self-destructive; toxic; unsafe; virulent; worldling; *x-ing; ydrad [arch.]; zero safety;*

**mortar** *(n. cement for bricks)*: adhesive; bonding material; cement; *daub; epoxy;* fixative; grout; *hold;* ichthyocolla; joint cement; kit; lithocolla; mastic; *nail; one;* paste; parget; *quince-mucilage; red grout;* slime; tempered ~; untempered ~; *viscous; weld; xenograft;* yoke; zip together;

**mortgage** *(n.)*: antichresis; bank ~; construction loan; debt; *extending;* financing; fixed-rate ~; grubstake; home ~; imprest; installment ~; jumbo ~; junior ~; *key loan;* loan; miniperm; *nonconforming ~;* open ~; package ~; *quick loan; refinancing;* second ~; take-out loan; underadvance; variable-rate ~; wadsett; *xfer; yearly payment;* z-bond;

**Moslem** *(adj.)*: Arab; Bedouin; *Carmathian;* dervish; *eastern; fakir; group; hafiz;* Islamic; *jihad;* Koranic; *Karmathian; liberal ~;* Muslim; Mohammedan; *non-Christian; Ottoman;* paynim; Quran-believing; *Qarmatian; religious;* Sunni; Shiite; *Turkish; Umayyad; view; Wahabi; xenophagy; Yeziti;* Zaidi;

**mossy** *(adj.)*: abundant; busky; cespitose; dense; enfoliated; fertile; grassy; green; herbaged; infoliated; jungly; *knotgrass-covered;* lush; moss-covered; *neosharpiella;* overgrown; plush; *quitch-grass covered;* rich; swardy; turfy; unspoiled; verdurous; *wooded; xerophilious; yellow-green;* zea-filled;

**most** *(adj.)*: almost all; bulk; biggest; ceiling; *determined;* extent; fairly; full (capacity); greater part; highest; *immoderate; jump; kop;* largely; limit; largest; majority; maximum; most; nearly all; *nth* degree; overmost; preponderance; *quorum; reach;* supreme; top; utmost; uttermost; *virtually;* vertex; weight; *xtry.;* yondmost; zenith; [*Ant.* minimal]

**mote** *(n.)*: amount; bit; chip; drop; *ens;* fragment; granule; grain; *hunk;* iota; jot; kernel; *lump;* morsel; nugget; ounce; particle; *quantity; remnant;* speck; *tidbit;* unit; *vestige; wad;* XAG*; yod; zum [arch.];*

**mother** *(n.)*: ancestor; biological ~; child-bearer; dam [zoo.]; *earth ~;* female parent; genetrix; *head; individual; jane; kinfolk; lady;* (mom)my; (ma)mmy; nanny; old lady [off.]; parent; *quite motherly; relative;* super-mom [joc.]; sweet ~; *trainer; unwed ~;* venter; woman who bore; *xtry. ~;* young ~; *zaftig;* [*see* parent; nurse]

**motherly** *(adj.)*: affectionate; baby-loving; caring; doting; enate; female; gentle; *her;* intimate; *jane;* kind; loving; maternal; nurturing; overprotective; parental; protective; *quality time; reassuring;* selfless; tender; unselfish; *virtuous;* warm; *xtry;* yearnful; *zero selfishness;*

**motion** *(n.)*: action; activity; bestirring; bustle; conveying; commotion; drift; dynamics; *excitement;* flurry; going; gesture; hydrokinetic; hustle and bustle; impulse; jee; kinetic; kinematic; locomotion; movement; mobility; momentum; *non-stationary; ongoing;* progress; quickening; relocation; shifting; stirring; transportation; *underway; velocity;* vagility; wave; working; *xfer; yede;* zipping; [*Ant.* motionlessness]

**motion** *(v.)*: advance; ask; bid; beckon; counsel; *desire;* encourage; extend; flag; give recommendation; gesture; *hold up;* importunate; indicate; *juration; kibitz [Yid.];* look to; move; nominate; nod; offer; propose; *quicken;* recommend; suggest; submit; signal; tender; urge; *vocalize;* wave; *want; xuld [arch.]; yearn; zealously ~;*

**motionless** *(adj.)*: at rest; becalmed; calm; dead still; easeful; fixed; frozen; *grinded to a halt;* hushed; idle; immobile; inanimate; jarless; *kept ~;* lying; lifeless; made still; non-moving; on hold; peaceful; placid; quiet; restful; stationary; still; tranquil; unmoving; vegetative; waiting; *x'ed;* yet to move; *zero motion;* [*Ant.* mobile]

**motivate** *(v.)*: activate; arouse; bestir; cause; compel; drive; encourage; excite; fire up; goad; get excited about; hearten; induce; incite; inspire; ignite; inflame; inspirit; jar; kindle; lead; move; nudge; *overexcite;* provoke; prompt; quicken; rouse; rally; stimulate; stir up; *trigger; undertake; upset;* vivify; whet; work up; *xuld [arch.];* yerk; *zing;* [*see* enthuse]

**motivation** *(n.)*: aim; animus; bestirring; compulsion; drive; enthusiasm; force; goal; heartbeat; hidden agenda; inspiration; justification; kindling; leading; mainspring; moving spirit; nudge; objective; provocation; quickening; reason; resolve; stimulus; stirring; *triggering;* urgency; *vitality;* will; *xuld [arch.]; yearning; zeal;*

**motive** *(n.)*: aim; basis; cause; design; end; foundation; goal; grounds; heart; hidden agenda; intention; justification; key reason; lure; motivation; *notion;* object; purpose; *quickening;* reason; stimulus; *trigger;* ulterior ~; underlying reason; *volition;* will; *xuld [arch.]; yearning; zeal;*

**motto** *(n.)*: axiom; byword; catch-phrase; dictum; device; expression; formula; guideline; hackneyed saying; idiom; jingle; *known ~;* locution; maxim; message; *neology; oracle;* phrase; quote; rule; slogan; saying; tag line; utterance; *verse;* watchword; *xenagogy; Yogism; zeteticism;*
**mound** *(n.)*: anthill; acclivity; bank; bluff; clump; collection; drift; embankment; fell; gathering; heap; hill; *incline;* jebel; kame; knoll; koppie; loma; lump; mass; motte; molehill; nab; oser; pile; quantity; quire; rise; ruck; stack; tussock; tuffet; *upslope;* versant; wad; *XL;* yunga; *zillions;*
**mount** *(v.)*: ascend; accumulate; boost; climb; develop; elevate; escalate; fly up; go up; get on; grow; heighten; heap; increase; jump up; *keep rising;* lift; move upward; *nudge higher;* overclimb; progress; pile; *quantum increase;* rise; *straddle;* scale; sur~; swell; transcend; upclimb; verge upward; wax higher; *xfer; yain* [arch.]; zoom up;
**mountain** *(n.)*: alp; berg; crag; djebel; elevation; foothill; guyot; hump; hill; highlands [pl.]; high place; inselberg; jebel; jokul; knoll; lofty height; mound; mount; nub; *orology;* peak; prominence [geog.]; *quantity; range;* summit; tor; upland; versant; volcano; vertex; white-capped peak; *Xiao; Yablonovvy;* zenith;
**mountainous** *(adj.)*: alpine; bumpy; craggy; *djebel; enlarged;* full of hills; giant; hilly; highland; *inselberg;* jagged; knolly; *lumpy;* mountainy; montane; nubby; *orology;* peak-filled; *quantity;* rugged; rocky; subalpine; tumulous; upland; versant; *wold; xalpine;* yunga-covered; *zenith;*
**mountaintop** *(n.)*: apex; brow; crest; *destination;* extremity; *farthest point; greatest height;* height; head; high point; *increase; jut;* kop; limit; lofty height; *maximum;* nib; *nunatak;* outcrop; peak; pinnacle; *quoif; ridge;* summit; top; tip; tor; upper extremity; vertex; *way up; xtry; yonder point;* zenith;
**mourn** *(v.)*: anguish; bemoan; bewail; be sad; cry; despair; elegize; fret; feel sad; grieve; gnash teeth; howl; *inconsolable; judder;* keen; lament; moan; noise; outcry; pine; quail; remorse; repent; sorrow; shed tears; *tearful;* ululate; *unhappy; vociferate;* weep; wail; *x-out;* yowl; yammer; yawp; yearn; *zing;* [*Ant.* make merry]
**mourner** *(n.)*: ailer; anguisher; bellower; bemoaner; crier; despairer; elegist; *fretter;* griever; howler; *inconsolable; joyless;* keener; lamenter; moaner; noiser; outcrier; pallbearer; *piner;* quailer; reuer; sorrower; *tearful;* ululator; *very sad;* weeper; wailer; *x'ed out;* yowler; yawler; *zero comfort;* [*Ant.* merrymaker]
**mournful** *(adj.)*: anguishing; broken-hearted; cast down; doleful; emotional; elegaic; forlorn; grief-stricken; gut-wrenching; heartbroken; heart-wrenching; inconsolable; joyless; keening; lamentable; lachymose; lachtymable; lugubrious; miserable; *noisome; negative;* overcast; plaintive; piteous; quailing; rueful; sorrowful; sad; sullen; tearful; unhappy; very sad; wailful; woeful; *x'ed;* yearnful; yowling; *zestless;* [*Ant.* merry]
**mouth** *(n.)*: aperture; beak; *bite; big ~;* chops; cavity; delta; entrance; flaps; gate; gums; gob; *the* hatch [slang]; *hole;* inlet; jaws; kisser [slang]; lips; maw; mug; *nozzle;* orifice; opening; os; portal; quadrate; *recess; savor;* trap [slang]; *teeth; underlip; voice; well; xerochilia;* yap; *zippered lips;*
**move** *(n.)*: action; advance; budge; conveyance; commigration; displacement; emigration; fare; going; *haul;* immigration; jee; *jump;* jill [naut.]; kinesis; *locomotion;* movement; motion; mobilization; migration; maneuver; nudge; *ongoing;* progress; push; pull; quickening; run; reposition; relocation; rearrangement; redistribution; stir; shift; step; shuffle; transport; transfer; unkenneling; venture; walk; xfer; xenization; xenotransplant; yead; zugzwang [chess];
**move** *(v.)*: act; advance; bestir; budge; convey; do; drift; displace; edge; flow; fly; go; get; hasten; *immigrate;* jump; jet; journey; *kindle;* locomote; maneuver; mobilize; migrate; nudge; navigate; *overrun; ongoing;* pass; proceed; progress; plod; position; quicken; reposition; relocate; run; stir; shift; stream; sail; scoot; travel; traverse; transport; transfer; transition; transplant; unkennel; *underway;* voyage; venture; verge; walk; wend; xfer; yede; yerk; zip; [*see* impel]

**movement** *(n.)*: activity; actuation; bestirring; bustle; course; current; conveyance; commotion; dynamism; expedition; flow; flurry; flight; flux; going; gesture; grass roots ~; hydrokinetic; hustle and bustle; impulse; influx; *jee;* kinetisis; locomotion; motion; mobility; mobilization; *non-stationary;* outflow; passage; quickening; relocation; stirring; shifting; stream; tide; travel; transferal; transportation; *upsurge;* velocity; working; wending; xfer; *yede;* zipping; [*Ant.* motionlessness]

**mow** *(v.)*: abscind; bob; cut; chop; crop; *dock;* exscind; foreshorten; *grate;* hack; incide; *jag;* knock down; *lop;* mulch; nip; obtruncate; pare; poll; *quash;* recise; shear; trim; *undercut;* vell; *whittle;* x-sect; yerk; zip;

**much** *(adj. + adv. + pron.)*: abundant; a lot of; bunch; bounteous; considerable; copious; disproportionate; excess(ive); extensive(ly); fruitful; great; galore; heaps; immense; jumbo; *king-sized amounts;* lots; loads; many; numerous; overmuch; plenty; plural(ity); quantitative; *replete; rich;* several; tons; uberous; voluminous; wantless; *x.;* yards; zillions;

**mud** *(n.)*: argil; *bemire;* clay; crud; dirt; *earth;* filth; glaur; gunk; hog wallow; *iron-clay; jet; kaolin; lutarious;* muck; mire; nast; ooze; peat bog; quagmire; red soil; sludge; slush; silt; slime; slop; *turf;* urry; *vile;* wet dirt; wallow; waste; *xysma; yellow soil; zonal soil;*

**muddy** *(adj.)*: *awful;* bemired; besmirched; collied; cruddy; covered (in mud); dirty; *earthy;* feculent; filthy; glaury; grubby; gunky; hazy; impure; jarbled; kallowed; lutulent; limous; muddied; mucky; miry; *nasty;* oozy; opaque; puggy; plashy; quaggy; roily; sludgy; slushy; slimy; sloppy; swampy; turbid; unclean; uliginous; *unwashed; vile;* well-muddied; *xysmic;* yucky; *zwishy;*

**muffle** *(v.)*: *alleviate;* bind up; cushion; cover; dampen; dull; deaden; enwrap; *fix;* gag; hush; *inclose; jacket;* keep quiet; lessen; mute; muzzle; *noise reduction;* overlay; prevent; quiet(en); reduce; soften; shush; stifle; silence; tone down; upbind; *veil;* wrap; *whisper;* x-bind; *yoke;* zeroize; [*Ant.* magnify]

**muggy** *(adj.)*: airless; *boiling;* clammy; damp; dank; *enkindled;* full-hot; *gross;* humid; icky; jejune; *kindled; languid;* moist; *non-fresh;* oppressive; pluvious; *quenchless;* rorid; sultry; stuffy; sticky; steamy; stifling; torrid; uncomfortable; *vaporous;* wettish; *xerothermic;* yucky; *zealless;*

**multiply** *(v.)*: augment; accumulate; amplify; become larger; breed; climb; crescendo; *develop;* expand; enlarge; flourish; grow; heighten; increase; jump up; *keep growing;* largen; magnify; *not decrease;* overflow with; proliferate; quadruplicate; reproduce; rocket; shoot up; swell; skyrocket; snowball; take off; upshoot; *volume;* wax greater; XL; *yain [arch.];* zoom up;

**multi-purpose** *(adj.)*: adaptable; bendable; changeable; convertible; *doable;* exchangeable; flexible; *geared to change;* handy; interchangeable; *jump;* key; *labile;* multi-use; non-fixed; open; polyergic; protean; *queachy [arch.];* reversible; switchable; transformable; useful; versatile; workable; *x-able;* yielding; *zet [dial.];*

**multitude** *(n.)*: assemblage; amassment; bunch; crowd; company; drove; *ekklesia [G.];* forgathering; flock; group; horde; ingathering; jam [slang]; kit [coll.]; lot; legion; mass; mob; number; overabundance; pack; press; quantity; ruck; rabble; swarm; throng; *unit;* volume; wisp; *xtry. crowd; yelm;* zillions;

**mundane** *(adj.)*: average; boring; banausic; commonplace; dull; dreary; everyday; flat; *generic;* ho-hum; insipid; jejune; known-by-all; lackluster; monotonous; nondescript; ordinary; ponderous; quotidian; routine; standard; tedious; uninteresting; vapid; wearisome; xtr. boring; yawnful; zestless; [*Ant.* magnificent]

**murder** *(n.)*: assassination; bloodshed; butchery; cold-blooded ~; disposal; elimination; extermination; finishing off; gunning down; homicide; *infanticide; jabbing;* killing; liquidation [joc.]; manslaughter; massacre; *neutralizing;* obliteration; premeditated ~; purging; quashing; rubbing out; slaying; taking one's life; unlawful killing; vitiation; wasting [slang]; x-ing out; *yanking down; zapping;*

**murder** *(v.)*: annihilate; assassinate; bump off [slang]; butcher; commit ~; cut off; dispose of; destroy; eliminate; exterminate; finish off; gun down; *homicide; immolate; jab;* kill; knock off [slang]; liquidate [joc.]; massacre; *neutralize;* obliterate; purge; quash; rub out; slay; smite; take one's life; terminate; *unseat;* vitiate; waste [slang]; x-out; *yank down;* zap;

**murderer** *(n.)*: annihilator; assassin; butcher; cut-throat; destroyer; executioner; eradicator; expunger; *finisher;* gunman; hackster; hired gun; hit man; *impenitent killer; jabber;* knifer; knifeman; killer; *lyncher;* manslayer; mankiller; murderess [fem.]; mass ~; ninja; *obliterator;* predator; quencher; ripper; slayer; slaughterer; serial killer; strangler; terminator; *undoer;* victimizer; vitiator; waster; widow-maker; *x-er; yegg;* zapper;

**murderous** *(adj.)*: atrocious; bloodthirsty; cutthroat; destructive; deathful; deadly; evil-intentioned; fiendish; gory; homicidal; *insidious; jaded;* kill-crazy; lethal; malevolent; nefarious; odious; pestilent; *quad;* ruthless; slaughterous; savage; treacherous; *uncivilized;* violent; wicked; *xenophobic; yeffell* [arch.]; *zero-mercy;* [Ant. moral]

**murky** *(adj.)*: *adularescent;* beclouded; cloudy; dim; dark; enclouded; foggy; gloomy; hazy; inclouded; *jumbled; kettle-black;* lowery; muddy; murksome; nebulous; obscure; poorly-visible; *qually* [arch.]; roily; shadowy; tenebrous; turbid; unclear; vague; *wispy; xenon cloud; yucky;* zero-zero;

**murmur** *(n.)*: *accusations;* bellyaching; complaint; carping; decrying; *exploding;* fussing; grumbling; gripe; honing; inveighing; jangling; knocking; lambasting; muttering; moaning; maundering; murmuring; niggling; objections; protests; quetching; repining; rumble; squawking; susurration; *tearing into; unhappiness;* vituperation; whining; *xuld [arch.];* yawping; zinging;

**murmur** *(v.)*: *accuse;* balk; bellyache; complain; carp; criticize; disparage; decry; *explode;* fuss; grumble; gripe; hone; harangue; impugn; inveigh; jangle; knock; lambaste; mutter; moan; maunder; nitpick; niggle; object; pick; protest; pule; quetch; quarrel; repine; remonstrate; squawk; susurrate; talk; *ululate;* vituperate; whine; *xuld [arch.];* yawp; zing;

**murmurer** *(n.)*: *accuser;* balker; bellyacher; complainer; carper; critic; disparager; *explode;* fusser; fault-finder; grumbler; griper; grouser; grievant; haranguer; impugner; jangler; knocker; kvetch; lambaster; moaner; nitpicker; objector; protester; quarreler; repiner; remonstrator; slammer; *talker; undoer;* vituperator; whiner; *xuld [arch.];* yawper; zoilus;

**muscle** *(n.)*: ability; brawn; capability; dint; energy; force; gusto; heftiness; horsepower; intensity; *jet-power; kilowatt;* lustiness; meat; might; *natural strength; overpower;* physique; power; *qualifications;* robustness; strength; thew; *usefulness;* vigor; wherewithal; *xenium; yare;* zip;

**muscular** *(adj.)*: athletic; brawny; beefy; *capable; durable;* enormous; fit; firm; great; hulky; iron(-bodied); *jusqu'au bout [F.];* keen; lusty; mighty; *nervy; obstinate;* powerful; *quality;* robust; sinewy; strong; tough; thewy; unflagging; vigorous; well-set; *x-strong;* yauld; *zippy;*

**mush** *(n.)*: *admixture;* bagasse; concoction; curd; dough; *essence;* fine purée; goop; grume; hominy; intermixture; jam; kasha; loblolly; mash; *non-solid;* oatmeal; pulp; purée; paste; porridge; *quagmire;* rag pulp; samp; slop; soup; thick liquid; *ugali; viscousmatter;* watery substance; *xtr. blended; yan; zuppe [It.];*

**music** *(n.)*: air; attunement; *ballad;* chorus; canticle; composition; chords; ditty; dirge; *easy-listening ~; folk ~;* fantasia; gallimaufry; harmony; intermezzo; jingle; *kasida; lullaby; love song;* melody; notes; *overture; postlude; prelude; pop ~; performance;* quadrille; rhapsody; refrain; *sound;* song; strain; tune; *unfinished symphony;* vocalization; *violin ~;* woodnote; *xylophone music;* yed; *zouk;*

**musical** *(adj.)*: accordant; blending; choral; canorous; dulcet; euphonic; euphonous; fine-toned; golden-voiced; harmonic; instrumental; *joyful;* keen-sounding; lyrical; lilting; melodic; melodious; *notes;* orchestral; pleasing; philharmonic; *quality;* rhythmic; songlike; sweet-sounding; symphonic; tuneful; *uplifting;* vocal; virtuosic; well-sounding; *xylophonic; yed; zero discordance;*

**musician** *(n.)*: accompanyist; artiste; bard; bandsman; caroler; concertist; composer; diva [fem.]; entertainer; *fiddler;* gleeman; harmonist; instrumentalist; jammer; jongleur; *keyboardist; lutist; lyricist;* minstrel; *negro minstrel; organist;* performer; player; pianist; *quartetist;* recitalist; symphonist; singer; soloist; tunester; troubadour; *trumpeter; ukulele player;* vocalist; virtuoso; warbler; *wind-instrumentalist; xylophonist;* yodeler; zitherist;

**muster** *(v.)*: assemble; aggregate; bring together; congregate; drum up; employ; flock; gather; *hurry;* initiate; *join; kindle;* line up; mobilize; marshal; *negotiate;* organize; position; *quicken;* rally; summon; throng; unite; *venture; work;* xfer; *yede; zone;*

**musty** *(n.)*: antiquated; bad-smelling; *corrupt;* decaying; *eroding;* fusty; gamy; hoared; ill-smelling; *jading;* ketty; *labefaction;* moldy; mildewy; mucid; nidorous; *nasty;* old; outdated; peccant; queering; rank; stuffy; stale; *tainted;* unventilated; *unpleasant;* vinnewed; welking; *xylaria; yellowed; zapped;*

**mutability** *(n.)*: alterability; *bendability;* changeableness; deviating; erraticism; fickleness; *going back and forth; hopping around;* inconstancy jerkiness; *kedging; lacination;* movability; mutableness; non-steadiness; oscillation; pendulating; *quivering;* rearranging; shifting; turning; unstableness; variability; wavering; *x-ing;* yo-yoing; zigzagging;

**mutable** *(adj.)*: alterable; *bendable;* changeable; deviative; editable; erratic; ever-changing; flexible; *growable; hopping around;* inconstant; jerky; kaleidoscopic; *labile;* modifiable; moveable; non-fixed; *oscillating;* protean; *quirky; revisable;* switchable; turnable; unfixed; unstable; variable; wavering; *x-ing;* yeasty; *zero constancy;*

**mutate** *(v.)*: alter; *bend;* change; contort; deform; distort; *evolve; fluctuate; gnarl; garble; hideous; innovate; jump; kink; lurch;* modify; metamorphose; morph; novate; *overhaul;* per~; *queer;* reform; reshape; shift; turn; transform; transmute; transmogrify; undergo change; vary; warp; xenomorph; *yaw; zigzag;*

**mutation** *(n.)*: alteration; *bending;* change; deviation; deformity; distortion; evolution; fluctuation; *gnarling; garbling;* heterogenesis; innovation; *jumping; kinesis;* lethal ~; *lycanthropy;* morphing; mutant; metamorphosis; novelty; *overhaul;* per~; *queerness;* reforming; reshaping; shift; transformation; trans~; transmogrification; *undergoing change;* variation; warping; xenomorphism; *yawing; zigzagging;*

**mute** *(adj.)*: aphonic; becalmed; calm; dumb; *exanimate; faded; gentle;* hushed; inarticulate; *jarless; keeping quiet; low;* mum; non-speaking; nonverbal; over-quiet; *peaceful;* quiet; *resting;* speechless; soft; soundless; silent; taciturn; unvoiced; uncommunicative; unheard; unspeaking; voiceless; whist; wordless; *x'ed; yareless;* zero sound;

**mutilate** *(v.)*: amputate; butcher; bemangle; contort; chop up; disfigure; *exscind; fissure;* garble; hurt; hash; hack(le); injure; *jab; knife;* lacerate; maim; mar; mangle; *notch;* olate; pull apart; *quade* [arch.]; rend; ruin; scar; spoil; tear asunder; twist; uglify; victimize; wreck; *x-sect;* yank apart; *zap;*

**mutilator** *(n.)*: *archfiend;* butcher; crusher; disfigurer; *executioner; felon;* garbler; hurter; injurer; *Jack the Ripper;* knife-man; lacerater; maimer; mangler; *no-good;* outlaw; perpetrator; *quade* [arch.]; ruiner; slasher; tearer; uglifier; victimize; wrecker; *x-sect; yegg; zapper;*

**mutinous** *(adj.)*: averse; *breakaway;* contumacious; disloyal; defiant; evil-intentioned; faithless; guileful; honorless; insurrectional; *jadish; knavish;* lawless; mutineering; non-loyal; *opportunistic;* perfidious; *quisling;* rebellious; seditious; treacherous; traitorous; treasonous; unfaithful; violent; wicked; *x-ing; yieldless; zero honor;*

**mutiny** *(n.)*: armed *conflict; breach; coup d'état* [F.]; defiance; émeute; *fight;* gainstanding; high treason; insubordination; insurrection; jacquerie; *kicking at;* lèse majesté [F.]; *misbehavior;* noncompliance; overthrow; perfidy; *questioning;* rebellion; revolt; sedition; takeover; treason; uprising; violence; *war; xgression;* yieldlessness; *zero obedience;*

**mutiny** *(v.)*: arise; buck; contravene; challenge; commit treason; defy; dissent; disobey; *err;* flout; gainstand; have rebellion; insurrect; *jump ship; kick at; leave; misbehave; non-compliance;* overthrow; pay no regard to; *quad;* rise up; rebel; revolt; stand against; subvert; throw off (yoke); usurp; uprise; *violate;* withstand; *x-gress; yieldless; zero obedience;*

**mutt** *(n.)*: animal; bitch [fem.]; cur; dog; *elkhound;* feist; *greyhound;* hound; *Irish setter; junkyard dog; K-9* [slang]; lapdog; mongrel; night-dog; *organism;* pooch; *quadruped;* retriever; sheepdog; terrier; *ululator;* vizsla; watchdog; *xolotl;* yellow dog; *zerda;* [see dog]

**mutter** *(v.)*: *accuse;* bellyache; carp; chunter; decry; *explode;* fuss; grumble; hone; inveigh; jangle; *kvetch* [Yid.]; land on; maunder; moan; nitpick; object; pule; quibble; repine; sigh; snarl; *talk;* utter; vituperate; whine; *xuld [arch.];* yawp; zing;

**mutual** *(adj.)*: associated; bilateral; consensual; common; corresponding; complementary; communal; cooperative; collaborative; dependent; equidependent; fellow; give-and-take; harmonious; inter~; interdependent; joint; *keenly felt; linked;* mutually-agreed; non-competitive; *own;* participatory; *qualified;* reciprocal; shared; symbiotic; twin; two-way; united; *vicissitudinous;* wholly; *xenobiotic;* yoking; *zero one-sidedness;*

**mutuality** *(n.)*: agreement; affinity; bilateralism; commonality; dependence; empathy; equidependence; fellow feeling; give-and-take; harmony; interdependence; joining; kinship; like-mindedness; meeting of the minds; non-competitiveness; oneness; partnership; *quality;* rapport; solidarity; togetherness; unity; *voluntariness; willingness; xenia; yung* [Chin.]; yoke; *zero-disagreement;*

**mysterious** *(adj.)*: arcane; baffling; cabalistic; dark; esoteric; furtive; guarded; hidden; inscrutable; *jumbled;* known to few; *labyrinthine;* mystical; mystifying; not revealed; odd; perplexing; quiet; recondite; secret(ive); strange; top-secret; transcendental; unsolved; unexplained; veiled; wildering; xtry.; yet unexplained; *zero explanation;* [*Ant.* manifest]

**mystery** *(n.)*: arcanum; black ~; curiousness; crime; conundrum; dark ~; detective story; enigma; *fuddlement;* great ~; hidden thing; inscrutableness; irresolution; jigsaw puzzle; kept secret; *little-known;* mysterious puzzle; non-disclosed fact; obscure fact; puzzle; question; riddle; secret; tricky question; unexplained thing; vagueness; whodunnit; X; yet undisclosed fact; zinger; [*Ant.* manifestation]

**mystic** *(n.)*: astrologer; bewitcher; clairvoyant; diviner; enchanter; fortune-teller; geomancer; haruspice; *incantation;* jadoo-wallah; *karakia [Maori];* lithomancer; medium; necromancer; oracle; psychic; *quad;* rhabdomancer; seer; telepathist; *ungodly;* voodooist; wizard; xylomancer; yogist; zodiacist;

**mystical** *(adj.)*: awe-inspiring; baffling; cabalistic; deep; esoteric; furtive; gnomic; hidden; inexplicable; *jumbled;* known to few; *labyrinthine;* magical; mystifying; numinous; oracular; puzzling; queer; recondite; strange; transcendent; unexplained; unknown; unknowable; veiled; wildering; *xenomorphic; yieldless; zany;*

**mystification** *(n.)*: amazement; bafflement; confusion; disorientation; enclouding; farrago; gastness; hiddenness; incomprehension; jumble; *knottiness; labyrinthine;* misunderstanding; non-comprehension; obscurity; puzzlement; *quizzical;* raveling; stupefaction; turmoil; uncertainty; vexation; wilderment; *xtry. mess; yo-yo; zero-understanding;*

**mystify** *(v.)*: amaze; baffle; bewilder; confound; discomfit; encloud; fuddle; flummox; gravel; hamper; incloud; jumble; kittle; lose; mix up; *mind-boggling;* nonplus; obscure; puzzle; perplex; quiz; *ravel;* stump; tangle; *unknown;* vex; wilder; *x; yo-yo; zero understanding;*

**mystique** *(n.)*: appeal; air; beauty; charm; chemistry; draw; enchantment; fascination; feminine ~; geasa; *hold;* inscrutability; *je ne sais quoi* [F.]; *kinch;* loveliness; mysteriousness; magic; nature; *overwhelming;* pull; *quality;* reaction; spell; temperament; unusualness; *voluptuousness; way; xtry. charm; yearning; zap;*

**myth** *(n.)*: account; apologue; *bedtime story;* creation; delusion; epic; fable; fairy tale; fiction; ghost story; hallucination; invention; imposture; journal; *kept tradition;* legend; lore; mythic story; *narrative;* oral legend; phantasm; quasi-reality; retelling; romantic legend; story; saga; superstition; tale; tradition; unproven account; version; written folklore; xenodocheionology; yarn; *zero truth;*

**mythical** *(adj.)*: air-built; *bogus;* chimerical; dreamt-up; epic; fictional; fabled; folkloric; gestic; highly imaginary; imaginary; just imagined; *known in fables;* legendary; made-up; mythic; mythological; nonexistent; *oft-retold;* phantasmal; quasi- ~; romanticized; supposed; talked-about; unreal; vichus; well-imagined; *xtry.;* yichus; zoomythic;

# N

**nail** *(n.)*: * annular ~; brad; common ~; door~; *eye bolt;* finishing ~; floor ~; fastener; galvanized ~; hob~; *hardware;* iron spike; joist; *keep together;* lost-head ~; masonry ~; marline-spike; *nailhead;* oval brad; piton; penny ~; paal; quarter-inch ~; roofing ~; spike; stake; six-penny ~; tack; ten-penny ~; tent spike; *U-bolt;* veneer pin; wire ~; xyston; *yoke;* zinc-coated ~;

**nail** *(v.)*: *assault;* bang; clock; conk; countersink; deck; *expunge; flail; get;* hammer; hit; impact; jab; knock; *lam;* mash; *nab;* overhit; punch; pound; quab; rap; strike; thwack; *undo; veney;* whack; *x-sect; yedder;* zonk;

**naïve** *(adj.)*: artless; benighted; childlike; dewy; easily-deceived; foolish; gullible; hoaxable; innocent; inexperienced; juvenile; know-nothing; lacking understanding; *moronic;* naive; non-aware; oblivious; Pickwickian; *quacky;* raw; simple; trusting; unaware; unwise; verdant; wareless; *xtry. dumb;* youthful; *zoned out;*

**naked** *(adj.)*: *au naturel* [F.]; bare; buck- ~; clothesless; disrobed; exposed; *flaunted; flagrant;* garbless; *heedless;* immodest; indecent; *jade; kinky;* laid bare; lewd; manifest; nude; open; obscene; peeled; *quad;* revealed; stripped; scanty; stark- ~; *tout ensemble* [F.]; unadorned; unclad; uncovered; undressed; visible; without clothes; x-rated; *yet uncovered; zero clothes;* [see plain]

**nakedness** *(n.)*: *the* altogether; bareness; clotheslessness; denudedness; disrobement; exposure; *flagrancy;* garblessness; *heedlessness;* indecency; immodesty; *jadedness; kinkiness;* lewdness; manifestation; nudity; obscenity; peeling away; *quad; the* raw; shame; scantiness; toplessness; uncovering; undress; *vulgarity; wantonness; x-rated; yet uncovered; zero clothes;*

**name** *(n.)*: * alias; appellation; by~; baptismal ~; Christian ~; designation; *entitled;* first ~; family- ~; given ~; handle [slang]; hypocorism; identity; identifier; *jurisdiction;* known by; label; last ~; moniker; middle ~; maiden- ~; nick~; nomen(clature); *overtitle;* pet ~; pen ~; *quiring;* representation; sur~; tag; title; *undercover ~;* vocable; word; xenonym; *yu* [Chin.]; zoon; [see authority; reputation]

**name** *(v.)*: *assign;* brand; call; christen; dub; designate; denominate; entitle; forename; give title to; hail as; identify; indicate; *jurisdiction; known as;* label; *mis~;* nick~; nominate; ordain; phrase; *quiring;* refer to; saddle with [slang]; style; sur~; tag; term; *use; vocable; word; xenonym;* yclept; *zoon;*

**name-calling** *(n.)*: abuse; belittlement; contempt; derision; *execration;* fleering; gibing; heckling; insults; jab; knocking; ludifaction; mockery; *nastiness;* opprobrium; pillory; quibbing; ridicule; scoffing; taunting; *unkindness;* verbal abuse; wiping; *x-ing; yocking;* zinging;

**namely** *(adv.)*: a.k.a.; by name; called; designated; explicitly; for example; *given the title;* hailed as; i.e.; *just call one;* known as; *labeled;* more specifically known as; namely; *one;* particularly; *qualified as;* referred to as; specifically; scilicet; that is; *use;* viz.; widely known as; *xenonym;* you know him as; *zero in;*

**nanny** *(n.)*: *au pair* [F.]; *bonne* [F.]; babysitter; caretaker (-giver); duenna; *educator; forewoman;* governess; home teacher; *instructress; jefe;* keeper; *leader;* mammy; mistress; nannie; nanna; nursemaid; *overseer;* principle caretaker; *quartermaid;* rectress; sitter; *trainer;* tutoress; *undershepherd; vicereine;* wet nurse; *xenagogue;* yaya; *zookeeper [joc.];*

**nap** *(n.)*: aestivation; *asleep;* blanket drill; cat~; doze; estivation; forty winks; *grogginess;* hibernation; idleness; *jadedness;* kip; loafing; Morpheus; *nod off;* obdormition; period of sleep; quiet time; repose; rest; shuteye; snooze; siesta; *time of rest;* unconsciousness; vegetation; wink; *x-sleep; yawning;* zizz;

**napkin** *(n.)*: *animetta;* brown paper ~; cloth ~; dinner ~; *eating;* folded ~; fabric ~; *gorget;* handkerchief; *item; jaconet;* kertch; linen; mouth-wipe; *napery; object;* paper ~ (-towel); *querche* [arch.]; rag; serviette; towel(ette); *unused ~; vandyke;* washcloth; *xanthation;* yellow ~; *zet [dial.];*
**narrate** *(v.)*: articulate; bespeak; cite; chronicle; describe; declaim; expatiate; fable; give; *herald;* iterate; inform; *jaw;* keep speaking; *lecture;* mouth; novelize; orate; pronounce; quote; recount; retell; relate; recite; rhetorize; say; state; speak; tell; unfold a story; utter; voice; word; *xenophonia; yak;* zay [dial.];
**narration** *(n.)*: articulation; bespeaking; citing; declaiming; echoing; fabling; giving; *heralding;* iteration; *jaw; keep coming; lecture;* mentioning; novelizing; oration; pronouncing; quotation; recounting; retelling; reading; relation; recitation; saying; stating; speaking; story-telling; telling; utterance; voicing; wording; *xenophonia;* yarn-spinning; *zay [dial.];*
**narrator** *(n.)*: addresser; book-reader; commentator; declarer; discourser; diseur; enunciator; fabler; *gabber; herald;* informer; *jabberer;* key speaker; lecturer; *man; mentioner;* narratage; orator; prelector; proser; quoter; relator; speaker; storyteller; talker; teller; utterer; verbalist; voice(over); worder; *xenophobia;* yarner; *zeug;*
**narrow** *(adj.)*: attenuated; boxed in; contracted; dinky; elongated; fine; gaunt; hairbreadth; incapacious; jimp; knife-blade thin; limited; lean; meager; minute; non-ponderous; overthin; pencil-thin; petite; quite thin; restricted; slim; slender; strait; thin; undersized; virgate [bot.]; wiry; wafer-thin; XF; yea wide; *zero extra room;*
**narrow** *(v.)*: attenuate; become slenderer; contract; constrict; diminish; decrease; exiguous; extenuate; fall off; get thinner; *halve; impair; jump down; knock down;* lessen; minimize; narrow down; *outgo;* peter out; quail; reduce; slenderize; straiten; thin; taper; *undersize; vanish;* wane; welk; XS; *yield;* zero in;
**narrow-minded** *(adj.)*: anti-change; biased; closed-minded; diehard; dogmatic; ever-narrow; firm; *grim;* hidebound; insular; intolerant; *jaw-set; keep-it-the-same;* limited; *mind made-up;* narrow; old-fashioned; parochial; provincial; *querulous;* resistant-to-change; stubborn; *traditionalist;* unprogressive; ultra-conservative; *vieux jeu* [F.]; willful; *x-grained;* yieldless; *zero give;*
**nasty** *(adj. hateful)*: antagonistic; belligerent; contemptuous; dastardly; despiteful; evil; fiendful; galsome; hateful; inimical; jaded; kindless; loathsome; mean; nefarious; odious; pernicious; querulous; rancorous; spiteful; terrible; unkind; vindictive; wicked; *xenophobic;* yucky; zoilean; [Ant. nice]
**nasty** *(adj. unpleasant)*: awful; bad; contemptible; disagreeable; distasteful; execrable; foul; gross; horrible; invidious; jarring; kindless; lousy; loathsome; miserable; nauseating; objectionable; offensive; odious; pitiful; pathetic; *quad;* repulsive; sickening; stomach-turning; terrible; unappetizing; unsavory; unlikable; undesirable; unpleasant; vile; wicked; *xenophobic;* yucky; *zero pleasure;*
**nation** *(n.)*: *area;* body politic; country; duchy; domain; dominion; empire; free state; fatherland; government; homeland; irredenta; *jurisdiction;* kingdom; land; motherland; native land; nation-state; *old country;* people; polity; power; *queendom;* realm; republic; state; superpower; territory; *United States; Vaterland* [G.]; weal; world power; *xerifdom; yard;* zemstvo [Rus.]; [*see* country; government; kingdom]
**national** *(adj.)*: all-nation; across-the-nation; *bloodline;* civil; country-wide; domestic; endemial; ethnic; federal; gentilitious; home-born; indigenous; internal; interior; *jingoistic;* kingdom-wide; local; lineal; *municipal;* native(-born); nationwide; *occupant;* public; patriotic; *quiritian* [L.]; residential; racial; *statewide;* territorial; *ubeity;* villager; whole-nation; *xenophile;* yokel; *zonal;*
**national** *(n.)*: aboriginal; blood- ~; citizen; dweller; ethnic; full-blood ~; fellow citizen; gentilic; habitant; inhabitant; indweller; inlander; *jingoist; kipper* [Aus.]; local; legal citizen; *mainlander;* native; *occupant;* person; people [pl.]; *quiritian* [L.]; resident; subject; *townsfolk; ubeity;* voter; whole-nation; *xenophile;* yokel; zonal; [Ant. non-citizen]
**nationalism** *(n.)*: ardor; *burning;* civism; devotion; enthusiasm; fervor; flag-waving; fanaticism; *gung-ho;* hundred-percenter; *imperialism;* jingoism; keenness; love of country; loyalty; *mania; militancy;* national pride; overpatriotism; obsession; patriotism; *quickness; readiness;* spirit; *thrilled;* ultra~; vehemence; wholeheartedness; xenophobia; yahooism; zealotry;

**nationality** *(n.)*: ancestry; background; bloodline; country; citizenship; descent; ethnicity; folk; gentility; heritage; indigenousness; *jingoism;* kindred; lineage; *mores;* nation; origin; people; *quarter;* residency; race; stock; strain; tribe; *ubiety; votership; wellspring; x-link; yoni* [Skr.]; *zoe;*
**native** *(adj.)*: aboriginal; born-there; blood-; connatural; domestic; ethnic; *from there;* genetic; homeborn (-bred); indigenous; inborn; *jake; kipper* [Aus.]; local; *municipal;* native-born; natural (-born); national; original; primal; *quiritian* [L.]; *residential; subject;* tribal; unacquired; villager; *whole-blooded; xenophile; yokel; zonal;* [*Ant.* non-native]
**native** *(n.)*: aboriginal; blood-national; countryman; dweller; ethnic; fellow citizen; *gentleman;* habitant; indigene; *jake; kipper* [Aus.]; local; *mainlander;* native; national; *occupant;* person; *quiritian* [L.]; resident; subject; tribesman; *townsfolk; ubeity;* villager; whole-blooded ~; *xenophile; yokel; zonal;* [*Ant.* non-native]
**nativity** *(n.)*: advent; arrival; birth; coming; delivery; debut; entrance; *forthcoming;* generation; hatching; inception; *jump off; kickoff; labor;* manifestation; nascence; origination; presentation; *quickening;* rising; start; *travail;* ushering in; *unveiling; visitation; welcoming; xenogenesis; yielding; zygogenesis;*
**natural** *(adj.)*: animate; basic; bodily; biological; carnal; corporeal; created; *direct;* earthly; fleshly; God-given; human; healthy; inborn; innate; inherent; instinctive; jejune; *knee-jerk;* living; mortal; material; normal; naturalistic; ordinary; organic; physical; quotidian; regular; raw; secular; temporal; tangible; unsaved; unprocessed; *veridical;* worldly; wild; *xenenthesis;* yet unadulterated; zoetical; [*Ant.* nonorganic]
**nature** *(n. character)*: attributes; *badge;* character(istic); constitution; disposition; essence; fiber; grain; heart; inclination; intrinsicality; *jist; kind;* lineament; makeup; nature; overall makeup; property; personality; quality; reality; suchness; spirit; temperament; tendency; tenor; underlying character; *virtue;* way; xenenthesis; *yetzer* [Heb.]; *zoe;* [*see* essence]
**nature** *(n. creation)*: all that is; *brute matter;* creation; *down here; the* earth; flora and fauna; God's earth; hyle; inartificiality; *jungle; the* kingdom of the living; landscape; Mother Nature; natural world; outdoors; omneity; physical world; *quite;* realm of this world; *scenery;* this world; *trees and forests; the* universe; *vast universe;* world; *the* wild; *xtry.;* yeard [Scot.]; *zoa;*
**naughtiness** *(n.)*: acting up; bad behavior; contravention; disobedience; error; evil; foul behavior; godlessness; headstrongness; ill conduct; iniquity; *jadedness;* knavishness; lawlessness; misconduct; mischief; non-obedience; orneriness; poor conduct; perverseness; *quad;* refractoriness; sin; troublemaking; transgression; unruliness; violation; wrongdoing; *xgression;* yieldlessness; *zero obedience;* [*Ant.* niceness]
**naughty** *(adj.)*: atrocious; bad; contrary; disobedient; defiant; devilish; evil-minded; froward; godless; headstrong; ill-behaved; *jaded;* knavish; lawless; mischievous; nasty; ornery; pernicious; *quad;* refractory; sinful; transgressive; unruly; villainous; willful; wrong(ful); *xgressing;* yieldless; *zero obedience;* [*Ant.* nice]
**nausea** *(n.)*: airsickness; butterflies; car sickness; disgust; discomposure; *ejection;* feeling sick; gagging; heaving; illness; *jaculation;* kecking; *lose one's supper;* mal de mer; motion sickness; nauseant; *oust;* puking; queasiness; qualmishness; retching; squeamishness; (sea) sickness; throwing up; upset stomach; uneasiness; vomiting; wooziness; *xuld* [arch.]; *yuckiness; zich* [arch.];
**nauseate** *(v.)*: affect; appall; bother; become sick; cause sickness; disgust; *enervate;* feel sick (to one's stomach); gross one out [slang]; horrify; indispose; jar; *keck; loathe;* make one sick; misaffect; *nauseous;* offend; peak; queasify [joc.]; repulse; sicken; turn one's stomach; unsettle; *vile;* weaken; *xuld* [arch.]; *yucky; zich* [arch.];
**nauseating** *(adj.)*: appalling; bad; contemptible; disgusting; execrable; fetid; gross; horrible; icky; intolerable; jarring; ketty; loathsome; mawkish; nasty; odious; offensive; putrid; queasifying [joc.]; repulsive; repugnant; sickening; stomach-turning; *terrible;* upsetting; vile; wambling; *x-bad;* yucky; *zorillo-like;*

**nauseous** *(adj.)*: airsick; barfish; carsick; *colorless;* disgustful; evil-affected; fulsome; green; heaving; ill; *jaculation;* kecking; *lightheaded;* mawmish; motion sick; nauseated; off; puky; *pale;* queasy; qualmish; retching; squeamish; (sea)sick; *turning stomach;* unsettled; vomitive; woozy; *xuld [arch.];* yucky; *zich* [arch.]; [*Ant.* nonaffected]

**nautical** *(adj.)*: aquatic; boating; bathymetrical; *channel;* deep-sea; *estuary; freshwater; grallatorial* [zoo.]; hydrographic; *inlet; jheel [Ind.]; keld;* limnetic; marine; maritime; navigational; nautic [poet.]; naval; natant; ocean-going; oceanic; pelagic; *quai;* river-going; seafaring (-going); sailing; transmarine; *undersea; voe;* water-borne; *xebec;* yachting; *Zee [G.];* [*Ant.* non-nautical]

**navigate** *(v.)*: advance; boat; cruise; cross; circum~; direct; edge; fare; find; guide; head; *igated;* journey; keep on course; lead; move; map; manage; *nightfare; orthodromy; outrun;* pass; plot; pilot; *quicken; reach;* seafare; sail; steer; traverse; use; vector; voyage; wayfare; wield; xfer; yacht; *zip;*

**navigation** *(n.)*: astro~; boating; control; coasting; circum~; direction; electronic ~; finding one's way; guidance; handling; helmsmanship; *igated; journeying; kiting;* luffing; movement; map-reading; navigating; orthodromics; plotting; piloting; pilotage; *quarter;* routing; steering; seafaring; transfretation; *underway;* vectoring; voyaging; wending; *xfer;* yarage; yachting; *zipping;*

**navy** *(n.)*: armada; armed forces; boats; battleships; convoy; division; *escort;* fleet; flotilla; flota; force; group; horde; *ironclads; junks; keelboats; longboats;* marine force; naval forces; *operation; PT boats; quinqueremes; R.N.;* squadron; ships; sea power; tonnage; task force; *U.S.N.;* vessels; warships; *xebecs;* yeomanry; *zebecs;*

**near** *(adj.)*: approaching; alongside; almost; about; adjacent; by; beside; bordering; close (to; by); drawn up to; *edging; fast by; going to come;* hard by; hot; intimate; impending; just about; *kept by;* local; more or less; neighboring; nigh; nearabout; nearby; next to; on(coming); proximate; proximal; *point-blank;* quite close; quasi-; related; similar; side by side; thereabout; toward; touching on; upon; upcoming; very close; vicinal; with; warm; well-nigh; *xferred; yede [arch.];* zeroing in on;

**near** *(v.)*: approach; border; close in on; draw nigh to; ease up to; enter upon; follow close; forthcome; go toward; hone in; impend; *juxtapose;* keep ~; localize; loom; lead up to; move close by; narrow; overhang; proximate; pass by; *quite close;* range; step up to; touch on; *upcoming;* verge on; wax close; *xfer; yede* [arch.]; zero in on;

**nearness** *(n.)*: approximation; adjacency; *by;* closeness; contiguity; *dearness; edging;* familiarity; *going to come;* hairsbreadth; immediacy; intimacy; *juxtaposition; kept by;* linking; location; localness; locality; mateyness; nighness; neighborhood; oncoming; proximity; parity; *quite close;* resemblance; relatedness; similarity; tightness; ubiety; vicinity; *well-nigh; xfer; yede [arch.];* zeroing in;

**neat** *(adj.)*: arranged; *beautiful;* clean(ly); clutter-free; dapper; elegant; freshened; fastidious; gemmy; hygienic; immaculate; just so; jimp [Br.]; kempt; *legible; lovely;* mess-free; natty; orderly; organized; ordered; over~; prest; picked-up; quaint; regimented; straitened up; snug; spruce; shipshape; tidy; trim; uncluttered; uniserial; very clean; well-kept; well-ordered; well-groomed; *xtry.;* yet unmessed; *zierlich [G.];* [*see* clean; *Ant.* neglected]

**neaten** *(v.)*: arrange; *bathe;* clean (up); declutter; expurgate; fix (up); *get clean;* houseclean; *immerse; jalap; keep up; launder;* make clean; ~ up; order; pick up; put in order; *quintessentialize;* rid of clutter; redd; straighten up; tidy; unclutter; *vacuum;* work on; *xylol; yellow soap; zierlich [G.];* [*Ant.* neglect]

**neatness** *(n.)*: adroitness; *beautify;* cleanness; dapperness; elegance; fastidiousness; gemminess; hygiene; immaculateness; *jimp [Br.]; kempt; legibility; loveliness; mess-free;* nattiness; orderliness; pristineness; quaintness; regimenting; snugness; sleekness; spiffiness; tidiness; trimness; unclutteredness; *very clean; well-kept; xtry.;* yet unmessed; zero mess; [*Ant.* non-orderliness]

**necessary** *(adj.)*: all-important; basic; compulsory; crucial; demanded; essential; fundamental; *grave; heavy;* indispensable; *jump to it;* key; lacking; mandatory; needful; necessitous; needed; obligatory; pressing; quantum; requisite; required; serious; top-priority; urgent; vital; wanted; without choice; *xtry.;* yet required; *zero option;* [*Ant.* non-compulsory]

**necklace** *(n.)*: * *adornment;* band; beads; chain; carcanet; choker; diamond ~; emerald ~; *finery;* gorget; gold ~; *heliotrope;* intaglio ~; *jewelry; kickshaw;* lace; lavaliere; lei; *locket; love beads;* medallion; neckband; ornament; pendant; pearl ~; *quaintry;* rivière; string; *trinket; uvarovite; valuables;* water sapphire ~; xtl. ~; yag; zonule;

**need** *(n.)*: absolute necessity; basic ~; constraint; demand; exigency; essential; fundamental ~; *got to (have);* having to; insistence; *juration;* known ~; lack; must; need-be; necessity; obligation; prerequisite; *quite ~ful;* requisite; requirement; stipulation; *task;* urge; urgent ~; *very needful;* want; xc.; yearning desire; *zero choice;* [*see* desire; poverty *Ant.* nonessential]

**need** *(v.)*: adjure; beg; call for; demand; exact; feel the ~ for; got to have; have to; insist; *juration; keenly desire;* lack; must have; necessitate; ought; pine; *quo minus [L.];* require; stipulate; *should;* thirst; *utter;* voice; want; *x-type;* yearn for; *zakon [Rus.];*

**needful** *(adj.)*: all-important; *big;* critical; demanded; essential; fundamental; *grave; heavy;* indispensable; *jump to it;* key; lacking; mandatory; needed; necessary; necessitous; obligatory; pressing; quantum; required; serious; top-priority; unforgoable; urgent; vital; *wanted;* weighty; *xtry.;* yet needed; *zero option;* [*Ant.* non-required]

**needle** *(n.)*: acantha; bristle; bodkin; barb; *cusp;* darner; dry point; *embroidery ~;* fid; fluke; fleam; graver; hairpin; hatpin; hypodermic ~; indicator; *instrument;* jigpin; knitting- ~; linchpin; lancet; mucro; nib; *object;* pin; point; prick(er); prickle; quadrille; quill; *razor-sharp;* sticker; sewing ~; sharp; tack; *unthreaded ~; Venus' comb; wimble;* xyston; yen-hok; zinger;

**needlework** *(n.)*: adorning; *broidery* [arch.]; crochet; embroidery; fancywork; *garter stitch;* handiwork; *interweaving; jacquard;* knitwork; laid work; mending; needlecraft (-point); orfrays; openwork; platting; petit point; quadro; quilting; rentering; stitching; sewing; tapestry; *using ornamentation; vest;* work; *weaving; x'ing;* yarn work; *zizz;*

**negative** *(adj.)*: adverse; bad; critical; disinclined; downbeat; disapproving; ever-critical; factious; gloomy; hypercritical; harsh; incompassionate; joyless; judgmental; knocking; low; loath; miserable; negativistic; opposed; pessimistic; querulous; resistant; skeptical; tetchy; unenthusiastic; unhopeful; uncheerful; vexed; *wary; xenophobic;* yucky; yieldless; zoilean;

**negativism** *(n.)*: antipathy; bucking; contrariness; disagreement; enmity; fatalism; gainsaying; hostility; impugnation; jangliness; *knocking;* loathing; malice; nastiness; opposition; polarity; querulousness; resistance; spite; *tetchiness;* unfriendliness; variance; withstanding; *xenophobia;* yawping; zoilism;

**negativist** *(n.)*: *antipathy;* balker; cynic; doubter; defeatist; doomsayer; Eeyore; fatalist; fearer; gloom-monger; hesitator; impugner; *jade;* killjoy; last-ditcher; misbeliever; naysayer; objector; pessimist; quarreler; rejecter; skeptic; terror-monger; unbeliever; *very disagreeable;* worrier; *x-er; yieldless; zoilean;*

**negativistic** *(adj.)*: anti-everything; balking; cynical; doubtful; down-on-everything; ever-doubtful; fearing; gloomy; hopeless; impugning; jaded; knocking; leery; mistrustful; negativist; objecting; pessimistic; *questioning;* rejecting; suspicious; terrormonging; unenthusiastic; *very disagreeable;* worrisome; xtry. ~; yawping; zoilistic;

**neglect** *(n.)*: abdication; abandonment; bypassing; carelessness; disregard; delinquency; error; forgetfulness; failure; going unattended; heedlessness; irregard; ignoring; inobservance; inattention; jumping over; *kesting;* listlessness; missing; negligence; oversight; omission; passing over; *quickly forgotten;* remissness; shirking; slight; thoughtlessness; unwariness; unfaithfulness; *vagueness;* wandering; xtry. irregard; *yemeles* [arch.]; zero responsibility;

**neglect** *(v.)*: abdicate; abandon; brush aside; *culpa;* disregard; elide; forget; fail; go over; *heedless;* ignore; irregard; jump over; *kest;* let go; miss; not take care of; overlook; omit; pass over; pretermit; *quickly forget; remiss;* slip; shirk; skip; slight; spurn; *toss aside; unfaithful; void;* want; *x-ing; yemeles* [arch.]; *zero responsibility;*

**neglected** *(adj.)*: abandoned; bypassed; cast aside; disregarded; dilapidated; elided; forgotten; gone over; half-done; ignored; jumped over; *kest;* let go; missed; not take care of; omitted; overlooked; passed over; *quickly forgotten;* run-down; skipped; tossed aside; uncared-for; unattended; unconsidered; vacated; want; x-ing; yemeles [arch.]; zero care;
**neglectful** *(adj.)*: abandoning; behindhand; careless; disregarding; dilatory; delaying; eliding; forgetful; fabian; *go unattended;* heedless; inattentive; *jim-jam; kim-kam;* lacking responsibility; lax; *missing;* neglective; negligent; *omitting;* procrastinating; quick-to-forget; remiss; slack; thoughtless; unmindful; unwatchful; very ~; without regard; *xtry. ~;* yet irresponsible; *zero responsibility;*
**negligence** *(n.)*: abdication; blunder; carelessness; delinquency; disregard; error; failure; going unattended; heedlessness; irresponsibility; inobservance; jumping over; *kesting;* laches; missing; neglect; overlooking; omission; preterition; procrastination; *quick to forget;* recklessness; slip; spurning; thoughtlessness; unfaithfulness; *vagueness; wrongdoing;* xtry. irregard; *yemeles* [arch.]; *zeallessness;*
**negligent** *(adj.)*: abdicating; behindhand; careless; disregardful; eliding; faithless; *go unattended;* heedless; irresponsible; *jim-jam; kim-kam;* lax; mismanaging; neglectful; *omitting;* procrastinating; quirky; remiss; slack; shirking; thoughtless; unreliable; undutiful; very neglectful; without regard; *xtry. ~;* yet irresponsible; *zero responsibility;*
**negotiate** *(v.)*: argue; arbitrate; battle; bargain; confer; chaffer; discuss; exchange words; fuss; *grapple;* haggle; have talks; interact; jangle; *key discussion; little chat;* meet about; naggle; open discussions; parley; quarrel; reason; speak with; talk; use diplomacy; vie; wheel and deal; work out; *x-purposes;* yak; *zero in;*
**negotiation** *(n.)*: arbitration; bargaining; conference; discussion; dialogue; deliberations; exchange; fussing; *gabbing;* haggling; heart-to-heart; huddle; interchange; jangle; *key ~; little chat;* meeting; negotiations; oral treaty; parley; powwow; quadrilogue; reasoning; roundtable; speech; talks; *uttering; vocalization;* words; *xenophonia;* yarn; *zero in;*
**neighbor** *(n.)*: abutter; *amigo* [Sp.]; borderer; buddy; brother; comrade; *defender; endeared;* fellow (man); friend; good-fellow; human being; intimate; *the* Joneses; kith [pl.]; *living soul;* mate; next door ~; one; person (one meets); *quarterer; resident;* soul; someone; tangent; *ubeity;* woman; *xenic;* yokefellow; *zoon;*
**neighborhood** *(n.)*: area; block; community; district; environs; *field; ground;* home area; in the area; *jagir [Asia]; kray [Rus.];* locality; *municipality;* nighness; nabe [slang]; outlying area; place; purlieus; quarter; region; section; street; suburb; *town;* ubeity; vicinity; ward; *x-sector; yard;* zone;
**neighboring** *(adj.)*: adjoining; bordering; *by;* close by; connected; down-one-door; environing; flush against; *go up to;* hard by; *interconnect;* joining; knitted; linked; local; meeting; nearby; next door; *opposite;* put together; *quite close;* roundabout; surrounding; touching; united; vicinal; *with; xenograft;* yoked; *zonal;*
**nerve** *(n. boldness)*: assertiveness; audacity; boldness; courage; daring; effrontery; fortitude; guts; hardiness; intrepidity; *jauntiness;* knightliness; lion-heartedness; manliness; nerviness; *obstinacy;* pluck; *quakeless; resolve;* spunk; self-assertion; strength; temerity; undauntedness; valiance; wherewithal; *xtry.; yung* [Chin.]; *zealousness;*
**nerve** *(n. neural transmitter)*: awareness; *bearing; connection;* dendrite; exteroceptor; *ending;* feeling; fascicle; ganglion; heartstring; impulse; interneuron; *jitters; know;* lemniscus; *mood;* neuron; *optic ~;* proprioceptor; *quick-response;* receptor; *ramus;* sensation; sensory ~; touch sensor; ulnar ~; vibe; *white matter; xmitter; yearning; zygomatic ~;*
**nervous** *(adj.)*: apprehensive; bothered; concerned; dreading; edgy; fearful; gutless; horrified; high-strung; *hesitant;* insecure; ill at ease; jittery; jumpy; keyed up; lily-livered; mistrusting; nerve-racked; overanxious; panicky; quivering; reluctant; restless; scared; skittish; tense; trepidant; *troubled;* terrified; uneasy; vexed; worried; *xenophobic;* yellow(-bellied); *zapped;* [*Ant.* nervy]

**nervousness** *(n.)*: anxiety; *burden;* care; cowardice; dread; exasperation; fear; gloom; horror; insecurity; jimjams; jitters; jitteriness; kiaugh [Scot.]; lather; mistrust; nervosity; over-anxiety; panic; phobia; paranoia; quaking; restlessness; stress; skittishness; trepidation; uneasiness; vexation; worry; *xenophobia;* yellow-belliedness; *zeallessness;*

**nest** *(n.)*: aerie; bed; bird's ~; covey; drey; den; dwelling; eyrie; fowl's ~; *grebe* ~; home; habitation; inhabitance; *jurisdiction; keep;* lodging; mud ~; nidus; *opening;* perch; place; pigeon-hole; *quarters;* roost; refuge; snuggery; tree ~; *ubeity;* vespiary; warren; *xerosere; young; zone;*

**nest** *(v.)*: abide; bide; build ~; cozy up; den; embosom; fit inside; *feather-line; go to live;* hide; inhabit; *jam;* keep house; lodge; make one's ~; nestle; nidificate; occupy; perch; *quarter;* reside; situate; settle; timber; *use; vault; wrap; xenize; yerde [arch.]; zone;*

**nestle** *(v.)*: affection; burrow; cuddle; croodle; cozy up; *draw close;* embrace; embosom; *fondle;* grip; hide; infold; *jam;* keep close; lie; make comfortable; nuzzle; *overply;* press; protect; *quash; rub;* settle; snuggle; tuck in; *upbind;* valentine; wrap; X; yoke up with; *zone;*

**net** *(n.)*: * app- ~; bolter; butterfly ~; cast ~; drag~; draw~; dredge; enmeshment; fish~; fly ~; gill ~; hallier; hair~; inmeshment; jute- ~; keep- ~; landing ~; mesh(work); mosquito ~; netting; network; osier ~; panter; pursenet; quail- ~; reticle; reticulation; seine; screen; trammel; toil; under ~; veil; web; wire netting; x-mesh; yair; zein- ~;

**netherworld** *(n.)*: abyss; below; *cavern; demi-monde* [F.]; erebus; fiery underworld; Gehenna; hell; Hades; *infernal; inframundane; jaw-hole;* kingdom of darkness; lower levels; *misery;* nether regions; outer darkness; *the* pit; *quenchless fire;* regions below; spirit world; Tartarus; underworld; *void;* world of darkness; xibalba; *yefell [arch.]; zone;*

**nettle** *(v.)*: aggravate; bother; cross; disturb; exasperate; frustrate; grate on; hassle; irritate; jangle; kindle; *livid;* miff; needle; *offend;* provoke; *quill;* rankle; stir up; tease; upset; vex; *weary; x-ing;* yerk; *zing;*

**neuter** *(adj.)*: asexual; bowdlerized; castrated; degenderized; eunuchized; epicene; fix; genderless; *half-and-half;* impotent; *jemmy;* kerned; *lukewarm;* make genderless; neutral; *objective;* poulardize [fem.]; *queenie; remove;* sexless; *truncate;* unsexed; *void of gender;* without gender; *x.; yet unalligned; zero;*

**neutral** *(adj.)*: *abstaining;* balanced; central; disinterested; dégagé; ever-peaceful; fence-straddling; gray; *halfhearted;* impartial; *just* ~; keep-out-of-it; lukewarm; latitudinarian; middle-of-the-road; mugwumpish; nonaligned; noncommittal; nonpartisan; objective; peace-loving; quite ~; removed; staying-out-of-it; standpat; taking neither side; unallied; unaligned; uninvolved; *vague;* wishy-washy; *x.;* yet unallied; zealless; [Ant. non-neutral]

**neutrality** *(n.)*: abstention; balance; *circumvention;* detachment; dispassion; *evasiveness;* fence-straddling; golden mean; *halfheartedness;* impartiality; juste milieu; keeping out; *leaving the conflict;* middle-of-the-road position; nonalignment; nonintervention; neutralism; objectivity; pacifism; quietism; refraining; staying out; taking neither side; uninvolvement; unbiasedness; *vague;* wishy-washiness; *x.; yet unallied;* zero alliances; [Ant. non-neutrality]

**new** *(adj.)*: added; beginning; brand- ~; contemporary; *de novo* [L.]; emergent; fresh; firsthand; fledgling; green; hot off the press; incipient; innovative; just out; just-released; *kickoff;* latest; modern; new-fangled; nascent; neoteric; novel; original; present-day; *quickened;* recent; renewed; spanking; twenty-first century; unused; up-to-date; ultramodern; virgin; *welcomed; xtr.;* young; *zygogenetic;*

**newborn** *(adj.)*: anew; brand new; baby; bantling; *calved;* days-old; eensie-weensie; fledgling; *green;* hatchling; infant; just born; *keeper;* little; moments-old; neonatal; new-wrought (-yeaned); *overly young; pint-sized; quickened;* recent; suckling; tiny; *ultranew;* very small; wee; *xenogenetic;* young; *zoe;*

**newness** *(n.)*: anew; brand-newness; contemporariness; dew-freshness; emergence; freshness; greenness; *hot-off-the-press;* incipience; innovation; *just out; kickoff;* lateness; modernness; novelty; originality; presentness; *quickening;* recentness; recency; strangeness; *today;* unusualness; uniqueness; virginity; *welcomed; xenogenetic;* youth; *zygogenetic;*

**news** *(n.)*: account; befalling; current events; coverage; developments; events; flash; goings-on; happenings; headlines; hard ~; information; intelligence; *just in;* *khubber* [Pers.]; *the* latest; local ~; material ~; ~flash; *oral report;* poop; press release; *quidnunc* [L.]; report; recent information; scoop; talk; tidings; update; *volume;* word; world ~; *Xinhua; yellow journalism;* zine;
**newsworthy** *(adj.)*: attention-getting; big; *critical;* deserving; eyebrow-raising; earthshaking; *focal;* great; grave; heavy; *interesting;* important; *journalist;* key; leading; major; noteworthy; *obligatory;* printable; paper-selling; press-worthy; *quantum; relevant; ratings;* significant; *salable;* top-rated; urgent; valuable; very important; weighty; worthy; *xtry.; yare;* zero in;
**nice** *(adj.)*: amiable; affable; agreeable; benign; cordial; congenial; delightful; exquisite; fine; friendly; good; genial; harmonious; hospitable; intentive; *jim dandy;* kind; likable; merciful; neighborly; openhanded; pleasant; polite; *queme;* regardful; sociable; sweet; thoughtful; uplifting; very friendly; warm; welcoming; xenial; yummy; *zestful;* [*Ant.* nasty]
**niceness** *(n.)*: amiableness; benevolence; compassion; consideration; congeniality; civility; decency; exquisiteness; favor; friendliness; graciousness; goodwill; humaneness; intentiveness; *joviality;* kindness; leniency; love; magnanimity; mercy; neighborliness; obligingness; pleasantness; quarter; regard; sweetness; thoughtfulness; unselfishness; virtuousness; warmth; xenia; yumminess; *zealousness;* [*Ant.* nastiness]
**nicety** *(n.)*: amenity; *bonus;* civility; courtesy; delicacy; dainty; daintrel; elegancy; favor; fine point; goody; *high-style; indulgence; jimp;* kindness; luxury; *manners;* nice things; *obligingness;* pleasantry; *quality;* refinement; subtlety; small point; tactfulness; urbanity; *virtue; well-treated;* xenium; *yeff [arch.]; zealous care;* [*Ant.* necessity]
**niche** *(n.)*: alcove; *area;* breach; bay; crevice; depression; exedra; fissure; forte; gap; hollow; incavation; interstice; jaw-hole; *khor* [Arab.]; *lacuna; mouth;* nook; opening; place; *pit;* quarry-pit; recess; role; snuggery; slot; secret place; *trench; umbilicus;* vug; *well; xystus pit;* yawn; zanja;
**nick** *(n.)*: ax-mark; break; cut; dent; etching; fissure; groove; hack; incision; indentation; jag; kerf; *laceration;* mark; notch; opening; pill-mark; *quadrisulcate; rut;* scratch; score; tick (mark); *undercut;* v-cut; *whack;* x; *yedder;* zip;
**nick** *(v.)*: ax; break; cut; dent; etch; fissure; graze; gouge; hack; incise; *jag;* kerf; *lacerate;* mark; notch; open; pill; *quadrisculate;* retrench; scratch; score; tick; *undercut; v-cut;* whack; whittle; *x-sect;* yerk; zip;
**nickname** *(n.)*: appellation; agnomen; brand; cognomen; designation; epithet; *first name; given ~;* handle; identifier; *jurisdiction; known by;* label; moniker; name; *overtitle;* pet name; *quiring;* representation; sobriquet; tag; unofficial name; vocable; *word;* xenonym; *yu* [Chin.]; *zoon;*
**night** *(n.)*: after-hours; bedtime; close of the day; dark; eve(n)(ing); fall of the sun; gloaming; *hibernating;* intense darkness; jet-black mid~; *kip;* late-night; lights-out; mid~; *moon;* nightfall; nighttime; obscurity; pitch-darkness; *quarter-moon; rest;* sunset; *soir* [F.]; twilight; *under the cover;* vesper(s); wee hours; *weeknight; xtr. dark;* yesternight; zero light;
**nightmare** *(n.)*: abstraction; bad dream; calamity; disaster; ephialtes; frightful dream; *ghastly;* hallucination; horror; incubus; *jag; knock-out blow; loss;* mar; night vision; omen; phantasm; *quandary; ruination;* scarebabe; torment; terror; upsetting dream; *upheaval;* vision; *woe; x-fix; yedder;* zinger;
**nimble** *(adj.)*: agile; brisk; *clever;* dexterous; energetic; fast; flexible; graceful; hurried; intense; *jiffy;* keen-footed; lithe; light-footed; mercurial; nippy; on the ball; pert; quick; rapid; swift; spry; supple; *timely;* ultrafast; volant; wimble; x-speed; yeasty; zippy; [*Ant.* non-graceful]
**nimbleness** *(n.)*: agility; briskness; celerity; dexterity; energy; fastness; gracefulness; hurriedness; intensity; jildi [mil.]; keenness; liveliness; *movement;* mercuriality; nippiness; *overhastiness;* promptness; quickness; rapidity; swiftness; *timeliness; uninhibited; velocity;* wimbleness; wit; *x-speed;* yeastiness; zip;
**nitpick** *(v.)*: attack; bellyache; complain; disparage; *equivocate;* fuss; gripe; harangue; inveigh; jangle; kvetch [Yid.]; land on; moan; niggle; object; pick; quibble; repine; split hairs; *tear into; unhappy;* vituperate; whine; *xuld [arch.];* yammer; zing;

**nitpicky** *(adj.)*: *attacking;* bellyaching; critical; dissatisfied; ever-grumbling; fussy; griping; hairsplitting; hard-to-please; implacable; joyless; knocking; logic-chopping; murmuring; nitpicking; over-picky; picky; quibbling; repining; scowling; trifling; unhappy; unsatisfied; vituperative; whiny; *xtry. critical;* yammering; zero joy; [*Ant.* nice]

**nobility** *(n.)*: aristocracy; bluebloods; court(liness); dignity; elite; family; gentry; high-born; illustriousness; junkers; jarldom; knightliness; lords and ladies; magnificence; noblesse; noble-mindedness; optimacy; overclass; patricians; pashadom [Turk.]; peerage; *queen's men;* respectability; seigniory; titled; trueborn; upper class; V.I.P.'s; well-bred; *xtry.;* younkers; *zayim;* [*Ant.* non-nobility]

   **Titles of nobility**: archduke; archduchess; baron(ess); count(ess); dame; duke; duchess; earl; emperor; empress; freiherr; freifrau; grand duke; grand duchess; *heir;* infante; infanta; jarl; king; knight; lord; margrave; margravine; marquis; noble; prince(ss); queen; regent; viscount; viceroy; vicereine; waldgrave;

**noble** *(adj.)*: aristocratic; blueblood; chivalrous; dignified; esteemed; freeborn; *of* family; gentry; gallant; high-born; ingenuous; junker; knighted; lordly; masterful; noble-born; nobiliary; optimate; patrician; *qualified;* respectable; *status;* titled; upper class (-crust); *vicomte* [F.]; well-born (-bred); *xtry.;* younker; *zamorin [Hind.];* [*Ant.* non-aristocratic]

**nobleman** *(n.)*: aristocrat; blueblood; *baron; count; duke; earl;* feudal superior; *grand duke; grandee;* gentleman; hidalgo [Sp.]; *important; jarl;* junker; knight; lord; *marquis; master;* noble; noblewoman [fem.]; optimate; patrician; palatine; *prince; queen; ruler; sir;* titled person; *upper crust; viscount; waldgrave; XO;* younker; *zayim;* [*Ant.* non-noble]

**noblewoman** *(n.)*: aristocrat; baroness; countess; duchess; dame; *elite; feudal lady;* grand duchess; gentlewoman; *heiress; important; jarl [fem.]; khanum* [Ind.]; lady; marquise; noble; optimate; patrician; *queen; royalty; silk-stocking;* titled woman; *upper crust;* viscountess; woman of breeding; *xtry; woman; younker; zayim;* [*Ant.* non-noble]

**noise** *(n.)*: acoustics; amplitude; *aloud;* bustle; blare; bedlam; clamor; clangor; clatter; din; dissonance; *echo;* feedback; fracas; fanfare; *groaning;* hubbub; hullabaloo; intonation; jangle; *knock;* loudness; *mutter; murmur;* noisiness; output; over~; pudder; peep; *quatch* [arch.]; racket; reverberation; sound; stridor; tumult; uproar; unquiet; verberation; vocable; voice; *warble; whisper; xenophonia;* yammer; *zoink;* [*Ant.* noiselessness]

**noise** *(v.)*: announce; bespeak; cry (out); declare; exclaim; fame; *growl;* holler; inform; *jubilate;* keen; loudly say; make known; notify; outcry; proclaim; *quote;* resonate; reverberate; shout; testify; trumpet; utter; vociferate; wail; *xenophonia;* yell; *zealously proclaim;*

**noisy** *(adj.)*: *audible;* boisterous; blaring; booming; clamorous; deafening; earsplitting; ear-offending; full-mouthed; grating; high-volume; intense; jarring; keen; loud; multisonous; noiseful; obstreperous; piercing; penetrating; plangent; quietless; raucous; strident; sharp; thunderous; unquiet; uproarious; voluminous; vociferous; *wailing; x-loud;* yelling; *zero quietude;* [*Ant.* non-noisy]

**nomad** *(n.)*: ambler; Arab; Bedouin; *camel-rider;* drifter; *emigrant;* floater; gadabout; gypsy; homeless; itinerant; journeyer; *Kenite; knight-errant;* landloper; migrant; night-wanderer; *oberration;* pilgrim; peregrinator; *quick-mover;* rover; roamer; rambler; sojourner; transient; tent-dweller; *unfixed;* vagrant; wanderer; *xerophile;* Yahgan; *zingaro* [It.]

**nomadic** *(adj.)*: ambling; *Bedouin;* circumforaneous; drifting; ever-moving; floating; gadding; *homeless;* itinerant; journeying; *keep moving;* landloping; migrating; noctivagant; non-stationary; *oberration;* pereginating; *quick-moving;* roving; *stray;* transient; tent-dwelling; *unfixed;* vagrant; wandering; *xerophilic; yawing;* zingaro;

**nominal** *(adj.)*: alleged; by name; considered; called; *deduced;* expected; *figurehead; guess; hollow;* in name only; just in name; known as; listed as; minimal; nuncupatory; ostensible; only in name; professed; presumed; *quasi;* reckoned; so-called; supposed; titular; unreal; *ventured;* would-be; *xenodiagnose;* yet in name only; *zero actuality;*

**nominate** *(v.)*: advance; bid; counsel; choose; designate; encourage; extend; forward; give recommendation; *hortatory;* importunate; *judge faithful; kibitz [Yid.]; look to;* motion; move; name; offer; propose; postulate; put forward; *quicken;* recommend; suggest; submit; select; tender; urge; vote on; *want; xuld [arch.]; yearn; zealously* ~;
**nonchalant** *(adj.)*: apathetic; blasé; casual; degage; easygoing; fancy-free; glib; happy-go-lucky; indifferent; jaunty; keg-meg; laid-back; mellow; non-concerned; offhand; pluckless; *quiet;* relaxed; smooth; turned-off; unconcerned; vapid; wareless; *xenarthrous;* yareless; zealless;
**nonconformist** *(n.)*: anarchist; beatnik; counteractant; dissenter; dissident; eccentric; free spirit; far-out; *guerilla; hippie;* individualist; *jaw-set; kabouter* [Du.]; larrikin; maverick; non-conformist; oppositionist; poissarde [fem.]; *queer;* renegade; rebel; radical; recusant; revolutionary; seditionary; square peg; troublemaker; unconformist; villain; wiggy; *x-grained; yieldless;* zealot;
**nonconformity** *(n.)*: abnormality; bizarreness; curiousness; difference; deviation; enigma; eccentricity; foible; *goofiness;* heterotype; irregularity; individuality; *jerkiness;* key difference; lawlessness; *misbelief; misbehavior;* noncompliance; nontraditionalism; oddity; peculiarity; quirk; recusancy; strangeness; transverseness; unconformity; variation; variance; weirdness; *xtry.; yaw; zero conformity;* [*Ant.* normality]
**nondenominational** *(n.)*: all-faith (-embracing); *broadminded;* cross-denominational; *denominations;* ecumenical; *faith community;* global; *heterogeneous;* interdenominational; joint; Judeo-Christian-Islamic; *keeping an open mind;* liberalistic; mutli-faith; nonsectarian; *one-world church;* polychurch; *quasi-Christian; receptive; sympathetic;* transdenominational; undenominational; universal; *Vatican II; W.C.C.; x-denominational; yielding; zero doctrinal position;*
**nondescript** *(adj.)*: average; boring; banal; common; dull; everyday; flat; frumpy; generic; general; humdrum; ho-hum; indescriptive; jejune; *known;* lackluster; mediocre; mundane; nondescript; ordinary; plain; prosaic; quotidian; regular; run-of-the-mill; simple; typical; uninteresting; uneventful; vanilla; *wearisome;* x; yawnsome; zestless;
**nonessential** *(adj.)*: adjunct; accessory; beyond-basics; conditional; contingent; dispensable; disposable; expendable; frivolous; gratuitous; hoity-toity; incidental; insignificant; inapposite; just-for-show; ketty; little; minor; needless; non-vital; off-the-subject; petty; quisquillos; redundant; superfluous; trivial; tertiary; throwaway; unnecessary; unneeded; unessential; unimportant; vain; worthless; xtr.; yet unneeded; zero-importance; [*Ant.* needful]
**nonexistence** *(n.)*: aught; blackness; cipher; desolation; emptiness; fiction; great abyss; *hollowness;* inexistence; imaginariness; irreality; incorporeity; *jack [slang]; kaput; lacking reality;* make-believe; nothing(ness); nil; naught; nonentity; non-being; nihility; oblivion; *pretense; quantity zero; rien [F.];* scratch; *thought-of;* unactuality; unreality; vacuity; void; *whimsical;* x; *yielded;* zero; [*see* death]
**nonexistent** *(adj.)*: air-built; blank; chimerical; dreamed-up; empty; fictive; fictional; gone; *hollow;* illusory; inexistent; imaginary; incorporeal; illusory; irreal; just imagined; keenly-imagined; lost; made-up; non-real; obliterated; phony; pretend; phantasmal; *quixotic;* relegated to the imagination; suppositious; *too fantastic;* unreal; void; without existence; *x;* yet inexistent; *zero reality;* [*Ant.* non-fictitious]
**noninterference** *(n.)*: abstention; broad-mindedness; co-existence; deregulation; endurance; forbearance; giving space; having; inaction; *justification; kind-heartedness;* laissez-faire; *mellowness;* nonintervention; noninvolvement; neutrality; overlooking; policy of ~; *quietness; removed;* silence; tolerance; uninvolvement; *vey separate; wide berth; x.;* yokelessness; zero interference;
**nonsense** *(n.)*: absurdity; baloney; balderdash; bunk; claptrap; drivel; eyewash; fiddle-faddle; flam; foolishness; flummery; folderol; gibberish; gobbledygook; hogwash; hooey; haver; idiocy; jabber; kibosh; looniness; malarkey; *niaiserie* [F.]; outlandishness; poppycock; piffle; quatsch; rubbish; slaver; stupidity; tripe; trumpery; twaddle; *unmeaningness; vain words;* whoopla; xenoglossy; yabber; *zeug* [G.];

**nonviolent** *(adj.)*: amicable; bloodless; congenial; diplomatic; dovelike; easeful; friendly; gentle; harmonious; irenic; judicious; keeping peace; *loving;* mild; nonaggressive; nonmilitant; *olive-branch bearing;* peaceful; quiescent; *restful;* serene; symphonious; tranquil; tame; unhostile; unwarlike; unagitated; violence-hating; wrathless; *xenophilious; yielding; zealous of peace;*

**nook** *(n.)*: area; alcove; breach; cranny; cubbyhole; den; exedra; fissure; gap; hole; incavation; jaw-hole; krater; *lacuna;* mouse hole; niche; opening; pit; pigeonhole; place; quoin; *quarry-pit;* recess; slot; *trench; umbilicus;* vug; *well; xystus pit;* yawn; zanja;

**noose** *(n.)*: ansa; braid loop; cord; collar; circle; *dule tress; ellipse; fiber;* gallows-rope; halter; hitch; hempen collar; hangman's ~; *instrument of punishment;* jig; kench; loop; lariat; *makeshift gallows;* necktie [slang]; O; parbuckle; *quviut;* riata; rope; slip knot; springe; tater; twine; *undo;* volt; *widdy; x-braid; yard rope; zein;*

**normal** *(adj.)*: average; basic; common; customary; conventional; daily; dull; everyday; familiar; general; habitual; intermediate; inelaborate; jejune; *known;* lackluster; mundane; medial; natural; ordinary; plain; quotidian; regular; routine; run-of-the-mill; standard; typical; usual; vanilla; wonted; *x-type; yawnish;* zestless [*Ant.* nonconformist]

**normality** *(n.)*: averageness; business-as-usual; commonness; customariness; decorousness; everyday life; familiarity; generalness; habitualness; intermediateness; inelaborateness; jejuneness; *known; lackluster;* mundaneness; *the* norm; normalcy; ordinariness; par; prevalence; quo; regularity; routineness; status quo; standardness; typicality; usualness; *vanilla;* wontedness; *x-type; yawn;* zestlessness;

**nose** *(n.)*: antlia [zoo.]; button ~; beezer; beak; bill; bridge; conk [slang]; *drip; errhine; front; great big ~;* honker; haustellum; intranasal; jut; kip; *lineament;* muzzle [zoo.]; *murr;* neb; nib; nasal passage; olfactory organ; proboscis; pecker; *quick-nosed;* retroussé ~; rhinarium [zoo.]; smeller; snout; schnoz [slang]; trunk [zoo.]; *tip; upturned ~; vomer;* whiffer; *xeromycteria; yead [arch.]; zit-nosed;*

**nosy** *(n.)*: *arbitrating;* butting in; curious; disturbing; encroaching; fishing; getting involved; horning in; inquisitive; invasive; jumping in; kibitzing; *looking for;* meddlesome; *non-respectful;* officious; prying; *questioning; restrain;* snooping; tampering; *unwanted;* violating; *whispering* ; *x;* yenta; zilch;

**notability** *(n.)*: acclaim; best mention; celebrity; distinction; eminence; fame; glory; honor; illustriousness; *jubilation; kudos;* legend; magnificence; notableness; notoriety; outstandingness; popularity; prestige; prominence; *quality;* recognition; status; *the* top; universal recognition; veneration; world-renown; *xtry.;* yichus; *zealous following;*

**notable** *(adj.)*: admirable; amazing; best; chief; celebrated; distinguished; especial; eminent; exceptional; focal; famous; great; highly regarded; important; jolly good; key; laudable; landmark; main; noteworthy; outstanding; prominent; *quantum* [L.]; remarkable; signal; significant; top; unrivaled; very good; well-known; wonderful; xtry.; *you-beaut* [Aus.]; *zestful;* [*Ant.* normal]

**notate** *(v.)*: annotate; *blazon;* chronicle; comment; denote; document; enter; *fabulize;* gloss; handwrite; inscribe; jot down; keep record; list; log; mark down; make notes; note; *overwrite;* put down; postil; quill; record; scribble down; take down; underwrite; *vellum;* write (down); *x;* yak; *zay;*

**notation** *(n.)*: annotation; book ~; comments; denotation; entry; footnote; gloss; handwriting; inscription; jotting; *kept record;* log entry; longhand; markings; note; *observations;* postil; *the* quill; remarks; scribbling; text; transcript; thoughts; *uncials; verbiage;* writing; words; *xiaozhuan; yellow journalism; zeug;*

**notch** *(n.)*: ax-mark; break; cut; dent; degree; etching; fissure; groove; grade; hack; incision; indentation; impression; jag; kerf; level; mark; nick; nock; nitch; opening; pill-mark; quadrisulcate; *rut;* rung; rabbet; score; slit; slash; score; step; tick (mark); *unit;* v-cut; whack; *x; yedder; zip;*

**notch** *(v.)*: *ax;* break; cut; dent; engrave; furrow; gash; groove; hack; indent; jag; kerf; *lacerate;* mark; nick; *open;* pock; puncture; *quadrisulcate;* recess; retrench; *rip;* slash; score; *tick;* undercut; *vell;* whack; *x-sect;* yerk; *zip;*

**note** *(n.)*: annotation; breve; bill of draft; business letter; comment; correspondence; communication; dispatch; e-mail; end~; epistle; foot~; fax; form letter; fan mail; *graving; hate mail;* interoffice memo; jotting; *kurvey;* letter; message; memo(random); marginal ~; musical ~; mail; notice; notation; observation; post; *quick ~;* remark; record; semibreve; sticky ~; *scribbling;* signed ~; telegram; *unopened ~; undelivered ~;* voucher; writing; *xfer;* yellow sticky ~; *zip code;*

**note** *(v.)*: acknowledge; be aware of; catch sight of; discern; examine; fix eyes on; give thought to; *hone in on;* inspect; jot down; ken; look; log; make out; notice; observe; perceive; *quick look;* remember; record; see; survey; spy; scrutinize; scan; take in; *understand;* view; watch; write; *x-ray vision;* yeme; zero in; [*see* notate]

**noteworthy** *(adj.)*: amazing; brilliant; capital; distinguished; extraordinary; fantastic; great; *highest;* incredible; impressive; jolly good; keen; laudable; major; notable; outstanding; prominent; *quantum* [L.]; remarkable; stupendous; tremendous; unrivaled; very good; wonderful; xtry.; *you-beaut* [Aus.]; zizzy; [*Ant.* normal]

**nothing** *(n.)*: aught; blankness; barrenness; blackness; cipher; duck; destitution; emptiness; *finished;* goose egg; *hollow;* inessentiality; jack [slang]; *kaput;* love; *lacking; mu* [Jap.]; naught; nil; naught; *peanuts;* quantity zero; *rien* [F.]; scratch; thing of naught; *used up;* void; whitespace; x; *yielded;* zero;

**notice** *(n. message)*: announcement; bill; bulletin; briefing; communication; dispatch; epistle; e-mail; fax; form letter; general notification; handout; interoffice memo; *jotting; kurvey;* letter; message; memo(random); note; office memo; poster; placard; *quick note;* report; sign; telegram; *unopened ~; undelivered ~; verbiage;* writing; *xfer; yellow envelope; zip code;*

**notice** *(n. regard)*: attention; acknowledgement; bearing (in mind); consideration; concentration; detection; esteem; focus; giving ~; heed; identification; *justness;* knowledge; looking; mindfulness; note; observation; perception; *quality;* regard; respect; seeing; thought; taking note; *unmitigated respect;* viewing; watching; *xtry.;* yeme; yeild; zeroing in; [*Ant.* neglect]

**notice** *(v.)*: acknowledge; behold; catch sight of; detect; eye; examine; espy; fix eyes on; find; gaze at; have in view; identify; inspect; *jarque;* ken; look; mark; mind; note; observe; perceive; pick up on; *quick look;* recognize; regard; see; sight; spot; take note; *understand;* view; watch; witness; *x-ray vision;* yeme; zero in; [*Ant.* neglect]

**noticeable** *(adj.)*: apparent; blatant; clear; conspicuous; distinct; explicit; eye-catching; flagrant; glaring; highly visible; in full view; *just plain to see;* kenspeckle; *lucid;* manifest; marked; notable; obvious; observable; perceptible; *quite obvious;* recognizable; salient; striking; transparent; unmistakable; unconcealed; visible; witnessable; *x-parent; yeme* [arch.]; zenithal; [*Ant.* non-conspicous]

**notification** *(n.)*: announcement; bulletin; broadcast; communication; declaration; dispatch; enunciation; forewarning; general dispatch; holding forth; indication; intimation; jactitation; *knowledge;* letter; mention; message; notice; *observation;* proclamation; public announcement; *quarterly report;* report; statement; telling; telegram; update; *utterance; verbalization;* warning; writ; *xenagogy;* yeme; zero in;

**notify** *(v.)*: advise; bid; call; communicate; disclose; enlighten; forewarn; give notice; hold forth; indicate; illuminate; *jaw; key in;* let out; mention; note; observe; proclaim; quoth; report; say; tell; update; utter; voice; witness; wire; warn; *xfer;* yak; *zero in;*

**notion** *(n.)*: aspiration; ambition; belief; compulsion; desire; estimation; fancy; gauging; hunch; idea; impulse; itch; imagination; *judgment; knowledge;* leaning; mindset; megrim; natural bent; opinion; perception; *quirk;* reaction; sentiment; thought; urge; view; whim(sy); *xenodiagnosis;* yen; *zeal;*

**notoriety** *(n.)*: acclaim; bigness; *beloved;* celebrity; distinction; eminence; fame; glory; honor(s); illustriousness; *jubilation;* kudos; legend; magnificence; note; name; outstandingness; popularity; prestige; *quality;* renown; respect; rumor; status; *talked-about;* universal knowledge of; veneration; world-renown; *xtry.;* yichus; *zealous love;*

**notorious** *(adj.)*: arrant; atrocious; bad; celebrated; contemptuous; disreputable; everywhere-known; evil; famous; flagitious; gestic; hated; iconic; infamous; *jaded;* known; legendary; much-hated; notour; noted; odious; prominent; *quantity;* recognized; sinister; talked-about; universally known; villainous; widely-known; *wanted; xtry.;* yichus; *zealously hunted;* [*see* evil; famous]
**nourishment** *(n.)*: alimentation; bread; comestibles; diet; daily bread; eating; food; groceries; *hash; health food;* intake; *junk food;* keep; *lunch;* meat; nutrition; *organic food;* pabulum; *quelque-chose [F.];* repast; sustenance; *table;* upkeep; viands; vitamins; *wheat;* xarque; yams; zakuski [Rus.];
**novel** *(adj.)*: avant-garde; brand-new; contemporary; different; ever-new; fresh; green; hot off the press; innovative; just out; *kickoff;* latest; modern; new; original; *prodigious; quick;* recent; refreshing; special; spanking; *terrific;* uncommon; unusual; unique; *virgin; welcomed;* xenogenetic; *young;* zygogenetic;
**novelty** *(n.)*: *anew;* brand-newness; contemporariness; *dew-freshness; ever-new;* freshness; greenness; *hot-off-the-press;* innovation; *just out; kickoff;* lateness; modernness; newness; originality; *present; quickening;* recentness; recency; strangeness; *today;* unusualness; uniqueness; virginity; *welcomed; xenogenetic;* youth; *zygogenetic;*
**novice** *(n.)*: amateur; beginner; cadet; disciple; empiric; first-timer; greenhorn; ham; inceptor; jackeroo; kook; learner; mentee; neophyte; newcomer; *one inexperienced;* pupil; *quick learner;* rookie; starter; trainee; tyro; undertaker; *venturer; wannabe;* xon; *yet inexperienced; zero experience;* [*Ant.* non-amateur]
**now** *(adv.)*: at once; at presence; bang! [slang]; currently; directly; ever-promptly; forthwith; *go fast;* hastily; immediately; just like that; keenly; lickety-split; momentarily; nonce; nowadays; on the spot; present time; promptly; pronto; quickly; right ~; straightway; this minute; *tour de suite* [F.]; undelayed; very quickly; without delay; *x-speed;* yet; *zero-delay;*
**nuance** *(n.)*: allusion; betokening; clue; denotation; *expression;* fine point; *giving indication;* hint; implication; insinuation; intimation; inference; innuendo; illation; *jab;* know; *leading into;* mention; nicety; overtone; postulation; quiddit; reference; suggestion; touch; undercurrent; undertone; vague express; *winking; xfer; yammering; zone;*
**nucleus** *(n.)*: axis; belly; center; core; dead-center; epicenter; fesse-point; *geological ~;* heart; hub; interior; inmost part; *just exactly centered;* kernel; *lodged;* middle; midpoint; midst; nave; omphalos; prokaryon; *quiddity;* rudiment; smack in the middle [slang]; triton; umbilic; *via media; within; x-section;* yolk; *zone;*
**nudge** *(v.)*: agitate; bump; butt; boost; *clobber;* dig; elbow; force; goad; heave; impel; jab; jog; jostle; knock; lean on; make; needle; *oblige;* push; prod; poke; prompt; quab; ram; shove; thrust; urge; veney; whack; *xuld* [arch.]; *yank;* zonk; [*see* remind]
**nugget** *(n.)*: *amount;* bit; banket; chunk; clump; daud; *ens;* fragment; gob; *gold ~;* hunk; ingot; junt; kernel; *karat;* lump; linget; morsel; mass; *nygot* [arch.]; ounce; piece; *quantity;* rock; small piece; tidbit; *unit; vestige;* wad; wedge; *xylon; yngot* [arch.]; *zum* [dial.]; [*see* gold]
**nuisance** *(n. irritation)*: annoyance; aggravation; bother; *cross;* disturbance; exasperation; frustration; grief; harassment; irritation; jangling; *kidding; livid;* menace; nagging; offense; pain in the neck; *queach* [arch.]; rankling; *steaming;* trouble; umbrage; vexation; woe; *x-ing;* yammering; *zinging;*
**nuisance** *(n. irritant)*: antagonist; aggravator; bother; crosser; drip; disturber; exasperator; frustration; grief; headache; harasser; itch; imp; irritant; jangler; *kidder; livid;* menace; nag; offense; pest(erer); pain in the neck; *queach* [arch.]; rankler; *steamer;* tease; trouble(r); umbrage; vexer; wrankler; *x-er;* yammerer; *zinger;*
**nullify** *(v.)*: annul; blank out; cancel; do away with; disannul; end; forswear; gainsay; halt; invalidate; *jump back;* kill; *leave;* make invalid; negate; overturn; put an end to; quash; revoke; reject; *stop;* terminate; *undo;* void; vitiatel withdraw; *x-ing;* yank; zero out;

**numb** *(adj.)*: anesthetized; analgetic; asleep; benumbed; clouded; deadened; dull; etherized; *frozen;* gone ~; heavy; hebetudinous; insensible; insensitive; insensient; jaded; knocked out; lacking feeling; made ~; numbed; obtundent; phlegmatic; paralyzed; *quiescent; resting;* stuporous; subdued; torpid; torpent; unfeeling; vegetative; without feeling; *xylocaine; yet without feeling;* zombie-like;
**numb** *(v.)*: anesthetize; benumb; cloud; deaden; dull; etherize; *freeze;* go ~; hebetate; insensitive; jade; knock out; lacking feeling; make ~; non-responsive; obtund; put out; *quiescent; reduce feeling;* sedate; stultify; turn ~; unfeeling; *very ~;* weaken; *xylocaine; yet without feeling;* zonk;
**number** *(n.)*: amount; *base amount;* count; cardinal ~; digit; *exponent;* figure; *grand total; gross amount;* high ~; integer; *jag; kit;* low ~; *minuend;* numeral; ordinal ~; *offset; portion;* quantity; rounded ~; sum(mand); tally; unit ~; volume; whole ~; weight; *x;* yield; *z;*
   **Numbers**: billion; duodecillion; eight; eleven; four; five; gazillion; hundred; jillion; kazillion; million; nine; one; quadrillion; six; seven; two; three; ten; undecillion; vigintillion; *x;* zero; zillion;
**numerous** *(adj.)*: abundant; bounteous; copious; disproportionate; excess(ive); fruitful; great; heaps; immense; jumbo; *king-sized amounts;* lots; loads; many; much; manifold; numbers; overabundant; overmuch; plenty; quantitative; rich; several; tons; uberous; voluminous; various; wantless; *x.; yards; zillions;* [*Ant.* negligible]
**nurse** *(n.)*: ∗ amah [Orient]; *belle;* caregiver; company ~; day ~; dry~; *EMS worker;* fostress; *girl;* head ~; health visitor [Br.]; intensive care ~; *jane; key personnel;* licensed practical ~; minister; medical ~; male ~ [masc.]; nurser; orderly; practical ~; private ~; qualified ~; R.N.; scrub ~; triage ~; unit ~; visiting ~; ward sister; wet ~; *xtr. care;* yaya; *zealous helper;* [*see* mother; midwife]
**nurse** *(v.)*: attend to; *bandage;* care for; doctor; *ease;* foster; give care; help; *interest; join in helping;* keep alive; look after; mind; minister; nurture; *oversee; perform; quality care; reach out;* see to; tend; take care of; *uphold; valet;* watch over; *xfer care;* yeme; *zealosly help;* [*see* feed; *Ant.* neglect]
**nursery** *(n.)*: arborist; botanical garden; cultivator; dendrologist; electro-horticulturalist; florist; floriculturist; greenhouse; garden; herbary; hothouse; horticulturalist; *individual; jardinière; keeper;* landscaping center; *main greenhouse;* nurseryman; orchardist; orangery; phytologist; quadrat; *rose garden;* sunroom; seller of plants; tree specialist; *undertaking; vendor; viniculturalist;* winter garden; xenic; *yardman; zet [dial.];*
**nut** *(n.)*: ∗ almond; acorn; Brazil ~; butter~; chestnut; dry-roasted pea~; earth~; filbert; goober; ger~; hazel~; ivory ~; jer~; kola; kipper- ~; *legume;* macadamia; monkey~; nigger toe [slang]; oil~; pea~; pecan; pistachio; Queensland ~; roasted ~; Spanish almond; *treat;* unsalted ~; *victuals;* wal~; *xtr. dry-roasted ~;* yar- ~; *zakuski [Rus.];* [*see* madman]
**nutrition** *(n.)*: aliment; bread; comestibles; diet; eating; food; groceries; health; intake; *justified; keep; lunch;* meat; nourishment; nutriment; *organic food;* provisions; *quelque-chose [F.];* repast; sustenance; *table; unprocessed food;* victuals; vitamins; *wheat; xarque; yams; zakuski [Rus.];*
**nutritious** *(adj.)*: alimental; advantageous; beneficial; commensal; dietetic; *expedient;* fine; good; healthy; *incredible;* just fine; keen; life-giving; mighty fine; nourishing; nutritive; okay; peachy; *quartful* [arch.]; right; salubrious; trim; *usable;* vitaminic; wholesome; yaul; zero detriment; [*Ant.* non-healthy]
**nutty** *(adj.)*: abnormal; batty; crazy; deranged; eccentric; funny; goofy; heterotypical; irregular; jokey; kooky; loony; mad; nuts; odd; peculiar; quacked; ridiculous; silly; screwy; *twisted;* unusual; very weird; weird; wacky; *xenomorphic; yokelish;* zany; [*Ant.* normal]
**nuzzle** *(v.)*: *affection;* bury; cuddle; cozy up; *cleave; draw close;* embrace; embosom; *fondle;* grip; hug; infold; *jam; keep close; love;* make comfortable; nestle; *overply;* press; *quash;* rub; snuggle; *tenderly hug; upbind; valentine; wrap; X; yoke up with; zone;*
**nymph** *(n.)*: alseid; brownie; crinaeae; *creature;* dryad; *elf;* fairy; genie; hamadryad; *imp;* jinni; korrigan; limnade; meliae; naiad; nixie; oread; pixie; *quasi-human;* river-nymph; sprite; sylph; sea- ~; tree-nymph; undine; vetter; wood-nymph; water nymph (-sprite); xana; *yokai [Jap.];* zana;

# O

**oar** *(n.)*: *apparatus;* boat ~; blade; canoe paddle; *double-banked; eight-oar;* feathered ~; gondolla scull; hand paddle; *implement; joeboat ~;* kayak paddle; *loom;* macon ~; *navy ~; outrigger ~;* paddle; quadruple scull; rower; scull; timber ~; unfeathered ~; *vessel; wash; xebec;* yulow; *zabra ~;*
**oarsman** *(n.)*: *after-guard;* bencher; bowman; boatman; *coxswain;* double sculler; *ensign;* ferrier; gob; gondolier; *hand; impressment;* jack-tar; keeler; lighterman; mariner; *man; navigator;* oar; paddler; punter; quad sculler; rower; sculler; strokesman; tar; *underling; voyager;* waterman; wherryman; xebec-mariner; yachtsman; zygite;
**oasis** *(v.)*: *asylum;* blissful place; cienega; desert spring; *Engedi; font;* gilgai; haven; idyll; island; *jubb [Heb.];* keld; *location; lake; mere;* namma hole; oasification; paradise; *querencia [Sp.];* refuge; sanctuary; spring; tropical ~; *underground pool; vlie;* watering hole; wadi; xanadu; yarkandi; zerzura;
**oath** *(n.)*: agreement; affirmation; adjuration; avouchment; *bond;* covenant; declaration; *ensuring;* forswearing; guarantee; hypothecation; *interpledging;* jurament; *kept promise; letter of commitment; making of vows;* non-conditional promise; obligation; pledge; promise; pollicitation; *qualified promise;* resolution; sworn statement; solemn ~; troth; testament; undertaking; vow; word (of honor); *x-one's heart; yafery* [arch.]; *zealous ~;*
**oatmeal** *(n.)*: *aliment;* bran-meal; *chow;* drank; *edible;* frumenty; gruel; hot ~; instant ~; *just-made ~;* kasha; loblolly; meal; mabela; mush; *nourishment;* oats; porridge; quick-oats; rolled oats; skilly; *table rations;* ugali; *viands;* wild oats; *xtr. hot ~; yan; zuppe [It.];*
**obduracy** *(n.)*: adamancy; bullishness; contrariness; doggedness; *entêté [F.];* firmness; grimness; hard-heartedness; intractability; immovability; *jaw-set; keeping; lastingness;* mulishness; *negativity;* obstinacy; obduration; pertinacity; *querulousness;* refractoriness; restiveness; self-will; tenacity; unyieldingness; *volition;* willfulness; *x-grained;* yieldlessness; *zero give;* [Ant. obsequiousness]
**obdurate** *(adj.)*: adamant; bullish; calloused; dogged; *entêté* [F.]; firm; grim; hard-hearted; impersuasible; immovable; jaw-set; *keep;* lithoid; mulish; non-moving; obstinate; *opinionated;* pertinacious; *querulous;* refractory; resolute; restive; strong-willed; self-willed; tenacious; unbending; *volitional;* willful; *x-grained;* yieldless; *zero give;* [Ant. obsequious]
**obedience** *(n.)*: acquiescence; bowing; blind ~; compliance; deference; execution; followership; fulfillment; giving in; heeding; implementation; jumping to it; keeping; listening; mindfulness; non-resistance; observance; obsequiousness; performance; *questionlessness;* regard; submission; tractability; upholding; vigilance; *willingness; xlation;* yielding; yieldedness; *zeal;*
**obedient** *(adj.)*: acquiescent; biddable; compliant; duteous; ever- ~; faithful; governable; heedful; implementing; *jump right to it;* keeping; kowtowing; law-abiding; morigerous; mindful; non-resistant; obsequious; *pliant; questionless;* regardful; right on it; submissive; subject; tractable; unresisting; *vigilant;* willing; *xtry;* yielded; *zealous;*
**obeisance** *(n.)*: admiration; bowing; consideration; deference; esteem; fear; genuflection; honor; homage; ingratiation; *justness;* kneeling; loyalty; *merit;* non-contempt; obsequiousness; praise; *quality;* respect; regard; salutation; submission; tribute; *unmitigated respect;* veneration; wonder; *xtry.;* yielding; *zero contempt;*
**obey** *(v.)*: abide; acquiesce; attend; bow; comply; conform; carry out; do; execute; follow; fulfill; give in; heed; humor; implement; jump (to it); keep; knuckle under; keel in; listen to; mind; not resist; observe; perform; *questionless;* regard; resign; submit; succumb; take orders; undertake; vigorously ~; *work; wholly; xlate;* yield; zip to it;

**obituary** *(n.)*: announcement of death; bill of mortality; casualty list; death record; epitaphic; *eulogy;* fatality list; *grave;* history; home-going announcement; *internment; just died; killed;* listing of deaths; mortality list; martyrology; necrology; necrologue; obit; posting of deaths; *quietus;* roster; roll; *salute;* testimonial; *undertaker; vault; written list; xat; yizkor [Heb.]; zet [dial.];*

**object** *(n.)*: article; *belonging; bauble;* commodity; doodad; entity; ens; feature; gizmo; gadget; *goods;* hoosywatsy; item; jib; kickumbob; *load; made thing; noun; ontology;* piece; *quintain; raw material; stuff;* thing; *utility; valuable; watchamacallit;* whatnot; widget; xylon; you-know-what; *Zeug [G.];*

**object** *(v.)*: *argue;* balk; cavil; complain; demur; disagree; differ; dissent; disapprove; except; expostulate; frown; fuss; gripe; gainsay; have a problem with; inveigh; jib; kick; *loath;* make objection; nitpick; oppose; protest; quibble; resist; raise ~ion; remonstrate; squawk; *strive against;* take issue; *urge against;* vituperate; vary; withstand; whine; *x-fire;* yawp; *zing;*

**objection** *(n.)*: argument; balking; complaint; disapproval; dissention; dispute; exception; expostulation; frowning; gripe; hang-up; impugnation; jeremiad; *kick;* low opinion; *murmuring;* nitpicking; opposition; protest; quarrel; resistance; *strife;* taking issue; unharmoniousness; variance; withstanding; *x-fire;* yammering; *za-zum [Rus.];*

**objective** *(n.)*: aim; aspiration; by-purpose; conation; design; end; function; goal; hope; high aim; intention; intent; journey's end; key reason; last stop; meaning; notion; object; purpose; point; quintain; reason; sake; target; *terminus ad quem* [L.]; ultimate aim; wish; will; x; *yearning; zero in;*

**obligate** *(v.)*: agree to; bind; constrain; demand; exact; force; *give ultimatum;* hold to; impose; *jurisdiction;* keep one to; *lean on;* make; necessitate; oblige; press; *quicken;* require; saddle with; twist one's arm; urge; use force; *violence;* wam; *xuld [arch.];* yoke; *zero way out;*

**obligation** *(n.)*: accountability; assignment; business; constraint; charge; commission; duty; engagement; errand; fealty; given duty; homage; incumbency; job; *key role;* liability; mission; necessity; obligating; promise; *quest;* responsibility; string; task; undertaking; vocation; work; xci.; *yoke; zealous task;* [Ant. option]

**obligatory** *(adj.)*: all-important; bounden; compulsory; demanded; essential; forced; given; hard-and-fast; inescapable; *jump to it;* key; legally-binding; mandatory; necessary; ordered; pressing; quantum; required; statutory; top-priority; urgent; vital; without appeal; *xuld [arch.]; yearnful; zero option;* [Ant. optional]

**oblige** *(v.)*: accommodate; bind; compel; coerce; duty-bind; exact; force; gratify; have to; indebt; indulge; *jurisdiction;* keep obligation; leave no option; make; necessitate; obligate; pressure; *quicken;* require; saddle with; twist one's arm; urge; use force; *violence;* wam; *xuld [arch.];* yoke; *zero way out;*

**obliterate** *(v.)*: annihilate; blot out; crush; destroy; demolish; disintegrate; expunge; exterminate; erase; *finish off; grind; havoc; incinerate; junk;* kill; lay waste; liquidate; level; *massacre;* nullify; overthrow; pulverize; quash; raze; smash; snuff out; *terminate;* unbuild; vaporize; wipe out; x; *yank down;* zap;

**obliteration** *(n.)*: annihilation; blotting out; crushing; destruction; expunction; extermination; *finishing off; grinding; havoc; incineration; junking;* killing; liquidation; *massacre;* nullification; overthrow; pulverization; quashing; *ruination;* snuffing out; termination; undoing; vaporization; wiping out; x-ing out; *yanking down; zapping;*

**oblivion** *(n.)*: aught; barrenness; cipher; desolation; emptiness; extinction; fiction; great abyss; *hollowness;* inexistence; *jack [slang]; kaput;* lethe; *make-believe;* nonexistence; nothingness; nihility; ought; *pulverization; quantity zero; rien [F.];* scratch; *thought-of;* unreality; void; *whitespace;* x; *yielded;* zero;

**oblivious** *(adj.)*: abstracted; benighted; clueless; deceived; elsewhere; faraway; gullible; half-conscious; ignorant; in the dark; incognizant; *juvenile; knowledge-deprived;* lost in thought; museful; naive; obtuse; preoccupied; Pickwickian; *quacky;* rapt; simple; totally ~; unmindful; unaware; verdant; wareless; *x-out;* yet unawares; zoned out; [Ant. open-eyed]

**obnoxious** *(adj.)*: abhorrent; boorish; cheeky; deplorable; execrable; foul; gruff; grating; horrible; in-your-face; insulting; insufferable; jangly; *kitsch;* loathsome; malodorous; nasty; offensive; perfidious; quite rude; reprehensible; rude; sickening; squalid; tasteless; uncouth; uncivil; vulgar; wretched; *x-bad;* yahoo; *zhlubby;*

**obscene** *(adj.)*: appalling; bawdy; coarse; disgraceful; explicit; erotic; filthy; goatish; heinous; indecent; jadish; kinky; lewd; mereticious; *nude;* offensive; promiscuous; perverted; pornographic; *quad;* raw; risque; smutty; shameful; tasteless; uncouth; vulgar; wicked; x-rated; *yucky; zhlubby;*

**obscenity** *(n.)*: *abomination;* blasphemy; curse; cussword; dirty word; expletive; foul language; *gross disrespect; hex;* impiety; invective; juration; *kitsch; lewd word;* malediction; naughty word; oath; profanity; *quadriliteral;* ribaldry; swearword; sacrilege; tasteless speech; ungodly language; vulgarity; wickedness; *x-rated speech;* yawp; *zinger;*

**obscure** *(adj.)*: adumbrate; abstruse; arcane; bedimmed; blurry; clouded; dark; enclouded; esoteric; fuliginous; gloomy; hidden; indistinct; jumbled; known to few; little-known; murky; mysterious; nebulous; opaque; *patchy;* quaggy; rayless; shadowy; tenebrous; unclear; unknown; undefined; vague; *wan; x; yucky; zero clarity;* [Ant. obvious]

**obscure** *(v.)*: adumbrate; block; becloud; bemask; bury; conceal; cover; cloud; darken; enshroud; eclipse; fog up; garble; hide; imbosk; jumble; keep hidden; *lay over;* mask; muddle; nubilate; obfuscate; obstruct; overshadow; put out of view; *quat* [arch.]; repress; shroud; suppress; tuck away; *under cover;* veil; wimple; *xenomorph; yird; zeroize;*

**observable** *(adj.)*: apparent; blatant; clear; discernible; evident; flagrant; glaring; highly visible; in full view; just plain to see; kenspeckle; *lucid;* manifest; noticeable; obvious; plain; perceptible; *quite obvious;* recognizable; salient; seeable; transparent; unmistakable; unhidden; visible; witnessable; *x-parent; yeme [arch.]; zenithal;* [Ant. obscured]

**observance** *(n.)*: affair; *beholding;* ceremony; custom; duty; exercise; formality; *gathering;* habit; holiday; institution; *jubilation;* keeping; *liturgy;* ministration; norm; observing; ordinance; ordinal; performance; practice; *quadrisacramentalism;* rite; ritual; service; sacrament; tradition; use; *vigil;* wont; *x-parent; yieldedness; zeal;*

**observant** *(adj.)*: alert; *bright;* careful; discerning; ever-watchful; *fine;* gazeful; heedful; hawk-eyed; intentive; *judicious;* keen-eyed; *looking;* mindful; *noticing;* observing; on the ball; perceptive; quick-eyed; regardful; sharp-eyed (-sighted); *trained eye;* ultra-careful; vigilant; watchful; *x-careful; yare; zero in;*

**observe** *(v.)*: acknowledge; attend; abide by; behold; catch sight of; detect; discern; examine; fix eyes on; gaze; *hone in on;* harken to; inspect; *jump to it;* ken; keep; look; make out; monitor; note; notice; *obey;* perceive; *quick look;* recognize; regard; see; spot; scrutinize; take in; *understand;* view; watch; witness; *x-ray vision; yeme; zero in;* [*see* obey; Ant. overlook]

**obsess** *(v.)*: absorb; beset; consume; dominate; engross; fill; fixate; grip; hold; involve; *jag;* kinch; *like;* monopolize; *narcosis;* occupy; preoccupy; possess; *quaffed;* rivet; spellbind; trouble; transfix; *under a spell;* vex; worry; *x-fix; yield; zone out;*

**obsession** *(n.)*: absorption; addiction; bemusement; captivation; domination; engrossment; fixation; *grip;* hang-up; *idée fixe* [F.]; *jag;* kinching; *like;* (mono)mania; *narcosis;* occupation; preoccupation; *quaffing;* riveting; spellbinding; transfixing; *under a spell; vegging out;* worry; *x-fixing; yieldedness; zeroing in;*

**obsolete** *(adj.)*: archaic; antiquated; behind the times; *ceased;* dated; discontinued; expired; formerly-used; *gone; has been;* inoperative; *junked; kaput;* long-retired; moribund; naff; outdated; outmoded; obsolescent; out-of-date; passé; past prime; *quondam;* retired; superseded; *terminated;* unfashioned; unused; *useless;* vestigial; worn-out; *x'ed; yesteryear; zero;*

**obstacle** *(n.)*: *aggravation;* barrier; cumbrance; difficulty; encumbrance; *frustration;* glitch; hurdle; impediment; impasse; jam; kink; *lodgment;* mountain; nuisance; obstruction; problem; quandary; roadblock; snag; trouble; *upset;* vigia; wall; x; *yard wall; zinger;*

**obstruct** *(v.)*: avert; block; barricade; cumber; deter; dam up; *delay;* encumber; frustrate; forestall; gum up; hinder; halt; hold back; impede; jam; keep (from); limit; make encumbered; *nullify;* obviate; prevent; quash; restrain; stop; thwart; *upset;* veto; withhold; *x; yank;* zilch; [*Ant.* open]

**obstruction** *(n.)*: arrest; barrier; blockage; barricade; cumbrance; difficulty; encumbrance; frustration; glitch; hindrance; impediment; jam; *keeping;* logjam; mountain; nuisance; obstacle; problem; *quandary;* roadblock; stumbling block; trouble; *upset;* vigia; wall; x; *yowler;* zilching; [*Ant.* opening]

**obtain** *(v.)*: acquire; attain; buy; bag [slang]; catch; collect; derive; *exact; earn;* fetch; find; get; gain; have; *intercept; inherit; jet;* kep; land; make off with; nab; net; own; procure; purchase; *quoff;* receive; reap; recover; secure; seize; take; usurp; *vest;* win; xfer; yank; zip away; [*Ant.* offload]

**obtainable** *(adj.)*: available; acquirable; buyable; derivable; easily obtained; findable; gettable; havable; *intercept;* just there for the taking; *keepable;* landable; makeable; nettable; open; procurable; purchasable; quite easily obtained; recoverable; seizable; takable; unclaimed; *vacant;* winnable; *xfer;* yours for the taking; *zero problem;* [*Ant.* out-of-reach]

**obtainment** *(n.)*: attainment; acquisition; buying; collection; derivation; *earning;* finding; getting; gain; having; *interception; inheritance; jetting;* keeping; landing; making off with; nabbing; owning; procurement; *quaffing;* reception; reaping; recovery; securing; seizing; taking possession; usurpation; *vesting;* winning; *xfer;* yanking; zipping away;

**obvious** *(adj.)*: apparent; blatant; clear; conspicuous; discernible; evident; explicit; flagrant; glaring; *highly visible;* in plain view; *just plain to see;* kenspeckle; *lucid;* manifest; noticeable; observable; overt; open; plain; *quite obvious;* recognizable; self-evident; shameless; transparent; unhidden; unconcealed; unmistakable; visible; well-pronounced; *x-parent; yeme [arch.]; zenithal;* [*Ant.* obscure]

**occasion** *(n.)*: affair; *ball;* chance; clip; chapter; *dance;* event; episode; experience; function; formal ~; gathering; happening; holiday; instance; incident; *jaunt; key event; lawn party;* meeting; notable event; opportunity; outing; occurrence; period; *quindene; reunion;* shebang; special ~; time; thing; *undertaking;* venture; wingding; *x-po; yong [arch.]; zet [dial.];*

**occasional** *(adj.)*: at times; *blue moon;* casual; *day;* erratic; episodic; fitful; *given;* here and there; incidental; infrequent; irregular; intermittent; just ~; *key times; little; moderately;* non-regular; now-and-then; occasional; once in a while; periodic; *quarterly;* recurrent; sporadic; spasmodic; scattered; *times;* uncommon; *variable;* without regularity; *xtr. special time; yong [arch.]; zero regularity;* [*Ant.* ordinary]

**occult** *(n.)*: astrology; black magic; conjuring; divination; demonism; devil-worship; enchantment; fortune-telling; *gyromancy;* hocus pocus; incantation; juju; *Keltic religion; legerdemain;* magic; necromancy; new age; obeah; psychicism; *quad;* rune; sorcery; theurgy; *ungodliness;* voodoo; witchcraft; *xylomancy; yogism; zodiac;*

**occultic** *(adj.)*: astrological; black; conjuring; demonic; evil; fortune-telling; *gyromantic; hexing;* incanting; *juju; Keltic religion;* luciferian; magical; new age; occulty; psychical; *quad;* runic; sorcerous; satanic; theurgic; unholy; voodooistic; witch; *xylomantic; yogist; zodiacal;* [*see* demonic]

**occupancy** *(n.)*: abode; biding; continuing; dwelling; domiciliation; *encampment; filled; going to;* habitation; inhabitancy; joint- ~; *keeping on;* lodging; living; *moving in;* no vacancy; occupation; possession; quartering; residence; residency; staying; tenancy; taking possession; use; *volume;* won; *winter-quarters; xfer; yearly contract; zero vacancy;*

**occupant** *(n.)*: abider; addressee; boarder; continuer; dweller; *encamper; feudatory; going to;* habitant; inhabitant; joint- ~; *keeper on;* lodger; *moving in; no vacancy;* occupier; possessor; quarterer; resident; stayer; squatter; tenant; user; *vassal; winter-quarterer; xferer;* year-rounder; *zone lessee;*

**occupation** *(n. invasion)*: annexation; *bondage;* capture; conquest; control; domination; expugnation; foreign takeover; *feat;* grabbing; *historic victory;* invasion; *jarring defeat;* knockout; *lordship;* military ~; national takeover; overtaking; occupying; possession; *quest; re-conquest;* seizure; takeover; usurpation; *victory; win; xfer; yong [arch.]; zapping;* [*Ant.* ousting]

**occupation** *(n. vocation)*: activity; assignment; avocation; business; career; craft; calling; duty; employment; field; *grind [slang]; handicraft;* industry; job; *key position;* livelihood; métier; *necessity;* operancy; profession; *quest;* responsibility; service; trade; task; undertaking; vocation; work; xci. *yoke; zealous duty;*
**occupational** *(adj.)*: *activity;* business; career-related; *duty;* employment-related; field-related; *grind [slang]; handicraft;* industrial; job-related; *key position; livelihood;* manufacturing; *necessary;* occupation-related; professional; *quest;* related; specialized; trade; *undertaking;* vocational; work-related; xci. *yoke; zealous duty;*
**occupy** *(v. fill one's time)*: abide; attend; busy; carry out; do; engage; employ; fill; go and do; hold attention; involve; *jam-pack;* keep busy; *lend oneself to;* man; *non-idle;* obsess; pre~; *questionless;* realize; spend; settle; take up; use; *vigor;* work; *xuld [arch]; yerde* [arch.]; zip to it;
**occupy** *(v. reside in)*: abide; bide; camp; continue; dwell; *encamp;* follow on; *go to;* habitate; inhabit; *jam;* keep on; live; move in; *nest;* overspread; overstay; overwinter; pause; populate; quarter; remain; reside in; stay; tarry; use; *voyage to;* wait; xenize; yerde [arch.]; *zip to;*
**occur** *(v.)*: arise; betide; come to pass; develop; ensue; fall; follow; go on; happen; hit; intervene; *jump up; kep;* light; materialize; *near; occasion;* proceed; *quicken;* rise; result; spring up; strike; take place; transpire; unfold; venture; *work; xpire; yield; zip;*
**occurrence** *(n.)*: affair; *befallen;* circumstance; case; development; event; experience; episode; falling; fact; *going on;* happening; incident; *juncture; kep; lot;* manifestation; matter; *new development;* occasion; phenomenon; *quicken;* realization; situation; thing; transpiration; unfolding; *venture; work; xpire; yield; zip;*
**ocean** *(n.)*: *archipelago;* briny blue; *channel; the* deep; expanse; fishpond [slang]; great sea; high seas; *inlet; jheel [Ind.];* keld; lagoon; marine; *narrows;* open sea; pond; *quai; reservoir;* sea; seven seas; tide [coll.]; *undercurrent; voe;* water; waves; *xyrisic; yeo;* Zee [G.]; [*see* river; lake]
**odd** *(adj.)*: abnormal; bizarre; crazy; deviant; erratic; eccentric; funny; freakish; gonzo; goofy; heterotypical; irregular; jokey; kooky; loony; mad; nonstandard; nutty; outrageous; outlandish; peculiar; quacked; queer; ridiculous; silly; screwy; strange; twisted; unusual; variant; wacky; weird; warped; xenomorphic; *yokelish;* zany; [*Ant.* ordinary]
**oddity** *(n.)*: aberration; anomaly; bizarrerie; curiosity; deviation; eccentricity; foible; freak; glitch; heterotypicality; idiosyncrasy; *joke;* kink; looniness; malformation; non-usualness; obliquity; peculiarity; quirk; rarity; strangeness; twist; unusualness; variation; weirdness; *xenomorph;* yaw; zaniness;
**oddness** *(n.)*: abnormality; bizarreness; craziness; deviation; eccentricity; foible; goofiness; heterotypicality; irregularity; inconsistency; *joke;* kookiness; looniness; malformation; non-usualness; oddity; peculiarity; queerness; ridiculousness; strangeness; twist; unusualness; variation; weirdness; *xenomorph;* yaw; zaniness; [*Ant.* normality]
**odor** *(n.)*: *aroma;* bad smell; contemptible smell; displeasing smell; effluvium; funk; foul smell; fetor; fetidness; galsome smell; horrible ~; *inhale;* joyless ~; *killing fumes;* loathsome smell; mephitis; malodorousness; niff; odorousness; pong; putridity; *quality;* reeking; smell; stench; stink; terrible smell; unsavoriness; vile ~; whiff; waft; *x-bad;* yucky smell; *zoril;*
**offend** *(v.)*: affront; anger; appall; bother; commit offense; disrespect; embitter; fume; gall; heat up; insult; jangle; kindle; *lose one's temper;* miff; niff; outrage; perturb; *quick-tempered;* rankle; slight; transgress; *tick off;* upset; violate; wrong; *xerothermic; yell; zap;*
**offense** *(n.)*: affront; abomination; bad thing; crime; difficulty; evil; foulness; guilt; hindrance; indignation; injustice; jangling; knocking; *loathsome behavior;* misdeed; niff; outrage; problem; perturbation; *quad;* resentment; sin; stumblingblock; transgression; umbrage; violence; wrong(doing); *x-gression; yetzer hara* [Heb.]; *zapping;*

**offensive** *(adj.)*: appalling; bawdy; cheeky; displeasing; embittering; foul; grody; hurtful; insulting; *jangly; kitsch;* loathsome; misbehaved; nasty; obnoxious; perfidious; quarrelsome; rude; sickening; squalid; tasteless; unpleasant; unflattering; vile; wretched; *x-bad;* yahoo; *zhlubby;* [*Ant.* okay]

**offer** *(n.)*: action; bid; counsel; deal; endeavor; final (-firm) ~; *gift;* hit [slang]; invitation; *juration; kibitz* [Yid.]; last ~; motion; movement; nomination; overture; proposition; proffer; *quicken;* recommendation; suggestion; tender; *urging; venture; want; xfer; yearning; zealous ~;*

**offer** *(v. proffer)*: advance; bid; come forward; dole; extend; furnish; give; hold out; invite; *just in case; kibitz* [Yid.]; lay at one's feet; make available; *now available;* outstretch hand; overture; *overbid;* outbid; ply; put forth; present; proffer; propose; propound; *quicken;* recommend; submit; set before; tender; urge upon; *underbid;* volunteer; *way; xuld [arch.]; yafe* [arch.]; *zero in;*

**offer** *(v. sacrifice)*: atone; burn; *conciliate;* do sacrifice; expiate; *fulfill;* give; *hecatomb;* immolate; *justify;* kill; lay on altar; make atonement; *night oblation;* offer up; present; *qualify;* reconcile; sacrifice; *take; undertake; victimize; worship; x-out;* yield up; *zealously ~;*

**offering** *(n. collection)*: accumulation; basket ~; collection; contribution; corban; donation; *evening ~;* freewill ~; gathering; gift; *heap;* ingathering; *jubilee ~; kit;* liberality; love ~; morning ~; *money;* number; *oblation;* passing the plate; quest [R.C.C.]; relinquishment; special ~; *store;* tithes and ~; *unhanding;* valuables; Wednesday-night ~; *xenium; yielding; zealous giving;*

**offering** *(n. sacrifice)*: atonement; *beast;* blood sacrifice; burnt ~; contribution; *drink ~;* evening oblation; expiation; *forfeiture;* gift; hecatomb; holocaust; immolation; *justification;* krioboly; *killing animal;* libation; mactation; night oblation; oblation; present; propitiation; *quitclaim;* reconciliation; sacrifice; *thank ~; undertaking;* victimation; *wave ~;* xenium; yielding; *yajna* [Hind.]; *zoid;*

  **Kinds of sacrifices**: animal sacrifice; burnt ~; corban; drink ~; food ~; guilt ~; heave ~; meat ~; peace ~; sin ~; thank ~; votive ~; wave ~; wood ~;

**office** *(n.)*: area; back ~; building; cubicle; corporate ~; desk; executive ~; front ~; facilities; government ~; home ~; industrial space; jakes; key location; *land ~;* location; *local ~;* main ~; *niche;* official location; place of business; quadrant; room; suite; sales ~; *trading post;* upstairs ~; *virtual ~;* workplace; *xy-coordinate; yamen* [Chin.]; *zone;* [see position]

**officer** *(n.)*: admiral; brass; centurion; commandant; commissioned ~; commander; deck ~; *ensign;* field ~; general; *hetman [Rus.]; irenarch [Gr.];* JAG ~; kick [slang]; line ~; leader; *lieutenant; major; marshal;* noncommissioned ~; naval ~; orderly ~; official; petty ~; *quartermaster;* rated man; staff ~; *top brass;* undermaster; vice-admiral; warrant ~; *x-chaser; yeoman;* zone ~;

  **Military officers:** admiral; brigadier general; captain; colonel; commodore; divisional general; field marshal; general; lieutenant; major; one-star general; petty ~; quartermaster; two-star general; vice admiral; warrant ~;

**official** *(adj.)*: appropriate; approved; authorized; bureaucratic; *bona fide;* correct; certified; *defensible;* endorsed; formal; good; homologated; *honored;* institutional; jural; *kosher;* legal; legit [slang]; legitimate; mandated; *non-forged;* on-record; proper; *qualified;* right; recognized; sanctioned; technical; *unopposed;* valid; well; *x-certified; yes; zero problem;*

**official** *(n.)*: agent; administrator; ambassador; bureaucrat; brass; consul; commissioner; commissary; delegate; diplomat; executive; functionary; government ~; hayward; intendant; jobs worth [Br.]; *kurveyor;* legate; leader; minister; notary; officer; proconsul; questman; representative; spokesman; statesman; trustee; *updater;* vice-consul; V.I.P.; *walking delegate; x-man; yamen* [Chin.]; zayim;

**officiate** *(v.)*: administer; be in charge; carry out; do; execute; fulfill; govern; have control; *implement; jurisdiction; keep;* lead; manage; minister; *name;* oversee; perform; preside; *questionless;* run; referee; superintend; solemnize; take charge; umpire; *validate; wherewithal; xlate; yeme; zealously fulfill;*

**often** *(adv.)*: a lot; *boundlessly;* commonly; daily; *every day;* frequently; *generally;* habitually; in many cases; just as oft as one can; *keep going;* lots of times; many times; numerous times; oft; oft(en)times; prevalently; quite ~; repeatedly; so ~; time and again; usually; very often; weekly; *xtr. times; yare; zealous;* [*Ant.* occasionally]

**oil** *(n.)*: \* antifriction; black gold; crude ~; chrism; dope [slang]; emollient; fuel ~; gasoline; grease; heavy ~; industrial-grade ~; *incense; juniper ~;* kerogen; lubricant; *lamp ~;* motor ~; multigrade ~; nonvolatile ~; nondrying ~; ~ -gas; *ointment; olive ~;* petroleum; *palm ~; quintessence;* rock ~; semidrying ~; train- ~; unction; *unrefined ~;* volatile ~; *vegetable ~; whale ~; xylitone; yalah;* zero ~;
**oil** *(v.)*: apply oil; begrease; *cover;* daub with grease; enlard; *fill;* grease; hand-spread; *infucate; jigger; key;* lubricate; lard; make greasy; overspread; put ~ on; *quick-lube;* rub ~ on; smear; tallow; use; *viscid;* wipe; xfer; yark; *zip;*
**oily** *(adj.)*: *adverse;* buttery; chrismal; *dangerous; endangering;* fatty; freshly-oiled; greasy; gunky; highly greasy; icky; just-oiled; *known risk;* lubricated; lubric(ous); *much-oiled; no traction;* oleaginous; pinguid; quite ~; regreased; slippery; slick; smooth; tallowy; unctuous; very slick; *viscous; wet; xtr. oil;* yolky; *zero traction;*
**ointment** *(n.)*: abirritant; balm; cream; demulcent; embrocation; *eyesalve;* fomentation; gel; harquebusade; inunctum; *jojoba; kamachili;* lotion; medication; *nard;* oil; palliative; palm oil; *quinine;* rub; salve; treatment; unguent; vulnerary; wash; xerogel; xeromyrum; *yellow balm; zinc ~;*
**old** *(adj.)*: aged; antiquated; age-old; ancient; bygone; *chronicled;* dated; decrepit; elderly; early; full-grown; *former;* geriatric; gray-headed (-haired); geezerly; hoary; historic; inveterate; immemorial; *jaded; kept;* long-standing (-lived); mature; not young; *nostalgic;* outdated; old (-fashioned); olden; prehistoric; past; *quondam;* ripe(ned); *retired;* senior; stricken in years; senile; time-honored (-worn); up in years; *used;* veteran; vintage; venerable; well-along in years; well-worn; *waning; weak;* XO; yellowed; *zillions of years old;*
**old-fashioned** *(adj.)*: antique; behind-the-times; *bygone days;* conservative; dated; *days gone by;* early-style; former; *good old;* horse-and-buggy; immemorial; *jaded; kept;* long-lived; mossgrown; nostalgic; old-style; old-time; old-school; outmoded; passé; *politically incorrect;* quaint; *retired;* superannuate; traditional; unfashionable; vintage; *vieux jeu* [F.]; well-aged; *Xanthian;* ye olde; *zero modernness;*
**oldness** *(n.)*: age(dness); anility [fem.]; antiquation; ancientness; *bygone;* caducity; dotage; decrepitude; elderliness; fullness of years; gray-headedness; golden years; hoary head; historicity; inveteracy; *jadedness; kept;* long life; maturity; *nostalgia;* old age; prehistory; *quondam;* ripeness; ricketiness; *retirement;* senescence; seniority; senility; *time;* up in years; venerability; *weakness; xtry, age;* years; *zillions of years;*
**ominous** *(adj.)*: adverse; bleak; brooding; cautionary; dismal; evil-looking; foreboding; gloomy; harbingering; ill-omened; inauspicious; *jarring; knee-knocking;* looming; menacing; non-encouraging; overcast; portentous; *quenching;* red-flag; sinister; threatening; unpromising; very ~; warning; *x-out;* yucky; zealless;
**omission** *(n.)*: absence; *blank;* culpa; delinquency; exclusion; ellipsis; *error;* failure; gap; *heedlessness;* ignoring; inobservance; jumping over; keeping out; lack; leaving out; missing; lapse; neglect; non-inclusion; omitting; oversight; passing over; *quit;* remissness; shirking; throwing out; ullage; *voidance;* want; *x-ing;* yemeles [arch.]; *zero inclusion;*
**omit** *(v.)*: *avoid;* bypass; cut out; disregard; elide; exclude; forget; go over; *have not;* ignore; jump over; knock off; leave out; miss; neglect; overlook; pass over; *quick-to-forget;* remember not; *remiss;* skip (over); toss out; *unfaithful;* void; withhold; x-out; *yemeles [arch.];* zeroize;
**omnipotence** *(n.)*: almightiness; boundless power; control; dominion; *ever-powerful;* fullness of power; *greatness;* highest power; infinite power; *justification; keen power;* limitless power; might; mastery; non-limitation; omnipotency; plenipotence; *qi; remarkable power;* supremacy; total power; ultimacy; *virtue; wherewithal; xtry. power;* yareness; *zero limitations;*
**omnipotent** *(adj.)*: almighty; all-powerful; *boundless;* completely powerful; *divine;* entheastic; *force;* greater than all; *High;* invincible; *justified; keenly powerful;* limitless; mighty; non-limited; omnificent; powerful; plenipotent; plenipotentiary; *qi; remarkable;* supreme; totally poweful; unstoppable; *very strong;* without limitation; *xtry. power;* yare; *zero limitations;*

**omnipresence** *(n.)*: ability to be everywhere at once; being everywhere; comprehensiveness; divine presence; everywhereness; *full power;* Godhood; *here;* immanency; *just everywhere; knowledge of all things;* limitlessness; majesty; *multipresence;* non-limitation; *omnipresential;* presence everywhere; *quality;* round the world; simultaneous presence everywhere; total immanence; ubiquity; *virtue; with us; xtry. ability; yere [Scot.];* zero limitations;

**omnipresent** *(adj.)*: all-pervading; *being everywhere;* capable of being in all places; *divinely present;* everywhere(-present); *ever-present; fully powerful;* Godlikeness; *here;* immanent; in all places; *just everywhere; know(s) all;* limitless; *multipresent;* non-limited; near; omnipresential; present everywhere; *quality; round the world;* simultaneously everywhere; *total immanence;* ubiquitous; *universal; virtue;* with us; *xtry, able; yere [Scot.];* zero limitation;

**omniscience** *(n.)*: absolute knowledge; *big picture;* complete knowledge; *divine knowledge;* entire knowledge; foreknowledge; full knowledge; *greater knowledge; highest;* infinite knowledge; *justification;* knowing all things; limitless knowledge; *manifest;* non-limited knowledge; omnipercipience; omnisciency; pansophy; perfect knowledge; *quality; right knowledge;* supreme knowledge; total knowledge; unlimited knowledge; *visible;* whole knowledge; *wist; xenagogy; yeme;* zero limitation;

**omniscient** *(adj.)*: all-knowing; *big picture;* completely knowledgeable; *divine;* everything-knowing; foreknowing; full awareness; *glorious; highest;* infinitely knowing; *justified;* knowing all things; limitless; *manifest;* non-limited; omniscious; omnipercipient; pansophical; *quality; rightly knows;* supremely aware; totally aware; unlimited; *visible; wist; xenagogic; yeme;* zero limitation;

**oneness** *(n.)*: accord(ance); bond; commonality; devotedness; empathy; fellowship; *glue;* harmony; inseparability; joint-bond; kinship; like-mindedness; mutuality; *nodding;* one-mindedness; one accord; parallelism; *quarrel-lessness;* rapport; solidarity; singleness; soleness; togetherness; unity; *voluntariness;* wholeness; *xenia; yedinstvo* [Rus.]; *zero division;*

**ongoing** *(adj.)*: abiding; *boundless;* continuous; constant; continual; chronic; *daily;* enduring; endless; forward-moving; going on and on; *hourly;* incessant; *jusqu'au bout* [F.]; *keeps going;* lasting; maintaining; nonstop; open-ended; perpetual; *quadrillion;* remaining; surviving; steady; *transcending;* uninterrupted; unceasing; *vast;* without end; *xferring;* year-round; *zillion;*

**onlooker** *(n.)*: audience; bystander; beholder; considerer; *crowd;* descrier; eyewitness; *forgathering;* gazer; *hearer;* innocent bystander; *janata [Asia];* keeker; looker-on; *man;* multitude; noticer; observer; person; passer-by; *quelet [arch.];* regarder; rubbernecker; spectator; televiewer; *throng; unbiased observer;* viewer; watcher; witness; *x.; yain [arch.]; zoa;*

**only** *(adj.)*: alone; *by oneself;* companionless; dearn; exclusive; first and last; *gone; hopeless;* isolated; just oneself; *kept alone;* lone; merely; non-accompanied; one (and ~); particular; *queer;* recluded; solitary; single; singly; sole; totally alone; unigenous; very much alone; without another; $x=1;$ yae zero accompaniment;

**only-begotten** *(adj.)*: alone-born; begotten alone; *complete; dearn;* exclusive; first and only; *given once; heterotypical;* isolated; just one; *kept alone;* lone-born; *merely;* non-accompanied; only-born; one and only; *particular; quantity: one; recluded;* sole-begotten; *totally alone;* unigenous; very much alone; without another; *xfer;* yae zero accompaniment;

**opaque** *(adj.)*: adiaphanous; beclouded; clouded; dark; dense; enclouded; fuliginous; gloomy; hidden; impermeable; impenetrable; *jet-dark; kettle-dark;* light-proof; murky; nontranslucent; nontransparent; obscure; *pitch-black; quite dense;* rayless; solid; turbid; tenebrous; untransparent; very dark; *wadd; x'ed; yucky;* zero light;

**open** *(adj. ajar)*: ajar; breach; cracked; cavernous; dehiscent; detached; dilated; extended; fissured; gaping; *hiation;* insecure; invitatory; just-opened; kept- ~; left ~; made ~; non-secured; opened; partly ~; quite ~; recluded; re-opened; screwed off; *torn* ~; unbayed; unbolted; uncapped; unscrewed; unlatched; unsecured; unshut; unclosed; vent; wide- ~; *x-out;* yawning; *zet [dial.];*

**open** *(adj. exposed)*: apparent; blatant; conspicuous; discernible; evident; exposed; flagrant; glaring; highly visible; in full view; *just plain to see;* kenspeckle; laid bare; manifest; noticeable; obvious; overt; plain; *quite obvious;* recognizable; seeable; transparent; unhidden; unmistakable; visible; wide- ~; *x-parent; yeme [arch.]; zenithal;* [*Ant.* obscure]

**open** *(v.)*: *ajar;* break open; breach; crack; distend; dilate; extend; expand; fissure; gape; hold ~; *in;* jimmy; jack; keep ~; leave ~; nake ~; *non-secured;* ope [poet.]; pry; *quickly ~;* reclude; re-open; swing ~; twist off; unbay; unbolt; uncap; unscrew; unlatch; unseal; unlock; uncork; unstop; unbar; ventilate; widen; *xfer* yawn; yaw; *zet [dial.];*

**opening** *(n.)*: aperture; break; breach; crack; doorway; entrance; embrasure; fenestra; fissure; gap(e); hole; incavation; jaw-hole; krater; *lacuna;* mouth; meatus; notch; ostium; orifice; pit; *quarry-pit;* rent; rupture; room; space; *tunnel;* unfolding; valley; ventage; *well; x-parent;* yawn; zanja;

**openly** *(adv.)*: apparently; blatantly; conspicuously; deliberately; expressly; freely; flagrantly; glaringly; *heedlessly;* intentionally; *just;* knowingly; lucidly; manifestly; noticeably; overtly; plainly; publicly; *quite;* roundly; saliently; shamelessly; *transparently;* unmistakably; visibly; wittingly; *XR;* yarely; zero secrecy;

**openness** *(n.)*: apertness; bluntness; candidness; directness; *ever-truthful;* fairness; frankness; *glasnost* [Rus.]; honesty; ingenuousness; jantiness; *keen ~; laying it out;* manifestation; non-concealment; overtness; plainness; *quite frank;* realness; sincerity; truth; transparency; understanding; verity; without secrecy; *x-parent; yet unhidden;* zero secrecy;

**operate** *(v.)*: activate; *busy;* control; do; drive; execute; function; govern; handle; *instruct;* jockey; keep (under control); lead; maneuver; manipulate; *nobble;* open up; *outperform;* perform; *quicken;* run; reactivate; start; supervise; take the oversight of; use; *vivify;* work; wreak; wield; *XO;* yeme; *zip;*

**operation** *(n.)*: *amputation;* brain ~; cutting open; *doctoring;* exploratory surgery; *fixing up; gastrotomy; hospitalization;* incision; *jejunostomy; the* knife; *laser surgery;* microsurgery; *neurosurgery;* op [slang]; outpatient surgery; procedure; *quick procedure;* reconstructive surgery; surgery; treatment; transplant; *under the knife;* vivisect; work; *xyster; yeme;* zooplasty;

**opinion** *(n.)*: angle; assessment; attitude; bias; belief; conviction; conclusion; decision; estimation; feeling; fancy; gauging; hunch; heart; idea; intuition; input; judgment; *knowledgeable assessment;* leaning; mind; notion; outlook; perspective; point of view; *quot homines tot sententiae* [L.]; reckoning; slight; slant; take; thoughts; *ule;* view(point); vantage (point); vote; vibe; whim; *xenodiagnosis; yaw; yankering; zeal;*

**opponent** *(n.)*: adversary; antagonist; bad guy; contender; combatant; disputant; enemy; foe; *garrison; hostile;* instigator; jangler; kemper; *legion; litigant;* match; nemesis; opposer; *the* opposition; *player;* quarreler; rival; striver; *traitor; troops;* underminer; *villain;* vier; *warling; xenic; yuon* [arch.]; *zeke [off.];*

**opportunity** *(n.)*: advantageous condition; break; chance; definite chance; excuse; fighting chance; feasibility; gamble; good chance; hope; *imaginable;* just a chance; kairos; likelihood; liberty; moment; *non-guaranteed;* occasion; prospect; potential; qualified chance; real chance; special ~; time; *uncertainty; viability;* window; *xtry. chance; yet possible; zet [dial.];*

**oppose** *(v.)*: argue; buck; contend with; contradict; challenge; disagree with; deny; dispute; expostulate; fight; gainsay; hinder; inhibit; jangle; kick at; lock horns [slang]; make fur fly; negate; object to; pick fight; quarrel; resist; stand against; take issue with; undo; undermine; vie; withstand; *x-purposes; yell; zap;*

**opposite** *(adj.)*: adverse; antithestical; back to back; converse; contradistinct(ive); contradictory; contrary; disparate; diametric(al); *exact ~;* facing; *gainsaying; hostile;* inverse; just the ~; *kicking; loathing;* most ~; *negative;* obverse; opposing; oppositional; polar; *quite different;* reverse; standing opposed; total ~; unsimilar; vis-à-vis; *withstanding; xtry. different; yaw;* zero agreement;

**opposition** *(n.)*: antipathy; bucking; competition; contrariness; contrariety; contention; disagreement; disputation; dissent; defiance; exception; enmity; fight; gainsaying; hostility; incongruity; jangling; kicking; loathing; malice; negativism; non-cooperation; objection; opposing; oppositeness; polarity; protestation; querulousness; resistance; rivalry; strife; *thumbs down;* unfriendliness; variance; withstanding; *x-fire;* yawping; *zeallessness;* [*Ant.* one-mindedness]

**oppress** *(v.)*: afflict; burden; control; conquer; domineer; enslave; force; govern; haunt; intimidate; *jurisdiction;* keep down; lord over; maltreat; master; *not reasonable;* overburden; overdrive; persecute; predominate; quell; repress; rule; subject; subdue; subjugate; tyrannize; use; vanquish; weigh; *xuld [arch.];* yoke; *zap;*

**oppression** *(n.)*: affliction; burden; control; domination; enslavement; forced submission; governance; hard bondage; intimidation; *jurisdiction;* keeping down; lording over; mastering; *not reasonable;* overburdening; predomination; persecution; quelling; repression; rule; subjection; subduing; subjugation; tyranny; *use;* vanquishment; weight of ~; *x-out;* yoke; *zap;*

**oppressive** *(adj.)*: authoritarian; brutal; cruel; domineering; exploitive; *evil;* fascistic; *gruff;* harsh; iron-fisted; *jaded;* kindless; loveless; monocratic; *nefarious;* overbearing; persecuting; *quite brutal;* repressive; suppressive; tyrannical; unreasonable; *violent; way too strict;* xenarchic; yieldless; *za-zum* [Rus.];

**optimistic** *(adj.)*: aspiring; bullish; bright; cheery; confident; desirous; expectant; full of hope; glass-is-half-full; hoping; idealistic; *just anticipating;* keen; *longing; mindful;* non-despairing; over-hopeful; positive; quixotic; rosy; sanguine; trusting; upbeat; visionary; wishful; *xel [arch.];* yearnful; zealous;

**optimum** *(adj.)*: *advantageous;* best; choicest; *delightfulest;* elite; finest; greatest; high-efficiency; incomparable; *just right;* keenest; *loftiest;* most desirable; nonpareil; optimal; premium; *quality; right;* superior; topmost; unexcelled; very best; winningest; xtry.; *yondmost;* zenithal;

**option** *(n.)*: alternative; *best ~;* choice; decision; determination; election; first ~; favorite; final judgment; *gauging; heart;* inclination; judgment; *knowledge; like; liberty; mind;* nomination; opportunity; pick; preference; pleasure; possibility; *quibble;* ruling; selection; take; top ~; *ultimatum;* verdict; vote; will; wish; *x; yes; zeal;* [*Ant.* obligation]

**optional** *(adj.)*: available; by choice; *choice;* discretionary; elective; freewill; *given the choice; heart; if one wants to; just want to; keenness; liking; minded;* non-compulsory; offered; possible; quite ~; refusable; selectable; *true desire;* unforced; voluntary; volitional; *willing; xel [arch.];* yare; *zero force;* [*Ant.* obligatory]

**oration** *(n.)*: address; bespeaking; communication; discourse; elocution; *filibuster; glossa;* homily; *inaugural address;* indiction; *jabbering; kerygma;* lecture; message; monologue; *narration;* oral address; proclamation; public speaking; pontification; *quotation;* recitation; speech; sermon; talk; utterance; vocalization; word(s); *xenophonia; yawner [off.]; zinger [slang];*

**orator** *(n.)*: addresser; *bombast;* communicator; declaimer; demagogue; expresser; fluent speaker; gabber; homilist; informer; jawsmith; keynote speaker; lecturer; *messenger; narrator;* oratress [fem.]; pontificator; proclaimer; *quoter;* remarker; speaker; speech-maker; talker; utterer; vocalizer; worder; *xenophonia;* yakker; *zeug [G.];*

**oratory** *(n.)*: ability; argumentation; bombast; communication skills; debate; eloquence; fluency; grandiloquence; holding forth; *interpretation; justification; knack;* language skills; mastery in speaking; magniloquence; *natural ability;* oral skills; orotundity; public speaking; persuasiveness; *quality;* rhetoric; speaking; speech-making; *talent; talking;* unfailing logic; verbal skills; wordcraft; *xenagogy; yeme; zealous words;*

**orchard** *(n.)*: arbor; arbustum; *apple ~;* basket; coppice; durian ~; *espalier;* firth; fruit farm; grove; hortyard; industrial ~; *Japanese garden; kitchen-garden; luxuriance;* motte; nemoral; *orangery;* plantation; queach; *rows of trees;* spinney; toft; umbrage; vineyard; wood(let); xystus; *yard;* zereba;

**ordain** *(v. appoint)*: anoint; appoint; bid; charge; consecrate; determine; decree; establish; *fix;* give authority; *hallow;* install; invest; *juration; keep;* lay hands on; mandate; name; order; ordinate; proclaim; place; *qualified; reinstate;* set up; set apart; separate; sanctify; tell; *unction;* vest; *word; xenagogy;* yark; zakon [Rus.];
**ordain** *(v. command)*: adjudge; bid; command; decree; enjoin; *force;* give command; *have;* instruct; *juration; kaleusmatic; lead;* mandate; necessitate; order; *pronounce; quo minus [L.];* require; stipulate; tell; *utter; voice; word; XO mandate;* yark; zakon [Rus.];
**ordeal** *(n.)*: aggravation; bind; complication; crucible; difficulty; experience; fix; grief; hassle; hardship; impasse; jam; kink; *load;* mess; nightmare; obstacle; problem; predicament; pickle; quandary; roadblock; situation; snag; spot; tight-spot; trouble; trial; unrest; urgent situation; vexation; woe; x-question; *yowler;* zinger;
**order** *(n. arrangement)*: array; arrangement; *bestowal;* collocation; consecutiveness; disposition; *echelon;* formation; grouping; harmoniousness; indexing; *judgment; kithe [Scot.];* lineup; method; matrix; number; organization; procession; queue; regularity; sorting; sequence; succession; system; *tier;* uniformity; *valuation;* way; *xfer; yield; zoning;*
**order** *(n. command)*: adjuration; behest; boss; command(ment); directive; demand; diktat; decree; edict; fiat; *governance; halidom;* instruction; injunction; juration; *keleusmatic;* law; mandate; *mittimus; necessitate;* official instruction; precept; pronouncement; *quo minus [L.];* requirement; statute; *tyranny;* utterance; ultimatum; unction; *voice;* word; *xenagogy; yelling;* zakon [Rus.];
**order** *(v. command)*: adjure; bid; command; charge; direct; demand; decree; enjoin; force; *govern; have;* instruct; *juration; kaleusmatic;* lay out; mandate; necessitate; ordain; prescribe; pronounce; *quo minus [L.];* require; say; *stipulate;* tell; *utter; voice;* word; xenagogy; yark; yell; zakon [Rus.];
**order** *(v. put in sequence)*: arrange; assort; *bestow;* categorize; distribute; *evaluate;* file; grade; hierarchize; index; *judge; kit;* list; methodize; make ~ed; neaten; organize; peg; place; *qualify;* rank; rate; sort; sequence; systemize; tabulate; unitize; valuate; *work; xfer; yield; zonate;*
**orderly** *(adj.)*: arranged; businesslike; continuous; disciplined; exacting; formulaic; *grid pattern; habitual;* in order; *just so; keen;* logical; methodical; neat; ordered; organized; painstaking; precise; *quasi-logical;* regimented; systematic; tidy; uniform; *vigilant;* well-ordered; *xtr. organized;* yare; zeroing in; [Ant. out-of-control]
**ordinance** *(n. church observance)*: affair; Biblical ~; ceremony; duty; exercise; formality; *gathering;* holy rite; institution; *jubilation;* keeping; *liturgy;* ministration; *nearness to God;* observance; performance; practice; *qualified; rite; ritual;* service; *sacrament; thing;* use; *virtue; word;* Xn. ~; *yielded to God; zet [dial.];*
**ordinary** *(adj.)*: average; basic; common; customary; dominant; everyday; familiar; general; habitual; *inelaborate;* jejune; *known; lackluster;* lowborn; mundane; normal; *original;* plain; quotidian; regular; routine; run-of-the-mill; standard; typical; usual; vanilla; *wonted; x-type; yawnish;* zestless; [Ant. odd]
**organization** *(n. arrangement)*: arrangement; blueprint; collocation; disposition; *establishment;* formation; grouping; hierarchy; indexing; *judgment; kithe [Scot.];* layout; lineup; method; matrix; number; neatness; order; procession; queue; regularity; sequence; succession; system; setup; structure; tidiness; *uniformity; valuation;* way it is organized; *x-structure; yield; zoning;*
**organization** *(n. association)*: agency; affiliation; association; alliance; business; body; brotherhood; club; company; coalition; confederacy; confederation; *department;* establishment; federation; group; guild; *horizontal union;* incorporation; joint coalition; *kongsi [Chin.];* league; *mutual interest group;* nexus; outfit; order; partnership; quinquevirate; registered guild; society; syndicate; trade union; union; *vertical union; workers' union; x-class;* yeald; zollverein;

**organize** *(v.)*: arrange; band together; build; coordinate; classify; categorize; catalog; distribute; evaluate; file; group; grade; handle; index; join forces; *kit;* list; methodize; manage; *notch;* order; place; put in order; *qualify;* re~; retrench; structure; sort; systemize; tabulate; unitize; valuate; work out; *xfer; yield; zonate;*

**origin** *(n.)*: advent; beginning; birth; creation; dawn; debut; extraction; entry; establishment; founding; genesis; heritage; inception; jump off; kickoff; lineage; *launching;* making; naissance; origination; production; *quickening;* rising; start; *take-off;* unveiling; ushering in; *verge;* welcoming; xenogenesis; youth; zygogenesis; [*Ant.* outcome]

**original** *(adj.)*: absolute first; beginning; commencing; debuting; earliest; first; *genesis;* homespun; *historical;* initial; *jump-off; kickoff; leading;* maiden; number one; oldest; pioneer; prototype; *quickened; rising;* starting; self-generated; *take-off;* unprecedented; underived; unretouched; virgin; *welcoming; xenogenesis; young; zygogenesis;*

**ornament** *(n.)*: adornment; beautification; cosmetic addition; decoration; embellishment; fandangle; fancy; filigreed; garnish; garniture; *highlight; incidental;* jewel(ry); *kit;* lovely embellishment; *magnificent; nicety;* ornamentation; pretty thing; *quaintry; ruby;* sequin; trim; tawdry; *upscale;* very fancy ~; *well-trimmed;* xtl. ~; *yclad [arch.];* zequine;

**ornament** *(v.)*: adorn; bedeck; *clothe;* decorate; embellish; fancify; garnish; habilitate; *inwrought;* jazz up; jewel; kit; *let be adorned;* make prettier; *nicer; outfit;* prettify; *quaintise* [arch.]; render lovely; spruce; trim; *use ornaments;* vest; *wear; xtry.; yclad [arch.]; zizz;*

**ornamental** *(adj.)*: adorning; bejeweled; beautifying; cosmetic; decorative; embellishing; fancy; garnishing; highlighting; improving; jeweled; *keenly ornamented;* luxurient; *much-decorated; nice;* ornamented; ornate; prettifying; *quaint;* ritzy; superficial; trimming; *upscale; very fancy; well-ornamented; xtry.; yet unsurpassed; zizzy;*

**ornate** *(adj.)*: attractive; adorned; beautiful; bedeckt; chichi; decorative; elaborate; extravagant; fancy; florid; flamboyant; gaudy; garish; high-wrought; intricate; jeweled; *keenly ornamented;* lavish; luxuriant; much-decorated; *nobby;* ornamented; overdone; pretty; plateresque; *quite ~;* ritzy; rococo; swanky; sumptuous; trimmed; upscale; Victorian; well-ornamented; *xtry.; yet unsurpassed;* zizzy; [*Ant.* ordinary]

**orphan** *(n.)*: abandoned child; *boy; bereft;* child; destitute child; *enfant [F.];* foundling; fatherless child; *girl;* home child; *individual; junior;* kid; little one; *lad; lass;* motherless child; *non-adopted;* orphaned one; parentless child; *quinquennarian; reject;* stray; tot; urchin; *vandal;* waif; warden; *xbred;* youth; *zero family;*

**orthodox** *(adj.)*: accurate; biblical; correct; doctrinally correct; *exact;* faithful; grounded; *honest; inerrant;* justifiable; known; legitimate; *most sound;* non-heretical; orthodoxical; proper; questionless; right; sound; true; unerring; valid; well-grounded; *x-parent; yes;* zero-error; [*Ant.* off-key]

**orthodoxy** *(n.)*: accuracy; biblical doctrine; correctness; doctrinal correctness; *exactness;* faithful teaching; groundedness; honest truth; inerrant truth; just the truth; keeping with the Bible; legitimacy; *most sound;* non-heresy; orthodox teaching; proper doctrine; *questionless;* right doctrine; rectitude; revealed truth; sound doctrine; truth; unerring doctrine; verity; *well-grounded; xtry. faithfulness; yet uncompromised;* zero error;

**ostracism** *(n.)*: alienation; blackballing; banishment; cold shoulder; disfellowship; exclusion; excommunication; *fugitation;* giving cold shoulder; having nothing to do with; isolation; *jinking;* keeping out; *loathing;* moving away from; non-acceptance; ostracizing; pushing away; proscription; quite [Sp.]; rejection; snubbing; shunning; turning away; unkindness; *vaulting;* withdrawal; *xenelasy; yarding* [arch.]; *zero fellowship;*

**ostracize** *(v.)*: avoid; alienate; blackball; banish; coldshoulder; disdain; debar; exclude; excommunicate; forbear; give cold shoulder; have nothing to do with; ignore; *jink;* keep out; leave out; make feel bad; not accept; *omit;* push away; proscribe; quit on; reject; snub; shun; spurn; turn away from; *unkind;* view with disdain; *walking papers; xenize; yard* [arch.]; *zero out;*

**outbreak** *(n.)*: alarming growth; boutade; breaking out; contagion; development; explosion; eruption; epidemic; flare-up; growth; *high;* irruption; *jump;* kickoff; large eruption; *mushrooming;* non-contained growth; outburst; pandemic growth; quick-spreading growth; rash; surge; *spread; threat;* upsurge; very widespread growth; wide-spread growth; *wildfire; xtry.; yedder; zoom;* [*Ant.* outcome]

**outburst** *(n.)*: *activity;* burst; breaking (forth); boutade; coursing; dehiscence; eruption; explosion; flow; gush; hurling; issue; jet; *ka-pow;* letting go; *movement; naid;* outbreak; pouring; *quickening;* rush; surge; spate; sudden ~; torrent; upsurge; vomiting; wave; *xfer; yead;* zipping;

**outcast** *(n.)*: alienated person; banished person; castaway; deportee; exile; expatriate; foreigner; forsaken one; *God-forsaken; heaved out; impulse; jettison; kithless;* leper; man without a country; *non-resident;* outsider; pariah; *quant;* reject; refugee; stranger; sent away one; *thrown out; unbefriended;* vagrant; *wale; xenelasy; ybanysshed* [arch.]*; zing;*

**outcome** *(n.)*: aftermath; byproduct; conclusion; consequence; derivative; effect; end result; finish; fate; fruit; *get;* harvest; impact; *just desserts; known outcome;* lattermath; *matter; necessarily;* outgrowth; offshoot; product; quantum effect; result; ramification; significance; sequent; termination; upshot; *validity;* work; wake; *xenagogy;* yield; *zeug [G.];*

**outdo** *(v.)*: *annihilate;* best; cap; do better; eclipse; exceed; *further;* go one better; *higher;* improve upon; *just pass; kill;* lick; master; *no contest;* one-up; outperform; outstrip; overshadow; pass by; *quash;* reach a higher level; rout; show up; trump; unseat; *vanquish;* win; worst; *x-cend; yet better;* zip past;

**outer** *(adj.)*: *apparent;* beyond; circumambient; displayed; *deportment;* external; exterior; extrinsic; facial; *general appearance;* hull; inlay; *just outside; known; looks; manifest;* non-internal; outward; *perceptible; quasi-aesthetic;* recognizable; superficial; topical; *unincorporated;* visible; without; x.; *yare; zenithal;*

**outflow** *(n.)*: afflux; blast; current; course; confluence; discharge; depletion; efflux; flux; flow; gush; hemorrhage; issue; jet(stream); *katabatic; leak;* movement; naid; outgo; outpouring; profluence; pouring; quell; rush; stream; tide; torrent; undercurrent; venting; vomiting; wash; *xfer;* yern; *zwoosh;*

**outlast** *(v.)*: *alive; beat;* continue; *dwell;* endure; follow; go on; hold out; *inhabit;* journey through; keep living; last longer; make it; not die; outlive; persevere through; *quality;* remain longer; survive; tarry longer; uphold; *voyage through;* weather; winter; *xenize; yerde [arch.];* zero harm;

**outlaw** *(n.)*: *assailant;* bad guy; bandit; criminal; deviant; evildoer; felon; gangster; highwayman; infractor; jailbird; knuck; lawbreaker; malefactor; no-good; offender; perpetrator; purloiner; *quad;* robber; scoundrel; thief; *underboss;* villain; wrongdoer; *xgressor;* yegg; *zhlub;* [*Ant.* officer]

**outlaw** *(v.)*: abolish; ban; cancel; censure; disallow; end; eliminate; forbid; get rid of; *halt;* illegalize; *jailbird;* kill; legally proscribe; make an end of; nix; *obstruct;* prohibit; proscribe; restrict; stop; suppress; terminate; undo; veto; *wipe out;* x-out; *yank;* zero out; [*Ant.* okay]

**outline** *(n.)*: arrangement; appearance; border; contour; delineation; encapsulation; edge; framework; form; figure; galbe; hem; itemization; J-curve; *kind;* limning; lineation; lineament; layout; marking out; nutshell; overview; outer edge; periphery; profile; *quat;* rough draft; relief; sketch; summary; syllabus; shape; *silhouette;* skeleton; thumbnail sketch; teaching ~; tracing; *useful ~; verge; winding; xy-curve; yaw; zag;*

**outline** *(v.)*: arrange; border; chart; contour; draw around; delineate; *encapsulate;* edge; frame; form; give main points; hem; itemize; J-curve; *kind;* limn; lineate; line out; lay out; make a rough draft; mark out; *nonlinear;* overview; plan through; *quat;* run through; relief; sketch; summarize; trace out; *use; verge;* write a summary; *xy-curve; yaw; zag;*

**outlive** *(v.)*: abide; *beat;* continue; *duration;* endure; follow; go on; hold on; *inhabit;* journey through; keep living; live longer; make it; not die; outride; outlast; overlive; perdure; *quantity;* remain alive; survive; supervive; tarry longer; uphold; *voyage through;* weather; *xenize; yerde [arch.];* zip past;

**outlook** *(n.)*: attitude; angle; bearing; belief; conception; cast; disposition; estimation; frame of mind; feeling; *ground;* heart; impression; idea; judgment; *ken;* leaning; mindset; mentality; notion; opinion; position; perspective; perception; point of view; *quot homines tot sententiae* [L.]; reckoning; sentiment; take; thinking; *ule;* view(point); way of thinking; *xenodiagnosis;* yaw; *zeal;*

**outmaneuver** *(v.)*: *action;* beat; cap; do better; excel; foil; gain advantage; *hors de combat [F.];* improve upon; *just pass; knock down;* lick; maneuver one in a corner; *no contest;* outdo; outperform; outrival; outvie; outflank; outgeneral; pass by; *quash;* rise above; surpass; transcend; top; unseat; *vanquish;* win; worst; *x-cend; yet better;* zip past;

**outnumber** *(v.)*: *amount;* beat; cap; dwarf; exceed; *further;* go beyond; have more; *higher; improve upon; just pass; kill;* lick; *more;* number more; outsize; outgun; pass by; *quantity;* rise above; surpass; top; *unseat; very much;* win; worst; *x-cend; yet superior;* zip past;

**outrage** *(n.)*: anger; abomination; *boiling point;* choler; crime; displeasure; defilement; enragement; fury; gall; hotness; infuriation; indignity; injustice; *jealous rage; kindling;* lividness; madness; malfeasance; *nettling; odiousness;* perturbation; quick-temperament; rage; shock; temper; trespass; *upset;* venting; violation; wrath; *xerothermia; yelling; zealousy* [arch.];

**outrage** *(v.)*: anger; boil; cross; disgust; enrage; fume; gall; *hot;* infuriate; incense; *jangle;* kindle; lose one's temper; madden; *nettle;* offend; perturb; *quick-tempered;* rile; steam; tick off; upset; vex; *wrath; xerothermic;* yell; *zealousy [arch.];*

**outsmart** *(v.)*: *annihilate;* beat; cap; defeat; ensnare; excel; foil; go beyond; *hoodwink;* insnare; jape; *knavery;* lick; master; *no contest;* outwit; outfox; put one over; *quiblin* [arch.]; rook; surpass; trick; unseat; verneuk; win; worst; *x-cend; yentz; zing;*

**outstanding** *(adj.)*: amazing; admirable; brilliant; commendable; chief; distinguished; exceptional; *finest;* great; highest; impressive; jim-dandy; keen; lofty; magnificent; main; noteworthy; overshadowing; prominent; pre-eminent; *quantum* [L.]; remarkable; superb; tremendous; top-flight; unequalled; very good; virtuous; wonderful; xtry.; *yichus;* zizzy; [Ant. ordinary]

**outward** *(adj.)*: aesthetic; apparent; beyond; circumambient; *dermal;* external; exterior; extrinsic; face; facial; *general appearance; hull;* integumental; *just outside; known; looks; manifest;* non-internal; observable; outside; outer; outlying; physical; *perceptible; quasi-aesthetic;* recognizable; surface; superficial; topical; *unincorporated;* visible; without; x.; *yare; zero internality;*

**outwit** *(v.)*: *annihilate;* beat; best; cap; defeat; excel; foil; go beyond; hornswaggle; improve upon; *just pass by; knock down;* lick; master; *no contest;* outfox; outsmart; outrival; outvie; outmaneuver; pass by; *quash;* rise above; surpass; triumph over; unseat; *vanquish;* win; worst; *x-cend;* yentz; zip past;

**oven** *(n.)*: athanor; burner; brick ~; cooker; convection ~; Dutch ~; electric ~; furnace; grate; heater; incinerator; *jet;* kiln; kettle-furnace; *limekiln;* muffle; microwave; *nut coal;* oast; potbelly stove; *quartz heater;* range; stove; toaster ~; tandoor; uniform-heat ~; *vulcan;* wood stove; wind-furnace; *xylopyrography; yellow-hot; zap;*

**over** *(prep.)*: above; atop; beyond; *climb;* directly above; elevated above; fixed (-far) above; gone above; high(er); *increased;* just above; *key;* lying on; *mounting;* north of; overhead; on (top of); *past;* quite higher; resting on; superincumbent; superior; *supra-;* top; *towering;* upper; *vertical;* way above; *xtr. high;* yonder; zenithal;

**overall** *(adj.)*: all-inclusive; broad; complete; comprehensive; *done;* entire; exhaustive; full; general; high; inclusive; *jim-bang; kept;* large-scale; main; non-limited; on-the-whole; panoramic; predominant; *qualified; reaching;* sweeping; synoptic; total; universal; *veritable;* whole; xtry.; yare; *zonal;*

**overbearing** *(adj.)*: authoritarian; bossy; controlling; domineering; *evil-hearted;* fascistic; grave; harsh; high-handed; Hitleresque; imposing; imperious; iron-fisted; *jaded;* kindless; loveless; magisterial; *nasty;* overweening; oppressive; pompous; *quede [arch.];* repressive; strict; strong; tyrannical; unreasonable; undemocratic; unassailable; *virulent; way too strict; xenophobic;* yieldless; *za-zum* [Rus.];

**overcast** *(adj.)*: acherontic; bleak; cloudy; dreary; enclouded; foggy; gloomy; gray; hazy; inclouded; joyless; *KH instability;* lowery; misty; nebulous; overshadowed; overclouded; puffy; *qually* [arch.]; *rain clouds;* sunless; turbid; umbered; vaporous; wispy; *xenon cloud; yellow cloud;* zero-zero;

**overcome** *(v.)*: *annihilate;* beat; conquer; defeat; expugn; foil; gain victory; *hammer; invincible; junk [slang];* knock out; lick; master; *neutralize;* overtake; overpower; prevail; quench; rise above; rout; subdue; squash; surmount; triumph (over); transcend; unseat; vanquish; win; worst; whoop; *x-ing; yank down;* zap;

**overconfident** *(adj.)*: arrogant; big-headed; cocky; cocksure; disdainful; egotistical; flatulent; gloating; heedless; haughty; inflated; *jackanapes; know-it-all;* lifted up; *magnificent;* narcissistic; overproud (-bold; -sure); proud; quick-to-boast; reassured; reckless; swelled; smug; temerarious; unabashed; unwary; vain; wrapped up in oneself; *x-proud; yelping; zero humility;*

**overextend** *(v.)*: add on too much; broaden too quickly; *continue;* draw out; extend too far; *further;* go beyond; *hang over;* increase beyond; jut; *keep going;* lengthen too much; make too long; *non-collapsed;* overstretch (-draw; -distend; -strain); protrude too far; *quantity;* reach beyond; stick out too far; strain; thrust out beyond; *up; vary;* wax too long; *XL; yet higher; zoom.*

**overhang** *(n.)*: *aslope;* brim; cornice; cliff; drop; edge; extension; eave; fall; flange; *glacial ridge;* hogh; impendence; jardang; *khud* [Ind.]; ledge; lap; mountainside; nip; outcrop; projection; *quoif;* ridge; spur; *top; upper ridge;* verge; *wax longer; XL;* yardang; *zenith;*

**overhang** *(v.)*: *aslope;* beetle; continue; draw out; drip; extend; flange; go beyond; hang over; increase; imbricate; impend; jut (out); *keep going;* lengthen; make longer; *non-collapsed;* obtrude; outstretch; project; protrude; *quantity;* reach forth; stick out; shoot; *stretch;* thrust out; *upgrade;* vary; wax longer; *XL; yield; zoom.*

**overhaul** *(v.)*: adjust; *better;* convert; develop; doctor; enhance; fix; go over; *help;* innovate; improve; *just better; key; lift; level;* modify; make over; new-make; *outdo; patch up; qualify;* redo; revamp; renovate; redesign; refurbish; switch; *sweeping changes;* transform; upgrade; vamp; *work; xenomorph; yaw; zigzag;*

**overlook** *(v.)*: absolve; blink at; close one's eyes to; dismiss; disregard; excuse; forgive; forget; fail to see; go over; hear nothing; ignore; *justify;* keep no account; let pass; miss; neglect; not hold accountable; omit; pardon; pass over; pay no mind; put away; *quick-to-forget;* remember not; remit; skip; shrug off; sleight; take no thought; *unvengefulness;* void; wink at; *x out;* yield to; *zero remembrance;* [Ant. observe]

**oversee** *(v.)*: administer; boss (around); be a steward of;control; direct; *execute; force;* govern; head; influence; judge; keep under control; lead; manage; *nobble;* officiate; *oppress;* procrate; *quell;* run; superintend; take the helm; *use; vanquish;* watch over; *XO;* yeme; *zayim;*

**overseer** *(n.)*: administrator; boss; chief; chairman; director; dean; executive; foreman; governor; head; intendant; jefe; keeper; leader; lord; manager; *night manager;* overman; procurator; principal; *quartermaster;* reeve; steward; supervisor; superintendent; trustee; undershepherd; vizer; viceroy; warden; XO; yardboss; zayim;

**overshadow** *(v.)*: adumbrate; bypass; block; beat; cap; cover; do better; eclipse; exceed; excel; *further;* go beyond; *higher;* improve upon; *just pass;* keep hidden; lick; mask; nubilate; obscure; outdo; outclass; pass by; *quash;* rise above; shroud; surpass; transcend; top; umbrate; veil; win; *x-cend; yet better; zip by;*

**oversight** *(n. omission)*: accident; blunder; culpa; delinquency; error; failure; going over; heedlessness; inattention; inobservance; ignoring; jumping over; *kink;* laches; lapse; missing; mistake; neglect; omission; overlooking; passing over; *quick to pass over;* remissness; slip-up; thoughtlessness; unmindfulness; *voidance;* want; *xtry. irregard; yemeles* [arch.]; *zero responsibility;*

**oversight** *(n. supervision)*: administration; bossing; control; dominion; empowering; faculty; government; headship; influence; jurisdiction; kingship; lordship; mastery; management; name; overseeing; power; *quo warranto* [L.]; responsibility; rule(rship); supervision; superintendence; *throne;* umpirage; *virtue;* warrant; weight; *XO;* yard; *zonal control;*

**overstep** *(v.)*: abuse; bypass; contravene; cross the line; disregard; exceed; *further;* go too far; *higher;* invade; *just too much; kill;* live dangerously; *misbehave; nerve;* outstep; pass; presume upon; *quite enough; rude;* step over the line; take liberties; transgress; *too far;* usurp; violate; *way out of line; x-cend; yerk; zoomed past;*

**overthrow** *(n.)*: annexation; bringing down; coup d'état; defeat; downfall; discomfiture; expugnation; forcing out; *getting rid of;* have the victory; insurgence; *jolting;* knock out; *lèse majesté* [F.]; mutiny; *noncompliance;* overpowering overturn; *push; questioning;* revolution; subversion; takeover; toppling; upheaval; violence; *won; x-ing; yanking down; zapping;*

**overthrow** *(v.)*: annihilate; bring down; conquer; defeat; depose; expugn; force out; *get rid of;* hammer; invade; *junk [slang];* knock out; lick; master; *neutralize;* oust; prevail; quash; remove; subvert; seize power from; topple; take over; unseat; vanquish; win over; *x-ing; yank down;* zap;

**overturn** *(v.)*: amend; bring to naught; capsize; disturb; dump over; *excite;* fall; flip over; go over; *have spill; improve; jolt;* knock over; *loop around;* move upside-down; *non-righted;* overset; *pivot; querl;* roll over; spin around; turn over; tip over; tump; upset; *violence; wrong side-up; xuld [arch.]; yerk; zet [dial.];*

**overview** *(n.)*: abridgement; brief; breviat; conspectus; condensation; *draft;* encapsulation; *framework;* general idea; gist; *heart;* idea; *jist; kernel; lifeblood; makeup;* newsbrief; outline; precis; *quintessence; recap;* summary; synopsis; thumbnail; *underneath;* vignette; *warp and woof; xenenthesis; yetzer* [Heb.]; *zoe [Gr.];*

**overwhelm** *(v.)*: astonish; awe; blow away; bog down; confound; drown; engulf; flood; *gape;* hold one's breath; inundate; *jolt;* knock over; load down; make to drown; nonplus; overload; overcome; overpower; perplex; *quite amazed;* render speechless; swamp; swallow up; take over; *under a load; very taxed;* whelm; weigh down; *xtry. pressure; yerk; zing;*

**own** *(v.)*: apprehend; *bear;* claim; control; *dwell in; embrace;* fully ~; get; gain; grip; have; hold; *inherit; just have;* keep; lay hold of; *monopolize; maintain; nab;* obtain; possess; *quantify;* retain; secure; take (possession of); use; *vaunt;* wield; win; *xfer; yain* [arch.]; zip out;

**owner** *(n.)*: apprehender; bearer; controller; deed-holder; *embracer;* full-owner; gainer; holder; inheriter; *joint- ~;* keeper; layer hold of; *monopolize; nabber;* obtainer; possessor; *qualifier;* ruler; securer; titleholder; *user; valid deed-holder;* wielder; winner; *xfer; yain [arch.]; zet [dial.];*

**ownership** *(n.)*: authority; belonging; control; *dhan; effects;* full ~; *got;* holding; *inheritance; jamindris* [Ind.]; joint- ~; keeping; legal ~; *monopoly; mine; non-disputed ~;* owning; possession; *quantity;* rights; *say;* title; *use; valuable;* winnings; ward; *xfer; yemsel [arch.]; zamindari [Ind.];*

**ox** *(n.)*: apis; aurochs; bullock; bovid; cow [fem.]; *creature;* draft- ~; *ennstal;* fatling; gaur; heifer; *Irish moiled; jument;* kouprey; *livestock;* musk ~; neat; *organism; polled shorthorn; quadruped;* red heifer; steer; sarlac; Tartary ~; urus; vu quang ~; water buffalo; xebu; yak; yoke [pl.]; zebu;

**oxidation** *(n.)*: atrophy; breakdown; corrosion; decomposition; disintegration; erosion; ferrugination; goethite; hydrolysis; iron oxide; *junk; killing;* labelfaction; mordication; *nulification;* oxidization; perjoration; queering; rust; spall; *tarnishing; turning to dust; undoing;* verdigris; weakening; *x-ing;* yellowing; zinc pest;

**oxidize** *(v.)*: atrophy; break down; corrode; disintegrate; erode; ferruginate; get rusty; hydrolyze; *iron oxide; junk; killing; labelfaction;* mordicate; *nulify;* oxidate; perjorate; queer; rust; spall; *tarnish;* turn rusty; *undo; verdigris;* weaken; *x-ing;* yellow; *zinc pest;*

# P

**pace** *(n.)*: amount; beat; clip; celerity; degree; *express;* flow; gait; hop; *impulse;* jog; *knots;* lick; movement; *nimbleness;* output; progress; quickness; rate; rapidity; speed; tempo; *uptempo;* velocity; *walking rate;* xfer rate; *yield; zip;*

**pacifism** *(n.)*: abstinence from war; *bloodless; calm;* dovishness; *ever-peaceful; for peace; gun control;* hatred of violence; idealism; juste-milieu; *keeping peace; love for peace;* makepeace *[arch.];* nonaggression; objection to war; peacefulness; *quiescence; romantic-notioned; Satyagraha; truce-making; uninvolvement;* violence-hating; war-hating; *xenophilia; yamen [Chin.];* zeal for peace; [*Ant.* pugnaciousness]

**pacifist** *(n.)*: anarcho- ~; *bloodless;* conscientious objector; dove; *ever-peaceful; for peace;* gun-hater; hater of violence; idealist; *justifier; keeper of peace;* lover of peace; man of peace; nonbelligerent; objector to war; peace-lover; peacenik; *Quaker; romantic-notioned; Satyagrahi; trucemaker; uninvolved;* violence-hater; war-hater; *xenophilous; yamen [Chin.]; zealot for peace;*

**pacifistic** *(adj.)*: anti-war; *bloodless; calm;* dovish; *ever-peaceful; for peace; gentle;* gun-hating; hating violence; idealistic; *justifying; keeping peace; loving;* makepeace *[arch.];* neutral; nonviolent; objecting to war; peace-loving; pacifist; *quiescent; romantic-notioned; Satyagrahi;* tame; unwarlike; violence-hating; war-hating; *xenophilious; yamen [Chin.];* zealous for peace; [*Ant.* pugnacious]

**pacify** *(v.)*: appease; allay; becalm; calm; conciliate; diffuse; demulce; ease; *fulfill;* gratify; hush; *indulge; justify; knock down;* lull; lenify; mollify; normalize; *overcome;* placate; propitiate; put at ease; quell; reconcile; resolve; satisfy; soothe; tranquilize; unruffle; *vanish;* win favor; x-out; *yield; zeroize;* [*Ant.* perturb]

**pack** *(n.)*: assemblage; bunch; bundle; batch; collection; crowd; drove; *envelope;* force; flock; group; horde; *ingathering;* jam [slang]; kennel; kit; lot; mob; number; oodles; passel; package; quantity; roundup; rally; set; stow; swarm; troop; thrave; *unit; volume;* wheen; *wolfpack; xuld [arch.];* yelm; *zoo;*

**pack** *(v.)*: arrange; bundle; bunch; box; cram; crunch; crowd; deposit; embox; fill; force; get in; *hammer;* infarce [arch.]; jam(-pack); *kibble;* load; *mash; niche;* overfill; overstuff; (pre)package; press; quash; ram; reorganize; repack; stow; store; settle; stuff; squeeze; tamp; *up thrust; volume;* wedge; wrap up; *xuld [arch.];* yelm; *zip;* [*Ant.* put away]

**package** *(n.)*: assemblage; box; bundle; bale; container; carton; drum; *delivery;* envelope; fardel; freight; *gift;* holder; item; *jar;* kirtle; letter; load; mailer; *multi~;* number; *overnight ~;* parcel; pack(et); *quire;* roll; shipping container; *trunk; unit;* value-pack; wrapper; wrapping; *xfer;* yellow mailer; *zonal delivery;*

**package** *(v.)*: arrange; box; bag; carton; deposit; embox; fill; get in; *have ~d;* include [arch.]; jam-pack; *kibble;* load; *mash; niche;* overfill; overstuff; pre- ~; pack; quash; ram; reorganize; repack; stuff; store; tamp; *up thrust; volume;* wrap; *xuld [arch.];* yelm; *zip;*

**pact** *(n.)*: agreement; *bond;* covenant; declaration; entente; formal agreement; guarantee; hypothecation; interpledging; joint-commitment; *kept promise;* league; mutual agreement; nonaggression ~; oath; pledge; promise; *qualified promise;* resolve; signed agreement; settlement; treaty; understanding; vow; word; *x-one's heart;* yafery [arch.]; *zealous agreement;*

**pad** *(n.)*: artist's sketch~; book; composition book; drawing pad; *engagement book;* four-subject notebook; *geometry ~;* history ~; *inventor's ~;* journal; *keep;* legal ~; memo~; note~; one-subject ~; *organizer;* pocket notebook; *pages; quarter-ream;* ring binder; scratch~; sketchbook; tablet; university-ruled ~; *vellum;* writing ~; *xylographica;* yellow ~; *zip-binder;*

528

**pad** *(v.)*: *amplify;* build up; cushion; cover; deposit padding; expand; fill out; guard; *highly protected;* insulate; jam-pack; *keep safe;* line; make safe; *noodles;* overstuff; package; protect; *quilted;* reinforce; stuff; take care of; upbuild; *vallate;* wad; wrap; *x-guard; yeme* [arch.]; *zone;*

**padding** *(n.)*: * *airy;* bubble wrap; cushioning; doublure; extra ~; filler; green styrofoam®; *highly padded;* insulation; *jute;* knee pads; lining; material; *noodles; overstuffed;* packaging; *quilted;* ribbed cardboard; stuffing; soft ~; tissue paper; unica; *Velostat;* wadding; *xillinous;* yarn; zero hardness;

**paddle** *(n.)*: attitude adjuster [slang]; boat oar; blade; canoe ~; *double-banked; eight-oar;* feathered oar; gondolla scull; hand ~; *implement; joeboat oar;* kayak ~; *loom;* macon oar; *navy oar;* oar; pandybat; quadruple scull; rower; scull; timber ~; unfeathered ~; *vane; wash; xebec;* yulow; *zabra oar;*

**pagan** *(adj.)*: *aboriginal;* barbaric; coarse; devilish; *evil;* foul; godless; Gentile; heathen; idolatrous; *jungli; kaf* [arch.]; lost; *mean;* neo~; *orisha-worshipping;* paganistic; *quad;* rude; savage; *tribal;* uncircumcised; uncivilized; unmoralized; ungodly; unevangelized; unchristian; vulgar; *wicked; xenon-worshipping; yantra;* zoolatrous;

**pagan** *(n.)*: animal-worshiper; *adulterer;* Baal-worshiper; chthonian; devil-worshiper; ecclesiolater; fetishist; *god-maker;* heathen; idolater; joss-worshiper; kore; lover of idols; moon-worshiper; neo- ~; orisha-worshiper; polytheist; paynim; *quad; rhabdomancer;* sun-worshiper; *temple-prostitute; unenlightened;* voodooist; worshiper; xoanon-worshiper; *Ymir-follower;* zoolater;

**paganism** *(n.)*: adultery; Baal-worship; covetousness; devil-worship; ethnicism; fetishism; false religion; *god-making;* heathenism; idolatry; joss-worship; *kore;* love of idols; moon-worship; neo- ~; orisha-worship; polytheism; *quad; rhabdomancy;* savageness; *theogony; unenlightenment;* voodoo; whoredom; xoanon-worship; *yantra;* zoolatry;

**paganistic** *(adj.)*: *aboriginal;* barbaric; coarse; devilish; *evil;* foul; *god-making;* heathenistic; heathenish; idolatrous; *jungli; kaf* [arch.]; lost; *mean;* neo-pagan; *orisha-worshipping;* pagan(ish); polytheistic; *quad; rude;* savage; *theogony;* uncivilized; ungodly; vile; *wicked; xoanon-worshipping; yantra;* zoolatrous;

**pageantry** *(n.)*: acclaim; bravura; celebration; display; elaborateness; fanfare; grandeur; hoopla; impressiveness; joyance; *kermis;* light show; magnificence; notoriety; *ostentation;* pomp; *quindene;* ritual; splendor; showiness; ticker-tape parade; *unveiling;* vernissage; *wingding; xtry.; yahoo!; zeal;*

**paid** *(adj.)*: *afforded;* bought; compensated; disbursed; expended; forked over; funded; financed; fulfilled; given; handed over; *indemnified; justified;* kicked in; laid out; made payment; *non-retention;* outlaid; *over~;* pre~; purchased; performed; ~ in full; *quit;* remitted; rendered; remunerated; requited; recompensed; re~; rewarded; satisfied; settled; taken care of; used; *vested;* weighed out; xfered; yielded; *zero-out one's debt;* [*Ant. payable*]

**pail** *(n.)*: aluminum ~; bucket; can; container; debe; *excavator bucket;* fire bucket; grain bucket; hod; ice bucket; *jug;* kit; lard bucket; *load;* milk ~; *nook;* oyster ~; plastic ~; *quinderkyn;* receptacle; scuttle; sand ~; tin ~; *utility ~;* vessel; water bucket; *xfer;* yard ~; *zeug [G.];*

**pain** *(n.)*: ache; agony; burning; biting; crick; cramp; chafing; discomfort; dolor; distress; excruciation; flare; grief; galling; hurt(ing); inflammation; irritation; *jabbing;* killing [slang]; *lumbago;* misery; nociception; *nagging ~; ordeal;* prick; pang; *piercing;* quab; rack; rawness; ranking; soreness; sting; smarting; suffering; twinge; tenderness; throe; throbbing; torment; *unpleasantness; uneasiness;* vexation; writhing; woefulness; *xiphodynia;* yaik [arch.]; zing; [*Ant.* painlessness]

**pain** *(v.)*: ache; *bother;* blast; crush; damage; endamage; fix [slang]; grieve; hurt; inflict ~; jeel; kill; *lift hand against;* makes one grieved; *nip; offend;* pang; *quash;* rack; scath; twinge; trouble; *upset;* victimize; wound; *x.; ydrad [arch.]; zap;*

**painful** *(adj.)*: aching; ailing; afflictive; agonizing; biting; burning; crampy; chafing; cutting; discomforting; dolorous; distressing; excruciating; frightful; grievous; hurting; irritated; inflamed; jabbing; killing [slang]; lancinate; miserable; nociceptive; *oppressive;* panging; piercing; *quivering;* raw; sore; smarting; stinging; sensitive; tender; throbbing; torturous; uncomfortable; vexing; wrenching; writhing; woeful; *xiphodynia; yowling;* zinging; [*Ant.* painless]

**pain-killer** *(n.)*: asperin; anodyne; bupivacaine; cinchocaine; dibucaine; ether; fentanyl; general anesthesia; halothane; ibuprofin; *jaded;* ketamine; laudanum; mefenamic acid; *medicine;* novacaine; naproxen; opiate; painkiller; paragoric; queller; ropivacaine; *sedative;* Tylenol®; ultra-short acting ~; vecuronium; *without feeling;* xylocaine; *yet numb;* zonker;

**painless** *(adj.)*: ache-free; *blunted;* comfortable; *doesn't hurt;* easy; facile; *gentle;* hassle-free; incredibly easy; *jarless; keen;* low-impact; mild; non-hurting; *okay;* pain-free; quite ~; *reasonable;* simple; sting-free; trouble-free; unproblematic; very easy; without pain; *xtry. simple;* yet ~; zero-pain; [*Ant.* painful]

**painstaking** *(adj.)*: assiduous; busy; careful; diligent; exacting; fastidious; *great detail;* hard; industrious; just so; keen; laborious; meticulous; nit-picking; onerous; punctilious; precise; *quiddle;* rigorous; scrupulous; solicitous; sedulous; thorough; tedious; *unhasty;* vigilant; *wholehearted;* xtry.; *yare;* zealous;

**paint** *(n.)*: acrylic ~; *backlight* ~; coat; cover; color(ant); colorwash; distemper; enamel ~; epoxy ~; exterior ~; finger~; glossy-finish ~; hue; house ~; *interior ~; japan;* kirtle; *krems;* latex ~; matte-finish ~; non-lead-based ~; oil(-color); pigment; primer; quick-drying ~; *rust-inhibiting ~;* spray ~; *stain;* tinting colors; tempera; top coat; undercoat; *varnish;* water color; *xanadu ~; yellow ~; zinc oxide ~;*

**paint** *(v.)*: apply; brush; coat; cover; *create;* depaint; daub; enamel; *furbish;* get ~ed; hand- ~; illustrate; *japan; kirtle;* leaded ~; *make;* non-leaded ~; over~; *prime;* portray; quick- ~; roller; render; swipe; smear; slap; spray~; transfer; use brush; underpaint; *varnish;* wipe; *xfer; yield; zinc oxide ~;*

**painter** *(n.)*: artist; brush artist; colorist; depainter; expressionist; futurist; *guy;* house ~; impressionist; *journeyman; kirtle;* limner; muralist; master; *neo-impressionist;* oil ~; portraitist; *quick-drying paint;* realist; Rembrandt; scenographer; *surrealist;* tinter; undercoat; verist; watercolorist; *Xia Gui; yamatoe [Jap.];* zoographer; Zeuxis;

**painting** *(n. art)*: art; brushwork; creation; depiction; *easel-piece;* fresco; grisaille; *handiwork;* illustration; *juvenilla;* kakemomo [Jap.]; landscape ~; mural; masterpiece; night-piece; oil ~; *objet d'art [F.];* portraiture; *quaintry;* relief- ~; secco; scenery- ~; tanka [Tib.]; *using the brush;* verism; work; *x-ray ~; yamatoe [Jap.];* zoography;

**painting** *(n. wall hanging)*: artwork; *brushwork;* canvas; depiction; easel-piece; fresco; grisaille; hanging; illustration; *juvenilla;* kit-cat; kamagraph; landscape; *likeness;* mural; masterpiece; night-piece; original; pastel; piece; portrait; picture; *quaintry;* representation; relief; still life; self-portrait; *thing; unfinished portrait;* vignette; watercolor; wall hanging; work (of art); *x-ray ~; yamatoe [Jap.];* zoograph;

**pair** *(n.)*: acoupling; both; brace; couple(t); case; duo; dyad; doublet; *even match; friends;* gemel; *hitched; harnessed; inseparable ~;* joining; kipple [Scot.]; link; match; marriage; *number; ordered ~;* partners; qualified ~; *reunite;* set; two(some); team; *united;* unit; *value-pack; wed; x-pair;* yoke; *zygo-;*

**pair** *(v.)*: *arrange;* bring together; bind; couple; double; *evenly match;* fix together; group by two; hook up; hitch; harness; *inosculate;* join; *knit;* link; match up; *network; order together;* put together; *quasi-fuse;* relate; *reunite;* stick together; team up; unite; *vise;* wed; *xenograft;* yoke; *zygo-;*

**palace** *(n.)*: *abode;* bastion; castle; court; *drawbridge;* escurial; fortress; *gates; headquarters; hold;* imperial ~; *jong* [Tib.]; konak; living quarters; mansion; *nest;* official residence; *place;* Quirinal; *residence;* royal ~; stronghold; *seraglio* [Turk.]; tower; turret; *ubiety;* vault; watchtower; *Xanadu; Yildiz Kiosk* [Turk.]; zwinger;

**palatable** *(adj.)*: appetizing; *bon!* [F.]; comestible; delicious; enjoyable; flavorful; good; gustable; heavenly; irresistible; *juicy;* keen; luscious; mouth-watering; nice; *outstanding;* pleasing; *quite good;* relishable; savory; tasty; *unbelievably good; very good;* wonderful; XF; yummy; zesty;

**pale** *(adj.)*: ashen; blurred; colorless; dim; drab; dull; etiolated; feeble; faded; faint; fair; grayish; hazy; insipid; *jejune; kalsomine;* light; muted; mealy; nitid; neutral; off-white; pallid; pastel; quite faint; reduced-intensity; sallow; subdued; soft; tallow-faced; uncolored; vague; wan; weak; white; *xanthocyanopic; yellowish; zero intensity;*

**palpable** *(adj.)*: apparent; blatant; clear; discernible; evident; flagrant; glaring; *highly visible; intentional; just plain to see;* kenspeckle; *lucid;* manifest; noticeable; obvious; plain; *quite obvious;* recognizable; seeable; transparent; unmistakable; visible; witnessable; *x-parent;* yeme [arch.]; zenithal;
**palpitate** *(v.)*: agitate; beat irregularly; *cadence;* drum; *excite;* flutter; go bump; heartthrob; *impact;* jutter; *knock;* lam; *move;* nubble; *overagitate;* pound; quiver; race; shudder; tremble; *upset;* vibrate; waver; *xuld [arch.];* yedder; zonk;
**palsy** *(n.)*: atony; becrippling; crippling; debilitation; *enfeebling; feebleness;* gameness; hemiplegy; incapacitation; jake-leg; *keeled over;* lameness; mobility-impaired; non-mobility; *obstructed;* paralysis; quadriplegia; *rendered immobile; spavined; thwarting;* unable; vulnerable; weakness; *x-out;* yedder; zero movement;
**paltry** *(adj.)*: austere; beggarly; chintzy; dinky; derisory; exiguous; feeble; *gnat-sized; hardly;* inadequate; insubstantial; *jejune;* ketty; little; meager; measly; negligible; overly small; petty; puny; pathetic; pitiful; *quantité négligeable* [F.]; runty; reduced; scanty; small; teeny; ungenerous; very small; wee; wretched; XS; *yea big; zero;* [Ant. prodigious]
**pamper** *(v.)*: *attend to;* baby; coddle; cosset; *do everything for; dote over; excessively ~;* fuss over; gratify; humor; indulge; *jump to it; keep; lavish;* mollycoddle; mother; nurse; overprotect; overindulge; pander; *quadle* [arch.]; *rave;* spoil; *take care of;* tend; *undertake; vigorously ~; worry too much; x-care;* yield to; *zip right to it;* [Ant. persecute]
**pamphlet** *(v.)*: advertisement; brochure; booklet; circular; double-fold; *essay;* flier; *gospel tract;* handbill; handout; *informational leaflet; journalism; key thoughts;* leaflet; *message; notations; opus;* paper; prospectus; quadrifoliate; reading matter; sheet; tract; unifoliate; *vignette; writing,* xenagogy; yeme; zeug;
**pan** *(n.)*: *ash~;* baking ~; bakeware; cake pan; cookware; dishpan; electric frying~; frying~; griddle; hotplate; iron skillet; jackshea; kettle; *lool;* milk~; nog; ovenware; pot; quart-pot; roaster; sauce~; skillet; *teapot; urn;* vessel; wok; xeo; yetling; ziti ~;
**pancake** *(n.)*: apple ~; battercake; blintz; blini; *crepe;* dosa; eggette; flapjack; flannel cake; fritter; fraise; griddlecake; hotcake; *injera;* johnnycake; knead-cake; *latke; memiljeon* [Kor.]; *nalesniki;* oatcake; potato ~; pikelet; quince-crepe; *rava dosa* [Ind.]; slapjack; short stack (pl.); silver dollar; *taita;* uttapam; *Viennese crepe;* wholewheat ~; *waffle;* xeo; yetling; zapote-crepe;
**pandemonium** *(n.)*: anarchy; bedlam; chaos; disorder; entanglement; farrago; gastness; havoc; intranquility; jumble; kerfuffle; *lunacy;* mayhem; non-orderliness; *obscurity;* pell-mell; *quandary;* restlessness; stupefaction; turmoil; upheaval; vexation; welter; *xtry. mess; yo-yo;* zoo; [Ant. peace]
**panel** *(n. council)*: advisory; board; council; cabinet; committee; diet; eldership; forum; group; *heads; illuminati;* jury; *kit;* legislative body; meeting; *nominative committee; organization;* presbytery; quinquevirate; ruling body; session; synod; team; tribunal; *union;* venire; vestry; *ward; xenocracy; yain* [arch.]; *zemstvo* [Rus.];
**panel** *(n. wooden pane)*: *acacia pane;* board; cross- ~; door- ~; *elm pane;* fiberglass ~; glass ~; hardboard ~; *ironwood pane; joined;* knobwood; lath; *maple pane; nemoral; one-by-four;* pane; quarter- ~; rectangle; section; timber; underlayment; veneer; wood ~; *xylon; yew pane; zingara pane;*
**panelist** *(n.)*: advisor; board member; council-member; diet member; expert; *elder;* forum participant; *group member; head; individual;* juryman; *kit;* legislative member; member; *nominative committee member;* official (~); panel member; *quinquevirate; ruling body;* session member; tribunal member; *union;* vestry member; *ward;* xenocrat; *yain* [arch.]; *zemstvo* [Rus.];
**pang** *(n.)*: ache; *biting;* cramp; discomfort; *excruciating;* flare; grief; hurt; intense pain; jab; kink; *lumbago;* misery; nip; *osteocope;* pain; prick; quab; rack; spasm; twinge; *unpleasantness;* vellication; wrenching; *xiphodynia; yaik* [arch.]; zing;
**panic** *(n.)*: alarm; *burden;* consternation; despair; *exasperation;* fright; *gloom;* horror; insecurity; jitters; kiaugh [Scot.]; *lily-livered;* mass ~; nervousness; over-anxiety; paranoia; quaking; riot; scare; stress; terror; uneasiness; vexation; worry; *xenophobia;* yellow-belliedness; *zeallessness;* [Ant. peace]

**pant** *(v.)*: aspirate; breathe; blow; *circulate air;* draw air; exhale; *feel out of breath;* gasp; huff; inhale; *judder; keep on;* labor to breathe; *mouth; no breath;* outblow; puff; pech; *quick breathing;* respire; *struggle; tongue hanging out; use oxygen;* ventilate; wheeze; *xuld [arch.];* yawn; zephyr;

**pantry** *(n.)*: ambry; butlery; back kitchen; closet; cupboard; dairy (house); *exedra;* food ~; *gallery; hollow; incavation; jars;* kitchen ~; larder; mess hall ~; niche; *open;* place; *quarter;* room; scullery; spence; *shelf;* tearoom; utility closet; *vicinity;* walk-in; x-section; yard; zeta;

**pants** *(n.)*: *attire;* britches; breeches; *blue jeans; bellbottoms;* chinos; cords; drawers; dungarees; *elephant bottoms;* flannels; *garment;* hose(n); *investment [arch.];* jeans; knee-breeches; knicker(bocker)s; loon ~; lederhosen; *menswear; nylon ~;* overalls; Oxford bags; pantaloons; plus fours; *quaintry [arch.];* rammies [Aus.]; *riding-breeches;* slacks; shorts; sweat~; slop; trousers; trunks; *underpants; vesture; wardrobe;* XL; yelek ; zoot ~;

**papal** *(adj.)*: apostolical; *bishop;* Catholic; *denominational; ecclesiastical;* Franciscan; Guelph; High Church; iconolatrous [derog.]; Jesuit; Knights of Columbus; *liturgical;* Mariolatrous [derog.]; *Nicene; Orthodox;* popish; papist; pontifical; *Quadragesimarian;* Romish; Romist; *sectarian;* transubstantiationist; ultramontane; Vatican; *worshipping;* Xaverian; Yagoua; *Zentrumspartei [G.];*

**paper** *(n.)*: * *article;* brown ~; copy ~; construction ~; drawing ~; etching ~; forel; folio; foolscap; graph ~; hemp ~; interleaf; jute- ~; kraft; leaf; letter ~; letterhead; mimeograph ~; note~; newsprint; onionskin; parchment; quire; quarto; ruled ~; scrap; sheet; school ~; stationery; typing ~; university-ruled ~; vellum; writing ~; xuan ~; yoshino ~ [Jap.]; zincograph ~;

**parable** *(n.)*: allegory; *book;* comparison; disimile; *emblematic;* figure; *general truth;* hyperbole; imagery; *juxtaposition; kingdom ~;* lesson; metaphor; *narrative; oral narrative;* picture; *quarto;* representation; simile; symbolic story; similitude; type; umbratic; vignette; word picture; *xenodocheionology; yarn;* zeugma;

**parachute** *(n.)*: annular ~; *apparatus;* brake chute; brolly [slang]; chute; canopy; drogue chute; *device;* elliptical; *flyer;* glider; harness; high-speed ~; *instrument;* jump chute; knapsack ~; light ~; MC-1B; naval ~; *open;* parapente; *quick-release ~;* round ~; *ripcord;* slider; T-10; umbrella [slang] vented ~; wing-loading ~; *xfer; yank;* zoom bag [slang];

**parade** *(n.)*: array; *band;* cavalcade; convoy; *celebration;* demonstration; display; dress ~; exhibition; fanfare; grand ~; *half-step;* infantry ~; *jatha* [Mos.]; *keeping pace;* line; march; motorcade; military ~; naval convoy; ostentation; pageant; procession; *quickstep;* royal ~; succession; show; ticker-tape ~; triumph [Rom.]; *uniformed men;* vaunting; war ~; *xfer; yomping; Zug [G.];*

**parade** *(v.)*: advance; *bear;* continue; demarch; exult; flaunt; go; hike; *interlope;* journey; *keep pace; lead; lope;* march; nauntle; *outwalk;* prance; *quicken; ramble;* strut; step; stride; tramp; triumph; *underway;* vaunt; walk; xfer; yomp; zigzag;

**paradise** *(n.)*: arcadia; blissful place; Cloud 9; dreamland; Eden; fairyland; Garden of Eden; haven; heaven; idyll; *jasper-walled city; kingdom;* la-la land; *merry old land;* never-never land; Oz; pleasance; Quivira; rose garden; sublimity; Shangri-La; seventh heaven; Trala-la; utopia; Vanhalla; wonderland; Xanadu; yarkandi; *Zion;* [Ant. perdition]

**paradox** *(v.)*: anamoly; antilogy; absurdity; bizarre fact; contradiction (in terms); disconformity; enigma; *farce; gap;* heterodoxy; inconsistency; incongruency; impossibility; *jangling; kicking at;* logical impossibility; *mystery;* nonsensical phrase; oxymoron; puzzle; quandary; *ridiculous;* seeming contradiction; technical impossibility; unconformity; *variation; without sense;* x-purposes; *yet inconsistent*; zero sense;

**paradoxical** *(adj.)*: anomalous; absurd; bewildering; contradictory; discrepant; enigmatic; *funny; glitchy;* having inconsistencies; inconsistent; *jangling; known discrepancies;* logically impossible; *mismatched;* nonsensical; oxymoronic; problematic; quirky; *ridiculous;* self-contradicting; *troubled;* uncoherent; varying; with discrepancies; *x-out;* yet containing inconsistencies; *zero consistency;*

**paragon** *(n.)*: apotheosis; *beau ideal* [F.]; case (in point); *distillation;* example; fugler; guide; holotype; ideal; jewel; *kept specimen;* lead; model; neotype; one to follow; paradigm; quintessence; representative; shining example; touchstone; ule; very model; working model; *xenagogue;* yardstick; *zealous;*

**paragraph** *(n.)*: article; body; block; clause; division; excursus; fragment; grouping; *hunk; indentation;* introductory ~; *jargon;* key ~; lead-in ~; *margin; notation;* operative ~; portion; *quantity; remnant;* section; segment; text; unit; verse; *wording;* x-mal [G.]; *yield;* zone;

**parallel** *(adj.)*: analogous; *balanced;* comparable; duplicate; equivalent; *following; going the same way;* homologous; identical; just the same; kindred; like; matching; non-differing; *one;* paralleling; *quae est eadem* [L.]; resembling; similar; twin; uniform; *verbatim; word-perfect; xerographed;* yoked; *zet;*

**paralysis** *(n.)*: atony; becrippling; crippling; debilitation; *enfeebling; feeble;* gameness; hemiplegy; incapacitation; jake-leg; *keeled over;* lameness; mobility-impaired; non-mobility; *obstructed;* palsy; paraplegia; quadriplegia; *rendered immobile;* stasis; *thwarting; unable; vulnerable;* weakness; *x-out; yedder;* zero movement;

**paralytic** *(adj.)*: ailing; becrippled; *broken;* crippled; disabled; debilitated; enfeebled; feeble; gimp; game; (hip)halt; hamstrung; handicapped; *injured;* immobilized; incapacitated; jake-legged; *keeled over;* lame; motionless; *maimed;* non-mobile; *overweak;* paralyzed; paralytical; palsied; palsical; quadriplegic; *reeling;* spavined; *tottering; unable;* vegetative; *weak; x-out;* yawing; *zeroized;*

**paralytic** *(n.)*: atony; becrippled man; cripple; disabled person; *enfeebled person; feeble;* gimp man; hemiplegic; incapacitated man; jake-leg; *knocked out;* lame man; *maimed;* non-mobile person; one sick of the palsy; palsied man; paraplegic; quadriplegic; *rendered immobile;* spavined man; *tottering; unable to walk;* vegetation; *weak;* x-out; *yedder;* zeroized;

**paralyze** *(v.)*: *afflict;* becripple; cripple; disable; *enfeeble; feeble;* game; hamstring; immobilize; impalsy; *jake-legged;* knock out; lame; maim; *neutralize;* obstruct; paralize; *query;* render inoperative; strike with palsy; stun; *stop; thwart; undo; victimize;* wing; *wound;* x-out; *yedder;* zap;

**paraphrase** *(v.)*: articulate differently; *bespeak;* change wording; do over; *different words;* express differently; *epanorthosis;* freely re-word; give using different words; *hyponym;* interpret; *just re-word;* key in; loosely translate; metaphrase; *new wording; over again;* phrase differently; quote loosely; recast; restate; re-word; rephrase; state differently; *translate;* use one's own words; *verbiage;* word differently; *xfer; yield; zet [dial.];*

**parasite** *(n.)*: *autoecism;* bug; bloodsucker; barnacle; cadger; clepto~; *chigger;* chinch; dependent; exploiter; endo~; freeloader; *foreign body;* giardia; *germ;* heterophyte; hyper~; horseleech; *insect; jigger;* klepto~; leech; micro~; *nit; obnoxious;* parasitical creature; *quad;* roundworm; scrounger; sanguisuge; taker; *tick; tapeworm;* uninvited guest [joc.]; *vermin;* victimizer; *wood tick; whipworm;* xeno~; *yellow cancerroot;* zoo~;

**parasitic** *(adj.)*: autoecious; blood-sucking; commensal; draining; exploitive; freeloading; grabby; helminthic; heteroecious; *insect; jigger;* klepto~; leech-like; living off another; micro~; non-independent; *obnoxious;* parasitical; *quad; ravening;* scrounging; tapeworm-like; *uninvited;* verminous; vampirical; *wolvish;* xeno~; *yellow cancerroot;* zapping;

**pardon** *(n.)*: acquittal; absolution; blotting out; clearing; cancelling; dismissal; disregarding; excusing; exculpation; exoneration; forgiveness; granting ~; *humaneness;* indemnification; justification; keeping no account; letting go; mercy; non-execution; overlooking; passing over; putting away; quittance; remittance; release; sparing; taking away; *unvengefulness;* voidance; wiping clean; *washing; x-ing out; yet forgiven;* zeroing out; [*Ant.* punishment]

**pardon** *(v.)*: acquit; absolve; blot out; clear; cancel; dismiss; disregard; excuse; exculpate; exonerate; forgive; grant ~; have mercy upon; indemnify; justify; keep no account; let go; make slate clean; *mercy;* non-execution; not hold accountable; overlook; pass over; put away; purge; quit; remit; release; remember no more; spare; show mercy; take away; *tolerate; unvengefulness;* void; wipe clean; *wash;* x out; *yielding;* zero out; [*Ant.* pardon]

**pardonable** *(adj.)*: absolvable; *bearable;* clearable; cancelable; defensible; excusable; forgivable; *grantable; humaneness;* inconsequential; justifiable; *keeping no account; legitimate; mercy;* non-binding; *okay; proper; quit;* removable; remittable; *sparing; tolerable;* understandable; venial; warrantable; *x out;* yet ~; *zero out;* [*Ant.* punishable]

**parent** *(n.)*: authority; ancestor; biological ~; *caring* ~; disciplinarian; dad [masc.]; engenderer; *elder;* folks [pl.]; father [masc.]; guardian; *head; in-laws; joint;* kinfolk [pl.]; *legal guardian;* mother [fem.]; matriarch [fem.]; nearest kin; originator; old man [masc.]; old woman [fem., both disrespectful]; progenitors; patriarch [masc.]; *quickener; relative;* sire [masc.]; step~; *single ~; trainer; undershepherd; Vater [G.];* warden; *x-linked; young ~; zaftig;*

**park** *(n.)*: *area;* botanical ~; commons; *district ~;* ecological ~; forest preserve; grove; garden; game reserve; *hamlet ~;* inner-city ~; *juvenile recreation area;* kid's playground; *lake;* mini~; national ~ (-forest; -reserve); *outing;* picnic area; playground; playing field; *quadrant;* recreational area; reserve; square; state ~; town ~; *urban ~; vest-pocket ~;* wildlife reserve; xystus; yard; *Yellowstone; zoological ~;*

**park** *(v.)*: abide; bide; camp; dwell; ensconce; *fix; go to;* hang one's hat; inhabit; *journey;* keep on; locate; lay; moor; *nest;* occupy; perch; place; position; *quarter;* relocate; rest; remain; situate; stay; set; tarry; *use; vest;* wait; *winter; xenize; yerde* [arch.]; zet [dial.];

**parlor** *(n.)*: antechamber; *beauty ~;* chamber; den; end room; frontroom; gallery; hall; inhabitance; *Jacobean bench;* keeping room; lounge; living room; *middle common room;* nook; observatory; place; quarters; room; sunroom; *TV room;* utility room; vestry; waiting room; xystum; *yu* [Chin.]; zeta;

**part** *(n.)*: aught; any; appurtenance; bit; cog; component; constituent; detail; division; element; fraction; faction; feature; *gob;* hunk; *half;* ingredient; item; installment; *jib;* kernel; lump; member; macrodivision; mite; *nugget;* ought; paring; portion; piece; parcel; quantity; rake-off; *remnant;* some; segment; section; share; tidbit; thing; *unit; vestige;* wedge; *x-mal [G.];* yngot [arch.]; zum [dial.];

**part** *(v.)*: alienate; break; cleave; divide; estrange; fork; fractionate; go separate ways; halve; incide; *jigsaw; knife;* laniate; make separate; *non-continuous;* open; partition; *quarter;* rend; rive; separate; *tear a~;* uncouple; unyoke; *vell; winnow; x-sect;* yawn; zone;

**partial** *(adj.)*: *any;* basic; constituent; deficient; elemental; factional; fractional; fragmentary; *growing;* halfway; incomplete; inconsummate; inadequate; imperfect; *just part; key;* limited; *mite;* non-complete; *ounce;* part; *quelque* [F.]; restricted; *rudimentary;* remnant; semi-completed; some; *tidbit;* unfinished; *vestigial; wee bit; x-mal [G.];* yet incomplete; zum [dial.]; [*see* biased; *Ant.* plenary]

**participant** *(n.)*: accomplice; *business partner;* contributor; contestant; doer; entrant; engager; fellow; group member; helper; involved individual; joiner; *knit; link up;* member; non-bystander; one involved; partaker; player; qualified contestant; runner; sharer; team member; user; *vier;* worker; *xel [arch.];* yokefellow; zealous ~;

**participate** *(v.)*: associate; attach; become a part; connect; commit; *do;* engage; *full-support;* get involved; humor; have a part; involve; indulge; join; *knit; link up;* make oneself a part; *non-bystander; offer;* partake; play; partner; *qualify;* run with; share; take part; unite with; *vie with;* work together with; *xfer;* yoke up; *zeal;*

**participation** *(n.)*: association; attachment; becoming part; contribution; connection; commitment; doing; engaging; enthusiasm; full support; getting involved; help; involvement; interest; indulgence; input; joining; *knitting; linking up;* membership; *nexus; oneness;* participating; playing; part(aking); *qualified ~;* running together; sharing; taking part; uniting; verve; working together; *xfer;* yieldedness; *zealous ~;*

**particular** *(adj.)*: appointed; *by name;* certain; designated; distinguished; distinct; exact(ing); especial; exceptional; *forementioned;* given; *hand-picked;* individual; *just;* known; *labeled;* marked; named; one; own; precise; peculiar; *qualifying;* respective; specific; singular; *tagged;* unique; *very;* well-chosen; *xtry.;* yarked; *zero in;* [*see* nitpicky]

**particular** *(n.)*: aspect; *basic part;* characteristic; condition; detail; exact ~; fact; fine point; *given detail;* highlight; individual detail; item; *just a fine point;* key aspect; little detail; minutiae [pl.]; *notable thing; object;* point; particularity; qualifier; requirement; specific(ation); thing; *understanding; virtue;* way; *x-factor; yetzer* [Heb.]; *zero in;*

**parting** *(n.)*: adieu; abandonment; breaking (away); cleavage; departure; desertion; exit; exodus; extrication; farewell; going; goodbye; hiatus; heave-ho; isolation; judicial separation; keeping separate; kissing goodbye; leaving; marching off; *non-accord;* opening; partitioning; quartering; quitting; rending; separation; sendoff; taking; uncoupling; unyoking; valediction; vacating; withdrawal; walking out; *xiphopagotomy; yawn;* zoning;

**partition** *(n.)*: apportionment; barrier; compartment; divider; espalier; fence; *garth;* hedge; immure; *jailhouse wall; kraal;* line of demarcation; mure; *non-permanent divider;* outer wall; obstruction; panel; *quickset hedge;* room divider; separator; *trellis;* utility wall; vallum; wall; *x-fence;* yard wall; zone;

**partition** *(v.)*: apportion; break up; chop up; compartmentalize; divide (up); establish boundaries; fractionate; fence off; *great divide;* halve; *inclusive; jurisdictions; kiosk; lop;* make into zones; *non-contiguous; outer wall;* parcel; quadrisect; regionalize; *rooms;* split; separate; subdivide; sectionalize; territorialize; *unyoke; vell;* wall off; *x-sect; yard;* zone;

**partner** *(n.)*: associate; bedfellow; co~; companion; cohort; counterpart; collaborator; *devoted friend;* equal; friend; good-fellow; helper; intimate; Jonathan; kith [pl.]; *loyal friend;* mate; *neighbor;* other half; pal; pardner [slang]; *quondam ~;* right-hand man; sidekick; teammate; *unfailing friend; votary;* workmate; *x-class;* yokefellow; *zealous friend;*

**partnership** *(n.)*: alliance; brotherhood; co~; coalition; cooperation; *devotion;* enterprise; friendship; firm; guild; *helping;* interest; joint venture; kinship; league; mateship; nexus; organization; partnering; quinquevirate; relationship; syndicate; trust; union; *vertical* union; *workers' union; x-class;* yoke; zollverein;

**party** *(n.)*: anniversary; bash; birthday ~; bacchanal; banquet; celebration; *display;* event; function; fete; festivity; gathering; garden ~; get-together; gala; house ~; hooley [Ire.]; *indulgence;* jamboree; jollification; *kitchenware ~; lawn ~;* merriment; masquerade; night ~; occasion; *pajama ~;* panegyris; *quindene;* revel-rout; revelry; shindig; soirée; social gathering; thrash; tea ~; *uplifting;* vernissage; whoop-de-doo; wingding; *wassail; x-po [slang]; yahoo!; zeal;*

**pass** *(n. official permission to enter)*: authorization; bus ~; boarding ~; badge; certificate; card; consent; credentials; clearance; ducet; daily ~; document; endorsement; family ~; fiat; government clearance; *homologating;* identification; *justification;* key; license; leave; metro ~; non-refundable ticket; okay; one-way ~; permit; papers; qualification; round-trip ticket; sanction; summer- ~; ticket; travelcard; unexpired ~; visa; voucher; variance; waiver; warrant; *xfer papers;* yellow ~; *zip card:*

**pass** *(v. move)*: advance; *budge;* come; drift; edge; flow; go; *hurry;* immigrate; journey; *kindle;* locomote; move; migrate; *nudge; overrun;* proceed; progress; pull ahead; quicken; relocate; shift; travel; traverse; *underway;* voyage; venture; walk; xfer; yede; zip;

**pass** *(v. overtake)*: accelerate past; bypass; beat; cap; dart past; excel; exceed; fly by; go beyond; hurtle past; inch past; jet past; kite past; leave behind; move past; *niddle;* overtake; outrun; outdo; outshine; outact; outstep; ~ one by; *quash;* rocket past; *rival;* surpass; transcend; top; usurp; *velocity;* whiz past; *x-cend; yonder;* zoom past;

**passage** *(n.)*: avenue; byway; corridor; defile; dirt road; esplanade; footpath; *glade;* highway; inlet; journey-way; kotal; lane; means; non-toll road; outlet; path(way); pass(ageway); *quo mode* [L.]; route; street; slype; trail; track; thoroughfare; *underpass;* vennel; way; xystus; *yong* [arch.]; *zwinger;*

**passenger** *(n.)*: airline ~; bus rider; commuter; *dependent;* excursionist; fare; goer; *human being; individual;* journeyer; kippage [pl. arch.]; *lad;* man; nonstop; one traveling; paying customer; person; *questor;* rider; *someone;* traveler; transit ~; ticket-holder; user; voyager; wayfarer; *xferer; young man; zip;*

**passion** *(n.)*: ardor; burning; commitment; devotion; enthusiasm; fervor; gusto; *heat;* heartiness; intensity; *joy;* keenness; love; mania; madness; *need;* obsession; passionateness; *quixotic;* romance; robustness; spirit; torch; *undying love;* vehemence; warmth; *xenophilia;* yareness; zeal;
**passionate** *(adj.)*: ardent; amorous; affectionate; breathless; burning; committed; devoted; emotional; fervent; fiery; gung-ho; hot; impassioned; intense; *jealous; jingoist;* keen; love-driven; mad; *non-apathetic;* overzealous; on fire; perfervid; quick; ready; romantic; spirited; torrid; unreserved; vehement; wholehearted; *xenocentric;* yare; zestful; zealous; [*Ant.* phlegmatic]
**passive** *(adj.)*: agreeable; acquiescent; biddable; compliant; docile; easy-going; flaccid; gentle; harmonious; happy; inactive; *jump right to it; keeping peace;* laid-back; meek; non-resistant; obedient; pliant; quiescent; reactive; submissive; servile; slavish; tractable; unassuming; unresisting; very submissive; willing; *xtry. obsequious;* yielding; *zero resistance;*
**past** *(adj.)*: anterior; bygone; citavant; dated; earlier; former; gone-by; historical; immemorial; *just before; known in the past;* last; *most recent; nee;* onetime; older; olden; prior; previous; preceding; quondam; retrospective; *starting;* then; *unseasonable;* very early; whilom; *x;* yesteryear; *zero currentness;* [*Ant.* present]
**paste** *(n.)*: adhesive; binder; bond(ing agent); cement; *daub;* epoxy; fixative; glue; *hold;* ichthyocolla; *jell; knit;* library ~; mucilage; meld; *nail; one;* plaster; quince-mucilage; rubber cement; stickum; *tack; unite; viscous;* wood glue; *weld; xenograft; yoke; zip;*
**pastor** *(n.)*: admonisher; Bible-teacher; bishop; chaplain; circuit rider; *declarer; Doomsday preacher;* expositor; elder; field preacher; *guide;* gospeler; herald; homilist; itinerant preacher; josser [Aus. slang]; *kerygma; leader;* lecturer; minister; messenger; man of God; *noiser;* orator; parson; preacher; pulpiteer; *quoter;* reverend; revivalist; speaker; sermonizer; servant of God; teacher; trumpeter; undershepherd; voicer; *warner; xenagogue; yeller [derog.]; zealous preacher;*
**pastorate** *(n.)*: appointment; bishoprick; chaplaincy; calling; *church; directorship;* eldership; *faculty;* governance; headship; *influence;* jurisdiction; keeping; leadership; ministry; *nomination;* office; oversight; position; pastorship; pastorage; pulpit; *qualification;* rule; stewardship; *trust; undershepherd; vote;* watch; *xenagogy; youth ~; zeal for the ministry;*
**pasture** *(n.)*: area; browse; clearing; downs eatage; field; grassland; ground; hill country; haugh [Scot.]; ile [Welsh]; *jebel; knoll;* lea; llano; meadow; *nature; outdoors;* prairie; pastureland; quadrat; range; sod; sheep ~; steppe; savanna; turf; upland; vega; *water meadow; xyris;* yard; *zea;*
**pat** *(n.)*: *action;* bump; click; drub; *elbow;* flick; *glump;* hit; impact; jab; knock; light tap; martel; nob; *overhit;* pitter-patter; *quab;* rap; smack; tap; *unquiet;* veney; whap; *x-sect;* yedder; zonk;
**pat** *(v.)*: *act;* buff; bat; click; drub; drum; *elbow;* flick; graze; hit; impact; impinge; jab; knock; lightly tap; martel; nob; *overhit;* percuss [med.]; quab; rap; smack; tap; *uppercut;* veney; whack; *x-sect; yerk;* zonk;
**patch** *(n.)*: area; bit; blotch; cover; dressing; eye- ~; elbow- ~; flap; fabric piece; gusset; *hood;* iron-on ~; insignia; *jacket;* knee- ~; lid; mend; new piece; overlay; piece; pirate ~; quilt- ~; reinforcement; small area; spot; sleeve insignia; *top; unit; veil;* wedge; *x-mal [G.]; yellow ~; zum [arch.];*
**path** *(n.)*: avenue; berme; byway; corridor; dirt road; esplanade; foot~; garden ~; horse ~; *ice road;* journey-way; kotal; lane; ley; means; *narrow ~;* outlet; pathway; passage; *quo mode* [L.]; road; sidewalk; street; trail; track; *underpass;* vennel; (walk)way; xystum; *yong* [arch.]; *zwinger;*
**pathetic** *(adj.)*: awful; bad; contemptible; disgraceful; despicable; execrable; feeble; grim; hopeless; heartbreaking; ill-favored; joyless; keen; lowly; lamentable; miserable; nasty; *odious;* pitiful; qualityless; risible; sad; sorry; terrible; utter; vile; wretched; xtry. bad; yucky; *zestless;*
**patience** *(n.)*: allowance; bearing; composure; *dispassion;* endurance; forbearance; graciousness; holding back; indulgence; *just waiting; keeping ~;* longsuffering; moderation; non-anxiety; over- ~; passivity; *quietness;* restraint; resignation; sufferance; tolerance; temperance; unhurriedness; *vasbyt;* waiting; *xtry. ~; yielding; zero irritation;*

**patient** *(adj.)*: accepting; bearing; composed; *dispassionate;* enduring; forbearing; gracious; *heart;* indulgent; *just wait; keeping patience;* longsuffering; merciful; non-anxious; over- ~; passive; *quiet;* restrained; resigned; stoic; self-controlled; tolerant; uncomplaining; vasbyt; willing to wait; *xtry. ~; yieldful; zero irritation;*

**patriarch** *(n.)*: ancestor; begetter; clan head; *dad;* elder; forefather; genitor; (great-) grandfather; head; hierarch; *inherited; judge; kin;* lineal father; male progenitor; *near of kin;* originator; progenitor; predecessor; *quarter;* respected head; *sire;* tribal head; *unilineal;* venerated father; *wise man; x-linked; yore; zet [arch.];*

**patriot** *(n.)*: advocate; autonomist; backer; civist; com~; devotee; enthusiast; extremist; flag-waver; fanatic; *gung-ho;* hundred-percenter; *impassioned;* jingo; *keen;* loyalist; *militant; minuteman;* nationalist; *obsessed;* partisan; *promoter; quick-to-arms; revolutionary;* supporter; separatist; spread-eagle; *total supporter;* ultranationalist; *votary; wholehearted;* xenophobe; *yahoo;* zealot;

**patriotism** *(n.)*: ardor; *burning;* civism; devotion; enthusiasm; fervor; flag-waving; fanaticism; *gung-ho;* hundred-percentism; *intensity;* jingoism; keenness; love (of country); loyalty; *militancy; mania;* nationalism; over~; obsession; pride in one's country; *quickness; readiness;* spirit; spread-eagleism; *thrilled;* ultranationalism; vehemence; wholeheartedness; xenophobia; yahooism; zealotry;

**patrol** *(n.)*: *around;* beat; border ~; circuit; duty; dogwatch; *enforcement; force;* guard; highway ~; investigation; jeep ~; *keep;* looking out; middle watch; night-watch; out-watching; perambulation; *questor;* rounds; sentry duty; tour; unit ~; vigil; watch; walk about; *xfer;* yard ~; zone ~;

**patrol** *(v.)*: *assure;* be around; check; defend; *enforce;* fend; guard; *hold;* insure; jaga; keep (watch); look after; make the rounds; *nestle;* overshadow; police; perambulate; *quia timet [L.];* regulate; safeguard; sweep; take care of; uphold; vallate; watch; walk about; *x-guard; yeme* [arch.]; *zealously watch;*

**patsy** *(n.)*: airhead; blockhead; chump; dupe; dumbbell; easy target; fool; greenhorn; harebrain; ignoramus; jackass; knucklehead; lame-brain; moron; nitwit; oaf; pea-brain; *quack;* rattlebrain; sucker; turkey; unsuspecting victim; victim; whipping-boy; *xtry. fool;* yo-yo; *zob;*

**pattern** *(n. blueprint)*: archetype; basis; blueprint; configuration; drawing; design; delineator; example; exemplar; fugler; guide; house plan; illustration; instructions; *ideal; jewel; key;* layout; model; *neotype;* outline; precedent; *quintessence;* rule; sketch; sample; template; ule; *virtual;* working drawing; *xenagogue;* yardstick; *zincograph;*

**pattern** *(n. repeating design)*: adornment; *background;* cosmetic design; design; embellishment; fashion; filigree; gadroon; *highlight; item; jig; kory;* lace- ~; motif; *nautical ~;* ornamentation; patterning; *quillons;* repeating design; scrollwork; theme; *unit;* vignette; weave; *x-pattern; yantra [Hind.];* zoophorus;

**pauper** *(n.)*: almsman; beggar; charity case; down-and-out; *empty-handed;* forgotten man; *gant;* have-not; hard-luck case; homeless person; indigent; impoverished person; javel; kern; low-income person; man in need; mendicant; needy person; *overcome;* poor person; *quisby; rags;* starveling; *tenuity [arch.];* underprivileged person; vagrant; welfare person; *xtry. poor; yowler; zero;*

**pause** *(n.)*: abeyance; break; cesura; delay; ease; forbearance; gap; hold; interlude; intermission; *jadedness; kip;* lag; lapse; lull; moratorium; *non-activity;* off-time; *peace;* quiet; rest; respite; stop; time-out; *unwinding;* vacation; wait; *x-rest; yawning; zizz;*

**pause** *(v.)*: *aestivate;* break; call time-out; delay; *ease;* forbear; go on break; hold; hesitate; idle; *just wait;* knock off; linger; *motionless;* nap; *off-time;* put on hold; quiet down; quit; rest; suspend; stop; take a break; tarry; *unwind;* vegetate; wait; *x-rest; yawn; zizz;* [Ant. proceed]

**paw** *(n.)*: animal foot; beetle-crusher; claw; dog; extremity; fore~; foot; *grip;* hind ~; *item; jag;* kicker; left ~; mitt; nail; *open ~;* pad; *quick;* right ~; sole; *toes;* ungula; *volar; webbed foot; x;* yads; *zet [dial.];*

**pay** *(n.)*: amount; base ~; compensation; defrayment; earnings; financial compensation; fruit; gross income; guerdon; hire; income; indemnity; just recompense; *kickback;* living wage; money; net ~; *overcompensation;* payment; paycheck; quittance; *quid pro quo* [L.]; remuneration; recompense; reward; salary; take-home ~; *unindebted;* virement; wage(s); xfer; yield; *zapping;*
**pay** *(v.)*: afford; buy; compensate; disburse; expend; forfeit; fork over; foot cost; fulfill; finance; give; guerdon; hand over; indemnify; *just recompense;* kick in; lay out; make payment; *non-retention;* outlay; *over~;* purchase; pre~; perform; pony up; quit; render; remit; recompense; remunerate; requite; re~; reward; spend; shell out; settle; tender; use; *vest;* weigh out; write check; xfer; yield; zero-out one's debt;
**payment** *(n.)*: annuity; allowance; budgeting; base pay; bonus; bounty; compensation; cash; commission; disbursement; defrayment; dividend; emolument; expense; earnings; finances; fee; fruit; gross income; guerdon; hire; imbursement; installment; income; *justification; kickback;* livelihood; liquidation; *minimum wage;* net pay; outlay; *outgo;* pre~; pay; purchase; quittance; quarterage; *quid pro quo* [L.]; recompense; remittance; reward; re~; royalty; salary; sum; satisfaction; settlement; stipend; transfer; take-home pay; *unindebted;* virement; wage(s); xfer; x-div.; yielding; *zapping;* [*see* judgment, price]
**peace** *(n.)*: amity; assurance; ataraxia; becalming; calm(ness); concord; composure; demilitarization; ease; friendliness; gentleness; harmony; idyll; *jarless;* keeping ~; lull; motionlessness; nonviolence; nonaggression; over-quietness; *order; olive branch;* peacefulness; peacetime; quiet(ude); quell; rest; reconciliation; still(ness); serenity; *shalom* [Heb.]; self-assurance; silence; tranquility; undisturbedness; *violence ended;* whisht; *xenophilia; yung* [Chin.]; zero hostilities; [*see* truce; reconciliation; *Ant.* pandemonium]
**peaceable** *(adj.)*: amicable; bloodless; congenial; dovelike; easeful; friendly; gentle; harmonious; irenic; *judicious;* keeping peace; lamblike; meek; mild; nonviolent; *orderly;* peace-loving; quiescent; reposeful; symphonious; tranquil; unhostile; *violence-hating;* wrathless; *xenophilious; yielding; zealous of peace;* [*Ant.* pugnacious]
**peaceful** *(adj.)*: accordant; becalmed; bloodless; calm; concordant; dovelike; easeful; friendly; gentle; hushed; harmonious; halcyon; idyllic; irenic; jarless; keeping peace; *luxurious;* motionless; nonviolent; nonbelligerent; non-aggressive; *orderly;* olive-branch bearing; peaceable; placid; quiescent; quiet; restful; still; serene; symphonious; tranquil; untroubled; unwarlike; *violence-hating;* well-disposed; *xenophilous; yielding;* zealous of peace; [*Ant.* pugnacious]
**peacefully** *(adv.)*: amicably; bloodlessly; calmly; *diplomatically;* easefully; friendlily; gently; harmoniously; idyllically; irenically; *jarless;* kindly; *luxuriously;* mildly; nonviolently; *obligingly;* peacefully; peaceably; quiescently; quietly; restfully; serenely; tranquilly; unbelligerently; *very ~;* without resistance; wrathlessly; *xenophilously; yieldingly;* zero violence; [*Ant.* pugnaciously]
**peacemaker** *(n.)*: arbitrator; balm; conciliator; diplomat; daysman; dove; *emissary; facilitator;* go-between; harmonizer; intermediary; intercessor; *justifier;* Kissinger; legate; mediator; negotiator; olive-branch offerer; peace-maker; pacificator; queller; reconciler; statesman; trucemaker; umpire; *violence-ender;* war ender; *xenophile; yamen* [Chin.]; zero hostility; [*Ant.* provoker]
**peak** *(n.)*: apex; brow; crest; climax; *destination;* extremity; *fastigium* [L.]; *greatest height;* hilltop; height; high point; *increase; important;* jut; kop; limit; lofty height; mountaintop; nib; nth degree; *overmost point;* pinnacle; *quoif;* rise; summit; tor; top; upper extremity; vertex; *way up; xtry; yonder point;* zenith;
**peal** *(n.)*: *alarm;* bong; clangor; chime; ding-dong; *echo;* flourish; gong; honk; *intonation;* jingle; knell; loud clang; music; *noise;* outcry; pealing; *quake;* ringing; sound; toll; *utterance;* voice [poet.]; *wheetle; x-ing; yammer; zing;*

**peasant** *(n.)*: agrarian; bumpkin; commoner; drudge; esne; farmer; grunt; husbandman; *hick;* ill-bred man; joskin; knave; liegeman; low-born; *masses* [pl.]; neif; *operant;* plebeian; peon; *quadrat;* rustic; serf; tike; underling; vassal; worker; xtr. *poor;* yokel; zhlub; [*Ant.* prince]

**peck** *(v.)*: *ate;* bite; *chomp;* dig; eat; *feed;* graze on; *have; intake;* jab; knab; *lance;* nibble; *overeat;* poke; pick; *quab; rip;* stab; *take;* use beak; *violence; wimble; xuld [arch.];* yaffle; zing;

**peculiar** *(adj.)*: abnormal; anomalous; bizarre; crazy; deviant; eccentric; extraordinary; funny; freaky; goofy; heterotypical; irregular; insane; jokey; kooky; loony; mad; nonstandard; nutty; outrageous; outlandish; particular; quacked; ridiculous; strange; screwy; twisted; unusual; unique; variant; weird; wacky; warped; xenomorphic; *yokelish;* zany; [*Ant.* plain]

**pedestal** *(n.)*: acropodium; base; column; dais; elevated platform; footstall; gallery; high place; *item; jack up; knoll;* low platform; marble ~; *montoir; necking; object;* plinth; platform; *quarter-arch;* raised platform; stand; socle; *thing;* understructure; *vertical;* wooden platform; *x-section; yew block;* zaccho;

**peel** *(n.)*: *apple ~;* bark; covering; cortex; *dermis;* epicarp; exocarp; *fringe; grape ~;* husk; hull; integument; jacket; *kiwi ~;* layer; *lemon ~;* membrane; *non-edible* pellicle; outer layer; peeling; *querl;* rind; skin; shuck; tegument; throw-away part; un~; *vacate; without; x.; yank;* zest;

**peel** *(v.)*: abscind; bare; bark; cut (-cast) off; divest; discase; denude; debark; decorticate; expose; flay; get skin off; husk; *incise; jerk off; kerf;* lay bare; make bare; nakedize; *off;* pare; *quick-husk;* remove; strip; shed; take off; undress; *vacate;* wear away; *xyster;* yank off; zip off;

**peer** *(n.)*: associate; buddy; colleague; coequal; compeer; *dude;* equal; fellow; *guy; human;* individual; *juror; kid;* like; match; mate; neighbor; *one; person; ~ group; qualified ~; regular guy;* rival; *same;* teammate; *unbiased; votary;* workmate; *x-class;* yealing; yokefellow; *'zactly [dial.];*

**peerless** *(adj.)*: A-1; best; choicest; *distinct;* elite; first; greatest; highest; incomparable; *jim-dandy;* keenest; leading; matchless; nonpareil; outstanding; prime; *quintessential; remarkable;* superior; top; unequalled; unrivaled; unmatched; ultimate; very best; without equal; xtry.; yondmost; zenithal;

**peeve** *(n.)*: annoyance; beef; complaint; dispute; exception; fuss; gripe; headache; irritation; jangling; kvetching; *locking horns;* murmuring; nuisance; objection; protest; plaint; problem; quarrel; repining; *strife; tussle; unharmoniousness;* vexation; *withstanding; x-fire;* yawp; *za-zum [Rus.];* [*Ant.* please]

**pen** *(n.)*: * *article;* ballpoint; calamus; clip-on ~; disposable ink~; erasable ink ~; fountain ~; felt-tip ~; graver; goosequill; gel ~; *handwrite;* ink~; *instrument; jot; keelvine; light ~;* marker; *nib; object; pencil;* quill; red-ink ~; stylus; stylograph; *tool; utensil; vessel;* writing utensil; *x-scriber; yellow ~; zeug;*

**pen** *(v.)*: author; *book;* compose; *create;* draft; enter; fabulize; *grave;* handwrite; indite; jot down; keep record; list; mark down; *make;* notate; originate; put down; quill; redact; set down; take down; underwrite; *vellum;* write; *x;* yak; zay;

**penalty** *(v.)*: affliction; *beating;* castigation; deserts; *execution; fee;* ferule; flogging; *garroting;* horsewhipping; infliction; just deserts; *keelhauling; lashing; make one pay;* nemesis; outcome; punishment; *quartering;* retribution; sentence; sanction; taking to task; *upbraiding; vengeance; wrath; whipping; xenagogy; yard [arch.]; zapping;*

**penance** *(n.)*: amends; *beating;* castigation; chastisement; discipline; expiation; flagellation; garroting; *Hail Marys; infliction;* just deserts; *keeping peas in one's shoes; lighting candles;* making up for; *non-grace; owe;* penalty; punishment; *quick-fix;* reparation; self-punishment; talion; *upbraiding; vengeance;* works; *x-ing; yard [arch.];* zero grace;

**penetrate** *(v.)*: auger; broach; bore; cut through; drive; drill; dig; empierce; enter; force through; go; gore; hole; impale; jab; knife; lance; make inroads; nail; open; pierce; puncture; *quill;* run through; stab; transfix; trans~; thirl; *undercut; ventilate;* wimble; *xylotomy; x-pierce;* yerk; zing;

**penetration** *(n.)*: *all the way through;* breach; breaking through; cutting through; drilling; entrance; forcing; getting through; *hole;* insertion; invasion; jabbing; *knife; lance; moving through; needle hole;* opening; piercing; puncturing; perforation; *quill;* running through; stabbing; thrusting; transfixion; *undercut; ventilate;* wimbling; *xylotomy; x-pierce;* yerk; zing;

**penitence** *(n.)*: attrition; about-face; brokenness; contrition; change of heart; despair; *ejulation;* feeling sorry; grief; humbling; *inveighing; juddering; keen; lamentation;* mourning; *non-stubbornness; outcry;* penitency; *quaking;* repentance; sorrow; turning; U-turn; *volte-face* [F.]; woefulness; *xtry, ruefulness; yamim nora'im* [Heb.]; zeal to get right; [*Ant.* presumption]

**penitent** *(adj.)*: apologetic; broken; contrite; despairing; *ejulation;* feeling sorry; grieving; humbled; heart-repentant; *inveighing; juddering;* keenly ~; lamenting; mourning; *non-stubborn;* outcrying; penitential; *quaking;* repentant; sorry; sorrowful; turning; U-turn; *volte-face* [F.]; woeful; *xtry.* ~; *yearning;* zealous to get right; [*Ant.* presumptuous]

**pensive** *(adj.)*: absorbed; brooding; cogitative; contemplative; deep in thought; deliberative; engrossed; fanciful; gazeful; heart-searching; introspective; judicial; *knowledge;* lost in thought; meditative; museful; notional; occupied; pondering; *questioning;* reflective; studious; thoughtful; understanding; *valuating;* wistful; *xenocratic; yearnful;* zetetic;

**pent-up** *(v.)*: arrested; bottled up; contained; *disallowed;* entrapped; fettered; girded; held back (-in); inhibited; *just* ~; kept in; locked in; manacled; *non-free; oppressed;* penned up; *quashed;* repressed; shut up inside; stifled; suppressed; trapped inside; unexpressed; *voiceless;* withheld; *x;* yarded; *zoster;*

**people** *(n.)*: *audience;* bodies; bourgeoisie; children (of Adam); crowd; citizens; common people; *demos* [Gr.]; everybody; folk(s); flesh; gentlefolk; gentry; general public; humans; humanity; humankind; individuals; inhabitants; janata [Asia]; kith; laity; men; man(kind); mob; masses; multitudes; natives; nation; ones; *oke* [S. Afr.]; persons; populace; public; *quorum;* residents; ruck; subjects; sea of humanity; third estate; *underlings;* vulgar; world; *xenic;* yokels; *zoa;*

**perceive** *(v.)*: apprehend; behold; comprehend; distinguish; detect; discern; espy; fathom; feel; grasp; *hear;* identify; judge; know; *look;* make out; mark; notice; observe; pick up on; *quantify;* recognize; realize; see; sense; take in; think; understand; view; watch; *xenodiagnose; yeme;* zero in; [*Ant.* pass over]

**perceptible** *(adj.)*: appreciable; *beholding;* clear; discernable; detectable; distinguishable; discriminable; estimable; evident; *findable;* graspable; *hearable;* identifiable; *judge;* knowable; *look;* measurable; *manifest;* noticeable; observable; perceivable; quantifiable; recognizable; seeable; traceable; understandable; visible; watchable; *x-parent; yare;* zero in;

**perception** *(n.)*: acuteness; awareness; *beholding;* clear-sightedness; comprehension; discernment; espying; envisionment; fathoming; grasp; *hearing;* heart-understanding; insight(fulness); identification; judgment; keenness; knowledge; *looking; light;* mindfulness; notice; noting; observation; perceptiveness; percipience; perceptibility; quick-sightedness; realization; sharpness; sense; *thought; taking note;* understanding; vision; wisdom; xtry. ~; *yeme [arch.];* zeroing in;

**perceptive** *(adj.)*: acute; aware; bright; clear-sighted; discerning; ever-watchful; far-sighted; *good; hawk-eyed;* insightful; judicious; keen; longsighted; mindful; *noticing;* observant; on the ball; percipient; perspicacious; quick; razor-sharp; sharp; sensitive; *trained eye;* understanding; vigilant; watchful; *wise; xtry.;* yepe; zero in;

**perch** *(v.)*: alight; balance; come to rest; dwell; esconse; fix; grab a spot; hang on; *inhabit;* juke; keep on; light; *make roost; nest;* occupy; park; quat; rest on; roost; sit; set; take a seat; *use; vajrasana;* well-situated; *x-chair; yerde* [arch.]; zet [dial.];

**perfect** *(adj.)*: accurate; blameless; blemishless; correct; complete; defectless; error-free; errorless; exact; flawless; guiltless; harmless; holy; infallible; inerrant; inerrable; impeccable; just right; *keen;* letter- ~; mistake-proof; non-flawed; offenseless; plu~; qualmless; righteous; spotless; sinless; taintless; unerring; virtuous; without flaw; *xtry.;* yet flawless; zero-defect;

**perfection** *(n.)*: absolute ~; blemishlessness; completion; *defectless;* exactness; flawlessness; goodness; harmlessness; holiness; infallibility; inerrancy; impeccability; *just right;* keenness; *letter-perfect; mistake-proof;* no flaw; *outstandingness;* perfectness; qualmlessness; righteousness; spotlessness; sinlessness; taintlessness; utter ~; virtuousness; *without flaw; xtry.;* yet flawless; zero defects;

**perform** *(v.)*: accomplish; bring about; carry out; complete; do; execute; fulfill; function; get done; heed; implement; jump (to it); keep; listen to; mind; not resist; obey; operate; put on; *questionless;* run; submit; transact; undertake; vigorously obey; work; *xlate;* yield; zip to it; [*see* act]
**performance** *(n.)*: act; achievement; array; behavior; *concert;* conduct; completion; doing; discharge; display; exhibition; floorshow; *gathering;* handling; implementation; *jamboree;* keeping; local show; manifestation; *nundination;* operation; presentation; performing; quality production; realization; ridotto; roadshow; show(ing); song and dance; trade show; theatrical ~; transaction; undertaking; vaudeville ~; vernissage; work; wingding; *xtry.; yield; zeal;*
**performer** *(n.)*: artist(e); actor; *bearer;* completer; doer; executant; entertainer; fulfiller; *get done;* heeder; implementer; *jump (to it);* keeper; *listen to; musician;* maker; *non-resister;* operator; perpetrator; player; practitioner; *qualified;* recitalist; showman; tackler; *unicyclist;* vaudevillian; worker; *xlate;* yielder; *zip to it;*
**perfume** *(n.)*: aroma; bal(sa)m; cologne; diapasm; essence; fragrance; *good-smelling ~; heavenly scent;* incense; jasmine; keora oil; *lavender;* musk; *myrrh;* nidor; odor; *parfum* [F.]; *quality scent;* redolence; scent; *toilet water; unforgettable aroma;* volatile oil; *whiff;* xanthoxylene; ylang-ylang; zedoary;
**perfume** *(v.)*: aromatize; *besprinkle;* cense; disseminate scent; essence; fragrance; give scent; heavily ~; imbue; infuse; *jet; keen smell;* lightly ~; make smell nice; mist; *naid; overspread;* permeate; *quick-spray; redolence;* scent; suffuse; spray; thurify; *unforgotten;* volatilize; *whiff; xuld [arch.];* ylang-ylang; zest;
**peril** *(n.)*: adversity; *bad;* chance; danger; endangerment; evil; *foreboding; fear; gnarly;* hazard; hurt; harm; imperilment; *injury;* jeopardy; known risk; *life-threatening;* menace; malificence; non-safety; *ominous;* perilousness; *questionable;* risk; self-risk; threat; unsafety; virulence; venturesomeness; warning; woe; "x"; *yeopartie* [arch.]; zero safety; [*Ant.* protection]
**perilous** *(adj.)*: adverse; bad; chancy; dangerous; endangering; foreboding; *gnarly;* hazardous; imperiled; jeopardous; *known risk;* life-threatening; menacing; nocuous; ominous; periculous; parlous; questionable; risky; self-hazarding; threatening; unsafe; very dangerous; woeful; *x.; ydrad [arch.];* zero safety; [*Ant.* protected]
**perimeter** *(n.)*: abuttal; boundary; coast; circumference; *dawn;* edge; fringe; frontier; *gate;* hem; inception; *jurisdiction; kept limit;* limit; margin; *narrow;* outskirts; outside; periphery; quadra; rim; side; threshold; ulterior; verge; without; *x-border;* yonder; zone;
**period** *(n.)*: amount of time; age; aeon; bit; cycle; *century;* dispensation; day; era; epoch; eon; *fortnight;* generation; *golden age;* hour; *heyday;* interval; *jiffy; juncture; kilocycle; lifetime;* moment; minute; month; millennium; *nanosecond; occasion;* phase; quarter; *run time;* span; time (span); timeframe; undetermined time ~; *vintage;* watch; week; x-time; yog [Ind.]; *years; zone;*
**periodic** *(adj.)*: at times; *before too long;* cyclical; *daily;* episodic; from time to time; *given times;* here and there; intervallic; just here and there; *known times; little while;* measured; *monthly;* now-and-then; occasional; periodical; *quarterly;* regular; scheduled; timed; *uncertain; volitional;* with regularity; x-time; yearly; zet [dial.];
**perish** *(v.)*: abate; be dead; cease; corrupt; die; decay; expire; fail; fall; go (home); go bad; *hazard;* invalidate; *jaws of death;* kick the bucket [slang]; *lifeless;* meet one's Maker; mortify; *non-living; over;* pass away; putrefy; quell; ruin; rot; succumb; spoil; terminate; up and die; *vanish;* wane; wither; "x"; yield one's spirit; *zapped;* [*Ant.* preserve]
**perishable** *(adj.)*: abating; brittle; corruptible; decomposable; expirable; failing; *going bad;* hydrolyzable; impermanent; *jading; ketty;* liable to spoil; *mortifying;* nondurable; oxidizable; putrefiable; *queering; rotting;* spoilable; temporal; unpreserved; unenduring; vitiatable; *welking;* xylaria; yellowing; zeroize; [*Ant.* preservable]
**perjure** *(v.)*: *allure;* bear false witness; con; deceive; equivocate; forswear; guile; hoodwink; invent; jape; knowingly lie; lie; misrepresent; nobble; *outlie;* pull wool over one's eyes; *quiblin* [arch.]; *rig;* speak untruth; tell falsehood; utter falsehood; verneuk; wangle; *xuld [arch.]; yentz; zing;*

**perjury** *(n.)*: *artfulness;* big lie; con; deception; equivocation; false witness; guile; hoax; inveracity; jactitation; knavery; lie (under oath); misrepresentation; non-truth; oath-breaking; promise-breaking; *quiblin [arch.];* represent falsely; stretch; tall tale; untruth; *verneuking;* whole cloth; *xuld [arch.];* yarn; *zinger;* [*Ant.* plain-dealing]

**permanence** *(n.)*: abidingness; *boundlessness;* continuance; continualness; durability; endurance; fadelessness; going on; holding; interminableness; *jusqu'au bout [F.];* keeps going; *longevity;* lastingness; *measureless;* non-cessation; *ongoing;* permanency; perpetuity; *quite long;* remaining; stability; time without end; unceasingness; *vastness; without end; x-cending; year-after-year; zero end;*

**permanent** *(adj.)*: abiding; *boundless;* continuing; ceaseless; durable; enduring; everlasting; fixed; fadeless; *forever;* going on forever; *hardy;* interminable; irradicable; immarcescible; *jusqu'au bout [F.];* keeps going; long-term; lasting; *measureless;* never-ending; ongoing; perpetual; *quadrillion;* remaining; steady; transcending; unceasing; unending; *vast;* without end; *x-cending;* year-after-year; *zero end;*

**permeate** *(v.)*: affect the whole; bespread; cover; diffuse; entincture; fill; flood; go through; *high;* infuse; imbue; impregnate; jam-pack; *kibble;* leave; make full; *non-localized;* overtake; perfuse; pervade; *quick-fill;* riddle; spread; saturate; suffuse; steep; take over; tincture; transfuse; utterly fill; *volume; waterlog; xfer;* yote; *zero room;*

**permeation** *(n.)*: all-pervading; *broad;* covering; dissemination; *expanding;* filling; going through; *high;* infusion; impregnation; *jam-pack; kibble;* loading; making full; *non-localized;* overtaking; overspreading; perfusion; pervasion; *quick-fill;* riddling; spreading; saturation; suffusion; taking over; utter ~; *volume; waterlogging; xfer;* yote; *zero room;*

**permission** *(n.)*: approval; authorization; allowance; assent; blessing; consent; clearance; *delight;* endorsement; favor; *freedom;* go-ahead; green light; hear to [reg.]; imprimatur; joint-permission; *knowingly allowed;* license; leave; *liberty;* licensure; *may;* nod; okay; permitting; *qualified yes;* rubber stamp; support; sufferance; sanction; thumbs up [slang]; unreluctance; vouchsafement; willingness; *warrant; x;* yes; *zealous ~;* [*Ant.* proscription]

**permissive** *(adj.)*: accommodating; broadminded; compliant; derelict; easy-going; free; *generous;* hands-off; indulgent; *justifying;* kindly dispositioned; lax; loose; lenient; liberal; mellow; non-judgmental; open-minded; progressive; *quell; reckless; soft;* tolerant; uncritical; very loose; willing to please; *xenial;* yielding; *zero opposition;* [*Ant.* proscriptive]

**permit** *(n.)*: authorization; *building ~;* certificate; document; endorsement; favor; go-ahead; hear to [reg.]; imprimatur; joint-permission; *knowingly allowed;* license; *may;* nod; okay; papers; pass; permission; *qualified yes; right;* sufferance; sanction; toleration; *unreluctance;* visa; warrant; *x;* yes; *zealous ~;* [*Ant.* proscription]

**permit** *(v.)*: allow; bless; consent to; *decriminalize;* enable; empower; facilitate; give permission; humor; have; indulge; *justify;* knowingly allow; let; make possible; *nod;* okay; pass; *qualify; ratify;* suffer; *sanction;* tolerate; *unhindered;* validate; vouchsafe; warrant; *x on the dotted line;* yield; *yes; zero opposition;* [*Ant.* proscribe]

**perpetual** *(adj.)*: abiding; *breakless;* continual; ceaseless; daily; enduring; everlasting; *fixed;* fadeless; *forever;* going on and on; *hourly;* incessant; *jusqu'au bout* [F.]; *keeps going;* lasting; measureless; never-ending; ongoing; permanent; *quadrillion;* remaining; repeated; steady; self-perpetuating; timeless; unceasing; unbroken; uninterrupted; *vast;* without end; *xferring;* year-round; *zero end;*

**perpetuity** *(n.)*: abiding; *breakless;* continuance; duration; endurance; endlessness; *forever;* going on; holding; imperishability; *jusqu'au bout [F.];* keeping; living on; *measureless;* non-ending; *ongoing;* perpetuation; *quadrillion;* remaining; survival; *timelessness;* uninterrupted existence; *vast; without end; x-cending; yet enduring; zero end;*

**perplex** *(v.)*: amaze; bewilder; confuse; discomfit; disconcert; *entangle;* flummox; fluster; gravel; hamper; *incoherent;* jumble; kittle; lose; moider; mystify; nonplus; obscure; puzzle; quiz; rattle; stump; tangle; unsettle; vex; wilder; *x; yo-yo; zero understanding;*

**persecute** *(v.)*: afflict; bully; cruciate; *crush;* disserve; evil-entreat; *foul-treatment; grieve;* hurt; harrow; harass; intimidate; injure; *imprison; jail; kill;* lift hand against; maltreat; molest; *needle;* oppress; punish; *quash;* rack; severely ~; torment; *unfairly treat;* victimize; vex; wreak havoc on; *xuld [arch.]; ydrad [arch.]; zap;* [*Ant.* pamper]

**persecution** *(n.)*: affliction; bullying; cruelty; *discrimination;* evil-entreatment; foul-treatment; *grief;* hurt; harassment; injury; intimidation; *jailing; killing; lifting hand against;* maltreatment; nocument; oppression; persecuting; *quashing; ruthlessness;* severe ~; torture; torment; unfair treatment; victimization; vexation; woe; wreaking havoc; *xuld [arch.]; ydrad [arch.]; zapping;* [*Ant.* pampering]

**persevere** *(v.)*: abide; brave; continue; determine; endure; follow after; go on; hang in; hold on; insist; just keep going; keep at it; live through; last; make it through; not give up; outface; persist; press on; *quicken;* remain; sustain; tough it out; *uphold; voyage on;* weather; *xtry.* ~; yield not; *zoom ahead;*

**perseverance** *(n.)*: abiding; assiduity; bulldog-tenacity; continuance; determination; endurance; foursquare; gumption; holding; indefatigableness; *jaw-set;* keeping at it; lasting; *mettle;* not giving up; obstinacy; *patience;* persistence; *quickening;* relentlessness; resolve; sticktoitiveness; tenacity; tirelessness; unweariedness; *volition;* willpower; *xtry.* ~; yieldlessness; *zealous continuance;*

**persist** *(v.)*: abide; bang away; continue; determine; endure; follow after; go on; hang in; insist; *journey on;* keep at it; live through; last; maintain; never give up; outface; persevere; *quicken;* remain; stick with it; *tenacious; uphold; voyage on;* weather; *x-cend;* yield not; *zero concession;*

**persistence** *(n.)*: assiduity; bulldog-tenacity; continuance; doggedness; determination; endurance; foursquare; gumption; holding; insistence; *jaw-set;* keeping at it; lasting; *mettle;* not giving up; obstinacy; perseverance; persistency; *quit-free;* resoluteness; steadiness; tirelessness; tenaciousness; unyieldingness; *volition;* wearilessness; willpower; *xtry.* ~; yieldlessness; *zealous continuance;*

**persistent** *(adj.)*: adamant; bound and determined; constant; determined; dogged; enduring; foursquare; firm; going on; hanging in; insistent; incessant; importune; indefatigable; *jusqu'au bout* [F.]; keeping on; lasting; *mulish;* never-ceasing; ongoing; persevering; perseverant; pertinacious; *quitting never;* resolute; relentless; steady; stout; tireless; tenacious; unremitting; unrelenting; undeterred; *volitional;* weariless; well-sustained; *x-cending;* yieldless; *zealous;*

**person** *(n.)*: anyone; being; character; *dude [masc.];* earthling; figure; gentleman [masc.]; guy [masc.]; human (being); individual; joe [slang masc.]; jill [slang fem.]; *kid;* living soul; man; mortal; *name;* one; personality; personage; pedestrian; *quadragenarian; resident;* soul; someone; Terran; *underling; villager;* worldling; woman [fem.]; *xenic; yokel;* zoon;

**personal** *(adj.)*: à deux; bosom; confidential; concealed; classified; delicate; exclusive; furtive; guarded; hidden; individual; *just between us;* kept to oneself *latent;* mysterious; non-public; own; private; quiet; respective; recondite; secret; top-secret; unseen; very private; *withheld; xeno-; yieldless; zero publicity;*

**personality** *(n.)*: attributes; behavior; character; constitution; composition; disposition; essence; fiber; fundamental; *gist;* heart; humor; hypostasis; individuality; *jist; kind;* lineament; makeup; nature; overall makeup; persona; qualities; *quirks;* reality; suchness; spirit; temperament; traits; underlying character; virtue; way; xenenthesis; *yetzer* [Heb.]; *zoe;*

**personification** *(n.)*: anthropomorphism; *becoming human;* characterization; distillation; epitome; exemplification; embodiment; *flesh-and-blood;* giving human attributes; humanization; incarnation; image; *just like; kind;* likening to man; making human; *metaphor; nature; one who personifies;* personifying; *qualities;* representation; *rendition;* speaking of in human terms; thinking of as human; use of human attributes; viewing as human; wording in human terms; *xenethesis; yet personal; zoon;*

**personify** *(v.)*: anthropomorphize; ascribe human qualities; body forth; characterize as human; *distillation;* embody; *flesh-and-blood;* give in human terms; humanize; incarnate; *just like; kind;* liken to a person; make human; *metaphorize; nature; one;* put in human terms; *qualities;* represent as human; speak of as human; think of as human; use human attributes; view as human; word in human terms; *xenenthesis; yet personal; zoon;*

**personnel** *(n.)*: attendants; *butlers;* crew; cortege; deputies; employees; faculty; *group; gofer;* (hired) hands; industrial workers; *jackmen; knaves;* laborers; ministers; *navvies;* office staff; people; professorate; *qualified ~;* recruits; staff; trained staff; underlings; valets; workers; workforce; *x-man; yeomen; zakai;*

**perspective** *(n.)*: angle; bearing; conception; disposition; evaluation; frame of mind; *ground; heart;* idea; impression; judgment; *known inclination;* leaning; mindset; notion; outlook; perception; point of view; *quot homines tot sententiae [L.];* reckoning; standpoint; take; *ule;* viewpoint; way of seeing it; *xenodiagnosis; yaw; zeal;*

**perspiration** *(n.)*: armpit *~;* brow-moisture; beads of sweat; cold sweat; dampness; droplets; desudation; diaphoresis; exsudation; forehead-sweat; *gleet;* hidrosis; *indrenched; juicy; kesting;* lather; *moisture;* mucksweat [Br.]; night-sweat; *ooze;* profuse sweat; *quite wet;* resudation; sweat(ing); sweat-drops; transudation; underarm *~; venting;* wetness; *xerosis; yote; zapped;*

**perspire** *(v.)*: *armpit;* bead up; break a sweat; *cold sweat;* drip; exude; *filter; flow;* get sweaty; hidrosis; *issue; juice; kest;* lather; *moisture; non-retention;* ooze; produce sweat; *quite wet;* resudate; sweat; transude; *underarm; vent;* work up a sweat; *xude; yote; zapped;*

**persuade** *(v.)*: argue; bring around; convince; cajole; coax; disabuse; encourage; *force;* gain; *help;* influence; induce; inveigle; incite; *justify; know;* lead into; motivate; make see; nobble; outtalk prevail on; *pressure; questionless;* re-educate; sell; sway; talk into; urge; *vie for;* win over; wile; *xel; yerk;* zorch;

**persuasion** *(n.)*: ability to persuade; assurance; belief; coaxing; conviction; cajolement; doctrine; determination; encouragement; faith; *genuine ~; hold;* inducement; *justification; knowledge; leading into;* making one see; mindset; non-doubt; opinion; persuading; point of view; parenesis; questionlessness; religious *~;* resolve; swaying; sureness; talking into; trust; urging; unwaveringness; view; winning over; wiles; *xel [arch.]; y'faith* [arch.]; *zorch;*

**persuasive** *(adj.)*: actuating; alluring; authoritative; believable; cogent; convincing; compelling; dominative; effectual; forceful; *great; hold;* influential; impelling; *jurisdiction; kingly;* logical; luring; motivating; moving; *name; overpowering;* powerful; predominative; *quo warranto [L.];* rational; seductive; swaying; touching; unctious; valid; weighty; *xuld [arch.]; yard; zonal control;*

**pervade** *(v.)*: affect the whole; bespread; cover; diffuse; encompass; fill; flood; *gorge;* honeycomb; infuse; imbue; jam-pack; *kibble;* load; make full; *non-localized;* overspread; permeate; perfuse; *quick-fill;* riddle; spread through; saturate; suffuse; take over; transfuse; utterly fill; *volume;* wedge in; *xfer; yote; zero room;*

**perverse** *(adj.)*: adulterated; bad; contorted; corrupt; distorted; depraved; evil; froward; godless; horrible; impure; jesuitistic; kinky; licentious; miscreant; *nefarious;* obstreperous; perverted; *quad;* reprobate; sinful; twisted; thrawn; ungodly; untoward; vile; warped; wicked; *x-rated;* yucky; *zhlubby;*

**perversion** *(n.)*: adulteration; badness; corruption; distortion; evil; frowardness; godlessness; horridness; iniquity; jesuitism; kinkiness; lewdness; misdirection; nefariousness; obstreperousness; pollution; perverseness; perversity; queeringness; reprobation; slanting; sinfulness; twisting; transgression; treachery; unrighteousness; violence; warping; wickedness; *x-rated; yuckiness; zhlubbiness;*

**pervert** *(n.)*: abomination; brute; beast; cur; deviant; degenerate; evildoer; fiend; *good-for-nothing; hedonist;* injurer; *jadish; knave;* lost soul; miscreant; *no-good;* offender; perverted person; *queer;* reprobate; sinner; transgressor; ungodly man; villain; wrongdoer; weirdo; *x-rated;* yahoo; *zhlub;* [*see* whoremonger]

**pervert** *(v.)*: adulterate; alter; bend; contort; corrupt; distort; entwist; foul up; garble; *harm;* injure; *jade;* knot; *louse up;* misapply; misrepresent; mutilate; *nullify;* obfuscate; pollute; permute; *quade* [arch.]; ruin; subvert; twist; *undo;* vary; warp; *xenomorph; yaw; zad;* [Ant. purify]

**pessimism** *(n.)*: apprehension; balking; cynicism; doubt; defeatism; doomsaying; *ever-doubting;* fear; gloom; hopelessness; incredulity; jadedness; *kiaugh [Scot.];* leeriness; misbelief; negativism; negativity; pure cynicism; questioning; *reservation;* skepticism; terrormonging; unbelief; *vacillation;* worry; *xtry. doubt; yieldlessness; zeroizer;* [Ant. positivism]

**pessimist** *(n.)*: *antipathy;* balker; cynic; doubter; defeatist; doomsayer; Eeyore; fearer; gloom-monger; hesitator; *impossible;* jade; knocker; *leery;* misbeliever; negativist; naysayer; objector; pure cynic; *questioner;* rejecter; skeptic; terror-monger; unbeliever; *very disagreeable;* worrier; wet blanket; *x-er; yieldless; zeroizer;* [*Ant.* positivist]

**pessimistic** *(adj.)*: abject; bleak; cheerless; cynical; dismal; downbeat; ever-doubtful; forlorn; gloomy; hopeless; in low spirits; joyless; knocking; lorn; morose; negativistic; *overcast;* pining; Q.B.I. [RAF slang]; *rejecting;* sad; sour; suspicious; troubled; unhopeful; very sad; woeful; xtry. ~; yawping; zoilistic; [*Ant.* positive-thinking]

**pest** *(n.)*: annoyance; bother; crosser; disturbance; exasperation; frustration; grief; hassle; irritant; irritation; imp; jangler; *kidder;* little imp; menace; nuisance; nag; *offence;* pain (in the neck); pesterer; *queach [arch.];* rankler; scourge; thorn in one's side; troublemaker; unnerving; vexation; weariness; *x-er;* yammerer; *zinger;* [*see* vermin]

**pester** *(v.)*: annoy; bug; bother; badger; chafe; disturb; exasperate; frustrate; grate (on); harass; irritate; jangle; *kid; livid;* menace; nettle; *offend;* peeve; *queach [arch.];* rankle; rile; *steam;* tease; taunt; unnerve; vex; weary; *x-ing;* yerk; *zing;* [*Ant.* please]

**pet** *(n.)*: animal; buddy; companion; *cat; dog; endeared;* fondling; (furry) friend; *good-fellow;* house~; intimate; *jerboa; kitten;* little friend; mascot; *newt; one;* pal; playmate; *puppy; quondam friend; rabbit;* sidekick; *trusted friend; unfailing friend;* varmint; watchdog; *xbreed;* yearling; *zoic;*

**pet** *(v.)*: *affection;* brush; caress; dally; embrace; feel; fondle; *gently ~;* hug; *inwrap; just barely touch;* knead; lightly touch; massage; move hand over; nuzzle; *overrun;* pat; *quab;* rub; run over; stroke; touch; *upstroke; voluptuary;* whisk; *xfer;* yank; *zip;*

**petition** *(n.)*: appeal; beseeching; cry; desire; demand; entreaty; *forewish;* grace; *humble entreaty;* intercession; imploration; *juration; kiddush [Heb.];* litany; making request; *nones;* orison; prayer; plea; *query;* request; supplication; suit; *telling;* urging; *vigil;* wish; *XQ;* yearning; *zikr* [Mos.];

**petition** *(v.)*: ask; appeal; beseech; call for; desire; entreat; *fawn; go begging; humbly ask;* implore; importune; *juration; keep asking;* look for; lobby; make request; *need;* obsecrate; plead; pray; *quiritation;* request; supplicate; *try to get;* urge; vocalize; wish; *XQ.;* yearn; *zealously plead;*

**petty** *(adj.)*: avaricious; base; cheap; churlish; dinky; exiguous; frivolous; grudging; hard-fisted; insignificant; inconsequential; jerkwater; *kooky;* little; minor; narrow-minded; niggling; over-stingy; paltry; quibbling; ridiculous; small(-minded); trifling; unimportant; uncharitable; *vile;* wretched; *xtry. ~; yieldless; zero generosity;* [*Ant.* pre-eminent]

**pew** *(n.)*: *area;* bench; back row; box ~; church ~; church-bench; chair; *deck-bench; exedra;* front row; *garden bench;* hold; Jacobean bench; kirk- ~; long bench; *mahogany ~;* niche; *object;* padded ~; *place; quiver leg;* row; seat; stall; slip; sedile; *thing;* upholstered ~; *vinyl-covered seat;* wooden ~; *x-chair; yewwood ~; zeug [G.];*

**phantom** *(n.)*: apparition; banshee; cacodemon; disembodied spirit; eidolon; fetch; ghost; haunt; illusion; imp; incorporiety; jumby; *kelpie;* lemures; materialization; nonmaterial being; oracle; phantasm; *quickened spirit;* revenant; shadow; terror; unsubstantiality; visitant; wraith; *xenenthesis; yaksha* [Ind.]; zumby;

**pharisaical** *(adj.)*: artificial; bogus; counterfeit; duplicitous; emulative; feigned; facile; guileful; hypercritical; insincere; Janus-faced; *knavery; lying;* make-believe; non-genuine; ostensible; phony; pharisaic; quacksalving; religious; superficial; self-righteous; tartuffian; two-faced; untruthful; verneuking; wangling; *xenophobic;* yentzing; *zelig;*

**Pharisee** *(n.)*: actor; bluffer; charlatan; counterfeit; dissembler; emulator; fraud; guiler; hypocrite; insincere person; *Jew; knavery;* law-keeper; make-believer; *master; nobbler; outside only;* pretender; play-actor; quacksalver; religious hypocrite; sectarian; self-righteous person; tartuffe; *teacher; unauthentic;* ventzer; whited sepulcher; *xenophobe;* yentzer; *zelig;*

**phase** *(n.)*: area; *basic ~;* chapter; developmental stage; degree; echelon; facet; grade; height; instar; juncture; *kind;* level; leg; manner; *notch;* operation; period; part; *quarter;* round; stage; season; tier; time; *unit;* variation; *way; x-class; y-level;* zone;
**phenomenon** *(n.)*: appearance; apparition; amazing thing; *befallen;* curiosity; development; experience epi~; fact; *going on;* happening; incidence; *jarring;* known ~; law (of the universe); manifestation; marvel; natural ~; notable thing; occurrence; paranormal occurrence; phenomena [pl.]; quite a thing; *rarity;* strange happening; thing; unexplained ~; *very strange;* wonder; xtry. ~; yet unexplainable ~; *zero explanation;*
**philosopher** *(n.)*: academian; *apologist; brahmin* [Ind.]; contemplator; contravertist; deipnosophist; epistemologist; fathomer; *guru;* hypothesizer; intellectual; *judge;* keen mind; logician; lover of wisdom; metaphysician; *nominalist;* oracle; philosoph(izer); *Platonist;* quodlibetarian; reasoner; *realist;* sophist; seeker; sage; *Socratist;* thinker; theorist; theoretician; *utilitarian; valuator;* wisdom-lover; *Xenophonean; yeme;* zetetic;
**philosophical** *(adj.)*: absorbed; abstract; brooding; contemplative; deep; eclectic; fanciful; gazeful; heady [slang]; ideological; idealistic; judicious; *Kantian;* logical; meditative; maieutic; metaphysical; *nominalistic;* oracular; pensive; profound; philosophic; quodlibetarian; quasi-philosophical; rational; Socratic; staid; theoretical; thoughtful; *understanding; valuating;* wise; xenphonean; *yearnful;* zetetical;
**philosophy** *(n.)*: attitude; *Aristotelianism;* beliefs; critical idealism; dogma; epistemology; *frame of mind; Gnosticism; Humanism;* ideology; intellection; *judgment; Kanteanism;* line; love of wisdom; mindset; mentality; metaphysics; *nominalism;* outlook; philosophicalness; *Platonism;* quodlibetary; reasoning; school of thought; sophistry; thinking; thought; theory; understanding; viewpoint; way of thinking; *Xenosphile; Yoga;* zetetic;
**phony** *(adj.)*: artificial; bogus; counterfeit; dissembling; deceitful; ersatz; false; fake; fictitious; fraudulent; feigned; falsified; forged; gag; guileful; hoax; imaginary; imitation; japed; kiddy; *lying;* make-believe; mendacious; non-real; *outfoxed;* pretend; plastic; phoney; quacky; quasi; replicated; rip off; spurious; sham; trick; unreal; *vain;* wily; *xeno-; yeggy; zero validity;*
**phony** *(n.)*: actor; bluffer; betrayer; charlatan; counterfeit; con artist; dissembler; deceiver; emulator; fake; fraud; forgery; guiler; hypocrite; hoaxer; imitation; imposter; jerry-sneak [Br.]; *kidder;* liar; make-believer; nobbler; *outer appearance;* pretender; quacksalver; rip-off arttist; sham artist; swindler; shyster; trickster; *unauthentic;* verneuker; wheeler-dealer; *x'ed out; yentzer; zelig;*
**physical** *(adj.)*: animate; bodily; carnal; corporeal; *down here;* earthly; fleshly; flesh-and-blood; *genuine;* human; innate; jejune; *known;* living; materiate; material; mortal; natural; ordinary; pertaining to the body; quotidian; regular; real; somatical; temporal; tangible; unspiritual; *vapid;* worldly; *xbred; yourself;* zoetical;
**pick** *(n.)*: appointment; best choice; choice; determination; election; first ~; favorite; *gauging;* hand-~ed; *heart;* inclination; judgment; *knowledge; like; mind;* nomination; option; one chosen; preference; pleasure; *quibble;* ruling; selection; top choice; ultimate choice; verdict; will; winner; *x; yes; zeal;*
**pick** *(v.)*: accept; *best choice;* choose; decide; determine; elect; favor; give choice; hand- ~; indicate; judge between; *know;* like; make selection; *nominate;* opt; prefer; *quibble;* resolve; select; settle on; take; *use;* vote; want; *well-chosen; x; yes; zealous for;*
**picky** *(adj.)*: *austere;* bellyaching; choosy; difficult; demanding; exacting; finicky; fussy; *griping;* hard to please; implacable; *just so;* knocking; logic-chopping; meticulous; nitpicky; over-finicky; particular; persnickety; quiddle; *repining;* selective; tough; unappeasable; very ~; whining; *xuld* [arch.]; yammering; *zero give;*
**picnic** *(n.)*: *activity;* barbeque; clambake; cook-out; *day trip;* event; excursion; field day; function; garden ~; *holiday;* indoor ~; junket; jaunt; kebab roast; lunch; meal; *nosh;* outing; *patio; quality time;* roast; Sunday School ~; trip; *unwind; victuals;* weenie roast; *xarque;* yard; *zugunruhe;*

**pictorial** *(adj.)*: artistic; *blowup;* color-picture; depicted; drawn; detailed; diagrammed; etching-filled; figurative; graphic; hieroglyphic; illustrated; illustrative; *just-pictures; kit-cat; likeness; masterfully illustrated; non-text;* only-pictures; photographic; *quality art;* representative; sketch-filled; textless; *umbratic;* virtu; visual; with pictures; wordless; *xylographic; you-beaut [Aus.]; zoom shot;*

**picture** *(n.)*: artwork; allegory; blowup; color ~; caricature; depiction; drawing; detail; diagram; etching; exposure; enlargement; figure; film; graphic (image); headshot; image; illustration; in-drawing; *juvenillo; kit-cat;* likeness; mugshot; metaphor; movie; *negative;* oil painting; photo(graph); portrait; painting; portrayal; *quattrocento;* representation; rendering; sketch; similitude; snapshot; simile; *tintype;* type; umbratic; view; vignette; *video;* wall ~; word ~; x-ray; yellowed photograph; zoom shot;

**picturesque** *(adj.)*: attractive; beautiful; charming; dainty; eye-catching; fair; gorgeous; highly ~; impressive; *joy-giving;* keen; lovely; magnificent; nice; *outstanding;* pretty; *photogenic;* quaint; romanticized; scenic; striking; *terrific; unsurpassed;* vivid; well-looking; xtry.; you-beaut [Aus.]; *zizzy;*

**piece** *(n.)*: amount; bit; component; chunk; collop; daud; element; fragment; fraction; granule; hunk; ingredient; junt; kernel; lump; mass; morsel; nugget; ounce; part; portion; percentage; quantity; remnant; scrap; slab; segment; section; tad; tidbit; unit; *vestige;* wad; wedge; *x-mal [G.]; yngot [arch.]; zum [arch.];*

**pierce** *(v.)*: auger; broach; bore; cut through; drive; drill; dig; empierce; enter; force through; gore; hole; impale; jab; knife; lance; make hole; nail; open; poke; puncture; penetrate; *quill;* run through; stab; transfix; trans~; thirl; *undercut; ventilate;* wimble; *xylotomy; x-pierce;* yerk; *zing;*

**piercing** *(adj.)*: acute; boring; cutting; driving; empiercing; forcing; *grievous; high-pitched;* intense; jabbing; knife-like; loud; *mince; nail;* opening; penetrating; *quick; resounding;* sharp; stabbing; transfixing; *undercut; ventilate;* window-rattling; *xyresic; x-pierce; yerk; zing;*

**piety** *(adj.)*: adoration; *belief;* contemplativeness; devoutness; devotion; earnestness; faithfulness; goodness; holiness; introspection; *jubilation; kneeling;* laud; moral goodness; *non-presumptuous; obeisance;* pietism; piousness; *quaking;* religiousness; strict devotion; thoughtful meditation; *uplifting;* virtuousness; worshipfulness; Xn.; *yearnfulness;* zeal; [Ant. profanation]

**pig** *(n.)*: animal; boar [masc.]; *Cheshire; Duroc;* entity; *farm animal;* farrow; grice; hog; *Indian wild boar;* jungle-hog; *Kenyan bush ~;* livestock; Landrace; Mangalitza; mammal; nestle-draf; oinker; porker; *quadruped; razorback;* sow [fem.]; swine; Tamworth; ungulate; Vietnam potbellied ~; warthog; wild boar; *x-breed;* yelt; *zoic;*

**pile** *(n.)*: amassment; bunch; boodle; bulk; collection; constellation; drift; embankment; full load; gobs; gathering; heap; hoard; *ingathering; juba [L.];* kit; lump; lots; load; mound; *number;* oodles; overabundance; potful; passel; quantity; quire; rick; raft; scads; stack; tussock; ton; *unit; volley;* wad; windrow; *XL;* yardful; *zillions;*

**pile** *(v.)*: amass; accumulate; bank; collect; cumulate; deposit; enlarge; *fill;* gather; heap; hoard; increase; *jump up; keep growing;* lay up; mound; *number; overgrow;* put; *quadruplicate;* reposit; stack; store up; stock~; *take off;* upbuild; *volume;* wax larger; *XL; yain [arch.]; zoom;*

**pilgrim** *(n.)*: *Arab; Bedouin;* camper; drifter; excursionist; *emigrant;* floater; gadabout; hadji [Mos.]; itinerant; journeyer; *knight-errant; landlouper;* migrant; newcomer; *oberration;* palmer; Puritan; *Quaker;* rover; rambler; sojourner; Separatist; traveler; *unfixed;* voyager; venturer; wayfarer; xenizer; Yahgan; *zingaro [It.];*

**pill** *(n.)*: aspirin; *antibiotic;* bolus; capsule; drug; *electuary;* febrifuge; *glycerol;* horse ~; *item; julep;* kibble; lozenge; medicine; nostrum; *oxacillin;* pellet; prescription; *quinine;* remedy; *supplement;* tablet; ule; virucide; *vitamin;* wonder drug; *xenobiotic; yanggona; zopissa [arch.];*

**pillage** *(v.)*: *appropriate;* boot; carry off; despoil; depredate; excoriate; forage; freeboot; gut; harrow; *incursion; junk; kidnap;* lay waste; loot; maraud; nobble; *overexploit;* prey upon; plunder; *quash;* ransack; rifle; ravin; ravage; rape; spoil; sack; take; *unlade;* violate; wreck; *xfer; yank; zap;*

**pillar** *(n.)*: ante; arch~; buttress; column; *doorpost; epistyle;* fulcrum; *gatepost;* herm; intercolumniation; jackstay; *kabber; load-bearing;* main support; *necking;* obelisk; pole; post; pilaster; queen post; rest; support; stanchion; trumeau; upright; vertical; *weight-bearing post; xystus; yard; zaccho;* zoophoric column;

**pillow** *(n.)*: * air ~; bolster; cushion; cow ~; down- ~; eiderdown ~; feather ~; foam ~; goosefeather ~; headrest; *item; jacketed ~;* kahili ~ [Haw.]; lumbar ~; memory-foam ~; *neck ~; overstuffed ~;* pillion; *pad; quilt;* rest; sofa ~; *support;* throw ~; *tick;* upholstery; velvet ~; *Winnipeg cushion; xillinous; yellow ~;* zafu;

**pilot** *(n.)*: aviator; airman; airline ~; ace; bush ~; co- ~; captain; driver; eagle; engineer; flyer; flier; flyboy [slang]; fighter ~; guide; governor; helmsman; high flier; hostler; *individual;* jet ~; kamikaze [Jap.]; leader; LAC; *master;* navigator; NFO; operator; plane operator; quirk [slang]; *ramjet ~;* steersman; steerer; timoneer; test ~; *user;* volplanist; wingman; *xenagogue; yeoman; zoomer;*

**pilot** *(v.)*: aviate; barnstorm; conduct; control; direct; escort; fly; guide; handle; *instruct;* jockey; keep on course; *lead;* make go; navigate; operate; *outfly;* plane; *quicken;* run; steer; take (flight); usher; veer; wing; *xuld [arch.]; yern;* zoom;

**pinch** *(v.)*: afflict; bite; constrict; draw together; ensphere; *force;* grab; *hurt;* inhibit; *jam;* knab; *limit;* make tighter; nip; over-tighten; pick up; *quash;* restrict; squeeze; tweak; tighten; *uncomfortable; vice;* wring; *xuld* [arch.]; yank; *zeroize;*

**pine** *(v.)*: ache; brood; crave; decline; ebb; fade away; get weaker; hunger; itch for; jade; *killing;* languish; mope; *not excel; overmuch sorrow;* pout; quail; *rot;* sulk; taper; *use up; vanish;* waste away; *xerosis;* yearn; zap;

**pink** *(adj.)*: * annatto; blush; cerise; coral; dusty rose; English ~; flesh-colored; florid; grey- ~; hot ~; incarnadine; Jacobean ~; *kermes-red;* livid ~; mallow- ~; magenta; neon ~; opera ~; old rose; primrose; pinkish; *Quaker drab;* rosy; rose; shell ~; salmon; shocking ~; tea rose; *undercooked; violet;* whitish- ~; *xanthoconite;* yellow madder; *zinc orange;*

**pinnacle** *(n.)*: apex; brow; climax; crest; culmination; *destination;* extremity; farthest point; greatest height; height; high point; *increase; important; jut;* kop; limit; mountaintop; nub; *overmost point;* peak; *quoif;* ridge; summit; top; upper extremity; vertex; *way up; xtry; yonder point;* zenith;

**pinpoint** *(v.)*: ascertain; bring to light; close in; determine; emplace; find; get; hone in; identify; isolate; *jab;* kithe [Scot.]; locate; make certain; narrow down; *obtain;* pin down; put one's finger on; *quick-to-find; range;* single out; track down; *uncover;* verify; work out; *x; ypointing;* zero in on;

**pioneer** *(n.)*: *abider;* backsettler; colonizer; colonist; dweller; explorer; frontiersman; globe-trotter; habitant; homesteader; immigrant; inhabitant; journeyer; *keeping; latecomer;* migrator; newcomer; *outlander;* plainsman; planter; *quarter; refugee;* settler; sooner; trailblazer; *use;* viator; wayfarer; woodlander; xmigrant; *yerde [arch.]; zip to;*

**pious** *(adj.)*: adorant; believing; contemplative; devout; earnest; fearing; godly; holy; holier-than-thou; introspective; *jubilating; kneeling;* laudatory; moralizing; *non-presumptuous; obeisance;* prayerful; *quaking;* reverent(ial); religious; saintly; sanctimonious; spiritual; thoughtful; *uplifting;* virtuous; worshipful; *Xn.; yielding; yearnful; zealous;*

**pipe** *(n. conduit)*: aqueduct; black ~; conduit; duct; drain~; electrical conduit; flume; gutter; galvanized ~; hose~; iron ~; *j-bend pipe; kyle;* line; main; nullah; outlet; pipeline; penstock; PVC; *quill* [arch.]; route; steel ~; spillway; tube; tail~; *underground ~line;* ventiduct; water ~; *x-ray tube;* Y-branch; *zanja;*

**pipe** *(n. flute)*: alto flute; bass flute; cornamute; dactylic flute; eunuch flute; flute; fife; gaita; halil; *instrument; jubal;* kaval; love ~; *musical instrument;* nay; ocarina; piccolo; quena; reed; shinobue; tanso; *union pipe; veuze; wind instrument;* xun; y-pipe; zuffolo;

**pirate** *(n.)*: *armed robber;* buccaneer; corsair; *captain; devil; evildoer;* freebooter; gob; harpy; *invader;* jack-tar; kill-cow; *lascar [Ind.];* mariner; nimmer; old salt; plunderer; picaroon; *questor;* robber; swashbuckler; sea-robber; thief; *underhanded;* villain; whaler; *xebec-mariner; yawler;* zebec;

**pit** *(n. hole)*: aperture; breach; cavity; crevice; crater; ditch; excavation; fissure; gap(e); hole; incavation; jaw-hole; krater; lacuna; maw; nook; opening; orifice; *pothole;* quarry- ~; recess; saw- ~; sump; trench; *umbilicus;* vug; well; *xystus* ~; yawn; zanja;

**pitch** *(v. reel)*: alternate; bounce; careen; dip; *exchange;* fluctuate; go up and down; heave; *instability;* jerk; keel; list; lurch; move up and down; nutate; oscillate; pull up and down; *quaddle;* reel; rock; sway; toss; *uneven;* vacillate; waver; *xfer;* yerk; *zigzag;*

**pitch** *(v. throw)*: *abandon;* betoss; cast; discharge; eject; fling; *give;* hurl; heave; impel; jetsam; kest; launch; lurch; *move; non-retention;* outthrow; propel; *quoit; recast;* sling; shoot; send; toss; upcast; vault; whip; *xuld* [arch.]; york; zing;

**pitcher** *(n.)*: amphora; beaker; container; crock; carafe; decanter; ewer; flagon; gallon jug; half gallon ~; *inurn; item;* jug; *kovsh* [Rus.]; lota; milk jug; *neck;* olla; *phial; quart container; receptacle;* skeel; *tea* ~; urn; urceolate; vessel; waterpot; *xeo;* yabba; *zun;*

**piteous** *(adj.)*: affecting; benevolent; clement; compassionate; dolorous; empathic; forgiving; forbearing; gracious; humane; *interested; joy-giving;* kind; lenient; merciful; non-harsh; over-gracious; propitious; pitying; quick-to-forgive; ready to forgive; sympathetic; sparing; tender-hearted; tolerant; tenderhearted; understanding; very kind; warm; *xenial; yearnful; yielding;* zealous to forgive; [*Ant.* pitiless]

**pitiful** *(adj.)*: abject; bleak; contemptible; disgraceful; doleful; execrable; forlorn; grim; hopeless; ill-favored; *jarring;* keen; lowly; lamentable; meager; miserable; nasty; odious; piteous; pitiable; pathetic; *quad;* rank; sorry; sad; terrible; unfortunate; vile; woeful; xtry. bad; yucky; *zestless;* [*Ant.* praiseworthy]

**pitiless** *(adj.)*: austere; barbaric; cruel; cold-hearted; disdainful; *excessive;* flint-hearted; *galsome;* heartless; incompassionate; jaded; knark; loveless; merciless; non-sparing; obdurate; pernicious; *querulous;* ruthless; stone-hearted; tearless; unpitying; unmerciful; unsparing; *violent;* without mercy; *xenophobic;* yieldless; *zestful;* [*Ant.* piteous]

**pittance** *(n.)*: *amount;* bit; bagatelle; crumb; drop (in the bucket); *ens;* fragment; *frivolous;* groat; handful; impertinence; jack; joke; kernel; little bit; *mere;* mite; modicum; nothing; ounce; peanuts; *pathetic; quiddle; remnant;* smidgen; trifle; *unimportant; vestige;* whit; whiffle; *XAG; yngot* [arch.]; zippo;

**pity** *(n.)*: *altruism;* benevolence; compassion; charity; clemency; *delicate love;* empathy; favor; grace; humaneness; identification; *jarred;* kindness; leniency; mercy; niceness; *overpiteousness;* pitying; quarter; ruth; sympathy; tender mercies; unmerited favor; *virtue; well-favored; xenophilia; yearning;* zeal to forgive; [*Ant.* pitilessness]

**pity** *(v.)*: ache for; bleed for; condole; commiserate; *delicately love;* express ~; empathize; feel (sorrow) for; favor; grieve for; have mercy; identify with; *just want to help; kindness;* love; *mercy; niceness; over-empathize;* put oneself in his shoes; *quarter;* rue; show concern; sympathize; *take up for;* understand; *virtue;* weep for; *xenophilia;* yearn for; *zealous to forgive;*

**placate** *(v.)*: appease; becalm; conciliate; calm; diffuse; ease; *fulfill;* gratify; hush; *indulge; justify; knock down;* lull; mollify; *nullify; overcome;* pacify; propitiate; quell; reconcile; render favorable; smooth; satisfy; tranquilize; unruffle; *vanish;* win favor; x-out; *yield;* zeroize;

**place** *(n.)*: address; area; abode; bearings; *county;* district; *environs;* field; fixation; footing; ground(-plot); habitat; immediate area; *jurisdiction; kray* [Rus.]; location; *municipality;* niche; office; position; point; quadrant; region; site; spot; scene; setting; *territory;* ubiety; venue; vicinity; whereabouts; xy-coordinate; *yard;* zone;

**place** *(v.)*: assign; arrange; bestow; *confer;* deposit; deploy; em~; fix; give; hand (over); impart; install; *juxtapose;* kit; lay; leave; locate; *move;* nest; offload; put; *qualify;* rest; stick; set; situate; stow; station; transfer; unhand; vest; *weigh;* xfer; *yield;* zet [dial.];

**placement** *(n.)*: arrangement; assignment; bearings; configuration; display; distribution; deployment; establishment; em~; format; fixing; grouping; hanging; installation; *juxtaposition; kithe* [Scot.]; location; manner of ~; non-concealment; order; placing; position; *quo mode* [L.]; rearrangement; setting; stationing; *transfer; ultrastructure; view;* way; whereabouts; *xfer; yield;* zetting [dial.];

**plague** *(n.)*: affliction; bane; blight; curse; difficulty; disease; evil; epidemic; fash; gall; hex; incantation; irritation; infestation; *infection;* jinx; *karakia [Maori];* larval ~; murrain; malady; misfortune; nuisance; outbreak; ordeal; pestilence; pox; pandemic; *qualm* [arch.]; rot; scourge; trouble; *upheaval;* visitation; *virulent disease; vermination;* woe; *x-disease; yellow blight; zauber [G.];*
 **Famous Plagues:** ambulatory ~; black death; bubonic ~; glandular ~; murrain; pneumonic ~; the scourge; septicemic ~; ten plagues; yellow fever;
**plague** *(v.)*: afflict; burden; bewitch; curse; distress; enchant; execrate; foment; get; grieve; harass; hex; imprecate; irritate; jinx; *karakia [Maori]; lash out;* menace; nettle; *overrun;* put curse (-spell) on; perplex; *quash; rile;* scourge; torment; trouble; upset; unnerve; vex; worry; witch; *xuld [arch.];* yerk; *zap;*
**plain** *(adj. obvious)*: apparent; blatant; clear; distinct; evident; explicit frank; forthright; glaring; *heedless;* in focus; intentional; *just plain to see;* kenspeckle; lucid; loud and clear; manifest; noticeable; naked; obvious; perceptible; quite obvious; recognizable; salient; transparent; unmistakable; visible; watchable; *x-parent; yare; zero-disguised;*
**plain** *(adj. ordinary)*: average; basic; common(place); dull; everyday; familiar; generic; general; ho-hum; homey; inelaborate; inglorious; jejune; known-to-all; lackluster; mundane; minimal; normal; non-fancy; natural; ordinary; pure; quotidian; regular; run-of-the-mill; simple; standard; straightforward; stripped; typical; unadorned; ugly; unattractive; unsophisticated; unembellished; vanilla; widely-used; *wonted; xtr. dull; yawnish;* zestless; [*Ant.* peculiar]
**plains** *(n.)*: area; butte; champaign; *desert;* estrade; flatlands; flood plain; grasslands; highveld; ile [Welsh]; *jebel;* karroo [Afr.]; llano; mesa; meadowlands; *nature;* open ~; prairie; pastureland; quadrat; range; steppe; savanna; tablelands; upland; veld; wilderness; *xyris; yard; zea;*
**plaintiff** *(n.)*: accuser; *bellyacher;* complaintant; claimant; disparager; delator; demandant; *explode;* fault-finder; grievant; *haranguer;* impugner; *jangler; kvetch;* litigant; murmurer; *nitpicker;* objector; petitioner; *the* prosecution; querent; remonstrator; suitor; *tear into; undoer;* vituperator; witness; *xuld [arch.]; yawper;* Zoilus;
**plan** *(n.)*: agenda; blueprint; conception; chart; design; drawing; diagram; engineering; foredesign; ground-work; game ~; *hope;* itinerary; *judgment; key location map;* layout; master ~; map; machination; *nisus;* outline; project; platform; *quick thinking;* resolution; schedule; scheme; schematic; strategy; strategem; tactics; *underlying* ~; visual; way; wile; x-chart; *yantra [Hind.]; zenithal projection;*
**plan** *(v.)*: arrange; birth; concoct; contrive; chart; devise; design; develop; engineer; formulate; get ready; hatch; intend; invent; *judge;* kiddy; lay out; machinate; map out; *notion;* organize; pre~; plot; prepare; *quick-thinking;* ruminate; scheme; schedule; strategize; think (up); *use brain; visualize;* work out (-up); *xenodiagnose; yeme;* zero in;
**planet** *(n.)*: asteroid; body; celestial body; *Draco;* earth; *Fornax;* globe; heavenly body; inferior planet; *Jovian* ~; *Krypton [fict.];* luminous body; marble; *Neptune;* orb; planetary body; planetoid; *quasar;* realm; red ~; satellite; sphere; *Terra; Uranus; vale;* world; *x-ray star;* yellow ~; *Zorcon [fict.];*
**planetary** *(adj.)*: astral; astronomical; *body;* cosmic; celestial; deep space; earth-wide; extraterrestrial; *four quarters of the earth;* global; galactic; heavenly; inter~; interstellar; intergalactic; intermundane; *jovial; kosmos;* lunar; metagalactic; *nebular;* outer space; orbital; planetwide; polygalactal; quasi-stellar; *relating to planets;* stellar; space; solar; terrestrial; universal; ultramundane; *vacuum;* worldwide; *x-ray star;* yonder; zonic;
**plank** *(n.)*: *acacia wood;* board; crossbeam; deal; *elm;* floorboard; gang~; hardboard; *ironwood;* joist; knee-timber; lumber; lath; *maple; nemoral;* one-by-four; panel; piece of wood; quarter-cleft; rafter; slat; stud; scantling; timber; two-by-four; underlayment; *veneer;* wood; *xylon; yew; zingara;*
**plant** *(n. factory)*: assembly line; business; company; *cannery; developer;* establishment; factory; group; *holding company;* industrial ~; *joint-venture; kongsi [Chin.];* location; manufactory; manufacturer; mill; national corporation; outfit; operation; production facility; quasi-public corporation; *refinery;* small business; shop; *tooling up; union shop;* venture; works(hop); *x12;* yard; *zaibatsu [Jap.];*

**plant** *(n. vegetation)*: annual; biennial; *bean;* cutting; *deciduous ~;* evergreen; flora; fern; greenery; greens; growth; herb; houseplant; herbage; *inflorescence;* jungle-growth; kerf; *legume; mushroom; notholaena;* organic ~; octander; plantlife; plantlet; pulse; phanerogam; quickset; *root;* seedling; shoot; triennial; undergrowth; underbrush; vegetation; verdure; vert; wort; *weed; xerad;* yarb [dial.]; *zymophyte;*
**plant** *(v.)*: *afforest;* bury; broadcast; cover; conceal; deposit; disseminate; entomb; establish; fix; ground; hide; heel in; im~; inseminate; inhume; inter; *jam;* kist; lodge; *move; make; nest; obscure;* put in; pot; *quat [arch.];* reset; resow; root; sow; seed; stand; set; seminate; transplant; *underfurrow; verge; whelm; xenotransplant;* yird; zet [dial.];
**plaster** *(n.)*: adhesive; binding; cement ~; dressing; *epithem;* fixative; gypsum; *hold;* ichthyocolla; joint compound; kit; lime mixture; mastic; mortar; *nail;* overlay; paste; ~ of Paris; *quince-mucilage;* roughcast; stucco; tempered cement; untempered cement; *viscous;* wattle and daub; *xenograft; yoke; zip together;*
**plate** *(n.)*: article; basin; china ~; dish; dinner ~; entremet; fine china; glass ~; *hot ~;* item; *jade dish;* kuel [Chin.]; loam ~; monkey dish; *Nyon ~; olla;* paper ~; platter; *quart-vessel;* round ~; side ~; trencher; *urn;* vessel; wooden ~; *xeo;* yandy; *Zurich ware;*
**plate** *(v.)*: anodize; aureate; brass- ~; bronze(- ~); cover; coat; chromate; chrome- ~; copper~; deaurate; engild; electro~; foil; foliate; gild; gold~; *have gold-plated;* inaurate; *jacket; kist;* leaf; metal; nickel- ~; overlay; platinize; *quicksilver;* roll; silver~; saffron; tin(- ~); *upbind;* vermeil; white gold- ~; *xfer;* yellow-gold encrust; zincify;
**plateau** *(n.)*: *area;* butte; campo; *dale;* estrade; flatland; grasslands; highland; *ile [Welsh];* jebel; karroo; level land; mesa; *nature;* open field; plains; puna; *quadrat;* range; steppe; table(land); upland; *veld;* wilderness; *xyris; yard; zea;*
**platform** *(n.)*: area; *the* boards; *catafalque;* dais; estrade; floor; gallery; *hall;* item; *jetty; kinema;* lower stage; main ~; *nook; overhang;* plinth; proscenium; *quarterdeck;* rostrum; raised ~; stage; stand; tribune; upper ~; *venue;* walk; wharf; *x-section; yard; zone;*
**platter** *(n.)*: argil ~: bisque tray; charger; carrier; dish; *entremet;* fish ~; gold ~; hot plate; ironstone ~; jasperware ~; *kuel [Chin.]; lazy Susan;* meat ~; *nickel-plated ~;* oval dish; plate; *quart-vessel;* round ~; salver; server; serving dish; trencher; (tea) tray; *unused ~; vessel;* waiter; *xorai;* yandy; *Zurich ware ~;*
**plausible** *(adj.)*: acceptable; believable; credible; down-to-earth; doable; *expected;* feasible; good enough; heady; intelligent; justifiable; *known;* logical; legitimate; likely; matter-of-fact; no-nonsense; *obtainable;* possible; probable; quite sensible; reasonable; realistic; sensible; tenable; *understandable; useful;* viable; valid; workable; *xtry. likely; yieldful; zero problem;*
**play** *(n.)*: act(ing); afterpiece; barnstorming; drama(tization); entertainment; *floorshow; gathering; hit;* indoor ~; *jamboree;* kid's ~; *lead;* musical; monodrama; not-for-profit ~; onstage performance; open-air ~; playlet; presentation; performance; production; pageant; *querencia [Sp.];* reenactment; skit; scene; stage ~; show; theatrical performance; *tragedy;* underacting; variety show; work; *xtry. performance;* youth group ~; *zet [dial.];*
**play** *(v. amuse)*: amuse oneself; behave playfully; cut up; disport; entertain oneself; frolic; fool (with); faddle; gambol; have fun; horse~; *interest;* join in; keep amused; laik [Br.]; mess with; *non-serious;* occupy oneself; participate; *quality time;* romp; rollick; sport; toy; trifle; *use; vivify;* wallow in; *xel; yerk; zealous;*
**play** *(v. use an instrument)*: amuse; busk; blow; chord; deploy; entertain; *force air through;* finger; gratify; handle; *instrument;* jam; *key in; let out a tune;* make music; *noise; outperform;* perform; *quality;* ring; strum; sound; serenade; tickle those ivories [joc.]; toot; use; *vocation;* work; *xuld [arch.]; yain [arch.]; zither;*
**playful** *(adj.)*: animated; arch; *bouncy;* carefree; desipient; excited; facetious; frisky; frolicsome; gamesome; high-spirited; impish; joking; jocose; jumpy; keyed up; lighthearted; lively; ludibrious; miscievous; non-serious; over-frisky; *outrageous;* quacky; rollicksome; sportive; teasing; trifling; unserious; *uninhibited;* very silly; witty; waggish; *xtry. ~;* yeasty; zizzy;

**plead** *(v.)*: ask; appeal; adjure; beseech; beg; conjure; desire; entreat; *foreadmonish;* go begging; *humbly ask;* implore; im~; intercede; *juration; kneel to;* lift up one's voice for; make request; *need;* obsecrate; petition; pray; *quiritation;* request; supplicate; throw oneself at one's feet; urge; *vocalize;* wish; *XQ.;* yearn for; *zealously beseech;*

**pleasant** *(adj.)*: agreeable; blithe; blissful; congenial; cheerful; convivial; delightsome; enjoyable; friendly; fun; good-natured; genial; gratifying; happy; heavenly; invigorating; jocund; joyous; keen; lovely; mellow; melodic; nice; of good cheer; personable; pleasing; pleasurable; *queme;* rewarding; satisfying; sapid; terrific; uplifting; *vivacious;* wonderful; *xenial; yeah!;* zizzy;

**pleasantness** *(n.)*: agreeableness; appeal; blissfulness; cheerfulness; delightfulness; enjoyableness; fineness; fun; goodness; gratification; happiness; invigoration; joyousness; keenness; loveliness; mellowness; melodiousness; niceness; *overjoyed;* pleasure; queme; richness; satisfaction; sapidity; thrill; urbanity; *vivaciousness;* wonderfulness; *xenia; yeah! zestfulness;*

**please** *(v.)*: appease; amuse; befit; content; delight; entertain; *enchant;* fulfill; gratify; humor; indulge; joy; keep happy; *like;* make happy; not dis~; oblige; overjoy; pamper; queme; rejoice; satisfy; suit; thrill; tickle; *uplift; very happy; wonderful; xtry.; yummy; zealous;* [*Ant.* peeve]

**pleasurable** *(adj.)*: agreeable; blissful; contenting; delightful; enjoyable; fun; good; gratifying; happy; heavenly; invigorating; joyous; keen; lovely; melodious; nice; out-of-this-world; pleasant; pleasing; *queme;* rewarding; satisfying; terrific; thrilling; uplifting; very good; wonderful; *xenial; yeah!;* zizzy; [*Ant.* painful]

**pleasure** *(n.)*: amusement; bliss; contentment; cheer; delight; enjoyment; ecstasy; fun; felicity; fulfillment; gratification; happiness; indulgence; joy; kicks; liking; merriment; niceness; overjoy; pleasure; queme; rapture; satisfaction; sensuality; titillation; *uplifted; vivacity; wonder; xanadu; yumminess;* zest; [*Ant.* pain]

**pledge** *(n.)*: affirmation; assurance; *bond;* commitment; declaration; *earnest;* forswearing; guarantee; hypothecation; *imprest;* jurament; *kept promise; letter of commitment; making of vows;* non-conditional promise; oath; promise; *qualified promise;* resolution; solemn oath; testament; troth; treaty; undertaking; vow; word (of honor); *x-one's heart; yafery* [arch.]; zealous ~;

**pledge** *(v.)*: assure; assert; adjure; bind to oath; covenant; deign; *ensure;* forswear; guarantee; give word; hypothecate; inter~; jurate; *keep word; legitimize;* make vow; *nobly ~;* oath; obligate; promise; *qualify;* resolve; swear; testify; *unconditionally ~;* vow; warrant; *x-ones heart; yafery [arch.]; zealously ~;*

**plentiful** *(adj.)*: abundant; bountiful; copious; disproportionate; excess(ive); fruitful; full; great; generous; heaps; immense; jumbo; *king-sized;* lots; lavish; many; much; numerous; overabundant; plenteous; quantitative; *replete;* rich; superabundant; surplus; superfluous; tons; uberous; unreserved; voluminous; vast; wantless; x.; *yards; zillions;*

**plenty** *(adj.)*: abundant; bounteous; copious; disproportionate; excessive; fruitful; great; galore; heaping; immense; jumbo; *king-sized;* lavish; many; much; numerous; overflowing; overabundant; overmuch; plentiful; quantitative; replete; rich; several; *tons;* uberous; voluminous; wantless; *x.; yards; zillions;*

**plenty** *(n.)*: abundance; bounty; copiousness; disproportion; excess; fruitfulness; greatness; heaps; immense(ness); *jumbo; king-sized amounts;* lots; loads; many; much; numerousness; overflow; overabundance; plentifulness; quantity; repleteness; *rich;* running over; superfluity; tons; uberousness; volume; *wantless; x.; yards; zillions;*

**pliable** *(adj.)*: adaptable; bendable; changeable; ductile; elastic; flexible; giving; hand-bendable; infirm; *jiggly; kinked;* limber; malleable; non-rigid; operable; pliant; *quick-flex;* resilient; rubbery; soft; tensile; unfirm; versatile; workable; willowy; withy; *xapuri;* yielding; *zingy;*

**pliant** *(adj.)*: accommodating; bendy; conformable; ductile; elastic; flexile; *give;* hand-bendable; infirm; *jiggly; knuckle;* lithe; manipulable; nimble; obedient; pliable; *queachy [arch.];* responsive; supple; springy; tractable; unfirm; variable; willowy; *xapuri;* yielding; *zingy;*

**plight** *(n.)*: adversity; bind; complication; calamity; dilemma; endangerment; fix; glitch; grief; headache; impasse; jam; kink; *load;* mess; *nuisance;* obstacle; pickle; predicament; quandary; rattle; strait; trouble; unholy mess; vexation; worry; *xtry. trouble; yuckiness; zhlubby;*

**plod** *(v.)*: advance; bumble along; clump; demarch; edge; footslog; go; galumph; hike; haul; *interlope;* journey; keep going; lumber; move; nudge; *outwalk;* pass through; *quicken; ramble;* slog; sling; trudge; *underway;* venture; wade; walk; xfer; yomp; *zigzag;*

**plot** *(n. piece of land)*: acre; back acre; croft; *division;* erf; farm; glebe; grounds; hide; hectare; *item; juger* [Rom.]; *khet* [Ind.]; land; lot; *manor; nook;* oxgang; plat; patch; parcel; quadrat; run; section; swidden; tract; thwaite; unit; virgate; *wedge; x-mal [G.];* yard(land); *zone;*

**plot** *(n. scheme)*: artifice; blueprint; cabal; conspiracy; design; enginery; foredesign; gambit; huggermugger; intrigue; jape; King's gambit; *layout;* machination; *notion;* outline; ploy; *quo mode* [L.]; ruse; scheme; treachery; under~; *usurpation;* villainy; wile; *x-chart; yantra [Hind.]; zenithal projection;*

**plot** *(v.)*: arrange; birth; brew; connive; conspire; cabal; devise; engineer; fabricate; *get* ideate; hatch; imagine; invent; *jockey;* kiddy; lay a ~; machinate; *notion;* navigate; originate; plan; *quick-thinking; ruminate;* scheme; think; *use brain; visualize;* work out; *xenodiagnose; yeme; zazen;*

**plow** *(n.)*: *apparatus;* breast- ~; *blade;* colter; dray- ~; *equipment;* foot~; gang- ~; harrow; *implement; j-groove; keel;* lister; middlebreaker; *nignay; object;* plough; *quat [arch.];* rake; swing- ~; tiller; trench- ~; *upturn; V-groove;* whip-stitch; *x-wide ~;* yoke; *zeug [G.];*

**plow** *(v.)*: *agriculture;* break up; cultivate; divide; entrench; furrow; grave; husband; harrow; intrench; *job;* keel; list; *labor; moil; newly ~ed;* open; plough; *quat [arch.];* (round)ridge; *score;* till; turn; upturn; *V-groove;* work; *x-cend; yoke; zeug;*

**ploy** *(n.)*: artifice; beguilement; con; device; deception; ensnarement; fake-out; gambit; hoax; imposture; japery; knavery; little game; maneuver; *nobbling; outfoxing;* plan; *quiblin [arch.];* ruse; racket; scheme; subterfuge; strategy; trick; tactic; *untruth;* verneuking; wile; *xuld [arch.];* yentzing; *zinger;*

**pluck** *(v.)*: abstract; *bring; capture;* draw; dehair; deplume; extract; fetch; grab; *haul;* intercept; jerk; kep; *lift;* make off with; nab; nip; obviate; pull; quill; remove; rip; snatch; take; tug; uproot; unplume; *vellicate;* whisk; *xuld [arch.];* yank; zip;

**plug** *(n.)*: *apparatus;* blockage; bung; bottle stopper; cork; dook; drain- ~; *encumbrance;* fipple; *gunk; hawse-plug; incumbrance;* jam; korke; lodgment; *mass; non-flowing;* obstruction; occlusion; *prevent;* quercus; rubber stopper; *rag;* stopper; stoppage; stopple; spile; tamkin; tap; *upset;* vigia; wad; *x; yieldless; zeroizer;*

**plug** *(v.)*: *arrested;* block; bung; cork; close; clog; dam up; encumber; fill; *gum up;* hinder; inhibit; jam in; *keep from;* load; make ~ged; *non-flowing;* obstruct; occlude; plug up; *quercus;* restrain; stop up; *thwart; upset; void;* wad up; *x-out; yieldless; zero flow;*

**plume** *(n.)*: apluster; beard; crest; decoration; *embellishment;* feather; goose-quill; hackle; *ibis-feather; jay-feather; kahili [Haw.];* lark-feather; mail [pl.]; *neossoptile; ornament;* plumage [pl.]; quill; remiges; scalpular; tuft; *uniform;* vibrissa; *wren-feather xema-feather; yellow finch-feather;* zoofulvin;

**plump** *(adj.)*: abundant; beefy; chubby; disproportionate; enlarged; full-figured; flabby; great; hefty; immense; jumbo-sized; king-size; large; massive; *noteworthy;* overweight; portly; pudgy; quantitative; round; rotund; sizable; tubby; *unwieldy;* voluminous; wide; XL; *Ymir;* zaftig;

**plunder** *(v.)*: appropriate; boot; *capture;* despoil; excoriate; freeboot; fleece; gut; harrow; *incursion;* jack; knock off [slang]; loot; maraud; nobble; overexploit; pillage; prey on; *quash;* ravin; raven; rob; rapine; ransack; sack; spoil; strip; take; *unlade;* violate; wreck; *xfer; yank; zap;*

**plunge** *(v.)*: *angle;* belly-whop; crash ~; dive; *eject;* fall; freefall; go down; *headlong;* immerse; jump down; jackknife; keel over; leap; make dive; nose-dive; *over the cliff;* plummet; quick-fall; running- ~; *reduce;* sink; submerge; tumble; turn downward; *under;* volt; whop; *x-cend; yank down;* zoom down;

**pocket** *(n.)*: * *area;* back ~; button ~; coat ~; dress ~; *eyeglass holder;* front ~; garment ~; hip pocket; inside ~; jacket ~; *knapsack ~; location; marsupium; nunny bag ~;* overall ~; pouch; pants ~; *quart-sized ~;* rear ~; shirt ~; trouser ~; utility ~; vest ~; watch ~; *XL ~; you [Chin.];* zip ~;

**poem** *(n.)*: acrostic; ballad; couplet; doggerel; elegy; free verse; georgic; hexastich; idyl; jingle; kasida; limerick; lyric; madrigal; nursery rhyme; ode; poetry; quatrain; rhyme; sonnet; triolet; unmetered ~; verse; virelay; *words; Xenphanean; Yeatsism;* zetetic;

**poet** *(n.)*: author; bard; composer; doggerelist; elegist; framer; *glossator;* humorist; improvisator; imbongi; jongleur; *kasida;* lyricist; laureateship; metaphrast; makar [Scot.]; minstrel; nursery rhymist; odist; poem writer; poetess [fem.]; poet laureate; poetaster; *quatrain;* rhymester; skald; songsmith; sonneteer; trouveur; *unpublished ~;* versifier; writer; *Xenphanes;* yedder; zetetic poet;

**poetic** *(adj.)*: acrostic; bardic; beautiful; cantable; colorful; descriptive; elegiac; expressive; flowing; graceful; *Homeric;* iambic; *jongleur;* Keatsian; lyrical; metaphrastic; melodic; metrical; non-prosaic; odic; poetical; *quadripartite;* rhythmic; *Shakespearean;* scaldic; *trouveur; unmetered poem;* versified; vivid; *wordsmith; Xenphanic; Yeatsian; zizzy;*

**point** *(n.)*: acicula; barb; beak; cusp; denticle; end; *fine ~;* goad; horn; *ice pick;* jag; *kiskari [Jap.];* knife~; lance; mucro; needle; nib; *oxgoad;* pin(head); prick(le); prong; piton; quill; razor-sharp ~; spine; spike; summit; tine; tip; termination; *ultra-pointy;* verge; *well-sharpened;* xyston; *yet undulled;* zenith;

**point** *(v.)*: aim; betoken; call attention to; *convey;* direct; *express;* fix on; guide; give direction; *head;* indicate; *jut;* kithe [Scot.]; lay forth; lead; make known; *notify; open up;* point out; *qualify;* reveal; reference; show; tell; take aim; train; *use sights;* view; way; *x-hairs; ypointing [arch.];* zero in;

**pointless** *(adj.)*: aimless; *by chance;* causeless; *draw of the hat;* empty; futile; groundless; hopeless; inane; jejune; keenly stupid; left to chance; meaningless; needless; of no use; purposeless; *quirky;* random; reasonless; senseless; totally arbitrary; useless; vain; without purpose; worthless; *x-out;* yet futile; *zero cause;*

**pointy** *(adj.)*: acute; barbed; cusped; denticled; edged; fine-edged; *graving;* highly pointed; *incisal;* jagged; keen; lanceolated; mucronate; nettled; over-sharpened; pointed; punctiform; quill-like; razor-sharp; sharp; spiky; tined; ultra-pointy; very sharp; well-sharpened; xiphoid; *yet undulled;* ziphoid;

**poise** *(n.)*: aplomb; balance; composure; carriage; deportment; dignity; elegance; equilibrium; fluency; grace; *high-style; impressive;* jimp; kinesics; loveliness; manner; mien; *nimbleness;* over-elegance; posture; *quickness;* refinement; self-control; smoothness; *tastefulness; unbroken;* voluble; *womanliness; xtry. ~; yaup; zierlichkeit [G.];*

**poison** *(n.)*: arsenic; aconite; bane; cyanide; *drug; effuvium; foxglove; grievance;* hemlock; inee; *jimsonweed;* kex; lewisite; *manihot; nicotine; orpiment;* prussic; pesticide; *quass;* ratsbane; spit-venom; toxin; upas; venom; wolfs-bane; xylostein; *yeara;* zootoxin;

**poison** *(v.)*: afflict; adulterate; arsenicate; befoul; contaminate; defile; destroy; empoison; envenom; exterminate; embitter; foul; *grime;* henbane; impoison; inquinate; impregnate; infect; *javel; kill;* lace; *murder;* nightshade; *outvenom;* pollute; quell; ruin; spoil; taint; undermine; venenate; vitiate; *warp;* xylostein; *yucky;* zap;

**poisonous** *(adj.)*: *adverse;* arsenious; baneful; contaminated; deadly; deleterious; envenomed; fatal; foul; *grievous;* harmful; injurious; infected; *jeopardous; killing;* lethal; malefic; noxious; *orpiment;* poison; perilous; *quelling;* ruinous; scatheful; toxic; unsafe; venenate; venomous; virulent; *wicked;* xylostein; *yeara;* zootoxic; [*see* corrupt]

**poke** *(v.)*: agitate; bump; *contact;* dub; elbow; force; goad; heave; impel; jab; knock; lean on; make; nudge; *overhang;* push; prod; quab; rap; *ram;* shove; thrust; urge; veney; whack; *xuld* [arch.]; *yank;* zonk;

**pole** *(n.)*: * *axle;* bar; caber; column; dowel; *epistyle;* flag~; *gatepost;* herm; intercolumniation; jackstay; *kabber; load-bearing;* mast; may~; newel; *object;* post; pylon; quarter-post; rod; shaft; stave; support; stanchion; telephone ~; tent ~; upright; virgulate; weight-bearing ~; *xystus;* yedder; zinc-coated rod;

**police** *(n.)*: authorities; bobbies [Br.]; cops; constabulary; *department;* enforcers; fuzz [off.]; gangbusters; highway patrol; *Interpol;* johnnies [Br.]; *kavass* [Turk.]; *the* Law; law enforcement; *marshal; nabbers* [Br. slang]; *officer;* policemen (-officers); *questura* [It.]; rangers; state troopers; smoky [slang]; *sheriff;* troopers; *undercover ~;* vice squad; *wolly [Br.];* xerif; *the* Yard [Scot.]; *zaptieh* [Turk.]; *zarp* [S. Afr.];

**police** *(v.)*: *arm; bind;* control; defend; ensure; enforce; fend; guard; hold to; insure; jaga; keep (safe); look after; monitor; *nestle;* overshadow; patrol; *quia timet [L.];* regulate; safeguard; take care of; uphold; vallate; watch; *x-guard; yeme* [arch.]; *zealously watch;*

**policy** *(n.)*: authoritative guideline; *the* book; code; directives; established practice; fundament; guideline; habit; instructions; *judgment; key policies;* line; *modus operandi* [L.]; method; *the* manual; *motto;* norm(al procedure); orders; operation; precedent; practice; pattern; procedure; *qualifier; the* rules; regulations; standard; system; tack; use; *verdict;* way of doing things; *xenagogy;* yardstick; *zakon [Rus.];*

**polish** *(n.)*: alkyd; burnish; coat; *Danish oil;* enamel; finish; gloss; glaze; glair; high-gloss finish; *inceration;* japan; *keen;* lacquer; luster; marine spar; nigrosine; *nail ~;* overglaze; polyurethane; *quartz sand; repolish;* shellac; sheen; shine; topcoat; urethane; varnish; wax; xesturgy; *yare; zinc flourosilicate;*

**polish** *(v.)*: apply ~; burnish; buff; *coat; dazzle; enamel;* furbish; *finish;* gloss; glaze; *high-gloss; inceration;* jigger; *keen;* lacquer; luster; lap; make shiny; *nigrosine;* overglaze; overpolish; overgild; planish; *polyurethane; quartz sand;* rub; shine; sleek; shellac; topcoat; *urethane;* varnish; wax; *xesturgy; yare; zinc flourosilicate;*

**polite** *(adj.)*: acceptable; amiable; benign; brought-up; courteous; civil(ized); deferential; *encouraging;* friendly; gracious; gentlemanly; *harmonious; interpersonal;* judicious; kind; *likable;* mannerly; nice; obsequious; *over- ~;* pleasant; proper; *queme;* respectful; sociable; thoughtful; tactful; urbane; very polite; well-mannered; *xenial;* yielding; *zero offense;* [Ant. poorly-mannered]

**politician** *(n.)*: aspirant; autocrat; bureaucrat; candidate; contender; congressman; dirty ~; demagogue; elected official; *favorite son;* geo~; highbinder; house leader; incumbent; jerrymanderer; *key official; lobbyist;* legislator; member of congress; minority leader; *nominee;* official; public servant; politicaster; *quango;* runner; representative; senator; solon; statesman; Tammany man; *upper house;* vote-getter; wealsman [derog.]; wannabe; *xenocrat; yes-man; zenocrat;*

**political** *(adj.)*: administrative; bureaucratic; congressional; diet-related; electoral; federal; governmental; heteronomous; institutional; judicatory; *kakistocratic;* legislative; *mayoral;* nomothetic; national; official; parliamentary; quasi-legislative; ruling; senatorial; *Hammany;* unicameral; viceroyal; wealsman; xenocratic; yard; zemstvo [Rus.];

**poll** *(n.)*: analysis; ballot; *breakdown;* census; *decennial census;* election; field study; *figures;* Gallup ~; *hand-raising;* inquiry; *judge; key survey;* listing; *mandated census;* nationwide ~; opinion ~; plebiscite; questionnaire; research; *results;* survey; town-wide survey; *undertaking; vox populi* [L.]; vote; *wishes; xenodiagnosis;* yearly ~; *zonal census;*

**poll** *(v.)*: ask; analyze; assess; *ballot;* canvass; do a ~; enquire; examine; evaluate; find out; get answers; *hunt for;* inquire; interview; investigate; *judge; knowledge;* look for; make query; *number;* opinion; probe; pose; question; request information; survey; sample; test; take census; uncover; view; want information; *XQ;* yeas and nays; *zero in;*

**pollutant** *(n.)*: adulterant; befoulment; contaminant; dirt; *evil;* filth; *grime;* hazardous material; impurities; *javelling; kallowing; loused up; manihot;* noxious substance; *organocide;* poison; pollution; *quade [arch.];* ruin; sullying; toxin; uncleanness; vileness; waste product; *xysma; yuckiness; zero cleanness;*

**pollute** *(v.)*: attaint; adulterate; abominate; blight; contaminate; dirty; defile; desecrate; empoison; foul; *go bad; hoar;* infect; *jade; ketty;* litter; lace; make unclean; *necrosis;* oxidize; poison; queer; ruin; spoil; sully; taint; *unclean;* violate; welk; *xylaria; yellow; zorch;* [Ant. purify]

**pollution** *(n.)*: adulteration; blight; contamination; defedation; empoisoning; fumes; *gray smog;* hazmat; inquination; *junk; kogai* [Jap.]; litter; *mess; noise* ~; noxious fumes; oxidation; polluting; photochemical smog; queerness; *ruination;* smog; toxic waste; unclean air; vog; welking; *xylaria; yellow air; zorch;* [*Ant.* purification]
**polygamist** *(n.)*: *adulterer;* bigamist; concubine-keeper; digamist; *err; femme-covert; gynaecceum;* hetaerist; *illegal; jarring; Koranic; libidnist; Mormon;* non-monogamist; *open-marriage;* polygynist; quadrigamist; *rake;* seraglio-keeper; trigamist; *unwise; variety;* womanizer; xenogamist; *Yeziti; Zaidi;*
**polygamous** *(adj.)*: *adulterous;* bigamous; concubine-keeping; digamous; *erring; femme-covert; gynaecceum;* hetaeristic; harem-keeping; *illegal; jarring; Koranic; libidnous; multi-wife;* non-monogamous; open-marriage; polygynous; quadrigamous; *rake;* seraglio-keeping; trigamous; *unwise; variety;* womanizing; xenagamous; *Yeziti; Zaidi;*
**polygamy** *(n.)*: *adultery;* bigamy; concubinage; digamy; *eight wives;* femme-covert; *gynaecceum;* hetaerism; harem-keeping; *illegal; jarring; Koranic;* leviration; marriages; multiple wives; non-monogamy; open marriage; polygyny; polybigamy; polyandry [fem.]; plural marriage; quadrigamy; *rake;* seraglio-keeping; trigamy; *unwise; variety;* womanizing; *wives;* xenogamy; *Yeziti; Zaidi;*
**pomp** *(n.)*: ado; bother; ceremony; display; extravagance; fanfare; grandeur; *hoopla; impressive; joyance;* kingly honor; *loftiness;* magnificence; *nundination;* ostentation; pageantry; ~ and circumstance; pretension; *quindene;* refulgency; show; splendor; to-do; *unparalleled;* vainglory; *wonder; xtry.; yahoo!; zeal;*
**pompous** *(adj.)*: arrogant; boastful; big-sounding; bombastic; condescending; disdainful; egotistical; flowery; flatulent; grandiose; high-sounding; imperious; *jackanapes; know-it-all;* lofty; magniloquent; narcissistic; ostentatious; orotund; pretentious; pontifical; quick-to-boast; *reassured;* splendid; self-important; showy; turgid; tumid; uppity; vain(glorious); wrapped up in oneself; *x-proud;* yelping; zero humility;
**pond** *(n.)*: arm; body (of water); carr; *deep;* estuary; fish~; gullet; hole; horse ~; *inlet; jheel* [Ind.]; kettle-hole lake; lake; mill~; *narrows;* ostiary; pool; *quai;* reservoir; salt ~; tarn; *underground pool; vlie [S. Afr.];* water (hole); wallow; *xyrisic; yeo; Zee [G.];*
**ponder** *(v.)*: analyze; brainstorm; consider; cogitate; contemplate; dwell on; debate; deliberate; evaluate; focus; gauge; *hypothesize; imagine; judge; know;* lucubrate; meditate; *notion; occur;* premeditate; pause; pore; puzzle over; question; reflect; study; think; use brain; valuate; weigh; *xenodiagnose; yeme; zazen;*
**pontificate** *(v.)*: address; bloviate; communicate; declare; express; *foresay;* go on; hold forth; impart; jabber; *key in;* lecture; mention; narrate; orate; preach; quoth; ramble; speak; talk; utter; vocalize; word; *xenophonia;* yak; *zeug [G.];*
**pool** *(n.)*: above-ground ~; bath; cistern; carr; collection; dead water; etang; fishpond; gilgai; horsepond; in-ground ~; *Jacuzzi®;* kettle-hole; lap pool; lido; lake; lagoon; linn; mere; natatorium; nausetorium; *Olypic swimming* ~; puddle; pond; ~side; *quai;* reservoir; swimming ~ (-hole); tarn; *underground* ~; vat; wading ~; *xyrisic; yeo; Zee [G.];* [*see* pond]
**pool** *(v.)*: accumulate; build; collect; come together; drain; *enlarge;* flow together; gather; heap up; *increase; jump up; keep growing;* lay up; mass; *naid; overflow;* puddle; pile up; *quicken;* reposit; settle; *travel;* upbuild; *volume;* wax larger; *XL; yern; zip together;*
**poor** *(adj.)*: abject; beggarly; bad off; *contemptible;* deprived; dirt- ~; destitute; desolate; empty-handed; forlorn; famished; gant; humble; hard-luck; impoverished; indigent; jejune; *keenly* ~; low-income; lowly; meager; modest; mean; moneyless; needy; overcome with poverty; poverty-stricken; penurious; penniless; *quisby; rags;* skint; suffering; tight; unfortunate; underprivileged; void; wanting; without; *xtry, destitute; yowling; zero;*
**pop** *(n.)*: airburst; bang; burst; crack; din; explosion; fulmination; going off; hit; implosion; *impact; jolt;* ka-pow; *let rip; mine;* noise; outburst; plop; plunk; pow; *quake;* rap; sound; thud; unleashing; vroom; wham; wallop; *xuld [arch.]; yield;* zonk;

**popular** *(adj.)*: admired; accepted; acclaimed; beloved; big; celebrated; dear-loved; ever-popular; familiar; favored; famous; fashionable; gestic; greatly loved; hot; highly regarded; illustrious; *jubilated over;* known (by all); liked; loved; magnifical; notable; *outstanding;* prevalent; *quality;* regarded; stylish; trendy; talked-about; universally known; vogue; well-liked; well-thought-of; widespread; *xtry.;* yichus; *zealously loved;*

**popularity** *(n.)*: acceptance; acclaim; admiration; *beloved;* celebrity; *distinction;* esteem; eminence; fame; favor (of the people); glory; honor; high regard; idolization; *illustriousness; jubilation; kudos;* likeableness; love; legend; *much-acclaimed;* notoriety; *outstanding;* public acclaim; *quality;* regard; recognition; renown; status; trendiness; *tribute; unmitigated ~;* vogue; veneration; *well-loved; xtry. ~;* yichus; *zealous love;*

**popularize** *(v.)*: advance; broadcast; circulate; disseminate; endorse; encourage; fame; get the word out; herald; *introduce; jar;* keep advertising; let be known; make popular; *notify;* overspread; promote; *quantity;* raise awareness; spread; tell others; *televise;* universalize; vulgarize; *widespread; xtr.; yet popular; zizzy;*

**populate** *(v.)*: accomplish; breed; colonize; crowd; *diffuse;* empeople; expand; fill; *gorge; have;* inhabit; invillage; *jam-pack;* keep house; live in; multiply; *non-deportation;* occupy; *over~;* people; *quantity;* replenish; repeople; stock; settle; take up residence; *use; volume; wedge in; xfer; yield; zillions;*

**porch** *(n.)*: *area; awning;* back ~; balcony; *covered entrance;* colonnade(-gallery); deck; entryway; forecastle [naut.]; gallery; hood; inclosed porch; jube; *knuckle balcony;* levee; lanai; *mirador;* narthex; out~; portico; piazza; parvis; quarterdeck [naut.]; rear porch; stoop; stoa; terrace; *upper deck;* veranda; *walkway; weather deck;* xyst; *yu [Chin.];* zayat;

**port** *(n.)*: anchorage; bay; berth; cove; dock; *exurb;* fishing town; *gangway;* harbor; haven; *inlet;* jetty; key town; landing; *location;* marina; mega~; *near-shore;* out~; port city; quay; riverside town; seaport; town; urban center; village; wharf; *xebec ~;* yacht landing; zone;

**portable** *(adj.)*: able to be moved; *borne along;* carriable; *dynamic;* easy-to-transport; *fold-up; goes;* handy; interchangeable; *janker; kurvey;* lightweight; movable; mobile; non-stationary; *on wheels;* pocket-sized; placeable; *quick-moving;* removable; *sailable;* transportable; unfixed; vest-pocket; wheelable; *xfer; yanker; zip;*

**portion** *(n.)*: allotment; bit; component; chunk; divvy; daud; element; fragment; fraction; granule; hunk; issuance; ingredient; junt; kernel; lump; mass; morsel; nugget; ounce; part; piece; percentage; quantity; ration; remnant; segment; section; share; tad; tidbit; unit; *vestige;* wad; *x-mal [G.]; yngot [arch.]; zum [arch.];*

**position** *(n. arrangement)*: arrangement; body ~; bearings; carriage; configuration; disposing; emplacement; fix; *form; ground;* how it's arranged; *immediate area;* jurisdiction; *kit;* location; maneuver; navigation; order; office; pose; place(ment); posture; *quadrant;* repositioning; stance; set; situation; *tactical ~;* ubiety; vicinity; whereabouts; *xfer; yard; zone;*

**position** *(n. rank)*: appointment; bearing; class; degree; estate; footing; grade; height; *importance;* job; *kind;* level; *mastery;* notch; office; order; place; quality; rank; standing; status; station; title; tier; *uniform;* varve; *way; x-class;* y-level; *zone;*

**position** *(v.)*: arrange; *bearings;* configure; dispose; emplace; fix; get into ~; hand-move; install; *jam; kit;* lay; locate; move; maneuver; navigate; order; pose; place; posit; posture; posturize; put; *quicken;* reposition; set; situate; take ~; *use; verge; work; xfer;* yede; zip;

**positive** *(adj.)*: assured; beyond doubt; certain; confident; definite; explicit; firm; guaranteed; highly confident; indisputable; just certain; keenly sure; like-minded; most certain; non-questionable; 100% certain; persuaded; promising; questionless; reliable; sure; true; unmistaken; very sure; without doubt; *xtry. ~; yes;* zero doubt;

**possess** *(v.)*: apprehend; bear; claim; control; dominate; embody; fill; gain; get; grip; have; hold; inherit; *just have;* keep; lay hold of; make one's own; *nab;* own; obtain; occupy; personally own; *quantify;* realize; retain; secure; take (possession of); use; *vaunt;* wield; win; *xfer; yain* [arch.]; zip out;
**possession** *(n.)*: asset; bequest; control; custody; *dhan;* energumen; filling; gaining; getting; holding; having; inheritance; *jamindris* [Ind.]; keeping; kit; *load;* mortmain; material asset; *needments;* ownership; *occupancy;* property; *quantity; resources;* substance; temporal; *use; valuable;* winnings; ward; *xfer; yemsel* [arch.]; *zamindari* [Ind.];
**possibility** *(n.)*: ability; aptness; *best bet;* chance; contingency; doableness; eventuality; feasibility; good chance; hope; *imaginable; improbability;* just a chance; known risk; likelihood; *maybe; non-guaranteed;* option; potential; prospect; plausibility; *qualified chance;* risk; scenario; *thinkable; uncertainty;* virtuality; *workability; xtry. chance; yet possible; zero doubt;*
**possible** *(adj.)*: achievable; able; *bearable;* capable; doable; earthly; feasible; gettable; humanly ~; imaginable; just ~; *keen;* likely; manageable; *maybe; no-nonsense;* obtainable; potential; plausible; performable; prospective; *qualified;* realistic; *sufficient;* thinkable; tenable; *usable;* viable; workable; *xtry.;* yet ~; *zero doubt;*
**post** *(n.)*: *archpillar;* baluster; bitt; bollard [both naut.]; column; door~; durn; *epistyle;* fence~; gate~; herm; intercolumniation; jackstay; kevel; *load-bearing;* main; newell ~; *octostyle;* pole; pylon; quarter- ~; rafter; support; stanchion; *tige;* upright; vertical; weight-bearing ~; *whipping ~; xystus;* yard; zoophoric column;
**post** *(v.)*: accredit; *books;* chalk up; denote; enter; fill in; file; get down; hand enter; imprint; journalize; keep in log; log; mark down; notate; *overwrite;* put down; *quill;* record; set down; take down; underwrite; *vell;* write (down); x; yak; zay;
**poster** *(n.)*: advertisement; announcement; bill; blowup; centerfold; circular; display ~; *eye-catching ~; full-color ~; giant ~;* hanging; information ~; *joint-ad;* king-sized ~; *leaflet;* magazine ~; notice; *object;* playbill; pin-up; picture; print; *quadrifoliate; red-letter announcement;* sign(board); *thing;* unifoliate ad; *vignette;* wall ~; wanted ~; XL ~; youth ad; zine ad;
**postpone** *(v.)*: adjourn; break; come back to; delay; defer; end for now; finish later; *go home;* hold off; hang; *interrupt; just over; knock off;* leave till later; make stall; *non-immediate;* over for now; put off; quit till later; reschedule; shelve; suspend; table; *unanimous motion to adjourn; vacate; waste time;* x; *yerde* [arch.]; *zero conclusion;*
**pot** *(n.)*: aluminum ~; boiler; broiler; cauldron; crock; dishpan; *electric fryingpan;* flesh~; fishkettle; *griddle; honey~; incinerator pan;* jackshea; kettle; *lool;* milkpan; nog; olla; *pan;* pipkin; quart-pot; roaster; sauce~; tagine; *tea~; urn;* vessel; wok; xeo; yetling; ziti pan;
**potage** *(n.)*: *alphabet soup;* broth; chowder; daube; *edibles;* fleshbroth; gipper; hotpot; Irish stew; jipper; kell; lobscouse; meal; mulligan stew; navarin; olio; pottage; pulp; pot-au-feu; *quibebe;* ragout; rabbit stew; stew; soup; tagine; *uneaten ~; venison stew; wonton soup;* xurpa; Yankee bean soup; *zuppe* [It.];
**potential** *(adj.)*: achievable; attainable; budding; capable; delitescent; efficacious; feasible; gettable; hypothetical; *imaginable;* just possible; known ~; latent; *the* makings; *may(be);* now-possible; obtainable; possible; procurable; *questionable;* reachable; realizable; securable; theoretic; theoretical; untapped; *viable;* would-be; *xfer; y potential* [sci.]; *zeta potential* [sci.];
**potential** *(n.)*: ability; aptitude; *become;* capacity; delitescence; efficacy; facility; faculty; *gift; hope; instinct; jurisdiction;* know-how; likelihood; means; makings; natural ability; opportunity; power; possibility; prospect; qualification; resources; sufficiency; *talent;* usefulness; virtuosity; wherewithal; *xenium; yare; zeal;*
**potion** *(n.)*: admixture; brew; blend; concoction; compound; drink; elixir; formula; *go-go juice; hypnotic ~;* intermixture; *juice; karakia* [Maori]; liquid; *love ~;* mixture; medicine; *nectar;* oil; philter; *quass;* remedy; recipé; serum; suspension; tonic; *ule; volatile substance;* witches' brew; *xenophobic;* yanggona; *zauber* [G.];

**potter** *(n.)*: artificer; *builder;* clay-worker; *designer;* earthen vessel-maker; fashioner; guildsman; hand-crafter; *individual;* jar-maker; *kaolin; laborer;* master ~; maker of pottery; *notoriety; operator;* pottery-maker; *qualified worker; ready worker;* skilled craftsman; trained ceramic worker; *useful;* vessel-maker; *workman; xtry.; yeoman; zaikai [Jap.];*
**pouch** *(n.)*: *article;* bag; canvas bag; coin ~; drawstring ~; *equipment;* fob; gunnysack; holder; inside pocket; jute sack; kitbag; *large ~; marsupium; nunny bag; overall pocket;* pocket; *quart-sized;* rear pocket; sack; *trouser pocket; utility bag;* velvet ~; *watch pocket; XL ~; yolk sac;* zip pocket;
**pounce** *(v.)*: attack; bound; come down; *capture;* dive; *ensnare;* fly upon; grapple; hop on; *invade;* jump on; *kemp;* leap; make attack; *nab; overtake;* plump; *quash; raid;* spring upon; tackle; upspring; vault; *waylay; xfer; yerk; zap;*
**pound** *(v.)*: assault; beat; buffet; clobber; drub; *efface;* flog; grind; hit; hammer; impact; jab; knock; lam; mash; nail; *overstrike;* punch; pummel; quab; rap; smite; strike; thump; thrash; uppercut; veney; wallop; *x-sect;* yedder; zonk;
**pour** *(v.)*: affuse; anoint; blow; burst; cascade; decant; dispense; discharge; disgorge; effuse; empty; flow; *fill;* gush; hurl; issue; jet; *keep flowing;* let fall; move; *naid;* out~; *put;* perfuse; *quicken;* rush; spill (out); stream; spew; transfuse; transfer; *tip; uprush;* vomit; well; xfer; yead; *zip;*
**pout** *(v.)*: agonize; brood; *carp;* despond; *elegiac;* fret; glower; huff; *incubate; joyless;* kick the dirt; languish; mope; *not happy;* over-ponder; pine; *question;* ruminate; sulk; think about; *unhappy;* vex; worry; xenodiagnose; yeme; zero in;
**poverty** *(n.)*: adversity; abject ~; beggary; *condition;* destitution; extreme ~; *famishment;* gutter; grinding ~; hardship; impoverishment; indigence; inadequacy; *jejuneness;* keen ~; lack; little; meagerness; mendicancy; *misery;* need; neediness; *overwhelming ~;* penury; pauperism; poorness; privation; *the* poorhouse; *quisby;* rags; scantiness; *tenuity* [arch.]; unprosperousness; *vulnerability;* want; xtry. ~; *yowling;* zero income;
**powder** *(n.)*: *anthrax;* baby ~; comminution; dust; empasm; filings; flakes; fine dust; granules; grindings; *gun ~;* grains; hair~; *item; jar; konite;* loose particles: mash; *non-toxic ~; obliterated;* particles; *quashed;* raspings; smeddum; sprinkles; shavings; *sawdust; substance;* talc; triturate; *unused; vanity;* white ~; *xeraphium; yttria; zineb;*
**power** *(n.)*: ability; authority; brawn; capability; cogence; control; dint; dynamo; energy; electricity; force; faculty; gusto; generant; heartiness; horsepower; intensity; influence; imperium; jet- ~; jurisdiction; keest; lustiness; might; muscle; mastery; manpower; means; *name;* oomph; potency; puissance; qi; resources; rule; strength; sufficiency; thewiness; *usefulness;* vim; vigor; *virtue;* wherewithal; *xenium; yare;* zip; zing; [*see* source; Ant. powerlessness]
**powerful** *(adj.)*: able(-bodied); brawny; cogent; compelling; durable; efficacious; empowered; forceful; great; husky; high-potency; influential; iron; *jusqu'au bout [F.];* keen; lusty; mighty; *nervy; obstinate; oaky;* potent; puissant; *quality;* robust; strong; tough; titanic; unflagging; vigorous; well-set; *x-strong;* yauld; *zippy;* [Ant. powerless]
**powerless** *(adj.)*: armless; *bad;* crippled; defenseless; disarmed; drained; enfeebled; effete; exhausted; feeble; frail; *gimp;* helpless; impotent; incapable; inert; *jejune; knocked out;* lame; much-weakened; non-potent; overweak; puny; pathetic; queachy [dial.]; *reduced;* scrawny; soft; strengthless; tired; unable; unmighty; vulnerable; weak; xtry. vulnerable; *yet without energy;* zapped; [Ant. powerful]
**practical** *(adj.)*: advisable; achievable; beneficial; constructive; down-to-earth; doable; expedient; effective; feasible; functional; good; helpful; *intelligent;* judicious; *keen;* logical; meet; no-nonsense; operational; operative; practicable; prudent; *quartful* [arch.]; realistic; sensible; sound; *tenable;* useful; utilitarian; viable; valuable; wise; workable; worthwhile; well-advised; *xtry. useful;* yieldful; *zero problem;* [*see* sensible]

**practicality** *(n.)*: advisability; achievability; benefit; constructive; doableness; expedience; effectiveness; feasibility; functionality; goodness; helpfulness; *intelligence;* judiciousness; *keenness;* logic; meetness; *no-nonsense;* operability; practicability; prudence; *quartful [arch.];* realism; reasonableness; sensibility; soundness; sense; *tenability;* usefulness; viability; value; workability; workableness; wisdom; *xtry. useful; yieldful;* zero problem;

**practice** *(n.)*: apprenticeship; basic training; conditioning; drill; dummy run; exercise; field ~; going over; habilitation; honing; improvement; job-training; knocking into shape; lessons; mock run; *night rehearsal;* on-the-job training; preparation; polishing; *qualification;* rehearsal; refining; readying; sharpening; training; tryout; *unlocking; upbringing;* versing; working with; xenagogy; yarking; *zealous instruction;*

**practice** *(v.)*: acclimate; become proficient; condition; drill; do over; exercise; *foster;* get better; go over; hone; improve; *jibe;* keep doing (-rehearsing); *learn;* make ready; *nurture; outfit;* prepare; polish; *qualify;* rehearse; refine; ready; sharpen; train; *use;* verse; work out; whet; *xenagogy;* yarken; *zealously train;*

**pragmatic** *(adj.)*: advantageous; beneficial; conducive; down-to-earth; expedient; favorable; good; helpful; inservient; judicious; *keen;* logical; meet; no-nonsense; operative; practical; *quartful* [arch.]; results-oriented; self-serving; *tenable;* utilitarian; viable; workable; *xtry. doable;* yieldful; *zero qualms;*

**pragmatism** *(n.)*: advantageousness; beneficialness; conduciveness; down-to-earthness; expedience; favorableness; *good;* helpfulness; inservience; judiciousness; *keenness;* logic; meetness; *no-nonsense;* operativeness; practicality; *quartful* [arch.]; realness; self-service; *tenability;* utilitarianism; viability; workability; *xtry. opportunism;* yieldfulness; *zero qualms;*

**praise** *(n.)*: accolades; adoration; acclaim; blessing; credit; commendation; devotion; exaltation; extolment; encomium; fame; glorification; honor; idolization; jubilation; kudos; laud; lifting up; magnification; *notoriety;* ovation; pangyrizing; *quality;* rejoicing; salute; singing; tribute; uplifting; veneration; worship; *xtry.; yichus;* zealous ~;

**praise** *(v.)*: adore; acclaim; applaud; bless; belaud; credit; commend; doxologize; extol; exalt; fame; glorify; honor; hail; idolize; jubilate; kneel before; laud; lift up; magnify; *note; over~;* pangyrize; *quiritation;* rejoice; resound; rave; salute; sing praises; thank; tout; uplift; venerate; worship; *xenophilia; yichus;* zealously ~; [*see* rejoice; sing; worship]

**praiseworthy** *(adj.)*: admirable; beloved; commendable; distinguished; estimable; favorable; fine; great; honorable; impressive; jake [Br.]; keen; laudable; meritorious; nice; outstanding; prized; *qualified;* remarkable; splendid; thank-worthy; ultra-good; virtuous; venerable; very good; worthy of praise; wonderful; xtry.; yichus; *zealously loved;* [*Ant.* pitiful]

**prank** *(n.)*: antic; beguilement; caper; cantrip; deception; escapade; farce; gag; hoax; imposture; joke; knavishness; lark; mischief; naughtiness; *outfoxing;* practical joke; quick trick; ruse; stunt; shenanigan; trick; *untruth; vandalism;* waggery; *xuld [arch.];* yock; zinger;

**prankster** *(n.)*: antics; bamboozler; caperer; clown; doer of practical jokes; *enigmatist;* farceur; gagster; ham; imp; joker; jokester; kidder; larrikin; merry-andrew; *nut; ornery;* practical joker; *quipster; riddler;* sporter; trickster; teaser; *unserious;* vandal; wag; *xtry. ~; yock;* zany;

**prattle** *(n.)*: absurdity; babble; chatter; drivel; empty words; fudge; gabble; guff; hot air; idle chatter; jabber; kelter; *lard;* mumbo-jumbo; nonsense; *outlandishness;* patter; queer speech; rambling; ranting; slaver; twaddle; talk; utterance; vain talk; wishwash; xenoglossy; yakking; *zeug* [G.];

**prattle** *(v.)*: announce; blather; chatter; dither; eloqute; fiddle-faddle; gab; haver; idly talk; jaw; keep talking; *loose tongue;* make conversation; natter; opine; prate; palaver; *quote;* rattle on; speak; talk; utter; voice; wag ones tongue; *xgress;* yakkety-yak; *zay* [dial.];

**pray** *(v.)*: appeal; ask; beseech; beg; call upon; deprecate; desire; entreat; *find out;* get before God; give thanks; humbly ask; intercede; inquire; implore; importune; jurate; kneel before God; *look to;* make request; *need;* obsecrate; petition; plead; query; request; supplicate; talk to God; tell God; *thank; urge;* vocalize; wish; *xenophagy;* yearn for; *zay [arch.];*

**prayer** *(n.)*: appeal; beseeching; benediction; call; cry; deprecation; *desire;* devotions; entreaty; *forewish;* grace; *humble entreaty;* intercession; importunity; imprecation; imploration; invocation; *juration; kiddush [Heb.];* litany; making request; nones; orison; obsecration; obtestation; petition; plea; *query;* request; rogation; supplication; *telling God;* urging; *vigil;* wish; *xenophagy;* yearning; *yizkor [Heb.]; zikr* [Mos.];

**pray-er** *(n.)*: asker; beseecher; beadsman; caller; daysman; entreater; *fearer of God; Godly man;* humble entreater; intercessor; jurator; *kneeler; laud;* maker of requests; man of prayer; *need;* offerer of prayers; petitioner; praying man; prayer warrior; requester; supplicant; *talker; urger;* vocalizer; wisher; *xenophagy;* yearner; *zay [arch.];*

**prayerful** *(adj.)*: adorant; beseeching; contemplative; devout; devotional; earnest; *fearing;* given to prayer; holy; interceding; imprecatory; importune; *juration; kneeling;* laudatory; *magnifying; non-presumptuous; on one's knees;* precatory; praying; petitionary; *quaking;* reverent; supplicatory; suppliant; *thoughtful; uplifting;* votive; worshipful; *Xn.;* yearnful; *zealous in prayer;* [Ant. prayerless]

**prayerless** *(adj.)*: abandoning prayer; *bad behavior;* careless; delinquent in prayer; *erroneous;* forgetful; *go without prayer;* heedless; inattentive; *jaded; knees unworn;* lax; *missing;* non-praying; neglectful; *omitting; prayer; proud;* quick-to-forget; remiss; slack; self-sufficient; *thoughtless;* unfaithful in prayer; void of prayer; without praying; *xtry. pride;* yet unpraying; *zero prayer;* [Ant. prayer]

**preach** *(v.)*: address; admonish; appeal; bespeak; cry; charge; declare; deliver; discourse; declaim; exhort; exposit; expound; foreadmonish; *gospel;* herald; harbinger; inform; inculcate; *jobation; kerygma;* lament; lecture; minister; noise; orate; proclaim; preachify; prophesy; quote the Bible; rant [derog.]; sermonize; speak; trumpet; tell; utter; urge; vocalize; vociferate; word; warn; *xenagogy;* yell; *zealously ~;*

**preacher** *(n.)*: *admonisher;* Bible-teacher; chaplain; circuit rider; *declarer;* discourser; *Doomsday ~;* expositor; evangelist; field ~; gospeler; herald; homilist; hot-gospeler; holderforth; itinerant ~; *josser [Aus. slang]; jargoneer [off.]; kerygma; kindler;* lecturer; lay- ~; messenger; minister; man of God; *noiser;* orator; open-air ~; pulpiteer; pastor; prophet; proclaimer; preacher-man [derog.]; *quoter;* revivalist; ranter [derog.]; speaker; sermonizer; servant of God; trumpeter; teacher; *utterer;* voicer; *warner;* xenagogue; *yeller [derog.];* zealous ~;

**preaching** *(n.)*: addressing; admonishment; application; Bible- ~; crying; charge; declaration; delivery; exhortation; expositing; field preaching; gospeling; homiletics; homily; hellfire-and-brimstone; injunction; inculcation; instruction; *jeremiad;* kerygma; lamentation; lecture; message delivery; noising; orating; open-air preaching; preaching; prophesying; quoting the Bible; ranting [derog.]; speaking; sermonizing; street-preaching; trumpeting; thundering; teaching; uttering; vocalizing; warning; xenagogy; *yelling; zealous ~;* [see sermon]

**preamble** *(n.)*: avant-propos; book introduction; comments; *discourse;* epigraph; exordium; forward; *genesis; handwriting;* introduction; inscription; *journal; kickoff;* lead-in; legend; monologue; note; overture; preface; prelude; prologue; *quotation;* remarks; start; *take-off;* unveiling; *verbiage;* welcome; *xiaozhuan; yede; zygogenesis;*

**precarious** *(adj.)*: ambiguous; borderline; chancy; dangerous; delicate; erratic; *fluctuating; giddy;* hairy; instable; iffy; jeopardized; *kooky;* labile; *moveable;* non-stable; on thin ice; parlous; questionable; risky; shaky; tippy; touch-and-go; unstable; unreliable; volatile; wobbly; *x-ing;* yo-yoing; *ziggety;*

**precaution** *(n.)*: admonishment; *beware;* caution; defensive measure; *equipping;* foresight; guarantee; *hue and cry;* insurance; *just in case; keep safe; looking ahead;* measure; *notification;* option; preventative measure; *questioning;* readiness; safeguard; tip; *urging; vatic;* warning; x-guard; yellow alert; zeal;

**precautionary** *(adj.)*: admonitory; advisory; backup; cautionary; defensive; deterrent; ensuring; foresighted; *guarding against; hue and cry;* insuring; just-in-case; *keeping safe;* looking ahead; *measures;* notification; optional; protective; preventative; pre-emptive; prognostic; *questioning;* readying; safeguarding; self-protecting; *thinking ahead; urging;* vatic; warning; wise; *x-guard; yepe; zealous alert;*

**precede** *(v.)*: antecede; antedate; be ahead of; come before; do(ne) before; exist first; forego; forerun; go before; guide; happen first; head; introduce; *just ahead;* keep ahead; lead; *move ahead; not before;* outrank; predate; preexist; *quondam;* run ahead; spearhead; take the lead; take place prior; usher; *venerate; way before;* xenagogue; *younger;* zet *[dial.];*

**precedence** *(n.)*: antecedence; *bigness; centrality;* dominance; exigency; eminence; first in order; greater importance; highest rank; importance; *justification; key;* lead; magnitude; most importance; *notoriety; outrank;* priority; primacy; *qualified;* rank; superiority; top-rating; urgency; vitalness; weight; *xtry.; yearning;* zero hour;

**precedent** *(n.)*: antecedent; bellwether; case (in point); *done before;* example; former instance; guide; *happen first;* instance; *justification; king's example;* lead; model; *non-changing standard;* original case; praxis; pattern; *qualified; representative;* sample; standard; *touchstone;* use; *venerated;* way it's been; *xenagogue;* yardstick; zet *[dial.];*

**precious** *(adj.)*: adored; beloved; cherished; costly; dear (bought); expensive; estimable; *fine;* greatly prized; highly-valued; invaluable; *judged worthy; king's ransom;* loved; meaningful; *nice;* of great price; prized; quality; ranking; revered; *steep;* treasured; *unequalled;* valued; valuable; worth it's weight in gold; *xtry.; yieldful; zestful;*

**precise** *(adj.)*: accurate; bona fide; correct; definite; dead-on; exact; factual; genuine; honest; infallible; justifiable; known; literal; meticulous; *mean it;* never-failing; *orderly;* particular; questionless; real; sure; true; unerring; veritable; well-defined; *x-parent; yes;* zero-error;

**precision** *(n.)*: accuracy; *bona fide;* correctness; dependability; exactness; factuality; genuineness; honesty; infallibility; *justification;* keenness; legitimacy; meticulousness; non-erring; *open;* particularity; *quaecumque sunt vera* [L.]; reliability; sureness; trustworthiness; trueness; unerringness; veracity; *well; xtry.; yes;* zero error;

**preclude** *(v.)*: *avert;* bar; cumber; debar; exclude; frustrate; forbid; *gum up;* hinder; inhibit; *jam;* keep (from); limit; *moderate; nullify;* obstruct; prohibit; quash; restrain; stop; turn away; *undo;* veto; withhold; *x;* yank; zero; zap; [*Ant.* permit]

**predator** *(n.)*: assailer; *bushwhacker; chaser; despoiler;* ensnarer; *foe; gunman;* hunter; huntsman; invader; *Jaeger* [G.]; killer; layer in wait; marauder; *nemesis; overtaker;* preyer; *quarry;* ravager; slayer; stalker; shark; tracker; *undertaker;* victimizer; vulture; wolf; *xenic;* yager; zapper; [*Ant.* prey]

**predestinate** *(v.)*: appoint; *beforehand select;* choose; determine; destine; decree; elect; foreordain (-choose; -appoint; -doom); *God-appointed; heaven-ordained; hand-pick;* institute; *judge; kismet; lay down; lot;* make; *necessitate;* ordain beforehand; predestine; predetermine; preordain; preselect; pre-elect; *quondam selection;* resolved by God; select; sovereignly choose; take; *unchangeable; verdict; willed by God; x-scending; yonder;* zero choice; [*see* foreknow]

**predestination** *(n.)*: appointment; *before-ordained;* choice; determination; destiny; decree; election; *established beforehand;* foreordination; *God-appointed; heaven-ordained;* inevitability; *judgment;* kismet; lot; *made to;* non-volition; ordaining beforehand; predetermination; preordination; preselection; pre-election; *quondam selection;* resolution of God; selection; sovereignty; *T.U.L.I.P.;* unchangeable plan of God; *verdict; will of God; x-cending; yonder;* zero choice; [*see* foreknowledge; Calvinism]

**predicament** *(n.)*: adversity; bind; complication; calamity; dilemma; dire straights; endangerment; fix; grief; headache; impasse; jam; kink; lot; mess; nuisance; obstacle; *ordeal;* plight; problem; quandary; rattle; strait; trouble; upheaval; vexation; woe; *xerotripsis; yuckiness; zhlubby;*

**predict** *(v.)*: augur; bode; calculate; divine; *declare;* envisage; forecast; foretell; foresee; give prophecy; hariolate; inform; *judge; kerygma;* lament; make a prediction; notify; orate; prophesy; portend; presage; *quain* [arch.]; read the future; see coming; second-guess; soothsay; tell the future; *utter;* vaticinate; warn; *xenagogy;* yell; zay *[arch.];*

**predictable** *(adj.)*: able to be asserted; assertable; affirmable; attributable; assumed; banal; calculable; calculable; determinable; expected; foreseeable; guaranteed; highly ~; in the cards; *judge;* knowable; likely; more than likely; not unexpected; obvious; probable; questionless; readily ~; sure; too ~; unchanging; very ~; without surprise; *xel [arch.]; yeme; zero surprise;*
**predominance** *(n.)*: authority; bulk; control; dominance; eminence; fame; greatest part; headship; influence; *jurisdiction; kingship;* leadership; majority; mastery; masterdom; *nobility;* overriding influence; predominancy; prevalence; *quo warranto* [L.]; rank; supremacy; superiority; top-position; upper hand; *veneration;* weight; *xtry.; yard;* zonal control;
**predominant** *(adj.)*: accepted; biggest; chief; dominant; eminent; frequent; greatest; highest; imperious; *jurisdiction;* key; leading; main; notable; overriding; prime; prevalent; *quintessential;* ranking; reigning; supreme; top; uppermost; *venerated;* weightiest; *xenenthesis; yet unsurpassed; zenithal;* [*see* usual]
**pre-eminence** *(n.)*: ascendancy; *best;* chief place; dominance; excellence; first place; greatness; highness; hagemony; influence; *jurisdiction;* key place; limelight; magnificence; No. 1 spot; overlordship; prominence; primacy; *quality;* renown; supremacy; top-importance; ultimacy; visibility; weightiness; *xtry.; yondmost; zenithal;*
**pre-eminent** *(adj.)*: above all else; *best;* chief; dominant; excellent; foremost; greatest; highest; incomparable; *jurisdiction; key;* leading; most importance; No. 1; over all; prominent; *quality;* ranking; reigning; supreme; top(most); ultimate; visible; weightiest; *xtry.; yondmost;* zenithal; [*Ant.* petty]
**preface** *(n.)*: avant-propos; beginning; commencement; *dedication;* epigraph; forward; *genesis; heading;* introduction; inscription; *journal; kickoff;* lead-in; legend; monologue; note; opening; preamble; prelude; prologue; proem; prolepsis; *quotation; remarks; start; take-off; unveiling; verbiage;* welcome; *xiaozhuan; yarken; zygogenesis;* [*Ant.* postscript]
**prefer** *(v.)*: aspire; *best choice;* choose; desire; elect; favor; give choice; have a preference; indicate; judge; *keen desire;* like better; love; make a choice; *nominate;* opt; pick; please; *questionless;* rather; select; take; *use;* vote for; want; *xel [arch.]; yearn for; zealous for;*
**preference** *(n.)*: aspiration; bias; choice; desire; druthers; election; first choice; favorite; great desire; heart's desire; inclination; judgment; *keen;* leaning; liking; mind; *notion; opinion;* pick; pleasure; penchant; partiality; *quibble;* ruling; selection; top choice; unneutrality; verdict; will; *x; yes; zeal;*
**pregnancy** *(n.)*: anticipation; brooding; conception; carrying; development; expectancy; formation; fertilization; *the* family way; gestation; gravidation; heaviness; impregnation; *jumboize; klutziness;* laden; maturation; nine months; *outbreeding;* parturiency; *quickening; reproduction; superfetation;* term; utero-gestation; *vivification;* waiting period; *xenogamy; young on the way; zygogenesis;*
**pregnant** *(adj.)*: anticipating; antenatal; brooding; carrying; *developing;* expecting; enceinte; fertilized; fecundated; gestating; great; gravid; heavy; impregnated; incubating; *jumbo-sized; klutzy;* laden; *multiplying; nascent;* one in the oven [slang]; parturient; *quickening; reproducing;* superimpregnated; *term;* utero-gestating; *vivifying;* with child; *xenogamous; young on the way; zygogenesis;*
**prejudge** *(v.)*: assume; *bias; chauvinism;* discriminate; expect; forejudge; generalize; *hatred; intolerance;* jump to conclusions; *klanism; leaning;* make stereotype; *narrow-minded; one-sided;* presume; prejudicate; *quick to judge; racism;* stereotype; take for granted; *unfair; valuate;* Waspish; *xenophobia; yahooism; zealotry;*
**prejudice** *(n.)*: *anti-Semitism;* bias; bigotry; chauvinism; discrimination; ethnocentrism; favoritism; *gall; hatred;* intolerance; jaundice; klanism; leaning; maltreatment; narrow-mindedness; one-sidedness; partiality; *quick to judge;* racism; supremism; segregationalism; tendentious; unfair; *vexation;* Waspish; xenophobic; *yahooistic; zealotry;*
**prejudiced** *(adj.)*: anti-Semitic; anti-black; biased; bigoted; chauvinistic; discriminatory; ethnocentric; favoring; *gall; hateful;* intolerant; jaundiced; *klanism;* low-thinking; *maltreat;* narrow-minded; one-sided; partial; quick-to-judge; racist; supremist; *terror;* unfairness; *vexation;* Waspishness; xenophobia; *yahooism; zealotry;*

563

**preliminary** *(adj.)*: advance; beginning; basic; commencing; debuting; exordial; first; groundwork; headmost; initiatory; introductory; initial; *jump-start;* kick-off; leading; makeready; opening; prefactory; prelusive; proemal; qualifying; readying; starting; *trial;* unveiling; *venture;* warm-up; *xon; yede; zip;*
**premature** *(adj.)*: advanced; before its time; *commencing early; done too early;* early; far ahead; green; half-baked; ill-timed; inopportune; *just too soon; keenly early; leading;* malapropos; *nonstandard;* out-of-season; preterm; *quick;* real early; soon; too early; untimely; unready; underdeveloped; very early; wrongly-timed; *xenogenesis; yarly* [arch.]; *zero hour;*
**premeditated** *(adj.)*: aforethought; by design; conscious; calculated; deliberate; ever-conscious; *forethought; glaring; highly visible;* intentional; intended; *just plain to see;* knowing; *liking;* meaningfully; non-accidental; on purpose; purposeful; (pre-)planned; quite intentional; *resolute;* studied; thought-out; unmistakingly; volitional; willful; witting; *xtry. planned; yearnful; zealous;*
**premium** *(adj.)*: A-1; best; choicest; *desirable;* elite; finest; greatest; highest; high-quality; *impressive; jim-dandy;* keenest; luxurious; loftiest; most desirable; No. 1; optimal; prime; quality; ritzy; superior; top; ultimate; *valuable;* world-class; xtry.; yondmost; zenithal; [Ant. poor-quality]
**premonition** *(n.)*: adumbration; bad sign; caveat; denotement; *ESP;* forewarning; *grasp;* herald; intuition; *judiciousness;* knowledge; *learn; misgiving;* notice; omen; oracle; presage; portent; presentiment; *quain [arch.];* red flag; sign; tip; *understanding;* vision; warning; *xylomancy;* yellow alert; *zero ignorance;*
**preoccupation** *(n.)*: absorption; bemusement; castle-building; concentration; domination; engrossment; fixation; *grip;* hold; *idée fixe* [F.]; involvement; *jag;* kinching; *like;* monomania; *narcosis;* obsession; preoccupation; *quaffing;* riveting; *rapt;* spellbinding; transfixing; unresponsiveness; *vegging out;* withdrawal; worry; wistfulness; *x-fixing; yieldedness; zeroing in;*
**preparation** *(n.)*: adaptation; arming; accustoming; bringing to readiness; conditioning; development; equipping; fitting; getting ready; groundwork; habilitation; homework; *instruction;* jibing [slang]; *knocking into shape;* lining out; making ready; *near-ready;* outfitting; priming; prepping; preparedness; qualification; readying; setting; suiting; training; *ultra-prepared;* versing; whetting; work (to do); *well-readied; xenagogue;* yarkening; *zealous ~;*
**preparatory** *(adj.)*: adaptive; basic; beginning; conditioning; dighting; equipping; foundational; grooming; habituating; instructive; *jibing [slang]; knocking into shape;* leading; making ready; *nearing readiness;* outfitting; opening; preliminary; parasceuastic; qualifying; readying; starting; training; *ultra-prepared;* versing; whetting; *xenagogic;* yarkening; *zealously ~;*
**prepare** *(v.)*: adapt; arm; accustom; bring to readiness; condition; cook up; dight; develop; establish; equip; fit; fix; get ready; groom; gear up; habilitate; *instruct;* jibe [slang]; knock into shape; line out; make ready; *nurture;* outfit; prime; pave the way; prep; qualify; ready; set; suit; train; *ultra-prepared;* verse; whet; whip up; *well-readied; xenagogue;* yarken; *zealously ~;*
**prerequisite** *(n.)*: accepted minimum; basic qualification; condition; criterion; demand; expectation; factor; gauge; habilitation; indispensable ~; *judgment standard;* key criterion; lowest expectation; must; necessity; obligation; precondition; qualification; requirement; stipulation; specification; *sine qua non* [L.]; terms; *ultimatum;* vital requirement; *want;* XO requirement; yarking; *zero option;*
**prerogative** *(n.)*: advantage; benefit; birthright; choice; due; entitlement; freedom; *gain;* honor; individual right; joy; key ~; license; *mind;* natural right; option; privilege; *questionless;* right; sole right; *treatment; use;* vantage; warrant; *x-div; yes; zeal;*
**presbytery** *(n.)*: advisory committee; board; body of elders; council; committee; diet; eldership; ecclesiastical council; forum; general council; *heads;* investigative committee; *jury; kit;* leadership; ministerial committee; *meeting; nominative committee;* ordination council; panel; presbyters; quinquevirate; religious board; session; synod; tribunal; *unit;* vestry; *ward; xenocracy; yain* [arch.]; *zemstvo [Rus.];*

**prescribe** *(v.)*: advise; bid; charge; direct; explain; exhort; fix; give orders; handle; indicate; instruct; justify; kibitz; lay down; mark out; *necessitate;* order; propose; *qualify;* recommend; suggest; stipulate; tell; *urge; voice; write out; xenagogy;* yield advice; *zealously exhort;*
**prescription** *(n.)*: advice; bidding; charge; doctor's orders; exhortation; formula; given orders; healing agent; instruction; justification; *key instructions; letter;* medical order; note; order; prescript; *qualification;* Rx; scrip; *transfer;* usage; *validated ~; written ~; xenagogy; yellow paper; zet* [arch.];
**present** *(adj.)*: at hand; being; current; contemporary; *durative;* existing; existent; *forthwith;* going on now; here and now; immediate; incumbent; just now; *known;* latest; modern; newest; *now;* of today; present-day; prevailing; *quickly;* right now; reigning; sitting; serving; this moment; today's; up-to-date; very newest; *without ado; x-speed; yet; zealously;* [Ant. past]
**present** *(n.)*: award; alms; bestowal; contribution; donation; endowment; favor; gift; handsel; impartation; *joy-giving;* kindness; liberality; largess; munificence; nicety; offering; presentation; peace offering; *quality gift; reward; surprise;* token; tribute; *unselfish gift;* vouchsafement; *white elephant gift;* xenium; *yeff* [arch.]; *zealous support;*
**present** *(v.)*: award; bestow; confer; donate; endow; furnish; give; gift; hand (over); impart; *jettison;* kit; leave; make a gift of; *non-retention;* offer; provide; *quicken;* render; show; set before; transfer; unhand; unveil; vest; *weigh; wave;* xfer; yield; *zip;*
**presentable** *(adj.)*: acceptable; bearable; condonable; decent; endurable; fit; good enough; *honorable; innocuous;* justifiable; *kosher; legitimate;* meet; not bad; okay; passable; questionless; respectable; satisfactory; sufferable; tolerable; unquestioned; valid; workable; *xtry.; yes; zero problem;*
**preservation** *(n.)*: assurance; bearing along; conservation; continuance; defense; eternalization; fending; guarding; holding on; immortalization; *jaga;* keeping; *looking after;* maintenance; non-destruction; *ongoing;* protection; perpetuation; *quia timet* [L.]; retention; safeguarding; salvation; taking care of; upholding; upkeep; *vallation;* well-being; *x-guard; yeming* [arch.] *zero termination;* [Ant. perishing]
**preserve** *(v.)*: *assure;* bottle up; conserve; continue; dry-salt; defend; ensconce; embalm; fend; guard; hold; insure; insulate; jaga; keep; look after; maintain; not use up; overshadow; protect; pickle; quick-freeze; reserve; retain; safeguard; save; sustain; shield; take care of; uphold; vallate; watch (over); ward; *well-kept; x-guard; yeme* [arch.]; *zero danger;* [Ant. perish]
**preside** *(v.)*: administer; bid; control; chair; direct; *evaluate; force;* govern; guide; head; instruct; judge; keep control; lead; moderate; *necessitate;* oversee; officiate; predominate; *queen;* run; rule; reign; supervise; take the lead; *uphold; voice;* wield authority; *xenagogue; yeme* [arch.]; *zakon* [Rus.];
**press** *(v.)*: apply pressure; bear down; compress; compel; depress; drive; exert pressure; force; flatten; grip; hug; impel; jam; kibble; lean; mash; nudge; overply; push; pressure; ply; quash; ram; squeeze; squash; tamp; upthrust; urge; *vice;* wring; weigh down; *xuld* [arch.]; *yerk; zone;* [see squash]
**pressure** *(n.)*: anxiety; burden; compression; demands; duress; emotional ~; force; goading; heaviness; intensity; jamming; *killing;* load; *make;* nagging; overburdening; overpressure; pull; *quash;* rigor; strain; tension; taxation; unrest; urging; vexation; weight; *x-stress; yank; zapping;*
**prestige** *(n.)*: acclaim; belovedness; clout; devotion; esteem; eminence; fame; greatness; glory; honor; importance; *jubilation;* kudos; laud; magnification; notability; *one-upmanship;* position; preeminence; *quality;* respect; regard; repute; status; standing; transcendence; uplifting; veneration; worthiness; *xtry.; yichus; zenith;* [Ant. pitifulness]
**prestigious** *(adj.)*: acclaimed; beloved; celebrated; distinguished; eminent; famed; great; high-ranking; illustrious; impressive; *jubilated over;* known; legendary; magnifical; notable; outstanding; prominent; *quality;* respected; significant; talked-about; universally known; venerated; well-known; world-famous; *xtry.;* yichus; *zealously loved;* [Ant. pitiful]
**presume** *(v.)*: assume; believe; conjecture; deduce; dare; expect; figure; guess; hypothesize; imagine; judge; *know;* live in the hope; make presumption; *notion;* opine; perceive; postulate; *question;* reckon; suppose; take for granted; think; *understand;* venture; wis; *xenodiagnose; yeme; zazen;* [Ant. prove]

**presumptive** *(adj.)*: apparent; believed; calculated; deemed; expectant; foreseen; granted; hoped-for; implicit; justifiable; *keenly awaiting;* likely; more than likely; non-proven; ostensible; probable; quite likely; reasonable; seeming; supposed; thought likely; unreasonably confident; verisimilar; waiting for; *xel [arch.];* yet probable; zealously awaiting; [*Ant.* proven]
**presumptuous** *(adj.)*: arrogant; bold; brash; confident; disrespectful; ever-bold; forward; gutsy; haughty; insolent; jaunty; know-it-all; lifted up; malapert; nervy; overconfident; presuming; *quick-to-act;* rash; self-assured; temerarious; unafraid; uppity; vain; willful; *xtry.;* yare; zero humility;
**pretend** *(adj.)*: *artificial;* bogus; counterfeit; dissembling; ersatz; false; fake; feigned; fictitious; fantasy; guileful; gag; hoax; imaginary; imitation; japed; kiddy; *lying;* make-believe; mendacious; non-real; *overactive imagination;* phony; quacky; quasi; replicated; spurious; sham; trick; unreal; vain; wily; *xeno-;* yeggy; zero validity;
**pretend** *(v.)*: act; affect; behave; be; bluff; claim; con; dream; dissemble; envision; fancy; feign; fake; fantasize; gammon; hoax; imagine; impersonate; *just make-believe; keep dreaming;* let on; *like;* make-believe; *non-reality;* overact; play at; play-act; *quasi;* romanticize; role-play; re-enact; simulate; sham; take on the part; use imagination; visualize; whimsy; *xfer;* yede; *zealously play at;*
**pretender** *(n.)*: actor; bluffer; con artist; capper; dreamer; dissembler; envisioner; feigner; faker; fantasizer; *guile;* hoaxer; hypocrite; imaginer; impersonator; *just make-believe; keep dreaming;* liar; make-believer; *non-reality; overact;* player; play-actor; phony; performer; quacksalver; romanticizer; role-player; shill; sham artist; *taker; usurper;* visualizer; *whimsy; xfer; yede; zealous imaginer;*
**pretense** *(n.)*: affectation; beguilement; cover; charade; deception; exhibition; fabrication; false pretense; game; hoax; invention; japery; knavishness; lie; make-believe; *non-reality;* ostentation; playacting; pretext; pretension; *questionable;* ruse; sham; subterfuge; showing off; trick; *untruth;* verneuking; wiliness; *xuld [arch.];* yentzing; zinger;
**pretentious** *(adj.)*: affected; bombastic; big-sounding; conceited; declamatory; exaggerated; flashy; grandiose; highfalutin; inflated; jazzy; *know-it-all;* lofty; lexiphanic; luxurious; magniloquent; narcissistic; overblown; ostentatious; pompous; *quick-to-boast;* rakish; showy; snobbish; swaggering; turgescent; tumid; unreal; vaunting; windy; *x-proud; yelping; zero humility;*
**pretty** *(adj.)*: attractive; beautiful; comely; charming; dainty; eye-catching; enchanting; fair; good-looking; handsome; heart-alluring; *irresistible; jolie laide [F.];* killing [slang]; lovely; *magnificent;* nice-looking; *ornate; outstanding;* purdy [dial.]; pleasing; pleasant; picturesque; quite beautiful; ravishing; striking; terrific-looking; *unsurpassed;* voluptuous; well-favored (-looking); *xtry.;* you-beaut [Aus.]; *zizzy;* [*Ant.* plain]
**prevail** *(v.)*: *annihilate;* beat; best; conquer; defeat; expugn; foil; get victory; *hammer; invincible; junk [slang];* kill; knock out; lick; master; *neutralize;* overcome; predominate; quench; rout; succeed; smite; surmount; triumph; take; unseat; vanquish; win (out); *x-ing; yank down;* zap;
**prevent** *(v.)*: avert; block; bar; ban; curb; cancel; cumber; disallow; deter; debar; encumber; estop; exclude; frustrate; foil; forestall; *gum up;* hinder; hamper; halt; head off; impede; inhibit; *jam;* keep (from); kibosh; limit; *let [arch.]; moderate;* nullify; obstruct; obviate; preclude; prohibit; quash; restrain; stop; thwart; *undo; upset;* veto; withhold; ward off; x; *yank;* zilch; [*Ant.* promote]
**preventative** *(adj.)*: averting; blocking; curbing; deterring; encumbering; foiling; guarding; hindering; inhibitive; interdictory; just-in-case; *keeping (from);* limiting; *moderating;* nullifying; obstructive; precautionary; preventive; prohibitive; prohibitory; protective; *quashing;* restraining; safeguarding; tutelary; *umbrella;* vigilant; withholding; xenophobic; *yanking;* zilching; [*Ant.* promotional]
**prevention** *(n.)*: avoidance; barring; cumbering; deterrence; encumbering; *exclusion;* foiling; *gum up;* halting; inhibition; *jam;* keeping (from); *limiting; mitigation;* nullification; obstruction; protection; preclusion; prohibition; quashing; restraint; stopping; thwarting; *undoing; veto;* warding off; x-ing; *yanking;* zilching; [*Ant.* promotion]

**preview** *(n.)*: antepast; before-the-fact viewing; cosmorama; day-in-advance viewing; examination; foretaste; *gone before; happening beforehand; inspection; jerque;* keek; look; *movie ~; new release; observe;* prelibation; prevue; *quick look;* research; sneak-peek; sample; taste beforehand; *unofficial ~;* viewing; vernissage; *watch ahead; xtry. opportunity; yet to come; zero concealment;*

**previous** *(adj.)*: aforetime; aforementioned; beforetime; ci-davant; *directly before;* earlier; ex-; erstwhile; former; foregoing; *gone before;* heretofore; *in time past;* just before; *known already;* last; most recent; *née;* one-time; preceding; prior; past; protatic; quondam; retrospective; sometime; then; *used; very early;* whilom; xel [arch.]; y-aforsayde [arch.]; zum; [Ant. posterior]

**price** *(n.)*: amount; asking ~; bulk ~; cost; charge; dollar figure; evaluation; fee; ferriage; garnish; going ~; *handling fee;* impost; jettage; keelage; list ~; markup; *money;* number; outlay; price-tag; quantity; quote; retail ~; sale ~; tab; unit ~; value; worth; wholesale ~; *x-tax;* yardage; *zakat;*

**priceless** *(adj.)*: *above all;* beyond price; costly; dear; expensive; *fine;* golden; helpful; highly-valued; invaluable; inestimable; *judged worthy; king's ransom; lovely;* more precious than gold; *non-estimable;* of great price; precious; *quality; rich; steep;* too precious for words; treasured; useful; valuable; without price; *xtry.; yieldful; zestful;*

**prick** *(v.)*: afflict; bore; *cut;* dig; empierce; *fix* [arch.]; goad; hurt; impale; jab; *knife;* lance; make hole; needle; open; poke; *quill;* run through; stick; thrust in; urticate; *ventilate;* wimble; *xyresic;* yerk; *zing;*

**prickle** *(n.)*: acantha; barb; cocklebur; distaff-thistle; *end;* firethorn; goat's-thorn; hawthorn; *impale;* jag; *keen-edged; lance;* musk thistle; needle; *ouch!;* point; quill; *rosebush;* spike; spine; thorn; urtica; *verge;* white-thorn; xanthium; yucca; *zizyphus;*

**prickly** *(adj.)*: acicular; aculeate; barbed; bristly; cusped; denticled; echinate; finely-barbed; glochidiate; highly pointed; *incisal;* jaculiferous; *keen;* lanceolated; multipoint; nettled; over- ~; pointy; quill-filled; *razor-sharp;* spiky; spiny; thorny; ultra-pointy; very sharp; well-nettled; xyresic; *yowch!; zinging;*

**pride** *(n.)*: arrogance; bigheadedness; boastfulness; conceit; condescension; cockiness; disdain; egotism; egocentricity; flatulence; fullness of self; gloating; haughtiness; high horse; imperiousness; impudence; immodesty; inflatedness; *jackanapes; know-it-all;* loftiness; magisterialness; narcissism; overconfidence; ostentation; overproudness; proudness; *quilicom* [arch.]; *ruff* [arch.]; smugness; self-righteousness; self-importance; self-exaltation; snobbery; stuck-upness; turgidity; uppityness; vanity; vainness; vainglory; wind; *xenophobia; yieldless; zero humility;* [Ant. pridelessness]

**priest** *(n. religious cleric)*: antistes; abbot; baccant; bishop; cleric; clergyman; curé; Catholic ~; dervis; diocesan; ecclesiastic; *flamen* [Rom.]; *"father";* grand prior; high ~; parish ~; presbyter; prior; hierarch; hiermonach; hierophant [Gr.]; intermediary; Jesuit ~; *joss-man* [Chin.]; kirkman [Scot.]; kahuna [Haw.]; *legate;* mediator; minister; man of the cloth; *negotiant;* overseer; parish ~; pontifex; priestess [fem.]; *pujari* [Hind.]; qumranite; rector; Roman Catholic ~; *sacramentalist;* santon [Turk.]; *teacher; ultramontane;* vicar; worker- ~; *Xaverian; yogi [Hind.];* zadokite; [see monk]

**priest** *(n. mediator)*: arbitrator; *bringer of peace;* conciliator; chief ~; daysman; *emissary;* facilitator; go-between; high ~; intermediary; judge; kohen; Levite; mediator; negotiator; *overseer;* peacemaker; *queller; referee; scribe;* tabernacle ~; *undershepherd;* vicar; worker; xenophile; yoke; zet [dial.];

**priesthood** *(n.)*: anointing; abbacy; bishoprick; calling; duty; employment; field; *go-between;* high ~; industry; *job; key position;* labor; ministry; *negotiation;* office; order; position; *quest;* role; service; temple service; *undertaking;* vocation; work; xci. yoke; zealous duty;

**priestly** *(adj.)*: *arbitrating; anointed;* bishoplike; clerical; *druidic;* ecclesiastic; flamenical; *go-between;* hieratic; high ~; intermediary; *justifying; Kohathite;* Levitical; mediatorial; negotiating; *official;* priestlike; parsonical; prelatic; *qualified;* religious; sacerdotal; theocratical; *undefiled; virtuous; worship; xci.; yonder; zonic;*

**primary** *(adj.)*: archical; biggest; chief; dominant; essential; foremost; greatest; highest; important; *judicial;* key; leading; major; No. 1; optimal; prime; principle; *quintessential;* ranking; supreme; top; utmost; *vital;* weighty; *xtry.; yondmost;* zenithal;
**prime** *(adj.)*: A-1; best; choicest; dominant; elite; finest; greatest; highest; important; *jim-dandy;* keenest; loftiest; most desirable; No. 1; optimal; premium; *quintessential;* ranking; select; top; unsurpassed; very best; world-class; xtry.; *yondmost;* zenithal; [*Ant.* poor]
**primitive** *(adj.)*: ancient; archaic; antediluvian; aboriginal; backward; basic; crude; dated; early; Folsom; generative; heathen; instinctive; *Jurassic; kipper [Aus.];* low-technology; *makeshift;* non-civilized; original; prehistoric; primal; primeval; *quintessential;* rough; simple; time-forgotten; uncivilized; unadvanced; unrefined; *vulgar;* way-old; XO; *ylem; zero-sophistication;* [*Ant.* present-day]
**prince** *(n.)*: adeling; *blueblood;* crown ~; dauphin; dynast; elector; emir [Turk.]; *firstborn;* grand duke; heir; his royal highness; *infante* [Sp.]; *junker;* kingling; knez [Rus.]; lord; *maharajah* [Ind.]; *master;* noble; *overseer;* prince regent; queen's son; *raja* [Ind.]; *regent;* son of the king; tsarevitch [Rus.]; uncrowned ~; vaivode; *warden; xabandar; younker; zayim;* [*Ant.* pauper]
**princess** *(n.)*: aristocrat; *blueblood;* czarevna [Rus.]; dauphine(ss); electress; *female;* grand duchess; heiress; her royal heiness; infanta; *junker;* king's daughter; lady; *maiden;* noblewoman; *overseer;* princess royal; queenling; royal ~; *silk-stocking;* tsarevna [Rus.]; *uncrowned ~;* viscountess; *woman; xtry.;* young maiden; zarevna [Rus.]; [*see* maiden; *Ant.* peasant]
**principal** *(adj.)*: absolute; big; chief; dominant; eminent; foremost; greatest; highest; important; *judicious;* key; leading; main; notable; overriding; prime; quintessential; ranking; supreme; top; ultimate; vital; weighty; *xenenthesis; yet unsurpassed;* zenithal; [*Ant.* petty]
**principality** *(n.)*: autocracy; borough; *bounds;* country; domain; enclave; *field;* governate; holding; *imperial;* jurisdiction; kingdom; land; monarchy; nation; *oligarchy;* princedom; power; *quadrant;* realm; sovereignty; territory; *unit;* viziership; ward; *xerifdom; yard; zone of influence;*
**principle** *(n.)*: axiom; belief; code; dictum; ethic; fundament; guideline; *horse sense;* ideal; institute; judgment; kernel of wisdom; lodestar; law; moral; *normative;* opinion; *organon;* postulate; qualm; rule; standard; truism; universal truth; veracity; wisdom; *xenagogy;* yardstick; zeteticism;
**print** *(v.)*: annotate; blazon; copy; duplicate; enface; engrave; *font;* grave; generate; handwrite; issue; imprint; jot; *kalotypography;* letterpress; mark; notate; offset; put down; publish; produce; quill; reproduce; replicate; re~; stamp; turn out; *underwrite; vignette;* write out; *xylograph;* yield; *zincograph;*
**prison** *(n.)*: *arrest;* behind bars; big house; bastille; brig [naut.]; cell; cage; confinement; correctional facility; detention; debtor's ~; dungeon; encagement; federal ~; *facility; fetters;* guardhouse; hold; incarceration; jail(house); keep; lockup; *labor camp;* maximum security; *manacles; nabbed;* oubliette; penitentiary; penal colony; panopticon; quod; roundhouse; rattle; state ~; slammer; solitary confinement; stir; tank [slang]; under lock and key; vile durance; ward; x; yard; zindan [Pers.]; *zipper [coll.];*
**prisoner** *(n.)*: arrestee; *behind bars;* convict; captive; detainee; *ex-convict;* fellow-prisoner; fiver; gaolbird [Br.]; hostage; inmate; internee; jailbird; kriegie [G.]; lagger; lifer; maximum security inmate; non-paroled ~; *oubliette;* POW; quod inmate; *rattle;* stir bird [slang]; trusty; *under lock and key;* villain; ward-bird [slang]; x,; yard bird [slang]; zebra [joc.]; zek [Rus.];
**private** *(adj.)*: à deux; behind-the-scenes; confidential; concealed; classified; *delicate;* exclusive; furtive; guarded; hidden; internal; intime; intimate; inconspicuous; *just between us;* kept to oneself; *latent;* mysterious; non-public; offstage; personal; quiet; respective; recondite; secluded; secret; surreptitious; top-secret; unseen; undisclosed; very ~; *withheld; xeno-;* yet undiscovered; *zero publicity;* [*Ant.* public]
**privately** *(adv.)*: apart; behind closed doors; confidentially; *delicately;* exclusively; furtively; *guarded;* hugger-mugger; internally; inconspicuously; *januis clausis* [L.]; *kept to oneself; latently;* mysteriously; not openly; *offstage;* personally; privily; quietly; q.t.; reconditely; secretly; surreptitiously; *top-secret;* unbeknownst; *veiled;* well-hidden; *xtr. security;* yet undiscovered; *zero publicity;* [*Ant.* publicly]

**privilege** *(n.)*: advantage; birthright; benefit; choice; due; entitlement; freedom; grant; honor; indulgence; *immunity;* joy; key ~; license; *mind; notion;* opportunity; option; prerogative; pleasure; *questionless;* right; sole right; *silver-spoon; treat; use;* vantage; warrant; *x-div; yes; zeal;*
**prize** *(n.)*: award; blue ribbon; crown; cup; decoration; *embellishment;* first ~; guerdon; gold cup; honor; handsome reward; *indemnity; incentive;* jackpot; *king's ransom;* laurel wreath; medal; meed; *Nobel Prize; Oscar;* plaque; payment; quittance; reward; recompense; satisfaction; trophy; title; *utu* [N.Z.]; victor's crown; winnings; xenium; yellow jersey [sports]; *Zion's crowns;*
**probability** *(n.)*: aptness; best bet; chance; degree of ~; expectation; fighting chance; good chance; hope; happening; *intention;* imminence; *just maybe;* known chance; likelihood; *maybe;* not *definite;* odds; prospect; potential; *questionableness; remote possibility;* statistical likelihood; true ~; *unsurprising;* verisimilitude; vraisemblance; *waiting; xel [arch.]; yet likely; zero chance;*
**probable** *(adj.)*: anticipated; apt; believed; calculated; deemed; expected; foreseen; *a* good chance; hoped-for; indubitable; *imminent; just waiting; keenly awaiting;* likely; most likely; not unlikely; ostensible; presumptive; promising; quite likely; ready; reasonable; seeming; thought likely; *unsurprising;* verisimilar; waiting for; *xel [arch.];* yet likely; zealously awaiting;
**probe** *(n.)*: audit; *bringing to light;* check; delving; examination; exploration; finding out; go-over; *hunt;* investigation; jerquing; *keeking;* look into; mission; nosing around; observation; probing; questioning; research; search; scrutinization; test; *understand; uncover; venture; work; XQ; yeme; zeroing in;*
**probe** *(v.)*: ascertain; *beseech;* comb; dig; delve; explore; find; go into; hunt; investigate; jerque; kithe; look into; make query; nose around; oppugn; prod; poke; query; research; search; test; *uncover;* venture; work on; *XQ.; yearn for; zero in;*
**problem** *(n.)*: adversity; ailment; aggravation; bind; complication; difficulty; dilemma; encumbrance; fix; glitch; grief; hardship; headache; hitch; incommodity; issue; impasse; jam; kink; little ~; mess; misfortune; nuisance; nightmare; obstacle; ordeal; predicament; plight; pickle; quandary; question; rattle; roadblock; strait; snag; spot; trouble; trial; tight spot; tar baby; upheaval; unrest; vexation; woe; x-question; *yowler;* zinger;
**procedure** *(n.)*: actions; approach; behavior; conduct; course of action; daily routine; *execution;* fashion; formal ~; game plan; how-to; instruction; *job; kept tradition;* line of attack; method; manner; *modus operandi* [L.]; *non-random;* order; operation; process; practice; *quo mode* [L.]; routine; system; steps; technique; *usage;* valid ~; way; *xenagogy; yare; zeroing in;*
**process** *(n.)*: actions; behavior; course; development; *execution; evolution;* fashion; *going; happening;* in the ~ of time; job; *key procedure;* line of attack; method; means; *natural ~;* operation; progression; procedure; *quo mode* [L.]; routine; *red tape;* string; series; tack; *underway; valid procedure;* way; *xenagogy; yare; zeug;*
**proclaim** *(v.)*: announce; broadcast; blazon; cry; declare; exclaim; fame; give out; herald; inform; *jobation; kerygma;* let out; make known; *message;* noise; outcry; orate; promulgate; preach; *quote;* rehearse; speak; shout; state; trumpet; tell; utter; vociferate; warrant; *xenagogy;* yell; *zealously ~;*
**proclamation** *(n.)*: announcement; bulletin; communication; declaration; edict; fiat; *give;* heralding; indiction; jactitation; *keynote address;* letter; message; notification; oration; pronouncement; *quotation;* ruling; revelation; statement; *testimonial;* utterance; verbalization; word; *xenagogy;* yeme; *zealous ~;*
**procrastinate** *(v.)*: abide; bide; *continue;* delay; drag one's feet; dilly-dally; extend; futz; fool around; goof off; hold off; hang around; idle; jauk; jack around; kick back; loiter; laze; lollygag; loaf; linger; mess around; *non-responsive; obstruct;* putter; piddle; prolong; quiddle; *remain;* stand around; stall; tarry; take one's time; *unresponsive;* veg out; waste time; *xenize; yerde [arch.]; zealless;*
**procrastination** *(n.)*: adjournment; break; *continuation;* delay; dilly-dallying; dalliance; extension; forbearance; gap; holdup; interval; jauking; keeping one waiting; lingering; lollygagging; *move slowly;* neglect; obstruction; putting off; postponement; *quietude;* remissness; stalling; tarrying; *unwinding;* vegetation; wait; *x-rest; yawning; zizz;* [*Ant.* promptness]

**procreate** *(v.)*: *accumulate;* beget; breed; bear young; *conceive;* develop; engender; father; flourish; generate; give birth to; grow; have offspring; increase; *join; kids; labor;* multiply; *nuptial fruit;* originate; produce; propagate; proliferate; *quicken;* reproduce; sire; spawn; turn out; thrive; *upbuild; venery;* whelp [zoo.]; *xenogenesis;* yield fruit; *zygogenesis;*

**procreation** *(n.)*: aphrodisia; begetting; birthing; breeding; *conception;* childbirth; delivery; engendering; fruit; generation; hatching; having offspring; incubation; *joining; kids; labor;* making; multiplication; nuptial fruit; origination; propagation; proliferation; *quantification;* reproduction; spawning; two becoming one; *undertaking;* venery; whelping [zoo.]; xenogamy; yielding fruit; zygogeneis;

**prod** *(n.)*: acuator; bestirrer; cattle ~; driver; electric cattle ~; foin; goad; harasser; *implement;* jabber; *kindle; lance; motivator;* needle; oxgoad; poker; prick; prong; *quickener;* ram; sticker; thruster; *urger;* valet; *whacker; xulder;* yerk [dial.]; *zapper;*

**prod** *(v.)*: actuate; bug; bestir; cause; coerce; drive; encourage; foment; goad; harass; hearten; incite; jab; kindle; lean on; move; make; nudge; *oblige;* push; provoke; prompt; poke; prick; quicken; ram; stir; stimulate; stab; thrust; urge; *veney;* whig; *xuld [arch.];* yerk [dial.]; *zonk;*

**prodigal** *(n.)*: *abuser;* big-spender; compulsive shopper; dissipater; effusive; extravagant spender; fritterer; good-for-nothing; high roller; indulger; *jaded; knave;* libertine; lavisher; misspender; no-good; overspender; profligate; *quick spender;* reprobate; squanderer; *thriftless; uncontrolled;* voluptuary; wastrel; wayward son; *xfer; yielder up; zeroizer;*

**produce** *(v.)*: assemble; build; beget; birth; bang out; construct; create; crank out [slang]; design; develop; engineer; engender; emit; export; fabricate; generate; give; hand make; incarnate; *job;* knock out; let out; manufacture; make; *new-built;* output; put together; pump out; quick-build; raise up; spawn; shape; supply; turn out; upbuild; volume- ~; work out; *xfer;* yield; *zealous production;*

**product** *(n.)*: aftereffects; byproduct; consequence; derivative; development; effect; fruit; goods; harvest; issue; just desserts; *known outcome;* lattermath; manufactured goods; *necessary outcome;* outcome; output; piece; production; quantum effect; result; sequent; *tale;* upshot; *volume;* workpiece; ware; *widget; xfer;* yield; *zeug [G.];*

**production** *(n.)*: assembling; building; construction; developing; effectuation; fabrication; generation; handiwork; incarnation; *JIT/JIC;* knocking out; *laboring;* making; manufacturing; *new-built;* output; producing; *quota;* raising; shaping; supply; turning out; upbuilding; volume ~; working up; *xfer;* yielding; *zipping out;*

**productive** *(adj. helpful)*: assistive; advantageous; assiduous; beneficial; busy; constructive; conducive; dynamic; edifying; fruitful; gainful; good; helpful; hard-working; industrious; *job;* keen; luxuriant; motivated; mobilized; not lazy; overdiligent; profitable; propitious; prolific; quick-to-help; *rewarding;* sedulous; tireless; useful; unslothful; vigorous; working; *xtry.;* yieldful; zippy;

**productive** *(adj. prolific)*: abundant; bountiful; *busy;* copious; diffuse; effusive; fruitful; generative; highly ~; inundant; *just keeps coming;* keenly ~; lush; luxuriant; *much; numerous;* overflowing; prolific; quantitative; rich; superabundant; thriving; *teeming;* uberous; very ~; wantless; *xtry.;* yieldful; *zillions;*

**productivity** *(n.)*: annual ~; bountifulness; *copiousness;* dynamic; efficiency; fruitfulness; generative ability; high ~; industriousness; *just abounding; keenness;* labor-efficiency; *making; non-idleness;* output; productiveness; quarterly ~; *quotas; ratio;* superabundance; throughput; top ~; usefulness; *volume;* work; *xtry. production;* yield; *zeal;*

**profane** *(adj.)*: appalling; abominable; blasphemous; corrupt; defiled; disrespectful; evil; foul (-mouthed); flippant; godless; *horrifying;* irreverent; impious; jaded; knowingly disrespectful; *loathsome;* maledictive; non-holy; offensive; polluted; perverted; *quad;* reproachful; sacrilegious; tainted; unholy; unclean; vulgar; violated; wicked; *x-rated; yieldless;* zero reverence; [*see* common; *Ant.* pious]

**profane** *(v.)*: abominate; abuse; blaspheme; curse; defile; debase; desecrate; execrate; foment; *goad; hate;* inquinate; *jade; kindle; loathe;* malign; not respect; offend; pollute; *quad;* revile; swear; taint; treat with irreverence; utter blasphemies; unhallow; violate; *wickedness; x-ing; yieldless; zing;*

**profanity** *(n.)*: *abuse; anathematizing;* bawdry; blasphemy; bad language; cursing; cussing; coarse language; dirty word; expletive; foul language; *gross disrespect; hex;* irreverence; invective; juration; *kitsch; lewd word;* malediction; *nasty language;* oath; obscenity; profaneness; *quadriliteral;* rude word; ribaldry; swearing; sacrilege; tasteless speech; ungodly language; vulgarity; vulgarism; *vernacular;* wickedness; *x-rated speech;* yawp; *zinger;*

**profession** *(n. admission)*: admission; affirmation; bearing witness; confession; declaration; enunciation; *fixing;* general announcement; holding forth; indication; *justification;* keen attestation; *language;* manifesto; notification; open attestation; proclamation; *quotation;* report; reassurance; substantiation; testimony; upholding; verbalization; word; witness; *x-certification;* yeme; *zero doubt;*

**profession** *(n. occupation)*: activity; area of expertise; business; career; craft; duty; employment; field; game [joc.]; handicraft; industry; job; *key position;* line of work; livelihood; métier; *necessity;* occupation; pursuit; position; *quest;* responsibility; service; trade; undertaking; vocation; work; xci. *yoke; zealous duty;*

**professional** *(adj.)*: authorized; businesslike; competent; career-related; diplomatic; expert; field-related; good; graceful; hand-skilled; industrial; job-related; knowledgeable; licensed; methodical; non-amateur; occupational; proficient; qualified; related to career; skilled; trained; *undertaking;* vocational; work-related; well-trained; workmanlike; xci. *yomanly; zealous duty;*

**professional** *(n.)*: authority; boffin; connoisseur; doyen [masc.]; doyenne [fem.]; expert; field expert; guru; hotshot; instructor; journeyman; knowledgeable person; leader; master; non-amatuer; old hand; pro; qualified expert; real expert; specialist; technician; *university grad;* veteran; whiz; *xtry.; years of experience; zet [dial.];*

**professor** *(n.)*: abecedarian; adjunct ~; *biology ~;* college ~; docent; doctor; educator; fugleman; faculty [pl.]; great mind; humanist [Scot.]; instructor; jr. college ~; *khosa [Hind.];* lecturer; learned man; master; *noetic; oracle;* Ph. D.; quodlibetarian; *researcher; regent;* scholar; teacher; theologian; university ~; *visiting ~;* wise man; xenagogue; *Yale ~; zetetic;*

**proficiency** *(n.)*: ability; adeptness; bravura; command; capability; competence; deftness; efficiency; expertise; flair; giftedness; habilitation; ingeniousness; *jimp;* knack; know-how; long suit; mastery; natural ability; *old-hand;* panurgy; prowess; quickness; real skill; skill; talent; *usefulness;* virtuosity; wherewithal; *xtry.; years of experience;* zest;

**proficient** *(adj.)*: able; adept; adroit; brilliant; capable; competent; deft; efficient; expert; fast; gifted; good; handy; incredible; jolly good; keen; *laudable;* masterful; notable; nimble; outstanding; practiced; qualified; remarkable; skilled; skillful; talented; up to; very good; wonderful; xtry.; *you-beaut [Aus.];* zippy; [*Ant.* pitiful]

**profit** *(n.)*: advantage; benefit; capital gain; dividend; earnings; favor; gain; help; increase; *justification;* keep; *lucre;* makings; net profit; obtainment; proceeds; quittal; quick buck; return; surplus; takings; use; upside; vantage; winnings; x-div; yield; *zillions;*

**profitable** *(adj.)*: advantageous; beneficial; constructive; conducive; desirable; expedient; fruitful; fair; gainful; good; helpful; hotsy; instrumental; jim dandy; keen; lucrative; money-making; nice; outstanding; productive; *questuary;* rewarding; salutary; serving; to be desired; useful; valuable; worthwhile; xtry.; yieldful; *zillions;* [*Ant.* profitless]

**profound** *(adj.)*: acute; awesome; big; clear-thinking; deep; extreme; enlightened; far-reaching; great; high; insightful; judicious; keen; learned; meditative; meaningful; noetic; overwhelming; pensive; perceptive; philosophical; prodigious; *quodlibetarian;* reflective; recondite; stupendous; thought-provoking; uncanny; very deep; weighty; wise; xtry.; yet unsurpassed; *zetetic;*

**profundity** *(n.)*: acuteness; awesomeness; brilliance; comprehension; depth; deepness; enlightenment; foresight; greatness; highness; insight; immensity; judiciousness; keenness; learning; meditation; *noetic;* oracularity; profoundness; perspicacity; *quodlibetarian;* reason; sagacity; tallness; understanding; *very deep;* wisdom; weight; xtry. wisdom; *yet unsurpassed; zetetic;*
**progress** *(n.)*: advancement; betterment; course; development; evolution; forward movement; growth; headway; improvement; journey; jumping ahead; *keeping up-to-date; leading edge;* movement; natural development; *ongoing;* progression; *quantum leap;* rising; revamping; rate of ~; stride; transition; *trend;* upswing; vamping; *work;* xtry. ~; *yain* [arch.]; zooming ahead;
**progress** *(v.)*: advance; become; continue; develop; evolve; forge ahead; go forward; grow; happen; increase; improve; jump; *keep going;* leap forward; move ahead; *non-static; ongoing;* proceed; *quantum increase;* run; ripen; rise; shape up; strengthen; spread; transition; take off; upgrade; venture on; wax greater; *xfer; yain* [arch.]; zoom ahead;
**progressive** *(adj.)*: advancive; advancing; becoming; continuing; developing; evolving; flowing; growing; heading somewhere; improving; journeying; keeps moving; leading (-edge); meliorative; moving forward; *non-static;* onward-moving; promotive; *quantum increase;* regressive; running on; ripening; rising; spreading; transitioning; transforming; *upgrade;* venturing on; waxing greater; *xfer; yain [arch.]; zooming ahead;* [see liberal]
**prohibit** *(v.)*: avert; block; bar; cumber; disallow; deter; estop; exclude; forbid; govern; halt; inhibit; illegalize; *jam;* keep (from); limit; make illegal; nix; outlaw; preclude; proscribe; quash; restrict; stop; thwart; *undo;* veto; withhold; *x; yank; zap;* [Ant. permit]
**prohibition** *(n.)*: arrestation; ban; court order; disallowing; debarment; exclusion; forbidding; government ban; holding back; interdict; illegalizing; jurisdictional bar; keeping out; lockout; making contraband; non-allowance; outlawing; proscription; prevention; *quite illegal;* restriction; sanction; tariff wall; *unlawful;* veto; withheld; *xtr. protection; ybarred [arch.]; zero entry;* [Ant. permission]
**prohibitive** *(v.)*: averting; blocking; baring; cumbering; disallowing; deterring; exclusive; forbidding; gouging; halting; inhibitive; *jamming;* keeping (from); limiting; much-limiting; nixing; overpriced; proscriptive; quashing; restrictive; stopping; thwarting; unreasonable; usurious; very ~; withholding; *x; yanking; zapping;* [Ant. permissive]
**project** *(n.)*: assignment; business; charge; commission; duty; errand; endeavor; fish to fry; goal; *homework;* intention; job; *key role;* labor; mission; necessity; obligation; purpose; *quest;* responsibility; service; task; undertaking; vocation; venture; work; xci.; *yoke; zealous task;*
**project** *(v.)*: *aslope;* beetle; continue; cast; *draw out;* extend; exsert; *further;* go beyond; hang over; impel; jut; kest; *keep going;* lengthen; make longer; *nudge;* outstretch; overhang (-extend); protrude; quoit; reach (forth); stretch; stick out; shoot; thrust out; *upcast; vary;* wax longer; *XL; yield; zoom.*
**projection** *(n.)*: *aslope;* beetling; continuance; *drawing out;* exsertion; extension; flange; *going beyond;* hang-over; *increase;* jettee; jut(ting); knob; lengthening; movement outward; nip; overhang; outthrust; protrusion; *quoif;* reach; spur; tuberosity; *upper ridge;* verge; *wax longer; XL;* yardang; *zenith.*
**prolific** *(adj.)*: abounding; bountiful; bounteous; copious; diffuse; effusive; fruitful; fertile; generative; hard-working; highly ~; inundant; *jam-packed;* keenly ~; lush; luxuriant; *lots; many; numerous;* overflowing; productive; propagative; profuse; quantitative; rich; superabundant; teeming; uberous; very ~; wantless; *xtry.;* yieldful; *zillions;*
**prolong** *(n.)*: add to; belabor; continue; draw (-drag) out; delay; extend; further; go on; hold out; increase; *jauk;* keep going; lengthen; make longer; *non-ceasing;* outstretch; put off; prolongate; protract; *quell;* run on; stretch out; tauten; temporize; *unfold; voluminous;* wax longer; *xuld [arch.]; yet again; zeal;*
**prominence** *(n.)*: acclaim; bigness; centrality; celebrity; distinction; eminence; fame; greatness; honor; importance; *jubilation; known;* legend; magnificence; notoriety; outstandingness; prominency; *quality;* renown; significance; status; tallness; *universally known;* veneration; weightiness; *xtry.;* yichus; *zealous love;*

**prominent** *(adj.)*: acclaimed; big; chief; conspicuous; distinguished; dominant; eminent; foremost; great; high-profile; important; *jutting out;* key; known; leading; major; notable; noticeable; outstanding; principle; quantum; renowned; significant; top; uppermost; visible; well-known; xtry.; yichus; zenithal; [*Ant.* petty]
**promiscuity** *(n.)*: abandonment; bawdiness; chambering; debauchery; easy virtue; *eroticism; evil;* fornication; fling; faithlessness; gross immorality; *harlotry; hedonism;* immorality; impurity; imprudence; infidelity; illicit sex; jadery; *kinkiness;* lewdness; looseness; mischief; naughtiness; odure; promiscuousness; profligacy; playing the harlot; *queanery;* revelry; sleeping around; (sexual) sin; *shamelessness;* treachery; unfaithfulness; unchastidy; venery; wantonness; whoredom; *x-rated behavior; youthful lust; zhlubbery;* [*Ant.* probity]
**promiscuous** *(adj.)*: abandoned; bawdy; coarse; disgraceful; explicit; erotic; filthy; gratuitous; heedless; indiscreet; indecent; jadish; *kinky;* licentious; lewd; mischievous; naughty; obscene; profligate; *quad;* revealing; seductive; smutty; sluttish; shameful; tantalizing; uncouth; vulgar; whorish; x-rated; *yucky; zero-modesty;* [*Ant.* proper]
**promise** *(n.)*: affirmation; bond; covenant; declaration; earnest; formal agreement; guarantee; hypothecation; ironclad ~; jurament; *kept ~;* legal agreement; mutual agreement; non-conditional ~; oath; pledge; pollicitation; *qualified ~;* resolution; sworn statement; testament; unconditional ~; vow; vouchsafe; word (of honor); *x-one's heart; yafery* [arch.]; zealous ~;
**promise** *(v.)*: adjure; assure; assert; bind to oath; covenant; deign; *ensure;* forswear; guarantee; give word; hypothecate; interpledge; jurate; *keep word; legitimize;* make vow; *nobly ~;* oath; obligate; pledge; *qualify;* resolve; swear; testify; understanding; vow; warrant; *x-ones heart; yafery* [arch.]; *zealously ~;*
**promote** *(v. advocate)*: advance; advocate; broadcast; bring about; circulate; disseminate; endorse; encourage; further; foster; get the word out; hype up; help; improve; jump; keep advertising; let be known; make known; nurture; overspread; popularize; plug; push; *quicken;* raise; support; subserve; strengthen; tell others; tout; uplift; *voice; widespread; xtr.; yell about;* zealously ~; [*Ant.* prevent]
**promote** *(v. graduate)*: advance; bump up; brevet; commend; *develop;* elevate; exalt; further; get promotion; graduate; *heighten;* increase; jump; kick upstairs [joc.]; lift up; move up; *next* lift; *outgrow;* pass on; *quantum increase;* raise; set; transcend; upgrade; *verge upward;* walk the platform; *xfer; yain [arch.]; zoom up;* [*Ant.* penalize]
**promotion** *(n.)*: advancement; brevet; continuance; development; elevation; exaltation; furtherance; graduation; heightening; improvement; increase; jump; kicking upstairs [joc.]; lifting up; moving up; nurturing; *onward;* preferment; *quantum leap;* raise; status increase; transcending; upgrade; *venturing ahead;* walking the platform; *xfer; yain [arch.]; zooming ahead;* [*Ant.* prevention]
**prompt** *(adj.)*: at the appointed time; before long; *current;* dead-on; direct; exact; fast; *going fast;* hastily; in short time; *Johnny-on-the-spot;* keeping good time; lickety-split; momentary; never-late; on-time; punctual; prest; quickly; right away; shortly; timely; undelayed; unhesitating; very punctual; without delay; xtry. ~; yare; *zero delay;* [*Ant.* procrastinatory]
**prompt** *(v.)*: affect; bring about; cause; drive; evoke; encourage; *foment;* get one to; goad; help; induce; inspire *jump-start;* kindle; lead to; motivate; nudge; occasion; provoke; precipitate; quicken; rouse; set off; stimulate; stir; trigger; urge; *vivify;* wreak; *xel* [arch.]; *yield;* zip into motion;
**prone** *(adj.)*: apt; bent; couchant; disposed; eager; favoring; gravitating toward; have a predisposition; inclined; *jee;* keen on; knocked flat; likely; leaning; moving; *nudging;* oriented; prostrate; propense; predisposed; quick; reclining; ready for; *rather;* supine; slanting; tending; usually tending; verging; wanting; *xel [arch.]; yawed; zealous;*
**pronounce** *(v.)*: articulate; bespeak; communicate; declare; enunciate; enounce; *form; give;* hold forth; intonate; judge; *key in;* let out; make known; *notify;* outline; proclaim; quoth; rehearse; relate; say; sound (out); tell; utter; voice; word; *xenophonia;* yak; zay [dial.];

**pronouncement** *(n.)*: announcement; assertion; bulletin; communication; decree; declaration; dictum; enunciation; edict; fiat; *governmental decree;* holding forth; indiction; judgment; *keynote address; letter;* message; notification; oration; proclamation; *quotation;* revelation; statement; *testimonial;* utterance; ukase; verdict; word; *xenagogy;* yeme; yell; *zealous message;*
**proof** *(n.)*: authentication; attestation; backup; confirmation; corroboration; certification; documentation; demonstration; data; evidence; exhibit; facts; grounds; hearsay evidence; hard facts; indication; indubitable evidence; justification; key evidence; legitimization; manifestation; notarization; obsignation; proven fact; qualification; reason (to believe); remonstrance; substantiation; support; surety; testimony; undeniable evidence; verification; witness; xtry. ~; *yes; zero doubt;*
**propaganda** *(n.)*: agitprop; brainwashing; conditioning; disinformation; doctrine; *education; fostering; giving instruction;* hype; hoopla; indoctrination; *journalism; knocking into;* lies; misinstruction; newspeak; *oppression;* propagandism; publicity; *qualification;* reindoctrination; rhetoric; *steeping;* training; *untruth; verbiage; writings;* Xinhua [Chin.]; *yellow journalism;* zhdanovism;
**propagate** *(v.)*: advance; breed; broadcast; continue; circulate; disseminate; extend; fecundate; generate; grow herald; issue forth; increase; *jump up; keep growing;* largen; multiply; *non-centralized;* outstretch; promulgate; proliferate; *quadruplicate;* reproduce; spread; transmit; *unfold; volume;* wax greater; *xmit;* yote; *zoom;*
**propel** *(v.)*: actuate; boost; cast; catapult; drive; eject; fling; force; fire; get moving; heave; impel; jet; kest; launch; move; nudge; *overthrow; pitch;* push; power; quant; ram; *rocket;* send, sling; shoot; thrust; upcast; vault; wale; *xuld* [arch.]; york; zorch;
**proper** *(adj.)*: appropriate; acceptable; adequate; approved; apposite; befitting; becoming; correct; due; ever-appropriate; fitting; good; honorable; idoneous; just; kosher; legitimate; meet; modest; *nice;* okay; official; polite; qualified; right; respectable; suitable; seemly; true; urbane; valid; well(-suited); *xtry.; yielded; zero problem;* [Ant. problematic]
**properness** *(n.)*: appropriateness; becomingness; correctness; decentness; etiquette; fitness; goodness; honorableness; idoneity; justness; *keenness;* legitimacy; modesty; *niceness;* orthodoxy; propriety; *qualification;* respectability; seemliness; suitableness; trueness; urbanity; validness; warrantedness; *xtry.; yenough* [arch.]; *Zufriedenheit* [G.];
**prophecy** *(n.)*: augury; anticipation; bodement; coming event; dream; divination; envisioning; expectation; foretelling; forecast; *God-given; heralding;* insight; *jeremiad;* known future event; lamentation; message; notification; oracle; omen; prediction; projection; presagement; *quain* [arch.]; revelation; saying; *sign;* telling the future; utterance; vision; vaticination; warning; *xenagogy; yammering; zay;* [*see* sermon]
**prophesy** *(v.)*: augur; address; admonish; bespeak; bode; cry; declare; divine; envisage; foretell; forecast; forebode; foresay; foreshow; foresee; give prophecy; herald; harbinger; inform; *indicate; jeremiad; kerygma;* lament; make a prediction; notify; orate; *omenate;* prophesy; preach; predict; project; prognosticate; portend; preominate; presage; *quain* [arch.]; reveal; speak; tell; utter; vaticinate; vocalize; warn; *xenagogic; yell; zay;* [*see* preach]
**prophet** *(n.)*: augur; boder; clairvoyant; dreamer; diviner; envoy; foreteller; forecaster; foreshower; God's man; herald; *instructor; jobation; kerygma;* lamenter; messenger; man (-mouthpiece) of God; *noiser;* oracle; orator; prophesier; preacher; predictor; presager; *quain* [arch.]; revelator; seer; sage; teller; *utterer;* voice; visionary; vates; wise man; *warner; xenagogue; yeller;* Zechariah;
**prophetic** *(adj.)*: augural; boding; clairvoyant; divinatory; expectant; fatidical; fey; foretold; God-revealed; heralding; insightful; *jeremiad;* known-beforehand; *lamented;* mantic; made known; *notifying;* oracular; prophetical; predictive; presageful; premonitory; precognative; *quain;* revelatory; sagely; *telling;* unveiling; vatic; warning; *xenagogic; yammered; zay;*

**propitiate** *(v.)*: appease; atone; becalm; conciliate; diffuse; dulcify; expiate; *fulfill;* gratify; *humor; hush;* immolate; *justify; knock down; lull;* mollify; make peace; *nullify;* oblate; offer; placate; pay; quell; reconcile; remit; satisfy; sacrifice; *tranquilize;* unruffle; *void;* win favor; *x-out; yield; zeroize;*
**propitiation** *(n.)*: appeasement; atonement; *becalming;* conciliation; dulcification; expiation; fulfillment; *getting right; hecatomb;* immolation; *justification; kwais kitir* [Arab.]; lustration; libation; making peace; mollification; *nullification;* oblation; offering; payment; placation; *quelling;* remittance; sacrifice; satisfactory payment; *transaction;* unruffling; *voidance;* winning favor; *x-ing out; yielding; zeroizing;*
**propitiatory** *(adj.)*: atonal; *becalming;* conciliatory; dulcifying; expiatory; fire-atoning; gratifying; *hushing;* immolative; *justifying; krioboly;* lustrational; mollifying; *nullifying;* oblational; piacular; piaculous; quelling; reconciatory; sacrificial; *tranquilizing;* unruffling; *voiding; winning favor;* x-ing out; *yielding; zeroizing;*
**proponent** *(n.)*: advocate; advancer; backer; champion; defender; encourager; exponent; friend; favorer; great supporter; helper; intercessor; justifier; keen supporter; lauder; *mate; no enemy; overcomer;* promoter; patron(ess); protagonist; partisan; *quickener;* representative; supporter; touter; upholder; voice; votary; well-wisher; *xtry. backer; yokefellow;* zealot;
**proportion** *(n.)*: amount; balance; cut; comparison; commensuration; degree; extent; figure; fraction; *gauge; half;* increase; *just allocation; key percentage;* level; measure; magnitude; number; *offset;* portion; percentage; part; quantity; relation; ratio; share; slice of the pie; total ~; units; volume; wedge; *x-mal [G.]; yield; zum [dial.];*
**proportionate** *(adj.)*: accordant; balanced; commensurate; corresponding; due; distributive; equitable; fair; germane; *half;* in proportion; *just the same; key percentage;* like; matching; non-differing; on a footing; prorated; *quae est eadem* [L.]; respective; same-portioned; *tantamount;* uniform; *volume; wedge; x-mal [G.]; yield;* zero variation;
**proposal** *(n.)*: advance; bid; counsel; draft; design; extension; final offer; game plan; *hortation;* invitation; *juration; kibitz [Yid.];* last offer; motion; nomination; offer; proposition; proffer; prospectus; *quicken;* recommendation; suggestion; submittal; *terms; urging;* valid offer; wish; *xfer; yearning; zealous ~;*
**propose** *(v.)*: advance; ask; bid; counsel; desire; encourage; extend; *foreadvise;* give recommendation; have a proposal; importunate; invite; *juration; kibitz [Yid.];* lay before; motion; move; nominate; offer; pop the question; put forward; present; proffer; postulate; *quicken;* recommend; suggest; submit; tender; urge; *vocalize; want; xuld [arch.];* yearn; zealously ~;
**propulsion** *(n.)*: *advance;* boost; compulsion; catapulting; driving; energy; force; going; heaving; horsepower; impulsion; jetting; jet ~; *knock;* locomotion; momentum; movement; *nudging; outshoot;* propelling; *quickening;* rocketing; *rate;* streaming; sailing; shooting; thrust; *underway;* velocity; *whipping; xuld [arch.]; yede* [arch.]; zip;
**prosecute** *(v.)*: arraign; bring suit against; charge; denounce; engage; follow through; go after; haul into court; indict; *judgment; keep;* litigate; make a legal claim against; *nab;* obtain by legal process; pursue; put on trial; *question; reprove;* seek redress; take action against; undertake legal action; *vengeance;* work to hang; *XQ; yawp; zet [dial.];*
**prosecution** *(n.)*: action; arraignment; bill of particulars; charge; denunciation; examination; following through; going after; hearing; indictment; judicial process; *keep;* litigation; making a claim against; *nabbing;* obtaining by legal process; pursuing; proceedings; quest; *reproof;* suit; trial; undertaking legal action; *vengeance;* working to hang; *XQ; yawp; zet [dial.];*
**proscribe** *(v.)*: avert; block; bar; ban(ish); cast out; disallow; estop; exclude; forbid; *get rid of;* halt; inhibit; interdict; *jettison;* keep (out); limit; make illegal; nix; outlaw; prohibit; quash; restrict; stop; thwart; *undo;* veto; withhold; *x;* yank; *zap;* [Ant. permit]

**proscription** *(n.)*: alienation; barring; condemnation; disallowing; debarment; exclusion; forbidding; government ban; holding back; interdiction; jurisdictional barring; keeping out; limitation; lockout; making contraband; non-allowance; outlawing; prohibition; *quite illegal;* restricting; shutting out; thwarting; *unlawful;* veto; withheld; *xenon-prohibition; ybarred [arch.];* zero entry; [Ant. permission]

**proselyte** *(n.)*: adherent; believer; convert; disciple; enthusiast; *evangelized;* follower; good follower; *holder;* imbiber; janissary; *kirsen [dial.];* liegeman; member; neophyte; *over;* professor; *qualified learner;* recruit; supporter; truster; *trainee; united; under;* votary; *won over; Xnize; yielder;* zealot;

**prospect** *(n.)*: aptness; belief; chance; degree of probability; expectation; fighting chance; good chance; hope; happening; imminence; *just maybe;* known chance; likelihood; *maybe; notion;* odds; outlook; probability; potential; *quite probable;* reasonable (-remote) chance; small hope; thinkability; *upcoming;* verisimilitude; *waiting; xel [arch.]; yet possible; zeal;*

**prospective** *(adj.)*: approaching; *believed;* coming; destined; eventual; expected; future; forthcoming; *guessed;* hoped-for; imminent; *just waiting; keenly awaiting;* latent; likely; long-awaited; more than likely; nearing; overdue; probable; promising; pending; quite probable; ready; soon-coming; thought likely; upcoming; verisimilar; waiting for; *xel [arch.];* yet probable; *zukunft [G.];*

**prosper** *(v.)*: achieve; advance; *attain;* boom; bloom; burgeon; come along well; do well; enlarge; fare well; flourish; go well; have success; increase; *jump up;* keep growing; luxuriate; make it; meet goal; not fail; obtain objective; prevail; pull off; *quantum increase;* reach goal; succeed; thrive; triumph; uprise; *victory;* work; *xtry.; yain [arch.]; zoom up;*

**prosperity** *(n.)*: affluence; auspiciousness; abundance; blessing; bounty; comfort; doing well; ease; felicity; flourishing; fortune; going well; good times; halcyon days; increase; *jewels; keen fortune;* (lap of) luxury; money; making it; *newfound success;* opulence; plenty; prosperousness; *quantum increase;* rising; riches; success; treasure; thriving; uberty; victory; wealth; wellbeing; weal; *xtry. ~; yain [arch.]; zillions [slang];* [Ant. privation]

**prosperous** *(adj.)*: affluent; blessed; comfortable; doing well; efficacious; flourishing; going well; *happy;* increased in goods; *jointly- ~; keenly ~;* loaded; moneyed; *non-failing;* on top; prospering; *quartful* [arch.]; rich; successful; thriving; *useful;* victorious well-to-do; wealthy; *xtry rich; yain [arch.]; zillions;* [Ant. poor]

**prostitute** *(n.)*: adulteress; bawd girl; call girl; courtesan; cocotte; doxy; escort; fornicator; gamester; harlot; hooker; hireling; *immoral woman; jade;* kittock; lady of the evening; mistress; meretrix; nightwalker; *obscene woman;* paramour; quean; rig; strange woman; slut; strumpet; streetwalker; trollop; trull; *unfaithful woman;* venal; whore; *x-rated woman;* yaud; *zhlub;*

**prostitute** *(v.)*: abuse; befoul; capitalize on; despoil; exploit; finagle; *get;* harm; ill-use; jockey; knock about; lig; misuse; *nobble;* overexploit; profit from; *questionable;* ravage; sell out; take advantage of; use; violate; victimize; walk all over; *x-out;* yeme; *zap;*

**prostitution** *(n.)*: adulteration; befoulment; corruption; debauchery; exploitation; fornication; *gross immorality;* harlotry; immorality; jadery; *kinkiness; lasciviousness;* malfeasance; naughtiness; odure; putage; *promiscuity;* playing the harlot; queanery; *revelry;* streetwalking; trafficking women; unchastidy; venery; whoredom; *x-rated behavior;* yielding; *zhlubbery;*

**prostration** *(n.)*: adoration; bowing; couching; debasement; devotion; *extolling;* falling down; groveling; homage; ingratiation; jacency; kneeling; lying; laying down; making oneself prostrate; *nod;* obeisance; proneness; *quiritation;* reverence; *submission;* sprawling; servitude; toadying; *under;* veneration; worship; *xenophilia;* yearning; *zeroizing;* [Ant. pride]

**protect** *(v.)*: aid; bulwark; cover; defend; ensconce; ensure; flank; fend; fortify; guard; harbor; hold; hide; insure; insulate; jaga; keep; look after; make safe; *nestle;* overshadow; *over~;* preserve; police; patrol; pavilion; *quia timet [L.];* refuge; *refortify;* safeguard; shelter; shield; take care of; uphold; vallate; watch (over); ward; *well-policed;* weather-fend; *x-guard; yeme* [arch.]; *zero danger;*

**protection** *(n.)*: auspices; armor; bulwark; covering; coverage; defense; ensuring; fending; fortification; guard; harborage; haven; insurance; incolumity; jaga; keeping; lee; *measures;* non-danger; *over~;* preservation; *quia timet* [L.]; refortification; refuge; rampart; safety; safeguard; shelter; safekeeping; self-defense; shield; security; *trustworthiness;* upholding; vallation; watchcare; well-being; *x-guard; yeming* [arch.]; zero danger; [*Ant.* peril]

**protest** *(n.)*: argument; balking; complaint; dispute; dissent; demonstration; *démarche* [F.]; exception; fuss; gripe; *harrowing;* impugnation; jeremiad; kicking; *locking horns;* murmuring; march; naysaying; objection; protestation; picketing; quarrel; remonstrance; strike; *trouble;* unharmoniousness; variance; walkout; *x-fire;* yelling; yammering; *za-zum [Rus.];* [*Ant.* promotion]

**protest** *(v.)*: argue; bemoan; complain; demur; disagree; differ; dissent; disapprove; except; frown; fuss; gripe; gainsay; have a problem with; howl; *insist;* jib; kick; *loath;* make objection; nitpick; object; oppose; picket; question; quarrel; resist; raise objection; remonstrate; squawk; speak out against; take issue; *urge against;* vituperate; vary; withstand; whine; *x-fire;* yawp; *zing;* [*Ant.* promote]

**prototype** *(n. example)*: archetype; basis; copied original; *design;* example; exemplar; fugler; guide; *holotype;* ideal; *jewel; key;* layout; model; neotype; original; pattern; *quintessence;* rule; specimen; standard; template; ule; *virtual; wax figure; xenagogue;* yardstick; *zincograph;*

**protrude** *(v.)*: aslope; beetle; continue; draw out; extend; exsert; expand; *fold out;* go beyond; *hang over;* increase; jut; *keep going;* lengthen; make longer; *non-collapsed;* obtrude; project; *quantity;* reach forth; stick out; thrust out; *upgrade; vary;* wax longer; XL; *yield;* zoom.

**proud** *(adj.)*: arrogant; big-headed; boastful; conceited; cocky; disdainful; egotistical; flatulent; gloating; haughty; imperious; inflated; *Jack-the-lad; know-it-all;* lifted up; *magnificent;* narcissistic; overconfident; over~; prideful; puffed up; quick-to-boast; reassured; swelled; self-exalting; supercilious; turgid; unhumbled; vain; wrapped up in oneself; *x-proud; yelping;* zero humility; [*Ant.* poor in spirit]

**provable** *(adj.)*: attestable; affirmable; *bearing out;* confirmable; demonstrable; defendable; declatable; evincible; fixable; *given; homologate;* incontestable; justifiable; *kithe [Scot.];* legitimate; maintainable; nailed down; *okay; proven;* qualifiable; real; supportable; testable; triable; unconfutable; verifiable; warrantable; x-certifiable; *yes;* zero doubt;

**prove** *(v.)*: authenticate; affirm; attest; bear out; confirm; clinch; corroborate; demonstrate; determine; document; *defend;* establish; evidence; evince; fix; give proof; homologate; illustrate; jerque; justify; kithe [Scot.]; legitimize; manifest; nail down; *okay;* provide evidence; probate; *questionless;* recheck; remonstrate; substantiate; show; set at rest; support; settle; sustain; try; uphold; verify; validate; warrant; x-certify; *yes;* zero doubt; [*Ant.* presume]

**proven** *(adj.)*: authenticated; affirmed; attested; borne out; confirmed; demonstrated; established; evinced; fixed; *guaranteed;* homologated; illustrated; jerqued; kithed [Scot.]; legitimized; *maintained;* nailed down; *okay;* proved; q.e.d.; questionless; reliable; sure; substantiated; shown; set at rest; tried (and true); upheld; verified; validated; warranted; well-proven; x-certified; *yes;* zero doubt; [*Ant.* presumed]

**proverb** *(n.)*: adage; axiom; byword; cliché; dictum; epigram; formula; guideline; generality; *hackneyed saying;* instruction; *judgment; koine;* law; maxim; neology; oracle; principle; platitude; quote; rule; saying; truism; tenet; universal truth; verse; wisdom; wise saying; *xenophonia; Yogism;* zeteticism;

**proverbial** *(adj.)*: axiomatic; aphoristic; *beloved;* celebrated; demonstrable; epigrammatic; famed; gnomic; high-profile; illustrious; *jubilated over;* known; legendary; mentioned often; notable; notorious [evil]; outstanding; popular; *quintessential;* reputed; stereotypical; typical; usual; venerated; well-known; *xtry.;* yichus; *zealously repeated;*

**provide** *(v.)*: allot; afford; bestow; confer; cater; care for; donate; endow; furnish; feed; favor; give; grant; hand over; help; impart; *jettison;* kit; keep (alive); leave; look after; make provision; *non-retention;* offer; outfit; present; procure; purvey; ply; *quarter;* render; supply; sustain; support; transfer; take care of; uphold; vest; victual; *weigh;* xfer; yield; *zip;*

577

**providence** *(n.)*: act of God; beneficence; circumstances; control of God; destiny; divine appointment; foreordination; God's working; *His will;* intervention of God; *judgment; knowledge; the* Lord's working; management; *manifest destiny; non-coincidental;* ordaining of God; omnipotence; overruling; providential workings; *qismat* [Arab.]; rule of God; sovereignty; superintendence; timely care; unsearchable workings of God; vocation; workings; will of God; *Xt.; Yahweh;* zonic intervention;

**province** *(n.)*: area; borough; county; district; division; earldom; *field;* grand duchy; hundred; *isolated area;* jurisdiction; *kray* [Rus.]; land; municipality; nomarchy; *oblast* [Rus.]; parish; precinct; part; quadrant; region; sector; territory; ubiety; viceroyalty; ward; *x-sector; yard; zillah* [Ind.]; zone;

**provision** *(n.)*: aliment; bestowal; care; daily ~; edibles; *endowment;* fare; *food; grant;* help; imparting; *just in time;* keeping; looking after; manna; meeting one's need; need; outfitting; purveyance; *quarter; rations;* sustenance; supply; taking care; upholding; *victuals;* watchcare; *xfer; yield; zero need;*

**provocation** *(n.)*: antagonizing; baiting; chafing; driving; excitement; frustration; goading; hassling; heartening; incitement; jarring; kindling; *lead;* motivation; move; needling; *offend;* provoking; promptore; *quickening;* riling; rousing; stirring; suggestion; temptation; *unnerving;* vexing; whetting; *xuld [arch.]; yerking; zinging;*

**provoke** *(v.)*: affect; aggravate; bestir; bother; cause; drive; excite; egg on; elicit; fire up; fan; frustrate; goad; hearten; hassle; incite; impel; instigate; induce; inflame; *jar;* kindle; light up; move; motivate; nudge; needle; offend; prod; prompt; pester; quicken; rouse; rile; stir; trigger; urge; vex; wake; work up; *xuld [arch.];* yerk [dial.]; *zing;* [*Ant.* prevent]

**proximity** *(n.)*: adjacency; *by;* closeness; *distance;* environs; *forthcoming; gone up to; happen;* immediacy; intimacy; juxtaposition; *kept by;* location; locality; localness; *more or less;* nearness; neighborhood; *oncoming;* propinquity; *quite close; relationship; soon; touching on;* ubiety; vicinity; *well-nigh; xfer; yede [arch.]; zeroing in;*

**proxy** *(n.)*: agent; assignee; broker; consul; delegate; deputy; emissary; fill-in; *ghost; herald;* internuncio; *joiner; kurveyor;* liaison; locum; messenger; negotiant; official representative; *partner; quod pro quo* [L.]; representative; substitute; stand-in; surrogate; temporary; understudy; vicar; *walking delegate; xfer; yamen [Chin.]; zwap [dial.];*

**prudence** *(n.)*: abstruseness; acumen; better judgment; common sense; caution; discretion; discernment; experience; foresight; good sense; horse sense; intelligence; insight; judiciousness; judgment; knowledge; logic; level-headedness; mindfulness; non-foolishness; *opportuneness;* perception; policy; *qui vive* [L.]; rationality; reasonableness; sense; sensibility; sagacity; thought; understanding; vigilance; wisdom; wis(eness); *xenagogy; yepe [arch.]; zeteticism;* [*Ant.* poor judgment]

**prudent** *(adj.)*: astute; advisable; *bright;* circumspect; discreet; discerning; expedient; ever-wise; farsighted; farseeing; *guarded; hesitant;* insightful; judicious; *keen;* longsighted; *museful; noetic;* oracular; prudential; perceptive; *quick-witted;* rational; sagacious; sensible; smart; tactical; understanding; *versed;* wise; *xenagogic;* yepe; *zetetic;* [*Ant.* poorly-judged]

**prune** *(v.)*: amputate; *bob;* crop; clip; cut (back); dress; dissever; exscind; *forehew; gouge;* hack; incide; incision; *jigsaw; kerf;* lop; *mulch; notch;* obtruncate; pare; *quadrisect;* remove; snip; trim; *unburden;* vell; whack off; *x-sect;* yerk; *zigsaw* [arch.];

**pry** *(v.)*: attempt to raise; bear on; crowbar; dig; elevate; force; get up; hoist; *impel;* jimmy; jack; *knock;* lever; make open; *muscle;* nose; open; poke; prize; *quicken;* raise; strong-arm; try to raise; use lever; *vie;* wrench; *xuld* [arch.]; *yank; zeal;*

**psalm** *(n.)*: anthem; ballad; carol; doxology; *étude; folksong;* gloria; hymn; inspirational; introit; *jingle;* kasida; laud; music; *notes; offertory;* praise song; quodlibet; refrain; (spiritual) song; *tune;* undersong; vocalization; warbling; *xylophone song;* yed; zemirah;

**psalmist** *(n.)*: author; bard; composer; doggerelist; elegist; framer; glorier; hymnist; hymn writer; inspirational songwriter; jongleur; kasida-writer; lyricist; music-writer; *noel;* odist; psalmographer; *quadrille;* rhymester; songwriter; tune-maker; *undersong;* versifier; writer; *xylophonist;* yedder; *zemirah;*
**pub** *(n.)*: ale-house; bar; cabaret; dramshop; establishment; fern bar; groghouse; hostelry; inn; joint; kiddleywink; lounge; mughouse; night-house; *open bar;* pothouse; *queme house;* rathskeller; saloon; tavern; *utility bar; vinery;* watering hole; *xenodocheum;* youth club; *zubrowka;*
**public** *(adj.)*: accessible; *body;* communal; civic; common; diffuse; exoteric; folk; general ~; high profile; intermutual; *joint;* known; local; municipal; non-private; open; public-domain; *quad; reported;* shared; town-owned; unrestricted; unclassified; village-owned; well-known; *xenic; yokel;* zonal; [*Ant.* private]
**public** *(n.)*: audience; body of citizens; community; citizenry; *demos* [Gr.]; electorate; folk; general ~; *hoi polloi* [Gr.]; inhabitants; *janata [Asia]; kith;* legal citizenry; masses; neighborhood; nation; *outlying;* people; populace; population; *quorum;* residents; society; townsfolk; urban population; village folk; voters; *well-known; xenic:* yokels; zone;
**publican** *(n.)*: assessor; *bureau;* collector; dunner; exiseman; federal ~; gabeler; *heartless ~;* IRS official; judge; khalsah [Ind.]; legal tax collector; money-collector; *non-sympathetic;* officer; public official; questor; receiver of taxes; *sheriff;* tax collector; *usurer;* vulture; worker; *xaraf;* yegg; zamindar [Ind.];
**publicity** *(n.)*: advertising; billing; broadcasting; circulation; coverage; dissemination; exposure; fame; free advertising; *glory;* hype; informing; *joint-advertisement;* kudos; letting it be known; media attention; marketing; notoriety; *overspread;* promotion; *quantity;* réclaim; spreading the word; transmission; *unleashing; veneration;* write-up; *xtry.;* yichus; *zealous ~;*
**publicize** *(v.)*: advertise; bill; broadcast; circulate; dispread; disseminate; expose; fame; get the word out; help others to know; *introduce; joint-advertisement; known;* let others know; make known; *notify;* openly report; publish; plaster; promote; politicize; *quarter-page ad;* release; raise awareness; spread; tell others; tout; televise; uphold; voice; write up; *xmit; yell;* zealously publish; [*Ant.* put away]
**publicized** *(adj.)*: advertised; *big-name;* commonly known; divulged; dispread; exposed; famed abroad; famous; greatly ~; high-profile; *infamous; joint-advertisement;* known; *legendary;* made known; *notorious;* openly reported; promulgated; published; proclaimed; *quarter-page ad;* revealed; *spoken of;* talked-about; universally known; voiced; well-known (-~); *xtry.;* yichus; *zealously ~;* [*Ant.* private]
**publicly** *(adv.)*: apparently; before all; blatantly; conspicuously; *distinctly;* explicitly; freely; glaringly; *high-profile;* in public; *just; knowingly;* lucidly; manifestly; noticeably; openly; overtly; patently; popularly; *quite;* recognizably; roundly; saliently; *transparently;* unmistakably; visibly; widely; wittingly; *XR;* yarely; zonally; [*Ant.* privately]
**publish** *(v.)*: announce; broadcast; circulate; declare; exclaim; fame; get the word out; help others to know; issue; *journalism; known;* let others know; make known; notify; openly declare; print; promulgate; publicize; *quarter-page ad;* report; spread; tell others; *televise;* uphold; *volume;* word; *xmit;* yell; zealously ~;
**puff** *(n.)*: airstream; breath; blast; billow; current; cloud; draught; emission; flaw; fluff; gust; headwind; indraft; jet stream; katabatic wind; levanter; moderate gale; notus; *overdraft;* poof; quiff; *respiration;* squall; tailwind; updraft; violent wind; wind; wisp; x-wind; *yaw;* zephyr;
**puff** *(v.)*: aerate; blow; bulge; bloat; *cough;* distend; enlarge; expand; fatten; gorge; huff; inflate; jet; *kest;* largen; mound; *nebular;* outblow; pant; poof; *quantum increase;* rise; swell; tumefy; *upbuild;* vent; wheeze; *XL;* yain [arch.]; *zoom up;*
**pull** *(v.)*: abstract; bring along; cant; draw; drag; extract; flounce; force; grab; heave; haul; intercept; jerk; kedge; lug; magnetize; nab; *outdrag;* pluck; quirk; remove; snatch; seize; take; tug; tow; *uncoif;* vellicate; wrench; *xuld* [arch.]; yank; *zip;* [*Ant.* push]
**pulp** *(n.)*: admixture; bagasse; concoction; dough; *essence;* fluff; goop; *hodgepodge;* intermixture; jelly; *keest; liquid;* mush; mash; *nectar;* oatmeal; pomace; pulpwood; purée; paste; *quagmire;* rag ~; soft mass; thick liquid; unhardened substance; *viscous matter;* wood-~; *xtr. blended;* yanggoma; *zeug;*

**pulpit** *(n.)*: ambo; bema; *chair* [arch.]; desk; *estrade;* faldstool; glass podium; hardwood ~; *item; jarahwood ~;* kiosk; lectern; *minbar; night stand; object;* podium; *quincewood ~;* rostrum; stand; soapbox; *teakwood ~; utility; varnished ~;* wooden ~; x-stand; *yew-wood ~; zebrawood ~;*
**pulsate** *(v.)*: agitate; beat; *cadence;* drum; *excite;* flutter; go bump; heartthrob; *impact;* judder; knock; lam; *move;* nubble; oscillate; pound; quiver; *quob* [arch.]; reverberate; sputter; throb; thrum; tick; *upset;* vibrate; wobble; *xuld [arch.];* yedder; zonk;
**pulse** *(n.)*: agitation; beat; blood flow; cadence; drumming; *excite;* fluttering; going bump; heartbeat; *impact;* judder; *knock;* laming; *movement;* nubbling; *overagitate;* pulsation; quob; rhythm; sputtering; thump; throb; *upset;* vibration; wobbling; *xuld [arch.];* yeddering; zonking; [*see* vegetable]
**pulverize** *(v.)*: annihilate; blot out; crush; comminute; demolish; disintegrate; expunge; exterminate; fragmentalize; grind; hammer; *incinerate; junk;* knock; lay waste; mash; mill; *nullify;* obliterate; purge; powder; quash; raze; smash; triturate; unbuild; vaporize; wipe out; *x-ing;* yank apart; zap;
**pump** *(v.)*: abstract; bring up; convey; carry; draw out; *expand;* force; get; *haul; inflate; janker;* kurvey; *lead;* move; *non-stationary; overcarry;* pass; *quantities;* raise; relay; remove; siphon; *suck out;* transfer; transport; uptake; vacuum- ~; work ~; xfer; *yield; zip;*
**punch** *(n.)*: assault; biff; blow; bash; clobber; clout; crack; cuff; clock; dash; deck; double-whammy; *efface;* flogging; *get;* hit; impact; jab; knock; knuckle sandwich; kidney- ~; lick; *mauling;* nevel; open-handed blow; *pow; quab;* rap; smite; strike; sock; swipe; shot; slug; thwack; uppercut; veney; whack; wallop; *x-sect;* yedder; zonk; [*see* beverage]
**punch** *(v.)*: assault; beat; box; buffet; clobber; clock; deck; drub; *efface;* flog; *get;* hit; hammer; *impact;* jab; knock; lam; mash; nevel; *overstrike;* pound; quab; rap; smite; strike; slug; thrash; thump; uppercut; veney; wallop; *x-sect;* yedder; zonk;
**punctual** *(adj.)*: absolutely on time; *bang!;* conscientious; dead-on; exact; *faithful; good;* heedful; in good time; just on time; keeping the arranged time; *literal; mindful;* never-late; on-time; on the dot; prompt; prest; quite ~; right on time; seasonable; sharp; timely; under the wire; very ~; without delay; xtry. ~; *yare; zero delay;* [*Ant.* procrastinatory]
**puncture** *(v.)*: *auger;* bore; *cut;* dirk; empierce; fix [arch.]; gore; hole; impale; jab; knife; lance; make hole; nail; open; pierce; perforate; prick; poniard; *quill;* run through; stab; stick; transfix; *undercut; ventilate;* wimble; *xylotomy;* yerk; *zing;*
**pungent** *(adj.)*: acrid; acidulous; biting; cutting; *distasteful;* extreme; fiery; gingery; hot; harsh; hardy; intense; jolting; keen; lively; *mighty strong; nippy;* overpowering; oniony; piquant; peppery; powerful; quite ~; robust; racy; sour; sharp; spicy; strong; tangy; tart; unsweetened; unpleasant; vivacious; vinegary; well-seasoned; *xtry.; yummy; yucky;* zesty; zippy; zingy; [*Ant.* plain]
**punish** *(v.)*: amerce; afflict; bring to justice; chastise; correct; castigate; condemn; discipline; damn; even the score; fleague; fine; *give stripes;* have redress; inflict punishment; imprison; *judge; keep locked up;* lay into; mulct; *necessitate; overdo;* penalize; *quittal;* reprimand; requite; *the* rod; spank; swinge; scourge; sentence; thrash; *upbraid; vengeance; whip; x-out;* yard [arch.]; zap; [*Ant.* praise; pardon]
**punishment** *(n.)*: affliction; amercement; beating; correction; castigation; chastisement; discipline; *deserts; execution;* ferule; flogging; *garroting;* horsewhipping; infliction; just deserts; *keelhauling;* lumps; lashing; mulct; maltreatment; nemesis; *overly harsh;* penalty; punishing; *quartering; the* rod; retribution; sanctions; sentence; suffering; taking to task; talion; thrashing; *upbraiding;* vengeance; whipping; *x-ing;* yard [arch.]; zapping; [*Ant.* praise; pardon]
**punitive** *(adj.)*: amendatory; *bringing justice;* corrective; castigatory; disciplinary; emendatory; *fleaguing;* grueling; *horsewhipping;* inflictive; justifictory; *keelhauling; lashing;* making one pay; *nexal; official; order-keeping;* penal; punitory; *quede [arch.];* retaliatory; *scourging; terrorizing;* upbraiding; vindicatory; *whip; wrath; x-ing;* yielding punishment; *zero tolerance;*

**puny** *(adj.)*: *abbreviated; baby;* compact; dinky; defenseless; eensie-weensie; feeble; frail; gimp; helpless; inadequate; *jejune;* knee-high; little; miniature; meager; negligible; overweak; petite; pygmean; pint-sized; *quantité négligeable* [F.]; runty; small; scrawny; tiny; undersized; underdeveloped; vulnerable; weak; XS; *yea big; zero;* [Ant. prodigious]

**puppet** *(n.)*: animal ~; body ~; carnival ~; dummy; *elephant ~;* finger ~; figure; fantoccini; glove ~ [Can.]; hand ~; *instant ~;* jumping-jack; *Judy; karakuri ningyo [Jap.]; llama ~;* marionette; moppet; mammet; neurospast; *ostrich ~;* poupeton; *Punch; quadruped ~;* rod ~; string ~; sock ~; table-top ~; *unicorn ~;* ventriloquist's dummy; water ~; *xoanon; yak ~; zebra ~;*

**puppy** *(n.)*: *animal;* bowwow; canine; cub; dog; *elkhound;* feist; *greyhound;* hound; *Irish setter; jackal; K-9 [slang];* lapdog; mutt; *newborn; organism;* pup; *pet; quadruped; retriever; sheepdog;* tail-wagger; *ululator; vizsla;* whelp; *xolotl;* young pup; *zerda;* [*see* dog]

**purchase** *(n.)*: acquisition; buy; catching; deal; emption; find; gain; having; in-store ~; investment; *junk; kind;* landing; *material;* netting; online ~; obtainment; procurement; *quantity;* receipt; retrieving; steal [slang]; taking; *thing; utility;* value; win; *xfer; yard sale ~; zet;*

**purchase** *(v.)*: acquire; buy; contract for; *deal; engage in sale; fetch;* get; *have;* invest; *jump at; kep;* lay out; make ~; *nab;* obtain; pick up; pay for; procure; quoff; redeem; sink money into; take home; *use money; vest;* wholesale; *xfer; yank; zet [dial.];* [Ant. purvey]

**pure** *(adj.)*: *absolute;* blameless; clear; clean; chaste; decent; essential; fair; fine; good; guiltless; honorable; innocent; immaculate; incorrupt; inviolate; *just;* keen; lily-white; mere; nice; non-mixed; 100% ~; plain; *quality;* qualmless; respectable; righteous; stainless; spotless; taintless; unpolluted; unadulterated; uncontaminated; untarnished; untainted; unmixed; unalloyed; unspoiled; unspotted; virgin(al); virtuous; vestal; white; wholesome; *xtry.;* yet unadulterated; *zero blemish;* [Ant. polluted]

**pureblood** *(adj.)*: absolutely pure; blood; completely; *derivation;* entirely; full-blood; *graded;* highbred; *incorrupt;* just; *keen; lily-white; mores;* non-mixed; 100% ~; purebred; pedigreed; *quite pure;* racially pure; *stock;* trueblood (-bred, -born); thoroughbred; unmixed; *very pure;* wholly; *x-link;* yet unadulterated; *zero admixture;* [Ant. polyethnic]

**purée** *(n.)*: admixture; blend; coulis; *diced finely;* emulsion; *formula;* goop; *hodgepodge;* intermixture; *jumble; ketchup; liquid;* mush; *nectar;* oatmeal; pulp; paste; *quagmire; raw pulp;* sauce; thick liquid; unhardened substance; *viscous matter;* wood-pulp; XF; yanggoma; *zuppe [It.];*

**purgative** *(n.)*: aparient; bowel-emptier; cathartic; *castor oil;* diarrheic; evacuative; eccoprotic; *flush-out;* gamboge; hydragogue; *insides; jalap; kesting;* laxative; mild ~; *medicine;* non-violent cathartic; *opener;* physic; purgament; *quinine;* relieving; scourer; *turpeth; ule;* violent cathartic; *white jalap; xenobiotic; yucky; zopissa [arch.];*

**purge** *(v.)*: abolish; *banish;* cleanse; clean out; depurate; expurgate; eliminate; eradicate; force out; get rid of; *heal; illegalize;* jalap; kill; liquidate; make an end of; nullify; oust; purify; put out; *quash;* rid; remove; root out; refine; stamp out; throw out; unload; *void;* wash (-wipe) out; x-out; *yank;* zeroize;

**purification** *(n.)*: ablution; bathing; cleansing; decontamination; depuration; detoxification; expurgation; februation; getting impurities out; headbath; *hallowing;* impurity-removal; *jalap; knee-bath;* lavation; lustration; mundification; *non-polluted;* outwashing; purgation; purging; purifying; *quintessentialize;* rinsing; refinement; sanctification; sanitization; taking out contaminants; *unpolluted; vacuation;* washing; *xylol; yellow soap; zinc oxide;* [Ant. pollution]

**purify** *(v.)*: absterge; bathe; cleanse; depurate; decontaminate, detoxify; demephitize; expurgate; edulcorate; flush; get impurities out; *hallow; implunge; jalap;* kill germs; lustrate; mundify; make pure; *non-polluted;* outwash; purge; *quintessentialize;* rinse; refine; sanctify; try (by fire); unsully; *vacuate;* wash; *xylol; yellow soap; zierlich [G.];* [Ant. pollute]

**purity** *(n.)*: absoluteness; blamelessness; cleanness; chastity; decency; essentiality; fairness; fineness; goodness; guiltlessness; honor; homogeneity; innocence; immaculacy; incorruptness; *justification;* keenness; *lily-white;* morality; non-mixture; *only;* pureness; plainness; *quality;* righteousness; singleness; soleness; taintlessness; unmixedness; uniformity; unspottedness; virtue; virginity; whiteness; wholesomeness; *xtry.; yet pure; zero blemish;* [*see* innocence; *Ant.* pollution]

**purple** *(adj.)*: amethyst; aubergine; bluish- ~; bepurpled; cimolite- ~; damson; empurpled; fuchsia; grape; gridelin; heather; heliotrope; impurpled; *jazel;* kingly ~; lavender; lilac; mauve; magenta; nigri- ~; orchid; plum; puce; purplish; queen's ~; royal ~; solferino; tare; *ultraviolet;* violet; wine; xeranthemum; *yellowish ~; zonnober ~;*

**purpose** *(n.)*: aim; by-purpose; *chief reason;* design; end; function; goal; high aim; intention; journey's end; key reason; *liking;* meaning; nisus; object(ive); point; quintain; reason; sake; target; use(fulness); *Thule* [L.]; *view;* wish; will; x; *yearning; zero in;*

**purposeful** *(adj.)*: adamant; bull-headed; constant; determined; dogged; doughty; ever-stubborn; firm; gritty; headstrong; indomitable; iron-willed; jaw-set; knowing; *lasting;* mulish; non-bending; obstinate; purposive; persevering; pertinacious; *quenchless;* resolute; strong-willed; tenacious; unwavering; volitional; willful; *x-grained;* yieldless; *zero give;* [*Ant.* purposeless]

**purse** *(n.)*: accessory bag; bag; clutch; caryall; day ~; ermine bag; *fanny pack;* grip; handbag; inro; *journey-sack;* kit bag; *luggage;* money- ~; *nécessaire* [F.]; organizer; pocketbook; *quiver;* reticule; shoulder bag; satchel; tote; utility case; valise; *vanity case;* wallet; *x-bag; yannigan;* zipper-bag;

**pursue** *(v.)*: *after;* be after; chase; dog; *engage;* follow; go after; hunt (down); hound; *interlope;* jack; *kill;* look for; make one's prey; *nimrod; open season;* press on; queue; run after; stalk; seek; track; trail; *undertake;* venture; *wild goose chase;* woo; *xfer; yager; zealously find;*

**pursuit** *(n.)*: attempt; business; chase; dogged ~; employment; following; game; hunt; hot ~; insecution; jerquing; *kith;* looking for; mission; *man-hunt; nosing around;* objective; persuance; quest; *rescue;* search; seeking out; tracking; *undertaking;* venture; *wild goose chase; x-search; yearn for; zetetic;*

**push** *(n.)*: assault; bump; boost; cram; driving force; exertion; force; goad; heave; impulsion; jab; jostle; jolt; kibbling; lamming; motivation; nudge; *ooch;* prod; *quant;* ram; shove; thrust; upthrust; violence; whack; *xowyn* [arch.]; yerk; *zonk;*

**push** *(v.)*: advocate; advance; budge; compress; depress; drive; exert pressure; force; flick; goad; heave; impel; jostle; jolt; kibble; lean; move forward; nudge; ooch; prod; press; propel; quant; ram; shove; shunt; thrust; upthrust; urge; *vice; whack; xowyn* [arch.]; yerk; *zonk;* [*Ant.* pull]

**put** *(v.)*: assign; *bestow; confer;* deposit; emplace; furnish; give; hand (over); impart; *juxtapose;* kit; lay; leave; *make rest; non-retention;* offload; place; *quicken;* rest; set; situate; stick; stow; transfer; unhand; vest; *weigh;* xfer; *yield;* zet [dial.];

**puzzle** *(n.)*: arcanum; *anagram;* brainteaser; conundrum; challenge; dilemma; enigma; fuddlement; game; *hidden thing;* inscrutableness; jigsaw ~; knot; logogriph; mystery; mindbender; non-disclosed fact; obscure fact; picture ~; poser; problem; question; quandary; riddle; rebus; stumper; telestich; unexplained thing; vagueness; word ~; *x.; yet undisclosed fact;* zinger;

**puzzle** *(v.)*: addle; baffle; boggle; confound; disconcert; *entangle;* fuddle; flummox; gravel; hamper; *incoherent;* jumble; kittle; lose; mystify; nonplus; obscure; pother; perplex; quiz; *ravel;* stump; tangle; *unorganized;* vex; wilder; *x; yo-yo; zero understanding;*

**puzzlement** *(n.)*: amazement; bafflement; confusion; disorientation; entanglement; *flurry;* gastness; *havoc;* incomprehension; jumble; kippage; lack of understanding; mystification; non-comprehension; *obscurity;* perplexity; quandary; *raveled;* stupefaction; turmoil; uncertainty; vexation; wilderment; *xtry.* mess; *yo-yo;* zero understanding;

# Q

**quack** *(n.)*: *actor;* bluffer; charlatan; con; *doctor; deceiver;* empiric; fake; fraud; grifter; hoaxer; huckster; haberdasher; imposter; jape; knave; *liar;* mountebank; medicaster; myropolist; nostrum; *oily;* phony; pretender; quacksalver; rip-off artist; snake-oil salesman; swindler; trickster; unlicensed practiticioner; verneuker; wheeler-dealer; *xenodiagnosis; yantzer; zinger;*

**quackery** *(n.)*: artfulness; beguilement; charlatanism; dabbling; empiricism; fraud; gulling; haberdashery; imposture; japery; kiddy; *lying;* mountbankery; nostrum; *opportunism; pet remedy;* quackism; racketeering; swindling; trickery; unlicensed practice; verneuking; wiliness; *xuld [arch.];* yanking one's chain; *zinger;*

**quadrant** *(n.)*: *untruther;* verneuker; wheeler-dealer; *xenodiagnosis; yantzer; zinger;* area; borough; county; district; division; element; fraction; field; ground; *hemisphere; imperial territory; jagir* [Asia]; *kaza* [Turk.]; locale; municipality; neighborhood; nome; *oblast [Rus.];* part; parcel; quarter; region; sector; section; territory; tetrarchy; *ubiety; vicinity; viceroyalty;* ward; x-sector; *yard;* zone;

**quadruped** *(n.)*: animal; beast; creature; domestic animal; *elk;* four-footed beast; game; *herbivore; insectivore;* jument; *koala;* living thing; *mammal; newt;* organism; *pony; quadru-pawed;* rodent; *reptile;* stock; tetrapod; ungulate; varmint; wilding; *xolotl; yearling;* zoic;

**quagmire** *(n.)*: *aikraw;* bog; carr; drain; everglade; fen; glade; haugh; inland marsh; *jheel* [Ind.]; kavir; *lagoon;* marsh; *nanoplankton; overgrown;* peatbog; quag; rosland; swamp; tarn; *usnea;* vlie [S. Afr.]; wetlands; xyrisic; yarpha; *zoocarpous area;*

**quail** *(v.)*: atrophy; abate; *break down;* consume; decline; deteriorate; diminish; dwindle; ebb; enfeeble; emasculate; exhaust; fade; fall; go down; hang back; impair; jade; *knock off;* languish; moderate; *narrow; outgo;* pine; quell; reduce; starve; subside; taper; *use up; vanish;* waste away; wane; wither; *xerosis; yield;* zap;

**quaint** *(adj.)*: appealing; antiquated; beautiful; charming; delightful; dainty; elegant; early-style; fair; good-looking; handsome; *interesting;* jimp; keen; lovely; *memorable;* nice; old-fashioned; picturesque; pleasant; quite charming; *refined; rural; scenic; traditional;* unusual; Victorian; wonderful; *xtry.; yesteryear; zierlich* [G.]; [Ant. queer]

**quake** *(v.)*: agitate; bestir; chatter; *convulse;* disquiet; *earthquake;* falter; fluctuate; *gyrate;* hurtle; *instability;* judder; knock; lurch; *move; nudge;* oscillate; pitch; quiver; rumble; shake; tremble; upheave; vacillate; wobble; *xuld [arch.];* yerk; zigzag; [Ant. quell]

**qualification** *(n.)*: adjuration; basic ~; condition; criterion; caveat; demand; expectation; fitness; gauge; habilitation; indispensable ~; *juration;* key ~; lowest expectation; *limitation;* must; mandatory ~; necessity; *obligation;* prerequisite; proviso; postulate; provision; qualified condition; requirement; requisite; rider; stipulation; specification; standard; top stipulation; ultimatum; vital condition; want; *XO requirement; yarking; zero option;*

**qualified** *(adj.)*: able; approved; accredited; board certified; competent; certified; deft; experienced; endorsed; fit; good; *has ability;* instructed; justified; knowledgeable; licensed; mighty; *means; may; natural ability;* on the level; *over~; proficient;* qualitied; readied; skilled; trained; up to; versed; well-able; *xtry. ~;* yarkened; *zealous;*

**qualifier** *(n.)*: adjustment; *bounds;* condition; demand; explanation; *foist;* guideline; *have;* imposition; *justification; keep confined;* limitation; modifier; *necessitate; ordinance;* particular; parameter; precondition; proviso; qualification; rule; restriction; rider; standard; stipulation; tempering; term; *ultimatum; variance; wording: XO requirement;* yardstick; *zero in;*

**qualify** *(v. modify)*: adjust; *bounds;* clear up; confine; delineate; explain; *foist;* give condition; *help to understand;* impose limitation; *justify; keep confined;* limit; make stipulation; modify; necessitate; narrow; *ordain;* parameterize; *qualification;* restrict; stipulate; temper; *uncloud; vary; work on; xenagogy;* yark; zero in;
**qualify** *(v. ready)*: authorize; become able; capacitate; dight; enable; fill the bill; get; hack it; *instruct;* justify; *keen;* let; make (ready); *nod;* outfit; pass; permit; *qualification;* ready; suit; sanction; train; *ultra-prepared;* validate; warrant; *xtr. training;* yarken; *zealously approve;*
**quality** *(n. character)*: attributes; *badge;* character(istic); condition; caliber; disposition; essence; fiber; feature; flavor; grade; heart; intrinsicality; *jist;* kind; lineament; makeup; nature; overall character; property; quale; reality; suchness; spirit; temperament; trait; *tendency;* underlying character; virtue; way; xenenthesis; *yetzer* [Heb.]; *zoe;*
**quality** *(n. degree of excellence)*: aspect; *bad; best;* caliber; class; degree; elevation; excellence; fineness; fashion; grade; height; *increase; judgment;* kind; level; mark; merit; notch; order; plateau; *par excellence* [F.]; *qualification;* rating; richness; superiority; tier; *unit;* value; virtue; workmanship; worth; *x-class; y-level; zone;*
**qualm** *(n.)*: apprehension; *bone;* compunction; conscience; doubt; ethics; foreboding; guilt; hesitation; issues; *jarred;* keen sense of guilt; *light of conscience;* misgiving; niggle; *nausea;* objections; problem; questions; reservations; scruple; trepidation; uneasiness; vacillation; worries; *x-ing; yieldedness; zeroing in;*
**quandary** *(n.)*: ailment; bind; complication; dilemma; *encumbrance;* fix; Gordian knot; headache; impasse; jam; kink; *load;* mess; nonplus; *obstacle;* predicament; problem; *quagmire;* rattle; strait; trouble; *upheaval;* vexation; worry; *xerotripsis; yuckiness; zhlubby;*
**quantitative** *(adj.)*: abundant; bounteous; copious; disproportionate; excessive; fantastic; *fruitful;* great; huge; immense; jumbo; *king-sized;* large; many; much; numerous; overmuch; overabundant; plentiful; quantities; *replete; rich;* substantial; several; tons; *tremendous;* uberous; voluminous; various; wantless; *x.; yards; zillions;*
**quantity** *(n.)*: amount; bulk; count; degree; extent; figure; force; group; horde; *ingathering;* jag; *kit;* level; load; measure; mass; number; *offset;* portion; part; quantum; quantulum; reckoning; range; size; sum; strength; score; total; tally; units; volume; whole; weight; *x; yard; z-score;*
**quarantine** *(n.)*: alienation; banishment; confinement; detachment; exclusion; forlorness; *grounding;* holding; isolation; *jailing;* keeping apart; lock up; *marabout;* non-inclusion; *outside;* penning up; quarantining; reclusion; seclusion; solitude; separation; *taking out; unsociability; veiling;* withdrawal; *x.;* yarding; *zone;*
**quarantine** *(v.)*: alienate; *apart;* banish; contain; confine; detach; exile; fence in; ground; hold; isolate; immure; *jail;* keep apart from; lock up; make isolated; *non-connected; outside;* pen up; *quant;* restrict; separate; sequester; shut up; take out; *under lock and key; veil;* ward; *x;* yellow flag; yard; *zone;*
**quarrel** *(n.)*: argument; bickering; contention; controversy; disagreement; dispute; embroilment; fight; feud; grappling; hassle; hostility; inaccordance; jangling; kagg; *locking horns; making fur fly;* negativism; odds; opposition; polemic; quibble; row; ruction; strife; squabble; spat; tiff; unharmoniousness; variance; wrangling; *x-fire;* yelling match; *zapping;*
**quarrel** *(v.)*: argue; bicker; contend; disagree; exchange words; fight; fuss; feud; grapple; gainsay; have words with; hassle; *inharmonious;* jangle; kick up dust; lock horns [slang]; make fur fly; niff; oppose; pick fight; quibble; resist; squabble; strive; tiff; *unharmonious;* vie; wrangle; *x-purposes;* yell; *zap;*
**quarreler** *(n.)*: arguer; bickerer; contender; disputer; disputant; embroiler; *enemy;* fighter; gainsayer; hassler; impugner; jangler; *knocker; lock horn;* militant; naysayer; objector; protester; *querulous;* resister; striver; troublemaker; *unfriendly;* vier; wrangler; *x-purposes;* yeller; *zapper;*

**quarrelsome** *(adj.)*: argumentative; belligerent; contentious; disagreeable; dissentious; emulous; factious; gainsaying; huffy; irritable; ill-tempered; jangly; knaggy; liverish; litigious; mean; nasty; ornery; pugnacious; querulous; resistant; ratiocinative; striving; shrewish; tetchy; umbrageous; vinegary; wranglesome; *xenophobic;* yieldless; zoilean;

**quarry** *(n.)*: *abandoned mine;* black coal mine; colliery; dig; excavation; flint mine; gravel pit: hole; incavation; *jaw-hole;* Klondike; lode; mine; *nugget;* open-pit mine; opencut; *operation;* pit; quarry-pit; rock ~; stone mine (-quarry); trench; *unearthing; vug; vein;* wheal; *xenolith; yawn; zanja;*

**quash** *(n.)*: *annihilate;* bash; crush; defeat; extinguish; flatten; grind; hush; immobilize; jam; kill; levigate; mash; nullify; overturn; put down; *press;* quell; repress; squelch; throttle; *undo;* void; wallop; x; yank down; zap;

**quay** *(n.)*: anchorage; berth; *coast;* dock; *estuary;* floating dock; *gangway;* harbor; *inlet;* jetty; key; landing; marina; mooring; *near-shore; oceanside;* pier; *quai* [F.]; *riverside;* slip; tie-down; *unloading area; voe;* wharf; *xebec dock;* yacht landing; *Zee* [G.]; [*see* harbor]

**queasiness** *(n.)*: airsickness; biliousness; butterflies; car sickness; disgust; discomposure; *ejection;* feeling sick; gagging; heaving; illness; *jaculation;* kecking; *lose one's supper;* motion sickness; mal de mer; nausea; *oust;* puking; qualmishness; retching; regurgitation; squeamishness; (sea) sickness; throwing up; uneasiness; vomiting; wooziness; *xuld [arch.]; yuckiness; zich* [arch.];

**queasy** *(adj.)*: airsick; bilious; carsick; disgustful; *ejective;* fulsome; green; heaving; ill; *jaculation; kecking; lightheaded;* mawmish; motion sick; nauseous; *off; pale;* pukish; qualmish; qualmy; retching; squeamish; sick; *turning stomach;* unsettled; vomitive; woozy; *xuld [arch.];* yucky; *zich* [arch.];

**queen** *(adj.)*: autocratrix; *begum* [Ind.]; consort; czarina [Rus.]; dame; empress; female sovereign; *governor;* highness; *imperial highness;* Juno; king's wife; kaiserin [G.]; lady; monarchess; majesty; matriarch; *noblewoman;* overseer; potentate; power; *princess;* queen dowager (-mother); ruler; regent; *rani* [Ind.]; sovereign; sultana; tsarina; *ultimate authority;* vicerine; *wheene* [arch.]; *xabandar; younker; zayim;*

**queenly** *(adj.)*: aristocratic; *blue-blooded;* commanding; dignified; excellent; fabulous; grand; highborn; impressive; Junoesque; kingly [masc.]; lofty; majestic; monarchal; noble; *outstanding;* pompous; queenlike; royal; regal; stately; *tsarish;* uncommon; virtuous; well-born; xtry.; yorkist; *zarish [arch.];*

**queer** *(adj.)*: abnormal; anomalous; bizarre; crazy; curious; different; deviant; erratic; enigmatic; eccentric; funny; freakish; gonzo; goofy; heterotypical; irregular; *jarring;* kooky; ludicrous; malformed; mad; marvelous; mysterious; non-usual; nonstandard; novel; odd; peculiar; quacky; queerish; quirky; ridiculous; strange; twisted; unusual; unconventional; variant; weird; xenomorphic; *yokelish;* zany;

**queerness** *(n.)*: abnormality; bizarreness; craziness; deviation; eccentricity; foible; goofiness; *heterotypical;* irregularity; *jokiness;* kookiness; looniness; malformation; non-usualness; oddness; peculiarity; quirk; *ridiculousness;* strangeness; twist; unusualness; variation; weirdness; *xenomorph;* yaw; zaniness;

**quell** *(v.)*: allay alleviate; appease; becalm; calm; dulcify; diffuse; ease; extinguish; flatten; gratify; hush; *indulge; jade;* keep down; lull; mollify; milden; nullify; overcome; overwhelm; pacify; put down; quench; quash; quiet; reduce; relax; still; soothe; suppress; tranquilize; tame; unruffle; vanquish; whish [Br.]; *well-pacified;* x-out; *yield;* zeroize; [*see* crush; *Ant.* quicken]

**quench** *(v.)*: appease; becalm; choke; calm; douse; extinguish; finish off; gratify; hush; immerse; *jam;* knock out; kill; *lull;* mitigate; nullify; overwhelm; *out;* put out; quell; reduce; snuff (out); slake; stifle; smother; satiate; *tame; turn off;* undo; void; wet; water; *x-out;* yote; zeroize; [*Ant.* quicken]

**quenchable** *(adj.)*: appeasable; beatable; conquerable; defeatable; extinguishable; *finish off; get doused; helpable;* immersible; *jammable;* knocked out; *lulling;* mitigable; *nullify; out; put out;* quellable; *reducible;* subduable; *tamable;* undone; voidable; wettable; *x-out; yote;* zeroizable;

**querulous** *(adj.)*: argumentative; bellyaching; contrary; discontented; divisive; emulous; factious; grumbling; hot-tempered; ill-tempered; jangly; knaggy; liverish; murmuring; negative; opposing; petulant; quarrelsome; repining; short-tempered; touchy; unsatisfied; vinegary; waspish; *xenophobic; yawping;* zoilean;
**querulousness** *(n.)*: antipathy; bitterness; contrariness; disagreement; enmity; factiousness; gainsaying; hostility; impugnation; jangling; *knocking;* loathing; malice; negativism; opposition; polarity; quarrelsomeness; rancor; rivalry; spite; *tetchiness;* unfriendliness; variance; withstanding; *xenophobia; yawping;* zoilism;
**query** *(n.)*: assize; beseeching; cross-examination; demand; enquiry; examination; feeler; grilling; *hunting for;* inquest; inquiry; *juration; know; looking for answers;* making ~; *nosing;* obsecration; official request; probe; questioning; request; seeking; test; *urge; vocalize; words;* XQ.; *yearn; zetetic;*
**query** *(v.)*: ask; beseech; cross-examine; dig; demand of; enquire; *find out;* grill; have questions; *hunt for;* inquire; interrogate; *juration; know; look for answers;* make ~; *nose;* obsecrate; oppugn; probe; question; quiz; request; seek; test; *urge; vocalize;* want; XQ.; *yearn; zetetic;*
**quest** *(n.)*: adventure; boat voyage; conquest; *directive;* expedition; endeavor; foray; *going;* hunt; inquest; journey; knight-errantry; lark; mission; *night voyage;* odyssey; operation; pursuit; qualified mission; *road;* search; trek; undertaking; venture; wayfaring; *xenization; yong* [arch.]; zugunruhe;
**question** *(n.)*: asking; *beseeching;* cross-examination; doubt; enquiry; *find out;* grill; *hunt for;* inquiry; *juration; know;* lead-in ~; mistrust; matter; *nosy;* oppugning; probe; query; quizzing; request; reservation; survey; suspicion; test; *uncertainty; voice;* what? who? x-question; XQ.; yes/no ~; *zetetic;* [*see* subject; doubt]
**question** *(v.)*: ask; beseech; cross-examine; drill; examine; *find out;* grill; *get; hunt for;* inquire; interrogate; *juration; know; look for answers;* make query; *nose;* obsecrate; oppugn; *obtain;* pose; probe; query; quiz; request; raise; seek; test; *urge; voice;* want; XQ.; *yearn; zetetic;*
**questionable** *(adj.)*: arguable; borderline; cannot be expected; contestable; controversial; doubtful; dubious; debatable; ever-doubtful; far-fetched; fishy; *grim;* hardly likely; improbable; implausible; iffy; *just unlikely; known unlikelihood; long shot;* much-doubted; not promising; not likely; one-in-a-million chance; probably not; querulent; *ridiculous;* suspect; totally unlikely; unlikely; unapt; unconvincing; unpromising; very unlikely; way-out; weak; xtry. chance; yet unlikely; *zero chance;* [*Ant.* questionless]
**questioner** *(n.)*: asker; *behest;* cross-examiner; driller; enquirer; examiner; *find out;* griller; *hard questions;* inquirer; interrogator; inquisitor; *juration; know;* lead ~; master ~; *nosy;* obsecrator; poser; prier; querist; quizzer; quizmaster; questionmaster; *requester;* seeker; tester; *urge; voice; work over; XQ; yearn; zetetic;*
**questionless** *(adj.)*: assured; beyond doubt; certain; definite; ever-firm; firm; guaranteed; highly confident; indisputable; incontestable; inarguable; incontrovertible; just sure; keenly sure; *legitimate;* mistake-proof; non-questionable; 100% sure; positive; quite sure; reliable; sure; true; unquestionable; undeniable; unmistaken; verified; without doubt; xtry. sure; *yes;* zero doubt; [*Ant.* questionable]
**queue** *(n.)*: array; arrangement; bank; column; chain; cue; descent; docket; *echelon;* file; *gamut;* how it's ordered; index; *job ~; key;* line (up); matrix; *nexus;* order; procession; *printer ~;* queueing; row; string; sequence; succession; train; tier; *unit order; vector;* waiting line; *x-line; yarn;* Zug [G.];
**quibble** *(v.)*: argue; bicker; cavil; dispute; equivocate; fuss; gainsay; hassle; *inharmonious;* jangle; kick up dust; lock horns [slang]; make a problem; negotiate; object; parley; quarrel; *resist;* squabble; trifle; *unharmonious;* vie; wrangle; *x-purposes;* yell; *zap;*
**quick** *(adj.)*: agile; accelerated; brisk; brief; *celerity;* dexterous; expeditious; fast; *geared up;* hurried; hasty; immediate; jildi [mil.]; keen; lightfooted; lickety-split; momentary; nimble; *on the double;* pronto; prompt; quicksilver; rapid; swift; speedy; turbo; *timely; ultrasonic;* volant; wimble; x-speed; yare; zippy; [*see* alive]

**quicken** *(v.)*: animate; awaken; breathe life into; bring to life; bestir; bolster; brisken; *come back;* disquiet; enliven; energize; ensoul; *fix;* give life; hearten; *heal;* invigorate; innerve; inspirit; insoul; jee; jar; kindle; liven; *life-giving;* move; make alive; *not dead;* overhaul; perk up; *quick;* revive; raise; revitalize; rouse; rejuvenate; resuscitate; stir; *thrive;* uplift; vitalize; vivify; wake; *xfer; yerk; zip; zoetic;* [Ant. quell]

**quickly** *(adv.)*: apace; at once; briefly; cursorily; directly; expeditiously; fast; *go fast;* hastily; immediately; just like that; keenly; lickety-split; momentarily; now; outright; on the spot; posthaste; quick(like); right away; straightway; soon; *tour de suite* [F.]; *undelayed;* very ~; without delay; *x-speed;* yet; yare; zestfully;

**quickness** *(n.)*: agility; acceleration; briskness; briefness; celerity; dexterity; expedition; fastness; *going;* haste; hurriedness; immediacy; jildi [mil.]; keenness; liveliness; mercuriality; nimbleness; overhastiness; promptness; quick-wittedness; rapidity; speed; tall stepping [slang]; *uninhibited;* velocity; *whipping; x-speed; yar;* zip;

**quicksand** *(n.)*: argil; bog; crud; dry ~; *ebbing sand;* fen; goop; gunk; *hog wallow; icky; jarring;* kaolin; *lutarious;* muck; mire; mixture; *nast;* ooze; pothole; quagmire; *red soil;* sludge; (sinking) sand; syrtis; *trap; unstable; vile;* wet sand; *xysma; yellow soil; zonal soil;*

**quiescent** *(adj.)*: at rest; *asleep;* becalmed; calm; dormant; easeful; fallow; *gentle;* hibernating; inactive; idle; inert; *jarless; keeping;* listless; latent; motionless; non-moving; out of action; peaceful; quiet; resting; recumbent; still; sluggish; sleeping; tranquil; unmoving; undisturbed; vacuous; workless; *x'ed;* yet to awaken; *zero activity;*

**quiet** *(adj.)*: allayed; becalmed; calm; dumb; docile; easeful; *furtive;* gentle; hushed; inaudible; inarticulate; idle; *jarless; keeping peaceful;* low-noise; mild; mute; noiseless; non-speaking; nonverbal; over-quiet; peaceful; quiescent; restful; resting; silent; speechless; soundless; soft; tranquil; taciturn; unspeaking; unvoiced; uncommunicative; unheard; voiceless; whist; wordless; *whispering; x'ed out; yareless; zitti* [It.];

**quietly** *(adj.)*: allayed; *becalmed;* calmly; docilely; easefully; *fallow;* gently; hushedly; inaudibly; inarticulately; idly; *jarlessly; keeping peaceful; lowly;* mutely; noiselessly; nonverbally; over- ~; peacefully; quiescently; restfully; silently; softly; tranquilly; taciturnly; *unvoiced;* voicelessly; whistly; *x'ed out; yarelessly; zitti [It.];*

**quietness** *(n.)*: absolute silence; *becalmed;* calmness; dumbness; emptiness; *fallowness;* gentleness; hush; inaudibility; *jarless; keeping peaceful; low;* muteness; noiselessness; over~; peacefulness; quiet; quiescence; restfulness; silence; tranquility; taciturnity; *unvoiced;* voicelessness; wordlessness; *x-ing out; yarelessness;* zero noise;

**quill** *(n.)*: aia- ~; barb; crest; *duck-feather; eiderdown;* feather; goose~; hackle; instrument; *jay- ~;* kahili [Haw.]; *lark- ~;* mail [pl.]; *nuptial plumage; neossoptile; oriole- ~;* plume; pen; *quail feather;* remiges; stylus; spine; tuft; teleoptile; utensil; vane; vibrissa; writing utensil; *xema- ~; yellow finch- ~;* zoofulvin;

**quilt** *(n.)*: Amish ~; bedspread; comforter; duvet; eiderdown; fuzzy blanket; goathair blanket; hyke; Italian ~; jersey blanket; kivver; *kaross* [S. Afr.]; log cabin ~; mohair blanket; *night time;* overblanket; patchwork ~; puff; quarter blanket; *ralli* ~; spread; throw; thermal blanket; *underblanket;* Victorian ~; wagga; *x-pattern; yellow* ~; zigzag ~;

**quintessence** *(n.)*: *attributes;* being; constitution; crux; distillation; essence; embodiment; fundamentality; flower; gist; heart; inbeing; inscape; inherence; jet; kernel; lifeblood; makeup; nature; nub; ontology; pith; *personification;* quiddity; root; substance; stuff; soul; thing; *underneath;* vitals; *warp and woof; xenenthesis;* yetzer [Heb.]; *zoe* [Gr.];

**quip** *(n.)*: answer; bon mot; clever reply; comeback; *defense; eccentricity;* funny remark; gibe; humor; *insult;* jest; jibe; kid; levity; *message;* nifty; one-liner; pun; quibble; retort; repartee; reply; riff; sally; smart remark; tease; *utterance; vexation;* wisecrack; witticism; *xuld [arch.];* yarn; zinger;

**quirk** *(n.)*: aberration; anomaly; bizarreness; craziness; deviation; eccentricity; foible; glitch; habit; happening; irregularity; *joke;* kink; looniness; malformation; non-usualness; oddity; peculiarity; queerness; *ridiculousness;* strangeness; twist; trait; unusualness; variation; weirdness; *xenomorph;* yaw; zaniness;

**quit** *(v.)*: abort; abandon; bail out; break off; cease; concede; cut short; discontinue; desert; desist; depart from; end; forbear; fold; give up; halt; hang up; interrupt; jib; jump off; kill; kibosh; leave (off); *moderate;* nullify; nash; opt out; pause; *quash;* resign; relent; stop; suspend; terminate; undo; *vacate;* walk out; wrap up; x; *yield;* zero;

**quite** *(adj.)*: absolutely; beyond doubt; completely; definitely; entirely; fully; *glaringly;* highly; indubitably; indeed; just; keenly; *literally;* most (certainly); notably; outright; precisely; *quodlibet* [L.]; really; surely; truly; terribly; utterly; very; wholly; 'xactly [slang]; *ywis* [arch.]; 'zactly [dial.];

**quitter** *(n.)*: abandoner; bolter; coward; conceder; deserter; defeatist; dropout; evacuator; forbearer; flat-leaver; goldbrick; *hang up; interrupter;* jilter; *killjoy;* loser; malingerer; negativist; *opt out;* poltroon; piker; pessimist; *quit;* resigner; runaway; shirker; *take off;* undedicated; *vacater;* washout; wimp; *x;* yellow belly; yielder; zero;

**quiver** *(n.)*: arrow case; bag; case; dart bag; *ebira* [Jap.]; fléchette case; *group;* holder; inclosure; jacket; *koleos [Gr.];* leather sleeve; *mure; nine-count; object;* pouch; quarrel-case; receptacle; sheath; *take-along case; utility case;* vessel; *wrap; xyston;* yadzutsu [Jap.]; *zipsleeve;*

**quiver** *(v.)*: agitate; bob; bestir; bicker; convulse; didder; *excite;* flutter; gyrate; hustle; *instability;* jiggle; judder; knock; *lurch; move;* nod; oscillate; palpitate; pitch; quaver; quake; rattle; shake; shudder; tremble; twitter; *upset; unstable;* vibrate; wobble; *xuld [arch.];* yerk; zigzag; [*see* worry]

**quiz** *(n.)*: assessment; *basic assessment;* check; *ditto;* exam; evaluation; *final (exam);* grilling; hearing; interrogation; *jam; kink; load;* make-up ~; midterm; *non-mandatory test;* oral exam; open-book ~; pop ~; questioning; responsions; scrutiny; test; *ungraded ~;* viva; written test; *x-examination; year-end exam; zero;*

**quorum** *(n.)*: amount; bare minimum; *count;* designated minimum; enough; fewest allowed; *general number;* half; ingathering; *just barely enough; kit;* lower limit; minimum; number required; needed amount; *one-quarter;* plenum; percentage; quorate; required number; smallest amount; *total percentage; unit;* voter-minimum; *workable minimum; x;* yet enough; *zum [dial.];*

**quota** *(n.)*: allotment; allowance; amount; apportionment; *budget;* count; designated amount; enforced minimum; firebote; grand total; *handling; ingathering;* job ~; known amount; limit; minimum; number; output allotment; (pro)portion; quantity; ration; size; sum; share; tally; total; *unitization;* volume; whole; *xfer;* yieldance; zoning;

**quotable** *(adj.)*: articulable; axiomatic; brilliant; catchy; declarable; expressible; *fantastic;* gnomic; great; *hold forth; incredible; jolly good;* keen; *lofty;* memorable; noteworthy; *outstanding;* proverbial; quoteworthy; repeatable; speakable; tellable; utterable; very good; well-worded; *xtry,; you-beaut* [Aus.]; *zero in;*

**quotation** *(n.)*: adducement; adage; byword; book citation; citation; dictum; excerpt; formulary; gobbet; *hackneyed saying;* instance; *judgment; koine;* line; maxim; narration; oral recitation; passage; pericope; quote; recitation; saying; selection; thought; tag; universal truth; verbiage; words; *xref; yed; zeteticism;*

**quote** *(v. cite)*: adduce; allude; *bespeak;* cite; declare; excerpt; forecite; give a quotation; *hold forth;* invoke; instance; *jaw; key in; let out;* mention; name; narrate; *over~;* parrot; *paraphrase;* quoth; recite; rehearse; retell; reference; repeat; say; tell; utter; *underquote; vouch* [arch.]; words; *xref;* yarn; yed; *zero in;*

# R

**rabbi** *(n.)*: abecedarian; bible-teacher; chief ~; decalogist; educator; fugleman; guide; herald; instructor; Jewish ~; *knowledge;* leader; master; mashgiah; *noiser;* orator; proclaimer; *quoter;* rebbe; rabbin; synagogue leader; teacher; talmudist; *utterer;* voicer; wise man; xenagogue; *yeller [derog.];* zaddik;

**rabbit** *(n.)*: angora ~; *animal;* bunny (~); brush ~; cottontail; *dwarf* ~; *elfin* ~; *Flemish lop; game;* hare; *Indian hare;* jack~; kit; lagomorph; lapin; leveret; *mini rex; Netherlands dwarf* ~; omilteme cottontail; pygmy ~; *quadruped;* robust cottontail; snowshoe hare; tri-colored Dutch ~; *untamed* ~; varying hare; wood ~; *warren; x-breed; yarkland hare; zoic;*

**rabble** *(n.)*: amassment; bunch; clamjamfry; canaille; dregs; *everybody;* flock; gang; horde; ingathering; jam [slang]; kit [coll.]; lower classes; mass; mob; multitude; number; *outcasts;* party; pack; *quantity;* riffraff; rout; scum; throng; *unit;* vermin; wisp; *xiaoren; yobs; zhlubs;*

**race** *(n. bloodline)*: ancestry; bloodline; country; clan; descent; derivation; ethnicity; extraction; family; *group;* genetics; heredity; *ilk; inherited; jus soli [L.];* kindred; lineage; *mores;* nation(ality); origin; people; pedigree; parentage; *quarter;* rod; *roots; relations;* stock; strain; tribe; *ubiety; variety; vein; white race; x-link; yoni [Skr.]; zoe;*

**race** *(n. competition)*: *affair; auto race;* battle; *boat-* ~; competition; contest; dash; derby; endurance ~; *event;* footrace; game; *Grand Prix;* hundred-yard dash; horse~; Indianapolis 500; *Isthmian* ~; *joust;* kermesse [Br.]; *lap; lampadedromy* [Gr.]; marathon; *night-* ~; *obstacle* ~; *Olympic* ~; pursuit; quest; run; relay; regatta; sprint; *struggle;* steeplechase; tournament; undertaking; venture; vying; *war;* xc.; *yacht* ~; *zip;*

**race** *(v.)*: accelerate; bolt; *battle;* charge; contend; compete; dash; dart; elan; flash; gallop; hasten; hurry; *interlope;* jog; *kite;* lope; move; *nimble; outrun; proceed;* quicken; run; sprint; tear; *uprush;* vie; whiz; *xuld [arch.];* yern; zip;

**racial** *(adj.)*: ancestral; blood; clannish; derivational; ethnic; family; genetic; hereditary; *inherited;* Japhetic; *Jewish;* kin-related; lineal; *mankind;* national; original; phyletic; *quarter;* race-related; stock-related; tribal; *unilineal; vein; white race; x-linked; yellow race; zygogenetic;*

**racism** *(n.)*: anti-Semitism; apartheid [S. Afr.]; bias; bigotry; chauvinism; discrimination; ethnocentrism; favoritism; *gall; hatred;* intolerance; jaundice; klanism; leaning; *minority-hating;* narrow-mindedness; *Nazism;* onesidedness; prejudice; *quick to judge;* racialism; supremism; segregationalism; *terror;* unfairness; ultranationalism; *vexation; White Supremism;* xenophobia; *yahooism; zealotry;*

**racist** *(adj.)*: anti-foreigner; *anti-Semitic;* biased; bigoted; chauvinistic; discriminatory; ethnocentric; fanatic; *galled; hater;* intolerant; jaundiced; *klansman;* lineage-hating; minority-hating; narrow-minded; *opinionated;* prejudiced; *quick-to-judge;* racialist; supremist; *terrorizing;* unfair; *vexing; White Supremist;* xenophobic; *yahooist; zealot;*

**racketeer** *(n.)*: abuser; beguiler; carpetbagger; defrauder; ensnarer; fraud; fake; gold-digger; hornswoggler; jape; knave; lawbreaker; money-grabber; nobbler; opportunist; profiteer; questuary; rooker; swindler; trickster; usurer; verneuker; weasel; *xgressor; yentzer* [Heb.]; *zinger;*

**radiance** *(n. brilliance)*: aura; brilliance; candescence; dazzle; effulgence; fulgency; glow; glory; halo; irradiance; *jumping light; keenness;* light; luminosity; *magic;* nitency; *overlight; phosphorescence;* radiation; radiancy; resplendence; refulgence; shine(-ing); splendor; twinkling; *ultraviolet light;* vividness; white light; *xenon light;* yellow light; *zodiacal light;*

**radiance** *(n. joyfulness)*: afterglow; brightness; cheer(fulness); delight; exhilaration; felicity; glow; happiness; intoxication; joy; *keenness;* lightheartedness; merriment; *niceness;* overjoy; pleasure; *queme;* rejoicing; sunniness; thrill; *uplifted;* vivacity; warmth; *xanadu; yeah!;* zestfulness;

**radiant** *(adj.)*: aglow; bright; beaming; cheerful; delighted; dazzling; exhilarated; effulgent; felicitous; fulgent; glowing; happy; illuminated; joyful; keen; lighthearted; luminous; merry; magnificent; nitid; overjoyed; pleased; *queme;* rejoicing; refulgent; sunny; shining; thrilled; transplendent; uplifted; vivacious; warm; *xtry.; yet undimmed;* zestful;

**radiate** *(v.)*: *aura;* beam; coruscate; diffuse; discharge; effuse; emanate; fan out; flare; glow; give off; *hurl;* impart; issue; incandesce; irradiate; *jump out; knock out;* lase; luster; make a discharge; *naid;* output; produce; phosphoresce; *quake;* release; shed; shine; twinkle; *throw;* unleash; *vection; waft; x-radiate;* yield; zap;

**radiation** *(n.)*: aura; atomic ~; beam; contamination; dispersion; *dose;* emission; emanation; energy; fallout; fluence; glow; heat; ir~; iridescence; isodose; *jeopardy; kilowatts;* light; mesons; *mutagen;* nuclear ~; orthovoltage; *output;* plutonium; quaking; rays; radioactivity; spreading; *stream; treatment; uranium;* V-particles; visible ~; waves; x-ray; x- ~; *yield;* zapping;

**radical** *(adj.)*: ardent; anarchist; besotted; crazed; drastic; extreme; extremist; fundamental; far-reaching; fanatical; great; *hearty;* intense; Jacobin; *keyed up;* large; leftist; major; militant; *notable;* overenthusiastic; passionate; *quantitative;* revolutionary; sweeping; *tremendous;* ultraistic; vehement; way-out; wild-eyed; *xenocentric;* yare; zealotic; [*Ant.* regular]

**radical** *(n.)*: activist; believer; campaigner; devotee; extremist; fanatic; *glory-seeker; huk* [Philippines]; insurrectionist; Jacobin; *kicker;* leftist; militant; nonconformist; objector; progressivist; quixote; revolutionary; *supporter; terrorist;* ultraist; votary; *Whig; xenocentrist;* Young Turk; zealot;

**radio** *(n.)*: air(waves); AM; broadcast; broadband; boombox; car ~; *channel; dial; electronics;* frequency; FM; *ground dipole;* ham ~; hi-fi receiver; *instrument;* J-Pole; Ku band; *loop aerial; monoliform; newscast; object;* portable ~; *quad antenna;* radiotelegraph; shortwave; transistor ~; transmission; transmitter; transponder; transceiver; *talk* ~; unit; UHF; vector; VHF; wireless; *x-mission; yagi; zero in;*

**raft** *(n.)*: *ark;* balsa; craft; dinghy; *eight-oar;* float; galiot; Halkett boat; inflatable ~; jangada; kelek; life ~; log- ~; moki; *neddy; outrigger;* pontoon float; *quadruple scull;* (rubber) ~; *scull; transportation; udema;* vessel; wooden ~; *xebec; youyou* [F.]; *zabra;*

**rafter** *(n.)*: angle ~; beam; crossbeam; deal; *elm beam;* four by four; girder; hardboard; hip ~; I-beam; joist; jack ~; king post; lumber; *maple beam; nemoral;* one-by-four; plate girder; queen post; rib; roof timber; strut; support beam; timber; two-by-four; underlayment; *veneer;* wood; *xylon; yew; zingara;*

**rag** *(n.)*: *article;* bath cloth; clout; cloth; chamois; drying ~; *engine oil* ~; flitter; *greasy* ~; hand towel; *item;* jaconet cloth; kersey cloth; linen cloth; mop; nylon cloth; old ~; painting ~; quentin cloth; rubbing cloth; shammy; schmatte; tatter; used ~; *vile;* wipe; *xfer; yucky old* ~; *zibeline;*

**rage** *(n.)*: anger; boil; choler; displeasure; enragement; fury; gall; hotness; infuriation; jealous ~; *kindling;* lividness; madness; *nettling;* outrage; perturbation; quick-temper; rampage; *storm;* temper; uproar; venting; wrath; *xerothermia; yelling; zealousy* [arch.]; [*see* trend; *Ant.* relaxedness]

**rage** *(v.)*: aggravate; break out; charge; drive; erupt; fume; go wild; *heat;* infuriate; *jump;* kindle; lose control; madden; *nettle;* outrage; prevail; *quick-tempered;* rave; rip; run wild; rampage; ravage; storm; tear; thunder; *upset;* vent; *violence;* wreak; *xerothermic; yell; zoom;* [*Ant.* relax]

**ragged** *(adj.)*: *awful;* bedraggled; choppy; coarse; disheveled; dog-eared; erratic; frayed; grubby; haggard; incomposed; jagged; keg-meg; *lousy;* messy; non-organized old; *pathetic;* quaggy; raggedy; rough-shod; shabby; slovenly; tattered; torn; unkempt; uneven; used; *vile;* worn; *x'ed;* yucky; zigzag;

**raid** *(n.)*: assault; bust; charge; drive; escalade; foray; *get;* hit; incursion; *jump; knock out;* lashing out; marauding; night ~; onrush; pillaging; *quick* ~; rush; reave; strike; surprise attack; sortie; sweep; *take; unrest;* veney; *violence;* war(fare); *x-fire; yed; zap;*

**raid** *(v.)*: attack; break into; *capture;* depredate; *escalade;* foray; gut; hit; harry; invade; *jump; knock; loot;* maneuver; *night* ~; overrun; *pillage; quab;* ransack; storm; sortie; sack; take; *unlade;* violate; warray; *xfer; yank; zap;*

**raider** *(n.)*: assaulter; attacker; *beater;* commando; defeater; *expugner;* freebooter; *grabber;* harrier; invader; *jabber; kemp;* looter; marauder; *Nazi storm trooper;* overcomer; pillager; plunderer; quester; robber; rapparee; ransacker; striker; storm trooper; *uninvited;* vanquisher; *warrior; xfer; yob;* zealot;

**rail** *(n.)*: area fence; barrier; banister; balustrade; *check~;* divider; enclosure; fence; guide- ~; guard~; hand~; in~; *jail;* kraal; line; mere-fence; *narrow fence;* obstruction; palisade; quarter-railing; railing; stair ~; sunk fence; taff~; toe~; utility fence; *Virginia fence; wall;* x-fence; yard fence; zigzag fence;

**rail** *(v.)*: affront; bemock; chide; deride; *execrate;* fleer; gibe; hiss; insult; jibe; knock; laugh at; mock; *name-calling;* objurgate; poke fun; quib; ridicule; scoff; taunt; utter against; vex; wipe; *xuld [arch.];* yock; *zap;*

**railer** *(n.)*: abuser; belittler; chider; denouncer; execrator; faulter; giber; humiliator; insulter; jeerer; kidder; laugher; mocker; niggler; offender; *pillory;* quipper; ridiculer; ribber; scoffer; teaser; *utterer;* vexer; *wiper; xuld [arch.];* yuker; *zapper;*

**railing** *(n.)*: aluminum handrail; banister; bar; balustrade; cockle-stair ~; *double ~;* extended balustrade; fence; grip; guide rail; guardrail; handrail; inrail; *Jersey barrier;* kempwood ~; *landing rail;* metal handrail; newel ~; outer ~; pulpit; quarter-railing; rail; steel ~; top-rail; uru ~; vert ~; wooden ~; *x-bar;* yew ~; zingana ~;

**railroad** *(n.)*: Alco®; boxcar; choo-choo (train); car; caboose; dinky; dining car; el; engine; freight train; gondola; handcar; iron horse; interurban; *J-line; K-line;* locomotive; line; monorail; *Northern Pacific;* observation car; passenger train; *queue;* railway; steam engine; train; tram road; *underground;* van; wagon-lit; *X'Trapolis; yard;* zenana;

   **Railroad Employees**: brakeman; conductor; dispatcher; engineer; fireman; gandy dancer; locomotive superintendent; plateman; railroad engineer; signalman; trackman; yardmaster;

**raiment** *(n.)*: apparel; attire; bedizenment; clothing; dress; daywear; duds; ensemble; finery; fashion; garb; garments; getup; habiliments; investiture; *jumper;* knitwear; *leatherwear; leisurewear; loungewear;* mufti; *menswear; national dress;* outfit; outerwear; playwear; *quaintry* [arch.]; rags; *regalia;* suit; togs; threads; *undergarments; uniform;* vesture; vestment; wardrobe; *womenswear; XL; yelek [Turk.]; zari;*

**rain** *(n.)*: *acid ~;* burst; *bad weather;* cloudburst; downpour; drizzle; *emanation;* fall; gullywasher; heavy ~; *hyetal;* inundation; *Jupiter Pluvius; knee-deep;* light (-latter) ~; mizzle; nucleation; night ~; outburst; precipitation; pour(ing rain); *quirlewind [arch.];* rains; rainfall; rainstorm; shower; serein; smir; spate; sleet; torrent; thundershower; *umbrella weather;* virga; wet weather; water; *xude; yellow ~; zonal rain;*

**rain** *(v.)*: *acid ~;* burst; come down; downpour; drizzle; *emanate;* fall; *gullywasher; hyetal;* inundate; *Jupiter Pluvius; knee-deep;* lightly ~; misle; mizzle; nucleate; *outburst;* precipitate; pour; *quirlewind [arch.];* rain down; shower; sprinkle; sleet; teem; *umbrella; virga;* weep [poet.]; wet; *xude;* yield ~; *zonal rain;*

**rainbow** *(n.)*: arch; bow; continuum; *dihexahedral prism; el;* fogbow; gamut; *glory;* hues; iris; ice bow; *jewel of the sky; keen;* lunar ~; marine ~; *nimbus; optical phenomenon;* prism; *quadrantal;* refraction; sunbow; spectrum; seadog; *transplendent; ultra-bright;* variegation; white ~; x-ray spectrum; *yanolite;* zonate;

**rainstorm** *(n.)*: *acid rain;* burst of rain; cloudburst; downpour; *electrical storm;* flaw; flashflood; gullywasher; heavy rain; *hurricane;* inundation; *Jupiter Pluvius; knot floater;* line squall; latter rain; *monsoon;* nucleation; outburst; pourdown; *quirlewind* [arch.]; rains(quall); storm; squall; thunderstorm; *umbrella weather;* virga; weather; *xude; yellow rain; zonal rain;* [*see* storm]

**rainy** *(adj.)*: abounding with rain; *bad weather;* cloudburst; drizzly; damp; *endrenched;* flawy; *gullywasher; heavy rain;* inclement; *Jupiter Pluvius; knee-deep; light rain;* moist; *nucleating;* over-rainy; pluvious; pouring; *quakeful;* raining; *rough;* soppy; sunless; showery; stormy; *torrential; umbrella weather; virga;* wet; *xude; yellow rain; zonal rain;* [*Ant.* rainless]

**raise** *(v.)*: advance; augment; amass; *arise;* boost; bring up; build; climb; construct; distend; develop; elevate; *further;* go up; hoist; heighten; hike; increase; jack up; kick upstairs; lift; move up; *new growth; overgrow;* put up; promote; pry; *quicken;* rise; rear; set higher; *soar;* take a turn up; uplift; upshoot; verge upward; wax higher; *XL; yain* [arch.]; *zoom up;* [*Ant.* reduce]
**rally** *(n.)*: assembly; banding together; caucus; convention; demonstration; event; forgathering; get-together; gathering; *horde;* ingathering; jamboree; kit [coll.]; *lot;* meeting; *number; opportunity;* party; pep ~; *quorum;* regathering; session; tourney; *unit; vestry;* wardmote; *x.; yain* [arch.]; *zayat [Burm.];*
**rally** *(v.)*: amass; bring together; congregate; call to arms; draw together; *encounter;* flock; gather; have a meeting; ingather; join together; *kindle;* link up; meet; marshal; muster; *negotiate; overcrowd; party; quorum;* reconvene; reunite; swarm; turn out; unite; *visit; work together; x.;* yoke; *zone;* [*see* recover]
**ram** *(n.)*: *animal;* bighorn; bellwether; *creature;* dall sheep; ewe [fem.]; fatling; gigot; hamel; Indian ~; jumbuck; karakul; lamb; mountain sheep; New Zealand ~; *ovine; Paschal ~; quadruped;* Rocky Mountain bighorn; sheep; tup; urial; *varmint;* wether; *x-breed;* yeo [Br.]; *zoic;*
**ram** *(v.)*: assault; bear down on; butt; *break;* cram; drive; *elbow;* force; gorge; heave; impel; jam; knock; *lunge; make; nudge; overthrow;* propel; quash; run; rocket; shove; stuff; thrust; *upcast; violence;* wedge; whack; *xuld [arch.];* york; *zip;*
**ramble** *(v.)*: *articulate;* babble; blather; chatter; double-talk; excurse; *fudge;* gab; gibber; gabble; haver; *idioglossa;* jabber; *kelter; lard;* maunder; natter; *outlandish;* prattle; prate; patter; *quatsch;* rant; rattle; slaver; twaddle; talk; utter; vocalize; witter; *xenoglossy;* yabber; yabble; *zeug [G.];* [*see* walk]
**rambunctious** *(adj.)*: agitated; boisterous; crazy; disorderly; disruptive; energetic; frolicking; *grating;* high-spirited; intemperate; jackanapes; *kicking;* loud; lively; misbehaved; noisy; overexcited; *pretty bad; querulous;* raucous; rumbustious; rowdy; strident; troublemaking; unruly; uproarious; vexatious; wild; *x-grained;* yeasty; zestful;
**ramification** *(n.)*: aftereffects; byproduct; consequence; complication; difficulty; effect; fruit; *get;* harvest; impact; *just desserts; known outcome;* lattermath; *matter; necessarily;* outcome; outgrowth; product; quantum effect; result; repercussion; significance; sequent; termination; upshot; *vamp;* work; wake; *xenagogy;* yield; *zeug [G.];*
**ramp** *(n.)*: acclivity; boat ~; climb; declivity; entry ~; exit ~; *fall;* grade; hill; incline; *jag; kink;* leaning board; moveable stairs; *natural slope; obliqueness;* pitched entryway; *quantity of slope;* rise; slope; shipway; *tilt;* upslope; *verge; way up; xy-gradient; yaw; zag;*
**rampant** *(adj.)*: all-pervading; broad; common; diffuse; endemic; epidemic; far-reaching; greatly spread; huge; immoderate; *joint; known world;* large-scale; multiplied; non-localized; out-of-control; pandemic; prevalent; quaquaversal; rife; runaway; *serious; threatening;* uncontrolled; ubiquitous; very ~; wild; widespread; *x-world; yet uncontrolled; zonic;* [*Ant.* restricted]
**ranch** *(n.)*: acreage; barnyard; cowboy ~; cattle ~; dude ~; *estancia* [Sp.]; farmstead; *grange;* homestead; horse farm; *institution; joclet;* keep; land; manor; *non-urban; old ~ house;* plantation; pony ~; *quinta;* rancho; stock farm; tract; *usable ~ land; villa;* working ~; western ~; *Xalapa;* yard; *zemledelie [Rus.];*
**rancher** *(n.)*: angus ~; buckeroo; cattleman; cowboy; cow-keeper; cattle ~; driver; drover [Aus.]; equestrian; *farmhand;* gaucho; herdsman; herder; *individual; Jehu;* knight-in-the-saddle; llanero [Sp.]; *muleteer;* neatherd; *outrider;* puncher; *quick draw;* ranch hand; rustler; stockman; *"Tex"; unsattled; vaquero* [Mex.]; wrangler; *x-breeder;* yeehaw; *Zorro;*
**rancid** *(adj.)*: awful; bad-smelling; corrupt; displeasing; effluvious; frowy; fetid; graveolent; *horrible;* ill-smelling; *jarring; ketty;* loathsome; malodorous; nauseating; olid; offensive; putrid; *queasy;* rank; stomach-turning; *terrible;* unpleasant; vile; whiffy; wicked; *x-bad;* yucky; zorillo-like; [*Ant.* redolent]

**random** *(adj.)*: arbitrary; by chance; chance; desultory; disorderly; draw of the hat; erratic; fortuitous; groundless; *guess;* habnab; *happen;* indiscriminate; *jumbled;* keg-meg; left to chance; motiveless; nonsystematic; orderless; purposeless; purely arbitrary; *quirky;* reasonless; senseless; subjective; *totally ~;* unsystematic; unmethodical; uncalculated; very arbitrary; wanton; *whim; x; yet indiscriminate;* zero reason;

**range** *(n.)*: ambit; area; array; breadth; compass; coverage; degree; diapason; expanse; extent; field; gamut; *height;* immediate ~; jurisdiction; *kray* [Rus.]; limit; magnitude; niche; outer limits; place; quantity; reach; scope; sphere; spectrum; territory; ubiety; vastness; ward; *x-section; yard;* zone;

**rank** *(adj.)*: awful; bad-smelling; corrupt; displeasing; effluvious; fetid; graveolent; horrible-smelling; icky; jarring; *ketty;* loathsome; malodorous; nauseating; odoriferous; putrid; *queasy;* rancid; smelly; *terrible;* unpleasant; vile; wicked; *x-bad;* yucky; zorillo-like; [*see* disgusting; *Ant.* redolent]

**rank** *(n.)*: arrangement; bracket; *brass;* class; commission; degree; echelon; elevation; estate; *first rate;* grade; height; *insignia; judgment; kabane* [Jap.]; *kind;* level; military ~; mark; *notch;* order; office; position; place; quality; ranking; status; sequence; station; title; tier; *uniform;* varve; *way; x-class;* y-level; *zone;*

**Military ranks**: admiral; airman; brigadier general; captain; corporal; colonel; commodore; commander; divisional general; ensign; field marshal; general; hauptmann [G.]; infantry leader; junior officer; *kanarang* [Pers.]; lance corporal (-sergeant); lieutenant; major; midshipman; *non-commissioned officer;* one-star general; petty officer; private; quartermaster; *rittmeister* [G.]; seaman; sergeant; two-star general; *unteroffizier* [G.]; vice admiral; warrant officer; yeoman;

**rank** *(v.)*: arrange; *bestow;* classify; categorize; distribute; evaluate; file; grade; *have;* index; judge; *kit;* list; methodize; *make; notch;* order; place; *qualify;* rate; sort; *tabulate;* unitize; valuate; weigh in; *xfer; yield;* zonate;

**ransack** *(v.)*: *assault;* boot; comb; carry off; despoil; excoriate; freeboot; forage; gut; harrow; *incursion; junk;* knock over; loot; lay waste; maraud; nobble; *overexploit;* pillage; plunder; *quash;* raid; rifle; ravage; spoil; sack; trash; take; *unlade;* violate; *whomp; xfer; yank; zap;*

**ransom** *(n.)*: amount; blackmail money; compensation; deliverance; exchange; *for; gold;* high price; *imbursement; jewels; kickback;* liberation money; money; *negotiation; outlay;* price; payment; payoff; quarterage; redemption-price; reward; release; sum; settlement; trover; *unmarked bills; virement;* wealth; *xfer; yielding;* zwap [dial.];

**ransom** *(v.)*: acquire; buy back; *change;* deliver; *deal;* exchange; emancipate; free; give ~; *hand over; invest; jockey; key trade;* liberate; *make deal; negotiation; obtain;* purchase; pardon; *quoff;* redeem; rescue; swap; trade; unshackle; *vest;* win back; *xfer; yield;* zwap [dial];

**rant** *(v.)*: *abuse;* bluster; complain; dote; declaim; explode; fume; growl; harangue; inveigh; jump down one's throat; *knock;* lambaste; mistreat; *nasty;* outburst; perorate; *quetch;* rage; shout; thunder; *ululate;* vent; vituperate; *wallop; xuld [arch.];* yell; *zing;*

**rape** *(n.)*: attack; abuse; *befoulment; crime;* defilement; disgrace; despoilment; exploitation; forcing; gang-rape; humiliation; *indignity;* incest; *jadishness; kinkiness; lust-crime;* molestation; *nefariousness; overtaking;* plundering; *quad;* ravishment; shame; statutory ~; tarnishing; *transgression; use;* violation; *wickedness; x-rated contact; yetzer hara* [Heb.]; zoonic behavior;

**rape** *(v.)*: attack; *abuse; befoul;* compromise; defile; disgrace; deflower; despoil; exploit; force; gang ~; humble; *infringe; jump; kinky;* lay with; molest; *nefarious;* overpower; plunder; *quad;* ravish; shame; take by force; *tarnish; use;* violate; wrench purity from; *x-rated contact; yank down; zing;*

**rapport** *(n.)*: affinity; bond; camaraderie; *delight;* empathy; fellowship; good relationship; harmony; identification; *joining;* kinship; link; mutuality; *nodding;* oneness; propinquity; *queme;* relationship; solidarity; togetherness; understanding; *voluntariness;* welcomeness; *xenia; yung* [Chin.]; *zealous agreement;* [*Ant.* rancor]

**rapture** *(n.)*: animation; bliss; cheerfulness; delight; elation; euphoria; felicity; glee; heaven; intoxication; jubilation; *keenness;* levity; merriment; *niceness;* overwhelming joy; pleasure; *queme;* ravishment; seventh heaven; transport; *uplifted; vivacity;* winsomeness; *xanadu; yeah!;* zestfulness; [*Ant.* ruefulness]

**Rapture** *(n.)*: advent; blessed hope; catching up; day of His coming; exit; ecstasy; flight; going up; home-going; *imminent return;* Jesus' coming in the clouds; *the King's coming; the* Lord's return; meeting in the air; *nabbing; the* out-gathering (of the saints); Parousia; *quick;* Return of Christ; Second Coming; snatching up; transport; *the* trumpet; *taking up;* uptaking; *verge upwards; whisking away; xfer; yank;* zipping up; zooming;

**rare** *(adj.)*: atypical; bare; costly; dear; exiguous; exceptional; few(-and-far-between); gant; hard to find; infrequent; introuvable; jimp; keenly ~; limited; little-found; meager; non-usual; obscure; precious; *queer;* recherché; scarce; sparse; scant(y); truly ~; uncommon; unusual; valuable; *wondrous; xtry.; you-beaut [Aus.];* zeep; [*Ant.* rich]

**rarity** *(n.)*: atypical item; barely-seen item; curiosity; dear thing; exiguity; find; gem; hard to find item; infrequently found thing; *jimp;* keenly sought-after item; little-found item; *marvel;* non-usual item; oddity; precious thing; *queer;* rare bird; scarcity; singularity; tenuity; uncommon thing; very rare item; *wonder; xtry.* piece; *you-beaut [Aus.]; zeep;*

**rascal** *(n.)*: agitator; blackguard; cad; devil; evildoer; firebrand; good-for-nothing; heel; *injurer;* jackanapes; knave; lowlife; menace; miscreant; ne'er-do-well; *outlaw;* polecat; questrel; rogue; rabble-rouser; rapscallion; scalawag; scoundrel; troublemaker; *ungodly person;* varlet; wretch; wrongdoer; *xiaoren;* yahoo; zhlub;

**rash** *(adj.)*: adventurous; brash; careless; determined; *eruptive;* foolhardy; *giddy;* hasty; impetuous; *jaunty;* knee-jerk; *ludicrous;* madcap; not-thought-out; over-hasty; precipitous; quick; reckless; reactive; sudden; thoughtless; temerarious; unconsidered; veloce; venturesome; wild; *x-ing; yare;* zealous; [*Ant.* rational]

**rash** *(n.)*: *ailment;* breaking out; chapping; dermal ~; erubescence; *fever; German measles;* hives; irritation; *jaundice; kibed;* lesion; *measles;* nirles; *ordeal;* pinkness; *quirk;* redness; reaction; skin ~; soreness; *tenderness;* uredo; *very sore; windsore;* xeroderma; *yarrish;* zits;

**rate** *(n.)*: amount; *bank* ~; current ~; degree; daily ~; *exchange* ~; flow; fastness; flux; frequency; *grade;* hourly ~; influx; incidence; *jump; key* ~; level; monthly ~; natural ~; occurrence; pace; percentage; quickness; rifeness; *repeating;* speed; tempo; transfer ~; *uptempo;* velocity; weekly ~; xfer ~; yield; yearly ~; YER; *zone;*

**rate** *(v.)*: arrange; assign; *bestow;* class(ify); categorize; catalog; distribute; evaluate; file; grade; *have;* index; *judge; kit;* list; methodize; *make; notch;* organize; order; pigeonhole; peg; place; *qualify;* rank; sort; systemize; tabulate; unitize; valuate; weigh; *xfer;* yield; *zonate;*

**ratify** *(v.)*: approve; accept; back; certify; decree; endorse; enact; formally approve; fall in; grant; homologate; indorse; *join in;* keep; legalize; make into law; *nod;* okay; obsignate; pass; *qualify;* recognize; rubber stamp; sanction; sign; *take; unanimously approve;* vote into law; validate; warrant; *x on the dotted line;* yes; *zealously approve;* [*Ant.* reject]

**rational** *(adj.)*: acceptable; balanced; commonsense; coherent; discursive; down-to-earth; evenhanded; expedient; fit; good; heady; intelligent; judicious; knowledgeable; logical; level-headed; lucid; matter-of-fact; no-nonsense; normal; *okay;* prudent; practical; quite sensible; reasonable; realistic; sensible; sound; sane; tenable; understandable; viable; valid; wise; *xenagogic; yepe; zero doubt;* [*Ant.* rash]

**rationalize** *(v.)*: authenticate; absolve; *back;* clear up; defend; excuse; figure out; give reasons; harmonize; insist it's okay; justify; *keep doing;* legitimize; make excuse for; *maintain;* naturalize; okay; palliate; *qualify;* reason out; substantiate; think through; uphold; validate; vindicate; warrant; *xenagogy;* yes; *zealously defend;*

**rattle** *(v.)*: agitate; berattle; bang; clatter; disquiet; *excite;* flutter; *growse [arch.];* hustle; *insecure;* jangle; knock about; *lurch; move; nudge; oscillate; play;* quake; rumble; shake; trouble; upset; vibrate; vex; vibrate; waggle; *xuld [arch.];* yerk; zonk;

**ravage** *(v.)*: assault; break; *carry off;* devastate; despoil; excoriate; freeboot; gut; harrow; *invade; junk; knock off [slang];* loot; lay waste; maraud; *nobble; overexploit;* pillage; plunder; *quash;* ruin; ransack; spoil; sack; *take; unlade;* violate; wreck; *xfer; yank; zap;* [*Ant.* rebuild]

**raven** *(n.)*: acalot; buceros; *bird;* crow; daw; Eurasian blackbird; forest ~; *fowl;* gracula; hooded ~; Indian ~; jackdaw; koo; little ~; magpie; night ~; ousel; piapiac; *quiscalus quiscula* [L.]; rook; *scavenger;* turdis; umber; *vulture;* white-necked bald ~; white-necked raven; xanthocephalus; yellow-bearded blackbird; zoic;

**ravenous** *(adj.)*: all-devouring; belly-pinched; craving; devouring; enhungered; famished; greedy; hungry; insatiable; jejune; *keenness;* lupine; *malnourished; needy;* overgreedy; panged; quenchless; rapacious; ravening; starving; *thirsty;* unappeasable; voracious; weak; wolfish; *xenorexic;* yearning; *zapped;* [*Ant.* replete]

**ravine** *(n.)*: abyss; arroyo; break; barranca; canyon; clough; defile; *excavation;* flood meadow; gorge; gulch; hollow; intervale; *Jackson Hole;* krantz; lowlands; *meadow;* nadir; opening; *pit; quarry;* rift; slade; *Tremola;* underlands; valley; water gap; *xyrisic;* yunga; *zanja;*

**ravish** *(v.)*: appreciate; *bliss; content;* delight in; enrapture; frolic in; gratify; have delight in; intoxicate oneself in; joy in; *kiss; like; merry; niceness;* overcome; please; *queme;* relish; rapture; satisfy; take pleasure in; *uplift; voluptuous;* wallow; *xtry.; yield; zestful;*

**ray** *(n.)*: *aura;* beam; beacon; *candescence;* diffusion; emission; emanation; flash; flow; flood; gleam; glimmer; *heat;* irradiation; *jet; kilowatt;* leam [Br.]; light; *moonbeam; nimbus; optic light;* patch; quiver; radiation; stream; shaft; sunbeam; twinkle; *ultraviolet ~; violet ~;* wave; x- ~; *yield;* zap;

**razor** *(n.)*: *apparatus;* blade; cutter; disposable ~; electric ~; edge; four-blade ~; Gilette®; hand ~; *instrument; jack knife;* kerfer; *loppers; metzenbaum; nipper;* one-blade ~; parer; quadruple-blade ~; razoredge; shaver; twin-blade ~; *unbearded; vell;* whetted edge; *xyrao* [Gr.]; *yakiba* [Jap.]; *zip;*

**reach** *(v.)*: arrive at; attain; border; become; come to; *do;* extend to; find; *far-reaching;* get to; gain; hit; *increase;* join to; *kep; land;* make; *nab;* overstretch; procure; *quicken to;* run into; stretch; touch; *unfold; victory;* win; *xfer; yain [arch.]; zoom to;*

**react** *(v.)*: answer; act; back answer; counter(act); cope; do; deal with; *express; feedback;* give response; handle; *impulse; judge; key; look;* meet; *notion; over~; perform; quicken;* respond; reciprocate; speak; take action; *utter; voice;* work; *x; yes; zero in;*

**reaction** *(n.)*: action; answer; behavior; backlash; counter~; contranitency; *double-take;* effect; feedback; feeling; *general reply;* handling; hit; impact; *judgment;* kickback; *look;* manner of behavior; *notion;* opinion; port; *quick-response;* response; riposte; sentiment; *spirit;* take; undercurrent; *verdict;* way of looking at it; *xtry. ~; yield; zealous reply;*

**read** *(v.)*: absorb; behold; comprehend; digest; examine; fix eyes on; fathom; gaze at; *hone in on;* interpret; *judge; know;* look at; make out; note; observe; peruse; pore over; *quick look;* recite; skim; study; see; scan; take in; understand; view; wade; *xfer; yeme; zero in;*

**readable** *(adj.)*: able to read; *be clear;* clear; comprehensible; discernable; easy-to-read; fair; fine; good enough; *handle it;* intelligible; *just plain;* knowable; legible; lucid; *make out;* neat; *obvious;* perceptible; *quality;* recognizable; straightforward; *transparent;* understandable; very clear; *watchable; x-parent; yare; zero confusion;*

**readiness** *(n.)*: alacrity; buxomness; capability; disposition; eagerness; facility; gameness; *hunger;* immediacy; *Johnny-on-the-spot;* keenness; kelter; liking; maturity; *nigh;* organization; preparedness; priming; quickness; readying; solicitousness; training; unreluctance; verve; willingness; *x-training; yare;* zeal; [*Ant.* reluctance]

**ready** *(adj.)*: alacritous; buxom; capable; disposed; due; desirous; equipped; eager; fit; fain; foresightful; geared up; game; girt; handy; instant; *impatient;* Johnny-on-the-spot; keyed up; keen; likely; minded; mature; *nigh;* organized; prepared; primed; poised; quick; readied; raring; set; solicitous; trained; up to; ultra-prepared; *vehement;* well-prepared (-readied); waiting; willing; *x-trained;* yare; zealous; [*Ant.* reluctant]
**ready** *(v.)*: adapt; become accustomed; capacitate; condition; dight; equip; fit; get ~; groom; gear up; habilitate; *instruct;* jibe [slang]; *knock into shape;* line out; make ready; *near-ready;* outfit; prepare; qualify; readjust; set; suit; train; *ultra-prepared;* verse; *well-readied; xenagogue;* yarken; *zealously ~;*
**real** *(adj.)*: actual; bona fide; certified; definite; existent; earnest; factual; genuine; honest-to-goodness); indubitable; justifiable; known; legitimate; material; never-failing; *ontic;* positive; pure; questionless; reliable; sincere; true; tangible; unerring; undeniable; veridical; veritable; *well-tried; x-parent; yes;* 'zactly [dial.];
**realistic** *(adj.)*: acceptable; accurate; authentic; believable; bearable; convincing; down-to-earth; expedient; fair; fitting; feasible; genuine; honest; intelligent; justifiable; *keen;* legitimate; moderate; meet; matter-of-fact; no-nonsense; obtainable; practical; prudent; plausible; passable; quite sensible; reasonable; rational; sensible; satisfactory; sufferable; true-to-life; tolerable; tenable; tough-minded; understandable; viable; valid; wise; workable; *x-real; yieldful; zero nonsense;* [*Ant.* ridiculous]
**reality** *(n.)*: actuality; being; certainty; demonstrability; entity; existence; factuality; genuineness; hypostasis; indubitability; *justness; knowledge;* literalness; materiality; non-fiction; *ontic;* precision; *quaecumque sunt vera* [L.]; realness; sureness; truth; undeniability; verity; whole truth; *x-parent;* yes; zero error;
**realization** *(n.)*: awareness; *belief;* comprehension; dawning; epiphany; fruition; grasp; *hitting on;* insight; *judgment;* knowledge; *light; lucubration;* materialization; notion; occurring; picking up on; *quite sure;* recognition; *sense; sober ~; thought; truth;* understanding; *valuation;* waking up; *xenodiagnosis; yeme;* zero doubt;
**realize** *(v.)*: actualize; admit; become aware; comprehend; dawn (on); envisage; figure; grasp; get it; hit on; incept; *judge;* know; *lucubrate;* meditate on; *notion;* own; occur; pick up on; *question;* remember; recognize; see; think of; understand; visualize; wake; *xenodiagnose; yeme; zazen;*
**realm** *(n.)*: area; ambit; branch; country; demesne; domain; dominion; department; empire; extent of influence; field; governance; hemisphere; imperium; jurisdiction; kingdom; land; monarchy; nation; *oligarchy;* purview; queendom [fem.]; royal jurisdiction; reach; sphere; scope; sovereignty; territory; *under one's authority;* viscounty; *world; xerifdom; yard;* zone of influence;
**reap** *(v.)*: acquire; bring in; cut; collect; develop; exact; fetch; find; gain; get; gather; garner; have; harvest; *incur; inherit; just desserts;* kirn [Scot.]; land; make; nab; net; obtain; procure; pick; *quoff;* receive; retrieve; secure; take in; usurp; *vest; wildcraft;* xfer; yank; zip away;
**reaper** *(n.)*: agriculturalist; binder; cutter; collector; *doer;* employee; farmhand; gleaner; gatherer; harvester; *indentured servant; jobholder;* kirner [Scot.]; laborer; manservant; neif; *operator;* picker; qualified farmhand; receiver; servant; toiler; *underling; vinedresser;* workman; *x-man;* yeoman; *zaikai;*
**rear** *(adj.)*: astern; back; baft; clear to the back; *dorsal;* end; foot; *gammon;* hind(ermost); *in the back;* jacksy; *keister;* latter part; nether part; *over;* posterior; quarterdeck; rearward; stern(ward); tail; *underside;* verge; waning; *xyz end; yondmost; Z-position;*
**rearrange** *(v.)*: alter; bemingle; change; doctor; exchange; fix; *grow; heighten;* innovate; improve; interchange; *jump; key to; lower;* move; mix up; *novate;* overhaul; permute; *qualify;* reorganize; reorder; revise; switch; trade; *upgrade;* vary; *warp; xenomorph; yaw;* zigzag;
**reason** *(n.)*: aim; account; argument; apologia; basis; cause; case; *drive;* defense; excuse; explanation; end; exposition; *force;* grounds; goal; *hypothesis;* idea; intention; justification; *key ~;* leading cause; motive; motivation; *notion;* occasion; objective; pretext; purpose; *quickening;* rationale; sense; thought; *ulterior motive;* vindication; wherefore; warrant; *xenodiagnosis; yeme;* zeal;

**reason** *(v.)*: adduce; argue; bring around; *brainstorm;* cogitate; consider; contend; deduce; demonstrate; evaluate; establish; expostulate; figure; gauge; *hypothesize;* imagine; infer; judge; justify; *know;* lucubrate; meditate; *notion; need; originate;* ponder; philosophize; point out; prove; question; rationalize; reflect; ratiocinate; remonstrate; study; solve; show; think; use brain; *valuate;* work out; win over; *xenodiagnose; yeme; zazen;*

**reasonable** *(adj.)*: acceptable; believable; bearable; commonsense; coherent; conscionable; decent; down-to-earth; defensible; evenhanded; endurable; expedient; fair; fitting; feasible; good enough; heady; intelligent; inexpensive; judicious; *knowledgeable;* logical; level-headed; legitimate; moderate; matter-of-fact; no-nonsense; ostensible; practical; plausible; quite sensible; rational; realistic; sensible; supportable; sufferable; sane; tolerable; tenable; understandable; viable; workable; *xenagogic; yepe; zero doubt;* [*Ant.* reasonless]

**reassure** *(v.)*: assure; bolster; comfort; dismiss all doubts; encourage; fillip; give confidence; hearten; inspire; *justify;* kindle; lift; make confident; make assured; *nail down; okay;* put at ease; *quicken;* raise spirits; settle; soothe; *take heart;* uplift; *vivify; well-assured; xuld [arch.]; yerk [dial.];* zealously assure;

**rebel** *(n.)*: arch~; anarchist; backstabber; criminal; dissident; evildoer; extremist; Frondeur; fifth columnist; guerrilla; *heretic;* insurgent; insubordinate; Jacobin; kicker; *leftist;* malcontent; militant; non-conformist; oppositionist; poissarde [fem.]; *questioner;* rebeller; recusant; revolutionary; revolutionist; seditionary; troublemaker; usurper; *vier;* withstander; *xenocentrist; yieldless;* zealot; [*see* nonconformist]

**rebel** *(v.)*: act in opposition; backtalk; backstab; cast off; contravene; defy; dissent; *evil;* flout; foment; gainstand; harden one's heart; insurrect; *jump ship;* kick; *lawless;* mutiny; not listen; overthrow; overturn; *perfidy; question;* revolt; resist; rise up; subvert; stiffen one's neck; stand against; strive against; throw off (yoke); usurp; undermine; uprise; *vie; violate;* withstand; *xgress; yieldless;* zealot; [*Ant.* regard]

**rebellion** *(n. disobedience)*: antinomianism; bad behavior; contravention; contumacy; disobedience; defiance; *ever-defiant;* flouting; frowardness; *general disregard; headstrongness;* insubordination; *jadedness; kicking;* lack of compliance; lawlessness; misbehavior; *mutiny;* noncompliance; naughtiness; obstinacy; *pigheadedness; questioning;* rebelliousness; refusal; refractoriness; stubbornness; sin; transgression; trespass; unyieldingness; usurpation; violation; waywardness; *xgression;* yieldlessness; *zapping;* [*see* sin; revolt; *Ant.* regard]

**rebellion** *(n. revolution)*: armed conflict; breach; coup d'état [F.]; defiance; emeute; *fight;* general uprising; high treason; insurrection; insurgence; jacquerie; *kicking at;* lèse majesté [F.]; mutiny; noncompliance; outbreak; overthrow; peasant revolt; putsch; *questioning;* revolution; revolt; rising up; subversion; treason; takeover; uprising; violence; war; *xgression;* yieldlessness; *yellow flu; zapping;*

**rebellious** *(adj.)*: antinomian; bad; contumacious; disobedient; defiant; ever-stubborn; flouting; *grim;* headstrong; insubordinate; incompliant; incorrigible; insurgent; *jaw-set; knocking;* lawless; mutinous; misbehaving; noncompliant; naughty; obdurate; pigheaded; querulous; refractory; recusant; self-willed; seditious; truculent; uncompliant; unsubmissive; unyielding; unruly; ungovernable; violating; wayward; *x-grained;* yieldless; *zero give;* [*Ant.* regardful]

**rebuke** *(n.)*: admonition; berating; censure; criticism; denunciation; excoriation; faulting; going-over; haranguing; increpation; jawing; knocking; lambasting; monitory; *nagging;* objurgation; *punishment; questioning;* reprimand; reproof; scolding; telling off; upbraiding; vituperation; *warning; xuld [arch.];* yelling at; *zapping;*

**rebuke** *(v.)*: admonish; berate; censure; correct; chide; chew out; castigate; denounce; excoriate; fault; flay; fulminate; give talking to; harangue; inveigh; jaw; knock; lambaste; lecture; lay into; *macerate;* nag; objurgate; *punish; question;* reprove; reprimand; reproach; scold; tell off; upbraid; vituperate; warn; wig [Br.]; *xuld [arch.];* yell at; *zap;* [*Ant.* rave]

**rebut** *(v.)*: answer; argue; back answer; counter; come back with; deny; disprove; *express; forcefully ~;* give answer; handle; invalidate; *judge wrong; key in;* lay to rest; make rebuttal; negate; overturn; prove wrong; *quash;* reply; rebuff; respond; retort; riposte; rejoin; return; surrebut; state; solve; tell; undo; voice confutation; word rebuttal; *x-out; yak; zeroize;* [*Ant.* receive]

**rebuttal** *(n.)*: answer; argument; back answer; comeback; counterstatement; defense; elenchus; *finding; general reply;* handling; impugnation; justification; *key comeback; letter; message;* negation; opposition; *pronouncement; questioning;* reply; response; rejoinder; refutation; repudiation; statement; sally; treatment; traversal; utterance; vindication; *witty reply; words; xtry. reply; yak;* zinger; [*Ant.* reception]

**recant** *(v.)*: annul; backpedal; back down; controvert; *change;* disavow; deny; *eat crow;* foreswear; go back; *hang up;* invalidate; *jump off; kest; leave;* make null and void; nullify; overturn; pull back; *palinody;* quitclaim; retract; renounce; revoke; swallow; set aside; take back; unsay; void; withdraw; x; yank; *zeroize;* [*Ant.* reaffirm]

**recantation** *(n.)*: abnegation; backpedaling; controversion; disavowal; denial; *eating crow;* foreswearing; going back; *hanging up;* invalidation; *jumping back; kesting;* leaving; making null and void; nullification; overturning; palinody; quitclaim; retraction; repudiation; setting aside; taking back; unsaying; voiding; withdrawal; x-ing; yanking; zeroization; [*Ant.* reaffirmation]

**recede** *(v.)*: abate; assuage; break; bate; contract; condense; decrease; decline; diminish; dissipate; dwindle; ease; ebb; fade; fall; go down; *hush; halt; impair; improve; jump down;* knock down; languish; lessen; lower; minish; moderate; minimize; *narrow; outgo;* peter out; quail; reduce; subside; shrink; taper off; *undo; vanish;* wane; withdraw; *xerosis;* yield; zap; [*Ant.* rise]

**receive** *(v.)*: acquire; admit; be given; come by; collect; draw; exact; fetch; get; have; inherit; *jet;* kep; let in; make receipt of; nab; obtain; procure; pick up; pocket; *quoff;* retrieve; secure; take; *usurp; valid;* win; *xfer; yank; zip away;* [*Ant.* reject]

**reception** *(n.)*: acceptance; *belief;* collection; *delivery;* embracing; feedback; greeting; homecoming; induction; imbibing; *jiving [slang];* keping; *leaving;* making receipt; non-refusal; open arms; picking up; *qualifying;* reaction; response; receipt; receiving; *securing;* taking (in); *unloading; validating;* welcome; *xfer;* yessing; *Zufriedenheit* [G.]; [*Ant.* rejection]

**receptive** *(adj.)*: approachable; agreeable; amenable; *blithe;* cooperative; disposed; *encouraging;* favorable; friendly; gracious; hospitable; interested; *just great;* kind(-hearted); *like putty;* minded; *non-opposed;* open; pervious; *quick to embrace;* regardful; responsive; recipient; sympathetic; tenderhearted; teachable; uncritical; very ~; warm; welcoming; *xenial;* yielding; *zealous;*

**recess** *(n. break)*: adjournment; break; coffee break; downtime; *ease;* forbearance; *gala day;* holiday; intermission; *journey's end; knock off;* leave; *motionlessness; night rest;* off-time; pause; *quiescence;* respite; suspension; time off; *unwinding;* vacation; wait; *x-rest; yawning; zwischenspiel* [music];

**recess** *(n. indentation)*: alcove; bay; cranny; (con)cavity; depression; embrassure; *fissure; grotto;* hollow; indentation; inset; *jaw-hole;* krater; *lacuna;* mouth; mew; nook; niche; opening; pit; *quarry-pit;* recessed area; socket; *tokonoma* [Jap.]; *unit;* vug; well; *xystus;* yawn; zanja;

**recipient** *(n.)*: addressee; acquirer; beneficiary; coferree; designatee; donee; *endued; fellow;* getter; heir; inheritor; joint- ~; *kepper;* legatee; *major ~; next-of-kin;* obtainer; one; parcener; payee; *quoff;* receiver; sole heir; taker; transferee; uncontested ~; *vessel;* winner; *xfer; yain* [arch.]; *zadruga;* [*Ant.* renderer]

**recitation** *(n.)*: address; bespeaking; communication; discourse; elocution; formal speech; *glossa;* homily; *indiction; jeremiad; kerygma;* lecture; monologue; narration; oration; performance; quotation; recital; speech; talk; utterance; vocalization; word(s); *xenophonia; yawner [off.]; zay [dial.];*

**recite** *(v.)*: articulate; bespeak; cite; declaim; echo; *foremention;* give; hold forth; iterate; *jaw; keep coming;* lecture; *mouth; mention;* name; narrate; orate; parrot; prelect; pronounce; quote; rehearse; retell; repeat; say; state; tell; trumpet; *unfold;* utter; voice; word; *xenophonia;* yak; zero in;

**reckless** *(adj.)*: abandoned; blasé; careless; dangerous; endangering; foolhardy; *gone mad;* haphazard; heedless; irresponsible; jaunty; keg-meg; *lunatic;* madcap; negligent; over-hasty; parlous; *precarious; questionable;* rash; slipshod; sloppy; slam-bang; thoughtless; uncontrolled; unsafe; venturous; wild; *x-ing; yieldless;* zany; [*Ant.* restrained]

**reckon** *(v.)*: assess; account; *believe;* consider; count; calculate; deem; esteem; evaluate; figure; gauge; hypothesize; imagine; judge; *know;* look at; make an estimation; number; opine; presume; *question;* regard; suppose; think; use brain; valuate; weigh; *xenodiagnose; yeme; zazen;*

**reckoning** *(n.)*: accounting; bookkeeping; computation; documentation; estimation; financial record-keeping; figuring; general ~; *house accounting;* judgment; keeping records; ledger-keeping; maintaining the books; number-crunching; office records; *payable;* quantitation; record-keeping; settlement; tabulation; *unpaid balance;* verification; weighing; *xaraf; yeme; zet [dial.];*

**recline** *(v.)*: *at rest;* bed down; cant; *down;* ease; fall; go down; humicubate; *idle; jacent; keep down;* lean; lay; lie (down); lounge; *move down; nap; non-erect;* overlie; prostrate; *quiet down;* rest; relax; repose; slouch; sprawl; *sit;* sidle; take ease; use bed; unwind; *vegetate; wait; x-rest;* yield; *zizz;*

**reclining** *(adj.)*: accumbent; *buoyed up;* cumbent; decumbent; downlying; *even;* flat; *going across;* horizontal; incumbent; jacent; *knocked out;* lying; leaning back; *motionless; non-erect;* on the ground; prostrate; prone; procumbent; *quasi-horizontal;* recumbent; resting; supine; transversal; un-erect; *very relaxed; way down;* x-axis; *yielded; zonked out;* [*Ant.* rectilinear]

**recluse** *(n.)*: anchoret; ascetic; *by oneself;* cenobite; dervis; eremite; *friar; gone off;* hermit; isolationist; *jubilarian; kithless;* loner; lone-wolf; marabout; mountain man; non-socialite; outcast; private person; *quietude;* reclusive; solitairian; seclusionist; stylite; *talapoin [Bud.];* unsocial; votary; withdrawn; *xenodochium; yokeless;* Zetetic;

**recognition** *(n.)*: acknowledgement; appreciation; *beholding;* comprehension; detection; establishment; fathoming; grasping; *having understanding of;* honor; identification; *judgment;* knowledge; kudos; *learning;* making out; noticing; noesis; observation; perception; placing; praise; *questionless;* realization; seeing; spotting; taking in; understanding; valuation; watching; *xenodiagnosis; yeme; zeroing in;* [*see* praise]

**recognize** *(v.)*: acknowledge; accept; appreciate; admit; be familiar with; comprehend; concede; distinguish; eye; fathom; get; grasp; grant; have appreciation for; identify; *judge;* know; *learn;* make out; notice; observe; perceive; pick out; *qualify;* realize; see; spot; single out; tell apart; understand; value; watch; *xenodiagnose; yeme;* zero in; [*Ant.* reject]

**recollect** *(v.)*: awaken memory; bethink; bring to mind; bear in mind; consider; dwell on; evoke; *foremembered;* get into one's head; hark back; imbibe; jog one's memory; keep a memory; look back; mind; not forget; open up memories; put to mind; *quicken mind;* remember; recall; reflect; reminisce; summon; think of; unlock; *venerate;* waken; *xfer; yet remembered; zero in;*

**recollection** *(n.)*: anamnesis; bearing in mind; cognizance; dwelling; evoking; flashback; going back; hypermnesia; impression; *jogging;* kept memory; looking back; memory; nostalgia; observation; *permanent memory; quick-to-remember;* remembrance; reflection; recall; reminiscence; *souvenir;* thought; *unaided recall; veneration; well-remembered; xfer; yesteryear; zum [dial.];*

**recommend** *(v.)*: advise; advocate; *bid;* counsel; commend; direct; exhort; encourage; foreadvise; give counsel; hail; instruct; judge; *kibitz [Yid.];* lead; motion; move; make ~ation; notify; nominate; name; offer one's opinion; propose; praise; *quicken; rede [arch.];* suggest; tender one's opinion; tell; urge; vouch for; *warn; xenagogy; yammer;* zero in; [*Ant.* resist]

**recommendation** *(n.)*: advice; advocacy; blessing; counsel; commendation; direction; exhortation; free advice; guidance; hortation; instruction; judgment; *kibizing [Yid.]; leading; mentorship; notification;* opinion; piece of advice; proposition; *quick advice;* recommending; suggestion; tip; testimonial; urging; voice (of support); word of advice; *xenagogy; yammering; zeroing in;*

**recompense** *(n.)*: amount; amends; base pay; bonus; compensation; damages; defrayment; due; earnings; emolument; financial remuneration; guerdon; hire; income; indemnification; just deserts; *kickback; lex talionis* [L.]; meed; *net pay;* overcompensation; payment; quittance; reward; remuneration; salary; satisfaction; take-home pay; tip; *unindebted;* virement; wages; xfer; yield; *zapping;*
**recompense** *(v.)*: afford; buy; compensate; disburse; expend; finance; foot cost; give; guerdon; hand over; indemnify; *justify;* kick in; lay out; make amends (-payment); *non-retention;* overcompensate; pay; quit; remunerate; reward; requite; repay; set right; tip; *tender; unhand; vest;* weigh out; *xfer;* yield; *zero-out ones debt;*
**reconcile** *(v.)*: appease; arbitrate; becalm; bring together; conciliate; *diffuse;* end conflict; fix; *gratify;* harmonize; iron out; intermediate; *join;* kiss and make up; legate; mollify; make peace; *nullify; overcome;* pacify; placate; propitiate; put right; quell; restore; square; settle one's differences; *tranquilize;* unruffle; *void;* win favor; *x-out; yield; zeroize;* [*Ant.* rankle]
**reconciliation** *(n.)*: appeasement; bringing together; conciliation; detente; ending of conflict; fixing; *gratification;* harmonization; intermediation; *joining; kiss and make up;* legation; mollification; making peace; *nullification; overcoming;* pacification; placation; propitiation; peacemaking; quelling; reconciling; restoration; squaring up; settling; *together again;* unruffling; *voidance;* winning favor; x-ing out; *yielding; zero variance;* [*see* atonement; *Ant.* rift]
**record** *(n.)*: account; archive; book; chronicle; cartulary; documentation; description; data; evidence; file; *get down;* history; information; journal; *kept ~;* log; megillah; muniment; notation; observations; proof; postea; *quill;* register; statement; testimony; tally sheet; transcript; *underwritten;* verification; veracity; witness; written account; *xenagogy;* yellow sheet [crim. law]; *zipper-book;*
**record** *(v.)*: annotate; *blazon;* chronicle; denote; enter; fill in; get down; handwrite; indicate; imprint; journalize; keep ~; log; mark down; notate; *overwrite;* put down; prerecord; quill; register; set down; take down; tape; underwrite; videotape; write (down); *x; yak; zay;*
**recourse** *(n.)*: alternative; avenue; backup plan; choice; decision; expediency; *function;* good option; help; *idea; justification; known ~;* legitimate option; move; *notion;* option; plan; path; *quick response;* route; resort; source of help; thing; *undertaking;* viable option; way out; *x-action; yeme* [arch.]; *zwinger;*
**recover** *(v.)*: advance; bounce back; convalesce; *deliver;* enhance; fix; get better; gain strength; heal; improve; *jump ahead;* knit; *laid up; look better;* mend; make progress; nurse to health; *optimize;* pull through; *quick-fix;* recuperate; rally; revive; rebound; rescue; stabilize; take a turn for the better; *undo; vamp;* wax stronger; *xtry. recovery; yele* [arch.]; *zet [dial.];* [*Ant.* regress]
**recovery** *(n.)*: advancement; betterment; convalescence; comeback; cure; *deliverance; enhancement;* fixing; getting better; healing; improvement; *jump ahead;* knitting; laying up; *looking better;* mending; miraculous ~; *nurturing; optimization;* pulling through; *quick-fix;* recuperation; rallying; revival; stabilization; survival; turnaround; upswing; upturn; vivification; waxing better; xtry. ~; *yeling* [arch.]; *zet [dial.];*
**recreation** *(n.)*: amusement; activity; *buffoonery; cheer;* diversion; disport; entertainment; enjoyment; fun; gaiety; hobby; idle amusement; jollity; *kick back;* leisure; mirth; *non-serious; overjoy;* pleasure; pastime; play; prolusion; quality time; relaxation; sport; tomfoolery; *unwind;* vacation; *whimsical; x-play; yeah!; zizz;*
**recreational** *(adj.)*: amusement; *buffoonery; cheering;* diversionary; entertainment; enjoyment; (for-)fun; *gaiety;* hobby; *idle amusement;* just for fun; *kicks;* leisure; *much enjoyment; non-serious; overjoy;* pleasure; play; quality time; *relaxation;* sport; *tomfoolery; unwinding;* vacation; *whimsical; x-play; yeah!; zizzy;*
**recruit** *(n.)*: apprentice; beginner; boot; cadet; debutant; draftee; enrollee; enlistee; first-timer; greenhorn; *hireling;* inductee; jackeroo; *kid;* learner; *mentee;* newcomer; newbie; *one;* pupil; *quick learner;* registered trainee; starter; trainee; *undertaker; venturer;* wannabe; *xon;* yardman; *zero experience;*

**recruit** *(v.)*: *admit;* bid; conscript; draft; enroll; enlist; find; get; hire; induct; *join; key people;* levy; muster; mobilize; *name; order;* press; put into service; *qualify;* register; raise; re-enlist; sign up; take; *use; venture;* write one's name down; *xfer; yede; zealously ~;* [*Ant.* remove]

**rectify** *(v.)*: amend; *better;* correct; doctor; emend; fix; get right; *harmonize;* improve; *jury-rig; kilter; level out;* make right; *neogenesis;* overhaul; put right; quick-fix; repair; restore; right; redress; set aright; tune up; unbend; unkink; *vamp;* work out; *x-fix; yield help; zero problems;* [*Ant.* rankle]

**recur** *(v.)*: *again;* be repeated; come back; duplicate; echo; flare up; *follow;* go again; happen again; iterate; *journeying on;* keep happening; *lasting;* maintain; *nonstop;* occur again; persist; *quadruplicate;* return; reappear; repeat; show up again; sustain; *tautolize; undergo again; verbigerate; wax stronger; x2; yet again; zero stopping;* [*Ant.* relent]

**recurrence** *(n.)*: atavism; *bearing;* coming back; duplication; *echo;* flare-up; going on; happening again; intermittence; iteration; *journeying on; keeps happening; likeness;* maintaining; *nonstop;* occurring again; persistence; *quadruplication;* repetition; recursion; reprise; reappearance; succession; *twice; undergoing again; verbigeration; without end; xerograph; yet again; zero stopping;* [*Ant.* rest]

**red** *(adj.)*: annatto; blood ~; brick ~; crimson; damask; envermeiled; flame- ~; gules; garnet; high ~; incarnadine; Japan ~; kermes- ~; lobster- ~; madder; maroon; Naples ~; orange- ~; puce; Quaker drab; ruby; scarlet; titian; umber- ~; vermillion; wine- ~; *xanthoconite;* yellowish- ~; *zinc orange;*

**redden** *(v.)*: *affect;* blush; become red; crimson; *develop;* encrimson; flush; grow red; *henna;* incarnadine; *jumping; kind of redden; laky;* mantle; make red; *non-pale;* overlay with red; pinken; *quite red;* ruddy; rubify; *shade;* turn red; *undergo;* vermilion; wax red; *xtr. red; yield redness; zet;*

**redeem** *(n.)*: atone; buy back; countervail; deliver; emancipate; exchange; free; give atonement for; *help;* indemnify; *justify; keep;* liberate; make free; *no condemnation; open;* purchase; *quicken;* release; restore; rescue; ransom; repurchase; save; transfer; use; *unshackle; vivify;* win back; *xfer; yonder-bound; Zion-bound;*

**redemption** *(n.)*: atonement; buying back; cleansing; deliverance; emancipation; final ~; *grace; heaven;* indemnification; justification; *know-so salvation;* liberation; *mercy;* new birth; *opening;* purchase; quickening; repurchase; ransom; salvation; *transformation; unshackling; vivification; washing;* Xt.; *yonder; Zion;*

**reduce** *(v.)*: abate; assuage; alleviate; break; bate; cut; curb; contract; condense; decrease; decline; diminish; drop; dissipate; dwindle; downsize; downscale; decimate; ease; ebb; fade; fall; go down; hush; halve; impair; *jump down;* knock down; lessen; lower; minish; moderate; mitigate; minimize; narrow; obtund; palliate; pare down; peter out; quail; recede; shrink; subside; taper; trim; *undo; vanish;* wane; waste; *xerosis;* yield; zap; [*Ant.* raise]

**reduction** *(n.)*: abatement; assuagement; alleviation; breaking; bating; curbing; contraction; condensation; cutback; decrease; decline; diminishment; diminution; dissipation; dwindling; decimation; easing; ebbing; fading; falling; going down; hushing; halving; improvement; jump down; knocking down; lessening; lowering; moderation; minimization; narrowing; obtunding; paring down; petering out; quelling; quailing; receding; reducing; subsiding; tapering; *undoing; vanishing;* waning; wasting; *xerosis*; yielding; zapping; [*Ant.* rising]

**redundancy** *(n.)*: *again;* battology; circumlocution; duplication; echoing; excess; *for the second time;* giving again; *heard twice;* iteration; *just said it; keeping it up;* logorrhea; mention again; nimiety; overabundance; pleonasm; *quadruplication;* repetition; superfluity; tautology; unneeded; verbigeration; *wordiness; xtr. time; yieldless; zillionth time;*

**redundant** *(adj.)*: already stated; again-mentioned; before-stated; conveyed twice; duplicated; echoed; *for the second time;* given again; *heard twice;* iterated; *just said it; keep it up;* logorrheic; much-repeated; mentioned again; needlessly ~; *over again;* perissological; pleonastic; *quadruplicate;* repetitive; superfluous; tautological; twice-mentioned; unneeded; verbigerating; *with repetition; xtr. time; yieldless; zillionth time;*

**reed** *(n.)*: arundo; bulrush; bamboo; cattail; cane; *durra; eelgrass;* flag; grass; haugh-grass; Indian ~; *jheel [Ind.];* kamish [Rus.]; lagoon-grass; mace-reed; *nanoplankton; overgrowth;* papyrus; quill; rush; stalk; seave; sedge; typha; *tall ~s; usnea;* vetiver-grass; water-flag; *xyris;* yedda; *zea;*

**reel** *(n.)*: *app;* bobbin; coil; cable-tier; capstan; *draw; enwrap;* filature; *gird;* hose ~; hasp; *intertwine;* jack; *knittle;* line-spool; metal ~; nylon spool; *organize;* pirn; quill; *roll;* spool; spindle; take-up; *utility ~; volution;* windle; wooden ~; *x-ing;* yarnwindle; zein-spool;

**reel** *(v. lurch)*: *amble;* bobble; coggle; didder; edge; falter; gimp; hobble; inch; jiffle; *keep swaying;* list; *move;* nutate; oscillate; pitch; quaddle; roll; stagger; stumble; spin; sway; totter; *uneven;* vacillate; wobble; whirl; *xfer;* yerk; *zigzag;*

**refer** *(v.)*: allude; advert; betake; cross-reference; direct; *express; footnote;* give reference to; have reference; indicate; indigitate; *jist; known;* link with; mention; make reference; *name; overtone;* point; quiddit; reference; submit; signify; touch on; *use;* vide; *word;* xref; *ypointing* [arch.]; zero in:

**referee** *(n.)*: arbitrator; *baseball ~;* commissaire; decision-maker; evaluator; final judge; *gauger;* honest broker; intermediary; judge; *kadi;* linesman; line judge; mediator; negotiant; official; presider; *qadi;* ref [slang]; *scorekeeper; settler;* timekeeper; third party; umpire; valuator; *weigher; XQ; yell; zamorin;*

**reference** *(n.)*: allusion; bearing; book ~; citation; cross reference; direct ~; end note; footnote; general ~; hint; indication; indirect ~; *jist;* key ~; location; mention; notation; overtone; pointer; quote; referring; suggestion; *touching on;* use; *vide;* word; xref.; *ypointing [arch.];* zero in;

**refine** *(v.)*: ameliorate; beautify; civilize; distill; decoct; develop; expurgate; enhance; *foster;* get impurities out; hone; *heat;* improve; *jump ahead; keen;* lixiviate; make pure; meliorate; *narrow;* optimize; purify; purge; perfect; polish; quintessentialize; revamp; smelt; subtilize; treat; upgrade; vamp; work on; whet; *xtry.; yarken; zaru;* [Ant. roughen]

**reflect** *(v.)*: *appear;* bend back; *carry;* deflect; echo; flash; give reflection; have image in; *image; jump; keen image; likeness;* mirror; *not absorb; object;* picture; *quintessentialize;* replicate; return; show reflection; throw back; *ultra-high reflectivity; vector; wave; xfer;* yield reflection; *zet [dial];*

**reflection** *(n.)*: appearance; bending back; catopter; deflection; echoing; flashing; *face; glass ~;* hand mirror ~; image; *jump; keen image;* likeness; mirror-image; *non-reversing ~; object;* picture; *quintessence;* resemblance; reflexion [Br.]; similitude; throwing back; *ultra-high reflectivity; vector;* waves; *xfer;* yielding reflection; *zet [dial.];*

**reflective** *(adj. introspective)*: absorbed; brooding; cogitative; contemplative; deep in thought; deliberating; engrossed; fanciful; gazeful; heart-searching; introspective; judicial; *knowledge;* lost in thought; meditative; museful; notional; occupied; pensive; quiet; reflecting; serious; thoughtful; thinking; understanding; *valuating;* wistful; *xenocratic; yearnful; zetetic;*

**reflective** *(adj. mirror-finished)*: *argentic;* brilliant; burnished; catoptric; chromatic; dazzling; enameled; furbished; glossy; highly polished; image-reflecting; just-polished; *keen image; lacquered;* mirror-finished; metallic; nicely-polished; over-polished; polished; quicksilvered; reflecting; specular; shiny; silvery; *throwing back images; undistorted;* varnished; well-polished; *xanthoconite;* ytterbic; *zinnobar;*

**reform** *(v.)*: amend; better; change (ways); correct; doctor; do better; enhance; fix; go straight; *help;* improve; *jib; key to; lower;* modify; meliorate; novate; overhaul; put right; *qualify;* revise; restructure; reorganize; switch; turn; *transform;* tweak; upgrade; vamp; *work; xenomorph; yaw; zigzag;*

**reformation** *(n.)*: amendment; betterment; change; difference; edition; fix; *growth; helping;* improvement; *jump; key changes; living right;* modification; melioration; *new behavior;* overhaul; permutation; *qualification;* revision; renovation; restructuring; redress; switch; turning (over a new leaf); upgrade; variation; *work; xenomorph; yielding; zeal to change;* [see repentance]

**refrain** *(n.)*: air; burden; chant; chorus; descant; epode; folderol; *gallimaufry;* heptastich; hexastich; hymn; intermezzo; jingle; *kasida;* laud; melody; *notes;* octastich; pentastich; quodlibet; reprise; strain; tetrastich; tune; theme; undersong; *vocalization; warbling; xylophone song; yed; zemirah;*

**refrain** *(v.)*: abstain; avoid; bow out; cease; desist; deny; *don't;* eschew; forbear; forego; give up; hold back; inhibit; just say no; keep from; leave off; make an end to; not do; *omit;* put up; quit; restrain oneself from; spare; terminate; *undo; voluntarily ~;* withdraw; x; *yieldless; zero;*
**refresh** *(v.)*: animate; brisken; boost; cool; cheer; delight; enliven; freshen; give life to; hearten; invigorate; jee; keel; liven; make alive; *nudge;* overjoy; perk up; quicken; revive; revitalize; rejuvenate; refreshen; stir; titillate; uplift; vitalize; waken; *xuld [arch.]; yerk;* zing up;
**refreshing** *(adj.)*: animating; boosting; cooling; delightful; energizing; freshening; good; heartening; invigorating; jarring; *keen;* livening; *making alive; neat; overjoying;* perking; quickening; refective; refreshful; revitalizing; strengthening; thirst-quenching; uplifting; vitalizing; vivifying; *wonderful; xuld [arch.]; yerk;* zestful;
**refuge** *(n.)*: asylum; bower; covert; city of ~; den; *defense; ensuring;* funk hole; getaway; hideaway; hiding place; hollow; haven; incolumity; *journey's end;* keep; lodgement; mattamore; non-danger; out of harm's way; place of rest; *quietude;* resting-place; sanctuary; shelter; safe haven; *taking in;* undercovert; very safe place; *well-being; xanadu;* yarkandi; zoar;
**refugee** *(n.)*: asylum-seeker; boat person; castaway; displaced person; evacuee; emigrant; expatriate; fugitive; *goer;* hider; homeless person; immigrant; *journeyer; kept; lodgement-seeker;* maroon; migrant; *non-settled persons;* outcast; *person; quit;* runaway; relocated person; seeker of refuge; transferee; uprooted person; vacater; war ~; xenizer; *yarkandi; zipped;*
**refusal** *(n.)*: abnegation; bucking; casting away; contravention; declining; denial; disobedience; exclusion; forbearance; flouting; *going against; hatred;* insubordination; *jilting;* knock-back [Scot.]; *like not to; mutiny;* non-acceptance; negative answer; obstinacy; *pitching; quitting;* rejection; snubbing; turning down (-away); unwillingness; *veto; withstand;* x-out; *yieldless; zero out;* [*Ant.* reception]
**refuse** *(n.)*: abatis; *bag; compost;* debris; *eliminate;* filth; garbage; *heap; items;* industrial waste; junk; ket; litter; mullock; *nihil* [L.]; offal; *pile;* quisquillous; rubbish; sweepings; trash; unwanted items; vuilnis; waste; *x-barrel; yucky; zero value;*
**refuse** *(v.)*: absolutely ~; brush off; buck; cast out; contravene; decline; deny; disobey; exclude; forbear; flout; flat ~; *go against; hate;* ignore; *jilt; keenly reject; like not to; mutiny;* not accept; nix; *oppose; pitch; quit;* reject; say no; snub; turn down (-away); utterly ~; *veto; withstand;* x-out; *yieldless; zero out;* [*Ant.* receive]
**refutation** *(n.)*: argument; answer; *back answer;* confutation; denial; disproof; elenchus; *forswearing; gainsaying;* hypobole; invalidation; *judicious reply; key answer; letter;* message; negation; nullification; opposition; *point;* proof to the contrary; quarrel; qualification; *reasoning;* rebuff; refutal; strong argument; *treatment;* unfailing logic; *verdict;* words; *xtry. ~; yes-answer; zeroizing;*
**refute** *(v.)*: abrogate; answer; back answer; confute; disprove; evert; *forcefully ~;* give answer; have answer; invalidate; *judge wrong; key in;* lay to rest; make rebuff; *meet;* negate; nullify; overthrow; prove wrong; *quash;* rebut; rebuff; show to be false; *tell;* undo; voice confutation; word rebuttal; *x-out; yak; zeroize;*
**regain** *(v.)*: acquire back; bring back; capture again; dispossess; *expropriate;* find again; get back; have back; *intercept; justify; kep;* liberate; make one's own again; *net again;* obtain back; procure again; *quoff;* recapture; retrieve; redeem; recover; salvage; take back; *undelete; vamp;* win back; xfer back; yank back; *zip back;*
**regal** *(adj.)*: authoritative; blueblooded; commanding; dignified; excellent; fine; grand; high-born; impressive; *judicious;* kingly; lordly; lofty; majestic; monarchal; noble; *ostentatious;* princely; proud; queenly [fem.]; royal; stately; *tsarish;* uncommon; valiant; well-born; xtry.; yorkist; *zarish* [arch.];
**regard** *(n.)*: attention; admiration; bearing; consideration; courtesy; dignity; deference; devoirs; esteem; fear; favor; good graces; honor; heed; interest; *justness; kneeling;* liking; mind; notice; obeisance; politeness; *quality;* respect(s); solicitude; salutation; thought; tribute; *unmitigated respect;* veneration; wonder; xtry.; yielding; *zero contempt;* [*Ant.* rudeness]

**regard** *(v.)*: acknowledge; admire; bow to; consider; deem; defer to; esteem; fear; favor; give honor; honor; heed; *idolize; just love;* kneel to; look up to; make obeisance to; notice; *obeisance;* prefer; *quality;* respect; recognize; revere; salute; think of; *unmitigated ~;* venerate; worship; *xtry.;* yield; *zero contempt;*
**regimentation** *(n.)*: assiduity; bossiness; control; discipline; exactitude; fastidiousness; governance; handling; imperiousness; *just so;* keeping order; *law;* meticulousness; narrowness; order(liness); precision; *questionlessness;* regulation; rigorousness; self-control; strictness; systemization; tight control; uniformity; *very ordered; well-regulated; xtry. exactness;* yieldlessness; *zero laxity;*
**regimented** *(adj.)*: assiduous; busy; careful; controlled; diligent; exacting; fastidious; *great detail;* hard(line); imperious; *just so; keen;* laborious; logical; methodical; military; nit-picking; orderly; precise; particular; *quiddle;* regulated; strict; systematic; tightly-controlled; uniform; very exacting; well-regulated; *xtry. exacting;* yare; *zero tolerance;*
**region** *(n.)*: area; borough; county; district; enclave; field; ground; geographic ~; *hemisphere; imperial district;* jurisdiction; *kray [Rus.];* land; municipality; nome; *oblast [Rus.];* province; quadrant; realm; sector; territory; tract; ubiety; viceroyalty; ward; *x-sector;* yard; zone;
**regional** *(adj.)*: area; borough-wide; citywide; divisional; district; *environmental; field;* geographic; *hemispheric; inclusive;* jurisdictional; *kray [Rus.];* locational; local; *limited;* municipal; nome-related; *oblast [Rus.];* provincial; quadrant-wide; region-specific; sectional; territorial; *ubiety;* vicinal; ward-related; *x-zone; yard-wide;* zonal;
**register** *(n.)*: account; book; catalog; directory; docket; enrollment; file; *get down; history;* inventory; journal; kept record; list(ing); log; ledger; kust; muniment; muster roll; notation; *names;* official list; posted roll; print-out; *quill;* roll; roster; record; *statement;* table; tally sheet; *underwritten; verification;* written account; *xenagogy;* yellow sheet [crim. law]; zipper-book;
**register** *(v.)*: admit; annotate; *book;* check; catalog; denote; enter; enroll; enlist; *facts;* get down; handwrite; indicate; imprint; journalize; keep record; list; matriculate; mark down; note; *overwrite;* put down; quill; record; sign up; set (down); take down; underwrite; *vellum;* write (down); *x; yak; zay;*
**registration** *(n.)*: admission; admittance; booking; check-in; *draft;* enrollment; filing; getting registered; *handling;* itemization; joint- ~; keeping record; list(ing); matriculation; *names;* official ~; pre- ~; posting; *qualification;* registering; recording; *roll;* signing up (-in); tabulation; *university ~; verification;* writing in; *xfer; yellow sheet; zet [dial.];*
**regress** *(v.)*: about-face; backslide; backset; change back; declension; escheat; fall back; go back to; hark back; *impede;* jump back; *knock back;* lapse; move back; *non-advancement; over again;* plunge; *quit;* revert; retrogress; slide back; turn back; *undo;* veer downward; worsen; *xfer;* yield again to; *zoom down;*
**regression** *(n.)*: about-face; backsliding; change back; declension; escheat; falling back; go back to; heading back; *impediment;* jump back; *knock back;* lapse; move backward; *non-advancement; over again;* plunge; *quitting;* reversion; return; retrogression; sliding; turnabout; *undoing; vacating;* waning; worsening; *xfer;* yield again to; *zoom downward;*
**regret** *(n.)*: attrition; bemoaning; compunction; deploration; embarrassment; feeling sorry; grief; heartache; *inveigh; juddering; keen; lamentation;* mortification; *non-innocence;* oversorrow; pangs of sorrow; qualms; remorse; regretfulness; repining; sorrow; *tearfulness;* unhappiness; voice of conscience; woefulness; *xtry. ruefulness; yamim; zealous repentance;* [Ant. rejoicing]
**regret** *(v.)*: anguish; apologize; bemoan; bewail; commiserate; deplore; *emotional anguish;* feel sorry for; grieve; heartache; *inveigh; hate; judder; keen;* lament; mourn; *non-innocence;* oversorrow; *plead guilty; quain [arch.];* rue; sorrow; think better of; *unhappy; voice my ~;* wish it never happened; *xtry. ruefulness;* yearn; *zealously repent;* [Ant. rejoice]
**regretful** *(adj.)*: apologetic; broken; contrite; compunctious; despairing; *ejulation;* full of regret; grieved; heart-repentant; inconsolable; *juddering;* keenly ~; lamenting; mourning; *non-stubborn;* outcrying; penitent(ial); *quaking;* rueful; remorseful; sorrowful; sorry; turning; unhappy; *volte-face [F.];* wistful; woeful; *xtry. ruefulness; yearning;* zealous to repent; [Ant. remorseless]

**regrettable** *(adj.)*: awful; bad; contemptible; disappointing; execrable; *foul;* grievous; heartbreaking; inopportune; joyless; *kind of sad;* lamentable; miserable; *not desirable; odious; a* pity; quite ~; reprehensible; sad; *a* shame; terrible; too bad; unfortunate; very bad; wrong; xtry. sad; *yearning; zealless;*
**regular** *(adj.)*: average; basic; common; customary; *daily;* even; everyday; familiar; generic; general; habitual; inelaborate; jejune; known; lackluster; mundane; normal; ordinary; plain; quotidian; routine; run-of-the-mill; standard; typical; usual; vanilla; well-known; wonted; *x-type; year-out; zero variation;* [*Ant.* rare]
**regularity** *(n.)*: alikeness; balance; consistency; duplication; evenness; flatness; generalness; habitualness; identicalness; *just alike; kept even;* likeness; mundaneness; monotony; method; normality; non-difference; ordinariness; orderliness; predictability; *quotidian;* routineness; sameness; steadiness; typicality; timed intervals; usualness; uniformity; *very constant; weekly; x-type; yearly;* zero variation;
**regulate** *(v.)*: adjust; administrate; box in; control; check; direct; ensure; fine-tune; govern; hold back; inspect; *jurisdiction;* keep in check; limit; monitor; moderate; normalize; oversee; police; qualify; regularize; rubricate; rein in; supervise; stabilize; safeguard; temper; uniformize; verify; watch over; *x-type;* yeme; *zealously watch;* [*Ant.* relax]
**regulation** *(n.)*: act; bylaw; command; code; directive; edict; formality; guideline; *halacha* [Heb.]; instruction; *jus gentium* [L.]; *keleusmatic;* law; mandate; *national law;* ordinance; precept; *quo minus* [L.]; rule; rubrication; standard; *technicality; ukase; voice; word;* XO mandate; *yardstick; zakon* [Rus.]; [*Ant.* relaxation]
**rehearsal** *(n.)*: *audition;* bench test; conditioning; drill; dry run; dress ~; exercise; field ~; going over; honing; improvement; *job;* knocking into shape; lessons; mock run; night ~; *outfitting;* practice; *qualification;* recital; run-through; stage test; trial; *unofficial run; versing;* walkout; walk-through; *xenagogy;* yarking; *zealous training;*
**rehearse** *(v.)*: *again;* become proficient; condition; drill; do over; exercise; *foster;* go over; hone; improve; *jibe;* knock into shape; *learn;* make ready; *nurture; outfit;* practice; *qualify;* repeat; reiterate; ready; say over; train; *use;* verse; work out; whet; *xenagogy;* yarken; *zealously train;*
**reign** *(n.)*: authority; *bishopric;* control; dominion; empery; *first;* government; headship; influence; jurisdiction; kingship [masc.]; leadership; lordship; (middle) management; *necessitation;* oversight; power; queenship [fem.]; rule; sovereignty; *total authority;* use of authority; *vizierate;* wardenship; *xenagogy;* yard; *zakon [Rus.];*
**rein** *(n.)*: *app;* bridle; cord; check~; closed ~; draw ~; *equipment; fasten; gear;* harness ~; halter; hackamore; horse- ~; inspan; jerk-line; knee-halter; (longe) line; loop ~; martingal; neck ~; *object; pet-leash;* quinsell; restraint; rope; romal ~; strap; side ~; tack; *unite;* vasquero ~; *webbing; xfer;* yard-rope; *yoke zein;*
**reject** *(v.)*: adjure; abnegate; blackball; boot out; cast out; disdain; denounce; decline; deny; decline; eliminate; exclude; expel; forbear; gainsay; hate; *indignation;* jilt; jettison; kick at; lay aside; make a ~ion; not accept; nix; naysay; oust; ostracize; *pitch; quit;* rebuff; refuse; recuse; spurn; snub; turn down (-away); throw away; turn down; utterly ~; veto; *withhold; wrath;* x-out; *yank;* zero out; [*see* abhor; persecute; *Ant.* receive]
**rejection** *(n.)*: abjuration; blackballing; casting aside; disdain; denunciation; declination; dismissal; denial; elimination; expulsion; forbearance; *giving the boot;* heave-ho; impugnation; jilting; *kesting; looking down on;* making a ~; non-acceptance; naysaying; ousting; ostracism; *pocket veto; quit;* refusal; recusation; spurning; snubbing; throwing away; turndown; utter ~; veto; walking papers; x'ing out; *yieldlessness; zeroing out;* [*see* persecution; *Ant.* reception]
**rejoice** *(v.)*: *applaud;* beam; bless; celebrate; cheer; delight; *dance;* elate; exuberate; exhilarate; exult; feel happy; glory; glee; gleam; hearten; *imparadised;* joy; jubilate; *kill the fatted calf;* lilt; *laugh;* make merry; *nowell;* overjoy; praise; party; *quiver;* radiate; revel; sing; shout; triumph; *thrill; uplift; vivify; wonder;* wallow in; *xanadu; yell; zealous;* [*see* praise; *Ant.* regret]

**rejoicing** *(n.)*: animation; bliss; cheer(fulness); celebration; delight; exultation; elation; euphoria; felicity; gladness; glee; happiness; intoxication; joy(fulness); jubilation; *keenness;* lightheartedness; merriment; *nowell;* overjoy; pleasure; *queme;* radiance; reveling; rapture; sunniness; satisfaction; thrill; *uplifted; vivacity*; winsomeness; *xanadu; yelling;* zestfulness; [*Ant.* regret]

**rekindle** *(v.)*: alight; burn again; combust; deflagrate; enkindle; fire up; get revived; hearten; ignite; incite; jar; kindle again; light again; *motivate; nudge;* overburn; provoke; *quick-match;* relume; rouse anew; revivify; stir-up; stoke; torch again; ustion; *vulcanize;* wake up; *xylophyrography; yearn; zap over;*

**relapse** *(n.)*: *again;* atavism; backslide; backset; change back; declension; escheat; falling back; go back to; heading back; *impediment;* jump back; *knock back;* lapse; move backward; *non-advancement; over again;* plunge; *quitting;* reversion; return; regression; retroversion; recidivism; setback; slide; turnabout; *undoing; vacating;* waning; *xfer;* yielding again; *zoom downward;* [*Ant.* recovery]

**relapse** *(v.)*: *again;* backslide; backset; change back; declension; escheat; fall back; go back to; hark back; *impede;* jump back; *knock back;* lapse; move back; *non-advancement; over again;* plunge; *quit;* revert; return; regress; retrovert; slide back; turn back; *undo;* veer downward; wane; *xfer;* yield again; *zoom downward;* [*Ant.* recover]

**relate** *(v. link)*: associate; bear on; connect; correlate; *draws; entwine;* fit with; goes together with; hook into; inter~; join; knit; link; makes connection; match; *network; offshoot;* pertain; *qualify;* refer; regard; set to; tie (into); unite; *v-link; with; xenograft;* yoke; *zip;*

**relate** *(v. tell)*: articulate; bespeak; convey; communicate; declare; express; *fit with;* give; hold forth; impart; indicate; *jaw; key in;* let out; mention; notify; observe; proclaim; quoth; relay; say; tell; utter; voice; word; *xenophonia;* yak; *zero in;*

**related** *(adj.)*: akin; agnate; associated; brethren; cognate; connected; concomitant; *daughter;* enate [both fem.]; family; flesh and blood; father [masc.]; german; *homologous;* interrelation; joined; kin(dred); linked; matching; *non-differing;* of a common root; parent; *qua est eadem* [L.]; relative; sister [fem.]; *tribe; ubeity;* very closely ~; *with; x-link;* yoked; *zero difference;*

**relation** *(n. connection)*: association; application; appurtenance; bearing; bond; connection; correlation; commonality; direct bearing; established link; family; grouping; *have to do with;* involvement; inter~; joint link; kinship; link; mutual bond; nexus; nearness; *oneness;* proximity; pertinence; propinquity; *qualification;* relationship; relevance; *share;* tie(-in); union; *v-link; with; x-connection;* yoke; *z-link;*

**relation** *(n. family)*: ∗ agnate; alliance; brethren; brother; blood relative; child; cousin; daughter; *established;* family (member); flesh and blood; father; grandparent; *horde;* interrelation; *junior;* kin(folk); living relative; mother; member of the family; near kinsman; niece; *oneness;* parent; *quarter-blooded;* relative; sister; tribesman; uncle; *vein;* wife; *x-link; y-chromosome; zet* [dial.];

**relationship** *(n.)*: association; bond; blood relation; brotherhood; connection; consanguinity; *dealings*; *enation;* family; german; *homologous;* interrelation; *joining;* kinship; link; *marriage;* nexus; *origin;* part; *qua est eadem* [L.]; relation; rapport; sisterhood; *shared;* tie; *ubeity; v-link; with; x-link;* yoke; *z-link;*

**relative** *(adj.)*: applicable; bearing; connected; comparative; directly related; *established; fit;* germane; homologous; important; joined; *key;* linked; material; *non-separate;* operative; proportional; pertinent; particular; *quo ad* [L.]; regarding; relevant; respecting; relating; significant; touching; to do with; unto; virtual; vis-à-vis; with regard to; *xfer;* yoked; *z-link;*

**relax** *(v.)*: aestivate; *abate;* break; breathe easy; calm down; *discontinue;* ease up; forbear; give rest; have a break; idle; *jadedness;* knock off; lounge; lie down; let up; loosen; mellow out; nap; *oversleep;* pause; quiet down; rest; release; slack off (-up); sit down; slacken; slumber; take it easy; unwind; unlax; vacation; wait; wind; *x-rest;* yawn; zizz; [*Ant.* rouse]

**relaxation** *(n.)*: *aestivation;* break; breathing easy; calm; *dolce far niente* [It.]; easing; forbearance; *gala day;* hold; idleness; *jaunt;* kip; leisure; letup; *moderation;* night rest; *oversleeping;* pause; quietude; recreation; rest; respite; slackening; time out; unwinding; vacation; wait; *x-rest; yawning;* zizz; [*Ant.* rigor]

**relay** *(v.)*: *assign;* bring; convey; deliver; *export;* forward; give; haul; impart; janker; kurvey; locomote; move; mail; *non-retention;* offload; pass on; *quarter-cart;* render; send; transfer; transmit; *uptake; vest; waft;* xfer; yanker [Br.]; zip;

**release** *(v.)*: allow to go; *bail out;* clear; discharge; *deliver;* emit; emancipate; free; fire; *get out; give freedom to;* hand over; issue; *jettison; kest;* liberate; loose; let go (-out); manumit; not detain; *open;* put out; quit; relinquish; set free; take out; unshackle; unchain; unhand; untie; unpen; unmoor; vent; *walk; xfer; yokeless; zoneless;*

**relent** *(v.)*: acquiesce; buckle; concede; desist; end; forbear; give in; halt; *indulge; jib;* knuckle under; leave off; *moderate;* not resist; *obey; pause;* quit; relinquish; stop; succumb; surrender; *terminate; undo; vacate;* withdraw; *white flag;* x; yield; *zeroize;* [*Ant.* resist]

**relentless** *(adj.)*: adamant; bound (and determined); constant; determined; dogged; enduring; firm; going on; hard; hell-bent; high-pressure; inexorable; incessant; inexhaustible; insistent; indefatigable; importune; *jusqu'au bout* [F.]; keeping on; lasting; merciless; never-tiring; obstinate; persistent; persevering; *quitting never;* resolute; steadfast; steady; tenacious; unrelenting; unyielding; unstoppable; unremitting; undeterred; very steady; weariless; *x-cending;* yieldless; zealous; [*Ant.* relenting]

**relevance** *(n.)*: application; bearing; connection; direct bearing; effect; fitness; germaneness; *heart;* importance; justification; keen ~; logical connection; meaning; *not unrelated; objective;* purpose; point; pertinence; quintessence; relation; significance; tie-in; use; value; weight; *xenenthesis; yet related; zeug [G.];*

**relevant** *(adj.)*: applicable; *ad rem* [L.]; belonging; befitting; connected; directly ~; *essential;* fitting; germane; having to do with; important; justified; keenly ~; logically connected; meshing; not unrelated; on the mark; pertinent; quintessential; related; significant; tied-in; useful; valuable; weighty; *xenenthesis; yet related; zeug [G.];*

**reliable** *(adj.)*: accurate; believable; committed; dependable; ever-faithful; faithful; guaranteed; honest; incontrovertible; *just; keen;* loyal; most faithful; never-failing; *open-and-shut case;* proven; questionless; responsible; steadfast; sure; trustworthy; unfailing; valid; well-trusted; *xtry;* yeomanly; *zero doubt;*

**reliance** *(n.)*: adherence; belief; confidence; dependence; entrusting; faith; hope; *immovability; just believe; knowledge; looking to; mainstay;* non-doubt; *overconfidence;* persuasion; questionlessness; resting; stand; trust; upholding; volitional faith; wholehearted ~; *xel [arch.]; y'faith* [arch.]; *zero-doubt;*

**relief** *(n.)*: abatement; alleviation; assistance; break; comfort; disburdening; deliverance; easefulness; freedom; giving assistance; help; *intercede; just-in-time;* kindness; lightening; letup; mitigation; *non-hindrance; opening;* palliation; quarter; reprieve; respite; support; taking the edge off; unburdening; venting; working to help; *xtry.; yielding; zero hindrance;*

**relieve** *(v.)*: alleviate; assuage; bail out; curtail; comfort; cure; deliver; disencumber; disburden; ease; free from grief; give assistance; help; *intercede; just-in-time; kindness;* lighten; lessen; lend a hand; mitigate; *not hinder;* off-load; palliate; *pitch in;* quiet; reduce; remove; rid; slacken; take the edge off; unburden; unlade; vent; work to help; *xtry.; yield;* zeroize;

**religion** *(n.)*: affiliation; beliefs; church; creed; confession; cult; denomination; doctrine; devotion; *ecclesiology;* faith; faction; group; good works; hierology; isagogics; *Jesus; know-so salvation;* liturgy; mainline denomination; *morals; non-atheism;* organization; persuasion; piety; *qualms;* ritualism; religiosity; rite; sect; system; theology; ule; values; viewpoint; virtue; wing; *Xavarian; Yoga; zootheism;* [*see* faith, Christianity]

    **Religions**: Anglican; Buddhism; Catholicism; Confucianism; Deism; Eastern Orthodox; Episcopalian; Fakirism; Gnosticism; Hinduism; Islam; Judaism; Karaite Judaism; Lutheranism; Methodism; Mormonism; Neo-evangelicalism; Orthodox; Protestantism; Presbyterianism; Quaker; Russian Orthodox; Rosicrucianism; Shintoism; Taoism; Theosophy; Unitarianism; Vedantism; Wesleyanism; Xinto; Yoga; Zen;

**religious** *(adj.)*: archiepiscopal; *believing;* clerical; congregational; denominational; devout; ecclesiastical; faithful; God-fearing; hierarchical; holier-than-thou; *indoctrinated;* jacobite; *kerygmatic;* liturgical; moralistic; *mystical; monastic;* numinous; orthodox; pious; priestly; prelatical; prayerful; *quoad sacra* [L.]; reverential; religiose; solemn; sectarian; sanctimonious; theistic; ultramontane; virtuous; worshipful; *Xavarian; yielded; zealous;* [*see* pious; *Ant.* reprobate]
**relinquish** *(v.)*: abandon; abdicate; abjure; break; bow out; back out; cut out; cast off; cede; desert; discard; disown; evacuate; forsake; forfeit; forswear; give up (-over); hand over; *ignore;* jettison; kest; leave; let go; *make an end;* not pursue; opt out; pitch; quit; renounce; resign; surrender; turn over; unload; vacate; waive; *xfer;* yield; *zero out;* [*Ant.* retain]
**reluctance** *(n.)*: aversion; *bashfulness;* caution; disinclination; *edginess;* foot-dragging; guardedness; hesitation; indisposition; jackalence; *keeping away;* lack of enthusiasm; mousiness; non-resolution; nolition; opposition; passive resistance; qualm; reticence; reluctancy; slowness; tottering; uncertainty; unwillingness; vacillation; wavering; *xenophobia;* yo-yoing; zeallessness;
**reluctant** *(adj.)*: averse; bucking; cautious; disinclined; *edgy;* faltering; guarded; hesitant; indisposed; jackalent; *keeping away;* laggard; loath; mousy; not eager; opposed; passively resistant; questioning; reticent; renitent; slow; tottering; unwilling; vacillating; wary; *xenophobic;* yarrow; zealless; [*Ant.* raring]
**rely** *(v.)*: accept; believe in; commit; count on; depend; entrust; *faith; give heart to;* have faith; inwardly trust; judge faithful; *know;* look to; *mainstay; non-doubt; overtrust;* put confidence in; *questionless;* rest in; stand on; trust; unwaveringly trust; very much ~; wholeheartedly ~; *x; y'faith* [*arch.*]; zealously embrace;
**remain** *(v.)*: await; bide; continue; dwell; endure; follow on; go on; hang around; inhabit; *just keep on;* keep; linger; maintain; not move; nest; outlast; persist; prolong; perpetuate; *quietude;* resume; stay; stick; tarry; uphold; *very last;* wait; *xenize;* yede; *zero movement;*
**remainder** *(n.)*: amount left over; balance; contingent; dividend; excess; *fraction; group;* holdover; item; *jag; kept;* leavings; net amount; oddments; portion remaining; quantity; remains; residue; rest; residual; residuary; surplus; *total;* unused amount; *volume; weight;* xtr.; yet remaining portion; *zum* [*dial.*];
**remake** *(v.)*: alter; build again; correct; change; do over; enhance; fix; *grow; heighten;* improve; *juvenate; key move; liven-up;* make over; novate; overhaul; *put right; qualify;* redesign; re-create; reform; revise; revamp; rework; renovate; switch; transform; upgrade; vamp; *work; xenomorph; yaw; zigzag;*
**remark** *(n.)*: answer; annotation; bespeaking; crack; comment; declaration; editorial; exclamation; *forementioning;* gloss; *hold forth;* interjection; insinuation; indication; *judgment; keying in;* language; mention; note; observance; pronouncement; *quote;* report; statement; *treatment;* utterance; voicing one's opinion; words; *xtry. ~;* yakking; zinger;
**remark** *(v.)*: answer; articulate; blurt out; bespeak; comment; declare; express; *foremention;* give comments; *have say;* interject; indicate; *jaw; key in;* let out; mention; note; observe; pipe up; *proclaim;* quoth; relate; say; tell; utter; voice; word; *xenophonia;* yak; zinger;
**remarkable** *(adj.)*: amazing; brilliant; breathtaking; commendable; distinguished; divine; exceptional; fantastic; great; heavenly; incredible; jim-dandy; keen; legendary; marvelous; notable; outstanding; praiseworthy; phenomenal; *quantum* [L.]; rememberable; superb; splendid; terrific; unbelievable; virtuous; wonderful; xtry.; *yippee!;* zizzy;
**remedial** *(adj.)*: advantageous; beneficial; curative; corrective; doctor-endorsed; effective; favorable; gainful; good; healing; iatric; *julep;* kinic; *lohock;* medicinal; *nostrum;* officinal; pharmaceutical; purgative; palliative; quinic; recuperative; restorative; salutary; therapeutic; useful; vulnerary; *worthwhile; xenobiotic; yieldful; zopissa* [*arch.*];
**remedy** *(n.)*: antidote; biologic; cure; drug; elixir; fix; *glycerol;* healing agent; *injection; julep; kinic;* lohock; medicine; natural cure; *oxacillin;* pharmaceutical; quick-fix; redress; serum; salve; treatment; ule; vaccine; wonder drug; xenobiotic; yanggona; *zopissa* [*arch.*];

**remedy** *(v.)*: amend; benefit; correct; cure; doctor; *ease;* fix; get working; help; harmonize; improve; *julep; kilter; level out;* mend; *neogenesis;* overhaul; patch up; quick-fix; repair; rectify; right; redress; set right; treat; *upbuild;* vamp; work on; *x-fix;* yield help; *zip back together;*

**remember** *(v.)*: awaken memory; bethink; bring to mind; bear in mind; consider; commit to memory; dwell on; evoke; *foremembered;* get into one's head; hark back; imbibe; insoul; jog one's memory; keep in mind; know; learn by heart; memorize; mind; not forget; open up memories; put to mind; *quicken mind;* retain; recall; recollect; reflect; reminisce; summon; think of; treasure; unlock; *venerate;* waken; *well-remembered; xfer; yet remembered;* zero in;

**remembrance** *(n.)*: attendance; bearing in mind; cognizance; commemoration; celebration; dwelling; evoking; flashback; going back; hypermnesia; impression; jogging; keeping in mind; looking back; memory; memorial; nostalgia; observation; past memory; *quick-to-remember;* recollection; reflection; retention; reminiscence; rote; *short-term memory;* thought; tribute; *unaided recall; veneration; well-remembered; xfer;* yesteryear; zeroing in;

**remind** *(v.)*: awaken memory; bethink; call to mind; *drop a reminder;* evoke; *foremembered;* give the cue; hint; *inform;* jog one's memory; keep in memory; let it be remembered; mind; mention; nudge; open up memories; put to mind; quicken ones memory; recall; summon; think of; *unlock;* verify; warn; *xfer; yet remembered;* zero in;

**reminisce** *(v.)*: awaken memories; bring to mind; conjure up memories; dwell on; evoke; *foremembered;* go back; *hit; insoul;* jog the memory; keep remembering; *know;* look back; mind; *not forgotten;* open up memories; put to mind; *quicken mind;* recollect; relive; remember; reflect; summon; think back; unlock; *venerate;* walk down memory lane; *xfer; yet unforgotten;* zero in;

**reminiscent** *(adj.)*: allusive; bringing to mind; conjuring; *dwelling on;* evocative; *foremembered; grand memories;* hinting; indicative; *jogging one's memory;* kept in remembrance; like; memoried; *not forgotten; opening up;* putting to mind; *quickening;* redolent; remindful; recollective; suggestive; thinking of; *unlocking; very ~; well-remembered; xfer; yet remembered;* zero in;

**remiss** *(adj.)*: abandoning; behindhand; careless; disregardful; dilatory; delaying; eliding; forgetful; fabian; good-for-nothing; heedless; inattentive; *jim-jam; kim-kam;* lacking responsibility; lax; *missing;* neglectful; negligent; overly-forgetful; procrastinatory; quick-to-forget; regardless; slack; thoughtless; unmindful; very neglectful; without regard; *xtry. ~;* yet irresponsible; *zero responsibility;*

**remission** *(n.)*: acquittal; absolution; amnesty; blotting out; clemency; clearing; disregard; excusing; exculpation; exoneration; forbearance; grace; *help;* indemnity; justification; kindness; leniency; mercy; non-prosecution; overlooking; pardon; quittance; remittance; reprieve; stay; taking away; *tabula rasa* [L.]; *unshackling;* voiding; *washing; x-ing out; yielding;* zeroing out; [see grace]

**remissness** *(n.)*: abdication; blunder; carelessness; disregard; delinquency; error; forgetfulness; failure; *good-for-nothing;* heedlessness; inattention; inobservance; irresponsibility; jumping over; *kesting;* listlessness; laches; lack; missing; mistake; neglect; negligence; omission; oversight; passing over; *quickness to forget;* recklessness; shirking; slight; slip-up; thoughtlessness; unfaithfulness; *vagueness; wandering; xtry. disregard; yemeles* [arch.]; *zero responsibility;*

**remit** *(v.)*: alleviate; bestow; cancel; disburse; dispatch; ease; expedite; furnish; free; give; hand (over); impart; *justify;* kit; lessen; make payment; *non-retention;* offer; pardon; provide; pay; *quantity;* reduce; release; render; supply; send; settle; satisfy; transfer; unhand; vail; weaken; weigh; xfer; yield; *zero out debt;*

**remittance** *(n.)*: acquittance; bestowal; conferral; disbursement; endowment; furnishing; giving; handing (over); imparting; *jettison; kit; liquidation;* making payment; *non-retention;* offering; provision; paying; quittance; rendering; supply; transferring; unhanding; *vail; weighing;* xferring; yielding; *zero out debt;*

**remnant** *(n.)*: amount; bit; balance; constituent part; detritus; element; fragment; fraction; few; *grain; group;* hunk; *iota;* jib; kernel; leftover; little part; leavings; morsel; minority; *nip;* ort; offcut; ounce; piece; part; percentage; *quantity;* residue; remainder; small amount; scrap; segment; trace; tinge; tidbit; umbrage; vestige; wit; *x-mal [G.]; yngot [arch.]; zum [arch.];*

**remorse** *(n.)*: attrition; brokenness; contrition; compunction; disgrace; emotional pain; feeling sorry; grief; guilt; heartache; *inveigh; juddering;* keen pain; *lamentation;* mortification; *non-innocence;* oversorrow; penitence; qualm; regret; remorsefulness; ruefulness; self-guilt; sorrow; *tearfulness;* unhappiness; voice of conscience; woefulness; *x-out; yamim; zeallessness;*

**remorseful** *(adj.)*: ashamed; broken; contrite; despairing; *embarrassed;* feeling sorry; grieving; heart-repentant; *inveighing; juddering;* keenly ~; lamenting; mourning; not proud; outcrying; penitent(tial); *quaking;* regretful; sorry; self-accusing; *tearful;* unhappy; *volte-face* [F.]; wistful; woeful; *x-out; yearning;* zealous to repent; [*Ant.* ashamed]

**removal** *(n.)*: abstraction; ablation [med.]; booting [slang]; clearing off; culling; deletion; disposal; elimination; extraction; erasure; freeing; getting rid of; hauling away; *impeachment;* junking; kicking out; leaving; lifting; moving out; *negate;* offloading; ousting; purging; *quitting;* removing; ridding; subtraction; taking away; transplanting; unloading; vacating; withdrawal; xfer; yanking; *zeroing out;*

**remove** *(v.)*: abstract; boot [slang]; clear; cull; delete; deduct; displace; eliminate; extract; erase; eradicate; *free; flee;* get rid of; haul away; *impeach; junk;* kick out; leave; lift; lop off; move out; *negate;* offload; oust; purge; *quit;* rid; subtract; take away; transplace; transplant; unload; vacate; withdraw; winnow; xfer; yank; *zero out;*

**rename** *(v.)*: assign new name; brand; change name; dub; *entitle; forename;* give new name to; hail as; *indicate; jurisdiction; known as;* label; *misname;* nickname; *ordain;* put a new name to; *quiring;* restyle; redesignate; style; surname; tag; *use; vocable; word; xenonym;* yclept; *zoon;*

**render** *(v.)*: afford; accord; bestow; confer; deliver; endow; furnish; give; hand (over); impart; *jettison;* kit; leave; mete; *non-retention;* offer; present; *quicken;* remit; supply; transfer; unhand; *vest; weigh;* xfer; yield; *zip;*

**rendition** *(n.)*: account; arrangement; brand; characterization; description; depiction; edition; expression; form; gloss; *harmonization;* interpretation; *justification; kind; literal translation;* metaphrase; *new version; optimization;* portrayal; presentment; *qualified rendering;* report; rendering; stylizing; translation; *update;* version; *wording; xlation; yielding; zay [dial.];*

**renege** *(v.)*: abrogate; break one's word; backword; backpedal; change mind; default; *err;* fail; go back; *honorless;* invalidate; jilt; *knowingly lie;* leave; lie; make void; not fulfill; *omit;* pull back; quit; refuse to honor; rescind; set aside; take back; unsay; verneuk; welch; *x-out; yentz; zeroize;*

**renounce** *(v.)*: abjure; abnegate; break with; cast off; disavow; disclaim; end; forswear; forsake; give up; hand over; invalidate; *jump off;* kest; kiss goodbye; leave; make relinquishment; not claim; *overturn;* pitch; quitclaim; repudiate; retract; relinquish; recant; surrender; shun; turn away; unsay; void; withdraw; x; *yield; zero claim;*

**renovate** *(v.)*: ameliorate; build up; better; completely redo; do over; enhance; embellish; furbish; fix up; gentrify; *help;* improve; *just do over; keen; leap;* make over; new-furnish; new-model; overhaul; prettify; *quick makeover;* remodel; refurbish; recondition; redo; reface; refit; soup up; titivate; upbuild; vamp (up); work on; *x-fix; yarken; zizzify;*

**renovation** *(n.)*: amelioration; building up; bettering; complete ~; development; enhancement; embellishment; furbishing; facelift; gentrification; *help;* instauration; improvement; *just do over; keen; leap;* makeover; new look; overhaul; *progress;* quick makeover; remodeling; refurbishment; reconditioning; refashioning; souping up; titivation; upbuilding; vamping (up); work; *x-fix; yarkening; zesting up;*

**renown** *(n.)*: acclaim; *beloved;* celebrity; distinction; eminence; fame; greatness; honor; illustriousness; *jubilation; kudos;* legend; magnificence; notoriety; note; *outstanding;* prominence; *quality;* reputation; repute; status; *talked-about;* universal admiration; veneration; world-renown; *xtry.;* yichus; *zealous love;*

**rent** *(n.)*: ablocation; back~; charter; due amount; *emphyteutic;* figure; *get for hire;* housage; installment; *jiggy [Br.]; keep;* lease; liferent; monthly ~; *number;* overpayment; payment; quit~; rental amount; sublease; total amount; usufruct; *value;* white- ~; x- ~; yearly ~; *z-score;*

**rent** *(v.)*: ablocate; buy time; charter; *due;* engage; *fetch;* get for hire; hire; *installment; jiggy [Br.]; keep;* lease; let; *monthly; nab;* obtain; pay ~ on; *quitrent;* render hire; sublet; sublease; tenant; take on; underlet; *value; white ~; xfer; yearly rent; z-score;*

**renunciation** *(n.)*: abjuration; abnegation; breaking with; casting off; disavowal; disclaiming; ending; forsaking; giving up; handing over; invalidation; *jumping off;* kesting; leaving; *making ~;* negation; *overturning;* palinody; quitting; quitclaim; repudiation; renouncement; surrender; turning away; unsaying; voiding; withdrawal; x-ing; *yielding; zero claim;*

**repair** *(n.)*: adjustment; *betterment;* correction; doctoring; darning; *establishment;* fix; *get working;* harmonization; improvement; *jury-rig; kilter; level out;* mending; *neogenesis;* overhaul; patch-up; quick-fix; reparation; service; tune-up; touch-up; *upbuilding;* vamp; work; *x-fix; yarken; zip back together;*

**repair** *(v.)*: adjust; *better;* correct; doctor; darn; emend; fix; get working; harmonize; improve; *jury-rig; kilter; level out;* mend; make good; *neogenesis;* overhaul; patch up; quick-fix; remedy; restore; rectify; right; set aright; service; stitch; set; tune up; touch up; tinker; *upbuild;* vamp (up); work on; *x-fix; yarken; zip back together;*

**repay** *(v.)*: acquit; balance; compensate; disburse; equalize; fix; give back; *hand over;* indemnify; *justify;* kick back; level out; make restitution; *non-indebted;* offset; pay back; *quid pro quo [L.];* requite; recompense; remunerate; reimburse; reward; settle up; square (up); *tender;* undo damage; vindicate; weigh out; *x-out; yield;* zero-out one's debt;

**repayment** *(n.)*: amends; becoming debt-free; compensation; drawback; equivalent; earnings; fixing; giving back; hire; indemnity; *justification;* kickback; leveling out; money-back; *non-indebted;* obligation; offset; payment; quittal; requital; recompense; remuneration; reimbursement; reward; refund; rebate; return; reparation; settlement; satisfaction; *total due; undo damage;* vindication; wages; *x-ing out; yield;* zeroing-out one's debt;

**repeal** *(n.)*: abrogation; annulment; abolishment; bringing to naught; canceling; disannulment; ending; *finishing off; going back;* halting; invalidation; *jumping back;* killing; *leaving; making void;* nullification; overturning; putting an end to; quashing; revocation; retraction; rescindment; reversal; stopping; turning over; *undoing;* voidance; withdrawal; *x-ing; yanking; zeroing out;*

**repeal** *(v.)*: abrogate; annul; abolish; bring to naught; cancel; disannul; end; *finish off; go back;* halt; invalidate; *jump back;* kill; *leave;* make an end; null(ify); overturn; put an end to; quash; revoke; retract; rescind; reverse; stop; turn over; take back; *terminate; undo;* void; vitiate; withdraw; *x-ing; yank; zero out;*

**repeat** *(v.)*: *again;* beat; copy; do again; duplicate; echo; *follow;* go on; hammer; harp; inculcate; iterate; imitate; *just like;* keep up; *likeness;* mimic; *non-original; over again;* parrot; *quadruplicate;* retell; recur; reiterate; reduplicate; replicate; restate; rehearse; say again; tell over; tautologize; utter again; verbigerate; *without end; xerograph; yieldless; zoomimic;*

**repel** *(v.)*: avert; beat back; chase off; drive back; defend; *estop;* fend off; get; hold off; indispose; *jar;* keep away; lick; make of no effect; nauseate; offend; oppose; prevent; parry; propulse; push back; quash; repulse; resist; stave off; turn away; upset; vitiate; ward off; withstand; *x-out; yieldless;* zilch; [*see* repulse]

**repent** *(v.)*: abhor; bewail; change mind (-heart); deplore; *emotional;* feel regret; go back; hate sin; *inveigh; judder; keen;* lament over; make about-face; *non-innocence; overturn; penitent; quain* [arch.]; regret; rue; sorrow; turn; *U-turn;* veer; wish it never happened; *xtry. sorrowful; yield; zealously ~;*
**repentance** *(n.)*: attrition; about-face; brokenness; contrition; change of heart; despair; *ejulation;* feeling sorry; grief; heart-repentance; *inveigh; juddering; keen; lamentation;* mourning; *non-stubbornness; outcry;* penitence; *quaking;* repenting; regret; sorrow; *sackcloth and ashes;* turning; turnaround; U-turn; *volte-face* [F.]; woefulness; *xtry. regret; yamim nora'im* [Heb.]; zeal to repent; [*see* remorse]
**repentant** *(adj.)*: apologetic; broken; contrite; despairing; *ejulation;* feeling sorry; grieving; heart-repentant; *inveighing; juddering;* keenly ~; lamenting; mourning; *non-stubborn;* outcrying; penitent(tial); *quaking;* regretful; rueful; remorseful; sorry; *tender-hearted;* turning; *U-turn; volte-face* [F.]; woeful; *xtry. sorrowful; yearning;* zealous to repent;
**repetition** *(n.)*: again and again; beating; copying; duplication; echo; following; going on; hammering; inculcation; iteration; imitation; *just like; keeping it up; likeness;* mimicking; noninterruption; *over again;* parroting; *quadruplication;* retelling; recurrence; reiteration; repeating; rote; saying again; telling over; uttering again; verbigeration; *without end; xerograph; yieldless; zoomimic;*
**repetitive** *(adj.)*: again; boring; cyclic; continuing; dull; emulative; flat; *gapless;* humdrum; iterant; iterative; jejune; *keeps going;* laborious; monotonous; non-exciting; ongoing; periodic; quotidian; routine; repeating; recurring; serial; tedious; uninteresting; *vapid;* wearisome; *xtr. times;* yawnful; *zestless;*
**replace** *(v.)*: alter; *better;* change; displace; exchange; fill in; follow; go instead; *heighten;* interchange; *jockey; key trade; let be exchanged;* make exchange; *novate;* outplace; put back; *quid pro quo* [L.]; return; replenish; restore; revise; supplant; swap; switch; substitute; supersede; trade; take the place of; upgrade; use instead; *vamp; work; xfer; yaw;* zwap [dial.];
**replenish** *(v.)*: accomplish; bring back; charge up; deliver; *energize;* fill; freshen; get replenished; *heighten;* imbue; *jam-pack; kit;* load up; make full; newly fill; *overfill;* put back; *quantify;* replace; refill; restore; restock; renew; stock up; top off; *unhand; volume; well-replenished; xfer; yield; zero space leftover;*
**replete** *(adj.)*: abounding; brimming; chock-full; dripping; effuse; full; fraught; gorged; heaping; inundated; jam-packed; *keenly full;* loaded; mounding; numerous; overflowing; packed; *quantity;* rife; rich; sated; stuffed; teeming; utterly full; very full; well-supplied; *xtra;* yote; *zillions;*
**reply** *(n.)*: answer; *backtalk;* counter; comeback; declaration; defense; *epistle;* evasive ~; explanation; *finding;* general ~; handling; input; judgment; *key input;* letter; message; *note;* outcome; *plea;* quotient; response; retort; rejoinder; riposte; rebuttal; statement; short ~; *treatment;* utterance; verdict; written ~; witty ~; *xtry.;* ~; yes-answer; zinger;
**reply** *(v.)*: answer; back answer; counter; come back with; declare; deal with; express; *echo;* figure out; give ~; handle; intimate; input; judge; *key in;* lay to rest; make reply; *note;* orate; *pipe up; quotient;* respond; retort; riposte; rejoin; return; rebut; say; state; snap back; tell; utter; voice; word; x; yes; zero in;
**report** *(n.)*: account; annual ~; bulletin; cahier; coverage; chronicle; description; document; enlightenment; full ~; general ~; handout; *how it is;* information; journal; *keeping abreast;* letter; monthly ~; notification; news; official report; proclamation; quarterly ~; record; story; statement; testimony; tale; update; version; word; weekly; *xfer;* yearly ~; *zeroing in;*
**report** *(v.)*: answer; announce; assert; bid; bear record; communicate; debrief; express; enlighten; familiarize; *facts; fame;* give account; hold forth; indicate; *jaw; key in;* let out; make ~; notify; observe; proclaim; quoth; relate; state; tell; utter; voice; word; *xfer ~;* yak; *zero in;*
**reprehensible** *(adj.)*: abominable; bad; contemptible; detestable; evil; foul; gross; horrid; ignoble; *jaded;* knavish; loathsome; miserable; nefarious; offensive; pathetic; *quad;* revolting; repugnant; sinful; shameful; terrible; uncouth; vile; wicked; *x-rated;* yucky; zhlubby;

**reprehension** *(n.)*: abomination; badness; contemptibleness; detestableness; evil; foulness; grossness; horridness; ignobleness; *jadedness;* knavishness; loathsomeness; miserableness; nefariousness; offensiveness; perfidiousness; *quad;* repugnance; shamefulness; terribleness; uncouthness; vileness; wickedness; *x-rating;* yuckiness; zhlubbiness; [*Ant.* rectitude]

**represent** *(v.)*: act for; betoken; connote; denote; designate; epitomize; emblemize; fill in for; give picture of; have meaning; indicate; *judge; key to; likened to;* mean; *notate;* omenate; picture; personate; *quiddit;* refer to; stand for; signify; symbolize; speak for; typify; use for; *under~;* visually depict; *word; x-type; yield; zay [arch.];*

**representation** *(n.)*: appearance; betokening; connotation; depiction; emblem; figure; graven image; *hewn image;* image; icon; *just like; keen resemblance;* likeness; mock-up; model; *notation; object;* presentment; picture; *quiddit;* replica; representment; symbol; simulacrum; token; type; *used for;* view; wooden image; *x-type; yield;* 'zactly [slang];

**representative** *(n.)*: agent; ambassador; bearer of tidings; consul; correspondent; commissary; diplomat; delegate; envoy; emissary; foreign minister; *genotype; herald;* intelligencer; internuncio; *jurisdictional ~; kurveyor;* liaison; legate; messenger; *member of Congress;* nuncio; negotiant; *official ~;* officer; proclaimer; proxy; *quidnunc [L.];* representer; substitute; spokesman; tidings-bearer; *updater; utterer;* vicar; voicer; walking delegate; *x-man; yamen* [Chin.]; *zip man;*

**repress** *(v.)*: *afflict;* bind; constrict; curb; control; crush; dominate; *enslave;* fetter; gag; govern; hold back; inhibit; jam; keep down; kill; limit; master; *nullify;* oppress; put down; quelch; quash; rein in; rule; shush; silence; suppress; subdue; stifle; tyrannize; use; vitiate; weigh; *x;* yoke; zap;

**repression** *(n.)*: *affliction;* binding; control; crackdown; domination; *enslaving;* fettering; governance; holding back; inhibition; jamming; keeping down; limiting; mastering; *nullification;* oppression; putting down; quashing; rule; suppression; tyranny; *using;* vitiation; weighing down; *x-ing;* yoking; zapping;

**reprieve** *(n.)*: alleviation; break; comfort; deliverance; easing; freedom; giving assistance; help; intermission; *just-in-time;* keen relief; liberation; mitigation; *non-hindrance; opening;* palliation; quarter; relief; respite; support; taking the edge off; *undergirding; vacation; week off; xtry.;* yielding; zero hindrance;

**reprimand** *(n.)*: admonishment; bashing; censure; chiding; denouncement; excoriation; flaying; going-over; harassment; increpation; jawing; knocking; lambasting; lashing; monitory; nagging; objurgation; pillory; *questioning;* rebuke; scolding; telling off; upbraiding; vitriol; warning; *xuld [arch.];* yelling at; *zapping;*

**reprimand** *(v.)*: admonish; berate; castigate; denounce; excoriate; flay; give talking to; harangue; inveigh; jump down one's throat; knock; lambaste; *macerate;* nag; objurgate; pillory; *question;* rebuke; revive; scold; tell off; upbraid; vituperate; warn; *xuld [arch.];* yell at; *zap;*

**reprisal** *(n.)*: attack; avengement; *blast;* counterattack; defense; evening the score; fighting back; getting back; hitting back; indemnification; justice; *knocking out;* lashing out; *malice; nastiness; obduracy;* payback; punishment; *quittal;* requital; retaliation; revenge; sanction; *take out; unrest;* vengeance; what is due; *xenophobia; yed; zap;* [*see* vendetta]

**reproach** *(n.)*: accusation; attainture; blame; criticism; disgrace; dishonor; embarrassment; flack; guilt(iness); humiliation; ignominy; infamy; indignity; *joylessness; kettiness;* loss of face; mortification; notoriousness; opprobrium; public disgrace; *quad;* reproach; rebuke; shame; stain; tarnishing; upbraid(ing); vitriol; wite; *xtry. shame;* yuckiness; zero honor;

**reproach** *(v.)*: attack; beef; chide; denounce; disparage; *embarrass;* fault; gripe; harangue; impugn; jangle; knock; lambaste; make criticism; nitpick; object; pan; question; revile; remonstrate; slam; traduce; upbraid; vituperate; whine; *xuld [arch.];* yell at; zing;

**reprobate** *(adj.)*: abandoned; adulterous; apostate; bad; corrupt; debauched; damned; evil; fornicative; godless; heinous; immoral; jaded; knavish; lascivious; lewd; libertine; meretricious; non-moral; obscene; profligate; *quad;* rejected; sinful; tainted; ungodly; vile; wicked; whorish; *x-rated; yucky; zipless;*

**reprobate** *(n.)*: abominator; bad man; castaway; criminal; degenerate; evildoer; fiend; godless person; hater of God; impenitent; jackanapes; knave; libertine; miscreant; no-good; offender; pervert; questrel; ribald; sinner; scoundrel; transgressor; *ungodly; villain;* wrongdoer; *xiaoren; yob; zero morals;*

**reproduce** *(v.)*: ape; borrow; copy; clone; counterfeit; duplicate; dub; emulate; echo; follow; forge; *geminate;* have children; imitate; *just like; keep; look alike;* mimic; mimeograph; make duplicates; *near; offprint;* parrot; personate; photocopy; produce; *quadruplicate;* replicate; repeat; spawn; transcribe; *use copier; virtual; watch closely;* xerograph; *yield; zincograph;*

**reproductive** *(adj.)*: *aphrodisiacal;* breeding; copulative; *duplicative; developmental;* egg-fertilizing; fertilizing; generative; *heterogamous; intimate;* joining; *knowing;* lovemaking; mating; *nuptial; natural;* offspring-producing; procreative; *quiff [arch.];* reproducing; regenerative; seminal; sex; *two becoming one; union-forming; venery; wedded; xenogenerative; yielding; zygotaxis;*

**reproof** *(n.)*: admonition; berating; correction; criticism; denunciation; excoriation; faultfinding; going-over; haranguing; increpation; indictment; *judgment;* knocking; lecture; monitory; nagging; objurgation; *punishment; questioning;* reprimand; reproval; scolding; telling off; upbraiding; vituperation; *warning; xuld [arch.];* yelling at; *zapping;*

**reprove** *(v.)*: admonish; berate; censure; chide; denounce; excoriate; fault; give talking to; harangue; inveigh; jaw; knock; lecture; make criticism; nag; objurgate; *punish; question;* revile; reprimand; scold; tell off; upbraid; vituperate; *warn; xuld [arch.];* yell at; *zap;*

**repulse** *(v. disgust)*: appall; *bring displeasure; contempt;* disgust; enrage; fill with contempt; gross one out; horrify; *indignation;* jar; *keck; loathe;* misaffect; nauseate; offend; perturb; *quad;* repel; revolt; sicken; turn one's stomach; upset; *vile;* ward off; *xuld* [arch.]; *yucky; zealously hate;*

**repulse** *(v. drive away)*: avert; beat back; chase off; drive away; *expugn;* fend off; get; hold off; *invincible; jar;* keep away; lick; make of no effect; nauseate; offend; prevent; parry; quash; repel; resist; stave off; turn away; upset; vitiate; ward off; withstand; *x-out; yieldless;* zilch;

**repulsive** *(adj.)*: abhorrent; bad; contemptible; despicable; disgusting; evil; foul; gross; ghastly; horrible; indecent; icky; jarring; ketty; loathsome; miserable; nasty; nauseating; offensive; pathetic; putrid; *queasy;* revolting; repugnant; sickening; stomach-turning; terrible; uncouth; unpleasant; vile; vulgar; wretched; wicked; *x-rated;* yucky; *zorillo;*

**reputable** *(adj.)*: aboveboard; blameless; creditable; dependable; ever-faithful; faithful; good; honest; highly regarded; incontrovertible; *just; keen;* law-abiding; moral; noble; of good repute; pure-hearted; questionless; reliable; respectable; sound; trustworthy; upright; very well thought-of; well-trusted; *xtry; yeomanly; zero doubt;*

**reputation** *(n.)*: acclaim; *badge; bad name;* character; disposition; esteem; fame; *good name;* honorableness; integrity; *justness; known for;* lineament; merit; name; opinion; popularity; *quality;* report; repute; standing; stature; testimony; underlying character; virtue; worth; *witness; xenenthesis.; yetzer* [Heb.]; *zoe;*

**repute** *(n.)*: account; *badge;* character; distinction; éclat; fair name; good report; high ~; importance; illustriousness; *justness;* kudos; looking up to; *merit;* notoriety; obeisance; popularity; *quality;* respect; reputation; renown; status; standing; tribute; *unmitigated respect;* veneration; worth; xtry. character; yielding; *zero contempt;*

**request** *(n.)*: appeal; behest; call; cry; desire; entreaty; *forewish;* give ~; *humble entreaty;* imploration; juration; *known need; looking for;* making request; *need; orison;* petition; plea; *query;* requisition; supplication; solicitation; *telling;* urging; *vocalizing;* wish; *XQ;* yearning; *zikr* [Mos.];

**request** *(v.)*: ask; appeal; beseech; beg; bid; call for; desire; entreat; file for; *get; hunt for;* implore; *juration;* know; *look for answers; lobby;* make ~; need; *obtain;* pose; probe; petition; plead; pray; prevail upon; query; question; quiz; raise; seek; supplicate; solicit; test; *urge; vocalize;* want; XQ.; *yearn; zetetic;*

**require** *(v.)*: adjure; bid; call for; compel; demand; entail; force; *govern;* have one; insist; *juration; kaleusmatic;* leave no option; mandate; make; mean; necessitate; need; oblige; obligate; order; pre~; prescribe; *quo minus [L.];* requisition; stipulate; tell; *urge; voice;* want; *XO mandate; yark; zakon [Rus.];*
**rescind** *(v.)*: abrogate; annul; *banish;* cancel; countermand; disannul; end; *finish off; go back;* halt; invalidate; *jump back;* kill; *leave; make void;* null(ify); overturn; put an end to; quash; repeal; revoke; retract; stop; take back; *undo;* void; withdraw; *x-ing; yank;* zero out;
**rescue** *(n.)*: aid; bail-out; breakout; *comfort;* deliverance; extrication; freeing; *getaway;* help; issuance; indemnification; jailbreak; *keeping safe;* liberation; manumission; *not allow to die; overprotect;* prison-break; protection; preservation; *quicken;* release; recovery; redemption; salvage; saving; salvation; transportation to safety; unshackling; *vivificate; well-protected; x-ported;* yanking from the jaws of death; *zero danger;*
**rescue** *(v.)*: aid; bail out; come to the aid; deliver; extricate; free; give life to; help; indemnify; *justified; keep one safe;* let loose; liberate; make free; *not allow to die; overprotect;* protect; preserve; *quicken;* release; recover; redeem; salvage; transport to safety; unshackle; *vivificate; well-protected; x-ported;* yank from the jaws of death; *zero danger;*
**research** *(n.)*: analysis; breakdown; checking; diagnostic; examination; field study; fact-finding; going over; *herborization;* investigation; *judgment;* knowledge(-gathering); lab analysis; look-over; microanalysis; *nosing;* overhaul; probe; query; researching; *results;* study; testing; *urinalysis;* volumetric analysis; work; winnowing; *xenodiagnosis;* yield results; *zootomy;*
**research** *(v.)*: analyze; bring under scrutiny; check out; consider; dissect; delve; examine; explore; find out; glean; get knowledge; have a look into; investigate; *judge; know;* learn; lucubrate; mug up; nose around; observe; probe; question; query; really study; study; try to understand; *test;* understand; vet; work on; *xenodiagnosis; yeme;* zero in;
**resemblance** *(n.)*: alikeness; analogy; *balance;* commonality; correspondence; duplication; dead ringer; equivalence; fashion; form; *gemination;* homogeneity; image; *just alike;* kinship; likeness; match; mirror-image; nearness; oneness; parallelism; *quasi-similitude;* reflection; similarity; similitude; sameness; semblance; spitting image; *twin;* uniformity; very image; *with comparison; xoanon; yet similar; zincograph;*
**resemble** *(v.)*: appear similar; *alike; akin;* bear resemblance to; compare; closely ~; duplicate; *equivalent;* favor; give impression of; have the likeness of; imitate; *just alike; kind of like;* look like; match; nearly ~; *owelty;* parallel; *quasi;* really look like; remind one of; seem like; smack of; take after; *uncanny resemblance;* very image; *with comparison; xoanon;* yield similarities; *zincograph;*
**resent** *(v.)*: abhor; begrudge; bear ill-will; contemn; disdain; deeply ~; envy; *fester about;* grudge; hate; hold against; *indignant; jealousy; kindless;* loathe; mind; not like; *offended; pshaw; querulous; reprobate; scorn;* take offense to; utterly loathe; vilipend; *wrathful; xenophobic; yucky; zero forgiveness;*
**resentment** *(n.)*: acrimony; animosity; anger; bitterness; contempt; disgust; displeasure; dudgeon; exasperation; fury; gall; hatred; indignation; ill-will; jadedness; *kindlessness; kindle;* loathing; malevolence; negativism; offense; pique; querulousness; resentfulness; rancor; spite; *tetchiness;* umbrage; venom; virulence; wrath; *xenophobia; yawping; zoilism;*
**reserve** *(n.)*: auxiliary; backup; cache; *deposit;* emergency; further amount; *gathering;* hoard; inventory; *just in case;* kept reserve; leftover amount; *more;* number in ~; *other; pack;* quantity in ~; reservoir; store; stockpile; *tertiary ~;* uplay; *volumes;* warehouse; xtr. amount; *yarded; zillions;*
**reserve** *(v.)*: allocate; bank; conserve; *deposit;* earmark; *fraction; gather;* hold back; *increase; just in case;* keep (back); lay up; make reservation; not use; *on hold;* preserve; put aside; *quantity;* retain; save (for a rainy day); set aside; take in ~; uplay; *vault;* withhold; *xtr.; yard; zet [dial.];*
**reside** *(v.)*: abide; bide; continue; dwell; exist; follow on; *go to;* hang one's hat; inhabit; *journey;* keep on; live; linger; lodge; *move in; nest;* occupy; pause; quarter; remain; stay; settle; sojourn; tarry; *use; voyage to;* wait; *winter;* xenize; *yerde* [arch.]; *zip to;*

**residence** *(n.)*: abode; address; building; cottage; dwelling (place); edifice; flat house; guest house; home; house; habitation; inhabitance; jacal; *kiosk;* living quarters; lodging; manse; messuage; manor; *nest;* outbuilding; place; quarters; roof; rent house; structure; summerhouse; townhouse; tenement; *utility apartment;* villa; *walk-up;* x-house; *yali; zwinger;*
**resident** *(n.)*: abider; boarder; continuer; dweller; *encamper; feudatory; going to;* habitant; inhabitant; joint-inhabitant; *keeper on;* lodger; *moving in; no vacancy;* occupant; possessor; quarterer; resider; stayer; squatter; tenant; user; *vassal; winter-quarterer;* xenizer; year-rounder; *zone lessee;*
**residue** *(n.)*: argal; buildup; chaff; deposit; drags; excess; filtrate; grouts; holdover; impurities; junk; kaff [dial.]; lees; matter; *non-wanted matter;* orgal; parings; quittor; remainder; remains; rest; substance; scum; silt; tartar; *unwanted;* vinasse; waste; *xysma; yuckiness; zero;*
**resign** *(v.)*: abandon; abdicate; break off; cease; demit; end; exit; forbear; give up; halt; hang up; interrupt; jump off; kiss goodbye; leave; *moderate; not stay;* opt out; part with; quit; relinquish; step down; surrender; terminate; *undo; vacate;* walk out; x; yield; *zero;*
**resist** *(v.)*: avoid; buck; baulk; contend against; defy; encumber; forbear; fight against; gainstand; hold off; insurrect; join the opposition; kick against; lock horns; militate; not abide; oppose; oppugn; propulse; protest; quarrel; refrain; repulse; stand against; turn away; uprise; *verses;* withstand; *x.;* yain [arch.]; *zealously withstand;* [*see* relent]
**resistance** *(n.)*: antipathy; bucking; baulking; contention; contrariness; defiance; exception; enmity; fight; forbearance; gainsaying; hostility; holding off; incongruity; jangling; kicking; keeping at bay; *loathing;* militation; non-cooperation; opposition; pushback; querulousness; rebellion; repulsion; standing against; *trouble;* uprising; *variance;* withstanding; *x-fire;* yieldlessness; *zeallessness;*
**resolute** *(adj.)*: adamant; bull-headed; constant; determined; dogged; doughty; ever-stubborn; firm; gritty; headstrong; indomitable; iron-willed; jaw-set; *keep up;* lasting; mulish; non-bending; obstinate; purposeful; persevering; pertinacious; quenchless; resolved; stubborn; strong-willed; steadfast; tenacious; unwavering; vehement; willful; *x-grained;* yieldless; zealous;
**resolution** *(n.)*: affirmation; *bond;* covenant; commitment; declaration; decision; determination; enaction; forswearing; guarantee; hypothecation; *insistence;* joint ~; *kept ~;* legislation; *making of vows;* non-conditional promise; oath; promise; pledge; *qualified pledge;* ruling; resolve; sworn statement; testament; unconditional ~; vow; word; *x-ones heart; yafery* [arch.]; *zealous oath;*
**resolvable** *(adj.)*: answerable; ascertainable; breakable; calculable; determinable; explainable; findable; gettable; *hashing out; iron out;* justifiable; knowable; *logical; making sense of; not hopeless;* openable; *perceivable; questionless;* reconcilable; solvable; *tellable;* uncoverable; *victory;* workable; xlate; yieldless; zero in;
**resolve** *(n.)*: adamancy; bulldog-tenacity; constancy; determination; endurance; firmness; gumption; headstrongness; indomitableness; *jaw-set;* keeping at it; lastingness; mettle; not giving up; obstinacy; perseverance; *quenchless;* relentlessness; resoluteness; sticktoitiveness; tenacity; unwaveringness; vehemence; willpower; *x-grained;* yieldlessness; zeal;
**resolve** *(v.)*: answer; break; crack; come to a decision; clinch; decide; determine; elect; figure out; find out; get to the bottom of; hash out; iron out; justify; *know;* lay to rest; make an end to; *nisus;* open up; put to rest; *questionless;* reconcile; solve; settle; *tell;* unravel; *victory;* work out; xlate; yieldless; zero in;
**resource** *(n.)*: ability; accumulation; bounty; buildup; backup; cache; deposit; emergency supply; font; goldmine; hoard; *issue; jewel; keep; lot;* means; mine; nest egg; overabundance; *power; quantity;* reserve; resources; source; supply; store; *treasure;* upbuild; *vein;* wherwithal; well(spring); wealth; *xenenthesis;* yield; zillions [slang];
**resources** *(n.)*: assets; ability; bounty; capital; capacity; disposable ~; earnings; funds; finances; gold; holdings; income; *jewels; krugerrands;* lucre; means; net assets; *opulence;* prosperity; *quantities;* reserves; revenue; substance; treasure; uberty; venture capital; wherwithal; working capital; *xenocurrency; yellow boy* [Br.]; zillions [slang];

**respect** *(n.)*: admiration; blessing; consideration; courtesy; dignity; deference; devoirs; due honor; esteem; fear; graciousness; honor; homage; high regard; intentiveness; *justness; kneeling;* laurels; mindfulness; non-contempt; observance; obeisance; politeness; *quality;* regard; reverence; repute; solicitude; salutation; tribute; thoughtfulness; urbanity; veneration; wonder; *xtry.;* yielding; *zero contempt;*
**respect** *(v.)*: acknowledge; admire; bow to; consider; defer to; dignify; esteem; fear; give honor; honor; idolize; *just love;* kneel to; kowtow; look up to; make obeisance to; notice; observe; prefer; praise; *quick to recognize;* regard; recognize; reverence; revere; salute; think of; uphold; venerate; worship; *xtry.;* yield; *zero contempt;* [*Ant.* revile]
**respectable** *(adj.)*: aboveboard; acceptable; blameless; creditable; decent; ethical; exemplary; fine; good; honorable; impeccable; just; *knightly;* laudable; moral; noble; okay; proper; principled; *qualified;* reputable; sound; trustworthy; upright; virtuous; well-respected; *xtry.; yichus; zero guile;*
**respecter** *(n.)*: acknowledger; *bow;* considerer; deferrer; esteemer; favorer; giver of favor; honorer; idolizer; *justifier; kneel to; liker; misuser; observer;* preferrer; *qualifier;* regarder; saluter; *treat differently; unjust;* venerator; *worshiper; xtr. favor;* yielder; *zealous;*
**respectful** *(adj.)*: affable; *bowing;* civil; courteous; considerate; duteous; deferential; esteeming; fearing; gracious; honoring; *illustrious; judicious; kind; kowtowing;* looking up to; mannerly; nice; obeisant; obsequious; polite; *queme;* reverent(ial); regardful; submissive; thoughtful; tactful; urbane; venerable; well-mannered; worshipful; *xenial;* yieldful; *zero offense;* [*Ant.* rude]
**respective** *(adj.)*: assigned; *by name;* certain; distinct; designated; exact; fixed; given; *hand-picked;* individual; *just;* known; *labeled;* marked; named; own; personal; particular; qualifying; relevant; separate; specific; singular; *tagged;* unique; *very; well-chosen; xtry.;* yarked; *zero in;*
**respond** *(v.)*: answer; back answer; counter; declare; deal with; express; *echo;* figure out; give ~; handle; intimate; input; judge; *key in;* lay to rest; make reply; *note;* orate; *pipe up; quotient;* reply; react; retort; rebut; say; state; tell; utter; voice; word; *x; yes; zero in;*
**response** *(n.)*: answer; action; argument; backtalk; comeback; counter(action); countermove; comment; declaration; defense; evasive reply; explanation; feedback; finding; general reply; handling; input; judgment; *key input; letter;* message; *notion;* outcome; opinion; presentment; *quotient;* reply; reaction; retort; rejoinder; riposte; statement; spoken ~; talking; *treatment;* utterance; verdict; witty reply; written ~; words; *xtry.; ~; yes-answer;* zinger;
**responsibility** *(n.)*: assignment; answerability; accountability; blame; burden; business; charge; commission; duty; dependability; encumbrance; errand; function; goal; guilt; handling; incumbency; job; key role; liability; mission; necessity; obligation; onus; place; post; purpose; *quest;* requirement; reliability; responsibleness; station; subjectability task; trustworthiness; undertaking; unction; vocation; work; weight; xci; yoke; *zealous task;* [see job]
**responsible** *(adj.)*: answerable; accountable; blamable; conscientious; dependable; *errant;* ever-faithful; faulted; faithful; guilty; *good;* held ~; in charge; *judged faithful; kept accountable;* liable; mature; never-failing; non-innocent; obliged; punishable; quite trustworthy; reliable; steadfast; subject to blame; trustworthy; trusted; to blame; unfailing; *valid;* well-trusted; *xfer;* yeomanly; *zero passing-the-buck;*
**responsive** *(adj.)*: answering; approachable; alert; *bestirred;* conscious; disquieted; echoing; favorably disposed; generally ~; heedful; interactive; inclined; *jarred;* knowing; liminal; mindful; *not closed;* open; perceptive; quick to react; responding; reactive; sensitive; syntonic; tenderhearted; understanding; very aware; wakeful; *x;* yielding; *zesty;*
**rest** *(n.)*: adjournment; bedrest; break; breather; calm; downlying; ease; forbearance; goof-off time; hold; idleness; *journey's end;* kip; leisure; lapse; lull; letup; *motionlessness;* night ~; *off;* pause; quiet(ude); relaxation; repose; respite; recess; suspension; slacking off; time out; tarrying; unwinding; vacation; wait; *x-rest; yawning;* zwischenspiel [mus.];

**rest** *(v.)*: adjourn; break; cease; do nothing; ease; forbear; go to sleep; hold; have a break; idle; *jadedness;* knock off; lounge; lie down; *motionless;* nap; *oversleep;* pause; quiet down; relax; repose; slack off; suspend; slumber; take it easy; unwind; vacation; wait; wind; *x-rest;* yawn; zizz;
**restaurant** *(n.)*: automat; beanery; brasserie; buffet; bistro; café; cafeteria; caterer; chop-house; commissary; diner; dining room; eatery; establishment; fonda; grill; hash house; inn; *joint;* kitchen; luncheonette; mess hall; *nightclub; oriental ~;* porterhouse; quick-lunch counter; refectory; steakhouse; snack bar; trattoria; tearoom; *urban café;* vent [arch.]; *Western steakhouse;* xenodocheum; *Yokohama steakhouse; zonal chain restaurant;*
**restful** *(adj.)*: all-composing; becalmed; calm; dreamy; easeful; *friendly; gentle; holiday;* idyllic; *jarless;* keeping peace; lulling; motionless; nonviolent; *orderly;* peaceful; quiet; relaxing; reposeful; serene; tranquil; undisturbed; *very ~; waveless; xenophilious; yielding; zealous of rest;*
**restitution** *(n.)*: amends; atonement; balancing; compensation; damages; expiation; *for;* giving back; *handing over;* imbursement; indemnification; *justification;* kickback; lex talionis [L.]; making amends; *money; non-indebted;* orfgild; paying back; payback; penitence; quittance; restoration; reparation; repayment; reddition; settlement; substitution; *transfer of funds; underpayment; virement;* wages; *xfer;* yielding amends; *zapping;*
**restless** *(adj.)*: agitated; antsy; bestirred; chafing; disquieted; disturbed; edgy; fidgity; *grousing;* high-strung; impatient; itchy; jittery; jumpy; keyed up; lacking sleep; malcontented; nervous; on edge; peaceless; qui vive [L.]; ruffled; shifting; skittish; squirmy; stirred; sleepless; twitchy; uneasy; unreposed; vacillating; wakeful; worked up; *xuld [arch.];* yeasty; *zestful;* [*Ant.* sleepy]
**restoration** *(n.)*: acquittal; bringing back; correction; change back; comeback; deraignment; exoneration; fixing; going back; giving back; healing; *improvement; justification; knitting; liberation;* melioration; *new;* overhaul; putting back; *quick-fix;* reinstatement; reconstitution; regaining; recovery; rehabilitation; reclamation; re-establishment; refurbishment; reddition; salvaging; taking back; undoing; undeleting; vamping; *warming over; xfer; yele [arch.]; zero damage;*
**restore** *(v.)*: acquit; bring back; correct; cure; change back; doctor; deraign; *exonerate;* fix; give back; heal; *improve; justify; knit; liberate; like new;* make like new; *nurse to health;* overhaul; put back; *quick-fix;* restore; reinstate; reconstitute; regain; replace; repair; rehabilitate; reclaim; recover; re-collect; re-establish; refurbish; salvage; take back; *touch up;* undo; undelete; vamp; win back; *xfer; yele [arch.]; zero retention;*
**restrain** *(v.)*: arrest; bind; bridle; contain; control; curb; check; detain; encumber; forbear; fetter; gyve; hold (back); hinder; halter; hog-tie; impede; inhibit; jail; keep; *let* [arch.]; limit; moderate; manacle; *narrow;* obstruct; prevent; pinion; qualify; restrict; stop; suppress; shackle; temper; *unliberated; veto;* withhold; x; yoke; *zoster;* [*see* forbid]
**restraint** *(n.)*: arrest; bonds; containment; control; continence; detainment; *encumbrance;* forbearance; fetter; gyve; holding back; handcuff; impedance; inhibition; jail; keeping; limit(ation); moderation; manacles; nippers; obstruction; prevention; prison; qualification; restriction; self-control; suppression; trammel; unexcessiveness *vetoing;* wall; withholding; *x-ing;* yoke; *zoster;*
**restrict** *(v.)*: *avert;* bar; ban; bind; block; confine; curb; circumscribe; control; disallow; demarcate; exclude; forbid; fetter; govern; hold (back); impede; *jam;* keep (from); limit; moderate; narrow; obstruct; outlaw; parameterize; pinion; prohibit; qualify; quarantine; restrain; suppress; straitjacket; temper; *undo; veto;* withhold; *x; yank; zero;*
**restriction** *(n.)*: *averting;* block; *clause;* condition; circumscription; disallowance; exclusion; forbidding; finiteness; *government ~;* hold(ing back); inhibition; injunction; *jam;* keeping (from); limitation; limit; moderation; narrowness; outlawing; proviso; parameter; prohibition; qualification; restraint; rider; stipulation; stricture; term; *ultimatum; veto;* withholding; *x; yanking; zero;*

**restrictive** *(adj.)*: *averting;* barring; confining; curbing; circumscriptive; controlling; disallowing; excluding; forbidding; fettering; *gumming up;* holding (back); inhibitive; *jamming;* keeping (from); limited; limitary; limiting; moderating; narrow; oppressive; pressing; qualifying; restrained; stinted; suppressive; tight; *undo;* very ~; withhold; *x; yank; zero freedom;*

**result** *(n.)*: aftermath; byproduct; consequence; derivative; effect; end; fruit; *get;* harvest; impact; issue; just desserts; *known outcome;* lattermath; *matter; necessarily;* outcome; product; quantum effect; ramification; resultant; reaping; repercussion; significance; sequent; termination; upshot; *validity;* work; wake; *xenagogy;* yield; *zeug [G.];*

**result** *(v.)*: arise; bring about; come of; cause; develop; ensue; follow; give rise to; happen; initiate; *jump-start; kindle;* lead to; leave; make; *nudge;* occasion; produce; *quicken;* redound; stem; trigger; unfold; *vivify;* work; *xuld [arch.];* yield; *zip into motion;*

**resultant** *(adj.)*: attendant; *after;* bringing about; consequential; distillate; ensuing; eventual; following; final; giving rise to; happening; *initiated; jump-start; kindled;* later; *make;* next; occurring; *outgrowth;* precipitate; *quickly following;* resulting; subsequent; sequacious terminating; ultimate; *vivified;* working out; *xfer;* yielding; *zum [dial.];*

**resume** *(v.)*: *again;* begin again; continue; carry on; do again; extend; follow on; go on; have another try; *iterate; journey on;* keep (up; on); *last;* make a fresh start; *non-stop; ongoing;* pick up; *quicken;* restart; recommence; return to; start over; take up; uphold; *voyage on; wax; xuld [arch.]; yede; zoom ahead;* [see start]

**resurrect** *(v.)*: awaken; bring back to life; come back; disquiet; emerge; enliven; *furbish; grave-opening; heal;* invigorate; *jar; keel;* live again; make alive; make a comeback; *no longer dead;* open grave; *proceed out of the grave;* quicken; raise; rise again; restore; revive; revivify; save; salvage; stir; *thrive; take out;* uprise; vivify; *victor;* wake; *x-out death;* yank; *zing up;*

**resurrection** *(n.)*: awakening; arising; bestirring; coming forth; comeback; disquieting; enlivening; first ~; grave-opening; *healing;* incitation; *jarring;* keeling; living again; making alive again; new life; opening of graves; open tomb; physical ~; quickening; rebirth; revivification; rising; restoration; rapture; salvation; second ~; tomb-opening; uprising; uptaking; vivification; victory over death; wakening; *Xn.* ~; *yonder; zoe;*

**retain** *(v.)*: *abide;* bear; carry; detain; engage; file; grip; hold (on to); inhibit; *impound; just keep;* keep; lay by oneself; maintain; not let go; own; possess; preserve; *quarantine;* remain; save; take; treasure; *think on;* uphold; *vigorously keep;* withhold; warehouse; *xtr. security;* yard; *zealously* ~; [*Ant.* relinquish]

**retaliate** *(v.)*: answer; avenge; *back;* counterstrike; do back; even the score; fix one; get back; hit back; *inflict; interchange; justice;* kill; *lex talionis [L.];* make counterstrike; *nemesis;* overreact; pay back; punish; *quick response;* reciprocate; revenge; strike back; take vengeance; *undo; vengeance;* wreak vengeance; *x-out; yet unavanged; zap;*

**retaliation** *(n.)*: answer; avengement; balancing; counterstrike; *doing;* evening the score; fixing; getting back; hitting back; *interchange;* justice; *killing; lex talionis* [L.]; making counterstrike; *nemesis; overreaction;* payback; punishment; quittal; reciprocation; striking back; settling the score; taking vengeance; *undone;* vengeance; wrath; *x-ing out; yet unavanged; zapping;*

**retard** *(v.)*: arrest; block; belate; bog down; curb; delay; decelerate; encumber; forestall; gum up; hinder; hold back; impede; impair; jam-up; keep back; lag; *limit;* make slow; *nullify;* obstruct; prevent; *quash;* restrain; slow (down); thwart; *undo;* upset; *vigia;* withhold; *x; yank; zilch;*

**retardation** *(n.)*: arrestation; blockage; curtailment; delaying; deceleration; encumbrance; forestalling; gumming up; hindrance; impedance; impairment; jam-up; keeping back; limitation; making slow; *non-speedy;* obstruction; prevention; *quashing;* retardment; slowness; thwarting; *undoing; vigia;* withholding; *x; yank; zilch;*

**retention** *(n.)*: *abiding;* bearing; confining; detainment; engaging; filing; grip; holding; imbibing; *just keep;* keeping; *learning;* maintaining; non-release; owning; possession; preservation; *quarantine;* retaining; saving; *thinking on;* upholding; *vigorous keeping;* withholding; *xfer;* yarding; *zealous keeping;* [*Ant.* relinquishment]
**retire** *(v.)*: abdicate; become ~d; cease working; discontinue work; exit the work force; *forsake;* give up work; *has-been; inoperative; junk; kaput;* leave; move off the scene; *naff;* obsolesce; put out to pasture; pension off; *quondam;* reach ~ment; stop working; superannuate; take one's leave; *useless; vestigial;* withdraw; *x'ed;* yield; *zero;* [*see* sleep]
**retract** *(v.)*: abrogate; backpedal; cancel; disannul; disavow; draw back; end; forswear; go back; halt; invalidate; *jump back;* kill; *leave;* make recall; null(ify); overturn; put an end to; quash; revoke; rescind; recall; recant; stop; swallow; turn over; take back; unsay; void; withdraw; *x-ing; yank;* zero out;
**retraction** *(n.)*: abrogation; backpedaling; cancellation; disannulment; disavowal; ending; forswearing; going back; halting; invalidation; *jumping back;* killing; *leaving;* making a recall; nullification; overturning; putting an end to; quashing; revocation; rescindment; recall; recantation; swallowing; taking back; unsaying; voidance; withdrawal; *x-ing; yanking;* zeroing out;
**retreat** *(n.)*: abandonment; backtracking; clearing out; drawing back; desertion; departure; evacuation; exit; flight; going; hightailing; *immigration; jetting; kesting;* leaving; moving out; *non-remaining; olate;* pulling out; quitting; running away; retiring; skedaddling; turning back; uprooting; vacating; withdrawal; *xfer;* yerning; zipping away;
**retreat** *(v.)*: abandon; backtrack; clear out; draw back; desert; depart; double back; evacuate; exit; flee; go; hightail; *incurve; jet; kest;* leave; move out; *not remain;* olate; pull out; quit; run away; retire; remove; recede; relinquish; skedaddle; turn back; uproot; vacate; vamoose; withdraw from; *xfer;* yern; zip away;
**retribution** *(n.)*: avengement; blood; comeback; despitefulness; evening the score; fixing; getting even; hitting back; indemnification; justice; *kindless;* lex talionis [L.]; malice; making good; *nastiness; obduracy;* payback; punishment; quittance; revenge; spite; settling the score; *terror; unkindness;* vengeance; wrath; *xenophobia; yucky; zap;*
**retrieve** *(v.)*: acquire; bring back; call back; *do;* extricate; fetch; field; get back; have; *intercept; join; kep; land;* make off with; net; obtain; procure; *quoff;* reclaim; restore; recover; recall; regain; secure; salvage; shag; take back; *usurp; vest;* win back; xfer; yank; zip away;
**retrieval** *(n.)*: acquisition; bringing back; calling back; delivery; extrication; fetching; getting back; having; *interception; joining; kep; landing;* mechanical ~; *net;* obtaining; procurement; *quoff;* reclamation; restoration; recovery; recall; salvage; taking back; *usurpation; vest; win;* xfer; yanking; *zip;*
**return** *(v.)*: about-face; bounce back; come back; draw back; *depart;* enter again; *find;* go back; give back; head back; *itinerate;* journey back; *knock back;* leave; make trip back; *navigate back; overturn;* put back; pass back again; *quit;* revert; reappear; reoccur; revisit; re-enter; *sail home;* turn back (-in); U-turn; venture home; *went; xfer; yede; zip back;*
**reveal** *(v.)*: appear; bare; break; come to light; disclose; divulge; display; exhibit; expose; evince; fully ~; give out; hold forth; indicate; *justify;* kithe [Scot.]; lay bare; manifest; make known; *noticeable;* open; present; *qualify;* release; show; tell; unveil; uncover; uncloak; unfold; *voice;* wave; x-ray; yield; zero-concealment;
**revelation** *(n.)*: apocalypse; baring; coming to light; disclosure; denouement; exhibition; full ~; *giving;* heralding; indication; *judgment;* knowing; *kithing;* letting one see; manifestation; non-concealment; oracle; opening up; presentation; *quain;* revealing; showing; *telling;* unmasking; unveiling; uncovering; vernissage; whole picture; *x-view;* yielding; zero-concealment;
**revenge** *(n.)*: avengement; balancing; comeback; despitefulness; evening the score; fixing; getting even; hitting back; indemnification; justice; *kindless;* lex talionis [L.]; malice; *nastiness;* offsetting; payback; punishment; quittal; retribution; retaliation; reprisal; spite; settlement; sweet ~; tit for tat; *terror; unkindness;* vengeance; wrath; *xenophobia; yucky; zap;*

**revenge** *(v.)*: avenge; bring to justice; come back; *despiteful;* even the score; fix; get (back); have vengeance; *inflict; justice* [arch.]; *kindless; lex talionis [L.];* make one pay; *nemesis;* offset; punish; pay back; *quittal;* requite; settle; take vengeance; *unkindness;* vindicate; *whip; x-out; yet unavenged;* zealously avenge;

**revengeful** *(adj.)*: avenging; bitter; cruel; despiteful; embittered; foul; galsome; hateful; implacable; jaded; kindless; loathsome; malicious; nasty; obdurate; *pernicious; quede* [arch.]; retaliatory; spiteful; *treacherous;* unforgiving; vengeful; vindictive; wreakful; *xenophobic; yucky; zealotic;*

**revere** *(v.)*: appreciate; bow to; cherish; defer to; esteem; exalt; fear; give honor; hold in high regard; idolize; *just love;* kneel to; look up to; make obeisance to; *notice; obeisance;* pay homage to; *quality;* regard; reverence; salute; think of; treasure; *unmitigated ~;* venerate; worship; *xtry.;* yield; *zero contempt;*

**reverence** *(n.)*: admiration; bowing; consideration; deference; esteem; fear; giving honor; honor; homage; high regard; idolization; *justness;* kneeling; laudation; *merit;* non-contempt; obeisance; piousness; *quality;* respect; regard; salutation; tribute; *unmitigated respect;* veneration; *wonder;* worship; *xtry.;* yielding; *zero contempt;*

**reverence** *(v.)*: admire; bow to; cherish; defer to; esteem; fear; give honor; honor; idolize; *just love;* kneel to; look up to; make obeisance to; nod; *obeisance;* praise; *quality;* respect; regard; salute; think of; *unmitigated ~;* venerate; worship; *xtry.;* yield; *zero contempt;*

**reverent** *(adj.)*: awed; *bowing;* courteous; deferential; esteeming; fearing; grave; God-fearing; humble; idolizing; in awe; *judicious; kneeling; loving;* mannerly; non-presumptuous; obsequious; polite; pietistic; prayerful; *queme;* reverential; respectful; solemn; submissive; *toadying; urbane;* venerative; worshipful; *xenial;* yieldful; *zero offense;*

**reversal** *(n.)*: about-face; abrogation; backup; change; derogation; exchange; eversion; flip; going other way; *hind end;* invalidation; inversion; jumping over; *key change; labile;* making overturn; *negation;* overturn; opposite; putting in reverse; *quashing;* repeal; reverse; swap; switch; turnaround; transposal; U-turn; *volte-face* [F.]; *wind; x-pose; yank;* zwap [dial.];

**reverse** *(adj.)*: alternate; antithesis; backward; contrary; converse; counterpoint; *derogated;* exchange; flip-flop; going the other way; *hind-end;* inverse; inverted; *jump back; key change; labile; modified;* negative; nadir; obverse; opposite; *polaric; quite opposite;* renverse; retrograde; switch; turning around; transposal; upside-down; void; volte-face; *vice versa;* wrong-way; *x-posal;* yaw; zwap [dial.];

**reverse** *(v.)*: about-face; abrogate; backpedal; change; derogate; exchange; evert; flip; go the other way; *heterogeneity;* invalidate; invert; jump over; *key change; labile;* make opposite; negate; overturn; put in ~; *quash;* repeal; rearrange; reorder; swap; switch; turn around; transpose; undo; *upside down;* void; wind; *x-pose; yank;* zwap [dial.];

**revert** *(v.)*: again; backslide; backset; change back; declension; escheat; fall back; go back to; hark back; *impede;* jump back; *knock back;* lapse; move back; *non-advancement; over again;* plunge; *quit;* retrovert; retrogress; return; slide back; turn back; *undo; veer downward;* wane; *xfer;* yield again to; *zoom downward;*

**review** *(n.)*: assessment; brief; capitulation; check; *data;* encapsulation; formal ~; going over; *heart;* inspection; judgment; *kernel; lifeblood; monthly ~;* newsbrief; overview; precis; *quintessence;* rundown; reconsideration; re-examination; summary; thumbnail; *underneath;* vignette; write-up; *xenenthesis;* yetzer [Heb.]; *zoe [Gr.];*

**review** *(v.)*: assess; analyze; audit; behold; check; diagnose; evaluate; *find;* go over; have a look; inspect; judge; keek; look over; make examination; notice; observe; overlook; pick over; pore; question; read; re-examine; scrutinize; study; take a look; *understand;* valuate; watch; *xenodiagnose; XQ;* yeme; *zero in;*

**revile** *(v.)*: attack; beef; chide; denounce; disparage; execrate; fault; gripe; harangue; impugn; jangle; knock; lambaste; *malign;* nitpick; object; pan; question; reproach; remonstrate; slam; traduce; upbraid; vituperate; whine; *xuld [arch.];* yell at; zing; [*Ant.* relish]

**revise** *(v.)*: alter; bend; blue-pencil; better; change; doctor; develop; edit; emend; fix; go over; *help;* innovate; improve; jib; *key to; lower;* modify; novate; overhaul; *put right; qualify;* redesign; remake; revamp; redact; switch; transform; tweak; tailor; upgrade; vary; vamp; *work;* xenomorph; yaw; zigzag;

**revision** *(n.)*: alteration; betterment; change; correction; difference; development; edition; emendation; *form; growth; heightening;* improvement; *juvenation; kind; lower version;* modification; new version; overhaul; permutation; *qualification;* revamping; recension; switch; substitution; tweaking; upgrade; update; variation; version; *wording change;* xenomorph; yaw; zigzag;

**revival** *(n.)*: awakening; bestirring; camp meeting; disquieting; enlivening; fire; *goading;* heartening; invigoration; jarring; kindling; *leading;* moving; *new zeal;* outpouring; pouring out; quickening; renewal; revitalization; rejuvenation; stirring; turning; uplifting; upheaval; vitalization; vivification; wakening; *xuld [arch.];* yielding; *zeal;*

**revive** *(v.)*: awaken; arouse; bestir; come alive again; disquiet; enliven; fire up; *goad;* hearten; ignite; jar; kindle; light on fire; make a comeback; *nudge; outpour;* perk up; quicken; rejuvenate; revitalize; revivify; rouse; rekindle; stir; *stoke; turn back;* uplift; vivify; vitalize; wake(n); *xuld [arch.];* yerk; *zap;*

**revocation** *(n.)*: abrogation; annulment; abolishment; *back;* canceling; disannulment; ending; forswearing; *going back;* halting; invalidation; *jumping back;* killing; *leaving; making void;* nullification; overturning; putting an end to; quashing; repeal; retraction; rescindment; recision; reversal; revokement; stopping; turning over; unsaying; voidance; withdrawal; *x-ing;* yanking; zeroing out;

**revoke** *(v.)*: abrogate; annul; back down (-out); cancel; disannul; end; forswear; *go back;* halt; invalidate; *jump back;* kill; *leave; made void;* null(ify); overturn; put an end to; quash; retract; recall; rescind; repeal; stop; take back; unsay; void; withdraw; *x-ing;* yank; zero out;

**revolt** *(n.)*: antagonism; backlash; challenge; defiance; émeute; failure to comply; general uprising; high treason; insurgence; jacquerie; *kicking at; lèse majesté [F.];* mutiny; noncompliance; obstinacy; perfidy; *questioning;* rebellion; riot; rising up; resistance; strike; treachery; treason; uprising; unyieldingness; *violence; waywardness;* xgression; yellow flu; zapping;

**revolt** *(v.)*: arise; break with; challenge; defy; *evil;* foment; gainstand; have rebellion; insurrect; *jump ship;* kick against; *lawless;* mutiny; *not listen;* offer resistance; protest; *question;* rebel; rise up; riot; strike; stand against; strive against; throw off (yoke); uprise; *vie; violate;* withstand; xgress; yieldless; zealot; [Ant. resign]

**revolution** *(n. rebellion)*: armed uprising; bouleversement; bloodless ~; contumacy; *coup d'état* [F.]; defiance; émeute; *fight; general disregard;* high treason; insurrection; jacquerie; *kicking at; lèse majesté* [F.]; *mutiny;* non-obedience; overthrow; peasant uprising; purge; quake; *quantum leap;* rebellion; revolt; subversion; treason; takeover; uprising; violence; war; *xgression;* yieldlessness; *zapping;*

**revolution** *(n. turning)*: *around*; backspin; circling; *downspin;* eddy; flipping; going around; gyration; hurtling; incurvation; *juttering; keeling;* looping; moving around; nutation; overturning; purling; querling; rotation; spin; turning; underspin; verticity; whirling; *x-ing; yede [arch.];* zipping around;

**revolutionary** *(n.)*: anarchist; backstabber; criminal; dissenter; extremist; Fenian [Ire.]; guerrilla; *huk* [Philippines]; insurrectionary; Jacobin; *kicker; loyal activist;* mutineer; maximalist; non-conformist; overthrower; poissarde [fem.]; *questioner;* rebel; revolutionist; seditionary; troublemaker; usurper; *villain;* withstander; xenocentrist; *yieldless;* zealot;

**revulsion** *(n.)*: aversion; *badness;* contempt; detestation; disgust; execration; foulness; gall; hatred; intense dislike; *jarring;* kindlessness; loathing; *malice;* nausea; odium; *perturbation; querulousness;* repugnance; *sickness; terribleness;* upset; vile; withdrawal; *xenophobia; yuckiness; zorillo;*

**reward** *(n.)*: award; blue ribbon; compensation; crown; cup; decoration; desert; *ending; favor;* guerdon; gift; gold cup; honeypot; honor; indemnity; incentive; jackpot; just deserts; *king's ransom;* laurel wreath; medal; meed; *Nobel Prize; Oscar;* prize; plaque; payment; quittance; requital; remuneration; recompense; satisfaction; trophy; title; *utu* [N.Z.]; *victory crown;* wage; "well done"; what is due; xenium; *yeff* [arch.]; yellow jersey [sports]; *Zion's crowns;* [Ant. retribution]

**reward** *(v.)*: award; bestow ~; compensate; crown; decorate; endow; *favor;* give ~; honor (with); issue award; *justly give ~; kit;* laurel; make presentation; *notable; outfit;* present; *quicken;* recognize; render; *satisfaction;* transfer award; *unhand;* vest; *weigh out;* xfer; *yield; zealously give ~;*

**rewarder** *(n.)*: awarder; blesser; compensator; crown-giver; decorator; *evaluator; favorer;* giver; honorer; indemnity-giver; judge; *king; laurel wreath;* medal-giver; *Nobel Prize; official;* prize-giver; *quittance;* requiter; *saluter;* trophy-giver; *utu [N.Z.]; victory crown;* "well done"; xenium; *yeff [arch.];* Zion's crowns;

**rib** *(n.)*: *appurtenance;* bone; *costae* [L.]; *cage;* dorsal ~ [zoo.]; *eleventh ~;* floating ~; fifth ~; *girder; heart;* intercostal; jib-bone; keel-beam; *leaf vein; manubrium;* neck; ogive; *part;* quadricostate; *rib cage;* rack; side; spare ~; true ~; third ~; upper ~; ventral ~ [zoo.]; *vertebrae;* whale bone; xiphocostal; Y-bone; ziphosternum;

**ribbon** *(n.)*: adornment; band; bow; cordon; caddis; decoration; *embellishment;* fillet; gimp; gingham ~; head ~; inkle; *jewel;* kincob ~; levantine ~; moiré ~; narrow piece; ornament(ation); obi; petersham; *prize; quilling;* riband; silk ~; sash; strip; tape; trimming; *untied ~;* velvet ~; wire ~; *xtr. wide ~;* yellow ~; *zonule;* [*see* award]

**rich** *(adj.)*: affluent; bountiful; comfortable; *dollars; endowed;* filthy ~; forehanded; *gold;* high-class; independently wealthy; jet set; *king's ransom;* loaded; moneyed; *means; notes;* opulent; prosperous; privileged; *quartful* [arch.]; rolling-in-the-dough; successful; sumptuous; treasure-filled; upper class; vested; wealthy well-off; well-to-do; *xtry. ~; yellow boy [Br.]; zillionaire;* [*see* extravagant]

**rid** *(v.)*: *abolish; banish;* clear; divest; dispose; empty; expel; free; get rid of; *halt;* illegalize; jettison; *kill;* liberate; make free from; nullify; oust; purge; *quash;* relieve; set free; throw out; unhand; unyoke; *void; wipe out;* x-out; *yank;* zeroize;

**ride** *(v.)*: *accelerate;* be borne; cycle; catch a train; chug along; *carried;* drive; *embark;* float; *fly;* go along; head; *impelled;* jeep; *kite;* locomote; move; *navigate;* operate; proceed; pass; *quick;* rest upon; *run;* sit on; sail; travel; *underway;* voyage; wend; xfer; yede; zip;

**ridicule** *(n.)*: abuse; belittlement; contempt; derision; *eruption;* fleering; gibing; heckling; insult; jeering; knocking; laughter; mockery; name-calling; opprobrium; pillory; quibbing; railery; ribbing; scorn; scoffing; teasing; taunting; *unkindness;* vexation; wiping; *x-ing;* yah; *zinging;* [*Ant.* respect]

**ridicule** *(v.)*: abuse; belittle; chide; deride; *execrate;* fleer; gibe; humiliate; heckle; hiss; insult; jeer; jibe; knock; laugh at; mock; *name-calling; offend;* pillory; pick on; quib; rail on; scorn; scoff; sneer; tease; taunt; utter against; verbally abuse; vex; wipe; *xuld [arch.];* yock; *zap;* [*Ant.* respect]

**ridiculous** *(adj.)*: absurd; asinine; bizarre; crazy; cockamamie; daft; *eccentric;* funny; farcical; far-fetched; goofy; haywire; incredible; impossible; illogical; *jokey;* kooky; laughable; ludicrous; mad; nutty; outrageous; preposterous; queer; risible; silly; strange; *tall;* unbelievable; unreasonable; *variant;* weird; whacky; *xenomorphic; yokelish;* zany; [*Ant.* realistic]

**ridge** *(n. grip)*: ambi; brim; crease; *dorsum;* edge; finger-grip; fold; grip; hand-grip; indentation; *jags;* knurl; lip; ledge; *mound;* notch; overlap; pleat; *porcated; querl;* rim; side-grip; tab; *unevenness; varix;* wrinkle; wale; *x-ing; yank;* zigzag grip;

**ridge** *(n. mountain ridge)*: arête; berm; crest; *dorsum;* drumlin; edge; esker; escarpment; fold; glacial ~; hogback; *ice ~;* jog; kaim; kotal; ledge; lip; mountainside; mountain pass; nek; outcrop; osar; pass; pleat; point bar; *quoif;* ridge; rim; saddle; serac; *top ~; upper ~;* verge; windrow; *Xiao;* yardang; *zone;*

**rift** *(n.)*: aperture; break; breach; crack; cleft; division; divide; estrangement; fracture; fissure; fork; gulf; gap; hiatus; interstice; *junction;* knapple; laceration; *moat;* non-continuum; opening; parting; *quadrisection;* rend; split; schism; tear; uncoupling; valley; *wedge; x-ing out;* yawn; zap; [*see* disagreement; *Ant.* reconciliation]

**right** *(adj.)*: accurate; appropriate; becoming; correct; definite; dead-on; exact; factual; fitting; genuine; good; honest; indubitable; just; kosher; legitimate; moral; never-failing; orthodox; proper; questionless; real; righteous; sound; suitable; true; unerring; veritable; valid; well-proven; *x-parent; yes;* zero-error;

**right** *(n. legal or moral claim)*: appurtenance; authority; benefit; birth~; claim; constitutional ~; droit; entitlement; freedom; *good reason;* God-given ~; holding; imperium; inalienable ~; jactitation; *known ~;* legal ~; moral ~; natural ~; option; property ~; perquisite; *questionless;* rights; say-so; tenable ~; unalienable ~; valid claim; warrant; *xfer; yard; zealous affirmation;*
**righteous** *(adj.)*: aboveboard; blameless; chaste; decent; ethical; faultless; good; godly; holy; honorable; impeccable; immaculate; just; *keen;* law-abiding; moral; non-sinful; outstanding; pure; perfect; qualmless; reputable; right; sinless; truehearted; upright; virtuous; worthy; *xia* [Chin.]; *yielded to God; zero-blame;*
**righteousness** *(n.)*: angelic; blamelessness; character; chasteness; decency; ethicalness; faultlessness; goodness; godliness; holiness; integrity; impeccability; justness; *kalokagathia* [Gr.]; *legitimacy;* morality; non-sinfulness; *over-scrupulousness;* probity; *quality;* rectitude; sinlessness; trueheartedness; uprightness; virtue; worthiness; *xtry; yieldedness to God; zero-blame;*
**rightful** *(adj.)*: authentic; bona fide; correct; definite; exact; factual; genuine; honest; indubitable; intended; just(ifiable); known; legitimate; meet; never-failing; *open;* proper; qualified; real; right; sure; true; unquestionable; valid; well-proven; *x-parent; yes;* 'zactly [dial.];
**rigid** *(adj.)*: adamant; bendless; changeless; dogged; ever- ~; firm; grim; hard; inflexible; *jaw-set; keep;* lasting; mulish; nonflexible; obstinate; petrous; *quality;* rock-solid; renitent; stiff; stubborn; solid; tough; unbending; unyielding; very rigid; *willful; x-grained;* yieldless; zero give; [*Ant.* rubbery]
**rigor** *(n.)*: asperity; brutality; cruelty; difficulty; extremeness; fierceness; *force;* graveness; harshness; intensity; *jabbing;* keenness; laboriousness; mercilessness; *nastiness;* onerousness; pitilessness; *quantitative;* rigidity; severity; toil; unrelentingness; vehemence weightiness; *xtry.; yondmost;* zeal;
**rigorous** *(adj.)*: arduous; backbreaking; challenging; difficult; exhausting; fatiguing; grueling; hard; intense; intensive; jading; killing; laborious; moiling; not easy; operose; pitiless; *quite hard;* rigid; rough; strenuous; toilsome; unrelenting; vehement; wearisome; *x-heavy; yare; zapping;* [*Ant.* relaxed]
**rim** *(n.)*: abuttal; border; brim; chine; circumference; *dawn;* edge; fringe; frontier; fore-edge; felly; gate; hem; inception; interface; *imbordered; jurisdiction; kept limit;* lip; ledge; margin; *narrow;* outskirts; perimeter; quadra; rand; *ridge;* skirt; threshold; ulterior; verge; *wheel ~; x-border; yonder;* zone;
**rind** *(n.)*: aril; bark; cortex; dermis; exocarp; *fringe; green;* hull; husk; integument; jacket; *kaffir ~; layer; lemon peel;* membrane; *non-edible;* outer layer; protective layer; peel; *quince skin; rough exterior;* skin; tegument; *throw-away part; unwanted part;* verge; *without; x.; yellow husk;* zest;
**ring** *(n. finger band)*: annulus; band; circle; circuit; diamond ~; eyelet; ferrule; *gold ~; gimbal;* grommet; hoop; incirclet; *jewelry; key ~;* loop; manil; *nose ~; orb;* parrel; quoit; ringlet; *silver ~;* terret; *trinket; unicircular;* vervel; *wedding band; x-radius; y-radius;* zonule;
**ring** *(n. noise)*: alarm; bell; bong; buzz; chime; chimb; ding(-dong); *echo; fweet!;* gong; hum; *intonation;* jingle; knoll; ka-ching; *loud ~;* music; *noise; output;* ping; peal; *quake;* reverberation; sound; toll; *tinkle;* tang; *tone; utterance; vibration;* voice [poet.]; wheetle; *x-ing; yammer;* zing;
**rinse** *(v.)*: ablute; bathe; cleanse; dip; expurgate; flush; get clean; hose (off; down); immerse; *jalap;* kill germs; launder; machine-wash; *neaten;* outwash; purify; *quintessentialize;* rid; synd; tub; unsully; *vat;* wash; *xylol; yellow soap; zierlich [G.];*
**riot** *(n.)*: anarchy; bedlam; commotion; disturbance; embroilment; emeute; fracas; general uprising; hullabaloo; insurrection; jacquerie; kick-up; *loud ~;* mayhem; noise; outrage; pandemonium; quarrel; revolt; sedition; tumult; uproar; uprising; violence; welter; xtry. uprising; *yelling; zoo;*
**riot** *(v.)*: attack; brawl; cast off; demonstrate; *enmity;* fight; gainstand; have uprising; insurrect; *jump ship;* kick; *lawless;* mutiny; *not listen;* overthrow; *perfidy; quake;* rebel; revolt; strive; throw off (yoke); uprise; *violence;* withstanding; *xgress; yieldless; zealot;*
**riotous** *(adj.)*: abandoned; baccchanal; bacchic; carefree; dissolute; drunken; extravagant; frolicsome; gratuitous; hedonistic; immoral; indulgent; intemperate; jovial; *kinky;* licentious; mischievous; noisy; orgiastic; playsome; *quad;* reveling; shameless; treasonable; unrestrained; *venery;* wanton; wild; *x-rated; yielded to the flesh;* zizzy;

**rip** *(v.)*: avulse; break; crack; cut; dilacerate; *eventerate;* fritter; gash; hackle; *incide;* jerk; *kedge;* laniate; lacerate; mutilate; *not together; open;* peel; part; *quarter;* rend; slit; shred; separate; slice; tear; unseam; *vell;* wrest; x-sect; yank apart; zip;

**ripe** *(adj.)*: able to be used; *blossomed;* complete; developed; edible; fit; full-grown; grown; *good;* harvestable; ideal; juicy; keen; *largened;* mellow; mature; nubile; omy; *over~;* pickable; perfect; qualified; ripened; ready; supple; timely; *unspoiled; very good;* well-ready; *XL;* yielded; *zapote;*

**ripen** *(v.)*: age; bring to perfection; come to peak; develop; *evolve; enlarge;* fully mature; grow ripe; *heighten;* increase; *jump up;* keep growing; largen; maturate; mature; mellow; *nourish; over~;* progress; perfect; *qualify;* ready; sprout; season; strengthen; *thrive;* upshoot; vegetate; wax greater; *XL; yain* [arch.]; *zoom up;*

**ripeness** *(n.)*: age; *blossomed;* completion; development; edibleness; fruition; goodness; harvestability; idealness; juiciness; keenness; *luxuriation;* maturation; mellowness; *near ~; over~;* perfection; peak; *quality;* readiness; suppuration; timeliness; *unspoiled; very good;* well-ready; *XL;* yielding; *zapote;*

**rise** *(v.)*: arise; ascend; augment; ascend; become higher; boost; climb; crest; develop; escalate; fly up; grow; go up; get up; heighten; hike; increase; jump up; *keep going up;* largen; levitate; mount; *nudge higher; originate;* progress; *quantum increase;* raise; rocket; shoot up; soar; skyrocket; stand; take off; upshoot; vault; wax greater; well; *XL; yain* [arch.]; zoom up; [*see* wake; *Ant.* recede]

**risen** *(adj.)*: arisen; *alive;* brought back; come forth; disquieted; exalted; *firstfruits;* gone up; *higher;* increased; jumped up; *kindled;* living; made alive; *not dead; out; performed;* quickened; raised; resurrected; sprung forth; *triumphant;* up; *victorious;* well-risen; *xfer;* yet alive; *zoetic;*

**risk** *(n.)*: adversity; bet; chance; danger; endangerment; fortuity; gamble; hazard; imperilment; jeopardy; known ~; liability; menace; maleficence; non-safety; opportunity; peril; *questionable;* risking; self- ~; threat; unsureness; unsafety; venture; wager; "x"; *yeopartie* [arch.]; zero safety;

**risk** *(v.)*: attempt; afford; adventure; bet; chance; dare; endanger; face; gamble; hazard; imperil; jeopardize; *known ~;* lay on the line; menace; *non-safety;* open to danger; peril; put at ~; *questionable;* run the ~; step out on a limb; take the ~; *unsafe;* venture; wager; *"x"; yeopartie [arch.];* zero safety;

**ritual** *(n.)*: amenities; buckram; ceremony; *duty;* exercise; formality; graces; holy rite; initiatory; *jubilee;* kept tradition; liturgy; mores; night ceremony; observance; practice; *quadrisacramentalism;* rite; religious ceremony; sacrament; tradition; tribal custom; *unchanged ~;* venerated custom; wont; *xtry. ~; yet traditional;* zet [dial.];

**rivalry** *(n.)*: antagonism; battle; bout; competition; dispute; emulation; enmity; fight; gall; hostility; inimicality; jealousy; *kampf* [G.]; locking horns; mêlée; noncooperation; opposition; *position warfare;* quarrel; resentment; struggle; striving; tussle; unfriendliness; vying; war; *x-fire;* yed; *zealous ~;*

**river** *(n.)*: arroyo; brook; creek; deluge; effluent; estuary; flood; freshet; flow; fluvial; gully; headwaters; inlet; *jheel [Ind.];* keld; lough; millstream; main stem; narrows; outlet; prong; quebrada; rill; rivulet; stream; tributary; torrent; *underground stream; voe;* waterway; *xyrisic;* yeo; Zee [G.]; [*see* sea; lake]

**riverside** *(n.)*: aquatic; bank; coast; dockside; edge; front; *gulf side; harbor side; inlet; jetty side; key side;* lakeside; lakefront; land's end; *millstream;* near shore; oceanside; pier side; quayside; riverbank; ripa; shore; *tidal; unhindered view; voe;* waterfront; waterside; *xyrisic;* yeo; Zee [G.];

**road** *(n.)*: avenue; boulevard; byway; course; corridor; drive; dirt ~; esplanade; expressway; freeway; footpath; footsteps; fashion; glade; gravel ~; gateway; highway; interstate; ice road; journey-way; *king's highway;* lane; mews; means; *main street;* non-toll road; outstreet; post ~; path(way); passage(way); parkway; queen's highway; roadway; route; street; thoroughfare; turnpike; thruway; toll ~; *underpass; vennel;* way; xystum; *yong* [arch.]; zwinger;

**roam** *(v.)*: amble; bum around; cruise; drift; expatiate; float; *flânerie* [F.]; go; gad; hoof; *interlope;* jaunt; knock about; lumber; mosey; meander; noctivagant; outwalk; promenade; *quicken;* ramble; rove; range; stray; stroll; saunter; tramp; travel; *underway;* venture; wander; xfer; yaw; zigzag;

**roar** *(n.) aloud;* bellow; blast; cry; discharge; exclamation; eruption; *fuss;* growl; holler; *inveigh;* jubilation; keen; loud ~; moan; mafficking; noise; outcry; *proclaim; quiritation;* rumble; reverberation; snarl; thundering; uproar: vociferation; wail; *xenophonia;* yowl; *zing;*
**roar** *(v.) aloud;* bellow; blast; cry; din; erupt; *fuss;* growl; holler; *inveigh; jubilate;* keen; *lament;* moan; maffick; noise; outcry; *proclaim; quiritation;* rumble; reverberate; snarl; thunder; *utter;* vociferate; wail; *xenophonia;* yowl; *zing;*
**roast** *(v.):* anneal; bake; broil; brown; cook; decrepitate; dry ~; *evenly ~;* fry; grill; heat; incinerate; jumbal; kiln-bake; *let bake;* make; *neal [arch.];* oven- ~; overheat; *prepare;* qualm [arch.]; rotisserie; sear; toast; torrefy; undercook; *very hot;* whip up; *xeo;* yark; *zap;*
**rob** *(v.):* abstract; burglarize; cabbage; deprive; despoil; *embezzle;* excoriate; filch; *grab;* hoist; hold up; heist; *impalm;* jack; *kleptomania;* lift; *loot;* mug; manavel [naut.]; nim; nobble; *obtain;* pilfer; purloin; pick-pocket; plunder; peculate; *quad;* reave; rifle; rip off; relieve; remove; steal; spoil; shoplift; swipe; stick-up; strip; take; thieve(rize); unpurse; *villany;* wrest; walk off with; *xfer; yank; zip away;*
**robbery** *(n.):* abstraction; burglary; breaking and entering; brigandage; caper; *crime;* deprivation; daylight ~; excoriation; extortion; filching; grand larceny; heist; holdup; housebreaking; highway ~; *impalming; identity theft;* job; kleptomania; larceny; mugging; nimming; *obtaining;* pilfering; purloining; petty larceny; *quad;* rip-off; stealing; shoplifting; theft; thievery; unpursing; *underhandedness;* violence; villainy; wresting; *xfer; yanking; zipping away;*
**robe** *(n.):* abaya; bath~; cloak; cassock; dalmatic; evening ~; frock; gown; housecoat; ihram; jerkin; kirtle; laticlave; manto; night-robe; overtunic; paranja [fem.]; *quaintry [arch.];* rochet; simar; soutane; tunic; tabard; under~; vestment; *ward~;* XL; yelek [Turk. fem.]; zimarra;
**robust** *(adj.):* able-bodied; burly; *capable;* durable; energetic; enduring; fit; great; husky; iron; *jusqu'au bout [F.];* keen; lusty; mighty; nervy; obstinate; oaky; powerful; *quality;* rugged; strong; tough; unflagging; vigorous; well-built; well-set; *x-strong;* yauld; zesty;
**rock** *(n.):* argillite; boulder; bed~; crag; clast; dibstone; *eaglestone;* formation; fieldstone; *flint;* granite; geode; *hairstone; igneous ~;* jackstone; klip; *kettle-stone; lapillus;* mineral; monolith; nugget; outcrop; pebble; *quartz;* river boulder; stone; *trap~;* uranite; volcanic ~; *whitestone; xenolith; yenite; zircon;*
**rock** *(v.):* alternate; astound; bank; coggle; disturb; *exchange;* fishtail; go back and forth; heel; *incline;* jolt; jee; keel; list; lean; lurch; move; nutate; oscillate; pitch; *quake;* reel; roll; sway; swing; shock; shoogle; tilt; teeter; upheave; veer; wag; *xuld* [arch.]; yaw; zag;
**rock and roll** *(n.):* acid rock; boogie woogie; contemporary music; death metal; emo; *electric guitar music;* folk rock; grunge; hard rock; heavy metal; indie ~; jazz-rock; *je-je* [F.]; jungle-music [derog.]; *keyboard; long-haired music;* metal; Mersey beat; mbanqanga [Afr.]; noise; new wave; *ode;* punk rock; pop music; psychedelic ~; *Quarrymen;* rock (music); soft rock; *syncopated; tune; underbeat; vocalization; wicked; xylophone; yé-yé* [F.]; *zouk;*
**rocky** *(adj.):* aggregate; bouldery; craggy; *dolomite; eaglestone;* flintlike; granitic; *hard;* igneous; jagged; *klip;* lithoid; lapideous; lithoid; monolithic; *nuggety; obsidian;* pebbly; petrous; quartzy; rocklike; rugged; stony; tough; *uranite;* volcanic; *whitestone;* xenolithic; yonnie-like; zircon-filled;
**rod** *(n.):* alpenstock; baton; bill; cane; dagger-staff; espantoon; ferule; godendag; hasta; *instrument;* jambee; kebbie; langet; malacca; nibby; officer's staff; pole; quarterstaff; rancoon; staff; tipstaff; *ununke* [Afr.]; *virgulate;* wad-staff; walking stick; *xylon;* yam stick; *zagaye;*
**role** *(n.):* appointment; *business;* charge; duty; *element;* function; *general function;* high calling; intent; identity; job; key role; *liability;* mission; *necessity;* obligation; office; occupation; part; place; purpose; position; persona; quarters; responsibility; station; task; undertaking; vocation; work; xci.; *yoke; zone;*
**roll** *(n. bread roll): angu bread;* bun; cross bun; dinner ~; *edible;* finger ~; *gingerbread;* hardtack; hard ~; *Italian bread; jannock;* kaiser ~; *light cake;* muffin; morning ~; *naan bread;* oat ~; pan dulce; *quick bread;* rusk; sweet ~; *toast; unleavened bread;* wheat ~; *x bun; yuan hsiao* [Chin.]; zwieback;

**roll** *(n. list of names)*: alphabetized list; book; catalog; directory; enumeration; enrollment; file; *given; history;* itemized ~; inventory; job ~; key listing; list(ing); muster ~; *mailing list;* names; *number;* ordered list; posting; print-out; *qualified list;* register; roster; record; *statement;* table; *unabridged list;* vita; written list; *x-list;* yellow sheet [crim. law]; *zet [dial.];*
**roll** *(v.)*: *around;* billow; becurl; bowl; curl; circle; *downward;* enwrap; flip; furl; gyrate; go around; hurl; hurtle; incurvate; *jee; keel;* loop; move; nutate; orb; purl; querl; revolve; rotate; sidle; spin; twirl; turn; tumble; troll; trundle; unwind; volt; whirl; wheel; wind; wheel; whirl; wind; wallow; wrap; *x-ing; yo-yo; zwoosh;*
**romance** *(n.)*: affection; *burning;* coquetry; dalliance; endearment; *fire; gentleness; gushiness; heat;* infatuation; involvement; *intimacy; joy;* keenness; love affair; *mania; nuptial precursor; obsession;* passion; *quixotic;* relationship; sweetness; tenderness; *undying love; vehemence;* warmth; *xenophilia;* yearning; zeal;
**romantic** *(adj.)*: amorous; becharmed; charming; cuddly; dreamy; emotional; extravagant; *enthralled;* fanciful; *fairytale;* gentle; gushy; *heart-smitten;* idealistic; *jealous;* kissy; loving; mushy; mad; nice; over- ~; passionate; quixotic; romance-filled; sentimental; sweet; snuggly; tender; utopian; *Valentine;* warm; *x-fixed; yearnful; zealous;* [Ant. revulsive]
**roof** *(v.)*: arched ~; barrel-arched ~; ceiling; curb- ~; dome; *eave; edifice;* flat ~; gable ~; gambrel ~; housetop; hip- ~; imbrex and tegula ~; *jut-* ~; knee- ~; lacunar; marquee; mansard ~; non-reflective solar panel ~; onion dome; *overhead;* pitched ~; *quoif;* rooftop; slope; slant ~; slate ~; tile ~; top; thatch ~; upper part; verge; wooden-shingle ~; *xanadu; yago* [Jap.]; *zenith;*
**room** *(n.)*: * antechamber; apartment; area; back~; bed~; berth; chamber; drawing ~; den; end ~; flat; front~; guest chamber; gallery; house~; hall; inhabitance; *john; kitchen;* keeping ~; lounge; living ~; middle common ~; nook; *observatory;* parlor; place; *play~;* quarters; residence; range; space; suite; sun~; TV ~; utility ~; vestry; ward(~); waiting ~; xystum; *yu* [Chin.]; zeta;
**roomy** *(adj.)*: abundant; ample; airy; big; capacious; commodious; disproportionate; extensive; full-size; giant; generous; huge; immense; jumbo-sized; king-size; large; massive; non-claustrophobic; open; oversize; prodigious; quantitative; *remarkable;* spacious; tremendous; uncramped; voluminous; wide; XL; *Ymir; zaftig;* [Ant. restrictive]
**root** *(n.)*: aerial ~; bulb; basis; corm; cause; derivation; earthnut; fine ~; fountainhead; fibrous ~; fibril; *ground;* hollow- ~; inducement; *jut;* knee ~; lead; *madumbi; nourishment; oca;* origin; plant ~; *quintessence;* radix; shoot; source; tuber; *underground;* vascular ~; *way down;* xylem; yamp; *zedoary;*
**roots** *(n. source)*: ancestors; ancestry; beginnings; *bloodline; clan;* derivation; *extraction;* family tree; forbearers; fathers; genesis; *heritage;* inception; *jet; kinfolk; line; making; nibiliary;* origin; progenitors; parentage; *quarter;* roots; *race;* source; *tribe; ultimate cause; venter; wellspring; x-link; yoni* [Skr.]; *zoe;*
**rope** *(n.)*: *abb;* braid; cord; cable(t); down-haul; earing; foretack; gantline; hemp; hank; halliard; *intertwined;* jack-line; jute; keel-rope; line; lanyard; mainsheet; nautical ~; osier ~; port- ~; painter; prolonge; qiviut; runner; restraint; *rigging;* strand; twine; tack; *uncoil;* vang; widdy; x-braid; yard- ~; zein;
**rot** *(v.)*: addle; break down; corrupt; decay; decompose; erode; fester; go bad; hoar; impair; *jade; ketty; labelfaction;* moulder; mortify; *necrosis; off;* oxidize; putrefy; queer; ruin; spoil; taint; *undo; vile;* welk; *xylaria;* yellow; *zorch;*
**rotate** *(v.)*: alternate; *backspin;* circle; do a circle; exchange; flip; go around; hurtle; interchange; jump; *keep going around;* loop; move around; nutate; orb; purl; pivot; querl; revolve; spin; swivel; turn; upsweep; volt; whirl; wheel; *x-ing; yede [arch.];* zip around;
**rotation** *(n.)*: alternation; backspin; cycle; circling; *downspin;* English; flipping around; gyration; hurtling; interchange; *juttering; keep turning;* looping; moving around; nutation; orbit; purling; querling; revolution; rotary; spin; turning; underspin; variation; whirl; *x-ing; yede [arch.];* zipping around;

**rotten** *(n.)*: addled; bad; broken down; carious; corrupt(ed); decayed; decomposed; evil; foul; fusty; fetid; gone bad; hoared; impaired; *jaded;* ketty; loathsome; moldy; no good; nasty; off; putrefied; putrid; peccant; perished; putrescent; queered; rancid; spoiled; stale; sour; tainted; unfresh; vile; well-rotted; wretched; wersh; *xylaria;* yecchy; *zilch;*
**rottenness** *(n.)*: autolysis; badness; bacterial decay; breakdown; corruption decay; dry rot; evil; foulness; *gangrene;* horridness; *ickiness; jadedness;* kettiness; labelfaction; morification; moldiness; nastiness; *opprobrium;* putrescence; putridity; putrefaction; *queasiness;* rancidness; rancidity; ruination; spoilage; tainting; unpleasantness; vileness; welking; wood rot; xylaria; yecchiness; *zapping;*
**rough** *(adj.)*: asperous; burly; brawny; bumpy; brutal; coarse; durable; difficult; enduring; forceful; good; husky; hard; hefty; irregular; jagged; knotty; lumpy; mighty; non-smooth; *offensive;* pitted; *quality;* rugged; rocky; strong; sturdy; tough; uneven; violent; well-built; *x-strong; yieldless; zippy;*
**round** *(adj.)*: annular; ball-shaped; circular; curved; cylindrical; discoid; encyclical; *elliptical;* falcade; globous; globular; hoop-shaped; *humped;* incirclet; *j-curve; kinch;* looping; *moving circularly;* nodular; orbicular; perispheric; *quasi-circular;* rounded; rotund; spherical; spheroidal; turning; unangular; verticil; winding; wheel-shaped; *x-radius; y-radius; zonical;*
**roundness** *(n.)*: annularity; ball-shape; circularity; curvature; disc-shape; encyclical shape; *falcade;* globularity; hoop shape; incirclet; *j-curve; kinch;* loop; *moving circularly;* nodularity; orbicularity; perisphericness; *quasi-circularity;* roundedness; rotundity; sphericity; sphericalness; turning; unangularity; verticil shape; wheel-shape; *x-radius; y-radius; zonicalness;* [*Ant.* rectangularity]
**rouse** *(v.)*: arouse; awaken; bestir; call up; disturb; disquiet; excite; fuel; fire up; goad; hearten; hype-up; incite; jar; kindle; liven; move; motivate; *nudge;* overexcite; provoke; quicken; revive; stir; trouble; upset; vivify; wake(n); *xuld [arch.];* yerk; *zing;* [*Ant.* relax]
**route** *(n.)*: avenue; boulevard; course; corridor; drive; expressway; freeway; footpath; *glade;* highway; interstate; journey-way; king's highway; lane; line; motorway; means; non-toll road; outstreet; path(way); parkway; *quo mode* [L.]; road; street; trail; track; turnpike; *underpass;* vennel; way; *xyst; yong* [arch.]; *zwinger;*
**routine** *(adj.)*: automatic; boring; beaten-path; customary; common; daily; everyday; frequent; general; habitual; inveterate; jake [Br.]; known; long-established; mechanical; normal; ordinary; perfunctory; quotidian; regular; scheduled; typical; usual; unvarying; *very ~;* wonted; *x-type; yearly; zero variation;* [*Ant.* rare]
**routine** *(n.)*: act; business; custom; course; daily business; established practice; fashion; general behavioral pattern; habit; ingrained action; *jake [Br.];* known pattern; long-established practice; manner; normal ~; *old ways;* pattern; practice; *quo mode* [L.]; regimen; schedule; tradition; *usage; very consistent:* way of doing things; *x-type;* yearly ~; *zero variation;*
**row** *(v.)*: actuate; bring along; conduct; convey; drive; *edge;* feather; *get;* heave; impel; *jet; kest; lead;* move; *navigate;* oar; paddle; propel; pull; *quant; race;* scull; transport; use oars; voyage; work the oars; *xfer; york; zip;* [see sail]
**rowdy** *(adj.)*: audacious; boisterous; crazy; disorderly; disruptive; *energetic;* frolicking; *grating;* high-spirited; intemperate; jackanapes; knavish; loud; lively; misbehaved; noisy; overexcited; *pernicious; querulous;* raucous; riotous; rambunctious; rough; strident; troublemaking; unruly; uproarious; vexatious; wild; *x-grained;* yeasty; *zealous;*
**royal** *(adj.)*: aristocratic; *authoritative;* blueblooded; commanding; dignified; excellent; fine; grand; high-born; imperial; *judicious;* kingly; lordly; majestic; monarchal; noble; *ostentatious;* princely; queenly [fem.]; regal; sovereign; *tsarish;* uncommon; valiant; well-born; xtry.; yorkist; *zarish* [arch.];
**royalty** *(n.)*: aristocracy; blue-bloodedness; command; dignity; excellence; fineness; gallantry; grace; honor; Highness; impressiveness; *judiciousness;* kingliness; loftiness; majesty; nobleness; *ostentation;* princeliness; pompousness; queenliness [fem.]; regality; sovereignty; *tsarishness;* uncommon; valor; *well-born; xtry.; yorkist; zarishness* [arch.];

**rub** *(v.)*: apply; anoint; agitate; abrade; butter; burnish; buff; caress; chafe; drag; dry~; embrocate; feel; frictionize; graze; grind; hand- ~; *irritate;* jigger; *knead; luster;* massage; *nuzzle;* overspread; polish; *quab;* relay; raze; *rubdown;* spread; smooth; smear; scrub; scour; triturate; *use; violent agitation;* wipe; wear down; *xfer;* yark; *zip;*

**rubble** *(n.)*: accident scene; broken fragments; chunks; debris; *elements;* fragments; *granules;* heap; *items;* junk; *ket; loppings; mass; nihil* [L.]; oddments; pieces; *quantity;* remains; ruins; stones; talus; *undone; vestiges;* wreckage; *x-mal [G.]; yucky; zone;*

**ruddy** *(adj.)*: *attractive;* blowzy; cerise; *dandy;* erubescent; flush; glowing; healthy-looking; incarnadine; juvenescent; *keen;* lusty; *madder; nourished; okay;* pinkish; pink-cheeked; *quite healthy;* reddish; rosy(-cheeked); red-faced; rubescent; sorrel; *trim; unimpaired;* very healthy; well-nourished; *xtry. healthy;* youthy; *zinc orange;*

**rude** *(adj.)*: abhorrent; appalling; bad-mannered; base; brutish; crude; coarse; crass; churlish; discourteous; disrespectful; evil; foul; gauche; homebred; impolite; ill-mannered; jaded; *kitsch;* loathsome; loutish; mean; nasty; obnoxious; offensive; pathetic; queer-mannered; reprehensible; raw; rough; sorry; shocking; terrible; tasteless; tactless; uncouth; uncivil; unrefined; vile; vulgar; wretched; wicked; *x-rated;* yokelish; zhlubby; [*Ant.* refined]

**rudeness** *(n.)*: abhorrence; baseness; crudeness; crassness; churlishness; discourtesy; disrespect; evil; foulness; gaucheness; horribleness; impoliteness; ill-manneredness; *jadedness;* kitsch; loutishness; meanness; nastiness; obnoxiousness; offensiveness; poor manners; *quad;* rawness; reprehension; roughness; surliness; terribleness; tactlessness; uncouthness; vileness; vulgarity; wretchedness; *x-rating;* yuckiness; zhlubbiness; [*Ant.* refinement]

**rue** *(v.)*: *abhor;* bewail; *condemn;* deplore; *emphatically regret;* feel sorry; grieve; hate; *inveigh; judder; keen;* lament; mourn; *non-innocence;* oversorrow; *plead guilty; quain* [arch.]; regret; sorrow; think better of; *unhappy; voice my* ~; wish it never happened; *xtry. sorrow;* yearn; *zealless;* [*Ant.* rejoice]

**rugged** *(adj. rough)*: asperous; bumpy; craggy; difficult; ever- ~; furrowed; grueling; gruff; harsh; irregular; jagged; knaggy; lapidarious; most difficult; non-smooth; onerous; pitted; quartzy; rough; rocky; stony; scabrous; tough; uneven; *villous;* wild; *xenolithic;* yieldless; *zero smoothness;* [*Ant.* refined]

**rugged** *(adj. strong)*: adamant; brawny; *capable;* durable; enduring; firm; good; hardy; iron; *jusqu'au bout [F.]; keen;* lusty; mighty; manly; *nervy; obstinate;* powerful; *quality;* rough; robust; strong; sturdy; tough; unflagging; *vigorous;* well-built; x-strong; yauld; *zippy;*

**ruin** *(v.)*: annihilate; break; crush; damage; devastation; efface; finish off; grind to dust; havoc; impoverish; *junk;* kill; lay waste; mangle; mar; nullify; olate; pull down; quash; ruinate; ravage; rack; raze; spoil; throw down; trash; unroot; vitiate; wreck; *x-ing;* yank down; zap; [*Ant.* remake]

**ruination** *(n.)*: annihilation; breaking; crushing; destruction; devastation; death; effacement; finishing off; grinding to dust; havoc; incapacitation; *junking;* killing; loss; laying waste; mashing; nullification; olation; pulling down; quashing; ruin; spoiling; trashing; undoing; vitiation; wreckage; *x-ing;* yanking down; zapping;

**rule** *(n. standard or law)*: act; bylaw; command; code; canon; directive; edict; *fatwa* [Mos.]; guideline; gauge; *halacha* [Heb.]; imperative; judgment; *keleusmatic;* law; mandate; measure; norm; ordinance; order; principle; qualifier; regulation; ruling; standard; statute; tenet; ukase; *verdict; word;* XO mandate; yardstick; *zakon* [Rus.];

**rule** *(n. dominion)*: authority; administration; *bishopric;* control; charge; command; direction; dominion; eminence; *eldership;* empery; first place; government; governance; headship; imperium; jurisdiction; kingship; leadership; lordship; management; monarchy; *necessitation;* oversight; power; *queenship;* reign; supervision; sovereignty; top position; *the* throne; use of authority; *vizierate;* wardenship; xerifdom; yard; *zakon [Rus.];*

**rule** *(v. oversee)*: administer; bid; control; command; direct; dominate; domineer; execute authority; *force;* govern; guide; head; instruct; judge; keep; lead; manage; master; *necessitate;* oversee; preside; predominate; *queen;* run; reign; superintend; take the lead; *usurp authority; voice;* wield authority; *xenagogue; yeme* [arch.]; *zakon* [Rus.];
**ruler** *(n. measuring stick)*: aluminum ~; *Biltmore stick;* carpenter's rule; desk ~; electronic tape measure; folding rule; gauge; *half-foot; instrument;* Jacob's staff; *kilometer;* line gauge; meter stick; measure; measuring tape; *nine-foot ~; object;* pole; plastic ~; *quantity;* rule; stick; steel ~; straightedge; tape measure (-line); utility ~; vara [Sp.]; wooden ~; *x unit;* yardstick; zigzag rule;
**ruler** *(n. one in charge)*: autocrat; authority; boss; chief; director; dynast; ethnarch; executive; *first;* governor; head; intendant; jarl; king; leader; lord; master; manager; nobleman; overseer; overlord; president; principal; prefect; patriarch; queen [fem.]; regent; rector; superior; superintendent; supervisor; taskmaster; *ultimate authority;* vizer; warden; warlord; xerif [Arab.]; *yokemaster;* zayim;
**rumor** *(n.)*: aspersions; blather; bruit; chatter; *defamation; evil-speaking;* furphy [Aus.]; gossip; *grapevine;* hearsay; *information;* juicy gossip; *khubber* [Arab.]; leak; *lies; mention;* news; on-dit; prattle; quidnunc; report; ~ *mill;* story; smear; tale; utterance; vicious ~; word; *xenophonia; yakking; zeroing in;*
**rumor** *(v.)*: announce; blather; bruit; badmouth; chatter; declaim; echo; fame; gossip; *holler; herald;* inform; iterate; *jaw; klubber [Arab.];* leak; mention; natter; noise; opine; prattle; quote; repeat; recite; say; smear; tell; tattle; talk; utter; voice; whisper; *xenophonia;* yarn; *zero in;*
**run** *(v. administer)*: administer; boss; control; drive; direct; *execute; force;* govern; head; influence; judge; keep under control; lead; manage; *nobble;* operate; oversee; pilot; prevail; *quell;* rule; superintend; take the oversight of; *use; vanquish; weight; XO;* yeme; *zero delta;*
**run** *(v. charge)*: accelerate; bolt; charge; dash; dart; elan; flash; gallop; hurtle; *inflow;* jog; *keep pace;* lope; move; *nimble;* out~; over~; *proceed;* quicken; rush; race; romp; sprint; streak; scurry; scamper; tear; trot; *uprush; velocity;* whiz; whip; *xuld [arch.];* yern; zip;
**runaway** *(n.)*: absconder; bolter; *cut out;* deserter; escapee; fugitive; *get away;* hooky-player; *infractor;* jail-breaker; *knuck;* leaver; man on the run; *not present;* outlaw; *on the run; price on one's head;* quitter; runner; refugee; skedaddler; shirker; truant; *unapprehended; vacate;* withdrawer; *xfer; yegg; zip away;*
**run-down** *(adj.)*: abandoned; broken down; contemptible; dilapidated; exhausted; feeble; *grungy;* haggard; in ruins; junky; *keg-meg; last legs;* messy; neglected; old; paltry; *quashed;* ramshackle; shabby; *shambles;* tatty; utterly forsaken; *vile;* worn-out; *x'ed;* yucky; zapped;
**runner** *(n.)*: athlete; bolter; courier; charger; contestant; candidate; dasher; darter; emissary; flasher; flier; goer; galloper; hurrier; harrier; *interloper;* jogger; *keep pace;* loper; lapper; mover; marathon ~; niddler; operator; *out~;* pacer; quickener; racer; rusher; sprinter; trotter; *uprusher; velocity;* whizzer; XC ~; yerner; zoomer;
**rupture** *(n.)*: aperture; break; bursting; crack; division; eruption; fissure; gap; hiatus; interstice; *jolt;* knapple; laceration; *mar; non-continuum; nova;* opening; parting; puncture; proruption; *quashing;* rift; rend; split; tear; *uncoupling; violence;* wham-bang; *x-ing out;* yawn; zap;
**rupture** *(v.)*: *apart;* burst; break; crack; dehisce; erupt; fissure; give; *hurl;* issue; jet; *ka-boom;* let go; *mar; non-continuum;* open; part; puncture; prorupt; *quicken;* rip; rend; split; tear; *uncouple; violence;* wham-bang; *x-ing out;* yead; *zap;*
**rural** *(adj.)*: agricultural; agrarian; bucolic; country; dairy farm; *esne;* farm(land); geoponic; georgic; husbandry; inurbane; *joskin; kolkhoz* [Rus.]; lowland; *manse;* non-urbanized; outland; predial; pastoral; *quaint;* rustic; sylvan; *tillage;* undeveloped; upland; viticultural; wheatland; *xeriscape®; yokelish; zemledelie* [Rus.];
**ruse** *(n.)*: act; beguilement; con job; deception; ensnarement; fraud; guile; hoodwinking; imposture; japery; knavishness; lie; maneuver; nobbling; outfoxing; pretext; *quiblin [arch.];* racket; sham; scam; trick; untruth; verneuking; wile; *xtry. plot;* yentzing; *zinger;*

**rush** *(n.)*: acceleration; breaking forth; charge; cascade; darting; descent; downflow; eructation; expedition; fountain; flight; flow; flare-up; gush; hurrying; hastening; inflow; jet; kiting; lash; mad ~; *non-restraint;* outflow; outbreak; offensive; pouring; quickening; race; scramble; seizing; tearing; torrent; *uprush; velocity;* whipping; *xuld [arch.];* yerning; zipping;
**rush** *(v.)*: accelerate; break forth; blitz; cruise; dart; erupt; expedite; fly; get moving; hurry; issue; jet; kite; light; move; *non-restrained;* outrun; pour; quicken; rip; race; speed; sally; tear; *uprush; velocity;* whip; *xuld [arch.];* yern; zip; [*Ant.* restrain]
**rust** *(n.)*: atrophy; breakdown; corrosion; decomposition; disintegration; erosion; ferrugination; goethite; hydrolysis; iron oxide; *junk; killing;* labelfaction; mordication; *nullification;* oxid(iz)ation; perjoration; queering; red oxide; rustiness; spall; *tarnishing; turning to dust; undoing;* verdigris; weakening; *x-ing;* yellowing; zinc pest;
**rust** *(v.)*: atrophy; break down; corrode; disintegrate; erode; ferruginate; get ~y; hydrolyze; infuscate; *junk; killing;* labelfaction; mordicate; *nullify;* oxidize; perjorate; queer; redden with ~; *redden;* spall; *tarnish;* turn ~y; *undo; verdigris;* weaken; *x-ing;* yellow; *zinc pest;*
**rust-colored** *(adj.)*: auburn; brick; bay; cupreous; dark orange; *embrowned;* ferruginous; goethite; *helianthin;* iron-red; *jack-o-lantern;* kelp; lateritous; *miniate; nacaret;* ocher; pumpkin; *queered;* rust; reddish-brown; russet; sepia; sorrel; terra cotta; testaceous; *umber; vermillion;* wadd; *xanthous;* yellow-brown; *zincite;*
**rustic** *(adj.)*: agrarian; bucolic; backwoods; country; cornpone; crude; dirt-farmer; exurbanite; farm; georgic; hinterland; hick [off.]; inurbane; *joskin; kolkhoz [Rus.];* loutish; mountain; natural; outland; predial; plain; pastoral; *quadrat;* rural; rough; simple; *tillage;* unrefined; *vulgar;* woodsy; *Xeriscape®;* yokelish; zhlubby;
**rustic** *(n.)*: agrarian; bumpkin; boor; backwoodsman; country bumpkin; chuff; dolt; exurbanite; farmer; funk; goff; hick; hillbilly; hoosier; *ignorant fellow;* joskin; kern; knuff; lout; larrikin; mountaineer; mountainer; non-urbanite; *oaf;* provincial; peasant; put; plebeian; plowboy; *quadrat;* rube; redneck; swain; tike; *unsophisticated; vassal;* whig [Br.]; *xtry.;* yokel; yap; yob; zhlub;
**rustler** *(n.)*: abactor; bandit; cattle- ~; desperado; *enemy;* filcher; gangster; horse thief; *intruder; jailbird;* knuck; livestock thief; *man;* nabber; outlaw; poacher; *quad;* robber; ravager; stealer; thief; *unscrupulous;* villain; waddy; *xiaoren;* yegg; *zhlub;*
**rust-proof** *(adj.)*: anti-rust; *bonded;* calorized; *double-coated;* electrogalvanized; fineamin-treated; galvanized; HDG-treated; *impermeable; joint-sealed; kept; low-rust; moisture-proof;* non-rusting; oxidation-resistant; protected; *quality;* rust-proofed; stainless; treated; undersealed; VCI-treated; well-protected; *xtr. ~; yieldless;* zinc-coated; [*Ant.* rusty]
**rusty** *(n.)*: atrophied; brownish-red; corroded; cankery; decomposed; disintegrating; eroded; ferruginated; *gerontic;* hydrolyzed; ironsick [naut.]; *jaded; ketty;* lateritious; *morticancy; necrosis;* oxidized; orange-rusted; *putrefied;* queered; rusted; reasty; salt-corroded; tarnished; unwonted; *verdigris;* wadd; weakened; *xylaria; yellow-brown; zinc pest;* [*see* slow; out-of-practice; *Ant.* rust-proof]
**rut** *(n.)*: aqueduct; *breach;* channel; cart- ~; depression; engraving; furrow; groove; hollow; impression; *jheel [Ind.];* kerf; leat; *microgroove;* narrow groove; *opening; pit;* quadrisulcate; runnel; slot; trough; track; trench; U-groove; vallation; ward; wheel- ~; *x-groove;* yawn; *zanja;*
**ruthless** *(adj.)*: atrocious; brutal; cruel; callous; devious; evil; fiendish; guileful; heartless; iniquitous; jaded; knavish; licentious; malicious; merciless; nasty; obdurate; pitiless; quasi-ethical; rapacious; sinister; savage; treacherous; unmerciful; vicious; wicked; *x-gressing;* yieldless; *zero morals;* [*Ant.* righteous]
**ruthlessness** *(n.)*: atrociousness; brutality; cruelness; deviousness; evil; fiendishness; guile; heartlessness; iniquitous; jadishness; knavishness; licentious; malicious; merciless; nastiness; obduracy; pitilessness; *quaintise* [arch.]; rapaciousness; savageness; treachery; unscrupulousness; viciousness; wickedness; *xgressing;* yieldlessness; *zero morality;* [*Ant.* righteousness]

# S

**sabbatical** *(n.)*: absence; break; *cruise;* day off; excursion; furlough; gap; hiatus; holiday; interruption; journey; *kept away;* leave; *misadventure; night voyage; off;* pause; paid holiday; quest; rest; retreat; *sojourn;* time off; *undertaking;* vacation; *week off; xenization; yong* [arch.]; *zugunruhe;*

**sabotage** *(n.)*: altering; blocking; crippling; disabling; despoiling; encankering; fouling up; gumming up; hamstring; harm; impairment; jamming; knocking out; lousing up; meddling; messing with; mischief; nobbling; obstruction; putting out of commission; *quab;* rigging; spoiling; subversion; tampering; undermining; vandalism; wrecking; *x-fire; yed;* zapping; [*Ant.* succor]

**sabotage** *(v.)*: alter; bollix; break; bewreck; cripple; disrupt; disable; despoil; encanker; fix; foul up; gum up; hamper; harm; hamstring; interfere; impair; incapacitate; jam; jury-rig; knock out; louse up; meddle; mess with; monkey with; nobble; obstruct; put out of commission; *quab;* rig; spoil; subvert; tamper; undermine; vandalize; wreck; *x-fire; yed;* zap; [*Ant.* succor]

**saboteur** *(n.)*: agent; adversary; bad guy; competitor; double agent; enemy; foe; guerilla; *hearer;* infiltrator; jobber; KGB agent; *looker;* mole; nark; outsider; plant; *quadruplator;* rival; spy; secret agent; terrorist; undercover agent; villain; *wiretapper; X; yard; zarp;* [*Ant.* succorer]

**sack** *(n.)*: *alligator-skin bag;* bag; canvas bag; drawstring ~; *earthbag;* flaxen bag; gunny~; holder; *in;* jute ~; kitbag; leather bag; *mailbag; moneybag; nunny bag; overnight bag;* pouch; poke; potato ~; *quiver;* receptacle; scrip satchel; saddlebag; tote; tow ~; utility bag; *velvet pouch;* wool~; x-bag; yannigan bag; zipper-bag; [*see* ransack]

**sackcloth** *(n.)*: *ashes;* burlap; coir; *coarse cloth; dust and ashes; ejulation;* flaxcloth; gunny; hopsack; horsecloth; *inveighing;* jute; kersey; *lamentation;* mourning clothes; *non-expensive cloth;* osnaburg; *pole-davy; quen;* rags; ramie; sisal; twinecloth; *upholstery cloth; volte-face; woefulness; weeping; xanthation; yard sack; zibeline;*

**sacrament** *(n.)*: act; *the bread and wine;* ceremony; custom; duty; exercise; formality; grace-giving rite; holy rite; institution; *jubilation;* keeping; *liturgy;* ministration; mass; *notion;* observance; ordinance; performance; practice; *quadrisacramentalism;* rite; ritual; religious ceremony; service; tradition; use; *viaticum;* wont; Xn. *observance; yeastless bread; zonic ordinance;*

**sacred** *(adj.)*: awe-inspiring; blessed; consecrated; dedicated; divine; *eternal; faultless;* great; holy; hallowed; inviolable; *just; kramat* [Arab.]; *laudable;* most ~; numinous; *outstanding;* purified; *quality;* revered; religious; sanctified; *timeless;* undefiled; untouchable; venerated; virtuous; worthy; *Xn.;* yielded (to God); zero-defect; [*Ant.* secular]

**sacrifice** *(n.)*: atonement; burnt offering; blood ~; *beast;* contribution; consecration; deprivation; drink offering; evening oblation; expiation; forfeiture; flow of blood; gift; guilt offering; hecatomb; holocaust; immolation; *justification;* krioboly; killing; libation; mactation; night oblation; offering; oblation; present; propitiation; *quitclaim;* ritual killing; ransom; slaughter; sacrificatory; thank offering; *undertaking;* victimization; wave offering; xenium; yielding; yajna [Hind.]; *zoid;*

   **Kinds of sacrifices**: animal ~; burnt ~; corban; drink offering; evening oblation; food offering; guilt offering; heave offering; meat offering; peace offering; sin offering; thank offering; votive offering; wave offering; wood offering;

**sacrifice** *(v.)*: atone; burn; consecrate; do ~; expiate; forfeit; *fulfill;* give; *hecatomb;* immolate; *justify;* kill; lay on altar; make atonement; *non-retention;* offer (up); present; *qualify;* reconcile; slay; take life; *undertake;* victimize; waive; *worship; x-out;* yield; *zealously offer;*

**sacrificial** *(adj.)*: atoning; *blood;* costly; conciliatory; *death;* expiatory; fire-atoning; gift; hecatombic; immolative; *justifying; krioboly;* libational; mactational; *nullifying;* oblational; oblatory; propitiatory; piacular; *quitclaim;* reconciliatory; religious; substitutional; sacrificatory; *thank-offering; undertaking;* vicarious; *wave offering; xenial;* yielded; *zoid;*

**sacrilege** *(n.)*: abomination; blasphemy; cursing; defilement; desecration; expletive; foulness; gross disrespect; *heresy;* irreverence; *juration; knavery; lewd word;* malediction; *non-respect;* offense; outrage; profanation; *quadriliteral;* ribaldry; strange fire; swearing; sin; transgression; unforgivable sin; violation; vitiation; wickedness; *x-rated speech;* yawp; *zinger;*

**sad** *(adj.)*: anguished; blue; broken-hearted; cast down; cheerless; crestfallen; downcast; dismayed; despondent; dejected; doleful; elegiac; forlorn; glum; grieved; heavy (of heart); inconsolable; joyless; *keening;* low; long-faced; miserable; melancholic; mournful; *negative; overcast;* poignant; piteous; *quivering;* rueful; sorrowful; saddened; tristful; tearful; tragic; unhappy; very ~; woeful; wistful; *xtr. ~;* yearnful; *zestless;* [Ant. satisfied]

**sadden** *(v.)*: affect; agonize; bother; bring to tears; cast down; dishearten; dismay; disturb; depress; demoralize; dispirit; eat at; fall; grieve; *hyp* [arch.]; *hopeless; inconsolable; joyless;* knock down; lower one's spirits; make sad; *negative;* oppress; pain; pall; plunge into sorrow; quench one's spirit; rend one's heart; sorrow; sink; trouble; upset; vex; wring heart; weigh upon; *xuld [arch.];* yearn; zestless; [Ant. satisfy]

**saddle** *(n.)*: Asian ~; *blanket;* camel-litter; drayman's ~; English ~; flexible ~; *gig;* horse- ~; *Indian ~; jug handle;* kajawah; *latigo;* military ~; *numnah;* oxhide ~; pannier; pack~; ped; pigskin; *pommel; quarter horse;* riding ~; seat; side ~; *tack(le);* upholstered ~; *voiturier ~;* Western ~; *x-rider;* yager ~; *zeug [G.];*

**sadistic** *(adj.)*: atrocious; beastly; cruel; devilish; evil; flagitious; *godless;* hurtful; inhumane; jackboot; kindless; loathsome; merciless; nasty; odious; perverse; *quad;* ruthless; severe; terrible; unmerciful; uncivilized; vicious; wicked; *xenophobic; yeffell* [arch.]; *zero-mercy;* [Ant. saintly]

**sadness** *(n.)*: anguish; blueness; bleakness; cheerlessness; crestfallenness; dolor; downheartedness; depression; despondency; *ejulation;* forlornness; grief; glumness; gloominess; heartbrokenness; hopelessness; heartache; inconsolableness; joylessness; katzenjammer; lowness; low spirits; melancholy; misery; negativism; overmuch sorrow; piteousness; *quivering;* ruefulness; regret; sorrow; sullenness; trouble; unhappiness; vapors; woe(fulness); *xtry. ~;* yearning; zestlessness; [Ant. satisfaction]

**safari** *(n.)*: adventure; big game hunt; *course; drive;* excursion; expedition; foray; grand expedition; hike; hunting trip; *itineration;* journey; jungle adventure; jeep ~; *kill;* lark; mission; night ~; outing; peregrination; quest; *ride;* search; trek; tour; *undertaking;* venture; walk *xfer;* yong [arch.]; zugunruhe;

**safe** *(adj.)*: alright; *blessed;* covered; delivered; ensconced; fine; fortified; good; garreted; guarded; harmless; harbored; hid; insured; insulated; innocuous; indemnified; just fine; kept; kosher; looked after; made ~; non-threatened; okay; protected; preserved; quite alright; risk-free; secure; safeguarded; taken care of; unharmed; unthreatened; very well; well(-protected); *xtry;* yet unendangered; *zero danger;* [Ant. susceptible]

**safe** *(n.)*: armored vault; bank ~; coffer; deposit box; *ebony chest;* firebox; gold depository; hidden vault; iron box; *jewel box;* keep; keister; lockbox; money box; night ~; *object;* protected vault; quarter-inch thick steel-walled ~; receptacle; strong-box; top-security ~; *utility box;* vault; wall ~; *xtr. protection; yadzutsu* [Jap.]; zechin;

**safeguard** *(n.)*: assurance; bulwark; cover; defense; *earthwork;* failsafe; guardship; *hold;* insulation; insurance; *just in case;* keep-safe; lunette; measure; *non-dangerous;* outwork; protection; palladium; *quarter guard;* rampart; security; safety net; upholding; vallation; wall; warren; *x-guard; yeming* [arch.]; *zero vulnerability;*

**safeguard** *(v.)*: assure; buffer; cloak; cover; defend; ensconce; ensure; flank; fend; fortify; guard; harbor; hold; hide; insulate; insure; jaga; keep safe; look after; make safe; *nestle;* overshadow; *overprotect;* protect; *quia timet [L.];* refuge; *refortify;* shield; secure; take care of; uphold; vallate; watch (over); *x-guard; yeme* [arch.]; *zero danger;*

**safety** *(n.)*: assurance; *buckler;* covering; defense; ensurance; freedom from danger; good; harmlessness; haven; insurance; incolumity; inviolability; *jaga;* keeping; lee; *mantlet;* non-danger; *overprotection;* protection; preservation; *quia timet* [L.]; refuge; security; safeness; safekeeping; trustworthiness; umbrella; *valor;* well-being; *x-guard; yeming* [arch.]; zero danger; [*Ant.* susceptibility]
**sag** *(v.)*: arch; buckle; bow; bend; curve; dip; droop; embow; ebb; fall; give way; hang; incline; *jiggle;* knuckle; lean; loll; make dip; nod; *overlap;* plop; quat; *rest;* slump; sink; trail; *uncinate;* verge; wilt; *x-curve;* yield; *zag;*
**saga** *(n.)*: account; adventures; *book;* chronicle; drama; epic; events; fable; fairytale; *ghost story;* history; imposture; *journal; king's ~;* legend; myth; narrative; novel; *oral narrative;* plot; *quarto;* retelling; story; tale; *unabridged story;* version; writing; xenodocheionology; yarn; *zipper book;*
**sail** *(n.)*: after-leech; ballooner; canvas; cross-jack; drabler; *endrol;* foresail; genoa; headsail; inner jib; jib; kite; lateen; luff; main~; mizzen; *navigable;* outer jib; parachute spinnaker; *quarter-sail;* royal; square~; spanker; top~; *unlace; veliferous;* wind~; *xebec;* yardarm; *zenith;*
**sail** *(v.)*: *adventure;* breeze; cruise; coast; cross; drift; dart; embark; edge; fare; float; ferry; fly; go; glide; head; *igated;* journey; jet; *kite;* luff; move; make for; navigate; *out~;* pilot; pass; ply; *quicken;* ride; run for; *reach;* slide; set ~; seafare; scud; *steam;* travel; traverse; *undergo;* voyage; wend; wing; *xfer;* yacht; *zip;* [*Ant.* stop]
**sailboat** *(n.)*: argosy; bajak; *boat;* clipper; cutter; dinghy; endrol; frigate; galleon; hooker; ironclad; jagger; junk [Jap.]; ketch; lateen; multihull; man-o-war; nickey; outrigger; praam; quarter galley; rigger; schooner; three-master; udema; *vessel;* vinco; windjammer; xebec; yawl; zarug;
**sailor** *(n.)*: able seaman; bluejacket; *captain;* doggerman; ensign; erk; *foretopman;* ferryman; first mate; gob; hand; helmsman; *impressment;* jack-tar; keeler; leatherback; mariner; navy man; navigator; oarsman; old salt; privateer; *pirate; questor;* rower; *rigger;* seaman; sea dog; shellback; swabbie; tar; *underling;* voyager; whaler; xebec-mariner; yardman; *yeoman;* zebec-mariner;
**saint** *(n.)*: *adherent;* believer; blood-washed ~; Christian; child of God; disciple; *delivered; elect;* fellow laborer; *forgiven;* God's child; heaven-bound believer; *in Christ;* justified man; *joint-heir;* kirsen [dial.]; lover of God; *man of God; new birth; orthodox;* possessor (of salvation); *quickened;* redeemed; righteous; saved person; *truster; unshackled man; victor; washed;* Xn.; *yonder-bound;* Zionite; [*Ant.* sinner]
**saint** *(v.)*: aggrandize; besaint; canonize; dub a saint; elevate to ~hood; exalt; *favor;* glorify; honor with ~hood; invest with ~hood; *jalap; keen;* lustrate; lionize; make a ~; number with the ~s; ordain a ~; *pray to; qualified; reconsecrate;* set apart; *title; uplift;* vest with ~hood; *worship; xtry.; yield; zet* [dial.];
**saintliness** *(n.)*: angelicalness; blamelessness; chasteness; Christlikeness; divineness; *eschewing evil;* faultlessness; godliness; holiness; impeccability; justness; kindness; *love;* morality; nobility; otherworldliness; piety; *quality;* rectitude; righteousness; spirituality; sanctitude; truthfulness; uprightness; virtue; wholesomeness; *xtry; yieldedness to God; zeal for God;* [*Ant.* sinfulness]
**saintly** *(adj.)*: angelic; blameless; chaste; Christlike; decent; ever-faithful; faithful; godly; holy; impeccable; just; *kind; loving;* moral; *noble;* otherworldly; pious; *quality;* righteous; saintlike; sanctified; sanctimonious; *truthful;* upright; virtuous; wholesome; Xn.; *yielded to God; zealous for God;* [*Ant.* sinful]
**sake** *(n.)*: account; benefit; cause; *deference;* end; final cause; good; gain; hide; interest; intent; *justification; keeping;* love; life; motive; nisus; objective; purpose; profit; *quality;* regard; reason; striving; *thing; usefulness; virtue;* welfare; well-being; *xtry,; yield; zoe* [Gr.];
**salary** *(n.)*: amount; base pay; compensation; defrayment; earnings; fee; gross pay; hire; income; job-pay; *kickback;* living wage; money; net pay; *overcompensation;* pay(rate); quittance; remuneration; rate of pay; settlement; take-home pay; *unindebted;* virement; wage(s); xfer; yield; *zapping;*

**sale** *(n.)*: auction; advertising campaign; buying; buyout; business; commerce; deal; discount; *exchange; for sale;* garage sale; *half-price;* intercourse; jumble-sale; *kommers* [G.]; *low-priced;* marketing promotion; *no-nonsense; on sale;* practique; pre~; promotion; *quarter-priced;* retail; *reduced;* selling; special; *savings;* trade; *unbelievable prices;* vending; vendue; *white ~; x-change;* yard ~; 0% down ~;
**salesman** *(n.)*: agent; *broker;* clerk; chapman; dealer; *exporter;* floorwalker; *grocer;* hawker; *importer;* jowter; kiddier; *let go for;* marketer; *non-commissioned ~;* operator; peddler; pedlar; pitchman; *qualified retailer;* representative; seller; salesclerk; salesperson; trader; traveling ~; tout; *telemarketer; used car ~;* vendor; wheeler-dealer; *xylonite;* yagger; *zyalde [arch.];*
**salon** *(n.)*: *artiste;* beauty ~; barbershop; coiffeuse; dresser; *establishment;* friseur's; gentleman's hairdresser; hairdresser; hair parlor; *incorporation; job; kudumi;* licensed beautician's; men's hair stylist [masc.]; nail ~; *outfit;* professional ~; *quaifer* [arch.]; *razor cutter;* stylist; *trimmer; uptown ~; village ~;* workplace; xerasia; YK; zone;
**salute** *(n.)*: acknowledgement; bow; credit; *deference;* esteem; favor; gesture; greeting; hello; hail; indication of respect; *justness;* kiss; laudation; *mark;* nod; observance; praise; *quality;* recognition; salutation; tribute; *unmitigated respect;* veneration; wave; X's and O's.; *yain [arch.];* zeal; [*Ant.* slight]
**salute** *(v.)*: acknowledge; acclaim; applaud; bow to; commend; compliment; cheer; *defer to;* esteem; favor; greet; hail; honor; indicate respect; *justness;* kneel to; kiss; look up to; make obeisance to; nod; *obeisance;* praise; *quality;* respect; regard; shake one's hand; *tribute; unmitigated respect;* venerate; wave; X's and O's.; *yain* [arch.]; zeal; [*Ant.* slight]
**salvation** *(n.)*: atonement; *a* born-again state; cleansing; deliverance; eternal life; everlasting life; expiation; forgiveness; final ~; *freedom;* grace; *heaven;* immortality; imperishableness; justification; keeping; *kingdom; know-so ~;* life (eternal); *liberation;* mercy; new birth; *one-way;* preservation; *purchase;* quickening; redemption; regeneration; rebirth; *ransom;* saving; salvaging; second birth; *setting free; transformation; unshackled;* vivification; washing; Xt.; *yonder;* Zion; [*see* deliverance; saved]
**salve** *(n.)*: abirritant; balm; cream; demulcent; embrocation; fomentation; gel; harquebusade; inunctum; *jojoba; kamachili;* lotion; medication; *nard;* ointment; palliative; *quinine;* rub; soothing lotion; skin cream; treatment; unguent; vulnerary; wash; xerogel; *yellow balm; zinc ointment;*
**salve** *(v.)*: appease; becalm; comfort; dulcify; ease; *fulfill;* give relief; gratify; hush; indulge; *justify; knock down;* lull; mollify; *nullify; overcome;* pacify; quell; relieve; soothe; treat; unruffle; *vanish;* win favor; x-out; *yield;* zeroize;
**same** *(adj.)*: alike; akin; another; *beforementioned;* consistent; comparable; duplicate; equivalent; equal; *further; geminated;* homogenous; homologous; identical; indistinguishable; invariable; isometric; just the same; kindred; like; matching; non-differing; *one;* parallel; *quae est eadem* [L.]; resembling; similar; such-like; synonymous; tie; tantamount; uniform; unchanged; unaltered; unimproved; unmodified; unvaried; verbatim; without difference; word-for-word; *xerographed;* yet the ~; zincograph; [*Ant.* sundry]
**sample** *(n.)*: apotheosis; bit; case (in point); chunk; *drop;* example; free ~; *gob;* hunk; instance; *jewel; kept specimen;* little piece; morsel; nugget; ort; piece; *quantity;* remnant; specimen; sampling; taste; unit; *vestige;* wedge; xylon; *yngot [arch.]; zum [dial.];*
**sanctification** *(n.)*: abstersion; blessing; consecration; cleansing; dedication; depuration; expurgation; februation; growth; hallowing; *improvement; jalap; keep growing;* lustration; making holy; *non-polluted; outwashing;* purification; *quintessentialize;* refining; sanctifying; *taintless; unsullying; vesting;* washing; x-ing out; *yielding; zierlich [G.];*
**sanctify** *(v.)*: *appropriate;* bless; consecrate; cleanse; devote; dedicate; depurate; expurgate; *free from sin;* grow; hallow; *improve;* jalap; *keep separate;* lustrate; make holy; mature; *nard;* ordain; purify; quintessentialize; refine; set apart; separate; *taintless;* unsully; vest; wash clean; *xfer; yield; zierlich [G.];* [*Ant.* secularize]

**sanction** *(v.)*: allow; authorize; approve; back; consent to; *decriminalize;* enable; endorse; facilitate; give permission; homologate; indorse; justify; knowingly allow; let; legalize; make possible; *nod;* okay; permit; *qualify;* ratify; suffer; support; tolerate; uphold; validate; warrant; x on the dotted line; yes; *zero opposition;*
**sanctimonious** *(adj.)*: austere; *big-headed;* censorious; devout; *egotistical;* flatulent; grandiose; hypocritical; holier-than-thou; inflated; *judgmental; know-it-all;* lofty; moralizing; *narcissistic;* over-pious; pious; *quick-to-boast;* religious; self-righteous; *turgid;* ultra-religious; *vainglorious;* worshipful; *Xn.; yielding; yearnful;* zealous; [*Ant.* self-effaced]
**sanctimony** *(n.)*: austerity; *big-headedness;* censoriousness; devoutness; *egotism;* flatulence; grandiosity; holiness; *inflatedness; judgmental;* kalokagathia [Gr.]; loftiness; moralization; *narcissism;* over-piousness; piety; *quickt-to-boast;* religiousness; religiosity; sanctimoniousness; *turgidity;* ultra-religiousness; *vainglory;* worshipfulness; *xtry;* yearnfulness; zeal; [*Ant.* self-effacement]
**sanctity** *(n.)*: absolute sacredness; blessedness; consecration; devoutness; *esteem; fear;* goodness; hallowedness; holiness; inviolability; *justness; kneeling; loftiness; merit;* nature of holiness; *obeisance;* privacy; purity; quality of solemnity; reverence; sanctitude; sacredness; *transcendence;* untouchableness; veneration; worthiness; xtry. heavenliness; *yet undefiled; zero contempt;*
**sand** *(n.)*: *aren;* beach ~; coastal ~; desert ~; emery; *filth;* grit; *grus; hazel-earth; item; jet;* kernels; *limestone; marl; nast; ocher;* particles; quartz ~; *quick~;* rock fragments; soil; top ~; *undersoil;* volcanic ~; white ~; *xysma;* yellow ~; *zonal soil;* [*see* dirt]
**sandal** *(n.)*: abarka; beach ~; clog; dress ~; espadrille; flip-flop; geta; huarache; *innersole;* jelly; kaparring; leather ~; *latchet;* mule; napa leather ~; open-toe; patten; quatros; Roman ~; shoe; slide; sabot; thong; *upper;* vamp ~; whang; x-sandal; yaga ~; *zori* [Jap.];
**sandy** *(adj.)*: arenarious; breccial; coarse-grained; detrital; *ecru;* fine-grained; grainy; granular; granulated; gritty; gravelly; *hardy; irregular; juiceless;* kernelled; lapideous; *marl; non-solid; ochrous;* pebbly; *quartz; rippling;* rock-strewn; sabulous; sanded; textured; trachytic; *uneven;* volcanic-ash; white-sanded; *xanthic;* yellow-sanded; *zet;*
**sane** *(adj.)*: able-minded; balanced; competent; clear-minded; discursive; *excellent;* fine; good; healthy; in one's right mind; just fine; keen-minded; lucid; levelheaded; mentally competent; normal; of sound mind; perfectly normal; quite ~; right-minded; rational; sound; thinking normally; understanding; very sound of mind; well-balanced; *xtry.; yaul; zero problem;* [*Ant.* sick]
**sanitary** *(adj.)*: aseptic; bathed; clean; disinfected; expurgated; fresh; germless; hygienic; immaculate; *jalap; kill germs;* laundered; machine-washed; nice; *okay;* purified; *qualmless; rinsed;* sanitized; sterile; taintless; uncontaminated; *virtuous;* well-sanitized; *xylol; yellow soap; zinc oxide;* [*Ant.* sullied]
**sanity** *(n.)*: able-mindedness; balance; competence; discursiveness; *excellence;* faculties; good sense; health; in one's right mind; *just fine; keenness;* lucidness; levelheadedness; marbles; mental competence; normality; *ordinariness;* power of reason; *quotidian;* rationality; right mind; reason; saneness; soundness of mind; thinking power; understanding; very sound mind; wit; *xtry.; yaul; zero problem;* [*Ant.* sickness]
**sap** *(n.)*: *alburnum;* balm; *calculary;* drippings; essence; fluid; gum; *health; issue;* juice; keest; liquid; matter; mucilage; nectar; out-drippings; pith; *quintessence;* resin; syrup; treacle; toddy; *utricle;* verjuice; wax; wood pitch; xylan; yacca gum; zep;
**sarcasm** *(n.)*: acerbity; bitterness; causticity; cynicism; derision; embitterment; facetiousness; gibing; humor; irony; jadedness; kindlessness; ludification; mordacity; narkiness; opprobrium; pyroticism; quick wit; scorn; spite; sardonicism; taunting; unkindness; virulence; wryness; *xuld [arch.]; yah;* zinging; [*Ant.* seriousness]
**sarcastic** *(adj.)*: acerbic; biting; bitter; caustic; cynical; derisive; dry; embittered; fleering; gibing; harsh; ironic; jaded; kindless; ludificatory; mordacious; mordant; narky; opprobrious; pyrotic; quick-witted; ridiculing; sardonic; sharp-tongued; taunting; trenchant; *ugly; unkind;* virulent; wry; *xuld [arch.]; yah;* zinging; [*Ant.* serious]

**sass** *(v.)*: argue; backtalk; cavil; disrespect; *erupt;* fuss; gainsay; hassle; *inharmonious;* jangle; kick up dust; lock horns [slang]; make a problem; niff; object; parley; quibble; retort; speak impudently; talk back; *unharmonious;* vie; wrangle; *x-purposes;* yell; *zap;* [*Ant.* submit]

**sassy** *(adj.)*: audacious; brash; bold-faced; cocky; discourteous; disrespectful; *effrontery;* feisty; fresh; glib; high-spirited; impudent; jaunty; *know-it-all;* lively; lippy; malapert; nervy; overbold; pert; *quite impertinent;* rude; saucy; spirited; temerarious; unabashed; vivacious; wise-acre; *x-proud; yieldless;* zizzy; [*Ant.* submissive]

**Satan** *(n.)*: Adversary; accuser; archenemy; Beelzebub; Belial; *the* corrupter; Devil; *the* Evil One; father of lies; god of this world; *Hell;* Instigator; *jab jab* [Carib.]; *Kali;* Lucifer; Mephisto(pheles); murderer; *Nick;* Old Serpent (-Scratch); Prince of Darkness; *quad;* ruler of darkness; serpent; *slanderer;* Tempter; Unholy One; Vile One; Wicked One; *Xargi; yeffell [arch.]; zar;* [*see* Devil; *Ant.* Savior]

**satanic** *(adj.)*: atrocious; bedeviled; bad; cruel; devilish; evil; foul; ghoulish; heinous; hell-bred; ignominious; *jaded; kindless;* luciferian; malevolent; Mephistophelean; nefarious; ogreish; pernicious; quad; ruthless; satanical; sinister; treacherous; ungodly; villainous; vile; wicked; *x-rated; yucky; zar-like;* [*Ant.* saintly]

**satiate** *(v.)*: appease; befit; content; cloy; delight; engorge; fill; gratify; gorge; glut; *have enough;* indulge; jam-pack; jade; *kibble;* load; make full; nauseate; overindulge; overfill; overdose; oversaturate; overstuff; pall; pack; quench; regale; satisfy; sate; surfeit; saturate; top off; *unreasonable; volumes;* weary; *xfer.; yain [arch.]; zero room left;* [*Ant.* starve]

**satire** *(n.)*: *abuse;* burlesque; caricature; derision; execration; fleering; gibing; humor; invectiveness; *imitation;* Juvenalianism; joke; *kidding;* lampoon(ery); mockery; nip; *opprobrium;* parody; pasquinade; quipping; ridicule; spoof; travesty; *unkindness;* vaudeville; wiping; wit; *x-ing;* yah; *zinging;*

**satirical** *(adj.)*: *abusive;* burlesque; caricatural; derisive; execrative; fleering; gibing; humorous; invective; Juvenalian; *kidding;* lampooning; mocking; *nipping; opprobrious;* parodical; quipping; ridiculing; sardonic; tongue-in-cheek; *unkind;* vaudevillian; witty; *x-ing;* yuking; *zinging;*

**satirist** *(n.)*: *abuser;* burlesquer; caricaturist; derider; execrator; *fleerer;* giber; humorist; imitator; Juvenal; joker; *kidder;* lampooner; mocker; nipper; *offender;* pasquinader; pasquiler; quipper; ridiculer; satirist; satirizer; scorner; *teaser; unkind;* wag; *x-er;* yuker; *zinger;*

**satisfaction** *(n.)*: approval; bliss; contentment; contentedness; delight; enjoyment; ecstasy; fulfillment; gratification; happiness; indulgence; indemnification; joy; justice; keen pleasure; liking; merriment; *niceness;* overjoy; peace of mind; pleasure; queme; redress; rapture; settlement; satisfying; self-enjoyment; titillation; *uplifted;* vindication; well-being; *xanadu; yummy; zest;*

**satisfactory** *(adj.)*: adequate; ample; bearable; cool [slag]; *decent;* endurable; enough; fine; good (enough); honky-dory; *impressive;* jake [Br.]; kosher; livable; minimal; normal; okay; passable; pleasing; *quantum* sufficient; satisfying; reasonable; sufficient; tolerable; unobjectionable; valid; well (enough); *xel [arch.]; yenough* [arch.]; *zero complaint;*

**satisfy** *(v.)*: appease; befit; content; complete; delight; execute; *enchant;* fulfill; fill; flatter; gratify; humor; indulge; ingratiate; *joy; jump to it;* keep happy; live up to; make happy; meet; not displease; overjoy; please; perform; quench; regale; remit; suit; satiate; sate; thrill; *uplift; victory;* win over; *xtry.; yummy; zip to it;*

**satisfying** *(adj.)*: agreeable; blissful; contenting; delightful; enjoyable; fulfilling; fine; gratifying; good; heartwarming; indulgent; joyful; keen; likeable; lovely; makes one happy; nice; okay; pleasing; pleasant; pleasurable; quenching; rewarding; suiting; *thrilling; uplifting;* voluptuous; well-satisfying; worthwhile; *xtry.; you-beaut* [Aus.]; yummy; *zestful;*

**saturate** *(v.)*: *absorb;* bloat; cover; drench; engorge; fill; gorge; *humectate;* inundate; jam-pack; *keep full;* load; make full; *non-dry;* overfill; permeate; pervade; perfuse; *quantum increase; riddle;* soak; spread; suffuse; totally fill; transfuse; utterly fill; *volume;* waterlog; *x-fill;* yote; *zero remaining space;*

**saturation** *(n.)*: absolute limit; bloating; capacity; drenching; engorgement; fullness; gorging; *height;* inundation; jamming; *kept full;* loading; *limit;* maximum capacity; *no room;* overload; overindulgence; permeation; *quantity;* repletion; repleteness; satiety; total ~; utterly filled; *volume;* wholly filled; *xtry.;* yoting; *zenith;*
**savage** *(adj.)*: aboriginal; barbaric; barbarous; cannibalistic; cruel; devilish; *evil;* fierce; ferocious; feral; godless; heathen; ill-mannered; jungli; kaf [arch.]; *lionlike;* mean; nasty; odious; pagan; *querulous;* rapacious; rude; *satanic;* tribal; truculent; uncivilized; uncouth; un-Christian; vicious; vile; warlike; wild; *xenophobic; yahoo; Zulu;* [Ant. sweet]
**savage** *(n.)*: aboriginal; barbarian; cannibal; devil; *enemy;* ferine; firewalker; *grim;* heathen; headhunter; Hun; *Hottentot;* Indian; jungli; *kill-crazy; lethal; medicine man;* native; non-Christian; *odious;* pagan; *querulous; rude;* spearman; tribesman; uncivilized person; vandal; wild man; warrior; *Xhosa;* yahoo; Zulu; [Ant. saint]
**save** *(v.)*: aid; bail out; come to the rescue; conserve; deliver; extricate; free; give life to; help; indemnify; *justified;* keep; liberate; loose; make free; *not lose; overprotect;* preserve; pocket; quicken; rescue; redeem; ransom; recover; reserve; salvage; spare; treasure; *unshackle; vivificate;* withhold; *x-ported;* yank from the jaws of death; *zero waste;* [*see* redeem; Ant. spend]
**saved** *(adj.)*: alive in Christ; born again, believer; blood-washed; blood-bought; Christian; cleansed; converted; *child of God;* delivered; elect; forgiven; glory-bound; God-fearing; gloriously ~; heaven-bound; in Christ; justified; kingdom-bound; *life eternal; mercifully saved;* non-condemned; *one of the redeemed;* purchased; quickened; redeemed; regenerate; reborn; salvaged; *son; transformed;* united in Christ; unshackled; *vivified;* washed; Xn.; *yonder-bound;* Zion-bound;
**savior** *(n.)*: aider; brave deliverer; champion; deliverer; extricater; freer; giver of life; hero; indemnifier; *justifier;* knight in shining armor; liberator; lifesaver; messiah; *noble;* overcomer; preserver; paladin; *quickener;* rescuer; redeemer; salvager; saviour; triumphant; *transporter;* unshackler; victor; white knight; *xia;* yanker from the jaws of death; *zealous hero;* [*see* Jesus Christ]
**savor** *(n.)*: aroma; bouquet; character; discrimination; essence; flavor; great taste; hint; intrinsicality; *juicy; keen ~;* liking; *m-m-m;* nature; *overall ~; palate;* quality; relish; savoriness; smell; taste; *unusual ~;* very good taste; way of tasting; *xenenthesis;* yumminess; zest;
**savor** *(v.)*: appreciate; bask in; cherish; delight in; enjoy; *fancy;* glory in; have; *invigorate;* joy in; *keen on;* love; luxuriate; *make one happy; nice; own;* please one; *queme;* relish; sip; take pleasure in; *uplift;* value; wallow in; *xtry.;* yearn for; *zestful;*
**say** *(v.)*: articulate; announce; assert; bid; bespeak; blurt; comment; convey; converse; delineate; disclose; divulge; declare; express; exclaim; enunciate; *fame; foremention; gab; give;* hold forth; impart; indicate; *jaw; key in;* let out; mention; noise; *note;* opine; observe; pronounce; quoth; relate; remark; report; rehearse; rumor; relay; speak; state; tell; utter; verbalize; voice; word; *xenophonia;* yak; *zero in;*
**saying** *(n.)*: adage; axiom; byword; cliché; dictum; expression; formulary; generality; *hackneyed saying;* instruction; *judgment; koine;* law; maxim; neology; oracle; proverb; quote; rule; saw; truism; universal truth; verse; wisdom; *xenophonia;* Yogism; zeteticism;
**scale** *(n. balance)*: *apparatus;* balance; *contrivance;* digital ~; electronic ~; fish ~; gauge; hydraulic ~; *instrument; just weights;* kitchen ~; *linear ~;* milligram ~; medical ~; *net weight;* object; postal ~; *quantity; read-out;* steelyard; *tip;* union ~; vernier; weight; weighing device; *xci.; yeme;* Zeug [G.];
**scale** *(n. scallop)*: armor plate; *bony plate;* cosmoid ~; denticle; *dragon ~;* escallop; fish-scale; ganoid ~; horny plate; *item; jack ~; karatin; keeled ~;* lamel; layer; *marlin ~; notch;* osteoderm; plate; platform ~; *quillfish;* rament; scute; scallop; toothed ~; upclimb; *veneer;* wing- ~; xerodermis; *yabby ~;* zander ~;
**scale** *(v.)*: ascend; become higher; climb; clamber; *develop;* elevate; *fly up;* go up; heighten; increase; jump up; *keep rising; largen;* mount; move upward; notch; overclimb; proceed; *queue;* rise; surmount; transcend; *upward;* verge upward; work one's way up; *xfer; yain* [arch.]; *zoom up;*

**scaly** *(adj.)*: armored; *bumpy;* crusted; ctenoid; *dry;* encrusted; flaking; fururaceous; ganoid; *hard;* inmailed; *jagged; karatin;* lamellar; lentiginous; mailed; *notched; overlapped;* peeling; *quat;* rough; squamous; *tough;* umbonate; *varix; well-steeled;* xerodermic; *yeme [arch.];* zoned;

**scandal** *(n.)*: aspersion; black mark; *cause célèbre* [F.]; disgrace; embarrassment; *fall;* -gate; humiliation; ignominy; *incident;* journalistic ~; knavery; loss of face; *mortification;* notorious *incident;* outrage; public outrage; *quad;* reproach; shame; tarnishing case; *upbraiding;* verecundity; wite; wrong; *xtry.* shocking; yuckiness; zero honor;

**scandalous** *(adj.)*: appalling; bad; contemptible; disgraceful; eyebrow-raising; embarrassing; flagitious; *guilty;* humiliating; ignominious; inexcusable; *jaded;* knavish; libelous; mortifying; notorious; newsworthy; outrageous; pathetic; *quad;* reproachful; shameful; shocking; tarnishing; unspeakable; vile; wicked; *xtry.* shameful; yucky; zero honor;

**scant** *(adj.)*: austere; bare; close; dear; exiguous; few(-and-far-between); gant; hard to find; insufficient; jimp; keenly ~; limited; measly; negligible; obscure; paltry; *queer;* rare; slight; sparse; thin; uncommon; very slight; wanting; *xtry.; you-beaut [Aus.];* zero; [*Ant.* sufficient]

**scapegoat** *(n.)*: Azazel; blame-taker; conveniently blamed party; *displacement; exchange;* fall guy; goat; human sacrifice; *immolation;* judgment-taker; *kaimakam [Turk.]; laazazeyl* [Heb.]; man blamed; *non-guilty;* one blamed; patsy; punishment-bearer; *quitclaim;* replacement; scape-goat; substitution; *target; used instead; vicarious;* whipping-boy; *xfer; yield; zwap [dial.];*

**scar** *(n.)*: abnormality; blemish; cicatrix; disfigurement; epidermic defacement; fibrosis [tech.]; *gash;* hypertrophic ~; injury; *jarble;* keloid; *laceration;* mar(k); *nevus; object;* pock mark; *quirk; rift;* stripe; *taint; ulcer; violent;* wound; wale; wem; *xanthoma;* yedder; zit ~;

**scarce** *(adj.)*: austere; bare; *curtailed;* dear; exceptional; exiguous; few(-and-far-between); gant; hard to find; infrequent; inadequate; jejune; keenly ~; little; meager; n'er; negligible; obscure; paltry; precious; *queer;* rare; sparse; scant(y); thin; uncommon; valuable; wanting; *xtry.; you-beaut [Aus.];* zero; [*Ant.* superabundant]

**scare** *(v.)*: affright; alarm; *bother; concern;* distress; dread; daunt; *exasperate;* frighten; gaster; horrify; intimidate; *jitters;* kiaugh [Scot.]; *languish;* make nervous; nerve; overburden; panic; quicken; *reluctant;* spook; terrify; unnerve; vex; worry; *xenophobia; yelping; zealless;* [*Ant.* settle]

**scary** *(adj.)*: alarming; bloodcurdling; chilling; creepy; distressing; disquieting; endangering; eerie; frightening; frightful; fearful; ghastly; horrifying; horrific; hair-raising; hairy; intimidating; *jittery;* knee-knocking; *lily-livered;* macabre; nerve-racking; *ominous;* petrifying; panicked; quivering; *rueful;* spine-chilling; terrifying; unsettling; unnerving; uneasy; *violent;* worrisome; *xenophobic; yellow-bellied; zealless;* [*Ant.* settling]

**scatter** *(v.)*: *away;* bestrew; break up; broadcast; circulate; disperse; diffuse; disband; disseminate; dissipate; effuse; fling; go away; hurl; intersperse; *jawp; known;* litter; let go; make to ~; *non-localized;* overspread; propagate; *quantity;* radiate; strew; spread; thinly spread; unleash; universalize; *very widespread;* whiffle; *widespread; xfer; yondmost; zillions;*

**scavenge** *(v.)*: accumulate; burrow; comb; collect; dig; *explore;* forage; go through; grub; garner; hunt for; investigate; *jerque;* kithe; look for; make a search; nose around; *obtain;* pursue; quest for; rummage; search; scrounge; track; *uncover; venture;* wade thru; *well-traced;* x-search; *yearn for;* zealously search;

**scavenger** *(n.)*: accumulator; *buzzard;* comber; digger; *explorer;* forager; grubber; hunter; hoarder; investigator; *jerque;* kither; looker; magpie; *noser; obtainer;* pursuer; packrat; questor; rummager; searcher; scrounger; tracker; *uncover;* vulture; wader; *x-search;* yearner; zealous searcher;

**scene** *(n.)*: area; backdrop; circumstance; district; environs; field; groundplot; *habitat;* immediate area; junction; *key site;* location; landscape; milieu; *niche; outside;* place; perspective; panorama; *quadrant;* region; site; setting; situation; terrain; ubiety; venue; vignette; view; whereabouts; *xy-coordinate; yard;* zone;

**scenery** *(n.)*: area view; background (-drop); countryside; drop; environment; field of view; geography; habitat; immediate area; *juncture; ken;* landscape; locale; *mise en scène* [F.]; nature; overlook; panorama; *quaint ~;* region; scene; setting; terrain; *ubiety;* view; vista; waterscape; xerosere; yonder; *zone;*
**scent** *(n.)*: aroma; balm; cense; delightful ~; essence; fragrance; good smell; *hint; incense;* joyous aroma; keen smell; *lovely smell; musk;* nidor; *nose;* odor; pleasant smell; quality; redolence; smell; (sweet) savor; terrific fragrance; unforgettable aroma; very pleasant aroma; whiff; *xtry. ~;* yummy ~; *zedoary;*
**scent** *(v.)*: aromatize; *besprinkle;* cense; *disseminate ~;* essence; fragrance; give ~; heavily ~; imbue; infuse; *jet; keen smell;* lightly ~; make smell nice; mist; *naid;* odorize; perfume; *quick-spray; redolence;* suffuse; spray; thurify; *unforgotten; very pleasant; whiff; xuld [arch.]; ylang-ylang; zest;*
**scepter** *(n.)*: *alpenstock;* baton; caduceus; *dagger-staff; emblem;* ferule; *godendag; hasta; insignia; jambee;* kingly ~; *langet;* mace; *nulla-nulla; officer's staff;* partisan; *quarterstaff;* rod; sceptre; staff; tipstaff; truncheon; *ununke* [Afr.]; verge; virgulate; wand; white staff; *xylon;* yard; *zagaye;*
**schedule** *(n.)*: agenda; blueprint; chart; calendar; date book; docket; *engineering;* foredesign; ground plan; *hatched;* itinerary; *job ~; key agenda;* list; master list; *notebook;* outline; plan; program; *quo mode [L.];* rota; regimen; scheme; timetable; *underlying plan; visual;* week outlook; work ~; *x-chart;* year outlook; *zenithal projection;*
**schedule** *(v.)*: allocate; assign; appoint; book; *chart; date;* enter; earmark; fit in; get in; have; *intend; jot down;* keep open; lay plans; list; make plans; map out; notate; organize; ordain; prearrange; pencil in; plan; *quick-planning;* register; slate; table; *use planner; visual;* write down; work out; *x-chart; yeme;* zet [dial.];
**scheme** *(n.)*: artifice; arrangement; blueprint; contrivance; conspiracy; design; engineering; foredesign; format; feint; game (plan); gambit; *hatch; hoax;* idea; jape; King's gambit; layout; master plan; *navigational chart;* operation; outline; order; plan; plot; ploy; play; *quo mode* [L.]; ruse; racket; rort; strategy; tactic; trick; underplot; *visual;* way; wile; *x-chart; yantra [Hind.]; zenithal projection;*
**scheme** *(v.)*: *analyze;* birth; conceive; concoct; devise; engineer; fabricate; *get;* hatch; invent; imagine; intrigue; *juggle;* kiddy; lay out; map out; machinate; *notion;* originate; plan; plot; *quick-thinking;* rig; set up; strategize; think; use brain; *visualize;* work up; *xenodiagnose; yeme; zazen;*
**schism** *(n.)*: aperture; break; breach; cleft; dichotomy; division; estrangement; faction; gap; hiatus; interstice; *junction;* knapple; *leaving; moving away;* non-continuum; *opening;* parting; *quadrisection;* rift; rend; split; *tear;* uncoupling; unharmoniousness; *veering; wedge; x-ing out;* yawn; *zap;* [Ant. solidarity]
**scholar** *(n.)*: academic; bookman; college professor; doctor; educator; fugleman; great mind; humanist [Scot.]; intellectual; jr. college professor; knowledgeable man; keen mind; *khoja* [Mos.]; learned man; man of letters; *noetic;* oracle; professor; polymath; quodlibetarian; researcher; savant; teacher; theologian; theoretician; university professor; *visiting professor;* wise man; xenagogue; *Yale professor; zetetic;* [Ant. student]
**scholarly** *(adj.)*: academic; bookish; collegiate; didactical; educated; erudite; *farsighted;* gifted; highbrow; intellectual; *judicious;* knowledgeable; learned; mentally astute; noetic; on the ball; pedagogical; profound; quick-witted; rational; smart; studious; scholar-like; ultra-smart; *valedictorian;* well-educated; wise; xenagogic; yaup; *zippy;* [Ant. simple]
**scholarship** *(n.)*: academics; book-learning; *the* classroom; discipleship; erudition; formal education; fostering; guidance; higher education; instruction; *junior college;* knowledge; learning; *mentoring;* nurturing; *oversight;* pedagogy; *qualification; readying;* study; scholarliness; teaching; training; upbringing; *versing; working with;* xenagogy; *yarking; zealous studying;*
**school** *(n.)*: academy; boarding ~; boy's ~; college; Christian ~; district ~; day ~; elementary ~; free~; finishing ~; grade (-grammar; -graduate) ~; halls; high ~; home ~; institution; institute; ivory tower; junior high ~; kindergarten; K-12; *lower ~;* middle ~; night ~; one-room ~house; pre~; private ~; parochial ~; primary ~; *quarter;* religious ~; reform ~; schoolhouse; trade ~; upper ~; vocational ~; vestibule ~; waldorf ~; *xenagogy;* year-round ~; *zone;*

**science** *(n.)*: analysis; body of knowledge; *chemistry;* discipline; examination; encyclopedy; findings; *geology;* hard ~; investigation; *jurimetrics;* knowledge; learning; microanalysis; natural ~; nano~; ology; *pseudo-* ~; pure ~; *quantum physics;* research; study; testing; *ufology;* volumetric analysis; *work; xylology; yield results; zootomy;*
  **Kinds of science**: astronomy; biology; chemistry; developmental biology; endochronology; fossilogy; geology; hydrology; ionics; jupitology; kinesiology; limnology; mineralogy; nematology; oceanography; physics; quantum physics; radiology; speleology; tectonics; urology; volcanology; windology; xylology; youthology; zoology;

**scientific** *(adj.)*: analytic; analytical; *biological; chemical;* disciplined; exact; exploratory; fact-finding; *great mind;* highly educated; investigative; inspective; *jurimetric; keen;* logical; methodical; *neuro~;* ordered; orderly; precise; questful; researching; systematic; technical; unromantic; very ~; well-educated; *xylological; yield results;* zetetic; [*Ant.* seat-of-the-pants]

**scientist** *(n.)*: analyst; analyzer; astronomer; biologist; chemist; doctor; experimenter; examiner; field worker; *geologist; highly educated;* intellectual; *jurimetricist; knowledge;* laboratory technician; man of science; mad scientist; microbiologist; natural scientist; *observer;* professor; physicist; qualified researcher; researcher; *scholar;* technician; urologist; volumetric analyst; *worker; xray-chrystallographer; yield reaults;* zoologist;

**scissors** *(n.)*: *aviation snips;* bandage ~; clippers; *ducktail snips; exscind;* forfex; *grass and hedge shears;* hedge clippers; *instrument; jack knife;* kitchen ~; loppers; metzenbaum ~; nail scissors; nippers; *offset snips;* paper ~; pinking shears; *pair;* pruner; *quadrisect;* rostrum; shears; snips [slang]; trimming ~; *universal snips; vell;* wool shears; x-sect; yerk; zip;

**scoff** *(v.)*: abuse; bemock; chaff; deride; *execrate;* fleer; gibe; heckle; hiss; inveigh; jibe; knock; laugh at; make fun (-sport); *name-calling; offend;* poke fun; pick on; *quip;* rail on; scorn; tease; taunt; utter against; verbally abuse; wipe; *xuld [arch.];* yock; *zap;*

**scoffer** *(n.)*: abuser; belittler; chider; derider; *execrator;* flouter; giber; heckler; insulter; jiber; knocker; laugher; mocker; niggler; offender; *pillory;* quipper; railer; scorner; teaser; taunter; *utterer;* vexer; *wiper; xuld [arch.];* yuker; zapper;

**scold** *(v.)*: admonish; berate; baste; chide; denounce; excoriate; flay; give talking to; harangue; inveigh; jaw; knock; lecture; *macerate;* nag; objurgate; *punish; question;* reprimand; reprove; rebuke; sermonize; tell off; upbraid; vituperate; *warn; xuld [arch.];* yell at; *zap;*

**scoop** *(n.)*: *article;* bail; burrower; cup; digger; dipper; *equipment;* feed ~; gouge; hand ~; *implement; jenkin;* keach; ladle; lade; measure; *nine oz. ~; object;* plastic ~; *pooper scooper; quantity; ration;* scooper; shovel; turf-spade; *tool;* utility ~; *volume;* workman's shovel; *xfer;* yielding; *zeug* [G.];

**scoop** *(v.)*: apportion; burrow; cup; dig; delve; draw; dip; dish; dollop; excavate; *furnish;* gouge; hollow out; hand dip; intrench; *jenkin;* keach; lade out; mole; *notch; open;* prospect; quarry; remove; scrape; shovel; serve; spoon; take up; use scoop; *venture;* work with ~; *xfer;* yield; zone;

**scope** *(n.)*: ambit; area; bounds; breadth; compass; degree; domain; diapason; extent; fullness; gamut; hugeness; immensity; jurisdiction; *known ~;* level; limit; magnitude; *neighborhood;* outlook; perspective; qua; range; reach; size; scale; *tier;* upper limit; vastness; width; *x-section; yard line;* zone;

**scorch** *(v.)*: *ablaze;* burn; char; deflagrate; *discolor; exsiccate;* flame-char; *gut; hurt;* incinerate; *jeopardize;* kindle; *light (up);* mar; neal; overburn; pyrolyze; *quick-match;* raze; sear; singe; torch; ustion; vesicate; *wound; xylophyrography; yearn;* zap;

**scorn** *(n.)*: abhorrence; *belittlement;* contempt; disdain; enmity; fleering; gall; hatred; ill-will; jeering; knocking; loathing; laughter; malice; odium; opprobrium; put-down; querulousness; ridicule; revulsion; scoffing; taunting; utter dislike; venom; *withstanding; xenophobia; yah;* zinging;

**scorn** *(v.)*: abuse; belittle; chide; deride; *execrate;* fleer; gibe; humiliate; insult; jeer; knock; laugh at; mock; *name-calling;* objurgate; pillory; quib; ridicule; scoff; sneer; taunt; utter against; vex; wipe; *xuld [arch.];* yock; *zap;* [*Ant.* salute]

**scorner** *(n.)*: abuser; belittler; chider; derider; denouncer; *execrator;* flouter; giber; humiliator; insulter; jeerer; kidder; laugher; mocker; niggler; offender; *pillory;* quipper; ridiculer; scoffer; taunter; *utterer;* vexer; *wiper; xuld [arch.];* yuker; *zapper;*

**scornful** *(adj.)*: angry; bitter; contemptible; despiteful; disdainful; derisive; embittered; foul; galsome; hateful; inimical; jaded; kindless; loathsome; mean; nasty; odious; pernicious; *quede* [arch.]; resentful; spiteful; terrible; unkind; virulent; wicked; *xenophobic; yucky; zealotic;*

**scoundrel** *(n.)*: agitator; blackguard; cad; devil; evildoer; firebrand; good-for-nothing; heel; *injurer;* jackanapes; knave; lowlife; menace; miscreant; ne'er-do-well; *outlaw;* polecat; questrel; rascal; rogue; rapscallion; scalawag; troublemaker; *ungodly person;* varlet; wretch; wrongdoer; *xiaoren;* yahoo; zhlub; [*Ant.* saint]

**scourge** *(n. whip)*: *affliction;* belt; cat-o-nine-tails; *device; equipment;* flogger; *grievance;* horsewhip; instrument of punishment; jower; knout; lash; mule-whip; *nail; overhit; punisher;* quirt; *rod;* razor strap; switch; swinge; thrasher; *unleash; vengeance;* whip; *xuld [arch.];* yerk; *zinger;*

**scourge** *(n. bane)*: annoyance; bane; blight; curse; displeasure; execration; evil; frustration; gadfly; hex; irritation; *jinx; karakia* [Maori]; *loathsome;* menace; nuisance; *offense;* pest; plague; *qualm* [arch.]; *ruination;* sorrow; trouble; umbrage; vexation; woe; *x-ing; yellow blight; zapping;*

**scourge** *(v.)*: afflict; beat; chastise; discipline; excoriate; flog; flagellate; gird; hit; inflict; *jeel;* knout; lash; lay stripes on; mark; *nail; overhit;* plow; punish; quirt; *rend;* stripe; thrash; *unleash;* victimize; whip; *xuld [arch.];* yerk; *zing;*

**scout** *(n.)*: agent; advance man; *beholder;* conductor; detective; emissary; forerunner; guide; *hearer;* investigator; *jobber;* knowledge-gatherer; lookout; mole; nark; outrider; pathfinder; quadruplator; reconnoiter; spy; spotter; trailblazer; undercover agent; vanguard; watch; *X; yard; zarp;*

**scout** *(v.)*: ascertain; blaze a trail; comb; discover; explore; find; go over; guide; have a look; hunt; investigate; jerque; keep in view; look at; locate; make a search; *nose;* observe; probe; patrol; *quest;* reconnoiter; search out; survey; traverse; uncover; view; watch; *x-search; yearn for; zealously ~;*

**scrap** *(n.)*: *amount;* bit; crumb; chip; daud; drop; *ens;* flake; fragment; *gob;* hunk; iota; jib; junt; jigger; kernel; little piece; morsel; modicum; nugget; ounce; ort; piece; part; *quantity;* remnant; ribbon; smidgen; small piece; tad; *unit; vestige;* whit; wedge; *xylon; yngot [arch.]; zum [dial.];*

**scrap** *(v.)*: abandon; betoss; chuck; cast off; discard; dispose of; dump; eliminate; free oneself of; get rid of; hurl; *incinerate;* junk; kest; *leave; move into garbage; non-valuable; oust;* pitch; *quoit;* recycle; rid oneself of; recycle; scuttle; trash; throw out; unload; *valueless;* waste; *x-out; yucky;* zero out;

**scrape** *(v.)*: abrade; bark; cut; dig; etch; file; graze; gouge; hack; *injure; jag; kerf;* lacerate; mark; nick; *open;* paw; *query;* rasp; rake; scour; scuff; skin; skim; scratch; *tear;* urticate; *violence;* wear away; wound; xyster; yeck; *zip;*

**scratch** *(n.)*: abrasion; boo-boo; cut; claw-mark; dig; etching; flesh wound; graze; gouge; *hurt;* injury; *jag; knock;* lesion; mark; nick; *opening;* prang; *query;* rasp; scrape; score; scrabble; tear; urtication; *violence;* wound; *xerophthalmia; yedder; zapping;*

**scratch** *(v.)*: abrade; bark; claw; carve; dig; etch; forehew; graze; gouge; hack; *itch; injure; jag; kerf;* lacerate; mark; nick; *open;* paw; *query;* rasp; rake; scrape; score; scuff; *tear;* urticate; *violence;* wound; *xerophthalmia;* yeck; *zip;*

**scream** *(v.)*: appeal; bellow; chirr; cry; *discharge;* exclaim; *fret;* growl; holler; howl; hoot; inveigh; *jubilate;* keen; loudly say; *moan;* make outcry; noise; outcry; *pule; quiritation;* roar; shrill; shriek; scream; screech; squall; trill; ululate; vociferate; vent; wail; *xenophonia;* yell; yowl; *zing;*

**scribble** *(n.)*: annotations; bescribbling; *characters;* doodle; etching; *form; glyphs;* handwriting; inscription; jotting; *kept records;* lettering; markings; mesy handwriting; niggle; *obscure; paragraph;* print; *the quill;* remarks; scribbling; scrawl; *text;* uncials; *verbiage;* writing; *xiaozhuan;* yod; *zeug [G.];*

**scribble** *(v.)*: annotate; bescribble; compose; doodle; dash off; enter; fabulize; get down; handwrite; imprint; jot; keep record; list; mark; notate; *overwrite;* put down; quill; redact; scrawl; scrabble; take down; *underwrite; vellum;* write (down); *x; yod; zay;*

**scribe** *(n.)*: annotator; book-copier; copyist; dialogue-writer; engraver; *fact-recorder;* glossator; *hedge-writer;* inscriber; journalist; *keeper;* letterer; man of letters; notater; observator; penman; quill-driver; replicator; scrivener; transcriber; *underwriter;* volumist; writer; *xerographer; yod; zincographer;* [*see* teacher]

**scroll** *(n.)*: autograph; book; banderole; *codex; copy;* document; epistle; *folio; graving;* hierogram; holograph; handscroll; inscription; *hournal; kept record;* letter; *leaf; the Law;* manuscript; *notation; octavo;* papyrus; parchment; paper roll; *Qumran;* roll; scriptures; tarp; text; uncial; vellum; writing; *xuan paper;* yellowed ~; *zay;*

**scrumptious** *(adj.)*: appetizing; *bon!* [F.]; *captivating;* delectable; delicious; enjoyable; exquisite; fine; flavorful; great-tasting; heavenly; irresistible; *juicy;* keen; luscious; mouth-watering; nice; *outstanding;* pleasing; palatable; *quite good; rewarding;* savory; tasty; tantalizing; *unbelievably good; very good; wonderful; xenial;* yummy; zesty; [*Ant.* sickening]

**scruple** *(n.)*: apprehension; *bone;* compunction; doubt; ethical consideration; foreboding; *guilt;* hesitation; issues; *integrity; jarred;* knowledge of right and wrong; leeriness; misgiving; niggle; objections; problem; qualm; reservations; second thought; trouble; uneasiness; *vacillation;* worries; *x-ing; yieldedness; zeroing in;*

**scrutinize** *(v.)*: analyze; behold; check out; consider; dissect; examine; fix eyes on; gaze; go over; *hone in on;* inspect; *judge; know;* look over; make out; monitor; *note;* observe; pore over; probe; *question;* review; run over; study; take in; *understand;* view; vet; watch; *xenodiagnose;* yeme; *zero in;*

**scrutiny** *(n.)*: analysis; beholding; check; close examination; dissection; examination; *find;* gazing; going-over; hunting; inspection; jerquing; *knowledge;* looking (over); meticulous going-over; *noting;* observation; poring over; *quest;* review; run-through; searching; trolling; *undertaking;* viewing; watching; *xenodiagnosis; yeme; zeroing in;*

**scum** *(n.)*: accumulation; buildup; crud; cremor; deposit; *emptying;* filth; froth; gunk; *horrid;* impurities; junk; *kaff;* lees; matter; nast; off-scouring; *ooze;* plaque; pond ~; quinoldine; residue; skin; tartar; *unwanted;* varve; waste; *xylene;* yacca gum; *zum* [dial.];

**scythe** *(n.)*: agricultural tool; blade; chopper; *device;* edge; falcate; grass-cutter; hedging bill; implement; *jelman* [Turk.]; kama; korambi; long-handled ~; mower; *navaja;* Ottoman sword; *panga;* quillons; reaping hook; sickle; *tool; utensil;* Venetian sword; war ~; *xiphoid;* yatagan; *zekill* [arch.];

**sea** *(n.)*: archipelago; *the* brine; briny blue; *channel; the* deep (blue sea); expanse; fishpond [slang]; great sea; high seas; *inlet; jheel* [Ind.]; keld; lagoon; main ~; *narrows;* ocean; open ~; offing; *palagic; quai;* reservoir; *the* seas; tide; thalassa; *undercurrent; voe;* water; waves; *xyrisic;* yeo; *Zee* [G.]; [*see* river; lake]

**seal** *(n.)*: affirmation; arms; blazon; boss; cachet; designation; emblem; figure; gold ~; hallmark; insignia; imprint; impression; *jack;* key; logo; mark; notation; official ~; pictogram; *quality ~;* representation; *ring ~;* signet; stamp; sigil; tag; *uncial;* verification; *vexillum;* wax ~; wafer; *X;* yacht ensign; *zeug;*

**seal** *(v.)*: affix seal; authenticate; *bond;* clinch; close; certify; confirm; decide; emboss; ensure; fasten; finalize; guarantee; hallmark; impress; *jointly-sealed; keep promise; lick;* make sure; mark; *notarize;* officially ~; pledge; *qualified promise;* resolve; stick shut; secure; settle; stamp; testify; *unconditional promise;* validate; wrap up; *x-one's heart; yafery* [arch.]; zet [dial.];

**séance** *(n.)*: awakening; bira; *black magic;* calling up the dead; *contact;* demonism; enchantment; *fortune-telling;* ghost-summoning; hailing the dead; incantation; *juju;* Keltic religion; legerdemain; magic; mediumism; necromancy; occultic summoning; powwow; *prayer; quad;* rhabdomancy; sitting; seance; summoning; theurgy; *the unknown; voodoo; witchcraft; xylomancy; yield; zombie;*

643

**sear** *(v.)*: alight; burn; brand; blister; char; cauterize; deflagrate; ensear; flame; grill; heat; harden; incinerate; *jade;* kindle; light (up); mark; *nightfire;* overburn; pyrotyze; *quicken; roast;* singe; scorch; toast; *ustion; vulcanize;* wilt; *xylopyrography; yellow; zap;*

**search** *(n.)*: attempt; burrowing; comb; delve; *effort;* exploration; find; forage; frisk; *goosechase;* hunt; investigation; inquest; jerquing; *kith;* looking; mission; man-hunt; nosing around; overlooking; pursuit; perquisition; poke around; quest; ransacking; rifle; rescue; shakedown; troll; *undertaking;* venture; *wild goosechase; x-search; yearn for; zetetic;*

**search** *(v.)*: ascertain; burrow; comb; discover; explore; find; forage; follow; fish; frisk; ferret; grope; *get;* hunt; investigate; inquest; jerque; kithe; look for; locate; leave no stone unturned; make a search; nose; overlook; probe; pursue; quest for; rake; rummage; ransack; rifle; seek; sweep; scour; scout; track; trail; try to find; uncover; unearth; *venture;* wade thru; *well-traced;* x-search; *yearn for; zealously ~;* [*Ant.* shroud]

**sea-serpent** *(n.)*: *animal;* basilisk; caddy; *creature;* dolichosaurus; elops; fire-breathing serpent; giant squid; hydra; ilomba [Zambia]; *Jormungandr* [Norse]; kraken; leviathan; Loch Ness monster; myrus; monster; naitaka; *Nessie;* ogopogo; plesiosaur; *quadrupedal creature; reptile;* sea monster; *thing; umibozu [Jap.]; varmint;* watery dragon; *xiphopagus;* yacumama; zeuglodon;

**seaside** *(n.)*: *area;* bank; beachfront; coastline; dockside; edge; foreshore; *front;* gulf front; hinterland; inception; *jetty; keys;* lido; lakeshore; leeshore; mudflat; nearshore ~; oceanside; plage; *quost* [arch.]; riviera; sands; shore(line); seashore; seacoast; seaboard; threshold; ulterior; verge; waterline; waterfront; *x-border; yonder; zone;*

**season** *(n.)*: appropriate time; *bit;* course; division of year; *day;* era; *fit time; geologic time;* hour; *holiday; itinerary;* juncture; *kilocycle;* lifespan; month; *nature;* occasion; period; quarter; *run;* suitable time; spell; span; time (of year); tide; *uptime; verge;* while; *week; x-time; year; Yuletide; zone;*

  **Seasons**: Autumn; Christmastime; Dry ~; Easter time; Fall; Harvest; Monsoon; Rainy ~; Seedtime; Spring; Summer; Winter; Yuletide.

**season** *(v.)*: add zing; bespice; *combine spices with;* devil; enliven; flavor; ginger; *high-seasoned;* imbue; improve; jazz up; *keen;* liven up; mull; *new-vamp; optimize;* pep up; pepper; *qualify; revamp;* spice; salt; tincture; use ~; vivify; *well-spiced; xfer; yarken;* zest;

**seat** *(n.)*: armchair; bench; chair; deck chair; easy chair; fiddleback; *furniture;* gig; hassock; ice cream chair; jump seat; kack [slang]; lawn chair; *milking stool; nursing chair;* ottoman; pillion; pew; queen's chair; recliner; stool; tuffet; *upholstery; vice chair;* wing chair; x-chair; yacht chair; *zeug [G.];*

**seat** *(v.)*: accommodate; be big enough for; contain; deposit; establish; fit; facilitate; grab a ~; hold; install; juke; *keep;* lay; locate; lodge; mount; nest; *oblige;* place; quat; rest; roost; set; sit(uate); take; *use chair; vajrasana; well-situated; x-chair; yark;* zet [dial.];

**seaworthy** *(adj.)*: A-1; *afloat;* buoyant; controllable; driftable; *easily floats;* fit for the sea; floatable; *going;* hoverable; inaquation; *jetting; kiting;* levitatable; maneuverable; navigable; oceangoing; passable; pilotable; *quickened; resting;* sea-worthy; seagoing; *transcending; upbear; volplaning;* waftable; *xuld [arch.];* yet unsinkable; *zooming;* [*Ant.* sinking]

**secede** *(v.)*: abandon; break away; come out of; disaffiliate; depart; end; exit; forsake; get out; *hang up; independence; jump off; kest;* leave; *migrate; nullify;* opt out; part; pull out; quit; resign; separate; take leave; terminate; *uproot;* vacate; withdraw; x.; *yead;* zip away; [*Ant.* stay]

**secession** *(n.)*: abandonment; breakaway; coming out; departure; *extrication; exiting;* forfeiture; getting out; *high treason; independence;* jumping off; *kesting;* leaving; *mutiny;* non-continuance; opting out; pullout; parting; *quitting;* resignation; separation; seceding; *taking leave; treason;* uncoupling; vacating; withdrawal; x.; *yanking; zipping away;*

**seclude** *(v.)*: alienate; banish; confine; detach; *distance;* exile; forsake the world; ground; hold; immure; isolate; *jail;* keep apart; lock up; make isolated; *not associate; outside;* pen up; quarantine; remove; separate; take away; *unsociable;* veiled; withdraw; x.; *yard; zone;*

**seclusion** *(n.)*: alienation; being alone; confinement; detachment; exclusion; forsaking the world; getting by oneself; hermitism; isolation; inaccessibility; *jejuneness;* kithlessness; loneness; moving away; non-inclusion; *out-of-the-way;* privacy; quarantine; quiet; reclusion; solitude; separation; *tranquility; unsociability; veiling;* withdrawal; *x.;* yokelessness; zipped away;

**secrecy** *(n.)*: anonymity; behind closed doors; confidentiality; concealment; covertness; deception; exclusiveness; furtiveness; *guarded;* hugger-mugger; hiding; imperceptibility; *just between us;* keeping secret; *lock and key;* mystery; non-disclosure; obscuration; privacy; privity; quietness; restriction; silence; seclusion; secretiveness; *top secret; the* unseen; veiling; *wariness; x; yieldless;* zero disclosure;

**secret** *(adj.)*: arcane; *baffling;* confidential; dark; evasive; exclusive; furtive; guarded; hush-hush; *internal; just between us;* kept-quiet; *locked;* mysterious; non-public; off-the-record; private; privileged; quiet; restricted; secretive; sensitive; top- ~; undisclosed; under wraps; veiled; *wary; xeno-; yieldless;* zero sharing;

**secret** *(n.)*: arcanum; black ~; confidence; concealment; dark ~; enigma; *furtiveness;* great mystery; hidden thing; inscrutableness; *just between us;* kept ~; little-known fact; mystery; non-disclosed item; *obscure fact; our little ~;* private matter; *question;* riddle; skeleton in the closet; *trick question;* undisclosed matter; veiled thing; well-kept ~; *x;* yet undisclosed fact; zero publicity;

**secretary** *(n.)*: assistant; *bookkeeper;* clerk; clerical worker; copyist; *dictation;* employee; filer; girl [fem.]; helper; *intern; junior apprentice;* keyboardist; liaison; minister; note-taker; office girl; personal assistant; *questor;* recording ~; secretaire; stenographer; typist; under~; viceroy; worker; *xaraf;* yeoman; *zaikat [Jap.];*

**secretive** *(adj.)*: arcane; baffling; cagey; cryptic; concealed; clandestine; covert; dark; deep-laid; esoteric; enigmatic; furtive; guarded; hidden; hush-hush; inexplicable; jumbled; *known-to-few; little-known;* mysterious; not revealed; obscure; private; quiet; recondite; secret; sly; stealthy; surreptitious; tight-lipped; undercover; underground; underhand; veiled; wary; *xeno-; yieldless; zero-publicity;* [Ant. salient]

**section** *(n.)*: area; apportionment; bit; chapter; chunk; division; element; fragment; *group;* hunk; item; *jib; key part;* lump; mass; *nugget; one;* part; piece; portion; quantity; *remnant;* segment; sector; subdivision; territory; unit; *vestige;* wedge; *x-mal [G.]; yngot* [arch.]; zone;

**secular** *(adj.)*: average; *basic;* common; desacralized; everyday; fleshly; generalized; hylic; irreligious; *Jesus-rejecting; kept separate;* lay; mundane; non-spiritual; nonreligious; ordinary; plain; profane; *quotidian;* regular; subcelestial; temporal; unreligious; very ~; worldly; *x-type; yet irreligious;* zero-religion; [Ant. sacred]

**secularize** *(v.)*: *abridge;* bowdlerize; censor; desacralize; edit God out; *fix; gag; hold back; inhibit; Jesus-rejecting; keep separate;* leave God out; make secular; not include God; omit religious references; *politically correct; quotidian;* remove God; strip God out of; temporalize; take out God; unspiritualize; *vitiate;* wrench religious connotations from; *x-out God;* yank religious references; *zero out;* [Ant. sanctify]

**secure** *(adj.)*: assured; bonded; *covered;* dependable; ensconced; fine; firm; fortified; flanked; guaranteed; guarded; harbored; insured; insulated; inalienable; *just fine;* kept safe; locked; made safe; non-jeopardized; okay; protected; *quartful* [arch.]; risk-free; safe; tight; unthreatened; unalienable; unappealable; very safe; well-protected; *xtry; you beaut* [Aus.]; zero danger; [Ant. shaky]

**secure** *(v.)*: assure; batten; *cover;* defend; establish; ensure; fasten; fix; fortify; guard; hold fast; insure; jaga; keep safe; lock; make safe; *nestle; overprotect;* protect; *quite safe;* reinforce; safeguard; take care of; tie down; trice; *uphold;* vallate; watch (over); *x-guard; yeme* [arch.]; *zero danger;* [see attach; obtain]

**security** *(n.)*: assurance; auspices; *bond;* certitude; *confidence;* defense; *ensured;* freedom from danger; guarantee; *harmlessness;* incolumity; *jaga;* keeping secure; lee; making safe; *mantlet;* non-danger; *overprotection;* protection; *querencia* [Sp.]; refuge; reassurance; safety; safekeeping; *trustworthiness;* unthreatened; *valor;* well-being; *x-guard; yeming* [arch.]; zero danger;

**sedate** *(v.)*: anesthetize; becalm; calm; drug; entrance; fix; give sedative; hit; idle; *jarless;* knock out; lull to sleep; milden; medicate; narcotize; opiate; put under; quiet; relax; soothe; settle one down; tranquilize; use sedative; *vulnery; wind down; x-out; yawn; zeroize;* [*Ant.* stimulate]

**sediment** *(n.)*: alluvium; buildup; *collection;* dregs; deposit; emptyings; feculence; grouts; *hunks;* impurities; *junk;* kaff [dial.]; lees; matter; *non-wanted matter;* orgal; pulp; quittor; residue; rape; silt; settlings; tartar; *unclean;* varve; vestiges; waste; *xysma; yuckiness; zero;*

**sedition** *(n.)*: agitation; *breach;* contumacy; defiance; extremism; fifth-column activity; *general disregard;* high treason; insurgence; *jumping ship; kicking at; lèse majesté* [F.]; mutiny; noncompliance; overthrow; perfidy; *quarrel;* rebellion; rabble-rousing; subversion; seditiousness; treason; troublemaking; uprising; *violence; war; xgression; yieldlessness; yellow flu; zapping;* [*Ant.* submission]

**seditious** *(adj.)*: alienating; breakaway; contumacious; disloyal; extremist; flouting; *grim;* highly treasonous; insurgent; *jumping ship; knocking;* lawless; mutinous; noncompliant; obdurate; perfidious; *querulous;* rebellious; revolutionary; subversive; treasonous; unsubmissive; violent; *wayward; x-grained;* yieldless; *zero regard;* [*Ant.* submissive]

**seduce** *(v.)*: allure; beguile; bait; coax; draw; debauch; entice; ensnare; fool; goad; hoodwink; inveigle; jape; *knavery;* lure; mislead; *nudge;* overpower; provoke; *quiblin [arch.];* rope in; suggest; sweet-talk; stir up; tempt; urge; vamp; woo; *xuld [arch.];* yerk; *zygotaxis;*

**seducer** *(n.)*: allurer; beguiler; charmer; debaucher; devil; enticer; fooler; fox; goader; hoodwinker; inveigler; japer; knave; lurer; misleader; *nudger;* old fox; prodder; *quiblin* [arch.]; rogue; seductress [fem.]; tempter; urger; vampire; wooer; wolf; *xuld [arch.]; yerker; zapper;* [*see* Devil; temptress]

**seduction** *(n.)*: allurement; bait; coaxing; debauchment; enticement; ensnarement; flirtation; gudgeon; hook, line and sinker; honeypot; inducement; incitement; japing; knavery; lure; misleading; *nudge;* overpowering; prodding; provocation; *quiblin* [arch.]; roping in; seducing; test; temptation; urging; vamping; wooing; *xuld [arch.]; yearning; zygotaxis [biol.];*

**seductive** *(adj.)*: alluring; beguiling; captivating; drawing; enticing; flattering; *gauche;* hypnotic; inviting; *jadish;* knavish; likable; motivating; magnetic; *naughty;* obscene; provocative; *quad;* rousing; *revealing;* suggestive; slinky; stimulating; tantalizing; tempting; *unchaste;* vulgar; wooing; *x-rated; yucky; zero-modesty;*

**seductress** *(n.)*: allurer; adulteress; beguiler; charmer; devil; enticer; ensnarer; flirt; *femme fatale* [F.]; goader; home-wrecker; inveigler; Jezebel; kittock; lady of the evening; meretrix; *naughty girl; outwitter;* prodder; quean; *roper;* she-devil; siren; seducer; temptress; tantalizer; user; vixen; vamp; wooer; *xtabay;* yaud; *zapper;* [*Ant.* saint]

**see** *(v.)*: *acknowledge;* behold; catch sight of; descry; distinguish; eye; examine; espy; face; fix eyes on; find; fleer; feast eyes on; gaze; have in view; inspect; *jerque;* keek; ken; look; make out; notice; note; observe; perceive; peek; peer; peep; *quick look;* recognize; survey; spy; scrutinize; take in; *understand;* view; watch; witness; *x-ray vision; yeme; zero in;* [*see* envision]

**seed** *(n.)*: aril; bulb; bean; core; *derivation;* endocarp; eggcase; fern; freestone; grain; germ(en); *hayseed;* insemination; *jujube ~;* kernel; legume; loment; *maize;* nut(let); nucleus; offspring; oilseed; pit; pip; pod; putamen; pyrene; pericarp; pyxis; *pine cone; quinquevalve;* rape~; stone; *tangerine ~;* utricle; *vista cherry ~;* wheat; *xanthspermous; yuzu ~; zeraim* [Heb.];
   **Types of seed**: apple ~; barley ~; cotton~; date ~; egusi; flax~; grapestone; hay~; Indian fig ~; juniper ~; kiwi ~; lint~; lotus ~; musk~; nectarine pit; oat~; poppy ~; quinoa ~; rape~; sesame ~; tomato ~; ugli® fruit ~; velvet bean; wheat ~; xigua ~; yam bean; zucchini ~;

**seek** *(v.)*: ask for; bid for; comb; chase; dig for; desire; *explore;* follow after; go after; get; hunt for; inquest; jerque; kithe; look for; make a search; nose out; *obtain;* pursue; quest for; request; search; strive for; try to get; *uncover;* venture after; work toward; *x-search;* yearn for; *zetetic;* [*Ant.* shun]

**seeker** *(n.)*: aspirant; adventurer; bidder; candidate; chaser; comber; desirer; digger; explorer; ferret; go-getter; hunter; inquirer; *jerque;* kither; looker; *much-sought; noser; obtainer;* petitioner; pursuer; perquisitor; quester; questant; questioner; querent; reseacher; solicitor; supplicant; searcher; tracker; *uncoverer;* venturer; wanter; wisher; *x-search;* yager; zetetic; [Ant. *the* sought]
**seethe** *(v.)*: agitate; boil; churn; decoct; estuate; effervesce; *ebullient;* foam; gently ~; heat; hard-boil; *irritate; jump;* kier; *liquid;* make boil; *nettle;* overheat; poach; parboil; *quicken;* rage; *rebullition;* simmer; stew; trouble; *upset; violent; vaporize;* wallop; *xeo; yerk;* zoutch; [*Ant.* settle]
**segment** *(n.)*: area; bit; chunk; division; element; fragment; *group;* hunk; installment; *jib; key piece;* lump; mass; *nugget; one part;* part; piece; percentage; quantity; *remnant;* section; slice; *tidbit;* unit; *vestige;* wedge; *x-mal [G.]; yngot* [arch.]; zone;
**segregation** *(n.)*: apartheid; apartness; *back-of-the-bus;* complete separateness; division; ethnic ~; *forking; gap; half and half;* isolation; *judicial separation;* keeping separate; *living apart;* making separate; non-integration; *ostracization;* parting; *quartering;* racial ~; separation; separateness; total separation; *unmixed; very separate; weeding out;* xenophobia; *yandy;* zero integration;
**seize** *(v.)*: apprehend; arrest; *bring;* capture; confiscate; commandeer; dispossess; divest; exact; fetch; grab; haul away; intercept; impound; *jump at;* keep; lay hold of; make off with; nab; obtain; procure; *quick;* reave; snatch; sequester; take; usurp; *violence;* wrest; *xfer;* yank; zip away; [*Ant.* surrender]
**seldom** *(adv.)*: almost never; barely; *cannot;* dearly *exception;* few; gauntly; hardly ever; infrequently; just occasionally; *keenly scarce;* leanly; meagerly; not often; only occasionally; paltrily; *quasi;* rarely; scarcely; tenuously; uncommonly; very ~; *wheenly* [arch.]; *xtry.; yet uncommonly*; zero;
**select** *(v.)*: accept; *best choice;* choose; decide on; elect; favor; go for; hand-pick; indicate; judge between; *keen on; like;* make a choice; *nominate;* opt; pick; prefer; *quibble;* resolve; settle on; specify; single out; take; *use;* vote; want; *well-chosen; x;* yes; *zealous for;*
**selection** *(n.)*: assortment; array; big selection; collection; diversity; extensive ~; full array; *grouping;* hodgepodge; heterogeneity; indication; jumble; keen assortment; *load;* large quantity; multiplicity; miscellany; mixture; mixed bag; mishmash; number; olio; options; pastiche; quantity; range; selecting; *ton; uberous;* variety; wide ~; wealth; xtry. ~; *yelm; zillions;*
**self-confidence** *(n.)*: assuredness; boldness; confidence; doughtiness; equability; fearlessness; gallantry; hubris; inflatedness; *jackanapes; know-it-all;* levelheadedness; *macho;* no fear; overconfidence; poise; presumption; *quick-to-boast;* resolution; self-assurance; temerity; *unafraid;* vouchsafement; *wrapped up in oneself; x-proud; yare;* zeal; [Ant. sheepishness]
**self-confident** *(adj.)*: assured; bold; confident; doughty; ever-confident; fearless; full of oneself; gallant; heroic; independent; inflated; *jackanapes; know-it-all;* lifted up; *macho;* never-fearing; overconfident; puffed up; quick-to-boast; resolute; sure of oneself; self-assured; temerarious; unafraid; very confident; *wrapped up in oneself; x-proud; yare;* zealous; [Ant. sheepish]
**self-control** *(n.)*: abstemiousness; *bringing under;* control; denial; eschewal; forbearance; *giving up;* holding back; inhibiting; *just say no;* keeping from; leaving off; meekness; moderation; non-indulgence; nephalism; *omission;* patience; *quitting;* restraint; self-discipline; self-restraint; temperance; unexcessiveness; voluntarily abstinence; willpower; *x;* yieldlessness; *zero;* [Ant. storminess]
**self-esteem** *(n.)*: arrogance; belief in self; confidence; dignity; egotism; fullness of self; *gloating;* haughtiness; inflated opinion of self; *jackanapes; know-it-all;* love of self; *me;* narcissism; overconfidence; pride; *quilicom* [arch.]; *reliance on self;* self-respect; self-worth; turgidity; *unhumbled;* vainness; wind; *xel [arch.]; yieldless;* zero humility; [Ant. self-doubt]
**selfish** *(adj.)*: avaricious; *begrudging;* churlish; *dissocial;* egotistic(al); *for oneself;* greedy; hoggish; inconsiderate; *jealous;* keenly ~; looking our for #1; mercenary; non-considerate of others; one-way; parsimonious; piggish; *quenchless;* regarding self; self-seeking; (-centered; -serving); thoughtless; tightfisted; unthoughtful; ungenerous; venal; wagamama; *xtry.* ~; yet avaricious; *zero concern for others;* [Ant. selfless]

**selfishness** *(n.)*: avariciousness; *begrudging;* churlishness; *dissocial;* egoism; egocentricity; *for oneself;* greed; hoggishness; inconsiderateness; *jealousy;* keen ~; looking out for #1; mercenariness; non-consideration; *own interests;* piggishness; *quenchlessness;* regarding self; self-seeking; (-centeredness; -interest); *thoughtlessness; unthoughtful;* venality; *wagamama; xtry. ~; yet avaricious; zero concern for others;* [*Ant.* selflessness]
**selfless** *(adj.)*: altruistic; big-hearted; Christlike; deferential; *endeared;* free-handed; giving; humble; high-minded; *ingenuous; joy-giving;* kind; loving; magnanimous; nice; others-oriented; philanthropic; quick-to-give; regardful; sharing; sacrificial; thoughtful; unselfish; *virtuous; well-natured; xenial;* yielding; *zealous of good works;* [*Ant.* selfish]
**selflessness** *(n.)*: altruistism; big-heartedness; Christlikeness; deference; *endeared;* free-handedness; generosity; high-mindedness; *ingenuousness; joy-giving;* kindness; love; magnanimity; nice; others-oriented; philanthropic; quickness to give; regardful; sacrificial; thoughtful; unselfish; *virtue; well-natured; xenial;* yielding; *zealous of good works;* [*Ant.* selfishness]
**self-pity** *(n.)*: *aggrieved;* blueness; cheerlessness; downheartedness; *ejulation;* feeling sorry for oneself; *grief; heartache; inconsolableness;* joylessness; *katzenjammer; languishing;* misery; moping; no joy; overmuch sorrow; pouting; pity-party; *quivering; remorse;* sadness; trouble; unhappiness; vapors; woe; *xtr. down; yearning; zestlessness;* [*Ant.* severity]
**self-righteousness** *(n.)*: arrogance; bigheadedness; conceit; disdain; egotism; flatulence; gloating; haughtiness; impudence; inflatedness; *jackanapes; know-it-all;* loftiness; magisterialness; narcissism; overconfidence; overproudness; pride; *quilicom* [arch.]; religiosity; smugness; superiority; turgidity; unctuousness; vainness; wind; *xenophobia; yieldlessness; zero humility;* [*Ant.* self-effacement]
**sell** *(v.)*: advertise; broker; carry; deal in; *ex; export;* furnish; *grocer;* hawk; hock; handle; *import;* job; *kiddier;* liquidate; merchandise; merchandize; market; nundinate; offer; outsell; oversell; *pitch;* peddle; purvey; pawn; *qualified sale;* retail; re~; supply; trade; traffic; unload; under~; *urge;* vend; wholesale; *x.;* yield; *zyalde* [arch.].
**seller** *(n.)*: agent; broker; business owner; chapman; dealer; distributor; exporter; floorwalker; furnisher; grocer; handler; importer; jobber; jagger; kiddier; *let go for;* merchant; marketer; monger; *négociant* [F.]; operator; peddler; purveyor; provider; *qualified re~;* retailer; re~; solicitor; storekeeper; supplier; trader; tradesman; trafficker; *utterer;* vendor; victualer; VAR; wholesaler; xylopolist; yarn man; *zyalde [arch.]* [*see* salesman; *Ant.* shopper]
**seminar** *(n.)*: assembly; *body;* conference; colloquium; discussion; educational class; forgathering; forum; gathering; *homily; ingathering;* joint conference; *kit [coll.];* lecture; meeting; night class; *oration;* presentation; *quantity;* roundtable; session; symposium; talk; *utterance; videoconference;* workshop; *xenophonia; yawner* [derog.]; *zone;*
**seminary** *(n.)*: academy; Bible college; college; divinity school; educational facility; *finishing school;* graduate school; halls; *higher education;* institution; ivory tower; junior ate [R.C.C.]; *knowledge; lower school; multiversity; night school; oracles;* preacher school (-factory) [slang]; *quarter;* religious school; scholasticate; school; theological institution; university; varsity [Br.]; *workshop; xenagogue; yeshiva* [Heb.]; *zone;*
**send** *(v.)*: airmail; *bus;* broadcast; bestow; convey; commission; deliver; dispatch; export; emit; e-mail; freight; forward; ferry; give; get; hurl; issue; impel; janker; *jet;* kurvey; launch; locomote; move; mail; *night delivery; overnight;* post; propel; quarter-cart; relay; ship; transport; transmit; transfer; thrust; upload; *van; waft;* xfer; xmit; *yield;* zip; [*Ant.* summon]
**senior** *(adj.)*: *adult;* boss; chief; dominant; elder; foremost; greatest; higher(-up; -ranking; -level); *important; judicious;* key; leading; main; notable; older; primary; quintessential; ranking; superior; supreme; top; upper; *vital; weighty; xenenthesis; yet unsurpassed; zenithal;* [*Ant.* subordinate]

**senior** *(n.)*: aged man; bearded man; codger; dotard; elder; father; fogey; golden-ager; geriatric; geezer [off.]; grandpa (-ma); hoary head; *individual; jack; knowledgeable individual; long-bearded man;* mature; Methuselah; nonagenarian; old (person; -timer; man; woman); octogenarian; patriarch; *quite old;* retiree; senior; sexagenarian; *time-worn;* up in years; veteran; white beard; *xtr. mature; years; zapped;* [*Ant.* suckling]

**seniority** *(n.)*: anciency; *best;* control; dominance; eldership; favor; greatness; highness; hegemony; influence; *jurisdiction; keenness;* lead; *magnitude; notableness;* old age; priority; *quality; reign;* superiority; *top;* ultimacy; *virtue;* weightiness; *XF;* years; *zenithal;* [*Ant.* subordination]

**sense** *(n.)*: awareness; bearing; brains; comprehension; discernment; detection; *experience;* feeling; gut reaction; horse ~; identification; insightfulness; *judgment;* knowledge; lucidity; mental grasp; nous; observation; perception; quickness; recognition; realization; sensation; sensitivity; sensibility; *taking in;* understanding; *vision;* wit; *xfer; yeme;* zeroing in;

**sense** *(v.)*: anticipate; become aware; can tell; discern; detect; *experience;* feel; find; grasp; have understanding; identify; *judge;* know; ken; *learn;* make out; *notice;* observe; perceive; pick up; *quicken;* recognize; realize; seem; *take in;* understand; *view;* wit; *xfer; yeme;* zero in;

**sensible** *(adj.)*: acceptable; believable; commonsense; coherent; down-to-earth; evenhanded; expedient; fair; feasible; good; healthy-minded; intelligent; judicious; knowledgeable; logical; level-headed; lucid; matter-of-fact; no-nonsense; objective; practical; practicable; prudent; plausible; quite ~; reasonable; rational; realistic; sound; sane; tenable; understandable; viable; wise; workable; well-thought-out; *xenagogic;* yepe; *zero doubt;* [*Ant.* senseless]

**sensitive** *(adj.)*: acute; aware; attentive; *bearing;* considerate; compassionate; caring; delicate; easily hurt; emotional; feelings; graciousness; hyper~; *inclined; judiciousness;* keen; love; mindfulness; niceness; nastic; over~; passable; precise; perceptive; *quick to sense;* responsive; soft(hearted); tender(-hearted); touchy; understanding; *virtue;* warm(hearted); *xenial;* yielding; *zero offence;*

**sensitivity** *(n.)*: attentiveness; *bearing;* consideration; compassion; care; delicateness; emotionalness; feelings; *graciousness;* hyper~; intuition; *judiciousness;* kindness; keenness; love; mindfulness; niceness; over~; passability; politeness; perception; *quick to help;* regardfulness; responsiveness; sympathy; thoughtfulness; understanding; *virtue;* warmth; *xenial; yielding; zero offence;*

**sensual** *(adj.)*: abandoned; animal; bodily; carnal; dissolute; erotic; fleshly; gamic; hedonistic; immoral; jadish; *kinky;* lewd; lustful; lascivious; *mischievous;* non-pure; obscene; pleasure-seeking; provocative; *quad;* ravishing; sensuous; sultry; stimulating; tantalizing; unchaste; voluptuous; wanton; *x-rated; yielded to the flesh;* zipless; [*Ant.* saintly]

**sensuality** *(n.)*: abandon; baseness; carnality; degradation; eroticism; filthiness; gratification; hedonism; indecency; jadishness; *kitsch;* lewdness; meanness; nefariousness; obscenity; provocativeness; *quad;* reprobation; sensualness; sexiness; tantilization; unchasteness; volupuousness; wantonness; *x-rated;* yuckiness; ziplessness; [*Ant.* saintliness]

**sentence** *(n. punishment)*: avengement; *blame;* condemnation; decision; determination; enunciation; finding; *give; gavel; hair shirt*; invocation; judgment; jankers; jail ~; *keep locked up; lay on one;* mandate; *notification; oracles;* punishment; pronouncement; *quantity;* ruling; sentence; *statement; telling;* utterance; verdict; word; *xfer clause; yeme; zeal;*

   **Kinds of punishment**: amercement; burning at the stake; beheading; chastisement; crucifixion; detention; dunking; death; exile; electric chair; fine; firing squad; fine; flogging; gating; guillotine; gas chamber; house arrest; hanging; incarceration; impalement; jail; keelhauling; life-imprisonment; lethal injection; necklacing; prison; quartering; spanking; stocks; scourging; stoning; torture; tar and feathering; whipping;

**sentence** *(v.)*: adjudge; *bid;* condemn; declare; doom; enunciate; find guilty; give punishment; *have;* invoke; impose; judge; *keep locked up;* lay down; mandate; necessitate; ordain; pass judgment; punish; pronounce; *qualify;* rule; *speak; tell;* utter; *verdict;* voice; weigh; *xfer; yard* [arch.]; *zakon* [Rus.];

**sentimental** *(adj.)*: affective; bathetic; cloying; disturbing; emotional; feeling; gushy; *hormonal;* inane; jarring; keenly ~; lachrymose; maudlin; novelettish; nostalgic; nauseating; over- ~; passionate; poignant; quixotic; romantic; sensitive; soupy; syrupy; sickening; touching; tender (-hearted); tearful; unrestrained; visceral; weepy; *xtry.* ~*; yet unquenched; zipless;*

**separate** *(adj.)*: apart; asunder; autonomous; broken; cleft; different; distinct; divided; disunited; *excluded;* free; *gapping;* heterogeneous; individual; independent; isolated; *jigsawed; knifed; laniated;* made separate; non-connected; *other; parted;* quinquefid; riven; solitary; split; two; unconnected; unattached; unrelated; varied; *wide-ranging; x'ed; yandied; zoned;*

**separate** *(v.)*: abstract; break; cleave; divide; detach; disconnect; divorce; disjoin; disassociate; disunite; decouple; diverge; extract; extricate; fork; fractionate; get out; halve; incide; isolate; *jigsaw; knife;* laniate; lixiviate; make ~; *non-continuous;* open; part; partition; parcel; *quarter;* rend; root out; remove; sever; segregate; split; sunder; sift; sort; *tear apart; unattached;* uncouple; unyoke; unmingled; *vell;* weed (out); winnow; *x-sect;* yandy; yawn; zone; [*Ant.* secure]

**separation** *(n.)*: abstraction; break(up); breach; cleavage; division; disjunction; disconnection; disunion; divorce; divergence; extraction; extrication; forking; gap; hiatus; *isolation;* judicial separation; keeping apart; leaving; marching away; *non-unity; opening;* parting; *quartering;* rending; subdivision; severance; split; sorting; taking apart; uncoupling; unyoking; vacating; withdrawal; weeding out; *xiphopagotomy;* yawn; zipping apart;

**sepulcher** *(n.)*: *area;* burial place; crypt; cave; dolmen; entombment; final resting place; grave; house of death; humation; interment; *jaw-hole;* kurgan; last home; mound; mausoleum; narrow house; ossuarium; plot; pit; pyramid; *quietus;* resting place; repository; sepulchre; tomb; underground; vault; *whited* ~*; xat;* yawn; *ziarat* [Mos.];

**sequence** *(n.)*: arrangement; *being;* course; *direction;* development; *evaluation;* format(ion); file; grouping; hierarchy; indexing; *judicial order;* keyed ~; lineup; method; number order; order; queue; rearrangement; succession; series; sorted order; train; *uniformity; valuation;* way; *xfer; yoked; zoning;*

**sequential** *(adj.)*: adjacent; back-to-back; consecutive; chronological; directly following in order; ensuing; following each other; going on; hard by; in order; incrementing; joining; kept-together; linked; methodical; numbered; ordered; one-after-the-other; placed together; queued; running; successive; succeeding; sequent; serial; touching; together; unbroken; uninterrupted; verging; without interruption; *xenograft;* yoked; *zero break;* [*Ant.* sensless]

**serious** *(adj.)*: acute; bound; crucial; dire; dead ~; earnest; foreboding; grave; grim; highly important; heavy; humorless; important; *judicious; keening;* life-and-death; momentous; major; needful; ominous; ponderous; po-faced; *quantum;* resolute; solemn; somber; sober(ing); soberminded; thoughtful; urgent; vital; weighty; *xtry.; yearnful;* zoetic; [*Ant.* sportive]

**seriousness** *(n.)*: acuteness; *burdensomeness;* criticalness; dead ~; earnestness; frankness; factuality; gravity; graveness; grimness; heaviness; importance; *judiciousness;* kidding aside; *life-and-death;* momentousness; needfulness; *ominous; pensiveness; quantum;* realness; seriousness; solemnity; sobriety; sobermindedness; truth; unction; verity; weightiness; *xtry.; yearnfulness;* zeal; [*Ant.* sportiveness]

**sermon** *(n.)*: address; bespeaking; communication; commentary; charge; declaration; discourse; elocution; exhortation; *filibuster; glossa;* homily; indiction; *jabbering; kerygma;* lecture; message; *midrash* [Heb.]; *notes;* oration; preaching; proclamation; preachment [derog.]; *quotation;* recitation; speech; sermonette; talk; utterance; vocalization; the Word; *xenophonia; yakking; zinger [slang];*

**serpent** *(n.)*: ∗ asp; adder; boa (constrictor); cobra; diamondback; emerald tree boa; firedrake; garter snake; horned viper; Indian python; jararaca; king cobra; large whip snake; moccasin; nedder; ophidian; python; queen snake; rattlesnake; *reptile;* snake; tree snake; *uraeus;* viper; water snake; *xenophidion;* yellow cobra; *zamenenis;*

**servant** *(n.)*: attendant; bond slave; bondman; bondmaid [fem.]; butler; chamberlain; cookmaid; demiurge; eunuch; errand-boy; factotum; flunky; footboy; *gofer* [slang]; gallopin; handmaid(en) [fem.]; help(er); hand; houseboy [masc.]; housemaid [fem.]; indentured servant; inferior; jackman; jong; knave; kitchen-maid [fem.]; kitchen-knave [masc.]; *khans amah* [Ind.]; lackey; man(servant) [masc.]; maid(servant) [fem.]; minion; menial; neif; nipper; outrider; porter; page; *personnel;* quarter-maid [fem.]; retainer; slave; scullion; servitor; subordinate; trusted ~; underservant; valet; varlet; worker; wench [fem.]; waiting-maid (-woman); x-man; yeoman; yardwoman [fem.]; zaikai; [*see* slave; employee; *Ant.* supervisor]

**serve** *(v.)*: attend assist; busy oneself; carry on activity; do; exert; function; grind; help; *industry; job;* keep; lackey; labor; minister; *night-work;* operate; obey; perform; *quick-to-obey;* render service; submit; tend; take care of; *use; valet;* wait (on); work for; *xfer;* yield to; *zealously ~;* [*Ant.* subdue]

**service** *(n.)*: attendance; assistance; bond- ~; burden; care; duty; daylabor; employment; exertion; effort; field ~; grunt-work; gainful employment; handi~; home~; hired labor; hard ~; help; industry; job; *kitchen ~;* labor; ministry; ministration; night-work; occupation; output; performance; production; *quantity output;* rigor; serving; toil; trade; *use;* vocation; work; *wrought; xtry. ~;* yardwork; *yakka* [Aus.]; *zealous labor;*

**session** *(n.)*: assembly; body; conference; discussion; *exchange;* forgathering; gathering; horde; ingathering; jam [coll.]; kit [coll.]; lot; lesson; meeting; negotiations; *opportunity;* pow-wow; palaver; *quorum;* regathering; sitting; summit; *turnout; unit meeting;* vestry; *wardmote; x.; yain* [arch.]; *zayat [Burm.];*

**set** *(adj.)*: absolute; bound; changeless; determinate; ever the same; fixed; guaranteed; having no change; immutable; irreversible; *just the same;* keeping the same; lasting; moveless; non-alterable; *obstinate;* permanent; quite ~; rigid; reverseless; static; *timeless;* unchangeable; unalterable; vested; written in stone; x-cending; yet the same; *zero change;* [*Ant.* switchable]

**set** *(n.)*: arrangement; assortment; bunch; *box;* collection; display ~; *edition;* full array; group; *hoard; items; juba* [L.]; kit; lot; layout; matrix; nexus; organized ~; panoply; *quantity;* range; series; selection; suite; *ton;* unit; varia; variety; *with; xtry. selection; yelm;* zet [dial.];

**set** *(v.)*: arrange; adjust; become permanent; confirm; congeal; deposit; establish; fix; get harder; gel; harden; *hold;* institute; incrassate; jell; kern; lay; leave; locate; make; *nail down;* ordain; organize; ossify; put; place; plant; pitch; pre-establish; preset; prefix; *quick-set;* rest; rigidify; settle; situate; stick; stow; stablish; take root; *unveil;* vest; wedge; *xfer;* yoke with; zet [dial.]; [*Ant.* switch]

**settle** *(v. balance out)*: adjust; become stationary; balance out; calm; compact; densify; ease; even out; fix; fall; firm up; go down; harmonize; *iron out; justify; knock down;* level out; moderate; make stable; normalize; *over;* pack (down); quieten; relax; rest; resolve; set; sink; subside; stabilize; stay; tamp; *unruffle;* vamp; work out; *xfer; yield;* zet [dial.]; [*Ant.* shake up]

**settle** *(v. colonize)*: *arrive;* abide; begin a colony; colonize; displace; establish; ensconce; fix; get to; homestead; immigrate; *journey; known;* live; migrate to; nestle; occupy; plant; put down roots; *quarter;* relocate; start a colony; stake a claim; transmigrate; *underway; voyage; warrant;* xenize; yede; zip;

**settle** *(v. resolve)*: affirm; become set; clear up; clinch; determine; establish; fix; get to the bottom of; hash out; iron out; justify; *know;* lay to rest; make an end to; *non-issue;* open up; pay; preresolve; quieten; resolve; reconcile; solve; set; take care of; unravel; verify; work out; *xlate; yieldless; zero in;*

**settlement** *(n. colony)*: *area;* burg; colony; community; dependency; eparchy; *fishing town;* governance; hamlet; imperial domain; *jurisdiction; kingship; land;* mandate; *nome;* outpost; protectorate; *queendom; region;* satellite; society; town; *under;* village; viceroyalty; *waywodeship [Turk.];* xenization; *yard; zone;*

**settlement** *(n. payment)*: arrangement; annuity; *bounty;* compensation; defrayal; emolument; *finances;* guerdon; *hire;* imbursement; *judgment;* kickback; liquidation; *minimum wage; net pay;* outlay; payment; quittance; remittance; repayment; satisfaction; trade-off; *unindebted;* virement; *wages;* xfer; yielding; *zapping;*

**settler** *(n.)*: *abider;* backsettler; colonizer; colonist; dweller; *emigrant;* frontiersman; *goer;* habitant; homesteader; immigrant; inhabitant; *journeyer; keeping; latecomer;* migrator; newcomer; *outlander;* pioneer; *quarter; refugee;* squatter; sooner; transmigrant; *use; voyager;* woodlander; xmigrant; *yerde* [arch.]; *zip to;*

**sever** *(v.)*: amputate; bisect; break; cut off; chop (off); dissever; divide; dismember; exscind; *fissure;* guillotine; hack (off); halve; incise; *jigsaw;* kerf; lop; *mince;* nip; obtruncate; part; *quarter;* rive; recise; split; separate; truncate; take off; undo; *vell;* whack off; x-sect; *yerk; zip off;* [*Ant.* secure]

**several** *(adj, pron.)*: abundant; a lot; bounteous; copious; disproportionate; excess(ive); fruitful; great; galore; heaps; immense; jumbo; *king-sized amounts;* lots; loads; many; much; numerous; overabundant; overmuch; plenty; plentiful; quantitative; quite a few; *replete;* sundry; tons; uberous; umpteen; voluminous; various; wantless; x-teen; *yards;* zillions; [*Ant.* solitary]

**severe** *(adj.)*: acute; brutal; cruel; catonian; difficult; dire; draconian; extreme; forceful; fierce; grave; grueling; harsh; hard; intense; *jabbing;* keen; *large;* merciless; major; *nasty;* onerous; powerful; parlous; painful; *quantitative;* rigorous; relentless; rough; strict; stern; serious; tremendous; unrelenting; very; virile; violent; weighty; xtry.; *yieldless;* zealous; [*Ant.* soft]

**severity** *(n.)*: asperity; brutality; cruelty; difficulty; extremeness; force; fierceness; graveness; harshness; intensity; *jabbing;* keenness; largeness; mercilessness; nastiness; onerousness; power; *quantitative;* rigor; strictness; sternness; tremendousness; *unrelenting;* violence; weightiness; xtry.; *yondmost;* zeal; [*Ant.* softness]

**sew** *(v.)*: *affix;* baste; *chain stitch;* darn; enseam; embroider; fimbriate; *garter stitch;* hem; *insertion stitch;* join; *knit;* Kat stitch; *lock stitch;* moss stitch; needle; *over~;* purl; quilt; renter; stitch; tack; tailor; use needle and thread; *vest;* welt; whipstitch; xenograft; yarn over; *zip together;*

**shack** *(n.)*: abode; bungalow; beach house; cottage; cabin; dwelling (place); dump; edifice; *frontroom;* grass hut; gunyah; hovel; hut; inhabitance; jacal; kya; kipsie [Aus.]; lean-to; lee; mud hut; Nissen hut; outbuilding; pandal; Quonset hut; residence; shelter; shanty; shed; *tent; utility apartment;* villa; wickup; *x-house;* yakutat hut; *zayat;*

**shackle** *(n.)*: ankle-band; band; bilboe; cuffs; *chain;* darbies; *enfettered;* fettering; gyve; handcuff; hand-fetter; hamper; irons; jail-bands; *keeping;* ligature; manacle; nipper; *oppression;* pinion; *quell;* restraint; stocks; trammel; *unliberated; vervel;* wristband; *Xica;* yoke; *zoster;*

**shade** *(n.)*: adumbration; *blackness;* covering; canopy; darkness; enclouding; *fuliginous;* gloom; hint; inumbration; *jettiness; keenness; lightlessness;* murkiness; nubulation; obscurity; penumbra; *quirkiness; raylessness;* shadow; tenebrosity; undertint; *very dim; wadd; xerophthalmic;* yeming; *zero light;*

**shade** *(v.)*: adumbrate; bedim; cloud; cover; crosshatch; color; dim; darken; encloud; fade; grey; hood; hatch; highlight; inumbrate; *jetty; kept shaded; lower light;* make darker; mark; nubilate; overshadow; obumbrate; overlay; over~; protect; *qualify; rayless;* shield; shade in; tint; umbrate; veil; *wimple; x;* yeme; *zero sun;*

**shadow** *(n.)*: adumbration; blackness; cover; darkness; enclouding; form; figure; galanty; gloom; heteroscian; image; *jettiness; kettle-black;* lightlessness; murkiness; nubulation; obscurity; *outline;* penumbra; *quirkiness;* raylessness; silouette; shade; tenebrosity; umbra; veil; *wadd; xerophthalmic;* yeme; *zero light;*

**shady** *(adj.)*: adumbrative; bosky; clouded; cool; canopied; dark; dim; dusky; enclouded; fuliginous; gloomy; *hooded;* inumbrate; *jetty; keen; lightless; mysterious;* nebulated; overshadowed; protected; panoplied; *quite ~; rayless; roofed;* shaded; shadowy; sheltered; tenebrous; umbrageous; veiled; well-shaded; *xtr. dim;* yeme [arch.]; zero sunlight; [*see* dishonest; *Ant.* sunny]

**shake** *(n.)*: agitation; bestirring; convulsion; disturbance; exciting; fluttering; gyration; hurtling; *incite;* jiggle; jigget; judder; knocking; *loosening;* movement; nutation; oscillation; palpitation; quake; rumble; shiver; shudder; succession; tremble; tremor; *upheaval;* vibration; wiggle; *xuld* [arch.]; yerk; zigzag;

**shake** *(v.)*: agitate; bestir; convulse; disturb; excite; flutter; gyrate; hurtle; *incite;* jiggle; judder; knock; *loosen;* move; nutate; oscillate; palpitate; quake; quiver; rumble; shiver; shudder; tremble; upset; vibrate; wobble; wiggle; *xuld* [arch.]; yerk; *zigzag;* [*Ant.* settle]

**shaky** *(adj.)*: aquiver; bouncy; capricious; doddery; erratic; flimsy; fluctuant; giddy; *hazardous;* instable; jumpy; *kooky;* loose; labile; *moveable;* non-stable; *out-of-control;* precarious; quivery; questionable; quavery; rickety; stormy; shaking; tenuous; tottery; unstable; unsteady; vacillating; wobbly; *x-ing; yo-yo;* ziggety; [*Ant.* stable]

**shallow** *(adj.)*: ankle-deep; *bitty;* centimeter-high; depthless; *easy;* fine-layered; *gone down; hairbreadth;* insubstantial; inches; just inches; knee-deep; low; light; meager; not deep; of little depth; pencil-thin; *quantité négligeable* [F.]; *reduced;* shoal; skin-deep; thin; *undersize;* very ~; wadable; *XS;* yea high; *zero depth;*

**shame** *(n.)*: ashamedness; abasement; abashment; bashfulness; contempt; disgrace; dishonor; debasement; degradation; disrepute; dispraise; disreputation; embarrassment; *fall;* guilt; humiliation; indignity; ignominy; infamy; ill repute; *joylessness; kettiness;* lowering; letdown; loss of face; mortification; *notorious incident;* opprobrium; public disgrace; pudency; *quad;* reproach; shamefulness; tarnishing; upbraiding; verecundity; wite; *x-out; yuckiness; zero honor;*

**shame** *(v.)*: abash; *ashamed;* belittle; bring reproach; chagrin; crush; disgrace; dishonor; embarrass; foreshame; *grieve;* humble; humiliate; *indignity; jackalent; knock down;* let down; lower; mortify; *nither* [arch.]; *out of countenance;* put down; *quieten;* reproach; *scandalize;* tarnish; *upbraid; vitiate;* wrong; *xtry. humiliated;* yield; *zero honor;*

**shameful** *(adj.)*: awful; appalling; bad; blameworthy; contemptible; contemptuous; disgraceful; dishonorable; execrable; embarrassing; flagitious; guilty; horrendous; ignominious; *jaded; ketty;* loathsome; miserable; nasty; opprobrious; pathetic; *quad;* reproachful; reprehensible; scurrilous; self-abasing; terrible; unacceptable; vile; wretched; *x-out;* yucky; *zero honor;*

**shameless** *(adj.)*: audacious; barefaced; brazen; clear; deliberate; explicit; flagrant; glaring; gross; high-handed; intentional; impudent; *just plain to see;* kenspeckle; *lucid;* malapert; noticeable; overt; patent; *quite obvious;* recognizable; salient; *terrible;* unashamed; unblushing; visible; without shame; witting; *x-parent;* yare; *zipless;* [*Ant.* shamefaced]

**shape** *(n.)*: arrangement; build; configuration; contour; cut; delineation; *exterior;* form; fashion; figure; guise; geometric ~; *heptagon;* image; impression; *just like; kind;* lineament; mode; *newly-formed;* outline; outward form; *object;* polygon; *quadrangle; rectangle;* structure; style; three-dimensional ~; *undecagon; view;* way; *x-shaped; y-shaped; z-shaped;* [*see* condition]

    **Kinds of shapes**: acute triangle; balbis; circle; cone; crescent; cube; cylinder; decagon; ellipse; hexagon; isogon; kite; lozenge; nonagon; octagon; oval; parallelogram; pentagon; polygon; pyramid; quadrangle; rectangle; rhombus; sphere; square; star; trapezoid; triangle; undecagon;

**shape** *(v.)*: arrange; build; cast; create; constitute; configure; design; efform; form; fashion; forge; give ~; hammer out; institute; *job;* knead; *lick into ~;* mold; make; model; *newly formed;* outline; *produce; quick-build;* remake; reform; style; sculpt; swage; take ~; tailor; transform; upbuild; *vamp;* whittle; *xenomorph;* yote; *zet* [dial.];

**shapeless** *(adj.)*: amorphous; blobby; changeable; dimensionless; erratic; formless; *gelatin-like;* hazy; inchoate; indistinct; ill-defined; jellyish; kaleidoscopic; loose; labile; multiversant; mutable; nebulous; *obscure; omniform;* protean; quasi-morphous; *revamping;* structure-less; transmutable; unformed; unshaped; unstructured; vague; wavy; *x-bodied; yielding;* zaggy; [*Ant.* shaped]

**shard** *(n.)*: *amount;* bit; crock(-shard); daud; *ens;* fragment; *gall;* hunk; *iota;* junt; *kernel;* lamia; morsel; *nugget; ounce;* potsherd; quill; rasping; sliver; splinter; *tidbit; under;* vestige; wedge; *xylon; zinger;*

**share** *(n.)*: allocation; apportionment; bestowal; consignment; distribution; *earmarked;* fraction; giving out; handing out; issuance; *just division; kit;* lot; measure; *non-transferable;* outfit; portion; part; quantum; ration; slice; set amount; *transferal;* unit; vesting; *weighing; xfer;* yielding; *zoning;*

**share** *(v.)*: allocate; *bestow;* cut in; divide (up); double up; evenly divide; fairly divide; go halves; *give;* have in common; impart; justly divide; *kit;* let have some; make communal; *non-selfish;* open up to all; partake with others; quantize; *render some;* split; *transfer some;* use together; *vest;* weigh; *xfer;* yield; zone;

**sharp** *(adj.)*: acute; barbed; cusped; denticled; double-edged; edged; fine-edged; *grinded;* harsh; *incisal;* jagged; keen(-edged); lanceolated; mucronate; nettled; over-sharpened; pointy; pointed; quill-like; razor- ~; spiky; sharpened; ~ -edged; tined; two-edged; unbated; ultra- ~; very ~; well-sharpened; xyresic; *yet undulled;* ziphoid; [*see* intelligent; *Ant.* smooth]

**sharpen** *(v.)*: acuminate; barb; cut; cuspidate; *double-edge;* edge; file; grind; hone; intensify; *jagged;* keen; *lanceolated;* make sharper; mill; *narrow;* oilstone; point; *quill-like;* resharpen; refine; spiculate strop; set; taper; *use file;* verge; whet; *xyster; yet undulled;* zap;

**sharpness** *(n.)*: acuteness; *barbed;* cutting ability; *distinctness;* edge; fineness; *grinding; highly pointed; incisal;* jaggedness; keenness; lanceolation; mucronation; *not blunted;* over- ~; pointedness; quickness; razor- ~; spikiness; *tined;* ultra-pointiness; *very sharp;* whetting; *xyresic; yet undulled;* zing; [*see* intelligence]

**shatter** *(v.)*: *annihilate;* break; bash; burst; crush; crumble; destroy; disintegrate; explode; fracture; fall apart; *grind;* hurt; *injure; junk;* krack; levigate; mash; *nullify; olate;* pulverize; *quash;* rupture; smash; *smithereens;* tear apart; *undone; violence;* wreck; *x;* yank apart; *zap;*

**shave** *(v.)*: *abridge;* barb; cut; dock; exscind; fleece; graze; *hack;* incise; *jag;* kerf; lop; mow; nip; *overcut;* pare; quick- ~; razor; shear; trim; *undercut; vell; well-shaven; xyrao [Gr.]; yakiba [Jap.]; zip off;*

**shear** *(v.)*: *abbreviate;* barb; clip; dock; exscind; fleece; *gouge;* hack; incide; *jag;* kerf; lop; mow; nip; *overcut;* poll; prune; quick-shave; raze; snip; shave; *shorn;* trim; *undercut;* vell; *well-shaven; xyrao [Gr.]; yakiba [Jap.]; zip off;*

**shears** *(n.)*: *aviation snips;* bandage ~; cutters; *ducktail snips; exscind;* forfex; grass and hedge ~; hedge clippers; *instrument; jack knife;* kitchen scissors; loppers; metzenbaum scissors; nippers; offset snips; pinking shears; pruner; *quadrisect;* rostrum; snips [slang]; scissors; *tool;* tin snips; *universal snips; vell;* wool ~; *x-sect; yerk;* zip;

**sheath** *(n.)*: *area;* blade-case; case; casing; dagger-case; encasement; falchion case; glaive-case; holder; holster; inclosure; jumbuck; knife-case; *koleos* [Gr.]; leather sleeve; *mure; non-exposed; obitori* [Jap.]; pocket; place; *quiver;* receptacle; scabbard; sleeve; *take-along case; utility case;* vessel; *wrap;* xiphoid ~; *yataghan case;* zipsleeve; zarf;

**sheathe** *(v.)*: *away;* back; cover; clothe; *disarm;* encase; *fix; go back;* hide; inclose; jacket; kit; *lay down;* mask; *non-exposed;* overlay; put in sheathe; *quiver;* return; replace; shroud; stow; scabbard; tog; *umbrate; veil;* wrap; *xfer;* yield; *zip away;* [*Ant.* show]

**shed** *(n.)*: agricultural ~; bothy; barn; bush house; carriage-house; cabin; depot; engine ~; farm ~; garden ~; hut; hovel; horse- ~; industrial ~; jacal; kiosk; lean-to; metal ~; nissen hut; outbuilding; poop house; *quarters; roof;* storage ~; shack; shanty; tool ~; utility ~; vinyl-sided ~; wood~; wain-house; x-house; yakutat hut; zayat;

**shed** *(v.)*: abandon; *bleed;* cast off; drop; divest; effuse; emit; exuviate; filter; flake off; *fall;* give; *hone;* issue; *jettison; kest;* lose; let fall; molt; *non-retention;* ooze; pour; *quit;* relinquish; spill; throw off; *unclothe;* vomit; weep; *xfer;* yield; *zip;*

**sheep** *(n.)*: animal; *argali;* bighorn; black ~; bellwether; crone; dall ~; ewe; fatling; flock [pl.]; gigot; houselamb; Indian ~; jumbuck; karakul; lamb; mountain ~; mufflon; *mutton;* New Zealand ~; *ovine;* Perendale; *quadruped;* ram [masc.]; shearling; tag; urial; *varmint;* woolly lamb; wether [masc.]; *x-breed;* yeo [Br.]; yowie; *zoic;*

**sheet** *(n.)*: *amount;* blank sheet; copy paper; *daud;* element; folio; flyleaf; *granule;* hunk; item; *junt;* kernel; leaf; *mass;* numbered ~; ounce; piece; page; paper; *quantity;* ream; slip; typing paper; *unit;* verto; *wad; x-mal [G.]; yngot [arch.]; zum [arch.];*

**shelf** *(n.)*: alcove; book~; bookcase; bottom ~; cratch; divided ~; étagère; flow rack; gray ~; holder; inset; industrial ~; *jar storage area;* kitchen ~; ledge; mantel~; *nook; open ~;* parts ~; *place; quadrilocular;* recess; rack; ridge; setback; sill; stowage; top ~; tack; utility ~; *vanity;* wall- ~; whatnot; *xtr. space; yellow book~; zark;*

**shelter** *(n. protection)*: abri; asylum; bothy; bower; bunker; bomb ~; cover(ture); canopy; dugout; *enclosure;* fortification; foxhole; *getaway;* haven; in-ground ~; *jaw-hole;* keep; lodgment; mattamore; *nest; outbuilding;* protection; *quarters;* refuge; safe haven; sanctuary; storm ~; shadow; sukkah; taking in; underground ~; vault; *wine-cellar; xtr. protection; yamen [Chin.]; zone;*

**shelter** *(n. shack)*: asylum; bower; booth; *barn;* cabin; dugout; edifice; *frontroom;* gunyah; hut; inhabitance; jacal; kya; lean-to; lee; makeshift ~; Nissen hut; outbuilding; pandal; Quonset hut; refuge; shack; temporary ~; tollbooth; *utility apartment;* villa; wickup; *x-house;* yakutat hut; *zayat;*

**shelter** *(v.)*: accommodate; bestead; cover; canopy; defend; ensconce; fend; guard; house; harbor; insulate; jaga; keep; look after; make safe; nestle; overshadow; protect; pavilion; quarter; refuge; shield; take in; uphold; vallate; watch (over); weather-fend; *x-guard; yeme* [arch.]; *zero danger;*

**shepherd** *(n.)*: animal herder; buttero; chief ~; cattleman; drover [Aus.]; escort; *flock caretaker;* grazier; guide; *goatherd;* herdsman; *individual; jumbuck;* keeper; leader; *man;* neatherd; overseer; pastor; *quadruped herder; ram;* sheepherder; shepherdess [fem.]; *transhumance;* under~; *vizer;* warden; woolgrower; watchcare provider; xenagogue; yak herder; zon [dial.];

**sheriff** *(n.)*: *authority;* baliff; chief; commissioner; *deputy(-sheriff);* enforcer; *fuzz [off.];* gendarme; *highway patrol;* inspector; *johnny [Br.];* keeper of the peace; *kotwal* [Ind.]; *the* Law; law officer (-man); marshal; *nabber* [Br.]; officer; police chief; *questura [It.];* ranger; *state trooper;* trooper; *under-sheriff;* viscount; *warden;* xerif; yeoman; zarp [S. Afr.];

**shewbread** *(n.)*: azyme; afikomen; (blessed) bread; consecrated bread; challah; dedicated bread; exhibition bread; *flatbread;* God's bread; holy bread; hallah; *item; jannock; kneading;* loaf; *lechem* [Heb.]; *loaves;* manna; naan; *offering;* priest's bread; *quick bread;* ritualistic bread; showbread; yemple bread; unleavened bread; *venerated;* wave-loaf; *xtr. holy;* yeastless bread; *zet [dial.];*

**shield** *(n.)*: armor; adarga; arms; buckler; *badge;* clipeum [Rom.]; coat of arms; defense; deflector; enarmes; escutcheon; *fortification;* guige; guard; gyron; hatchment; insignia; jaga; kite ~; *lantern ~;* mantlet; *national emblem; over-protected;* pavis; *protection;* quartering; rondache; screen; scutcheon; *scutum* [Rom.]; targe(t); umbo; *vallation;* witham ~; *x-shield;* yeelaman [Aus.]; Zulu ~;

**shield** *(v.)*: assure; *bring under protection;* cover; defend; ensconce; en~; fend; guard; hide; insulate; jaga; keep safe; look after; make safe; *nestle;* overshadow; *overprotect;* protect; *quia timet [L.];* refuge; shelter; safeguard; take care of; *uphold;* vallate; watch (over); ward off; weather-fend; *x-guard; yeme* [arch.]; *zero danger;* [Ant. strike]

**shift** *(v.)*: affect; alter; branch off; change; down~; deviate; exchange; flip; go; *hedge;* interchange; jump; jog; *keel;* lean; move; *new; obvert;* put; *querl;* rotate; switch; swing; swap; transfer; turn; upshift; vary; verge; wind; wend; xfer; yaw; zag;

**shine** *(n.)*: aura; brilliance; brightness; candescence; coruscation; dazzle; effulgence; fulgency; gleam; glow; glare; *halo;* irradiance; *jet; keenness;* luster; luminosity; *moonlight;* nitency; *overlight;* patina; radiance; sparkle; sheen; twinkle; *ultraviolet light;* vividness; white light; *xenon light;* yellow light; *zodiacal light;*

**shine** *(v.)*: *aura;* beam; brighten; burn; coruscate; cast light; dazzle; daze; effulge; emit light; enlighten; flash; flicker; fluoresce; glare; gleam; glisten; glitter; glow; *highlight;* illuminate; incandesce; irradiate; *jet;* kindle; light; luminesce; luster; make light; *nitency;* outshine; *polish; quiver;* radiate; sparkle; throw light; twinkle; *ultraviolet light; vividness;* waver; *x-ray;* yield light; zap; [see polish]

**shiny** *(adj.)*: aglow; brilliant; bright; burnished; chrome; ciré; dazzling; enameled; finished; flashing; glossy; gleaming; glistening; high-gloss; irradiative; *joyous; keen;* lambent; lacquered; mirror-like; *magnificent; metallic; non-matte;* over-polished; polished; *quality;* radiant; reflective; resplendent; shimmering; sparkly; sunny; transplendent; urethane-coated; vibrant; varnished; well-polished; wet-looking; *xesturgy; ytterbic;* zinnober;

**ship** *(n.)*: ark; aircraft carrier; boat; barge; *battle~;* craft; clipper; cruiser; *destroyer; E-boat;* frigate; ferry; *flag~;* galley; galleon; *gunboat;* hulk; ironclad; junk [Jap.]; *keelboat; ketch;* liner; man-o-war; naval ~; ocean liner; *PT boat;* q-ship; *quinquereme;* rigger; sea craft; steam~; superliner; transport; *tanker; udema;* vessel; watercraft; war~; *xebec;* yacht; *zabra;*

**ship** *(v.)*: airmail; bear; bring; bus; convey; deliver; export; freight; forward; ferry; get; haul; import; janker; kurvey; *load;* mail; *night shipment; over-carry;* pass; *pack; quarter-cart;* relay; send; transport; uptake; *van; waft;* xfer; yanker [Br.]; zip;

**shipping** *(n.)*: airfreight; boating; conveyance; cabotage; delivery; express; freight; ferriage; *going;* haulage; importation; international ~; janker; kurveying; lighterage; moving; *next-day ~;* ocean transport; post; *quick-delivery;* relocation; sending; sea-transport; transport; *underway; unshackled; voyage;* waftage; wagonage; xfer.; *yielding; zipping;*

**shipwreck** *(n.)*: accident; breakup; breakage; calamity; disaster-at-sea; destruction; *empty hull;* flotsam; gutted vessel; heap; *hull; injury; jetsam; ket;* loss; lagan; *mass;* naufrage; *obliteration;* pieces; *quashed;* ruin; remains; sunken ship; tragedy; undoing; violent end; wreckage; *x-mal [G.]; yanking down; zero;*

**shirk** *(v.)*: avoid; bilk; bludge; circumvent; dodge; evade; *foot-dragger;* get out of; hedge; *indirect;* jink; *keep away from;* let it go; malinger; not show up; *obviate;* put off; *quit;* run away; sidestep; scrimshank; skulk; tiptoe around; *unclear; vacillate;* wiggle out of; *xfer;* yern; zip away;

**shirker** *(n.)*: avoider; bludger; circumventer; dawdler; evader; foot-dragger; growtnol; hedger; idler; *jinker; kaynard* [arch.]; lazybones; loafer; malingerer; non-worker; *obviate;* procrastinator; quisby; *remiss;* slacker; sluggard; slouch; torpid person; *unmotivated; vacillate;* wastrel; *xenarthra;* yerner; *zealless;*

**shiver** *(v.)*: agitate; bicker; *chatter;* didder; *excite;* flutter; growse [arch.]; hustle; *instability;* judder; knock; *lurch; move; nudge;* oscillate; palpitate; quiver; quake; rattle; shudder; shake; tremor; tremble; *unnerved;* vibrate; wobble; *xuld [arch.];* yerk; *zigzag;*

**shock** *(n.)*: astonishment; blow; confounding; *charge;* devastation; emotional ~; electrocution; fright; great ~; horrific ~; impact; jolt; knock; kick; *lightning;* numbness; *ordeal; pain;* quake; rude awakening; surprise; scare; shake up; shatter; trauma; upset; *volts;* wake-up call; *xiphodynia; yank;* zap;

**shock** *(v.)*: alarm; bowl over; confound; devastate; dumbfound; electrify; flabbergast; gape; hold one's breath; impact; jar; jolt; knock wind out of one's sails; look aghast; make marvel; nonplus; overwhelm; overawe; phase; quake; render speechless; stun; shake up; take back; traumatize; unnerve; *vex;* wonder; *xtry.; yerk;* zap; [Ant. settle]

**shocking** *(adj.)*: appalling; bad; confounding; disgraceful; deplorable; distressing; *evil;* flabbergasting; grotesque; horrendous; indecent; jarring; *knocking down;* lamentable; most awful; nonplussing; outrageous; phasing; quaking; repulsive; scandalous; terrible; unbelievable; very bad; wicked; *x-rated;* yucky; *zapping;* [Ant. soothing]

**shoe** *(n.)*: * *abarka;* blucher; boot; clog; deck ~; dress ~; espadrille; footwear; footgear; galosh; high heels [fem.]; *innersole;* jelly; kitten heels [fem.]; loafer; moccasin; mule; napa ~; oxford; over~; pump; *quatros;* running ~; sandal; sneaker; tennis ~; *upper leather; vamp;* wingtip; wooden ~; *x-sandal; yoga sandal;* zocco;

**shoot** *(v.)*: *aim at;* assassinate; blow away; bolt; cast; catapult; discharge; dart; eject; elance; fire; fly; gun down; hurl; impel; jet; jut; kest; kill; launch; murder; nail [slang]; open fire; propel; pick off; plug; pip (Br.); pull the trigger; propel; quant; rocket; riddle; sling; snipe; *strike;* thrust; upcast; vault; *volley;* wale; *xuld* [arch.]; york; zap;

**shop** *(n.)*: *area store;* boutique; convenience store; depot; emporium; five-and-dime; flea market; grocery store; galleria; *house; industry; jumble- ~; key store; location;* market; mart; mill; *newsstand;* outlet; PX; quick mart; retail outlet; store; salon; trading post; *unit;* variety store; shoppe; work~; workplace; warehouse; *xtr. workspace; yard (sale); zoco* [Arab.];
**shop** *(v.)*: acquire; buy; bargain-hunt; *come by;* deal; *engage in sale; fetch; frequent;* go ~ping; hunt for bargains; *invest; jump at; kep;* look for; make purchases (-the rounds); *nab;* obtain; *overbuy;* patronize; purchase; pay for; procure; *quoff; receive;* sink money into; take home; *use money;* visit stores; window- ~; *xfer; yafe [arch.]; zealously acquire;* [Ant. sell]
**shore** *(n.)*: *abuttal;* beach; bank; brink; coast(line); *dockside;* edge; fringe; *gulf front;* hinterland; inception; *jetty side; key side;* lakeshore; margin; near~; oceanside; plage; *quost* [arch.]; riviera; shoreline; sea~ (-coast, -side); *threshold; undercurrent;* verge; waterline (-front, -side); *x-border; yeo; Zee [G.];*
**short** *(adj.)*: abbreviated; abridged; brief; badger-legged; contracted; concise; diminutive; elfin; fugacious; gnomish; half-pint; itsy-bitsy; *jot;* knee-high; little; miniature; midget; not long; *overly small;* petite; pygmy; quarter-length; *quick;* runty; small; stunted; scrubby; tiny; undersized; vertically challenged [joc.]; wee; XS; *yea big; Zwerg;*
**shortage** *(n.)*: absence; *big ~;* curtailment; deficiency; dearth; destitution; *empty;* falling short; famine; *gap; hardly enough;* insufficiency; just not enough; *known deficiency;* lack; meagerness; need; outage; paucity; privation; *quisby;* rareness; shortfall; scarcity; short supply; scantiness; *too little;* unavailability; ullage; *void;* want; *xtry. deficiency; yowling; zero sufficiency:* [Ant. superabundance]
**shortcoming** *(n.)*: area of failing; blemish; character flaw; deficiency; defect; *error;* failing; fault; flaw; *gap;* hamartia; imperfection; inadequacy; *jeofail; known deficiency;* limitation; *mistake; need; onus;* problem; quirk; *real problem;* shortfall; *transgression; trait; unperfected;* vice; weakness; *xgression; yet a problem; zero sufficiency:*
**shorten** *(v.)*: abbreviate; abridge; bob; cut; curtail; condense; contract; decrease; diminish; epitomize; foreshorten; *go down;* halve; impair; *jitney; knee-high;* lower; lessen; lop; minimize; nip off; *optimize;* pare; prune; quail; reduce; shrink; truncate; trim; *undersize; vell;* welk; *x-sect; yank; zeroize;* [Ant. stretch]
**shortness** *(n.)*: abbreviation; brevity; conciseness; compactness; diminutiveness; elfishness; fugaciousness; gnomishness; *half-pint; itsy-bitsy; jot;* knee-height; littleness; minuteness; non-lengthiness; *over- ~;* petite size; quarter-length; *quickness;* runtiness; smallness; tininess; undersize; *vertically challenged [joc.];* weeness; XS; *yea big; Zwerg;*
**shout** *(n.)*: acclamation; bellow; cry; *discharge;* exclamation; *fit;* growl; hoot; holler; howl; *inveighing; jubilation;* keen; loud shout; *lamentation;* moan; noise; outcry; proclamation; quiritation; resonation; reverberation; roar; shout; scream; shriek; thundering; ululation; uproar; vociferation; wail; whoop; *xenophonia;* yell; *zindabad;*
**shout** *(v.)*: acclaim; bellow; beckon; cry; call; declaim; exclaim; *fit;* growl; holler; hoot; howl; halloo; *inveigh; jubilate;* keen; loudly say; *moan;* noise; outcry; proclaim; promulgate; *quiritation;* resonate; reverberate; roar; scream; thunder; trumpet; ululate; vociferate; wail; whoop; *xenophonia;* yell; *zindabad;*
**shove** *(n.)*: assault; bump; boost; cram; driving force; exertion; force; goad; heave; impulsion; jab; jostle; jolt; kibbling; lamming; motivation; nudge; *ooch;* push; *quant;* ram; shot; thrust; upthrust; *violence;* whack; *xowyn* [arch.]; yerk; *zonk;*
**shove** *(v.)*: apply pressure; budge; bundle; compress; depress; drive; exert pressure; force; goad; heave; impel; jam; jostle; jolt; kibble; lean; move forward; nudge; ooch; push; propel; quant; ram; *shoot;* thrust; upthrust; *violence;* whack; *xowyn* [arch.]; yerk; *zonk;*
**show** *(n.)*: act; array; bravura; benefit; charade; carnival; drama; display; exhibition; floorshow; *gathering;* histrionics; *horse ~;* indication; *jamboree; kermis;* local ~; manifestation; *nundination;* occasion; performance; presentation; production; private ~ing; quality production; ridotto; road~; showing; song and dance; trade ~; theatre performance; *unveiling;* vernissage; variety ~; vaudeville ~; wingding; *xtry. ~; yield; zizz;*

**show** *(v.)*: array; appear; bear; come in sight; connote; display; depict; demonstrate; exhibit; exemplify; epitomize; expose; flaunt; flash; guide; hold out; indicate; illustrate; *justify;* kithe [Scot.]; lay out; manifest; make plain; *non-concealment;* open up; present; point out; *qualify;* reveal; spread out; set out; typify; unveil; uncover; vaunt; *wave; x-ray;* yield; *zet [dial.];* [*Ant.* shroud]
**showiness** *(n.)*: *amazingness;* bedazzlement; colorfulness; dazzle; extravagance; flashiness; flamboyance; gaudiness; garishness; high style; impressiveness; jazziness; kitschiness; *larger-than-life;* magnificence; *nice-looking;* ostentation; pickedness; *quasi-garrishness;* razzle-dazzle; spectacularness; spruceness; tawdriness; *uptown;* vanity; wildness; *xtry; you-beaut [Aus.];* zizziness; [*Ant.* simplicity]
**show-off** *(n.)*: *arrogant;* blusterer; coxcomb; dandy; exhibitionist; fanfaron; fop; gloater; huff; *inflated;* Jack-the-lad; know-it-all; loudmouth; magnificator; narcissist; *outdoer;* poseur; popinjay; princox; *petit-maitre* [F.]; quidnunc; roisterer; show-off; swaggerer; trumpeter; ululator; vaporer; vain fellow; *wallower; xtry. person; yelper; zero humility;*
**showy** *(adj.)*: adorned; *bedazzling;* conspicuous; dazzling; extreme; extravagant; flashy; foppish; flaunty; flamboyant; gaudy; garish; glorying; high style; impressive; jazzy; kitschy; larger-than-life; meretricious; magnificent; *nice-looking;* ostentatious; operatic; pretentious; quasi-garish; ritzy; raffish; spectacular; tawdry; uptown; vain; wild; xtry; you-beaut [Aus.]; zizzy; [*Ant.* simple]
**shred** *(n.)*: *atom;* bit; band; clip; cutting; *debris; element;* fragment; *grain;* hunk; *jot; knife;* laceration; morsel; narrow piece; offcut; *ounce;* peel; piece; *quarter;* ribbon; scrap; shaving; strip; shiver; tatter; tape; *unit;* vestige; whit; *x-sect; yod; zonule;*
**shred** *(v.)*: *abscind; bisect;* cut up; *destroy; exscind; forehew; graze;* hack; incise; *jag; knife; lacerate;* mince; make into ribbons; *notch;* operate shredder; *pare; quadrisect; ribbons;* slice; tear; use shredder; *vell;* waste; *x-sect; yerk; zip off;*
**shrewd** *(adj.)*: astute; artful; beguiling; Bismarckian; crafty; cunning; clever; devious; evasive; foxy; fraudful; guileful; *hidden;* ingenious; jady; knavish; *lying;* Maciavellian; non-trustworthy; *overwise;* pawky; *quaintise [arch.];* roguish; savvy; sagacious; subtle; sly; sneaky; tricky; unscrupulous; vulpine; wily; *xtry.;* yepe; *zinger;* [*Ant.* simple]
**shrewdness** *(n.)*: archness; artfulness; beguiling; Bismarckianism; craftiness; cunning; cleverness; deviousness; evasiveness; foxiness; fraudulence; guile; *hidden;* ingeniousness; jadishness; knavishness; *lying;* Machiavelism; nous; *outfoxing;* policy; *quaintise* [arch.]; roguishness; savvy; subtlety; slyness; sneakiness; trickiness; unscrupulousness; *vulpine;* wiliness; *xtry, cleverness;* yepship [arch.]; *zinging;* [*Ant.* simplicity]
**shrine** *(n.)*: arch; basilica; chapel; chorten [Bud.]; *dagoba* [Ind.]; enshrinement; fane; grotto; grove; holy place; high place; *inner sanctuary;* joss-house [Chin.]; kiack [Burm.]; long home; memorial; mausoleum; naos; oracle; ossuary; place of prayer; *qubba;* roodloft; stupa; topa; *upper room;* vihara [Bud.]; worship-place; *xtry. place; yele* [arch.]; zayat [Burm.].
**shrink** *(v.)*: abate; atrophy; become smaller; contract; downsize; decrease; dwindle; ebb; fade; grow smaller; *half-size; impair;* jump down in size; *keep ~ing;* lessen; minimize; make smaller; narrow; *outgo; palliate;* quail; recede; reduce; subside; shrivel; shorten; turn smaller; *undersized; vanish;* weaken; wane; wither; waste; *xerosis;* yield; zeroize; [*see* cower; *Ant.* stretch]
**shrivel** *(v.)*: anhydrate; bake dry; curl up; contract; dry up; deflate; emaciate; exsccate; flag; *go dry;* heat-dry; insolate; *juiceless;* kiln-dry; languish; mummify; non-hydrate; over-dry; parch; quail; *rainless;* shrink; torrefy; *undo;* vaporate; wither; wilt; wizen; *xerosis; yarrish;* zap; [*Ant.* swell]
**shroud** *(v.)*: *artfulness;* blanket; bury; conceal; cover; disguise; drape; darken; envelop; enfold; fold; garb; hide; inter; *jape;* keep hidden; lay over; mask; *non-recognizable;* obscure; overlay; put out of view; *quiet;* repress; swathe; suppress; tuck away; *unknown;* veil; wrap; *xenomorph; yashmak; zero recognition;* [*Ant.* show]

**shudder** *(v.)*: agitate; bicker; convulse; didder; *excite;* flutter; growse [arch.]; hustle; *instability;* jiggle; judder; knock; *lurch; move; nervous;* oscillate; palpitate; pitch; quiver; rattle; shake; shiver; tremble; tremor; *unnerved;* vibrate; waggle; *xuld [arch.];* yerk; zigzag;

**shun** *(v.)*: avoid; balk at; coldshoulder; debar; eschew; forbear; give cold shoulder; hold aloof; ignore; *jilt;* keep out; *look down on;* make feel bad; not accept; ostracize; proscribe; quit on; recoil from; reject; snub; shut out; turn away from; *unkind; veto;* withhold fellowship; *xenize; yard* [arch.]; *zero fellowship;*

**shut** *(adj.)*: *absolutely sealed;* bolted; closed; deadbolted; engaged; fastened; factory-sealed; glued; *hard fastened;* isolated; *jailed;* kept shut; latched; locked; made fast; non-opened; *new;* occluse; plastic-wrapped; *quite closed; reclosed;* sealed; tightly ~; unopened; *very tight;* wrapped; *x-tight;* yet ~; zippered;

**shut** *(v.)*: act; bolt ~d; catch; close; deadbolt; *engage;* fasten; *guard;* have locked; interlock; *jail;* keep ~d; latch; lock; make fast; *narrow;* occlude; push closed; *quickly ~;* reclose; secure; seal; slam; tighten; *unopened; vault; well-secured; x-tight; yank;* zip up;

**shy** *(adj.)*: apprehensive; bashful; coy; chary; demure; diffident; embarrassed; fearful; gentle; hesitant; introverted; insecure; jackalent; keenly ~; *lily-livered;* mortified; nervous; overmodest; petrified; quiet; reserved; reticent; self-effaced; sheepish; timid; unpretentious; verecund; withdrawn; *xenophobic;* yarrow; *zealless;* [Ant. sociable]

**shyness** *(n.)*: apprehension; bashfulness; coyness; diffidence; embarrassment; fearfulness; gentleness; hesitancy; introversion; insecurity; *jitteriness;* keen ~; *lily-liveredness;* mortification; nervousness; overmodesty; petrification; quietness; reservedness; self-effacement; sheepishness; timidity; unsureness; verecundity; withdrawal; *xenophobia;* yarowness; *zeallessness;* [Ant. sociability]

**sick** *(adj.)*: affected; ailing; bad; bedridden; consumptive; cankerous; cancerous; diseased; *disgusted;* evil-affected; frail; feverish; *galled; horrible;* ill; indisposed; infected; *jaundiced;* ketty; laid up; malaise; *morbillous;* nauseous; not well; off; poor health; qualmish; queasy; *rabid;* squeamish; sickly; tetched; taken ill; under the weather; unwell; unhealthy; vulnerable; weak; *x-disease; yellow; yucky; zich* [arch.]; [see deranged; Ant. sound]

**sicken** *(v.)*: appall; become sick; bother; cause sickness; disgust; enervate; fail; gross one out; horrify; indispose; jar; *keck; loathe;* make one sick; misaffect; nauseate; offend; peak; queasify [joc.]; repulse; *shock;* turn one's stomach; take ill; unsettle; upset; *vile;* weaken; worsen; *xuld* [arch.]; *yucky; zich* [arch.];

**sickly** *(adj.)*: ailing; ashen; bad; consumptive; diseaseful; etoliated; florid; feeble; frail; green; grim; ghastly; healthless; *horrible;* infirm; *jaundiced; keenly sick;* languid; lazar-like; livid; morbose; not well; off-color; pale; pallid; pasty; queasy; run-down; sick; shilpit; tallow-faced; unhealthy; unwell; unfit; valetudinarian; wan; weak; waxen; weakly; wanly; xanthocyanopic; yellowish; *zich* [arch.]; [Ant. sound]

**sickness** *(n.)*: ailment; bug; blight; *bout;* condition; disease; endemic (-epidemic) disease; *frailty; fever; germ;* health problem; hardship; illness; infirmity; *jaundice; kings evil;* lesion; malady; nausea; *ordeal;* pox; plague; queasiness; *remittent;* scourge; taint; *thorn in the flesh;* unhealthiness; upset; virus; woe; *x-disease; yellow fever;* zoonosis; [Ant. soundness]

**side** *(n.)*: angle; aspect; bank; border; back~; *coast;* dimension; down~; edge; element; *east ~;* flank; face(t); faction; front~; *good ~;* hind~; *issue; jag;* key; left ~; margin; *north ~;* outer edge; opinion; part(y); perimeter; quality; right ~; surface; *south ~;* top ~; under~; *up~;* verge; view; wale; *west ~; x-factor;* yonder; *zet [dial.];*

**side** *(v.)*: ally; *bind;* collaborate; confederate; defend; *enter into a league;* federate; give assistance; help; *involve;* join (forces); *knit;* league; make league; *non-aggression pact;* one; partner; *quick-to-help; reciprocal;* support; ~ with; team up with; unite; *vouch for;* work together; *xenophile;* yoke; *zealously support;*

**sidetrack** *(v.)*: avert; *backslide;* bear off; change direction; divert; derail; deter; distract; deflect; deviate; entangle; forestall; go off; head off; *inhibit; jink;* keep from; lose one's focus; move away; *non-attention; off-track;* preoccupy; put on the back burner; *quell;* redirect; reroute; sideline; throw off course; turn away; *unseat;* veer; *ward off; wander; xuld [arch.];* yank off course; *zag;*

**sideways** *(adj.)*: across; breadthways; crosswise; crabwise; dead level; edgewise; flat; *ground;* horizonal; incumbent; jacent; *knocked over;* longways; lengthwise; longwise; laying down; mean sea level; non-vertical; oblique; procumbent; *quasi-horizontal;* recumbent; sidewise; sidelong; turned; unsloping; *vegetating;* wide; west-east; x-axis; *yet on end; zero verticalness;*

**siege** *(n.)*: assault; besiegement; cordon; drawing around; encirclement; fight against; *gird;* hem in; inclosing; *jeopardy; kampf [G.];* laying ~; *march on; non-broken circle;* offensive; *placement of forces;* quarrel; 'round about; surrounding; starving out; *take on;* unrest; violence; war(fare); *x-fire; yard; zone;*

**siege** *(v.)*: *attack;* besiege; cordon; circle; cut off; contain; draw around; encircle; environ; frame; gird; hem in; inclose; *jeopardize;* kirtle; lay ~ to; *march on; non-broken circle;* overwhelm; put around; *quoil [dial.];* 'round about; surround; starve out; *take on;* unrest; *volt;* whelm; *x-fire;* yard; zone;

**sift** *(v.)*: aerate; bolt; cribble; drain; *elutriate;* filter; *grate;* hand- ~; *interstices; jiggety-sifter;* kitchen strainer; lixiviate; make separate; *non-combined;* operate ~er; pass through sieve; *pan;* quaff; riddle; ree; strain; screen; separate; transcolate; use ~er; *ventilate;* winnow; *xfer;* yandy; *zaru;*

**sifter** *(n.)*: *apparatus;* bolter; colander; chinnoise; cribble; *device; ethmoid;* filter; flour ~; *grate;* hand-held ~; *instrument;* jiggety sieve; kitchen strainer; lixiviator; mesh strainer; *net;* operation; percolator; *quaff;* riddle; strainer; sieve; screen; tammy; *utensil; ventilate;* wilch; *xfer;* yandy; *zaru;*

**sigh** *(n.)*: aspiration; *argh!;* breath; complaint; *depressed;* exhalation; *forlorn;* groan; huff; heavy breath; *inconsolable; jeremiad; kvetching;* lament; longing; moan; noisy exhalation; outbreath; *protest; quarimony;* repining; sob; sough; suspiration; *tussle;* underbreath; ventilation; whimper; *xfer;* yearning; *zero happiness;*

**sigh** *(v.)*: aspirate; breathe; *cry;* draw air; exhale; *forlorn;* groan; huff; *howl;* inhale; *judder; kvetch;* lament; moan; *noise;* outblow; puff; *quarimony;* respine; sob; sough; suspire; *tussle;* unhappy; ventilate; whimper; *xuld [arch.];* yearn; *zero happiness;*

**sight** *(n.)*: ability to see; appearance; *beholding;* clear ~; display; eyesight; eyeshot; field of vision; gazing; *highly visible;* image(ry); *judgment;* ken; looking; manifestation; naked eye; observation; *optical;* picture; photopia; *quick-sighted;* representation; range of view; seeing; scene; sighting; *taking in;* understanding; vision; view; vista; watching; xanthopsia; x-ray vision; Young-Helmholtz theory; zeroing in; [Ant. sightlessness]

**sign** *(n.)*: announcement; bulletin; *communication;* danger ~; expressway ~; freeway ~; guidepost; highway ~; information ~; junction ~; *km marker;* lettering; monopole ~; notice; *one-way ~;* placard; plaque; posted notice; *qualifier;* regulatory ~; road~; signage; signpost; street ~; traffic ~; unipole ~; *vignette;* warning ~; *xmit;* Yield ~; *zero in;*

**signal** *(n.)*: alert; beacon; cue; communication; denotation; expression; flag; flare; gesture; guidepost; green light; hand ~; heliograph; indication; *jibber;* knell; lantern; *light;* motion; nod; *outcry;* prompt; *quo minus [L.];* red flag; sign; ~ fire; *tell;* telltale sign; urge; *vociferate;* wink; wave; whistle; wigwag; warning; warison; *xfer;* yell; *zealously bid;*

**signal** *(v.)*: alert; beckon; bid; cue; communicate; denote; express; flag; fingerspell; gesture; give sign; hand ~; hint; hail; indicate; intimate; jibber; knell; key; let one know; motion; make sign; nod; *outcry;* prompt; *quo minus [L.];* radio; red flag; sign(ify); tell; urge; *vociferate;* wink; wave; wigwag; warn; *xfer;* yell; *zealously bid;*

**signature** *(n,)*: autograph; *backing;* co~; designation; *dotted line;* endorsement; formal ~; *graving;* handwritten ~; inscription; *initials;* John Hancock; key ~; *log;* mark; name; okay; *permission;* quiring; *register;* signed name; *transcription;* undersigning; *validation;* writing; X; *your name; zay;*

**significance** *(n.)*: all-importance; bigness; criticalness; degree; exigency; enormity; *focal;* gravity; greatness; heaviness; import(ance); *justification; key;* lead; magnitude; meaning; need; necessity; *obligation;* portentousness; press(ure); precedence; *quintessence;* requirement; relevance; seriousness; top-rating; urgency; vitalness; value; weight; *xtry.;* yearning; *zero hour;*
**significant** *(adj.)*: all-important; big; considerable; chief; central; dire; dominant; eminent; earthshaking; fundamental; focal; grave; great; heavy; high; important; *jump to it;* key; leading; main; major; momentous; noteworthy; outstanding; portentous; pressing; prominent; preeminent; pertinent; principal; quantum; relevant; substantial; supereminent; top-priority; urgent; ultimate; vital; weighty; worthy; xtry.; *yearnful;* zero hour; [*Ant.* small]
**signify** *(v.)*: allude; betoken; connote; denote; demonstrate; express; emblemize; foreshadow; give the idea; hint; indicate; illustrate; imply; *jibber; known;* let one know; mean; notate; *overemphasize;* picture; quiddit; reveal; represent; show; suggest; speak of; symbolize; typify; *utter;* very aptly show; *word; x-type; yield; zero in;*
**silence** *(n.)*: absolute ~; *becalmed;* calmness; dumbness; emptiness; *fallowness; gagged;* hush; inaudibility; inarticulateness; idleness; *jarless;* keeping quiet; lull; muteness; noiselessness; overquietness; obmutescence; peacefulness; quiet; quiescence; restfulness; silentness; speechlessness; tranquility; taciturnity; untalkativeness; voicelessness; wordlessness; *xtr. quiet; yarelessness;* zero noise; [*Ant.* stridence]
**silence** *(v.)*: *arrest;* bottle up; cork; choke; cut off; dampen; dummy up; extinguish; *finish;* gag; hush; *idle;* jam up; keep one quiet; kill; lull; muffle; muzzle; make stop; noiselessness; overawe; pipe down; quiet(en); quash; restrain; repress; shush; smother; stifle; stop; tongue-tie; *unvoiced; volume reduction; wordless; xtr. quiet; yield;* zeroize;
**silent** *(adj.)*: aphonic; becalmed; calm; dumb; docile; echoless; *fallow; gagged;* hushed; inaudible; inarticulate; idle; *jarless; kept quiet; laconic;* mum; mute; noiseless; non-speaking; nonverbal; over-quiet; peaceful; quiet; *resting;* speechless; soundless; taciturn; unspeaking; unvoiced; uncommunicative; unheard; voiceless; whist; wordless; *whispering; xtr. quiet; yareless; zitti* [It.]; [*Ant.* strident]
**silly** *(adj.)*: asinine; absurd; bizarre; childish; corny; crazy; daffy; daft; dumb; ditsy; dopey; egg-headed; eccentric; funny; foolish; goofy; giddy; hare-brained; hilarious; irrational; juvenile; kooky; loony; mad; nutty; outrageous; outlandish; peculiar; quacky; ridiculous; screwy; tomfoolish; twisted; unwise; vacuous; weird; wacky; warped; wild; *xtry. ~; yo-yo;* zany; [*Ant.* sensible]
**silver** *(adj.)*: argent; burnished; chrome; dove-gray; *electrum;* flat ~; gray; gleaming; hoar; iron-gray; *jeweled; keen;* lead-gray; lustering; metallic; nickel; *over-polished;* pearl-gray; *quarter;* reflective; silvery; tin-colored; *undimmed;* vermeil; well-polished; *xanthoconite; ytterbic;* zinnober;
**silver** *(n.)*: argent; billon; chrome; *Doré bullion; electrum;* fine ~; German ~; horn ~; *ingot; jewel-encrusted ~; keen;* luster; metallic; noble metal; *over-polished;* polished ~; pewter; *quarter;* refined ~; siller [Scot.]; *tarnished ~; unrefined ~;* vermeil; *white metal;* xanthoconite; *ytterbic;* zinnober;
**similar** *(adj.)*: alike; akin; as; analogous; *balanced;* close; comparable; congenial; *duplicate;* equivalent; favoring; *geminated;* homologous; identical; just the same; kindred; like; matching; non-differing; *one;* parallel; qua; resembling; related; same; such-like; semblable; *tantamount;* uniform; unvaried; very close; *word-perfect; xerographed;* yet the same; *zincograph;* [*Ant.* sundry]
**similarity** *(n.)*: alikeness; bond; comparison; comparableness; *duplication;* equivalence; fashion; form; gemination; homogeneity; image; *just alike; kind;* likeness; match; nearness; oneness; parallel; *quasi-similitude;* resemblance; similitude; sameness; tie-in; uniformity; very image; *with comparison; xerograph;* yet undistinguishable; *zincograph;*
**simple** *(adj.)*: artless; basic; bare; clean; clear; down-to-earth; easy; forthright; facile; generic; ho-hum; incomplex; *just ~;* kindergarten-level; lowbrow; mere; non-complex; non-fancy; naïve; oversimplified; plain; quick-and-easy; regular; *reasonable;* straightforward; simplified; too easy; uncomplicated; unsophisticated; uncomplex; verdant; wonted; *x-type;* yare; *zero complexity;* [*Ant.* spectacular]

**simplicity** *(n.)*: artlessness; bareness; crudeness; clarity; directness; easiness; ease; forthrightness; facileness; genericness; *ho-hum;* incomplexity; *just ~;* kindergarten-level; low level; mere simplicity; non-complexity; naïvity; oversimplification; plainness; *quick-and-easy;* rawness; rusticity; relaxedness; simpleness; smoothness; straightforwardness; transparency; unsophistication; uncompoundedness; verdancy; witlessness; *x-type;* yokelism; *zero complexity;*
**simplify** *(v.)*: abridge; boil down; condense; declutter; ease; foreshorten; generalize; *help;* improve; *just made easier;* keep simple; lower; make easier; *narrow down;* over~; overgeneralize; pare down; *quite simple;* reduce; streamline; shorten; throw light on; untangle; *very easy; way easy; xtr. simple; yet understandable; zero confusion;*
**simulate** *(v.)*: act out; bear likeness; create; copy; duplicate; emulate; feign; fake; go like; hoax; imitate; *just make-believe; keep pretending; live; like;* mock up; mimic; nearly reproduce; *overact;* pretend; play-act; *quasi;* replicate; reproduce; role-play; re-enact; sham; *take on the part;* use imagination; visualize; whimsy; *xfer;* yede; *zealously play at;*
**simulation** *(n.)*: acting out; *being;* creating; copying; duplication; emulation; fake; *guile; holotype;* imitation; *just like; keep;* look-alike; mock-up; mimicry; near reproduction; on-screen ~; pretending; *quasi;* reproduction; replication; recreation; sham; takeoff; *unreal;* virtual reality; *whimsy; xfer; yede; zero reality;*
**simultaneous** *(adj.)*: at the same time; *both;* concurrent; concomitant; co-occurring; done together; exactly the same moment; *featured together; going together;* holus-bolus; in sync (-step); jointly-timed; *keeping together; lickety-split; meanwhile; nonce;* occurring together; parallel; quite synchronized; right together; synchronized; stereo; synchronal; together; *unison; virtually ~;* with; *xtry. timing; yfere* [arch.]; *zwischenzug* [G.]; [*Ant.* separate]
**sin** *(n.)*: abomination; atrocity; bad; breach; crime; depravity; *debt;* evil; error; flagitiousness; foul-behavior; fallenness; fault; guilt(iness); godlessness; heinousness; iniquity; *jadedness;* knavishness; licentiousness; leaven; mischief; malice; malignity; misconduct; misdeed; naughtiness; nefariousness; obduracy; offense; peccability; perverseness; *quad;* rebellion; sinfulness; sin-debt; transgression; trespass; treachery; unrighteousness; villainy; violation; vice; wrong(doing); wickedness; *xgression; yetzer hara* [Heb.]; *zero righteousness;* [*see* immorality; *Ant.* sinlessness]
**sin** *(v.)*: abominate; breach; break law; *backslide;* commit ~; contravene; do wrong; disobey; *disregard;* err; fall; go astray; *harden one's heart;* infringe; *jaded; knavish;* leave the straight and narrow; lapse; misbehave; *neglect; naughty;* offend; *overstep;* pervert; *pay no regard to; quad;* rebel; slip; transgress; trespass; *unfaithful;* violate; wrong; *x-gress; yetzer hara* [Heb.]; *zero righteousness;*
**sincere** *(adj.)*: authentic; artless; bona fide; candid; definite; earnest; frank; genuine; grave; honest; heartfelt; ingenuous; *just; known;* legitimate; meant; non-fictional; open; pure; questionless; real; straight; serious; single-hearted; truthful; unmixed; unfeigned; veritable; wholly true; *x-parent; yare; zealous;* [*Ant.* superficial]
**sinew** *(n.)*: attaching fibers; bond-fiber; connective tissue; *dorsal radiocarpal;* elastic cartilage; fibers; fascia; *guts;* hamstring; *insides; joint; knee ~;* ligament; membrane; master- ~; nerve; *object; periodontal ligament; qiviut; radiocarpal ligament;* string; tendon; undertissue; vinculum; *willowy; xiphocostal;* y- ~; z-line;
**sinful** *(adj.)*: abominable; atrocious; bad; corrupt; criminal; devilish; decadent; depraved; evil; fiendish; foul; godless; heinous; iniquitous; *jaded;* knavish; licentious; mischievous; malicious; malevolent; naughty; nefarious; obdurate; ornery; profligate; peccant; pernicious; piacular; *quad;* rebellious; sinister; transgressive; unrighteous; unclean; unholy; villainous; vicious; wicked; wrong(ful); *xgressing;* yucky; *zymotic;* [*Ant.* sinless]
**sing** *(v.)*: *articulate;* break forth; boom; carol; croon; cantillate; discant; entertain; flute; glory; harmonize; intone; jodel; key in; let out; lullaby; make melody; *nonet; outbreak;* perform; quaver; resonate; serenade; trill; troll; utter; vocalize; warble; *well-sung; xoeoemei;* yodel; *ziraleet;*

**singer** *(n.)*: artist; alto; balladeer; baritone; bass; crooner; chorister; choir member; chanter; cantor; *duettist;* entertainer; folk ~; gospel ~; hymn ~; *intoner;* jingle ~; key ~; lead; melodist; minstrel; music makers; mastersinger; nightingale [fem.]; *opera ~;* performer; quirister; rhapsodist; songster; songstress [fem.]; serenader; soloist; soprano; tenor; utterer; vocalist; voice; volkslieder; warbler; *xenoligea;* yodeler; *ziraleet;*

**singing** *(n.)*: *attunement;* breaking forth; chanting; crooning; caroling; *ditty;* entertaining; folk ~; gaiety; harmony; intonation; *joy;* keying in; letting out; (making) melody; music; *notes;* opera; performing; psalmody; quadrille; resonating; song; trilling; *uttering;* vocalizing; vocalism; warbling; *xoeoemei;* yodeling; *ziraleet;* [*see* praise; choir; *Ant.* sadness]

**sink** *(v.)*: abate; bring low; crash; depress; droop; dive; drop; descend; decline; ebb; fall; go down; hang; hide; immerge; immerse; jump down; keel over; lower; lessen; make nose-dive; nose-dive; *over the cliff;* plunge; plummet; quick-fall; reduce; submerge; slump; scuttle; stoop; swamp; tumble; torpedo; *undo;* verge; whop; *x-cend; yield;* zoom down; [*Ant.* soar]

**sinless** *(adj.)*: aboveboard; blameless; clean; clear; dovelike; ethical; faultless; guiltless; holy; innocent; impeccable; irreproachable; *justified;* known-innocent; lamblike; *moral;* not guilty; offenseless; pure; perfect; questionless; righteous; spotless; taintless; unblamable; unguilty; unimpeachable; virtuous; white; witeless; *xtry.; yielded;* zero-guilt; [*Ant.* sinful]

**sinlessness** *(n.)*: arete; blamelessness; cleanness; *decency;* ethicalness; faultlessness; goodness; godliness; holiness; impeccability; justness; *kalokagathia* [Gr.]; *legitimacy;* morality; non-sinfulness; offenselessness; probity; purity; perfection; *quality;* righteousness; spotlessness; sanctification; saintliness; taintlessness; uprightness; virtuousness; witelessness; *xtry; yieldedness to God;* zero-guilt; [*Ant.* sinfulness]

**sinner** *(n.)*: abominator; bad man (-woman; -person); criminal; doer of evil; evildoer; fallen man; godless person; hater of God; injurer; impenitent; jackanapes; knave; lost person; misdoer; naughty person; nithing; offender; pervert; questrel; reprobate; ribald; scoundrel; scorner; transgressor; trespasser; *ungodly;* villain; villainess [fem.]; wrongdoer; worldling; wretch; *xiaoren; yob;* zero morals; [*see* liar; thief; murderer; adulterer; *Ant.* saint]

**sister** *(n.)*: *affiliate;* big ~; cousin; di-di [S. Asia]; elder ~; full-blood ~; *german;* half- ~; identical twin; *junior;* kid ~; kin(swoman); little ~; *ménage;* near kinswoman; older ~; *person; quedam* [arch.]; relative; relation; sis; *sibling;* twin ~; *uterine ~; virgin ~; woman; x-chromosome;* younger ~; *zoster* [arch.];

**sit** *(v.)*: alight; be seated; come to rest; crouch; *deposit;* ensconce; fix; grab a seat; have a seat; *incubate;* juke; *kick back;* locate; lay; *make rest; non-retention;* occupy; park; perch; place; quat; rest; relax; roost; set; situate; settle; squat; take a seat; *use chair; vajrasana; well-situated; x-chair; yark;* zet [dial.]; zazen; [*Ant.* stand]

**situate** *(v.)*: arrange; bestow; collocate; deposit; emplace; fix; *give; have;* impart; *jump up on;* kit; locate; *move; non-retention; offload;* place; position; *quick-set;* rest; set; stick; transfer; *unhand;* vest; *weigh;* xfer; *yield;* zet [dial.];

**situation** *(n.)*: *alentours* [F.]; *being;* circumstance; condition; case; details; development; event; estate; fix; fare; fact; guise; happening; incident; juncture; kilter; lot; manner; mode; *new development;* occurrence; order; particulars; posture; place; predicament; plight; position; quality; *result;* state; status; scene; tenor; tone; *unusual ~;* venue; vein; way; *xenenthesis; yield;* zero in;

**size** *(n.)*: amount; bigness; bulk; capacity; dimension; extent; fatness; greatness; hugeness; immensity; jumboness; *king-sized;* largeness; length; mass; measurement; magnitude; number; proportion; quantity; roominess; scope; tonnage; tallness; *unladen weight;* volume; voluminosity; weight; x-height; *yards;* zonal measurement;

**skeleton** *(n.)*: atomy; bones; compages; dead bones; endo~; frame; *ghastly;* human ~; infrastructure; joints; knee-bone; *lamella;* man's ~; notamy; ossa; *phalanges; quadra;* remains; rattlebones; *ribs;* structural frame; *tibia;* underframe; *vertebrate;* white ~; x-frame; *x-ray;* yellowy ~; *zygoma;*

**skeptic** *(n.)*: agnostic; balker; critic; cynic; doubter; disbeliever; *enquirer;* freethinker; *guarded; hesitator;* irresolute; *infidel;* jangler; knocker; *leery;* misanthropist; nonbeliever; oppugner; polemic; pessimist; Pyrrhonist; questioner; rejecter; somatist; truth-challenger; unsure; unbeliever; vacillator; *wet blanket; x-careful; yawper;* zetetic;
**skeptical** *(adj.)*: agnostic; *beware;* critical; cynical; doubtful; disbelieving; ever-cynical; faithless; guarded; hesitant; irresolute; *infidel;* jangling; knocking; leery; mistrustful; nonbelieving; oppugning; polemic; pessimistic; questioning; rejecting; suspicious; trustless; unsure; unbelieving; vacillating; wary; *x-careful; yare-handed;* zetetic; [*Ant.* sure]
**skepticism** *(n.)*: agnosticism; balking; cynicism; distrust; *ever-doubtful;* faithlessness; guardedness; hesitancy; irresolution; jangling; knocking; leeriness; mistrust; nonbelief; oppugning; Pyrrhonism; questioning; rejection; skepticalness; tough-mindedness; unbelief; vacillation; wariness; *x-careful; yare-handed;* zeteticism;
**sketchy** *(adj.)*: amorphous; blurry; cursory; dim; enclouded; fuzzy; gray; hazy; indefinite; ill-defined; incomplete; *jumpy; knocked out; lacking clarity;* murky; nebulous; nonspecific; obscure; perfunctory; quick-drawn; rough; superficial; turbid; undefined; vague; woolly; *xtry. fuzzy;* yet undefined; *zero clarity;* [*Ant.* specific]
**skill** *(n.)*: ability; adeptness; art; aptitude; bent; craft(smanship); command; capability; cunning; deftness; expertise; experience; flair; forte; familiarity; finesse; gift; genius; handicraft; habilitation; instinct; *jack-of-all-trades;* knack; know-how; long suit; mastery; manual skill; masterfulness; natural ability; occupation; proficiency; praxis; prowess; qualification; quality; readiness; skillfulness; sleight; talent; usefulness; virtuosity; wherewithal; way; *xenium;* yaup; *years of experience;* zest;
**skillful** *(adj.)*: adroit; able; adept; artful; accomplished; brilliant; commanding; capable; deft; expert; familiar; gifted; good; handy; heaven-gifted; incredible; jolly good; knowledgeable; *laudable;* masterful; notable; nimble; outstanding; *old hand;* proficient; qualified; remarkable; seasoned; skilled; talented; unequalled; virtuosic; wonderful; xtry.; *you-beaut [Aus.];* zippy; [*Ant.* skilless]
**skin** *(n.)*: animal ~; bark [joc.]; back; cutis; complexion; dermis; epidermis; flesh; fell; *goatskin;* hide; integument; jacket; *kangaroo skin;* lamina; layer; membrane; natural covering; outer surface; pelt; parfleche; pellicle; *quarry [zoo.];* rind; revetment; surface; sheathing; tegument; tannage; *undertone;* vellum; whang; *xerdermia;* yellow ~; *zest;*
**skin** *(v.)*: abrade; bark; cut; decorticate; debone; excoriate; flay; graze; husk; *incise;* julienne; *knife;* lash; mince; *negate;* open; peel; pare; *quick-husk;* rasp; remove ~; strip; take ~ off; uncase; vell; whittle; xyster; yerk; zip;
**skinny** *(adj.)*: attenuated; bony; constricted; delicate; emaciated; frail; gaunt; half-starved; insubstantial; jimp; knife-blade thin; lean(-fleshed); lank(y); meager; malnourished; narrow; overthin; pencil-thin; *quantité négligeable [F.];* ribby; slim; scrawny; scraggy; thin; underfed; virgate [bot.]; wiry; wasted; XF; *yieldless; zero body fat;* [*Ant.* stout]
**skip** *(v.)*: avoid; bound; cut; caper; disregard; demivolt; elide; exclude; forget; frolic; go over; gambol; hop over; ignore; jump over; jete; *kest;* leave out; leap; miss; neglect; omit; over~; pass over; piaffe; *quick-to-forget;* romp; scamper; tittup; upleap; vault; *waltz; x-ing; yemeles [arch.]; zero responsibility;*
**skirt** *(n.)*: ∗ *apparel;* ballet tutu; *culhottes;* divided ~; *dress;* evening gown; farthingdale; grass ~; hoop ~; *infinite dress;* jupe; kirtle; *kilt;* lappa; midi; mini~; *non-slit ~;* over~; poodle ~; *quadrille dress;* rah-rah ~; split ~; sarong; tube ~; tutu; under~; valance; wraparound; XL; *yukata;* zari;
**skull** *(n.)*: area; block; brain; bonce [Br.]; cranium; death head; epicranium; *face; forehead;* Grim Reaper; head; *item;* jole [zoo.]; *kopf [G.];* lambda; *memento mori;* noggin; occiput; pannikel; *quadrigeminal;* region; skeleton head; *temple;* upper extremity; vertex; white ~; x-bones; yead [arch.]; *zenith;*

**sky** *(n.)*: air; atmosphere; *the* blue; clouds; canopy; deep blue ~; ether; expanse; empyrean; firmament; first heaven; fug [slang]; *gray skies;* heavens; horizon; ionosphere; *jumbo cloud;* KH *instability; layer;* mid-heaven; mackerel ~; mesosphere; noonday ~; *night ~;* open-skies; *polluted ~; quarter moon; region; red skies;* stratosphere; *thermosphere;* upper atmosphere; vault of heaven; welkin; *weather; xerosere;* yonder; zenith;
   **Kinds of skies**: blue ~; clear ~; cloudy ~; dawn ~; mackerel ~; morning ~; midnight ~; night ~; red ~; sunrise; sunset;

**slab** *(n.)*: *amount;* bit; chunk; daud; *ens;* fragment; *granite ~;* hunk; *item;* junt; *kernel;* lump; mass; *nugget; ounce;* piece; portion; panel; plait; quantity; *remnant;* shingle; section; table(t); *unit; vestige;* wedge; *x-mal [G.]; yngot [arch.];* zum [arch.];

**slack** *(adj.)*: abdicating; behindhand; careless; disregardful; dilatory; eliding; forgetful; faithless; goldbricking; heedless; irresponsible; inattentive; *jim-jam; kim-kam;* lax; messy; neglectful; overpermissive; pithless; questionable; remiss; shirking; slighting; spurning; thoughtless; unreliable; very neglectful; without regard; *xtry. ~;* yet irresponsible; *zero responsibility;* [*Ant.* sedulous]

**slacker** *(n.)*: avoider; bum; circumventer; dawdler; evader; foot-dragger; goof-off; growtnol; goldbrick; hedger; idler; *jinker; kaynard* [arch.]; lazybones; loafer; malingerer; non-worker; *obviate;* procrastinator; quisby; *remiss;* shirker; sluggard; trifler; *unmotivated; vacillate;* wastrel; *xenarthra;* yerner; *zealless;*

**slam** *(n.)*: assault; bump; clobber; deck; *efface;* flap; *get;* hit; impact; jolt; knock; lick; mash; nevel; *open-handed blow;* punch; *quab;* ram; strike; smack; thump; thwack; uppercut; veney; whack; *x-sect;* yedder; zonk;

**slam** *(v.)*: assault; bash; crash; cuff; dash; *efface;* flop; *get;* hit; impact; jam; knock; lam; mash; nail; *overstrike;* pound; quab; rap; smack; strike; thwack; uppercut; *veney;* whack; *x-sect;* yerk; zonk; [*see* insult]

**slander** *(n.)*: aspersion; backbiting; calumny; character assassination; defamation; denigration; evil-speaking; false words; gossip; *hearsay;* insult; injure; jaunder; *klatsch;* libel; mudslinging; malediction; name-calling; obtrectation; putting down; *quidnunc;* running down; slurring; smearing; traducement; tarnishing; unfair criticism; vilification; *wickedness; x-ing;* yellowing; *zeroization;*

**slander** *(v.)*: asperse; backbite; belittle; blast; badmouth; bespatter; calumniate; criticize; defame; denigrate; *execrate;* falsely accuse; gossip about; harangue; insult; jab; knock; libel; malign; name-call; obloquy; put down; *quib;* run down; slur; smear; tarnish; traduce; *use;* vilify; wipe; *xuld* [*arch.*]; yellow; *zap;*

**slanderer** *(n.)*: asperser; backbiter; calumniator; defamer; denigrator; disparager; detractor; dispraiser; evil-speaker; false accuser; gossip; hatchet man; insulter; jaunderer; knocker; libeler; maligner; mudslinger; name-caller; *over-critical;* put down; *quib;* railer; smearer; traducer; tarnisher; *unfair;* vilifier; *wicked; x-ing;* yellower; *zeroizer;*

**slanderous** *(adj.)*: abusive; backbiting; calumnious; defamatory; disparaging; evil-speaking; foul; gossipy; harmful; insulting; injurious; jabbing; keenly ~; libelous; maledictive; malicious; non-truthful; *obnoxious;* pejorative; *quad;* ridiculing; slandering; scurrilous; traducent; tarnishing; *untrue;* vilifying; *wicked; x-ing;* yellowing; *zeroizing;*

**slant** *(n.)*: angle; acclivity; bias; crook; camber; decline; descent; declivity; *elevation;* fall; gradient; gore; glacis; heel; hill; incline; inclination; *italics;* jag; keel; lean; *mountainside; natural slope;* obliqueness; pendence; pitch; proneness; *quantity of slope;* rise; slope; steepness; skew; tilt; upslope; unevenness; verge; vector; wind; *xy-gradient;* yaw; zigzag;

**slap** *(n.)*: assault; blow; cuff; dash; *efface;* flap; *get;* hit; impact; jab; knock; lick; *mauling;* nob; open-handed blow; punch; *quab;* rap; smack; spank; swat; thwack; *uppercut;* veney; whap; *x-sect;* yedder; zonk;

**slap** *(v.)*: assault; boff; cuff; dash; *elbow;* flail; *get;* hit; impact; *jab;* knock; lick; *mash;* nail; *overhit;* pelt; quab; rap; smack; strike; swat; thwack; *uppercut;* veney; whack; x-sect; yedder; zonk;

**slaughter** *(v.)*: annihilate; butcher; battue; cut up; destroy; execute; expunge; finish off; gun down; *homicide;* immolate; *jab;* kill; *liquidate;* massacre; *neutralize;* obliterate; put to death; quarter; run through; slay; smite; terminate; *unseat; victimize;* wipe out; x-out; *yank apart;* zap;

**slave** *(n.)*: attendant; bond slave; bondman; captive; drudge; esne; eunuch; flunky; galley- ~; *grunt;* helot; handmaid(en) [fem.]; inferior; jong; jackslave; *khansamah* [Ind.]; laborer; man(servant) [masc.]; maid(servant) [fem.]; neif; odalisque [fem.]; pawn; peon; *quelled; retainer;* servant; serf; thrall; underservant; vassal; worker; *Xica;* yokefellow; *zaikai;* [*Ant.* subjugator]

**slavery** *(n.)*: *assiento;* bondage; burden; bondservice; captivity; compulsory labor; drudgery; enslavement; forced labor; fetters; grip; hard bondage; helotism; hardship; inthrallment; *job; keeping down;* labor; mancipation; niefdom; oppression; *overlabor;* peonage; *quelling;* repression; slave-labor; servitude; servility; subjection; shackles; toil; thralldom; *under;* vassalage; work; xibalo; yoke; *Zeug [G.];* [*Ant.* subjugation]

**slay** *(v.)*: annihilate; butcher; bump off [slang]; cut off; destroy; eliminate; expunge; finish off; gun down; *homicide;* immolate; *jab;* kill; *liquidate;* murder; massacre; *nip;* obliterate; put to death; purge; quench; run through; smite; slaughter; terminate; *unseat;* vitiate; waste [slang]; wipe out; x-out; *yataghan;* zap;

**sleep** *(n.)*: aestivation; *asleep; bedtime;* beauty ~; catnap; *coma;* doze; deep ~; dormancy; estivation; forty winks; *grogginess;* hibernation; idleness; *jadedness;* kip; loafing; *motionlessness; Morpheus;* nap; night-rest; obdormition; oversleeping; peacefulness; quiet time; repose; rest; rack; slumber; shuteye; siesta; *twilight sleep; trance;* unconsciousness; vegetation; wink; wakelessness; *x-sleep; yawning;* zizz; [*Ant.* sleeplessness]

**sleep** *(v.)*: aestivate; *asleep;* bed down; *bunk;* crash; catnap; doze; estivate; fall asleep; get shuteye; hit the sack; hibernate; idle; *jaded;* knock off; kip [Br.]; loaf, *Morpheus;* nap; nod off; oversleep; pass out; *quiet time;* repose; rest; retire; slumber; snooze; take nap; turn in; *unconscious;* vegetate; *wink; x-sleep; yawn;* zonk (out); zizz; [*Ant.* stir]

**sleeper** *(n.)*: aestivator; bedder; catnapper; dozer; estivator; *flâneur* [F.]; groggy-head; hybernator; idler; *john-a-nods;* kipper; loafer; *Morpheus;* napper; nodder; oversleeper; *passed out;* quisby; rester; reposer; relaxer; slumberer; snoozer; sleepyhead; snorer; sleeping beauty; *take a nap; undersleeper;* vegetator; winker; *x-sleep;* yawner; zombie;

**sleepiness** *(n.)*: *apathy;* bleariness; comatose; drowsiness; exhaustion; fatigue; faintness; grogginess; heaviness of eyes; hypersomnia; inertia; jetlag; kef; languor; lassitude; lethargy; mopishness; nappiness; nodding; overtiredness; oscitancy; *pooped; quiet; rest;* somnolence; stupor; tiredness; torpor; *unenthusiasm; vapidity;* weariness; *wooziness; xenarthrous;* yawning; *zonked out;* [*Ant.* sleeplessness]

**sleepless** *(adj.)*: alert; awake; bestirred; *can't sleep;* disturbed; ever-alert; *fired up; get up;* having no sleep; insomnious; *jarred; kept awake;* lacking sleep; *much-stirred;* non-sleeping; nidgetty; overtired; peaceless; *qui vive* [L.]; restless; stirred; tireless; unsleeping; unreposed; vigilant; wakeful; weariless; *xuld [arch.];* yawnless; *zestful;* [*Ant.* sleepy]

**sleeplessness** *(n.)*: alertness; bestirring; *can't sleep;* disquietude; excitement; *fired up; get up; hyped up;* insomnia; jactitation; keeping awake; *laying there awake; much-stirred;* non-sleepiness; oscitancy; problem sleeping; *quickening;* restlessness; stirring; tirelessness; unrest; unweariness; vigilance; wakefulness; *x-awake;* yawnlessness; zippiness; [*Ant.* sleepiness]

**sleepy** *(adj.)*: aweary [lit.]; bushed; beat; bone-weary; comatose; drowsy; drained; dog-tired; exhausted; faint; fatigued; groggy; haggard; half dead; inert; jaded; knocked-out; lethargic; moribund; noddy; overtired; oscitant; pooped; phlegmatic; *quiescent;* run down; slumberous; somnolent; tired; unrested; vegetative; weary; *xenarthrous;* yawny; zapped; [*Ant.* sleepless]

**slice** *(n.)*: amount; bit; cut; deal; element; fragment; gash; *granule;* hunk; *item;* junt; *kernel;* lump; morsel; nugget; *ounce;* piece; portion; quantity; *remnant;* sliver; slab; section; serving; tad; tidbit; unit; *vestige;* wedge; *x-mal [G.]; yngot [arch.]; zum [arch.];*

**slice** *(v.)*: abscind; bisect; cut; carve; dissever; exscind; *forehew;* gash; hack; incise; *jag; knife;* lop; mince; miter; notch; obtruncate; prescind; *quadrisect;* retrench; slit; slash; split; sever; trim; *unseam; vell;* whack; *x-sect;* yerk; *zip off;*

**slide** *(v.)*: avalanche; backslide; coast; delapse; drag; *elance;* fly; flow; glide; glissade; hydroplane; *ice skate;* jet; kite; lapse; move; *natant; outsoar;* plane; *quicken;* run; rush; slip; skate; sail; skid; toboggan; *uprush;* volplane; whiz; *xuld [arch.];* yern; zip;

**slight** *(adj.)*: attenuated; brief; bit; constricted; dinky; exiguous; feeble; fractional; gaunt; gradual; hardly; insubstantial; jimp; *knee-high;* little; minor; meager; narrow; overthin; petty; quite small; remote; ribby; slim; small; subtle; thin; unimportant; very little; wee; wiry; weedy; wafer-thin; XF; yet small; *zero body fat;* [*Ant.* sizable]

**slight** *(v.)*: affront; brush off; coldshoulder; disregard; exclude; flout; give cold shoulder to; humiliate; ignore; *jink;* keep out; look through; *loathe;* move away from; not acknowledge; offend; push away; *quite [Sp.];* reject; snub; turn away from; *unkindness; veto;* wispy; x-out; *yard [arch.]; zero fellowship;* [*Ant.* salute]

**slim** *(adj.)*: attenuated; bony; constricted; delicate; elongated; fine; fleshless; gracile; hairbreadth; insubstantial; jimp; *knife blade-thin;* lean; meager; narrow; overthin; petite; *quantité négligeable* [F.]; ribby; slender; svelte; thin; unsubstantial; virgate [bot.]; willowy; XF; *yieldless; zero body fat;* [*Ant.* stout]

**slime** *(n.)*: *awful; bemire;* crud; discharge; excretion; emission; fluid; goop; glop; gunk; goo(k); horrid stuff; icky stuff; *issue;* jelly; *ketchupy substance; liquid;* muck; mire; *nast;* ooze; *pus;* quagmire; resin; sludge; sliminess; *tacky; thick;* urry; viscous matter; *wet matter; xysma;* yucky stuff; *zook;*

**slimy** *(adj.)*: *awful;* boggy; coagulated; *disgusting; evil;* feculent; gunky; gooey; gooky; *hoggish;* icky; jellied; *kaolintic;* lutulent; mucky; miry; muculent; nasty; oozy; puggy; quaggy; resinous; *repulsive;* scummy; sludgy; *sticky;* turbid; uliginous; viscous; well-muddied; *xysmic;* yucky; *zwishy;* [*see* unpleasant]

**sling** *(v.)*: *abandon;* betoss; cast; discharge; eject; fling; *go;* hurl; impel; jaculate; kest; launch; lob; *move; non-retention; outthrow;* pitch; propel; *quoit;* rocket; send; shoot; throw; upcast; vault; whip; *xuld* [arch.]; york; zip;

**slip** *(v.)*: *accelerate; blunder;* coast; delapse; *elance;* fall; fly; glide; hydroplane; *inaquate;* jet; kite; lose one's footing; move smoothly; *natant; outsoar;* plane; *quicken; ride;* run; slide; skid; trip; *uprush;* volplane; whiz; *xuld [arch.];* yern; zip;

**slippery** *(adj.)*: *adverse;* buttery; *chancy;* dangerous; *endangering;* frozen-over; glib; glare; glossy; glazed; greasy; *hazardous;* icy; *jeopardous;* known risk; lubrous; *muddy; no traction;* oily; polished; quite ~; *risky;* slick; smooth; *treacherous;* unctuous; verk slick; wet; *xysmic;* yet unsalted; zero traction;

**slit** *(n.)*: aperture; breach; cut; crack; division; *exect;* fissure; gash; graze; gap; hole; incision; kerf; laceration; *microtear;* nick; notch; opening; piercing; *quarter-cut;* rip; rend; *riven;* slot; slice; scoring; tear; *unseam;* vent; wound; *x-section;* yedder; *zip open;*

**slit** *(v.)*: ax; break; cut; divide; exect; *fissure;* gash; graze; hack; incise; *jag;* knife; *lacerate; miter;* nick; notch; open; *prescind; quadrisect;* rive; rend; slice; *tear; unseam;* vent(ilate); *wound; x-sect;* yerk; zip;

**slither** *(v.)*: approach; *budge;* belly-crawl; creep; crawl; *dart;* edge; *flow;* glide; *hitch;* inch; *jee; kite;* lumber; move; *nudge; outrun;* plod; *quaddle;* run; roll; slink; scrawl; slideslip; *twist; underway; venture;* wriggle; wind; worm; *xfer;* yaw; zigzag;

**sliver** *(n.)*: *amount;* bit; crock(-shard); daud; *ens;* fragment; *gall;* hunk; *iota;* junt; *kernel;* lamia; morsel; *nugget; ounce;* potsherd; quill; *remnant;* splinter; shard; *tidbit; under; very shiny;* wedge; *xylon; zinger;*
**slob** *(n.)*: anarchic person; bum; clutter-bug; dirtbag; *entangled;* filthy person; grung-bucket; *higgledy-piggledy;* incomposed individual; jumbled person; *keg-meg;* louse; mess; non-cleanly individual; *orderless; pell-mell; quaggy;* rumpled person; sloven; tangled mess; unkempt person; *vexing;* wild-man; *x'ed;* yob; zhlub;
**slogan** *(n.)*: ad ~; byword; catch-phrase; distinctive phrase; expression; *formulary;* great saying; *hackneyed saying; idiom;* jingle; known ~; locution; motto; *neology; oracle;* phrase; quote; recognized saying; saying; tag line; *utterance; verse;* watchword; *xenagogy;* Yogism; *zeteticism;*
**slope** *(n.)*: acclivity; angle; bias; cant; chute; drop; declivity; escarpment; fall; grade; gore; hill; incline; *jag; kink;* lean; mountainside; *natural ~;* obliqueness; pendence; pitch; *quantity of slope;* rise; slant; steepness; tilt; talus; upslope; verge; versant; *wind; xy-gradient;* yaw; *zigzag;*
**sloppy** *(adj.)*: anarchic; bedraggled; cluttered; careless; disorganized; disheveled; entangled; frowzy; grungy; higgledy-piggledy; incomposed; jumbled; keg-meg; littered; messy; neglected; orderless; pell-mell; quaggy; rumpled; slipshod; slovenly; tangled; untidy; *vexing;* wild; *x'ed;* yucky; zoo-like; [*Ant.* spruce, shipshape]
**slot** *(n.)*: aperture; breach; cut; crack; *deposit; eye-hole;* fissure; gap; groove; hole; incision; keyway; laceration; *microtear;* narrow opening; opening; peephole; *quarter-inch opening; return;* receptacle; slit; thin hole; trench; *uncovered;* vent; window; *x-section;* yawn; *zip open;*
**slothful** *(adj.)*: abulic; bone-lazy; casual; droopy; ergophobic; fainéant; groggy; half-hearted; indolent; *jog-trot;* kef; lazy; mopish; non-motivated; otiose; pepless; phlegmatic; quiescent; remiss; slack; torpid; unmotivated; unindustrious; vapid; workshy; *xenarthrous;* yareless; zealless; [*Ant.* sedulous]
**slothfulness** *(n.)*: abulia; blahness; casualness; droopiness; ergophobia; faintness; grogginess; half-heartedness; indolence; *jadedness;* kef; laziness; mopishness; non-diligence; oscitancy; peplessness; quiescence; remissness; sloth; torpor; unenthusiasm; vapidity; weariness; *xenarthrous;* yarelessness; zeallessness; [*Ant.* sedulousness]
**slow** *(adj.)*: arrested; bovine; creeping; crawling; decelerated; dilatory; delayed; dawdling; draggy; easy; flagging; gradual; heavy; inanimate; inactive; inching; impeded; indolent; *jog-trot;* kef; lagging; leisurely; languid; moving slowly; not fast; obstupefactive; poky; quiescent; retarded; sluggish; time-consuming; tortoiselike; tardigrade; unhurried; *vapid; weary; xenarthrous;* yareless; zealless; [*Ant.* swift]
**slow down** *(v.)*: arrest; brake; cut one's speed; decelerate; ease off; *forestall;* go slow; hold back; impede; jam-up; keep back; lose speed; make slower; *non-accelerate;* obstruct; put on the brakes; palliate; quieten; retard; reduce speed; slow; slacken; take it easy; unlax; *verge;* withhold; x; *yank; zeroize;* [*Ant.* speed up]
**slowly** *(adv.)*: adagio [It.]; bit by bit; cautiously; delayed; ever-so- ~; flaggingly; gradually; heavily; inch by inch; inchmeal; indolently; *jog trot; kef;* languidly; leisurely; lingeringly; moderately; non-hurriedly; not fast; *over-slow;* pokily; quite ~; retardedly; sluggishly; tardily; tediously; tardigradous; unhurriedly; unspeedily; very ~; with leisureliness; *wearily; xenarthra;* yarelessly; zeallessly; [*Ant.* swiftly]
**slowness** *(n.)*: acedia; bovinity; caution; dilatoriness; dullness; delay; dawdling; easiness; foot-dragging; gradualness; heaviness; indolence; *jog trot; kef;* lagging; leisureliness; languidness; moderate speed; *non-rushed;* obstupefaction; pokiness; quiescence; retardation; sluggishness; tardiness; unhurriedness; *vapidity; weariness; xenarthra;* yarelessness; zeallessness; [*Ant.* speed]
**sluggard** *(n.)*: apathetic fellow; bum; clock-watcher; droil; ergophobe; fainéant; growtnol; goof-off; half-hearted worker; idler; *jog trot; kaynard* [arch.]; loafer; lazy person; lubber; layabout; lazybones; laggard; mope; nebbish; otiose man; pepless fellow; quisby; *remiss;* snail; slothful man; slacker; shirker; torpid person; *unmotivated; vagabond;* wastrel; *xenarthra; yareless; zealless;* [*see* bum; freeloader]

**sluggish** *(adj.)*: abeyant; benumbed; creeping; draggy; droopy; easygoing; flagging; groggy; half-hearted; indolent; jaded; kef; lethargic; languid; moribund; non-motivated; oscitant; otiose; pepless; phlegmatic; quiescent; retarded; slow(-footed); slothful; torpid; unmotivated; unenthusiastic; vapid; workshy; *xenarthrous;* yareless; zealless; [*Ant.* sedulous]

**sluggishness** *(n.)*: apathy; blahness; complacency; creeping; dullness; droopiness; drowsiness; *exhaustion;* faintness; feebleness; grogginess; heaviness; irresponsiveness; jadedness; kef; lethargy; languishment; laziness; lassitude; lentitude; mopishness; *numbness;* oscitancy; peplessness; *quiescence; resistance;* slothfulness; slowness; torpidity; unenthusiasm; vapidity; weariness; *xenarthrous;* yarelessness; zeallessness; [*Ant.* sedulousness]

**slum** *(n.)*: alley; bad neighborhood; cabbage town; dive; dump; ethnic enclave; favela; ghetto; Hooverville; imijondolo; *Judengasse* [G.]; *Karjan* [Morocco]; *Lusnynai* [Lithuania]; minority neighborhood; *mellah* [Arab.]; *neighborhood; Orangi Town* [Pakistan]; poor neighborhood; *quartier* [F.]; run-down neighborhood; shantytown; skid row; *trailer park;* urban dump; *villas miseria* [Argentina]; wrong side of the tracks; x-sector; yard; zone;

**sly** *(adj.)*: artful; beguiling; cunning; clever; deceptive; evasive; foxy; guileful; hugger-mugger; illusory; jady; knavish; *lying;* misleading; non-trustworthy; *oblique;* pawky; *quaintise [arch.];* roguish; subtle; sneaky; tricky; underhanded; vulpine; wily; *xtry.;* yepe; *zinger;* [*Ant.* simple]

**slyness** *(n.)*: artfulness; beguiling; cunning; cleverness; deceptiveness; evasiveness; foxiness; guile; *hidden;* illusiveness; jiggery-pockery; knavishness; *lying;* Machiavelism; non-trustworthiness; *outfoxing;* pawkiness; *quaintise* [arch.]; roguishness; subtlety; sneakiness; trickiness; underhandedness; *vulpine;* wiliness; *wise as serpents; xtry, cleverness;* yepship [arch.]; *zinging;* [*Ant.* simplicity]

**small** *(adj.)*: abbreviated; baby; compact; concise; dinky; diminutive; dwarfed; eensie-weensie; fine; gnat-sized; half-pint; itsy-bitsy; *jot;* knee-high; little; low; minute; miniature; modest; negligible; one-horse; puny; petite; pygmy; pint-sized; *quantité négligeable* [F.]; runty; rinky-dink; reduced; scant; short; shrimpy; smallish; tiny; teeny; undersized; very small; wee; XS; young; *yea big; zero;* [*Ant.* sizable]

**smallness** *(n.)*: abbreviation; brevity; compactness; conciseness; dinkiness; dwarfism; exiguity; fineness; fewness; feebleness; gnat-likeness; humbleness; insignificance; inconsiderableness; jejuneness; *knee-high;* littleness; minuteness; meanness; negligibility; naggle; over-smallness; puniness; paucity; pettiness; *quantity;* runtiness; scantiness; slightness; tininess; teeniness; unimpressiveness; unimportance; *very small;* weeness; weakness; *XS; yea big; zero;*

**smart** *(adj.)*: astute; academic; bright; brainy; brilliant; clever; discerning; educated; farsighted; genius; gifted; highbrow; high I.Q.; intelligent; intellectual; ingenious; judicious; keen; learned; *muser;* nimble-witted; on the ball; perceptive; quick(-witted); *rocket scientist;* sharp; scholarly; thinking; ultra-smart; *valedictorian;* witty; well-informed; well-educated; x-smart; yaup; *zippy;* [*see* knowledgeable; wise; *Ant.* simple]

**smash** *(v.)*: annihilate; bash; collide; crash; crush; destroy; *explode;* flatten; grind; hurt; *immobilize;* jam; kill; lam; levigate; mash; *nullify; overpower;* pulverize; quash; ruin; squash; throttle; tamp; *undo;* vanquish; wreck; x; yank down; zap;

**smear** *(n.)*: *attainting;* blot(ch); blemish; coloration; discoloration; eyesore; flaw; *gaum; halftone;* infucation; jaup; *ketchup ~; line;* mark; naeve; *off-color;* patch; *quirk; ring;* spot; smudge; smirch; tarnish; taint; unsightly ~; *vice;* wem; xanthochromia; xanthosis; yellow; zona;

**smear** *(v.)*: apply; anoint; besmear; begrime; butter; cover; coat; daub; distribute; even out; extend; fan out; fill; gaum; hand- ~; infucate; *jigger; kirtle:* lay on; mantle; muddy; *non-containment;* overspread; paint; perfuse; plaster; *quab;* rub; smooth; spread; smirch; ted; transfer; utterly cover; *use; volume;* wipe; xfer; *yain* [arch.]; *zero containment;* [*see* slander]

**smell** *(n.)*: aura; aroma; bad ~; bouquet; cense; *delightful (-displeasing)* ~; emanation; effluvium; essence; fume; fetor; fragrance; *good (-gallsome)* ~; hint; incense; *joyful (-joyless)* ~; *keen (-killing)* ~; *lovely (-loathsome)* ~; musk; mephitis; nidor; niff; odor; olfaction; perfume; quality; reeking; redolence; stench; scent; spice; savor; trace; trail; *unsavoriness; very nice (-vile)* ~; whiff; waft; *xtry.* ~; *yummy (-yucky)* ~; zedoary; zoril;

**smell** *(v. emit odor)*: air; bad-smelling; come out; *detect;* exude; emit odor; funk; give off odor; have ~; *intolerable; jarring; kest; lungful;* make odor; niff; offend; pong; *quill [arch.];* reek; stink; *terrible;* unleash odor; *vile; whiffy; xuld [arch.];* yield; *zap;*

**smell** *(v. whiff)*: apprehend; breathe in; *circulate;* draw in; detect; *encounter; follow one's nose;* get whiff of; have a ~; inhale; *just a whiff;* know; *lungful;* make out; nose; *notice;* olfact; perceive; pick up; *quill [arch.]; recognize;* sniff; sense; take in; use nose; *ventilate;* whiff; wind; *xfer; yummy; yucky; zero in;*

**smelly** *(adj.)*: awful; bad-smelling; *contemptible;* displeasing; evil-smelling; effluvious; foul; fetid; fulsome; graveolent; *horrible;* ill-smelling; *jarring; ketty; loathsome;* mephitic; malodorous; niffy; nauseating; odoriferous; olid; offensive; putrid; *queasy;* rancid; reeking; rank; stinky; *terrible;* unpleasant; vile; whiffy; wicked; *x-bad;* yucky; zorillo-like; [*see* disgusting, *Ant.* sweet-smelling]

**smile** *(n.)*: array of teeth; beam(ing); *cute* ~; *dentition; expression;* face lit up; grin; gleam; *happy; intoxicated; joy;* keen ~; *lovely* ~; mug; million-dollar ~; *nice* ~; overbite; *overjoyed; pleased; quite happy; radiant;* simper; smirk; teeth; toothy grin; underbite; upturned mouth; *very happy; winsome* ~; *xtr. happy;* yellow-toothed ~; *zeal;* [*Ant.* scowl]

**smile** *(v.)*: *act happy;* beam; crack a ~; *delight; enjoy;* flash ~; grin; gleam; glow; *happy; intoxicated; joy; keyed up;* light up; make a ~; *nice* ~; *overjoyed;* put a smile on; *quite happy;* radiate; smirk; show pearly whites; simper; shine; *toothy grin;* upturn mouth; *very happy; winsome* ~; *xtr. happy;* yellow-toothed smile; *zeal;* [*Ant.* scowl]

**smite** *(n.)*: assault; blow; clobber; clout; crack; clock; dash; deck; *efface;* flagellation; *get;* hit; impact; jolt; knock; lick; lam; *mauling;* nob; *open-handed blow;* punch; *quab;* rap; slap; strike; smack; sock; slam; spank; thwack; thump; uppercut; veney; whack; wallop; *x-sect;* yedder; zonk;

**smite** *(v.)*: assault; beat; clobber; cut off; destroy; defeat; exterminate; execute; expunge; flail; flog; finish off; gun down; hit; immolate; jab; knock; kill; lam; mash; murder; nail; obliterate; punch; purge; quench; run through; strike; slay; terminate; uppercut; *vaporize;* wallop; wipe out; x-out; *yedder;* zap;

**smoke** *(n.)*: atomization; *aura;* breath; *bank;* cloud; contrail; dust cloud; exhaust; fumes; fog; gas; gauze; gloom; haze; *incloud; jumbo cloud; KH instability; London fog;* mist; miasma; nimbus; *overcast;* puff; pollution; *quasi-vaporous; rain cloud;* steam; smog; *thundercloud; umbered;* vapor; wisp; *xenon cloud; yellowy cloud;* zirconium cloud;

**smoke** *(v.)*: *atomize;* bogue; billow; cure; *dusty;* exhaust; fume; gas; haze; incloud; *jumbo cloud; KH instability;* light up; make smoke; nubilate; obnubilate; puff; *quasi-vaporous;* reek; smolder; *turbid;* use cigarettes; vapor; wisp; *xenon cloud;* yield ~; *zwoosh;*

**smoky** *(adj.)*: *adularescent;* billowy; cloudy; dusty; encloued; foggy; fumy; gloomy; gray; hazy; included; *jumbo clouded; KH instability;* lour; murky; misty; nebulous; obscure; *overclouded;* puffy; *qually [arch.];* reeky; steamy; smoke-filled; turbid; umbered; vaporous; wispy; *xenon cloud; yellowy cloud;* zero-zero;

**smolder** *(v.)*: *alight;* burn; combust; deflagrate; enkindle; fume; glow; *heat;* ignite; *jeopardize;* kindle; light (up); *miskindle;* neal; overburn; *pyric; quick-match;* roast; smoulder; smoke; torrefy; ustion; *vulcanize; waste; xylopyrography; yearn; zap;*

**smooth** *(adj.)*: acomous; bald; buff; buttery; creaseless; creamy; deburred; even; easy; flat; fine; flowing; glabrous; glib; *horizontal;* ironed (out); jointless; *kibbled;* lubric; *legato [mus.];* mild; non-bumpy; *open;* planar; quite ~; rollered; smoothened; silky; tabulate; unwrinkled; unrough; unrumpled; unlined; unobstructed; very ~; wrinkleless; wrinkle-free; *x-smooth;* yet wrinkleless; zero wrinkles;

**smooth** *(v.)*: *align;* burnish; bulldoze; compress; deburr; dub; even (out); flatten; glib; *horizontal;* iron; *jam down; knock down;* level; make flat; *nullify; oiled;* plane; *quash;* roller; smoothen; steam roll; take wrinkles out; unwrinkle; uncrumple; *very flat; wrinkle-free; xuld [arch.];* yerk; zeroize; [Ant. scrunch]

**smoothness** *(n.)*: acomia; baldness; creaminess; deburring; evenness; fluency; fineness; flow; glassiness; glabrousness; horizontalness; ironing; *jamming; keenness;* levelness; *much-flattened;* non-bumpiness; *oiliness;* planarity; *quite smooth;* regularity; sleekness; silkiness; tabulation; unobstruction; velvetiness; volubility; *wrinkle-free;* x-smooth; *yet without wrinkles; zero wrinkles;*

**smother** *(v.)*: asphyxiate; *bind;* choke; deprive of oxygen; extinguish; *finish off;* gag; hush up; *incapacitate;* jugulate; kill; *lynch;* muffle; *nullify;* overwhelm; *put out;* quell; quench; restrict; suffocate; stifle; throttle; *undo; void; whirken* [arch.]; *xuld [arch.]; yote; zeroize;*

**smug** *(adj.)*: arrogant; big-headed; condescending; disdainful; egotistical; full of oneself; gloating; haughty; inflated; *jackanapes; know-it-all;* lifted up; *magnificent;* narcissistic; overconfident; puffed up; quick-to-boast; *reassured;* self-confident; think highly of oneself; unabashed; vainglorious; wrapped up in oneself; *x-proud; yelping; zero humility;* [Ant. self-effacing]

**smuggle** *(v.)*: act; bring in illegally; convey unlawfully; *deliver;* export illegally; freight in secretly; get in; haul illegally; import illegally; *janker;* kite; *lug;* move; *non-legal;* operate; pass; *quarter-cart;* run; rustle sneak in; traffic; unlawfully import; *van;* work; xfer; *yanker [Br.];* zip away;

**snake** *(n.)*: \* asp; boa (constrictor); cobra; diamondback; emerald tree boa; firedrake; garter ~; horned viper; Indian python; jararaca; king cobra; large whip ~; moccasin; nedder; ophidian; python; queen ~; rattlesnake; *reptile;* serpent; tree ~; *uraeus;* viper; water ~; *xenophidion;* yellow cobra; *zamenenis;*

**snap** *(v.)*: *amputate;* break; cut; crack; dissever; exscind; fracture; *get broken;* halve; incise; *jerk;* kerf; *lop; mince;* nip; obtruncate; part; *quarter;* recise; sever; split; separate; take off; undo; *vell; whack off;* x-sect; *yerk;* zip;

**snare** *(n.)*: artifice; *bear-trap; con;* deception; entrapment; foxtrap; farce; flimflam; gin; harepipe; illusiveness; illaqueation; inmeshment; Judas-kiss; kelong; lace; live trap; mantrap; malversation; mouse-trap; mesh; net; *outfox;* pitfall; pot; *quiblin [arch.];* ruse; springe; trap; toil; *undoing;* verneuking; weely; weir; *xuld [arch.]; yentzing; zinger;*

**sneak** *(v.)*: *amble;* budge; creep; *drift;* edge; *furtive;* gimp; *hide;* inch; jiffle; *keep quiet;* lumber; move quietly; nightwalk; *obambulate [arch.];* pussyfoot; prowl; quietly move; *relocate;* slip; slink; steal (away); sidle; skulk; tiptoe; tippytoe; *use stealth; very slow;* worm; xfer; *yaw;* zip;

**sneaky** *(adj.)*: arch; beguiling; crafty; deceitful; devious; evasive; furtive; guileful; *hidden;* insidious; jesuitical; knavish; *lying;* misleading; mischievous; non-trustworthy; *outsmart;* pawky; *quiet;* roguish; subtle; sly; shrewd; scheming; tricky; unscrupulous; vulpine; wily; weaselly; *xtry.; yepe; zinger;* [Ant. straightforward]

**sneer** *(v.)*: *abuse;* belittle; contemn; deride; *execrate;* fleer; gibe; hiss; insult; jibe; knock; laugh at; mock; *name-calling; offend;* pillory; quib; ridicule; scoff; turn nose up at; utter against; verbally abuse; wag head; *xuld [arch.];* yock; *zap;*

**sneeze** *(n.)*: achoo; burst; *blow;* convulsive force; *'choo!;* discharge; eruption; *forceful ~; going off; hurling;* issue; *jet;* ka-choo; *letting go; mucus;* neese; *outburst; peppered; quickening;* release; rhonchus; sneezing; sternutation; *tickle; upsurge;* violent emission; *wham~; xuld [arch.]; yead; zap;*

**snow** *(n.)*: arctic ~; blanket; corn ~; *cold;* drift; *ewden-drift* [arch.]; flurry; *flake;* graupel; hail; ice; *Jack Frost; kittly-benders; low temperature;* mantle of ~; névé; *oversnow;* powder-snow; *piste; quern [arch.];* red ~; snowfall (-drift; -bank; blanket); *thawless ~;* unthawing ~; *verglas;* white; *xue [Taiwan]; yowndrift [arch.]; zero degrees;*

**snowstorm** *(n.)*: arctic blizzard; blizzard; *cold front;* driven snow; *ewden-drift [arch.]; flurry;* graupel; hailstorm; ice storm; *Jack Frost; knot floater; line squall;* mantle of snow; nivosity; onslaught; pirry; *quirlewind [arch.];* rough weather; snow squall; tempest; upheaval; *violent storm;* white-out; white squall; *xue [Taiwan]; yowndrift [arch.]; zinger;*

**snowy** *(adj.)*: arctic; blizzardy; *cold;* drifty; *ewden-drift [arch.];* flurried; *graupel;* haily; icy; *Jack Frost; kittly-benders; low temperature;* mantled; nival; niveous; *oversnow;* powdery; quite ~; *red snow;* snow-covered (-crowned); *thawless;* unmelted; *verglas;* wintery; white; *xue [Taiwan]; ycie* [arch.]; zero degrees;

**snuggle** *(v.)*: *affection;* bury; cuddle; cozy up; croodle; cleave; *draw close;* embrace; embosom; *fondle;* grip; hug; infold; *jam; keep close; love;* make comfortable; nestle; nuzzle; *overply;* press; *quash; rub;* snug up; settle; *tenderly hug; upbind; very cozy;* wrap; *x;* yoke; zone;

**soak** *(v.)*: absorb; bedrench; bathe; *cover;* drench; *encompass;* fill; flood; gorge; humectate; indrench; immerse; imbibe; jawp; *keep wet; lie in;* madefy; macerate; marinate; *non-dry;* overload; plunge; permeate; *queven [arch.];* ret; saturate; souse; steep; sop; *soggy;* take in; *undried; vapor;* wet; water- ~; waterlog; *xtr. wet;* yote; *zet [dial.];*

**soar** *(v.)*: ascend; breeze; coast; dart; escalate; fly; glide; hover; *issue;* jet; kite; light; move; *navigate;* overfly; plane; *quicken;* rise; rocket; shoot; streak; take flight; upbear; volplane; wing; *xuld [arch.];* yern; zoom; [*see* swoop; float; *Ant.* sink]

**sob** *(v.)*: *attrition;* bawl; blubber; boo-hoo; cry; despair; erupt into tears; *feel sorrow;* grieve; howl; *inveigh; judder;* keen; lachrymate; moan; *noise; outweep; pout; quistle [arch.];* roar; sigh; snivel; tear; *ululate; vociferate;* whimper; weep; *xtr. sad;* yowl; *zealless;* [*Ant.* sing]

**sober** *(adj.)*: abstemious; *back to normal;* coherent; dry; earnest; free from intoxication; grave; heavy; *himself;* in one's right mind; *jarred;* keen-minded; level-headed; mellow; non-intoxicated; ominous; ponderous; *quick-witted;* right-minded; sober-minded; somber; temperate; unintoxicated; uninebriated; *vigilant;* wineless; *xtr. serious;* yare-handed; *zesty;* [*Ant.* sloshed]

**soberness** *(n.)*: abstemiousness; *back to normal;* coherence; dryness; earnesty; freedom from intoxication; gravity; healthy mind; *in one's right mind; jarred;* keen-mindedness; level-headedness; mellowness; non-intoxication; *ominousness;* ponderousness; *quick-witted;* right mind; sobriety; somberness; temperance; unintoxicatedness; uninebriatedness; *vigilance;* winelessness; *xtr. seriousness;* yare-handedness; *zero intoxication;*

**social** *(adj.)*: associational; *body;* collective; companionable; communal; convival; *departmental;* established; *fraternal;* group; gregarious; horizontal; interactive; *joint; kongsi [Chin.];* league; mutual; *nexus;* organizational; public; *quinquevirate;* relational; societal; *troop;* urbane; *vertical union; way of life; xenial; yeald; zonta;*

**socialize** *(v.)*: acculturate; behave toward; converse; deal; enrich; fraternize; get together; hobnob; interact; interrelate; interface; intermingle; *join; keep company;* link up; mingle; *non-isolated; over-friendly;* party; *qua [L.];* relate; schmooze; treat; *utter; verbalize;* work; *xenia; yeme; zero in;*

**society** *(n.)*: association; affiliation; brotherhood; body; civilization; community; culture; confraternity; citizenry; confederation; club; dwellers; establishment; federation; fraternity; fellowship; guild; group; habitancy; institution; joint coalition; *kongsi* [Chin.]; league; mutual interest group; nexus; organization; open ~; public; partnership; quinquevirate; *registered guild;* strata; syndicate; trade union; troop; union; *vertical union;* way of life; workers' union; *x-class;* yeald; youth organization; zollverein; zonta;

**socket** *(n.)*: *aperture;* bay; cavity; depression; *eye- ~; fitment;* gudgeon; glene; genoid; hollow; incavation; jack; *krater;* lacuna; mouth; *niche;* ouch; opening; port; pod; plug; quabing; recess; slot; tool jack; *universal joint;* vug; well; *x-type;* yawn; *zone;*

**soft** *(adj.)*: airy; *bouncy;* comfortable; cottony; ductile; downy; elastic; easy; fluffy; fleecy; flexible; flabby; gentle; *half-volume;* infirm; jiggly; *kind;* limber; lenient; malleable; mild; mellow; nappy; nice; nesh; nubile; over-soft; overstuffed; plush; pliant; pliable; padded; pillowy; quilted; rubbery; supple; spongy; squashy; tender; unhardened; unctuous; velvety; weak; xillinous; yielding; *zero hardness;* [*Ant.* solid, severe]

**soften** *(v.)*: alleviate; bate; curb; cushion; demulce; ease; emolliate; fade; get easier; *hush;* intenerate; *jump down; keep soft;* lessen; mull; malaxate; mellow; melt; mitigate; mollify; numb; obtund; palliate; quell; reduce; subside; tenderize; temper; unsteel; *una corda [mus.];* vanish; weaken; *xillinous;* yield; *zeroize;* [*Ant.* stiffen, strengthen]

**softness** *(n.)*: airiness; *bounciness;* comfort; delicacy; easiness; emollescence [metals]; fluffiness; gentleness; *hirsute;* infirmness; jiggliness; *keen ~;* limberness; malleability; mildness; nappiness; over- ~; pliability; *quilted; reclining;* suppleness; tenderness; unctuousness; velvetiness; weakness; xillinousness; yieldedness; *zero hardness;* [*Ant.* severity]

**sojourn** *(n.)*: abiding; brief visit; continuance; *dwelling;* encampment; foray; flight; *going to;* honeymoon; hadj; inhabiting; journey; *keeping on;* lingering; mission; *nesting;* overnighter; peregrination; quest; residing; stay; tarrying; *undertaking;* vacation; visit; waiting; xenization; *yatra* [Hind.]; zugunruhe; [*see* wander; adventure]

**sojourn** *(v.)*: abide; bide; continue; dwell; *encamp; endure;* follow on; *go to;* hang one's hat; inhabit; *journey;* keep on; live; linger; lodge; *move in; nest;* occupy; pause; peregrinate; quarter; remain; reside; stay; settle; tarry; *use;* visit; wait; *winter;* xenize; yerde [arch.]; *zip to;*

**soldier** *(n.)*: army man; boy [slang]; combatant; doughboy [slang]; dragoon; enlisted man; foot ~; fighting man; G.I.; grenadier; halberdier; home guard; infantryman; janissary [Turk.]; kern; knight; lancer; legionnaire; (military) man(-at-arms); minuteman; mercenary; musketeer; marine; *noncommissioned officer; officer;* private; pikeman; paratrooper; *quartermaster;* regular; rifleman; serviceman; sword-man; trooper; *uniformed men;* velite [Rom.]; *veteran;* warrior; *xiphos-bearer;* yeoman; *zoauve;*

**solemn** *(adj.)*: august; awe-inspiring; *big;* ceremonial; dour; earnest; formal; grave; great; heavy; humorless; important; *judicial; key;* lugubrious; momentous; noble; *ominous;* ponderous; *quantum;* reverential; serious; sober-faced; sacred; somber; thoughtful; unsmiling; venerative; weighty; *xttr.; yearnful;* zoetic;

**solid** *(adj.)*: adamant; bone-hard; concrete; dense; ever-rigid; firm; granitelike; hard; inflexible; jam-packed; kiln-hardened; lithoid; marblelike; non-pliant; oaky; petrous; *quartz;* rigid; rock- ~; stiff; tough; unyielding; very ~; well-built; x-hard; yieldless; *zero give;* [*Ant.* soft]

**solution** *(n.)*: answer; *band-aid ~;* conclusion; deciphering; explanation; fix; general ~; handling; interpretation; justification; key; logical ~; means; *note;* opening up; permanent ~; quick ~; resolution; short-term ~; settlement; *treatment;* uncovering; *victory;* way out; *xtry.; ~; yes-answer; zeroing in;*

**solvable** *(adj.)*: answerable; ascertainable; breakable; calculable; decipherable; explainable; findable; gettable; *hashing out; iron out;* justifiable; knowable; *logical; making sense of;* not a problem; openable; *perceivable; questionless;* resolvable; reconcilable; settlable; soluble; *tellable;* uncoverable; *victory;* workable; *xlate; yieldless; zero in;*

**solve** *(v.)*: answer; ascertain; break; crack; calculate; clear up; decipher; elucubrate; expose; explain; figure out; find out; get (to the bottom of); hash out; interpret; iron out; justify; know; lay to rest; make sense of; *naw [dial.];* open up; put to rest; *questionless;* resolve; settle; *tell;* uncover; unravel; untangle; *victory;* work out; *xlate; yieldless; zero in;*

**son** *(n.)*: adopted ~; boy; child; decendant; eldest ~; filial; *fils* [F.]; firstborn ~; *guy;* heir; *increase;* junior; *kid;* lad; manchild; newborn ~; natural ~; only-begotten ~; *progeny; quilpe [arch.];* relative; scion; stripling; *step ~;* tyke; teenage ~; *urchin;* virile; whelp; *xbred;* youngster; zon [dial.];

**song** *(n.)*: anthem; arrangement; ballad; carol; canticle; composition; chorus; cantata; chantey; ditty; descant; doxology; dirge; even- ~; étude; folk~; gallimaufry; hymn; harmony; *inspirational;* jingle; kasida; love~; lullaby; melody; medley; notes; ode; opus; offertory; piece; psalm; quadrille; refrain; recessional; strain; sonnet; serenade; sonata; shanty; tune; under~; vocalization; work- ~; war ~; warbling; *xylophone ~;* yed; zemirah; [*see* music]

**songwriter** *(n.)*: author; bard; composer; cleffer; doggerelist; elegist; framer; *glossator;* hymnist; hymn writer; inspirational songwriter; jongleur; kasida-writer; lyricist; librettist; music-writer; minstrel; *noel;* odist; psalmist; poet; *quadrille;* rhymester; song-writer; tune-maker; *undersong;* versifier; writer; *Xanrof;* yedder; zemirah-writer;
**soon** *(adv.)*: anon; betimes; before long; by and by; briefly; coming shortly; directly; erelong; *first thing; geared up;* hurriedly; imminently; just a little while; keenly; lickety-split; momentarily; *now; near;* over~; *overnight;* presently; presto; quickly; rapidly; shortly; *tout de suite* [F.]; upcoming; very ~; without delay; *wikiwiki* [Haw.]; *xtr. quick;* yarely; zippily;
**soothe** *(v.)*: appease; assuage; becalm; calm; conciliate; diffuse; demulce; ease; *fulfill;* gratify; hush; *indulge; justify; knock down;* lull; mollify; *nullify;* obtund; placate; propitiate; quell; reconcile; resolve; satisfy; smooth; soften; tranquilize; unruffle; *vanish;* win favor; x-out; *yield; zeroize;* [Ant. stimulate]
**soothing** *(adj.)*: appeasing; becalming; calming; comforting; diffusing; easeful; *fulfilling;* gentle; hushing; irenic; *justifying;* kind; lulling; mellow; mild; nice; obtundent; peacful; pleasant; quiet; relaxing; soft; tender; tranquil; unruffling; *very ~; without harshness; xtr. soft; yield; zeroize;* [*Ant.* stirring]
**sophistication** *(n.)*: acculturation; bringing (-being) up to par; civilization; decorum; elegance; fineness; good manners; high refinement; improvement; *jobation;* knowledgeableness; *loveliness;* mannerliness; *non-barbarity; overelegance;* propriety; *quaintness;* refinement; style; *tastefulness;* urbanity; *versing;* wordliness; *xtry.; younker;* zero barbarity; [*Ant.* simplicity]
**sorcerer** *(n.)*: alchemist; astrologer; bewitcher; conjurer; clairvoyant; diviner; enchanter; fortune-teller; geomancer; haruspice; *incantation;* jadoo-wallah; *karakia [Maori];* lithomancer; magician; mystic; medium; necromancer; new ager; occultist; psychic; *quad;* rhabdomancer; soothsayer; spiritualist; seer; theurgist; *ungodly;* voodooist; wizard; warlock; xylomancer; *yogist;* zodiacist;
**sorcery** *(n.)*: alchemy; astrology; black magic; conjuration; divination; enchantment; fortune-telling; geomancy; hocus pocus; incantation; juju; *Keltic religion; legerdemain;* magic; necromancy; occult; palmistry; *quad;* rune; soothsaying; theurgy; *ungodliness;* voodoo; wizardry; witchcraft; *xylomancy; yogism;* zodiac; [*see* divination]
**sore** *(adj.)*: aching; bruised; bloody; crampy; discomforting; excruciating; feeling bad; grievous; hurting; inflamed; *jabbing;* killing [slang]; *laceration;* miserable; *nippy; ouch!;* painful; *quivering;* raw; smarting; stinging; sensitive; tender; uncomfortable; *violent;* wrenching; *xiphodynia; yipes!;* zinging;
**sorrow** *(n.)*: anguish; attrition; burden; cheerlessness; distress; *ejulation;* forlornness; grief; heartbrokenness; inconsolableness; joylessness; katzenjammer; lamentation; mourning; *negativism;* overmuch ~; *piteousness; quivering;* ruefulness; regret; sorrowfulness; trouble; ululation; *vapors;* woe; *xtr. sad;* yearning; *zestlessness;*
**sorrow** *(v.)*: anguish; bewail; bemoan; be sad; cry; despair; *express grief;* feel sad; grieve; howl; *inconsolable; judder;* keen; lament; mourn; *noise;* outcry; *pine;* quail; regret; *repent;* shed tears; torment; *tearful;* ululate; *vociferate;* weep; wail; *xtr. sad;* yowl; *zing;* [*Ant.* sing]
**sorrowful** *(adj.)*: anguished; broken; cast down; distressed; elegiac; forlorn; grief-stricken; grieved; heartbroken; inconsolable; joyless; keening; low; lamentable; miserable; mournful; negative; *overcast;* piteous; *quivering;* regretful; rueful; sad; sorrowing; tristful; tearful; unhappy; upset; very sad; woeful; *xtr. sad;* yearnful; *zestless;*
**sort** *(n.)*: *analysis;* brand; breed; category; cast; designation; denomination; estate; fashion; genre; group; genus; *heading;* ilk; *jack;* kind; lot; label; make; manner; model; mold; *nature; name;* order; phylum; persuasion; *quarter;* rank; rating; species; strain; style; stripe; type; *unit;* variety; way; *x-class;* year-class; *zoological classification;*
**sort** *(v.)*: assort; arrange; alphabetize; break down; brand; catalog; categorize; classify; collate; divide; evaluate; file; group; have ~ed; index; *judge; kit;* list; make groups; *nicely order;* order; organize; put in order; *qualify;* rank; separate; sequence; systematize; tabulate; unitize; *valuate;* weed (out); *xfer;* yandy; *zone;*

**soul** *(n.)*: anima; being; consciousness; core; distillation; essence; entity; existence; fundamentality; *gist;* heart; inner-being; individual; immaterial part; inner man; jiva [Hind.]; kernel; *ka* [Egy.]; life; *makeup;* noncorporeal part; *ontology;* person; psyche; quintessence; *root;* self(-consciousness); *spirit; thing; underneath;* vital force; *within; xenenthesis;* yetzer [Heb.]; *zoe* [Gr.];

**soul-winning** *(n.)*: *action;* biblical witnessing; conversion; door-knocking; evangelism; fervency for souls; Gospel presentation; Great Commission; house visitation; *inviting people; Jesus;* knocking doors; leading souls to Christ; missionary work; *ministry;* neighborhood outreach; outreach; personal ~; *quest for souls;* reaching the lost; *salvation;* trying to win souls; *undertaking;* visitation; winning souls; witnessing; *xenagogy; yede;* zeal for souls;

**sound** *(adj.)*: accurate; *assured;* bona fide; concrete; dependable; ever-faithful; firm; good; healthy; hearty; infallible; justifiable; *keen;* legitimate; most faithful; non-shaky; orthodox; *perfect;* quatch; rock-solid; reliable; solid; trustworthy; tried-and-true; unfailing; unshakeable; veritable; well-tried; *xtry.; yieldless; zero problem;* [*Ant.* shaky]

**sound** *(n.)*: acoustics; *aloud;* bustle; blare; bedlam; clamor; clatter; din; euphony; fracas; feedback; fanfare; *groaning;* hubbub; hullabaloo; intonation; *jangle; knock;* loudness; *mutter; murmur;* noise; *overnoise;* pudder; peep; quatch [arch.]; reverberation; resonance; sonant; sonance; sonority; tone; uproar; unquiet; verberation; vocable; voice; *warble;* whisper; *xenophonia;* yammer; *zoink;* [*Ant.* silence]

**soundness** *(n.)*: accuracy; *bona fide;* concreteness; dependability; excellence; firmness; goodness; health; heartiness; infallibility; justifiableness; *keenness;* legitimacy; *most faithful;* non-shakiness; orthodoxy; *perfection; quartful [arch.];* reliability; stability; strength; trustworthiness; truth; unshakableness; verity; weal; *xtry.; yieldless; zero problem;* [*Ant.* shakiness]

**soup** *(n.)*: alphabet ~; broth; bisque; consommé; chowder; cream ~; *decoction; edibles;* fleshbroth; gumbo; homemade ~; hot ~; *Italian wedding ~; julienne;* kettle-broth; *liquid;* milk-pottage; noodle ~; okasi; *oxtail soup;* pottage; potage; *quibebe; repast; stock;* thick ~; *unopened can of ~;* vichyssoise; *wonton soup;* xurpa; Yankee bean ~; zuppe [It.];

**sour** *(adj.)*: acidic; acidulous; biting; cutting; disagreeable; extreme; *frowzy; gone off;* harsh; intense; jolting; keen; lemony; much-soured; *nippy;* overpowering; pungent; quarred; *rancid;* sourish; strong; tangy; tart; unsweetened; unpleasant; vinegary; well-soured; *xtry. ~; yucky;* zesty; zingy; [*Ant.* sweet]

**source** *(n.)*: *advent;* basis; beginning; cause; cache; derivation; extraction; font; fountain; foundation; grounds; heart; hoard; inducement; *issue; justification; kickoff;* lode; mine; *nibiliary;* origin; *proceeding;* quarry; root; reserve; re~; starting point; store; stock; spring; supply; *traduction;* underlying cause; vein; venter; well(spring); *xenenthesis;* yoni [Skr.]; *zygogenesis;*

**sovereign** *(adj.)*: autonomous; absolute; *boss;* controlling; dominant; eminent; free; foremost; greatest; highest; independent; in control; *jurisdiction;* key; kingly; leading; loftiest; most high; maximal; No. 1; outstanding; overriding; prime; predominant; *queenly;* ranking; self-determining; supreme; top(most); ultimate; *vital;* weighty; xtry.; *yet unsurpassed;* zenithal;

**sovereignty** *(n.)*: authority; *bishopric;* control; dominion; empery; first place; governance; headship; influence; jurisdiction; kingship; lordship; monarchy; *ne plus ultra* [L.]; oversight; power; providence; queenship [fem.]; reign; rule; supervision; supreme power; *the* throne; umpirage; *vizierate;* wardenship; workings; *xenagogy;* yard; zenith; [*Ant.* servitude]

**sow** *(v.)*: *afforest;* bury; bestrew; bescatter; broadcast; cover; conceal; dibble; deposit; disseminate; entomb; establish; fix; ground; hide; heel in; implant; inseminate; intersperse; inhume; inter; *jacket;* kippin; lodge; *move; make; nuzzle;* overspread (-scatter); plant; propagate; *quat [arch.];* reset; re~; seed; scatter; seminate; throw seed; *underfurrow; verge;* whelm; *xenotransplant;* yird; zet [dial.];

**space** *(n. area)*: area; berth; capacity; dimensions; extent; field; ground; hugeness; immediate ~; jurisdiction; *kray* [Rus.]; *legroom;* latitude; leeway; municipality; niche; neighborhood; open ~; place; qua; quarters; room; range; span; territory; ubiety; volume; ward; *x-section; you* [Chin.]; *zone;*

**space** *(n. cosmos)*: aerospace; blackness of ~; cosmos; deep ~; ether; four corners of the universe [poet.]; galaxy; heavens; infinity; *Jupiter and beyond;* kosmos; last frontier; macrocosm; *nebula;* outer ~; planets; *quasar; rocket;* stars; second heaven; *trail;* universe; vacuum of space; world; *x-ray galaxy; yu* [Chin.]; *zone;*

**spacious** *(adj.)*: abundant; ample; airy; big; capacious; commodious; disproportionate; extensive; full-size; giant; generous; huge; immense; jumbo-sized; king-size; large; massive; *not cramped;* open; oversize; prodigious; quantitative; roomy; sizable; tremendous; uncramped; voluminous; wide; XL; *Ymir; zaftig;* [Ant. snug]

**span** *(n.)*: arch; breadth; clearance; depth; distance; expanse; farness; gap; height; interconnect; *juncture; knots;* length; mileage; *nitch [Scot.];* overall length; parsecs; *quantity;* reach; size; traverse; *units;* vault; width; wideness; *xenograft;* yardage; *zone;*

**span** *(v.)*: arch; bridge; connect; cross; *do;* extend; fix together; go across; hook up; interconnect; join; *knit;* link; move across; *nitch [Scot.];* overlie; pass over; *quicken;* reach across; reunite; set together; tie together; traverse; unite; vault; *wed; xenograft;* yoke; zet [dial.];

**spank** *(v.)*: afflict; beat; belt; blister; chasten; chastise; discipline; *educate;* flail; flog; *guide;* hit; *inflict; jolt;* knock; lick; *maul; nail; open ones eyes;* paddle; quab; *rap;* strap; switch; thrash; train; tan one's hide; take to the woodshed; *use the rod; virge;* whoop; whip; wallop; *x-sect; yedder; zonk;* [Ant. salute]

**spanking** *(n.)*: attitude adjustment; beating; blistering; *the* belt; chastening; chastisement; caning; corporal punishment; discipline; *education;* flogging; *guidance;* hide-tanning; *infliction; jankers [mil.]; knoppler;* licking; *much-needed ~; nailing;* over-the-knee ~; paddling; quabbing; *the* rod; strapping; tanning; using the rod; virge; whooping; whipping; *x-sect; yard* [arch.]; *zonking;* [Ant. salute]

**spare** *(v.)*: allow to go; *bail out;* cut loose; deliver; except; free; give mercy; have mercy; *indemnify; justify;* keep safe; loose; let off; *mercy;* not condemn; *overabundant;* preserve; *quicken;* release; reserve; restore; save from; show mercy; turn loose; uphold; *vivificate;* waive; *xtr.; yield; zero selfishness;*

**spark** *(n.)*: arc; blue ~; coruscation; discharge; ember; electrical ~; flash; glint; *hot;* incineration; *jag; kindle;* luminous particle; *match flame; nightfire; overburn;* particle; *quick-match;* rising ~; sparkle; twinkle; *ustulation; volcano; welding ~; xfer;* yellow ~; *zap;* [see fire]

**spark** *(v.)*: alight; blow sparks; coruscate; deflagrate; emit sparks; flare up; glint; *heat;* ignite; *jump;* kindle; light(en); make sparks; *nightfire; overburn; pyre; quick-match;* rekindle; *start;* sparkle; throw sparks; *upward; verge; whoosh; xfer; yellow ~; zap;*

**sparse** *(adj.)*: austere; bare; *close;* dear; exceptional; few(-and-far-between); gant; hard to find; infrequent; inadequate; jimp; keenly ~; light; meager; measly; nippet; obscure; paltry; *queer;* rare; scarce; scant(y); thin; uncommon; valuable; *wheen* [arch.]; *xtry.; you-beaut [Aus.]; zero;* [Ant. superabundant]

**speak** *(v.)*: articulate; address; bespeak; communicate; declare; declaim; express; enunciate; *foremention;* gab; *give;* hold forth; impart; indicate; intimate; jaw; *key in;* let out; mention; *notify;* noise; observe; orate; pronounce; pipe up; quoth; relate; remark; ramble; say; state; tell; utter; verbalize; voice; word; *xenophonia;* yak; *zero in;* [Ant. shut up]

**speaker** *(n.)*: addresser; *blurter;* communicator; declaimer; demagogue; expresser; fluent speaker; gabber; guest ~; homilist; informer; jabberer; jawsmith; keynote ~; lecturer; *man;* mouthpiece; *narrator;* orator; pontificator; proclaimer; public ~: *quoter;* ranter; remarker; speech-maker; spokesman; talker; utterer; vocalizer; worder; *xenophonia;* yakker; *zeug [G.];*

**spear** *(n.)*: assegai; *blade;* cateia; demi-lance; espontoon; fishspear; gaff; harpoon; halberd; impaler; javelin; *knife;* lance; *magari-yari [Jap.];* needle; *offensive weapon;* pike; point; poker; *qiang* [Chin.]; rapparee; spontoon; tragula; uchine; *verutum [Gr.]; weapon;* xyston; *yari [Jap.];* zaghaya;

**special** *(adj.)*: amazing; best; celebrated; distinguished; especial; elite; exclusive; extraordinary; famous; great; highly regarded; important; *jolly good;* key; *king;* laudable; main; notable; outstanding; prime; prominent; *queen;* remarkable; reserved; significant; top; uncommon; unique; very ~; wonderful; xtry.; *you-beaut* [Aus.]; *zaikai [Jap.];*

**specific** *(adj.)*: *assigned; by name;* certain; designated; distinguished; distinct; definite; exact(ing); exceptional; especial; explicit; *focused;* given; *hand-picked;* individual; identifiable; *just;* known; limited; marked; named; *one;* particular; precise; peculiar; *qualifying;* respective; singular; tagged; unique; unambiguous; *very;* well-defined; *xtry.;* yarked; *zero in;*

**specification** *(n.)*: arrangement; blueprint; condition; description; details; exact definition; expectation; fine point; gauge; habilitation; instruction; *judgment;* key ~; limitation; measurement; notation; orders; plan; proviso; provision; qualifications; requirement; stipulation; specifying; terms; vitals; wanted design; *x-required; yardstick; zero option;*

**specify** *(v.)*: assign; *best choice;* choose; designate; denote; earmark; forechoose; give choice; *hand pick;* indicate; indigitate; *judge; know;* label; mention by name; name; ordain; point out; qualify; refer to; signify; show; stipulate; tag; *utter; use;* vest; *well-chosen; x; yield name; zero in;*

**speck** *(n.)*: *atom;* bit; blot; chit; crumb; dot; *engrained;* fleck; freckle; fragment; germ; grain; *hair;* iota; jaup; kink; little mark; mark; naeve; ounce; (pin)point; pip; pimple; polka-dot; particle; quirk; *round spot;* speckle; spot; tittle; unsightly spot; very small piece; wale; wem; X; *yedder;* zona;

**spectator** *(n.)*: attestant; beholder; considerer; *crowd;* descrier; eyewitness; *fan;* gazer; *gathering; group;* hearers; inspectors; janata [Asia]; keeker; looker-on; *multitude;* mass; *nonplayers;* onlooker; percipient; *quelet [arch.]; regarder;* seer; *sightseer; throng;* unbiased observer; viewer; watcher; witness; *x.; yain [arch.]; zoa;* [*see* fan]

**spectrum** *(n.)*: array; breadth; continuum; *dihexahedral prism;* extent; full array; gamut; hues; iris; *jumble; key;* line ~; matrix; nexus; outlay; prism; palette; *queue;* range; rainbow; spread; *train;* ubiety; variety; *water-gall;* x-ray ~; *yield;* Zeeman effect;

**speculate** *(v.)*: assume; bet; conjecture; deduce; estimate; figure; guess; hypothesize; imagine; judge; *know;* lucubrate; muse; *notion; occur;* presume; *question;* reckon; suppose; think; theorize; *use brain; venture;* wonder; *xenodiagnose; yeme; zazen;* [*Ant.* substantiate]

**speculation** *(n.)*: assumption; bet; conjecture; deduction; estimation; figuring; guess; hypothesis; imagining; judgment; *knowledge;* lucubration; musing; *notion; occurring;* presumption; *question;* reckoning; supposition; surmise; thought; theory; *use brain; view;* wondering; *xenodiagnosis; yeme; zazen;* [*Ant.* substantiation]

**speech** *(n.)*: address; bespeaking; communication; discourse; declamation; dithyramb; elocution; expression; formal ~; *filibuster; glossa;* homily; *inaugural address;* indiction; jeremiad; *kerygma;* lecture; message; monologue; manner of speaking; *narration;* oration; oratory; public address; proclamation; pontification; parlance; philippic; *quotation;* recitation; rhetoric; sermon; statement; spiel; talk; utterance; vocalization; *valediction;* word(s); *xenophonia; yawner [off.]; zinger [slang];* [*Ant.* speechlessness]

**speechless** *(adj.)*: astonished; awestruck; bowled over; confounded; cat's got one's tongue; dumbstruck; *enchanted;* flabbergasted; gaping; hushed; inarticulate; incredulous; jolted; knocked for six; looking aghast; mute; non-speaking; nonplused; nonverbal; overwhelmed; perplexed; quiet; rapt; surprised; stunned; shocked; thunderstruck; unspeaking; uncommunicative; voiceless; wonderstruck; wordless; *xtry.; yareless; zitti* [It.]; [*Ant.* strident]

**speechlessness** *(n.)*: absolute quiet; bowling over; confoundedness; dumb(founded)ness; *extinguished; fallow;* gaping; holding one's tongue; inability to speak; *jarless;* keeping quiet; *lull;* muteness; non-speech; over-quietness; perplexity; quietness; *resting;* silence; taciturnity; *unspoken;* voicelessness; wordlessness; *xtry.; yerking; zero speech;* [*Ant.* speech]

**speed** *(n.)*: agility; acceleration; briskness; celerity; clip; dexterity; expedition; fastness; grease [slang]; haste; hurriedness; *intensity;* jildi [mil.]; keenness; liveliness; lightfootedness; movement; *Mach;* nimbleness; *overhastiness;* precipitance; promptness; quickness; rapidity; speediness; swiftness; tall stepping [slang]; *uninhibited;* velocity; *whipping; x-speed; yar;* zip; [*Ant.* slowness]

**spell** *(n.)*: anathema; bewitchment; charm; curse; cantrip; conjuration; demonifuge; enchantment; execration; fascination; glamour; hex; hypnosis; incantation; invocation; juju; jinx; *karakia* [Maori]; *lethe;* magic; malediction; night-spell; *out;* pox; *prayer; plague;* qualm [arch.]; *reliquary;* summoning; *trance; under;* voodoo; witchery; weird [Scot.]; *x-fix;* yoga trance; *zauber* [G.];
**spend** *(v.)*: allot; bestow; buy; consume; disburse; drop; drain; deplete; expend; exhaust; fork over; give (out); hand out; invest; *jiggy [Br.]; kill;* lay out; lavish; *mis~; make payment; non-retention;* outlay; pay out; *quaff;* run through; squander; splurge; throw away; use (up); unload; *vest;* waste; *xfer; yield;* zap; [*Ant.* save]
**spendthrift** *(n.)*: abuser; big-spender; compulsive shopper; dissipater; *extravagant spender;* fritterer; *giver;* high roller; *incontinent; justifier; kill;* lavisher; losel; misspender; *non-retention;* overspender; prodigal; profligate; *quick spender; reckless;* squanderer; spender; *thriftless; unthrifty; vanish;* wastrel; waster; wastethrift; *xfer; yielder up; zeroizer;* [*Ant.* skinflint]
**spice** *(n.)*: additive; bite; color; *dill;* élan; flavor; gusto; herb; hotness; hot ~; ingredient; *jigger;* kick; liveliness; *mace;* nippiness; oomph; punch; pizzazz; *quantity;* relish; seasoning; snap; tang; *unit;* vigor; *wedge; xacuti;* yarb [dial.]; zest; zing; zip;
**spice** *(v.)*: add zing; bespice; color; devil; enliven; flavor; give a kick; *hotness;* improve; jazz up; *keen;* liven up; mull; *new-vamp; optimize;* pep up; pepper; *quintessentialize; revamp;* season; ~ up; *salt;* tincture; use ~; vivify; *well-spiced; xfer; yarken;* zest;
**spicy** *(adj.)*: *ablaze;* burning; curried; deviled; exciting; extreme; flavorful; fiery; gingery; hot; intense; jolting; keenly ~; lively; *mouth on fire;* nippy; oniony; piquant; peppery; quite hot; racy; strong; tangy; *unpleasant; vivacious;* well-seasoned; *xtry.;* yarb-filled [dial.]; zesty; [*Ant.* savorless]
**spike** *(n.)*: annular nail; brad; calk; *duplex; eye bolt;* fastener; galvanized ~; hobnail; iron ~; joist; *knife;* lance; *marline-spike;* nail; oval brad; point; piton; paal; quill; rurp; stake; tent ~; *U-bolt;* veneer pin; wire nail; xyston; *yoke;* zinc-coated nail;
**spill** *(n.)*: accident; bung; catastrophe; drip; dribble; discharge; effusion; flow; gathering; *heap;* inundation; *juicy; kettle-hole;* leakage; mishap; *non-dry;* overflow; overrun; puddle; *quai;* run-over; slash; slick; spillage; spill-over; *tarn; underground ~; vat;* wet spot; *xyrisic; yeo; zone;*
**spill** *(v.)*: *affuse; bump;* course; cascade; dump; drop; discharge; effuse; flow; fall; gush; *head out;* influx; *jet;* knock over; let fall; make ~; *non-retention;* overflow; overrun; overspill; outpour; pour; *quick-fall;* run out; splatter; stream; slosh; *tumble;* throw; *use up; vent;* wash; *xuld [arch.]; yield;* zip out;
**spin** *(n.)*: alternation; backspin; cycle; circling; *down~;* eddy; english; furling; gyration; going around; hurtling; *interchange;* jurtling; *keep turning;* looping; movement; nutation; orbit; purling; querling; rotation; spinning; turning; twirling; *up~;* volting; whirl; *x-ing; yede [arch.];* zipping around;
**spin** *(v.)*: *around;* back~; becurl; circle; *downward;* eddy; flip; furl; gyrate; go around; hurtle; incurvate; *jee; keel;* loop; move around; nutate; orb; purl; querl; reel; roll; rotate; revolve; swirl; twirl; turn; trill; *under~;* upsweep; volt; whirl; whorl; wheel; *x-ing;* yede; zwoosh; zip; [*Ant.* stop]
**spirit** *(n.)*: anima; apparition; being; consciousness; core; distillation; essence; energy; entity; fundamentality; ghost; heart; immaterial part; inner man; jumby; *ka* [Egy.]; life-consciousness; manes; non-corporeal part; *oomph;* presence; personality; quintessence; revenant; *soul; thing;* undead; vital force; verve; wraith; *xenenthesis; yetzer [Heb.];* zip; zumby;
**spiritual** *(adj.)*: aery; bodiless; *celestial;* divine; ethereal; eternal; fey; Godward; godly; heavenly-minded; immaterial; *Jesus; kramat [Arab.]; lofty;* mystical; numinous; noncorporeal; nonphysical; otherworldly; preternatural; *quoad sacra* [L.]; religious; spiritually-minded; supernal; supernatural; transcendent; transmundane; ultramundane; unearthly; unworldly; *virtuous;* worshipful; *xtry.; yonder;* zoic;
**spirituality** *(n.)*: angelicalness; blamelessness; Christlikeness; character; divineness; *ever-faithful;* fear of God; godliness; heavenly-mindedness; impeccability; justness; *keenness; love;* morality; *nobleness;* other-worldliness; piety; purity; *quality;* religiousness; righteousness; saintliness; *truthfulness;* uprightness; virtue; walk with God; *Xty.; yieldedness;* zaddik [Heb.];

**spite** *(n.)*: animosity; bitterness; contempt; dislike; enmity; fight; gall; hostility; ill-will; jadedness; *knocking;* loathing; malice; nastiness; odium; polarity; querulousness; rancor; rivalry; spitefulness; *tetchiness;* unkindness; virulence; withstanding; xenophobia; *yawping; zoilism;*
**spiteful** *(adj.)*: atrocious; bitter; contemptible; despiteful; disdainful; embittered; foul; galsome; hateful; inimical; jaded; kindless; loathsome; malicious; mean; nasty; odious; pernicious; querulous; resentful; scornful; sore; splenetic; terrible; unkind; ugly; vengeful; wicked; xenophobic; *yucky; zoilean;*
**splash** *(v.)*: *aqua;* bespatter; *cover;* dabble; douse; *emit;* flick; *get wet; hurl;* indrench; jaup; ker-plash; lap; madefy; *non-dry;* overwhelm; plash; *quench; ripple;* spatter; splatter; swash; sprinkle; *throw; undried;* vault; wet; *xuld [arch.];* yote; *zip;*
**splinter** *(n.)*: amount; billet; crock(-shard); daud; *ens;* flinder; *gall;* hunk; *iota;* junt; *kernel;* lamia; morsel; *nugget;* offshoot; piece; quill; rift; *remnant;* sliver; shard; *tidbit; under; vestige;* wedge; wood ~; *xylon; zinger;*
**split** *(n.)*: *apart;* break; breach; cleft; division; divorce; exscinding; fork; fissure; gap; grike; hiatus; incision; *isolation; judicial separation;* keeping separate; leaving; *marching away; non-unity; opening;* parting; quinquefid; rift; rent; separation; tear; unyoking; *vacating;* wedge; *x-section;* yawn; zipping apart;
**split** *(v.)*: ax; bisect; break; branch; bifurcate; cleave; divide; divorce; exect; fissure; fork; *gap;* hack; halve; hew; incise; *jigsaw; knife;* lop; *miter; nick;* open; part; prescind; quadrifurcate; recise; rive; rip; sever; separate; slice; tear in two; truncate; unyoke; vell; whack; wedge; x-sect; yerk; *zip; zone;*
**spoil** *(v. despoil)*: appropriate; boot; *carry off;* despoil; excoriate; freeboot; gut; harrow; *incursion; junk; knock off [slang];* loot; maraud; *nobble; overexploit;* pillage; plunder; *quash;* ransack; rob; ravage; sack; take; *unlade;* violate; whomp; xfer; yank; zap;
**spoil** *(v. go bad)*: addle; break down; corrupt; decay; erode; fester; fail; go bad; hoar; impair; *jade; ketty; labelfaction;* mortify; *necrosis; off;* oxidize; putrefy; queer; rot; ruin; *sink;* taint; turn; *undo; vile;* welk; *xylaria;* yellow; *zorch;*
**spoil** *(v. indulge)*: accommodate; baby; coddle; cater to; cosset; dote over; epicurize; fuss over; gratify; humor; indulge; *justify;* keep happy; let; mollycoddle; *nod;* oblige; pander; pamper; *quell;* regale; relish; revel; ruin; suffer; splurge; satisfy; tolerate; take pleasure in; treat; *unhindered;* volutate; wallow; wreck; *xuld [arch.];* yield to; *zero opposition;*
**spoils** *(n.)*: *assets;* booty; cache; *doubloons; emeralds;* fortune; goods; gain; *hoard;* ill-gotten gains; *jewels; king's ransom;* loot; *lares and penates; money; moolah; notes; obol;* plunder; pickings; prey; pillage; prize; quarry; reward; riches; swag; *stolen goods;* treasure; *uberty;* valuables; wealth; *x-div;* yield; *zechins;*
**spontaneous** *(adj.)*: artless; *bang!;* cueless; direct; extemporaneous; free; gut; *haphazard;* impulsive; just as it comes up; *keen; like that;* momentary; natural; off-the-cuff; on the fly; out-of-nowhere; *put on the spot; quick;* reflexive; spur-of-the-moment; *think-as-you-go;* unprompted; voluntary; winging it; *xtry.; yare; zip;*
**spool** *(n.)*: *app;* bobbin; coil; cable-tier; capstan; *draw; enwrap;* filature; *gird;* hose reel; hasp; *intertwine;* jack; *knittle;* line-reel; metal reel; nylon ~; *organize;* pirn; quill; reel; spindle; take-up; utility ~; *volution;* windle; wooden ~; *x-ing; yarn-gatherer;* zein- ~;
**sport** *(n.)*: athletics; activity; ballgame; competition; disport; diversion; exercise; field ~; gymnastics; game; *horseplay;* intervarsity; junior varsity; *knockabout [Br.];* lacrosse; match; non-competitive ~; Olympics; pastime; playoff; pursuit; *quiz; round; rivalry;* (summer) sports; team game; *training; upmanship;* varsity; winter ~; X Games; yannigan; *zorbing;*
**spot** *(n.)*: abnormality; blot(ch); blemish; blister; blaze; chit; dot; dapple; defect; eyesore; fleck; freckle; ferntickle; flaw; *grease ~; hue; ingrained;* jaup; kink; *line;* mark; mottle; mote; macula; naeve; *ocellate;* pimple; polka-dot; patch; pip; quirk; *round ~; ring;* speck; stain; smudge; splotch; *tarnish;* unsightly ~; vice; verruca; wart; welt; wale; wem; X; *yedder;* zona;

**spot** *(v.)*: *alter;* bespot; bedrop; bespeckle; color; *checker;* dot; dapple; drop; embrue; fleck; ground in; *hue;* imbrue; *jaup; kink; line;* mark; maculate; *naeve; ocellate;* punctulate; *quirk; ruddle;* stain; speckle; *tarnish; unsightly;* variegate; *write; x; yellow; zone;* [*see* see]
**spotless** *(adj.)*: absterged; blameless; blemishless; clean; chaste; dirt-free; decent; expurgated; fair; fine; guiltless; honorable; immaculate; innocent; *just right;* keen; lily-white; *moral;* nice; orderly; pure; pristine; qualmless; righteous; sparkling; stainless; taintless; unspotted; unstained; virtuous; white; without spot; *xtry.;* yet untainted; *zero blemish;* [*Ant.* spotted]
**spotlight** *(v.)*: accentuate; bring to the fore; concentrate on; draw attention to; emphasize; focus; give emphasis to; highlight; illumine; *jump out;* keep emphasis on; lay emphasis upon; make more noticeable; *notice; overemphasize;* point up; *quite overstress; red letter;* stress; *target;* underscore; *value; weight; xtry. emphasis; yed;* zero in;
**spotty** *(adj.)*: abnormal; bespotted; blotchy; brindled; chit-filled; dappled; dotted; eyespotted; freckled; *grease-stained;* herky-jerky; irregular; *jaupy; kinked; large spots;* mottled; marked; naevose; *ocellate;* pimply; polka-dot; patchy; *quirky; ringed;* spotted; speckled; stippled; splotchy; tabby; unregular; variegated; wealy; whaly; *X; yedder;* zitty; [*Ant.* spotless]
**spouse** *(n.)*: ally; best friend; better half; beloved; bride [fem.]; companion; dear one; *endeared;* fellow(helper); goodman [masc.]; goodwife [fem.]; helper; helpmate [fem.]; honey; husband [masc.]; intimate; joint-partner; kith [pl.]; love; mate; marriage partner; nuptial partner; other half; partner; *quixotic; romance;* sidekick; soul mate; *trusted friend; upholder; very special;* wife [fem.]; *xenophile;* yokemate; *zoon;* [*see* husband, wife]
**spout** *(n.)*: avenue; bibcock; blowhole [zoo.]; channel; chute; column; discharge; duct; emission point; funnel; fountain; geyser; *hydrant; instrument;* jet; *key; location;* mouth; nozzle; *neck;* opening; outline; petcock; *pipe; quantity control;* release; rose; stream; spurt; tap; tube; *unit;* valve; water~; *x-switch; yield; zeug;*
**spout** *(v.)*: accelerate; burst; course; cascade; discharge; emit; flow; gush; hurl; issue; jet; *kite;* leap; *move; naid;* outpour; pour out; *quicken;* rush; spew; spurt; shoot; throw; *uprush;* vomit out; wash; *xuld [arch.];* yield; *zwoosh;*
**spray** *(v.)*: atomize; besprinkle; cannonade; discharge; emit; flow; gush; hurl; issue; jet; *kite;* light ~; mist; naid; *overspread;* plash; *quench;* ret; squirt; splatter; splash; sprinkle; *throw; uprush;* vaporize; wet; *xuld [arch.]; yote; zip;*
**spread** *(v. smear)*: apply; anoint; besmear; butter; cover; coat; daub; distribute; even out; extend; fan out; fill; glaze; *grease;* hand- ~; infucate; *jigger; kirtle:* lay on; mantle; *non-containment;* over~; *oil;* perfuse; plaster; *quab;* rub; smooth; smear; slather; scatter; ted; transfer; utterly cover; *use; volume;* wipe; xfer; *yain [arch.]; zero containment;*
**spread** *(v. proliferate)*: advance; broaden; broadcast; cover; disburse; extend; expand; fan out; grow; *heighten;* increase; *jump up; keep growing;* largen; multiply; *non-centralized;* outstretch; over~; *outgrow;* proliferate; permeate; propagate; *quadruplicate;* rise; reach; stretch; scatter; suffuse; take off; travel; telecast; *thrive;* unfold; *volume;* wax greater; widen; *XL;* yote; *zoom;* [*Ant.* shrink]
**spring** *(n. fountain)*: artesian well; beginning; brine- ~; baths; cascade; cistern; discharge; emanation; font; fount(ain); geyser; head~; hot ~; issue; jet; keld; *lake;* mineral ~; *namma hole;* origin; *procession; qanat;* resource; *reservoir;* spout; source; thermae; *upsurge;* venter; well~; water~; *xenenthesis;* yoni [Skr.]; *zemzem;* [*see* source]
**sprinkle** *(v.)*: asperge; be~; christen; dot; dash; dew; drizzle; disperse; effuse; flock; freckle; get wet; *humectate;* intersperse; jawp; *keep wet; lap;* mist; mizzle; moisten; *non-dry; overspread;* plash; pepper; *queven [arch.];* rain; resperse; splash; spatter; splatter; scatter; sparge; spray; spritz; tinkle; trickle; *undried; vapor;* wet; xpn.; yote; *zip;*

**sprout** *(v.)*: arise; bud; burgeon; climb; develop; emerge; flourish; grow; germinate; *have;* issue forth; jump up; *keep growing;* luxuriate; mature; *nourish;* offshoot; push up; pop up; *quantum growth;* rise; shoot; spring; *take off;* upshoot; vegetate; wax greater; XL; *yain* [arch.]; *zoom up;* [*Ant.* shrink]

**spurn** *(v.)*: alienate; blackball; cast away; disdain; exclude; forbear; give cold shoulder; hold in contempt; ignore; jilt; kick; look down on; make feel bad; not accept; nix; ostracize; push away; quit on; reject; snub; turn away from; *unkind; veto;* ward off; *xenize; yard* [arch.]; *zero out;*

**spy** *(n.)*: agent; beagle; CIA agent; double agent; detective; emissary; fink; *gazer; hearer;* informant; informer; infiltrator; intelligence [pl.]; *jobber;* KGB agent; *looker;* mole; nark; *observer;* outsider; plant; peacher; quadruplator; reconnoiter; scout; secret agent; saboteur; tout [slang]; undercover agent; vedette; watcher; *wiretapper;* X; *yard; zarp;*

**spy** *(v.)*: *appear incognito; bug;* closely watch; descry; espy; eavesdrop; face; gaze; have a look; inform; infiltrate; *jerque;* keep eye on; look; listen; mole; nark; overhear; observe; peek; peach; *quietly observe;* reconnoiter; see; scout; *take in; undercover;* view; watch; *wiretap; worm;* X; *yeme; zero in;*

**spying** *(n.)*: agents; *beholding;* CIA; detective work; espionage; *finding;* government intelligence; human intelligence; intelligence; *jobbing;* KGB; *looking;* military intelligence; *nark; observation;* peaching; quadruplation; reconnaissance; scouting; *sabotage;* touting [slang]; undercover work; *vedette; wiretapping;* X; *yard; zarp;*

**squad** *(n.)*: army; band; crew; detachment; *elect group;* force; group; *host; ingathering; jam* [slang]; *kit* [coll.]; lot; mass; maniple; *men;* number; out-crew; party; posse; quantity; roundup; rally; rabble; set; team; unit; *variety;* workforce; x-men; *yokefellows; zouave;*

**squander** *(v.)*: abuse; blow; consume; dissipate; eat (up); exhaust; *extravagant;* fritter away; go through; *hand away; incontinent; just give away;* kill; lavish; *lose;* misspend; misuse; *non-retention;* overspend; pour down the drain; *quaff; reduced;* scatter; slather; *spend;* throw away; use up; *vanish;* waste; *xfer; yield up; zeroize;* [*Ant.* save]

**squanderer** *(n.)*: *abuser;* big-spender; compulsive shopper; dissipater; *extravagant spender;* fritterer; *giver;* high roller; *incontinent; jack; kill;* lavisher; losel; misspender; *non-retention;* overspender; prodigal; *quick spender; reckless;* spendthrift; *thriftless; unthrifty; vanish;* wastrel; waster; wastethrift; *xfer; yielder up; zeroizer;* [*Ant.* saver]

**square** *(n.)*: *area;* box; cube; *diamond;* equilateral; four-sided figure; geometric ~; *heptagon; item; joined; kind; lozenge; mathematics; non-circular; orange ~;* polygon; parallelogram; quadrangle; quadrilateral; rectangle; rectangular; rhombus; *shape; squircle;* tetragon; unit ~; vector-drawn ~; *white ~; xyxy; yellow ~;* zenzic; [*Ant.* sphere]

**squash** *(v.)*: apply pressure; annihilate; bear down; bash; crush; cram; compact; compress; defeat; depress; extinguish; exert pressure; flatten; grind; hush up; hold down; *hurt; injure;* jam; kibble; kill; levigate; mash; *nullify;* overply; put down; press; quash; ram; squeeze; squish; squelch; smash; tamp; *upthrust; vice;* wreck; *xuld* [arch.]; *yerk; zap;*

**squeeze** *(v.)*: apply pressure; bear down; clutch; clamp; compress; constrict; depress; extrude; express; flatten; force; grip; hug; *impel;* jam; kibble; *levigate;* mush; *nullify; overcome;* press; quash; ram; squash; squish; scrunch; tamp; *upthrust; vice;* wedge; wring; *xowyn* [arch.]; *yank down; zap;*

**stab** *(v.)*: *afflict;* bore; bayonet; cut; dig; empierce; *fix* [arch.]; go in; gore; hole; impale; jab; knife; lance; make hole; nail; open; poke; pierce; penetrate; *quill;* run through; stick; spear; transfix; thrust in; *undercut; ventilate;* wound; *xylotomy;* yerk; *zing;*

**stability** *(n.)*: abiding; balance; constancy; consistency; continuity; dependability; evenness; endurance; firmness; fixedness; gaplessness; high degree of ~; immovability; *juste millieu* [F.]; keeping steady; lastingness; moderation; non-varying; trustworthiness; persistence; permanence; *quenchless;* regularity; relentless; steadiness; *trueness;* uniformity; unbrokenness; veracity; waverlessness; *x-cending;* yieldlessness; *zero deterring;* [*Ant.* shakiness]

**stabilize** *(v.)*: alleviate; ballast; balance; calm; correct; counterbalance; *decelerate;* equalize; fix; give stability to; harmonize; *improve; just keep it steady; keep;* level; maintain; make stable; normalize; ossify; poise; palliate; *quiet;* regularize; steady; tranquilize; uphold; *vanquish; wind down; x-out; yield; zeroize;* [*Ant.* shake up]

**stable** *(n. barn)*: *area;* barn; *cowshed;* dairy ~; ecurie; *farm; grange;* hostry; horse ~; inclosure; jacal; kipsie [Aus.]; livery- ~; *milking barn; nitch;* outbuilding; place; *quinta;* red barn; *receptacle;* stall; *two-story barn;* utility building; vaccary; *woodshed; x-house; yakutat hut; zayat;*

**stable** *(adj. steady)*: abiding; balanced; constant; dependable; even; fixed; gapless; highly ~; inexorable; *jusqu'au bout* [F.]; *keeping up;* lasting; measured; non-changing; never-ending; ongoing; persistent; perpetual; *quenchless;* regular; relentless; steady; stabile; trustworthy; uniform; unfaltering; unwavering; undeviating; unbroken; very consistent; without deviation; waverless; *x-cending;* yieldless; *zero change;* [*Ant.* shaky]

**stack** *(n.)*: accumulation; amassment; batch; bunch; cluster; collection; deposit; *enlargement;* full load; gathering; group; heap; *ingathering; juba* [L.]; kit; load; mound; number; *overabundance;* pile; quantity; respository; *ream;* stockpile; tussock; *unit;* volume; wad; wagonload; *xtry. pile;* yelm; *zet [arch.];*

**stack** *(v.)*: amass; accumulate; bank; build up; collect; cumulate; deposit; enlarge; *fill;* gather; heap; increase; *jump up; keep growing;* lay up; mound; *number; overgrow;* pile; *quadruplicate;* reposit; store up; stockpile; *take off;* upbuild; *volume;* wax larger; XL; *yain* [arch.]; *zoom;*

**staff** *(n. rod)*: alpenstock; baton; bill; crook; cane; dagger- ~; engel~; ferule; field- ~; grain~; hand~; *instrument;* jambee; kebbie; langet; malacca; nibby; officer's ~; pole; pack~; quarter~; rod; stick; shepherd's ~; tipstaff; *ununke* [Afr.]; *virgulate;* wad- ~; walking stick; *xylon;* yam stick; *zagaye;*

**stage** *(n. platform)*: area; *the* boards; center ~; dais; elevated ~; floor; *the* footlights; gallery; *hall; in front of everyone; job;* kinema; lower ~; *limelight;* main ~; *nook; overhang;* platform; plinth; proscenium; *quarterdeck;* rostrum; raised platform; stand; soapbox; tribune; upper platform; *venue;* wooden platform; *x-section; yard; zone;*

**stagger** *(v.)*: alternate; bewilder; *bending;* creep; crawl; dither; edge; falter; gimp; hobble; halt; inch; *jiffle; knock;* limp; lurch; *move; non-stable;* oscillate; *plod;* quaddle; reel; stumble; sway; totter; *uneven;* vacillate; wobble; *xfer;* yaw; zigzag; [*see* bewilder]

**stagnant** *(adj.)*: at rest; becalmed; calm; dead; eased; fixed; groggy; heavy; inactive; jibbed; *kaput;* lifeless; motionless; non-agitated; non-progressing; obsolescent; passive; quiet; relaxed; still; torpid; unstirred; vegetative; *waiting; x'ed;* yet unmoving; *zero movement;* [*Ant.* stirred]

**stagnate** *(v.)*: abate; becalm; calm; cease to flow; decline; ease; fester; go stale; halt; idle; jade; *kaput;* languish; minish; not budge; obsolesce; *putrefy;* quail; recede; stand; sit; stop; *unstirred;* vegetate; wane; *xerosis;* yield; *zeroize;* [*Ant.* stir]

**staid** *(adj.)*: assured; *bendless;* composed; calm; cool; collected; demure; even-keeled; firm; grave; *heavy;* invariable; jarless; *keep going;* long-faced; matter-of-fact; non-volatile; *overconfident;* poised; quiet; resolute; steady; sedate; self-assured; tranquil; unruffled; very ~; weighty; *xttr. calm;* yieldless; zoetic; [*Ant.* stirred]

**stain** *(n.)*: abnormality; blot(ch); blemish; coloration; discoloration; eyesore; flaw; *grease spot; halftone;* infucation; ironmold; jaup; *ketchup* ~; lentigo; mark; naeve; *off-color;* patch; *quirk; ring;* spot; smudge; smear; tarnish; taint; unsightly ~; *vice;* wem; xanthochromia; xanthosis (discoloration of skin); yellow; *zona;* [*see* vilify]

**stain** *(v.)*: attaint; blot; blemish; color(ate); discolor; dye; embrue; engrain; *fleck;* ground in; *hue;* imbrue; infucate; japan; *key to; line;* mark; *non-washable; off-color;* put ~ on; *quirk;* ruddle; stain; spot; soil; tinge; tarnish; *unsightly;* vat-dye; wem; *xanthene;* yellow; *zone;*

**stairs** *(n.)*: *approach;* back~; cockle- ~; *downward* ~; *escalator;* flight; greeze; halfpace; increment; *joint; keep going up;* landing; *mark;* newel; outside ~; perron; quarterpace; rungs; stairway; (spiral) staircase; steps; *tier;* upward ~; *venture;* winders; *xfer;* yomp; *zip;*

**stale** *(n.)*: *awful;* bad; crusty; decaying; *eroding;* fusty; *green;* hoared; impairing; jejune; ketty; limp; moldy; musty; *nasty;* off; old; *overgrown;* peccant; queering; rotting; soured; tainted; *unpleasant;* vinnewed; welking; *xylaria;* yellowed; *zapped;*

**stall** *(n.)*: alcove; box ~; booth; compartment; crib; coop; *division;* enclosure; fold; *greens- ~;* hok; inclosure; *jail;* kraal; loosebox; mew; *narrow;* oxstall; pen; *quarters;* room; *stable; stockyard;* tigh [dial.]; utility pen; vollery; wynd [dial.]; *xystus;* yard~; zariba;

**stall** *(v.)*: *adjourn; block;* cumber; delay; detain; dally; encumber; fore~; go slow; hold up; hesitate; inhibit; jauk; keep; kill time; linger; *moderate; non-hurried;* obstruct; pause; prolong; *quit;* restrain; slow down; tarry; use time; *veto;* wait; waste time; x; *yank; zap;* [*Ant.* speed]

**stalwart** *(adj.)*: able-bodied; brawny; courageous; dauntless; energetic; fearless; gallant; great; husky; iron; *jusqu'au bout [F.];* knightly; lusty; muscular; *nervy;* obstinate; powerful; *quality;* rugged; sturdy; stout; tough; unflagging; vigorous; well-set; x-strong; yeomanly; *zippy;*

**stalwart** *(n.)*: advocate; backer; champion; defender; endorser; frontrunner; guardian; hero; heavyset; *indefatigable; jubilant;* knight; loyalist; mainstay; *non-loser;* overcomer; protector; paladin; *queller;* rescuer; supporter; tower of strength; Titan; upholder; vanquisher; warrior; *xtry.; yeoman;* zealot;

**stamina** *(n.)*: ability; *bearing;* constitution; determination; endurance; energy; fortitude; forbearance; grit; hardiness; indefatigability; *jaw-set;* keest; liveliness; make-up; *not giving up;* oomph; patience; pith; *quintessence;* resilience; strength; sufferance; tolerance; unyieldingness; vigor; wherewithal; willpower; *x-scend;* yieldlessness; zip; [*Ant.* softness]

**stamp** *(v.)*: affix mark; brand; cancel; certify; date- ~; *designate;* enface; en~; fix; grave; hand- ~; impress; *justify; ken- ~;* label; legitimize; mark; *notate;* over~; print; press; *qualify;* rubber ~; reconfirm; seal; signet; substantiate; *token;* use ~; validate; *watermark; x-certify; yes; zet [dial.];*

**stand** *(n.)*: adjustable ~; alcove; booth; canterbury; cubicle; display ~; easel; frame; *gadget;* gazebo; holder; hut; *instrument; jib;* kiosk; *leg;* music ~; neap; news~; *object;* outbuilding; portable ~; pavilion; pagoda; quadripod; rest; support; stall; shack; tripod; tetrapod; tollbooth; unipod; *vice;* wooden ~; x- ~; *yew-wood ~; zayat* [Burma]:

**stand** *(v.)*: arise; abide; be on one's feet; bear up; cock up; *continue;* defy; dwell; erect; *free-standing;* get up; hoist; halt; inhabit; *jump up; keep;* locate; make erect; not move; oppose; *overcome;* position; *quite erect;* rise; rear up; remain; situate; set upright; stay; take a ~; uprise; upend; *unseated; vertical;* with~; *xfer; yain [arch.]; zip up;* [*see* tolerate; *Ant.* sit]

**standard** *(adj.)*: average; basic; common; customary; dominant; everyday; familiar; general; habitual; *inelaborate;* jejune; *known; lackluster;* mundane; normal; ordinary; plain; quotidian; regular; routine; run-of-the-mill; settled upon; typical; usual; vanilla; *wonted; x-type; yawnish;* zestless; [*Ant.* special]

**standard** *(n.)*: accepted ~; average; benchmark; criterion; degree; established ~; fashion; fundament; guideline; hallmark; ideal; judgment ~; *key;* level; model; norm; *organizational ~;* pattern; quality; rule; rank; specification; touchstone; ule; vital condition; working rule; *XO requirement;* yardstick; *zero option;* [*see* flag]

**standpoint** *(n.)*: attitude; angle; bearing; belief; conception; disposition; evaluation; frame of mind; *ground;* heart; impression; judgment; *known inclination;* leaning; mindset; notion; outlook; opinion; perspective; point of view; *quot homines tot sententiae [L.];* reckoning; sentiment; take; *urge;* view(point); way of thinking; *xenodiagnosis;* yaw; *zeal;*

**standstill** *(n.)* abeyance; break; cessation; cul-de-sac; deadlock; draw; dead end; end of the road; full stop; gridlock; holdup; impasse; jam; *keep;* logjam; Mexican standoff; *non-operation;* pause; *quietus;* rest; stalemate; standoff; *time out; unwinding; void;* wait; *x-rest; yawning;* zero productivity;

**stanza** *(n.)*: acatalectic; *bob;* couplet; cinquain; canto; *chorus;* dimeter; division; epode; fit; glyconian; hexameter; irregular verse; *jingo; kasida;* line; monostich; *meter; neck verse;* ogdoastich; pentstich; portion; quatrain; regular verse; staff; stave; triplet; tetrastich; unit; uneven verse; verse; *words; xtr. verse; yo fu [Chin.]; zemirah;*

**star** *(n. astral)*: astral; asterisk; burst; cor; *cluster;* day~; dwarf ~; extragalactic ~; Fomahant; *galaxy;* heavenly body; illuminant; *Jewish ~;* K-class ~; light; luminary; mullet; molet; magnetar; morning ~; neutron ~; nova; *North Star; open cluster;* pulsar; pentagram; pentacle; *polar ~; pole- ~; Polaris;* quasar; red ~; sun; stellar object; *sideral;* technetium; *unclassified ~;* vesper; white ~; x-ray ~; yellow ~; *zenith ~;*
**star** *(n. stage performer)*: actor; actress; big name; celebrity; diva; entertainer; film ~; Grammy®-award winner; hero; idol; jeune premier; kid ~; lead; leading man (-lady); luminary; movie ~; name; onstage performer; pop hero; personality; *querencia [Sp.];* rock ~; singer; super- ~; thespian; *universally known;* vedette; well-known ~; *xtry.;* young ~; *zealously loved;*
**stare** *(v.)*: angrily ~; behold; catch sight of; descry; eyeball; face (down); fleer; fix eyes; gaze; gaup; glare; gape; gawk; glower; *hone in on;* inspect; *judgment;* ken; look; leer; make eyes; notice; outstare; outface; ogle; peer; pore; *quick look;* regard; *stony look;* scowl; take in; *unkind eye;* view; watch; *x-ray vision;* yawn; zero in;
**starry** *(n.)*: astral; burst-filled; bespangled; constellated; *dazzling; empyreal;* flickering; glittery; *heavenly;* instarred; *impressive; K-class;* lustrous; many-starred; *nova; open cluster; pentacled;* quasar-filled; *radiant;* star-studded; (star-)spangled; starred; sideral; stellar; star-spangled; twinkling; *undimmed; vespertine;* well-starred; *xtr. stars; yellow-starred;* zodiacal; [*Ant.* starless]
**start** *(n.)*: advent; beginning; commencement; dawn; debut; establishment; embarkment; founding; first; genesis; getgo; *hatching;* inception; initiation; instigation; introduction; jump off; jump~; jackrabbit ~; kickoff; launching; *making;* naissance; onset; outset; origin; opening; point of embarkation; *quickening;* rise; rising; start-up; setting up; take-off; triggering; undertaking; *unveiling;* ushering in; *verge; welcoming; xenogenesis; youth; zygogenesis;* [*Ant.* summation]
**start** *(v.)*: activate; begin; commence; debut; embark; establish; form; found; generate; go; *hatch;* initiate; instigate; institute; jump-start; kick off; launch; lead off; make a start; *newly ~;* originate; proceed; push- ~; *quicken;* reactivate; rise; set out; sally; turn on; trigger; undertake; unleash; venture out; *work out; xenogenesis; yield; zip;* [*Ant.* stop]
**startle** *(v.)*: alarm; affright; bowl over; confound; disconcert; excite; frighten; gaster; horripilate; impact; jolt; knock aback; look aghast; make jump; nonplus; overawe; phase; panic; *quicken;* rattle; surprise; take aback; unnerve; *vex;* wonder; *xtry.;* yerk; zap;
**starvation** *(n.)*: austerity; belly-pinching; *crisis;* dearth; emptiness; famish(ment); famine; *going without;* hunger; inanition; jejuneness; *keenness of appetite;* lack; longing; malnourishment; need; over-hungry; pangs; *quenchless;* ravenousness; *shortage; thirst;* undernourishment; vacuity; want; xenorexia; yearning; *zero food;* [*Ant.* satiation]
**starve** *(v.)*: abstain; be in want; clem; deprive; die; eat nothing; expire; fail; famish; go without food; *hunger; inanition; jaws of death;* kill with hunger; lack nourishment; *much-deprived;* not eat; *omit;* perish; quell; ruin; succumb; terminate; undernourish; *vanish;* want; waste away; xerophagy; yield one's spirit; zap; [*Ant.* satiate]
**state** *(n. condition)*: appearance; *being;* condition; development; estate; fashion; fettle; guise; happening; health; *incident; juncture;* kilter; level; manner; *new development;* order; posture; place; plight; position; quality; repair; situation; status; shape; tenor; tone; *unusual ~;* vein; way; *xenenthesis; yield; zero in;*
**state** *(v.)*: articulate; assert; asseverate; bespeak; communicate; convey; declare; express; enounce; *frame;* give; hold forth; indicate; intimate; *jaw; key in;* let out; mention; make known; name; noise; notify; observe; pronounce; proclaim; quoth; remark; relate; say; speak; tell; utter; verbalize; voice; word; *xenophonia;* yak; *zero in;*
**statement** *(n.)*: assertion; announcement; avowal; affidavit; bulletin; communication; declaration; enunciation; facts; *give;* holding forth; indiction; jactitation; judgment; *keynote address;* letter; message; notification; oration; pronouncement; proclamation; *quotation;* report; summation; testimonial; utterance; verbalization; word; witness; *xenagogy;* yeme; yell; *zealous message;*

**station** *(n. office)*: area; base; *bus ~;* center; depot; *environs;* footing; ground; home office; installation; job; *kray [Rus.];* locus; location; level; main office; *niche;* office; position; place; post; *quadrant;* region; stop; spot; standing; terminal; *train ~;* ubiety; *venue;* whereabouts; xy-coordinate; *yard;* zone;
**station** *(n. position)*: appointment; berth; class; degree; employment; estate; *first rate;* grade; height; *importance;* job; *kind;* level; *mastery; notch;* office; position; place; quality; rank; standing; status; title; tier; *uniform;* varve; work; *x-class;* y-level; *zone;*
**station** *(v.)*: assign; base; commission; deposit; establish; fix; garrison; hand (over); install; *join;* keep; lodge; leave; locate; move; nest; *offload;* place; post; *qualify; rest;* set; situate; transfer; unhand; vest; *weigh;* xfer; *yield;* zet [dial.];
**stationary** *(adj.)*: at rest; bolted down; changeless; dead; ever the same; fixed; glued down; halted; holding; immobile; inert; jibbed; *kaput;* lifeless; motionless; non-moving; on hold; parked; peaceful; quiet; resting; static; still; sitting; stopped; suspended; stagnant; tarrying; tranquil; unmoving; vegetative; waiting; *x'ed;* yet to move; *zero movement;*
**statue** *(n.)*: artwork; acrolith; bust; carving; colossus; depiction; engraving; figure(ine); graven image; *god; head; handiwork;* image; *Jupiter;* koruru; likeness; monument; *niche;* object; piece; *quartz work;* representation; sculpture; torso; *unveiled work;* virtu; wood carving; xylograph; xoanon; yaksha; zoophorus;
**status** *(n.)*: attributes; achievement; bearing; condition; cachet; degree; estate; fare; guise; grade; *happening;* importance; *juncture;* kilter; lot; level; manner; *new development;* order; place; position; prestige; quality; rank; state; station; tenor; *unusual ~;* vein; way; worth; *xenenthesis;* yield; zero in; [*see* importance]
**staunch** *(adj.)*: adamant; bendless; committed; devoted; died-in-the-wool; ever-rigid; firm; gritty; hard; inflexible; *jarless; keep;* loyal; mulish; nonflexible; obstinate; petrous; quite firm; rigid; resolute; stalwart; solid; sound; tough; unbending; unyielding; very strong; well-grounded; *x-grained;* yieldless; *zero give;* [*Ant.* swaying]
**stay** *(v.)*: abide; bide; continue; dwell; exist; endure; follow on; go on; hang around; inhabit; *journey;* keep on; linger; lodge; maintain; nest; occupy; pause; quarter; remain; settle; tarry; uphold; *visit;* wait; *winter;* xenize; yerde [arch.]; *zip to;* [*Ant.* skedaddle]
**steady** *(adj.)*: abiding; balanced; constant; dependable; even; fixed; *going on;* highly ~; inexorable; *jusqu'au bout* [F.]; keeping up; lasting; measured; non-changing; never-ending; ongoing; persistent; perpetual; *quenchless;* regular; relentless; stable; trustworthy; uniform; unfaltering; unwavering; undeviating; unbroken; very consistent; without deviation; *x-cending;* yieldless; *zero change;* [*Ant.* shaky]
**steal** *(v.)*: abstract; burglarize; burgle; cabbage; deprive; excoriate; filch; *grab;* hoist; hold up; *impalm;* jack; *kleptomania;* klick [Scot.]; lift; *loot;* mug; manavel [naut.]; nim; nobble; *obtain;* pilfer; purloin; pick-pocket; pectulate; *quad;* rip off; rob; shoplift; swipe; stick-up; thieve(rize); *take;* unpurse; *villainy;* wrest; walk off with; *xfer;* yank; *zip away;*
**stealth** *(n.)*: artfulness; beguiling; covertness; deception; evasiveness; furtiveness; guardedness; *hidden;* insidiousness; Jesuitry; *knowledge-less;* lurking; mysteriousness; non-detection; outfoxing; prowling; quietness; reconditeness; subtlety; secrecy; trickiness; underhandedness; *veiled;* wiliness; *xtry, cleverness;* yepship [arch.]; *zinging;* [*Ant.* salience]
**stealthy** *(adj.)*: arcane; beguiling; clandestine; concealed; covert; dark; esoteric; furtive; guarded; hidden; impenetrable; *Jesuitry; knowledge-less;* lurking; mysterious; not revealed; obscure; private; quiet; recondite; surreptitious; secret(ive); top-secret; undiscovered; undercover; veiled; without detection; *xeno-; yieldless;* zany; [*Ant.* salient]
**steep** *(adj.)*: abrupt; big; colossal; *dizzy;* elevated; formidable; great; high; immense; *jumbo;* king-size; long; mile-high; *massive;* narrow; oblong; precipitous; *quarter-mile high;* real big; *rising;* sizable; tall; towering; upright; vertical; way up high; *xy-height; y-axis;* zenithal; [*see* expensive]

**steeple** *(n.)*: *apex;* belfry; church ~; *cupola; divine;* epi; finial; *great point;* high point; *item; jut; kop; limit;* minaret; needle; *obelisk;* point; pinnacle; *quoif;* ridge; spire; turret; upper extremity; vertex; *white ~; Xn. church; yonder point;* zenith;
**stem** *(n.)*: axis; branch; chat; culm; caudex; *divarcation; extremity;* floral axis; *grafted ~;* haum; *ironwood;* jackstraw; kex; leafstalk; *maple trunk;* neck; offshoot; peduncle; quill; rod; rachis; stalk; shoot; stock; trunk; *upright; vimineous;* withe; xylem; yard [arch.]; *zamia;*
**step** *(v.)*: advance; *bear along;* continue; demarch; edge; *enter; fare;* go; hike; *increment;* journey; *keep pace;* lumber; move; march; night-walk; outwalk; pace; proceed; *quicken;* ramble; stride; tread; traipse; *underway;* venture; walk; xfer; yomp; *zip;*
**sterile** *(adj. disinfected)*: aseptic; bleached; clean; cleansed; disinfected; expurgated; fresh; germ-free; hygienic; immaculate; *jalap; killed germs;* laundered; machine-washed; nice; *okay;* purified; *qualmless;* radiation-cleansed; sterilized; sanitary; shipshape; spic-and-span; tidied up; unsullied; undefiled; uncontaminated; unsoiled; *virtuous;* washed; well-scrubbed; *xylol; yellow soap; zinc oxide;* [Ant. soiled]
**sterile** *(adj. infertile)*: arid; barren; childless; desolate; empty; effete; *eunuch;* fixed; gelded; *heirless;* infertile; jejune; *kept from bearing;* lacking; *most ~;* neutered; non-bearing; olated; *poor; quenched;* resourceless; spayed; *teemless;* unfruitful; verdureless; wanting; *xylol;* yeld; *zero fruit;*
**sterilize** *(v.)*: antisepticize; bleach; boil; cleanse; disinfect, decontaminate; elute; fumigate; get rid of germs; hygienize; *immaculate; jalap;* kill germs; *launder;* make germ-free; neutralize; outwash; purify; pasteurize; *quench;* rid of germs; sanitize; *tub;* unsully; *vacuum;* wipe; *xylol; yellow soap; zierlich [G.];*
**stern** *(adj. harsh)*: austere; brutal; cruel; dour; exacting; firm; grim; harsh; hardhearted; intense; *jarless;* kindless; *loveless; meticulous; nasty;* overbearing; peremptory; *quashing;* rigid; strict; severe; terrible; unrelenting; very strict; *weighty;* xtry. austere; yieldless; *zero mercy;* [Ant. soft]
**stern** *(adj. rear)*: astern; back; baft; clear to the back; *dorsal;* end; foot; *gammon;* hind; *in the back; jacksy; keister;* latter part; nether part; *over;* posterior; quarterdeck; rear; sternward; ship's rear; tail; *underside; verge; waning; xyz end; yondmost; Z-position;*
**sternness** *(n.)*: austerity; brutality; cruelty; dourness; exactingness; firmness; grimness; harshness; intensity; *jarlessness;* kindlessness; *lovelessness;* meanness; *nastiness;* overbearing; peremptoriness; *quashing;* rigor; strictness; severity; terribleness; *unrelenting; very strict; weighty;* xtry. austerity; *yieldlessness; zero mercy;* [Ant. softness]
**stew** *(n.)*: *alphabet soup;* broth; chowder; daube; *edibles;* fleshbroth; gipper; hotpot; Irish ~; *jipper;* kell; lobscouse; mulligan ~; navarin; olio; potage; *quibebe;* ragout; rabbit ~; soup; salmi; slumgullion; smoor; tagine; *union; venison stew; wonton soup; xurpa; Yankee bean soup;* zarzuela;
**stew** *(v.)*: agitate; braise; boil; cook; decoct; estuate; *foam;* gently ~; heat; *irritate; jump;* kier; *liquid; move; navarin;* overheat; poach; parboil; *quicken;* rage; *rebullition;* simmer; smoor; trouble; *upset; violent; vaporize;* wallop; xeo; *yerk;* zoutch;
**steward** *(n.)*: administrator; boss; chamberlain; director; *employee;* foreman; governor; head(man); intendant; jefe; keeper; leader; manager; *night manager;* overseer; procurator; *quartermaster;* reeve; supervisor; seneschal; trustee; undershepherd; viceroy; warden; XO; yardmaster; *zayim;*
**stewardship** *(n.)*: administration; *bishopric;* control; direction; *eldership;* full control; government; governance; headship; intendancy; jurisdiction; keepership; leadership; lordship; management; *necessitation;* oversight; procuration; power; *queenship;* rule; running; supervision; superintendence; *taking the lead;* use of authority; *vizierate;* ward; *xenagogy;* yard; zonal jurisdiction;
**stick** *(n.)*: arm; branch; chat; *dogwood branch; extremity;* faggot; *grafted branch;* hickory ~; *ironwood;* jackstraw; kipper; limb; *maple branch;* nicky; osier; plash; *quaker;* rame; stave; shoot; sprig; switch; twig; tendril; *upas ~; vimineous;* withe; wattle; *xylem; xenograft; yard* [arch.]; *zamia;*
**stick** *(v.)*: adhere; affix; agglutinate; attach; bond; cement; cohere; cling; *dovetail; embed;* fasten; fix; glue; grip; hold (together); hang; *imbed;* join; *knit;* keep; latch; mount; *nail; oneness;* paste; put; *quick-dry;* remain; stay; secure; tack; unite; *viscous;* weld; wed; *xenograft; yoke; zip;* [Ant. separate]

**stickiness** *(n.)*: adhesiveness; bonding; cohesiveness; *diatancy; emplastic; fixing;* gumminess; goopiness; gluiness; gooeyness; *heaviness; ichthyocolla; join; knit;* lentor; mucilaginousness; *non-separable;* ooziness; pitchiness; *quince-mucilge;* ropiness; syrupiness; tackiness; tenacity; *unite;* viscosity; viscidity; *weld; xenograft; yoke; zip;*

**sticky** *(adj.)*: adhesive; bonding; clinging; clottish; dauby; emplastic; *fixing;* gummy; glutinous; goopy; gluey; gooey; *heavy; ichthyocolla; join; knit;* lentous; mucilaginous; *non-separable;* oozy; pitchy; *quince-mucilage;* ropy; syrupy; sizy; tacky; tenacious; *thick; unite;* viscid; viscous; *weld; xenograft; yoke; zip;*

**stifle** *(v.)*: abate; bind; curb; dampen; end; force to end; garrote; hold back; inhibit; jam; keep in check; limit; muffle; nullify; oppress; put down; querken; repress; restrain; suppress; suffocate; stop; throttle; terminate; use; vitiate; weigh; *x;* yoke; zap;

**stigma** *(n.)*: abasement; blot; *contempt;* disgrace; embarrassment; *fall; grief;* humiliation; ignominy; *joyless; ketty;* loss of face; mark; *nota* [L.]; opprobrium; public disgrace; *quad;* reproach; shame; tarnishing; *upbraiding;* verecundity; wite; xtry. shame; *yuckiness;* zero honor;

**still** *(adj.)*: at rest; becalmed; calm; dead- ~; easeful; fixed; *gentle;* hushed; inanimate; idle; immobile; jarless; *kept* ~; lifeless; motionless; non-moving; on hold; peaceful; placid; quiet; restful; silent; serene; sitting; tranquil; untroubled; unmoving; vegetative; waiting; *x'ed;* yet to move; zero motion; [*Ant.* stirred]

**still** *(v.)*: allay; alleviate; appease; anesthetize; becalm; calm; diffuse; ease; *fix; gratify;* hush; *intercept; jarless; knock down;* lull; mitigate; milden; mollify; normalize; *overcome;* pacify; quiet; quell; relieve; redress; repress; soothe; settle; sedate; tranquilize; unruffle; *vanquish; wind down; x-out; yield; zeroize;* [*Ant.* stir]

**stimulate** *(v.)*: arouse; bestir; cause; disquiet; excite; fire up; *goad; hearten;* incite; jar; jolt; kindle; liven; motivate; *nudge; overexcite;* perturb; provoke; pique; quicken; rouse; stir; titillate; *upset;* vitalize; wake; *xuld [arch.];* yerk; zest up; [*Ant.* soothe]

**sting** *(v.)*: *afflict;* bite; *cut into;* dig; empierce; *force through;* gore; hurt; injure; impale; jab; *knife;* lance; *mince;* needle; *open;* pierce; puncture; *quill;* run through; stick; transfix; tingle; urticate; *ventilate;* wound; *x-pierce;* yerk; *zing;*

**stinginess** *(n.)*: *accumulation;* begrudging; cheapness; dollar-hoarding; economicalness; frugality; *good husbandry;* hoarding; illiberality; *Jack Benny;* knippering; laggardness; miserliness; niggardliness; over-frugality; penny-pinching; *quick-to-save; reluctance;* strait-handedness; skimpiness; tight-fistedness; ungenerosity; *very miserly; wary;* xtry. ~; *yieldlessness;* zero-generosity; [*Ant.* selflessness]

**stingy** *(adj.)*: avaricious; begrudging; cheap; dollar-conscious; economical; frugal; grudging; hard-fisted; illiberal; jejune; *knippering;* laggard; miserly; niggardly; overcautious; penny-pinching; *quick-to-refuse;* reluctant; sparing; scrimping; thrifty; tight(fisted); ungenerous; *vacillating;* wary; xtr. ~; yieldless; *zero-generosity;* [*Ant.* selfless]

**stink** *(n.)*: aroma; bad smell; contemptible smell; displeasing smell; effluvium; fetor; foul smell; fetidness; funk; galsome smell; horrible ~; *inhale;* joyless ~; *killing fumes;* loathsome smell; mephitis; malodorousness; niff; odor; pong; putridity; quality; reeking; smell; stench; terrible smell; unsavoriness; vile ~; whiff; waft; *x-bad;* yucky smell; *zoril;*

**stink** *(v.)*: air; *bad-smelling; come out; detect;* emit odor; fester; give off odor; have small; *intolerable; jarring; kest; lungful;* make odor; niff; offend; pong; *quill [arch.];* reek; smell; turn bad; unleash odor; *vile; whiffy; xuld [arch.];* yield an odor; *zap;* [*Ant.* savor]

**stipulate** *(v.)*: agree; bargain for; contract; demand; enumerate; *force;* give terms; have a clause; indicate; itemize; *juration; key stipulation;* lay out; make a condition; name condition; oblige; postulate; provide; qualify; require; specify; tell; *terms; utter; voice;* warrant; *x;* yark; zero in;

**stipulation** *(n.)*: agreed condition; binding condition; catch; condition; demand; expectation; *factor; fine print;* given; habilitation; indispensable condition; *juration;* key ~; limitation; legal agreement; must; mandated condition; necessity; *obligation;* prerequisite; proviso; provision; qualification; requirement; specification; terms; understanding; *ultimatum;* vital requirement; *warrant; XO requirement; yarking; zero option;*
**stir** *(v. arouse)*: arouse; awaken; bestir; call up; disquiet; excite; enkindle; foment; goad; hearten; incite; ignite; jar; kindle; *lead;* move; motivate; nudge; overexcite; perturb; provoke; quicken; rouse; roil; stimulate; trouble; unsettle; *upset; vex;* wake(n); whet; *xuld* [arch.]; yerk; zing; [*Ant.* sedate]
**stir** *(v. churn)*: agitate; blend; churn; disturb; *excite;* fold; go around; *harrow;* intermix; jabble; kirn [Scot.]; *lash;* mix; nudge; *overmix;* paddle; queach; remix; rouse; scramble; turn; trouble; unsettle; *vex;* whip; whisk; *xuld [arch.];* yerk; zing;
**stock** *(n.)*: amassment; accumulation; buildup; collection; deposit; *enlargement;* forgathering; group; gathering; hoard; inventory; jam [slang]; kit [coll.]; lot; mass; number; overflow; pile; quantity; reserve; stash; store; supply; stash; takings; *upbuild;* volume; wheen; *xuld [arch.]; yield;* zillions;
**stock** *(v.)*: accumulate; buy; carry; deal in; *exchange;* fill up; *got;* have (available); hoard; inventory; *job;* keep (in store); lay up; maintain; *number; over~;* provide; *quantify;* replenish; shelve; store; supply; sell; trade in; upbuild; *vend; wares; x-div; yield; zet* [dial.];
**stomach** *(n.)*: abdomen; belly; crop; *digestive; eat;* front; gut; gizzard; *huge ~;* ingluvies [zoo.]; *jelly-belly;* kyte; *load;* midsection; maw; midriff; mesothorax; *notum [zoo.];* omasum [zoo.]; *organ;* pot [slang]; paunch; pannel [zoo.]; *qualmish;* rumen [zoo.]; sack [slang]; tummy; underbelly; venter; wame; *waist; xtr. big ~; yellow-bellied; zone;*
**stone** *(n.)*: *agate;* boulder; bedrock; crag; dornick; *dib~; eagle~;* formation; field~; granite; *hair~; igneous rock;* jack~; klip; *kettle- ~; lapillus;* mineral; monolith; nugget; outcrop; pebble; *quartz;* rock; shale; sand~; toad~; uranite; volcanic rock; white~; xenolith; yenite; zircon;
 **Kinds of stone:** alum~; blood~; chalk~; dib~; eagle~; fairy~; gypsum~; horn~; ink~: jack~; kettle- ~; lime~; mandle~; needle~; onyx; pebble~; quartz ~; rag~; sand~; toad~; ulexite; whin~; xenotime; yuksporite; zircon;
**stone** *(v.)*: attack; bombard; chuck rocks; *destroy; execute;* flail; *get;* hurl rocks; *impact;* jolt; kill; lapidate; maul; nubble; *overhit;* pelt; pummel; *quab; ruin; strike;* throw stones; *undone; volley;* wallop; *xuld [arch.];* yedder; zonk;
**stony** *(adj.)*: aggregate; bouldery; craggy; *dense; eaglestone;* flinty; granitic; hard; igneous; *jaggy;* klip; lithoid; lapideous; marblelike; monolithic; *nuggety; obdurate;* pebbly; petrous; quartzy; rocky; stonelike; scopulous; tough; *uranite;* volcanic; *whitestone;* xenolithic; yonnie-like; zircon-filled; [see unemotional]
**stoop** *(v.)*: *acquiesce;* bend; crouch; dip; enfold; fold; *geniculate;* hunker; incline; *jag;* knuckle; kneel; lean over; *move down;* namaste; *overbend; patronize;* quat; *refold;* squat; turn down; *under; vary;* wind; *xtr. bent; yield; zag;* [see condescend]
**stop** *(v.)*: abort; abandon; avast; arrest; belay; block; cease; desist; discontinue; end; forbear; fold; give up; halt; interrupt; jib; *jam;* kill; leave off; make an end; *non-moving;* obstruct; prevent; quit; resign; relent; suspend; stifle; surcease; terminate; undo; veto; walk off; *x; yield; zero;* [*Ant.* start]
**stoppable** *(adj.)*: avertable; blockable; *cease; discontinue; escapable;* foldable; *give up; halt;* interruptible; jammable; killable; *leave off; motionless;* needless; *obstruct;* preventable; *quit; relent;* suspendible; terminable; undoable; *veto;* within one's power to stop; *x; yieldable; zero;* [*Ant.* steadfast]
**store** *(n.)*: *area ~;* boutique; convenience ~; corner ~; chain ~; commissary; depot; department ~; emporium; franchise; farmer's market; fish market; grocery ~; *hoard; inventory; jumble-shop; key ~; location;* market; mart; *newsstand;* outlet; plaza; PX; quick mart; retail outlet; shop; supermarket; showroom; trading post; *unit;* variety store; warehouse; *xtr. storage; yard sale; zoco* [Arab.];

**store** *(v.)*: accumulate; bank; collect; deposit; emplace; file; gather; hold on to; inventory; *jam;* keep; lay up; mount up; *nest; overabundance;* pack away; put in storage; *quantity;* reposit; stow; stockpile; tidy away; *upbuild; volume;* warehouse; *xfer;* yain [arch.]; zet [dial.];

**storehouse** *(n.)*: *area;* arsenal; building; cattery; depot; entrepot; facility; godown; granary; haven; *icehouse; junction; kura* [Jap.]; loft; magazine; *nine-story ~; ordnance;* promptuary; *quick storage;* repository; silo; storeroom; stockroom; terminal; unit; vault; warehouse; *xtr. storage;* yurt; *zone;*

**storm** *(n.)*: *agitation; after- ~;* blizzard; cloudburst; cyclone; downpour; dust ~; electrical ~; flaw; flashflood; fury; gale; groundswell; gullywasher; hurricane; inundation; ice ~; Idaho rain~; *Jupiter Pluvius; knot floater;* line squall; monsoon; nor'easter; onslaught; pirry; *quirlewind* [arch.]; rain~; squall; snow~; sand~; tempest; thunder~; typhoon; upheaval; virga; weather; wind~; white-out; windflaw; *xuld [arch.]; yern; zinger;*

**storm** *(v.)*: *agitate;* bestorm; break out; clamor; *crash;* downpour; erupt; fulminate; fume; go crazy; hail; *heat;* infuriate; *jar;* kindle; *lightning; monsoon; noise;* outrage; *pummel;* quake; rage; squall; thunder; toss; *unleash;* vent; *violence;* wreak havoc; *xuld [arch.];* yedder; *zap;*

**stormy** *(adj.)*: agitated; angry; boisterous; blustery; blizzardy; cyclonic; drizzly; enraged; flawy; furious; gusty; hostile; inclement; impetuous; *Jupiter Pluvius; knot floater; line squall;* monsoonal; nimbose; over-boisterous; pandemoniac; quakeful; rainy; rough; raging; storming; squally; tempestuous; tumultuous; thundery; turbulent; unstable; violent; wild; windy; *xude; yond [arch.]; zinging;* [*Ant.* serene]

**story** *(n.)*: anecdote; account; apologue; allegory; book; conte; chronicle; drama; epic; episode; fable; fairytale; folktale; fiction; fish ~; *ghost ~;* history; historical novel; imposture; journal; *kappa book;* legend; lore; myth; narrative; nonfiction; novel; *oral* narrative; parable; play; portrayal; plot; *quarto;* record; retelling; report; saga; short ~; tale; *unabridged ~; underplot;* version; work; writing; xenodocheionology; yarn; *zipper book;*

**storyteller** *(n.)*: account-giver; *author;* book-reader; commentator; declarer; discourser; enunciator; fabler; fabulist; fantasist; *giver;* humorist; informer; *jabberer;* key speaker; lecturer; mythologist; magsman; Münchausen; narrator; orator; proser; *quoter;* raconteur; relator; shannachie; taleteller; utterer; voice; worder; *xenagogue;* yarn-spinner; *zeug;*

**stove** *(n.)*: athanor; burner; cooker; *device;* electric ~; Franklin ~; gas ~; heater; incinerator; *jet;* kerosene ~; *limekiln;* muffle; microwave; *nut coal;* oven; potbelly ~ *quartz heater;* range; stovetop; tandoor; uniform-heat ~; *vulcan;* wood ~; *xeo; yellow-hot;* zay [dial.];

**straight** *(adj.)*: aligned; arrow- ~; bendless; curveless; direct; erect; even; flat; gun-barrel ~; horizontal; in a line; jagless; kink-less; linear; level; *made straight;* non-curved; on the level; pale; quite ~; rectilinear; right; straightened; true; unbent; upright; unwarped; vertical; virgate; waveless; *x-straight;* yawless; *zero curvature;* [*see* honest; direct; *Ant.* slanted]

**straighten** *(v.)*: align; become straight; comb; conk; draw out; disentangle; defrizz; extend; flatten; get straight; *have no kinks; in a line; jagless;* keep elongated; *lengthen;* make straight; neaten; outstretch; put straight; *quite straight;* rectify; set straight; ~ out; take bends out; tauten; unbend; uncurl; unkink; untwist; *vertical; waveless; x-straight; yawless; zero kinks;* [*Ant.* skew]

**straightforward** *(adj.)*: *absolute;* blunt; candid; direct; easy; frank; forthright; freespoken; genuine; gun-barrel straight; honest; inelaborate; *just regular; knowable; low-impact;* matter-of-fact; non-subtle; open; plain(-spoken); prosaic; *quick; rudimentary;* self-explanatory; straight (-shooting); truthful; upfront; very ~; well-defined; *x-type; yet facile; zestless;* [*Ant.* sly]

**straightness** *(n.)*: alignment; bendlessness; curvelessness; directness; erectness; evenness; flatness; *guided;* horizontalness; *in a straight line;* jaglessness; *kink-less;* linearity; *levelness; made straight;* non-curvature; *outright;* planar; *quite straight;* rectitude; *straight and narrow;* trueness; uprightness; verticality; wavelessness; *x-straight;* yawlessness; *zero zigzag;*

**strain** *(n. burden)*: anxiety; burden; care; distress; exertion; force; grief; heaviness; intensity; *jimjams; kiaugh [Scot.];* load; *misery;* nervous tension; overstrain; pressure; pull; pression; *quash; rigor;* stress; tension; *undergo;* vexation; weight; *x-stress; yank; zapping;*
**strain** *(v. exert oneself)*: attempt; bear down; *compete;* distend; exert; force; grind; hammer; *intense; jerk;* keep trying; labor; make an effort; *not easy;* overtax; push oneself; *quash; rigorous;* stretch; strive; struggle; try hard; tax; *undertake; venture;* work at; *xuld [arch.]; yerk; zealously endeavor;*
**strain** *(v. filter)*: *aerate;* bolt; cribble; drain; elutriate; filtrate; *grate;* hand ~; *interstices; jalee; kitchen ~er;* lixiviate; make separate; *non-combined; ooze;* pass through sieve; quaff; riddle; sift; screen; sieve; separate; transcolate; *use ~er; ventilate;* winnow; *xfer;* yandy; *zaru;*
**strange** *(adj.)*: abnormal; atypical; antic; bizarre; curious; crazy; different; enigmatic; eccentric; foreign; funny; freakish; freaky; gonzo; goofy; heterotypical; irregular; incongruent; jokey; kooky; ludicrous; left-field; mysterious; malformed; nonstandard; nutty; odd; outré; peculiar; queer; ridiculous; screwy; *twisted;* unusual; uncharacteristic; unfamiliar; *variant;* wacky; weird; xenomorphic; *yawed;* zany; [*Ant.* standard]
**strangeness** *(n.)*: abnormality; bizarreness; curiousness; craziness; difference; enigma; foreignness; funniness; freakishness; goofiness; *heterotypical;* irregularity; incongruency; *jokiness;* kookiness; looniness; malformation; non-usualness; oddness; peculiarity; queerness; ridiculousness; screwiness; twist; unusualness; variation; weirdness; *xenomorph;* yaw; zaniness;
**stranger** *(n.)*: alien; *auslander* [G.]; barbarian; *Czech; Dane; distant;* émigré; foreigner; guest; habitué; immigrant; journeyer; *kwai-lo* [Chin. off.]; *lodger; Mexican;* non-resident; non-Israelite; outsider; outlander; peregrintor; *quidam; refugee;* strange man; tramontane; unco; visitor; *Welshman;* xenic; *yonder; Zambian;*
**strangle** *(v.)*: asphyxiate; *bind;* choke; deprive of oxygen; extinguish; *finish off;* gag; garrote; *hush;* incapacitate; jugulate; kill; *lynch; murder; nullify;* overlay; *overwhelm; put out;* quackle; quench; *repress;* suffocate; smother; strangulate; stifle; scrag; throttle; *undo; void;* wring (one's neck); whirken [arch.]; *xuld [arch.]; yote; zeroize;*
**strangulation** *(n.)*: asphyxia(tion); *binding;* choking; deprivation of oxygen; extinguishment; *finishing up;* gagging; garroting; *hushing up; incapacitation;* jugulation; killing; *lynching; murdering;* necktie party; overlaying; *putting out;* quenching; *repression;* suffocation; smothering; throttling; *undoing; voiding;* wringing; *x-ing; yote; zeroizing;*
**strategist** *(n.)*: attack planner; behind-the-scenes operator; contriver; deviser; engineer; framer; general; *hatcher; idea;* japer; King's gambit; *lucubrator;* master ~ (-mind); *naval ~;* orchestrator; planner; *quo mode [L.]; racketeer;* schemer; tactician; *unmatched; visionary;* war ~; *x-chart; yantra [Hind.]; zinger;*
**strategy** *(n.)*: approach; attack plan; blueprint; battle plan; conception; design; engineering; foredesign; gambit; game-plan; *hatch;* idea; jape; King's gambit; line of attack; maneuver; master plan; *naval ~;* orchestration; plan; ploy; plot; *quo mode* [L.]; ruse; racket; strategem; scheme; tactic; *underlying plan; visual;* way; wile; *x-chart; yantra [Hind.]; zonal ~;*
**straw** *(n.)*: *alfalfa;* bedstraw; crabgrass; dry feed; ensilage; fodder; *festucous;* grass; hay; ile; *Japanese millet;* kemple; lovegrass; meslin; *natural grass;* ozier; provender; parabuntal; quill; reed; shilf; tow; *unprocessed grass; vegetation;* wicker; *xyris;* yedda; *zacate;*
**stray** *(adj.)*: abandoned; *barren;* cast off; disgarded; erratic; forsaken; *gadabout;* homeless; *itinerate; jaunt; kest;* lost; misplaced; neglected; on-the-street; *pathetic; quite alone;* roving; street-dwelling; transient; *unwanted;* vagrant; wandering; *x out; yet unwanted; zero care;*
**stray** *(v.)*: amble; become lost; change; drift; err; float; get lost; go amiss; *hike; interlope;* june; *keep looking;* lose one's way; meander; noctivagant; obambulate; peregrinate; *quicken;* roam; saunter; traipse; turn from; *underway;* venture off; wander; *xfer;* yaw; *zigzag;*

**streak** *(n.)*: *abnormality;* band; blotch; blemish; *coloration;* dash; discoloration; element; *fess; gash;* hint; infucation; *jaup; kenmark;* line; lode; mark; *naeve; off-color; patch; quirk;* ray; suggestion; strake; smear; smudge; touch; trail; *unsightly ~;* vein; wale; *xanthochromia; yellow;* zona;
**streak** *(v.)*: accelerate; bolt; cruise; dart; flash; go (fast); glide; hasten; *issue;* jet; kite; light; move; niddle; outstrip; *progress; quicken;* rip; rocket; shoot; speed; tear; *uprush; velocity;* whiz; *xuld [arch.];* yern; zip;
**stream** *(n.)*: arroyo; brook; creek; confluence; *deep;* effluent; freshet; gully; *headwaters;* influx; *jheel [Ind.];* keld; logan; millstream; nant; outlet; prong; quebrada; river; rivulet; spout; streamlet; tributary; torrent; *underground river; voe;* water(way); *xyrisic;* yeo; Zee [G.];
**street** *(n.)*: avenue; boulevard; causey; course; corridor; drive; esplanade; freeway; *going;* highway; interstate; journey-way; king's highway; lane; mews; *main drag;* non-toll road; outstreet; path(way); paseo; queen's highway; road; side road; strip; thoroughfare; through ~; *underpass;* vennel; way; xystum; *yong [arch.];* zwinger;
**strength** *(n.)*: ability; adamancy; brawn; capability; cogence; dint; durability; energy; endurance; force; greatness; gusto; hardiness; horsepower; intensity; *jet-power;* keest; kick; lustiness; might; muscle; *natural ability; oomph;* power; potency; qi; robustness; ruggedness; sufficiency; sturdiness; thewiness; toughness; *usefulness;* vim; vigor; wherewithal; *xenium;* yield strength; zip; [*Ant.* softness]
**strengthen** *(v.)*: augment; amplify; build; boost; bolster; brace; beef up; concentrate; develop; enhance; empower; edify; fortify; grow; help; heighten; increase; intensify; jump up; *keep growing;* largen; magnify; nourish; *overgrow;* proliferate; *quadruplicate;* reinforce; support; solidify; toughen; temper; *triple;* uplift; undergird; vest; wax stronger; *XL; yain [arch.]; zoom up;* [*see* encourage; *Ant.* soften]
**strenuous** *(adj.)*: arduous; burdensome; challenging; difficult; demanding; exhausting; fatiguing; grueling; hard; intense; jading; killing; laborious; moiling; not easy; operose; painful; *quite hard;* rigorous; spirited; taxing; tiresome; tough; *unrelenting;* vigorous; wearisome; *x-heavy; yary;* zapping; [*Ant.* simple]
**stress** *(n.)*: anxiety; angst; burden; crunch; disquietude; emotional ~; force; fretting; grief; hassle; heaviness; hypertension; intensity; inquietude; jimjams; kiaugh [Scot.]; load; *misery;* nerves; overburdening; overstrain; overpressure; pressure; *quash;* restlessness; stress; strain; tension; taxation; unrest; vexation; weight; *x-stress; yank;* zapping;
**stress** *(v.)*: accentuate; bring out; concentrate on; draw attention to; emphasize; focus on; give emphasis to; highlight; *italicize; jump out;* keep emphasis on; lay emphasis upon; make more noticeable; *notice; overemphasize;* point out (-up); play up; *quite over~; red letter;* spotlight; thrust; underscore; *value; weight; xtry. emphasis; yed;* zero in; [*Ant.* soften]
**stressful** *(adj.)*: arduous; anxious; burdensome; challenging; distressful; demanding; exhausting; fatiguing; fierce; grueling; hectic; hairy; high-pressure; harried; intense; jittery; knotty; *load; major;* nail-biting; operose; pressure-filled; quivering; rough; strenuous; tense; taxing; traumatic; unnerving; vexing; weighty; *xtr. ~; yemelich [arch.]; zapping;*
**stretch** *(v.)*: adapt; broaden; become longer; *change; continue;* draw out; elongate; expand; extend; flex; grow; *hold out;* inflate; increase; jut; *keep elongated;* lengthen; make longer; *nimble;* out~; outspread; overspan; pull; protract; *quantum increase;* reach; span; strain; tauten; tenter; unfold; *vary;* widen; *xapuri; yield; zip;* [*see* exaggerate; *Ant.* shrink]
**stretchy** *(adj.)*: adaptable; bouncy; contractile; ductile; elastic; expandable; flexible; gummy; *give; hevea;* infirm; jiggly; *keep pulling;* latex; lithe; malleable; non-rigid; *over-*extensile; pliant; *quivering;* rubbery; resilient; springy; stretchable; tensile; unfirm; *versatile;* whippy; *xapuri;* yielding; *zingy;*
**strew** *(v.)*: *abandon;* be~; besprinkle; broadcast; cast; distribute; dot; dust; *emit;* fleck; *give out;* hurl; intersperse; *jaculate; kest;* litter; *make a mess; non-contained;* overspread; pepper; *quoit;* resperse; straw; scatter; sprinkle; spread; throw; *upcast; vault; whip; xuld [arch.];* yote; *zoochory;* [*Ant.* stockpile]

**strict** *(adj.)*: authoritarian; austere; bossy; commanding; controlling; domineering; demanding; dictatorial; exacting; firm; grave; harsh; imperious; *jaded;* kindless; *lordly;* meticulous; narrow; overbearing; precise; peremptory; *quede [arch.];* repressive; rigorous; stern; stringent; true; tyrannical; unyielding; *verdical; weighty; xenagogic;* yieldless; *za-zum* [Rus.]; [*Ant.* soft]

**strife** *(n.)*: argument; altercation; bickering; brawl; battle; contention; discord; dissension; embroilment; fighting; gainsaying; hairsplitting; inaccordance; jangling; kagg; *locking horns; making fur fly;* negativism; odds; opposition; *polemic;* quarreling; rivalry; striving; trouble; unharmoniousness; *unpleasantness;* variance; wrangling; *x-fire;* yed; *zapping;* [*Ant.* solidarity]

**strike** *(n.)*: assault; blow; clout; crack; clobber; clock; deck; *efface; flogging; get;* hit; impact; jolt; knock; licking; lam; *mauling;* nob; nevel; open-handed blow; punch; *quab;* rap; smite; slap; smack; sock; slam; shot; spank; thwack; uppercut; veney; whack; wallop; *x-sect;* yedder; zonk;

**strike** *(v.)*: assault; beat; clobber; conk; deck; dash; *efface;* flail; *get;* hit; impact; jab; knock; lam; mash; nail; *overstrike;* punch; quab; rap; smite; sock; smack; slam; thump; thwack; uppercut; veney; whack; x; yedder; zonk;

**striking** *(adj.)*: arresting; breathtaking; conspicuous; dazzling; eye-catching; forceful; great; highly visible; impressive; jarring; kenspeckle; *lucid;* marked; noticeable; outstanding; prominent; *quite obvious;* remarkable; salient; stunning; transparent; unmistakable; visible; wondrous; xtry.; *yeme [arch.]; zenithal;*

**string** *(n.)*: app; bow~; braid; cord; draw~; *entangle;* fiber; filament; flax; *goldthread;* halter; *intertwine;* jute; knittle; line; lace; ligature; lash; microfiber; natural fiber; organzine; ply; packthread; *qiviut;* rope(-yarn); strand; thread; twine; *uncoil;* vang; warp; woof; watap; *xylem;* yarn; zein;

**strip** *(n.):* [see stripe]

**strip** *(v.)*: abrade; bare; cast off; decorticate; divest; discase; denude; debark; expose; flay; get skin off; husk; *isolate; jerk off; kerf;* lay bare; make bare; nakedize; *off;* peel; pare; *quick-husk;* remove; shed; skin; take off; undress; *vacate;* wear away; *xyster;* yank off; zip off;

**stripe** *(n.)*: aspect; band; bar; cingulum; diagonal ~; *edge;* fess; *gash;* hairline; *impression; jot; key marking;* line; marking; *notch;* one-inch ~; pinstripe; pale; *quillstroke;* row; ribbon; strip; streak; striation; *thin-striped;* underlining; vitta; weal; wale; *wing bar* [zoo.]; *x'ed;* yellow ~; zonule;

**striped** *(adj.)*: array; banded; brindled; broad- ~; cingulate; diagonally ~; *edged;* fessed; graybanded; horizontally ~; *impressions;* jagged- ~; *key markings;* lined; *marked;* narrow-banded; *one-inch stripe;* pinstriped; paly; *quillstroke;* ribbed; ribboned; streaked; striated; thin-striped; *upstroke;* vitta; veined; waled; *x'ed; yellow- ~;* zonated; zebrine; zebroid; [*Ant.* solid, spotted]

**strive** *(v.)*: attempt; argue; bicker; battle; clash; contend; compete; dispute; endeavor; fight; gainsay; grapple; have words with; *impugn;* jarring; kemp; lock horns [slang]; make an effort; make fur fly; *negate;* oppose; pick fight; quarrel; resist; seek; struggle; try; tangle; undertake; vie; wrestle; war; withstand; war; *x-purposes;* yell; zap; [*Ant.* support]

**stroke** *(v.)*: *act;* brush; caress; dally; *down~;* embrace; feel; fondle; gently ~; hug; *inwrap; just barely touch; kemb;* lightly touch; massage; move hand over; nuzzle; *overrun;* pet; *quab;* rub; run over; sweep; touch; *up~; voluptuary;* whisk; *xfer; yank; zip;*

**strong** *(adj.)*: adamant; able-bodied; brawny; compelling; capable; courageous; durable; energetic; enduring; forceful; firm; fortified; fit; great; hulky; herculean; husky; impregnable; influential; iron; *jusqu'au bout* [F.]; keen; lusty; lasting; mighty; muscular; non-weakened; overpowering; powerful; potent; quality; rugged; robust; reinforced; sturdy; solid; tough; unbreakable; unflagging; vigorous; well-built; x-strong; yauld; *zesty;* [see big; courageous; inflexible; *Ant.* soft]

**stronghold** *(n.)*: acropolis; base; bastion; blockhouse; castle; citadel; donjon; *defense; enclosure;* fort(ification); fortress; garrison; headquarters; hold; *imperial palace; jong* [Tib.]; keep; *laager;* muniment; martello; motte and bailey; nest; outpost; octagon; propugnacle; palace; *quarters;* refuge; redoubt; rath; safehold; sconce; tower; *unbeatable;* vault; watchtower; walls; ward; *x-house; yamen* [Chin.]; zwinger;

**strongman** *(n.)*: Atlas; ape; big guy; brute; bruiser; crusher; dynamo; *energy; fit; force;* gorilla; he-man; hulk; Hercules; ironside; *jungle-man;* kemp; *lusty;* muscleman; mesomorph; man's man; *non-weakling; oaky;* power-house; *quite strong;* rocky; Samson; strong-man; titan; Ulysses; *very strong man;* weightlifter; *xia; yauld; zero weakness;* [*Ant.* sissy]

**structure** *(n.)*: architecture; building; construction; complex; design; edifice; epi~; frame; formation; *girders;* house; *institution; job; kamienica;* layout; makeup; matrix; *nine-story ~;* office building; palazzo; quadriplex; rearrangement; scheme; super- ~; tower; *unit; vertical ~; wing; x-frame; yardhouse; z-bar;*

**structure** *(v.)*: arrange; build; construct; configure; constitute; dispose; design; *erect;* form; fix; *generate;* hierarchize; *intend; join; kit;* lay out; make; *newly formed;* organize; plan; pose; *qualify;* rearrange; set up; *turn out; upbuild; vamp;* work; *xfer; yield;* zet [dial.];

**struggle** *(n.)*: affray; battle; conflict; contest; dispute; effort; fight; great effort; grapple; hassle; *intense ~; joust;* kagg; *labor;* mêlée; *non-peaceful;* occursion; *push;* quarrel; resistance; rivalry; striving; tug-of-war; unrest; vying; warfare; wrangling; *x-fire;* yed; *zapping;*

**struggle** *(v.)*: agonize; brawl; contend; dispute; endeavor; fight; grapple; have trouble; *intense; jarring;* kick; labor; make effort; *nasty;* oppose; *push; pull;* quarrel; resist; strive; scuffle; tangle; *use great effort;* vie; wrestle; *x-purposes; yell; zap;*

**strum** *(v.)*: *affect;* brush; *caress; do; entertain;* fiddle; finger; graze; *handle; instrument; jam;* kittle [joc.]; *lead guitar;* make music; *non-discord; outperform;* play; pluck; *quality; run fingers over;* stroke; thrum; twang; tickle [joc.]; *use; vibrate;* whisk; *xfer; yield; zing;*

**strut** *(v.)*: amble; bounce; cavort; demarch; *enter;* flounce; gambol; hitch; *inch;* jounce; *keep pace;* lope; march; nauntle; outwalk; prance; parade; *quicken;* romp; step; swagger; swank; stride; titup; *underway;* venture; walk; xfer; yomp; *zip;* [*Ant.* slog]

**stubborn** *(adj.)*: adamant; bull-headed; contumacious; determined; dogged; ever-stubborn; firm; grim; headstrong; insistent; inflexible; intractable; intransigent; iron-willed; jaw-set; *keep; lasting;* mule-headed; mulish; non-bending; obstinate; obdurate; *opinionated;* pigheaded; pertinacious; *querulous;* rigid; refractory; resolute; restive; resistant; stiff-necked; strong-willed; self-willed; stiff-necked; tenacious; unbending; unyielding; *volitional;* willful; *x-grained;* yieldless; *zero give;* [*see* proud; *Ant.* submissive]

**stubbornness** *(n.)*: adamancy; bull-headedness; contumacy; determination; *ever-stubborn;* firmness; grimness; headstrongness; hard-heartedness; inflexibility; immovability; *jaw-set; keeping; lastingness;* mule-headedness; non-yieldedness; obstinacy; pigheadedness; pertinacity; *querulousness;* rigidity; resolution; self-will; steadfastness; tenacity; tenaciousness; unyieldingness; *volition;* willfulness; *x-grained;* yieldlessness; *zero give;* [*see* pride; *Ant.* submissiveness]

**student** *(n.)*: apprentice; abecedarian; academian; bookworm; cadet; college ~; day ~; *education;* freshman; gleaner; high schooler; *individual;* junior; *kindergartener;* lowerclassman; learner; letterman; mentee; night student; observer; pupil; protégé(e); philomath; *querier; researcher;* studier; sophomore; senior; swot; trainee; tutee; undergraduate; upperclassman; *varsity player;* wonk; *xenagogy; youth; zealous learner;* [*Ant.* schoolmaster]

**studious** *(adj.)*: academic; bookish; concentrative; diligent; erudite; *focused; genius; hard-working;* intellectual; *judicial;* knowledgeable; learned; meditative; noetic; *occupied;* pensive; *quiet;* reflective; scholarly; thoughtful; understanding; versed; well-read; *xenocratic;* yaup; *zetetic;* [*Ant.* simple]

**study** *(n.)*: analysis; attention; analyzation; breakdown; check; diagnostic; examination; field research (-of ~); focus; *finding;* going over; headwork; immersion; investigation; *judgment;* knowledge; look-over; lucubration; meditation; *nisus;* overhaul; probe; query; research; scrutiny; testing; *understanding;* valuation; winnowing; *xenodiagnosis;* yield results; *zootomy;*

**study** *(v.)*: analyze; bone; cram; consider; dissect; elucubrate; examine; explore; find out; glean; get knowledge; *hear of;* investigate; *judge; know;* learn; lucubrate; mug up; *naw [dial.];* observe; probe; question; query; research; scrutinize; smatter; swot; try to learn; understand; vet; work on; *xenodiagnosis; yeme; zero in;*

**stuff** *(n.)*: articles; appurtenance; belongings; commodities; chattels; *duffel bag;* effects; equipment; feedstock; goods; gear; habiliments; hyle; items; junk; kit; *load;* material; matter; needments; objects; possessions; property; paraphernalia; personal effects; quintessence; *quintessence;* raw material; substance; supplies; things; tackle; *unit;* valuables; warp and woof; *xenenthesis; yannigan; zeug* [G.];

**stuff** *(v.)*: *absolutely ~;* block up; crush; depress; engorge; force; fill; gorge; heave; impel; jam (-pack); kibble; load; mash; *niche;* overfill; pack; quash full; ram; squeeze; squash; tamp; *upthrust; very full;* wad; wedge; *xuld* [arch.]; *yerk; zip;*

**stumble** *(v.)*: *amble;* blunder; belly-flop; creep; *drag;* err; fall; gimp; hobble; inch; jiffle; *kink;* limp; lurch; misstep; *non-stable; oscillate;* pitch; quaddle; reel; stagger; slip; totter; trip; *uneven;* vacillate; wobble; *xfer;* yaw; *zigzag;*

**stumblingblock** *(n.)*: *arrest;* barrier; cumbrance; difficulty; encumbrance; *frustration;* glitch; hindrance; impediment; impasse; jam; kink; *lodgment;* monkey wrench; nuisance; obstacle; offense; pitfall; problem; quandary; roadblock; rock of offense; snag; stumbling block; trouble; *upset;* vigia; wall; x; *yowler; zinger;*

**stump** *(n.)*: *abbreviated;* base; butt; cut-off; *dogwood tree ~;* end; frustum; *gnarl;* hunk; *incomplete part; jog;* knob; kippin [Ire.]; lop; *mound;* nub; *oak tree ~;* partial treetrunk; quat; remains; remnant; stub; tree- ~; *ungrinded ~;* vestige; *wooden;* xylon; yew ~; zuche;

**stump** *(v.)*: addle; baffle; confuse; discomfit; *entangle;* flummox; gravel; hamper; *incoherent;* jumble; kittle; lose; mystify; nonplus; obscure; puzzle; perplex; quiz; *ravel; scramble;* tangle; *unknown;* vex; wilder; *x; yo-yo; zero understanding;* [Ant. shed light]

**stun** *(v.)*: astound; bedazzle; bewilder; confound; daze; dumbfound; *excite;* flabbergast; floor; gape; hold one's breath; impact; impress; jolt; knock down; look aghast; make marvel; nonplus; overawe; phase; paralyze; *quite amazed;* rattle; shock; startle; traumatize; upset; *vex;* wonder; *xtry.; yerk;* zap; [see zap]

**stunt** *(n.)*: act; buffoonery; *behavior;* coup; deed; exploit; feat; *go;* heroic act; *intrepidity;* job; *knavishness; laudable;* move; *nobbling;* operation; prank; performance; *quiblin [arch.];* ruse; sleight; trick; *undertaking;* venture; wile; *x-action; yentzing; zinger;*

**stunt** *(v.)*: arrest; bedwarf; curb; dwarf; encumber; frustrate; *gum up;* hinder; inhibit; *jam;* keep (from); *let* [arch.]; make little; *non-growth;* obstruct; prevent; *quash;* restrict; slow down; thwart; *undo; vex;* withhold; *x; yank; zeroize;* [Ant. spawn]

**stupefy** *(v.)*: addle; amaze; astonish; bemuse; befuddle; confuse; daze; dumbfound; *dumbstruck;* enchant; entrance; flabbergast; *gone;* hebetate; hypnotize; inebriate; *jaw-fallen;* keel one over; lay out; mesmerize; mystify; nonplus; overawe; perplex; *quaff;* render speechless; stun; shock; startle; tongue-tied; taken back; *uncommunicative;* veg out; wack out; *x-out; yikes!;* zonk; zombify; zone out;

**stupid** *(adj.)*: air-headed; bumbling; bone-headed; brainless; clownish; crazy; dense; dumb; egg-headed; foolish; gullible; goofy; harebrained; idiotic; jackass; knot-headed; lame-brained; moronic; nit-witted; outrageous; pea-brained; quacky; ridiculous; senseless; slow; thick(-headed); unthinking; vacuous; witless; *xtry. dumb; yokelish;* zany; [see ridiculous; Ant. sensible]

**stupidity** *(n.)*: asininity; brainlessness; craziness; dumbness; egg-headedness; foolishness; gullibility; goofiness; hebetude; idiocy; jackassery; kookiness; ludicrousness; madness; naivety; outrageousness; preposterousness; quackery; ridiculousness; senselessness; thoughtlessness; unteachability; vertigo; witlessness; *xtry. ~; yokelishness;* zaniness; [Ant. sensibleness]

**stupor** *(n.)*: abstraction; bemusement; confusion; daze; entrancement; fuddling; grayout; haze; incoherence; *inebriation;* jag; knocked out; lethe; laid out; mesmerism; narcosis; *numbness;* out (of touch); preoccupation; *quaffing;* reverie; stupefaction; sopor; spell; *stoned;* trance; unconsciousness; *under;* vexation; whacked (out); xanthoxylin; yarked; zonking;
**sturdy** *(adj.)*: able-bodied; brawny; *capable;* durable; enduring; firm; fit; great; husky; iron; *jusqu'au bout [F.]; keen;* lusty; lasting; mighty; non-frail; obstinate; powerful; *quality;* rugged; strong; solid; stout; strapping; tough; unflagging; vigorous; well-built; x-strong; yauld; *zippy;* [*Ant.* soft]
**style** *(n.)*: approach; brand; cast; designation; décor; estate; form; fashion; *genus;* habiliment; ilk; *jack;* kind; literary ~; manner; model; mold; nature; order; pattern; *quality;* romanticism; sort; type; taste; *unit;* variety; way; *x-class;* year-class; *zeal;*
**stylish** *(adj.)*: *awesome;* big; current dandy; ever- ~; fashionable; faddish; grody; hip; in; jaunty; keen; *latest;* modish; nardy; *outstanding;* popular; quite faddish; rakish; snappy; trendy; tony; up-to-date; voguish; with-it; xtry.; you-beaut [Aus.]; zazzy;
**suave** *(adj.)*: attractive; boss [slang]; charming; cultured; debonair; elegant; fine; gracious; genteel; high style; impeccable; jemmy; *kempt; lovely;* mannered; natty; over-polite; polished; *quaint;* refined; stylish; smooth; slick; sleek; sophisticated; *tidy;* urbane; vogue; well-mannered; xtry.; yuppyish; zippy; [*Ant.* sorry]
**subconscious** *(adj.)*: alluded to; *brain;* concealed; directed; eluded to; flashed; *given;* hidden; intuitive; *just momentary; known;* led into; mind-affecting; notional; *oblique;* planted; *quick-flashed;* redolent; subliminal; *tacit;* unconscious; *vague;* without awareness; *xfer; yet unconscious; zonked out;*
**subdue** *(v.)*: annihilate; annex; bring under subjection; beat; conquer; capture; defeat; dominate; enslave; force; *gain mastery;* hold down; *invincible; jam;* knock out; lick; master; *neutralize;* overpower; oppress; prevail; quash; repress; subjugate; subject; triumph (over); unseat; vanquish; worst; xeno-dominate; yoke; zap; [*Ant.* succumb]
**subject** *(n.)*: area; basic theme; central theme; discipline; emphasis; focus; *gist; heart;* idea; *jet;* key topic; leitmotif; main topic; matter; notion; overriding ~; premise; *quintessence; root;* ~ matter; topic; underlying ~; *vital;* weight; xenenthesis; *yaw;* zone;
**subject** *(v.)*: *affect;* bring under subjection; cause to undergo; dominate; expose; enslave; foist; force; *gain victory; hammer;* impose upon; *jam; knock out;* lay open to; make one endure; *no choice;* overcome; ply; prevail on; put on; quench; repress; saddle with; subjugate; take over; unseat; vanquish; whelm; *xeno-dominate; yoke; zap;*
**subjugate** *(v.)*: assume control over; beat; bring under subjection; conquer; crush; defeat; dominate; expugn; enslave; force to submit; grind into submission; hold down; *intimidate; junk [slang];* keep down; lick; master; *neutralize;* overcome; overpower; oppress; occupy; prevail; quell; quash; repress; rule; subdue; suppress; subject; take (over); triumph (over); unseat; *under;* vassalize; vanquish; win; worst; whip; *xeno-dominate; yoke;* zap; [*Ant.* succumb]
**submerge** *(v.)*: absorb; bathe; bury; baptize; cover; dunk; dip; dive; drown; demerse; engulf; flood; go under; *hide;* immerse; jump in; *keelhaul;* lower; move down into; nosedive; overwhelm; plunge; put under; plant; *queven* [arch.]; *rinse;* submerse; sink; *totally under; under (the water);* verge; whelm; *xuld [arch.]:* ybaptized [arch.]; *zet [dial.];*
**submission** *(n.)*: acquiescence; biddableness; compliance; deference; execution; followership; fulfillment; giving in; heeding; implementation; *jumping to it;* kneeling; listening; mindfulness; non-resistance; obedience; obsequiousness; passivity; *questionlessness;* regard; resignation; submissiveness; timidity; unreluctance; vigilance; willingness; *xlation;* yieldedness; *zeal;* [*Ant.* sedition]
**submissive** *(adj.)*: acquiescent; accommodating; biddable; compliant; deferential; duteous; ever-obedient; following; governable; heedful; implementing; *jump right to it;* kneeling; kowtowing; law-abiding; mindful; meek; non-resistant; obedient; obsequious; passive; questionless; regardful; resigned; subservient; surrendered; tractable; unresisting; *vigilant;* willing; *xtry;* yielded; *zealous;* [*Ant.* self-willed]

**submit** *(v.)*: abide by; bow; comply; conform; do; execute; follow; fulfill; give in; heed; implement; jump (to it); knuckle under; keel in; kowtow; listen to; mind; not resist; obey; perform; *questionless;* regard; resign; succumb; truckle; take orders; *toe the line;* undertake; vigorously obey; *work; wholly yield; xlate;* yield; zip to it;

**subsequent** *(adv.)*: after; behind; coming after; directly following; ensuing; following; going next; henceforth; in pursuit of; just behind; *kept behind;* later (on); *much ~;* next; *over;* past; posterior; *quickly following; resulting;* since; thereafter; *ulterior;* very next; whenceforth; *x-list;* yonder; *Z-position;*

**subside** *(v.)*: abate; assuage; alleviate; break; bate; calm; curb; contract; condense; decrease; decline; diminish; dissipate; dwindle; ease; ebb; fade; fall; go down; hit a downturn; *impair; improve; jump down;* knock down; languish; lessen; lower; minish; moderate; mitigate; *narrow; outgo;* peter out; quell; quail; recede; reduce; shrink; sink; taper; *undo; vanish;* wane; waste; *xerosis;* yield; zap; *zeroize;* [*Ant.* swell]

**subsist** *(v.)*: abide; bide; consist; continue; dwell; exist; eke out a living; fare; go on; get by; hang on; inhere; just make it; keep going; live; manage (to survive); not die; *occupy;* perdure; *quick;* remain; survive; stay alive; tarry; *uphold; vitality; work; xenize; yerde* [arch.]; *zoe;* [*Ant.* starve]

**substance** *(n.)*: atoms; being; body; constitution; distillation; essence; feedstock; gist; hyle; heart; inbeing; jet; keest; lifeblood; makeup; material; matter; nature; nub; ontology; pith; quintessence; quiddity; raw material; stuff; soul; thing; tangibility; *underneath;* vitals; warp and woof; *xenenthesis;* yetzer [Heb.]; *zeug [G.];*

**substantial** *(adj.)*: appreciable; big; bonny; considerable; corporeal; concrete; dramatic; extensive; formidable; great; generous; handsome; impressive; jumbo-sized; king-size; large; material; major; *noteworthy;* oversize; prodigious; quantum; real; rock solid; substantive; sizable; significant; tangible; *unwieldy;* vast; vital; well; whopping; xtry.; *yet unsurpassed; zillions;* [*Ant.* scanty]

**substantiate** *(v.)*: authenticate; bear out; certify; confirm; demonstrate; document; establish; fix; give proof; homologate; illustrate; justify; kithe [Scot.]; legitimize; make sure; nail down; notarize; objectify; prove; *questionless;* reconfirm; show; sustain; try; testify; uphold; verify; warrant; x-certify; *yes; zero doubt;* [*Ant.* shoot down]

**substitute** *(adj.)*: alternate; backup; changed; displaced; delegated; exchanged; fill-in; ghost; *have instead;* in place; interchanged; *instead; in place;* jibbed; *kaimakam [Turk.];* lieutenant; *makeshift; new;* other; proxy; *quid pro quo [L.];* replacement; stand-in; subrogate; surrogate; trade-in; *used instead;* vicarious; *willing ~; xfer; yielded;* zwapped [dial.];

**substitute** *(n.)*: alternate; backup; change-out; deputy; exchange; fill-in; *go instead; have instead; instead;* jib; *kaimakam* [Turk.]; locum; *lamb; make switch;* next best thing; other; proxy; *quid pro quo* [L.]; replacement; stand-in; subrogate; surrogate; succedaneum; scapegoat; trade-in; understudy; vicar; *work; xfer; yield;* zwap [dial.];

**substitute** *(v.)*: alternate; barter; change; displace; exchange; fill in for; go instead; have instead; interchange; jib; *kaimakam [Turk.]; locum;* make a switch; *novate;* offer in exchange; put instead; quick-swap; replace; switch; swap; trade; take the place of; use instead; *vicarious; work;* xfer; *yield;* zwap [dial.];

**substitution** *(n.)*: alternation; barter; change; displacement; exchange; *for;* going instead; having instead; interchange; jib; *kaimakam [Turk.]; locum;* making a switch; *novate; overhaul;* putting instead; *quick-swap;* replacement; switch; swap; subrogation; trade; *use instead; vicarious; work;* xfer; *yield;* zwap [dial.];

**substitutional** *(adj.)*: alternate; alternative; bartered; commutative; delegated; exchanged; for; given in exchange; *handed over;* interchanged; instead of; *jockey; key trade;* locum; *modified; novate;* on behalf of; proxied; *quid pro quo* [L.]; replaced; substitutionary; succedaneous; traded; *used instead;* vicarious; *work; xfer; yielded;* zwaped [dial];

**subtle** *(adj.)*: artful; beguiling; crafty; cunning; devious; evasive; furtive; guileful; *hidden;* illusive; ingenious; jesuitical; knavish; low-profile; Maciavellian; non-obvious; obscure; pawky; *quiet;* roguish; shrewd; sly; tricky; underhanded; vulpine; wily; *xtry.;* yepe; *zinger;* [*Ant.* simple]

**subtlety** *(n.)*: artfulness; beguiling; craftiness; cunning; deviousness; evasiveness; furtiveness; guile; *hidden;* illusiveness; jesuitry; knavishness; *lying;* Machiavelism; *nuance; outfoxing;* policy; *quietness;* roguishness; subtleness; shrewdness; slyness; trickiness; underhandedness; *vulpine;* wiliness; *xtry, cleverness;* yepship [arch.]; *zinging;* [*Ant.* simplicity]

**subtract** *(v.)*: abstract; *betake;* cast out; deduct; except; fall off; get rid of; *halve; integer; jump down;* knock off; lessen; minus; *negative; off;* put back; *quantity;* remove; reduce; *shrink;* take away; unload; *void out;* withdraw; x-out; yank; zeroize; [*Ant.* supplement]

**suburb** *(n.)*: *area;* bedroom community; burb [slang]; conurbation; *district; development;* environs; exurb; faubourg; greenbelt; *hamlet; invillaged;* junction; kirk-town [Scot.]; *location;* municipality; near-city community; outskirts; *place; quarter;* residential area; suburbs; town; urban vicinity; *vicinity; ward;* x-urb; *yard; zone;*

**subversive** *(adj.)*: antiestablishment; breakaway; *Bolshevik;* clandestine; dissident; eroding; fifth column; government-subverting; hole-and-corner; insurrectionary; *Jacobin; knotty; low-profile;* mutinous; non-loyal; overthrow-minded; private; *questionable;* revolutionary; rebellious; secretive; traitorous; treacherous; undermining; *veiled;* weakening; *xenophilious; yanking down; zeroizing;* [*Ant.* supportive]

**succeed** *(v.)*: achieve; advance; attain; boom; bloom; burgeon; come along well; do well; effectuate; fare well; flourish; go well; have success; *increase; jump up;* keep growing; luxuriate; make it (-good); meet goal; not fail; obtain objective; prosper; prevail; pull off; qualify; reach goal; *self-made;* thrive; triumph; uprise; *victory;* work; *xtry.;* yain [arch.]; zoom up; [see replace; *Ant.* sink]

**success** *(n.)*: achievement; attainment; burgeoning; boffo; complete victory; doing well; éclat; felicity; flourishing; fortune; fulfillment; favorableness; going well; *heightening;* increase; *jumping up;* keen ~; luxury; making it; non-failure; obtainment; prosperity; prosperousness; qualification; reaching one's goal; successfulness; *succès fou* [F.]; turn out well; thriving; utter ~; victory; working; weal; xtry. ~; *yain [arch.]; zillions;* [*Ant.* setback]

**successful** *(adj.)*: accomplished; burgeoning; completed; celebrated; doing well; efficacious; flourishing; felicitous; favorable; famed; going well; happy; in good case; jointly- ~; keenly ~; lucrative; *making it;* noteworthy; overcoming; prosperous; *quartful* [arch.]; rewarding; rich; succeeding; self-made; thriving; triumphal; *useful;* victorious working; well-to-do; *xtry; yieldful; zillions;* [*Ant.* sinking]

**successive** *(adj.)*: adjacent; back-to-back; consecutive; directly following; ensuing; following each other; *going along;* hard by; in order; joining; kept-together; linked; methodical; neighboring; ordered; one after the other; placed together; *quite orderly;* rotating; sequential; succeeding; touching; together; unbroken; *uninterrupted; unfolding;* verging; without interruption; *xenograft;* yoked; *zero break;*

**successor** *(n.)*: after-comer; beneficiary; co-heir; descendant; *estate;* fellow- ~; *getter;* heir; inheritor; joint-heir; *kepper;* legal ~; *ménage;* next-of-kin; obtainer; parcener; *quoff;* rightful heir; tanist; uncontested heir; *valuables; will;* xmit; *yain [arch.];* zadruga;

**succumb** *(v.)*: acquiesce; bow; bend; cede; come under; compromise; do; defer; *expire;* fall in; give in; heed; indulge; *jump (to it);* knuckle under; keel in; listen to; mind; not resist; obey; perform; *questionless;* relent; submit; surrender; *toe the line;* undertake; *voided;* work; xlate; yield; *zero-resistance;* [*Ant.* surmount]

**suck** *(v.)*: absorb; bring in; *collect;* draw; drink; *extract; fill; get; have;* inhale; intake; *juice;* knock down; *lap up;* milk; *nip;* osmose; *partake;* quaff; reabsorb; resorb; sook; siphon; tap; take in; uptake; vacuum; *whiff; xfer;* yaffle; *zip in;*

**sudden** *(adj.)*: abrupt; breakneck; *confounding;* dramatic; expeditious; fast; *greased lightning;* hasty; impulsive; just like that; *keen; lightning-fast; mercurial; not expected;* overhasty; precipitate; quick; quantum; rapid; swift; surprise; *time;* unexpected; *very fast;* without notice; *xtry.;* yar; *zippy;* [*Ant.* slow]

**suddenly** *(adv.)*: abruptly; bang!; *currently;* directly; ever-promptly; fastly; *greased lightning;* hastily; impulsively; instantly; just then; keenly; lickety-split; *momentarily; non-expectedly;* out of the blue; plumb; presto; poof!; quickly; rapidly; straightway; *twinkling of an eye;* unexpectedly; unawares; very quickly; without warning; *whammo; xtry.;* yare; zip!; [*Ant.* slowly]

**suddenness** *(n.)*: abruptness; *breakneck speed; confounding;* dramatic speed; expeditiousness; fastness; greased lightning; hastiness; impulsiveness; *just like that; keenness;* lightning-speed; *mercurial; not expected;* overhastiness; precipitation; quickness; rapidity; swiftness; surprise; *time;* unexpectedness; *very fast; without notice; xtry.;* yar; *zippiness;* [*Ant.* slowness]

**sue** *(v.)*: *action;* bring suit against; charge; demand; entreat; file suit; go to court; *have;* implead; indict; *judgment; key;* litigate; libel; make a legal claim against; *non-criminal action;* obtain by legal process; prosecute; pursue; *quo minus* [L.]; *require;* seek recompense; take to court; undertake legal action; *voice complaint; win judgment; xfer; yieldless; zero recourse;*

**suffer** *(v. allow)*: allow; bear; consent to; *do;* enable; endure; facilitate; go along with; humor; indulge; judge okay; knowingly allow; let; make possible; not oppose; okay; permit; put up with; *qualify; rationalize;* sanction; tolerate; undergo; *validate;* warrant; *x on the dotted line;* yield; *zero opposition;*

**suffer** *(v. hurt)*: agonize; anguish; bear; *bleed; cut; cry;* distress; endure; experience pain; feel pain; grieve; hurt; *inconsolable; judder; keen;* lament; languish; make hurt; *noise; outcry;* pain; *quail; regret;* smart; sorrow; *tearful;* undergo ~ing; *vociferate;* writhe; *x-out;* yowl; *zing;* [*Ant.* stop]

**suffering** *(n.)*: agony; anguish; burden; chafing; discomfort; distress; dolor; excruciating pain; *feeling bad;* grief; galling; gnawing; hurt(ing); heartache; inflammation; injury; *jabbing;* killing [slang]; *laceration;* misery; *nip; ouch!;* pain; persecution; *Passion; quivering;* rack; ranking; soreness; stinging; torture; torment; *unpleasantness; uneasiness;* vexation; *violence;* wrenching; writhing; woe; *xiphodynia; yelling; zing;*

**suffice** *(v.)*: avail; be sufficient; content; *do; enough;* fill the bill; gratify; hack it; *indulge;* just do fine; keep happy; *like;* meet the requirements; not displease; *overjoy;* please; qualify; *reach;* suit; satisfy; *thrill; uplift; victory; well; xtry.;* yield a profit; *zero problem;*

**sufficiency** *(n.)*: adequacy; amplitude; ability; *brawn;* capability; capacity; deftness; efficacy; faculty; *genius;* habilitation; *influence; jurisdiction;* know-how; *legerdemain;* means; *natural ability; okay;* proficiency; potential; plentitude; qualification; resources; self- ~; sufficientness; satisfactory; *talent; unction;* virtuosity; wherewithal; *xenium; yaup* [arch.]; *zero need;* [*Ant.* shortness]

**sufficient** *(adj.)*: adequate; ample; able; *bountiful;* capable; due; enough; efficacious; full-able; fine; good; *handsome; influence;* jake [Br.]; *keen;* legitimate; means; no less; okay; proficient; plenty; qualified; respectable; self- ~; satisfactory; sufficing; tolerable; unobjectionable; very ample; well; *xenium; yenough* [arch.]; *zero need;* [*Ant.* short]

**suffocate** *(v.)*: asphyxiate; block up; burke; choke; deprive of oxygen; extinguish; *finish off;* gag; *hush; incapacitate;* jugulate; kill; *lynch;* muzzle; *nullify;* overlay; *put out;* quackle; quench; repress; squelch; smother; stifle; throttle; *undo; void;* wring (one's neck); *xuld* [arch.]; *yote; zeroize;*

**suffocation** *(n.)*: asphyxia(tion); burking; choking; deprivation of oxygen; extinguishment; *finishing off;* gagging; garroting; *hushing up; incapacitation;* jugulation; killing; *lynching;* muzzling; *nullification;* overlaying; *putting out;* quenching; *repression;* strangulation; smothering; throttling; *undoing; voiding;* wringing; *x-ing; yote; zeroizing;*

**suggest** *(v.)*: advise; bid; counsel; direct; exhort; foreadvise; give counsel; hint; intimate; *judge; kibitz* [Yid.]; lead; mention; make suggestion; notify; offer one's opinion; postulate; propound; *quicken;* recommend; submit; set forth; tender one's opinion; urge; volunteer; *warn; xenagogy; yammer; zero in;* [*Ant.* state]

**suggestion** *(n.)*: advice; *befriending;* counsel; direction; exhortation; free advice; guidance; hortation; hint; idea; intimation; insinuation; judgment; *kibizing* [Yid.]; *leading;* motion; *notion;* opinion; piece of advice; proposal; *quick advice;* recommendation; suggesting; tip; *urging;* voice; word of advice; *xenagogy; yammering; zeroing in;*

**suicide** *(n.)*: autocide; assisted ~; blowing oneself away; *crime;* dispatching; ending it all; felo-de-se; *gun;* hari-kari; hanging oneself; *immolation; junshi* [Jap.]; killing oneself; *liquidation;* murdering oneself; *non-living; obliteration;* para~; putting an end to it; *quelling; run through;* self-destruction (-immolation; -annihilation); taking one's life; *unseat; violence;* wasting own life; *x-out; yataghan; zap;*

**suitability** *(n.)*: appositeness; aptness; adequacy; becomingness; correctness; desirability; expediency; fitness; goodness; helpfulness; idoneousness; justification; *kosher;* legitimacy; meetness; niceness; *okay;* properness; qualification; rightness; seemliness; *tolerability;* usefulness; validity; worthiness; *xtry.; yielded; zealous;*

**suitable** *(adj.)*: apposite; apt; adequate; befitting; correct; due; expedient; fitting; good; helpful; idoneous; just; *kosher;* legitimate; meet; not out-of-place; okay; proper; qualified; right; seemly; *tolerable;* useful; valid; well-suited; *xtry.; yielded; zealous;*

**suitor** *(n.)*: admirer; beau; caller; *date;* esquire; fellow; gallant; heartthrob; inamorato; joe [slang]; knight in shining armor; lad; *loverboy;* man; noble ~; *one;* paramour; quester; Romeo; sweetheart; swain; torch; *unmarried;* valentine; wooer; *x-linked;* young man; *zon [dial.];*

**sulfur** *(n.)*: *aluminum sulfide;* brimstone; common ~; *dithiane;* element; ever-burning; *foul-smelling; gunpowder;* hepar; *iron sulfide; jarring;* kibrit; *lead sulfide;* mineral; mercaptan; $Na_2SO_4$; *oleum; polysulfide; quad;* realgar; sulphur; *thiol; unpleasant;* volcanic sulfur; *wicked;* xanthate; *yellow ~;* zoogen;

**sulk** *(v.)*: agonize; brood; contemplate; dwell on; *evaluate;* fret; grumble; huff; *incubate; joyless;* kick the dirt; languish; mope; *not happy;* object; pout; *question;* repine; self-pity; *scowl;* think unhappy thoughts; *upset;* vex; worry; *xenodiagnose; yeme; zero in;* [Ant. sing]

**sulky** *(adj.)*: aggravated; broodish; cheerless; dumpy; elegiac; fretful; glowering; heavy; ill-tempered; joyless; kicking the dirt; languishing; mopey; non-happy; over-sad; petulant; pouty; *quivering;* repining; self-pitying; trustful; unhappy; vexed; woeful; *xtry. displeasure; yearnful;* zestless; [Ant. sunny]

**sullen** *(adj.)*: angry; bleak; broody; cross; dark; dour; *embittered;* fuming; gloomy; heavy; intractable; ill-humored; joyless; *kindless;* lugubrious; morose; nettled; overcast; perturbed; *Q.B.I.;* resentful; sour; sore; somber; tenebrous; uncheerful; vexed; weary; *xenophobic; yucky; zealless;* [Ant. sunny]

**sullenness** *(n.)*: anger; bleakness; brooding; crossness; dourness; *embittered; fuming;* gloominess; heaviness; intractableness; joylessness; *kindlessness;* lugubriousness; moroseness; negativism; *overcast;* perturbation; *Q.B.I.;* resentfulness; sourness; silence; somberness; *ticked off;* uncheerfulness; vexation; wearifulness; *xenophobia; yuckiness; zeallessness;*

**sultry** *(adj.)*: airless; burning; clammy; damp; *enkindled;* full-hot; *gross;* humid; icky; *jejune; kindled; loathsome;* muggy; nasty; oppressive; pluvious; quenchless; roasting; steamy; sun-baked; torrid; uncomfortable; *vaporous;* warm; *xerothermic;* yucky; *zapping;*

**sum** *(n.)*: amount; bottom line; count; *deal;* entirety; figure; *gist; heart; itemization;* jag; *kit;* level; load; measure; mass; number; *overall;* portion; part; quantity; reckoning; range; size; summation; total; tally; units; volume; whole; weight; *x; yard; z-score;*

**summarize** *(v.)*: abridge; boil down; condense; capsulize; do a summary; epitomize; encapsulate; foreshorten; go over; *heart; idea; jist;* knock down; lessen; minimize; *nutshell;* outline; precis; perorate; quickly review; recap; review; recapitulate; sum up; synopsize; thumbnail; *use summary; vitals;* words; *xenenthesis; yetzer [Heb.]; zoe [Gr.];*

**summary** *(n.)*: abridgement; brief; breviat; condensation; capsulization; compendium; capitulation; digest; encapsulation; fundamentality; general idea; heart; idea; jist; *kernel; lifeblood;* main idea; nutshell; newsbrief; overview; outline; precis; profile; peroration; *quintessence;* review; recap; reduction; summarization; summation; sketch; synopsis; thumbnail; upshot; vignette; *warp and woof; xenenthesis;* yetzer [Heb.]; *zoe [Gr.];*
**summit** *(n.)*: apex; acme; brow; climax; crest; *destination;* extremity; *farthest point;* greatest height; height; high point; hilltop; *increase; jut;* kop; limit; mountaintop; nib; outcrop; peak; pinnacle; *quoif; roof;* spire; top; upper extremity; vertex; *way up; xtry; yonder point;* zenith; [*see* discussion; meeting]
**summon** *(v.)*: assemble; ask one to come; arraign; beckon; bid; convoke; call; cry; desire; evoke; foregather; gather; gesture; holler; invite; *jar;* knell; *let know;* motion; muster; nempne; order; organize; page; petition; preconize; *quantify;* rally; rouse; request; signal; send for; tell; *utter; urge;* vociferate; *will; xfer;* yell; *zealously bid;* [*Ant.* send]
**summons** *(n.)*: arraignment; bidding; citation; call; court order; directive; entreatment; fiat; garnishment; high court order; inducement; juror ~; knell; legal ~; monition; nempne; order; process; *questioning;* request; subpoena; *scire facias* [L.]; ticket; *ultimatum;* vocation; venire; writ; *xfer;* yellow slip; *zealous bidding;*
**sumptuous** *(adj.)*: abundant; bountiful; costly; classy; deluxe; extravagant; excessive; fabulous; gorgeous; grand; high-class; immoderate; indulgent; *jet-set;* kingly; luxurious; lavish; magnificent; never-wanting; opulent; plush; *quartful* [arch.]; rich; ritzy; resplendent; spectacular; splendid; *tremendous;* upscale; voluptuous; wealthy; xtry.; *yet unsurpassed; zierlich* [G.];
**sun** *(n.)*: aubade; *brightness; body;* corona; daystar; *energy;* full sun; *glow;* heliacal; illuminant; jewel of the sky [poet.]; king of day [poet.]; luminary; light; midday ~; noonday ~; *orb;* Pheobus; photosphere; *quite sunny;* rising ~; setting ~; Sol; *star; thermoluminescence;* ultraviolet; *vivid ~;* winter ~; *xtr. bright;* yellow ~; *zonne* [arch.];
**Sunday** *(n.)*: advent; *blessed day; the* Christian Sabbath; *church day;* dominical; day of rest; *Easter ~;* first day of the week; God's day; holy day; *interval; Jesus;* kirk-day [Scot.]; *the* Lord's day; *morning; new week; off-day; period;* Quadragesima; rest day; Sabbath; *time of the week; unique; venerated; Whit ~; weekend;* Xn. Sabbath; *Yeshua;* Zion's Hope;
**sunny** *(adj.)*: aglow; balmy; bright; clear; cheerful; *delightful;* effulgent; fair; fine; gleaming; happy; hot; insolated; joyful; *keen;* luminous; light; *magnificent;* merry; nice; optimistic; pleasant; *quenchless;* radiant; sunlit; sun-drenched; sunshiny; toasty; unclouded; upbeat; *vivacious;* warm; *xerothermic;* yellow-hot; zestful; [*Ant.* stormy]
**sunrise** *(n.)*: A.M.; break of day; crack of dawn; dawn; daybreak; dayspring; daylight; *early morn;* first light; forenoon; going up of the sun; half-light; *initial; jump off; kick off;* light (of day); morning; *night's end; opening; picturesque; quickening;* rising of the sun; *rooster;* sunup; *time; tomorrow; up-going of the sun;* very early; *wake up call; xtry,; yestermorn; yeender; zone;* [*Ant.* sunset]
**sunset** *(n.)*: *after hours;* blaze; bedtime; close of the day; dusk; day's end; evening; eventide; eve; fall of the sun; gloaming; *hibernation; idleness; jammies; kip; late-night; moonlight;* night(time); nightfall; *overnight;* P.M.; *q.n.; rest;* sundown; setting of the sun; twilight; *unconsciousness;* vespers; *wink; x-ing; yester-evening; zone;* [*Ant.* sunrise]
**sunshine** *(n. illumination)*: apricity; brightness; *candescence;* daylight; effulgence; fulgency; glory; glare; haze; illumination; *joyance; keenness;* light of the sun; midday sun; natural light; oriency; prefulgency; *quite bright;* rays; sunlight; transplendency; *utter shine;* vividness; warmth of the sun; *xenon light;* yellow light; *zodiacal light;* [*Ant.* shadow]
**super** *(adj.)*: amazing; big; chief; divine; extraordinary; fantastic; great; heavenly; incredible; jolly good; keen; laudable; marvelous; mighty; notable; outstanding; prodigious; *quantum* [L.]; remarkable; stupendous; superhuman; ~ -duper; terrific; tremendous; unequalled; *ultra-;* very good; virtuous; wondrous; xtry.; you-beaut [Aus.]; *zestful;*

**superb** *(adj.)*: amazing; *bon!* [F.]; bang-up; capital; charming; divine; excellent; extraordinary; fabulous; great; heavenly; incredible; jolly good; keen; lovely; marvelous; nice; outstanding; praiseworthy; quality; remarkable; splendid; super; stupendous; terrific; unequalled; very good; wonderful; xtry.; *yeah!;* zizzy; [Ant. sorry]

**superintendent** *(n.)*: administrator; boss; chief; chairman; director; dean; executive; foreman; governor; head; intendant; jefe; keeper; leader; lord; manager; *night manager;* overseer; procurator; principal; *quartermaster;* reeve; supervisor; steward; trustee; undershepherd; viceroy; warden; XO; yardboss; zayim;

**superior** *(adj.)*: ascendant; better; bigger; choicer; dominant; exceptional; foremost; finer; greater; higher; hegemonic; incomparable; *just plain better;* keener; loftier; leading; much higher; nicer; nobler; outstanding; over; prepotent; preponderant; preeminent; predominant; *quality; reigning;* supreme; top-quality; unequalled; very much improved; worthier; weightier; XF; yet unsurpassed; *zenithal;* [Ant. second-rate]

**superiority** *(n.)*: ascendancy; *best;* control; dominance; excellence; *foremost;* greatness; hegemony; incomparability; *just plain better; keenness;* lead; might; *notability;* overlordship; preeminence; predominance; primacy; *quality;* reign; supremacy; *top;* ultimacy; virtue; worthiness; weightiness; *XF; yet unsurpassed;* zenithal; [Ant. servanthood]

**supersede** *(v.)*: assume; *betake;* change; displace; exchange; follow; go in place; *have instead;* invalidate; *jockey; key replacement; leave behind;* make obsolete; *nullify;* override; overtake; outmode; put in place; *quid pro quo* [L.]; replace; supplant; succeed; take the place of; unseat; usurp; *vamp; work; xfer; yaw; zwap [dial.];*

**supplant** *(v.)*: appropriate; arrogate; *betake;* commandeer; displace; depose; dethrone; expropriate; force out; grab; *hold; intercept; jockey; keep;* lay hold of; make off with; *nobble;* overthrow; oust; put in place; *quid pro quo [L.];* replace; seize; take the place of; undermine; usurp; *villainy;* wrest; *xfer;* yank away; *zwap [dial.];*

**suppose** *(v.)*: assume; believe; consider; deduce; expect; feel; guess; gather; hypothesize; imagine; judge; *know;* look upon as; maintain; *notion;* opine; presume; postulate; posit; *qua* [L.]; reckon; speculate; suggest; think; theorize; understand; venture; wis; *xenodiagnose; yeme; zazen;*

**supposition** *(n.)*: assumption; belief; conclusion; conjecture; deduction; expectation; feeling; guess; hypothesis; idea; judgment; *know; lucubration; musing;* notion; *opine [arch.];* presumption; postulation; pre~; *qua [L.];* reckoning; speculation; theory; understanding; *venture; wis; xenodiagnose; yeme; zazen;*

**suppositional** *(adj.)*: assumed; belief-based; conjectural; deductive; estimated; *feeling;* guessed; given; hypothetical; imaginary; *just suppose; knowledgeable; lemma; minded;* notional; not proven; opinionative; putative; Q.E.D.; reckoned; speculative; supposed; theoretical; unproven; virtual; *what if...; xenagogic; yankering; zealous;*

**surplus** *(adj.)*: additional; bonus; *copious; de trop* [F.]; extra; further; *gratuitous; heightened;* increased; joining; *king-sized amounts;* leftover; more; net; over; plus; *quantities;* remaining; spare; *too;* unused; *volume; wealth;* x.; yet more; *zillions;*

**surplus** *(n.)*: abundance; bounty; copiousness; disproportionate; excess; *flood;* generous amount; galore; heap; immensity; jumbo amount; *king-sized amount;* lots; loads; liberality; multiplicity; much; many; numerousness; overabundance; plethora; preponderance; profusion; quantities; repleteness; superabundance; tons; uberty; volumes; wealth; x.; *yards; zillion;* [Ant. shortfall]

**superficial** *(adj.)*: artificial; bogus; cursory; duplicitous; external; feigned; false; facile; glib; hollow; insincere; Janus-faced; knee-deep; *lying;* mendacious; make-believe; non-genuine; on the surface; outward; phony; quick; roundabout; surface; skin-deep; *trivial;* unreal; vain; wooden; wangling; *xtry. hypocritical; yentzing; zelig;* [Ant. sincere]

**superintendent** *(n.)*: administrator; boss; chief; chairman; dean; director; executive; foreman; governor; head; intendant; jefe; keeper; leader; manager; night manager; *nazir [Mos.]*; overseer; principal; *quartermaster;* rector; supervisor; top brass; *taskmaster;* undershepherd; viceroy; warden; XO; *yardboss;* zayim;

**supernatural** *(adj.)*: angelic; abnormal; bodiless; celestial; divine; demonic; ethereal; fey; firmamental; godlike; ghostly; hyperphysical; heavenly; holy; incorporeal; immaterial; *jarring; kramat [Arab.]; lurid; mystical;* numinous; noncorporeal; otherworldly; preternatural; paranormal; *queer; realm;* spiritual; supernal; superhuman; transcendent; transmundane; unnatural; unearthly; unworldly; *visitant;* weirdward; *xtry.; yonder;* zoic; [*Ant.* sublunary]

**superstition** *(n.)*: accepted belief; belief; *cultural belief;* delusion; *erroneous belief;* freet [Ire.]; folklore; fear; *ghost story;* hunch; idea; irrational fear; *juju; knowledge;* legend; lore; myth; notion; old wives' tale; pishogue; *queer belief; religious fallacy;* shibboleth; tall tale; unfounded fear; *version; writing; xenodocheionology; yarn;* zoophobia;

**supervise** *(v.)*: administer; boss (around); be a steward of; control; direct; *execute; force;* govern; head; influence; judge; keep under control; lead; manage; *nobble;* oversee; procurate; *quell;* run; superintend; take the helm; *use; vanquish; weight;* XO; yeme; zayim; [*Ant.* submit]

**supervisor** *(n.)*: administrator; boss; chief; chairman; director; executive; foreman; floorwalker; governor; head; intendant; jefe; keeper; leader; manager; *night manager;* overseer; procurator; principal; *queen [fem.];* ruler; superintendent; top brass; *taskmaster; tyrant; ultimate authority;* viceroy; warden; XO; yardmaster; zanjero;

**supper** *(n.)*: aliment; bread; cuisine; dinner; evening meal; food; *groceries; haute cuisine;* ingesta; junket; keep; *lunch;* meat; meal; nourishment; *organic food;* provisions; *quelque-chose [F.];* repast; sustenance; third meal; *unassimilated food;* victuals; *wheat;* xarque; yams; ziti;

**supplement** *(v.)*: add on; append; better; complement; *develop;* enhance; fill out; fortify; further; *give more;* help; increase; improve; join; *keen;* link; make better; *new; offer;* put together; *quantity;* round out; reinforce; step up; tag on; tack on; unite; *vest; with; xtr.; yoke; zip;*

**supplemental** *(adj.)*: additional; auxiliary; bonus; contributory; *different;* extra; further; gainful; helpful; increased; joining; *keen; linking;* more; new; other; plus; *quantities;* reinforcing; supplementary; surplus; tack-on; *unused; volumes; with;* xtr.; yet more; *zeug;*

**supplicate** *(v.)*: appeal; beseech; call on; desire; entreat; *forewish;* go ask; *humbly ask;* implore; importune; *just keep asking; keep asking; look for;* make request; *need;* obsecrate; petition; *quiritation;* request; seek; solicit; *try to obtain;* urge; *vocalize;* want; *XQ.;* yearn for; *zealously entreat;* [*Ant.* supply]

**supplication** *(n.)*: appeal; beseeching; cry; *desire;* entreaty; *forewish;* grace; *humble entreaty;* intercession; importunity; imploration; juration; *kiddush [Heb.];* litany; making request; nones; orison; prayer; petition; plea; *query;* request; solicitation; suit; *telling God;* urging; *vigil;* wish; *XQ;* yearning; *zikr* [Mos.]; [*Ant.* supply]

**supplier** *(n.)*: area ~; buyer; contributor; distributor; equipper; furnisher; *forager;* giver; *handing (out);* issuer; *jettison; kit; lender;* manciple; *non-retention;* outfitter; provider; provisioner; quartermaster; renderer; seller; storekeeper; transferer; *unhand;* vester; victualer; *weigh; xferer;* yielder; *zonal ~;*

**supply** *(n.)*: amassment; buildup; collection; deposit; endowment; fund; furnishment; *group;* hoard; ingathering; jam [slang]; kit [coll.]; lode; lot; mass; number; overflow; provision; quantity; reserve; resource; source; stock; takings; *upbuild;* volume; wheen; *xuld [arch.];* yield; *zillions;* [*Ant.* shortage]

**supply** *(v.)*: allot; bestow; contribute; cater; distribute; deliver; equip; furnish; give; hand (out); issue; *jettison;* kit; *lend;* make provision; *non-retention;* outfit; provide; *quarter;* render; regale; sell; transfer; *unhand;* vest; *weigh;* xfer; yield; *zip;* [*Ant.* secure]

**support** *(n. permission)*: approval; assent; backing; blessing; consent; defend; *delight;* endorsement; favor; *freedom;* go-ahead; green light; hear to [reg.]; imprimatur; joint-permission; keeping; license; leave; *liberty; may;* nod; okay; permission; *qualified yes; right;* sufferance; sanction; sustentation; subvention; thumbs up [slang]; unreluctance; vouchsafement; willingness; *xtr. helpful;* yes; *zealous ~;*
**support** *(n, buttress)*: abutment; assistance; buttress; brace; base; butment; backing; column; crutch; cooperation; *distribute;* encouragement; foundation; fulcrum; flying buttress; funding; girding; holding up; help; *investment;* joist; *keeping;* leg; lending aid; maintenance; *nail; object;* pillar; prop; patronage; *quick help;* reinforcement; stanchion; sympathy; sponsorship; *taking on;* undergirding; (-pinning; -prop; -writing); vang; vote of confidence; *wall; well-supported; xfer; yes vote;* zealous ~;
**support** *(v, financially back)*: abet; back; bankroll; come to the aid; dole out; disburse funds to; endow; finance; fund; foot cost; get behind; help; habilitate; invest in; *just-in-time;* keep; lend aid; maintain; *nurture; overpay;* pay for; patronize; *quick; recompense;* subsidize; sponsor; take on (for ~); underwrite; vouch for; *well-supported; xfer;* yield ~; *zet [dial.];*
**support** *(v. hold up)*: assist; bear; buttress; bolster; back; brace; carry; *deliver;* encourage; *for;* give assistance; hold up; help; *improve;* janker; keep; *load-bearing;* maintain; *nail; over- ~;* prop up; *quick-to-help;* relieve; revet; sustain; shoulder; take part of burden; uphold; undergird; underprop; *verify; well-sustained; xfer;* yomp; *zero hindrance;*
**supposed** *(adj.)*: apparent; alleged; assumed; believed; commonly thought; credited; deemed; expected; evident; *figure;* generally accepted; hypothetical; imagined; *j'accused; known; looks;* meant; non-confirmed; ostensible; presumed; perceived; putative; *questionable;* reputed; seeming; thought; theoretical; unconfirmed; verisimlar; *word; xel [arch.];* yet unconfirmed; *zero proof;* [*Ant.* sure]
**supposition** *(n.)*: assumption; belief; conclusion; deduction; expectation; feeling; guess; hypothesis; idea; inkling; *judgment; knowledge;* lemma; *mind;* notion; *opinion;* presumption; postulation; *qua [L.];* reckoning; supposing; theory; understanding; *view;* working theory; *xenodiagnosis; yankering; zealous belief;* [*Ant.* surety]
**suppress** *(v.)*: abate; burden; crush; control; dominate; extinguish; enslave; force; govern; hush; hold back; inhibit; jam; keep down (-back); levigate; master; neutralize; oppress; prevent; put down; quell; repress; subjugate; subdue; stifle; tame; tyrannize; use; victimize; weaken; withhold; *x;* yoke; zap; [*Ant.* succumb]
**suppression** *(n.)*: arrestation; burdening; control; domination; extinguishment; enslaving; forced compliance; governing; hushing; inhibition; *jamming;* keeping down; levigation; mastering; neutralizing; oppression; putting down; prevention; putting down; quelling; repression; subjugation; taming; tyranny; unseating; victimization; weakening; withholding; *x-ing;* yoking; zapping; [*Ant.* succumbing]
**supreme** *(adj.)*: absolute; almighty; best; chief; choicest; dominant; elite; finest; greatest; highest; imperative; inimitable; *jim-dandy;* keenest; loftiest; most high; maximal; No. 1; optimum; premium; prime; quintessential; ranking; superior; superlative; sovereign; top(most); ultimate; *valedictorian;* world-class; xtry.; yondmost; zenithal; [*Ant.* smallest]
**sure** *(adj.)*: assured; beyond doubt; certain; definite; dependable; evident; firm; guaranteed; highly confident; indisputable; incontestable; incontrovertible; ironclad; just ~; keenly ~; *legitimate;* mistake-proof; non-questionable; 100% certain; positive; quite ~; questionless; reliable; self-evident; true; unfailing; undeniable; unmistaken; verified; without doubt; xtry. ~; yes indeed; zero doubt; [*Ant.* shaky]
**surface** *(n.)*: *area;* appearance; boundary; coat; covering; dimension; exterior; even ~; façade; flat ~; face; *gradient;* hull; integument; *jaggy ~; key;* level ~; *margin; nominal;* outside; plane; *quality;* rind; side; shell; topside; upside; veneer; *wall; x-factor; yonder; zet [dial.];*

**surface** *(v.)*: arise; become evident; come out; dawn; debouch; emerge; egress; flow out; get out; happen; issue; *journey; known; look;* materialize; *non-hidden;* occur; proceed out of; *quicken;* rise up; show up; turn up; upspring; venture out; *walk out; xfer;* yede; zip out;
**surge** *(n.)*: acceleration; burst; breaking forth; coursing; dehiscence; deluge; eruption; flow; gush; hurling; issue; jet; *ka-pow;* letting go; *movement; naid;* outburst; pouring; *quickening;* rush; spate; stream; torrent; upsurge; vomiting; wave; *xfer; yead;* zwoosh;
**surge** *(v.)*: accelerate; burst; break forth; course; deluge; erupt; flow; flood; gush; hurl; issue forth; jet; *ka-pow;* let go; *move; naid;* outburst; pour; *quickening;* rush; rise; stream; torrent; upsurge; vomit; well up; *xfer; yead;* zwoosh;
**surgery** *(n.)*: amputation; brain ~; cutting open; *doctoring;* exploratory ~; *fixing up;* general ~; *heart ~; hospitalization;* intensive care; *jejunostomy;* the knife; *laser ~;* micro~; *neuro~;* operation; op [slang]; outpatient ~; procedure; *quick procedure;* reconstructive ~; surgical procedure; treatment; *under the knife;* vivisect; work; *xyster; yeme;* zooplasty;
**surly** *(adj.)*: abrupt; brusque; churlish; disrespectful; emulous; feisty; gruff; harsh; impolite; *jaded;* kindless; liverish; mean; nastiness; ornery; peevish; quick-tempered; rude; short-tempered; truculent; unfriendly; vinegary; waspish; *xenophobic;* yieldless; *zhlubby;* [Ant. sweet]
**surpass** *(v.)*: advance past; beat; cap; do better; eclipse; excel; exceed; *further;* go beyond; *higher;* improve on; *just pass;* kill; lick; master; *no contest;* outclass (-do -race; -shine; -perform); pass by; *quash; rout;* speed past; transcend; top; unseat; *vanquish;* worst; *x-cend; yet better;* zip past; [Ant. succumb]
**surprise** *(n.)*: amazement; blow; bombshell; confounding; disbelief; eye-opener; flabbergasting; gastness; *hit;* incredulity; jolt; keeling over; *look aghast;* marveling; *nonplus;* overwhelming; puzzlement; quake; rattle; revelation; shock; taking back; unbelief; *very impressed;* wonderment; *xtry.;* yerk; zonking;
**surprise** *(v.)*: astound; alarm; bowl over; confound; daze; *excite;* flabbergast; floor; gape; hit; impact; impress; jolt; knock down; look aghast; make marvel; nonplus; overawe; phase; quake; rattle; stun; startle; take aback; *unbelievable; virtually astound;* wonder; *xtry.;* yerk; zap;
**surrender** *(n.)*: acquiescence; bow; bend; (con)cession; ceding; capitulation; deferring; *ending;* forfeiture; giving up; handing over; *indulging; jumping off;* knuckling under; laying down arms; *making peace; nonsuccess;* obedience; parting with; quittance; relinquishment; resignation; reddition; submission; throwing in the towel; *unvictorious; void;* white flag; *xfer;* yielding; *zapped;* [Ant. subjugation]
**surrender** *(v.)*: acquiesce; admit defeat; bow; bend; (con)cede; capitulate; defer; deliver; *end;* forfeit; give up (-in); hand over; *indulge; jump off;* knuckle under; lay down arms; make concession; negotiate terms of ~; obey; part with; quit; relinquish; resign; succumb; submit; throw in the towel; *unvictorious; void;* withdraw claim; wave the white flag; *xfer;* yield; *zapped;* [Ant. seize]
**surround** *(v.)*: *all around;* begird; beset; besiege; beleaguer; blockade; circle; *contain;* draw around; encircle; envelop; enclose; environ; encompass; encase; frame; gird; gherao; hem in; hedge; inclose; incase; *Jordan curve;* kirtle; leaguer; loop around; move around; mure; *non-broken circle;* outline; put around; *quarantine;* ravel; siege; sandwich; swallow; twine; *upwind;* volt; wrap; wall in; *xfer;* yard up; zone;
**survey** *(n.)*: analysis; *breakdown;* census; citywide ~; *count;* decennial census; evaluation; field study; Gallup poll; hone in; *inquiry; judgment;* key ~; listing; local ~; mandated census; nationwide ~; opinion poll; poll; popular opinion; questionnaire; research; rating; *results;* sampling; town-wide ~; *undertaking;* vox pop; *view;* write-up; *xenodiagnosis;* yield results; *zonal census;*
**survey** *(v.)*: assess; appraise; analyze; ask; behold; consider; distinguish; examine; evaluate; enquire; find out; gaze; go over; *hone in on;* inspect; inquire; judge; *keep eyes on;* look; make out; make inquiry; note; observe; *opinion;* probe; poll; question; query; review; reconnoiter; study; scrutinize; scan; sample; take in; take census; *understand;* view; watch; *xenodiagnose;* yeme; *zero in;*

**survival** *(n.)*: abiding; bearing through; continuance; duration; endurance; *follow;* getting through; holding out; imperishability; *journeying through;* keeping on; long-standingness; making it; not dying; outliving; perseverance; *qualification;* remaining; survivorship; sustaining; *toleration;* unyieldingness; victory; weathering; *x-scend;* yieldlessness; *zero harm;* [*Ant.* succumbing]

**survive** *(v.)*: *alive;* bear through; bear up; continue; dure; endure; emerge; fare well; go on; get through; hold out (on); *imperishability;* journey through; keep living; live (through); last; make it; not die; outlive; outlast; overlive; outride; persevere; *qualify;* remain (alive); stay alive; subsist; triumph over; uphold; *victory;* weather; winter; *xenize; yieldless; zero harm;* [*Ant.* succumb]

**survivor** *(n.)*: *alive;* bearer; continuer; *dure;* endurer; emerger; finalist; *go on;* hanger-on; *imperishability; journeyer through;* kept alive; living; *make it; not die;* outliver; overcomer; perseverer; *qualified;* relict [biol.]; subsister; survivalist; trooper; *tough; upholder;* victor; weatherer; *xenizer; yieldless; zero harm;*

**susceptibility** *(n.)*: affectability; bent; capability; disposition; endangerment; *frailness; get;* hazard; inclination; jeopardy; known risk; liability; menace; non-immunity; openness; predisposition; proneness; *qualification;* receptiveness; risk; susceptibleness; threat; *unprotected;* vulnerability; weakness; *xenenthesis; yaw; zero defense;*

**susceptible** *(adj.)*: at risk; *bent;* capable of being affected; disposed; endangered; *frail; get;* have the inclination; inclined; jeopardized; keenly ~; liable; *menaced;* non-immune; open; predisposed; prone; *qualified;* receptive; susceptible; subject; threatened; unprotected; vulnerable; *weak; xenenthesis; yaw; zero defense;* [*Ant.* safety]

**suspect** *(adj.)*: apprehensive; *beclouded;* confusing; doubtful; dubious; *equivocal;* fishy; *guarded;* highly ~; incredulous; *just not sure; kiaugh [Scot.];* lacking certainty; *misgivings;* not sure; odd; *puzzling;* questionable; *reticent;* suspicious; shady; trustless; uncertain; unsure; *very unlikely; wavering; xtry,* ~; yet unconformed; *zero certainty;* [*Ant.* sure]

**suspect** *(n.)*: accused; believed guilty party; charged party; defendant; enquiree; *figure; guilty;* he that is accused; inquiree; *jalouse [Scot.];* key ~; likely guilty individual; *malefactor;* non-convicted; *offender;* possibly guilty party; questionee; respondent; subject; *transgressor;* unconvicted; villain; wrongdoer; *x;* yet unconvicted; *zero in;*

**suspect** *(v.)*: assume; believe; conjecture; construe; deduce; expect; figure; guess; hold; have a theory; imagine; jalouse [Scot.]; *keen suspicion; likely;* misgive; make a presumption; *notion; occur;* presume; *question; reckon;* suspect; suppose; think; theorize; *understand;* venture to guess; wager; *xenodiagnose; yeme; zero confirmation;*

**suspend** *(v.)*: act; buoy; carry; dangle; *equipoise;* float; *gibbet;* hang; hover; hold; *impend; just hanging;* keep up; loom; make to hang; *nail up;* overhang; put up; *pendulous; quat;* rest; swing; *tie up; up in the air;* volplane; waft; *x-out; yede; zero gravity;* [*see* postpone]

**suspense** *(n.)*: anticipation; anxiety; *burden;* concernment; cliff-hanging; disquiet; expectation; excitement; fretting; great anticipation; hopefulness; heebie-jeebies; incertitude; jitteriness; kiaugh [Scot.]; lather; *misgiving;* nervousness; over-anxiety; pins and needles; *questionableness;* restlessness; stress; trepidation; titillation; unrest; vexation; wondering; *xel [arch.];* yearning; *zeal;*

**suspension** *(n.)* abeyance; break; ceasing; dangling; discontinuance; deferment; *ending;* floatation; forbearance; giving a break; hangup; hovering; holdup; inactivity; *jerk away;* keeping up; looming; letup; motionlessness; non-operation; overhanging; pensility; pendulousness; pause; postponement; quieting; rest(ing); suspending; swinging; stoppage; surcease; time out; *up in the air;* vacation; waiting; *x-rest;* yawning; *zero productivity;*

**suspicion** *(n. mistrust)*: apprehension; *bothered;* captiousness; distrust; doubt; *ever-mistrustful;* fishiness; guardedness; hesitancy; iffiness; jealousy; keen ~; leeriness; mistrust; non-trust; over- ~; paranoia; querulence; *reluctance;* suspiciousness; *tentativeness;* untrustworthiness; umbratiousness; *vacillation;* wariness; *xenophobia;* yare-handedness; *zärtlich [G.];*

**suspicion** *(n. theory or belief)*: assumption; belief; conjecture; deduction; educated guess; estimation; feeling; guess; hunch; hypothesis; idea; *judgment;* keen imagination; *lemma;* mind; notion; opinion; postulation; qualified guess; reckoning; speculation; theory; *urge;* view; *wild guess; xenodiagnosis; yankering; zeal;* [Ant. surety]
**suspicious** *(adj.)*: apprehensive; accusatory; borderline; captious; dark; doubtful; dubious; distrustful; dubious; ever-leery; fishy; guarded; hesitant; highly ~; iffy; incredulous; jealous; keenly ~; leery; mistrustful; non-trustworthy; open-to-doubt; over- ~; paranoid; querulent; questionable; *reluctant;* suspect; shiftless; *tricky;* uncertain; untrustworthy; umbratious; very ~; wary; *xenophobic;* yare-handed; *zärtlich* [G.]; [Ant. shady]
**sustain** *(v.)*: abide; assist; bear; continue; carry on; do; endure; *fix;* go on; hold; help; *incur; journey on;* keep up; look after; maintain; *non-stop;* outlast; preserve; *quicken;* remain; suffer; subsist; support; *tarry;* uphold; undergo; *voyage on;* wage; *xtr. steady;* yield not; *zero cessation;* [see feed; Ant. stop]
**swaddle** *(v.)*: array; bind; bundle; clothe; draw around; enwrap; fold; gird; hug; inwrap; *jacket;* kirtle; lash; mummify; *nurture;* overwind; put around; *quoil* [arch.]; ravel; swathe; tie; twine; upbind; volt; wrap; *x-ing; yard; zone;*
**swagger** *(v.)*: amble; bluster; crow; *delight in self;* exhibition; flounce; flaunt; flourish; gloat; gasconade; hector; *intimidate;* jactitate; *know-it-all;* lock step; magnificate; *narcissist;* ostentate; piaffe; parade; prance; *quidnunc;* roister; saunter; strut; tittup; ululate; vaunt; wamble; *xtry. proud;* yelp; *zestful;*
**swallow** *(v.)*: absorb; bolt; consume; down; drink; engulf; eat up; *finish off;* gulp; *have;* ingest; imbibe; ingurgitate; *jam down;* knock back; *lap up; munch; nip;* overwhelm; pop; quaff; raven; *receive;* swig; scarf; take down; uptake; *victual;* wash down [slang]; wolf; *xfer;* yolp; *zip down;*
**swamp** *(n.)*: aikraw; bog; carr; drainage area; everglade; fen; glade; haugh; inland marsh; *jheel* [Ind.]; kavir; *lagoon;* marsh; moor; *nanoplankton; overgrown;* peatbog; pocosin; quagmire; rosland; *reeds;* slough; tarn; tule; *usnea;* vlie [S. Afr.]; wetlands; xyrisic; yarpha; *zoocarpous area;*
**swampy** *(adj.)*: alluvial; boggy; carr-like; damp; *everglade;* fenny; gouty; *heavy; icky; jheel [Ind.];* kavir-like; lutose; *loamy;* marshy; miry; *never-dry; oozy;* paludal; peaty; quaggy; *reedy;* sloughy; spongy; *turbid;* uliginose; *vlie [S. Afr.];* washy; watery; xyrisic; *yucky; zoocarpous;*
**swarm** *(n.)*: amassment; bunch; bees; bugs; cluster; cloud; drove; *en masse;* flight; group; horde; hotch [Scot.]; ingathering; jam [slang]; kit [coll.]; lot; mass; number; overabundance; pack; passel; quantity; ruck; rally; squad; throng; *unit; volume;* wisp; *xtry. number; yardful; zillions;* [see plague]
**sway** *(n.)*: authority; bearing; control; clout; dominion; effect; faculty; governance; hold; influence; jurisdiction; kingship; leverage; mastery; name; oversight; power; pull; *quo warranto [L.];* rule; strength; *throne;* upper hand; *virtue;* weight; *xuld [arch.];* yard; zorch;
**sway** *(v.)*: arch; bend; bow; curve; dip; *enfold;* flex; go back and forth; hunch; incline; jump; knuckle; lean; move; nutate; oscillate; ply; quat; rock; stoop; swing; swoop; tilt; undulate; vacillate; wave; *xy-curve;* yield; yawl zigzag; [see convince; rule; influence]
**swear** *(v.)*: affirm; bind to an oath; covenant; deign; *ensure;* forswear; guarantee; give word; hypothecate; interpledge; jurate; *keep word; legitimize;* make vow; *nobly ~;* oath; obligate; pledge; promise; *qualify;* resolve; solemnly promise; testify; *unconditionally ~;* vow; warrant; *x-ones heart; yafery [arch.]; zealously ~;* [see curse]
**swearword** *(n.)*: anathema; blasphemy; curse; cussword; dirty word; expletive; execration; foul language; *gross disrespect; hex;* invective; juration; *kitsch; lewd word;* malediction; *nasty language;* oath; profanity; *quadriliteral;* ribaldry; swearing; sacrilege; tasteless speech; ungodly language; vulgarism; *vernacular;* wickedness; XXXX; yawp; *zinger;*
**sweat** *(n.)*: armpit ~; brow-moisture; beads of ~; cold ~; dampness; droplets; desudation; diaphoresis; exsudation; forehead-sweat; *gleet;* hidrosis; *indrenched; juice; kesting;* lather; moisture; muck~ [Br.]; night- ~; ooze; perspiration; *quivering;* resudation; sweating; sweat-drops; transudation; underarm ~; *venting;* wetness; *xerosis; yote; zapped;*

**sweat** *(v.)*: *anguish;* bead up; *cold ~;* drip; exsude; *flow; grind;* hidrosis; *issue; juice; kest; lose; moil; non-retention;* ooze; perspire; *quiver;* resudate; secrete; transude; *underarm; vent;* work up a ~; *xude; yote; zapped;* [see worry]

**sweet** *(adj. nice)*: agreeable; amiable; benign; charming; darling; delightful; enjoyable; fine; gentle; honeyed; honey- ~; *intimate;* jaggery; kindhearted; lovable; melting; merciful; nice; obliging; pleasant; *quick to help;* regardful; softhearted; sugary; satisfying; thoughtful; tender(hearted); touching; unselfish; very kind; warm; xenial; *yielding; zuccary* [arch.]; [*Ant.* sour]

**sweet** *(adj. sugary)*: ambrosial; *be honeyed;* candied; dulcified; edulcorated; fructose-sweetened; *glazed;* high-sugar; ingratiated; jaggery; *keen-tasting; luscious;* maple-sugared; *nectarous;* over-sweetened; powder-sugared; *quiniva;* rendered ~; sugary; sacchariferous; tasting of sugar; *unsalted;* very ~; with sugar; xylose-added; *yummy; zuccary* [arch.]; [*Ant.* sour]

**sweeten** *(v.)*: add sugar; behoney; become sweet; candy; dulcify; disembitter; edulcorate; embellish; fructose-sweeten; *granulated sugar;* honey; ingratiate; improve; *jaggery; keen-tasting; luscious;* make sweeter; milden; *nice; over~;* put sugar in; *quiniva;* render sweet; sugar(coat); *table sugar;* upgrade; *very sweet; with sugar; xylose-added; yummy; zuccary [arch.];*

**sweetheart** *(n.)*: amoret; angel; beloved; babe; buttercup; boyfriend [masc.]; cutie; darling; dear; dove; esquire [masc.]; flame; gallant [masc.]; girlfriend [fem.]; honey(-bun); heartthrob; inamorato; Juliet [fem.]; kitten [fem.]; love(r); lovebird; leman; love-lass; lamb; ladylove; mavourneen [Ire.]; mistress [fem.]; *nice; other;* precious; pet; prince charming [masc.]; *querida* [Sp. fem.]; *querido* [Sp. masc.]; Romeo [masc.]; sweetie(-pie); sugar; true love; torch; *undying love;* valentine; wooer; *XOXO; young love; zitella [It. fem.];* [*Ant.* sworn enemy]

**sweetness** *(n. kindness)*: agreeableness; benevolence; compassion; dulcoration; edulcoration; favor; goodness; *helpfulness; indulgence; joviality;* kindness; love; mercifulness; niceness; obligingness; pleasantness; *quick to give;* regard; sugar(iness); thoughtfulness; tenderness; unselfishness; *virtuousness;* warmth; xenia; *yearning; zealousness;* [*Ant.* sourness]

**swell** *(v.)*: augment; bloat; bulge; billow; balloon; crescendo; distend; dilate; engorge; enlarge; expand; fatten; gorge; greaten; grow; heighten; inflate; increase; *jut; keep growing;* largen; mound; *nodular;* overdistend (-develop; -saturate); *overblown; outblown;* puff up; poof; plump; protuberate; *quantum increase;* rise; soak; saturate; tumefy; tumulate; *upgrow* [arch.]; *venticrose;* wax great; waterlog; *XL; yain* [arch.]; *zoom;* [*Ant.* shrink]

**swelling** *(n.)*: augmentation; bloating; bulging; crescendoing; distension; enlarging; ectasia; fattening; growth; heightening; inflating; increase; intumescence; *jutting; kibe;* largeness; mounding; *nodular;* overdistension; protuberance; puffing; *quantum increase;* rising; soaking; tumefaction; *upgrowth* [arch.]; *venticrose;* waxing great; *XL; yain [arch.];* zooming; [*Ant.* shrinkage]

**swerve** *(v.)*: alter; bend; curve; careen; deviate; el; fold; gybe; go off; hook; incline; *jag;* knuckle; *left turn;* move; *nonlinear; offset; pull;* quat; reel; swing; sheer; turn; *uncinate;* veer; wander; *xy-curve;* yaw; zag;

**swift** *(adj.)*: agile; accelerated; brisk; breakneck; *celerity;* dexterous; expeditious; fast; *greased lightening;* hurried; *instant(aneous); jiffy; keen;* lissome; lightning-fast; mercurial; *moving;* nimble; on the double; pronto; prompt; quick; rapid; speedy; turbo; *timely; ultrasonic speed;* volant; wimble; x-speed; yar; zippy; [*Ant.* slow]

**swim** *(v.)*: *advance;* backstroke; bathe; crawl; dive; *drift;* dip; drift; dog-paddle; dive; *edge;* float; glide; have a ~; *impel; jet; keep going; leap in;* move; *navigate; natant; out~;* paddle; *quick;* race; stream; (side)stroke; skinny-dip; traverse; *underway;* voyage; wade; *wend; waft; xfer; yede; zip;*

**swimmer** *(n.)*: *aquatics;* backstroker; bather; dipper; dog-paddler; diver; *edge;* floater; *gold medalist; him; her; impel; jet; keep going; life guard;* mover; *natant;* Olympic ~; paddler; professional ~; *quick; rip across the water;* skinny-dipper; traverser; *underway;* voyager; wader; *xfer; yede;* zipper;

**swindle** *(v.)*: *allure;* bilk; bunco; cheat; defraud; ensnare; fool; finagle; gyp; grift; hornswoggle; insnare; jape; *kid; lie;* mislead; nobble; outfox; put one over; *quiblin* [arch.]; rook; shyster; sucker; trick; *use;* verneuk; weasel; *xuld [arch.]; yentz; zing;*
**swindler** *(n.)*: *allurer;* beguiler; con artist; cheat; deceiver; defrauder; ensnarer; fraudster; guiler; grifter; hoaxer; huckster; imposter; jackal; knave; liar; misleader; no-good; open liar; phony; quacksalver; rook; shyster; trickster; untruther; verneuker; wangler; weasel; *xgressor;* yarn-spinner; *yentzer* [Heb.]; *zinger;*
**swing** *(v.)*: alternate; *back and forth;* change; dangle; *exchange;* fluctuate; go back and forth; *hang;* interchange; *jump; keep wavering;* lash; move; nutate; oscillate; pendulate; pivot; *quiver;* rock; sway; switch; shift; turn; undulate; up~; vacillate; whirl; wave; *x-ing; yo-yo; zoom;*
**switch** *(v.)*: adjust; alter; *better;* change; convert; *correct;* do a switcheroo; exchange; flick; fix; give in exchange; *heighten;* interchange; *jump; key to; lower;* modify; modulate; *novate;* overhaul; *permute; qualify;* replace; rearrange; shift; swap; substitute; turn; trade; upgrade; vary; *work; xenomorph; yaw; zigzag;* [*see* thrash]
**swollen** *(adj.)*: aggrandized; bloated; blown up; bulging; chubby; distended; engorged; enlarged; fat; gibbous; high-blown; intumesce; inflated; *jutting; king-sized;* large; magnified; nodular; over-blown; puffy; *quantum increase;* raised; swelled; tumid; turgescent; *upbuilt;* ventricose; well-swollen; waterlogged; XL; *yain [arch.]; zoomed up;* [*Ant.* shrunken]
**swoop** *(v.)*: alight; *attack;* bear down; crash five; descend; dive; *evolation;* fly down; fall; go down; *headlong dive; immerge;* jump down; *kite;* lunge; make dive; nosedive; *outfly;* plunge; plummet; quick-fall; rocket; sweep; soar; take dive; *under;* volplane; wing; whoosh; *xuld [arch.]; yern;* zoom;
**sword** *(n.)*: aor; blade; broad~; cutlass; *dagger;* damaskin; épée; *Excalibur;* falchion; glaive; hanger; *harpé; instrument;* Japanese ~; katana; long~; *machete; no-dachi [Jap.];* Ottoman ~; poniard; *quillons;* rapier; saber; scimitar; short~; Toledo; trusty ~; uni~; *Venetian sword;* winyard; *weapon;* xiphos; *yataghan;* zweihander; [*see* Bible]
**symbol** *(n.)*: *arms;* badge; blazon; brand; character; crest; coat of arms; designation; emblem; ensign; figure; glyph; hierogram; heraldry; insignia; icon; indication; image; imprint; initial; ideogram; *jack;* key; logo; letter; mark; notation; numeral; *object;* picture; pictogram; *quarter;* representation; sign(et); seal; stamp; shield; token; uncial; *uppercase; vexillum; wafer;* X; *yacht ensign; zeug;*
**symbolic** *(adj.)*: allegorical; betokening; curiologic; descriptive; emblematic; figurative; glyphic; hieroglyphic; illustrative; *just ~;* kuriologic; *likening;* metaphoric; *non-literal; obscured;* pictorial; *quarto;* representative; symbolical; signaling; typical; tokenistic; umbratical; vignette; *word-picture; xenodoceionological; yarn;* zeugmatic;
**symbolism** *(n.)*: adumbration; betokening; comparison; designation; *example;* figuration; *glyphics;* hieroglyphics; illustration; imagery; *just like;* kuriology; likening; meaning; *notice; oracle;* pictures; *quain [arch.];* representation; symbolization; typology; tokenism; *umbrage; very image;* word pictures; *xenenthesis; yichus; Zeug [G.];*
**symbolize** *(v.)*: add up to; betoken; connote; denote; epitomize; emblemize; *for;* give picture of; have meaning; indicate; *jobation; key to; limn;* mean; *notate;* omenate; picture; *quiddit;* represent; signify; show; stand for; typify; *use for;* visually depict; *word; x-type; yield; zay [arch.];*
**symmetrical** *(adj.)*: alike; *axisymmetic;* balanced; commensurable; *duplicate;* equiponderant; equilibrated; even; *finished;* geometrically ~; harmonious; holohedral; isonomic; justified; keeping balance; *kilter;* level; matching; mirror-image; *non-difference;* omniparous; proportioned; quite balanced; right-looking; symmetric; *together;* uniform; *varying not;* well-balanced; *xy-balanced; yet alike;* zygomorphic; [*Ant.* skewed]
**symmetry** *(n.)*: alikeness; balance; correspondence; duplication; evenness; equilibrium; *finished;* geometric ~; harmony; identicalness; isonomy; *just alike; knotted score;* likeness; levelness; match; *non-difference;* omniparity; proportion; *quits;* regularity; sameness; *togetherness;* uniformity; *varying not; well-balanced; xy-balanced; yet alike;* zero imbalance;

**sympathetic** *(adj. understanding)*: agreeable; benevolent; compassionate; concerned; condolent; delicate; empathetic; friendly; *forgiving;* gentle; humane; identifying; *joining;* kind(-hearted); loving; merciful; nice; over-empathizing; pitying; *quick to help;* regardful; sensitive; thoughtful; tender(hearted); understanding; very kind; warmhearted; *xenial; yielding; zealous to help;* [*Ant.* soulless]

**sympathize** *(v.)*: ache; agree with; back; condole; commiserate; *dear;* empathize; feel for; grieve with; have compassion; identify; *join; kindness;* love; *mercy; niceness;* over-empathize; pity; *quick-to-understand;* relate to; sorrow; side with; *tender;* understand; *virtue; warmth; xenial;* yearn; *zealous to help;*

**sympathy** *(n.)*: affinity; benevolence; compassion; clemency; condolences; delicateness; empathy; forgiveness; grace; goodwill; heart; humanity; interest; involvement; *joy-giving;* kindness; loving-kindness; leniency; mercy; niceness; oneness; pity; pathos; quarter; ruth; readiness to forgive; support; tenderness; understanding; *virtue; warmth; xenia;* yearning; *zeal to help;* [*Ant.* severity]

**symptom** *(n.)*: attribute; basis for belief; clue; *denotement;* element; feature; good indication; *hint;* hallmark; indication; *justification;* key ~; lineament; manifestation; mark; *nature; object;* prodrome; quality; recognizable sign; (sure) sign; trait; telltale sign; undeniable sign; *very good indication;* way; x-factor; *yetzer;* zero in;

**symptomatic** *(adj.)*: assertive; associated; bespeaking; characteristic; demonstrative; denotive; expressive; evidential; figural; *giving;* hinting; indicative; *jaw; key in;* leading to believe; manifesting; notifying; *outlining;* pointing to; *quoth;* redolent; suggestive; telling; *uttering;* verifying; *wording; xenophonia; yielding; zeroing in;*

**synagogue** *(n.)*: assembly; *beyt knesset* [Heb.]; congregation; *designation;* esnoga; forgathering; gathering; house of worship; Hebrew center; *ingathering;* Jewish ~; kenessa; local ~; meeting place; *number;* Orthodox Jewish ~; place of assembly; *quorum;* Reformed Temple; shul; temple; *unit; vestibule;* worship house; *xenagogy;* Yiddish; *zayat* [Burm.];

**synonymous** *(adj.)*: alike; *balanced;* commensurate; close in meaning; *duplicate;* equivalent; *fairly ~;* generally the same; homologous; *identical; just the same;* kindred; like-meaning; matching; non-differing; one and the same meaning; polyonomous; *parallel; quit the same;* resembling; same-meaning; *similar; tantamount;* undiffering; very close in meaning; *word; xerographed;* yes; zero variation;

**synopsis** *(n.)*: abridgement; brief; breviat; compendium; capitulation; draft; encapsulation; foreshortening; general idea; *heart; idea; jist; kernel; lifeblood; makeup;* newsbrief; overview; outline; precis; profile; *quintessence;* rundown; summary; survey; thumbnail; *underneath;* vignette; *warp and woof; xenenthesis;* yetzer [Heb.]; *zoe* [Gr.];

**system** *(n.)*: approach; behavior; course of action; design; *execution;* fashion; *guidelines;* habitude; *ingenius ~; job;* key; line of attack; method; *modus operandi* [L.]; *notion;* order; operation; procedure; *quo mode* [L.]; routine; scheme; technique; *usage; vein;* way; *xenagogy;* yet unconventional ~; *zet* [dial.];

**systematic** *(adj.)*: analytical; businesslike; careful; disciplined; exacting; formulaic; *grid pattern;* habitual; industrious; *just so; keen;* logical; methodical; *non-random;* orderly; ordered; painstaking; precise; *quasi-logical;* regimented; rigid; regular; systematical; systematized; tedious; uniform; *unemotional; vigilant;* well-regulated; *xtr. organized; yare; zeroing in;* [*Ant.* sloppy]

**systematize** *(v.)*: arrange; *base of logic;* configure; collate; display; distribute; *exhibit;* fix; group; hierarchize; index; *judge; kit;* lay out; make plans; *nicely order;* order; organize; place; put in order; prepare; *qualify;* rank; rearrange; sort; systemize; *tabulate;* unitize; *valuate;* work; *xfer; yield; zonate;*

# T

**tab** *(n.)*: annotation; *bit;* card; designation; earmark; flap; *gusset;* hangtag; index ~; *jut; key;* label; marker; *name;* overlap; piece; pull- ~; *qualification; remnant;* stub; thumb ~; tag; *unit; voucher;* white ~; *xfer;* yellow ~; *zone;* [*see* bill]

**tabernacle** *(n.)*: *architecture;* basilica; chapel; cathedral; *dagoba* [Ind.]; Ebenezer [Br.]; fane; God's house; holy place; house of worship (-God); habitation; inner sanctuary; *joss-house* [Chin.]; *kiack* [Burm.]; *the* Lord's house; minster; naos; oracle; place of worship; pavilion; *qubba; roodloft;* sanctuary; tent; temple; *upper room; vihara* [Bud.]; worship-house; *Xn. church; yele* [arch.]; *zayat* [Burm.];

**table** *(n.)*: *analogion;* bench; coffee ~; card ~; dining ~; desk; end ~; folding ~; *furniture;* gate leg ~; head ~; imbenching; jacaranda ~; kitchen ~; ledge; lap desk; *mensal;* night ~; nightstand; *overhang;* patio ~; quercine ~; round ~; surface; tray ~; tea ~; teapoy; trolley; utility ~; vanity ~; workbench; work~; xy- ~; yew-wood ~; zebrawood ~;

**table** *(v.)*: adjourn; *break;* come back to; defer; end for now; finish later; get back to; hold off; hang; *interrupt; just over; knock off;* lay aside; make stall; *non-immediate; over for now;* put aside; postpone; quit till later; *reschedule;* shelve; take up again later; *use later; void;* wait; *x; yerde* [arch.]; zero conclusion;

**tablet** *(n.)*: *article; bit;* chunk; *daud;* engraving ~; *fragment;* granite ~; hunk; inscribed ~; *junt;* kettlestone ~; *lump;* marble ~; monolith; *needlestone ~; object;* plane; piece of stone; *quartz;* rock slab; stone ~; slab; slate; table(ture); *uncut; volcanic rock;* wedge; *xenolith; yenite; zum* [arch.];

**taboo** *(adj.)*: abominable; anathema; bad; banned; censored; disallowed; excluded; forbidden; *gauche;* horrid; highly offensive; inappropriate; *jadish; kapa* [Haw.]; lewd; *malapropos;* nefandous; noa; nonpermissible; *non dit* [F.]; off-limits; prohibited; *questionable;* restricted; socially unacceptable; *shocking; sacred;* tabu; unacceptable; unspeakable; unmentionable; vulgar; *withheld;* x-rated; *ybarred* [arch.]; *zhlubby;* [*Ant.* tolerable]

**taciturn** *(n.)*: aloof; bashful; coy; distant; *embarrassed; few words;* gentle; holding one's peace; introverted; jackalent; keeping quiet; *little on words;* meek; nonverbal; over-quiet; *private;* quiet; reserved; silent; shy; timorous; uncommunicative; verecund; withdrawn; *xenophobic;* yarrow; *zitti* [It.]; [*Ant.* talkative]

**tackle** *(n.)*: articles; belongings; burton; commodities; dress; equipment; furnishings; gear; habiliments; items; *junk* [slang]; kit; *load;* matter; needments; objects; paraphernalia; *pulleys; quantity;* rigging; *ropes;* stuff; tack; trappings; *utensils;* valuables; *wares;* wanigan; *xenenthesis; yannigan; zeug* [G.];

**tackle** *(v.)*: attack; block; body-slam; cast down; dive; *eject;* force down; foreseize; grapple; hurl; impel; jump; knock down; leap on; *make one hit the floor; nobble; overthrow;* pounce; push down; quant; ram; seize; slam; shove; take down; throw; *undo; vault;* wale down; *xuld* [arch.]; yank down *zing;*

**tacky** *(adj.)*: appalling; boorish; cheesy; despicable; *evil;* foul; gauche; horrid; impolite; jadish; kitsch; low; mean; nasty; ostentatious; poor taste; quite rude; rude; scurrilous; tactless; unfashionable; vulgar; wanting of taste; *x-rated;* yucky; zhlubby; [*Ant.* tasteful]

**tact** *(n.)*: amiableness; *benignancy;* care; consideration; discretion; diplomacy; elegance; fragility; graciousness; heed; inoffensiveness; judgment; kid gloves; *lovingkindness;* mindfulness; *manners;* non-offensiveness; over-politeness; politesse; *queme;* regard; sensitivity; tactfulness; thoughtfulness; urbanity; virtuosity; wisdom; *xenagogically; yepe;* zero offense; [*Ant.* tactlessness]

**tactful** *(adj.)*: amiable; *benign;* careful; considerate; diplomatic; delicate; discreet; discerning; ever-careful; fabian; gracious; heedful; inconspicuous; inoffensive; judicious; kind; *loving;* mindful; *mannerly;* non-direct; nice; over-careful; polite; politic; pleasant; *queme;* regardful; sensitive; tasteful; urbane; very careful; wise; *xenagogic;* yepe; *zärtlich [G.];* [*Ant.* tactless]

**tactic** *(n.)*: approach; blueprint; conception; course of action; design; engineering; foredesign; gambit; *hatch;* idea; jape; King's gambit; line of attack; maneuver; master plan; *notion;* orchestration; plan; *quo mode [L.];* ruse; strategy; tack; *underlying plan; visual;* way; wile; x-chart; *yantra [Hind.]; zenithal projection;*

**tactician** *(n.)*: attack planner; *blueprint;* contriver; deviser; engineer; field marshal; general; *hatcher; idea;* japer; King's gambit; *lucubrator;* master ~; machinator; *naval ~;* orchestrator; planner; *quo mode [L.]; racketeer;* strategist; tactical strategist; *unbeatable; visionary;* war strategist; x-chart; *yantra [Hind.];* zinger;

**tag** *(n.)*: attached ~; appellation; badge; card; designation; decal; earmark; *first name; green ~;* hangtag; indicator; identification ~; *jut; key;* label; marker; name ~; *orange ~;* price ~; *qualification;* red ~; sticker; sticky ~; tab; ticket; unit marker ~; voucher; white ~; xfer ~; yellow ~; *zonal ~;*

**tail** *(n.)*: appendage; back; brush ~; *bushy ~;* cue; *caudal; dock;* extremity; empennage; fan; flag [zoo.]; *goat ~;* heterocercal; *item; jackal ~; keister; limit;* member; *node;* outer limit; posterior; plumage; queue; rear appendage; rectrices; scut; sickle ~; train; *uttermost; vertebrate;* wagger; *xiphoid; yak ~;* zoofuvin;
  Kinds of *tailed*: bob-tailed; bushy-tailed; cotton-tail; devil-tailed; dovetailed; fishtailed; fork-tailed; long-tailed; nick-tailed; pigtailed; ponytailed; rat-tail; short-tailed; thick-tailed; wide-tailed;

**tailor** *(n.)*: *artificer;* busheler; clothingmaker; clothier; dressmaker; expert ~; fitter; garmentmaker; haberdasher; *industrial workman; journeyman; key worker; laborer;* maker of clothes; needleworker; outfitter; pricklous [derog.]; *qualified ~;* retrofitter; suit-maker; tailoress [fem.]; *underling; versed;* workman; *xtry.;* yeoman; *zakai [Jap.];*

**tailor** *(v.)*: adapt; alter; accommodate; *better;* cut; customize; doctor; enhance; fashion; fit; gear to; *hem;* improve; *jib;* key to; *lengthen;* make (to order); modify; needle; overhaul; prepare; qualify; readjust; retrofit; refit; suit; tailor-make; upgrade; vary; work; *well-tailored; xfer; yield; zip;*

**tailspin** *(n.)*: *around and around;* backspin; circling; dive; downward spiral; *eddy;* (free)fall; going down; hurtling; incurvation; *jump; keckle;* loop; moving downward; nosedive; *out-of-control;* plunge; *querl;* roll; spiral; spin; tail spin; tumble; underspin; volt; whirl; x-ing; *yede [arch.];* zwoosh;

**taint** *(v.)*: adulterate; attaint; blemish; contaminate; corrupt; defile; deprave; decay; empoison; foul; *go bad; hoar;* infect; impregnate; jade; *ketty;* lace; mortify; *necrosis;* oxidize; pollute; poison; queer; ruin; spoil; sully; tarnish; tincture; *undo;* vitiate; welk; *xylaria;* yellow; *zorch;*

**take** *(v.)*: appropriate; accept; betake; bring; capture; confiscate; commandeer; carry; dispossess; divest; draw; deprive; exact; extract; expropriate; extort; fetch; grab; get; gain; have; haul away; intercept; impound; jump at; keep; lay hold of; make off with; nab; obtain; procure; pocket; *quirk;* receive; remove; seize; snatch; sequester; transume; transport; use; usurp; undertake; *vellicate;* wrest; xfer; yank; yomp; zip away; [*see* purchase]

**takeover** *(n.)*: annexation; buyout; conquest; coup; *coup d'état* [F.]; capture; domination; dispossession; expugnation; *feat;* grab; gain; hostile ~; invasion; incorporation; joining; knockout; *lordship;* merger; national ~; overthrow; occupation; overtaking; putsch; *prevail; quest;* re-conquest; seizure; subjugation; triumph; usurpation; *victory; win;* wresting; *xfer; yong [arch.];* zapping;

**tale** *(n.)*: account; *book; chronicle; drama;* epic; fable; fairytale; *ghost story; historical fiction;* imposture; *journal; kappa book;* legend; myth; narrative; *oral narrative;* parable; *quarto;* retelling; report; story; saga; thriller; *unabridged story;* version; *writing;* xenodocheionology; yarn; *zipper book;*

**talebearer** *(n.)*: aspersion-caster; backbiter; chatterbox; defamater; echoer; *famer;* gossip; *hearsay;* idle chatterer; jaunderer; kimmer; *loose-tongue;* magpie; newsmonger; *obtrectation;* prattler; quidnunc; rumormonger; slanderer; tattler; *utterer; voice;* whisperer; *xiaoren;* yenta; zeroizer; [*Ant.* truth-teller]

**talent** *(n.)*: ability; adeptness; bent; capability; dower; deftness; expertise; flair; forte; gift; habilitation; instinct; *jimp;* knack; long suit; mastery; métier; muse; natural ability; *occupation;* proficiency; qualification; readiness; skill; *training;* usefulness; virtuosity; wherewithal; *xenium; yaup* [arch.]; zest;

**talented** *(adj.)*: accomplished; brilliant; commanding; capable; deft; expert; familiar; gifted; good; handy; heaven-gifted; incredible; jolly good; knowledgeable; *laudable;* multi~; masterful; notable; outstanding; *old hand;* proficient; qualified; remarkable; seasoned; top-notch; unequalled; virtuosic; wonderful; xtry.; *you-beaut [Aus.]; zealous;*

**talk** *(v.)*: address; bespeak; blurt; chat; converse; communicate; declare; discuss; declaim; express; flap the lips; gab; have words; interject; indicate; inform; jabber; *key in;* lecture; mention; natter; negotiate; narrate; orate; parley; pontificate; prate; quoth; quip; remark; ramble; rant; relate; rap; speak; state; tell; utter; voice; vocalize; word; *xenophonia;* yak; *zeug* [G.]

**talkative** *(adj.)*: articulate; bombastic; babbling; conversational; communicative; chatty; disclosive; effusive; fluent; garrulous; gabby; *high-sounding;* incessant; *jabbering; kelter;* lengthy; loquacious; long-winded; logorheic; multiloquous; mouthy; *nonstop;* ongoing; pompous; prating; quantitative; running on; rambling; sociable; talky; uttering; verbose; windy; *xenoglossic;* yaketty; zealous; [Ant. taciturn]

**talker** *(n.)*: addresser; blusterer; chatterer; communicator; declarer; expresser; *foresayer;* gabber; *hollerer;* informer; jabberer; *kerygma;* lecturer; mentioner; narrator; orator; pontificator; prater; *quibbler;* rambler; ranter; speaker; teller; utterer; vocalizer; worder; windbag; *xenophonia;* yakker; *zeug [G.];*

**tall** *(adj.)*: altitudinous; big; considerable; colossal; *disproportionate;* erect; elongated; elevated; ectomorphic; *full-height;* great; giant; high(-reaching); immense; *jumbo;* king-size; long; lank; leptosome; *massive; narrow;* oblong; *overlong;* perpendicular; portrait; *quantitative;* rangy; *rising;* steep; sizable; standing; towering; upright; uplifted; vertical; *whopping; xy-height;* y-axis; zenithal; [Ant. tiny]

**tame** *(adj.)*: approachable; broken; bridled; compliant; domesticated; docile; ever-calm; friendly; gentle; governable; heedful; insipid; *jarless;* kept under control; lamblike; meek; mild; non-wild; obedient; placid; quelled; reclaimed; submissive; spiritless; tamed; trained; unresisting; vanquished; well-trained; *xtry trained;* yielded; zeroized;

**tame** *(v.)*: acclimize; break; bridle; cicurate; control; civilize; domesticate; ease; *friendly; govern;* hush; *insipid; jarless;* keep in line; lull; moderate; *neutralize;* overcome; pacify; quieten; quell; repress; subdue; train; tranquilize; unruffle; *vanquish; willing; x-out;* yoke; zeroize;

**tameable** *(adj.)*: able to tame; breakable; conquerable; domesticable; educable; *enslavable; forcible;* governable; handlable; *instructable;* judged ~; *keen;* lickable; masterable; *neutralizable; overpower;* possible to tame; *quell;* restrainable; subduable; tamable; trainable; unresisting; vanquishable; *well-trained; xeno-dominative;* yielding; *zero resistance;*

**tamer** *(n.)*: animal trainer; beast- ~; circus trainer; domesticator; discipliner; *enslaver;* formal ~; *governor;* habituator; instructor; *judge; knowledgeable;* lion- ~; master; *neutralizer;* obedience trainer; *pedogogue; queller; ruler;* subduer; trainer; unit trainer; *vet;* worker with animals; *xeno-dominator;* yokemaster; zookeeper;

**tamper** *(v.)*: alter; bewreck; corrupt; doctor; encanker; fiddle; fix; gum up; horn in; interfere; impinge; jam; jury-rig; *knock;* louse up; meddle; mess with; monkey with; nobble; *obstruct;* play around with; *quirk;* rig; rework; sabotage; spoil; tinker; *undo;* vary; wreck; *xenomorph; yank apart; zeroize;*

**tan** *(adj.)*: almond; beige; brownish-white; cream; dark tan; ecru; fawn; *gray-brown;* hazel; *imbrowned;* java; *khaki;* light brown; magnolia; natural; *off-white;* pale brown; *queen's brown; russet;* sandy; tawny; *umber; Vandyke;* whitish-brown; xanthomelanoid; yellowish- ~; zerda- ~;

**tangible** *(adj.)*: actual; bona fide; concrete; definite; existing; factual; genuine; hard; indubitable; *justifiable;* known; legitimate; material; *non-abstract;* obvious; physical; quantifiable; real; solid; substantial; tactile; unerring; undeniable; visible; *well-tried; x-parent;* yes; *zero question;*

**tangle** *(n.)*: *anarchy;* bind; contortion; complication; chaos; disarrangement; entanglement; farrago; gnarl; hodgepodge; intertanglement; jumble; knot; labyrinth; mess; node; *ordeal;* problem; *puzzle;* quandary; ravel; snarl; twist; tousle; *umbilication; voluble;* weave; xyloma; *yaw;* zigzag; [*see* fight]
**tangle** *(v.)*: *abstruse; burden;* contort; catch; disarrange; entangle; entwine; foul up; gnarl; hook; inter~ (-twine; -weave); intwine; jumble; knot; louse up; mess; node; *overcomplicate;* pleach; *quirky;* ravel; snarl; tousle; twist; *unstraightened; voluble;* weave; x; *yarn;* zigzag; [*see* fight]
**tangled** *(adj.)*: abstruse; byzantine; convoluted; complex; difficult; en~; fouled up; gnarled; *hard;* intertwined; intricate; jumbled; knotted; labyrinthine; maze-like; nodated; overcomplicated; perplexing; puzzling; *question-filled;* ramified; snarled; tangly; unsolvable; vexatious; wildering; *xenagogic; yucky;* zany; [*Ant.* tangle-free]
**tangy** *(adj.)*: acidulous; biting; cutting; *distasteful;* extreme; *forceful; grapefruit;* harsh; intense; jolting; keen; lemony; *much-soured;* nippy; overpowering; pungent; quite ~; racy; sour; strong; tart; unsweetened; unpleasant; vinegary; well-soured; *xtry.* ~; *yummy;* zesty; zingy; [*Ant.* tasteless]
**tanner** *(n.)*: artificer; buckskin ~; *currier;* deerskin ~; *expert;* fleecer; *guildsmanl* hide-worker; *individual;* jucten-maker; *kip manl* leathermaker; leatherworker; maker of leather; napa-producer; oxhide worker; pelt-worker; *quriboilly;* rawhide maker; skinner; tawer; *union worker; versed;* worker with leather; *xero dermicl* yuft-tanner; zug-producer;
**tantalize** *(v.)*: allure; bestir; charm; draw; entice; flatter; get attention of; hold captive; induce; *jill-flirt; keen on;* lure; make desire; *nudge;* overstimulate; provoke; *quiblin;* rouse; stimulate; seduce; tempt; tease; torment; *unattainable; very attractive;* wink; *xuld [arch.]; yerk; zizzy;*
**tantamount** *(adj.)*: as good as; basically; close; duplicate; equivalent; *fairly equal; generally the same;* homologous; identical; indistinguishable; just the same; *kindred;* like; matching; non-differing; *one;* parallel; practically; *quae est eadem* [L.]; resembling; same; *truly: unvaried;* virtually the same; *working; xenenthesis;* yet undistinguishable; *zero-difference;*
**tantrum** *(n.)*: anger-fit; burst; choler; display of bad temper; *displeasure;* explosion; fit; freakout; gall; hissy fit; invective; jumping fit; *kindling; lividness;* meltdown; *nettled;* outburst; philippic; pet; *quake;* rage; storm; tiff; temper ~; unmitigated rage; venting; *widdrim* [arch.]; *xerothermia; yelling; zero calmness;*
**tap** *(n.)*: *action;* bump; click; drum; *elbow;* flick; *glump;* hit; impact; jab; knock; *lick; martel;* nob; open-handed blow; pat; *quab;* rap; strike; smack; thump; tick; *unquiet;* veney; whack; *x-sect;* yedder; zonk;
**tap** *(v.)*: *act;* bang; bat; click; drum; drub; *elbow;* flick; graze; hit; impact; impinge; jar; knock; lightly hit; martel; *nail; overhit;* pat; percuss [med.]; quab; rap; strike; slap; touch; tick; thrum; thump; *unquiet;* veney; whack; *x-sect; yerk;* zonk;
**taper** *(v.)*: attenuate; become thinner; condense; diminish; extenuate; fall off; get thinner; *halve; improve; jump down; knock down;* lessen; make thinner; narrow; *only narrower;* pare down; peter out; quail; reduce; slenderize; slim down; thin; *undersized; vanish;* wane; *XS; yield;* zeroize; [*Ant.* thicken]
**tar** *(n.)*: asphalt; bitumen; blacktop; cement; *driveway;* earth-pitch; *freeway; gravel; highway surface; infrastructure;* judaicum; karabe of Sodom; *lane;* macadam; maltha; *naphtha;* otta seal; pavement; pitch; *quick-setting concrete;* resin; roadway; street; slime; screed; tarmac; traprock; uintaite; *viscid;* wearing course; wood tar; *xystus; yong [arch.];* zaguan;
**tar** *(v.)*: asphalt; bituminize; blacktop; cover with tar; daub with tar; *embrocate; fan out; get tar on;* hot ~; *infucate;* judaicum; karabe of Sodom; lay ~ on; *make ~red; non-concrete based coat;* overspread with tar; pitch; *pave;* quab; resurface; *reapply;* spread tar on; slime; *smear;* tarmac; uintaite; *viscud;* wipe tar on; *xfer; yong [arch.];* zaguan;
**tardy** *(adj.)*: *abeyance;* behind schedule; belated; *cumbered;* dilatory; delayed; deferred; ever-late; fashionably late; *gradual;* hindered; impeded; jauking; keeping one waiting; late; moratory; non-timely; overdue; postponed; past-due; past-time; procrastinatory; quite late; *remiss;* slow; too late; unpunctual; unseasonable; untimely; *vapid; workshy; xenarthrous; yareless; zealless;* [*Ant.* timely]

**target** *(n.)*: aim; archery ~; bullseye; bogey; clout; drogue; design; end; *figure;* goal; gold; *hope;* intention; *journey's end; key; level;* mark; *notion;* objective; *purpose;* quintain; *range;* shooting ~; training ~; *ultima view;* wish; x; yearning; zero in;

**target** *(v.)*: aim at; *bring into range;* close (in); direct; draw a bead; *endeavor;* fix(ate); focus on; go for; hone (in); *intend; jaeger;* kithe [Scot.]; level; mark; nock; *obtain a bead;* point; pinpoint; *quick-aim;* range; sight; single out; train; take aim; *use sights; view;* work out; *x-y coordinate; ypointing;* zero in;

**tarnish** *(v.)*: attaint; blemish; corrupt; discolor; *efface;* foul; *go off-color; harm;* infect; jade; *ketty;* louse up; mar; *necrosis;* oxidize; *pollute; queer;* ruin; stain; taint; tincture; *undo;* vitiate; welk; *xylaria;* yellow; *zorch;* [*see* vilify]

**tarry** *(v.)*: abide; await; bide; continue; dwell; dally; endure; follow on; go on; hang around; inhabit; idle; *journey;* keep on; live; linger; lodge; maintain; *nest;* occupy; pause; procrastinate; quarter; remain; stay; tide over; *visit;* wait; *xenize;* yerde [arch.]; *zip to;* [*Ant.* take off]

**task** *(n.)*: assignment; business; charge; commission; duty; errand; function; goal; *handling;* incumbency; job; *key role;* liability; mission; necessity; obligation; purpose; quest; responsibility; *station;* thing to do; undertaking; vocation; work; xci.; *yoke;* zealous ~;

**taskmaster** *(n.)*: administrator; boss; chief; disciplinarian; enslaver; foreman; governor; headman; intendant; *jarl;* kingpin; *leader;* master; *night manager;* overseer; *principal; quartermaster;* ruler; slave-driver; Simon Legree; tyrant; *ultimate authority;* viceroy; workmaster; XO; *yokemaster;* zayim;

**taste** *(n.)*: after~; bite; character; discrimination; essence; flavor; *good ~;* hint; intrinsicality; *juicy; keen ~;* liking; mouthful; morsel; nature; *overall ~;* perception; *palate;* quality; relish; savor(iness); smack; tincture; *unusual ~; very good ~;* way of tasting; *xenenthesis; yummy;* yucky; *zest;*

**taste** *(v.)*: appraise; bite; *chew;* delibate; drink; eat; experience; evaluate; feed; gustate; have; ingest; judge; knab; lick; munch; nibble; *overeat;* partake; *quill* [arch.]; relish; sample; sip; savor; smack; try; *undereat; victual;* wolf; *xerophagy;* yaffle; *zip down;*

**tasteful** *(adj.)*: aesthetic; beautiful; classy; discriminating; discerning; elegant; fashionable; genteel; graceful; *high-society;* in good taste; judicious; *keen; lovely;* mannerly; nice; *overelegant;* proper; pleasant; *quaint;* refined; sophisticated; *tactful;* urbane; very ~; with good taste; XF; *younker; zierlich [G.];* [*Ant.* tacky]

**tasteless** *(adj.)*: appalling; boorish; crude; despicable; effete; foul; gauche; horrid; indecent; jadish; kitsch; low; mean; nasty; offensive; off-color; poor taste; quite rude; rude; scurrilous; tacky; tactless; uncouth; vulgar; wanting of taste; *x-rated;* yucky; zhlubby; [*see* bland; *Ant.* tasty]

**tasty** *(adj.)*: appetizing; *bon!* [F.]; *captivating;* delicious; dainty; delectable; enjoyable; flavorful; good; gustable; heavenly; irresistible; *juicy;* keen; luscious; mouth-watering; nectarous; *outstanding;* pleasing; palatable; quite good; relishable; savory; sapid; tantalizing; *tempting;* toothsome; *unbelievably good; very good;* wonderful; *xtry.;* yummy; zesty; [*Ant.* tasteless]

**tattered** *(adj.)*: awful; bedraggled; *chaotic;* disheveled; *effaced;* frayed; grubby; haggard; incomposed; jagged; keg-meg; *lousy;* messy; non-organized old; *pathetic;* quaggy; ragged; raggedy; rough-shod; shabby; slovenly; tatty; torn; unkempt; unkempt; uneven; *used; vile;* worn; *x'ed;* yucky; *zany;* [*Ant.* tidy]

**tattle** *(v.)*: *assert;* blab; blow the whistle; betray; *convey;* disclose; *expose;* fink; gossip; *hearsay;* inform; jaunder; *kibitz;* let one know; mention; notify; *opine;* prate; *quidnunc;* rat; snitch; squeal; tell; utter; *vocalize; whistleblower; x-gress;* yak; zero in;

**tattler** *(n.)*: aspersion-caster; bigmouth; blabbermouth; cummer; defamater; echoer; fink; gossiper; *hearsay;* idle chatterer; informer; informant; jaunderer; kibitz; *loose-tongued;* magpie; newsmonger; *obtrectation;* prater; quidnunc; rumormonger; rat; slanderer; snitch; tattletale; tongue-wagger; *utterer; vicious voice;* whistle-blower; *xiaoren;* yakker; *zeroizer;*

**taunt** *(v.)*: abuse; bemock; chide; deride; *execrate;* fleer; gibe; heckle; hiss; insult; jibe; kid; knock; laugh at; mock; *name-calling; offend;* pillory; poke fun; quib; ridicule; rag; scorn; tease; utter against; verbally abuse; wipe; *xuld [arch.];* yock; *zap;*

**taut** *(adj.)*: ataunt; *bound tightly;* cinched; drawn-out; extended; firm; *greatly tightened;* hard-fastened; inflexible; *just as tight as can be;* kept ~; long; made ~; no slack; overtight; outstretched; pulled; quite tight; rigid; stiff; stretched; tight; tense; unrelaxed; very tight; widened; x-tight; yanked tight; *zero slack;*

**tavern** *(n.)*: ale-house; bar; cabaret; dramshop; establishment; fern bar; groghouse; hostelry; inn; joint; kiddleywink; lounge; mughouse; night-house; open bar; pub; *queme;* roadhouse; saloon; taproom; *utility bar; vinery;* watering hole; *xenodocheum;* youth club; *zubrowka;*

**tax** *(n.)*: assessment; bite; back ~; charge; custom; duty; excise; flat ~; fee; gabelle; head ~; income ~; jettage; keyage; levy; mulct; nuisance ~; octroi; poll ~; property ~; *quarterage;* rate; *revenue;* sales ~; taxation; tribute; tariff; *usury;* vigorish; withholding; x-int; yardage; zakat [Mos.];

**tax** *(v.)*: assess; appropriate; bill; charge; demand; excise; exact; fine; *get; garnish;* have; impose; *jettage;* levy; mulct; *non-exempt;* over~; prorate; *press; quarterage;* require; reassess; surcharge; *squeeze;* take; *unpaid ~; valuate;* withhold; x-int. receipt; yank away; zakat [Mos.];

**tax collector** *(n.)*: assessor; *bureau;* collector; cessor; debt collector; exciseman; federal ~; gabeler; *heartless ~;* IRS official; *jarl;* khalsah [Ind.]; *law;* money-collector; *non-sympathetic;* officer; publican; questor; receiver of taxes; *sheriff;* taxer; tide-waiter; *usurer;* vulture [slang]; *warren; xaraf;* yeoman; zamindar [Ind.];

**tax-exempt** *(adj.)*: allowed; *bondless;* clear; duty-free; exempt; free; *gratis; hold;* illeviable; indecimable; *justified;* kirset [arch.]; levy-free; *mulct-free;* non-taxable; *off; pro bona* [L.]; quite tax-free; revenue-free; scot-free; tax-free; taxless; untaxed; *void;* without tax; *xenium-free; yokeless;* zero-rate [*Ant.* taxable]

**teach** *(v.)*: acquaint; admonish; *bring up;* condition; catechize; disciple; educate; explain; expound; enlighten; foster; fugle; guide; ground; home school; instruct; inculcate; ingrain; illuminate; indoctrinate; *jobation; knock into;* lecture; *mis~;* mentor; *narrate;* open one's eyes; prime; pedagogue; qualify; ready; school; train; tutor; *unlock;* verse; work with; xenagogue; *yak; zealously instruct;* [*see* learn]

**teachable** *(adj.)*: admonishable; *biddable;* counselable; coachable; docible; educable; easily taught; *following;* guidable; heedful; interested; instructable; *jump into it;* keen-minded; *listening;* mentorable; non-stubborn; open; *persuadable;* quick-to-learn; receptive; submissive; showable; trainable; unresisting; *very interested;* willing to learn; *xenagogic;* yielded; zealous to learn;

**teacher** *(n.)*: abecedarian; *biology ~;* coach; doctor; educator; expounder; fugleman; faculty [pl.]; guide; governess [fem.]; headmaster; instructor; *jobation; kindergarten ~;* lecturer; master [masc.]; *narrator;* orienter; overseer; pedagogue; preceptor; professor; *qualifier;* rabbi; regent; schoolmaster [masc.]; tutor; trainer; *undershepherd; vice principle; worker;* xenagogue; *Yiddish professor; zoology professor;* [*Ant.* trainee]

**team** *(n.)*: assemblage; army; A- ~; band; body; crew; company; detachment; *electorate;* faction; fellows; gang; group; horde; host; ingathering; jam [slang]; kit [coll.]; lineup; mass; members; *number;* outfit; party; panel; *quantity;* roundup; *randem;* side; squad; staff; troop; unit; varsity; wisp; working staff; x-unit; *yoke; zonal ~;*

**teammate** *(n.)*: ally; amigo; buddy; comrade; crewmate; colleague; *defender; encourager;* fellow; good-fellow; helper; *intimate;* joint-laborer; kith [pl.]; *loyal friend;* mate; *neighbor; other player;* partner; *qualified helper; runner;* supporter; team member; unfailing friend; votary; workmate; *xenophile;* yokefellow (-mate); *zealous friend;*

**tear** *(n. teardrop)*: *affected;* bead; brine; *crying; crocodile ~s;* drop(let); eye drop; falling drop; globule; *hurting; inundation;* joy-tears; *keening; limpid fluid;* mass; *misty-eyed; not happy; outburst;* pearl [poet.]; *quantity;* rheum; *rain;* salty ~; teardrop; *unhappy; very sad;* water-drop; *xude;* yelm; *zum* [dial];

**tear** *(n. rip)*: aperture; break; crack; dilaceration; *efforce; fissure; frittering;* gash; hole; interstice; *jagged;* knapple; laceration; *mutilate;* nick; opening; parting; *quadrisection;* rent; rip; rift; rupture; split; tearing; unseaming; *veering; wresting; x-section out;* yawn; *zipping;*

**tear** *(v. rend)*: abscind; avulse; break; crack; dilacerate; eventerate; fritter; *gouge;* hackle; *incide;* jerk; *kedge;* laniate; lacerate; *mangle; not together; open;* part; *quarter;* rend; rip; rive; shred; separate; take apart; unseam; *vell;* wrest; x-sect; yank apart; zip;
**tearful** *(adj.)*: *affected;* aggrieved; bawling; crying; despondent; emotional; forlorn; grief-stricken; howling; inconsolable; joyless; keening; lachrymose; maudlin; mournful; *negative;* over-sentimental; pathetic; quivering; rueful; sad; sentimental; sobbing; sniveling; teary; *unhappy;* very sad; weepy; woeful; *xtr. sad; yearnful; zestless;* [*Ant.* tearless]
**teary-eyed** *(adj.)*: affected; bleary-eyed; crying; disturbed; emotional; feeling; gut-wrenching; hysterical; *inspired;* jarring; keenly tearful; lachrymose; misty-eyed; novelettish; overwhelmed; passionate; *quixotic; romantic;* sentimental; teary; *unrestrained;* visceral; weepy; *xtry. ~; yet unquenched; zealous;* [*Ant.* tearless]
**tease** *(v.)*: abuse; banter; bedevil; chaff; dally; exasperate; fleer; flirt; gibe; harry; insult; inveigh; jest; josh; joke; kid; laugh at; make fun (-sport) of; nettle; needle; *offend;* poke fun; pick on; quip; razz; rib; scoff; toy; twit; taunt; tantalize; torment; utter against; vex; wipe; *xuld [arch.];* yock; *zap;* [*see* flirt]
**teasing** *(n.)*: abuse; banter; badinage; chaffing; derision; exasperation; fleering; gibing; harrying; insulting; jesting; joshing; joking; kidding; laughing; making fun (-sport); needling; name-calling; *offending;* poking fun; quipping; ribbing; repartee; sport; taunting; uttering against; vexing; wiping; *xuld [arch.];* yocking; zapping; [*see* flirtation]
**technique** *(n.)*: actions; approach; behavior; conduct; course of action; deftness; efficiency; fashion; form; going about it; handiness; ingenuity; *job;* knack; line of attack; learned procedure; method; manner; *new ~;* order; operation; procedure; process; *quo mode* [L.]; routine; system; tack; *usage; virtuosity;* way; xenagogy; *years of experience; zet [dial.];*
**technological** *(n.)*: advanced; *brand-new;* computerized; *developed;* electronic; *fancy; ground-breaking;* high-tech; highly developed; industrial; *just out; know-how; leap;* mechanical; next-generation; *operational;* progressive; *quantum electronics;* refinement; scientific; technologic; technicological; ultra-sophisticated ~; *vibronics;* wireless; *X12; years ahead of it's time; zizzy:*
**technology** *(n.)*: advancement; *button-operated;* circuitry; computers; cutting edge ~; *devices;* electronics; equipment; expertise; *faradic;* gadgetry; highly advanced ~; *instrumentation; just out;* knowledge; leading-edge ~; leading ~; machinery; modern ~; new ~; optoelectronics; *powered;* quantum electronics; refinement; skill; sophistication; science; technological advancement; ultra-sophisticated ~; *vibronics;* wisdom; *X12; years ahead of it's time; zizzy:*
**tedious** *(adj.)*: *arduous;* boring; banausic; *cheerless;* dull; ever- ~; flat; *generic;* humdrum; insipid; jejune; *keep going;* laborious; monotonous; non-exciting; operose; ponderous; quotidian; repetitive; soporific; tiresome; uninteresting; vapid; wearisome; *xtry. tiresome;* yawnful; *zestless;* [*Ant.* thrilling]
**tedium** *(n.)*: arduousness; boredom; *cheerlessness;* dullness; dreariness; ennui; flatness; grind; humdrum; insipidity; jejuneness; *keep going;* laboriousness; monotony; non-excitement; operoseness; ponderousness; *quotidian;* repetitiveness; soporific activity; tediousness; *uninteresting;* vapidity; wearisomeness; *xtry. boredom;* yawnfulness; *zestlessness;* [*Ant.* thrill]
**teem** *(v.)*: abound; brim; bustle; cram; crawl; *do well;* emanate; fill; flood; *gorge;* hotch [Scot.]; inundate; jam-pack; *keen;* load; multiply; *nourish;* overflow; overabound; pullulate; pack; *quantity;* reproduce; *rife;* swarm; stuff; throng; *upsurge; volume; wax great; xtry.;* yain [arch.]; *zillions;*
**teenage** *(adj.)*: adolescent; boylike [masc.]; callow; *developing;* early; *fresh;* green; hastive; *immature;* juvenile; kiddish; *little;* maturing; nubile; *over-confident;* pubescent; *quite young;* raw; *sweet sixteen;* teen-age; underage; vernal; *wee; XS;* youthful; *zit-faced;*
**teenager** *(n.)*: adolescent; bobby soxer [fem.]; *child;* damsel [fem.]; *eighteen-year old; fifteen-year old;* guy [masc.]; gal [fem.]; high-schooler; *individual;* juvenile; junior miss [fem.]; kid; lad [masc.]; lass [fem.]; minor; *nineteen-year old;* older kid; pubescent; quincearian; rose [fem. slang]; *seventeen-year old;* teen; *underage; virgin; vandal;* whippersnapper; *xbred;* youngster; youth; *zit-faced kid;*

**television** *(n.)*: *the* air(waves); boob tube; box; *broadcast;* cathode ray tube; *cable;* display; *electronics;* flat screen TV; goggle box; high definition ~; idiot tube; *jansky;* Kinescope; LCD display; monitor; *newscast; networks; onscreen;* panel; pay TV; *program; quad; rabbit ears;* screen; show; TV; tube; UHF; video; *viewing;* VHF; wide-screen TV; *x-rated; yagi; zoo TV;*

**tell** *(v.)*: articulate; address; announce; assert; bid; bespeak; communicate; comment; convey; declare; delineate; disclose; express; fill in; get across; have a word; inform; impart; indicate; intimate; *jaw; key in;* let out; mention; notify; noise; observe; opine; pronounce; proclaim; quoth; relate; remark; report; rumor; relay; say; state; talk; utter; voice; word; *xenophonia;* yak; *zero in;*

**temper** *(n.)*: anger; bad mood; crossness; displeasure; *enragement;* fractiousness; gall; hotness; ire; *jealous rage; kindling;* lividness; mood; madness; *nettling; outrage;* pique; *quick-temperament;* rage; *steamed; temperament; upset;* violent ~; wrath; *xerothermia; yelling; zealousy* [arch.];

**temper** *(v.)*: alleviate; bate; curb; diminish; ease; fade; go down; *hush;* improve; *jump down;* knock down; lessen; lighten; moderate; *narrow; outgo;* palliate; quell; reduce; soften; tone down; *undo; very much lessen;* wane; *xerosis;* yield; *zeroize;* [*see* harden]

**temperament** *(n.)*: attitude; bent; bias; character; disposition; emotional; erratic; *feeling; ground;* humor; inclination; *judgment;* kidney; leaning; makeup; nature; outlook; personality; propensity; quality of mind; *reaction;* spirit; tendency; unpredictable; volatile; way; *xenodiagnosis;* yaw; *zeal;*

**temperamental** *(adj.)*: argumentative; bad-tempered; contrary; disagreeable; emulous; factious; fractious; grouchy; hard to get along with; huffy; irascible; jangly; kindless; *loud-mouthed;* mean; nasty; ornery; petulant; querulous; resistant; snappish; tempestuous; umbrageous; volatile; waspish; *xenophobic;* yieldless; zoilean; [*Ant.* tame]

**temperance** *(n.)*: abstinence; abstemiousness; *bowing out;* control; denial; eschewal; forbearance; *giving up;* holding back; inhibiting; *just say no;* keeping from; leaving off; meekness; moderation; non-indulgence; nephalism; *omission;* prohibitionism; *quitting;* restraint; refraining; self-control; self-denial; temperateness; teetotalism; *undoing;* voluntarily abstinence; *withdrawal; x;* yieldlessness; *zero;*

**temperate** *(adj.)*: abstemious; balanced; controlled; disciplined; even-tempered; ever- ~; *even;* equitable; fair; governed; holding back; intermediate; judicious; *keeping from;* lukewarm; level; moderate; mild; non-excessive; *omitting;* proportionate; *quite reasonable;* restrained; regulated; soberminded; self-restrained; sparing; tempered; unassuming; *voluntary discipline;* well-controlled; *xtry.* ~; yepe; *zero extremes;*

**temperature** *(n.)*: actual ~; body heat; coolness; climate; degrees; *extreme ~;* frigidity; *gradient;* hotness; heat index; inside ~; *Joule effect;* kryometer reading; level of heat; mercury reading; *nippiness;* outside ~; *polar; quicksilver;* reading; *severity;* thermometer reading; *underarm ~; very hot;* warmth; *xeric; yield; zero degrees;* [*see* fever]

**tempestuous** *(adj.)*: agitated; angry; boisterous; blustery; chaotic; disturbed; enraged; fierce; gusty; hostile; hard; inclement; impetuous; intense; jouncy; *killer; lousy;* mad; nimbose; nidgetty; *outraged;* peaceless; quakeful; rough; raging; stormy; turbulent; tumultuous; unstable; unbridled; volatile; violent; *windy;* wild; wrathful; *xuld [arch.]; yucky;* zippy; [*Ant.* tranquil]

**template** *(n.)*: archetype; basis; blueprint; configuration; cut-out; *depiction;* example; exemplar; fugler; guide; *holotype; illustration; jewel;* key; *kind;* lead; master; model; mold; *neotype;* original; pattern; *quintessence;* rule; representation; stencil; sample; type; ule; *virtual; way; xenagogue;* yardstick; *zincograph;*

**temple** *(n.)*: *architecture;* basilica; chapel; cathedral; *dagoba* [Ind.]; Ebenezer [Br.]; fane; God's house; grotto; holy place; house of worship (-God); *heiau* [Hawaii]; inner sanctuary; *joss-house* [Chin.]; *kiack* [Burm.]; *the* Lord's house; minster; *mandir* [Hind.]; naos; oracle; palace; place of worship; *pantheon;* pagoda; qubba; roodloft; sanctuary; shrine; tabernacle; *upper room; vihara* [Bud.]; worship-house; *Xn.* church; *yele* [arch.]; *zayat* [Burm.];

**temporal** *(adj.)*: animate; bodily; corporeal; carnal(-minded); *delusory;* earthly; evanescent; fleshly; fleeting; *globe;* human; impermanent; *just secular; katchha [Ind.];* living; material; mortal; mundane; momentary; natural; non-spiritual; ordinary; of this earth; passing; quotidian; *regular;* short-lived; temporary; this-worldly; terrestrial; unstable; unspiritual; under the sun; volatile; worldly(-minded); *xenenthesis;* yielded to the flesh; zoetical; [*Ant.* transmundane]

**temporary** *(adj.)*: acting; *ad hoc* [L.]; brief; *cutcha* [Ind.]; done quickly; ephemeral; evanescent; episodic; fleeting; for a time; *going for a short time;* having limited duration; interim; impermanent; jackleg; *katchha* [Ind.]; limited; lasting a short while; makeshift; momentary; non-permanent; only ~; provisional; provisory; passing; quick; *real brief;* short-term; temporal; transitory; transient; unstable; volatile; while waiting; *x-itory;* yet fleeting; *zwischnzug* [G.];

**tempt** *(v.)*: allure; beguile; bait; coax; draw; deceive; entice; ensnare; fool; goad; hoodwink; induce; incite; jape; *knavery;* lure; mislead; *nudge; outwit;* prod; provoke; *quiblin [arch.];* rope; seduce; tantalize; *test;* urge; *vie;* wheedle; *xuld [arch.];* yerk; *zygotaxis;*

**temptation** *(n.)*: allurement; bait; coaxing; drawing; deception; enticement; ensnarement; forbidden fruit; gudgeon; hook, line and sinker; honeypot; inducement; incitement; japing; *knavery;* lure; misleading; *nudge; outwitting;* prodding; provocation; *quiblin* [arch.]; *roping;* seduction; test; tantalizing; trap; urging; *vie;* wooing; *xuld [arch.];* yearning; *zygotaxis [biol.];*

**tempter** *(n.)*: allurer; beguiler; charmer; devil; debaucher; enticer; fooler; fox; goader; hoodwinker; inciter; japer; *knave;* lurer; misleader; *nudger; outwitter; old fox;* prodder; *quiblin* [arch.]; *roper;* seducer; temptress [fem.]; urger; *vier;* wooer; *xuld [arch.];* yerker; *zapper;* [*see* Devil; temptress]

**temptress** *(n.)*: allurer; adulteress; beguiler; charmer; devil; enticer; flirt; *femme fatale* [F.]; fornicatress; goader; home-wrecker; inveigler; Jezebel; kittock; lady of the evening; meretrix; *naughty girl; outwitter;* prodder; quean; *roper;* seductress; she-devil; tempter; tigress; tantalizer; user; vixen; vamp; wooer; *xtabay;* yaud; *zapper;*

**tenable** *(adj.)*: acceptable; believable; credible; defensible; excusable; feasible; good; *holding;* intelligent; justifiable; *known;* logical; maintainable; no-nonsense; okay; *obtainable;* plausible; quite sensible; reasonable; sound; *true;* understandable; valid; workable; *xtry.; yieldful; zero problem;*

**tenacious** *(adj.)*: adamant; bull-headed; contumacious; determined; dogged; ever-stubborn; firm; grim; headstrong; insistent; jaw-set; keeping; lasting; mulish; non-yielding; obstinate; persistent; *quenchless;* resolute; stubborn; steadfast; tireless; unyielding; *volitional;* willful; *x-grained;* yieldless; *zero give;* [*Ant.* tractable]

**tenacity** *(n.)*: assiduity; bulldog- ~; continuance; determination; doggedness; endurance; firmness; gumption; holding; indefatigableness; *insistence; jaw-set;* keeping at it; lastingness; mulishness; non-yieldedness; not giving up; obstinacy; perseverance; persistence; *querulousness;* relentlessness; resoluteness; steadfastness; tenaciousness; unyieldingness; *volition;* willpower; *xtry. effort;* yieldlessness; *zealous continuance;* [*Ant.* tractability]

**tenant** *(n.)*: apartment resident; boarder; *customer;* dweller; *end user;* feudatory; *grantee;* holder; inhabitant; *job-holder; keener;* lessee; *mesne* lessee; lodger; *non-owner;* occupant; paravail; quarterer; renter; *ryot* [Ind.]; socager; sublessee; tacksman; tabler; usufructary; *vassal;* weekly renter; *xtr. person;* year-rounder; *zone lessee;*

**tend** *(v.)*: attend; busy oneself; care (for); do; *exert; function;* give attention to; help; *industry; job;* keep; look after; minister; mind; nurse; *operate; obey; perform; quick-to-obey;* run; serve; take care of; *use; valet;* wait (on); watch over; *xfer;* yeme; *zealously ~;*

**tendency** *(n.)*: affinity; bent; bias; cast; disposition; desire; drift; *enthusiasm;* favor; general inclination; heart; inclination; *judgment;* keenness; leaning; mind; movement; notion; natural bent; *outlook;* predisposition; penchant; proneness; proclivity; propensity; *quality; reckoning;* slant; spirit; trend; urge; *vein;* way; warp; *xenenthesis;* yankering; yaw; *zeal;*

**tender** *(adj.)*: affectionate; bleeding-heart; *brotherly;* caring; dear; delicate; ever-gentle; flexible; gentle; gentling; heart-warming; infirm; immature; jiggly; kind; loving; mild; nice; nubile; oversoft; pleasant; *quilted; responsive;* soft; supple; sympathetic; sweet; softhearted; touching; unhardened; velvety; warm; *xillinous;* yielding; young; *zero hardness;* [*Ant.* tough]

**tenderhearted** *(adj.)*: amiable; bighearted; compassionate; caring; *dear;* endearing; forgiving; good-natured; humane; introspective; *jovial;* kindhearted; loving; merciful; nice; *obliging;* pleasant; *quick to help;* regardful; sympathetic; sweet; softhearted; tender; thoughtful; unselfish; very kind; warm; xenial; *yielding; zealous of good works* [Tit. 2:4];

**tenderness** *(n.)*: affection; bleeding heart; care; *devotion;* endearment; feelings; gentleness; heart; insolidity; intimacy; *juvenescence;* kindness; love; mildness; niceness; oversensibility; pure love; *quietness; responsiveness;* sweetness; softness; sensitivity; tenderheartedness; unselfishness; *virtue;* warmth; *xenial;* yearning; youthfulness; zeal; [*Ant.* tenderness]

**tenor** *(n.)*: attributes; *badge;* character; drift; essence; fiber; gist; heart; intention; jist; kind; lineament; makeup; nature; overall makeup; property; quality; reality; spirit; temperament; tone; underlying character; *virtue;* way; xenenthesis; *yetzer* [Heb.]; *zoe;* [*see* essence]

**tense** *(adj.)*: apprehensive; anxious; burdensome; concerned; distressing; edgy; fretful; grilling; grueling; heavy; hairy; high-strung; intense; jumpy; jittery; knotty; *load; moody;* nervous; nerveracking; overwrought; overanxious; overstrung; pressure-filled; quivering; restless; stressful; taxing; uneasy; uptight; vexing; worrisome; *xenophobic; yemelich* [arch.]; *zapping;*

**tension** *(n.)*: anxiety; burden; concern; disquietude; exertion; emotional stress; force; grief; hassle; heaviness; hypertension; intensity; jimjams; knottiness; load; mental strain; nervous ~; overstrain; pressure; pull; *quash;* rack; stress; strain; tensity; tenseness; tautness; taxation; tenseness; unrest; vexation; weight; worry; *x-stress; yank; zapping;*

**tent** *(n.)*: *awning;* bivvy; camping ~; circus ~; *canopy; cover;* dwelling; enclosure; exhibition ~; fairgrounds ~; ger; *huppa [Heb.];* inclosure; *jaga* ~; kibitka; lodgement; marquee; nylon camping ~; *overcanopy;* pavilion; pup ~; *quarters;* ridge ~; shelter ~; shade; tabernacle; teepee; tupek; umbrage; velarium; wigwam; *xystus;* yurt; zipper-tent; *zayat;*

**tenuous** *(adj.)*: aerial; baseless; cloud-built; doubtful; embryonic; feeble; groundless; hazy; insubstantial; *jackleg; keeling;* lame; microcosmic; non-potent; overweak; poor; questionable; *rickety;* shaky; *tottery;* unconvincing; unsubstantiated; vague; weak; xtry. weak; yet unconfirmed; *zero confirmation;* [*Ant.* trustworthy]

**terminate** *(v.)*: abort; annihilate; butcher; bump off [slang]; close; cease; cut off; destroy; end; finish; gun down; halt; immolate; *jab;* kill; leave off; make an end; murder; *nip;* obliterate; purge; quench; run through; stop; slay; smite; take one's life; *unseat; vaporize;* wipe out; x-out; *yank down;* zap;

**termination** *(n.)*: abortion; annihilation; breakoff; cessation; discontinuation; death; ending; elimination; extermination; finishing off; *gunning down;* halting; *internment; jabbing;* killing; liquidation; mortality; *nullification;* obliteration; purging; quenching; *ruination;* stopping; smiting; taking of life; undoing; vaporization; wiping out; x-ing out; *yank down; zapping;*

**terrible** *(adj.)*: awful; abominable; baneful; corrupt; dreadful; execrable; frightful; godless; horrible; intolerable; jaded; knavish; lousy; malevolent; nasty; odious; pernicious; *quad;* ruthless; sinful; tragic; treacherous; unrighteous; villainous; vile; wicked; wrong(ful); *x-gressing;* yucky; *zhlubby;* [*Ant.* terrific]

**terrific** *(adj.)*: amazing; brilliant; capital; divine; excellent; exceptional; fantastic; fabulous; great; grand; heavenly; incredible; jim-dandy; keen; likable; laudable; marvelous; notable; outstanding; praiseworthy; quality; remarkable; superb; splendid; tremendous; unbelievable; unequalled; very good; virtuous; wonderful; xtry.; *you beaut* [Aus.]; *zizzy;* [*Ant.* terrible]

**terrify** *(v.)*: alarm; *burden; care;* distress; daunt; *exasperate;* frighten; gaster; horrify; intimidate; *jitters;* kiaugh [Scot.]; *languish;* make nervous; nerve; overburden; panic; quicken; *red alert;* scare; terrorize; unnerve; vex; worry; *xenophobia; yelping; zealless;* [*Ant.* thrill]

**territory** *(n.)*: area; bounds; county; district; domain; extent; enclave; field; ground; holding; *imperial district;* jurisdiction; *kray* [Rus.]; location; land; municipality; nome; *oblast [Rus.];* province; parish; precinct; part; quadrant; region; section; sector; space; tract; township; tetrarchy; terrain; ubiety; viceroyalty; ward; *x-sector;* yard; zone;
 Kinds of territories: administrative district; burrough; canton; constituency; colony; district; domain; duchy; emirate; federal district; governorate; hamlet; imperial province; jarldom; kingdom; land; monarchy; municipality; nation; oblast; parish; province; quarter; queendom; region; satrap; sector; state; subdistrict; tetrarchy; uyezd [Rus.]; viceroyalty; ward; xerofdom; zone;
**terror** *(n.)*: alarm; affright; *burden;* cowardice; dread; evil; fear; fright; gastness; horror; insecurity; jitteriness; kiaugh [Scot.]; *lily-livered; mistrust;* nervousness; over-anxiety; panic; quaking; *reluctance;* scaredness; stress; shock; *trepidation;* uneasiness; vexation; worry; *xenophobia;* yellow-belliedness; *zeallessness;* [*Ant.* tranquility]
**terrorism** *(n.)*: agri~; bombing; *clash;* daunter; *evil;* frightening; gastering; harrying; intimidation; *jitters; killing; lashing out;* making afraid; narco~; oppression; panicmongery; *quarreling;* revolutionism; suicide bombing; terror(izing); unlawful combat; violence; *wickedness; xenophobia; yell;* zealotry;
**terrorist** *(n.)*: attacker; agri- ~; bomber; criminal; *cell group;* daunter; *enemy;* frightener; guerrilla; harrier; intimidator; jafar [Mos.]; killer; lasher out; murderer; narco~; oppressor; panicmonger; *quarreler;* revolutionary; suicide bomber; terrormonger; unlawful combatant; urban ~; victimizer; *warfare; xenophobic; yeller;* zealot;
**terrorize** *(v.)*: attack; bully; cause terror; distress; daunt; *endanger;* frighten; gaster; harry; intimidate; *jitters;* keep down; *lash out;* make afraid; nerve; oppress; panic; *quicken;* repress; scare; terrify; unnerve; vex; worry; *xenophobia; yell; zap;*
**terse** *(adj.)*: abrupt; brief; brusque; concise; curt; direct; economical; fugacious; gruff; *harsh;* insignificant; infinitesimal; insubstantial; itsy-bitsy; inadequate; insufficient; *jitney; just little;* knee-high; laconic; miniature; neat; *overly small;* pithy; *quick;* reduced; short; succinct; snappy; sententious; to the point; unloquacious; very small; wee; *XS; yea big; zero;* [*Ant.* talkative]
**test** *(n.)*: assessment; analysis; acid ~; *basic assessment;* check; cross-examination; *difficulty;* exam(ination); evaluation; experiment; final (exam); field ~; grilling; hearing; interrogation; inspection; *jam; kink; load;* midterm; make-up ~; *non-mandatory ~;* oral exam; ordeal; open-book ~; pop quiz; proving; probe; pre~; probation; post~; quiz; responsions; road~; scrutiny; standardized ~; testing; trial; take-home ~; *ultimate ~;* viva; written examination; xenodiagnosis; year-end exam; *zetetic;* [trial]
**test** *(v.)*: assess; analyze; bear out; check; determine; examine; experiment with; evince; field ~; give ~; *homologate;* investigate; jerque; *kithe [Scot.];* legitimize; make certain; *nail down; okay;* prove; probe; *question;* re-test; substantiate; try; *uphold;* verify; *warrant;* xenodiagnose; *yes; zero doubt;*
**testament** *(n.)*: agreement; bond; covenant; declaration; *ensuring;* forswearing; guarantee; hypothecation; *interpledging;* jurament; *kept promise; letter of commitment; making of vows;* non-conditional promise; oath; promise; pact; *qualified promise;* resolution; solemn agreement; *treaty;* unconditional promise; undertaking; vow; will; word (of honor); *x-one's heart; yafery [arch.]; zealous promise;*
**testify** *(v.)*: attest; bear witness; certify; depone; declare; establish; *fix;* give sworn statement; homologate; inform; *justify; know;* kithe [Scot.]; *legitimize;* make known; notify; observe; proclaim; *questionless;* relate; say swear; tell; *utter;* vouch; witness; x-certify; *yes; zealously affirm;*
**text** *(n.)*: article; body; content; discourse; *edition; form; glyphs; handwriting;* inscription; *journalism; kapnography;* letters; main body; message; material; manuscript; microprint; notation; original writing; prose; passage; print; *quotation;* reading material; script; type; transcript; *used words;* version; words; writing; *xiaozhuan; yellow journalism; zeug;*

**texture** *(n.)*: *attribute;* body; consistency; character; distillation; embodiment; feel; grain; handle [Br.]; *intrinsic; jist;* keest; *like;* makeup; nature; *organization; pat;* quale; runniness; roughness; surface; smoothness; touch; *uneven ~; velvetiness;* weftage; way of feeling; *xenenthesis; yetzer [Heb.]; zeug [G.];*
**thank** *(v.)*: appreciate; acknowledge; bless; *conscious; due to;* express gratitude; *forever thankful;* give thanks; *heartfelt thanks;* indebted; *jubilate;* kiss; *laud; mindful; mahalo* [Haw.]; not forget; owe; offer ~s; praise; *quick-to-thank;* recognize; salute; show gratitude; *think on; ta [Br.]; understand; value;* welcome; *xenium; yet thankful; zealously ~;*
**thankful** *(adj.)*: appreciative; beholden; conscious; duly ~; evangelian; full of gratitude; forever ~; grateful; *happy;* indebted; *joyful;* kind-thoughted; *lavishing praise;* mindful; much obliged; non-forgetful; obliged; pleased; quite grateful; remembering; satisfied; thanking; *understanding;* very ~; welcoming; *xtry. ~;* yielding thanks; *zealous to give thanks;* [*Ant.* thankless]
**thankfulness** *(n.)*: appreciativeness; appreciation; *beholden;* credit; *deo gratias* [L.]; expression of thanks; *forever thankful;* gratitude; gratefulness; gramercy; *honor;* indebtedness; *joy;* kind-thoughtedness; *love;* mindfulness; non-forgetfulness; obliging; praise; *quick-to-thank;* recognition; spirit of thanksgiving; thanks(giving); *understanding; very thankful;* wah [Asia]; *xtry. gratitude;* yielding thanks; *zeal;* [*Ant.* thanklessness]
**thankless** *(adj.)*: absent-minded; bad-mannered; churlish; disregardful; eliding; forgetful; grumbling; heedless; ingrate; ill-remembered; ingrate; *jaded; kindless;* loutish; miserable; non-appreciative; oblivious; praiseless; quick-to-forget; *remiss; rude;* self-centered; thoughtless; unappreciative; ungrateful; unthankful; very unmindful; without thanks; wretched; *xgressing; yemeless [arch.]; zero appreciation;* [*Ant.* thankful]
**thanksgiving** *(n.)*: appreciation; blessing; credit; delivering of thanks; expression of thanks; *forever thankful;* gratefulness; giving of thanks; *honor;* indebtedness; *joy;* kind-thoughtedness; *love;* mindfulness; non-forgetfulness; outpouring of gratitude; praise; prayer of ~; *quick-to-thank;* recognition; spirit of thankfulness; thanks; *understanding; very thankful; wholehearted thanks; xtry. gratitude;* yielding thanks; *zeal;* [*see* praise; *Ant.* thanklessness]
**thaw** *(v.)*: ablate; become soft; colliquate; defrost; de-ice; ease; flow; give; *heat up;* ice-out; *jump down;* keep *~ing;* liquefy; melt; mollify; *non-hardened;* oversoften; *palliate; quick-defrost;* reheat; run; *recede;* soften; tenderize; unfreeze; *vanish;* warm; *xfer;* yeet; *zeroize;*
**theater** *(n.)*: amphitheatre; arena; auditorium; acting; bioscope; *Broadway;* coliseum; cinema; concert hall; drama; dinner ~; drive-in; edifice; *entertainment;* footlights; farce; grandstand; histrionism; hall; house; *ice rink; judgment hall;* kinema; *kabuki* [Jap.]; lyceum; libretto; *lecture hall;* multiplex; megaplex; movie house; music hall; nabe; *naumachy* [Rom.]; nickelodeon; odeum; odea; opera house; ozoner; playhouse; plays; picture house; *performance;* quad; *round ~;* stage; silver screen; theatre; troupe; *upper `circle;* venue; *vaudeville;* Wendy house; *XXX theater;* yard; zone;
**theatrical** *(adj.)*: acting; big-screen; cinematic; dramatic; expressive; emotive; exaggerated; *emotive;* feigning; *gut-wrenching;* hammy; histrionical; *inspired; jarring;* keenly ~; lush; melodramatic; *novelettish;* overdramatic; on-stage; operatic; performing; *quixotic; romantic;* scenic; stage-related; theatric; thespian; unreal; vaudeville; *weepy; xtry. ~; yearnful;* zealous;
**theft** *(n.)*: abstraction; burglary; breaking and entering; brigandage; *crime;* deprivation; excoriation; extortion; embezzlement; filching; grand larceny; hoist; heist; holdup; housebreaking; *impalming; identity ~; jailable crime;* kleptomania; larceny; mugging; michery; nimming; *obtaining;* pilfering; purloining; petty larceny; *quick-fingered;* robbery; stealing; shoplifting; thievery; unpursing; *underhandedness;* violence; villainy; wresting; *xfer;* yanking; *zipping away;*
**theme** *(n.)*: area; burden; central ~; design; donnée; emphasis; focus; *gist; heart; hobby horse;* idea; *jet;* keynote; leitmotif; motif; matter; notion; overriding ~; premise; *quintessence;* rubric; subject (matter); topic; thesis; underlying subject; *vital; weight; xenenthesis;* yaw; *zone;*

**theologian** *(n.)*: apologist; Bible college professor; Christian ~; doctor; defender of the faith; ecclesiastic; *fugleman;* great mind; harmonist; *instructor; judge; kerygmatic;* leading ~; lecturer; master ~; *noetic; oracle;* professor; Ph. D.; quodlibetarian; *researcher;* scholar; theologist; theolog [derog.]*;* university professor; *visiting ~; writer; xenagogue; youth pastor; zetetic;*
**theological** *(adj.)*: apologetical; biblical; creedal; doctrinal; ethereal; ecclesiological; faith-related; God-related; hierological; isogogic; *Jesus-related; kerigmatic; learning about God;* ministerial; *non-secular; orthodox; pneumatological; pastoral;* quodlibetical; religious; scriptural; spiritual; theologic; ultramundane; *virtue; Word of God; Xn.; youth-ministry related; zetetical;*
**theology** *(n.)*: apologetics; beliefs; conviction; creed; doctrine; divinity; dogma; ecclesiology; *following;* God science; hierology; isogogics; *Jesus; kerygma; knowledge; learning;* moral ~; natural ~; oracles; position; quodlibetary; religion; study; systematic ~; science of God; theologism; theodicy; understanding; viewpoint; *word; xenagogy; youth-ministry related; Zionism;*
    **Disciplines of theology**: angelology; anthropology; apologetics; bibliology; Christology; covenantology; demonology; dispensationalism; ecclesiology; eschatology; familiology; hamartiology; hermeneutics; Israelology; missiology; pnematology; satanology; soteriology; theology proper;
**theoretical** *(adj.)*: abstract; belief-based; conjectural; deductive; *estimated;* fanciful; guess; hypothetical; idealistic; *just suppose; knowledgeable;* logical; metaphysical; notional; not proven; opinionative; proofless; Q.E.D.; reckoned; speculative; suppositional; supposed; seeming; theoretic; thought-to-be; untested; unproven; untried; virtual; *what if...; xenagogic; yankering; zealous;* [*Ant.* true]
**theorize** *(v.)*: assume; bet; conjecture; deduce; estimate; figure; guess; hypothesize; imagine; judge; *know; lucubrate;* muse; *notion; occur;* propound; presume; *question;* reckon; speculate; suppose; think; *use brain; venture; wis; xenodiagnose; yeme; zazen;*
**theory** *(n.)*: assumption; belief; conjecture; deduction; educated guess; estimation; figuring; feeling; guess; hypothesis; idea; judgment; *knowledge; lemma;* mind; notion; opinion; postulation; premise; proposal; *presumption;* qualified opinion; reckoning; speculation; thought; theorem; *urge;* view; way of thinking; *xenodiagnosis; yankering; zeal;*
**therapeutic** *(adj.)*: advantageous; beneficial; calming; curative; *doctor-endorsed;* effective; favorable; gainful; healing; iatric; *julep;* kinic; *leg therapy;* medicinal; *nostrum; outstanding;* profitable; quinic; relaxing; remedial; restorative; salutary; tonic; useful; vulnerary; valuable; worthwhile; *xenobiotic; yieldful; zopissa [arch.];*
**therapy** *(n.)*: analysis; *backrub;* cure; *doctoring;* electro- ~; exercises; *foot ~; group ~;* healing; heat- ~; hydro~; *industry; julep; knack; leg ~;* ministration; massage- ~; natural ~; *oil massage;* physical ~; psycho~; *quinic;* rehab(ilitation); shock ~; spa ~; treatment; *ule;* vulnerary; work; xylo~; x-ray ~; *yanggona;* zoo~;
**thick** *(adj.)*: ample; broad; chunky; congealed; deep; dense; *extensive;* fat; full-bodied; *great;* hefty; inpissated; jellied; *king-sized;* large; massive; non-watery; oatmealy; *prodigious; quantitative; rotund;* stocky; thickset; thickened; unthinned; *voluminous;* wide; *x-axis;* yearned; zoomed out; [*Ant.* thin]
**thicken** *(v.)*: *add to;* become thick; congeal; coagulate; condense; densify; expand; firm up; gel; harden; inspissate; jell(ify); knot; lump; make hard; *non-fluid;* obdure; ossify; pectize; quarle; *reinforce;* set; solidify; stiffen; thick; *unyielding; viscid;* waulk; whip; *xerogel;* yearn; zet [dial.]; [*Ant.* thin]
**thicket** *(n.)*: arbor; boscage; brake; bushes; brush; bush; covert; copse; *dendroid;* exuberance; firth; grove; hedges; intervale; *juba bush; kalmia; lantana;* motte; nemoral; overgrowth; *plants;* queach; *rosa;* spinney; shaw; shrubbery; thorn-bushes; underbrush; vegetation; woods; *xylopia; yawshrub; zereba;*
**thickness** *(n.)*: *area;* breadth; conpissation; deepness; density; extent; fullness; girth; heaviness; inpissation; jellification; *king-sized; largeness;* mucilaginousness; *non-watery;* overall ~; ply; prodigiousness; *quantity;* rotundity; span; stiffness; solidity; thickening; *unthinned;* viscosity; width; wideness; *x-axis; yearned; zoomed out;* [*Ant.* thinness]

**thief** *(n.)*: armed man; bandit; burglar; brigand; crook; dip; extortionist; filcher; gangster; highwayman; hustler; heister; intruder; *jailbird;* knuck; kleptomaniac; larcenist; mugger; nimmer; outlaw; prowler; pick-pocket; pirate; *quad;* robber; stealer; shoplifter; *thug; unscrupulous;* villain; waddy; *xiaoren;* yegg; *zhlub;* [Ant. trooper]

**thin** *(adj.)*: attenuated; bony; constricted; delicate; elongated; ectomorphic; fine; frail; gracile; hairbreadth; insubstantial; jimp; knife blade-thin; lean; lank(y); little; meager; narrow; overthin; overextended; paper-thin; pencil-thin; petite; *quantité négligeable [F.];* ribby; slim; slender; stringy; trim; twiggy; threadlike; underweight; virgate [bot.]; weedy; wafer-thin; XF; *yieldless; zero body fat;* [Ant. thick]

**thin** *(v.)*: attenuate; become ~ner; condense; *diet;* downsize; decoagulate; extenuate; fade; get ~ner; *halve;* impair; *improve;* jump down; *knock down;* lose weight; make ~ner; narrow; overextend; pare down; quail; reduce; slenderize; slim down; taper; *undersized; vanish;* wane; waste; XS; *yield;* zeroize; [Ant. thicken]

**thing** *(n.)*: article; aspect; baggage; belonging; bauble; commodity; doodad; *equipment;* entity; feature; gadget; *goods;* hoosywatsy; item; jib; jingbang; kickumbob; *load;* matter; *noun;* object; particular; piece; *quelque chose* [F.]; *raw material;* some~ tidbit; utensil; *valuable;* whatnot; widget; xylon; you-know-what; *zeug [G.];* [*see* things]

**things** *(n.)*: articles; belongings; commodities; chattels; duffel; effects; equipment; feedstock; goods; gear; habiliments; items; junk; kit; *load;* material; matter; needments; objects; odds and ends; possessions; property; paraphernalia; personal effects; quintessence; *quantity;* rigging; stuff; substance; supplies; tackle; trappings; utensils; valuables; *wares; wanigan; xenenthesis; yannigan; zeug* [G.];

**think** *(v.)*: analyze; brainstorm; cogitate; consider; contemplate; concentrate; calculate; concoct; compute; conceive; dwell; devise; deem; evaluate; figure; focus; fabricate; guess; gauge; hatch; hypothesize; invent; imagine; judge; *know;* logicalize; meditate; muse; mull; *notion;* occur; ponder; question; reason; ruminate; study; theorize; trow; use brain; valuate; visualize; wonder; weigh; *xenodiagnose; yeme;* zero in;

**thinker** *(n.)*: academic; analyzer; brain [slang]; brainstormer; cogitator; contemplator; concoctor; deliberator; deviser; deep ~; evaluator; figurer; genius; highbrow; intellectual; inventor; imaginer; judger; keen ~; logician; muser; nestor; originator; ponderer; philosopher; planner; questioner; reasoner; reflector; reckoner; smarty [slang]; scholar; studier; theorizer; *ultra-smart;* valuator; whiz (kid); wonder-kid; wonderer; weigher; wise man; *xenagogue; yauper; zetetic;* [Ant. tomfool]

**thinness** *(n.)*: attenuation; boniness; constriction; delicacy; exility; emaciation; fineness; gauntness; *hairbreadth;* insubstantiality; jimpness; *knifeblade-thin;* leanness; lankness; littleness; macilency; meagerness; marasmus; narrowness; non-ponderosity; over-thinness; peakishness; *quantité négligeable [F.];* ribbiness; slimness; slenderness; skinniness; scrawniness; slightness; tininess; unsubstantiality; *virgate [bot.];* wispiness; wiriness; *XF; yieldless; zero body fat;* [Ant. thickness]

**thirst** *(n.)*: aridity; ambition; burning dryness; desire; craving; dryness; dehydration; desire; eagerness; fancy; great ~; hankering; *insatiable ~;* itch; jejuneness; keenness; longing; lust; *mouth-dryness;* need; *over-thirsty;* parchedness; polydipsia; passion; quenchlessness; *rainlessness; siccatation;* thirstiness; *under-hydrated;* vacuity; want; waterlessness; xerotes; yearning; *zapped;*

**thirst** *(v.)*: aspire; ache; burn with desire; crave; desire; eagerly desire; fancy; got to have; hope for; itch; *just got to have; keenly desire;* long for; must have; need; *order;* pant; *quest for;* relish; seek; *thirstiness; urge; velleity;* want; *xel [arch.];* yearn for; *zeal;*

**thirsty** *(adj.)*: athirst; arid; bone-dry; chapped; dry; dehydrated; evaporated; fountainless; gone dry; *greedy;* hasky; inthursted; jejune; kibe; *lusting; mouth-dry;* non-watered; overhot; parched; quenchless; rainless; scorched; thirsting; unwatered; under-hydrated; vaporated; withered; xerothermic; yearning; zapped;

**thorn** *(n.)*: acantha; bur; barb; cocklebur; distaff-thistle; *end;* fire~; goat's- ~; haw~; *impale;* jag; jujube; *keen-edged; lance;* musk thistle; nettle; *ouch!;* point; *quill; rosebush;* spike; spine; thistle; urtica; *verge;* white- ~; xanthium; yellow ~; *zizyphus;*

**thorny** *(adj.)*: acicular; barbed; briery; brambly; cocklebur-riddled; denticled; echinate; full of thorns; *goat's-thorn;* hedge-nettled; *irritating;* jaculiferous; *keenly sharp; lanceolated;* mucronate; nettly; over-prickly; prickly; quill-filled; *rough;* sharp; spiny; thistly; urtica-filled; *very sharp;* well-nettled; *xyresic; yellow thorn; zinging;*

**thorough** *(adj.)*: all-encompassing; aggregate; broad; complete; comprehensive; detailed; entire; exhaustive; full; good and ~; *high;* inclusive; in-depth; *just dandy; keep going;* leaving-no-stone-unturned; methodical; non-abridged; out-and-out; painstaking; *quiddle,* rigorous; sweeping; systematic; scrupulous; total; through-and-through; utter; unmitigated; *veritable;* whole; *xtry.; yare; zealous;*

**thought** *(n. idea)*: *approach;* brainchild; concept; determination; evaluation; fancy; fabrication; *genius;* hunch; idea; inspiration; impression; judgment; *knowledge;* lucubration; musing; mentation; notion; observation; *opinion;* perception; *quick thinking;* reflection; speculation; stroke of genius; thinking; theory; using ones brain; *valuation;* weighing; *xtry ~; yeme* [arch.]; *zazen* [Bud.];

**thought** *(n. thinking)*: analysis; attention; brainwork; cogitation; consideration; contemplation; concentration; deliberation; evaluation; figuring; focus; *genius;* headwork; imagination; intellection; judgment; *knowledge;* lucubration; meditation; mentation; *notion;* observance; *on one's mind;* pondering; *questioning;* reckoning; reflection; rumination; study; speculation; thinking; using one's brain; *valuating;* weighing; *x-examine; yeme* [arch.]; *zazen* [Bud.];

**thoughtful** *(adj.)*: attentive; benevolent; considerate; deferential; *endearing; friendly;* good-natured; gracious; helpful; *introspective; judicial;* kind(-hearted); loving; mindful; nice; obliging; polite; quick-to-help; regardful; selfless; sensitive; tenderhearted; unselfish; very kind; warmhearted; well-natured; xenial; yielding; zealous of good works [Tit. 2:4]; [*Ant.* thoughtless]

**thoughtfulness** *(n. consideration)*: attention; benevolence; consideration; deference; *endearing;* favor; goodness; helpfulness; *introspection; judiciousness;* kindness; love; mercifulness; niceness; obligingness; politeness; quickness to help; regard; selflessness; solicitude; sensitivity; tenderheartedness; unselfishness; *virtuousness;* warmth; xenia; yieldedness; zealousness to help; [*Ant.* thoughtlessness]

**thoughtfulness** *(n. contemplativeness)*: absorption; brooding; contemplativeness; deepness of thought; engrossment; fancifulness; gravity; heedfulness; heart- ~; introspection; *judging; knowledge;* lucubration; musing; *notional;* occupation; pensiveness; preoccupation; *questioning;* reflectiveness; regard; studiousness; thinking; understanding; valuation; wistfulness; weightiness; *x-examination; yearnful; zeteticism;* [*Ant.* torpidity]

**thoughtless** *(adj.)*: absent-minded; brainless; careless; distracted; empty-headed; forgetful; giddy-brained; *goffish;* harebrained; inconsiderate; inattentive; insensitive; insensate; *Jehu;* knuckle-headed; *lackadaisical;* mindless; neglectful; over-forgetful; perfunctory; *quirky;* reckless; regardless; selfish; thick-skinned; tactless; unthoughtful; unthinking; vacant-minded; without regard; *x-out;* yonderly; *zero thought;* [*Ant.* thoughtful]

**thrash** *(v.)*: assault; beat; batter; clobber; drub; *efface;* flog; give whipping; hit; impact; *jab;* knout; lick; maul; nubble; *overstrike;* pummel; quab; rap; smite; thresh; thwack; *uppercut;* veney; wallop; *x-sect;* yedder; zonk;

**thread** *(n.)*: app; *braid;* cord; drawstring; *entangle;* fiber; filament; *gold~;* halter; *intertwine;* jute; knittle; line; monofilament; natural fiber; organzine; pack~; *qiviut;* rope-yarn; string; strand; tram; *uncoil;* vang; warp; woof; *xylem;* yarn; zein;

**threat** *(n.)*: adversity; *beware;* commination; danger; duress; endangerment; forewarning; grim warning; hazard; imperilment; jeopardy; known ~; *life-threatening;* menace; non-safety; *ominous;* peril; *questionable;* risk; self-risk; threatening; ultimatum; *vatic;* warning; "x"; *yeopartie* [arch.]; *zero security;*

**threaten** *(v.)*: aggress; bully; bluster; blackmail; coerce; daunt; endanger; force; give notice; hector; intimidate; imperil; jeopardize; *kiaugh;* lay open; menace; notify; open to danger; pressure; *quicken;* ramp; scare; terrorize; threat [poet.]; utter threats; *victimize;* warn; *xenophobia; yell threats at; zap;*
**threatening** *(adj.)*: aggressive; baleful; comminatory; dangerous; endangering; foreboding; gloomy; hostile; imperiling; jeopardous; *kiaugh;* life- ~; menacing; minacious; nasty; ominous; perilous; *questionable;* risky; scary; threatful; unfriendly; violent; worrisome; *x.;* yet hazardous; *zero comfort;*
**thresh** *(v.)*: *abstract;* beat; buffet; cull out; drub; *extract;* flail; gin; hit; impact; *jab;* knock; lam; maul; nubble; *overstrike;* pommel; quab; *remove;* sort; separate; sift; thrash; *uncouple;* veney; whack; winnow; *x-sect;* yandy; *zonk;*
**threshold** *(n.)*: abuttal; brink; coast; dawn; doorway; edge; fringe; frontier; gateway; *hem;* inception; *jurisdiction; kept limit;* limit; margin; *near;* onset; perimeter; quadra; rim; *start; tolerance;* ulterior; verge; *without; x-border; yonder; zone;*
**thrift** *(n.)*: austerity; begrudging; cheapness; dollar-saving; economy; economicalness; frugality; good husbandry; hoarding; illiberality; *Jack Benny;* knippering; laggardness; miserliness; niggardliness; over-frugality; parsimony; *quick-to-save; reluctance;* scrimping; strait-handedness; thriftiness; unwastefulness; *very miserly; wary; xtry. ~; yieldlessness; zero-generosity;*
**thrifty** *(adj.)*: austere; begrudging; careful; conservative; dollar-conscious; economical; frugal; grudging; hesitant; illiberal; judicious; *kitsch; laggard;* meager; niggardly; overcautious; parsimonious; pennywise; provident; *quick-to-refuse;* reluctant; sparing; tight-fisted; unwasteful; *vacillating;* wary; *xtry. ~; yieldless; zero-generosity;*
**thrill** *(n.)*: animation; bliss; cheer; delight; excitement; exhilaration; felicity; glee; hilarity; intoxication; joy; kick; lightheartedness; merriment; nice feeling; overjoy; pleasure; quaver; rapture; sensation; *seventh heaven;* tingle; transport; uplift; *vivacity;* winsomeness; *xtry ~; yeah!;* zestfulness; [*Ant.* terror]
**thrill** *(v.)*: *affect;* animate; bless; bestir; cheer; delight; excite; exhilarate; fascinate; glory; glee; hearten; invigorate; joy; jubilate; *kick;* lift; move; *nowell;* overjoy; *prickles;* quiver; rouse; stir; titillate; uplift; vivify; wow; *xtry; yell; zestful;* [*see* praise; *Ant.* terrify]
**thrilling** *(adj.)*: animating; arousing; breathtaking; captivating; delightful; exciting; exhilarating; electric; fun; gripping; heart-stirring; intriguing; inviting; intoxicating; jolting; kicking; lovely; moving; mind-blowing; *nice;* overwhelming; pleasing; quivering; riveting; stimulating; sensational; (soul-)stirring; titillating; thrill-a-minute; uplifting; vitalizing; winsome; *xtry; yeah!;* zestful; [*Ant.* tedious]
**thrive** *(v.)*: advance; boom; bloom; burgeon; come into full bloom; do well; develop; enlarge; experience growth; flourish; grow; heighten; increase; jump up; *keep growing;* luxuriate; make it (-good); mushroom; *nourish;* outgrow; prosper; proliferate; *quantum increase;* ripen; rise; sprout; succeed; *teem;* upspring; vegetate; wax greater; *xtry. growth; yain* [arch.]; *zoom up;*
**throat** *(n.)*: *air passage;* bronchial tube; craw; *canal;* duct; esophagus; fauces; gullet; glottis; hatch [slang]; *ingest;* jugulum; *kex;* larynx; *mouth;* neck; nasopharynx; oesophagus; oropharynx; pharynx; pipe; *quill; resonate; stem;* trachea; throat-pipe; thrapple; *uvula;* voicebox; windpipe; *x; yoke; zoe;*
**throb** *(v.)*: agitate; beat; *cadence;* drum; *excite;* flutter; go bump; heart~; *impact;* jutter; knock; lam; *move;* nubble; *overagitate;* pulsate; quiver; quab; race; resonate; *rhythm;* shutter; thump; *upset;* vibrate; waver; *xuld* [arch.]; *yedder; zonk;*
**throng** *(n.)*: assemblage; bystanders; crowd; company; drove; *eyewitnesses;* forgathering; group; gathering; horde; ingathering; jam [slang]; kit [coll.]; lookers-on; mass; multitude; mob; number; onlookers; press; quantity; rally; rabble; spectators; turnout; *unit; viewers;* wisp; *x.; yain* [arch.]; *zoo;*
**throng** *(v.)*: amass; *burden;* crowd (around); densify; *encumber;* flock; flood; fill in; gather 'round; horde; inundate; jam; *kibble;* load; mass; *no room;* overcrowd; press; pack in; quash; rally; swamp; take up all the space; unite; *volume;* wedge in; *x-people; yield; zero space leftover;*

**through** *(adv.)*: across; amid(st); by (way of); cross; during; done; *endure;* full- ~; *go; heart;* in(side); *just ~; keep going; longwise; middle; nonstop;* over; past; *quite;* right ~; sheer (-straight) across; throughout; transversal; using; via; within; widthways; *while; xversal; yare; zet* [dial.];

**throw** *(v.)*: abandon; betoss; bowl; cast; chuck; catapult; discharge; eject; fling; flick; flip; flop; give toss; hurl; impel; jaculate; kest; launch; lob; *move; non-retention;* over~; out~; pitch; pelt; peg; *quoit; recast;* sling; shoot; send; toss; upcast; vault; wale; whip; *xuld* [arch.]; yend; *zing;*

**thrust** *(n.)*: acceleration; boost; blow; butt; casting; celerity; drive; discharge; ejection; force; *going;* heave; impulse; jet; jaculation; *knock;* launch; momentum; nudge; *overcast; oust;* pass(ado); push; propulsion; quickening; rush; ramming; remise; shove; shot; tierce; upthrust; veney; whipping; *xuld* [arch.]; *yank;* zip;

**thrust** *(v.)*: actuate; accelerate; boost; cast; drive; discharge; eject; exsert; force; fling; fire; go; give force; heave; impel; jet(tison); kest; lunge; launch; move; nudge; *overthrow;* push; propel; quant; ram; rocket; remise; shove; throw; upcast; vault; wale; *xuld* [arch.]; york; *yank;* zip;

**thump** *(v.)*: *assault;* batter; bump; clonk; clump; drub; *elbow;* flail; give whack; hit; impact; jab; knock; lam; make impact; nail; *overhit;* pound; quab; rap; smack; thud; thwack; undercut; *veney;* whack; *x-sect;* yerk; zonk;

**thunder** *(n.)*: *act of God;* booming; crashing; clap; crack; din; electrical storm; fulminating; fulguration; fork lightning; *gullywasher;* heat lightning; *ionization; jolt;* kaboom; loud noise; *lightning; monsoon;* noise; *outburst;* poom; *quake;* rumbling; storm; thunder-clap; *upper atmospheric lightning;* voltage; *whistler; Xevioso; yell;* zap; [*see* lightning]

**thundercloud** *(n.)*: angry cloud; black cloud; cloud; dark cloud; *early warning; fog;* gloom; haze; ice cloud; *jumbo cloud; KH instability;* lightning cloud; *miasma;* nimbus; *overcast;* omen; pall; *quasi-vaporous;* rain cloud; storm cloud; thunderhead; *umbered;* vapor; water vapor; warning sign; *xenon cloud; yellowy cloud; zirconium cloud;*

**thunderstorm** *(n.)*: *agitation; after-storm;* booming; crashing; din; electrical storm; fury; fulmination; *gullywasher;* heavy rain; inundation; *Jupiter Pluvius; knot floater;* lightning storm; *monsoon; nor'easter;* onslaught; pirry; quaking; rainstorm; rumbling; storm; thundersquall; tempest; upheaval; violent storm; weather; windstorm; white-out; white squall; windflaw; *x-current; yern; zinger;*

**thwart** *(v.)*: avert; athwart; baffle; block; bring to naught; confound; check; defeat; disconcert; discomfit; encumber; foil; frustrate; gum up; hinder; halt; impede; *jam;* keep (from); *limit;* mess up; nullify; outsmart; perplex; prevent; quash; ruin; stop; spoil; throw a monkey wrench into; upset; void; ward off; *x; yank;* zeroize;

**ticket** *(n.)*: authorization; admission; affidavit; boarding pass; bus pass; card; *chit;* ducet; daily pass; endorsed ~; family ~; game pass; *handbill; itinerary; journey;* key pass; leave; metro pass; non-refundable ~; nontransferable ~; one-way ~; pass; *qualification;* round-trip ~; summer-pass; supersaver; travelcard; unexpired ~; voucher; warrant; *xfer;* yellow ~; *zoo ~;*

**tickle** *(v.)*: arouse; brush; bestir; chuck; *cootchie-cootchie;* delectate; excite; finger; give a thrill; *ha ha;* incite; *irritate; jolly;* kittle; lightly touch; make laugh; nettle; *outburst;* pat; quisquose; rouse; stroke; titillate; touch lightly; thrill; *urge;* vellicate; whet; *xtr.* ticklish; *yuk; zing;*

**ticklish** *(adj.)*: acutely sensitive; *boff; chuckly;* delicate; easily-tickled; *funny;* giggly; high-strung; hypersensitive; infirm; *jolly;* keenly sensitive; *laughable;* miffy; *nicker;* over~; precarious; quisquose; responsive; sensitive; tickly; tender; titillative; unstable; vellicative; whimsical; *xtr. ~; yuk; zing;*

**tide** *(n.)*: afflux; bore; counter~; deluge; eagre; ebb(~); flood (~); flux; *gush;* high ~ (-water); influx; inrush; incoming ~; *jawp; keep rising;* low ~; level; lee- ~; *moon; movement;* neap; outflow; *plateau; quantity;* rip~; reflux; rush; surge; swelling; sea level; spring- ~; torrent; upsurge; upwelling; *varve;* waterflow; *x-wave; yeo; zwoosh;*

**tidal wave** *(n.)*: *amassment;* bore; *comber;* deluge; eagre; *flood;* groundswell; heave; *internal wave; jaw; keld;* long sea; massive wave; *node;* ocean wave; *plash;* quake; roller; surge; tsunami; undulation; upsurge; *vacillation;* wave; *x-wave;* yeast; *zwoosh;*
**tidy** *(adj.)*: arranged; *beautiful;* cleanly; clutter-free; dapper; *elegant;* fastidious; gemmy; hygienic; immaculate; just so; kempt; *lovely;* mess-free; neat; natty; ordered; orderly; organized; picked-up; quaint; regimented; spruce; straitened up; shipshape; trim; uncluttered; very clean; well-ordered; well-groomed; *xtry.; yet unmessed; zierlich* [G.];
**tidy** *(v.)*: arrange; *bathe;* clean; declutter; expurgate; fix; groom; get in order; houseclean; *immerse; jalap; keep up; launder;* make clean; neaten; order; pick up; put in order; *quintessentialize;* rid of clutter; redd; sweep; straighten up; spruce up; trim up; unclutter; *vacuum;* work on; *xylol; yellow soap; zierlich [G.];*
**tie** *(v.)*: attach; affix; bind; connect; clinch; do up; entwine; frap; fasten; gird; hog~; interlock; interweave; join; knot; link; mount; *network; occupy;* put together; *quasi-fuse;* relate; rope; restrain; secure; tie in; unite; *vise;* wed; *xenograft;* yoke; *zip;*
**tier** *(n.)*: array; bed; class; category; continuum; degree; deck; echelon; elevation; floor; grade; height; *increase;* journey level; *kind;* level; *mark;* notch; nexus; order; plane; plateau; *queue;* rank; stratum; story; *title;* underlayer; varve; *way; x-class; y-level;* zone;
**tight** *(adj.)*: ataunt; bound ~; close; compact; close-fitting; cramped; constricted; drum-~; difficult; *extended;* fast; fitted; greatly ~ened; hard and fast; inflexible; jammed; kept taut; leak-proof; made ~; narrow; non-spacious; overstretched; pulled ~; pinching; quite ~; restrictive; snug; skintight; straitened; taut; tightened; unrelaxed; very ~; way too ~; *XS;* yanked ~; zip-~;
**tighten** *(v.)*: *anchor;* bind; cinch; constrict; compress; draw; *extended;* fasten; gird; hold tighter; *inflexible; jam;* keep within bounds; localize; make tighter; narrow; nip; outstretch; pinch; *quite tight;* rein in; restrict; squeeze; stretch; straiten; tighten; tauten; *unrelaxed; very tight;* wring; winch; x-stretch; yank; *zero slack;*
**tightness** *(n.)*: *absolute;* binding; closeness; compactness; constriction; drum- ~; exclusiveness; fastness; *greatly tightened;* hardness; inflexibility; *jam;* keeping taut; lack of slack; *much-tightened;* non-spaciousness; overstretching; pulling; *quite tight;* restrictiveness; snugness; tautness; unrelaxed state; *very tight; way too tight; x-stretch; yanked tight; zero slack;*
**tile** *(n.)*: * adobe; bathroom ~; ceramic ~; delft ~; earthen ~; floor ~; flooring; *gutter ~;* heat-resistant ~; imbrication; inlay; jasper ~; kitchen ~; linoleum; marble ~; non-slip ~; overlay; *pan~;* quarle; quadrel; quarry ~; *rotovinyl;* surface; tiling; underlayment; vinyl ~; wall ~; *xtr. wide ~;* yellowware ~; zellige;
**tilt** *(n.)*: angle; bias; *crooked;* diagonal; elevation; fall; gradient; heel; incline; *jag; kink;* lean; list; *move; natural slope;* obliqueness; pitch; *quantity of slope;* rise; slant; turn; upslope; verge; *wind; xy-gradient; yaw;* zigzag;
**tilt** *(v.)*: angle; bias; cock; cant; dip; elevate; fall; go down; heel; incline; *jag; kink;* lean; list; move up (-down); *nudge; obliqueness;* pitch; *quantity of slope;* raise; recline; rake; slant; slope; turn; *upslope;* verge; *wind; xy-gradient; yaw; zag;*
**time** *(n.)*: age; bit; bout; bide a wee; *the* clock; century; *down ~; delay;* day; date; duration; dispensation; era; eon; Father Time; flash; fourth dimension; fortnight; *generation;* hour; horary; instant; jiffy; juncture; *kilocycle;* life~; moment; minute; month; millennium; nanosecond; occasion; overtime; olympiad; period; point; quarterly; *run ~;* season; second; spell; shift; time-span; *up~; Universal Time;* vintage; while; wait ~; watch; week; x-time; year; *Yukon ~;* zone ~;
**time-honored** *(n.)*: age-old; *behavioral;* customary; cultural; common; conventional; dominant; expected; established; familiar; general; historic; inveterate; jake [Br.]; known; long-established; main; normal; *natural;* ordinary; predominant; *qualified;* routine; standard; traditional; usual; venerated; well-established; *x-cultural; ye olde; zealous tradition;*

**timeless** *(adj.)*: abiding; ageless; boundless; changeless; durable; deathless; enduring; eternal; fixed; fadeless; *great; hallowed;* interminable; *jusqu'au bout [F.];* keeps going; lasting; *measureless;* never-ending; olamic; perpetual; perdurable; *quadrillion; remaining;* sempiternal; transcendent; undying; venerable; without end; *XO;* year-after-year; *zillion;*

**timely** *(adj.)*: absolutely on time; before it's too late; convenient; dead-on; exact; fit; *good; honorable;* in good time; just in time; keenly-timed; *literal; meet;* never-late; on-time; *on the dot;* punctual; prompt; prest; quite ~; right on time; seasonable; sharp; timeful; *unhesitating;* very ~; well-timed; xtry. ~; yare; *zero delay;*

**timid** *(adj.)*: apprehensive; bashful; coy; diffident; embarrassed; fearful; gentle; hesitant; introverted; jackalent; keenly shy; lily-livered; mortified; meek; nervous; overmodest; petrified; quiet; reserved; shy; sheepish; timorous; unpretentious; verecund; withdrawn; *xenophobic;* yarrow; *zealless;* [*Ant.* temerarious]

**timidity** *(n.)*: apprehension; bashfulness; coyness; diffidence; embarrassment; fearfulness; gentleness; hesitancy; introversion; jackalence; *keen ~;* lily-liveredness; mortification; meekness; nervousness; overmodesty; pudency; quietness; reservedness; shyness; sheepishness; timidness; unsureness; verecundity; withdrawal; *xenophobia;* yarowness; *zeallessness;* [*Ant.* temerity]

**tingle** *(n.)*: arousing; bestirring; chill; ding; excitement; frill; growse; *goose bumps;* heebie-jeebies; inciting; jangle; kindle; *laughing; moving; nudging; over-agitation;* prickle; quaver; rousing; sensation; shiver; tingling; tickle; thrill; *unsettling;* vibration; wow; *xuld [arch.];* yerk; zing;

**tingle** *(v.)*: arouse; bestir; *chill; disquiet;* excite; feel a ~; growse; have a tingly feeling; incite; *jar;* kindle; *lead; move; nudge; over-agitate;* prick; quiver; rouse; shiver; shudder; tickle; titillate; tinkle; *thrill; upset;* vibrate; wow; *xuld [arch.];* yerk; zing;

**tiny** *(adj.)*: *abridged;* bitty; compact; diminutive; dwarfed; eensie(-weensie); fine; germinal; half-pint; infinitesimal; *jitney;* knee-high; little; microscopic; minute; miniature; negligible; not very big; *overly small;* puny; petite; pygmy; pint-sized; *quantité négligeable* [F.]; runty; *reduced;* small; subatomic; teeny; trivial; undersized; ultra-short; very small; wee; XS; *yea big; zero;*

**tip** *(n. gratuity)*: advantage; acknowledgement; bonus; *change;* douceur; extra; freebee; favor; 15%; gratuity; *honorarium;* incentive pay; *joy-giving;* kindness; liberality; leftover change; money; *nicety; offering;* pour-boire; perk; perquisite; *quantity;* riptowell; show of appreciation; *twenty percent; unselfish ~; vouchsafement; wage;* xenium; yeff [arch.]; *zealous gift;*

**tip** *(n. point)*: apex; barb; beak; cusp; denticle; end; extremity; fine point; *greatest height;* head; high point; *increase;* jut; kop; limit; mountaintop; needle; nib; nose; *over-sharpened;* point; peak; quill; *razor-sharp point;* summit; spike; top; termination; upper extremity; vertex; *well-sharpened; xtr sharp.; yonder point;* zenith;

**tipsy** *(adj.)*: addled; boozy; besotted; crocked; drunk; *entranced;* fuddled; giddy; heady; inebriated; jingled; kaylied; lit up; maudlin; nappy; over; pickled; quaffed; reeling; smashed; tanked; unsteady; under the influence; *vineous;* woozy; *xanthoxylin;* yarked; zonked;

**tiptoe** *(v.)*: atiptoe; be careful; creep; *drift;* edge; *flow;* go on ~; *hide presence; inch;* jiffle; *keep going;* lurk; *light-footed;* move (carefully); *non-speedy; obambulate;* pussyfoot; prowl; quietly walk; *reptant;* sneak; slip; tippy-toe; *undetected; very careful;* walk on eggshellls; *xfer; yede; zigzag;*

**tirade** *(n.)*: anger-fit; burst; choler; diatribe; explosion; fit; freakout; gall; hissy fit; huff; invective; jumping fit; *kindling;* lecture; meltdown; *nettled;* outburst; philippic; pet; *quake;* rage; storm; tantrum; tiff; unmitigated rage; venting; *widdrim* [arch.]; *xerothermia;* yelling fit; *zero calmness;*

**tire** *(v.)*: *abate;* bleed; consume; deplete; exhaust; finish; fatigue; get tired; hone; *impair;* jade; knock out; lessen; *minimize; nullify;* overtax (-spend); poop out; quail; run out; spend; tap out; use (up); vacate; wipe out; *xerosis; yield;* zap; [*Ant.* energize]

**tired** *(adj.)*: aweary [lit.]; bushed; beat; bone-weary; *comatose;* drowsy; drained; dog- ~; draggy; exhausted; faint; fatigued; groggy; haggard; half dead; *indolent;* jaded; knocked-out; lethargic;

*moiled;* noddy; oscitant; overwrought; pooped; plum- ~; *quiescent;* run-down; sleepy; spent; somnolent; tuckered; toilworn; unrested; *vapid;* weary; worn out; wrung out; wiped out; *xenarthrous;* yawnish; zapped;

**tiresome** *(adj.)*: arduous; backbreaking; challenging; difficult; exhausting; fatiguing; grueling; hard; intense; irksome; jading; killing; laborious; moiling; not easy; overtaxing; plaguing; *quotidian;* rigorous; strenuous; tedious; unrelenting; unrestful; *very hard;* wearisome; *x-heavy;* yawnful; *zapping;*

**tithe** *(n.)*: assessment; *bestowal;* charge; contribution; church-money; duty; excise; firstfruits; first tenth; God's due; *head tax; income duty; investment in eternity; Jehovah's due;* kirk-money; *the Lord's ~;* money; *non-negotiable;* one-tenth; percentage; *quantity due;* remittal; support; tenth; teind [Scot.]; *unhand; valuables; withholding;* xenium; yield; zakat;

**tithe** *(v.)*: act; bestow; contribute; decimate; expend; *fulfill;* give (10%); *hand over; impart; invest in eternity; joyfully give; kick in; lay out; mete; not withhold;* offer; pay the ~; *quantity;* remit; render *support;* the ~; teind [Scot.]; tenth; ten percent; unhand; *vest; weigh out; xfer; yield;* zakat;

**title** *(n. heading)*: annotation; blurb; caption; cutline; comment; description; designation; epigraph; footer; *go by;* heading; inscription; *journalism; key;* legend; message; notation; outline ~; preamble; *quotation;* remark; rubric; subtitle; subheading; tag; *uncials; verbiage;* writing; words; *xiaozhuan;* yield; *zeug;*

**title** *(n. name)*: appellation; baptismal name; Christian name; designation; entitlement; forename; given name; handle [slang]; identifier; *jurisdiction; known by;* label; moniker; name; *over~;* proper name; *quiring;* representation; surname; tag; *undercover name;* vocable; *word;* xenonym; *yu [Chin.]; zoon;*

**title** *(n. property deed)*: absolute interest; bureau-issued ~; *charter;* deed; evidence of ownership; *file;* government-issued ~; house ~; *item; justification; key document;* legal ~; land ~; manorial ~; *notarized ~;* ownership papers; property ~ deed; *questionless;* recorded ~; rights; *scroll;* title deed; *upheld;* valid ~; *writing;* xfer papers; *yellowed ~; zeug;*

**toast** *(v.)*: *apply heat;* brown; cook; dry; ensear; fire-dry; griddle; *golden;* heat; *incinerate; jumbal; kindle;* lightly ~; make golden brown; *neal [arch.];* overburn; pan-broil; *quick-bake;* roast; scorch; singe; *torch; undercook; vulcanize;* warm; *xeo; yark; zap;*

**today** *(adv.)*: at present; before sundown; currently; day; directly; even now; for now; *going on now;* hodiernal; immediately; just now; *known;* late this afternoon; *momentarily;* now(adays); on the douoble; presently; *quite soon;* right now; *soon;* this day; *undelayed; very quickly; without delay; x-speed;* yet this day; *zero-delay;*

**toddle** *(v.)*: amble; bobble; coggle; daddle; *edge;* flounce; go slow; galumph; hobble; inch; jiffle; *keep going;* lumber; limp; mosey; nutate; *overstride;* patter; plod; quaddle; rove; scuffle; shuffle; stagger; stumble; totter; *underway; venture;* wobble; waddle; *xfer; yomp;* zigzag;

**toe** *(n.)*: * appendage; big ~; *club ~;* digit; dactyl; extremity; foot; fissiped; *goer;* hallux; *item; jut; kicker;* little ~; middle ~; *nub;* nail; *object;* phalanges; pettitoe [zoo.]; *piggy;* quadridigitate; *right foot; soma;* tootsy; talon; *ungula; volar; webbed ~; xfer; yads;* zygodactyl;

**together** *(v.)*: accompanying; banded ~; bound; connected; combined; *dovetailed;* entwined; fastened; fixed; fused; *glued;* hitched; inseparable; joined; knitted; linked; married; merged; *networked;* one; put ~; *quasi-fused;* reunited; secured; tied; united; *vise;* with; wedded; *xenograft;* yoked; *zipped;*

**togetherness** *(n.)*: attachment; bond; closeness; devotedness; endearment; friendship; fellowship; *glued;* hitching; inseparability; intimacy; joining; knitting; link; marriage; merging; *network;* oneness; putting together; *quasi-fuse;* reunion; solidarity; tie; unity; union; *vise; with one another;* wedding; *xenograft;* yoking; *zero separation;*

**tolerable** *(adj.)*: acceptable; bearable; *co-existing;* decent; endurable; fair; fine; good; *humor;* inoffensive; jake [Br.]; *kosher;* livable; minimal; manageable; not bad; okay; passable; *quantum sufficit* [L.]; reasonable; sufficient; *tolerated;* unoffensive; veritable; welcome; well; *xenial; yenough* [arch.]; *zero opposition;*

**tolerance** *(n.)*: acceptance; broad-mindedness; co-existence; disregard; endurance; forbearance; giving space; having; indulgence; *justification; kind-heartedness;* lenience; leeway; mellowness; *non-judgmental;* open-mindedness; patience; *questionlessness;* reception; sufferance; toleration; understanding; *vasbyt;* willingness to endure; *xenia;* yieldedness; *zero opposition;*

**tolerant** *(adj.)*: accommodating; accepting; broadminded; co-existing; *deferential;* enduring; forbearing; *generous;* hands-off; indulgent; *justifying; kind-hearted;* latitudinarian; lenient; lax; mellow; non-judgmental; open-minded; patient; placable; *quell;* receptive; stoic; tolerating; uncritical; uncomplaining; vasbyt; willing to put up with; *xenial;* yielding; *zero opposition;*

**tolerate** *(v.)*: abide; accept; allow; bear; bide; brook; co-exist with; countenance; close one's eye's to; dure; endure; forbear; give permission; have; indulge; *justify;* keep going along with; live with; *maintain; nod;* outride; put up with; permit; *quiet;* receive; suffer; stomach; stand; take; understand; *vouchsafe;* warrant; wink at; *xenial;* yield; *zero problem;* [see allow]

**toleration** *(n.)*: abidance; bearing; charity; *dure;* endurance; forbearance; grace; having; indulgence; *justification;* kindness; lenience; mellowness; *non-judgmental;* okaying; putting up with; placability; *questionlessness;* reception; softness; stoicalness; tolerance; understanding; *vasbyt;* winking; *xenia;* yieldedness; *zero opposition;*

**toll** *(n. fee)*: assessment; *bill;* charge; chiminage; duty; excise; fee; *gabelle;* head tax; *impost;* jettage; keelage; levy; mulct; *nuisance tax; octroi;* passage; quayage; *revenue;* surcharge; tax; usage fee; vigorish; *wharfage; xenium; yardage; zakat* [Mos.];

**toll** *(n. ringing)*: alarm; bong; chime; clangor; ding-dong; *echo; fweet!;* gong; *hum; intonation;* jingle; knoll; loud ringing; music; *noise; operation;* peal; *quake;* ring(ing); sound; tang; *utterance;* voice [poet.]; *warning; x-ing; yammer; zing;*

**tomb** *(n.)*: arch; burying-place; crypt; cave; dolmen; entombment; final resting place; grave; house of death; humation; home; interment; *jaw-hole;* kurgan; last home; mound; mausoleum; narrow house; ossuarium; plot; pit; *quietus;* resting place; repository; sepulcher; tumulus; undercroft; vault; *whited sepulcher; xat; yawn; ziarat* [Mos.];

**tombstone** *(n.)*: arch; burial plaque; cenotaph; cross; cemetery marker; cairn; dolmen; *epitaph;* footstone; gravestone; headstone; heap; *indicator;* joint marker; *knoll-marker; land marker;* monument; marker; memorial; mausoleum; mound; *necropolis;* obelisk; plaque; pillar; *quartz headstone;* remembrance; stone (marker); shrine; tomb; *urn; vault plaque; whinstone; writing;* xat; *yard stone;* ziarat [Mos.];

**tone** *(n.)*: air; attitude; blend; bearing; character; cast; disposition; emphasis; feeling; grain; hint; hue; intonation; *jingle; key; leaning;* manner; nature; over~; posture; quality; resonance; sound; shade; sentiment; tinge; tenor; timbre; under~; voice; value; way; *xfer; yaw; zeal;*

**tool** *(n.)*: apparatus; battery-powered ~; contrivance; device; *electric ~; fix;* gadget; hardware; hand ~; implement; instrument; *jack;* kit [pl.]; *leveling ~;* means; non-power ~; *object;* power ~; *quomode* [L.]; *ratchet; screwdriver; tackle;* utensil; *vise;* wood ~; *xyster;* Yankee push drill; *zeug* [G.];
  **Types of tools**: awl; box wrench; chisel; drill; edger; file; gimlet; hammer; hacksaw; ice pick; jack; keyhole saw; lathe; level; miter box; nail-gun; open-end wrench; plane; pliers; quannet; ratchet; rasp; ratchet; ruler; router; saw; screwdriver; square; tape measure; trowel; utility knife; vise; wrench; xyster; Yankee push drill; zigzag rule;

**toot** *(n.)*: *alarm;* beep; blow; bleep; choo-choo; declare; *echo;* fweet!; *gong;* honk; hoot; *intonation; jow; knoll;* loud ~; *music;* noise; ooga ooga; peep; proclaim; *quake;* ring; sound; tootle; tweet; trumpet; *utterance;* vweet!; whistle; whoot; *xtr. loud ~; yammer; zap;*

**tooth** *(n.)*: *alveolar;* bicuspid; buck~; cuspid; chomper [slang]; dentitcle; *denture;* eye~; fore~; fang; grinder; *horse ~;* incisor; jaw- ~; jag; *Korff;* laniary; lower ~; molar; milk- ~; nipper; odontoid; pearl [slang]; quadricuspid; *razor;* snaggle~; smile [pl.]; *tusk;* upper ~; *vampire teeth; wisdom ~; xanthdont;* yellow ~; zygodont;
  **Kinds of *tooth(ed)***: buck-tooth; big-toothed; cheek-tooth; gold-toothed; master-tooth; saw-tooth; sharp-toothed; sweet-tooth; wang-tooth; yellow-toothed;

**top** *(adj.)*: apical; A-1; *atop;* best; choicest; crowning; dominant; elite; finest; first(-rate); foremost; greatest; head; highest; *impressive; jim-dandy;* keenest; loftiest; leading; maximal; No. 1; overmost; prime; preeminent; primary; *quality;* ruling; superior; select; super-; supreme; topmost; ultimate; uppermost; *valedictorian;* world-class; winningest; xtry.; yondmost; zenithal;

**top** *(n.)*: apex; brow; crest; crown; cap; dominant position; *end; extremity; furthest; first;* greatest height; high point; head; *increase; important; jut;* kop; limit; lofty height; mountaintop; maximum; meridian; nib; *overmost point;* peak; pinnacle; *quoif;* roof; summit; tip(-top); topside; upper extremity; vertex; *way up; xtry; yonder point;* zenith;

**top** *(v.)*: ascend; beat; cap; do better; eclipse; exceed; finish; go beyond; head; improve upon; *junk [slang];* kill; lick; master; *no contest;* outdo; outperform; pass by; *quash; rout;* surpass; transcend; unseat; *vanquish;* win; worst; *x-cend; yondmost;* zip past;

**topic** *(n.)*: area; basic theme; central theme; design; emphasis; focus; *gist; heart;* idea; *jet;* keynote; leitmotif; main ~; motif; matter; notion; overriding ~; premise; *quintessence; root;* subject (matter); theme; underlying subject; *vital; weight; xenenthesis;* yaw; *zone;*

**top view** *(n.)*: aerial view; bird's-eye view; crow's nest view; down-looking view; eagle's-eye view; from the sky; gull's-eye view; *high-up; in the air; jay's view;* kestral's view; looking down; *mountaintop; north;* overview; perspective; *quite high;* raven's-eye view; satellite picture; top-down view; *upper;* view from above; *way up; xema; yonder;* zenithal view;

**Torah** *(n.)*: *authoritative text;* Bible; canon; divine revelation; *Exodus;* five Books of Moses; God's Word; Heptateuch; inspired Word; *Jehovah's Word; Kabbalah;* Law (of Moses); Mosaic Law; Nevim; Old Testament; Pentateuch; *quick and powerful;* revelation; Scriptures; Tanach; *unadulterated Word; version;* Word (of God); *Xn. Bible; yesod mora* [Heb.]; *Zechariah;*

**torch** *(n.)*: acetylene ~; brand; blow~; cresset; *droplight; enkindle; emit;* firebrand; flambeau; *glow;* hand ~; incendiary; *jacklight; kindle;* light; *mussal* [Ind.]; *nuptial ~;* oxyacetylene ~; *oil lamp;* propane ~; *quick-match; rushlight; shining;* torchlight; tiki ~; tede; *uplight; visual;* wall ~; welding ~; *xenon lamp; yellow light; zircon light;*

**torment** *(n.)*: agony; anguish; burden; chafing; distress; dolor; excruciation; foul-treatment; gnawing; grief; galling; hurt; ill-treatment; *jabbing; killing; loss;* misery; *nip;* ordeal; oppression; pain; persecution; *quivering;* rack; ranking; suffering; throe; trial; tribulation; *unhappiness;* vexation; *violence;* woe; *xiphodynia; yipes!;* zing;

**torment** *(v.)*: afflict; brutalize; cause suffering; distress; excruciate; *flog;* grieve; hurt; injure; ill-treat; inflict damage; jeel; kill by inches; lift hand against; maim; *nocument;* oppress; pain; persecute; *quail* [arch.]; rack; smite; scath; trouble; torture; *undo;* vex; wreak havoc; *x.; ydrad [arch.]; zap;* [Ant. aid]

**tormentor** *(n.)*: afflicter; bane; curse; devil; *executioner;* flogger; giver of pain; grand inquisitor; hazer; inflictor; jeeler; *kick;* lasher; menace; *nocument;* oppressor; persecutor; *questioner;* riler; scourge; torturer; *unkind;* victimizer; whip-master; *x-out; yager; zapper;*

**tornado** *(n.)*: agitation; baguio [Sp.]; cyclone; dust devil; eddy; funnel cloud; gustnado; hurricane; ill wind; *Jupiter Pluvius; khamsin* [Egy.]; *line squall; monsoon; nor' easter; Oklahoma rainstorm;* precession; *quirlewind* [arch.]; rotary storm; spout; storm; twister; typhoon; *upheaval;* vortex; whirlwind; waterspout; *xuld* [arch.]; *yern; zwoosh;*

**torpid** *(adj.)*: *apathetic;* blah; comatose; dull; enervated; faint; groggy; heavy; inactive; *jaded;* kef; lethargic; mopish; non-motivated; oscitant; pepless; quiescent; retarded; sluggish; *tired;* unambitious; vapid; weary; *xenarthrous;* yareless; zapped;

**torpor** *(n.)*: apathy; blahness; comatoseness; dullness; enervation; faintness; feebleness; grogginess; heaviness; indolence; inertia; jadedness; *kef;* languor; mopishness; nappiness; oscitancy; peplessness; *quiescence; rest;* slothfulness; torpidity; unenthusiasm; vapidity; weariness; *xenarthrous;* yarelessness; zeallessness;

**torrid** *(adj.)*: ardent; burning; candent; *dry;* enkindled; fiery; grilling; hot; inflammative; jejune; *kindled;* like an oven; *muggy; non-stop;* overhot; passionate; parched; quenchless; roasting; scorching; torrefied; unquenched; *vaporous;* warm; xerothermic; yellow-hot; *zealous;*
**torture** *(n.)*: affliction; agony; brutalization; cruel and unusual punishment; *distress;* excruciation; foul-treatment; *grief;* hurt; inhumane treatment; infliction; jeeling; killing by inches; lashing; maiming; maltreat; *nocument;* oppression; *ordeal;* persecution; pain; *quale* [arch.]; rack; suffering; torment; *undoing;* victimizing; wreaking havoc; x-ing; *yanking around; zapping;*
**torture** *(v.)*: afflict; brutalize; cruciate; do bodily harm; excruciate; endamage; *frighten;* give one "the works"; haze; hurt; inflict pain; jeel; *kick; kock;* lash; make suffer; maltreat; *nocument;* oppress; persecute; pain; *quale* [arch.]; rack; scath; strappado; torment; undo; vex; victimie; wreak havoc; work over; *whip; x-out; yank around; zap;*
**torturer** *(n.)*: afflicter; brutalizer; cruciater; devil; *executioner;* flogger; giver of pain; grand inquisitor; hazer; inflictor; inquisitor; jeeler; *killer;* lasher; *mangler; nocument;* one who tortures; persecutor; *questioner;* rack-operator; scourge; sadist; tormenter; *Undertaker;* victimizer; whip-master; *x-out; yager; zapper;*
**toss** *(v.)*: abandon; betoss; bung; cast; chuck; *discard;* eject; fling; flip; *give;* hurl; impel; *jetsam;* kest; launch; lob; *move; non-retention; overpitch;* pitch; *quoit; recast;* sling; shy; throw; upcast; vault; whip; *xuld* [arch.]; york; *zing;*
**total** *(adj.)*: absolute; all-encompassing; aggregate; arrant; broad; big; complete; comprehensive; definitive; entire; full; global; *high;* inclusive; *jim-bang; known; length-and-breadth;* mass; non-abridged; overall; out-and-out; plenary; panoptic; *quantified; ranging;* sweeping; summative; thorough; unmitigated; unreserved; utter; unbroken; unedited; unqualified; unmitigated; veritable; whole; *x-total;* yare; *zealous;*
**total** *(n.)*: amount; bottom line; bulk; count; degree; extent; figure; force; group; grand ~; horde; *ingathering;* jag; *kit;* level; load; measure; mass; number; *overall;* portion; part; quantum; reckoning; range; sum(mation); sub~; totality; tally; units; volume; whole; *x; yard; z-score;*
**total** *(v.)*: add up; aggregate; *bulk;* count up; calculate; compute; determine ~; *equal;* figure up; get ~; group; have the ~; indicate ~; *join;* keep running ~; lump together; merge; *number; overcount;* put together; quantify; reckon; sum up; totalize; tally; *unite; valuate;* work out ~; *x-total; yeme; zum [dial.];*
**totalitarian** *(adj.)*: authoritarian; autocratic; bossy; controlling; dictatorial; *evil-hearted;* fascistic; grave; high-handed; iron-fisted; imperious; *jaded;* kindless; loveless; magisterial; *nasty;* oppressive; peremptory; *quad;* repressive; strict; strong; tyrannical; undemocratic; *virulent;* weighty; xenophobic; yieldless; *za-zum* [Rus.];
**totalitarianism** *(n.)*: authoritarianism; bossiness; control; despotism; dictatorship; *evil-heartedness;* fascism; garrison state; high-handedness; imperiousness; *jadedness; kindlessness;* lovelessness; *militarism; Nazism;* oppression; peremptoriness; *quad;* reign of terror; strictness; suppression; tyranny; unchecked power; *virulence;* weightiness; xenophobia; yieldlessness; *za-zum [Rus.];*
**totally** *(adv.)*: absolutely; altogether; broadly; completely; dead; entirely; fully; globally; hundred-per-cent; inclusively; *just ~; keenly; largely;* macroscopically; non-partially; one-hundred percent; perfectly; plenarily; quite; roundly; sweepingly; thoroughly; utterly; veritably; wholly; *xtry.;* yarely; *zero incompletion;*
**totter** *(v.)*: alternate; bowl along; creep; crawl; didder; daddle; edge; falter; gimp; hobble; inch; jiffle; *keep advancing;* limp; mosey; nutate; oscillate; plod; quaddle; *reel;* stagger; teeter; topple; *uneven;* vacillate; wobble; *xfer;* yaw; zigzag;
**touch** *(v.)*: abut; affect; brush; contact; caress; connect; depress; embosom; feel; fondle; graze; handle; *haptic;* intersect; join; kiss; knock; link to; meet; *nudge; overhandle;* pat; palpate; quab; rub; stroke; tap; *use; veney;* whisk; *xenograft; yank; zonk;*

**touching** *(adj.)*: affecting; beautiful; caring; dear; emotional; *feeling;* gentle; heart-warming; impressive; intimate; joy-giving; *kind;* loving; moving; nice; over-soft; *pleasant; quixotic; romantic;* stirring; sweet; tender; *understanding;* very ~; warm; *xtry.;* yielding; young; *zero hardness;*

**touchy** *(adj.)*: argumentative; awkward; bad-tempered; crotchety; disagreeable; delicate; easily upset; fractious; grumpy; hypersensitive; irritable; jangly; knaggy; liverish; moody; nasty; oversensitive; prickly; quick-tempered; rankling; sensitive; short-tempered; tetchy; thin-skinned; tricky; umbrageous; vinegary; wranglesome; *xenophobic;* yieldless; *za-zum [Rus.];*

**tough** *(adj.)*: adamant; burly; brawny; callous; durable; enduring; firm; good; hard(y); hefty; ironlike; inviolable; *jusqu'au bout [F.]; keen;* (long-)lasting; leathery; mighty; muscle-bound; *nervy;* obstinate; powerful; *quality;* rugged; rigid; rough; strong; sturdy; solid; tenacious; unflagging; unbreakable; vigorous; well-built; *x-strong;* yieldless; *zippy;* [*Ant.* tender]

**toughen** *(n.)*: anneal; build up; callous; *develop;* enharden; firm up; fortify; get tougher; harden; indurate; *jade;* kern; *lapidify;* make tough; *not soft;* overharden; *prop; qualify;* reinforce; strengthen; temper; undergird; vulcanize; wax tough; *x-strong; yieldless; zet [dial.];* [*Ant.* tenderize]

**tour** *(n.)*: adventure; break; *cruise;* drive; excursion; foray; guided ~; holiday; itineration; journey; *kayak trip;* leisure ~; *misadventure; night voyage;* outing; pleasure trip; quest; road trip; *retreat;* sightseeing ~; trip; *undertaking;* vacation; visit; *week off; xenization; yong* [arch.]; zugunruhe; [*see* assignment]

**tour** *(v.)*: analyze; *behold;* check out; cruise; descry; examine; fix eyes on; go to; have a vacation in; inspect; *jerque;* ken; look; make a ~; *note;* observe; probe; *qualified look;* recognize; see; survey; travel to; *understand;* vacation in; watch; *xQ; yeme;* zero in;

**tourist** *(v.)*: adventurer; *bus tour;* commuter; drifter; excursionist; explorer; forayer; goer; hosteller; holidaymaker [Br.]; itinerant; journeyer; jaunt; knight of the road [joc.]; leisure visitor; migrant; *metic; nonimmigrant; overnighter;* peregrinator; pilgrim; quester; roamer; rover; sight-seer; traveler; tourer; *undertaker;* vacationer; wayfarer; world-traveler; *xenizer;* yachter; *zingaro [It.];*

**tournament** *(n.)*: athletic ~; battle; competition; derby; event; face-off; field game; game; *happening; interplay; joust;* kemp; *luctation* [arch.]; match; meet; national ~; *opponents;* playoff; *quarrel;* round robin; *rivalry;* sport; set; tourney; *upmanship; vying;* war games; X Games; *yed; zealous competition;*

**toward** *(prep.)*: approaching; by; closer to; drawn up to; en route to; facing; *gone up to;* hard by; in the direction of; *just to; kept by; localize;* moving in that direction; near; over against; *proximate;* quite close; right by; *reaching; side by side;* towards; to; thitherward; unto; verging on; well-nigh; *xferred; yede [arch.];* zeroing in on;

> **Varieties of *towards***: airward; backward; coastward; downward; eastward; earthward; frontward; Godward; homeward; heavenward; inward; landward; leeward; leftward; manward; northward; outward; poleward; rearward; rightward; seaward; shoreward; skyward; southward; thitherward; upward; us-ward; westward; windward; zenithward;

**towel** *(n.)*: *article;* bath ~; cloth; dish ~; dishcloth; dishrag; *edge;* face cloth; *green ~;* hand ~; *item; jaconet;* kitchen ~; linens [pl.]; *monogrammed ~;* napery; *object;* paper ~; quilted paper ~; rag; roller ~; swimming ~; terry cloth ~; tea ~; *unsoiled ~; velvety;* washcloth; *XL ~;* yellow ~; *zeug;*

**tower** *(n.)*: *acropolis;* belfry; bell ~; bastille; campanile; crow's nest; donjon; erection; fortress; gopuram; high ~; high-rise; ivory ~; *jong [Tib.];* keep; lookout ~; martello; nest; *needle;* observation tower; pylon; *quarters;* rath; spire; skyscraper; turret; *unit; vault;* watch~; *x-structure; yamen* [Chin.]; ziggurat;

**town** *(n.)*: *area;* burg; clachan [Scot.]; crossroads; country ~; dorp; exurb; *fishing ~; ghost ~; gates;* hick ~; home~; hill~; hamlet; *invillaged;* junction; kirk- ~ [Scot.]; kraal [Hottentot]; kibbutz [Isr.]; *location;* municipality; market ~; *native ~;* outpost; one-horse town; place; *quarter;* rancho; rube ~; shire; settlement; thorp; township; tank ~; urban area; village; whistle stop [slang]; *ward; xa* [Vietnam]; yokel town; *zone;* [*see* city]

**toxic** *(adj.)*: *adverse;* *bad;* contaminated; deadly; evil; fatal; *grievous;* harmful; injurious; *jeopardous;* *killing;* lethal; malefic; noxious; *odious;* poisonous; *quelling;* *ruinous;* *spoiled;* tainted; unsafe; virulent; *wicked;* xenobiotic; *yeara;* zootoxic;

**toy** *(n.)*: amusement; bauble; child's plaything; *doll;* entertainment; *fun;* game; gimcrack; *hooseywatsy;* *item;* jimcrack; *jack-in-the-box;* *jump rope;* knack; kickshaw; *kazoo;* leisure; *moving ~;* novelty; *object;* plaything; *popgun;* *pinwheel;* quelkshaw; *rocking horse;* *sport;* trifle; *unused ~;* *vanity;* wooden ~; *whirlygig;* *xylon;* yo-yo; *zoetrope;*

**trace** *(n.)*: *allusion;* bit; clue; drop; evidence; footstep; ghost; hint; indication; intimation; jot; *kernel;* lead; leftover; mark; nuance; *ounce;* pointer; *piece;* quantity; remnant; relic; shadow; sign; semblance; suggestion; tip-off; tinge; token; track; umbrage; vestige; whit; *x-item;* *yod;* *zum [dial.];*

**track** *(v.)*: ascertain; *be after;* chase; *discover;* explore; follow; go after; hunt; *investigate;* *jerque;* *kithe;* look for; make a search; nose out; *overtake;* pursue; quest for; *rake;* search; stalk; sleuth; trail; trace; uncover; venture after; *well-traced;* *x-search;* *yearn for;* zero in;

**tract** *(n.)*: advertisement; brochure; booklet; *Chick ~;* double-fold; *essay;* flier; flysheet; gospel ~; handout; informational leaflet; *journalism;* *key thoughts;* leaflet; literature; *message;* *notations;* *opus;* pamphlet; quadrifoliate; reading matter; *salvation ~;* trifold; unifoliate ~; *vignette;* *writing;* xenagogy; *yeme;* zeug;

**trade** *(n. profession)*: activity; assignment; business; career; craft; duty; employment; enterprise; field; *grind [slang];* handicraft; industry; job; *key position;* living; métier; *necessity;* occupation; profession; *quest;* responsibility; service; *task;* undertaking; vocation; work; xci. *yoke; zealous duty;*

**trade** *(n. swap)*: alternation; barter; buying and selling; change; conversion; deal; exchange; even ~; flip; giving in ~; hand-over; interchange; *jockeying;* key trade; *link;* market; network; *overhaul;* put right; *quid pro quo [L.];* reversal; replacement; reciprocation; switch; swap; substitution; transposal; upgrade; *vary;* work; xfer; *yaw;* zwap [dial];

**trade** *(v.)*: alternate; barter; change; *deal;* exchange; *for;* *give;* *get;* *hock;* interchange; *jockey;* *key ~;* let have for; make a ~; *negotiate;* *over~;* permute; *quick-change;* replace; substitute; switch; swap; sell; transfer; traffic; upgrade; *vamp;* *wissel [arch.];* xfer; *yaw;* zwap [dial.];

**tradition** *(n.)*: accepted way; behavior; custom; daily routine; established practice; folk ways; general behavioral pattern; habit; institution; *jake [Br.];* kultur [G.]; long-established ~; manner; mores; norm; old ways; practice; *quo mode [L.];* ritual; society; social behavior; traditional way; usage; values; *venerated;* ways; *x-cultural;* *ye olde;* *zealous ~;*

**traditional** *(n.)*: accepted; *behavioral;* customary; conventional; conservative; dominant; established; familiar; general; habitual; inveterate; jake [Br.]; known; long-established; main; normal; ordinary; prevalent; *qualified;* regular; standard; time-honored; usual; *unwritten;* venerated; well-established; *x-cultural;* *ye olde;* *zealous tradition;*

**traffic** *(n.)*: automobiles; buildup; business; bumper-to-bumper ~; cars; congestion; density; *engines;* flow of ~; *gridlock;* hustle and bustle; highway ~; interstate ~; *jam;* *kit;* load; movement; night ~; *onslaught;* people; *quantity;* rush hour ~; street ~; ~ flow; *unit;* vehicles; volume; *weekend ~;* xfer; yards; zooming along;

**tragedy** *(n.)*: adversity; blow; breakup (-down); calamity; catastrophe; cataclysm; cave-in; disaster; debacle; devastation; evil; fiasco; flop; grief; heartbreak; hammer blow; infelicity; *judgment;* killer; loss; misfortune; nightmare; ordeal; predicament; quake; ruin; shock; traumatic experience; upheaval; violence; woe; *x-ing;* yedder; zinger;

**tragic** *(adj.)*: awful; baneful; calamitous; disastrous; *execrable;* frightful; grim; horrible; heartbreaking; ill-fated; inauspicious; *just horrible;* *keening;* lamentable; misfortunate; *negative;* oversorrowful; pitiable; *quad;* *rueful;* sorrowful; sad; tragical; tear-filled; terrible; unfortunate; very sad; wretched; *x-ing;* *yucky;* *zealless;*

**trail** *(n.)*: avenue; berme; corridor; dirt road; esplanade; footpath; groove; hiking ~; horse path; *ice road;* journey-way; kotal; lane; ley; means; mountain pass; marked ~; narrow path; outlet; path(way); pass(age); *quick way;* rut; road; *strip; street;* track; trailway; *vennel;* way; wagon ~; *xystum; yong [arch.];* zwinger;

**train** *(v.)*: admonish; bring up; coach; disciple; drill; educate; foster; guide; home school; instruct; *jobation; knock into;* lecture; mentor; *nurture;* orient; prepare; prime; pedagogue; qualify; ready; raise; show; teach; *unlock;* verse; work with; xenagogue; *yak; zealously instruct;*

**trainer** *(n.)*: abecedarian; *basic ~;* coach; driller; drillmaster; educator; fugleman; guide; headmaster; instructor; *jobation; khosa* [Hind.]; leader; master; *nurturer;* overseer; pedagogue; preparer; *qualifier; regent;* schooler; tamer; teacher; tutor; *under-teacher; varsity coach; worker;* xenagogue; *yokemaster; zealous ~;*

**training** *(n.)*: admonishment; bringing along; coaching; discipling; discipline; drilling; education; educating; fostering; guidance; home schooling; instruction; *jobation; knowledge;* lecturing; lessons; mentoring; nurture; on-the-job ~; preparation; qualification; readying; schooling; teaching; *unlocking; upbringing;* versing; work; xenagogy; yarking; *zealous instruction;*

**trait** *(n.)*: attribute; *badge;* characteristic; detail; element; ethos; feature; *good quality;* highlight; ingredient; *jist;* key feature; lineament; mark; *nature; object;* property; quality; reality; *side;* thing; undeniable quality; virtue; way; *x-factor; yetzer* [Heb.]; *zero in;*

**traitor** *(n.)*: arch~; betrayer; Benedict Arnold; collaborationist; double-crosser; *evildoer; fiend;* guiler; *honorless;* insurgent; Judas; *knave;* lawbreaker; mutineer; *non-loyal;* opportunist; plotter; quisling; renegade; rebel; snake; turncoat; *traditor;* treasonist; *unloyal;* villain; wicked; *xfer; yegg; zero loyalty;*

**trample** *(v.)*: *attack;* beat; break down; crush; charge; dash across; *endamage;* flatten; grind; *harm;* injure; *jump on; kick down; levigate;* mash down; *nullify;* overrun; *pulverize;* quash; run down (-over); squash; stampede; tread underfoot; *underfoot* violate; walk on; *xuld [arch.];* yern; *zoom over;*

**trance** *(n.)*: abstraction; astonishment; bemusement; catalepsy; daze; enchantment; entrancement; fugue; gibbered; haze; incoherence; *inebriated;* jag; *knocked out;* lethe; mesmerization; nystagmus; out (of touch); preoccupation; *quaffing;* rapt; stupor; spell; torpor; *under;* vexation; whacked (out); *xanthoxylin; yarked;* zonked;

**tranquil** *(adj.)*: all-composing; becalmed; calm; docile; easeful; *friendly;* gentle; hushed; harmonious; idyllic; jarless; *keen; lovely;* motionless; mild; nonviolent; oblivious; peaceful; placid; quiet; restful; still; serene; trouble-free; untroubled; vacuous; waveless; *xenial; yielding; zet [dial.];*

**tranquility** *(n.)*: accordance; becalming; calm(ness); docility; ease; friendliness; gentleness; harmony; idyll; jarlessness; keeping peace; lull; motionlessness; nonviolence; over-quietness; obliviousness; peace; quiet; rest; repose; stillness; serenity; tranquilness; *untroubled;* vacuity; whisht; *xenophilia; yung* [Chin.]; zero hostilities;

**tranquilize** *(v.)*: anesthetize; becalm; calm; drug; ease; *fix;* give sedative; *hush;* intoxicate; *jarless;* knock out; lull; lay out; milden; mollify; normalize; *overcome;* put under sedation; quell; quiet down; relax; sedate; tame; *undisturbed; vulnery; wind down; x-out; yawn; zeroize;*

**tranquilizing** *(adj.)*: ataractic; barbiturate; calming; drowsing; easing; fatigue-inducing; gentling; hushing; hypnotic; inducing sleep; jading; knock-out; lenitive; mollifying; narcotic; opiate; putting to sleep; quietening; relaxing; soothing; sedative; sleep-inducing; soporific; taming; *unexciting; vulnerary;* wearying; *x-ing; yawnful;* zonking;

**transfer** *(v.)*: aliene; assign; bring; carry; convey; cede; deliver; deed over; extradite; forward; furnish; give; haul; hand over; impart; janker; kit; *lug;* leave with; move; *non-retention; over;* pass (on); *quicken;* relocate; relay; render; ship; send; shift; transport; turn over; uptake; *vest; waft;* xfer; yanker; *zip;*

**transferal** *(n.)*: assignment; bringing; conveyance; ceding; delivery; extradition; forwarding; furnishing; giving over; handover; impartation; jankering; kitting; *lugging;* movement; *non-retention; over;* passing (on); *quickening;* relocation; relay; sending; shipment; shift; transfer; uptaking; *vestment; wafting;* xfer; *yanker;* zipping;

**transform** *(v.)*: alter; become; change; develop; evolve; *fluctuate;* go into; *heighten; innovate;* jump; *key changes; leap;* mutate; modify; metamorphose; novate; *overhaul;* permute; *qualify;* reform; revamp; switch; shift; turn into; transmute; upgrade; vary; *work; xenomorph; yaw; zigzag;*
**transformation** *(n.)*: alteration; becoming; change; conversion; deviation; development; evolution; flip-flop; *growth;* hemimetabolous; immutation; *jumping; key changes*; leap; metamorphosis; makeover; *newness;* overhaul; permutation; quantum leap; remake; revision; revamping; revolution; renovation; replacement; switch; swap; shift; substitution; shift; transmutation; transfiguration; transmogrification; upgrade; variation; *warping;* xenomorphism; *yaw; zigzag;*
**transgress** *(v.)*: abominate; break law; contravene; do wrong; disobey; err; fall; go astray; have sin; infringe; *jaded; knavish;* leave the straight and narrow; misbehave; not obey; offend; pervert; *quad;* rebel; sin; trespass; *unfaithful;* violate; wrong; *x-gress; yetzer hara* [Heb.]; *zero righteousness;*
**transgression** *(n.)*: atrocity; breach; crime; debauchery; evil; fault; guilt(iness); heinousness; iniquity; *jadedness; knavishness;* licentiousness; mischief; naughtiness; offense; perverseness; *quad;* rebellion; sin; trespass; unrighteousness; violation; wrongdoing; *xgression; yetzer hara* [Heb.]; *zymosis;*
**transgressor** *(n.)*: abominator; bad man; criminal; doer of evil; debtor; evildoer; fallen man; godless person; hater of God; injurer; jackanapes; knave; law-breaker; malefactor; naughty person; offender; pervert; questrel; ribald; sinner; trespasser; *ungodly;* villain; wrongdoer; *xiaoren; yob; zero integrity;*
**transient** *(n.)*: *Arab;* bum; *circulator;* drifter; *emigrant;* floater; gypsy; gadabout; homeless; itinerant; journeyer; *Kenite landlouper;* migrant; nomad; *oberration;* pilgrim; peregrinator; *quick-mover;* rover; roamer; rambler; sojourner; stroller; transient; tent-dweller; traveler; *unfixed;* vagrant; wanderer; wayfarer; Wandering Jew; *xerophile;* Yahgan; *zingaro* [It.]
**transition** *(n.)*: alteration; becoming; betterment; change; conversion; development; evolution; flux; growth; *heightening;* improvement; jump; key change; *link;* modification; metabasis; *newness;* overhaul; permutation; qualification; realignment; shift; transfer; transformation; upheaval; variation; *warping;* xfer; xenomorph; *yaw; zigzag;*
**transition** *(v.)*: adjust; become; change; develop; evolve; flow; grow into; *heighten;* improve; jump; *key to; link;* move; novate; overhaul; permute; *qualify;* revamp; switch; shift; turn into; transform; upgrade; *vary;* work into; xfer; *yaw; zigzag;*
**translate** *(v.)*: adapt; bring into; carry over; convert; decipher; explain; *form;* give; have rendered; *harmonize;* interpret; *jump to;* key to; *letters;* metaphrase; *newly ~; over;* put in; *qualify;* render; say (in); transliterate; transpose; transfer; *understand; vamp;* word in; xlate; yield; *zay [dial.];*
**translation** *(n.)*: adaptation; bilingual text; conversion; deciphering; depiction; explanation; edition; equivalent; form; gloss; *harmonization;* interpretation; *justification;* key; literal (-loose) ~; metaphrase; non-literal ~; new version; *optimization;* paraphrase; passing over; qualified rendering; rewording; rendering; rendition; *superscription;* transcription; transliteration; transposal; *update;* version; word-for-word ~; wording; xlation; *yielding; zay [dial.];* [*see* Bible; perversion]
  **Bible Versions:** ASV; BLE; CEV; Douay; ESV; FFB; GNB; HCSB; ISV; Jerusalem; KJV; Lamsa; MLB; NASV; NEB; NIV; NKJV; OSB; Quaker; RSV; SEB; TLB; UKJV; VIW; Wycliff; YLT;
**translucent** *(adj.)*: *apparent;* blurry; cloudy; diffusing; enclouded; frosty; *glowing;* hydrophanous; *identifiable; jaspery; keep lighted;* lucent; milky; murky; non-opaque; opalescent; pearly; quasi-transparent; *rays;* semi-transparent; semi-diaphanous; translucid; umbered; *visible; waych; x-lucent; yeme [arch.]; zero clarity;*
**transmission** *(n.)*: airing; broadcast; communication; dissemination; emission; flow; giving out; *hurl;* impartation; intercommunication; *jawp; kilowatts; letting out;* metathesis; *notice;* overspreading; propagation; *quantity;* radio ~; signal; sending; transfer; transmittal; telecast; unicast; vesting; *via satellite; widespread;* xmission; *yielding;* zonal ~;

**transmit** *(v.)*: *air;* beam; broadcast; communicate; download; electronically send; *emit;* forward; give; *hurl;* issue; impart; *janker;* kurvey; *let out;* multiplex; *notify;* output; pass along; put on the air; *quick; radio;* radiate; send; transfer; televise (-cast); uplink; upload; vest; *via satellite;* wire; xmit; *yield; zip;*

**transparency** *(n.)*: apparentness; *bombycinousness;* clearness; diaphanousness; *evident; filminess;* glassiness; hyalescence; *identifiableness; just plain; keenly visible;* lucidity; *marked;* non-opaqueness; pellucidity; *quickly seen;* relucence; sheerness; transparence; *uncolored;* vitreosity; *well-defined; x-parent; yeme [arch.]; zero confusion;*

**transparent** *(adj.)*: apparent; *bombycinous;* clear; colorless; diaphanous; evident; *filmy;* glasslike; hyalescent; *identifiable; just plain;* keenly visible; lucid; luculent; light-pervious; *marked;* non-opaque; *obvious;* pellucid; *quickly seen;* relucent; see-through; translucid; transpicuous; uncolored; vitreous; *well-defined; x-parent; yeme [arch.]; zero confusion;*

**transpire** *(v.)*: arise; betide; come to pass; develop; ensue; fall; follow; go on; happen; intervene; *jump up; kep;* light; materialize; *near;* occur; proceed; *quicken;* rise; result; spring up; take place; unfold; venture; *work; xpire; yield; zip;*

**transplant** *(v.)*: attach; bed; consign; deplant; engraft; emigrate; fix; graft; *hand-move;* ingraft; imbed; *jump; kurvey; locate;* move; *new location; over;* put elsewhere; *quicken;* relocate; replant; shift; transfer; uproot; *venture; work;* xeno~; *yede; zip;*

**transport** *(v.)*: *airlift;* bring; bear; bus; cart; carry; convey; deliver; *export;* extradite; freight; forward; ferry; *fly;* give; get; haul; *import;* janker [Br.]; *jet;* kurvey; locomote; move; mail; *navigate; offload;* port; quarter-cart; relay; ship; send; take; transfer; uptake; van; waft; wheel; xfer; yomp; zip;

**transportation** *(n.)*: airmail (-lift); busing; carting; carrying; conveyance; conveying; delivering; delivery; express delivery; freight; ferriage; going; haulage; international delivery; *jump;* kurveying; logistics; moving; mass transit; *nonstop;* over-the-road ~; public ~; quick-delivery; relocation; shipping; transference; transporting; transit; *underway;* voyaging; wagoning; wheelbarrowing; xylophory; *yede; zipping;*

 **Types of transportation**: airplane; boating; busing; car; carting; dirigible; eighteen-wheeler; electric train; ferry; freight train; hot air balloon; locomotive; ocean-liner; railroad; shipping; trucking; train; van; wagoning; zeppelin;

**trap** *(n.)*: artifice; booby ~; *catch;* death~; deception; entrapment; enmeshment; fox~; farce; flimflam; gin; harepipe; illusiveness; illaqueation; inmeshment; Judas-kiss; kelong; lace; live ~; mouse- ~; man~; mesh; malversation; net; *outfox;* pitfall; pot; *quiblin [arch.];* ruse; snare; trick; *undoing;* verneuking; weely; weir; *xuld [arch.]; yentzing; zinger;*

**trap** *(v.)*: apprehend; betrap; capture; catch; deceive; ensnare; entrap; fool; get; hook in; imprison; *jail; keep; lure;* lay hold; mesh; nab; net; overtake; pick up; *quiblin [arch.]; rig;* seize; trammel; tangle; usurp; *vanquish; wrest; x.;* yard; *zing;*

**trappings** *(n.)*: accessories; adornments; bells & whistles; *comforts;* decorations; external signs; frills; finery; gear; habiliments; indications; *jewels; key evidence;* luxuries; marks; niceties; outward signs; plusses; quaintries; reflections; signs; things; trimmings; underlying signs; *valuables; wealth; xtras; yet unsurpassed; zizz;*

**trash** *(n.)*: abatis; bilge; *bag;* castoffs; debris; *eliminate;* filth; garbage; *heap; industrial waste;* junk; ket; litter; mullock; *nihil* [L.]; offscouring; offal; *pile;* quisquillous; refuse; rubbish; recyclables; scrap; sweepings; throw-away items; unwanted items; vuilnis; waste; *x-barrel; yucky; zero value;*

**trashy** *(adj.)*: awful; base; cheap; cheesy; chintzy; dumpy; *embarrassing;* faulty; gimcrack; horrible; inferior; junky; keg-meg; lousy; miserable; no-good; *otious;* poor; paltry; quisquillous; rubblishy; shoddy; substandard; tin-pot; third-rate; unprime; *vile;* wretched; *x-bad;* yucky; zero-quality;

**trauma** *(n.)*: anguish; *blast;* crisis; disturbance; distress; devastation; emotional shock; forlornness; grief; horrific shock; impact; jarring; jolt; knock; *lowness;* mental shock; nervous breakdown; ordeal; pain; quake; *restlessness;* shock; stun; traumatism; upset; *worry; xiphodynia; yank;* zap; zonk;

**traumatic** *(adj.)*: awful; *blast;* calamitous; disturbing; distressing; devastating; emotionally disturbing; *forlorn;* grueling; harrowing; hard; intense; jarring; *knocking; low;* mentally shocking; nervous; *overwrought;* painful; quaking; *restless;* shocking; stunning; troubling; upsetting; vexing; *worrisome; xiphodynia; yearnful;* zapping;

**travel** *(v.)*: advance; betake oneself; come to; commute; draw (near); emigrate; fare; fly; go; head; hike; itinerate; immigrate; journey; *kite;* locomote; migrate; move; navigate; nightfare; *outrun;* proceed; pass; peregrinate; *quicken;* relocate; reach; sail; sally; traverse; tour; trek; *underway;* voyage; wayfare; xenize; *yede* [arch.]; *zip;*

**traveler** *(v.)*: adventurer; Bedouin; commuter; drifter; excursionist; explorer; farer; forayer; goer; (hitch-)hiker; itinerant; journeyer; knight of the road [joc.]; losel; migrant; *nomad; overnighter;* peregrinator; pilgrim; passenger; questor; roamer; rover; rider; *sojourner;* traveler; tourist; trekker; *undertaker;* visitor; vacationer; voyager; wayfarer; xenizer; *yachter;* zingaro [It.];

**traverse** *(v.)*: across; bridge; cross; *drift over; emigrate;* fly over; go over; *hurry;* intersect; juncture; *kindle;* lie across; move over; navigate; overlap; pass over; *quicken; run;* range over; span; travel over; transverse; *underway;* venture across; *walk;* xfer; *yede;* zip over;

**travesty** *(n.)*: alteration; bad representation; corruption; distortion; exaggeration; false representation; gross misrepresentation; horrid version; inflation; jaded ~; knockoff; lousy representation; misrepresentation; non-realistic portrayal; *offense;* parody; perversion; *queering; reproduction;* slanting; twisting; unrealistic picture; *version;* warping; *xtry. ~; yucky;* zero accuracy;

**treacherous** *(adj.)*: artful; betraying; backstabbing; crooked; deceitful; disloyal; dastardly; evil; faithless; guileful; honorless; insidious; jadish; knavish; lying; malevolent; mutinous; non-loyal; *opportunistic;* perfidious; quisling; roguish; ruthless; seditious; shiftless; traitorous; unfaithful; violent; wicked; *x-ing; yeggy;* zero honesty;

**treachery** *(n.)*: artfulness; betrayal; crookedness; deceit; disloyalty; evil; evasiveness; faithlessness; guile; honorlessness; infidelity; jadery; knavery; lying; malevolence; mutiny; non-loyalty; *opportunism;* perfidy; quisling; roguery; sedition; treason; traitorousness; unfaithfulness; violence; wickedness; *x-ing; yegginess;* zero honesty;

**treason** *(n.)*: armed conflict; betrayal; *coup d'état* [F.]; desertion; disloyalty; *ever-defiant;* fifth-column activity; *general disregard;* high ~; insurrection; *jump ship; kicking at;* lèse majesté [F.]; mutiny; noncompliance; overthrow; prodition; perfidy; quislingism; rebellion; rising up; sedition; subversion; treachery; uprising; violence; *war;* xgression; *yieldlessness;* zapping;

**treasonous** *(adj.)*: averse; *breakaway;* contumacious; disloyal; defiant; evil-intentioned; faithless; guileful; honorless; insurrectional; *jadish; knavish;* lawless; mutinous; non-loyal; *opportunistic;* perfidious; *quisling;* rebellious; seditious; treacherous; traitorous; unfaithful; violent; wicked; *x-ing; yieldless;* zero honor;

**treasure** *(n.)*: abundance; bounty; cache; *dollars;* delight; *estate;* fortune; gold; hoard; inventory; *jewels; king's ransom;* lucre; money; material wealth; *nest egg;* opulence; possessions; pride and joy; pearl of great price; *quantities;* riches; substance; stockpile; silver and gold; ~ trove; uberty; valuables; wealth; *xenocurrency; yellow boys* [Br.]; zillions [slang];

**treasurer** *(n.)*: accountant; bursar; bookkeeper; chamberlain; cash-keeper; *depositor;* economist; financial secretary; geo-economist; *hoard-keeper; investor; jewel-keeper;* keeper of the books; *ledger;* moneybag-holder; number-cruncher; officer; purser; paymaster; *questor;* record keeper; reckoner; secretary; trustee; *underling;* verifier; warden; xaraf; *yeme;* zaikai [Jap.];

**treasury** *(n.)*: assets; bank; coffers; *deposit box;* exchequer; fisc; *gold;* hanaper; *iron chest;* jewels; keep-chest; lockbox; money bin; *night safe; opulence;* purse; *quantities;* repository; repertory; riches; strongroom; store; trove; treasure house; undercroft; vault; *war chest; xaraf; yadzutsu [Jap.];* zechins;
**treat** *(n.)*: additional frill; blessing; bonus; choice morsel; dainty; delight; delicacy; extravagance; frippery; frill; goody; *heavenly;* indulgence; just-for-fun ~; *kindness;* luxury; morsel; nicety; *overplus;* pleasure; *quaintry;* reward; special ~; tidbit; undeserved favor; *very nice gesture; windfall;* xtr.; *year-end bonus;* zest;
**treat** *(v.)*: act towards; behave toward; consider; care for; deal with; doctor; entreat; favor; give attention; handle; interact with; *justify; keep (under control);* look after; manage; minister to; nurse; *overhaul; perform; qua* [L.]; respond to; regard; *supervise;* take care of; use; *vamp;* work; xtr. attention; *yeme; zet [dial.];*
**treatise** *(n.)*: argument; book; composition; discourse; dissertation; essay; *form; graving;* handiwork; *inscription; journal; kapnography;* literature; letter; leader; monograph; *note;* opus; *opinion;* pandect; paper; *the quill;* review; research paper; study; thesis; tractate; term paper; *uncials;* vignette; writing; work; *xiaozhuan; yellow journalism; zeug;*
**treatment** *(n. care)*: assistance; basic care; care; doctoring; *easing;* fix; giving of help; handling; help; intercession; *just-in-time; keen care; lead;* medication; medicine; *nursing;* operation; policy; prescription; *quick-fix;* regimen; strategy; surgery; therapy; upholding; *vamp;* work; xtr.; *care; zealous help;*
**treatment** *(n. dealings)*: actions; behavior toward; consideration; dealings; *execute;* favor; goings on; handling; interaction; *jockeying; keeping (under control); leading;* manner; ministration; management; *navigation; overhaul;* processing; performance; *qua [L.];* regard; *supervision;* treating; usage; use; *vamping;* working; xtr. attention; *yeme; zet [dial.];*
**treaty** *(n.)*: agreement; *bond;* covenant; declaration; entente; forswearing; guarantee; hypothecation; interpledging; joint-commitment; *kept promise;* league; mutual agreement; nonaggression pact; oath; pact; *qualified promise;* resolve; signed agreement; settlement; truce; understanding; vow; word; *x-one's heart; yafery [arch.]; zealous agreement;*
**tree** *(n.)*: acer; arboret; bole; conifer; *cherry ~;* dottard; espalier; evergreen; fruit ~; *ginkgo;* hickory; ironwood ~; juniper ~; *kurrajong [Aus.];* lemon tree; maple ~; neem; oak ~; pollard; peach ~; quaker ~; redwood ~; sapling; *sycamore ~;* timber; *ulmaceae [L.];* varnish ~; willow ~; *xanthoxylon; yew;* zanthoxylum;
  **Kinds of trees**: apple; birch; cedar; dogwood; elm; evergreen; fig; fir; ginkgo; hickory; ironwood; juniper; kumquat; larch; maple; myrtle; nutmeg; oak; palm; pine; poplar; quaker; redwood; sycamore; teak; upas; varnish; walnut; willow; ximenia; yew; yulan; zamia
**trek** *(v.)*: advance; *bearing;* come to; direct one's course; *embark;* fare; go; hike; *immigrate;* journey; *kite;* locomote; make a journey; migrate; navigate; *outrun;* peregrinate; pass; *quicken;* relocate; sally; travel; *undergo;* venture; voyage; wayfare; xfer; *yacht; zip;*
**trellis** *(n.)*: arbor; basketwork; cross-hatching; duplex ~; *enclosure;* frame; grating; grille; hanging-plant support; iron ~; jalee; *ketwork;* lattice(work); meshwork; *network;* open framework; pergola; *quadra;* rack; *support;* trelliswork; treillage; *unit;* vine ~; wattle; wooden ~; x-mesh; yard ~; *zone;*
**tremble** *(v.)*: agitate; bicker; convulse; didder; *excite;* flutter; grimace; hustle; *inquietude;* judder; jitter; knock (knees); lose it; *move; nudge;* oscillate; palpitate; quake; rattle; shake; shudder; shiver; twitter; tremor; *unnerved; unstable;* vibrate; wobble; waggle; *xuld [arch.];* yerk; *zigzag;*
**tremendous** *(adj.)*: amazing; big; colossal; disproportionate; enormous; fantastic; fat; great; gigantic; huge; humongous; immense; incredible; jumbo-sized; king-size; large; magnificent; noteworthy; outstanding; oversize; plenteous; prodigious; quantitative; remarkable; substantial; terrific; titanic; uncanny; unbelievable; vast; whopping; weighty; XL; *you-beat [Aus.]; zenithal;*

**tremor** *(n.)*: agitation; bestirring; *convulsion;* disquieting; earthquake; faltering; growse [arch.]; heaving; inquietude; judder; jostle; knocking; lurch; *movement; nudge;* oscillate; pitch; quake; rumble; shake; trembling; upheaval; vibration; wobbling; *xuld [arch.];* yerk; *zigzag;*

**trench** *(n.)*: abysm; breach; channel; ditch; dugout; excavation; furrow; fosse; gully; hollow; incavation; jaw-hole; kerf; leat; moat; notch; outwork; pit; quadrisulcate; rut; slit ~; sondage; trough; U-groove; vallum; ward; *xystus pit;* yawn; zanja;

**trench** *(v.)*: *abstract;* burrow; channel; dig out; ditch; excavate; furrow; grub; hollow; incise; *jenkin;* kip; *lower;* mole; notch; open; put ~ in; quarry; rill; shovel; take out earth; *tunnel;* undermine; *vacate;* work; *xfer; yede;* zanja;

**trend** *(n.)*: ardor; bias; craze; design; desire; *enthusiasm;* fashion; fad; fever; general inclination; high fashion; hysteria; in thing; inclination; *jaunty;* keenness; kick; look; love; mania; notion; new ~; obsession; passion; quirk; rage; style; thing; urge; vogue; whim; *x-fervor;* yankering; zeal;

**trendy** *(adj.)*: awesome; bad; current; cool; dandy; extreme; fashionable; faddish; grody; hip; in; jaunty; keen; *latest;* modish; *modern;* nardy; new-fashioned; *outstanding;* popular; quite faddish; rakish; stylish; snappy; terrific; up-to-date; voguish; with-it; xtry.; you-beaut [Aus.]; zooty;

**trespass** *(n.)*: atrocity; breach; contravention; crime; debauchery; encroachment; evil; fault; godlessness; heinousness; infraction; iniquity; *jadedness; knavery;* licentiousness; misdeed; misconduct; noncompliance; nonfeasance; offense; peccability; *quad;* rebellion; sin; transgression; unlawful entry; unrighteousness; violation; wrongdoing; *xgression; yetzer hara* [Heb.]; *zymosis;*

**trespass** *(v.)*: act badly; breach; commit ~ do wrong; defy; *disregard;* encroach; fall; go wrong; *heinous;* infringe; infract; intrude; interlope; *jaded; knavish;* lapse; misbehave; *neglect;* overstep; offend; *pay no regard to; quad;* rebel; sin; transgress; *unfaithful;* violate; *wrong; x-gress; yetzer hara* [Heb.]; *zero obedience;*

**trespasser** *(n.)*: abominator; bad person; criminal; doer of evil; evildoer; fallen man; godless person; gate-crasher; hater of God; intruder; interloper; impenitent; jackanapes; knave; lost person; misdoer; nithing; offender; *pervert;* questrel; ribald; sinner; transgressor; *ungodly;* villain; wrongdoer; *xiaoren; yob; zero permission;*

**trespassing** *(n.)*: advancing upon; breaching; crossing the line; *disregard;* entrenchment; flouting; going into; horning in; infringing; intruding; interloping; impinging; *jurisdiction; knavery; lapsing;* making inroads into; nonfeasance; overstepping; pourpresture; *quad;* rebellion; squatting; transgression; usurpation; violation; wrongful entry; *xfer; yieldless; zero permission;*

**trial** *(n.)*: adversity; burden; complication; calamity; difficulty; distress; experience; fix; grief; hardship; incommodity; jam; kink; *load;* misfortune; *nuisance;* ordeal; problem; *quandary;* rattle; strait; trouble; tribulation; test; upheaval; vexation; woe; worry; *xerotripsis; yuckiness; zinger;* [*see* tribunal]

**tribe** *(n.)*: ancestry; brethren; blood relations; clan; connection; descent; ethnic group; family ; gens; group; heredity; in-group; *jus soli [L.];* kinfolk; kith; line; *mores;* nation; near of kin; *outfit;* people; phratry; *quarter;* race; rod; stock; troupe; tribal community; *ubiert; vein; wheen; x-link; yoni [Skr.];* zone;

   **Tribes of Israel**: Asher; Benjamin; Dan; Ephraim; Gad; Issachar; Joseph; Judah; Levi; Manasseh; Naphtali; Reuben; Simeon; Zebulon;

   **American Indian tribes**: Apache; Blackfoot; Cherokee; Comanche; Crow; Dakota; Euchee; Flathead; Gwichin; Hopi; Iroquois; Jicarilla; Kickapoo; Lucayan; Mohawk; Navaho; Oneida; Paiute; Quarai; Red; Seminole;Tupi; Ute; Vicam; Wanapum; Xega; Yellowknife; Zapotek;

**tribal** *(adj.)*: ancestral; blood; clannish; derivational; ethnic; family; genetic; hereditary; *inherited; jus soli [L.];* kin-related; lineal; *mankind;* national; original; phyletic; *quarter;* racial; stock-related; tribe-related; *unilineal; vein; within; x-linked; yoni [Skr.]; zygogenetic;*

**tribulation** *(n.)*: adversity; bind; calamity; difficulty; endangerment; fiery trial; grief; hardship; incommodity; jam; kettle of fish [slang]; *load;* misfortune; *nuisance;* ordeal; problems; *quandary;* rigor; suffering; trouble; trial; upheaval; unrest; vexation; woe; *xerotripsis; yuckiness; zhlubby;*
**Tribulation** *(n.)*: *adversity; bowl judgments; calamity;* Daniel's 70th Week; earth's final judgment; final judgment; Great ~; *horrific; intense trouble;* Jacob's trouble; judgment of God; *keening; lamenting; misfortune; the* next age; *ordeal; punishment; quandary; retribution of God;* seven-year ~; Seventieth Week; time of Jacob's trouble; unmixed wrath of God; *vial judgments;* world-judgment; wrath of God; *x-out;* Yahweh's wrath; *Zion's trouble;*
**tribunal** *(n.)*: arbitration; bench; bar; court; district court; ecclesiastical court; eyre; forum; gemot; hearing; inquisition; judgment seat; kings court; *kangaroo ~;* law court; manorial court; night court; open ~; *piepoudre;* quarter session; rota; session; trial; *United States Supreme Court;* venue; wardmote; *xabandar;* youth court [Can.]; *zamorin [Hind.];*
**tributary** *(n.)*: arm; branch; contributor; *dependent;* estuary; freshet; gully; *headwaters; inferior; jheel [Ind.]; kill* [Du.]; lough; millstream; narrows; offshoot; *passage;* quebrada; rivulet; rill; stream(let); *trickle; underground stream; voe;* wadi; *xyrisic;* yeo; *Zee [G.];*
**tribute** *(n.)*: acknowledgement; blood money; bepraisement; consideration; commendation; deference; duty; excise; esteem; encomium; fee; flattery; gift; gratitude; homage; honor; impost; idolizing; just desserts; kneeling; laudation; memorial; *notability;* obeisance; payment; panegyric; *quality;* recognition; respect; salutation; tax; unmitigated respect; veneration; *wonder; xtry.; yielding;* zero contempt;
**trick** *(n.)*: allurement; artifice; beguilement; con; deception; defrauding; device; ensnarement; fraud; feat; guile; hoax; imposture; japery; knavishness; knack; lie; misleading; nobbling; outfoxing; ploy; prank; *quicksand;* ruse; stunt; scam; sleight; subterfuge; trickery; trap; untruth; verneuking; wile; *xuld [arch.];* yentzing; *zinger;*
**trick** *(v.)*: *allure;* beguile; con; cheat; deceive; dupe; ensnare; fool; gyp; guile; hoodwink; insnare; jape; kid; lie to; mislead; nobble; outfox; put one over; *quiblin* [arch.]; rook; shyster; trap; *utter falsehood;* verneuk; wangle; *xuld [arch.];* yentz; *zing;*
**trickery** *(n.)*: artfulness; beguiling; crookedness; cheating; cozenage; dupery; deceit; deception; ensnarement; fraudulence; guile; honorlessness; improbity; jadery; jugglery; knavery; lying; misleading; non-truthfulness; *opportunism;* perfidy; questionableness; roguery; skullduggery; shadiness; treachery; underhandedness; villainy; wiliness; *x-ing;* yegginess; *zinger;*
**trickiness** *(n.)*: artfulness; beguiling; craftiness; cleverness; deviousness; deceitfulness; evasiveness; foxiness; guile; *hidden;* ingenuity; Jesuitry; knavishness; *lying;* Machiavelism; non-trustworthiness; *outfoxing;* policy; *quaintise* [arch.]; roguishness; subtlety; shrewdness; trickery; unscrupulousness; *vulpine;* wiliness; *xtry, cleverness; yepship* [arch.]; *zinging;*
**trickle** *(v.)*: *abate;* bleed; come out; dribble; drizzle; drip; emit; filter; gleet; *hemorrhage;* issue; *just a little;* kest; leak; *move; non-retention;* ooze; *pour; quicken;* run slowly; seep; spill; secrete; transude; *uprush; vomit;* weep; *xfer;* yote; *zip;*
**tricky** *(adj.)*: artful; beguiling; crafty; devious; deceptive; ensnaring; foxy; fraudulent; guileful; *hallucinatory;* illusive; insidious; jady; knavish; *lying;* misleading; non-trustworthy; *outfox;* pawky; *quirky;* rough; roguish; sneaky; subtle; tough; touchy; *thorny;* two-faced; underhanded; vulpine; wily; *xtry.;* yepe; *zinger;*
**trifle** *(n.)*: *amount;* bit; bagatelle; crumb; drop; *ens;* fragment; groat; hair; impertinence; jack; joke; kernel; little bit; mite; modicum; nothing; ounce; pittance; *quiddle; remnant;* smidgeon; tidbit; *unimportant; vestige;* whit; whiffle; XAG; *yngot [arch.];* zippo;
**trifle** *(v.)*: amuse oneself; belittle; coquet; dally; *ease;* fool around; fritter; *go on;* hang around; idle; jerk around; *knock;* lightly treat; mess (around); not take seriously; *obstruct;* piddle; quiddle; *ridicule;* scoff; treat lightly; use up; *veg out;* waste time; wink at; *xenize;* yerk around; *zealless;*

**trifling** *(adj.)*: airy; *blithering;* cursory; *dubious;* empty; frivolous; *gossamery;* hairsplitting; insignificant; jerkwater; ketty; little; marginal; minor; negligible; nominal; otiose; petty; paltry; quisquillous; ridiculous; small; slight; trivial; token; unimportant; vain; wee; XS; *yokelish; zilch;*
**trim** *(adj.)*: arranged; *beautiful;* clean; dapper; elegant; fit; gemmy; hygienic; immaculate; jimp [Br.]; kempt; lean; *mess-free;* neat; orderly; prest; proper; quaint; regimented; spruce; sleek; tidy; uncluttered; very clean; well-kept; *xtry.;* yet unmessed; *zierlich* [G.];
**trim** *(v. cut)*: abridge; bob; cut; clip; crop; *doll up;* edge; fettle; give ~; hack; incide; *jag; kerf;* lop; make even; *neaten;* obtruncate; pare; poll; prune; *quadrisect;* rip; shear; snip; take off; undo; vell; whittle; *x-sect; yerk; zip off;*
**trim** *(v. decorate)*: adorn; bedeck; *clothe;* decorate; embellish; fancify; garnish; habilitate; inwrought; jazz up; kit; *let be adorned;* make prettier; *nicer;* ornament; prettify; prank; pretty up; *quaintise* [arch.]; render lovely; ready up; *ribbon;* spruce; titivate; *use ornaments;* vest; *wear; xtry.; yclad* [arch.]; *zizz;*
**Trinity** *(n.)*: Almighty; Beginning and End; Creator; Divine Triad; *essence;* Father, Son, and Holy Ghost; Godhead; Holy ~; Hypostasies; *I AM; Jehovah;* King Eternal; Lord; Most High; *nature of God;* one God in Three Persons; Persons of the ~; *quintessence;* Ruler; Supreme Being; Triunity; Triad; Three in One; Unity of Three Persons; Virtue; Wise God; *xenenthesis; Yahweh;* Zion's Hope; [see God]
**trinket** *(n.)*: *article;* bauble; bijou; bric-a-brac; costume jewelry [pl.]; chachka; decoration; embellishment; fandangle; folderol; gewgaw; gaud; *habiliment; item;* junk jewelry [pl.]; knickknack; *lovely ornament; merchandise;* novelty; nicknack; ornament; pretty thing; play jewelry; *quaintry; roundlet; sequin;* toy jewelry; tawdry; *useless item;* valueless object; whatnot; *yannigan; zircon;*
**trip** *(n.)*: adventure; *boat ride;* cruise; drive; errand; excursion; foray; flight; getaway; holiday; *itineration;* jaunt; journey; *knight-errantry;* leisure tour; misadventure; mission; *night voyage;* outing; peregrination; quest; ramble; retreat; ride; spree; sortie; tour; trek; *undertaking;* voyage; weekend excursion; *xenization; yong* [arch.]; zugunruhe;
**trip** *(v.)*: *affect;* belly-whop; crash dive; cause to stumble; dive; err; fell; go down; *headlong; injure; jolt;* knock down; lose balance; misstep; make stumble; *nose-dive; over;* plunge; *quick-fall; ravel;* stumble; sprawl; supplant; tumble; trip up; unsettle; *volt; whop; x-cend; yank down; zoom;*
**trite** *(adj.)*: antiquated; bathetic; clichéd; dated; empty; familiar; *generic;* hackneyed; inane; jejune; *known;* lackluster; musty; nugacious; overused; old; pedestrian; *quondam;* ready-made; stale; tired; time-worn; used; unoriginal; very dated; worn out; xtry. unimaginative; yellowed; *zero imagination;*
**triumph** *(n.)*: *achievement;* brilliant victory; conquering; conquest; championship; domination; debellation; exultation; feat; glory; gain; historic ~; *invincibleness;* jubilee; knockout; landslide victory; mastery; *nike* [G.]; overcoming; prevailing; prize; *quashing;* rejoicing; success; total victory; uncontested ~; victory; victoriousness; win(ning); *xtry. win; yell; zing;*
**triumph** *(v.)*: *annihilate;* beat; conquer; defeat; exult; foil; *gut;* have victory; *invincible; joy;* knock out; kill; lick; master; *neutralize;* overcome; prevail; quash; rout; succeed; subjugate; trounce; unseat; vanquish; win; worst; *x-ing; yank down;* zap;
**triumphant** *(adj.)*: ascendant; *best;* conquering; champion; dominant; exultant; *famous;* glorious; *heroic; invincible;* jubilant; *kemp; leading;* master; non-defeated; overcoming; prizewinning; prevalent; prevailing; predominant; *quashing;* rejoicing; *ruling;* successful; triumphal; undefeated; unbeaten; vanquishing; victorious; winning; *xtry.; yelling;* zealous;
**trivial** *(adj.)*: asinine; *blithering;* cheap; desipient; empty; frivolous; futile; good-for-nothing; hoity-toity; insignificant; inconsequential; irrelevant; jerkwater; ketty; little; minor; nugatory; negligible; *obscure;* petty; peripheral; picayune; quisquillous; ridiculous; small; secondary; trifling; unimportant; vain; worthless; XS; yeasty; *zilch;*
**triviality** *(n.)*: asininity; buffoonery; complete unimportance; desipience; emptiness; frivolity; frivolousness; fiddle-faddle; gewgaw; *goofiness;* hoity-toity; insignificance; inconsequence; irrelevance; joke; jazz; kettiness; littleness; lightness; marginality; meanness; negligibility; nifle;

nonsense; niff-naff; *obscureness;* pettiness; piffle; quirkiness; *ridiculousness;* smallness; slightness; song; trivialness; trifle; unimportance; vanity; whiffle; *xs;* yock; zilch;

**troop** *(n.)*: army; battalion; company; corps; division; encampment; force; garrison; host; infantry; junior service [Br.]; *kerns;* legion; military; multitude; number; outfit; platoon; quarter-guard; regiment; soldiers; taxis [Rom.]; tanks; unit; vanguard; warriors; x-force; *yeald;* zouave;

**tropical** *(adj.)*: ascian; balmy; calid; *delightful;* equatorial; *fine; golden; hot; islands;* jungly; *Keys; luxurious; magnificent;* neo~; ocean; *overgrown;* paradisiacal; pantropic; quite balmy; *region;* sub~; sunny; tepid; tropic; *unfrozen; virtual paradise;* warm; *xtr. balmy; yellow-sun; zoographical region;*

**trouble** *(n.)*: adversity; bind; breakdown; burden; calamity; complication; difficulty; distress; dilemma; danger; endangerment; encumbrance; fix; glitch; grief; hardship; hard times; headache; hitch; incommodity; impasse; inconvenience; jam; kink; kettle of fish [slang]; load; misfortune; mess; nuisance; obstacle; *ordeal;* problems; predicament; plight; pickle; quandary; rattle; strait; stew; stalemate; snag; spot; tribulation; trial; test; upheaval; unrest; vexation; woe; worries; *xerotripsis; yuckiness; zhlubby;*

**trouble** *(v.)*: aggrieve; ail; agitate; bother; burden; concern; disturb; exasperate; *excite;* frustrate; grieve; harass; irritate; impose; jangle; *kindle;* lose sleep over; menace; nettle; overburden; perturb; *quake;* rile; stir; torment; upset; vex; worry; *xuld [arch.]; ydrad; zero peace;*

**troublemaker** *(n.)*: agitator; blackguard; cad; devil; evildoer; firebrand; good-for-nothing; heel; instigator; jackanapes; knave; kempy; lowlife; menace; miscreant; ne'er-do-well; *outlaw;* polecat; pest; questrel; rascal; rogue; rabble-rouser; ringleader; scalawag; transgressor; *ungodly person;* varlet; vexer; wretch; wrongdoer; *xiaoren;* yahoo; zhlub;

**troublesome** *(adj.)*: adverse; annoying; bothersome; burdensome; complicated; difficult; exasperating; formidable; grievous; hard; irksome; jarring; knotty; lousy; *miserable;* noisome; onerous; problematic; quisquose; rattling; straitened; trying; troubling; unpleasant; vexatious; worrisome; *xerotripsis; yucky; zhlubby;*

**trough** *(n.)*: *aqueduct;* bin; box; crib; channel; ditch; entrenchment; feeding trough; feeder; feedbag; gully; gutter; holder; hack; hopper; *impression;* jube; kneading trough; launder; manger; nullah; *outlet; pit;* qanat; rut; sluice; trench; tray; *u-groove;* vale; *vessel;* watering-trough; *x-groove;* yard- ~; zanja;

**truce** *(n.)*: armistice; break; breather; ceasefire; cessation of hostilities; declaration; end of hostilities; *fains* [arch.]; *guarantee;* hypothecation; interval; interlude; joint-agreement; *keep; lapse;* letup; moratorium; negotiation; oath; peace; pact; quittance; respite; reprieve; settlement; treaty; understanding; vow; *word; x-one's heart; yafery [arch.]; zero-aggression;*

**true** *(adj.)*: actual; accurate; authentic; bona fide; correct; definite; exact; earnest; factual; faithful; genuine; good; honest; heartfelt; indubitable; justifiable; known; legitimate; *mean it;* never-failing; open; ontic; precise; proper; qualified; questionless; real; right(ful); reliable; so; sincere; truthful; trustworthy; unquestionable; veritable; valid; well-tried; *x-parent; yes;* 'zactly [dial.];

**truly** *(adv.)*: absolutely; assuredly; beyond doubt; certainly; definitely; easily; fully; factually; genuinely; honestly; indeed; indisputably; justifiably; *keenly;* literally; most (certainly); nothing else but; *outright;* positively; quite; really; surely; sincerely; truthfully; undoubtedly; verily; without doubt; 'xactly [slang]; *ywis [arch.];* 'zactly [dial.];

**trumpet** *(n.)*: aida ~; alpenhorn; bugle; cornet; clarion; *dawn bugle; euphonium;* flugelhorn; German bugle; horn; hazora; *instrument;* jubil; key-bugle; lituus; matin ~ *neat-horn; ophicleide;* post horn; quadrivalve; rams-horn; shofar; sackbut; *signal;* trump; *unvalved horn; voice- ~; wind instrument; xylophone; yak-horn;* zinke;

**trumpet blast** *(n.)*: alert; blare; blast; bugle-call; chamade; display; *erupt;* fanfare; flourish; *go off;* horn-blast; herald; *indication;* jubil-blast; *key signal; letting out; music;* noise; *outblow; prompting;* qeren; reveille; sounding; shofar-blast; sennet; trump; trumpeting; tuck(et); tantara; *urging;* voice of the trumpet [poet]; whiffle; *xuld [arch.]; yakamik;* zinke-blast;

**truncate** *(v.)*: abbreviate; bisect; bob; cut; chop; dissever; dislimb; exscind; foreshorten; *gouge;* hew; hack; incide; jigsaw; knock off; lop off; *maim; notch;* obtruncate; prune; *quarter;* retrench; shorten; trim; take off; *undo; vell;* whack off; x-sect; *yerk; zigsaw* [arch.];
**trunk** *(n.)*: ark; box; chest; case; cassone; depository; *equipment;* footlocker; *garment bag;* hutch; iron chest; *journey-sack;* keister; locker; *luggage; marilda [Aus.]; nécessaire* [F.]; overnight case; portmanteau; *quinderkyn [arch.];* receptacle; suitcase; strongbox; travel case; treasure chest; utility case; valise; wardrobe ~; *x-bag;* yakdan; *zipper-bag;*
**trust** *(n.)*: adherence; belief; confidence; dependence; entrusting; faith; hope; *investment; just believe;* keeping; *looking to; mainstay;* non-doubt; overconfidence; persuasion; questionlessness; reliance; stand; true faith; *ule;* volitional faith; wholehearted ~; *xel [arch.]; y'faith* [arch.]; *zero-doubt;*
**trust** *(v.)*: accept; believe; confess; commit; depend on; embrace; expect; follow; *faith;* give heart to; have faith in; hold; inwardly believe; judge faithful; keep faith in; *know;* look to; *mainstay;* never doubt; *over~;* put faith in; profess; *persuaded; questionless;* rely; rest in; repose; stand on; take into one's heart; unwaveringly ~; very much ~; wholeheartedly ~; *y'faith [arch.];* zealously embrace; [see faith]
**trusting** *(adj.)*: *artless;* benighted; childlike; dewy; easily-deceived; foolish; gullible; honest; innocent; ignorant; *juvenile; knowledge-deprived;* lacking deceit; *moronic;* naive; non worldly-wise; open; Pickwickian; *quite ~;* reliant; simple-hearted; too ~; unsuspecting; verdant; wareless; *xtry. childlike;* youthful; *zero wisdom;*
**trustworthiness** *(n.)*: accuracy; believability; credibility; consistency; correctness; dependability; ethicalness; faithfulness; genuineness; honesty; infallibility; justifiableness; *kosher;* loyalty; *most faithful; never-failing; open-and-shut case;* proven ~; questionlessness; reliability; sureness; steadfastness; trustiness; unfailingness; veritableness; *well-trusted; xtry;* yeomanliness, *zealous;*
**trustworthy** *(adj.)*: accurate; believable; credible; consistent; correct; dependable; ever-faithful; faithful; good; genuine; honest; infallible; justifiable; known; loyal; most faithful; never-failing; *open-and-shut case;* principled; questionless; reliable; sure; steadfast; true; trusty; unfailing; veritable; well-trusted; *xtry;* yeomanly; *zealous;*
**truth** *(n.)*: actuality; accuracy; *bona fide;* certainty; dinkum oil [N.Z.]; exactness; fact(uality); faithfulness; genuineness; *the* gospel ~; honesty; indubitability; *justice;* knowledge; literalness; legitimacy; *meticulousness;* naked ~; *ontic;* precision; *quaecumque sunt vera* [L.]; quite so; reality; straightforwardness; sincerity; sureness; trueness; truthfulness; unambiguity; verity; veracity; whole ~; *x-parent; yes; zero error;* [Ant. talebearing]
**truthful** *(adj.)*: actual; accurate; bona fide; correct; definite; dependable; exact; earnest; factual; frank; genuine; honest; ingenuous; just; *kyriolexy;* literal; matter-of-fact; *mean it;* non-fiction; open; precise; plain; *qualified;* real; straight; sincere; true; unerring; uncolored; veritable; valid; veridical; *well-tried; xtry.; yes;* 'zactly [dial.];
**truthfulness** *(n.)*: actuality; accurateness; bluntness; candor; correctness; definiteness; earnestness; exactitude; frankness; faithfulness; goodness; genuineness; honesty; integrity; justness; kyriolexy; *legitimacy;* morality; non-deceitfulness; openness; probity; plain-dealing; *quaecumque sunt vera* [L.]; reliability; straightforwardness; truth; trustworthiness; uprightness; veracity; *well-trusted; xtry; yieldedness to God;* zero guile;
**try** *(n.)*: attempt; bid; crack; dare; effort; endeavor; full-blown effort; go; *hazarding; intent;* jab; kemp; *like to; move; nisus* [L.]; *offer;* push; proffer; quest; *retry;* shot; stab; trial; undertaking; venture; whirl; *xuld [arch.]; yearning; zeal;*
**try** *(v.)*: attempt; assay; bid; contend for; dare; endeavor; essay; follow after; go for; hazard; *intend; jeopardize;* kemp; *like to;* make an effort; *nitency; offer;* push for; proffer; *question [arch.];* road-test; risk; strive; seek; tackle; test; undertake; venture; work at; wing it; *xuld [arch.]; yearn; zealously endeavor;*

**tub** *(n.)*: *area;* bath(~); basin; baptistery; container; cauldron; *dryfat; ewer;* footbath; *get clean;* hot ~; *iron vat;* Jacuzzi®; knap; leach- ~; *mashing-* ~; nap; *oil bath;* punch bowl; *quinderkyn;* receptacle; reservoir; spa; sitz bath; tank; utility tank; vessel; vat; wash~; whirlpool; *xtr.-wide* ~; *yellow bath~;* zone;

**tube** *(n.)*: ajutage; black pipe; cardboard ~; chute; conduit; duct; efflux ~; flume; gutter; hose(pipe); *irrigation canal; j-bend pipe; kyle;* line; main; *nullah;* outlet; pipe; *quill* [arch.]; roller; *route;* steel pipe; tubing; *underground pipeline;* ventiduct; vein; water pipe; *x-ray tube;* yardbeam; *zanja;*

**tuck** *(v.)*: *act;* bunch; crease; crinkle; double; enfold; fold; gather; *hem;* insert; jam; kilt; lodge; make fold; *nudge;* overfold; put; quill; ram; rumple; shove; stick; thrust; upbind; volt; wedge; *xuld [arch.]; yerk;* zip;

**tumor** *(n.)*: abscess; bulge; cyst; dermoid; emerod; furuncle; growth; hemorrhoid; hunch [arch.]; intumescence; jarble; knot; lump; lipoma; mass; nodule; osteoma; protuberance; *quirk;* rising; ranula; swelling; terminthus; ulcer; vomica; wen; xanthogranuloma; *yedder;* zoocyst;

**tumult** *(n.)*: anarchy; agitation; bedlam; commotion; disturbance; embroilment; fracas; furor; fuss; *gastness;* havoc; hoopla; hullabaloo; insurrection; *jangle;* kick-up; loud ~; mayhem; nitty; noise; outcry; pandemonium; *quandary;* riot; racket; rumpus; shouting; to-do; upheaval; uproar; *violence;* welter; xtry. uprising; *yo-yo;* zoo;

**tumultuous** *(adj.)*: agitated; angry; boisterous; confused; disorderly; embroiled; frantic; grueling; hectic; incoherent; jouncy; *kick-up; loud;* mad; noisy; outrageous; peaceless; quaking; riotous; restless; stormy; turbulent; tumultuary; unrestrained; volatile; wild; *xuld [arch.]; yelling;* zany;

**tune** *(n.)*: air; *ballad;* composition; ditty; euphony; folksong; *gallimaufry;* harmony; *inspiration;* jingle; *kasida; low pitch;* melody; *notes;* ode; piece; *quodlibet;* refrain; song; tunes; undersong; *variation;* warble; *xylophone song;* yed; *zemirah;*

**tune** *(v.)*: adjust; attune; bring into line; calibrate; dispose; equalize; fine- ~; fix; gear to; harmonize; improve; *jury-rig;* key to; *level off;* make aligned; *non-fixed;* overhaul; proportion; *quick-fix;* regulate; rectify; set; synchronize; tram; tweak; *upbuild;* vamp; *work on; xfer;* yark; zet [dial.];

**tunic** *(n.)*: abaya; bathrobe; caftan; dalmatic; evening robe; frock; gilet; housecoat; ihram; jerkin; kirtle; laticlave; manto; night-robe; overtunic; paranja [fem.]; *quaintry [arch.];* robe; simar; tabard; undergarment; vestment; *ward~; XL; yelek* [Turk. fem.]; zimarra;

**tunnel** *(n.)*: adit; burrow; bore; channel; corridor; chute; duct; escape ~; *furrow; groove; hallway;* interconnection; *j-bend; kanat* [Arab.]; level; mineshaft; narrow passageway; open ~; outlet; passage(way); pit; *qanat* [Arab.]; *railroad* ~; shaft; subway; subterranean passage; *tube;* underpass; underground passageway; ventiduct; winze; warren; *xystus;* Y-tunnel; *zanja;*

**tunnel** *(v.)*: *advance;* burrow; channel; dig; delve; excavate; *furrow;* grub; hollow; hole; *intrench; jenkin;* kip; *lower;* mole; *notch; open; prospect;* quarry; *remove dirt;* scoop; shovel; *trench;* undermine; *venture;* worm; *xfer; yede; zanja;*

**turbid** *(adj.)*: *ambiguous;* blurry; cloudy; confused; dark; dense; enclouded; foggy; feculent; gray; hazy; indefinite; jarbled; kallowy; lutulent; muddied; murky; nebulous; obscure; puggy; quaggy; roiled; shadowy; thick; unclear; vague; woolly; *xeroophthalmic;* yucky; *zero-clarity;*

**turbulence** *(n.)*: agitation; bumpiness; bounciness; commotion; disturbance; discomposure; disquietude; enragement; fluctuation; furor; *grueling;* havoc; inclemency; instability; jumpiness; knocking; *lousiness;* motion; moil; non-calmness; over-agitation; peacelessness; quaking; roughness; storminess; turmoil; turbulency; unrest; violence; welter; *xuld [arch.]; yuckiness;* zippiness;

**turbulent** *(n.)*: angry; blustery; bumpy; bouncy; chaotic; disturbed; enraged; fierce; frantic; grueling; hostile; hard; intense; jumpy; jarring; *killer; lousy; maddening;* nidgetty; *out-of-whack;* peaceless; quaking; restless; rough; raging; stormy; tumultuous; tempestuous; uncontrolled; unstable; violent; weltering; wild; *xuld [arch.];* yeasty; zippy;

**turgid** *(adj.)*: arrogant; bombastic; conceited; dull; egotistical; florid; grandiloquent; high-sounding; impressive; Johnsonian; know-it-all; lofty; magniloquent; noble-sounding; orotund; pompous; *quantitative;* rhetorical; swelling; tumid; uppity; verbose; well-sounding; *x-proud; yammering; zesty;*

**turmoil** *(n.)*: anarchy; bedlam; chaos; disorder; entanglement; farrago; gastness; havoc; intranquility; jumble; kerfuffle; *lunacy;* mayhem; non-orderliness; *over-agitation;* pandemonium; *quandary;* rage; stupefaction; tumult; unruliness; vexation; welter; *xtry. mess; yo-yo;* zoo;
**turn** *(n.)*: angle; bend; curve; corner; crook; dip; el; fold; *geometric curve;* hook; hairpin ~; inflection; jog; jag; knee; knuckle; kink; left ~; *move; meandering; nonlinear;* ogee; oxbend; parabola; quat; quarter ~; right ~; round; stoop; twist; U- ~; verge; wag; wind; xy-curve; yaw; zig; zag;
**turn** *(v.)*: angle; alter(nate); bend; bear; curve; convert; crank; change; churn; dip; enfold; fold; flip; go around; gyrate; hurtle; incline; jag; knuckle; left ~; *loop;* move around; meander; nutate; obvert; overturn; purl; querl; revolve; rotate; roll; spin; swerve; twist; twirl; torque; transform; upsweep; veer; whirl; wheel; *x-ing;* yaw; zig; zag;
**turncoat** *(n.)*: absconder; backstabber; Benedict Arnold; collaborator; deserter; defector; *evildoer; fiend;* fifth columnist; guiler; *honorless;* insurgent; Judas; *knave; liar;* mutineer; *non-loyal; opportunist;* plotter; quisling; rat; snake; seditionist; traitor; *unloyal; villain; wicked; xfer; yegg; zero loyalty;* [*see* hypocrite]
**turnpike** *(n.)*: avenue; artery; bypass; beltway; conduit; causeway; divided highway; expressway; freeway; *going;* highway; interstate; journey-way; king's highway; lane; motorway; non-toll road; *outstreet;* pike; queen's highway; route; superhighway; thruway; *underpass; vennel;* way; *xyst;* yong [arch.]; *zwinger;*
**turquoise** *(adj.)*: aqua(marine); blue-green; cyanic; dark ~; *electric blue; French racing blue;* green-blue; *hyacinth; igneous rock; jade; kyanite;* light ~; medium ~; Nile blue; ocean blue; pale ~; peacock blue; *queen's blue;* robin egg blue; sea-green; teal; *ultramarine;* viridian; *watchet; xyris; yew-green; zaffer;*
**tusk** *(n.)*: *antler;* barb; boar ~; cornicle; *dentate;* elephant ~; *eyetooth;* fang; gagtooth; *gore;* horn; ivory; jabber; *knag;* laniary; moose ~; nape; *ox horn;* point; projection; *quadricorn; rack;* sabre tooth; tooth; tine; *unicorn horn; violent;* wild boar ~; walrus ~; *xanthdontous;* yak horn; *zygodont;*
**tutor** *(n.)*: after-school trainer; *basic instructor;* coach; discipler; educator; *fugleman;* guide; helper; instructor; *job trainer; knock into;* lecturer; mentor; *narrator;* orienter; pedagogue; *qualifier;* regent; schooler; trainer; tutorer; teacher; *undershepherd; verser; worker;* xenagogue; *yield; zealous trainer;*
**tutor** *(v.)*: acquaint; *bring up;* coach; disciple; educate; foster; guide; *home school;* instruct; *job training; knock into;* lecture; mentor; *narrate; open one's eyes;* prime; pedagogue; qualify; ready; school; teach; *unlock;* verse; work with; xenagogue; *yak; zealously train;*
**twig** *(n.)*: arm; branch; chat; *dogwood branch; extremity;* faggot; *grafted branch; hickory branch; ironwood;* jackstraw; kipper; *limb; maple branch;* nicky; osier; plash; *quaker;* rame; runner; stick; stave; shoot; sprig; switch; tendril; *upas ~; vimineous;* withe; wattle; *xylem;* young shoot; *zamia;*
**twilight** *(n.)*: *after hours; blaze;* crepuscule; dusk; evening; fall of the sun; gloaming; *half-light; idleness;* just before dawn; *kip; late-night;* morning ~; nightfall; *overnight;* P.M.; *q.n.; rest;* sunset; time after sunset; *unconsciousness;* vespers; *wink; x-ing; yester-evening;* zone;
**twine** *(n.)*: *abb;* braid; cord; *draw; en~;* fiber; gantline; henequin; *item;* jute; knittle; line; *mainsheet; natural fiber;* organzine; packthread; qiviut; rope; string; thread; *uncoil;* vang; watap; x-braid; yarn; zein;
**twinkle** *(v.)*: *aura;* blink; coruscate; dance; effluge; flash; flicker; gleam; glisten; glitter; glimmer; halo; illuminate; *jiffy;* kindle; luster; *move; nitency; outshine; patter;* quiver; reflect; shimmer; sparkle; spangle; throw light; *ultraviolet light; vividness;* wink; *x-ray; yield light; zap;*
**twirl** *(v.)*: *around; backspin;* circle; *downward;* eddy; furl; go around; *hurtle;* incurvate; *jee; keel;* loop; move around; nutate; orb; purl; querl; rotate; revolve; spin; twizzle; upsweep; volt; whirl; *x-ing;* yede; *zip;*
**twist** *(v.)*: *alternate;* becurl; coil; convolute; *distort;* entwist; entwine; fold around; glomerate; hankle; intwist; *join;* keckle; *loop;* meander; *nonlinear;* overwind; *prewind;* querl; rotate; ravel; roll; rove; spiral; skew; screw; turn; twine; tweak; torque; twizzle; unscrew; volt; wind; *x-ing; yaw;* zigzag;

**twitch** *(n.)*: *anxiety;* brief jerk; convulsion; didder; *excite;* flinch; flick; *gyrate;* hitch; involuntary movement; jerk; judder; *kick; lurch;* movement; *non-epileptic convulsion; oscillate;* paroxysm; quiver; *rattle;* spasm; *shaking;* tic; tremble; *unstable;* vellication; wince; *xuld [arch.];* yank; *zag;*
**twitch** *(n.)*: *anxiety;* briefly jerk; convulse; didder; *excite;* flinch; flick; *gyrate;* hitch; involuntarily move; jerk; judder; *kick;* lurch; move; *nod; oscillate;* paroxysm; quiver; *rattle;* shudder; shake; tic; tremble; *unstable;* vellicate; wince; *xuld [arch.];* yank; zag;
**tycoon** *(n.)*: *authority;* baron; boss; chief; director; entrepreneur; financier; governor; head; intendant; jefe; kalhuna; kingpin; lord; magnate; mogul; nabob; overseer; plutocrat; queen [fem.]; ruler; ringleader; supervisor; top-dog; *ultimate authority;* vizer; warden; XO; *yokemaster;* zayim;
**type** *(n. kind)*: *area;* brand; breed; bracket; class(ification); category; cast(e); designation; denomination; estate; form; fashion; feather; genre; group; genus; grade; heading; ilk; *jack;* kind; label; make; manner; model; nature; *name;* order; phylum; persuasion; *quarter;* rank; rating; sort; species; strain; style; stripe; technique; *unit;* variety; *way; x-class; year-class; zoo~;*
**type** *(n. picture)*: adumbration; betokening; characterization; comparison; designation; *example;* foreshadow; foretoken; figure; *glyph;* harbinger; illustration; image; *just like;* key ~; likeness; model; *notice; oracle;* picture; presage; pretype; prefiguration; *quain [arch.];* representation; shadow; sign; token; *umbrage;* very image; *word; xenenthesis; yichus; Zeug [G.];*
**typical** *(adj.)*: average; basic; common(place); customary; characteristic; dominant; dull; daily; everyday; familiar; generic; general; habitual; inveterate; jejune; *kuriologic;* long-established; *lackluster;* mundane; normal; ordinary; plain; quotidian; regular; standard; traditional; usual; vanilla; wonted; *x-type; yawnish;* zestless;
**typically** *(adv.)*: as a rule; by and large; commonly; customarily; dominantly; essentially; frequently; generally; habitually; in general; *jejunely; known;* largely; mostly; normally; ordinarily; *prevalently; quotidian;* regularly; *standard;* traditionally; usually; *very common;* wontedly; x-type; yawnish; zestlessly;
**typify** *(v.)*: allude to; betoken; characterize; demonstrate; epitomize; exemplify; embody; foreshadow; foretoken; give picture of; *herald;* illustrate; instantiate; indicate; *justify; kithe [Scot.]; likened to;* manifest; *name; open up;* personify; picture; portend; point out; *qualify;* represent; suggest; show forth; signify; speak of; token; *unveil; vaunt; way; x-type; yield; zay [arch.];*
**typo** *(n.)*: accident; boo-boo; copy-error; defect; error; flaw; goof-up; *howler [Br.];* inaccuracy; *jumble;* key mix-up; louse-up; mistake; misprint; *non-purposive;* oversight; problem; *quirk; real mess-up;* slip-up; typographical error; unintentional mistake; *violation; wrong; xmit error; yaw; zinger;*
**typology** *(n.)*: adumbration; betokening; comparison; designation; *example;* figuration; *glyphics; have meaning;* illustration; imagery; *just like;* kuriology; likening; meaning; *model; notice; oracle;* pictures; *quain [arch.];* representation; symbolism; type; tokenism; *umbrage;* very image; word pictures; *xenenthesis; yichus; Zeug [G.];*
**tyrannical** *(adj.)*: arbitrary; bossy; controlling; dictatorial; despotic; domineering; evil-hearted; fascistic; grinding; harsh; iron-fisted; *jaded;* kindless; lordly; magisterial; *nasty;* oppressive; overbearing; peremptory; *quede [arch.];* repressive; strict; totalitarian; tyrannic; unreasonable; unassailable; *virulent; way too strict; xenophobic;* yieldless; *za-zum* [Rus.];
**tyranny** *(n.)*: autocracy; absolutism; brute force; cruelty; despotism; enslavement; fascism; *gauleiter;* harshness; Hiterism; iron-fistedness; *jadedness;* kindlessness; lording over; monocracy; *Nazism;* oppression; police state; *quenching;* rule by force; severity; totalitarianism; unchecked power; *violence; warlord; xenarchy;* yieldlessness; *za-zum [Rus.];*
**tyrant** *(n.)*: autocrat; absolute ruler; boss; commander; dictator; despot; executive; *Führer [G.];* governor; head; intendant; jemander [Ind.]; king; leader; lord; master; *Negus [Afr.];* overlord; oligarch; potentate; prefect; queen [fem.]; ruler; superior; superintendent; supervisor; tsar; tormentor; usurper; vizer; *warlord;* XO; *yokemaster;* zayim;

# U

**ugliness** *(n.)*: awfulness; badness; contortedness; deformity; evil-favoredness; frightfulness; ghastliness; grotesqueness; homeliness; hideousness; ickiness; *jackal-faced; knarled;* loathsomeness; monstrousness; misshapenness; monstrosity; nastiness; non-attractiveness; offensiveness; plainness; queerness; repulsiveness; repugnance; *sickening;* terribleness; unsightliness; unattractiveness; vileness; *warped; xerophthalmic;* yuckiness; *zit-faced;*

**ugly** *(adj.)*: appalling; bad-looking; contorted; disgusting; evil-favored; eye-offending; *eyesore;* foul-looking; grotesque; homely; hideous; ill-favored; *jackal-faced; knarled;* loathsome; monstrous; misshapen; nasty; nauseating; offensive; odious; plain; plug- ~; queer; repulsive; sickening; shocking; terrible; unattractive; unsightly; vile; wicked; *xerophthalmic;* yucky; *zit-faced;*

**ultimate** *(adj.)*: A-1; best; choicest; concluding; decisive; elite; eventual; finest; final; greatest; highest; incomparable; *just the best;* keenest; loftiest; last; most desirable; No. 1; optimum; prime; quintessential; *remarkable;* superior; super-; top; unsurpassed; *vital;* world-class; winningest; xtry.; yondmost; zenithal;

**ultimatum** *(n.)*: adjuration; behest; command; demand; enjoining; final demand; *governance;* heavy demand; injunction; juration; *kicker; last word;* mandate; necessity; order; *precept; quo minus [L.];* requirement; stipulation; *threat;* ultimatum; *voice;* warning; word; *XO mandate; yelling; zakon [Rus.];*

**umpire** *(n.)*: arbitrator; *baseball* ~; commissaire; decision-maker; *evaluator;* final judge; *gager;* honest broker; intermediary; judge; *kadi;* linesman; line judge; mediator; negotiant; official; presider; qadi; referee; *scorekeeper; settler;* timekeeper; *unquestioned;* valuator; *weigher; XQ; yeller; zamorin;*

**unable** *(adj.)*: armless; *badly equipped;* crippled; deficient; enfeebled; effete; exhausted; feeble; frail; *gimp;* helpless; impotent; incapable; inept; incompetent; *jejune; knocked out;* lame; much-weakened; not equal to; overweak; powerless; queachy [dial.]; *reduced;* scrawny; *soft;* tired; unendowed; unqualified; vulnerable; weak; xtry. vulnerable; *yet without energy;* zapped; [Ant. unflagging]

**unabridged** *(adj.)*: all-inclusive; big; broad; comprehensive; complete; detailed; exhaustive; full-length; *general; grand; high;* inclusive; *jim-bang; kept intact; long version; major;* non-abridged; overall; *perfect; quantified; real;* sheer; total; uncut; unedited; *veritable;* whole; XL; yare; *zero abridgment;*

**unacceptable** *(adj.)*: awful; bad; *crummy;* deficient; exceptionable; falling short; *greatly in need;* halfmeasure; intolerable; *just not good enough;* keenly improper; lame; most ~; non-satisfactory; objectionable; poor; *questionable; rotten;* short; too little; unallowable; unsatisfactory; very ~; wanting; wrong; xtry. *deficient; yet ~; zero sufficiency;*

**unaccompanied** *(adj.)*: (all) alone; *a cappella* [It.]; by oneself; companionless; desolate; *empty;* friendless; forlorn; *grieved; hopeless;* isolated; just oneself; kithless; lone(some); *miserable; non-accompanied;* on one's own; *piteous; quit on; reclusive;* single; solitary; *tearful;* unchaperoned; unassisted; unattended; very alone; without accompaniment; *xtry. lonely; yet ~; zero accompaniment;*

**unaffiliated** *(adj.)*: autonomous; bondless; *control;* disassociated; empowered; free; governing oneself; *headship;* independent; *justified; kept free;* liberated; managing own affairs; non-affiliated; non-allied; non-subjugated; open; particularistic; quite independent; ruling self; self-governing; totally ~; unassociated; unrelated; unallied; unconnected; *very ~; warranted; xtry. isolated;* yokeless; *zero connection;*

**unalterable** *(adj.)*: absolute; bendless; changeless; determinate; ever the same; fixed; firm; *grim;* hard-core; irreversible; intransmutable; immutable; *just the same;* keeping the same; *lasting;* moveless; never-changing; non-alterable; *obstinate;* permanent; quite ~; rigid; static; *timeless;* unwavering; unchangeable; very fixed; written in stone; *x-cending;* yet the same; *zero change;* [Ant. upgradeable]

**unambiguous** *(adj.)*: apparent; blatant; clear; categorical; definite; direct; explicit; express; forthright; glaring; highly understandable; impossible to miss; *just plain to see;* kenspeckle; lucid; manifest; non-ambiguous; not obscure; overt; open; plain; perspicuous; quite obvious; *recognizable;* straightforward; transparent; unequivocal; unmistakable; understandable; univocal; very clear; without ambiguity; xtl. clear; yet understandable *zero-ambiguity;* [Ant. unclear]

**unambitious** *(adj.)*: apathetic; *blasé;* complacent; droopy; *easygoing;* fainéant; groggy; half-hearted; indolent; *jog trot;* kef; lazy; mopish; non-motivated; otiose; pepless; quiescent; *remiss;* slothful; shitless; torpid; unenthusiastic; unmotivated; unaspiring; *vapid;* workshy; *xenarthrous;* yareless; zealless;

**un-American** *(n.)*: anti-American; antipatriotic; betraying; *Benedict Arnold;* Communist; disloyal; *enemy; foreign; grossly ~;* honorless; incivist; jadish; *knavish; loyalist; mutinous;* non-patriotic; opposed to America; *perfidious; quisling; royalist;* subversive; *treacherous;* unpatriotic; *venomous; wicked;* xenophilic; Yankee-hating; *zero honor;*

**unanimity** *(n.)*: agreement; bond of harmony; cohesion; *done by all;* everyone; fellow feeling; general agreement; harmony; in one accord; joint approval; kinship; like-mindedness; mutuality; *nodding;* oneness; *per curium [L.]; questioned by none;* ratification by all; single-mindedness; total agreement; unity; unison; voting by all; *widespread agreement; xel [arch.]; yedinstvo* [Rus.]; *zealous oneness;*

**unanimous** *(adj.)*: agreed (by all); be in accord; common; *done by all;* endorsed by all; *fallen in;* granted by all; held by all; indorsed by all; jointly approved; kept by all; like-minded; minded by all; non-divided; one-hundred percent; *per curium* [L.]; *questioned by none;* ratified by all; shared-by-everyone; *together;* unchallenged; unified; voted by all; with one voice; *xel [arch.]; yedinstvo* [Rus.]; *zealously approved by everyone;* [Ant. undecided]

**unappetizing** *(adj.)*: awful; bad; contemptible; disagreeable; distasteful; execrable; foul; gross; horrible; invidious; jarring; kindless; loathsome; miserable; nasty; nauseating; objectionable; *poor; quad;* repulsive; stomach-turning; terrible; unpleasant; unpalatable; unsavory; vile; wicked; *xtry. gross;* yucky; *zero pleasure;*

**unappreciative** *(adj.)*: absent-minded; *bad;* churlish; disregardful; eliding; forgetful; gratitude-neglecting; *heedless;* ill-remembered; *jaded; kindless; lax;* most ~; non-appreciative; *owe nothing;* praiseless; *quick-to-forget; remiss; spirit of ingratitude;* thankless; unthankful; ungrateful; very unmindful; without thanks; *xgressing; yemeles [arch.]; zero appreciation;*

**unarmed** *(adj.)*: armless; barehanded; *crippled;* defenseless; exposed; *fine;* guardless; helpless; inermous; justiciable; *knocked out;* liable; *much at risk;* naked; open (to attack); pregnable; *queachy* [dial.]; *reduced;* susceptible; totally harmless; unprotected; unshielded; unweaponed; unarmored; unguarded; vulnerable; weaponless; *xtry. vulnerable;* yet defenseless; *zappable;*

**unashamed** *(adj.)*: *abusing;* brazen; contumacious; defiant; ever-defiant; flagrant; griefless; hard-hearted; hardened; impenitent; *jaded; kicking;* lawless; *misbehaving;* non-repentant; obdurate; *pigheaded; querulous;* remorseless; shameless; *transgressing;* unabashed; unembarrassed; unrepentant; unremorseful; *violating;* wayward; *xgression;* yieldless; *zero repentance;*

**unashamedly** *(adv.)*: apparently; brazenly; conspicuously; deliberately; expressly; flagrantly; glaringly; heedlessly; intentionally; justifiably; knowingly; lucidly; manifestly; noticeably; overtly; patently; *quite;* remorselessly; shamelessly; *transparently;* unabashedly; visibly; wittingly; *XR;* yarely; zonally;

**unattainable** *(adj.)*: *aloof;* beyond reach; closed to; denied; *excluded;* far; *gone;* hopeless; inaccessible; *just can't have; kept from;* lost to; most ~; non-obtainable; not for sale; out-of-reach; prohibited; quite ~; *remote; secluded;* too much for; unreachable; unrealistic; unachievable; *very unlikely; without a chance;* X; yet ~; *zero access;*

**unattractive** *(adj.)*: awful; bad-looking; contemptible; disagreeable; evil-favored; *eyesore;* foul-looking; gross; homely; ill-favored; *jarring; kindless;* lousy; mousy; nasty; ordinary; plain (-looking); queer-looking; repelling; sorry-looking; terrible; unsightly; unlovely; unappealing; uninviting; vile; wretched; *xerophthalmic;* yucky; *zit-faced;* [see ugly]

**unavailable** *(adj.)*: already taken; absent; busy; booked; cannot be had; definitely ~; engaged; full; flat chat [Aus.]; gone; *hard-to-find;* in use; inaccessible; just not available; kept from; lost to; *married;* not available; occupied; overbusy; preoccupied; quite ~; reserved; spoken for; taken; unattainable; *vain;* well-occupied; *x-out;* yern; *zero availability;* [*Ant.* unclaimed]

**unavoidable** *(adj.)*: assured; bound to; certain; destiny; expected; foreordained; fated; guaranteed; *happening for sure;* inevitable; inescapable; ineludible; *just certain;* kismet; *literal;* manifest; necessary; obvious; preordained; predictable; quite sure; really certain; sure; shunless; totally sure; unchangeable; very sure; wholly ~; *'xactly; yes; zero option;*

**unbalanced** *(adj.)*: asymmetrical; *bent;* crooked; disproportionate; *erratic;* flim-flam; *grotesque;* hunchbacked; incongruous; jim-jam; kim-kam; lopsided; malapportioned; non-symmetical; out-of-balance; proportionless; queer-looking; *repandous;* sloping; *top-heavy;* uneven; unsymmetrical; *variable;* without symmetry; *xy-discordant;* yawed; zad; [*Ant.* uniform]

**unbearable** *(adj.)*: agonizing; beyond the pale; *calamitous; distressing;* excruciating; egregious; far too much; grueling; hard; intolerable; insufferable; just too much; *killing;* lamentable; more than one can bear; not bearable; over-the-top; past bearing; quite ~; rough; rigorous; severe; too much; unacceptable; unendurable; very hard; *weighty;* xtry.; yet insufferable; *zero tolerance;*

**unbelief** *(n.)*: apprehension; agnosticism; atheism; *baffling;* cynicism; *confusion;* doubt; disbelief; distrust; *equivocalness;* faithlessness; fear; *getting nervous;* hesitation; iffiness; incredulity; infidelity; *jitteriness; kiaugh [Scot.];* leeriness; lack of faith; misbelief; mistrust; misgivings; non-belief; *over-anxiety;* pessimism; question; reservation; skepticism; suspicion; trepidation; uncertainty; *vacillation;* worry; wavering; *xtry. doubt; yieldlessness;* zero confidence; [*see* astonishment; *Ant.* understanding]

**unbelievable** *(adv.)*: amazing; astounding; astonishing; bizarre; crazy; daft; extraordinary; far-fetched; goofy; hard to believe; incredible; inconceivable; jokey; kooky; loony; laughable; marvelous; mind-boggling; nutty; outrageous; outlandish; odd; peculiar; quacked; remarkable; ridiculous; stupendous; silly; screwy; twisted; unlikely; unthinkable; *variant;* wonderful; xtry.; yuk yuk; zany; [*Ant.* unquestioned]

**unbeliever** *(n.)*: agnostic; atheist; balker; critic; Christ-rejecter; doubter; disbeliever; denier; *enquirer;* freethinker; ganako; hellion; *heretic;* infidel; jackeen; knocker; lost man (person); man of the world; nonbeliever; non-Christian; oppugner; polemic; questioner; rejecter; skeptic; transgressor; unsaved person; vacillator; worldling; *xiaoren; yob;* zetetic;

**unbelieving** *(adj.)*: anti-Christian; blasphemous; Christ-rejecting; disbelieving; earthly-minded; faithless; godless; heathen; irreligious; indevout; infidel; jackeen; *knavish;* latitudinarian; lost; misbelieving; non-believing; overcredulous; pagan; *profane;* questioning; reprobate; secular; *transgressing;* unfaithful; undevout; unsaved; *vile;* worldly-minded; worshipless; *x-gressing; yieldless;* zero-faith; [*Ant.* understanding]

**unbending** *(adj.)*: adamant; bendless; constant; determined; ever-rigid; firm; grim; hard; inflexible; jaw-set; *keep;* loyal; mulish; nonflexible; obstinate; pertinacious; *querulous;* rigid; stubborn; stiff(-necked); strong(-willed); tough; unyielding; very rigid; willful; *x-hard;* yieldless; zero give; [*Ant.* unfirm]

**unbiased** *(adj.)*: anti-discriminatory; *blameless;* correct; disinterested; equitable; fair; good; honest; impartial; just; keeping justice; *legitimate;* moral; non-discriminatory; nonpartisan; neutral; objective; plain-dealing; *quality;* righteous; square; true; unprejudiced; virtuous; *wholly ~; xtry. just; yet ~; zero-bias;* [*Ant.* unfair]

**unbiblical** *(adj.)*: amiss; bad; *confused;* defective; extra-biblical; false; *groundless;* heretical; heterodox; incorrect; *jim-jam; kim-kam; lying;* mistaken; non-biblical; off base; *problematic; questionable; repudiated;* spurious; *tricky;* unscriptural; unorthodox; untrue; *variant;* wrong; *xtr. bad; yawed; zero-truth;*

**unborn** *(adj.)*: awaiting birth; baby; *child;* developing; expected; embryonic; future; fetal; growing; heretofore ~; infant; *just developing; kid; little;* maturing; not born; *ovule; progressing; quantum increase; ripening;* still-in-the-womb; *thriving;* unbirthed; *vitellus;* womb-inhabiting; *xenogenetic;* yet to be; zoon;

**unbreakable** *(adj.)*: ageless; bullet-proof; *continuous;* durable; everlasting; firm; *going on;* Herculean; indestructible; *jarless; keeps;* lasting; *mighty;* non-breakable; *ongoing;* permanent; *quality;* rock-solid; shatterproof; *tough; timeless;* unperishable; *very strong;* well-built; *x-cending; year-after-year; zero destruction;*

**unbreathable** *(adj.)*: awful; bad; choking; *deadly; evil;* foul; gaseous; horrendous; harmful; irrespirable; *jeopardous; killing;* loathsome; malevolent; noxious; offensive; polluted; *quad;* repugnant; suffocating; terrible; toxic; unendurable; vile; wretched; *x-out; yucky; zero tolerance;*

**unbroken** *(adj.)*: all together; always; *broad;* complete; continuous; *durable;* entire; endless; enduring; full; gapless; *high;* intact; jointless; *keep going;* lineal; macroscopic; non-abridged; ongoing; perfect; perpetual; *quality;* repeated; steady; total; undivided; uninterrupted; veritable; whole; *xtr.-good-condition; yare; zero breaks;* [*Ant.* unusable]

**uncaring** *(adj.)*: *aloof;* businesslike; callous; cold; cruel; disinterested; emotionless; frigid; *glaring;* hard-hearted; indifferent; jaded; knark; loveless; matter-of-fact; non-sympathetic; *objective;* pitiless; *quiet;* ruthless; steel-like; soulless; tough; unfeeling; *viewless;* withdrawn; *xerothalmic; yieldless;* zealless;

**unceasing** *(adj.)*: abiding; breakless; ceaseless; continual; *daily;* endless; fixed; *forever;* going on and on; *hourly;* incessant; *jusqu'au bout* [F.]; *keeps going;* lasting; *maintaining;* never-ending (-ceasing); ongoing; perpetual; *quadrillion;* repeated; steady; timeless; uninterrupted; unending; *vast;* without end; *xferring;* year-round; *zillion;*

**uncensored** *(adj.)*: allowed; boundless; completely free; *doable; enabled;* free; *go; have; indulged; justified;* kept; *liberty; most free;* non-censored; open; *permitted;* quite ~; restriction-free; *say anything;* totally ~; tolerated; unrestricted; uncontrolled; very free; without censorship; *xtry. freedom;* yet without censorship; *zero bounds;* [*Ant.* unallowed]

**uncertain** *(adj.)*: ambiguous; beclouded; confused; clouded; doubtful; equivocal; elusive; foggy; fuzzy; gray; hazy; iffy; imprecise; indecisive; irresolute; inconclusive; jerky; *kiaugh [Scot.];* leery; muddled; nebulous; not sure; obscure; parlous; precarious; questionable; *risky;* shaky; tentative; unsettled; unsure; unconfirmed; unclear; up-in-the-air; vague; vacillating; weak-minded; without certainty; wavering; *xtry. ambiguous;* yet unascertained; *zero certainty;* [*Ant.* unmistaken]

**uncertainty** *(n.)*: apprehension; ambiguity; bewilderment; confusion; doubt; dubiety; equivocalness; fogginess; fear; grayness; homonymy; hesitation; irresolution; indecisiveness; inconclusiveness; iffiness; jerkiness; kiaugh [Scot.]; leeriness; muddiness; non-certainty; nervousness; obscurity; precariousness; question; risk; reservation; shakiness; tentativeness; trepidation; uncertainness; unbelief; vagueness; waffling; *xtry. doubt; yet uncertain;* zero confidence;

**unchangeable** *(adj.)*: absolute; always-the-same; bound; changeless; determinate; ever the same; fixed; guaranteed; having no change; irreversible; immutable; *just the same;* keeping the same; lasting; moveless; non-alterable; *obstinate;* permanent; quite ~; rigid; reverseless; static; set; *timeless;* unalterable; vested; written in stone; *x-cending;* yet the same; *zero change;* [*Ant.* unpredictable]

**unchanging** *(adj.)*: alike; ageless; boundless; consistent; changeless; determinate; even; equal; fixed; *glorious;* homogenous; invariable; just the same; kept the same; like; matching; non-varying; ongoing; permanent; *quae est eadem* [L.]; rigid; same; steady; static; timeless; uniform; unvarying; very consistent; without change; *x-cending;* yieldless; *zero change;* [*Ant.* unpredictable]

**uncharacteristic** *(adj.)*: atypical; aberrant; bizarre; curious; different; deviant; enigmatic; erratic; freaky; gonzo; heterotypical; irregular; *jarring; kooky; loony; mysterious;* non-characteristic; out-of-character; odd; peculiar; Pickwickian; queer; *rare;* strange; *twisted;* unusual; variant; weird; *xenomorphic; yo-yoish;* zonky; [*Ant.* usual]

**uncivilized** *(adj.)*: aboriginal; barbaric; backward; crude; *devilish; evil;* feral; godless; heathen; ill-mannered; jungli; kaf [arch.]; loutish; mean; nasty; outlandish; pagan; *queer;* rough; rude; savage; tameless; uncouth; unchristian; underdeveloped; vulgar; wild; *xenophobic; yahoo; zhlubby;* [*Ant.* urbane]
**unclean** *(adj.)*: adulterated; besmirched; contaminated; defiled; dirty; *erring;* foul; grimy; *hateful;* impure; infected; immund; *javelled; kollowed;* loathsome; maculate; nasty; non-kosher; offensive; polluted; *quad;* reprehensible; sullied; sinful; tainted; unwashed; unwashen; vile; wretched; *x;* yucky; *zero cleanness;* [*Ant.* unsullied]
**unclear** *(adj.)*: amorphous; blurry; cloudy; dim; equivocal; fuzzy; *general;* hazy; indistinct; indefinite; indistinguishable; ill-defined; indiscernable; imprecise; indefinable; *jellyish; kedging;* lour; misty; nebulous; obscure; problematic; *qually* [arch.]; *really difficult;* smoky; shadowy; turbid; uncertain; undefined; vague; wispy; *xtry. difficult; yet indistinguishable; zero clarity;* [*Ant.* unambiguous]
**unclothed** *(adj.)*: the altogether; bare; clothesless; disrobed; exposed; *flaunted; filthy;* garbless; *heedless;* indecent; immodest; *jade; kinky;* laid bare; lewd; *manifest;* naked; obscene; open; peeled; *quad;* revealed; stripped; scanty; stark naked; *tout ensemble* [F.]; undressed; unclad; visible; *without clothes;* x-rated; *yucky; zhlubby;* [*see* plain]
**uncluttered** *(adj.)*: arranged; bare; clean; clutter-free; dapper; *elegant;* fastidious; gemmy; hygienic; immaculate; jimp [Br.]; kempt; *lovely; mess-free;* neat; organized; orderly; picked-up; quaint; regimented; straitened up; shipshape; tidy; uniserial; very clean; well-kept; *xtry.; yet ~; zierlich* [G.]; [*Ant.* untidy]
**uncombed** *(adj.)*: *awful;* bedraggled; *cluttered;* disheveled; entangled; frowzy; grubby; haggard; intertwined; jumbled; knotted; *ludicrous;* messy; non-organized; outlandish; poky; quaggy; ruffled; scraggly; straggly; tangled; unkempt; untidy; *vile;* windswept; *x'ed;* yucky; *zany;*
**uncomfortable** *(adj.)*: apprehensive; awkward; bothered; bad; comfortless; difficult; distressing; edgy; embarrassing; fretful; grueling; hesitant; hurting; insecure; ill at ease; jittery; knotty; *lamentable;* miserable; nervous; overanxious; painful; problematic; *quirky;* rough; self-conscious; tense; troubled; uneasy; unpleasant; vexed; worried; *xenophobic; yemelich* [arch.]; *zapped;*
**uncommon** *(adj.)*: austere; bare; curious; distinctive; dear; exceptional; extraordinary; few(-and-far-between); geason; hard to find; infrequent; jimp; keenly ~; little-known (-seen); meager; most ~; non-usual; obscure; outstanding; peculiar; queer; rare; scarce; *totally foreign;* unusual; very ~; valuable; *wheen* [arch.]; xtry.; you-beaut [Aus.]; *zero;* [*see* precious; *Ant.* usual]
**uncommonly** *(adv.)*: atypically; barely; curiously; distinctly; exceptionally; extraordinarily; found rarely; greatly; hardly ever; infrequently; jimply; known to few; *leanly;* meagerly; not commonly; obscurely; peculiarly; *queerly;* rarely; remarkably; seldom; *tenuously;* unusually; unfrequently; very (seldom); *wheenly* [arch.]; *xtry.; yet ~; zero typicality;*
**uncompromising** *(adj.)*: adamant; bendless; committed; dependable; ever-faithful; faithful; good; hard; inflexible *jaw-set; keep;* loyal; most faithful; never-failing; obdurate; pertinacious; quite adamant; rigid; stubborn; true; unbending; very rigid; with fidelity; *xtry.;* yieldless; *zero compromise;*
**unconcerned** *(adj.)*: apathetic; blithe; carefree; calm; cool; careless; casual; complacent; dispassionate; easygoing; foolhardy; *gay;* happy-go-lucky; indifferent; improvident; jaunty; *keg-meg;* listless; laid-back; limpid; mellow; nonchalant; offhand; peaceful; *quiet;* relaxed; serene; thoughtless; unworried; unflappable; unmindful; unsympathetic; *vapid;* wareless; *xenarthrous;* yareless; zealless;
**unconditional** *(adj.)*: absolute; all-out; *bonded;* categorical; definite; ever-effective; firm; guaranteed; *heroic;* irrevocable; *just positive; kit and caboodle;* limitless; most certain; non-conditional; outright; pure; quite irrevocable; resounding; sure; total; termless; unqualified; unmitigated; unreserved; veritable; without provisos (-reservation); *x on the dotted line; yafery* [arch.]; *zero conditions;*
**unconfessed** *(adj.)*: awaiting judgment; biding; continuing; *due;* enduring; *fault; guilty;* hanging on; iniquitous; *justified;* kept; lingering; left over; *miscreant;* non-confessed; outstanding; pending; *quite sinful;* remaining; still remaining; tarrying; undealt-with; *vile;* wicked; *xfer; yet ~; zero confession made;*

**unconfirmed** *(adj.)*: assumed; alleged; believed; conjectured; deduced; expected; *feeble; guessed;* groundless; hearsay; invalidated; indefinite; *just thought; keenly-imagined; led to believe;* much-believed; non-confirmed; only hearsay; presumed; questionable; rumored; supposed; thought; tenuous; unverified; unproven; vague; without grounds; *xtr. doubt;* yet ~; *zazen;* [*Ant.* upheld]

**unconscionable** *(adj.)*: amazing; bizarre; *crazy;* disagreeable; *evil;* fantastic; fanciful; far-fetched; *grossly unacceptable;* hard-to-believe; implausible; inconceivable; just unimaginable; *kooky;* ludicrous; mind-boggling; non-believable; outrageous; preposterous; *questionable;* ridiculous; shocking; *terrible;* unthinkable; unreasonable; unbelievable; *ungodly;* vaporous; *wild; xtry.;* y.; *za-zum* [Rus.];

**unconscious** *(adj.)*: asleep; blacked out; comatose; down for the count; estivating; fallen ~; *fainted; gone;* half-awake; insensible; *just asleep;* knocked out; *laid out;* mindless; numb; necromorphous; out (cold); passed out; quiet; *resting;* sleeping; *taking a nap;* unawake; under; vegetative; wakeless; *x-sleep;* yet to be conscious; zonked out;

**unconsciousness** *(n.)*: asleep; blacking out; coma; deep sleep; estivation; falling unconsious; *gone;* hibernation; insensibility; *just asleep;* knocking out; *laid out; motionless;* necromorphosis; *out (cold);* passing out; quietute; *resting;* sopor; *taking a nap; unawake; vegetation;* wakelessness; *x-sleep; yet to wake;* zonking out;

**unconventional** *(adj.)*: alternative; avant-garde; bizarre; crazy; deviational; experimental; enigmatic; far-out; goofy; heterotypical; irregular; innovative; *jokey;* kooky; *loony;* maverick; nonconformist; non-traditional; original; odd; off-key; offbeat; peculiar; quirky; queer; *ridiculous;* strange; *totally weird;* unorthodox; variant; weird; way-out; *xtry.; yawed;* zany; [*Ant.* usual]

**uncooperative** *(adj.)*: adverse; balky; contumacious; disobedient; ever-stubborn; flouting; *grim;* headstrong; inflexible; jaw-set; *knocking; lousy attitude;* mulish; non-bending; obstructive; pigheaded; querulous; resistant; stubborn; tenacious; unyielding; very stubborn; willful; *x-grained;* yieldless; *zero give;* [*see* proud; *Ant.* unresisting]

**uncoordinated** *(adj.)*: awkward; bumbling; clumsy; dowdy; *étourderie* [F.]; fumbly; gangly; graceless; gimpy; heavy-handed; inelegant; jumbly; klutzy; lumbering; maladroit; non-graceful; oafish; plumbeous; *quirky; rube;* socially inept; troublesome; ungainly; ungraceful; *vexatious;* wooden; *xtry. inept;* yokelish; zhlubby;

**uncouth** *(adj.)*: abhorrent; base; coarse; degraded; evil; filthy; gauche; gross; horrendous; indecent; ill-mannered; *jaded;* kitsch; lewd; loathsome; mean; miserable; nefarious; offensive; obscene; perverted; pathetic; *quad;* repugnant; rude; rough; squalid; tasteless; tactless; unclean; unrefined; vulgar; wretched; *x-rated;* yucky; zhlubby; [*Ant.* urbane]

**uncover** *(v.)*: ascertain; bare; bring to light; come across; discover; expose; evince; find out; *get;* hold forth; identify; *jump into;* kithe [Scot.]; lay bare; learn; make known; *notice;* open; pinpoint; *qualify;* reveal; show; turn up; unveil; uncloak; unearth; *venture upon; watch; x-search; yead;* zero-concealment;

**undaunted** *(adj.)*: audacious; brave; courageous; daring; enterprising; fearless; gallant; heroic; impervious; *jarless; knightly;* lion-hearted; *manly;* never-fearing; *obstinate;* plucky; questful; resolute; stout; temerarious; unflinching; undisturbed; valorous; *wherewithal; xtry.; yare; zealous;* [*Ant.* unnerved]

**undecided** *(adj.)*: ambiguous; borderline; changing; double-minded; dithering; ever-changing; fickle; *going back and forth;* hesitant; indefinite; irresolute; indeterminate; *jumping; kaleidoscopic;* lacking decisiveness; mutable; not settled; obscure; open; pendulating; questionable; reluctant; shaky; teeter-tottering; unsure; undetermined; unsettled; vacillating; wavering; *x-ing;* yet ~; *zero decisiveness;* [*Ant.* unanimous]

**undeniable** *(adj.)*: assured; beyond doubt; certain; definite; evident; firm; guaranteed; highly confident; indisputable; incontestable; irrefutable; incontrovertible; just sure; keenly sure; *legitimate;* mistake-proof; non-questionable; 100% sure; patent; questionless; reliable; sure; true; unquestionable; unarguable; verified; without doubt; xtry. sure; *yes;* zero doubt; [*Ant.* unproven]

**undercurrent** *(n.)*: *afflux;* backflow; crosscurrent; deflow; ebb; flow back; gush; headwind; influx; jetstream; *kickback; liquid;* movement back; naid; opposing flow; *profluence; quell;* reflux; reflow; stream; tide; undertow; underset; *vomiting;* wash; x-current; *yern;* zwoosh;
**underestimate** *(v.)*: assess too low; belittle; consider too low; disappreciate; disprize; disvalue; estimate too low; figure too low; give too low a value; *humiliate;* insult; *jibe; knock; low estimate;* misjudge; misdeem; misprize; not esteem; *off;* put down; *quib;* ridicule; set at naught; think too little of; trivialize; undervalue (-rate); *underquote;* value too low; wipe; *xuld [arch.];* yock; zeroize;
**undergird** *(v.)*: *assist;* buttress; bolster; brace; carry; *double;* encourage; fortify; give assistance; hold up; help; *improve;* janker; keep up; lend support; maintain; *nail; overprotect;* prop up; *quick-to-help;* reinforce; support; strengthen; toughen; underprop; uphold; upbear; *vest; well-sustained; xfer;* yomp; zero hindrance; [*Ant.* undermine]
**underground** *(adj.)*: all- ~; belowground; buried; covered; deep in the earth; endogenic; *funeralized;* grounded; hypogene; hypogeal; in the earth; *jacketed; kist;* lying under the surface; *mantled;* not above ground; *overlayed;* put in the ground; *quarried;* recessed in the earth; subterranean; subterraneous; tucked in the earth; undersurface; *verge; whelmed; xenotransplanted;* yet ~; *zet [dial.];* [see secretive; hidden]
**undermine** *(v.)*: attenuate; bring down; controvert; damage; disserve; discredit; destabilize; erode; frustrate; *grieve;* hurt; impair; injure; jeel; knock the bottom out of; lessen influence; make ineffective; *nonplus;* overthrow (-turn); *perfidy; question;* ruin; subvert; tear down; undercut; undo; usurp; vandalize; weaken; *x-out;* yank down; zeroize; [*Ant.* undergird]
**underscore** *(v.)*: accentuate; *bring out;* call attention to; draw attention to; emphasize; feature; give emphasis to; highlight; *italicize; important; jump out;* keep focus on; lay stress upon; mark; *noticeable;* overemphasize; point out (-up); *quite emphasize;* red-underline; stress; *triple- ~;* underline; *value; weight; x-emphasis; yed;* zero in; [*Ant.* underemphasize]
**understand** *(v.)*: apprehend; absorb; *aware;* believe; comprehend; command; conceptualize; discern; *expect;* fathom; grasp; get; grip; gather; glom; have understanding; incept; imbibe; *judge;* know; ken; learn; latch on; make out (-sense); naw [dial.]; *own;* perceive; pick up; *questionless;* realize; see; take; *unmysterious; visualize;* wot; wist; *xenodiagnosis;* yeme; zero in;
**understandable** *(adj. comprehensible)*: apparent; absorbable; *basic;* clear; comprehensible; discernable; explicit; easy-to-understand; fathomable; graspable; *handle it;* intelligible; *just plain;* knowable; learnable; logical; lucid; manifest; non-confusing; obvious; perceivable; pellucid; plain; questionless; recognizable; simple; straightforward; self-explanatory; transparent; unambiguous; uncomplicated; very easy; well-structured; *xparent;* yet ~; zero confusion; [*Ant.* unexplainable]
**understandable** *(adj. justified)*: admissible; allowable; *becoming;* correct; defensible; explainable; excusable; forgivable; *good; helpable;* indemnifiable; justifiable; *kosher;* legitimate; maintainable; necessary; okay; proper; quite ~; reasonable; suitable; *tolerable;* uncondemned; valid; warrantable; *xferable;* yet ~; zero problem; [*Ant.* unforgivable]
**understanding** *(n. comprehension)*: apprehension; awareness; *belief;* comprehension; command; conception; discernment; erudition; fancy; fix; grasp; grip; *hindsight;* insight; illumination; judgment; knowledge; ken; learning; *light;* mental apprehension; *notion; ownership;* perception; perceptiveness; percipience; *quick-sighted;* realization; sense; *take; thought; unmysterious;* visualization; wisdom; xtry. ~; *yeme [arch.];* zero problem; [*Ant.* uncertainty]
**understanding** *(n. sympathy)*: altruism; benevolence; compassion; *deeply ~;* empathy; feeling; forgiveness; grace; heart; identification; *joy-giving;* kindness; loving-kindness; leniency; mercy; niceness; oneness; pity; pathos; quarter; ruth; sympathy; tolerance; uncallousness; *virtue;* warmth; *xenia;* yearning; *zeal to forgive;*

**understate** *(v.)*: *assess too low;* belittle; curtail; devalue; estimate too low; figure too low; give too low an opinion; *hold too low; insult; jibe; knock; low estimate;* minimize; make little of; not state correctly; *off;* play down; *questionable;* reduce to nothing; set at nought; tone down; trivialize; underestimate; underrate; value too low; whitewash; xtr. *mild; yet ~d; zeroize;* [Ant. underscore]

**undertaker** *(n.)*: administrator; burial supervisor; cemetery worker; *director;* embalmer; funeral director; grave digger; headstone salesman; interrer; *job;* keeper; *lych-gate;* mortician; *necropolis;* ossuarium director; pollinctor; qualified mortician; *repository;* supervisor; tombstone-seller; upholder; vault-keeper; worker; *xat;* yard manager; *ziarats;*

**undertaking** *(n.)*: assignment; business; charge; commission; chore; duty; enterprise; errand; *function; goal;* handling; handiwork; *incumbency;* job; *key role;* liability; mission; necessity; obligation; post; purpose; *quest;* responsibility; striving; task; unction; vocation; work; xci.; *yoke; zealous task;*

**underwater** *(adj.)*: aquatic; awash; abyssopelagic; bathymetrical; below-surface; (completely) covered; deep-sea; *engulfed;* flooded; *grallatorial* [zoo.]; hydrospace; immersed; *just below; keld;* limnetic; marine; neritic; oceanic; pelagic; *quai;* river(-bottom); submarine; sea; sub-aquatic; subaqueous; submerged; thalassic; undersea; *voe;* water-dwelling; *xyrisic; yeo; Zee* [G.];

**undeserved** *(adj.)*: *absolutely ~;* by grace; completely ~; discriminatory; *excessive; false;* gracious; *humane;* inequitable; inordinate; justiceless; *kindness;* lacking merit; *munificent; merciful;* non-earned; not deserved; obtained-by-grace; purely gracious; quite ~; *ruth;* so ~; totally ~; unwarranted; unmerited; unearned; undue; unfair; *very unwarranted;* without merit; xtr. *measure of grace;* yet ~; *zero merit;*

**undesirable** *(adj.)*: awful; adverse; bad; contemptible; disagreeable; distasteful; *de trop* [F.]; execrable; foul; gross; horrible; invidious; jarring; kindless; lousy; loathsome; miserable; nasty; nauseating; non-desirable; *non grata* [L.]; objectionable; offensive; *poor; quad;* repulsive; sickening; stomach-turning; terrible; unwanted; unenviable; unwelcome; unpleasant; vile; wicked; xtr. ; yucky; *zero pleasure;*

**undetectable** *(adj.)*: *à perte de vue* [F.]; *behind the scenes;* concealed; *disguised;* ever-invisible; furtive; *ghostlike; hidden;* imperceptible; invisible; *jape;* kept out of view; *low-visibility;* mysterious; non-detectable; obscure; perceived not; quite unperceived; real quiet; silent; secretive; transparent; unperceivable; unnoticeable; veiled; without notice; xtry. ~; yet undiscovered; zero perception; [Ant. unhidden]

**undeveloped** *(adj.)*: adolescent; baby-stage; childhood-stage; depauperate; developing; early-stage; fledgling; green; hastive; immature; juvenile; kiddish; little; maturing; not fully grown; *over-young;* puerile; partial; *quite young;* rudimentary; small; tender; underdeveloped; unripe; vernal; wee; XS; young; *zero maturity;*

**undiluted** *(adj.)*: absolute; *biggest;* complete; distilled; *entire;* full-strength; *genuine;* highest-concentration; intense; *just; kept at full-strength; lacking dilution;* maximum-strength; neat; non-diluted; one-hundred percent; pure; *potent; quality;* robust; straight; *total;* unmixed; unweakened; virgin; whole; *x-tra strength;* yet ~; *zero admixture;*

**undisputed** *(adj.)*: acknowledged; beyond question; certain; definite; established; firm; granted; held by all; irrefutable; irrefragable; *just plain as day;* known by all; *legitimate;* manifest; non-disputed; open; *positive;* questionless; recognized; self-evident; *true;* undeniable; veritable; well-established; xtr. *certain;* yet ~; zero doubt; [Ant. unsettled]

**undisturbed** *(adj.)*: all-composing; becalmed; calm; docile; easeful; friendly; gentle; harmonious; idyllic; *jarless; keeping peace; likeable;* motionless; nonviolent; *orderly;* peaceful; quiescent; quiet; restful; still; tranquil; untroubled; *violence-free; waveless; xenial; yieldful; zealous of peace;* [Ant. upset]

**undo** *(v.)*: abrogate; annul; blot; cancel; delete; eliminate; eradicate; efface; erase; fix; get rid of; *halt;* invalidate; *junk;* kill; kibosh; *let go;* make an end of; nullify; negate; *obliterate;* purge; quash; rid; rub; scratch; strike; terminate; unmake; void; *wipe out;* x; *yank;* zero out;

**undoing** *(n.)*: abasement; breakup; cessation; collapse; downfall; end; fall; *going down;* humiliation; invalidation; *jaws of death; killing;* liquidation; mortality; nullification; overthrow; perishing; *quietus;* ruination; subversion; termination; unravel; vanishing; waterloo; *x-ing out; yielding up; zonking out [slang];*
**undress** *(v.)*: *abare* [arch.]; bare; cast off; disrobe; divest; denude; denudate; doff; expose; *flaunt;* get undressed; *have no clothes on; indecent; jerk off clothes; kinky;* lay bare; make bare; molt; nakedize; *nudation; overexpose; open;* peel; *quad;* remove clothes; strip; take off; unclothe; unapparel; *vaunt; without clothes; x-rated;* yank off; zip off;
**undue** *(adj.)*: *above;* beyond reason; *crazy;* disproportionate; excessive; far above; gratuitous; inappropriate; inordinate; *jumbo; king-sized; large; more than enough;* not needed; out-of-place; poorly chosen; *questionable;* ridiculous; *substantial;* too much; unwarranted; undeserved; unjustifiable; unneeded; very high; wrong; xtry.; yet unwarranted; *zero suitability;*
**unearth** *(v.)*: *abstract;* bring out; come up with; dig up; disinter; discover; excavate; exhume; expose; find; get out; happen upon; *intrench; jenkin;* kithe [Scot.]; locate; mine; *no longer hidden;* open; pull out; *quarry;* reveal; *show;* take out; uncover; *venture upon;* work with spade; *xfer; yede; zanja;*
**unearthly** *(adj.)*: abnormal; bizarre; creepy; disturbing; eerie; fearful; ghastly; hair-raising; intimidating; jarring; knee-knocking; lurid; macabre; nerve-racking; ominous; paranormal; peculiar; queer; *reluctant;* supernatural; terrifying; unnatural; vexatious; weird; *xenophobic; ydrad* [arch.]; zonic; [Ant. usual]
**uneasiness** *(n.)*: apprehension; *bothered;* care; dismay; discomposure; *exasperation;* fear; gloom; hesitation; insecurity; jitters; kiaugh [Scot.]; lack of easiness; misgiving; nervousness; over-anxiety; panickiness; quaking; reluctance; stress; trepidation; unrest; vexation; worry; *xenophobia; yellow-belliedness; zeallessness;* [Ant. undauntedness]
**uneasy** *(adj.)*: anxious; apprehensive; bothered; concerned; disturbed; distressed; edgy; fretful; gutless; hesitant; insecure; ill at ease; jittery; jumpy; keyed up; lily-livered; *moody;* nervous; overanxious; perturbed; peaceless; quaky; restless; squirmish; troubled; uncomfortable; vexed; worried; *xenophobic; yemelich* [arch.]; *zapped;* [Ant. undaunted]
**uneducated** *(adj.)*: *amateur;* badly schooled; childlike; deprived; empty-headed; *foolish;* gullible; *hillbilly;* ignorant; ill-educated; *juvenile;* knowledge-deprived; lumpen; lacking education; moronic; non-educated; oblivious; poorly educated; *quirky;* rude; simple; *tutorless;* unlearned; uninstructed; untaught; unschooled; verdant; wide-eyed; *xtry. ignorant;* yokelish; zhlubby;
**unemotional** *(adj.)*: affectless; aloof; businesslike; cold; composed; detached; dispassionate; emotionless; flinty; glacial; hard; inexpressive; impassive; inexcitable; jaded; knark; loveless; matter-of-fact; nonemotional; objective; pokerfaced; passionless; *quiet;* repressed; steel-like; spiritless; tough; unfeeling; unmoved; vapid; withdrawn; wooden; *xerothalmic;* yareless; zombie-like;
**unemployed** *(adj.)*: axed; booted out; canned; dismissed; *expelled;* fired; gone *job-hunting;* hard-core unemployed; idle; jobless; *kicked out;* looking for employment; *mostly out of work;* non-employed; out-of-work; *pink-slipped; quashed; removed from position;* searching for a job; technologically ~; unworking; *void;* without employment; *x'ed out;* yet ~; *zero employment;*
**unending** *(adj.)*: abiding; breakless; continual; ceaseless; day and night; endless; everlasting; fixed; *forever;* gapless; *hourly;* infinite; *jusqu'au bout* [F.]; *keeps going;* lasting; *maintaining;* nonstop; never-ceasing; ongoing; perpetual; *quadrillion;* relentless; repeated; steady; *timeless;* undying; unceasing; unbroken; *vast;* without end; *xferring;* year-round; *zillion;*
**unequal** *(adj.)*: asymmetrical; biased; *contrary;* dissimilar; disparate; *erratic; flawed; great disparity;* heterogeneous; inequitable; incongruous; incommensurate; imbalanced; *justiceless; knavish;* lopsided; mismatched; nonsimilar; one-sided; off-balance; partial; *queer; reverse;* slanted; tilted; unbalanced; unequivalent; uneven; unfair; variable; warped; wrongful; *xenomorphic; yawed; zero equality;* [Ant. unbiased]

**unequalled** *(adj.)*: amazing; *the* best; choicest; distinguished; extraordinary; fantastic; great; highest; incomparable; *jim-dandy;* keenest; leading; matchless; nonpareil; outstanding; peerless; *quantum* [L.]; remarkable; superior; top; unmatched; unparalleled; unrivaled; *very good;* without equal; xtry.; *yondmost; zenithal;*

**unerring** *(adj.)*: accurate; *bearing true;* certain; correct; definite; error-free; flawless; faultless; good; *honest;* infallible; inerrant; impeccable; immaculate; *justifiable; keenly accurate; legitimate;* mistake-proof; non-fallible; 100% sure; perfect; positive; question-less; reliable; sure; true; unmistaken; unimpeachable; veritable; verifiable; *well-tried; x-parent; yes;* zero-defect; [*Ant.* unsound]

**unethical** *(adj.)*: artful; bad; crooked; disreputable; dishonorable; evasive; *evil;* fraudulent; guileful; honorless; ignoble; jackleg; knavish; lying; misconducted; non-credible; opportunistic; perfidious; quasi-ethical; ruthless; shady; treacherous; unscrupulous; unprincipled; venal; wily; *x-ing;* yeggy; *zero honesty;* [*Ant.* upright]

**uneven** *(adj.)*: asperous; asymmetrical; bumpy; crooked; disproportionate; disparate; *erratic;* flim-flam; *grotesque;* hunchbacked; irregular; jaggy; kim-kam; lopsided; mismatched; malapportioned; non-symmetrical; out-of-balance; proportionless; queer-looking; rough; sloping; *top-heavy;* unfair; unbalanced; unsymmetrical; varying; without symmetry; *xy-discordant;* yawed; zad; [*Ant.* uniform]

**uneventful** *(adj.)*: average; boring; commonplace; dull; *empty;* flat; generic; humdrum; insipid; jejune; *known;* lackluster; mundane; non-exciting; ordinary; plain; quotidian; routine; standard; typical; unexciting; uninteresting; vapid; wearisome; *xtry. boring;* yawnful; zestless;

**unexplainable** *(adj.)*: arcane; baffling; cabalistic; dark; enigmatic; furtive; *guarded;* hidden; inexplicable; *jumbled; knotted; labyrinthine;* mysterious; non-understandable; *odd;* past finding out; puzzling; *question; recondite;* searchless; transcendental; unsearchable; unaccountable; veiled; wildering; *xtry.; yieldless; zero understanding;* [*Ant.* understandable]

**unfair** *(adj.)*: *abominable;* biased; crooked; discriminatory; disingenuous; dishonest; *evil;* false; foul; *godless; gap; hardly fair;* inequitable; incommensurate; inordinate; invidious; justiceless; *knavish;* lopsided; *mismatched;* nonequitable; nonobjective; one-sided; partial; *quad; ruthless;* slanted; tilted; unjust; unrighteous; undeserved; unsportsmanlike; *venal;* wrongful; warped; *xiaoren; yeggy; zero justice;* [*Ant.* unbiased]

**unfaithful** *(adj.)*: adulterous; betraying; backstabbing; crooked; disloyal; evil; false; faithless; guileful; honorless; inconstant; jadish; knavish; lying; mutinous; non-loyal; *opportunistic;* perfidious; quisling; recreant; seditious; traitorous; treacherous; untrue; violent; wicked; *x-ing; yeggy; zero honesty;* [*Ant.* unfailing]

**unfaithfulness** *(n.)*: adultery; betrayal; cuckoldry; debauchery; disloyalty; *evil;* faithlessness; *gross infidelity; harlotry;* infidelity; *jadery; kinkiness;* lasciviousness; *looseness; mischief;* non-faithfulness; *offense;* promiscuity; *queanery;* revelry; sin; treachery; ungodliness; venery; whoredom; *x-rated behavior; yielding; zhlubbery;*

**unfaltering** *(adj.)*: adamant; *bull-headed;* constant; determined; ever-steady; firm; *going on;* high-resolved; indefatigable; *jusqu'au bout* [F.]; keeping up; lasting; mulish; never-faltering; ongoing; persistent; *quenchless;* resolute; steady; tenacious; unwavering; unshaken; unwearying very firm; well-resolved; *x-cending;* yieldless; *zero give;* [*Ant.* unsteady]

**unfamiliar** *(adj.)*: alien; *bizarre; curious;* different; exotic; foreign; *groping;* heterotypical; irregular; *jokey; kooky; left-field;* mysterious; new; odd; peculiar; queer; recherché; strange; *too strange;* unacquainted; unversed; unknown; unaccustomed; unaware; *variant;* weird; *xenomorphic; yawed*; zany;

**unfashionable** *(adj.)*: antiquated; behind the times; *ceased;* dated; expired; far-out; *gone off the scene;* has-been; inoperative; junked; kaput; long-retired; moribund; naff; out(dated); passé; queer; *retired; superseded; terminated;* unpopular; uncool; *vestigial;* worn-out; *x'ed; yesteryear; zero;* [*Ant.* up-to-date]

**unfasten** *(v.)*: *apart;* break off; come apart; detach (from); disconnect; disengage; ease; free; get apart; *have open; isolate; jerk apart; knock apart;* loose(n); make separate; *non-attached;* open; part; *quarter;* release; slacken; separate; take off; unattach; unbutton; uncatch; unclasp; uncouple; undo; unfix; ungird; unhook; unlace; untie; unsnap; unyoke; unzip; unloose(n); untether; *vell; wide open; x-sect; yandy;* zip open; [*Ant.* unite]

**unfathomable** *(adj.)*: arcane; beyond comprehension; countless; deep; ever-mysterious; fathomless; great; *high;* inconceivable; incomprehensible; *just too high;* kithless; limitless; mind-blowing; non-fathomable; *over one's head;* profound; quantum; *ridiculous; real hard; stupefying;* too deep (-great); unthinkable; unimaginable; ungraspable; unconscionable; unknowable; vast; *wild;* xtry.; y.; *zero understanding;* [*Ant.* understandable]

**unfavorable** *(adj.)*: adverse; bad; contrary; disagreeable; detrimental; execrable; foul; grievous; harmful; inauspicious; ill-favored; jarring; kindless; lousy; miserable; negative; objectionable; poor; *quad;* recalcitrant; severe; terrible; undesirable; very bad; wicked; *xtry. bad;* yucky; *zero pleasure;*

**unfeasible** *(adj.)*: *absurd;* beyond realistic; contrary to reason; doomed to failure; *extraordinary; fat chance;* grim; hopeless; impractical; impossible; inoperable; idealistic; just impossible; *knot-headed;* Laputan; ludicrous; *mad;* non-practical; out of question; pie-in-the-sky; questionable; quixotic; ridiculous; *shaky;* totally ~; unworkable; unrealistic; untenable; unviable; *virtually ~;* without a chance; *x;* yet untenable; zero chance; [*Ant.* useful]

**unfeeling** *(adj.)*: aloof; businesslike; cold; callous; disinterested; emotionless; frigid; glacial; heartless; hard(-hearted); hardened; insensitive; indurate; jaded; knark; loveless; matter-of-fact; non-sympathetic; obtuse; pitiless; *quiet;* repressed; steel-like; tough; tearless; unsympathetic; unmoved; uncaring; unaffected; *viewless;* wooden; *xerothalmic;* yieldless; zombie-like; [*see.* numb]

**unfit** *(adj.)*: amiss; bad; *contrary;* deficient; erroneous; faulty; *groundless;* highly inappropriate; improper; incorrect; inappropriate; *jim-jam; kim-kam;* lousy; mismatched; malapropos; non-suited; out-of-place; poor; questionable; reprehensible; *substandard;* terrible; unbecoming; unseemly; un(be)fitting; unsuitable; *vile;* wrong; *xgressing;* yucky; *zero propriety:*

**unfold** *(v.)*: appear; become visible; come; develop; disclose; disentangle; emerge; expand; extend; fan out; *grow;* happen; irrupt; *jump in;* kithe [Scot.]; lay open; materialize; manifest itself; *non-concealed;* open (up); outstretch; progress; *quicken;* reveal; spread (out); tell; unwrap; unfurl; unroll; *visible;* widen; *xfer;* yede; *zip out;* [*Ant.* upbind]

**unforeseen** *(adj.)*: accidental; beyond knowing; chance; concealed; destinal; extraordinary; fluky; fortuitous; fated; *great;* hidden; inadvertent; indeterminate; inconceivable; *just didn't know;* known to none; *little known;* mysterious; non-anticipated; out of the blue; precipitant; quite ~; *remarkable;* sudden; surprising; *took one by surprise;* unintended; unexpected; unanticipated; veiled; without warning; xtry.; yet ~; *zero understanding;*

**unforgettable** *(adj.)*: amazing; big; celebrated; distinguished; extraordinary; fantastic; great; highly ~; impressive; *just amazing;* keen; like no other; memorable; notable; outstanding; permanently etched in memory; quite ~; recallable; remarkable; special; significant; tremendous; *unforgotten;* very ~; worth remembering; xtry.; *yet unforgotten; zero forgetting;* [*Ant.* unmemorable]

**unforgivable** *(adj.)*: abominable; beyond forgiveness; condemnable; damnable; execrable; flagitious; *guilty; horrendous;* inexcusable; inexpiable; indefensible; irremissible; *jailable; keeping record; loathsome;* mortal; non-justifiable; over the line; punishable; *quad;* reprehensible; scandalous; *tarnishing;* unjustifiable; unwarrantable; unpardonable; very indefensible; *wicked; xtry.;* yet inexcusable; zero grace; [*Ant.* understandable]

**unforgiving** *(adj.)*: angry; avenging; bitter; cruel; despiteful; embittered; foul; galsome; hateful; implacable; jaded; kindless; loathsome; malicious; nasty; obdurate; pitiless; *quede* [arch.]; resentful; spiteful; *treacherous;* ungracious; vengeful; wicked; *xenophobic;* yucky; zealotic; [*Ant.* understanding]

**unfortunate** *(adj.)*: adverse; bad; calamitous; disturbing; disadvantaged; disastrous; evil; fateful; fortuneless; grievous; hapless; inauspicious; ill-fated; Jonahesque; *killing;* luckless; lamentable; misfortunate; *nebbich* [Yid.]; ominous; pitiable; queer-lucked; regrettable; sad; sorry; successless; terrible; unhappy; unlucky; very bad; woeful; xtry. bad; *yucky; zero luck;*
**unfounded** *(adj.)*: absurd; baseless; causeless; delusory; erroneous; foundationless; false; groundless; highly questionable; idiopathic; just for no reason; *keenly off;* lacking basis; misconceived; made-up; not justified; off base; phantasmal; questionable; reasonless; speculative; shaky; tenuous; uncaused; unsupported; unsubstantiated; unbacked; unconvincing; unconfirmed; unvalidated; *vague;* without foundation; weak; *xtry.;* yet unconfirmed; *zero foundation;* [Ant. unquestionable]
**unfriendly** *(adj.)*: antagonistic; belligerent; contentious; dour; enemy; fractious; grumpy; galsome; hostile; inimical; jingoish; kindless; *loathsome;* malicious; nasty; odious; pugnacious; quarrelsome; rough; standoffish; threatening; uncongenial; unsociable; violent; warlike; *xenophobic; yieldless; zealotic;*
**unfruitful** *(adj.)*: arid; addle; barren; childless; desolate; destitute; devoid; empty; effete; forlorn; gaunt; heirless; infertile; jejune; *kept from bearing;* lacking; meager-fruited; non-bearing; olated; paltry; *quenchless;* resourceless; sterile; teemless; unverdant; unfertile; unproductive; verdureless; wanting; without issue; *xerarch;* yieldless; *zero fruit;*
**ungainly** *(adj.)*: awkward; bumbling; clumsy; dowdy; *étourderie* [F.]; fumbly; gangly; gawky; gimpy; heavy-handed; inelegant; jumbly; klutzy; lumbering; maladroit; non-graceful; oafish; plumbeous; *quirky; rube;* socially inept; troublesome; ungraceful; uncoordinated; *vexatious;* wooden; *xtry. inelegant;* yokelish; zhlubby;
**ungodliness** *(n.)*: abomination; badness; corruption; debauchery; evil; fallenness; godlessness; heinousness; iniquity; *jadedness; knavishness;* licentiousness; mischief; naughtiness; obduracy; perverseness; *quad;* rebellion; sin(fulness); transgression; unrighteousness; virulence; wickedness; *xgression; yetzer hara* [Heb.]; *zymosis;* [Ant. unworldliness]
**ungodly** *(adj.)*: abominable; bad; corrupt; debauched; evil; errant; foul; godless; heinous; iniquitous; *jaded; knavish;* licentious; mischievous; naughty; obdurate; perverse; *quad;* rebellious; sinful; transgressing; unrighteous; virulence; wicked; *xgressing;* yucky; *zymotic;* [Ant. unworldly]
**ungraceful** *(adj.)*: awkward; bumbling; clumsy; cumbersome; dowdy; *étourderie* [F.]; fumbly; graceless; hulky; inelegant; jumbly; klutzy; lumbering; maladroit; non-graceful; oafish; ponderous; *quirky; rube;* socially inept; stiff; troublesome; ungainly; unwieldy; unlovely; undignified; uncouth; *vexatious;* wooden; *xtry. bad;* yokelish; zhlubby;
**unhappiness** *(n.)*: anguish; blueness; cheerlessness; discontentedness; downheartedness; emptiness; forlornness; grief; heartache; inconsolableness; joylessness; katzenjammer; lowness; melancholy; misery; negativism; overmuch sorrow; piteousness; *quivering;* restlessness; ruefulness; sadness; sorrow; trouble; uncheerfulness; unfulfillment; vapors; woe; *xtry. sad; yearning;* zestlessness;
**unhappy** *(adj.)*: *affected;* anguished; blue; blissless; cheerless; crestfallen; discontent(ed); displeased; dissatisfied; downcast; elegaic; forlorn; glum; grief-stricken; grieved; heartbroken; heavy (of heart); inconsolable; joyless; keening; low; lachrymose; melancholic; miserable; mournful; negative; overcast; poignant; *quivering;* rueful; sad; sorrowful; sore displeased; tristful; upset; uncheerful; unsatisfied; very sad; woeful; wistful; *xtry, displeasure; yearnful;* zestless; [Ant. uplifted]
**unharmed** *(n.)*: all right; bodily intact; complete; *dandy;* entire; fine; good; healthy; intact; just fine; *kept intact; lovely; most ~;* non-injured; okay; perfectly fine; preserved; pristine; *quartful* [arch.]; *right;* safe (and sound); totally fine; unscathed; uninjured, unhurt; undamaged; unmolested; very well; whole; *xtry.;* yet ~; *zero harm;*
**unhealthy** *(adj.)*: ailing; adverse; bad; cachectic; detrimental; damaging; evil-affected; foul; germy; hazardous; harmful; infirm; ill; innutritious; injurious; jeopardous; *killing;* languishing; morbose; noisome; noxious; ominous; peccant; pestilent; quite ~; *rotten;* risky; sickly; toxic; unsound; unhealthful; unhygienic; unwholesome; vile; weakened; way bad [slang]; *xtry. bad; yucky; zero nutrition;*

**unholy** *(adj.)*: abominable; bad; cruel; devilish; evil; foul; guilty; heinous; iniquitous; jaded; kindless; luciferian; malevolent; nefarious; *odious;* pernicious; quad; ruthless; satanic; sinister; terrible; unrighteous; unchristian; villainous; vile; worldly; wicked; *xgressing; yeffell* [arch.]; *zarlike;* [*Ant.* unworldly]

**unhurried** *(adj.)*: arrested; ambling; *backward;* casual; crawling; dallying; easy; flagging; gradual; halting; hasteless; half-hearted; indolent; inching; *jog trot;* kef; leisurely; laggard; *moderate;* non-rushed; obstupefactive; poky; quiescent; relaxed; retarded; slow; tortoiselike; unaccelerated; *vapid; weary; xenarthrous;* yareless; zealless;

**unification** *(n.)*: adjoining; binding; combining; drawing together; engrafting; fusing; getting together; hitching; interconnecting; joining; knitting; linking; marriage; merger; non-separation; oneness; putting together; *quasi-fuse;* reunification; singleness; solidarity; tying together; uniting; union; *victory;* wedding; *xenograft;* yoking; *zipping together;* [*Ant.* ungluing]

**uniform** *(adj.)*: alike; *balanced;* consistent; *duplicate;* even; flat; gapless; homologous; indistinctive; invariable; just the same; kindred; like; matching; non-differing; of one kind; parallel; *quae est eadem* [L.]; regular; set; same; similar; single; *tantamount;* unvarying; very similar; well-regulated; *xerographed;* yet the same; zero-variation; [*Ant.* uneven]

**uniform** *(n.)*: attire; army ~; blues; battle dress; clothing; costume; camouflage; dress (~; blues; grays); fatigues; garb; getup; gear; grays; habiliments; *issue; insignia; jumper;* khakis; kit; livery; monkey suit [slang]; military ~; *national dress;* outfit; panoply; *quaintry* [arch.]; regalia; regimentals; suit; *troop; threads; uniformity;* vesture; workwear; whites; *XL; yelek [Turk.]; zari;*

**uniformity** *(n.)*: alikeness; accord; balance; conformity; duplication; evenness; flatness; gaplessness; homogeny; identicalness; *just alike;* keeping; likeness; match; non-difference; oneness; parallelism; *quits;* regularity; sameness; similitude; symmetry; *tedium;* unity; *very similar;* wholeness; *xerograph; yet the same;* zero variance; [*Ant.* unevenness]

**unimaginable** *(adj.)*: arcane; amazing; beyond imagination; contrary to reason; deep; ever-mysterious; fathomless; great; hard to comprehend; *high;* indescribable; inconceivable; incomprehensible; *just too high;* kithless; *limitless;* mind-blowing; non-fathomable; *over one's head;* phenomenal; profound; quantum; ridiculous; stupefying; too deep (-great); unthinkable; unfathomable; untold; un-dreamed-of; vast; wondrous; xtry.; y.; *zero understanding;*

**unimaginative** *(adj.)*: average; boring; commonplace; dull; everyday; flat; *generic;* ho-hum; insipid; jejune; *known;* lackluster; mundane; non-imaginative; ordinary; ponderous; quotidian; routine; run-of-the-mill; standard; tedious; uninteresting; uninspired; unoriginal; vapid; wearisome; *xtr. boring;* yawnful; zestless;

**unimportant** *(adj.)*: *absurd;* back-burner; common; dumb; diminutive; exiguous; frivolous; futile; *goofy;* hoity-toity; insignificant; inconsequential; irrelevant; jerkwater; ketty; lowly; little; minor; marginal; nonessential; nugatory; *obscure;* petty; peripheral; picayune; puny; quisquillous; *ridiculous;* small; secondary; sideline; trivial; trifling; tangential; unneeded; vain; worthless; *XS; yokelish; zilch;* [*Ant.* urgent]

**unimpressive** *(adj.)*: average; basic; common; center; dinky; disinteresting; everyday; familiar; generic; ho-hum; inelaborate; *juste-milieu* [F.]; *known;* lackluster; minor; mediocre; non-exceptional; no big deal; ordinary; puny; plain; quotidian; rinky-dink; regular; run-of-the-mill; simple; standard; typical; unexceptional; unremarkable; *via media* [L.]; wonderless; *xy-median;* yawnsome; zestless; [*Ant.* unbelievable]

**unintentional** *(adj.)*: accidental; by accident; coincidental; chance; done by accident; *erroneous;* fateful; fortuitous; *goof-up;* haphazard; inadvertent; just by chance; *kink;* lucky; mistaken; non-intentional; nonscheduled; *opportune;* purposeless; quite by accident; random; *surprise;* totally unexpected; unintended; unplanned; unexpected; unwitting; unscheduled; unmeaning; unpremeditated; *via accident;* without intending; *xtry. circumstance;* yet unexpected; *zero planning;*

**uninterested** *(adj.)*: apathetic; bored; cool; casual; cold(-hearted); complacent; disinterested; emotionless; flinty; *gone to sleep;* hard(-hearted); indifferent; jaded; knark; loveless; matter-of-fact; nonchalant; non-sympathetic; objective; pococurante; *quiet;* repressed; supercilious; turned-off; unenthused; uncaring; unsympathetic; unfeeling; uncommitted; viewless; withdrawn; *xerothalmic;* yareless; zealless;

**union** *(n.)*: alliance; affiliation; amalgamation; blend; brotherhood; combination; coalescence; confederation; craft ~; *defense ~;* encompassment; fusion; federation; group; guild; hookup; intermixture; interminglement; integration; incorporation interspersion; inosculation; industrial ~; joining; joint coalition; knot; league; mix(ture); mergence; mingling; marriage; meld; muddling; *node;* overmixing; organization; pouring together; partnership; *queaching [arch.];* relatedness; society; throwing together; trade ~; union; uniting; vertical ~; wedding; worker's ~; *xenograft;* yoke; zollverein;

**unique** *(adj.)*: all one's own; beyond compare; characteristic; distinctive; especial; *famous; great;* heterotypical; idiosyncratic; individual; identifying; inimitable; incomparable; *just one; known by;* legendary; matchless; notable; one-of-a-kind; peculiar; particular; proper; quite ~; recognizable; special; signature; *sui generis* [L.]; trademark; unmistakable; unambiguous; very ~; without parallel; *xtry.;* yet unreproduced; *zany;* [*Ant.* usual]

**uniqueness** *(n.)*: anotherness; *brand;* characteristicness; distinctiveness; eccentricity; *famousness; greatness; heterotypical;* individuality; individualism; inimitableness; incomparability; *just one; known characteristic; legendary;* mark; notableness; originality; peculiarity; particularity; quirk; recognized trademark; singularity; trademark; unlikeness; *variation; well-known; xtry.;* yet unreproduced quality; *zaniness;* [*Ant.* usualness]

**unison** *(n.)*: accordance; bond of harmony; concert; *dovetail;* everyone; fellowship; general agreement; harmony; in one accord; jointly; kinship; like-mindedness; mutuality; *nodding;* oneness; one accord; put together; *questionless; reunited;* synchronization; simultaneousness; togetherness; unity; union; *voluntariness;* with one voice; *xtry. harmony; yung [Chin.];* zeal;

**unit** *(n.)*: amount; assembly; bit; component; cluster; dose; division; denomination; entity; fraction; group; *hundredweight;* item; junt; kernel; lot; measure; module; node; object; piece; portion; quantity; *regiment;* set; section; segment; thing; unitized portion; *volume;* wedge; xunit; *yard; zum [arch.];*

    **Types of measuring units**: amp; bushel; centimeter; cc; degree; dram; ephah; foot; gallon; gram; hour; inch; joule; kilogram; liter; meter; mile; net ton; ounce; pint; pound; quart; quincupedal; rayl; square inch; toise; uncia; volt; watt; xunit; yard; zak;

    **Types of military units:** army; battalion; brigade; company; contingent; corps; detachment; division; flank; formation; group; legion; outfit; patrol; platoon; quaternion; regiment; troop; section; squad(ron); unit; wing;

**unite** *(v.)*: adjoin; attach; affix; band; bind; bond; connect; combine; draw together; entwine; engraft; fasten; fix; fuse; glue; graft; hitch; interlock; interconnect; intermix; inosculate; join; knit; knot; link; marry; merge; meld; *nail; network; oxreim;* put together; *quasi-fuse;* relate; re~; stick; secure; splice; set to; tie; tack; unify; *vise;* wed; weld; *xenograft;* yoke; zip; [*Ant.* unattach]

**united** *(adj.)*: accordant; allied; bound; combined; connected; conjunct; division-free; entwined; engrafted; federated; fused; gathered; grouped; hinged; hooked; indivisible; integrated; interwoven; inseparable; joint; knotted; linked; merged; non-separated; one; put together; *quasi- ~;* reunited; stuck-together; together; tied; unscattered; unseparated; unsevered; unified; *very ~;* wedded; *xenograft;* yoked; *zero division;* [*Ant.* unattached]

**United States of America** *(n.)*: America; *Boston;* Country; Continental U.S.; Columbia [poet.]; *Delaware; E. Pluribus Unum;* Fifty States; *Georgia;* Home of the Brave; *Indiana; Jacksonville; Kentucky;* Land of the Free; melting pot; Nation; *Ohio; purple mountain majesties; Queens;* Republic; *the* States; *Tennessee;* United States; *the* Union; U.S. (A.); *Virginia;* Washington D.C.; *the White House; Xenia;* Yankeedom; Yankeeland [both slang]; *Zanesville;*

    **U.S. States:** Alabama; Connecticut; Delaware; Florida; Georgia; Hawaii; Iowa; Kentucky; Louisiana; Missouri; New York; Ohio; Pennsylvania; Rhode Island; South Carolina; Tennessee; Utah; Vermont; Washington;

**unity** *(n.)*: agreement; accord; blending; bond; cohesion; commonality; camaraderie; *delight;* empathy; fellowship; good relations; harmony; inseparableness; joining; kinship; like-mindedness; mutuality; non-separateness; oneness; partnership; *quality of oneness;* rapport; single-mindedness; solidarity; togetherness; unison; unanimity; unitedness; union; *voluntariness;* widespread agreement; wholeness; *xenia;* yielding; *yedinstvo* [Rus.]; *yung* [Chin.]; *zeal;* [*Ant.* unharmoniousness]

**universal** *(adj.)*: all-inclusive; across-the-board; broad; common; comprehensive; *done everywhere;* everywhere; entire; full; general; global; galactic; *high;* inclusive; international; *joint;* known-to-all; limitless; mass; not limited; overall; planetary; pandemic; quaquaversal; 'round-the-world; sweeping; total; thorough; unanimous; unrestricted; veritable; worldwide; whole; *x-global;* yare; *zoneless;*

**universe** *(n.)*: all that is; *bailiwick;* cosmos; creation; *deep space;* everything; full creation; *galaxy;* God's ~; heavens and earth; *including all; jimbang;* kosmos; *length-and-breadth;* macrocosm; nature; outer space; planets and stars; *quasar; 'round;* second heaven; totality; *universal;* vast ~; world; whole ~; *x-ray galaxy; yonder; zoneless;*

**university** *(n.)*: academy; *alma matter;* boys college; college; degree-granting institution; educational center; four-year college; graduate school; halls of education; institution; ivy league school; junior college; *knowledge; lower school;* multiversity; night school; normal school; *Oxford;* place of higher learning; *quarter;* residential college; school; *seminary;* trade school; technical ~; upper school; varsity [Br.]; vocational school; village ~; work college; *xenagogue;* yard; *yeshiva* [Heb.]; *zone;*

**unkempt** *(adj.)*: *awful;* bedraggled; chaotic; disheveled; entangled; frowzy; grotty; haggard; incomposed; jumbled; keg-meg; lousy-looking; mangy; non-organized; outlandish; poky; quaggy; rumpled; scruffy; shabby; scraggly; slovenly; tousled; uncombed; untidy; *vile;* wimpled; windswept; wild; *x'ed;* yucky; *zany;*

**unkind** *(adj.)*: awful; atrocious; bad; cruel; despiteful; embittered; evil-affected; foul; gruff; hard; hateful; heartless; inimical; jaded; kindless; loathsome; loveless; malicious; mean; nasty; odious; pernicious; pitiless; *quede* [arch.]; rancorous; ruthless; spiteful; terrible; tawdry; unloving; unchristian; ugly; vindictive; virulent; wicked; *xenophobic; yucky; zealotic;* [*Ant.* understanding]

**unkindness** *(n.)*: animosity; badness; cruelty; dislike; evil; foulness; godlessness; hostility; harshness; ill-will; *jangling;* kindlessness; loathsomeness; meanness; malice; nastiness; odiousness; perniciousness; querulousness; rancor; ruthlessness; spitefulness; terribleness; unfriendliness; virulence; wickedness; *xenophobia;* yuckiness; *zoilism;*

**unknowable** *(adj.)*: arcane; beyond knowing; cabalistic; deep; ever-mysterious; fathomless; great; *high;* inconceivable; incomprehensible; just too high; kithless; *limitless;* mind-blowing; non-fathomable; *over one's head;* profound; past knowing; quantum; *ridiculous;* sealed; too great; unrevealed; unimaginable; unfathomable; vast; *wonderful;* xtry.; *y.; zero understanding;* [*Ant.* understandable]

**unknowingly** *(adj.)*: accidentally; blindly; carelessly; *deceived; easily-deceived;* feeble-mindedly; gullibly; heedlessly; ignorantly; innocently; imperceptibly; inadvertently; just accidentally; *keenly unaware;* lightly; mistakingly; naïvely; obtusely; obliviously; *peasantly;* quite by accident; remissly; simply; stupidly; thoughtlessly; unawares; unwittingly; unbeknownst; unintentionally; verdantly; without knowledge; *xtry. ignorant;* yet unawares; *zero knowledge;*

**unknown** *(adj.)*: anonymous; beclouded; concealed; *cryptic;* dark; ever-mysterious; esoteric; fameless; *guessed;* hidden; ignotus; indefinite; indeterminate; *just don't know;* kithless; little known; mysterious; not known; nameless; new; obscure; *open-ended;* puzzling; quite ~; renownless; strange; sealed; top secret; unfamiliar; unidentified; undetermined; undefined; unspecified; unrevealed; veiled; without certainty; X; y.; *zero understanding;* [*Ant.* understood]

**unlawful** *(adj.)*: actionable; banned; barred; contraband; criminal; disallowed; excluded; extralegal; forbidden; government-banned; held back; illegal; justiciable; kept from; lawless; *misguided;* not allowed; nixed; *nudum pacum* [L.]; non-permissible; outlawed; prohibited; punishable; *questionable;*

restricted; shut out; *sinful;* transgressive; unallowed; unauthorized; unlicensed; unconstitutional; *verboten* [G.]; wrongful; *x-ed; ybarred* [arch.]; *zapoviednik* [Rus.]; [*Ant.* unprohibited]
**unleash** *(v.)*: allow to go free; *bondless;* clear; discharge; emancipate; free; *give freedom to;* have go free; *issue; just let go; kest;* loose; let go; *manumit; non-restrained;* open; put on the loose; *quit;* release; set free; take out; unyoke; uncork; *volley; walk; xfer; yokeless; zoneless;*
**unleavened** *(adj.)*: azymous; *baked without leaven;* containing no yeast; de-yeasted; employing no yeast; free of leaven; *godly;* heavy; *impeccable; just; kosher;* leaven-free; *matstsah* [Heb.]; non-leavened; no-yeast; *omitted;* prepared without yeast; quite yeastless; *righteous; Sabbath-acceptable;* totally yeast-free; *taintless;* unyeasted; unraised; unfermented; *virtuous;* without yeast; *x-out;* yeastless; *zero leaven;*
**unlikely** *(adj.)*: absurd; bleak; cannot be expected; doubtful; ever-doubtful; far-fetched; *grim;* hardly likely; improbable; *just ~; known unlikelihood; long shot;* much-doubted; not promising; not likely; one-in-a-million chance; probably not; questionable; remote; seemingly false; totally unpromising; implausible; unapt; unconvincing; unthinkable; very ~; way-out; weak; xtry. chance; yet implausible; *zero-chance;*
**unlimited** *(adj.)*: all-comprehensive; *ad infinitum* [L.]; boundless; ceaseless; *durable;* endless; fadeless; global; highest degree; illimitable; infinite; interminate; *jusqu'au bout [F.];* keeps going; limitless; measureless; never-ending; open(-end); plenary; perpetual; *quantum libet* [L.]; *remaining;* supreme; termless; unqualified; unbounded; unconfined; unreserved; unmitigated; unrestricted; vast; without limit; *x-cending; year-after-year; zillions;*
**unload** *(v.)*: alleviate; bring down; clear; disburden; deonerate; disencumber; discharge; debark; ease; empty; *finish;* get off shoulders; hand off; *improve;* jettison; *kest;* load off; lighten; move off; *non-burdened;* offload; put down; *quaff;* remove; relieve; set down; take off wagon; transfer; unlade; unpack; *vacate;* without burden; *xfer;* yead; *zero load;*
**unlock** *(v.)*: *ajar;* bare; clear; disengage; expose; expound; emancipate; free; give access to; *hand over;* illuminate; *justify; key;* liberate; loose; make usable; *non-tight;* open; provide access; *quit;* release; reveal; set free; take off; unbar; unchain; unshackle; unleash; unfasten; *volley; walk; xfer; yokeless; zoneless;*
**unloved** *(adj.)*: abhorred; *badly treated;* contemned; detested; despised; *enemy; forsaken; gall;* hated; ill-treated; *jaded; kindless;* loathed; loveless; made to feel ~; not liked; openly ~; *poorly treated; quick-to-loved;* reviled; spurned; treated with contempt; unbeloved; unpopular; unpreferred; unprized; unvenerated; *venom; withstood; xenophobia; yucky; zero love;*
**unlucky** *(adj.)*: adverse; bad; calamitous; disadvantaged; evil-starred; fortuneless; grievous; hapless; hard-luck; ill-fated; inauspicious; Jonahesque; *killing;* luckless; misfortunate; *nebbich* [Yid.]; overly bad; pitiable; queer-lucked; regrettable; sorry; successless; terrible; unfortunate; unhappy; unfavored; unblessed; very bad; wretched; xtry. bad; *yucky; zero luck;* [*Ant.* ultra-lucky]
**unmanageable** *(adj.)*: awkward; bulky; cumbersome; difficult; *étourderie* [F.]; flighty; *great;* hard; hairy; irrepressible; impossible; incorrigible; jumbly; klutzy; *labor-intensive;* mind-boggling; non-manageable; out-of-control; problematic; quite ~; rampant; raging; rowdy; *sticky; too hard;* unrestrained; untamable; unbridled; uncontrolled; unruly; vexatious; wieldless; wild; *x;* yet ~; *zero ability;* [*Ant.* under control]
**unmindful** *(adj.)*: absentminded; blind to; careless; disregardful; eliding; forgetful; *giddy;* heedless; inattentive; just not thinking; *keenly unaware;* lax; listless; mindless; neglectful; offhand; oblivious; perfunctory; *quirky;* reckless; remiss; slack; thoughtless; unaware; very neglectful; without regard; *xtry. ~;* yet irresponsible; *zero attention;*
**unmistakable** *(adj.)*: apparent; blatant; clear; discernible; deliberate; evident; explicit; flagrant; glaring; *highly visible;* implicit; just plain to see; kenspeckle; loud and clear; manifest; noticeable; obvious; plain; quite obvious; recognizable; seeable; self-evident; transparent; unconcealed; visible; well-defined; *x-parent; yeme* [arch.]; *zenithal;* [*Ant.* unclear]

**unmixed** *(adj.)*: absolute; bare; concentrated; dilutent-free; *entire;* full-strength; *genuine;* highest degree; intense; *just; kept pure; lacking dilution;* most potent; non-diluted; one-hundred percent; potent; pure; *quality; robust;* straight; sheer; taintless; undiluted; virgin; whole; *x-tra strength;* yet undiluted; *zero admixture;*
**unmotivated** *(adj.)*: apathetic; abulic; blasé; *complacent;* draggy; *easygoing;* fainéant; groggy; half-hearted; indolent; indifferent; *jog trot;* kef; lazy; *mawmish;* non-motivated; otiose; phlegmatic; quiescent; *remiss;* slothful; torpid; unambitious; unmoved; unenthusiastic; vapid; workshy; *xenarthrous;* yareless; zealless;
**unmovable** *(adj.)*: absolute; adamantine; bolted down; changeless; definite; ever the same; fixed; *guaranteed;* hard; immovable; irremovable; *just the same;* kept the same; lasting; made firm; non-moveable; nailed down; obstinate; permanent; quite firm; rigid; stationary; *timeless;* unmovable; vested; without change; *x-cending; ypight* [arch.]; *zero movement;* [Ant. unfixed]
**unnamed** *(adj.)*: anonymous; *baffling;* concealed; *disguised; empty;* faceless; guess who; hidden; innominate; John Doe [masc.]; Jane Doe [fem.]; known to none; *little known;* mysterious; nameless; not-named; *one; person; quidam* [L.]; *revealed to none;* secret; *top secret;* unknown; unidentified; undisclosed; undesignated; unspecified; veiled; without name; X; you-know-who; Y.Z. [Br.]; *zero identity;*
**unnatural** *(adj.)*: artificial; *bogus;* contranatural; *dissembling;* emulative; factory-made; false; fake; *grotesque;* heterogeneal; inorganic; imitation; junky; *kinky;* laboratory-produced; man-made; manufactured; non-natural; odd; processed; preternatural; queer; refined; synthetic; *trick;* unreal; *vain;* well-refined; *xtr.-processed; yonder; zero reality;*
**unnecessary** *(adj.)*: additional; *bonus;* contributory; dispensable; *de trop* [F.]; extra; expendable; *further;* gratuitous; *has been;* inessential; junk; *kaput;* leftover; *most ~;* nonessential; needless; not needed; obviated; *plus;* quite ~; redundant; replaceable; superfluous; supervacaneous; *too much;* unessential; unneeded; unjustified; valueless; worthless; xtr.; yet unneeded; *zero need;* [Ant. urgent]
**unneeded** *(adj.)*: additional; bonus; contributory; *de trop* [F.]; extra; *further;* gratuitous; *hoards;* inessential; just too much; *king-sized amounts;* leftover; more; needless; overmuch; plus; *quantities; remaining;* superfluous; surplus; too much; unnecessary; unessential; *very; with;* xtr.; *yards; zero need;*
**unnoticed** *(adj.)*: *abandoned;* bypassed; camouflaged; disregarded; elided; forgotten; furtive; gone over; *heedless;* ignored; imperceptible; jumped over; *known not;* looked over; missed; neglected; overlooked; passed over; *quickly forgotten; remiss;* skipped; stealthy; *totally ~;* unapparent; unnoted; unseen; unperceived; *viewless; went over; x-ing;* yet ~; *zero notice;*
**unobtainable** *(adj.)*: *absolutely ~;* beyond reach; contraband; disallowed; excluded; forbidden; government-banned; hopeless; inaccessible; just not available; kept from; lost to; *maddening;* non-obtainable; off-limits; out-of-reach; prohibited; quite ~; restricted; shut out; totally inaccessible; unattainable; unavailable; *verboten* [G.]; withheld; *x'ed; ybarred [arch.]; zero change;*
**unoccupied** *(adj.)*: available; bare; blank; claimable; deserted; empty; free; forsaken; gettable; havable; inane; just there for the taking; *keepable; leftover; most accessible;* non-occupied; open; procurable; quite available; readily available; spare; tenantless; uninhabited; untenanted; unsettled; vacant; wasting; *xtra;* yet available; *zero occupant;* [Ant. unavailable]
**unoffended** *(adj.)*: affable; benignant; charitable; deferential; easy-going; forbearing; forgiving; gracious; hard-to-offend; indulgent; *joyous;* kind-hearted; *loving;* mellow; not offended; okay; propitious; *quite mellow; reasonable;* sweet; tolerant; *unhurt;* very gracious; willing to put up with; *xenial;* yet to be offended; *zero offense;* [Ant. upset]
**unofficial** *(adj.)*: affable; black-market; casual; degage; easy(going); familiar; furtive; *goofy;* hush-hush; informal; inofficial; just casual; *known to few;* loose; mellow; non-official; on-the-sly; officious; private; popular; quasi-official; *quiet;* relaxed; secretive; technically ~; unannounced; unrecognized; unconfirmed; *veiled;* without official recognition; *x-out;* yet unconfirmed; *zero recognition;*

**unopened** *(adj.)*: *absolutely sealed;* bolted; closed; deadbolted; engaged; fastened; factory-sealed; glued; *hard fastened; interlocked; jailed;* kept shut; latched; locked; made fast; non-opened; *new;* occluse; plastic-wrapped; *quite closed; reclosed;* sealed; shut; sealed; tightly shut; unaccessible; *very tight;* wrapped; *x-tight;* yet ~; *zet [dial.];* [*Ant.* unclosed]

**unoriginal** *(adj.)*: adopted; borrowed; copied; derived; emulated; fusty; gotten elsewhere; heavily borrowed; imitative; just borrowed; *klicked [Scot.];* look-alike; mimetic; non-original; old-hat; *overheard;* plagiarized; *questionable;* reproduced; stolen; taken; unimaginative; verbigerated; well-imitated; *xeroxed;* yet to be creative; *zero creativity;* [*Ant.* unique]

**unowned** *(adj.)*: available; buyable; claimable; *doable;* easily purchased; for sale; free; gettable; *havable; item;* just came available; *keepable; leftover; market;* non-claimed; obtainable; open; on the market; procurable; purchasable; quite obtainable; readily available; *sellable;* takable; up for grabs; unsold; unclaimed; *vacant; workable; xtra;* yet ~; *zero ownership;*

**unpack** *(v.)*: *act;* bring out; clear; discharge; empty out; *finish;* get ~ed; *hold forth; inside; just-opened; kest;* load off; move in; *non-burdened;* open; offload; put away; *quannet;* remove; *set out;* take out; unload; unwrap; *vacate; work; xfer;* yank out; *zip off;*

**unpaid** *(adj.)*: arrears; *balance due;* collectible; due; *elided; forestalled; gone unattended; have debt;* in arrears; *jadish; kept open;* late; *missed payment;* non-satisfied; owed; overdue; outstanding; payable; past due; quite overdue; remaining; still owed; tardy; unsettled; unremitted; untendered; unrepaid; very late; *weight; xtr. late;* yet ~; *zero satisfaction;*

**unparalleled** *(adj.)*: *amazing;* best; choicest; *distinct;* elite; first; greatest; highest; incomparable; *jim-dandy;* keenest; *king;* leading; matchless; nonpareil; never-paralleled; one-of-a-kind; peerless; *queen; remarkable;* superior; top; unequalled; unrivaled; *valedictorian;* without equal; xtry.; yondmost; zenithal; [*Ant.* usual]

**unpardonable** *(adj.)*: abominable; beyond forgiveness; *contemptible;* disgraceful; damnable; execrable; flagitious; *guilty;* hell-damning; inexcusable; irremissible; *jailable; killable; loathsome;* mortal; non-justifiable; over the line; punishable; *quad;* reprobate; soul-damning; *tarnishing;* unforgivable; very indefensible; *wicked; xtry.;* yet inexcusable; zero grace; [*Ant.* understandable]

**unpatriotic** *(adj.)*: un-American; anti-American; antipatriotic; betraying; *Benedict Arnold; Communist;* disloyal; *enemy; fifth-column; grossly un-American;* honorless; incivist; jadish; *knavish; loyalist; mutinous;* non-patriotic; opposed to America; *perfidious; quisling; royalist;* subversive; *treacherous;* un-American; *venomous; wicked;* xenophilic; Yankee-hating; *zero honor;*

**unpleasant** *(adj.)*: awful; annoying; abhorrent; bad; contemptible; crummy; displeasing; disagreeable; distasteful; execrable; foul; gross; grievous; hard; horrible; invidious; irksome; jarring; kindless; lousy; loathsome; miserable; nasty; nauseating; objectionable; offensive; odious; poor; quisquose; repulsive; sickening; stomach-turning; terrible; unpleasing; unlikable; undesirable; unsavory; unappetizing; vile; wicked; *xerotripsis;* yucky; *zero pleasure;*

**unplowed** *(adj.)*: allowed to rest; become dormant; cultivation-free; dormant; *eased;* fallow; gone untouched; *hold;* inactive; jejune; *kept ~; left ~;* most uncultivated; non-cultivated; out-of-action; *plowless;* quiescent; resting; still ~; totally uncultivated; unused; unworked; uncultivated; untilled; unfarmed; virgin; workless; wild; *x'ed;* yet ~; *zero activity;*

**unplug** *(v.)*: abstract; break flee; clear; deobstruct; deoppilate; extract; eliminate; free from obstruction; get rid of; *help; isolate;* jerk out; *knock out;* loose; *move; negate;* open; pull loose; *quit;* remove obstructions; separate; take away blockage; uncork; unstop; vacate; winkle out; *xfer;* yank out; *zero blockage;*

**unpolished** *(adj.)*: anti-glare; basic; cloudy; crude; dull; *everyday;* flat; glossless; gauche; humdrum; inelegant; *juste-milieu [F.]; klutzy;* lusterless; lackluster; matte; nonglare; nonglossy; non-shiny; ordinary; plain; quite flat; rough; simple; stripped; *typical;* unvarnished; unimpressive; *vulgar;* without polish; *xy-median; yawnish;* zestless;

**unpolluted** *(adj.)*: axenic; blameless; clean; decent; ever-pure; fair; fine; good; honorable; incorrupt; inviolate; *justified;* keen; lily-white; *moral;* nice; *outstanding;* pure; *quality;* respectable; spotless; taintless; untainted; unspoiled; unsullied; virginal; wholesome; *xtry.;* yet ~; *zero pollution;* [*Ant.* unclean]

**unprecedented** *(adj.)*: amazing; breathtaking; cutting-edge; *done first;* extraordinary; first-time-ever; *great;* highly experimental; incredible; *jim-dandy; keen;* legendary; marvelous; never-before-attempted; new; outstanding; phenomenal; *quantum* [L.]; remarkable; stupendous; tremendous; unexampled; very new; wondrous; xtry.; yet unattempted; *zero precedence;* [*Ant.* usual]

**unpredictable** *(adj.)*: alterable; *bouncy;* changeable; deviable; erratic; fluctuating; fickle; giddy; *haywire;* instable; inconstant; jumpy; kaleidoscopic; labile; mutable; non-stable; out-of-control; protean; precarious; questionable; random; shaky; tottery; unsteady; uncertain; variable; volatile; wavering; x-ing; yo-yo; ziggety; [*see* dangerous; crazy; unsafe; *Ant.* unchanging]

**unprepared** *(adj.)*: absolutely ~; bowled over; caught off-guard; dazed; extemporized; flat-footed; grossly ~; haphazard; ill-prepared; jolted; *knocked down;* lacking readiness; most ~; not ready; off-the-cuff; precipitate; quite ~; rattled; reckless; surprised; totally ~; unready; very surprised; *worried; x-out;* yet ~; *zero preparation;*

**unprofitable** *(adj.)*: aimless; bootless; *crazy;* deleterious; disadvantageous; empty; failed; futile; fruitless; gainless; harmful; ineffectual; improsperous; *jejune;* keenly stupid; losing; meaningless; non-beneficial; otiose; pointless; profitless; *quirky;* reasonless; rewardless; senseless; successless; totally pointless; unfruitful; unsuccessful; unproductive; unavailing; unprosperous; useless; vain; valueless; wasted; wasteful; worthless; *x'ed;* yieldless; zero-profit; [*Ant.* useful]

**unprotected** *(adj.)*: apt; at risk; brittle; crippled; defenseless; exposed; feeble; guardless; helpless; indefensible; justiciable; *knocked out;* liable; lame; much-weakened; non-helpable; naked; open; powerless; *queachy* [dial.]; *reduced;* susceptible; *tired;* unguarded; unarmed; vulnerable; weak; weaponless; wide-open; *xtry.* exposure; yawnish; zapped;

**unproved** *(adj.)*: assumed; believed; conjectural; deduced; experimental; flimsy; groundless; hypothetical; investigational; *just a hypothesis; keen idea;* lacking proof; *malinformed;* not proven; opinionative; proofless; Q.E.D.; reckoned; speculative; trial; tentative; theoretical; unproven; untested; untried; *virtual;* without grounds; *xtry.* tentative; yet unproven; *zero proof;*

**unprovoked** *(adj.)*: *absurd;* baseless; causeless; *dirty; excessive;* for no reason; groundless; *hateful;* idiopathic; just for no reason; *kindless; lame excuse;* motiveless; malicious; nonsensical; out of the blue; *pernicious;* quite ~; reasonless; senseless; *totally ~;* unprodded; uncalled-for; unwarranted; *virulent;* without provocation; *xtry.;* yet senseless; *zero-justification;* [*Ant.* unendangered]

**unquestionable** *(adj.)*: absolute; beyond doubt; conclusive; definite; ever-firm; firm; guaranteed; highly certain; irrefutable; inarguable; indisputable; incontrovertible; just sure; keenly sure; *legitimate;* mistake-proof; non-questionable; 100% sure; positive; questionless; reliable; sure; true; undeniable; unarguable; verified; without doubt; xtry. sure; *yes;* zero doubt; [*Ant.* unclear]

**unrelated** *(adj.)*: antithetic; *by chance;* chance; distinct; discrete; disconnected; detached; extraneous; foreign; *groundless; having no connection;* irrelative; isolated; irrelevant; *jumbled; keg-meg; lacking any relation;* mismatched; non-related; other; purely arbitrary; *quinquefid;* random; separate; tangential; *totally ~;* unassociated; unconnected; very different; *worlds apart; x'ed; yandied; zero relationship;*

**unrelenting** *(adj.)*: adamant; *bear through;* constant; determined; dogged; enduring; firm; going on; hard; hell-bent; high-pressure; inexorable; incessant; inexhaustible; insistent; indefatigable; incessant; importune; *jusqu'au bout* [F.]; keeping on; lasting; merciless; nonstop; never-ceasing; obstinate; persistent; persevering; *quitting never;* relentless; resolute; steadfast; steady; tenacious; unyielding; unremitting; undeterred; *very steady;* weariless; *xtry.;* yieldless; zealous;

766

**unreliable** *(adj.)*: astable; bad; capricious; careless; doubtful; disregardful; erratic; eliding; fly-by-night; false; faithless; *giddy;* heedless; inaccurate; instable; insubstantial; irresponsible; jumpy; knavish; labile; lax; *mistaken;* non-reliable; negligent; off-base; precarious; questionable; remiss; risky; shaky; slack; tottery; undependable; unsound; unstable; unsubstantial; unfaithful; variable; wonky; *x-ing;* yet irresponsible; *zero reliability;* [*Ant.* unfailing]

**unresolvable** *(adj.)*: *alienated;* beyond solving; conflicting; discomfiting; enigmatic; *fruitless;* grim; hopeless; irreconcilable; irresoluble; immitigable; irresolvable; *just ~; known impossibility; lasting;* mysterious; non-resolvable; out of the realm of understanding; perplexing; Q.B.I. [RAF slang]; revanchist; stumping; too hard; unsolvable; unreconcilable; vexing; wildering; *x;* yet unexplainable; *zero solution;*

**unrestrained** *(adj.)*: abandoned; boundless; crazy; disorderly; epidemic; free; *giddy;* hog-wild; incontinent; jungli; *kaf* [arch.]; loose; madcap; non-restrained; out-of-control; prodigal; *quite ~;* rampant; running wild; reinless; reckless; *savage;* too much; unbridled; uncontrolled; ungoverned; unchecked; uninhibited; violent; wild; *xtry. wild;* yet ~; zany;

**unrighteous** *(adj.)*: atrocious; bad; corrupt; debauched; evil; errant; foul; godless; heinous; iniquitous; *jaded; knavish;* licentious; mischievous; naughty; ornery; pernicious; *quad;* rebellious; sinful; transgressing; ungodly; villainous; wicked; *xgressing; yucky; zymotic;* [*Ant.* upright]

**unrighteousness** *(n.)*: atrocity; badness; corruption; debauchery; evil; fallenness; fault; godlessness; heinousness; iniquity; *jadedness; knavishness;* licentiousness; mischief; naughtiness; orneriness; perverseness; *quad;* rebellion; sin(fulness); transgression; ungodliness; villainy; wickedness; *xgression; yetzer hara* [Heb.]; *zymosis;* [*Ant.* uprightness]

**unsafe** *(adj.)*: adverse; bad; chancy; dangerous; endangering; foreboding; gnarly; hazardous; insecure; jeopardous; *known risk;* life-threatening; menacing; nocuous; ominous; precarious; questionable; risky; self-hazarding; threatening; unsecure; venturesome; woeful; *x.;* yet ~; *zero safety;* [*Ant.* unendangered]

**unsatisfactory** *(adj.)*: awful; bad; *crummy;* deficient; *empty;* falling short; *greatly in need;* halfmeasure; insufficient; inadequate; just not good enough; keenly ~; lacking; lame; *missing something;* non-satisfactory; *out;* poor; *questionable; rotten;* short; shy; too little; unacceptable; unsufficing; *under;* very ~; wanting; wrong; *xtry. deficient;* yet ~; *zero sufficiency:*

**unsatisfied** *(adj.)*: anguished; belly-aching; complaining; dissatisfied; discontented; *enraged;* fussing; grieved; heavy (of heart); inconsolable; joyless; *knocking;* low; miserable; negative; overcast; *outstanding; poignant;* quermonious; repining; sad; tristful; unfulfilled; unmet; very sad; woeful; wistful; *xtry. unhappy; yearnful; zestless;*

**unsaved** *(adj.)*: astray; *bad;* condemned; Christless; doomed; damned; eternally lost; fallen; faithless; guilty; *goat;* hell-bound; infidel; irregenerate; *judged; knavish;* lost; *misbelieving;* natural; non-regenerate; *off-course;* punishable; *quite lost;* reprobate; *sinner;* totally lost; unreached; unregenerate; unredeemed; unforgiven; unconverted; unjustified; *void of understanding;* wayward; without Christ; *xci.;* yet accountable; *zero hope;*

**unsearchable** *(adj.)*: abstruse; beyond knowing; bewildering; complicated; deep; *expansive;* furtive; *grueling;* hidden; intricate; inscrutable; *jarring;* knotty; labyrinthine; mysterious; non-understandable; overwhelming; past finding out; perplexing; *queer; recondite;* shadowy; tough; too great; unfathomable; veiled; wildering; *xenagogic; yieldless; zany;* [*Ant.* understandable]

**unseasonable** *(adj.)*: at the wrong time; badly timed; *crazy; dumb;* erroneous-timed; foul-timed; *grossly improper; highly inappropriate;* ill-timed; inopportune; *just out-of-place; kooky; lousy;* mistimed; not timely; out-of-place; premature; poorly-timed; *questionable; ridiculous; stupid;* totally out-of-place; untimely; unusual; very ~; wrongly-timed; *xtry. poor; yieldless; zany:*

**unseemly** *(adj.)*: awful; bad; *coarse;* dreadful; *earthy;* foul; gross; horrendous; improper; inappropriate; indecorous; just wrong; kitschy; lousy; misbecoming; *misguided;* not proper; out-of-place; poor; questionable; reprehensible; rude; shocking; tasteless; unbecoming; unseemly; unbefitting; uncouth; untoward; unsanctioned; vile; wrongful; *xgressing;* yucky; *zhlubby;*

**unseen** *(adj.)*: *à perte de vue* [F.]; behind the scenes; concealed; disguised; *evasive; faint; furtive; ghostlike;* hidden; invisible; imperceptible; *jape;* kept out of view; latent; low-lying; mysterious; non-observable; obscure; out-of-sight; private; *quietly;* recondite; see-through; transparent; undetected; unperceivable; veiled; well-hidden; x-parent; *yeme [arch.];* zero perceptibility; [*Ant.* unhidden]
**unselfish** *(adj.)*: altruistic; big-hearted; Christlike; deferential; *endearing;* fair; free-handed; giving; humanitarian; impartial; just; kind; loving; magnanimous; nice; others-oriented; philanthropic; quick-to-give; regardful; selfless; self-sacrificing; thoughtful; ungrudging; virtuous; *well-natured; xenial;* yielding; *zealous of good works;*
**unselfishness** *(n.)*: amiableness; benevolence; consideration; deference; *endearing;* favor; graciousness; humanitarianism; impartiality; kind-heartedness; love; mercifulness; niceness; obligingness; philanthropy; *quick to give;* regard; selflessness; thoughtfulness; ungrudgingness; virtuousness; warmth; *xenia; yearning; zealousness;*
**unsightly** *(adj.)*: awful; blemished; crude; disgusting; evil-favored; foul-looking; gross; hideous; ill-favored; *jackal-faced; knarled;* loathsome; monstrous; nasty; offensive; poor-looking; queer-looking; revolting; shocking; terrible; uncomely; ugly; vile; *wicked; xerophthalmic;* yucky; *zero beauty;*
**unskilled** *(adj.)*: artless; awkward; amateur; *bungling;* callow; dilettante; experience-deprived; fresh; footless; green; haphazard; inept; inexpert; improficient; inexperienced; inconversant; incompetent; jackleg; *kyu [Jap.];* less proficient; maladroit; menial; non-proficient; *over-green;* pathetic; quasi-skilled; raw; skilless; *tedious;* untalented; untrained; unpracticed; unversed; unhandy; unmechanical; verdant; wanting; *xtr. klutzy;* young and inexperienced; *zero skill;*
**unsociable** *(adj.)*: antisocial; belligerent; contentious; dour; distant; enemy; *fierce;* grumpy; galsome; hostile; inimical; *jeopardizing;* kindless; *loathsome;* mean; nasty; nongregarious; odious; pugnacious; quarrelsome; rough; standoffish; threatening; unfriendly; unsocial; violent; warlike; *xenophobic; yieldless; zealotic;*
**unsolvable** *(adj.)*: arcane; baffling; confounding; discomfiting; enigmatic; *fruitless;* grim; hopeless; inexplicable; irreconcilable; just ~; *known impossibility; ludicrous;* mysterious; non-resolvable; out of the realm of understanding; perplexing; Q.B.I. [RAF slang]; *ridiculous;* stumping; too hard; unresolvable; vexing; wildering; x; yet unexplainable; *zero solution;*
**unsound** *(adj.)*: amiss; blemished; bad; chancy; defective; erroneous; faulty; flawed; fallacious; groundless; hazardous; imperfect; incorrect; inadequate; illogical; jeopardous; *kaput;* lousy; messed up; non-stable; on the blink; problematic; questionable; rickety; shaky; specious; troublesome; unstable; untrustworthy; *volatile;* weak; wobbly; *x-out; yo-yoish; zany;* [*Ant.* unfailing]
**unspeakable** *(adj.)*: abominable; awesome; beyond words; cannot be uttered; dark; divine; extraordinary; *forbidden;* ghastly; heinous; heavenly; indescribable; inexpressible; incommunicable; ineffable; *just can't say; known only to me;* lofty; magnificent; non-utterable; *overwhelming; profound;* quite ~; reprehensible; remarkable; shocking; stupendous; taboo; unutterable; unpronounceable; unnameable; unrepeatable; *vulgar;* wondrous; xtry.; yet ~; *zero words;* [*Ant.* utterable]
**unspoken** *(adj.)*: assumed; *believed;* connoted; *dark;* ever-silent; forethought; *guessed;* hushed; inarticulate; inaudible; intimated; *judged;* kept quiet; *led to believe; mum;* non-verbal; *obscure;* presumed; quiet; referred to; silent; tacit; unsaid; unexpressed; unvoiced; unstated; understood; voiceless; wordless; *xtry. quiet;* yet unexpressed; zero verbalizing; [*Ant.* uttered]
**unstable** *(adj.)*: astable; bouncy; crazy; disturbed; divergent; dangerous; erratic; fluctuating; giddy; hinky; haywire; hazardous; instable; jumpy; jeopardous; kaleidoscopic; labile; moody; mutable; non-stable; out-of-control; precarious; questionable; random; rickety; risky; shaky; tottery; temperamental; unsteady; unpredictable; volatile; wavering; wobbly; x-ing; yo-yo; ziggety; [*see* dangerous, crazy; *Ant.* uniform]

**unsteady** *(adj.)*: alterable; bouncy; changeable; capricious; disturbed; erratic; fluctuating; flitty; giddy; hinky; inconstant; irregular; jumpy; kooky; loose; lubric; mutable; non-stable; out-of-control; precarious; quavering; random; shaky; tottering; unstable; uneven; vacillating; wavering; wobbly; *x-ing;* yo-yoing; ziggety; [*Ant.* unwavering]

**unstoppable** *(adj.)*: abort-proof; *bold;* ceaseless; *constant;* dauntless; ever-resolute; firm; fated; *going on;* herculean; irresistible; inexorable; indomitable; invincible; *jusqu'au bout* [F.]; *keeps going; lasting; mulish;* necessary; non-stoppable; onward-marching; persevering; *quitting never;* resistless; relentless; steadfast; sure; *tough; tenacious;* unrelenting; unpreventable; unyielding; *very steady; weathering; xtry.;* yieldless; *zealous;*

**unsuccessful** *(adj.)*: aborted; bootless; crushed; defeated; empty; failed; foiled; frustrated; futile; fruitless; gainless; hollow; *hopeless;* ineffectual; ineffective; improsperous; *jejune;* keenly ~; lacking a profit; meaningless; non-beneficial; otiose; pointless; profitless; *quirky;* reasonless; senseless; successless; totally pointless; useless; unavailing; unprosperous; unfruitful; unprofitable; unproductive; vain; valueless; wasted; worthless; *x'ed;* yieldless; zero-profit; [*Ant.* useful]

**unsuitable** *(adj.)*: amiss; bad; *contrary;* deficient; erroneous; faulty; *groundless;* highly ~; improper; inapposite; incommodious; inappropriate; incorrect; incompetent; ineligible; inept; insufficient; inadequate; just not right; *kitsch;* lousy; mismatched; malapropos; misbecoming; non-suited; out-of-place; poor; questionable; reprehensible; *substandard; totally ~;* unfit; unbefitting; unconjugal; unseemly; unqualified; *vile;* wrong; *xgressing;* yucky; zero propriety:

**unsung** *(adj.)*: almost forgotten; anonymous; barely remembered; *careless;* disregarded; *elided;* forgotten; *gone over; horribly-treated;* irrenowned; ignored; *jumped over;* known to few; little known; lost; missed; neglected; overlooked; passed over; *quick-to-forget; remiss;* silent; taken-for-granted; uncelebrated; unappreciated; unrecognized; unacknowledged; unpraised; *void; want; x-ing; yet ~; zero recognition;* [*Ant.* unforgotten]

**unsympathetic** *(adj.)*: austere; businesslike; cold; callous; disinterested; emotionless; flinty; glacial; heartless; hard(-hearted); indifferent; jaded; knark; loveless; matter-of-fact; non-sympathetic; obdurate; pitiless; *quiet;* ruthless; steel-like; tough; thick-skinned; unfeeling; uncaring; *viewless;* withdrawn; without mercy; *xerothalmic; yieldless;* zealless; [*Ant.* understanding]

**unsystematic** *(adj.)*: arbitrary; by chance; chance; disorderly; erratic; fortuitous; groundless; haphazard; indiscriminate; jumbled; keg-meg; left to chance; motiveless; nonsystematic; orderless; planless; pell-mell; *quirky;* random; reasonless; senseless; subjective; systemless; *totally ~;* unmethodical; uncalculated; very arbitrary; wanton; *whim; x; yet indiscriminate; zero reason;*

**untangle** *(v.)*: *arrange;* brush; correct; comb; disentangle; disencumber; disembroil; extricate; enucleate; free; fix; get out; *hatchel; improve; justify; kinkless;* loose; make right; neaten; outwind; open; put right; quannet; release; separate; straighten; take a comb to; *tangle-free;* unravel; unwind; unloose; unsnarl; *vamp;* work out; *xfer; yarn-comb; zero entanglements;*

**unthankful** *(adj.)*: *absent-minded; bad;* churlish; disregardful; eliding; forgetful; gratitude-neglecting; *heedless;* ingrate; *jaded; kindless; lax; missed;* non-appreciative; *owe nothing;* praiseless; *quick-to-forget; remiss; spirit of ingratitude;* thankless; unappreciative; ungrateful; very unmindful; wretched; *xgressing; yemeless [arch.]; zero appreciation;*

**unthinkable** *(adj.)*: amazing; beyond reason; *crazy;* disagreeable; extraordinary; fantastic; far-fetched; *ghastly;* hard to believe; inimaginable; inconceivable; *jarring; kooky;* ludicrous; mind-blowing; non-believable; outrageous; preposterous; *questionable;* ridiculous; *stupefying; terrible;* unconscionable; unimaginable; vaporous; *wild; xtry.;* y.; *za-zum* [Rus.];

**untiring** *(adj.)*: adamant; bound; contumacious; determined; ever-persevering; firm; grim; headstrong; insistent; jaw-set; *keep; lasting;* mulish; never-tiring; obstinate; persistent; *querulous;* resolute; relentless; steadfast; tireless; unrelenting; unyielding; vigorous; weariless; *xel [arch.];* yieldless; *zero give;* [*Ant.* unenthusiastic]

**untrustworthy** *(adj.)*: artful; bad; crooked; dishonest; evil-hearted; fly-by-night; fraudulent; guileful; honorless; ignoble; jady; knavish; lying; misconducted; non-credible; opportunistic; perfidious; quasi-ethical; roguish; shady; shifty; treacherous; unscrupulous; unprincipled; unethical; venal; wily; *x-ing;* yeggy; *zero honesty;* [*Ant.* unfailing]

**unusable** *(adj.)*: *absolutely ~;* bad; broken; *cracked; crummy;* defective; effectless; functionless; fruitless; good-for-nothing; *horrible;* insufficient; *just no good;* kaput; lacking; missing something; non-usable; out-of-order; otiose; pointless; profitless; *questionable; ridiculous;* sorry; *smashed; substandard;* too unreliable; useless; unemployable; unfit; unsuitable; valueless; worthless; *xtry. deficient; yieldless; zero usability;* [*Ant.* usable]

**unusual** *(adj.)*: abnormal; bizarre; curious; different; distinctive; enigmatic; eccentric; exceptional; freaky; freakish; funny; fantastic; *foreign;* goofy; heterotypical; irregular; *jarring;* kooky; ludicrous; *mysterious;* novel; odd; peculiar; queer; remarkable; strange; special; too strange; uncharacteristic; uncommon; unconventional; unexpected; uncanny; unnatural; variant; weird; way-out; xtry.; yet unknown; zany; [*Ant.* usual]

**unvarying** *(adj.)*: alike; balanced; consistent; constant; dry; even; fixed; *good;* homologous; invariable; just the same; kept the same; like; matching; non-changing; ongoing; perpetual; *quae est eadem* [L.]; regular; reliable; steady; true; unwavering; very steady; without change; *xerographed;* yet the same; *zincograph;* [*Ant.* unalike]

**unwanted** *(adj.)*: abhorred; *balked at; cast out;* disliked; *de trop* [F.]; *extra;* frowned upon; *gall;* hated; *ill-treated; jilted; kicked at;* loathed; misliked; not wanted; *outlawed; ostracized;* poorly received; *quite disliked; reproached; surplus; taken an aversion to;* undesired; unwished for; unwelcome; unneeded; vilipended; *without desire; xenophobic; yucky; zero desire;*

**unwavering** *(adj.)*: abiding; bendless; constant; determinate; even-keeled; fixed; foursquare; *going on;* high-resolved; indefatigable; *jusqu'au bout* [F.]; *kragdadig* [S. Afr.]; lasting; mulish; non-changing; ongoing; pertinacious; *quenchless;* resolved; stable; tenacious; unfaltering; undeviating; uninterrupted; very firm; well-resolved; *x-cending;* yieldless; *zero give;* [*Ant.* unsteady]

**unwholesome** *(adj.)*: abominable; bad; corrupt; debauched; evil; foul; godless; horrible; inappropriate; insalubrious; *jadish; kitsch;* lewd; misbecoming; non-suitable; obscene; peccant; questionable; reprehensible; sinful; shocking; tasteless; unhealthy; ungodly; unseemly; vile; wicked; *xgressing;* yucky; *zero propriety:* [*Ant.* upright]

**unwholesomeness** *(n.)*: abomination; badness; corruption; debauchery; evil; foulness; godlessness; horribleness; inappropriateness; insalubrity; *jadishness; kitsch;* lewdness; *misbecoming;* non-suitableness; obscenity; peccancy; questionableness; reprehensibility; sinfulness; tastelessness; unhealthiness; ungodliness; unseemliness; vileness; wickedness; *xgression;* yuckiness; *zero propriety:* [*Ant.* uprightness]

**unwieldy** *(adj.)*: awkward; bulky; cumbersome; difficult; *étourderie* [F.]; fumbly; graceless; hulky; inelegant; jumbly; klutzy; lumbering; maladroit; non-graceful; oafish; ponderous; *quirky; rube;* socially inept; troublesome; ungainly; ungraceful; *vexatious;* wooden; *xtry. ungainly;* yokelish; zhlubby;

**unwilling** *(adj.)*: averse; bucking; cautious; disinclined; *edgy;* fractious; grudging; half-hearted; hesitant; indisposed; jackalent; kicking (and screaming); laggard; loath; mousy; non-willing; opposed; *poor attitude; questioning;* reluctant; sullen; stubborn; *tough;* unenthusiastic; unconsenting; vacillating; wary; *xenophobic;* yarrow; zealless; [*Ant.* unreluctant]

**unwillingness** *(n.)*: aversion; *bashfulness;* contrariness; disinclination; *edginess;* flat refusal; great opposition; hesitation; headshaking; indisposition; jackalence; kicking; *loath;* mousiness; nolition; opposition; protestation; qualm; reluctance; refusal; sullenness; stubbornness; *timidity;* uncooperativeness; vacillation; wavering; *xenophobia;* yo-yoing; zeallessness;

**unworthy** *(adj.)*: abominable; bad; contemptuous; disgraceful; execrable; flagitious; grossly undeserving; good-for-nothing; hollow; heinous; inadequate; insufficient; ineligible; indign; junky; ketty; lacking; lousy; meritless; noughty; non-worthy; otiose; paltry; quisquillous; reproachful; sorry; shameful; *terrible;* undeserving; unvalued; unbefitting; vile; valueless; wrong; worthless; without merit; *x-bad;* yet unmerited; unqualified; *zero worthiness;*

**unwrap** *(v.)*: *act;* bare; cast off; detangle; expose; fold back; get wrapping off; *husk; inside; just-~ped; knock off;* loosen; let out; manifest; make bare; *nakedize;* open; peel; *quannet;* remove wrapping; rip open; strip; take off; unfold; unravel; unwind; uncoil; unreel; *vacate;* work out; *xfer;* yank off; *zip off;* [*Ant.* upbind]

**upbeat** *(adj.)*: animated; bubbly; cheerful; delightful; effervescent; exuberant; fun; genial; happy; intoxicated; joyful; jovial; *keyed up;* lighthearted; merry; *nice;* optimistic; positive; *queme;* radiant; sunny; thrilling; uplifting; vivacious; winsome; *xanadu;* yeasty; zestful; [*Ant.* unhappy]

**upbraid** *(v.)*: admonish; berate; blame; castigate; denounce; excoriate; flay; give talking to; harangue; impugn; jaw; knock; lecture; *macerate;* nag; objurgate; *punish; question;* rebuke; reprove; reprimand; rake over the coals; reproach; revile; scold; tell off; *urge;* vituperate; *warn; xuld* [arch.]; yell at; *zap;*

**upbringing** *(n.)*: admonishment; adolescence; breeding; background; brought up; childhood; cultivating; disciplining; development; direction; education; fostering; grooming; home training; instruction; *jobation; knowledge; lessons;* mentoring; nurturing; ontogeny; preparation; parenting; *qualification;* rearing; raising; schooling; training; *unlocking; versing;* working with; *xenagogy;* youth; *zealous instruction;*

**upgrade** *(v.)*: advance; better; convert; develop; enhance; *fix;* graduate; *heighten;* improve; jib; *key to; lift;* modify; modernize; novate; overhaul; *put right; qualify;* revise; revamp; raise; switch; *transform; trade;* update; vamp; *work; xfer; yarken; zenith;*

**uplifting** *(adj.)*: agreeable; bright; cheerful; delightful; encouraging; felicitous; glad(some); happy; heartening; invigorating; joyful; *keen;* lovely; moving; *nice;* optimistic; positive; *queme;* radiant; sunny; stirring; thrilling; upbeat; vivacious; winsome; *xanadu; yeah!* zestful; [*Ant.* unhappy]

**upright** *(adj.)*: aboveboard; blameless; conscientious; decent; ethical; faultless; good; honorable; impeccable; just; *keen;* law-abiding; moral; noble; *overscrupulous;* principled; *qualmless;* righteous; reputable; respectable; sinless; trustworthy; upstanding; virtuous; well-principled; xtry.; yet untilted; *zero lean;* [*see* vertical; *Ant.* underhanded]

**uprising** *(n.)*: aggression; *breach;* coup d'état [F.]; civil disobedience; defiance; émeute; *fight;* general ~; high treason; insurrection; jacquerie; *kicking at;* lèse majesté [F.]; mutiny; noncompliance; overthrow; perfidy; putsch; *quake;* revolt; rebellion; revolution; riot; subversion; treason; takeover; upheaval; violence; *war; xgression; yieldlessness; zealotry;*

**uproar** *(n.)*: anarchy; ado; bedlam; ballyhoo; commotion; disturbance; ebullience; fracas; furor; fuss; flap; gaff; havoc; hoopla; hullabaloo; insurrection; jangle; kick-up; loud ~; mayhem; nitty; noise; outrage; outcry; pandemonium; *quandary;* riot; racket; rumpus; shouting; tumult; upheaval; vexation; welter; xtry. uprising; *yo-yo; zoo;*

**uproot** *(v.)*: averruncate; *break; cut out;* dig up; disinter; displace; deracinate; extract; force out; grab; haul away; *invade;* jerk out; *kill; lay waste;* move; *nullify; obliterate;* pull out; pluck up; quash; root; rip out; remove; *subvert;* tear out; transplant; unroot; *violence;* wrest; weed out; xenotransplant; yank out; *zap;*

**upset** *(adj.)*: aggravated; beside oneself; cross; distraught; disturbed; exasperated; flustered; grieved; hot; incensed; jittery; jumping mad; knocked over; livid; mad; nettled; outraged; peeved; quick-tempered; raging; steamed; sad; shook-up; sore; temperamental; troubled; unglued; vexed; wrathful; *xerothermic; yond* [arch.]; *zealousy* [arch.]; [*Ant.* unoffended]

**upset** *(v.)*: aggravate; boil; cross; disturb; exasperate; fluster; grieve; *hot;* incense; jar; jangle; jolt; kindle; lose one's temper; madden; needle; outrage; perturb; *quick-tempered;* rile; shock; steam; tick off; unnerve; vex; wind up; *xerothermic; yell; zealousy [arch.];*
**upshot** *(n.)*: aftereffects; byproduct; consequence; consummation; derivative; development; effect; end result; fruit; *get;* harvest; impact; *just desserts; known outcome;* lattermath; *matter; necessarily;* outcome; product; quantum effect; result; significance; sequent; termination; unraveling; *validity;* working out; wake; *xenagogy;* yield; *zeug [G.];*
**upside-down** *(n.)*: arsy-varsy; backward; bottom-up; capsized; downside-up; end-up; flipped; *gone awry;* hindside-up; inverted; *just reversed; keeled over; lopsided; mixed-up;* non-righted; overturned; *pinnacle-down; quacked;* reversed; resupinate; resupine; switched; topsy-turvy; tapsalteerie [Scot.]; upturned; *vice versa;* wrong-way up; *xuld [arch.];* yerk; *zwap [dial.];*
**upstart** *(n.)*: arriviste; boy; budding young capitalist; *capitalist; developing;* entrepreneur; first-timer; greenhorn; howdy-doody; *individual;* jackeen; Johhny-come-lately; *kid;* latecomer; mushroom; newcomer; nobody overnight success; *obscure; parvenu [F.]; quick;* rookie; skip-jack; *tyro;* unknown; *venturer; wannabe; xon;* young pup; *zip;*
**urban** *(adj.)*: anti-agrarian; big-city; built-up; city; developed; *exurb;* factory-filled; *ghetto;* heavily populated; inner-city; *jurisdictiona; kirk-towner; limits;* metropolitan; non-rural; oppidan; overpopulated; populated; *quarter; residential;* street; *slum; suburban;* town; urbanized; *village; ward; xtr.* built-up; Yonkers; zonal; [*Ant.* underdeveloped]
**urbane** *(adj.)*: amiable; affable; *bon ton* [F.]; civilized; cultured; courteous; debonair; elegant; fair-spoken; fashionable; gracious; gentlemanly; genteel; gallant; high class; handsome; *interpersonal;* jimp [Br.]; *kind; kulturny* [Rus.]; *lovely;* (mild-)mannered; mannerly; nice; obliging; polite; polished; quaint; refined; sophisticated; suave; stylish; tactful; thoughtful; *ultra-sophisticated;* very polite well-mannered (-bred; -raised; refined); *xtry.; younker; zero civility;* [*Ant.* uncouth]
**urbanite** *(n.)*: *anti-agrarian;* burg-dweller; city-dweller; city-slicker; city folk [pl.]; dude; exurbanite; *factory-worker; ghetto person;* hamlet-dweller; inhabitant of the city; *jounker;* kirk-town resident [Scot.]; *land-lubber;* metropolitan; non-rustic; oppidan; *person; quite sophisticated;* resident of the city; socialite; townfolk; urban dweller; villager; *worker; xtr.* built-up; yuppie; *zonal occupant;*
**urchin** *(n.)*: *adolescent;* beggar; child; dandiprat; elf; *fellow;* guttersnipe; gamin; hellion; imp; jackanapes; katzenjammer; keelie; *lad;* mudlark; nipper; *orphan;* puck; *quinquennarian;* ragamuffin; scamp; street kid; tramp; unruly child; vagrant; *vandal;* waif; *wretch; xiaoren;* youth; *zon [dial.];*
**urge** *(n.)*: aspiration; ache; big desire; craving; desire; drive; eagerness; fancy; great desire; hankering; impulse; itch; *just want to;* keen desire; longing; motivation; notion; *need; obsession;* panting; *quick; rage;* strong ~; thirst; urging; velleity; wish; *xenenthesis; yen;* yearning; yankering; *zeal;*
**urge** *(v.)*: adjure; admonish; beseech; bear on; beg; compel; chivvy; desire; exhort; force; goad; hurry; *hortatory;* implore; impel; insist; importunate; *juration; kneel and plead;* lean on; make; motivate; nudge; *order;* press(ure); prod; ply; *quicken;* recommend; supplicate; tell; *utter; vie;* warn; wish; *xuld [arch.];* yearn; yen; *zealously ~;* [*see* encourage]
**urgency** *(n.)*: all-importance; bigness; criticalness; direness; exigency; emergency; fundamental importance; gravity; heaviness; imperativeness; import(ance); *justification; key; life-threatening;* major importance; need; necessity; *obligation;* press(ure); precedence; *quintessence; requirement;* seriousness; *terribly important; unparalleled;* vitalness; weight; *xtry.;* yearning; *zero hour;* [*Ant.* unimportance]
**urgent** *(adj.)*: all-important; burning; crucial; critical; compelling; dire; exigent; essential; extreme; first priority; grave; heavy; imperative; important; *jump to it;* key; life-or-death; major; matter of life or death; needful; necessary; *obligatory;* pressing; paramount; priority; *quintessential;* required; serious; sore; stat [med.]; top priority; *unparalleled;* vital; weighty; *xtry.; yearnful; zero hour;* [*see* emergency; *Ant.* unimportant]

**urine** *(n.)*: *acidic;* body waste; chamber-lye; discharge; emiction; excreta; *furosemide; going; had to go;* issue; jigg [reg.]; keytonuria; *land* [arch.]; micturation; *nephritical; outpouring;* piddle; *quad; relief;* sig; tinkling; urea; *vile substance;* waste; water; wee-wee; *xanthine;* yellow fluid; zigg;

**urn** *(n.)*: ash ~; bisque; container; carafe; crock; ceramic pot; depository; decanter; earthenware vase; funeral ~; Grecian ~; holder; *item; inurn;* jar; kist; lota; Ming vase; *nesting ~;* ossuary; olla; pot; pitcher; *quarterfoil;* receptacle; samovar; table vase; urceole; vase; vessel; waterpot; *xerophyte;* yabba; zun;

**usable** *(adj.)*: available; applicable; beneficial; controllable; convenient; deployable; employable; exercisable; exploitable; functional; *governable;* handleable; helpful; handy; *invaluable; justifiable; keenly utilizable; legitimate;* manipulable; *nearby; non-wasted;* operable; practical; quite ~; *running; ready;* serviceable; *tenable;* utilizable; *viable;* workable; *xferable; yain [arch.]; zero problem;* [*Ant.* unusable]

**use** *(n.)*: adaptability; application; activity; benefit; convenience; custom; deployment; employment; exercise; exploitation; function(ality); good; harnessing; implementation; jockeying; *key employment;* legal right; *misuse;* manipulation; *nobbling;* operability; operation; *overuse;* practice; point; practicability; profit; *qualification;* role; service; trick; utility; utilization; value; work; worth; *x-div;* yield; *zet [dial.];*

**use** *(v.)*: adapt; avail; apply; benefit from; control; deploy; drive; *do;* employ; exercise; exploit; fall back; get benefit from; handle; harness; *implement;* jockey; *keep; lig;* make use of; manipulate; *nobble;* operate; overuse; ply; parlay; put to use; *qualify;* run; *set to use;* take advantage of; utilize; *vocation;* work; wield; *xuld [arch.]; yain* [arch.]; *zeal;*

**used** *(adj.)*: aged; *behind-the-times;* cast off; discarded; exploited; *faded;* galled; hand-me-down; *in mothballs; junky; kept;* long-retired; much- ~; not new; old; *over~;* pre-owned; *quondam;* reconditioned; second-hand; third-hand; used up; very experienced; worn; well- ~; *x-old; yellowed; zet [dial.];* [*Ant.* unused]

**useful** *(adj.)*: advantageous; beneficial; constructive; conducive; desirable; efficacious; efficient; effectual; expedient; functional; gainful; good; helpful; handy; instrumental; *jim dandy;* keen; *lovely;* meritorious; nice; operative; productive; *quality;* relevant; salutary; serviceable; *terrific;* usable; utilizable; valuable; worthwhile; xtry.; yieldful; *zestful;* [*Ant.* useless]

**usefulness** *(n.)*: advantage; benefit; beneficialness; conduciveness; desirability; efficaciousness; effectualness; expedience; functionality; gain; helpfulness; handiness; instrumentality; *jim dandy;* keenness; *loveliness;* merit; niceness; operativeness; productivity; *quality;* relevance; serviceableness; *terrific;* utilization; value; worth; xtry.; yield; *zero waste;* [*Ant.* uselessness]

**useless** *(adj.)*: aimless; bootless; counterproductive; disserviceable; empty; futile; fruitless; good-for-nothing; hopeless; impractical; ineffectual; ineffective; *joyless; kaput;* lame; meaningless; no good; of no use; pathetic; pointless; *Q.B.I. [RAF slang]; ridiculous;* senseless; *terrible;* unusable; unworkable; unproductive; unsuccessful; vain; valueless; worthless; wasted; *x-out;* yeld; *zero use;* [*Ant.* useful]

**usher** *(n.)*: attendant; bridesman; *butler;* chamberlain; commissionaire; doorman; escort; fellow; guide; groomsman; helper; *individual;* jacketed ~; *keeper;* lackey; man; *neif;* ostiary; porter; quarter-waiter [Br.]; *reliable;* servant; *tend;* usherer; usherette [fem.]; valet; *worker; xenagogue;* yeoman; zaikai;

**usher** *(v.)*: attend; bring (in); conduct; direct; escort; *facilitate;* guide; help; *instruct; jump to it; keep;* lead; move; navigate; oversee; *point; quicken; run;* seat; take down the aisle; tend; *useful; valet;* wait on; *xenagogy; yeme [L.]; zero in;*

**usual** *(adj.)*: average; broad; common; customary; day-to-day; dominant; everyday; familiar; general; habitual; inveterate; inconspicuous; jejune; known-to-all; long-established; mainstream; mundane; normal; ordinary; par (for the course); prevalent; plain; quotidian; regular; standard; same (old); status quo; typical; used; vanilla; well-established; wonted; *x-type; yawnsome; zestless;* [*Ant.* unusual]

**usually** *(adv.)*: as a rule; by and large; commonly; chiefly; *dominantly;* essentially; frequently; generally; habitually; in general; *just the norm; known;* largely; mainly; mostly; normally; ordinarily; principally; popularly; primarily; *quotidian;* regularly; routinely; *standard;* typically; *unoriginally; universally; very common;* widely; wontedly; *x-type; yawnsome; zestless;* [*Ant.* unusually]

**usualness** *(n.)*: averageness; business-as-usual; commonness; *daily routine;* everyday life; familiarity; generalness; habitualness; *inelaborateness;* jejuneness; *known; lackluster;* mundaneness; norm(ality); normalcy; ordinariness; par; quo; regularity; routineness; status quo; typicality; *unsurprised; vanilla;* wontedness; *x-type; yawn;* zestlessness; [*Ant.* unusualness]

**usurp** *(v.)*: assume; arrogate; break bounds; commandeer; dispossess; encroach; grab; *have;* intercept; *jump at;* keep; lay hold of; make off with; nab; obtain; procure; *quick; rebel;* seize; take; *use;* violate; wrest; xfer; yank; zip away;

**usury** *(n.)*: anatocism; advantage; *benefit;* charge; duty; exploitation; extortion; fee; *gain;* handling charge; interest; *jettage; keyage;* loan-sharking; markup; net interest; overcharge; profit; *quarterage;* return; shylocking; *turnover;* usage fee; *vigorish;* withholding; x-int; yield; *zakat [Mos.];*

**utility** *(n.)*: advantage; benefit; convenience; *desirable;* effectiveness; favor; gain; helpfulness; improvement; *jump;* kinch; *lead; makings; non-difficult;* obtainment; profitableness; *quite handy;* relevance; serviceable; *takings;* usefulness; value; *worthwhile;* x-div; yield; *zippity;*

**utilize** *(v.)*: avail oneself of; benefit from; control; develop; *do;* employ; *function; govern; get benefit from;* harness; *implement;* jockey; *keep; lig;* make use of; *nobble;* operate; put to use; *qualify;* run; set to use; take advantage of; use; *vocation;* work; *xuld [arch.]; yoke; zero waste;*

**Utopia** *(n.)*: arcadia; blissful place; Cloud 9; dreamland; Elysium; fairyland; *Garden of Eden;* (hog) heaven; haven; idyll; *Jasper-walled city; kingdom;* la-la land; *merry old land;* never-never land; nirvana; Oz; paradise; *queme;* rose garden; Shangri-La; sublimity; Trala-la; *utopian community;* Vanhalla; wonderland; Xanadu; yarkandi; Zion;

**utopian** *(n.)*: arcadian; blissful; best; *Cloud 9;* dreamy; elysian; fantastic; Garden-of-Eden; heavenly; idyllic; idealistic; joyous; *keen; lovely;* marvelous; *notional;* optimistic; paradisiacal; paradisean; *perfect;* quixotic; rosy; romantic; sublime; *terrific;* ultimate; *very great;* wonderful; *Xanadu; yarkandian; zealous;* [*Ant.* unenviable]

**utter** *(adj.)*: absolute; broad; complete; consummate; downright; entire; flat-out; full; gross; *high;* inclusive; *jimbang; keen; large;* most; *notable;* outright; perfect; *quite;* real; rank; sheer; total; thorough; unreserved; veritable; whole; *xtry.; yes; zealous;*

**utter** *(v.)*: articulate; bespeak; communicate; convey; declare; express; exclaim; enunciate; formulate; *give;* hold forth; *indicate; jaw; key in;* let out; mention; *notify;* noise; observe; pronounce; proclaim; quoth; relate; remark; rehearse; relay; say; speak; state; say; tell; *understate;* voice; verbalize; word; *xenophonia;* yak; *zero in;*

**utterable** *(adj.)*: articulable; bestowable; communicable; declarable; disclosable; expressible; *formable;* givable; *holler;* impartable; *jaw;* knowable; *lamentable;* mentionable; nameable; *oratory;* pronounceable; *quotable;* repeatable; speakable; tellable; *useable;* vocable; *worded; xenophobia;* yak; zero in; [*Ant.* unspeakable]

**utterly** *(adv.)*: altogether; absolutely; beyond doubt; completely; downright; entirely; fully; flatly; far and away; *glaringly;* highly; indubitably; just; keenly; *literally;* most (certainly); *notably;* outright; positively; quite; really; surely; soundly; totally; unreservedly; very; wholly; 'xactly [slang]; *ywis* [arch.]; 'zactly [dial.];

**uxorious** *(adj.)*: adoring; *becharmed; caring;* devoted; doting; excessively devoted; fond; fussing; *groveling;* henpecked; indulgent; *jumping to it; keen;* loving; meek; non-resistant; obsequious; overly-devoted; *passive; quixotic;* regardful; submissive; toadying; unresisting; *valentine;* worshipping; *xtry. devotion; yearnful; zealous;* [*Ant.* unloving]

# V

**vacant** *(adj.)*: abandoned; available; barren; clear; desolate; deserted; empty; evacuated; free; forsaken; gone; gant; *hollow;* inane; jejune; *kaput;* lacking; *moved out;* non-occupied; open; *plain;* quit; *relocated;* spare; tenantless; teemless; unused; uninhabited; unoccupied; void; vacated; without inhabitant; *x; yeld; zero;*

**vacate** *(v.)*: abandon; be off; clear out; depart; displace; desert; evacuate; exit; flee; go; hightail; immigrate; jilt; kiss goodbye; leave; migrate; not remain; olate; part; pull out; quit; remove; skedaddle; take leave; uproot; vanish; withdraw; xfer; yead; zip away;

**vacation** *(n.)*: absence; break; Christmas ~; *cruise;* day off; day trip; escape; excursion; furlough; *flight;* getaway; holiday; hiatus; *honeymoon;* itineration; journey; *kip;* leisure time; leave; liberty [nav.]; mini- ~; *night voyage;* off-time; *personal day;* paid ~; pleasure tour; quest; retreat; sabbatical; sojourn; shore leave [nav.]; trip; tour; *travel;* time off; *unwind;* voyage; visit; week off; *xenization; yong* [arch.]; zugunruhe;

**vacillate** *(v.)*: alternate; bobble; crisscross; change; dither; *erratic;* fluctuate; go back and forth; hem and haw; *interweave;* jag; jump; *kedge;* librate; meander; nutate; oscillate; pendulate; *quiver;* reel; reciprocate; shift; swing; sway; shilly-shally; turn; twist; teeter; totter; undulate; vary; waver; waffle; *x-ing;* yo-yo; zigzag;

**vacillation** *(n.)*: alternation; bobbling; changing; dithering; *erraticism;* fluctuation; going back and forth; *hesitation;* instability; indecision; joggling; *kedging;* libration; meandering; nutation; non-stability; oscillation; pendulating; *quivering;* reeling; shifting; turning; unstableness; vacillating; wavering; waffling; *x-ing;* yo-yoing; zigzagging;

**vagabond** *(n.)*: almsman; beggar; cadger; derelict; *estivator;* floater; gadabout; hobo; *idler;* javel; knockabout; landlouper; mendicant; no-good; *oberration;* panhandler; *quisby;* rolling stone; scavenger; tramp; *urchin;* vagrant; wanderer; wretch; *xenarthra; yahoo; zhlub;* [*see* sluggard]

**vagary** *(n.)*: aberration; bidding; crotchet; caprice; deviance; erraticism; fancy; general desire; hankering; impulse; jumpiness; *kinkiness;* liking; mood; notion; obliquity; pleasure; quirk; *reckoning;* shift; *thought;* urge; velleity; whim(sy); *xenenthesis;* yen; *zeal;*

**vagrancy** *(n.)*: alms-taking; begging; cadging; destitution; *errantry;* forlornness; gadding; homelessness; itinerancy; *javel; kern;* loafing; mendicancy; nomadism; oberration; peregrination; panhandling; *quisby;* roaming; scavenging; transience; *urchin;* vagrantness; wandering; *x-iency; yahoo;* zaanaim;

**vagrant** *(n.)*: alms-taker; bum; cadger; drifter; *estivator;* fugitive; gadabout; hobo; homeless person; *idler; javel;* kern; landlouper; mendicant; no-good; *oberration;* peregrinator; panhandler; *quisby;* rolling stone; scavenger; tramp; urchin; vagabond; wastrel; wretch; *xenarthra; yahoo; zhlub;*

**vague** *(adj.)*: ambiguous; blurry; clouded; dim; enclouded; equivocal; fuzzy; foggy; fuliginous; faint; gray; hazy; indefinite; indistinct; ill-defined; *jellylike;* kaleidoscopic; loose; murky; nebulous; obscure; obfuscatory; poorly defined; quaggy; rough; sketchy; shadowy; turbid; umbratic; unclear; undefined; unapparent; unclarified; unfocused; veiled; woolly; *xerophthalmic;* yet unclear; *zero clarity;* [*Ant.* visible]

**vagueness** *(n.)*: ambiguity; blurriness; cloudiness; dimness; equivocality; fuzziness; fogginess; grayness; haziness; indefiniteness; indistinctness; *jellylike; kaleidoscopic;* looseness; murkiness; nebulousness; obscurity; poor definition; quagginess; roughness; sketchiness; shadowiness; turbidity; unclearness; veil; woolliness; *xeroophthalmia; yuckiness; zero clarity;* [*Ant.* visibility]

**vain** *(adj.)*: arrogant; big-headed; boastful; conceited; disdainful; egotistical; flatulent; gloating; haughty; imperious; inflated; *jackanapes;* know-it-all; lofty; *magnificent;* narcissistic; ostentatious; overproud; proud; quick-to-boast; *reassured;* self-important; stuck-up; turgid; unhumbled; vaunting; vainglorious; wrapped up in oneself; *x-proud; yelping; zero humility;*

**vainly** *(adv. proudly)*: arrogantly; boastfully; conceitedly; disdainfully; egotistically; flatulently; gloatingly; haughtily; imperiously; *jackanapes; know-it-all;* loftily; *magnificently;* narcissistically; ostentatiously; proudly; *quick-to-boast; reassuredly;* self-righteously; turgidly; unhumbly; vauntingly; *wrapped up in oneself; x-proud;* yelpingly; zero humility;

**vainly** *(adj. unsuccessfully)*: aimlessly; bootlessly; cursedly; *desolately;* emptily; futilely; gainlessly; hopelessly; ineffectually; in vain; jejunely; *kaput;* lucklessly; meaninglessly; non-beneficially; otiosely; pointlessly; *quirkily; reasonless;* senselessly; to no avail; unsuccessfully; unprofitably; valuelessly; without success; *x'ed;* yieldlessly; *zero-profit;*

**valet** *(n.)*: attendant; butler; chamberlain; demiurge; employee; footman; gillie; house steward; indentured servant; *Jeeves;* keeper; lackey; minister; manservant; naperer; offsider; pantler; quarter-waiter; *retainer* [arch.]; servant; *trusty servant;* underservant; *varlet;* waiter; x-man; yeoman; *zaikai;*

**valiance** *(n.)*: adventurousness; boldness; chivalry; daring; enterprise; fearlessness; gallantry; hardiness; intrepidity; *jarless;* knightliness; lion-heartedness; manfulness; mettle; nobleness; *obstinacy;* pluck; *quakeless; resolve;* strength; spirit; *tenacity;* undauntedness; valantness; valor; warproof; *xtry. ~; yung* [Chin.]; zealousness;

**valiant** *(adj.)*: audacious; brave; courageous; daring; enterprising; fearless; gallant; heroic; intrepid; *jarless;* knightly; lion-hearted; manly; noble; *overconfident;* plucky; questful; *resolute;* stout; strong; *tenacious;* unafraid; undaunted; valorous; *wherewithal; xtry.;* yare; zealous; [*Ant.* vexed]

**valid** *(adj.)*: authentic; acceptable; bona fide; binding; cogent; correct; credible; defensible; efficacious; factual; genuine; honest; inspected; justifiable; *known;* legitimate; merited; non-counterfeit; official; okay; proper; qualified; real; sure; sound; true; unerring; veritable; well-tried; *x-parent; yes;* 'zactly [dial.]; [*Ant.* void]

**validate** *(v.)*: authenticate; bear out; confirm; demonstrate; establish; fix; give proof; homologate; illustrate; justify; kithe [Scot.]; legitimize; make legal; notarize; okay; prove; *questionless;* rubber-stamp; reconfirm; substantiate; show; sustain; try; uphold; verify; warrant; x-certify; *yes; zero doubt;* [*Ant.* void]

**validation** *(n.)*: authentication; bearing out; confirmation; demonstration; establishment; final check; giving of proof; homologation; illustration; justification; *kithe [Scot.];* legitimization; making legal; notarization; okay; proof; *questionlessness;* reconfirmation; seal; stamp of approval; testimonial; upholding; verification; warrant; x-certification; *yes; zero doubt;* [*Ant.* voiding]

**valley** *(n.)*: *arroyo;* basin; cirque; dale; dingle; depression; *excavation;* flood meadow; glen; gorge; hollow; intervale; *Jackson Hole;* kar; krantz; lowlands; lap; *meadow;* notch; *opening; pit;* quarry; ravine; slade; trough; underlands; vale; water gap; *xyrisic;* yunga; *zanja;* [*Ant.* vertex]

**valor** *(n.)*: audacity; bravery; courage; daring; enterprise; fearlessness; fortitude; gallantry; heroism; intrepidity; *jarless;* knightliness; lion-heartedness; manliness; nerve; *obstinacy;* prowess; *quakeless; resolve;* stoutness; stalwartness; *tenacity;* undauntedness; valiance; wherewithal; *xtry. ~;* yareness; zeal;

**valorous** *(adj.)*: adventurous; bold; chivalrous; dauntless; enterprising; fearless; gallant; hardy; intrepid; *jarless;* knightly; lion-hearted; manly; never-fearing; *obstinate;* plucky; questful; *resolute;* strong; spirited; stalwart; *tenacious;* unflinching; unfrightened; valiant; *wherewithal; xtry.;* yare; zealous;

**valuable** *(adj.)*: advantageous; admired; beneficial; costly; dear(-bought); expensive; estimable; *favorable; fine;* good; golden; helpful; highly-valued; important; invaluable; judged worthy; *king's ransom; lovely;* meaningful; much-admired; *nice;* of great price; precious; pricey; prized; quality; rich; respected; sought-after; treasured; useful; valued; worthwhile; worthy; worth it's weight in gold; *xtry.; yieldful; zestful;* [*Ant.* valueless]

**value** *(n.)*: assessment; book ~; cost; dearness; excellence; evaluation; face ~; fair-trade; fineness; goodness; highness; importance; *judgment; known ~;* list price; merit; net worth; *opinion;* price; quality; regard; significance; treasure; unit price; usefulness; valuation; validity; virtue; worth; *xenodiagnosis; yield; zenith;* [*see* cost]

**value** *(v.)*: assess; appraise; *believe;* consider; deem; determine; evaluate; esteem; figure; gage; hold; *importance;* judge; *knowledge;* list; make out; measure; *number; overestimate; overrate;* put a ~ on; prize; quantize; regard; reckon; surmise; treasure; *underestimate; unerrate;* valuate; weigh; *XQ; yardstick; zamorin;*

**values** *(n.)*: aretaics; attitudes; beliefs; convictions; code of ethics; *doctrine;* ethics; family ~; *godliness;* honor; ideals; *judgments; kalokagathia* [Gr.]; *legitimacy;* morals; mores; *nobility;* old-time ~; principles; priorities; qualities; rules; sense of decency; standards; tenets; *uprightness;* virtues; way of life; *xtry.; yichus; zeal;*

**vandal** *(n.)*: aggressor; bad kid; criminal; desecrator; delinquent; evildoer; fiend; *graffiti;* hooligan; hood(lum); instigator; injurer; juvenile delinquent; *kern;* lowlife; marauder; nicker; *offender;* prankster; *quade [arch.];* rabble-rouser; ruffian; spoiler; troublemaker; thug; *undoer;* varlet; vandalizer; wrecker; *xiaoren;* yob; youthful offender; *zapper;*

**vandalism** *(n.)*: abuse; breaking; cruelty; defacement; desecration; destruction; evil; fiendishness; graffiti; hooliganism; harm; injury; iconoclast; juvenile delinquency; jeel; *knocking; loss;* mischief; naughtiness; *offense;* prank; *quashing;* ruining; ravagement; spoiling; trashing; undoing; *uglification;* violence; wrecking; wrongdoing; *x-ing;* yobbery; *zapping;*

**vandalize** *(v.)*: abuse; break; *commit offense;* deface; desecrate; despoil; destroy; endamage; *fiend; graffiti-painting;* harm; injure; impair; jeel; *knock down;* lay waste; mar; *nicker; offend;* prang; *quade* [arch.]; ravage; ruin; spray paint; spoil; tear up; trash; uglify; vandalise [Br.]; *vitiate;* wreak havoc; wreck; *x-gress;* yob; *zap;*

**vanish** *(v.)*: *abate;* become invisible; cease to be seen; disappear; dematerialize; evaporate; ebb; fade (away); go away; hide; immaterialize; just disappear; keep out of view; *killed;* leave no trace; melt away; not be found; *out of sight;* pass off the scene; *quick-vanish;* recede; sink away; turn invisible; *unseen;* vaporize; withdraw; wither; *xeromatous; yield;* zip away; [see perish]

**vanity** *(n. pride)*: arrogance; bigheadedness; conceit; disdain; egotism; fullness of self; gloating; haughtiness; imperiousness; immodesty; inflatedness; *jackanapes; know-it-all;* loftiness; magisterialness; narcissism; overconfidence; ostentation; pride; *quilicom* [arch.]; *ruff* [arch.]; self-importance; snobbery; turgidity; *unhumbled;* vainness; vainglory; wind; *xenophobia; yieldless;* zero humility;

**vanquish** *(v.)*: annihilate; beat; conquer; defeat; expugn; foil; gut; hammer; *invincible; junk [slang];* kill; lick; master; massacre; *neutralize;* overcome; overtake; prevail; quench; quash; rout; subjugate; smite; triumph (over); unseat; vitiate; worst; whoop; *x-ing; yank down;* zap;

**vanquishment** *(n.)*: achievement; brilliant ~; conquering; conquest; championship; domination; debellation; exultation; feat; glory; gain; historic ~; *invincibleness;* jubilee; knockout; *lordship;* mastery; *nike* [G.]; overcoming; prevailing; prize; *quashing;* reward; success; triumph; uncontested ~; victory; victoriousness; win(ning); *xtry. win;* yell; zing;

**vapor** *(n.)*: atomization; brume; breath; cloud; dew; exhalation; exhaust; fog; fume; gas; gauze; haze; *incloud; jumbo cloud; KH instability; London fog;* mist; nimbus; *overcast;* puff; pother; *quasi-vaporous;* reek; rack; steam; smoke; *thundercloud; umbered;* vapour; *veil;* wisp; *xenon cloud; yellowy cloud; zirconium cloud;*

**vaporize** *(v. evaporate)*: atomize; boil; become vapor; change into vapor; disseminate; evaporate; fumigate; fog; gasify; *heat up;* incloud; *jumbo cloud;* kier; *lour;* mist; nebulize; oxygenate; pass off into vapor; *quicken;* ret; spray; turn into vapor; *upset;* vanish; wallop; *xuld [arch.]; yield;* zoutch;

**vaporize** *(v. destroy)*: annihilate; blot out; crush; destroy; demolish; disintegrate; expunge; exterminate; finish off; gasify; *havoc; incinerate; junk;* kill; lay waste; liquidate; level; *massacre;* nullify; overthrow; pulverize; quash; raze; smash; snuff out; terminate; unbuild; *vitiate;* wipe out; *x-ing; yank down;* zap;

**vaporous** *(adj.)*: aeriform; beclouded; cloudy; dim; enclouded; ethereal; foggy; fumy; gaseous; hazy; included; insubstantial; *jumbo clouded; KH instability;* lour; misty; nebulous; obscure; puffy; *qually* [arch.]; reeky; steamy; smoky; turbid; unclear; vapory; wispy; *xenon cloud; yellowy cloud; zero-zero;*

**variable** *(adj.)*: alterable; adjustable; *bendable;* changeable; capricious; deviating; erratic; flexible; fluctuating; fickle; *growable;* herky-jerky; inconstant; irregular; jerky; kaleidoscopic; labile; mutable; movable; non-fixed; oscillating; patchy; protean; precarious; positionable; *questionable;* random; switchable; stochastic; temperamental; unsteady; uneven; unpredictable; unfixed; varying; wavering; *xenomorphic;* yo-yo; ziggety;
**variance** *(n.)*: alteration; *big difference;* change; conflict; difference; discrepancy; edition; far cry; *growth;* heterogeneity; incompatibility; inconsistency; incongruity; *jumping;* key difference; *leeway* modification; nonagreement; oppugnancy; otherness; permutation; qualification; revision; shift; transformation; unharmoniousness; unconformity; variation; *warping; xenomorph; yaw; zigzag;*
**variant** *(n.)*: alternate; adaptation; branch-off; change; deviation; divergence; *edition; fluctuation; growth;* heterogeneity; improvement; *jumping;* kind; *lowering;* modification; mutation; new strain; obliquation; permutation; *quirk;* revision; sort; type; *upgrade;* variation; *warping; xenomorph; yaw; zigzag;*
**variation** *(n.)*: alteration; adaptation; branching off; change; deviation; difference; disparity; edition; fluctuation; gradual change; hade; heterogeneity; inconstancy; jumping around; *key change; lowering;* modification; mutation; nonconformity; otherness; particularization; permutation; qualification; revision; shift; transformation; unconformity; variance; vagary; variant; *warping; xenomorph;* yaw; *zigzag;*
**variety** *(n. assortment)*: assortment; array; big selection; collection; diversity; extensive ~; full array; *grouping;* hodgepodge; heterogeneity; *interesting ~;* jumble; keen assortment; *load;* large quantity; multiplicity; miscellany; mixture; mixed bag; number; olio; options; pastiche; quantity; range; selection; smorgasbord; *ton; uberous;* variations; wide selection; wealth; xtry. selection; *yelm; zillions;*
**variety** *(n. type)*: *analysis;* brand; breed; class; category; cast; designation; estate; fashion; form; feather; genre; group; genus; genotype; heading; ilk; *jack;* kind; lot; label; make; manner; model; mold; nature; order; phylum; persuasion; *quarter;* rank; rating; sort; species; strain; style; stripe; type; *unit;* variation; *way; x-class; year-class; zoological classification;*
**various** *(adj.)*: assorted; bounteous; contrasted; different; diverse; erratic; full-gamut; *great variety;* heterogeneous; inconsonant; incompatible; jumbled; *kinds;* lots; mixed; many; miscellaneous; numerous; of all kinds; plentiful; *quantity; ranging;* sundry; several; *tons;* unlike; unsimilar; varied; wide-ranging; *xtry.; yards; zillion;*
**varnish** *(n.)*: alkyd; buff; coat; *Danish oil;* enamel; finish; gloss; glaze; high-gloss finish; *inceration;* japan; *keen;* lacquer; marine spar; nigrosine; oil ~; overglaze; polish; quality coating; *resin;* shellac; spirit ~; topcoat; tung oil; urethane; veneer; wax; *xesturgy; yare; zinc flourosilicate;*
**varnish** *(v.)*: apply ~; burnish; buff; coat; daub; enamel; furbish; finish; gloss; glaze; *high-gloss; inceration;* japan; *keen;* lacquer; make shiny; *nigrosine;* overglaze (-polish); polish; *quartz sand;* rub; shellac; topcoat; use ~ on; veneer; wax; *xesturgy; yare; zinc flourosilicate;*
**vary** *(v.)*: alter; branch off; change; deviate; edit; fiddle with; *grow; heighten;* innovate; improve; jib; *key to; lower;* modify; novate; overhaul; *put right;* qualify; revise; switch; shift; turn; transform; *upgrade;* veer; warp; *xenomorph; yaw; zigzag;*
**vase** *(n.)*: azalea; bottle; container; *depository;* earthenware ~; flowerpot; gombroon; holder; *inurn;* jar; jug; *jardinière* [F.]; *kelebe* [Gr.]; *koro* [Jap.]; *lily ~; Ming ~; narcissus; olla;* pot; planter; pottery; *quarrefoil;* rose ~; *sculptured ~;* table ~; urn; vessel; wildflower ~; *xerophyte;* yabba; zun;
**vast** *(adj.)*: astronomical; abundant; big; boundless; capacious; colossal; disproportionate; enormous; extensive; expansive; fantastic; great; gigantic; huge; immense; jumbo-sized; king-size; large; massive; never-ending; oversize; prodigious; quantitative; *remarkable;* sizable; substantial; tremendous; unlimited; voluminous; wide; whopping; XL; *yet unbounded; zaftig;*

**vastness** *(n.)*: amplitude; bigness; capaciousness; disproportion; enormity; extent; expansiveness; fullness; greatness; hugeness; immensity; infinitude; jumboness; *kazillion;* largeness; magnitude; *never-ending;* overlargeness; prodigiousness; quantity; roominess; size; tremendousness; *unbelievable;* vastitude; wideness; XL; *yet unbounded; zillion of miles;*

**vat** *(n.)*: * ale- ~; basin; cistern; cask; container; cauldron; crucible; dryfat; *enormous ~;* font; grape press; holding tank; iron ~; *jumbo-sized ~;* kier; keeve; kettle; *leach-tub;* mashing-tub; nap; oil ~; press; pot; *quinderkyn;* reservoir; receptacle; steeper; tub; tun; tank; utility tank; vessel; wine- ~; *winepress; xeres ~; yayin ~; zun;*

**vault** *(n.)*: armored ~; bank ~; coffer; deposit box; *ebony chest;* firebox; *gold;* hidden ~; iron box; *jewel chest;* keep; keister; lockbox; money box; *no access; object;* protected ~; quarter-inch thick steel-walled ~; receptacle; repository; safe; strong-box; top-security ~; utility box; *valuables;* wall safe; *xtr-reinforced ~; yadzutsu [Jap.]; zechin;*

**veer** *(v.)*: alter; bend; curve; careen; deviate; el; fold; go off; hook; incline; jibe; knuckle; *left turn;* modulate; move off; *nonlinear;* offset; pull; quat; rove; swerve; slue; turn; *uncinate;* verge; wind; *xy-curve;* yaw; zag;

**vegetable** *(n.)*: artichoke; bean; crop; *deciduous plant;* edible; flora; fern; food; garden plant (-green); herb; *item;* julienne ~; *kiwi;* legume; *melon; non-animal;* organic ~; produce; plant; *quickset;* root; steamed ~; *salad greens; tomato;* uncooked ~; veggie [slang]; winter ~; *xerad;* yield; zymophyte;
   **Type of vegetables**: artichoke; bean, carrot, dulse; eggplant; fennel; gourd; green bean, haricot bean; iceberg lettuce; jalapeño; kale; lettuce; maize; nopal; onion; potato, quandong; radish, spinach; tomato; turnip; udo; velvet bean; watercress; xanthosoma; yam; zucchini;

**vegetarian** *(adj.)*: anti-carnivorous; baccivorous; *cabbage-eating;* dietarily ~; ethically ~; fruitarian; granivorous; graminvorous; herbivorous; *in vitro; just vegetables; keep from meat;* lacto~; meatless; miagre; naturalist; no-meat; ovolacto~; plant-eating; phytivorous; phytophagous; quercivorous; raw ~; semi- ~; *Tamil;* uncarnivorous; vegetable-eating; vegan; without meat; *xanthosoma; yam-eating;* zero meat;

**vegetarian** *(n.)*: *abstainer;* baccivore; *cabbage-eater;* dietary ~; ethical ~; fruitarian; granivore; herbivore; herbalist; *in vitro; just vegetables; keep from meat;* lacto~; meat-abstainer; naturalist; non-carnivore; ovolacto~; plant-eater; phytivore; quercivore; raw ~; semi- ~; *Tamil; uncarnivorous;* vegetable-eating; vegan; *without meat; xanthosoma; yam-eater;* zero meat;

**vegetate** *(v. grow)*: advance; blossom; climb; develop; enlarge; flourish; germinate; grow; hibernate; *heighten;* increase; *jump up; keep growing;* luxuriate; mature; *nourish; overgrow;* progress; *quantum growth;* rise; sprout; shoot up; take root; *thrive;* upshoot; *vivify;* wax greater; XL; *yain* [arch.]; *zoom;*

**vegetate** *(v. sleep)*: aestivate; bed down; *crash;* do nothing; estivate; fall asleep; get shuteye; hibernate; idle; just sit; knock off; loaf; merely exist; nap; *oversleep;* pass the time; *quiet;* repose; sleep; take nap; *unconscious;* vegetate; wait; *x-sleep; yawn;* zonk (out);

**vegetation** *(n.)*: annual; budding; biennial; cutting; crops; *deciduous plant;* evergreen; flora; fern; greenery; greens; growth; herbage; houseplant; herbage; *inflorescence;* jungle-growth; kerf; legume; maquis; *notholaena;* organic plant; plant; quickset; *root;* seedling; shoot; triennial; undergrowth; verdure; wort; *weed; xerophyte;* yarb [dial.]; *zymophyte;*

**vehemence** *(n.)*: ardor; alacrity; burning; commitment; devotion; enthusiasm; energy; eagerness; fervency; fervor; force; gusto; heartiness; intensity; *joy;* keenness; liveliness; mercilessness; might; *necessity;* overzealousness; passion; *quickness;* readiness; relish; spirit; savor; stridency; tigerlike ferocity; *ultra-zealous;* vigor; wholeheartedness; *x-fervor;* yareness; zeal;

**vehement** *(adj.)*: ardent; burning; committed; devoted; enthusiastic; eager; fervent; gung-ho; hearty; intense; impassioned; *jumping;* keen; lively; motivated; mad; merciless; *no holds barred;* overzealous; passionate; perfervid; quick; ready; spirited; strident; tigerish; unreserved; vigorous; wholehearted; *xenocentric;* yare; zealous; zestful;

**veil** *(n.)*: aridas ~; byssine ~; cloth; covering; curtain; drape; *enshroud;* facecloth; face covering; guise; hanging; Islamic ~; *inveiled; jaconet; kittel* [Heb.]; kredemnan; *layer;* mantilla; napkin; netting; outer ~; *pongee ~; quale; rajshahi ~;* shemogh; shroud; silk ~; tire; *under cover;* veiling; wimple; *xanthation; yashmak* [Mos.]; *Zaidi ~;*
**veil** *(v.)*: *artfulness;* bemask; conceal; cloak; cover; disguise; enshroud; *facade, garb;* hide; *incognito;* imbosk; *jape;* keep hidden; lay low; mask; *non-recognizable;* obscure; put out of view; *quat* [arch.]; *repress;* shroud; *tuck away; under cover;* vizand; wimple; *xenomorph; yashmak;* zero recognition;
**vein** *(n.)*: artery; arteriole; blood vessel; capillary; duct; *efflux; flow;* gate~; *hose;* innominate artery; jugular; *kurvey;* lode; *line;* main artery; neck- ~; *outlet;* pulmonary ~; passage; *quart; route;* saphena; tube; *units;* vena; venule; varicose; varix; *way; xfer; Y-branch; zoicic;*
**velocity** *(n.)*: acceleration; briskness; celerity; dexterity; expedition; fastness; gait; hurriedness; impetus; jildi [mil.]; keenness; liveliness; momentum; movement; nimbleness; *overhastiness;* pace; quickness; rapidity; rate; speed; tempo; *uninhibited speed; volant; whipping; x-speed; yar;* zippiness;
**vendetta** *(n.)*: avengement; attack; battle; crusade; dispute; embroilment; feud; grudge; hostilities; *ill-will; justice; jihad* [Mos.]; *killing-spree; luctation* [arch.]; mêlée; *negation;* occursion; personal feud; quarrel; retaliation; revenge; *strife;* total war; *unrest;* vengeance; war; *x-ing out;* yed; *zapping;*
**vendor** *(n.)*: *advertiser;* broker; business owner; chapman; dealer; distributor; exporter; *furnisher;* grocer; handler; importer; jobber; jagger; kiddier; *let go for;* merchant; marketer; monger; *négociant* [F.]; operator; peddler; purveyor; provider; qualified retailer; retailer; reseller; seller; supplier; trader; tradesman; trafficker; *utterer;* victualer; VAR; wholesaler; xylopolist; yarn man; *zyalde [arch.];*
**veneer** *(n.)*: appearance; aesthetics; bemasking; covering; deception; exterior; façade; facing; fascine; guise; *hidden;* inlay; *jape; kept hidden;* layer; mask; *not real;* overlay; outside; paneling; *qua [arch.];* resurfacing; surface; topcoat; *unreal;* vizand; verisimilitude; wainscot; wall paneling; xylotechnigraphy; yare; *zero recognition;*
**venerate** *(v.)*: admire; bow to; consider; defer to; esteem; fear; favor; give honor; honor; idolize; *just love;* kneel to; look up to; make obeisance to; *note; obeisance;* prefer; praise; *quality;* respect; regard; revere; salute; think of; *unmitigated respect;* value; worship; *xtry.; yield; zero contempt;*
**veneration** *(n.)*: admiration; *bowing;* consideration; dignity; deference; devoirs; esteem; fear; giving of honor; honor; homage; high regard; idolization; *justness; kneeling;* love; *merit;* non-contempt; obeisance; praise; *quality;* respect; regard; repute; reverence; *salutation;* tribute; *unmitigated respect;* venerability; worship; *xtry.;* yielding; *zero contempt;*
**vengeance** *(n.)*: avengement; blood; comeback; counterattack; despitefulness; evening the score; fixing; getting back; hitting back; *implacableness;* justice; *kindless; lex talionis* [L.]; malice; *nastiness; obduracy;* payback; punishment; quittal; retaliation; reprisal; retribution; revenge; spite; settling the score; sweet revenge; terror; *unkindness;* vindication; wrath; *xenophobia; yucky; zap;*
**vengeful** *(adj.)*: avenging; bitter; cruel; despiteful; embittered; foul; galsome; hateful; implacable; jaded; kindless; loathsome; malicious; nasty; obdurate; *pernicious; quede* [arch.]; revengeful; spiteful; *treacherous;* unforgiving; vindictive; wreakful; *xenophobic; yucky; zealotic;*
**vengefulness** *(n.)*: acrimony; bitterness; cruelty; despitefulness; embitterment; festering; gall; hatefulness; implacableness; jadedness; kindlesness; *loathsomeness;* malice; nastiness; obduracy; *perniciousness; quede [arch.];* revengefulness; spite; *terror;* unkindness; vindictiveness; wickedness; *xenophobia; yuckiness;* zeal to avenge;
**venom** *(n.)*: animal poison; bane; cobra ~; deadly poison; evil; fatal poison; *grievous;* habu ~; *inee; jararaca; kex;* lethal poison; moccasin ~; noxiousness; ophidian ~; poison; *quass;* rattlesnake ~; snake ~; spit- ~; toxin; *upas;* virulence; water snake ~; *xylostein; yeara;* zootoxin; [see malice]
**venomous** *(adj.)*: à la mort [F.]; baneful; contaminated; deadly; deleterious; envenomed; fatal; foul; *grievous;* harmful; injurious; *jeopardous; killing;* lethal; malefic; nocuous; *orpiment;* poisonous; *quelling;* rancorous; scatheful; toxic; unsafe; virulent; *woeful; xylostein; yeara;* zootoxic; [see corrupt]

**vent** *(n.)*: aperture; air-hole; break; crack; chimney; discharge; escape; exhaust; flue; gap; grate; hole; incavation; intake; jaw-hole; *khor [Arab.];* louver; micro- ~; naris; outlet; opening; orifice; pipe; *quarter-inch opening;* register; spout; *thing;* uptake; ventilator; *wind way;* weep hole; *x-vent;* yawn; zanja;
**verbal** *(adj.)*: audible; bespoken; *communicative;* declarative; enunciated; *force; gab;* hearable; *identifiable; judicable; key in;* lexical; lingual; morphemic; nuncupatory; noised; nuncupative; oral; pronounced; parol; *quoted;* rhetorical; spoken; stated; told; uttered; unwritten; vocal; voiced; word-of-mouth; *xenophonia; yak; ziraleet;* [Ant. voiceless]
**verbalize** *(v.)*: articulate; bespeak; comment; convey; declare; discuss; express; form into words; gab; have words; indicate; *jaw; key in;* let out; mention; notify; noise; observe; put into words; quoth; relate; remark; say; speak; tell; utter; voice; vocalize; word; *xenophonia;* yak; *zero in;*
**verbatim** *(adj.)*: accurately; *believably;* correctly; dead-on; exactly; faithfully; flawlessly; faithfully; *genuine; highly accurate;* identical; just right; *keen; kyrilexy;* literal; letter-perfect; *meticulous;* non-flawed; *over-particular;* perfectly; precisely; quoted; reliably; strict; true; unerringly; verily; word-for-word; word perfect; 'xactly [slang]; *ywis* [arch.]; 'zactly [dial.];
**verge** *(n.)*: approach; border; brink; coast; *dawn;* edge; frontier; fringe; *gate;* hem; inception; *jurisdiction; kept limit;* limit; margin; *narrow;* outskirts; perimeter; quadra; rim; *side;* threshold; ulterior; virge; *without; x-border; yonder; zone;*
**verification** *(n.)*: authentication; bearing out; check; confirmation; demonstration; establishment; final certification; giving of proof; homologation; illustration; insurance; justification; *knowing;* legitimization; making sure; notarization; okay; proof; *questionless;* reconfirmation; substantiation; testimonial; upholding; validation; warrant; warrent; x-certification; *yes; zero doubt;* [Ant. voidance]
**verify** *(v.)*: authenticate; bear out; check; confirm; demonstrate; establish; fix; give proof; homologate; illustrate; justify; kithe [Scot.]; legitimize; make sure; nail down; okay; prove; *questionless;* reconfirm; substantiate; show; sustain; try; uphold; validate; warrant; x-certify; *yes; zero doubt;* [Ant. void]
**verily** *(adv.)*: actually; accurately; beyond question; correctly; definitely; exactly; factually; faithfully; genuinely; honestly; indubitably; *justifiably;* knowledgably; literally; most truly; nothing else but; of a truth; precisely; quite; really; surely; truly; truthfully; unquestionably; veritably; with truth; 'xactly [slang]; *ywis* [arch.]; 'zactly [dial.];
**vermin** *(n.)*: annoyance; bug; cockroach; dog; *earwig;* flea; grub; *herbivore;* insect; irritant; *jointworm; kaleworm;* louse; maggot; nuisance; *oligochaete;* pest; parasite; *quab;* rat; slime; trouble; *undesirable;* varmint; worm; weasel; *xyleborus;* yuck; *zyzzogeton;*
**vernacular** *(n.)*: argot; buzzword; colloqialism; dialect; expression; familiar language; glossa; household words; informal speech; idiomatic language; jive; *kitschy;* language; lingo; *modern;* native speech; ordinary language; popular usage; *quirk; rendition;* speech; slang; talk; usage; *verlan* [F.]; vulgar language; words; *xenography;* yawp; *zaumnyi* [Rus.]; [see cussword]
**versatile** *(adj.)*: adaptable; bendable; changeable; convertible; *doable;* exchangeable; flexible; generally able; handy; interchangeable; *jump; key; labile;* multipurpose; multi-use; non-fixed; open; polyergic; protean; *queachy [arch.];* reversible; switchable; transformable; useful; variable; workable; *x-able;* yielding; *zet [dial.];*
**versatility** *(n.)*: adaptability; bendableness; changeability; convertibility; ductility; elasticity; flexibility; give; handiness; impressionability; *jumping;* keenness; limberness; multi-usefulness; non-rigidity; *operativeness;* pliability; *quantity;* resourcefulness; stretchiness; transformability; usefulness; variableness; workableness; *xtry. uses;* yieldedness; *zet [dial.];*
**verse** *(n. passage of scripture)*: address; Bible reference; chapter and verse; *content; division;* extract; excerpt; *finding;* God's Word; Holy Bible; item; jewel; KJV; locus classicus [L.]; *message; nugget; oracle;* passage; pericope; portion; quotation; reference; Scripture; section; segment; selection; text; *unit;* verset; words; *x-mal [G.]; yesod mora [Heb.];* Zech.;

**verse** *(n. poetry)*: acrostic; ballad; couplet; doggerel; ditty; elegy; free verse; georgic; hexastich; iamb; jingle; kyrielle; limerick; lyric; metrical language; madrigal; nursery rhyme; orthometry; poetry; *poem;* quatrain; rhyme; sonnet; triolet; unmetered poem; versification; *words; Xenphanean; Yeatsism; zetetic;*

**verse** *(n. stanza)*: acatalectic; *bob;* couplet; cinquain; canto; *chorus;* dimeter; division; epode; fit; glyconian; hexameter; irregular ~; *jingo; kasida;* line; monostich; *meter; neck ~;* ogdoastich; pentstich; portion; quatrain; regular ~; stanza; staff; stave; triplet; tetrastich; unit; uneven ~; *versicle; words; x-mal [G.]; yo fu [Chin.]; zemirah;*

**versed** *(adj.)*: acquainted; adept; *brilliant;* conversant; deep-versed; experienced; familiar; fluent; good; hard-bitten; informed; intimate; *jolly good;* knowledgeable; *laudable;* moderated; matured; not ignorant; outstanding; proficient; qualified; real good; skilled; seasoned; trained; tempered; up-to-date; very familiar; well-versed (-read, -informed); xtry.; *you-beaut [Aus.]; zippy;*

**version** *(n.)*: account; adaptation; brand; change; conversion; description; edition; form; gloss; *harmonization;* interpretation; iteration; *justification;* kind; literal translation; metaphrase; modification; new ~; *optimization; perversion;* paraphrase; portrayal; *qualified rendering;* report; revision; rendering; rendition; renovation; style; translation; update; variation; variant; variety; written ~; word-for-word translation; *xlation; yielding; zay [dial.];* [*see* Bible; variation]

**vertex** *(n.)*: apex; apogee; brow; crest; crown; *destination;* extremity; farthest height; greatest height; height; high point; *increase; jut;* kop; limit; mountaintop; *nib; overmost point;* peak; pinnacle; *quoif; ridge;* summit; top; upper extremity; very top; *way up; xtry; yonder point;* zenith; [*Ant.* valley]

**vertical** *(adj.)*: apeak; *bendless;* columnar; decurrent; erect; endwise; endways; *fixed; geometrically normal;* high; intersecting at right angles; jutting; *kept upright;* linear; mile-high; *non-horizontal;* orthotropic; on end; perpendicular; plumb; quite erect; right-angle; rampant [heraldry]; standing; sheer; straight-up; transverse; *tall;* upright; upend; up and down; upstanding; *vertically;* wholly standing; *xtr. straight;* y-axis; zenith-ward;

**vessel** *(n.)*: ark; box; bowl; boat; container; craft; depository; *ewer; firkin;* Grecian urn; holder; *iron chest;* jug; kist; *lockbox;* marine ~; navy ~; *ocean-going ~;* pot; pyx; *quinderkyn;* receptacle; ship(ping container); trunk; urceole; vasculum; vehicle; wooden crate; *xebec; yabba [Jam.];* zun; [*see* ship]

**vestige** *(n.)*: allusion; bit; clue; daud; drop; evidence; footstep; glimmer; hint; indication; intimation; *junt;* kernel; leftover; mark; nugget; ounce; piece; *presence; quantity;* remnant; relic; shadow; sign; trace; umbrage; visual clue; wit; *x-particle; yngot [arch.]; zum [dial.];*

**vestigial** *(adj.)*: atrophic; *bits-and-pieces; ceased;* dated; expired; functionless; *gone;* holdover; inoperative; *junked; kaput;* leftover; moribund; nonfunctioning; obsolete; past prime; *quondam;* remaining; surviving; *token;* useless; vestige; worn-out; *x'ed; yesteryear; zero use;*

**vestment** *(n.)*: alb; black gown; cincture; chasuble; cloth; dalmatic; dress; ecclesiastical robe; frock; garb; habiliment; ihram; jerkin; kirtle; liturgical garment; mantle; mozzetta; *nabedrennik;* outer garment; pallium; pontificals; *queen's robe;* robe; surplice; stole; tunic(le); uniform; vesture; *wardrobe; Xaviarian ~; yedder; zucchetto;*

**veteran** *(adj.)*: adept; battle-ready; competent; certified; deft; experienced; expert; familiar; *great;* habilitated; highly experienced; *instructor;* job-trained; knowledgeable; *legendary;* master; *no stranger;* old-hand; professional; qualified; ripened; retired; seasoned; skilled; trained; tried-and-tested; understanding; versed; weathered; *xenagogic; years of experience; zest;*

**veteran** *(n.)*: *army retired;* battle-experienced ~; campaigner; *discharged;* ex-soldier; former soldier; G.I,; hero; *infantry retired; janissary; kern; legend;* marine; *navy ~;* old soldier; POW; quondam soldier; retired military; *soldier; trainer; unsung hero;* vet; war hero; warhorse; *x-soldier; yeoman; zoauve;*

**vex** *(v.)*: aggravate; burden; chivy; confuse; distress; exasperate; frustrate; grieve; harrow; irritate; jangle; *kiaugh [Scot.]; livid;* menace; nonplus; *oppress;* perplex; *queach [arch.];* rankle; stump; trouble; torment; upset; *victimize;* wilder; *x-ing; yearn; zing;*

**vexation** *(n.)*: annoyance; adversity bind; burden; consternation; difficulty; distress; exasperation; frustration; grief; hardship; incommodity; jam; kink; *load; misfortune;* nuisance; obstacle; problem; *quandary;* rattle; strait; trouble; upheaval; vesation; woe; worries; *xerotripsis; yuckiness; zhlubby;*
**vexatious** *(adj.)*: annoying; adverse; burdensome; calamitous; difficult; distressing; exasperating; frustrating; grievous; hard; irritating; jarring; knotty; *lousy; messy;* noisome; onerous; problematic; pesky; quisquose; rattling; saddening; troublesome; trying; unpleasant; vexing; woeful; *xerotripsis; yucky; zhlubby;*
**viability** *(n.)*: achievability; *believability;* credibility; doableness; effectiveness; feasibility; goodness; *helpfulness; intelligence;* judiciousness; *keenness;* logic; meetness; *no-nonsense;* obtainability; practicality; *quartful [arch.];* reasonableness; sensibility; tenability; usefulness; validity; workability; *xtry. effectiveness; yieldful; zero problem;*
**viable** *(adj.)*: achievable; acceptable; *believable;* credible; doable; effective; feasible; good (enough); *helpful; intelligent;* judicious; *keen;* logical; meet; no-nonsense; obtainable; practical; quite sensible; reasonable; realistic; sensible; tenable; useful; valid; workable; worthwhile; *xtry. effective; yieldful; zero problem;*
**vial** *(n.)*: acetabulum; bottle; bowl; cruse; cruet; container; decanter; *ewer;* flask; *galipot; holder; inurn;* jar; kit; lachrymatory; mazer; *neck; olla;* phial; *quart-vessel;* receptacle; *soldier [slang];* test tube; *urn;* vessel; winchester; *xeo;* yan; zun;
**vibrant** *(adj.)*: alive; animated; bright; brilliant; bubbly; colorful; dazzling; dynamic; energetic; enthusiastic; florid; frisky; glowing; high-energy; healthy; intense; *jovial;* keen; lively; *motivated;* nippy; *over-active;* pert; quickened; radiant; robust; spirited; *thrilling; upbeat;* vivacious; warm; *xtry;* yeasty; zesty; [*Ant.* vapid]
**vibrate** *(v.)*: agitate; bicker; chatter; didder; *excite;* flutter; growse [arch.]; hustle; *instability;* jiggle; knock; librate; move; nutate; oscillate; palpitate; quiver; rattle; shake; shudder; tremble; *unstable;* vacillate; wobble; *xuld [arch.];* yerk; *zigzag;*
**vicarious** *(adj.)*: alternate; bartered; commutative; delegated; exchanged; for; given in exchange; *handed over;* interchanged; instead of; *jockey; key trade; locum; modified; novate;* on behalf of; proxied; *quid pro quo* [L.]; replaced; substitutionary; succedaneous; traded; *undeserved; varied; work; xfer; yet for another;* zwapped [dial];
**vice** *(n.)*: atrocity; blemish; corruption; crime; debauchery; depravity; evil; fault; failing; godlessness; *heinousness;* iniquity; *jadedness; knavishness;* licentiousness; malfeasance; naughtiness; offense; perverseness; *quad;* rebellion; sin; transgression; unrighteousness; violation; vileness; wrongdoing; *xgression; yetzer hara* [Heb.]; *zymosis;*
**vice versa** *(adv.)*: alternately; backward; conversely; *different;* exchanged; flipped around; *go other way; heterogeneity;* inverted; just the opposite; *key trade; labile;* make it the other way; *negate;* opposite order; other-way-around; put the other way; *quo [L.];* reversed; swapped; turned around; *upside down;* vice-versa; *wrong way; xfer; you know what I mean; zwapped* [arch.];
**vicinity** *(n.)*: area; block; community; district; environs; foreground; general area; habitat; immediacy; *just about there; kehal* [Heb.]; locality; locale; *more or less;* neighborhood; outlying area; proximity; quadrant; region; surrounding area; territory; ubiety; vicinage; *well-nigh; xfer; yede [arch.];* zone;
**vicious** *(adj.)*: animalistic; brutal; cruel; dreadful; evil; ferocious; grievous; hostile; horrible; inhuman; junglish; kill-crazy; lionlike; mean; merciless; malefic; nasty; obnoxious; pernicious; *querulous;* raving; rancorous; rapacious; savage; terrible; unrestrained; violent; wild; *xtry. mean;* yahoo; *zoilean;*
**viciousness** *(n.)*: aggressiveness; brutality; cruelty; destructiveness; evil; ferociousness; grievousness; harshness; intensity; *jeopardizing; killing;* lion-likeness; meanness; mercilessness; nastiness; odiousness; pugnaciousness; *querulousness;* rapaciousness; savageness; terribleness; uncivility; violence; wildness; *xenophobia;* yelling; Zulu;

**victim** *(n.)*: agonizer; anguisher; butt; chump; casualty; *dead;* endurer; fatality; gazingstock; harmed party; injured party; *judderer;* kill; lamenter; martyr; nockingstock; object; prey; quarry; *rueful;* stooge; sufferer; target; *undergoer; victimized;* wretch; wounded; *x;* yowler; *zeroed in;*

**victor** *(n.)*: award-winner; beater; conqueror; champion; champ; defeater; dominator; expugner; frontrunner; *great;* hero; *invader; jubilant;* kemp; laureate; master; non-loser; overtaker; overcomer; prevailer; *quasher; ruler;* subjugator; subduer; triumpher; undefeated champ; vanquisher; winner; *xtry.;* yell; *zealous;* [Ant. vanquished]

**victorious** *(adj.)*: ascendant; *best;* conquering; champion; dominant; exultant; favored; glorious; *heroic;* invincible; jubilant; *kemp; leading;* master; non-defeated; overcoming; predominant; prevalent; prevailing; *quashing; ruling;* successful; triumphant; undefeated; unbeaten; vanquishing; winning; *xtry.; yelling;* zealous; ]Ant. vanquished]

**victory** *(n.)*: *achievement; brilliant ~;* conquering; conquest; championship; domination; debellation; exultation; feat; glory; gain; *historic ~; invincibleness;* jubilee; knockout; *lordship;* mastery; *nike* [Gr.]; overcoming; prosperity; prevailing; prize; *quashing; reward;* success; triumph; *uncontested ~;* upper hand; victoriousness; win(ning); *xtry. win; yell; zing;* [Ant. vanquishment]

**view** *(n.)*: angle; aspect; bearing; *big picture;* conception; disposition; evaluation; fancy; *ground; heart;* idea; impression; judgment; *knowledge;* leaning; mindset; notion; outlook; observation; perspective; point of view; panorama; prospect; quadriform; reckoning; standpoint; take; *ule;* viewpoint; way of seeing it; watch-point; *xenodiagnosis; yaw; zeal;*

**view** *(v.)*: assess; behold; consider; check out; descry; examine; face; fix eyes on; feast eyes on; gaze; have a look; inspect; *judge;* keep looking; look; make out; note; observe; perceive; peek; pan; ponder; *quick look;* regard; reconnoiter; see; survey; scrutinize; take in; *understand;* visualize; watch; *x-ray vision;* yeme; *zero in;*

**viewing** *(n.)*: antepast; baring; broadcast; cosmorama; debut; display; exhibition; exposition; full ~; gaze; *hone in;* inspection; *just-for-show; keek;* look; manifestation; non-concealment; oracle; preview; *private ~;* premiere; presentation; *quick look;* revelation; sneak peek; screening; showing; showcase; taking in; unveiling; uncovering; vernissage; whole picture; *x-view;* yielding; zero-concealment;

**viewpoint** *(n.)*: angle; assessment; belief; conviction; *conclusion;* decision; estimation; feeling; fancy; gauging; hunch; idea; judgment; *knowledge;* leaning; mind; notion; opinion; outlook; perspective; point of view; *quot homines tot sententiae* [L.]; reckoning; slant; take; thoughts; *unbiased ~;* view; vantage point; way of thinking; *xenodiagnosis; yaw; zeal;*

**vigilance** *(n.)*: alertness; attentiveness; *beware;* cautiousness; carefulness; *discernment; ever-watchful; fabian;* gingerness; heedfulness; intentiveness; *judicious;* keeping watch; leeriness; mindfulness; noticing; observation; precaution; quickness; regard; *suspicion;* tending; ultra-carefulness; vigor; watchfulness; wariness; *x-careful;* yare-handedness; *zeal;*

**vigilant** *(adj.)*: alert; attentive; *beware;* careful; discerning; ever-watchful; fabian; guarded; heedful; intentive; judicious; keeping in mind; leery; mindful; noticing; observant; on guard; precautious; quick-witted; regardful; *suspicious; tending;* ultra-careful; vigorous; watchful; wary; *x-careful;* yare-handed; *zärtlich* [G.];

**vigilante** *(n.)*: avenger; *battler;* crusader; *disputer;* enforcer; folk hero; *grudge;* hero; *ill-will; justice;* knight; *luctation* [arch.]; *mêlée;* nullifier; *occursion;* punisher; quarreler; retaliator; *strife; total war;* urban warrior; vengeance-taker; *vendetta;* warrior; *x-ing out; yed;* zapper;

**vigor** *(n.)*: ardor; brio; briskness; commitment; drive; exuberance; élan; ferocity; gusto; heartiness; intensity; *joyfulness;* kick; lustiness; muscle; *non-laziness;* oomph; pith; power; punch; *quickness;* robustness; spirit; thewiness; ultra-zealousness; vim; verve; wholeheartedness; *x-fervor;* yare; zest;

**vigorous** *(adj.)*: ambitious; brisk; committed; dynamic; enthusiastic; energetic; fervent; gung-ho; hearty; intense; jaunty; keen; lusty; motivated; *nippy;* overzealous; passionate; quick; raring; spirited; tigerish; unreserved; vehement; wholehearted; *xtry;* yare; zealous;

**vile** *(adj.)*: abominable; awful; base; brutish; bad; crude; coarse; detestable; despicable; evil; filthy; foul; godless; gauche; gross; horrid; indecent; ill-mannered; jaded; kitsch; lewd; licentious; miserable; mean; nasty; nauseating; obnoxious; odious; putrid; pathetic; *quad;* repugnant; rude; sordid; sleazy; sorry; tasteless; tactless; uncouth; unholy; vulgar; wretched; *x-rated;* yucky; zhlubby; [*see* savage; *Ant.* virtuous]

**vileness** *(n.)*: abomination; baseness; crudeness; degradation; evil; filthiness; gaucheness; godlessness; horridness; indecency; *jadedness;* kitsch; lewdness; meanness; nefariousness; offense; putridity; *quad;* reprehension; shamefulness; terribleness; uncouthness; vulgarity; wretchedness; *x-rating;* yuckiness; zhlubbiness; [*Ant.* virtue]

**vilify** *(v.)*: asperse; badmouth; calumniate; defame; denigrate; demonize; excoriate; falsely accuse; give bad name; harangue; insult; impugn; jab; knock; libel; malign; name-call; obloquy; put down; pan; *quib;* run down; slam; slander; slur; traduce; tarnish; *use;* vilipend; wipe; *xuld [arch.];* yellow; *zap;*

**village** *(n.)*: *assemblage;* burg; clachan; crossroads; country town; dorp; exurb; *fishing town; ghost town;* hamlet; *invillaged;* junction; kirk-town [Scot.]; kraal [Hottentot]; *location;* municipality; market town; *native town;* one-horse town; *oppidum* [Rom.]; place; pueblo; *quarter;* rancho; shire; settlement; town; *urban center;* vill; whistle stop [slang]; *Xenia;* yokel town; *zone;*

**villain** *(n.)*: antagonist; arch-enemy; bad guy; criminal; deviant; enemy; evildoer; felon; gangster; *highwayman;* injurer; *jailbird;* knuck; lawbreaker; malefactor; no-good; outlaw; perpetrator; public enemy; *quad;* rogue; scoundrel; transgressor; *underboss;* violator; wrongdoer; *xgressor;* yob; *zhlub;*

**villainous** *(adj.)*: abominable; bad; corrupt; diabolical; evil; fiendish; guileful; heinous; iniquitous; jaded; knavish; lawless; malevolent; nefarious; odious; pernicious; *quad;* ruthless; sinister; treacherous; unscrupulous; vile; vicious; wicked; *xgressing; yucky; zymotic;* [*Ant.* virtuous]

**vindicate** *(v.)*: acquit; absolve; bear out; clear; deraign; declare not guilty; destigmatize; exonerate; exculpate; free; give absolution to; hold not-guilty; indemnify; justify; *kithe;* let go; make absolution; *non-guilty; open;* prove (innocence); propugn; quit; remove blame; revenge; restore; *support;* totally acquit; undo damage; validate; withdraw charges; *x-out; yele [arch.];* zero out charges;

**vindication** *(n.)*: acquittal; bearing out; clearing; discharge; exoneration; exculpation; freedom; guiltlessness established; holding not guilty; indemnification; justification; *kithing;* loosing; making absolution; name-clearing; *opening;* proof; quittance; restoration; restitution; setting free; total acquittal; upholding; vindication; *vengeance;* withdrawal of charges; *x-ing out; yele [arch.];* zero guilt;

**vindictive** *(adj.)*: avenging; bitter; cruel; despiteful; embittered; foul; galsome; hateful; implacable; jaded; kindless; loathsome; malicious; nasty; obdurate; *pernicious; quede* [arch.]; revengeful; rancorous; spiteful; *treacherous;* unforgiving; vengeful; wreakful; *xenophobic; yucky; zealotic;*

**vindictiveness** *(n.)*: acrimony; bitterness; cruelty; despitefulness; embitterment; festering; gall; hatefulness; implacableness; jadedness; kindlesness; *loathsomeness;* malice; nastiness; obduracy; *perniciousness; quede* [arch.]; revengefulness; spite; *treachery;* unkindness; vengefulness; wickedness; *xenophobia; yuckiness;* zeal to avenge;

**vine** *(n.)*: azal ~; branch; creeper; climber; dureza ~; elbing ~; *fern;* grape~; hop~; *item;* jalap; kudzu; liana; muscadine; *niagara; object; plant;* quamoclit; quarter~; *red grape;* stem; shoot; trailer; tendril; *uveous;* Virginia creeper; wax ~; wortling; *xylem; yage; zebrina;*

**vinedresser** *(n.)*: agriculturalist; *botanist;* cultivator; *dureza; elbing grower;* farmer; grape-grower; horticulturalist; *intercrop; jillaroo [fem.];* kellersman; land-worker; *man;* nurseryman; orchardist; planter; quintra keeper; *reaper;* sower; tiller; underfarmer [arch.]; vigneron; viniculturalist; wine grower; *xarel-lo;* yardman; *zéta;* [*see* gardener]

**vineyard** *(n.)*: arboretum; botanical garden; cru; *clos* [F.]; chateau; dureza ~; elbing ~; fruit vine; grapevines; himrod grape ~; *interlaken;* jardin; keller; lagrein ~; merlot ~; niagara grape ~; onaka grape ~; plantation; quinta; red grape ~; sunken garden; *trellis; uveous;* vignette; vinery; *vines;* winery; wine producer; *xeres;* yard; zéta ~;

**vintage** *(n.)*: agricultural yield; age; bracket; collection; crop; dividend; day; era; epoch; fruit(age); farm crop; grapes; gathering; generation; harvest; ingathering; *juglans;* kirning [Scot.]; land yield; *making; nurse crop;* origin; production (year); period; proceeds; *quantities;* reaping; *season;* takings; time period; *underutilized ~;* vine-yield; *wine;* xarel-lo; yield; year; *zéta;*

**violate** *(v.)*: abuse; break; contravene; defy; despoil; encroach; flout; go against; hurt; infract; infringe; *jaded; knock;* lapse; mistreat; not obey; offend; overstep; pay no regard to; *quad;* ravage; rape; *sin;* transgress; trespass; *use; upset;* victimize; wrong; *x-out; yank down; zeroize;*

**violation** *(n.)*: abuse; breach; contravention; disobedience; disregard; encroachment; failure to comply; flouting; *guilt; harm;* infraction; infringement; *jadedness; kicking at;* lack of compliance; lapse; misuse; misbehavior; noncompliance; outlawry; offense; profanation; *quad;* rebellion; *sin;* transgression; trespass; *unyieldingness;* violating; wrongdoing; *x-gression;* yieldlessness; *zero compliance;*

**violence** *(n.)*: atrocity; aggression; bloodshed; brutality; cruelty; destruction; evil; ferocity; force; gruesomeness; gore; harm; inclemency; injury; *jeopardy;* killing; lethalness; murder; malevolence; nastiness; odiousness; perniciousness; quashing; riotousness; storminess; sadism; treachery; tumultuousness; tempestuousness; turbulence; upheaval; viciousness; volatility; wildness; *war; xuld [arch.]; yanking down; zealotry;*

**violent** *(adj.)*: aggressive; bloody; brutal; beastly; bloodthirsty; cruel; destructive; evil; fierce; ferocious; gory; hostile; impetuous; injurious; inclement; jeopardizing; killing; lethal; murderous; nasty; odious; pernicious; pitiless; quaking; riotous; raging; rapacious; stormy; sadistic; treacherous; tempestuous; turbulent; unpeaceful; unstable; uproarious; vicious; volatile; wild; warlike; *xuld [arch.]; yieldless;* zoonic;

**virgin** *(adj.)*: abstinent; blameless; chaste; decent; ever-new; fallow; fresh; *good;* honorable; innocent; inviolate; immaculate; initial; jejune; *kid; lily-white;* moral; new; 100% pure; pure; *qualmless;* respectable; righteous; spotless; single; taintless; undefiled; uncontaminated; unadulterated; unused; unknown; virginal; virtuous; vestal; wholesome; *xtr. ~;* yet unused; *zitella [It.];*

**virgin** *(n.)*: *adolescent;* belle; celibate; damsel; *ever-new;* fair maiden; girl; honorable girl; innocent girl; *jejune; kid;* lass; lady-in-waiting; maiden; nymphet; *old maid;* pure woman; quedam [fem.]; rose [slang]; single girl; tomato [slang]; *unmarried;* vestal; *woman; x-chromosome;* young lady; *zitella* [It.];

**virginity** *(n.)*: abstinence; bachelordom; chastity; dewiness; freshness; girlhood; honor; innocence; immaculacy; *justness; keenness; lily-white;* maidenhood; newness; originality; purity; *questionless;* righteousness; stainlessness; taintlessness; undefilement; virtue; *wholesomeness; xtry; yieldedness to God; zeal for purity;*

**virtual** *(adj.)*: almost; about; basically; close to; comparative; *detailed;* essential; fundamental; generally; honorary; implicit; just about; *known as; like;* more or less; near; 100% realistic; practical; potential; quasi; roughly; realistic; simulated; touching on; unofficial; very nearly; well-nigh; *xtry close; yede [arch.]; zeroing in on;*

**virtue** *(n.)*: arete; blamelessness; chastity; divinity; decency; excellence; fairness; fineness; goodness; honor; integrity; justness; *kalokagathia* [Gr.]; *likeness to God;* morality; non-sinfulness; *over-scrupulousness;* probity; purity; profitableness; quality; righteousness; rectitude; sinlessness; taintlessness; uprightness; usefulness; virtuousness; wholesomeness; *xtry; yieldedness to God; zeal for God;* [Ant. vice]

> **Virtues**: accountability; benevolence; courage; diligence; earnestness; fidelity; goodness; honesty; integrity; justness; kindness; love; mercy; nobleness; orderliness; patience; quietness; reliability; self-discipline; truthfulness; unselfishness; vitality; wisdom; yeomanliness; zeal;

**virtuous** *(adj.)*: angelic; blameless; clean; chaste; continent; decent; ethical; exemplary; fair; fine; good; guiltless; honorable; innocent; immaculate; just; keen; lily-white; moral; noble; *over-scrupulous;* pure; qualmless; righteous; stainless; spotless; taintless; unblemished; unspotted; upright; upstanding; very good; wholesome; *white;* xtry.; yeomanly; *zero blemish;* [Ant. venal]

**viscous** *(adj.)*: adhesive; bonding; clinging; clottish; dauby; emplastic; full-bodied; gummy; glutinous; goopy; gluey; gooey; heavy; incrassated; jellified; *knit;* lentous; mucilaginous; *non-separable;* oozy; pitchy; *quince-mucilage;* ropy; sticky; tacky; tenacious; thick; *unite;* viscid; *weld; xenograft; yoke; zip;*

**vise** *(n.)*: angle clamp; bar clamp; clamp; *device; equipment;* furniture clamp; grip(per); hand~; iron clamp; joint clamp; *jaws; kit;* lever ~; machinists ~; *nutcracker; object;* press; *quash; retain;* squeezer; shop ~; tourniquet clamp; *tool; tight;* U-clamp; *vice [var.];* woodworker's ~; *x-hold; yoke; zeug [G.];*

**visibility** *(n.)*: apparentness; beholding; conspicuousness; clarity; discernibility; evidence; eyeshot; field of view; *gazing;* horizon; high ~; *identifiably; just plain;* ken; line of vision; *low ~;* manifestation; *noticeable;* observation; outlook; perception; palpability; plainness; profile; prominence; plain view; *quick-to-sight;* recognition; range of view; sight; scope of ~; *top view;* unmistakableness; view; vista; watchability; *x-hairs; yonder;* zone of vision;

**visible** *(adj.)*: apparent; beholdable; conspicuous; clear; discernable; detectable; evident; eye-catching; forthright; glaring; highly ~; identifiable; just plain as day; kenspeckle; *lucid;* manifest; marked; noticeable; observable; obvious; perceivable; plain; palpable; patent; *quite obvious;* recognizable; seeable; *transparent;* unmistakable; unobscured; viewable; watchable; *x-parent; yeme [arch.]; zoom in;*

**vision** *(n. dream)*: abstraction; *appearance;* bemusement; chimera; dream; entrancement; fantasy; *ghost;* hypnologic image; imagery; *jag; knocked out;* lethe; *mesmerism;* night ~; oracle; pipe dream; prophecy; *quain;* revelation; sweven; trance; *unconsciousness;* view; *woolgathering; x-fix; yield; zoned out;* [see aspiration]

**vision** *(n. sight)*: ability to see; *beholding;* clear ~; *discernment;* eyeshot; eyesight; field of ~; *gazing; high-visibility;* image; *just see;* ken; *looking; light-sensitive; manifestation;* naked eye; *night- ~;* observation; optics; perception; photopia; *quick-sighted;* range of view; sight; sense of seeing; *taking in;* understanding; view; visual range; watching; *xanthopsia; x-ray ~;* Young-Helmholtz theory; *zeroing in;*

**visionary** *(adj.)*: ahead-of-one's-time; *boding;* creative; dreaming; enthusiastic; envisioning; eye-minded; futurist; far-seeing; fanciful; great-minded; highly imaginative; inventive; imaginative; *John-a-dreams; keen-dreaming;* looking-ahead; *mantic;* notional; oracular; prophetic; quixotic; romantic; seeing-ahead; thinking; *unrealistic;* vatic; way-ahead-of-one's-time; *xtry.;* yeasty; *zealous;*

**visionary** *(n.)*: abstract-thinker; boy wonder; brain; creative person; dreamer; enthusiast; futurist; fancier; great ~; great mind; highbrow; imaginer; John-a-dreams; keen-dreamer; *luminary;* mastermind; nonpareil; oracle; prophet; quixote; romantic; seer; thinker; *unrealistic;* vision; whiz (kid); *xtry.; yield; zealous;*

**visit** *(n.)*: appointment; brief ~; call; dropping by; *excursion;* fellowship; friendly ~; *go;* housecall; *itineration; join;* klatch; leisurely ~; mini-vacation; *night out;* outing; pleasure trip; *quest;* ride; stopover; sojourn; stay; trip; *unwind;* vacation; weekend trip; time; *xenization; yong* [arch.]; zugunruhe;

**visit** *(v.)*: appear; attend; betake oneself; come to see; call on; drop in on; enter in; frequent; fly; go to; head; haunt; itinerate; intrude; journey to; *kite;* land in on; make a ~; navigate; nightfare; *outrun;* pop in; *quicken;* re~; see; sail; sojourn; stay; travel; *underway;* voyage; wayfare; *xfer; yede* [arch.]; *zip;*

**visitation** *(n.)*: address; biblical witnessing; canvassing; door-knocking; evangelism; *flier distribution;* going door-to-door; house ~; handing out tracts; *inviting people; Jesus;* knocking doors; literature distribution; *ministry;* neighborhood outreach; outreach; *pursuit; questing; relate;* soul-winning; telling others about Christ; tract distribution; *undertake;* visiting; witnessing; winning the lost; *xenagogy; yede;* zealous witnessing;

**visitor** *(n.)*: arrival; alien; boarder; company; caller; drop-in; denizen; entrant; friend; foreigner; frequenter; guest; gate crasher; house guest; *habitué* [F.]; invitee; incomer; intruder; journeyer; key guest; lodger; *latecomer;* moocher; newcomer; outsider; person; quarterer; questor; roamer; sightseer; stranger; tourist; unexpected guest; visitant; wayfarer; *xenos* [Gr.]; *yokefellow; zingaro [It.];*

**visor** *(n.)*: adjustable ~; brim; blind; cover; drop ~; eyeshade; eyeshield; flange; filter; *gear;* hat ~; *item; jut; keep sun off;* light filter; lip; moveable ~; non-reflective ~; overhang; poke; *qualifier;* rim; shade; top ~; umbriere; vizor; ventrail; *wimple; xtr. protection;* yellow-tinted ~; *zero sun;*
**visual** *(adj.)*: artistic; beholdable; *color;* diagrammatic; eye-catching; figurative; graphic; *highly ~;* illustrative; *just-pictures;* key ~; *likeness;* manifest; noticeable; optical; pictorial; *quality art;* representative; seeable; *textless; unobscured;* visible; watchable; x-parent; *yeme [arch.];* zoom shot;
**visualize** *(v.)*: anticipate; apprehend; bring to mind; contemplate; conceive; dream of; envision; fancy; foresee; get idea; *hypothesize;* imagine; image; just see; *know; lucubrate;* meditate; *notion;* objectify; picture; prevision; *quick-sighted;* realize; see; think; use brain; view; watch; *xenodiagnose; yeme; zazen;*
**vital** *(adj.)*: all-important; basic; critical; crucial; dire; exigent; essential; fundamental; grave; heavy; imperative; important; *jump to it;* key; life-or-death; major; necessary; *obligatory;* paramount; quintessential; required; serious; terribly important; urgent; very key; *weighty; xtry.; yearnful; zero hour;* [*Ant.* vain]
**vitality** *(n.)*: animation; brio; compulsion; drive; energy; force; gusto; heartiness; intensity; *joie de vivre* [F.]; kick; liveliness; might; *natural life force;* oomph; power; *quickness;* robustness; strength; thewiness; ultra-zealousness; vim; vigor; verve; wholeheartedness; *x-fervor;* yare; zip; [*Ant.* vapidity]
**vitalize** *(v.)*: animate; boost; cheer; disquiet; energize; enliven; *freshen;* give life; hearten; *heal;* invigorate; jee; keel; liven up; make alive; *non-stagnant; overhaul;* pep up; quicken; revitalize; rejuvenate; strengthen; *thrive;* uplift; vivify; wake; *xuld [arch.]; yerk;* zing up;
**vitriol** *(n.)*: abuse; bashing; bitterness; contempt; denunciation; excoriation; faultfinding; gall; hatred; increpation; judgment; knocking; lashing; maliciousness; *nitpicking;* objurgation; *punishment; questioning;* reproach; sarcasm; telling off; upbraiding; venom; vituperation; whingeing [Br.]; *xuld [arch.];* yelling at; *zapping;*
**vivid** *(adj.)*: active; bright; brilliant; colorful; clear; dazzling; effulgent; fulgent; gleaming; graphic; high-colored; intense; imaginative; *joyous;* keen; lambent; magnificent; nitid; orthochromatic; powerful; *quick;* radiant; rich; shining; splendid; transplendent; utterly ~; vibrant; *wondrous; xtry.; yellow;* zesty; [*Ant.* vapid]
**vivify** *(v.)*: animate; bring to life; bestir; cheer; disquiet; enliven; *freshen;* give life to; hearten; invigorate; *jar;* kindle; liven; *life-giving;* make alive; *not dead; over-agitate;* perk up; quicken; revive; revitalize; stir; *thrive;* uplift; vitalize; wake; *xuld [arch.]; yerk;* zoetic;
**vocal** *(adj.)*: audible; *aloud;* by word of mouth; choral; clamorous; *distinct;* enunciatory; *fine; gettable;* hearable; identifiable; *judicable; knowable;* loud; *listenable; manifest;* noisy; oral; pronounced; *quality;* recognizable; spoken; sonant; singing; *traceable;* uttered; unwritten; verbal; voiced; worded; *xenophonic; yaked; zeroing in;* [*Ant.* voiceless]
**vocalize** *(v.)*: articulate; bespeak; communicate; declare; enunciate; *foremention; give;* hold forth; indicate; intone; *jaw; key in;* let out; modulate; noise; observe; pronounce; quoth; relate; recite; speak; sing; tell; talk; utter; voice; word; *xenophonia;* yammer; *zero in;*
**vocation** *(n.)*: activity; assignment; business; career; craft; charge; commission; duty; employment; enterprise; field; *grind [slang]; handling;* industry; job; *key position;* livelihood; labor; métier; *necessity;* occupation; profession; *quest;* responsibility; service; trade; task; undertaking; venture; work; xci.; *yoke; zealous duty;*
**vociferate** *(v.)*: *appeal;* bellow; call; cry; *discharge;* exclaim; *erupt; fret;* growl; holler; *inveigh; jubilate;* keen; loudly say; make an outcry; noise; outcry; protest; *quiritation;* roar; shout; *thunder out;* ululate; *vocalize;* wail; xenophonia; yell; *zindabad;*
**vogue** *(n.)*: ardor; big thing; craze; design; desire; *enthusiasm;* fashion; fad; fever; general inclination; high fashion; hysteria; in thing; inclination; *jaunty;* keenness; look; love; mania; notion; obsession; popular; quirk; rage; style; trend; thing; urge; very in; whim; *xtry.;* yankering; zeal;

**voice** *(v.)*: articulate; bespeak; convey; communicate; declare; express; *foremention; gab; have say;* indicate; *jaw; key in;* let out; make known; noise; observe; pronounce; proclaim; quoth; relate; remark; say; speak; tell; utter; verbalize; word; *xenophonia;* yak; *zero in;*

**void** *(adj.)*: annulled; bad; cancelled; disapproved; erroneous; *expired;* flawed; groundless; *horrible;* invalid; illegitimate; *just not acceptable; killed; lousy; mistaken;* null; non-valid; *old; objectionable; pathetic; quad;* rejected; spurious; turned down; unapproved; unacceptable; voided; wrong; *x-out;* yucky; *zero validity;* [*Ant.* valid]

**void** *(n.)*: abyss; barrenness; cavity; desolation; emptiness; empty space; *four corners of the universe;* great abyss; hollowness; inexistence; *jack [slang]; kaput;* lack; *missing;* nonexistence; nothingness; ought; outer-space; *phantom; quantity zero; rien [F.];* scratch; *thought-of;* unreality; vacuity; vacancy; whitespace; x; *yielded;* zero;

**void** *(v.)*: annul; *bereft;* cancel; disannul; end; *finish off; go back;* halt; invalidate; *jump back;* kill; *leave; make void;* nullify; overturn; put an end to; quash; revoke; retract; rescind; stop; terminate; *undo;* vitiate; withdraw; *x-ing;* yank; zero out; [*Ant.* validate]

**volatile** *(adj.)*: airy; alterable; bouncy; capricious; changeable; disturbed; *dangerous;* explosive; erratic; fickle; fluctuating; giddy; *hazardous;* haywire; inconstant; irregular; jumpy; kaleidoscopic; labile; mutable; non-stable; out-of-control; precarious; quirky; random; shaky; tumultuous; unstable; unpredictable; violent; vacillating; wild; wavering; *x-ing; yo-yo;* ziggety;

**volcanic** *(adj.)*: ablaze; burning; combustible; *destructive;* explosive; eruptive; etnean; flammivomous; *glowing;* high-flaming; ignivomous; *jarring; kindled;* lava-flowing; molten; magmatic; *natrocarbonatite; overhot; oceanic;* pumiceous; *quaking;* rhyolitic; *smoking;* tuffaceous; ustorious; Vesuvian; *white-hot; xenochlore; yellow-hot; zapping;*

**volition** *(n.)*: accord; bidding; choice; decision; *enthusiasm;* free will; general desire; *hope; heart;* inclination; *just want to; keenness;* liking; mindset; notion; option; pleasure; preference; *quiritation; reckoning;* self-will; *true desire;* urge; velleity; will; *xenenthesis;* yearning; *zeal;*

**volitional** *(adj.)*: according to choice; by choice; choosing; deliberate; elective; freewill; *general desire;* heart-chosen; inclined; *just want to; keenness;* liking; *minded;* not by constraint; of the will; purposeful; *quiritation; reckoning;* self-willed; *true desire; urge;* volitive; willing; willful; *xenenthesis;* yearning; *zeal;*

**volley** *(n.)*: assault; barrage; bombardment; cascade; discharge; drumfire; expulsion; fire; fusillade; gun; hit; *inundation; jolt; kesting;* lobbing; *mortaring;* nonstop barrage; onslaught; pommel; *quash; raid;* simultaneous discharge; shower; salvo; torrent; *unleashing;* vaulting; wale; *xuld [arch.]; yed;* zipping;

**volume** *(n. amplitude)*: amplification; amplitude; bigness; clamorousness; decibels; elevation; fullness; greatness; highness; intensity; *jacked up; kilowatts;* loudness; largeness; magnitude; noise; *outsound;* phon; plenitude; quantity; *roaring;* sound ~; *turned up;* unquietness; voluminosity; watts; *x-loud;* yelling; *zero quietness;*

**volume** *(n. book)*: album; book; copy; digest; *edition;* folio; *gazetteer;* hardcover; *imprinting; journal; kappa book;* literature; manual; novel; octavo; publication; quarto; *revision;* storybook; text(book); *unpublished work;* vade-mecum; work; xylographica; *yearbook; zipper-book;*

**volume** *(n. space)*: area; berth; capacity; cubature; dimensions; extent; field; *ground;* hugeness; immediate ~; *jurisdiction; kray [Rus.];* largeness; measurements; *number; oblast [Rus.];* place; quantity; room; space; territory; ubiety; vastness; ward; *x-section; you [Chin.]; zone;*

**voluminous** *(adj.)*: abundant; big; bounteous; copious; capacious; disproportionate; enormous; excessive; *fat; fantastic;* great; huge; immense; jumbo; king-size; large; loads; lots; massive; many; much; numerous; overflowing; overabundant; overmuch; plentiful; quantitative; roomy; sizeable; several; tons; uberous; vast; various; wantless; *x.; yards; zillions;*

**voluntary** *(adj.)*: advised; by choice; chosen; conscious; deliberate; decided; elected; freewill; favored; gratuitous; *heart;* intentional; *just want to; knowing; like to;* meditative; meant; nonconscripted; on purpose; optional; purposeful; planned; purposive; quite intentional; *resolved;* selected; thought-out; unpaid; unforced; volitional; volunteer; willing; willful; wageless; *xel [arch.];* yare; zealous;

**volunteer** *(adj.)*: *autonomous; brave; choice;* discretionary; elective; freewill; gracious; gratuitous; helping; *independent;* joining; *kind; like to; made available;* non-mandatory; offered; proffered; *quick-to-help;* resolved to help; self-acting; totally ~; unasked; unreluctant; unpaid; uncompelled; unpressured; volitional; volunteering; voluntary; willingly offered; *xel [arch.]; yes;* zealous;

**volunteer** *(n.)*: abettor; backer; candy striper; *doer;* enlistee; free help; giver of help; helper; *individual;* joiner; *kindhearted; like to; mate;* non-paid helper; offerer of services; profferer; *partner; quick-to-help;* recruit; sympathizer; *taken;* unpaid worker; *volitional;* willing helper; *xel [arch.];* yokefellow; zero pay;

**volunteer** *(v.)*: *agree;* be available; choose; decide; enlist; freely assist; give; help; indicate desire to help; join up; *kindness; like to;* make oneself available; *notion;* offer services; put name one's down; *quick-to-help;* resolve; sign-up; step forward; tell; *unpaid; volition;* want to help; willingly help; *xel [arch.]; yes; zealous for;*

**voluptuous** *(adj.)*: attractive; beautiful; cute; desirable; erotic; foxy; gorgeous; hot; irresistible; *juicy;* knock-out; luscious; lascivious; man-catching; nubile; *obsessed;* provocative; promiscuous; *quixotic;* ravishing; sensual; sensuous; tantalizing; *unchaste;* venerous; whorish; *x-rated; yearnful;* zesty; [*Ant.* vile]

**vomit** *(n.)*: *ambergris;* barf; chunder; disgorge; discharge; ejection; *emesis;* flow; gushing; heaving; issue; jaculation; kecking; lost supper; *mess;* nausea; outflow; puke; *queasiness;* regurgitation; sickness; spewing; throw up; upchuck; vomition [med.]; wambling; *xuld [arch.]; yucky; zich [arch.]*

**vomit** *(v.)*: *abandon;* barf; chunder; disgorge; eject; feed the fish [joc.]; *gag;* gush; heave; issue; jaculate; keck; lose one's supper; *move; nausea; oust;* puke; *queasy;* regurgitate; ralph; sick up; spew; throw up; upchuck; *vault;* wamble; *xuld [arch.]; yield; zing;*

**voracious** *(adj.)*: avaricious; belly-pinched; craving; devouring; edacious; famished; gluttonous; hungry; half-starved; insatiable; *jejune; keen;* limitless; *malnourished; needy;* openmouthed; over-hungry; piggish; quenchless; rapacious; starving; *thirsty;* unfed; vacuitous; weak; *xenorexic;* yearning; *zealous;*

**voracity** *(n.)*: avarice; belly-pinching; craving; *desire* edacity; famishment; gluttony; greed; hunger; insatiability; *jejuneness; keenness;* lust; *malnourishment; non-subdued; over-hungry;* piggishness; quenchlessness; rapaciousness; rapacity; starvation; *thirst; undernourished;* voraciousness; vacuitousness; weakness; *xenorexic;* yearning; *zeal.*

**vortex** *(n.)*: *around; baguio* [Sp.]; cyclone; counterflow; downward spiral; eddy; funnel cloud; gyration; helix; involute; *Jupiter Pluvius; khamsin* [Egy.]; *loop;* maelstrom; nutation; *Oklahoma rainstorm;* precession; querl; rotation; spout; swirling; spinning; tornado; twirling; turbillion; *undercurrent;* volute; whorl; whirlwind; willy [naut. slang]; weel; waterspout; *xuld [arch.]; yern; zwoosh;*

**votary** *(n.)*: adherent; believer; convert; devotee; *enthusiast;* follower; *gung-ho;* habitué; ideologue; janissary; *kirsen [dial.];* liegeman; member; neophyte; *obsessed;* proselyte; *quiritian [L.];* recruit; supporter; *trainee;* upholder; vower; *won over; Xnize; yielder;* zealot;

**vote** *(n.)*: absentee ballot; ballot; choice; decision; election; favoring; gall; hand ~; indication; judgment; *keenness; logroll;* majority ~; *non placet [F.];* opinion; poll; pick; preference; plebiscite; *questioning;* referendum; suffrage; selection; show of hands; *take; usage;* voice; write-in ballot; X; *yes; zeal for;*

**vote** *(v.)*: accept; ballot; cast ballot; choose; decide; elect; favor; give choice; hand ~; indicate; judge; *keen on; like;* make choice; *nominate;* opt; pick; *questionless;* resolve; select; take; *use;* voice opinion; *want; weigh;* X; *yes; zealous for;*

**voter** *(n.)*: *absentee ~;* balloter; ballot caster; citizen; constituent; decider; elector; factionary; *give;* homager; informed citizen; *judge; knowledgeable;* legal citizen; member; national; *oppidan;* polee; *quiritian* [L.]; resident; registered ~; suffragist; taxpayer; *ubeity;* villager; write-in ~; *x-er; yes- ~; zonal;*
**vouch** *(v.)*: assure; attest; back; confirm; certify; declare; ensure; forswear; guarantee; hypothecate; *indicate;* jurate; *kept promise; letter of commitment;* make sure; *non-conditional promise; obligate;* pledge; promise; *qualify; resolve;* swear; testify; undertake; underwrite; vouchsafe; verify; witness; warrant; *x-one's heart; yafery* [arch.]; *zealously confirm;*
**voucher** *(n.)*: authorization; *bill;* confirmation; coupon; draft; endorsed ~; *form;* government ~; *handbill;* indication; IOU; joint ~; *key paperwork;* letter; *monition;* nontransferable ticket; note; navicert; obsignation; promissory note; paper; quitus; receipt; signed ~; ticket; *unexpired ticket;* verification; warrant; yellow ticket; *zet [dial.]:*
**vow** *(n.)*: agreement; affirmation; assurance; blood oath; covenant; contract; commitment; declaration; *engagement;* forswearing; guarantee; hypothecation; ironclad oath; jurament; *kept promise; letter of commitment; making of vows;* non-conditional promise; oath; obligation; pledge; promise; *qualified promise;* resolution; sworn statement; solemn oath; testament; troth; unconditional promise; vouchsafing; word (of honor); *x-one's heart; yafery* [arch.]; zealous ~;
**vow** *(v.)*: adjure; assure; assert; bind to oath; covenant; deign; *ensure;* forswear; guarantee; give word; hypothecate; interpledge; jurate; *keep word; legitimize;* make vow; *nobly ~;* obligate; oath; promise; pledge; *qualify;* resolve; swear; testify; *unconditionally ~;* vouchsafe; warrant; x-ones heart; *yafery [arch.]; zealously ~;*
**voyage** *(n.)*: adventure; boat trip; cruise; *drive;* excursion; expedition; flight; *going; hadj* [Mos.]; itineration; journey; knight-errantry; *look-in;* mission; migration; *night ~;* outing; ocean ~; peregrination; quest; ride; sail; sojourn; trip; tour; *undertaking;* venture; wayfaring; xenization; *yatra* [Hind.]; zugunruhe; [*see* adventure]
**voyage** *(v.)*: advance; boat; cruise; cross; draw (near); *embark;* fare; go; head; itinerate; journey; *kite;* leave for; move; navigate; *outrun;* pass; ply; *quicken;* reach; sail; seafare; steam; travel; traverse; trek; *underway;* venture; wayfare; xenize; yacht; *zip;*
**vulgar** *(adj.)*: abhorrent; appalling; base; boorish; crude; coarse; crass; degraded; despicable; evil; filthy; foul; gauche; gross; horrid; indecent; jadish; kitsch; lewd; low-minded; mean; miserable; nefarious; nasty; offensive; obscene; perverted; perfidious; *questionable;* rude; ribald; scurrilous; tasteless; tactless; uncouth; unholy; vile; wicked; wanton; *x-rated;* yucky; zhlubby; [*Ant.* virtuous]
**vulgarity** *(n.)*: abhorrence; baseness; crudeness; degradation; evil; filthiness; gaucheness; horridness; indecency; *jadishness;* kitsch; lewdness; meanness; nefariousness; obscenity; perfidiousness; *quad;* repugnance; scurrility; terribleness; uncouthness; vileness; vulgarness; wretchedness; *x-rating;* yuckiness; zhlubbiness;
**vulnerability** *(n.)*: Achilles' heel; assailability; brittleness; challengeability; crushability; defenselessness; exposure; frailness; *guardless;* helplessness; indefensibility; justiciableness; *knock out point;* liability; *much-weakened;* non-ability; openness; pregnability; *quirk; reduced ability;* susceptibility; superableness; *tiredness;* unpreparedness; vulnerableness; vincibility; weakness; *xtry.* openness; yielding; zapped; [*Ant.* vallation]
**vulnerable** *(adj.)*: at risk; brittle; challengeable; crushable; defenseless; exposed; expugnable; endangered; *en prise* [F.]; frail; guardless; helpless; indefensible; justiciable; *knocked out;* liable; much-weakened; non-helpable; naked; open; pregnable; *queachy* [dial.]; *reduced;* susceptible; superable; *tired;* unprotected; unguarded; vincible; weak; weaponless; wide-open; *xtry.* open; yielding; zappable; [*Ant.* vallated]
**vulture** *(n.)*: accipiter; buzzard; condor; *duckhawk;* Egyptian ~; *falcon;* griffon ~; honey-buzzard; *Indian hawk;* john-crow; king ~; lammergeyer; *merlin;* neophron; osprey; palm-nut ~; *quab;* raptor; scavenger; turkey ~; upland buzzard; *varmint; wildlife; xema; yarak;* zopilote;

# W

**waddle** *(v.)*: amble; bundle; coggle; *duck walk;* edge; flounder; gimp; hobble; joggle; *keel;* lumber; move from side to side; *non-stable;* oscillate; paddle; quaddle; rock; shuffle; sway; toddle; *uneven;* vacillate; waggle; *xfer;* yaw; zigzag;

**wade** *(v.)*: advance; bundle; cross; drudge; *edge;* ford; gump; go through; haul; *inch;* jiffle; *keep going;* lumber; move through; negotiate; *outwalk;* pass through; plod; quaddle; *relocate;* slog; sling; slosh; trudge; *underway; venture;* waft; weather; *xfer;* yead; zigzag;

**wag** *(v.)*: agitate; brush; *circle;* didder; *excite;* flap; go back and forth; hustle; *instability;* jiggle; judder; keep moving; lash; move; nutate; oscillate; pendulate; *quagswag* [arch.]; reel; shake; switch; sway; twitch; *upset;* vacillate; waggle; wiggle; wave; *xuld [arch.];* yerk; zwish;

**wage** *(n.)*: amount; base pay; compensation; *defrayment;* earnings; finances; *fruit;* gross pay; hire; income; job-pay; *kickback; livelihood; money; minimum wage;* net pay; *overcompensation;* pay(ment); quittance; remuneration; recompense; reward; salary; take-home pay; *unindebted;* virement; wages; xfer; yield; *zapping;*

**wager** *(n.)*: ante; bet; chance; dice-roll; exacta; *faites vos jeux [F.];* gamble; game; high stake; *indulging;* jeopardy; *kitty;* loo; lay ~; longshot; monet; noddy; *odds;* parlay; pledge; perfecta; punt; quinella; risk; *roll of the dice;* stake; set; *take of chance; up the ante;* venture; wagering; *xiaoren; Yarborough;* zet [dial.];

**wagon** *(n.)*: *apparatus;* buggy; cart; coach; covered ~; chuck ~; dray; *encoach;* farm wagon; gig; hay wagon; handcart; *Italian coach;* janker; *jinrickshaw; karrozzin;* landau; mailcoach; noddy; ox-wagon; pull-cart; prairie schooner; quadricycle; rig; red ~; *stagecoach;* truck; unsprung cart; vehicle; wagonette; wain; *x-port;* yanker [Br.]; *zip;*

**wail** *(n.)*: aggrieve; bemoan; bewail; cry; dirge; exclamation; ejulation; forlorn cry; grief; howl; inveigh; *judder;* keen; lament; mourn; moan; noise; outcry; pule; quiver; quiritation; roar; shout; sob; *tears;* troat; ululation; vociferation; wrawl; *xenophobia;* yowl; zing;

**wail** *(v.)*: *appeal;* bellow; cry; despair; erupt into tears; *fuss;* grieve; howl; *inveigh; judder;* keen; lament; moan; noise; outcry; pule; *quistle [arch.];* roar; sob; shed tears; squall; tear; ululate; *vociferate;* weep; wrawl; *xenophthalmia;* yowl; *zowie;*

**wait** *(n.)*: adjournment; breather; break; continuance; delay; *ease;* forbearance; gap; holdup; interval; jauking; keeping; killing time; lingering; lull; lag; lapse; moratorium; night rest; *off-time;* pause; procrastination; quietude; rest; suspension; time out (-lag); *unwinding; vacation;* whiling away time; *x-rest; yawning; zizz;*

**wait** *(v.)*: await; abide; bide; break; continue; dally; drag; delay; expect; endure; follow on; *go on;* have patience; hold on (-out); hang on; idle; just ~; keep; kill time; linger; lag; lapse; *maintain; not hasten;* occupy; pause; procrastinate; pend; *quiet;* remain; rest; stay; sit on (-out); tarry; *use; veg out;* while away; watch; *x-pire; yerde [arch.]; zero impatience;*

**waive** *(n.)*: abandon; brush aside; concede; defer; *end;* forgo; forfeit; give up; hand over; ignore; *jump off;* knuckle under; lay down; make relinquishment; not claim; opt out; part with; quit; relinquish; surrender; throw out; *unload;* voluntarily give up; *withdraw; xfer;* yield; *zero out;*

**waiver** *(n.)*: abdication; *besides;* charter; disclaimer; dispensation; exemption; free pass; government ~; *handbill;* immunity; *judgment; kesting;* letting off; mandated exception; nullification; official ~; *protection;* quittance; relinquishment; special status; ticket; *unaffected;* variance; voidance; writ; *xfer; yet unaffected; zero effect;*

**wake** *(v.)*: arouse; awaken; bestir; call up; disturb; disquiet; excite; *fire up;* get up; hearten; incite; jog; kindle; *lead; move; nudge;* overagitate; *provoke; quicken;* rouse; stir; *trouble; upset; vex;* waken; *xuld [arch.];* yerk; *zing;*

**walk** *(n.)*: amble; bearing; crossing; demarching; *expedition; flânerie* [F.]; *gait;* hike; interloping; journey; *keeping pace;* lumbering; march; meander; night- ~; obamulation; promenade; parade; procession; *quickening;* ramble; stroll; saunter; treading; *underway;* venture; walk; *xfer;* yomping; *zipping;*
**walk** *(v.)*: amble; advance; bumble along; creep; continue; drift; demarch; edge; *flow;* footslog; fare; gad; gravitate; go; hoof; hike; haul; *inch;* jaywalk; journey; *keep pace;* lumber; lilt; mosey; mince; move; march; night-walk; negotiate; overstride; preambulate; progress; pass; promenade; prance; *quicken;* ramble; roam; step; stroll; saunter; strut; traipse; tramp; transcend; tread; travel; trek; *underway;* visit; venture; wander; xfer; yomp; *zigzag;* [*see* run]
**walkway** *(n.)*: archway; arcade; boardwalk; corridor; catwalk; duckboard; esplanade; footpath; gateway; hiking trail; *ice road;* journey-way; *kotal;* lane; mall; *non-toll road;* outlet; pathway; pedway; *quo mode* [L.]; route; rope-walk; sidewalk; stoa; skywalk; trail; travelator; *underpass;* vennel; walk; xystus; *yong* [arch.]; zaguan;
**wall** *(n.)*: *area wall;* barrier; bulkhead; brick ~; contramure; divider; enceint; fence; firewall; *great divide;* hedge; immure; jetty; krantz; *kraal;* levee; *load-bearing ~;* mure; mudwall; merlon; *non-passable;* obstruction; outwall; outer ~; partition; panel; parapet; perpend; party~; *quickset hedge;* retaining ~; separator; stone-wall; traverse; utility wall; vallum; walling; xystum; yard wall; *zariba;*
    **Famous walls**: Antonine ~; Bamboo Curtain; Berlin ~; Communards' ~; Democracy ~; Erdene Zuu Monastery ~; Flodden ~; Great ~ of China; Hadrian's ~; Iron Curtain; Jerusalem ~; King's ~; London ~; Servian ~; Trajan's ~; Via Anelli ~; Wailing ~; Walls of Jericho; York city walls; Zimbabwe Walls;
**walled** *(adj.)*: attack-resistant; bulwarked; castle-walled; double-walled; enwalled; fenced; fortified; *gate;* high-walled; inwalled; *jardang; kept out; line of defense;* made defensible; *non-vulnerable;* obstruction; protected; quadruplicated; ramparted; strong-walled; thick-walled; unassailable; vallated; wall-protected; *x-fence;* yarded; *zoned;*
**wallet** *(n.)*: *article;* billfold; *bankroll;* coin pouch; day purse; *elk hide ~; fanny pack; gear;* holder; *item;* jag; *kit;* leather ~; money-clip; *nécessaire* [F.]; organizer; purse; *quantity;* receptacle; scrip; tri-fold ~; *utility case;* valise; *walrus skin ~; x-bag; yannigan;* zipper- ~;
**wallow** *(v.)*: *agitate;* bathe; bask; *contentment;* delight in; *enjoy;* flounder; glory; *have a get down;* indulge; joy; *kvell;* loll; love; mire down; nestle; *overjoyed;* pleasure in; querl; roll; revel; swim; thrash; tumble; take pleasure; *unhindered;* volutate; wade; welter; *xuld [arch.]; yerk;* zeal;
**wander** *(v.)*: amble; bat around; continue; drift; divagate; expatiate; float; go around; hit the road; *interlope;* june; jaunt; keep going around; lumber; mill about; mosey; meander; migrate; noctivagant; obambulate; peragrate; peregrinate; *quicken;* roam; rove; ramble; stray; saunter; traipse; travel; *underway;* venture; walk; wayfare; *walk; xfer;* yaw; zigzag;
**wanderer** *(n.)*: Arab; Bedouin; carouser; drifter; *emigrant;* floater; gypsy; gadabout; homeless; itinerant; journeyer; *knight-errant; landlouper;* migrant; nomad; *oberration;* pilgrim; *quick-mover;* rover; roamer; sojourner; transient; tent-dweller; *unfixed;* vagrant; wayfarer; *xerophile;* Yahgan; *zingaro* [It.]
**wandering** *(n.)*: ambling; *bouncing;* continuing; discursion; excursion; floating; grassation; *hiking; interloping;* juning; keep moving; lumbering; meandering; moseying; noctivagence; obamulation; pererration; *quickening;* rambling; roving; straying; traipsing; *underway;* venturing; walking; *xferring; yawing;* zigzagging;
**wane** *(v.)*: abate; bate; contract; decrease; decline; diminish; dissipate; dwindle; ease; ebb; fade; fail; go down; *hush;* impair; jade; knock down; languish; lessen; lower; minish; moderate; mitigate; *minimize; narrow; outgo;* peter out; *pall; pine;* quail; recede; reduce; shrivel; shrink; subside; taper off; *undo; vanish;* waste; *xerosis;* yield; zap; [*Ant.* wax]
**want** *(n.)*: ambition; anxiety; aspiration; aching; *bidding;* craving; covetousness; desire; desideratum; *enthusiasm;* fancy; greed; hankering; hope; hubris; hunger; itching; *intention; impulse; juration;* keen desire; lust; longing; *mania; need;* notion; optation; pruriency; pining; *quest; restlessness; search;* strong desire; thirst; urge; velleity; volition; wish; will; whim(sy); *xel [arch.];* yearning; yen; *zeal;*

**want** *(v.)*: aspire; avarice; ache; bid; covet; crave; desire; drive; desiderate; *eagerly desire;* fancy; got to have; hanker; hope for; hone; itch; *just got to have; keen desire;* lust after; long for; *mine; need; order;* pant; *please; quest for; reach for;* seek; thirst for; *urge; velleity;* wish; would like; welcome; *xel [arch.];* yearn for; yammer; *zeal;*

**wanton** *(adj.)*: abandoned; bad; carefree; dissolute; errant; extravagant; frolicsome; foolhardy; gratuitous; heedless; hedonistic; intemperate; immoral; indulgent; jadish; *kinky;* licentious; lewd; loose; lascivious; libertine; ludibrious; mischievous; negligent; orgiastic; playsome; playful; *quad;* reckless; riotous; shameless; sybaritic; *terrible;* unrestrained; unchaste; uninhibited; venery; wild; *x-rated; yielded to the flesh;* zizzy; [*Ant.* wholesome]

**wantonness** *(n.)*: abandon; bacchanalia; carousing; depravity; evil; frolicsomeness; gratuitousness; hedonism; intemperance; japery; knavery; licentiousness; looseness; lasciviousness; looseness; mischievousness; naughtiness; obduracy; playfulness; *quad;* revelry; reckless abandon; shamelessness; trespass; unrestraint; venery; wildness; wickedness; *x-rating; yetzer hara* [Heb.]; *zero restraint;* [*Ant.* wholesomeness]

**war** *(n.)*: aggression; armed conflict; arms; battle; belligerency; conflict; combat; clash; crusade; civil ~; dispute; encounter; embroilment; fight; fray; guerrilla ~fare; *gunnery;* hostilities; holy ~; irregular ~fare; *invasion; jihad* [Mos.]; *kampf* [G.]; *luctation* [arch.]; mêlée; naval ~fare; nuclear ~; onslaught; occursion; operations; position ~fare; quarrel; run-in; revolutionary ~; religious ~; struggle; total ~; trench ~fare; two-front ~; *unrest;* vying; *violence;* warfare; *x-fire;* yed; *zapping;*

**war** *(v.)*: attack; battle; contend; clash; dispute; duke it out [slang]; engage; fight; grapple; *have it out with;* invade; jangle; kemp; levy ~; make ~ with; *naysay;* oppose; pick fight; quarrel; resist; squabble; strive; struggle; tangle; take up arms against; *unharmonious;* vie; wage ~; *x-purposes; yain* [arch.]; *zap;*

**warden** *(n.)*: *authority; bloke;* curator; custodian; constable; defender; ensurer; forester; guardian; game ~; *helper;* intendant; *jail-master;* keeper; *lookout;* manager; *non-sympathetic;* overseer; protector; prison ~; *quarterman;* ranger; steward; superintendent; tutelar; upholder; verderer; waldgrave; *xabandar; yeoman of the guard; zeloter;*

**wardrobe** *(n. armoire)*: armoire; bureau; cabinet; closet; chest; chiffonier; chifforobe; dresser; *enrobing; furniture; footlocker;* garderobe; highboy; *investient* [arch.]; *jumper;* keep; lowboy; locker; *mahogany cabinet;* nacelle; organizer; pine ~; *quadrilocular;* rosewood ~; storage closet; trunk; *utility;* vitrine; walk-in; *xylograqphy; yew ~;* zeta;

**wardrobe** *(n. clothes)*: apparel; *boyswear;* clothing; dress; *enrobing;* finery; garments; habiliments; *investient* [arch.]; *jumper;* knitwear; *loungewear; menswear; national dress;* outfits; *palliament* [arch.]; *quaintry* [arch.]; raiment; suit; threads [slang]; *uniform; undergarments;* vesture; *weeds* [arch.]; *XL; yelek* [Turk.]; *zari;*

**warehouse** *(n.)*: area ~; building; cattery; depot; entrepot; *facility;* godown; *house;* icehouse; jumble-shop; *kura* [Jap.]; *large ~; mandi* [Asia]; magazine; *niche; ordnance;* promptuary; *quick storage;* repository; storehouse; storeroom; stockroom; tool shed; unit; *volume;* wareroom; *xtr. storage;* yurt; *zone;*

**wares** *(n.)*: articles; *batch;* commodities; *delivery;* equipment; furnishings; goods; house~; habiliments; items; *junk; kaffir truck;* line; merchandise; *necessities;* objects; products; *quantity; refurbished items;* stock; supplies; stuff; things; *useful goods;* vendables; *wanigan; x-stock;* yard goods; *zeug* [G.];

**warlike** *(adj.)*: aggressive; belligerent; bellicose; confrontational; destructive; *evil; enemy;* fierce; galsome; hostile; inimical; *jingoist; killing; liverish;* militaristic; martial; non-peaceful; nasty; odious; pugnacious; quarrelsome; *rancorous; ruthless;* savage; treacherous; unfriendly; unpeaceful; unpacific; unpeacable; violent; vicious; warring; *xenophobic; yieldless; zealotic;* [*Ant.* well-natured]

**warm** *(adj.)*: aglow; balmy; calid; cozy; *decoct;* enkindled; full-warm; glowing; heated; hand-hot; incandescent; jejune; *kindled;* lukewarm; mild; *muggy; non-cooled;* overwarmed; pleasant; parching; quenchless; *roasting;* sunny; summery; toasty; tepid; uncomfortable; *vaporous;* well-heated; *xerothermic;* yellow-hot; *zeta-warmed;* [*see* friendly; *Ant.* wintry]

**warm** *(v.)*: anneal; bask; bake; cook; decrepitate; expose to heat; *flame; gas-heated;* heat; *incinerate; jet heater; kindle a fire under; let cook;* microwave; neal; oven- ~; put a flame under; quick-bake; reheat; *steam;* tepefy; *undercook; vulcanize;* warm up; *xeric;* yark; *zap;*

**warmth** *(n.)*: *aflame;* burning; calidity; *deflagration;* estuance; excadescence; fieriness; glow; heat; incandescence; *just right; kerosene heat; latent heat; muffle;* nealing; overheat; *pyre;* Q [phys.]; *roasting; scorching heat;* tepor; toastiness; *temperature;* ustulation; *volcanic ~;* warmness; *xeric; yellow-hot; zapping;* [*Ant.* wintriness]

**warn** *(v.)*: alert; alarm; admonish; advise; bode; caution; counsel; *dissuade;* exhort; fore~; give warning; help; inform; *jeopardy; knowledge;* let one know; make known; notify; noise; opine; presage; precaution; premonish; prewarn; previse; *quicken; relate; remind;* signal; tell; tip off; threaten; urge; *vocalize;* word; xenagogy; yellow alert; zero in; [*see* arouse]

**warning** *(n.)*: alert; alarm; advisory; admonishment; *beware;* caution; caveat; commination; *distress; emergency;* forewarning; foretoken; grim ~; hue and cry; injunction; *jeopardy;* klaxton; larum; monition; *monitory;* notification; *omen;* precaution; *quivering;* red alert; sign(al); siren; tip; *urging; vatic;* word of caution; xenagogy; yellow alert; *zealous alert;*

**warp** *(v.)*: adulterate; alter; bend; contort; distort; entwist; foul up; garble; *harm;* injure; *jade;* knot; *louse up;* mutate; misrepresent; *nullify; obloquoy; oppress;* pervert; *quade* [arch.]; ruin; skew; twist; *undo;* vary; wring; *xenomorph; yaw; zad;*

**warrant** *(n.)*: authorization; *backing;* clearance; document; doquet; exequatur; *freedom;* green light; *high authority;* imprimatur; joint-permission; *knowingly allowed;* license; *mittimus;* naked ~; order; okay; papers; permission; *quittance; right;* sanction; search ~; thumbs up [slang]; *unopposed;* validation; written authorization; *x-pass;* yes; *zealous okay;*

**warranty** *(n.)*: assurance; *bond;* commitment; declaration; ensuring; forswearing; guarantee; hypothecation; *interpledging;* jurament; *kept promise;* letter of commitment; *making of vows;* non-conditional ~; oath; pledge; *qualified promise;* resolution; solemn oath; testament; unconditional guarantee; vow; written guarantee; *x-one's heart; yafery* [arch.]; *zealous promise;*

**warrior** *(n.)*: army man; battler; combatant; crusader; defender; duelist; *enlisted man;* fighter; gladiator; hoplite [Gr.]; infantryman; janissary [Turk.]; knight; lansquenet; legionnaire; military man; mercenary; *noncommissioned officer; officer;* pikeman; *quartermaster;* retiarius; soldier; swordsman; *trooper; uniformed men;* velite [Rom.]; warfighter; *xiphos-bearer; yardbird; zoauve;*

**wart** *(n.)*: abnormality; bump; *cyst;* distension; excrescence; flaw; growth; hump; imperfection; jog; knob; lump; mound; nodule; nub; outgrowth; protuberance; plantar ~; *quirk; raised area; swelling; tumor;* umbo; verruca; wem; *xanthomata; yedder; zoocyst;*

**war-torn** *(adj.)*: *assaulted;* battle-scarred; battle-weary; *crumbling;* devastated; *effaced; fighting;* gutted; harrowed; *impaired; junked; kemp; laid waste; marauded; nasty;* over-damaged; pillaged; *quashed;* ravaged; *shattered;* torn; uprooted; *violence;* war-ravaged; *x-fire; yanked down; zapped;*

**wary** *(adj.)*: alert; *beware;* cautious; chary; distrustful; ever-careful; fabian; guarded; heedful; *informed;* judicious; keeping in mind; leery; mistrustful; *nervous;* overcautious; precautious; prudent; quick-witted; regardful; suspicious; *thoughtful;* ultra-careful; vigilant; watchful; x-careful; yare-handed; *zärtlich* [G.]; [*Ant.* wareless]

**wash** *(v.)*: ablute; bathe; clean; cleanse; disinfect, degrease; deterge; elute; flush; get clean; hose (off; down); *immerse; jalap;* kill germs; launder; machine- ~; *neaten;* out~; purify; *quintessentialize;* rinse; scrub; scour; *shower;* tub; unsully; vapor-clean; wipe; *xylol; yellow soap; zierlich [G.];*

**waste** *(n. excrement)*: argol; *buffalo chips;* composture; dung; excrement; feces; guano; *horsedung; intestinal discharge;* jakes; *keytonuria; laystall;* manure; night soil; ordure; poop; *quisquillous;* refuse; sewage; stool; turd [vulg.]; *urine;* void; waste-matter; xysma; *yuckiness; zigg [vulg.];*

**waste** *(n. garbage)*: abatis; *brush; bag;* compost; discharge; effluent; elimination; filth; garbage; *heap; items;* industrial ~; junk; ket; litter; mullock; nuclear ~; offscouring; offal; *pile;* quisquillous; refuse; rubbish; recyclables; scrap; sweepings; trash; unwanted items; vuilnis; waste product; wastrel; *x-barrel; yucky; zero value;*
**waste** *(v.)*: abuse; blow; consume; dissipate; exhaust; fritter away; go through; *hand away; incontinent; just give away;* kill; lavish; *lose;* misspend; misuse; *non-retention;* overspend; pour down the drain; *quaff; reduced;* squander; *spend;* throw away; use up; *vanish; wasteful; xfer; yield up; zeroize;*
**wastebasket** *(v.)*: aluminum ~; bin; can; circular file [joc.]; container; dustbin; *eliminate; fly-tipping;* garbage can; *holder; heap pile; indoor trash bin;* junk bin; *kitchen garbage;* litter bin; *metal dumpster; nihil [L.];* office garbage; *pushcart; quisquillous;* rubbish bin; recycling bin; receptacle; skip; trash can (-bin); *unwanted items; vessel;* wastepaper basket; wheelie bin; waste container; *x-barrel;* yard bin; *zero out;*
**wasteful** *(adj.)*: *abundant; abusive; blasé;* careless; *disorganized;* extravagant; fulsome; *garbage;* heedless; inefficient; *junk-producing; knowingly ~;* lavish; mismanaged; non-frugal; over- ~; profligate; prodigal; quite ~; *reckless;* sloppy; thriftless; unthrifty; uneconomical; very careless; wild; *xtr. waste; yareless; zero efficiency;* [Ant. wise]
**wastefulness** *(n.)*: *abundance; abusiveness; blasé;* carelessness; *disorganization;* extravagance; fulsomeness; great waste; heedlessness; inefficiency; *junk-production; knowingly wasteful;* lavishness; liberality; mismanagement; non-frugality; over- ~; profligality; *quite wasteful; reckless;* sloppiness; thriftlessness; unthriftiness; *very careless;* waste; *xtr. waste; yarelessness; zero efficiency;* [Ant. wisdom]
**watch** *(v.)*: attend to; behold; catch sight of; descry; distinguish; examine; eye; espy; face; fix eyes on; find; fleer; feast eyes on; gaze at; guard; *hone in on;* inspect; *judge;* keep an eye on; look at (-after); make out; mark; mind; notice; note; observe; perceive; peer; pay attention to; *quick look;* recognize; see; spectate; stare at; spy on; take in (-care of); tend; *understand;* view; witness; *x-ray vision; yeme; zero in;* [*see* protect]
**watchful** *(adj.)*: alert; attentive; *beware;* careful; discerning; ever-watchful; fabian; guarded; heedful; intentive; judicious; keeping in mind; leery; mindful; *noting;* observant; on guard; precautious; quick-witted; regardful; *suspicious; tending;* ultra-careful; vigilant; watching; wary; *x-careful;* yare-handed; zealous; [Ant. wareless]
**watchfulness** *(n.)*: alertness; *beware;* cautiousness; *discernment; ever-watchful; fabian;* gingerness; heedfulness; intentiveness; *judicious;* keeping watch; leeriness; mindfulness; *noting;* observation; precaution; quickness; regard; *suspicion;* tending; ultra-carefulness; vigilance; wariness; *x-careful;* yare-handedness; *zeal;*
**watchman** *(n.)*: armed sentry; beefeater; cordon; defender; eunuch; footguard; guard(ian); hyperaspist; jaga; keeper; lookout; musketeer; night-watchman; outguard; patrol; quarterman; rear-guard; sentry; tower-guard; *uniformed sentry;* vigil; watch(er); *xiphos-bearer;* yeoman of the guard; *zoauve;*
**watchtower** *(n.)*: *acropolis;* bastille; crow's nest; donjon; *enclosure;* fort; garrison; high tower; *ivory tower; jong [Tib.];* keep; lookout tower; martello; nest; outpost; observation tower; pylon; *quarters;* rath; refuge; stronghold; sconce; tower; *unbeatable;* vault; watchtower; walls; wick; ward; *x-house;* yamen [Chin.]; zwinger;
**water** *(n.)*: aqua; bottled ~; back~; bath~; cold ~; drinking ~; distilled ~; dampness; *drink; elluent;* fluid; fresh~; flood~; gulch ~; $H_2O$; ice ~; *juniper water;* keld ~; liquid; light ~; moisture; moistness; melt~; natural spring~; *open !;* purified ~; *quay* ~; rain ~; river- ~; rose~; salt ~; sea ~; spring~; tap ~; tide- ~; *under~;* vadose; Vichy ~; wetness; white ~; well ~; wateriness; *Xingu; yeo;* ziment ~; zeon;
**watertight** *(adj.)*: airtight; *bonded;* caulked; drip-proof; *enclosed;* floodproof; gasketed; hermetic; impermeable; *joint-sealed; kaolin-lined;* leak-proof; moisture-proof; non-leaking; *o-ring;* payed; quite ~; raintight; stormtight; sealed; tight-sealed; unleaking; *vinyl-coated;* waterproof; *xenoy; yieldless;* zero-leak;

**watery** *(adj.)*: aqueous; bedashed; *cold;* drippy; diluted; endrenched; fluidic; gushy; hydric; imbrued; juicy; *kept ~;* liquidy; moist; madefied; matted; non-dry; *oozy;* plashy; *quaggy;* runny; soaked; soggy; sodden; shilpit; thin; undried; vapored; watered-down; weak; *xtr. ~;* yoted; *zeon;* [*Ant.* waterless]

**wave** *(n. a billow)*: *amassment;* billow; breaker; comber; curl; *deep;* eagre; float; groundswell; heave; internal ~; jaw; *keld;* ladies' fingers [slang]; *lap;* mushburger; *movement; nautical movement;* ocean ~; *plash; quake;* ripple; roll(er); rip curl; seawave; surge; surf; swell; tidal ~; *tsunami;* undulation; upsurge; *vacillation;* whitecap; wake; wavelet; *x-wave;* yeast; *zwoosh;*

**wave** *(v.)*: *acknowledge;* beckon; brandish; *call;* dip; *express;* flap; flutter; gesture; go back and forth; *hail; indicate; jiggle;* keep moving; *lilt;* move; motion; *nod;* oscillate; *pay regards; quiver;* ripple; signal; sway; twitch; undulate; *vacillate;* wiggle; wag; *xfer; yaw;* zigzag;

**waver** *(v.)*: alternate; *bend; bounce;* crisscross; change; dither; *exchange;* fluctuate; *go back and forth; hesitate; interweave;* jag; jump; *kedge; laciniate;* meander; nutate; oscillate; pendulate; *quiver;* ramble; reciprocate; shift; swing; sway; shilly-shally; turn; twist; teeter; totter; undulate; vacillate; waver; *x-ing;* yo-yo; zigzag;

**wavy** *(adj.)*: *anguine;* back-and-forth; curvy; crenulate; disturbed; *erratic;* flexuous; going back and forth; hankled; irregular; *jagged; kedging; lilting;* moiré; not straight; oscillating; *ply; querly;* ripply; rolling; sinuous; sinuate; serpentine; surgy; tabbied; undulate; unde; vermicular; wiggly; winding; wavering; *x-wave;* yawing; zigzag; [*Ant.* waveless]

**wax** *(n.)*: * *alnight;* bees~; buildup; cere; commosis; cerumen; *dip;* ear~; fragranced ~; *glob;* hardened ~; inceration; Japan ~; klister; lipid; mineral ~; motan ~; *non-scented ~;* ozocerite; paraffin ~; propolis; quick-melting ~; residue; sealing- ~; *substance;* tallow; undercoat; vegetable ~; white- ~; *xesturgy;* yellow ~; *zopissa;*

**wax** *(v.)*: apply ~; burnish; buff; cere; *coat; cerated; do;* enamel; furbish; *finish;* gloss; glaze; *high-gloss; inceration;* jigger; *keen;* luster; make shiny; *nigrosine;* overglaze; *overpolish;* polish; *quartz sand;* rub; shine; topcoat; *urethane;* varnish; *work on;* xesturgy; *yare; zinc flourosilicate;*

**way** *(n.)*: avenue; *broad way;* course; direction; *esplanade;* footpath; fashion; gate~; high~; *itinerary;* journey- ~; king's high~; lane; means; manner; *narrow ~;* orientation; path(~); *quo mode* [L.]; road; *street;* track; *underpass;* vector; *walk~; xystus; yong* [arch.]; *zwinger;*

**wayward** *(adj.)*: *abandoned to vice;* bad; capricious; defiant; disobedient; errant; forward; foul; *godless;* headstrong; insubordinate; intractable; jaded; *knavish; lewd; misguided;* noncompliant; naughty; ornery; prodigal; *quad;* rebellious; refractory; self-willed; truculent; unruly; uncontrollable; usurpative; *vagabond;* wayward; wanton; willful; wrongheaded; *xgressing;* yieldless; *zizzy;* [*Ant.* well-behaved]

**weak** *(adj.)*: anile; brittle; *curtailed; crippled; drained;* debilitated; defenseless; enfeebled; effete; feeble; frail; flaccid; flimsy; floppy; faint; forceless; gimp; helpless; incapable; inert; infirm; impotent; jejune; *knocked out;* limp; lustless; lame; much-weakened; nesh; nugatory; non-potent; over~; old-womanish; *overfatigued; overspent;* pathetic; puny; powerless; *queachy* [dial.]; rickety; reduced; scrawny; soft; torpid; trifling; *tired;* unable; unhardy; unsound; unsteadfast; unmighty; vulnerable; wimpy; washy; xtry. ~; *yawnish; zapped;*

**weaken** *(v.)*: attenuate; abate; *break down;* curtail; *cut;* decline; deteriorate; diminish; dwindle; debilitate; enervate; ebb; enfeeble; exhaust; erode; fade; flag; fall; go down; *halt;* impair; jade; *knock off;* languish; lessen; moderate; *narrow; negate; outgo; pall;* quail; reduce; subside; taper; undercut; undermine; *vanish;* wane; wither; *xerosis; yield;* zap;

**weakling** *(n.)*: *afraid;* baby; coward; dastard; *ever-fearful;* featherweight; gutless ~; hesitator; *insecure;* jellyfish; *kitten-hearted; lily-livered;* milquetoast; nebbesh; *overanxious;* pipsqueak; pushover; *quiverer; recreant;* sissy; scaredy-cat; trembler; *unmanly; vexed;* wimp; *xiaoren;* yellow-belly; zob; [*Ant.* weightlifter]

**weakly** *(adj.)*: anile; brittley; *crippled; drained;* effetely; feebly; frailly; flimsily; faintly; gimply; helplessly; impotently; inertly; *jejunely; knocked out;* lamely; limply; *much-weakened;* nugatorily; over~; powerlessly; *queachily* [dial.]; *reduced;* scrawnily; softly; torpidly; unsteadily; vulnerably; wimpily; xtry. weak; *yawnishly; zero energy;* [Ant. well-built]

**weakness** *(n.)*: Achilles' heel; brittleness; caducity; defenselessness; debility; deficiency; enfeeblement; effeteness; feebleness; frailty; faintness; flimsiness; flaccidity; fragility; foible; failing; *gimp;* helplessness; impotency; inanition; inability; inertness; infirmity; impotence; *jejuneness; knocking out;* lameness; limpness; *much-weakened;* non-ability; openness; powerlessness; pregnability; quirk; *reduced ability;* susceptibility; softness; scrawniness; torpor; *unprotected;* valetudinarianism; vulnerability; vincibility; weakside; wimpiness; *xtry. ~; yielding; zapped;* [Ant. wherewithal]

**wealth** *(n.)*: affluence; bounty; capital; *dollars;* estate; fortune; gold; holdings; *income; jewels; krugerrands* lucre; money; means; mammon; millions; *notes;* opulence; prosperity; possessions; pelf; *quantities;* riches; substance; treasure; uberty; valuables; wherewithal; wealthiness; *xenocurrency; yellow boy [Br.];* zillions [slang]; [Ant. want]

**wealthy** *(adj.)*: affluent; bountiful; comfortable; *dollars; endowed;* filthy rich; *golden;* high-class; independently ~; jet set; *king's ransom;* loaded; moneyed; *means; notes; opulent;* prosperous; privileged; *quartful* [arch.]; rich; successful; treasure-filled; upper class; vested; well off; *xenocurrency; yellow boy [Br.];* zillionaire; [see extravagant]

**wean** *(v.)*: ablactate; acclimate; alienate; become ~ed; *conform;* delactate; dissuade; discourage; ease; *familiarize; fit in;* get off; *habilitate;* inure; *jibe [slang];* kitted; line out; move onto; *not needed; off;* prepare; qualify; reconcile; switch to; *train; used;* verse; *well-adjusted;* xenize; yarken; *zealously ready;*

**weapon** *(n.)*: arms; armament; battle implement; combat tool; *destruction;* equipment; equipage; firearm; *gun;* hand ~; *instrument; javelin;* killing ~; *lance;* munitions; *nuclear ~;* ordnance; panoply; *quarterstaff;* ranged ~; small arms; side arms; *sword;* secret ~; tackle; *tool;* Uzi; unit; violence; weaponry; *xiphos; y-gun; zweihander;*

  **Weapons**: arrow; atomic bomb; axe; battleaxe; bayonet; bazooka; blowgun; boomerang; bomb; broadsword; catapult; cannon; club; crossbow; cutlass; dagger; dart; dynamite; épeé; flail; flamethrower; grenade; halberd; iaito; javelin; knife; lance; longsword; mace; machinegun; mortar; musket; ninja star; nuclear bomb; one-handed sword; pike; pistol; quarterstaff; rapier; rifle; slingshot; spear; sword; tank; tomahawk; Uzi; vechevoral; war hammer; xiphos; yataghan; zweihander;

**weaponry** *(n.)*: arms; armaments; battle implements; combat tools; devices of war; engines of war; *equipment;* firearms; gunnery; guns; hoplology; instruments of war; *javelins; killing implements; load;* munitions; *missilery; musketry; nuclear weapons;* ordnance; panoply; *quantity;* repository; stockpile; *tools; utility; volume;* weapons; *xiphos; y-gun; zweihander;*

**wear** *(v. don)*: adorn; bear; bedeck; carry; clothe; dress; don; enrobe; *fancify;* gird; garb; gussy up; have on; invest; indue; jacket; kit; *loungewear; make prettier; nice;* outfit; *overdress;* put on; prink; *quaintise [arch.];* reapparel; rig; sport; trim; uniform; vest; *work; xuld [arch.]; yclad* [arch.]; zip on;

**wear** *(v. wear away)*: abrade; attrit; burn out; consume; deteriorate; efface; erode; fray; fret; gobble up; gnaw away; *halve; impair; jump down;* knock down; lessen; minimize; *negate;* out~; over~; *pall;* quail; rub off; spend; *threadbare;* use; *vanish;* wear out (-away; -down); weaken; *x-out; yield; zeroize;*

**weariness** *(n.)*: *apathy;* bleariness; *comatose;* drowsiness; exhaustion; fatigue; grogginess; heaviness; inertia; jetlag; kef; lethargy; mopishness; nappiness; oscitancy; *peplessness; quiet; rest;* sleepiness; tiredness; *unenthusiasm; vapidity;* weakness; *xenarthrous;* yawning; *zonked out;*

**wearisome** *(adj.)*: arduous; backbreaking; challenging; demanding; exhausting; fatiguing; grueling; hard; intense; jading; killing; laborious; moiling; not easy; operose; *painful; quite hard;* rigorous; strenuous; toilsome; tiresome; tedious; uneasy; *very hard;* wearying; *x-heavy;* yawnful; *zapping;*

**weary** *(adj.)*: aweary [lit.]; bushed; beat; *comatose;* drained; dog-tired; exhausted; faint; fatigued; *groggy;* haggard; half dead; *indolent;* jaded; knocked-out; lethargic; listless; *moiled;* noddy; overwrought; overspent; pooped; *quiescent;* run down; spent; tired; unrested; *vapid;* worn out; wrung out; wiped out; *xenarthrous;* yawnish; zapped;

**weary** *(v.)*: *awearied;* bleed; consume; drain; defaticate; do in; exhaust; fatigue; frazzle; *grueling;* hone; *impoverish; jade; kaput;* lessen; make tired; *nullify; overspend; put out;* quail; run out of energy; sap; tire (out); tucker; use up all one's energy; *void;* wear; wipe out; *xerosis; yield;* zap;

**weave** *(v.)*: *abstruse;* braid; crisscross; *disarrange;* entwine; *fabricate;* gnarl; hook; inter~; intertwine; join; knit; lace; merge; network; *overcomplicate;* plait; quill; raddle; *snarl;* tangle; twist; twine; thrum; twill; tie; unite; *voluble; woven;* x; *yarn over;* zigzag;

**web** *(n.)*: airstring; *bolter;* cob~; *dusty cob~;* enmeshment; fibroin; gossamer; gauze; *handiwork;* inmeshment; *joining; keep-net; line;* mesh; network; *object; panter; quad;* reticle; spider ~; silk; snare; tela; *umbrella; veil;* weft; x-mesh; *yair; zone;*

**webbed** *(adj.)*: attached; *broad;* connected; ducklike; enmeshed; fin-footed; *girded; hitched;* interconnected; joined; *knitted;* knot; linked; membraned; non-separated; *oldsquaw;* palmate; palmiped; *quasi-palmate;* reticular; semi-palmate; *together; united; vulpanser;* webby; *xenograft;* yoked; *zero separation;*

**web-footed** *(adj.)*: aliped; *broad; connected;* duck-footed; *eider;* fin-footed; goose-footed; *hitched; interconnected;* join-toed; *knitted; linked;* membrane-toed; *non-separated; oldsquaw;* palmate; paddle-footed; *quack; reticular;* syndactyl; totipalmate; *united; vulpanser;* webbed-footed; web-toed; *xenograph;* yoked; *zero-separation;*

**wed** *(v.)*: adjoin; bind; conjoin; *dearly beloved;* exchange vows; elope; *fix;* get hitched; have; inter~; join; knit together; knot; lead to the altar; marry; *nuptial;* one; *pair (off);* quest; reunite; settle down; take; tie the knot; unite; *vows;* wive; *x.;* yoke with; *zonam solvere* [L.];

**wedding** *(n.)*: *the* altar; *bridal;* ceremony; church ~; Christian ~; civil ~; destination ~; *double ~;* espousal; *elopement; feast; festivities;* grand ~; gunshot ~; *huppah* [Heb.]; hitching; *Italian ~;* joining; knot-tying; *life-long union;* marriage (feast); nuptials; nowes; *opetide; proposal; postnuptial; queen-gold; rite; reception;* solemnization; tying the knot; union; uniting; vows; white ~; *x;* yoking; *zonam solvere* [L.]; [*see* marriage]

**wedge** *(n.)*: *article;* block; chock; chunk; *doorstop; equipment;* forelock; gib; gad; hunk; iron ~; jam; kyle; *lump; mass; nugget; object;* (pie) piece; quoin; quinnet; *rubber doorstop;* slice; splitter; sphenoid; triangle; trig; *unit;* voussoir; wood-splitting ~; *xylon; yngot* [arch.]; *Zeug* [G.];

**wedge** *(v.)*: *apply pressure;* bear down; cram; depress; *exert pressure;* force; gorge; heave; impel; jam; kibble; lodge; mash; *nudge;* overstuff; pack; press; quash; ram; stuff; thrust; upthrust; *violence;* whack; *xuld* [arch.]; yerk; zonk;

**wedlock** *(n.)*: alliance; *affinity;* bond; connection; *deuterogamy; espoused; frankmarriage;* getting together; *hymeneal;* intermarriage; joining; knot; league; marriage; nuptials; *oneness;* partnership; *queen-gold; relationship;* spousals; *tying the knot;* union; vows; *wedding; x;* yoke; *zonam solvere* [L.];

**weed** *(n.)*: * ash~; bugle~; cotton~; duck~; *eel-grass;* furrow~; gout~; horse~; iron~; jimson~; knap~; loco~; mat~; nit~; ox-eye; pond~; quack grass; ragwort; snake~; tare; *undergrowth;* vetch; white~; xeranthemum; yaw~; zizany;

**weep** *(v.)*: *attrition;* bawl; blubber; cry; despair; erupt into tears; *feel sorrow;* grieve; howl; *inveigh; judder;* keen; lament; lachrymate; moan; *noise;* outcry; *outweep; pout; quistle* [arch.]; roar; sob; snivel; shed tears; squall; tear; *ululate; vociferate;* wail; whimper; *xenophthalmia;* yowl; yawp; *zowie;*

**weigh** *(v.)*: assess; *burden;* consider; determine weight; deem; evaluate; figure; gauge; *hold; ideate;* judge; *know;* librate; measure; *notion; out~;* ponderate; put on scale; *quote;* reckon weight; surmise poundage; tip the scales; use scale; valuate; weigh out; *xtr. careful; yeme; zet* [dial.];

**weight** *(n.)*: avoirdupois [joc.]; burden; cumbrance; difficulty; dead ~; encumbrance; *full- ~;* gross ~; *grams;* heaviness; heft; hindrance; *imposition; judging; kilograms;* liveweight; lading; mass; net ~; oppression; poundage; pounds; ponderance; ponderosity; quantity; reckoned ~; specific gravity; tonnage; tare; unladen ~; volume; weighing; xci. *yoke; zeugma [Gr.];*
**weightless** *(adj.)*: airy; buoyant; *condition;* driftable; ethereal; frail; floatable; *going;* hoverable; insubstantial; *jetting; kiting;* light; *microgravity; no gravity; outer space; planing; quickened; resting;* slight; suspendable; totally ~; *upbearing; volplaning;* waftable; wispy; *xuld [arch.]; yet floating;* zero gravity; [ *Ant.* weighty]
**weightlessness** *(n.)*: airiness; buoyancy; *condition;* driftability; ethereality; floatability; *going;* hoverability; inaquation; *jetting; kiting;* lightness; levity; microgravity; no gravity; *outer space; planing; quickened; resting;* suspendibility; total ~; *upbearing; volplaning;* waftability; *xuld [arch.];* yet floating; zero gravity; [ *Ant.* weightiness]
**weird** *(adj.)*: abnormal; bizarre; crazy; different; eldritch; erratic; enigmatic; eccentric; funny; freakish; gonzo; goofy; heterotypical; irregular; jokey; kooky; loony; mad; mysterious; malformed; nonstandard; nutty; odd; peculiar; queer; ridiculous; strange; screwy; screwball; twisted; unusual; unconventional; variant; wacky; xenomorphic; *yawed;* zany; zonky;
**weirdness** *(n.)*: abnormality; bizarreness craziness; *difference; enigma;* funniness; goofiness; *heterotypic;* irregularity; *jokiness;* kookiness; lunacy; madness; mysteriousness; nonsensicality; oddness; peculiarity; queerness; ridiculousness; strangeness; twistedness; unusualness; variance; wackiness; *xtry.; yaw;* zaniness;
**welch** *(v.)*: abort; bilk; *con;* disappoint; default; evade; fail; go back on; *honorless; impropriety; jackal; knowingly lie;* lapse; *misrepresent;* not honor; omit; *poor; quit;* renege; skip; stiff; *take back;* undo; violate; welsh; *x-out; yieldless; zing;*
**welcome** *(adj.)*: appreciated; *blessed; cherished;* delightful; embraced; *friendly;* gladly received; halse; *indebted; joyous;* kindly received; longed-for; *manners; not forget;* owe; prized; *quick-to-receive;* refreshing; respected; saluted; timely; understand; valued; wanted; *xenium; yet thankful; zealously ~;*
**welcome** *(v.)*: appreciate; *bless;* cordially ~; desire; embrace; *friendly;* greet; gladly receive; halse; *include;* joy over; kindly greet; *long for; manners;* not forget; *one;* praise; *quick-to-receive;* receive; salute; take in; understand; value; want; warmly ~; *xenium; yearn for; zealously ~;*
**weld** *(v.)*: attach; bond; braze; connect; diffusion- ~; electron-beam ~; fuse; gas- ~; *hitch;* induction ~; join; *knit;* link; laser- ~; *make oxy-fuel ~; nonseparable; one;* put together; *quasi-fuse;* ravel; solder; spot ~; tack ~; ultrasonic ~; *v-butt joint;* wed; x-ray ~; yoke; *zip;*
**welfare** *(n.)*: advantage; best interests; *care;* daily ~; *enjoyment; fitness;* good; health(fulness); happiness; interests; *joy; keeping;* living; *meaning good; needs; overall good;* protection; quality of life; *round-the-clock;* safety; soundness; sakubrity; *total health; unworried;* vigor; wellbeing; weal; *xtry. care; yaul;* zero danger; [ *Ant.* wounding]
**well** *(adj. healthy)*: able-bodied; *brawny; capital;* dandy; entire; fit; fine; good; healthy; *incredible;* just fine; keen; lusty; mighty fine; nurtured; okay; peachy; peak; *quartful* [arch.]; robust; right; sound; swell; strong; trim; thriving; tip-top; unimpaired; vibrant; whole; *xtry.;* yaul; zippy; [ *Ant.* weak]
**well** *(n. cistern)*: artesian well; basin; cistern; draw- ~; *exploration ~;* font; *fountain; gush;* headspring; issue; *jubb* [Heb.]; keld; *lake;* mickery; namma hole; *oil ~;* pump ~; Persian ~; quell; qanat; reservoir; spring; source; step~; sluice; *tank;* underground ~; vat; watering hole; wishing ~; water ~; *XO; YP; zemzem;*
**wellspring** *(n.)*: *ajutage;* brine-spring; cascade; cistern; *derivation; estuary;* fountain(head); fount; geyser; headspring; issue; jet; keld; *lake;* mockery; namma hole; origin; *proceeding; qanat;* root; *reservoir;* spring; spout; source; *traduction; uprush;* venter; well-head; waterspring; *xenenthesis; yoni* [Skr.]; *zemzem;*

**westerner** *(n.)*: American; *Belgian;* Caucasian; *Dane;* European; *Frenchman;* gweilo [Chin.]; Hesperian; *Italian; Jutlander;* kabloona [Innuit]; *Londoner;* man from the West; *Norwegian;* one from the West; *Portuguese; questor;* Rhode Islander; *Spaniard; Scot; Tennessean; Utahan; Virginian;* white man; *xanthocroic; Yugoslavian; zoon;*
**westernize** *(adj.)*: Americanize; become western-like; Christianize; civilize; develop; Europeanize; *forge ahead;* get modernized; *help;* Hellenize; industrialize; *jump ahead; kirkify; leading edge;* modernize; *naturalize;* occidentalize; *progress; quality of life; renovate; streamline; transform; upgrade; vamp;* Westernize; *xform; Yankify; zoom ahead;*
**wet** *(adj.)*: aqueous; bedashed; *clammy;* damp; drenched; doused; dripping; dewy; embrocated; flooded; gushy; hydric; hydrated; humective; imbrued; indrenched; *irriguous;* juicy; *kept ~; liquidy;* moist; madefied; matted; non-dry; *oozy;* plashed; *quaggy;* roric; rainy; soaked; soggy; sopping; sodden; sopping *~; tear-stained;* undried; vapored; watered; watery; waterlogged; washy; *xerophobic;* yoted; *zwoosh;* [Ant. waterless]
**wet** *(v.)*: *aqua; affusion;* bedew; bedash; bedrench; *clean;* dampen; douse; drench; embrocate; *fill; flood; get one wet;* humectate; imbrue; indrench; jawp; *keelhaul; launder;* moisten; madefy; *non-dry; overwhelm;* plash; quench; ret; rinse; soak; spray; sprinkle; splash; *tear-stained; torrential; undried; urinate;* vapor; water; *xfer water;* yote; *zigg;*
**whale** *(n.)*: *animal;* blue ~; *beast; creature;* cete; cow [fem.]; cetin; dwarf sperm ~; *enormous;* finback; gray ~; gam [pl.]; humpback ~; irrawaddy; *jument;* killer ~; *leviathan;* minke ~; *Moby Dick;* narwhal; orca; pilot ~; *quale* [arch.]; rorqual; sperm ~; toothed ~; *underwater creature;* very large; white ~; *xtr. large; Yangtze dolphin;* ziphoid;
**wharf** *(n.)*: anchorage; berth; *coast;* dock(side); *estuary;* floating dock; *gangway;* harbor; *inlet;* jetty; key; landing; marina; mooring; *near-shore; oceanside;* pier; quay; *riverside;* slip; tie-down; *unloading area; voe;* waterfront; *xebec dock;* yacht landing; *Zee [G.];*
**wheat** *(n.)*: *article;* bread ~; bran; cereal grain; *crop;* durum; einkorn; emmer; frumentarious; grain; hard ~; Indian dwarf ~; *jute;* kernel; *load;* Marquis ~; *notwheat; organic;* Polish ~; *queatch* [arch.]; rivet ~; spelt ~; tuft; unthreshed ~; *volume;* wheaten; winter ~; *xanthophyll;* yelm; zea mays;
**wheel** *(n.)*: alloy ~; auto ~; blackwall; caster; car ~; cart- ~; disteel ~; engine ~; felly; *going;* hubless ~; *hubcap;* inner tube; *jeep ~; karrozzin ~;* leading ~; Mansell ~; *noddy ~;* orb; pedrail ~; penumatic tire; *quele* [arch.]; rim; roller; rubber tire; *sidewall;* trundle; tire; truckle; *ultimate ~; vehicle ~;* whitewall; *xfer; yanker ~; zoom;*
**wherewithal** *(n.)*: ability; *background; brawn;* capability; deftness; dowry; expertise; *endowment;* faculty; facility; funds; gift; genius; habilitation; *instinct; jurisdiction;* know-how; knack; legerdemain; means; makings; money; natural ability; *opportunity;* power; qualification; resources; sufficiency; skill; talent; usefulness; virtuosity; way; wealth; *xenium; yare; zeal;*
**whet** *(v. sharpen)*: acuminate; barb; cut; cuspidate; *double-edge;* edge; file; grind; hone; *instrument; jagged;* keen; *lanceolated;* make sharper; *narrow; oilstone;* point; *quill-like;* resharpen; sharpen; spiculate; *taper; ultra-sharp; verge; well-sharpened; xyster; yet undulled; zap;* [Ant. wear]
**whet** *(v. stimulate)*: arouse; bestir; *coax;* disquiet; excite; fire up; goad; *hearten;* incite; jar; kindle; *lead;* motivate; *nudge; overexcite;* provoke; quicken; rouse; stimulate; tingle; *unloose; vivify;* wake; *xuld [arch.];* yerk; zing; [Ant. weary]
**whetstone** *(n.)*: *acuminate;* burrstone; blade-sharpener; chopper; dicer; emery wheel; file; grinder; grindstone; hone; *instrument; jagged;* kern-stone; knife-grinder; *levigation;* millstone; *non-dull;* oilstone; *point;* quern-stone; quetstone; rubstone; ragstone; sharpener; *tool; ultra-sharp; verge;* whetter; whet-slate; *xyst; yet undulled; zap;*
**whim** *(n.)*: aspiration; *bent;* caprice; crotchet; desire; *emotion;* fancy; *got to;* hankering; impulse; *judgment; knowledge;* leaning; megrim; notion; optation; perception; quirk; reaction; sentiment; thought; urge; vagary; whimsy; *xenodiagnosis;* yen; *zeal;*

**whimper** *(v.)*: anguish; bemoan; cry; despair; *express sorrow; feel sorrow;* groan; heave a sigh; *inconsolable; judder;* keen; lament; moan; *noise;* outcry; *pout;* querk; *rumble;* sob; snivel; *tear;* utter cry; *vociferate;* whine; *xenophthalmia;* yammer; *zowie;*
**whimsical** *(adj.)*: amusing; blithe; capricious; *daft;* entertaining; erratic; fanciful; funny; goofy; humorous; imaginative; impulsive; jocular; kooky; lighthearted; moody; notional; off-the-wall; playful; quirky; random; silly; tongue-in-cheek; unpredictable; variable; witty; *xtry.;* yen; zany; [*Ant.* weighty]
**whine** *(n.)*: *appeal;* bellyache; complaint; drone; *exclamation;* fretting; groan; howl; *inveighing; jubilation;* keen; lamentation; moan; noise; outcry; pule; quiritation; *roar;* squawk; tone; ululation; vituperation; whimper; *xuld [arch];* yowl; *zing;*
**whine** *(v.)*: accuse; bellyache; complain; cry; decry; *explode;* fuss; groan; hone; holler; inveigh; jangle; kvetch [Yid.]; land on; moan; nitpick; object; pule; quibble; repine; squawk; *tear into;* ululate; vituperate; whimper; *xuld [arch.];* yell; zing;
**whip** *(n.)*: *affliction;* bull~; cat-o-nine-tails; crop; *device;* equipment; flogger; *gird;* horsewhip; *instrument;* jower; knout; koorbash; lash; mule-whip; *nail; overhit;* punisher; quirt; riding ~; *rod;* scourge; thrasher; thong; tawse; *unleash; vengeance;* whipcord; *xuld [arch.];* yerk; *zinger;*
**whip** *(v.)*: afflict; beat; belt; chastise; *draw; efface;* flog; flay; flagellate; gird; hit; inflict; *jeel;* knout; lash; larrup; lambaste; lay stripes on; mark; *nail; overhit;* plow; punish; quirt; *rend;* scourge; thrash; tawse; *unleash; victimize;* wale; *xuld [arch.];* yerk; *zing;* [*see* afflict]
**whirl** *(n.)*: *alternation; becurled;* curl; *downspin;* entwisting; frizz(le); gyrating; helix; hank; *intwisting; jag; kink; looping; meandering; nonlinear; overwound;* pin curl; querl; ringlet; spiral; swirl; twist; twirl; upwinding; volute; whorl; *x-ing; yaw;* zigzag;
**whirl** *(v.)*: *around;* becurl; curl; circle; *downspin;* eddy; furl; gyrate; hurtle; incurvate; *jee; keel;* loop; move around; nutate; orb; purl; querl; rotate; spin; swirl; twirl; turn; upsweep; volt; whorl; wheel; *x-ing;* yede; zip around;
**whirlpool** *(n.)*: *around;* backset; counterflow; current; *downward spiral;* eddy; funnel; gurge; *hurling;* incurvation; *jee; keel; loop;* maelstrom; nutation; *orb;* purling; querl; rotary; swirl; twirl; turbillion; undercurrent; vortex; whirl; willy [naut. slang]; weel; *x-ing; yede; zwoosh around;*
**whirlwind** *(n.)*: *agitation; baguio* [Sp.]; cyclone; dust devil; eddy; funnel cloud; gustnado; hurricane; ill wind; *Jupiter Pluvius; khamsin* [Egy.]; *line squall; monsoon; nor' easter; Oklahoma rainstorm;* precession; *quirlewind* [arch.]; rotary storm; rainspout; spout; *storm; spiral;* tornado; twister; tourbillion; *upheaval;* vortex; wind tunnel; waterspout; *xuld [arch.]; yern; zwoosh;*
**whisper** *(n.)*: aspiration; breath softly; *comment; divulge; express; fuss;* gentle speech; hushed tones; insuserration; *just a whisper; kept low;* low tones; muttering; murmuring; non-voiced words; *opining; psst!;* quiet ~; *roun* [arch.]; susurrus; soft speech; talking quietly; undertone; *unvoiced; vocalization;* whisper; *xfer; yawping; zeroing in;*
**whisper** *(v.)*: asperation; breathe; *comment;* divulge; express; fuss; gently say; *hushed;* insuserrate; *jaw;* keep low; *low-volume;* mutter; muffle; *non-voiced; opine; psst!;* quietly say; *roun* [arch.]; say softly; tell softly; utter softly; *under one's breath;* vocalize; word; *xfer;* yawp; zero in;
**whisperer** *(n.)*: aspersion-caster; backbiter; chatterbox; defamater; echoer; *famer;* gossip(er); hisser; informer; jaunderer; kimmer; *loose-tongued;* murmurer; newsmonger; *obtrectation;* prattler; quidnunc; rumormonger; slanderer; tattler; utterer; *vicious voice;* wagger; *xiaoren;* yenta; *zeroizer;*
**whistle** *(n. noisemaker, tooter)*: *article;* blower; cornamute; dog ~; *device;* equipment; foghorn; gazoo; horn; *instrument; jubal;* kazoo; klaxon-horn; *love flute; musical note;* noisemaker; *object;* penny whistle; quail-pipe; *recorder;* steam ~; tooter; *union pipe;* veuze; whiffler; *xirula;* yell; zarah;
**whistle** *(n. toot)*: alarm; beep; blow; bleep; clangor; choo-choo; din; *echo; fweet!; gong;* honk; hoot; *intonation; jow; knoll;* loud toot; *music;* noise; ooga ooga; peep; *quake;* ring; sound; shrill; toot(le); tweet; *utterance;* vweet!; whiffle; *xirula; yammer; zap;*

**white** *(adj.)*: alabaster; albino; bleached; *blanc* [F.]; blank; Chinese ~; colorless; Dutch ~; eggshell; flat ~; fair; *glowing;* grayish; hoar; ivory; jasmine- ~; *kaolin;* lily- ~; *light;* milk~; milky; niveous; off- ~; pearl ~; pure ~; pale; *quit* [arch.]; rhetizite; snow ~; snowy; true ~; uncolored; *unblemished; vanilla;* whited; xanthochroic; yellowish-white; zinc white;

**whiten** *(v.): albescent;* bleach; blanch; blench; *candescent;* dealbate; decolorize; discharge; etiolate; fade; grow pale; *hue; industrial bleach; javel water; kalsomine;* lighten; make white; *non-colored;* obliterate; pale; *quite white;* remove color; *stain-remover;* take color out; uncolor; *vanish;* whitewash; *whited; xanthochroic; yellow-remover; zero color;*

**whiteness** *(n.)*: absolute white; *blanched;* colorlessness; cleanness; dealbation; etolation; *fadedness;* gleaming ~; hueless; hoarness; intinctivity; *javel water; kalsomine;* lightness; *most white; non-colored; only white;* paleness; purity; *quite white; real white;* snowiness; taintlessness; unsulliedness; *very white;* white *xanthochroic; yet pure; zero color;* [see purity]

**whitewash** *(v.): artfulness;* bemask; cover up; disguise; explain away; *feign;* gloss over; hide the truth; *imbosk; justify;* keep hidden; lie about; misrepresent; *non-truth;* obscure; pass over; put a nice face on; *qualify; repress;* suppress; sweep under the carpet; tuck away; *under wraps;* veil; withhold; *xenomorph; yashmak; zero honesty;* [see whiten]

**whittle** *(v.): artwork; barb;* carve; chip; dig; diminish; erode; fashion; *grave;* hew; inscup; *jag;* kerf; lessen; mold; *notch; overcut;* pare; quinse; shave; sculpt; trim; undermine; *v-groove;* work; *xylography; yerk; zip off;*

**whiz** *(v.)*: accelerate; breeze; cruise; dart; elan; fly; glide; hurtle; *issue;* jet; kite; light; move; *nippy; outrun; proceed; quicken;* rip; streak; shoot; tear; *uprush; velocity;* whip; *xuld [arch.];* yern; zoom;

**whole** *(adj.)*: aggregate; all(-encompassing); *broad;* big; complete; collective; comprehensive; *done; detailed;* entire; exhaustive; full; gross; *high;* intact; indivisible; integral; jimbang; *kept intact;* length-and-breadth; lump; mass; macroscopic; non-abridged; overall; panoramic; perfect; plenary; *quantified; ready;* sheer; total; thorough; unabridged; undivided; uncut; universal; unbroken; unedited; veritable; wide-ranging; *xtry.;* yare; *zet [dial.];*

**wholehearted** *(adj.)*: all-out; *burning;* complete; dedicated; enthusiastic; full; fervent; gung-ho; hearty; impassioned; *jumping in;* keen; *loyal;* motivated; *mad; never-failing;* overzealous; passionate; quick; ready; spirited; *thrilled;* unreserved; vehement; *wholly; xenocentric;* yare; zealous;

**wholeness** *(n.)*: aggregation; bigness; completeness; *done;* entireness; fullness; *gross; high;* indivisibility; *jimbang; kept intact;* length-and-breadth; mass; non-abridgement; *overall;* panorama; perfection; *quantity; round;* soundness; totality; thoroughness; unbrokenness; veritableness; whole; *xtry.;* yare; *zero division;*

**wholesome** *(adj.): appropriate;* beneficial; clean; chaste; decent; *ethical;* fit; good; healthful; innocent; jackalent; *kid-appropriate; legitimate; lovely;* moral; nice; *old-fashioned;* pure; *quality;* respectable; salubrious; taintless; upright; virtuous; *well; Xn.; yet unspoiled; zero-raunch;* [Ant. whorish]

**wholesomeness** *(n.): appropriateness;* beneficialness; cleanness; chasteness; decency; *ethicalness;* fitness; goodness; healthfulness; innocence; jackalence; *keenness; legitimacy;* morality; niceness; *old-fashioned ~;* purity; *quality;* respectability; salubrity; taintlessness; uprightness; virtue; wholesome goodness; *well; Xn.; yet unspoiled; zero-raunch;*

**wholly** *(adv.)*: altogether; *broad;* completely; downright; entirely; fully; far and away; generally; *highly;* integrally; inclusively; *jimbang; keep; lump;* macroscopically; *non-abridged;* outright; overall; 100%; perfectly; purely; quite; roundly; stark; soundly; totally; thoroughly; throughly; through and through; throughout; utterly; very; well; whole hog; wholesale; *xtry.;* yare; *zealously;*

**whore** *(n.)*: adulteress; bawd girl; courtesan; doxy; escort; fornicator; gamester; harlot; hooker; hireling; immoral woman; jade; kittock; lady of the evening; mistress; meretrix; nymphomaniac; *obscene woman;* prostitute; quean; rig; strange woman; slut; strumpet; trollop; trull; *unfaithful woman;* venal; wench; working girl; *x-rated woman;* yaud; *zipless;*

**whoredom** *(n.)*: adultery; bawdiness; cuckolddom; *concupiscence;* debauchery; *evil; enticements;* fornication; gross immorality; *godlessness;* harlotry; hooking; immorality; jadery; *kinkiness;* lasciviousness; *looseness; mischief; naughtiness;* odure; prostitution; playing the harlot; queanery; revelry; sexual sin; *shamelessness;* trollopy; unfaithfulness; unchastidy; uncleanness; venery; whoring; wenching; *x-rated behavior; yielding to sin; ziplessness;* [*see* sin]

**whoremonger** *(n.)*: adulterer; belswagger; carouser; debauchee; evil man; fornicator; *gigolo;* home-wrecker; immoral-man; john [slang]; *keeper or a mistress;* libertine; lecher; libidnist; mistress-keeper; *(married) man;* non-faithful; *outparamour;* playboy; philanderer; palliard; *quad;* rake; satyr; two-timer; unfaithful man; vow-breaker; womanizer; wencher; *x-rated;* yoke-breaker; *zipless;*

**wicked** *(adj.)*: abominable; bad; corrupt; depraved; diabolical; evil; fiendish; flagitious; godless; heinous; iniquitous; *jaded; knavish;* licentious; malevolent; nefarious; odious; pernicious; perverse; *quad;* rebellious; ruthless; sinful; sinister; scurrilous; treacherous; unrighteous; ungodly; villainous; wrong(ful); *xgressing;* yucky; *zero morals;* [*Ant.* well-intentioned]

**wickedness** *(n.)*: abomination; badness; crime; corruption; debauchery; depravity; evil; flagitiousness; godlessness; heinousness; iniquity; *jadedness; knavishness;* licentiousness; mischief; malignity; nefariousness; odiousness; perverseness; *quad;* rebellion; sin(fulness); transgression; turpitude; unrighteousness; villainy; wrongdoing; *xgression; yetzer hara* [Heb.]; *zero morality;*

**wide** *(adj.)*: askant; broad; capacious; *disproportionate;* extensive; edgewise; flat; far-reaching; *great;* horizontal; *immense;* jacent; *king-sized;* lengthways; lengthwise; lateral; laterally; landscape; large; *massive;* not thin; obtuse; oblique; prodigious; quantitative; *roomy;* sideways; sidewise; spread-out; sidelong; *tremendous; unusual; vast;* widened; *width-wise;* XL; *yawning;* zoomed out;

**widen** *(v.)*: augment; broaden; *cross-widened;* dilate; debouch; enlarge; expand; extend; flare; fan out; greaten; grow; *heighten;* increase; jumboize; *keep growing;* largify; make wider; *newly-widened;* outspread; *post-expansion; quantum increase; revamp;* spread; swell; thicken; upbuild; *very wide;* wax bigger; XL; *yawn; zoom;* [*Ant.* wane]

**wideness** *(n.)*: amount; area; breadth; coverage; distance across; extent; *fullness;* girth; gage; hugeness; *jurisdiction; king-sized;* latitude; measurement; *not thin; oversize;* purview; qua; range; reach; span; size; thickness; *unit width;* volume; width; x-width; *yard;* zone;
    **Breadths**: fingerbreadth; footbreadth; hairbreadth; hairsbreadth; handbreadth; handsbreadth;

**widespread** *(adj.)*: all-pervading; broad; common; diffuse; extensive; *epidemic;* far-reaching; far-flung; general; huge; *international; indiscriminate; joint; known world;* large-scale; major; non-localized; overall; pandemic; prevalent; predominant; pervasive; quaquaversal; rife; rampant; regnant; *serious; trans-world;* universal; very ~; wide-reaching; *x-world; yonder; zonic;*

**widow** *(n.)*: *alone;* bereft woman; *citess;* dowager; *elderly lady; female;* griever; hag; *individual; joyless; kimmer;* little old widow-woman; *madam; Nain;* old woman; *poor woman;* queen-mother [royalty]; relict; suttee; *tantie;* unhappiness; *vidual;* widow-woman; *woman; war ~; x-out;* young ~; *Zaraphath;*

**width** *(n.)*: area; breadth; capacity; diameter; extent; fullness; girth; hugeness; immensity; jumboness; *king-sized;* length; measurement; *non-vertical;* overall ~; prodigiousness; quantity; reach; span; thickness; *underlying ~;* volume; wideness; *x-coordinate; yardage;* zoomed out;

**wield** *(v.)*: *ability;* brandish; carry; control; command; display; exhibit; flaunt; flash; flourish; *grip;* handle; have; *impressive; jockey;* keep; kithe [Scot.]; lay hold on; manage; *nobble; operate;* ply; *quicken;* reveal; show; tote; use; unsheathe; vaunt; wave; *xuld [arch.];* yield; *zip out;*

**wiener** *(n.)*: *all-American;* ballpark frank; Coney (island); chili dog; dog; *eats;* frank(furter); *German sausage;* hot dog; *Italian sausage;* jegget; *knockwurst; lomo; mortadella; nutrition; onions;* pigs in blankets; *quelque-chose [F.]; refreshment;* sausage; tube steak [slang]; *uncooked hotdog;* Vienna sausage; weenie; *xarque; Yankee stadium; zakuski* [Rus.];

**wife** *(n.)*: *amoret;* better half; beloved; betrothed; bride; consort; companion; concubine; dame; dutch; *endeared;* feme; feme-covert; *frau* [G.]; goodwife; helpmeet; housewife; homemaker; helper; *hausfrau* [G.]; *intimate; jealous ~;* kadin [Mos.]; love; mate; marriage partner; mistress; madam; Mrs.; misses; *newlywed; old woman* [slang]; partner; *queen;* rib [joc.]; spouse; soul mate; stepwife; slave wife; *trusted ~;* ux.; *vrouw* [S. Afr.]; woman; *xanthippe;* yokemate; *zaftig;*

**wig** *(n.)*: *artificial hair;* bob-wig; covering; *dark-haired ~; extension;* full-bottom; false hair; *gris;* hairpiece; headdress; *imitation hair;* jasey [slang]; *katsura* [Jap.]; *locks;* mop; *non-real; overcovering;* periwig; peruke; postiche; powdered ~; *quiff;* rug; scratch; shimmy; toupee; tete; *unreal;* vallancy; wiglet; *xerasia; yellow-haired ~; zapata;*

**wiggle** *(v.)*: agitate; bicker; *convulse;* didder; *erratic;* flutter; *gyrate;* hustle; *instability;* judder; jiggle; *knock; lurch; move; nudge;* oscillate; *pitch;* quaver; rattle; shake; shimmy; squirm; sway; twist; twitter; twitch; *unstable;* vacillate; wag(gle); wriggle; worm; wriggle; *xuld* [arch.]; yaw; zigzag;

**wild** *(adj.)*: animalistic; brutish; bestial; boisterous; crazy; disorderly; disruptive; *evil;* feral; fierce; ferocious; *grievous;* haywire; haggard; harsh; hog-wild; inhuman; irregular; jungli; *kaf* [arch.]; loutish; lionlike; mad; non-domesticated; natural; nasty; noisy; outrageous; out-of-control; passionate; *querulous;* reckless; rampant; rough; rip-roaring; sylvatic; savage; terrible; turbulent; tempestuous; unbridled; untamed; unrestrained; unmanageable; uncontrolled; undomesticated; vicious; violent; wildish; *xtry.;* yahoo; zany; [Ant. well-behaved]

**wilderness** *(n.)*: arid region; barren land; backwoods; badlands; bush; *country;* desert; desolate land; *emptiness;* forest; grassless place; *howling ~;* ile [Welsh]; jungle; *kavir* [Pers.]; *lowveld* [S. Afr.]; mesa; non-cultivated area; outback; plains; *Qattara;* rough country; savanna; steppe; *trackless; uninhabited land;* veld; *vast ~;* wilds; wildwood; xerarchy; *yews; Zahara;*

**wildlife** *(n.)*: animals; animalia; beasts; big game; *birds;* creatures; domestic animals; *elk;* fauna; game; herbivores; insectivores; juments; *koalas;* life forms; mammals; *nature;* organisms; *ponies;* quadrupeds; *rabbits;* small game; *turtles; ungulates;* vertibrates; wildings; *xeme; yearlings;* zoics;

**wildness** *(n.)*: anarchy; brutishness; bestiality; craziness; disorderliness; disruptiveness; *evil;* fierceness; ferociousness; *grievousness;* harshness; inhumanness; irregularity; jungliness; *kaf [arch.];* loutishness; lionlikeness; madness; non-domestication; outrageousness; passion; *querulousness;* recklessness; rampancy; roughness; savageness; terribleness; turbulency; tempestuousness; unbridledness; unrestrainedness; unmanageability; viciousness; violence; wildishness; *xtry.; yahoo;* zaniness;

**wiliness** *(n.)*: artfulness; *beguiling;* craftiness; cunning; deviousness; evasiveness; foxiness; guile; *hidden;* illusiveness; insidiousness; jadishness; knavishness; *lying; mendacity;* non-trustworthiness; *outfoxing;* pawkiness; *quaintise* [arch.]; roguishness; subtlety; slyness; sneakiness; shrewdness; trickiness; underhandedness; *vulpine;* weaseliness; *xtry, cleverness; yepship* [arch.]; zinging;

**will** *(n. desire)*: aspiration; bidding; choice; choosing; desire; delight; *enthusiasm;* fancy; free will; general desire; hope; heart; inclination; *judgment;* keen desire; longing; liking; mind; notion; *obsession;* pleasure; *quality; reckoning;* self-will; *tendency;* urge; volition; vagary; velleity; will; wish; want; whim(sey); *xenenthesis;* yen; yearning; *zeal;*

**will** *(n. last testament)*: article; *bereft;* covenant; *document; express ~;* filed ~; given ~; *hope; intentions; jointure; key document;* last will and testament; *mention;* nuncupative ~; official ~; probate; *qualified; reckoning;* settlement; testament; uncontested ~; valid ~; (written) ~; *xfer; yellowed paper; zet* [dial.];

**will** *(v.)*: aspire; avarice; bid; covet; desire; *eagerly desire; fancy;* go to; hope to; intend to; *just going to; keen desire;* long for; *mine; need; order;* plan to; please to; *quest for; reach for;* shall; *thirst for;* urge; *velleity;* want to; would like to; *xel* [arch.]; *ye'se* [arch.]; *zeal;*

**willful** *(adj. deliberate)*: *aware;* by design; conscious; deliberate; ever-conscious; *forethought; glaring; highly visible;* intentional; *just plain to see;* knowing; *liking;* meaningfully; non-accidental; on purpose; peccant; purposeful; quite intentional; *resolute;* studied; thought-out; unmistakingly; voluntary; witting; willing; with design; *xtry. planned; yearnful;* zealous;

**willful** *(adj. stubborn)*: adamant; bull-headed; contumacious; determined; dogged; ever-stubborn; firm; grim; headstrong; insistent; inflexible; iron-willed; intractable; jaw-set; *keep; lasting;* mule-headed; non-yielding; obdurate; pigheaded; *querulous;* rigid; refractory; resolute; stubborn; strong-willed; self-willed; stiff-necked; tenacious; unbending; unyielding; *volitional; without yielding;* x-grained; yieldless; *zero give;* [*Ant.* willing]

**willing** *(adj.)*: agreeable; *burning desire;* cooperative; desirous; eager; favorable; game; have desire; inclined; *joy;* keen; *longing for;* minded; *not disinclined;* of a mind to; pleased; quick; ready; set; too happy; unreluctant; very ~; *want; xtry. happy;* yare; *zealous;* [*Ant.* wary]

**willingness** *(n.)*: agreeableness; aptness; *burning desire;* cooperativeness; desirousness; eagerness; favorableness; gameness; *heart;* inclination; *joy;* keenness; *love; minded;* non-reluctance; *obliging;* pleasure; quickness to comply; readiness; self-determination; towardness; unreluctance; ungrudgingness; voluntariness; willing heart; *xtry. ~; yare;* zeal; [*Ant.* wariness]

**wilt** *(v.)*: anhydrate; *bow;* collapse; droop; dry up; exsiccate; fade; *go dry;* hang; insolate; *juiceless; knuckle;* languish; mummify; non-hydrate; over-dry; parch; quail; *rainless;* shrivel; sag; torrefy; *under-water;* vaporate; wither; wane; *xerosis; yarrish;* zap;

**wily** *(adj.)*: artful; *beguiling;* crafty; cunning; devious; evasive; foxy; fraudful; guileful; *hidden;* illusive; insidious; jady; knavish; *lying;* misleading; mischievous; non-trustworthy; *outfox;* pawky; *quaintise [arch.];* roguish; subtle; sly; sneaky; shrewd; tricky; underhanded; unscrupulous; vulpine; weaselly; *xtry.;* yepe; *zinger;*

**win** *(v.)*: annihilate; beat; conquer; defeat; expugn; foil; *gain victory;* hammer; *invincible; junk [slang];* kill; knock out; lick; master; *neutralize;* overcome; prevail; quench; rout; succeed; triumph; take; unseat; vanquish; worst; whoop; *x-ing; yank down;* zap;

**wince** *(v.)*: *aback;* balk; blench; cringe; draw back; *edgy;* flinch; go back; *hesitate; involuntary;* jump; *kick; lose courage;* move back in fear; *nervous; ouch; palter;* queck; quail; recoil; *react;* shrink; shy away; tremble; *uneasy; vexed;* withdraw; *xuld [arch.];* yerk; *zip aback;*

**wind** *(n. breeze)*: airstream; breeze; blast; boreas; current; cross~; draft; east ~; foehn; favonian; flaw; gust; gale; head~; indraft; jetstream; katabatic ~; levanter; land-breeze; moderate gale; north ~; night- ~; notus; *overdraft;* puff; quarter-wind; *rotary winds;* scud; south ~; southeaster (-wester); trade ~; tail~; updraft; undercurrent; violent ~; Vayu [Hind.]; west ~; waft; westerly; williwaw; x-wind; *yaw;* zephyr;

**wind** *(v. coil)*: alternate; becurl; bend; coil; curl; crank; *do wrap;* entwist; furl; glomerate; hankle; intwist; involute; *jag;* keckle; loop; meander; *nonlinear; over~; prewind;* querl; ravel; roll; reel; spiral; snake; sinuate; twist; upwind; volt; wrap; *x-ing; yaw;* zigzag;

**winding** *(adj.)*: anfractuous; bendy; curvy; curving; *dither;* entwisted; fluctuating; glomerate; hankled; intwisted; indirect; *jagged;* keckled; loopy; meandering; *nonlinear; over~; ply;* querled; reeling; snaky; twisty; unstraightened; volted; windy; *x-ing; yawed;* zigzaggy;

**window** *(n.)*: awning ~; box ~; bay ~; casement; double ~; embrasure; fenestra; glass; hopper ~; industrial ~; Jesse ~; kitchen ~; lancet; *multi-lit ~;* non-glare ~; opening; oriel; portal; pane; porthole; quarrel; roof ~; skylight; tilt and turn ~; *unopened ~;* ventana; windowpane; windshield; x-om; yard; zeta ~;

**windy** *(adj.)*: airish; aeolian; breezy; blustery; boisterous; *cyclonic;* drafty; eolian; flawy; gusty; *howling; inclement; jet stream;* katabatic; *line squall;* moderately ~; *not calm;* over-windy; puffy; *quarter-wind;* rough; raging; stormy; squally; turbulent; tempestuous; *uncontrolled; violent;* windswept; *x-wind; yaw;* zephyrous; zephyry; [*see* winding; *Ant.* windless]

**wine** *(n.)*: ∗ alcohol; blood of grapes; burgundy; chablis; champagne; *drink; dago; effervescence;* fermented grape juice; florence; grape juice; gamay; hermitage; ice~; jug ~; kabinett; Lambrusco; merlot; new wine; Nebbiolo; *oinos [Gr.];* Orvieto; Port ~; quadrimium; red ~; sherry; table ~; *unmixed ~;* vino; white ~; xeres; *yquem [F.]; yayin [Heb.];* zinfandel;

**winepress** *(n.)*: *apparatus;* basket press; continuous screw press; *device; equipment;* foot-press; grape press; horizontal screw press; *item; juicer; kern; lenos* [Gr.]; manual ~; *niagara; oenology;* press; *quern; receptacle;* squuzer; turn-press; *unit; vat; vintage;* wine press; wring; *xeres; yeqeb* [Heb.]; *zinfandel;*
**wing** *(n.)*: appendage; alae; bird-wing; *canard;* delta ~; eagle's ~; fore~; feathers; fan; gull~; hackle; ibis ~; *jay ~; kite;* limb; membrane- ~; *night hawk; oriole ~;* pinna; pinion; plane; quadrinodal; rogallo; sweepback; *tarsel;* under~; van; *wingtip; xema ~; yearn [arch.]; zoofulvin;*
   Kinds of **winged**: four-winged; gold-winged; gull-winged; long-winged; net-winged; short-winged; six-winged; two-winged; wide-winged;
**wink** *(v.)*: *allure;* blink; bat; close eye; *dally;* eye~; flutter; flip eyelid; glint; *hint; inveigle; jaw ~ing; keen on; lashes;* move eyelid; nictate; oeiliad; *play; quick ~; rouse;* squint; twinkle; *tip a ~; use eyelid; volitant;* whiz; *xuld [arch.];* yerk; zip;
**winner** *(n.)*: award-winner; beater; conqueror; champion; champ; defeater; dominator; expugner; frontrunner; *great;* hero; *invader; jubilant;* kemp; laureate; master; non-loser; overtaker; overcomer; prevailer; *quasher; ruler;* subjugator; subduer; triumpher; undefeated champ; victor; worster; *xtry.; yell; zealous;*
**winnow** *(v.)*: agitate; betoss; cast in the air; disturb; eventilate; fan; *get done;* hackle; *insufflate; jet; kest; labor;* make separate; *neat; over-agitate;* part; *quicken;* remove chaff; separate; scutch; *trouble; toil; upset;* ventilate; wim; *xuld [arch.];* yandy; *zephyr;*
**winter** *(n.)*: *arctic;* bleak mid~; cold season; depth of ~; December; *extreme temperatures;* February; frigid months; frost; *gelidity;* hard ~; *hibernal;* icy season; January; *keen; low temperatures;* midwinter; *nippiness; overcold; polar; quivering;* raw weather; snowy weather; *season; unheated; very low temperatures;* wintertime; wintertide; *Xmas [off.]; Yuletide;* zero weather;
**wipe** *(v.)*: absterge; *bathe;* clean; dry; erase; *friction;* give rub; hand-wipe; *in hand; jigger; Kleenex®; luster;* mop; *nard;* overspread; polish; *quab;* rub; spread; swab; sluff; smear; towel-dry; *use; violent agitation;* wash; *xfer;* yark; zip;
**wire** *(n.)*: armored cable; *BX;* cable; cord; copper ~; *direct-buried cable;* electrical ~; feed; guywire; *house ~;* insulated ~; jumper; *kilovolt;* line; lead; *multiwire;* nanowire; *ohm;* priming-wire; power line; *quantum; Romex®;* strand; shielded ~; *transmission line;* underground cable; *voltage;* wiring; *xfer;* Y-cable; *zap;*
**wiry** *(adj.)*: attenuated; bony; constricted; delicate; elongated; fine; gangly; hairbreadth; insubstantial; jimp; knife blade-thin; lean; lanky; meager; narrow; overthin; pencil-thin; *quantité négligeable* [F.]; ribby; skinny; stringy; thin; underweight; virgate [bot.]; willowy; XF; *yieldless; zero body fat;* [Ant. wide]
**wisdom** *(n.)*: abstruseness; acumen; *better judgment;* common sense; caution; discretion; discernment; experience; foresight; good sense; horse sense; intelligence; insight; judiciousness; judgment; knowledge; level-headedness; *maxim;* non-foolishness; *overwiseness;* prudence; *quick-witted;* rationality; reasonableness; sense; sensibility; sagacity; sapience; thought; understanding; *value;* wiseness; *xenagogy; yepe [arch.]; zeteticism;* [Ant. witlessness]
**wise** *(adj.)*: astute; *advised;* bright; circumspect; discreet; discerning; ever-wise; farsighted; farseeing; *great; heaven-gifted;* insightful; judicious; *knowledgeable;* longsighted; *museful; noetic;* oracular; over~; prudent; *quick-witted;* rational; sagacious; sensible; sapient; smart; *thinking;* understanding; *versed;* well-thought-out; wise-hearted; *xenagogic;* yepe; *zetetic;* [Ant. witless]
**wisecrack** *(n.)*: answer; *backtalk;* clever reply; comeback; *defense; eccentricity;* funny remark; gibe; humor; *insult;* jibe; kid; levity; *message;* nifty; one-liner; pun; quip; retort; reply; sally; smart remark; tease; *utterance; vexation;* witticism; *xuld [arch.];* yarn; zinger;
**wish** *(n.)*: ambition; bidding; craving; desire; *enthusiasm;* fancy; general desire; hope; hankering; hunger; inclination; itching; *just want to;* keen desire; longing; *mind;* notion; need; optation; pleasure; *quest; reckoning;* self-will; strong desire; true desire; urge; volition; velleity; will; want; whim(sy); *xenenthesis;* yearning; zeal;

**wish** *(v.)*: aspire; ache; bid; crave; desire; *eagerly desire;* fancy; got to have; hope for; itch; *just got to have; keen desire;* long for; make a wish; *need; order;* pant; *please; quest for; reach for;* seek; thirst for; *urge; velleity;* want; *xel [arch.];* yearn for; *zeal;*
**wishful** *(adj.)*: aspiring; aspirant; *believing;* craving; desirous; eager; fancying; *gung-ho;* hopeful; hungry; itching; *just want it;* keen; longing; *minded;* notional; optative; prurient; *questful; reckoning;* solicitous; *truly want; urge; volitional;* wanting; willing; *xenenthesis;* yearnful; *zealous;*
**wishy-washy** *(adj.)*: alternating; *back and forth;* changing; dithering; *erratic;* fluctuating; *going back and forth;* hesitant; irresolute; jellyfish-like; *kedging; lacking decisiveness;* mutable; non-resolute; oscillating; pathetic; quasi-resolute; reluctant; spineless; teeter-tottering; unmanly; vacillating; weak-minded; waffly; watered-down; *x-ing;* yo-yoish; zigzagging;
**wit** *(n.)*: astuteness; brightness; cleverness; dexterity; esprit; *funniness;* genius; humor; ingenuity; jocularity; keenness; *levity; mirth;* nimble-wittedness; outfoxing; policy; quick-wittedness; repartee; sharpness; *trickiness; underhandedness; vulpine;* wittiness; *xtry, ~; yepship [arch.];* zeal;
**witch** *(n.)*: astrologist; bewitcher; charmer; diviner; enchantress; fortune-teller; *gastromancer;* hag; *incantation;* jinx; korrigan; lamia; medium myalist; night hag; necromantist; old witch; occultist; pythoness; *palm-reader; quad; rhabdomancer;* soothsayer; sorceress; tagati; *ungodly;* vexer; witch-woman; white ~; *xylomancer;* yenta; zodiacist; [see sorcerer]
**witchcraft** *(n.)*: alchemy; black magic; conjuring; divination; enchantment; fortune-telling; geomancy; hocus pocus; incantation; juju; *Keltic religion; legerdemain;* magic; myalism; necromancy; new age; occult; *palmistry; quad;* rune; *rhabdomancy;* sorcery; soothsaying; tagati; *ungodliness;* voodoo; witchery; wizardry; xenomancy; *yogism; zodiac;*
**witch doctor** *(n.)*: astrologer; bewitcher; conjurer; diviner; enchanter; *fortune-teller;* geomancer; healer; inyanga; jadoo-wallah; kahuna [Haw.]; *lithomancer;* medicine man; *necromancer;* obeah doctor; *psychic; quad; rhabdomancer;* shaman; theurgist; *ungodly;* voodooist; witchman; xenomancer; *yogist; zodiacist;*
**with** *(prep.)*: alongside; among; amid; accompanying; beside; by; *combined; drawn together; escorting;* flanking; *gotten;* here ~; in the presence of; joined to; *knit together;* linked; midst; next to; *on;* present ~; *quality time;* right next to; side-by-side ~; there~; together ~; using; *vicinity;* withal; *x.;* yoked ~; *zero separation;*
**withdraw** *(v. retreat)*: abandon; back out; clear out; draw (back); depart; evacuate; exit; flee; go back; *hightail; immigrate; jet; kest;* leave; move out; *not remain;* olate; pull out; quit; retreat; retire; remove; skedaddle; take out; *uproot;* vacate; walk out; *xfer;* yank out; zip away;
**withdraw** *(v. take out money)*: abduce; abstract; *bank;* clear; draw (out); deduct; eliminate; extract; *free; flee;* get rid of; haul away; *interval; jettison; knock off;* leave; *lop off;* minus; *negate; overdraw;* purge; *quit;* rid; recede; subtract; take away; transplace; unload; vacate; *winkle out;* xfer; yank; *zero out;*
**withdrawal** *(n.)*: abandonment; backing out; clearing out; drawing back; departure; evacuation; flight; going back; *hightailing; immigration; jetting; kesting;* leaving; moving out; *non-remaining; olate;* pullback; pulling out; quitting; retreat; recall; skedaddling; taking out; *uprooting;* vacating; withdrawing; *xfer;* yanking; zipping away;
**wither** *(v.)*: anhydrate; bake dry; *chap;* dry up; dehydrate; exsiccate; fade; *go dry;* heat-dry; insolate; *juiceless;* kiln-dry; languish; mummify; non-hydrate; over-dry; parch; quail; *rainless;* shrivel; shrink; sear; torrefy; *undone;* vaporate; wilt; wizen; *xerosis; yarrish;* zap;
**withered** *(adj.)*: anhydrated; *arid;* baked-dry; *chapped;* dried; dehydrated; desiccated; exsiccated; flaccid; *gone dry;* heat-dried; insolated; juiceless; kiln-dried; languished; mummified; marcescent; non-hydrated; over-dried; parched; *quenchless; rainless;* shriveled; sun-dried; sere; torrefied; *unwatered;* vaporated; wilted; wizen; wrinkled; wizened; xeromatous; *yarrish;* zapped;

**witness** *(n.)*: attester; bystander; confirmer; deponent; eyewitness; *faithful ~;* gazer; hostile ~; hearer; *informant; jerque;* kibitz; looker-on; *minder;* noticer; observer; onlooker; passer-by; *quidnunc; regarder;* spectator; seer; scrutinizer; spy; testifier; testimony; *uncoverer;* viewer; witnesser; watcher; *x-viewer; yeme;* zero in;
**witness** *(v.)*: attest; behold; bear ~; certify; declare; espy; establish; *find; fix;* give sworn statement; homologate; inform; *justify; know;* kithe [Scot.]; *legitimize;* make known; notify; observe; proclaim; *questionless;* relate; see; speak out; substantiate; say so; testify; tell; *utter;* view; vouch; verify; watch; x-certify; *yes; zealously affirm;* [*see* see, say; affirm]
**witnessing** *(n.)*: attesting; biblical witnessing; conversion; door-knocking; evangelism; fervency for souls; Gospel presentation; house visitation; *inviting people; Jesus;* knocking doors; leading souls to Christ; missionary work; *ministry;* neighborhood outreach; outreach; personal ~; *quest for souls;* reaching the lost; soul-winning; trying to win souls; *undertaking;* visitation; winning souls; *xenagogy; yede;* zeal for souls;
**witty** *(adj.)*: amusing; bright; clever; deft; entertaining; funny; *gifted;* humorous; intelligent; jokey; keen-witted; *laugh-a-minute;* mentally astute; nimble-witted; on the ball; *perceptive;* quick-witted; *real funny;* smart; sharp-witted; *tongue-and-cheek; uproarious;* very sharp; whimsical; *x-smart;* yare-handed; *zippy;*
**wizard** *(n.)*: astrologer; bewitcher; conjurer; diviner; enchanter; fortune-teller; geomancer; haruspice; *incantation;* jadoo-wallah; *karakia [Maori];* lithomancer; magician; necromancer; oracle; psychic; *quad;* rhabdomancer; sorcerer; theurgist; *ungodly;* voodooist; warlock; xylomancer; *yogist;* zodiacist;
**wizardry** *(n.)*: alchemy; black magic; conjuring; divination; enchantment; fetishism; geomancy; hocus pocus; incantation; juju; *Keltic religion; legerdemain;* magic; necromancy; occult; *psychic; quad;* rune; *rhabdomancy;* sorcery; theurgy; *ungodliness;* voodoo; witchery; *xylomancy; yogism;* zodiac;
**wobble** *(v.)*: *alternate;* bob; coggle; didder; *erratic;* fluctuate; growse [arch.]; hop; *instability;* jiggle; *knock; lurch; move; nod;* oscillate; pitch; quaver; reel; shake; shimmy; totter; *unstable;* vacillate; wabble; *xuld [arch.];* yerk; zigzag;
**wobbly** *(adj.)*: *alternating;* bouncy; bobbling; capricious; diddery; erratic; fluctuating; giddy; *hazardous;* instable; jumpy; *kooky;* loose; *moveable;* non-stable; out-of-control; precarious; quavering; rickety; shaky; shoogly [Scot.]; tottering; unstable; unbalanced; vacillating; wobbling; wavering; *x-ing; yo-yo;* ziggety; zig-zaggy;
**woe** *(n.)*: anguish; bleakness; crestfallenness; distress; *ejulation;* forlornness; grief; hopelessness; heartache; inconsolableness; joylessness; katzenjammer; lowness; misery; *negativism;* overmuch sorrow; piteousness; *quivering;* ruefulness; sorrow; trouble; trial; unhappiness; vapors; woefulness; *xtry. grief; yearning; zestlessness;* [*see* calamity; *Ant.* wonderment]
**woeful** *(adj.)*: awful; baleful; crestfallen; downhearted; doleful; elegiac; forlorn; glum; gloomy; hapless; inconsolable; joyless; keening; lachrymose; low; miserable; mournful; morose; negative; noisome; overcast; pitiable; pathetic; *quivering;* rueful; sorrowful; sullen; troubled; unhappy; very sad; woebegone; *wretched; xtr. bad;* yearnful; zealess; [*Ant.* wonderful]
**wolf** *(n.)*: arctic ~; beast; black ~; canine; cub; cajota; carnivore; coyote; demi- ~; Ethiopian ~; fox; fiend; gray ~; hyena; *isatis;* jackal; killer; lobo; mad dog; maned ~; *night ~; organism;* predator; prairie ~; *quadruped;* red ~; she- ~ [fem.]; timber ~; *ululator; vulpine;* whelp; wolfess [fem.]; wild beast; *xenocyon;* yabbi; zorro;
**wolfish** *(n.)*: all-devouring; bestial; bloodthirsty; canine; doggish; doglike; extortionate; foxlike; fiendish; grabby; hound-like; hungry; inhuman; jackalesque; *killing;* lupine; mongrel; mean; nasty; omnivorous; predatory; *quadrupedal;* ravening; rapacious; savage; sharklike; terrible; *uncouth;* vulpine; voracious; vulturous; wolflike; wolvish; *xolotl;* Yorkshire terrier-like; *zerda;*

**woman** *(n.)*: *amoret; adult;* beauty; belle; chick [slang]; citess; cummer [Br.]; daughter; dame [off.]; distaff; *effeminate;* female; femme; gal; girl; gentlewoman; *her;* housewife; *individual;* jane [slang]; kimmer [Br.]; *kinswoman;* lady; maid; madam; ma'am; mistress; matron; nymph [poet.]; *nullipara; one;* peri; *quaedam* [arch.]; *queen; red-head;* sister; squaw [Am. Ind.]; she-male [slang]; señora [Sp.]; *termagant; temptress; unmanly; virgin; vrouw* [Du.]; weaker vessel; womenfolk [pl.]; *x-chromosome; young lady;* zaftig; [see girl, wife; broad]
   **Female names**: Abigail; Betty; Cheryl; Deborah; Esther; Francine; Gertrude; Helen; Irene; Jennifer; Kim; Lisa; Mary; Nancy; Olivia; Patricia; Quisilla; Rachel; Sarah; Tricia; Ursula; Valerie; Wilma; Xanthe; Yvonne; Zoe;
**womanhood** *(n.)*: adulthood; *age; blossoming;* condition of being a woman; development; *effeminacy;* femaleness; flower of ~; girlhood; gentlewomanliness; *her; individual maturity; jeune fille [F.];* kinswoman; ladylikeness; maturity; muliebrity; matronhood; matronship; *nymphishness; of age; peri;* quinceañera; *readiness; sisterliness; tenderness; unmanliness; virtue;* womanliness; x-chromosome; *young womanhood; zaftig;*
**womankind** *(n.)*: *adults; beauties; chicks [slang];* distaff; *ever-womanly;* females; fairer sex; girls; *hers; housewives; individuals;* janes [slang]; kimmers [Br.]; *the* ladies; maids; nymphs [poet.]; *ones; peris; quaedams* [arch.]; *queens; red-heads;* sisters; *termagants; unmanly; virgins;* women(folk); weaker sex; *x-chromosome; young ladies; zaftigs;*
**womanliness** *(n.)*: *attractiveness; beauty;* charm; decorum; delicateness; *effeminacy;* femininity; girlishness; gentleness; gentle~; *hers; inobtrusiveness; jeune fille [F.]; kins~;* ladylikeness; maidenliness; muliebrity; nymphishness; *over- ~; prissiness; quietness; ravishing; sissiness; sweetness; softness;* tenderness; unmanliness; *voluptuousness;* womanishness; x-chromosome; yokemate; zaftig;
**womanly** *(adj.)*: *attractive; beautiful;* charming; *delicate;* ever-womanly; feminine; girlish; gynic; gentle(~); *her; inobtrusive; jeune fille [F.]; kins~;* ladylike; maidenly; muliebrile; *meek;* nymphish; *over-womanly;* petticoat [dated]; *quiet; quedam* [arch.]; *ravishing;* she-; *sweet; soft; tender;* unmanly; *virtuous; voluptuous;* womanlike; womanish; x-chromosome; *young woman; zaftig;*
**womb** *(n.)*: abdomen; belly; cervix; *development;* endometrium; *front; gut; home; inside;* jagung [Kor.]; kelder [arch.]; *laden;* matrix; *notum [zoo.];* oven [slang]; *pelvis; place;* quern; rahim [Turk.]; stomach [slang]; *tummy;* uterus; venter; wame; *xfer;* yoni [Skr.]; zone; zigong [Chin.];
**wonder** *(n.)*: awe; amazement; astonishment; bedazzlement; confounding; disbelief; dazzlement; enthrallment; fascination; gaping; gastness; holding one's breath; incredulity; *joy;* keenness; looking aghast; marvel; musing; *nonplus; overwhelmed;* prodigiousness; *quake; rendered speechlessness;* stupefaction; surprise; terror; unbelief; *very impressed;* wonderment; *xtry;* yerk; zowie!;
**wonderful** *(adj.)*: amazing; astonishing; brilliant; capital; commendable; divine; excellent; exceptional; fantastic; fabulous; great; grand; grandiose; glorious; heavenly; incredible; impressive; jim-dandy; keen; lofty; laudable; marvelous; magnificent; masterful; noteworthy; notable; outstanding; prodigious; praiseworthy; *quantum* [L.]; remarkable; superb; splendid; spectacular; terrific; tremendous; unbelievable; very good; wondrous; xtry; yippee!; zizzy; [Ant. woeful]
**wood** *(n.)*: *acacia;* boards; cordage; *cedar;* deal; *elm;* firewood; *gopher ~;* hardwood; *ironwood; juniper;* kindling; kemp; lumber; *maple; mahogany; nemoral; oak;* planks; plywood; *pine; quassia; redwood;* soft~; seer-wood; timber; trees; underbrush; vert; *veneer;* wenge; xylem; *xylon; yew; zingana;*
   **Kinds of wood**: acacia- ~; brush~; candle~; dead~; elm~; fiddle~; gopher~; hare~; iron~; jarah~; knob~; larch~; musk~; oak- ~; pine~; quince~; rose~; sycamore- ~; teak~; uru- ~; virola ~; worm~; xanthoxylon capense; yellowwood; zebrawood;
**wooden** *(adj.)*: *acacia;* birchen; beechen; cedar; *driftwood; elm; fur; gopherwood;* hardwood; hickory; *ironwood; jaracanda; knobwood;* ligneous; made of wood; mahogany; *natural;* oak(en); pine; quassia; rosewood; *sycamore-wood;* timber; *uru-wood; veneer;* wood; *walnut;* xyloid; yew; *zebrano;*
**woods** *(n.)*: arbor; bosket; boscage; bush; coppice; covert; *dense woods;* espalier; forest; firth; grove; greenwood; heath; holt [poet.]; hurst [Br.]; *ironwood trees;* jungle; kumquats; luxuriance;

*maple trees;* nemoral; overgrowth; pinewood; pineland; queach; *rain forest;* scrub; trees; timberland; underwood; virgin forest; *vegetation;* wood(land); *the* wild(wood); wilderness; *ximenia; yews; zamia;*

**woodwork** *(n.)*: art; *business;* carving; carpentry; design; engraving; fancy ~; graving; hewing; handiwork; industry; job; joinery; *know-how;* lignography; millwork; *nice;* oak carving; piece; *quinse; routing;* skill; tooling; *use;* veneer; wood carving; xylograph; xoanon; yew carving; *zebrawood;*

**woodworker** *(n.)*: artist; bas-relief artist; carver; craftsman; chiseler; dry pointist; engraver; fashioner; graver; hand-crafter; inlayer; joiner; *kapnographer;* lignographer; master craftsman; *niellist; originator;* pyrographer; quinser; *router;* scroll-worker; sculptor; tooler; *user; venerrer;* woodcrafter; xylographer; yew-carver; *zingana;*

**woodworking** *(n.)*: art (of ~); bas-relief; chiseling; carpentry; carving; *craft;* dry point; engraving; *fashioning;* graving; *handiwork;* industry; joinery; *knack;* lignography; millwork; *negative; object;* pyrography; *quinse; routering;* sculpting; skill; timber-work; tooling; talent; *unmanufactured; virtu;* wood engraving; xylography; yew-carving; zoophorus;

**woody** *(adj.)*: arbustive; *abundant;* bosky; cespitose; dense; elmy; forested; green; *gnarly;* herbaged; infoliated; jungly; *knotty;* lush; luxuriant; meadowy; mossy; moss-covered; nemorous; overgrown; plush; *quaker-tree covered;* rich; sylvan; swardy; timbered; unspoiled; verdurous; wooded; xylary; yewy; zamia-covered;

**wool** *(n.)*: angora; báinín; cashmere; combed ~; dyed ~; ewe- ~; fleece; felt; gare; *hair;* Indian ~; jersey; kemp; kersey; knickerbocker yarn; lambs~; mohair; merino; *New Zealand ~; ovine;* Persian ~; qiviut; ratteen; serge; sheeps ~; tartan; *tweed;* undyed ~; virgin ~; vicuna; worsted; weft; *xillinous;* yarn; zibeline;

**woolen** *(adj.)*: angora wool; *brocade;* cashmere; *delaine;* ewe-wool; fleecy; gare; *hairy;* Indian wool; *jersey;* knitted; lanate; lanifice; ligneous; made of wool; neat; *ovine;* Persian wool; *quilled;* ratteen; serge; *twilled;* undyed wool; virgin-wool; wool(y); *xillinous;* yarny; zibeline;

**woolly** *(adj.)*: *abounding in hair;* bushy; *curly;* downy; *ewe-wool;* fleecy; flocculent; *gris;* hairy; *Indian wool; jubate;* kempy; lanate; *maned; non-bald;* overgrown; puffy; *quiff;* really furry; shaggy; tufty; unpolled; villous; wooly; woolen; *xerasia; yellow-haired; zapata;*

**word** *(n.)*: *articulation;* breath; *by~;* catch~; *declare;* expression; *fore mention; gab;* hyponym; idiom; jargon; ketch- ~; language; loan~; *mouth;* nomenclature; *onomatopoeia; pronunciation;* quatch; remark; speech; semantics; term; terminology; thought; utterance; verbiage; wordage; *x-word; yawping; zero in;*

**wording** *(n.)*: articulation; *best choice of words;* choice of words; diction; expression; formulation; *grammar; heart; idioms;* jargon; *ketch-word;* language; manner of speaking; *neology;* order of words; phrasing; phraseology; *quatch [arch.];* rhetoric; sentence structure; semantics; terminology; usage; verbiage; wordage; way of putting it; *xfer; yawping; zero in;*

**wordy** *(adj.)*: articulate; bombastic; big; chatty; diffuse; effusive; *florid;* garrulous; *high-sounding;* incessant; *jabbering; kelter;* lengthy; long-winded; multiloquous; *nonstop;* ongoing; prolix; prosy; quantitative; running on; *sizeable;* talkative; uttering; verbose; word-filled; *xenoglossic;* yaketty; *zealous;* [Ant. wordless]

**work** *(n.)*: action; burden; craft; drudgery; daylabor; employment; effort; exertion; field ~; grunt~; gainful employment; handi~; home~; hired labor; hard ~; industry; job; *kitchen ~;* labor; manual labor; moil; night-work; occupation; output; performance; production; *quantity output;* rigor; service; slave labor; toil; trade; *use;* vocation; working; *wrought; xtr. labor;* yard~; yakka [Aus.]; *zealous labor;*

**work** *(v.)*: act; busy oneself; craft; carry on activity; do; drudge; effect; exert; function; grind; hustle; *industry; job;* keep at; labor; moil; *night-work;* operate; *outwork; overwork;* produce; plod; ply; put out; plug away; *quietly ~; run; rigor;* slave; strive; serve; slog; *sweat;* toil; *use; volunteer;* wield; *wrought; xfer; yardwork;* zealously ~;

**workable** *(adj.)*: achievable; banausic; credible; doable; effective; feasible; functional; good; helpful; *intelligent;* judicious; *keen;* logical; meet; no-nonsense; operative; practical; quite sensible; reasonable; realistic; sensible; tenable; useful; viable; worthwhile; *xtr. work; yieldful; zero problem;*
**worker** *(n.)*: artificer; associate; apprentice; (busy) beaver; breadwinner; craftsman; co-worker; cowhand; doer; drudge [derog.]; day laborer; employee; fellow laborer; floozy [derog.]; farm hand; gofer [slang]; grunt [derog.]; hireling; hand; help; industrial worker; jobholder; jack; *kitchen worker;* laborer; moiler; menial; navvy [Br.]; operator; performer; producer; *qualified laborer;* retainer; roustabout; servant; staff member; subordinate; toiler; tradesman; underling; unskilled laborer; *vassal;* workman; *xylographer;* yeoman; *zaikai [Jap.];*
**works** *(n.)*: actions; *bid;* capability; doings; efforts; faculty; good works; hard work; industry; *just deserts;* kindnesses; labors; *merit;* natural ability; own effort; power; qualifications; *resources;* self-righteous acts; things one does; *undertaking;* virtue; work; *xuld [arch.];* your own effort; *zeal;*
**world** *(n.)*: all the ~; blue marble [poet.]; *ball; cosmos;* domain of man (-Satan); earth; *field;* globe; geosphere; God's footstool; humanity; *inhabitants; joint nations of the ~;* known ~; *large-scale;* middle-earth; natural ~; orb; *our ~; the* planet; *quaquaversal; real ~;* sea of humanity; Terra; universe; vale (of tears); *the* whole ~; *xtry.;* yeard [Scot.]; *zoa;*
**worldliness** *(n.)*: animate; badness; corporeality; carnal-mindedness; *down here;* earthliness; fleshliness; *globe;* humanness; irreligiousity; *just secular; knowledge; life down here;* materialness; naturalness; non-spirituality; ordinariness; physicality; profaneness; *questionable;* secularism; temporality; unspirituality; vileness; worldly-mindedness; *xenenthesis;* yieldedness to the flesh; *zoetical;*
**worldly** *(adj.)*: animate; bodily; corporeal; carnal-minded; *down here;* earthly; fleshly; *globe;* human; irreligious; *just secular; knowledgeable; life down here;* material; mortal; mundane; natural; non-spiritual; ordinary; of this earth; physical; profane; *quite ~; routine;* sublunary; secular; temporal; this-worldly; terrestrial; unspiritual; under the sun; vile; worldly-minded; *xenenthesis;* yielded to the flesh; *zoetical;*
**worldview** *(n.)*: *angle;* belief; conception; *deduction;* estimation; *fancy; ground; hypothesis;* idea; *judgment; knowledge; lemma;* mindset; notion; outlook; paradigm; *qua [L.];* reckoning; standpoint; theory; understanding; view of life; *Weltanschauung* [G.]; *xenenthesis; yeard [Scot.]; zonic outlook;*
**worldwide** *(adj.)*: all-inclusive; *big; broad;* common; comprehensive; *diffuse;* earth-wide; *four quarters of the earth; far-reaching;* global; *human;* international; *joint-national; known world;* large-scale; mondial; *the nations; over all the earth; overall;* planetary; planetwide; panhuman; quaquaversal; *relating to the whole world; spherical;* terrestrial; trans-world; universal; *very widespread;* whole-earth; *xtry.;* yonder; *zonic;*
**worm** *(n.)*: * army~; blood~; canker~; dracunculus; earth~; flat~; glow~; grub; heart~; inch~; joint~; kale~; larva; lug~; meal~; maggot; nematode; oligochaete; palmer~; quab; rag~; sand~; tape~; uncinaria; vermicule; velvet~; whip~; xenoturbella; yamamai; zygolobus;
**worm** *(v.)*: *advance;* burrow; creep; channel; dig; delve; edge; *find way in;* grub; hollow; hole; inch; *jenkin;* kip; *lower;* mole; *notch; open; prospect;* quarry; *remove dirt;* sneak; slither; tunnel; trench; undermine; *venture; way in; xfer; yede* zigzag;
**worn** *(adj.)*: *attrition;* battered; crumbling; diminished; effaced; faded; foot~; fore~; galled; hoary; hackneyed; impaired; *jaded;* knee- ~; *kaput;* lessened; much-used; napless; overused; over~; out- ~; old; passé; quite ~; run down; retired; secondhand; *shot;* tattered; time~; threadbare; trite; used (up); very old; ~ out; weathered; well- ~ (-used); weather-beaten; *x-old; yellowed; zero usefulness;* [see old]
**worrier** *(n.)*: alarmist; brooder; Cassandra; doomsayer; *exasperated;* fussbudget; fretter; fatalist; gloom-monger; *horrified;* insecure; *jittery;* kiaugher [Scot.]; lily liver; *mistruster;* nervous; over-anxious; panicker; pessimist; prophet of doom; *quitter; reluctant;* stresser; *terror-monger; uneasy;* vexer; worrywart; *xenophobia;* yellow-belly; *zealless;*

**worry** *(n.)*: anxiety; alarm; brooding; burden; care; dread; distress; *exasperation;* fear; gastness; horror; insecurity; jitters; kiaugh [Scot.]; *lily-livered; mistrust;* nervousness; over-anxiety; panic; preoccupation; quaking; *reluctance;* stress; *scared;* terror; trepidation; uneasiness; vexation; worriment; *xenophobia;* yellow-belliedness; *zeallessness;*
**worry** *(v.)*: agonize; affright; brood; be nervous; concern; dread; despair; distress; eye askance; fear; fret; get anxious; have qualms; *intimidated; jumpy; knees knocking;* lose courage; misgive; *nervous wreck; overwhelm;* panic; quiver; *recoil;* scare; *shake;* tremble; take fright; *uneasy; unnerved; vulnerable;* weigh down; wig out; *xenophobic; ydrad; zoophobic;*
**worse** *(adj.)*: ancillary; augmented; *below;* crummier; *compounded;* declining; ever- ~; fouler; gone down; half as good; inferior; junkier; *keeps getting ~;* lesser; lower; much lower; not as good; outranked; outclassed; poorer; *quite ~;* retrograde; retrogressive; shoddier; sorrier; subordinate; tin-pot; *under;* viler; waur; weaker; *x-out;* yuckier; *zapped;* [Ant. worthier]
**worsen** *(v.)*: augment; *broaden;* compound; deteriorate; decline; degenerate; escalate; flare; fall; grow worse; get worse; *heighten;* intensify; impair; jump down; *keep getting worse;* lessen; lower; *multiply; mount; narrow; negate; outgo;* pall; quail; regress; revert; sink; take a turn for the worse; *undo;* verge downward; wax worse; weaken; *x; yield;* zap;
**worship** *(n.)*: adoration; adulation; blessing; celebration; devotion; divine service; exaltation; extolling; falling down; glorification; homage; honor; *idolatry;* jubilation; kneeling; laud(ation); love; magnify; *never-failing love;* obeisance; praise; prostration; *quiritation;* reverence; *song of praise;* tribute; uplifting; veneration; vespers; worshipping; *xenophilia;* yearning; *zeal;*
**worship** *(v.)*: adore; bow (the knee); bless; celebrate; devote; exalt; extol; fall down; give praise to; glorify; honor; idolize; jubilate; kneel; knee-tribute; lift up; laud; love; magnify; *night oblation;* obeisance; praise; prostrate oneself; pay homage; *quiritation;* revere; reverence; sing praises; serve; *thank; tribute;* uplift; venerate; *worth; xenium;* yearn for; *zealously praise;* [*see* praise; sing]
**worshipful** *(adj.)*: adorant; blessing; contemplative; devout; deferential; extolling; *earnest;* fearing; grave; God-fearing; honoring; holy; humble; *introspective; jubilating; kneeling;* laudatory; magnifying; *non-presumptuous; obeisance;* prayerful; pious; *quaking;* reverent; reverential; solemn; thoughtful; *uplifting;* venerative; worshipping; *Xn.;* yielding; yearnful; zealous;
**worshiper** *(n.)*: adorer; blesser; celebrant; devotee; extoller; follower; glorifier; homager; honorer; hallower; idolizer; Jehovist; kneeler; lauder; magnifier; *night oblation;* offerer; praiser; pangyrist; *quiritation;* rejoicer; reverer; sacrificant; singer; *thanker;* uplifter; venerator; *worship; xenium;* Yahwist; *zealous praiser;*
**worst** *(adj.)*: absolute ~; bottom of the list; baddest [improper]; crummiest; *deteriorated;* extreme ~; evilest; foulest; grimmest; *horrible;* ickiest; *jaded; knavish;* lousiest; least; most inferior; nastiest; orneriest; poorest; *quality zero;* rottenest; shoddiest; sorriest; *terrible; utterly; unhealthiest;* vilest; wickedest; *x-out;* yuckiest; *zero;* [Ant. worthiest]
**worth** *(n.)*: assessment; book value; cost; *desert;* excellence; evaluation; *figure; gauging;* goodness; highness; importance; *judgment; known value;* list price; merit; nobility; *opinion;* price; quality; regard; *surmising; take;* usefulness; value; virtue; worthiness; *xenodiagnosis; year-end audit; zero-defect;*
**worthiness** *(n.)*: admirableness; *brilliance;* caliber; desert; deserving; excellence; fineness; goodness; high quality; impressiveness; *judgment;* keenness; loftiness; merit; nobility; notoriety; *opinion;* praise~; quality; *remarkableness; superiority; transcendence; unsurpassed;* value; virtue; worth; *xtry; you-beaut [Aus.]; zero-defect;* [Ant. worthlessness]
**worthless** *(adj.)*: *absurd;* bad; cheap; *crummy;* draffish; *empty;* futile; fruitless; good for nothing; hollow; insignificant; junky; ketty; lousy; meritless; non-worthy; otiose; paltry; quisquillous; rubbishy; sorry; shoddy; trivial; threepenny; useless; unimportant; unsalable; vain; valueless; vile; wretched; *xiaoren;* yieldless; *zero worth;* [Ant. worthy]

**worthlessness** *(n.)*: *absurdity;* bad quality; cheapness; draffishness; emptiness; futility; *good for nothing;* hopelessness; insignificance; junkiness; kettiness; lousiness; meritlessness; nugacity; otiosity; paltriness; putidness; *quisquillous;* rubbish; sorriness; triviality; uselessness; unusefulness; valuelessness; vileness; vanity; wretchedness; *x'ed; yuckiness;* zero worth; [*Ant.* worthiness]
**worthwhile** *(adj.)*: advantageous; beneficial; constructive; deserving; efficacious; expedient; fine; gainful; good; helpful; instrumental; justified; keen; *lucrative;* merited; meaningful; nice; *outstanding;* productive; *quality;* rewarding; salutary; *terrific;* useful; valuable; worthy; xtry.; yieldful; *zestful;* [*Ant.* worthless]
**worthy** *(adj.)*: appropriate; apposite; best-suited; befitting; condign; deserving; eligible; efficient; fit(ting); good; highly deserving; idoneous; justified; keenly ~; legitimate; meriting; *notable; outstanding;* proper; qualified; right; suitable; *true;* up for; *valuable;* well-suited; worthwhile; *xtry.;* yichus; *zestful;* [*Ant.* worthless]
**wound** *(n.)*: affliction; abrasion; ailment; burn; bruise; boo-boo; cut; contusion; damage; *evil;* flesh ~; gash; gall; hurt; head injury; harm; injury; jab ~; knife ~; lesion; laceration; maim; mar; *mischief;* nick; *offense;* prang; query; *riven;* sore; scratch; stab- ~; tear; ulcer; violence; welt; wheal; *xanthogranuloma;* yedder; *zapping;*
**wound** *(v.)*: afflict; bruise; burn; cause suffering; damage; endamage; fix [slang]; *grieve;* hurt; harm; injure; impair; inflict ~; jeel; *kick; knock; lift hand against;* maim; *nocument; offend;* persecute; pain; quail [arch.]; ruin; scathe; *trouble; unsafe;* victimize; wreak havoc; *wrong; x.; ydrad [arch.]; zap;*
**wrap** *(v.)*: *around;* bind; begird; bundle; coil; *cover;* draw around; drape; enwrap; enfold; encircle; embrace; enclose; enswathe; fold; gird; hug; inwrap; infold; inclose; jacket; kirtle; loop; lash; ligate; mummify; *nonlinear;* overwind; put around; *quoil* [arch.]; roll; ravel; swaddle; swathe; *tie; twine;* upbind; volt; wind; *x-ing;* yard; *zone;*
**wrath** *(n.)*: anger; *bitterness; boiling;* crossness; choler; displeasure; enragement; fury; gall; hotness; infuriation; incensement; ire; *jealous rage; kindling;* lividness; madness; *nettling;* outrage; perturbation; quick-temperament; rage; *steaming;* temper; upset; unmixed wrath; venting; wrathfulness; *xerothermia;* yelling; *zealousy* [arch.];
**wreck** *(n.)*: accident; bang-up; collision; crash; disaster; error; fender-bender; *goof-up;* hit; impact; jolt; kink; *lapse;* mishap; *nasty;* ordeal; pile up; *quirk;* ramming into; smash; *trouble; upset; violent;* wrack; *x; yipes!; zing;*
**wreck** *(v.)*: annihilate; break; crush; destroy; demolish; efface; fracture; ground; harm; injure; *jab;* knock apart; *lacerate;* mar; mangle; *non-working;* olate; prang; pull down; quash; ruin; smash; shatter; scupper; sabotage; subvert; tear up; torpedo; uproot; vitiate; wreak havoc; *x-ing;* yank down; *zap;*
**wrestle** *(v.)*: *altercate;* brawl; contend; *dispute; engage;* fight; grapple; *hold; intense; jolt;* kemp; *labor;* mud- ~; *negate;* oppose; *push; pull;* quarrel; *resist;* struggle; strive; tussle; tag- ~; *use moves;* vie; wrassle; *x-plex; yain [arch.]; zap;*
**wretch** *(n.)*: *âme-de-boue* [F.]; beggarly fellow; creature; crum; devil; derelict; dirt bag; *enfant terrible* [F.]; fallen one; good-for-nothing; have-not; insect; *junky;* knark; lowlife; louse; miserable ~; miscreant; nithing; n'er-do-well; outcast; profilgate; poor soul; *queer sight;* rapscallion; runnion; rakeshame; sad case; sorry fellow; thing; unfortunate (-unprincipled) person; vile person; wastrel; worm; *xiaoren;* yob; zero;
**wretched** *(adj.)*: abject; bleak; bad; crummy; dejected; dismal; despicable; evil; forlorn; foul; flea-bitten; glum; hopeless; hapless; ignoble; *junky; kindless;* low; lorn; lousy; miserable; mean; nasty; opprobrious; pathetic; poor; pitiful; piteous; *quad;* rakish; sorry; shameful; terrible; unnoble; unblessed; vile; woeful; xtr. bad; yucky; *zero goodness;*
**wriggle** *(v.)*: agitate; bestir; contort; didder; *exagitate* [arch.]; flip; *growse* [arch.]; hustle; *instability;* jiggle; *knock; lurch;* move around; *nudge;* oscillate; *pitch;* quiver; *riggle* [arch.]; squirm; twist; *unstable;* vacillate; writhe; wiggle; *xuld [arch.];* yerk; *zigzag;*

**wring** *(v.)*: *apply pressure;* bear down; compress; dispunge; entwist; force out; *grasp; hug;* intort; jam; *keep pressure; levigate;* mush; *nullify; overply;* press; quash; *roll;* squeeze; twist; *unmoisten; volt;* wrench; *x; yank; z-twist;*

**wrinkle** *(n.)*: agedness; *bend;* crease; crinkle; cockle; corrugation; doubling; enfolding; fold; gathering; *hem;* infolding; *j-bend;* kirtle; line; *marcescence; non-rigid;* overfold; pleat; *plissé;* quadriplanar; ripple; rimple; rumple; ridge; rugate; ruck; skin- ~; *scrunch;* tuck; undercrease; *volt;* whelk; *x-ing; yard; zone;*

**wrinkle** *(v.)*: *age;* bunch up; crease; crumple; crinkle; corrugate; double; enfold; fold; gather; *hem;* infold; *j-bend;* kirtle; lap over; make fold; *non-smooth;* overlap; pleat; pucker; quill; ruck; rumple; scrunch; tuck; turn; undercrease; volt; wrap; *x-ing;* yank; *zone;*

**wrinkled** *(adj.)*: *aged;* bunched up; creased; crumpled; crinkly; dried-up; enfolded; folded; gathered; *haggard;* infolded; *j-bend;* kirtled; lined; *marcescent;* non-smooth; overdried; plissé; pruney; prunelike; pleated; quilled; rumpled; rugose; scrunched; tucked; undercreased; volted; wrinkly; withered; wizened; *xeromatous;* yanked; *zapped;* [*Ant.* wrinkle-free]

**writ** *(n.)*: arraignment; bidding; bailpiece; billet; citation; court order; directive; detainder; elegit; fiat; *given order; holy* ~; interpellation; juror summons; *keleusmatically;* latitat; monition; notice; order; process; paper; *questioning;* request; summons; subpena; *scire facias* [L.]; ticket; *urging;* vocation; venire; written order; *xfer;* yellow slip; *zet [dial.];*

**write** *(v.)*: annotate; address; author; blazon; compose; chronicle; correspond; draft; denote; enter; expatiate; enface; engrave; emblazon; etch; fabulize; grave; hand~; indite; inscribe; indicate; imprint; jot; keep record; log; mark; *make;* notate; *over~;* pen; put down; print; quill; redact; record; register; scribble; scrawl; sign; scratch; take down; transcribe; under~; *vellum;* write down; *x; yak; zay;* [*Ant.* white out]

**writer** *(n.)*: author; blazoner; columnist; commentator; co-author; columnist; copyist; dialogue- ~; essayist; fabulizer; glossator; ghost~; hedge- ~; inscriber; journalist; *keeper of journal;* leafleteer; man of letters; makar [Scot.]; novelist; observator; penman; playwright; pamphleteer; quill-driver; remarker; scribe; transcriber; *underwriter;* volumist; wordsmith; *Xenophon; yellow journalist; zay [dial.];*

    **Famous authors**: Alcott; Boswell; Chaucer; Dickens; Emerson; Faulkner; Goethe; Hemingway Irving; Joyce; Keats; Longfellow; Milton; Nikolai; Osborne; Poe; Quarles; Roberts; Shakespeare; Tennyson; Updike; Verne; Whitman; Xenophon; Yeats; Zola;

**writhe** *(v.)*: agonize; anguish; *burn;* contort; *discomfort; distress; excruciating; feel bad;* grieve; gall; hurt; *inflammation;* jerk; *killing [slang];* lament; *misery; nip; ouch!;* pain; *quiver;* rack; squirm; suffer; twist; thrash; *unpleasantness;* vacillate; wriggle; wrench; *xiphodynia;* yerk; *z-twist;*

**writing** *(n.)*: autograph; *book;* characters; composition; commentary; calligraphy; caption; document; engraving; essay; epistle; etching; epigraph; epitaph; form; graving; glyphs; handwriting; hieroglyphics; inscription; journalism; kapnography; longhand; literature; letter(ing); legend; letterpress; mark(ing)s; notation; note; niggle; oeuvre; *observations; opus;* prose; paragraph; piece; *the* pen; *the* quill; *roll; revision;* sentence; scribbling; superscription; scripture; text; thoughts; uncials; verbiage; writing; work; *xiaozhuan;* yellow journalism; *zeug;*

**wrong** *(adj.)*: amiss; bad; confused; defective; deficient; erroneous; false; fallacious; groundless; heretical; inaccurate; incorrect; jim-jam; kim-kam; *lying;* mistaken; misguided; misunderstood; misconceived; not true; off base; peccant; *queer; repudiated;* spurious; specious; *trick;* untrue; unsound; *void of truth;* wrongful; *x-gressing; yawed; zero-truth;* [*see* sinful; *Ant.* well-proven]

**wrongdoing** *(n.)*: atrocity; badness; criminality; delict; debauchery; error; fault; godlessness; heinousness; iniquity; *jadedness; knavishness;* licentiousness; mischief; misdeed; naughtiness; offense; perverseness; *quad;* rebellion; sin; transgression; unrighteousness; violation; wrong; *xgression; yetzer hara* [Heb.]; *zymosis;* [*see* wickedness]

# X

**Xanadu** *(n.)*: arcadia; Asgard; blissful place; Cloud 9; dreamland; Elysium; fairyland; *Garden of Eden;* (hog) heaven; haven; idyll; *Jasper-walled city; kingdom;* la-la land; *merry old land;* never-never land; nirvana; Oz; paradise; *queme;* rose garden; Shangri-La; sublimity; Trala-la; Utopia; *utopian community;* Vanhalla; wonderland; Walhall; Xanadu; yarkandi; *Zion;*

**xanthic** *(adj.)*: aureate; buff; citron-yellow; dandelion; ecru; foliomort; goel; gold; honey; Indian yellow; jonquil; king's yellow; lemon (-colored); marigold; Naples yellow; orpiment; primrose; quince; royal yellow; sulfur-colored; topaz-yellow; uranite; vitelline; wan; xanthous; yellow; *zivolo;*

**xanthippe** *(n.)*: Amazon; battleaxe; crab; devil-woman; *evildoer;* fishwife; grimalkin; hellcat; *incessant;* Jezebel; *knocker;* lamia; monster; nag; ogress; princess; quarreler; rude woman; shrew; she-devil; termagant; *unkind;* virago; witch; xantippe; yenta; *zaftig;*

**xanthochroic** *(adj.)*: Aryan; blond-haired; Caucasian; European; fair-skinned; *Germanic;* Hesperian; Indo-European; Japhetic; *kabloona* [Innuit]; light-skinned; *Monacan;* Nordic; Occidental; paleface [Am. Ind.]; *Québecois; Russian; Scandinavian; Teutonic; Ukrainian; Viennese;* white; xanthochroid; *Yugoslav; Zeelander;*

**xanthochroid** *(n.)*: Aryan; buckra; Caucasian; *Dane;* European; fair-skinned; *German; Hungarian;* Indo-European; Japhethite; *kabloona* [Innuit]; *light-skinned; Monacan;* Nordic; Occidental; paleface [Am. Ind.]; *Québecan; Russian; Scandinavian; Teuton; Ukrainian; Viennese;* white; xanthochroic; *Yugoslav; Zeelander;*

**xanthous** *(adj.)*: amber; beige; canary; dandelion; ecru; fallow; foliomort; goel; honey; Indian yellow; icterus; jaundice; king's yellow; lemon (-colored); marigold; Naples yellow; ocherous; primrose; quince; royal yellow; sallow; topaz-yellow; uranite; vitelline; wan; xanthic; xanthochromatic; yellowish; *zivolo;*

**xenophile** *(n.)*: alien-lover; benefactor; *charitable; delighter in;* émigré-lover; foreigner-lover; *goodwill;* helper; immigrant-lover; *journeyer; kind to foreigners;* lover of strangers; *merciful;* non-xenophobic; *openhanded;* person who loves foreigners; *quarterer;* receiver of strangers; stranger-lover; *tolerant; unbigoted;* visitor-welcomer; welcomer; xenophiliac; *yield;* zealous; [*Ant.* xenophobe]

**xenophilia** *(n.)*: amiableness; benevolence; cordiality; *deference; entertainment;* friendliness; goodwill; hospitality; *invitation; joy;* kindness; love of strangers; munificence; neighborliness; openhandedness; propitiousness; *quarter; regard; reception; sociability;* tolerance; *unbigoted; virtuousness;* warmth; xenophily; *yieldedness; zealousness;* [*Ant.* xenophobia]

**xenophilous** *(adj.)*: alien-loving; benevolent; *congenial; delighter in;* émigré-loving; friendly; gregarious; hospitable; immigrant-loving; *journeyer;* kind; love of strangers; *merciful;* non-xenophobic; outsider-loving; *personable;* quite friendly; relisher of foreigners; stranger-loving; *tender-hearted;* unbigoted; visitor-welcoming; welcoming; warm; xenial; *yearn; zero hostility;* [*Ant.* xenophobic]

**xenophobe** *(n.)*: anti-foreigner; anti-Semitic; bigot; *biased;* chauvinist; discriminator; ethnocentrist; fearer of strangers; *gall-monger; hater of foreigners;* intolerant person; *jingo;* Jew-hater; klansman; *loather; malice-bearer;* narrow-minded person; *Nazi; opinionated;* partisan; *prejudiced; quiverer;* racist; sectarian; supremist; *terrorizer; unloving; vexer;* white supremist; xenophobe; *yahoo;* zenophobe; [*Ant.* xenophile]

**xenophobia** *(n.)*: apartheid; bias; bigotry; contempt; discrimination; ethnocentrism; enmity; fear; *gall;* hatred (of foreigners); intolerance; jingoism; klanism; *loathing;* malice; narrow-mindedness; *Nazism;* overpatriotism; prejudice; *quivering;* racism; sectarianism; supremism; *terror;* unfairness; *vexation;* white supremism; *worry;* xenophobia; yahooism; zenophobia; [*Ant.* xenophilia]

**xenophobic** *(adj.):* anti-foreigner; bigoted; chauvinistic; discriminatory; ethnocentric; foreign-hating; *galled; hatful;* intolerant; jaundiced; *klansman; loathing; malicious;* narrow-minded; *overpatriotic;* prejudiced; *quick to judge;* racist; supremist; *terrorizing;* unfair; *vexing;* White Supremist; xenophobic; *yahooist;* zenophobic; [*Ant.* xenophilous]

**xeric** *(adj.):* anhydrous; arid-region; barren-land; *chapped;* desert; dry-climate; evaporated; *fountainless; grassless;* hot-climate; insitient; jejune; kibe; low-moisture; moisture-deprived; non-watered; overhot; parched; quenchless; rainless; savanna-type; torrid-zone; unthirsty; *vaporated;* warm-climate; xerothermic; *yellow-hot; zapped;*

**xerography** *(n.):* autotypography; *book printing;* chromotypography; duplication; electrophotography; flexography; Gestetner; hectography; imprinting; *justification;* kalotypography; lithography; mimeographing; *non-printable blue;* offset printing; photocopying; *quarto;* reproduction; stereotypography; typography; *ukiyo-e [Jap.];* vitrography; woodblock printing; xeroprinting; *yakusha-e [Jap.];* zincography;

**xiphoid** *(adj.):* aor-shaped; bladelike; cutlass-like; daggerlike; ensiform; *fine-edged;* gladiate; *highly pointed; incisal; jagged; keen-edged;* long and pointy; *mucronate;* needle-shaped; *over-sharpened;* punctiform; *quill-like;* rapier-like; sword-shaped; *tined; ultra-pointy; very sharp; well-sharpened;* xiphoidian; yataghan-like; ziphoid;

**x-rated** *(adj.):* adulterous; base; crude; degrading; explicit; fornicative; fleshy; gauche; horrid; indecent; jadish; kinky; lewd; meretricious; *nude;* obscene; pornographic; *quad;* raunchy; sleazy; tasteless; trashy; uncouth; vulgar; whorish; x-certificate [Br.]; *yucky; zipless;*

**x-ray** *(n.):* arthrogram; beam; chest ~; *depiction;* encephalogram; fetoscope; grenz ray; heart cavity ~; irradiation; *joint ~;* K-electron; *leg ~;* microradiograph; negative; *object;* picture; *pyelogram;* qualimeter; (roentgen) ray; radiograph; radiation; *sonogram; technology;* urogram; venogram; wave; xeroradiograph; *yield;* zeugmatograph;

**xylographer** *(n.):* artist; bas-relief artist; carver; craftsman; chiseler; dry pointist; engraver; fashioner; graver; hand-crafter; inlayer; joiner; *kapnographer;* lignographer; master craftsman; *notcher; originator;* pyrographer; quinser; *router;* scroll-worker; sculptor; tooler; *user; venerrer;* woodworker; xylographist; yew-carver; *zingana;*

**xylography** *(n.):* artwork; bas-relief; chiseling; carving; *craft;* dry point; engraving; *fashioning;* graving; *handiwork;* inlaying; *joinery; kapnography;* lignography; *masterpiece; negative; object;* pyrography; *quinse; routering;* sculpting; tooling; *unmanufactured;* virtu; woodworking; xyloglyphy; xylopyrography; yew-carving; zoophorus;

**xylophone** *(n.):* amadinda; bala(fon); *bells;* carillon; *dulcimer; electronic keyboard; fangxiang [Chin.];* glockenspiel; *hammer dulcimer;* idiophone; *instrument;* jublag; kaffir piano; lamellaphone; marimba; *nebel;* orchestral ~; *percussion instrument; quijada; ranatek;* straw fiddle; tinglik; ugal; *vibraphone; wooden bars;* xylorimba; *yu [Chin.];* zylophone;

**xyrisic** *(n.):* aikraw; bog; bayou; carr; *damp;* everglade; fen(land); glade; haugh; inland marsh; *jheel* [Ind.]; kavir; *lagoon;* marsh(land); moor(land); morass; *nanoplankton; overgrown;* peatbog; quag(mire); rosland; *reeds;* swamp(land); slough; salt marsh; tarn; *usnea;* vlie [S. Afr.]; wetlands; xyrisic; yarpha; *zoocarpous area;*

**xyster** *(n.):* abrasion; bone scraper; *chamfering tool; dough scraper; edge-rounding tool;* file; *grater;* hand scraper; *implement; jack plane; knife; linishing;* medical scraper; *needle file; ovate handaxe;* pull scraper; *quannet;* raspatory; scraper; scalping-iron; *tool; unifacial tool; varnish scraper; wall scraper;* xyst; *yeck; zeug [G.];*

**xystus** *(n.):* arcade; boardwalk; corridor; *drive;* esplanade; *footpath;* gallery; *highway; ice road;* journey-way; *kotal;* lane; mall; *non-toll road;* outlet; piazza; promenade; *quo mode* [L.]; route; stoa; slype; terrace; *underpass;* vennel; walkway; xyst; *yong* [arch.]; zwinger;

# Y

**yacht** *(n.)*: *America's cup ~;* boat; craft; day sailer; esnecca; felucca; *galley; hooker;* ice ~; jacht; *ketch;* luxury boat; motor ~; *narrow boat;* one-design class ~; pleasure boat; *quarter galley;* racing ~; sailboat; sand ~; super~; *trimaran; udema;* vessel; watercraft; *xebec;* yaught [var.]; yawl; *zeaught* [Scot. arch.];

**yak** *(n.)*: aurochs; bovid; cow [fem.]; *creature;* domesticated ~; dzo; *ennstal;* fatling; gnu; highland ~; indicus; jomo; kouprey; longhaired ox; musk ox; n'dama; ox; *polled shorthorn; quadruped;* red heifer; sarlac; Tibetian ~; urus; vu quang ~; wild ~; xebu; yakow; zebu;

**yammer** *(v.)*: *accuse;* bellyache; complain; demur; *explode;* fuss; grumble; gripe; harangue; hammer; hone; holler; inveigh; impugn; jangle; knock; *kvetch* [Yid.]; lambaste; land on; murmur; nitpick; object; protest; quarrel; repine; *snarl; tear into; ululate;* vituperate; whine; *xuld [arch.];* yell; yawp; zing;

**yank** *(v.)*: abstract; avulse; bob; cant; draw; drag; extract; flounce; force; grab; heave; haul; intercept; jerk; kedge; lug; *move;* nab; *outdrag;* pull; pluck; quirk; remove; snatch; seize; take; tear; tug; *uncoif;* vellicate; wrench; wimple; *xuld* [arch.]; yerk; *zip;*

**yard** *(n.)*: acre; back~; barn~; court(~); curtilage; *dale;* enclosure; exclosure; field; front ~; grass; grounds; haugh [Scot.]; inclosure; *jebel; knoll;* lawn; lot; meadow; *nature; outdoors;* patch of grass; quadrat; *range;* school~; side~; sward; turf; *upland;* vega; *water meadow; xyris;* yarrow; zea;

**yarn** *(n.)*: app; bay~; bouclé; crewel; dyed ~; *entangle;* fiber; *goldthread;* halter; inkle; jersey; knittle; line; *microfiber; natural fiber; organzine;* packthread; qiviut; rope- ~; strand; skein; spun- ~; saxony; *slip;* thrum; thread; *uncoil; vang;* wool; *xylem; yarnlike;* zein;

**yaw** *(n.)*: alteration; bias; change; driftage; deviation; *el; fluctuation;* going off; heading away; incline; *jumping off; knocking off;* leaning; movement; *not on course; oscillation; path; quat; route;* sway; turn; *updating;* variation; waftage; *xenomorph;* yawing; zigzag;

**yaw** *(v.)*: alter; bend; curve; careen; deviate; el; fold; go off; hook; incline; jibe; knuckle; *left turn;* modulate; move off; *nonlinear;* offset; pull; ply; quat; rove; reel; swerve; slue; turn; tilt; undulate; verge; veer; wind; *xy-curve;* yaw off; zag;

**year** *(n.)*: annum; a; *B.C.;* calendar ~; *Draconic ~; era;* fiscal ~; Gregorian ~; *hour;* interval; Julian ~; kilocycle; leap ~; metonic ~; *new ~;* one ~; period; *quarter; run time;* school ~; solar ~; summer; twelvemonth; *timespan; upcoming ~; vintage ~;* winter; *x-time; yearlong;* zeir [Scot.];

**yearling** *(n.)*: animal; baby; child; *darling; enfant [F.];* firstling; fledgling; *girl;* hatchling; *infant; just new;* kitling; little animal; *miniature;* nestling; offsping; *peewee; quite new; recent arrival;* suckling; *tot; ungrown;* very young one; whelp; *xbreed;* youngling; *zoic;*

   **Specific young animals**: billy; bunny; calf; chick; colt; cosset; cub; cria; cygnet; dogie; duckling; fawn; filly; fledgling; foal; gosling; heifer; joey; kid(ling); kit(ten); lamb; leveret; nymph; owlet; piglet; pup(py); pullet; poult; shoat; whelp;

**yearly** *(adj.)*: annual; by the year; coming yearly; *continuously; deciduous;* every year; *forever; going on and on;* held ~; *incessantly; jusqu'au bout [F.]; kept going; lastingly; maintaining; non-ceasingly;* once-a-year; perennial; *per annum* [L.]; quotennial; recurrent; *steadily;* twelve-monthly; *unceasingly;* vintage; *without end; xferring;* year on year; *zone;*

**yearn** *(v.)*: ache; burn; crave; desire; *eagerly desire; fancy;* got to have; hanker; hope for; itch; *just got to have; keen desire;* long for; moon; need; *order;* pant after; *quest for; reach for;* seek; thirst for; urge; *velleity;* want; wish; *xel [arch.];* yammer; *zealously desire;*

**yeast** *(n.)*: active dry ~; *agent;* barm; bottom ~; baker's ~; brewer's ~; *chametz* [Heb.]; dough- ~; enzyme; ferment; granulated ~; hartshorn; instant ~; *ingredient; jast* [Swed.]; *killer ~;* leaven; *monocalcium phosphate;* newing; *overleaven;* pre-cultured ~; *quickener;* rising agent; saccharomyces; top ~; *unprocessed ~;* vegemite; wort; *xiao* [Chin.]; *yest* [arch.]; zyme;

**yell** *(n.)*: acclamation; bellow; blare; cry; call; *discharge;* exclamation; *eruption; fretting;* growl; holler; hoot; howl; *inveighing; jubilation;* keen; loud shout; *lamentation;* moan; noise; outcry; *proclamation;* quiritation; resonation; reverberation; roar; shout; scream; shriek; thundering; ululation; *uproar;* vociferation; wail; whoop; *xenophonia;* yowl; *zindabad;*

**yell** *(v.)*: acclaim; *appeal;* bellow; beckon; boom; cry; call; *discharge;* exclaim; *erupt; fret;* growl; holler; hoot; howl; *inveigh; jubilate;* keen; loudly say; *lament;* moan; noise; outcry; *proclaim; quiritation;* resonate; reverberate; roar; shout; scream; shriek; thunder; ululate; vociferate; vent; wail; whoop; *xenophonia;* yowl; *zindabad;*

**yeller** *(n.)*: *appealer;* bellower; crier; declaimer; exclaimer; fretter; growler; howler; hollerer; hooter; inveigher; *jawer;* keener; lamenter; moaner; noiser; out-crier; proclaimer; *quiritation;* roarer; shouter; screamer; shrieker; *town-crier;* ululator; voicer; wailer; *xenophobia;* yowler; *zindibad;*

**yellow** *(adj.)*: aureate; buff; canary; citron-yellow; dandelion; ecru; fallow; foliomort; gamboge; gold; honey; Indian yellow; jonquil; king's yellow; lemon; marigold; Naples yellow; ocherous; primrose; quince; royal yellow; saffron; straw-colored; topaz-yellow; uranite; vitelline; *wan;* xanthic; yellowish; *zante;*

**yellowish**: aurate; buttery; citrine; creamy; dandelion-colored; ecru; fallow; golden; honey-colored; *Indian yellow;* jonquil; *king's yellow;* lutescent; luteolous; marigold; *Naples yellow;* ocherous; primrose; quince; *royal yellow;* sallow; sandy; tartrazine; uranitic; vitelline; *wan;* xanthochromatic; yellowy; *zante;*

**yen** *(n.)*: ambition; bidding; craving; desire; *enthusiasm;* fancy; general desire; hankering; inclination; *just want to; keenness;* longing; *mind;* notion; optation; *pleasure; quiritation; reckoning;* self-will; *thirst;* urge; velleity; wish; whim; *xenenthesis;* yearning; zeal;

**yeti** *(n.)*: abominable snowman; bigfoot; chuchunya; *creature;* drill; *entellus;* Fouke Monster; gorilla; hibagon; *indri;* Jonesville monster; Kang Admi; Lake Worth monster; monster; nuk-luk; Old Yellow Top; *primate; quasi-human; rhesus;* sasquatch; *ts'emekwes;* uakari; vari; wildman; *xenopithicus;* yowie; *zoic;*

**yield** *(v. succumb)*: acquiesce; bow; bend; (con)cede; comply; conform; defer; *execute;* follow; give in; heed; implement; indulge; *jump;* knuckle under; keel in; kowtow; listen to; mind; not resist; *obey; perform; questionless;* relent; relinquish; succumb; surrender; *turn; take; undertake; vigorously obey;* wholly give; *xfer; yes; zero resistance;*

**yieldedness** *(n.)*: acquiescence; bowing; compliance; co-operation; deference; execution; following; giving in; heeding; *implementation; jumping to it;* keeping; listening; mindfulness; non-resistance; *obedience; performance; questionlessness;* relenting; relinquishing; succumbing; *turning; taking; upholding; vigorous obedience;* willingness; *xlation;* yielding; *zero resistance;* [*Ant.* yieldlessness]

**yieldless** *(adj.)*: adamant; bull-headedness; contumacious; determined; ever-stubborn; firm; grim; headstrong; inflexible; jaw-set; knaggy; liverish; mule-headed; non-bending; obstinate; pigheaded; persistent; *quarrelsome;* resistant; rigid; stubborn; tenacious; unbending; unyielding; vinegary; willful; *x-grained; yed; zero give;* [*Ant.* yielded]

**yieldlessness** *(n.)*: adamancy; bull-headedness; contumaciousness; doggedness; endurance; firmness; grimness; hardness; inflexibility; *jaw-set;* knagginess; liverishness; mule-headedness; non-yieldedness; obstinacy; persistence; *quarrelsomeness;* resistance; rigidness; stubbornness; tenacity; unyieldedness; *vinegariness;* willfulness; *x-grained;* yed; *zero give;* [*Ant.* yieldedness]

**yip** *(v.)*: arf; bark; cry; *discharge;* exclaim; *fuss;* growl; howl; *inveigh; jubilate;* keen; latrate; mewl; narr; outcry; pule; *quibble;* ruff; speak; *troat;* ululate; vociferate; woof; *xenophonia;* yap; yelp; *zing;*

**yoke** *(n.)*: acoupling; brace; breech-harness; crossbar; coupling; cattle- ~; duo; doubletree; *draught;* encumbrance; frame; gemel; harness; head ~; halter; hitched team; inspan; joining; kipple [Scot.]; *linked;* match; *marriage;* neap- ~; oxbow; *oppression;* pair; quoiler; *repression;* set; tackle; team; *united;* vu quang ~; withers yoke; *x-pair;* yellow; *zeugma* [Gr.]; [bondage]

**yoke** *(v.)*: attach; bind; couple; connect; *double;* entwine; fasten; *group;* hitch; interconnect; inosculate; join; knit; link; marry; merge; *network; oxreim;* put together; pair; *quasi-fuse;* relate; reunite; secure; set to; tie; unite; *vise;* wed; *xenograft; yoking;* zip;
**yokefellow** *(n.)*: ally; associate; buddy; co-laborer; companion; *devoted friend; endeared;* friend; good-fellow; helper; intimate; Jonathan; kith [pl.]; *loyal friend;* mate; *neighbor; ouboet [S. Afr.];* partner; *quondam friend;* roommate; supporter; teammate; unfailing friend; *voice; watcher; xenophile;* yokemate; *zealous friend;*
**yokel** *(n.)*: agrarian; bumpkin; boor; backwoodsman; country bumpkin; chuff; dolt; *egghead;* farmer; funk; goff; hick; hillbilly; ignoramus; joskin; kern; knuff; lout; larrikin; mountaineer; mountainer; numbskull; oaf; provincial; peasant; put; plebeian; plowboy; quack; rube; rustic; redneck; swain; tike; *unsophisticated; vassal;* whig [Br.]; *xiaoren;* yap; yob; zhlub;
**yonder** *(prep.)*: after; beyond; clear of; distant; extralimitary; further; farther; gone over (past); *hereafter;* in another place; just past; *kilometers beyond;* longer; more; next; over; outside; past; quite farther; *reach;* surpassing; there; ulterior; *very far;* within view; x.; yon(d); *zooming past;*
**young** *(adj.)*: adolescent; babyish; callow; childish; *developing;* early; fledgling; fresh; green; growing; hastive; immature; juvenescent; kiddish; little; maidenly [fem.]; new(born); *over-young;* puerile; *quite young;* raw; small; tiny; tender; unadult; unripe; vernal; wee; *XS;* youthful; youthy; *zero-experience;*
**youngster** *(n.)*: adolescent; boy [masc.]; child; *daughter [fem.]; enfant [F.]; freshman;* girl [fem.]; *high-schooler;* infant; junior; juvenile; kid; lad [masc.]; lass [fem.]; minor; *newborn; one;* puerile; *quincearian; ruddy; student;* teenager; *undergraduate; vandal;* whippersnapper; woungster; *xbred;* youth; *zit-faced kid;*
**youth** *(n. a child)*: adolescent; boy; child; *developing child; enfant* [F.]; *fellow;* girl [fem.]; *hatchling; immaturity;* juvenile; junior; kid; lad; lass [fem.]; minor; neophyte; non-adult; *one; offspring; preschooler;* quinquennarian; *ruddy ~;* sapling; schoolboy; sprout; tyke; teenager; urchin; *vandal;* waif; *xbred;* youngster; young man; *zon [dial.];*
**youth** *(n. youngness)*: adolescence; boyhood [masc.]; babyhood; childhood; development; early years; formative years; girlhood [fem.]; greenness; *hatchling;* immaturity; infancy; juvenility; juvenescence; juniority; kidhood [joc.]; *little;* may; nonage; newborn; *over-young;* puberty; pubescence; *quite young; rawness;* schooldays; springtime of life; tenderness; underdevelopment; unripeness; verdancy; weanling; *XS;* youngness; youthfulness; *zero-experience;*
**youthful** *(adj.)*: adolescent; boyish [masc.]; callow; *dollish;* early; ever-young; fresh-faced; girlish [fem.]; hastive; immature; juvenile; juvenescent; kidlike; little; maidenly [fem.]; nubile; *over-young;* pubescent; *quite young;* raw; small; tender; teenage; underage; vernal; *weak; XS;* young; youthy; yeasty; *zero-experience;*
**yowl** *(n.)*: *appeal;* bewailing; cry; caterwaul; dirge; exclamation; forlorn cry; grieving; howl; inveigh; *judder;* keen; lament; mourn; moan; noise; outcry; pout; quiritation; *regret;* shout; *tears;* ululation; vociferation; wail; weeping; whine; whimper; *xenophobia;* yowl; yawl; yammer; *zing;*
**yowl** *(v.)*: aah!; bawl; bemoan; cry; despair; erupt into tears; *feel sorrow;* grieve; howl; *inveigh; judder;* keen; lament; moan; *noise;* outcry; *pout; quistle [arch.];* roar; squall; *tear;* ululate; vociferate; wail; *xenophthalmia;* yawp; *zowie;*
**yucky** *(adj.)*: awful; bad; cruddy; disgusting; disagreeable; evil; foul; gross; grungy; gunky; horrid; icky; *junky;* ketty; lousy; mucky; mawkish; noxious; nauseating; offensive; putrid; *queasy;* repulsive; sickening; terrible; unpleasant; vile; wretched; x-bad; yecchy; *zorillo;* [*Ant.* yummy]
**yummy** *(adj.)*: appetizing; *bon!* [F.]; *captivating;* delicious; enjoyable; flavorful; good; heavenly; irresistible; *juicy;* keen; luscious; mouth-watering; *m-m-m;* nice; *outstanding;* pleasing; palatable; *quite good; rewarding;* savory; scrumptious; tasty; *unbelievably good; very good; wonderful; xenial;* yum-yum; zesty; [*Ant.* yucky]

# Z

**zaniness** *(n.)*: absurdity; buffoonery; craziness; confusion; disorder; eccentricity; foolishness; foolery; giddiness; goofiness; helter-skelter; inanity; juvenility; kookiness; ludicrousness; madness; nonsensicality; outlandishness; preposterousness; quackery; ridiculousness; senselessness; stupidity; turmoil; unusualness; vexation; weirdness; *xtry. mess; yo-yo;* zanyism;

**zany** *(adj.)*: absurd; batty; crazy; daft; eccentric; funny; goofy; hilarious; humorous; insane; jokey; kooky; loony; mad; nutty; outrageous; peculiar; quacked; ridiculous; silly; screwy; topsy-turvy; twisted; unstable; *variant;* weird; wacky; wild; *xtry.;* yo-yo; zonky;

**zanyism** *(n.)*: absurdity; bizarreness; craziness; daftness; eccentricity; funniness; goofiness; hilarity; *insanity;* joke; kookiness; looniness; madness; nuttiness; outrageousness; preposterousness; quackiness; ridiculousness; silliness; screwiness; twistedness; *unstable; vexation;* weirdness; *xtry.;* yock; zonkiness;

**zap** *(v. drain)*: abate; bleed; consume; deplete; drain; diminish; eat; expend; exhaust; fade; go down; *halt;* impair; *jump down; knock down;* languish; lessen; moderate; *negate;* outgo; *pall;* quail; reduce; suck dry; taper; use up; *vanish;* wane; wither; *xerosis; yield up;* zero out;

**zap** *(v. shoot)*: annihilate; blast; blitz; *cremate;* discharge; destroy; emit; exterminate; electrocute; fire; *get; hit;* impact; jolt; kill; laser; maser; *nail* [slang]; obliterate; phase; *quash; ray;* stun; shock; shoot; *terminate; undo;* vaporize; waste; wipe out; *x-ray; yank;* zing;

**zapped** *(adj.)*: aweary [lit.]; bushed; *comatose;* drained; exhausted; faint; fatigued; *groggy;* half dead; *indolent;* jaded; knocked-out; lethargic; *moiled;* noddy; overspent; pooped; *quiescent;* run down; spent; tired; unrested; *vapid;* wiped out; *xenarthrous; yawnish;* zonked out;

**zeal** *(n.)*: ardor; bustle; commitment; devotion; enthusiasm; fervor; gusto; heart; intensity; *joie de vivre [F.];* keenness; liveliness; mania; *nationalism; obsession;* passion; *quickness;* robustness; spirit; *thrill;* urgency; vehemence; wholeheartedness; *x-fervor;* yareness; zealousness;

**zealless** *(adj.)*: apathetic; blasé; complacent; dull; etiolated; fainéant; groggy; half-hearted; indolent; jaded; kef; listless; mopish; non-motivated; oscitant; pepless; quiescent; *remiss;* spiritless; torpid; unenthusiastic; vapid; weary; *xenarthrous;* yareless; zapped; [*Ant.* zealous]

**zeallessness** *(n.)*: apathy; blahness; *complacency;* disinterest; etiolation; ennui; faintness; grogginess; half-heartedness; indolence; jadedness; kef; listlessness; mopishness; non-motivation; oscitancy; peplessness; *quiescence; remiss;* spiritlessness; torpidity; unenthusiasm; vapidity; weariness; *xenarthrous;* yarelessness; *zapped;* [*Ant.* zealousness]

**zealot** *(n.)*: activist; advocate; believer; campaigner; crusader; devotee; enthusiast; extremist; fanatic; *glory-seeker; huk* [Philippines]; insurrectionist; Jacobin; jingo; *kicker;* loyal activist; militant; nationalist; objector; patriot; quixote; radical; revolutionary; *supporter; terrorist;* ultra- ~; votary; Whig; *xenocentrist;* Young Turk; zealoter;

**zealotry** *(n.)*: ardency; burning; civism; devotion; extremism; fervency; fanaticism; *glorying;* heartiness; impassionedness; *joy;* keenness; liveliness; militancy; nationalism; obsession; patriotism; *quickness;* radicalism; spirit; *trueness;* ultranationalism; vehemence; wholeheartedness; *xenophobia;* yareness; zealotry;

**zealous** *(adj.)*: ardent; avid; burning; committed; devoted; enthusiastic; eager; fervent; gung-ho; hearty; impassioned; *jingoist;* keen; *loyal;* motivated; *nationalistic;* overzealous; obsessed; *on fire;* passionate; quick; ready; spirited; *thrilled;* unreserved; vehement; wholehearted; *xenocentric;* yare; zestful; zealful; [*Ant.* zealless]

**zealousness** *(n.)*: ardency; bustle; commitment; devotedness; exuberance; fervency; *gung-ho;* heartiness; impassionedness; *joy;* keenness; love; mania; *nationalism; overzealousness;* passion; *quickness;* readiness; spirit; *thrill;* ultra- ~; vigor; wholeheartedness; *x-fervor;* yareness; zeal; [*Ant.* zeallessness]

**zenith** *(n.)*: apex; acme; brow; climax; crest; *destination;* extremity; *farthest point;* greatest height; height; high point; *increase; jut;* kop; limit; meridian; maximum; *nib; overmost point;* peak; pinnacle; *quoif; ridge;* summit; top; up; vertex; *way up; xtry; yonder point;* zenithal point;

**zephyr** *(n.)*: air(flow); breeze; current; draft; *east wind;* foehn; gentle breeze; *headwind;* indraft; jet stream; katabatic wind; light wind; moderate gale; north wind; notus; near gale; *overdraft;* puff; pleasant breeze; quarter-wind; *rotary winds;* south wind trade wind; undercurrent; Vayu [Hind.]; (west) wind; westerly; waft; x-wind; *yaw;* zonda;

**zephyrous** *(adj.)*: airish; breezy; *crosswind;* drafty; eolian; flawy; gusty; *howling; inclement; jet stream;* katabatic; *light wind;* moderately windy; *not calm; over-windy;* puffy; *quarter-wind; rough;* squally; *turbulent; undercurrent; very breezy;* windy; x-wind; *yaw;* zephyry; zephrous;

**zeppelin** *(n.)*: airship; blimp; craft; dirigible; *engine;* fire balloon; *Graf ~;* hydrogen blimp; *Hindenburg;* investigator; *jumbo balloon; K-class;* lighter-than-air craft; montgolfier; *Norge; observation balloon;* pilot balloon; *quicken;* rockoon; ship; sausage [slang]; *transport; unidentified object;* vessel; *weather balloon; x-port; yonder;* zep;

**zero** *(n.)*: aught; blank; *barren;* cipher; duck; *destitute;* empty; *finished;* goose egg; *hollow; integer;* jack [slang]; *kaput;* love; mu [Jap.]; naught; nothing; nil; oh; *pinyin ling* [Chin.]; quantity ~; rien [F.]; scratch; *slashed ~; trailing ~; used up; void; without;* x; *yielded;* zilch;

**zest** *(n.)*: animation; ardor; boldness; bang; bite; color; devotion; dynamism; excitement; enthusiasm; fire; gusto; hardiness; intensity; *joie de vivre [F.]; jolt;* kick; liveliness; *mirth; not dull;* oomph; pizzazz; piquancy; passion; *quickening;* robustness; relish; spice; *thrill; upbeat;* verve; *warmth; x-fervor;* yareness; zing; [*see* spice]

**zestful** *(adj.)*: animated; bubbly; cheerful; dynamic; effervescent; exuberant; fun; glowing; happy; intoxicated; joyful; keen; lighthearted; merry; mirthful; *nice;* optimistic; passionate; *queme;* radiant; sunny; thrilling; upbeat; vivacious; winsome; *xanadu;* yeasty; zealous; zippy; [*Ant.* zealless]

**zesty** *(adj.)*: alive; bold; colorful; cheerful; dynamic; energetic; effervescent; frisky; flavorful; *gusto;* high-spirited; intense; jaunty; kedge; lively; lusty; much-spiced; *intense;* nippy; overactive; peppy; quickened; robust; spirited; *thrilled; upbeat;* vivacious; warm; *xtry;* yauld; yeasty; zippy; zestful; zingy;

**zetetic** *(adj.)*: absorbed; brooding; contemplative; deep; eclectic; fanciful; gazeful; heady [slang]; ideological; judicious; *Kantian;* logical; meditative; maieutic; metaphysical; *neo-Platonic; occupied;* philosophic(al); pensive; quodlibetarian; quasi-philosophical; rational; Socratic; staid; theoretical; thoughtful; *understanding; valuating;* wise; *xenocratic; yearnful;* zetetical;

**zhlub** *(n.)*: agrarian; bumpkin; boor; backwoodsman; country bumpkin; chuff; dolt; *egghead;* farmer; funk; goff; hick; hillbilly; ignoramus; joskin; kern; knuff; lout; larrikin; mountaineer; mountainer; numbskull; oaf; provincial; peasant; put; plebeian; plowboy; quack; rube; rustic; redneck; simpleton; *turkey; unsophisticated; vassal;* whig [Br.]; *xiaoren;* yokel; yap; yob; zob;

**ziggurat** *(n.)*: acropolis; bastille; campanile; donjon; *enclosure; fort; garrison;* high tower; ivory tower; *jong [Tib.];* keep; lookout tower; martello; *needle;* observation tower; pyramid; *quarters;* rath; spire; tower; *Ur; vault;* watchtower; *x-structure; yamen* [Chin.]; zikkurat;

**zigzag** *(adj.)*: alternating; bent; crisscross; crooked; *dithering;* extravagating; fluctuating; flexuous; *gnarly; hackly;* irregular; indirect; jagged; jig-a-jig [mil.]; *kedged; laciniate;* meandering; nonlinear; oscillating; ply; *quivering;* reeling; reciprocate; swerving; snaking; serpentine; sawtooth; twisting; *uneven;* vacillating; wigwagging; winding; *x-ing;* yawing; zigzaged; zigzaggy;

**zigzag** *(n.)*: alternation; *bending;* crisscross; crankle; deviating; extravagate; fluctuation; flexing; *gnarly; hackly;* interweave; jaggedness; *kedging; laciniation;* meandering; *nonlinear;* oscillation; *pendulation; quivering;* reeling; staggering; swerving; squirming; snaking; turning; twisting; *unevenness;* vacillation; wigwag; *x-ing;* yaw; zigzaggery;

**zigzag** *(v.)*: alternate; *angle;* bend; crisscross; *dither; entwist;* fluctuate; go back and forth; *hump;* interweave; jag; *kedge; laciniate;* meander; *nonlinear;* oscillate; pendulate; ply; *quiver;* reel; sinuate; *turn;* twist; undulate; vacillate; *veer;* wigwag; *x-ing;* yaw; zig and zag;

**zing** *(n.)*: ardor; bang; bite; *color;* dynamism; dash; energy; flair; gusto; heartiness; intensity; jolt; kick; life; *might;* nip; oomph; punch; pizzazz; *qui;* razzmatazz; snap; spirit; tang; *uncommon heartiness;* vitality; *wow; xuld [arch.]; yareness;* zip; zest; zizz;

**zinger** *(n.)*: anecdote; banter; comeback; *canard* [F.]; *derision; exaggeration;* funny; gag; humor; *insult;* joke; jest; jab; jape; kidding; levity; *mockery;* nifty; one-liner; pun; quip; reply; riddle; shocker; trick; tease; *utterance; vexation;* witticism; *xuld [arch.];* yock; zanyism;

**Zion** *(n.)*: *al-Quds* [Arab.]; Beth David; *the* City (of David); *district; exurb;* Faithful City; *governmental seat;* Holy City; *Ir David;* Jerusalem; *key city; location;* Mt. Zion; *national capital; the* Old City; *place;* Queen City of the Earth; *Rusalimum* [Egy.]; Sion; *town; Urusalim* [Egy.]; *village; ward; Xn. quarter; Yerushalayim* [Heb.]; Zion's Hill; [*see* heaven]

**zip** *(n.)*: agility; *brawn;* capability; dint; energy; forcefulness; gusto; heartiness; intensity; *jet-power; kilowatt;* lustiness; might; *natural ability; omnipotence;* potency; *qualifications;* robustness; strength; spirit; thewiness; *usefulness;* vim; vigor; whamo; *xenium; yare;* zing;

**zip** *(v.)*: *accelerate;* blast; burst; barrel; book; blitz; breeze; cruise; dart; *elan;* fly; go (fast); glide; hurtle; *issue;* jet; kite; light; move; *nippy; outrun; progress; quicken;* rip; rush; rocket; race; run; rip; speed; streak; soar; tear; *uprush; velocity;* whiz; whip; whoosh; *xuld [arch.];* yern; zoom;

**zipper** *(n.)*: attach; *bind;* closed-ended ~; *device; engage;* fastener; fly; *gripper;* hook and eye ~; invisible ~; jacket ~; *keep closed; latchet;* metallic ~; nylon ~; open-ended ~; pull ~; *quick-zip; rivet;* snap; trouser ~; unzipped ~; Velcro®; white ~; *XL ~; YKK®;* zip-fastener;

**zipper** *(v.)*: attach; bind; connect; *close; do;* entwine; fasten; *get together;* hitch; interlock; join; knit; link; latch; merge; *not apart;* open; put together; *quasi-seal;* reunite; secure; seal; *tie;* unite; *Velcro®;* wed; *xenograft;* yoke; zip;

**zippy** *(adj.)*: agile; brisk; *celerity;* dexterous; expeditious; fast; *greased lightening;* hurried; *instant; jiffy; keen;* lively; mercurial; nimble; *on the double;* pronto; quick; rapid; swift; *timely; ultrasonic speed;* volant; wimble; x-speed; yar; zappy; [*Ant.* zealless]

**zit** *(n.)*: abnormality; *acne;* blemish; blackhead; *condition;* dot; eruption; flaw; growth; hydatis; imperfection; *jarble;* kibe; *lump;* mark; milium; node; oil acne; pimple; quat; *raised area;* spot; *tumor;* ulcer; umbo; vesicle; wheal; whitehead; *xanthoma; yedder; zitty;*

**zitty** *(adj.)*: acned; bespotted; *chit-filled;* dotted; eyespotted; *freckly; growth;* hydatis-filled; *imperfect; jarbled;* kibe-filled; *lacunose;* marked; naevose; oil-acned; pimply; papulous; pock-faced; quat-faced; *red-spotted;* spotted; tubercle-filled; umbo-sporting; *unsightly;* verrucose; whelky; *xanthomatous; yeddery;* zit-filled; zit-faced;

**zodiac** *(n.)*: astrology chart; baldrick; constellation chart; divination; enchantment; fortune-telling; gridle; genethliac; horoscopy; I-Ching [Chin.]; *juju; Keltic religion; legerdemain; magic;* new age; nativity; occult; prediction; *quad; rune;* star-gazing; sorcery; *theurgy; under a sign;* voodoo; witchcraft; *xylomancy; yogism;* zodiac;

    **Zodiac symbols**: Aquarius; Aries; Cancer; Capricorn; Gemini; Leo; Libra; Pisces; Sagittarius; Scorpio; Taurus; Virgo;

**zodiacal** *(adj.)*: astrological; *baldrick;* celestial; divinatory; extrapolative; fortelling; gridle-related; horoscopic; *informative; juju; kurbeying; legerdemain;* magical; message-yielding; necromantic; oracular; predictive; premonitory; *quad;* revelatory; *the* stars; *telling; under a sign;* vatic; *warning; xylomantic; yielding;* zodiac-related;

**zoic** *(n.)*: animal; brute; creature; domestic animal; *elk;* fauna [pl.]; game; *herbivore; insectivore;* jument; *koala;* life form; *mammal; non-vertebrate;* organism; *pony;* quadruped; *rodent; sea animal; tiger;* ungulate; *vertibrate;* wildlife [pl.]; *xeme; yearling;* zooid;

**zombie** *(n.)*: animated body; automatan; body; corpse; cadaver; creature; dead person; draugr; *enchanted corpse;* fiend; *ghoul; haint; imp; jumbie;* ket; living dead; mummy; monster; *necroanimation;* one back from the dead; *pall;* quickened cadaver; rotting corpse; sleepwalker; *terror;* undead; vampire; walking dead; wight; *xiphopagus; yaksha [Ind.];* zomby;

**zonal** *(adj.)*: area; borough-wide; citywide; divisional; district; *environs; field; ground; hemispheric; inclusive;* jurisdictional; *kray [Rus.];* locational; *limited;* municipal; nome-related; *oblast [Rus.];* provincial; quadrant-wide; regional; region-specific; sectional; territorial; *ubiety;* vicinal; ward-related; *x-zone; yard-wide;* zonic; zonary;

**zone** *(n.)*: area; belt; clime; district; element; field; *ground; hemisphere; inclusive;* jurisdiction; *jagir* [Asia]; *kray* [Rus.]; location; municipality; nome; *oblast [Rus.];* place; part; quadrant; region; range; sphere; section; sector; territory; ubiety; vicinity; ward; *x-zone; yard;* zonelet; zilla; zona;

**zone** *(v.)*: apportion; break up; compartmentalize; divide (up); *environs;* fractionate; fence off; *group off;* halve; *inclusive;* jurisdiction; *kiosk; line out; make separate; non-contiguous;* organize into zones; partition; *quadrisect;* regionalize; sectionalize; sector; subdivide; territorialize; *unyoke; vell;* wall off; *x-sect; yard;* zonate;

**zoo** *(n.)*: animal park; beasts; collection; children's ~; *domestic animals; engaged; fauna [pl.];* game farm; *habitat; institution;* juments; *koalas; life forms;* menagerie; *non-profit organization;* petting ~; quadrat; *reserve;* safari park; *tigers; ungulates;* vivary; wildlife park; *xenopus; yearlings;* zoological park;

**zookeeper** *(n.)*: animal warden; *beekeeper;* caretaker; director; *employee;* feeder; gamekeeper; head ~; intendant; *jefe;* keeper; leader; manager; *night manager;* overseer; procurator; *quartermaster;* reeve; steward; *trustee; undershepherd; viceroy;* warden; *XO;* yardmaster; zoologist;

**zoolatry** *(n.)*: animal-worship; beast-worship; creature-worship; *doctrine; evil; false religion; gods;* heathenism; idolatry; *joss-worship; kore;* love of animal gods; *monkey-worship; neo-paganism;* offerings to animals; paganism; *quad; reincarnation;* sacrifice to animals; *teaching; ungodliness; voodoo;* worship of animals; xenon-worship; *yantra;* zoism;

**zoological** *(adj.)*: animalistic; biological; bestial; conservational; *dreadful; elephantine;* faunal; *genetic; herpetological; ichthyological; junglish; kaf [arch.];* lionlike; mammalian; *natural;* organic; *physiological; quadruped;* reptilian; *scientific; taxonomical; uakari;* veterinary; wild; *xeroseric; yak-related;* zoonic;

**zoologist** *(n.)*: animal scientist (-doctor); biologist; creature scientist; doctor; *elephant doctor;* farrier; general veterinarian; herd tester; *ichthyologist;* jungle-animal expert; keeper; life scientist; marine biologist; mammalogist; *neontologist; ophiologist; ornithologist;* professor; *quail; reptile specialist;* specialist; scientist; *taxonomist;* unlicensed animal doctor; veterinarian; wildlife expert; *xenoparasite specialist; yardmaster;* zoonomist; zoologer;

**zoology** *(n.)*: animal science; bioscience; biology; creature-science; *discipline;* ecology; farriery; genetics; *herd testing; ichthyology;* jungle-animal studies; *kangaroo studies; life science; marine biology; mammalogy; neontology; ophiology; ornithology; primatology; quail expert;* research; science; taxonomy; *uakari studies; veterinary medicine;* wildlife studies; xenology; *yak-care;* zoology;

**zoom** *(v.)*: accelerate; burn; blitz; bolt; cruise; dart; fly; go (fast); glide; hurry; *issue;* jet; kite; light; move; niddle; outstrip; *progress; quicken;* rush; rocket; rip; shoot; soar; swoosh; streak; tear; *uprush; velocity;* whip; whoosh; whiz; *xuld [arch.];* yern; zip;

**zymurgy** *(n.)*: alcoholization; brewing; concoction; distillation; extillation; fermentation; *gleaning;* homolysis; *intoxification; jag; kirsch;* leavening; making alcohol; *negus; operation;* purification; *quality;* refining; *still operation; turning out;* using a still; vinivication; wine-making; *xenenthesis;* yeasting; zymology;

# Appendix A
# Abbreviations Used in this Book

The following abbreviations are used in this volume.

| | | | | | |
|---|---|---|---|---|---|
| *adj.* | adjective | *Heb.* | Hebrew | *p.p.* | past participle |
| *adv.* | adverb | *Hind.* | Hindu | *p.t.* | past tense |
| *Am. Ind.* | American Indian | *hist.* | history | *Pers.* | Persia |
| *ant.* | antonym | *Ind.* | India | *R.C.C.* | Roman Catholic |
| *Arab.* | Arabic | *interj.* | interjection | | Church |
| *arch.* | archaic | *Ire.* | Ireland | *reg.* | regional |
| *Aus.* | Australia | *Isr.* | Israel | *rel.* | religious |
| *biol.* | biology | *It.* | Italy | *Rom.* | Roman |
| *bot.* | botanical | *Jam.* | Jamaica | *Rus.* | Russian |
| *Br.* | British | *Jap.* | Japanese | *S. Afr.* | South African |
| *Bud.* | Buddhism | *Jew.* | Jewish | *Scand.* | Scandinavian |
| *Bur,* | Burmese | *joc.* | jocular | *sci.* | scientific |
| *Can.* | Canada | *Kor.* | Korea | *Scot.* | Scottish |
| *Carib.* | Caribbean | *L.* | Latin | *Skr.* | Sanskrit |
| *Celt.* | Celtic | *lit.* | literary | *Slav.* | Slavic |
| *Chin.* | Chinese | *masc.* | masculine | *Sp.* | Spanish |
| *coll.* | colloquial | *med.* | medical | *Swed.* | Swedish |
| *conj.* | conjunction | *Mex.* | Mexican | *tech.* | technical |
| *derog.* | derogatory | *mil.* | military | *Tib.* | Tibet |
| *dial* | dialect | *Mos.* | Moslem | *Turk.* | Turkey |
| *Eng.* | England | *mus.* | musical | *U.S.* | United States |
| *Du.* | Dutch | *myth.* | mythological | *v.* | verb |
| *Egy.* | Egyptian | *n.* | noun | *var.* | variant spelling |
| *err.* | erroneous | *naut.* | nautical | *vulg.* | vulgar |
| *F.* | French | *nav.* | naval | *xfer* | transfer |
| *fem.* | feminine | *neg.* | negative | *xmit* | transmit |
| *fict.* | fictional | *Nor.* | Norwegian | *XQ.* | cross-question |
| *Fin.* | Finland | *N.Z.* | New Zealand | *xtr.* | extra |
| *G.* | German | *off.* | offensive | *xtry.* | extraordinary, |
| *Gael.* | Gaelic | *pfn.* | personification | | extraordinarily |
| *geog.* | geography | *phys.* | physics | *Yid.* | Yiddish |
| *geom.* | geometry | *pl.* | plural | *zoo.* | zoological |
| *Gr.* | Greek | *poet.* | poetic | | |
| *gram.* | grammatical | *prep.* | preposition | | |
| *Haw.* | Hawaii | *pron.* | pronoun | | |

# Appendix B
# Bibliography

The author acknowledges the following sources used in the compilation of this book:

1. *The American Heritage Dictionary of the English Language, Fourth Edition.* Boston: Houghton Mifflin Company, 2000.

2. *The American Heritage Dictionary of the English Language, Second College Edition.* Boston: Houghton Mifflin Company, 1982.

3. Elwell, Walter (Ed,), *Evangelical Dictionary of Theology, Second Edition,* Cumbria: Baker Book House Company, 2001.

4. *Encarta Word English Dictionary,* New York: St. Martin's Press, 1999.

5. Kleinedler, Steven (Supervising Ed.), *Webster's New College Dictionary, Third Edition,* Boston: Houghton Mifflin Hardcourt, 2005.

6. *Merriam-Webster's Collegiate dictionary, Eleventh Edition,* Springfield: Merriam-Webster, 2003.

7. *The New Oxford American Dictionary, Second Edition,* New York: Oxford University Press, 2005.

8. Simpson, John (Ed.). *The Oxford English Dictionary.* Oxford: Oxford University Press, 1990.

9. Stevenson, Angus (ed.). *The Oxford American Dictionary, Third Edition.* New York: Oxford Press, 2010.

10. Webster, Noah. *American Dictionary of the English Language.* San Fransisco: Foundation for Christian Education, 1828.

11. *Websters Third New International Dictionary, Unabridged.* Springfield: Merriam-Webster, 1986.

Consulted in the final review stage of this book:

1. Dictionary.com, LLC., an IAC company.
    2013-2014 <http://www.thesaurus.com>

2. Thesaurasize.com., Next Wave Services.
    2013-2014 <http://www.thesaurasize.com>

Made in United States
Cleveland, OH
29 January 2025

13884181R00457